HANDBOOK OF LATIN AMERICAN STUDIES: No. 58

A Selective and Annotated Guide to Recent Publications in Art, History, Literature, Music, Philosophy, and Electronic Resources

VOLUME 59 WILL BE DEVOTED TO THE SOCIAL SCIENCES: ANTHROPOLOGY, ECONOMICS, GEOGRAPHY, GOVERNMENT AND POLITICS, INTERNATIONAL RELATIONS, SOCIOLOGY, AND ELECTRONIC RESOURCES

EDITORIAL NOTE: Comments concerning the *Handbook of Latin American Studies* should be sent directly to the Editor, *Handbook of Latin American Studies*, Hispanic Division, Library of Congress, Washington, D.C. 20540.

HANDBOOK OF LATIN AMERICAN STUDIES: NO. 58

HUMANITIES

Prepared by a Number of Scholars
for the Hispanic Division of The Library of Congress

LAWRENCE BOUDON, *Editor*
KATHERINE D. McCANN, *Assistant Editor*

2002

UNIVERSITY OF TEXAS PRESS   *Austin*

International Standard Book Number: 0-292-70910-2
International Standard Serial Number: 0072-9833
Library of Congress Catalog Card Number: 36-32633
Copyright © 2002 by the University of Texas Press.
All rights reserved.
Printed in the United States of America.

Requests for permission to reproduce material
from this work should be sent to:
Permissions, University of Texas Press,
Box 7819, Austin, Texas 78713-7819.

First Edition, 2002

The paper used in the publication meets
the minimum requirements of American National
Standard for Infomation Sciences—Permanence
of Paper for Printed Library Materials,
ANSI Z39.48-1984. ∞

CONTRIBUTING EDITORS

HUMANITIES

Edna Acosta-Belén, *University of Albany, SUNY*, LITERATURE
Maureen Ahern, *The Ohio State University*, TRANSLATION
Severino J. Albuquerque, *University of Wisconsin-Madison*, LITERATURE
Félix Angel, *Inter-American Development Bank*, ART
Uva de Aragón, *Florida International University*, LITERATURE
Barbara von Barghahn, *George Washington University*, ART
Dain Borges, *University of Chicago*, HISTORY
John Britton, *Francis Marion University*, HISTORY
Francisco Cabanillas, *Bowling Green State University*, LITERATURE
Sara Castro-Klarén, *The Johns Hopkins University*, LITERATURE
Walter Aaron Clark, *University of Kansas*, MUSIC
Don M. Coerver, *Texas Christian University*, HISTORY
Wilfredo H. Corral, *University of California at Davis*, LITERATURE
Edith B. Couturier, *Independent Scholar*, HISTORY
Edward Cox, *Rice University*, HISTORY
Sandra Cypess, *University of Maryland*, LITERATURE
Jennifer L. Eich, *Loyola Marymount University, Los Angeles*, LITERATURE
César Ferreira, *University of Oklahoma*, LITERATURE
Francisco J. Fonseca, *Princeton University*, ELECTRONIC RESOURCES
José Manuel García-García, *New Mexico State University*, LITERATURE
Magdalena García-Pinto, *University of Missouri-Columbia*, LITERATURE
John D. Garrigus, *Jacksonville University*, HISTORY
Miguel Gomes-Ocampo, *University of Connecticut*, LITERATURE
Gilberto Gómez, *Wabash College*, LITERATURE
Lance R. Grahn, *Marquette University*, HISTORY
María Cristina Guiñazú, *Lehman College-CUNY*, LITERATURE
Michael T. Hamerly, *Brown University*, HISTORY
Robert Haskett, *University of Oregon*, HISTORY
José M. Hernández, *Professor Emeritus, Georgetown University*, HISTORY
Rosemarijn Hoefte, *Royal Institute of Linguistics and Anthropology, The Netherlands*, HISTORY
Joel Horowitz, *Saint Bonaventure University*, HISTORY
Regina Igel, *University of Maryland*, LITERATURE
Clara Alicia Jalif de Bertranou, *Universidad Nacional de Cuyo, Argentina*, PHILOSOPHY
Peter T. Johnson, *Princeton University*, ELECTRONIC RESOURCES
Erick D. Langer, *Georgetown University*, HISTORY
Pedro Lastra, *State University of New York at Stony Brook*, LITERATURE

Asunción Lavrin, *Arizona State University at Tempe*, HISTORY
Alfred E. Lemmon, *Historic New Orleans Collection*, MUSIC
Peter S. Linder, *New Mexico Highlands University*, HISTORY
Maria Angélica Guimarães Lopes, *University of South Carolina*, LITERATURE
Cristina Magaldi, *Towson University*, MUSIC
Carol Maier, *Kent State University*, TRANSLATIONS
Claire Martin, *California State University, Long Beach*, LITERATURE
Teresita Martínez-Vergne, *Macalester College*, HISTORY
Daniel Masterson, *Unites States Naval Academy*, HISTORY
David McCreery, *Georgia State University*, HISTORY
Joan E. Meznar, *Eastern Connecticut State University*, HISTORY
Elizabeth Monasterios, *State University of New York at Stony Brook*, LITERATURE
Naomi Hoki Moniz, *Georgetown University*, LITERATURE
José M. Neistein, *Brazilian-American Cultural Institute, Washington*, ART
José Miguel Oviedo, *University of Pennsylvania*, LITERATURE
Suzanne B. Pasztor, *University of the Pacific*, HISTORY
Daphne Patai, *University of Massachusetts, Amherst*, TRANSLATIONS
Anne Pérotin-Dumon, *Pontificia Universidad Católica de Chile*, HISTORY
Charles A. Perrone, *University of Florida*, LITERATURE
José Promis, *University of Arizona*, LITERATURE
James Radomski, *California State University, San Bernardino*, MUSIC
Susan E. Ramírez, *DePaul University*, HISTORY
Jane M. Rausch, *University of Massachusetts-Amherst*, HISTORY
Oscar Rivera-Rodas, *University of Tennessee, Knoxville*, LITERATURE
Humberto Rodríguez-Camilloni, *Virginia Polytechnic Institute and State University*, ART
Mario A. Rojas, *Catholic University of America*, LITERATURE
Kathleen Ross, *New York University*, TRANSLATIONS
Oscar Sarmiento, *State University of New York at Potsdam*, LITERATURE
William F. Sater, *California State University, Long Beach*, HISTORY
Jacobo Sefamí, *University of California, Irvine*, LITERATURE
Susan M. Socolow, *Emory University*, HISTORY
Barbara A. Tenenbaum, *Hispanic Division, The Library of Congress*, HISTORY
Juan Carlos Torchia Estrada, *Consultant, Hispanic Division, The Library of Congress*, PHILOSOPHY
Lilián Uribe, *Central Connecticut State University*, LITERATURE
Thomas Whigham, *University of Georgia*, HISTORY
Stephen Webre, *Louisiana Tech University*, HISTORY
Stephanie Wood, *University of Oregon*, HISTORY

SOCIAL SCIENCES

Juan M. del Aguila, *Emory University*, GOVERNMENT AND POLITICS
Benigno E. Aguirre-López, *Texas A&M University*, SOCIOLOGY
Amalia M. Alberti, *Independent Consultant, San Salvador*, SOCIOLOGY
G. Pope Atkins, *University of Texas at Austin*, INTERNATIONAL RELATIONS
Melissa H. Birch, *University of Kansas*, ECONOMICS
Jacqueline Braveboy-Wagner, *The City College-CUNY*, INTERNATIONAL RELATIONS
Roderic A. Camp, *Claremont-McKenna College*, GOVERNMENT AND POLITICS

William L. Canak, *Middle Tennessee State University*, SOCIOLOGY
Gustavo Enrique Cañonero, *Independent Consultant*, ECONOMICS
César Caviedes, *University of Florida*, GEOGRAPHY
Marc Chernick, *Georgetown University*, GOVERNMENT AND POLITICS
Jeffrey Cohen, *Pennsylvania State University*, ANTHROPOLOGY
Harold Colson, *University of California-San Diego*, ELECTRONIC RESOURCES
Lambros Comitas, *Columbia University*, ANTHROPOLOGY
William Van Davidson, *Louisiana State University*, GEOGRAPHY
David Dent, *Towson University*, GOVERNMENT AND POLITICS
Gary S. Elbow, *Texas Tech University*, GEOGRAPHY
Damián J. Fernández, *Florida International University*, INTERNATIONAL RELATIONS
Michael Fleet, *Marquette University*, GOVERNMENT AND POLITICS
James W. Foley, *University of Miami*, ECONOMICS
Jeffrey Franks, *International Monetary Fund*, ECONOMICS
Daniel W. Gade, *University of Vermont*, GEOGRAPHY
Eduardo Gamarra, *Florida International University*, GOVERNMENT AND POLITICS
José Zebedeo García, *New Mexico State University*, GOVERNMENT AND POLITICS
Ivelaw L. Griffith, *Florida International University*, GOVERNMENT AND POLITICS
Kevin Healy, *Inter-American Foundation*, SOCIOLOGY
Darrin Helsel, *University of Maryland*, SOCIOLOGY
John Henderson, *Cornell University*, ANTHROPOLOGY
Silvia María Hirsch, *Trenton State College*, ANTHROPOLOGY
William Keegan, *Florida Museum of Natural History*, ANTHROPOLOGY
Roberto Patricio Korzeniewicz, *University of Maryland*, SOCIOLOGY
Susana Lastarria-Cornhiel, *University of Wisconsin-Madison*, SOCIOLOGY
Paul Lewis, *Tulane University*, GOVERNMENT AND POLITICS
Robert E. Looney, *Naval Postgraduate School*, ECONOMICS
Peggy Lovell, *University of Pittsburgh*, SOCIOLOGY
Markos J. Mamalakis, *University of Wisconsin-Milwaukee*, ECONOMICS
Tom L. Martinson, *Auburn University*, GEOGRAPHY
Nohra Rey de Marulanda, *Inter-American Development Bank*, ECONOMICS
Betty J. Meggers, *Smithsonian Institution*, ANTHROPOLOGY
Keith D. Muller, *Kent State University*, GEOGRAPHY
Deborah Nichols, *Dartmouth College*, ANTHROPOLOGY
Robert Palacios, *The World Bank*, ECONOMICS
David Scott Palmer, *Boston University*, GOVERNMENT AND POLITICS
Ransford W. Palmer, *Howard University*, ECONOMICS
Jorge Pérez-López, *US Department of Labor*, ECONOMICS
Timothy J. Power, *Florida International University*, GOVERNMENT AND POLITICS
Catalina Rabinovich, *Independent Consultant, Chevy Chase, Maryland*,
  ECONOMICS
Martín Rama, *The World Bank*, ECONOMICS
Joanne Rappaport, *Georgetown University*, ANTHROPOLOGY
Dereka Rushbrook, *Independent Consultant*, ECONOMICS
René Salgado, *Independent Consultant*, GOVERNMENT AND POLITICS
David W. Schodt, *St. Olaf's College*, ECONOMICS
Russell E. Smith, *Washburn University*, ECONOMICS
Paul Sondrol, *University of Colorado, Colorado Springs*, GOVERNMENT AND
  POLITICS
Dale Story, *University of Texas at Arlington*, INTERNATIONAL RELATIONS

CONTENTS

HISTORY

LITERATURE

MUSIC

PHILOSOPHY: LATIN AMERICAN THOUGHT

INDEXES

EDITOR'S NOTE

I. GENERAL AND REGIONAL TRENDS

IN THE SHORT TIME that I have served as editor of the *Handbook of Latin American Studies,* one trend has become patently obvious: that we are observing a veritable explosion in scholarly publications on Latin America, the vast majority of which are produced in the region itself. Moreover, it is not just in terms of quantity that the scholarship has increased, but in quality, as well. Scholars are better trained, have access to better information, in part due to the spread of the Internet, but also because of the expansion of libraries and research centers. The result of this burgeoning trend is that the *Handbook* must become increasingly selective regarding what is annotated in the print version, as well as in *HLAS Online.* That said, the focus of the Editor's Note for *HLAS 58* will be on recent trends in historical scholarship.

As the new millennium begins, the historiography of Latin America is branching out in new directions, some of which appeared in the last several years, while others are decidedly new and welcome. Overall, the quality of the scholarship in the field continues to improve, although one contributing editor lamented a "growing trend among large commercial publishing houses. These presses are increasingly printing histories, particularly biographies, intended for popular audiences without any indication of sources" (p. 415). While the quote refers specifically to Argentina, the trend toward more popular-oriented historical works of little value to scholars can be seen elsewhere in the region. Notwithstanding, it is encouraging that historical research is experiencing something of a boom in Latin America, the result of the consolidation of democratic regimes in most countries and an increase in the number of rigorously trained scholars. One contributing editor noted the"increasing professionalization" of historiography in Mexico (p. 191), a statement which could be applied equally throughout the region.

One of the more notable trends is the growing focus on regional and local history, relying in some cases on little-known archives. In Venezuela, the contributing editor reports that there is a "proliferation of high-quality regional and local studies" (p. 363), while in Mexico, historical research is being done on individual states, cities and towns. Of particular interest for Mexico are the works on the early revolutionary period in the states of Guanajuato (item **1392**), Michoacán (item **1514**), and Tlaxcala (item **1529** and item **1405**). In Colombia, the five-volume *Historia General del Huila* (item **2564**) "reveals the value of a regional focus when studying a country composed of loosely united regions" (p. 370). Additionally, Posada Carbó contributed to our understanding of the Caribbean coast with his well- researched survey of that region from 1870 to 1950 (item **2597**). Finally, Doering and Lohman Villena's history of Lima (item **2658**) "represents one of the best urban histories of the past decade by two of Peru's finest historians" (p. 384).

A second area in which historiography is breaking new ground is in the study of women and gender. While the attention is not new, the scholarship is, as one contributing editor put it, "belatedly maturing" (p. 257). Outstanding general works include two by Pareja Ortiz, one on the daily life of Sevillian women in the Americas (item **946**), and the other on marriage laws in the Spanish empire (item **945**).

An ongoing but growing topic of research is the history of immigration, particularly of groups previously ignored or understudied. It should not be surprising, perhaps, that the rise to power of Peruvian President Alberto Fujimori has prompted scholars to focus on the Japanese in Peru. In that vein, the work of the late Japanese-Peruvian sociologist Fukumoto (item **2655**) will be the benchmark for years to come. Also interesting is Ortíz Sotelo's study of the small Croatian community in Peru (item **2687**). In Brazil, studies on Portuguese and German immigration appeared (items **3299**, **3321**, and **3319**), as did works on less-studied groups such as the Syrians (item **3336**) and the Jews (items **3245** and **3284**). While the quantity of scholarship on immigration in Argentina decreased somewhat in the past several years, it did diversify in terms of the groups and topics studied. For instance, while works on Italian immigration are hardly new, Cibotti's contribution (item **2855**) focuses on how they maintained a sense of ethnic identity. In a similar vein, Bjerg examines the Danes (item **2825**), while Jozami attempts to ascertain the number of Muslims in Argentina (item **2934**). Broader, regional works include those on British immigration to the Western Hemisphere (item **786**), the Japanese in Latin America, the US, and Canada (item **829**), and Kitroeff's groundbreaking study of the Greeks in the Americas (item **1031**).

A related theme is that of forced migration, or slavery as it is more commonly known. This topic continues to occupy a central spot in historical research and is benefitting from what one contributing editor termed "renewed interest" in the English-speaking Caribbean. Eltis' study (item **1843**) stands out in that he argues that the role of the British in the slave trade has been "grossly underexaggerated" (p. 257). Another historian noted the "fresh interpretations" of research on 18th-century French Caribbean slave society and the impact of revolutionary upheaval (p. 258). Abundant scholarship on slaves, slave resistance, and runaway slave communities has been published recently in Brazil. Two outstanding works tackle the plight of ex-slaves following abolition (item **3345**) and the meaning of "freedom" (item **3312**). Reis and Dos Santos have compiled a collection of diverse essays on runaway slave communities (item **3180**), while other historians focused on quilombos (items **3230** and **3275**), and slaves and ex-slaves in the army (item **3283**).

Before turning to literature, art, and music, I would like to highlight some of the more interesting and unusual trends in Latin American historiography over the past several years. This all too brief survey should not be considered exhaustive, rather a tantalizing taste of what is being written and published. One encouraging trend, as noted by the Cuban historian, is the appearance of two quality biographies of legendary guerrilla leader Ernesto "Che" Guevara, one by Jon Lee Anderson (item **2043**), who remains objective despite exaggerating his role in the Cuban Revolution. The other, by noted scholar of the left Jorge Castañeda (item **2052**), unveils new information on Guevara and, while not as good as Anderson's work, is still a vast improvement over most previous biographies. In Peru, meanwhile, the 1995 conflict with Ecuador prompted a flurry of works on the history of the border dispute. Of these, two stand out: Denegri Luna's treatise on the diplomacy, treaties, and military conflicts between the two countries since colonial times (item **2653**), and Yepes' study on the US-sponsored McBride Commission, upon which Peru relied to validate its territorial claims (item **2709**).

An interesting new trend in Argentine historiography is occurring in the field of political history, where efforts are being made not simply to describe and interpret events, but to uncover the processes behind them. Scholars are trying to determine how politicians attracted votes, how the voters were mobilized, and how the elections were carried out. In one such work, Alonso studies elections in Buenos Aires during the period in which the Radical Party began challenging the Conservatives (1890-98), concluding that they not only were competitive, but reasonably fair (item **2802**). In addition, scholars are studying the Argentine political parties on a regional level, such as Lacoste's works on the Radicals (item **2947**) and Socialists (item **2946**) in the province of Mendoza.

With the new millennium in sight, Brazilian historians turned their attention recently to reforms in certain cities carried out at the turn of the 20th century. Rio de Janeiro is spotlighted, in particular. Meade (item **3300**) examines the conflicts that arose due to "modernization," noting that while the poor lost most of the battles, they did win a few. Chalhoub (item **3249**) looks at the destruction of slums in an effort to combat yellow fever, while Rocha (item **3320**) views the same event and its resultant marginalization of the poor. Other cities whose reforms were studied include Santos (item **3287**), Campinas (item **3288**), and Fortaleza (item **3313**).

In Mexican historiography, a couple of trends noted in previous volumes continued in *HLAS 58*. Works on the Porfiriato and other events of the 19th century are beginning to shed light on the struggle between the central government and some of the country's regions, a theme common to much of Latin America following independence. In addition, economic history continues to blossom, with scholars studying a range of topics, from the difficulties of establishing a telephone system in Mexico City (item **1291**) to the relationship between the country's industrial-business class and the state following the Revolution (items **1487** and **1489**).

Finally, two works annotated in this volume stand out for different reasons, one for its contribution to an understudied country, Haiti, and the other for its bold and controversial revision of an historical event in Bolivia. Relying on his knowledge of 20th-century Haitian literature, Dash compares and contrasts the views that Haitians had of the US, and vice versa, placing them within a political context (item **1782**). Mendoza, meanwhile, generated considerable controversy in his book, *La mesa coja* (item **2735**), arguing that the 1809 declaration of independence was part of an elite plan to establish the capital in La Paz, rather than La Plata (Sucre).

In the relatively new but rapidly growing field of ethnohistory, scholars continue to try to unravel the mysteries of the preconquest civilizations. In Mesoamerica, one noteworthy new discovery is that the indigenous peoples in the northern regions possessed "much more complex societies than once believed; . . . were less isolated from the peoples of the center than previously assumed; and once Spaniards began settling in these regions, the central Mexican colonists who accompanied them brought more of 'Mesoamerica' along with them." (Haskett and Wood, p. 83).

With this volume of the *Handbook*, the chapter on Spanish American general literature draws to a close, with the resignation of long-time contributing editor Sara Castro-Klarén. Ironically, this comes at a time when the scholarship in that field is growing so much that it became increasingly difficult to select works for inclusion in *HLAS 58*. Of those that were, Castro-Klarén noted with approval the continued study of women writers, a new focus on gay studies, and a return to the essay.

An interesting trend underscored by another retiring contributing editor, Edna Acosta-Belén, is the growing tendency for bilingual writers from Puerto Rico to engage in what she calls "crossover" writing, to take advantage of markets in both English and Spanish. What is interesting in the case of Rosario Ferré, is her decision to write books in English and then rewrite them in Spanish, rather than have them translated. The result is similar, but not identical works in the two languages. The Spanish versions, *La casa de la laguna* (item **3566**) and *Vecindarios excéntricos* (item **3567**) were reviewed in this volume.

A noteworthy and welcomed byproduct of the wave of scholarship marking the 300th anniversary of the death of Mexican intellectual and prodigy, Sor Juana Inés de la Cruz (1648-95), was an increased interest in the writings of women in the colonial era, in general. A number of symposia were organized in the mid-1990s and some produced edited proceedings (items **3457** and **3469**). Other scholars put together anthologies on colonial women, as well as well-documented editions of unpublished materials (item **3471**). A good example of how literature reflects the society in which it is written is occurring in Colombia, whose civil war became more ferocious in the 1990s, fueled in part by the hugely profitable trade in illicit drugs. The violence surrounding the drug trade has found its way into the novels of two established writers: Darío Jaramillo Agudelo's *Novela con fantasma* (item **3644**) and Plinio Apuleyo Mendoza's *Cinco días en la isla* (item **3646**). In addition, Antonio Caballero's reissue of his work *Sin remedio* (item **3642**) contains an extremely pessimistic view of the situation, but also seeks to find meaning amid the violence.

It is important to note the passing, at the end of 1996, of renowned Chilean author José Donoso, followed closely by the death of his wife, Pilar. Prior to his death, Donoso was able to complete the edits on his final novel, *El mocho* (item **3716**), which synthesizes the various themes that had obsessed him over the course of his productive literary career. In the field of art, publications from Mexico and Argentina continue to dominate the Hispanic world, but quality works from Colombia, Venezuela, and Uruguay are increasing in number and scope. A monumental, seven-volume set from Mexico documents that country's artwork in collections around the world (item **174**). The work, *México en el mundo de las colecciones de arte*, spans 3,000 years. One trend observed during this biennium is the growing interest in the illegal trafficking of art. Daniel Schávelzon's *El expolio del arte en la Argentina* explores not only that topic, but also theft and vandalism (item **291**).

In Brazil, contributing editor José Neistein notes the continued focus on 20th-century art, with just three publications on the 19th century, and only two on the colonial period. He reviews seven theoretical or reference works, including one on the impact of European modernity on Brazil (item **395**) and a collection of essays on Brazil's self-discovery (item **393**). In addition, he highlights a number of publications dedicated to particular artists, regions, or time periods, such as the two works on Lygia Clark (items **410** and **420**).

Turning briefly to the colonial era, it is significant to note the proliferation of works on historic monuments in Mexico, many of which have been the subject of restoration projects. In addition, new attention is being paid to the 16th century, in particular the little-examined impact of humanism on decorative art, such as the Casa del Deán in Pueblo (item **27**). On a broader scale, the exceptional *Arquitectura colonial iberoamericana,* by Graziano Gasparini *et al.,* stands out and deserves special mention (item **12**), as does the encyclopedic volume *Pintura, escultura y artes útiles en Iberoamérica, 1500-1825* (item **19**).

Works on music in *HLAS 58* reflected the variety of genres and eras being studied in Latin America and the Caribbean, including a healthy examination and recording of colonial music. In the Caribbean, Cuban composer Esteban Salas (1725-1803) is the focus of articles by Robert Stevenson in the *Inter-American Music Review* (item **4812**) and Victoria Eli Rodríguez in the *Revista Musical de Venezuela* (item **4811**). Farther south, attention is being paid to 17th- and 18th-century musical practices in Jesuit missions, as seen in works by Gerardo Huseby *et al.* (item **4817**), Piotr Nawrot (items **4820** and **4821**), and Victor Rondón (item **4867**). A major Brazilian contribution to the study of colonial music is Régis Duprat's work on the musical holdings of the Museu da Inconfidência in Ouro Preto, Minas Gerais (item **4896**). In Mexico, there is a continuing fascination with *mariachis,* not only from a musical perspective, but historical and anthropological, as well, once again highlighting the interdisciplinary nature of Latin American studies. Works by Jesús Flores y Escalante and Pablo Dueñas Herrera (item **4752**), Alvaro Ochoa (item **4764**), and Jorge Chamorro Escalante (item **4745**) appear in this volume.

II. CLOSING DATE

The closing date for works annotated in this volume was mid-2000. Publications received and cataloged at the Library of Congress after that date will be annotated in the next humanities volume, *HLAS 60.*

III. ELECTRONIC ACCESS TO THE *HANDBOOK*

Web Site

On January 18, 2001, the Hispanic Division of the Library of Congress unveiled the Portuguese version of *HLAS Online.* The web site can be accessed at http://lcweb2.loc.gov/hlas/portugues/hlashome.html. The Portuguese homepage features a description of the *Handbook of Latin American Studies* and includes links to the translated search page, help menu, and feedback page, as well as to acknowledgements and copyright information. With the addition of Portuguese, *HLAS Online* is now available in three languages, including English and Spanish.

Online Public Access Catalog

HLAS records from Volumes 50 onward may be searched through the Library of Congress online catalog. This search method allows the use of limits, such as language and date of publication, and provides options for printing, saving, and emailing search results. Please see http://catalog.loc.gov/help/database.htm for instructions and more information.

IV. CHANGES FROM PREVIOUS HUMANITIES VOLUME

General

Beginning with this volume, the end-of-chapter Journal Abbreviation lists have been eliminated in favor of providing more space for annotated entries. As always, all journals indexed in a volume can be found in the Title List of Journals Indexed and the Abbreviation List of Journals Indexed located at the back of each volume.

History

For the 19th and 20th centuries chapter, Dr. Peter Linder assumed full responsibility for the Venezuela section. Thomas Whigham, University of Georgia, collaborated with Joel Horowitz for the section on Argentina, Paraguay, and Uruguay. David McCreery collaborated on the Brazil chapter, contributing annotations for works on the Empire period. Daniel Masterson, US Naval Academy, took over responsibility for section on 19th and 20th century Peruvian history.

Literature

Jennifer Eich, Loyola Marymount University, Los Angeles, took over responsibility for the colonial period chapter. For the chapter on 20th-century prose fiction, Will Corral, University of California, Davis, prepared the section for Central America. Gilberto Gómez, Wabash College (Indiana), collaborated on the Andean countries section, annotating works of Colombian and Venezuelan literature. Claire Martin, California State University, Long Beach, collaborated on the River Plate countries section, contributing annotations for the Argentine literature section. For the poetry chapter, Miguel Gomes took over responsibility for Colombia and Venezuela. Oscar Sarmiento, Potsdam College (New York), covered the Chile section. Sandra Cypess, University of Maryland, collaborated on the drama chapter, preparing the annotations for Mexico and Central America.

Music

Robert Stevenson retired after many years of service to the *Handbook*. For this volume, four new contributors were recruited. James Radomski, California State University, San Bernardino, covered the Mexico section. Walter Clark, University of Kansas, canvassed the works for Colombia, Ecuador, Peru, and Venezuela. Cristina Magaldi, Towson University (Maryland), assumed responsibility for Argentina, Bolivia, Brazil, Chile, Paraguay, and Uruguay. Alfred Lemmon, Historic New Orleans Collection, contributed annotations for the Central America and Caribbean section.

Philosophy

Clara Bertranou, Universidad Nacional de Cuyo (Argentina), contributed several annotations for this chapter.

V. ACKNOWLEDGMENTS

In August 1999, the Library of Congress implemented a new Integrated Library System, resulting in the need for an entirely new method of producing the print version of the *Handbook of Latin American Studies*. At the same time, efforts were underway at the Library of Congress to create an XML-based document-type definition (DTD) for bibliographies. Thanks to this auspicious turn of events, the *Handbook* accepted an opportunity to serve as the prototype for the first implementation of the LCbib DTD. (Further discussion of the use of DTDs at the Library of Congress can be found on the web at http://www.loc.gov/marc/marcsgml.html/.)

HLAS 58 is the first edition to be produced using the XML-based system. We are grateful to the members of the Library of Congress staff who served on the HLAS/XML-DTD Bibliographic Working Group: Belinda Urquiza, Ardie Bausenbach, and Andy Lisowski of the Automation Planning and Liaison Office; Marla Banks of Information Technology Services, and Cheryl Graunke of the Network Development and MARC Standards Office. Their many hours of hard work and their willingness to learn the intricacies and eccentricities of *Handbook* style brought this project to a successful conclusion.

Others at the Library of Congress were no less vital to the creation of a new *HLAS* print production system. It would have been impossible to undertake this project without the interest and generous support of Peter Young, Chief of the Cataloging Distribution Service. Randy Barry (NDMSO) and David Williamson (APLO) lent their invaluable knowledge of MARC and the ILS to the creation of a series of reports indicating editorial inconsistencies in *Handbook* citations. Special thanks are also due to ITS staff members, Jane Mandelbaum, Ken Carpenter, and Tom McCready.

Handbook staff rely upon the able assistance of high school work-study students from the metropolitan Washington DC community to complete a wide variety of projects. During the past year, Cynthia Acosta's work consistently bore the unmistakable stamp of her intelligence and maturity. Finally, we would like to thank our Library of Congress managers, Winston Tabb and Carolyn Brown, and the chief of the Hispanic Division, Georgette Dorn, for their continued support of the *Handbook* and its staff.

Lawrence Boudon, *Editor*
Katherine D. McCann, *Assistant Editor*

HANDBOOK OF LATIN AMERICAN STUDIES: No. 58

ELECTRONIC RESOURCES

PETER T. JOHNSON, *Bibliographer for Latin America, Spain, and Portugal, Princeton University*
FRANCISCO J. FONSECA, *Assistant to the Bibliographer for Latin America, Spain, and Portugal, Princeton University*

THE SECTION ON ELECTRONIC RESOURCES consists of two parts: the first covers electronically formatted sources accessible on CD-ROM or diskette, and the second part covers materials accessible through the Internet. Bibliographical, reference, and subject-specific titles appear in the two sections. Given the interdisciplinary nature of research, some social science works with content useful to the humanities and history are cited.

During the past three years, the volume of electronically formatted information being produced in Latin America grew tremendously; and perhaps more significantly, access to such information became more widespread throughout the region. Certainly the lowering of costs for cutting CD-ROMs and the growing access to computers throughout Latin America contributed to this trend. Recognition and acceptance of electronic resources in higher education, as well as in the workplace, suggest that the coming years will witness even greater quantities of electronic information. Most of these materials continue to be bibliographic and statistical databases in multimedia format. The digitization of full texts is still quite rare, largely due to the substantial costs of software, text preparation, and the scanning itself. The limited commercial market also influences the choice of materials to be made available. Currently, the majority of CD-ROMs and web sites that describe their materials as full text offer scanned page images; less expensive to produce, these images are also less useful as they do not allow keyword or fixed-field vocabulary searching. Latin American equivalents of JSTOR (*http://www.jstor.org/*) or the University of Michigan's Digital Library Project (*http://www.si.umich.edu/UMDL/*) have yet to be created.

Bibliographic resources emerged early on as favored materials to offer on CD-ROM or on diskette. This continues to be true, though libraries are increasingly providing on-line access to their public catalogs via the Internet. Specialized documentation centers operating in the public and private sectors also offer their catalogs or subject bibliographies in electronic format. Bookdealers in Spain, Argentina, Mexico, and the US have created their own databases, most of which provide a listing of in-print books and serials of interest to the academic world.

A notable trend in the world of electronic information is the increased access to full-text documents, first with single serial titles, and now with thematic collections of out-of print books, government documents, and pamphlets. The most important of these initiatives is DIGIBIS, Publicaciones Digitales from the Fundación Histórica Tavera in Spain (*http://www.digibis.com/*). Now focused on bringing to a broader readership the fundamental or "classic" texts that heretofore were found only in large research libraries, DIGIBIS offers nine series ranging from primary sources written in the colonial period to legal materials, along with works devoted to indigenous issues, thematic histories, and linguistics. This important advance in access to scarce texts offers images rather than full-text searchable capacity. Some limited indexing of contents does allow for more efficient searching.

Accounting for a small amount of the total output is the mixed media CD-ROM designed for didactic purposes, but with some utility for scholarly research. These works tend to offer limited bibliographic information, emphasize fragments of texts, or create their own secondary text to link together illustrated matter and sound recordings. These CD-ROMs occasionally provide access to photographic archives and motion picture clips that otherwise are extremely difficult to obtain. Judging from the range of such works currently on the market, far greater attention to scholarly interests is necessary before such products can be considered useful for more than introductory purposes.

Technological constraints are a continuing problem with all of these electronic materials. Often difficult to install, or operating with software now considered obsolete, CD-ROMs and diskettes all too frequently are not compatible with current technology. Built-in expiration dates also can be troublesome. Eventually such flaws in design and writing will diminish, but until then, information in this format, like other forms of publishing, offers a wide range of quality.

CD-ROMs AND DISKETTES

1   Archivo, testimonio: documentos históricos sobre Argentina ante el nazismo y el fascismo, 1930–1960. Buenos Aires: Delegación de Asociaciones Israelitas Argentinas, Centro de Estudios Sociales, 1995? 1 computer laser optical disc.

Historical memory projects on human rights issues in Latin America are generally focused on the 1960s–80s. Delegación de Asociaciones Israelitas Argentinas (DAIA) uncovered an extensive array of manuscripts, pamphlets, official documents, and newspaper and magazine articles concerning Argentina's association with Nazi Germany and anti-Semitism. Searchable by keyword, personal name, and organization. System requirements: IBM-compatible PC 486/Windows 3.1 or 95.

2   Bases de datos bibliográficos UNIRED 2000. 2da. edición. Buenos Aires: Ministerio de Economía y Obras y Servicios Públicos, 1999. 1 computer laser optical disc.

Based primarily upon the collections of 96 Argentine government agencies, the 600,000+ citations cover topics in the social sciences, history, architecture, and the environment. Provides various search strategies, including a subject approach. Valuable resource primarily for the official government publications, especially prior to 1945. System requirements: IBM-compatible PC/MS-DOS 6.0/Windows 3.1.

3   Catálogo colectivo de fondo antiguo, siglos XV–XIX, de la Asociación de Bibliotecas Nacionales de Iberoamérica (ABINIA). Madrid: Chadwyck-Healey España, 1995. 1 computer laser optical disc.

Contains bibliographic records from 22 national libraries in Latin America, Spain, and Portugal for monographs published up to and including the year 1900. Allows searching by author, corporate author, title, publisher, place and year of publication, subject, and library. Detailed information on which libraries have copies of a particular monograph can be viewed from the full-record display. Search categories, help messages, and menus can be displayed in English, Spanish, or Portuguese. System requirements: IBM-compatible PC 286+/MS-DOS 3.1+.

4   Centenário 1997: Academia Brasileira de Letras. Rio de Janeiro: Sony Music Entertainment (Brasil), 1997? 1 computer laser optical disc.

A good biographical and bibliographical resource for queries about the members of the Academia Brasileira de Letras. A special section on Machado de Assis provides a bibliography as well as some historical context of the period. System requirements: IBM-compatible PC/Pentium 75+/Windows 3.1 or Macintosh Performa+/System 7.

5   Cien años de cine mexicano, 1896–1996. Mexico: CONACULTA, 1999. 1 computer laser optical disc.

A comprehensive and efficient collection of biographical and bibliographical information with access by subject, director, and actor. Overviews of motion pictures include over 5,000 synopses, with many film clips. Also provides general information on film industry. System requirements: IBM-compatible PC 486+/MS-DOS/Windows 95/soundcard.

6   Colección Clásicos Tavera. Serie I: Iberoamérica en la historia; Vol. 9: Textos clásicos de la historia de Cuba. Madrid: Fundación Histórica Tavera/DIGIBIS, 1999. 1 computer laser optical disc.

A collection of 64 books, government documents, and pamphlets concentrating on 19th- and early-20th-century Cuban history, politics, and society. Included are works by José Antonio Saco and Enrique José Varona. Scanned complete texts are searchable by either terms in the works' title, author, and imprint, or, for more precise searching, by terms appearing in compiler-generated indices for each work. Because the texts are provided as images, the database does not provide keyword searching of the texts themselves. A useful gathering of many works basic to the period. System requirements: IBM-compatible PC/MS-DOS 6.0/Windows 3.1.

7   Foreign Broadcast Information Service Electronic Index. New Canaan, Conn.: NewsBank/Readex. 2 computer laser optical discs. <http://wnc.fedworld.gov/>

Cumulation of the indexes to the FBIS *Daily Reports* (see *HLAS 54:48*); the reports provide translations of texts from the print and broadcast media on an extensive array of subjects. CD-ROM set covers 1977–96 (when FBIS became Worldnews Connection, a web-based resource: http://wnc.fedworld.gov/). The site offers keyword searches and provides basic bibliographic information for locating the full text in the microform set.

8   Handbook of Latin American Studies CD-ROM, v. 2.0: HLAS/CD. vols. 1–55, 1936–1996. Madrid: Fundación MAPFRE América; Washington, D.C.: The Library of Congress, 1999. 1 computer laser optical disc.

Although the web version provides a more up-to-date version of the *Handbook* and allows some differences in searching and printing, for some users the CD-ROM with its 270,000 citations has specific advantages,

not the least of which is speed. Search options enable simple and sophisticated inquiries with a range of limit options. Regardless of access means, *HLAS* remains the best qualitative resource for nearly all phases of research. System requirements: IBM-compatible PC 486/Windows 3.1+. See *HLAS 56:14* for the review of *HLAS/CD, v. 1.0*. For a review of *HLAS Online*, the web version of the *Handbook*, see *HLAS 56:27*.

9   Sintesoft biografías, historia, geografía y cultura de la República Argentina el ateneo. Buenos Aires: Universal Soft S.A., 1997. 1 computer laser optical disc.

This extensive gathering of biographical information on major and many minor Argentine figures provides short entries with enough detail to place the individuals within a broader context. A separate section offers short essays on many historical and cultural topics up to the 1930s. Some entries include cartographic, video, and audio content. System requirements: IBM-compatible PC 486/Windows 95.

DATABASES

10   Datastream International. Waltham, Mass.: Thompson Financial, 199-. <http://www.datastream.com/>

Datastream provides international historical financial information, including equities, bonds, futures, options, commodities, indices, and economic indicators, derived from over 5,000 organizations in 50 countries. Latin American coverage is limited to Argentina, Brazil, Chile, Colombia, Ecuador, Peru, and Venezuela. Coverage of particular topics and dates varies from country to country; generally, coverage for Latin America begins in the 1970s. Information is gathered from national statistical offices, central banks, and other government agencies, as well as from nongovernmental and international organizations, such as the IMF and OECD. Results can be formatted in a variety of ways, such as reports, time series, graphs, or according to the user's preferences. While learning to search the database is tedious and documentation is limited, an excellent guide is available at http://www.princeton.edu/~econlib/ds/. Operates as a web-based subscription with password access. Updated daily.

11 The Economist Intelligence Unit (E.I.U.) Country Reports and Country Profiles. London: Economist Intelligence Unit Limited, 2001. <http://www.eiu.com/>

These reports and profiles (1996–) provide analysis of historical (1960s–), political, societal, infrastructural, and economic trends covering Latin American and Caribbean countries. The profiles are revised and updated annually, while the reports are quarterly; includes analysis of current trends and a two-year forecast. In HTML and PDF formats with full layout and graphics. Also available in CD-ROM and Lotus Notes format.

ART

SPANISH AMERICA
Colonial
General, Middle America, and the Caribbean

BARBARA VON BARGHAHN, *Professor of Art History, George Washington University*

HISTORIC MONUMENTS, many of which have been the subjects of restoration projects in Veracruz, Morelos, Jalisco, the Yucatán, Michoacán, and Oaxaca, have figured prominently in recent scholarly works on Mexican art history (items **25, 28, 29, 34, 35, 36, 42, 46, 47, 49, 53, 54, 59,** and **60**). Such architectural studies, continuing in the tradition of those by Manuel Toussaint and George Kubler, are important to the development of the field. New investigations of secular architecture offer a counterbalance to the considerable number of studies on 18th-century churches and they are indeed a welcome addition to scholarship which has encompassed conservation and archeology (items **30, 41, 50,** and **54**).

Equally significant have been the forays into 16th-century architecture, including the little explored humanist impact upon decorative programs such as the Casa del Deán in Pueblo (item **27**). Such fruitful examinations contribute to our understanding of the melding of ideas that occurred due to the convergence of cultures in the Americas. Most importantly, investigations of religious orders in Mexico help define the advocational interests of a nation. Complementing current work on the social evolution of Mexico are the broader analyses of Franciscan, Oratorian, Dominican, and Jesuit endeavors. Three excellent studies not only describe the structures built under the aegis of dominant orders, but also provide the names of ecclesiastical patrons, their interest in specific advocational images, and even the function of liturgy as it relates to the structural form of notable complexes (items **32, 45,** and **52**).

The bountiful field of Mexican iconography receives attention, but not enough. Many architectural studies provide excellent surveys of a site, but analysis of the symbolism in sacred art is more often than not abbreviated. Technical examination and analysis of style demand a more comprehensive discussion of the imagery and ideas presented in major altarpieces. Citations of exegetical literature, rarely found in current works, would clarify issues regarding the selection of specific subjects. A Carmelite institution, for example, can be thoroughly analyzed regarding the evolution of its architectural components and restoration; the same study can be resplendently illustrated, inclusive of its chapel altarpieces, while failing to make a single mention of Saint Teresa of Ávila, whose writings provide the basis for examining Carmelite pictorial themes. Santiago Sebastián was among the first to recognize the need to emphasize iconography in Mexican art historical research. He is gone, however, and the challenge remains to fill in these theoretical lacunae.

Almost as severe as the lack of books containing "symbolic content" is the dearth of monographs on major Mexican masters. Encyclopedic picture books contribute greatly to the photographic record of Mexican art history and are often visually striking in their grouping of painters and sculptors (items 55 and 43). The information they contain on the stylistic development of masters and their workshops, however, is superficial. Two texts provide important documentary information on colonial portraits (item 33) and the marriages of 16th and 17th century artisans (item 26). Another focuses on the polychrome wooden sculpture in the Museo Nacional del Virreinato de Tepotzlán, and it contains superb material on workshops and the social and religious milieu of colonial sculptors (item 40).

The decorative arts have received attention this biennium, with fine investigations of colonial lacquer (item 48) and works of tortoise shell (item 57). Also worthy of note are two texts on the silver of the Canary Islands (item 22) and Guatemala (item 64).

The issue of synchronism continues to be a subject of scholarly polemic, with a relevant study regarding the impact of precolumbian and colonial Mexico on Spain that should inspire further work on the topic (item 44). Panama also has been the focus of investigation, including an in-depth analysis of its post-17th-century social structure (item 61). A recent study of the architecture of the Caribbean before World War II describes the civic and religious buildings, also including significant information about waves of migrations (item 62). Two outstanding collections of essays merit special attention from researchers: a volume on Cuba edited by Felipe Préstamo y Hernández with articles concerning architecture and urbanization over four centuries (item 63), and the papers of the *1991 International Symposium on Historic Preservation for Puerto Rico and the Caribbean* (item 67).

As usual, the reference items this year encompass a wide variety of topics, each of which contributes to knowledge about Mexico, Central America, and the Caribbean. One of the most outstanding is the bibliography compiled by José Guadalupe Victoria, which lists Mexican colonial publications dating between 1521 and 1990 (item 58). Though illness this year has precluded writing a lengthier commentary, it is obvious from a perusal of the corpus of new books to be annotated for *HLAS 60* that scholarship in the field continues to be most impressive. A note of appreciation is given to Pilar Díaz, a PhD candidate (Bolivian painting) at George Washington Univ. for her collaboration in the preparation of this review.

GENERAL

12 Arquitectura colonial iberoamericana.
Coordinación de Graziano Gasparini. Caracas: Armitano Editores, 1997. 565 p.: bibl., ill. (some col.)

Monumental deluxe anthology lives up to the high standard of the best Armitano publications. With chapters written by leading authorities in the field, the work offers a well-documented and beautifully illustrated overview of the development of architecture and urbanism in the Americas during the Spanish colonial period. A major achievement of contemporary scholarship, it will most likely remain the single most comprehensive treatment of the subject for years to come. Spectacular color photographs complement the texts throughout and together with the architectural plans and archival documents (many of which are reproduced here for the first time) constitute an unparalleled resource. Abundant notes provide additional useful commentaries as well as a guide to other primary and secondary sources. Also includes an extensive bibliography organized by country. [H. Rodríguez-Camilloni]

Bermúdez, Jorge R. Gráfica e identidad nacional. See item 757.

13 **Coloquio Internacional de Historia del Arte, *17th, Zacatecas, Mexico, 1994.*** Arte, historia e identidad en América: visiones comparativas. v. 1–3. México: Univ. Nacional Autónoma de México, Instituto de Investigaciones Estéticas, 1994. 3 v.: bibl., ill. (Estudios de arte y estéticas; 37)

Multivolume work consists of proceedings from the XVII Coloquio Internacional de Historia del Arte. The collected essays represent a good cross-section of the state of the art of current research. For a review of individual paper by Rodríguez-Camilloni, see *HLAS 56:206.* [H. Rodríguez-Camilloni]

14 **Congreso Internacional para la Conservación del Patrimonio Cultural, *1st, Riobamba, Ecuador, 1994.*** Primer Congreso Internacional de Conservación del Patrimonio Cultural. Quito: ICOMOS, 1994. 203 p.: bibl., ill.

Proceedings from the First International Congress for the Conservation of Cultural Heritage organized by the International Council on Monuments and Sites (ICOMOS) in Riobamba, Ecuador, in 1994. Includes transcription of important documents such as the Charter of Venice (1964) and the Norms of Quito (1967). A useful methodology for the structural analysis of historic monuments is presented in the case study "La iglesia de las hermanas agustinas de la Encarnación [de Quito]" by Placencia (p. 93–122). Conservation recommendations in other chapters apply to historic monuments, urban environments, and national parks.[H. Rodríguez-Camilloni]

15 **Encyclopedia of Latin American and Caribbean art.** Edited by Jane Shoaf Turner. New York: Grove's Dictionaries, 1999. 782 p., xl p. of plates: ill. (some col.), maps. (Grove encyclopedias of the arts of the Americas)

This outstanding publication, covering Latin America and the Caribbean, is an essential reference source for English-speaking readers at all levels. By far the most comprehensive book of its type to date. Reliable biographical entries contributed by leading authorities in the field include the most important artists and architects active in the American viceroyalties. Individual biogra-

phies provide an excellent guide for further reading. [H. Rodríguez-Camilloni]

16 **Fane, Diana *et al.*** Converging cultures: art & identity in Spanish America. Edited by Diana Fane. New York: Harry N. Abrams, 1996. 320 p.: bibl., ill. (some col.), index.

Nicely illustrated companion catalog to the exhibition of the same title held at the Brooklyn Museum, N.Y. (March 1-July 14, 1996), Phoenix Art Museum (Dec. 14, 1996-Feb. 23, 1977), and Los Angeles County Museum of Art (March 30-June 8, 1997) explores the evolution of Spanish American viceroyalties of New Spain (Mexico) and Peru through 250 works including paintings, sculptures, costumes, textiles, furniture, domestic and religious objects, as well as illustrated manuscripts. Scholarly essays by various authors examine issues of identity as expressed and reflected in a wide range of objects and images representative of indigenous contributions and European imported culture. Individual entries for the works of art provide basic data on provenance, date, medium, and dimensions. [H. Rodríguez-Camilloni]

17 **Gutiérrez, Ramón and Cristina Esteras.** Territorio y fortificación: Vauban, Fernández de Medrano, Ignacio Sala y Felix Prosperi : influencia en España y América. Traducción de *Veritable manière de bien fortifier de Mr. de Vauban* por Gerard Jalain Badoux y Danielle Steffen. Madrid: Tuero, 1991. 326 p.: bibl., ill., index, maps. (Col. Investigación y crítica; 6)

Important contribution to the history of fortifications in Latin America during the Spanish colonial period. Examines in detail the impact of the designs and theoretical writings of the famous French military engineer Sébastien le Prestre de Vauban (1633–1707) on the formation of the Real Colegio de Ingenieros Militares in Spain and the practice of military engineering throughout Latin America during the 17th-18th centuries. Also considers the work of Spanish military engineers Sebastián Fernández de Medrano (1646–1705) and Ignacio de Sala (d. 1755), who played a decisive role in disseminating Vauban's ideas. Historical maps and illustrations from fortification treatises of the time constitute a rich visual corpus for future studies. [H. Rodríguez-Camilloni]

18 **Hardoy, Jorge Enrique; Margarita Gutman; and Sylvio Mutal.** Impacto de la urbanización en los centros históricos de Iberoamérica: tendencias y perspectivas. Madrid: Editorial MAPFRE, 1992. 536 p.: appendix, bibl., ill., tables. (Col. Ciudades de Iberoamérica; 15. Col. MAPFRE 1492)

Monumental work by leading urban historians represents substantial revision of *Impacto de la urbanización en los centros históricos latinoamericanos* originally published in 1983 by Hardoy and Dos Santos in collaboration with Gutiérrez and Rofman. Text concentrates on three major topics: 1) an adjustment of theoretical and practical approaches to the rehabilitation of historic centers with an emphasis on policy; 2) the identification of the main threats that historic centers, towns, and cities will face in the future; and 3) the presentation of selected initiatives carried out during the last decade. Well documented with an abundance of footnotes, an appendix of statistical tables, illustrations, and exhaustive bibliography. [H. Rodríguez-Camilloni]

19 **Pintura, escultura y artes útiles en Iberoamérica, 1500–1825.** Coordinación de Ramón Gutiérrez. Madrid: Cátedra, 1995. 444 p.: bibl., ill., indexes. (Manuales arte Cátedra)

Encyclopedic volume with contributions by leading scholars in the field offers a reliable general survey of Latin American colonial painting, sculpture, and the decorative arts. Five introductory chapters discuss socioeconomic background that conditioned artistic production in American colonies, and provide a conceptual framework for the studies that follow. In the second, third, and fourth sections, chapters discuss development of colonial painting, sculpture, and decorative arts, respectively, by country or region. Even though the 402 b/w photographs are not integrated with the texts, they represent a valuable visual reference. Comprehensive bibliography divided by chapters is an indispensable source. [H. Rodríguez-Camilloni]

20 **Platería iberoamericana: Fundación Santillana, junio-septiembre 1993.** Madrid: Fundación Santillana, 1993. 116 p.: bibl., ill. (some col.), index.

Handsome companion catalog to the exhibition with the same title held at the Fundación Santillana (Madrid, 1993). Brief, informative text traces history of silver mining and silver-smithing in viceregal Mexico and Peru, with special reference to Cerro de Potosí in Bolivia. The catalog itself, divided into two sections—"platería religiosa" and "platería civil"—describes each of the silver works with basic information concerning their provenance, dimensions, and present location. Works from public and private collections in Peru, Argentina, Uruguay, Colombia, and Bolivia are well represented. Several fine quality color photographs permit a good appreciation of the works. Includes a useful glossary and bibliography by Isabel Ruiz de Elvira Serra. [H. Rodríguez-Camilloni]

21 **Rípodas Ardanaz, Daisy.** Iconografía de la justicia en hispanoamérica colonial. (*Rev. Hist. Derecho*, 22, 1994, p. 319–330, ill.)

Well-illustrated iconographic study examines the representations of the emblem of Justice in the Spanish American colonies derived from European printed sources such as the treatises by Vicenzo Cartari (1556), Cesare Ripa (1593), and Jean Baudoin (1636). As a powerful reminder of the authority invested upon viceregal heads of states and church, images of Justice are shown to have been prominently displayed on public monuments such as catafalques erected in the Cathedral of Lima on the occasion of the deaths of King Philip IV (1966) and the Archbishop don Diego Antonio de Parada (1781). For historian's comment, see item 957. [H. Rodríguez-Camilloni]

22 **Rodríguez, Gloria.** La platería americana en la isla de La Palma. Spain: Servicio de Publicaciones, Caja General de Ahorros de Canarias, 1994? 175 p.: bibl., ill. (some col.). (Servicio de Publicaciones de la Caja General de Ahorros de Canarias; no. 174. Arte; 18)

Descriptive catalog of ecclesiastical silver work of colonial America from various collections in the Canary Islands. The author provides valuable biographical information on donors and their professional activity. Documents the chronology of the objects, their centers of origin, and the circumstances of their arrival in Spain.

23 **Sólo angeles: iconografía angélica en el arte colonial iberoamericano, noviembre-diciembre 1995.** Buenos Aires:

Museo de Arte Hispanoamericano Isaac Fernández Blanco, 1995. 32 p.: col. ill.

Small exhibition catalog devoted to angels as represented in South American colonial art, including some fine examples of the famous *ángeles arcabucareos* (archangels with muskets) from the Cuzco School. The introductory essay by Horacio Botalla and Marta Sánchez is a good overview of the different iconographic themes and their sources. The color reproductions of paintings, sculptures, and silverworks from public and private collections are mainly useful as visual references and should be studied together with Mujica Pinilla's earlier, more detailed work on the subject. See also *HLAS 56:198*. [H. Rodríguez-Camilloni]

24 **Viñuales, Graciela María et al.** Iberoamérica, siglos XVI-XVIII: tradiciones, utopías y novedad cristiana. 1. ed. española. Madrid: Ediciones Encuentro, 1992. 306 p.: bibl., ill. (some col.). (Pueblos y culturas)

Splendid multiauthored volume is an important addition to Ediciones Encuentro of the Biblioteca Quinto Centenario. Fourteen erudite chapters offer comparative visions of the development of architecture and urbanism in the Spanish and Portuguese American colonies, emphasizing the viceroyalties of Mexico and Peru. Selected studies reflecting a variety of methodological approaches to the subject include "Nuevos espacios para el culto" by Viñuales, "El convento urbano" by Gutiérrez and Maeder, and "Santuarios de peregrinación" by Nicolini. Excellent visual material consisting of color plates, b/w photographs, and architectural drawings accompanies the texts. Includes a comprehensive bibliography arranged by chapter. [H. Rodríguez-Camilloni]

MEXICO

25 **Adopte una Obra de Arte, 1992–1994.** Textos de Cristina Artigas de Latapí. México: s.n., 1994. 142 p.: col. ill.

Results of the restoration projects carried out between 1992–94 under the auspices of the program "Adopt a Work of Art." Consists of a catalog, organized by region, of more than 100 paintings (the majority of projects) and architectural monuments restored in Jalisco, Morelos, the Yucatán, Coahuila, Michoacán, Veracruz, and Oaxaca. Lists the individuals who adopted the work

and contains good color photographs, many of which show prerestoration condition.

26 **Archivo General de la Nación (Mexico).** Catálogos de documentos de arte en el Archivo General de la Nación, México. Ramo, matrimonios, tercera parte. México: Univ. Nacional Autónoma de México, Instituto de Investigaciones Estéticas, 1995. 1 v. (Catálogos de documentos de arte; 18.)

The third and final volume of the Catálogos de documentos de arte contains matrimonial testimonies of individuals whose profession is related to Mexican art. Contains ca. 1500 documents dated principally between the 17th-18th centuries. Professions include painters, carpenters, furniture makers, gilders, metal workers, silversmiths, weavers, textile workers, and masons. Includes name and profession indices.

27 **Arellano, Alfonso.** La Casa del Deán: un ejemplo de pintura mural civil del siglo XVI en Puebla. México: Univ. Autónoma de México, 1996. 185 p.: bibl., ill. (some col.). (Colección de arte; 48)

An excellent documentary study with color photographs of the murals in the Casa del Deán, which represent a series of sibyls and triumphal carts. Provides a formal analysis and iconographic interpretation of the imagery. A plan of the house indicates the location of each object.

28 **Arquitectura en el Valle de San Luis Potosí: cuatrocientos años.** San Luis Potosí, Mexico: Multiva Grupo Financiero: Fondo Cultural Bancen, 1992. 131 p.: bibl., ill.

Study by a group of young architects from San Luis de Potosí concerned with the artistic patrimony of their city. Brief but well-researched commentaries describe the development of Potosí architecture from its 16th-century origins to the present day. Text is accompanied by contemporary color photographs, historical illustrations, and a few early photographs.

29 **Artigas H., Juan B.** Metztitlán, Mexico: arquitectura del siglo XVI. México: Univ. Nacional Autónoma de México, 1996. 188 p.: bibl., ill. (some col.), maps.

Excellent and well-documented account of 16th-century architecture in Metztitlán, Hidalgo, written by a professional architect and accomplished scholar. Describes

Metztitlán's geographic history and the technical construction and development of its architecture. Also provides a contemporary analysis. Contains thorough photographic documentation, colonial maps, contemporary ground plans and elevations of churches, as well as renderings of architectural details and mural decorations.

30 Ayala Alonso, Enrique. La casa de la ciudad de México: evolución y transformaciones. México: Consejo Nacional para la Cultura y las Artes, 1996. 275 p.: bibl., ill.

This study goes beyond a formal description and esthetic analysis of house design in Mexico to offer an interpretation based on the complex network of economic, social, and cultural relations. Begins with an analysis of the indigenous home and lifestyle and continues into postrevolutionary, modern, and contemporary periods of historic transition, during which a new conception of urban space developed offering greater possibilities for individual expression. Contains many b/w plates of colonial city plans, 19th-century plans and photographs, and 20th-century photographs up to the 1980s.

31 Azar, Héctor. San Angel, entre las horas detenido. México: Miguel Angel Porrúa, Grupo Editorial, 1996. 225 p.: bibl., ill. (some col.).

Poetic account of the past and present history of San Angel. Color photographs of contemporary tourist markets and details of cacti mix with historic illustrations and images of colonial works of art and architecture. Aims to entice the senses with past and present images of lush gardens and succulent tropical fruits.

32 Carlos Casas, Bernardo. Semblanza historica de la parroquia de Tlaltenango: 1544–1991, 447 aniversario de ser carato. Guadalajara: Dirección de Publicaciones de la Univ. de Guadalajara, 1991. 77 p.: bibl., ill.

Evangelical guide, geographical and historical account, and description of Franciscan endeavors in Tlaltenango. Mentions the founding of the Virgin of the Rosary and the transfer and coronation of the Virgin of Guadalupe. Lists priests who served in Tlaltenango since 1600. Concludes with statements summarizing recent changes and the current issues to be addressed in the diocese.

33 Ciancas, María Ester and **Bárbara Meyer.** La pintura de retrato colonial, siglos XVI-XVIII. México: Instituto Nacional de Antropología e Historia: Museo Nacional de Historia, 1994. 243 p.: bibl., ill., indexes. (Colección Catálogos)

Catalog of the portraits in the National History Museum, which is the most important collection of colonial portraits in Mexico. A small b/w illustration of each work is accompanied by explanatory text and, in some cases, the biographical dates of the individuals portrayed. Provides date, material, size, and provenance. Also contains a biographical list of artists and illustrations of their signatures in the collection, as well as an index of colonial painters from the 16th-18th centuries and some from the 19th-20th centuries.

34 Conservación del patrimonio monumental: quince años de experiencias: conclusiones de los simposios del Comité Mexicano del ICOMOS, 1987–1994. México: Instituto Nacional de Antropología e Historia, 1996. 111 p. (Serie Manuales)

Conclusions of the symposia held by the Mexican Committee of the International Council on Monuments and Sites (ICOMOS), which took place from 1978–94. Under discussion were Querétaro, Guanajuato, Morelia, La Trinidad, Tepotzlán, Cuernavaca, Puebla, Mérida, and Zacatecas, among others.

35 Echame una manita!: Centro Histórico 1991–1994. México: Fideicomiso del Centro Histórico de la Ciudad de México, 1994. 126 p.: col. ill.

Collaborative survey records the restoration processes of the city's colonial, 19th- and 20th-century monuments. Contains information on the number of buildings in Mexico City classified and slated to be classified as monuments, percentages of financial contributions, and types of restoration projects. Also examines the participation of city residents in restoration projects and the impacat of the projects on them. Chapters discuss particular sections of the city, the esthetic of urban harmony, the improvement of the public market, and the problems of vehicular traffic. Good color photographs, some full-page.

36 Garrido Cardona, Martha Lis. Monumentos coloniales religiosos del Istmo de Tehuantepec. México: Instituto Nacional de Antropología e Historia, 1995. 172 p.: bibl., ill., maps. (Serie Monumentos históricos)

Catalog of 31 colonial churches in the 22 population centers of the Tehuantepec and Juchitán districts. The introduction provides geographical and historical background, as well as a summary of the social and political culture of the area. The catalog consists of a brief historical account of each church, a b/w photograph, physical description, and information on the interior pictorial works.

37 González Gamio, Angeles. El patrimonio rescatado. México: Depto. del Distrito Federal, 1993. 220 p.: col. ill.

The restoration and remodeling of several important buildings in the historic center of Mexico City is part of a program oriented towards using monuments as modern working environments: banks, artistic spaces, commercial establishments, conference centers, or homes. Magazine-style color photographs show before-and-after states of the restoration projects. Some of the projects examined are the Antiguo Colegio Real de Minas, which today is the Association of Engineers; the Antiguo Colegio de San Ildefonso, now the University Museum; and an 18th-century home, now the renowned Café Tacuba.

38 Gruzinski, Serge. El águila y la sibila: frescos indios de México. Fotografías de Gilles Mermet. Barcelona: M. Moleiro Editor, 1994. 196 p.: bibl., ill. (chiefly col.).

Fascinating study about the frescos executed in Mexico by indigenous artists during Spain's domination, in particular those at Actopan, Ixmiquilpan, Texamachalco, and Puebla. Includes an additional section on Mexican convents. Text is beautifully complemented by excellent photographs. Examines the frescos as the meeting ground of different "cosmovisions." Within them, European and Amerindian mentalities collide in subtle visual metaphors of complex sensibility, often with fascinating results. [F. Angel]

39 La magia del grabado: guía de la exposición; colecciones de la antigua Academia de San Carlos. México: Univ. Nacional de México, 1994. 30 p.: ill. (some col.).

Interesting brochure about the 1994 exhibition that focused on the development of engraving and its practice in Mexico at the Academy of San Carlos, presented at the Colegio of San Idelfonso in Mexico. The exhibit had a didactic character, and the publication reflects this throughout, explaining chemical and general workshop procedures of the profession. [F. Angel]

40 Maquívar, María del Consuelo. El imaginero novohispano y su obra: las esculturas de Tepotzotlán. México: Instituto Nacional de Antropología e Historia, 1995. 174 p., 21 leaves of plates: bibl., ill. (some col.). (Colección Obra diversa)

Study of the polychrome wooden sculpture in the collection of the Museo Nacional del Virreinato de Tepotzlán. Describes the development and organization of sculpture workshops, rules and regulations for sculptors, and influences upon imagery. Also provides an analysis of wood and pigment. Examines the social, artistic, and religious life of colonial sculptors.

41 Mentz, Brígida von *et al.* Haciendas de Morelos. México: Instituto de Cultura de Morelos: Consejo Nacional para la Cultura y las Artes, 1997. 412 p.: bibl., ill. (some col.).

Comprehensive study by a group of scholars explores the development, expansion, and economic impact of haciendas in the state of Morelos, especially those connected to the sugar industry. Illustrated with contemporary color photographs, 19th- and early-20th-century photographs, and maps. Also includes much archival data.

Mínguez, Víctor. Los reyes distantes: imágenes del poder en el México virreinal. See item **1173.**

42 Morelia: patrimonio cultural de la humanidad. Recopilación de Silvia María Concepción Figueroa Zamudio. México: Univ. Michoacana de San Nicolás de Hidalgo: Gobierno del Estado de Michoacán: Ayuntamiento de Morelia, 1995. 317 p.: bibl., ill. (some col.).

Collective endeavor by scholars from the region, this study captures the essence of this prestigious colonial city. Well-documented chapters lavishly illustrated with color photographs and some 19th- and early-20th-century photographs and prints reveal an elegant and refined ensemble of civic and religious architecture in perfect harmony with its surrounding plazas and gardens. Colonial paintings of religious processions and portraits of ecclesiastical figures reveal Morelia's history. In the late-19th-century paintings by Mariano de Jesus, the city's plazas, churches, and church interiors are brought to life by images of strolling couples, street vendors, and women washing laundry in city fountains. The heroes of the Independence are presented with driving force in the 20th-century murals by Alfredo Zalce.

43 Museo Nacional del Virreinato (Mexico). Pintura novohispana: Museo Nacional del Virreinato, Tepotzotlán. t. 3, Siglos XVII-XX, segunda parte. Tepotzotlán, Mexico: Asociación de Amigos del Museo Nacional del Virreinato, 1996. 1 v.: bibl., ill. (some col.).

Third and final volume of a catalog of the paintings in the National Museum of the Viceregal period. Over 300 works are represented by excellent color photographs, with date, size, state of conservation, and transcription of texts. Volume is divided into images of saints, female portraits, male portraits, and miscellaneous works that include altar frontals, coats of arms, and maps. For review of t. 1, see *HLAS 54:101*. For review of t. 2, see *HLAS 56:114*.

44 Nafarrate Mexía, Enrique. Influencia de la arquitectura de México en la de España. Guadalajara, Mexico: Editorial Conexión Gráfica, 1996. 123 p.: bibl., ill., maps.

A brief but thought-provoking study of the reverse influence of Mexican architecture on that of Spain's during the colonial era. For example, the author says that the characteristic organization of prehispanic religious centers around large plazas, as seen at Palenque, Teotihuacan, and Chichenitza, was transferred first to Mexican and then to Spanish architecture. Also identifies Americanized architectural elements and decorative motifs in buildings in Murcia, Olivia, and in the Canary Islands. Contains a few photographs with drawings of mostly architectural details.

45 El oratorio filipense en Guanajuato, 200 años: y los precursores jesuitas. Recopilación de José Luis F. Díaz Ramírez. Guanajuato, Mexico: Gobierno del Estado de Guanajuato, 1994. 269 p.: bibl., ill. (some col.).

Includes a brief history of the church of La Compañia, its celebrations, and its 1993 restoration. The history of San Filipo Neri consists of extensive documentary accounts of the church's foundation, administration, and current activity. Devotes a section to San Filipo Neri's art museum, facsimile reproductions of 18th-century decrees, testimonies, church inventories, and other documents. Illustrated with large color photographs.

46 Ortiz Lanz, José Enrique. Piedras ante el mar: las fortificaciones de Campeche. México: Gobierno del Estado de Campeche: Consejo Nacional para la Cultura y las Artes, 1996. 177 p.: bibl., ill. (Biblioteca básica del sureste)

Historical survey of the fortifications of Campeche which have defined and given character to the city since its founding in 1540. Analyzes the political and economic factors that affected their transformation. Contains a bibliography, but no footnotes. Includes some photographs.

47 Palacios de gobierno en México. Dirección y coordinación general de Carmen Valles Septién. México: CVS, 1996. 179 p.: bibl., col. ill.

Vol. II completes the survey of the Palaces of Government in Mexico with its studies of Aguascalientes, Campeche, Chihuahua, Durango, Guanajuato, Jalisco, Chiapas, Quintana Roo, Baja California, and others. Intended for general public, this collective study by several scholars of Mexican architecture combines historical descriptions, commentaries, and color images of exteriors and interiors.

48 Pérez Carrillo, Sonia. La laca mexicana: desarrollo de un oficio artesanal en el Virreinato de la Nueva España durante el siglo XVIII. Madrid: Alianza Editorial: Ministerio de Cultura, Dirección General de Cooperación Cultural, 1990. 223 p.: bibl., ill. (some col.).

Survey and catalog of Mexican laquer works. Describes the materials and procedures used in laquer work, its origin and development in Mexico, and known specialists in colonial workshops. Abundant color photographs and details.

49 Proyecto Santo Domingo: memoria de la primera etapa. Oaxaca de Juárez, Mexico: Secretaría de Desarrollo Turístico del Estado de Oaxaca, 1995. 139 p.: col. ill.

The first part of this work consists of several interviews in which state government officials discuss the restoration of the Santo Domingo complex. The second part consists of a letter to King Philip II by the Bishop of Oaxaca, Fray Bernardo de Albuquerque, about the "problem" of the indigenous population, along with other letters.

50 Rubio Mañé, Jorge Ignacio. La casa de Montejo en Mérida de Yucatán. Mexico: Banco Nacional de México, 1995. 146 p.: ill. (some col.).

Well-documented historical study of the illustrious 16th-century mansion of Don Francisco de Montejo, the founder of the old capital of the Yucatán. Only the magnificent plateresque façade remains, which stands as the most splendid and valuable example of colonial civic architecture today. Originally published in 1941, this new edition contains a study by Michael Toussaint that examines the artistic importance of the Casa de Montejo in relation to similar works of colonial civic architecture in Mexico.

51 Ruiz Gomar, Rogelio *et al.* Un pintor manierista: Baltasar de Echave Ibía. Edición y prólogo de Francisco Vidargas. México: Textos Dispersos Ediciones, 1995. 69 p.: bibl., ill. (Historia del arte)

In this valuable study, Rogelio Ruiz Gomar, Gibson Danes, and Elisa Vargas Lugo explore the life and work of the mannerist Mexican painter, Baltasar de Echave. In addition, Nelly Sigaut contributes an essay on the brother of Baltasar, Manuel de Echave. One hopes that this much needed contribution to the study of 17th-century Spanish American artists will inspire further work in this area. [F. Angel]

52 Santiago Silva, José de. Atotonilco. México: Ediciones la Rana: Instituto de la Cultura del Estado de Guanajuato, 1996. 313 p.: bibl., facsims., ill. (some col.), indexes.

Elaboration of a 1985 study retraces history of the Church of Jesús Nazareno and development of its intricate pictorial plan of Renaissance emblematic iconography, Golden Age mysticism, and indigenous sensitivity. Excellent photographic documentation of the rich mural decoration, most of which was done by the colonial mestizo artist Miguel Antonio Martínez de Pocasangre. Contains plans of the church and surrounding building compound, and a diagram locating the scenes represented in the Calvary chapel.

53 Suárez Aguilar, Vicente and Heber Ojeda Mas. Arqueología histórica en la ciudad de Campeche. Campeche, Mexico: Univ. Autónoma de Campeche: SEP, FOMES, 1996. 207 p.: bibl., ill., maps.

Study of the archeological investigation of three 19th-century architectural constructions in the city of Campeche: the portals of San Francisco Plaza, the former public prison of Campeche, and a subterranean vault.

54 Terán Bonilla, José Antonio. La construcción de las haciendas de Tlaxcala. México: Instituto Nacional de Antropología e Historia, 1996. 396 p.: bibl., ill. (1 folded), maps. (Colección científica; 311)

Provides a deeper understanding of the use and structural evolution of haciendas in Tlaxcala, viewing them as architectural entities directly linked to economic production. A technical study with definitions of terms and diagrams illustrating the construction of roofs and domes and the types of tools used.

55 Tovar de Teresa, Guillermo. Repertorio de artistas en México: artes plásticas y decorativas. v. 1, A-F. México: Grupo Financiero Bancomer, 1995. 1 v.: bibl., ill. (some col.).

A selection of highlights of Mexico's artistic heritage from the 16th-20th century is illustrated by beautiful color plates in this alphabetically arranged catalog of Mexican painters, architects, photographers, and decorative arts. Personal statements or erudite observations about the artists precede biographical summaries. With a prologue by Octavio Paz and texts by accomplished academics, this survey, the first in a set of three volumes, is a visual and intellectual celebration of Mexico's continuing artistic achievements. For comment on vol. 2, see item **56.**

56 **Tovar de Teresa, Guillermo.** Repertorio de artistas en México: artes plásticas y decorativas. v. 2, G-O. México: Grupo
Financiero Bancomer, 1996. 1 v.: bibl., ill.
(some col.).

According to the opening statement,
these volumes, sponsored by Grupo Financiero Bancomer, reunite artists relevant
to the development and evolution of the
decorative and plastic arts (also architecture) in Mexico since colonial times. Beautifully printed with excellent color reproductions. For comment on vol. 1, see item 55.
[F. Angel]

57 **Trabajos mexicanos de carey: siglos
XVII y XVIII.** México: La Cartuja,
1996. 53 p.: bibl., col. ill. (Ensayos sobre artes
decorativas; 1)

Color catalog with brief descriptions
of decorative objects made with tortoise
shell. An oriental influence is characteristic
of these boxes and chests, which were produced with much popularity during the
Baroque period. Includes introductory essay
by José Ignacio Aldama González with references.

58 **Victoria, José Guadalupe.** Una bibliografía de arte novohispano. Colaboración de Pedro Angeles Jiménez, Norma Fernández Quintero y María Teresa Velasco de
Espinosa. México: Univ. Nacional Autónoma
de México: Instituto de Investigaciones Estéticas, 1995. 364 p.: bibl., indexes. (Apoyo a
la docencia; 2)

Comprehensive and systematic bibliography of Mexican colonial art publications
and documents from 1520–1990 compiled by
a distinguished and accomplished academic.
Goes beyond previous bibliographies of Mexican colonial art in scope and professionalism, and includes themes largely ignored until now. Categories include architecture,
painting, sculpture, industrial and decorative
arts, engraving, theory and criticism, conservation and restoration, history of cities and
their monuments, catalogs and exhibitions,
maps, and guides.

59 **Yanez Díaz, Gonzalo.** Desarrollo urbano virreinal en la región Puebla-
Tlaxcala. Puebla, Mexico: División de Estudios de Posgrado e Investigación de la
Facultad de Arquitectura, Univ. Nacional
Autónoma de México, 1994. 225 p.: appendices, bibl., ill. (some col.), index.

Well-defined study of urban architectural development demonstrates the union
of indigenous and Spanish cultures in the
Puebla and Tlaxcala regions. Illustrates how
conquistadors and colonizers adopted
scheme of prehispanic regional relations.
Chapters are oddly preceded by contemporary picturesque watercolors of colonial
churches. Appendices contain transcriptions
of several colonial documents from the General Archive of the State of Tlaxcala and
color aerial views of churches and their
plazas.

60 **Yanez Díaz, Gonzalo** *et al.* Revita-
lización de centros históricos. Durango, Mexico: Presidencia Municipal de Durango: Instituto Nacional de Antropología e
Historia, 1994. 81 p.: bibl. (El municipio del
siglo XXI. Serie editorial)

Originates from a symposium on this
theme initiated to create a base of analysis
of the past and present situation of the cultural patrimony of the city of Durango. This
is the first volume of articles in a series.
Some of the topics addressed in the brief essays are the promotion of colonial culture,
anthropology and revitalization, the city in
the environment of modern culture, social
implications of revitalization, and the pros-
pect of urban archeology of Durango's historic center.

CENTRAL AMERICA AND
THE CARIBBEAN

Arellano, Jorge Eduardo. Historia de la pintura nicaragüense. See item 213.

61 **Castillero Calvo, Alfredo.** Arquitectura, urbanismo y sociedad: la
vivienda colonial en Panamá—historia de un
sueño. Panamá: Biblioteca Cultural Shell,
1994. 392 p.: bibl., graphs, ill., tables.

Panama in the late-17th century was
essentially an elitist society. This comprehensive study examines that society from
the perspective of the quality of the material
culture of home environments, drawing comparisons to European cosmopolitan centers.
Sees the home and its surrounding urban
environment as an expression of social ambition. Contains some reproductions of colonial city plans, several 19th-century photographs and illustrations, inventories, reconstructions of dwellings, archeological
remains, and graphs and tables.

62 Crain, Edward E. Historic architecture in the Caribbean Islands. Gainesville: Univ. Press of Florida, 1994. 265 p.: bibl., ill. (some col.), index.

Well-illustrated general survey describes the historic architecture of the area constructed before WWII. Organizes architectural examples according to building types: residences, military facilities, public and institutional buildings, and religious buildings. Short introductory chapters and brief descriptions take into consideration influential factors such as geography, climate, early Amerindian occupation, European and African immigration, emancipation, and immigration from Asia.

63 Cuba: arquitectura y urbanismo. Recopilación de Felipe J. Préstamo y Hernández. Introducción por Marcos Antonio Ramos. Miami, Fla.: Ediciones Universal, 1995. 476 p.: bibl., ill., maps. (Colección Arte)

Edited by Préstamo y Hernández, an architectural historian at the Univ. of Miami who began his career at the Univ. of La Habana, this volume is composed of a series of articles written by Cuban architects, art critics, engineers, and historians during the first half of the 20th century. This historical analysis examines the cultural and artistic processes that shaped the development of Cuban architecture and urban planning for more than four centuries. Generously illustrated with 19th- and 20th-century photographs and maps of plazas, forts, monuments, and fountains.

64 Esteras Martín, Cristina. La platería en el reino de Guatemala, siglos XVI-XIX. Guatemala: Fundación Albergue Hermano Pedro, 1994. 347 p.: bibl., ill. (some col.).

Catalog of about 150 pieces of ecclesiastical silver work from the kingdom of Guatemala which are now in various collections in Guatemala and elsewhere. Contains jewel-studded chalices, elaborately worked crucifixes, silver-tooled cups, crowns, lecturns, and other ecclesiastical objects. Introduction provides a concise historical chronology and information on silver workers. Catalog entries of the objects contain descriptions and information on their makers.

Fonk, Hans. Curaçao: architectuur en stij = Curaçao: architectural style. See item **246.**

65 Gaitán, Héctor. Centro histórico de la ciudad de Guatemala. Guatemala: Ediciones Artemis-Edinter, 1995. 132 p.: bibl., ill. (Historia)

Written for a general audience, the author narrates the history, development, and present condition of churches, civic architecture, and historic homes in Guatemala City.

66 Gutiérrez, Samuel A. Historia y vicisitudes de un cabildo: del primer cabildo de tierra firme al palacio municipal republicano. Panamá: Academia Panameña de la Historia, 1993. 48 p.: bibl., ill., maps.

Brief study of the establishment of city and town councils in the New World, the earliest being in Panamá in 1503. Also contains an analysis of the neoclassical Municipal Palace and a short description of parallels between the town council of Panamá and those of the Rio de la Plata region. Contains some historical photographs, engravings, and plans.

67 International Symposium on Historic Preservation for Puerto Rico and the Caribbean, 2nd, San Juan, Puerto Rico, 1991. Conferencias. Recopilación por Milagros Flores Román. San Juan: Servicio Nacional de Parques, 1991. 238 p.: bibl., ill.

Series of papers presented as part of the quincentenary celebration of the discovery of the Americas. Some of the topics addressed are the work of Antonio Gaudí in the world patrimony of UNESCO, the collection of the Art Museum of Ponce, the historic preservation of Puerto Rico, Cuban colonial fortifications, the reconstruction of lighthouses in Puerto Rico, and the Military Architecture Archive in San Juan.

68 Medendorp, Clazien. Gerrit Schouten, 1779–1839: botanische tekeningen en diorama's uit Suriname = Gerrit Schouten, 1779–1839: botanical drawings and dioramas from Surinam. Amsterdam: Koninklijk Instituut voor de Tropen; Paramaibo: Stichting Surinaams Museum, 1999. 160 p.: ill. (many col.).

Attractive exhibition catalog indexes all known drawings and dioramas by Surinamese artist Gerrit Schouten. First provides biographical information on Schouten and discusses his art work in relation to the work of other artists then living in Suriname (including Maria S. Merian). Then describes his dioramas of Amerindian camps, slave dances, and plantations, etc. Volume also includes work by Schouten's contemporary, John Henri Lance. [R. Hoefte]

69 Santo Domingo y sus monumentos coloniales. Recopilación de Luis Scheker Ortíz; textos de Salomé Frías; fo-

tografías de Freddy Pérez; traducción de Larissa Veloz = Santo Domingo and its colonial monuments. Santo Domingo: Ediciones Pasado, 1992. 127 p.: col. ill., maps.

Survey text, in both English and Spanish, written for the general reader. Contains passable photographs.

South America

HUMBERTO RODRÍGUEZ-CAMILLONI, *Professor and Director, Henry H. Wiss Center for Theory and History of Art and Architecture, College of Architecture and Urban Studies, Virginia Polytechnic Institute and State University*

THE LAST BIENNIUM witnessed the passing away of one of the great Latin Americanist scholars of all times, Dr. George Alexander Kubler, Sterling Professor Emeritus of the History of Art at Yale University, on Oct. 3, 1996. Many of Kubler's pioneer works, including *The Religious Architecture of New Mexico in the Colonial Period and Since the American Occupation* (1940; see *HLAS 06:746*), *Mexican Architecture of the Sixteenth Century* (1948; see *HLAS 14:1723*), and *Art and Architecture in Spain and Portugal and their American Dominions, 1500–1800* with Martin Soria (l959; see *HLAS 23:1421*), established a solid foundation for future scholarship in the field of Spanish colonial art, which Kubler was largely responsible for legitimizing in the US. Accordingly, many of the items reviewed in this and previous volumes of *HLAS* are a tribute to his legacy. It is therefore with the deepest respect and appreciation that this section is dedicated to him.

Both quantitatively and qualitatively, the items reviewed here represent important advances of scholarship in the field. Well-documented monographs with high-quality illustrations, state-of-the-art museum exhibitions, and excellent critical catalogs allow an appreciation and better understanding of the rich Spanish colonial artistic and architectural heritage of the Americas. More rigorous research and a wider range of methods of analysis and interpretation reflect the formal academic training of a new generation of scholars. While new factual data continues to accumulate, comparative visions clarify the unique contributions of individuals and societal groups across space and time.

Encyclopedic volumes with contributions by teams of leading scholars, such as *Pintura, escultura y artes útiles en Iberoamérica, 1500–1825* (item **19**) and *Encyclopedia of Latin American & Caribbean art* (item **15**), provide necessary information biographical information for artists and architects active in the Spanish viceroyalties, among other topics. Special mention must be made of Graziano Gasparini et al., *Arquitectura colonial iberoamericana*, a monumental deluxe anthology that is a triumph of contemporary scholarship (item **12**). By far the most ambitious publication on the subject in recent years, the work is an outstanding contribution to the artistic literature of Spanish and Portuguese America.

Studies devoted to architecture and urbanism account for the largest number of titles, while others deal with painting, sculpture, and the decorative arts. Expanding on the earlier work by Alcides Parejas Moreno and Virgilio Suárez Salas' *Chiquitos: historia de una utopía* (1992; see *HLAS 54:2442*), *Las misiones jesuíti-*

cas de Chiquitos, edited by Pedro Querejazu, is an exceptional publication containing a wealth of documentation on extant and lost Jesuit mission churches in the province of Chiquitos, today's department of Santa Cruz, Bolivia (item **104**). Not only do fine quality color plates document the art and architecture of these missions churches today, but the inclusion of the complete Photographic Archive of Chiquitos consisting of 467 b/w historic photographs makes it an invaluable resource for scholars.

German Téllez Castañeda's *La arquitectura colonial de Santa Cruz de Mompox* is a revelation of a little-known but significant Spanish colonial town on the Magdalena river in Colombia (item **88**). The main text, complemented with stunning color plates, captures the distinctive character of the historic religious and secular buildings of the town, constituting an impressive architectural corpus comparable to other Caribbean coastal cities like Cartagena, Colombia, and Coro, Venezuela. Equally important in this context is Graziano Gasparini's *Coro: patrimonio mundial,* celebrating the 1993 inclusion of the city in UNESCO's World Heritage List (item **84**). Incorporating new material from recent research, this publication contributes a wealth of visual and documentary material that complements the earlier book by the same author, *La arquitectura colonial de Coro* (1961; see *HLAS 24:1698*).

Military and rural architecture are well represented by Ramón Gutiérrez and Cristina Esteras' *Territorio y fortificación: Vauban, Fernández de Medrano, Ignacio Salas y Félix Prósperi: influencia en España y América* (item **17**) and Benjamín Barney and Francisco Ramírez's *La arquitectura de las casas de hacienda en el Valle del Alto Cauca* (item **81**). The first title examines in detail the impact of the design and theoretical writings of the famous French military engineer Sébastien le Prestre de Vauban (1633–1707) on the formation of the Real Colegio de Ingenieros Militares in Spain and the practice of military engineering throughout Latin America during the 17th and 18th centuries. In addition to the critical study by the authors, the book includes a valuable transcription of four major documentary sources by Du Fay (1702), Fernández de Medrano (1699), Sala (1743), and Prósperi (1744), making them available together for the first time. The second title fills a void in the artistic literature of colonial Spanish South America by focusing attention on the rarely discussed topic of rural architecture, marking the culmination of a survey of hacienda houses in the Valley of Alto Cauca, Colombia, and providing an architectural history and much needed complement to socioeconomic research on the subject.

Exemplary among the titles devoted to painting and sculpture is *Arte y fe: colección artística agustina Colombia* by Rodolfo Vallín Magaña et al., documenting the impressive restoration of religious art undertaken by the Taller de Restauración de San Agustín in Bogota (item **80**). The critical catalog contains 541 entries of important works executed during the Spanish colonial period and later under the patronage of the Augustinian order.

The magnificent collection of colored drawings in *Trujillo del Perú a fines del siglo XVIII* deserves separate commentary (item **101**). Now complete, the set of nine volumes reproducing in facsimile the colored drawings commissioned by Bishop Martínez de Compañón during his residence in Trujillo, Peru, from 1779–89, makes available a unique visual encyclopedia of far-reaching importance for disciplines beyond art and architectural history. The complementary study by Pablo Macera, Arturo Jiménez Borja, and Irma Franke, *Trujillo del Perú: Baltazar Martínez Compañón; acuarelas; siglo XVIII,* offers the best scholarly research of these drawings to date (item **98**).

Even though studies on decorative arts represent the smallest number of works reviewed here, there is increasing interest in research in this area. In particular, colonial silverwork has been the subject of important publications in Peru and Ecuador in recent years. For example, thanks to the archival research of Jesús Paniagua Pérez and his colleagues in Quito (items **106, 107,** and **108**), much more is now known about the activities of the guild of silversmiths in that city and elsewhere in Ecuador during the 17th and 18th centuries. At the same time, Carlos F. Duarte's *Mobiliario y decoración interior durante el período hispánico venezolano* offers the most comprehensive history of furniture and decorative arts in Venezuela during the Spanish colonial period (item **83**).

Outstanding critical catalogs that have accompanied major exhibitions of Spanish colonial art in the US and abroad include *Converging cultures: art & identity in Spanish America,* edited by Diana Fane (item **16**); *Platería iberoamericana: Fundación Santillana, junio-septiembre 1993* (item **20**); *La Plata del Plata* (item **77**); *Potosi: Colonial Treasures from the Bolivian City of Silver,* by Pedro Querejazu *et al.* (item **114**); and *Iglesia Museo Santa Clara, 1647* (item **86**). These publications set high standards of scholarship, offering comprehensive discussions of the works in their historical context. The inclusion of bibliographies with primary and secondary sources adds to their usefulness.

The 49th International Congress of Americanists, held in Quito, Ecuador, July 7–11, 1997, included the symposium "Art and Architecture of Colonial Latin America: Comparative Visions," chaired by Clara Bargellini from the Instituto de Investigaciones Estéticas, UNAM. This event sought an understanding of Spanish colonial art through a comparative vision of expressions from different regions to assess similarities and differences iniconographic, technical, and other issues. It is anticipated that the papers presented by a group of distinguished scholars (several of which dealt with South American topics) will be published in the near future.

From September 15–16, 2000, the symposium "Circa 1700: Architecture in Europe and the Americas" was held in the National Gallery of Art, Washington, DC. Sponsored in conjunction with the splendid exhibition "The Triumph of the Baroque: Architecture in Europe, 1600–1750," the program included a presentation by Francisco Stastny, "From Fountain to Bridge: Hispanism and Baroque Projects between 1650 and 1746 in Lima." The Center for Advanced Studies in the Visual Arts will publish this and other papers from the meeting in a forthcoming volume of the National Gallery of Art's *Studies in the History of Art* under the editorial direction of Henry A. Millon.

Finally, mention should be made of the noteworthy exhibition "Santos: Substance & Soul" at the Arts and Industries Building, Smithsonian Institution, Washington, DC, from September 17, 2000-March 31, 2001. Sponsored by the Smithsonian Center for Materials Research and Education, this fine exhibition examines from different points of view the images of saints from Mexico, Ecuador, Bolivia, Puerto Rico, Brazil, and the Philippines, from the colonial period and later. The exhibition places special emphasis on the need to appreciate these sculptural and painted images beyond their religious meaning to include the craft involved in their creation, evidence of their use, and ultimately, their preservation and deterioration as physical objects. Specialized scientific techniques, including material analysis and use of infrared and ultraviolet light and X-rays, permit viewers to better appreciate the works and celebrate many threads in contemporary American culture. Each piece in the exhibition is reproduced in a handsome color illustration with a complete descriptive caption in the companion publication, "Exhibition Objects List." Designed as a traveling exhibition, it is scheduled to open at the National

Hispanic Cultural Center of New Mexico in Albuquerque on June 22, 2001, and at the Museo de Arte de Puerto Rico in San Juan on December 14, 2001, thus contributing to the dissemination of an important aspect of Spanish and Portuguese colonial art of the Americas.

CHILE, ARGENTINA, PARAGUAY, AND URUGUAY

70 **Barroffio Burastero, Raúl.** El rescate de las murallas de Montevideo. (*Bol. Hist. Ejérc.*, 287/290, 1993, p. 131–162, bibl., ill., map)

Brief study documents the field work of a rescue mission to locate and preserve the remains of the fortification walls of Montevideo dating from the 17th-18th centuries. A labor of love initiated by the author in 1989 with the help of an interdisciplinary team of professionals, it is a rare example of historic archeology in Uruguay. Because the city has lost most of its architecture from the Spanish colonial period, this is an extremely important effort worthy of the full support of the Comisión del Patrimonio Histórico y Cultural de la Nación, officially charged with the nomination of national historic landmarks. This pioneer work will serve as an indispensable reference for future studies.

71 **Briones, Luis** and **Pedro Vilaseca P.** Pintura religiosa en Tarapacá: fe y color en el desierto. Santiago?: Editora e Impresora Cabo de Hornos, 1983? 117 p.: bibl., ill. (some col.).

Presents groundbreaking research on Spanish colonial paintings from little-known churches in southern Andean towns formerly belonging to the Peruvian province of Tarapacá, including Socoroma, Parinacota, Pachama, Pachica, Carquima, and Huaviña. Examines the religious iconography of selected examples of canvas and mural painting, placing them in their historical framework and establishing relationships to the Cuzco and Altiplano schools. Color and b/w photographs of uneven quality.

72 **La Cuadrícula en el desarrollo de la ciudad hispanoamericana: el caso de Córdoba.** v. 1, 1573–1810. v. 2, Córdoba 1810–1916. Córdoba, Argentina: Instituto del Ambiente Humano, Facultad de Arquitectura y Urbanismo, Univ. Nacional de Córdoba, 1987–90. 2 v.: bibl., ill., maps (some folded).

Valuable urban history of Córdoba traces development of the city's Spanish colonial gridiron plan from 1573–1810 (vol. 1) and 1810–1916 (vol. 2). Provides a wealth of visual documentation. Particularly useful is the detailed analysis of individual urban blocks with plans and elevation and perspective drawings, many prepared specially for this publication. Unfortunately, the b/w photographs have not reproduced well due to poor paper quality. Provides footnotes, but offers no general bibliography.

73 **Giuliano, Juan Carlos.** Arquitectura de La Rioja hasta 1880. v. 1. La Rioja, Argentina: Editorial Canguro, 1993. 1 v.: ill., map, photos. (Col. Libro riojano/Ministerio de Cultura y Educación, Secretaría de Cultura de la provincia de La Rioja)

Short history of the architecture of La Rioja from prehistoric times and its Spanish foundation in 1591 until 1880. Discusses Spanish colonial period of 1591–1810 in p. 20–46, including the plan of the city and a selection of religious and secular buildings. While historic data is sparse, work complements b/w photographs of extant architectural details with plans, sections, and elevations. Gives special attention to materials of construction and structural details.

74 **Gori, Iris** and **Sergio Barbieri.** Empresas sacras en la Iglesia de la Compañia de Jesús de Córdoba, Argentina. Córdoba, Argentina: s.n., 1992. 1 v. (unpaged): ill. (some col.).

Handsome large portfolio consisting of loose b/w photographs and color plates documents complete set of 50 polychromed rectangular panels in high relief representing Christian emblems decorating the interior frieze of the Jesuit church of La Compañía in Córdoba, Argentina. Bilingual Spanish-English text discusses the iconography of each of the panels, providing useful insights about their meaning and possible relationship to earlier printed sources.

75 **Gori, Iris** and **Sergio Barbieri.** Teresa
de Jesús: divino y humano junto. Córdoba, Argentina: Cantico Ediciones, 1993.
1 v. (unpaged): ill. (some col.).

Large portfolio follows format of earlier work by same authors (see item **74**), this
time documenting 16 17th-century canvases
from the Cuzco School depicting the life of
Saint Theresa of Jesus. Presumably all originally acquired in 1744 by the convent of San
José de Carmelitas Descalzas in Córdoba, Argentina, a few of these paintings are now in
other museums in the same city. Concise
bilingual Spanish-English text describes each
of the paintings comparing the iconography
to other similar works in Peru and elsewhere
in South America. On the basis of stylistic
analysis, the authors attribute the paintings
to a follower of the well-known Cuzco
painter José Espinoza de los Monteros. B/w
photographs are of uneven quality, but color
plates provide valuable details.

76 **Larrauri, Elsa** *et al.* Alta Gracia:
evolución histórica y desarrollo
urbano-arquitectónico. Córdoba, Argentina:
Centro de Estudios de Historia Urbana Argentina y Latinoamericana, Facultad de Arquitectura y Urbanismo, Univ. Nacional de
Córdoba, 1992. 156 p.: bibl., ill., maps.

Popular edition documents historic
evolution and architectural development of
Alta Gracia in the prov. of Córdoba from
Spanish colonial period to the present. Highlights important role played by the Jesuit order in the construction and management of
the original Spanish colonial *estancia*, which
served as nucleus to the town, as a critical
factor in the subsequent growth of the town
as a regional agricultural center. Visual documentation, including plans and b/w photographs, was not reproduced well due to the
poor quality of the paper.

López Anaya, Jorge. Historia del arte argentino. See item **275.**

Oliveira Cézar, Lucrecia de. Aristóbulo del
Valle. See item **2996.**

77 **La Plata del Plata.** Buenos Aires: s.n.,
1992. 63 p.: bibl., col. ill.
Companion catalog to exhibition with
the same title organized by the Municipalidad de la Ciudad de Buenos Aires in celebration of the quincentennial of the discovery of
the Americas. Representative examples of co-

lonial silverwork from Peru, Alto Peru (Bolivia), and Argentina in the important collections of the municipal museums Isaac Fernández Blanco, José Fernández, and Brig.
Gen. Cornelio de Saavedra are illustrated in
good b/w and color photographs, accompanied by descriptive captions. Provides historical background in brief texts by Marta
Sánchez and Ana María Cousillas covering
the topics "Los Plateros en el Río de la
Plata," "Platería Religiosa," "Platería Civil,"
"Platería Rural," and "Platería Pampa y Mapuche."

78 **Sahady Villanueva, Antonio; Patricio
Duarte Gutiérrez;** and **Myriam Wais-
berg I.** La vivienda urbana en Chile durante
la época hispana: zona central. Dibujantes de
Jhon Acevedo Tapia *et al.* Santiago: Depto. de
Historia y Teoría de la Arquitectura, Facultad
de Arquitectura y Urbanismo, Univ. de
Chile, 1992. 219 p.: bibl., ill., maps.

Well-documented survey of colonial
residences in Santiago, La Serena, San Felipe,
and Rancagua consisting of floor plans, elevations, sections, and perspective drawings.
Major emphasis is given to morphological
analysis of individual buildings supplemented with historical information about
their origins and later transformations to the
present day. The bibliography includes an
important list of published and unpublished
sources.

79 **La salvaguarda del patrimonio je-
suítico: seminario post congreso
Posadas 1994.** II Congreso Internacional de
Rehabilitación del Patrimonio Arquitectónico y Edificación. Posadas, Argentina:
Ediciones Montoya, 1995. 238 p.: bibl., ill.
Proceedings from the II Congreso held
in Posadas, Misiones, in 1994, predominantly
but not exclusively devoted to the preservation of Jesuit mission churches in Argentina.
Includes discussion of theoretical and technical issues by experts in the field using well-
documented case studies. Transcribes the
Declaración de Mar del Plata, summarizing
recommendations for preserving the world's
cultural heritage on a continuing basis.

COLOMBIA AND VENEZUELA

80 **Arte y fe: colección artística agustina
Colombia.** Investigación y textos de
Rodolfo Vallín Magaña y María Victoria
Gálvez Izquierdo. Bogotá: Provincia de Nues-

tra Señora de Gracias, 1995. 207 p.: bibl., col. ill.

Deluxe catalog documents impressive restoration of religious art by the Taller de Restauración de San Agustín in Bogota, promoted by the Augustinian Province of Nuestra Señora de Gracia. Part of this initiative was the restoration of the church of San Agustín in 1980–86 under direction of architect Germán Téllez Castañeda, who gives an account of this undertaking in the introduction. While an adjoining Spanish colonial monastic complex was lost to demolition earlier this century, the inventory of 1797 reproduced in "Anexo 2" provides a clear idea of the rich artistic treasures that once belonged to the Augustinian community. Additionally, the inventory serves as a valuable documentary reference for the works assembled in the catalog. Included in the 541 entries are important works executed during the Spanish colonial period and later under the patronage of the Augustinian order. Excellent color photographs are accompanied by captions providing basic curatorial data and brief iconographic descriptions.

81 **Barney, Benjamín** and **Francisco Ramírez.** La arquitectura de las casas de hacienda en el Valle del Alto Cauca. Fotografías de Fernell Franco. Bogotá: El Ancora Editores, 1994. 167 p.: bibl., ill. (some col.), maps on lining papers.

Handsome monograph marks the culmination of a survey of hacienda houses from the Valley of Alto Cauca initiated by authors in 1987. Important contribution to the study of South American colonial rural architecture from an art historical point of view and a much needed complement to widely published socioeconomic research on the subject. Separate chapters with generous notes discuss the setting, function, building techniques, and form of the hacienda houses. Comprehensive bibliography includes suggestions for further reading and lists documentary sources in regional archives. The catalogue raisonné features 20 hacienda houses, each illustrated with fine site plans; elevation drawings; and color photographs, which, unfortunately, are of relatively poor quality.

82 **La Casa del Marqués de San Jorge, Santafé de Bogotá: colección de arte y objetos coloniales.** Bogotá: Fondo de Promo-

ción de la Cultura, 1993. 110 p.: bibl., ill. (some col.).

Handsome small publication celebrates the 1993 opening of the exhibition of Spanish colonial art from the Banco Popular collection in the Casa del Marqués de San Jorge in Bogota. An excellent example of 17th-century domestic architecture since its restoration in 1972, the house served as an archeological museum and headquarters of the Fondo de Promoción de la Cultura. The new installation of colonial art in the Salón San Jorge helps restore the original cultural background of the residence. A short biography of the most notable owner, don Jorge Lozano de Peralta, Marqués de San Jorge (d. 1793) is followed by a fully illustrated, descriptive catalog of the art collection, including paintings, sculptures, silverwork, liturgical objects, and furniture. Fine quality color and b/w photographs.

83 **Duarte, Carlos F.** Mobiliario y decoración interior durante el período hispánico venezolano. Caracas: Armitano Editores, 1980? 567 p.: appendix, bibl., ill. (some col.).

Major work by leading art historian pays a worthy tribute to Alfredo Machado Hernández (1887–1946), founder of the Museo de Arte Colonial in Caracas, and fills an important void in the field. By far the most comprehensive history of furniture and decorative arts in Venezuela during the Spanish colonial period. With painstaking care, author fully describes and attempts to place in original architectural contexts, a representative corpus of works from public and private collections not easily available to researchers. Clear organization by chronological order, covering 17th century to 1812, permits an appreciation of the development of styles across time and the changing tastes of colonial society. Abundant b/w and color illustrations complement informative text. Appendix provides a compilation of historic documents of vital importance, including detailed inventories of houses that represent a cross section of the upper and middle classes.

Espinosa, José María. José María Espinosa: abanderado del arte y de la patria. See item **320.**

84 Gasparini, Graziano. Coro: patrimonio mundial. Caracas: Armitano, 1994. 190 p.: bibl., ill. (some col.).

Deluxe edition by renowned architectural historian celebrates 1993 inclusion of the city in UNESCO's World Heritage List. Complements rather than supersedes earlier book by same author, *La arquitectura colonial de Coro* (1961) (see *HLAS 24:1698*), with an additional wealth of visual material, including spectacular full-page color photographs of colonial monuments and their environs. Lucid text, both factual and analytical, incorporates material from recent research and argues for a sound policy of historic preservation in the city of Coro. Several architectural plans have been redrawn for this edition and are supplemented with reconstruction drawings and historic photographs. See also item **85**.

Gil Tovar, Francisco. El arte colombiano. See item **321**.

85 González Batista, Carlos. Coro, donde empieza Venezuela. Coro, Venezuela: Caracas Paper Company, 1994. 79 p.: bibl., ill. (some col.), photos.

Brief, handsomely illustrated introduction to the city of Coro on the occasion of its 1993 inclusion in UNESCO's World Heritage List contains historic b/w photographs and contemporary full-color illustrations of the city's religious and secular buildings as well as urban spaces. Provides a historical overview of Coro and describes its architecture and recent historic preservation work undertaken by the Venezuelan authorities. See also item **84**.

86 Iglesia Museo Santa Clara, 1647. Bogotá: Colcultura; Instituto Colombiano de Cultura Hispánica, 1995. 160 p.: ill. (some col.), index.

Museum catalog sets high standard as first in a series intended to reflect the completion of comprehensive inventories of art collections undertaken by the Instituto Colombiano de Cultura. Fully documents art collection of the 17th-century church of Santa Clara in Bogota, the first major restoration work completed by the Instituto between 1969–83. Specially noteworthy are the nave elevation drawings used to locate the paintings, sculptures, and altarpieces within their architectural context. Individual catalog entries by Jaime Gutiérrez Vallejo provide basic curatorial and descriptive information, complemented by good quality b/w and color photographs. Two sections discuss iconography of angels in colonial painting and different columnar supports of the altarpieces.

87 Mújica, Elisa. Las casas que hablan: guía histórica del barrio de la Candelaria de Santafé de Bogotá. Bogotá?: Corporación La Candelaria; Biblioteca Nacional de Colombia; Colcultura, 1994. 198 p.: bibl., col. ill.

Not an art historical study, but a literary narrative of the history of Colombia since the Spanish colonial period and throughout the 19th century as told by the streets and buildings of the Barrio de la Candelaria in Bogota. Major emphasis on the social milieu and the lives of the principal historical figures who shaped the country. Handsome colored drawings serve as visual vignettes of settings and scenes described in the text.

88 Téllez, Germán. La arquitectura colonial de Santa Cruz de Mompox. Bogotá: El Ancora Editores, 1995. 166 p.: bibl., ill. (some col.).

This lavishly illustrated book by distinguished restoration architect presents the beautiful, but little known, Spanish colonial town of Santa Cruz de Mompox (or Mompos) on the Río Grande de la Magdalena. Stunning color plates capture distinctive character of Caribbean regional style in historic religious and secular buildings, also found in coastal cities such as Cartagena, Colombia, and Coro, Venezuela. Text, intended as a personal reading and critical interpretation of the town, refers to several historical sources and provides a solid formal analysis of the buildings and their urban spaces. Makes suggestive visual comparisons between brick and stucco houses of Mompox and similar fenestration treatments with iron railings in Spanish Andalusian towns such as La Campana, Ubeda, and Seville. Raises concern about recent trend resulting in the repainting of façades in garish colors, striking to the eye but not always historically authentic.

PERU, ECUADOR, AND BOLIVIA

89 Adoum, Rosángela et al. Panorama urbano y cultural de Quito. Quito: Dirección General de Planificación, Municipio del Distrito Metropolitano de Quito; Sevilla, Spain: Consejería de Obras Públicas y Transportes, Junta de Andalucía, Ministerio de Asuntos Exteriores de España, 1994. 238 p.: ill. (some col.). (Serie Quito; 10)

Vol. 10 in the Serie Quito features case studies relevant to the study of the city's Spanish colonial art and architecture. Varying in scope and thematic content, these include: "Quito colonial, en prosa y poesía," by Peralta and Estrella; "El comercio de antigüedades y obras de arte en Quito," and "La restauración de un monumento: la Antigua Universidad," by Fondello. "Quito: cartografía y descripciones urbanas," by Burbano, offers a brief history of the urban development of the city from Spanish colonial period to the present, illustrated with historic plans not well reproduced in b/w. Pt. VI contains a useful account of the principal historical museums in the city with an outline of their collections. For reviews of other volumes in the series, see *HLAS 56:182,* (no. 1); *HLAS 56:177,* (no. 2); item **109,** (no. 4); *HLAS 56:178,* (no. 5); item **2185,** (no. 6); item **96,** (no. 7); and item **95,** (no. 9).

90 Arequipa II. Lima: Instituto Nacional de Cultura, Dirección General de Inventario, Catalogación e Investigación del Patrimonio Cultural, 1993. 126 p.: bibl., ill. (some col.), maps. (Serie sobre el inventario del patrimonio artístico mueble; 3)

Follows format of first volume (1989, see *HLAS 54:223*). Comprehensive photographic survey includes paintings, sculptures, and liturgical artifacts from major religious monuments of colonial Arequipa and vicinity, including Santa Catalina, San Agustín, Santa Teresa, Santa Marta, Yanahuara, Characato, Caima, and the private collection of the Banco Central de Reserva. Small, poor quality b/w photographs are useful only as visual reference, better color reproductions appear in p. 119–121. Captions identify subject matter, medium, measurements, location, and state of conservation for each work.

91 Banco Central del Ecuador. Museo. Catálogo de la sala de arte colonial. Quito: Museo Nacional del Banco Central del Ecuador, 1995. 35 p.: col. ill. (Catálogos de los Museos del Banco Central del Ecuador; 3)

Brief, elegant catalog features major

Spanish colonial paintings and sculptures from the Quito School in the collection of the Museo Nacional del Banco Central (Ecuador). Stunning color reproductions attest to the fine quality of these works, representative of the religious transformation and cultural syncretism of European and American heritages. Bilingual Spanish-English texts by Rafael Cordero and Holguer Jara Chávez offer an introduction to the social milieu of the period.

92 Baptista Gumucio, Mariano. La fe viva: misiones jesuíticas de Bolivia. La Paz: Fundación Cultural Quipus, 1994. 199 p.: bibl., ill. (some col.).

Elegant publication by journalist Baptista Gumucio and photographer Peter McFarren provides solid introduction to topic. Presents historic development of Jesuit missions of Chiquitos, entered in UNESCO's World Heritage List in 1990, in a well-crafted text complemented by prints and drawings from 19th century. Appropriately dedicated to Bishop Antonio Eduardo Bösl and Swiss architect Hans Roth in recognition of their major contributions to the restoration and conservation of many of these churches. Color photographs are an outstanding testimony to the decorative beauty of the churches of Santa Ana, Concepción, San Ignacio de Velasco, San Rafael, San Miguel, San Javier, and San Ignacio de Moxos, and of contemporary life that perpetuates a religious tradition. See also item **104.**

93 Benavente Velarde, Teófilo. Pintores cusqueños de la colonia. Colaboración del artista Alejandro Martínez Frisancho. Lima: Municipalidad del Qosqo, 1995. 222 p.: bibl., ill. (some col.). (Historia del arte cusqueño)

Posthumous publication pays tribute to distinguished Cuzco art historian who taught at the Escuela Superior Autónoma de Bellas Artes Diego Quispe Tito. Text offers a wealth of documentation on the artists whose work defined the important Cuzco School of painting during Spanish colonial period. Organization follows strict chronological order by century, including extensive lists of artists and their known works with useful reproductions of their respective autographs. Biographical data compiled mostly from secondary sources is complemented with brief descriptions of pictorial techniques and the iconography of their major works. Provides detailed information in separate chapters on better-known 17th- and 18th-century painters such as Diego Quispe Tito, Basilio de Santa Cruz Pumaqallo, and Basilio Pacheco. Color and b/w reproductions are extremely uneven, but an important visual reference for future studies nonetheless.

94 Benito, José Antonio. Candarave cristiano: la construcción de la iglesia parroquial en los libros de inventarios, 1777–1977. (*Rev. Arch. Arzobispal Arequipa*, 2, 1995, p. 45–78, bibl.)

Presents history of construction and subsequent transformations of the parish church of San Juan Bautista de Candarave in the prov. of Tarata and southernmost dept. of Tacna, Peru, through transcription of inventories dating from 1655–1977. Documentation from the Archivo Arzobispal de Arequipa and the Archivo Diocesano de Tacna provides detailed information about building's condition, works of art, and religious ornaments found in its interior.

95 Bonilla, Efrén et al. Quito, transformaciones urbanas y arquitectónicas. Quito: Dirección de Planificación I. Municipio de Quito; Sevilla, Spain: Consejería de Obras Públicas y Transportes, Junta de Andalucía, 1994. 237 p.: ill. (some col.). (Serie Quito; 9)

Ninth vol. in the Serie Quito is devoted to the analysis of the various master plans proposed for the control of urban growth of Quito, beginning with the Plan Regulador of 1945 and the subsequent Planos Generales of 1967, 1973, and 1981. Fully illustrated with b/w photographs and urban plans, the multi-authored text overviews current planning strategies monitored by the Dirección de Planificación of Quito's municipal government. Chapter by Bustamante and Cifuentes discusses guidelines for urban rehabilitation and restoration of historic monuments. For reviews of other volumes in the series, see *HLAS 56:182*, (no. 1); *HLAS 56:177*, (no. 2); item **109**, (no. 4); *HLAS 56:178*, (no. 5); item **2185**, (no. 6); item **96**, (no. 7); and **89**, (no. 10).

96 Bustamante, Teodoro et al. Quito, comunas y parroquias. Quito: Dirección de Planificación, I. Municipio de Quito,

Ecuador; Sevilla, Spain: Consejería de Obras Públicas y Transporte, Junta de Andalucía; Ministerio de Asuntos Exteriores de España, 1992. 237 p.: bibl., ill., maps. (Serie Quito; 7)

Seventh volume in the Serie Quito is devoted to the study of the communes and rural parishes surrounding the city of Quito. Contributions by different authors reflect demographic, socioeconomic, and historic approaches to urban planning. Some chapters were originally written as technical reports under the Plan Maestro de Rehabilitación de las Areas Históricas de Quito for the Dirección de Planificación. Diagnostic assessments of present condition of communes and rural parishes are accompanied by recommendations for rehabilitative interventions. Important documentation on individual rural buildings will be of interest to urban geographers and planners. For reviews of other volumes in the series, see *HLAS 56:182*, (no. 1); *HLAS 56:177*, (no. 2); item **109**, (no. 4); *HLAS 56:178*, (no. 5); item **2185**, (no. 6); item **95**, (no. 9); and item **89**, (no. 10).

97 Escudero-Albornoz, Ximena. Neptalí Martínez: la permanencia del arte colonial. Quito: Ediciones Fundación El Comercio, 1996. 103 p.: bibl., facsims., ill. (some col.), ports.

Life and oevre of a wood sculptor who continues to work in the tradition of the "Escuela Quiteña" and is therefore much sought after for restoration projects as well as original work. Born in 1910, Martínez still was active at the time of publication of this book. His artistry embellishes churches and showcases homes of the city. [M.T. Hamerly]

Fernández, José Abel. Grabadores en el Perú: bosquejo histórico 1574–1950 con una muestra de 130 xilografías. See item **348**.

98 Macera, Pablo; Arturo Jiménez Borja; and Irma Franke. Trujillo del Perú: Baltazar Jaime Martínez Compañón; acuarelas; siglo XVIII. Lima: Fundación del Banco Continental, 1997. 254 p.: bibl., col. ill., map.

Deluxe edition celebrates purchase by the Banco Continental from Sotheby's in New York of two splendid volumes containing a partial duplicate set of the collection of colored drawings commissioned by Bishop Martínez Compañón during his residence in Trujillo, Peru, between 1779–89 (see item **101**). First volume, titled *Trajes y costum-*

bres de las misiones acuarelas: siglo XVIII, corresponds to Vol. 2 in Madrid's Royal Library, even though it only consists of 64 watercolors; while Vol. 2, titled *Pájaros/Acuarelas/Siglo XVIII,* corresponds to Vol. 7 in Madrid's Royal Library yet only consists of 56 watercolors, including 53 birds, one insect, one bat, and one precolumbian textile (see also *HLAS 50:249* and *HLAS 48:1663*). Erudite texts by scholars from three disciplines discuss drawings from historical, artistic, and iconographic points of view that will serve as a foundation for future studies of this extraordinary corpus of images. All 120 drawings are reproduced in color, permitting comparisons with other known contemporary copies in the Royal Library of Madrid and the National Library in Bogota.

99 **Maguiña Gómez, César.** El convento franciscano de Chiclayo. (*Bol. Lima,* 17:98, marzo/mayo 1995, p. 19–26, bibl., photos)

Already threatened by demolition in 1949 when Harold E. Wethey (*Colonial architecture and sculpture in Peru;* see *HLAS 15:580*) documented the Franciscan church and monastery in the northern coastal town of Chiclayo, this article attempts to rescue from oblivion the extant remains of the main and second cloisters of this important religious institution. Dating from the second half of the 16th century, the main cloister with its brick and stucco single story of pointed arches is unique in Peru. Archival documentation shows indigenous population from local *pueblo de indios* contributed money and labor for construction of monastic complex. Makes strong case for urgent implementation of a restoration project approved by the Instituto Nacional de Cultura in 1986, but never carried out.

100 **Málaga Medina, Alejandro.** La iglesia de Quequeña: joya de la arquitectura mestiza. (*Rev. Arch. Arzobispal Arequipa,* 1, 1994, p. 83–102, photo)

The history of the parish church of Nuestra Señora de la Concepción in the town of Quequeña situated 25 kilometers to the SE of Arequipa is told through inventories dating from the 18th century and later. The present building, completed in 1769, is a fine example of white sillar masonry construction characteristic of the regional style of Arequipa and nearby towns. More descriptive than analytical, the text is a good source of information on the condition of the church and its artistic treasures from the colonial period to the present. Unfortunately, only one b/w photograph of a panoramic view of the town showing the church from a distance is supplied.

Martínez Borrero, Juan; Carmen Ugalde de Valdivieso; and Juan Cordero Iñiguez. De lo divino y lo profano: arte cuencano de los siglos XVIII y XIX. See item **2242.**

101 **Martínez Compañón y Bujanda, Baltasar Jaime.** Trujillo del Perú. v. 4–5, 7–9. Madrid: Ediciones Cultura Hispánica, 1989–1991. 5 v.: appendix.

Volumes complete the publication of the magnificent collection of colored drawings commissioned by Bishop Martínez Compañon during his residence in Trujillo, Peru between 1779–89. A rare pictorial record from the Spanish colonial period originally deposited in Madrid's Royal Library, its reproduction in facsimile now makes it more easily available to scholars and the general public. Material depicted in these volumes consists of fruit trees, palm trees, flowers, and herbal fruits (Vol. 4); medicinal herbs (Vol. 5); birds (Vol. 7); fish, amphibians, and seashells (Vol. 8); and antiquities and archeology of the northern coast of Peru: plans of pre-Inca and Inca remains (mostly from Chimu sites), ceramics, metal work, and textiles (Vol. 9). Even though the quality of the drawings varies, pointing to the intervention of different hands, the entire set is a remarkable and unique encyclopedic visual corpus of far reaching importance for many disciplines beyond art and architectural history. For description of other volumes, see *HLAS 50:249* and *HLAS 48:1663.*

102 **Mesa, José de.** La influencia de Flandes en la pintura del area andina. (*Rev. Hist. Am.,* 117, enero/junio 1994, p. 61–82, bibl., ill.)

Brief study reviews important influence of Flemish art on development of Spanish colonial painting in Andean regions of Peru (Cuzco), Bolivia (Sucre), and Ecuador (Quito). From 16th century onwards and throughout 18th century, Flemish paintings and prints from Antwerp were imported to the New World in large quantities, thus becoming readily available to local artists and their shops. Representative works by de Vos, Baptista Danielson, Forchaudt, and copies of Rubens and van Dyck are examined in this context. Also documents activity of Jesuit painter De la Puente (b. Malines, 1586), who travelled to Peru around 1620 and left signed works in Trujillo, Lima, Cuzco, and Juli.

103 Mito y simbolismo en los Andes: la figura y la palabra. Recopilación de Henrique Urbano. Cusco, Perú: Centro de Estudios Regionales Andinos Bartolomé de las Casas, 1993. 323 p.: bibl., ill. (Estudios y debates regionales andinos; 84)

Unusual anthology of essays by different authors examines myth and symbolism in visual arts and literature during Spanish colonial period. Introduction by Henrique Urbano surveys research methods on the study of signs and symbols and their meaning. Focused essays represent solid models of iconographic analysis and interpretation. Topics dealing with paintings include "Las túnicas incas en la pintura colonial" by Iriarte; "La representación en el siglo XVI: la imagen colonial del Inca" by Cummins; "El arte de la nobleza inca y la identidad andina" by Stastny; and "La plástica colonial y sus relaciones con la Gran Rebelión" by Estenssoro. Suggestive architectural study by Barnes, "Un análisis de la iconografía y la arquitectura andina en una iglesia colonial: San Cristóbal de Pamachiri (Apurímac-Perú)," investigates continuity of Inca traditions during early Spanish colonial period. All essays include extensive footnotes, good illustrations, and useful bibliographies.

104 Molina Barbery, Plácido et al. Las misiones jesuíticas de Chiquitos. Edición y recopilación de Pedro Querejazu. Fotografías de Plácido Molina Barbery et al. La Paz: Fundación BHN, Línea Editorial; La Papelera, 1995. 718 p.: bibl., ill. (some col.), maps, plans.

Monumental multi-authored work pays tribute to Plácido Molina Barbery, who championed the conservation of the extant Jesuit mission churches in the prov. of Chiquitos, now the Santa Cruz dept. Contains a wealth of documentation pertaining to the churches of San Javier, San Ignacio (demolished in 1948), San Miguel, San Rafael, San José, Santa Ana, Santiago, Santo Corazón, San Juan, and Concepción, including the pub-

lication of the complete Photographic Archive of Chiquitos consisting of 467 b/w photographs. Individual chapters provide a comprehensive view of mission life during the period of Jesuit administration (1691–1767 and thereafter). Features several splendid, well-illustrated essays dealing specifically with the art, architecture, and urbanism of the missions. Specially noteworthy is the photographic essay, "Visiones de la utopía hoy" (p. 565–549) compiled by Querejazu with beautiful color plates documenting art and architecture of mission churches today. Excellent companion to Parejas Moreno and Suárez Salas' *Chiquito: historia de una utopía* (see *HLAS 56:202*) and Bösl's *Una joya en la selva boliviana: la restauración del templo colonial de Concepción* (see *HLAS 56:181*). See also item **75.** Exhaustive bibliography. Indispensable reference work.

105 Núñez Zeballos, Alejandro Málaga. Erección de la Catedral de Arequipa. (*Rev. Arch. Arzobispal Arequipa*, 1, 1994, p. 103–119)

Chronological summary traces the history of the creation of the diocese of Arequipa in 1609 under the pontificate of Paul V. Also includes full transcription of the papal bull authorizing the erection of the Cathedral of Arequipa in a Spanish translation from the Latin dated Oct. 11, 1619 preserved in the Archivo Arzobispal de Arequipa (p. 104–119).

106 Paniagua Pérez, Jesús. Algunas piezas identificadas de la platería Quiteña del siglo XVIII. (*An. Mus. Am.*, 4, 1996, p. 107–118, bibl., photos)

Important contribution to the study of silverwork in colonial Quito offers a rare group of signed and dated pieces of religious art that may be compared with other contemporary works. According to the author, "The intention is thereby to attempt to facilitate further research into the silversmith's art in the city in question, since activity in this field in Quito would seem to [be] a good deal more extensive than what was assumed to be the case until quite recently."

107 Paniagua Pérez, Jesús and Deborah Truhan. Nuevas aportaciones a la platería azuaya de los siglos XVI y XVII. (*Rev. Complut. Hist. Am.*, 21, 1995, p. 57–70, table)

Recent research at the Archivo Nacional de Historia, Sección del Azuay, expands on the pioneer study by Paniagua Pérez, *La plata labrada en la Audiencia de Quito (la Provincia de Azuay), siglos XVI-XIX* (León: Univ. de León, Secretariado de Publicaciones, 1989). Adds several new names to list of known silversmiths in the city of Cuenca and vicinity during 16th-17th centuries. Newly discovered documents, including inventories and testaments of the time, provide important information on tools and techniques used by artisans. In some instances, silversmiths who travelled from Cuenca to Quito and Lima were found to be engaged in other commercial activities including the sale of pewter and cloth. Also documents for the first time the activity of indigenous silversmiths living in Cuenca between 1592–1702, suggesting they were a larger part of the artistic community than previously believed.

108 Paniagua Pérez, Jesús and **Gloria M. Garzón Montenegro.** Las sagas familiares en el gremio de plateros quiteños del siglo XVII. *(Bol. Mus. Inst. Camón Aznar,* 63, 1996, p. 121–143, photos)

Excellent study looks at the activities of the guild of silversmiths in Quito during the 18th century. Original archival research at the Archivo Histórico Nacional in Quito yields wealth of documentation concerning several silversmithing families (e.g., Binueza, Albán y Palis, Castillo, Murillo, López de Solís, and Ruiz), reflecting the craft's importance as a major occupation of the time. Detailed discussion of legislation governing the guild and hierarchical organization and responsibilities of officers. The brotherhood of San Eloy and its important role in the silversmiths' church, La Merced, is also described.

109 Peralta, Evelia. Quito: guía arquitectónica. Quito: Dirección de Planificación, I.; Andalucía, Spain: Junta de Andalucía, 1991. 238 p.: bibl., ill. (some col.). (Serie Quito; 4)

Fourth volume in the Serie Quito follows same format as previous volumes. Fully illustrated guide to architecture of the city of Quito and vicinity is not restricted to buildings dating from Spanish colonial period. Provides essential information for each

building, including location, date, name of architect or architects (if known), and present function. Additional texts for each entry focus primarily on description and historical data. Useful urban plans facilitate location of buildings within their respective districts. The clarity of the presentation makes it a model for guides to cities throughout Spanish America. For reviews of other volumes in the series, see *HLAS 56:182,* (no. 1); *HLAS 56:177,* (no. 2); *HLAS 56:178,* (no. 5); item **2185,** (no. 6); item **96,** (no. 7); item **95,** (no. 9); and item **89,** (no. 10).

110 Pérez, David. Los franciscanos a través del arte en la Audiencia de Charcas. *(Arch. Ibero-Am.,* 57:225/226, enero/dic. 1997, p. 809–860, appendix, bibl., ill., photos)

Survey of Spanish colonial art and architecture in Bolivia pertaining to the Franciscan order. The text, somewhat disjointed, reads more as a series of encyclopedia entries than a continuous narrative. Draws heavily from secondary sources, but also includes references to archival documents in the Archivo Nacional de Bolivia, the Archivo de la Casa de la Moneda in Potosí, Tarija, and Sucre. Appendix lists works related to the Franciscan order in major museums of Bolivia.

111 Pérez Morera, Jesús. El árbol genealógico de las órdenes franciscana y dominica en el arte virreinal. *(An. Mus. Am.,* 4, 1996, p. 119–126, bibl., photos)

Discusses iconography of the geneaological trees of the Dominican and Franciscan orders as depicted in architectural decoration and painting during the Spanish colonial period. Cited examples include the famous decoration of polychromed plaster of the *sotocoro* of the church of Santo Domingo in Oaxaca, Mexico (1657) and the monumental canvas (10 x 10 m.) by Espinoza de los Monteros in the monastery of San Francisco, Cuzco (1655). The specific source for the Cuzco painting is identified as the engraving titled "Epilogue of the Franciscan Order" by the Flemish artist De Lode, dated 1626. Used as instruments of propaganda, these representations emphasized the parallels between the two religious orders, whose apostolic mission in the New World enjoyed the full support of the Spanish Crown.

112 Prado Heuderbert, Javier. Lima: arquitectura y escultura religiosa virreynal. Prólogo y textos de Juan Gunther. Edición de Ignacio Prado Pastor. Lima: s.n., 1996. 261 p.: bibl., ill.

Deluxe edition consisting primarily of a photographic album from the author's private collection celebrates inclusion of the historic center of Lima in UNESCO's World Heritage List. The cathedral and sagrario, parish churches, monasteries, convents, and other religious institutions are discussed in the first six chapters, while a shorter, additional seventh chapter is devoted to secular buildings. With the exception of a few contemporary color photographs that mark the chapter title pages, the large corpus of b/w photographs provides a valuable visual record of the rich colonial architectural heritage of the city from the late-19th century to the present. Includes images of important buildings lost to neglect and demolition. Informative texts derived from secondary sources, but also incorporating some of the most recent research introduce each of the monuments.

113 Proyecto—inventario y catalogación del patrimonio artístico mueble. Lima: Instituto Nacional de Cultura, Dirección de Conservación del Museo Nacional, Unidad de Administración de Colecciones, 1986. 135 p.: bibl., ill.

Companion volume to Rogger Ravines' *Cajamarca: arquitectura religiosa y civil* (1983, see *HLAS 50:252*). Provides comprehensive inventory of altarpieces, paintings, sculptures, furniture, and liturgical objects of the major religious monuments of colonial Cajamarca, including the cathedral and sagrario, and churches of San Francisco, Belén, La Concepción, La Recoleta, San José, and Jesús. Description of each work includes subject matter, medium, measurements, location, and state of conservation.Also includes art collections of José Dammert Bellido and Andrés Zevallos. Text concludes with transcription of a notarial document dated Dec. 4, 1632, signed by painter Leonardo Jaramillo for work on an altarpiece (*retablo*) in a church of the city. Small, poor quality b/w photographs are useful as visual reference only.

Querejazu, Pedro. El dibujo en Bolivia: dibujos, 1900–1950. See item **303.**

114 Querejazu, Pedro et al. Potosí: colonial treasures from the Bolivian city of silver. New York: Americas Society, 1997. 152 p.: bibl., ill. (some col.).

Beautifully illustrated companion catalog to exhibition of the same title (American Society Art Gallery; New York, 1997) is a fine overview of the legendary "Bolivian City of Silver" and its colonial treasures. Bilingual texts written by preeminent Bolivian art historians Escobari, Gisbert, de Mesa, and Querejazu, trace the historic development of Potosí since its foundation in 1545 and its growth as one of the great silver mining towns in the Americas during Spanish colonial period and its significance as a major marketplace and artistic center for architecture, painting, sculpture, and silverwork. The consistent high quality of the works featured in the exhibition attests to a rich artistic legacy that led to Potosí's well-deserved recognition by UNESCO in 1985 as a World Heritage Site. A selected bibliography of primary and secondary sources offers excellent suggestions for further reading.

115 Ramos Sosa, Rafael. La sillería coral de Santo Domingo de Lima. (*Arch. Esp. Arte*, 271, 1995, p. 309–316, appendix, photos)

New research reveals that Juan Martínez de Arrona was the sculptor of the choir stalls of the church of Santo Domingo in Lima, a work previously attributed to other masters. The notarial document attesting to this fact, transcribed in an appendix, shows that Arrona received payment for his work from the Domincan friars in 1603, thus making these choir stalls the earliest in Peru. Stylistically, the Dominićan choir stalls can now be firmly related to Arrona's other major known sculptural work in Lima, the wooden high relief figures of Christ and the Apostles behind the chest of drawers (*cajonería*) of the Cathedral of Lima (1608).

116 Redescubramos Lima: Iglesia de San Pedro. Lima: Fondo Pro Recuperación del Patrimonio Cultural de la Nación, 1996. 61 p.: bibl., ill. (some col.).

Fine publication sponsored by Banco de Crédito del Perú follows format of catalog *Los Cristos de Lima* (1991) in the same series (see *HLAS 56:185*). Five well-written essays closely examine architecture and art of the

Jesuit church of San Pedro (formerly La Compañía) in Lima, offering a balanced treatment of historic data, iconography, formal analysis, and interpretation. Excellent color photographs by Giannoni Succar complement text and permit an appreciation of one of the most important colonial churches of Lima and its artistic treasures.

117 San Cristóbal, Antonio. El carpintero Diego de Medina. (*Rev. Arch. Gen. Nac.,* 13, 1996, p. 95–131, appendix)

Complementary study to item **118**, documents the work of master carpenter Diego de Medina (d. 1652), who was active in Lima during the first half of the 17th century. Medina's only known extant work, the wonderful coffered ceiling of wood and the ante-sacristy of San Agustín in Lima (1643) was but one of several important architectural projects that he executed for religious institutions in the city. Contractual documents preserved in the Archivo General de la Nación (fully transcribed here) show that Medina worked on the wooden ceilings (*artesonados*) of the church of Nuestra Señora del Carmen (1645–51) and of the church of Santa Clara (1648). For this last project, which turned out to be the most ambitious of his entire professional career, consisting of a seven-part lavishly decorated *artesonado*, Medina was paid the handsome sum of "21,000 pesos a de ocho reales." Even though none of these works survive today, the new findings in the notarial archives significantly expand our knowledge of the contribution of this master builder to the architecture of 17th-century Lima.

118 San Cristóbal, Antonio. El carpintero mudéjar Bartolomé Calderón. (*Rev. Arch. Gen. Nac.,* 12, 1995, p. 99–128, appendices)

Research in the notarial archives of the Archivo General de la Nación in Lima sheds light on the work of the little-known master carpenter Bartolomé Calderón. The design and construction details of several *artesonados* (ornamental wooden ceilings) for church hospitals and other religious institutions between 1623–35 show that Calderón contributed significantly to maintaining the *mudéjar* tradition in Lima during the first half of the 17th century. Full texts of building contracts signed by Calderón with

the Hospital of Santa Ana and Hospital of San Andrés are transcribed in a documentary appendix. See also item **117**.

San Cristóbal, Antonio. La construcción de la Iglesia de la Soledad. See item **2338**.

119 San Cristóbal, Antonio. Las fachadas barrocas de Ayacucho. (*An. Mus. Am.,* 4, 1996, p. 127–136, photos)

Useful morphological analysis identifies some of the formal elements that distinguish of the 17th- and 18th-century church facades of Ayacucho in the central Andes of Peru. The author's insistence on the use of the stylistic label "baroque" for these designs is unfortunate, however, since they are found to be closer in spirit to the art of the Renaissance (sometimes with Mannerist tendencies) and should be more correctly identified as representative of an original regional style.

San Cristóbal, Antonio. Ignacio Martorell y las torres de la Catedral de Lima. See item **2339**.

120 Saranyana, Josep-Ignasi and **Ana de Zaballa.** Influencias joaquinistas en la iconografía franciscano-cuzqueña del siglo XVII. (*Arch. Francisc. Hist.,* 85 : 1/4, Jan./Dec. 1992, p. 441–460)

Close iconographic reading of the Cuzco School painting "The Prophecy" hanging in the main cloister of the monastery of San Francisco in Cuzco leads to a search for its European visual and written sources. The unusual painting depicting a winged St. Francis surrounded by the Sybil of Erithrea, St. Bonaventura, St. John the Evangelist, and Joachim de Fiore Abbot has been attributed to the circle of 17th-century painters Basilio de Santa Cruz, Marcos Rivera, and Juan Zapata Inca. Even though the authors were unsuccessful in locating a European print that may have been used as a source of inspiration, they are convinced the iconography in question betrays a familiarity with the writings of St. Bonaventura and Bartholomaeus De Pisa.

Vega Vega, Wilson. José María Vargas: bibliografía. See item **2117**.

19th and 20th Centuries

FÉLIX ANGEL, *Curator, Cultural Center, Inter-American Development Bank*

THE NUMBER OF ART PUBLICATIONS produced in Latin America and the Caribbean continues to increase, fortunately without any fundamental changes in the seriousness and quality of the publications. Works from countries such as Argentina and Mexico not only outnumber those from other countries in the region, but also offer readers a wider variety of essays, art criticism, and art history while providing clearer evidence of in-depth and detailed research. With the exception perhaps of Cuba, monographs are still a favorite format among art entrepreneurs, but most of them leave the reader with a suspicious feeling.

Advanced art historical research in Mexico and Argentina are well represented by two publications. The first is an outstanding and monumental work, *México en el mundo de las colecciones de arte,* an impressive set of seven volumes documenting Mexican art treasures in collections throughout the world (item **174**). The book, which spans 3,000 years, provides a fine overview of Mexico's extraordinary cultural resources in all periods of its history. The second is a publication dedicated to the private art collection of Eduardo Constantini—consisting mostly of 20th-century art—which went on public view for the first time in 1996 in Buenos Aires (item **278**).

Despite the predominance of Argentina and Mexico, art history research and publication in some countries, such as Uruguay, Colombia, and Venezuela, has continued to broaden significantly its scope. Their bibliographies contain topics not seriously considered before, such as Alvaro Medina's *El arte colombiano de los años veinte y treinta* (item **329**), and Santiago Londoño's *Historia de la pintura y el grabado en Antioquia* (item **328**). In addition, it is satisfactory to have found from smaller countries like Costa Rica, a book as unpretentious and well documented as Eugenio Zavaleta's *Los inicios del arte abstracto en Costa Rica, 1958–1971* (item **229**), and from Haiti, the similarly well-prepared *50 années de peinture en Haïti, v. I, 1930–1950* (item **241**). Both are valuable examples of regional developments that need to be examined carefully in light of the great imbalances that exist among the countries of the Americas and their respective artistic transformations.

Collecting important works of art is still a prerogative of the wealthy, although money is not necessarily the only condition for amassing an important collection. In Latin America and the Caribbean, the state and the Church have traditionally collected cultural objects, including art, with a few notable exceptions in the corporate and private sector. Individual collectors are rare and, in some countries, virtually nonexistent. As with art publications, the important private collectors seem to spring from the same countries with healthy editing and printing industries. Institutional collecting of Latin American and Caribbean art outside the region is not as popular as one could wish.

An interesting publication related to collecting but dealing with another serious problem is Daniel Schávelzon's *El expolio del arte en la Argentina,* which addresses illegal trafficking, robbery, and vandalism of art works (item **291**). Although most countries have official policies and have signed international agreements that have been effective primarily in the cases of precolumbian art, most Latin American and the Caribbean countries still lack efficient legislation and controls. As globalization advances and these countries are increasingly exposed to an inquisitive international scene, they will unavoidably be interacting in areas where they have little experience.

The visual arts continue to be one of the most dynamic areas of expression in a territory characterized by unparalleled cultural pluralism. Increasing, and sometimes unscrupulous, commercialism is an inevitable component of the entire phenomenon. For this reason, it is important to recognize the efforts that attempt to define and analyze the visual arts in the region, as well as to demand from the reader a higher capacity for understanding. Many of the books reviewed in this chapter will undoubtedly contribute to the achievement of these goals.

GENERAL

121 América Latina '96. Buenos Aires: Museo Nacional de Bellas Artes, 1996. 160 p.: ill. (some col.).

Catalog representing a variety of art trends from Argentina, Brazil, Colombia, Chile, Mexico, Peru, Uruguay, and Venezuela documents an exhibition at the Museo Nacional de Bellas Artes in Buenos Aires in 1996, under the sponsorship of Citibank, Argentina. Coordinated by Jorge Gluzberg, each country invited to the exhibit also had an individual curator. Justo Pastor Mellado, Federica Palomero, Paulo Herkenhoff, and José Ignacio Roca are some of the authors whose presentations accompany the catalog. Fully illustrated in color.

122 Art d'Amérique latine, 1911–1968. Paris: Musée national d'art moderne: Centre Georges Pompidou, 1992. 523 p.: bibl., ill. (some col.), index.

French catalog for the exhibition on Latin American art (1911–68) with a small section on architecture organized by The Museum of Modern Art, New York, and presented at the Pompidou Center in Paris in 1992 (also in New York and at the 1992 World's Fair in Seville). Originally conceived as an event to commemorate the quincentennial, this effort may be interpreted as an attempt by MOMA to silence criticism about its reluctance, apart from a few examples, to include Latin American artists in the museum's permanent collections. The various texts written for the catalog follow the curatorial script, focusing on specific subjects. Beautifully produced, with lovely illustrations and superb printing. See also *HLAS 56:271.*

123 Bayón, Damián. Pensar con los ojos: ensayos de arte latinoamericano. 2. ed. México: Fondo de Cultura Económica, 1993. 400 p.: index. (Colección Tierra firme)

Selection made by Bayón of writings about Latin American art, divided in two main groups: precolumbian and colonial art, and modern and contemporary. Anthology does not follow a chronological order giving preference to genre, although original date of the articles and sources are indicated. Book covers more than 20 years of writings by the Argentine critic and historian.

Bermúdez, Jorge R. Gráfica e identidad nacional. See item **757.**

124 Latin American women artists = artistas latinoamericanas: 1915–1995. Guest curator Geraldine P. Biller. Essays by Bélgica Rodríguez, Edward J. Sullivan, and Marina Pérez de Mendiola. Milwaukee, Wis.: Milwaukee Art Museum, 1995. 198 p.: bibl., ill. (some col.).

Catalog of the exhibit sponsored by the Philip Morris Companies, organized by the Milwaukee Art Museum. Pérez de Mendiola provides perhaps the best and most enlightening text. As a whole, the exhibit appears to be extremely uneven due to the questionable inclusion of certain artists and the notable absence of other, more relevant artists. The personal preferences of the curators and advisors are too obviously perceived. Illustrated in b/w and color. Complemented with annotations about each of the 35 artists included.

125 Traba, Marta. Hombre americano a todo color. Bogotá: Editorial Univ. Nacional; Uniandes, 1995. 187 p., 46 p. of plates: ill. (some col.).

Originally scheduled for publication in Caracas in 1975, this book was finally published 20 years later in Bogotá. Fifteen separate short essays about Latin American artists, among them José Luis Cuevas, Rodolfo Abularach, Fernando de Szyszlo, Agustín Fernández, and Luis Caballero make up the text of this publication. The book reflects Traba's idea of the multifaceted, often contradictory Latin American as seen through the arts, in opposition to what many would consider a defined personality or cultural character. Illustrated in color with accompanying biographical notes on every artist.

MEXICO

126 **A México.** Barcelona: Generalitat de Catalunya, Dept. de la Presidència; Comissió Amèrica i Catalunya 1992; Monterrey, Mexico: Museo del Estado de Nuevo León; Museo de Monterrey, 1991. 176 p.: ill. (some col.).

On the occasion of the visit of the President of Catalonia to Mexico in Dec. 1991-Jan. 1992, the Generalitat and the Comissió Amèrica i Catalunya organized this exhibition, which included nine artists: three Mexicans (Tamayo, Felguerez, Cuevas), three Catalonians who emigrated to Mexico (Bartolí, Peyrí, Rojo), and three Catalonians who live and work in Catalonia (Casamada, Guinovart, Amat). In addition to solid biographical information, the carefully assembled publication includes many articles by prestigious art critics and literary figures, such as Marta Traba, Octavio Paz, and Alvaro Mutis. Montserrat Galí Boadella's essay on the cultural relationship between Catalonia and Mexico, particularly during the Spanish Civil War, is noteworthy. Well illustrated in b/w and color. In Catalan and Spanish.

127 **Aguirre, Carlos.** Newton en el D.F. México: Galería de Arte Mexicano; Museo de Arte Carrillo Gil, 1991. 1 v. (unpaged): ill. (some col.).

Good compilation of color images by artist Carlos Aguirre, presented at the Museo de Arte Carrillo Gil and the Galería de Arte Mexicano in Mexico City. Exhibition included paintings and installations.

128 **Aire de familia: colección de Carlos Monsiváis.** México: Consejo Nacional para la Cultura y las Artes; INBA; Museo de Arte Moderno, 1995. 99 p.: bibl., ill. (some col.).

Catalog of an exhibition of 212 caricatures ranging from Joaquín Heredia to Francisco Toledo (the oldest dating from 1845), from the collection of Carlos Monsiváis, presented at Mexico's Museo de Arte Moderno in 1995. Texts by the collector himself and by Teresa del Conde and Rafael Barajas. Barajas' essay entitled "Un país que no conoce su rostro está condenado a la caricatura" ("A country that does not know its own face is condemned to be a caricature") summarizes the intention of the exhibit and exhibitor. Monsiváis longs for a Mexican society with more self-criticism and humor.

129 **Andrade, Lourdes.** Para la desorientación general: trece ensayos sobre México y el surrealismo. México: Editorial Aldus, 1996. 189 p.: bibl., ill. (some col.), map. (Col. Las horas sitadas)

According to author, purpose of work is to unite a number of manifestations of Mexico's image as depicted in the essays, poems, paintings, and objects by various surrealists who had contact with Mexico and Mexican culture. Attempts to explain significance and symbolic meaning of Mexico's role within the Parisian group.

130 **Anguiano, Raúl.** Anguiano por Anguiano = Anguiano by Anguiano. Pachuca, Mexico: Univ. Autónoma del Estado de Hidalgo, 1997. 133 p.: ill. (some col.).

Bilingual monograph on Anguiano based on autobiographical documentation kept by the wife of the artist. In addition to Anguiano's recollections, includes a number of photographs taken mostly at professional moments, a checklist of the exhibition, a synthetic biography, and a list of his awards and commissions. Published as companion piece to the 1997 exhibition of graphic works at the Univ. Autónoma del Estado de Hidalgo.

131 **Antología del paisaje mexiquense.** Toluca, Mexico: Instituto Mexiquense de Cultura, 1995. 150 p.: bibl., ill. (some col.), map.

Landscape painting has been a favorite genre for Mexican artists. This publication accompanied an exhibit at the Instituto Mexiquense de Cultura in 1995, covering 175 years of activity in the field in Mexico. Catalog reflects various curatorial approaches associated with the genre: a historic panorama, perspective and tridimensionality, physical and geographical aspects, and symbolism. Illustrated in b/w and color, with brief biographical notes on the artists.

132 Arte en barro: tipos mexicanos, escenas costumbristas; Tlaquepaque, Jalisco. Coordinación de investigación y textos de Gutierre Aceves Piña. Fotografía de Gerardo Suter. Edición y coordinación general de Carlos Beltrán. Guadalajara, Mexico: Bancentro, 1994. 143 p.: bibl., col. ill.

Focuses on clay figures produced in the area of San Pedro Tlaquepaque (Jalisco) that have become part of the great popular tradition of Mexican folk art. A text by Pantaleón Panduro traces roots of this tradition to second half of the 19th century. Texts in English and Spanish pay tribute to the late Fernando Gamboa, from whose collections many of the pieces were selected.

133 Arte popular mexicano: cinco siglos. Coordinación del catálogo de Olga Sáenz González. México: Antiguo Colegio de San Ildefonso, 1996. 237 p.: bibl., col. ill.

Contains 10 essays on various aspects of 500 years of Mexican popular arts. Nicely annotated and illustrated in color, work accompanied 1996 exhibition at Colegio de San Ildefonso in Mexico City. Excellent introduction to the subject for the general reader.

134 Autorretrato en México: años 90. Investigación de Enrique Franco Calvo. México: La Sociedad Mexicana de Arte Moderno: Instituto Nacional de Bellas Artes, 1996. 127 p.: col. ill.

Catalog of the 1996 invitational organized by the Museo de Arte Moderno in Mexico City, featuring 71 self-portraits created for the event by the invited artists. Enrico Franco Calvo introduces the works, which are all reproduced in color.

135 Balmori, Santos. Reflejo del ritmo: antología de Santos Balmori. Recopilación de Helena Jordán de Balmori. México: Univ. Nacional Autónoma de México, Coordinación de Humanidades, 1997. 117 p.: ill. (some col.).

Compilation of 111 works of the artist by his second wife, Helena Jordán, with introduction by Alberto Dalla. Demonstrates artist's many influences and stylistic changes throughout his career.

136 Bayón, Damián. Hacia Tamayo. México: Fundación Olga y Rufino Tamayo; Fondo de Cultura Económica, 1995. 127 p.: col. ill. (Tezontle)

Citing Pierre Francastel, Bayón makes a journey into Rufino Tamayo's vast body of work, selecting only those (little more than 70) he deems most appropriate to help identify and clearly distinguish the distinct visual elements that make Tamayo an innovator and a great artist. He starts as early as 1928 and ends around 1986. The book makes a visit to an imaginary museum of Tamayo's work.

137 Casimiro Castro y su taller. México: Gobierno del Estado de México; Instituto Mexiquense de Cultura; Fomento Cultural Banamex, 1996. 204 p.: bibl., ill. (some col.).

Catalog of an exhibition of Casimiro Castro's works presented at the Palacio Iturbide in Mexico, and later at the Museo José María Velasco in Toluca in 1996. Exhibition gathered more than 200 works owned by one of the artist's former pupils. While best known for his lithographs of the Mexican railroad, this exhibit presented different aspects of the 19th-century academic artist, expanding the traditional perception of his work. Texts by Carlos Monsiváis, Maria Elena Altamirano, and four other authors help us to understand his role in the formation of the country's artistic national identity. Beautifully illustrated in color.

138 Cauduro, Rafael. Rafael Cauduro: dibujos. México: Consejo Nacional para la Cultura y las Artes, Instituto Nacional de Bellas Artes; Museo Nacional de la Estampa; Lotería Nacional para la Asistencia Pública, 1995. 63 p.: ill. (some col.).

Catalog of the exhibition of 55 drawings by Cauduro held at the Instituto Nacional de Bellas Artes (Mexico, 1995). Presentation by Gerardo Estrada. Introduction by Beatriz Vidal, and essay by Ricardo Garibay. Illustrated in color and b/w.

139 Clausell, Joaquín. Joaquín Clausell y los ecos del impresionismo en México. México: Patronato del Museo Nacional de Arte; Consejo Nacional para la Cultura y las Artes, 1995. 192 p.: bibl., ill. (some col.).

Publication related to exhibition of the same name presented at the Museo Nacional de Arte (Mexico, July-Oct. 1995), with texts by curator Jorge Alberto Manrique ("Impresionismo y Modernidad en México") and others. Essays contextualize Clausell's work within Mexican art scene using as reference, among other components, the work of his contemporaries including Diego Rivera. Well documented and illustrated in color.

140 Cohen, Eduardo. Hacia un arte existencial: reflexiones de un pintor expresionista. México: Univ. Nacional Autónoma de México, 1993. 192 p.: bibl. (Bitácora de poética; 4)

Essays written by Cohen, the Mexican painter, between 1985–90, as a result of several workshops he gave on the theoretical aspects of art, based on his personal experience as an artist.

141 Coloquio Internacional de Historia del Arte, 20th, Puebla, Mexico, 1996. Patrocinio, colección y circulación de las artes. Edición de Gustavo Curiel. México: Univ. Nacional Autónoma de México, 1997. 826 p.: bibl., ill. (Estudios de arte y estética; 46)

Rida Eder introduces this fascinating compilation of 39 papers presented at the 20th Coloquio International de Historia del Arte, celebrated at the Univ. of Puebla in 1996. Themes are divided into three areas: patronage, collecting, and circulation of the work of art. The extraordinary variety of presentations centered around three activities inherent to the role of the arts, rarely the subject of any analysis in Latin America, makes this work particularly enlightening. Themes range from role of religious orders in the colonial Americas to censorship at the 1963 and 1964 São Paulo Biennials.

142 Contactos en el límite de la arquitectura y la escultura. México: Banamex Fomento Cultural Banamex A.C., 1994. 48 p.: ill. (some col.).

Interesting, concise publication documenting exhibit sponsored by Banamex about the relation, or proximity, between architecture and sculpture, organized at the initiative of architect Agustín Hernández. Eight artists including Manuel Felguerez and Sebastián, and two teams of architects: Legorreta Arquitectos and TEN Arquitectos, combined their talents in this exhibition of 47 works, presented at the Museo Rufino Tamayo in Mexico City. Excellent color reproductions complemented with short biog-

raphical sketches and brief references to the artists' work.

143 Cortázar, Roberto. Antiguo futuro: Roberto Cortazár. México: Praxis Arte Internacional, 1996. 57 p.: ill. (some col.).

Catalog of the 1996 exhibition of 25 mixed media works by Cortázar at Galería Praxis, with texts by José Luis Cuevas and Rafael Tovar y de Teresa.

144 Creación en movimiento: arquitectura, escultura, fotografía, gráfica, medios alternativos, multimedia, pintura, video; séptima muestra de becarios, 1995/1996. México: Museo de Arte Contemporáneo; FONCA, 1997. 57 p.: ill. (some col.).

Catalog of an exhibition representing Mexican art at the end of the millennium— with the participation of 57 young artists— according to Verónica Volkow, who wrote the presentation. Artists' proposals involve a variety of fields, from painting, printmaking, photography, and sculpture to architecture, video, and alternative media. Illustrated in color and b/w, with biographical sketches of the artists. See also item **145.**

145 Creación en movimiento: becarios 1992–1993; arquitectura, escultura, fotografía, pintura, video. Mexico: FONCA, 1994. 39 p.: ill. (some col.).

Catalog of an exhibition at the Museo Carrillo Gil (Mexico City, 1994) of the fourth generation of fellows at the Fondo Nacional para la Cultura y las Artes. Forty-one artists were invited, representing a variety of media including photography and installation art.

146 Cuevas, José Luis. Gigantes y fantasmas del maestro Cuevas. Mexico: ITESM Campus Estado de Mexico, 1994. 1 v. (unpaged): ill. (some col.).

Catalog of an exhibition of drawings by José Luis Cuevas presented at ITESM's Campus Estado de Mexico in 1994, on occasion of his 60th birthday. Includes 36 drawings on the theme of the "Giant"; 23 on other themes. Texts by various authors, including Margarita Michelena and Mariano Rivera.

147 Diálogos insólitos: arte objeto. México: Sociedad Mexicana de Arte Moderno, 1997. 112 p.: bibl., ill. (some col.).

Exhibition and resulting catalog focus on 43 artists who have executed tridimensional works. Well-known and lesser-known artists are united in their pursuit of the "object" as an artistic alternative to traditional sculpture. Includes brief biographical statements.

148 Diego Rivera y el arte de ilustrar. México: Museo Dolores Olmedo Patiño, 1995. 108 p.: bibl., col. ill.

Catalog of the second temporary exhibition at the Museo Dolores Olmedo Patiño in Mexico City, dedicated to a little known facet of Diego Rivera: the art of illustration. Nearly 100 works were shown, some of them never before exhibited. Presentation by Dolores Olmedo; introduction by José Suáres; essays by Jorge Alberto Manrique and Armando Torres Michúa.

149 Emerich, Luis Carlos. Nueva plástica mexicana. Entrevistas por Enrique Franco Calvo. Producción y deseño de Magda González Villareal. México: Diana, 1997. 227 p.: bibl., col. ill.

Book covers 45 artists born between 1940–70, selected as outstanding examples of Mexico's creativity during the second half of 20th century. Good survey of contemporary Mexican art emphasizes painting and sculpture, but also includes some draftsmen and engravers. Contains excellent reproductions and photos of the artists along with their biographies, which serve as the backdrop for interviews with a number of Mexican critics and historians, such as Teresa del Conde, Patricia Ortiz Monasterio, and Víctor Sandoval.

150 Expresión plástica: 35 artistas en Veracruz. Veracruz, Mexico: Gobierno del Estado de Veracruz; Instituto Veracruzano de Cultura, 1995. 224 p.: ill. (some col.). (Col. Arte)

Catalog of 1995 exhibition organized by the government of Veracruz and the Instituto Veracruzano de Cultura to honor the state of Veracruz. All artists were born or live in the area, which was the criteria for the exhibition. Includes a short commentary on the work of each artist.

151 Felguérez, Manuel. Felguérez: el límite de una secuencia. Monterrey, Mexico: Museo de Arte Contemporáneo de Monterrey, 1997. 78 p.: bibl., ill. (some col.).

Catalog of a 1997 exhibition of 37 paintings and sculptures by Felguérez at the Museo de Arte Contemporáneo de Monterrery demonstrates the traditionally high quality of this museum's publications. Fully illustrated in color and with complete information on the exhibited works. Also includes a concise illustrated retrospective of career highlights and accomplishments showing the evolution of the artist's style.

152 Frank, Patrick. Posada's broadsheets: Mexican popular imagery, 1890–1910. Albuquerque: Univ. of New Mexico Press, 1998. 264 p.: bibl., ill., index.

Close examination of Posada's work in context, including shocking crimes, executions, folkloric subjects, bandits, the coming of the Revolution, sources of Posada's style, etc., which help in understanding his spontaneous working-class outlook.

153 Frérot, Christine. El mercado del arte en México, 1950–1976. México: INBA, 1990. 227 p.: bibl., ill. (some col.). (Serie Investigación y documentación de las artes. Segunda época. Artes plásticas)

Updated version of Frérot's doctoral thesis on the social, economic, and political conditions of the relatively newly formed art market in Mexico, viewed from an international perspective. Focuses on years 1970–76 (during presidency of Luis Echeverría), which were crucial in market development. Well documented, the book provides a rare look at the economics of Latin American art. Illustrated in b/w and color, with generous notes and good bibliography.

154 Goldman, Shifra M. Contemporary Mexican painting in a time of change. Foreword by Raquel Tibol. Albuquerque: Univ. of New Mexico Press, 1995. 229 p.: bibl., ill., index.

Provocative book on the role of figurative artists (known as Nueva Presencia and Interioristas) in Mexico during 1960s. Their work demonstrated an interest in the human figure while they distanced themselves from the social realism of preceding generations. Good analysis of the era's sociopolitical scene and conflicting currents of nationalism and internationalism. Excellent bibliography and notes. Illustrated in b/w.

155 Gómez del Campo, Carmen and Leticia Torres Carmona. En memoria de un rostro: Isabel Villaseñor. México: LOLA de México, 1997. 94 p.: bibl., ill. (some col.).

Brief biography of the Mexican model, actress, singer, poet, playwright, painter, printmaker, and rural teacher, within the framework of her own life and against the backdrop of work of other contemporary personalities. Besides her husband and teacher, many characters make cameo appearances in Villaseñor's life such as the photographer Manuel Alvarez Brazo, the Russian film director Eisenstein, and model Angelina Beloff.

156 Gómez Serrano, Jesús. José Guadalupe Posada: testigo y crítico de su tiempo; Aguascalientes, 1866–1876. Mexico: Univ. Autónoma de Aguascalientes; SEP, Subsecretaría de Educación Superior e Investigación Científica, 1995. 195 p.: bibl., ill. (some col.).

In 18 chapters the work offers a historic perspective on the years 1866–76 in Mexico through life of printmaker Posada. Points out many events and characters that had an impact on Posada's life, including his brother, Cirilo, and his move from Aguascalientes to León in 1872. Very entertaining, with good information sources. Illustrated in b/w.

157 González Camarena, Jorge. Universo plástico. México: Democracia Ediciones, 1995. 110 p.: bibl., ill. (some col.).

Presents a global vision of the life and work of the Mexican painter, sculptor, illustrator, and muralist González Camarena who died in 1980. Illustrated in color and b/w. Texts by María Teresa Favela Fierro with prologue by Miguel Alvarez González.

158 González Mello, Renato. Orozco: ¿pintor revolucionario? México: Univ. Nacional Autónoma de México, Instituto de Investigaciones Estéticas, 1995. 97 p.: bibl., ill. (some col.), index. (Cuadernos de historia del arte; 45)

González Mello's provocative essay questions the original date of the famous Orozco painting "Despojo Humano" ("Driftwood") in the collection of the Museo Carrillo Gil in Mexico City. The painting is usually considered to have been completed in 1915. If, however, the painting was done around 1926–28, as the author suggests, this would change the traditional interpretation of Orozco's work in relation to the sociopolitical context. Essay emphasizes Orozco's antagonism toward revolutionary ideals and his frustration with the power of political

agendas to shape the direction of the arts in Mexico.

159 La Guía artes de Mexico: museos, galerías y otros espacios del arte. Coordinación general del proyecto de Antonieta Cruz. México: Artes de México y del Mundo, 1995. 318 p.: col. ill., index.

Complements *Museos de la ciudad de México* (item **186**). This particular guide not only covers museums but also commercial galleries and other art spaces, such as bookstores, frame shops, and restaurants in Mexico City, Monterrey, Guadalajara, and Oaxaca. First-hand cultural and entertainment guide for any visitor.

160 Homenaje a Rodolfo Nieto: 1936– 1985. Monterrey, Mexico: Museo de Arte Contemporáneo de Monterrey, 1995. 179 p.: bibl., col. ill.

Bilingual catalog of the exhibition-tribute to the artist (who died in 1985), held to commemorate 10th anniversary of his death. Includes essay by Jaime Moreno Villarreal explaining Nieto's work and influences, from Dubuffet to Picasso. However, as with most artists from Nieto's generation, the strongest influence, particularly during his last 10 years, is one not mentioned here—Tamayo himself. Lavishly illustrated in color with complete checklist and short biography.

161 Iconografía de David Alfaro Siqueiros. México: Instituto Nacional de Bellas Artes; Centro Nacional de Investigación, Documentación, e Información de Artes Plásticas; Fondo de Cultura Económica, 1997. 166 p.: ill.

Fascinating collection of photographic documentation related to life and work of one of Mexico's three great muralists. Work offers a better understanding of Siqueiros as an artist, a man, and a historic figure; and of the people who surrounded him. Profusely illustrated in color and b/w. Includes a biographical chronology.

162 Imágenes y visiones: arte mexicano, entre la vanguardia y la actualidad. Spain: Centro Galego de Arte Contemporánea, 1995. 222 p.: ill. (some col.).

Excellent catalog of exhibition of the same name presented at the Centro Galego de Arte Contemporánea (Spain, 1995). The works of 15 artists from three generations, including Guatemalan-born Carlos Mérida and Rufino Tamayo, were selected in part for the evocative connotations of what can be identified as "Mexican." Texts include those of Carlos Monsiváis and Erika Billeter. Complemented with biographical and technical data, and excellent color reproductions.

163 Jose Luis Cuevas, el ojo perdido de Dios. Recopilación de Jorge Toribio. Toluca, Mexico: Univ. Autónoma del Estado de México, 1997. 180 p., 52 plates: bibl., ill. (Colección Arte y artistas; 2)

Compilation of writings by the Mexican artist about how he began to write and how he formed relationships with colleagues and various intellectuals throughout his life. Toribio has complemented Cuevas' texts with additional material extracted from articles by such writers as Marta Traba and Elena Poniatowska. Offers an intimate portrait of rivalries and friendships. Illustrated in b/w.

164 Joyas de la pintura mexicana: exposición temporal inaugural. Monterrey, Mexico: Museo de Monterrey, 1994. 52 p.: col. ill.

Exhibit catalog reproduces first-class works of several Mexican master painters, from 19th-century Hermenegildo Bustos to Rufino Tamayo. The photographs, all very good, justify exhibition's title. Worthwhile for the reproductions and their documentary value.

165 Kahlo, Frida. The diary of Frida Kahlo: an intimate self-portrait. Introduction by Carlos Fuentes. Essay and commentaries by Sarah M. Lowe. New York: H.N. Abrams; México: La Vaca Independiente S.A. de C.V., 1995. 295 p.: bibl., ill. (some col.), index.

Carlos Fuentes writes passionately and brilliantly about Frida Kahlo in the introduction of this book, which reproduces the pages and drawings of Kahlo's personal diary. Sarah M. Lowe, who wrote the commentaries and the essay, provides a more balanced view. Work is a curious gathering of thoughts and feelings, observations and annotations, and indeed makes the reader feel that he/she is entering forbidden and intimate territory. A deep realm, at times tender and dark, the book will probably make Kahlo's many fans eager to dive in.

166 Kirking, Clayton; Luis Carlos Emerich; and Jorge Esquinca. Roberto Márquez: fragmentos del tiempo. Monterrey, Mexico: Museo de Arte Contemporáneo de Monterrey, 1997. 146 p.: bibl., col. ill.

Catalog of an exhibit at Museo de Arte Contemporáneo de Monterrey, which included paintings and mixed media, makes evident that little has changed in Márquez's work over last 10 years. Complete checklist and color illustrations.

167 Un listón alrededor de una bomba: una mirada sobre el arte mexicano; André Breton. México: Instituto Nacional de Bellas Artes, 1997. 208 p.: bibl., ill. (some col.), map.

Breton's well-known phrase about Frida Kahlo's work provides the title for the catalog to the exhibition held at the Museo Casa Estudio Diego Rivera y Frida Kahlo in Mexico City, commemorating Breton's 1939 exhibition of Mexican art in Paris. In the form of an anthology, texts by Rivera, Breton, Luis Cardoza y Aragón (besides Breton and Kahlo) are reunited as a tribute to the founder of French surrealism, and to his connection with Mexican art and two of its more illustrious figures.

168 Luna, Andrés de. La pintura de Enrique Estrada. México: Instituto Nacional de Bellas Artes; Fundación Cultural Bancomer, 1998. 135 p.: ill. (some col.).

Publication is a complement to retrospective exhibition presented by the artist at the Palacio de Bellas Artes (Mexico City, 1994). Profusely illustrated in color.

169 Luna Arroyo, Antonio. González Camarena. México: Ciencia y Cultura Latinoamérica, 1995. 166 p.: bibl., ill. (chiefly col.). (Colección Biografías. Serie Pintores.)

Luna's analysis of Jorge González Camarena—which relies heavily on artist's transcriptions and statements—attempts to place his importance in Mexican art beyond his most significant—or at least better known—work, the mural "La Fusión de Dos Culturas." González Camarena occupies third place among Mexican muralists in terms of square footage of surface painted; however, his recognition does not equal this numeric statistic.

170 **Luna Arroyo, Antonio.** Ramos
Martínez. México: Salvat Ciencia y
Cultura Latinoamerica, 1994. 156 p.: bibl.,
ill. (some col.). (Artistas latinoamericanos)

According to author, this is the second
formal study and the most complete on life
and work of Alfredo Ramos Martínez, who
Luna Arroyo claims to be the "educator" of
the Mexican artistic Renaissance. Illustrated
with 26 reproductions in color.

171 **Maestros del arte contemporáneo en
la colección permanente del Museo
Rufino Tamayo.** México: Américo Arte Editores; Fundación Olga y Rufino Tamayo; Instituto Nacional de Bellas Artes, 1997.
259 p.: bibl., col. ill.

Superb catalog of the equally exquisite
international collection of the Museo Rufino
Tamayo in Mexico City. In the introduction,
Gerardo Estrada points out that the texts by
Alberto Ruy Sánchez and Manuel Larrosa
discuss the museum as a whole, including its
natural and sociocultural environment, its
development, and its future. Provides a concise vision of contemporary Western art.
Each work reproduced is accompanied by a
comprehensive annotation and complete
technical data, conservation record, and exhibition history.

172 **Malvido Arriaga, Adriana.** Nahui
Olin: la mujer del sol. México: Diana,
1993. 175 p., lxiv p. of plates: bibl., col. ill.,
indexes.

Tells story of Nahui Olin (whose real
name was Carmen Mondragon). Prologue is
by Elena Poniatowska who calls the author
"woman, mother, and reporter." In turn
Malvido calls Olin "poet, painter, and muse."
In reality, Olin was an exotic, mysterious and
complex beauty with extraordinary, wonderful eyes, animal appeal, and an upper-class
upbringing; a colorful character of the times.
During 1920–30s, Olin's association—not
necessarily professional—with the muralists,
and in particular with Dr. Atl and with photographers such as Manuel Alvarez Bravo,
Antonio Garduño, and Edward Weston,
among others, produced audacious results for
them. Work is entertaining despite poor layout. Reproductions confirm that the real talent of Ms. Olin was not in the plastic arts.

173 **Máscaras en el Poliforum.** México: Poliforum Siqueiros, 1996. 78 p.: ill.

The mask, an element deeply rooted

in many societies, and particularly strong in
the Mexican popular tradition, is the theme
of this catalog. Includes the works of many
contemporary artists who applied their talents and individual creative visions to contribute to an exhibition entitled Por Amo
al Arte (For the Love of Art), at the famous
Siqueiros' Polyforum. Particularly noteworthy are the excellent color reproductions and
biographical sketches of the participants.

174 **México en el mundo de las colecciones
de arte.** v. 1–7. México: El Gobierno de
la República, 1994. 7 v.: bibl., ill. (some col.),
maps.

Massive survey of Mexican art in
collections throughout the world. Each volume contains hundreds of color illustrations
and good bibliographies. Excellent quality
printing. All volumes were meticulously assembled and include annotations indicating
sources of the illustrations.

175 **Mexico. Secretaría de Hacienda y
Crédito Público.** Colección pago en especie de la Secretaría de Hacienda y Crédito
Público, 1992–1993: catálogo. México: Secretaría de Hacienda y Crédito Público, 1994.
294 p.: col. ill.

Well-printed volume registers contributions (many of them very good) made to
the Mexican government by Mexican artists
who decided to pay their taxes with art
works of their own creation. This original
concept allows the Secretaría de Hacienda to
organize exhibitions within its own facilities
as well as to lend the pieces to other institutions for temporary exhibitions, thereby contributing to the dissemination of the Mexican artists' works. Nearly 140 artists are
represented in this book, which includes a
color reproduction for each work and a short
biographical sketch of each artist. See also
item **178.**

176 **Morales, Rodolfo.** Un tema que se
repite: obra gráfica 1994 a 1997. Oaxaca, Mexico: Fundación Cultural Rodolfo
Morales, 1997. 51 p.: bibl., ill. (some col.).

Catalog of first exhibition of the
graphic work (lithography and silkscreen) by
the Oaxacan artist held at the foundation
that bears his name. Includes introductory
text by Edward Sullivan in both English and
Spanish, complete checklist, and color illustrations.

177 Moyssén L., Xavier; Fausto Ramirez; and **Israel Cavazos Garza.** Un homenaje a Alfredo Ramos Martínez, 1871–1946. Monterrey, Mexico: Museo de Arte Contemporáneo de Monterrey, 1996. 160 p.: bibl., col. ill.

Bilingual catalog of the 1996 retrospective exhibition of 74 works of Ramos Martínez, commemorating 50th anniversary of the artist's death and 400th anniversary of the foundation of the city of Monterrey where the artist was born. Excellent color reproductions.

178 **Mexico. Secretaría de Hacienda y Crédito Público.** Muestra de la colección pago en especie: José Chávez Morado, Raúl Anguiano, Rafael Coronel, Luis Nishizawa, Ricardo Martínez, Roger von Gunten, Manuel Felguérez, Vicente Rojo. México: Secretaría de Hacienda y Crédito Público, 1992. 89 p.: col. ill.

Catalog of the exhibition organized in 1992 with selections from the art collection of the Secretaría de Hacienda y Crédito Público, consisting of works received as payment for taxes, a program initiated in 1975. Illustrated in color, with texts by Raquel Tibol, Rafael Sámano, and others. See also item **175.**

179 **Los Murales del Palacio de Bellas Artes.** México: Américo Arte Editores; Consejo Nacional para la Cultura y las Artes; Instituto Nacional de Bellas Artes, 1995. 213 p.: bibl., ill. (chiefly col.).

Complements other publications related to the Palacio de Bellas Artes de México. Concentrates primarily on the murals executed by the Mexican school of muralists, including Rivera, Orozco, and Tamayo. The group of color illustrations depicting the murals is preceded by a short essay, which includes rare, b/w photographic archival material.

180 **Museo Biblioteca Pape. Exposición, 62nd, Monclova, Mexico, 1995.** Los maestros latinoamericanos de la colección del Museo José Luis Cuevas. Monclova, Mexico: Museo Biblioteca Pape, 1995. 32 p.: col. ill.

Catalog of the exhibition presented at the Museo Biblioteca Pape in Juárez, featuring 47 selected works from the Museo José Luis Cuevas collection. Exhibition included other artists of Cuevas' generation such as Colombian Alejandro Obregón, Nicaraguan Armando Morales, and Peruvian Fernando de Szyszlo. Cuevas' wife Bertha, who is the director of the museum, wrote the introduction.

181 **O'Higgins, Pablo.** Pablo O'Higgins: un compromiso plástico. México: Museo Dolores Olmedo Patiño, 1995. 84 p.: chiefly col. ill.

Catalog of the exhibition inaugurating temporary exhibition program at the Museo Dolores Olmedo Patiño in Mexico City. Features 66 works by the North American artist who emigrated to Mexico in 1924, honoring 91st anniversary of his birth. Includes presentation by Dolores Olmedo, and essays by José Suárez Sánchez (director of the museum) and Gilberto Bosques Saldívar. Chronology by Francisco Reyes Palma.

182 **Orozco Romero, Carlos.** Carlos Orozco Romero: propuestas y variaciones. México: Instituto Nacional de Bellas Artes, 1996. 88 p.: bibl., ill. (some col.).

Short monograph on the Mexican artist who died in 1984 examines his career and stylistic traits. Of the many texts, the two by Luis-Martin Lozano and Carlos Blas Galindo are the most enlightening about artist's life and work. Well printed and illustrated, mostly in color.

183 **Ortiz Angulo, Ana.** La pintura mexicana independiente de la Academia en el siglo XIX. México: Instituto Nacional de Antropología e Historia, 1995. 149 p.: bibl., ill. (Colección Científica; 302)

The author, a pupil of the late scholar Justino Fernandez, from whom she had borrowed the title for her research, makes a very conscientious and well-documented effort to analyze the painting produced in Mexico outside the officialdom of the San Carlos Academy, particularly between 1810–1910. Illustrated, but reproductions are not of the same good quality as the text, which focuses primarily on Hermenegildo Bustos and José María Estrada.

184 **Otras rutas hacia Siqueiros: un simposio organizado por CURARE, and** other organizations. México: Instituto Nacional de Bellas Artes; CURARE, Espacio Crítico para las Artes, 1996. 302 p.: bibl., ill., maps.

Compilation of the papers presented at the symposium organized by CURARE as

199 Salón de Arte Bancomer, 1st, Mexico City, 1995. 95 Salón de Arte Bancomer. México: Fundación Cultural Bancomer, 1995. 88 p.: col. ill., ports.

Catalog of an exhibition of 34 invited artists and 58 works (selected by a panel of four advisors) sponsored by Grupo Financiero Bancomer of Mexico based on the idea of maintaining an alternative display space for progressive artists who are outside the commercial circle. Includes introduction by Olivier Debroise about the origins and modern meaning of a "salon." Illustrated in color and completed with checklist and a short biography of the artists.

200 Salón de Triunfadores, 1st, Aguascalientes, Mexico, 1996. Salón de Triunfadores: 30 años de arte joven. México: Instituto Nacional de Bellas Artes, 1996. 115 p.: ill. (some col.).

Catalog of the exhibition commemorating 30th anniversary of the national competition for art students organized in the city of Aguascalientes. From its relatively simple origins, the competition has evolved into the more complex competition that it is today. Raquel Tibol writes a short essay about the evolution of the event and her personal relation to it.

201 Sánchez Hernández, Sergio. Fuentes para el estudio de Gerardo Murillo, Dr. Atl. México: Univ. Nacional Autónoma de México, Coordinación de Humanidades, Dirección General de Publicaciones, 1994. 133 p.: bibl.

Author summarizes book with his four objectives: 1) to provide a research guide to Dr. Atl's own archives, which had been unavailable for many years; 2) to complement the information contained in the archives of Silvino Macedonio González; 3) to make known other information available in various institutions and museums; and 4) to publish a bibliography of writings by and about Dr. Atl.

202 Santiago, José de. Jesús Gallardo. Guanajuato, Mexico: Gobierno del Estado de Guanajuato, 1994. 146 p.: bibl., ill. (some col.). (Serie Artistas de Guanajuato)

Nicely printed book focuses on work of local artist Jesús Gallardo. Links Gallardo—mainly a landscape artist with an illustrative vein—with the Mexican landscape tradition.

Excellent color illustrations; however, work is repetitive.

203 60 años TGP: Taller de Gráfica Popular. México: Consejo Nacional para la Cultura y las Artes; Instituto Nacional de Bellas Artes, 1997. 55 p.: ill.

Commemorative publication on occasion of the 60th anniversary of the TGP, which can be credited for encouraging and maintaining interest in the graphic arts in Mexico. Antonio Rodríguez explains the contribution of the TGP to Mexican art, and Jesús Alvarez Amaya provides a brief history of the Taller.

204 Siqueiros, David Alfaro. Siqueiros en la colección del Museo Carrillo Gil. México: Instituto Nacional de Bellas Artes, 1996. 130 p.: bibl., ill. (some col.).

Color illustrated, bilingual catalog of the works of Siqueiros (paintings, drawings, and prints) in the collection of the Museo de Arte Carrillo Gil issued on occasion of 1996 celebrations organized to commemorate 100th anniversary of artist's birth. Ana Garduño writes of the semblance of friendship that existed between Siqueiros and Dr. Carrillo Gil. Includes a catalog list with commentaries on the works, illustrated with photographs from the Siqueiros archive showing how the artist relied on the use of photographic images to compose some of his most complex murals.

205 Siqueiros, David Alfaro. Siqueiros por Siqueiros. México: Museo Dolores Olmedo Patiño, 1996. 125 p.: bibl., chiefly col. ill.

Despite its title, José Juárez, Irene Herner, and Arnoldo Martínez Verdugo present the work of Siqueiros through the unifying theme of the self-portrait, a recurrent theme for the artist during his career. Siquieros' skills as a painter, draftsman, and muralist are presented well, despite other more arguable aspects of the essays. The variety of techniques represented by the different works illustrates the interest in Siqueiros for his technical mastery of art. Excellent chronology and a satisfying number of illustrations make this catalog a good introduction to the complex personality of the Mexican master.

206 Tibol, Raquel. José Clemente Orozco. México: Galeria Enrique Guerrero, 1998. 55 p.: ill. (some col.).

Catalog of the 1998 exhibition (shown in Bogotá and Mexico City) of 30 works by Orozco, which according to Raquel Tibol offer a view of Orozco's changing esthetic interests between 1910–48. The watercolors from 1910–13 are outstanding. Illustrated in color, with complete checklist and biography of the artist.

207 Volkow, Verónica. La mordedura de la risa: un estudio sobre la obra gráfica de Francisco Toledo. México: Editorial Aldus, 1995. 77 p.: ill. (some col.). (Col. Las horas situadas. Serie Iluminaciones)

More than a "study", the book is a poetic digression on the graphic work of Francisco Toledo. Divided into 17 themes, with many illustrations in color and b/w.

208 Zalce, Alfredo. Alfredo Zalce: artista michoacano. Morelia, Mexico: Gobierno del Estado de Michoacán; Instituto Michoacano de Cultura; México: Secretaría de Educación Pública; Instituto Politécnico Nacional, 1997. 199 p.: bibl., col. ill.

Contributors to this study of Zalce's works include Augusto Isla, Teresa del Conde, Berta Taracena, Graciela Kartofel, and Armando Torres Michúa. Explores the various facets of Zalce's works as reflected in his murals, easel painting, printmaking, drawing, and sculpture, along with his commitment to using both technical and esthetic means to advance social transformation. Good illustrations, with a chronology of the artist and checklist of works. See also item **209**.

209 Zalce, Alfredo. Zalce total. Mexico City: Instituto Nacional de Bellas Artes, 1995. 126 p.: ill. (chiefly col.).

Catalog of the 1995 traveling retrospective of 243 works (in different media) by Alfredo Zalce, covering more than seven decades of the artist's work, organized under the initiative of the Instituto Nacional de Bellas Artes in cooperation with other institutions. Alberto Hijar wrote the main text entitled "Frontera de la Modernidad." Well illustrated in color and complemented with a chronology about the artist. See also item **208**.

210 Zepeda del Valle, Juan Manuel. La obra mural de Diego Rivera en la capilla de Chapingo. Mexico: Univ. Autónoma Chapingo, Dirección de Patronato Universitario, Dirección de Centros Regionales, 1993. 112 p.: bibl., ill.

Provides a detailed explanation of the Rivera murals at Chapingo, with a mostly didactic intention about their meaning, without engaging in esthetic digressions. Very useful guide for any student interested in Mexican muralism. Illustrated in color with a drawing plan of the chapel.

211 Zurian, Tomás. Rosario Cabrera: la creación entre la impaciencia y el olvido. México: Instituto Nacional de Bellas Artes, 1998. 139 p.: bibl., ill. (some col.).

Pioneering study that accompanied 1998 exhibition dedicated to the life and work of the enigmatic female painter who was the first Mexican woman to exhibit in Paris. Cabrera developed a career dedicated to teaching art to indigenous children, retiring eventually to anonymity. The essay by Tomás Zurian, complemented with a chronology by Carla Zurian, are first steps in deciphering the personality of this artist still shrouded in mystery.

CENTRAL AMERICA

212 Album de grabados en madera. 2. ed. San José: Ministerio de Cultura, Juventud y Deportes, Editorial de la Dirección de Publicaciones, 1996. 1 v. (unpaged): ill.

Sixty-two wood engravings by some well-known Costa Rican artists of mid-century are reproduced in this publication on the occasion of the 25th anniversary of Costa Rica's Ministerio de Cultura, Juventud y Deportes. The artists included are Francisco Amighetti, Francisco Zúñiga, Manuel de la Cruz González, Carlos Salazar Herrera, Gilbert Laporte, Teodorico Quirós, and Adolfo Sáenz. No essays or annotations accompany the illustrations.

213 Arellano, Jorge Eduardo. Historia de la pintura nicaragüense. 5. ed., rev. y ampliada. Managua: s.n., 1994. 188 p.: bibl., ill.

Original text of this volume (now in its fifth edition) has been revised, updated, and enlarged since it first appeared in 1974. Due to the traditional lack of art historians in Nicaragua dedicated to the study of plastic arts, book remains a first-rate guide to country's developments in painting since colonial times. Illustrated in b/w. For a review of the 1990 edition, see *HLAS 52:332.*

214 Art-en Costa Rica, 1996: directorio de la plástica costarricense = Guide of Costa Rican fine arts. San José: Art Directo, 1996. 190 p.: ill. (some col.).

Practical, commercially oriented directory of artists active today in Costa Rica. Over 80 artists are included, each with biographical information, personal photograph, reproduction of one work (painting, sculpture, print, etc.), and address.

215 Bienal de arte de Panamá Cervecería Nacional, 4th, Panamá, 1998. Cuarto bienal de arte de Panamá Cervecería Nacional. Panamá: Museo de Arte Contemporáneo, 1998. 113 p.: facsims., photos.

Color catalog of event sponsored by Cervecería Nacional in Panama following success of salons organized by same company since 1984. Includes introductions by Irene Escoffery, Mónica Kupfer, and Ramón Oviero. Fernando Toledo received first prize. Forty-seven works (paintings, sculptures, mixed media) were selected for this edition of the Biennial, illustrating latest trends in Panamanian art.

216 Bienal de pintura Centroamérica y Panamá, Museos del Banco Central de Costa Rica, 1992. Bienal de pintura Centroamérica y Panamá. San José: Museo de Arte Costarricense, 1992. 40 p.: ill.

Catalog of painting competition organized by the Museo de Arte Costarricense in San José in 1992. Nineteen artists were selected for the event. The biographical data of each artist appears with a b/w reproduction of the work. The only prize awarded went to Carlos Montenegro of Nicaragua. Panama did not participate in this event.

217 Bienal de pintura nicaragüense Fundación Ortiz-Gurdián, 1st, Managua, 1997. Bienal de pintura nicaragüense Fundación Ortiz-Gurdián. Managua: Fundacion Ortiz-Gurdián, 1997. 97 p.: col. ill.

Catalog of the 1997 exhibition and invitational held at the Rubén Darío Theater in Managua provides an indication about the state of the arts in the country up to that year. Complemented with short biographical

sketches of the participating artists and color reproductions of the works on exhibit.

218 González Palma, Luis. Luis González Palma. Introducción de María Christina Orive. Edición de Sara Facio. Buenos Aires: Azotea Editorial Fotográfica, 1993. 82 p.: bibl., chiefly ill. (some col.). (Col. del sol)

First book from Azotea Editorial Fotográfica introduces work of González Palma in a bilingual edition. Orive presents the art of this Guatemalan architect and artist, whose work is focused on installations using photographic images and collages.

219 Herrera, Fabio. Fabio Herrera: gesto, signo, materia. San José: Museo de Arte Constarricense, 1996. 59 p.: col. ill.

Bilingual catalog of the exhibition at the Museo de Arte Costarricense, curated by Efraím Hernández, who also wrote the retrospective essay.

220 López R., J. Evaristo and **Longino Becerra.** Honduras, visión panorámica de su pintura. Tegucigalpa: Baktun Editorial, 1994. 245 p.: bibl., ill. (some col.).

General view of history of painting in Honduras concentrates on the 20th century, with emphasis on contemporary artists. Due to the scarcity of material about the subject in Central American countries, book is definitely welcome, more as a reference for the current situation than as a serious study. Bibliography is poor, and the sources documenting factual information are flawed which perhaps explains historic inaccuracies and errors of interpretation. Illustrated in color.

221 Rodríguez, Bélgica. Arte centroamericano: una aproximación. Caracas: Editorial Ex Libris, 1994. 119 p.: bibl., photos.

Forty-five artists (the oldest being Teodorico Quiroz) from five Central American countries are represented in this book, each with an accompanying illustration of a work and a short biographical sketch. An introduction and five different essays, one for each country, form the main text. This is a general panorama of modern and contemporary art in the region, indicating at the same time, in broad terms, some of the individual achievements and problems of a social, cultural, and economic nature.

222 **Rojas González, José Miguel.** Museo de Arte Costarricense. San José: Museo de Arte Costarricense, 1996. 142 p.: bibl., ill. (some col.).

Catalog of selected works in museum's collection (from late 1800s to contemporary artists), divided thematically (portraiture and landscape), and stylistically (figurative and expressionist, abstract and geometric art). Introductory essay traces the history of the museum since its creation in 1977.

223 **Sobalvarro, Orlando.** Sobalvarro. Nicaragua: Galería CODICE, 1995. 134 p.: bibl., ill. (some col.). (Libros de la plástica nicaragüense; 1)

Monograph on Sobalvarro with texts by Julio Valle-Castillo (painting), and Maria Dolores G. Torres (sculpture), complemented with an anthology of opinions about him by arts and letters personalities such as Pablo Antonio Cuadra, Raquel Tibol, Marta Traba, José Gómez Sicre, and Rodrigo Peñalba. Includes numerous reproductions of works in both disciplines (mostly executed in the 1990s), which might give the impression that Sobalvarro is primarily a painter, showing a consistency in 1990s not seen in previous periods. For review of No. 2 in the series, see item **226.**

224 **Torres, María Dolores G.** La modernidad en la pintura nicaragüense, 1948–1990. Managua: Banco Nicaragüense, 1996. 261 p.: bibl., ill. (some col.). (Col. cultural Banco Nicaragüense. Serie arte nicaragüense)

Commendable effort by author, under sponsorship of the Banco Nicaragüense de Industria y Comercio, to present a panoramic view of the development of painting in Nicaragua beginning with the year in which Rodrigo Peñalba assumed the directorship of the Escuela Nacional de Bellas Artes of Managua. The book is divided into nine chapters, and is complemented with biographical profiles of the artists. Profusely illustrated, mostly in color. This updated perspective is a welcome addition to the sparse bibliography on Nicaraguan art.

225 **Trujillo, Guillermo.** Guillermo Trujillo: mito y metamorfosis. Curaduría de Raquel Tibol. México: Fundación Olga y Rufino Tamayo, 1997. 82 p.: bibl., ill. (some col.).

Catalog of 1997 exhibition of 37 works (painting, works on paper, tapestries, and sculptures) dedicated to the artist and architect Trujillo held at Museo Rufino Tamayo in Mexico as part of the Masters of Latin American Art series. Includes a presentation by Panama's Ambassador Eloy Alfaro, and Raquel Tibol's compilation of critical excerpts outlining Trujillo's long and dedicated career. Complemented with a chronology by Carmen Alemán. Fully illustrated in color and b/w. The artist, well known for his penetrating and moody humor, has annotated every work with a witty commentary.

226 **Valle-Castillo, Julio.** Saravia. Managua: Codice Galería de Arte Contemporáneo, 1996. 133 p.: ill. (some col.). (Libros de la plástica nicaragüense; 2)

No. 2 of the series *Libros de la plástica nicaragüense* published by Galería Códice, volume is dedicated to Fernando Saravia, painter and sculptor. Saravia is considered to be the most prolific sculptor in Nicaragua. Book indicates, however, that Saravia's most interesting work is the abstract series he painted from the mid-1960s to the mid-1970s, influenced by Spanish informalism. For review of No. 1 in the series, see item **223.**

227 **Visión del arte contemporáneo en Guatemala.** v. 3. Guatemala: Patronato de Bellas Artes de Guatemala, 1996. 1 v.: bibl., ill.

Catalog of the third exhibition on Guatemalan art held at the Museo Nacional de Arte Moderno (Guatemala) focused on the generations of the 1970s to the present. Exhibition sponsored by the Patronato de Bellas Artes with the idea of revitalizing the role of the museum in the community. Includes texts by curator Rossina Cazali and Antonio Morales Santos explaining the situation of the arts during the years considered. Illustrated in b/w.

228 **Yuscarán, Guillermo.** Velásquez: the man and his art. Tegucigalpa: Nuevo Sol Publications, 1994. 302 p.: bibl., ill. (some col.), index.

Biography of the primitive artist as recollected through his own words and secondary sources. Author parallels Velásquez's life and work with contemporaneous historical events. At the time of publication, this was the only known complete biography of the artist. Illustrated in color and b/w.

229 Zavaleta Ochoa, Eugenia. Los inicios del arte abstracto en Costa Rica, 1958–1971. San José: Museo de Arte Costarricense, 1994. 211 p.: bibl., ill. (some col.).

Excellent study of beginnings of Costa Rican abstract art pays tribute to the pioneering role of its seminal figure, Manuel de la Cruz González, clarifying the origins of his work after he left the country to escape political reprisal. Makes evident the connection between González and the Venezuelan geometric-abstractionists. Well documented and illustrated, although mostly in b/w, work is one of the best studies on the subject published so far in Central America.

THE CARIBBEAN

230 Aguilera, Alejandro. Heroes de uso y otras reliquias. México: Galería Ramis Barquet, 1996? 1 v. (unpaged): col. ill.

Catalog of the 1996 exhibition of sculptures, paintings, and constructions by Aguilera at Galería Ramis Barquet in Mexico City. Includes a bilingual text by Osvaldo Sánchez.

231 Arte de nuestra América. Bogotá: Banco de la República, 1997. 71 p.: col. ill.

Illustrated catalog of the 1997 exhibition of 50 selected works representing same number of Latin American and Caribbean artists, from Diego Rivera to José Bedía, at the Biblioteca Luis Angel Arango in Bogotá. All works belong to the Casa de las Américas. Complemented with biographical sketches of the artists.

232 Arte dominicano, artistas españoles y modernidad: 1920–1961. Textos de María Ugarte y Jeannette Miller. Santo Domingo: Centro Cultural Hispánico, Instituto de Cooperación Iberoamericana, 1996. 79 p.: ill. (some col.).

Catalog of the 1996 exhibition at the Centro Cultural Hispánico de Santo Domingo analyzes the impact of the arrival, around 1940, of a group of Spanish painters fleeing the Spanish Civil War. Maria Ugarte

explains the role of the Spaniards in the development of Dominican art, while Jeannette Miller traces the developments of modern art in the country around the 1920s. Illustrated in color with biographical summaries of the artists included.

233 Bedia, José. José Bedia. México: Galería Ramis F. Barquet; Ninart, Centro de Cultura, 1992. 1 v. (unpaged): ill. (some col.).

Catalog of the exhibition of the artist held at Galería Ramis Barquet and NINART in Mexico City, undated. Includes an essay by Edward Sullivan, in English and Spanish.

234 Bienal de La Habana, 6th, 1997. El individuo y su memoria: sexta bienal de la Habana = L'individu et sa mémoire. Paris: Association française d'action artistique; Naço, 1997. 289 p.: col. ill., index.

Bilingual catalog (Spanish-French) of the 1997 Havana Biennial at which 176 artists from 45 countries on all the continents participated. Event focused on themes of the individual and memory. The purpose, in the words of Llilian Llanés, was to call attention to the role of historic memory as a means to preserve and defend cultural identity in a contemporary world suffering from collective amnesia. Good color reproductions and texts about each participating artist make this catalog a good documentary of the entire biennial.

235 Bienal de San Juan del Grabado Latino americano y del Caribe. Cátalogo general. San Juan: Instituto de Cultura Puertorriqueña, 1992. 1 v.: ill.

There were 269 engravings selected for this convocation of the oldest and only biennial in Spanish America dedicated solely to printmaking. Catalog reproduces works complemented with biographical summaries of the participants. As with the previous catalogs published, this is an excellent reference for those interested in recent developments of the technique throughout Latin America.

236 Boxer, David and Veerle Poupeye. Modern Jamaican art. Kingston: Ian Randle Publishers, 1998. 192 p.: bibl., col. ill., index.

Two essays, the first by Boxer originally published in 1982 and the second by Poupeye covering the current Jamaican art scene, are united in this volume which gives an overview of Jamaican art since the early 1920s. Work's most outstanding feature is the excellent selection of more than 150 color illustrations representing most relevant artists. Complemented with biographical summaries of the artists.

237 Campeche, Oller, Rodón: tres siglos de pintura puertorriqueña = Campeche, Oller, Rodón: three centuries of Puerto Rican painting. San Juan: Instituto de Cultura Puertorriqueña, 1992. 164 p.: bibl., ill. (some col.).

Eight different texts by various authors—among them Marta Traba and Rafael Squirru—are gathered on occasion of the exhibit of the same name (with 28 works total), organized by the Instituto de Cultura Puertorriqueña. Complemented with numerous reproductions in color, chronologies, and bibliographies about each of the three featured artists.

238 Catálogo de las obras de arte en la colección del Ateneo Puertorriqueño. Textos de Arturo V. Dávila, Osiris Delgado Mercado, and Myrna Rodríguez. San Juan: Ateneo Puertorriqueño, 1996. 224 p.: bibl., ill. (some col.).

1996 catalog of artworks in the collection of the Ateneo Puertorriqueño, an institution that since its creation in 1876 has been linked to the core of intellectual life and nationalist spirit in Puerto Rico. Divided into 10 chapters, the first is dedicated to the 18th and 19th centuries; four refer to painting, drawing, printmaking, stained glass, and sculpture in the 20th century; and the remaining five discuss other categories, such as portraiture of illustrious Puerto Ricans. Each work reproduced is appropriately annotated. Many of the works received awards in competitions held at the Ateneo. Although collection is uneven, catalog provides a panoramic view of the development of Puerto Rican arts.

239 Cinco artistas cubanos. Buenos Aires: Der Brücke Ediciones, 1994. 25 p.: col. ill. (Col. Cuadernos de arte; 27)

No. 27 in the series Colección Cuadernos de arte. The five artists are Gustavo Acosta, Arturo Cuenca, Jorge Pantoja, Pedro Pérez, and Rubén Torres Llorca. Several works by each of them are reproduced in color along with a chronology of their activity, making this cuaderno a promotional publication.

240 Cincuenta artistas plásticos cubanos. La Habana: Ediciones UNIÓN, Unión de Escritores y Artistas de Cuba, 1996. 102 p.: col. ill. (Cuba y Puerto Rico)

Catalog of exhibition presented by Adelaida de Juan in Puerto Rico of works by contemporary artists who are members of the Asociación de Artistas Plásticos, of the la Unión de Escritores y Artistas de Cuba. Includes biographical data on artists and color reproductions of the works. Selection is interesting because the installations so popular in Cuba in recent years are conspicuously absent, but includes painting, drawing, and sculpture.

241 50 années de peinture en Haïti. v. 1, 1930–1950. Port-au-Prince: Fondation culture création, 1995. 1 v.: bibl., ill. (some col.).

Vol. 1 of a project covering Haitian art between 1930–80, undertaken by the Musée d'art haitien and Fondation culture création. Main essay explains the impact of circumstances and sociohistorical situations surrounding the national artistic scene during years considered, including topics such as indigenous heritage and the Cuban avant-garde. Includes chronologies for historic, artistic, literary, and theatrical events during the years considered.

242 Colección de arte latinoamericano = Latin American art collection. Ponce, Puerto Rico: Museo de Arte de Ponce, 1993? 184 p.: bibl., ill. (some col.).

The Ford Foundation sponsored the publication of this bilingual illustrated catalog of selected works from the Latin American collection of the Museo de Arte de Ponce, with emphasis on Puerto Rican artists. The museum owns the most important collection of Western art among the island countries of the Caribbean basin. Introductory text on José Campeche and Francisco Oller by René Taylor; overview of Puerto Rican art by Carmen Ruiz de Fischler; and annotations by Marimar Benítez. The publication's layout is disappointing.

243 Collazo, Carlos. Carlos Collazo, 1956–
1990: exposición homenaje. San Juan:
Antigo Arsenal de la Marina Española, 1994.
52 p.: bibl., ill. (some col.), ports.

Catalog of the 1994 exhibition honoring memory of the artist who was an active
member of Puerto Rico's vanguard on many
fronts, including photography, design, and
filmmaking, in addition to painting and
drawing. Marimar Benítez provides an
overview of both the artist's work and the
man. Illustrated in color with archival photo-
documentation in b/w. Includes several
statements about the artist by friends and
intellectuals.

**244 Crónicas americanas: obras de José Be-
día.** Textos de Judith Bettelheim, Orlando Hernández, and Charles Merewether.
Monterrey, Mexico: Museo de Arte Contemporáneo de Monterrey, 1997. 178 p.: bibl., ill.
(some col.).

Bilingual catalog of 1997 exhibition of
José Bedía at Museo de Arte Contemporáneo
de Monterrey, the first exhibit at the museum dedicated to a Cuban artist (who
worked in Mexico before moving to the US).
Handsomely illustrated in b/w and color,
complemented with texts by Judith Bettelheim, Orlando Hernández, and Charles
Merewether, each focusing on a different
aspect of Bedía's work.

245 Echevarría, Gustavo César. Antología
de un artista, Raúl Martínez. La Habana: Casa Editora Abril, 1994. 105 p.: bibl.,
col. ill. (Pinos nuevos. Ensayo)

Pocket-book edition of Echevarría's essay on work and life of the artist who during
1950s was a member of the Los Once group
and who founded the circle Tiempos Nuevos.
Martínez is credited with renewing forces in
the intellectual life of Cuba during the
1950s, later becoming one of the most important graphic designers of the Revolution.

246 Fonk, Hans. Curaçao: architectuur en
stij = Curaçao: architectural style.
Text by Ruud van der Neut. Editorial production by Nicole Henriquez and Anko van der
Woude. Willemstad, Netherlands Antilles:
Stichting Curaçao Style, 1999. 194 p.: bibl.,
ill., photos.

Beautifully produced coffee-table book
provides insight into evolution of Curaçao's
historic architecture and highlights modern

architecture and contemporary art. Showcases different historic quarters of Willemstad, *kunuku* and plantation houses, non-
residential buildings, and seaside hotels.
Includes over 300 color plates. [R. Hoefte]

247 Geron, Cándido. Oviedo: vida, obra y
proyección internacional = Oviedo: his
life, work and international projection. Santo
Domingo: s.n., 1995. 134 p.: col. ill.

For a book that is intended to present
Oviedo's work to a wider audience, this publication leaves much to be desired, although
the effort can be appreciated. Information
mingled with unnecessary praise and excessive detail serves no purpose, leaving doubts
about the accuracy of the interpretation. Illustrated in color and b/w. No bibliography.

**248 Los hijos de Guillermo Tell: artistas
cubanos contemporáneos.** Caracas:
Consejo Nacional de la Cultura; Museo de
Artes Visuales Alejandro Otero, 1991. 49 p.:
ill. (some col.).

Catalog of exhibition held at the
Museo de Artes Visuales Alejandro Otero in
Caracas in 1991 (also shown at the Banco de
la República de Colombia), featuring 15 contemporary Cuban artists belonging to the
newest generation. Curators Gerardo Mosquera and Graciela Pantín wrote the text explaining the circumstances and motivations
engulfing young Cuban artists, and the
meaning of their artistic expressions in relation to the Cuban reality and international
influences.

**249 La hoja liberada: el portafolios en la
gráfica puertorriqueña.** San Juan: Instituto de Cultura Puertorriqueña, 1996. 70 p.:
bibl., ill. (some col.).

Catalog of the 1996–97 exhibition (at
Instituto de Cultura Puertorriqueña in
Puerto Rico and New York's Museo del Barrio), dedicated to the history of graphic portfolios in Puerto Rico since they first appeared
in San Juan in 1951. Teresa Tío, the guest curator, included 38 out of the nearly 90 artists
who have participated in 180 portfolios produced in Puerto Rico in the last 45 years. Tío
also wrote the main essay explaining the development of graphics and pointing out individual contributions to the field by Puerto
Rican artists. With some illustrations, checklist, and sources.

250 **Levine, Robert M.** Cuba in the 1850s: through the lens of Charles DeForest Fredricks. Tampa: Univ. of South Florida Press, 1990. 101 p.: bibl., ill., index.

Presents a collection of mostly mid-19th-century photographs of Havana. [B. Aguirre-López]

251 **Lucas, Eugenio.** Eugenio Lucas Velázquez en la Habana: Madrid, 20 febrero-21 abril 1996. Madrid: Fundación Cultural MAPFRE Vida, 1996. 149 p.: bibl., ill. (some col.).

Catalog of the 34 paintings from Havana's Museo Nacional de Bellas Artes, originally from the collection of Rafael Carvajal, Marques de Pinar del Rio, who inaugurated the museum in 1955. Manuel Crespo Larrazábal wrote the insightful text, which sheds light on the Spanish painter whose work shows strong influence from Goya, and who was active in the third quarter of the 19th century. Excellent reproductions with complete data.

252 **Martínez, Juan A.** Cuban art and national identity: the Vanguardia painters, 1927–1950. Gainesville: Univ. Press of Florida, 1994. 189 p.: bibl., ill. (some col.), index.

Provides detailed account of the contribution of the avant-garde Cuban artists to overall picture of Caribbean art. Publication's value lies in the fact that many sources of information difficult to obtain were consulted and systematically evaluated. For sociologist's comment, see *HLAS 57:4867.*

Marvel, Thomas S. Antonin Nechodoma, architect 1877–1928: the Prairie School in the Caribbean. See *HLAS 57:4871.*

253 **Morel, Yoryi.** Yoryi Morel: recreador delirante. Santo Domingo: Museo de Arte Moderno, 1997. 55 p.: col. ill.

Catalog of the 1997 exhibition at the Museo de Arte Moderno in Santo Domingo in tribute to Yoryi Morel, a pioneer of Dominican art. Brief texts by Virginia Goris, Antonio Guadalupe, Roberto Flores, José Perdomo, and Luichy Martínez, among others. Includes complete checklist and illustrations. Of little academic value.

254 **Mujeres artistas: protagonistas de los ochenta.** Puerto Rico: s.n., 1991? 127 p.: bibl., ill. (some col.).

Thirty-five women artists active in Puerto Rico (most of them born in Puerto Rico) presented their works in a 1990 exhibition shown in San Juan and Santo Domingo. Professor Myrna Rodríguez offers a clear and concise historic perspective of the situation of the arts for women in the island up to present day. In her introduction, Dominican critic Marianne de Tolentino explains the visual interests of each artist. Each artist is represented with a color or b/w illustration.

255 **Mundo soñado: joven plástica cubana.** Madrid: Consorcio Casa de América, 1996. 92 p.: ill. (some col.).

Catalog of the intriguing exhibition organized by the Fundación Ludwig de Cuba following an initiative by the Ateneo Americano de la Casa de América in Madrid and curated by Helmo Hernández Trejo. Includes a number of reproductions in color and a complete technical checklist.

256 **Novecento cubano: la naturaleza, el hombre, los dioses.** Milan: Edizioni Cronodata, 1995. 95 p.: col. ill.

Catalog of the Cuban exhibition presented in Italy with the sponsorship of the Cuban Embassy. Selections for the exhibition came from the 20th-century holdings of the Museo Nacional de Cuba. Exhibition included modern masters such as Lam and Peláez, in addition to some interesting contemporary artists not very well known internationally.

257 **Pintura europea y cubana: en las colecciones del Museo Nacional de La Habana.** Madrid: Fundación Cultural MAPFRE Vida, 1997. 214 p.: bibl., col. ill.

This publication is the third of a trilogy of exhibitions undertaken by Spain's Fundación Cultural MAPFRE Vida, highlighting the holdings of the Museo Nacional de Cuba. The other two are *Pintura Española del Siglo XIX del Museo de Bellas Artes de La Habana* (1995) and *Eugenio Lucas Velázquez en La Habana* (see item **251**). The commentary by Calvo Serraller points out the encyclopedic character of the museum, which includes a variety of European schools as well as a number of Cuban artists trained in the academic tradition. The broad scope may explain the unevenness of the collection, although there are some exceptional pieces by artists such as Corot, Daubigny, José de Ribera, Francesco Guardi, and a number of German and English portraits of great quality including two by George Romney. Olga López Núñez wrote the essay related to colonial painting in Cuba. María del Carmen Rippe Moro and Miguel Luis Núñez Gutiérrez provide a brief history of the museum. Good color reproductions.

Price, Richard and **Sally Price.** Executing culture: museé, museo, museum. See *HLAS 57:890.*

258 **Roche-Rabell, Arnaldo.** Arnaldo Roche Rabell. México: Museo de Arte Moderno, 1995. 99 p.: bibl., ill. (some col.).

Insightful catalog of exhibition held at the Museo de Arte Moderno de México, Feb. 23-May 28, 1995. Curated by Alejandro Gallo, with texts by Teresa del Conde and Edward J. Sullivan. Good color reproductions and a complete checklist.

259 **Santería aesthetics in contemporary Latin American art.** Edited by Arturo Lindsay. Washington: Smithsonian Institution Press, 1996. 306 p.: bibl., ill. (some col.), index, maps.

Gathers texts exploring the relationship between Santería and esthetics. Essays by artists, scholars, and religious leaders are dedicated mostly to Cuba, with one essay on Brazil and others on various Caribbean artists. Interest in the subject, currently a frequent theme in specialized art publications, is growing among artists who feel related to Afro-American culture in general. Despite some irregularity in the book's content, probably due to the complexity of themes, this work serves as a good introduction to the topic from a contemporary perspective. Profusely illustrated; contains a useful glossary of terms and generous notations.

260 **Shared visions: celebrating the 50th anniversary of the University of the West Indies.** Barbados: Canoe Press, Univ. of the West Indies, 1997. 87 p.: col. ill.

Catalog of exhibition organized on occasion of the UWI Golden Jubilee, with works by 37 artists representing the university campuses in Jamaica, Barbados, and Trinidad and Tobago. Exhibit traces, indirectly, the historical evolution of the institution. Also includes brief mention of mural work and indoor and outdoor sculpture done by some artists who could not be included in the traveling show.

261 **Wifredo Lam: pasión y magía sobre papel.** Santiago: Museo Nacional de Bellas Artes, 1995. 53 p.: ill. (some col.).

Catalog of the traveling exhibition of 47 paintings and 35 prints, many never exhibited outside Cuba, presented at the Museo Nacional de Bellas Artes in Chile (and previously in Mexico and Argentina), during April-May of 1995. Exhibit was curated and organized by the Museo Nacional de Cuba. Texts include an essay by Roberto Comas Amate and Lam's biographical sketch, illustrated with family photographs. Includes color reproductions and a complete checklist.

SOUTH AMERICA
Argentina

262 **Aberastury, Gabriela.** Gabriela Aberastury: 43 años de pintura, dibujo, y grabado. Buenos Aires: Clásica Producciones, 1990. 83 p.: ill. (some col.).

Booklet primarily compiles illustrated samples of the artist's work in the abstract field, developed over several decades. Includes introductory note by Rafael Squirru written in the critic's characteristically spirited style.

263 **Alonso, Carlos.** Carlos Alonso: el pintor caminante y otros temas, 1980–1994. Bogotá?: Colcultura, 1994. 48 p.: ill. (some col.).

Catalog of exhibition held at the Museo Nacional de Colombia, in conjunction with Argentina's attendance at the 1994 Feria Internacional del Libro in Bogotá. Includes two texts written 20 years apart: an excerpt from a book by Marta Traba, and another from a work by Jorge López Anaya. Essays help contextualize Alonso's painting, which is full of allusions to the dehumanization of man. Fully illustrated in color, with a biographical summary.

264 **Asociación Argentina de Críticos de Arte.** Historia crítica del arte argentino. Dirección general de la obra de Osvaldo Svanascini. Buenos Aires: Dirección de Relaciones Externas y Comunicaciones, TELECOM Argentina, 1995. 305 p.: bibl., ill. (some col.).

Interesting collection of essays on various aspects, periods, and tendencies in the plastic arts in Argentina from 19th century to date. Includes essays on a number of individual artists written by a group of members of the Asociación Argentina de Críticos de Arte. Horacio Safons wrote one of the most interesting pieces on development of art criticism in Argentina, origins of which can be traced to the second quarter of the 19th century. Illustrated in color, with numerous notes and sources.

265 100 años de gráfica en Rosario y su región. Rosario, Argentina: Escuela de Bellas Artes, Facultad de Humanidades y Artes, Univ. Nacional de Rosario, 1994. 119 p.: bibl., ill.

Unpretentious publication is a complement to the activities developed by the Escuela de Bellas Artes of the Univ. de Rosario on occasion of the First Miniprint Biennial of 1994. All 41 artists included have been active in that city, although several were born elsewhere. Includes 112 illustrations.

Cosmelli Ibáñez, José Luis. Historia de la cultura argentina. See item **2865.**

266 40 dibujantes argentinos. Buenos Aires: Ediciones Actualidad en el Arte, 1987. 323 p.: ill.

Closing statement makes clear that book is not an anthology or a general overview of the state of drawing in Argentina; rather, it unites 40 Argentine artists who practice the technique of drawing, most of whom are little known outside Argentina. The biographical data on each artist is useful; however, quality of b/w illustrations leaves much to be desired. Essays by six Argentine critics (Osiris Chiérico, Sarah Guerra, Elba Pérez, Osvaldo Seiguerman, Raúl Vera Ocampo, and Rodolfo Bretones) complement the publication, which is a collective effort.

267 Cuatro aspectos de la pintura argentina contemporánea. Buenos Aires: Fondo Nacional de las Artes, 1997. 100 p.: col. ill.

Guillermo Whitelow introduces this rigorous selection of works by 12 Argentine painters, from Xul Solar to Silvia Young, who represented Argentina at the Latin American Pavillion of Madrid's ARCO in 1997. Fermín Fèvre and Whitelow wrote the individual presentations for the artists. Illustrated in full color and complemented with biographical profiles.

268 Exposición de Artes Visuales DAIA, 1st, Buenos Aires, 1996. I Exposición de Artes Visuales DAIA: con subasta. Buenos Aires: Fundación Amigos de DAIA, 1996. 258 p.: ill. (some col.).

Bilingual catalog of the works by Argentine artists offered in auction to benefit the Fundación Amigos de DAIA (Delegación de Asociaciones Israelitas Argentinas) in 1996, which coincided with the reopening of the Casa de la Cultura de la Ciudad de Buenos Aires. More than 60 artists are represented, including a good number of the well known and recognized. Color reproduction of works by each artist.

269 Fader, Fernando. Fernando Fader: 1872 [i.e. 1882]–1935. Buenos Aires: Zurbarán Ediciones, 1995. 1 v. (unpaged): col. ill.

Catalog of sixth exhibition organized in 1995 by Zurbarán, a commercial gallery in Buenos Aires, to honor the artist on the 60th anniversary of his death. Works included covered four major periods of the artist's work, including his earlier periods in Mendoza and Munich. Presentation by Ignacio Gutiérrez. All works are reproduced.

270 Fèvre, Fermín. Treinta años de arte argentino: una visión parcial. Argentina: Fundación Petto Ruti, 1997. 204 p.: bibl.

Fèvre has compiled more than 100 articles previously published between 1967–96 in catalogs of individual or collective exhibitions of Argentine art. Since the articles support Fèvre's ideas about the work of art, he warns that his experience is not intended to substitute the viewer's personal interpretation. Work lacks illustrations and explanatory notes.

271 Forner, Raquel. Raquel Forner. Buenos Aires: Centro Cultural Recoleta, 1998. 87 p.: bibl., col. ill.

Color-illustrated catalog of the 1998 retrospective exhibition at the Centro Cultural Recoleta, honoring Forner, indisputably the most prominent female painter from Argentina between 1930–70. Her closest biographer, Guillermo Whitelow, wrote the introduction.

272 Gutiérrez Zaldívar, Ignacio. El paisaje en el arte de los Argentinos. Buenos Aires: Zurbarán Ediciones, 1994. 85 p.: bibl., col. ill.

Brief review of landscape as a theme being practiced by Argentine artists from

Johann Moritz Rugendas to lesser-known contemporary painters. Includes personal statements from the artists.

273 Herencia italiana en el arte de Córdoba: 60 artistas plásticos de origen italiano. Siena, Argentina: Pugliese, 1991. 144 p.: col. ill.

"In Argentina too, the history of art is packed with Italian last names," says Giusseppe Damis, consul of Italy in Córdoba, when referring to the exhibition organized by his office and presented at the Galería de Arte Jaime Conci. Catalog boasts a color reproduction and a short biography of each participant, all of whom are of Italian descent, the main criteria for inclusion. Texts by Nelly Perazzo and Domingo Biffarella.

274 Lazzari y los maestros de la plástica boquense: a cien años de la llegada de Alfredo Lazzari y a veinte años de la muerte de Benito Quinquela Martín. Buenos Aires: Museo Municipal de Artes Plásticas Eduardo Sívori, 1997. 1 v. (unpaged): col. ill.

After a prologue by Rafael Squirru, the poet Carlos Semino writes about the exhibition of 21 artists belonging to the so-called "Escuela de La Boca" at the Museo Sívori in Buenos Aires. The term applies to those painters and sculptors for whom the old Buenos Aires harbor was a frequent theme. The neighborhood of La Boca has always been associated with economic growth and the immigration boom of Buenos Aires, and also carries sociopolitical connotations. Illustrated in color and complemented with short biographies of the artists selected.

275 López Anaya, Jorge. Historia del arte argentino. Buenos Aires: Emecé Editores, 1997. 413 p., 32 p. of plates: bibl., ill., index.

Described as a work of historic synthesis, book analyzes different currents and tendencies in Argentine art between 1795 and the postmodern period. Most of the book is dedicated to the 20th century. With a selected bibliography, generous annotations, and some illustrations in b/w, the book is especially helpful to university students unfamiliar with Argentina's art development.

276 Maldonado, Tomás. Tómas Maldonado: escritos preulmianos. Recopilación y selección de textos de Carlos A. Méndez Mosquera y Nelly Perazzo. Buenos Aires: Ediciones Infinito, 1997. 134 p.: bibl., ill. (some col.). (Biblioteca de diseño)

Méndez Mosquera and Perazzo have selected 18 revealing articles (including a short interview) written by Maldonado before joining the Hochschule für Gestaltung de Ulm in West Germany in 1954 as a professor and vice dean. Maldonado's eurocentric ideas influenced the new generation of Argentine artists, graphic designers, and architects between mid-1940s and mid-1950s. He became a seminal figure in the Argentine avant-garde and an active member of the Buenos Aires "Concrete" art movement. This collection of his writings clarifies the many directions taken by Argentine art during the immediate postwar period.

277 Museo Eduardo Sívori: exposición de patrimonio, 1900–1960, primera parte; primeros premios de pintura en los Salones Municipales, 1945–1995. Buenos Aires: Municipalidad de la Ciudad de Buenos Aires, 1996. 1 v. (unpaged): col. ill.

Catalog of the 1996 exhibition of works from the collection of the Museo Sívori in Buenos Aires, showing development of the plastic arts in Argentina (starting with Sívori himself). Exhibition groups artists into three general categories: people's artists, concrete artists, and city painters. Contains complete checklist and an additional list of those artists who received awards in the municipal salons starting in 1945; also includes listing of jury members.

278 Museo Nacional de Bellas Artes (Buenos Aires). La colección Costantini en el Museo Nacional de Bellas Artes. Buenos Aires: MNBA, 1996. 210 p.: col. ill.

Catalog of the superb private art collection of Eduardo Costantini, exhibited in public for the first time at the Museo Nacional de Bellas Artes (Buenos Aires, 1996). Illustrated in full color with an introductory presentation by Jorge Gluzberg, catalog follows the order of the presentation of the collection for didactic purposes. Organized in order of Forerunners, Surrealism, Social Painting, and Constructivist currents, collection reflects the taste and perceptions that have predominated among Southern Cone collectors interested in modern and contemporary art.

279 Noé, Luis Felipe. Luis Felipe Noé: pinturas 60–95 en el Museo Nacional de Bellas Artes, Buenos Aires, Argentina. Argentina: IMPSAT, 1995. 95 p.: bibl., ill. (some col.).

Catalog of the anthological exhibition of the artist, a founding member of the Grupo Neofigurativo (1961) who abandoned painting for almost a decade before taking it up again in 1974. Curated by Jorge Glusberg, exhibit is divided into 10 chronologically successive stages, complemented with excellent color reproductions, bibliography, and statements by other figures of the times.

280 Obras del Museo Municipal de Bellas Artes Juan B. Castagnino. Rosario, Argentina: Secretaría de Cultura y Educación, Municipalidad de Rosario, 1997. 79 p.: bibl., col. ill.

Catalog of selected works in the collection of Rosario's municipal museum published in 1996, in anticipation of the celebration of museum's 60th anniversary. Illustrated in color, reproducing—with few exceptions—works by Argentine artists such as Pettoruti, Berni, and Lino Enea Spilimbergo.

281 Los 80 en el MAM: instalaciones de 27 artistas. Textos de Silvia de Ambrosini and Alina Molinari. Buenos Aires: MAM, 1991. 61 p.: ill. (some col.).

Catalog of the project developed by Silvia de Ambrosini and Alina Molinari at the Museo de Arte Moderno of Buenos Aires, presented from April 8-May 8, 1991. Project consisted of 27 installations by artists representative of the Buenos Aires art scene during the 1980s. Each proposal is reproduced in color along with original sketch and a summary of each artist's career.

282 Páez, Oscar. Páez. Buenos Aires: Der Brücke Ediciones, 1995. 1 v. (unpaged): bibl., ill. (some col.). (Col. cuadernos de arte)

Jorge Gluzberg presents (in Spanish with an English translation) the work of Oscar Páez on the occasion of his exhibition in Buenos Aires in 1995. The booklet, however, seems to be intended for more than just one exhibition since it forms part of the *Cuadernos de arte* collection published by Der Brücke Ediciones. Good color reproductions.

283 Páez de la Torre, Carlos and **Celia Terán.** Lola Mora: una biografía. Buenos Aires: Planeta, 1997. 286 p.: bibl., ill.

Well-documented and objective biography of the singular and prolific Argentine sculptress whose personality and work scandalized Buenos Aires, giving her a reputation far beyond reality. Mora's talents and a government scholarship took her to Rome at the end of the 19th century, where she became the toast of town. She died penniless in Buenos Aires in 1936, spanning 69 years of fame and success, recognition, rejection, and oblivion. All aspects of her life are depicted in this book, which at the same time offers a fine description of the social, artistic, and political life of Buenos Aires during the city's golden years. Illustrated in b/w.

284 Perazzo, Nelly and **Mario H. Gradowczyk.** Esteban Lisa, 1895–1983: Esteban Lisa con un texto de Fermín Fèvre. Buenos Aires: Fundación Esteban Lisa, 1997. 79 p.: bibl., ill. (some col.).

Monographic study of work of the marginal artist who, along with Juan del Prete and other figures, may be considered one of the initiators of abstract art in Argentina. Illustrated in color and b/w.

285 Pettoruti, Emilio. Emilio Pettoruti. Buenos Aires: Salas Nacionales de Exposición; Buenos Aires?: Fundación Pettoruti, 1995. 172 p.: ill. (some col.).

Catalog of retrospective and anthological exhibition of work of Emilio Pettoruti (1892–1971), presented under the patronage of the Argentine government at the Palais de Glace in Buenos Aires in 1995, as a preview to its itinerary in the US and Europe. Texts by Rafael Squirru, Eleanor Heartney, and Jacques Lassaigne. Presentation by Tomás Roberto Días Varela, President of the Fundación Pettoruti, and additional research and biographic synopsis by Cristina Díaz Varela. Profusely illustrated in b/w and color. Superb presentation; undoubtedly one of the most accurate studies on the Argentine master.

286 Polesello, Rogelio. Polesello: progresiones. Buenos Aires: Asociación Amigos de Salas Nacionales y Artes Visuales, 1995. 115 p.: bibl., ill. (some col.).

Publication that accompanied the artist's anthological exhibition at Palais de

Glace in Buenos Aires, from October 5–29, 1995. Excellent reproductions (not in strict chronological order) assert Polesello as a versatile and ingenious visual artist who has managed to update his geometric vocabulary through four successive decades in accordance with the tendencies of the international art scene, without losing his originality.

287 Recurrencias: arte argentino de la generación de los 80. Caracas: Museo de Arte Contemporáneo de Caracas Sofía Imber, 1997. 48 p.: ill. (some col.). (Catálogo; 127)

Catalog of the exhibition presented at the Museo de Arte Contemporáneo de Caracas Sofía Imber as part of a government initiative to promote the art of Argentina (1994–98) in Venezuela. Unites nine artists belonging to a generation, all approximately 50 years old. The curatorial concept is focused on the sign-like imagery developed by all artists selected. The catalog is well illustrated in color and contains a brief biography of the participants.

288 Rodríguez, Artemio. Artes plásticas en la Córdoba del siglo XIX. Córdoba, Argentina: Univ. Nacional de Córdoba, 1992. 298, 22 p. of plates: bibl., ill.

Relatively complete account of the situation of the arts in Córdoba province, and in particular in the city of the same name, from private academies to art galleries, as well as institutions and artists. Interesting historic panorama with many bibliographic references in every chapter. Includes some b/w illustrations.

289 Romero Brest, Jorge. Así se mira el arte moderno. Buenos Aires: Beas Ediciones, 1993. 142 p.: bibl., ill. (Colección Así se hace—)

Although not stated in the book, this collection of short digressions on abstraction and cubism by one of the pre-eminent theoreticians on contemporary art in Argentina had to have been originally written during the 1960s. For the same reason, it serves as a reference for more radical ideas about what the course of visual arts could be, developed much later by Romero Brest before his death in 1989.

290 San Martín, María Laura. Breve historia de la pintura argentina contemporánea. Buenos Aires: Editorial Claridad, 1993. 389 p.: bibl., ill., index. (Col. Breve historia)

A preliminary note of this handbook explains its intention to publicize work of Argentine painters, without preferences or exclusions. Illustrated in b/w, publication is a useful source of basic information about 20th-century Argentine painters and the influences that they might have experienced. Complemented with an alphabetical listing of the artists.

291 Schávelzon, Daniel. El expolio del arte en la Argentina: robos y tráfico ilegal de obras de arte. Buenos Aires: Editorial Sudamericana, 1993. 191 p.: bibl., ill.

Traces illegal trafficking of art works, which intensified in Argentina between 1980–92. Author blames ambition of unscrupulous thieves stimulated by activity of the art black market. He also blames inefficient legislation and the incapacity of the official bureaucracy to act by itself. One of the most important thefts occurred at the cathedral of Rosario, which had its monstrance sold to the public in 1978. Works by El Greco, Goya, Renoir, Gaugin, and a number of Argentine artists, including decorative works from countless sources and public monuments, are still missing or vandalized.

292 Segui, Antonio. Antonio Segui: exposición retrospectiva 1958–1990. Buenos Aires?: Museo Nacional de Bellas Artes, 1991. 188 p.: bibl., ill. (some col.).

Excellent catalog published on occasion of Segui's retrospective of 129 works at the Museo Nacional de Bellas Artes (Buenos Aires, 1991) with texts by Damián Bayón and Edward Shaw. Catalog familiarizes reader with the artist's work both thematically and chronologically. Complemented with a biographical sketch and numerous photographs in color and b/w.

293 Segui, Antonio. Antonio Segui: hombre de ciudades. México: Museo Rufino Tamayo, 1997. 81 p.: bibl., ill. (some col.).

Catalog of the exhibition of 60 works held at the Museo Rufino Tamayo in Mexico, including paintings, reliefs, and sculptures covering a span of 23 years. Selection illustrates Segui's evolution and consistency. Presentations by Raquel Tibol and Ana María

Escallón are accompanied by illustrations in color.

294   Seis décadas de arte argentino. Seminario coordinado por Edward Shaw. Buenos Aires: Univ. Torcuato Di Tella, 1998. 213 p.

Record of second seminar organized by Univ. Di Tella to disseminate the contributions of Argentine artists during the last six decades (1940s-90s). Twenty-four participants from different sectors in the art community: artists, critics, historians, art dealers, etc., offer their opinions about the most relevant works produced during a particular decade. Interesting exercise that intentionally avoids any definitive conclusions.

295   Sendra, Rafael. El joven Berni y la Mutualidad Popular de Estudiantes y Artistas Plásticos de Rosario. Rosario, Argentina: UNR Editora, 1993. 111 p.: bibl., ill. (some col.).

Sendra writes an almost fictional account of the early days of painter Antonio Berni (during the 1930s) and his association with the group in charge of renovating the arts in the city of Rosario, known as La Mutual. His sources include his interviews with surviving members of the group and many newspapers and magazine articles from the time. Includes some color and b/w reproductions.

296   Squirru, Rafael F. Libros y libros, cuadros y cuadros: ensayos breves. Morón, Argentina: Univ. de Morón, 1995. 285 p.: ill.

The 56 articles previously published in *La Nación* (Buenos Aires) between 1992–94 comprise the content of this book by the prolific Argentine art critic. Includes articles about artists such as Pettoruti and Botero, and others with themes such as the underestimated public, or idealism and illusion. Does not include many illustrations, but is entertaining.

297   Vega, Jorge de la. Jorge de la Vega. Madrid: Fundación Arte y Tecnología, 1996. 185 p.: bibl., col. ill.

Illustrated catalog of 1996 De la Vega retrospective exhibition at Fundación Arte y Tecnología in Madrid, comprising 37 works from 1948–70, offers a complete panorama of artist's evolution. Silvia de Ambrosini presents the artist's work. Contains a biographical chronology, bibliography, and several songs written by the artist.

298   Veinte años: 361 imágenes contra los crímenes de ayer y de hoy. Buenos Aires: s.n., 1996. 361 p.: ill.

Volume is a visual statement against the crimes committed during Argentina's 1970s military regime. More than 300 artists participated in the project (five of them disappeared in Argentina's Dirty War). The artists and their families financed the publication that serves as the catalog for the exhibition presented at Buenos Aires' Plaza de Mayo (March, 1996). After that, the exhibition was shown in other cities such as Rosario and São Paulo. In the introduction, Miguel Briante summarizes the intentions of the exhibition with an excerpt from his book entitled *No al indulto, obediencia debida y punto final* (1989).

299   20 obras maestras: arte argentino del siglo XX. Buenos Aires: Banco Velox, 1996. 84 p.: bibl., col. ill.

Beautiful, well-printed catalog of the exhibition held on occasion of the 1996 IDB Annual Meeting in Buenos Aires at the Museo Nacional de Arte Decorativo. Includes works by Antonio Berni, Alfredo Guttero, and Xul Solar from the 1920s and 1930s. Text by Marcelo E. Pacheco places this superb selection in context.

Bolivia

300   El fin de los márgenes: Fernando Casas, Keiko Gonzales, Guiomar Mesa, Ejti Stih, Sol Mateo, Gaston Ugalde, Valcarcel; siete artistas de Bolivia en el Museo de Arte Contemporáneo, Santiago de Chile, abril 1996. Catálogo y textos de Juan Cristóbal McLean *et al.* Santiago: Museo de Arte Contemporáneo, 1996. 1 v. (unpaged): bibl., ill. (some col.).

Catalog of exhibition of seven young artists from Bolivia held at the Museo de Arte Contemporáneo de Chile in Santiago offers an indication of the new directions taken in Andean visual arts. While most exhibition catalogs attempt to document a particular group, the various texts included here are not necessarily connected or integrated. The biographical data is not consistent. The numerous reproductions, however, say more about the work of the artists than anything else.

301 **Fundación Cultural EMUSA: memoria, 1974–1994; Empresa Minera Unificada Sociedad Anónima.** La Paz: Fundación Cultural EMUSA, 1994. 256 p.: ill. (some col.).

Institutional history of the activities undertaken by the Fundación EMUSA (Empresa Minera Unificada Sociedad Anónima) in La Paz between 1974–94 to promote the visual arts. Documents all exhibitions of the Bolivian artists (over 400) and international artists presented by the foundation. Also describes a great variety of complementary activities. Organized by technique and illustrated in color with an introduction about the Bolivian contemporary art scene by Teresa Gisbert de Mesa. Jacobo Libermann provides a short essay on the significance of the EMUSA art gallery; Roberto Valcárcel explains operation of the gallery.

302 **Pacheco, María Luisa.** María Luisa Pacheco, pintora de los Andes. La Paz: La Papelera, 1993. 1 v. (unpaged): bibl., chiefly col. ill.

Illustrated catalog of the exhibition organized by the Spanish Embassy in Bolivia, presented at the Museo Nacional de Arte (La Paz, Oct. 1993) and later in the city of Santa Cruz de la Sierra (1994). With few exceptions, all works come from the personal collection of the artist's daughter, M.E. Pacheco de Azcamunz. Introductory texts by Valeria Paz, Roberto Valcárcel, and Leopoldo Castedo.

303 **Querejazu, Pedro.** El dibujo en Bolivia: dibujos, 1900–1950. La Paz: Fundación BHN, 1996. 118 p.: bibl., ill. (some col.).

Querejazu should be credited for trying to revive Bolivia's weak tradition in drawing. A well-intentioned first effort, this book may provide a stepping stone to further research. After a meager introduction on the origins of drawing in Bolivia and its practice in the Peruvian Viceroyalty, Querejazu provides a general overview of the subject from colonial times to the end of the 19th century. The focus of the book, however, is a selection of drawings from different periods in a private collection of La Paz, mainly 20th-century artists active until mid-century, such as Arturo Borda and Maria Luisa Pacheco. Profusely illustrated in color and b/w.

Chile

304 **Arte textil contemporáneo en Chile.** Textos de Margarita Alvarado et al. Santiago: Museo Nacional de Bellas Artes, 1996. 97 p.: bibl., ill. (some col.).

Interesting catalog examines the work of 20 artists who use fiber for their visual proposals, all but one of whom are women. Text traces Chilean textile tradition to precolumbian times. Educational from a technical viewpoint, and illustrated in color with brief biographical notes.

305 **Arte y colección: grandes maestros de la pintura chilena.** Santiago: s.n., 1996. 234 p.: col. ill.

Color-illustrated catalog of 1995 exhibition held at Galería Jorge Carroza of works collected by the private sector. Selection focuses on artists active from mid-19th to mid-20th century, showing the artistic and institutional consolidation of the fine arts in Chile, from Thomas Somerscales to Pedro Luna. Interesting selection not frequently seen due to its private character. Number of works by Juan Francisco González and Arturo Gordon equals that of the remaining 24 artists featured in the exhibit. Three brief texts dedicated to the themes of collecting, investing in art, and the exhibition itself introduce the selection.

306 **Bravo, Claudio.** Claudio Bravo: visionario de la realidad. Santiago: Museo Nacional de Bellas Artes, 1994. 117 p.: bibl., ill. (some col.).

Catalog of exhibition held at the Museo Nacional de Bellas Artes (Santiago, March-May 1994), covering more than 30 years of painting and drawing. Text by curator Edward J. Sullivan. Excellent printing, beautifully illustrated, and complemented with biographical and bibliographical data and collectors' list. Good visual reference for those interested in Bravo's work.

307 **Códice Mallok-O.** Santiago: Grupo Mallok-O, 1994. 105 p.: bibl., ill. (some col.).

Catalog of Grupo Mallok-O exhibition held at the Museo de Arte Contemporáneo de Chile (Dec. 1994-Jan. 1995) describes in text and photographs the process developed by artists Félix Lazo, Juan Enrique Gabler, and Patricio Flaño in the conception and execution of their installations. The trend has been embraced enthusiastically throughout the 1990s by a large number of Latin American artists.

308   Duclos, Arturo. El ojo de la mano. Santiago: Osculum Infame Editores, 1995. 78 p.: bibl., ill. (some col.).

Catalog of exhibition of Arturo Duclos (Santiago, 1959) at the Museo Nacional de Bellas Artes in Santiago in 1995, divided in three "portfolios." Texts by Dan Cameron, Guillermo Machuca, Nelly Richard, and an interview with the artist by Adriana Valdés.

309   Emar, Juan. Juan Emar: escritos de arte, 1923–1925. Recopilación, selección e introducción de Patricio Lizama A. Santiago: Dirección de Bibliotecas, Archivos y Museos, Centro de Investigaciones Diego Barros Arana, 1992. 170 p.: appendices, bibl., ill. (Escritores de Chile; 2)

Compilation of articles written between 1923–25 by Chilean Juan Emar (whose real name was Alvaro Yáñez Bianchi). Emar was a diplomat, novelist, and journalist in Santiago who, after his stay in Paris, became an art critic and theoretician of the Montparnasse Group, considered by many to be the movement that broke with the post-academic tradition in Chile in the 1920s. Patricio Lizama A., who wrote a brief introduction to the book, selected the writings and placed them in context. Divided intelligently into three sections—articles about art, art criticism, and notes about art—the work allows readers to establish the literary and philosophical intent of every subject. Work also has two appendices, one of short biographies of the artists mentioned, and the other a chronological listing of the articles that appeared in *La Nación,* the newspaper for which the texts were originally written.

310   Girolamo, Giulio di. Giulio di Girolamo: 75 años de labor artística. Santiago: Museo Nacional de Bellas Artes, 1992. 47 p.: ill. (some col.), maps.

Short profile of Italian artist who in 1948, at age 46, emigrated with his family from Rome to Santiago. His work might be associated with Italian decorative movement, and within this field his work is not exactly innovative, although it is proficient. However, he did bring his Italian schooling and technical knowledge to Chile, especially in the areas of graphic design, mosaics, and fresco techniques. Booklet is a convenient reference source from the biographical and visual perspectives.

311   Machuca, Guillermo and **Justo Pastor Mellado.** Arte joven en Chile: 1986–1996. Santiago: Museo Nacional de Bellas Artes, 1997. 91 p.: ill. (some col.).

Catalog of exhibition presented at the Museo Nacional de Bellas Artes as a survey of the latest conceptual art tendencies in Chile. Eleven artists were selected for the rigor of their theoretical research and the originality of their bidimensional and tridimensional solutions.

312   Pablo Burchard, 1875–1964: un pintor fundamental. Textos de Gema Swinburn P. and Francisco González V. Santiago: Corporación Cultural de las Condes, 1996. 20 p.: bibl., ill. (some col.).

Brief monograph on the Chilean modernist Burchard on occasion of the retrospective, and a commemorative exhibition of Chilean artists in honor of him, organized by the Corporación Cultural de las Condes in Santiago. Illustrated in color, with texts and a graphic chronology.

313   Schultz, Margarita. La obra escultórica de Marta Colvin: rosa de los vientos. Santiago: Hachette, 1993. 120 p.: bibl., ill. (some col.), photos.

Personal tribute by the author to the Chilean sculptress who is in great part responsible for the introduction of abstract geometric sculpture in Chile. Includes numerous photographs, all b/w, and a list of the most important public commissions. Lacks critical analysis and information about Colvin's development.

314   Tacla, Jorge. Self-feeder: Jorge Tacla. Garza García, Mexico: Galería Ramis Barquet, 1996. 1 v. (unpaged): ill. (some col.).

Catalog of the exhibition presented by the artist (who has lived in New York since 1981) at Galería Ramis Barquet in Mexico City, under the name of "Self-Fed." Contains a bilingual, introductory essay by Richard Vine entitled "Thought in the Wilderness" ("El Pensamiento en el Desierto"), good biographical information about the artist, and excellent color reproductions.

315 **Verdugo, Patricia.** Conversaciones con Nemesio Antúnez. Santiago: Ediciones ChileAmérica, 1995. 143 p.: ill. (some col.), photos.

Recollections of Antúnez's life and work compiled by Verdugo in interviews with the artist recorded a short time before his death. Text is very informal and personal. For non-Chileans or those not familiar with Antúnez's career, however, book might seem excessively local in scope. Illustrated with photographs of family and friends, and some secondary pieces of Antúnez's work.

Colombia

316 **Arte para Bogotá.** Bogotá: Editorial Univ. Nacional, 1997. 271 p.: ill., index.

Illustrated catalog of 1995 invitational organized by Bogotá's Alcaldía Mayor, with the objective of rediscovering and re-evaluating importance of public areas in the Colombian capital. Sixty-eight projects by almost as many architects, sculptors, and conceptual artists were presented. Ten were selected by the jury, all related to different avenues, parks, and other urban locations in Bogotá. Interesting contest showing artists' awareness and imagination when making a visual proposition affecting public space.

317 **Caballero, Luis.** Luis Caballero: obra sobre papel. Textos del catálogo de Camilo Calderón Schrader. Bogotá: Banco de la República; Biblioteca Luis Angel Arango, 1995. 110 p.: ill.

Camilo Calderón writes the introduction to this catalog of drawings by Luis Caballero exhibited at the Biblioteca Luis Angel Arango in Bogotá during June-Aug. 1995. Many of the works were discovered at the artist's studio after his death and had not been seen before. Selection contains a large group of intimate and personal sketches and undated drawings that more correctly belong in the category of "studies," but nevertheless corroborate Caballero's innate capacity to draw by conveying his sensitive and emotionally charged identification with the medium. Illustrated in b/w and color.

318 **Caballero, Luis.** Luis Caballero: sin título, 1966–1968. Bogotá: Museo Nacional de Colombia, 1997. 111 p.: bibl., col. ill.

Catalog of the exhibition organized by Bogotá's Museo Nacional around the "Polyptic," the work for which Luis Caballero won first prize at the Coltejer Biennial in Medellín in 1968. The work has been known traditionally as the Chamber of Love, although it seems the artist never intended to put a title to any of his works. The "Polyptic" was presented at the biennial in an incomplete form, and this exhibition presents it in its entirety for the first time. The many illustrations provide a clear indication of Caballero's early visual and erotic concerns, which prevailed as a characteristic note in his work throughout his career.

319 **Cárdenas, Jorge** and **Jesús Gaviria Gutiérrez.** Eladio Vélez: libretas de dibujo, 1927–1931. Bibliografía preparada por Miguel Escobar Calle. Medellín, Colombia: Fondo Editorial, Univ. EAFIT, 1997. 133 p.: bibl., chiefly col. ill. (Col. El arte en Antioquia ayer y hoy; volumen 1)

The editorial fund of Medellín's Univ. EAFIT has made possible the publication of the sketches of Eladio Vélez contained in 10 "libretas" or booklets, executed by the artist during his four-year European journey. Booklets Nos. 5, 6, and 7 are the least satisfactory, but the others demonstrate the artist's capacity for capturing in drawing the essence and visual structure of the subjects. No. 10 is exemplary. Artist Jorge Cárdenas, Vélez's student and current owner of the booklets, gives an account of his teacher's experiences in Europe. The book is illustrated and contains a short biographical chronology and bibliography.

320 **Espinosa, José María.** José María Espinosa: abanderado del arte y de la patria. Bogotá: Museo Nacional de Colombia, 1994. 64 p.: bibl., ill. (some col.).

Catalog for the exhibition organized by the Museo Nacional de Colombia on the work of José María Espinosa, one of the few early-19th-century Nueva Granada artists belonging to what is today Colombia. In his triple role as soldier, artist, and chronicler, Espinosa left one of the most memorable legacies in Spanish America from the time of the war for independence, including a few portraits of Simón Bolívar whom he knew personally and scenes of some of the most crucial battles. Includes numerous illustrations, mostly in b/w, and bibliographic material.

321   Gil Tovar, Francisco. El arte colombiano. 3. ed. Bogotá: Plaza & Janes Editores-Colombia, 1985. 191 p.: bibl., ill. (Selección Cultura colombiana; SCC 3. Arte)

Already in its third edition, this panorama of the arts in Colombia is an excellent "pocket book" for those wishing to familiarize themselves with the subject. In a clear and straightforward style, the Spanish-born Gil Tovar provides a general overview of the development of Colombian plastic arts, from precolumbian times to the present. The book has a few b/w illustrations and a good bibliography.

322   Iriarte, María Elvira. Historia de la serigrafía en Colombia. Bogotá: Univ. Nacional de Colombia, 1986. 107 p.: bibl., col. ill.

This first, brief study gives a precise account of the development of silk screening for artistic purposes in Colombia. Although silk screening was known and practiced in Colombia for commercial use since the early 1930s, it was not until 1969, according to Iriarte, that the technique was systematically utilized as a graphic media with artistic intent. The bulk of the book is dedicated to the decade 1970–80, in which Iriarte recognizes two different stages (1970–74 and 1975–78), and a third (beginning in 1979) that probably has continued up to this day. Complemented with 20 small reproductions. Bibliography is scarce but practical.

323   Jaramillo, Carmen María and María Iovine Moscarella. Carlos Rojas. Bogotá: Ediciones El Museo, 1995. 179 p.: bibl., ill. (some col.).

First publication of Ediciones El Museo dedicated to the geometric abstractionist painter, one of the few artists (and probably the most consistent) in Colombia who adhered to this tendency in the 1960s. Jaramillo wrote the text, dividing the sections chronologically, stylistically, and thematically. Moscarella wrote the chronology. Well illustrated, mostly in color.

324   Jaramillo, Lorenzo. Lorenzo Jaramillo: exposición retrospectiva. Bogotá: Banco de la República; Biblioteca Luis Angel Arango, 1995. 87 p.: bibl., ill. (some col.). (Col. Exposiciones, col. retrospectivas)

Catalog of the 1995 post-mortem retrospective exhibition at Bogotá's Biblioteca Luis Angel Arango honoring one of the most interesting and promising personalities that emerged in Colombian art during the 1980s. Throughout his short and intense career, L. Jaramillo produced—according to critic Germán Rubian who also wrote the concise essay introducing artist's work—nearly 1,000 pieces, 600 of which can be considered mature and completed works. María Clara Martínez is the author of a well-documented and succinct biography and bibliography. Includes a detailed checklist and abundant illustrations in color and b/w showing consistency of Jaramillo's work in painting, drawing, and printmaking.

325   Jaramillo, Luciano. Luciano Jaramillo: otra mirada. Bogotá: Banco de la República; Biblioteca Luis Angel Arango, 1997. 87 p.: ill. (some col.).

Catalog of 1997 retrospective exhibition of 88 works (mostly paintings and drawings) organized by the Biblioteca Luis Angel Arango in Bogotá as a tribute to the artist who passed away in 1984 at 46 years of age. Publication includes texts by Camilo Calderón Schrader and Germán Rubiano Caballero, and a chronology by Gloria Martínez. The entire checklist is included, along with numerous color and b/w illustrations. This is the most complete publication—if not the only one—in existence about the Colombian figurative expressionist whose early work seems to be the most interesting of his career.

326   Londoño Vélez, Santiago. Débora Arango: vida de pintora. Bogotá: Ministerio de Cultura, República de Colombia, 1997. 241 p.: bibl., ill.

Monograph honoring one of Colombia's more controversial painters, whose expressionistic work during the 1940s-50s was frequently surrounded by scandal and motivated angry personal attacks in the press. On occasion this led to the closing of several of her exhibitions, but her contribution was finally recognized in the 1980s. Arango's painting, both provocative and daring, usually deals with political, religious, and moral issues, although she also practiced more conventional themes such as portraiture, still life, and landscape. Supported by good documentation and illustrated in b/w, this book is part of a great effort by Londoño, whose research focused on the arts of the region of Antioquia, revitalizing an almost-forgotten field.

327 Londoño Vélez, Santiago. El grabado en Antioquia. Bogotá: Banco de la República; Medellín, Colombia: Museo de Arte Moderno de Medellín, 1990. 31 p.: bibl., ill. (some col.).

Santiago Londoño writes the text of this booklet published in 1993 to accompany the exhibition of the same name, organized by the Museo de Arte Moderno de Medellín and the Banco de la República. The essay serves more as a documentary review than esthetic criticism of the development of graphic arts in the province of Antioquia since early-19th century. Valuable for those interested in Latin American graphic arts, particularly due to the paucity of similar studies. Illustrated in b/w with a few color images. For review of an additional work on Antioquian painting and printmaking by Londoño, see item **328.**

328 Londoño Vélez, Santiago. Historia de la pintura y el grabado en Antioquia. Medellín, Colombia: Editorial Univ. de Antioquia, 1995. 266 p.: bibl., col. ill., indexes. (Señas de identidad)

Centers exclusively on techniques of painting and printmaking as practiced by the artists in Antioquia. The historic framework ranges from colonial times to mid-20th century. Londoño's study differs from the traditional, centralist perspective of Bogotá's critics. Well documented, this work received a Colcultura award. For review of an additional work on Antioquian printmaking by Londoño, see item **327.**

329 Medina, Alvaro. El arte colombiano de los años veinte y treinta. Bogotá: Colcultura; Instituto Colombiano de Cultura Hispánica 1995. 360 p.: bibl., ill. (Premios nacionales de cultura, 1994)

This detailed study received one of the 1994 national history awards in Colombia. Satisfactorily illustrated in b/w and well documented, this publication is fundamental for anyone interested in understanding early-20th-century Colombian art through its indi-

vidual artistic figures and sociological context.

330 Museo Nacional de Colombia. Arte para la historia: 170 años; promesas de donación/proyectos de adquisición; anhelos del Museo Nacional por una colección más rica en sus 170 años. v. 1. Bogotá?: Museo Nacional de Colombia, 1993. 1 v.: ill. (some col.).

Catalog of the 1993 exhibition celebrating the 170th anniversary of the founding of the Museo Nacional de Colombia. Selection includes artworks from all periods to the present, and features some artworks designated as gifts to the institution.

331 Once maestros de la pintura andina. Bogotá: Propal, 1998. 174 p.: ill. (some col.).

Volume focuses on 11 artists from the Andean region, as part of the series of calendars by Productora de Papel, S.A. dedicated to the work of well-known Colombian artists. Each artist is represented with several illustrations in color and a biographical career summary.

332 Pedro Nel Gómez: 80 años al servicio del arte, la cultura y su pueblo. Medellín, Colombia: Univ. de Antioquia, 1981. 66 p.: bibl., ill. (some col.).

The Univ. of Antioquia organized a tribute to Gómez, and this modest publication was produced to document his contribution to Colombian art. Nine different texts previously published by an array of intellectuals and writers such as Angel Guido, Enzo Carli, Efe Gomez, and Ciro Mendía are reunited here, complemented with the artist's explanation of his mural work.

333 Poesía de la naturaleza. Textos de Juan Luis Mejia Arango, Miguel Escobar Calle, and Roberto Luis Jaramillo. Medellín, Colombia: Compañía Suramericana de Seguros, 1997. 160 p.: bibl., ill. (some col.).

Suramericana commissioned this exhibition dedicated to studying evolution of landscape painting in the Antioquia region beginning with late-18th century. Texts are accompanied by acceptable color illustrations.

334 Rodríguez, Ofelia. Ofelia Rodríguez. Garza García, Mexico: Galería Ramis Barquet, 1994. 1 v. (unpaged): bibl., col. ill.

Catalog of the 1994 exhibition of unspecified number of "boxes" by O. Rodríguez at Galería Ramis Barquet in Mexico City, with text by Alberto Ruy-Sánchez and Edward Lucie-Smith.

335   Serrano, Eduardo; Fabio Giraldo Isaza; and John Stringer. Darío Morales. Bogotá: El Sello Editorial, 1993. 255 p.: bibl., ill. (some col.).

Profusely illustrated monograph on Morales may reaffirm the idea that he was more a draftsman than a painter or sculptor, although he realized many works in both techniques. Two themes dominate Morales' work: the female nude and the relationship between model and artist. His studied eroticism is aseptic, however, and comes across more as an artificial formalism, leaving doubts about which idea was more important for Morales. Includes a chronology and bibliography.

336   Urdaneta, Alberto. Alberto Urdaneta, vida y obra. Bogotá: Banco de la República, Depto. Editorial, 1992. 38 p.: ill. (some col.).

Catalog of an exhibition of 367 works (paintings, engravings, photographs, drawings, caricatures, sketches, murals, etc.) held at Biblioteca Luis Angel Arango (1992). Urdaneta (1845–87) was a cultivated man committed to many endeavors: military man, architect, artist, and photographer, but above all, a man of letters and the founder of four newspapers. His last, *Papel Periódico Ilustrado,* gathered in its time the most prestigious figures of Bogotá's intelligentsia, becoming a classic in Colombia's journalism. Includes texts describing Urdaneta's accomplishments and selected writings from the period.

337   Wiedemann, Guillermo. El legado de Guillermo Wiedemann. Bogotá: Banco de la República; Biblioteca Luis Angel Arango, 1994. 86 p.: bibl., col. ill.

Catalog of the exhibition held at the Biblioteca Luis Angel Arango in Bogotá presenting works donated by Wiedemann's widow to the Museo Nacional de Colombia and the aforementioned library, on occasion of 25th anniversary of the artist's death. All works belonged to the personal collection of the German-born artist (1905–69). Text by Iriarte and a summarized biography. All works seem to have been reproduced in color, showing Wiedemann's evolution from a tropical, expressionistic, figurative style to a geometric abstract one.

Ecuador

338   Castro y Velázquez, Juan. Manuel Rendón Seminario, 1894–1980: catálogo razonado. Guayaquil, Ecuador: Comité del Centenario del Nacimiento del Pintor Manuel Rendón Seminario, 1995. 350 p.: ill. (some col.).

Catalog raissoné of the work of Manuel Rendón, a pioneer modernist in Ecuador and the Americas, published on occasion of the centenary of the artist (Guayaquil, 1894). This book is the most complete study on Rendón to date. Many scholars have overlooked the artist when analyzing the context of modernity in 20th-century Latin America. Well documented, book traces the career of Rendón since his beginnings with the school of Paris in 1916, his flirtation with *indigenismo* at the end of the 1930s, and his final and definitive journey into geometric abstraction from early 1940s to his death in 1980. An important effort with excellent results.

339   Colvin, Jean and Alfredo Toaquiza. Pintores de Tigua = Indigenous artists of Ecuador. Washington: Organization of American States, 1996. 1 v. (unpaged): col. ill.

Booklet dedicated to a group of indigenous painters from Tigua (a village in the Ecuadorian Andes), on occasion of the 1996 exhibition at the OAS in Washington, DC. The work, in the artists' own words, describes the reality of indigenous life now and in the past. Text describes introduction of painting in the town 25 years ago and how its practice has contributed to the quality of life.

340   De la inocencia a la libertad: arte cuencano del siglo XX = From innocence to liberty: Cuencan art of the 20th century. Edited by Andrés Abad Merchán. Cuenca, Ecuador: Ediciones del Banco Central del Ecuador, 1998. 280 p.: bibl., col. ill.

Fifteen authors analyze different facets of the arts produced in Cuenca since the 19th century, through the work of 180 artists born or active in the city, the site of one of the few existing art biennials in Latin America. Well illustrated in color.

Escudero-Albornoz, Ximena. Neptalí Martínez: la permanencia del arte colonial. See item **97.**

341 Gilbert, Araceli. Araceli. Quito: Banco del Progreso, 1995? 182 p.: bibl., ill. (some col.), index.

Illustrated volume traces career of one of Ecuador's more prolific women artists, a forerunner in introduction of geometric tendencies in that country in early 1950s. Ecuador's Banco del Progreso commissioned the book. Text by Lenín Oña is perhaps too laudatory. Chronology is intended to place Gilbert's work within the general events of the plastic arts and literature, and 20th-century political circumstances. Content is overselected and general.

342 Lee Tsui, Pablo; Florencio Compte Guerrero; and Claudia Peralta González. Testimonio y memoria de la arquitectura histórica de Guayaquil. 2nd. ed. ampliada. Guayaquil, Ecuador: Univ. Católica de Santiago de Guayaquil, 1996. 273 p.: appendix, bibl., ill. (some col.), maps.

Some architectural gems have survived in late-20th-century Guayaquil, including the home of Vicente Rocafuerte, the second president of Ecuador (1835–39). Volume is a stunning testimony to the city's architectural history. Text and illustrations are complementary and highly informative. Second edition of *Patrimonio arquitectónico y urbano de Guayaquil* (1989). [M.T. Hamerly]

Martínez Borrero, Juan; Carmen Ugalde de Valdivieso; and Juan Cordero Iñiguez. De lo divino y lo profano: arte cuencano de los siglos XVIII y XIX. See item **2242.**

343 Museo-Archivo de Arquitectura (Ecuador). El arte ecuatoriano de hoy. Quito: Museo-Archivo de Arquitectura, 1995. 127 p.: bibl., ill. (some col.), index.

Catalog of exhibition of 21 contemporary artists held at the Museo-Archivo de Arquitectura (Quito, 1995) on occasion of the celebration of the festival entitled "La Huella de Europa, Ecuador 95." Includes brief information about all artists.

344 Rodríguez Castelo, Hernán. Panorama del arte ecuatoriano. Quito: Corporación Editora Nacional, 1993. 167 p.: bibl. (Biblioteca ecuatoriana de la familia; 9)

Pocket version synthesis of other books by the author on the same subject. In four chapters (precolumbian, colonial, republican, and 20th century), author gives a capsulated summary of what Ecuadorian art has been, from the past to the present, in a simple style intentionally suitable for high school students, hence its interest. Complemented with a short bibliography and a glossary of terms for those unfamiliar with the artistic and architectural field.

Vega Vega, Wilson. José María Vargas: bibliografía. See item **2117.**

Paraguay

Escobar, Ticio. A gravura popular, outra imagem da guerra. See item **3085.**

345 Plá, Josefina; Olga Blinder; and Ticio Escobar. Arte actual en el Paraguay, 1900–1995: antecedentes y desarrollo del proceso en las artes plásticas. 2. ed. Asunción: Ediciones IDAP, 1997. 197 p.: ill. (some col.).

J. Plá, O. Blinder, and T. Escobar offer different and complementary perspectives on 20th-century development of the arts in Paraguay. Timelines, bibliographies, summarized biographies of the artists mentioned, and a selection of articles written between 1952–95 by a variety of authors add to the reference value of this updated study on Paraguayan art.

Peru

346 Bienal Iberoamericana de Lima, 1st Lima, 1997. Primera Bienal Iberoamericana de Lima. Lima: Tele 2000, 1997. 241 p.: col. ill., music.

Impressive, full-color catalog of event organized in celebration of Lima's 1997 nomination as Plaza Mayor de la Cultura Ibero americana by the Union of Iberoamerican Capitals. Twenty Iberoamerican countries were invited to participate. Peru was represented with nine artists. The biennial was divided into several areas or salons, including 40 specially invited "masters." Good reference source for trends currently in vogue in Latin America.

347 Braun-Vega, Herman. Herman Braun-Vega. Madrid: Minsterio de Cultura, Dirección General de Bellas Artes y Archivos, 1992. 83 p.: col. ill.

Catalog of anthological exhibition of paintings, drawings, and prints by Peruvian-born and Paris resident Braun-Vega, at the Antiguo Museo Español de Arte Contemporáneo (Madrid, 1992), covering 1950–91. Includes texts by various authors reflecting long-term friendships with the artist. Good quality printing, many illustrations.

348 Fernández, José Abel. Grabadores en el Perú: bosquejo histórico 1574–1950 con una muestra de 130 xilografías. Lima: s.n., 1995. 228 p.: bibl., ill.

Described by the author as a "historic sketch," this compilation of texts about the development of printmaking in Peru since the early stages of the colonial period is profusely illustrated, and constitutes an excellent summary of graphic arts activities in the country. An explanatory text about the technical aspects of engraving makes this book a useful and didactic publication.

349 Llona, Ramiro. Ramiro Llona: 1973–1998. Lima: Pontificia Univ. Católica del Perú; Museo de Arte de Lima, 1998. 354 p.: bibl., col. ill.

Voluminous exhibition catalog of 183 paintings and works on paper and graphics, covering 25 years of work, with excellent color reproductions. Villacorta's essay traces the many influences present in Llona's work: Gorky, Matta, Lam, and Diebenkorn, among others; while Kuspit refers to it as a postmodern amalgam of modernist ideas.

350 Museo Municipal de Arte Contemporáneo (Cuzco, Peru). Catálogo de Mario Soto Sayhua. Qosqo, Peru: Municipalidad del Qosqo, 1995. 76 p.: ill. (some col.).

One hundred works from the private collection of Dr. Luis Rivera Dávalos, donated to the municipality of Cuzco, led to the founding of a museum of contemporary art. As with most private collections, this one reveals taste and artistic inclinations of its patron. With a few exceptions, most works are by local commercial and untrained artists. A colloquial text by Manuel Gibaja animates the reader to relate freely with the works, which are predominantly figurative and folkloric. The term "contemporary" is perhaps a little too ambitious for the group.

351 Vinatea Reinoso, Jorge. Vinatea Reinoso: 1900–1931. Catálogo y textos de Luis Eduardo Wuffarden. 2. ed. Lima: Telefónica del Perú; Patronato de Telefónica, 1997. 373 p.: ill. (some col.).

Volume dedicated to Jorge Segundo Vinatea Rinoso, painter, watercolorist, draftsman, and caricaturist (Arequipa, 1900) whose early death at age at 31 halted a promising career. The best of Vinatea's work stems from indigenist current of Peruvian art, and in this vein he executed his most inspired paintings.

Uruguay

352 Anastasía, Luis Víctor. Figari, lucha continua. Cronología anotada por Walter Rela. Montevideo: Istituto Italiano di Cultura in Uruguay; Academia Uruguaya de Letras; Libros Gussi, 1994. 301, p.: ill. (some col.).

One of the most complete and satisfactory studies on the life, times, and work of Pedro Figari, covering all aspects of his personality and career. Contains excellent documentation and annotated chronology by Walter Rela, and some archival photographic reproductions. For a review of *Figari: XXIII Bienal de São Paulo*, see item **356.**

353 Barradas/Torres-García: agosto-setiembre-1995. Coordinación del Depto. Cultural de la Embajada de Uruguay en la República Argentina. Buenos Aires?: Cultura de la Nación Argentina; Museo Nacional de Bellas Artes de Buenos Aires, 1995. 120 p.: ill. (some col.), indexes.

Catalog of the Buenos Aires exhibition of the work of Rafael Barradas (102 works) and Joaquín Torres García (126 works) at the Museo Nacional de Bellas Artes, in 1995. Presentation by Julio María Sanguinetti. Essays by Jorge Gluzberg and Angel Kalemberg, with chronologies on both artists. Generously illustrated, mostly in color.

354 Bausero, Luis. Manuel Rosé. Montevideo: Ediciones Lucía Ametrano Galería de Arte, 1990. 181 p.: ill. (some col.).

Volume produced by Lucía Ametrano in tribute to the artist on occasion of the exhibit organized and presented at her art gallery in Montevideo in 1990. Includes many color and b/w reproductions of Rosé's work, as well as 17 texts by various authors (from as early as 1925), but Bausero wrote the majority. Each book (1,000 copies) is complemented with three photo-lithographs based on original drawings by the author.

355 Blanes Viale, Pedro. P. Blanes Viale: 1878–1926. Palma de Mallorca, Spain: Caixa de Balears Sa Nostra, 1992. 194 p.: bibl., ill. (some col.).

Catalog (in Spanish and Catalan) of the 1992 exhibition dedicated to the artist at the Centre de Cultura de Palma de Mallorca, Blanes Viale's place of origin. Includes presentations by Carlos Blanes Nouvilas and Maria Luisa Torrens. Essay by José María Pardo. All works are reproduced in color with clear annotations and complete data. Sources are well indicated and biographical information is enhanced with photo-documentation. See also item **365.**

356 Figari, Pedro. Figari: XXIII Bienal de São Paulo. Buenos Aires: FINAMBRAS, 1996. 204 p.: bibl., ill. (some col.).

Illustrated catalog of Figari's exhibition of more than 80 paintings at the Uruguay-Argentina pavilion of the São Paulo Biennial, with presentation by Jorge Castillo. For a review of *Figari, lucha continua,* see item **352.**

357 Heine, Ernesto. 12 pintores uruguayos. Montevideo?: Impr. Gordon, 1995. 84 p.: bibl., ill. (some col.). (Artistas de América y de España)

It is not clear what kind of criteria was used in uniting the 12 Uruguayan artists featured in this book. The artists represent various styles and generations, from Francisco Matto (1911) to Clever Lara (1952) and Alvaro J. Montañéz (1958). Biographical data is useful for anybody interested in Uruguayan art. Illustrated in b/w and color.

358 Italia en el arte uruguayo: exposición realizada en ocasión de la visita del presidente de Italia Oscar Luigi Scalfaro. Montevideo: Museo Nacional de Artes Visuales, 1995. 43 p.: ill. (some col.).

Catalog of the exhibition presented at the Museo Nacional de Artes Visuales de Montevideo, on occasion of the visit of the President of Italy. Forewords by President José María Sanguinetti, President Oscar Luigi Scalfaro, and Angel Kalenberg. As title suggests, artists represented in the exhibition (covering 19th and 20th century) are Italian nationals, immigrants, or Uruguayans who have had a direct relation with Italy through

ancestry or education. Illustrated in color with short biographical sketches of each artist.

359 Iturria, Ignacio. Ignacio Iturria. Buenos Aires: Fundación Praxis para la Difusión del Arte, 1994. 52 p.: col. ill.

Bilingual catalog of exhibition held at Fundación Praxis in Buenos Aires includes texts by Albino Dieguez Videla and Olga Larnaudie, among others. Illustrated in color, and complemented with a biographical sketch.

360 Kalenberg, Angel. Damiani. Montevideo: Galería de la Matriz, 1993. 212 p.: ill. (some col.).

A short text explains the metaphysical character of Damiani's work. The rest of the book is dedicated to reproducing Damiani's paintings, drawings, and collages with excellent illustrations in color and b/w covering 1956–92. Includes a chronology and a short biographical summary.

361 Laroche, Walter E. C. Arzadun, 1888–1968: su tiempo, su obra; derrotero para una historia del arte en el Uruguay. Prólogo de Edmundo Narancio. Montevideo: Museo y Archivo Ernesto Laroche, 1995. 71 p.: bibl., ill. (some col.).

Judicious biographical research about the Uruguayan modernist attempts to place Arzadun's contribution in relation to both the modernist esthetic current of his time and the Uruguayan art scene. Sparsely illustrated.

362 Montevideo y la plástica. Montevideo: Intendencia Municipal de Montevideo, 1996. 107 p.: bibl., ill. (some col.), map.

In 1996 Montevideo was declared the Cultural Capital of Ibero-America. On that occasion, the Intendencia Municipal de Montevideo published this book, and to echo the celebration, 11 exhibitions were organized to focus on the connection between the artists and the city. Featured artists range from Torres García and Figari to younger, contemporary artists. Alicia Haber, Ola Larnaudie, and Joan van dev Berghe wrote the essays. Illustrated in b/w and color.

363 Peluffo Linari, Gabriel. Historia de la pintura uruguaya. v. 1–8. Montevideo: Ediciones de la Banda Oriental, 1986–1992. 8 v.: bibl., ill. (some col.).

Series of eight booklets focusing exclusively on painting in Uruguay follows a chronological development up to the 1930s. Conceived as a didactic text, the format is simple and clear, and the booklets are well documented and illustrated. Extremely useful and highly recommended for any student interested in the art of the Río de la Plata region or Latin American art in general.

364 Peluffo Linari, Gabriel. El paisaje a través del arte en el Uruguay. Montevideo: Edición Galería Latina, 1995. 190 p.: ill. (some col.), maps.

Focuses on landscape as a genre allowing analysis in the context of social, political, and cultural conditions of Uruguayan society. Begins with 18th century when landscape achieves its own autonomy as a subject, although in the Americas its practice begins more as the result of scientific and geopolitical interests. Comprised of six chapters and clear notes indicating sources, and 211 illustrations in color and b/w.

365 Pereda, Raquel. Blanes Viale. Montevideo: Fundación Banco de Boston, 1990. 189 p.: bibl., ill. (some col.).

Extensively detailed and groundbreaking biographical study of life and work of Pedro Blanes Viale, the Uruguayan artist who died in 1926 and whose work can be linked to that of Spain's Santiago Rusiñol and Anglada-Camarasa. Sources are well documented. Contains numerous reproductions of artist's work, and photo-documentation of his personal life in b/w and color. Excellent source for understanding Uruguayan art at the beginning of the century and artist's contribution to the visual arts of his country. See also item **355.**

366 Torres, Augusto. Augusto Torres. Organized by the Embajada de España and Instituto de Cooperación Iberoamericana. Montevideo: Museo Torres García; Cabildo de Montevideo, 1994. 1 v. (unpaged): bibl., ill. (some col.).

Biographical summary of Torres by Patricia Betancur (with whom Torres' widow collaborated) paints an emotionally controlled picture, domestic at times, of his life and work, always under the shadow of his father, the great modernist master Joaquín Torres García. Illustrated in color and b/w.

367 Torres-García, Joaquín. Historia de mi vida. Barcelona: Paidós, 1990. 234 p., 8 p. of plates: ill., port.

This book, originally published in Montevideo in 1939, chronicles artist's life up to his return to Uruguay in 1934. Written in third person, work is a delightful "must read" for any artist, critic, historian, or collector of Latin American art or modern art in general. Torres-García gives a colorful account of his career, his stays in New York and Barcelona, the people he met and those who helped him, his views about life and art, and much more. Illustrated with sketches of the master himself.

368 Zorrilla de San Martin, José Luis. José Luis Zorrilla de San Martin, 1891–1991. Montevideo: Museo Nacional de Artes Visuales, 1992. 95 p.: bibl., ill. (some col.).

Published for the 1992 retrospective at the Museo Nacional de Artes Visuales de Montevideo, book honors the artist (sculptor and painter) who passed away at age 100. The exhibit was organized by María Luisa Torrens, Director of Culture of the Uruguayan government, who wrote one of the two essays that appear in the publication. The other was written by Roberto de Espada. Illustrated in color and b/w.

Venezuela

369 Banco Central de Venezuela. Banco Central de Venezuela: colección de arte, 1940–1996. Caracas: Banco Central de Venezuela, 1997. 332 p.: bibl., ill. (some col.), indexes.

Annotated and illustrated catalog of the art collection of the BCV, divided into two sections corresponding to 19th a 20th centuries. Includes a unique group of Camille Pisarro's watercolors acquired by the bank in 1965; it is believed that the French impressionist executed the paintings during his stay in Venezuela. Roberto Montero Castro presents the collection and traces its history. Collection is representative of the evolution of the visual arts in Venezuela, with an emphasis on painting.

370 Becerra, Milton. Milton Becerra. México: Galería Ramis Barquet, 1996. 1 v. (unpaged): bibl., col. ill.

Catalog of the exhibition held in 1996 at Galería Ramis Barquet of Mexico City, with an introduction (in English and Spanish) by Colombian Alvaro Medina. All 12 works, inspired by the objects and symbols used by the Amazonian tribes, are reproduced in color. Includes a biographical resume of the artist.

371 Botero, Fernando. Botero: donación del artista para el Museo de Arte Contemporáneo de Caracas Sofía Imber. Caracas: Museo de Arte Contemporáneo de Caracas Sofía Imber, 1996. 96 p.: bibl., ill. (some col.). (Catálogo; 124)

Catalog of artist's most recent exhibition at MACCSI, including a donation of 15 sculptures, five works already in the collection of the museum, and 20 new color drawings on canvas. Beautifully illustrated in color, with a text by Roberto Guevara.

372 Boulton, Alfredo. Alejandro Otero. Caracas: O. Ascanio Editores, 1994. 174 p.: bibl., ill. (some col.).

Author warns about "personal" tone of this book due to his lifelong friendship with the painter. The author's access to Otero's personal archive after the artist's death is reflected in this publication and adds to the value of additional material (letters, photos, and artworks) already in Boulton's possession, dating from Otero's move to Paris in mid-1940s. Good selection of illustrations showing the constant evolution and transformation of Otero's work until the time of his death. For additional studies on Alejandro Otero and his work, see items **385** and **386.**

373 Boulton, Alfredo. Manuel Cabré. Caracas: Macanao Ediciones, 1989. 120 p.: ill. (some col.).

Four texts about Cabré, "the painter of the Avila," are united in this volume which pays a personal and emotional tribute to one of the forerunners of Venezuela's regional modernism. Excellent color reproductions.

374 Brandt Pérez, Mary. Mary Brandt: pinturas, dibujos y grabados, 1950–1985. Text by Roberto Guevara. Caracas: Galería de Arte Nacional, 1995. 79 p.: ill. (some col.).

Catalog of the anthological exhibition of paintings, drawings, and prints, 1950–1985, held at Galería de Arte Nacional in Caracas, during June-Aug., 1995, on occasion of the 10th anniversary of the artist's death. Well illustrated in color and b/w. Includes extensive annotations and solid chronology.

375 Calzadilla, Juan. Pedro Angel González. Caracas: Armitano Editores, 1996. 230 p.: bibl., ill. (some col.).

Excellent study elaborates on a critical analysis of the work of González, a singular figure in Venezuelan 20th-century modernism whose work is characterized by his dedication to landscape painting. Throughout his life, he maintained a constant insecurity toward his own work, thinking it was anachronistic and out of the mainstream of European modernism, which he confessed he did not understand. He stopped painting for 10 years, then returned to his craft in 1936 to realize his best compositions in a regional, realistic style. He established his own vision of the Venezuelan landscape in a style that can be characterized as nationalist, in tune with the dominant direction taken by Latin American art at the time. Beautifully illustrated in color, with autobiographical texts and a selected bibliography.

376 Esteva Grillet, Roldán. Para una crítica del gusto en Venezuela. Caracas: Fundarte, 1992. 200 p.: bibl., index. (Col. Cuadernos de difusión; 186)

In nine essays, each related to a different time frame, author analyzes diverse aspects of Venezuelans' cultural behavior in regard to what the author considers "taste." Witty and amusing, often sarcastic and colloquial, book does not lose perspective of the historical context. A curious x-ray of Venezuelan idiosyncrasies.

377 Fundación Polar (Venezuela). Catálogo: colección de arte Fundación Polar. Caracas: Fundación Polar, 1995. 1 v. (unpaged): col. ill. (Col. Artistas)

Catalog of Venezuelan art collection owned by foundation created by Polar Enterprises comes in the form of a binder to which one can add new entries in the future to keep it updated as the collection grows. Each work in the collection—which is mostly 20th-century—is reproduced in color on separate, alphabetically organized cards that contain technical data and a short critical commentary.

378 Gramcko, Elsa. Elsa Gramcko: una alquimista de nuestro tiempo; muestra antológica, 1957–1978. Textos de Elizabeth Schön, Juan Carlos López Quintero, and Juan Calzadilla. Caracas: Galería de Arte Nacional, 1997. 62 p.: bibl., ill. (some col.). (Publicación; 172)

Juan Carlos López Quintero is the curator of this anthological exhibition of Gramcko's work, covering years between her early geometric abstractions (1957) to her late informalist period (1974). Several of works selected had never been seen before. Includes complete checklist and excellent color reproductions. Catalog is complemented with an illustrated chronology by Cruz Barceló Cedeño and an interview given by the artist in 1976.

379 Herrera Toro, Antonio José. Antonio Herrera Toro, 1857–1914: final de un siglo. Caracas: Galería de Arte Nacional, 1995. 168 p.: ill. (some col.).

Detailed catalog of the exhibition—to date the most comprehensive—on the Venezuelan artist whose work belongs to the last quarter of the 19th century, organized by the Galería de Arte Nacional, Caracas, in 1995. Texts by Francisco Da Antonio, Anna Gradowska, and Marian Caballero de Borges. Well illustrated in b/w and color. Well documented.

380 Jezierski, Karin. Pintores del Zulia. Caracas: Lagoven, 1995. 95 p.: bibl., ill. (some col.). (Cuadernos Lagoven)

Ten painters are united in this book, which attempts to survey work by painters outside Caracas. Includes individual notes and a biographical summary on each artist. Illustrated in color.

381 Los maestros del Círculo de Bellas Artes: homenaje a Luis Alfredo López Méndez; exposición itinerante. Caracas: Fundación Galería de Arte Nacional, 1993. 100 p.: bibl., ill. (some col.). (Catálogo; 137)

Catalog of the traveling exhibition organized in 1993 by the Galería de Arte Nacional in Caracas as a tribute to the 92nd birthday of the artist. Included more than 80 works by the founders of the Círculo de Bellas Artes (1912). El Círculo is credited with the introduction of modernism to Venezuelan art. Nicely illustrated in color, with good bibliography.

382 Michelena, Juan Antonio. Juan Antonio Michelena, un testigo de la gloria. Caracas: Consejo Nacional de la Cultura; Fundación Museo Arturo Michelena, 1994? 60 p.: bibl., ill. (some col.). (Catálogo / Fundación Museo Arturo Michelena; 7)

Catalog of exhibition researched and organized by the Fundación Museo Arturo Michelena in Caracas, which identified approximately 30 original paintings by this forerunner of Venezuelan art, and one of the first Venezuelan painters of the Third Republican Period. Essay on the artist by Francisco Da Antonio. Evelyn Ramos Guerrero gives a general overview of the portraits painted by Michelena. Natalia Díaz places artist in context. Good color reproductions and additional archival material make this publication of great value.

383 Navarro, Pascual. Pascual Navarro: imágenes y percepciones de un tiempo. Caracas: Consejo Nacional de la Cultura Fundación Museo Arturo Michelena, 1994. 67 p.: ill. (some col.). (Catálogo / Fundación Museo Arturo Michelena; 5)

Catalog of the 1994 traveling exhibition organized by Fundación Museo Arturo Michelena in Caracas. Navarro died in 1985 and is considered one of the forerunners of geometric abstraction in Venezuela, although he returned to figurative work in the mid-1950s, which is the subject of the essay by Cruz Barceló Cedeño. Good biographical research and archival documentation make this catalog very useful. Illustrated in color and b/w.

384 Noriega, Simón. Ideas sobre el arte en Venezuela en el siglo XIX. Mérida, Venezuela: Univ. de Los Andes, Ediciones del Rectorado, 1993. 92 p.: bibl.

Author's intention is to fill some voids in the critical history of Venezuelan art. Six chapters cover period from pre-dawn of independence to Guzmán Blanco. Lacks illustrations but offers a concise bibliography.

385 Otero Rodríguez, Alejandro. Alejandro Otero: las estructuras de la realidad. Textos de María Elena Ramos et al. Caracas: Fundación Museo de Bellas Artes, 1991. 67 p.: ill.

Catalog of Alejandro Otero exhibition held at the Museo de Arte Moderno Jesús Soto in Ciudad Bolívar, from Dec. 1990-Feb. 1991. Curated by Maria Helena Ramos, who also wrote most of the texts in the catalog.

Mariana Figarella, Federica Palomero, and Katherine Chacón contributed additional texts and Douglas Monroy wrote the chronology. For additional studies on Alejandro Otero and his work, see items **372** and **386.**

386   Otero Rodríguez, Alejandro. Papeles biográficos: memorias de infancia. Prólogo de Efraín Inaudy Bolívar. Cronología de Carlos Yusti. Upata, Venezuela: Fondo Editorial Predios, 1994. 163 p. (Predios testimonio)

Published six years after the artist's death, this is the last volume in a trilogy of autobiographical recollections. Otero writes in a simple, unpretentious way, giving a first-hand account of himself up to the time he enrolled in the Escuela de Artes Plásticas. For additional studies on Alejandro Otero and his work, see items **372** and **385.**

387   Pardo, Mercedes. Mercedes Pardo: moradas del color. Caracas: Fundacion Galería de Arte Nacional, 1991. 180 p.: bibl., col. ill.

Formative monograph on Mercedes Pardo, one of Venezuela's pioneering women artists who dared to join the contemporary art scene of Venezuela when she joined the Escuela de Artes Plásticas y Aplicadas in Caracas in 1941. Includes essays by María Fernanda Palacios, Elizabeth Schon, and Gloria Carnevali; and chronology and bibliography by Luisa Pérez Gil. Fully illustrated in b/w and color, book follows evolution of Pardo's work through its many stylistic variations and expressions, although she is better known outside Venezuela for her geometric work.

388   Quintana Castillo, Manuel. Manuel Quintana Castillo: bañarse en el mismo río. Caracas: CONAC, 1997. 76 p.: bibl., ill. (some col.).

Catalog of the traveling exhibition (Colombia, Mexico, and US) organized by Venezuela's Consejo Nacional de la Cultura. Juan Carlos Palenzuela introduces artist's work starting from mid-1950s. Publication includes five articles by Quintana on various subjects. Complemented with a biographical chronology and checklist. Illustrated in color.

389   Reverón, Armando. Armando Reverón: luz y cálida sombra del Caribe; exposición itinerante 1996–1997. Textos de Katherine Chacón, Rafael Arráiz Lucca, and Edgardo Rodríguez Juliá. Caracas: Consejo Nacional de la Cultura, 1996. 140 p.: bibl., ill. (some col.).

Bilingual catalog of traveling exhibition (Colombia, Dominican Republic, Costa Rica, Puerto Rico, and Venezuela) curated by the Fundación Museo Armando Reverón. Illustrated in b/w and color. Texts include four critical essays, a chronology of 15th-19th century Latin America, and a bibliography.

390   Rivas, Bárbaro. Bárbaro Rivas, imágenes y revelaciones: exposición homenaje en el centenario de su nacimiento, 1893–1993. Caracas: Fundación Galería de Arte Nacional, 1993. 82 p.: bibl., ill. (some col.). (Catálogo; no. 139)

Catalog of the exhibition organized on occasion of 100th anniversary of artist's birth. Essays by Anita Tapias, Francisco Da Antonio, Miguel Von Dangel, and William Niño Araque are quite revealing about the strange, frequently disconcerting, and enchanting vision of an artist who lived in an unquestioned, multidimensional world. With complete checklist and selected color reproductions, this publication should serve as a model for exhibition catalogs.

391   Vega, Marta de la. Angel Hurtado. Prólogo de Jesús Soto. Caracas: Armitano Editores, 1994. 312 p.: bibl., ill. (some col.).

Monograph on artist who alternated between painting and cinematography, and who lived in Paris and then in Washington for many years before settling in the Margarita Island off the Venezuelan shore. Book concentrates on his work as a painter, going back to artist's beginnings in the town of El Tocuyo where he was born in 1927. From this rural reality, Hurtado's interest in landscape evolved to his present-day work. Excellent reproductions, good bibliography and biblio-filmography, and a clear text make this book a prime source for understanding Hurtado's life and work.

392   Voces y demonios de Armando
      Reverón: cuentos, anécdotas, pen-
samientos. Recogidos por Juan Calzadilla.
Caracas: Alfadil Ediciones, 1990. 136 p.:
bibl., ill. (Col. Orinoco; 25)

An interesting collection of stories and anecdotes about Armando Reverón told by those who knew him, including many personalities of the arts and letters. Valuable descriptions of Reverón's life and character.

BRAZIL

JOSÉ M. NEISTEIN, *Executive Director, Brazilian-American Cultural Institute, Washington, DC*

AS IN RECENT VOLUMES, the overwhelming majority of publications selected for this chapter examine various aspects of 20th-century Brazilian art. In addition, art publishing in Brazil remains proportionally the same as in past years with regard to the fields covered and, while there are few works available on some topics, all of the publications reviewed this biennium deserve the attention of scholars.

Seven theoretical and reference works were annotated and, among them, a few stand out due to the limited bibliography in this field. The impact of European modernity on Brazil (item **395**) heads the list, followed by the fine essays on Brazil's self-discovery (item **393**). The essays on Brazil's perception of the century are an original contribution to the literature (item **397**). Finally, the selected, annotated bibliography of art in Brazil is the most comprehensive work of its kind published to date in a single volume (item **398**).

Only two publications have been included for the colonial period. Of these, the rarest and most unusual describes a special expedition in the 18th century in search of examples and specimens of Brazilian flora and fauna (item **400**).

Just three items deal with the 19th century. One covers the architecture of sugar mills (item **402**), the second discusses Rio de Janeiro watercolors by Robert Pierce (item **404**), and the third examines the European vision of Brazilian landscapes and cityscapes (item **403**)

Several works on individual artists, regions, and time periods deserve special mention. Lygia Clark is the focus of two recent publications (items **410** and **420**). The catalog of Lasar Segall's works is one of the finest and most detailed studies of the expressionist master (item **408**), while avant-garde in Bahia is the subject of a broad study (item **426**). A long overdue monograph on Victor Brecheret is very welcome (item **417**), as is a fascinating essay on Siron Franco (item **405**). Tomás Santa Rosa, one of the most significant pioneers of 20th-century Brazilian set and costume design, is the well-chosen subject of a work reviewed here (item **407**). The visual conceptualization of Brazil by its own artists provides an important perspective on the Brazilian art world (item **416**), while a historical study of the artistic milieu of São Paulo in the 1940s and 1950s provides the reader with an original and creative examination of the period (item **419**).

The regions of Brazil have lately been the focus of a number of studies; the work on Rio Grande do Sul (item **423**) is a case in point. Hélio Oiticica's influence on Brazilian postmodernism is examined in item **412,** while Afro-Brazilian arts, artists, and traditions are the focus of two major publications: items **441** and **442.**

Three books stand out among the seven covering architecture and city planning. First, the monograph on Ramos de Azevedo (item **436**); second, the survey of contemporary Brazilian architects (item **433**); and, third, the one-volume collection of essays on Porto Alegre and its planning (item **434**). The guide to Rio's architectural heritage is another useful and welcomed resource (item **435**).

The catalog of Brazilian popular art (item **429**) offers a broad panorama of the field, while *Brazilian Naïf Art of Today* is a good reference for the esthetic trends of that category (item **430**). *Density of Light: Contemporary Brazilian Photography* presents an in-depth look at six photographers; (item **431**) and *Retratos de Família: Leitura da Fotografia Histórica,* a historical view of immigrant families, offers a tool for visual anthropology (item **432**).

Among the entries in the miscellaneous category, the introduction to the National Library of Rio de Janeiro (item **450**) stands out. *Tempos de Grossura: o Design no Impasse* (item **444**) is a welcomed data source, while the profile of Mato Grosso's artistic identity (item **455**) is a new approach. Brazilian graphic designers (item **445**) are introduced here as an eclectic group of varying interests. Meanwhile, *Images of the Unconscious from Brazil* (item **452**) contributes to the international body of literature on art as a path to emotional and psychological health. Finally, *Revista do Patrimônio Histórico e Artístico Nacional* (item **454**) provides an excellent source for relevant essays on restoration and preservation.

REFERENCE AND THEORETICAL WORKS

Encyclopedia of Latin American and Caribbean art. See item 15.

393 Internationale Junifestwochen Zürich, *1992.* Brasilien: Entdeckung und Selbstentdeckung. Bern, Switzerland: Benteli Verlag, 1992. 527 p.: bibl., ill. (some col.).

This catalog for the 1992 Zürich exhibition on Brazil is one of the most comprehensive works published to date on the history and arts of Brazil. Ranging from the early-16th century to the early 1990s, the included texts by an array of the finest historians, art critics, sociologists, art historians, and anthropologists examine the discovery and self-discovery of Brazil. A wealth of reproductions and photographic materials. Text in German only.

394 Lima, Sérgio Cláudio F. A aventura surrealista. v. 1, Iniciação ao surrealismo. Campinas, Brazil: Editora da Univ. Estadual de Campinas; São Paulo: Fundação para o Desenvolvimento da Unesp; Petrópolis, Brazil: Editora Vozes, 1995. 1 v.: bibl., ill. (some col.).

Fine contribution to the literature on surrealism both in general and in Brazil. Sharp insights, dialectical discussions of the international bibliography in the field, and a number of pertinent illustrations both in the visual arts and in literature.

395 Modernidade e modernismo no Brasil. Organização de Annateresa Fabris. Campinas, Brazil: Mercado de Letras, 1994? 160 p.: bibl. (Coleção Arte—ensaios e documentos)

Through sharply focused insights and critical commentary, this collection of essays examines the often contradictory means by which European modernity found its entry into Brazil and adapted to the country's particular requirements. Modernist autonomy is critiqued in favor of a more scholarly, diversified approach using new methods and documentation. Discusses 20th-century Brazilian intellectual and artistic life within this context.

396 Morais, Frederico. Cronologia das artes plásticas no Rio de Janeiro: da missão artística francesa à geração 90, 1816, mil oitocentos e dezesseis a mil novecentos e noventa e quatro, 1994. Rio de Janeiro: Topbooks, 1995. 559 p.: bibl., indexes.

Accurately describes each event or project that occurred during the period indicated; a large number of solo and group shows are registered, as well as hundreds of artists. A unique source for future research information.

397 Naves, Rodrigo. A forma difícil: ensaios sobre arte brasileira. São Paulo: Editora Atica, 1996. 285 p.: bibl., ill. (some col.).

In an attempt to understand the nature of Brazilian art, Naves has written essays on five artists—Debret, Guignard, Volpi, Segall, and Amilcar de Castro. With very few exceptions, Brazilian art has always been shy and ambivalent in its depictions. The author attributes this ambivalence to a poorly defined sociability, as shown through the country's history. In his own essays, Naves is not ambivalent; indeed, his insights are well articulated, even when they are polemical. An original contribution to the interpretation of the history of Brazilian art.

398 Neistein, José M. A arte no Brasil dos primórdios ao século vinte: bibliografia seleta, anotada. [Art in Brazil from its beginnings to modern times: a selected, annotated bibliography.] Washington, DC: Brazilian-American Cultural Institute; São Paulo: Livraria Kosmos Editora, 1997. 538 p.: bibl.

A meaningful contribution to the literature on the history of art in the Americas. Subjects covered range from reference and theoretical works through urban planning and folk art to Afro-Brazilian and Indian traditions. Each section is introduced by an annual summary of the related publishing history and important art-related events. In Portuguese and English.

399 II Arte Atual Paraibana. João Pessoa, Brazil: Fundação Espaço Cultural da Paraíba, 1990. 1 v. (unpaged): ill. (some col.).

Nearly 100 artists have been selected and included in this survey of current artists active in the state of Paraíba in 1990. Various trends are represented, predominantly the neorepresentational. Includes short biographies of the artists and one work of each reproduced in color.

COLONIAL PERIOD

O Brasil dos viajantes. See item 3157.

400 Fauna e flora brasileira, século XVIII = Brazilian fauna and flora, 18th century. Pesquisa histórica de Isa Adonias; pesquisa

científica e botânica de Arline Souza de Oliveira e Carmem Lúcia de Almeida Ferraz; ornitologia de Dante Luís Martins Teixeira; ictiologia de Gustavo Wilson Nunan. Rio de Janeiro: Spala Editora, 1986. 280 p.: bibl., ill. (some col.), maps.

Attributed to 18th-century Italian naturalist Antonio Land, who worked for Mato Grosso Governor Luiz de Albuquerque, these 116 drawings of Brazilian fauna (78) and flora (38) survived a devastating fire at the House of Insua in Portugal; many other drawings were destroyed. The specimens illustrate the "Philosophical Expedition" of 1765–70, which mainly explored Mato Grosso and Pará (Amazonia), detailing one of the most fascinating evolutionary histories of plant life on earth. This now rare book includes scientific and historical explanatory texts, first-rate iconography, and color reproductions of the highest quality.

401 Maia, Tom and **Thereza Regina de Camargo Maia.** Ouro Preto. Introdução de Francisco Iglésias. Rio de Janeiro: Expressão e Cultura, 1994. 91 p.: bibl., ill.

To celebrate the bicentennial of the "Inconfidência Mineira", this book, illustrated by china ink drawings, describes important secular and religious monuments of Ouro Preto. Includes introduction and descriptions in Portuguese, Spanish, French, English, German, and Russian.

19TH CENTURY

402 Antigos engenhos de açúcar no Brasil. Introdução e história dos engenhos e legendas de Fernando Tasso Fragoso Pires; estudo arquitetônico de Geraldo Gomes. 2a ed. Rio de Janeiro: Editora Nova Fronteira, 1994. 206 p.: bibl., ill. (some col.), col. maps.

As early as the first half of the 16th century, the Portuguese introduced sugar mills (*engenhos*) to Brazil, mainly in Pernambuco, Bahia, and Rio de Janeiro. A relevant chapter of Brazilian architecture was written on the mansions and chapels of the *engenhos*, particularly throughout the 19th century. This encompassing study was long overdue. Includes many color photographs and text in Portuguese and English.

403 Belluzzo, Ana Maria de Moraes. O Brasil dos viajantes. v. 3, A construção da paisagem. São Paulo: Metalivros; Rio de

Janeiro: Odebrecht, 1994. 1 v.: bibl., ill. (some col.), col. maps, indexes.

Many 19th-century European travelers and naturalists focused on the scientific classification of nature in Brazil. This diverse group of visitors viewed and described Brazilian landscapes and cityscapes from a wide variety of perspectives. While many minute details were faithfully reproduced from specimens or sites examined, imagination also seemed to have played a role in descriptions of Brazil's natural and architectural wonders. Drawings and watercolors were the major media. Belluzzo's text provides an account of this varied group of travelers, biographical information on many artists, and dozens of color and b/w reproductions. For geography specialist's comment on vol. 1, see *HLAS* 57:2387. For historian's comment on catalog of exposition, see item **3157.**

404 Pearce, Robert. Aquarelas: feitas durante a viagem ao Brasil da H.M.S. Favorite em 1819 e 1820. Introdução e análise descritiva das estampas por Max Justo Guedes. Salvador?, Brazil: Banco da Bahia Investimentos; Rio de Janeiro: Livraria Kosmos Editora, 1991. 39 p.: col. ill.

In 1819, H.M.S. Favorite left England for the Cape of Good Hope, stopping in Brazil on its outbound and homeward voyages. Gathered here are the watercolors of the coasts of Rio de Janeiro, Pernambuco, and principally Bahia, that Lieutenant Robert Pearce produced during those stopovers. Descriptions in Portuguese translation.

20TH CENTURY

405 Ades, Dawn. Siron Franco: figuras e semelhanças, pinturas de 1968 a 1995. Prefácio de Ferreira Gullar. Rio de Janeiro: Editora Index, 1995. 240 p.: bibl., ill. (some col.).

Siron Franco's painting blends humans and animals in many variations, at times demonstrating their profound relationship, at other times denouncing human cruelty. Franco's work depicts metaphors of the unconscious and a surreal memory of Central Brazil. Over 200 excellent color reproductions illustrate his rich output from the mid-1960s to the mid-1990s. Includes extensive biography and bibliography, and perceptive text by Dawn Ades.

406 Arte moderna brasileira: uma seleção da Coleção Roberto Marinho. Curadoria e textos de Paulo Venancio Filho. São Paulo: Museu de Arte de São Paulo Assis Chateaubriand; Rio de Janeiro: Coleção Roberto Marinho, 1994. 146 p.: bibl., ill. (some col.), index.

A fine and varied selection of 20th-century Brazilian art includes almost 100 works by virtually all major artists. Excellent color reproductions. Well-informed introductory essay by curator.

407 Barsante, Cássio Emmanuel. A vida ilustrada de Tomás Santa Rosa. Rio de Janeiro: Fundação Banco do Brasil: Bookmakers, 1993. 160 p.: ill. (some col.)

Although a legitimate painter in his own right, Tomás Santa Rosa is best known as one of the most significant pioneers in Brazilian 20th-century set and costume design, and one of the finest book illustrators and cover designers. This long overdue monograph does justice to his numerous contributions in these fields and also as a painter. Good variety of color and b/w reproductions and period photographs. Lucid text describes his struggles and accomplishments.

408 D'Alessandro, Stephanie. Still more distant journeys: the artistic emigrations of Lasar Segall. With contributions from Reinhold Heller and Vera D'Horta = Por caminhadas ainda mais distantes: as emigrações artisticas de Lasar Segall de Stephanie D'Alessandro; com contribuições de Reinhold Heller e Vera D'Horta. Chicago, Ill.: David and Alfred Smart Museum of Art, 1997. 284 p.: bibl., ill. (some col.).

Exhibition catalog devoted to the entire output of Lasar Segall is currently the most comprehensive overview of the artist and his work. The exhibition itself, one of the most complete retrospectives of Segall ever displayed, was seen only in Chicago and New York. Texts cover Segall's immigration to Germany (1905) and to Brazil (1924), and his artistic biography, highlighting his participation in the Dresdner Sezession as a key figure in the development of German expressionism and his subsequent significance in Brazilian modernism. Includes supplementary documentation, as well as a large number of photographs, ephemera, and publications. The exhibition included over 220 paintings, watercolors, prints, and drawings; virtually all of them are reproduced here in color or b/w.

409   Escallon, Ana Maria and **Damián Bayón.** Gerchman. Rio de Janeiro: Gabinete de Arte do Rio de Janeiro, 1994. 211 p.: bibl., ill. (some col.), map.

Gerchman is one of the most creative neorealistic, urban painters in postwar Brazil. This deluxe edition unites insightful texts and many top quality color reproductions of his works from the mid-1960s to the mid-1990s.

410   Fabbrini, Ricardo Nascimento. O espaço de Lygia Clark. São Paulo: Editora Atlas, 1994. 292 p.: bibl., ill.

Lygia Clark was one of the most significant avant-garde artists in Brazil after WWII. Her ideas continue to stimulate younger artists, critics, art historians, and the art world at large. Thanks to her influence, painting, sculpture, art therapy, and wearable art experienced new prospects in Brazil and abroad. This in-depth study covers all aspects of her creativity. A chronology, list of works in national and international collections, bibliography, and illustrations complete this welcome publication.

411   Fabris, Annateresa. O futurismo paulista: hipóteses para o estudo da chegada da vanguarda ao Brasil. São Paulo: Editora Perspectiva: Edusp, 1994. 305 p.: bibl., ill. (Estudos; 138. Arte)

Examines Marinetti's visit to Brazil and its implications for understanding the various paths that modernism took in Brazil after the 1922 Week of Modern Art (*Semana de Arte Moderna*). Exploration of "futurismo paulista" focuses on Papini, Soffici, Oswald de Andrade, Menotti Del Picchia, and Mario de Andrade. Author implies that futurism defines the spirit of early modernism in São Paulo, which, in the 1930s, evolved into discussions on Brazilian society. Includes valuable bibliographic information. Original scholarly contribution to the field.

412   Favaretto, Celso F. A invenção de Hélio Oiticica. São Paulo: Edusp: FAPESP, 1992. 234 p.: bibl., ill. (some col.). (Texto & arte; 6)

Oiticica often said that his pieces were nonprogrammed programs or "programs in progress." He represents the most fertile example of experimentalism in Brazilian art from 1950s-70s. Favaretto's approach to his work combines broad information with deep esthetic evaluations of Oiticica's paintings, environmental art, audio-visual and cinematic experiments, special structures, behavioral propositions from the delirious to conceptual lucidity, to his highly personal reinvention of 20th-century art. Details Oiticica's seminal influence on Brazilian postmodernism. Includes valuable bibliography and many illustrations in b/w and color. The most comprehensive study of the artist to date.

413   Geraldo, Sheila Cabo. Goeldi, modernidade extraviada. Rio de Janeiro: Diadorim: ADESA, 1995. 172 p.: bibl., ill.

In-depth study of Osvaldo Goeldi, the expressionist master of 20th-century Brazilian printmaking. Uses the modernist inquiry, "What is Brazilian art?" to scrutinize Goeldi's expressionism. Also analyzes the relationship between Goeldi and the modernists who underestimated him. Extensive bibliography, b/w reproductions.

414   Hélio Oiticica. Curated by Guy Brett *et al.* Rio de Janeiro: Centro de Arte Hélio Oiticica, 1997? 277 p.: bibl., ill. (some col.).

Catalog of the traveling exhibition dedicated to the artist whose work pioneered many innovations in Brazilian art after 1950. Includes texts in both English and Portuguese written by five different authors, with a selection of the artist's own work from 1960-80. Many color and b/w photographs document Oiticica's unconventional visual proposals. [F. Angel]

415   Ianelli, Arcangelo. Ianelli: 50 anos de pintura = 50 years of painting. Idealização, realização e coordenação geral de Lloyds Bank Plc, Depto. de Marketing Institucional. Brazil: O Departamento, 1993. 79 p.: bibl., ill. (some col.).

Distinguished Brazilian critics review 50 years of Ianelli's creativity. Illustrates all periods with color reproductions. Documents artist's life with many photographs. Includes biographical notes and a complete list of solo and group shows.

416 Klintowitz, Jacob. Os novos viajantes. São Paulo: Serviço Social do Comércio, 1993. 159 p.: ill. (some col.).

Shows how Brazil is seen, felt, and perceived by her own artists. Text introduces and discusses the vision of Siron Franco, Ana Maria Pacheco, Francisco Brennand, Franz Krajcberg, Antonio Hélio Cabral, Israel Pedrosa, João Câmara, Roberto Magalhães, and Maria Bonomi. Includes many color reproductions.

417 Klintowitz, Jacob. Victor Brecheret, modernista brasileiro = Victor Brecheret, a Brazilian modernist. Coordenação geral de Marilisa Rathsam. São Paulo: MD-Comunicação e Editora de Arte, 1994? 157 p.: ill. (some col.).

Through his sculptural work, Brecheret became a seminal figure in the establishment of Brazilian modernism. In Paris, where he lived for 20 years, Brecheret absorbed some of the main trends of modernism and brought these ideas to Brazil, having transformed them in a personal way, blending cubism and art deco statements of great sensitivity and elegance. Text discusses his impact on Brazil, his contribution to modern art in Brazil, and the many controversies he and his work sparked. His universal relevance has been gradually accepted.

418 Lemos, Fernando. Desenhumor: anos 50. São Paulo: Empório Cultural, 1991. 1 v. (unpaged): all ill. (Coleção Branco e preto; 2 v.)

Lemos (b. 1920), a native of Lisbon, has lived in São Paulo since 1953. A pioneer of surrealism in Portugal, he gradually distanced himself from Breton and surrealism altogether and started producing humorous drawings in tune with new graphic alternatives. He published his b/w drawings in *Revista Manchete, Revista da Semana,* and *Revista Sombra,* some illustrating literary texts. The São Paulo Biennial played an important role in his life, and he, in turn, influenced many young Brazilian artists. Short biography included.

419 Lourenço, Maria Cecília França. Operários da modernidade. São Paulo: HUCITEC: Edusp, 1995. 322 p.: bibl., ill. (some col.), indexes. (Estudos urbanos; 9. Série Arte e vida urbana; 3)

This is a minutely detailed history of the artistic milieu of São Paulo in the 1940s-50s. At that time many of the tensions and contradictions that followed the 1922 Week of Modern Art were resolved allowing for the establishment of institutions to promote modern art and support artists, as well as to provide a legacy for future generations. Meanwhile, the artists themselves matured, gaining a certain level of professional recognition, while also achieving a more profound understanding of the issue of national identity. A wealth of information and a great contribution to a historical and theoretical re-evaluation of the period. Includes a variety of illustrations in color and b/w, a rich bibliography, and name and work indexes.

420 Milliet, Maria Alice. Lygia Clark: obra-trajeto. São Paulo: Edusp, 1992. 203 p.: bibl., ill. (Texto & arte; 8)

Lygia Clark (1920–88) refused any esthetic or stylistic classification of her work. She accepted only the evaluations of those who understood the sensitivity that was necessary for her to create a painting or an attitude. Maria Alice Milliet is just such a careful reviewer. In this examination of Clark's entire body of work, Milliet is interested in Clark's dialectic, in the tension she experienced between the inside and the outside. An original interpretative contribution to a better understanding of this "creative-recreative" seminal personality in Brazilian avant-garde from the 1950s-80s. Interviews, bibliograpy and b/w photographs and reproductions.

421 O Modernismo no Museu de Arte Brasileira: pintura. São Paulo: Fundação Armando Alvares Penteado, 1993. 1 v. (unpaged): col. ill.

Homage to the centennial of Mario de Andrade (1893–1945), this exhibition displayed some of the best examples of Brazilian modernist painting, including canvasses by Lasar Segall, Anita Malfatti, Di Cavalcanti, Ismael Nery, Tarsila do Amaral, Portinari, Guignard, Pancetti, Cicero Dias, Flávio de Carvalho, and John Graz. Notes on the artists. Excellent color reproductions.

422 Monteiro, Vicente do Rego. Vicente do Rego Monteiro, pintor e poeta. Rio de Janeiro: 5a. Cor Editores, 1994. 299 p.: bibl., ill. (some col.).

Monteiro's work was influenced by a

number of different styles and movements: futurism, cubism, Japanese woodblock prints, African tribal art, Brazilian baroque, indigenous art from Marajó island, and the School of Paris (he was the finest Brazilian representative of the latter). He was also a poet, participated in the Semana de Arte Moderna 1922, and became, over the following decades, one of the most accomplished Brazilian artists of this century. An array of the finest Brazilian and French intellectuals, critics, and art historians contributed texts to this book. Includes excellent reproductions and an extensive bibliography.

423   Pieta, Marilene Burtet. A modernidade da pintura no Rio Grande do Sul. Porto Alegre, Brazil: Sagra-DC Luzzatto Editores, 1995. 16 p. of plates, 273 p.: bibl., ill. (some col.).

Modern painting in Rio Grande do Sul has a recent history. Academic painters appeared there towards the end of the 19th century; a more scholarly form of art history started only in the 1970s. This pioneering study gathers information on the several esthetic currents present in the state during the past 40 years, analyzing them in their historical, social, and artistic contexts. Demonstrates the search, from an artistic perspective, for a regional identity within the Brazilian context. Short bibliographies of artists, reproductions in color and b/w. A welcome publication.

424   Portinari Leitor. Curadoria de Annateresa Fabris e Cacilda Teixeira da Costa. São Paulo: Museu de Arte Moderna de São Paulo, 1996. 58 p.: bibl., ill. (some col.).

Portinari had diverse literary interests; the works of Machado de Assis and Cervantes fascinated him. He accepted offers to illustrate "Memorias Póstumas de Brás Cubas," "O Alienista," and "Don Quijote," as well as Hans Staden's 16th-century writings, "Two Trips to Brazil." In all of them Portinari expresses—in different media—his great talent as an illustrator and illuminator. Thanks to these 1997 exhibitions, a special and seldom seen side of Portinari's work is revealed.

425   Projeto Portinari. Resumo. Projeto Portinari. Rio de Janeiro: O Projeto, 1993. 52 leaves: ill., maps.

The Portinari Project, unique in Brazil for its scope, is the best research institution of its kind in the country. In addition to classifying 5,300 paintings, drawings, and prints of one of the most significant Brazilian artists, the project also gathered 25,000 documents that provide a profile of the views and concerns of the artist's generation. This work describes the development of the project, detailing its mission, methodology, and collections. The Portinari Project is available at http://www.candidoportinari.com.br/.

426   Risério, Antonio. Avant-garde na Bahia. São Paulo: Instituto Lina Bo e P.M. Bardi, 1995? 259 p.: bibl., ill. (Pontos sobre o Brasil)

"Toward the province against the province" was the artistic and intellectual refrain in 1950s Bahia. Many musicians, composers, architects, photographers, painters, and sculptors found a new home in Bahia stimulating young artists in all media towards the "new", and in turn being stimulated by them. This textbook, filled with photographs, gives an account of the invigorating days of Bahian avant-garde.

427   Segall, Lasar. Lasar Segall: textos, depoimentos e exposições. Biblioteca Jenny Klabin Segall, Museu Lasar Segall, Instituto Brasileiro do Patrimônio Cultural-IBPC, Secretaria de Cultura da Presidência da República. 2a. ed., rev. and amplified. São Paulo: Associação Cultural de Amigos do Museu Lasar Segall, 1993. 134 p.: bibl., ill.

A compilation of texts by Lasar Segall, including some works never before published, a catalog essays, articles published in the daily press, interviews with the Brazilian press, and a statement from the artist to the Associated American Artist Galleries in New York, 1948. Also includes a short biography, a list of his major shows, and a basic bibliography. A welcome research source.

428   Serpa, Ivan. Ivan Serpa: retrospectiva, 1947–1973. Rio de Janeiro: Centro Cultural Banco do Brasil, 1993. 99 p.: bibl., ill. (some col.).

Ivan Serpa (1923–73), an artist active in the avant-garde movement in Rio de Janeiro in the 1950s-60s, experimented with representational and abstract art through concretism and gestual expressionism. This catalog, a retrospective of his work 25 years after his premature death, sheds new light on a constantly questioning, intellectual artist. Includes many excellent color reproductions and a selected bibliography.

FOLK ART

429 **Beuque, Jacques van de.** Brasilianische Volkskunst: Werke aus der Sammlung Casa do Pontal = Brazilian popular art: exhibits from the Casa do Pontal collection. São Paulo: Câmara Brasileira do Livro, 1994. 127 p.: chiefly col. ill. (Brasiliana de Frankfurt)

This collection of Brazilian folk art, one of the finest extant, was displayed at the 46th Frankfurt Book Fair, 1994. All the pieces exhibited are described and reproduced here. The focus is on baked clay figurines and wood carved pieces, some with color and some b/w. The works are from several states, primarily in the Northeast, and cover the principal themes: daily life, occupations, leisure, folklore, religion, dancing, and music. Text elaborates on the esthetics and sociology of popular art in Brazil.

430 **Finkelstein, Lucien.** Zeitgenössische naive Malerei aus Brasilien = Brazilian naïf art of today. São Paulo: Câmara Brasileira do Livro, 1994. 128 p.: col. ill. (Brasiliana de Frankfurt)

Over 100 color reproductions show the full spectrum, both in styles and subjects, of current Brazilian naïf art. All of the paintings shown are part of the collection of the Brazilian International Museum of Naïf Art of Rio de Janeiro. Introductory essay discusses the concept, background, and esthetics of this art form, which has a particularly rich tradition in Brazil.

PHOTOGRAPHY

431 **Herkenhoff, Paulo.** Die Dichte des Lichts: zeitgenössische brasilianische Fotografie = Density of light: contemporary Brazilian photography. São Paulo: Câmara Brasileira do Livro, 1994. 127 p.: bibl., ill. (some col.). (Brasiliana de Frankfurt)

For an exhibition at the 46th International Book Fair, which featured Brazil, Herkenhoff, the curator, selected six photographers. He believes that the work of this group demonstrates the trauma of history, each one expressing the losses, passions, wounds, and scars in his or her own personal way. The photographers, Claudia Andujar, Mário Cravo Neto, Miguel Rio Branco, Rosangela Rennó, Luiz Braga, and Paula Trape, are among the best in Brazil. Reproductions in color and b/w.

432 **Leite, Miriam Moreira.** Retratos de família: leitura da fotografia histórica. São Paulo: EDUSP: FAPESP, 1993. 192 p.: bibl., ill. (some col.). (Texto & arte; 9)

By examining the work of a large number of photographers of immigrant families, the author documents the social uses and artistic dimensions of photography in Brazil from approximately 1890–1930. Supplemented with testimonies of travelers and artists such as Richard Burton and Jean Baptiste Debret, who describe everyday life in 19th-century Brazil. Also uses methods of visual anthropology to achieve a better understanding of historical photography. Includes bibliography and many reproductions.

CITY PLANNING, ARCHITECTURE, AND LANDSCAPE ARCHITECTURE

433 **Arquitetos do Brasil = Architects from Brazil.** Prefácio de Sergio Bernardes; organização de Angela Brant. Rio de Janeiro: Salamandra, 1995. 213 p.: ill. (some col.).

Subsidized by nearly 50 engineering and architecture offices from all over Brazil, this book offers an overview of the Brazilian construction market, including commercial sites, government buildings, private homes— in the city, at the beach, and in the mountains—, schools, hospitals, apartment buildings, factories, embassies, and so forth, as well as city planning in various states of the country. Information on individual architects is also provided.

434 **Estudos urbanos: Porto Alegre e seu planejamento.** Organização de Wrana M. Panizzi e João F. Rovatti. Porto Alegre, Brazil: Editora da Univ., Univ. Federal do Rio Grande do Sul; Prefeitura Municipal de Porto Alegre, 1993. 373 p.: bibl., ill., maps.

Several scholars discuss the methodology of urban studies, a major concern in Brazil, where over 70 percent of the population lives in cities. Here the focus is Porto Alegre and its recent structural changes, new cultural spaces, the port and the city, political and economic conditions, positivistic traditions, rural and gaúcho traditions, and alternative city planning, housing, and transportation. The most wide-ranging study of its kind in Brazil.

435 Guia do patrimônio cultural carioca: bens tombados = Rio's heritage guide.
Rio de Janeiro: Rio Prefeitura da Cidade, Secretaria Municipal de Cultura, Turismo e Esportes, Depto. Geral do Patrimônio Cultural, 1992. 138, A-N p.: ill., index, 91 maps.

Minutely detailed guide to the buildings, parks, and monuments of Rio and its suburbs. Concise and accurate descriptions with maps to locate each item. Of great help to historians and art historians. Includes many b/w photographs, but lacks bibliography.

436 Lemos, Carlos Alberto Cerqueira.
Ramos de Azevedo e seu escritório. São Paulo: Pini Editora, 1993. 165 p.: bibl., ill. (some col.).

Francisco de Assis Ramos de Azevedo, civil engineer and architect, built hundreds of government, commercial, and residential buildings in the city of São Paulo. Working on his own projects and on those of other architects, he defined the city's profile from the late 1870s-late 1920s. His funeral was comparable to that of a head of state. This detailed, well-illustrated work describes his life and projects and includes hundreds of his plans.

437 Lina Bo Bardi. Coordenação editorial de Marcelo Carvalho Ferraz. São Paulo: Empresa das Arte: Instituto Lina Bo e P.M. Bardi, 1993. 333 p.: bibl., ill. (some col.).

A chronological catalog of the work of architect Lina Bo Bardi. The text, written by Bo Bardi in her unique style, describes her projects and reveals her personal philosophy and thoughts on various subjects including Brazil. Born and raised in Italy, she adopted Brazil as her home, restoring many buildings of historical interest and influencing a generation of architects, playwrights, moviemakers, and designers. Her life, projects, watercolors, photographs, and designs are richly documented here. Most of the catalog's illustrations were drawn from her archives.

438 Oscar Niemeyer. Redacción de Josep Maria Botey y Miquel Dalmau; fotografía de Toni Cumella y Ramón Sirvent. Barcelona: Fundació Caixa de Barcelona, 1990. 266 p.: bibl., ill. (some col.).

Luxurious catalog of a major Niemeyer exhibition includes a representative selection of his projects from initial drafts to finished products, a wealth of color and b/w photographs, along with facsimiles of the architect's manuscripts which detail his ideals and concerns.

439 Pelourinho, centro histórico de Salvador, Bahia: a grandeza restaurada = Pelourinho, historic district of Salvador, Bahia: the restored grandeur. Editação de Nelson Cerqueira. Textos de Jorge Amado *et al.* 3a. ed. Salvador, Brazil: Fundação Cultural do Estado da Bahia, 1995. 120 p.: bibl., ill. (some col.), col. map.

The Pelourinho (pillory) is the heart of the largest historic district in Brazil. This neighborhood has the largest concentration of baroque churches and secular buildings in the New World. In the past, its elegant mansions and townhouses were home to the aristocracy of Bahia, and in the 18th century it served as an auction place for slaves. A large number of decayed buildings have been restored with historical accuracy and creative artisanry. Today the Pelourinho is a major cultural center. This account of the Pelourinho's restoration is complemented with many color photographs.

440 Toledo, J. Flávio de Carvalho: o comedor de emoções. São Paulo: Editora Brasiliense; Campinas, Brazil: Editora da UNICAMP, 1994? 850 p.: bibl., ill., index.

Biography of Brazilian architect Flávio de Carvalho (1899-1973), a controversial, mercurial figure who became a symbol of audacity and irreverence while his fame spread throughout Brazil. His towering presence was a part of all artistic gatherings deemed important by him in Brazil, England, and France. In spite of his conspicuous presence and his initiatives which ranged from designing men's attire to designing houses for tropical climates, Carvalho might be forgotten if not for this extensive and well-researched examination of his works and personality. [R. Igel]

AFRO-BRAZILIAN AND INDIAN TRADITIONS

441 Araújo, Emanoel. Afro-brasilianische Kultur und zeitgenössische Kunst = Art in Afro-Brazilian religion. São Paulo: Câmara Brasileira do Livro, 1994. 127 p.: bibl., ill. (some col.). (Brasiliana de Frankfurt)

In 1994, Brazil was the theme country at the Frankfurt Book Fair, which included a major exhibition on art in Afro-Brazilian religions. This exhibit catalog ranges from 19th-century European visions of black Africans in Brazil to contemporary statements of Afro-Brazilian artists with a representative selection of works in a variety of media. Includes illustrations of nearly all items discussed.

442 Os herdeiros da noite: fragmentos do imaginário negro. Textos de Ricardo Ohtake. São Paulo: Pinacoteca, Seu Museu, 1994. 70 p.: bibl., ill. (some col.).

This exhibition commemorated the 300th anniversary of Palmares, the general headquarters of slave resistance established under the leadership of the legendary hero Zumbi. The goal of the exhibit was not an explanation of black culture, but rather an attempt to provide a frame of reference for appreciating the influence of African culture on Brazilian arts: popular music, painting and sculpture, folk feasts, rituals, and religions. Includes color and b/w photographs and reproductions, and a variety of introductory texts.

MISCELLANEOUS

443 Arte no Metrô: São Paulo, Brasil. Pesquisa e redação de Leonor Amarante. São Paulo: Companhia do Metropolitano de São Paulo, Governo do Estado de São Paulo, 1994. 155 p.: bibl., ill. (some col.).

Contemporary public art plays an expressive role in urban spaces; it offers a means of humanizing the cities. The artwork displayed in the São Paulo metro is designed to provide the thousands of daily passengers with a source of esthetic enjoyment through an exposure to Brazilian contemporary art. It is also an effective way of involving commuters with contemporary cultural expression. This book contains a number of theoretical essays about and color reproductions of the artwork displayed on stations walls, platforms, etc. Also includes all technical and biographical information in Portuguese and English.

444 Bardi, Lina Bo. Tempos de grossura: o design no impasse. São Paulo: Instituto Lina Bo e P.M. Bardi, 1994. 79 p.: ill. (some col.). (Pontos sobre o Brasil)

The basic principle behind this anthology by prominent Brazilian artists, scholars, and intellectuals, is that a deeper understanding of the lower strata of a society will lead to a better understanding of the country as a whole. In this case, the area under study is the northeast of Brazil. Studies a large variety of artifacts in all possible media. Many color and b/w reproductions.

445 Bienal de Design Gráfico ADG, 2nd, São Paulo, 1994. 2a. Bienal de Design Gráfico ADG 94: 04 a 22 de maio de 1994, Museu da Imagem e do Som. Associação dos Designers Gráficos. São Paulo: Museu da Imagem e do Som: ADG, 1994? 80 p.: ill. (some col.).

In the past three decades, Brazilian graphic designers have been developing their own national style. This handsome catalog of the Second Biennial of Graphic Design (São Paulo) displays a variety of commercial art samples, from the most elegant to the most aggressive, from the most conservative to the most humorous. No bibliography. Excellent color reproductions. Basic information on the designers.

446 Brandão, Ignácio de Loyola. Luz no êxtase: vitrais e vitralistas no Brasil = Light on ecstasy: Brazil's stained glass windows and artists. Fotografías de Ary Diesendruck. São Paulo: Dórea Books and Art, 1994. 95 p.: bibl., ill. (some col.). (Biblioteca EUCATEX de cultura brasileira)

Introduces various European schools of stained-glass window making, then discusses the introduction of stained glass to Brazil toward the end of the 19th century and its subsequent development from traditional religious and secular subjects—many of them national themes—to contemporary abstraction. Many good color reproductions. Includes glossary of technical terms.

447 Ferreira, Orlando da Costa. Imagem e letra: introdução à bibliologia brasileira: a imagem gravada. São Paulo:

Edusp, 1994. 509 p.: bibl., ill., indexes, maps. (Texto & arte; 10)

The result of a lifetime spent studying the history of bookmaking and graphic arts, this work provides an in-depth examination of book printing and illustration in Brazil. This was to be the first part of a more comprehensive work; sadly, Ferreira died before finishing the second part. Even so, this is a unique reference work notable for its wealth of information both in word and image. Includes indexes of names and subjects and a list of illustrations.

448 Fundação Pierre Chalita (Maceió, Brazil). Fundação Pierre Chalita: um exercício de guarda. Pesquisa e texto de Fernanda de Camargo-Moro. Maceió, Brazil: Salgema Indústrias Químicas, 1991. 105 p.: col. ill.

Artist in his own right, musician, architect, professor, and collector Pierre Chalita (b. 1930) converted his residence in Maceió, Alagoas, into a foundation where he assembled his collection of Brazilian sacred art. His collection, one of the most complete in the country, focuses particularly on the 17th and the 18th centuries. This work offers a good, but only partial presentation of the collection.

449 Gaudenzi, Tripoli. Memorial de Canudos = The Canudos memorial. Salvador, Bahia: Fundação Cultural do Estado da Bahia, 1993. 251 p.: ill. (some col.), col. maps.

Canudos and its legendary hero Antônio Conselheiro went down in Brazilian history as a chapter of nearly inconceivable violence and destruction in Bahia (1869). Using oil paintings, drawings, and mixed media on paper, and drawing on extensive research, Gaudenzi, a well-established Bahian artist, depicts the battle with realism and compassion. Excellent introduction by José Calasans, an authority on the history of Canudos.

450 Herkenhoff, Paulo. Biblioteca Nacional: a história de uma coleção. Fotografias de Pedro Oswaldo Cruz. Rio de Janeiro: Editora Salamandra, 1996. 263 p.: bibl., ill. (some col.), maps (some col.).

The National Library of Rio de Janeiro and its collections are unsurpassed within Latin America and it is among the best libraries in the world. In writing the history of its collections, the author describes the strengths of each section of the distinguished library, established by King John VI of Portugal in 1810. This luxurious edition offers a wealth of reproductions and an extensive bibliography.

451 A luz da pintura no Brasil. Coordenação de Reynaldo Valinho Alvarez e Rodrigo Otávio De Marco Meniconi; Texto de Pedro Martins Caldas Xexéo, Quirino Campofiorito e Reynaldo Valinho Alvarez. Rio de Janeiro: Centro da Memória da Eletricidade no Brasil, Memória da Eletricidade, 1994. 95 p.: col. ill.

Small textbook-like anthology of the history of painting in Brazil focusing on the use of light from the 17th century to the mid-1990s. Explores the impact of modern electricity. Uses examples from the collection of the Museu Nacional de Belas Artes. Color reproductions of uneven quality.

452 Mavignier, Almir da Silva. Bilder des Unbewussten aus Brasilien = Images of the unconscious from Brazil. São Paulo: Câmara Brasileira do Livro, 1994. 127 p.: ill. (some col.). (Brasiliana de Frankfurt)

In the mid-1940s, the occupational therapy section of the Engenho de Dentro Psychiatric Hospital in Rio de Janeiro started to hold painting and modeling workshops for clients diagnosed as schizophrenics. The workshops proved to be a successful part of treatment. Their works reveal much about the human psyche. As Jean Dubuffet wrote: "Here we can witness artists work in a completely pure and genuine form." This book compiles examples of great impact.

453 Palácio Itamaraty, Brasília, Rio de Janeiro. Textos de João Hermes Pereira de Araújo, Silvia Escorel e André Aranha Corrêa do Lago. São Paulo: Banco Safra, 1993. 319 p.: bibl., ill. (some col.), maps.

The Brazilian Ministry of External Relations has an unrivaled collection of Brazilian art, including the decorative arts, dating from the 17th-20th century. The collection is displayed both in the old Itamaraty Palace in Rio and in the new Itamaraty in Brasília, itself a landmark in modern Brazilian architecture. Illustrations in this work cover only a fraction of the holdings. Several essays provide a wealth of information.

454 *Revista do Patrimônio Histórico e Artístico Nacional.* No. 24, 1996. Cidadania. Brasília?: Instituto do Patrimônio Histórico e Artístico Nacional, Ministério da Cultura.

This issue of *Patrimônio* includes a number of articles and essays on restoration and preservation of both the past and the present for future generations, and for the sake of an affirmative vision and concept of cultural identity. Art historians, architects, anthropologists, archeologists, historians, city planners, sociologists, philosophers, cinema historians, poets, novelists, musicologists, technicians in various fields, and photographers contributed to this unique source of study on the theoretical and practical levels of preservation of cultural, artistic, historical, and intellectual patrimony.

455 **Rosa, Maria da Glória Sá; Maria Adélia Menegazzo; and Idara Negreiros Duncan Rodrigues.** Memória da arte em Mato Grosso do Sul: histórias de vida. Campo Grande, Brazil: Projeto Memória da Arte em Mato Grosso do Sul, 1992. 338 p.: bibl., ill.

This book was planned as, and to some extent it is, a systematic register of artistic creativity in the state of Mato Grosso do Sul. It is also a study in cultural identity within context of Brazil's search for its unique identity. May provide a point of departure for future, in-depth studies. Short bibliography.

HISTORY

ETHNOHISTORY
Mesoamerica

ROBERT HASKETT, *Associate Professor of History, University of Oregon*
STEPHANIE WOOD, *Assistant Professor of History, University of Oregon*

THE SPLENDORS OF INDIGENOUS INTELLECTUAL achievements, the complexities of precontact cosmological constructions, the iron hard reality of resistance to Spanish invasions, military and cultural, the rhythms of native life before and after the Iberian intrusion; all this and much more has captivated the many scholars whose work is represented in these pages. The Nahuas (above all the Aztecs) and the Mayas (especially the lowlanders) persist as the leading ethnohistorical characters in this academic drama. Here recent scholarship has been graced by the appearance of Graulich's compelling study of Montezuma (item **505**); Carrasco's important new reading of the "Aztec Empire" in his *Estructura política del Imperio Tenochca* (item **475**); a new, expanded, and updated edition of Sharer's comprehensive *The Ancient Maya* (item **593**); and a thought-provoking study of the "cult of the dead" among the middle and late formative Maya by McAnany (item **542**). Thematically, a sustained interest in the sacred world is highlighted by the significant work of McKeever Furst (item **544**) and by seven notable articles collected in *De hombres y dioses* (item **491**). Calendrical analyses such as the impressive monographic treatment created by Malmström in his *Cycles of the Sun, Mysteries of the Moon* (item **540**), food (item **601**), costume (item **570**), marriage and kinship (item **543**), and Graulich's compelling *Myths of Ancient Mexico* (item **506**), an examination of myth and history in the Mesoamerican past, all enrich the corpus.

Yet as far as the Aztec empire is concerned, the focus continues to shift from a preoccupation with a kind of homogenized, Valley of Mexico-centered imperial history to a far more nuanced approach alive to a great variation of regional experiences. This trend is most impressively represented in *Aztec Imperial Strategies* (item **470**). Carrasco's rereading of the empire's structure, and the attention he pays to the often slighted *altepetl* of Texcoco and Tlacopan, is part of this same process. Gillespie additionally shows us some of the colonial manipulation of the supposed "Triple Alliance" organization in her contribution to *Native Traditions in the Postconquest World* (item **551**).

Thematic diversity can be found among studies of the postconquest situation. Our current sample does not include as many synthetic monographs as in the past. But those which do appear here, such as Piho's posthumous *Iztapalapan durante la conquista* (item **558**); two more information-packed volumes in Zavala's cycle of publications (items **606**); Horn's deft, Nahuatl record-based study of indigenous and

Spanish society in Coyoacan (item **518**); excellent articles by Chance (item **476**), Ouweneel (item **554**), and Gasco (item **500**); and Nebel's study of the evolution of the cult of the Virgin of Guadalupe (item **552**) are all worthy additions to the literature. While Taylor's monumental, prize-winning *Magistrates of the Sacred* is not precisely a work of ethnohistory, its detailed examination of local religious beliefs, practices, and of clergy-parishioner relations makes it an essential resource (item **594**). Of equal merit is the recently published Quincentenary anthology entitled *Native Traditions of the Postconquest World* (item **551**). For the Maya, Quezada's *Pueblos y caciques yucatecos* makes a real contribution (item **561**). Restall's *The Maya World* will have a major and lasting impact on the field (item **567**). More than any previous scholar of the postconquest Yucatan, Restall has expertly mined Mayan-language sources, from notarial records to primordial titles, to present us with a more thoroughly indigenous-centered reading.

Collectively and in conjunction with the larger number of scholarly articles falling into this category, these works strengthen our grasp of the reality of postconquest cultural durability, something not expected or acknowledged by those who for so long were convinced that native cultures were fundamentally destroyed by the influx of Europeans and their ways.

Two mainstays of ethnohistorical literature have been the publication of critically presented facsimiles of codices and of transcribed and translated alphabetic records in the indigenous tradition. This has remained true of the current sampling, which includes beautifully realized studies of components of the Borgia group (item **481**), the historical-genealogical *Códice Cozcatzin* (item **482**), the *Códice Durán* (item **493**), the Cuicatec *Códice de Tepeucila* (item **514**), and analyses provided by Alcina Franch (items **457** and **458**), León-Portilla (item **480**), Yoneda (item **605**), and by Batalla Rosado (items **464, 465, 466, 467,** and **468**). In our current sampling the efforts of Fray Bernardino de Sahagún are not represented by as many independent investigations as in the past, but his *Primeros memoriales* is featured in two different forms (items **461** and **583**), and many other scholars continue to mine and interpret his work in the course of their varied ethnohistorical investigations (item **473**). The labors, life, and times of indigenous participants in the creation of the Sahaguntine corpus and other similar materials have been brought to life (items **527** and **513**).

Among postconquest alphabetic texts, the late Arthur J.O. Anderson and Susan Schroeder's two-volume publication of recently discovered manuscripts written by Chimalpahin stands out (item **477**). It is a fitting monument to Anderson, one of the greatest and most talented proponents of Nahuatl studies of the 20th century. Of virtue, too, are Spores' offering of documents related to colonial Oaxaca (item **484**), transcriptions of mundane Nahuatl-language records in the journal *Estudios de Cultura Náhuatl* (items **532** and **533**), the *Libro de los guardianes y gobernadores de Cuauhtinchan (1519–1640)* (item **534**), and Christensen's examination of Cristóbal del Castillo's Nahuatl-language history of the Mexica migration (item **478**). Additionally, Restall presents us with a valuable broadly based overview of evolving indigenous written expression during the Spanish era (item **566**).

A number of other topical concentrations deserve recognition here. Gender studies ranging across the pre- and postconquest eras continue to proliferate, exhibiting an expanding menu of issues and methodologies. A recent anthology entitled *Indian Women of Early Mexico* covers a range of different times, places, and topics (see *HLAS 56:471*). Several other authors have contributed outstanding pieces of scholarship in the area of gender, including Hendon (items **511** and **512**) and Klein (item **528**), and gender assumes a major analytical role in other works as well (items **547, 573,** and **585**). Theater and public ritual receive continued attention (items **509, 536,** and **568**). A number of studies push beyond the Nahuas, the Mayas, and even the peoples of Oaxaca to bring the Huasteca, the Populucas, Otomíes, and Totonacs on to the analytical stage, most notably in Martínez's *Codiciaban la tierra: el despojo agrario en los señoríos de Tecamachalco y Quecholac (Puebla, 1520–1650)* (item **541**) and an investigation of Sonora entitled *Wandering Peoples* (item **565**; see also items **496, 579,** and **580**).

Another important event has been the appearance of a consequential series of monographic studies published by Mexico's Centro de Investigaciones y Estudios Superiores en Antropología Social (CIESAS). All are regionally focused case studies, ranging from Ruz's ethnohistorical investigation of Tabasco (item **582**), Romero Frizzi's inquiry into the evolution of Oaxaca's indigenous communities (item **577**), and de Vos' treatment of the evolving experiences of the indigenous peoples of Chiapas (item **602**), to Hu-DeHart's analysis of Yaqui adaptation and resistance to the Spanish presence in their homeland (item **519**) and Radding's study of the Sonoran O'Odham and Teguima peoples from 1520–1830 (item **564**). All of these books sweep over a broad expanse of temporal terrain, from precontact times through the end of the viceregal era, and in some cases beyond, allowing for a vital rather than static understanding of the dynamic forces driving cultural evolution, cultural preservation, and sometimes outright cultural resistance. All include documentary appendices and, as a bonus, contain vivid illustrations.

Two of these authors, Hu-Dehart and Radding, are concerned with regions and peoples not customarily defined as part of "Mesoamerica." This volume's ethnohistory section contains several other studies of peoples not always seen as Mesoamericans (items **474, 553, 575,** and **588**), Phil C. Weigand and Acelia García de Weigand's compelling *Los orígenes de los caxcanes y su relación con la guerra de los nayaritas: una hipótesis* is of special note (item **603**). Yet exactly what "Mesoamerica" was at any given time has long been open to discussion, debate, and redefinition with an eye to the changing cultural situation over vast periods of time. Several of the authors represented in this chapter grapple with the issue of "what is Mesoamerica" or challenge us to do this ourselves, most notably Malmström (item **540**), McKeever Furst (item **544**), López Austin and López Luján (item **537**), and Sprajc (item **608**).

Whether or not Sonora, Chihuahua, or the Gran Chichimeca can ever be truly considered part of a cultural Mesoamerica, work on the peoples who inhabited the north echoes many of the same broad issues connected with the evolution of indigenous societies of better known peoples—Aztecs, Mayas, Zapotecs, and Mixtecs. We are discovering that the northern peoples had much more complex societies than once believed; that they were less isolated from the peoples of the center than previously assumed; and that once Spaniards began settling in these regions, the central Mexican colonists who accompanied them brought even more of "Mesoamerica" along with them. And we must not forget that the inhabitants of the basin of Mexico, above all the Aztecs, celebrated their ancestral roots among the Chichimeca of fabled Aztlan.

This volume's bibliography includes descriptions of a number of anthologies, many of them based on the fruits of scholarly conferences and colloquia (such as the aforementioned *Aztec Imperial Strategies* and *Native Traditions in the Postconquest World*). The precontact era receives the lion's share of attention in them, but many move into the postconquest era as well; Mayanists, students of Oaxaca, and of the Nahuas are all represented. Thematically the articles range widely and touch on many of the specific topics already covered here. Two volumes dedicated to the work of Jacques Soustelle under the joint editorship of Jacqueline de Durand-Forest and Georges Baudot contain an especially high-powered assemblage of scholarship (items **548** and **549**). A few of the collections were long in production and admittedly are based on scholarship from the 1980s at the latest (items **485, 486, and 487**) and Yet we include them here because they contain vital work by important investigators, much of which can still be seen as making important intellectual and material contributions. Our strategy has been to give as full an accounting as possible of the contents of all of these anthologies to alert interested scholars to the great thematic and methodological variety of the work contained in them.

Looking at the entire corpus of work represented in these pages, we are encouraged by the continued strength of the diverse field of Mesoamerican Ethnohistory. If in quantity postconquest material is somewhat less well represented than it has been in the past, the work reviewed here continues to make methodological and interpretive innovations. The persistent appearance of high quality presentations of codices and of analytically supported transcriptions and translations of other forms of ethnohistorical documentation can be justly celebrated. So, too, can ongoing efforts to include on our menu of worthy topics of Mesoamerica the experiences of indigenous groups who have traditionally received less attention than the Aztecs and the Mayas. Scholars of the precontact era (as well as the postconquest) are testing us with new or deepened cross-disciplinary approaches, and it is not uncommon to find diverse collections of insights from archeology, art history, and ethnography joining forces with more heavily document-based ethnohistory (items **471** and **525**). As we continue to create new methodological syntheses, we must always remember that considerations of the impact of time, space, race, ethnicity, gender, class, and specific cultural traditions will inform and underlie theoretical constructs. Finally, we need to realize, as so many of our authors do, that the Spanish invasion was not so much a stark historical watershed as only one of many key points in the ongoing evolution of Mesoamerican indigenous society, as different peoples came into contact and conflict, as some new elements entered existing cultural streams while others were rejected, modified, or ignored.

456 **Alberti Manzanares, Pilar.** Mujeres sacerdotisas aztecas: las cihuatlamacazque mencionadas en dos manuscritos inéditos. (*Estud. Cult. Náhuatl*, 24, 1994, p. 171–217, bibl., facsims.)

Study of two previously unpublished, closely related manuscripts, presented here in facsmile and translation, entitled "Noticias de las Vestales Mexicanos escrita por Don Carlos de Sigüenza y Góngora año de 1684" and "Daré noticia de las doncellas que al modo de las Virgines Vestales consagraban los yndios para el servicio y culto de sus templos" (n.d., author unknown). The documents, held in the collection "Memorias de Nueva España" of the Real Academia de la Historia de Madrid, provide information about the selection, training, and functions

of priestesses in precontact central Mesoamerica.

457 **Alcina Franch, José.** Códices mexicanos. Madrid: Editorial MAPFRE, 1992. 353 p.: bibl., ill., index. (Col. Lenguas y literaturas indígenas; 1. Col. MAPFRE 1492)

This study, completed in 1990, is intended as an overview and introduction to the diverse treasury of pre- and postcontact indigenous Mexican manuscripts, with chapters on materials from the Nahuas, Borgia group, Zapotecs, Mixtecs, Mayas, and other cultures. An update and expansion of the compiler's famous 1955 essay of a similar nature (see *HLAS 22:500*). Limited coverage of ethnohistorical studies from the 1970s and 1980s.

458 Alcina Franch, José. Tláloc y los Tlaloques en los códices del México Central. (*Estud. Cult. Náhuatl*, 25, 1995, p. 29–43, bibl., ill.)

Study of the many varying iconographic representations of Tlaloc in codices covering a wide area of central Mesoamerica. Discusses, as well, the character of Tlalocan and the nature of the tlaloque. Many useful illustrations.

459 Anders, Ferdinand and **Maarten Evert Reinoud Gerard Nicolaas Jansen.** Mexiko: alte Handschriften beginnen zu sprechen [Mexico: ancient scripts begin to talk]. München: Staatliches Museum für Völkerkunde in München, 1999. 96 p.: bibl., ill. (some col.).

Excellent color plates of pictorial folding manuscripts and line drawings provide a fascinating insight into precolumbian Mixtec culture. Included are the Códices Fejérváry Mayer, Laud, Cospi, Borgia, Vindobonensis, Nuttall, Vaticanus, Dresdensis, and Codex Porfirio Díaz. Emphasizing the significance of recent technology, which facilitates increased study of these ancient manuscripts, the accompanying well-written text, translations, and interpretations make this volume a valuable addition to Mexican ethnography and ethnohistory. [C. Converse]

460 Anderson, Arthur J.O. Las mujeres extraordinarias de Chimalpahin. (*Estud. Cult. Náhuatl*, 25, 1995, p. 225–237, bibl.)

Study of passages from Chimalpahin's work which describe women who played unusual roles in the dynastic histories of the peoples of precontact central Mexico, in contrast to the education and functions such women were ideally expected to fulfill. Includes parallel sections of pertinent Nahuatl text with author's translations into Spanish.

461 Anderson, Arthur J.O. Los *primeros memoriales* y el *Códice Florentino*. (*Estud. Cult. Náhuatl*, 24, 1994, p. 49–91)

Valuable comparative examination of the *Primeros Memoriales*, based on information gathered in the Texcocan subject *altepetl* of Tepepulco, and the *Florentine Codex*, heavily influenced by Tlatelolcan informants. The author painstakingly identifies and discusses a process of evolution that reveals much about the methodology, attitudes, and purposes of Sahagún, as well as the nature of

the information conveyed by indigenous informants. See also item **583**.

462 Antropología, historia e imaginativa: en homenaje a Eduardo Martínez Espinosa. Edición de Carlos Navarrete y Carlos Alvarez A. Tuxtla de Gútierrez, Mexico: Gobierno del Estado de Chiapas, Consejo Estatal de Fomento a la Investigación y Difusión de la Cultura DIF-CHIAPAS/Instituto Chiapaneco de Cultura, 1993. 353 p.: bibl., ill., maps. (Serie Antropología)

An eclectic anthology of principally archeological studies, this festschrift focuses on Chiapas and its neighbors. One of the more notable ethnohistorical contributions, by Francisco Beristáin Bravo, centers on the records surrounding the Dominican church in the Zoque pueblo of Osumacinta (now under water). For a critical analysis by Jan de Vos exploring the history vs. legend of the stoning of Las Casas and his expulsion from San Cristóbal, see **488**.

463 Arnold, Philip P. Paper ties to land: indigenous and colonial material orientations to the Valley of Mexico. (*Hist. Relig.*, 35:1, Aug. 1995, p. 27–60, facsims.)

Interesting, if somewhat uneven, study of the ritual implications of paper among the precontact Nahua and the impact of different ideas about paper and written records arriving with the Spaniards, above all Franciscans such as Fray Bernardino de Sahagún.

464 Batalla Rosado, Juan José. Datación del *Códice Borbónico* a partir del análisis iconográfico de la representación de la sangre. (*Rev. Esp. Antropol. Am.*, 24, 1994, p. 47–74, bibl., ill.)

Exacting study of representations of blood, uncovering two main styles, all with the aim of gauging the extent of postconquest acculturative influence (or lack of it) on the codex and those who produced it.

465 Batalla Rosado, Juan José. El ejercicio violento del poder durante la colonia (siglo XVI) a partir del análisis de las imágenes de los códices mesoamericanos. (*Estud. Hist. Soc. Econ. Am.*, 12, 1995, p. 15–35, facsims.)

Author ably decodes images depicting the physical punishment of indigenous people at the hands of individual Spaniards and mestizos, both lay and religious. Documents include the *Relación Geográfica de Tlaxcala, Códice Cuevas, Códice Kingsborough, Códice Osuna, Códice Indígena de algunos pueblos del Marquesado del Valle n.o 29, Códice Azoyú n.o 1, Códice Vaticano A,* and the *Códice de San Juan Teotihuacan.*

466 Batalla Rosado, Juan José. La pena de muerte durante la colonia—siglo XVI—a partir del análisis de las imágenes de los códices mesoamericanos. (*Rev. Esp. Antropol. Am.,* 25, 1995, p. 71–110, bibl., facsims.)

Exacting interpretation of pictorial representations of executions found in a number of postconquest codices. Author determines that, while noble Spaniards were customarily beheaded, noble indigenous men and women were hanged, a fate considered to be degrading for people of this status but serving as a powerful warning to others of the same class. The author also offers some well-founded suggestions for the reinterpretation and redating of some of the codices, such as the Códice de Tlatelolco.

467 Batalla Rosado, Juan José. Prisión y muerte de Motecuhzoma, según el relato de los códices mesoamericanos. (*Rev. Esp. Antropol. Am.,* 26, 1996, p. 101–120, bibl., facsims.)

Well-mounted comparison of the depiction of Motecuhzoma's detention and death, as presented in conquerors' chronicles and indigenous codices. While Spanish sources deemphasize coercion and blame the Aztecs for their ruler's death, pictorial representations in several postconquest codices emphasize physical restraints put on the tlatoani and his murder by the conquerors. Includes a discussion of the possible role played by Tlaxcalan enmity toward the Aztecs in the graphic representation of Motecuhzoma's fate.

468 Batalla Rosado, Juan José. Teorías sobre el origen colonial del Códice Borbónico: una revisión necesaria. (*Cuad. Prehispánicos,* 18/21, 1991/94, p. 5–42, ill.)

Summarizes a licentiate thesis on the dating of the only Mexica codex of possible prehispanic origin, which the author concurs actually comes from the colonial era. He also argues, however, against European influence.

469 Baudot, Georges. Nezahualcóyotl, príncipe providencial en los escritos de Fernando de Alva Ixtlilxóchitl. (*Estud. Cult. Náhuatl,* 25, 1995, p. 17–28)

Intriguing analysis of the depiction of Nezahualcóyotl by Ixtlilxochitl, and of two poems included in the latter's work attributed to the earlier Texcocan ruler. Author suggests that Ixtlilxochitl was using Nezahualcóyotl and his poetry as vehicles to establish an apocalyptic presentiment—and therefore the legitimacy—of the establishment of Catholic Spanish rule.

470 Berdan, Frances F. *et al.* Aztec imperial strategies. Washington, D.C.: Dumbarton Oaks Research Library and Collection, 1996. 400 p.: appendices, bibl., ill., indexes, maps.

Important collection of articles by well-known scholars which, in combination, stress the importance of "place-oriented studies" as correctives to the more typical homogenized, urban-oriented, and Valley of Mexico-centered depiction of the Aztec empire. The impressive work contained in this excellent volume, which includes a series of detailed appendices centered on provincial description and organization, presents new interpretations of the extent of the Aztecs domains, imperial strategies, economic relations between core and provinces, and the significance of artistic expression and writing systems in the sociopolitical ideology of the empire. For archeologist's comment, see *HLAS 57:32.*

471 Blanton, Richard E. *et al.* A dualprocessual theory for the evolution of Mesoamerican civilization. (*Curr. Anthropol.,* 37:1, Feb. 1996, p. 1–14, bibl., map, tables)

Blanton *et al.* present a demanding and important proposal for a new approach to the analysis of sociocultural evolution in which corporate systems are emphasized. Joyce and Winter (item **525**) explore an actor-based model of the development of urban society at Monte Albán between 500 BC and AD 800 in which nobles manipulated ideology, control of ritual knowledge, and inter-regional conflict in such a way that non-elites responded positively by increasing family size, enlarging craft specialization, and expanding agricultural production. A number of noted scholars provide commentary on these articles, to which the authors reply. Includes a lengthy bibliography. For anthropologist's comment, see *HLAS 57:34.*

472 Bonifaz Nuño, Rubén. Cosmogonía antigua mexicana: hipótesis iconográfica y textual. México: UNAM, Coordinación de Humanidades, Seminario de Estudios Prehispánicos para la Descolonización de México, 1995. 155 p., 111 p. of plates: bibl., ill.

Collection of revisionist essays, some previously published, aimed at promoting author's hypothesis that the human-serpentine complex is an elementary and pervasive feature of Mesoamerican creation belief, dating from Olmec times and reaching its culmination in Aztec expression. Strongly indicts US scholarship on the Olmecs, heatedly refuting the jaguar interpretation, among others. Employs some traditional ethnohistorical sources but also argues that the plastic arts be read as texts, even in preference to colonial indigenous documents that, he charges, are "all suspect of falsehood" (&quotødos sospechosos de falsedad," p. 125) due to the influence that the European invaders had upon native writers.

473 Burkhart, Louise M. A doctrine for dancing: the prologue to the *Psalmodia christiana. (Lat. Am. Lit. Rev.,* 11:1, Spring 1995, p. 21–33)

Superb analytical essay in which the author finds compelling evidence for indigenous agency in the composition of the *Psalmodia* by analyzing the language and imagery of its unorthodox (from the strictly Spanish Catholic point of view) catechism. On this basis, she suggests ways in which Christian teachings could have been given more thoroughly Nahua interpretations by the native audience.

474 Campos Rodríguez, Patricia *et al.* Comunidades indígenas en Guanajuato: pasado y presente de los chichimecas. Edición de Isauro Rionda Arreguín. Guanajuato, Mexico: Archivo General del Gobierno del Estado de Guanajuato, 1996. 107 p.: bibl.

Brief anthology includes noteworthy ethnohistorical contributions on 16th-century "Chichimeca" pueblos near Guanajuato and San Miguel Allende, with some attention to more recent conditions. Authors

employ a cautious utilization of primary sources, aimed at clarifying the identity and cultural hallmarks of indigenous groups in this region.

475 Carrasco, Pedro. Estructura político territorial del Imperio tenochca: la triple alianza de Tenochtitlan, Tetzcoco y Tlacopan. México: Colegio de México, Fideicomiso Historia de las Américas; Fondo de Cultura Económica, 1996. 670 p.: bibl., indexes, maps. (Hacia una nueva historia de México)

An impressive tome with a solid footing in primary research. Extracts careful detail on the political geography of the Tenochca empire. After exploring the tripartite structure as illuminated in annals, chronicles, and codices, follows that broad regional organization, tracing information about tributary veins in each area and in the outlying reaches of the empire. Also includes a fascinating study of the human groups (warriors, colonists, public works laborers, merchants, and ceremonial participants) who facilitated the functioning of the empire. Provides helpful name and place indices.

476 Chance, John K. The barrios of colonial Tecali: patronage, kinship, and territorial relations in a central Mexican community. (*Ethnology/Pittsburgh,* 35:2, Spring 1996, p. 107–139, bibl., tables)

Substantially realized search for the origins and nature of barrios in this Puebla-region indigenous community, based heavily on surviving parish registers as well as other forms of archival documentation. Discusses such indigenous forms as the *teccalli, calpulli,* and *tlaxilacalli* and the possible relationships (or lack of them) between these precontact entities and the colonial-era "barrio" in Tecali. Most significant contribution is a painstaking discussion of sociocultural themes related to barrio-level life and organization. For ethnologist's comment, see *HLAS 57:43.* For archeologist's comment, see *HLAS 57:711.*

477 Chimalpahin Cuauhtlehuanitzin, Domingo Francisco de San Antón Muñón. Codex Chimalpahin: society and politics in Mexico Tenochtitlan, Tlatelolco, Texcoco, Culhuacan, and other Nahua altepetl in central Mexico: the Nahuatl and

Spanish annals and accounts collected and recorded by don Domingo de San Antón Muñón Chimalpahin Quauhtlehuanitzin, v. 1-2. Norman: Univ. of Oklahoma Press, 1997. 2 v.: bibl., index. (The civilization of the American Indian series; 225)

Essential two-volume translations of recently discovered examples of Chimalpahin's work held by the Bible Society Library at Cambridge Univ., given in parallel with transcriptions of Nahuatl texts. In both volumes, brief introductions by Schroeder provide useful information about Chimalpahin and his work. In v. 1, Ruwet provides as well a "Physical Description of the Manuscripts." An important addition to the growing body of indigenous language records and accounts in translation.

478   Christensen, Alexander F. Cristóbal del Castillo and the Mexica *exodus*. (*Americas/Franciscans*, 52:4, April 1994, p. 441-464)

Fascinating, significant study of Castillo's Nahuatl-language history of the Mexica migration. Ably linking its narrative form to Old Testament models, author ferrets out important clues to the intellectual context of the account, its purpose(s), and its intended audience(s). Useful comparisons are made to Guamán Poma's nearly contemporary Andean account.

479   Ciudad Suárez, María Milagros. Los lacandones: *hombres de guerra*, siglo XVI. (*An. Acad. Geogr. Hist. Guatem.*, 68, 1994, p. 229-256)

Valuable synthetic study of the various efforts—both peaceful and military—made by the Spanish to pacify the Lacandones, paying attention as well to indigenous responses.

480   Códice Alfonso Caso: la vida de 8-Venado, Garra de Tigre (Colombino-Becker I). Introducción de Miguel León Portilla. México: Patronato Indígena, 1996. 110 p.: bibl., ill.

Significant publication issued in commemoration of the 100th anniversary of the birth of Alfonso Caso, who first posited the now widely accepted belief that the Colombino and Becker I Codices were actually fragments of the same codex centered on the life of the Mixtec ruler 8-Deer. Includes a beautiful facsimile reuniting the fragments in the

sequence suggested by Caso, under the new commemorative name Códice Alfonso Caso.

481   Códice Borgia. Madrid: Sociedad Estatal Quinto Centenario; Vienna?: Akademische Druckund Verlagsanstalt; México: Fondo de Cultura Económica, 1993. 2 v. in case: bibl., col. facsims., ill. (Códices mexicanos; 5)

Handsomely realized study of this key member of the Borgia Group of pictorial manuscripts, part of a projected series intended to cover all of its five components (see item **483**). Here, the editors provide a stunning facsimile of the original along with a detailed, revisionist analysis of the gods and rites featured in the manuscript. An important contribution.

482   Códice Cozcatzin. Estudio y paleografía de Ana Rita Valero de García Lascuráin. Paleografía y traducción de los textos nahuas de Rafael Tena. México: Instituto Nacional de Antropología e Historia; Puebla, Mexico: Benemérita Univ. Autónoma de Puebla, 1994. 112 p.: bibl., ill., maps + 34 p. of col. facsims. (Códices mesoamericanos; 4)

Significant study and stunning facsimile of a postconquest "historical genealogical" manuscript from a town in the Valley of Mexico containing descriptions of lands said to have been given out by Itzcoatl in 1439, historical information about prehispanic rulers of Tenochtitlán and Tlatelolco, Tenochtitlán's conquest of Tlatelolco in 1473, genealogical information about Xochimilco, and some limited astrological information.

483   Códice Vaticano B.3773. Madrid: Sociedad Estatal Quinto Centenario; Vienna?: Akademische Druck- und Verlagsanstalt; México: Fondo de Cultura Económica, 1993. 1 folded strip (96 p.), 1 accompanying volume (382 p.): col. facsim. (Códices mexicanos; 4)

Dense analysis of this stunning pictorial manuscript, one of the five components of the Borgia Group. First in a projected series of codex studies, it consists of a vivid reproduction of the document and a thorough commentary investigating the ways in which concepts of time, the calendar, the cosmos, and deities are presented. See also item **481**.

484 Colección de documentos del Archivo General de la Nación para la etnohistoria de la Mixteca de Oaxaca en el siglo XVI. Recopilación de Ronald Spores. Nashville, Tennessee: Vanderbilt Univ., 1992. 104 p.: indexes. (Vanderbilt University publications in anthropology; 41)

Valuable presentation of documentary transcriptions from the Indios, Mercedes, and General de Parte collections of Mexico's National Archive. Of great utility to ethnohistorians, anthropologists, and others interested in early colonial Mixtec culture and the impact of Spanish systems and ways on this society.

485 Coloquio de Documentos Pictográficos de Tradición Náhuatl, *2nd, Museo Nacional de Antropología, 1985.* Segundo y Tercer Coloquios de Documentos Pictográficos de Tradición Náhuatl. Recopilación de Jesús Monjarás-Ruiz, Emma Pérez-Rocha y Perla Valle Pérez. México: Instituto Nacional de Antropología e Historia, 1996. 455 p.: bibl., ill., maps. (Serie Arqueología. Col. científica; 249)

Twenty-three articles originating in meetings staged in Mexico in 1985 and 1987. Of special interest are several studies of Techialoyan manuscripts (*San Antonio Techialoyan, San Simón Calpulalpan, Códice de Tepozotlán*) as well as an interpretation of representations of plants in this documentary genre. Among other things, the combined volume also includes studies of the *Códice de San Juan Teotihuacán*, the *Códice Sierra*, the *Mapa de Coatlinchan*, the *Mapa de San Antonio Calpulalpan*, and several lienzos from the Puebla region.

486 Coloquio de Historia de la Religión en Mesoamérica y Areas Afines, *2nd, Mexico City, 1990.* Coloquio. Recopilación de Barbro Dahlgren Jordan. México: UNAM, Instituto de Investigaciones Antropológicas, 1990. 295 p.: bibl., ill., maps.

Anthology of 20 brief scholarly articles addressed to the main theme of the title, arranged in several topical sections: "Mayas, Nahuas, Dioeses, Santos y Hombres-Mito, Mitos de Fundación," and "Otros Aspectos Religiosos." Specific papers within each section range temporally from prehispanic era through recent ethnographic studies. Articles of special interest to Mesoamerican ethno-

historians include a well-argued comparison between reliefs found at the early classic site of Izapa, Chiapas, and the first two sections of the Popul Vuh; an examination of the Popul Vuh as well as more recent, even more obviously Christian-infiltrated traditions from the Maya world; a linguistical/historical analysis of key passages from the Ritual de las Bacabes; a comparison of New Guinean beliefs in female deities associated with the agricultural cycle with similar ones found in precontact Nahua conceptions; a study drawing information from Durán's *Historia* about rituals involving widows and children of slain warriors; an analysis of descriptions and rituals of the Tlaloc complex as found in both colonial chronicles and tales from various places in modern Mexico; a presentation of suggestive evidence for a tradition of the "return of a white, bearded deity" among the peoples of 16th-century Colorado River area similar to the Quetzalcoatl story; a comparison of a story collected in the del Sur of Guerrero between October 1929 and May 1930 with similar information contained in colonial-era lienzos and codices; an examination of 14 replies from Valley of Oaxaca communities to question 14 of the Relación questionnaire, which concerned religious beliefs and rituals; and a brief discussion of beliefs and rituals connected with chiles. For comment on the third colloquium, see item **487.**

487 Coloquio de Historia de la Religión en Mesoamérica y Areas Afines, *3rd, Mexico City, 1990.* Coloquio. Recopilación de Barbro Dahlgren Jordan. México: UNAM, Instituto de Investigaciones Antropológicas, 1993. 338 p.: bibl., ill.

Anthology of 29 brief articles addressed to the organizing theme of the book and originating in a scholarly gathering in Mexico City in 1990. Articles of interest to ethnohistorians of Mesoamerica include: a short study of confession among the Mexica; a study of the symbolism of conches in prehispanic central Mesoamerica; Barba de Piña Chan's analysis of Mexica beliefs connected with childbirth and death in childbirth; a thoughtful consideration of evangelical efforts to instruct the indigenous people of central Mexico about salvation by impressing them with images of tormented sinners; an analysis of the use of medicinal plants by

Catholic missionaries in the northwest, as well as commercial trade in these commodities; Quezada's study of colonial curanderos and their manipulation of Christian saints and the devil; and a comparison between prehispanic and colonial indigenous beliefs in the relationship between illness and sexual deviance and similar beliefs in modern Pachiquitla, Hidalgo. For comment on the second colloquium, see item 486.

488 Congreso Internacional de Mayistas, 1st, San Cristóbal de Las Casas, Mexico, 1989. Memorias del Primer Congreso Internacional de Mayistas. v. 1, Inauguración, homenajes, lingüística, lingüística y textos indígenas, antropología social y etnología. v. 2, Mesas redondas, arqueología, epigrafía. v. 3, Conferencias plenarias, arte prehispánico, historia, religión. México: UNAM, 1992–1994. 3 v.: bibl., ill., maps.

The ethnohistorical contributions to these important proceedings, based largely on original archival research, include a piece by de Vos (also published in *Antropología, historia, e imaginativa*). For a review of the latter, see item 462.

489 Cruz, Víctor de la. Los nombres de los días en el calendario Zapoteco *Piye* en comparación con el calendario Nahua. (*Estud. Cult. Náhuatl*, 25, 1995, p. 149–176, bibl., tables)

Exacting analysis of the 20-day signs of the Zapotec ritual calendar. Author moves beyond mere description, using comparisons between the Nahua and Zapotec signs and systems to suggest that a variety of specific calendrical structures resulted mainly from linguistic and regional variations traceable to a common conceptual point of origin.

490 Danforth, Marie Elaine; Keith P. Jacobi; and Mark Nathan Cohen. Gender and health among the colonial Maya of Tipu, Belize. (*Anc. Mesoam.*, 8:1, Spring 1997, p. 13–22, ill., map, tables)

Painstakingly thorough analysis of skeletal remains of 16th- and 17th-century Mayan men and women from the cemetery of Tipu, an archeological site in west-central Belize. Results of the analysis of skeletal remains are compared with extant ethnohistorical data, allowing the authors to offer significant verification of, as well as some corrections to, our knowledge of the intersec-

tion of gender, health, and culture change among the colonial Maya. For archeologist's comment, see *HLAS 57:186*.

491 De hombres y dioses. Coordinación de Xavier Noguez y Alfredo López Austin. Michoacán, Mexico: El Colegio de Michoacán; Zinacantepec, México: El Colegio Mexiquense, 1997. 326 p.: bibl., ill.

Collection of seven significant articles by scholars such as Graulich, López Austin, and Taube. Chronologically organized, the chapters consist of an analysis of iconographic representations of the maize god among the Olmec and its spread among other peoples of Mesoamerica, a discussion of evidence for decapitation rituals found in recent excavations of the Casa del Marqués del Apartado in central Mexico City (the site of a prehispanic temple), a study of late postclassic central Mexican astrological and calendrical symbolism connected with pulque, death, the night, and the *tzitzimime*, an examination of the iconography of the famous "Mexican Calendar Stone" and the *Teocalli de la Guerra Sagrada*, two chapters on the functions of myth and ritual, and a study of modern Papago ritual from the area encompassed by parts of Arizona and Sonora.

492 De la Garza, Mercedes *et al.* Los Mayas: su tiempo antiguo. Edición de Gerardo Bustos y Ana Luisa Izquierdo. México: UNAM, Instituto de Investigaciones Filológicas, Centro de Estudios Mayas, 1996. 325, [1] p., [2] folded leaves: bibl., ill., maps (some col.).

Collection of 10 scholarly articles examining everything from the geography and physical anthropology of the Maya zone to the history, social organization, linguistics and epigraphy, ritual and religion, science, and art. Based on studies prepared for a series of conferences running from 1983–88, which is reflected in the lack of citations of more recent secondary literature in the combined bibliography.

Doolittle, William E. Indigenous development of Mesoamerican irrigation. See *HLAS 57:2540*.

493 Duran, Diego. Códice Duran. Proyecto y textos de Electra y Tonatiúh Gutiérrez. México: Arrendadora Internacional, 1990. 1 v.: col. ill.

Beautiful presentation of the illustrations from Durán's well-known work. Editor's introduction presents a brief physical description of the illustrations, as well as a biography of Durán and his work, but high quality reproductions of the illustrations themselves, along with descriptive captions, dominate the work.

494 Durand-Forest, Jacqueline de. Algunas observaciones sobre el *diario* de Chimalpahin Quauhtlehuanitzin. (*Estud. Cult. Náhuatl*, 25, 1995, p. 417–423)

Short but meaty overview of the form, contents, and chronology of folios 72–94 of Manuscript 220 of the Goupil Aubin Collection, National Library of Paris. A key section of Chimalpahin's *Diario* serves as an introduction for a revised translation, in Spanish, presented in parallel to the Nahuatl. Revision of a version originally published by the same author in 1987 as *Compendium de Historia Precolombina*.

495 Elferink, Jan G. R.; José Antonio Flores; and Charles D. Kaplan. The use of plants and other natural products for malevolent practices among the Aztecs and their successors. (*Estud. Cult. Náhuatl*, 24, 1994, p. 27–47, bibl., tables)

Engaging investigation of the beliefs, practices, and products employed for purposes of killing or harming enemies, or for attracting unwilling members of the opposite sex. The role of the *nahualli*, in this case defined as sorcerer, and the impact of Spanish ideas of "good" and "bad" are considered, as are the ways in which "malevolent practices" evolved during the colonial period and beyond.

496 Escobar Ohmstede, Antonio. Los pueblos indios en las Huastecas, México, 1750–1810: formas para conservar y aumentar su territorio. (*CLAHR/Albuquerque*, 6:1, Winter 1997, p. 31–68, map, tables)

Serious, well-executed, archive-based study of late-colonial agrarian matters in indigenous communities in a lesser known region.

497 Esponda Jimeno, Victor Manuel. El K'awaltic: las ordenanzas de Oxchuc del Visitador Jacinto Roldán de la Cueva, 1674. (*Anu. Inst. Chiapaneco Cult.*, 1992, p. 187–205, bibl., photos)

Fascinating piece presenting a transcription and discussion of a 17th-century set of ordinances for the conduct of civil and sacred corporate indigenous life in Chiapas. Equally important is the intriguing description of the way in which these ordinances were transformed into a community charter, a sacred book of "Our Lord" in Oxchuc tradition which became the object of yearly rituals still performed today.

498 Estudios del México antiguo. Coordinación de Beatriz Barba de Piña Chán. México: Instituto Nacional de Antropología e Historia, 1996. 162 p.: bibl.,. ill., maps. (Serie Historia. Col. científica; 315)

Informative series of public lectures by noted scholars, including Barba de Piña Chan's exploration of the grandmother figure in Quiche culture, particularly as illustrated in the Popol Vuh and some Olmec-Maya bas reliefs at Izapa, which may take the concept back as far as 300 BC; Folan's survey of excavations at Calakmul, Campeche, a site with impressive and telling classic period tombs; Piña Chan's revisionist study of one of the Cacaxtla, Tlaxcala, murals which he believes represent ritual sacrifice linked with Quetzalcoatl and, therefore, the death and rebirth of Venus; Macías Goytia's revelations about the cultural life highlighted by excavations at Huandacareo in the basin of Cuitzeo, Michoacan; Olivé Negrete's exploration of the elusive meaning of Aztlan; Valle de Revueltas' summary of her research on Tepetlaoztoc, part of Acolhuacan; Heyden's considerations regarding the fate of 16th-century writings of Sahagún and Durán; and Pérez-Rocha's summary of her work on colonial agrarian issues in the jurisdiction of Tacuba.

499 Fernández Valbuena, José A. Mirroring the sky: a postclassic K'iche-Maya cosmology. Drawings by Jorge L. Sánchez and Melinda A. Goelz. Lancaster, Calif.: Labyrinthos, 1996. 107 p.: bibl., ill., maps.

Intriguing archeoastronomical study in which the role of cosmological symbolism is analyzed in relation to an elite K'iché ideology of rule in Utatlán, Guatemala.

500 Gasco, Janine. Cacao and economic inequality in colonial Soconusco, Chiapas, Mexico. (*J. Anthropol. Res.*, 52:4, Winter 1996, p. 385–409, bibl., graphs, maps, tables)

Convincing study in which the author examines how indigenous social structures were affected by the region's participation in the world economic system through cacao production. Contrary to what might be expected, she discovers and describes regionally and temporally variant patterns of both social leveling and increasing social stratification, with the former more common through the late-18th century and the latter seen more often by the early-19th century.

501 Gillespie, Susan D. and **Rosemary A. Joyce.** Gendered goods: the symbolism of Maya hierarchical exchange relations. (*in* Women in prehistory: North America and Mesoamerica. Philadelphia: Univ. of Penn. Press, 1997, p. 189–207, ill.)

Thought-provoking, ambitious comparative analysis based on readings of monuments and hieroglyphic texts from the classic period, documents from early Spanish period, and modern ethnographic material, all examined in relation to a model developed in the study of contemporary culture in eastern Indonesia. Uncover suggestive patterns in the gendered language and representation found in rituals involving wife-providers and wife-receivers among the Maya.

502 González Rodríguez, Luis. Thomás de Guadalaxara, 1648–1720: misionero de la Tarahumara, historiador, lingüista y pacificador. (*Estud. Hist. Novohisp.*, 15, 1995, p. 9–34, appendix, bibl.)

Detailed examination of the life of the Jesuit Thomás de Guadalaxara contains some ethnohistorical information but concentrates principally on the character and career of this missionary to the Tarahumara. Includes a résumé of the *Crónica de la Sierra Tarahumara,* coauthored by Guadalaxara and a fellow Jesuit, José Tardá, and a brief documentary appendix.

503 González Torres, Yólotl and **Juan Carlos Ruiz Guadalajara.** Diccionario de mitología y religión de Mesoamérica. Madrid: Larousse, 1991. 250 p.: bibl., ill., maps. (Referencias Larousse)

Handy ethnohistorical and ethnographic reference work with a broad, though not exhaustive, geographical base. Logically, Nahua and Maya entries are most numerous, but Huichol, Mixtec, Otomí, Tarascan, Totonac, and Zapotec material also appears. Author provides cross-references, cultural identifiers, and scientific names, when appropriate; indicates sources of information only occasionally, but includes a bibliography at the end.

504 Good, Catharine. Salt production and commerce in Guerrero, Mexico: an ethnographic contribution to historical reconstruction. (*Anc. Mesoam.*, 6:1, Spring 1995, p. 1–13, bibl., maps, photos)

Useful suggestions for reconstructing prehispanic or colonial salt production and for evaluating the role of oral tradition for preserving technical information. Interesting finding is the prevalent role of women in salt-making and trading. For archeologist's comment, see *HLAS 57:70.*

505 Graulich, Michel. Montezuma, ou, L'apogée et la chute de l'empire aztèque. Paris: Fayard, 1994. ix, 520 p.: bibl., ill., indexes, maps.

Skillful chronological narrative, relying on ethnohistorical sources, of the history of the Aztec empire, with particular attention to the relatively lightly studied reign of Montezuma (1502–1520). Provides some attention to controversial issues, such as the Aztecs' predictions of the coming of the Spanish, Quetzalcoatl's expected return, and conflicting stories about Montezuma's death. One interesting chapter examines the daily life of the Mexican sovereign.

506 Graulich, Michel. Myths of ancient Mexico. Translated by Bernard R. Ortiz de Montellano and Thelma Ortiz de Montellano. Norman: Univ. of Oklahoma Press, 1997. xii, 370 p.: ill., maps. (The civilization of the American Indian series; 222)

Innovative study, drawing on extensive ethnohistorical and ethnographical materials, of the mythology of the Toltecs and the Aztecs, with broader Mesoamerican comparisons, including the Popol Vuh of the Quiché Maya. Finds recurring themes in origin stories of light and darkness, sacrifice, expulsion and wanderings, and arrival in a Promised Land. Analysis includes considerations of myth vs. history.

507 Guernsey Allen, Anne E. A stylistic analysis of the *Codex Cozcatzin:* its implications for the study of post-conquest Aztec manuscripts. (*Estud. Cult. Náhuatl,* 24, 1994, p. 255–281, bibl., facsims.)

This partly pictorial, partly textual (Spanish and Nahuatl) codex was connected with a land repatriation case brought before the Audiencia in 1572 by the Tlalelocan-area community of San Sebastian Coyutlan. Submitting the document to intensive analysis, the author finds strong evidence that the conventions of secular precontact-style pictographic writing were passed on for at least 60 years following the Spanish invasion.

508 Hamannn, Byron. Weaving and the iconography of prestige: the royal gender symbolism of Lord 5 Flower's/Lady 4 Rabbit's family. (in Women in prehistory: North America and Mesoamerica. Philadelphia: Univ. of Penn. Press, 1997, p. 153–172, ill.)

Reasoned interpretive analysis of Monte Albán's Tomb 7, Tombs 1 and 2 at Zaachila, and Codex Nuttall (p. 33–35) focusing on the meaning and intent of representations of weaving linked with royal women and men. Author finds assertions of gender parallelism, complementarity, and equality. Weaving techniques, the spread of the Mixteca-Puebla style, and the implications of interdynastic marriage are also discussed.

509 Harris, Max. The dramatic testimony of Antonio de Ciudad Real: indigenous theatre in sixteenth-century New Spain. (Colon. Lat. Am. Rev., 5:2, Dec. 1996, p. 237–251)

Suggestive study of dances, plays, and "military theater" (such as large-scale pageants featuring combat between moros y cristianos) based mainly on the richly detailed late-16th-century accounts of Antonio de Ciudad Real. Harris ably uncovers possible "hidden transcripts" of resistance and "indigenous patriotism" in Ciudad Real's descriptions, which are placed in a larger comparative context.

Harris, Max. Moctezuma's daughter: the role of la malinche in Mesoamerican dance. See HLAS 57:735.

510 Haskett, Robert Stephen. Paper shields: the ideology of coats-of-arms in colonial Mexican primordial titles. (Ethnohistory/Society, 43:1, Winter 1996, p. 99–127)

Interpretation of the sociocultural meanings of Spanish-style coats-of-arms described or depicted in primordial titles from the Huejotzingo and Cuernavaca regions.

511 Hendon, Julia A. Hilado y tejido en las tierras bajas mayas en la época prehispánica: tecnología y relaciones sociales de la producción textil. (Yaxkin/Tegucigalpa, 13:1/2, enero/dic. 1995, p. 57–70, bibl.)

Brief but meaty article focused on the Valley of Copán, which argues that fine textile production for elite consumption was carried out in domestic settings in or near elite residences. Evidence points to noble women as the principal producers of this kind of specialized product. Closely related to author's later work described in item **512.**

512 Hendon, Julia A. Women's work, women's space, and women's status among the classic-period Maya elite of the Copán Valley, Honduras. (in Women in prehistory: North America and Mesoamerica. Philadelphia: Univ. of Penn. Press, 1997, p. 33–46, maps, table)

Notable investigation of the gendered meanings of artifacts found in the nonruling-class elite Sepulturas sector of Copán. Concentrating on the "women's work" of food preparation and textile production, identifies key sociocultural patterns, including the gendering of space and the importance of the labor activities performed by elite women. For related article, see item **511.**

513 Hernández de León-Portilla, Ascensión. Hernando de Ribas: intérprete de dos mundos. (Rev. Lat. Pensam. Leng., 2:2b, 1995/96, p. 477–493)

Well-researched biography of this important, trilingual product of the Colegio de Santa Cruz de Tlatelolco, who left a lasting imprint on the work of Fray Alonso de Molina, Fray Juan de Gaona, and Fray Juan Bautista. Informative analysis of the intellectual products of these scholars is included.

514 Herrera Meza, María del Carmen and Ethelia Ruiz Medrano. El Códice de Tepeucila: el entinatado mundo de la fijeza imaginaria. México: Instituto Nacional de Antropología e Historia, 1997. 83 p.: bibl., ill. (some col.).

This virtually unknown codex, housed in the Archivo General de Indias, is related to a 16th-century judicial suit pitting the Cuicatec people of Tepeucila (Oaxaca) complaining of excessive tribute assessments against their encomendero, Andrés de Tapia. Particularly fascinating here is the story of the tactics employed by Tapia's lawyers, who tried mightly to discredit the pictorial as a "true" record, and the revealing forensic wrangling over exactly how to interpret the codex as acceptable evidence in a court case. Thoughtful analysis and commentary.

515 Heyden, Doris. Los guerreros y la muerte. (Anuario/INAH, 1, 1995, p. 51–58, bibl.)

Brief, descriptive synthesis of information drawn from Sahagún and Durán about warriors and their ceremonies (sacrificial and funerary) among the Mexica.

516 Hill, Robert M. Eastern Chajoma (Cakchiquel) political geography: ethnohistorical and archaeological contributions to the study of a late postclassic highland Maya polity. (*Anc. Mesoam.*, 7:1, Spring 1996, p. 63–87, bibl., maps, photos)

Well-crafted historical geography of a Cakchiquel polity on the eve of the Spanish invasion. Uses a mixture of early colonial ethnohistorical documents, some in Cakchiquel, as well as archeological surveys to postulate the date of Chajoma's foundation, its geographic extent, its political organization, and its population.

517 Historia antigua de México. v. 2, El horizonte clásico. v. 3, El horizonte posclásico y algunos aspectos intelectuales de las culturas mesoamericanas. México: Consejo Nacional para la Cultura y las Artes; UNAM; M.A. Porrúa, 1995. 2 v.: bibl., ill., maps.

Solid collection of essays with geographical and cultural breadth, pulling data from archeological, ethnohistorical, and ethnographical sources to provide a panorama of the postclassic cultures of Mesoamerica. Covers the following zones: the Gulf (Ochoa), Oaxaca (González Licón and Márquez Morfín), highland Maya (Iglesias Ponce de León and Ciudad Ruiz), lowland Maya (Rivera Dorado), the West (Michelet), central highland Toltec stage (Noguez), central highland Chichimec stage (Reyes García and Odena Güemes), central highland Triple Alliance stage (Obregón Rodríguez), the central North (Brambila), and Chihuahua (Guevara Sánchez). Remaining chapters explore Mesoamerican cultural hallmarks, including systems of exchange (Lorenzo), writing, calendars, and number systems (Ayala Falcón), religion, magic, and cosmovision (López Austin), and art (Pasztory). For archeologist's comment on vol. 1, see *HLAS* 57:82 and for comment on vol. 2, see *HLAS* 57:83.

518 Horn, Rebecca. Postconquest Coyoacan: Nahua-Spanish relations in Central Mexico, 1519–1650. Stanford, Calif.: Stanford Univ. Press, 1997. 370 p.: bibl., ill., index, maps.

Innovative and deft examination of Nahua-Spanish interaction in numerous settings, with an eye to the implications for cultural change, particularly in Nahua communities. Explores jurisdictional, political, and economic questions in notable depth. Employs both Spanish and Náhuatl-language sources in great number.

519 Hu-DeHart, Evelyn. Adaptación y resistencia en el yaquimi: los yaquis durante la colonia. Traducción de Zulai Marcela Fuentes Ortega. Revisión de traducción de Teresa Rojas Rabiela. Tlalpan, Mexico: CIESAS; Col. Alpes, Mexico: INI, 1995. 124 p.: bibl., ill. (some col.), maps (some col.). (Historia de los pueblos indígenas de México)

Handsome Spanish-language presentation of important work on the Yaqui during the Spanish era as they faced Jesuit missionization and the later secularization of the missions, sometimes responding with resistance and rebellion. A valuable documentary appendix, consisting heavily of ecclesiastical correspondence, covers the years 1533–1765. For ethnologist's comment, see *HLAS* 57:742.

520 Ibarra García, Laura. La visión del mundo de los antiguos mexicanos: origen de sus conceptos de causalidad, tiempo y espacio. Guadalajara, Mexico: Univ. de Guadalajara, 1995. 268 p.: bibl., ill. (Col. Fin de milenio)

Uses a dense discussion of Jean Piaget's "genetic theory" as a point of departure for consideration of Aztec concepts of human life, death, nature, the cosmos, time, and space.

The Indian in Spanish America: centuries of removal, survival, and integration; a critical anthology. See item 4989.

521 Jiménez, Gloria Martha. La chontalpa en el siglo XVI. (*Am. Indíg.*, 54:1/2, enero/junio 1994, p. 63–89, bibl.)

Straightforward study of the waves of Spanish invasion and settlement experienced by the Maya-Chontal of Tabasco, focusing on their resistance and later incorporation into the encomienda system and the process of Catholic evangelization.

522 Johansson K., Patrick. Análisis estructural del mito de la creación del sol y de la luna en la variante del *Códice Flo-*

rentino. (Estud. Cult. Náhuatl, 24, 1994, p. 93–123)

Rereading of the well-known story of the creation of the Sun and Moon, employing analytical methodology proposed by Claude Lévi-Strauss. This dense study, which analyzes the text line by line, explores the purposes and evolution of "mythic" structure, expressions of duality, time, and space.

523   Johansson K., Patrick. El discurso náhuatl de la muerte. *(Rev. Lat. Pensam. Leng.,* 2:2b, 1995/96, p. 503–514, ill.)

Succinct investigation of the theme of the title, carried out in relation to texts and terminology dealing with death in such well-known sources as the *Cantares Mexicanos,* the *Romances de los señores de la Nueva España,* and the Florentine Codex.

524   Joseph, de San Buenaventura, fray. Historias de la conquista del Mayab, 1511–1697. Edición, paleografía, introducción y notas, Gabriela Solís Robleda, Pedro Bracamonte y Sosa. Mérida, Mexico: Univ. Autónoma de Yucatán, Facultad de Ciencias Antropológicas, 1994. 230 p.: bibl., ill., folded map.

Welcome first publication of a little-known account completed in 1725 by this member of the Franciscan order. Includes Fray Joseph's version of a chronicle purportedly written by the famous shipwrecked Spaniard-turned Maya war leader, Gonzalo Guerrero, as well as accounts of the first waves of the conquest of the Yucatán, the conversion of the Chontales, and the conquest of the Itza by 1697. Editors' valuable introduction discusses the veracity of the claims made about Guerrero's account, the ethnohistorical significance of the entire work, its historical context, and the identity of its author.

525   Joyce, Arthur A. and **Marcus Winter.** Ideology, power, and urban society in pre-Hispanic Oaxaca. *(Curr. Anthropol.,* 37:1, Feb. 1996, p. 33–86, bibl., ill., map)

For annotation, see item **471.**

526   Joyce, Rosemary A. and **Susan A. M. Shumaker.** Encounters with the Americas. Photographs by Hillel S. Burger. Cambridge, Mass.: Peabody Museum of Archaeology and Ethnology, 1995. 87 p.: bibl., ill. (some col.).

Richly illustrated catalog accompanied the renovated exhibition at Harvard's Peabody Museum. Like the exhibition, the catalog is divided into three parts: the age of encounter between indigenous and Spanish peoples; the classic Maya; and cultural survival in the contemporary world among the highland Maya of Guatemala, the Kuna people of Panama, and Amazonian societies. The authors present their own synthetic treatments of these subjects, supported by well-selected testimony from the actors themselves, such as Hernando Cortés, Sahagún's informants as presented by *The Broken Spears,* and recorded testimony from contemporary indigenous peoples.

527   Karttunen, Frances E. Cuicapixqueh: Antonio Valeriano, Juan Bautista de Pomar, and Náhuatl poetry. *(Lat. Am. Indian Lit. J.,* 11:1, Spring 1995, p. 4–20)

Engaging paired biographical sketches of Juan Bautista de Pomar, mestizo author of Texcoco's *Relación Geográfica* and compiler of precontact-style verse, and of Antonio Valeriano, scholarly product of the Colegio de Santa Cruz of Tlatelolco, key aide to Fray Bernardino de Sahagún, and *gobernador* in turn of his home community of Azcapotzalco and of the indigenous sector of Mexico City. In highlighting Valeriano's many important contributions, also debunks his supposed authorship of the *Nican mopohua* account of the apparition of the Virgin of Guadalupe, and questions his role in the compilation of the *Cantares Mexicanos.*

528   Klein, Cecelia F. Fighting with femininity: gender and war in Aztec Mexico. *(Estud. Cult. Náhuatl,* 24, 1994, p. 219–253, bibl., facsims., photos)

Reasoned analysis of numerous colonial sources, seeking an understanding of the Aztecs' gendering of war and their ambivalence toward female aggressiveness. Concludes that the ideology allows for some gender parallelism but also exhibits an intrinsic assymetricality that bolstered the power and authority of men and the sovereignty of the state.

529   Laitner Benz, Karen and **Bruce F. Benz.** Las condiciones culturales y ambientales en la Reserva de la Biosfera Sierra de Manantlán en tiempo de la Conquista: una perspectiva de los documentos etnohistóricos secundarios. (*Estud. Hombre*, 1, nov. 1994, p. 15–45, appendix, bibl., map, tables)

Analysis, somewhat in the style of a historical geography, of the provinces of Amula, Milpa, and the Tepetitango (modern Jalisco) in the 16th century with the intent to recover information about indigenous society in the region on the eve of the conquest.

530 Latin American Indian Literatures Association. Symposium. *12th, Universidad Nacional Autónoma de México, 1995.* Messages and meanings. Edited by Mary H. Preuss. Lancaster, Calif.: Labyrinthos, 1997. 222 p.: bibl., ill. (Latin American Indian literatures)

Eclectic conference proceedings spanning time periods with papers on the Maya zone, central Mexico, and Central and South America. Of special note to ethnohistorians of Mesoamerica are Gubler's study of two lesser known books of Chilam Balam; Andueza's exploration of the content of the songs of Dzitbalché; Aguilera's new reading of the patron goddess of the 18th-week of the *tonalpohualli* in the Codex Telleriano-Remensis; Bernal-García's study of toponyms in the *Historia Tolteca-Chichimeca*; Ruhnau's analysis of Chimalpahin's theological discourses in his *Diferentes historias originales*; Brotherston's rethinking of codex genres and methods of reading them, with attention to pre-Columbian origins of alphabetic scripts; Iwaniszewski's revisionist study of Mexica concepts of time in 16th-century sources; and, Rincón Mautner's examination of "place-becoming" in Coixtlahuaca Basin codices.

531 León Portilla, Miguel. Aportaciones recientes sobre: sociedad y cultura indígenas en el México colonial; la perspectiva de los testimonios en Náhuatl. (*Estud. Cult. Náhuatl*, 24, 1994, p. 455–474)

Informative critical discussion of J. Lockhart's *The Nahuas after the conquest* (*HLAS 54:518*), as well as the work of several of his students set in a broader historiographical context: *Colonial Culhuacan, 1580–1600* by S.L. Cline (*HLAS 50:511*); *Indigenous rulers: an ethnohistory of town government in colonial Cuernavaca* by R. Haskett (*HLAS 54:488*); and *Chimalpahin & the kingdoms of Chalco* by S. Schroeder (*HLAS 54:565*).

532 León Portilla, Miguel. Una comunicación en Náhuatl sobre tributos: Tlaxcala, 1546. (*Estud. Cult. Náhuatl*, 25, 1995, p. 253–261, facsim.)

Careful historico-linguistic analysis of a brief Nahuatl document from Tlaxcala. It is significant due to its rarity: an unequivocally early alphabetic text. Includes a facsimile, transcription, and translation.

533 León Portilla, Miguel. Un cura que no viene y otro al que le gusta la india Francisca: dos cartas en náhuatl de la Chontalpa, Tabasco, 1579–1580. (*Estud. Cult. Náhuatl*, 24, 1994, p. 139–170, facsims.)

Extensive commentary on the form, content, and meaning of two late-16th-century Nahuatl documents from a predominantly Chol-speaking region. Also discusses the reasons for the use of Nahuatl in this area. Facsimiles, transcriptions, and translations of the two documents are included.

534 Libro de los guardianes y gobernadores de Cuauhtinchan, 1519–1640. Paleografía, introducción y notas de Constantino Medina Lima. Mexico: CIESAS, 1995. 178 p.: bibl., col. ill., indexes.

Valuable transcription, translation, and brief analysis of important, mainly Nahuatl-language, annals from this community in the Puebla region. Document includes a wealth of information on the political and religious history of the community during the first century or so after Spanish colonization.

535 Long, Janet Towell. De tomates y jitomates en el siglo XVI. (*Estud. Cult. Náhuatl*, 25, 1995, p. 239–252, bibl.)

Straightforward study of these two types of tomatoes, paying attention to taxonomy, methods of cultivation, role in commerce and tribute, and spread of the fruits to the Mediterranean world, primarily Spain and Italy.

536 Lopes Don, Patricia. Carnivals, triumphs, and rain gods in the New World: a civic festival in the city of México-Tenochtitlán in 1539. (*Colon. Lat. Am. Rev.*, 6:1, June 1997, p. 17–40)

Deft study explaining how and why a celebration staged in the new main plaza of Mexico City commemorating the Franco-Spanish treaty of 1538 could have been infused by indigenous participants with "pagan" rites in the same year that later saw the public execution for idolatry of Don Carlos of Texcoco.

537 López Austin, Alfredo and **Leonardo López Luján.** El pasado indígena. México: Colegio de México, Fideicomiso Historia de las Américas; Fondo de Cultura Económica, 1996. 305 p.: bibl., ill., maps. (Hacia una nueva historia de México)

Divides indigenous peoples into three major units: 1) "Aridamérica" (including central and southern California, the Sonora coast, the Great Basin of Nevada, Utah, and northwestern Arizona, the Apache area, a small part of southern Texas, and a large portion of northern Mexico); 2) "Oasisamérica" (covering parts of northern Mexico, southeastern California, all of Arizona, almost all of Utah, more than half of New Mexico, and the southwestern corner of Colorado); and 3) "Mesoamérica" (defined, in part, as taking in the peoples of 16 linguistic families: Hokanocoahuilteca, Chinanteca, Otopame, Oaxaqueña, Mangueña, Huave, Tlapaneca, Totonaca, Mixe, Maya, Yutoazteca, Tarasca, Cuitlateca, Lenca, Xinca, and Misumalpa). Proceeds with an overview of the Mesoamerican preclassic, classic, epiclassic, and postclassic periods.

538 Luque Alcaide, Elisa. El juicio sobre la *segunda conquista* en el III Concilio Mexicano, 1585: la guerra de los Chichimecas. (*in* Las raíces de la memoria: América Latina, ayer y hoy, quinto encuentro debate = Amèrica Latina, ahir i avui, cinquena trobada debat. Coordinación de Pilar García Jordán *et al.* Barcelona: Univ. de Barcelona, 1996, p.103–115)

Enlightening discussion of a debate on the justice of the war against the Chichimecas and its conclusions carried out at the prompting of Mexico City's *cabildo* during the Third Mexican Council.

539 Madrid, Blanca Mireya Lara. La resistencia indígena frente a la evangelización: Sinaloa en los siglos XVI y XVII. (*in* Congreso de Historia Regional de Sinaloa, *10th, Culiacán Rosales, México?, 1994.* Historia y Región. Culiacán Rosales, México: Univ. Autónoma de Sinaloa, Facultad de Historia, 1996, p. 78–85)

Brief discussion of indigenous resistance—violent and clandestine—to Catholic evangelization as well as resulting internal conflicts in affected communities and the techniques employed by Jesuit missionaries in their efforts to convert and instruct the native peoples.

540 Malmström, Vincent H. Cycles of the sun, mysteries of the moon: the calendar in Mesoamerican civilization. Austin: Univ. of Texas Press, 1997. 295 p.: bibl., ill., index, maps.

Engagingly written revisionist argumentation regarding the ancient origins of the "Maya" calendars, which this author posits to have originated in Izapa, Soconusco, and then spread to other peoples of Meso america. Draws from intensive interdisciplinary research in astronomy, history, and geography to identify the "calendars' cradle" on the Pacific slope and to trace their diffusion over time and space. Also relies on extensive "alignments and orientation" analyses made across Mesoamerica, plus linguistic and pottery distribution patterns. Impacts Olmec studies, among others. Refutes Chinese and East Indian origins for the Mesoamerican calendar.

541 Martínez, Hildeberto. Codiciaban la tierra: el despojo agrario en los señoríos de Tecamachalco y Quecholac, Puebla, 1520–1650. México: CIESAS, 1994. 305 p.: ill.

Impressive study, based on a significant amount of archival research in Mexico, Spain, and the US, of the process of land dispossession experienced by the Popoluca, Nahua, and Otomi inhabitants of the Puebla region.

542 McAnany, Patricia Ann. Living with the ancestors: kinship and kingship in ancient Maya society. Austin: Univ. of Texas Press, 1995. 229 p.: bibl., ill., index, maps.

Rethinking concepts of the "cult of the dead" and &quotåcestor worship," this archeological, ethnohistorical, and ethnographic study posits a compelling thesis that the middle and late formative Maya began communing with the deceased and keeping their remains close, attaching them to the land and other natural resources, which led to a growing inequality and provoked factional disputes. Focus is on K'axob, a site in Belize, but the analysis has implications that reach out geographically as well as forward in time. For archeologist's comment, see *HLAS* 57:102.

543 McCaa, Robert. Matrimonio infantil, *Cemithualtin,* (familias complejas) y el antiguo pueblo Nahua. (*Hist. Mex.,* 46:1, julio/sept. 1996, p. 3–70, appendix, bibl., tables)

Exacting analysis of the by now well-known early postconquest Nahuatl-language censuses from Morelos, indicating that very early marriages were frequent among the region's Nahua inhabitants. Author discusses relationships between members of complex households, as well, and provides a lengthy analytical appendix.

544 McKeever Furst, Jill Leslie. The natural history of the soul in ancient Mexico. New Haven, Conn.: Yale Univ. Press, 1995. 240 p.: bibl., ill., index, maps.

Fascinating examination of Mexica thought and belief (ca. 1200–1519) regarding the soul, utilizing iconographic and ethno-historical sources but also giving special consideration to the influence of natural environments on ideology. Cultural concepts of special note here include the Nahua *yolia, ihiyotl,* and *tonalli.* Author saves the *nahualli* for future study.

545 Megged, Amos. Poverty and welfare in Mesoamerica during the sixteenth and seventeenth centuries: European archetypes and colonial translations. (*CLAHR/Albuquerque,* 6:1, Winter 1997, p. 1–29, map)

Appropriately considers influence exerted by both the European concepts and the local situation, in this case Chiapas and Guatemala, in shaping the nature of indigenous *cofradías* (confraternities). Emphasizes the Maya but provides central Mexican comparisons.

546 Megged, Amos. Right from the heart: Indians' idolatry in mendicant preachings in sixteenth-century Mesoamerica. (*Hist. Relig.,* 35:1, Aug. 1995, p. 61–82)

Well-crafted study of Dominican interpretations and definitions of idolatry in 16th-century Chiapas. Includes an insightful analysis of Maya religious terminology as defined (and transformed) by Domingo de Ara in his two c.1560 dictionaries, the *Arte de la lengua Tzendal,* and the *Vocabulario en lengua Tzendal.*

547 Milbrath, Susan. Gender and roles of lunar deities in postclassic central Mexico and their correlations with the Maya area. (*Estud. Cult. Náhuatl,* 25, 1995, p. 45–93, bibl., ill.)

Systematic comparative analysis of precontact representations of deities with lunar associations (complemented by colonial and contemporary ethnographic information) arguing that the moon was seen as bisexual, changing its gender as it moved through its phases. Demonstrates how gendered portrayals of lunar deities were linked to gender ideology applied to human society.

548 Mille ans de civilisations mésoaméricaines: des Mayas aux Aztèques; mélanges en l'honneur de Jacques Soustelle. v. 1, Danse avec les dieux. Paris: L'Harmattan, 1995. 1 v.: bibl., ill.

First in two-volume anthology in homage to Jacques Soustelle with remembrances from Baudot, Durand-Forest, and Matos Moctezuma, plus an additional memory of Georgette Soustelle by León-Portilla. Substantive chapters include: "A School of Sculptors at Chichen Itza, Yucatán, Mexico," by Greene Robertson; "Déambulations rituelles et arcours cosmique: le groupe de la croix de Palenque," by Baudez; "Les rituels du jeu de balle dans l'épigraphie maya," by Davoust; "Rites sacrificiels Mayas," by Fettweis-Vienot"; Identity in the Quiche Theater," by Edmonson; "Les figures du guerrier et du roi dans le 'Rabinal Achi:' une version maya du couple celeritas/gravitas," by Breton; "Les fruits du chêne: les Mayas face á la christianisation," by Ruz; "Perception synchronique de la nation de la personne dens les sociétés mayas: le cas mochó," by García-Ruiz; "Sub umbra floreo," by Nelken-Terner; "Un rey ilustrado, promotor de las primeras exploraciones arqueológicas en América," by Ballesteros Gaibrois; "Le renouveaude l'américanisme en Nouvelle-Espagne dans la seconde moitié du XVIIIe siécle," by Roulet; and, "La recherche archéologique dans les archives inédites de la commission scientifique du Mexique, 1864–1867," by Duclot-Renaud. For review of vol. 2, see item **549.**

549 Mille ans de civilisations mésoaméricaines: des Mayas aux Aztèques; mélanges en l'honneur de Jacques Soustelle.

v. 2, La quête du cinquième soleil. Paris: L'Harmattan, 1995. 1 v.: bibl., ill.

Important collection of 29 articles presented in honor of Jacques Soustelle and written in French, Spanish, and English by leading scholars. The work is divided into several topical sections. Pt. 1, "Les Aztèques, Ethnohistoire et nahuatl;" "Reflection on the Translation of the Florentine Codex" by Dibble; "Here it is Told...," an analysis of the anonymous Nahuatl account of the apparition of the Virgin of Guadalupe, Nican mopohua by Anderson; "Ballades Chichimèques des seigneurs du temps jadis," a study of songs from the Cantares Mexicanos by Baudot; Saurin's study of Nahuatl descriptions of divinities of the Florentine Codex, "Un exemple de discours sur le corps chez les Aztèques: Les devinettes;" "Vers une bibliothèque nahuatl informatisée ver une procédure de vérification des lectures des images Aztèques," a brief but useful example of his ongoing textual analysis by Thouvenot; and "Le vocabulaire du don en Nahuatl," another mainly linguistic study of several related Nahuatl verbs by DeHouve. Part 2, "Les Aztèques, Histoire et civilisation" contains: "Lienzos, cartes et plans" by Galaza; "Codex Telleriano-Remensis 25–28: Essai d'interprétation" by Vollemaere; "La Cronica X: algunas consideraciones mas" by Romero Galván; "La Brevisima Relación de Bartolomé de las Casas y La Historia de las Indias de Nueva España de Fray Diego Durán" by Vázquez Chamorro; "Premiers chroniqueurs Acolhuas" by Lesbre; "The Aztec Process of Expansion: Methods and Motivations" by Davies; "Repeticiones de nombres personales entre los miembros de la familia real azteca" by Van Zantwijk; "Les réformes politiques de Motecuhzoma II" by Graulich; "Sur quelques aspects mathématiques des computs meso-américains" by Eisinger; "L'Éducation de jeunes dans la société Aztèque selon les Huehuetlatolli—'témoignages de l'ancieene parole'" by Leander de Silva; "Ethno-ornithologie de l'Aigle royal (aguila chrysaetos canadensis) au sein de la civilisation Aztèque" by Gilonne; and "Referencias sobre Telmelican y Santiago Zapotitlan en documentos coloniales [Sierra Madre del Sur de Guerrero]" by Vega Sosa. Finally Pt. 3, entitled "Religion et Cosmologie," includes: "El agua: universo de significaciones y realidades en Mesoamérica" by León-Portilla; "En torno a la cosmovisión mexica: viejas ideas, nuevas hipótesis" by Alcina Franch; "Three Fragmentary Aztec Monuments Dedicated to the Solar Cult: Iconographic Interpretations" by Nicholson; "War and Sacrifice in Mexica State Sculpture" by Baquedano and James; "Mexico's Persistent Quechquemitl: From Ritual Attire to Village Apparel" by Rieff Anawalt; "The Sacrifice of Nanahuatzin: The Coroner's Report and Mesoamerican Iconography" by McKeever-Furst; "La représentation des rituels dans le Tonalamatl du Codex Borbonicus" by Quiñones Keber; "Xipe Totec: Who Was He, Where did He Come From?" by Heyden; "Nouvelles considérations sur 'Tlaloc'" by Durand-Forest; "Feu et lumières dans le Mexique précolombien" by Köhler; and "Jours de fête au quotidien" by Fournier. For review of vol. 1, see item **548.**

550 Motolinía, Toribio. Memoriales: libro de oro (MS JGI 31). Edición crítica, introducción, notas y apéndice de Nancy Joe Dyer. México: El Colegio de México, Centro de Estudios Lingüísticos y Literarios, 1996. 588 p.: bibl., ill. (Biblioteca novohispana; 3)

Important introduction analyzes the writings of Motolinia that comprise his *Memoriales* (1527–49), contained within the Libro de Oro (JGI 31, Benson Latin American Collection, Univ. of Texas, Austin). Examines the audience, European and indigenous sources, style, languages employed (Spanish, Latin, Nahuatl), and history of the manuscript. Earlier Spanish-language editions of the *Memoriales* are out of print; this one offers a transcription closer to the original.

551 Native traditions in the postconquest world: a symposium at Dumbarton Oaks, 2nd through 4th October 1992. Edited by Elizabeth Hill Boone and Tom Cummins. Washington, D.C.: Dumbarton Oaks, 1998. 487 p.: bibl., ill., index.

Important anthology marking, but not celebrating, the Columbian Quincentenary, directing attention to indigenous cultural responses to the Spanish intrusion in Mexico and Peru, utilizing as much as possible native documents and sources, and exploring mentalities. While we can benefit from the analysis and methodology in all contributions to this volume, items certain to interest Mesoamericanists include: Hill Boone, "Introduction," for the volume's orientation; Laiou, "The Many Faces of Medieval Colonization," for background, analysis of colonization as process, and its multiple forms; Lockhart, "Three Experiences of Culture Contact: Nahua, Maya, and Quechua," for special attention to language change as a reflection of broader cultural evolution in key areas; Hill Boone, "Pictorial Documents and Visual Thinking in Postconquest Mexico," for an examination of the endurance of these forms in 16th-century Nahua culture; Wood, "The Social vs. Legal Context of Nahuatl Títulos," for an examination of community self-representation in native manuscripts and pictorials in the eighteenth century; Gillespie, "The Triple Alliance: A Postconquest Tradition," for an explanation of the colonial manipulation of the symbolic triadic organization for a new historical tradition; Burkhart, "Pious Performances: Christian Pageantry and Native Identity in Early Colonial Mexico," for a study of the Nahuas' reshaping of Christian ritual; Karttunen, "Indigenous Writing as a Vehicle of Postconquest Continuity and Change in Mesoamerica," for an examination of Nahua and Maya writing traditions into the present, including evidence of women's lesser but possibly significant role; and, Cummins, "Native Traditions in the Postconquest World: Commentary," for concluding reflections on the interrelated elements of text (written, performative, visual, auratic, and so on), image, discourse, language, traditions, identity, and colonialism.

552 Nebel, Richard. Santa María Tonantzin, Virgen de Guadalupe: continuidad y transformación religiosa en México. México: Fondo de Cultura Económica, 1995. 441 p.: bibl., ill., indexes. (Sección de obras de historia)

Much appreciated Spanish translation of Nebel's fine study of the evolving cult of the Virgin of Guadalupe, originally published in 1992 as *Santa María Tonantzin, Virgen de Guadalupe: religiöse Kontinuitat un Transformation in Mexiko* (see HLAS 54:1138). This more accessible version offers an excellent complement to Stafford Poole's *Our Lady of Guadalupe* and includes a facsimile, translation, and analysis of the Nahuatl *Nican mopohua* account.

Nutini, Hugo G. Mesoamerican community organization: preliminary remarks. See HLAS 57:759.

553 Odena Güemes, Lina. La cuestión chichimeca: planteamiento y fuentes de estudio. (*Anuario/INAH*, 1, 1995, p. 15–42, bibl., ill., map)

Proposes a more exacting study of the peoples generally labeled "chichimeca," both in terms of their role as migrants and settlers in central Mesoamerica and with respect to the true nature of indigenous culture in the so-called "Gran Chichimeca." In this preliminary study, the most significant available ethnohistorical sources are discussed and a scheme of analysis is suggested.

554 Ouweneel, Arij. From *tlahtocayotl* to *gobernadoryotl*: a critical examination of indigenous rule in 18th-century central Mexico. (*Am. Ethnol.*, 22:4, Nov. 1995, p. 756–785, bibl., maps)

Excellent research piece in which the author investigates *Gobernadoryotl* as an adaptive, evolutionary expression of the same kind of sociopolitical power once enjoyed by preconquest lords. Also includes a wealth of information about the relationships of *caciques* and *cacicazgos* to this system. For ethnologist's comment, see HLAS 57:760.

555 Ouweneel, Arij. El pasado seguía en Antonio Pérez: envidias de testamentos de un indígena mexicano. (*Colon. Lat. Am. Rev.*, 6:1, June 1997, p. 71–96)

Significant new study of Pérez's allegedly idolatrous activities in central New Spain, emphasizing their political dimensions. Adds many important new insights into an episode studied earlier by such scholars as Serge Gruzinski.

556 Pardo, Osvaldo F. Bárbaros y mudos: comunicación verbal y gestual en la confesión de los nahuas. (*Colon. Lat. Am. Rev.*, 5:1, 1996, p. 25–53)

Sophisticated study of the barriers to verbal communication in the 16th century between clergy and indigenous people in the sacrament of confession, a problem "solved" by the acceptance of nonverbal communication as a permissible mode of expression.

557 Paz, Josef. The vicissitude of the alter ego animal in Mesoamerica: an ethnohistorical reconstruction of tonalism. (*An-*

thropos/Freiburg, 90:4/6, 1995, p. 445–465, bibl.)

Thoughtful article proposes that tonalism and nagualism were preserved in popular religious practices in central Mesoamerica, but were suppressed in Aztec imperial religious ideology because they were considered to be too "democratic," allowing everyone access to the sacred without resort to elite religious specialists.

558 **Piho, Virve.** Iztapalapan durante la Conquista. México: Instituto Nacional de Antropología e Historia, 1996. 267 p.: bibl., ill. (2 folded), maps. (Col. científica; 319. Serie Historia/Instituto Nacional de Antropología e Historia)

Posthumous publication of this carefully researched and detailed investigation into the Spanish conquest as seen from Iztapalapan, site of fierce resistance which turned to alliance with the invaders. Includes a study of glyphs in an effort to clarify the derivation of the toponym, still a matter of debate. Also gives considerable attention to maps and routes.

559 **Porro, Antonio.** O messianismo Maya no período colonial. São Paulo, Brazil: FFLCH-USP, 1991. 284 p.: bibl., ill., maps. (Antropologia; 17)

A fascinating little collection of excerpts from primary sources relating to Guatemala, the Yucatán, and Chiapas, from the 16th-18th centuries, illustrating the author's hypothesis of a recurring Maya messianic or millenarian response to the Spanish invasion and occupation.

560 **Quezada, Noemí.** Congregaciones de indios y grupos étnicos: el caso del Valle de Toluca y zonas aledañas. (*Rev. Complut. Hist. Am.*, 22, 1995, p. 141–165, bibl., map, table)

Study of the *congregación* process in this important center of colonial indigenous society, at its best when it ties specific trajectories of congregation and indigenous responses to regionalized cultural and ecological factors.

561 **Quezada, Sergio.** Pueblos y caciques yucatecos, 1550–1580. México: Colegio de México, Centro de Estudios Históricos, 1993. 228 p.: bibl., ill., index, maps.

Impressive, revised doctoral dissertation that explores the impact of the Spanish presence on indigenous Yucatecan political and territorial institutions. Revisits known primary source material but with new questions and interpretations, and with the intention of defining more precisely the *batab, batabil, halach uinic, tzucub,* and *cuchcabal.* Tracks their evolution into colonial entities, such as *caciques, pueblos, cacicazgos,* and provinces through a critical period of change.

562 **Quiñones Keber, Eloise.** Creating the cosmos: the myth of the four suns in the Codex Vaticanus A. pt. 2. (*Lat. Am. Indian Lit. J.*, 12:2, Fall 1996, p. 192–212)

Straightforward comparative interpretation of the "Myth of the Four Suns," highlighting its unique aspects as narrated in this particular codex, which the author believes can be explained by linking the document's origin to the Puebla region. For comment on part one of this study, see item **563**.

563 **Quiñones Keber, Eloise.** Painting the Nahua universe: cosmology and cosmogony in the Codex Vaticanus A. pt. 1, Introduction and translation. (*Lat. Am. Indian Lit. J.*, 11:2, 1995, p. 183–205)

Discussion of the images and commentary presented on folios 1v-7r of this postconquest codex, closely related to (but not identical to) the Codex Telleriano-Remensis. A translation of extensive glosses originally added in Italian is included; the document was prepared for an Italian patron, possibly by or on behalf of the Mexican Dominican Pedro de los Ríos. Author continues her analysis in item **562**.

564 **Radding Murrieta, Cynthia.** Entre el desierto y la sierra: las naciones o'odham y tegüima de Sonora, 1530–1840. México: CIESAS; INI, 1995. 213 p.: appendix, bibl. (Historia de los pueblos indígenas de México)

Excellent study of the indigenous peoples of what is now called Sonora, concentrating on the effects of the waves of military, Jesuit, and civil intrusions. Indigenous responses, ranging from mediated acceptance as a form of cultural preservation, to recourse to legal channels, to outright rebellion and resistance assume major importance in the ongoing discussion. Includes a useful documentary appendix.

565 **Radding Murrieta, Cynthia.** Wandering peoples: colonialism, ethnic spaces, and ecological frontiers in northwestern Mexico, 1700–1850. Durham, N.C.: Duke Univ. Press, 1997. 424 p.: bibl., ill., index, maps. (Latin America otherwise)

Impressively researched social-ecological and ethnohistorical study of Sonora, Mexico, which includes some material on prehispanic and early colonial times, although the principal thrust is late and attention is directed to the emergence of an internally differentiated peasant class. Highlights issues of ethnicity, community, gender, production, and diverse responses to colonial hegemony. For historian's comment, see item **1530.**

566 **Restall, Matthew.** Heirs to the hieroglyphs: indigenous writing in colonial Mesoamerica. (*Americas/Franciscans*, 54:2, Oct. 1997, p. 239–267, tables)

Informative discussion of the evolution of indigenous written expression, paying attention to precontact forms and precedents as well as to the postcontact situation. Author's emphasis on Mixtec and Yucatec Mayan records, as well as the better studied Nahuatl genres, is a significant contribution.

567 **Restall, Matthew.** The Maya world: Yucatec culture and society, 1550–1850. Stanford, Calif.: Stanford Univ. Press, 1997. 455 p.: bibl., ill., index, maps.

Sophisticated study resting on a foundation of the analysis of postcontact indigenous language documentation ranging from notarial records to primordial titles. Author is interested in charting the persistence and evolution after the Spanish invasion of the Maya *cahob*, or self-governing communities, as well as the *chibal*, or extended family lineage. He does so with skill and aplomb, producing a major work of ethnohistorical analysis.

568 **Revueltas, Eugenia.** Texto y representación: el teatro misionero y la interculturalidad. Comentario por Evodio Escalante. (*in* Tradición e identidad en la cultura mexicana. Zamora, Mexico: El Colegio de Michoacán; Consejo Nacional de Ciencia y Tecnología (CONACYT), 1995, p. 357–377)

Examines religious theater of the first half of the 16th century, especially with regard to the differences between texts and performances, and the colonial adaptations that

the friars had to make to the medieval European Christian traditions. A commentary by Evodio Escalante follows, with additional references to Andrés de Olmos and his theatrical work, *Juicio final.*

569 **Reyes García, Cayetano.** El altepetl y la reproducción de la cultura Náhua en la época colonial. Comentario por Ethelia Ruiz Medrano. (*in* Tradición e identidad en la cultura mexicana. Zamora, Mexico: El Colegio de Michoacán; Consejo Nacional de Ciencia y Tecnología (CONACYT), 1995, p. 271–304, bibl.)

Examines ways in which the Nahuas were able to persist as a distinct people. In author's view, the surviving *altepetl* were the vessels through which the Nahuas were able to preserve, adapt or, in other words, reproduce the mundane aspects of daily life that are the essential components of culture. The commentary makes additional remarks about recent scholarship based on Nahuatl-language records.

570 **Rieff Anawalt, Patricia.** Aztec knotted and netted capes: colonial interpretations vs. indigenous primary data. (*Anc. Mesoam.*, 7:2, Fall 1996, p. 187–206, bibl., ill., photos, tables)

Unravels the tangled and confused skein of references to types of capes worn by Aztec notables. Probing far beyond standard Spanish sources to examine textual, archeological, and pictorial evidence from indigenous records, author is able to confirm the existence of two important forms—the tie-died blue cape of the emperors and the netted cape worn mainly by lesser, though still prominent, figures—and links them to iconographic assertions of status, descent, and divine patronage.

571 **Rincón Mautner, Carlos.** The 1580 Plan Topographique de Santa María Ixcatlan, Oaxaca: a description and commentary. (*Lat. Am. Indian Lit. J.*, 12:1, Spring 1996, p. 43–66)

Informative study of this pictographic document from an Ixcatec-speaking community glossed in Spanish and Nahuatl, including boundary descriptions, information on the history of founding lineages, and the ancestral ownership of land. Commentary examines the Plan in light of the debilitating effects of encomienda labor in gold mining, demographic decline, and indigenous efforts to resettle as many of their traditional lands as possible in the later-16th century.

572 Rincón Mautner, Carlos. The notes and sketch of Lienzo Seler 1 or Mapa de Santa María Ixcatlan, Oaxaca, Mexico: description and commentary. (*Lat. Am. Indian Lit. J.*, 12:2, Fall 1996, p. 146–177)

More than just a descriptive piece, the author sets in a firm ethnohistorical context what can be discerned about the by now lost original from a brief study carried out by Walter Lehmann in 1905. A transcription and translation of Lehmann's notes is included.

573 Rodríguez-Shadow, María and Robert Dennis Shadow. Mujer, religión y muerte en el pensamiento nahua prehispánico. (*in* Primer anuario de la dirección de etnología y antropología social de INAH. México: Instituto Nacional de Antología e Historia, 1995, p. 43–49, bibl.)

Thought-provoking though brief, this worthy article considers the implications of Nahua beliefs associated with the fate of women dying during childbirth. Maintains that gender-specific religious ideology served to socialize women, while at the same time, it upheld a growing privileging of the male over the female in a militaristic society.

574 Román Gutiérrez, José Francisco. Los Chichimecas: notas sobre cacería y nomadismo. (*in* Tradición e identidad en la cultura mexicana. Zamora, Mexico: El Colegio de Michoacán; Consejo Nacional de Ciencia y Tecnología (CONACYT), 1995, p. 89–111, bibl.)

This careful reading of 16th-century Spanish chronicles reveals the penetration of ideas and practices from more sedentary groups and their adaptation to hunting and nomadic life. Discusses the origin of the term Chichimeca. [E. Couturier]

575 Román Gutiérrez, José Francisco. Los indígenas de Juchipila alrededor de 1540–1547. (*Estud. Jalisc.*, 23, feb. 1996, p. 21–29)

Highlights the role of the Caxcanes of Juchipila and Zacatecas peoples in the Mixtón War in Nueva Galicia, suggesting that, despite differences in sociopolitical organization, these groups shared some religious beliefs and an oppositional attitude toward the Spanish presence. Also argues that Caxcan

caciques played a fundamental role that has been overshadowed by Las Casas' defense of Don Francisco Tenamaztle of Nochistlán.

576 Romero Frizzi, María de los Angeles. Las batallas y las ideas: la conquista de Oaxaca, 1519–1560. (*Anuario/INAH*, 1, 1995, p. 69–87, bibl.)

A rethinking of indigenous responses, such as alliance and rebellion, to the Spanish invasion of Oaxaca, utilizing records in Spanish. Also considers the intriguing case of the Zapotecs' possible decoration and veneration of a Spaniard's skull.

577 Romero Frizzi, María de los Angeles. El sol y la cruz: los pueblos indios de Oaxaca colonial. Tlalpan, Mexico: CIESAS; Col. Alpes, Mexico: INI, 1996. 291 p.: appendix, bibl., ill. (some col.), maps (some col.). (Historia de los pueblos indígenas de México)

A solid contribution to an impressive series that recognizes indigenous agency in Mexican colonial history. Covers Oaxaca from the eve of the Spanish invasion through the late-18th century, encompassing origins, social organization, the prolonged conquest period, tribute rearrangements, evangelization, rebellions, history (re)writing, negotiated relationships with Spanish power, economic change, social and cultural change, more rebellion, land struggles, and other themes. Among other records worthy of note in the documentary appendix are the undated *títulos* of four pueblos in the Sierra Zapoteca and a bill of sale in Zapotec, dated 1703.

578 Roth Seneff, Andrew. Etnocentrismo narrativo y la *Historia Tolteca Chichimeca.* (*Estud. Cult. Náhuatl*, 24, 1994, p. 125–137, bibl.)

Offering a new interpretation of the apparent ethnocentrism of the *Historia*, the author sees in the account powerful evidence for a redefinition of the basis of ruling legitimacy in precontact (and by extension postconquest) Cuauhtinchan.

579 Ruiz Medrano, Carlos Rubén. Rebeliones indígenas en la época colonial: el tumulto indígena de Papantla de 1767. (*Mesoamérica/Plumsock*, 17:32, 1996 p. 339–353)

Excellent analysis of rioting in this Totonac community. Probes the causes and underlying intent of the indigenous uprising.

Details of the quality and pressures of daily life in the community are revealed.

580 Ruvalcaba Mercado, Jesús. Vacas, mulas, azúcar y café: los efectos de su introducción en la Huasteca, México. (*Rev. Esp. Antropol. Am.*, 26, 1996, p. 121–141, bibl.)

Straightforward and informative study of the tempo and sociocultural impact of the introduction of new crops, such as sugar cane and livestock into the Huasteca. In the last pages of the article the author moves to a consideration of coffee agriculture and peasant resistance in the 19th and 20th centuries.

581 Ruz, Mario Humberto. *Desfiguro de naturaleza:* los nobles de Ocozocuautla y los laboríos del Valle de Xiquipilas en 1741. (*An. Antropol.*, 29, 1992, p. 397–436, graphs, map)

Excellent study of social relations in Zoque communities of 18th-century Chiapas, uncovering a wealth of valuable, multigenerational genealogical information. In addition, the author ably surveys strategies used to gain freedom from indigenous tribute obligations, including assertions of noble social status, movement to surrounding estates, or marriage to non-indigenous people, a process referred to as *desfiguro de naturaleza*.

582 Ruz, Mario Humberto. Un rostro encubierto: los indios del Tabasco colonial. México: Ciesas; INI, 1994. 352 p.: bibl., ill. (some col.). (Historia de los pueblos indígenas de México)

Excellent overview of a lesser studied region, utilizing broad archival resources and encompassing the period from the eve of the Spanish conquest through the era of Independence. Documentary appendices include pieces from the 16th, 17th, 18th, and 19th centuries.

583 Sahagún, Bernardino de. Primeros memoriales. Facsim. ed. Norman: Univ. of Oklahoma Press; Madrid: Patrimonio Nacional and the Real Academia de la Historia, 1993. 1 v. (unpaged): ill. (some col.). (The civilization of the American Indian series; v. 200, pt. 1)

Beautiful glossy color facsimile of this early and crucial manifestation of Sahagún's work with indigenous informants recording information about precontact society and culture. See also item **461.**

584 Salinas Flores, Oscar. Tecnología y diseño en el México prehispánico. México: Facultad de Arquitectura, Centro de Investigaciones de Diseño Industrial, UNAM, 1995. 223 p.: bibl., ill., maps. (Col. Arquitectura ; 9)

Interesting synthesis draws together important topics, combining succinct commentary with excellent illustrations, many drawn from codices. [J. Britton]

585 Sampson, Elisa and **Vera Tudela.** Fashioning a *cacique* nun: from saints' lives to Indian lives. (*Gend. Hist.*, 9:2, Aug. 1997, p. 171–200)

Rooted in archival research and theoretically complex, this essay examines ecclesiastical testimony on issues of sexuality and race in response to an 18th-century proposal to found a convent in Mexico City for elite indigenous women. Gives attention to policy and practice as they impacted indigenous women.

586 Santabella, Sylvia. *Nican Motecpana:* Nahuatl miracles of the Virgin of Guadalupe. (*Lat. Am. Indian Lit. J.*, 11:1, Spring 1995, p. 34–54)

Discusses the 17th-century corpus of Guadalupan texts as propaganda designed to spread the influence of the Virgin's cult, as well as discussing the probable origins of the 1649 Nahuatl text of *Huei Tlamahuicoltica*. As the title suggests, author makes a contribution here by highlighting the less well-studied depiction of miracles in the second section of that document, and provides a transcription and English translation of miracles one, eight, and eleven.

587 Schmid, Catherine and **Mary Swift.** Filling in the gaps: a Nahuatl will and its translation. (*Lat. Am. Indian Lit. J.*, 11:1, Spring 1995, p. 55–70)

Linguistic, orthographic study of a will dating from 1714. The content of the will, part of the Univ. of Texas' Benson Latin American Collection, is of potential use to ethnohistorians.

588 Schöndube, Otto. El pasado de tres pueblos: Tamazula, Tuxpan y Zapotlán. Guadalajara, Mexico: Univ. de

Guadalajara, Dirección General Académica, 1994. 518 p.: bibl., ill., maps. (Libros de tiempos de ciencia; 7)

Principally an archeological study but with added information from ethnohistorical sources. Illuminates little-known sites in modern Jalisco, in the northwestern-most corner of the Tarascan dominion and a regional source for silver, which probably provided the incentive for early Spanish penetration. Substantiates some cultural links with the Basin of Mexico.

589   Schwaller, John F. Small collections of Nahuatl manuscripts in the United States. (*Estud. Cult. Náhuatl*, 25, 1995, p. 377–416)

Another installment in this author's series of essential guides to repositories holding Nahuatl documents. Included here: the Thomas Gilgrease Museum of Tulsa, Oklahoma; The William L. Clements Library of the Univ. of Michigan; The Univ. of New Mexico; Princeton Univ. Library; Univ. Research Library, Dept. of Special Collections, Univ. of California, Los Angeles; the Huntington Library; the Sons of the Republic of Texas Collection of the Univ. of Texas, San Antonio; listings from the Library of Congress Manuscript Division; the Museum of Natural History/Smithsonian Museum; the Huntington Free Library/Library of the Museum of the American Indian; and the Hispanic Society of America.

590   Sepúlveda y Herrera, María Teresa. Anales mexicanos. Puebla, Tepeaca, Cholula. Colección antigua 229. México: Instituto Nacional de Antropología e Historia, 1995. 106 p.: bibl., ill., map. (Fuentes)

Critical edition of previously unpublished 1847 copy of Nahuatl-language annals (1524–1634) originally collected by Guillermo Dupaix. A transcription and Spanish translation of the document is followed by a full facsimile, and the book ends with a transcription of Faustino Galicia Chimalpoca's version (in Spanish) of the *Anales de Tepeaca* (1528–1634).

591   Shadow, Robert D. and **María Rodríguez-Shadow.** Aztec slavery: a historical panorama of anthropological perspectives. (*in* Amerikaner wider Willen: Beiträge zur Sklaverei in Lateinamerika und ihren folgen. Herausgegeben von Rüdiger

Zoller. Frankfurt: Vervuert Verlag, 1994, p. 161–173)

Critically reviews 20th-century scholarship on prehispanic Aztec slavery or *tlacoliztli*, concluding with an enumeration of slavery's core features as drawn from the most convincing research.

592   Sharer, Robert J. The ancient Maya. 5th ed. Stanford, Calif.: Stanford Univ. Press, 1994. 924 p.: bibl., ill., index.

Another fine synthesis and update on Mayan studies, now one-fourth longer than the previous edition, owing to the continuing proliferation of research and excavations and the author's reorganization and revisions of the opus, including, for example, a much expanded discussion of cultural history and new material on language and writing. For archeologist's comment, see *HLAS 57:131*.

593   Sharer, Robert J. Daily life in Maya civilization. Westport, Conn.: Greenwood Press, 1996. 249 p.: bibl., ill., index, map. (The Greenwood Press "Daily life through history" series, 1080–4749)

More accessible for the nonspecialist than *The Ancient Maya*, yet written by the same author and drawing from the same recent research in archeology, ethnohistory, ethnography, epigraphy, and other fields. Constructs a chronological overview from the archaic through the late postclassic periods, including narrations about successive rulers and their activities in key sites. Daily life material lodges more in the subsequent chapters on economy, society, government, religion, writing and calendars, and arts and crafts.

594   Šprajc, Ivan. Venus, lluvia y maíz: simbolismo y astronomía en la cosmovisión mesoamericana. México: Instituto Nacional de Antropología e Historia, 1996. 176 p.: bibl., ill. (Serie Arqueología. Col. científica ; 318)

Revised Master's thesis convincingly broadens the base of substantiation for the conceptual complex identified by other scholars, associating rain, maize, and the planet Venus. Explores cultures across Mesoamerica and over time, probing astronomical, ethnohistorical, and ethnographic information to clarify the meaning of the complex.

595 Taylor, William B. Magistrates of the sacred: priests and parishioners in eighteenth-century Mexico. Stanford, Calif.: Stanford Univ. Press, 1996. 882 p.: bibl., ill., index, maps.

While not fundamentally an ethnohistorical study, in this impressively detailed investigation into the lives and attitudes of late-colonial Mexican secular clergy, author also deftly reveals the nature of late-colonial, village-level religious devotion, *cofradías*, lay officials, town government, and the causes of conflicts between villagers and their *curas*. For colonial historian's comment, see item **1201.**

596 Temas mesoamericanos. Coordinación de Sonia Lombardo y Enrique Nalda. México: Instituto Nacional de Antropología e Historia; Dirección General de Publicaciones del Consejo Nacional para la Cultura y las Artes, 1996. 509 p.: bibl., ill., maps. (Col. Obra diversa)

Diverse anthology treating prehispanic themes, including: agriculture, quotidian technology, Tarascan metallurgy, lowland Maya non-market exchange, 16th-century militarism, Triple Alliance organization and structure, Tenochca tribute organization, the northern frontier, the trans-Tarascan zone, central Mexican and highland Maya interaction, sculpture, calendars, and cosmovision. Another chapter of special worth for ethnohistorians, "El registro de la historia," offers a brief overview of the historical record in its various forms across time and space, with special attention to epigraphy and codices.

597 Tena, Rafael. La religión mexica. México: Instituto Nacional de Antropología e Historia, 1993. 99 p.: appendix, ill. (Col. Divulgación)

Brief overview, ideal for Spanish-speaking undergraduates, of Mexica religion as officially professed in the capital city just prior to European contact. Drawing from ethnohistorical sources, one of the principal chapters, an appendix, and a series of illustrations all aim to identify deities.

598 Tlatelolco a través de los tiempos: 50 años después, 1944–1994. v. 2, Etnohistoria. México: Instituto Nacional de Antropología e Historia, 1996. 1 v.: bibl., ill. (Etnohistoria. Arqueología)

Second volume in a series comprised of reissues of the following articles: "Migraciones de los mexica," by Acosta Saignes, "Algunas notas sobre organización social de los tlatelolca," by A. Espejo y A. Monzón, "La fecha de la conquista de Tlatelolco por Tenochtitlan," by Caso, and López Sarrelangue's "Los tributos de la parcialidad de Santiago Tlatelolco," the latter a careful, localized study of the operation of the colonial tribute. All of the articles deserve the attention of modern ethnohistorians.

599 Tschohl, Peter. Der Pochtekenbericht in Sahagúns *Historia general:* zwischen altaztekischer Wirklichkeit, Mitteilung in Tlatelolco, Sahagúnscher Redigierung und ethnohistorischer Auslegung. Berlin: Gebr. Mann, 1998. 364 p.: bibl., ill., maps. (Indiana. Beiheft; 14)

In a highly specialized monograph, Tschohl presents methodology and analyses of Sahagún's complex report on the Aztec *pochteca,* or traveling merchants, of Tlatelolco. Points out pitfalls of previously published interpretations and translations. Tschohl, who spent decades in ethnohistorical research, provides a wealth of detailed descriptions of heroic campaigns, administrative functions, and ritual culture of the commercial aristocracy of the *pochteca.* [C.K. Converse]

600 Universitätsbibliothek Eichstätt (Germany). Die Bücher der Maya, Mixteken und Azteken: die Schrift und ihre Funktion in vorspanischen und kolonialen Codices; Katalog. Edited by Carmen Arellano Hoffmann and Peer Schmidt. Frankfurt am Main, Germany: Vervuert, 1998. 535 p.: bibl., ill. (some col.), index, maps. (Schriften der Universitätsbibliothek Eichstätt, 0724–6579; 34)

With this catalog of facsimiles of codices preserved at Catholic University, Eichstätt, 12 experts in precolumbian ethnohistory, cultural geography, and indigenous languages provide introduction to precolumbian and early colonial indigenous "communications technology." Editors emphasize significance of nonglossographic systems, hieroglyphs, pictographs, and Andean notation systems such as *tocapu* and *quipu.* Well-written articles are documented and include bibliographies. [C.K. Converse]

601 Vargas Pacheco, Ernesto. Síntesis de la historia prehispánica de los mayas chontales de Tabasco-Campeche. (*Am. Indíg.*, 54:1/2, enero/junio 1994, p. 15–61, bibl., maps, photos)

Systematic discussion of the nature and evolution of Chontal culture to the time of the Spanish invasion. Employs a range of ethnohistorical sources, including *Relaciones Geográficas* and major Spanish-era accounts.

602 Velasco Lozano, Ana María Luisa. La alimentación entre los mexicas. (*Anuario/INAH*, 1, 1995, p. 59–68, bibl.)

Extracts information from the writing of Sahagún and Durán about the foods of the postclassic Mexica, listing the flora and fauna of land and water, emphasizing their variety and nutritive value and people's rational use of natural resources.

603 Vos, Jan de. Vivir en frontera: la experiencia de los indios de Chiapas. Tlalpan, Mexico: Centro de Investigaciones y Estudios Superiores en Antropología Social, 1994. 313 p.: appendix, bibl., ill. (some col.), maps. (Historia de los pueblos indígenas de México)

An overview of the history of the indigenous peoples of Chiapas from just prior to the Spanish invasion through the early-20th century. Makes excellent use of primary sources and includes a large appendix with Spanish-language documents and oral tradition spanning 1527–1986.

604 Weigand, Phil C. and **Acelia García de Weigand.** Un legado prehispánico del municipio de Magdalena. (*Estud. Jalisc.*, 29, agosto 1997, p. 5–15, ill.)

Reconstruction based on existing archeological remains and the historical record of Xochitepec, stronghold of indigenous resistance leader Guaxícar, until its capture by Spanish forces in 1542. Details of Guaxícar's struggle against the Spanish invasion of New Galicia are included.

605 Weigand, Phil C. and **Acelia García de Weigand.** Los orígenes de los caxcanes y su relación con la guerra de los nayaritas: una hipótesis. Zapopan, Mexico: El Colegio de Jalisco, 1995. 94 p.: bibl., ill., maps. (Ensayos jaliscienses)

Painstaking study of the origins of the Caxcanes, their possible relations with Chalchihuite culture, and their participation in the Mixtón War and later postconquest struggles. Work offers important new insights and is solidly based on archeological and ethnohistorical sources.

606 Yoneda, Keiko. Migraciones y conquistas: descifre global del mapa de Cuauhtinchan núm. 3. México: Instituto Nacional de Antropología e Historía, 1996. 476 p.: bibl., ill., maps. (Colección Científica; 289. Serie Etnohistoria)

A careful deciphering of one of a series of 16th-century pictographic manuscripts from Cuauhtinchan, Puebla, with an analysis of the historiographical tradition of the document (covering events from the 12th-16th centuries) and its place in the broader category of Mesoamerican writing systems. Where possible, translates pictographical material into Nahuatl expressions with assistance from the related *Historia tolteca chichimeca*.

607 Zavala, Silvio Arturo. El servicio personal de los indios en la Nueva España, 1636–1699. v. 6, 1636–1699. v. 7, 1700–1821. México: Colegio de México, Centro de Estudios Históricos; Colegio Nacional, 1994–1995. 2 v.

Two more volumes of Zavala's extremely valuable work, organized topically as in the past and offering commentaries, digests, and descriptions of archival documentation, other primary sources, and pertinent secondary works. Each volume also includes documentary appendices, such as material related to the construction of Mexico City's cathedral (vol. VI, appendix C) and digests of documents held in the Municipal Archive of Saltillo and the Archivo del Ayuntamiento de Monterrey (vol. VII, appendix B). With these volumes, Zavala has extended his work to the point of Independence, and provided investigators in many specific specialties with a wonderful resource.

608 Zeitlin, Judith F. Historia política del sur del Istmo de Tehuantepec durante la época colonial. (*Cuad. Sur/Oaxaca*, 3:6/7, enero/agosto 1994, p. 25–45, bibl., photos)

Enlightening study of the manner in which a sense of community survived in postconquest Tehuantepec, and the roles played by its *caciques* as heads and symbols of the corporate group. Some discussion of uprisings staged in 1660 and 1715.

South America

SUSAN E. RAMÍREZ, *Professor of History, DePaul University*

THE WORK OF HISTORIANS of indigenous groups in the Americas included in *HLAS 58* prompts three suggestions for future research in the field. First, more primary sources should be published, either in the text or in an appendix (items **646, 672, 673, 684, 686,** and **699**). In that regard, the exemplary effort in this chapter is the series of volumes published by Tovar Pinzón of 16th-century accounts (*relaciones* and Visitas) of Colombia (item **2179**). Volume 2, on the Caribbean provinces of Santa Marta and Cartagena, should be used as a model (item **713**). Some accounts contain European observations on the political, economic, social, and, occasionally, religious organization of the indigenous peoples (items **650, 668, 693,** and **729**) Such sources also tell a great deal about the worldview of the European writers and the nature of the encounters. Encomienda grants, tribute lists (item **666**), letters (items **614, 631, 656, 703,** and **727**) court cases, investigations (item **623**), and records of idolatry campaigns (item **651**) also are welcome. Publication increases availability for those who cannot easily gain access to primary documents.

Second, analysis of ethnic groups should not always be defined by modern geographical borders. Many of the peoples whom historians seek to describe and understand placed less emphasis on territorial demarcations than on kinship and alliance-based boundaries. The Inca empire, for example, relied on social and hegemonical frontiers rather than clearly delineated physical borders. By studying a group within modern political boundaries, historical societies become segmented in an artificial manner. The historical societies studied should themselves inform us as to how they defined the geographic limits of their own groups (items **652, 696, 707, 714, 731,** and **745**).

Third, in certain cases there is sufficient material to begin cross-cultural comparisons (item **640**) or, equally as important, to begin placing ethnic groups within a wider context (item **708**). Thus, there should be more studies about how the Pastos (item **626**) can be compared with the Chachapoyas (items **672** and **744**). Or, alternatively, how the Inca compared with the Maya. Or, more broadly, how the Inca empire (items **650, 677, 721, 740,** and **741**) and compared with and contrasted to other empires. Or, more universally, how an Andean chiefdomship, or *curacazgo*, compared with Asian and African chiefdomships. Such studies would attract broader readership to these research efforts and help bring into the mainstream questions, concerns, and conclusions of historians.

609 Almeida Reyes, Eduardo. Los yumbos de Rumicucho. Quito, Ecuador: Ediciones Abya-Yala, 1993. 33 p.: bibl., ill., maps.

Short study of the Yumbos of Rumicucho (Ecuador). Folklore and present-day ethnography serve as a source to understand the group's history. Uses census data from 1990s and chroniclers from as early as 1573. Text is accompanied by several photographs, drawings, and maps.

610 Amazônia: etnologia e história indígena. Organização de Eduardo Batalha Viveiros de Castro and Manuela Carneiro da Cunha. São Paulo: Núcleo de História Indígena e do Indigenismo: Fundação de Amparo à Pesquisa do Estado de São Paulo, 1993. 431 p.: bibl., ill., maps. (Série Estudos)

Presents 15 papers first presented in 1987 at a conference entitled, "Pesquisas recentes em etnologia e história indígena da amazonia." Organizes research in four units:

history; kinship; cosmology, war and names; and ecology. For ethnologist's comment, see *HLAS* 57:946.

611 Amazonian Indians from prehistory to the present: anthropological perspectives. Edited by Anna Roosevelt. Tucson: Univ. of Arizona Press, 1994. 438 p.: bibl., ill., index.

Compilation of articles on native inhabitants of the Amazon. Pt. 1 traces important ethnohistorical transition, a period of convulsive change in indigenous societies during European conquest and colonization from the 16th-20th century. During this time, many groups had to adapt to greatly changed circumstances, some forms of society disappeared, and new ones developed. Pt. 2 deals with subsistence, health, and reproductive strategies of Amazonian Indians; and impact of historical, political, and socioeconomic factors on their changing forms. Pt. 3 addresses influence of Amazonian peoples' changing ecological, economic and social contexts on ideology and organization.

612 Andrade Padilla, Claudio. La rebelión de Tomas Katari. Sucre, Bolivia: IPTK/ CIPRES, 1994. 287 p.: bibl., ill. (Serie Reflexión etnohistorica; 2)

Presents a document-based biography of Katari, the "Gran Kuraka," and an analysis of popular participation in the rebellion. Women, forgotten native leaders, and communities are protagonists in this story of resistance to Spanish colonial rule and repression.

613 Angles Varga, Víctor. Pacárectambo y el origen de los Incas. Cusco, Perú: V. Angles Vargas, 1995. 613 p.: bibl., ill. (some col.), indexes.

Analyzes origin myths and histories of Incas. Includes chapters on toponyms, *tambos* (inns), religion, calendars, celebrations, and important places such as Pacárectambo and Cuzco. Written for a popular audience.

614 Ares Queija, Berta. Tomás López Medel: trayectoria de un clérigo-oidor ante el Nuevo Mundo. Guadalajara, Spain: Institución Provincial de Cultura "Marqués de Santillana," 1993. 598 p.: bibl. (Virrey Mendoza; 4)

An important, serious, and well-documented biography of López Medel, a clergyman and royal official of the Spanish crown in the 16th century. Pt. I follows López

Medel from Spain to southern Mexico and Yucatan, and New Granada. His life serves as background for analysis and comprehension of his writings, including *De los tres elementos*, a natural history, and administrative reports. Pt. II publishes López Medel's letters, ordinances, instructions, and *De los tres elementos*.

615 Arruti, José Maurício Andion. Morte e vida do nordeste indígena: a emergência étnica como fenômeno histórico regional. *(Estud. Hist./Rio de Janeiro*, 15, jan./junho 1995, p. 57–94, bibl., table)

A long, well-documented study of the creation or invention of ethnic identity by indigenous groups in northeastern Brazil. Gives equal space to colonial and republican history. The struggle over land tenure and territory is a constant throughout and contributes to the establishment of a feeling of community.

616 Barragán Romano, Rossana *et al.* Guía de archivos para la historia de los pueblos indígenas en Bolivia. La Paz: Plural Editores: Ministerio de Desarrollo Humano, Secretaría Nacional de Asuntos Etnicos, Géneros y Generacionales, 1994. 116 p.: bibl., maps. (Historias)

Indispensable tool for research on indigenous peoples of the Audiencia of Charcas and the Republic of Bolivia. Because of the jurisdiction of Charcas, documents cover parts of Chile, Paraguay, Argentina, Uruguay and Brazil. Presents standard information, such as address, archive director, work conditions, and coverage, for both civil and ecclesiastical repositories.

617 Basso, Ellen B. The last cannibals: a South American oral history. Austin: Univ. of Texas Press, 1995. 335 p.: bibl., ill., index.

Third book in a series on Kalapalo narrative discourse uses nine stories collected between 1967–82 to interpret Kalapalo history. Primarily concerned with what these stories can tell us about a particular native history, how individuals are remembered, and meanings given to decisions and choices made in the past.

618 Bastidas Valecillos, Luis. La conquista española y la resistencia indígena en el imaginario del campesino merideño. *(Bol. Antropol./Mérida*, 29, sept./dic. 1993, p. 33–40, bibl.)

Attempts to characterize encounter between indigenous peoples and Europeans during an early phase of colonization in the area of Merida, Venezuela. Touches on passive resistance (flight and suicide) and European images of natives and their culture.

619 Bauer, Brian S. The development of the Inca state. Austin: Univ. of Texas Press, 1992. 201 p.: bibl., ill., index.

Innovative work challenges traditional views of Inca state development; suggests that incipient state growth in the Cuzco region was marked by the gradual consolidation and centralization of political authority in Cuzco, rather than resulting from a single military victory. Analyzes processes of political, economic, and social change, based on historical, ethnographic, and archeological data.

620 Bauer, Brian S. and **David S.P. Dearborn.** Astronomy and empire in the ancient Andes: the cultural origins of Inca sky watching. Austin: Univ. of Texas Press, 1995. 235 p.: bibl., ill., index, maps.

This joint project of an astrophysicist (Dearborn) and an archeologist (Bauer) was written for the use of astronomers, archeologists, and historians. Includes sufficient background information for readers with little or no knowledge of the Andes. Text sheds new light on relationship between Inca cosmology and social structure.

621 Bello Maldonado, Alvaro. La comisión radicadora de indígenas, su paso por la Araucanía, 1866–1929. (*Nütram/Santiago,* 9:34, 1993/94, p. 33–43)

The colonization of Araucania from 1866 to 1929, much like the experience in the Andes during the 16th and 17th centuries, resulted in the Mapuche losing their way of life. Despite resistance, they were reduced to nucleated villages (*reducciones*), and their lands were usurped and taken as part of a plan to "civilize" them.

622 Berg, Hans van den. La *Crónica continuada de la provincia de San Agustín del Perú* de Juan Teodoro Vázquez. (*Yachay/Cochabamba,* 12:22, 1995, p. 57–80, bibl., facsim.)

A catalog of topics covered in the chronicle by Vázquez (*HLAS 54:2423*). Among the most important topics are the lives of certain monastery members and the

missions. Ethnic groups mentioned are the Mojos, Tacanas, Apolistas, Lecos and Chiriguanos.

623 Berg, Hans van den. El *Memorial de las cosas del Pirú tocantes a los indios* del agustino Rodrigo de Loayza, 1586: crónica del fracaso de un proyecto colonial. (*Yachay/Cochabamba,* 12:22, 1995, p. 9–56, facsim., tables)

Pt. 1 summarizes the "Memorial" of Rodrigo de Loayza in outline form and pt. 2 transcribes it. Much of the argument foreshadows in a general way that of Phelipe Guaman Poma de Ayala's *Letter to the King.* More of these primary sources should be published to make them available to scholars who cannot visit the repositories.

624 Betanzos, Juan de. Narrative of the Incas. Translated and edited by Roland Hamilton and Dana Buchanan from the Palma de Mallorca manuscript. Austin: Univ. of Texas Press, 1996. 344 p.: bibl., ill., index, maps.

A chronicle that has been judged the "single most authentic document of its kind." Based on testimonies from descendants of Inca kings, who in the 1540s-50s still remembered the oral history and traditions of their ancestors. Beginning in 1551, Betanzos transcribed their memories and translated them from Quechua by order of Viceroy Antonio de Mendoza. Pt. I covers Inca history prior to the Spanish arrival and Pt. II deals with the conquest to 1557, mainly from the Inca point of view. For translation specialist's comment, see item **4670.**

625 Cajias, Martha and **Claudia Ranaboldo.** El manejo de la medicina casera en la provincia de Pacajes del Departamento de La Paz. (*in* Reunión Anual de Etnología, *6th, La Paz?, 1992.* Actas. La Paz: Museo Nacional de Etnografía y Folklore, 1993, t. 1, p. 37–49, tables)

A report on the use of household remedies among the peasantry of Pacajes, Bolivia. Provides lists of plants and other remedies for common ailments of both humans and livestock. Emphasizes important role of peasant women in collecting, storing, and using these remedies.

626   Calero, Luis Fernando. Chiefdoms under siege: Spain's rule and native adaptation in the southern Colombian Andes, 1535–1700. Albuquerque: Univ. of New Mexico Press, 1997. 233 p.: bibl., ill., index, maps.

A disappointing study of the Pastos, Quillacingas, and Abads in Southern Colombia between 1535–1700. Chapters focus on precolumbian inhabitants, ecology, Spanish land acquisition, colonial labor and tribute impositions, and the encomienda. Although based on several data-filled visitas, text is riddled with problems, ranging from unsupported interpretations to factual errors. For historian's comment, see item **2162.**

627   Calizaya Velásquez, Zenobio. Proceso etno-histórico de la región intersalar. (*in* Reunión Anual de Etnología, *6th, La Paz?, 1992*. Actas. La Paz: Museo Nacional de Etnografía y Folklore, 1993, t. 1, p. 25–36)

Brief essay on the peoples who lived in one zone of today's modern Bolivia. Mentions the Uros, Chipaya and the Puqinas. Half of the work describes archeological remains (*pukaras*, or fortifications) in the area. Lacks footnotes.

628   Camacho Sánchez, Miguel. Encuentro y síntesis de dos culturas. (*Bol. Hist. Antig.*, 786, julio/sept. 1994, p. 669–689)

More an essay than a traditional scholarly article, work cites well-known published primary sources, such as Columbus' diary, in reviewing contact between Europeans and native Americans from 1492-present.

629   Canahuire Ccama, J. Alfonso. Historia social de Ichu: un pueblo mitimae en altiplano peruano. Puno, Perú: Federación Folklórica Departamental de Puno, 1993. 58 p., 5 leaves: bibl., ill.

A mimeographed local social history of Ichu (Puno), identified as a mitimae town of the Andean high plain. Organizes story chronologically from pre-Incan to recent times. Includes descriptions of rituals and dances.

630   Cañedo-Argüelles Fábrega, Teresa. Las reducciones indígenas en el sur andino: estrategias de producción y sus efectos en el medio ambiente. (*Rev. Complut. Hist. Am.*, 21, 1995, p. 123–140, bibl., facsim.)

Well-written history of indigenous and Spanish agricultural production in the Valley of Moquegua. Highlights factors affecting product substitution process from traditional crops such as maiz, coca, and chili peppers to olives, wheat, alfalfa, and European cattle.

631   Cartas de frontera: los documentos del conflicto interétnico. Recopilación de Marcela Tamagnini. Río Cuarto, Argentina: Univ. Nacional de Río Cuarto, Facultad de Ciencias Humanas, 1995. 356 p.: facsims.

Letters from the Archivo de San Francisco lend a voice to the indigenous peoples who lived in a frontier region of Argentina along the Cuarto River in the second half of the 19th century. Includes letters from natives, priests who lived in *reducciones* (nucleated villages) of Villa de Mercedes and Capitán Sarmiento, and political and military authorities, among others. Some important themes are evangelization of the Indians, Franciscan missionary foundings, *reducciones*, civil-military relations, expeditions, the Rebellion of 1784, the War of the Triple Alliance, caciques, inter-ethnic relations, haciendas, and captives.

632   Castillo, Eduardo. Informe sobre investigación histórico-legal de las tierras huilliches. (*Nütram/Santiago*, 9:34, 1993/94, p. 7–31)

Dense article catalogs laws, decrees, and regulations concerning lands in the south of Chile. Shows how legal dispositions progressively allowed the state and individuals to appropriate Indians' traditional lands, under the guise of incorporating the indigenous peoples into "civilized" society.

633   Castrillón Arboleda, Diego. Trazo histórico de Yanaconas y su templo la cultura guambiana. (*Bol. Hist. Antig.*, 786, julio/sept. 1994, p. 691–698, bibl.)

Short article, based on primary and secondary sources, on the history of the town of Yanaconas, near Popayan, Colombia. Traces origins of people to prehispanic times. Focuses on town's church and its potential as a tourist attraction.

634   Chaim, Marivone M. A política indigenista no Brasil. (*Clio Hist./Recife*, 15, 1994, p. 141–152)

A brief outline of Portuguese and Brazilian legislation about indigenous peoples, from 16th-20th century, emphasizing its ambiguity and its consequences for native population.

Choque Canqui, Roberto and **Esteban Ticona Alejo.** Jesús de Machaqa: la marka rebelde. See item **2716.**

635 **Cieza de León, Pedro de.** Crónica del Perú. pt. 4, v. 3, pts. 1–2, Guerra de Quito. Recopilación de Laura Gutiérrez Arbulú. Lima, Perú: Pontificia Univ. Católica del Perú, Fondo Editorial: Academia Nacional de la Historia, 1994. 2 v.: bibl., index. (Colección Clásicos peruanos)

Third volume of *The Civil Wars of Peru,* which is Pt. 4 of the *Chronicle of Peru,* by a keen observer of 16th-century Andean life and customs. Narrates consequences of the New Laws (1542), including the rebellion led by Gonzalo Pizarro against the first viceroy, Blasco Núñez Vela. Reports on actions of Governor Cristóbal Vaca de Castro; the Real Audiencia; and groups of conquistadors from Cuzco, Arequipa, Charcas, Bogotá, and Quito.

636 **Cieza de León, Pedro de.** Crónica del Perú. pt. 4, v. 2, Guerra de Chupas. Recopilación de Gabriela Benavides de Rivero. Lima: Pontificia Univ. Católica del Perú, Fondo Editorial, 1994. 1 v.: indexes.

Penultimate work by Cieza about the second civil war between Don Diego de Almagro ("el mozo") and Licenciado Cristóbal de Castro (representing the Crown) for the governorship. Retells story that culminated in the bloody battle of Chupas (16-IX-1542), describing the assassination of Francisco Pizarro; the exploration of Nueva Granada, Rio de la Plata and Amazonas; the arrival of the Viceroy Núñez Vela; and the last moments of the rebellion of Manco Inca in Vilcabamba. Description of rebellion indicates subtle sympathy for Andean cause.

637 **Claros Arispe, Edwin.** Juan Polo Ondegardo: pionero en temas de religión autóctona. (*Yachay/Cochabamba,* 12:22, 1995, p. 81–98, bibl., facsim.)

Short introduction to life and work of the Licenciado Polo de Ondegardo presents information in outline form for easy reference. Although *ceques* are discussed, does not mention of the work of R. Tom Zuidema, the leading authority on the topic.

638 **Cloudsley, Tim.** El tiempo y el mito en la dialética entre los mundos amazónico y andino en el Perú precolombino. (*Anthropologica/Lima,* 13, 1995, p. 81–89)

Short paper centers on hypothesis that Andean societies and cultures originated in the tropical eastern jungles. Based on archeological and anthropological writings.

639 **Cook, Anita Gwynn.** Wari y Tiwanaku: entre el estilo y la imagen. Lima: Pontificia Univ. Católica del Perú, Fondo Editorial, 1994. 344 p.: bibl., ill.

Study is based primarily on a pottery analysis. Text is followed by an extensive bibliography and plates showing ceramics and iconography.

640 **Corona Sánchez, Eduardo.** Teotihuacan y Tiwanaku: dos formaciones de estado. (*Pumapunku/La Paz,* 4:8, enero 1995, p. 88–114, bibl., ill., maps)

Attempts to compare Teotihuacan and Tiwanaku civilizations, based mostly on secondary sources. Focuses on evolution, centralized dominance, and resource use.

641 **Cronistas que describen la colonia: las relaciones geográficas, la extirpación de idolatrías.** Recopilación de Francisco Carrillo. Lima: Editorial Horizonte, 1990. 216 p.: bibl., ill., map. (Enciclopedia histórica de la literatura peruana; 5)

Contains excerpts from chroniclers describing Peru during colonial times. Includes partial texts of Luis de Morales, Hernando de Santillán, Juan de Matienzo, Fray Reginaldo de Lizárraga, Miguel Cabello Valboa, Gregorio García, José de Acosta, Bernabé Cobo, Antonio de León Pinelo, Fray Buenaventura de Salinas y Córdova, Hernando de Avendaño, and Pablo José de Arriaga, among others.

642 **Dalmau i Jover, Antoni.** De l'Anoia a l'Amazones: el pare Bartomeu d'Igualada. Barcelona: Fundació Salvador Vives i Casajuana, 1993. 184 p.: bibl., ill. (Publicacions de la Fundació Salvador Vives Casajuana; 114)

Flattering biography of a 19th-century missionary who spent part of his life in the Colombian Amazon. Father Bartomeu is portrayed as an explorer, ethnographer, preacher, builder of convents, and defender of the weak.

643 **Encuentro de Cosmovisión Andina "La Cruz Cuadrada", *1st, La Paz, 1994.*** La cruz escalonada andina: aproximación al pasado y presente. v. 1–2. La Paz: Editor Centro de Cultura, Arquitectura y Arte Taipinquiri, 1995. 2 v.: ill., indexes.

Volume contains nine papers presented at a conference held in May 1994. Topics include the precolumbian past, the search for identity, interpretations of the Andean world, Andean mysticism, geometry and mathematics, and Andean calendars. Individual papers focus on such varied themes as the archeology of Tiwanaku, precolumbian architecture, solar eclipses, and modern Bolivian identities. Absent from the proceedings are contributions by scholars who have written on the same topics, such as R. Tom Zuidema and Gary Urton.

644 Espacio, etnias, frontera: atenuaciones políticas en el sur del Tawantinsuyu, siglos XV-XVIII. Recopilación de Ana María Presta. Sucre, Bolivia: Antropólogos del Surandino, 1995. 360 p.: bibl., ill., maps. (Ediciones ASUR; 4)

Compilation of well-researched, previously published papers on the southern Andes over four centuries. Chapters cover such ethnic groups as the Qharaqhara and Churumatas, and such places as Pilaya and Paspaya, Oronccota, Ayopaya, Mizque, and Tarija.

645 Estenssoro, Juan Carlos. Los Incas del Cardenal: las acuarelas de la colección Massimo. (*Rev. Andin.*, 12:2, 1994, p. 403–426, bibl., ill.)

Important study on the provenance of a series of watercolor drawings, among which appear pictorial representations of the Incas and one colla (queen). Analysis is a model for the careful and critical study of such sources.

Ethnicity, markets, and migration in the Andes: at the crossroads of history and anthropology. See *HLAS 57:1040.*

Etnohistoria del Amazonas. See *HLAS 57:928.*

646 Etnohistória dos índios potiguara. Recopilación de Frans Moonen and Luciano Mariz Maia. João Pessoa, Brazil: Procuradoria da República na Paraíba: Secretaria da Educação e Cultura do Estado da Paraíba, 1992. 409 p.: bibl., maps.

A study of the history of the Potiguara people of Paraíba, Brazil, who at the time of the work's publication numbered 6,000. Their history is summarized from contact in the 16th century through 1992. More than half of the book reproduces reports and documents about the society and culture.

647 Feijoo Seguin, María Luisa. Los charrúas y sus creencias: Pt. II. (*Hoy Hist.*, 11:65, sept./oct. 1994, p. 25–34, facsims.)

Brief overview of belief system of the Charrúas of Uruguay. Topics include religion, medicine, shamanism, and ancestor worship. Arrogantly toned article has no explicit time frame and uses uneven sources uncritically. Pt. I found in *Hoy Hist.*, 11:64, julio/agosto 1994, p. 25–35.

648 Ferreiro, Juan Pablo. El Chaco en los Andes: churumatas, paypayas, yalas y ocloyas en la etnografía del oriente jujeño. (*Poblac. Soc.*, 2, dic. 1994, p. 3–23)

Asks basic question: what exactly constitutes an ethnic group? Reviews literature on the Churumatas and other associated peoples to answer question. Evidence includes quotes from 16th-century encomienda grants.

649 Findji, María Teresa. Movimiento indígena y recuperación de la historia. (*in* Latinoamérica: enseñanza de la historia, libros de textos y conciencia histórica. Buenos Aires: Alianza Editorial; FLACSO; Frankfurt: Georg Eckert Instituts, 1991, p. 155–171)

Describes a Colombian project called "Mapas parlantes" (Speaking maps), designed to evoke historical memory of contemporary indigenous peoples. Distinction between history written by academics and history accessible to peoples through oral tradition is integral to argument.

650 Galdós Rodríguez, Guillermo. Reflexiones y confrontaciones etnohistóricas. Arequipa, Peru: Univ. Nacional de San Agustín: Talleres del Centro de Artes Gráficas, 1995. 225 p.: bibl., ill.

Ethnohistorical account of southern end of the Inca empire, specifically interrelated area of Qollasuyo and Cuntisuyo, is based on archival documents and secondary sources. Finds reciprocity, redistribution and exchange within complex ethnic groups beginning in 1532, but not between the Inca and other groups. Chapters include information on reducciones, encomiendas, and ritual. Republishes text, with analysis, of the *visita* (inspection) of Atico and Caravelí (1549).

651 García Cabrera, Juan Carlos. Ofensas a dios; pleitos e injurias: causas de idolatrías y hechicerías, Cajatambo, siglos XVII-

XIX. Cusco, Peru: CBC, 1994. 560 p. (Monumenta Idolatrica Andina; 1)

A welcome volume on campaigns against idolatry in Peru. Most of the book is dedicated to reproducing transcribed primary documents from the section *Hechicerías e Idolatrías* of the Archbishop's Archive in Lima. Most documents are from the 17th century, three are from the 18th century, and one is from later.

652 García-Moro, Clara. Reconstrucción del proceso de extinción de los Selknam a través de los libros misionales. (*An. Inst. Patagon./Ser. Cienc. Hum.*, 21, 1992, p. 33–46, bibl., graphs, maps, tables)

Concise study of the Selknam (Ona) peoples of Tierra del Fuego (southern Argentina and Chile), based largely on records of two Salesian missions established in late-19th century, covers period through end of second decade of the 20th century. Argues that European-introduced diseases and departure from nomadic way of life after contact led to extinction of group. Uses data to produce demographic profiles of population.

653 Gisbert, Teresa. El señorío de los Carangas y los chullpares del Río Lauca. (*Rev. Andin.*, 12:2, 1994, p. 427–485, bibl., ill., maps, photos)

Long article on the señorío of the Caranga people, who, in the 16th century, lived in what is now Bolivia. Uses Spanish chronicle accounts, secondary sources, and archeological findings to show a compelling similarity between decorations woven into textiles and designs found on burial structures (*chullpas*) near the Lauca river. Suggests that iconography symbolized political hegemony and alliances.

654 González Coll, María Mercedes and María Emilia Pérez Amat. Problemática de la cultura de contacto en la frontera sur: enfoque etnohistórico. Bahía Blanca: Depto. de Humanidades, Univ. Nacional del Sur, 1994. 121 p.: bibl., ill., maps.

A team-produced study of early-19th century inter-ethnic relations in the southern part of present Buenos Aires prov.

655 Guarisco, Claudia. Entre la obediencia y la evasión: el tributo indígena en el Ecuador del siglo XIX. (*Allpanchis/Cusco*, 26:46, segundo semestre 1995, p. 11–43, bibl.)

Concise history of tribute collection in Ecuador in the first half of the 19th century, based on solid work in the national archives, shows that tribute collection depended on force. Eventually, a constellation of factors, including flight and evasion by indigenous peoples, self-interest of hacienda owners, a weak state bureaucracy, and alternative forms of government revenue eliminated tribute system.

656 Guillén Guillén, Edmundo. La guerra de reconquista Inka. Lima: E. Guillén Guillén, 1994. 357 p.: bibl., ill., indexes, maps.

Noted author, who has published on related topics, recounts history of Incas defending their sovereignty between 1536–72. Story begins at end of Huayna Capac's reign, and traces his successor's interactions with the Spanish from Cajamarca through the siege of Cuzco to Vicabamba. Transcriptions of 16th-century letters and accounts follow text.

657 Hernández, Isabel. Los indios de Argentina. Madrid: Editorial MAPFRE, 1992. 335 p.: bibl., indexes, maps. (Colecciones MAPFRE 1492)

An overview of the history of indigenous peoples in Argentina, based mainly on secondary sources. Colonization, resistance, the "conquest of the desert," and the Chaco campaigns receive considerable attention.

658 Herrera Angel, Marta. Espacio y poder: pueblos de indios en la provincia de Santafé, siglo XVIII. (*Rev. Colomb. Antropol.*, 31, 1994, p. 33–62, bibl.)

A well-documented study of the breakdown of the colonial policy of segregation through the *república de indios* and the *república de españoles*. Shows how the Church in the *pueblo de indios* brought "whites" and "Indians" into contact with each other and follows contact into early-19th century, when pueblos were turned into *parroquias* (parishes) and *"indios"* were replaced by mestizos.

História dos índios no Brasil. See *HLAS 57:962.*

659 História pré-colonial do Brasil. Organização de Ivan Alves Filho. Rio de Janeiro: Europa Editora, 1993. 248 p.: bibl., ill., maps.

Compilation of 13 articles on precolonial and colonial history of indigenous peoples of Brazil is organized into three chronological parts. Precolonial topics include art and agriculture. Colonial history section emphasizes encounter between indigenous peoples and Europeans. Final section discusses identity.

660 Huarochirí: ocho mil años de historia. v. 2. Lima: Municipalidad de Santa Eulalia de Acopaya, 1992. 1 v.: bibl.

A compilation of regional histories, published by the Concejo Distrital of Huarochirí. Articles cover both colonial and national periods. Several contributions deal with curacas and various forms of resistance. Others detail community life and values. For annotation of vol. 1, see *HLAS 57:635.*

661 Huidobro Bellido, José. Apuntes sobre una teoría: Murra y la verticalidad ecológica. (*in* Reunión Anual de Etnología, 6th, La Paz, 1992. Actas. La Paz: Museo Nacional de Etnografía y Folklore, 1993, t. 1, p. 51–60, bibl., graphs)

Short article analyzes the universality of John V. Murra's archipelago model. Some of the author's objections to Murra's work and his suggested alternative hypothesis are based on European preconceptions and do not take into consideration recent ethnohistorical research on the Andes.

662 Huidobro Bellido, José. El estado despótico de Tiwanaku: un análisis político, económico y social. (*Pumapunku/ La Paz,* 4:8, enero 1995, p. 161–188, bibl., ill., map, photo, tables)

A panoramic overview of the evolution of Tiwanaku civilization, influenced by Karl Wittfogel's ideas on hydraulic societies. Mentions that Tiwanakans had a system of writing (based on statuary) and that climate change initiated the decline of the civilization.

The Indian in Spanish America: centuries of removal, survival, and integration; a critical anthology. See item **4989.**

663 Jiménez Villalba, Félix. La iconografía del Inca a través de las crónicas españolas de la época y la colección de keros y pajchas del Museo de América de Madrid. (*An. Mus. Am.,* 2, 1994, p. 5–20, bibl., ill.)

A tightly written article explores the basis of legitimacy of the Incas as found in nine Spanish chronicles and as depicted in indigenous iconography on ceremonial drinking vessels. Weak section on succession is followed by a strong discussion of iconography and ideology.

664 Kaulicke, Peter. Historia general del Perú. v. 1, Los orígenes de la civilización andina. Lima: Editorial Brasa, 1994. 1 v.: bibl., ill., index, maps.

Handsome first volume of a three-tome set on the history of Peru covers origins of human habitation through the formative and Chavín periods. Work is clearly organized and footnoted; and contains many helpful charts, maps, and photographs. Excellent starting point for any serious consideration of the Andean past. For citations of other vols., see items **712** and **721.**

665 Lalueza, C. et al. Linajes mitocondriales de los aborígenes de Tierra del Fuego y Patagonia. (*An. Inst. Patagon. /Ser. Cienc. Hum.,* 23, 1995, p. 75–86, appendix, bibl., graph, photo, tables)

Technical article is based on DNA analysis of populations in southern Chile. Scientific analysis shows two major groups or lineages of people (of a total possible number of four), which leads authors to hypothesize two waves of independent migration into the area.

666 Landázuri N., Cristóbal. Los curacazgos pastos prehispanicos: agricultura y comercio, siglo XVI. Otavalo, Ecuador: Instituto Otavaleño de Antropología; Quito: Ediciones del Banco Central del Ecuador, 1995. 229 p. (some folded): bibl., ill. (Colección Pendoneros; 13)

A study of the curacazgos in the northern Andes, based on primary and secondary documents, archeological findings, and ethnographic studies. Describes environment and agriculture, and discusses interchange and the Inca conquest. Includes a selection of primary documents (tribute list, wills, and court cases).

667 Langebaek, Carl Henrik. La elite no siempre piensa lo mismo: indígenas, estado, arqueología y etnohistoria en Colombia, siglos XVI a inicios del XX. (*Rev. Colomb. Antropol.,* 31, 1994, p. 121–143, bibl.)

Historiographic analysis of works that describe and study the "Indian" in Colombia since the 16th century. Argues that the different elite groups who wrote about indigenous life did so to promote their own biases and interests. Suggests that historians study "white" society, while anthropologists and archeologists study the "Indian." Also sees this division in the organization of Colombian museums.

668 Langebaek, Carl Henrik. Mercados, poblamiento e integración etnica entre los muiscas, siglo XVI. Bogotá: Banco de la República, 1987. 168 p.: bibl., ill. (Colección bibliográfica. Antropología.)

Based largely on periodic colonial visitas, text focuses on social and economic aspects of the Muiscas people of Colombia in the 16th century. Highlights production of goods and types of interchange.

669 Langebaek, Carl Henrik. Mindalaes, balsas y la relevancia del imperialismo Inca en el sur de Colombia. (*Cespedesia/Cali*, 18:61, julio/dic. 1991, p. 73–92, bibl.)

Provocative article, based on both primary sources and secondary literature, argues that long distance trade or exchange with the Inca had minimal effect on the social evolution of cacicazgos in southern Colombia. This argument contrasts with C.T. Patterson's hypothesis that the characteristics of southwestern Colombian societies were determined by relations with imperial Cuzco.

670 Laraia, Roque de Barros. Los indios de Brasil. Madrid: MAPFRE, 1993. 260 p.: bibl., ill. (Colecciones MAPFRE 1492)

Chronological synthesis of the history of the indigenous peoples of Brazil, beginning with a short chapter on the pre-1500 era. Follows the Tupinambá and others from colonial through modern times. An annotated bibliography follows. The tone of the text is captured in pictures of the smiling and the naked.

Latin American Indian Literatures Association. Symposium. *12th, Universidad Nacional Autónoma de México, 1995.* Messages and meanings. See item **530.**

León de d'Empaire, Arleny. Felipe Salvador Gilij: nuevas perspectivas americanas en la crónica dieciochesca. See item **912.**

671 León Solís, Leonardo. Guerras tribales y estructura social en la Araucanía, 1760–1780. (*Rev. Cienc. Soc./Valparaíso*, 39, 1994, p. 91–110)

Presents overview of two conflicts: the Araucanian-Spanish War, and the struggle between Araucanian leaders and their followers between 1760–80. Discusses such topics as the basis of power of indigenous leaders, the formation of alliances between lineages, the establishment of tribal federations, and the manipulation of relations with Spanish and criollos on the frontier of Biobio.

672 Lerche, Peter. Los Chachapoya y los símbolos de su historia. Lima: P. Lerche, 1995. 133 p.: appendix, bibl., ill.

A short history of the Chachapoya peoples of northern Peru. This book was inspired by a primary document from the personal archive of Humberto Arce Burga. Manuscript concerns Inca descendants, living in Levanto, who petition the Crown to be exonerated from paying tribute. For their services, the emperor Charles V gives them a coat of arms in 1545. Appendix includes excerpts from the document.

673 Livro das canoas: documentos para a história indígena da Amazônia. Organização de Márcio Meira. São Paulo: Núcleo de História Indígena e do Indigenismo: Fundação de Amparo à Pesquisa do Estado de São Paulo, 1993. 239 p.: bibl. (Série Documentos)

Transcription of the *Livro das canoas*, a manuscript from the Arquivo Público do Estado do Pará, includes information from 17th-19th centuries and provides important first-hand data on people, places, and events of the Amazonian region. Descriptions of captured indigenous peoples in the Rio Negro and Japura rivers between 1739–55 are especially interesting. Mentions by name several dozen ethnic groups (and lists them on p. 17–18).

674 Londoño L., Eduardo. Los muiscas en las crónicas y los archivos. (*Rev. Colomb. Antropol.*, 31, 1994, p. 105–120, bibl.)

Interesting article on the value of Spanish chronicles vis-à-vis archival documents for the study of Colombian ethnohistory. Concludes that both types of sources are problematic and must be used with caution. Gives good examples of cross-cultural misreporting using concepts of wealth and political organization and hierarchy.

675 **Lyon, Patricia J.** The more things change... (sic). (*Lat. Am. Anthropol. Rev.*, 6:1, Spring 1994, p. 29–32, bibl.)
A short but useful overview of coca production and use in the 16th century. Shows that if the demand for coca declines, the supply will decline as well.

676 **Malengreau, Jacques.** Sociétés des Andes: des empires aux voisinages. Paris: Editions Karthala, 1995. 454 p.: bibl., graphs, maps. (Collection "Hommes et sociétés")
Structured overview of Andean civilization since 12,000 B.C.E. describes Incas in terms of myth, cosmology, political and economic organization, and technology. Colonial history includes sections on *ayllus*, *kurakas*, identity, tribute, and haciendas. One-half of the book deals with modern history, including agrarian reforms of the 1960s-70s, development of the state, and Andean culture.

677 **Malpass, Michael Andrew.** Daily life in the Inca empire. Westport, Conn.: Greenwood Press, 1996. 193 p.: bibl., ill., index, map. (The Greenwood Press "Daily life through history" series, 1080–4749)
Looks at everyday life in the Inca empire, based on current research. Reconstructs Inca way of life using information on life-cycle events, food and drink, dress and ornaments, recreation, religious rituals, the calendar, and the labor tax. Timeline of Inca history, glossary of terms, and bibliography make the work appropriate for classroom use.

678 **Manzi, Liliana M.** Actividades en los sitios de agregación selk'nam según las crónicas: ¿hay alguna evidencia arqueológica? (*Cuad. Inst. Nac. Antropol. Pensam. Latinoam.*, 14, 1992/93, p. 217–235, bibl.)
Discusses the hunter-gatherer families of Isla Grande of Tierra del Fuego; their subsistence strategies; and the ritual, social, and economic motivations for meeting periodically in larger groups between 1880 and 1924.

679 **Marín Silva, Pedro.** Etnolingüística e historiografía de la región de los ríos Putumayo, Caquetá y Caguán. (*Maguaré/ Bogotá*, 9:10, 1994, p. 80–104, facsims., map, table)
Aims to help define an ethnolinguistic group for presentation to the Colombian Congress for the territorial re-ordering mandated by the Constitution of 1994. Includes a discussion of languages and dialects, and missionary efforts in the area.

680 **Martínez Martín, Carmen.** Las reducciones de los pampas, 1740–53: aportaciones etnogeográficas al sur de Buenos Aires. (*Rev. Complut. Hist. Am.*, 20, 1994, p. 145–167)
Reviews gradual extension of European influence on the pampas between 1740–53, based largely on mission records. Highlights difficulty of exploration and the slow and late pace of evangelization. For colonial historian's comment, see item **2469.**

681 **Martínez Neira, Christian.** Colonización extranjera y recuperación territorial en la Araucanía, el caso de los terrenos al oriente de Gorbea, 1883–1910. (*Nütram/Santiago*, 8:30, 1992, p. 5–26, tables)
A short history, based on both primary and secondary sources, of a Chilean government attempt to establish a Dutch-Boer colony in Araucania in the early-20th century. The 19 original immigrant families faced lack of infrastructure and local hostility. Most were rapidly replaced by national settlers.

682 **Martinic Beros, Mateo.** Los Aónikenk: historia y cultura. Punta Arenas, Chile: Ediciones de la Univ. de Magallanes, 1995. 387 p.: bibl., ill. (some col.), indexes, map.
The history of the Aónikenk people from prehispanic times to their extinction, based on both primary and secondary sources. Describes impact of the horse and alcohol on this culture and society. Second part of book is dedicated to a description of their customs and way of life.

683 **Martinic Beros, Mateo.** Cementerios y tumbas rurales en Magallanes. (*An. Inst. Patagon./Ser. Cienc. Hum.*, 23, 1995, p. 5–40, appendix, bibl., maps, photos, tables)
A singular article which presents an inventory of 19th- and 20th-century tombs in

southern Chile. Among the findings are two distinct styles of burial—one for indigenous peoples and one for foreigners, especially the British. Presents data using photos and a long appendix.

684 Maruyama, Makoto and **Yoshiki Kobayashi.** Hatun Puna 1710–1712: documents relating to the origin of an Andean community based economically on pure pastoralism in Puno, Peru. Tokyo: Univ. of Tokyo, Komaba, Graduate School of Arts and Sciences, Dept. of Advanced Social and International Studies, 1996. 54 p.: bibl., ill., maps. (Working papers; 68)

Welcome attempt by an ethnographer to interpret and publish a primary document from the early-18th century on migration and pastoralism in the Hatun Puna near the pueblo of Acora. Forward by Makoto Maruyama puts document into a broader disciplinary context. Transcribed manuscript contains information on cattle tending, migration to and from La Paz, abusive indigenous authorities, and the titling of an *estancia* (cattle station).

685 Michieli, Catalina Teresa. Antigua historia de Cuyo. San Juan, Argentina: Ansilta Editora, 1995. 99 p.: bibl., map.

A local history of the Cuyo region from first Spanish contact, based on both primary and secondary sources. Indigenous population concentration in *reducciones*, demographic collapse, pastoralism, and commerce with Chile during the 17th century are topics covered.

686 Morales Méndez, Filadelfo. Sangre en los conucos: reconstrucción etnohistórica de los indígenas de Turmero. Caracas: Fondo Editorial Tropykos, 1994. 207 p.: bibl., ill., indexes, maps.

An archeological and ethnohistorical study of the Indians of Turmero, based on published primary and secondary sources. Useful colonial section summarizes information on demographic collapse, impact of the Spanish *requerimiento* (the requirement) on indigenous liberties, struggle over land, and encomienda. Appendices reprint Spanish colonial documents such as the *requerimiento*, and others on the treatment of indigenous peoples.

687 Mota, Lúcio Tadeu. As guerras dos índios Kaingang: a história épica dos índios Kaingang no Paraná, 1769–1924. Maringá, Puerto Rico: Editora da Univ. Estadual de Maringá, 1994. 285 p.: bibl., ill., maps.

A regional study of the Kaingang, indigenous peoples of Paraná (Brazil), between 1769–1924, based on primary and secondary sources. Subjects covered include geography; demography; and precolonial, colonial, and postcolonial history. Resistance is an important theme.

688 El mundo ceremonial andino. Recopilación de Luis Millones y Yoshio Onuki. Lima: Editorial Horizonte, 1994. 299 p.: bibl., ill. (Etnología y antropología; 8)

This handsome volume publishes the proceedings of the XVI Simposio Internacional de la Fundación Taniguchi (Japan, 1992). Papers deal with ceremonial life during the early formative period in Ecuador, ceremonial construction on the North Coast and highlands of Peru, and rituals of the past and present.

689 Muratorio, Blanca. Diálogos de mujeres, monólogo de poder: género y la construcción del sujeto colonial en la Alta Amazonia. (*ANDES Antropol. Hist.*, 6, 1994, p. 241–263, bibl.)

Ethnohistorical study of the Canelo in Ecuadorian Amazon from advent of the Liberals in 1895 through 1980s focuses primarily on women, especially on Francisca Andi and "her song," analyzed by Muratorio for its historical as well as cultural, mother/daughter, researcher/informant meanings and significance. [M.T. Hamerly]

690 Murra, John V. Did tribute and markets prevail in the Andes before the European invasion? (*in* Ethnicity, markets, and migration in the Andes: at the crossroads of history and anthropology. Edited by Brooke Larson and Olivia Harris with Enrique Tandeter. Durham, N.C.: Duke Univ. Press, 1995, p. 57–72)

A masterful treatise on the nature of exchange in the Andes, which subtly rejects Western concept of "commercialization." Murra leaves the exact nature of the exchanges vague and subject to further research.

691 Nacuzzi, Lidia R. *Nómades* versus *sedentarios* en Patagonia, siglos XVIII-XIX. (*Cuad. Inst. Nac. Antropol. Pensam. Latinoam.*, 14, 1992/93, p. 81–92, bibl., map)

A well-written article on relationship between indigenous nomads and sedentary populations (both Christian and indigenous) in Patagonia from the 18th century into the 19th century. Primary focus is economic exchange. Argues that Christian populations could not have settled successfully without help from local indigenous populations.

Native traditions in the postconquest world: a symposium at Dumbarton Oaks, 2nd through 4th October 1992. See item 551.

692 Negro, Sandra. La persistencia de la visión andina de la muerte en el virreinato del Perú. (*Anthropologica/Lima*, 14, 1996, p. 121–141, bibl.)

A well-written, organized overview and summary of Andean attitudes about death, based on published Spanish chronicles and idolatry records. Article would be more helpful to scholars with more extensive footnoting.

693 Orbell, John. Los herederos del cacique Suaya, historia colonial de Ráquira, 1539–1810. Bogotá: Banco de la República, 1995. 312 p.: appendices, bibl., ill., index, maps, tables. (Colección bibliográfica)

Straightforward, document-based monograph is centered on the colonial history (1539–1810) of the town of Ráquira (Colombia). Focuses on factors that modified indigenous concepts of the world and their social organization. Chapters deal with setting, population, tribute, conversion, and land tenure. Summarizes data in tables and maps, and appendices include various transcribed visitas.

694 Pacheco, Diego and **Edgar Guerrero Peñaranda.** Machas, Tinkipayas y Yamparas: provincia Chayanta, Norte de Potosí. Sucre, Bolivia: CIPRES, 1994. 167 p.: bibl., ill. (some col.) (Serie Reflexión etnohistorica; 1)

Multi-ethnicity and identity in three *ayllus* of the province of Chayanta form the structure of this team-produced study. Summarizes data in numerous tables and maps. Emphasizes 19th and 20th centuries.

695 Palermo, Miguel Angel. La etnohistoria en la Argentina: antecedentes y estado actual. (*Runa/Buenos Aires*, 20, 1991/92, p. 145–150)

A useful overview of the ethnohistory of Argentina. Lists the major contributions of individuals in the field. Also discusses wider issues of definition and methodology.

696 Paraíso, Maria Hilda Baqueiro. Amixokori, Pataxó, Monoxó, Kumanoxó, Kutaxó, Kutatoi, Maxakali, Malali e Makoni: povos indígenas diferenciados ou subgrupos de uma mesma nação?; uma proposta de reflexão. (*Rev. Mus. Arqueol. Etnol.*, 4, 1994, p. 173–187, bibl., tables)

Uses anthropological, linguistic, historical, and archeological data to argue that certain tribes were subgroups of the Tikmu'nu nation in the 18th and 19th centuries. These peoples lived in what today are the states of Bahia, Minas Gerais, and Espirito Santo.

697 Paternosto, César. The stone and the thread: Andean roots of abstract art. Translated by Esther Allen. Austin: Univ. of Texas Press, 1996. 293 p.: bibl., ill., index, map.

Shows that precolumbian tectonic forms (especially as found in sculpture and weaving) appear to be an overlooked source, or anticipation, of much of the art of the 20th century. Second part of book deals with artifacts as American art and addresses reception of ancient tectonics in the 20th century. Emphasizes intense relationship that some members of the New York School (particularly Barnett Newman and Adolph Gottlieb) had during 1940s with the aboriginal arts of the North American part of the hemisphere and thus the affinities between their work and the work of the older Torres García in Montevideo, at the other end of the continent. For archeologist's comment, see *HLAS 55:691*. For art specialist's comment, see *HLAS 56:315*.

698 Pease G.Y., Franklin. Las lecturas del Inca Garcilaso y su información andina. (*Histórica/Lima*, 18:1, julio 1994, p. 135–157, bibl.)

Briefly discusses sources of information used by Garcilaso to write his chronicles. Raises questions about which chronicler borrowed or transcribed from whom, and the reliability of the information.

699   Penazzo de Penazzo, Nelly Iris and **Guillermo Tercero Penazzo.** Wot'n: documentos del genocidio Ona. v. 1–3. Buenos Aires: Ediciones Arlequín de San Telmo, 1995. 3 v.: bibl., ill., maps.

This three-volume set underscores the demise of the Ona people, a hunting and gathering people, who lived on an island of Tierra del Fuego. The premise is that European land occupation, in this caseby Salesian missionaries and various large agricultural enterprises, resulted in ethnocide. Lists of property grants and transfers are accompanied by detailed maps. Discusses the indigenous population and reducciones. All three vols. reproduce many documents describing the society.

700   Perera, Miguel Angel. La mirada perdida: etnohistoria y antropología americana del siglo XVI. Caracas: Monte Avila Editores Latinoamericana, 1994. 294 p.: bibl., ill. (Estudios)

Details impact that discovery of America had on the philosophy and sciences of the Western world. Discusses Cristóbal Colón, Amerigo Vespucci, Bartolomé de las Casas, and several other observers, assessing the effect of their writings on literature, history, government, and science.

701   Pérez de Micou, Cecilia. La etnohistoria en los estudios paleoetnobotánicos de cazadores recolectores: presentación de un caso. (*Cuad. Inst. Nac. Antropol. Pensam. Latinoam.*, 15, 1994, p. 225–235, bibl.)

Methodologically significant article exemplifies the effectiveness of a multidisciplinary approach. Uses ethnohistorical, ethnographic, and archeological research strategies to identify seven tubers and roots that served as food for hunters and gatherers on the Patagonian steppes of Argentina.

702   Pi Hugarte, Renzo. Los indios de Uruguay. Madrid: Editorial MAPFRE, 1993. 355 p.: bibl., ill., indexes. (Colecciones MAPFRE 1492)

An overview of the history of the indigenous peoples of Uruguay from prehispanic times. The Charrúa, Chaná, and Guaraní ethnic groups receive special attention. Some important topics covered include

missionary efforts among the Guaraní, destruction of cultures, and acculturation.

703   Polia, Mario. Siete cartas inéditas del Archivo Romano de la Compañía de Jesús, 1611–1613: huacas, mitos y ritos andinos. (*Anthropologica/Lima*, 14, 1996, p. 209–259, bibl.)

Useful publication reprints seven of the annual letters written by Jesuit fathers in the early-17th century, showing their attempts to extirpate idolatry. Describes rituals, sacrifices, ancestor worship, and other aspects of Andean religion. Extensive footnotes clarify concepts and note other descriptions of phenomena.

704   Polia, Mario and **Fabiola Chávez Hualpa.** Ministros menores del culto, shamanes y curanderos en las fuentes españolas de los siglos XVI-XVII. (*Anthropologica/Lima*, 11, enero 1994, p. 7–48, bibl., graph, tables)

Compiles information from 22 primary sources (mostly chronicles) about specialized practitioners of traditional Andean religion in the 16th-17th centuries. Organized like a catalog for easy reference, but this presentation leads to some repetition. Includes some references to contemporary practices.

705   Ponce de León Paiva, Antón. The wisdom of the ancient one: an Inca initiation. Woodside, Calif.: Bluestar Communications, 1995. 118 p.: ill.

First-person account of a spiritual journey to learn the knowledge of the Inca ancestors. The Quechua-speaking author describes initiation rites in the Andes.

706   Ponce Sanginés, Carlos. Arthur Posnansky y su obsesión milenaria: biografía intelectual de un pionero. Bolivia: Producciones CIMA, 1994. 233 p.: bibl., ill.

An intellectual biography of Arthur Posnansky (1873–1946), a pioneer in Bolivian archeology who studied Tiwanaku with a passion. Posnansky is credited with the establishment of national parks and the introduction of the automobile in his adopted homeland. Contains numerous photos and a complete bibliography of his writing.

707   Portugal, Ana Raquel Marques da Cunha Martins. Síntese analítica da concepção de *ayllu* em crônicas do século

XVI. (*Estud. Leopold.*, 32:148, julho/agôsto 1996, p. 87–101, bibl.)

Analyzes changing notion of the word *ayllu*, based on the writings of six Spanish chroniclers. Shows how the word changes from one that implies family, lineage, or social group to one that has an implicit or explicit territorial dimension. This metamorphosis may explain why many colonial historians of the Andes are confused by the term.

708 **Powlison, Paul Stewart.** La mitología yagua: tendencias épicas en una mitología del Nuevo Mundo. Versión castellana de Marlene Ballena Dávila. Yarinacocha, Perú: Instituto Lingüístico de Verano, 1993. 148 p.: bibl., map. (Comunidades y culturas peruanas; no. 25)

Presents the mythology and oral traditions of the Aguarunas. Compares various versions, placing them in the wider context of South American mythology.

709 **Prada Ramírez, Fernando.** El khipu incaico: de la matemática a la historia. (*Yachay/Cochabamba*, 12:21, 1995, p. 9–38, bibl., facsims., ill., map)

Studies the functions of the *quipu* (an Inca record-keeping device, based on knotted strings) and how, ultimately, the information in the *quipu* was recorded in writing to safeguard indigenous rights to land, water, and other resources. Avoids issue of whether or not the *quipu* represented a system of writing. Also relates the *quipu* to the *ceque* system of Cuzco.

710 **Priegue, Celia Nancy.** Aspectos históricos en el conocimiento científico de los pueblos indígenas pampeano-patagónicos. Bahía Blanca, Argentina: Depto. de Humanidades, Univ. Nacional del Sur, 1992. 55 leaves: bibl., ill.

A study of the indigenous peoples of Patagonia and Pampa, based on both primary and secondary sources. Uses linguistic and ethnographic observations to review and reassess earlier reports and interpretations.

711 **Rabinovich, Ricardo David.** La juridización de la relación paterno-filial en el Tawantinsuyu tardío. (*Rev. Hist. Derecho*, 21, 1993, p. 209–223)

A short, non-analytical article that extracts tenets of family law of the Tawantinsuyu mostly from Spanish chronicles. Occasionally cites secondary or archeological sources to confirm European observations.

712 **Ravines, Róger.** Historia general del Perú. v. 2, Las culturas preincas. Lima: Editorial Brasa, 1994. 1 v.: bibl., ill., index, maps.

Vol. 2 of a three-tome set which covers Peruvian archeology from 200 B.C.E. to (but not including) the Incas. Examines cultures and styles, legendary kingdoms, prehispanic militarism, Huari culture, and historic señoríos (chieftainships) in detail. Maps, charts, photographs, and tables complement the text, written by one of Peru's recognized authorities. For annotations of other vols., see items **664** and **721.**

713 **Relaciones y visitas a los Andes, siglo XVI.** v. 2, Región del Caribe. Bogotá: Colcultura: Instituto Colombiano de Cultura Hispánica, 1993. 1 v.: bibl., ill., maps. (Colección de historia de la Biblioteca Nacional)

Produced under the direction of noted Colombian historian, this series is dedicated to publishing all early accounts (*relaciones* and visitas) of two regions. Vol. 2 describes the Caribbean provinces of Santa Marta and Cartagena, starting with a report on the Valley of Pacabueyes of 1533 in Santa Marta and an account of Pedro de Heredia from the same year for Cartagena. For review of all four vols., see item **2179.**

714 **Restrepo Arcila, Roberto A.** Instituciones sociales, políticas y económicas del Tawantinsuyu. (*Pumapunku/La Paz*, 4:8, enero 1995, p. 115–138, graphs, ill., map, photo)

A basic, largely unfootnoted, review of the features of Tawantinsuyu organization. Discusses the "sacred cross" and political hierarchy, among other topics. Problems with the analysis include the romanticizing of some aspects of the organization, giving the *ayllu* a territorial base, and stating that the land was divided (literally) into three parts for the community, the state, and the Church.

715 **Robins, Nicholas A.** El mesianismo y la rebelión indígena: la "Rebelión de Oruro" en 1781. Traducción de Luz Mariela Escobar R. La Paz: Hisbol, 1997. 192 p.: bibl.

Using primary and secondary documents, closely examines the uprising of Oruro in 1781. Argues that the rebellion was two distinct movements: one of creoles and mestizos who planned, initiated, and executed the uprising against the Spanish; and the second involving indigenous peoples. Finds that collaboration proved short lived because of different goals. Includes sections on millenarian movements and Bourbon reforms.

716 Rodríguez, Carlos Armando. Los estudios sobre la historia prehispánica del suroccidente de Colombia y el noroccidente del Ecuador. (*Cespedesia/Cali*, 18:61, julio/dic. 1991, p. 93–136, bibl.)

Historiographical article on the archeology and ethnohistory of southwestern Colombia and northwestern Ecuador chronologically lists important authors and area or ethnic group that each studied. The disproportionate attention paid to archeology may reflect the state of research of these two disciplines. Extensive bibliography will help anyone contemplating research in these areas.

717 Santos-Granero, Fernando. Etnohistoria de la Alta Amazonia: siglos XV-XVIII. Quito: Ediciones ABYA-YALA, 1992? 305 p.: bibl., maps. (Colección 500 años; 46)

An ethnohistorical study of the peoples of the Amazon from precontact times to the end of the 18th century. Each of the 12 chapters focuses on a theme, examined chronologically. Topics include exchange, contact between the Incas and Amazonian populations, first Spanish expeditions into the area, colonial policy, Franciscan and Jesuit missionaries, disease, indigenous resistance, the rebellion of Juan Santos Atahuallpa, and identity. For ethnohistorian's comment, see *HLAS 57:1013*.

718 Sarramone, Alberto. Catriel y los indios pampas de Buenos Aires. Azul, Argentina: Editorial Biblos, 1993. 371 p.: bibl., ill., maps.

Recounts conquest of indigenous peoples by immigrant Europeans in 18th- and 19th-century Argentina. Describes frontiers and attacks, caciques, and customs of the Pampas. The life of Juan Catriel "El Viejo" and his descendants personalizes the regional history.

719 Scarzanella, Eugenia. Fotografías de indios: misioneros salesianos y documentación etnográfica de Tierra del Fuego. (*in* Fronteras, etnias, culturas: América Latina, siglos XVI-XX. Organización de Chiara Vangelista. Quito: Ediciones Abya-Yala, 1996, p. 149–168, photos)

A revelatory piece on the use of photographs at a Salesian missionary station and school in Tierra del Fuego in late-19th and early-20th centuries. Shows how photographs were used to document conversion and to undo stereotypes of the Onas, Alcalufes, and Yaganes, who were rapidly disappearing. Includes examples with long commentaries. Some of the pictures are detailed enough to be of ethnographic interest.

720 Seminario Internacional de Etnohistoria del Norte del Ecuador y Sur de Colombia, *1st, Popayán and Cali, Colombia, 1994.* Memorias. Edición de Guido Barona Becerra and Francisco Zuluaga R. Cali: Editorial Facultad de Humanidades, 1995. 395 p.: bibl. (Colección Historia y sociedad)

A compilation of conference papers on the ethnohistory of northern Ecuador and southern Colombia. Methodological issues predominate; verticality, myth and history, and ritual are among other themes discussed.

721 Silva Santisteban, Fernando and **Róger Ravines.** Historia general del Perú. v. 3, Los incas. Lima: Editorial Brasa, 1994. 1 v.: bibl., ill., index, maps.

Third volume of a three-tome set is dedicated to a description and analysis of the Inca empire. Topics covered include origins, expansion, the empire, agriculture, architecture, weaving, mining, transportation, war, and *quipus* (a record-keeping system based on knotted strings). For citations of other vols., see items **664** and **712.**

722 Silva Sifuentes, Jorge E. El imperio de los cuatro suyos. 1. ed. Lima: Fondo Editorial de COFIDE, 1995. 265 p.: bibl. (Asuntos culturales Cofide)

A synthesis of Inca civilization written for non-specialists. Outlines Inca history chronologically from Manco Capac to Francisco Pizarro's capture of Atahualpa. Describes civilization using social, political, economic, and religious categories. Also describes Cuzco and other provincial administrative centers.

723 Stehberg, Rubén and Victor Lucero.
Evidencias de coexistencia entre cazadores de lobos y aborígenes fueguinos a principios del siglo XIX en Isla Desolación, Shetland del Sur, Antártica. (*Serie Cient.*, 45, 1995, p. 67–88, bibl., map, photos, table)

A report about the 1995 field season during which four seal hunting camps dating from the early-19th century were excavated. The presence of indigenous implements in two of the camps suggests that indigenous peoples joined in the activities.

724 Sullivan, William. The secret of the Incas: myth, astronomy, and the war against time. New York: Crown Publishers, 1996. 421 p.: bibl., ill., index, maps.

"This book is the story of an experiment," to quote the author (p. 12). Focuses on myth as the key to understanding the Incas' past. Many conclusions differ from those of standard scholarly literature. Some examples that run counter to orthodox views on Andean peoples are the notion that Andean myth recounts significant precessional events; the view that the three worlds of Andean cosmology were understood, on one level, as locations on the celestial sphere, united by the Milky Way; and the idea that Andean peoples not only had names for all the planets visible to the unassisted eye, but also associated them with important deities. Uses ethnoastronomical studies of Gary Urton and R. Tom Zuidema.

725 Tavel, Iván. Anello Oliva, 1598: un intérprete de quipucamayos. (*Yachay/Cochabamba*, 12:22, 1995, p. 99–110, bibl., facsim.)

Brief work provides a biography of the chronicler Anello Oliva and a discussion of his work. His chronicle contains information on illustrious Jesuits, and on the Incas and the Spanish conquest. Critically analyzes the ethnohistorical information of his writings.

726 Téllez Lúgaro, Eduardo. De incas, picones y promaucaes: el derrumbe de la *frontera salvaje* en el confín austral del Collasuyo. (*Cuad. Hist./Santiago*, 10, dic. 1990, p. 69–86)

Takes up question of the demarcation of the southern frontier of the Tahuan-

tinsuyu. Accepts the Maipo River as the dividing line, but argues that it was not clearly drawn and that some, if not all, of the "civilized" Picones to the north of the river and the "savage" Promaucases to the south were the same people. [M.T. Hamerly]

727 Téllez Lúgaro, Eduardo. De tehuelches, césares y australidades: una relación postrera de Nicolás Mascardi S.J., 1673. (*Mapocho/Santiago*, 35, primer semestre 1994, p. 265–276)

Short article sketches the life of a missionary to southern Chile, Nicolás Mascardi. Recounts what is known of his life, and transcribes one of his letters, dated circa 1673. This letter mentions the indigenous inhabitants of the area, hunting and gardening activities, and relations with government officials and other priests.

728 Tenório, Maria Cristina. A coleta de vegetais entre os indígenas na época do contato com o europeu. (*Clio Arqueol./Recife*, 1:10, 1994, p. 81–101, bibl.)

Based largely on chronicles and travelers accounts, article notes that indigenous Brazilians supplemented gardening by gathering wild fruits and vegetables (such as bananas, coconuts, and manioc). Concludes that cultivation never completely replaced gathering.

729 Tovar Pinzón, Hermes. El saber indígena y la administración colonial española: la visita a la provincia de Mariquita de 1559. (*Anu. Colomb. Hist. Soc. Cult.*, 22, 1995, p. 9–33, tables)

Well-written and organized description of Honda, Chapaima, and Calamoyma (prov. of Mariquita), based on a 1559 *visita* (administrative inspection). Analyzes ecology, demography, and economic system of indigenous peoples to highlight two points: 1) the appropriative nature of colonialism, and 2) the rapidity of change between first contact with Europeans and the date of the visita.

730 Trelles Aréstegui, Efraín. Linajes y futuro. Lima: SUR: Otorongo, 1994. 190 p.: bibl., ill.

An unfootnoted, but well-informed explanatory essay on the misinterpretations between Spaniards and indigenous peoples during (and after) the encounter in the Andes.

Especially considers how two ethnic groups initially misjudged and continue to misunderstand each other.

Universitätsbibliothek Eichstätt (Germany). Die Bücher der Maya, Mixteken und Azteken: die Schrift und ihre Funktion in vorspanischen und kolonialen Codices; Katalog. See item 600.

731 Uribe, María Victoria. Los Pasto y etnias relacionadas: arqueología y etnohistoria. (*in* Area septentrional andina norte: arqueologia y etnohistoria. Otavalo, Ecuador: Instituto Otavaleño de Antropología; Quito: Ediciones del Banco Central del Ecuador, 1995, p. 367–438, bibl., ill., maps, tables)

Lengthy, well-documented article on the Pastos of southern Colombia and northern Ecuador from the 9th-17th centuries. Refutes idea that political units were small, isolated, self-sufficient, local enclaves characterized by a simple and stable internal organization. Brings together archeological, ethnohistorical, and linguistic data to show that there was much exchange and contact with neighboring peoples. See also item **732.** There is some overlap between the two articles (by the same author) which appear in the same volume.

732 Uribe, María Victoria. Los Pasto y la red regional de intercambios de productos y materias primas: siglos IX a XVI D.C. (*in* Area septentrional andina norte: arqueologia y etnohistoria. Otavalo, Ecuador: Instituto Otavaleño de Antropología; Quito: Ediciones del Banco Central del Ecuador, 1995, p. 439–458, facsims., ill., map)

A study of the inhabitants of the Pasto region from the 9th-15th centuries, based on archeological and historical analyses. Mentions regional economic production and exchanges. On the last point, relies heavily on F. Salomon's work on indigenous merchants, or *mindalaes*. However, work pays little attention to motives and mechanisms of exchange, the dates and provenance of the information, and where historical evidence is written. See also item **731.**

733 Uzcátegui Andrade, Byron. Los llanganates y la tumba de Atahualpa. Quito: Abya-Yala: Instituto Panamericano de Geografía e Historia, Sección Nacional del Ecuador, 1992. 171 p.: bibl., ill., map.

A short inquiry into the final resting place of the Inca Atahualpa placed in the broader context of imperial and encounter history. Author believes that the grave will be found on or near Cerro Hermoso, a pre-Inca and Inca sacred site.

734 Uzcátegui M., César. Una aproximación al estudio de la política indigenista venezolana en el siglo XIX. (*Montalbán/Caracas*, 28, 1995, p. 195–207, bibl.)

Catalogs various 19th-century laws on indigenous land holdings. Does not attempt to verify to what extent these laws and decrees were observed and implemented.

735 Vargas Paliza, Ernesto. Lawata: comunicación retruecano y mnemotecnico inka, siglos XVII—XVIII; ensayo de cultura andina para la historia de Cusco. Cuzco, Peru: E. Vargas P.: El Distribuidor, Los Andes, 1994. 112 p.: bibl., ill.

Studies the use of a type of flute called *lawata.* The flute, made from a condor bone, invokes the Andean people to return to their *wakas* (deities) and, as such, played a role in the rebellion of 1780.

736 Vargas Sarmiento, Patricia. Los embera y los cuna: impacto y reacción ante la ocupación española, siglos XVI y XVII. Bogotá: Instituto Colombiano de Antropología: CEREC, 1993. 199 p.: bibl., maps, tables. (Serie Amerindia; no. 6)

A regional study of indigenous resistance to Spanish colonialism during the 16th-18th centuries, based on archival research, oral history, and secondary literature. The protagonists of the story include the Embera, the Burumia, the Tule, and the Carauta, who all lived near the Atrato river. Data on *parcialidades, encomenderos*, and population are presented in tables. Several maps illustrate the text.

737 Vega, Juan José. Túpac Amaru y sus compañeros. v. 1–2. Qosqo, Peru: Municipalidad del Qosqo, 1995. 2 v. (507 p.): bibl., ill., index.

Part One of a three-part study of José Gabriel Túpac Amaru and the rebellion he led presents his biography, followed by that of his companion Micaela Bastidas. Final part provides information about Túpac Amaru's collaborators in the rebellions in Cuzco (Qosqo), Arequipa, Ayacucho, Puno, and Lambayeque.

738 Villalobos R., Sergio. La vida fronteriza en Chile. Madrid: Editorial MAPFRE, 1992. 435 p.: bibl., ill., index, maps. (Colecciones MAPFRE 1492)

A welcome, serious study of frontier life in Tarapacá and Araucanía. Reviews physical landscape and forms of its exploitation, and indigenous inhabitants for each region. Also includes extensive description of Araucanians' struggle and resistance. Based solidly on manuscript collections in Chile and Spain. See also items **2415** and **2401.**

739 Villanueva Sotomayor, Julio. El Tahuantinsuyu: la propiedad privada y el modelo curacal de producción. Lima: Ediciones Luciérnaga, 1994. 269 p.: maps.

A popular text on Andean history from the earliest hunter-gatherers to the beginning of colonial times. Develops a model of the *curacal* mode of production. Posits that *curacas*, as elites, appropriated the best lands and formed large, privately held haciendas before Spanish arrival.

740 Villarías Robles, Juan J.R. El fetichismo de la fuente etnohistórica fiable: teorías y textos del debate sobre el estado incaico y la comunidad andina (primera parte). (*Rev. Indias,* 55:203, enero/abril 1995, p. 175–202)

An excellent, two-part article reviews the differing interpretations of the nature of the economic structure of the Inca empire and examines the sources on which each argument is based. Maintains that the various authorities culled evidence to support their own views, rather than basing their conclusions on all of the (sometimes vague or contradictory) available material. For bibliographic citation for pt. 2 of this work, see item **741.**

741 Villarías Robles, Juan J.R. El fetichismo de la fuente etnohistórica fiable: teorías y textos del debate sobre el estado incaico y la comunidad andina (segunda parte). (*Rev. Indias,* 55:204, mayo/agosto 1995, p. 301–331, tables)

See item **740.**

742 Visión de los otros y visión de sí mismos: descubrimiento o invención entre el Nuevo Mundo y el viejo? Recopilación de Fermín del Pino and Carlos Lázaro. Madrid: Consejo Superior de Investigaciones Científicas, 1995. 373 p.: bibl., ill. (Colección Biblioteca de historia de América; 12)

A serious, well-crafted collection of essays first presented at a seminar during 1992–93 centers on identity. Analysis of the texts by José de Anchieta, Acosta, and Polo de Ondegardo lead to new understandings about cannibals in Brazil. Jesuit writings inform about the Chaqueños and their resistance to colonialism. Texts by F. Núñez de Pineda Bascuñán and Fray Juan Falcón offer contrasting views on Araucanian society. Also analyzes papers of the Malaspina Expedition for new insights. Other papers present research on the *indigenismo* movement and nationalism in 19th-20th centuries.

743 Yapu Gutiérrez, Freddy. El Titi: tradición mito y leyenda del Lago Titicaca. (*in* Reunión Anual de Etnología, 6th, La Paz?, 1992. Actas. La Paz: Museo Nacional de Etnografía y Folklore, 1993, t. 1, p. 61–71, bibl.)

A short essay, based on dictionaries, chronicles, and secondary sources, explores the meaning and significance of the word *titi.* Finds that the word refers to a gray cat indigenous to the area of Titicaca. The word is associated with fertility in the myth, oral history, and religious beliefs of the inhabitants of the Altiplano.

744 Zanabria Zamudio, Rómulo. Visión castrense del antiguo Perú. Qosqo, Peru: Municipalidad del Qosqo, 1994. 242 p.: bibl., ill.

A study of the Central Andes reviews Chavín, Sechin, Parakas, Nazca, Recuay, Moche, Vicus, Tiwanaku, Wari, Chimu, Chachapoyas, and Inca history. Particular attention is given to geography, interethnic group conflict, and the army of the Incas.

745 Zanolli, Carlos Eduardo. Estructuración étnica de la Quebrada de Humahuaca: el caso de los Omaguacas; estudios preliminares. (*Poblac. Soc.,* 1, dic. 1993, p. 67–78)

Attempts to identify and delimit what is meant by the term *Omaguacas* in 16th century primary sources. Shows that the word has both a demographic and a territorial basis.

746 **Zucchi, Alberta.** Las migraciones Maipures: diversas líneas de evidencias para la interpretación arqueológica. (*Am. Negra*, 1, junio 1991, p. 113–138, bibl., maps, tables)

Article on the expansion of the Maipure ethnolinguistic group presents a new model of the migration of the Piapoco. Based on archeological, ethnohistorical, and linguistic analyses and oral history.

Zuluaga Gómez, Víctor. Vida, pasión y muerte de los indígenas de Caldas y Risaralda. See *HLAS 57:1145.*

GENERAL HISTORY

JOHN BRITTON, *Gasque Professor of History, Francis Marion University*

THIS TWO-YEAR HARVEST of books and articles on general topics yielded some welcome contributions, especially on the immigration experience, nationalism, and economic history. The expected decline in the quantity of publications on the early colonial period with the passing of the Quincentennial did not mean that the quality of work on this era diminished to any appreciable extent.

The field of social history benefitted from several outstanding publications that applied a healthy diversity of approaches to the task of understanding day-to-day existence, especially in the colonial period. López Cantos examined public entertainment, such as fiestas, in the colonial era as a means of probing the lifestyles of several social strata (item **916**). Martinelli Gifre analyzed early methods of communication between native Americans and the Spanish ranging from translation to physical gestures (item **924**), and Mira Caballos discussed the small group of native Americans who were transported to and lived in Spain in the 1500s (item **935**). Martínez's arresting examination of the evolution of styles of dress traced fashion from the 16th-19th centuries (item **794**).

A quartet of authors concentrated on the signs of disruption and unrest that began to appear in the 18th century. Gallegos' survey of society under the Bourbon Reforms pointed out the stresses and strains evident in law enforcement, the legal system, and native American communities (item **841**). Merino and Newson provided a scholarly overview of the consequences of the expulsion of the Jesuit order from their mission systems in North and South America (item **933**). In a refined work of synthesis, McFarlane assessed the causes of several major revolts in the last decades of the colonial period with an emphasis on local grievances as the driving forces behind the likes of Tupac Amaru and Hidalgo (item **1005**).

The role of women in Latin American history continues to receive much-needed attention. Reviewed in the previous volume, but meriting further mention here is Lavrin's subtle and substantial critique of Spanish American women's writing in the 1970s-80s (see *HLAS 56:1068*). In this biennium, outstanding studies appeared on topics from the early colonial period to the late-20th century. Pareja Ortiz contributed two valuable colonial era studies: a specialized examination of the daily life of Sevillian women in the Americas (item **946**), and a survey of marriage laws under the Spanish empire (item **945**). Economic and political issues were at the forefront of two impressive articles: Monteón examined the burdens placed upon women in the Great Depression of the 1930s and the debt crises of the 1980s (item **1034**), and Luna continued her consistently fine work in gender studies with an analysis of women's political participation (item **1033**). Many publications in this recent surge in gender history have challenged the usefulness of the Marianismo-machismo dichotomy. Exploring and enlarging the innovations in this area, French and James assembled a collection of well-researched articles based on sensitive and sophisticated approaches to the study of gender in the work place, the union hall, and the realm of politics. In their introductory and concluding essays, they point out promising directions in research and conceptualization that have large ramifications in this area (item **1003**).

Nationalism, a topic that has received little attention in Latin American history in recent decades, re-emerged in this biennium in the work of scholars following the lead of David Brading, whose prescient and impressive 1991 synthesis, *First America*, examined the colonial era sources of Creole national identity in Mexico and Peru (see *HLAS 54:941*). In this biennium, Brading extended his study of nationalism into the late 19th and 20th centuries in a perceptive essay (item **760**). Entrena Durán emphasized the function of populism in Brazil, Argentina, and Mexico through the coalescence of the nation-state in these three countries in the 1930s-40s (item **1030**). Bermudez's innovative study traced the development of the graphic arts in Latin America from the colonial period into the early 20th century. His interpretation reveals that national identity began to play a significant role in the graphic arts in the early 1800s (item **757**).

One of the major benefits of the flood of publications related to the Quincentennial was the large number of books and articles on the subject of immigration. Editorial MAPFRE was a leader in this important field and deserves special recognition for its prolific role in immigration history, as well as in many areas in Latin American history and international history in general. The long list of MAPFRE publications constitutes a historiographical accomplishment of significant proportions that will have a lasting influence on the understanding of the interactions of many nations and peoples. Five excellent examples of this type of contribution can be found in this biennium's list on immigration history: Albonico's book on the Italians in the Americas from Columbus to Valentino (item **748**), Jones' survey of British immigration to the Western Hemisphere (item **786**), Yanaguida's much-needed discussion of the movement of Japanese to Latin America, the US, and Canada (item **829**), Kitroeff's path-breaking work on Greeks in the Americas (item **1031**), and Morner's magisterial overview of immigration throughout the region (item **802**).

Other authors contributed to the growing bibliography on this topic. Klich and Lesser's article on Middle Eastern immigrants (item **1032**) and Vilar's examination of Jewish immigration from Morocco (item **1024**) covered topics rarely studied while Yanez Gallardo and Biagini examined familiar ground by using new approaches. Yanez Gallardo produced two books: one, a quantitative study of general Spanish immigration in the 19th and 20th centuries (item **830**), and the second, an examination of kinship networks in Catalonian migration to the Americas (item **1025**); and Biagini appropriately infused intellectual history into immigration studies with his exploration of the growing Spanish interest in Argentina in the last decades of the 19th century (item **2822**).

Perhaps as a reflection of the economic turmoil of recent years, a number of scholars have focused on economic history. Vila Vilar wrote an exemplary study of the activities of two merchant families in Peru and Spain of the late 1500s and early 1600s (see *HLAS 56:2511*). Yeager employed the concepts of neoinstitutional economics to explain the Spanish Crown's decision to favor the encomienda over slavery as a labor source (item **993**). Two historians give serious, in-depth treatment to often overlooked, but important topics. Río Moreno details the significance of the pig in the Spanish conquest (item **956**), and Smith explores the use of the tomato from the preconquest period into the 19th century (item **817**). Footpaths and railroads symbolize the evolution of transportation systems through the colonial era to the middle of the 1800s as covered in the superior synthesis by Gutiérrez Alvarez (item **776**). Dore contributed a thought-provoking examination of the social and ecological repercussions of mining in Latin America (item **767**), while Haber rendered a pointed critique of the concept of dependency in his articulate introduction to the New Economic History (item **777**). Three important studies of foreign economic influences in the region appeared: Riguzzi's article on the Latin American reaction to the intrusions of US business interests from 1870–1914 (item **1013**), Bottcher's historiographical summation of published works on the role of British merchant houses in the region from 1760–1860 (item **759**), and Jones' overview of British trade and investment in the region (item **785**). Finally, in an exceptional work of synthesis, Salvatorre adroitly analyzed three surges of economic reform: the Bourbon era of the 1700s, mid-19th-century liberalism, and the neoliberalism of recent years (item **812**).

GENERAL

747   Adams, Jerome R. Notable Latin American women: twenty-nine leaders, rebels, poets, battlers, and spies, 1500–1900. Jefferson, N.C.: McFarland & Co., 1995. 191 p.: bibl., index, maps.

Straightforward and brief biographical sketches of 29 women including Doña Marina, Juana Inés de la Cruz, Manuela Sáenz, and Leopoldina of Brazil.

748   Albònico, Aldo and **Gianfausto Rosoli.** Italia y América. Traducción de la segunda parte de Margarita Hernando de Larramendi. Madrid: Editorial MAPFRE, 1994. 449 p.: bibl., indexes, maps. (Col. MAPFRE 1492. Col. Europa y América; 8)

Impressive work of synthesis examines important and seldom-covered subjects. First half (by Albònico) deals with Italian presence in the Americas as projected by cultural images and individual personalities from Columbus to Mussolini to Valentino. Second half, by Rosoli, is an historical account of Italian immigration emphasizing policies of the Italian government and condition of Italian communities in the US, Argentina, and Brazil. Although lacking footnotes, authors' bibliographical essay is helpful.

749   Alvarez, Jesús Timoteo and **Ascensión Martínez.** Historia de la prensa hispanoamericana. Colaboración técnica de Enrique Ríos Vicente. Madrid: Editorial

MAPFRE, 1992. 348 p.: bibl., ill., indexes. (Col. Realidades americanas; 10. Col. MAPFRE 1492)

Broad synthesis ranging from colonial era to the 1980s serves as a useful introduction to an important and often neglected topic. Over 260 of the text's 323 pages are devoted to the independence era and the national period, and are organized in a country-by-country format.

750   Alvarez Gila, Oscar. Bibliografía sobre emigración y presencia religiosa navarra en la América contemporánea. (*Anu. Estud. Am.*, 51:1, 1994, p. 267–286)

Unique bibliographical essay focuses on 19th and 20th centuries and covers the missionary activities of several orders including Capuchin, Franciscan, Dominican, and Jesuit. Also includes a biographical section.

751   Alvarez Gila, Oscar. Cultura, nacionalidad y pasaporte: consideraciones sobre las "sociedades étnicas" como fuente para el estudio de la emigración europea a América. (*Ibero-Am. Arch.*, 21:1/2, 1995, p. 3–20)

Thoughtful reconsideration of European immigration to the Americas over last two centuries features methodology and historiography.

752   Arrom, Silvia Marina. Rethinking urban politics in Latin America before the populist era. (*in* Riots in the cities: popular politics and the urban poor in Latin

America, 1765–1910. Wilmington, Del.: Scholarly Resources Inc., 1996, p. 1–16)

Introduction to collection of essays offers challenging interpretation of the role of urban crowds in Latin America before 1910. Argues that urban masses used public celebrations as well as rebellions to exert pressure on elites.

753 Avilesinos en América. Dirección de Baudilio Barreiro Mallón. Avilés, Spain: Casa Municipal de Cultura, 1992. 326 p.: bibl., ill. (Col. En/torno; 3)

Statistical studies of immigration patterns and biographical sketches dating from the early 1500s to the early 1900s. Included in biographies are Pedro Menéndez de Avilés of colonial Florida and José Menéndez, a pioneer in 19th-century Patagonia.

754 Bagú, Sergio. Perspectivas de la historiografía latinoamericana. (*Bol. Am.*, 36:46, 1996, p. 55–65)

Stimulating discussion of recent trends in Latin American historiography including the application of the scientific method and economic theory as well as the ideas of commentators such as Domingo Maza Zavala, Paul Kennedy, and Jared Diamond.

755 Banco de España. La formación de los bancos centrales en España y América Latina, siglos XIX y XX. v. 1–2. Madrid: Banco de España, Servicio de Estudios, 1994. 2 v.: bibl., ill. (Estudios de historia económica, 0213–2702; 29–30)

Scholarly essays on an important topic tend to concentrate on 19th and early-20th centuries in Spain, Mexico, and Argentina, with additional coverage of Brazil, the Andean nations, and the Caribbean. Contributions are footnoted and some have useful bibliographies.

756 Barcia, María del Carmen. La esclavitud moderna en la historiografía americana, 1974–1994. (*Hist. Soc./Valencia*, 19, 1994, p. 129–139, facsims.)

A trenchant review of major publications organized in the following categories: theoretical works, demography and statistics, economics, and social history.

757 Bermúdez, Jorge R. Gráfica e identidad nacional. México: Univ. Autónoma Metropolitana-Xochimilco, 1994. 204 p.: bibl., ill.

Impressive, succinct interpretation of the development of graphic art in Latin America from colonial period to early-20th century. Examines postcards, popular press, and photographs.

758 Bonnichon, Philippe. Los navegantes franceses y el descubrimiento de América, siglos XVI, XVII y XVIII. Traducción de Irene Echevarría Soriano. Madrid: Editorial MAPFRE, 1992. 389 p.: bibl., ill., indexes, maps. (Col. Mar y América; 17. Col. MAPFRE 1492)

Synthesis of French role in the Americas and impact of the Americas on France. Examines not only the exploratory expeditions but also settlements in Guiana, the Caribbean, and Canada. Three of Bonnichon's 14 chapters assess the French intellectual response to the Americas as reflected in philosophy, literature, and science.

759 Böttcher, Nikolaus. Casas de comercio británicas y sus intereses en América Latina, 1760–1860: estado y problemas de la investigación actual. (*Ibero-Am. Arch.*, 22:1/2, 1996, p. 191–241, bibl.)

Useful historiographical survey of the work of British commercial houses in Latin America, arranged by country. Cognizant of the issues surrounding the concept of informal imperialism, author provides a careful, even-handed discussion of the major published works in this area.

760 Brading, D.A. Nationalism and state-building in Latin American history. (*Ibero-Am. Arch.*, 20:1/2, 1994, p. 83–108)

Thoughtful and thought-provoking essay traces nationalism in Latin America from its creole roots in 18th and 19th centuries to full blown "romantic" nationalism in the 20th century as reflected in works of Rodó, Vasconcelos, Ugarte, Gamio, and others.

761 Carroll, Patrick. Recent literature on Latin American slavery. (*LARR*, 31:1, 1996, p. 135–147)

Informative review essay provides capsule summaries of the findings of leading scholars in the field. Examines macro-historical works by Inikori and Engerman, Meillassoux, Solow, and Thornton, together with more specialized studies by Blanchard, Bush, and Pérez.

Castro de la Mata, Ramiro and **Nils D. Noya T.** Coca: erythroxylum coca; erythroxylum novogranatense; bibliografía comentada. See *HLAS 57:4539.*

762 Centro de Estudios Regionales Andinos Bartolomé de Las Casas (Peru). La venida del reino: religión, evangelización y cultura en América, siglos XVI-XX. Recopilación de Gabriela Ramos. Cusco, Peru: Centro de Estudios Regionales Andinos Bartolomé de Las Casas, 1994. 435 p.: bibl. (Cuadernos para la historia de la evangelización en América Latina, 1012–2737; 12)

Historical essays exploring the interaction of European Catholicism and native American peoples include considerable archival research while pursuing a diversity of topics.

763 Chevalier, François. L'Amérique Latine: de l'indépendance à nos jours. 2. éd. Paris: Presses universitaires de France, 1993. 723 p.: bibl., ill., index, maps. (Nouvelle Clio, 0768–2379)

Senior French Mexicanist updates his handbook on contemporary Latin American history first published in 1977 (see *HLAS 40:2148*). For each region an annotated core bibliography, list of research tools, chronology, and statistics are introduced by a brief survey on the period in light of recent literature, pointing to innovative approaches and agendas for future research. Reflects throughout on Latin America as a culture born out of the Iberian matrix, on the emergence of an "Ibero-American modernity," and on the interplay of slow tempo and catalytic processes. [A. Pérotin-Dumon]

764 Coloquio Internacional de Heráldica, 7th, Cáceres, Spain, 1991. Las armerías en Europa al comenzar la Edad Moderna y su proyección al Nuevo Mundo: actas. Organización de la Académie internationale d'héraldique. Edición coordinada por Faustino Menéndez Pidal de Navascués. Madrid: Dirección de Archivos Estatales, 1993. 459 p.: bibl., ill. (some col.).

Features 24 historical essays on this highly specialized topic encompassing Spain, Portugal, Latin America, and several European countries. Contains numerous illustrations.

765 Congreso Internacional sobre los Dominicos y el Nuevo Mundo, 4th, Bogotá, 1993. Los Dominicos y el Nuevo Mundo, siglos XVIII-XIX: actas. Edición de José Barrado Barquilla. Salamanca, Spain: Editorial San Esteban, 1995. 647 p., 16 p. of plates: bibl., index. (Monumenta histórica iberoamericana de la Orden de Predicadores; 6)

Contains 27 historical studies covering a variety of topics, but focusing largely on conflicts and crises involving the Catholic Church and several governments.

766 Cuesta Domingo, Mariano. Extremadura y América. Madrid: Editorial MAPFRE, 1992. 350 p.: bibl., ill., indexes, maps. (Col. Las Españas y América; 8. Col. MAPFRE 1492)

Focuses on the Spanish conquest, with Cortez and the Pizarro brothers as the central characters. Based on published works.

767 Dore, Elizabeth. Una interpretación socio-ecológica de la historia minera latinoamericana. (*Ecol. Polít.*, 7, mayo 1994, p. 49–68)

Bold, provocative overview of the social consequences and ecological impact of mining in Latin America from early colonial era in New Spain and Peru to 1980s Amazon Basin gold rush. Based on published studies and thoroughly footnoted.

768 Elkin, Judith Laikin. Colonial origins of contemporary anti-Semitism in Latin America. (*in* The Jewish diaspora in Latin America: new studies on history and literature. New York: Garland Publ., 1996, p. 127–141, bibl.)

Finely honed interpretive essay links modern anti-Semitism with aggressive conquest-era Catholicism.

769 Elkin, Judith Laikin. Exploring the Jewish archipelago in Latin America. (*LARR*, 30:3, 1995, p. 224–238, bibl.)

Informative review essay examines recent growth in the historical studies of Jewish communities in Latin America, with particular attention to Argentina, Cuba, Mexico, and Brazil.

770 Eltis, David and **David Richardson.** The "numbers game" and routes to slavery. (*Slavery Abolit.*, 18:1, April 1997, p. 1–15, table)

Valuable historiographical overview of recent findings on African slave trade emphasizes resources available in the database at the W.E.B. Du Bois Institute at Harvard University.

771 **Familia y vida privada en la historia de Iberoamérica: seminario de historia de la familia.** Coordinación de Pilar Gonzalbo Aizpuru y Cecilia Andrea Rabell. México: El Colegio de México, Univ. Nacional Autónoma de México, 1996. 550 p.: bibl., ill. (some col.), index.

Collection of 22 well-researched studies covers early colonial era into early-20th century. Many are based on archival research; all are thoroughly footnoted. A 43-page index enhances volume's value. Approximately half of the studies deal with Mexico.

772 **Fisher, John R.** El americanismo en Gran Bretaña durante los últimos 25 años, con especial referencia al período colonial. (*in* Del este al oeste al encuentro de otros mundos: líneas actuales de investigación; actas del cincuentenario de la Escuela de Estudios Hispano-Americanos, CSIC. Sevilla: CSIC, 1993, p. 35–49, appendices, table)

Brief, informative survey of the growth in Latin American studies in Great Britain from 1967–92 discusses specific academic disciplines and publications.

Forment, Carlos A. Socio-historical models of Spanish-America democratization: a review and reformation. See *HLAS 57:4544.*

773 **Forum international des sciences humaines (Paris).** De los imperios a las naciones: Iberoamérica. Dirección de Antonio Annino, Luis Castro Leiva y François-Xavier Guerra. Zaragoza, Spain: IberCaja, Obra Cultural, 1994. 620 p.: bibl.

Important set of 25 essays covers political, economic, social, and cultural history of Latin America from colonial era into late-20th century. Contributors include D.A. Brading, Francois-Xavier Guerra, Josefina Vázquez, Antonio Annino, and Luis Castro Leiva.

774 **García de la Herrán Muñoz, María del Carmen** and **María del Mar Graña Cid.** Notas bibliográficas para el estudio del franciscanismo en la América contemporánea, siglos XIX-XX. (*Arch. Ibero-Am.,* 57:225/226, enero/dic. 1997, p. 3–65, bibl.)

Extensive 50-page listing of published works on the history of the Franciscans, organized in the following categories: general, missions, convents, biographies, spiritual works, and linguistic works and dictionaries

(in indigenous languages). Helpful introductory essay.

775 **García del Pino, César.** Vikingos, españoles, genoveses, franceses y holandeses en América. Morelia, Mexico: Depto. de Historia Latinoamericana, Instituto de Investigaciones Históricas, Univ. Michoacana de San Nicolás de Hidalgo, 1994. 127 p.: bibl., ill. (Col. Alborada latinoamericana; 5)

Miscellaneous essays span the centuries from the Vikings to Piet Heyn to the Cuban Navy's actions against German submarines in 1943.

776 **Gutiérrez Alvarez, Secundino-José.** Las comunicaciones en América: de la senda primitiva al ferrocarril. Madrid: Editorial MAPFRE, 1993. 424 p.: bibl., ill., maps. (Col. Realidades americanas; 17. Col. MAPFRE 1492)

Admirable attempt to synthesize an important topic, study ranges from 16th to 19th centuries and covers ocean transportation, interoceanic transit across the Central American isthmus, various colonial roads to mines and ports, and the 19th-century emergence of railroads.

777 **Haber, Stephen.** Economic growth and Latin American economic historiography. (*in* How Latin America fell behind: essays on the economic histories of Brazil and Mexico, 1800–1914. Stanford, Calif.: Stanford Univ. Press, 1997, p. 1–33, bibl.)

Hard-hitting critique of dependency theory also explains some of the basic methods used by practitioners of the New Economic History led by John Coatsworth. Also discusses role of 1992 conference at Stanford Univ. in injecting New Economic History into the work of Latin American historians.

778 **Hahner, June E.** Recent tendencies in the historiography of woman in Latin America. (*Not. Bibliogr. Hist.,* 28:160, jan./março 1996, p. 50–59)

Concise, thoughtful essay points out the importance of and the need for comparative studies in women's history.

779 **Herrera, Luis Alberto de.** La Revolución Francesa y Sudamérica. 2. ed. Montevideo?: República Oriental del Uruguay, Camara de Representantes, 1988. 281 p.: bibl., ill. (Serie Teorización política; 2)

Collection of 15 essays on connections between the French Revolution and South

America also includes a 10-page introduction by Walter Santoro. Reflects Herrera's interest in modern political and intellectual history.

780 Hilton, Sylvia L. and Ignacio González Casasnovas. Fuentes manuscritas para la historia de Iberoamérica: guía de instrumentos de investigación. Suplemento. Madrid: Fundación Histórica Tavera, 1997. 350 p.: indexes.

Supplement adds 1,343 manuscript collection guides to the 3,729 included in the 1995 publication (see *HLAS 56:716*). Also continues the six indexes used in the first publication.

781 Historia social de las ciencias en América Latina. Coordinación de Juan José Saldaña. México: UNAM, Coordinación de Humanidades; UNAM, Coordinación de la Investigación Científica; M.A. Porrúa, 1996. 541 p.: bibl., ill. (Problemas educativos de México)

Valuable collection of 14 articles plus impressive introductory essay by Saldaña constitutes important contribution in an area too often left on the periphery. Contributions span the preconquest, colonial, and national periods. Contain useful bibliographies.

782 The human tradition in modern Latin America. Edited by William H. Beezley and Judith Ewell. Wilmington, Del.: SR Books, 1997. 277 p.: bibl., index. (Latin American silhouettes)

Reworks classic biographical approach to social-political history. Covers 1780 to present. Intended for the classroom.

783 International Federation of Latin American and Caribbean Studies. Congress. 6th, Warsaw, 1993. Memorias. Foro Temático 9: Las relaciones América Latina—España. Foro Temático 12: Los europeos (no-ibéricos) en la historia latinoamericana. Rio de Janeiro: UERJ, 1994. 98 p.: bibl., tables.

Spanish and Latin American historians contributed to this thematic collection of 10 essays on relationships between Spain and Latin America, mainly in late-19th and much of 20th century. Also contains three essays on other European influences: Marxism-Leninism, ideologies of European immigrants, and German influence in the Chaco War. A diverse and valuable collection.

784 Izard, Miquel and Javier Laviña. Maíz, banano y trigo: el ayer de América Latina. Barcelona: EUB; Les Punxes Distribuidora, 1996. 195 p.: bibl. (Humanidades; 16)

Polemical treatment of the plight of the indigenous populations under colonial-era aggressive Spanish expansionism and US imperialism thereafter. Brief, vitriolic summary of this point of view.

785 Jones, Charles A. El Reino Unido y América: inversiones e influencia económica. Madrid: Editorial MAPFRE, 1992. 259 p.: bibl., indexes. (Col. Europa y América; 4. Col. MAPFRE 1492)

Well-organized synthesis of the history of British trade and investment in the Americas including Canada and US as well as Latin America. Divides chronology of economic history into three phases: early- to middle-19th century, 1860–1920, and 1920-present. Informative 14-page bibliographic essay.

786 Jones, Maldwyn Allen. El Reino Unido y América: emigración británica. Madrid: Editiorial MAPFRE, 1992. 382 p.: bibl., maps, indexes. (Col. Europa y América; 5. Col. MAPFRE 1492)

General survey of British immigration to the Americas from 1500s to 1990 includes Canada and US as well as Latin America. Based on scholarly monographs and published sources, this outstanding work provides broad synthesis of major topic in international history.

787 Jornadas de Andalucía y América, 8th, Univ. de la Santa María de Rábida, Seville, 1988. Propiedad de la tierra, latifundios y movimientos campesinos: actas. Edición de Bibiano Torres Ramírez. Sevilla, Spain: Junta de Andalucía, Consejería de Agricultura y Pesca; Huelva, Spain: Excma. Diputación de Huelva; El Monte. Caja de Huelva y Sevilla; Univ. de Santa María de la Rábida, 1991. 383 p.: bibl.

Important collection of 15 well-researched studies on rural history from colonial era to 20th century includes specialized works on Andalucía, Mexico, the Andean region, and Brazil.

788 Jornadas Presencia de España en América—Aportación Gallega, 1st, Pazo de Mariñán, Spain, 1987. Actas.

Madrid: Editorial Deimos, 1989. 760 p.: bibl., ill.

Essays examine several topics with some emphasis on immigration, covering colonial period to 20th century.

789 Keen, Benjamin. A history of Latin America. 5th ed. Boston: Houghton Mifflin Co., 1996. 622 p.: bibl., ill., index, maps.

Revision of standard college textbook includes new sections on the European arrival in America, NAFTA, and the Colombian "drug lords."

790 Kirby, Peadar. Ireland and Latin America: links and lessons. Dublin: Trócaire; Gill and MacMillan, 1992. 192 p.: bibl., index, maps. (Trócaire world topics; 2)

Essays explore role of the Irish and Ireland in Latin America, emphasizing the Catholic Church in 1970s and 1980s. Not a definitive study, but suggestive of some important issues.

791 Labandeira Fernández, Amancio. Introducción a las tipobibliografías hispanoamericanas. Madrid: Fundación Histórica Tavera, 1997. 44 p. (Serie Fuentes Bibliográficas Tavera)

Brief overview of the history of printing and bibliographic publication in Latin America features extensive, informative footnotes. Includes a chapter on José Toribio Medina.

792 Lerman Alperstein, Aída. Ideas y proyectos de la integración latinoamericana: siglo XIX y primera mitad del siglo XX. (*Mundo Nuevo/Caracas,* 17:3/4, julio/dic. 1994, p. 307–324)

Sweeping overview of various efforts to unify Latin America outlines main characteristics of several leaders of international stature from Bolívar to Perón. Based on published works.

793 Malamud, Carlos *et al.* Historia de América: temas didácticos. Madrid: Editorial Universitas, 1993. 525 p.: bibl.

Survey text on Latin American history from indigenous societies of preconquest era to late-20th century. Strongest coverage on social and economic history.

794 Martínez Carreño, Aída. La prisión del vestido: aspectos sociales del traje en América. Bogotá: Planeta Colombiana Edi-

torial, 1995. 203 p.: bibl., ill. (Col. Ariel historia)

Serious historical study of area ignored by most scholars. Combines cultural and economic factors to explain rich diversity in the evolution of styles of dress for men and women. Although beginning with colonial era, focus is on 19th century and emergence of "traje nacional." Much commentary deals with Colombia. Research base includes archival work and contemporary publications as well as historical monographs.

795 Martínez del Peral Fortón, Rafael. Las armas blancas en España e Indias: ordenamiento jurídico. Madrid: Editorial MAPFRE, 1992. 277 p.: bibl., ill. (Col. MAPFRE 1492. Col. Armas y América; 5)

Sweeping history of the development of swords, bayonets, and related weaponry from the late-Middle Ages to 19th century contains many useful descriptions and is nicely illustrated.

796 Martínez Montiel, Luz M. Negros en América. Madrid: Editorial MAPFRE, 1992. 372 p.: bibl., indexes. (Col. América, crisol; 2. Col. MAPFRE 1492)

Historical survey of African peoples in the Americas ranges geographically from British North America to Spanish South America and chronologically from early colonial era to 20th century. Over half of text deals with African-American cultures within modern nations of the Western Hemisphere. Intended for the general reader, work has few footnotes and a sparse bibliography.

797 Medina, Miguel Angel. Los dominicos en América: presencia y actuación de los dominicos en la América colonial española de los siglos XVI-XIX. Madrid: Editorial MAPFRE, 1992. 353 p.: bibl., facsims., indexes, maps. (Col. Iglesia católica en el Nuevo Mundo. Col. MAPFRE 1492)

Introduction to history of the Dominican order in Spanish America is divided into six sections: the Caribbean and Venezuela, New Spain, Central America, New Granada, Peru-Ecuador, and southern South America. Each section discusses order's arrival and its evangelization and educational activities. Includes some archival research.

798 Meyer, Eugenia. Los nuevos caminos de la historia oral en America Latina. (*Hist. Fuente Oral,* 13, 1995, p. 97–102)

Widely respected pioneer in the field persuasively defends oral history as a valuable source for the study of all levels of society.

799 **Mirelman, Victor A.** Los sefardíes en Latinoamérica después de la independencia. (*Sefárdica/Buenos Aires*, 11, sept. 1996, p. 55–88, photos)

General overview of Jewish presence throughout Latin America focuses on Curaçao community and its influence in the circum-Caribbean, as well as on Jewish populations in Brazil and Argentina. Chronological focus is on century after 1830. Extensive footnotes indicate secondary sources used.

800 **Mompradé, Electra L.** and **Tonatiúh Gutiérrez O.** Imagen de América. Prólogo y Elías Trabulse. México: Transportación Marítima Mexicana, 1996. 385 p.: bibl., ill. (some col.), maps.

Profusely illustrated, glossy-paged volume includes work of well-known artists and cartographers from late 1400s to late 1800s, covering both South and North America. Text consists of brief introductory comments and quotations from writers who were the contemporaries of the artists and cartographers.

801 **Morgan, Philip D.** The cultural implications of the Atlantic Slave Trade: African regional origins, American destinations and New World developments. (*Slavery Abolit.*, 18:1, April 1997, p. 122–145)

Synthesis of recent demographic research on connections between origins and American destinations of African slaves emphasizes difficult questions involving cultural continuity. Stresses Brazil, the Caribbean, and North America.

802 **Mörner, Magnus.** Aventureros y proletarios: los emigrantes en Hispanoamérica. Madrid: Editorial MAPFRE, 1992. 220 p.: bibl., ill., indexes, maps. (Col. América 92; 11. Col. MAPFRE 1492)

Valuable work encapsulates research and analysis of one of the foremost authorities on immigration history. Based on extensive reading of published studies, this relatively brief text furnishes a stimulating overview of the role of immigration from the colonial era into the last half of the 20th century.

803 **Mörner, Magnus.** El impacto de los productos latinoamericanos en la cultura material de Suecia con anterioridad a 1810. (*Jahrb. Gesch.*, 32, 1995, p. 231–256)

Careful study of presence of Latin American products such as silver, tobacco, potatoes, and sugar in Sweden makes excellent use of Swedish sources.

804 **Morón, Guillermo.** Hispanoamérica y Brasil en la historia general de América. (*in* Congresso das Academias da História Ibero-Americanas, *4th, Lisboa and Porto, Portugal, 1994.* Actas. Lisboa: Academia Portuguesa da História, 1996, p. 633–648, bibl.)

Very broad overview of Brazil's place in the history of the Western Hemisphere.

805 **Navarra y América.** Coordinación de José Andrés-Gallego. Madrid: Editorial MAPFRE, 1992. 521 p.: bibl., ill. (Col. Las Españas y América; 13. Col. MAPFRE 1492)

Social and economic history are the basic themes in study spanning five centuries. Includes archival research but lacks index.

806 **Núñez Jiménez, Antonio.** Un mundo aparte: aproximación a la historia de América Latina y el Caribe. Madrid: Ediciones de la Torre, 1994. 462 p.: bibl., index, map. (Col. Nuestro mundo; 32. Serie Historia)

General survey text is highlighted by biographical sketches of individuals such as Túpac Amaru, Miranda, Bolívar, Martí, and Castro.

807 **Palmié, Stephan.** A taste for human commodities: experiencing the Atlantic system. (*in* Slave cultures and the cultures of slavery. Knoxville: Univ. of Tennessee Press, 1995, p. 40–54, bibl.)

Intriguing exercise in the macrohistory of slavery examines distinctions between capitalist and noncapitalist manifestations. Based on monographs and published sources.

808 **Pereña, Luciano.** Genocidio en América. Madrid: Editorial MAPFRE, 1992. 401 p.: bibl., ill., indexes. (Col. Realidades americanas; 9 Col. MAPFRE 1492)

Extensive examination of debate concerning defeat and destruction of native

American cultures. Concentrates on testimonies of Fernández de Oviedo and Bernal Díaz del Castillo as well as Aztec and Inca accounts. Also traces evolution of the controversy through works of Las Casas, Teodoro de Bry, Juan de Solórzano, Servando Teresa de Mier, and others, from the 1500s to the 20th century. Includes 55 of de Bry's illustrations.

809 Rickenberg, Michael. Caudillos y caudillismo: la presentación del tema en los libros escolares latinoamericanos de historia. (*in* Latinoamérica: enseñanza de la historia, libros de textos y conciencia histórica. Buenos Aires: Alianza Editorial; FLACSO; Frankfurt: Georg Eckert Instituts, 1991, p. 172–193)

Survey discussion of caudillo image in textbooks and more specialized works emphasizes periodization and themes of climate, charisma, violence, and regionalism. Selections tend to concentrate on Bolivian and Mexican textbooks.

810 Rodríguez González, Jesús Jerónimo. Asturias y América. Madrid: MAPFRE, 1992. 339 p.: bibl., ill., indexes. (Col. las Españas y América; 12. Col. MAPFRE 1492)

Synthesis of the influence of Asturias in the Americas from 16th-20th centuries emphasizes period since 1800. Includes chapters on Asturian economic, cultural, and political contributions and on Asturian associations in the Americas. Draws largely from secondary sources.

Ruiz de Azúa y Martínez de Ezquerecocha, María Estibaliz. Vascongadas y América. See item **960.**

Sáenz-Díez, Juan Ignacio. Los riojanos en América. See item **963.**

811 Safford, Frank. Applying Moore's model to Latin America: some historians' observations. (*in* Agrarian structure & political power: landlord & peasant in the making of Latin America. Pittsburgh, Pa.: Univ. of Pittsburgh Press, 1995, p. 177–181)

Sophisticated summary of several efforts to apply Barrington Moore's conceptual framework to Latin America. Examines a range of conclusions that, in general, reveal more variety than consistency in the structural base of political power and, at most, rather limited landowner control of the state.

812 Salvatore, Ricardo D. Tres discursos de mercado en America Latina, 1750–1990. (*Rev. Hist. Am.*, 117, enero/junio 1994, p. 83–117, bibl.)

Useful discussion of language and the ideas of three economic reform movements: the Bourbon reforms, classic (or 19th-century) liberalism, and 20th-century neoliberalism. Last section contains a comparative analysis of these three versions of liberalism, constructed from the findings of a wide selection of economists and writers on economic topics.

809 Salvatore, Ricardo D. and **Carlos Aguirre.** The birth of the penitentiary in Latin America: toward an interpretive social history of prisons. (*in* The birth of the penitentiary in Latin America: essays on criminology, prison reform, and social control. Austin: Univ. of Texas Press, 1996, p. 1–43)

Innovative, exploratory essay on the evolution of prison systems in Latin America considers European and North American influences, the encroachment of modernity through growth of export economies, and conflicting perceptions of social order and acceptable behavior. Drawn from a wide range of monographs and interpretive studies.

814 Samara, Eni de Mesquita. A mulher e a família na historiografia latino-americana recente. (*Anos 90*, 1:1, maio 1993, p. 23–47, bibl.)

Overview of recent trends in family and women's history in Latin America devotes about half of text to 19th-century Brazil. Effectively contrasts earlier findings of Freyre with more recent works by Flora, Leite, Saffioto, Hahner, Graham, and others.

815 Schoultz, Lars. Beneath the United States: a history of U.S. policy toward Latin America. Cambridge, Mass.: Harvard Univ. Press, 1998. 476 p.: bibl., maps.

Excellent and well-written history of US foreign policy toward Latin America emphasizes often depreciative view that Washington statesmen had of their neighbors to the south. Based on extensive research of correspondence, speeches, and other foreign policy-related statements. Useful for specialists, undergraduates, and anyone interested in US/Latin American relations. [L. Boudon]

816 **Schwarzstein, Dora.** La historia oral en América Latina. (*Hist. Fuente Oral*, 14, 1995, p. 39–50)

Informative discussion of the development of oral history throughout the region with emphasis on Mexico, Argentina, and Costa Rica. Also comments on some problems associated with the "popularization" of oral history.

817 **Smith, Andrew F.** The tomato in America: early history, culture, and cookery. Columbia, S.C.: Univ. of South Carolina Press, 1994. 224 p.: bibl., ill., indexes.

Serious scholarly study traces biological origins of the tomato and evolution of human attitude toward its use from preconquest western South America, the Central America isthmus, and Mexico to 16th-century Europe. Then follows path of the tomato back across the Atlantic to 19th-century US. Also identifies another possible route for the tomato from the Caribbean to southeastern US. Drawn from scientific, medical, and historical works as well as traditional cookbooks.

818 **Soldevilla Oria, Consuelo.** Cantabria y América. Madrid: Editorial MAPFRE, 1992. 365 p.: bibl., ill., indexes, maps. (Col. Las Españas y América; 6 Col. MAPFRE 1492)

Broadly interpretive survey covers 1492–1950 and emphasizes 19th- and 20th-century Cantabrian migration to Cuba and Mexico.

819 **Symposium Internacional de Historia de la Masonería Española, 6th, Zaragoza, Spain, 1993.** La masonería española entre Europa y América. v. 1–2. Zaragoza, Spain: Gobierno de Aragón, Depto. de Educación y Cultura, 1995. 2 v.: bibl.

Articles cover wide range of topics in Latin American and European 19th- and 20th-century Freemasonry. Although focus is on Spanish Freemasonry, 14 contributions deal specifically with Latin America. In addition, several articles in the "Relaciones Internacionales" section have significance for the Western Hemisphere. Well researched and contain ample footnotes.

820 **Szuchman, Mark D.** The city as vision: the development of urban culture in Latin America. (*in* I saw a city invincible: urban portraits of Latin America. Wilmington, Del.: Scholarly Resources Inc., 1996, p. 1–31)

Carefully measured essay provides informative introduction to urban history in Latin America from preconquest Tenochtitlán through the colonial era to 19th-century Buenos Aires to 20th-century "Leviathan" metropolises of São Paulo and Mexico City.

821 **Tanodi de Chiapero, Branka María.** Grafística precolombina e hispano-americana. Córdoba, Argentina: Centro Interamericano de Desarrollo de Archivos, 1992. 163 p.: bibl., ill.

Overview of writing in the Americas begins with precolumbian pictographs. Brief section on Hispanic paleography serves as introduction to 16th- and 17th-century cursory styles. [S. Socolow]

822 **Tarragó, Rafael Emilio.** The pageant of Ibero-American civilization: an introduction to its cultural history. Lanham, Md.: Univ. Press of America, 1995. 125 p.: bibl., ill., index, maps.

Brief text accomplishes what the title promises. Tarrago gives the student a clear, readable introduction to Latin American culture in seven chapters arranged chronologically from the conquest to the late-20th century.

823 **Tilly, Charles.** Contention and the urban poor in eighteenth- and nineteenth-century Latin America. (*in* Riots in the cities: popular politics and the urban poor in Latin America, 1765–1910. Wilmington, Del.: Scholarly Resources Inc., 1996, p. 225–242, bibl., graph)

Concluding essay presents innovative, flexible conceptual framework for analysis of urban riots that encompasses both general similarities and divergent tendencies in these movements. A valuable contribution to comparative history.

824 **Topik, Steven.** Culture, economy, and coffee. (*LARR*, 32:1, 1997, p. 125–138)

The cultural and economic consequences of the coffee production are only two of several themes explored in this succinct review essay that covers Chiapas to the Amazon.

825 **Tordesillas y sus consecuencias: la política de las grandes potencias europeas respecto a América Latina, 1494–1898.**

Edición de Bernd Schröter y Karin Schüller. Frankfurt am Main: Vervuert; Madrid: Ibero americana, 1995. 260 p.: bibl.

Geopolitical ramifications of the Treaty of Tordesillas and subsequent European rivalries form the central themes in this volume of 15 well-researched historical essays. Topics include Spanish-British confrontation on the Mosquito Coast, Spanish-Russian rivalry in North America, European commercial rivalry in 19th-century Mexico, and 1860s French intervention in Mexico.

826 Triano, María Antonia. El Archivo General de Indias de Sevilla: historia del edificio, sus fondos y utilización. (*Anuario/Sucre*, 1996, p. 471–481, table)

Compact, convenient, rather terse overview of the history of the archive from the late 1500s to the 1980s.

827 Vallenilla, Nikita Harwich. From Jerusalem to Megalopolis: urban centers in Latin America; an historical perspective. (*in* International Congress of Americanists, 48th, Stockholm, 1994. Threatened peoples and environments in the Americas = Pueblos y medios ambientes amenazados en las Américas. Stockholm: Institute of Latin American Studies, Stockholm Univ., 1995, v. 1, p. 139–154, bibl.)

Brief, general survey of urban history from preconquest period to the 20th century.

828 Vilar, Juan Bautista. Los murcianos y América. Madrid: Editorial MAPFRE, 1992. 488 p.: bibl., ill., indexes. (Col. Las Españas y América; 9. Col. MAPFRE 1492)

Exceptionally well-researched work draws on archival sources to trace migrations and activities of Murcians and their descendants in America. Chronology extends from the 15th to the 20th centuries.

829 Yanaguida, Toshio and María Dolores Rodríguez del Alisal. Japoneses en América. Madrid: Editorial MAPFRE, 1992. 348 p.: bibl., indexes, maps. (Col. América, crisol de pueblos; 5. Col. MAPFRE 1492)

Much-needed pioneering study of Japanese immigration to the Western Hemisphere, including Latin America (with emphasis on Peru and Mexico), US, and Canada. Discusses anti-Japanese movements and complications arising out of World War II.

830 Yáñez Gallardo, César. La emigración española a América, siglos XIX y XX: dimensión y características cuantitativas. Colombres, Spain: Archivo de Indianos, 1994. 274 p.: bibl., ill. (Col. Cruzar el charco; 12)

Heavily quantitative examination of immigration includes thorough discussions of statistical sources and several revealing categories of analysis including professional standing, age, gender, and regions of origin (within Spain). Also examines migration, return, net balance of immigration, and the "golondrina" phenomenon. Several charts and graphs support text.

831 Zavala, Silvio Arturo. Ensayos iberoamericanos. Mérida, Mexico: Dirección General de Extensión, Univ. Autónoma de Yucatán, 1993. 164 p. (Yucatán, raíces y expresión de su identidad)

Collection of 10 of Zavala's essays and lectures focusing on historical importance of the Quincentennial. Includes "¿El castellano, lengua obligatoria?"

COLONIAL

832 Abad Pérez, Antolín. Los franciscanos en América. Madrid: Editorial MAPFRE, 1992. 318 p.: bibl., ill., indexes, maps. (Col. Iglesia Católica en el Nuevo Mundo; 11 Col. MAPFRE 1492)

Convenient survey of Franciscans in colonial Spanish America combines regional and chronological organization. Lacks footnotes but contains useful bibliographies following each chapter.

833 Acevedo, Edberto Oscar. Reflexiones en torno a la primera evangelización de América. (*Invest. Ens.*, 44, enero/dic. 1994, p. 15–34, bibl.)

General essay on "spiritual climate" and the attitude of priests toward conversion of indigenous peoples during early 1500s. Based largely on published monographs.

834 Acevedo, Edberto Oscar. El sentido de la colonización de Hispanoamérica según la historiografía americana contemporánea. (*Rev. Hist. Am. Argent.*, 17:33/34, 1993/94, p. 11–36)

Broad overview of interpretations of the colonial period by several 19th- and 20th-century Latin American historians including Benjamín Vicuna Mackenna, José Manuel

Groot, and Carlos Pereyra. Emphasizes influences of liberalism and positivism.

835 Acham, Karl. Os grandes descobrimentos ibéricos e seu impacto na revisão da opinião européia sobre o mundo. (*Rev. SBPH*, 8, 1993, p. 3–16)

General survey of the impact of European encounter with the Americas on life and thought in Europe. Emphasizes ideas on race, political and social organization, and international law.

836 Acosta, Vladimir. El continente prodigioso: mitos e imaginario medieval en la Conquista americana. Caracas: Univ. Central de Venezuela, Ediciones de la Biblioteca, 1992. 464 p.: bibl., ill.

Extensive, detailed, and sometimes stimulating study of the myths that preoccupied the conquistadores. Based on original texts of the conquest period.

837 Aguiar y Acuña, Rodrigo de and Juan Francisco de Montemayor y Córdova y Cuenca. Sumarios de la recopilación general de leyes de las indias occidentales. Presentación de José Luis Soberanes Fernández. Prólogo de Guillermo F. Margadant. Estudio introductorio de Ismael Sánchez Bella. México: UNAM, Instituto de Investigaciones Jurídicas, Depto. de Publicaciones; Fondo de Cultura Económica, 1994. 792 p. (Sección de obras de política y derecho)

Publication of 1677 document with introduction by Ismael Sánchez Bella.

838 Alonso Baquer, Miguel. Generación e la conquista. Madrid: Editorial MAPFRE, 1992. 266 p.: bibl., indexes. (Col. Armas y América; 3. Col. MAPFRE 1492)

Condensed sketches of the conquistadors emphasize biography more than sociological or cultural analysis. Based on published monographs.

839 Altez, Rogelio. Las Casas de la conquista: inglobación, anexión, expropiación de territorios y su legitimación en las estrategias de conquista española; breve estudio a través de la capitulación de Bartolomé de Las Casas, 1520. (*Montalbán/ Caracas*, 28, 1995, p. 91–118, bibl.)

Interpretive study places the Crown's 1521 agreement with Las Casas within the context of Spanish law and religious practices. Based on published sources.

840 Álvarez Peláez, Raquel. La descripción de las aves en la obra del madrileño Gonzalo Fernández de Oviedo. (*Asclepio/ Madrid*, 48:1, 1996, p. 7–25)

Close analysis of Oviedo's commentary on bird life in the Americas, placed within the context of the writings of other 16th-century naturalists.

Amado, Janaína and Luiz Carlos Figueiredo. No tempo das caravelas. See *HLAS 57:2385.*

841 Andrés Gallego, José. Quince revoluciones y algunas cosas más. Madrid: Editorial MAPFRE, 1992. 368 p.: bibl., ill., index. (Col. América 92; 10 Col. MAPFRE 1492)

Well-researched, sophisticated examination of 1760s unrest provides valuable portraits of cross-sections of colonial society during the time of change and stress associated with the Bourbon reforms. Concentrates on the condition and actions of the indigenous peoples, law enforcement, the problem of justice, and growing impact of cultural and commercial influences from outside the Spanish empire. Numerous footnotes indicate author's use of archival research and relevant published works.

842 Anes y Alvarez de Castrillón, Gonzalo. La Corona y la América del siglo de las luces. Madrid?: Marcial Pons; Asociación Francisco López de Gómara, 1994. 185 p.: bibl. (La Corona y los pueblos americanos; 8)

Nicely written survey of 18th-century Spanish Empire. Extensive footnotes contain a healthy mixture of secondary and primary sources.

843 Archivo General de Indias. Coordinación de Pedro González García. Barcelona, Spain: Lunwerg Editores; Madrid: Ministerio de Cultura, Dirección General del Libro, Archivos y Bibliotecas, 1995. 328 p.: bibl., ill. (some col.), col. maps. (Col. Archivos europeos)

Oversized, profusely illustrated introduction to world-famous archive is designed for the general reader but also includes information useful for beginning scholars. Individual chapters cover archival contents for the age of exploration in America, la Casa de Contratación, and the Consejo de Indias.

844 Archivo General de Indias (Spain). Catálogo de las consultas del Consejo de Indias. v. 11, 1662–1668. Sevilla, Spain: Diputación Provincial, 1994. 1 v.: bibl., index. (V centenario del descubrimiento de América; 11)

Useful publication for scholars interested in the operations of the Consejo de Indias. Includes extensive, valuable index.

845 Archivo General de Indias (Spain). Catálogo de las consultas del Consejo de Indias. v. 12, 1669–1675. Sevilla, Spain: Diputación Provincial, 1995. 1 v.: bibl., indexes. (V centenario del descubrimiento de América; 12)

Continuation of vol. 11 (see item **844**). Covers 1669–75 and contains useful index of personal and place names, government offices, and key words such as encomienda, *armas, deudas,* and *navios.*

846 Archivo General de Simancas (Spain). Colón en Simancas. Edición de Demetrio Ramos Pérez. Valladolid, Spain: Sociedad V Centenario Tratado de Tordesillas, 1995. 382 p. (Col. de historia)

Reproduces several documents from the Archivo General de Simancas relevant to Columbus, mainly concerning his four voyages to America. Editor Ramos Pérez provides extensive and useful commentary.

847 Arróniz, Othón. La despertar científico en América: la vida de Diego García de Palacio; documentos inéditos del Archivo de Sevilla. Prólogo de Octavio Castro López. Jalapa, México: Univ. Veracruzana, Gobierno del Estado de Veracruz, 1994. 223 p.: bibl., ill.

Biographical study of the navigation specialist and government official, based on archival research. Thoroughly footnoted. Publishes 20 archival documents of central importance to García de Palacio's career.

848 Asociación de Archiveros de la Iglesia en España. Congreso. 8th, Córdoba, Spain, 1992. Memoria Ecclesiae V: órdenes religiosas y evangelización de América y Filipinas en los archivos de la Iglesia; santoral hispano-mozárabe en España; actas. Edición de Agustín Hevia Ballina. Oviedo, Spain:

Asociación de Archiveros de la Iglesia en España, 1994. 412 p.: bibl., ill.

Volume describes church archives useful to scholars specializing in the history of missions and relations between Europeans and native Americans during the colonial period. Some entries also cover the work of the Church in the Philippines and in 19th-century Cuba.

849 Ávila Hernández, Rosa. El tribunal de la inquisición y su estructura administrativa. (*Novahispania/México,* 1, 1995, p. 45–109, ill.)

Broad survey of institutional components of the Inquisition consisting largely of descriptions of the duties of major and minor officials. Based on archival research.

850 Barbosa Sánchez, Araceli. Sexo y conquista. México: Univ. Nacional Autónoma de México, 1994. 171 p.: bibl. (500 años después; 17)

Low-key, analytical discussion of sexual practices in the conquest era offers valuable perspective on a controversial subject. Exposes biases of the chroniclers; re-examines the role of Malinche and indigenous females in general; and offers careful discussions of Aztec sexual practices before the European arrival.

851 Barral Gómez, Ángel. Rebeliones indígenas en la América española. Madrid: Editorial MAPFRE, 1992. 311 p.: bibl., indexes. (Col. Armas y América; 11 Col. MAPFRE 1492)

Effective, largely narrative survey of indigenous uprisings throughout the colonial period, based on secondary sources.

852 Beceiro, Juan Luis. La mentira histórica desvelada: genocidio en América? Madrid: Editorial Ejearte, 1994. 638 p.: bibl., index.

Large, broad, sometimes rambling defense of Spanish colonial policies makes extensive use of quotations from published works. Chief focus is compilation of opinions and judgments on controversial topics.

853 Behrendt, Stephen D. Crew mortality in the transatlantic slave trade in the eighteenth century. (*Slavery Abolit.,* 18:1, April 1997, p. 49–71, tables)

Detailed, well-researched analysis of

survival rates among crews of British and French slave ships is based largely on data available at the W.E.B. Du Bois Institute. Includes eight tables along with a readable text.

854 Blanco Fernández de Caleya, Paloma. Los herbario de las expediciones científicas españolas al Nuevo Mundo. (*Asclepio/Madrid*, 47:2, 1995, p. 185–209)

Survey of the herbaria of the Real Jardín Botánico in Madrid is organized primarily in terms of 18th- and 19th-century scientific expeditions to Spanish America that built these collections. Footnotes draw from published sources.

855 Bordejé y Morencos, Fernando de. El escenario estratégico español en el siglo XVI, 1492–1556. Madrid: Editorial Naval, 1990. 224 p.: bibl., ill. (some col.), index, maps. (Gran Armada; 8)

Examination of the naval, military, political, and religious factors in Spanish policy focuses on Europe and the Mediterranean, but includes commentary on the Americas.

856 Bradley, Peter T. Navegantes británicos. Madrid: Editorial MAPFRE, 1992. 347 p.: bibl., indexes, maps. (Col. Mar y América; 13. Col. MAPFRE 1492)

Brisk, three-part narrative of activities of British ships in American waters from 1500s to 1700s. Pt. 1 traces careers of John Hawkins, Francis Drake, and their countrymen in the Caribbean. Pt. 2 deals with Walter Raleigh, Henry Hudson and settlement of British colonies in North America. Pt. 3 traces Hawkins, Drake, George Anson, and other explorer-interlopers in South American waters. Brief bibliography; lacks footnotes.

857 Brenes Rosales, Raymundo. Interpretaciones historicas en torno al descubrimiento de America. (*Rev. Hist. Am.*, 117, enero/junio 1994, p. 7–22, bibl.)

This exercise in categorization places many better-known historians of this period in a series of historiographical schools that reflect the recent controversies surrounding the events and aftermath of 1492.

858 Buelna Serrano, María Elvira. Modernidad y contramodernida de la Compañia de Jesús. (Costelaciones [sic] de modernidad: anuario conmemorativo del V Centenario de la llegada de España a América. México: UNAM, Unidad Azcapotzalco, División de Ciencias Sociales y Humanidades, 1990, v. 2, p. 49–78, bibl.)

Broad interpretation of Jesuits' role in New Spain in light of their contradictory commitments to learning and the life of social action, while operating within a hierarchical structure and defending their landed estates against 1700s Bourbon reforms. Synthesis based on published materials. Extensive bibliography.

859 Burkholder, Mark A. and **Lyman L. Johnson.** Colonial Latin America. 2nd ed. New York: Oxford Univ. Press, 1994. 360 p.: bibl., ill., index.

Textbook intended for college survey courses incorporates recent scholarship of much value for more advanced students. Uses standard political and economic approach enhanced by sharply focused sections on labor, the Church, and social life.

860 Calero, Francisco. Jerónimo Münzer y el descubrimiento de América. (*Rev. Indias*, 56:207, mayo/agosto 1996, p. 279–296)

Succinct biographical and intellectual study of Münzer includes analysis of his 1493 letter to King John II of Portugal regarding America.

861 Cartay Angulo, Rafael. Historia de la alimentación del nuevo mundo. v. 1–2. Mérida, Venezuela: R. Cartay, 1991. 2 v.: bibl.

Nicely organized study of the origins and evolution of food production and distribution in the Americas includes extensive sections on indigenous and Iberian contributions plus shorter examinations of African and non-Iberian European influences. Draws from wide array of published sources in anthropology, geography, economics, and history, as indicated in extensive footnotes.

862 Casas, Bartolomé de las. Cartas y memoriales. Edición de Paulino Castañeda *et al.* Madrid: Alianza Editorial, 1995. 439 p.: bibl., index. (Obras completas/Bartolomé de las Casas; 13)

Continuation of publication of works by Las Casas contains 57 documents ranging from 1516–66. Includes useful index.

863 Casas, Bartolomé de las. Indian freedom: the cause of Bartolomé de las Casas, 1484–1566; a reader. Translations and notes by Francis Patrick Sullivan. Kansas City, Mo.: Sheed & Ward, 1995. 371 p.: bibl., indexes.

Intended for classroom use, work contains 47 pages from *Las Casas' life of Columbus* plus 24 other selections.

864   Castilla Urbano, Francisco. El mal de la historia: el descubrimiento de Rafael Sánchez Ferlosio. (*Rev. Indias*, 56:206, enero/abril 1996, p. 243–255)

Historiographical and philosophical commentary on the writings of Sánchez Ferlosio regarding the Spanish conquest.

865   Castillo Martos, Manuel and **Mervyn Francis Lang.** Metales preciosos— unión de dos mundos: tecnología, comercio y política de la minería y metalurgia ibero americana. Prólogo de José Rodríguez de la Borbolla Camoyán. Sevilla, Spain: Muñoz Moya y Montraveta Editores, 1995. 224 p.: bibl., ill. (Serie Ciencias)

Brief, convenient synthesis of the histories of mining and metallurgy within their economic context in the colonial period.

866   Castrillo Mazeres, Francisco. El soldado de la conquista. Madrid: Editorial MAPFRE, 1992. 316 p.: bibl., ill., index, maps. (Col. Armas y América; 4. Col. MAPFRE 1492)

Profile of conquest soldiers in terms of origins, values, psychology and *cualidades negativas*. Includes some quantitative analysis but lacks footnotes.

867   Cerezo Martínez, Ricardo. El meridiano y el antimeridiano de Tordesillas en la geografía, la náutica y la cartografía. (*Rev. Indias*, 54:202, sept./dic. 1994, p. 509–542, ill., maps)

Close examination of the worldwide implications of the Treaty of Tordesillas, based on a careful reading of published sources.

868   Chaliand, Gérard. Mirrors of a disaster: a chronicle of the Spanish military conquest of America. Translated by A.M. Berrett. Watertown, Mass.: Blue Crane Books, 1994. 257 p.: bibl., ill., index.

Fast-paced, dramatic account of the conquests of Mexico and Peru is intended for general readership. Also includes some discussion of recent historiographical issues and lengthy quotations from published historical documents.

869   Colección documental del descubrimiento, 1470–1506. v. 1–3. Madrid: Real Academia de la Historia; Consejo Superior de Investigaciones Científicas; Fundación MAPFRE América, 1994. 3 v.: bibl., indexes.

Massive collection of documents centering on Columbus and his voyages. Pérez de Tudela's 197-page introductory essay provides incisive commentary on many Columbian controversies.

870   Colón de Carvajal, Anunciada and **Guadalupe Chocano Higueras.** La Cartuja y los Colón. (Historia de La Cartuja de Sevilla: de ribera del Guadalquivir e recinto de la Exposición Universal. Sevilla, Spain: Turner; Sociedad Estatal Universal de 1992, División Cultural, Recinto de La Cartuja, 1989, p. 83–108, facsims., plates)

In-depth discussion of the Columbus family and its archive in the Carthusian monastery.

871   Colón de Carvajal, Anunciada and **Guadalupe Chocano Higueras.** Cristobal Colón: incógnitas de su muerte 1506–1902; primeros almirantes de las Indias. v. 1–2. Madrid: Consejo Superior de Investigaciones Científicas, 1992. 2 v.: bibl., ill. (some col.), indexes, maps, ports.

Traces controversy surrounding the remains of Columbus over four centuries. Vol. 1, the main text, is thoroughly footnoted and contains numerous illustrations. Vol. 2 consists of supporting documents.

872   Columbus, Christopher. Diario del primer viaje de Colón. Edición de Demetrio Ramos Pérez y Marta González Quintana. Granada, Spain: Diputación Provincial de Granada, 1995. 434 p.: bibl., ill. (some col.), index. (Vardas polo)

New edition of the diary with informative introduction by Ramos Pérez.

873   Congreso Hispano-Portugués, *1st, Salamanca, Spain, 1992.* Las relaciones entre Portugal y Castilla en la época de los descubrimientos y la expansión colonial. Edición de Ana María Carabias Torres. Salamanca, Spain: Ediciones Univ. de Salamanca, Sociedad V Centenario del Tratado de Tordesillas, 1994. 372 p.: bibl., ill. (some col.), maps. (Estudios históricos y geográficos; 92. Acta Salmanticensia)

Careful scholarship and considerable archival research typify most of the 27 contributions, which span the period from the Treaty of Tordesillas to 1640.

874 Consejo Superior de Investigaciones Científicas (Madrid). Documentos sobre política lingüística en Hispanoamérica, 1492–1800. Compilación, estudio preliminar y edición de Francisco de Solano. Madrid: Consejo Superior de Investigaciones Científicas, 1991. 294 p.: bibl., ill., index. (Col. Tierra nueva e cielo nuevo; 32)

Collection of 129 documents on the interaction of linguistics and indigenous policy in the colonial era includes editor's thoughtful and substantial 67-page introduction.

875 Cortés Alonso, Vicenta. Los archivos diocesanos en América: su organización y la investigación. (*Rev. Arch. Arzobispal Arequipa*, 1, 1994, p. 31–44)

Somewhat mistitled article discusses diocesan archives in Barcelona with some brief references to archives in Latin America.

876 Davidson, Miles H. The Toscanelli letters: a dubious influence on Columbus. (*CLAHR/Albuquerque*, 5:3, Summer 1996, p. 287–310)

Incisive, detailed refutation of historical validity of the Toscanelli letter. Concludes that Toscanelli probably did not write the letter, and that the letter (whoever wrote it) had no influence on Columbus.

877 Diaz Diaz, Rafael Antonio. Historiografía de la esclavitud negra en América Latina: temas y problemas generales. (*Am. Negra*, 8, dic. 1994, p. 11–29, bibl.)

Helpful essay covers publications from 1970s to the early 1990s and deals with slave trade, historical character of slavery, slave resistance, and emancipation.

878 Durston, Alan. Un regimen urbanístico en la América hispana colonial: el trazado en damero durante los siglos XVI y XVII. (*Historia/Santiago*, 28, 1994, p. 58–115, bibl.)

Sophisticated interpretation of the ideas and values underlying Spanish colonial urban policies, based on a careful and critical reading of colonial texts as well as the work of modern historians.

879 Egmond, Florike and Peter Mason. Armadillos in unlikely places: some unpublished sixteenth-century sources for New World *Rezeptionsgeschichte* in Northern Europe. (*Ibero-Am. Arch.*, 20:1/2, 1994, p. 3–52, bibl., ill.)

Insightful and entertaining examination of Dutch writers' often imaginative descriptions of animal life in the Americas including various sea monsters and a "cyclops." Findings are based on close reading of Dutch archival manuscripts. Includes 15 illustrations.

880 Eltis, David and David Richardson. West Africa and the transatlantic slave trade: new evidence of long-run trends. (*Slavery Abolit.*, 18:1, April 1997, p. 16–35, graphs, tables)

Probing demographic study of the regional origins of slaves shipped from Africa to the Americas from 17th-19th centuries. Emphasizes importance of the Gold Coast (Ghana) and Benin as points of origin and declining percentage of women in the slave populations from 1700s to 1800s.

881 Emiliani, Jorge Roberto. Manual de administración indiana. Córdoba, Argentina: J.R. Emiliani, 1994. 336 p.: bibl.

Sketchy outline of Spanish colonial administration, drawn from published sources.

882 Encuentros de Historia y Arqueología, 8th, San Fernando, Spain, 1992. Andalucía en América, América en Andalucía: actas. San Fernando, Spain: Ayuntamiento de San Fernando, Fundación Municipal de Cultura, 1993? 182 p.: bibl., ill., maps. (Col. Actas, encuentros, congresos)

Wide range of essays includes studies on shipbuilding and architecture.

883 Eugenio Martínez, María Angeles. Encadenados a los "topos:" ordenamiento sobre esclavitud indígena. (*Ibero-Am. Arch.*, 20:3/4, 1994, p. 247–278, appendices)

Competent survey of colonial law concerning native American slavery from 1533–60 is based on archival research and includes relevant documents in five appendices.

884 **Fernández Alvarez, Manuel.** Europa y
América en la política imperial de
Carlos V. (*Correspondance/Cáceres*, número
especial 1994, p. 21–33, ill., photos)
Succinct general study of the foreign
policy of Charles V with section devoted to
Spain's empire in America.

885 **Fernández Pérez, Paloma.** Impacto
social del comercio colonial en la
metropoli: los comerciantes de Cádiz en la
época del auge y caída del imperio español en
America, 1700–1812. (*Histórica/Lima*, 18:2,
dic. 1994, p. 287–316, appendix, bibl., tables)
Impressive study of 18th-century
Cádiz merchants combines archival research
and statistical analysis. Includes discussion
of capital accumulation and family connections, together with a biographical appendix.

Fisher, John R. El americanismo en Gran Bretaña durante los últimos 25 años, con especial referencia al período colonial. See item
772.

886 **Fisher, John R.** Los cambios estructurales en la carrera de Indias en el
período borbónico. (*Rev. Hist. Naval*, 12:47,
1994, p. 21–34)
Well-organized overview of Spanish
trade policies identifies numerous commercial fluctuations and economic weaknesses
in late 1700s. Valuable synthesis, but lacks
footnotes.

887 **Fisher, John R.** Ciencia y comercio en
Hispanoamérica durante el período
borbónico. (*Cuad. Sur Hist./Bahía Blanca*,
26, 1996, p. 3–15, bibl.)
Challenging thought-piece assesses
impact of scientific expeditions on resource
use and economic development in the Bourbon Reform era.

888 **Galán García, Agustín.** Financiación
de las expediciones de misioneros a las
Indias Occidentales. (*Arch. Hist. Soc. Jesu*,
63:126, Jul./Dec. 1994, p. 261–281)
Impressive study of methods and
cycles of financing missionary expeditions to
Spanish America from 1580s-1760s. Extensive primary research.

889 **Galera, Andrés** and **Marcelo Frias.**
Félix de Azara y Georges Lucien
Leclerc: dos formas de iluminar la naturaleza
americana. (*Asclepio/Madrid*, 48:1, 1996,
p. 27–36)

Descriptive commentary on the work
of two late-18th-century naturalists.

890 **Gámez Amián, Aurora.** El comercio de
Málaga con América, 1765–1820: una
ocasión perdida. (*Rev. Indias*, 55:205,
sept./dic. 1995, p. 635–656, graphs, tables)
Solid archival research and thorough
quantitative analysis establish a firm foundation for this examination of a little-studied
area in colonial trade.

891 **García López, Aurelio.** Miseria y aventura: un estudio de la emigración a
América durante el período de la Casa de
Austria a través de las fuentes locales.
Guadalajara, Spain: Excmo. Diputación Provincial, 1995. 265 p.: bibl. (Varios; 14)
Portrait of immigration from Spain to
America is based on archival research. Discusses motives, material possessions, and religious outlooks of the immigrants. Detailed
footnotes will aid scholars. Also contains a
selection of 15 documents.

892 **García Oro, José.** Fray Juan de
Quevedo, OFM, primer obispo de
Tierra Firme: un confidente del Cardenal
Cisneros. (*Arch. Francisc. Hist.*, 85:1/4,
Jan./Dec. 1992, p. 39–75, appendix)
In-depth biographical study based on
archival research is thoroughly footnoted
and includes six relevant documents.

893 **García Tapia, Nicolás.** En busca de
tesoros bajo el mar: invenciones de
equipos para bucear en América. (*Rev. Indias*, 55:203, enero/abril 1995, p. 7–31, facsims.)
Fine article traces experimental efforts
by inventors Giuseppe Bono in the 1580s and
Jeronimo de Ayanz in early 1600s to supply
air to divers for extended periods of time.
Based on primary research. Includes several
illustrations.

894 **Gil, Juan.** Cara y cruz de La Cartuja
en la época del Descubrimiento. (*in*
Historia de La Cartuja de Sevilla: de ribera
del Guadalquivir a recinto de la Exposición
Universal. Sevilla, Spain: Turner; Sociedad
Estatal Universal de 1992, División Cultural,
Recinto de La Cartuja, 1989, p. 83–108, fac-
sims., plates)
Detailed examination of monastics'
role in early 1500s Americas includes discus-

sions of archival documents and several illustrations.

895 Gómez Gómez, Lorenzo. San Martín de Valdeiglesias en el descubrimiento de América. Madrid: Talleres Industria Gráfica de Leganés, 1992. 162 p.: bibl., ill, maps.

Local history and biography dominate this highly specialized study of the conquest era. Based on published works.

896 Gómez Pérez, María del Carmen. El sistema defensivo americano: siglo XVIII. Madrid: Editorial MAPFRE, 1992. 259 p.: bibl., ill., indexes. (Col. MAPFRE 1492. Col. Armas y América; 9)

Well-organized analysis of the Spanish army in America in the Bourbon Reform period deals with recruitment, weaponry and other equipment, medical care, religious services, and budgetary matters. Draws from both archival sources and published monographs.

897 González Bueno, Antonio. La utilidad de la flora americana en el proyecto expedicionario de la España Ilustrada. (*Asclepio/Madrid*, 48:2, 1995, p. 79–90)

Examination of late-1700s, early-1800s botanical expeditions concludes that these efforts did not achieve their goal of fully developing colonies' economic potential, but did advance scientific knowledge to some extent. Based on published sources.

898 González González, Francisco José. Astronomía y navegación en España: siglos XVI-XVIII. Madrid: Editorial MAPFRE, 1992. 283 p.: bibl., ill., indexes. (Col. Mar y América; 3. Col. MAPFRE 1492)

Impressive specialized examination of connections between astronomy and navigation within context of Spanish science, in particular, and European science in general. Includes chapter on navigation and nautical astronomy textbooks used in the period.

899 González Pujana, Laura. Estudio comparativo del conocimiento astronómico en los cronistas de la América andina. (*Rev. Complut. Hist. Am.*, 20, 1994, p. 75–85)

Pioneering exploratory essay deals with early chroniclers' discussions of indigenous astronomical observations.

900 González-Ripoll Navarro, María Dolores. A las órdenes de las estrellas: la vida del marino Cosme de Churruca y sus expediciones a América. Preámbulo de Francisco de Solano. Madrid: Fundación Banco Bilbao-Vizcaya; Consejo Superior de Investigaciones Científicas, 1995. 187 p.: bibl. (Monografías; 8)

Careful biographical study of 18th-century scientist/traveler from Guipuzcoa, a leading figure in map-making expeditions from the Straits of Magellan to the Antilles. Based on extensive archival research.

901 Guillamón Alvarez, Francisco Javier. Institutional reform and municipal government in the Spanish Empire in the eighteenth century. (*Itinerario/Leiden*, 20:3, 1996, p. 109–123)

Examines interaction between enlightened absolutism and administrative system. The change triggered by the Bourbon reforms transformed a patrimonial state into a nationalist monarchy. The reforms, in turn, led the monarchy to seek agents that could implement innovative policies. [R. Hoefte]

902 Hartmann, Peter Claus. Der Jesuitenstaat in Südamerika, 1609–1768: eine christliche Alternative zu Kolonialismus und Marxismus. Weissenhorn, Germany: Anton H. Konrad, 1994. 174 p.: bibl., ill. (some col.), indexes, maps.

Using diverse and controversial eyewitness accounts, as well as international secondary sources, author examines positive and negative influences affecting indigenous peoples of the "Jesuit state." Concludes that, although eurocentric and paternalistic, the "Jesuit state" proved to be a fascinating religious and socioeconomic experiment that provided a more peaceful environment than was available to indigenous peoples elsewhere in North or South America during the colonial period and afterwards. [C.K. Converse]

903 Hernández Sánchez-Barba, Mario. El mar en la historia de América. Madrid: Editorial MAPFRE, 1992. 343 p.: bibl., indexes. (Col. Mar y América; 7. Col. MAPFRE 1492)

In a promising effort to synthesize the history of sea power and ships in the early colonial era, author examines the roles of exploration, trade, naval campaigns, port cities, and islands in the imperial matrix. Unfortunately, lacks footnotes and annotated bibliography is limited.

904 Izard, Miquel. Perpetuar el embeleco o rememorar lo ocurrido. (*Bol. Am.,* 36:46, 1996, p. 243–257, bibl.)

Pessimistic meditation on conquest era emphasizes use of force and culture of violence.

905 Jackson, Robert H. Race/caste and the creation and meaning of identity in colonial Spanish America. (*Rev. Indias,* 55:203, enero/abril 1995, p. 149–173, tables)

Examines ethnicity and caste system in 1790s-early 1800s Sonora and in 19th-century Cochabamba, concluding that frequently made racial categorizations are often too easily accepted by historians and social scientists. Perceptive examination of gap between historical documents and social reality.

906 Jara, Álvaro. La nueva sociedad colonial americana: un panorama trisecular. (*Rev. Chil. Hist. Geogr.,* 161, 1994/95, p. 73–98, graphs)

General essay includes demography, economic organization, inter-colonial trade, and government and private finances. Includes graphs, but no footnotes or bibliography.

907 Jornadas de Andalucía y América, 10th, Univ. de Santa María de la Rábida, Sevilla, 1991. Los cabildos andaluces y americanos: su historia y su organización actual; actas. Edición de Bibiano Torres Ramírez. Sevilla, Spain: Impr. Galán, 1992. 482 p., 3 leaves of plates: bibl.

Eighteen historical essays deal specifically with Cartagena de Indias, Guatemala, and the Yucatán. Also includes generic studies of the cabildo. Essays are generally based on archival research.

908 Junta de Andalucía (Spain). Consejería de Cultura. Andalucía en América: el legado de ultramar. Barcelona, Spain: Lunwerg Editores, 1995. 234 p.: bibl., ill. (some col.), maps (some col.).

A wide variety of contributions make up this edited volume, including some interesting essays on New World fortifications and architecture.

909 Klein, Herbert S. Las finanzas americanas del Imperio Español: 1680–1809. Traducción de Isabel Vericat. México: Instituto de Investigaciones Dr. José María Luis Mora: Univ. Autónoma Metropolitana-Iztapalapa, 1994. 178 p.: bibl., ill. (Historia económica)

Important synthesis brings together Klein's archival research and his thorough reading of published monographs. He examines three administrative areas: the Viceroyalty of Peru, the Audiencia of Charcas, and the Viceroyalty of New Spain. Interpretive concluding chapter contrasts the rise of New Spain with the decline of Peru.

910 Klein, Herbert S. and Stanley L. Engerman. Long-term trends in African mortality in the transatlantic slave trade. (*Slavery Abolit.,* 18:1, April 1997, p. 36–48, graphs, tables)

Quantitative study draws from published monographs and Du Bois Institute data to pose some thoughtful generalizations concerning the decline of slave mortality rates after 1700.

911 Las Heras, Isabel J. and María C.R. de Monteagudo. La España y los españoles del descubrimiento y la conquista de América. Prólogo de Carlos S.A. Segreti. Córdoba, Argentina: Centro de Estudios Históricos, 1992. 208 p.: maps.

Interesting treatment of conquest period emphasizes Spanish perspective and is intended for a popular audience. No bibliography and few footnotes.

912 León de d'Empaire, Arleny. Felipe Salvador Gilij: nuevas perspectivas americanas en la crónica dieciochesca. Caracas: Univ. Católica Andrés Bello, Cátedra Fundacional Monseñor Mariano Talavera y Garcés, 1993. 139 p.: bibl.

Explanation and analysis of late-18th-century writings of Gilij in the fields of ethnology and natural history.

913 Lépori de Pithod, María Estela. El descubrimiento de América visto desde España en el siglo XVII. (*Rev. Hist. Univ.,* 6, 1994, p. 67–85)

Interesting discussion of evaluations by leading 17th-century writers of American colonization's place in Spanish history. Focuses on Luis Cabrera de Córdoba, Diego Saavedra Fajardo, and Miguel Alvarez Osorio.

914 Lockhart, James. The merchants of early Spanish America: continuity and change. (*Ibero-Am. Arch.*, 20:3/4, 1994, p. 223–245)

Stimulating historiographical essay on the evolution of practices and policies of colonial merchants examines the scholarly works of Hoberman, Otte, Borchart, Kicza, and Socolow.

915 Lohmann Villena, Guillermo. Los americanos en las órdenes nobiliarias. v. 1–2. 2a. ed. Madrid: Consejo Superior de Investigaciones Científicas, 1993. 2 v. (Col. Biblioteca de historia de América; 7)

Family background sketches of more than 1,000 colonial members of six noble orders. Extensive introductory essay provides useful historical overview for both specialists and general readers.

916 López Cantos, Angel. Juegos, fiestas y diversiones en la América española. Madrid: Editorial MAPFRE, 1992. 332 p.: bibl., index. (Colecciones MAPFRE 1492)

Important contribution to social history and popular culture, this work examines festivals, games, and other forms of public entertainment within context of Spanish American colonial society. Employs a conceptual framework placing the Crown and its administrators at the top of the hierarchy that sponsored these events, but also gives considerable attention to the spectators/participants who came from middle and lower sectors of society. Quite extensive coverage ranges from solemn religious festivals to carnival to theatrical productions to sporting events. Based on impressive combination of archival sources and published scholarly works.

917 Lucena Salmoral, Manuel. Piratas, bucaneros, filibusteros y corsarios en América: perros, mendigos y otros malditos del mar. Caracas: Grijalbo, 1994. 313 p.: bibl., ill., indexes. (Tierra nuestra)

Well-written synthesis of published works on piracy features sharply etched biographical portraits. Thoroughly footnoted.

918 Luque Alcaide, Elisa and **José Ignacio Saranyana.** La Iglesia Católica y América. Madrid: Editorial MAPFRE, 1992.

371 p.: bibl., indexes. (Col. Iglesia católica en el Nuevo Mundo; 10 Col. MAPFRE 1492)

Solid survey of Catholic Church's first century in Spanish America has a particularly effective chapter on Creole culture and education. Contains useful 34-page bibliographical essay.

919 Malaspina '92: I jornadas internacionales Madrid-Cádiz-La Coruña, 17–25 de septiembre de 1992. Edición y coordinación de Mercedes Palau Baquero y Antonio Orozco Acuaviva. Cádiz, Spain: Real Academia Hispano-Americana, 1994. 413 p.: bibl., ill., index, maps.

Publishes proceedings of 1992 conference on the Malaspina Expedition. Contains something for almost everyone interested in 18th-century scientific expeditions to the Americas or to the Pacific. Work is well edited and profusely illustrated; almost all contributors are eminent scholars. [M.T. Hamerly]

920 Marchena Fernández, Juan. Ejército y milicias en el mundo colonial americano. Madrid: Editorial MAPFRE, 1992. 323 p.: bibl., ill., indexes, maps. (Col. Armas y América; 10 Col. MAPFRE 1492)

Well-organized, clearly written institutional study of the Spanish military primarily during the Bourbon Reform era. Based on considerable archival research and extensively footnoted.

921 Marchena Fernández, Juan and **María del Carmen Gómez Pérez.** La vida de guarnición en las ciudades americanas de la Ilustración. Madrid: Ministerio de Defensa, 1992. 326 p.: bibl., ill. (Publicaciones de defensa)

Thorough examination of 18th-century Spanish defensive preparations and military construction is based on extensive archival research. Includes appropriate illustrations and maps, and extensive discussions of daily life in the fortified cities. Also examines financial costs of the large-scale defense systems.

922 Márquez Macías, Rosario. La emigración española a América, 1765–1824. Oviedo, Spain: Univ. de Oviedo, Servicio de Publicaciones, 1995. 283 p.: bibl., ill.

Demographic study of the migration process with extensive chapter on quantification, including origins and destinations.

Uses both archival sources and recently published monographs.

923 Martín Acosta, María Emelina. El dinero americano y la política del Imperio. Madrid: Editorial MAPFRE, 1992. 333 p.: bibl., index. (Col. Relaciones entre España y América; 5. Col. MAPFRE 1492)

Impressive study examines Crown's use of the silver and gold of the Americas during its ill-fated ventures in European power struggles from early 1500s to mid-17th century. Based heavily on archival research.

924 Martinelli Gifre, Emma. La comunicación entre españoles e indios: palabras y gestos. Madrid: MAPFRE, 1992. 321 p.: bibl. (Col. Idioma e Iberoamerica; 8. Col. MAPFRE 1492)

Stimulating study examines cultural, linguistic, political, psychological, and philosophical dimensions of initial communications between native Americans and the Spanish. Considers physical gestures as well as the work of interpreters, the dictates of government, and Church policy. No footnotes, but end-of-chapter bibliographies indicate sources.

925 Martínez, José Luis. Enrique Otte, descubridor. (*Ibero-Am. Arch.*, 20:3/4, 1994, p. 437–444)

Extended commentary on publications of German-Spanish historian Otte on the colonial era, especially his innovative work on the lives of Spanish immigrants to the New World.

926 Martínez, Milagros. El mundo allende los mares: mitos y fábulas transplantadas a América, siglos XV y XVI. (*Hist. Cult./Lima*, 22, 1993, p. 11–25, bibl.)

Interesting exploration of the myths and fables employed by the Europeans in their early efforts to understand the Americas. Drawn from secondary sources.

927 Martínez de Codes, Rosa María. De la reducción a la plantación: la utilización del esclavo negro en las haciendas jesuitas de la América española y portuguesa. (*Rev. Complut. Hist. Am.*, 21, 1995, p. 85–122)

Synthesizing an important topic, combines several published studies to develop a comprehensive portrait of African slavery on Jesuit estates in Peru, New Granada, Quito,

New Spain, and Brazil. Includes evaluations of religious instruction and the living and working conditions of the slaves.

928 Martínez Gutiérrez, Gregorio. Gaspar de Villaroel, OSA: un ilustre prelado americano; un clásico del derecho indiano, 1587–1665. Valladolid, Spain: Ed. Estudio Agustiniano, 1994. 236 p.: bibl., ill., index. (Estudios de historia agustiniana; 3)

Traces life of the Spanish cleric from childhood to position as Archbishop of Charcas. More descriptive than analytical. Based mainly on secondary sources.

929 Martínez-Hidalgo, José María. Las naves del descubrimiento y sus hombres. Madrid: Editorial MAPFRE, 1991. 288 p.: bibl., ill., indexes, ports. (Col. Mar y América; 5. Col. MAPFRE 1492)

Details of construction and operation of Columbus' ships in the 1490s and of 19th- and 20th-century reconstructions of these vessels constitute main themes of this specialized study. Based on extensive reading of available sources, but not footnoted.

930 Martínez Shaw, Carlos. La emigración española a América, 1492–1824. Colombres, Spain: Archivo de Indianos, 1994. 278 p.: bibl., ill. (Col. Cruzar el charco; 11)

Intelligent synthesis of Spanish emigration to the Americas includes both narrative and quantitative approaches and an interpretive chapter on the motives for emigration.

931 Maura, Juan Francisco. *Ilustraciones de la Casa de Niebla:* una nota histórica sobre el *predescubrimiento* de Cristóbal Colón. (*CLAHR/Albuquerque*, 5:3, Summer 1996, p. 311–332, appendix, facsims.)

Discusses document apparently containing evidence that Columbus traveled to England and then to America in early 1480s. Traces historiography of this theory. Convenient compilation, but not definitive.

932 Medalfe Rojas, Ronaldo and Lorena Loyola Goich. Músicos y cantores: interlocutores de la sociedad colonial americana. (*Cuad. Hist./Santiago*, 13, dic. 1993, p. 55–67)

Interesting interpretive study of the role of indigenous musicians and singers as intermediaries in the complex relationship between the Spanish conquerors and the general indigenous population. Concentrates on 16th century and draws from scholarly monographs and published documents.

933 Merino, Olga and **Linda A. Newson.** Jesuit missions in Spanish America: the aftermath of the expulsion. (*Rev. Hist. Am.*, 118, julio/dic. 1994, p. 7–32, tables)

Commendable synthesis of the impact of the expulsion of the Jesuits on the various missions they had established from California to Paraguay to Chile. Based on an extended survey of published monographs.

934 Minería y metalurgia: intercambio tecnológico y cultural entre América y Europa durante el período colonial español. Edición de Manuel Castillo Martos. Sevilla, Spain: Muñoz Montoya y Montraveta Editores, 1994. 503 p.: bibl., ill. (Serie Ciencias)

Contains 21 essays divided into four parts. Pt. 1 deals with native American/European relations; remaining three parts focus on the technology and economics of mining. Several essays are based on archival research.

935 Mira Caballos, Esteban. Aproximación al estudio de una minoría etnica: indios en la España del siglo XVI. (*Hispania/Madrid*, 56:194, 1996, p. 945–964)

Innovative examination of the economic, cultural, and religious conditions of native Americans brought to Spain in the 1500s. Based on archival research.

936 Mira Caballos, Esteban. Los prohibidos en la emigración a América, 1492–1550. (*Estud. Hist. Soc. Econ. Am.*, 12, 1995, p. 37–53, table)

Legal and administrative history of the regulation of migration into Spanish America emphasizes three basic categories of restrictions: religious, political, and social (marginal social groups and criminals). Includes commentary on the special status of the Portuguese. Based on considerable archival research.

937 Monteiro, Jacinto. Atentado contra Colombo nos Açores. Lisboa?: Secretaria Regional da Educação e Cultura, Direcção Regional dos Assuntos Culturais, 1994? 143 p.: bibl., ill.

Explores circumstances of the hostile reception of Columbus in the Portuguese

Azores on his return voyage in Feb. 1493. Extensive footnotes include archival references.

938 Mörner, Magnus. La emigración canaria a Indias dentro del contexto español. (*in* Coloquio de Historia Canario-Americana, 10th, Las Palmas, Spain, 1992. Actas. Las Palmas, Spain: Ediciones del Cabildo Insular de Gran Canaria, s.d., v. 1, p. 469–491, bibl.)

This convenient scholarly overview of Canary Islanders' emigration during the colonial period contains a useful bibliography.

939 Mörner, Magnus. Ethnicity, social mobility and mestizaje in Spanish American colonial history. (*in* Iberische Welten: Festschrift zum 65. Geburtstag von Günter Kahle. Vienna: Böhlau Verlag, 1994, p. 301–314)

Mörner's typically frank comments on the work of his critics such as John Chance and William Taylor made this brief, but stimulating, review of publications in social and ethnic history even more valuable.

940 Mörner, Magnus. Spanish historians on Spanish migration to America during the colonial period. (*LARR*, 30:2, 1995, p. 251–267, tables)

Survey of recent publications on Spanish migration to America includes a much-needed overview of recent regional emigration studies.

941 Mota Murillo, Rafael. Documentación franciscana en el Archivo de Indias: nueva serie de la sección Indiferente, 1601–1650. (*Arch. Francisc. Hist.*, 85:1/4, Jan./Dec. 1992, p. 177–282)

A listing with brief, helpful descriptions of the contents of 794 documents. Also provides introductory comments for each of the nine categories of documents used to organize the listing.

942 Muriel, Josefina. Las mujeres de Hispanoamérica: época colonial. Madrid: Editorial MAPFRE, 1992. 353 p.: bibl., ill., index. (Col. Realidades americanas; 8. Col. MAPFRE 1492)

Carefully structured synthesis based on extensive study of published monographs plus some archival sources examines the role of women in preconquest societies and the conquest itself. Uses regional approach emphasizing New Spain and Peru. Thoroughly footnoted.

943 Navarro García, Luis. El falso Campillo y el reformismo borbónico. (*Temas Am.*, 12, 1995, p. 5–14)

Detailed and highly critical textual commentary on *Nuevo sistema de gobierno económico para la América* (see *HLAS 42: 1833*), and some pointed observations regarding authorship. Footnotes convey dimensions of the historiographical controversy.

944 Navarro García, Luis. Fundación de poblaciones en las Indias españoles en el siglo XVIII. (*in* Congreso Histórico sobre Nuevas Poblaciones, 5th, *La Luisiana, Spain and Cañada Rosal, Spain, 1992.* Las nuevas poblaciones de España y América. Córdoba, Spain: Junta de Andalucía, Consejería de Cultura y Medio Ambiente, 1994, p. 37–52)

Historical and geographical survey of the expansion of Spanish colonial communities from the Canary Islands to Chihuahua to Chile. Drawn from published sources.

945 Pareja Ortiz, María del Carmen. Un aspecto de la vida cotidiana: la mujer ante el matrimonio en la legislación de Indias. (*Rábida/Huelva*, 9, marzo 1991, p. 9–21, ill.)

Impressive archival research and clarity of prose characterize this important study of the legal foundations of marriage in colonial Spanish America.

946 Pareja Ortiz, María del Carmen. Presencia de la mujer sevillana en Indias: vida cotidiana. Sevilla, Spain: Diputación Provincial de Sevilla, 1994. 287 p.: bibl., ill. (some col.).

Perceptive study in women's history draws heavily from archival records to document women's place in general migration from Seville to the Americas from 1550–1650. Topics covered include marriage, family life, and religiosity. Also includes colorful illustrations from contemporary works of art.

947 Pérez Fernández, Isacio. Bartolomé de las Casas: contra los negros?; revisión de una leyenda. Madrid: Editorial Mundo Negro; México: Ediciones Esquila, 1991. 268 p.: bibl., ill.

In the first of two studies on the theme of Las Casas and African slavery,

author examines evolution of the presumption that the European champion of the native Americans was &quotâti-Negro," and then proceeds to attack this "legend." Combination of archival research, historical synthesis, logical argumentation, and scholarly citations combine to make a strong case for author's interpretation. For comment on second study, see item **948.**

948 Pérez Fernández, Isacio. Fray Bartolomé de las Casas, O.P.: de defensor de los indios a defensor de los negros. Salamanca, Spain: Editorial San Esteban, 1995. 227 p.: bibl., indexes. (Monumenta histórica iberoamericana de la Orden de Predicadores; 8)

Second study on this theme examines nuances in attitude and actions of Las Casas toward African slavery. Solid research and persuasive argumentation reinforce conclusions reached by author in his first study. See item **947.**

949 Pérez Turrado, Gaspar. Las armadas españolas de Indias. Madrid: Editorial MAPFRE, 1992. 303 p.: bibl., ill., indexes, maps. (Col. Mar y América; 2. Col. MAPFRE 1492)

Well-organized synthesis of the evolution of the Spanish navy's organization, resources, and operations in the American colonies from the late-16th to the 17th centuries. Includes chapters on naval vessels and crews, finance, and operations against pirates and filibusters.

950 Phillips, William D., Jr. Recent works on the exploration and settlement of Latin America. (*LARR*, 32:1, 1997, p. 265–271)

Useful review essay covers several books published in connection with the Quincentennial.

951 Piqueras, Ricardo. Un indio vale casi como un caballo: utilización indígena en las huestes del XVI. (*Bol. Am.*, 36:46, 1996, p. 275–297)

General consideration of indigenous peoples' roles in several expeditions, mostly in northern South America. Based largely on published sources with some archival research.

952 **Provencio Garrigós, Lucía.** La emigración murciana a América durante el siglo XVI: catálogo de pasajeros. Murcia, Spain: V Centenario, Comisión de Murcia, 1993. 291 p.: bibl., ill. (Col. Carabelas. Ensayo; 10)

Much more than a catalog, book includes nearly 200 pages of historical text and statistical analysis, supported by charts, graphs, and extensive footnotes.

953 **Ramírez, Susan E.** Indian and Spanish conceptions of land and tenure. (*in* International Congress of Americanists, *48th, Stockholm, 1994.* Colonizacíon agrícola y ganadera en América, siglos XVI-XVIII: su impacto en la población aborigen. Quito: Ediciones Abya-Yala, 1995, p. 191–224)

Uses archival sources to examine contrasting perspectives on land use and land ownership by indigenous peoples and the Spanish in colonial Andean America. Provides interesting insights to indigenous perspective.

954 **Ramos Garrido, Estrella.** El papel del azogue en la industria minera en España y en las Indias. (*CLAHR/Albuquerque,* 5:2, Spring 1996, p. 151–194, table)

Thorough discussion of the Spanish mercury monopoly includes information on mercury mining and its use in the purification of silver. Research draws from Archivo General de Indias in Spain and the Fugger Archive in Germany.

955 **Remesal, Agustín.** 1494, la raya de Tordesillas. Valladolid, Spain: Junta de Castilla y León, Consejería de Cultura y Turismo, 1994. 153 p., 65 p. of plates: bibl., col. ill., col. maps.

Remesal's trenchant essay anchors this volume that includes the text of the treaty and illustrations from several relevant maps.

956 **Río Moreno, Justo L.** El cerdo: historia de un elemento esencial de la cultura castellana en la Conquista y colonización de América, siglo XVI. (*Anu. Estud. Am.,* 53:1, 1996, p. 13–35, graphs)

Serious scholarly study of a neglected but important subject: the place of the pig in the Spanish conquest. Uses archival sources, relevant secondary sources, and a perceptive grasp of dietary studies and economic history to present an outstanding essay.

957 **Rípodas Ardanaz, Daisy.** Iconografía de la justicia en hispanoamérica colonial. (*Rev. Hist. Derecho,* 22, 1994, p. 319–330, ill.)

Interesting examination of the symbolic representation of justice in paintings, book illustrations, statues, and other art work. Well-illustrated with research based on colonial-era publications. For art historian's comment, see item **21.**

958 **Rodríguez Nozal, Raúl.** La *Oficina Botánica,* 1788–1835: una institución dedicada al estudio de la flora americana. (*Asclepio/Madrid,* 48:2, 1995, p. 169–183)

Administrative study of the Oficina Botánica emphasizes its shortcomings in promoting economic and scientific development. Based on primary and secondary sources.

959 **Rodríguez Nozal, Raúl** and **Antonio González Bueno.** Las colonias al servicio de la ciencia metropolitana: la financiación de las "floras americanas," 1791–1809. (*Rev. Indias,* 55:205, sept./dic. 1995, p. 597–634, graphs, tables)

Archival research and quantitative analysis highlight examination of Spanish Crown's effort to raise funding for publication of a study of American flora in the waning years of the colonial era.

960 **Ruiz de Azúa y Martínez de Ezquerecocha, María Estibaliz.** Vascongadas y América. Madrid: Editorial MAPFRE, 1992. 388 p.: bibl., indexes. (Col. Las Españas y América; 7. Col. MAPFRE 1492)

Surveys the role of Basques in the Americas, devoting eight of 11 chapters to colonial period. Examines Basque participation in government, Church, and economic activities.

961 **Ruiz Jurado, Manuel.** "Enviados por todo el mundo..." (*Paramillo/San Cristóbal,* 14, 1995, p. 723–737)

Discusses psychology and ideology of Jesuits' missionary work in 1500s and 1600s, with some references to Latin American missions.

962 **Ruiz Rivera, Julián Bautista** and **Manuela Cristina García Bernal.** Cargadores a Indias. Madrid: Editorial MAPFRE, 1992. 395 p.: bibl., index. (Col. Relaciones

entre España y América; 12. Col. MAPFRE 1492)

Examines the role of merchants within the confines of the Casa de la Contratación and the Consulado de Cargadores a Indias from the 16th-18th centuries. Work of synthesis based on published monographs.

963 Sáenz-Díez, Juan Ignacio. Los riojanos en América. Madrid: Editorial MAPFRE, 1992. 354 p.: bibl., ill., indexes, map. (Col. las Españas y América; 10. Col. MAPFRE 1492)

Social history of colonial-era migrants from La Rioja is based mainly on published sources. Contains a chapter on José Antonio Manso de Velasco, who was Viceroy of Peru from 1745–61.

964 Sala Catalá, José. Ciencia y técnica en la metropolización de América. Madrid: Doce Calles; Consejo Superior de Investigaciones Científicas, 1994. 346 p.: bibl., ill. (some col.), index, maps. (Theatrum machinae. Historia de las técnicas)

Engaging, three-part interpretive study of science and engineering in the colonial period. Pt. 1 emphasizes Mexico City aqueducts and storm drainage; pt. 2, the work of architect Constantino Vasconcelos in Lima; and pt. 3, the scientific projects of Maurice of Nassau in Olinda in the period of Dutch control.

965 Saleh, Jaime M. Gobierno, derecho y administración de justicia en Hispanoamérica en la época colonial. (Bol. Acad. Nac. Hist./Caracas, 77:307, agosto/sept. 1994, p. 65–98, bibl.)

Brief overview of Spanish colonial government drawn from well-known sources. Translation of an essay originally written in Dutch.

966 Sánchez, Joseph P. Los dibujos de Pedro de Ledesma, 1626: modos y maneras de pescar la ostra y otro modo y segura invención para que una o dos personas abajen fondo del mar. (CLAHR/Albuquerque, 4:2, Spring 1995, p. 167–211, ill.)

Description and analysis of a document originally located in the Museo Naval de Madrid, which contains instructions for fishing and for the recovery of shipwrecks. Reprints 14 of Ledesma's illustrations.

967 Sánchez-Arcilla Bernal, José. Las ordenanzas de las Audiencias de Indias, 1511–1821. Madrid: Dykinson, 1992. 509 p.: bibl.

Well-edited volume brings together a sampling of laws and ordinances from 1511–1821. Introduction gives appropriate background for each case.

968 Sánchez Bella, Ismael; Alberto de la Hera; and Carlos Díaz Rementería. Historia del derecho indiano. Madrid: Editorial MAPFRE, 1992. 407 p.: bibl., index. (Col. MAPFRE 1492. Col. Relaciones entre España y América; 11)

Survey of the basic elements of Spanish law regarding indigenous peoples includes 12 essays on topics ranging from historiography, formation of the concept *derecho indiano*, government of indigenous institutions, and economic/commercial institutions. Essays have short bibliographies, but no footnotes.

969 Sánchez Gil, Víctor. Controversia sobre la Comisaría General de Indias en el siglo XVII. pt. 1. (Arch. Francisc. Hist., 85:1/4, Jan./Dec. 1992, p. 367–440, appendix)

Microhistorical examination of middle level of Franciscan bureaucracy emphasizes controversies, but also includes institutional history and 17 relevant documents.

970 Sánchez González, Antonio. Medinaceli y Colón: la otra alternativa del descubrimiento. Madrid: Editorial MAPFRE, 1995. 334 p.: bibl., ill., indexes. (Col. Relaciones entre España y América; 25. Col. MAPFRE 1492)

Detailed examination of political and property resources of the Medinaceli family and especially of the relationship between Luis de la Cerda (Medinaceli), the Spanish Crown, and Christopher Columbus in the preparations for the latter's first voyage to the Americas. Also provides a family tree for the Medinacelis.

971 Santos Hernández, Angel. Los jesuitas en América. Madrid: Editorial MAPFRE, 1992. 381 p.: bibl., maps. (Col. Iglesia Católica en el Nuevo Mundo; 5. Col. MAPFRE 1492)

Well-organized summary of the rise and fall of the Jesuits in the colonial era concludes with their expulsion in the 1760s. Over half of text is a region-by-region survey extending from New Spain to Paraguay and Argentina. Also examines Jesuit missions, schools, and scientific work. Based on secondary accounts; well-footnoted.

972 Santos Martínez, Pedro. Características, métodos y procedimientos de la evangelización hispana en América. (*Invest. Ens.*, 44, enero/dic. 1994, p. 35–65, ill.)

Helpful synthesis of historical studies dealing with methods employed by early missionaries, including use of pictures (*método picto-ideográfico*) and linguistics. Based on published works.

973 Sargiotto, Elena. Matrimonio y sexualidad en Hispanoamérica colonial: tesis historiográficas recientes en los Estados Unidos. (*in* Páginas sobre Hispanoamérica colonial: sociedad y cultura. Buenos Aires: PRHISCO-CONICET, 1994, v. 1, p. 109–127)

Useful survey of books and articles dealing with ethnicity, parental control of marriage, domestic life, and cultural values related to sexuality.

974 Seed, Patricia. "Are these not also men?": the Indians' humanity and capacity for Spanish civilisation. (*J. Lat. Am. Stud.*, 25:3, Oct. 1993, p. 629–652)

Places Spanish debate concerning humanity of indigenous peoples within an imperial environment in which the voices of the indigenous peoples themselves were not heard and the terms of the debate were determined by European values and political considerations. An effective summation of the school of thought that is generally critical of the role of the Spanish.

975 Sepúlveda, Juan Ginés de. Historia del Nuevo Mundo. Introducción, traducción y notas de Antonio Ramírez de Verger. 2. ed. en "Alianza universidad," nueva ed. rev. Madrid: Alianza Editorial, 1996. 241 p.: bibl., index, maps. (Alianza universidad; 495)

Convenient paperback edition of the classic work includes 20-page introduction, explanatory footnotes, and an index of proper names.

976 Serrano Mangas, Fernando. Función y evolución del galeón en la carrera de Indias. Madrid: Editorial MAPFRE, 1992.

251 p.: bibl., ill., indexes. (Col. Mar y América; 9. Col. MAPFRE 1492)

Detailed discussion of the design, construction, and performance of the Spanish galleon includes a chapter on cannons. Combines archival research with published sources and includes several helpful illustrations.

977 Siebzehner, Batia B. La universidad americana y la Ilustración: autoridad y conocimiento en Nueva España y el Río de la Plata. Madrid: MAPFRE, 1994. 268 p.: bibl., indexes. (Colecciones MAPFRE)

Essay in intellectual history focuses on academic and administrative life of the Real y Pontificia Univ. de México and the Univ. Nacional de Córdoba. Effectively evaluates impact of the Bourbon reforms and the Enlightenment on the two institutions utilizing secondary sources and a wide-ranging knowledge of this era in America and Europe.

978 Silva, Hernán A. La estructuración del comercio y la navegación desde el Río de la Plata a Cuba. (*Anu. Estud. Am.*, 51:2, 1994, p. 61–73, tables)

The expansion of exports—mainly salted meats—from Rio de la Plata to Havana is thoroughly documented in well-written article combining narrative description with statistics. Covers 1790s. Based on archival and published sources.

979 Solano, Francisco de. La expansión urbana ibérica por América y Asia: una consecuencia de los Tratados de Tordesillas. (*Rev. Indias*, 61:208, sept./dic. 1996, p. 615–636, bibl.)

Comparative history on a general level contrasts methods of urban settlement employed by the Spanish and Portuguese in a variety of locations.

980 Stapells Johnson, Victoria. Las irónicas circunstancias que rodearon el naufragio de la capitana de Nueva España en 1641: tragedia en la barra de Sanlúcar. (*Rev. Hist. Naval*, 14:52, 1996, p. 7–17, map)

Well-written article uses archival sources to document the bureaucratic and natural causes of the sinking of the ship *San Pedro y San Pablo*. Adroitly examines this disaster as an indicator of the problems that beset mid-1600s Spanish colonial system.

981 Tarragó, Rafael Emilio. La financiación de las ciencias y las expediciones científicas en Hispanoamérica bajo los Borbones. *(in* Seminar on the Acquisition of Latin American Library Materials, *38th, Guadalajara, Mexico, 1993.* Technology, the environment, and social change. Albuquerque, N.M.: SALALM; Univ. of New Mexico, 1995, p. 45–70, bibl.)

Useful summary of government-financed scientific expeditions that surveyed a variety of subjects: botany, mining technology, and vaccination. Based on secondary sources.

982 Taviani, Paolo Emilio. Cristóbal Colón—dos polémicas. Coordinación y traducción de Guiliana Dal Piaz. México: Nueva Imagen, 1991. 117 p.: bibl., ill., maps.

Taviani, an Italian historian and biographer of Columbus, focuses on two basic points: 1) a cogent explanation of Columbus' Italian roots, and 2) a discussion of the various locations for his first landing in the Caribbean, concluding that San Salvador is the most likely spot.

983 Tejerina, Marcela Viviana. La lucha entre España y Portugal por la ocupación del espacio: una valoración alternativa del Tratado de San Ildefonso de 1777. *(Rev. Hist./São Paulo,* segundo semestre, 1996, p. 31–39, bibl.)

Well-organized synthesis of the geopolitical and economic impact of the Treaty of San Ildefonso in the large frontier region of the Río de la Plata.

984 Torres Ramírez, Bibiano. La Marina en el gobierno y administración de Indias. Madrid: Editorial MAPFRE, 1992. 272 p.: bibl., ill., indexes. (Col. Mar y América; 14. Col. MAPFRE 1492)

Brief account of the exploratory, economic, and technical functions of Spanish shipping followed by a lengthy biographical listing of the officers who also served in high government positions. Lacks scholarly methodology.

985 Universidad del País Vasco (Spain). Comerciantes, mineros y nautas: los vascos en la economía americana. Edición de Ronald Escobedo Mansilla, Ana de Zaballa Beascoechea y Oscar Alvarez Gila. Vitoria,

Spain: Servicio Editorial, Univ. del País Vasco, 1996. 390 p.: bibl.

Essays cover wide range of economic activities in the colonial era, focusing on Venezuela, the Caribbean, and Peru. Most are based on extensive archival research.

986 Universidad del País Vasco (Spain). Euskal Herria y el Nuevo Mundo: la contribución de los vascos a la formación de las Américas. Edición de Ronald Escobedo Mansilla, Ana de Zaballa Beascoechea y Oscar Alvarez Gila. Vitoria, Spain: Servicio Editorial, Univ. del País Vasco, 1996. 681 p.: bibl., ill.

Wide variety of subjects and historical approaches characterize this compilation of essays devoted largely to the colonial period. Major topical categories include conquest and colonization, civil administration, education and culture, and a special section on Alonso de Ercilla. Essays contain useful footnotes; most are based on archival research.

987 Universidad Nacional Autónoma de México Instituto de Investigaciones Históricas. Conquista y comida: consecuencias del encuentro de dos mundos. Coordinación de Janet Towell Long. México: UNAM, 1996. 539 p.: bibl., ill.

Valuable, stimulating collection deals with diet and food preparation in Spain and the Americas on the eve of the conquest, and with the interaction of food and diets in the colonial era. Also examines a variety of alcoholic beverages as well as cookbooks and recipes. The 30 contributions exhibit unusually high quality of research and analysis.

988 Vargas Machuca, Bernardo de. Milicia indiana. Presentación de Oscar Rodríguez Ortiz. Caracas: Biblioteca Ayacucho, 1994. 126 p. (Col. Claves de América; 17)

Handbook for Spanish military commanders of largely indigenous units, this 1599 publication offers insights on colonial society and geography as well as on internal dynamics of the army.

989 Viforcos Marinas, María Isabel. La América española a través de las *Relaciones* de Cabrera de Córdoba, 1599–1614. *(Estud. Humaníst. Geogr. Hist. Arte,* 16, 1994, p. 139–155, tables)

Highly focused reading of Cabrera de Córdoba's account of events and trends in the Spanish colonies and their impact on the

Spanish court. Offers numerous examples of the flow of information across the Atlantic to Spain.

990 Vitar, Beatriz. La *otredad* lingüística y su impacto en la conquista de las Indias. (*Rev. Esp. Antropol. Am.*, 26, 1996, p. 143–165, bibl.)

Examines the interaction of Spanish and indigenous languages, including the work of the Jesuits, European presumptions of linguistic superiority, and the role of interpreters in the conquest. Based on a healthy mix of primary and secondary sources.

991 Weddle, Robert S. Changing tides: twilight and dawn in the Spanish Sea, 1763–1803. College Station: Texas A&M Univ. Press, 1995. 352 p.: bibl., ill., index, maps. (Centennial series of the Association of Former Students, Texas A&M University; 58)

Well-organized and clearly written, this volume, the third part of a history of the Gulf of Mexico in the Spanish colonial era, rests on a thorough integration of secondary publications with the author's archival research. The first part of series is *Spanish Sea: Gulf of Mexico in North American discovery* (1985); second part is *The French thorn: rival explorers in the Spanish Sea, 1682–1762* (1991).

992 Yaranga Valderrama, Abdón. Los *reducciones*, uno de los instrumentos del etnocidio. (*Rev. Complut. Hist. Am.*, 21, 1995, p. 241–262, appendices, facsim., maps, tables)

Negative assessment of the role of Spanish *reducciones* in colonial Peru, based on primary and secondary sources. Includes maps and charts, and publishes five documents tending to reinforce author's thesis.

993 Yeager, Timothy J. Encomienda or slavery?: the Spanish Crown's choice of labor organization in sixteenth-century Spanish America. (*J. Econ. Hist.*, 55:4, Dec. 1995, p. 842–859, bibl., graph, tables)

In a perceptive, interpretative essay, author argues that the Spanish Crown established the encomienda to secure control over the American colonies and to gain immediate revenues—policies that proved shortsighted in terms of need for investment in large-scale projects and promotion of long-term economic growth.

INDEPENDENCE AND 19TH CENTURY

Baer, Werner and **Kent Hargis.** Forms of external capital and economic development in Latin America, 1820–1997. See *HLAS 57:1250.*

994 Castillo Meléndez, Francisco; Luisa J. Figallo Pérez; and **Ramón María Serrera Contreras.** Las Cortes de Cádiz y la imagen de América: la visión etnográfica y geográfica del Nuevo Mundo. Cádiz, Spain: Servicio de Publicaciones, Univ. de Cádiz, 1994. 504 p.: bibl., ill.

Early 19th-century archival documents are accompanied by brief but instructive introductory essays.

995 Cervera Pery, José. La marina española en la emancipación de Hispanoamérica. Madrid: Editorial MAPFRE, 1992. 290 p.: bibl., ill., indexes, maps. (Col. Mar y América; 11. Col. MAPFRE 1492)

Engaging combination of institutional and narrative history unfortunately lacks depth in footnotes. Bibliography includes several archival sources.

996 Chust Calero, Manuel. La abolición del régimen colonial americano en las cortes de Cádiz: el caso de la encomienda. (*in* Tiempos de Latinoamérica. Castellón de la Plana, Spain: Univ. Jaume I, 1994, p. 113–138)

Connects political conditions in Spain and America in a scholarly examination of the origins of the 1811 movement to abolish the encomienda.

997 Chust Calero, Manuel. De esclavos, encomenderos y mitayos: el anticolonismo en las Cortes de Cádiz. (*Mex. Stud.*, 11:2, Summer 1995, p. 179–202)

Impressive study of challenges to some key policies of the Spanish imperial system posed by representatives of the American colonies relies heavily on Cortes-published records. Also examines Spanish political conditions and some international—especially British—influences.

998 Contreras Pérez, Francisco. Un mecanismo financiador de la emigración contemporánea de andaluces a Iberoamérica. (*Rev. Hist. Contemp.*, 6, junio 1995, p. 61–94, bibl., tables)

Well-researched and carefully reasoned

examination of migrants' motives and of methods of financing immigration from Andalucía to Latin America (mainly Argentina, Brazil, and Cuba) from 1880–1900.

999 Díaz Cid, Manuel Antonio and Fidencio Aguilar Víquez. Ilustración e independencia en Hispanoamérica. Puebla, Mexico?: Ediciones de la Univ. Popular Autónoma del Estado de Puebla, 1992. 190 p.: bibl., maps.

Sweeping, provocative assessment of ideological roots of the independence movements stresses the Enlightenment as a motivating force, in general, and Protestantism, Masonry, and individual quests for power as particular forces. Based mainly on published sources with some information from primary documents. For a more interpretive approach, see item **1000.**

1000 Díaz Cid, Manuel Antonio and Fidencio Aguilar Víquez. Sociedades de pensamiento e independencia. Puebla, Mexico: Ediciones de la Univ. Popular Autónoma del Estado de Puebla, 1990? 177 p.: bibl., ill., maps.

Descriptive listing of late-18th-century intellectual societies connects this general trend to early-19th-century independence revolts. Based on published monographs. See also item **999.** For philosophy specialist's comment, see item **4955.**

Falcón, Fernando. La política militar de Carlos III y su impacto en el proceso de independencia de Venezuela. See item **2527.**

1001 Fernández, Delfina. Ultimos reductos españoles en América. Madrid: Editorial MAPFRE, 1992. 344 p.: bibl., indexes, maps. (Col. Armas y América; 7. Col. MAPFRE 1492)

Impressive archival research buttresses carefully focused study of last stages of Spanish resistance to independence revolutions of the 1810s-1820s.

1002 Gandía, Enrique de. La independencia de América y las sociedades secretas. Santa Fe, Argentina: Ediciones Sudamérica Santa Fe, 1994. 427 p.: bibl.

Self-proclaimed polemical study stresses influence of Masonry on José de San Martín and on independence movement in general.

1003 The gendered worlds of Latin American women workers: from household and factory to the union hall and ballot box. Edited by John D. French and Daniel James. Durham, N.C.: Duke Univ. Press, 1997. 320 p.: bibl., ill., index. (Comparative and international working-class history)

Collection of well-researched articles effectively combines gender history and labor history and includes specialized studies of Argentina, Brazil, Chile, Colombia, and Guatemala. Each article is thoroughly footnoted, revealing broadly-based sources including interviews, memoirs, and government publications, as well as authors' extensive reading in comparable published studies and theoretical literature. Editors also contribute introductory and concluding essays rich in historiographical and methodological insights.

1004 Interethnische Beziehungen in der Geschichte Lateinamerikas [Interethnic relations in the history of Latin America]. Herausgegeben von Heinz-Joachim Domnick, Jürgen Müller und Hans-Jürgen Prien. Frankfurt am Main: Vervuert, 1999. 255 p.: bibl. (Acta coloniensia; 3)

Twelve well-researched and well-written papers cover a variety of relevant topics concerning interethnic contacts and relations. Topics include the role of European ethnocentrism in Christian missionary efforts, Bourbon reforms and ethnicity in New Mexico and the role of minorities during the revolutionary period, the impact of shipwrecked African slaves on the indigenous population of Esmaraldas, African slaves and the law in colonial Uruguay, the significance of ethnicity and class for women during the colonial period, studies of national and foreign trade in South and Central America during the 19th century, ethnicity and racism in Cuba, and modern Guatemalan nationalism versus indigenous traditionalism. [C. Converse]

Jackson, Robert H. Race/caste and the creation and meaning of identity in colonial Spanish America. See item **905.**

1005 McFarlane, Anthony. Rebellions in late colonial Spanish America: a comparative perspective. (*Bull. Lat. Am. Res.,* 14:3, Sept. 1995, p. 313–338)

Valuable synthesis filters several interpretations to produce a nuanced, coherent essay. Points out that rebellions in Spanish America were driven by their own sets of circumstances and causes separate from instabilities of Napoleonic Europe, and that independence era should be understood in this largely American context. Thoroughly footnoted.

1006 Náter, Laura. En busca de reconocimiento: la independencia de América Latina y la política española, 1820–1823. *(Hist. Mex.,* 45:4, abril/junio 1996, p. 704–735, appendix)

Concise account of Spanish Cortes discussions on the recognition of the newly independent Spanish American governments. Appendix has considerable detail on many Spanish American delegates.

Park, James William. Latin American underdevelopment: a history of perspectives in the United States, 1870–1965. See *HLAS 57:1417.*

1007 Paz Sánchez, Manuel de and **Manuel Hernández González.** La esclavitud blanca: contribución a la historia del inmigrante canario en América, siglo XIX. Santa Cruz de Tenerife, Spain: Centro de la Cultura Popular Canaria, 1992. 211 p.: bibl., ill. (Taller de Historia; 13)

Narrative, interpretive, and quantitative history are effectively combined in this well-researched account of migration of Canary Island peasants to Cuba, Puerto Rico, Venezuela, and Uruguay. Last 100 pages contain reproductions of relevant documents.

1008 Pérez O., Eduardo. Guerra irregular en la América Meridional, s.s. XVIII-XIX: ensayo de historia social comparada con España y la Nueva Granada. v. 1. Tunja, Colombia: Academia Boyacense de Historia; Univ. Pedagógica y Tecnológica de Colombia, 1994. 1 v.: bibl., ill. (some col.), maps.

Ambitious effort in comparative history seeks to identify popular roots and political consequences of irregular (or guerrilla) warfare in Spain, New Granada, Peru, northern Argentina, Paraguay, and southern Brazil. Basic information drawn from published monographs and documents as indicated in extensive footnotes and lengthy bibliography. Vol. 1 of an extended study on this topic.

1009 Pérez Tomás, Eduardo E. De columbina haereditate, 1492–1810. v. 2. México: Instituto Panamericano de Geografía e Historia, 1993. 1 v.: bibl., index.

Pt. 3 of Vol. 2 concludes this unique survey history of colonial Hispanic America by concentrating on the years 1797–1810, the activities of Francisco Miranda, and role of the British in the independence of Venezuela, Brazil, and Argentina. Based on research in Spanish archives and Britain's Public Records Office. For annotation of vol. 1, see *HLAS 56:952.*

1010 Pumar Martínez, Carmen. La primera renuncia española al colonialismo: 1.820 o el regreso de los patriotas americanos. *(Estud. Hist. Soc. Econ. Am.,* 12, 1995, p. 133–140)

Study of the influence of liberalism in Spain during Napoleonic era and its aftermath focuses on the return of "American patriots" to their homelands in the Western Hemisphere. Combines research in Spain's Archivo General de Indias and the British Museum.

1011 Rathbone, Richard. The Gold Coast, the closing of the Atlantic slave trade, and Africans of the diaspora. (*in* Slave cultures and the cultures of slavery. Knoxville: Univ. of Tennessee Press, 1995, p. 55–66, bibl.)

Valuable synthesis of 19th-century post-slave trade era emphasizes return of African-Caribbean and African-Brazilian peoples to the Gold Coast (Ghana).

1012 Las revoluciones hispánicas: independencias americanas y liberalismo español. Dirección de François-Xavier Guerra. Madrid: Editorial Complutense, 1995. 292 p.: bibl. (Cursos de verano de El Escorial; 93–94)

Well-organized group of essays, some by respected specialists, examines typology, sociology, and ideology of the early-19th-century revolutions as well as problems of nationhood and establishment of governmental institutions. Engagingly written essays will appeal to both scholar and general reader.

1013 Riguzzi, Paolo. ¿Arte o comercio, poesía o industria?: la presencia económica de EU en América Latina, 1870–1914; visiones y actitudes latinoamericanas. (*in* Estados Unidos desde América Latina: sociedad, política y cultura. México: Instituto de Investigaciones Dr. José María Luis Mora; Centro de Investigación y Docencia Económicas, El Colegio de México, 1995, p. 159–182)

Perceptive and non-polemical summary of the expansion of US economic interests in Latin America, based on examination of recent publications and archival research in Mexico.

1014 Rivadulla Barrientos, Daniel; Jesús Raúl Navarro García; and **María Teresa Berruezo.** El exilio español en América en el siglo XIX. Madrid: Editorial MAPFRE, 1992. 417 p.: bibl., ill., indexes. (Col. Relaciones entre España y América; 14. Col. MAPFRE 1492)

Three essays on Spanish exiles examine the role of liberal exiles during the independence period, the activities of the Carlists from 1830s-1870s, and republican activities over the last third of 19th century. All based on healthy mixtures of archival research and published monographs.

1015 Rivas, Ricardo Alberto. Historiadores del siglo XIX y la historia de América. La Plata, Argentina: Univ. Nacional de La Plata, Facultad de Humanidades y Ciencias de la Educación, 1995. 123 p.: bibl.. (Serie Estudios/investigaciones; 26)

Convenient introduction to historiography of 19th-century Latin America employs both thematic and chronological discussions. Emphasizes emergence of national historiographies—especially in Chile, Brazil, and Argentina—in middle- and late-19th century and, in particular, the writings of Chilean Diego Barros Arana.

1016 Rodríguez O., Jaime E. La independencia de la América española. México: El Colegio de México; Fideicomiso Historia de las Américas; Fondo de Cultura Económica, 1996. 308 p.: bibl., maps. (Serie Ensayos / Fideicomiso Historia de las Américas. Sección de obras de historia)

Masterful synthesis of the independence era organized around fundamental themes: state of the Spanish empire, origins of the revolutionary movements, and beginnings of representative government. Author uses a region-by-region approach in coverage of civil strife, military campaigns, and final achievement of independence.

Rodríguez Ozán, María Elena. Las ideologías de los inmigrantes europeos en América Latina. See item **5036.**

1017 Schröter, Bernd. Los comienzos de la diplomacia prusiana en América del Sur de 1816 a 1820. (in Tordesillas y sus consecuencias: la política de las grandes potencias europeas respecto a América Latina, 1494–1899. Frankfurt: Vervuert; Madrid: Iberoamericana, 1995, p. 91–99)

Prussian commercial diplomacy in Brazil, Argentina, and the Banda Oriental is central focus of well-organized study based on research in German archives.

1018 Selser, Gregorio. Cronología de las intervenciones extranjeras en América Latina. v. 1, 1776–1848. Mexico: UNAM, Centro de Investigaciones Interdisciplinarias, 1994. 1 v.: bibl., index. (Cuadernos del CIIH. Serie Fuentes; 12)

Combines day-by-day listing of foreign interventions, including diplomatic, military, and economic influences, with author's often provocative commentary on each item.

1019 Semprún, José and **Alfonso Bullón de Mendoza Gómez de Valugera.** El ejército realista en la independencia americana. Madrid: Editorial MAPFRE, 1992. 346 p.: bibl., indexes, maps. (Col. Armas y América; 8. Col. MAPFRE 1492)

General history of Spanish military during wars of independence contains both a survey of institutional factors and a narrative of the fighting. Chapters on guerrilla warfare and ideological motivations are especially thought-provoking. Sparsely footnoted; brief bibliography.

1020 Sotomayor, Teresa Maya. Estados Unidos y el panamericanismo: el caso de la I Conferencia Internacional Americana, 1889–1890. (Hist. Mex., 45:4, abril/junio 1996, p. 759–781)

Interesting account of Pan-American Conference in Washington emphasizes archival research grounded in correspondence between Mexico's representative Matias Romero and Mexican Foreign Minister Ignacio Mariscal.

1021 Uribe, Víctor M. The enigma of Latin American independence: analyses of the last ten years. (LARR, 32:1, 1997, p. 236–255)

Informative historiographical essay covers 14 books published from 1986–94, and includes commentary on several important scholarly articles.

1022 Valdaliso, Jesús María. La flota mercante española y el tráfico con América en la segunda mitad del siglo XIX. (*Rev. Hist. Naval,* 13:49, 1995, p. 7–37, appendix, bibl., graphs, maps, tables)

Examines changing nature of Spanish trade with America (Cuba, Puerto Rico, the independent Latin American nations, and the US) giving special attention to transition from sail to steam and to importance of the Basques. Contains numerous tables, charts, and maps.

1023 Vásquez, George L. La historiografía latinoamericana del siglo XIX: el caso de tres historiadores ilustres: Andrés Bello, Diego Barros Arana y Bartolomé Mitre. (*Histórica/Lima,* 20:1, julio 1996, p. 131–153, bibl.)

Examination of the historical writing of three leading 19th-century figures includes both textual analysis and relevant and revealing biographical information. Thoroughly footnoted.

1024 Vilar, Juan Bautista. La emigración judeo-marroquí a la América Latina en la fase pre-estadística, 1850–1880. (*Sefárdica/Buenos Aires,* 11, sept. 1996, p. 11–54, photos, tables)

Extensive survey of published monographs and documents, combined with archival research, produces informative account of Jewish immigration from Morocco, at first focused on Brazil, then Argentina, and later on other Latin American countries.

1025 Yáñez Gallardo, César. Saltar con red: la temprana emigración catalana a América ca. 1830–1870. Madrid: Alianza Editorial, 1996. 272 p.: bibl. (Alianza América; 37)

Effective historical sociology of migration from Catalonia to the Americas—especially to Cuba, Puerto Rico, and Argentina—emphasizes importance of family networks. Impressive combination of archival research and broad reading of parallel migration studies; thoroughly footnoted.

20TH CENTURY

1026 Avni, Haim. Postwar Latin American Jewry: an agenda for the study of the last five decades. (*in* The Jewish diaspora in Latin America: new studies on history and literature. New York: Garland Publ., 1996, p. 3–19, bibl., table)

Stimulating analytical examination of the historiography of modern Jewry in the region, organized into political, social, and economic themes. Also includes suggestions for future research.

Baer, Werner and **Kent Hargis.** Forms of external capital and economic development in Latin America, 1820–1997. See *HLAS* 57:1250.

1027 Bernecker, Walther L. ¿Punto de partida hacia la modernidad?: América Latina a finales de la Segunda Guerra Mundial. (*Stud. Hist. Hist. Contemp.,* 13/14, 1995/96, p. 149–166)

Sophisticated overview of political and economic tendencies in Latin America from late 1940s to 1950s. Stresses initial impetus toward democracy, followed by return to right-wing dictatorships. Includes interesting commentary on the US role.

1028 Bushnell, David. Feminismo filatélico: imágenes de la mujer en sellos de la Argentina, Colombia, Cuba y Estado Unidos, 1893–1994. (*Bol. Am.,* 37:47, 1997, p. 77–90, ill., tables)

Analytical and entertaining article offers insights into politics and popular culture of nations under study.

1029 Cárdenas, Eduardo. La Iglesia hispanoamericana en el siglo XX, 1890–1990. Madrid: Editorial MAPFRE, 1992. 305 p.: bibl., indexes. (Col. Iglesia católica en el Nuevo Mundo; 6. Col. MAPFRE 1492)

Competent, brief survey of the Catholic Church set within political and social context of early- to mid-20th-century Latin America. Tends to be more encyclopedic than interpretive and pays little attention to liberation theology and competition with Protestantism.

Díaz Fuentes, Daniel. Crisis y cambios estructurales en América Latina: Argentina, Brasil y México durante el periodo de entreguerras. See *HLAS* 57:1300.

1030 Entrena Durán, Francisco. Los populismos y la formación del estado-nación en América Latina. (*Anu. Estud. Am.*, 53:1, 1996, p. 101–121)

Intriguing interpretation of populism in Brazil during the Vargas era, in Argentina under Perón, and in Mexico in the Cárdenas years. Sees populism in these contexts as an essential element in the consolidation and legitimization of the nation-state. Well-organized and convincingly presented study.

García Zarza, Eugenio. La emigración española a Iberoamérica, 1946–90: estudio geográfico. See *HLAS 57:2413.*

1031 Kitroeff, Alexander. Griegos en América. Traducción de Isabel M. Romero. Madrid: Editorial MAPFRE, 1992. 296 p.: bibl., indexes. (Col. América, crisol de pueblos; 4. Col. MAPFRE 1492)

Pioneering synthesis offers a topical overview of a heretofore neglected subject. Concentrates on 20th-century patterns ranging from Canada to South America and includes themes such as geographical distribution of immigrants, maintenance of Greek identity and ethnic institutions, and the Greek Orthodox Church. The footnotes and bibliography feature Greek sources.

1032 Klich, Ignacio and Jeffrey H. Lesser. *Turco* immigrants in Latin America. (*Americas/Franciscans*, 53:1, July 1996, p. 1–14)

Well-informed, brief overview of an area previously neglected in ethnic and immigration studies. Authors explain their somewhat reluctant use of the term *turco* and the diversity within this arbitrary grouping of immigrants from the Middle East. Tends to dwell on Argentina and Brazil and relies on published sources as indicated in ample footnotes.

Lehmann, David. Struggle for the spirit: religious transformation and popular culture in Brazil and Latin America. See item **3289.**

1033 Luna, Lola G. Estado y participación política de mujeres en América Latina: una relación desigual y una propuesta de análisis histórico. (*in* Mujeres y participación política: avances y desafíos en América Latina. Bogotá: TM Editores, 1994, p. 29–44)

Important overview of women's role in 20th-century politics. Considers participation of women under four types of regimes: oligarchic, populist, military, and democratic. Also develops a conceptual framework for various types of political participation. Based on a survey of recently published books and articles.

1034 Monteón, Michael. Gender and economic crises in Latin America: reflections on the Great Depression and the debt crisis. (*in* EnGENDERing wealth and well-being: empowerment for global change. Boulder, Colo.: Westview Press, 1995, p. 39–62)

Stimulating pioneering study of women's role in two major economic crises: the 1930s Great Depression and 1980s debt crisis. Survey of published studies indicates that improvements in employment conditions for women have come slowly because of the resiliency of male domination in the workplace.

Park, James William. Latin American underdevelopment: a history of perspectives in the United States, 1870–1965. See *HLAS 57:1417.*

Pons Muzzo, Gustavo. Estudio histórico sobre el protocolo de Río de Janeiro: el Ecuador, país amazónico. See *HLAS 57:4041.*

1035 Prothero, R. Mansell. Malaria in Latin America: environmental and human factors. (*Bull. Lat. Am. Res.*, 14:3, Sept. 1995, p. 357–365, bibl.)

Carefully considered account details increase of malaria in Latin America since 1980s. Although author considers many possible causes, human migration into malaria-prone areas resulting from economic development (the Amazon basin) and migration driven by political instability (Central America) seem to be the primary factors. Discusses areas where malaria outbreaks have received prompt responses by government health officials (e.g., Costa Rica and Venezuela).

Riguzzi, Paolo. ¿Arte o comercio, poesía o industria?: la presencia económica de EU en América Latina, 1870–1914; visiones y actitudes latinoamericanas. See item **1013.**

Rodríguez Ozán, María Elena. Las ideologías de los inmigrantes europeos en América Latina. See item **5036.**

1036 Samper K., Mario. El estudio histórico comparado de las caficulturas latino americanas: breve reseña bibliográfica, con énfasis en el cambio tecnológico-social. (*Rev. Hist./Heredia,* 31, enero/junio 1995, p. 195–209)

Brief, somewhat overly selective discussion of the historiography of coffee cultivation stresses comparative studies from early 1960s-early 1990s.

1037 Taracena Arriola, Arturo. Agela, 1925–1933: la Asociación General de Estudiantes Latinoamericanos de París. (*Cuad. Marcha,* 9:95, junio 1994, p. 66–79, ill.)

Excellent portrait of important, but heretofore little studied, episode in Latin American intellectual history traces coalescence and dissolution of a young, idealistic group of students in Paris. Generally leftists and anti-imperialists, these writers took outspoken stands on current issues before embarking on their careers in literature, politics, and the professions. The group included Miguel Angel Asturias, Carlos Quijano, and León Debayle Sacasa.

1038 Townsend Ezcurra, Andrés. Patria grande: pueblo, parlamento e integración. Lima: Editorial e Imprenta DESA, 1991. 339 p.: bibl.

Mainly a narrative account of effort to develop a Latin American parliament from 1960s-80s, with some historical background. Author, a participant in the movement, offers some probing insights.

1039 Wright, Thomas C. América Latina en la época de la Revolución Cubana: un intento de interpretación. (*Rev. Chil. Hist. Geogr.,* 160, 1992/93, p. 177–185)

Perceptive general essay updates Wright's interpretation of the impact of Fidel Castro's revolution discussed in his book *Latin America in the era of the Cuban Revolution* (see *HLAS 55:3881*). Focuses on causes and effects of the revolution's diminishing influence.

1040 Zapata, Francisco. Autonomía y subordinación en el sindicalismo latino-americano. México: El Colegio de México; Fondo de Cultura Económica, 1993. 171 p.: bibl. (Serie Ensayos / Fideicomiso Historia de las Américas. Sección de obras de historia.)

Pointed assessment of Latin American labor movement written with a critical perspective on rapid changes associated with 1980s debt crisis and privatization. Well-organized text includes brief case studies of Bolivia, Chile, Peru, Argentina, Brazil, and Mexico. Argues that Latin American labor movement must devise new ideological and organizational approaches to deal with massive changes of recent years.

MEXICO
General and Colonial Period

ASUNCIÓN LAVRIN, *Professor of History, Arizona State University at Tempe*
EDITH B. COUTURIER, *Independent Scholar*

TRADITIONAL AND WELL-TRIED APPROACHES characterize the general books on the historiography of Mexico as it stood in the early-to-mid-1990s, as well as works focusing on the colonial period. There were few thematic or methodological surprises in this biennium.

The general histories focus on cities (item **1064**), housing (item **1067**), regions (item **1070**); or study one of a few select themes, such as women (items **1073** and **1054**) or the political roots of the Mexican state (item **1061**). As usual, we have placed guides to archives, documentary collections, anthologies, collections of essays resulting from conferences, or individual compilations in the General section, as long as they cover a significant period of time. Good examples are the festschrift in honor of Jean-Pierre Berthe (item **1051**) and the volume on ecclesiastical sources for Mexican social history edited by Connaughton and Lira (item **1058**). A special tribute is owed to Father Lino Canedo's latest and posthumous archival review (item **1047**), which demonstrates his lifetime interest in unearthing and organizing sources for future research.

Resources and guides that cover only limited time periods or small areas, such as a municipality or a city, are found in the Colonial section. See, for example, the 20-year guide to the municipality of Colima (item **1092**) or the notarial records of Toluca (item **1104**). The second guide to personal cases and writings scrutinized and sometimes banned by the Inquisition has a place of singular importance (item **1044**). This rich source for 17th-century counterculture contains writings of a literary nature, sermons, and processes of investigation against individuals. All the preceding works testify to the vigorous engagement of local and regional historians in understanding their own past and promoting its interpretation.

Established areas of economic history, such as internal trade, mining, commodity prices, and the hacienda-market relationship form a solid core of information in works reviewed this biennium (items **1146, 1174,** and **1197**). New and useful directions of research, such as hacienda ownership analysis, the contributions of the indigenous population to trade rather than agriculture, the muleteer industry, and the relevance of regional markets offer a fresh perspective. Among them, the works of Garavaglia and Grosso (items **1131** and **1133**), as well as those of Ibarra (items **1150** and **1151**) deserve special mention.

Ethnographic studies are enriched by revisionist works on the role of indigenous peoples in the economy and the economic impact of labor and landownership systems on indigenous populations. For example, Jeremy Baskes challenges traditional interpretations of *repartimiento* (item **1098**), Grosso clarifies peon-patrón relationships through case studies (item **1143**), and Menegus defines the differences between Indian and Spanish market activities (item **1172**). In-depth studies of indigenous communities are missing this biennium. However, studies of the class split between caciques and macehuales (item **1113**) and indigenous rebellions indicate a continuous expansion of ethnographic studies at the local level. Equally important, in a similar direction, are the studies of the population of African descent. The works annotated here are an indication of renewed interest in this topic, further highlighted by several national conferences. Garavaglia and Grosso's study of mestizaje and class suggests the need to use contemporary colonial definitions and understandings of race and class (item **1132**).

Ecclesiastical history has enough sample studies of religious orders to reassure readers that the genre is still being cultivated. However, it is religious evangelization and the lives of men and women within the faith that compel attention. Francisco Morales' re-examination of the process of evangelization helps in understanding the accommodation between Christian and non-Christian beliefs (item **1178**), while Corcuera de Mancera points to problems plaguing that process (item **1118**). Evangelization made few inroads in more remote areas such as Nayarit, according to Mylene Péron (item **1186**), and this clarifies, in part, the root of the rebellions chronicled by Itarch Ramón (item **1188**) and Macleod (item **1163**). Within the Catholic tradition, the study of familial religiosity by Loreto (item **1159**) and devotional practices by Mazín (item **1168**) stand out as new trends of analysis. The substantive study of the clergy by Taylor (item **1201**) turns the interest of colonialists to the secular church, which has so far remained in an ancillary position.

Mazín's study of the Michoacán cathedral cabildo and Trasloheros' study of the episcopacy of Michoacán Bishop Marcos Ramírez de Prado reinforce this trend (items **1167** and **1205,** respectively).

Studies of women and gender relations were limited in scope, mostly amplifying established knowledge on honor and sexuality. A literary analysis on the meaning of Malinche extends the debate on this challenging figure (item **1137**).

Among the materials annotated in the *HLAS* section now called North, rather than North and Borderlands, we find a number of publications issued by institutions in the northern states. These works provide tangible evidence of the high level of activity in the field of northern Mexican history; activity that includes conferences and historical research.

Works reviewed this biennium seem to strengthen a revisionist view of land tenure. It appears that the prior picture of domination of the land by haciendas failed to take into account the true complexity of land tenure, particularly the existence of small- and medium-sized landholders and the strength of the communities that supported them. The works of Cynthia Radding (items **1257** and **1259**) are particularly important in this respect, as well as in their elucidation of mission history. Among others, the works by Romero on Sonora (item **1264**) and Osante on Nuevo Santander (item **1252**) contribute to our understanding of this phenomenon. Robert Jackson's continued critiques of the mission system through careful analysis of population figures (item **1242**), meanwhile, represent an important addition to our understanding of indigenous-white relations.

Contributions focusing on the history of California include a new collection of original works called *Contested Eden* (item **1228**) and León Portilla's collection of articles about Baja California (item **1247**). Another notable work on California is the careful study of San Juan Capistrano by Haas (item **1239**). A new edition of the letters of Palau from California provides a documentary contribution (item **1253**). Discussion of the reasons for the failure of Gálvez's colonization project provides another interesting perspective on the nature of Spanish control over California (item **1217**). Finally, a study of the missions of Junípero Serra constitutes an original contribution to the mission history of California (item **1223**).

Notable also is the augmented depth of understanding of local communities. Cheryl Martin's work on Chihuahua provides an important new view of a northern colonial city. This work (item **1251**) underscores the possibilities in writing local histories of the north. It is based on one small part of an enormous microfilming project carried out by the Univ. of Texas system for the northern states of Mexico, making primary materials available for the use of scholars at their own institutions. David Brading provides another study of a colonial town in the north with his work on the origins of the mining community of Catorce (item **1103**).

Thanks to new research, a far more interesting and nuanced history of the northern regions is emerging. One hopes to see this trend continue well into the future.

GENERAL

1041 A Dios lo que es de Dios. Coordinación de Carlos Martínez Assad. México: Aguilar, 1995. 415 p.: bibl., ill. (Nuevo siglo)

Essay collection explores mostly 19th- and 20th-century Roman Catholic personalities and historical issues. Serious effort to write nonpolitical history from an ecclesiastical viewpoint. [AL]

Aboites Aguilar, Luis. Norte precario: poblamiento y colonización en México, 1760–1940. See item **1215**.

La agricultura en tierras mexicanas desde sus orígenes hasta nuestros días. See *HLAS* 57:4557.

1042 Alvarez, Manuel. Historia de la astronomía en México. México: SEP—FCE, 1986. 260 p.: ill. (La Ciencia desde México, 4)

Thirteen essays on the history of astronomy in Mexico. Those covering the preconquest period and colonial history are of greater interest than those covering later periods. Accessible information for those interested in the history of sciences. [AL]

1043 Una aproximación a Puerto Vallarta. Edición de Jaime Olveda. Zapopan, Mexico: Colegio de Jalisco, 1993. 161 p.: bibl., maps.

Eight articles on the history and development of Puerto Vallarta from the prehispanic era to contemporary times. Includes essays on tourism, urban growth, and migration. [D. Coerver]

1044 Archivo General de la Nación (Mexico). Catálogo de textos marginados novohispanos: Inquisición, siglos XVII. México: El Colegio de México: Archivo General de la Nación (México): Fondo Nacional para la Cultura y las Artes, 1997. 806 p.: indexes.

Annotated catalog of a variety of texts scrutinized by the Inquisition in the 17th century. Includes personal narratives, legal depositions, poems, etc., offering an excellent source for researching the social and cultural history of the colonial baroque period. [AL]

1045 Barragán López, Esteban. El proceso de ladinización en la sierra de Tamazula. (*Estud. Jalisc.*, 27, feb. 1997, p. 5–22)

Charts the process of cultural change in this region on the borders of Jalisco and Michoacán from the time of the Spanish invasion to the 1990s. Considers such topics as the effects of epidemic disease, congregation, Catholic evangelization, independence, and the dynamic process of changing land tenure. [AL]

1046 Becerril, Leticia Román de. Chiapas, kaleidoscopio histórico: siglos de historia, remembranzas y consideraciones: semblanzas de Belisario Domínguez como hombre, médico y héroe. México: Gernika, 1995. 251 p.: bibl., ill., maps.

Popular treatment of the history of Comitán, Chiapas, and a laudatory sketch of a native son. [D. Coerver]

1047 Canedo, Lino Gómez. Archivos históricos de México. Advertencia y notas de Ernesto de la Torre Villar. Madrid: Fundación Histórica Tavera; México: Univ. Nacional Autónoma de México, Instituto de Investigaciones Históricas, 1997. 189 p. (Documentos Tavera; 5)

Posthumous publication of noted Franciscan historian updates his previous archival surveys. Since national, state, local, and private archives have made tremendous advances since the 1970s, this volume should assist investigators. Describes the archives, outlines the sections, and provides inclusive dates and the number of volumes in each repository. [EBC]

1048 Careaga Viliesid, Lorena and **Luz del Carmen Vallarta Vélez.** Quintana Roo: historiografía regional, instituciones y fuentes documentales. Chetumal, Mexico: Editora Norte Sur, 1996. 182 p.: bibl.

Review of scholarly works, printed primary sources, and archival sources related to the history of Quintana Roo from colonial times to the contemporary era. Also includes comments on institutional projects aimed at reconstructing the region's past. [D. Coerver]

1049 Congreso Internacional de Historia Regional Comparada, 4th, *Univ. Autónoma de Ciudad Juárez, 1993.* Actas. Juárez, Mexico: Univ. Autónoma de Ciudad Juárez, 1995. 1 v.: bibl., ill.

Compilation of presentations from the Fourth International Congress of Comparative History. Although the case for comparative history is unclear, this mixed bag of essays has some interesting readings, mostly on the history of northern Mexico. Sections on colonial literary texts and the praxis of contemporary primary schools in northern Mexico exemplify the bric-a-brac nature of these volumes. [AL]

1050 Congreso Nacional de Historia Regional, 8th, *Culiacán, Mexico, 1992.* Contribuciones a la historia del noroccidente mexicano: memoria del VIII Congreso Nacional de Historia Regional. Compilación de Guillermo Ibarra Escobar y Ana Luz Ruelas. Culiacán, Mexico: Univ. Autónoma de

Sinaloa, Escuela de Historia, 1994. 340 p.: bibl., ill.

Emphasizing the 20th century, the papers from this Congress are of variable quality, but there is a considerable contribution to the history of mining in the Northwest. Topics include family, political, and labor history. Some papers based on secondary sources. [EBC]

1051 Des indes occidentales à l'Amérique latine: à Jean-Pierre Berthe. Textes réunis par Alain Musset et Thomas Calvo. Fonenay-aux-Roses, France: ENS éditions Fontenay/Saint-Cloud, 1997. 2 v. (690 p.): bibl., ill. (Sociétés, espaces, temps, 1258–1135)

This celebration of Prof. Jean-Pierre Berthe's dedication to the history of colonial Mexico contains 47 essays by distinguished historians of Europe and the Americas. Essays focus on colonial subjects, with several works on the 19th century and on Spain. The essays are grouped into six categories: Space and Territory; Chronicles of Daily Life; Intellectual and Religious Life; Labor and Silver; Political Life and the Pursuit of Power; Images and Texts. An interview with Professor Berthe delves into his intellectual formation. The high quality of the contributions merits special attention and commendation. Colonialists should be aware of this excellent publication. [AL]

1052 Escobar Ohmstede, Antonio. Del gobierno indígena al Ayuntamiento constitucional en las Huastecas hidalguense y veracruzana, 1780–1853. (*Mex. Stud.*, 12:1, Winter 1996, p. 1–26)

Studies the internal structure of the government of an indigenous town prior to independence and the changes that occurred thereafter. Posits that the economic base of the republican municipalities was very thin, but they still provided a base for power struggles. Between 1820–40, the elite in most municipalities consolidated their power over smaller towns and over the indigenous population, despite much resistance. [AL]

1053 Estado de México: tras la huella de su historia. Coordinación de Elvia Montes de Oca Navas y María del Pilar Iracheta Cenecorta. Toluca, Mexico: H. Ayuntamiento Constitucional 1994–1996 de

Toluca; Colegio Mexiquense, 1996. 284 p.: bibl., ill.

Collection of essays covers colonial, 19th-century, and Revolutionary topics. Includes studies of the role of Mexican peasants and workers in the Revolution, and of socialist education in Mexico state during the 1930s. [D. Coerver]

Familia y vida privada en la historia de Iberoamérica: seminario de historia de la familia. See item **771.**

1054 Florescano, Enrique and Susan Swan. Breve historia de la sequía en México. Xalapa, Mexico: Univ. Veracruzana, Dirección Editorial, 1995. 246 p.: bibl., ill. (Biblioteca)

Based on the research of many scholars, work includes charts identifying years of drought and their length and impact. Explores regional differences and the effects of "El Niño." Provides material not easily accessible to historians. [EBC]

1055 Flujos comerciales y de transporte: un panorama histórico. Sanfandila, Mexico: Instituto Mexicano del Transporte, Secretaría de Comunicaciones y Transportes, 1995. 163 p.: bibl., ill., maps. (Documento técnico, 0188–7114; 13)

Global history about the relationship between transportation, commerce, and economic growth. [D. Coerver]

1056 Foro para la Historia de Fresnillo, 5th, Fresnillo, Mexico, 1994. Memoria. Fresnillo, Mexico: AFEHYAC, 1996. 280 p.: bibl., ill.

Disparate collection of papers relating to the colonial, 19th-century, and contemporary history of Fresnillo and Zacatecas. [D. Coerver]

1057 Fuentes bibliográficas para el estudio de la historia de Campeche. Coordinación general de Aída Amine Casanova Rosado, colaboración de Adriana Rocher Salas. Campeche, Mexico: Univ. Autónoma de Campeche, Direc. de Serv. Educ. de Apoyo, Coordinación de Publicaciones, 1994. 133 p. (Colección Raíces campechanas. Serie Acervo documental)

Annotated list of printed sources for the study of Campeche includes books and journals. Twenty-seven libraries were consulted. [AL]

1058 Las fuentes eclesiásticas para la historia social de México. Coordinación de Brian F. Connaughton Hanley y Andrés Lira González. México: Univ. Autónoma Metropolitana: Instituto de Investigaciones Dr. José Luis Mora, 1996. 420 p.: bibl., 2 maps.

Thoughtful collection of essays on the rich research material for social history available in ecclesiastical archives. Twenty-two historians study diocesan *juzgado* (ecclesiastical court) records, parochial archives, reports of diocesan visits, religious pamphlets, and similar sources, aptly mixing source analysis and examples from their own investigations. Based on recognition that church records, because of their inclusive nature, are essential for understanding key features of Mexican social and political history. Commendable effort. [AL]

1059 Garibay Alvarez, Jorge. Guía de fuentes documentales parroquiales de México. Madrid: Fundación Histórica Tavera, 1996. 99 p.: bibl. (Documentos Tavera; 3)

Useful guide to the main sources of the ecclesiastical history of Mexico. Describes, in general terms, the contents of the archives in all bishoprics, highlighting their strength by historical periods. [AL]

1060 González y González, Luis. La magia de la Nueva España. Mexico: Clío, 1995. 231 p.: bibl., ill. (some col.), index. (Obras completas de Luis González y González; t. 3)

A collection of essays by a master storyteller. González endows history with an air of familiarity and ease that makes his writing suitable for all readers. In this book he covers themes from preconquest times to independence. [AL]

1061 Guerrero, Omar. Las raíces borbónicas del estado mexicano. México: Univ. Nacional Autónoma de México, Coordinación de Humanidades, Dirección General de Publicaciones, 1994. 315 p.: bibl.

Written from the viewpoint of a political scientist, this study examines the transformation of the Mexican state from its origins in a society of estates to a modern bureaucratic organization. Thorough review and explanation of the development of various governmental agencies. Partly based on a wide variety of secondary sources and on the Viceregal correspondence in the AGN. [EBC]

1062 Guía general de archivalia. Aguascalientes, Mexico: Archivo Histórico del Estado de Aguascalientes, 1996. 86 p.: ill.

Basic archival guide, including thematic coverage and organizational scheme of each Fondo. Includes inventory of photograph, map, newspaper, and book holdings of the archive. [D. Coerver]

1063 La historia hoy. México: Facultad de Filosofía y Letras, Univ. Nacional Autónoma de México, 1993. 201 p. (Memoria del coloquio)

Proceedings from a colloquium at the College of History at UNAM. Essays cover the state of history and its teaching at UNAM rather than topics on Mexican history itself. [D. Coerver]

1064 Jiménez Pelayo, Agueda. Santa Rosalía y Ayutla: vida cotidiana y economía, 1780–1925. Zapopan, Mexico: Colegio de Jalisco; Guadalajara, Mexico: Secretaría de Desarrollo Rural, 1995. 191 p.: bibl., ill., map.

Microhistory of two small towns in Jalisco, a cradle of families with Pelayo as surname. Provides demographic and economic data, and sketches of daily life, mostly in the 19th century. [AL]

1065 Kearney, Milo and Anthony Knopp. Border cuates: a history of the U.S.-Mexican twin cities. Illustrated by Peter Gawenda. Austin: Eakin Press, 1995. 336 p.: bibl., ill., map.

A discussion of the unusual nature of the Mexico-US border, which spawned twin cities on both sides of the frontier. Begins with a brief review of the colonial period and growth of US forts constructed to counterbalance already existing Mexican towns. Continues through the 19th century and concludes with a review of the events of the 1990s. [EBC]

1066 Kuri Camacho, Ramón. Chignahuapan y su historia. 2. ed. Mexico: H. Ayuntamiento de Chignahuapan, Mexico: Secretaría de Cultura del Gobierno del Estado de Puebla; Benemérita Univ. Autónoma de Puebla, 1996. 362 p.: ill.

Exploration of a region in Puebla's Sierra Norte by a native son. Discusses historical development beginning in the prehispanic era and attempts to explain socioeconomic and political trends in today's Chignahuapan. [D. Coerver]

Lathrop, Jacqueline Phillips. Ancient Mexico: cultural traditions in the land of the feathered serpent. See *HLAS 57:92.*

The legacy of Mesoamerica: history and culture of a Native American civilization. See *HLAS 57:94.*

1067 López Moreno R., Eduardo. La vivienda social: una historia. Mexico: Univ. de Guadalajara: Univ. Católica de Lovaina: ORSTOM: Red Nacional de Investigación Urbana, 1996. 507 p.: bibl., ill.

Global history of urban property and urban development in Guadalajara from the 1500s—1990s. Author studies ownership patterns, private entrepreneurship, and the role of the state as a promoter of urban growth and real estate ownership. Well-documented social and urban history. Commendable for its interdisciplinary approach. [AL]

1068 Martínez Assad, Carlos R. Breve historia de Tabasco. México: Colegio de Mexico, Fideicomiso Historia de las Américas; Fondo de Cultura Económica, 1996. 232 p.: bibl., ill. (Serie Breves historias de los estados de la República Mexicana. Sección de obras de historia)

General survey from colonial era to the early 1990s. Includes discussion of cultural and social developments, as well as the state's political and economic history. [D. Coerver]

1069 Michoacán desde afuera: visto por algunos de sus ilustres visitantes extranjeros, siglos XVI al XX. Coordinación de Brigitte Boehm de Lameiras, Gerardo Sanchez Díaz y Heriberto Moreno García; fotografía de Carlos Blanco; fotografía documental de Ricardo Sánchez González. Zamora, Mexico: El Colegio de Michoacán: Gobierno del Estado de Michoacán: Instituto de Investigaciones Históricas, 1995. 469 p.: bibl., col. ill.

Beautifully illustrated coffee-table book contains excerpts of impressions of the region written by the most illustrious visitors to Michoacán. [AL]

1070 Moreno García, Heriberto. Haciendas de tierra y agua en la antigua Cienega de Chapala. Zamora, Mexico: Colegio de Michoacán, 1989. 396 p.: bibl., maps.

Detailed agricultural study of the region of Michoacán bordering the Ciénaga of Chapala, also traces the varied connections of the region to Jalisco. A model regional history with genealogical information based on local sources, including summaries of land titles. Author's vision of hacienda development is based on family histories. Covers both agriculture and stock breeding, and analyzes the qualities of owners and renters. Ranges from the 16th century through 1867. [EBC]

1071 Núñez Becerra, Fernanda. La Malinche: de la historia al mito. México: Instituto Nacional de Antropología e Historia, 1996. 191 p.: bibl. (Colección Divulgación)

Reviews the historical evolution of La Malinche's representations in the writings of leading historians, playwrights, novelists, poets, and essayists. Also alludes to the condition of indigenous peoples in Mexico, but does not make a clear connection between the two themes. [AL]

1072 Pérez Luque, Rosa Alicia. Catálogo de documentos para la historia de Guanajuato en el Archivo General de Indias. Guanajuato, Mexico: Archivo Histórico de Guanajuato: Univ. de Guanajuato, 1991 [i.e. 1993]. 107 p.: col. ill.

Guide to materials on Guanajuato available in Seville. Author scanned 190 packets of documents finding over 7,500 pages of information, mostly on the late-18th century. [AL]

1073 Ramos Escandón, Carmen. Quinientos años de olvido: historiografía e historia de la mujer en México. (*in* Las raíces de la memoria: América Latina, ayer y hoy, quinto encuentro debate = Amèrica Llatina, ahir i avui, cinquena trobada debat. Coordinación de Pilar García Jordán *et al.* Barcelona: Univ. de Barcelona, 1996, p. 565–585)

Survey of the historiographical literature on Mexican women written during the 20th century. Although not complete, it is a useful guide. [AL]

1074 Recuento histórico bibliográfico de la minería en la región central de México. Coordinación de José Alfredo Uribe Salas. Morelia, Mexico: Univ. Michoacana de San Nicolás de Hidalgo, Instituto de Investigaciones Históricas, Depto. de Historia de

México, 1994. 271 p.: bibl., ill. (Estudios de historia mexicana; 2)

Five essays about mining in the states of Hidalgo, Michoacán, Guanajuato, Mexico, and the Tasco district. Begins with brief essays summarizing the history of the important mining centers, followed by a comprehensive bibliography. [EBC]

1075 Rendón Garcini, Ricardo. Breve historia de Tlaxcala. México: El Colegio de México; Fideicomiso Historia de las Américas; Fondo de Cultura Económica, 1996. 182 p.: bibl., ill. (Serie Breves historias de los estados de la República Mexicana)

Basic survey from precolumbian era to contemporary times. Aimed at a popular audience. [D. Coerver]

1076 Sepúlveda y Herrera, María Teresa. Catálogo de la colección de diarios de José Fernández Ramírez. México: Instituto Nacional de Antropología e Historia, 1994. 149 p.: bibl., ill. (Serie Documentos)

Guide to the 42 volumes of notes taken by the notable 19th-century bibliographer and historian José Fernández Ramírez during his research stints in Europe. The diaries contain copies of original documents from the precolumbian and colonial eras, as well as his own historical writings. [AL]

1077 Toluca, Mexico: su historia, sus monumentos, su desarrollo urbano. Recopilación del Programa de Investigación Cultural. Toluca de Lerdo, Mexico: H. Ayuntamiento de Toluca; Univ. Autónoma del Estado de México, 1996. 331 p.: bibl., ill.

Collection of symposium papers covers the history of Toluca since colonial times. Includes essays on the development of the city's architectural heritage and on historiographical and archival sources related to Toluca's past. [D. Coerver]

1078 Tovar Ramírez, Aurora. Mil quinientas mujeres en nuestra conciencia colectiva: catálogo biográfico de mujeres de México. Mexico: Documentación y Estudio de Mujeres, 1996. 781 p.: bibl.

Biographical capsules of 1,500 women born up to but not beyond 1925, and who distinguished themselves in the arts or the sciences. Well indexed and with a list of the sources used for information. Attempts to create a collective memory of women. [AL]

1079 Valladolid-Morelia, 450 años: documentos para su historia, 1537–1828. Selección, introducción, paleografía, notas y apéndices de Ernesto Lemoine Villicaña. Morelia, Mexico: Editorial Morevallado, 1993. 260 p.: bibl., ill., 2 folded maps.

Brief but useful collection of documents on Valladolid. Includes previously unpublished and little-known sources, of which the most important are a description of the Bishopric of Michoacán in 1619 and the conversion of Indian congregations in 1601. [AL]

1080 Veracruz: primer puerto del continente. Recopilación de Alejandro de Antuñano Maurer. México: ICA: Fundación Miguel Alemán, 1996. 253 p.: bibl., ill. (some col.), maps (some col.).

Beautifully illustrated coffee-table book contains informative articles about Veracruz by Elías Trabulse and Inés Herrera, among others. Includes political, scientific, economic, and cultural history of the city and its impact on the nation and the world. [EBC]

1081 Warren, Richard. Entre la participación política y el control social: la vagancia, las clases pobres de la ciudad de México y la transición desde la colonia hacia el Estado nacional. (*Hist. Graf.*, 6, 1996, p. 37–54, table)

Discusses how the treatment of "vagos," or unemployed poor urban masses, in Mexico changed from the late colonial period to the early years of the republic. Factional politics used the threat of urban disorder to define their own meanings of popular representative governments and "equality." [AL]

1082 Yoma Medina, María Rebeca and **Luis Alberto Martos López.** Dos mercados en la historia de la ciudad de México: el Volador y la Merced. Mexico: Secretaría General de Desarrollo Social, Depto. del Distrito Federal; Instituto Nacional de Antropología e Historia, 1990. 253 p.: bibl., ill. (Colección Divulgación)

Provides information about two markets and their relationship to each other and to the history of two sections of the city. Based on the Mexico City archives, beginning with the colonial period and ending about 1900. [EBC]

Zorrilla, Luis G. Relaciones políticas, económicas y sociales de México con el extranjero. See *HLAS 57:4138*.

COLONIAL
General

Abadie-Aicardi, Aníbal. La tradición salmantina en la Real y Pontificia Universidad de México, 1551–1821. See item **5065**.

1083 Adeva Martin, Ildefonso and **Carmen J. Alejos Grau.** Fuentes de inspiración de la *Regla cristiana breve* de Fr. Juan de Zumárraga, OFM. (*Arch. Francisc. Hist.*, 85:1/4, Jan./Dec. 1992, p. 77–98)

Establishes the intellectual sources of Zumárraga's *Brief Christian Rule*—a marker of his spirituality—and indicates that Tomas Aquinas, Saint Bonaventura, and John Gerson were some of his inspirational foundations. [AL]

1084 Alanís Boyso, José Luis. Padrones coloniales de población del estado de México: catálogo documental. Toluca, Mexico: Gobierno del Estado de México, Secretaria de Finanzas, 1995. 207 p.: ill.

Lists the population census of 18 towns in the state of Mexico between 1786 and 1809. Provides round figures of numbers of inhabitants and racial classification. Useful source. [AL]

1085 Alvarado Gómez, Antonio Armando. Comercio interno en la Nueva España: el abasto en la ciudad de Guanajuato, 1777–1810. México: Instituto Nacional de Antropología e Historia, 1995. 165 p.: bibl., ill. (Serie Historia / Instituto Nacional de Antropología e Historia)

Studies the nature, sources, and movement of supplies to the town of Guanajuato in the last decades of the colonial period. Examines the impact of the Bourbon economic reforms on one of the richest towns of New Spain. A strong study of internal colonial trade based on archival sources. [AL]

1086 Alves, Abel A. Brutality and benevolence: human ethology, culture, and the birth of Mexico. Westport, Conn.: Greenwood Press, 1996. 247 p.: bibl. (Contributions in Latin American studies, 1054–6790; no. 8)

Cultural anthropology of the conquest and the establishment of the colonial system in the 16th century. Explores basic human sentiments—wonderment, hatred, brutality, compassion—using both the Aztec and the Spanish prisms. Food, justice, benevolence, and gender are the venues used to examine the behavior of indigenous and Spanish peoples. [AL]

1087 Andrés-Gallego, José. El abastecimiento del México, 1761–1786: semejanzas y diferencias entre la Nueva España y la España Europea. (*Rev. Indias*, 57:209, enero/abril 1997, p. 113–140)

Deals with the provision of staple foods in Mexico City through the mechanisms of *pósito* and *alhóndiga*. Focuses on provision during years of scarcity and the use of other edibles as a means of survival. Also comments on diet, hunger, and disease. [AL]

1088 La antigua Oaxaca-Cuilapan: desaparición histórica de una ciudad. Textos de Víctor Jiménez, Rogelio González y Joaquín Galarza. México: Codex Editores, 1996. 79 p.: bibl. + 1 envelope (13 leaves: col. ill.). (Tule)

Contains several essays and testimonials on the city of Oaxaca. An excellent example of technical virtuosity in printing. [AL]

1089 Archer, Christon I. Insurrection-reaction-revolution-fragmentation: reconstructing the choreography of meltdown in New Spain during the Independence era. (*Mex. Stud.*, 10:1, Winter 1994, p. 63–98)

Commendable revisionist view of the period 1816–21. Dispels notion that these were years of military inactivity, a version of history created by early Mexican historians. Archer presents a picture of gradually diminishing royalist strength and its desperate efforts to fight disaffected guerrilla groups and local elites who saw no further use for Spanish taxation and centralized domination. [AL]

1090 Archer, Christon I. Politicization of the army of New Spain during the War of Independence, 1810–1821. (*in* The origins of Mexican national politics, 1808–1847. Wilmington, Del.: SR Books, 1997, p. 11–37)

Analyzes causes of various actions carried out by Army leaders and the Audiencia between 1808–21 and addresses the reasons that many in the army joined Agustín de Iturbide. [AL]

1091 Archivo Histórico del Municipio de Colima. Archivo de la villa de Colima de la Nueva España, siglo XVI. t. 1. Colima, Mexico: Archivo Histórico del Municipio de Colima, 1995. 1 v.

Summarizes transcriptions of 250 notarial deeds from the municipality of Colima between 1535–74. Indexed and amplified with historical notes, these documents reflect daily life in the earliest years of the town. Very useful. [AL]

1092 Archivo Histórico del Municipio de Colima. Fondos del siglo XVIII. t. 1, 1703–1713; t. 2, 1714–1724. Colima, Mexico: Archivo Histórico del Municipio de Colima, 1995. 2 v.: indexes. (Pretextos; 12–13)

Annotated catalog of the holdings of the municipal Archive of Colima between 1700–24. Includes topographic and onomastic indexes. [AL]

1093 Arenas, Isabel. La mujer encomendera en Yucután (México), siglo XVIII. (in Encuentro de la Ilustración al Romanticismo, 7th, Cádiz, 1993. La mujer en los siglos XVIII y XIX. Coordinación de Cinta Canterla. Cádiz, Spain: Univ. de Cádiz, 1993, p. 149–164)

Brief survey of female encomienda holders in Yucatán, where the King did not escheat them until 1785. [AL]

1094 Arnal Simón, Luis. El presidio en México en el siglo XVI. México: Facultad de Arquitectura, Univ. Nacional Autónoma de México, 1995. 320 p.: bibl., ill., maps. (Colección Arquitectura; 7)

Appealing, well-executed history of the presidios, which were founded in the 16th century as venues for the process of conquest, assimilation of the indigenous population, defense, and geographical expansion. Excellent maps and architectural illustrations. [AL]

1095 Arróniz, Othón. Dos ensayos históricos. Prólogo de José González Sierra. Xalapa-Enríquez, Mexico: Univ. Veracruzana, Gobierno del Estado de Veracruz, 1995. 236 p.: bibl.

Part of a collection that reissues the works of the noted philologist, writer, and historian of Veracruz and Córdoba. This volume highlights his essays on the naval battle for San Juan de Ulúa (1568) and the treaties of Córdoba (1821–22). [AL]

1096 Arróniz, Othón. Teatro de evangelización en Nueva España. México: Univ. Nacional Autónoma de México, 1994. 275 p.: bibl., index.

Traces the birth of religious theater, introduced by the Franciscans to aid the indigenous conversion to Christianity. Also includes Dominican and Jesuit pieces written for the same purpose. Appendix contains several excerpts. Tribute to Arróniz, a well-known philologist. [AL]

1097 Artís Espriu, Gloria. Familia, riqueza y poder: un estudio genealógico de la oligarquía novohispana. México: Centro de Investigaciones y Estudios Superiores en Antropología Social (CIESAS), 1994. 157 p.: bibl., ill. (Colección Miguel Othón de Mendizábal)

Based on data on 23 elite families, author provides a general view of marriage transactions and preservation of property and status. Largely legal study with pedagogical uses. [AL]

1098 Baskes, Jeremy. Coerced or voluntary?: the *repartimiento* and market participation of peasants in late colonial Oaxaca. (*J. Lat. Am. Stud.*, 28:1, Feb. 1996, p. 1–28)

Revisionist study of the *repartimiento.* Argues that credit provided by *alcalde* to the Indians answers the problematic issues raised by merchandise sales. *Repartimiento* should be understood as "a system of consumer and producer credit designed for colonial situations when other arrangements were not feasible." Challenging essay. For ethnologist's comment, see *HLAS 57:699.* [AL]

Baudot, Georges. Utopia and history in Mexico: the first chroniclers of Mexican civilization, 1520–1569. See *HLAS 57:30.*

1099 Bermúdez Gorrochotegui, Gilberto. Historia de Jalapa, siglo XVII. Xalapa, Mexico: Univ. Veracruzana, 1995. 428 p.: bibl., ill. (Biblioteca)

Based on local notarial and parochial archives. Highlights the demographic profile of the area, the landownership patterns, the administration of nearly a dozen sugar mills, the slave trade, and the activities of the numerous small actors within the region's economic networks. Makes available much information for further analysis or for a global synthesis of the economy of New Spain. [AL]

Beuchot, Mauricio. Panorama de la historia de la filosofía novohispana. See item **5072.**

1100 Blázquez, Adrián and **Thomas Calvo.** Guadalajara y el Nuevo Mundo: Nuño Beltrán de Guzmán, semblanza de un conquistador. Guadalajara, Spain: Institución Provincial de Cultura "Marqués de Santillana", 1992. 287 p.: bibl., maps. (Virrey Mendoza; 3)

Brief biography of Nuño de Guzmán, conqueror of New Galicia, is followed by a broad selection of documents that allow reader and researcher to judge this much debated figure. Contains documents related to his administration, the sale of Indian slaves; his *residencia* judgement, and several testimonies of witnesses to his career. The compilers attempt an objective introduction pointing to achievements as well as execrable character qualities. [AL]

1101 Borah, Woodrow. The revenues of curate of Tejupan in the late colonial period. (*Ibero-Am. Arch.*, 20:3/4, 1994, p. 337–356, tables)

Microhistory of a curate's income in Indian towns. Details of income sources reveal the economic ties between Indian community and the local church. [AL]

1102 Brading, D.A. Mexican silver mining in the eighteenth century: the revival of Zacatecas. (*in* Mines of silver and gold in the Americas. Edited by Peter Bakewell. Aldershot, Great Britain; Brookfield, Vt.: Variorum, 1997, p. 303–319)

Reviews the various actions undertaken by the lay population and the clergy to christianize the poor, isolated, and overwhelmingly indigenous population of Mendoza. Requests to state and Church authorities for aid seemed to be endless.

1103 Brading, D.A. Poder y justicia en Catorce, 1779–1805. (*Relaciones/Zamora*, 69, invierno 1997, p. 91–120, photo)

Revisits the creole-gauchupin conflict in the narrative of the establishment of the mining community of Catorce. Follows the path of conflict and almost Byzantine intrigue over questions of control of government and military. Also published in English in *Ibero-Amerikanisches Archiv*, 20:3/4, 1994, p. 357–380. [EBC]

1104 Bribiesca Sumano, María Elena. Catálogo de protocolos de la notaría no. 1 Toluca. v. 7, 1634–1761. Toluca, Mexico: Ediciones del Gobierno del Estado de México, 1995. 1 v.: ill. (v. 7: Colección Textos y apuntes; 39)

Useful annotated catalog of the notarial records of Toluca between 1643 and 1761. Geographical onomastic and subject indexes are complemented by a glossary of colonial terms. [AL]

1105 Buenaventura Zapata y Mendoza, Juan. Historia cronológica de la noble ciudad de Tlaxcala. Transcripción paleográfica, traducción, presentación y notas de Luis Reyes García y Andrea Martínez Baracs. Tlaxcala, Mexico: Univ. Autónoma de Tlaxcala, Secretaría de Extensión Universitaria y Difusión Cultural: Centro de Investigaciones y Estudios Superiores en Antropología Social, 1995. 746 p.: bibl., ill. (Colección Historia: Serie Historia de Tlaxcala; 4)

First publication of the complete text of this chronicle of Tlaxcala by a 17th-century Tlaxcalan noble, finished by a family friend. This bilingual text in Spanish and Nahuatl is of great value for ethnohistorians and historians. [AL]

1106 Calderón, Francisco R. Historia económica de la Nueva España en tiempo de los Austrias. Mexico: Fondo de Cultura Económica, 1988. 711 p.: bibl., ill. (Sección de obras de economía)

Synthesis of known sources and authors, this work covers precolumbian and colonial Mexico. Some chapters are more social than economic history, and chapters on trade, the exchequer, agriculture, mining, artisans, and industries contain much information suitable for general readers rather than scholars. [AL]

1107 Calvo, Thomas. De una esclavitud a otra en México: estudios de casos, siglos XVI y XVII. (*Relaciones/Zamora*, 18:70, primavera 1997, p. 129–157, graph, tables)

Contrasts Indian and African slavery in Guadalajara and offers anecdotal material on African slaves. [AL]

1108 Carrillo Cázares, Alberto. Las juntas teológicas de México sobre la Guerra Chichimeca, 1569–1575.

(*Relaciones/Zamora*, 18:70, primavera 1997, p. 105-128)

Studies the ethical theories developed by theologians between 1569-75 to justify the wars with the Chichimecs. Dominicans opposed the wars; other orders approved of it. In 1585 the official posture of the church was to use persuasion, not war, against the Chichimecs. [AL]

1109 Carrillo Cázares, Alberto. Michoacán en el otoño del siglo XVII. Fotografía de Ricardo Sánchez González. Zamora, Mexico: El Colegio de Michoacán: El Gobierno del Estado de Michoacán, 1993. 516 p.: bibl., ill. (some col.).

Based on a previously unpublished and assumed lost census of the bishopric of Michoacán ordered by Bishop Francisco Aguiar y Seijas (1679-82) and carried out in 1680-81. Author uses census to paint a broad picture of Michoacán society, emphasizing ecclesiastic institutions and religious practices. Expensive edition; profusely illustrated. Census included as an appendix. [AL]

1110 Carrillo Cázares, Alberto. Parecer de algunos teólogos de México sobre la justicia de la guerra contra los indios Chichimecas. (*Relaciones/Zamora*, 18:70, primavera 1997, p. 209-214)

Transcribes theological statements on the "just war" against rebellions by Chichimec Indians in the late-1560s. [AL]

1111 Castro Gutiérrez, Felipe. Nueva ley y nuevo rey: reformas borbónicas y rebelión popular en Nueva España. Zamora, Mexico: Colegio de Michoacán; México: Univ. Nacional Autónoma de México, Instituto de Investigaciones Históricas, 1996. 288 p.: bibl., ill. (Colección Investigaciones)

Based in part on a recently discovered collection of legal documents in the Biblioteca de la Real Academia de Historia in Madrid, this revisionist version of the reasons for the 1767-68 rebellions in Michoacán, San Luis Potosí, and Guanajuato argues that the expulsion of the Jesuits did not cause the rebellions, but that they derived from the ethnic, social, and political organization of people in the villages and towns. [EBC]

1112 Castro Gutiérrez, Felipe. La rebelión de los indios y la paz de los españoles. Tlalpan, Mexico: CIESAS, 1996. 170 p.: bibl., ill. (some col.). (Historia de los pueblos indígenas de Mexico)

Abundantly illustrated, popularly written account of the Indian rebellions and the varying Spanish attempts to mediate or to repress them. Rebellions reminded the Spaniards that they were not dealing with a passive and obedient population, and caused them to moderate their demands for tribute, personal service, and work in the mines. [EBC]

1113 Chance, John K. The caciques of Tecali: class and ethnic identity in late colonial Mexico. (*HAHR*, 76:3, Aug. 1996, p. 475-502, bibl.)

Excellent study of the cacique class in the eastern Nahua towns of Tecali, close to Puebla. Caciques traced their status to land grants dating back to 1591. Challenged by macehual pressure from below, and increasingly hispanized themselves, caciques were not impervious to change. They succeeded in maintaining their status by heightening their ethnicity and distancing themselves from macehuales and castas. [AL]

1114 Chávez Carbajal, María Guadalupe. Negros y mulatos libres en Michoacán. Comentario por Alvaro Ochoa Serrano. (*in* Tradición e identidad en la cultura mexicana. Zamora, Mexico: El Colegio de Michoacán; Consejo Nacional de Ciencia y Tecnología (CONACYT), 1995, p. 393-414, map)

The search for blacks and mulattoes in the population of Michoacán yields significant rates in small towns and establishes the presence of this racial component since the late-16th century. [AL]

1115 Comas, Juan. El mestizaje cultural y la medicina novohispana del siglo XVI. Edición a cargo de J.L. Fresquet Febrer y J.M. López Piñero. Valencia, Spain: Univ. de Valencia, Instituto de Estudios Documentales e Históricos sobre la Ciencia, 1995. 296 p.: bibl. (Cuadernos valencianos de historia de la medicina y de la ciencia; 48. Serie A, Monografías; 48)

Essay collection on the history of medicine in New Spain. Assumes that the 16th century was a period in which precolumbian and European notions of medicine made important exchanges. Attention is given to Nahua notions of medicine, testimonials in codices, the teaching of medicine, and medical books printed in Mexico in the 16th century. [AL]

1116 Commons de la Rosa, Aurea. Las intendencias de la Nueva España. México: Univ. Nacional Autónoma de México, 1993. 253 p., 7 folded leaves: bibl., maps. (Espacio y tiempo; 4)

Concerned with the geographical definition of the intendancies and their administrative structure. Excellent maps make this work a useful tool for historical geography. [AL]

1117 Contreras Sánchez, Alicia del C. Capital comercial y colorantes en la Nueva España, segunda mitad del siglo XVIII. Zamora, Mexico: El Colegio de Michoacán: Univ. Autónoma de Yucatán, 1996. 212 p.: bibl., ill. (some col.), 6 folded maps. (Colección Investigaciones)

Based on a rich collection of primary sources. Useful illustrations. Emphasizes the importance of commercial capital, forced labor, transportation, and royal policy. [EBC]

1118 Corcuera de Mancera, Sonia. El fraile, el indio y el pulque: evangelización y embriaguez en la Nueva España (1523–1548). México: Fondo de Cultura Económica, 1991. 307 p., 8 leaves of plates: bibl., ill. (some col.). (Sección de obras de historia)

Even though the theme of drunkenness is rather ancillary to this work, the methodical analysis of the process of evangelization and its European theological bases makes it worthwhile reading. [AL]

1119 De Rojas, José Luis. Al César lo que es del César: Alonso de Zorita y los estudios sobre la organización política y social del centro de México. (*Relaciones/Zamora*, 18:70, primavera 1997, p. 63–103, appendix, bibl.)

Rojas makes a careful review of Zorita's description of the Mexican lords and their categories and prerogatives. He notes serious contradictions and a tendency to side with the indigenous natural hierarchies, believing them to be just and harmonious. Rojas also exposes how historians have misinterpreted Zorita's information and asks for more critical studies of his data. [AL]

1120 Díaz Cruz, Manuel J. El indio en la documentación colonial: Chiapas en el siglo XVII. (*in* Las raíces de la memoria: América Latina, ayer y hoy, quinto encuentro debate = Amèrica Llatina, ahir i avui, cinquena trobada debat. Coordinación de Pilar García Jordán et al. Barcelona: Univ. de Barcelona, 1996, p. 23–36, bibl., graph, map)

Bemoans lack of historical documentation emanating from indigenous sources. This rapid demographic survey of Chiapas rescues some population data from Spanish archives. [AL]

1121 Diego-Fernández Sotelo, Rafael. La primigenia audiencia de la Nueva Galicia, 1548–1572: respuesta al cuestionario de Juan de Ovando por el oidor Miguel Contreras y Guevara. Versión paleográfica. Zamora, Mexico: El Colegio de Michoacán; Guadalajara, Mexico: Instituto Cultural Ignacio Dávila Garibi, Cámara Nacional de Comercio de Guadalajara, 1994. 459 p.: bibl. (Colección Fuentes)

Questionnaire and answers to the founding *oidores* and other witnesses of the New Galicia Audencia by first *visitador*. A rare document completely transcribed that allows historians to learn about the administrative processes in an early Audiencia (1548–72), which was later reorganized to conform to more standard procedures and the situation of New Galicia after mid-century. [AL]

1122 Documentos lingüísticos de la Nueva España. Altiplano central. México: Univ. Nacional Autónoma de México, Instituto de Investigaciones Filológicas, Centro de Lingüística Hispánica, 1994. 808 p.: bibl., ill., indexes, map. (Serie Documentos lingüísticos de la Nueva España; 1)

Even though the purpose of this work is to illustrate the development of the Spanish language in colonial Mexico, historians will appreciate the 320 writing samples. Extracted from a variety of archival sources, the writings cover many aspects of daily life: letters, testimonials of misbehavior, petitions for favors, denunciations of witchcraft, and so forth. [AL]

1123 Encuentro Nacional de Afromexican-istas, *3rd, Colima, Mexico, 1992.*
Memoria. Recopilación de Luz María Martínez Montiel y Juan Carlos Reyes G. Colima, Mexico: Gob. del Estado, Instituto Colimense de Cultura: Culturas Populares, Nuestra Tercera Raíz, Consejo Nacional para la Cultura y las Artes, 1993. 229 p.: bibl.

Collection of essays derived from third national conference of historians of the African presence in Mexico. Although few of these essays provide new information about the African element in Mexico, this work provides a useful summary of the current state of research on this topic. [AL]

1124 Ensayos sobre la Ciudad de México.
v. 2, La muy noble y leal ciudad de México. México: Depto. del Distrito Federal: Univ. Iberoamericana: Consejo Nacional para la Cultura y las Artes, 1994. 1 v.: bibl., ill.

Collection of essays on the history of Mexico City by well-known historians includes such topics as urban design, the city council, the Church, and educational institutions. For general, rather than specialized, readership. [AL]

1125 Fernández Repetto, Francisco and Genny Negroe Sierra. Una población perdida en la memoria: los negros de Yucatán. Mérida, Mexico: Univ. Autónoma de Yucatán, Dirección General de Extensión, 1995. 77 p.: bibl., ill. (Yucatán, raíces y expresión de su identidad. Serie Sociedad, historia y cultura. Documentos de investigación; 1)

General survey of the black and mixed-race population of the city of Mérida. The most useful part of this brief work is the statistical information on the marriages of this group between 1567 and 1797. [AL]

1126 Fernández Rodríguez, Pedro. Los dominicos en el contexto de la primera evangelización de México, 1526–1550. Salamanca, Spain: Editorial San Esteban, 1994. 308 p.: bibl., ill., maps. (Monumenta histórica iberoamericana de la Orden de Predicadores; v. 3)

Chronological history of the Dominican Order. Re-examines the issue of the anti-indigenism of Fr. Domingo de Betanzos seeking a revindication of this figure. [AL]

1127 Flinchpaugh, Steven. Economic aspects of the viceregal entrance in Mexico City. (*Americas/Franciscans*, 52:3, Jan. 1996, p. 345–365)

Study of the economic and political aspects of the celebrations held to observe viceregal visits to Mexico City. Interesting approximation of daily life history. [AL]

1128 Flores Olea, Aurora. El procurador general y el cabildo de la ciudad de México en el siglo XVII, 1600–1650. (*Novahispania/México*, 2, 1996, p. 73–91)

Follows the activities of the attorney for the cabildo of Mexico City during the 17th century. The cabildo opposed the Church's position on labor allocations (*repartimiento*). [AL]

1129 Gálvez, María Angeles and Antonio Ibarra. Comercio local y circulación regional de importaciones: la Feria de San Juan de los Lagos en la Nueva España. (*Hist. Mex.*, 46:3, enero/marzo 1997, p. 581–616, bibl., graphs, tables)

Study of the merchant fair of San Juan de los Lagos in an effort to understand the trade mechanics of an internal regional market. Ties the origin and meaning of the fair to the worship of an image of the Virgin Mary. Analyzes the economic impact of the fair on the region, based on the moneys sent between 1792 and 1808. Notes the increasing importance of the fair within the region of Guadalajara until its official termination for political reasons in 1810. [AL]

1130 Gálvez Jiménez, Mónica Leticia.
Celaya: sus raíces africanas. Guanajuato, Mexico: Ediciones La Rana, 1995. 140 p.: bibl., ill., maps. (Nuestra cultura)

Study of the African roots of the town of Celaya in central Mexico. Provides a valuable analysis of the baptismal and matrimonial records of Afro-mestizos in the 17th and 18th centuries. [AL]

1131 Garavaglia, Juan Carlos and Juan Carlos Grosso. Las alcabalas novohispanas, 1776–1821. Mexico: Archivo General de la Nación, Dirección del Archivo Histórico Central: Banca Cremi, 1988. 247 p.: bibl., ill.

Received in the Library of Congress in 1994, this useful study of the alcabala tax provides students of colonial fiscal policies with a useful compilation of sources, as well as explanations of tax collection procedures. [AL]

1132 Garavaglia, Juan Carlos and **Juan Carlos Grosso.** Criollos, mestizos e indios: etnias y clases sociales en México colonial a fines del siglo XVIII. (*Secuencia/México*, 29, mayo/agosto 1994, p. 39–80, bibl., graphs, ill., tables)

A discussion of the meaning of *mestizaje* seeks to clarify the ongoing historical debate on the significance of race versus class in late colonial Mexico. Ethnic affiliation is understood here as largely a result of auto-definition in a multiracial society with many biological mixtures. Using the 1791 census of Tepeaca and other demographic sources, the authors match declared ethnicity to occupation; they also study marriage patterns and residence patterns concluding that colonial society was a complex knot of "representations" based on many variables manipulated by the historical actors. A thoughtful evaluation that avoids polarizations and attempts a balanced assessment of a difficult subject. [AL]

1133 Garavaglia, Juan Carlos and **Juan Carlos Grosso.** Indios, campesinos y mercado: la región de Puebla a finales del siglo XVIII. (*Hist. Mex.*, 46:2, oct./dic. 1996, p. 245–278, map, tables)

Study of the economic role of indigenous people in the provision of food to three towns in the bishopric of Puebla at the end of the colonial period. Concludes that indigenous people contributed substantially to the provision of cattle, agricultural products, and salt, and were more than simply providers of labor. [AL]

1134 García Bernal, Manuela Cristina. Haciendas y tributo en Yucatán: el reglamento de 1786 y la controversia en torno a los indios luneros. (*CLAHR/Albuquerque*, 6:2, Spring 1997, p. 121–141)

Discusses the hotly debated 1786 reform of tribute collection that imposed a standard cash tax over all Indians. This reform was met with strong resistance from landowners, especially as it affected Indians who worked only on Mondays in exchange for the use of land. The enforcement of the tax worked to the detriment of the Indians. [AL]

1135 García Morales, Soledad. Hacendados y capitales: análisis de proprietarios de la región de Coatepec, Veracruz, 1790–1810. Xalapa, Mexico: Univ. Veracruzana, Dirección Editorial, 1994. 137 p.: bibl., ill. (Biblioteca)

Interesting study of four hacienda owners in the region of Coatepec, Veracruz, in the late colonial period. Focuses on the acquisition of the properties, their administration, the manner of obtaining credit, and general management. This prosopography identifies two types of landowners: traditionalist and reformist, the latter being new arrivals influenced by the Enlightenment. Both types sought stability and security in their operations and relations with the indigenous people. Largely based on notarial archives. [AL]

García Targa, Juan. Arqueología colonial en el área maya: aspectos generales y modelos de estudio. See *HLAS 57:208.*

1136 Gil Blanco, Emiliano. La realidad del tráfico veracruzano y su contraste con las políticas de los consulados de Sevilla y México. (*Novahispania/México*, 2, 1996, p. 161–210)

Study of the policies and interests guiding the Consulados of Seville and Mexico in regard to flow of fleets, saturation of merchandise, contraband, and collection of taxes. Discusses problems created by contradictions between the dictates of the Crown and the business interests of local merchants. [AL]

1137 Glantz, Margo. La Malinche, sus padres y sus hijos. México: Facultad de Filosofía y Letras, Univ. Nacional Autónoma de México, 1994. 230 p.: bibl., ill. (Colección Jornadas)

Provocative collection of essays by literary critics and historians on the real, the symbolic, and the mythological Malinche, Cortes' mistress during the conquest of Mexico. Highly recommended as a heuristic analysis of this much-debated feminine figure. [AL]

1138 Gonzalbo Aizpuru, Pilar. De la penuria y el lujo en la Nueva España: siglos XVI-XVIII. (*Rev. Indias*, 56:206, enero/abril 1996, p. 49–74)

Describes and comments on important issues in the social history of New Spain. Beginning with the perceived necessity of a hierarchical society composed of rich and poor as expressed in laws and sermons, continuing with the requirement of voluntary poverty on the part of a few, and concluding the first part with a discussion of the significance of charity in the relationship between rich and poor. A qualitative examination of dowries and of wills of those who died intestate reveals the shifting importance of jewelry, household goods, furniture, art works, and clothing. [EBC]

González Rodríguez, Luis. Thomás de Guadalaxara, 1648–1720: misionero de la Tarahumara, historiador, lingüista y pacificador. See item **502.**

1139 González y González, Luis. Atraídos por la Nueva España. t. 2. México: Clío, 1995. 196 p.: bibl., ill. (Obras completas de Luis González y González; t. 2)

Part of a series of the complete works of well-known historian Luis González. Contains five early essays on colonial historians and historiography written in his captivating synthetic style. [AL]

1140 González y González, Luis. Jerónimo de Mendieta: vida, pasión y mensaje de un indigenista apocalíptico. Zamora, Mexico: Colegio de Michoacán, 1996. 172 p.: bibl.

Taking advantage of the abundant literature on this noted Franciscan, Luis González y González has selected five clusters from the writings of Mendieta of particular ethnographic and historical interest. Included in this work are prayers, fiestas, addresses of mothers to daughters and of fathers and sons, and materials about the conversion process. Thoughtful introduction by the editor provides essential background. [EBC]

1141 Grafenstein, Johanna von. Nueva España en el Circuncaribe, 1779–1808: revolución, competencia imperial y vínculos intercoloniales. México: Univ. Nacional Autónoma de México, Coordinación de Humanidades, Centro Coordinador y Difusor de Estudios Latinoamericanos, 1997. 378 p.: bibl., maps. (Nuestra América; 46)

Study of the influence of US and Haitian independence on the Caribbean due to the political and economic interconnections of the region. Argues for understanding the region as a geographical and historical unity.

Mostly concerned with the financial and trade effects of the US and Haitian wars of independence on the economies of the colonies and the new nations of the area, and, especially, on the economy of Mexico. [AL]

1142 Grajales Porras, Agustín. La población de la intendencia de Puebla en las postrimerías del régimen colonial. (Secuencia/México, 29, mayo/agosto 1994, p. 127–152, bibl., ill., tables)

Panoramic view of the composition of Puebla's population, examining the entire intendancy. Provides information on individual ethnic groups and a useful global table. [AL]

1143 Grosso, Juan Carlos. Campesinos, poblados de hacienda y producción indígena en el entorno agrario de Tepeaca en la segunda mitad del siglo XVIII. (Anu. IEHS, 11, 1996, p. 11–37, bibl.)

A new investigation and analysis of indigenous villagers and hacienda workers in Tepeaca finds that rural laborers had a share of the market for certain commodities, petitioned for and received a *fundo legal* of significant size from hacienda lands, and hacendados frequently owed back wages that might be interpreted as an exchange for rental of productive lands. Peons' debts often resulted from agreements to work on the hacienda in exchange for wage advances. Confirms some of Gibson's findings for the Valley of Mexico. Based on a series of case studies, this work is not quantitative. [EBC]

1144 Gutiérrez Lorenzo, María Pilar. De la Corte de Castilla al Virreinato de México: el conde de Galve, 1653–1697. Guadalajara, Spain: Excma. Diputación Provincial, 1993. 194 p.: bibl., ill., maps. (Varios; 12)

Although well-documented, this biography falls short of doing justice to a critical period in colonial history. Nevertheless, it does shed light on this venal and vain Viceroy. [AL]

1145 Hassig, Ross. Mexico and the Spanish conquest. London; New York: Longman, 1994. 215 p.: bibl., maps. (Modern wars in perspective)

Readable account of the history of central Mexico and Tenochtitlan prior to its conquest by Spain and the conquest itself. Suitable for general readers and undergraduate reading, this book is based on the author's solid knowledge and does not simplify its topic. For archeologist's comment, see *HLAS* 57:77. [AL]

1146 Hausberger, Bernd. La minería novo-hispana vista a través de los "libros de cargo y data" de la Real Hacienda. (*Estud. Hist. Novohisp.*, 15, 1995, p. 36–66, bibl., tables)

Important and rich article refines the earlier TePaske and Klein work on colonial treasuries (*Ingresos y egresos de la Real Hacienda de Nueva Espana,* 1986) with emphasis on the smaller Reales de Minas. Efforts to separate the figures on silver produced by smelting and those produced by mercury will help to determine more accurately the periods of profitability for the mines. Points out that although the small mines produced much of the wealth of New Spain, the wholesale merchants, such as Manuel Aldacó and the Count of Jala, made the truly large profits. Compares Peruvian mine production to that of New Spain. [EBC]

1147 Hernández Aparicio, Pilar. Fray Marcos Ramírez de Prado, OFM: obispo de Michoacán, 1640–1666. (*Arch. Francisc. Hist.*, 85:1/4, Jan./Dec. 1992, p. 303–332, appendices)

Examines life of this distinguished 17th-century bishop of Michoacán, whose death prevented him from becoming archbishop of Mexico. Dwells on the administration of his diocesis and the terms of his episcopal visits. [AL]

1148 Herrejón Peredo, Carlos. Los orígenes de Guayangareo-Valladolid. Zamora, Mexico: El Colegio de Michoacán; Morelia: Gobierno del Estado de Michoacán, 1991. 226 p.: bibl.

Through a detailed discussion of the original name of the city of Valladolid, author provides much information on the local history of the city and the area in the 16th century. [AL]

Hu-DeHart, Evelyn. Adaptación y resistencia en el yaquimi: los yaquis durante la colonia. See item **519.**

1149 Huerta Jaramillo, Ana María D. Los boticarios poblanos, 1536–1825: un estudio regional sobre el ejercicio farmacéutico y su despacho. Puebla, Mexico: Gobierno del Estado de Puebla, Secretaría de Cultura, 1994. 281 p.: bibl., ill. (Colección Portal poblano; núm. 8)

Despite unevenness in the development of its topic—largely due to the unavailability of archival sources—this is a useful work on a relatively unexplored topic. Of interest to social historians. [AL]

1150 Ibarra, Antonio. Conspiración, desobediencia social y marginalidad en la Nueva España: la aventura de Juan de la Vara. (*Hist. Mex.*, 47:1, julio/sept. 1997, p. 5–33)

Lively recreation of an 18th-century conspiracy against the Crown (1794). The story centers on one of the conspirators and dwells on the meaning of official fear of disorder and revolt; social inequality and discontent; and the mechanisms that trigger disobedience and indictment. [AL]

1151 Ibarra, Antonio. Mercado urbano y mercado regional en Guadalajara, 1790–1811: tendencias cuantitativas de la renta de alcabalas. (*in* Circuitos mercantiles y mercados en Latinoamérica, siglos XVIII-XIX. México: Instituto de Investigaciones Dr. José María Luis Mora; Instituto de Investigaciones Históricas UNAM, 1995, p. 100–135, graphs, tables)

Using two different sources for the collection of alcabala for the Guadalajara region between 1790 and 1811, author attempts a new hypothesis to explain strong urban market in Guadalajara. He sees a heavy demand from other areas for merchandise and a strong consumption of regional products in the internal markets as the reasons for the dynamism of Guadalajara's economy throughout the period under review. Highly technical article. [AL]

1152 Jiménez Codinach, Estela Guadalupe. México: su tiempo de nacer, 1750–1821. México: Fomento Cultural Banamex, 1997. 301 p.: bibl., ill.

Surveys the last years of the viceroyalty, and the insurgency period up to independence. A felicitous blend of social and political history makes this a recommendable work. The lavish illustrations make it a treasure trove of visual information. [AL]

1153 Jiménez Gómez, Juan Ricardo. Mercedes reales en Querétaro: los orígenes de la propiedad privada, 1531–1599. Querétaro, Mexico: Univ. Autónoma de Querétaro, Facultad de Derecho, Centro de Investigaciones Jurídicas, 1996. 433 p.: bibl.

Informative introduction describes the first two decades of Querétaro's history as an

Indian republic. The Spanish presence arrived after mid-century. Using archives from Querétaro, Mexico City, Guadalajara, and Spain, author has transcribed grants of land, water, and milling rights in Querétaro and its surroundings. [EBC]

1154 Juárez, Abel. Las redes de poder de una oligarquía regional. (*Bol. Am.*, 35:45, 1995, p. 201–219)

Two unconnected papers conflated in one article deal with the successful career of Genoese trader Juan Bautista Franyutti and his partners and the Indian rebellion of 1787. The setting is the region of Acayucan, near Coatzacoalcos, the southern coastal gate to Oaxaca and the isthmus. [AL]

1155 Knaut, Andrew L. Yellow fever and the late colonial public health response in the port of Veracruz. (*HAHR*, 77:4, Nov. 1997, p. 619–644, graph, ill.)

Study of the health conditions of the port of Veracruz in the late-18th century. Details medical concepts of the time and public health initiatives by the cabildo and the consulado to improve health and the environment and to protect the city's trade. [AL]

1156 Lavrin, Asunción. La celda y el siglo: epístolas conventuales. (*in* Mujer y cultura en la colonia hispanoamericana. Recopilación de Mabel Moraña. Pittsburgh: Instituto Internacional de Literatura Iberoamericana, Univ. of Pittsburgh, 1996, p. 139–159)

Follows the late-17th-century correspondence between the abbess of the Mexico City convent of San José de Gracia and a female patron, disclosing domestic and political aspects of conventual life and life in the cities of Mexico and Puebla. Based on archival sources. [AL]

1157 Lenkersdorf, Gudrun. La resistencia a la conquista española en los altos de Chiapas. (*in* Chiapas: los rumbos de otra historia. México: Centro de Estudios Mayas del Instituto de Investigaciones Filológicas y Coordinación de Humanidades (UNAM); Centro de Investigaciones y Estudios Superiores en Antropología Social; Centro de Estudios Mexicanos y Centroamericanos; Guadalajara, Mexico: Univ. de Guadalajara, 1995, p. 71–85, maps)

Chronicles the first encounter of Spaniards and indigenous peoples in what is today

Chiapas, stressing the resistance of the latter. [AL]

1158 León Portilla, Miguel. La flecha en el blanco: Francisco Tenamaztle y Bartolomé de las Casas en lucha por los derechos de los indígenas, 1541–1556. México: Editorial Diana, 1995. 202 p., 8 p. of plates: bibl., ill. (some col.), index.

History of the 1541 indigenous rebellion in Zacatecas. This book dwells on the Spanish exile of its leader, Tenamaztle, and his alliance with Fr. Bartolomé de las Casas in a joint appeal for redress. [AL]

1159 Loreto López, Rosalva. Familial religiosity and images in the home: eighteenth-century Puebla de Los Angeles, Mexico. (*J. Fam. Hist.*, 22:1, Jan. 1997, p. 26–49, ill., photos)

Author studies art within the domestic sphere as an example of the religiosity of 18th-century Puebla. Paintings had an educational role as well as being excellent examples of the religious imagery and messages of the period. Novel approach to art as part of social history. [AL]

1160 Lozano Armendares, Teresa. El chinguirito vindicado: el contrabando de aguardiente de caña y la política colonial. México: Univ. Nacional Autónoma de México, 1995. 355 p.: bibl. (Serie de historia novohispana / Instituto de Investigaciones Históricas; 51)

Social history of the preparation, legalization, consumption, and illegal trade of the most popular alcoholic beverage in New Spain. Based on archival sources, focuses mostly on the 18th century. [AL]

1161 Lozano Armendares, Teresa. Tablajeros, coimes y tahúres en la Nueva España ilustrada. (*Estud. Hist. Novohisp.*, 15, 1995, p. 67–86)

Deals with gambling, gamblers, and half-hearted efforts from viceregal authorities to end what was seen as a "social plague." [AL]

1162 Luna Díaz, Lorenzo Mario. Historia de la universidad colonial: avances de investigación. México: Univ. Nacional Autónoma de México, Coordinación de Humanidades, Centro de Estudios sobre la Universidad, 1987. 115 p.: bibl. (La Real Universidad de México, estudios y textos; 1)

Collection of short historiographical

essays on the Real y Pontificia Universidad de México. Maintains that despite a number of previous attempts, the history of the university needs to be systematically researched using rigorous methodology. [AL]

1163 MacLeod, Murdo J. Motines y cambios en las formas de control económico y político: los acontecimientos de Tuxtla. (*in* Chiapas: los rumbos de otra historia. México: Centro de Estudios Mayas del Instituto de Investigaciones Filológicas y Coordinación de Humanidades (UNAM); Centro de Investigaciones y Estudios Superiores en Antropología Social; Centro de Estudios Mexicanos y Centroamericanos; Guadalajara, Mexico: Univ. de Guadalajara, 1995, p. 87–102)

Detailed narrative of a local Indian rebellion in Tuxtla, 1693, preceding the better known rebellion of 1712. Stresses the intensity of factional competition among Spaniards for indigenous labor and tribute, the strong control of the alcaldes mayores over economic resources, and the forced sales of merchandise after the 1680s. These factors placed a heavy burden on a dwindling indigenous population, provoking this and other rebellions. [AL]

1164 Malvido, Elsa. El barroco y las ofrendas humanas en Nueva España. (*Rev. Indias*, 54:202, sept./dic. 1994, p. 593–610, table)

Explores offerings of body parts or pieces of clothing as relics as part of colonial baroque religious culture, and introduces the reader to Christian and indigenous rituals surrounding death. [AL]

1165 Marichal, Carlos. El comercio, la fiscalidad y el crédito en el virreinato de la Nueva España, 1760–1820: bibliografía reciente. (*in* Historia y economía: un nuevo diálogo. México: DGAPA; Facultad de Economía de la UNAM; Claves Latinoamericanas, 1996, p. 247–280, bibl.)

Reviews bibliographic production on the economy of New Spain during the last 60 years of the viceroyalty. Includes works written largely between the late-1960s and the early-1990s. The survey comprises the Bourbon reforms and their impact on trade, tax policies, and credit. Overlooks many important works in English and in Spanish and falls short of being a comprehensive review. [AL]

1166 El marqués: don Juan Antonio de Urrutia y Arana, marqués de la villa del Villar del Aguila. Recopilación de Ignacio R. Frías Camacho. Querétaro, Mexico: H. Ayuntamiento de Querétaro, 1994. 250 p.: bibl., ill.

Eulogistic biography of the second marquis of Villar del Aguila. Has a small but interesting collection of archival family documents. [AL]

1167 Mazín Gómez, Oscar. El cabildo catedral de Valladolid de Michoacán. México: El Colegio de Michoacán, 1996. 499 p.: bibl., ill. (some col.), map. (Colección Investigaciones)

Thorough study of the cathedral cabildo—the ruling body of the Episcopal church—in the important diocesis of Michoacán. Covers the entire colonial period. The cabildo is analyzed as a collegiate body aware of its historical identity, its responsibilities and duties, and its relationship with the bishop. Traces important nuances in the evolution of this body. Sustained by strong archival research, this is a commendable history of a key part of the secular church. [AL]

1168 Mazín Gómez, Oscar. Culto y devociones en la catedral de Valladolid de Michoacán, 1586–1780. Comentario por Alberto Carrillo Cázarez. (*in* Tradición e identidad en la cultura mexicana. Zamora, Mexico: El Colegio de Michioacán; Consejo Nacional de Ciencia y Tecnología (CONACYT), 1995, p. 305–356, appendices)

Thorough study of the forms of public worship and devotional practices in the city of Valladolid, and the role played in orchestrating both by the ecclesiastical cabildo of the cathedral church. Important for the study of religious thought. [AL]

1169 Meissner, Jochen. De la representación del reino a la Independencia: la lucha constitucional de la élite capitalina de México entre 1761 y 1821. (*Hist. Graf.*, 6, 1996, p. 11–35, graph, tables)

Elegant discussion of elite political representation from the colonial regime to the newly established republic. Proposes that new elite for the late-18th century had power and representation in the Mexico City Cabildo and that it regarded itself as a link between Crown and Viceroyalty. As such, the elite believed in its credibility as a power-holder in the political crisis of 1808. Although this position was unsuccessful, the attempt was vindicated in the final chapter of the struggle for independence in 1821. [AL]

1170 Melville, Elinor G.K. Environmental change and social change in the Valle del Mezquital, Mexico, 1521–1600. (An expanding world; 17) (in Agriculture, resource exploitation, and environmental change. Edited by Helen Wheatley. Aldershot, Great Britain; Brookfield, Vt.: Variorum, 1997, p. 69–98, tables)

Posits that intense sheepgrazing leading to important ecological changes, coupled with demographic decline, resulted in key changes in the character of land ownership in Mezquital. Careful assessment of the interaction of these factors leads Melville to believe that neither a planned policy nor economic changes unleashed by the conquest are the exclusive determinants of a latifundia system in this area. Latifundia was the solution to the problem of an abused environment. [AL]

1171 Menegus Bornemann, Margarita. Las comunidades productoras de sal y los mercados mineros: los casos de Taxco y Temascaltepec. (in Reunión de Historiadores de la Minería Latinoamericana, 1st, Zacatecas, México, 1990. Actas. México: Instituto Nacional de Antropología e Historia, 1994, vol. 4, p. 21–31, map)

Discussion of tensions between the indigenous communities that produced salt for the Taxco mining area and the mine owners. Indians evaded price controls by several means, creating serious supply problems for miners. [AL]

1172 Menegus Bornemann, Margarita. La participación indígena en los mercados del Valle de Toluca a fines del período colonial. (in Circuitos mercantiles y mercados en Latinoamérica, siglos XVIII-XIX. México: Instituto de Investigaciones Dr. José María Luis Mora; Instituto de Investigaciones Históricas UNAM, 1995, p. 136–157, graphs, map, tables)

Study of indigenous participation in the provisioning of markets in the Toluca region at the end of the 18th century. Posits that Indians were very active in the regional markets, while Spaniards preferred the city of Mexico, the mining centers of the Bajío, and other mining regions. [AL]

1173 Mínguez, Víctor. Los reyes distantes: imágenes del poder en el México virreinal. Castelló, Spain: Univ. Jaume I: Servei de Publicacions, Diputació de Castelló, 1995. 201 p.: bibl., ill. (some col.). (Biblioteca de les aules; 2)

Interesting study of royal iconography and ephemeral architecture in the graphic arts and in popular celebrations in honor of the Spanish kings. [AL]

1174 Miño Grijalva, Manuel. La manufactura colonial: la constitución técnica del obraje. México: El Colegio de México, Centro de Estudios Históricos, 1993. 204 p.: bibl., ill. (Jornadas; 123)

Study of the technical aspects of textile production in Quito and New Spain. Considers machinery, wool and cotton production, and changes in the production process at the end of the colonial period. Based on archival sources. [AL]

1175 Miranda Godínez, Francisco. El mestizaje, un proyecto de Tomás López Medel y una experiencia de Vasco de Quiroga. Comentario por Gaspar Aguilera. (in Tradición e identidad en la cultura mexicana. Zamora, Mexico: El Colegio de Michoacán; Consejo Nacional de Ciencia y Tecnología (CONACYT), 1995, p. 247–270)

Comparison of the ideas of Tomás López Medel, lawyer and royal official, with those of Vasco de Quiroga on the organization and treatment of indigenous peoples under Spanish legal and social premises. Lopéz Medel proposed a cultural *mestizaje* but, unlike Quiroga, he accepted the notion of the inferiority of indigenous cultures. [AL]

1176 Monségur, Jean de. Las nuevas memorias del capitán Jean de Monségur. Recopilación, prólogo e introducción de Jean-Pierre Berthe; traducción de Florence Olivier, Blanca Pulido e Isabelle Véricat. México: Univ. Nacional Autónoma de México, Instituto de Investigaciones Históricas, 1994. 251 p.: bibl., maps. (Serie Historia novohispana; 50)

Translation into Spanish of an important early-18th-century report on the social and economic conditions of New Spain by a Frenchman at the service of Spain. The report offered many suggestions on improving the trade and economy of New Spain. [AL]

1177 **Morales, Francisco.** Evangelización y culturas indígenas: reflexiones en torno a la actividad misionera de los franciscanos en la Nueva España. (*Arch. Francisc. Hist.*, 85:1/4, Jan./Dec. 1992, p. 123–157, appendix, table)

Fascinating analysis of early Franciscan texts in Nahuatl, which were used for the evangelization of the first generation of Nahua-Mexica people. Author argues that Franciscans accepted and used spaces and symbols of non-Christian beliefs in their activities, and accommodated their teachings to some aspects of precolumbian religion and discursive style. [AL]

1178 **Morales, Francisco.** Mexican society and the Franciscan Order in a period of transition, 1749–1859. (*Americas/Franciscans*, 54:3, Jan. 1998, p. 323–356, graph, tables)

Broadly conceived and executed essay delivers a bird's-eye view of the evolution of the Franciscan Order and the religious vocation of Mexican men from 1749–1859. Posits that under pressure of secularization, the decline of the order began in the late-18th century. Useful and interesting survey. [AL]

1179 **Moreno, Justo L. del Río** and **Lorenzo E. López y Sebastián.** El trigo en la ciudad de México: industria y comercio de un cultivo importado, 1521–1564. (*Rev. Complut. Hist. Am.*, 22, 1996, p. 33–51, bibl., graphs, tables)

Sixteenth-century cabildos sought to ensure adequate production of wheat by granting monopolies to encomenderos, who, for their part, were slow to overcome scarcity of tools, beasts of burden, and individuals familiar with planting wheat. Indigenous peoples, by the middle of the century, increasingly participated in commerce rather than agriculture, further frustrating the encomenderos who needed their labor. [EBC]

1180 **Ngou-Mve, Nicolás.** El Africa bantú en la colonización de México, 1595–1640. Madrid: Consejo Superior de Investigaciones Científicas: Agencia Española de Cooperación Internacional, 1994. 197 p.: bibl., ill., maps. (Monografías; 7)

Survey of the slave trade of Bantú origins to Mexico, mostly in the 16th century. Deals with *asiento* contracts, viceregal policies, number of imports, and market trends. [AL]

1181 **El ocaso novohispano: testimonios documentales.** Recopilación de D.A. Brading; traducción de Antonio Saborit. México: INAH: Dirección General de Publicaciones del Consejo Nacional para la Cultura y las Artes, 1996. 338 p.: bibl. (Sello Bermejo)

Publication of documentary sources of great importance for the last years of Spanish rule, especially for shedding light on the insurgency. Includes an account of forced labor in the mines of Guanajuato, Miguel Dominguez' investigations of the *obrajes* in Querétaro, and various documents revealing Spanish prejudice against Creoles. [EBC]

1182 **Olmos Sánchez, Isabel.** Movimientos migratorios España América: aproximaciones a un caso concreto; el México colonial tardío, 1787–1821. (*Estud. Hist. Soc. Econ. Am.*, 13, 1996, p. 123–145, tables)

Study of immigration from Spain to its colonies in the late colonial years and the period of independence wars. Numbers are small and most of the migrants were merchants, ecclesiastics, bureaucrats, and military men. [AL]

1183 **Olveda, Jaime.** Colima a finales del siglo XVIII. (*Secuencia/México*, 29, mayo/agosto 1994, p. 81–100, bibl., ill., tables)

Overview of the region of Colima and its economic, social, and political features at the end of the colonial period. Informative synthesis that does not change the view of Colima as a backwater area, study nevertheless underlines current interest in regional history. [AL]

1184 **Ortiz Escamilla, Juan.** Las élites de las capitales novohispanas ante la Guerra Civil de 1810. (*Hist. Mex.*, 46:2, oct./dic. 1996, p. 325–357)

Analyzes the different strategies deployed by the key provincial capitals in the face of the Hidalgo revolt. Whether friendly or hostile, none of the cities were the same after 1810 due to the ascendancy to power of the new urban elites. [AL]

1185 **Pérez-Rocha, Emma.** Ciudad en peligro: probanza sobre el desagüe general de la ciudad de México, 1556. México: Instituto Nacional de Antropología e Historia, 1996. 148 p.: bibl., ill. (Colección científica; 314, Serie Historia)

Paleographic transcription of an investigation on the feasibility of draining the city of Mexico; carried out in 1556. A considerable number of witnesses were indigenous groups who provided information on pre-columbian methods of controlling floods. [AL]

1186 Péron, Myléne. Dos visitas episcopales del siglo XVII en la Sierra de Nayarit. (*Relaciones/Zamora*, 69, invierno 1997, p. 41–76, map, photo)

Using the reports of two 17th-century episcopal visits to Nayarit, author reconstructs patterns of resistance to Spanish penetration and conversion to Christianity. The reports of Bishop Juan Ruiz Colmenares (1642) and Juan de León Garabito (1679) are the basis for this interesting article. [AL]

1187 Pita Moreda, María Teresa. Los predicadores novohispanos del siglo XVI. Salamanca, Spain: San Esteban, 1992. 310 p.: bibl. (Los Dominicos y América; 9)

Excellent study of the Dominican Order in the 16th century. Avoids a chronological account giving the reader instead a methodical analysis of the institutional, social, and economic organization of the order. To the prototypes of the urban and the rural convents, Pita Moreda adds a balanced assessment of the missionary activities. [AL]

1188 Pitarch Ramón, Pedro. Una versión tzeltal de la rebelión indígena de 1712, y sus razones. (*Anu. IEI*, 4, 1991/93, p. 151–173, bibl.)

Indigenous version of the 1712 revolt. Text was provided recently to Pitarch by an Indian community. Of great interest to ethnohistorians. Useful final comments. [AL]

1189 Los precios de alimentos y manufacturas novohispanos. Coordinación de Virginia García Acosta. Tlalpan, Mexico: Centro de Investigaciones y Estudios Superiores en Antropología Social; México: Instituto de Investigaciones Dr. José María Luis Mora, 1995. 299 p.: bibl., graphs, ill., tables.

Attempts to revive the neglected history of the prices of products in New Spain. In nine essays, several researchers examine the sources and methodology for the history of prices and the cycles of prices for staple products and manufactures. Also includes a special study of merchandise and prices in the 16th century. Rich in tables and raw data as well as analysis, this is a welcome addition to the economic history of the period. [AL]

1190 Quezada, Noemí. Sexualidad, amor y erotismo: México prehispánico y México colonial. México: Plaza y Valdés: Univ. Nacional Autónoma de México, 1996. 303 p.: bibl.

Study of a wide range of erotic and sexual topics in Aztec and colonial Mexican society, although there is no direct connection between them. Uses literary texts and ethnographic and archival sources. Good coverage of basic themes explained in a pedagogical style. The bibliographical sources are limited to works in Spanish or translated into Spanish. [AL]

1191 Relaciones geográficas de 1792. Estudio introductorio, transcripción y notas de Lourdes M. Romero Navarrete y Felipe I. Echenique March. México: Instituto Nacional de Antropología e Historia, 1995. 231 p.: ill. (Colección científica; 295)

Mostly previously unpublished geographical descriptions of a variety of jurisdictions in central New Spain, written in the early 1790s. [AL]

1192 Romero de Solís, José Miguel. Robar caballos y cometer incesto: el caso de Diego Jerónimo Flores. (*Estud. Jalisc.*, 27, feb. 1997, p. 23–35)

Utilizing the story of a humble Indian accused of stealing horses and living in concubinage, author tries to rescue from anonymity the daily life of poor people in late-16th- century Guadalajara and promote further research on that subject. [AL]

1193 Romero Sotelo, María Eugenia. Minería y guerra: la economía de Nueva España, 1810–1821. México: El Colegio de México: Univ. Nacional Autónoma de México, 1997. 292 p.: bibl., ill., index.

Well-researched, lucid account of the mining industry in war and peace. Especially informative on policy, the book provides a review of mining practices before the wars of independence, during the time of the insurgency, and the period after 1816 when conditions began to return to normal. Discusses questions such as the mining of silver, supplying the mines, and conditions and attitudes of the workers. [EBC]

Rosati Aguerre, Hugo. El imperio español y sus fronteras: Mapuches y Chichimecas en la segunda mitad del siglo XVI. See item **2411.**

1194 Sacristán, María Cristina. Locura y disidencia en el México ilustrado, 1760–1810. Zamora, Mexico: El Colegio de Michoacán; México: Instituto Mora, 1994. 281 p.: bibl., ill. (Colección Investigaciones)

Novel study of madness in late colonial Mexico, based on the records found in Inquisition, Criminals and Prisons sections of the AGN. Madness is understood as a behavior challenging religious discourse, rather than as a mental condition. Thus, this is a cultural, not a medical history. [AL]

1195 Sánchez de Aguilar, Pedro. Informe contra idolorum cultores del obispado de Yucatán. 5. ed. Valladolid, Mexico: Ediciones del Instituto Cultural Valladolid, 1996. 122 p.

Reissue of 17th-century treatise on indigenous idolatry. Latin-Spanish edition. [AL]

1196 Sennhauser, Rudolf Widmer. Veracruz y el comercio de harinas en el Caribe español, 1760–1830. (Estud. Hist. Soc. Econ. Am., 13, 1996, p. 107–122, tables)

Deals with the supply of flour from New Spain to the Spanish Caribbean and the role of the merchant elite of Veracruz, who controlled this trade. [AL]

1197 Silva Riquer, Jorge. Tendencias de los granos básicos del diezmo en los partidos de Zamora, Valladolid, Puruándiro, Maravatío y Zitácuaro, Michoacán: 1660–1803. (in Circuitos mercantiles y mercados en Latinoamérica, siglos XVIII-XIX. México: Instituto de Investigaciones Dr. José María Luis Mora; Instituto de Investigaciones Históricas UNAM, 1995, p. 179–231, graphs, map, tables)

Quantitative study of the fluctuations in wheat, corn, and bean prices in three key areas of the bishopric of Michoacán in the 17th-18th centuries. An increased production of these staple foods indicates a rising demand by an ever-increasing population and the development of a more complex market within Michoacán and beyond its boundaries. [AL]

1198 Solano, Francisco de. Las voces de la ciudad: México a través de sus impresos, 1539–1821. Madrid: Consejo Superior de Investigaciones Científicas, 1994. 400 p.: bibl., ill. (Colección Biblioteca de historia de América; 9)

Comprehensive listing of nearly 1,000 printed works from Mexico City includes bandos, constitutions, regulations, sermons, and reports of festivities. [EBC]

1199 Spanoghe, Sander. Los salarios dentro del sistema del repartimiento forzoso en el Valle de México, 1549–1632. (Anu. Estud. Am., 54:1, enero/junio 1997, p. 43–64, tables)

Study of salaries paid to Indians engaged in forced repartimiento between 1550–1632. Author considers the nominal salary, which continued to increase; differences in payment among Indian and Spanish employers; mining and agricultural salaries; salaries for skilled vs. unskilled labor, etc. Concludes that given the tax burden weighing on the working people, the salary meant little in terms of providing them with a better living condition by European standards. [AL]

1200 Suárez Argüello, Clara Elena. Camino real y carrera larga: la arriería en la Nueva España durante el siglo XVIII. México: Centro de Investigaciones y Estudios Superiores en Antropología Social; Ediciones de la Casa Chata, 1997. 350 p.: appendices, bibl., graphs, tables.

Welcome and much-needed study of muleteers concludes that transport of commodities by well-organized mule teams bound the regions of New Spain together. Special concentration and detail on the transport of tobacco in the year 1800. Based on the rich collections of the AGN, the author reveals materials about the organization of the teams, ownership, routes, costs, and the social worlds of the men dedicated to this work. [EBC]

1201 Taylor, William B. Magistrates of the sacred: priests and parishioners in eighteenth-century Mexico. Stanford, Calif.: Stanford Univ. Press, 1996. 882 p.: bibl., ill., index, maps.

Extensive and in-depth study of the Episcopal church covers politics, economics, and the spiritual and social life of late-Bourbon Mexico. Begins with a description of regalist policies and the secularization of parishes, and concludes with a discussion of priests and the Mexican Insurgency. Among topics discussed are issues of cruelty and deference in relationships between parishoner and priest, changing elite visions of Indians, and alterations in rural communities. Compares parish priests to other ecclesiastical powers, and includes life histories of priests. Of particular interest is the often startling modifications in the use of symbols of Santiago and Guadalupe. Encyclopedic in the breadth and depth of the sources explored. For ethnohistorian's comment, see item **595**. [EBC]

1202 Torales Pacheco, María Cristina.
Suegro comerciante, yerno financiero: Gabriel de Iturbe y su empresa mercantil en Nueva España, 1797–1812. (*Ibero-Am. Arch.*, 22:1/2, 1996, p. 73–102, appendices, bibl., tables)
Describes familial ties and multinational commercial activities in the context of the liberal Bourbon economy by relating details surrounding two generations of one Basque family. Useful illustration of elite strategies of familial survival through employment of relatives, marriage of cousins, cooperation between siblings in acquiring posts, and occupation of social, military, financial, and bureaucratic positions of rank. [EBC]

1203 Torre Villar, Ernesto de la. Las congregaciones de los pueblos de indios: fase terminal—aprobaciones y rectificaciones. México: Univ. Nacional Autónoma de México, 1995. 343 p.: bibl., ill. (Serie Historia novohispana; 54)
Transcribes the documentation on *congregaciones* (the relocation of indigenous towns) between 1603–25 as recorded by Pedro de Campos Guerrero. Erudite introduction by a well-known historian. Very useful for colonial historians. [AL]

1204 Traslosheros H., Jorge E. Estratificación social en el reino de la Nueva España, siglo XVII. (*Relaciones/Zamora*, 59, verano 1994, p. 45–64, table)
Using two classic legal sources, the *Recopilación de Leyes de Indias* and Solorzano's *Política Indiana*, author argues for the definitional importance of blood, birth, and corporate affiliation in adjudicating status, honor, and privileges to colonial people. [AL]

1205 Traslosheros H., Jorge E. La reforma de la iglesia del Antiguo Michoacán: la gestión episcopal de fray Marcos Ramírez de Prado, 1640–1666. Michoacán, Mexico: Univ. Michoacana de San Nicolás de Hi-

dalgo/Escuela de Historia/Secretaría de Difusión Cultural, 1995. 1 v.: bibl., maps.
Thorough study of the activities and reform campaign waged by the Bishop of Michoacán, Fr. Marcos Ramírez de Prado, during the terms of his bishopric, 1640–66. The internal administration of his church, the internal disciplining of the clergy, and the morals of the community were among his priorities. Based on archival research, this work offers dependable, precise information. [AL]

1206 Traslosheros H., Jorge E. El templo de este mundo o de cómo fue reformada la Iglesia del antiguo Michoacán, 1640–1666. (*Estud. Michoacanos*, 5, 1994, p. 19–37, bibl.)
Author analyzes the meaning of the reforms adopted in the bishopric of Michoacán by Bishop Fr. Marcos Ramírez de Prado between 1640–66. Argues that Ramírez de Prado symbolizes the spirit of the secular church in mid-colonial times as he tried to centralize, integrate, and organize his domain, which represented a spiritual reality beyond this world. [AL]

1207 Valk, Juutlje van der. Chastity as legal empowerment: the province of Tetepango, Mexico, 1750–1800. (*in* The legacy of the disinherited: popular culture in Latin America; modernity, globalization, hybridity and authenticity. Amsterdam; CEDLA, 1996, p. 93–111, bibl.)
Using a sampling of cases brought to the ecclesiastic courts by indigenous women, author establishes that personal sexual honor was very meaningful to this sector of the population, particularly in preventing "their household[s] from breaking up". Adds one more meaning to the definitions of honor in colonial Mexico. [AL]

1208 Victoria Ojeda, Jorge. Mérida de Yucatán de las Indias: piratería y estrategia defensiva. Mérida, Mexico: Depto. de Comunicación Social del H. Ayuntamiento de Mérida, 1995. 274 p.: bibl., ill.
Narrative history of defensive strategies against piracy. Of interest to military historians. [AL]

1209 Viqueira, Juan Pedro. Las causas de una rebelión india: Chiapas, 1712. (*in* Chiapas: los rumbos de otra historia. México: Centro de Estudios Mayas del Instituto de Investigaciones Filológicas y Coordinación de Humanidades (UNAM); Centro de Investigaciones y Estudios Superiores en Antropología Social; Centro de Estudios Mexicanos y Centroamericanos; Guadalajara: Univ. de Guadalajara, 1995, p. 103–143)

Thorough analysis of the 1712 rebellion. Examines the anatomy and dynamics of the *chiapaneco* society, its demographic configuration, and its economic structures. Also looks carefully at differing Spanish and Indian circumstances. Cites an agricultural crisis between between 1707–12, political factionalism among Spaniards, indigenous discontent, and tributary extortions as the leading reasons for the revolt. Suggests that Indians rebelled to be free of the Spanish administration and to gain tribute exemptions. Their actions were kindled by syncretic religious beliefs and took place in a complex economic and social medium. [AL]

Vos, Jan de. Vivir en frontera: la experiencia de los indios de Chiapas. See item **603.**

Weckmann, Luis. El milenarismo de Fray Bernardino de Sahagún. See item **5101.**

1210 Weigand, Phil C. La población negra del occidente de México según el censo de Menéndez, 1791–1793. (*in* Tradición e identidad en la cultura mexicana. Zamora, Mexico: El Colegio de Michoacán; Consejo Nacional de Ciencia y Tecnología (CONACYT), 1995, p. 381–391, bibl., tables)

Argues for the recognition of an African component to the late-18th-century population of Jalisco, mostly as mixed with whites and Indians. [AL]

1211 Yasumura, Naoki. Justicia y sociedad rural en Michoacán durante la época colonial. (*Estud. Michoacanos*, 6, 1995, p. 139–186, bibl.)

Fascinating analysis of the evolution of the concepts of "legal" and "useful" land ownership, using one case in Michoacán. Argues that the legal framework changed between the mid-17th and mid-18th centuries, by which time productivity became foremost to crown policy and legal experts. Landownership that had been secure in the 1670s could be legally challenged in the 1770s, often to the detriment of indigenous communities. Commendable study. [AL]

1212 Yrolo Calar, Nicolás de. La Política de escrituras. México: Instituto de Investigaciones Históricas, Univ. Nacional Autónoma de México, 1996. 299 p.: ill., tables (Serie Historia Novohispana; 56)

Very useful re-edition of the 1605 treatise on writing notarial documents by a contemporary expert with 30 years of experience. Excellent guide for colonial historians preceded by a very well-crafted introductory study by Martínez López-Cano. Highly recommended for researchers. [AL]

1213 Yuste, Carmen. Alcabalas filipinas y géneros asiáticos en la Ciudad de México, 1765–1785. (*in* Circuitos mercantiles y mercados en Latinoamérica, siglos XVIII-XIX. México: Instituto de Investigaciones Dr. José María Luis Mora; Instituto de Investigaciones Históricas UNAM, 1995, p. 87–99, tables)

Studies the general characteristics of the commercial flux between the Philippines and New Spain using information from the accounts of Mexico City customs houses. While not a competitor to the Atlantic trade, the oriental market, nonetheless, drained investments and capital from the former and maintained its own financial rhythm. [AL]

Zaballa Beascoechea, Ana de and **Josep-Ignasi Saranyana.** La discusión sobre el joaquinismo novohispano en el siglo XVI en la historiografía reciente. See item **5102.**

1214 Zárate Toscano, Verónica. La muerte de un noble novohispano: el Conde de Regla. (*Obradoiro Hist. Mod.*, 5, 1996, p. 183–199, bibl.)

Based on primary and extremely rare secondary sources, this account of the death of the richest man in 18th-century New Spain identifies public and private aspects of this event, and describes the ceremonies and actions of crown and clergy in marking this milestone. [AL]

North

1215 Aboites Aguilar, Luis. Norte precario: poblamiento y colonización en México, 1760–1940. México: Colegio de México, Centro de Estudios Históricos: Centro de Investigaciones y Estudios Superiores en Antropología Social, 1995. 312 p.: bibl., maps.

Study of the main territorial occupation and population trends of the vast region of northern Mexico. Studies commercial routes, mining development, indigenous resistance, and infiltration of North American capitalist enterprises to determine population policies between the 18th- and mid-20th centuries. [AL]

1216 Altable Fernández, Francisco I. El proyecto colonizador de don José de Gálvez en la Baja California. (*in* Simposio de Historia y Antropología Regionales, *6th, La Paz?, 1995?* Memorias. La Paz, Mexico: Univ. Autónoma de Baja California Sur, 1995, p. 33–38)

Thoughtful analysis of the failure of the colonization project for Baja California. Reasons cited in the study include the failure to secularize the competitive and well-established mission system, poor soil, lack of rainfall, and better opportunities for settlers in other northwestern regions. [EBC]

1217 Amao, Jorge. Mineros, misioneros y rancheros de la antigua California. México: INAH: Plaza y Valdés, 1997. 168 p.: bibl., ill., maps.

Emphasizes the role of mining in encouraging the secular settlement of Lower California. Points out that José de Gálvez favored mining over missionary activities because the former provided greater financial resources to the Crown. [EBC]

1218 Arricivita, Juan Domingo. Apostolic chronicle of Juan Domingo Arricivita: the Franciscan mission frontier in the eighteenth century in Arizona, Texas, and the Californias. v. 1–2. Berkeley, Calif.: Academy of American Franciscan History, 1996. 2 v.: bibl., index.

An annotated translation of an 18th-century chronicle describing the work of the Franciscan College of Propaganda Fide of Santa Cruz de Querétaro. Makes available primary source material of exceptional interest for the history of the northern missions. Valuable information for ethnohistorians. [EBC]

1219 Ayres, James E. The archaeology of Spanish and Mexican colonialism in the American Southwest. With contributions by Leo R. Barker *et al.* Ann Arbor, Mich.: Society for Historical Archaeology, 1995. 133 p.: bibl. (Columbian quincentenary series)

Bibliography with introductory essays appears to be a relatively comprehensive treatment of printed sources for both archeology and ethnohistory. Organized by states,

it includes site identifications and describes major problems and issues. [EBC]

1220 Bernabeu Albert, Salvador. La frontera califórnica: de las expediciones cortesianas a la presencia convulsiva de Gálvez, 1534–1767. (*in* Estudios (nuevos y viejos) sobre la frontera. Madrid: Consejo Superior de Investigaciones Científicas, Centro de Estudios Históricos, Depto. de Historia de América, 1991, p. 85–118)

Explores the maritime expansion of the Spaniards in Mexico through a variety of published primary sources and a thorough exploration of secondary sources. Emphasis on the crucial role of ships in the discovery and conquest of the Californias. Contains much detail about naval history. [EBC]

1221 Bernabeu Albert, Salvador. La religion ofendida: resistencia y rebeliones indígenas en la Baja California Colonial. (*Rev. Complut. Hist. Am.*, 20, 1994, p. 169–180)

Thoughtful effort to conceptualize the conflicts between friars and Indians concludes that Indians viewed the physical punishment inflicted, particularly by the Dominicans, as an offense to be revenged, while the friars intended it as only a correction. [EBC]

1222 Bernabeu Albert, Salvador. Trillar los mares: la expedición descubridora de Bruno de Hezeta al noroeste de América, 1775. Preámbulo de Francisco de Solano. Madrid: Fundación Banco Bilbao-Vizcaya: Consejo Superior de Investigaciones Científicas, 1995. 241 p.: bibl., maps. (Monografías; 9)

Publication of a diary of an expedition of 1775 to explore the northern Pacific. Introduction describes the process of undertaking the voyage, the men involved, and expedition's goals. [EBC]

1223 Borges, Pedro. Características de las fundaciones juniperianas. (*Arch. Francisc. Hist.*, 85:1/4, Jan./Dec. 1992, p. 463–487)

Based on the published letters of Friar Junípero Serra and responses to them, author reviews the special characteristics of the Upper California missions. Serra's insistence on adequate military protection, adherence to urbanization plans, and the enclosure of Indians in mission compounds distinguish these missions from others. Also provides a survey of mission life and describes conflicts that arose when ecclesiastical authorities forced friars to move to different locations against their wishes. [EBC]

1224 Brooks, James F. "This evil extends especially...to the feminine sex": negotiating captivity in the New Mexico borderlands. (*Fem. Stud.*, 22:2, Summer 1996, p. 279–309)

Modifies our ideas of gender relations and ethnic boundaries on the New Mexico frontier. Provides life histories of captives and underlines their important role in negotiating diplomatic and economic relationships. [EBC]

1225 Bugarín, José Antonio. Visita de las misiones del Nayarit 1768–1769. Recopilación de Jean Meyer. México: Centro de Estudios Mexicanos y Centroamericanos: Instituto Nacional Indigenista, 1993. 255 p.: bibl.

Visita document produced by the priest sent to report on the vacated Jesuit missions in 1768–69 has especially abundant ethnohistorical materials on conversion. Introduction by Jean Meyer furnishes the context on missions and religious anthropology. Compares Nayarit with the demographic disasters of California and other missionary provinces. [EBC]

1226 Castañeda, Carmen. Historia de la sexualidad al norte de la Nueva España. (*Clío/Culiacán*, 12, sept./dic. 1994, p. 7–18)

Continuation of the author's previous work on sexuality with a study of cases from Guadalajara. Concludes that the Church would not severely punish men for violations of its rules. The importance attributed to the preservation of marriages led the Church to impose only fines for sexual transgressions. [EBC]

1227 Churruca Peláez, Agustín et al. El sur de Coahuila en el siglo XVII. Torreón, Mexico: Editorial del Norte Mexicano, 1994. 318 p.: bibl., ill., maps.

Collection of primary sources from various Mexican archives is used as a basis for divulging data about the Laguna region. Valuable for information about ecclesiastical history. Includes inventories of slaves in church institutions. [EBC]

1228 Contested Eden: California before the gold rush. Edited by Ramón Gutiérrez and Richard J. Orsi. Berkeley: Univ. of California Press, 1998. 407 p.: bibl., ill., index, maps. (California history sesquicentennial series; 1)

One of a series of books written to celebrate the 150th anniversary of the admission of California to the Union, emphasizes the natural environment, the history of the Indians, exploration, and social and economic history, rather than the traditional institutional studies of mission and presidio. Takes advantage of the latest research and includes contributions by leading scholars. [EBC]

1229 Cramaussel, Chantal. Ilegítimos y abandonados en la frontera norte de la Nueva España: Parral y San Bartolomé en el siglo XVII. (*CLAHR/Albuquerque*, 4:4, Fall 1995, p. 405–438, graphs, tables)

Rich demographic and social study examines the fate of illegitimate and abandoned children, comparing figures from an agricultural town and a mining town, in addition to examining the general population history. Seeks to determine when (by seasons of the year or times of famine) and by which ethnic groups children were abandoned. Relates these figures to the differing social conditions of the parents' ethnic groups. Compares figures with those found by Thomas Calvo for Guadalajara (see *HLAS 56:1129*). [EBC]

1230 Curiel, Guadalupe. La historia de Texas en la Biblioteca Nacional de México, 1528–1848: bibliografía comentada. Colaboración técnica de Aurora Serrano Cruz. México: Univ. Nacional Autónoma de México, 1994. 237 p.: bibl., ill. (Serie Bibliografías / Instituto de Investigaciones Bibliográficas)

Generously annotated bibliography of the history of Texas to 1848 places works in context and includes brief biographies of authors. Entries are arranged chronologically. Contains reproductions of the *portadas* of many books. [AL]

1231 Del Río, Ignacio. El fin de un régimen de excepción en Baja California: la expulsión de los jesuitas. (*in* Simposio de Historia y Antropología Regionales, 6th, La Paz², 1995² Memorias. La Paz, Mexico: Univ. Autónoma de Baja California Sur, 1995, p. 19–24)

Exciting account of the expulsion of the Jesuits describes the process and suggests that land disputes had exacerbated matters.

Suggests that the decision to expel the Jesuits emerged from rampant regalism. [EBC]

1232 Echenique March, Felipe I. La conquista espiritual de las Californias: un ensayo de sus principales paradigmas. (*Estud. Front.*, 31/32, mayo/agosto/sept./dic. 1993, p. 101–133, bibl.)

A careful analysis of the Jesuit chronicles reveals that the "spiritual" conquest destroyed customary subsistence habits of indigenous peoples that had made peaceful and ingenious use of scarce resources. [EBC]

1233 Epistolario de Zacatecas, 1549–1599. Recopilación de José Enciso Contreras. Zacatecas, Mexico: Ayuntamiento de Zacatecas, 1996. 443 p.: bibl. (Serie Elías Amador)

Transcription of letters written about Zacatecas in the 16th century from various manuscript collections. Essential source materials for the history of mining. [EBC]

1234 La expansión del septentrión novohispano, 1614–1723. t. 1, Algunos personajes y sus contribuciones. t. 2, Apéndice documental. México: Instituto de Investigaciones Sociales, UNAM; Saltillo, México: Instituto Estatal de Documentación de Coahuila, 1997. 2 v.: bibl., ill., maps.

Biographical histories of 17th-century men who contributed to the imperial venture. Includes reproductions of diaries and reports; also includes location of additional sources. Uses sources from Spanish and Mexican archives. [EBC]

1235 Flores Clair, Eduardo. El lado oscuro de la plata: la vida en los reales mineros novohispanos a finales del siglo XVIII. (*Anu. Estud. Am.*, 54:1, enero/junio 1997, p. 89–106)

Study of the many forms of daily entertainment in the mining towns of New Spain. Author sees bullfights, gambling, and public celebrations as forms of popular culture idiosyncratic to mining towns. [AL]

1236 Frank, Ross. Economic growth and the creation of the vecino homeland in New Mexico, 1780–1820. (*Rev. Indias*, 61:208, sept./dic. 1996, p. 743–782, graphs, tables)

History of late colonial New Mexico based on tithe records and population statistics informs us that the original alliance between the Pueblo Indians and the Hispanic or vecino (non-Indian) colonists against the no-

madic Indians became less important as the Hispanic populations rose, and the Indian population declined. [EBC]

1237 Gerhard, Peter and W. Michael Mathes. Peregrinations of the Baja California mission registers. (*Americas/Franciscans*, 52:1, July 1995, p. 81–88)

History of the fate of the baptismal, marriage, and death records kept by Jesuit, Franciscan, and Dominican friars for Lower California. Only 45 percent of these have been located. Includes list of those that can be found in repositories in the US. [EBC]

1238 Gradie, Charlotte M. Jesuit missionaries and native elites in northern Mexico, 1572 to 1616. Storrs, Conn.: Univ. of Conn., Center for Latin American & Caribbean Studies; Providence, RI.: Brown Univ., Center for Latin American Studies; Amherst: Univ. of Massachussetts, Latin American Studies Program, 1997. 23 p. (Latin American Studies Consortium of New England Occasional papers; 8)

Thoughtful essay on Jesuit practices and Tepehuan reactions. Missionaries' policy of restricting intertribal warfare resulted in danger to themselves and the loss of status for Indian leaders. Describes conflicts between chief and shamans; also discusses customs of warfare. [EBC]

1239 Haas, Lisbeth. Conquests and historical identities in California, 1769–1936. Berkeley, Calif.: Univ. of California Press, 1995. 294 p.: bibl., ill., maps.

Study of the Mexican population of Upper California especially around San Juan Capistrano. Addresses culture, economics, and social life. [EBC]

1240 Hausberger, Bernd. La vida diaria de los padres jesuitas en las misiones del noroeste de México: un acercamiento a la historia cotidiana colonial. (*in* Simposio de Historia y Antropología de Sonora, *20th, Hermosillo, Mexico, 1995.* Balance de dos décadas de producción historiográfica en los simposios de historia y antropología, 1975–1995. Hermosillo, Mexico: Univ. de Sonora, Instituto de Investigaciones Históricas, 1996, p. 53–104, bibl.)

Well-organized description of the pleasures and difficulties of life on the frontier based on Jesuit letters. Covers questions such as food, illness, medical treatment, solitude, guests, and the adaptation of European

Jesuits to life on the frontier. Describes their disappointment with their inability to convert the Indians thoroughly. Spent much of their time on nonmissionary activities such as providing food and housing and resolving linguistic problems. [EBC]

1241 Hendricks, Rick. La presencia de Tlalpujahuenses en la reconquista de Nuevo México. (*Relaciones/Zamora*, 18:70, primavera 1997, p. 193–206)

Discusses 12 men, all important figures in the mining community of Tlalpujahua, Michoacán, who joined Diego de Vargas in the reconquest of New Mexico. The 12 married well and came to form part of the New Mexico elite. [EBC]

1242 Jackson, Robert H. Grain supply, congregation, and demographic patterns in the missions of northwestern New Spain: case studies from Baja and Alta California. (*J. West*, 36:1, Jan. 1997, p. 19–25, photos, tables)

Based on a statistical analysis of grain production and population at six California missions, concludes that food supply had little impact on demographic success or on the ability to attract converts to the missions. The correlation between grain supply and population found in Europe does not appear to apply to California. [EBC]

1243 Jackson, Robert H. and Edward Castillo. Indians, Franciscans, and Spanish colonization: the impact of the mission system on California Indians. Albuquerque: Univ. of New Mexico Press, 1995. 221 p.: bibl., ill.

Well-documented study demonstrates that conditions within the California missions caused high mortality rates among the Indians. [EBC]

1244 Jiménez, Alfredo. El lejano norte español: cómo escapar del *American West* y de las *Spanish Borderlands*. (*CLAHR/Albuquerque*, 5:4, Fall 1994, p. 381–412)

Intelligent and informed discussion of the ways in which historians have conceptualized the Spanish imperial presence as it spread throughout the north. Proposes dropping the Boltonian word "borderlands," and adopting "far north" or "lejano norte" when discussing the areas along the traditional Boltonian borderlands and the frontier. [EBC]

1245 Jones, Oakah L., Jr. Rescue and ransom of Spanish captives from the *indios bárbaros* on the northern frontier of New Spain. (*CLAHR/Albuquerque*, 4:2, Spring 1995, p. 128–148, map)

This description of the ransoming of Spanish, casta, Native American, and Mexican captives begins with Vargas' reconquest of New Mexico in 1692, describes changes in the system by Teodoro de Croix in 1778, and continues through the mid-19th century. Discusses the difficulties of finding relatives and integrating former captives into their old communities. [EBC]

1246 Knaut, Andrew L. The Pueblo Revolt of 1680: conquest and resistance in seventeenth-century New Mexico. Norman, Okla.: Univ. of Oklahoma Press, 1995. 260 p.: bibl., ill., index, maps.

Succint but well-told story of the Pueblo Revolt, popularly written and based on published primary and secondary sources. Uses insights developed by ethnohistorians. Emphasizes Spanish brutality. [EBC]

1247 León Portilla, Miguel. La California mexicana: ensayos acerca de su historia. México: Univ. Nacional Autónoma de México, Instituto de Investigaciones Históricas; Mexicali, B.C.: Univ. Autónoma de Baja California, Instituto de Investigaciones Históricas, 1995. 308 p.: bibl., ill., maps. (Serie Historia novohispana; 58)

Collection of previously published essays on Baja California by a master of Mexican history and ethnohistory. Includes a new autobiographical introduction and an epilogue, examining Baja California from the perspective of various frontier theories. Included are essays on the Dominicans, Franciscans, and explorers. A valuable overview of the history of Baja California. [EBC]

1248 Longinos Martínez, José. Diario de las expediciones a las Californias de José Longinos. Recopilación de Salvador Bernabéu. Aranjuez, Spain: Doce Calles, 1994. 315 p.: bibl., ill. (some col), maps. (Theatrum Naturae. Serie Textos clásicos)

Beautifully illustrated report of a naturalist in California from 1789. Demonstrates the increasing level of interest in scientific matters and the difficulties confronting scientists of the era. [EBC]

1249 López Castillo, Gilberto. Ranchos de la llanura costera de la provincia de Culiacán, 1691–1765. (*Clío/Culiacán*, 12, sept./dic. 1994, p. 53–67, bibl., map, table)

Offers a revision of the history of landed property in one of the northern areas of the Viceroyalty by a study of land records indicating the continuity of indigenous property and small, family-owned ranchos on the coast of Culiacán. The only larger properties were those of mule breeders and suppliers to the mines. [EBC]

1250 MacCameron, Robert. Environmental change in colonial New Mexico. (An expanding world; 17) (*in* Agriculture, resource exploitation, and environmental change. Edited by Helen Wheatley. Aldershot, Great Britain; Brookfield, Vt.: Variorum, 1997, p. 219–241)

Study of the environmental impact of Spanish settlement in colonial New Mexico. Includes land and forest usage, introductions of crops, animals and material culture, and exchange with Pueblos. Posits that New Mexico experienced a *sui generis* layered environmental change. [AL]

1251 Martin, Cheryl English. Governance and society in colonial Mexico: Chihuahua in the eighteenth century. Stanford, Calif.: Stanford Univ. Press, 1996. 282 p.: bibl., index.

A valuable addition to the historical literature on late colonial Mexico and the very modified impact of the Bourbon reforms. Solidly based on research in the well-preserved local archives, the author investigates how a large city on the northern frontier differed from other cities in New Spain. Particularly rich in materials on labor and ritual. [EBC]

1252 Osante, Patricia. Orígenes del Nuevo Santander (1748–1772). México: Univ. Nacional Autónoma de México, Instituto de Investigaciones Históricas; Ciudad Victoria: Univ. Autónoma de Tamaulipas, 1997. 300 p.: bibl., index, maps. (Serie Historia novohispana; 59)

Both quantitatively and qualitatively, this book delivers more than the title promises. Beginning with the earliest Spanish efforts to colonize the area north and east of Querétaro, continuing to the attacks against José Escandón and his ultimate vindication

in 1776. Especially strong on the politics of conquest and settlement, describing viceregal administrations, colonial policies, as well as the actions of Hispanic settlers. [EBC]

1253 Palóu, Francisco. Cartas desde la península de California, 1768–1773. Transcripción y recopilación de José Luis Soto Pérez. México: Editorial Porrúa, 1994. 557 p.: ill., indexes. (Biblioteca Porrúa; 112)

This new edition of letters corrects errors of two previous editions. A valuable primary source for the period in California history between the expulsion of the Jesuits and the establishment of the Franciscans. Editor adds material from the AGN and the newly organized and indexed archives of the Franciscan Province of Michoacán. [EBC]

1254 Pearcy, Thomas L. The smallpox outbreak of 1779–1782: a brief comparative look at twelve borderland communities. (*J. West*, 36:1, Jan. 1997, p. 26–37, graphs, map, photos, tables)

Study of parish registers of 12 communities reveals mestizo populations suffered equally with Indians, and did not possess increased immunity from smallpox. Concludes that the greatest mortality occurred when people lived in close proximity to one another. [EBC]

1255 The Presidio and militia on the northern frontier of New Spain: a documentary history. v. 2, pt. 2, The central corridor and the Texas corridor, 1700–1765. Tucson: Univ. of Arizona Press, 1997. 1 v.: bibl.

This documentary history contains original and annotated translations of documents dealing with presidios. Contains materials for the history of discovery, conquest, and settlement of the central corridor of eastern Nueva Vizcaya, New Mexico, and Texas between 1700–65. [EBC]

1256 Los puertos noroccidentales de México. Coordinación de Jaime Olveda y Juan Carlos Reyes Garza. Zapopan, Mexico: Colegio de Jalisco; Colima: Univ. de Colima; México: Instituto Nacional de Antropología e Historia, 1994. 269 p.: bibl., ill.

A collection of essays on the history of the ports of Mexico's northwest. This is a novel idea that merits development as a new path in economic, regional, and urban history. [AL]

1257 Radding Murrieta, Cynthia. Comparative frontiers: domination and changing ethnic boundaries in Northern Mexico, 1750–1850. (*ANDES Antropol. Hist., 6, 1994,* p. 265–272)

Cumulation of an enormous amount of recent research in a new conceptualization of the conflicts between sedentary Indian populations of Sonora and Sinaloa and nomadic peoples. Explains the slow process of the transformation of Indian polities into peasant communities. [EBC]

1258 Radding Murrieta, Cynthia. Etnia, tierra y Estado: la nación ópata de la sierra sonorense en la transición de Colonia a República, 1790–1840. (*in* Simposio de Historia y Antropología de Sonora, *19th, Hermosillo, Mexico, 1994.* Memorias. Hermosillo, Mexico: Instituto de Investigaciones Históricas de la Univ. de Sonora, 1994, v. 1, p. 105–142)

Studies the land structure and the process of land appropriation suffered by the Opata nation. Under pressure since the Bourbon reforms, the poorest peasants lost ground to their own leaders and Mexican land-grabbers during the first four decades after independence. [AL]

1259 Radding Murrieta, Cynthia. Wandering peoples: colonialism, ethnic spaces, and ecological frontiers in northwestern Mexico, 1700–1850. Durham, N.C.: Duke Univ. Press, 1997. 424 p.: bibl., ill., index, maps. (Latin America otherwise)

Balanced and thorough work on colonial and early-19th-century Sonora and Sinaloa combines historical and ethnohistorical methodologies, narratives, statistical data, and analysis of the changing relations among Indians, villagers, miners, missionaries, and the state. Describes and analyzes the changes in Indian communities. Discussion of the transition between colony and independent Mexico provides a vision of changes and continuities. Exceptionally wide collection of sources. For ethnohistorian's comment, see item **565.** [EBC]

1260 Ramenofsky, Ann F. The problem of introduced infectious diseases in New Mexico: A.D. 1540–1680. (*J. Anthropol. Res.,* 52:2, Summer 1996, p. 161–184, bibl., ill., map, tables)

On the basis of an analysis of the proper conditions for the transmission of diseases and a careful reading of the documents, author suggests that, contrary to the accepted wisdom, the native population of upland New Mexico did suffer from diseases before the re-entry of the Spaniards after the 1680 rebellion. Useful article in explaining the conditions under which parasites thrive and cause mortality to human populations. [EBC]

1261 Ramírez Meza, Benito and **Fabiola Ibarra Díaz.** Los gobernadores de las provincias de Sonora y Sinaloa durante la época colonial: la gestión de Juan Claudio de Pineda, 1763–1770. (*in* Simposio de Historia y Antropología de Sonora, *19th, Hermosillo, Mexico, 1994.* Memorias. Hermosillo, Mexico: Instituto de Investigaciones Históricas de la Univ. de Sonora, 1994, v. 1, p. 181–195, bibl.)

Study of the governorship of Juan Pineda describes the series of crises of the 1760s in the northwest, including lack of mercury, decline of the mines, attacks by nomadic Indians, as well as the loss of Mission properties (as distinct from Jesuit holdings) after the expulsion of the Jesuits. Although Pineda is remembered for his military contributions, he also took censuses, established a *real caja* in Los Alamos, and distributed land to colonists. [EBC]

1262 Río, Ignacio del. La aplicación regional de las reformas borbónicas en Nueva España: Sonora y Sinaloa, 1768–1787. México: Univ. Nacional Autónoma de México, Instituto de Investigaciones Históricas, 1995. 236 p.: bibl., ill. (Serie Historia novohispana; 55)

Assesses the local impact of the Bourbon reforms on northwest Mexico and sheds light on the effectiveness—or lack thereof— of the reform plan. [AL]

1263 Río, Ignacio del. El problema de la escasez de moneda en Sonora y la política borbónica. (*in* Simposio de Historia y Antropología de Sonora, *19th, Hermosillo, Mexico, 1994.* Memorias. Hermosillo, Mexico: Instituto de Investigaciones Históricas de la Univ. de Sonora, 1994, v. 1, p. 197–211, bibl.)

Interesting interpretation of one of José de Gálvez' policies encouraging the coinage of money in the northwest. Concludes that this policy made Northerners less dependent on the *situado* and encouraged the development of a semi-autonomous regional economy. [EBC]

1264 Romero, Saúl Jerónimo. De las misiones a los ranchos y haciendas: la privatización de la tenencia de la tierra en Sonora, 1740–1860. Hermosillo, Mexico: Gobierno del Estado de Sonora, Secretaría de Educación y Cultura, 1991. 237 p.: bibl., ill.

Argues that before the mid-19th century, the state of Sonora was populated by small and medium landowners and also had communal and ejido land. This process of land tenure began toward the end of the 18th century. Work is based on property registers made between 1770–1829. [EBC]

Ruvalcaba Mercado, Jesús. Vacas, mulas, azúcar y café: los efectos de su introducción en la Huasteca, México. See item **580.**

1265 Sánchez, Joseph P. Nicolás de Aguilar and the jurisdiction of Salinas in the province of New Mexico, 1659–1662. (*Rev. Complut. Hist. Am.*, 22, 1996, p. 139–159)

Another interpretation of an Inquisition case previously treated by France Scholes. Civil officials clashed with Franciscan friars over the use of Indian labor and the performance of Kachina dances. Interesting discussion of church-state relations and the rights and customs of indigenous peoples. [EBC]

1266 Tyler, Daniel. The Spanish colonial legacy and the role of hispanic custom in defining New Mexico land and water rights. (*CLAHR/Albuquerque*, 4:2, Spring 1995, p. 149–165, map)

Establishes the role of local customs in defining legal water rights in the isolated colony. Argues that the effort of the state of New Mexico to impose a different system of water allocation rights, providing for water to be diverted from the most recent grantees, would destroy community solidarity. [EBC]

1267 Valdés, Carlos Manuel. La gente del mezquite: los nómadas del noreste en la colonia. Tlalpan, Mexico: CIESAS; INI, 1995. 279 p.: bibl., ill. (some col.). (Historia de los pueblos indígenas de México)

Part of an ambitious project to write the history of the indigenous peoples of Mexico, this work, is based on abundant primary materials primarily from the Saltillo archives, as well as other sources in Coahuila, Nuevo León, and parts of Chihuahua. Discusses attitudes of other groups towards indigenous peoples. Abundantly illustrated. [EBC]

Vitar, Beatriz. Las fronteras "bárbaras" en los virreinatos de Nueva España y Perú. See item **2130.**

Independence, Revolution, and Post-Revolution

BARBARA A. TENENBAUM, *Mexican Specialist, Hispanic Division, Library of Congress; Editor in Chief, Encyclopedia of Latin American History and Culture*
DON M. COERVER, *Professor of History, Texas Christian University*
SUZANNE B. PASZTOR, *Assistant Professor of History, University of the Pacific*

INDEPENDENCE TO REVOLUTION

SCHOLARLY WRITING ON MEXICAN HISTORY from 1810–1910 continues to rise to new heights and address new subjects. Since the mid-1980s, the field has become ever more sophisticated, moving sharply away from the hagiography characteristic of earlier times. Such improvements are not simply due to its increasing professionalization, as noted in *HLAS 56*, but to other factors at work in both Mexico and the US.

This biennium Mexican research reflects new concerns about democratic processes and institutions, as well as a new interest in immigrants, highlighting, for a change, their beneficial contributions to life in their adopted Mexican homeland.

Particularly noteworthy among the works reviewed here is the charming book by Sano on Japanese sailors shipwrecked off the coast of Mazatlán (item **1352**). On the cultural side, Mexican historians are exploring an ever-widening assortment of source materials including traditional calendars, visitor's cards, newspaper advertisements, and Mexican versions of books that had originated abroad (items **1269, 1320, 1333, 1339,** and **1367**). As historians continue to delve into such previously untapped resources, their interpretations will deepen our understanding of Mexico's past.

Researchers' interest in politics continues, but different themes have moved to the forefront. As predicted in *HLAS 56*, scholars are looking somewhat more objectively at the Porfiriato, particularly at the construction and maintenance of political control, a thread first articulated by Laurens Perry in his *Juarez and Díaz: machine politics in Mexico* (see *HLAS 42:2229*). Articles on Yucatan during the Caste War; voting in the state of Mexico; Porfirian political networks; and local political and spiritual leaders in Chihuahua, Puebla, and Veracruz, among others, study how localities reacted to events and demands from the center (for example, items **1278, 1345, 1347,** and **1363**). If this worthy trend first noted in *HLAS 54* continues, historians can look forward to a more comprehensive picture of the struggle between central control and provincial/local aspirations. In another important trend, historians are finally beginning to look at Mexican indigenous peoples as protagonists of their own history, rather than solely as victims in peril. A number of new studies examine the role of indigenous peoples in local and national politics during independence, the Caste War, the Reform, and the French Empire (for example, items **1279** and **1268**) and Especially interesting is the daring article by Velasco Avila on the indigenous in Nuevo México who took Mexican mestizos hostages, but left those from the US alone (item **1324**).

Economic historians are also hard at work. This biennium saw impressive essays on previously neglected financial, fiscal, and trade issues. These scholars are locked in struggle with the cultural historians, particularly in the US. Each group hotly contests the assumptions, evidence, and arguments of the other, as occurred during an especially rancorous Mexican Studies Committee meeting at the American Historical Association Convention in 1997. This controversy is not precisely new and is destined to continue as more aspects of Mexican history are carefully studied. In the meantime, scholars should consider the merits and weaknesses of the vast array of ideological interpretations, ranging from dependency to econometrics, found in recent historical studies on a variety of topics: railroads, public works, free-standing British companies, the Banco de México, copper, gold, and silver money; and a recalculation of national income (items **1287, 1297, 1317, 1325,** and **1349**). The period also saw two excellent and likely-to-be-definitive essays by Knowlton on the *ejido* and by Wells on henequen (items **1312** and **1370** respectively). [BT]

REVOLUTION AND POST-REVOLUTION

Regional history continues to attract scholars who are increasingly focusing their research on the political dynamics of the post-revolution period. Heather Fowler Salamini explores the continuing interest in the revolutionary period (item **1301**), while Raymond Buve (item **1405**) examines the revolutionary process in Tlaxcala. Studies of the early revolutionary period focus on Guanajuato (item **1392**), Tlaxcala (item **1405**), and Veracruz (item **1476**). Contributing to an understanding of the

1930s and 1940s are studies of Michoacán (item **1515**) and item **1428**), Puebla (item **1575**), and Tamaulipas (item **1379**).

In the field of labor history, the relationship between miners' unions and the Revolution is explored in Gonzales (item **1454**), while Jonathan C. Brown provides an important analysis of Mexican oil workers and the expropriation of 1938 (item **1400**). Studies by Jeffrey Bortz (item **1395**), Dora Elvia Enríquez Licón (item **1434**), and Michael Snodgrass (item **1559**) highlight the relationship between labor movements and the state during the 1920s and 1930s. Ignacio Rabelo Ruiz de la Peña inventories documents on Tabasco's labor movement (item **1527**).

Research on Mexico's economic history persists as a popular theme. Elsa Margarita Gracida Romo provides a good overview of Mexico's industrial growth (item **1461**), while Jesús Méndez Reyes examines economic policy during the Madero years (item **1503**). Juan Barragán (item **1384**), María del Carmen Collado (item **1422**), and Felícitas López Portillo (items **1487** and **1489**) provide good studies of the relationship between Mexico's industrial-business class and the state in the post- revolutionary period.

Women's history continues to attract scholars. Ana Lau Jaiven provides a useful historiographical survey highlighting primary and secondary works relating to women's experiences in the Mexican Revolution (item **1479**). Martha Eva Rocha Islas uses documents from the Archivo de la Secretaría de la Defensa Nacional to profile female participants in the Revolution (item **1537**), while Andrés Reséndez Fuentes discusses the differences between *soldaderas* and female soldiers (item **1532**). Explorations of Mexico's women's movement and of the political activities of contemporary Mexican women are the subject of works by Marta Lamas *et al.* (item **1477**) and Carmen Ramos Escandón (item **1530**). An interesting study of homosexuality by Rob Buffington is a hopeful sign that some scholars may be expanding their focus to the more general field of gender studies (item **1403**).

A notable interest in Church-state relations, particularly the Cristero Rebellion, characterized the last biennium. Celestino Barradas concludes his multivolume study of the Church in Veracruz (item **1383**). María de la Luz Martínez Rojas examines relations between the Church and the Madero, Huerta, and Carranza administrations (item **1319**). Regional explorations of the Cristero movement focus on Aguascalientes (item **1545**) and Jalisco (items **1417; 1472;** and **1555**) among others.

Mexican diplomatic history has likewise attracted considerable attention of late. Oscar Flores Torres (item **1441**), Carlos Illades (item **1308**) and Marina Zuloaga Rada (item **1593**) explore relations between Mexico and Spain and between Mexico and its Spanish residents during the Revolution. Diplomatic dealings between Mexico and the US during the 1920s is the topic of articles by Daniela Spenser Grollová (item **1562**) and Pedro Castro (item **1418**). Alan Knight analyzes the emergence of a Mexican-US alliance in the years before World War II (item **1474**), and Stephen Niblo examines how wartime cooperation with the US influenced Mexico's postwar development policy (item **1511**). Jurgen Buchenau provides an excellent general study of Mexico's relationship with Central America (item **1402**), while articles by José Antonio Serrano Ortega (item **1554**) and Thomas D. Schoonover (item **1551**) provide more specific studies of the same theme. Finally, Mexico's Secretary of Foreign Relations has produced an interesting photographic history of Mexican diplomacy in the decades after World War I (item **1382**).

Several notable works produced in the last biennium do not fit into the above categories. John W. Sherman (item **1556**) and Ricardo Pérez Montfort (item **1519**) provide important studies of the Mexican right. Mary K. Vaughan has produced an excellent study of educational politics in the post-revolutionary era (item **1577**). New analyses of Zapata and Zapatismo can be found in Samuel Brunk (item **1401**) and Francisco Piñeda Gómez (item **1521**). Arnaldo Córdova provides an important study of the Maximato (item **1427**), while Marjorie Becker revises the "myth of secular redemption" surrounding Cárdenas and his agrarian reform program (item **1389**). Finally, Robert Buffington breaks new ground with a study of the political significance of prison reform during the Revolution (item **1404**). [DC and SP]

INDEPENDENCE TO REVOLUTION

1268 Abramo Lauff, Marcelo and **Yolanda Barberena Villalobos.** El estadio: la prensa en México, 1870–1979. México: Instituto Nacional de Antropología e Historia, 1998. 272 p.: bibl., indices. (Fuentes)

Listing of every newspaper published throughout Mexico during the decade that saw the death of Juárez, the presidencies of Sebástian Lerdo y Tejada and Porfirio Díaz, and substantial diplomatic problems with the US. Important source.

1269 Aguila M., Marcos Tonatiuh. El liberalismo mexicano y la sucesión presidencial de 1880: dos ensayos. México: Univ. Autónoma Metropolitana, Unidad Azcapotzalco; M.A. Porrúa Grupo Editorial, 1995. 174 p.: bibl., ill. (Las Ciencias sociales)

Uses cartoons from the period to explain Mexican politics during this critical era. Discusses the historiography of various scholars of the time, from Cosío Villegas to Reyes Heroles to Krauze and Knight.

1270 Aguilar Rivera, José Antonio. Oposición y separación de poderes: la estructura nacional institucional del conflicto 1867–1872. (*Metapolítica/México*, 2:5, enero/marzo 1998, p. 69–92)

Discusses Emilio Rabasa's view of the constitutionality of two major events during the Restored Republic: the asking and granting of emergency authority and the factional conflict between the states. Concludes that Mexico was barely a constitutional liberal state during the 120 months between the end of the Empire and the Porfiriato.

1271 Alanís Enciso, Fernando Saúl. La promoción de la inmigración de trabajadores agrícolas asiáticos a Yucatán, 1880–1910. (*Secuencia/México*, 37, enero/abril 1997, p. 79–94, bibl.)

Examines the recruiting of Asians, including Japanese and Koreans, to work in the henequen agribusiness. Readers need to look at the statistics carefully, since the census totals for 1910 and 1920 probably will be revised substantially.

Amador Zamora, Edgar Abraham. Entrando en órbita: las relaciones económicas México-Estados Unidos, 1821–1910, y la función de los poderes regionales. See *HLAS 57:4063*.

1272 Anna, Timothy E. Forging Mexico: 1821–1835. Lincoln, Neb.: Univ. of Nebraska Press, 1998. 330 p.: bibl., index.

In this work, which is more historiography than monographic history, the author discusses various conventional theories and interpretations concerning the evolution of Mexican federalism and its role in "forging Mexico." Although the author accepts the lasting impact of federalism throughout Mexican history, he does not link it to popular nationalism and resistance as do Thomson and Mallon among others.

1273 Aquino Sánchez, Faustino A. Intervención francesa, 1838–1839: la diplomacia mexicana y el imperialismo del librecambio. México: Instituto Nacional de Antropología e Historia, 1997. 340 p.: bibl. (Serie Historia)

Surpasses all previous studies in drawing connection between intervention and financial interests. Carefully details how Mexico's financial weakness played into the hands of its invaders. Also adds much on the diplomatic side. Worthy addition to Barker's classic works.

1274 Ávila, Alfredo. Diplomacia e interés privado: Matías Romero, el Soconusco y el Southern Mexican Railroad, 1881–1883. (*Secuencia/México*, 38, mayo/agosto 1997, p. 51–76, bibl., ill.)

Discusses the role of Romero and US President Ulysses S. Grant in negotiations with the US and Guatemala for a treaty fixing the Mexican-Guatemalan border in preparation for building a railroad. Despite diplomatic success, the proposed line linking Chiapas to the US ultimately failed for lack of funds.

1275 Azuela, Luz Fernanda and **Rafael Guevara Fefer.** La ciencia en México en el siglo XIX: una proximación historiográfica. (*Asclepio/Madrid*, 50:2, 1998, p. 77–105)

Bibliographic essay on major works on Mexican science published between 1895–1996 provides excellent introduction to the field and its debates. Discusses studies of scientific societies, scientific theories, and histories of disciplines such as botany, biology, geology, and pharmacy.

1276 Barrera Bassols, Jacinto. El caso Villavicencio: violencia y poder en el Porfiriato. México: Alfaguara, 1997. 311 p.: bibl. (Extra Alfaguara)

Compelling in-depth analysis of an obscure, but important, incident of the Porfiriato. During the traditional Independence Day festival in 1897, Arnulfo Arroyo hit President Díaz on the back of the neck and was immediately set upon by the crowd. Arroyo was later murdered in jail by "hoodlums" thought to be police. The chief of police committed suicide and several of his men were sent to jail, among them, Antonio Villavicencio, the focus of this study.

1277 Bartra, Armando. El México bárbaro: plantaciones y monterías del sureste durante el Porfiriato. México: El Atajo, 1996. 516 p.: bibl., ill. (Col. El carril de la flor)

Penetrating look at southern Mexico's "tropical" agriculture of tobacco, coffee, chicle, and rubber uses archival sources and foreign visitors' accounts. Stresses interactions between German owners and Mexican workers.

1278 Beltrán López, Dina and **Marco Antonio Berrelleza Fonseca.** A las puertas de la gloria: las elecciones de 1909 en Sinaloa. Culiacán, México: Univ. Autónoma de Sinaloa, Archivo Histórico; Dirección de Investigación y Fomento de Cultura Regional, 1997. 173 p.: bibl., ill.

Relates remarkable reaction in Sinaloa to Porfirio Díaz's interview with James Creelman. Argues that the state sought a democratic route in its 1909 elections, a pre-cursor to the movement characteristic of Mexico today.

1279 Cárdenas Gutiérrez, Salvador. La construcción del imaginario social *república representativa* en la folletería mexicana: 1856–1861. (*Hist. Mex.*, 48:3, enero/marzo 1999, p. 523–566, bibl.)

Interesting study of the relationship between newspapers and pamphlets, and of the latter's role in persuading and often creating public opinion. Focuses specifically on the debate surrounding the promulgation of the 1857 Constitution, but omits the salient connection between *folletos* and *pronunciamentos*.

1280 Castelán Rueda, Roberto. La fuerza de la palabra impresa: Carlos María de Bustamante y el discurso de la modernidad, 1805–1827. México: Fondo de Cultura Económica/Univ. de Guadalajara, 1997. 389 p.: bibl., index. (Sección de obras de historia)

Long overdue look at a key architect of Mexican liberalism concentrates on the rhetorical edifice Bustamante constructed, and examines how his successors used his works for their own post-revolutionary purposes. Includes interesting material on how Bustamante consistently manipulated the facts to suit his own ideas, and zeros in on his creation of myths such as the heroic insurgent Indian and virtuous insurgent creole women (the Corregidora being just one example), along with his saintly Morelos in contrast to the vile Calleja.

1281 Castillo Troncoso, Alberto del. Entre la criminalidad y el orden cívico: imágenes y representaciones de la niñez durante el Porfiriato. (*Hist. Mex.*, 48:2, oct./dic. 1998, p. 277–320, bibl., facsims., photo)

Fascinating study of how the perceived need to elevate the "Mexican race" during the Porfiriato led to concerns over the proper upbringing of children. Also discusses the role of photography in alerting readers to the menace of delinquency. Concludes with an articulation of the model Mexican child. Strongly recommended.

1282 Cerutti, Mario. Gran propiedad y organización de la agricultura en el norte de México: la experiencia de La Laguna, 1870–1920. (*Humanitas/Monterrey*, 26, 1999, p. 539–557, bibl., tables)

Case study of a Basque entrepreneur who arrived in northern Mexico in the 1870s and became one of the largest *hacendados* in the La Laguna area. Insists that merchant investment by immigrant Spaniards, rather than demographic growth, created the region's wealth.

1283 Chaoul Pereyra, María Eugenia. La instrucción municipal, un espejo de la ciudad: la gestión educativa del Ayuntamiento de México, 1867–1896. (*Anu. Estud. Urbanos*, 1999, p. 180–214, bibl., graphs, maps, tables)

Examines public education supported by the Ayuntamiento prior to the beginning of its takeover by the national government in 1896. Contends that the municipal council had offered a variety of course options, including night schools to provide literacy classes for adults. Includes helpful charts and maps for social historians.

1284 Chowning, Margaret. Wealth and power in provincial Mexico: Michoacán from the late colony to the Revolution. Stanford, Calif.: Stanford Univ. Press, 1999. 477 p.: bibl., ill., index, maps.

Highly original work places the growth of an important state in the national and, at the same time, familial environment. Argues that the Reform must be seen in the context of a general economic upturn begun in the 1840s.

1285 Colección documental sobre la independencia mexicana. Compilación de Eric Van Young. Traducción de Roberto de la Torre Salcedo. México: Univ. Iberoamericana, 1998. 386 p.: ill., indices.

Superb guide to a collection of documents from 1746–1823 given to Univ. Ibero americana by philanthropist Manuel Arango Arías. Volume contains many papers relating to Miguel Hidalgo and family, as well as a large group devoted to independence. Excellent indices make this work a model of its kind. Recommended.

1286 Connaughton, Brian F. Conjuring the body politic from the *corpus mysticum:* the post-independent pursuit of public opinion in Mexico, 1821–1854. (*Americas/Franciscans,* 55:3, Jan. 1999, p. 459–479)

Fascinating analysis of the Mexican transformation of the medieval concept of the *corpus mysticum* into a rationale and

metaphor of Mexican independence and subsequent political events. Must reading for scholars of the 19th century.

1287 Connolly, Priscilla. El contratista de Don Porfirio: obras públicas, deuda y desarrollo desigual. México: El Colegio de Michoacán; Univ. Autónoma Metropolitana-Azcapotzalco; Fondo de Cultura Económica, 1997. 423 p., 32 p. of plates: bibl., ill., maps. (Sección de obras de historia)

Long overdue biography of Lord Cowdray (Weetman Pearson), Porfirio Díaz's preferred agent for public works projects. Likely to be the seminal work on the physical manifestations of Porfirian progress. Highly recommended. See also item **1335.**

1288 Coppel, Ernesto. El camino a la Tierra Prometida. Mazatlán, Mexico: s.n., 1998. 179 p.

Loving account of how a Jewish family from Poland, whose progenitor Isaac Coppel Kolschezki came to settle in Mazatlán in 1855, became part of that city's Christian elite. Thanks to the business acumen of successive generations, their shoe and luggage factory and real estate enterprises established the family's considerable fortune. Valuable contribution to the debate on immigration.

1289 Covarrubias, José Enrique. Visión extranjera de México, 1840–1867. v. 1, El estudio de las costumbres y de la situación social: Mühlenpfordt, Sartorius, Fossey, Domenech, Biart y Zamacois. México: UNAM; Instituto de Investigaciones Doctor José María Luis Mora, 1998. 1 v.: bibl. (Serie Historia moderna y contemporánea; 31)

Vol. 1 of projected two-volume set records observations of six foreign travelers concerning Mexican society during one of the most obscure periods of Mexican history. Analyses are interesting, but work lacks commentary about the travelers' lives and education prior to arrival in Mexico. Until such data becomes available, their writings have limited value as primary sources.

1290 Cruz Barney, Oscar. El régimen jurídico del corso marítimo: el mundo indiano y el México del siglo XIX. México: UNAM, 1997. 568 p.: appendix, bibl. (Serie C—Estudios históricos; 64)

Study of "corsairs," or ships that were licensed by their government to defend shipping and pursue pirates. Explains laws regulating such activities up to the 19th century, when an independent Mexico issued them to protect its commerce. Substantial appendix follows the laws on this activity beginning in the 16th century. Important work for historians studying trade.

1291 Cuchí Espada, Víctor. La ciudad de México y la Compañía Telefónica Mexicana: la construcción de la red telefónica, 1881–1902. (*Anu. Estud. Urbanos*, 1999, p. 118–158, bibl., maps, tables)

Shows the difficulties in erecting a telephone system in Mexico City, given the problems of shifting subsoil and the determination that the system fill the needs of only those sufficiently well off to subscribe. Provides invaluable material for scholars looking at the social structure of Mexico City during the Belle Epoque. Highly recommended.

1292 Deaton, Dawn Fogle. The decade of revolt: peasant rebellion in Jalisco, Mexico, 1855–1864. (*in* Liberals, the Church, and Indian peasants: corporate lands and the challenge of reform in nineteenth-century Spanish America. Edited by Robert H. Jackson. Albuquerque: Univ. of New Mexico Press, 1997, p. 37–64, graphs)

Excellent reminder of the instability of the country's most important area after Mexico City during a crucial period. Argues against the simple explanation of peasant revolt as a reaction against land expropriation, and looks to other factors that complicated the picture such as drought and a cholera epidemic in 1850s and a typhoid epidemic in the early 1860s.

1293 Demard, Jean Christophe. Río Nautla: étapes de l'intégration d'une communauté française au Mexique, 1833–1926. Prez-sur-Marne, France: D. Guéniot, 1999. 351 p.: bibl., ill., maps.

Fascinating in-depth study from *the* historian of French immigration to Mexico. Using documentation drawn almost exclusively from French sources, author details a group that came to Mexico as early as 1826 and settled in Jicaltepec, Veracruz, because of its excellent location on the Nautla River. Recommended.

Destino México: un estudio de las migraciones asiáticas a México, siglos XIX y XX . See item **1432.**

1294 Di Tella, Torcuato S. National popular politics in early independent Mexico, 1820–1847. Albuquerque: Univ. of New Mexico Press, 1996. 383 p.: bibl., index.

Author, an Argentine sociologist, focuses on the period before 1832. Less here on popular politics and more on inter-governmental and political squabbling. Good section on social stratification.

1295 Don Porfirio presidente—, nunca omnipotente: hallazgos, reflexiones y debates, 1876–1911. Compilación de Romana Falcón y Raymundus Thomas Joseph Buve. México: Univ. Iberoamericana, Depto. de Historia, 1998. 572 p.: bibl. (El pasado del presente)

Excellent compilation of 18 essays devoted to the Porfiriato. Especially recommended are Marichal on the 1888 debt conversion, Buve on conflict in the countryside, and Leticia Reina on the autonomy of indigenous villages. Major contribution to a reevaluation of a complex period.

1296 España y el Imperio de Maximiliano: finanzas, diplomacia, cultura e inmigración. Recopilación de Clara Eugenia Lida. Presentación de Andrés Lira. México: Colegio de México, Centro de Estudios Históricos, 1999. 362 p.: bibl., index, maps.

Thorough study of Spain's role in Mexican affairs during the 1860s, with excellent essays on the debt, diplomacy, the Spanish view of Mexican culture as seen in France, and the identity of the Spanish community in Mexico. Also includes collection of short biographies of the leading players. Excellent contribution.

1297 Ferrocarriles y vida económica en México, 1850–1950: del surgimiento tardío al decaimiento precoz. Coordinación de Sandra Kuntz Ficker y Paolo Riguzzi. México: El Colegio Mexiquense; Ferrocarriles Nacionales de México; Univ. Autónoma Metropolitana Xochimilco, 1996. 383 p.: bibl., ill.

Six essays approach the history of Mexican railroads from the perspective of the "new economic history." See especially Soto's essays on the relationship between industry and railroads in Monterrey, and Grunstein Dickter on the difference in approach between the *científicos* and the Carrancistas; however, all essays are important and well done. Recommended. See also items **1357** and **1313**.

1298 Figueroa Esquer, Raúl. Entre la intervención oculta y la neutralidad estricta: España ante la guerra entre México y Estados Unidos, 1845–1848. México: ITAM; Secretaría de Relaciones Exteriores, 1999. 574 p.: bibl., index.

Well-researched study of diplomacy during the Mexican-American War contains analyses that go far beyond the scope indicated in the title. Points out differences between Spanish ministers Angel Calderón de la Barca (husband of Fanny) and his successor, Salvador Bermúdez de Castro. Must reading for scholars seeking to understand that crucially important war.

1299 Forte, Riccardo. Liberalismo y sistema electoral a finales del siglo XIX: análisis comparativo de los casos mexicano y argentino. (*Metapolítica/México*, 2:5, enero/marzo 1998, p. 39–68)

Pioneering effort to understand Mexico (and Argentina) in a Hemispheric context. Looking at voting, political centralization, economic modernization, and relation between the immigrant and national population, author concludes, not surprisingly, that Argentina's mass immigration rather than Mexico's mestizo and indigenous poor was the leading factor in the differences between the two systems. However, work does not discuss key element: the political education the newcomers brought with them.

1300 Fowler, Will. Tornel and Santa Anna: the writer and the caudillo, Mexico, 1795–1853. Westport, Conn.: Greenwood Press, 2000. 308 p.: bibl., index. (Contributions in Latin American studies, 1054–6790; 14)

Makes persuasive case that José María Tornel y Mendívil, spin-doctor for Antonio López de Santa Anna, was an important figure in his own right, both as a politician and a writer. Emphasizes the "great man" school of history, but forces the reader to conclude that the first political generation of independent Mexico boasted a substantial crew of extraordinary personalities.

1301 Fowler-Salamini, Heather. The boom in regional studies of the Mexican revolution: where is it leading? (*LARR*, 28:2, 1993, p. 175–190)

Good survey and analysis of seven works published in the 1980s and early 1990s. Demonstrates that regional studies of the Revolution are underscoring the importance of peasant/popular uprisings, while adopting new theoretical approaches gleaned from social history and ethnography.

1302 French, William E. Imagining and the cultural history of nineteenth-century Mexico. (*HAHR*, 79:2, May 1999, p. 249–267)

Looks at a number of recent studies to explain how interpretations of cultural and gender identity formations contribute to understanding Mexican history. As such, provides a brief, but useful survey of what has been done thus far. Leaves open the question of whether a national state can promote individual identity, particularly in struggles with stronger powers.

1303 Frías Sarmiento, Eduardo. Historia del alumbrado eléctrico en Culiacán, 1895–1920. Culiacán, Mexico: Dirección de Investigación y Fomento de Cultura Regional, H. Ayuntamiento de Culiacán, 1999. 114 p.: bibl., facsims. (Col. Los premios)

One of the first studies of electricity in a Mexican state. Author writes from an economics perspective; there is no attempt to look at this facet of modernization from a social standpoint.

1304 García Gutiérrez, Blanca Estela. La cosmovisión conservadora en México a mediados del siglo XIX: una retrospectiva a través de la prensa. (*Iztapalapa/México*, 18:43, enero/junio 1998, p. 27–50, bibl., facsims.)

In-depth look at the development of a conservative ideology from the appearance of *El Tiempo* to the beginnings of *El Universal*. Drawing on theories of Benedict Anderson, argues that the conservatives did not envision a return to a glorious past but rather a "resignification" of it in a climate of "liberal" scorn.

1305 García Roldán, María del Mar. Expedientes en el A.G.I. sobre las misiones de Sonora y Sinaloa a comienzos del siglo XIX. (*Arch. Ibero-Am.*, 57:225/226, enero/dic. 1997, p. 107–126, tables)

Helpful guide to information concerning Franciscan missions in Sonora and Sinaloa contained in documents preserved in the Archivo General de Indias for that order's activity in Jalisco and Querétaro. Lists some of the materials found there, particularly concerning indigenous peoples and their conversion.

Gómez Serrano, Jesús. José Guadalupe Posada: testigo y crítico de su tiempo; Aguascalientes, 1866–1876. See item **156.**

1306 Güemez Pineda, Arturo. Comunidades indígenas rebeldes y colonización en Yucatán: la paradójica solución a un proyecto criollo. (*Relaciones/Zamora*, 69, invierno 1997, p. 163–195, maps, photo, table)

Shows how Yucatecan creoles, much like the Spaniards and Mexicans living in the northernmost fringes of the Provincias Internas, planned for colonization of the area north of the Río Hondo in Belize as a means of checking British expansion. Because the schemes failed, the area became a "refugee zone," particularly during the Caste War. This outcome paradoxically resulted in slowing British colonization of more of the area.

1307 Hacienda y política: las finanzas públicas y los grupos de poder en la primera República Federal Mexicana. Edición de José Antonio Serrano Ortega y Luis Jáuregui. Zamora, Mexico: El Colegio de Michoacán; México: Instituto Mora, 1998. 369 p.: bibl., ill. (Col. Memorias)

Twelve new essays on public finance resulting from a seminar held at the Colegio de Michoacán. Fine introductory essay on the state of the field by the co-editors. Something here for everyone, from a look at the struggle over revenues collected by the tobacco monopoly (José Antonio Serrano Ortega) to the maintenance of income in the northern state of Sonora, from colony to republic (Saúl Jerónimo Romero).

1308 Illades, Carlos. Presencia española en la Revolución Mexicana, 1910–1915. México: Facultad de Filosofía y Letras, UNAM; Instituto de Investigaciones Dr. José María Luis Mora, 1991. 182 p.: bibl., ill.

Highlights the experiences of propertied Spaniards in Mexico from the Porfiriato to the Revolution. Discusses diplomatic and economic relations between Spain and Mexico, Spanish migration during the nineteenth century, anti-Spanish xenophobia, and the response of Spaniards and the Spanish government to revolutionary events. Based on Mexican archival sources.

1309 Illades, Carlos. Los trabajadores y la República: el Gran Círculo de Obreros de México en las fiestas cívicas. (*JILAS/Bundoora*, 5:1, July 1999, p. 1–14)

Fascinating exploration of how a workers' organization developed its own secular festivals and adopted its own heroes, namely Juárez and Zaragoza. The Gran Círculo's venture into this public sphere came to be emulated by both succeeding labor movements and the Mexican state.

1310 Jiménez P., Blanca M. and Samuel Villela. Los Salmerón: un siglo de fotografía en Guerrero. México: Instituto Nacional de Antropología e Historia, 1998. 204 p.: bibl., photos (Obra diversa)

Combines family history with that of photography in an understudied state beginning in 1890. Of special note are the pictures Armando Salmerón took of the Revolution in the south, including a magnificent Zapata (March 1914).

Jiménez Pelayo, Agueda. Santa Rosalía y Ayutla: vida cotidiana y economía, 1780–1925. See item **1064.**

1311 Johns, Michael. The city of Mexico in the age of Díaz. Austin: Univ. of Texas Press, 1997. 142 p., 16 p. of plates: bibl., ill., index, maps.

Strange anti-Porfirista depiction of social conditions in the city without reference to major actors such as Weetman Pierson or to other major cities during the same era. Offers only the "official history," demonstrating Díaz's lack of concern for everyone except his cronies.

1312 Knowlton, Robert J. El ejido mexicano en el siglo XIX. (*Hist. Mex.*, 48:1, julio/sept. 1998, p. 71–96, bibl.)

Excellent survey of history and definition of *ejido* in Mexico. Shows that *ejido* meant different things in Spain and Mexico and that different regimes understood it differently, as well. Curiously, the author shows that even during the Revolution, breaking up *ejidos* continued. Highly recommended for use with graduate students.

1313 Kuntz Ficker, Sandra. Empresa extranjera y mercado interno: el Ferrocarril Central Mexicano, 1880–1907. México:

Colegio de México, 1995. 391 p.: bibl., ill., index.

Extensive landmark study of Mexico's most important railroad line from its inception to its takeover by the Mexican government. Includes massive statistical studies of the railroad's effect on agricultural and mineral production. Concludes that the railroad could modernize Mexico only to the extent that the rest of society permitted. See also items **1357** and **1297**.

1314 Kuntz Ficker, Sandra. Mercado interno y vinculación con el exterior: el papel de los ferrocarriles en la economía del porfiriato. (*Hist. Mex.*, 45:1, julio/sept. 1995, p. 39–66, bibl., map, tables)

Analysis of cargo statistics for Mexico's main railroad companies. Challenges John Coatsworth's scholarship by arguing that railroads built during the Profiriato were not solely intended to link Mexico with outside markets. Railroads also contributed to Mexico's own growth and internal development.

1315 Landavazo, Marco Antonio. La urbanización demográfica: en el noreste mexicano, siglo XIX. (*Anu. Espacios Urbanos*, 1997, p. 157–179, bibl., maps, tables)

Based mostly on published sources, author concentrates on secondary cities, some of which had been *cajas reales* during the colonial period. Study does not take into account the 1848 loss of the far northern territory, nor does it consider the continuation or severing of economic ties regardless of the change of sovereignty.

1316 Lapointe, Marie. La política indigenista de Maximiliano en Yucatán. (*Saastun/Mérida*, 3, dic. 1997, p. 47–66, map, photo)

Focusing on the activities of Imperial Commissioner José Salazar Illaregui in Mérida, author throws doubt on the belief that the indigenous people supported the Austrian-born Emperor. Although the Empire decreed some progressive laws for indigenous people nation-wide, those statutes never were published in Mérida because of pressure from landlords, on one hand, and rebellious Maya still active in the Caste War, on the other.

1317 Liehr, Reinhard and **Mariano E. Torres Bautista.** Las *free-standing companies* británicas en el México del Porfiriato, 1884–

1911. (*Hist. Mex.*, 47:3, enero/marzo 1998, p. 605–653, bibl., graphs, map, table)

Authors add a new element to the mix of foreign investment during the Porfiriato: the 154 free-standing British companies (companies registered on the London stock exchange but run mostly in the country of operation) doing business in Mexico between 1884–1910. These companies bought mines, land, and even other firms to sell in Great Britain. Confirms Tischendorf's statistics (see *HLAS 24:3583* and *HLAS 26:685*). Clear stage between 1884–92 (top 1890–92); decline 1898–1900. Reaugmented in 1901, reaching its height in 1907. Also challenges Katz's view that British investment went only to the center and south (*The Cambridge history of Latin America*, v. 5, New York: Cambridge Univ. Press, 1968, p. 3–78).

1318 Ludlow, Leonor. La disputa financiera por el Imperio de Maximiliano y los proyectos de fundación de instituciones de crédito, 1863–1867. (*Hist. Mex.*, 47:4, abril/junio 1998, p. 765–805, bibl., tables)

Investigates the founding of Mexico's first bank and notes that British and French interests gave four bank projects, including a bank of emission, to the Regency and the Emperor. Links projects to the French ministry of the treasury and to colonial plans for Argentina, Brazil, Chile, and Peru. Provides a list of loans by commercial banking firms to mining and textile mills and their involvement in internal debt and diplomatic conventions.

1319 Martínez Rojas, María de la Luz. Relaciones iglesia-Estado en los gobiernos de Madero y Carranza. (*J. Hist. Occidente*, 13, 1990, p. 199–215, bibl.)

Establishment of the Partido Católico Nacional at the end of the Porfiriato set the stage for good relations during the Madero and Huerta administrations. Considering the Church to be an ally of Huerta, Carranza was more combative, but ultimately chose a conciliatory stance.

1320 Massé Zendejas, Patricia. Simulacro y elegancia en tarjetas de vista: fotografías de Cruces y Campa. México: Instituto Nacional de Antropología e Historia, 1998. 136 p.: bibl., photos. (Col. Alquima)

One of a series of books on 19th-century Mexican photography. Volume looks at photographs made by the commercial house of Cruces y Campa for calling cards. Collection includes even the calling card of Gen. Porfirio Díaz. Important work for social history.

1321 Masson, René. René Masson dans *Le trait d'union*: journal français universel. Préface de Thomas Calvo. Sélection et prologue de Françoise Dasques. México: UNAM, Instituto de Investigaciones Bibliográficas; Centre français d'études mexicaines et centraméricaines, 1998. 321 p.: bibl. (Historia)

First-ever collection of articles from this prominent liberal newspaper that circulated in Mexico City from 1849–74. Masson often has been mentioned by other historians, Jacqueline Covo in particular, but never has been showcased so prominently before. Volume would have been greatly improved had the selections been translated into Spanish.

1322 Memorias e informes de jefes políticos y autoridades del régimen porfirista, 1883–1911: Estado de Veracruz. Coordinación de Soledad García Morales y José Velasco Toro; Colaboracíon de Francisca Lilí Canales. Veracruz, Mexico: Univ. Veracruzana, 1997. 6 v.: maps

Fills an important gap in the understanding of how Porfirians centralized an important state. It is hoped that the project will continue until the period is fully covered, since few 20th-century documents appear here.

1323 Méndez Reyes, Salvador. El hispanoamericanismo de Lucas Alamán, 1823–1853. Toluca, Mexico: Univ. Autónoma del Estado de México, 1996. 311 p.: bibl.

Interesting and welcome summary of Alamán's writings on the rest of Latin America. Puts Alamán in his true context as a statesman as well as a conservative politician.

1324 Mexico. Comisión Pesquisidora de la Frontera del Norte. En manos de los bárbaros. Recopilación de Cuauhtémoc Velasco Avila. México: Breve Fondo Editorial, 1996. 158 p. (Acervo)

Rare look at the other side of the "noble Indian" depicted in Mexican official history. These tales of Mexicans held in captivity among the indigenous peoples indicate that tribes in Nuevo México, for whatever

reasons, did not capture *norteamericanos*. These accounts beg for comparison with those of the US and Argentina during the same time period.

Meyer, Jean A. Religión y nacionalismo. See item **5092.**

1325 La moneda en México, 1750–1920. Coordinación de José Antonio Bátiz Vázques y José Enrique Covarrubias. México: Instituto Mora; El Colegio de Michoacán; El Colegio de México; Instituto de Investigaciones Históricas-UNAM, 1998. 234 p.: bibl., ill. (Lecturas de historia económica mexicana)

Title dates notwithstanding, collection concentrates on the 19th century. Includes two interesting essays on the troublesome *moneda de cobre*, three on provincial mints, and one on the use of paper money. Invaluable for both economic and social historians.

1326 Morales, Francisco. Los Franciscanos ante los retos del siglo XIX mexicano. (*Arch. Ibero-Am.*, 57:225/226, enero/dic. 1997, p. 781–807, graphs, tables)

Indicates that the secularization of Franciscans should not be considered as stemming from an invitation for them to leave their order, but rather as a response to the "vida claustral" of the period. Many of these religious people simply became priests in parishes under the authority of the local bishop. Nevertheless, by 1856 there were 388 Franciscans in 69 convents, and another 222 living in six convents and four missions.

Moreno García, Heriberto. Haciendas de tierra y agua en la antigua Cienega de Chapala. See item **1070.**

1327 Moreno García, Heriberto. Implementos y herramientas agrícolas en el norte de Michoacán, 1826–1910. (*Relaciones/Zamora*, 59, verano 1994, p. 83–111)

Uses hacienda inventories to survey technological development in Michoacán's agricultural sector.

1328 Nelen, Yvette. De illustere heren van San Pablo: lokaal bestuur in negentiende-eeuws Mexico; Tlaxcala, 1823–1880 [The illustrious gentlemen of San Pablo: local government in nineteenth-century Mexico; Tlaxcala, 1823–1880]. Leiden, The Netherlands: Onderzoekschool CNWS, School voor Aziatische, Afrikaanse en Amerindiaanse

Studies, Univ. Leiden, 1999. 346 p.: maps. (CNWS publications, 0925–3084)

Dissertation on the development of the *ayuntamiento* of San Pablo Apetatitlán. Pt. 1 studies the functioning of the *ayuntamiento* in the 19th century, and the background and careers of local officials. Pt. 2, describes chronologically the *ayuntamiento's* internal and external policies. The author argues that this study challenges the idea that Mexico was ungovernable in the 19th century. Includes a four-page summary in English. [R. Hoefte]

1329 Pacheco, Carlos and **Manuel Sánchez Facio.** La controversia acerca de la política de colonización en Baja California. Prólogo de Paolo Riguzzi. Mexicali, Mexico: SEP; Univ. Autónoma de Baja California, 1997. 334 p.: bibl., ill., index. (Col. Baja California, nuestra historia; 12)

Documental study of Mexican plans to prepare Baja California for colonization in an environment still characterized by mistrust and fear following the loss of Texas, the war with the US, and the French intervention. Idea concocted by Secretario de Fomento Carlos Pacheco and assistant Sánchez Facio was to use British rather than US colonists. Essential work for understanding both the history of Baja California and Mexican immigration policy.

1330 Pacheco, José Emilio and **Andrés Reséndez.** Crónica del 47. México: Clío, 1997. 95 p.: bibl., ill. (some col.), maps.

Although easy to dismiss as another picture book published by Editorial Clío, Pacheco's luminous prose, coupled with Reséndez's research, make this a stand-out. For example, authors note that Mexico is to the US as Ireland to England and Poland to Russia. Should be translated for classroom use by English-language students.

1331 Pérez Montfort, Ricardo; Alberto del Castillo Yurrita; and **Pablo Piccato.** Hábitos, normas y escándalo: prensa, criminalidad y drogas durante el Porfiriato tardío. México: Ciesas; Plaza y Valdes Editores, 1997. 210 p., 16 p. of plates: bibl., ill.

Three excellent essays on the underside of Porfirian "progress." Pérez Montfort covers press coverage of crime; Piccato, the connections between alcoholism and illegality; and Castillo, the use of forbidden drugs including the popular "mariguana."

1332 Pérez-Rayón Elizundia, Nora. México 1900: la modernidad en el cambio de siglo; la mitificación de la ciencia. (*Estud. Hist. Mod. Contemp. Méx.*, 18, 1998, p. 41–62)

Study of the elite idea of modernity as publicized in two contemporary newspapers—*El Imparcial* and *Diario del Hogar*—and fought in the Catholic paper *El Tiempo*. Most interesting are the descriptions of future scientific progress represented by advances in sea travel, ballooning, and the emergence of the automobile, and by the new beliefs in the efficacy of statistics, mass vaccination, and even the electric cannon.

1333 Pérez Salas C., María Esther. Genealogía de *Los mexicanos pintados por sí mismos.* (*Hist. Mex.*, 48:2, oct./dic. 1998, p. 167–207, bibl., ill.)

Important article discusses the gestation of the fashion for depicting current life in a *costumbrista* style. Traces the technique back to the English in 1840–41, but does not discuss the period's romance with the "folk" that began with the German romantics in 1830s.

1334 Pérez Toledo, Sonia. Los hijos del trabajo: los artesanos de la ciudad de México, 1780–1853. México: Colegio de México, Centro de Estudios Históricos; Univ. Autónoma Metropolitana Iztapalapa, 1996. 300 p.: bibl., ill., index, maps.

Ground-breaking study of the artisans in Mexico during a significant period of transformation. Concludes that their numbers and their percentage of the population stayed about the same over time, but that their conditions of life and work changed significantly. Contains important statistical material useful to any scholar working on those years. Highly recommended.

1335 Perló Cohen, Manuel. El paradigma porfiriano: historia del desagüe del Valle de México. México: Programa Universitario de Estudios Sobre la Ciudad, Instituto de Investigaciones Sociales; M.A. Porrúa Grupo Editorial, 1999. 314 p.: bibl., ill., map. (Las ciencias sociales)

Well-documented examination of the struggle to construct drainage works in a perpetually-flooding capital. Sees Don Porfirio as Faust in the drama of Mexican development, and argues that the plan to drain Mexico City was just as much a bid for more political and social control as a response to scientific and salutary imperatives. Good companion to Connolly's work—see item **1287**.

1336 La política del disenso: la "polémica en torno al monarquismo"; México, 1848–1850, ... y las aporías del liberalismo. Compilación e introducción de Elías José Palti. México: Fondo de Cultura Económica, 1998. 471 p.: bibl. (Sección de obras de historia)

Interesting guide to Mexican political and legal thought in the mid-19th century. Compiler has grouped editorials from major newspapers into such themes as popular sovereignty and the innate problems of republicanism and federalism. Highly valuable for those studying the evolution of democracy in Mexico.

1337 Posada, José Guadalupe. Primicias litográficas del grabador José Guadalupe Posada: 134 ilustraciones. Selección y notas de Francisco Antúnez. 2. ed. Aguascalientes, Mexico: Depto. Editorial del Instituto Cultural de Aguascalientes, 1999. 1 v.: ill., facsims.

Collection of cartoons and religious images drawn by Mexico's most famous pre-revolutionary lithographic artist, José Guadalupe Posada. Reprint of a volume published in Aguascalientes in 1952 (see *HLAS 18:481*), the centenary of Posada's birth. Volume includes his work during his days at Aguascalientes and León beginning in 1871. Many of the images feature religious symbols (including holy cards for funerals) or wrappers for cigar boxes. Excellent addition to the copious studies of the famed engraver.

1338 Los pueblos indios y el parteaguas de la independencia de México. Coordinación de Manuel Ferrer Muñoz. México: Instituto de Investigaciones Jurídicas, Univ. Nacional Autónoma de México, 1999. 362 p.: bibl., indices. (Serie Doctrina jurídica; 2)

Nine essays concerning Mexico and its indigenous peoples during the 19th century, three written by Ferrer Muñoz. Interesting pieces include María Bono López on the inclusion of indigenous terms in dictionaries of the time.

1339 Quiñónez, Isabel. Mexicanos en su tinta: calendarios. México: Instituto Nacional de Antropología e Historia, 1994. 149 p.: bibl., ill. (Col. Obra diversa)

Wonderful key to the *mentalité* of 19th-century Mexicans. Traces the development of the *calendarios* and their publishers from their 17th-century origins to 1900, complete with explanations and political and social satire. A must for those who study the 19th century.

1340 Rodríguez Centeno, Mabel M. Borrachera y vagancia: argumentos sobre marginalidades económica y moral de los peones en los congresos argícolas mexicanos del cambio de siglo. (*Hist. Mex.*, 47:1, julio/sept. 1997, p. 103–131, bibl.)

Interesting look at how *hacendados* regarded their laborers, as revealed in agrarian congresses held in Tuxtla Gutiérrez in 1896 and in Tulancingo in 1904–05. Stresses the differences between "el México antiguo" and "el México moderno." Not surprisingly, the *hacendados* were concerned about bad habits that led to early deaths in the countryside and the loss of laborers. Curiously, while *hacendados* saw *peones* as passive in 1905, these "victims" would rise up in the Mexican Revolution just a few years later.

1341 Rodríguez García, Martha. La guerra entre bárbaros y civilizados: el exterminio del nómada en Coahuila, 1840–1880. Saltillo, Mexico: CESHAC, 1998. 288 p.: bibl., maps. (Expedientes itinerantes)

Long-overdue study of a taboo subject. Author places developments in the context of the debate over what is barbaric and what is civilized, and on how this debate impacted on the destruction of certain indigenous tribes, including the Kickapoo, whose solemn reception by Maximilian was immortalized in the beautiful painting "Vista de la Embajada de Indios Kickapoos al Emperador Maximiliano" by Jean-Adolphe Beaucé. Recommended.

1342 Rodríguez Kuri, Ariel. La experiencia olvidada: el ayuntamiento de México; política y gobierno, 1876–1912. México: El Colegio de México, Centro de Estudios Históricos; Univ. Autónoma Metropolitana-Azcapotzalco, 1996. 301 p.: bibl.

Work provides not only a thoughtful analysis of the *ayuntamiento* process but also an important examination of Mexico City's development during those years. Major contribution to the history of "la capital" is also of interest for the historiography of emerging interest in democratic principles in late *fin-de-siècle* Mexico.

1343 Román Alarcón, Rigoberto Arturo. Comerciantes extranjeros de Mazatlán, 1880–1910. Culiacán, Mexico: Colegio de Bachilleres del Estado de Sinaloa, 1998. 138 p. (Col. Crónicas; 17)

Through use of notary records, author has constructed a useful survey of foreign businesses in the most important port on Mexico's Pacific Coast. Very important for the study of the growth of capital and industry nationwide. Surprisingly, few of the merchants were *norteamericanos*.

1344 Rublúo, Luis. Retrato de Vicente García Torres. Pachuca, Mexico: Gobierno del Estado de Hidalgo, Sistema de Educación Pública de Hidalgo, Consejo Estatal para la Cultura y las Artes, 1997. 138 p.: bibl. (Col. Orígenes)

Although there is a street named for him in Coyoacán, Vicente García Torres, founder of the important 19th-century Mexico City newspaper *El Monitor Republicano*, is relatively little known. Contains a short biography and some new documentation indicating García Torres' bravery during the Mexican-American War and his friendship with most of the leading thinkers of the day.

1345 Rugeley, Terry. Rural political violence and the origins of the Caste War. (*Americas/Franciscans*, 53:4, April 1997, p. 469–496, maps)

Author argues that, beginning in 1800, competition over scarce resources led to numerous petitions by settlements to escape the tax and labor lists of other communities. Once the revolt of 1840 led by Santiago Imán had established Yucatán as independent, smaller units began their armed quest for more autonomy as well. The sustained fighting prepared residents for the Caste War that followed and continued even after the central conflict had been suppressed. Excellent contribution to Caste War literature. Article is part of entire journal issue devoted to the Caste War.

1346 Rugeley, Terry. Yucatán's Maya peasantry and the origins of the Caste War. Austin: Univ. of Texas Press, 1996. 243 p.: bibl., index, maps.

Social history that challenges earlier views of the Caste War. Examines the development of the social, political, and economic structure of the Yucatán during the first half of the 19th century and profiles four towns involved in the Caste War. Emphasizes the eroding status of Maya elites as a key to the revolt.

1347 Salinas Sandoval, María del Carmen. Política y sociedad en los municipios del Estado de México, 1825–1880. México: El Colegio Mexiquense, A.C., 1997. 340 p.: bibl., ill.

Large-scale analysis of voting and other aspects of democracy in an extremely important state. By focusing on *municipios*, author indicates how society on the local level changed after independence. Also devotes much attention to events surrounding the Revolution of Tuxtepec in 1876. Should be read in conjunction with Laurens Perry's work on political maneuvers during part of the same time period. For comment on Perry's work, see *HLAS 42:2229*.

1348 Salmerón Castro, Alicia. Política y redes sociales a fines del siglo XIX: el caso de Rosendo Pineda. (*TRACE/México*, 32, dic. 1997, p. 48–55, photo)

Approaches the Porfiriato from the perspective of the development of its political machine. Shows how Pineda, a native of Juchitán, Oaxaca, who arrived in the capital in 1884 at age 29, used his contacts back home to create a stronghold of Porfirian power.

1349 Salvucci, Richard J. Mexican national income in the era of independence, 1800–40. (*in* How Latin America fell behind: essays on the economic histories of Brazil and Mexico, 1800–1914. Stanford, Calif.: Stanford Univ. Press, 1997, p. 216–242, bibl., tables)

Authoritative look at the question of Mexico's failure to grow from the late-colonial period to the 1840s. Also contains an analysis of previously accepted figures for national income. A must read for any scholar of the period.

1350 Sánchez Andrés, Agustín. La crisis de 1898 en el horizonte y las relaciones hispano-mexicanas. (*Cuad. Hispanoam.*, 577/578, julio/agosto 1998, p. 45–58, bibl.)

Uses archival sources to show that, from 1895–97, Mexico and Spain had similar interests in keeping Cuba under Spain and away from the US, and in dampening the fires of revolution in the Caribbean. Also comments on the actions of the Spanish community in Mexico.

1351 Sánchez Silva, Carlos. Indios, comerciantes, y burocracia en la Oaxaca poscolonial, 1786–1860. Oaxaca, Mexico: Instituto Oaxaqueño de las Culturas; Fondo Estatal para la Cultura y las Artes; Univ. Autónoma Benito Juárez de Oaxaca, 1998. 235 p.: bibl. (Serie Dishá. Col. Historia)

Archival study builds on the work of William Taylor and others to indicate how Oaxaca fared in the transition from colony to republic. Emphasizes that rebellion was only one form of resistance as indigenous groups sought to keep others from their communities.

1352 Sano, Yoshikazu. Vida en México de trece náufragos japoneses, 1842. México: Artes Gráficas Panorama, 1998. 126 p.: ill. (some col.), col. maps.

Using Japanese sources, relates the story of 13 Japanese sailors who arrived in La Paz, Baja California Sur, on June 29, 1842, after having been rescued by Mexicans. Accompanied by glorious illustrations showing the Japanese understanding of what they had seen on Mexico's western coast from Cabo San Lucas down to Mazatlán.

1353 Schell, William, Jr. Money as commodity: Mexico's conversion to the Gold Standard, 1905. (*Mex. Stud.*, 12:1, Winter 1996, p. 67–89, graphs)

Important contribution for understanding the 1907–08 economic crisis that helped undermine the Porfirian regime. Shows that the purchase of Mexican silver pesos due to the conversion made Mexico more dependent on foreign capital markets and on US economic cycles. Also notes that most of Mexico's silver pesos were used in East Asia, among many other important findings. Highly recommended.

1354 Solares Robles, María Laura. El bandidaje en el Estado de México durante el primer gobierno de Mariano Riva Palacio, 1849–1852. (*Secuencia/México*, 45, sept./dic. 1999, p. 27–62, bibl., graphs, ill.)

In-depth look at the miscreants of the state of Mexico. Using data from the Archivo General de la Nación, author constructs statistical information for 1845 concerning the distribution of crimes among professions, ages, and married vs. unmarried men. No mention of that classic work of fiction *Los bandidos del Río Frío* by Riva Palacio's friend, Manuel Payno y Flores. For comment on Payno y Flores' work, see *HLAS 25:4311*.

1355 Solares Robles, María Laura. Una revolución pacífica: biografía política de Manuel Gómez Pedraza, 1789–1851. México: Instituto de Investigaciones Dr. José María Luis Mora; Acervo Diplomático de la Secretaría de Relaciones Exteriores; Querétaro, Mexico: Consejo Estatal para la Cultura y las Artes del Gobierno del Estado de Querétaro, 1996. 310 p.: bibl., port.

Long overdue biography of the "always bridesmaid" of the early republic. Author says much more about the political maneuvers of the period, concentrating on personalities of the Mexican elite. Somewhat useful.

1356 Speckman Guerra, Elisa. Ideas y representaciones en torno al castigo: un acercamiento a la literatura popular mexicana de fines del siglo XIX. (*Haciendo Hist.*, 1:1, enero 1999, p. 6–15, ill., photos)

A Foucault-influenced look at how judicial punishment was depicted in the popular press. Although Mexican law forbade bodily mutilation in the cause of justice, popular drawings and *corridos* dwell on the physical punishments of incarceration, the last hours of the condemned, and the difficulties of burying the corpses in consecrated ground.

1357 Summerhill, William. Transport improvements and economic growth in Brazil and Mexico. (*in* How Latin America fell behind: essays on the economic histories of Brazil and Mexico, 1800–1914. Stanford, Calif.: Stanford Univ. Press, 1997, p. 93–117, bibl., tables)

Economic analysis of the railroad and its contribution to the growth of national economies. Contends that, at least for Brazil, the new mode of transportation actually lessened dependence on foreign economies. Rips into Kuntz Ficker's and Riguzzi's argument that railroads in Mexico were not positive developments since they did not foster a railroad industry by asserting that they had no such effect in the US either. Substantial contribution to the ongoing debate. For comment on Kuntz Ficker and Riguzzi's work, see item **1297**. See also item **1313**.

1358 Tenenbaum, Barbara A. Mexico, so close to the United States: unconventional views of the nineteenth century. (*LARR*, 30:1, 1995, p. 226–235)

Reviews eight works dealing primarily with 19th-century Mexico. Includes a compilation of documents on Nayarit covering the period from the early-19th century to 1940, and a regional history of Veracruz from the late Porfirian era to the 1960s.

1359 Tenorio Trillo, Mauricio. Mexico at the world's fairs: crafting a modern nation. Berkeley: Univ. of California Press, 1996. 373 p.: bibl., ill., index. (The new historicism; 35)

Cosmopolitan approach frames the issue within a more international setting than is common in works about a single Latin American country. Recommended.

1360 Thomson, Guy P.C. and David Gerald LaFrance. Patriotism, politics, and popular liberalism in nineteenth-century Mexico: Juan Francisco Lucas and the Puebla Sierra. Wilmington, Del.: Scholarly Resources, 1999. 420 p.: bibl., ill., index, maps.

Outstanding contribution to studies of popular liberalism. Constructs an in-depth portrait not only of Juan Francisco Lucas, but also of a coffee-growing region whose residents managed to maintain their way of life through their militant embrace of national liberalism.

1361 Tortolero, Alejandro. Les hommes et les ressources naturelles dans le bassin de Mexico: l'innovation technologique et son impact dans un milieu rural, Chalco, 1890–1925. (*Ann. hist. sci. soc.*, 52:5, sept./oct. 1997, p. 1085–1113, maps, tables)

Traces water problems of a well-known, but outlying part of Mexico City. Discusses the disputes over the Chalco, which included even how to characterize it (was it a "lake" or a "swamp?"). Article also valuable for relating how the use of technology by the powerful enabled them to get their way during the Porfirian period, to the extent that damage to the delicate ecological balance had become permanent even before the Zapatista revolt fought for land claims.

1362 Trujillo Bolio, Mario A. Operarios fabriles en el Valle de México, 1864–1884: espacio, trabajo, protesta y cultura obrera. México: Colegio de México; Centro de

Investigaciones y Estudios Superiores en Antropología Social, 1997. 385 p.: bibl., ill., index.

First major study to examine not only the nature of the working class in the Valley of Mexico, but also how workers lived. Concentrates on their organizations and also provides insights on popular culture. Confirms Haber's thesis that textile production proceeded despite political instability. Little discussion of the topic within an evolutionary historical context.

1363 Vanderwood, Paul J. The power of God against the guns of government: religious upheaval in Mexico at the turn of the nineteenth century. Stanford, Calif.: Stanford University Press, 1998. 409 p.: bibl., ill., index, maps.

Writing in a narrative style reminiscent of Womack's *Zapata and the Mexican Revolution* (see *HLAS 32:1737*), author explains a series of 1890s uprisings in Tomóchic, in the border state of Chihuahua, against the Porfirians' determination to dictate who would control the land and the future. Pushed forward by the belief in folk saint Teresa Urrea, indigenous people and mestizos led by Cruz Chávez fought government troops to preserve their way of life. Surprisingly, author makes no mention of another such movement in Brazil occurring at the same time, which was immortalized first by Da Cunha and then by Vargas Llosa.

1364 Velasco, Jesús. La derrota despierta la conciencia: la prensa de la Ciudad de México ante el Tratado de Guadalupe Hidalgo en 1848. (*Estud. Filos. Hist. Let.*, 14:50/51, otoño/invierno 1997/98, p. 77–96, bibl.)

Minimal account of how the Mexico City press reacted to the Treaty of Guadalupe Hidalgo. Content presented seems to echo Charles Hale's original thesis in *Mexican Liberalism in the Age of Mora*, and does not identify consistently the self-interest of many of the actors involved. For comment on Hale's work, see *HLAS 36:2026*.

1365 Viajes de michoacanos al norte. Edición de Alvaro Ochoa Serrano. Morelia, Mexico: Instituto Michoacano de Cultura; Zamora, Mexico: Colegio de

Michoacán, 1998. 159 p.: bibl., ill., indices, maps. (Col. Testimonios)

Small volume contains excerpts from travel accounts dating from 1893–1926 by three men from Michoacán: Ramón Sánchez Muñiz, Salvador Sotelo Arévalo, and Isaac Gallegos Cervantes. Important corrective to the usual Mexican fascination with foreigners who visited, rather than with Mexicans who went abroad. Very important for students of Mexican economic development.

1366 Victoria, José Guadalupe; Beatriz Ruiz Gaytán; and Mario Pérez Torres. Tlatelolco en la historia de México. México: Secretaría de Relaciones Exteriores; Univ. Nacional Autónoma de México, 1994. 53 p.: bibl. (Cuadernos del acervo histórico diplomático)

Three essays explore the evolution of Tlatelolco as a cultural space. Focus is on colonial and 19th-century themes.

1367 Vida cotidiana: Ciudad de México, 1850–1910. Recopilación de Cristina Barros y Marco Buenrostro. México: Consejo Nacional para la Cultura y las Artes; Lotería Nacional para la Asistencia Pública; Univ. Nacional Autónoma de México; Fondo de Cultura Económica, 1996. 195 p.: bibl., ill. (Sección de obras de historia)

Excellent "picture book" includes a short introduction to newspaper articles and reproductions of advertisements for everything from public baths to dancing. Required reading for both scholars of Mexico City and social historians, and just the thing for classroom use.

1368 Villa Guerrero, Guadalupe. Riqueza en suelo eriazo: la industria guayulera y los conflictos interregionales de la elite norteña en México. (*Secuencia/México*, 46, enero/abril 2000, p. 93–120, bibl., graphs, ill., map, tables)

Important article on the little-studied agribusiness of rubber cultivation from San Luis Potosí north into Texas during first years of the 20th century. Author shows how investors, both Mexican and foreign, developed cultivation in an area previously devoted only to cotton. When the Madero family, the largest Mexican holder of rubber properties, launched the Revolution in 1910, the coalition fractured and the foreign investors went elsewhere. Recommended.

Vos, Jan de. Vivir en frontera: la experiencia de los indios de Chiapas. See item **603**.

1369 Weiner, Richard. Competing market discourses in Porfirian Mexico. (*Lat. Am. Perspect.*, 26:1, Jan. 1999, p. 44–64, bibl.)

Author analyzes statements about "the market" by the *científicos*, the Partido Liberal Mexicano (PLM), and the social Catholics. Curiously, the *científicos* had a state capitalist view of a market needing intervention by a government motivated by national concerns, whereas the PLM came to see the market as enslaving workers and the Social Catholics vilified it as the creator of social inequality and worker oppression.

1370 Wells, Allen. Henequen. (*in* The second conquest of Latin America: coffee, henequen, and oil during the export boom, 1850–1930. Austin: Institute of Latin American Studies, Univ. of Texas Press, 1998, p. 85–124, tables)

Definitive essay shows how the international price of henequen affected every aspect of life in Yucatán, and how henequen fitted into the web of international capitalism. Following the Mexican Revolution and World War I, sisal grown in East Africa and Java would spell the end of the international henequen trade.

Zorrilla, Luis G. Relaciones políticas, económicas y sociales de México con el extranjero. See *HLAS 57:4138*.

1371 Zubirán, Norma. La "guerra chica" en el Sotavento durante la intervención francesa. (*Estud. Hombre*, 9, 1999, p. 153–169, map)

Interesting look at the Gulf Coast south of Veracruz during the French intervention. Sketches the activities of a population determined not to surrender to the invaders and which remained in liberal hands throughout the conflict. Speculates somewhat unconvincingly that this resistance was a factor in Napoleon III's decision to pull his troops out of the country.

REVOLUTION AND POST-REVOLUTION

Abramo Lauff, Marcelo and **Yolanda Barberena Villalobos.** El estadio: la prensa en México, 1870–1979. See item **1268**.

1372 **Abreu Ayala, Arturo E.** Madrazos en *el trópico.* Villahermosa, Mexico: A.E. Abreu Ayala, 1995. 212 p.: bibl., index.

Polemical account of contemporary politics in Tabasco. Focuses on the activities of the late governor Carlos Madrazo and his son Roberto. Praises both for challenging the centralism of the PRI system.

1373 **Aceves Lozano, Jorge E.** *et al.* Historia y testimonios orales. Coordinación de Cuauhtémoc Velasco. México: Instituto Nacional de Antropología e Historia, 1996. 209 p. (Col. Divulgación. Serie Historia)

Collection of papers presented at an oral history conference. Includes comments on state of oral history in Mexico, and on methodological approaches and problems. Also contains examples of the application of the oral history method.

1374 **Acosta Díaz, Vladimir.** La lucha agraria en Veracruz. v. 2-3. Xalapa, Mexico: Gobierno del Estado de Veracruz, 1992-1994. 2 v.: ill.

Final installments in survey of the struggle over agrarian reform in Veracruz. Focuses on state-level League of Agrarian Communities and its interaction with a succession of PRI governors. Covers the founding of the League in 1923 to the early 1990s.

1375 **Actores sociales en un proceso de transformación: Veracruz en los años veinte.** Coordinación de Manuel Reyna Muñoz. Xalapa, Mexico: Univ. Veracruzana, 1996. 246 p.: bibl.

Eight essays highlight the development of the labor movement in Veracruz. Also includes an essay on the occupation of this port city during the De la Huerta rebellion and an essay on attempts to create a new educational system based on revolutionary goals.

1376 **Aguascalientes (Mexico). Archivo General Municipal.** Archivo General Municipal: catálogo temático. v. 1, Acequias. Acueductos y canales. Aeropuertos. Aguas. Fuentes y regadíos. Agricultura. Alumbrado público y asociaciones. Aguascalientes, Mexico: Archivo General Municipal, 1996. 1 v.: ill.

Basic list of documents with brief explanation of the themes they cover.

1377 **Alperóvich, M.S.** La revolución mexicana en la interpretación soviética del período de la *guerra fría.* (*Hist. Mex.*, 44:4, abril/junio 1995, p. 677–690, bibl.)

Survey and analysis of Soviet historiography. Demonstrates the degree to which Soviet Cold-War interpretations of the Revolution were ideology-bound and lacking in academic rigor.

1378 **Alvarado, Salvador.** Mi actuación revolucionaria en Yucatán. México?: S.D.N., 1990. 210 p. (Biblioteca del oficial mexicano; 6)

Well-known general discusses and defends the revolutionary program he introduced in the Yucatan in the face of local opposition. First published in 1918.

1379 **Alvarado Mendoza, Arturo.** El portesgilismo en Tamaulipas: estudio sobre la constitución de la autoridad pública en el México posrevolucionario. México: Colegio de México, Centro de Estudios Sociológicos, 1992. 390 p., 16 p. of plates: bibl., ill., maps.

Detailed analysis of the political activities of Emilio Portes Gil in his native state during the 1920s. Demonstrates the extent to which Mexico's post-revolutionary political system (based on corporatism and presidentialism) was a product of the local consolidation of power.

1380 **Anaya Merchant, Luis.** La construcción de la memoria y la revisión de la Revolución. (*Hist. Mex.*, 44:4, abril/junio 1995, p. 525–536, bibl.)

Examination of the major ideas advanced by three historians in their studies of the Mexican Revolution: Adolfo Gilly (*La revolución interrumpida*, see HLAS 36:2119 and HLAS 56:1479), Arnaldo Córdova (*La ideología de la revolución mexicana*, see HLAS 36:2104), and Ramón Eduardo Ruíz (*México: la gran rebelión*, see HLAS 46:2276).

1381 **Angeles Contreras, Jesús.** Jesús Silva Espinosa: primer gobernador maderista del Estado de Hidalgo. Pachuca, Mexico: Presidencia Municipal de Pachuca, Hgo., 1994. 78 p.: ill.

Brief biography of the provisional governor of Hidalgo appointed by Madero in November 1910. Silva spent almost as much time in jail (November 1910-May

1911) as in the governorship (May 1911-November 1911). Little insight into Silva's activities as governor other than his feud with Madero over local political appointments which led to his forced resignation.

Azuela, Luz Fernanda and **Rafael Guevara Fefer.** La ciencia en México en el siglo XIX: una proximación historiográfica. See item **1275.**

1382 Bandera al viento: imágenes de la diplomacia mexicana, 1930–1952. México: Secretaría de Relaciones Exteriores, 1996. 191 p.: bibl., ill., index.
Photographic history of Mexican diplomacy in the decades after World War I.

1383 Barradas, Celestino. Historia de la Iglesia en Veracruz. v. 3. Xalapa, Mexico: Ediciones San José, 1990? 1 v.: bibl., ill.
Concludes multi-volume work on the Church in Veracruz, covering the period from 1920–89. For a review of vol. 2, see *HLAS 56:1414.*

1384 Barragán, Juan and **Mario Cerutti.** Juan F. Brittingham y la industria en México, 1859–1940. Monterrey, Mexico: Urbis Internacional, 1993. 199 p.: bibl., ill.
Extensively illustrated examination of the role played by North American entrepreneur John Brittingham in the modernization and industrialization of northern Mexico, especially Monterrey. Drawing on personal and political contacts, Brittingham prospered in both the Porfirian and post-Revolutionary periods, playing a leading role in the banking, glass, and cement industries and helping to lay the foundations for two of Mexico's current industrial giants, CEMEX and VITRO.

1385 Barragán López, Esteban. La *rancherada* en México: sociedades en movimiento, anónimas y de capital variable. *(Relaciones/Zamora,* 69, invierno 1997, p. 121–162, bibl., ill., maps, photo)
Historical exploration of Mexico's rancheros and ranchero communities. Explores the origins and characteristics of rancheros and examines the cultural representations of this sector of Mexican society.

1386 Bartolomé, Miguel Alberto. Indians and Afro-Mexicans at the end of the century. (*in* Changing structure of Mexico: political, social, and economic prospects. Ar-

monk, N.Y.: M.E. Sharpe, 1996, p. 299–306, bibl.)
Brief overview of the problem of defining racial and ethnic categories. Focus is on indigenous groups, especially the impact of government programs on them.

1387 Bastian, Jean Pierre. Una ausencia notoria: la francmasonería en la historiografía mexicanista. (*Hist. Mex.,* 44:3, enero/marzo 1995, p. 439–460, bibl.)
Survey of literature on the 19th century, the Porfiriato, and the Revolution. Suggests ways to better incorporate the theme of freemansory into Mexican history.

1388 Bazant, Jan. Historia de la deuda exterior de México, 1823–1946. Prólogo de Antonio Ortiz Mena. 3. ed. México: Colegio de México, 1995. 282 p.: bibl., index. (Nueva serie; 3)
Third edition of a work first published in 1968 (see *HLAS 31:3235.*) Explores the elaboration of Mexico's external debt after independence and concludes with a discussion of the 1946 agreements that finally settled Mexico's 19th-century debt.

Beato, Guillermo. Grupos sociales dominantes: México y Argentina, siglos XIX-XX. See item **2819.**

1389 Becker, Marjorie. Setting the Virgin on fire: Lázaro Cárdenas, Michoacán peasants, and the redemption of the Mexican Revolution. Berkeley: Univ. of California Press, 1995. 188 p.: bibl., index, maps.
Provides convincing revision of the "myth of secular redemption" surrounding Lázaro Cárdenas and his program of land distribution to the campesinos. Operating on a "stripped-down image of land-hungry peasants," Cárdenas and his supporters underestimated the difficulty of gaining peasant allegiance to the post-revolutionary government and initially failed to understand that they were confronting a cultural as well as an economic problem as they tried to extend revolutionary hegemony.

1390 Bernal Tavares, Luis. Vicente Lombardo Toledano y Miguel Alemán: una bifurcación en la revolución mexicana. México: Facultad de Filosofía y Letras, UNAM; Centro de Estudios e Investigación para el Desarrollo Social, 1994. 199 p.: bibl.

Traces the political careers of two "fundamental figures" of the Revolution, both of whom thought that Mexico's future lay in modernization through industrialization. Although Lombardo supported Alemán for the presidency in 1946, the "bifurcation" soon took place as each had a different vision of the proper road to modernization.

1391 Between two worlds: Mexican immigrants in the United States. Edited by David G. Gutiérrez. Wilmington, Del.: Scholarly Resources, 1996. 271 p.: bibl. (Jaguar books on Latin America; 15)

Collection of 11 essays dealing with both the historical and contemporary aspects of Mexican emigration to the United States. Work is divided into three parts: "Historical Antecedents," "Political and Cultural Contestation," and "Contemporary Perspectives." Good introduction for each entry.

1392 Blanco, Mónica Alejandra. Revolución y contienda política en Guanajuato, 1908–1913. México: Colegio de México, Centro de Estudios Históricos; Univ. Nacional Autónoma de México, Facultad de Economía, 1995. 226 p.: bibl., index, maps.

Lamenting the lack of historical studies on Guanajuato in the early stages of the Revolution, the author provides an excellent study of Maderista politics at the state and local levels. The focus is on political action and elections, including contests for the governorship in 1911 and for the national congress in 1912. Military action was not important in the state in making the transition to the Madero era, but there were a number of local revolts against Madero.

1393 Bloch, Avital H. and Servando Ortoll. ¡Viva México! ¡Mueran los yanquis!: the Guadalajara riots of 1910. (*in* Riots in the cities: popular politics and the urban poor in Latin America, 1765–1910. Wilmington, Del.: Scholarly Resources Inc., 1996, p. 195–223, facsims.)

Examination of two nights of large-scale rioting on Nov. 10–11, 1910. Led by middle-class elements, especially students, the riots were not connected to the Revolution that would soon begin but rather reflected the growing anti-Americanism and anti-Protestant feeling of the late Porfiriato.

1394 Bonnett Vélez, Diana. Los informes de los cónsules mexicanos en Colombia...unas relaciones diplomáticas difíciles 1926–1936. (*Tierra Firme,* 14:55, julio/sept. 1996, p. 457–487, bibl.)

Explores the reactions of Mexican diplomatic officials to the Church-state question in Colombia at a time when Mexico itself was struggling with the same issue. Includes an examination of how Mexican officials reacted to Colombian opinion on Mexican church reform.

1395 Bortz, Jeffrey. The genesis of the Mexican labor relations system: federal labor policy and the textile industry, 1925–1940. (*Americas/Franciscans,* 52:1, July 1995, p. 43–69)

Using the textile industry as a case study, discusses the use of the "contrato-ley," a labor contract that could be applied to an entire industry and enforced through presidential decree. This practice made the federal government the ultimate arbiter in labor relations while providing protection to industrialists and state support to labor leaders. Challenges the pro-Labor image of Cárdenas, who sided with the industrialists on major issues such as wages and hours.

1396 Bracamonte Allaín, Jorge. Modernización y ciudadanía: la experiencia de la Ciudad de México, 1870–1930. (*Allpanchis/Cusco,* 29:49, primer semestre 1997, p. 87–113, bibl.)

Examination of the differential impact of the process of urbanization and suburbanization on the "popular," middle, and elite classes of Mexico City. Work is evenly divided between pre-and post-1910 periods. Urban planning was largely left in private hands and the Revolution had little immediate effect on the problems of urbanization.

Brachet-Márquez, Viviane de. The dynamics of domination: State, class, and social reform in Mexico, 1910–1990. See *HLAS 57:4571.*

Brachet-Márquez, Viviane de and Margaret S. Sherraden. Austérité budgétaire, état de bien-être et changement politique: le cas des politiques de santé et d'alimentation au Mexique, 1970–1990. See *HLAS 57:3005.*

1397 Brennan, James P. Industrial sectors and union politics in Latin American labor movements: light and power workers in

Argentina and Mexico. (*LARR*, 30:1, 1995, p. 39–68, bibl.)

Comparative study of the political activity of labor unions in one sector of the post-World War II economy. Argues for a more multi-faceted and less ideology-bound examination of trade union politics in Latin America. For Argentine historian's comment, see item **2835**.

1398 Brewster, Keith. *Caciquismo* in rural Mexico during the 1920s: the case of Gabriel Barrios. (*J. Lat. Am. Stud.*, 28:1, Feb. 1996, p. 105–128, map, photo)

Inquiry into the nature and meaning of boss rule in the post-revolutionary era, with a focus on one of Puebla's most successful leaders.

1399 Britton, John A. Political pilgrimage and the Mexican Revolution. (*SECOLAS Ann.*, 26, March 1995, p. 67–76)

Explores travels to Mexico by US intellectuals during the 1920s-30s. Observations of the Revolution by people such as Ernest Gruening, Carlton Beals, Frank Tannenbaum, and Anita Brenner were not always favorable, despite careful attempts by the Mexican government to "guide" their tours of the country.

1400 Brown, Jonathan C. Los trabajadores y el capital foráneo en la industria petrolera mexicana. (*Secuencia/México*, 34, enero/abril 1996, p. 93–128, bibl., ill.)

Depicts Mexico's oil expropriation as part of an internal dynamic: the struggle of Mexican oil workers for economic security.

1401 Brunk, Samuel. Emiliano Zapata: revolution & betrayal in Mexico. Albuquerque: Univ. of New Mexico Press, 1995. 360 p.: bibl., index, maps, ports.

Emphasizing the man rather than the movement, the author provides an excellent political biography of Zapata. Concludes that Zapata was successful as a local and regional leader but could not make the transition to national leadership, primarily because of the activities of his urban advisors in late 1914 and early 1915. See author's earlier work in *HLAS 56:1422.*

1402 Buchenau, Jürgen. In the shadow of the giant: the making of Mexico's Central America policy, 1876–1930. Tuscaloosa: Univ. of Alabama Press, 1996. 287 p.: bibl., ill., index, map.

Thorough study of the endogenous and external factors that have shaped Mexico's dealings with the Central American republics. Asserts that Mexico's policy has reflected both its status as a "middle power" between Central America and the United States, and its desire to assert a leadership role in the region.

1403 Buffington, Robert. *Los Jotos:* contested visions of homosexuality in modern Mexico. (*in* Sex and sexuality in Latin America. New York: New York Univ. Press, 1997, p. 118–132)

Interesting exploration of the meaning of sexual "deviance" in Porfirian and postrevolutionary Mexico. Argues that both criminologists and male prison inmates politicized homosexuality, but in significantly different ways.

1404 Buffington, Robert. Revolutionary reform: capitalist development, prison reform, and executive power in Mexico. (*in* The birth of the penitentiary in Latin America: essays on criminology, prison reform, and social control. Austin: Univ. of Texas Press, 1996, p. 169–193)

Surveys prison policy under Porfirio Díaz and highlights changes made by 1916–1917 Constitutional Convention. Argues that the debate on prison reform reflected a more general struggle over the parameters of executive power.

1405 Buve, Raymundus Thomas Joseph. El movimiento revolucionario en Tlaxcala. Tlaxcala, Mexico: Univ. Autónoma de Tlaxcala, Secretaría de Extensión Universitaria y Difusión Cultural; México: Univ. Iberoamericana, Depto. de Historia, 1994. 589 p.: bibl.

Sixteen articles explore the advent of the Revolution and its process in Tlaxcala. Includes pieces on theoretical and historiographical considerations, as well as comparative analyses of the Revolution in other Mexican states.

1406 Cabrera, Luis. Revolución e historia en la obra de Luis Cabrera: antología. Recopilación y estudio introductorio de Eugenia Meyer. México: Fondo de Cultura

Económica, 1994. 363 p.: bibl. (Vida y pensamiento de México)

Compilation of works of the noted Carrancista official and ideologue who continued his career as a journalist and his running commentary on the Revolution until his death in 1954. Compiler provides an extended and excellent introduction.

1407 Calderón Mólgora, Marco and **Martín Sánchez Rodríguez.** Cambio social y transformaciones políticas en Jacona, Michoacán: una propuesta de esquema, 1920–1992. (*Relaciones/Zamora*, 61/62, invierno/primavera 1995, p. 13–30, bibl., map, tables)

Traces changes in the local political order and in the local political culture of a municipality in northwestern Michoacán. Local government was dominated by a PRI-connected agrarian elite until the 1980s, when a variety of opposition groups challenged their control. Contested local elections led to the opposition seizure of public buildings and even the creation of a parallel administration.

1408 Caminos de hierro. Coordinación general y diseño de Martha Elena León. México: Sector Comunicaciones y Transportes; Ferrocarriles Nacionales de México, 1996. 238 p.: bibl., ill. (some col.), col. map.

Copiously illustrated popular treatment of the legacy of the Mexican railroad.

1409 Capella, María Luisa. Lázaro Cárdenas y la no intervención en el caso español. (*Leviatán/Madrid*, 61, otoño 1995, p. 151–158)

Analysis of the international response to the refusal by the Cárdenas administration to go along with the League of Nation's efforts to isolate the Spanish Civil War, which the Mexican government felt interfered with normal relations with the legally-constituted republican government. The Mexican position found little support among the nations of Europe or Latin America.

1410 Caraveo Estrada, Baudilio B. Historias de mi odisea revolucionaria: la revolución en la sierra de Chihuahua y la Convención de Aguascalientes. Presentación de Jesús Vargas Valdez. Chihuahua, Mexico: Doble Hélice Ediciones, 1996. 428 p.: ill.

Personal recollections by a supporter of Madero, a member of the Villista forces, and a Villista delegate to the Convention of Aguascalientes.

1411 Carbó Darnaculleta, Margarita. ¡Viva la tierra y libertad!: la utopía magonista. (*Bol. Am.*, 37:47, 1997, p. 91–100)

Discussion of the failure to combine Magonismo with the Zapatista movement. Magonismo represented a non-bourgeois political alternative, but its internationalism ultimately clashed with the localism and traditionalism of Zapatismo.

1412 Cárdenas García, Nicolás. La quimera del desarrollo: el empacto económico y social de la minería en El Oro, Estado de México,1900–1930. México: Instituto Nacional de Estudios Históricos de la Revolución Mexicana, 1996. 87 p.: bibl., ill.

Brief sketch of a mining community that experienced a brief but intense boom around the turn of the century. Includes discussions of economic and technologial developments, and labor relations. Explores the implications of extractive development driven by foreign investment.

1413 Cariño Olvera, Martha Micheline. La pesca y el cultivo de perlas en la región de La Paz, 1870–1940: su impacto socioeconómico. (*Siglo XIX/Monterrey*, 5:13, sept./dic. 1995, p. 27–48, map)

Examination of the social and economic impact of the pearl industry on the La Paz area. Most of the work deals with the pre-1910 period. Concludes that the industry had an important effect on economic diversification, capital accumulation, and market development.

1414 Carrillo Rojas, Arturo et al. La revolución en Sinaloa. 1. ed. de COBAES. Culiacán, Mexico: Colegio de Bachilleres del Estado de Sinaloa, 1994. 169 p.: bibl. (Col. Crónicas)

Collection of five essays without any central theme. Most deal with the 1910–1920 period.

1415 Casillas de Alba, Martín. La villa de Chapala: los promotores, sus inversiones y un inspirado escritor, 1895–1933. México: Banca Promex, 1994. 145 p.: bibl., ill. (some col.).

Nostalgic study of the early development of Chapala, with the emphasis on social and economic changes. Some of Chapala's greatest growth took place during the turbulent first decade of the Revolution. Numerous illustrations and lots of atmosphere.

1416 Castellanos, José Alfredo. Fuentes históricas para el estudio del municipio de Acolman. 1. ed. en español. Chapingo, Mexico: PIHAAA, CIESTAAM, Univ. Autónoma Chapingo, 1996. 81 p.: ill.

Nonexhaustive inventory of archival and secondary sources related to the history of a municipality in Mexico State. Covers colonial era and 19th and 20th centuries.

1417 Castillo Girón, Víctor Manuel. La Cristiada: desarrollo y efectos en el suroeste de Jalisco. (Estud. Jalisc., 18, nov. 1994, p. 47–62)

Describes the experiences of four municipalities, using archival material and oral interviews. Examines the local issues leading to the revolt, the nature of the fighting, and the means by which peace was achieved.

1418 Castro, Pedro. La intervención olvidada: Washington en la rebelión delahuertista. (Secuencia/México, 34, enero/abril 1996, p. 63–91, bibl., ill.)

Describes the role of the United States in Obregón's successful campaign against de la Huerta. Aid in the form of war material, transit privileges on American soil, an arms embargo against rebels, and help in ending the rebel blockade of Tampico were decisive in Obregón's victory.

1419 Cavazos Guzmán, Luis. Historia de la seguridad social en Nuevo León. Monterrey, Mexico: Instituto Mexicano del Seguro Social, Dirección Regional Norte, Delegación Nuevo León, 1997. 93 p., 39 leaves of plates: bibl., ill.

Official, institutional history of Mexico's national health care system, with a focus on one northern state.

1420 Cheibub, José Antonio. Mobilizing and sustaining collective action in the Mexican Revolution. (Polit. Soc./Marxism, 23:2, June 1995, p. 243–258)

Analysis of the different patterns of mobilizing for collective action as exemplified by the Federal Army under Victoriano Huerta, the Zapatista movement, and the Constitutionalist Army (both Carrancista and Villista) during the 1913–15 period. Central thesis is that each movement's mobiliza-

tion method affected its subsequent development and orginal objectives.

1421 Collado, María del Carmen. Admiración y competencia: la visión empresarial mexicana sobre Estados Unidos, 1920–23. (in Estados Unidos desde América Latina: sociedad, política y cultura. México: Instituto de Investigaciones Dr. José María Luis Mora; Centro de Investigación y Docencia Económicas, El Colegio de México, 1995, p. 269–284)

Examination of how Mexican business sectors viewed the US during the period when Washington did not recognize the Obregón regime. While there was no uniform business view, there was widespread admiration for US business success and the relationship between business and government. Many Mexican businesses hoped that US pressure on Obregón would strengthen their position vis-à-vis the new revolutionary government.

1422 Collado, María del Carmen. Empresarios y políticos, entre la restauración y la revolución, 1920–1924. México: Instituto Nacional de Estudios Históricos de la Revolución Mexicana, 1996. 381 p.: bibl., ill., index.

Detailed exploration of the relationship between Mexico's business class (bankers, industrial and commercial magnates) and the government of Alvaro Obregón. Discusses the process by which these elites sought to accommodate themselves to the post-Revolutionary state.

1423 Confederación Nacional Campesina. México: PRI, Coordinación Nacional de Estudios Historicos, Políticos y Sociales, 1993. 530 p.: bibl., ill., index. (La esencia de la nación)

Brief history of the Confederación Nacional Campesina from its founding in 1938 to 1993. Narrative is organized around the Confederation's national congresses and the administrations of the general secretaries.

1424 El conflicto entre la Gran Bretaña y México por la expropiación petrolera: documentos del Foreing [sic] Office, 1938–1942. Recopilación y traducción de Olaf Christiansen. México: Editorial ASBE, 1997. 296 p.

Series of British newspaper articles

and documents that describe Great Britain's approach to the oil controversy in Mexico.

1425 Congreso Internacional de Historia Regional Comparada, 4th, Univ. Autónoma de Ciudad Juárez, 1993. Actas. v. 2. Juárez, Mexico: Univ. Autónoma de Ciudad Juárez, 1995. 1 v. (770 p.): bibl., ill.

Diverse collection of papers exploring the Revolution in northern Mexico and various contemporary themes, including education, foreign investment, and the Church.

1426 Cordero Oliveros, Inmaculada. Exilio español e imagen de España en México. (*Leviatán/Madrid*, 62, invierno 1995, p. 115–139)

Examines the generally negative image of Spain held by most Mexicans due to public education and the impact of Spanish Civil War exiles on this image. Although government policy and the Mexican intellectual elite supported the Republican exiles, it was much more difficult to create a positive image of the exiles among the general public.

1427 Córdova, Arnaldo. La revolución en crisis: la aventura del maximato. México: Cal y Arena, 1995. 552 p.: bibl., index.

Important study of the Maximato (1928–34) sees Cardenismo as the culmination of—rather than the replacement for—many important political developments under Calles. Concludes that there were "important differences" but also "essential overlaps" between Calles and Cárdenas. Cardenismo would not have been possible without the Maximato. By the same author, see also *HLAS 36:2104* and *HLAS 44:2167*.

1428 Cortés Zavala, María Teresa. Lázaro Cárdenas y su proyecto cultural en Michoacán, 1930–1950. Morelia, Mexico: Univ. Michoacana de San Nicolás de Hidalgo, 1995. 256 p.: bibl., ill. (Col. Centenario; 2)

Explores the role of culture and cultural politics in the aftermath of the Revolution. Discusses Cárdenas' cultural projects, both as governor of Michoacán and as Mexico's president. Surveys cultural developments in Michoacán and explores the work of several local novelists.

1429 Costa-Amic, Bartomeu. León Trotsky y Andreu Nin: dos asesinatos del stalinismo; aclarando la historia. San Pedro Cholula, Mexico: Altres-Costa-Amic, 1994. 158 p.: ill.

The author—a Spanish Republican exile in Mexico—briefly narrates his political activities in the 1930s and 1940s, including his role in the granting of asylum to Leon Trotsky. Most of the work is an annex of related correspondence, photos, and newspaper articles.

1430 Covo, Jacqueline. El periódico al servicio del cardenismo: *El Nacional*, 1935. (*Hist. Mex.*, 46:1, julio/sept. 1996, p. 133–161, bibl.)

Study of the official Mexican state newspaper during the first year of the Cárdenas presidency. Demonstrates the ways in which the newspaper sought to increase Cárdenas' popularity and encourage readers to act on behalf of Mexico's revolutionary agenda.

1431 Delgado Wise, Raúl. Hacia una interpretación de la nacionalización de la industria petrolera mexicana. (*Anuario/Xalapa*, 10, 1995, p. 123–145, tables)

Places the rise and fall of Mexican oil production leading up to nationalization in 1938 within the wider context of the global oil industry and the strategies being pursued by the major international oil companies. Concludes with an examination of the problems confronted by PEMEX as the Mexican oil industry had to switch from an external to an internal orientation.

1432 Destino México: un estudio de las migraciones asiáticas a México, siglos XIX y XX . Recopilación de María Elena Ota Mishima. México: El Colegio de México, Centro de Estudios de Asia y Africa, 1997. 438 p.: bibl., ill., maps.

Contains 10 essays on Asian immigrants who came to Mexico mostly in 20th century. Includes studies of Japanese, Koreans, Arabs, Palestinians, Filipinos, and even Sikhs from India. Rosario Cardiel Marín's essay on the Chinese in Baja California also is of interest. Provides a different picture for a country usually thought of as extremely homogeneous.

1433 Díaz de Kuri, Martha and Lourdes Macluf. De Líbano a México: crónica de un pueblo emigrante. Mexico: Gráfica, Creatividad y Diseño, 1995. 284 p.: bibl., ill., index.

Traces the role of the Lebanese in Mexico from the first substantial arrival of immigrants in the early Porfiriato to the establishment of the Lebanese embassy in Mexico in 1947. The immigrants entered primarily through Gulf Coast ports and quickly spread throughout Mexico, often forming their own barrios in urban areas. Extensive illustrations.

1434 Enríquez Licón, Dora Elvia. Colima en los treinta: organizaciones obreras y política regional. México: Consejo Nacional para la Cultura y las Artes, 1994. 154 p. (Regiones)

Explores the growth of a regional workers' movement and its relationship to the Mexican state. Details the process by which Colima's unions were ultimately subordinated to central authority.

1435 Espejel López, Laura. El Cuartel General Zapatista, 1914–1915: documentos del Fondo Emiliano Zapata del Archivo General de la Nación. México: Instituto Nacional de Antropología e Historia, 1995. 2 v.: bibl., indexes. (Colección Fuentes)

Valuable reference work is a partial catalog of documents contained in the Fondo Emiliano Zapata in the Archivo General de la Nación. The Fondo is not a collection of Zapata's personal correspondence but rather a collection of the correspondence of the Cuartel General, the coordinating organ for the Zapatista movement. The documents cataloged deal almost exclusively with 1914–15 and are arranged in chronological order only. Excellent introduction.

1436 Esquivel Obregón, Toribio. Toribio Esquivel Obregón: una visión sobre la economía de México de 1891 a 1945; recopilación hemerográfica. México: Biblioteca Francisco Xavier Clavigero, Univ. Iberoamericana, 1997. 454 p.

Collection of newspaper articles by and about Esquivel Obregón, who served as Huerta's treasury secretary. Emphasizes his economic thought.

1437 Figueroa Torres, Carolina. Señores vengo a contarles—: la Revolución Mexicana a través de sus corridos. México: Secretaría de Gobernación, Instituto Nacional de Estudios Históricos de la Revolución Mexicana, 1995. 197 p.: bibl., ill. (some col.).

Provides a general narrative of revolutionary developments from 1908–20, interspersed with numerous illustrations and parts of *corridos*. The 32 *corridos* forming

the basis for the narrative are reproduced in full at the end of the work.

1438 El fin del proyecto nacionalista revolucionario. Coordinación de Jorge Basurto y Aurelio Cuevas. México: Instituto de Investigaciones Sociales, Univ. Nacional Autónoma de México, 1992. 145 p.: bibl. (Sociedad y política)

Collection of essays dealing with the end of the "nationalist revolutionary project," which represented a revolutionary commitment to nationalism, worker and peasant protection, a preference for domestic capital, an expanding welfare state, and the state as chief modernizing agent. The project went into decline in the 1940s, hit a crisis stage in the 1970s, and was completely undone by the reforms of the 1980s.

1439 Flores Arellano, Nélida and **América Wences Román.** Doña María de la O: una mujer ejemplar. Coordinación de Carlota Botey Estapé. Chilpancingo, Mexico: Univ. Autónoma de Guerrero; México: Centro de Estudios Históricos del Agrarismo en México, 1992. 79 p.: bibl., ill. (Precursores del agrarismo; 8)

Biography of a woman active at both the regional (Guerrero) and national level in the agrarian movement and the organization of women. Work is an effort to revive the "Precursores del agrarismo" series started by the now-defunct Centro de Estudios Históricos del Agrarismo en Mexico.

1440 Flores Magón, Ricardo. Ricardo Flores Magón: el sueño alternativo. Recopilación y estudio introductorio de Fernando Zertuche Muñoz. México: Fondo de Cultura Económica, 1995. 257 p.: bibl., ports. (Vida y pensamiento de México)

Good selection of documents on Magonismo, including a brief biography of Ricardo Flores Magón and a history of his movement.

1441 Flores Torres, Oscar. Revolución Mexicana y diplomacia española: contrarevolución y oligarquía hispana en México, 1909–1920. México: Instituto Nacional de Estudios Históricos de la Revolución Mexicana, Secretaría de Gobernación, 1995. 467 p.: bibl., ill. (Investigación)

Examines the complex relationships and interactions among the Spanish colony in Mexico, the Spanish government, Spanish domestic political forces, the Mexican government, the different revolutionary factions, and the US. While the Spanish government followed a vacillating and sometimes contradictory policy when confronted by revolutionary changes, the Spanish colony was almost uniformly antirevolutionary although some pragmatically switched their support to Carranza.

1442 Franco Nájera, Evila. Evila Franco Nájera, a pesar del olvido. México: Instituto Nacional de Estudios Históricos de la Revolución Mexicana, 1995. 84 p.: bibl., ill. (Testimonio)

Reminiscences of a "liberal, Catholic, and revolutionary" schoolteacher who tried to bring education to the less-developed areas of her native state of Guerrero. The daughter of a Porfirian bureaucrat, she established a "proletarian" school for the poor.

1443 Fujigaki Cruz, Esperanza. Las haciendas y la revolución en México, 1910–1920. (*Invest. Econ.*, 221, julio/sept. 1997, p. 129–152, tables)

Study of 11 haciendas in five northern border states which had been extended credit by the Caja de Préstamos in the late Porfiriato. Located in areas of considerable military acitivity, most of the haciendas suffered destruction and market dislocation and wound up being intervened or administered by the Caja.

1444 García Ramírez, Sergio. Los personajes del cautiverio: prisiones, prisioneros y custodios. México: Secretaría de Gobernación, 1996. 319 p.: bibl., ill. (some col.), photos.

Photographic profile and official treatment of Mexico's penal history.

1445 García Torres, Guadalupe. El movimiento cristero en la memoria colectiva de los pueblos: Jiquilpan, Cojumatlán y Sahuayo. (*J. Hist. Occidente*, 13, 1990, p. 233–265, photos)

Exploration of the Cristero Rebellion in Guanajuato through the words of several participants.

1446 García Ugarte, Marta. La propuesta agraria de Venustiano Carranza y los sonorenses, 1915–1929. (*Estud. Filos. Hist. Let.*, 41, verano 1995, p. 31–47)

Examination of the impact—or lack of it—of agrarian reform on the large landhold-

ings in the state of Querétaro. Concludes that presidents from Carranza through Calles were more concerned with agricultural progress than agrarian reform.

1447 Garciadiego Dantan, Javier. Rudos contra científicos: la Universidad Nacional durante la Revolución mexicana. México: Colegio de México, Centro de Estudios Históricos; UNAM, Centro de Estudios sobre la Univ., 1996. 455 p., 40 p. of plates: bibl., ill., index.

Thorough, well-researched history of UNAM from its contemporary founding to 1920. Explores the relationship of the university to the Mexican government and demonstrates the extent to which UNAM mirrored the major conflicts that were part of Mexico's revolutionary history.

1448 Garro, Elena. Revolucionarios mexicanos. México: Grupo Editorial Planeta, 1997. 183 p. (Seix Barral)

Collection of articles by prominent Mexican novelist. Includes biographical sketches of Ricardo Flores Magón and Francisco Madero, as well as articles on the interim government of Francisco León de la Barra and on the Tragic Ten Days.

1449 Ginzberg, Eitan. Integración social y política: Lázaro Cárdenas, gobernador de Michoacán. (*Cuad. Am.*, 10:58, julio/agosto 1996, p. 60–91)

As governor of Michoacán from 1928–32, Cárdenas confronted a society of diverse interest groups, many of them non-revolutionary. In order to carry out major reforms without provoking class conflict, Cárdenas employed three approaches to promote social and political integration: ideological, statist, and charismatic. Concludes that the lessons learned at the state level were later employed successfully by Cárdenas as president.

1450 Glockner Corte, Fritz. Un pueblo en campaña. Mexico: El Atajo Ediciones, 1995. 205 p. (El carril de la flor)

Chronicle of the 1994 presidential campaign by one of the media managers for Cuauhtémoc Cárdenas. Takes dim view of the coverage provided by the mass media, especially television.

1451 Gojman de Backal, Alicia. Los *Camisas Doradas* en la época de Lazaro Cárdenas. (*Can. J. Lat. Am. Caribb. Stud.*, 20:39/40, 1995, p. 39–64)

Work is not so much a detailed examination of the Camisas Doradas as it is a discussion of the various factors leading to an upswing in nationalism, xenophobia, antisemitism, and anticommunism during the 1930s. One of the prime goals of the Camisas Doradas was the overthrow of the administration of Cárdenas, who suppressed the group and exiled its leader, Nicolás Rodríguez, in early 1936.

1452 Gómez Tepexicuapan, Amparo and **Alfredo Hernández Murillo.** Manuscrito de la Junta Revolucionaria de Puebla. Mexico: INAH, Museo Nacional de Historia, 1993. 50 p.: bibl., ill.

Reproduction of the manuscript and photos presented to Francisco Madero upon his visit to Puebla in July 1911. The manuscript and photos cover the activities of the Revolutionary Junta of Puebla from Feb.-July 1911. First installment in a proposed series of publications commemorating the 50th anniversary of the establishment of the Museo Nacional de Historia in 1944.

1453 Gomezcésar Hernández, Ivan. Sonora y Arizona: apuntes para una historia. (*Estud. Soc./Hermosillo*, 5:10, julio/dic. 1995, p. 9–26)

Discusses new approaches to or ways of rethinking the binational history of Sonora and Arizona, emphasizing contradictory characteristics introduced by the frontier condition, the presence of large numbers of Sonorans in southern Arizona, and the transborder indigenous populations.

1454 Gonzales, Michael J. U.S. copper companies, the mine workers' movement, and the Mexican Revolution, 1910–1920. (*HAHR*, 76:3, Aug. 1996, p. 503–534, tables)

Study of interactions among miners' unions, revolutionary leaders, and copper companies in Sonora. After 1915, Constitutionalists sided with miners against foreign investors, thus definitively drawing these workers into the Constitutionalist movement. See also *HLAS 56:1482.*

1455 González, Gilbert G. Company unions, the Mexican consulate, and the Imperial Valley agricultural strikes, 1928–1934. (*West. Hist. Q.*, 27:1, Spring 1996, p. 53–73)

Re-evaluation of the efforts to organize workers in the Imperial Valley in the violent 1928–34 period. Concludes that Mexican consuls played an important role in organizing workers into more conservative unions affiliated with Mexico's national workers' confederation, the CROM. Through these actions, the consuls supported the growers as well as local, state, and federal officials.

1456 González Filizola, Enrique Martín. Una Victoria perdida: relatos de este lado del tablero. Cd. Victoria, Mexico: Univ. Autónoma de Tamaulipas, Instituto de Investigaciones Históricas, 1994. 149 p.: bibl., ill.

Extensively illustrated study of several landholding families in the area around Ciudad Victoria, Tamaulipas. Most of the work is devoted to the Porfirian period, with only a brief final chapter on the post-1910 period.

1457 González Marín, Silvia. Historia de la hacienda de Chapingo. Chapingo, México: Univ. Autónoma Chapingo, CIESTAAM, 1996. 193 p.: bibl., ill.

Thorough study tracing the evolution of a Texcoco hacienda from the colonial period to 1923, the year of its expropriation. Discusses territorial development, economic activities, and ownership.

1458 González Pérez, Alvaro. El general Francisco J. Múgica y su participación en la educación. Mexico: Univ. Autónoma Chapingo, 1991. 82 p.: bibl., ill.

Explores the efforts of a prominent revolutionary figure to bring about reforms in Mexico's educational system. Discusses Múgica's educational agenda as governor of Tabasco, as a representative to the Constitutional Convention of 1916–17, and as governor of Michoacán.

1459 González y González, Luis. Pueblo en vilo: microhistoria de San José de Gracia. 5a ed. en español. Zámora, Mexico: Colegio de Michoacán, 1995. 442 p.: ill., maps. (Col. Clásicos)

Fifth edition of González's classic work of regional history.

1460 González y González, Luis. La ronda de las generaciones. México: Clío, 1997. 348 p.: bibl., ill., index. (Obras completas de Luis González y González; 6)

Exploration of six generations of prominent Mexicans whose lives spanned the Reforma, Restored Republic, Porfiriato, Revolution, and Cárdenas era.

1461 Gracida Romo, Elsa Margarita. El programa industrial de la Revolución. México: UNAM, Facultad de Economía, Instituto de Investigaciones Económicas, 1994. 145 p.: bibl.

Traces the path of Mexico's industrial development from the Porfiriato to the early 1960s.

1462 Guía del archivo de testimonios familiares y documentos históricos. Torreón, Mexico: Univ. Iberoamericana, Plantel Laguna, 1995. 51 p.: ill., indexes.

Well-written guide to archive containing materials dealing with the Laguna region from the late Porfiriato to the present.

1463 Hale, Charles A. Los mitos políticos de la nación mexicana: el liberalismo y la revolución. (*Hist. Mex.*, 46:4, abril/junio 1997, p. 821–837)

Explores the meaning and interpretations of liberalism and of the revolutionary ideal in Mexico's post-Reform history.

1464 Henderson, Peter V.N. Recent economic and regional histories of the Mexican revolution. (*LARR*, 30:1, 1995, p. 236–246)

Review and analysis of five recent works, including monographs by Stephen Haber, Jonathan Brown, and Dana Markiewicz, and edited volumes by Thomas Benjamin and Mark Wasserman, and by Eric Van Young.

1465 Hernández Chávez, Alicia. De la economía a la economía nacional, 1926–1940. (*in* Cincuenta años de historia en México: en el cincuentenario del Centro de Estudios Históricos. México: Colegio de México, Centro de Estudios Históricos, 1991, v. 1, p. 315–327)

Focusing on the Plan Sexenal of 1933 and the Plan Nacional de Desarrollo of 1935, author describes how the concept of a national economy emerged in response to changes in the international economy and to internal social transformations resulting from the Revolution. A national market and a major role in the economy for the state would be basic features of this national economy.

1466 Hernández Z., Enrique. Juan Espinosa Bávara: soldado de la revolución, constituyente de Querétaro y periodista liberal. Tepic, Mexico?: Cambio XXI Fundación Nayarit, 1993. 107 p.: ill. (Serie Historia)

Biography of regional figure who supported the Carrancista cause between 1913–16, served at the Constitutional Convention of 1916–17, and played a key role in transforming the territory of Tepic into the state of Nayarit.

1467 Historia general de Sonora. v. 4, Sonora moderno, 1880–1929. 2. ed. Hermosillo, Mexico: Gobierno del Estado de Sonora, 1997. 1 v.: bibl., ill., maps. (Sonora)

Nine pieces on Porfirian and revolutionary Sonora by various authors. Topics include: modernization and economic development, the indigenous and Chinese communities, Maderismo and Constitutionalism, and post-revolutionary reconstruction.

1468 Historiadores de México en el siglo XX. Recopilación de Enrique Florescano y Ricardo Pérez Montfort. México: Consejo Nacional para la Cultura y las Artes; Fondo de Cultura Económica, 1995. 558 p.: bibl. (Sección de obras de historia)

The first part of this work offers biographical sketches of historians, including their contributions to the profession. The second part features historians' responses to a questionnaire exploring how they entered the profession and the highlights of their professional development.

1469 Isidro Fabela: pensador, político y humanista, 1882–1964. Coordinación de María Teresa Jarquín Ortega. Zinacantepec, Mexico: El Colegio Mexiquense; Instituto Mexiquense de Cultura, 1996. 516 p.: bibl., 1 ill., maps.

Collection of articles exploring the life, thought, and writings of a prominent revolutionary and Mexican diplomat.

1470 Jáuregui de Cervantes, Aurora. El mineral de La Luz, Guanajuato: trayecto histórico. Guanajuato, Mexico: Univ. de Guanajuato, 1996. 184 p.: bibl., ill., maps. (Col. Otro tiempo)

Explores the development of a silver mining region from the mid-19th century to the 1970s, with attention to the effect of historical events on the community of La Luz.

**1471 Jiquilpan, 1920–1940: memoria pueb-
lerina.** Recopilación de Guillermo
Ramos Arizpe y Salvador Rueda Smithers.
Mexico: Centro de Estudios de la Revolución
Mexicana Lázaro Cárdenas, Archivo de His-
toria Oral, 1994. 596 p.: ill.

Oral history of the town of Jiquilpan
in the state of Michoacan based on more
than 200 interviews held between 1980–87
with persons born between 1895–1920. Each
chapter has an introduction followed by extensive quotations from the interviews. Topics include: immigration to and return from
the United States, the Cristero rebellion, and
the agrarian reform of the 1930s.

1472 Jrade, Ramón. La organización de la
Iglesia a nivel local y el desafío de los
levantamientos cristeros al poder del Estado
revolucionario. (*Estud. Hombre*, 1, nov. 1994,
p. 65–80)

Focusing on the state of Jalisco, demonstrates how differences in the agrarian context, parish organization, and local politics
explain the differing local allegiances during
the Cristero rebellion. The accelerated establishment of parishes by the archdiocese of
Guadalajara had helped to preserve the traditional role of the parish as the center of rural
life in many areas.

1473 Katz, Friedrich. The demise of the old
order on Mexico's haciendas, 1911–
1913. (*Ibero-Am. Arch.*, 20:3/4, 1994, p. 399–
435)

Contends that upper-class resentment
of Madero was primarily based on his administration's inability to prevent the breakdown
of the old order in the countryside which, in
turn, reflected a breakdown in most of the old
Porfirian mechanisms of control. Madero's
agrarian reform was limited and never threatened the large landowners.

1474 Knight, Alan. México y Estados
Unidos, 1938–1940: rumor y realidad.
(*Secuencia/México*, 34, enero/abril 1996,
p. 129–153, bibl., ill.)

Study of various factors influencing
Mexico's foreign policy during the last years
of the Cárdenas presidency. Despite tensions
caused by the oil expropriation, the US and
Mexico forged a strong alliance as World War
II approached.

1475 Knight, Alan. Punto de vista; revisionismo y revolución: México compara-
do con Inglaterra y Francia. (*Bol. Inst. Hist.*

Ravignani, 10, segundo semestre 1994, p. 91–
127)

Useful exploration of the historiography and revisionist ideas pertaining to the
English, French, and Mexican revolutions.

1476 Koth, Karl B. Madero, Dehesa y el cientificismo: el problema de la sucesión
gubernamental en Veracruz, 1911–1913. (*Hist.
Mex.*, 46:2, oct./dic. 1996, p. 397–424, bibl.)

Examines Madero's failure to gain political control over Veracruz. In resorting to
Porfirian political practices in the search for a
new governor, Madero demonstrated his lack
of committment to a democratic revolution.

1477 Lamas, Marta et al. Building bridges:
the growth of popular feminism in
Mexico. Translated by Ellen Calmus. (*in* The
challenge of local feminisms: women's movements in global perspective. Boulder, Colo.:
Westview Press, 1995, p. 324–347, photos,
table)

An exploration of Mexico's women's
movement in the contemporary era.From a
middle-class movement developed during the
1970s, Mexican feminism has evolved into a
more popular and activist movement that
crosses class lines and places more emphasis
on female political participation. For political scientist's comment, see item *HLAS*
57:3067.

1478 Lamas Lizárraga, Mario Alberto. El
ferrocarril sudpacífico y la formación
social regional, 1905–1917. (*in* Simposio de
Historia y Antropología de Sonora, *19th,
Hermosillo, Mexico, 1994.* Memorias. Hermosillo, Mexico: Instituto de Investigaciones
Históricas de la Univ. de Sonora, v. 2, p. 51–
63, bibl., tables)

Discusses the importance attached to
the construction of a railway line from Guay-
mas to Guadalajara. The South Pacific Railway brought economic and social integration
to Mexico's northwest, contributing to the
creation of a distinct region.

1479 Lau Jaiven, Ana. Las mujeres en la revolución mexicana: un punto de vista
historiográfico. (*Secuencia/México*, 33,
sept./dic. 1995, p. 85–102, bibl., ill.)

Survey and analysis of writings by and
about women of the late Porfirian and revolutionary periods. Examines primary works by
female journalists and writers, as well as
more academic works produced since the
Revolution.

1480 Lempérière, Annick. Los dos centenarios de la independencia mexicana, 1910–1921: de la historia patria a la antropología cultural. (*Hist. Mex.*, 45:2, oct./dic. 1995, p. 317–352, bibl.)

Analysis of celebrations held during the Porfiriato and the Obregón presidency. While the first centenary featured "official" history and sought to justify the Díaz regime, the second celebration was more cultural, taking its cue from the work of Mexican intellectuals to reconstruct Mexico's indigenous past.

1481 León Morales, Ramón. La posrevolución en Colima: historia regional del partido del estado, 1917–1967. Colima, Mexico: Univ. de Colima, 1993. 169 p.: bibl. (Cuadernos de historia regional/Universidad de Colima)

Political history of the state of Colima organized around governorships and presidential elections. Emphasis is on the role of central authorities in determining state politics, with official party chiefs serving as intermediaries between central authorities and state administrators. Based on local and state archives.

1482 Leriche Guzmán, Luis Fernando. Isla del Carmen: la historia indecisa de un puerto exportador; el caso de la industria camaronera, 1947–1982. Campeche, Mexico: Gobierno del Estado de Campeche; Univ. Autónoma del Carmen; Instituto de Cultura de Campeche, 1995. 226 p.: ill., maps. (Serie Historia. Palo de tinte)

After considerable background on the local history, geography, and economy, author traces the shrimping industry from its 1947 origins as a major economic undertaking to its transfer from the private sector to cooperatives in July 1982. Government was actively involved throughout the process, but even extensive government aid could not offset the problems of a monocultural, exporting economy.

1483 Lerner Sigal, Victoria. Espionaje y revolución mexicana. (*Hist. Mex.*, 44:4, abril/junio 1995, p. 617–643, bibl.)

Preliminary study of Villista spies operating along the US-Mexico border during the Revolution. A formal espionage corps, individual male and female spies, and Mexican consular officials all played a role in the spy network.

1484 Liwerant, Judit Bokser. Cárdenas y los judíos: entre el exilio y la inmigración. (*Can. J. Lat. Am. Caribb. Stud.*, 20:39/40, 1995, p. 13–37)

After a review of Mexican immigration policy in the 1920s and 1930s, which was largely driven by considerations of economics and assimilation, author addresses the Mexican response to the problem of admitting Jewish refugees. The Cárdenas administration's reaction was influenced by the forced repatriation of Mexicans from the US and by the large influx of refugees from the Spanish Civil War.

1485 Llerenas, Fidelina G. and Jaime Tamayo. El levantamiento delahuertista: cuatro rebeliones y cuatro jefes militares. Guadalajara, Mexico: Univ. de Guadalajara, 1995. 136 p.: bibl. (Col. Fin de milenio. Biblioteca Movimientos Sociales)

Revisionist view of the traditional interpretation of 1923 revolt as a reaction against Obregón's imposition of Calles. Authors study four different regional revolts between 1923–24, all with different leaders and provoked by different causes: Rómulo Figueroa in Guerrero, Enrique Estrada in Jalisco, Guadalupe Sánchez in Veracruz, and Fortunato Maycotte in Oaxaca. Rebels failed because of a lack of central control or unifying program. Adolfo de la Huerta played only a "decorative role" in the armed movement against Obregón.

1486 Loaeza, Soledad. Perspectiva para una historia política del distrito federal en el siglo XX. (*Hist. Mex.*, 45:1, julio/sept. 1995, p. 99–158, bibl.)

An exploration of the political habits and characteristics of Mexico's capital city and its inhabitants. Focuses on electoral trends and on the formation of interest groups and social movements. Illustrates the variety of Mexico City's political history.

1487 López Portillo T., Felícitas. Estado e ideología empresarial en el gobierno alemanista. México: UNAM, 1995. 374 p.: bibl. (Serie Nuestra América; 50)

Explores Mexico's experience with import-subsitution industrialization through the eyes of the Mexican business class. Discusses the agendas of Mexico's major business organizations and evaluates their position on state intervention, state-labor relations, and other issues.

1488 López Portillo T., Felícitas. México y Venezuela: un vistazo diplomático. (*Tierra Firme,* 14:55, julio/sept. 1996, p. 489–507)

Provides a view of Venezuela's internal affairs in the post-WW II era through an exploration of the confidential reports of Mexican ambassadors.

1489 López Portillo T., Felícitas. La revolución de 1910: ¿burguesía nacional o justicia social? (*in* Burguesías en América Latina. México: Univ. Autónoma de México, 1993, p. 107–136)

Examines the economic program of Miguel Alemán as part of Mexico's continuing struggle to promote industry and create a Mexican industrial class. Suggests continuity between the presidencies of Cárdenas and Alemán.

1490 Lorenzo Monterrubio, Carmen. Felipe Angeles: una vida de controversia. Pachuca, Mexico: Consejo Estatal para la Cultura y las Artes de Hidalgo, Centro de Investigación, 1995. 31 p.: bibl., ill. (Cuadernos hidalguenses; 4)

Brief biography of a prominent and controversial revolutionary figure. Explores Angeles' image through the eyes of both critics and supporters.

1491 Lorey, David E. The revolutionary festival in Mexico: November 20 celebrations in the 1920s and 1930s. (*Americas/Franciscans,* 54:1, July 1997, p. 39–82, ill.)

Focuses on the changes in the way Revolution Day was celebrated from 1920–40 as a way of providing new insights into political consolidation, social change, and daily life. Contends that such an examination shows new tensions in the postrevolutionary order and how such tensions could be resolved through public ritual.

1492 Loyo, Engracia. La empresa rendentora: la casa del estudiante indígena. (*Hist. Mex.,* 46:1, julio/sept. 1996, p. 99–131, bibl., tables)

Explores the impact of a school established during the Calles years to "civilize" Mexico's indigenous peoples. Ultimately, the school failed in its mission of integrating the indigenous population and creating indigenous teachers, while it reinforced a broader historical trend in which Mexico's

Indians have been treated as less than fully human.

1493 Luna Zamora, Rogelio. La historia del tequila, de sus regiones y sus hombres. México: Dirección General de Publicaciones del Consejo Nacional para la Cultura y las Artes, 1991. 302 p.: bibl., ill. (Regiones)

Study of the development of the tequila industry in Jalisco. Explores the evolution of an entrepreneurial class devoted to maguey production and tequila-making, and the commercialization and marketing of tequila on the local, national, and global levels.

1494 Mac Gregor Campuzano, Javier. Browderismo, unidad nacional y crisis ideológica: el partido comunista mexicano en la encrucijada, 1940–1950. (*Iztapalapa/México,* 15:36, enero/junio 1995, p. 167–184, bibl., photos)

Examination of the "crisis years" of the Mexican Communist Party under the leadership of Dionisio Encina. Influenced variously by the Communist International, "Browderism," the Soviet Union, and labor leader Vicente Lombardo Toledano, the party found it difficult to reorganize itself and to formulate a program as the Mexican Revolution moved to the right.

1495 Macías Richard, Carlos. Vida y temperamento: Plutarco Elías Calles. v. 1, 1877–1920. México: Instituto Sonorense de Cultura; Gobierno del Estado de Sonora; Fideicomiso Archivos Plutarco Elías Calles y Fernando Torreblanca; Fondo de Cultura Económica, 1995. 1 v.: bibl., ill., index. (Vida y pensamiento de México)

Citing the lack of an exhaustive biography of Calles, author provides a detailed discussion of the personal and political evolution of this key figure. Vol. 1 of a projected two-volume study covers the period to 1920. Based on extensive archival sources. See also *HLAS 54:1462.*

1496 Mantilla Gutiérrez, Jorge. La influencia cubana en la revista socialista *Tierra de Yucatán,* 1918–1923. (*in* Caribbean Studies Association Conference, *19th, Mérida, Mexico, 1994.* Actas. Mérida, Mexico: Facultad de Ciencias Antropológicas, Univ. Autónoma de Yucatán, 1995, p. 237–245)

Brief treatment of a Yucatán weekly

that suggests a link between Cuban and Yucatecan intellectuals.

1497 Márquez Carrillo, Jesús. Cátedra en vilo: apuntes y notas de historia universitaria poblana. Puebla, Mexico: Centro de Estudios Universitarios, Univ. Autónoma de Puebla, 1992. 165 p.: bibl., ill. (Col. Pasajes; 2)

Collection of essays dealing with forerunners to and the current Universidad Autónoma de Puebla. Considerable attention to the involvement of the institution and its students in political activities.

1498 Martínez Barreda, Alonso. Los Redo: una familia empresarial posrevolucionaria. (Clío/Culiacán, 12, sept./dic. 1994, p. 105–114)

Traces the economic fortunes of a prominent Porfirian clan. Despite revolution and political change, three generations successfully built and preserved an extensive economic empire based in Sinaloa.

1499 Martínez Jiménez, Alejandro. La educación primaria en la formación social mexicana, 1875–1965. Prólogo de Arturo Bonilla Sánchez. Mexico: Univ. Autónoma Metropolitana-Xochimilco, División de Ciencias Sociales y Humanidades, Depto. de Relaciones Sociales, 1996. 417 p.: bibl., ill., tables.

Theoretical look at the development of elementary education in Mexico. Links the politics of education to Mexico's capitalist economic development and explores the realtionship between changing educational agendas and Mexican society.

1500 Matute, Alvaro. Bucareli en el debate histórico. (Secuencia/México, 28, enero/abril 1994, p. 65–79, bibl., ill.)

Discussion of the historiography on the Mexican side of the highly-disputed Bucareli agreements of 1923. Divides commentators into three groups or "generations," ranging from contemporaries of the event to a third generation composed primarily of academics. Limited discussion of individual works, particularly of the third generation.

1501 Matute, Alvaro. Las dificultades del nuevo estado. México: Colegio de México, Centro de Estudios Históricos, 1995. 313 p.: bibl., index. (Historia de la Revolución Mexicana; 7. 1917–1924)

The second of three volumes covering the 1917–24 period in this series on the Rev-

olution. Vol. 7 covers the first three years of the Carranza administration as it tries to establish a "new state" and "national space" in the face of internal and external pressures. Work is divided into three major parts: international, national, and regional. See HLAS 48:2172 for vol. 8 in the series by same author.

1502 Mayer, Leticia. El proceso de recuperación simbólica de cuatro héroes de la revolución mexicana de 1910 a través de la prensa nacional. (Hist. Mex., 45:2, oct./dic. 1995, p. 353–381, bibl., table)

Study of five newspapers and their treatment of four revolutionary figures: Madero, Zapata, Carranza, and Villa. Explores how each man became a part of the myth of the Mexican Revolution after his death, with Zapata ultimately assuming the position as the most important symbol of the Revolution.

1503 Méndez Reyes, Jesús. La política económica durante el gobierno de Francisco I. Madero. México: Instituto Nacional de Estudios Históricos de la Revolución Mexicana, 1996. 166 p.: bibl., ill.

Examines Madero's economic ideas and his approach to various economic issues, including labor-management relations, agrarian reform, and fiscal policy. Argues that Madero's economic policies fell somewhere between 19th-century Liberalism and a more modern interventionism.

1504 Meyer Cosío, Francisco Javier. El final del porfirismo en Guanajuato: elites en la crisis final, septiembre de 1910-junio de 1911. 1. ed. en la Col. Nuestra cultura. Guanajuato, Mexico: Gobierno del Estado de Guanajuato, 1993. 70 p.: bibl., ill. (Nuestra cultura)

Excellent state-level study that is part of a projected larger work covering the period from 1893–1913. Concludes that the Madero revolution had little effect on state elites who maintained their control over the state government until the militarization brought on by the Huerta regime in 1913.

1505 Millon, Robert Paul. Zapata: the ideology of a peasant revolutionary. 2nd ed. New York: International Publishers, 1995. 163 p.: bibl., index.

Work—originally published in 1969—examines the ideology and program of the Zapatista movement. Goes beyond the agrarian issue to discuss the other economic, social, and political reforms proposed by the Zapatistas. Concludes that the program was "anti-feudal, bourgeois-democratic, and anti-imperialist in spirit."

1506 Moguel, Josefina. Venustiano Carranza, primer jefe y presidente. Coahuila de Zaragoza, Mexico: Gobierno del Estado de Coahuila, 1995. 165 p.: bibl., ill.

Brief political biography published on the 75th anniversary of the death of Carranza. Emphasis is on the shaping of the Constitutionalist army, the Constitution of 1917, and Carranza's efforts at state-building. Author is head of the Carranza archive at Condumex.

1507 Moreno, Daniel A. Los hombres de la Revolución. México: Secretaría de la Defensa Nacional, 1995. 285 p.: bibl., ill. (Biblioteca del oficial mexicano; 2)

Brief biographical sketches of some 40 revolutionary figures, including intellectual precursors and political and military leaders.

1508 Moreno García, Heriberto. Guaracha: tiempos viejos, tiempos nuevos. 2. ed. Zamora, Mexico: El Colegio de Michoacán, 1994. 309 p.: bibl., ill. (Col. Investigaciones)

Revised edition of work first published in 1980. Traces the evolution of an hacienda in Michoacán through its transformation into an ejido in the Cárdenas years. For another study of the Guaracha hacienda, see *HLAS 54:1500.*

1509 Múgica Martínez, Jesús. Francisco J. Múgica, constituyente 1916–1917. Morelia, Mexico: s.n., 1994. 111 p.: bibl., ill.

Commemorative work discusses the role played by the prominent revolutionary figure in drafting the more radical provisions of the 1917 Constitution.

1510 Nava Moreno, Joaquín. Heliodoro Castillo Castro, general zapatista guerrerense: relato testimonial. Ajuchitlán, Mexico: Ediciones El Balcón, 1995. 199 p.: ill.

Reminiscences of a colonel and secretary to a zapatista general who died in March 1917. Testimonial was not completed until early 1980s when Colonel Nava was almost 90.

1511 Niblo, Stephen R. War, diplomacy, and development: the United States and Mexico, 1938–1954. Wilmington, Del.: Scholarly Resources, 1995. 320 p.: bibl., ill., index. (Latin American silhouettes)

Excellent study of the origins of Mexico's rapid industrialization development program and how it went astray. Emphasis is on how wartime cooperation led to unprecedented levels of US influence on the economy and investment after the war. A blend of war, industrialization, domestic conservatism, and US pressure shifted the Revolution to the right.

1512 Nuncio, Abraham *et al.* Fundidora, diez años después: para que no se olvide—. Recopilación de Sandra Arenal. Monterrey, Mexico: Univ. Autónoma de Nuevo León, 1996. 232 p.: ill.

Historical reflections on Monterrey's smelter, founded in 1900 and closed in 1986. Primarily a collection of personal memoirs by former workers and others connected to the plant.

1513 Ochoa Rodríguez, Héctor Porfirio. La acción social de los estibadores manzanillenses, 1919–1922. Colima, Mexico: Archivo Municipal de Colima, 1992. 39 p.: bibl. (Pretextos; 1)

Study of the effort to organize the stevedores in the port city of Manzanillo beginning with the strike of 1919. The stevedores achieved their main goal of having only union workers hired to unload cargo, but were dependent on constantly changing political alliances at the local and state levels.

1514 Oikión Solano, Verónica. El constitucionalismo en Michoacán: el periodo de los gobiernos militares, 1914–1917. México: Consejo Nacional para la Cultura y las Artes, 1992. 602 p.: bibl., ill., maps. (Regiones)

Excellent state-level study of the impact—or the lack of impact—of constitutionalism. A series of constitutionalist military governors failed to implement significant agrarian reform and did little to try to improve the economy, which was in a state of continuing crisis. Efforts at centralization restricted the governors, culminating in the rigged 1917 elections that put Pascual Ortiz Rubio in the governorship.

1515 Oikión Solano, Verónica. Michoacán en la vía de la unidad nacional, 1940–1944. México: Instituto Nacional de Estudios Históricos de la Revolución Mexicana, Secretaría de Gobernación, 1995. 487 p.: bibl., ill., maps.

Detailed study of Michoacán during the governorship of Félix Ireta Viveros. Emphasizes the connections between local and national political processes and argues that, despite the popularity of Cardenismo in Michoacán, Ireta embraced the agenda of the Avila Camacho administration.

1516 Oropeza, Manuel González. La discriminación en México: el caso de los nacionales chinos. (*in* Jornadas Lascasianas, *6th, Mexico City, 1996.* La problemática del racismo en los umbrales del siglo XXI. México: UNAM, Instituto de Investigaciones Jurídicas, 1997, p. 47–56)

Discussion of anti-Chinese activity during the Revolution and the 1920s, including the efforts of various groups to expel the Chinese from Mexico.

1517 Ortoll, Servando. Rosalie Evans y los informantes de Alvaro Obregón. (*Estud. Hombre,* 1, nov. 1994, p. 101–113)

Re-examines the murder of US landowner Rosalie Evans in Puebla state in 1924 using three letters found in the archives of the National Catholic Welfare Conference, the official organization of US bishops. Questions "official version" of the incident, which described it as a common crime, and speculates that the three letters may have wound up in the archive to justify Obregón's assassination in 1928.

1518 Pacheco Ladrón de Guevara, Lourdes C. et al. Cien revoluciones: Nayarit, memoria oral. Tepic, Mexico: Univ. Autónoma de Nayarit, 1995. 373 p.: ill.

Excerpts from 100 oral interviews, most dealing with themes from the post-1920 period.

1519 Pérez Montfort, Ricardo. *Por la patria y por la raza:* la derecha secular en el sexenio de Lázaro Cárdenas. México: Facultad de Filosofía y Letras, Univ. Nacional Autónoma de México, 1993. 228 p.: bibl. (Col. Seminarios)

Exploration of the political right. Argues that a nationalism inspired by totalitarian thought emanating from Central Europe constituted an important opposition force to the Cárdenas administration. Includes documents related to Mexico's rightist groups.

1520 Pérez Rosales, Laura. Anticardenismo and anti-Semitism in Mexico, 1934–1940. (*in* The Jewish diaspora in Latin America: new studies on history and literature. New York: Garland Publ., 1996, p. 183–197, bibl.)

Study of two right-wing Mexican newspapers that sought to undermine Cárdenas by equating his reforms with communism and with Jewish "plots."

1521 Pineda Gómez, Francisco. La irrupción zapatista, 1911. México: Ediciones Era, 1997. 247 p.: ill., maps. (Col. Problemas de México)

Extensively researched exploration of the emergence of Zapatismo. Presents Zapatismo as a phenomenon transcending local boundaries and reflecting national developments.

1522 Piñera Ramírez, David and Jorge Martínez Zepeda. Baja California, 1901–1905: consideraciones y datos para su historia demográfica = Considerations and data for its demographic history. Tijuana, Mexico: Univ. Autónoma de Baja California; México: UNAM; San Diego, Calif.: San Diego State Univ., 1994. 334 p.: bibl., ill., indexes.

Exhaustive compilation of birth, marriage, and death records. Intended as a resource for demographic and social historians.

1523 Portilla, Santiago. Una sociedad en armas: insurrección antirreeleccionista en México, 1910–1911. Dibujo cartográfico de Ignacio Márquez Hernández. México: Colegio de México, Centro de Estudios Históricos, 1995. 652 p.: bibl., ill. (some col.), index.

Good overview of the decisive role played by the "popular armed forces" in the overthrow of the Díaz regime. Excellent collection of maps as well as some useful chronologies.

1524 Los primordiales del 36: testimonios de los protagonistas del reparto agrario en La Laguna. Durango, Mexico: Secretaría de Educación, Cultura y Deporte; Dirección General de Culturas Populares, Unidad Regional Norte-La Laguna, 1994. 145 p. (Col. Identidad duranguense)

Recollections of ejido members involved in the land redistribution program of 1936 in the Laguna region. Part one contains interviews with ejido members; part two is a combination of written testimonies, essays, and articles.

1525 **Profesor y general Antonio Ireneo Villarreal, 1879–1944: homenaje en el
50 aniversario de su muerte.** Textos recogidos por Celso Garza Guajardo. Monterrey,
Mexico: Univ. Autónoma de Nuevo León,
1994. 133 p.: bibl.
Brief biography of a durable revolutionary. Extensive use of Villarreal's correspondence and decrees to illustrate his activities.

1526 **Rabadán Figueroa, Macrina.** Discurso
vs. realidad en las campañas antichi-
nas en Sonora, 1899–1932. (*Secuencia/
México*, 38, mayo/agosto 1997, p. 77–94,
bibl., ill.)
Explores the nature of anti-Chinese
sentiment and argues that, despite the negative images, Sonora's Chinese population was
an accepted and integral part of Sonoran society.

1527 **Rabelo Ruiz de la Peña, Ignacio.**
Bosquejo histórico del movimiento
obrero: fuentes documentales para el estudio
del movimiento obrero en Tabasco. Villahermosa, Mexico: Univ. Juárez Autónoma de
Tabasco, 1996. 192 p.: bibl.
General survey of the workers' movement in Tabasco, accompanied by a descriptive list of documents relating to this theme
and contained in the Archivo General de la
Nación.

1528 **Ramírez Flores, José.** La revolución
maderista en Jalisco. México: Univ. de
Guadalajara; Centre d'études mexicaines et
centraméricaines, 1992. 185 p.: bibl. (Col. de
documentos para la historia de Jalisco; 1)
Posthumous reconstruction of
Ramírez; account of the early stages of the
Revolution in Jalisco.

1529 **Ramírez Rancaño, Mario.** La revolución en los volcanes: Domingo y Cirilo
Arenas. México: Instituto de Investigaciones
Sociales, UNAM, 1995. 283 p.: ill., maps.
Attempts to dispel the "black legend"
that regional leaders Domingo and Cirilo
Arenas betrayed the principles of the Plan of
Ayala by switching to Carranza in 1917, a
move that led to the killing of Domingo by
the Zapatistas. Cirilo, in turn, was executed
in 1920 by Carrancista officials. Operating
primarily in Tlaxcala, the brothers maintained their commitment to agrarian reform
throughout their revolutionary careers.

1530 **Ramos Escandón, Carmen.** Women's
movements, feminism, and Mexican
politics. (*in* The women's movement in Latin
America: participation and democracy.
Edited by Jane S. Jaquette. Boulder, Colo.:
Westview Press, 1994, p. 199–221)
Good summary of women's political
participation since the Revolution. Demonstrates the extent to which women have
increased the frequency and changed the nature of their participation since 1970. Will-
ingess to articulate gender-specific concerns
while varying the forms of women's organization are hallmarks of today's women's
movement. For political scientist's comment,
see *HLAS 57:3103*.

1531 **Religión, política y sociedad: el sinarquismo y la Iglesia en México; nueve
ensayos.** Coordinación y recopilación de
Rubén Aguilar V. y Guillermo Zermeño P.
México: Univ. Iberoamericana, Depto. de
Historia, 1993. 310 p.: bibl., ill. (El pasado del
presente)
Series of essays on the Catholic Right.
Most selections are regional in scope and focus on the 1937–1945 era, when synarchism
first emerged in Mexico. Also includes an interesting essay on the role of women in the
synarchist movement.

1532 **Reséndez Fuentes, Andrés.** Battle-
ground women: *soldaderas* and female
soldiers in the Mexican Revolution. (*Ameri-
cas/Franciscans*, 51:4, April 1995, p. 525–
553, table)
Drawing a firm distinction between
"female soldiers" and "*soldaderas*," author
compares and contrasts the various roles
played by women in the military campaigns
of the different revolutionary groups. The
soldaderas differed from the female soldiers
in terms of their functions, status in the
armed forces, and social background. The involvement of women of both categories
peaked during the military campaigns of the
1913–1915 period.

1533 **La responsabilidad del historiador:
homenaje a Moisés González Navarro.**
Coordinación y recopilación de Shulamit
Goldsmit y Guillermo Zermeño P. México:
Univ. Iberoamericana, Depto. de Historia,
1992. 292 p.: bibl., ill.
Series of essays by Mexican and North
American scholars reflecting on the work of

an important Mexican historian. Highlights the importance of González Navarro's writings, especially in the field of social history. Includes several essays inspired by his work.

Retana Tello, Ismael Reyes. México frente al arbitraje internacional: el caso de El Chamizal. See *HLAS 57:4111.*

1534 Ricardo Flores Magón: Programa del Partido Liberal y Manifiesto a la nación. México: Instituto Nacional de Estudios Históricos de la Revolución Mexicana, Secretaría de Gobernación, 1992. 41 p.: ill.

Work consists of a brief biography of Flores Magón followed by the complete text of the Liberal Party Plan of 1906.

1535 Riera Llorca, Vicenç. Els exiliats catalans a Mèxic. Edició a cura de Josep Ferrer i Costa i Joan Pujadas i Marquès. Barcelona: Curial, 1994. 386 p.: index. (La Mata de jonc; 29)

Author, a Catalan exile himself, provides a personal and historical narrative of the Catalan exiles from the Spanish Civil War who settled in Mexico. Discussion includes descriptions of exile publications, activities and political organizations. Appendices contain a census of the exiles with background information and a list of business enterprises begun by the exiles.

1536 Rivas Hernández, Ignacio. La política administrativa de Félix Ortega en el partido sur de la Baja California. (*in* Simposio de Historia y Antropología Regionales, 5th, *La Paz?, 1994?* Actas. La Paz, México: Univ. Autónoma de Baja California Sur, 1994, p. 75–82)

Explores the response of a local merchant class to the struggle between Carranza and the Convention.

1537 Rocha Islas, Martha Eva. El archivo de veteranas de la revolución mexicana: una historia femenina dentro de la historia oficial. (*in* América Latina contemporânea: desafios e perspectivas. Organização de Eliane Geraindo Dayrell e Zilda Márcia Gricoli Iokoi. Rio de Janeiro: Expressão e cultura; São Paulo: Edusp, 1996, p. 619–635)

A look at women's experiences during the Revolution based on information contained in the Archivo de la Secretaría de la Defensa Nacional. Most female participants were middle class, single, and had a teaching

background. Their activities in the Revolution were varied and often included work as propagandists and spies.

1538 Rodríguez, Miguel. Chicago y los charros: ritos y fiestas de principios de mayo en la Ciudad de México. (*Hist. Mex.,* 45:2, oct./dic. 1995, p. 383–421, bibl.)

Explores first-of-May celebrations held in Mexico City from the early-20th century to 1952. Discusses the forms that such celebrations took and suggests how they reflected the growing influence of workers' groups.

1539 Rodríguez Hernández, Gina. Niños trabajadores mexicanos, 1865–1925. México?: Fondo de la Naciones Unidas para la Infancia; Instituto Nacional de Antropología e Historia, 1996. 96 p.: bibl., ill.

Photographic history of child labor in Mexico.

1540 Romero, Saúl Jerónimo. La incorporación del pueblo al proceso electoral de 1910. México: Instituto Nacional de Estudios Históricos de la Revolución Mexicana, Secretaria de Gobernación, 1995. 40 p.: bibl., ill.

Brief study of the 1910 presidential election, including the failed candidacy of Bernardo Reyes. Author sees Madero's candidacy as providing a means of expression for the politically marginalized.

1541 Romero Hernández, David Eduardo. Enemistades rancheras, bandolerismo y procesos de modernización. (*Estud. Jalisc.,* 27, feb. 1997, p. 47–67)

General exploration of the history of Mazamitla, Jalisco, with an emphasis on the 19th and 20th centuries. Emphasizes agrarian conflict and Mazamitla's more recent transformation to a modern economy.

1542 Sabido Méndez, Arcadio. Los hombres del poder: monopolios, oligarquía y riqueza Yucatán, 1880–1990. Mérida, Mexico: Univ. Autónoma de Yucatán, 1995. 316 p.: bibl. (Tratados; 2)

Revised thesis in sociology. Reviews the many changes that have affected the Yucatan in the last century, including the composition of the oligarchy, and concludes that the area has always been controlled by an oligarchy monopolizing economic and political power.

1543 Sáenz Arriaga, Joaquín and **Alicia Olivera de Bonfil.** El movimiento tradicionalista en México. (*J. Hist. Occidente,* 13, 1990, p. 267–283, bibl.)

A look at the Catholic Church in post-revolutionary Mexico. Focuses on the evolution of the Church since Vatican II, with attention to the activities of both the conservative and reformist branches.

1544 Sáenz Carrete, Erasmo. Santa María del Oro, Durango, y su región: una breve historia. México: Potrerillos Editores; H. Ayuntamiento Constitucional de El Oro, 1995. 189 p.: bibl., ill., map. (Col. Historia regional)

Basic history of a mining community in northern Mexico with brief remarks on the post-revolutionary era. Highlights the physical and economic development of El Oro and its environs.

1545 Salmerón Castro, Alicia. Un general agrarista en la lucha contra los cristeros: el movimiento en Aguascalientes y las razones de Genovevo de la O. (*Hist. Mex.,* 44:4, abril/junio 1995, p. 537–579, bibl.)

Study of the Cristero Rebellion from the perspective of a Zapatista general. Surveys the various conflicts inherent in the rebellion and argues that, in combatting the Cristeros, de la O was supporting the state-building project of Sonoran leaders.

1546 Salmerón Castro, Fernando I. La revolución y taretan. (*Estud. Michoacanos,* 6, 1995, p. 263–298, bibl., tables)

Surveys developments in a Michoacán municipality from 1913–30. While little change came to Taretan during this period, the stage was set for land reform.

1547 Samaniego López, Marco Antonio. Prensa y filibusterismo en los sucesos de 1911. (*Estud. Front.,* 33, enero/junio 1994, p. 125–155, bibl.)

Analysis of the Magonista incursion into Baja California, using principal California newspapers of the time. Explores the motives of editors and owners of these newspapers as a key to understanding this event.

1548 Sandoval, Guillermo and **Jorge Mantilla.** Felipe Carrillo Puerto: ensayo biográfico; vida y obra. Mérida, Mexico: Ediciones de la Univ. Autónoma de Yucatán, 1994. 225 p.: bibl., ill.

Laudatory biography of famous Yucatecan revolutionary with the emphasis on his educational and agrarian reforms.

1549 Santoyo, Antonio. La mano negra en defensa de la propiedad y el orden: Veracruz, 1928–1943. (*Secuencia/México,* 28, enero/abril 1994, p. 81–97, bibl., ill.)

Traces the growth of a *cacicazgo* led by Manuel Parra Mata. Through the cultivation of political alliances and the use of force, Parra successfully resisted the radical agrarianism of Gov. Adalberto Tejada and the popular agrarianism of Lázaro Cárdenas.

1550 Sariego Rodríguez, Juan Luis. Historia minera de Chihuahua. (*Siglo XIX/Monterrey,* 5:13, sept./dic. 1995, p. 7–26, map, table)

Overview of the mining industry in Chihuahua during the 20th century, organized along three "production models:" small or independent operators, medium-size firms, and large-scale, often foreign-owned, operations. The three models do not represent sequential stages of development, but rather have co-existed throughout the period.

1551 Schoonover, Thomas D. Los intereses europeos y estadounidenses en las relaciones México-Guatemala, 1850–1930. (*Secuencia/México,* 34, enero/abril 1996, p. 7–30, bibl., ill.)

Explores the ongoing border dispute between Mexico and Guatemala. Several European countries, as well as the Central American republics, sought to shape the outcome of this dispute.

1552 Sentíes, Yolanda. Adolfo López Mateos, senador de la república, 1946–1952. Toluca, Mexico: Instituto Mexiquense de Cultura, 1993. 234 p.: bibl., ill.

Collection of documents tracing López Mateos' path to the Senate.

1553 Serrano Alvarez, Pablo. La cooperativa de salineros de Colima: de la organización a la acción y lucha social, 1924–1953. (*in* La sal en México. Colima, Mexico: Univ. de Colima; México: Consejo Nacional para la Cultura y las Artes, Dirección General de Culturas Populares, 1995, p. 163–175)

Describes the formation, governing principals, and initial activities of the saltworkers' cooperative.

1554 Serrano Ortega, José Antonio. México y la fallida unificación de Centroamérica, 1916–1922. (*Hist. Mex.*, 45:4, abril/junio 1996, p. 843–866)

Analysis of relations between Mexico and Central America during the Carranza and Obregón years. Mexico's goal was a Central American union that would help limit the influence of the US in Latin America.

1555 Shadow, Robert D. and María J. Rodríguez-Shadow. Religión, economía y política en la Rebelión Cristera: el caso de los gobiernistas de Villa Guerrero, Jalisco. (*Hist. Mex.*, 43:4, abril/junio 1994, p. 657–699, bibl.)

Demonstrates that the Cristero Rebellion generated a variety of responses. Socioeconomic and political factors, not the religious question, were most important in determining the response to the Cristero challenge in this municipality.

1556 Sherman, John W. The Mexican right: the end of revolutionary reform, 1929–1940. Westport, Conn.: Praeger, 1997. 154 p.: bibl., index.

Important study of the Cárdenas era focusing on a neglected aspect of Mexico's political history. Details the origins and development of the secular and Catholic right, and the nature of rightist opposition to the revolutionary state.

1557 Simposio de Historia, *5th, Mexicali, Mexico, 1992.* V Simposio de Historia: días 12–13 Junio 1992, Mexicali, Baja California. Mexicali, Mexico: Instituto de Investigaciones Históricas del Estado de Baja California, 1992. 1 v.: bibl., ill.

Proceedings of the Fifth Symposium on Regional History held in Mexicali revolving around the theme, "The Mexican Revolution in Baja California, 1910–1920." The Magonista invasion of 1911 receives the greatest amount of attention.

1558 Smith, Michael M. *Carrancista* propaganda and the print media in the United States: an overview of institutions. (*Americas/Franciscans*, 52:2, Oct. 1995, p. 155–174)

Examination of the propaganda apparatus organized and reorganized by the Carranza administration from 1913–20 in an effort to influence the views of both English-speaking and Spanish-speaking populations

in the US. Concludes that the Carranza administration was generally effective in manipulating the print media in support of its diplomatic goals.

1559 Snodgrass, Michael. La lucha sindical y la resistencia patronal en Monterrey, México, 1918–1940 = The union struggle and employer resistance in Monterrey, Mexico, 1918–1940. Monterrey, Mexico: Archivo General del Estado de Nuevo León, 1996. 93 p.: bibl. (Serie Orgullosamente bárbaros; no. 17)

Bilingual account of the development of unionism in an important industrial city, with a focus on steelworkers and glassworkers. Emphasizes worker-employer relations during the Cárdenas administration.

1560 Sosa Elízaga, Raquel. Los códigos ocultos del cardenismo: un estudio de la violencia política, el cambio social y la continuidad institucional. México: UNAM; Plaza y Valdés Editores, 1996. 579 p.: bibl., ill.

Attempts to decipher the "codes of violence" operating during the Cárdenas regime by analyzing internal and external pressures. Sees the two greatest threats to the regime embodied in Saturnino Cedillo and Juan Andrew Almazán; their defeat came at the cost of toning down the social movement initiated by Cárdenas. Agrarian violence was the most important constant of the Cárdenas years.

1561 Soto Blanco, Cecilia. Ceremonial en el Zócalo: notas sobre la resistencia obrera. México: s.n., 1993. 325 p.: bibl.

Partisan chronicle of various labor actions, primarily strikes. Despite the title, coverage is not restricted to actions at the Zócalo or even in the Federal District. Period covered extends to 1992.

Sotomayor, Teresa Maya. Estados Unidos y el panamericanismo: el caso de la I Conferencia Internacional Americana, 1889–1890. See item **1020.**

1562 Spenser Grollová, Daniela. Uso y abuso de la ideología en las relaciones políticas entre Estados Unidos y México durante los años veinte. (*Secuencia/México*, 34, enero/abril 1996, p. 31–61, bibl., ill.)

Study of methods used by US investors to block Mexico's implementation of reforms contained in the 1917 Constitution. Argues that "anti-Bolshevism" colored US diplomatic relations with Mexico until the end of the decade.

1563 Taylor Hansen, Lawrence Douglas.
¿Charlatán o filibustero peligroso?: el papel de Richard "Dick" Ferris en la revuelta magonista de 1911 en Baja California. (*Hist. Mex.*, 44:4, abril/junio 1995, p. 581–616, bibl.)

Review of the activities of a California journalist and businessman linked to revolutionary activity. Argues that Ferris was neither a key figure in a US plot to annex Baja California, nor was he simply a publicity seeker.

1564 Taylor Hansen, Lawrence Douglas.
Gunboat diplomacy's last fling in the New World: the British seizure of San Quintin, April 1911. (*Americas/Franciscans*, 52:4, April 1996, p. 521–543, maps)

Study of the brief (17 hours) and bloodless British intervention at the port of San Quintín, Baja California. The landing by a small contingent of British marines was in response to a threatened Magonista attack on the port and prompted protests from both Mexican and US officials.

1565 Taylor Hansen, Lawrence Douglas. La repatriación de mexicanos de 1848 a 1980 y su papel en la colonización de la región fronteriza septentrional de México. (*Relaciones/Zamora*, 69, invierno 1997, p. 197–212, photo)

Traces the ongoing efforts of the Mexican government to support the repatriation of Mexicans from the US and settle them in northern Mexico. Until the mid-1970s, Mexico generally provided some sort of assistance (land, free transportation) to those seeking repatriation. Approximately half of work deals with post-1910 period.

1566 Taylor Hansen, Lawrence Douglas. La revuelta magonista de 1911 en Baja California: acontecimiento clave en el desarrollo del sentimiento nacional entre la población peninsular norteña. (*Front. Norte*, 7:13, enero/junio 1995, p. 25–47)

Examines impact of the Mexican Liberal Party (PLM) 1911 revolt on the development of nationalism and cultural identity in an isolated, frontier region. Although the anarcho-communist philosophy of the Mago-

nistas was probably too sophisticated for most of the inhabitants of the area, the Liberal revolt was still the most significant factor in the development of nationalist sentiment.

1567 Taylor Hansen, Lawrence Douglas. La toma y subsecuente pérdida de Agua Prieta en abril de 1911: un momento de gran expectativa y desilusión para el movimiento rebelde en el norte. (*in* Simposio de Historia y Antropología de Sonora, *19th, Hermosillo, Mexico, 1994.* Memorias. Hermosillo, Mexico: Instituto de Investigaciones Históricas de la Univ. de Sonora, 1994, v. 2, p. 17–35, bibl.)

Military account of the brief capture of Agua Prieta by Sonoran rebels. This victory convinced Porfirio Díaz to begin peace negotiations with Maderista rebels.

Tenenbaum, Barbara A. Mexico, so close to the United States: unconventional views of the nineteenth century. See item **1358.**

1568 Tenorio Trillo, Mauricio. The cosmopolitan Mexican summer, 1920–1949. (*LARR*, 32:3, 1997, p. 224–242)

Reviews seven books on political, social, and cultural themes that span two decades of Mexican history. Includes analyses of biographical works on Andrés Molina Enríquez and Covarrubias, and of studies that highlight the American attraction to Mexico during this era.

1569 Tenorio Trillo, Mauricio. 1910 Mexico City: space and nation in the city of the *Centenario*. (*J. Lat. Am. Stud.*, 28:1, Feb. 1996, p. 75–104, maps)

A "tour" of the capital and an exploration of the meanings inherent in the various projects for expanding and improving it. In their plans for Mexico City and the centennial celebration, Porfirian elites revealed their desire for an ideal, modern city that embraced their own notions of progress.

1570 Tiempos y espacios laborales: II Encuentro Nacional de Mujeres Legisladoras. México: Honorable Cámara de Diputados, LV Legislatura, Secretaría de Gobernación, Archivo General de las Nación, 1994? 96 p.: chiefly ill.

Collection of photos depicting the changing labor roles of women in the early years of the Revolution. Photos are good but often undated; captions are brief and not particularly informative.

1571 Tortolero, Alejandro. Historia agraria y medio ambiente en México: estado de la cuestión. *(Not. Hist. Agrar.*, 11, enero/junio 1996, p. 151–178, appendix, bibl., table)

Historiographical survey of hacienda studies with an eye toward understanding Mexico's environmental history and current environmental problems. Underscores the importance of an interdisciplinary approach to Mexico's environmental history.

1572 Tuñón, Julia. Estados Unidos en el cine mexicano de los años de oro: entre el avasallamiento y el ninguneo. *(in* Estados Unidos desde América Latina: sociedad, política y cultura. México: Instituto de Investigaciones Dr. José María Luis Mora; Centro de Investigación y Docencia Económicas, El Colegio de México, 1995, p. 300–321)

Examination of the influence of North Americans on and their depiction in Mexican films during the "golden years" of the 1940s. Contrasts the considerable North American impact on the Mexican film industry to its limited impact on Mexican films, which often contained negative North American stereotypes.

1573 Urquizo, Francisco Luis. Recuerdo que—: visiones aisladas de la Revolución. v. 2–3. Ed. exclusiva para el Ejército Mexicano. México: Secretaría de la Defensa Nacional, 1993. 2 v.: ill. (Biblioteca del oficial mexicano; 2, 4)

Disjointed reminiscences of Carrancista general with the emphasis on the common soldier in the revolutionary ranks. Vols. 2 and 3 cover the period from 1914–17.

1574 U.S.-Mexico borderlands: historical and contemporary perspectives. Edited by Oscar Jáquez Martínez. Wilmington, Del.: Scholarly Resources, 1995. 264 p.: bibl. (Jaguar books on Latin America; no. 11)

Excellent collection of scholarly essays and primary documents. Covers 1830s-1990s, with the emphasis on the post-1910 era. Work is divided into seven sections, each covering a key issue in borderlands history. Good introduction to each entry.

1575 Valencia Castrejón, Sergio. Poder regional y política nacional en México: el gobierno de Maximino Avila Camacho en Puebla, 1937–1941. México: Instituto Nacional de Estudios Históricos de la Revolución Mexicana, 1996. 179 p.: bibl., ill. (Investigación)

Analyzes Camacho's campaign for the governorship of Puebla and his efforts to build alliances with workers, peasants, and the political and economic elites. Explores the links between local power and national politics during the Cárdenas years.

1576 Valle Herrera, Ramona del. El conflicto religioso mexicano a través de la prensa argentina. *(Rev. Hist. Am. Argent.*, 17:33/34, 1993/94, p. 37–70)

Examines the coverage of the Cristero Rebellion in the Argentine press, using two newspapers from Buenos Aires and two from Mendoza. Work is more an overview of the Church-state conflict in Mexico between 1926–29, using newspaper sources, than a review of newspaper coverage of the crisis.

1577 Vaughan, Mary K. Cultural politics in revolution: teachers, peasants, and schools in Mexico, 1930–1940. Tucson: Univ. of Arizona Press, 1997. 262 p.: bibl., index, maps.

Innovative study of the cultural legacy of the Mexican Revolution, using the story of rural schools. Focuses on Puebla and Sonora and the attempt by the central government to implement socialist education and to advance its nationalist agenda. Stresses the importance of negotiation among national and local leaders, teachers and peasants.

1578 Vázquez Alfaro, Guillermo Gabino. Zapata, Carranza y Villa, precursores agrarios: Emiliano Zapata y el movimiento zapatista en el agrarismo mexicano y la ley agraria del *6 de enero de 1915.* México: Editorial PAC, 1995. 329 p.: bibl.

Work is two separate studies, detailing the evolution of Zapata's thought on the agrarian question, his activities related to land reform, and the eventual development of the Agrarian Law of 1915.

1579 Venustiano Carranza: testimonios; a 75 años de su fallecimiento. Saltillo, Mexico: Gobierno del Estado de Coahuila, 1995. 296 p.: bibl., ill.

Most of the work is a collection of essays by contemporaries of Carranza analyzing his military policy, foreign relations, economic/financial actions, and his revolutionary views and activities. The remainder is made up of thirteen documents spanning the years 1913–20. Well illustrated.

Victoria, José Guadalupe; Beatriz Ruiz Gaytán; and Mario Pérez Torres. Tlatelolco en la historia de México. See item **1366.**

1580 Villaneda, Alicia. Juana Belén Gutiérrez de Mendoza, 1875–1942: justicia y libertad. México: Documentación y Estudios de Mujeres, 1994. 92 p.: bibl., ill.

Biography of perennial dissident who was successively a Liberal, Maderista, and Zapatista. Frequently jailed, she pioneered in educational reform, agrarian reform, indigenismo, and feminism.

1581 Villegas Moreno, Gloria. Los confines de la utopía. (*Hist. Mex.*, 46:4, abril/junio 1997, p. 839–869, bibl.)

Study of the 1909 vice-presidential campaign between Bernardo Reyes and Ramón Corral. Official fears of conflict resulted in Reyes' withdrawal from the race and underscored the antidemocratic nature of the Porfiriato.

1582 Visión histórica de la frontera norte de México. t. 5, De la revolución a la Segunda Guerra Mundial. t. 6, La frontera en nuestros días. 2da edición. Mexicali, Mexico: Univ. Autónoma de Baja California, Centro de Investigaciones Históricas UNAM-UABC, 1994. 2 v.: ill., maps, ports.

Two installments in a six-volume work on the border. Articles explore the Revolution in the border states, the effects of Prohibition, the Depression, and World War II in the border zone, Cardenista reform in northern Mexico, and general economic, political, and cultural developments affecting the border since 1945.

Vos, Jan de. Vivir en frontera: la experiencia de los indios de Chiapas. See item **603.**

1583 Vuurde, Rob van. Los Países Bajos, el petróleo y la Revolución Mexicana, 1900–1950. Amsterdam: Thela Publishers, 1997. 160 p.: appendices, bibl., tables.

Examines relations between Holland and Mexico, focusing on the Royal Dutch/Shell Oil Company from its entry into Mexico through the expropriation of 1938 to the settlement of 1947. Concludes that the company generally favored direct negotiations

with the Mexican government, rather than appealing for help from the Dutch government, which attached primary importance to maintaining cordial relations with Mexico.

1584 Wager, Stephen J. The Mexican military approaches the 21st century: coping with a new world order. (*in* Mexico faces the 21st century. Westport, Conn.: Greenwood Press, 1995, p. 59–76)

Description of military developments in the closing decades of the 20th century, with limited discussion of future developments. Sees the military continuing its emphasis on civic action, crisis management, and antidrug activity, and identifies several factors inhibiting growth in military power such as available funding.

1585 Women of the Mexican countryside, 1850–1990: creating spaces, shaping transitions. Edited by Heather Fowler-Salamini & Mary Kay Vaughan. Tucson: Univ. of Arizona Press, 1994 253 p.: bibl., ill., index, map.

Collection of thirteen essays—nine of which relate to the post-1910 period—examining the role of women and gender relations as rural families make the transition from an agrarian to an industrial society. The nine essays are organized around two themes: Rural Women and Revolution in Mexico and Rural Women, Urbanization, and Gender Relations.

1586 ... y la revolución volvió a San Angel. México: Instituto Nacional de Estudios Históricos de la Revolución Mexicana de la Secretaría de Gobernación con la Delegación Alvaro Obregón del Departamento del Distrito Federal, 1995. 81 p.: bibl., ill.

Brief history of the municipality of San Angel. Most of the work deals with the post-1910 period and ends with the assassination of President-Elect Obregon in July 1928. Well illustrated.

1587 Yankelevich, Pablo. Las campañas pro México: estrategias publicitarias mexicanas en América Latina, 1916–1922. (*Cuad. Am.*, 49, enero/feb. 1995, p. 79–95)

Examination of propaganda efforts by the Carranza and Obregón administrations aimed at countering negative publicity from US sources as well as promoting a positive image of revolutionary Mexico. Title is somewhat misleading, as most of work deals with Carrancista activities in Argentina, Brazil, and Chile.

Yankelevich, Pablo. La diplomacia imaginaria: Argentina y la Revolución Mexicana 1910–1916. See item **3073.**

1588 Yankelevich, Pablo. Una mirada argentina de la revolución mexicana: la gesta de Manuel Ugarte, 1910–1917. (*Hist. Mex.*, 44:4, abril/junio 1995, p. 645–676, bibl.)

Explores the echoes of the Mexican Revolution in Argentina through the thought and writings of a staunch supporter of Carranza's Constitutionalist movement. Ugarte was a proponent of Latin American unity and he saw the Revolution as a struggle against US aggression.

1589 Zapata Vela, Carlos. Conversaciones con Heriberto Jara. México: Costa-Amic Editores, 1992. 222 p.: ill.

Recollections by a participant in the Mexican Revolution. Jara served as a military leader, member of the 1917 Constitutional Congress, and post-revolutionary politician.

1590 Zebadúa, Emilio. El banco de la Revolución. (*Hist. Mex.*, 45:1, julio/sept. 1995, p. 67–98, bibl.)

Good survey of the events and obstacles that led up to the creation of a national bank in 1925. Examines the attempts by revolutionary leaders to establish an institution separate from Mexico's private banks, thus helping to affirm the country's financial autonomy.

1591 Zebadúa, Mará et al. La nueva historia de Nuevo León: historia, economía y sociedad. Recopilación de Rocío González Maíz y José Antonio Olvera Sandoval. Monterrey, Mexico: Ediciones Castillo, 1995. 229 p.: bibl.

Collection of seven regional studies without a central theme. Most deal with the post-1910 period, with the emphasis on rural and industrial topics.

Zorrilla, Luis G. Relaciones políticas, económicas y sociales de México con el extranjero. See *HLAS 57:4138.*

1592 Zuleta Miranda, María Cecilia. Alfonso Reyes y las relaciones México-Argentina: proyectos y realidades, 1926–1936. (*Hist. Mex.*, 45:4, abril/junio 1996, p. 867–905)

Explores the attempts by a prominent Mexican intellectual to strengthen ties with Argentina in the era between the two World Wars. Although commercial links between the two countries increased, political and financial obstacles hampered most projects, while both countries were compelled to focus their diplomatic efforts on the Great Powers.

1593 Zuloaga Rada, Marina. La diplomacia española en la época de Carranza: iberoamericanismo e hispanoamericanismo, 1916–1920. (*Hist. Mex.*, 45:4, abril/junio 1996, p. 807–842)

Explores the specific attempts of Spain to promote pan-hispanism. Mexico's revolutionary ideology ultimately clashed with Spain's idea of Iberoamericanism, while conservative Spanish governments complicated attempts at closer relations between the two countries.

CENTRAL AMERICA

DAVID MCCREERY, *Professor of History, Georgia State University*
STEPHEN WEBRE, *Professor of History, Louisiana Tech University*

INCREASINGLY SOLID RESEARCH and greater awareness by scholars of theoretical and methodological trends outside the region continue to characterize Central American historiography. In the largely untapped area of cultural history, a major event is Whisnant's study of Nicaragua from the preconquest era to the struggle to appropriate Sandino's memory (item **1622**). Notable also in this field is the substantial body of work on Costa Rica produced both individually and collectively by Molina Jiménez and Palmer (items **1610, 1613,** and **1729,** among others). The question of gender, both in its broadest sense and conceived more narrowly as "women's" history, is receiving greater attention. In quite diverse ways, Rodríguez (item **1616**) and Lobo (item **1646**) both examine sexual deviance and marriage in Costa Rica, while new works by Macpherson (item **1722**) and Aubry (item **1595**) address the condition of women in Belize and urban Chiapas respectively.

For the colonial period, the perennial theme of Spanish-indigenous relations is well represented by Dakin and Lutz's unusual collection of Nahuatl-language petitions from 16th-century Guatemala (item **1635**), and in MacLeod's sensitive reconstruction of a 1693 native uprising in Tuxtla, Chiapas (item **1650**). Missionary activities on the colonial frontier are the subject of important new studies by Black on Honduras (item **1627**) and Castillero Calvo on Panama (item **1630**). Miscegenation as both a biological and a cultural process is addressed for Guatemala by Luján Muñoz (item **1647**) and Rodas (item **1662**), and for Costa Rica by Acuña León and Chavarría López (item **1624**) and Meléndez Chaverri (item **1624**). Finally, two important personages of the Bourbon era are the subjects of major new biographies: merchant Juan Fermín de Aycinena by Brown (item **1628**) and Guatemalan Archbishop Pedro Cortés y Larraz by Martín Blasco and García Añoveros (item **1652**).

Scholars of the national period continue to devote much attention to familiar political topics, but recent works reflect newer concerns, such as inquiries into state-labor relations by Miller (item **1726**) and Trujillo Bolio (item **1760**); cross-class alliances by Gould (item **1700**) and Vargas (item **1763**); democracy by Gudmundson (item **1703**) and Merino del Río (item **1725**); and state violence by Alvarenga (item **1673**) and Holden (item **1709**). A particularly new direction, at least for Central America, appears in Rocío Tábora's study of masculinity and political violence in 19th-century Honduras (item **1759**).

The study of social history remains largely concerned with issues of race and ethnicity. Palmer looks at how Central American intellectuals used social Darwinism and eugenics to explain national development and nationhood (item **1736**), and Taracena Arriola and Piel have edited a first-rate collection of essays on ethnicity and the state in the various republics (item **1711**). Related country studies include Gudmundson's comparison of Guatemala and Costa Rica (item **1704**), Taracena Arriola's well-documented study of separatism in Guatemala's western highlands (item **1621**), Gould's examination of official mestizo-centered ideology in Nicaragua (item **1701**), and Howe's discussion of Kuna resistance in early-20th-century Panama (item **1710**). Afro-Central American experience is the subject of new works by Martínez Montiel (item **1615**), Chomsky (item **1686**), and Murillo Chaverri (item **1733**).

There has been a revival of interest in the history of communications. Studies of radio, such as those by Almorza (item **1672**) and Castillo (item **1682**), are in their infancy, but Vega Jiménez's study of early Costa Rican newspapers is impressive (item **1765**). Also, the Spanish government recently funded a number of railroad histories in the region (items **1698, 1712,** and **1752**).

In addition to these specific areas, the past few years have witnessed many welcome additions to the essential national bibliographies of the isthmian republics. In Guatemala, for example, classic works on the revolutionary period (1944–54) are reappearing, including those by Cardoza y Aragón (item **1681**), Galich (item **1697**), and León Aragón (item **1717**). Also, some participants have offered their personal memories for the first time, notably Bauer Paiz (item **1677**) and Ruiz Franco (item **1750**). El Salvador's long nightmare of the 1980s has found capable historians in Byrne (item **1680**) and Lungo (item **1721**), whose general accounts are complemented by more narrowly focused works by Danner (item **1690**), Keune (item **1714**), Quezada and H.R. Martínez (item **1745**), and Moroni Bracamonte (item **1732**). For Honduras, higher standards of documentary research—evident elsewhere, too—are reflected in Euraque's major study of the role of the northern coast in shaping the country's political evolution (item **1694**), as well as in new accounts of the 1954 banana strike by Argueta (item **1675**) and Barahona (item **1746**).

Political changes in Nicaragua in the 1990s have not diminished historians' interest in Augusto C. Sandino, who is the subject of an important new biography by Wünderich (item **1768**), as well as of shorter studies by Dospital (item **1692**) and Schroeder (item **1754**). Students of more recent history will appreciate the interesting, if predictable, memoirs of Violeta Chamorro (item **1685**), as well as Sobel's careful calculation of Contra aid (item **1758**). Finally, Costa Rica continues to offer innovative work of good quality, including a flourishing of the cultural histories referred to in the introductory paragraph, and a number of recent works on urban history, such as those of Quezada Avendaño (item **1744**), Cerdas Albertazzi (item **1684**), Palmer (item **1612**), and Fernández Esquivel (item **1603**).

GENERAL

1594 Arellano, Jorge Eduardo. Historia básica de Nicaragua. v. 1, El mundo aborigen; la conquista; la pax hispánica. Managua: Fondo Editorial CIRA, 1993. 1 v.: bibl., ill., maps.

First of three-volume general history of Nicaragua provides detailed account of prehispanic, conquest, and colonial periods. Extensive bibliography contains both primary and secondary references. Essential for the period.

1595 Aubry, André. Miedo urbano y amparo femenino: San Cristóbal de las Casas retratada en sus mujeres. (*Mesoamérica/Plumsock*, 15:28, dic. 1994, p. 305–320, graph, maps, tables)

Fear of Indian attacks, population collapse, natural disasters, and political conflicts shaped urban geography of San Cristóbal. Labor demands and political and social violence tended to move men around the countryside, while women remained in urban areas, "assuring the continuity of the urban refuge."

1596 Browning, John. Un obstáculo imprescindible: el indígena en los siglos XVIII y XIX. (*in* Encuentro Nacional de Historiadores (Guatemala), 2nd, Guatemala, 1995. Memorias. Guatemala: Univ. del Valle de Guatemala, 1996, p. ix-xxvi)

Brief overview of elite attitudes toward Guatemala's indigenous population, emphasizing repeated assimilationist proposals from late-18th to late-19th century. Since conquest, creole view has been dominated by dual motifs of Indian as labor source and as feared, inscrutable other.

1597 Centeno García, Santos. Historia del pueblo negro caribe y su llegada a Hibueras el 12 de abril de 1797. Tegucigalpa: Univ. Nacional Autónoma de Honduras, Editorial Universitaria, 1996. 116 p.: bibl. (Col. Antropología; 1)

Broader scope than title suggests. Readable essays on Garífuna history and culture, and on role of Hondurans of African descent in general. Lacks documentation.

1598 Dejour, Dominique. Condiciones sanitarias y de vida en la Mosquitia, 1492–1850. (*Wani/Managua*, 17, sept. 1995, p. 3–13, bibl., facsims.)

Extract from French doctoral thesis in medicine examines history of difficult health and medical conditions on Nicaragua's Caribbean coast from conquest to arrival of Moravian missionaries. Fails to answer question posed: why, despite Sandinista improvements, do indigenous peoples continue to think of past as better than present?

1599 Encuentro Nacional de Historiadores, Guatemala, 2nd, Univ. del Valle de Guatemala, 4–6 de diciembre de 1995. Memoria. Guatemala: Univ. del Valle de Guatemala, 1996. 447 p.: bibl., ill.

Twenty-five randomly arranged, short

pieces of varying quality. Particularly useful are Wagner's "La crisis del fin del siglo XIX," several pieces on women's history, and Esquit's study of landholding and ethnic conflict in Tecpán, Guatemala (item **1601**). Several useful contributions are noted separately.

1600 Encuentros con la historia. Recopilación de Margarita Vannini. Managua: Instituto de Historia de Nicaragua, Univ. Centroamericana; México?: Ccntro Francés de Estudios Mexicanos y Centroamericanos, 1995. 382 p.: bibl., ill., maps.

Collected presentations from four-month institute for Nicaraguan teachers and researchers (Managua, 1993). Contributions on Nicaragua include: Romero Vargas on state and society in colonial period; Casanova Fuertes on internal conflicts of 1840s; Herrera Cuarezma on external actors and the conflict of 1855–57; Gould on *mestizaje*, and on popular movements; Walter on *somocismo*; and Wünderich on Sandino's nationalism and spiritualism. Also includes papers on history and historical method by Pérez Brignoli, Fonseca Corrales, Acuña Ortega, and Romero Vargas; and on the Central American context by Pérez Brignoli, Fernández Molina, Taracena Arriola, and Samper Kutschbach.

1601 Esquit, Edgar. La lucha por la tierra y el origen del conflicto étnico entre indígenas y ladinos: Tecpán Guatemala, 1750–1858. (*in* Encuentro Nacional de Historiadores (Guatemala), *2nd, Guatemala, 1995.* Memorias. Guatemala: Univ. del Valle de Guatemala, 1996, p. 57–72, bibl.)

Despite formal prohibitions, by 1800 more than 40 percent of Guatemala's ladino population lived in indigenous communities. In Tecpán, Guatemala, an abundance of communal lands combined with ladinos' value as mediators with external interests kept conflict to a minimum until 1817, when ladinos attempted to title land they previously rented. Legal changes following independence strengthened their position, not only in Tecpán but throughout the country.

1602 Euraque, Darío A. San Pedro Sula: de villorrio colonial a emporio bananero, 1536–1936. Tegucigalpa: Univ. Nacional Autónoma de Honduras, Editorial Universitaria, 1995. 62 p.: bibl. (Col. Cuadernos universitarios; 89)

Excellent, short "macroeconomic" history of San Pedro Sula region, northern Honduras' late 19th- and early 20th-century export center, and more recently locus of national industrialization efforts. Concludes with brief comparison between San Pedro Sula and Tegucigalpa.

1603 Fernández Esquivel, Franco. La Plaza Mayor: génesis de la nación costarricense. Cartago, Costa Rica: Editorial Cultural Cartaginesa; Uruk Editores, 1996. 335 p.: bibl., ill., maps.

Presents history of Costa Rica as seen from central plaza of Cartago, economic hub and site of key political events and colonial justice, religious and civic festivals. Mostly treats natural disasters, such as volcanic eruptions and floods, as tangentially linked to the plaza. Interesting approach.

1604 Fonseca Corrales, Elizabeth. Centroamérica: su historia. San José: Facultad Latinoamericana de Ciencias Sociales; Editorial Universitaria Centroamericana (EDUCA), 1996. 379 p.: bibl., ill., maps, plates.

Up-to-date synthesis, based on recent scholarship and condensed from six volume *Historia general de Centroamérica* (*see HLAS 56:1633*). Intended for use in secondary and university-level courses.

1605 Historia de El Salvador. v. 1–2. San Salvador?: Ministerio de Educación, 1994. 2 v.: ill. (some col.), maps (some col.).

Well-done, if necessarily summary, treatment of El Salvador's history from conquest to 1870s (vol. 1), and 1870s-1980s (vol. 2), meant for secondary school use. Includes contributions from well-known anthropologists, historians, and economists.

1606 Historia general de Guatemala. t. 3, Siglo XVIII hasta la independencia, t. 4, Desde la República Federal hasta 1898. Guatemala: Asociación de Amigos del País, Fundación para la Cultura y el Desarrollo, 1994? 2 v.: bibl., ill. (some col.), maps (some col.).

Part of massive, multi-volume history of Guatemala with dozens of contributing authors. Vol. 3 covers late-18th century and independence. Vol. 4 treats period from Federal Republic to 1898. Includes sections on politics and government, society, economy, regional history, and culture. Beautifully produced, with many prints and photographs and a unified bibliography. Constitutes new standard for multi-volume histories of Central America.

The legacy of Mesoamerica: history and culture of a Native American civilization. See *HLAS 57:94.*

1607 Lutz, Christopher H. *et al.* Territorio y sociedad en Guatemala: tres ensayos históricos. Guatemala: Centro de Estudios Urbanos y Regionales, Univ. de San Carlos de Guatemala, 1991. 125 p.: bibl.

Includes essays on differences during colonial period in land ownership and settlement between Guatemala's "Indian" west and "ladino" east, on regional development of Los Altos at end of colonial period, and on changes in Guatemalan family during 20th century.

1608 Meléndez Chaverri, Carlos. La independencia de Centroamérica. Madrid: Editorial MAPFRE, 1993. 267 p.: bibl., index. (Col. Independencia de Iberoamérica; 12 Col. MAPFRE 1492)

Excellent overview of independence based largely on secondary sources and some newspapers. Includes chronology of events for 1808–48 and short biographical sketches of chief participants. Part of "Colección Independencia de Iberoamérica," financed by Spain's Fundación MAPFRE.

1609 Mena García, María del Carmen. Temas de historia panameña. Prólogo de Alfredo Figueroa Navarro. Panamá: Editorial Universitaria, 1996. 460 p.: bibl.

Presents collection of previously published essays by distinguished specialist. Contributions on early colonial period include studies and documents on: themes of religiosity and death in Pedrarias' will; early encomienda in Panama (2 studies); Pedrarias and Laws of Burgos (*HLAS 52:1396*); abandonment of Nombre de Dios and founding of Portobelo (*HLAS 52:1397*); royal treasury in 16th-century Panama (2 studies; for one, see *HLAS 50:1348*); 1550 revolt launched in Nicaragua by Pedrarias' grandsons, Pedro and Hernando de Contreras (2 studies); and bureaucracy and power in 16th century. Other items are synthetic treatments of Central America in the 19th-20th centuries, bibliography of urban history (unrelated to Panama), and polemic on 1989 US invasion to oust dictator Manuel Noriega.

1610 Molina Jiménez, Iván. Él que quiera divertirse: libros y sociedad en Costa Rica, 1750–1914. San José: Editorial de la Univ. de Costa Rica, Ciudad Universitaria, Rodrigo Facio; Heredia, Costa Rica: Editorial de la Univ. Nacional, Campus Omar Dengo, 1995. 240 p.: bibl., ill. (Col. Nueva historia)

Well-documented examination of book trade and book culture in 18th- and 19th-century Costa Rica, by one of the country's most innovative young historians.

1611 Nicaragua en busca de su identidad. Edición de Frances Kinloch Tijerino. Managua: Instituto de Historia de Nicaragua, Univ. Centroamericana, 1995. 619 p.: bibl., ill.

Handsomely produced volume of 33 papers from interdisciplinary conference on nationalism and identity in Managua (May 1995). Contributions represent range of recent Nicaraguan inquiry into what it means, and has meant, to be Nicaraguan. Entries touch on art; literature; education; church; ethnic relations; emergence of nation-state, political parties, and political institutions; and, of course, *sandinismo*.

1612 Palmer, Steven Paul. Prolegómenos a toda historia futura de San José, Costa Rica. (*Mesoamérica/Plumsock*, 17:31, junio 1996, p. 181–213, maps)

Overview of historical development of San José, from mid-18th century to 1900, based on secondary sources and author's archival work. Ties city's history to broader currents of Latin American urban historiography and shows link between different views of development and current ideological concerns.

1613 El paso del cometa: estado, política social y culturas populares en Costa Rica, 1800/1950. Recopilación de Iván Molina Jiménez y Steven Palmer. San José: Editorial Porvenir; Plumsock Mesoamerican Studies, 1994. 232 p.: bibl., ill., map. (Col. Ensayos)

Collection of essays on popular culture in Costa Rica explore darker recesses of plebeian and peasant behavior. Contributors include Rodríguez Sáenz on rape and incest; Marín Hernández on prostitution; Naranjo Gutiérrez on banditry; Edelman on ethnicity, class, gender, and pacting with the devil; Acuña Ortega on nationalism and working class consciousness; Molina Jiménez on popular panic inspired by 1910 visit of Halley's comet; and Palmer on heroine abuse. For sociologist's comment, see item *HLAS 57:4735.*

1614 Pérez Alonso, Manuel Ignacio. Fuentes documentales para la historia de Nicaragua en archivos y bibliotecas del extranjero: conferencia. Dictada por Manuel Ignacio Pérez Alonso en el Simposio sobre la Documentación Histórica de Nicaragua, organizado por el Instituto de Cultura en la Biblioteca Nacional de Nicaragua el 17 de agosto de 1991. Managua: Impr. UCA, 1995. 30 p.: ill.

Survey, with user notes, of Nicaraguan material available in Archivo General de Indias and other Spanish archives, Vatican archives, British Public Record Office, US National Archives, Bancroft Library, and Archivo General de la Nación, Mexico.

1615 Presencia africana en Centroamérica. Coordinación de Luz María Martínez Montiel. México: Consejo Nacional para la Cultura y las Artes, 1993. 292 p.: bibl. (Claves de América Latina)

Presents survey history of Africans and descendants in Central America. Country-specific essays (including Belize and Panama but omitting Guatemala) follow introductory overview. Chapters on Panama and Nicaragua are based on archival research, whereas others summarize secondary sources somewhat competently.

1616 Rodríguez, Eugenia. Tiyita Bea lo que me han echo: estupro e incesto en Costa Rica, 1800–1850. (*Anu. Estud. Centroam.,* 19:2, 1993, p. 71–88, tables)

Examines 13 cases of rape and incest as part of larger project on marriage and family in central valley of Costa Rica from 1750–1850. Finds that Church and state preferred marriage, but fines and imprisonment were also imposed. Women shared blame, except when minors were involved or when violence was evident.

1617 Sáenz Carbonell, Jorge Francisco. Don Joaquín de Oreamuno y Muñoz de la Trinidad: vida de un monárquico costarricense. San José: Editorial Univ. Estatal a Distancia, 1994. 295 p.: bibl., ill., map.

Biography of important independence-period monarchist and leader of Iturbide partisans in Cartago. Examines not only participation in events of 1821–23, but also activities in colonial period, private life, and commercial and military endeavors.

1618 Sánchez, Consuelo. La conformación étnico-nacional en Nicaragua. México: Instituto Nacional de Antropología e Historia, 1994. 383 p.: bibl., maps. (Serie Antropología)

Covers history of Nicaraguan people from prehispanic times to mid-19th century. Argues that differing impact of European imperial activity reinforced existing cultural differences between native inhabitants of Pacific and Atlantic regions. Lacks both introduction and conclusion.

1619 Sibaja Chacón, Luis Fernando *et al.* La industria: su evolución histórica y su aporte a la sociedad costarricense. San José: Cámara de Industrias de Costa Rica, 1993. 251 p.: bibl., ill. (some col.).

History of industry in Costa Rica funded by Cámara de Industrias. Pt. 1 examines development of artisan handicrafts from preconquest to end of 19th century, and industrial development in first half of 20th century. Pts. 2 and 3 focus on post-World War II period, especially impact of Central American Common Market and crisis of 1980s. Solid work with considerable statistical data.

1620 Taracena Arriola, Arturo. Génesis del movimiento separatista en Los Altos de Guatemala, 1806–1829. (*Rev. Hist./Heredia,* 29, enero/junio 1994, p. 7–60, tables)

Details construction of conscious regional identity among elites of Quezaltenango, Guatemala, from the forming of Ayuntamiento de Españoles in 1805 and Diputación Provincial in 1813. Emphasizes federation politics in 1820s and temporary frustration of separatist designs.

1621 Taracena Arriola, Arturo. Invención criolla, sueño ladino, pesadilla indígena: Los Altos de Guatemala; de región a Estado, 1740–1850. Antigua, Guatemala: Centro de Investigaciones Regionales de Mesoamérica; San José: Porvenir, 1997? 435 p., 11 leaves of plates (7 folded): bibl., ill., index.

Supported by rural small holders, creole and ladino elites of Quezaltenango, Guatemala, sought autonomy for western

highlands, first as part of Mexico, then as independent state in Central American Federation. Attributes failure to elite's refusal to include indigenous majority in schemes, except
as taxpayers and cheap labor.

1622 Whisnant, David E. Rascally signs in
sacred places: the politics of culture
in Nicaragua. Chapel Hill: Univ. of North
Carolina Press, 1995. 582 p.: bibl., ill., index,
maps.

Wide-ranging look at culture over time
and space in Nicaragua, from preconquest to
present. Pt. 1 treats history of national culture to end of 19th century. In pt. 2, four
chapters focus on culture under Somoza and
Sandinistas. Topics addressed include unau-
thorized removal of archeological treasures
during the 19th century, cultural politics
surrounding Rubén Darío and Augusto C.
Sandino, and gender relations and "cultural
recalcitrance." Worth reading.

1623 Zaporta Pallarés, José. Religiosos mer-
cedarios en Panamá, 1519–1992: con
testimonios históricos de Tirso de Molina.
Madrid: Revista Estudios, 1996. 294 p.: appendix, bibl., ill.

Offers materials for history of Mercedarian order in Panama. Present on isthmus from 1519–1861, order returned in 1980
to work among Panama City's poor. Eclectic
combination of colonial documents, biographical notes, and recent testimony, including
eyewitness account of 1989 US invasion,
whose impact author compares to 1671 sack-
ing of city by pirate Henry Morgan.

COLONIAL

1624 Acuña León, María de los Angeles and
Doriam Chavarría López. Cartago colonial: mestizaje y patrones matrimoniales,
1738–1821. (*Mesoamérica/Plumsock*, 17:31,
junio 1996, p. 157–179, maps, tables)

Analyzes more than 4,500 marriage
records for Costa Rica's colonial capital. Reveals strong tendency toward exogamy among
city's various racial groups, facilitating miscegenation and formation of multiracial society.
However, most unions, especially among
Spanish elites, remained endogamous.

1625 Alvarenga Venutolo, Patricia. Resistencia campesina y formación del
mercado de bienes básicos: Cartago, 1750–

1820. (*Rev. Hist./Heredia*, 31, enero/junio
1995, p. 41–67)

Although only rarely engaging in open
conflict, peasant producers in late-colonial
Costa Rica successfully resisted efforts, especially by Cartago's municipal authorities, to
coerce them into expanded commitment to
market production on terms dictated by consumer groups. Economic autonomy of producers, scarcity of cash, and relative weakness of state all seen as characteristic of
primitive stage of market evolution at time
of independence.

1626 Barón Castro, Rodolfo. Reseña
histórica de la villa de San Salvador:
desde su fundación en 1525, hasta que recibe
el título de ciudad en 1546. 2. ed. San Salvador: Dirección de Publicaciones e Impresos,
1996. 307 p.: bibl., ill., indexes, maps (some
col.).

Welcome new edition of classic work,
first published 1950, features biographical
sketch of Barón Castro (1909–86), Salvadoran
diplomat and one of country's most important historians of 20th century. Originally
noted in *HLAS 16:1589* by Howard Cline.

1627 Black, Nancy Johnson. The frontier
mission and social transformation in
western Honduras: the Order of Our Lady
of Mercy, 1525–1773. Leiden, Netherlands;
New York: E.J. Brill, 1995. 206 p.: bibl., index, maps. (Studies in Christian mission,
0924–9389; 14)

Significant contribution to Central
American ecclesiastical history and ethnohistory. Heart of study focuses on missionary
interaction with Lenca people of Tencoa district. Fills important gap in literature for the
Lenca, colonial Honduras, and the Mercedarian order.

1628 Brown, Richmond Forrest. Juan Fermín de Aycinena: Central American
colonial entrepreneur, 1729–1796. Norman:
Univ. of Oklahoma Press, 1997. 215 p.: bibl.,
ill., index.

Most powerful man in late-colonial
Guatemala is subject of long-needed scholarly biography, largely based on privately
held family papers. Rich account of 18th-
century economic and political life. Major
work.

1629 Carrillo Padilla, José Domingo. Lectura de historiografía: la conquista de México y Centroamérica. (*Estudios/USAC*, 1, 1995, p. 61–79, bibl.)

Response to polemics surrounding Columbian Quincentenary. Surveys both classic and recent secondary literature on conquest, with particular reference to Central America. Emphasizes regional and chronological variations, and especially contribution of native collaboration to historical outcome.

1630 Castillero Calvo, Alfredo. Conquista, evangelización y resistencia: ¿triunfo o fracaso de la política indigenista? Panamá: Editorial Mariano Arosemena; Instituto Nacional de Cultura, 1995. 494 p.: bibl., maps. (Col. Ricardo Miró. Premio ensayo; 1994)

Sophisticated study of Spanish-indigenous relations on Panamanian frontier from conquest through 19th century. Based on extensive archival research, country's most distinguished contemporary historian argues that persistence of unsubjugated frontiers on both eastern and western ends of isthmus was due to inconsistencies in Spanish indigenist legislation; methodological weaknesses of missionaries; and lack of coherent, effective frontier strategy throughout colonial period. Despite scarcity of ethnohistorical work on Panama, noteworthy for attempt to make sense of resistance from native point of view. Major work.

1631 Castro Vega, Oscar. Pedrarias Dávila, la ira de Dios. San José: Litografía e Impr. LIL, 1996. 191 p.: bibl., ill.

Readable short biography of Pedro Arias de Avila y Puñonrostro (1440–1531), better known to history as Pedrarias, early governor of Panama and Nicaragua. Gives due credit for successful efforts to establish Spanish presence in eastern Central America, but does not challenge Pedrarias' well-established reputation for treachery, ruthlessness, and cruelty.

1632 Chaverri, María de los Angeles. El repartimiento de trabajo como causa de la protesta social en la Honduras colonial: el caso de Texíguat. (*Paraninfo/Tegucigalpa*, 3:5, julio 1994, p. 71–104, bibl., map)

From mid-16th century to end of colonial period in Honduras, *repartimiento* was the principal mechanism for mobilizing indigenous labor and an important link in symbiotic relationship between district magistrates and both creole landowners and mine operators. Native population resisted in many ways, including mob violence in extreme cases.

1633 Ciudad Suárez, María Milagros. El Colegio de Doncellas: una institución femenina para criollas, siglo XVI. (*Mesoamérica/Plumsock*, 17:32, 1996, p. 299–314)

Study of boarding school established in Santiago de Guatemala for orphaned creole girls emphasizes institutional aspects, seen as reflecting prevailing norms and expectations of proper female behavior.

1634 Contreras Reynoso, J. Daniel. Guatemala: fundación y traslados. Guatemala: Ministerio de Cultura y Deportes, 1991. 24 p.: bibl. (Col. Ixim)

Early history of Santiago de Guatemala (Antigua), based on well-known sources. More original of two brief essays disputes traditionally accepted version of city's founding, in particular precise date, and seriously questions reliability of early-17th-century historian Antonio de Remesal.

1635 Dakin, Karen and **Christopher H. Lutz.** Nuestro pesar, nuestra aflicción: tunetuliniliz, tucucuca; memorias en lengua náhuatl enviadas a Felipe II por indígenas del Valle de Guatemala hacia 1572. México: UNAM, Centro de Investigaciones Regionales de Mesoamérica, 1996. 209 p.: bibl., facsims., maps, tables.

Nahuatl-language documents written in 1572 and addressed to crown by indigenous municipalities contain complaints regarding Spanish abuses and other problems. Native voices add to our understanding of social and economic transformations occurring in central Guatemalan highlands in first century after conquest. Nahuatl was lingua franca in this Maya region, but its use instead of Spanish was probably tactical error; apparently petitions were never read, much less acted upon. Bilingual edition contains copious notes and substantial historical introduction. Originals are in the Archivo General de Indias, Seville. For ethnohistorian's comment, see *HLAS 56:427*.

1636 Esgueva Gómez, Antonio. La Mesoamérica nicaragüense: documentos y comentarios. Managua: Univ. Centroamericana, 1996. 321 p.: bibl., ill.

Documentary extracts, primarily from Gonzalo Fernández de Oviedo y Valdés' *Historia general y natural de Indias*, relating to origins of Nicaragua's native peoples; and to indigenous culture, society, and economy at time of Spanish conquest.

1637 Fletes Díaz, Ramón *et al.* Para comprender la historia colonial: diccionario de términos. Tegucigalpa?: s.n., 1994. 134 p.: bibl.

Useful glossary, with succinct definitions, of terms commonly encountered in colonial documents. Some terms are peculiar to Central America, but most are applicable to all of Spanish empire.

1638 Fortune, Armando. Obra selecta. Recopilación y prólogo de Gerardo Maloney. Panamá: Instituto Nacional de Cultura, Dirección Nacional de Publicaciones y Comunicación, 1994. 370 p.: bibl. (Col. Dabaibe)

Reprinted essays on experience of blacks in Panama, including, among others, "El esclavo negro en el desenvolvimiento económico de Panamá (1501–1532);" "Los negros cimarrones en Tierra Firme;" "El negro en la vida y cultura colonial de Panamá;" and "El prejuicio y la discriminación como causa de disturbios y conflictos de la personalidad." All based on published primary and secondary sources.

1639 Fowler, William R., Jr. La población nativa de El Salvador al momento de la conquista española. (*Universidad/San Salvador*, 119:1, mayo/agosto 1994, p. 5–28, tables)

Important study, originally published in 1988, reprinted for Salvadoran readers. Previously noted in *HLAS 52:1382* and *HLAS 53:188*.

García Targa, Juan. Arqueología colonial en el área maya: aspectos generales y modelos de estudio. See *HLAS 57:208*.

1640 González Vásquez, Fernando. Colón en Cariay: indagando en el encuentro ocurrido en 1502. San José: Ministerio de Cultura, Juventud y Deportes, 1995. 80 p.: bibl., ill., maps.

Focusing on Christopher Columbus' brief September 1502 sojourn at Cariay, or Cariari (today Puerto Limón), author draws on historical, archeological, and ethno-graphic evidence to explore meaning of first encounter on Costa Rican soil between natives and Europeans.

1641 Guatemala. Audiencia. Libro de los pareceres de la Real Audiencia de Guatemala, 1571–1655. Edición y estudio preliminar por Carlos Alfonso Alvarez-Lobos Villatoro y Ricardo Toledo Palomo. Guatemala: Academia de Geografía e Historia de Guatemala, 1996. 371 p.: bibl., ill., index. (Biblioteca Goathemala; 32)

Register of audiencia rulings in response to individual and corporate petitions, transcribed from original manuscript volume in Guatemala City's Archivo General de Centro América, with useful introduction. Rich source on affairs and concerns of colonial elites in late-16th and early-17th centuries.

Güemez Pineda, Arturo. Comunidades indígenas rebeldes y colonización en Yucatán: la paradójica solución a un proyecto criollo. See item **1306**.

1642 Hawkins, Timothy P. José de Bustamante and the preservation of Empire in Central America, 1811–1818. (*CLAHR/Albuquerque*, 4:4, Fall 1995, p. 439–463)

Tentative reassessment of Central America's independence-era captain general. Questioning traditional portrayal as repressive tyrant, argues for nuanced view of Bustamante against backdrop of contemporary events not only on isthmus, but also in Spain and Mexico.

1643 Johnston Aguilar, Mario René. De Santiago de Guatemala a la villa de la antigua Guatemala, transformación y vida social ante una crisis. Guatemala: Univ. del Valle de Guatemala, 1997. 182 p.: appendices, bibl., graphs, maps, tables.

Well-documented study of Guatemala's former capital, from the 1773 earthquake to 1820. "Unnecessary" relocation in late 1770s of administrative functions and other important activities, along with much of population, did not, despite authorities' intentions, lead to city's disappearance. Even so, population dropped from approximately 30,000, stabilizing around 7,000; economic, social, and spatial hierarchies were subverted; and assaults, drunkenness, prostitution, and vagrancy all increased.

1644 Kupperman, Karen Ordahl. Providence Island, 1630–1641: the other Puritan colony. Cambridge; New York: Cambridge Univ. Press, 1993. 393 p.: bibl., index.

Thoroughly researched account of attempt by English Protestants to establish colony on Old Providence Island (Santa Catalina, off the coast of Nicaragua). Planted in 1630, colony failed to prosper for reasons author develops with clarity and erudition, and was wiped out by the Spanish in 1641. Failure, of course, did not end British interest in the Caribbean or in the Central American coast. Major work. For British Caribbean historian's comment, see *HLAS 56:1890.*

1645 Lehnhoff, Dieter. El maestro de capilla durante la época colonial en Guatemala. (*in* Encuentro Nacional de Historiadores (Guatemala), 2nd, *Guatemala, 1995.* Memorias. Guatemala: Univ. del Valle de Guatemala, 1996, p. 163–176)

Cathedral and parish choir masters presented as principal agents for propagation of European musical forms in colonial Guatemala.

1646 Lobo, Tatiana. Entre Dios y el diablo: mujeres de la colonia; crónicas. San José: Editorial de la Univ. de Costa Rica, 1993. 148 p.: bibl., ill.

Argues that not all women in colonial Costa Rica fit the stereotype of *beata* tied to kitchen, "who made love while saying the beads on a rosary." Fictionalizes material from notary and church records, including stories of orphans robbed and marital promises breached, lost honor, adultery and incest. Worth reading.

1647 Luján Muñoz, Jorge. Estratificación social y prejuicios a finales del siglo XVIII: un ejemplo de diferentes actitudes en Guatemala y en España. (*in* Encuentro Nacional de Historiadores (Guatemala), 2nd, *Guatemala, 1995.* Memorias. Guatemala: Univ. del Valle de Guatemala, 1996, p. 177–189)

Official responses to 1782 petition by prominent colonial architect Bernardo Ramírez to be declared "Spanish" despite African ancestry illustrate how attitudes toward estate, race, and class differed between Spain and Guatemala.

1648 Luján Muñoz, Jorge. Los vascos en el comercio del Reino de Guatemala al final del período colonial. (*An. Acad. Geogr. Hist. Guatem.,* 66, 1992, p. 9–16, bibl.)

Based on familiar secondary sources, brief overview of Basque immigrants' role in late-colonial Guatemala emphasizes the Aycinera, Irisarri, and Barrundia families. For a more substantial treatment of the Aycinenas, see item **1628.**

1649 MacLeod, Murdo J. Depopulation, dispersed settlement, old and new resources, and native American resistance in colonial Central America. (*in* International Congress of Americanists, 48th, Stockholm, 1994. Colonizacíon agrícola y ganadera en América, siglos XVI-XVIII: su impacto en la población aborigen. Quito: Ediciones Abya-Yala, 1995, p. 31–48)

Review of Central American evidence in light of recent scholarship on indigenous accommodation to postconquest demographic and environmental changes. Argues that native peoples synthesized traditional and exogenous practices, taking advantage of abundance of land, scarcity of labor, and availability of new resources (notably wild cattle) to insulate themselves against excessive colonial exploitation.

1650 MacLeod, Murdo J. Motines y cambios en las formas de control económico y político: los sucesos de Tuxtla en 1693. (*Mesoamérica/Plumsock,* 15:28, dic. 1994, p. 231–251)

Analysis of 1693 indigenous rebellion in Tuxtla, Chiapas, reconstructs narrative on basis of primary record. Seeks to explain both event itself and severity of Spanish response, citing growing monopolization of provincial economy by *alcaldes mayores,* among other factors.

1651 Maldonado Polo, J. Luis. Los recursos naturales de Centroamérica: el origen de la expedición botánica al reino de Guatemala. (*Asclepio/Madrid,* 48:2, 1995, p. 45–66)

Brief account of preparations in Mexico for 1795 visit to Guatemala by famed naturalists José Longinos Martínez and José Mociño, and painter Vicente de la Cerda, as concluding phase of more extensive Expedición Botánica de Nueva España. Based on materials in Spanish and Mexican archives, emphasizes administrative and financial difficulties.

1652 Martín Blasco, Julio and Jesús María García Añoveros. El arzobispo de Guatemala: don Pedro Cortés y Larraz, Belchite 1712, Zaragoza 1786; defensor de la justicia y de la verdad. Belchite, Spain: Exmo. Ayuntamiento de Belchite (Zaragoza), 1992. 466 p.: bibl., ill., maps.

Long-needed study of 18th-century Guatemalan prelate best remembered for his much-analyzed pastoral *visitas* (1768–70) and his vigorous opposition to relocating colony's capital following earthquake of 1773. Presents detailed discussion of these episodes, complemented by attention to previously little-known pre- and post-Guatemala career, documents, and illustrations.

1653 Meléndez Chaverri, Carlos. Las migraciones y procesos de mestizaje: el caso de la Costa Rica colonial. (*Rev. Arch. Nac. Hist. Azuay*, 66, 1992, p. 39–49, tables)

Based on familiar published sources, sketches broad outlines of Costa Rica's demographic evolution in colonial period, with emphasis on demonstrating population's racially diverse origins, dismissing as fable the traditional claim that Costa Ricans today are predominantly of Spanish decent.

1654 Mena García, María del Carmen. Estructura demográfica de Veragua en el siglo XVIII (y III). (*Anu. Estud. Am.*, 52:1, 1995, p. 229–260, tables)

Third and final installment of 1756 census of Veragua district, Panama. For a review of the first installment of the census, see *HLAS 56:1668*.

1655 Mena García, María del Carmen. Recursos agrícolas y ganaderos de Panamá en los origenes de la colonización. (*in* International Congress of Americanists, *48th, Stockholm, 1994*. Colonización agrícola y ganadera en América, siglos XVI-XVIII: su impacto en la población aborigen. Quito: Ediciones Abya-Yala, 1995, p. 49–89)

Valuable introduction. Crops and livestock in early Panama supplied not only colony's inhabitants, but also transient personnel. Efforts to establish wheat and wine failed, leading to dependence on Peru, but Panama eventually produced abundant maize, beans, rice, and variety of fruits and vegetables, both indigenous and imported.

Stockraising predominated, reflecting minimal labor requirement; presence of extensive, well-watered grasslands; and colonial elites' latifundist aspirations; but province continued to import mules for service on transit route.

1656 Morel de Santa Cruz, Pedro Agustín. Costa Rica en 1751: informe de una visita. San José: V.M. Rojas, 1994. 161 p.: ill., indexes.

Record of pastoral *visita* conducted in 1751 by newly arrived bishop of Nicaragua, whose diocese at that time included Costa Rica. First published in 1900 by Costa Rica's scholarly bishop Bernardo Augusto Thiel, present edition by Vérnor M. Rojas is based on Thiel's and includes that historian's notes, comments, and statistical extracts. Rich in data on ecclesiastical and spiritual life, but also on trade, agriculture, and, especially, population.

1657 Musset, Alain. Mosquitos, piratas y cataclismos: las transformaciones de la red urbana en América Central, siglos XVI-XVIII. (*Yaxkin/Tegucigalpa*, 13:1/2, enero/dic. 1995, p. 5–36, facsims., maps)

Rambling discourses on colonial urbanization, with emphasis on factors accounting for failure of some settlements and relocation of others, notably Nombre de Diós; Panama City; León, Nicaragua; and Santiago de Guatemala, which was relocated three times (1527, 1541, and 1773).

1658 Palma Murga, Gustavo. El valle central de Guatemala en el siglo XVI: tierra, identidad y presión colonial. (*Estudios/USAC*, 2, dic. 1993, p. 39–60, bibl.)

Overview of early development of Guatemala's central valley, focusing on reasons for its primacy in colonial Central America and on its distinctive patterns of settlement, land tenure, and ethnic relations.

1659 Papeles de Panamá, siglo XVIII. Recopilación de Pablo Macera. Paleografía de Fernanda Atauchi Cusi *et al.* Lima: Univ. Nacional Mayor de San Marcos, Seminario de Historia Rural Andina, 1993. 186 p., 2 leaves of plates: maps. (Fuentes de historia social americana; 19)

Seven documents on Panama, dated 1774–88, published with brief introduction. Location of originals not identified, but apparently were abandoned in Charcas (La Paz,

Bolivia) by itinerant cleric. Includes local descriptions and *visitas,* extensive report on situation of church on isthmus, and extensive analysis of expenses to royal treasury at Panama City.

1660 Peláez Almengor, Oscar Guillermo. En el corazón del reino: el Cabildo de la Nueva Guatemala 1779. (*Estudios/USAC,* 1, 1995, p. 85–91)

In 1779 document opposing royal order forcing artisans to abandon destroyed capital for recently established Guatemala City, municipal council analyzes economic realities affecting period's manufactures, including established sources of supply and demand for labor, raw materials, and other goods and services.

1661 Potthast-Jutkeit, Barbara. Dos grandes potencias europeas y un pequeño pueblo indígena: la costa de Mosquitos entre los imperios coloniales de España y Gran Bretaña. (*in* Tordesillas y sus consecuencias: la política de las grandes potencias europeas respecto a América Latina, 1494–1899. Frankfurt: Vervuert; Madrid: Iberoamericana, 1995, p. 43–59)

Useful overview of Mosquito Coast's role in British-Spanish relations, focusing on 18th century, stresses difference of outlook between authorities in London and British officials and entrepreneurs in the Caribbean. Relies heavily on author's *Die Mosquitoküste im Spannungsfeld britischer und spanischer Politik, 1502–1821* (Cologne and Vienna, 1988).

1662 Rodas, Isabel. Mujeres: mediadoras en la circulación de los bienes y posiciones sociales durante el período colonial. (*in* Encuentro Nacional de Historiadores (Guatemala), 2nd, Guatemala, 1995. Memorias. Guatemala: Univ. del Valle de Guatemala, 1996, p. 271–288, bibl.)

Important essay provides fresh insights on women, families, elites, rural society, and process of *mestizaje.* Case study of 17th-century "ruralized" creole Argueta Santizo family shows how, despite geographic isolation, members used marriage and land to maintain social and racial identity, although, as number of descendants increased, many passed out of Spanish elite via inter-racial unions.

1663 Romero Vargas, Germán. Las sociedades del Atlántico de Nicaragua en los siglos XVII y XVIII. Managua: Fondo de Promoción Cultural-Banic, 1995? 322 p.: bibl. (Col. cultural Banco Nicaragüense. Serie histórica)

Draws on extensive research in archives in Europe and Central America. Describes Nicaragua's Atlantic coast and its people, tracing impact over time of British presence. Long-needed complement to earlier *Las estructuras sociales de Nicaragua en el siglo XVIII* (HLAS 54:1681), which focused only on Spanish-controlled Pacific region. Major work.

1664 Rubio Sánchez, Manuel. La influencia de la masonería en la vida política del reino de Guatemala: primer parte, 1717–1821. (*An. Acad. Geogr. Hist. Guatem.,* 68, 1994, p. 71–98)

Lengthy, sparsely documented essay finds no evidence for Masonic "influence" mentioned in title, but admits that key enlightenment and independence-era figures—among them Jacobo de Villaurrutia, Antonio García Arredondo, Antonio de Liendo y Goicoechea, Antonio de Larrazábal, and Gabino Gainza—may have been masons.

1665 Sagastume F., Alejandro Salomón. Historia de una frontera olvidada: establecimientos ingleses en Honduras. (*in* Estudios (nuevos y viejos) sobre la frontera. Madrid: Consejo Superior de Investigaciones Científicas, Centro de Estudios Históricos, Depto. de Historia de América, 1991, p. 119–161, map)

Useful overview of British activities in Bay Islands and on Honduran coast emphasizes 17th-18th centuries. Includes information on neighboring regions and on Spanish responses. Based chiefly on Spanish manuscript sources.

1666 Sánchez, Evelyne. Las élites de Nueva Guatemala, 1770–1821: rivalidades y poder colonial. (*Mesoamérica/Plumsock,* 17:31, junio 1996, p. 129–156, photo)

Study of Guatemalan elites in final decades of colonial era emphasizes contradictions among province's most powerful families, focusing on those affiliated with Consulado de Comercio and cabildo of Guatemala City. Factions, which tended to align around attitudes toward commercial policy, were effectively exploited by colonial officials, preventing emergence of unified elite position in resistance to royal authority.

Sansonetti, Vito. Quemé mis naves en estas montañas: la colonización de la altiplanicie de Coto Brus y la fundación de San Vito de Java. See *HLAS 57:2496.*

1667 Solórzano, Juan Carlos. El comercio de Costa Rica durante el declive del comercio español y el desarrollo del contrabando inglés: período, 1690–1750. (*Anu. Estud. Centroam.*, 20:2, 1994, p. 71–119, bibl.)

First half of 18th century saw "radical transformation" of Costa Rica's economy as decline in Spanish fleet system impoverished Panama, previously a dominant trading partner. Producers attempted many adaptations, most significantly growing exchange of cacao for illicit imports from English in Jamaica and Dutch in Curaçao.

1668 Turcios, Roberto. Los primeros patriotas: San Salvador, 1811. San Salvador: Ediciones Tendencias, 1995. 236 p.: bibl.

Based on published sources, readable account of Nov. 1811, uprising in San Salvador. Seen not as premeditated blow for independence, but as spontaneous expression of popular resentment, occasioned by local manifestations of imperial crisis and influenced by elite rhetoric and intrigues.

1669 Werner, Patrick S. Los reales de minas de la Nicaragua colonial y la ciudad perdida de Nueva Segovia. Managua: Instituto Nicaragüense de Cultura, 1996. 104 p.: bibl., ill.

Study of mining activity in early colonial Nicaragua claims successful identification of ruins of 16th-century boom town Nueva Segovia. Draws on both archeology and history, arguing multidisciplinary approach is indispensable for further progress on this topic.

NATIONAL

1670 Adams, Richard N. Etnicidad en el ejército de la Guatemala liberal, 1870–1915. Guatemala: FLACSO, 1995. 67 p.: bibl. (Debate; 30)

After 1871, Guatemala's liberal government sought to create all-ladino army for modernization and social control, but found predominance of indigenous element in pop-

ulation made goal impossible. Recruiting records from San Marcos reveal markers commonly used to indicate "race."

1671 Alexander, Robert Jackson. Presidents of Central America, Mexico, Cuba, and Hispaniola: conversations and correspondence. Westport, Conn.: Praeger, 1995. 277 p.: bibl., index.

Snippets of public talks, interviews, and correspondence by regional leaders, in and out of office. Each country chapter is prefaced by short overview of recent political history. More than 100 of book's 277 pages deal with Costa Rica.

1672 Almorza, Antonio. Historia de la radiodifusión guatemalteca. Guatemala: s.n., 1994. 206 p.: ill.

Presents early history of radio broadcasting, advertising, and programming in Guatemala, based chiefly on oral accounts and remembrances. Includes mixture of narrative, quotes, documents and photographs.

1673 Alvarenga Venutolo, Patricia. Cultura y ética de la violencia: El Salvador, 1880–1932. San José: EDUCA, 1996. 371 p.: bibl. (Col. Rueda del tiempo)

Commonly in collaboration with local authorities, Salvadoran elites used terror to divide and control peasant and indigenous communities in late-19th century. After 1912 a shift to reliance on repressive force of National Guard reduced tensions within peasant communities, promoting more unified response to outside demands, while participation in Ligas Rojas provided rural population with valuable political experience.

Araúz, Celestino Andrés. Panamá y sus relaciones internacionales. See *HLAS 57:4139.*

1674 El Archivo Municipal de Patzicía: cuadro de organización e inventario general. Guatemala: Instituto de Investigaciones Históricas, Antropológicas y Arqueológicas, Univ. de San Carlos de Guatemala, 1994. 56 p.

Guide to administrative and legal materials in municipal archives of Patzicía, Guatemala. Most documentation is from 20th century, but some from 19th century, especially from town government.

1675 Argueta, Mario. La gran huelga bananera: 69 días que conmovieron a Honduras. Tegucigalpa: Editorial Universitaria, 1995. 270 p.: bibl. (Col. Realidad nacional; 42)

By 1954 US State Dept. records, newspapers, and interviews reveal shift in Honduras away from enforced stability of Cariato and Cold War toward modest economic modernization and political opening. Broad "middle" and "popular" sectors cooperated with banana workers to force traditional elites to yield concessions such as Labor Code.

1676 Arias Gómez, Jorge. Farabundo Martí. San José: EDUCA, 1996. 296 p.: bibl., ill. (Col. Rueda del tiempo)

Revised and expanded version of "biography" of Agustín Farabundo Martí. Originally published in 1972 (*HLAS 36:2234*), book is chiefly overview of labor-political conflicts during the 1910s-20s, touching only occasionally on Martí. Argues Martí broke with Sandino over Sandino's contacts with Mexican government, which Mexico's Communist party opposed.

1677 Bauer Paiz, Alfonso and **Iván Carpio Alfaro.** Memorias de Alfonso Bauer Paiz: historia no oficial de Guatemala. Guatemala: Rusticatio Ediciones, 1996. 452 p.: indexes, ports.

Memoirs of prominent Guatemalan lawyer and politician heavily involved (when not in exile) in local events from 1930s-80s. Based on taped interviews, which Bauer Paiz subsequently edited and annotated, and on written remembrances. Useful for alliances and conflicts among shifting political elites during the period covered.

1678 Bossche, Stefan van den. Een kortstondige kolonie: Santo-Tomas de Guatemala, 1843–1854; een literaire documentaire = A short-lived colony: Santo-Tomas de Guatemala, 1843–1854; a literary documentary. Tielt, Belgium: Lannoo, 1997. 236 p.: bibl., ill.

Fast-paced history of a forgotten Belgian colony is written from both a Flemish and a literary perspective. In Pt. 1 author relates how financial mismanagement and a high mortality rate doomed the attempt to establish a Belgian foothold on the Central American coast. Pts. 2 and 3 focus on a journey of a Belgian delegation to the ruins of the colony in 1939 and on a trip by the author in 1997. Based on poetry and song texts, travel accounts, letters, and Belgian archival sources. [R. Hoefte]

Boxt, Matthew A. Interesting litter: notes on unexpected historical finds at Sarteneja, an ancient Maya site in northern Belize. See *HLAS 57:169.*

1679 Brentlinger, John. The best of what we are: reflections on the Nicaraguan revolution. Amherst: Univ. of Massachusetts Press, 1995. 383 p.: bibl., ill., index, map.

Personal impressions of Nicaraguan Revolution based on six trips over seven years. Standard *internacionalista* fare, apart from last chapter on years 1991–92 addressing some FSLN mistakes.

1680 Byrne, Hugh. El Salvador's civil war: a study of revolution. Boulder, Colo.: Lynne Rienner Publishers, 1996. 255 p.: bibl., index, map.

Attempt to "understand as fully as possible the social, political, economic, and human dynamics that gave rise to a revolutionary conflict," written by ex-political director of Committee in Solidarity with the People of El Salvador (CISPES). Argues that FMLN survived by maintaining overall unity, something "counterrevolutionary coalition" was unable to do. For political scientist's comment, see *HLAS 57:3162.*

1681 Cardoza y Aragón, Luis. La revolución guatemalteca. La Antigua Guatemala, Guatemala: Editorial del Pensativo, 1994. 215 p.: bibl.

Reprint of 1955 classic (*HLAS 19:4269*) attributes failure of 1944–54 Revolution to incapacity of "national bourgeoisie" to develop and lead genuine revolutionary undertaking. Superseded in some areas by subsequent research, the book nevertheless maintains value. Includes new introduction by Alfonso Bauer Paiz.

1682 Castillo, Manuel J. Mi Panamá de ayer. Panamá: s.n., 1990? 154 p.: ill.

Memoir by journalist, bureaucrat, and diplomat active in early radio broadcasting and sports promotion. View of Panamanian history from Colón.

1683 **Cazali Avila, Augusto.** La autonomía universitaria como legado de la revolución del 20 de octubre de 1944. (*Estudios/ USAC*, 3, nov. 1994, p. 11–30, bibl.)

Brief survey of Guatemala's Univ. of San Carlos in late-19th and early-20th century shows how lack of autonomy exposed institution to repeated political interventions. New government granted university autonomy in Nov. 1944.

1684 **Cerdas Albertazzi, José Manuel.** El marco socio urbano de los obreros manufactureros josefinos, 1930–1960. (*Rev. Hist./Heredia*, 29, enero/junio 1994, p. 89–123, map, tables)

Between 1930 and 1960 residential areas of San José moved from city center as businesses took over. At same time residential areas differentiated along class lines. Assumes intimate knowledge of San José's urban geography.

1685 **Chamorro, Violeta; Sonia Cruz de Baltodano; and Guido Fernández.** Dreams of the heart: the autobiography of President Violeta Barrios de Chamorro of Nicaragua. New York: Simon & Schuster, 1996. 352 p.: ill., index, map.

Interesting if self-serving memoir by former president of Nicaragua, "always guided by the selfless desire to improve the lot of [her] countrymen." Details workings of non-Sandinista opposition to Somoza through 1979, and conflicts during 1980s between right and Sandinista regime. Accuses opponents after 1990 of "scurry[ing] to hide under the skirts of the U.S. Congress or White House."

1686 **Chomsky, Aviva.** Afro-Jamaican traditions and labor organizing on United Fruit Company Plantations in Costa Rica, 1910. (*J. Soc. Hist.*, 28:4, Summer 1995, p. 837–855)

Struggling to create world for themselves on Costa Rica's banana plantations, West Indian workers drew on "British" identity, Protestant non-conformist sects, and Africa-based religious forms such as obeah and myalism. Covers background for 1910 strike, largely ignored by Costa Rican labor movement both then and now.

1687 **Chomsky, Aviva.** West Indian workers and the United Fruit Company in Costa Rica, 1870–1940. Baton Rouge: Louisi-ana State Univ. Press, 1996. 315 p.: bibl., ill., index, map.

History of UFCO's Atlantic coast operations in Costa Rica from perspective of largely West Indian labor force. Examines formation of enclave economy, including role of West Indian labor, subsistence production, and health problems as occasion of worker-company misunderstandings. Also studies workers' cultural and political lives apart from, and sometimes in conflict with, company, and how West Indians and UFCO figured in Costa Rican nationalist thought and politics.

1688 **Creedman, Theodore S.** El gran cambio: de León Cortés a Calderón Guardia. San José: Editorial Costa Rica, 1996. 264 p.: bibl.

Claims that 1900–40s were not golden age of genesis of Costa Rican democracy. Rather, corrupt system of fraudulent elections and economic status quo eventually collapsed of own weight, leading to reforms led by Rafael Angel Calderón Guardia, Víctor Sanabria, and Manuel Mora. Suggests that 1948 successful alliance continued and expanded upon Calderón's efforts.

1689 **Cuestas Gómez, Carlos Humberto.** Cotito, crónica de un crimen olvidado. Panamá: Litho Editorial Chen, 1993. 161 p.: bibl., ill.

Recounts 1941 attack by Panamanian police on German-speaking Swiss colonists. Apparently unable to differentiate Germans from Swiss, government accused victims of being spies and fifth columnists despite membership in Peace Mission Movement, a religious sect committed to primitive communalism.

1690 **Danner, Mark.** The massacre at El Mozote: a parable of the Cold War. New York: Vintage Books, 1994. 304 p.: bibl., ill., map.

Thorough account of Dec. 1981 massacre of villagers by Salvadoran armed forces includes details of subsequent cover-up. Guerrillas acknowledged many civilian victims were rebel supporters, but El Mozote was Protestant stronghold unreceptive even to liberation theology. Good overview of military, death squad, and guerrilla violence in early 1980s.

1691 Delgado Fiallos, Aníbal. Rosa: el político. Tegucigalpa?: Editorial Cultura, 1994. 80 p.: bibl. (Col. Premios)

Based chiefly on Ramón Rosa's writings, essay argues project for national capitalism and centralized state was frustrated by members of Rosa's liberal faction too devoted to theoretical liberties. Rosa is seen as only politician of his time with sense of future direction for Honduras.

1692 Dospital, Michelle. La herencia mexicana en la lucha sandinista de los años 20 en Nicaragua. (*Secuencia/México*, 30, sept./dic. 1994, p. 117–129, bibl., ill.)

Argues experience in Mexico influenced Sandino's political thought by convincing him of importance of "national dignity, patriotism, and antiimperialism," and of the need for labor legislation. Draws no connection between Sandino's program in Nicaragua and Mexican anarcho-syndicalism.

1693 Ensayos olvidados sobre don Ricardo Jiménez. Prólogo y recopilación de Eugenio Rodríguez Vega. San José: Univ. Autónoma de Centro América, 1994. 218 p.

Eight essays by various authors on aspects of thought and personality of Costa Rican statesman and writer Ricardo Jiménez Oreamuno, followed by 100 p. of selected texts. Since Jiménez was president three times in early 20th century, his ideas and policies contributed to development of Costa Rican democracy.

1694 Euraque, Darío A. Reinterpreting the Banana Republic: region and state in Honduras, 1870–1972. Chapel Hill: Univ. of North Carolina Press, 1996. 268 p.: bibl., ill., index, maps.

Major work focusing on Honduras' northern coast challenges traditional assumption that dominant position of foreign banana companies in region precluded significant, active role for local capitalists and workers. New understanding emerges of "military populism" and other peculiar features of 20th-century Honduran political history.

1695 Euraque, Darío A. Zonas regionales en la formación del Estado Hondureño, 1830s-1930s: el caso de la Costa Norte. (*Rev. Centroam. Econ.*, 13:39, sept./dic. 1992, p. 65–97, tables)

Looks at regional histories of Honduras, the intersection of regions with world economy, and specifically, the development of Honduras' northern coast. Although largely controlled by US capital, expansion of banana exports after 1870 funded tardy development of national state.

1696 Fleer, Peter. Arbeitsmarkt und Herrschaftsapparat in Guatemala, 1920–1940 [Labor market and power structure in Guatemala, 1920–1940]. Frankfurt am Main; New York: P. Lang, 1997. 277 p.: bibl., ill., maps. (Hispano-Americana, 19)

Methodically researched study examines the activities of the state, which depended on highly labor-intensive coffee production and export, in the proletarianization of the indigenous population. Peasants practicing subsistence agriculture and minifundistas lost their land or access to land and moved from the traditional patronage system through a period of debt peonage to labor recruitment utilizing vagrancy laws. Concludes that the exploitative character of labor relations was a response to external market factors, internal ethnic segregation and monopoly of power during the covered period. Noting that the highland peasant population had developed an actual culture of resistance, at least on local levels, observes that the peasants never managed to organize politically. From colonialism and patronage to the modern liberal economic model and the freedom of the labor market, the Guatemalan peasants' lot did not improve. [C. Converse]

1697 Galich, Manuel. Por qué lucha Guatemala: Arévalo y Arbenz, dos hombres contra un imperio. 2a ed. Guatemala: Ministerio de Cultura y Deportes de Guatemala, Editorial Cultura, 1994. 374 p.: ill.

Reprint of angry 1956 account of Guatemalan Revolution written by top-level participant. Focuses on events leading up to 1954 rather than on overthrow of Arbenz regime, which occurred while author was ambassador to Argentina and therefore not in the country.

1698 García, Marcela Alejandra. Los ferrocarriles de la República de Honduras. (*Anu. Estud. Am.*, 53:1, 1996, p. 123–151, graphs, maps, tables)

Provides overview of history and operation of railroads in Honduras from 19th century to present, based on limited secondary sources. Largely institutional history, focusing on banana company railroads.

1699 Gómez Díez, Francisco Javier. La política guatemalteca en los orígenes de la "década revolucionaria": la asamblea constituyente de 1945. (*Rev. Indias*, 55:203, enero/abril 1995, p. 127–147)

Provides detailed analysis of composition and activities of assembly that produced Guatemala's 1945 "revolutionary" constitution, based on session records. Votes for illiterates and "religious question" were particularly controversial issues. Radical left did not recognize importance of peasants and Indian population to revolutionary process.

1700 Gould, Jeffrey L. La alianza frustrada: los socialistas y la oposición, Nicaragua, 1946–1950. (*Anu. Estud. Centroam.*, 19:2, 1993, p. 51–69)

Divided by anti-communism and class and cultural differences in late 1940s, bourgeois forces and the left-wing Partido Socialista Nicaragüense (PSN) failed to align to overthrow mutual enemy, dictator Anastasio Somoza García. Success of Somoza's *populismo obrerista* and indecision of US embassy permitted him to survive until US support was regained in 1950.

1701 Gould, Jeffrey L. Y el buitre respondió: "aquí no hay indios"; la cuestión indígena en Nicaragua occidental, 1920–1954. (*Mesoamérica/Plumsock*, 16:30, dic. 1995, p. 327–354)

Nineteenth-century liberals and 20th-century intellectuals helped to develop an "inclusive" national ideology positing Nicaragua as a mestizo nation, denying separate identity to Indians. Even Augusto C. Sandino downplayed ethnic differences and supported *indohispano* unity against imperialism.

1702 Grandin, Greg. The strange case of "la Mancha Negra": Maya-State relations in nineteenth-century Guatemala. (*HAHR*, 77:2, May 1997, p. 211–243)

Sees community as "contested arena" and argues that resulting "divisions, contradictions, and relations" contributed to cultural survival and self-awareness, rather than conceding to external pressure. In village, struggle for common land and scheme to locate textile mill show how appeal to outside power sources by different factions enlarged community's resources for resistance.

1703 Gudmundson, Lowell. Lord and peasant in the making of modern Central America. (*in* Agrarian structure & political power: landlord & peasant in the making of Latin America. Pittsburgh, Pa.: Univ. of Pittsburgh Press, 1995, p. 151–176)

Part of collection applying Barrington Moore's ideas on "dictatorship and democracy" to Latin America, in this case Costa Rica. Detailed, subtle examination of post-WWII Costa Rica seems to support part of Moore's thesis on socioeconomic differentiation and democracy, but author warns against mechanically applying ideas.

1704 Gudmundson, Lowell. Tierras comunales, públicas y privadas en los orígenes de la caficultura en Guatemala y Costa Rica. (*Mesoamérica/Plumsock*, 17:31, junio 1996, p. 41–56, facsims., maps)

Shows how *censo enfiteusis* (long-term rent) was used in mid-19th-century Guatemala and Costa Rica to acquire land from indigenous communities for early coffee development. Intended as compromise, system quickly gave way to simple private property and, therefore, loss of community lands.

1705 Guía del Archivo Guerras Centroamericanas, 1827–1912. Coordinación de Guadalupe Rodríguez de Ita. Presentación de Roberto Marín. México: Secretaría de Relaciones Exteriores; Instituto Mora, 1995. 125 p.: bibl. (Archivo histórico diplomático mexicano)

Guide to documents dealing with conflicts in Central America in archive of Mexican Ministry of Foreign Relations.

1706 Handy, Jim. Enfrentándose al pulpo: nacionalismo económico y cambio político en Guatemala y Costa Rica en la década de 1920. (*Mesoamérica/Plumsock*, 17:31, junio 1996, p. 11–39)

Reports that US diplomats routinely pressured Central American administrations to act illegally to favor US private interests, including the United Fruit Company. Efforts were more aggressive and successful in Guatemala. Costa Rica's more open political and economic environment guarded the country against US influence.

1707 Harbury, Jennifer. Bridge of courage: life stories of the Guatemalan *compañeros* and *compañeras*. Updated ed. Mon-

roe, Me.: Common Courage Press, 1995.
275 p.: map.

Personal histories of participants in
1980s-90s guerrilla movements against
Guatemala's military regime, collected by a
US citizen who lost Guatemalan husband in
struggle, and prefaced by scathing history of
Guatemala since 1930s by Noam Chomsky.
Simplistic and not on par with similar pub-
lished remembrances from El Salvador and
Nicaragua.

1708 Harrison, Benjamin. The United
States and the 1909 Nicaragua Revolution. (*Caribb. Q.*, 41:3/4, Sept./Dec. 1995,
p. 45–63)

"From the first day he became Secretary of State," Philander Knox set out to
remove Nicaragua's president José Santos
Zelaya (1893–1909) for racist reasons, to promote US business, and because Zelaya fili-
bustered in Central America after Roosevelt
opted for Panama over Nicaragua for canal
route. Local US businesses were allies, not
instigators. Based on US State Dept. records.

1709 Holden, Robert H. Constructing the
limits of state violence in Central
America: towards a new research agenda. (*J.
Lat. Am. Stud.*, 28:2, May 1996, p. 435–459)

Discusses government-sponsored violence in history of state formation in Central
America, looking at upward displacement of
power from caudillos to the state, central
role of subaltern collaboration with agents
of state violence, and internationalization
of violence as US involvement grew in 20th
century.

1710 Howe, James. La lucha por la tierra en
la costa de San Blas, Panamá, 1900–
1930. (*Mesoamérica/Plumsock*, 16:29, junio
1995, p. 57–76, map, photo)

Describes how Kuna responded to
threats to their land from, at different times,
Afro-Panamanian and Colombian peasants,
large-scale US capital, and nation-state intent on asserting hegemony over countryside. Such problems continue, as does Kuna
resistance based on negotiation, direct action, and resorting to external help.

**1711 Identidades nacionales y estado mo-
derno en Centroamérica.** Recopilación
de Arturo Taracena A. y Jean Piel. San José:
Editorial de la Univ. de Costa Rica, 1995.
281 p.: bibl., ill., maps. (Col. Istmo)

Excellent collection of short essays,
some original and some translated, on state
and ethnicity in 19th-century Central America. Contributors include Demyky, Gudmundson, Taracena, Acuña, Palmer, Lindo-
Fuentes, Barahona, Woodward, Euraque,
Little-Siebold, Lauria, and Gould.

1712 Juárez, Orient Bolívar. El ferrocarril de
Nicaragua: historia y liquidación; informe. Precedido de una sinopsis histórica
del Ferrocarril de Nicaragua escrita por O-
rient Bolívar Juárez. Managua: Comisión de
Liquidación, 1997. 135 p.: bibl., ill., maps.

Presents short history of the construction, operation, and decline of Ferrocarril de
Nicaragua, focusing on deactivation of line
after 1990. Blames failure on *entreguista*
policies of Adolfo Díaz, plundering by Somoza, and inactivity of Sandinista and
Chamorro governments.

1713 Karlen, Stefan. *Make the Escuela
Politécnica as near like West Point as
possible:* Jorge Ubico and the professionalization of the Guatemalan military, 1931–1944.
(*Ibero-Am. Arch.*, 20:1/2, 1994, p. 109–151,
bibl.)

Guatemalan president Jorge Ubico
(1931–44) sought professionalization to
make military more efficient, but failed to
appreciate how this process contributed to
development of independent institutional
identity. Disaffected younger officers became
plotters in 1944 revolt against Ubico and his
loyal high command.

1714 Keune, Lou. Sobrevivimos la guerra: la
historia de los pobladores de Arcatao
y de San José Las Flores. Fotografías de Piet
den Blanken. San Salvador: Adelina Editores,
1995. 276 p., 1 folded leaf: map, ports.

Micro-study of two settlements in El
Salvador's Chalatenango dept. describes how
population survived civil war by taking refuge in *monte* during worst of fighting, then
repopulating towns in 1984–86. Text interweaves and links individual accounts to similar topics. Based on extended interviews.

1715 Konrad, Edmond G. Nicaragua durante
los 30 años de gobierno conservador,
1857–1883: la familia Zavala. (*Mesoamérica/
Plumsock*, 16:30, dic. 1995, p. 287–308,
map, tables)

Efforts by Nicaraguan president
Joaquín Javier Zavala (1879–83) to promote

national development were frustrated by inability to overcome shortage of domestic capital and by Zavala's unwillingness to share power with newly emerging socioeconomic groups.

Krenn, Michael L. The chains of interdependence: U.S. policy toward Central America, 1945–1954. See *HLAS 57:4174.*

1716 León, Jorge. Fuentes y uso de datos del movimiento marítimo y comercio exterior de Costa Rica entre 1821–1900. San José: Centro de Investigaciones Históricas de América Central, Univ. de Costa Rica, 1995. 145 p.: bibl. (Serie Trabajos de metodología; 5)

Introduces sources and problems for study of Costa Rican maritime history. Presents wide, if eclectic, array of statistical tables and charts on such topics as ship movements and seaborne exports. Also includes case study of 19th-century shipping firm William Le Lacheur and Son.

1717 León Aragón, Oscar de. Caída de un régimen: Jorge Ubico—Federico Ponce; 20 de octubre de 1944. Guatemala: FLACSO, 1995. 497 p.: bibl.

Reprint of detailed examination of events surrounding 1944 overthrow of Guatemalan president Jorge Ubico, focusing on 108-day Federico Ponce Vaides regime and based on newspapers and "what I personally saw." Author, among students who made contact with Honor Guard, understands chief political contradiction between wartime Allied goals and internal repression. Claims he never imagined events would go as far as they did.

1718 Little Siebold, Todd. Guatemala y el anhelo de modernización: Estrada Cabrera y el desarrollo del Estado, 1898–1920. (*Anu. Estud. Centroam.,* 20:1, 1994, p. 25–41, graphs, tables)

Revisionist argument maintains that Guatemalan President Manuel Estrada Cabrera (1898–1920) laid groundwork for future economic development by broadening access of liberal reforms such as schools, telegraphs, and health care, to general population. Dictator sought to counteract effects of spread of coffee industry by increasing food production, but was unable to end inflation that plagued period.

1719 Longley, Kyle. The sparrow and the hawk: Costa Rica and the United States during the rise of José Figueres. Tuscaloosa: Univ. of Alabama Press, 1997. 253 p.: bibl., ill., index.

Extensively documented study stresses Figueres' ability to manipulate symbols and service influential contacts, which afforded Costa Rica space to pursue nationalist agenda, resisting US domination without provoking US intervention.

1720 López García, Víctor Virgilio. La Bahía del Puerto del sol y la masacre de los garífunas de San Juan. Tegucigalpa?: s.n., 1994. 88 p.: ill.

Shows how internal divisions in Garifuna community of San Juan, Honduras, played out in "party" terms, Liberals versus Nationalists, culminating in 1937 massacre of opponents of Tiburcio Carías' seizure of power. Some Garifuna used "party" to even personal scores and seek local power. Based on local oral history.

1721 Lungo, Mario. El Salvador in the eighties: counterinsurgency and revolution. Edited with an introduction by Arthur Schmidt. Translated by Amelia F. Shogan. Philadelphia: Temple Univ. Press, 1996. 246 p.: bibl., index, map.

Views Salvadoran insurgency of 1980s as "negotiated revolution," with adaptation and innovation more important than ideology to left's successes. Presents nuanced history of changes over time in positions of both FMLN and government-US bloc, especially ARENA, and two sides' eventual mutual approximation.

1722 Macpherson, Anne S. Viragoes, victims and volunteers: creole female political cultures and gendered State policy in 19th-century Belize. (*in* Belize: selected proceedings from the second interdisciplinary conference. Lanham, Md.: Univ. Press of America, 1996, p. 23–44, bibl.)

Lumber trade skewed demography and gender relations in 19th-century Belize City, granting even slave women considerable autonomy while men were absent for months in forests. But consolidation of politicized female community was compromised by divisions of race and class, and by conflicts among women of impoverished popular classes.

1723 Madriz, José and **Adolfo Altamirano.**
Por Nicaragua, por el Partido Liberal,
por el general Zelaya: polémica histórica. Recopilación de Orient Bolívar Juárez. Managua: Impresiones y Troqueles, 1995. 281 p.:
bibl., ill. (Publicación Banco Mercantil)
Reproduces four turn-of-century tracts
by José Madriz against Nicaraguan president
José Santos Zelaya (1893–1909), and four by
Adolfo Altamirano in support of Zelaya.
Madriz argues Zelaya betrayed principles of
liberalism; Altamirano sees efforts to apply
doctrinaire theories to real world as counter-
productive.

1724 Mencos, Mario Alberto. La Guatemala
de ayer: cartas a un mi amigo. Guatemala de la Asunción: Librerías Artemis-
Edinter, 1995. 134 p.: ill.
Costumbrista remembrances of early-
20th-century Guatemala City, complemented by photographs from period.

1725 Merino del Río, José. Manuel Mora y
la democracia costarricense: viaje al
interior del Partido Comunista. Heredia,
Costa Rica: Editorial Fundación UNA, 1996.
223 p.: bibl.
More than just elections, democracy
in Costa Rica has involved complex development of ideas and experience, to which Costa
Rican Communist Party has made important
contributions. As principal theorist of Costa
Rican communism, Manuel Mora helped
construct "a political system of civilized tolerance with an advanced social orientation."

1726 Miller, Eugene D. Labour and the wartime alliance in Costa Rica, 1943–
1948. (*J. Lat. Am. Stud.*, 25:3, Oct. 1993,
p. 515–541)
Detailed analysis of pre-1948 state-
Church-labor relations. Alliance of Rafael
Angel Calderón Guardia's Partido Republicano Nacional, Catholic Church, and Communist Party-CTCR provided favorable environment for labor organizing and passing
modern Labor Code, but Cold War tensions
soon prompted Church to end cooperation
and form anti-Communist labor federation.

1727 Moberg, Mark. Crown colony as Banana Republic: the United Fruit Company in British Honduras, 1900–1920. (*J. Lat.
Am. Stud.*, 28:2, May 1996, p. 317–381)
In early-20th-century Belize, colonial

administrators eagerly submitted colony's
material resources and labor power to demands of United Fruit Company, "to the
detriment of local banana production."

1728 Molina Jiménez, Iván. Viviendas y
muebles: el marco material de la vida
doméstica en el valle central de Costa Rica,
1821–1824. (*Rev. Hist. Am.*, 116, julio/dic.
1993, p. 59–91, tables)
Examines houses and furniture of
different social groups in Costa Rica, based
on post-mortem records. Finds generally
low level of wealth made houses simple
and furniture scarce, but, for same reason,
items were often focus of inheritance disputes.

1729 Molina Jiménez, Iván and **Steven
Palmer.** La voluntad radiante: cultura
impresa, magia y medicina en Costa Rica,
1897–1932. San José: Editorial Porvenir;
Plumsock Mesoamerican Studies, 1996.
159 p.: bibl., ill.
Uses histories of immigrant Catalan
printer and Cuban medical charlatan to examine conflicting cultural currents in early-
20th-century Costa Rica. Printer epitomized
successful "self-made" man, but failed when
attempted more socially prestigious occupation of coffee sales. Charlatan exploited social space for "miracles, marvels, and magic"
present even in modernizing Costa Rica of
1930s.

1730 Morazán, Francisco. Escritos del General Francisco Morazán. Recopilación
y ordenación por Carlos Meléndez Chaverri.
Tegucigalpa: Banco Central de Honduras,
1996. 411 p.: bibl.
Compiles some 200 public documents
spanning years 1825–42, written by Morazán
or in his name, including "Apuntes sobre
la Revolución de [1]829." Introduction discusses additional items known or thought
to exist but not reproduced here.

1731 Morgan, Henry G. Vistas de Costa
Rica. San José: Comisión del Centenario de la Democracia Costarricense, 1989.
105 p.: chiefly ill.
Photographs of early 1890s Costa Rica,
originally published in Boston in 1892. Re-
arranged here, with added short descriptive
and historical texts. Focuses mostly on San
José and other towns of central valley.

1732 Moroni Bracamonte, José Angel and **David E. Spencer.** Strategy and tactics of the Salvadoran FMLN guerrillas: last battle of the Cold War, blueprint for future conflicts. Westport, Conn.: Praeger, 1995. 212 p.: bibl., ill., index, maps.

Offers "nuts and bolts" description of FMLN strategy and tactics, with attention to organization, weapons, equipment, communications, logistics, and training. Includes detailed analyses of specific battles. Essentially a handbook for military aspects of guerrilla war.

1733 Murillo Chaverri, Carmen. Identidades de hierro y humo: la construcción del ferrocarril al Atlántico, 1870–1890. San José: Editorial Porvenir, 1995. 160 p.: bibl., ill.

Joins history and anthropology to view construction of Atlantic railroad as "forge" of Costa Rican national identity for elites as well as migrant and immigrant workers. Pays particular attention to ethnic relations among laborers in line camps. Unusual approach.

1734 Olander, Marcia. Costa Rica in 1948: Cold War or local war? (*Americas/Franciscans*, 52:4, April 1994, p. 465–493)

Uses State Dept. records to suggest, against much recent scholarship, that US did not purposefully intervene in 1948 Costa Rican uprising. Argues Washington was not forewarned of uprising, misunderstood rebels' intent, denied Costa Rican government's requests for US mediation, and did not immediately recognize rebels.

Pakkasvirta, Jussi. Un continente, una nación?: intelectuales latinoamericanos, comunidad política y las revistas culturales en Costa Rica y en el Perú, 1919–1930. See item **2688.**

1735 Palmer, Steven Paul. Confinement, policing, and the emergence of social policy in Costa Rica, 1880–1935. (*in* The birth of the penitentiary in Latin America: essays on criminology, prison reform, and social control. Austin: Univ. of Texas Press, 1996, p. 224–253)

Excellent preliminary look at the development of prisons and policing in turn-of-century Costa Rica. Shows how shift from penal colonies to urban penitentiary, meant as instrument of positivist rehabilitation,

failed as this institution mainly housed rotating population of minor offenders.

1736 Palmer, Steven Paul. Racismo intelectual en Costa Rica y Guatemala, 1870–1920. (*Mesoamérica/Plumsock*, 17:31, junio 1996, p. 99–121)

Costa Rican intellectuals used social Darwinism and eugenics to laud racially homogeneous nation, whereas, given predominance of Indian population, Guatemalan counterparts emphasized assimilation. Good analysis of concepts of "race" and "social Darwinism" as understood at that time.

1737 Panamá en sus usos y costumbres. Recopilación de Stanley Heckadon Moreno. Panamá: Editorial Universitaria, 1994. 683 p.: bibl., ill. (Biblioteca de la cultura panameña; 14)

Presents 38 pieces of varying length by assorted 19th- and 20th-century authors on topics such as Chinese and "Hindu" immigration; subsistence farming in Indian and Negro communities; urbanization; politicization of indigenous population; language, folklore, women, and peasant culture; Carnival, cockfights, and lottery.

1738 Pattridge, Blake D. The Catholic Church and the closed corporate community during the Guatemalan Revolution, 1944–1954. (*Americas/Franciscans*, 52:1, July 1995, p. 25–42)

Examines pressures on *cofradías* during revolutionary period. After 1944, large number of foreign priests entered country, many at odds with traditional practices, as was new Catholic Action movement. Spread of political parties provided alternative venue for local power struggles.

1739 Pattridge, Blake D. La Universidad de San Carlos de Guatemala en el régimen conservador, 1839–1871: penuria, reforma y crecimiento. (*Mesoamérica/Plumsock*, 16:30, dic. 1995, p. 265–286, photos, tables)

Surveys development and problems of Univ. of San Carlos during conservative "Thirty Years," compared to earlier liberal Academia de Estudios. Not dominated by reaction, university subscribed to periodicals in English and French to keep abreast of new ideas, and offered courses in natural sciences and economics.

1740 Pearcy, Thomas L. Panama's Generation of '31: patriots, praetorians, and a decade of discord. (*HAHR*, 76:4, Nov. 1996, p. 691–719, graphs, tables)

In years after Generation of '31 took power, middle-class political fragmentation and lower-class economic desperation created ongoing "crisis of hegemony" that produced "state of exception," ushering in "progressive assumption of power" by police. Military began to play dominant role in Panamanian politics in 1940s, not 1960s.

1741 Peters, Gertrud. La evaluación de las fuentes históricas censales-agropecuarias en Costa Rica: el censo agrícola e industrial de 1905. (*Rev. Hist./Heredia*, 31, enero/junio 1995, p. 213–235, tables)

Shows how 1905 census can be source for Costa Rica's agrarian history. Extensive tables summarize key census information for Heredia province.

1742 Piel, Jean. El departamento del Quiché bajo la dictadura liberal, 1880–1920. Guatemala?: FLACSO Guatemala; Centro de Estudios Mexicanos y Centroamericanos, 1995. 164 p.: bibl., ill., map, tables.

Based on research in national and departmental archives, examines regional and local activities of liberal state in Guatemala's highland El Quiché dept. during 1880–1920, including day-to-day administration, labor mobilization, apparatus of institutionalized violence, and education. Includes surveys of available documentation, appended documents, and extensive statistical tables.

1743 Potthast-Jutkeit, Barbara. El impacto de la colonización alemana y de las actividades misioneras moravas en la Mosquitia, durante el siglo XIX. (*Mesoamérica/Plumsock*, 15:25, dic. 1994, p. 253–288, ill., map, photos)

Account of German missionary and colonization schemes in Moskitia, based mainly on published German-language sources. Details failure of both state-sponsored and private colonization projects, in contrast to relative success of Moravian missions which adapted better to local conditions.

1744 Quesada Avendaño, Florencia. Los del Barrio Amón: marco habitacional, familiar y arquitectónico del primer barrio residencial de la burguesía josefina, 1900–1930. (*Mesoamérica/Plumsock*, 17:31, junio 1996, p. 215–241, map, photos, tables)

Describes development and architecture of elite neighborhood in northern San José. Finds tendency toward functional specialization of rooms and influence of imported European models. Includes interesting photographs and information on styles and building materials. Based on limited number of oral histories.

1745 Quezada, Rufino Antonio and Hugo Roger Martínez. 25 años de estudio y lucha: una cronología del movimiento estudiantil. San Salvador: s.n., 1995. 126 p.: ill.

Short history of Salvadoran student movement from 1970s-early 1990s, written by two of movement's leaders. Presents chronological catalog of groups, alliances, conflicts, and victims. Little analysis.

Ramírez, Sergio. Hatful of tigers: reflections on art, culture, and politics. See item **4681**.

1746 Rivera, Julio César et al. El silencio quedó atrás: testimonios de la huelga bananera de 1954. Recopilación de Marvin Barahona. Tegucigalpa: Editorial Guaymuras, 1994. 418 p.: bibl., ill. (Col. Talanquera)

Excellent brief overview of 1954 banana strike, based chiefly on newspaper research, followed by *testimonios* of seven leaders and participants. Very useful.

1747 Rodríguez, Jorge. Los salesianos en Nicaragua: Casa de Granada, 1876–1994. Edición de Jorge Eduardo Arellano. Managua: J. Rodríguez, 1994. 311 p.: bibl., ill.

Detailed but poorly organized history of Salesians in Nicaragua, including short biographies of notable Salesian fathers. Many quotes but no sources. Uniformly hostile to Sandinistas.

1748 Rojas, Margarita; Margarita Tórrez; and José Antonio Fernández. Acceso a la tierra y actividades económicas en cinco comunidades del occidente nicaragüense: el censo de 1883. (*Rev. Hist./Managua*, 3/4, 1994, p. 21–31, bibl., photos, tables)

Brief overview of patterns of land-ownership and use in Nicaraguan communities of Diriamba, Niquinohomo, San Juan de Oriente, El Rosario, and La Paz, based on 1883 agricultural censuses. Towns differed in access to land and in relative holdings of national, communal, and private property, with cash cropping concentrated on larger holdings.

1749 Rubio Sánchez, Manuel. Historial del cultivo de la grana o cochinilla en Guatemala. Guatemala: Tip. Nacional, 1994. 324 p.: appendix, bibl.

History of cultivation and export of cochineal from Guatemala, heavily laced with long extracts from documents and travelers' accounts. Includes 100 p. documentary appendix. More raw materials compilation than finished analysis, but valuable to 19th-century specialists.

1750 Ruiz Franco, Arcadio. Fermentos de lucha: hambre y miseria en Guatemala, 1944–1950. Guatemala: Editorial Universitaria, Univ. de San Carlos de Guatemala, 1993. 226 p. (Col. Editorial Universitaria; 91)

Written in 1949, describes daily life of Guatemala City's skilled workers and their efforts to organize before and during October Revolution. Disjointed and fragmented, but worth reading for sense of immediacy.

1751 Sáenz Carbonell, Jorge Francisco. Historia diplomática de Costa Rica, 1821–1910. San José: Editorial Juricentro, 1996. 672 p.: bibl., maps.

Survey of Costa Rican diplomatic history. While teaching future diplomats, author noted profound ignorance of subject, which he attributes to country's lack of professional foreign service. Includes biographical data on chief foreign policy officials.

1752 Santamaría García, Antonio. Los ferrocarriles de servicio público nicaragüense, 1870–1990. (*Anu. Estud. Am.*, 52:1, 1995, p. 117–143, map, tables)

Presents history of Nicaraguan railroad projects, only one of which succeeded. Finds that viable schemes were state-supported projects concentrated on Pacific coast, where available traffic and low construction costs promised relatively easy profits.

1753 Schmölz-Häberlein, Michaela. Continuity and change in a Guatemalan Indian community: San Cristóbal-Verapaz, 1870–1940. (*HAHR*, 76:2, May 1996, p. 227–248)

Studies landowner-Indian relations in San Cristóbal-Verapaz, Guatemala, under Reforma liberals, emphasizing effects of changes in land titling and spread of coffee cultivation. German immigrants and local ladinos benefited, while Indians lost land and were converted into cheap labor, provoking resistance and flight.

1754 Schroeder, Michael J. Horse thieves to rebels to dogs: political gang violence and the State in the Western Segovias, Nicaragua, in the time of Sandino, 1926–1934. (*J. Lat. Am. Stud.*, 28:2, May 1996, p. 383–434, map, photo)

Detailed treatment of political origin and effect of bandit violence on Nicaragua's northern frontier that argues violence was tied to shift from local *caudillo* power to development of effective central state. Sandino adopted many traditional bandit methods for political purposes.

1755 La separación de Panamá de Colombia y el surgimiento de la república, 3 de noviembre de 1903. Estudio introductorio y antología por Patricia Pizzurno de Araúz. Panamá: Instituto Nacional de Cultura, Archivo Nacional de Panamá, 1995. 110 p.

Brief history of separatist movements in Panama against Colombia, followed by anthology of documents and short first-person accounts of 1903 independence movement.

1756 Sieder, Rachel. Honduras: the politics of exception and military reformism, 1972–78. (*in* Authoritarianism in Latin America since independence. Westport, Conn.: Greenwood Press, 1996, p. 109–132)

Argues roots of Honduras' unusual reformist military regime lay in country's integration into world economy under US monopoly capital instead of under local export bourgeoisie. Military and organized labor developed as political actors from 1950s, but, because of US influence, ORIT-aligned labor, local manufacturing capital, and military all supported 1972 coup and subsequent populist reforms. For political scientist's comment, see *HLAS 57:3209.*

1757 Smutko, Gregorio. La presencia capuchina entre los miskitos, 1915–1995. Cartago, Costa Rica: Imprenta A.G. Covao; Coedición entre la Univ. de las Regiones Autónomas de la Costa Caribe Nicaragüense y la Vice Provincia de los Capuchinos de América Central y Panamá, 1996. 290 p.: bibl., ill., maps.

Well-researched, balanced amateur history of Indian-state-Church relations on Nicaragua's Caribbean coast during 1980s.

1758 Sobel, Richard. Contra aid fundamentals: exploring the intricacies and the issues. (*Polit. Sci. Q.*, 110:2, Summer 1995, p. 287–306, tables)

Identifies sources of funding for US-sponsored anti-Sandinista forces in 1980s Nicaragua, calculating amount provided versus amount Contras actually received, and considering whether funding violated US law. Concludes that, if one supported Reagan administration policies, Contras were a bargain, but many transactions were questionable and some plainly illegal. For international relations specialist's comment, see *HLAS 57:4200.*

1759 Tábora, Rocío. Masculinidad y violencia en la cultura política hondureña. Tegucigalpa: C.H. Honduras; Centro de Documentación de Honduras, 1995. 129 p.: bibl.

Examines political violence and *caudillismo* in turn-of-century Honduras from perspective of relationship between violence and masculinity. Half of book devoted to gender theories and social psychology. Uses autobiographies to analyze social attitudes toward masculine violence. Approach novel to Central American historiography.

Tack, Juan Antonio. Ilusiones y realidades en las negociaciones con los Estados Unidos de América. See *HLAS 57:4205.*

1760 Trujillo Bolio, Mario A. Historia de los trabajadores en el capitalismo ιιicaragüense, 1850–1950. México: Centro de Estudios Latinoamericanos, Facultad de Ciencias Políticas y Sociales, UNAM, 1992. 232 p.: bibl.

Schematic and predictable within standard Marxist framework, but brings together material from numerous secondary sources about labor history. Offers more detail for years after 1929 and role of PTN. Relies heavily on Pérez Bermúdez and Guevara López's *El movimiento obrero en Nicaragua* (see *HLAS 50:1437*).

1761 Turcios, Roberto. Autoritarismo y modernización: El Salvador, 1950–1960. San Salvador: Ediciones Tendencias, 1993. 221 p.: bibl.

Finds causes of 1969 "Soccer War" in economic and political developments of 1950s. Despite efforts of state and young military officers to diversify economy, El Salvador's dependence on coffee continued, and coffee elites remained politically dominant. Based on newspapers and government documents.

1762 Valle, Víctor Manuel. Siembra de vientos: El Salvador, 1960–69. San Salvador: CINAS, 1993. 554 p.: appendix.

Personal view of Salvadoran politics in 1960s by former student leader and founder of Movimiento Nacional Revolucionario, based on interviews of author by Salvadoran graduate student Jeannette Cecilia Noltenius. Useful for political history in general, and for involvement of university and MNR in particular. Valuable features are documentary appendix and postscript reflecting on 1980s crisis. For political scientist's comment, see *HLAS 55:2971.*

1763 Vargas, Oscar-René. Floreció al filo de la espada: el movimiento de Sandino, 1926–1939; once ensayos de interpretación. Prólogo de Carlos Tünnermann Bernheim. Managua: Centro de Estudios de la Realidad Nacional; Centro Nicaragüense de Escritores, 1995. 529 p.: bibl. (Col. Centenario)

Weakness of Nicaraguan proletariat and strong cross-class attraction of anti-imperialism allowed sectors of *pequeña burguesía* to gain influence with Sandino. With US out, Sandino failed to grasp that chief contradiction had shifted to bourgeoisie and that negotiations now served their interests and those of President Juan Bautista Sacasa.

1764 Vargas Llosa, Alvaro and **Santiago Aroca.** Riding the tiger: Ramiro de León Carpio's battle for human rights in Guatemala. Miami: Brickell Communications, 1995. 255 p.: ill.

Highly favorable (self-)portrait of human rights activist who became president of Guatemala following legislative coup against predecessor Jorge Serrano Elías (1991–93). Based on interviews with Vargas Llosa and Aroca, includes flattering prologue and epilogue and reprinted dispatches from Guatemala.

1765 Vega, Patricia. De la imprenta al periódico: los inicios de la comunicación impresa en Costa Rica, 1821–1850. San José: Editorial Porvenir, Programa Latinoamericano de Periodismo, 1995. 225 p.: bibl.

Thoroughly researched, detailed his-

tory of early printing and press in independent Costa Rica. Includes information on
production process and distribution system,
contents of early newspapers, and writers
and readers.

**1766 Velásquez Carrera, Eduardo Antonio
and Oscar Guillermo Peláez Almengor.** Economía urbana y periodización histórica de Guatemala: dos estudios. Guatemala: Centro de Estudios Urbanos y
Regionales, Univ. de San Carlos de
Guatemala, 1993. 77 p.: bibl.

Based on secondary sources, essay by
Velázquez Carrera focuses on periodization
of economic development and urbanization.
Peláez Almengor uses archival material to
discuss urban economy of late-19th-century
Guatemala City, emphasizing city's meat
supply.

1767 Villegas Hoffmeister, Guillermo. Testimonios del 48. v. 2, San Isidro de El
General en llamas. San José: Editorial Costa
Rica, 1996. 1 v.: ill. (v. 2: Biblioteca Col. de
periodismo reportajes extraordinarios)

Costa Rica's 1948 civil war reflected in
personal accounts from both sides of fighting
around San Isidro de El General.

1768 Wünderich, Volker. Sandino: una biografía política. Managua: Editorial
Nueva Nicaragua, 1995. 367 p.: bibl., plates.

Based heavily on US and German
diplomatic materials, readable scholarly biography of Augusto C. Sandino distinguishes
between man and myth.

1769 Yuscarán, Guillermo. Gringos in Honduras: the good, the bad, and the ugly.
English ed. Tegucigalpa: Nuevo Sol Publicaciones, 1995. 154 p.: bibl., ill., map.

Based on secondary sources, presents
short biographies in English of eclectic selection of "gringos" associated with Honduran
history, including John Lloyd Stephens,
William Walker, O. Henry, Lee Christmas,
and Wilson Popenoe.

1770 Zelaya, Gustavo. El legado de la Reforma Liberal. Tegucigalpa: Editorial
Guaymuras, 1996. 132 p.: bibl. (Col. Códices)

Examines ideas underlying Honduras'
19th-century liberal reform, with particular
attention to Ramón Rosa, Marco Aurelio
Soto, and Adolfo Zúñiga. Addresses sociohistorical context, connections between positivism and liberalism, and how ideas laid basis for dependent capitalism and "progress."
Ambitious for length, but worth reading.

THE CARIBBEAN, THE GUIANAS, AND THE SPANISH BORDERLANDS

EDWARD L. COX, *Associate Professor of History, Rice University, Houston*
ANNE PÉROTIN-DUMON, *Professor of History, Pontificia Universidad Católica de Chile*
JOHN D. GARRIGUS, *Professor of History, Jacksonville University*
JOSÉ M. HERNÁNDEZ, *Professor Emeritus of History, Georgetown University*
ROSEMARIJN HOEFTE, *Head, Department of Caribbean Studies, Royal Institute of
Linguistics and Anthropology, The Netherlands*
TERESITA MARTÍNEZ-VERGNE, *Professor of History, Macalester College*

THE BRITISH CARIBBEAN

AS WAS THE CASE with previous volumes of the *Handbook*, important trends in
the publications reviewed this biennium seem to indicate that the state of writing
on the English Caribbean is alive and well. While no single publication stands out
as truly remarkable, there are a number of highly important studies that deserve
special mention. Ramesar's *Survivors of Another Crossing: A History of East Indians in Trinidad, 1880–1946* is a well-documented and cogently argued text that

presents interesting portraits of East Indians in late-19th- and early-20th-century Trinidad (item **2089**), while Campbell's *The Young Colonials: A Social History of Education in Trinidad and Tobago, 1834–1939* evaluates the quality of education that young Trinidadians received in the 100 years after slavery's abolition (item **1949**). B. Moore's *Cultural Power, Resistance, and Pluralism: Colonial Guyana, 1838–1900* commendably treats the multi-ethnic situation in Guyana, where the pattern of divisiveness that was a distinct feature of the immediate postslavery era remained largely intact and became institutionalized by the end of the 19th century (item **2005**). In a well-researched and well-argued article, J. Scott portrays the efforts of sailors and slaves to bridge the artificial boundaries that nation-states created in the Caribbean (item **1919**), while R. McDonald's fruitful use of a stipendiary magistrate's diary provides an insider's commentary on societal strains during the apprenticeship period (item **2000**).

The belatedly maturing state of the discipline relative to the study of women and gender is amply demonstrated through the works of a number of authors. Bush (item **1873**), Jabour (item **1983**), Gaspar (item **1850**), and Beckles (item **1871**) provide interesting dimensions on slave women's experiences including resistance, work conditions, and health and reproductive matters. The 20th-century landscape is wonderfully illuminated through the contributions of Vassell (item **2101**), French (item **2065**), and Woolford (item **2107**), who point to the efforts women made to become politically active despite official policy aimed at keeping them in traditional roles. If this research trend continues, we can expect an increasing number of worthwhile works on these themes as scholars explore aspects of society that for too long have gone unattended.

In a gradual shift from previous years, renewed interest in Atlantic slavery suggests that scholars are becoming increasingly dissatisfied with the state of scholarship surrounding this important, though contentious, subject. Eltis addresses the matter head-on by using his own study as a springboard for an assault on normally accepted notions regarding the volume of the trade and British involvement in it during the 17th century (item **1843**). He concludes that previous studies grossly underexaggerated the role of the British. Gragg and Burnard are more specific, limiting the focus of their useful studies to the volume and workings of the trade in early Barbados and Jamaica, respectively (items **1851** and **1834**).

The crucial transition from slavery to full freedom continues to attract the attention of scholars. In addition to McDonald's work cited above, Shelton (item **2030**) and Troillot (item **2037**) have made worthwhile contributions to our understanding of this phase of the Caribbean experience through their studies of St. Kitts and Dominica. Particularly impressive are Troillot's and McDonald's compelling arguments and their thorough use of the reports and diaries of two different stipendiary magistrates.

The experiences of newer immigrants continue to garner attention. Mention has already been made of Ramesar's important work on indigenous peoples in Trinidad (item **2089**). Mohamed's article constitutes a fascinating study of the emergence of a Portuguese business community in Guyana (item **1979**); Menezes provides a comprehensive examination of the sociopolitical history of the entire Portuguese community in the country (item **2003**); while Shepherd and Basdeo analyze the experiences of indigenous peoples on Jamaica and Guyana, respectively (items **2031** and **1990**).

Finally, efforts to place the experiences of early Bermuda colonists within the larger North American context have led to the publication over the past few years of a number of fruitful and highly important studies. Bernhard's article shows that, although slaves on Bermuda rebelled throughout the period of slavery's existence, punishment was vastly different from that experienced by their counterparts on the other Caribbean islands (item **1831**). Through the use of probate records, Metz provides a fascinating glimpse of wealth and material culture in 18th-century Bermuda (item **1906**). Similarly, Bowen and Jarvis (item **1872**) and Barka and Harris (item **1830**) have put archeological findings to excellent use, enhancing our understanding of lifestyles, food usage, and general fortifications on the island. As scholars seek to understand more fully the Bermudian variant of the early British North American colonies, we will see more in-depth studies of a colony often neglected by the literature. [ELC]

FRENCH AND DANISH CARIBBEAN AND FRENCH GUIANA
For scholars, guides to resources provide invaluable assistance. Historians of the Virgin Islands have given us two excellent research tools: Highfield and Tyson's *Slavery in the Danish West Indies: a Bibliography* (item **1792**); and its companion book of selected texts, *The Kamina Folk* (item **1827**). Drawing on unique sources, these works offer fresh interpretations of the institution of slavery in the 18th-century Danish West Indies. Highfield identifies patterns of accommodation and resistance (item **1897**), while Olwig examines the possible African origins of modes of social insertion (item **1910**). David's "L'histoire religieuse de Martinique au XVI-Ième siècle" constitutes another important research tool for the study of the Lesser Antilles and French Guiana in the 17th century (item **1839**).

Fresh avenues of research have been opened for the further exploration of 18th-century French Caribbean slave society and the impact of revolutionary upheaval. Geggus delineates the place of females within the slave population and shows that sexuality placed them in an ambiguous position with respect to their masters (item **1890**). He also skillfully traces the origins of the naming of Haiti (item **1788**). Combining the resources of social, economic, and cultural history, Garrigus describes a landed, rural, free-colored elite threatened by rising racial prejudice (item **1887**), while Pérotin-Dumon stresses the political nature of claims, strategies, and alliances made by Guadeloupian slaves and free-coloreds in the 1790s (item **1913**). *Sugar and Slavery, Family and Race* makes a felicitous selection in English of Dessalles' testimony on the end of a planter elite in Martinique (item **1964**). To Nelly Schmidt we owe the authoritative biography of the famous abolitionist Victor Schoelcher (item **2024**); her editing of his correspondence throws light on his private persona (item **2028**). Cottias and Fitte-Duval have begun exploring the origins of the persistent political marginalization of Caribbean women by analyzing the legal and cultural meaning of the abolition of slavery from a gender perspective (item **1781**).

Turning to other areas of research, ecobiologist Hatzenberger shows the importance of imported species in Guadeloupe's flora during the 1790s, even in woods that were not cleared (item **1896**); her study exemplifies a recent trend toward environmental history. So, too, does Bégot's sophisticated reading of reactions to the tropical landscape of Martinique in the early 1800s, exhibiting both physiocratic interest and emerging romanticism (item **1941**).

The origins of Caribbean history-writing and the meaning of the past during different eras are topics receiving more attention, as shown by three works: Buffon's insightful account of the work of Lacour, Guadeloupe's most prominent 19th-century historian (item **1944**); Pérotin-Dumon's article on 20th-century French

Caribbean historiography, its plantation society paradigm, and Haitian nationalism in contrast to the quests of Martinique and Guadeloupe for identity (item **1813**); and Nesbitt's survey on the treatment of Delgrès, a key military figure in the Guadeloupe uprising of 1802, in historical and political literature (item **1808**).

To the historiography of the 20th century, a lasting contribution has been made by Dash's *Haiti and the United States: National Stereotypes and the Literary Imagination* (item **1782**), which places Haitian and US perceptions of each other in political context. By focusing on the Church in politics, Chathuant documents a shady page of Guadeloupe's past during World War II (item **2055**). Finally, we are grateful to publishing houses that have reprinted a number of classics, each with a scholarly introduction; in particular: Capt. Bruneau's *Histoire véritable de certains voyages périlleux et hasardeux sur la mer, 1599*, the oldest narrative of a French voyage to the Caribbean (item **1832**); Baron de Wimpffen's travel in St. Domingue at the end of the ancien régime, *Haïti au XVIIIe siècle* (item **1928**); and Lacroix's lucid memoirs of the war of Haitian independence, *La Révolution de Haïti* (item **1901**). [APD & JDG]

DUTCH CARIBBEAN

In the last decade or so, important gaps in the extant historiography have been filled by a remarkable number of informative dissertations on various socio-economic and cultural topics. During the last couple of years this trend has been even more pronounced: not one senior scholar has recently produced a monograph of any historiographical importance.

Archeological studies of the precolumbian period on the Dutch Caribbean islands form one of the most fruitful areas of research. See for example Versteeg and Ruiz (*HLAS 55:521*) and Versteeg and Rostain (*HLAS 57:336*) for the results of excavations on Aruba.

As expected, slavery and plantation studies continue to dominate the historiographical scene. In his dissertation, Henk den Heijer studies an underexposed part of Dutch economic history: the vicissitudes of the West India Company (WIC) in West Africa (item **1852**). He challenges the notions that the slave trade was the WIC's *raison d'etre* and that the company was a commercial failure. Nevertheless, the WIC did transport many slaves to the Caribbean and Lenders' revised dissertation describes the efforts of the Moravians to preach the gospel to them (see *HLAS 56:1837*). Not all the Caribbean islands depended on plantations, as is shown by Luc Alofs, who chronicles slavery on Aruba (see *HLAS 56:1805*). A volume edited by Gert Oostindie for the first time examines antislavery and abolitionism in the Netherlands and the Dutch colonies in the Americas, Asia, and Africa (see *HLAS 56:2143*). In yet another dissertation, Ellen Klinkers looks at the transition from slavery to apprenticeship to full freedom in Suriname (item **1986**). The final volume on slavery is very different in character: Elmer Kolfin studies the visual representation of slavery in Suriname by analyzing contemporary engravings, lithos, and drawings (item **1802**).

Three studies fill gaps in the field of cultural history. Rutgers' revised dissertation is an extensive cultural history of the Netherlands Antilles and Aruba concentrating on oral and written literature (item **1817**). Rosalia has written a dissertation on the repression of tambú in Curaçao and the impact of this censorship on Afro-Antillian life (item **1816**). Meel has done a masterful job editing, annotating, and introducing the writings of Jan Voorhoeve, a linguist, anthropologist, and cultural activist concerned with Suriname (item **2103**).

Two general histories of Suriname and the Netherlands Antilles and Aruba are also reviewed this biennium. The history of Suriname by journalist Hans Buddingh' is not an unqalified success (item **1776**). *Geschiedenis van de Antillen* *[History of the Antilles]* thematically introduces the history of the six Dutch Antillian islands (item **1789**). This work is the sibling of *Geschiedenis van Suriname* *[History of Suriname]* (1993), which covers Suriname's history (see *HLAS 55:4696*). Finally, the University of Suriname has launched a new journal entitled *Journal of Social Sciences* that includes English-language essays on the humanities and social sciences. [RH]

PUERTO RICO

With the recent centennial of the US invasion of Puerto Rico and Cuba, Puerto Rican historians decreased their output of studies on labor, migration, and status; made apparently permanent inroads into new research areas, such as women, urban life, and racial politics; and prepared for the plethora of works on discourse analysis that will ensue as the colonial relationship is re-examined.

Traditional themes continue to capture the attention of both established historians and some newcomers. Migration studies in the past few years include the conventional narratives of European insertion into the island's economy, such as works by Chinea (item **1957**), Cifre de Loubriel (item **1958**), and Casablanca (item **1950**), as well as interdisciplinary work on Puerto Rican migration to the US, namely *The Commuter Nation: Perspectives on Puerto Rican Migration* edited by Torre, Rodríguez Vecchini, and Burgos (item **2059**). The ever-present status issue is covered by Castro and Cubano Iguina, who discuss the economic considerations of 19th-century party affiliates (items **1953** and **1959**), while d'Alzina Guillermety looks at the juridical aspects of the autonomist position (item **1960**). Examining the more recent political scene, Mari Bras and Morris offer explanations for the intensity, if not the popularity, of the separatist position (items **2081** and **1997**). Almost as if to revive labor studies, Pérez Velasco and Baronov produced a lengthy unannotated bibliography of sources on the late-19th- and 20th-century labor movement (item **2088**).

In response to changing theoretical tendencies and to fill existing historical lacunae, a number of new themes have appeared over the past few years. In the field of women's studies, Barceló Miller (item **2047**) and Colón, Mergal, and Torres (item **2058**) have published, respectively, a narrowly focused account of the women's suffrage movement and a general history of women's political and economic participation in the early-20th century. Urban life, in its many manifestations but localized in San Juan, is explored by Ayala in his survey of masonic lodges (item **1938**), by Rivera Rivera in her narrative of the successes and failures of the charity system (item **2021**), by Kinsbruner in his exploration of racial prejudice through housing patterns (item **1985**), by Matos Rodríguez in his rich description of working class daily life (item **1996**), and by Mayo Santana, Negrón Portillo, and Mayo López in their ongoing analysis of the lives of slaves and freedmen and women (item **1997**). The last three works are outstanding in their use of sources, their insights into daily life, and their examination of the broader Latin American and Caribbean context.

As has been the case for several years, discourse analysis, subaltern studies, and other theoretical perspectives have promoted a rereading of familiar sources and revisiting of old affairs. Picó (item **2013**), Matos Rodríguez (item **1995**), Clark (item **2057**), Rigau-Pérez (item **2020**), and Santiago-Valles (item **2022**) have probed texts to explore such varied topics as the desires and expectations of common people, the impressions of a traveler, the debate over prohibition, the force of authoritarian politics, and resistance on the part of the marginalized classes. The status controversy has also benefitted from discourse analysis, less so in García-Passalacqua's *Hegemón: otredad y mismidad de la otra cara* (item **2070**), and enormously in Doris Sommer's "Puerto Rico a flote: desde Hostos hasta hoy" (item **2034**), an imaginative celebration of the Puerto Rican capacity for keeping options open. Finally, Fernández-Aponte (item **2064**) and García (item **1970**) offer a glimpse of the quality that one hopes will mark the inevitable copious production in the next few years. [TMV]

CUBA, THE DOMINICAN REPUBLIC, AND THE SPANISH BORDERLANDS

The material received for review this biennium exceeded 350 items, indeed an avalanche of historical writings, published sources, and historiographical essays. Unfortunately, quality did not entirely measure up to quantity and, for this reason, in addition to space limitations, only a portion of the items received will be reviewed here.

Despite the outpouring of average or below average publications, the biennium was graced by the appearance of the first biographies of Ernesto Che Guevara worthy of that name (items **2043** and **2052**). Curiously enough, both biographers, Jon Lee Anderson and Jorge Castañeda, are men who are sympathetic to the almost mythical guerrilla fighter. Both nonetheless resisted the temptation to write just another panegyric and honestly provided the readers with the pertinent facts, regardless of their nature. In due time their works will surely be superseded by others based on a broader documentation and a longer perspective. But both have made important contributions to the largely undistinguished historiography of the Cuban Revolution.

Significant biographies were also written on other figures, such as the legendary Spanish conqueror Hernando de Soto and his almost 4,000-mile expedition across the Southeastern US in the 16th century. With his monumental study, Hudson has made it possible for the first time to map De Soto's daring journey with a reasonable degree of approximation (item **1933**). Duncan, for his part, has produced the best biography of De Soto to date (item **1931**). Future investigators will no doubt improve on these two books, but these have set the current standard.

Those interested in pre-Castro Cuba will have to take into account Salwan's study of the corruption of the Cuban press (item **2092**), as well as Carr's article on sugar mill occupations and Soviets in Cuba after the 1933 fall of the Machado dictatorship (item **2050**). These two are noteworthy publications that certainly deserve to be singled out.

At the same level, generally speaking, is the output of Spanish historians, who have continued to examine various aspects of 19th-century Cuba. One of the most interesting of these studies is Paz Sánchez's long article on the inauspicious beginning of the 1895–98 Cuban War of Independence in the western half of the island (item **2012**). Nationalistic Cuban historians probably will not be pleased with some of Paz's disclosures, as they will most certainly reject the findings of Castellano Gil in his volume on Spanish Masonry in Cuba (item **1952**). Castellano, a member of the Center for Historical Studies on the Spanish Masonry, dismisses as tendentious and politically inspired most of what Cubans have written on the subject. As his conclusions gain currency, the history of the Masonry in Cuba will have to be rewritten. His work is based on a doctoral dissertation and his scholarly apparatus is impressive. No Cuban has ever researched the subject as thoroughly as he has.

In addition to the works of the Spaniards, valuable contributions were also made by Father Manuel Maza, S.J. (item **1806**) and Father José Luis Sáez, S.J. (items **1917, 1819,** and **1806**), who have persevered in their efforts to fill gaps and break new ground in the histories of the Catholic Church in Cuba and the Dominican Republic. This biennium, however, they have not been alone and have been joined by Martínez-Fernández, who published a conscientious article on Church-state relations and nationality in 19th-century Dominican Republic (item **1994**). This is indeed a most welcome development. [JMH]

GENERAL

1771 Adélaïde-Merlande, Jacques and **Jean-Paul Herview.** Les volcans dans l'histoire des Antilles. Paris: Karthala, 1996. 229 p.

A judicious selection of writings on the Montagne-Pelée, Martinique, and the Soufrière, Guadeloupe, reminds us that volcanoes have been observed and studied since the 18th century. [APD]

1772 Anthony, Michael. Historical dictionary of Trinidad and Tobago. Lanham, Md.: Scarecrow Press, 1997. 670 p.: bibl., maps. (Latin American historical dictionaries; 26)

Author claims to have included well-known individuals like Eric Williams and C.L.R. James, as well as less well-known figures like Sookoo. In addition to citing individuals such as Princess Margaret, who merely visited Trinidad and Tobago, he has included names of horses, ships, games, etc., while omitting major figures such as Francis De Ridder. Of some use nonetheless. [ELC]

1773 Association of Caribbean Historians. Conference. *25th, Mona, Jamaica, 1993.* West Indies accounts: essays on the history of the British Caribbean and the Atlantic economy in honour of Richard Sheridan. Edited by Roderick Alexander McDonald. Kingston: The Press, Univ. of the West Indies, 1996. 388 p.: bibl., ill., index.

Collection of essays written by former students, colleagues, and friends to honor a preeminent economic historian of the Caribbean. Covering period 1650–1850, essays encompass a broad range of topics, with major focus on various aspects of slavery and imperial relations during those years. Excellent introductory essay on Sheridan's contributions to Caribbean economic history. Extremely useful. [ELC]

Barthélemy, Gérard. Dans la splendeur d'un après-midi d'histoire. See *HLAS 57:795.*

1774 Bonniol, Jean-Luc. La couleur comme maléfice: une illustration créole de la généalogie des "Blancs" et des "Noirs." Paris: A. Michel, 1992. 304 p.: bibl., index. (Bibliothèque de synthèse; 1158–6591)

Shows that the whitening of the population that occurred in Les Saintes (Guadeloupe) after 1848 resulted from departure of former slaves and freedmen from the islands, rather than an influx of French settlers as popularly assumed. Anthropologist with a historical bent reflects on ways in which barriers between whites and blacks based on phenotypic differences have been culturally constructed while at the same time contested and reshaped by miscegenation. Based on fieldwork in La Désirade and Les Saintes. [APD]

1775 Brereton, Bridget. Gendered testimony: autobiographies, diaries, and letters by women as sources for Caribbean history. Mona, Jamaica: Dept. of History, Univ. of the West Indies, 1994. 20 p.: bibl. (Elsa Goveia memorial lecture; 1994)

Concentrating on writings of Maria Nugent, Mary Prince, Mary Seacole, Anna Mahase, Sarah Norton, and Adella Archibald, author shows how greater and systematic use of records left by women can enhance our understanding of Caribbean history. Mahase, Morton, and Archibald are especially important for showing changing marriage patterns for Indo-Trinidadian girls and impact of Canadian missionaries on the lives of Indo-Trinidadian women. [ELC]

1776 Buddingh', Hans. Geschiedenis van Suriname [History of Suriname]. Utrecht, The Netherlands: Het Spectrum, 1995. 424 p.: bibl., ill., index.

Journalistic account of the history of

Suriname from the first attempts at colonization to 1994 is based on secondary sources. Coverage of topics is rather uneven; author pays much attention to slavery and abolition thereof and to Maroon society and history. Second part is devoted to 20th-century political and socioeconomic developments. The second and third editions of this work were published in 2000. [RH]

1777 Burton, Richard D.E. La famille coloniale: la Martinique et la mère patrie, 1789–1992. Paris: L'Harmattan, 1994. 308 p.: bibl.

Innovative sociological study examines central idea underpinning France's political relationship with its colony: that of a mother who granted freedom to her sons. This idea draws its success from actual role played by women as mothers in modern Caribbean societies. [APD]

1778 Canino Salgado, Marcelino J. Dorado, Puerto Rico: historia, cultura, biografías y lecturas. Dorado, P.R.: Administración Municipal del Dorado, 1993. 426 p.: bibl., photos.

Study of the history and cultural peculiarities of the northern Puerto Rican town of Dorado was commissioned for 150th anniversary of its founding. Sources include government correspondence, newspaper articles, and folklore. Contains short biographies of leading figures, statistical information, and photographs. [TMV]

1779 Cassá, Roberto. Directorio de archivos de la República Dominicana. Madrid: Fundación Histórica Tavera, 1996. 110 p.: appendix. (Documentos Tavera; 1)

An indispensable tool for researchers of the history of the Dominican Republic. [JMH]

1780 Chauleau, Liliane. Il était une fois Saint-Pierre. Préface de Françoise Lacroix. Fort-de-France: Société des amis des archives et de la recherche sur le patrimoine culturel des Antilles, 1994. 119 p.: ill. (some col.), maps (some col.).

Beautiful album reproduces maps and other iconographic sources documenting history of first port city in Lesser Antilles from its 17th-century origins to its destruction by the 1902 eruption of the Montagne Pelée volcano. [APD]

1781 Cottias, Myriam and **Annie Fitte-Duval.** Femme, famille et politique dans les Antilles Françaises de 1828 a nos jours. (*Caribb. Stud.*, 28:1, 1995, p. 76–100)

Welcome examination of female civil and political rights during the transition from slavery to free society. Sets rich agenda for future research on the restrictions placed on women by the Napoleonic Civil Code and the emergence of the "respectable motherhood" model in lieu of the right to vote (granted to freed men in 1848, but to women only in 1946). Authors note that such practices led to women's participation in voluntary associations and charities but, with a few exceptions, marginalized them from politics. [APD]

1782 Dash, J. Michael. Haiti and the United States: national stereotypes and the literary imagination. 2nd ed. New York: St. Martin's Press, 1997. 182 p.: bibl., index.

Highly stimulating history of Haitian and US perceptions of each other as seen in each country's literature from 1850s-1990s. Dash sets these texts in political context and repeatedly demonstrates the narrow line between "imaginative" and "objective" descriptions of Haiti by US writers. This critical perspective, combined with the author's knowledge of 20th-century Haitian literature, makes this study a particularly valuable one. [JDG]

1783 Derkx, Jo. Netherlands Antilles and Aruba: a bibliography 1980–1995. Leiden, The Netherlands: KITLV Press, 1996. 591 p.: indexes. (Caribbean bibliographies)

Contains 4,152 entries on Netherlands Antilles and Aruba and on Dutch Antillean and Aruban communities abroad. Includes titles published from 1980-July 31, 1995, and is based on the collections of the Royal Institute of Linguistics and Anthropology in Leiden, The Netherlands. Includes entries on monographs, articles, novels, poetry, and juvenile literature, as well as on unpublished manuscripts. Indexes of personal names, geographical names, and subjects. [RH]

Eeuwen, Daniel van and **Yolande Pizetty-van Eeuwen.** ¿Existen estados en el Caribe? See *HLAS 57:3244.*

1784 Emmer, Pieter C. The Dutch in the Atlantic economy, 1580–1880: trade, slavery and emancipation. Aldershot, England; Brookfield, Vt.: Ashgate, 1998. 394 p.:

bibl., index, maps. (Variorum collected studies series; CS614)

Collection of 11 articles originally published between 1977–96, brought up-to-date. Topics include the Dutch and the making of the Atlantic system, the West India Company, Dutch (slave) trading, abolitionism, and different forms of plantation labor. [RH]

1785 Emmer, Pieter C. De Nederlandse slavenhandel, 1500–1850 [The Dutch slave trade, 1500–1850]. Amsterdam: Arbeiderspers, 2000. 259 p.: bibl., ill., index.

Divided into eight parts covering Dutch slave trade in the Atlantic world, discusses the Middle Passage, demand for slaves in the Caribbean, the trade's profitability, and abolition and emancipation. Final part asks whether The Netherlands has a debt of honor as a result of this trade. Although very brief bibliographies for each part are included, the main sources for this work remain unclear. Much of the text seems to be syntheses of work of other scholars. [RH]

1786 Fergus, Howard A. Montserrat: history of a Caribbean colony. London: Macmillan Caribbean, 1994. 294 p.: bibl., ill., index, maps.

Though not extensively documented, work makes available important information and elucidates many aspects of island's history. Contains excellent material on Chief Minister Rueben Meade for example, and includes information on natural disasters, labor and politics, and economic development. Particularly strong for slavery period and 20th century. Includes chapter on arts and culture. [ELC]

1787 Fernández Méndez, Eugenio. Crónicas de las poblaciones negras en el Caribe Francés. Traducción y notas por Manuel Cárdenas Ruiz. San Juan: Centro de Estudios Avanzados de Puerto Rico y el Caribe con la colaboración de la Editorial de la Univ. de Puerto Rico, 1996. 393 p.: bibl., ill.

Welcome translation of selected well-known narrative sources documenting history of French Lesser Antilles from its 17th-century origins. Comprehensive introductions place each text and author in context. [APD]

1788 Geggus, David Patrick. The naming of Haiti. (*NWIG,* 71:1/2, 1997, p. 43–68, bibl.)

Leading expert on colonial Haiti probes origins of name adopted at independence in 1804. Tentatively assigns choice of this self-consciously indigenous American name to Louis Boisrond Tonnerre, a French-educated, but strongly anti-European, individual who was Dessalines' secretary. Argues convincingly that "Haiti" appealed to revolutionaries because it was neither European nor African. Drawing on French and Spanish historians, leaders of the anti-French struggle in early-19th century identified the nearly extinct original inhabitants of the island with resistance to slavery and colonization. [JDG]

1789 Geschiedenis van de Antillen: Aruba, Bonaire, Curaçao, Saba, Sint Eustatius, Sint Maarten = History of the Antilles: Aruba, Bonaire, Curaçao, Saba, St. Eustatius, St. Maarten. Edited by Leo Dalhuisen *et al.* Zutphen, The Netherlands: Walburg Pers, 1997. 176 p.: bibl., ill. (some col.), index, maps.

In one of the few books describing the history of the six Dutch Antillan islands as an entity, Antillean and Dutch authors and editors adopt a thematic approach. In 10 chapters they discuss historical sources, ecology and population, Amerindian history, slavery, European influences, colonial and foreign relations, Antillean cultural and political identity, the May 1969 revolt in Curaçao, relations among the six islands, and migration. Intended as a general introduction to the history of the Dutch Antilles. [RH]

1790 Haïti à la une: une anthologie de la presse haïtienne de 1724 à 1934. v. 2, 1870–1908. v. 3, 1909–1915. v. 4, 1915–1921. Port-au-Prince: Imprimeur II, 1993. 3 v.

Desquiron pursues his methodical inquiry on the Haitian press, combining data on each newspaper and its political stance or literary importance with a selection of articles covering major national and international events. Vol. 2 analyzes and illustrates the life of 30 daily papers active from 1870–1908. Vol. 3 focuses on years preceding US intervention. Vol. 4, on years 1915–21, presents range of public opinion on US occupation in its beginnings. For annotation of vol. I, see *HLAS 56:1827.* [APD]

1791 Harris, Edward C. Bermuda forts, 1612–1957. Hamilton?: Bermuda Maritime Museum Press, 1997. 358 p.: bibl., ill. (some col.), index, maps.

Of immense value to archeologists and the general public, this carefully crafted book with copious drawings and photographs of forts constructed on Bermuda in the 17th-18th centuries provides excellent portrayal of importance of this colony to the British and the great efforts they made to keep it within their power. [ELC]

1792 Highfield, Arnold R. and George F. Tyson. Slavery in the Danish West Indies: a bibliography. St. Croix, US Virgin Islands: The Virgin Islands Humanities Council, 1994. 96 p.: indexes.

The result of a long-term project conducted by the Society of Virgin Islands Historians in collaboration with various institutions such as the University of the Virgin Islands and the Royal Archives in Copenhagen, this excellent research tool lists and annotates: 1) historiographical studies on slavery and slave trade (legal regime, conditions, education, emancipation, religion rebellions, free blacks, and free coloreds); 2) documentary sources and fiction; 3) location of materials listed, both in the Virgin Islands and abroad. Especially useful on 18th-century narratives by Danes. Detailed subject and author indexes. See also item **1827.** [APD]

1793 Historia general de la Iglesia en América Latina. v. 4, Caribe. Salamanca, Spain: Ediciones Sígueme, 1995. 1 v.: bibl., indexes. (El Peso de los días; 14)

Multi-authored, highly sophisticated volume on history of religious institutions and policies in the Caribbean covers four salient themes: the Catholic Church and Spanish colonialism, the churches (Catholic and Protestant) and slavery, the churches and the decolonization process, and relations between the churches and the dictatorial governments supported by the US (Batista of Cuba, Trujillo of the Dominican Republic, and Duvalier of Haiti). Authors often combine findings of published monographs with their own research in primary documents. [J. Britton]

1794 History Gazette. No. 65, Feb. 1994. The colonial foundations of race relations and ethno-politics in Guyana by Percy Hintzen. Turkeyen, Guyana: Univ. of Guyana, History Society.

Well-argued article contends that deliberate policies in colonial period explain continuing racial tensions in the nation. Ethnically oriented institutions, policies, and political parties reflected the ethnic polarization among workers and management. Exploitation in the plantation complex continues to frustrate efforts at unifying a nation-state where ethnicity is increasingly less revelant. [ELC]

1795 Hoogbergen, Wim. Afrosurinam. (*in* Presencia africana en el Caribe. México: Consejo Nacional para la Cultura y las Artes, 1995, p. 571–661, bibl., photos, tables)

Comprehensive introduction to Afro-Suriname history and culture is divided into five parts. Pt. 1 looks at Dutch expansion in the Caribbean. Pt. 2 focuses on the plantation colony, demographics of slavery, and the social and religious life of the slaves. Pt. 3 discusses marronage; while pt. 4 details slave insurrections, guerrilla wars, and peace treaties with the different Maroon groups. Final part considers Creole and Maroon development following abolition of slavery in 1863. [RH]

1796 Inikori, Joseph E. Slavery and the rise of capitalism. Mona, Jamaica: Dept. of History, Univ. of the West Indies, 1993. 33 p.: bibl. (Elsa Goveia memorial lecture; 1993)

Argues that Britain's protoindustrial growth between 1650–1850 was response to pressures and opportunities emanating from the Atlantic slave trade. Hence, 19th-century capitalist economy expanded to capture important part of larger world market. Draws on theories of Immanuel Wallerstein and modifies somewhat Eric Williams' main conclusions. Brief, highly important, work. [ELC]

1797 Inniss, Probyn, Sir. Historic Basseterre: the story of a West Indian town. Basseterre, Saint Kitts and Nevis: P. Inniss, 1985. 84 p.: bibl., ill.

Short book by native Kittitian who later became governor. Despite title, deals with history of entire island. Useful chronology and addition of photographs make this volume an improvement over earlier edition. Shows important economic and social role that Basseterre has played in island's history. [ELC]

1798 James, Willie. St. Lucia, land of intriguing romances. 2nd ed. St. Lucia: Mayers Printing Co., 1996? 51 p.: ill., 1 map.

Brief but interesting booklet on Saint Lucia's French heritage. Discusses the history of the name of Castries, the preference on the island for French priests, and the continuing legacy of French creole culture and language. [ELC]

1799 Jesse, Charles. Outlines of St. Lucia's history. 5th ed. Castries?: St. Lucia Archaeological and Historical Society, 1994. 122 p.: bibl., ill., index, maps.

Brief popular history, intended for a general audience, draws primarily on colonial reports and 17th–19th century books to provide excellent synopsis of major events and forces that shaped the island's history to 1960. Author has written extensively on various aspects of island's past. [ELC]

1800 Johnson, Howard. The Bahamas from slavery to servitude, 1783–1933. Gainesville: Univ. Press of Florida, 1996. 218 p.: bibl., index, map.

Highly important scholarly treatment of Bahamian socioeconomic history in post-emancipation period. In addition to examining last phases of slavery in both rural and urban settings, looks at export economies of salt, cotton, pineapples, and sponges, and their roles in emergence of mercantile middle class. Concludes that partly because of flawed governmental policies, workers ended up in servitude and ultimately migrated to Miami. [ELC]

1801 Johnson, Howard. The Bahamas in slavery and freedom. Kingston: Ian Randle Publishers; London: James Currey Publishers, 1991. 184 p.: bibl., index.

Initially published as independent essays, chapters cover islands' slow, painful transition from slavery to freedom. Included are examinations of the trucking system, organization and control of labor during and after slavery, role of merchant class in controlling labor, and 20th-century consequences of this control, including migration of Bahamians to Florida. [ELC]

1802 Kolfin, Elmer. Van de slavenzweep en de muze: twee eeuwen verbeelding van slavernij in Suriname [The slave whip and the muse: two centuries of representation of slavery in Suriname]. Leiden, The Netherlands: KITLV Press, 1997. 184 p.: bibl., ill. (some col.), index. (Caribbean series; 17)

First study of contemporary engravings, lithos, and drawings depicts two centuries of slavery in Suriname. Work shows how representation of slaves changed over time: first they were depicted as economic objects; later as exotic human beings. Also gives attention to abolition debate and its influence on contemporary art. This impressive work, placed in a Caribbean and North American context, contains more than 140 illustrations including 28 color plates. [RH]

1803 Lafleur, Gérard. La distillerie Bologne: du sucre au rhum. (*Bull. Soc. hist. Guadeloupe*, 103, 1995, p. 75–110, appendices, facsim., map)

Well-researched and multifaceted study of one of Guadeloupe's earliest sugar plantations reconstitutes estate, buildings, and equipment; lists the owners; and describes organization of slave and then free workers since 17th century. Longitudinal approach allows one to follow major transitions in sugarcane processing up to today's rum distillery. Supplemented by Schnakenbourg's study; see item **2027**. [APD]

1804 Lampe, Armando. Breve historia del cristianismo en el Caribe. Alajuelita, Costa Rica: CEHILA-América Central; Chetumal, Mexico: Univ. de Quintana Roo, 1990. 207 p.

Overview of history and present role of Christianity in the Caribbean is divided into 12 chapters. Topics include Amerindian religions, missionary activities, slavery, role of religion in the Haitian Revolution, Catholicism and the dictatorships of Trujillo and the Duvaliers, Christianity and the Cuban Revolution, the Lavalas Movement in Haiti, decolonization and Christianity, ecumenism, and the growth of Pentecostalism. [RH]

1805 The Lesser Antilles in the age of European expansion. Edited by Robert L. Paquette and Stanley L. Engerman. Gainesville: Univ. Press of Florida, 1996. 383 p.: bibl., ill., index.

Outgrowth of papers presented at conference marking Columbus' quincentennial and centering around new societies formed as a result of culture contact. Essays focus on precolumbian peoples of the Lesser Antilles and their earliest encounters with Europeans; imperial rivalries and wars and their impact on settlement patterns; and local societies, slavery, trade, and abolition. Highly useful. [ELC]

1806 Maza, Manuel. Iglesia cubana: cinco siglos de desafíos y respuestas. (*Estud. Soc./Santo Domingo*, 28:99, enero/marzo 1995, p. 65–112)

Short summary is objective and as free of prejudices as is humanly possible. [JMH]

1807 National symbols of St. Martin: a primer. Edited by Lasana M. Sekou. 2nd ed. Philipsburg, St. Martin: House of Nehesi Publishers, 1996. 173 p.: bibl., ill., index, maps.

Useful portraits of individuals who made major contributions to island's history. Includes slaves and revolts in which they participated, emancipation, and 20th-century developments. Also contains a useful section on the island's natural history. [ELC]

1808 Nesbitt, F.T. Nick. Aperçu de l'historiographie au sujet de Louis Delgrès. (*Bull. Soc. hist. Guadeloupe*, 110, 1996, p. 9–37, bibl.)

Intelligent analysis of how Delgrès, a leading figure of 1802 Guadeloupe uprising, was treated (or ignored) by 19th- and 20th-century historiography and public opinion. Stresses two key events: Lacour's publication of *Histoire de la Guadeloupe* (1855) and Henri Bangou's early contribution to the Communist newspaper *L'Etincelle* (1950–52). With the former, Delgrès acquired historical status; with the latter, his cause became emblematic of an anticolonial consciousness. Also describes novelist Maryse Condé's more recent, iconoclastic approach, returning a measure of humanity to this mythical hero. [APD]

1809 Nicholls, David. From Dessalines to Duvalier: race, colour, and national independence in Haiti. Rev. ed. New Brunswick, N.J.: Rutgers Univ. Press, 1996. 357 p.: bibl., index, map.

New edition of a valuable survey of Haitian history that first appeared in 1979 (see *HLAS 44:2491*). Nicholls died in 1996, and changes to the original book appear to be limited to a new, 41-page preface that summarizes political events in the country from 1986–94. [APD]

1810 Nicholson, Desmond V. Antigua and Barbuda forts. St. John's?: Museum of Antigua and Barbuda, 1994? 41 p.: bibl., ill., index, maps.

This small book is of enormous importance for understanding the islands' defense system from the 17th–19th centuries. Provides detailed description and discussion of fortifications at different times, and includes interesting sketches as well as list of various regiments in Antigua to 1850s. Useful for military historians and individuals interested in heritage tourism. [ELC]

1811 Nicolas, Armand. Histoire de la Martinique. v. 1–2. Paris: L'Harmattan, 1996. 2 v.: maps.

Directed to a broad audience, presents a standard version of the history of Martinique from its origins. Notable for providing the first attempt at a comprehensive treatment of the first half of the 20th century. [APD]

1812 Oostindie, Gert. Het paradijs overzee: de Nederlandse Caraïben en Nederland [Paradise overseas: the Dutch Caribbean and The Netherlands]. 2nd ed. Amsterdam: B. Bakker, 1998. 385 p.: bibl., ill., indexes, maps.

Collection of four original and six previously published (and revised) essays on some major themes in Dutch Caribbean history. Topics include slavery, decolonization and nationalism, migration, and Dutch Caribbean identity. Central question is how a cluster of different societies has developed through the centuries with such "remarkable ambivalence," being simultaneously Dutch and Caribbean. Intended for a general audience. [RH]

1813 Pérotin-Dumon, Anne. Les ancêtres d'Aimé Césaire et d'Alexis Leger: l'historiographie des Antilles Françaises, 1970–

1990. (*Anu. Estud. Am.*, 52:2, 1995, p. 289–316)

Companion to author's 1994 article (see *HLAS 56:1849*) carries her historiographical analysis to the present decade. Rather than focusing solely on investigations of slave plantation society as is the usual practice in such essays, here author reviews how recent historical works in many subfields have contributed to debates about identity in Francophone Caribbean. In addition to describing the best work on slave and revolutionary periods in Haiti, Martinique, and Guadeloupe, article summarizes recent scholarship on 19th- and 20th-century political, cultural, and social history, as well as the best of published genealogy and local history. [JDG]

1814 The Puerto Ricans: a documentary history. Edited by Kal Wagenheim and Olga Jiménez de Wagenheim. Princeton, N.J.: M. Wiener Publishers, 1994. 338 p.: bibl., ill., index.

Paperback edition and updated version of previous work of same title (1973). Includes excerpts from writings of historians, anthropologists, journalists, essayists, poets, politicians, bureaucrats, and others, providing a chronological account of the island's five centuries of colonial domination. This version includes a few newspaper articles from the early 1990s by Kal Wagenheim. [TMV]

1815 Romero Estébanez, Leandro S. La Habana arqueológica y otros ensayos. La Habana: Editorial Letras Cubanas, 1995. 242 p.: bibl., ill.

Collection of well-written and erudite essays, easy to read and certainly worth reading. [JMH]

1816 Rosalia, René Vicente. Tambu: de legale en kerkelijke repressie van Afro-Curaçaose volksuitingen [Tambu: the legal and religious repression of an Afro-Curaçaoan popular expression]. Zutphen, The Netherlands: Walburg Pers, 1997. 388 p.: bibl., ill.

Informative dissertation looks at formal and informal repression of Tambu and consequences of this repression for Afro-Antillan cultural life. The repression provoked open and hidden rebellion, and changed the character of Tambu; yet Tambu

was never completely eliminated on Curaçao. Includes one-page, poorly translated summaries in English and also Papiamentu. Careful editing would have enhanced the readability of this study. [RH]

1817 Rutgers, Wim. Beneden en boven de wind: literatuur van de Nederlandse Antillen en Aruba. Amsterdam: De Bezige Bij, 1996. 468 p.: bibl., indexes.

Revised dissertation offers an extensive cultural history of the Netherlands Antilles and Aruba, concentrating on their oral and written literature in Papiamentu, Dutch, Spanish, and English. [RH]

1818 Sáez, José Luis. Cinco siglos de la Iglesia en Santo Domingo: panorama general. (*Estud. Soc./Santo Domingo*, 28:99, enero/marzo 1995, p. 9–39)

Excellent summary of evolution of the Dominican church throughout five centuries of its existence. [JMH]

1819 Sáez, José Luis. La iglesia y el negro esclavo en Santo Domingo: una historia de tres siglos. Santo Domingo: Patronato de la Ciudad Colonial de Santo Domingo, 1994. 621 p.: bibl., index. (Colección Quinto centenario. Serie Documentos; 3)

This anthology of 165 documents, many of them previously unpublished, is indispensable. Most are ecclesiastical documents, usually preceded by a historical introduction relating the context in which they were produced. Author has also written a scholarly introduction to the volume as a whole, which while failing to address some critical issues, is balanced, objective, and not hampered by *lascasismo*. [JMH]

1820 Sainte-Rose, Monique. Gabriel Debien. (*Ann. Antill.*, 27, 1988/91, p. 4–20)

Useful biographical data is followed by compilation of 230 references to publications by French pioneer of Caribbean colonial studies. Although often erudite and biased, and in need of revision, Debien's works remain amazing for their insights and variety of themes. [APD]

1821 Sandiford, Keith A.P. and **Earle H. Newton.** Combermere School and the Barbadian society. Barbados: The Press, Univ. of the West Indies, 1995. 178 p.: bibl., ill., index.

Written by two former students of perhaps one of the Caribbean's most famous educational institutions, book elucidates school's evolution and analyzes its contribution to the development of Barbadian society. Although scarcity of adequate documentation results in an uneven treatment of different periods, work examines roles of various headmasters and their administrations in the school's evolution. Additionally, work places Combermere, and the changes it underwent, within the larger framework of societal changes that Barbados experienced. Useful case study. [ELC]

1822 Saunders, Hartley Cecil. The other Bahamas. Nassau: Bodab Publishers, 1991. 477 p.: bibl., ill.

Highlights African involvement in development of Bahamas. Includes interesting biographical sketches of various individuals of African ancestry with their contributions to islands' growth, especially in political realm. Makes fruitful use of local newspapers and legislative journals. Somewhat unbalanced portrait of "the true Bahamian." [ELC]

1823 Slicher van Bath, B. H. De bezinning op het verleden in Latijns Amerika, 1493–1820: auteurs, verhalen en lezers [Reflection on the Latin American past, 1493–1820: authors, stories, and readers]. Groningen, The Netherlands: Reco, 1998. 762 p.: bibl.

Historiographical study of colonial Latin America groups more than 1,800 authors together according to a number of variables including employment, ethnic and national background, their use of sources, and size and type of study. Also discusses the readers of historical works. This volume is perhaps not easy to read from cover to cover, but offers interesting perspectives on this topic. [RH]

1824 Statia silhouettes. Edited by Julia G. Crane. New York: Vantage Press, 1999. 604 p.: bibl., ill., maps.

Collection of 22 life histories based on fieldwork conducted between1985–87 in Saint Eustatius. Interviewees ranged in age from early 20s to 80s. No fixed questionnaire was used because it was hoped that each person would talk freely and emphasize those things he/she thought important. According

to the editor, stories reveal a greater interest in African-American heritage and slavery than on other Dutch Caribbean islands. [RH]

1825 University of the West Indies (Mona, Jamaica). Inside slavery: process and legacy in the Caribbean experience. Edited by Hilary Beckles. Foreword by Woodville K. Marshall. Mona, Jamaica: Canoe Press, Univ. of the West Indies, 1996. 154 p.: bibl., index, port.

Contains lectures presented at Cave Hill from 1987–93 to honor memory of Elsa Goveia, a highly regarded Caribbean historian. Themes and topics include Thistlewood's Journals (Douglas Hall), slave conditions in Barbados and other islands (Richard Sheridan), slavery and freedom in Brazil and Louisiana (Rebecca Scott), and Emancipation Day celebrations after 50 years (Bridget Brereton). Useful. [ELC]

1826 Vertovec, Steven. "Official" and "popular" Hinduism in diaspora: historical and contemporary trends in Surinam, Trinidad and Guyana. (*Contrib. Indian Sociol.*, 28:1, 1994, p. 123–148, bibl.)

Important article traces development of "official" Hinduism in the Caribbean. Examines religious backgrounds and early social conditions of migrants from India, and describes Hindu religious activities in Trinidad, Guyana, and Suriname from most "official" to most "popular" modes of practice. Concludes that Caribbean Hindu traditions are currently in the process of transformation and will continue to undergo changes. [RH]

1827 Virgin Islands Humanities Council. The Kamina folk: slavery and slave life in the Danish West Indies. Edited by George F. Tyson and Arnold R. Highfield. St. Thomas, US Virgin Islands: Virgin Islands Humanities Council, 1994. 246 p.: bibl., ill., index.

Companion to the bibliography on the same topic (see item **1792**), work provides access to superb 18th- and 19th-century printed sources on slavery in the Danish Caribbean, most of them translated from Danish. Much less well-known than their English and French counterparts, these texts often bring fresher and more detailed information from a variety of informants—missionaries, administrators, overseers, physicians. [APD]

1828 Watterson, Gerald G. Tobago heritage: drawings of the island's past. Port of Spain: Script-J Printers Ltd., 1993. 57 p.: chiefly ill.
Portrayal of Tobago's architectural heritage includes depictions of forts, "great houses" of various architectural styles on different estates, modest homes, old windmills, windmill towers incorporated in homes, and churches. [ELC]

EARLY COLONIAL

1829 Appleby, John C. English settlement in the Lesser Antilles during war and peace, 1603–1660. (in The Lesser Antilles in the age of European expansion. Gainesville: Univ. Press of Florida, 1996, p. 86–104, table)
Well-documented article casts much light on activities of English merchants in early settlement of islands. Using data from sources other than traditionally consulted Admiralty records, author demonstrates full scope of mercantile activity in supplying colonies with slaves and provisions; hence the emergence of vast, important commercial empire by mid-17th century. [ELC]

1830 Barka, Norman F. and Edward C. Harris. The 1993 archaeological investigations at Castle Island, Bermuda. (Bermud. J. Archaeol. Marit. Hist., 6, 1994, p. 1–80, bibl., map, photos, tables)
Discusses buildings and artifacts found at one of four 17th-century forts, used until 1820s, on a two-acre site on eastern end of island. Interesting maps and drawings. Among items found are coins (including some "Hogge Money"), buttons, ceramics, tobacco pipes, glass, nails. [ELC]

1831 Bernhard, Virginia. Bids for freedom: slave resistance and rebellion plots in Bermuda, 1656–1761. (Slavery Abolit., 17:3, Dec. 1996, p. 185–208)
While slave runaways were few because of island's small size and isolated location, Bermuda had its share of 17th- and 18th-century rebellions and rebellion scares. Punishment for ringleaders was physical markings. Poisoning scares and other forms of protest also occurred. As salt mining increased in the 18th century, escape efforts by boat increased. Concludes that causes of revolts generally match those in the rest of the region, i.e., economic hardships and political and religious turmoil. Important. [ELC]

Bowen, Joanna and Michael Jarvis. Provisioning systems in the New World: the British colony of Bermuda. See item 1872.

1832 Bruneau de Rivedoux, Jean-Arnaud, capitaine. Histoire véritable de certains voyages périlleux et hasardeux sur la mer, 1599. Édition, présentation et notes de Alain-Gilbert Guéguen. Préface de François Belloc. Paris: Editions de Paris; Harmonia mundi, 1996. 126 p.: bibl., ill. (Voyages et récits)
Welcome reprint of one of the oldest sets of narratives (eight short texts) of French voyages to the Caribbean in late 1500s. The author, a captain operating from La Rochelle, describes the islands, his privateering raids and encounters with the Caribs, and his trade along the European Atlantic Coast. [APD]

1833 Bulletin de la Société d'histoire de la Guadeloupe. Nos. 107/108, 1996. Personnes et familles à Sainte-Croix au XVIIe siècle par Aimery Caron. Basse-Terre: Archives départementales avec le concours du Conseil général de la Guadeloupe.
Compiled by senior historian of US Virgin Islands, lists main archival sources (and some transcriptions) on islands' colonial beginnings. Includes locations and names of key contacts. Invaluable research tool for social historians and genealogists. [APD]

1834 Burnard, Trevor. Who bought slaves in early America?: purchasers of slaves from the Royal African Company in Jamaica, 1674–1708. (Slavery Abolit., 17:2, Aug. 1996, p. 68–92)
An examination of the profiles of 1,405 individuals who purchased slaves and 105 separate transactions concludes that large purchasers, often officeholders, merchants, or large planters, dominated the market. Urban merchants, especially those based in Port Royal, were important purchasers. Market became increasingly complex over time, with specialized merchants becoming more pronounced. Very useful. [ELC]

1835 Cabrera, Gilberto R. Puerto Rico y su historia íntima, 1500–1996. v. 1., Siglos XVI, XVII y XVIII. San Juan: G.R. Cabrera, 1997. 1 v.: bibl, ill., maps.
Not an "historia íntima" at all, work is a chronological account, based on printed sources, of the tenure of governors in first three centuries of Puerto Rican history. [TMV]

1836 Campbell, P.F. Some early Barbadian history. St. Michael, Barbados: Caribbean Graphics & Letchworth Ltd., 1993. 269 p.: bibl., index, map.

Rather than a history of early-17th-century Barbados, work is a collection of essays, "some of them correcting and revising articles" that author had previously published. Intended for readers interested in 17th-century living conditions on the island. People are given center stage with focus on Richard Ligon, the Holdips, the Walronds, Sir William Dutton, and some of the Barbadian immigrants to South Carolina. Also contains text of an anonymous 1741 work entitled *Memoirs of the first settlement of the island of Barbados.* [ELC]

1837 Camus, Michel Christian. Flibuste et pouvoir royal. (*Rev. Soc. haïti.*, 49:175, mars 1993, p. 5–15)

Describes limited success of French crown in its attempts to curb undisciplined behavior of buccaneers after having continuously relied on them during 17th-century wars in the Caribbean. Despite problems of discipline and authority, the French would continue to rely on pirates through much of the 18th century. [APD]

1838 Damiani Cósimi, Julio. Estratificación social, esclavos y naborías en el Puerto Rico minero del siglo XVI: la información de Francisco Manuel de Lando; ensayo de cuantificación y transcripción paleográfica. San Juan: Depto. de Historia, Centro de Investigaciones Históricas, Univ. de Puerto Rico, Recinto de Río Piedras, 1994. 154 p.: bibl., tables. (Cuadernos de investigación histórica; 1)

Using information gathered by Governor Francisco Manuel de Lando in 1530, author compares San Juan and San Germán, the two Spanish settlements in Puerto Rico. Statistical tables corroborate that social stratification responded to availability of thousands of Indian workers, Indian and African slaves, and presence of a few hundred government officials and colonists in high and low occupations. Pamphlet includes a full transcription of the document itself. [TMV]

1839 David, Bernard. L'histoire religieuse de Martinique au XVIIème siècle. (*Ann. Antill.*, 27, 1988/91, p. 21–75)

Written by a specialist on the topic, this research tool for Martinique's early history combines: 1) an annotated bibliography on the history of the Church and religious practices; 2) a critical survey of the field as a whole, informed by the author's extensive research and insights; and 3) a selection of previously unknown documents from the Jesuit collection in the Vatican Archives on slave evangelization in 17th-century Lesser Antilles and French Guiana. [APD]

1840 De Verteuil, Anthony. Martyrs and murderers: Trinidad, 1699. Port of Spain: A. de Verteuil, 1995. 179 p.: bibl., ill., maps.

Interesting and lively, though general, treatment of Roman Catholic missionaries in Trinidad who were massacred by local indigenous peoples. Also discusses search for the "murderers" and subsequent glorification of the martyrs. [ELC]

1841 Deive, Carlos Esteban. La Española y la esclavitud del indio. Santo Domingo: Fundación García Arévalo, 1995. 442 p.: bibl., ill., index. (Serie documental; 3)

A scholarly work focusing on Indian slaves brought to work on Hispaniola from other parts of the New World. Also devotes attention to the slave trade thus generated. [JMH]

1842 Deive, Carlos Esteban. Tangomangos: contrabando y piratería en Santo Domingo, 1522–1606. Santo Domingo: Fundación Cultural Dominicana, 1996. 264 p.: bibl., ill., maps.

Re-examines Spanish policies that forced depopulation of northern Hispaniola in early-17th century. While based on archival materials and filled with new insights, author fails to put his conclusions in the context of European imperial ambitions at the time. [JMH]

1843 Eltis, David. The British transatlantic slave trade before 1714: annual estimates of volume and direction. (*in* The Lesser Antilles in the age of European expansion. Gainesville: Univ. Press of Florida, 1996, p. 182–205, tables)

Bemoaning the relative paucity of archival studies on the British slave trade since Philip Curtin's 1969 work (see *HLAS* 32:1146), author presents detailed statistics for Caribbean and British North America that seek to show magnitude of 17th-century British trade in that region. Suggests changes in ebb and flow over time, especially to particular islands. [ELC]

1844 Eltis, David. The total product of Barbados, 1664–1701. (*J. Econ. Hist.*, 55:2, June 1995, p. 321–338, bibl., tables)

Using trade statistics and figures from island's customs books, provides estimate of total and per capita product for Barbados for 1665, 1666, and 1699–1701. Concludes that Barbados' per capita product was one-third to two-thirds higher than that of England and Wales, while per capita exports were well above Chesapeake colonies. [ELC]

1845 Emmer, Pieter C. *Jesus Christ was good, but trade was better:* an overview of the transit trade of the Dutch Antilles, 1634–1795. (*in* The Lesser Antilles in the age of European expansion. Gainesville: Univ. Press of Florida, 1996, p. 206–222)

Overview of Dutch expansion in the Lesser Antilles. Author blames metropolitan policy, demographic weakness, and limited naval power for the lack of success in establishing a thriving plantation sector in the Americas. After 1675 Dutch merchants profited from a neutral position vis-à-vis the imperial rivalries in the Atlantic and focused on strengthening their position in the transit trade. Saint Eustatius especially prospered in late-18th century. [RH]

1846 Engerman, Stanley L. Europe, the Lesser Antilles, and economic expansion, 1600–1800. (*in* The Lesser Antilles in the age of European expansion. Gainesville: Univ. Press of Florida, 1996, p. 147–164, tables)

Concludes that while 17th-century Lesser Antilles were more important to Europe than Greater Antilles, the situation reversed itself from the 18th century onwards. Despite their diminished status over time, Lesser Antilles continued to play an important role in settlement and trade and production patterns of Caribbean. Unable to measure conclusively their contribution to the Industrial Revolution. [ELC]

1847 Games, Alison F. Opportunity and mobility in early Barbados. (*in* The Lesser Antilles in the age of European expansion. Gainesville: Univ. Press of Florida, 1996, p. 165–181, tables)

Useful update of issues raised in Richard Dunn's work (see *HLAS 34:2019*). Treat-

ment of early Barbados society shows how planter elite became firmly established by late-17th century. Demonstrates nexus among migration, labor, and land acquisition in both presugar and postsugar Barbadian society; also shows how monied newcomers were able to use available opportunities for social advancement. [ELC]

1848 García Regueiro, Ovidio. Oro y población: la producción aurífera cubana, 1518–1542. Madrid: Fundación Centro Español de Estudios de América Latina, 1994. 381 p.: bibl.

Despite title, work is actually an attempt to quantify Cuba's gold production in early colonial period. Supplements information provided by Earl Hamilton in his classic work *American treasure and the price revolution in Spain, 1501–1650* (1934), but contains little else. [JMH]

1849 Gardyner, George. The generall description of America or the New World. Edited by Arnold R. Highfield and Alfredo E. Figueredo. Christiansted, US Virgin Islands: Antilles Press, 1993. 32 p.: bibl., index, map.

Welcome scholarly edition of 17th-century guide gives brief description of each Caribbean island individually, including settlers and indigenous population. Written by the son of a prominent English family who traveled to the recently settled English colonies in North America and the Caribbean and wished to establish a colony of his own in the Bahamas. [APD]

1850 Gaspar, David Barry. From "the sense of their slavery": slave women and resistance in Antigua, 1632–1763. (*in* More than chattel: black women and slavery in the Americas. Indianapolis: Indiana Univ. Press, 1996, p. 218–238, table)

Examines role of slave women in various revolts and other forms of protest in early Antigua. Argues for recognition of their profound commitment to get out of bondage through these acts. [ELC]

1851 Gragg, Larry. "To procure Negroes": the English slave trade to Barbados, 1627–60. (*Slavery Abolit.*, 16:1, April 1995, p. 65–84)

In important revision of findings of previous historians, author concludes that although Dutch had strong presence in 17th-century Barbados trade, they supplied island with relatively few slaves. Rather, individual English traders were main suppliers from 1640s-60s. Provides useful information on length of voyages and slave prices. [ELC]

1852 Heijer, Henk den. Goud, ivoor en slaven: scheepvaart en handel van de Tweede Westindische Compagnie op Afrika [Gold, ivory and slaves: shipping and commerce of the Second West India Company in Africa]. Zutphen, The Netherlands: Walburg Pers, 1997. 444 p.: appendix, bibl., ill., map, tables.

Important, economics-oriented history of the Westindische Compagnie (WIC) on the West African Coast. Questions whether slave trade was WIC's most important and lucrative business; also challenges notion that WIC was a failure. Author gives little attention to sociocultural aspects of the trade and to *how* WIC trade actually was conducted. Includes eight-page summary in English. Unfortunately, work is poorly edited. [RH]

1853 Instituto de Historia de Cuba. Historia de Cuba. v. 1, La colonia: evolución socioeconómica y formación nacional; de los orígenes hasta 1867. La Habana: Editora Política, 1994. 1 v.: bibl., ill., maps.

Vol. 1 of a five-volume attempt to produce a general history of Cuba incorporating research done in last few years. Socioeconomic events, art, religion, literature, and science—subjects which by authors' own admission have been relatively neglected—are to be emphasized. In this volume, the treatment of some 19th-century figures such as Father Félix Varela and of subjects such as origins of the Cuban independence movement leaves much to be desired. [JMH]

1854 Kiple, Kenneth F. and Kriemhild C. Ornelas. After the encounter: disease and demographics in the Lesser Antilles. (*in* The Lesser Antilles in the age of European expansion. Gainesville: Univ. Press of Florida, 1996, p. 50–67, table)

Re-examines data on numbers of indigenous inhabitants at Columbus' arrival, and manner in which contemporary and modern historians have treated these data. Confirms difficulty in obtaining accurate data for precolumbian inhabitants and early European and African arrivals. Discusses waves of epidemics and various diseases that negatively affected early populations, and highlights role of yellow fever from 1600s to introduction of Africans. [ELC]

1855 Klooster, Wim. Illicit riches: Dutch trade in the Caribbean, 1648-1795. Leiden, The Netherlands: KITLV Press, 1998. 283 p.: bibl., ill., index, maps. (Caribbean series; 18)

Noteworthy study of transit trade in the Caribbean presents alternative view of Dutch seaborne empire. Argues that Dutch illegal inter-imperial commerce with Spanish, English, and French colonies was far more important than historians have realized. According to author, this Caribbean contraband trade, revolving around the entrepôts in Curaçao and Saint Eustatius helped Dutch survive 17th-century loss of most of their territorial empire in the Western Hemisphere. [RH]

Landers, Jane. An eighteenth-century community in exile: the *floridanos* in Cuba. See item **1902.**

1856 Le Riverend, Julio. Problemas de la formación agraria de Cuba: siglos XVI-XVII. La Habana: Editorial de Ciencias Sociales, 1992. 296 p.: bibl. (Historia de Cuba)

A Marxist perspective on agrarian history of Cuba. Author acknowledges that this initial study of the subject is based on limited sources. [JMH]

1857 Ly, Abdoulaye. La Compagnie du Sénégal. Nouv. éd. rev. et augm. Paris: Karthala; Dakar: Ifan Ch. A. Diop, 1993. 379 p., 16 p. of plates: bibl., ill. (Col. Hommes et sociétés)

Welcome reprint of unsurpassed study of the first French slave trading company in West Africa (1673–96). Company attempted to challenge the de facto Dutch monopolistic supply to the French islands. Documents company's activities in the context of early transatlantic trade, the variety of traded items, and organization of trading posts; and shows that chronic shortage of capital led to the company's downfall and its replacement by privileges in slave trade granted to main Atlantic ports in early-18th century. [APD]

Maurer, Bill. Colonial policy and the construction of the commons: an introduction. See *HLAS 57:867.*

Metz, John D. The dynamics of settlement in Devonshire Parish, Bermuda. See item 1907.

1858 Nicholson, Desmond V. Heritage landmarks: Antigua and Barbuda. Antigua: Museum of Antigua and Barbuda, 1994. 53 p.: ill.

Intended to provide visitors with some background to the islands, work is truly a "heritage tourism" project that benefits tourists and historians alike. Though brief, contains useful information on buildings, forts, people, and shipwrecks on the former important British possession. Most entries deal with 16th–17th centuries. [ELC]

1859 Page, Willie F. The Dutch triangle: the Netherlands and the Atlantic slave trade, 1621–1664. New York: Garland Pub., 1997. 297 p.: bibl., ill., index, maps. (Studies in African American history and culture)

Study of European expansion and role of The Netherlands in the Atlantic slave trade is divided into five chapters. The first two discuss Dutch history and European expansion in Africa. The third focuses on Dutch in Brazil, the Guianas, and the Caribbean. Final chapters look at early settlement of New Netherland and the life of Africans there. Intended as a text for undergraduate students of African and African-American history. [RH]

1860 Pierre, Fritz. Le commerce de la viande à Saint-Domingue aux XVIIème et XVIIIème siècles: l'ère des bouchers, 1695–1710. (Rev. Soc. haïti., 51:183, mars 1995, p. 25–38; 51:186, déc. 1995, p. 1–18; 52:189/190, sept./déc. 1996, p. 1–19; and 52:192, juin 1997, p. 37–61)

Traces evolution of French royal policy on butchers and local supply of fresh meat in Saint-Domingue. Provides insights on livestock trade with Santo Domingo and on official attempts to encourage establishment of livestock corrals in the mountains. [JDG]

Rossi, Máximo, Jr. Praxis, historia y filosofía en el siglo XVIII: textos de Antonio Sánchez Valverde, 1729–90. See item 5139.

1861 Szaszdi Nagy, Adam. Los guías de Guanahaní y la llegada de Pinzón a Puerto Rico. Valladolid, Spain: Casa Museo de Colón; Seminario Americanista de la Univ. de Valladolid, 1995. 208 p.: bibl., maps. (Cuadernos colombinos; 19)

Re-examines Columbus' diary to determine native guides' role in tracing route followed in the first inter-island reconnaissance. Concludes that Columbus depended on Arawak navigational knowledge, as Columbus himself states in his diary, and that his journal entries regarding his wanderings are accurate. Based on this understanding and corroborating it through other sources, Szaszdi argues that Martín Alonso Pinzón "discovered" Puerto Rico (which Columbus called Baneque in the journal) when the Pinta became separated from the other two ships. [TMV]

1862 Tarragó, Rafael Emilio. Experiencias políticas de los cubanos en la Cuba española, 1512–1898. Barcelona: Puvill Libros, 1996. 260 p.: bibl., ill. (Biblioteca universitaria Puvill. Historia y cultura de Hispanoamérica; 2)

Although some of the author's opinions and conclusions are quite debatable, he analyzes process of Cuban independence from an unusual perspective that deserves serious consideration. [JMH]

LATE COLONIAL AND FRENCH REVOLUTIONARY PERIODS

1863 Amores Carredano, Juan Bosco. El joven Arango y Parreño: origen del proyecto político-económico de la sacarocracia habanera, 1786–1794. (Temas Am., 12, 1995, p. 25–33)

Sound piece of historical writing, well thought-out and researched. [JMH]

1864 Archibald, Douglas. Tobago, "melancholy isle." v. 2, 1770–1814. Port-of-Spain: Westindiana, 1995. 1 v.

Though short on documentation and interpretation, contains wealth of information on Tobago during the revolutionary period. An engineer by training, author has used local archives and other official sources to great advantage. Of some use. [ELC]

1865 Arzalier, Francis. Déportés haïtiens et guadeloupéens en Corse, 1802–1814. (Ann. hist. Révolut. fr., 3/4:293/294, juillet/déc. 1993, p. 469–490, bibl.)

Solid research on some 600 black and colored men, mostly professionals, who were deported from Haiti and Guadeloupe for their revolutionary involvement. Arzalier shows how a repressive policy was combined with a (failed) project to develop the island of Corsica using a convict labor force. [APD]

1866 Auguste, Claude B. André Rigaud: leader des anciens libres. (*Rev. Soc. haïti.*, 52:188, juin 1996, p. 30–40; 52:191, juin 1997, p. 1–29; 52:193, sept. 1997, p. 1–27; and 52:194, déc. 1997, p. 13–22)

Detailed narrative of relations between the French government and Rigaud, the mulatto general who became the caudillo of one-third of colonial Haiti before being politically and militarily outmaneuvered by Toussaint Louverture. Drawing on Napoleonic archives and classics of Haitian historiography, Auguste focuses mainly on period around France's failed 1802 expedition to reconquer the island. [JDG]

1867 Balcácer, Juan Daniel and **Manuel Antonio García Arévalo.** La independencia dominicana. Madrid: Editorial MAPFRE, 1992. 243 p.: bibl., ill., indexes, map. (Col. Independencia de Iberoamérica; 7. Col. MAPFRE 1492)

Carefully written and researched introduction for the uninitiated. An unpretentious but useful contribution. [JMH]

1868 Barbotin, Maurice. Conamama: camp de la mort en Guyane pour les prêtres et les religieux en 1798. Paris: L'Harmattan, 1995. 239 p.: bibl., ill.

Based on a careful critique of the documentation, work examines one aspect of the grim beginning of French Guiana as a place for France's convicts and political prisoners during the French Revolution. Describes deportation of some 300 priests and a few nuns and their internment in camps, of which Conamama was the harshest. [APD]

1869 Bardin, Pierre. La famille Fougeu de Saint-Domingue. (*Généal. hist. Caraïbe*, 74, sept. 1995, p. 1416–1417)

New genealogical research is informed by social history. Traces parallel branches of the Fougeu family in the 18th century that were separated by the "color barrier." [APD]

1870 Barka, Norman F. Citizens of St. Eustatius, 1781: a historical and archaeological study. (*in* The Lesser Antilles in the age of European expansion. Gainesville: Univ. Press of Florida, 1996, p. 223–238, map)

Draws on documentary and archeological research to reconstruct population of Saint Eustatius at the time of the sack by Admiral George Rodney in 1781. Finds evidence of a strong British presence, both numerically and culturally, which suggests the extent of British citizens' complicity in the contraband traffic to the north. [RH]

Barka, Norman F. and **Edward C. Harris.** The 1993 archaeological investigations at Castle Island, Bermuda. See item **1830.**

Beahrs, Andrew. "Ours alone must needs be Christians": the production of enslaved souls on the Codrington Estates. See *HLAS 57:796.*

1871 Beckles, Hilary. Black female slaves and white households in Barbados. (*in* More than chattel: black women and slavery in the Americas. Indianapolis: Indiana Univ. Press, 1996, p. 111–125, table)

Concentrating on experiences of domestic slaves in Barbados, particularly housekeepers, contends that despite their "special" status, they nevertheless were exploited more than field hands and rebelled at various times. Yet few would have preferred the life of a field hand since domestic slaves were more likely to obtain their freedom. [ELC]

1872 Bowen, Joanna and **Michael Jarvis.** Provisioning systems in the New World: the British colony of Bermuda. (*Bermud. J. Archaeol. Marit. Hist.*, 6, 1994, p. 81–94, graphs)

Based largely on archeological findings at Tucker House in Bermuda, with additional information from four other sites, shows that Bermuda remained dependent on the outside world much longer than its counterparts in New England and the Chesapeake Bay, which achieved a relatively high level of self sufficiency in provisioning. [ELC]

1873 Bush, Barbara. Hard labor: women, childbirth, and resistance in British Caribbean slave societies. (*in* More than chattel: black women and slavery in the Americas. Indianapolis: Indiana Univ. Press, 1996, p. 193–217)

Argues that harsh labor conditions for slave women negatively affected their reproductive capabilities. Low birth rate was also caused by women's conscious decisions to exercise control over their reproductive capacities in a way that would be detrimental to their masters' interests. Hence, it should be remembered that resistance took various forms and should be studied from a number of perspectives, especially in a gendered context. [ELC]

Cabrera, Gilberto R. Puerto Rico y su historia íntima, 1500–1996. See item **1835.**

1874 Campo del Pozo, Fernando. Fray Agustín Beltrán de Caicedo, Prefecto Apostólico de Curaçao, 1715–1838: defensor de los negros y del Archiduque Carlos. (*Paramillo/San Cristóbal*, 14, 1995, p. 613–647, map)

Supplement to biographies of Agustín Beltrán de Caicedo by W.M. Brada (*Prefect Caysedo 1715–1738*, 1950) and J. Benigno Van Luijk (see *HLAS 24:4102*) is based on newly found archival documents. Examines Beltrán's role in the contraband trade of cacao and tobacco with Dutch merchants and as protector of black Catholics. He had to resign in 1694 and returned to Europe. In 1715 he was named prefect of the missions in Curaçao, Aruba, Bonaire, Saint Eustatius, and Saint Kitts. He baptized more than 4,000 individuals, mostly blacks and mulattoes. [RH]

1875 Camus, Michel Christian. Lettres d'Haïti à l'Abbé Grégoire. (*Rev. Soc. haïti.*, 52:191, mars 1997, p. 3–10)

Contains extracts of hitherto unpublished letters from prominent Haitians to the most famous and influential French abolitionist to survive the French Revolution. Reveals the enormous respect with which Grégoire, the "new Las Casas" as two of his correspondents dubbed him, was regarded in Haiti. Also reveals enthusiasm of early Haitian elite for Grégoire's vision of a racial equality rooted in assumption of French cultural superiority. [JDG]

1876 Cauna, Jacques de. Quelques aperçus sur l'histoire de la franc-maçonnerie en Haïti. (*Rev. Soc. haïti.*, 52:189/190, sept./déc. 1996, p. 20–33)

Overview of history of freemasonry in Saint-Domingue/Haiti notes importance of contacts in Bordeaux and in England's New World colonies for emergence of a rich network of masonic lodges and networks for French colonists in 1760s-70s. Unlike other works on the subject, follows freemasonry into national period, noting dissolution of ties to France and emergence of a distinctive

Haitian organization with formal links to the government. [APD]

1877 Cormack, William S. Legitimate authority in revolution and war: the French Navy in the West Indies, 1789–1793. (*Int. Hist. Rev.*, 18:1, Feb. 1996, p. 1–27)

Original and welcome approach to question of political authority in revolutionary times, in colonies distant from the metropolis. Documents involvement of French Navy stationed in Lesser Antilles during conflict between royalists and patriots, and relates how different commanders "tried to use their ships" to preserve, restore, or alter the legitimacy of the state. [APD]

1878 Craton, Michael. The Black Caribs of St. Vincent: a reevaluation. (*in* The Lesser Antilles in the age of European expansion. Gainesville: Univ. Press of Florida, 1996, p. 71–85, photo)

General treatment, drawing mostly on secondary sources, of the historical perception and treatment of Black Caribs. Author questions whether or not events of 1763–97, when Black Caribs were finally transported to Roatan, were significant in the creation of the Garifuna people/nation. [ELC]

1879 Craton, Michael. Reembaralhando as cartas: a transição da escravidão para outras formas de trabalho no Caribe britânico, 1790–1890. (*Estud. Afro-Asiát.*, 28, out. 1995, p. 31–83, bibl.)

Examination of gradual changes in labor systems in British Caribbean colonies from slavery's heyday to late-19th century concludes that gradualism rather than radicalism was the order of the day. Slaves were protopeasants and protoproletarians, while apprentices and their followers were subjected to domination and control similar to slaves. Immigration, missionary policies, and political reform all constituted part of same gradual shuffling of the pack. [ELC]

1880 Drescher, Seymour. The long goodbye: Dutch capitalism and antislavery in comparative perspective. (*in* The Lesser Antilles in the age of European expansion. Gainesville: Univ. Press of Florida, 1996, p. 345–367)

Incorporates The Netherlands into a comparative perspective to test the general theoretical framework linking capitalism to antislavery. Concludes that neither a dynamic 17th-century nor a sluggish 18th-century economy stimulated Dutch abolitionism. Argues that abolitionism is linked primarily not to economic developments, but rather to the communal expansion of individual rights and liberty. [RH]

Emmer, Pieter C. *Jesus Christ was good, but trade was better:* an overview of the transit trade of the Dutch Antilles, 1634–1795. See item **1845.**

Engerman, Stanley L. Europe, the Lesser Antilles, and economic expansion, 1600–1800. See item **1846.**

1881 Fick, Carolyn E. The French Revolution in Saint-Domingue. (*in* A turbulent time: the French Revolution and the Greater Caribbean. Bloomington: Indiana Univ. Press, 1997, p. 51–77, maps)

Useful overview of the Haitian Revolution by author of an important book (see *HLAS 54:1903*) on the subject. Traces "combination of mutually reinforcing factors" that resulted in France's official abolition of slavery in its most valuable sugar plantation colony. Fick sees revolutionary ideology as far less important than the political turmoil the French Revolution generated in the colony. For her, abolition of slavery occurred because a "self-determined, massive slave rebellion" coincided with presence in Saint-Domingue of a "practical abolitionist" named Sonthonax, sent by Paris to resolve colonial troubles. [JDG]

1882 Foubert, Bernard. L'affaire Perrigny: un drame familial à Saint-Domingue sous la Revolution. (*Rev. Soc. haïti.,* 52:188, juin 1996, p. 1–29)

Relates story of the collapse of a prominent planting family in early years of the French Revolution. Ironically, the Perrigny family was better able to deal with rebellious slaves and emerging leadership of free men of color than with poor white employees and neighbors who had the Perrignys arrested in 1793 on suspicion of plotting counterrevolution with slave leaders. [JDG]

1883 Foubert, Bernard. Un agenais a Saint-Domingue: l'habitation Couderq en 1791. (*Rev. Soc. haïti.,* 51:183, mars 1995, p. 1–23, maps)

Uses notarial contracts to reconstruct short career of a relatively poor colonist, fo-cusing on his efforts, together with his free black housekeeper and partner, to expand from livestock raising to coffee planting in late 1780s. [JDG]

1884 Gainot, Bernard. Le Général Laveaux, Gouverneur de Saint-Domingue, député néo-jacobin. (*Ann. hist. Révolut. fr.,* 61:278, oct./déc. 1989, p. 433–454)

Based on Laveaux's original correspondence, this solid piece of research demolishes stereotypes by throwing light on the principles that guided Saint-Domingue's last governer, a liberal aristocrat, in his policy of accommodation with Toussaint Louverture, who was then in full ascent as leader of the Haitian Revolution. [APD]

1885 Garate Ojanguren, Montserrat. Comercio ultramarino e Ilustración: la Real Compañía de La Habana. Prólogo de Carlos Martínez Shaw. San Sebastián, Spain: Real Sociedad Bascongada de los Amigos del País, 1994. 442 p.: bibl., ill. (Col. Ilustración vasca; 6)

First-rate monograph on a crucial, but thus far largely neglected, subject. [JMH]

1886 Gardes, Gilbert. Nicolas-Germain Léonard, 1744–1793, écrivain guadeloupéen: 250e anniversaire de sa naissance et réédition de son roman *Lettres de deux amants.* (*Bull. Soc. hist. Guadeloupe,* 103, 1995, p. 65–74)

Much-needed study on Guadeloupe's most famous writer of the period traces his creole family origins, his career as a judge, and his literary success in Europe. Offers insightful analysis of his works, which combine a social critique of his native slave society with a melancholy view of male-female relationships and of landscapes, very much in a pre-Romantic vein. [APD]

1887 Garrigus, John D. Colour, class and identity on the eve of the Haitian Revolution: Saint-Domingue's free coloured elite as *colons américains.* (*Slavery Abolit.,* 17:1, April 1996, p. 20–43, graphs, maps, tables)

Insightful study yields important new findings on pivotal class of free-coloreds in Saint-Domingue at end of the ancien régime. Traces trajectories of three prominent families from a parish in the island's southern peninsula—occupations, sources of prosperity, social and family ties—for over half a century. The group's marked ascent to the landed rural class was threatened by growing racial discrimination, leading some to assume revolutionary leadership in the 1790s and to retain a French identity up to the early 1800s. [APD]

1888 Gaspar, David Barry. Ameliorating slavery: the Leeward Islands Slave Act of 1798. (*in* The Lesser Antilles in the age of European expansion. Gainesville: Univ. Press of Florida, 1996, p. 241–258)

Provides political and philosophical background on landmark legislation that profoundly impacted process of slave amelioration in the Leewards. Following analysis of Act's provisions, contends that legislation was passed locally only grudgingly because of imperial threats of slave trade abolition. Hence Act constitutes important milestone in antislavery movement. [ELC]

1889 Geggus, David Patrick. The Great Powers and the Haitian Revolution. (*in* Tordesillas y sus consecuencias: la política de las grandes potencias europeas respecto a América Latina, 1494–1899. Frankfurt: Vervuert; Madrid: Iberoamericana, 1995, p. 113–125)

Useful treatment of the Haitian Revolution from standpoint of international relations. Describes Spanish officials' range of responses, from "perfect neutrality" in spite of rebels' royalist rhetoric to siding with the British against the French army led by Toussaint Louverture in Haiti. Concludes that "despite contemporary and modern claims ... the new Haitian state did not prove a direct threat to neighboring slave regimes." [APD]

1890 Geggus, David Patrick. Slave and free colored women in Saint Domingue. (*in* More than chattel: black women and slavery in the Americas. Indianapolis: Indiana Univ. Press, 1996, p. 259–278)

Excellent overview by scholar who has done the most to reveal nature of slave life and plantation society on eve of the Haitian Revolution. Draws on his previous studies of plantation inventories, colonial censuses, and other sources to describe how creole and African women lived in, worked under, and fought against slavery. Also provides a solid overview of the position of free women of color. See also item **1922.** [APD]

1891 Geggus, David Patrick. The slaves and free-coloreds of Martinique during the age of the French and Haitian Revolutions:

three moments of resistance. (*in* The Lesser Antilles in the age of European expansion. Gainesville: Univ. Press of Florida, 1996, p. 280–301, map)

Focuses on three attempted rebellions that took place in Martinique's main towns, accompanied by slave resistance in the countryside. A rigorous critique of available documentation allows author to provide evidence of direct links with Haitian Revolution, but also to place these uprisings within the context of a series of Caribbean slave insurrections that were influenced by the nascent antislavery movement. (See "Revue historique," 597, jan./mars 1996, p. 105–132, for a French version of this article.) [APD]

1892 Gerbeau, Hubert and **Jean Benoist.** Victor Hugues: les neutres et la Révolution française aux Antilles. (*Caribena/ Martinique*, 3, 1993, p. 13–35, bibl.)

Good synthesis of role played by famous commissary who ruled Guadeloupe during the Revolution, based on correspondence between Hugues and authorities of neighboring neutral islands and on Pérotin-Dumon's previous publications on the topic. [APD]

1893 Goguet, Antoine and **Marie Goguet.** Lettres d'amour créoles: des événements de Saint-Domingue à la Restauration. Présentation et notes par Marie-France Barrier et Jean-Marie Williamson. Paris: Karthala, 1996. 175 p.

Correspondence between husband and wife—he an officer, she a planter—who married in the last, tumultous days of Saint-Domingue. Letters express couple's moving concern for each other and their capacity to face the hardship and separation brought about by war. [APD]

Groot, Silvia W. de. Charting the Suriname Maroons, 1730–1734. See *HLAS 57:838.*

1894 Guide du négociant à Saint-Pierre: Années 1786–1787. Edition par Jacques Petitjean-Roget. (*Ann. Antill.*, 28, 1991/94, p. 47–66)

These selected and annotated pages from the memoirs of a young French merchant who conducted business in Saint-Pierre, Martinique, provide detailed information on the sale of his cargo and transportation of colonial staples back across the

Atlantic. One would hope for publication of the manuscript in full. [APD]

1895 Gutiérrez del Arroyo, Isabel. La política y la Ilustración. Río Piedras, P.R.: Centro de Investigaciones Históricas, Univ. de Puerto Rico; Editorial de la Univ. de Puerto Rico, 1995. 305 p.: bibl. (Obras completas / Isabel Gutiérrez del Arroyo; 1)

Basically an unrevised and much welcome reprint of *El reformismo ilustrado en Puerto Rico*, Gutiérrez del Arroyo's principal contribution to Puerto Rican history (see *HLAS 19:3766*). That work, originally published in 1953, became a model for historians because of its use of sources, especially Secretary-to-the-Governor Pedro Tomás de Córdova's *Memorias geográficas, históricas, económicas y estadísticas de la Isla de Puerto Rico*. Author both relies on and questions Córdova's account of the political, administrative, economic, and social impact of the Bourbon reforms and enlightened despotism in Puerto Rico. [TMV]

1896 Hatzenberger, Françoise. Paysage de la Guadeloupe à la fin du XVIIIe siècle d'après le poète créole Léonard. (*Rev. fr. hist. Outre-Mer*, 83:310, 1996, p. 61–82)

Combining a pre-Romantic sensibility toward nature with a physiocratic interest in agronomy, creole poet Nicolas-Germain Léonard proves to be a rich informant for a biobotanist examining forest clearing and soil erosion after more than a century of agricultural exploitation. Hatzenberger's analysis of the descriptions of landscapes in Léonard's *Lettre sur un voyage aux Antilles* yields important data on tropical secondary vegetation. Identifies a blending process of native species (some in fact from the American continent) with imported ones (some particulary aggressive), and shows that at end of 18th century, Guadeloupe's humid central mountain forests had been impacted more significantly by colonization than previously believed. [APD]

Heijer, Henk den. Goud, ivoor en slaven: scheepvaart en handel van de Tweede Westindische Compagnie op Afrika [Gold, ivory and slaves: shipping and commerce of the Second West India Company in Africa]. See item **1852**.

1897 Highfield, Arnold R. Patterns of accommodation and resistance: the Moravian witness to slavery in the Danish

West Indies. (*J. Caribb. Hist.*, 28:2, 1994, p. 138–164)

Based on the regular evaluations and rigorous critique of Moravian missionaries' work, this comprehensive article focuses on their essential role in these colonies, where in a period of 70 years they converted 54 percent of the slaves. In order to understand slave response, defined as a mixture of accommodation and resistance, article first analyzes Moravian theology and social ethics, which focus exclusively on individual spiritual concerns. Author stresses some unique features of missionaries' pedagogy such as full integration of converted slaves into the Moravian community, teaching in slaves' vernacular Danish language, and an emphasis on literacy. Also documents signs of resistance: the persistence of African languages, cults, and dances. See also items **1910** and **1905**. [APD]

Instituto de Historia de Cuba. Historia de Cuba. See item **1853**.

1898 Jarvis, Michael. The Henry Tucker House: 280 years of Bermudian history. (*Bermud. J. Archaeol. Marit. Hist.*, 6, 1994, p. 151–167, appendix, facsim.)

Focuses on a single house and on the different people—all Tuckers or close relatives—who lived in/owned it over time. Although house is best known for being inhabited by Henry Tucker (1775–1807) who was island president, many of the residents were fixtures in Bermuda's 18th-century society. Author hopes that portraits of these other residents would provide a more balanced view of the house and of Bermuda. [ELC]

1899 Johnson, Howard. Slave life and leisure in Nassau, Bahamas, 1783–1838. (*Slavery Abolit.*, 16:1, April 1995, p. 45–64)

Posits that the conflict between masters and slaves over latter's use of leisure time reflected the changing relationship between the groups in a town that Loyalists dominated politically, but never completely controlled. Slaves' residential independence and impersonal contractual relations in urban setting increasingly superseded 18th-century paternalist intimacy. [ELC]

1900 Kafka, Judith. Action, reaction and interaction: slave women in resistance in the south of Saint Domingue, 1793–1794. (*Slavery Abolit.*, 18:2, Aug. 1997, p. 48–72)

Narrowly focused examination of resistance by women slaves in early years of Haitian Revolution is based closely on documents collected by the French revolutionary commissioner Polverel. Specifically discusses active vs. passive resistance, arguing that although gender shaped the ways that women fought slavery, their actions cannot be separated from the resistance of other members of the slave population. [JDG]

Klooster, Wim. Illicit riches: Dutch trade in the Caribbean, 1648–1795. See item **1855.**

1901 Lacroix, Pamphile, vicomte de. La Révolution de Haïti. Édition présentée et annotée par Pierre Pluchon. Paris: Karthala, 1995. 525 p.: bibl., map. (Relire)

Drawing on archives and notes from interviews he had brought back from Haitian war of independence, a former high-ranking officer with a liberal bent offered in 1819 a first analysis of what happened and its significance: the strength demonstrated by an army of liberation, European troops plagued by yellow fever, the coming of a new era and society for Haiti. Pluchon provides solid introduction and annotations on author, who gave an account of the first major colonial war lost by the French. [APD]

1902 Landers, Jane. An eighteenth-century community in exile: the *floridanos* in Cuba. (*NWIG*, 70:1/2, 1996, p. 39–58, bibl.)

Sheds considerable light on links between Florida and Cuba since early-16th century. [JMH]

1903 Lee, T. van der. Curaçaose vrijbrieven 1722–1863: met indices op namen van vrijgelatenen en hun voormalige eigenaren [Curaçaoan manumission permits, 1722–1863: with indexes on personal names of freed persons and their former owners]. The Hague: Algemeen Rijksarchief, 1998. 670 p.: bibl., indexes. (Onderzoeksgids)

Comprises manumission letters from 1722 to abolition of slavery in 1863. Each description contains the name, age, sex, and race of the slave, reason for release, the amount paid, and name of the owner as far as is known. Compiler has consulted records from archives of Aruba, Bonaire, and Curaçao dating from 1722–1845 (deposited in the Public Record Office in The Hague) and records from 1845–63 in the archive of the Ministry of Colonial Affairs. Includes indexes on names of freed men and women and their former owners. [RH]

1904 Little, Thomas J. George Liele and the rise of independent black Baptist churches in the Lower South and Jamaica. (*Slavery Abolit.*, 16:2, Aug. 1995, p. 188–204)

Fascinating story of former slave who established black Baptist congregations in South Carolina, Georgia, and Jamaica in late-18th century. Highlights successes and failures in Jamaica at a time when missionary activity among slaves was still in its infancy. [ELC]

1905 Meier, Gudrun. Preliminary remarks on the Oldendorp manuscripts and their history. (*in* Slave cultures and the cultures of slavery. Knoxville: Univ. of Tennessee Press, 1995, p. 67–77, bibl.)

Very useful scholarly introduction to 3,000-page manuscript left by Moravian minister who, in 1767–68, was sent to report on the mission in the Danish West Indies. Oldendorp documented in a unique manner "the islands' geographical and biological characteristics and the ethnographic, linguistic, medical, and legal features of their societies," particularly by interviewing slaves about their lives. See also items **1910** and **1897.** [APD]

1906 Metz, Cara Anne Harbecke. Wealth in Bermuda during the eighteenth century: a view from the probate inventories of the colonial capital of St. George's. (*Bermud. J. Archaeol. Marit. Hist.*, 6, 1994, p. 95–109, map, tables)

Through examination of preliminary data from probate records for St. George's, concludes that Bermuda's consumer revolution peaked about 1740, after which time stagnation set in. A comparison of records from Bermuda with those for Annapolis, Md., for the same time period, suggests that the island's maritime economy promoted a greater diversity in available consumer goods. [ELC]

1907 Metz, John D. The dynamics of settlement in Devonshire Parish, Bermuda. (*Bermud. J. Archaeol. Marit. Hist.*, 6, 1994, p. 110–128, graphs, maps)

Drawing on nine assessments and over 100 wills from the parish, author provides in-depth analysis of settlement patterns of Bermuda. Assessments from 1698–1798 show parish-wide changes in land tenure over time. Wills from 1640–1798 contain information specific to dynamics of these changes. Concludes that changes in land-holding show responses to stress from plantation growth and the diminished availability of land and resources. Land tenure, however, remained stable throughout 17th century. [ELC]

1908 Mosneron-Dupin, Joseph. Moi, Joseph Mosneron, armateur négrier nantais, 1748–1833: portrait culturel d'une bourgeoisie négociante au siècle des Lumières. Edition par Olivier Pétré-Grenouilleau. Rennes, France: Editions Apogée; Paris: Diffusion PUF, 1995. 238 p.: bibl., ill. (Collection Moi—)

Mosneron's memoirs illustrate a merchant's life in the golden age of France's major slave-trading port, his austere values, and his persistence. As a young captain, he introduces us to the experience of voyages to the African coast and to the commercial circles of Caribbean colonial ports. [APD]

1909 Olivares, Itamar. La cession de Santo-Domingo à la France, 1795–1802. (*Mélanges/Madrid*, 30:2, 1994, p. 49–75)

Based on archives of the French foreign ministry, provides good overview of complex situation in Santo Domingo when it officially became French following defeat of the Spanish in 1795. Focuses on rivalry between Roume, the French agent appointed to occupy Saint-Domingue, and Gen. Toussaint Louverture, who successfully unified the whole island under his de facto authority in 1801. Only the landing of the Napoleonic expeditionary corps under Gen. Leclerc in 1802 ended Toussaint's ambitions, leading to withdrawal of French occupants from the island. [APD]

1910 Olwig, Karen Fog. African cultural principles in Caribbean slave societies: a view from the Danish West Indies. (*in* Slave cultures and the cultures of slavery. Knoxville: Univ. of Tennessee Press, 1995, p. 23–39, bibl.)

Offers fresh and sophisticated perspective on slave culture. Drawing from first-hand testimony of C.G.A. Oldendorp, a Moravian missionary who conducted interviews with Danish West Indian slaves in 1767–68, author refutes a monolithic notion of slave resistance against an oppressive system. Argues that instead: 1) African cultural principles and practices informed slaves' re-

sistance responses; 2) those principles and practices involved need to form a variety of ties within the social hierarchy the slaves encountered; and 3) these ties included kin-like relationships of dependency with masters and more experienced slaves. See also items **1905** and **1897**. [APD]

1911 Oostindie, Gert and **Alex van Stipriaan.** Slavery and slave cultures in a hydraulic society: Suriname. (*in* Slave cultures and the cultures of slavery. Knoxville: Univ. of Tennessee Press, 1995, p. 78–99, bibl., table)

Case study of slavery focuses on ecology, in particular water. The struggle to construct and maintain the *polder* hydraulic system determined the Suriname slaves' living and working conditions. Authors call attention to many spheres of life in which Surinamese slaves confronted challenges and options different from those facing slaves in other parts of the Caribbean. [RH]

1912 O'Shaughnessy, Andrew. Redcoats and slaves in the British Caribbean. (*in* The Lesser Antilles in the age of European expansion. Gainesville: Univ. Press of Florida, 1996, p. 105–127)

Examines islands' demand for British soldiers and military up to time of American Revolution as result of fear of slave revolts. Evaluates the provisions that island legislatures made for accommodating troops, their conditions of service, and "problem" of their presence which exacerbated civilian/military disputes. [ELC]

1913 Pérotin-Dumon, Anne. Free-coloreds and slaves in revolutionary Guadeloupe: politics and political consciousness. (*in* The Lesser Antilles in the age of European expansion. Gainesville: Univ. Press of Florida, 1996, p. 259–279, map)

Stimulating re-examination of early revolutionary events in Guadeloupe. Reviews various goals of whites, free people of color, and slaves in the context of an emerging revolutionary culture of patriotic societies, popular demonstrations, federation ceremonies, militia service, and public petitions. In spite of attempts by white and free-colored masters to maintain slavery, revolutionary ideology and politicization of Guadeloupean social relations rapidly dissolved the bonds of slavery up to 1794 when events in Saint-Domingue led the French to abolish the institution. [JDG]

1914 Quintanilla, Mark S. Late seventeenth-century indentured servants in Barbados. (*J. Caribb. Hist.*, 27:2, 1993, p. 114–128)

Draws heavily on wills, census data, assembly records, baptismal and marriage registers, and vestry records to piece together material on 1685 Monmouth Rebels who went to Barbados. Concludes that none of the rebels were part of the Redlegs community by 1715, and that very few resided in Barbados by that time. Speculates that as political prisoners they obviously had important connections that permitted them greater mobility than poor servants. [ELC]

1915 Reinders Folmer-van Prooijen, C. Van goederenhandel naar slavenhandel: de Middelburgse Commercie Compagnie 1720–1755 [From commodities trade to slave trade: the Middelburgse Commercie Compagnie 1720–1755]. Middelburg, The Netherlands: Koninklijk Zeeuws Genootschap der Wetenschappen, 2000. 222 p.: appendix, bibl., graphs, ill., table.

Traditional study of the Middelburgse Commercie Compagnie (MCC) describes company's business operations and focuses on its change from the commodities trade to the slave trade. From 1720–55 the MCC made a total of 173 trading journeys with 38 ships of its own. Includes a 25 p. summary in English. [RH]

1916 La Révolution française et Haïti: filiations, ruptures, nouvelles dimensions. v. 1–2. Port-au-Prince: Société haïtienne d'histoire et de géographie; Editions H. Deschamps, 1995. 2 v.: bibl., ill., index.

Presented at a conference in Haiti to commemorate the 1989 bicentennial of the French Revolution, these papers represent an excellent selection of works published over the past 20 years by specialists on slavery in 18th-century Saint-Domingue and the transatlantic slave trade. New research is represented by Pierre H. Boulle's examination of restrictions placed on free blacks residing in France, which tended to make their status similar to that of slaves; Bernard Foubert's "Statut social et statut foncier dans la plaine des Cayes sous la Révolution," which documents how granting garden plots to slaves led to their freedom and land ownership; Serge Daget's work on the last French slave shipments to the Antilles (1815–32);

Jacques Cauna's new biographical data on Polverel, a *commissaire* of the Convention nationale sent to Guadeloupe in 1793 who worked for economic reconstruction and the creation of a landed class of freedmen; and Paul Lachance's study of the composition and social relations of Saint-Domingue refugees in New Orleans in 1809. [APD]

1917 Sáez, José Luis. Jesuitas europeos e hispanoamericanos en Santo Domingo, 1650–1767. (*Arch. Hist. Soc. Iesu*, 65:129, Ian./Iun. 1996, p. 31–99)

Work provides substantial source material, but fails to fill the gap in the history of the Jesuits in the Dominican Republic. [JMH]

1918 Saugera, Eric. Bordeaux, port négrier: chronologie, économie, idéologie, XVIIe-XIXe siècles. Biarritz, France: J & D éditions; Paris: Karthala, 1995. 382 p., 8 p. of plates: bibl., ill. (some col.), index.

Written by best contemporary specialist on French slave trade, well-researched study throws light on how the leading 18th-century metropolitan port claimed a growing share of this trade, especially in 1780s, and then of the contraband slave trade in early 1800s. [APD]

1919 Scott, Julius S. Crisscrossing empires: ships, sailors, and resistance in the Lesser Antilles in the eighteenth century. (*in* The Lesser Antilles in the age of European expansion. Gainesville: Univ. Press of Florida, 1996, p. 128–143)

Due to a commonality of interests among peoples who placed national goals secondary to their own and their survival, sailors and smugglers were frequent international travelers, especially during wartime. Their actions, and those of runaway slaves who also crossed national boundaries, demonstrate the importance of commonality of space in Lesser Antilles despite artificial political divisions. [ELC]

1920 Selig, Robert A. The French capture of St. Eustatius, 26 November 1781. (*J. Caribb. Hist.*, 27:2, 1993, p. 129–143)

Brief, interesting account of circumstances surrounding island's capture by the French in 1781. Important as a smuggling station and as a supply point of goods for nascent US, island was captured by French because of tactical errors by British forces. Ultimately island's importance decreased after its return to the Dutch in 1784. [ELC]

1921 Shepherd, Verene A. Livestock farmers and marginality in Jamaica's sugar-plantation society: a tentative analysis. (*Soc. Econ. Stud.*, 41:2, June 1992, p. 183–201, bibl.)

Marginalized for their involvement in livestock farming at a time (18th century) when sugar was king, farmers made individualistic and pragmatic efforts, with limited results, to achieve upward social mobility. Accomodationists at best, they used their wealth and education to seek acceptance by whites, not to challenge dominant ideology. [ELC]

1922 Socolow, Susan M. Economic roles of the free women of color of Cap Français. (*in* More than chattel: black women and slavery in the Americas. Indianapolis: Indiana Univ. Press, 1996, p. 279–297, tables)

Primary archival research on elites and urban life in Latin America. Uses 315 notarial contracts from 18th-century Cap Français to describe economic roles played by free women of color in colonial Haiti's most dynamic city. Shows that some women of color were shopkeepers, landlords, and real estate investors, as well as higglers and servants. Also traces careers of some of these extraordinary figures. See also item **1890.** [APD]

1923 Steel, M.J. A philosophy of fear: the world view of the Jamaican plantocracy in a comparative perspective. (*J. Caribb. Hist.*, 27:1, 1993, p. 1–19)

Study of proslavery ideology of Jamaican planters from 1780s-1830 contends that Jamaicans' fear of revolts was greater than their US southern counterparts' because of local demographic situation. Potential British assistance in suppressing slave insurrections was largely responsible for their loyalty. Negrophobia and stereotypical views of blacks operated side-by-side with tolerance for miscegenation. [ELC]

1924 Stipriaan, Alex van. An unusual parallel: Jews and Africans in Suriname in the 18th and 19th centuries. (*Stud. Rosenthaliana*, 31:1/2, 1997, p. 74–93, ill., tables)

Discusses history of Jewish and African immigrants in light of 18th- and 19th-century economic developments in Suriname. Close personal and economic contact

between Jews and Africans existed from the beginning; author argues that remarkable parallels link the two groups. After the indigenous population, Jews and Africans lived in Suriname the longest, and both groups experienced integration and emancipation in society at large in the 19th century. [RH]

Tarragó, Rafael Emilio. Experiencias políticas de los cubanos en la Cuba española, 1512–1898. See item **1862.**

1925 Thibaudault, Pierre. Echec de la démesure en Guyane: autour de l'expédition de Kourou; une tentative européenne de réforme des conceptions coloniales sous Choiseul. Saint-Maixent-l'Ecole, France: P. Thibaudault, 1995. 504 p.: bibl., ill., maps.

Good narrative on settlement project launched to make up for the defeat in the Seven Years War includes selection of original sources. Presents important data on: 1) those who launched the project, the circumstances and magnitude of the failure, and its human cost; and 2) the 17,077 participants in the expedition, including their names, dates and places of embarcation, occupations, dates and places of birth, parents' names, and family connections among them. [APD]

1926 Thoden van Velzen, H.U.E. Dangerous ancestors: ambivalent visions of eighteenth- and nineteenth-century leaders of the eastern Maroons of Suriname. (Slave cultures and the cultures of slavery. Knoxville: Univ. of Tennessee Press, 1995, p. 112–144, bibl.)

Examines use and abuse of power in Suriname's Maroon societies. Explores experiential contradictions of resistance on borderlands between Maroons and Dutch colonial state. Explains complex moral dilemmas of Maroon historiographical praxis in relation to power itself. [RH]

1927 Thornton, John K. "I am the subject of the King of Congo": African political ideology and the Haitian Revolution. (*J. World Hist.*, 4:2, Fall 1993, p. 181–214)

Important article discusses ideology of kingship in the late-18th-century civil wars in the Kingdom of Kongo. Notes that leaders of the Haitian Revolution may have used specific religious symbols and specific acts of violence to convince slaves from this region to join their war against French colonists. Importantly, uses this African perspective on revolutionary events to explain why creole leaders had such limited control over African soldiers, and why they had such difficulty creating a centralized state after Haitian independence. [JDG]

1928 Wimpffen, Alexandre-Stanislas, baron de. Haïti au XVIIIe siècle: richesse et esclavage dans une colonie française. Édition présentée et annotée par Pierre Pluchon. Paris: Karthala, 1993. 317 p.: bibl., ill., index, maps. (Relire)

New edition of Wimpffen's 1797 publication is accompanied by a general essay on Saint-Domingue's economy and society by Pluchon, the most extensively published living French scholar of colonial Haiti. Wimpffen, an army officer from the Rhineland, was sympathetic to both Enlightenment humanitarianism and the profits produced by the plantation system. He provides a valuable and highly readable critique of this colony on the eve of the great slave revolution. [JDG]

1929 The wreck of the ten sails. Edited by Margaret E. Leshikar-Denton. George Town, Grand Cayman: Cayman Islands National Archive; Cayman Free Press, 1994. 95 p.: ill. (Our islands' past; 2)

To commemorate the 200-year anniversary of the event, this publication of some original correspondence and other documents sheds light on circumstances surrounding the wreck of 10 ships that were part of a 1794 convoy. Letters are mostly from squadron leader and other naval leaders about the event, salvage operations, and other related matters. [ELC]

Zips, Werner. Schwarze Rebellen: Afrikanisch-karibischer Freiheitskamp in Jamaica. See *HLAS 57:919.*

SPANISH BORDERLANDS

1930 Caron, Peter. "Of a nation which the others do not understand": Bambara slaves and African ethnicity in colonial Louisiana, 1718–60. (*Slavery Abolit.,* 18:1, April 1997, p. 98–121)

Article is key for unlocking identities and communal development of New World Africans. [JMH]

1931 Duncan, David Ewing. Hernando de Soto: a savage quest in the Americas. Norman: Univ. of Oklahoma Press, 1996. 608 p.: bibl., ill., index, maps.

An admirable *tour de force* that will need to be consulted by future biographers of the Spanish conquerer. Impeccable scholarship and documentation. [JMH]

1932 Hann, John H. A history of the Timucua Indians and missions. Foreword by Jerald T. Milanich. Gainesville: Univ. Press of Florida, 1996. 399 p.: bibl., index, maps. (Ripley P. Bullen series)

Author is the premier historian of Native American groups that lived in Florida during period of European colonization. This work—a solid, ground-breaking, in-depth study of the Timucua—is as scholarly and illuminating as his previous works. [JMH]

1933 Hudson, Charles M. Knights of Spain, warriors of the sun: Hernando de Soto and the South's ancient chiefdoms. Athens: Univ. of Georgia Press, 1997. 561 p.: bibl., ill., index, maps.

This monumental work, a blending of archeology and history, is the most thorough study of De Soto's expedition produced since the 1930s. For the first time De Soto's journey can be laid on a map and tied to specific archeological sites. [JMH]

Landers, Jane. An eighteenth-century community in exile: the *floridanos* in Cuba. See item **1902.**

1934 Manucy, Albert C. Sixteenth-century St. Augustine: the people and their homes. Gainesville: Univ. Press of Florida, 1997. 160 p.: bibl., ill., index, maps.

Author is the leading architectural interpreter of Saint Augustine. In this work he goes back in time to describe buildings and backyards of early Spanish settlers and the Timucua influence on this architecture. An accurate, broadly synthetic, and readable book. [JMH]

1935 Milanich, Jerald T. Florida Indians and the invasion from Europe. Gainesville, Fla.: Univ. Press of Florida, 1995. 290 p.: bibl., ill., index, maps.

Based on the best modern historical research on the Timucua and other Florida indigenous groups, work relates their decline and extinction. [JMH]

19TH CENTURY

1936 Afroz, Sultana. The unsung slaves: Islam in plantation Jamaica. (*Caribb. Q.,* 41:3/4, Sept./Dec. 1995, p. 30–44)

Tracing Islam's presence in Jamaica to slavery period, provides useful revision to generalized accounts of religious experiences and activities of slaves. However, one may query the evidence supporting the assertion that the slave uprising of 1831, commonly known as the Baptists War, constituted a Jihad against Christianity. [ELC]

Allen, Rose Mary. Resistance as a creative factor in Curaçaoan culture. See *HLAS* 57:788.

1937 A.M. Chumaceiro Az.: praktizijn-journalist-publicist; onpartijdig pionier op Curaçao [A.M. Chumaceiro Az: lawyer-journalist-publicist; impartial pioneer in Curaçao]. Edited by Henny E. Coomans and Maritza Coomans-Eustatia. Bloemendaal, The Netherlands: Stichting Libri Antilliani, 1998. 608 p.: photos.

This "labor of love" on Abraham Mendez Chumaceiro (1841–1902) is divided into two parts. Pt. 1 consists of seven articles detailing Chumaceiro's life and work, and contemporary Curaçaoan society. Pt. 2 is devoted to reprints of his work on Curaçao and Aruba, published between 1879–95. Includes photographs of late-19th-century Curaçao. [RH]

Arubaans akkoord: opstellen over Aruba van vóór de komst van de olieindustrie [Aruban accord: essays on Aruba before the oil industry]. See item **2044.**

1938 Ayala, José Antonio. La masonería de obediencia española en Puerto Rico, en el siglo XIX. Murcia, Spain: Univ. de Murcia, 1991. 368 p.: bibl., ill., maps. (Cuadernos; 32)

Thorough survey of Spanish-affiliated Masonic lodges in Puerto Rico. Treats Freemasonry as a social phenomenon with ideological incursions into religion, politics, colonialism, slavery, education, social assistance, etc. Includes glossary of terms and lists of lodges and members. [TMV]

Balcácer, Juan Daniel and **Manuel Antonio García Arévalo.** La independencia dominicana. See item **1867.**

1939 Baldrich, Juan José. Cigars and cigarettes in nineteenth-century Cuba. (*Rev. Rev. Interam.*, 24:1/4, 1994, p. 8–35, graphs)

Bold attempt to qualify the usual categorization of Latin America and the Caribbean as a purveyor of raw materials and foodstuffs to the 19th-century industrial world is at best partially successful. [JMH]

1940 Baud, Michiel. Patriarchy and changing family strategies: class and gender in the Dominican Republic. (*Hist. Fam.*, 2:4, 1997, p. 355–377, bibl.)

Uses case study (1870–1930) of a village in the Cibao to illustrate importance of patriarchal ideologies for class and gender relations. Argues that analysis of family strategies should take into account the context of class relations in the countryside and influence of hegemonic ideologies on gender relations within rural families. According to author, these factors formed the basis for rural families' specific strategies and also for diverging and often contradictory attitudes among individual family members. [RH]

Beckles, Hilary. Black female slaves and white households in Barbados. See item **1871.**

1941 Bégot, Danielle. Nature et révolution sous les tropiques: le paysage martiniquais vu par le préfet colonial Pierre-Clément de Laussat. (*Bull. Soc. hist. Guadeloupe*, 106, 1995, p. 23–36)

In a well-written and insightful study of the diary of an important 17th-century governor of Martinique, Bégot shows that the "landscaped portrait" of island's tropical nature reveals primarily Laussat himself. Author traces Laussat's sensitivity and interest in climate and plant life to his formative years and readings during the ancien régime. [APD]

Berleant-Schiller, Riva. From labour to peasantry in Montserrat after the end of slavery. See *HLAS* 57:797.

1942 Berleant-Schiller, Riva. The white minority and the emancipation process in Montserrat, 1807–32. (*NWIG*, 70:3/4, 1996, p. 255–281, bibl., tables)

Contends that examination of behavior of whites on Montserrat during crucial emancipation period reveals much more heterogeneity than previously assumed. Yet unified stance against free-coloreds' rights, and whites' "institutional and individual resistance to the emancipation process" demonstrates more solidarity than author admits. For anthropologist's comment, see *HLAS* 57:798. [ELC]

Besson, Jean. Land, kinship, and community in the post-emancipation Caribbean: a regional view of the Leewards. See *HLAS 57:806.*

Bilby, Kenneth M. Swearing by the past, swearing to the future: sacred oaths, alliances, and treaties among the Guianese and Jamaican Maroons. See *HLAS 57:809.*

1943 Blanco Rodríguez, Juan Andrés and **Coralia Alonso Valdés.** Presencia castellana en el Ejército Libertador Cubano, 1895–1898. Valladolid, Spain: Junta de Castilla y León, Consejería de Educación y Cultura; Zamora, Spain: UNED Zamora, 1996. 220 p.: bibl., ill. (Estudios de historia)

Excellent study clearly demonstrates the change in the Spanish perspective on the Cuban wars of independence. [JMH]

1944 Buffon, Alain. Regard d'un historien créole sur la Révolution: Auguste Lacour, 1805–1869. (*Bull. Soc. hist. Guadeloupe,* 106, 1995, p. 49–90)

Important study—the first of its kind—of Guadeloupe's most eminent 19th-century historian examines his training, view of history, method, and sources used. Second part analyzes Lacour's reading of the Revolution—the most sensitive theme for his generation, discussing the events that Lacour himself emphasized and those he ignored, as well as the familial relations captured in his writing. [APD]

1945 *Bulletin de la Société d'histoire de la Guadeloupe.* Nos. 104/105, 1995. La Banque de la Guadeloupe et la crise de change, 1895–1904: pt. 2. par Christian Schnakenbourg. Basse-Terre: Société d'histoire de la Guadeloupe.

Pt. 2 of in-depth study of state-controlled colonial bank's policy of favoring increased circulation of paper money to remedy major international sugar crisis, and policy's failure. Focuses on three structural forces affecting Bank's policy: the sugar mill planter lobby, the market, and the state. Shows that: 1) the Bank was too lenient with credit toward an increasingly indebted sugar-producing sector; 2) although sugar mill lobby strongly influenced Bank policy, it could not alone trigger a crisis of such magnitude; 3) if origin of Bank crisis was undeniably the world sugar crisis affecting other tropical economies, its 1897 climax was due

to a specific financial situation in Guadeloupe; 4) in 1895 a noninterventionist state began to assert control over Bank's management to end excessive facilities previously offered to sugar producers; and 5) a new crisis in 1904 led new Bank management to observe sugar producers with a mixture of pragmatism and rigor. For annotation of Pt. 1, see *HLAS 56:2085.* [APD]

Bush, Barbara. Hard labor: women, childbirth, and resistance in British Caribbean slave societies. See item **1873.**

1946 Cabrera Déniz, Gregorio José. Canarios en Cuba: un capítulo en la historia del archipiélago, 1875–1931. Las Palmas, Spain: Ediciones del Cabildo Insular de Gran Canaria, 1996. 461 p.: bibl. (Historia)

Well-written and researched comparative study. [JMH]

1947 Caddy, John Herbert. The St. Lucia diary of Lt. J.H. Caddy, R.A.: Sept 14th, 1833-April 22nd, 1834. Edited by B.H. Easter. 2. ed. rev. Castries: St. Lucia Archaeological and Historical Society, 1995. 46 p.: ill.

Brief, but highly important diary of individual who served in the Windward command in early-19th century. Reveals much about diarist's experiences and observations on eve of emancipation, the military regimen, and the conditions faced by soldiers. [ELC]

1948 Camille, Michael A. Population and ethnicity of Belize, 1861. (*in* Belize: selected proceedings from the second interdisciplinary conference. Lanham, Md.: Univ. Press of America, 1996, p. 45–63, bibl., tables)

Utilizing data from first comprehensive population survey for Belize conducted by Britain in 1861, author demonstrates population growth in 19th century and residential clustering along ethnic lines. Gender imbalances resulted from skewed male involvement in economic activities such as timber extraction in certain regions. Inelegant documentation. [ELC]

1949 Campbell, Carl C. The young colonials: a social history of education in Trinidad and Tobago, 1834–1939. Barbados: Press, Univ. of the West Indies, 1996. 387 p.: bibl., index.

Argues that in content and orientation

islands' educational system during colonial period was geared more to the metropole than to the local situation. Uses career and initiatives of J.O. Cutteridge, British educational official in Trinidad, to portray the occasional absurdity of the system. Highlights religious bodies' meaningful role in building schools and in other educational activities. Concludes that despite problems, education did provide a mechanism for upward social mobility and for overcoming barriers imposed by race, class, or ethnicity. Includes list of island scholars from late-19th century through 1939. [ELC]

1950 Casablanca, Marie-Jeanne. L'émigration corse à Porto Rico. Corte, France: Editions Le signet, 1993. 246 p.: bibl., maps.

Adds European source material to María Dolores Luque de Sánchez's previous work on Corsican immigration to Puerto Rico (see *HLAS 52:1778*). Establishes overpopulation and soil depletion in Corsica as push factors, and attributes immigrant success to extensive experience in agriculture and trade. [TMV]

1951 Casanovas Codina, Joan. Movimiento obrero y lucha anticolonial en Cuba después de la abolición de la esclavitud. (*Bol. Am.*, 35:45, 1995, p. 23–41)

Interesting conceptualization of pro-independence attitude assumed by Cuban labor movement after 1890. Author's categorization of Martí's movement as the "left wing" of Cuban separatism is untenable. [JMH]

1952 Castellano Gil, José Manuel. La masonería española en Cuba. Prólogo de José A. Ferrer Benimeli. Tenerife, Spain: Centro de la Cultura Popular Canaria, 1996. 415 p.: bibl., ill. (Taller de historia; 19)

The author, himself a Mason, takes to task the Cubans who have written about the history of Freemasonry on the island, criticizing them for their lack of scholarship and for being merely "pseudohistorians." Author is right in most cases. [JMH]

1953 Castro, María de los Angeles. El autonomismo en Puerto Rico, 1808–1898: la siembra de una tradición. (*Secuencia/México*, 31, enero/abril 1995, p. 5–22, bibl., ill.)

Examines autonomist ideology from its first formulation in the instructions given to the Puerto Rican delegates to the Cortes in early-19th century, through the objectives of the liberal reformist commissioners to the Junta Informativa of 1867, and to party politics in the 1870s-80s. Argues that in the past century, like today, political affiliation responded to economic conditions; the 1870s assimilationist current, therefore, must be seen more as a holding pattern than as a definitive stance. Permanent union with US, author laments, has facilitated substitution of the "nationalism conducive to the creation of an independent nation-state" with a "cultural and sports-oriented nationalism." [TMV]

1954 Céspedes, Carlos Manuel de. Carlos Manuel de Céspedes: el diario perdido. Estudio de Eusebio Leal Spengler. La Habana: Editorial de Ciencias Sociales, 1992. 302 p.: bibl., ill., indexes. (Historia de Cuba)

Important contribution to the literature on the Cuban wars of independence relates the inner thoughts of the man who started them. [JMH]

1955 Chaffin, Tom. Fatal glory: Narciso López and the first clandestine US war against Cuba. Charlottesville: Univ. Press of Virginia, 1996. 282 p., 10 p. of plates: bibl., ill., index, map.

Focuses primarily on López's place in US domestic politics. Challenging traditional view of López, author maintains that he was a creature of both southern and northern interests. Well written and extensively researched. [JMH]

1956 Chanderbali, David. A portrait of paternalism: Governor Henry Light of British Guyana, 1838–48. Turkeyen, Guyana: D. Chanderbali, 1994. 277 p.: bibl., index, maps.

Mid-19th-century history of Guyana gives particular emphasis to labor situation, importation of East Indians, government policy towards them and other labor groups, and policies of Governor Light. Author concludes that despite Governor Light's benevolence, the difficult situation in which he found himself compounded his problems and contributed to his somewhat unfavorable image. [ELC]

1957 Chinea, Jorge L. Race, colonial exploitation and West Indian immigration in nineteenth-century Puerto Rico,

1800–1850. (*Americas/Franciscans*, 52:4, April 1994, p. 495–519, tables)

Situates West Indian immigration of people of color in expanding economy—considered at the time as a necessary evil. Explains politics of race as fear on the part of Spanish officials that migrants would contribute to revolutionary abolitionist and reformist movements. Immigration ceased after 1840. [TMV]

1958 Cifre de Loubriel, Estela. La formación del pueblo puertorriqueño: la contribución de los isleño-canarios. San Juan: Centro de Estudios Avanzados de Puerto Rico y el Caribe, 1995. 498 p.: facsims., ill., maps.

Fourth of author's studies dedicated to immigrant groups in 19th-century Puerto Rico is based on data for 2,068 men and 655 women. Author tallies origin, location, occupation, personal data, and citizenship choice (US or Spanish) following the Treaty of Paris. As has become her trademark, she offers a brief biographical sketch for each person. [TMV]

Craton, Michael. Reembaralhando as cartas: a transição da escravidão para outras formas de trabalho no Caribe britânico, 1790–1890. See item **1879.**

1959 Cubano Iguina, Astrid. Política radical y autonomismo en Puerto Rico: conflictos de intereses en la formación del Partido Autonomista Puertorriqueño, 1887. (*Anu. Estud. Am.*, 51:2, 1994, p. 155–173)

Argues that *hacendados* were not the founding members of the Partido Autonomista; rather, this movement was propelled by urban groups indirectly affected by economic crisis caused by drop in sugar prices. Autonomists' liberal republicanism interested planters only minimally; planters' main concern was to escape fiscal demands of a reorganized Spanish treasury. [TMV]

1960 D'Alzina Guillermety, Carlos. Evolución y desarrollo del autonomismo puertorriqueño, siglo XIX. San Juan: Univ. Politécnica de Puerto Rico, 1995. 339 p.: bibl., ill.

Juridical study examines the shift toward autonomist position in Puerto Rico. After analyzing major legal instruments that regulated colonies' political relationship to Spain, author considers international, metropolitan, local, and even individual forces and

figures, to explain why autonomy became the Spanish solution to the "Cuban problem" in the face of US intervention. [TMV]

1961 De Asturias a América: Cuba, 1850–1930; la comunidad asturiana de Cuba. Coordinación de Pedro Gómez Gómez. Colombres, Spain: Archivo de Indianos; Principado de Asturias, 1996. 335 p.: bibl., ill., maps.

Studies Asturian presence in Cuba from different scholarly perspectives. [JMH]

1962 De Verteuil, Anthony. And then there were none: a history of the Le Cadre family in the West Indies. 2nd ed. Port of Spain, Trinidad: Litho Press, 1992. 186 p.: bibl., ill.

Drawing on "intimate letters and writings" of Le Cadre family including two autobiographies and numerous poems and letters, author presents interesting portrayal of members of Creole family with branches in Martinique and Trinidad. Three generations of the family were active in Caribbean affairs. First published in 1974, this expanded, updated, and corrected version covers mostly the 19th-century Trinidad branch. [ELC]

1963 De Verteuil, Anthony. The Germans in Trinidad. Port of Spain: A. de Verteuil, 1994. 231 p.: bibl., ill., indexes, maps.

Work is not a comprehensive treatment of Germans in Trinidad. Rather, after treating in general terms the entire German community and its origins, book concentrates on five families—Stollmeyer, Siegert, Urich, Boos, and Graff—that emigrated to Trinidad before 1875 and later became involved in various aspects of life on the island. [ELC]

1964 Dessalles, Pierre. Sugar and slavery, family and race: the letters and diary of Pierre Dessalles, planter in Martinique, 1808–1856. Edition and translation by Elborg Forster and Robert Forster. Baltimore: Johns Hopkins Univ. Press, 1996. 322 p., 4 p. of plates: bibl., ill., index, map. (Johns Hopkins studies in Atlantic history and culture)

Two senior historians of ancien régime societies have deftly translated and introduced selected pages of this extraordinary diary left by a planter of old lineage who lived through momentous changes in Caribbean society and economy. For annotation of the original diary, see *HLAS 48:2503.* [APD]

Duharte Jiménez, Rafael. Cuba: identidad cultural, mestizaje y racismo; encuentros y desencuentros de la cultura cubana. See *HLAS 57:4820.*

1965 Epailly, Eugène. Une page d'histoire du bagne de Guyane: Alfred Dreyfus, déporté dans l'enfer du Diable. Cayenne?: s.n., 1995. 152 p.: bibl., ill. (some col.).

Maps, photographs, and archival sources document the place where this French officer, a victim of anti-Semitic paranoia in fin-de-siècle France, spent four years of his life as a result of unjust condemnation. [APD]

1966 Estrade, Paul. José Martí, ¿una biografía imposible? (*Rev. Indias,* 55:205, sept./dic. 1995, p. 573–595)

Author claims that while production of a true biography of Martí is possible, it is unlikely to be written at least for the time being. Contradictory political attitudes and the lack of critical approach to the subject prevent such a work from becoming a reality. [JMH]

1967 Ferrer, Ada. Esclavitud, ciudadanía y los límites de la nacionalidad cubana: la Guerra de los Diez Años, 1868–1878. (*Hist. Soc./Valencia,* 22, 1995, p. 101–125, facsim., photo)

One of the best and more conscientious studies thus far of race relations in the Cuban liberating army during the Ten Years' War (1868–1878). [JMH]

1968 Frustier, Pierre et al. Clermonthe, affanchie en 1833. (*Généal. hist. Caraïbe,* 74, sept. 1995, p. 1407–1409)

In a genealogical study based on social history, authors reconstruct life of a female slave before and after her emancipation. [APD]

1969 Galloway, J.H. Botany in the service of empire: the Barbados cane-breeding program and the revival of the Caribbean sugar industry, 1880s-1930s. (*Ann. Assoc. Am. Geogr.,* 86:4, Dec. 1996, p. 682–706, bibl., ill., maps, photos)

Through examination of cane-breeding program on Barbados in late-19th century when authorities sought to replace Bourbon cane with disease-resistant species, author traces diffusion of this species to other islands. Argues that cane-breeding enhanced

the role of Royal Botanic Gardens at Kew in promoting economic botany and history of agricultural science, while simultaneously helping to shape British imperial policy. [ELC]

1970 García, Gervasio Luis. Strangers in Paradise?: Puerto Rico en la correspondencia de los cónsules norteamericanos, 1869–1900. (*Op. Cit./Río Piedras,* 9, 1997, p. 27–55)

Attempts to exorcise from the Puerto Rican psyche the spirit of 1898, the year Puerto Rico was occupied by US military forces. Establishes that US consular agents had commented on the commercial potential of the island decades prior to the invasion, to which territorial and political interests were added in late 1890s. The invasion of Puerto Rico, therefore, was not an incidental offshoot of the so-called Spanish-American War. Article also faces squarely the embarrassment that the initial welcome of US forces by island residents still causes Puerto Ricans. Avoiding the all-too-common practice of citing dramatic shows of patriotism, author prefers to somberly point out naive expectations at the end of Spanish rule. [TMV]

1971 García González, Vicente. Vicente García: leyenda y realidad. Selección e introducción de Víctor Manuel Marrero. La Habana: Editorial de Ciencias Sociales, 1992. 456 p.: bibl. (Palabra de Cuba)

Best-researched work produced thus far on this controversial figure of 19th-century Cuba. However, author did not succeed in overcoming his regionalistic prejudices in assessing the General's actions. [JMH]

1972 García Rodríguez, Gloria. La esclavitud desde la esclavitud: la visión de los siervos. Prólogo de Salvador E. Morales. México: Centro de Investigación Científica Ing. Jorge L. Tamayo, 1996. 251 p.: bibl., index.

Unique anthology of statements by slaves as they appear in judicial proceedings extant in the Archivo Nacional de Cuba. Also includes letters written by the slaves to the governor of Cuba asking for the redress of grievances against their masters. Worth reading. [JMH]

1973 Le grand tournant de l'école en 1853: documents officiels et correspondance privée. Edition par Bernard David et Léo Elisabeth. (*Ann. Antill.,* 28, 1991/94, p. 3–46)

Selected documents from French colonial archives show that clergy appointed by abolitionist government of Second Republic attempted to promote schools in Martinique for recently emancipated boys and girls. Also demonstrates the opposition that the policy encountered from a colonial administration appointed by a Third Empire whose sole aim was to maintain an agricultural labor force. [APD]

1974 Guicharnaud-Tollis, Michèle. Regards sur Cuba au XIXe siècle: témoignages européens. Paris: L'Harmattan, 1996. 351 p.: bibl., index. (Recherches et documents. Amériques latines)

Welcome contribution to a field that thus far has been dominated by North American perspectives. [JMH]

1975 Hector, Michel. La participation populaire dans la crise 1843–1848. (*Rev. Soc. haïti.*, 51:186, déc. 1995, p. 39–59; 52:193, sept. 1997, p. 29–48; and 52:194, déc. 1997, p. 23–50)

Reinterpretation of the Piquet revolt draws on contemporary journalism and classic Haitian historiography. Rather than seeing these armies of cultivators as tools of the mulatto elite (following Thomas Madiou, Pauleus Shannon, and others), Hector argues that resistance movements were autonomous and should be regarded as part of the long process of peasant formation that began with first successful revolt against colonial slavery. [JDG]

1976 Hidalgo Paz, Ibrahím. El Partido Revolucionario Cubano en la isla. La Habana: Editorial de Ciencias Sociales, 1992. 213 p.: bibl. (Col. de estudios martianos)

Good introduction to the Partido Revolucionario Cubano, a subject requiring much research before any conclusions can be reached. [JMH]

1977 Higman, B.W. Slave population and economy in Jamaica, 1807–1834. Kingston: The Press, Univ. of the West Indies, 1995. 327 p.: bibl., ill., index, tables.

First published in 1976 (see *HLAS 40:2983*), work is a masterful analysis of the dynamics of slave labor in the economic growth of early-19th-century Jamaica. Discusses various characteristics of slave and free-colored population including mortality, birth rates, manumission, distribution, and

structure, as well as jobs performed on island as a whole. Contains excellent statistical tables and new introduction by author. See also item **1978**. [ELC]

1978 Higman, B.W. Slave populations of the British Caribbean, 1807–1834. Kingston: The Press, Univ. of the West Indies, 1995. 781 p.: bibl., ill., index.

Reprint of work that originally appeared in 1984 (see *HLAS 48:2517b*). Excellent and thorough treatment of major demographic aspects of British Caribbean slavery from abolition of slave trade to slave emancipation. Draws heavily on extensive data available from slave registration returns for various islands to provide comparative perspective of nature of slave life. Excellent tables and figures. Essential for serious scholars of the region. See also item **1977**. [ELC]

1979 *History Gazette.* No. 60, Sept. 1993. The establishment of the Portuguese business community in British Guiana by Khalleel Mohamed. Turkeyen: Univ. of Guyana.

Despite their limited resources, the Portuguese established superiority in retail trade. Strained relations ensued between them and Creoles who resented unsavory practices of Portuguese shopkeepers. Tensions mounted in 1840s, prompting grievances that Creoles' mentors belatedly sought to redress. Important work. [ELC]

1980 Holt, Thomas C. "A essência do contrato": a articulação da raça, gênero e economia na política de emancipação britânica, 1838–1866. (*Estud. Afro-Asiát.*, 28, out. 1995, p. 9–30, bibl.)

Discussion of emancipation process in British Caribbean suggests that discourse on emancipation was based on premise of existence of Great Contract between Great Britain and its colonies, similar to personal liberty and equality present in classical liberal ideology. Shows how Jamaican special interest groups, particularly planters, fostered emancipation policies that veered from liberal beginnings to dependence on state intervention. [ELC]

1981 Hove, Okke ten and **Frank Dragtenstein.** Manumissies in Suriname, 1832–1863 [Manumissions in Suriname, 1832–1863]. Utrecht, The Netherlands: Centrum voor Latijns-Amerikaanse en Caraïbische Studies, Univ. Utrecht; Instituut ter Bevordering van de Surinamistiek, 1997. 441 p.: bibl., ill. (Bronnen voor de studie van Suriname; 19)

Authors used several, often incomplete sources to compile this register, which includes names of all 6,364 slaves who were manumitted in Suriname between 1832 and July 1, 1863 (abolition of slavery). Includes list of all manumitted slaves, a list of changes in personal names, as well as indexes on names of the manumitted, the owners or manumitters, plantations, and changes in personal names. This useful reference work also gives a history of manumission in Suriname. [RH]

1982 **Iglesias García, Fe.** Contratados peninsulares para Cuba. (*Anu. Estud. Am.*, 51:2, 1994, p. 93–112, tables)

Shows that slavery impacted the work of free immigrants, even if they were native Spaniards. [JMH]

Instituto de Historia de Cuba. Historia de Cuba. See item **1853.**

1983 **Jabour, Anya.** Slave health and health care in the British Caribbean: profits, racism and the failure of amelioration in Trinidad and British Guiana, 1824–1834. (*J. Caribb. Hist.*, 28:1, 1994, p. 1–26)

Using reports from parliamentary papers related to Trinidad and British Guiana, concludes that disease-ridden environment, demanding work loads, and inadequate diets militated against slaves' health. Further, miserliness and racism caused both planters and slave advocates to overlook evidence of malnutrition and illness; thus, proposed measures for improving slave health and achieving natural increase were ineffective. [ELC]

Jarvis, Michael. The Henry Tucker House: 280 years of Bermudian history. See item **1898.**

Johnson, Howard. Slave life and leisure in Nassau, Bahamas, 1783–1838. See item **1899.**

1984 **Johnson, Whittington B.** The Amelioration Acts in the Bahamas, 1823– 1833: a middle ground between freedom and antebellum slave codes. (*J. Bahamas Hist. Soc.*, 18, Oct. 1996, p. 21–32, facsims., photo)

Accepting the notion that Bahamas Amelioration Acts were hardly revolutionary, author concludes that they nonetheless

brought about improvements for slaves, who occupied a position somewhat better than their counterparts in the US South. By 1830s, Bahamian slaves were decidedly better off than those in US, where repressive measures increasingly were being promulgated. [ELC]

Jolivet, Marie José. De "l'habitation" en Guyane: éléments de réflexion sur la question identitaire créole. See *HLAS 57:849.*

1985 **Kinsbruner, Jay.** Not of pure blood: the free people of color and racial prejudice in nineteenth-century Puerto Rico. Durham, N.C.: Duke Univ. Press, 1996. 176 p.: bibl., ill., index, maps.

Based on examination of housing patterns in San Juan and demographic data from four of its 19th-century *barrios*, work provides a much-needed exploration of racial prejudice in Puerto Rico. Challenges commonplace denial of racial discrimination up to the present by showing that free people of color had limited economic, social, and political opportunities to advance their status. [TMV]

1986 **Klinkers, Ellen.** Op hoop van vrijheid: van slavensamenleving naar Creoolse gemeenschap in Suriname, 1830–1880 [In hope of liberty: from slave society to Creole community in Suriname, 1830–1880]. Utrecht, The Netherlands: Vakgroep Culturele Antropologie, Univ. Utrecht, 1997. 229 p.: bibl., ill., index, maps. (Bronnen voor de studie van Afro-Surinaamse samenlevingen: 0922–3630; 18)

Dissertation discusses transition from slavery to emancipation through detailed study of the final three decades of slavery, the 10-year period of apprenticeship, and the first seven years of complete freedom. Examines influence of enslavement on newly liberated slaves, and how they rebuilt their lives after abolition. Based on archival sources in Suriname, The Netherlands, and Germany; most important sources are the reports by Moravian Brethren. Includes three-page summary in English. [RH]

1987 **Lazarus-Black, Mindie.** John Grant's Jamaica: notes towards a reassessment of courts in the slave era. (*J. Caribb. Hist.*, 27:2, 1993, p. 144–159)

Drawing heavily on late-19th-century document by jurist who heard cases in Jamaica, author concludes that island afforded excellent opportunity for "paupers and princes to tell their stories." Despite privileged social position of elites, law occasionally protected rights of poor, female, and enslaved. Fails to discuss instances in which complaints by the marginalized classes did not reach the courts. Interesting corrective on legal system. [ELC]

Lee, T. van der. Curaçaose vrijbrieven 1722–1863: met indices op namen van vrijgelatenen en hun voormalige eigenaren [Curaçaoan manumission permits, 1722–1863: with indexes on personal names of freed persons and their former owners]. See item **1903.**

1988 Legêne, Susan. De bagage van Blomhoff en Van Breugel: Japan, Java, Tripoli en Suriname in de negentiende-eeuwse Nederlandse cultuur van het imperialisme [The baggage of Blomhoff and Van Breugel: Japan, Java, Tripoli and Suriname in the 19th-century Dutch culture of imperialism]. Amsterdam: Koninklijk Instituut voor de Tropen, 1998. 468 p.: bibl., ill.

Well-written, but unconvincing dissertation on incorporation of ideas about non-Western cultures in The Netherlands in 19th century. Based on experiences and material legacies of the related Blomhoff and Van Breugel families in Suriname, North Africa, and Asia. Part of the book is devoted to Gaspar van Breugel, an absentee plantation owner who has written extensively about Suriname and (abolition of) slavery. [RH]

1989 Lewis, Andrew. "An incendiary press": British West Indian newspapers during the struggle for abolition. (*Slavery Abolit.,* 16:3, Dec. 1995, p. 346–361)

Argues that even most liberal newspapers did not wish to promote a slave insurrection, despite claims to the contrary by their opponents. However, newspapers inadvertently fueled slave discontent that eventually became uncontrollable and helped foster abolition. [ELC]

Lowes, Susan. "They couldn't mash ants": the decline of the white and non-white elites in Antigua, 1834–1900. See *HLAS 57:862.*

1990 Mangru, Basdeo. A history of East Indian resistance on the Guyana sugar estates, 1869–1948. Lewiston, N.Y.: Edwin Mellen Press, 1996. 370 p.: bibl., index, map. (Caribbean studies; 4)

Denying concept of East Indian docility and conservatism, author argues that their militancy, especially on sugar estates where they were exploited, demonstrates their willingness and ability to champion their rights. Links this trait to aggressive nature of their 20th-century political efforts to enhance material conditions of workers. [ELC]

1991 Marimon i Riutort, Antoni. Els balears en les guerres de Cuba, Puerto Rico i les Filipines. Barcelona: Barcanova, 1996. 126 p.: bibl., index. (Barcanova Educació)

Well-documented study on a little-researched subject. [JMH]

1992 Martínez-Fernández, Luis. The Havana Anglo-Spanish Mixed Commission for the Suppression of the Slave Trade and Cuba's *emancipados. (Slavery Abolit.,* 16:2, Aug. 1995, p. 205–225)

While not a ground-breaking piece of historical writing, work is still highly recommendable. [JMH]

1993 Martínez-Fernández, Luis. Political change in the Spanish Caribbean during the United States Civil War and its aftermath, 1861–1878. (*Caribb. Stud.,* 27:1/2, Jan./June 1994, p. 37–64)

Argues that an unlikely alliance among Cuban reformists, separatists, planters, professionals, abolitionists, and slaveowners formed in support of the Union forces during the US Civil War due to the evident collapse of slavery in the hemisphere. Likewise, during Cuba's Ten Years' War, revolutionaries adopted an abolitionist stance because US support appeared so necessary to their success. Puerto Rican Liberals, on the other hand, with less at stake and less influence in the metropolis than the Cuban elite, maintained a more inflexible stance toward reform throughout the period. [TMV]

1994 Martínez-Fernández, Luis. The sword and the crucifix: Church-State relations and nationality in the nineteenth-century Dominican Republic. (*LARR,* 30:1, 1995, p. 69–93, bibl.)

Carefully written and researched work relates convincingly why the Catholic Church became a bastion of Dominican nationality in the 19th century and continued in this role well into the 20th century. [JMH]

1995 Matos Rodríguez, Félix V. "Keeping an eye a patriot and the other an emigrant": an introduction to the "Lecture on Porto Rico" by Charles Chauncy Emerson. (*Rev. Rev. Interam.*, 23:3/4, otoño/invierno 1993, p. 26–50)

Transcribes lecture given by Charles Chauncy Emerson (brother of Ralph Waldo) in Concord, Mass., in 1833. In a brief introduction, Matos Rodríguez places the piece within the genre of travel literature and identifies three common strategies of representation of such accounts evident in the lecture: 1) centering on the landscape, 2) edenic references, and 3) focus on a civilizing mission. [TMV]

1996 Matos Rodríguez, Félix V. Street vendors, pedlars, shop-owners and domestics: some aspects of women's economic roles in nineteenth-century San Juan, Puerto Rico, 1820–1870. (*in* Engendering history: Caribbean women in historical perspective. New York: St. Martin's Press, 1995, p. 176–193, tables)

Shows that working-class women of color participated actively in San Juan's economic life—as food vendors, peddlers, shop owners, laundresses, seamstresses, midwives, etc. Although the state and the local authorities continuously tried to regulate their activities, poor working women actively defended their income-earning opportunities. Article is rich in its description of the daily life of the urban working class. [TMV]

1997 Mayo Santana, Raúl; Mariano Negrón Portillo; and Manuel Mayo López. Cadenas de esclavitud—y de solidaridad: esclavos y libertos en San Juan, siglo XIX. San Juan: Centro de Investigaciones Sociales, Univ. de Puerto Rico, Recinto de Río Piedras, 1997. 204 p.: bibl.

An expanded version of an earlier work on urban slavery by two of the authors (see *HLAS 54:2065*), this volume places Puerto Rican forced labor in the vast historiography on New World labor systems, racial categories, rural and urban lifestyles, household patterns, and economic transformations. Identifies key issues in slave studies; explains their relevance to the Puerto Rican case; and describes the experience of San Juan's emancipated slaves based on the city's *libro de contratos de libertos* (freedmen and -women contracts register). See also item **1998.** [TMV]

1998 Mayo Santana, Raúl; Mariano Negrón Portillo; and Manuel Mayo López. Esclavos y libertos: el trabajo en San Juan pre- y post-abolición. (*Rev. Cienc. Soc./Río Piedras*, 30:3/4, mayo 1995, p. 1–48, tables)

Authors establish growing specialization of labor under slavery in urban areas. Cooks, seamstresses, and other skilled workers attained a degree of financial independence and stood a better chance of buying their freedom. After abolition, freedmen and -women continued working at these jobs, and rural workers migrated to the cities in search of relatives and employment opportunities. Article is inserted in current historiography of slavery, coerced/forced labor, and the meaning of freedom. Also see *HLAS 54:2065.* [TMV]

1999 McDonald, John and Ralph Shlomowitz. Mortality on Chinese and Indian voyages to the West Indies and South America, 1847–1874. (*Soc. Econ. Stud.*, 41:2, June 1992, p. 203–240, appendix, bibl., tables)

Authors conclude that inadequate supervision accounted for higher mortality rates for Chinese than for East Indians on voyages, and for slave over non-slave voyages. Administrative measures such as adequate screening of migrants and reducing overcrowding resulted in lower mortality. Regression analysis shows mortality related to length of voyages and to seasons and ports of departure. [ELC]

2000 McDonald, Roderick A. "Birth-pangs of a new order": special magistrate John Anderson and the apprenticeship in St. Vincent. (*in* The Lesser Antilles in the age of European expansion. Gainesville: Univ. Press of Florida, 1996, p. 324–344, map)

Drawing on a diary kept by this observant individual, work provides fascinating glimpse of four-year experiment in preparing ex-slaves for full freedom. Important commentary on society at crucial juncture, especially as Anderson speaks powerfully of conflicts over labor assignment, color, and ethnicity. Thus, diary depicts crisis experienced by that society during transition from slavery to freedom, and painful birth of free society. [ELC]

2001 Mejía de Fernández, Abigail. Vida de Máximo Gómez en Santo Domingo. Santo Domingo: ONAP, 1995. 76 p.: bibl.

Interesting for its feminine perspective on the life of the general. [JMH]

2002 Mendieta Costa, Raquel. Cultura: lucha de clases y conflicto racial, 1878–1895. La Habana: Editorial Pueblo y Educación, 1989. 92 p.: bibl.

Includes three very informative essays on black-white relations during the decades following abolition of slavery in Cuba. [JMH]

2003 Menezes, Mary Noel. The Portuguese of Guyana: a study in culture and conflict. S.l.: s.n., 1993? 226 p.: bibl., ill.

Interesting sociopolitical history of new immigrants that contributed meaningfully to development of Guyanese society. A descendant of these migrants and an established authority on Portuguese presence in Guyana, author provides fullest treatment to date on important aspect of Guyanese history. Examines migration, and their departure from cane fields for commercial activity. Viewed as distinctly separate and avoiding inter-ethnic marriage, the Portuguese maintained cultural strivings in multi-ethnic society. Notes their cultural contributions to music, song, arts, sports, and politics. Ends in 1920s when Guyana's political status changed. [ELC]

2004 Montoro, Rafael. Discursos y escritos. Prefacio de José Manuel Hernández. Compilación e introducción de Rafael E. Tarragó. Miami: Editorial Cubana, 1999. 530 p.

Selected collection of speeches and writings of a leading proponent of Cuban autonomy from Spain and an elected deputy in the Spanish Cortes in late 1800s. Includes preface by José Manuel Hernández and a biographical introduction by Rafael Tarragó who argues that Montoro is one of Cuba's "most unjustly ignored" historical figures. [L. Boudon]

2005 Moore, Brian L. Cultural power, resistance and pluralism: colonial Guyana 1838–1900. Kingston: The Press, Univ. of the West Indies; Montreal: McGill-Queen's Univ. Press, 1995. 376 p.: bibl., ill., index, maps.

Seeks to determine manner in which colonial elite used culture and consensus of values to maintain their hegemony, and examines responses of the subordinate groups to these initiatives and nature of the resulting cultural fabric. His conclusion—that 19th-century Guyanese society consisted of a number of "discrete cultural sections which shared very little with one another other than a common commitment to making money in the plantation society"—suggests the presence of acquisitive materialism that now inhibits growth of consensus-building mechanisms at the national level. [ELC]

2006 Moore, Dennison. Origins & development of racial ideology in Trinidad: the black view of the East Indian. Tunapuna, Trinidad and Tobago: Chakra Publishing House, 1995. 330 p.: bibl., ill., index.

Examines 19th-century, especially indentureship period, antecedents to 20th-century race prejudice in Trinidad. Discusses prevalence of race issues in present-day politics, with the capitalist mode of production, class and state ideologies, and churches all contributing to continued racial tensions. [ELC]

2007 Naranjo Orovio, Consuelo and Mercedes Valero González. Trabajo libre y diversificación agrícola en Cuba: una alternativa a la plantación, 1815–1840. (*Anu. Estud. Am.*, 51:2, 1994, p. 113–133)

A not-entirely successful attempt to diminish the importance of the "fear of the black" in colonial Cuba. [JMH]

2008 Navarro García, Jesús Raúl. Un ejemplo de censura en el Puerto Rico decimonónico: la carta al Duque de Wellington de Jorge D. Flinter, 1829. (*Anu. Estud. Am.*, 51:2, 1994, p. 261–271)

Transcribes George D. Flinter's entire 1829 letter to the Duke of Wellington, which was censored by *La Gaceta de Puerto Rico*, the metropolitan government's spokespiece on the island. Flinter, a Spanish citizen of Irish origin, fled Venezuela during the war of independence and advocated recognition of the former colonies. His objective—to contain what he viewed as social disorder—was behind this posture, but watchful colonial authorities suppressed a lengthy paragraph on the subject. [TMV]

2009 Ojeda, Dolores Bessy. Francisco Leyte Vidal. Santiago de Cuba: Editorial Oriente, 1988. 251 p.: bibl., ill., indexes, maps.

Leyte Vidal participated in Cuban wars of independence and was involved in politics in early days of the Cuban republic. The publication of his papers and biography are important contributions to the study of these events. [JMH]

Oostindie, Gert and **Alex van Stipriaan.** Slavery and slave cultures in a hydraulic society: Suriname. See item **1911.**

2010 Opatrný, Josef. Los cambios socioeconómicos y el medio ambiente: Cuba, primera mitad del siglo XIX. (*Rev. Indias*, 56:207, mayo/agosto 1996, p. 367–386)

Although based primarily on printed and secondary sources, work is interesting because of its subject: the deforestation caused by development of the Cuban sugar industry in first half of the 19th century. [JMH]

2011 Partido Revolucionario Cubano. Sección Puerto Rico. Memoria de los trabajos realizados por la Sección Puerto Rico del Partido Revolucionario Cubano: 1895 a 1898. San Juan: José Celso Barbosa y Alcalá, 1993. 250 p.: ill.

Shows conclusively that at least one group of Puerto Ricans actively lobbied Washington for US invasion of their island in 1898. [JMH]

2012 Paz Sánchez, Manuel de. Julio Sanguily y Garritte, 1846–1906, y los alzamientos de febrero de 1895 en el occidente de Cuba. (*Rev. Indias*, 56:207, mayo/agosto 1996, p. 387–428)

Dwells on aspects of the Cuban uprising of Feb. 1895 that historians usually do not discuss. Based on ample archival sources. Author also is quite familiar with the pertinent Cuban literature. [JMH]

2013 Picó, Fernando. Contra la corriente: seis microbiografías de los tiempos de España. Río Piedras, P.R.: Ediciones Huracán, 1995. 189 p.: bibl.

Six narratives on the lives of "historically unimportant" figures (an African-descent family from slavery to freedom, an alleged separatist landowner, a Jesuit priest, a powerful local strongman, an anti-imperialist journalist, a popular outlaw) are woven together through vital statistics, records of the acquisition of property, descriptions of political activity, and the like. This work is author's response to postmodernist allegation that historical texts are another form of fiction. Actually, unearthing and analyzing primary data, he argues, is a more productive undertaking than engaging in debates. [TMV]

2014 Piniella Corbacho, Francisco. La Empresa Mercantil de Correos Marítimos de La Habana, 1827–1851: aproximación a los usos náuticos en la primera mitad del siglo XIX. Cádiz, Spain: Servicio de Publicaciones, Univ. de Cádiz, 1995. 566 p.: bibl., ill., maps.

A significant contribution to our knowledge of maritime transportation between Cuba and Spain during the period. This doctoral dissertation truly deserves the *apt cum laude* distinction that it was awarded. [JMH]

2015 Piqueras Arenas, Josep Antoni. La revolución democrática, 1868–1874: cuestión social, colonialismo y grupos de presión. Madrid: Ministerio de Trabajo y Seguridad Social, 1992. 848 p.: bibl. (Col. Ediciones de la Revista de Trabajo; 37)

Although exhaustively researched, book is too detailed and not well written. Work does not focus on Cuba directly; rather, it studies the powerful influence of Cuban proslavery interests in the fight against reforms and abolition carried on by Valencia's urban patriarchs. [JMH]

2016 Portuondo Zúñiga, Olga. Esclavitud o independencia: disyuntiva del liberalismo criollo oriental de la isla de Cuba en 1836. (*Secuencia/México*, 29, mayo/agosto 1994, p. 153–170, bibl., table)

Proves conclusively that slavery hampered Cuban separatism long before the beginning of the wars of independence. [JMH]

2017 Prince, Mary. The history of Mary Prince, a West Indian slave. Related by herself. Edited with an introduction by Moira Ferguson. Preface by Ziggi Alexander. Ann Arbor: Univ. of Michigan Press, 1993. 124 p.: bibl., ill., map.

Interesting and highly valuable first-person narrative of a woman slave who details her experiences in Bermuda and Antigua and also in Britain where she was employed by abolitionist Thomas Pringle. Sheds light on women's roles and experiences, and on slave system in islands. Prince was first known woman who rebelled from slavery and wrote her own account. First published in 1831, work was eagerly embraced by antislavery groups. [ELC]

Ramesar, Marianne D. Soares. Survivors of another crossing: a history of East Indians in Trinidad, 1880–1946. See item **2089.**

2018 Richardson, Bonham C. Detrimental determinists: applied environmentalism as bureaucratic self-interest in the *fin-de-siècle* British Caribbean. (*Ann. Assoc. Am. Geogr.*, 86:2, June 1996, p. 213–234, graph, map, photos)

Through examination of official policies toward British Caribbean at end of 19th century, concludes that most officials promoted expeditious rationale of longstanding Caribbean social order in which inferiority of blacks could be maintained. By emphasizing oversimplified dichotomies of white over black, officials used their authority to propagate their views of racial superiority. [ELC]

2019 Richardson, Bonham C. A "respectable" riot: Guy Fawkes Night in St. George's, Grenada, 1885. (*J. Caribb. Hist.*, 27:1, 1993, p. 21–35)

Important article links riot to worsening economic conditions and protest against unrepresentative government. Notes, however, that sugar had already fallen out of grace and colonial administrators exaggerated possibilities for political unrest. Hence, riot is more "manifestation of class differences, political frustrations and ambiguities, and inter-island contrasts at that time." [ELC]

2020 Rigau-Pérez, José G. Surgery at the service of theology: postmortem cesarean sections in Puerto Rico and the Royal Cédula of 1804. (*HAHR*, 75:3, Aug. 1995, p. 377–404)

Through a transcription of the royal *cédula* requiring removal of fetuses from presumably dead women for purposes of baptism, author explores the "practical" violence with which Enlightenment-period rulers approached their subjects. A detailed description of the impact of the decree on its colonial objects (surgeons, priests, and families) reveals the complex chain of communication between political and social actors in early-19th-century Puerto Rico. Incidentally, the *cédula* sheds light on notions of death and becomes a source for studying the medical profession as well. [TMV]

2021 Rivera Rivera, Antonia. El estado español y la beneficencia en el Puerto Rico del siglo XIX. Santo Domingo: Editorial El Cuervo Dorado, 1995. 235 p.: bibl., ill. (Col. Cuadernos humanísticos; 3)

Complete chronological narrative account of Spanish government's efforts to administer the system of charity in 19th-century Puerto Rico is based on Spanish archival sources. [TMV]

San Miguel, Pedro Luis. Los campesinos del Cibao: economía de mercado y transformación agraria en la República Dominicana, 1880–1960. See item **2093.**

2022 Santiago-Valles, Kelvin A. "Forcing them to work and punishing whoever resisted": servile labor and penal servitude under colonialism in nineteenth-century Puerto Rico. (*in* The birth of the penitentiary in Latin America: essays on criminology, prison reform, and social control. Austin: Univ. of Texas Press, 1996, p. 123–168, facsim., map, photos)

Resistance (smuggling, sabotage, flight) on the part of subaltern groups to precapitalist forms of labor extraction impeded the maturation of wage-based exploitation. Thus, penal confinement could not be calculated economically and remained an ineffective method of imposing order on colonial society. Presents novel argument that rests on a Foucauldian reading of printed primary sources. [TMV]

2023 Schmidt, Nelly. L'engrenage de la liberté: Caraïbes-XIXe siècle. Aix-en-Provence, France: Univ. de Provence, 1995. 360 p.: bibl., index.

Written by specialist on French abolition, offers comparative approach to similar processes throughout the Caribbean. Stresses impact of British abolitionist policy on the French, as well as the specific characteristics of the French policy: authorities and former masters kept a tight grip on the enfranchised labor force which showed no massive movement of desertion or refusal to work. Indentured workers were hired to lower the cost of labor. [APD]

2024 Schmidt, Nelly. Victor Schoelcher et l'abolition de l'esclavage. Paris: Fayard, 1994. 440 p.: appendix, bibl., index.

First-rate study of the Protestant merchant whose wide travel experience and liberal convictions made him France's most impressive abolitionist and architect of the 1848 decree of abolition. Schmidt analyzes his social and political thought and its origins—from Abbé Grégoire to Fourier. She traces Schoelcher's impact in the French Antilles: his conversion into an iconic figure and his action inspiring a new republican colonial doctrine, or *schoelchérisme*. She follows his subsequent career as an indefatigable and impartial advocate of human rights, a feminist, and a republican politican who introduced important reforms in colonial administration and whose competence in colonial economy and labor force organization was widely influential. The appendix is a rich source that shows Schoelcher to be a gifted writer, whose lucidity and sophistication are noted by the author. See also items **2028** and **2025**. [APD]

2025 Schmidt, Nelly. Victor Schoelcher: une conscience de la République au XIXe siècle. (*in* La terre et la cité: mélanges offerts à Philippe Vigier. Paris: Créaphis, 1994, p. 251–264)

Drawing on her own extensive work on the abolitionist, Schmidt provides a crisp synthesis of Schoelcher's political activity and its underlying vision. Schoelcher's activity focused first on abolishing slavery during the Second Republic, then on putting the regimes of the colonies on an equal basis with France (the assimilationist policy) during the Third Republic. See also items **2024** and **2028**. [APD]

2026 Schmidt-Nowara, Christopher. "Spanish" Cuba: race and class in Spanish and Cuban antislavery ideology, 1861–1868. (*Cuba. Stud.*, 25, 1995, p. 101–122)

Shows persuasively how revolution in Spain and Cuba in 1868 shattered the Cuban reformist vision of a gradual abolition of slavery. [JMH]

2027 Schnakenbourg, Christian. Note complémentaire sur l'histoire industrielle et financière de l'usine Bologne, 1873–1887. (*Bull. Soc. hist. Guadeloupe*, 110, 1996, p. 39–53)

Economic historian completes Lafleur's history (see item **1803**) of oldest sugar factory in Guadeloupe. From its brief decade as sugar *central* in 1870s to its liquidation, this work documents the history of the factory, including venture capital, cane supply, railway and other transportation, its relationship with neighboring sugar estates, and advanced technical equipment. Shows that the enterprise underutilized its produc-

tive capacity throughout its history, as it failed to attract all the cane produced in the region. [APD]

2028 Schoelcher, Victor. La correspondance de Victor Schoelcher. Présentation par Nelly Schmidt. Paris: Maisonneuve et Larose, 1995. 379 p.: ill., index.

Most of these letters were sent to Ernest Legouvé, Schoelcher's close friend throughout his life, and are preserved in the Archives de la Martinique. The letters reveal the private man, keen on music and the arts and a person of deep humanitarian sensitivity. See also items **2024** and **2025**. [APD]

2029 Serrano, Violeta. La Intendencia de Hacienda en Cuba. La Habana: Editorial Academia, 1990. 102 p.: bibl.

One of the few available monographic studies on the subject. [JMH]

2030 Shelton, Robert S. A modified crime: the apprenticeship system in St. Kitts. (*Slavery Abolit.*, 16:3, Dec. 1995, p. 331–345, tables)

Focusing on apprenticeship period, shows degree of continuity that existed between that period and the slavery period. Examines work stoppages and how they were handled, punishments for minor infractions, and difficulties that stipendiary magistrates faced. [ELC]

2031 Shepherd, Verene A. Transients to settlers: the experience of Indians in Jamaica, 1845–1950. Leeds, England: Peepal Tree; Univ. of Warwick, 1994. 281 p.: bibl., ill., index, maps.

Contests the notion that East Indians in 19th- and 20th-century Jamaica lacked "cultural visibility" and were the most depressed of the East Indian communities in the Caribbean. Demonstrates that they maintained a distinct cultural identity despite the marginal position that they were alloted in society, especially in the political sphere. Useful work. [ELC]

2032 Skrekiboekoe: boek der verschrikkingen; visioenen en historische overleveringen van Johannes King [Skrekiboekoe: book of horrors; visions and historical traditions by Johannes King]. Edited by Chris de Beet. Utrecht, The Netherlands: Centrum voor Latijns-Amerikaanse en Caraïbische Studies, Univ. Utrecht; Instituut ter Bevordering van de Surinamistiek, 1995.

334 p.: bibl, map, photos. (Bronnen voor de studie van Afro-Suriname; 17)

Extensive edition of the writings of Johannes King, a 19th-century Maroon missionary who stood with one foot in the world of Christianity and the other in Maroon culture. Work contains King's descriptions of his dreams and visions, and episodes from the history of his family and of Maroon society in general. Edition is based on handwritten manuscript located in Herrnhut, Germany. Text is preceded by useful introduction placing King's work in the context of his biography, the Moravian mission, and 19th-century Maroon society. [RH]

Small, Stephen. Racial group boundaries and identities: people of 'mixed-race' in slavery across the Americas. See *HLAS* 57:4553.

Small islands, large questions: society, culture, and resistance in the post-emancipation Caribbean. See *HLAS* 57:900.

2033 Société d'histoire de la Guadeloupe. Cahier de marronnage du Moule, 1845–1848. Edition par Ghislaine Bouchet, Josette Fallope et Jacques Adéläide-Merlande. Basse-Terre: Société d'histoire de la Guadeloupe, 1996. 1 v.: ill., index, map.

Welcome publication of an invaluable municipal document. These 119 declarations reporting maroon slaves submitted by slave owners from Guadeloupe's most active sugar-exporting region reveal that, on the eve of the 1848 abolition of slavery, *marronnage* was more widespread than previously thought. [APD]

2034 Sommer, Doris. Puerto Rico a flote: desde Hostos hasta hoy. (*Op. Cit./Río Piedras*, 9, 1997, p. 253–262)

Author celebrates Puerto Rico's ambivalence with respect to its political status (the most recent manifestation of which occurred in Dec. 1998, when a less-than-unequivocal "no" was the response to a referendum proposing annexation to the US). She parallels this survival strategy to Hostos' own capacity to move within his desire for autonomy and his admiration for Spanish learning—to "float" among "insoluble tensions [that] are dynamic sites of construction." [TMV]

Steel, M.J. A philosophy of fear: the world view of the Jamaican plantocracy in a comparative perspective. See item **1923.**

2035 Stipriaan, Alex van. Between state and society: education in Suriname, 1850–1950. (*in* Mediators between state and society. Hilversum, Netherlands: Verloren, 1998, p. 57–86, photos, table)

Focuses on role of formal education in state and society formation in Suriname. Argues that education translated interests of the colonial state to the local population while at the same time providing careers for the articulate dissidents it produced. Yet education was not simply a state-supervised vehicle for keeping colonial society under control; in the process, the white monopoly was gradually eroded and the state became the driving force of socio-ethnic competition. Moreover, education played a part in the emergence of nationalism. [RH]

Stipriaan, Alex van. An unusual parallel: Jews and Africans in Suriname in the 18th and 19th centuries. See item **1924.**

Tarragó, Rafael Emilio. Experiencias políticas de los cubanos en la Cuba española, 1512–1898. See item **1862.**

Thoden van Velzen, H.U.E. Dangerous ancestors: ambivalent visions of eighteenth- and nineteenth-century leaders of the eastern Maroons of Suriname. See item **1926.**

2036 Tisnes J., Roberto M. El Ilustrísimo Señor Don Dionisio González de Mendoza, Gobernador Eclesiástico de Puerto Rico y Santiago de Cuba, Vice-Presidente del Escorial y Auditor de la Rota. (*Bol. Acad. Puertorriq. Hist.*, 13:43, enero 1992, p. 41–104)

Detailed narrative account of conflict between Church and civil authorities in mid-19th-century Puerto Rico. Contextualizes the "schism" that occurred due to conflicting jurisdictions over appointive powers by comparing Church-state relations, and specifically the application of the *patronato* in Spain and in the colonies. [TMV]

2037 Trouillot, Michel-Rolph. Beyond and below the Merivale paradigm: Dominica's first 100 days of freedom. (*in* The Lesser Antilles in the age of European expansion. Gainesville: Univ. Press of Florida, 1996, p. 305–323, tables)

Uses reports compiled by colored stipendiary magistrate William Lynch to provide analysis and commentary on working of apprenticeship on Dominica. Arguing that Lynch's findings are representative of entire island, concludes that substantial numbers of ex-slaves were absent from estates during first months of full freedom, leading planters to enlist aid of magistrates to evict them. Planters established significant linkage between labor and rent as mechanism to induce adequacy of labor short of eviction. Suggests need for similar detailed analyses for other islands. [ELC]

2038 Vink, Steven. Suriname door het oog van Julius Muller: fotografie 1882–1902 [Suriname through the eye of Julius Muller: photography, 1882–1902]. Amsterdam: Koninklijk Instituut voor de Tropen; Paramaribo: Stichting Surinaams Museum, 1997. 95 p.

Valuable collection of photographs by the Suriname photographer Julius Muller (1846–1902) is culled from collection of the Tropenmuseum (of the Royal Tropical Institute in Amsterdam). In more than 50 photos, Muller gives his view of social and economic life in Paramaribo and outlying districts in final decades of 19th century. [RH]

Vuurde, Rob van. Engeland, Nederland en de Monroeleer, 1895–1914: Europese belangenbehartiging in de Amerikaanse invloedssfeer [England, The Netherlands, and the Monroe Doctrine, 1895–1914: European protection of interests in the American sphere of influence]. See item **2104**.

2039 Weiss, John McNish. Free black American settlers in Trinidad, 1815–16. London: McNish & Weiss, 1995. 52 p.: bibl., maps.

Author's attempt to locate ethnohistorical material on ancestors who settled on Trinidad in early 19th century led to this short but useful publication covering entire group of free black settlers. Includes list of names of settlers, their US origins where available, land grants they received, and their military company. [ELC]

Woolford, Hazel M. Gender and women in Guianese politics, 1812–1964. See item **2107**.

Zequeira Sánchez, Mario and **Isabel Valdivia Fernández.** El papel del cultivo del café para le sociedad y la economía cubana. See *HLAS* 57:4947.

20TH CENTURY

2040 Alarcón Ramírez, Dariel. Memorias de un soldado cubano: vida y muerte de la Revolución. Edición e introducción de Elizabeth Burgos-Debray. Barcelona: Tusquets Editores, 1997. 354 p.: index. (Col. Andanzas; 295 Memorias)

Author is a Cuban defector and former intelligence agent who claims that he never was a Communist, merely a *fidelista*. Reader will have to decide the extent to which he may be believed. [JMH]

2041 Albizu Campos, Pedro. La palabra como delito: los discursos por los que condenaron a Pedro Albizu Campos, 1948–1950. Edited by Ivonne Acosta. San Juan: Editorial Cultural, 1993. 184 p.: ill.

Compilation of 12 speeches, as recorded by the police stenographer, for which Albizu Campos was convicted of breaking Law #53, which prohibited words and actions directed against the insular government of Puerto Rico. Editor suggests there is no correlation between inflammatory language in each of the orations, which were used as evidence for 12 separate charges, and the length of the sentences imposed. [TMV]

Allen, Rose Mary. Curaçaoan women's role in the migration to Cuba. See *HLAS* 57:787.

2042 Ameringer, Charles D. The Caribbean Legion: patriots, politicians, soldiers of fortune, 1946–1950. University Park: Pennsylvania State Univ. Press, 1996. 180 p.: bibl., ill., index, map.

Commendable effort to reduce a myth to historical proportions. Interesting reading. [JMH]

2043 Anderson, Jon Lee. Che Guevara: a revolutionary life. New York: Grove Press, 1997. 814 p.: bibl., ill., index, maps.

Author obviously admires Guevara and thus tends to exaggerate his role in the Cuban Revolution; however, he has managed a degree of objectivity sufficient for production of the best biography of the guerrilla thus far. Author's research is wide and deep, his work is careful and meticulous, and he always remains close to the facts. Few will continue to venerate the memory of Guevara after reading this book. See also items **2052** and **2099**. [JMH]

2044 Arubaans akkoord: opstellen over Aruba van vóór de komst van de olieindustrie [Aruban accord: essays on Aruba before the oil industry]. Edited by Luc Alofs, Wim Rutgers, and Henny E. Coomans. Bloemendaal, The Netherlands: Libri Antilliani, 1997. 271 p.: ill., photos, tables.

Includes 30 essays in memory of Johan Hartog, founding father of Aruban historiography. Volume lacks coherence, as authors sketch a variety of topics concerning Aruban history in the pre-oil era (i.e., before 1924). Discusses Aruba's history as found in archives, museums, and monuments; the Amerindian legacy; the West India Company; legal history; education; economic and cultural history; and representation. [RH]

2045 Bangou, Henri. Mémoires du présent: témoignages sur une société créole de l'après-guerre à nos jours. Point-à-Pitre, Guadeloupe: Jasor, 1991. 251 p., 16 p. of plates: ill.

Rich autobiography of Guadeloupe's most prominent leftist politician since 1960s. Of modest origins, Bangou retraces his early career as a physician concerned with the poor, his lifetime affiliation with the Communist Party, and successful career as MP and mayor of Guadeloupe's first city, in a complex political setting both Caribbean and French. [APD]

2046 Barbados: thirty years of independence. Edited by Trevor A. Carmichael. Kingston: Ian Randle Publishers, 1996. 294 p.: bibl., ill., index.

Collection of 11 essays by scholars and business and other professionals examines island nation's performance during its 30 years of independence. Topics include the economy, political system, and educational development. [ELC]

2047 Barceló Miiler, María de Fátima. La lucha por el sufragio femenino en Puerto Rico, 1896–1935. San Juan: Centro de Investigaciones Sociales; Río Piedras, P.R.: Ediciones Huracán, 1997. 239 p.: bibl.

Thorough account of efforts of Puerto Rican women to obtain the right to vote. Author is careful to place the suffragist campaign in the complicated context of party politics, the colonial condition, and traditional attitudes toward women. In 1929 Puerto Rico became the second Latin American country to allow women into the polling place. [TMV]

Baud, Michiel. Patriarchy and changing family strategies: class and gender in the Dominican Republic. See item **1940.**

2048 Bertram, Arnold. P.J. Patterson: a mission to perform. Kingston: AB Associates and Supreme Printers and Publishers, 1995. 133 p.: bibl., ill., index.

Brief, interesting, and revealing first biography of Jamaica's prime minister. A political colleague of Patterson, author served as his special advisor at the time this book was being written. Author used Patterson's papers and interviewed family members and associates. [ELC]

2049 Bordes, Ary. Un médecin raconte: une vie, une carrière. v. 1. Port-au-Prince: Editions H. Deschamps, 1989. 1 v. (Col. Témoin)

A Haitian physician critiques implementation of public health programs in Haiti from 1950–70, with international organizations relying uncritically on a corrupt government. These memoirs vividly evoke the extreme conditions of poverty, malnutrition, and innumerable pathologies endured by Haitian people. [APD]

Bulletin de la Société d'histoire de la Guadeloupe. See item **1945.**

Cabrera Déniz, Gregorio José. Canarios en Cuba: un capítulo en la historia del archipiélago, 1875–1931. See item **1946.**

Campbell, Carl C. The young colonials: a social history of education in Trinidad and Tobago, 1834–1939. See item **1949.**

2050 Carr, Barry. Mill occupations and soviets: the mobilisation of sugar workers in Cuba, 1917–1933. (*J. Lat. Am. Stud.,* 28:1, Feb. 1996, p. 129–158, table)

Thoroughly demolishes most of the legends fabricated about the role of the Partido Comunista de Cuba in the establishment of soviets in the Cuban sugar mills and estates after the 1933 collapse of the Machado dictatorship. [JMH]

2051 Cassá, Roberto. Conformación de las fuerzas políticas en la transición posdictatorial de República Dominicana. (*Ibero americana/Stockholm,* 25:1/2, 1995, p. 73–98)

Lucid account of the factors that shaped political forces in the Dominican Republic after the fall of Trujillo. [JMH]

2052 Castañeda, Jorge G. *Compañero:* the life and death of Che Guevara. New York: Alfred A. Knopf, 1997. 456 p.: index, photos.

Author regards Guevara as an icon of his own generation, and this fact is reflected in the book. He is not as familiar with Cuban history as he might have been, and he tends to overstate Guevara's role in the Cuban Revolution. Nevertheless, he has unearthed new information about Guevara and generally has remained faithful to the facts. The biography is not as good as Anderson's (see item **2043**), but better than many others. [JMH]

2053 Charles, George Frederick Lawrence.
The history of the labour movement in St. Lucia, 1945–1974: a personal memoir. Edited by Didacus Jules and Lawrence Poyotte. Castries, St. Lucia: Folk Research Centre, 1994. 98 p.: ill.

The author, a prominent labor leader and later government minister, offers an insider's perspective on the political system during the island's crucial transitional period of decolonization. Recounts difficulties faced by labor movement in promoting universal adult suffrage and the right to paid leave for workers. Very useful. [ELC]

2054 Chase, Ashton. Guyana—a nation in transit: Burnham's role. Georgetown?: A. Chases, 1994. 186 p.: ill.

More than simply a biography of Forbes Burnham, the political leader who led Guyana to independence and remained at the political helm for many years. Provides wider backdrop on Guyana's economic and social history and on political activities and aspirations of the nation as a whole. Completed in 1989, book suffers somewhat from absence of revisionist perspectives of Burnham that appeared over the past eight years. A contemporary and comrade-in-arms of Burnham, author's sympathy is obvious. [ELC]

2055 Chathuant, Dominique. Dans le sillage de la marine de guerre: pouvoir et Eglise en Guadeloupe, 1940–1943. (*Bull. Soc. hist. Guadeloupe,* 103, 1995, p. 40–64, appendix, facsims.)

Insightful and well-researched piece on Guadeloupe's political history during

WWII documents the colony's gradual shift from *Vichysme* to *Gaullisme,* departing on many points from accepted official version. Focuses on key ecclesiastical personalities and on incidents involving political and naval authorities, aptly conveying the strange, volatile situation that ensued as the colony was cut off from France. [APD]

2056 Chathuant, Dominique. Eglise et vie politique en Martinique et en Guadeloupe: notes sur un histoire à construire. (*Cah. Adm. Outre-Mer,* 6/7, 1995, p. 19–35)

Useful contribution for understanding role of the Church and religion in political history of WWII. Analyzing well-chosen and documented incidents, author shows that both *vichistes* and *gaullistes* courted the ecclesiastical hierarchy and called on popular religiosity to strengthen their position. [APD]

2057 Clark, Truman R. Prohibition in Puerto Rico, 1917–1933. (*J. Lat. Am. Stud.,* 27:1, Feb. 1995, p. 77–97)

Explains launching of prohibition in 1917 and its demise in 1933 as strictly a function of Puerto Rico's colonial status. Puerto Ricans voted for the measure, the author argues, out of loyalty to the US and (in the case of the Partido Socialista and Partido Unión) to party leaders. The measure's failure resulted only from the difficulties of enforcement and not from opposition on the part of island parties. [TMV]

2058 Colón, Alice; Margarita Mergal; and
Nilsa Torres. Participación de la mujer en la historia de Puerto Rico: las primeras décadas del siglo veinte. New Brunswick: Rutgers, State Univ. of New Jersey, 1986. 66 p.: bibl., ill.

Brief, straightforward account of struggle for women's rights in early-20th century covers entrance of women into labor force, their political mobilization, and their limited successes. Although targeting a young reading public, booklet is solidly researched and carefully argued. [TMV]

2059 The commuter nation: perspectives on
Puerto Rican migration. Edited by Carlos Antonio Torre, Hugo Rodríguez Vecchini, and William Burgos. Río Piedras, P.R.: Editorial de la Univ. de Puerto Rico, 1994. 401 p.: bibl.

Key scholars provide comprehensive coverage of central issues in historiography of Puerto Rican migration to US. Includes chapters on economic forces, family life, impact on women, education, literature, music, return migration, and political status. Excellent bibliography. [TMV]

2060 Cox, Edward L. Religious intolerance and persecution: the Shakers of St. Vincent, 1900–1934. (*J. Caribb. Hist.*, 28:2, 1994, p. 208–242)

Studies discrimination against an Afro-Caribbean religious group in early-20th century. Members were fined and imprisoned for holding religious meetings and engaging in religious ceremonies that authorities had outlawed. This religious persecution constituted a form of social and political control. [ELC]

De Asturias a América: Cuba, 1850–1930; la comunidad asturiana de Cuba. See item 1961.

2061 Diocèse des Gonaïves (Haiti). Commission Justice et paix. La répression au quotidien en Haïti, 1991–1994. Direction de Gilles Danroc et Daniel Roussière. Paris: Karthala; Port-au-Prince: H.S.I., 1995. 298 p.: ill. (some col.), maps.

Key observers continue to document the contemporary plight of the Haitian people and their difficulty in establishing a viable democracy and economy. These reports, written for human rights organizations on behalf of the Comission Justice et paix of the Catholic Diocese of Gonaïves, focus on the terror and repression affecting the rural area of the Artibonite around the time of the Cédras coup, and constitute an invaluable source for future historians of those years. [APD]

2062 Edwards, Harriet. The Colonial Office response to the Trevor Williams 1947 report on conditions in Trinidad. (*J. Caribb. Hist.*, 28:1, 1994, p. 84–98)

Suggests that the report by Williams, whose investigation was sponsored by a British newspaper, was not markedly different from Moyne Commission's, and received lukewarm support from Parliament. Internal memos reveal that financial considerations prevented the British government, however receptive it was to the idea of change and improving working conditions, from taking meaningful action. [ELC]

2063 Epailly, Eugène. Francis Lagrange, bagnard, faussaire génial. Cayenne?: s.n., 1994. 171 p.: bibl., ill. (some col.).

Intended for a wide audience, but also useful for research, work presents a lively picture of Devil's Island in the 1940s and of one of the last convicts, a well-known figure. A talented artist, Lagrange illustrated the work with his own paintings. [APD]

2064 Fernández Aponte, Irene. El cambio de soberanía en Puerto Rico: otro '98. Madrid: Editorial MAPFRE, 1992. 438 p.: bibl., ill., indexes. (Col. Independencia de Iberoamérica; 8. Col. MAPFRE 1492)

Uses primary documents and contemporary literature to flesh out the "other '98," the more human aspects of the change in Puerto Rico's sovereignty. Although she covers the expected themes—political dislocations, worker unrest, the 1899 hurricane, emigration, modifications in trade policy, agricultural restructuring, educational reform -, she focuses on people's reactions to change and the daily struggle to adjust to circumstances, rather than on government-level decisions and macro effects. [TMV]

2065 French, Joan. Women and colonial policy in Jamaica after the 1938 uprising. (*in* Subversive women: women's movements in Africa, Asia, Latin America and the Caribbean. Atlantic Highlands, N.J.: Zed Books Ltd., 1995, p. 121–146, tables)

Argues that conservative feminism imported from Great Britain found expression in various colonial development and welfare acts passed before and after the Moyne Commission Report. By promoting the idea that the roles and obligations of men and women fell into separate spheres, report recommendations and adopted policies had a profound impact on middle- and working-class women. [ELC]

2066 Fuente García, Alejandro de la. Raça e desigualdade em Cuba, 1899–1981. (*Estud. Afro-Asiát.*, 27, abril 1995, p. 7–43, bibl., graphs, tables)

Although race and racial inequality are difficult subjects to approach from the perspective of 20th-century US, the author is far more objective and dispassionate than most of his predecessors. For sociologist's comment, see *HLAS 57:4831*. [JMH]

2067 Furniss, H.W. Seule l'intervention étrangère peut réformer le régime haïtien. (*Rev. Soc. haïti.*, 182, déc. 1994, p. 17–51)

Welcome publication of a confidential 1909 report to the Dept. of State from the US Ambassador to Haiti. After a thorough diagnosis of Haiti's plight, the black liberal diplomat concludes by advocating foreign intervention to bring about structural change, rather than the imposition of customs controls—the solution adopted two years earlier in the case of Santo Domingo. [APD]

2068 Gaillard, Roger. La république exterminatrice. v. 5, Le grand fauve. Port-au-Prince: R. Gaillard, 1995. 1 v.

Haiti's senior political historian adds a new volume to his history of Haiti, as it can be reconstituted from the press. Volume focuses on years surrounding the US intervention, stressing particularly the weakness of the state as epitomized by General Nord-Alexis' defeat of the democratic forces that rallied around Joseph-Anténor Firmin in 1902. Nine years later Nord-Alexis himself would be replaced by another military figure. [APD]

Galloway, J.H. Botany in the service of empire: the Barbados cane-breeding program and the revival of the Caribbean sugar industry, 1880s–1930s. See item **1969.**

2069 García, María Cristina. Havana USA: Cuban exiles and Cuban Americans in South Florida, 1959–1994. Berkeley: Univ. of California Press, 1996. 290 p.: bibl., index.

Useful as a general survey, though it does contain some errors. Work is not altogether fair-minded, and some of the names mentioned in the Cubanology section do not belong there. [JMH]

2070 García-Passalacqua, Juan M. Hegemón: otredad y mismidad de la otra cara. San Juan: Editorial Cultural, 1994. 136 p.: bibl., ill. (Col. Ambos mundos)

Analyzing more than 100 texts produced by what author considers the US establishment, he identifies six paradigmatic changes in the colonialist discourse toward Puerto Rico. The US saw the island first as a "problem," then as a "model," a "dilemma," and a "challenge." The relationship reached a "crisis" point in 1972–84, and seemed to

be heading toward "solution" after 1984 and up to the time of writing. At stake throughout the century has been recognition of a separate Puerto Rican nationality. Author concludes that despite Hegemón's attempts to absorb Puerto Rico into "sameness," the island has maintained its "otherness." [TMV]

Gleijeses, Piero. Cuba's first venture in Africa: Algeria, 1961–1965. See *HLAS 57:4241.*

Gleijeses, Piero. Truth or credibility: Castro, Carter and the invasions of Shaba. See *HLAS 57:4243.*

Grant, Rudolph W. Politics, religion and education: the Canadian Presbyterian Church and the struggle over schools in Guyana. See *HLAS 57:3274.*

2071 Guerrero, Miguel. Trujillo y los héroes de junio. Santo Domingo: M. Guerrero, 1996. 342 p.: bibl., ill., index.

Account of consequences of the Cuban-organized anti-Trujillo expeditions that landed in the Dominican Republic on June 14 and 20, 1959. Lack of footnotes indicating sources is a drawback. [JMH]

2072 History Gazette. No. 72, Sept. 1994. International perceptions of the People's Progressive Party by 1953 by James G. Rose and John Williams. Turkeyen, Guyana: Univ. of Guyana, History Society.

Negative perceptions of People's Progressive Party (PPP) by British and US before 1953 came to head at elections. Argues that because Janet Jagan and other leaders of PPP were labelled communists by US intelligence community, concerns and uneasiness grew in minds of imperial powers in post-WWII era of rigid international poles and emerging Cold War, when Caribbean basin was deemed strategically important by Western powers. [ELC]

2073 Howe, Glenford D. In the crucible: race, power and military socialization of West Indian recruits during the First World War. (*J. Caribb. Stud.*, 10:3, Summer/Fall 1995, p. 163–181)

Analyzes manner in which civilian volunteers were turned into professional soldiers and ways in which racism affected their adjustment to army life. [ELC]

2074 Howe, Glenford D. West Indian blacks and the struggle for participation in the First World War. (*J. Caribb. Hist.*, 28:1, 1994, p. 27–62)

In this carefully argued article, author uses British West Indian newspapers to evaluate local participation in the war. Locals saw participation in war as means of showing their loyalty and as bargaining chip for enhanced political participation. [ELC]

2075 Ibarra Guitart, Jorge Renato. La SAR: dictadura, mediación y revolución, 1952–1955. La Habana: Editorial de Ciencias Sociales, 1994. 85 p.: bibl. (Pinos nuevos. Ensayo)

Author's heavily ideological perspective mars what might have been a useful first approach to the subject. [JMH]

Irish, J.A. George. Life in a colonial crucible: labor and social change in Montserrat, 1946-present. See *HLAS 57:3297.*

2076 Issa, Suzanne. Mr. Jamaica, Abe Issa: a pictorial biography. Edited by Jackie Ranston. Kingston: S. Issa, 1994. 188 p.: photos.

Compiled by Issa's daughter, this popular book, with a generous supply of interesting photographs, highlights the life of an individual who played a major role in the development of Jamaica's tourist and hotel industries and served as a member of parliament. Extremely important. [ELC]

2077 Jarvis, Kelvin A. The Historical Society of Trinidad and Tobago, 1932–1955. (*Rev. Rev. Interam.*, 25:1/4, enero/dic. 1995, p. 45–71, appendices, table)

Traces history of the Historical Society of Trinidad and Tobago from its founding in 1932 by Dr. K.S. Wise, Surgeon General, to its subsequent focus on cultural issues, local history, and archeological sites under Eric Williams' leadership in 1950s. Provides lists of speakers and topics they covered, publications of the Society, and membership data. [ELC]

2078 Klerk, C.J.M. de. Cultus en ritueel van het orthodoxe Hindoeïsme in Suriname: de immigratie der hindostanen in Suriname [Cultus and ritual of orthodox Hinduism in Suriname: the immigration of Hindustani in Suriname]. The Hague: Amrit, 1998. 539 p.: bibl., photos, tables.

Extremely useful reprint of two classic works by Father C. de Klerk on the community of contract laborers from British India and their descendants in Suriname. The first part comprises his dissertation (1951) on rituals of orthodox Hindus in Suriname in the first half of the 20th century. The second part, on the immigration of indentured laborers from India, was first published in 1953 and still is considered a standard work. Includes a brief introduction to the life and work of De Klerk and a number of photographs of him in Suriname. [RH]

2079 Maldonado, A.W. Teodoro Moscoso and Puerto Rico's Operation Bootstrap. Gainesville: Univ. Press of Florida, 1997. 262 p.: bibl., ill., index.

Highly personal and admiring commissioned biography of the architect of Puerto Rico's 1940s-50s industrialization program relies heavily on interviews and personal papers made available by Moscoso's family. For international relations specialist's comment, see *HLAS 57:4269.* [TMV]

2080 Malone, Shelley Boyd and **Richard Campbell Roberts.** Nostalgic Nassau: picture postcards, 1900–1940. Nassau?: Nassau Nostalgia, 1991. 63 p.

Reproduces, with brief annotations, picture postcards of the Bahamas from between 1900–40. Portrays some interesting aspects of the history of the country. [ELC]

Mangru, Basdeo. A history of East Indian resistance on the Guyana sugar estates, 1869–1948. See item **1990.**

2081 Mari Brás, Juan. Patria y universo: ideas y sentimientos de un puertorriqueño libre. Mayagüez, P.R.: Causa Común Independentista, Proyecto Educativo Puertorriqueño, 1993. 272 p.: ill.

The author, one of the most respected Puerto Rican independence leaders, presents an eloquent defense of the separatist option published just prior to the 1993 plebiscite. Rejecting the vote as a solution to the "status question," he proposes activism on the part of *independentistas* as a way to sway other Puerto Ricans, the US government, and the international community to support decolonization. He introduces his position with reflections on the political trajectories of Pedro Albizu Campos, Eugenio María de Hostos, and his own. [TMV]

2082 Marqués Dolz, María Antonia. The nonsugar industrial bourgeoisie and industrialization in Cuba, 1920–1959. (*Lat. Am. Perspect.*, 22:4, Fall 1995, p. 59–80, bibl.)

Focuses on the development of non-sugar industry in prerevolutionary Cuba. One of the few studies of its kind. [JMH]

2083 Martin, Tony. Jews to Trinidad. (*J. Caribb. Hist.*, 28:2, 1994, p. 244–257)

Useful study of Jewish community and presence in Trinidad from 1916–40. Argues that community increased considerably in late 1930s as war clouds hovered over Europe. Details assistance efforts for those who relocated to Trinidad, especially activities of the American and local Jewish communities and organizations. [ELC]

Martínez-Fernández, Luis. The sword and the crucifix: Church-State relations and nationality in the nineteenth-century Dominican Republic. See item **1994**.

Menezes, Mary Noel. The Portuguese of Guyana: a study in culture and conflict. See item **2003**.

2084 Michel, Georges. Charlemagne Péralte and the first American occupation of Haiti = Charlemagne Péralte: un centenaire, 1885–1985. Translated by Douglas Henry Daniels. Dubuque, Iowa: Kendall/Hunt Pub. Co., 1996. 88 p., 1 folded leaf of plates: bibl., ill.

Valuable selection of original documents vividly illustrates the 1919 capture of a famous leader, as well as other less well-known aspects of the *caco* insurrection against US troops underway since the previous year. [APD]

2085 Montejo Arrechea, Carmen. El Club Atenas: contexto y propósitos. (*Estud. Hist. Soc. Econ. Am.*, 12, 1995, p. 165–178)

Fair, albeit superficial, description of this predominantly black association is followed by a somewhat tendentious discussion of its fight against racial discrimination throughout Cuba's republican period. [JMH]

Moore, Dennison. Origins & development of racial ideology in Trinidad: the black view of the East Indian. See item **2006**.

2086 Morris, Nancy. Puerto Rico: culture, politics, and identity. Westport, Conn.: Praeger, 1995. 205 p.: bibl., index, maps.

Explores how local political elites have shaped Puerto Rican identity during almost a century of US involvement. Traces Island's political trajectory in its relations with US (pt. 1), and reproduces verbatim interviews with selected political leaders to identify elements that contribute to Puerto Ricans' sense of nationhood (pt. 2). Concludes that, despite pervasiveness of US cultural norms and the pressure to assimilate, Puerto Rican identity remains resilient to this day (pt. 3). [TMV]

2087 Naranjo Orovio, Consuelo and **Armando García González.** Medicina y racismo en Cuba: la ciencia ante la inmigración canaria en el siglo XX. Prólogo de Raquel Alvarez Peláez. Santa Cruz de Tenerife, Spain: Centro de la Cultura Popular Canaria, 1996. 205 p.: bibl., indexes. (Taller de historia; 18)

Work is well researched, but written from the perspective of half a century later. Analysis of historical evidence is faulty; authors do not make clear how the work of the Cuban scientists influenced immigration legislation. [JMH]

2088 Pérez Velasco, Erick J. and **David Baronov.** Bibliografía sobre el movimiento obrero de Puerto Rico, 1873–1996. San Juan: Ediciones Cildes, 1996. 112 p.

Unannotated bibliography for study of Puerto Rico's labor movement is divided into writings by workers, workers' press, reactions to labor movement, government documents, and academic research. Refers readers to depositories for primary sources. [TMV]

2089 Ramesar, Marianne D. Soares. Survivors of another crossing: a history of East Indians in Trinidad, 1880–1946. St. Augustine, Trinidad and Tobago: Univ. of the West Indies, School of Continuing Studies, 1994. 190 p.: bibl., ill. (some col.), index, maps, ports.

Excellent scholarly work, with many worthwhile pictures of East Indian migrants and their descendants, explores the roles and fortunes of this ethnic group. Of particular interest are the details about those who remained after expiration of their indentureship: occupations; savings; land acquisition; religious, social, economic, and political activities; and overall impact on Trinidadian society. Highly recommended. [ELC]

2090 Römer, Amado E.J. Korsou den siglo XX: desaroyo di un pueblo òf tragedia? [Curaçao in the 20th century: development of the population or tragedy?]. Curaçao: Amado E.J. Römer, 1997. 172 p.: bibl., photos, tables.

Chronological overview examines social, demographic, economic, cultural, and religious changes in 20th-century Curaçao. Characterizes years 1900–35 as a period of transition. Major political and socioeconomic changes took place after WWII. Growing self-awareness in 1960s culminated in the revolutionary upheaval of May 30, 1969. Concludes that since 1975 no major ideological or structural changes have taken place. Includes 10-page summary in English. [RH]

2091 Sablé, Victor. Mémoires d'un foyalais: des îles d'Amérique aux bords de la Seine. Paris: Maisonneuve et Larose, 1993. 267 p.: bibl.

Notwithstanding their self-serving aspect, these political memoirs of a Martinique political figure, a member of the colored bourgeoisie and a lawyer by training, provide historians with important testimony of a generation whose decisive action in favor of *départementalisation* stemmed from their adhesion to *France libre* during WWII. Beautifully written and filled with interesting observations on 20th-century Martinican society. [APD]

2092 Salwen, Michael B. The dark side of Cuban journalism: press freedom and corruption before Castro. (*in* Communication in Latin America: journalism, mass media, and society. Wilmington, Del.: Scholarly Resources, Inc., 1996, p. 139–154)

Examines an aspect of Cuban journalism that Cuban writers understandably rarely mention. Author demonstrates that bribes and subsidies were widespread in pre-Castro mass media system, although he fails to cover the subject completely. [JMH]

2093 San Miguel, Pedro Luis. Los campesinos del Cibao: economía de mercado y transformación agraria en la República Dominicana, 1880–1960. San Juan: Decanato de Estudios Graduados e In-

vestigacion; Editorial de la Univ. de Puerto Rico, 1997. 374 p.: bibl., ill.

Major contribution to the histories of the Dominican Republic, the Caribbean, and Latin American peasantries raises important interpretative questions. [JMH]

2094 Sancho, T. Anson. The Green way: a biography of Hamilton Green. Georgetown?: s.n., 1996? 132 p.: bibl., ill.

Overly sympathetic treatment of individual who emerged as important force in Guyana's politics from 1950s onwards. Author's failure to include dates in discussion assumes erroneously that readers will locate material within larger historical landscape. [ELC]

2095 Saunders, Gail. The 1958 general strike in Nassau: a landmark in Bahamian history. (*J. Caribb. Hist.*, 27:1, 1993, p. 81–107)

Excellent analysis of underlying causes of strike. Argues that the well-planned strike started as dispute between cab workers and tour companies and eventually escalated to massive proportions. Strikers called for labor, constitutional, electoral, and social reforms avidly supported by returning students and other migrants. Colonial Office accession to demands, especially constitutional reform, reflects power of the movement, a blending of race and class consciousness. [ELC]

2096 Schmidt, Hans. The United States occupation of Haiti, 1915–1934. New foreword by Stephen Solarz. New Brunswick, N.J.: Rutgers Univ. Press, 1995. 303 p.: bibl., ill., index, map.

Welcome reprint of the authoritative scholarly work on the topic, the first to make use of then recently opened US archival sources. Gives balanced account of the intervention, occupation, and its legacy. For international relations specialist's comment, see *HLAS 57:4292*. For annotations of the first edition, see *HLAS 34:2137* and *HLAS 36:2372*. [APD]

2097 Shannon, Magdaline W. Jean Price-Mars, the Haitian elite and the American occupation, 1915–1935. New York: St. Martin's Press, 1996. 186 p.: bibl., index.

Less than a full biography of Haiti's charismatic nationalist leader and most gifted 20th-century writer, this volume covers period that includes publication of *Ainsi parla l'oncle* (1928) up to his political defeat as president following US withdrawal. Uses Price-Mars' career as a prism for viewing US occupation's political and intellectual impact on Haiti. Focuses on his political commitment to organizing Haiti and mobilizing the press, and his international campaign during early years of US occupation (1916–18). Elaborates on the tenets of his thought: respect for the religious culture of the peasants but lucid criticism of Haitian elites' lack of civic responsibility, and a practical approach toward national unity, including denouncing the prejudices of light-skinned Haitians toward darker Haitians. Written by Price-Mars' American translator. Draws on Haitian, French, and US printed and archival materials. [APD]

Shepherd, Verene A. Transients to settlers: the experience of Indians in Jamaica, 1845–1950. See item **2031.**

2098 Singh, Kelvin. Conflict and collaboration: tradition and modernizing Indo-Trinidadian elites, 1917–56. (*NWIG*, 70:3/4, 1996, p. 229–253, bibl.)

Bemoaning influence that modernizing elites exercised over traditional East Indian cultures, author makes strident call for creation of new Indo-Trinidadian cultural forms that can meaningfully fit into larger cultural milieu of American civilization while simultaneously "maintaining the poise, dignity, and gracefulness that are characteristic of traditional Indian cultural forms." [ELC]

Sommer, Doris. Puerto Rico a flote: desde Hostos hasta hoy. See item **2034.**

Stipriaan, Alex van. Between state and society: education in Suriname, 1850–1950. See item **2035.**

2099 Taibo, Paco Ignacio. Ernesto Guevara: también conocido como el Che. México: Planeta, Editorial J. Mortiz, 1996. 860 p.: bibl., ill. (Horas de Latinoamérica)

Although passable as a literary work and perhaps entertaining, cannot be compared to recent biographies by Anderson (item **2043**) and Castañeda (item **2052**). [JMH]

2100 University of the West Indies (Mona, Jamaica). Garvey: his work and impact. Edited by Rupert Lewis and Patrick E. Bryan. Mona, Jamaica: Institute of Social and Economic Research & Dept. of Extra-Mural Studies, Univ. of the West Indies, 1988. 334 p.: bibl., ill., index.

Contains some papers presented at conference held in Jamaica to mark centenary of Garvey's birth. Aim was to link Garvey's vision with political reality of blacks in Jamaica and the wider world in late-20th century. Contributors are all highly regarded Garvey scholars. Topics include black ethnicity, black political involvement in postemancipation Jamaica, women in Garvey's movement, Garvey and cultural development in Jamaica, mass organizing, and race and economic development. [ELC]

2101 University of the West Indies (Mona, Jamaica). Voices of women in Jamaica, 1898–1939. Compiled by Linnette Vassell. Mona, Jamaica: Dept. of History, Univ. of the West Indies, 1993. 45 p.

Brief selection of writings provides insights into diverse experiences and opinions of women in early 20th-century Jamaica. Their comments on issues ranging from politics to social welfare indicate how they sought to influence the realities they faced, and how their lives were shaped by class, race, gender, and nationality. Especially helpful in obtaining framework for understanding Caribbean and Jamaican feminist perspective. [ELC]

2102 Verstegen, M.A.M. Inpakken onder schijnwerpers: de prijs van het Surinaamse leger [Packing up in the floodlights: the price of the Suriname army]. Amsterdam: Van Soeren, 1997. 104 p.: ill., index.

Former top Dutch government official gives his account of negotiations leading to Suriname's independence in 1975. Highlights discussions on formation of a Surinamese army—the *sine qua non* condition of independence for the Suriname administration. Written in a rather journalistic style. [RH]

2103 Voorhoeve, Jan. Op zoek naar Surinaamse normen: nagelaten geschriften van Jan Voorhoeve, 1950–1961 [In search of Suriname standards: posthumous writings of Jan Voorhoeve, 1950–1961]. Edited by Peter Meel. Utrecht, The Netherlands: Centrum voor Latijns-Amerikaanse en Caraïbische Studies, Univ. Utrecht; Instituut ter Bevordering van de Surinamistiek, 1997. 625 p.: appendix, bibl., photos. (Bronnel voor de studie van Suriname; 20)

Annotated selection of journals, letters, reports, and lectures of Jan Voorhoeve (1923–83) on Suriname demonstrates his versatile scholarly work as a linguist and Bible translator, cultural anthropologist, and man of letters, as well as his many cultural activities relating to Suriname. Meel, in a useful introduction, places Voorhoeve's life and work in the context of Suriname's sociocultural history in the postwar period. Significant contribution to 20th-century history of Suriname. [RH]

2104 Vuurde, Rob van. Engeland, Nederland en de Monroeleer, 1895–1914: Europese belangenbehartiging in de Amerikaanse invloedssfeer [England, The Netherlands, and the Monroe Doctrine, 1895–1914: European protection of interests in the American sphere of influence]. Amsterdam: De Bataafsche Leeuw, 1998. 593 p.: bibl., ill., index.

Well-written thesis on British and Dutch government reactions to, and press commentaries on, the emergence of the American sphere of influence in Latin America and the Caribbean. Divided into four parts, first sections evaluate interests of both countries in the region and their de facto recognition of the American sphere of influence. Last parts are case studies of European actions against Venezuela and Mexico. Study ignores the Latin American side of the debate. Includes English summary. [RH]

2105 Waltmans, Henk and Geert Groothoff. Aruba, Curaçao en Bonaire aan het begin van de twintigste eeuw [Aruba, Curaçao, and Bonaire in the early twentieth century]. Hilversum, The Netherlands: Verloren, 1999. 96 p.: appendix, bibl., ill., photos.

Collection of facsimiles of articles on the Netherlands Antilles from the 9th (Curaçao Special, 1905), 11th (Bonaire Special, 1907), and 15th (Aruba Special, 1911) volumes of the periodical *Neerlandia*. Includes sketchy introduction to socioeconomic and political situation in the Netherlands Antilles from 1900–10 and on the Antilles group of the General Dutch Association (ANV, Algemeen Nederlands Verbond). [RH]

2106 Williams, Gary. Prelude to an intervention: Grenada 1983. (*J. Lat. Am. Stud.*, 29:1, Feb. 1997, p. 131–169, map)

In addition to material from US State Dept. telegrams and other Grenada documents in US National Archives, author uses interviews with US Ambassador Milan Bish and other principals to enhance understanding of crucial pre-intervention period. Errs in assuming that lack of US ambassadorial presence on island translated into absence of US intelligence-gathering apparatus. [ELC]

2107 Woolford, Hazel M. Gender and women in Guianese politics, 1812–1964. (*Guyana Hist. J.*, 111, 1991, p. 13–26)

Focuses on legislation and institutions that excluded women from the franchise, women's supportive role in politics, and their eventual active role as politicians. Also speculates on reasons for low participation of women as candidates. Emphasizes the period after 1940. [ELC]

2108 Worcester, Kent. C.L.R. James and the development of a Pan-African problematic. (*J. Caribb. Hist.*, 27:1, 1993, p. 54–80)

Thought-provoking article regards James' relationship to Pan-African movement as "heterodox, episodic, and in certain respects, problematic—but neither hesitant nor qualified." Examination of James' life is essential to explanation of key difficulties in defining his Pan-Africanism. Concludes that one needs to look beyond Pan-Africanism to understand James' approach to world affairs and his political praxis. [ELC]

Zequeira Sánchez, Mario and Isabel Valdivia Fernández. El papel del cultivo del café para le sociedad y la economía cubana. See *HLAS 57:4947.*

2109 Zonzon, Jacqueline. Ouvrons l'œil sur notre ville: pochette pédagogique. Clichés de Monique Judick et Alexander Miles. Cayenne: Archives départementales de Guyane, Service éducatif; Société des amis des archives et de l'histoire de la Guyane, 1994. 1 portfolio (52 leaves).

Volume of 50 photos is a pleasant introduction to the history of Cayenne, French Guiana's capital city, during the first half of 20th century. [APD]

SPANISH SOUTH AMERICA
General

MICHAEL T. HAMERLY, *Special Project Librarian, John Carter Brown Library, Brown University*

2110 **Arias Altamirano, Luis.** Iglesias parroquiales de la Arquidiócesis de Guayaquil. v. 1. Guayaquil, Ecuador: Editorial Arquidiocesana Justicia y Paz, 1996. 864 p.

Upon completion, this work will be a monumental history of the Archdiocese of Guayaquil—a parish-by-parish account that is based on many years of original research. A treasure trove of data, but unfortunately not indexed. [MTH]

2111 **Guardino, Peter** and **Charles Walker.** Estado, sociedad y política en el Perú y México entre fines de la colonia y comienzos de la republica. (*Histórica/Lima,* 18:1, julio 1994, p. 27–68, bibl.)

Compares and contrasts social, economic, and political developments in Mexico and Peru proper during late colonial, independence, and early national periods. In a bibliographically well-informed, methodologically interesting, and thought-provoking work, the authors, both Peruvianists, critique existing paradigms of the class structure of the two colonies/countries, and propose a new model in which the Túpac Amaru movement becomes "una revolución burguesa inconclusa." [MTH]

2112 **Klaiber, Jeffrey.** Estudios recientes sobre la iglesia en Perú, Bolivia y Ecuador: un balance historiográfico. (*Histórica/Lima,* 19:2, dic. 1995, p. 251–280, bibl.)

Cogent review of literature published during second half of 20th century on Church history of the Central Andean republics. Organized thematically. Includes discussion of studies of Protestant activities. Strong on Peruvian and Bolivian materials, less so on Ecuadorian works. [MTH]

2113 **Lavallé, Bernard.** Bibliografía francesa sobre el Ecuador, 1968–1993: ciencias humanas, sociales y de la tierra. Quito: Cor-

poración Editora Nacional, 1995. 156 p.: index. (Biblioteca de ciencias sociales; 46)

Lists 1,479 French works on Ecuador in the humanities, social sciences, and natural sciences from 1968–93. Some of the works listed, including those in history and related disciplines, have previously gone unnoticed; hence the importance of this timely and well-done bibliography. Indexed by subject, personal name, and place names. [MTH]

2114 **Morelli, Federica.** Doing historical research in Quito: a guide to archives and libraries. (*Itinerario/Leiden,* 18:2, 1994, p. 143–147)

Useful update on status and location of historical archives and research libraries in Quito. [MTH]

2115 **Perry, Richard O.** The frontiers of South America. (*J. West,* 34:4, Oct. 1995, p. 41–47, map, photos)

Insightful overview of the role of frontiers in the history of South America from the Spanish conquest and initial Portuguese incursions through the early-20th century. Also compares and contrasts the frontiers of North America with those of South America. [MTH]

2116 **Vega Vega, Wilson.** Bibliografía del Dr. Carlos Manuel Larrea. (*Memoria/SEIHGE,* 2, 1991/92, p. 261–286)

Lists 253 publications of the late Ecuadorian bibliographer and historian Carlos Manuel Larrea in chronological order, from 1907–88. [MTH]

2117 **Vega Vega, Wilson.** José María Vargas: bibliografía. (*Memoria/SEIHGE,* 1, 1989/90, p. 181–244)

Registers 839 publications of the late Ecuadorian art historian in chronological order, from 1925–1988. [MTH]

Colonial Period

MICHAEL T. HAMERLY, *Special Project Librarian, John Carter Brown Library, Brown University*
SUSAN M. SOCOLOW, *Professor of History, Emory University*
LANCE R. GRAHN, *Associate Professor and Chair of the Department of History, Marquette University*

WE HAVE HAD TO PARE our introductory remarks once again because the onslaught of noteworthy publications on Spain's former colonies in South America continues unabated. There were not nearly as many new books this time around, however, at least not in English. Regrettably it was also a period that saw the demise of a number of distinguished colonialists.

There was little in the way of truly general works. Specialized studies continue to prevail. Even the two especially noteworthy general works are general only in the geographic sense; thematically they are specialized. The first is the closing volume of an Andean history project: *Ethnicity, Markets, and Migration in the Andes: At the Crossroads of History and Anthropology,* individual contributions to which are reviewed in this chapter. This work is the "revised, updated English-language edition" of *La participación indígena en los mercados surandinos* (see *HLAS 50:709*). [MTH]

VENEZUELA

The recent historiography on colonial Venezuela featured here represents two broad categories: regional or local history and the prelude to independence. Neither focus in and of itself is a new departure. But each is represented by fine examples of conscientious research and careful argumentation. Regarding the first group, the overlapping concerns with the collection of data and its explication produced a set of high quality works that especially examined the origins, activities, and influence of local societal sectors, particularly of the elite. For example, Picón-Parra's encyclopedic treatment of Mérida understandably emphasizes the local elite even as it promotes the study of the genealogical and social history of the province (items **2143** and **2144**). Langue, consciously limiting his study to the elite of Caracas, examines the city's internal tensions caused by concerns over regional dominance in a changing political and economic landscape (item **2138**).

Langue's essay also represents the second category of concentration—the evolving dynamics of conflict and accommodation that, from a perspective of hindsight, disrupted colonial stability and propelled the colony toward political independence. Ramón Aizpurua's important study of smuggling in the southern Caribbean demonstrates that Venezuelan merchants and consumers developed their own networks of trade that rivaled, if not replaced, legal networks in response to commercial instability (item **2131**). *Los pardos libres en la colonia y la independencia* (item **2149**) and *José Leonardo Chirino y la insurrección de la serranía de Coro* (item **2137**) advance the role of Afro-Venezuelans in creating a political climate conducive to independence. And Tomás Polanco Alcántara personalizes this tendency toward independence in his biography of Francisco Miranda (item **2145**). Miquel Izard, however, argues that conflict in the llanos prompted by the oligarchy's efforts to expand their economic control and to eliminate the Maroon example of popular autonomy actually set the stage for independence a century earlier (item **2136**).

Two other works deserve special mention here. The collection of essays *Químeras de amor, honor y pecado en el siglo XVIII venezolano* engagingly contemplates the realities of love, marriage, and sexuality in Venezuelan society (item **2147**). Charles Nicholl's *The Creature in the Map* is a superb account of Walter Raleigh's failed search for the fabled El Dorado in the late-16th century (item **2142**).

NUEVA GRANADA

Valuable studies of social and daily life in the New Kingdom of Granada dominate entries in *HLAS 58*, illustrating an engaging creativity and maturity within recent Colombian historiography. For example, Pablo Rodríguez's *Sentimientos y vida familiar en el Nuevo Reino de Granada, siglo XVIII* (item **2180**) and Diana Luz Ceballos Gómez's *Hechicería, brujería e Inquisición en el Nuevo Reino de Granada* (item **2163**) explore quotidian realities of family life and belief systems, respectively, with insight and sensitivity. Though less overtly social, even the monographs of Guido Barona Bacerra (item **2159**) and Renán Silva (item **2183**) effectively frame human existence, the former within the hardening economic situation of Popayán and the latter within the New Granadan academy. Documentary collections such as Tovar Pinzón's four-volume *Relaciones y visitas a los Andes, siglo XVI* (item **2179**), the *Cabildos de San Juan de Pasto, 1573–1579* (item **2161**), and the *Indice de dotes, mortuorias y testamentos existentes en las notarías de Santafé de Bogotá* (item **2168**) help to secure the permanence of the archival foundation for such monographs.

Secondarily, the history of the Caribbean provinces received considerable attention in this biennium. Ceballos Gómez's book is the most noteworthy of this group. But others, though more traditional, also provide useful accounts of society there. Two works present the viceregal government's intent to invigorate colonial society in the north with bold colonization schemes (items **2158** and **2172**). Others, focusing more exclusively on Cartagena city and province, probe the indigenous and African history of the area (items **2173, 2177,** and **2182**). And the late Alvaro Jara, one of the most respected Latin American historians of his generation, examined the fiscal health of the Cartagena treasury (item **2169**). [LRG]

QUITO

Turning to Ecuador, the increase in the quality as well as the quantity of studies continues to be impressive. In fact it has become almost impossible to stay abreast of the flood. Two not so new journals need to be added to the list of historical periodicals: *Memoria*, Sociedad Ecuatoriana de Investigaciones Históricas y Geográficas, 1 (1989–1990) ; and *Revista del Centro Nacional de Investigaciones Genealógicas y Antropológicas*, 1 : 1 (marzo 1981) . The first journal does not appear to be very promising, but the second does. The most significant of the new monographs are: Andrien's superb *The Kingdom of Quito, 1690–1830* (item **2188**); Estrella's magnificent *La "Flora Huayaquilensis" de Juan Tafalla* (item **2208**); Herzog's wholly novel *La administración como un fenómeno social* (item **2217**); Lavallé's revisionist *Quito et la crise de l'alacaba, 1580–1600* (item **2231**); and Tardieu's richly textured *Noirs et nouveaux maîtres dans les "vallées sanglantes" de l'Équateur, 1778- 1820* (item **2263**). Unfortunately, Estrella, who was almost single-handedly revolutionizing the history of science in and scientific expeditions to Ecuador, died in 1996. The increasing internationalization of Ecuadorian studies is best exemplified by Herzog, an Israeli scholar, who literally burst on to the scene in the mid-1990s with three books, published in Spain (item **2217**), Ecuador (item **2219**), and Germany (item **2218**), respectively.

PERU

In Peru the new journal, the *Revista del Archivo Arzobispal de Arequipa* (1994–) is exceptionally important. Carlos J. Díaz Rementaría, the author of *El cacique en el Virreinato del Perú: estudio histórico-jurídico* (*HLAS 44:2582*) died in 1996. For an appreciation of his *oeuvre*, see Hampe Martínez's "In memoriam: Carlos J. Díaz Rementaría (1947 1996)," *Jahrbuch für Geschichte von Staat, Wirtschaft und Gesellschaft lateianamerikas*, 34, 1997, p. 15–20.

The most important of the new and recent books are clearly Damian's multidisciplinarian *The Virgin of the Andes* (item **2288**), J.M. Williams' excellent edition of several of Pedro de Peralta Barnuevo's writings (item **2328**), Sala i Vila's major contribution to the literature on the Túpac Amaru rebellion (item **2335**), the beautiful to view and delightful to read *Santa Rosa de Lima y su tiempo* (item **2292**), and Varón Gabai's pathbreaking work on the financial empire of the Pizarros (item **2345**). As for articles, especially impressive are Aldana Rivera's piece on the participation of indigenas in the market economy of Paita (item **2271**), Cahill's studies of health care in Lima (item **2278**) and popular religion in Cuzco (item **2279**), Dougnac Rodríguez's work on water rights in the valleys of Lima (item **2289**), Huertas' model study of Zaña (item **2310**), Iwasaki Cauti's essay on the all too human Luisa Melgarejo de Soto (item **2311**), and Stavig's novel study of indigenous sexual and marital beliefs and practices (item **2341**).

ALTO PERÚ

Turning to Alto Perú, we note with regret the 1994 passing of María Eugenio del Valle de Siles, the editor of Francisco Tadeo Diez de Medina's *Diario del alzamiento de indios conjurdos contra la Ciudad de Nuestra Señora de La Paz, 1781* (item **2361**). Only a handful of new books appeared, the most novel of which was Rossells' *La gastronomía en Potosí y Charcas* (item **2385**). There were a substantial number of important articles, on the other hand. At the usual risk of being invidious, those that strike this contributor as especially significant are: Gutiérrez Brockington's two studies of the quasi-forgotten Corregimiento of Mizque (items **2357** and **2358**); Lema's and Meruvia's essays on the *yungas* (items **2371** and **2380**, respectively); the several extracts from López Beltrán's Columbia University doctoral dissertation on the elite of 17th-century La Paz (items **2373, 2376,** and **2374**) and and the usual solid contributions by Santamaría (items **2387** and **2388**) and Tandeter (items **2394, 2395,** and **2396**).

CHILE

The field continues to be dominated by national scholars, two of the greatest of whom are no longer with us. Rolando Mellafe died in 1995, and Alvaro Jara in 1998. However, the Spanish historian Francisco de Solano, who also died recently (in 1996), left us new major sets of coeval sources, *Relaciones económicas del Reino de Chile, 1780* (item **2410**) and *Relaciones geográficas del Reino de Chile, 1756* (1992). The most important of the recent monographs are Foerster's *Jesuitas y*

mapuches, 1593–1767 (item **2403**), unfortunately written in postmodernistic qualitative discourse—an idiom desperately in need of desobfuscation—Villalobos'
more easily digested *La vida fronteriza en Chile* (item **738**), both of which are revisionist studies. The best of the somewhat reduced crop of articles were Larrain's
re-examination of the terms of trade during the second half of the colonial period
(item **2404**) and Salinas Meza's pioneering study of "La violencia conyugal y el rol
de la mujer en la sociedad chilena tradicional" (item **2412**). [MTH]

RIO DE LA PLATA

Social history continues to be an important topic for historians of the Rio de la
Plata region. Of note is the work of Aguirre and Petit on apprentices (item **2419**),
those of Martínez de Sánchez on urban meat supply and dress (items **2467** and
2468, respectively), Porro and Barbero on material culture (item **2480**), and Ferreiro
on Jujuy encomenderos (item **2442**). Work on land and labor, another important
topic within the region's historiography, continues to result in generally high quality research. Especially interesting are the article by Garavaglia and Gelman (item
2446), the works by Azcuy Ameghino (item **2426**) and the "Azcuy group" (item
2427), Barba (item **2428**), and Birocco (item **2434**), as well as studies concentrating
on the northwestern and northeastern interior by López de Albornoz (items **2457**
and **2458**), Mata de Lápez (items **2470** and **2471**), J.C. Pistoia (item **2478**), and
Rivarola Paoli (item **2486**).

   Interest continues in local and long-distance trade in the region (Alvarez Pantoja (item **2422**), Bellotto (item **2429**), Bentancur (item **2431**), Palomeque (item
2477), Silva (item **2495**) and Tejerina (item **2501**)). Also noteworthy are two studies
of political organization by E.O. Acevedo (item **2418**) and Bentancur (item **2430**).
Missions and frontiers continue to be of interest to several scholars, with a new
focus on relations between Spaniards and indigenous peoples along the frontier
(A.M. Acevedo (item **2416**), Alemán (item **2420**), Areces (item **2425**), Neumann
(item **2475**), Ras (item **2483**), and Santamaría (item **2489**)); and in Jesuit and non-
Jesuit attempts at extending their missions outside of the famous Misiones region
(Machón (item **2462**), Martínez Martín, (item **2469**), Maeder (item **2463**), and B.H.
Pistoia (item **2478**)). Not to be overlooked is Lucía Gálvez's synthesis of everyday
life in the Jesuit missions (item **2445**). Another productive field is that of historical
demography, as demonstrated by a number of works reviewed this biennium
(Boleda (item **2435**), Ghirardi de Millar (item **2448**), and Ulloa (item **2502**)).

   We applaud the publication of primary sources, including Cardiel's *Breve
relación de las misiones del Paraguay* (item **2436**), *Cartas y documentos coloniales
de Mendoza* (item **2438**), Maziel's *De la justicia del tratado de límites* (item **2472**),
and Varanda's *Miscelánea histórico-política* (item **2503**), a new contribution to
paleography by Tanodi de Chiapero, (item **2500**) and several fine bibliographies and
catalogs (Delgado and Martínez (item **2439**) Gabbi and Martín de Codoni (item
2444), Melia and Nagel (item **2473**), and Santos Martínez (item **2465**)). The fine
attempt at popular synthesis of the colonial history of the region undertaken by
Luna is also worthy of note (item **2461**).

   Some other tendencies worthy of note include a slow increase in studies that
extend our knowledge of the region into the 17th century. Although women's history is almost absent from the articles reviewed here, there is a notable increase in
the number of women working on different aspects of the region's history. Lastly,
the high quality of articles on more distant part of the region and on Paraguay and
Uruguay is an encouraging sign. [SMS]

GENERAL

2118 Bravo Acevedo, Guillermo. Historiografía de la empresa económica jesuita en Hispano América colonial. (*Universum/Talca*, 10, 1995, p. 5–16, bibl., ill.)

Reviews literature on economic activities of the Jesuits throughout Spanish America during colonial period. Discusses most of the major and some of the minor studies. [MTH]

2119 Congreso de Manifestaciones Religiosas en el Mundo Colonial Americano, *1st, Tlaxcala, Mexico, 1991.* Manifestaciones religiosas en el mundo colonial americano. v. 1–2. México: Centro de Estudios de Historia de México Condumex; INAH, Dirección de Estudios Históricos; Univ. Iberoamericana, Depto. de Historia, 1993. 2 v.: bibl.

Major set of original, mostly insightful, and occasionally innovative, essays on multiple aspects of the role of ordinary men and women, and nuns, in the religious life of colonial Spanish America. Examines the multifaceted manifestations of religion in daily life, especially in Mexico and Peru, from 16th-18th centuries. For literary specialist's comment, see item **3456.** [MTH]

2120 Cortés Alonso, Vicenta. El Padre Lino Gómez Canedo y los archivos: aportes a la historia hispanoamericana. (*Arch. Ibero-Am.*, 57:225/226, enero/dic. 1997, p. 861–872)

An appreciation of the career of the extraordinarily productive Lino Gómez Canedo and of his many contributions to the historiography of the colonial period. Father Lino contributed to the *Handbook of Latin American Studies* for many decades. Among his basic works is the still indispensable *Los archivos de la historia de América: período colonial español.* See *HLAS 25:3043* and *HLAS 28:416.* [MTH]

2121 Demélas-Bohy, Marie-Danielle. Modalidades y significación de elecciones: generales en los pueblos andinos, 1813–1814. (Historia de las elecciones en Iberoamérica, siglo XIX: de la formación del espacio político nacional. Coordinación de Antonio Annino. Buenos Aires: Fondo de Cultura Económica, 1995, p. 291–313, tables)

Comparative study examines reaction of Spanish towns, ethnically mixed communities, and indigenous *pueblos* in what are now Ecuador, Peru, and Bolivia, to the call for elected representatives as stipulated in the Constitution of Cádiz. Interesting contribution to the history of elections and early flirtations with "democracy" in the Andean region. [MTH]

2122 Erauso, Catalina de. Lieutenant nun: memoir of a Basque transvestite in the New World. Translated from the Spanish by Michele Stepto and Gabriel Stepto. Foreword by Marjorie Garber. Boston: Beacon Press, 1996. 80 p.

English version of *Historia de la monja alférez* (1988), the "autobiographical" account of a Basque woman who fled convent life in Spain; made her way to the Indies disguised as a page boy; and spent 22 years as a soldier in the colonies, mostly in Chile and the Perus, in early 17th century. Traditionally rejected as a work of fiction, Catalina de Erauso's story has been verified—to the extent that verification is possible—as well as authenticated by recent scholarship. [MTH].

Ethnicity, markets, and migration in the Andes: at the crossroads of history and anthropology. See *HLAS 57:1040.*

2123 Fritz, Samuel. Diario. Presentado por Hernán Rodríguez Castelo. Quito: Academia Ecuatoriana de la Lengua; Academia Nacional de Historia del Ecuador, 1997. 154 p.: bibl., map.

New edition of a work that heretofore has been easier to obtain in English (*Journal of the travels and labours of Father Samuel Fritz in the River of the Amazons between 1688 and 1723* (1922)) than in the original Spanish. A major source for the study of the historical geography of the Upper Amazon Basin as well as for the history of the Jesuit missions in the area. [MTH]

2124 Garner, Richard L. Long-term silver mining trends in Spanish America: a comparative analysis of Peru and Mexico. (*in* Mines of silver and gold in the Americas. Edited by Peter Bakewell. Aldershot, Great Britain; Brookfield, Vt.: Variorum, 1997, p. 225–262, graphs, tables)

Useful summary of a considerable body of quantifiable data regarding mine output in colonial Mexico and the Perus (Lower and Upper), and inputs, especially labor, re-

quired to sustain the production of silver.
[MTH]

2125 Hampe Martínez, Teodoro. El libro en el Virreinato del Perú: siglos XVI-XVII. (*in* Páginas sobre Hispanoamérica colonial: sociedad y cultura. Buenos Aires: PRHISCO-CONICET, 1995, v. 2, p. 11–23, appendix, table)

This study is similar to one that appeared in *HAHR* (73:2, May 1993, p. 211–233), on which see *HLAS 54:2380*. In this regard, it will be recalled that Hampe Martínez tends to publish his work in multiple venues and versions. [MTH]

2126 Mazzeo, Cristina Ana. Tradición y modernidad en el comerciante peruano a fines del XVIII: un estudio comparativo. (*Rev. Arch. Gen. Nac.*, 12, 1995, p. 147–160)

Compares careers of Mexican Pedro Romero de Terreros, the aristocracy of Zacatecas, the Anchorena family of Buenos Aires, and Peruvian José Antonio de Lavalle y Cortés in order to establish strategies employed by merchants of the late colonial period to survive and prosper in the face of the major changes taking place in their world. Fascinating study enriches the pioneering historiography upon which it is built. [MTH]

2127 Navarro, José Gabriel. Estudios históricos. Recopilación de Wilson Vega. Presentación de Jorge Salvador Lara. Quito: Aymesa; Academia Nacional de Historia, 1995. 536 p. (Col. Grupo Aymesa)

Welcome compendium of a number of Navarro's lesser-known contributions to the historiography of the colonial period. Although Navarro (1881–1965) is best remembered as the pioneer art historian of Ecuador, he also cultivated a number of other historical genres. This anthology includes his pathbreaking and still basic *Epigrafía quiteña* (1918), his works on the descendants of Atahualpa and on the municipality in the Spanish colonies, five essays on the Franciscans in the Americas, and miscellaneous essays on the history of the road to Esmeraldas. [MTH]

2128 Ramón, Armando de. Rol de lo urbano en la consolidación de la Conquista: los casos de Lima, Potosí y Santiago de Chile, 1535–1625. (*Rev. Indias*, 55:204, mayo/agosto 1995, p. 391–419)

Comparative study of Lima, Potosí,

and Santiago during consolidation of Spanish conquest and first century of the colonization of the future Peru, Bolivia, and Chile is interesting for its focus on the role of the city as intermediary between the Crown and the conquered. [MTH]

2129 Tardieu, Jean-Pierre. La mano de obra negra en las minas del Perú colonial, fines del s. XVI-comienzos del s. XVII: de los principios morales al oportunismo. (*Histórica/Lima*, 19:1, julio 1995, p. 119–144, bibl., map)

Well-informed review, with new archival data, on utilization of slave labor in the gold mines of southern Ecuador and the silver mines of Upper and Lower Peru. [MTH]

2130 Vitar, Beatriz. Las fronteras "bárbaras" en los virreinatos de Nueva España y Perú. (*Rev. Indias*, 55:203, enero/abril 1995, p. 33–66)

Comparative study of the Spanish occupation of northern New Spain (or the Gran Chichimeca and beyond) and of the "cattle frontier" of Tucumán in the Río de la Plata (an area "menaced" by the Guaycuru). Includes new archival data on the history of the Tucumán region and adds to our knowledge of the little-known Guaycuru and the eventual Spanish occupation of the Chaco. [MTH]

VENEZUELA

2131 Aizpurua, Ramón. Curazao y la costa de Caracas: introducción al estudio del contrabando de la provincia de Venezuela en tiempos de la Compañía Guipuzcoana, 1730–1780. Caracas: Academia Nacional de Historia, 1993. 417 p.: bibl. (Biblioteca de la Academia Nacional de la Historia. Fuentes para la historia colonial de Venezuela; 222)

Important study of the dynamics of smuggling and influence of illicit trade on the development of late colonial Venezuelan economy. Tied into the ebb and flow of both international war and the Caracas company, contraband trafficking in hides, mules, tobacco, and cacao, exchanged for products such as comestibles, textiles, and slaves, reflected regional commercial norms. Smuggling therefore developed its own infrastructure that paralleled and even overlapped legal networks of provincial exchange and influence. [LRG]

2132 Antonio de Berrío: la obsesión por El Dorado. Estudio preliminar y selección documental de José Rafael Lovera. Caracas: Petróleos de Venezuela, 1991. 477 p.: bibl., ill. (Col. V centenario del encuentro entre dos mundos,1492–1992, 1498–1998)

A collection of nearly 40 documents related to Berrío's governorship of Trinidad and his quest for El Dorado in central Venezuela (Guiana) in the 1580s and 1590s. Already in his 50s when he and his family migrated to the New World to assume the territorial and political legacy left him by his wife's uncle, the great New Granadan conquistador Gonzalo Jiménez de Quesada, Berrío's late adult life illustrated the power of the El Dorado myth among Spaniards and Britons alike; Berrío and Walter Raleigh crossed swords in 1595 when the latter first sought the fabled area. Berrío's late career also demonstrates the continuation of the conquest era through late-16th century. Handsomely printed and nicely illustrated with reproductions of De Bry engravings. A useful companion to this book is Charles Nicholl's study of Raleigh's expedition, *The Creature in the Map,* see **2142.** [LRG]

2133 Arcila Farías, Eduardo and **Federico Brito Figueroa.** Política colonizadora y desarrollo de la propriedad territorial en Venezuela. Mérida, Venezuela: Univ. de Los Andes, Consejo de Publicaciones, 1997. 87 p.: bibl. (Col. Ciencias sociales. Serie Historia)

Republishes essays by two of Venezuela's premier historians, Eduardo Arcila Farías and Federico Brito Figueroa, which originally appeared in 1968 and 1973, respectively. Both continue to be useful introductory surveys of land tenure patterns, not only in colonial Venezuela but throughout Spanish America with their sketches of private, communal, corporate, and state land ownership. [LRG]

2134 Avellán de Tamayo, Nieves. En la ciudad de El Tocuyo: 1545–1600. v. 1–2. Caracas: Academia Nacional de la Historia, 1997. 2 v.: bibl., ill. (some col.), indexes. (Biblioteca de la Academia Nacional de la Historia. Fuentes para la historia colonial de Venezuela; 232–233)

Called an homage to the city of El Tocuyo, which was established in 1545 and ceased to exist 400 years later, the work is more a comprehensive encyclopedia of the city's 16th-century history than an analytical treatment. Yet, as an informational "vision of the complex process of formation, growth, and permanence" of a city established by first-generation Venezuelan conquerors, this 2-volume work is fundamental. [LRG]

2135 Hernández González, Manuel. Los campesinos canarios en el valle de Caracas, 1780–1810. (*Montalbán/Caracas,* 28, 1995, p. 63–82, bibl., table)

Although the substantial Canary Islander presence in the valley of Caracas declined in the late-18th century as a result of growth of the peninsular population, pressures on the land there, and opportunities in the Llanos, tensions between immigrant smallholders and the oligarchy grew in response to the expansion of coffee and indigo production. Still, as local notarial records demonstrate, the Canary Islander community in the Caracas region maintained a strong sense of collectivity and played an important role in the transformation of the social and economic landscape. [LRG]

2136 Izard, Miquel. Pensando en el sur: el Llano en el siglo XVII. (*Anu. Estud. Am.,* 51:1, 1994, p. 65–89, appendices)

Typical of Izard's clarity and command of sources, this examination of colonial dynamics in the Venezuelan Llanos argues that overlapping battles for cimarron autonomy, expansion of pasturage and herding, and mid-17th-century oligarchical domination set the stage for fateful conflict in the late-18th century. [LRG]

2137 José Leonardo Chirino y la insurrección de la Serranía de Coro de 1795: insurrección de libertad o rebelión de independencia; memoria del simposio realizado en Mérida los días 16 y 17 de noviembre de 1995. Mérida: Univ. de Los Andes: Univ. Central de Venezuela: Univ. del Zulia: Univ. Nacional Experimental Francisco de Miranda, 1996. 225 p.: bibl.

Important collection of 15 essays examines not only the 1795 slave insurrection in Coro and the leadership of José Leonardo Chirino, but also the larger role and purpose of popular rebellion in late colonial Venezuelan society and politics as a precursor to independence. [LRG]

2138 Langue, Frédérique. El círculo de las alianzas: estructuras familiares y estrategias económicas de la élite Mantuana, siglo XVIII. (*Bol. Acad. Nac. Hist./Caracas,* 78:309, enero/marzo 1995, p. 97–121)

Based solidly in primary documentation from the Archdiocesan Archive of Caracas and an impressive array of secondary sources, this study of an "authentically creole" subset of the *caraqueña* elite—those so designated because of their wives' clothing—places its foundations in the cacao economy, its regional character, and its anti-peninsular stance. Nonetheless, the essay best explains both the means (reliance upon the concept of honor and friendship) and roles of marriage (joining together family wealth and bloodlines) in cementing relationships between powerful families but which, ironically, came also to weaken the dominant influence of the planter elite. [LRG]

2139 Leal, Ildefonso. El libro parroquial más antiguo de Los Teques, 1777–1802: libro primero de matrimonios y de gobierno de la Iglesia San Felipe Neri. Los Teques, Venezuela: Alcaldia y Concejo Municipal del Municipio Guaicaipuro; Oficina del Cronista, 1994. 290 p.: ill.

Source book provides transcripts of parish records useful for constructing late colonial social history. Secondarily, this documentary collection reflects the local impact of Bourbon reformism. [LRG]

2140 Moreno Pérez, Amado. Los pueblos de doctrina y las encomiendas en el poblamiento de Mérida: siglos XVII, XVIII, XIX. (*Fermentum/Mérida,* 1:1, mayo/agosto 1991, p. 19–39, appendices, ill., map)

Tabular appendices complement Nelly Velásquez's "Los resguardos de indios en la Provincia de Mérida, siglo XVII" (see item **2155**) and Edda Samudio's "El resguardo indígena en Mérida, siglos XVI al XIX" (see item **2153**). Moreno's overview reiterates that the basis for changes in the region's demographic and land-use patterns in the colonial period was the shift from an emphasis on evangelization to one on the export-oriented economy. [LRG]

2141 Navarro de Andriaensens, José María. Configuración textual de la *Recopilación historial de Venezuela* de Pedro de Aguado. Caracas: Academia Nacional de la

Historia, 1993. 309 p.: bibl. (Biblioteca de la Academia Nacional de la Historia. Fuentes para la historia colonial de Venezuela; 223)

Important critical analysis of Pedro de Aguado's famous 1581 *Recopilación historial de Venezuela* explicates chronicle's language and semiotics, use of character and characterization, narrative style, and metaphorical significance. Navarro emphasizes the text as a construction built by both chronicler and reader, with linguistic and interpretive tools of communication. Work is a useful companion to previous editorial notations on the text by Jerónimo Becker (1918/1919), Juan Friede (1957, *HLAS 20:2708a*), and Guillermo Morón (1987). [LRG]

2142 Nicholl, Charles. The creature in the map: a journey to El Dorado. New York: W. Morrow and Co., 1996. 398 p.: bibl, ill., index, maps.

A highly readable and authoritative account of Walter Raleigh's failed expedition up the Orinoco river to find the fabled El Dorado in mid-1595. Based largely on first-hand accounts such as the Raleigh's own *The Discoverie of Guiana,* Francis Sparry's testimony, and the author's retracing of Raleigh's route, the book not only recounts the expedition itself but also explicates the cultural myth of El Dorado that animated explorers and conquerors like Raleigh and the Spaniard Antonio de Berrío. See also item **2132**. [LRG]

2143 Picón-Parra, Roberto. Fundadores, primeros moradores y familias coloniales de Mérida, 1558–1810. v. 3, Los primeros moradores, 1560–1600. Caracas: Academia Nacional de la Historia, 1993. 1 v.: bibl., index. (Biblioteca de la Academia Nacional de la Historia. Fuentes para la historia colonial de Venezuela; 224)

Comprehensive biographical encyclopedia for genealogical and social history of Mérida prov. in the late-16th century. Like its companion volume (item **2143**), this is a superb reference tool that provides considerable detail about family members. [LRG]

2144 Picón-Parra, Roberto. Fundadores, primeros moradores y familias coloniales de Mérida, 1558–1810. v. 4, Otras familias coloniales, 1601–1810. Caracas: Academia Nacional de la Historia, 1993. 1 v.: bibl., index. (Biblioteca de la Academia Nacional de la Historia. Fuentes para la historia colonial de Venezuela; 224)

Continuation of large project to provide a comprehensive biographical encyclopedia for the genealogical and social history of Mérida prov. Like its earlier companion volume (item **2144**), this is a superb reference tool that provides considerable detail about family members. [LRG]

2145 Polanco Alcántara, Tomás. Francisco de Miranda: ¿Ulises, don Juan o don Quijote? 2. ed. venezolana. Caracas: Editorial Ex Libris, 1997. 332 p.: bibl., ill., maps.

Handsomely illustrated biography by renowned scholar and diplomat seeks to understand human dimensions of the man whose political actions, the author asserts, separated Venezuela's national period from its colonial past. Miranda ultimately emerged as a tragic quixotic figure who could not realize his visionary idealism. [LRG]

2146 Ponce de Behrens, Marianela. El ordenamiento jurídico y el ejercicio del derecho de libertad de los esclavos en la provincia de Venezuela, 1730–1768. Caracas: Academia Nacional de la Historia, 1994. 309 p.: bibl., index. (Biblioteca de la Academia Nacional de la Historia. Fuentes para la historia colonial de Venezuela; 226)

Reproduces 10 groups of documents (*expedientes*) related to slaves gaining their freedom in mid-18th-century Venezuela. Documents had reposed in the Registro Principal del Distrito Federal (Caracas) before being transferred to the national archives. Useful for understanding Hispanic slavery in general, publication is concerned primarily with illustrating legal and regulatory framework of slavery and ways in which slaves used the legal system to earn their freedom. A helpful survey of the administrative context precedes the collected documents. [LRG]

2147 Quimeras de amor, honor y pecado en el siglo XVIII venezolano. Recopilación de Elías Pino Iturrieta. Caracas: Editorial Planeta Venezolana, 1994. 290 p.: bibl. (Voces de la Historia)

Engaging anthology of seven essays examines sociocultural realities of daily life for individual Venezuelans. Two essays explore divorce, one within an aristocratic marriage and one for a free-black couple. Two essays utilize biography to analyze love, honor, and

matrimony within black and *casta* societies. The other three examine sociopolitical dynamics of disjunction between popular standards of sexual morality and actual behavior. [LRG]

2148 Rodrigo Bravo, Fernando. Las elites militares en Venezuela, 1760–1810. (*Estud. Hist. Soc. Econ. Am.*, 12, 1995, p. 505–585, tables)

Collection of summary military service records of nearly 100 officers ranging in rank from cadet to colonel, and of testamentary transcriptions drawn from the Archdiocesan Archive for 33 persons, not all of whom belong to the military but judged to belong to the social elite. [LRG]

2149 Rodríguez, Manuel Alfredo. Los pardos libres en la colonia y la independencia: discurso de incorporación como individuo de número de la Academia Nacional de la Historia. Caracas: Academia Nacional de la Historia, 1992. 53 p.: bibl.

Published version of Rodríguez's presentation upon his election to numerary status in Venezuela's Academia Nacional de la Historia in 1992. Celebrates role of free blacks in building the late-18th-century political society that then pursued national independence. [LRG]

2150 Rodríguez Mirabal, Adelina C. Latifundio ganadero y conflictos sociales en los llanos de Apure, 1700–1800. Caracas: Fondo Editorial Tropykos, Facultad de Ciencias Económicas y Sociales, 1995. 201 p.: bibl.

This sequel to *La formación del latifundio ganadero en los llanos de Apure, 1750–1800* (1987) can be read as both a historical and economic geography of the Venezuelan *llanos* and a socioeconomic approach to agricultural development there. Central to author's argument is her contention that the consequent land tenure patterns of expanding cattle ranching reflected a growing social restiveness in the area. [LRG]

2151 Rojas, Reinaldo. El conflicto Iglesia-encomenderos en el poblamiento colonial de la región barquisimeto, 1530–1718. (*Estud. Hist. Soc. Econ. Am.*, 12, 1995, p. 429–439, map, table)

Overview most useful for its conciseness, work provides a chronological, geographical, and topical framework into which larger works, such as those of Avellán de

Tamayo (see *HLAS 56:2245*) and Rojas (see item **2152**) can be fit. [LRG]

Rojas, Reinaldo. La economía de Lara en cinco siglos: una aproximación a su estudio. See *HLAS 57:1971.*

2152 **Rojas, Reinaldo.** Elites y propiedad territorial en Barquisimeto, provincia de Venezuela, siglo XVIII. (*Estud. Hist. Soc. Econ. Am.,* 12, 1995, p. 441–458, bibl., maps, tables)

Chronological survey of elite dominance in Barquisimeto from the mid-16th century through the 1700s adds social and genealogical information to burgeoning sources of data for history of Barquisimeto. For fuller treatments of the social history of Barquisimeto, see Avellán de Tamayo (*HLAS 56:2245*) and Rojas (item **2151**). [LRG]

2153 **Samudio A., Edda O.** El resguardo indígena en Mérida, siglos XVI al XIX. (*Paramillo/San Cristóbal,* 11/12, 1992/93, p. 7–90, bibl., maps, tables)

For annotation, see item **2140.**

2154 **Vásquez de Ferrer, Belín.** Una élite regional: los comerciantes de Maracaibo en tiempos de crisis y ruptura con el realismo hispánico, 1780–1821. (*Islas/Santa Clara,* 107, enero/abril 1994, p. 82–98, table)

Arguing that the merchants built upon their economic influence to establish dominance over local and regional politics in the late Bourbon period, author nicely sketches the spatial, mercantile, and personal networks centered in Maracaibo. Local commitment to this capitalist system that linked interior and exterior markets fostered regional autonomy and dominated views both for and against independence. [LRG]

2155 **Velázquez, Nelly.** Los resguardos de indios en la Provincia de Mérida: siglo XVII. (*Fermentum/Mérida,* 1:1, mayo/agosto 1991, p. 7–18, bibl., tables)

See items **2140** and **2153.**

2156 **Venezuela en el siglo de las luces.** Coordinación de María Carmen Mena García. Recopilación de María Angeles Eugenio Martínez y María Justina Sarabia Viejo. Sevilla, Spain: Muñoz Moya y Montraveta Editores, 1995. 329 p.: bibl., ill., map. (Biblioteca americana. Serie Historia)

Wide-ranging anthology of 11 articles on late-colonial Venezuela examines subjects as diverse as indigo production and professorial conflicts. Although held together largely by focus on 18th century, essays provide solid analyses of economic and social topics. [LRG]

NUEVA GRANADA

2157 **Academia Colombiana de Ciencias Exactas, Físicas y Naturales.** Tratados de minería y estudios geológicos de la época colonial 1616–1803. Recopilación, transcripción y notas de Guillermo Hernández de Alba y Armando Espinosa Baquero. Bogotá: Academia Colombiana de Ciencias Exactas, Físicas y Naturales, 1991. 91 p.: bibl.. (Col. Enrique Pérez-Arbeláez; 4)

Transcriptions, accompanied by short introductions, of mining and mineralogical treatises from Luis Sánchez de Aconcha (1616), Angel Díaz (1803), and Juan José D'Elhuyar (1786). Collection focuses on late-18th-century mining reform with Díaz's study of the Supía silver mines in Popayán and Elhuyar's description of the emerald mines of Muzo. [LRG]

2158 **Archivo General de la Nación (Colombia).** Dos colonizaciones del siglo XVIII en la Sierra Nevada de Santa Marta. Transcripciones paleográficas de José Agustín Blanco Barros. Bogotá: Archivo General de la Nación, 1996. 38 p. (Documentos en busca de investigador; 2)

Transcriptions of documents related to the foundation of government-sponsored colonies in Santa Marta prov.: the short-lived San Sebastián de Rábago, authorized by Viceroy Jose Alonso Pizarro in March 1750, and the more successful San Carlos de San Sebastián, ordered established by Charles III in 1786 and implemented by Viceroy Antonio Caballero y Góngora in 1787. Both efforts to expand the permanent Spanish presence in Santa Marta reflect Bourbon activism, while the latter also illustrated Enlightenment experimentation, as the new colonists included a group from Philadelphia. [LRG]

2159 **Barona Becerra, Guido.** La maldición de Midas en una región del mundo colonial: Popayán, 1730–1830. Cali, Colombia: Editorial Facultad de Humanidades, Univ. del Valle; Fondo Mixto para la Promoción de la

Cultura y las Artes del Cauca, 1995. 335 p.: bibl., ill., maps.

Provocative explication of the regional economy of 18th-century Popayán assigns structural and moral meaning to the development of mining and agriculture in the province. Solid analyses of economic indicators such as rural real estate transactions, coca prices, and gold production lend validity to the conclusion that Enlightenment-era expansion of Atlantic capitalism in the province fostered economic contradiction and ambiguity there, including the *desmonetización* of the countryside. [LRG]

2160 Borrego Pla, Carmen. Encomiendas y rentas en la gobernación de Cartagena de Indias, 1675. (*Anu. Estud. Am.*, 52:2, 1995, p. 235–249, tables)

Presentation of data drawn from 1675 document "Testimonio y Relación de Encomiendas que Tiene la Provincia de Cartagena," found in the Archivo General de Indias. Sixty-nine settlements in the districts of Cartagena, Tolú, and Mompox contained a total of 1,103 tributaries. Only the Mompox indigenous population showed an increase at the time. Table of encomiendas includes names of encomenderos and both the kind and value of indigenous tribute. A second table details the grants of these encomiendas. [LRG]

2161 Cabildos de San Juan de Pasto, 1573–1579. Recopilación de Emiliano Díaz del Castillo Zarama. Bogotá: Academia Colombiana de Historia, 1995. 458 p.: appendices, indexes. (Biblioteca de historia nacional; 143)

Important collection of transcribed minutes of town council meetings in the 1570s. These reports both detail and illustrate municipal life in Pasto, from the politically mundane, as on March 23, 1577, when the council met only to decide there was nothing to discuss and adjourned; to the important, as the Feb. 13, 1577, meeting illustrates with its discussion of personnel, religious, fiscal, and jurisdictional issues. A number of appendices listing various office holders and three indexes facilitate use of the meeting reports. [LRG]

2162 Calero, Luis Fernando. Chiefdoms under siege: Spain's rule and native adaptation in the southern Colombian Andes,

1535–1700. Albuquerque: Univ. of New Mexico Press, 1997. 233 p.: bibl., ill., index, maps.

Solid but traditional study of encomienda regime in the Pasto area in the 16th and 17th centuries. Relies heavily on data derived from official inspection tours to the region and reinforces standard conclusions about the encomienda, such as metropolitan efforts to regulate it, local abuse of its prerogatives, and indigenous resistance to its deleterious effects. For ethnohistorian's comment, see item **626.** [LRG]

2163 Ceballos Gómez, Diana Luz. Hechicería, brujería, e Inquisición en el Nuevo Reino de Granada: un duelo de imaginarios. Bogotá: Editorial Univ. Nacional, 1994. 249 p.: appendices, bibl., ill.

Important contribution to the social history of the New Kingdom and Cartagena de Indias, in particular. Spanish efforts first to comprehend and then control, if not eliminate, indigenous and African forms of alleged magic, whether religious or medical, illustrated imperial imperatives of domination and cultural transformation of subject peoples. First half of book establishes definitions and structures within which confrontation of Spanish and non-Western belief systems clashed. Second half provides a series of illustrative case studies. A glossary and documentary appendices augment the text. [LRG]

Cicala, Mario. Descripción histórico-topográfica de la Provincia de Quito de la Compañía de Jesús. See item **2203.**

Espinosa, José María. José María Espinosa: abanderado del arte y de la patria. See item **320.**

2164 Guzmán, Angela Inés. Poblamiento e historias urbanas del Alto Magdalena Tolima: siglos XVI, XVII y XVIII. Bogotá: Ecoe Ediciones, 1996. 236 p.: bibl., ill., maps.

Geographically based survey of colonial town formation in Tolima dept.. in the central Magdalena River valley. Centered on Ibagué, this urban history is especially useful for its utilization of the perspectives of cartography and urban planning. [LRG]

2165 Herrera-Angel, Marta. Poder local, población y ordenamiento territorial en la Nueva Granada, siglo XVIII. Bogotá:

Archivo General de la Nación, 1996. 181 p.: bibl., ill. (Serie Historia; 2)

Fine political geography of central Nueva Granada (Santa Fe prov.) was originally prepared as a master's thesis. Demonstrates how changing property boundaries and land use both illustrated and activated shifts in social power relationships. For example, the dislocation of indigenous communities helped weaken the *corregidores de naturales,* which, in turn, facilitated the rise of other local administrators and jurisdictions and quickened the pace of miscegenation and citizenship expansion. [LRG]

2166 Indice de documentos para la historia de la antigua gobernación de Popayán: Archivo Histórico de Quito. Dirección general de la investigación de William Jaramillo Mejía. Bogotá: Instituto Colombiano de Cultura Hispánica, 1996. 561 p.: indexes. (Col. Indices; 3)

Useful guide to documents concerning Popayán located in various *fondos* of the Sección General of Ecuador's Archivo Nacional de Historia. The largest group of cited documents comes from the Fondo Popayán, but entries range from sections Alcabalas to Vínculos y Mayorazgos. Most of the documents date from late-18th century. Includes onomastic and geographical indices. A companion volume, *Indice de documentos para la historia de la antigua gobernación de Popayán: Archivo Histórico Nacional de Colombia* has also been published. See item **2167.** [LRG]

2167 Indice de documentos para la historia de la antigua gobernación de Popayán: Archivo Histórico Nacional de Colombia. Recopilación de Jorge Tomás Uribe Angel. Bogotá: Instituto Colombiano de Cultura Hispánica, 1996. 364 p.: indexes. (Col. Indices; 4)

Useful guide to documents concerning colonial Popayán located in various *fondos* of Colombia's Archivo Histórico Nacional. Entries range from sections Abastos to Real Hacienda. As with the companion Ecuadorian index, *Indice de documentos para la historia de la antigua gobernación de Popayán: Archivo Histórico de Quito* (see item **2166**), most of the documents date from late-18th century. Includes onomastic and geographical indices. [LRG]

2168 Indices de dotes, mortuorias y testamentos existentes en las notarías de Santafé de Bogotá. Bogotá: Instituto Colombiano de Cultura Hispánica, 1994. 527 p.: index. (Col. Indices; 1)

Exhaustive index of wills, dowry agreements, and death notices found in the First, Second, and Third notarial offices of Bogotá, 1550–1819, which will facilitate social and genealogical history. Entries are chronologically arranged, with added notations of notarial office, scribe, and documentary location. An onomastic index supplements the guide. [LRG]

2169 Jara, Álvaro. El financiamiento de la defensa en Cartagena de Indias: los excedentes de las Cajas de Bogota y de Quito, 1761–1802. (*Historia/Santiago,* 28, 1994, p. 117–182, graphs, tables)

Important study by a dean of Latin American economic history examines treasury subsidies transferred to Cartagena de Indias in late-18th century. Paralleling his and John J. TePaske's monographic study of the royal treasury of Bogotá (*Las finanzas del Imperio español en el siglo XVIII: el Virreinato de Nueva Granada; la Caja Central de Santa Fe de Bogotá; ingresos y egresos, 1700– 1808*—forthcoming), Jara provides statistics on imperial fiscal transfers, defense expenditures, and the structure of treasury income in Cartagena; argues for the usefulness of such quantitative studies; and shows that subsidies formed a significant portion of annual treasury revenue but seldom fully paid for defense costs. [LRG]

2170 Jaramillo Mejía, William and Jorge Tomás Uribe Angel. Indices de documentos para la historia de Antioquia. Bogotá: Instituto Colombiano de Cultura Hispánica, 1994. 310 p.: index. (Col. Indices; 2)

Index of documents found in the "Colonia" section of Colombia's Archivo Histórico Nacional relating to cities and towns located in current Antioquia dept. [LRG]

2171 Jones Mathers, Constance. Santa Marta gold: Spaniards in Colombia, 1526–1536. (*CLAHR/Albuquerque,* 4:3, Summer 1995, p. 287–310, map)

Useful English-language survey of early (1526–36) history of Santa Marta focuses on the administration of García de

Lerma and its failures to pacify hostile indigenous peoples and to establish a stable polity. After a decade of existence, the colony was chiefly important for being the starting point for the Gonzalo Jiménez de Quesada expedition to the interior highlands in 1536. [LRG]

2172 Mora de Tovar, Gilma. Poblamiento y sociedad en el Bajo Magdalena durante la segunda mitad del siglo XVIII. (*Anu. Colomb. Hist. Soc. Cult.,* 21, 1993, p. 40–62, tables)

Unlike previous two centuries, 1700s were years of demographic growth and quickened miscegenation. This trend paralleled Bourbon emphasis on colonization schemes such as those entrusted to José Fernando Mier y Guerra in the Caribbean provinces of Nueva Granada. Such projects would not only congregate an increasingly free population for purposes of improved administrative control, but would also strengthen viceregal security and provide landholders with stable labor. [LRG]

2173 Navarrete, María Cristina. Historia social del negro en la colonia: Cartagena, siglo XVII. Cali, Colombia: Univ. del Valle, 1995. 128 p.: bibl., ill., maps.

Brief study contributes to both history of slavery and social history of Cartagena de Indias, especially for relatively overlooked 17th century. Most useful as a concise summation of standard conclusions, such as centrality of black labor in the local economy and society and utilization of racism, evangelization, and force to control black populations. See also item **2174.** [LRG]

2174 Navarrete, María Cristina. Prácticas religiosas de los negros en la colonia: Cartagena, siglo XVII. Cali, Colombia: Univ. del Valle, Editorial Facultad de Humanidades, 1995. 174 p.: bibl. (Col. Historia y Sociedad)

Meticulous, objective study of religious practices among blacks in Cartagena during 1600s is based on several years of archival research, especially in Inquisition records, in Spain and Colombia. This work, and author's companion study (see item **2173**), are exceptionally important works that contribute signficantly to the social history of Afro-Colombians. [MTH]

2175 Ocampo López, Javier. La rebelión de las alcabalas: el primer grito de rebeldía contra el impuesto a las ventas, 1592.

Bogotá: Ecoe Ediciones: Univ. Pedagógica y Tecnológica de Colombia, 1995. 119 p.: appendix, bibl., ill. (Novísima historia; no. 1)

A concise review of the 1592–94 cabildo-led protest against sales taxes in the highland city of Tunja. Essay places the unsuccessful struggle for municipal autonomy and prerogatives at the convergence of tensions between indigenous peoples and colonists, creoles and peninsulars, and colony and empire created by the maturation of Spanish rule in Nueva Granada. A documentary appendix completes the book. [LRG]

2176 Ortiz de la Tabla Ducasse, Javier. Cartas de cabildos hispanoamericanos. Audiencia de Santa Fe. v. 1, Santa Fe de Bogotá, siglos XVI-XIX. Sevilla, Spain: Escuela de Estudios Hispano-Americanos, Consejo Superior de Investigaciones Científicas, 1996. 1 v.: indexes. (Publicaciones de la Escuela de Estudios Hispano-Americanos de Sevilla; no. general 386)

A component of the Escuela de Estudios Hispano-Americanos' ongoing series of guides to municipal documents in the Archivo General de Indias, Seville, that began in 1974. This volume is the first of two dedicated to the Audiencia of Santa Fe (Nueva Granada). Its contents, dealing with the capital of Santa Fé de Bogotá, are drawn exclusively from the Audiencia de Santa Fé section of the archives, covering *Legajos* 1–1261 and the years 1542–1819. Indexes of personal and place names and topics augment book's usefulness. [LRG]

2177 Palacios de la Vega, Joseph. Diario de viaje entre los indios y negros de la Provincia de Cartagena en el Nuevo Reino de Granada, 1787–1788. Edición e introducción de Gerardo Reichel-Dolmatoff. 2. ed. Barranquilla, Colombia: Ediciones Gobernación del Atlántico, 1994. 141 p. (Col. Historia)

First published in 1955 under the editorship of Gerardo Reichel-Dolmatoff (see *HLAS 20:2730*), this newly reissued first-person account of the Franciscan friar's work among indigenous peoples and blacks in the San Jorge River valley again stands out as a telling portrayal of life and culture in southern Cartagena prov. The work highlights the continuing difficulties of evangelization, the complex character of society in the region, and the policy concerns of Archbishop-Viceroy Antonio Caballero y Góngora. [LRG]

2178 Porro Gutiérrez, Jesús María. Venero de Leiva: gobernador y primer presidente de la Audiencia del Nuevo Reino de Granada. Valladolid, Spain: Secretariado de Publicaciones, Univ. de Valladolid, 1995. 341 p.: bibl., maps. (Serie: Historia y sociedad; 51)

A valuable and singular in-depth biographical treatment of the first president of the Audiencia of Nueva Granada who governed from 1563–72. Important for early history of Nueva Granada, as Venero de Leiva's administration illustrates imposition of royal government in the colony and its jurisdictional structure, as well as the resulting conflict between the encomenderos' self-interest and metropolitan intent. [LRG]

2179 Relaciones y visitas a los Andes, siglo XVI. v. 1–4. Bogotá: Colcultura; Instituto Colombiano de Cultura Hispánica, 1993–1996? 4 v.: bibl., ill., maps. (Colección de historia de la Biblioteca Nacional)

Impressive multi-volume anthology of transcribed letters, Visitas, and *relaciones* detailing early colonial places and societies in the greater Andes from Quito in the south to Santa Marta in the north. Vol. 1 examines Panamá, Antioquia, Quito, and Popayán; vol. 2, (*Región del Caribe*; see item **713**), treats Santa Marta and Cartagena; vol. 3, (*Región Central-Oriental*), focuses on Trinidad and 16th-century Nueva Granada as a whole; and vol. 4, (*Región del Alto Magdalena*), studies Mariquita, Neiva, and Ibagué. These documents were collected and edited by a premier Colombian historian. [LRG]

2180 Rodríguez, Pablo. Sentimientos y vida familiar en el Nuevo Reino de Granada, siglo XVIII. Bogotá: Editorial Ariel, 1997. 339 p.: bibl., ill. (Ariel historia)

A valuable study of late-18th-century family and social structure in urban Nueva Granada clarifies contours of domestic life in the colony. Utilizing data from Cartagena de Indias, Tunja, Medellín, and Cali, but not Bogotá, Rodríguez sketches patterns of fundamental phases and institutions of social life: childhood, old age, widowhood, and marriage, divorce, and annulment. Conclusions such as the overwhelming feminine makeup of widowhood, the continuing employment of the elderly, and domestic abuse as the principal cause of divorce demonstrate vital character of the home and illustrate impor-

tant social attitudes within the body politic. [LRG]

2181 Rueda Méndez, David. Las encomiendas de Santiago de las Atalayas, siglo XVII. Tunja, Colombia: Univ. Pedagógica y Tecnológica de Colombia, 1996. 104 p.: bibl., ill.

Institutional case study of encomienda regime provides a local illustration of its ethnic, political, and economic patterns from the *llanos* region of Nueva Granada. Although the system's labor exactions were ultimately self-defeating, encomiendas around Santiago de las Atalayas in the Meta River basin lasted for a century from 1588–1684. [LRG]

2182 Ruiz Rivera, Julián Bautista. Los indios de Cartagena bajo la administración española en el siglo XVII. Bogotá: Archivo General de la Nación, 1996. 187 p.: bibl. (Serie historia; 3)

Useful and foundational overview of indigenous populations in the prov. of Cartagena in the 16th and 17th centuries follows standard structure of Visitas, encomiendas, tribute and personal service, and evangelization. [LRG]

Saladino García, Alberto. El papel de Francisco José de Caldas en la divulgación de la ciencia moderna en Nueva Granada. See item **5161.**

2183 Silva, Renán. Universidad y sociedad en el Nuevo Reino de Granada: contribución a un análisis histórico de la formación intelectual de la sociedad colombiana. Bogotá: Banco de la República, 1992. 477 p.: bibl. (Col. bibliográfica Banco de la República. Historia colombiana)

Careful and detailed portrayal of the professorial community and scholarly culture in the New Kingdom. Rightly insisting that intellectual development in Nueva Granada is not limited to the era of Charles III, despite an analytical focus on the Enlightenment, Silva traces growth of the university corporation over the entire colonial period in terms of numbers, identity, and influence. [LRG]

2184 Suárez Pineda, Rafael. Los caballeros conquistadores y sus ejecutorias: comentarios críticos sobre la conquista, trancurridos 500 años del descubrimiento de

América. Bogotá: Instituto Colombiano de Cultura Hispánica, 1996. 549 p.: bibl.

Encyclopedic overview of the conquest era in Nueva Granada. Work is organized topically and includes chapters on religion, government, justice and commercial laws, public works, health, education, and public finance, as well as on "Los Conquistadores." [LRG]

Zuluaga Gómez, Víctor. Vida, pasión y muerte de los indígenas de Caldas y Risaralda. See *HLAS 57:1145.*

QUITO

2185 Aguilar, Paúl *et al.* Enfoques y estudios históricos: Quito a través de la historia. Quito: Dirección de Planificación, I. Municipio de Quito; Sevilla, Spain: Consejería de Obras Públicas y Transporte, Junta de Andalucía; Madrid: Ministerio de Asuntos Exteriores de España, 1992. 237 p.: bibl., ill. (some col.). (Serie Quito; 6)

Exceptionally important set of original essays delineates and elucidates multiple aspects and various periods of the history of the capital. Well written and researched. For reviews of other volumes in the series, see *HLAS 56:182,* (no. 1); *HLAS 56:177,* (no. 2); item **109** (no. 4); *HLAS 56:178,* (no. 5); and items **89,** (no. 10); **95,** (no. 9); and **96,** (no. 7). [MTH]

2186 Anda Aguirre, Alfonso. Indios y negros bajo el dominio español en Loja. Quito: Ediciones Abya-Yala, 1993. 311 p.: bibl.

Consists of research notes and transcriptions of sources on indigenous peoples—focusing especially on *caciques* and communes—and on black slaves in the *corregimiento* of Loja. Drawn from notarial records, the Enrique Vacas Galindo collection, and the Archivo Nacional de Historia. Incorporates author's "La trata de los negros en Loja." See also *HLAS 52:2078.* [MTH]

2187 Andrien, Kenneth J. Corruption, self-interest, and the political culture of eighteenth-century Quito. (*in* Virtue, corruption, and self-interest: political values in the eighteenth century. Bethlehem, Pa.: Lehigh Univ. Press; London; Toronto: Associated University Presses, 1994, p. 270–296)

Preview of chapters seven and eight of

author's work *The Kingdom of Quito* (see item **2188**) includes case studies of regimes and machinations of Presidents Juan de Sosaya (1707–16), José de Araujo y Río (1736–47), and José García de Leon y Pizarro (1778–84). [MTH]

2188 Andrien, Kenneth J. The kingdom of Quito, 1690–1830: the State and regional development. Cambridge; New York: Cambridge Univ. Press, 1995. 255 p.: bibl., ill., index, maps. (Cambridge Latin American studies; 80)

Well-researched, structured, and articulated study of demographic and economic events and developments in the three major regions (northern and central highlands, southern highlands, and central and southern coast) and in the three primary cities of Quito, Cuenca, and Guayaquil. Also studies political economy of the colony at large, from 1690s epidemics through establishment of the nation-state in 1830. Draws heavily on Royal Treasury data. One of the most important economic studies of the Audiencia of Quito yet attempted. [MTH]

2189 Aráuz, Maritza. El mestizaje en las sociedades rurales en la costa ecuatoriana: Montecristi y Jipijapa. (*Quitumbe/ Quito,* 9, junio 1995, p. 37–54, bibl.)

Preliminary study examines utilization of declarations of *mestizaje* to escape payment of tribute and to improve one's socioeconomic status by individuals who apparently were members of the indigenous elite of the Ecuadorian central coast. See also items **2206, 2215, 2223, 2264,** and **2267.** [MTH]

2190 Archivo Municipal de Quito. Actas del cabildo colonial de la ciudad de la Inmaculada Concepción de Loja de 1547 a 1812. Investigación, recopilación, transcripción y relato histórico de Alfonso Anda Aguirre. Quito: Archivo Municipal de Quito, 1995 357p.: bibl., ill., indexes. (Publicaciones del Archivo Municipal de Quito; 38)

Brings together the few surviving minutes from the colonial period for the cabildo of Loja. Includes various *actas* from 1547–1812, and the only complete book of Cabildo minutes apparently in existence: the fourth, from 1774–80. [MTH]

2191 Ares Queija, Berta. Relación del licenciado Michael de la Torre, Quito 1574. (*in* Colección nuestra patria es America: la cultura en la historia. Recopilación de Jorge Nuñez Sánchez. Quito: Editora Nacional, 1992, v. 8, p. 13–32, bibl.)

With an introduction by Ares Queija, publishes a 1574 petition to the crown by the pastor of the Cathedral of Quito in which the prelate argues in favor of teaching Spanish to all indigenous peoples so that they might be catholicized and civilized more easily and thoroughly. Interestingly enough, De la Torre cites the indigenous peoples of Portoviejo as an example, so early had some of the ethnic groups of the central coast acculturated linguistically. [MTH]

Arias Altamirano, Luis. Iglesias parroquiales de la Arquidiócesis de Guayaquil. See item **2110.**

Arosemena, Guillermo. El fruto de los dioses. See *HLAS 57:2018.*

2192 Arteaga, Diego. Juan Chapa y su legítima mujer Magdalena Caroayauchi: una familia india en Cuenca, s. XVI-XVII. (*Rev. Arch. Nac. Hist. Azuay*, 10, 1996, p. 7–60, appendix, bibl.)

This carefully crafted study of an apparently unusually successful native family in Cuenca during late-16th, early-17th centuries is an exceptionally important contribution to the ethnic and urban history of the early colonial period, inasmuch as the role of indigenous peoples in the economy and society of Spanish towns barely has begun to be studied in Ecuador. [MTH]

2193 Beerman, Eric. Pintor y cartógrafo en las Amazonas: Francisco Requena. (*An. Mus. Am.*, 2, 1994, p. 83–97, ill.)

Reproduces the 10 watercolors and eight maps drawn by Requena between 1778–85 while serving on the Cuarta Partida de Límites. Excerpted from Beerman's *Francisco Requena: la expedición de límites: Amazonia, 1779–1795* (Madrid: Compañia Literaria, 1996). [MTH]

2194 Borchart de Moreno, Christiana Renate. Beyond the *obraje:* handicraft production in Quito toward the end of the colonial period. (*Americas/Franciscans*, 52:1, July 1995, p. 1–24)

Pioneering essay on a largely neglected aspect of the colonial economy: the domestic, guild, and workshop production of handicrafts other than woolen textiles. Focuses mostly on northern and central highlands, and on the late colonial period because of the existence of a source group (the *libros de guías*) that sheds light on the subject. Examines a wide variety of manufactured products, emphasizing primarily the production of cotton textiles. For Spanish-language version, see item **2196.** See also item **2199.** [MTH]

2195 Borchart de Moreno, Christiana Renate. Llamas y ovejas: el desarrollo del ganado lanar en la Audiencia de Quito. (*in* International Congress of Americanists, *48th, Stockholm, 1994.* Colonizacíon agrícola y ganadera en América, siglos XVI-XVIII: su impacto en la población aborigen. Quito: Ediciones Abya-Yala, 1995, p. 153–190, maps)

Breaking new ground, reviews evidence on the distribution and utilization of llamas, alpacas, vicuñas, and guanucos in prehispanic and early Hispanic Ecuador. Notes their virtual disappearance of the animals by the end of the 1500s and describes the introduction, propagation, and utilization of sheep and their wool. [MTH]

2196 Borchart de Moreno, Christiana Renate. Más allá del obraje: la producción artesanal en Quito a fines de la colonia. (*Memoria/MARKA*, 5, 1995, p. 1–34, bibl.)

Spanish-language version of article annotated in item **2194.** [MTH]

2197 Borchart de Moreno, Christiana Renate and **Segundo E. Moreno Yánez.** Las reformas borbónicas en la Audiencia de Quito. (*Anu. Colomb. Hist. Soc. Cult.*, 22, 1995, p. 35–57, bibl.)

Important review and solid digest of the impact of Bourbon administrative, fiscal, and military reforms on the colony as a whole and on its several regions. Original research as well as recent historiography. [MTH]

2198 Burgos Guevara, Hugo. Primeras doctrinas en la Real Audiencia de Quito, 1570–1640: estudio preliminar y transcripción de las relaciones eclesiales y misionales de los siglos XVI y XVII. Quito: Ediciones ABYA-YALA, 1995. 488 p.: bibl., ill.

Publishes—mostly for the first time—31 *relaciones* dating from 1552–1648 and covering themes ranging from the organization and staffing of the Diocese of Quito to complaints of *caciques, indios principales,* and *pueblos* regarding abuses by the clergy. A major set of primary materials not only for Ecuadorian church history but more importantly for study of the interaction between conquerors and conquered and the persistence of autochthonous beliefs and practices during the early colonial period. Includes a solid introductory study. [MTH]

2199 Büschges, Christian. Crisis y reestructuración: la industria textil de la real Audiencia de Quito al final del período colonial. *(Anu. Estud. Am.,* 52:2, 1995, p. 75–98)
    Systematic study of the textile industry throughout the highlands during the late-18th and early-19th centuries. Examines the home or "cottage" industry, in addition to the better-known manufacturing sector or *obrajes.* Based on original research as well as existing studies. See also items **2194** and **2196.** [MTH]

2200 Büschges, Christian. "Las leyes del honor": honor y estratificación social en el distrito de la Audiencia de Quito, siglo XVIII. *(Rev. Indias,* 57:209, enero/abril 1997, p. 55–84)
    Original essay examines the meaning and significance of honor among the elites of the late colonial period. Defines honor as "a concept of social distinction and exclusion," and the elites as the titled nobility (the *hidalgos*—those generally reputed to be "noble", particularly descendants of *conquistadores* and/or *primeros vecinos*) and their immediate families. Also examines the control exercised by the nobility over their children's marriages. Those excluded or petitioned to be excluded were considered unsuitable marriage partners for the nobility. The agency of exclusion in these cases was the civil tribunal of the Audiencia, no comparable cases having been found by the author in the ecclesiastical archives of Quito. See also item **2201.** [MTH]

2201 Büschges, Christian. La nobleza de Quito a finales del período colonial, 1765–1810: bases jurídicos y mentalidad social. *(Procesos/Quito,* 10, 1997, p. 43–61)
    Original essay focuses on the composition and definition of the elites (resident peninsular as well as creole) of Quito and the northern and central highlands. Excerpted

from previous work, see *HLAS 56:2320.* See also item **2200.** [MTH]

2202 Cevallos García, Gabriel. Historia nacional del Ecuador, edición bilingüe = bilingual edition. Cuenca, Ecuador: Romlacio Editor, 1992? 399 p.: ill.
    New bilingual edition of a standard history of Ecuador includes section on country's prehistory by Juan Cordero Iñiguez. Chronologically updated by Antonio Lloret Bastidas. Enriched with numerous illustrations. Previous Spanish-language editions were published in 1967 and 1987. For review of 1987 edition, see *HLAS 52:2413.* [MTH]

2203 Cicala, Mario. Descripción histórico-topográfica de la Provincia de Quito de la Compañía de Jesús. Quito: Instituto Geográfico Militar, 1994. 669 p.: ill.
    First Spanish-language version, and first complete edition in any language, of Cicala's 1771 *Descrizione istorico-física de la Provincia del Quito,* heretofore known only through excerpts. Italian Jesuit who spent nearly 23 years (1743–67) in the future Ecuador provides minute description of the Audiencia of Quito. Exceptionally important historical geography source. Includes chapters on Popayán and Pasto and their districts. [MTH]

2204 Cipolletti, María Susana. Lacrimabili statu: indianische Sklaven in Nordwestamazonien, 17.-20. Jahrhundert. (Beiträge zur Kulturgeschichte des westlichen Südamerika. Opladen, Germany: Westdeutschler Verelag, 1990, p. 207–226)
    Exploratory essay on the nature and practice of slavery among Upper Amazon Basin ethnic groups from 16th-20th centuries focuses especially on inter-ethnic relations between the Tucano, Zaparo, and Omagua. For Spanish-language version of article, see *Revista de Indias* (Madrid), 55:205, sept./dic. 1995, p. 551–571. [MTH]

2205 Costales, Piedad Peñaherrera de and **Alfredo Costales Samaniego.** Viracochas y peruleros. Quito: Xerox, 1995. 219 p.: bibl.
    Biographical dictionary of 434 Spaniards who participated in the conquest of the future Ecuador, more specifically those who accompanied Almagro, Alvardo, and Benalcázar. Useful but far from complete. [MTH]

2206 Cruz Zuñiga, Pilar. Mestizos e indígenas en la Real Audiencia de Quito: segunda mitad del siglo XVIII. (*Quitumbe/Quito*, 9, junio 1995, p. 89–115, bibl., graphs)

Tabulates and analyzes demographic, economic, and social characteristics of mestizos according to data presented in petitions of mestizaje and related sources. See also items **2189, 2215, 2223, 2264,** and **2267.** [MTH]

2207 Donoso Vallejo, Alegría. Sinopsis histórico del Santuario de Guápulo. (*Mus. Hist.*, 63, 1996, p. 89–125, bibl., ill.)

Overview of the history of the centuries-old Sanctuary of Guápulo on the outskirts of Quito, while useful, fails to address the relationship between Spanish saints and Andean deities. [MTH]

2208 Estrella, Eduardo. La "Flora Huayaquilensis" de Juan Tafalla: crónica e iconografía de una expedición silenciada, 1779–1808. 2nd. ed. Guayaquil, Ecuador: Banco del Progreso; Jardín Botánico de Guyaquil, 1995. 323 p.: bibl., facsims., plates.

Not a true second edition of the *Flora Huayaquilensis* (described in item **2209**), but rather an augmented version of Estrella's history of and introduction to the original work. Nonetheless, study is welcome for its expansion of our knowledge of this little-known botanical expedition, and for its reprinting of some of the reproductions (52 out of 217) of the coeval illustrations of flora of coastal Ecuador, thereby making them more widely available. [MTH]

2209 Estrella, Eduardo; Jorge Núñez; and Jorge Salvador Lara. Flora huayaquilensis: la Expedición Botánica de Juan Tafalla a la Real Audiencia de Quito, 1799–1808. Quito: Ediciones Abya-Yala; Centro Cultural Artes, 1991. 103 p.: bibl., ill., maps. (Col. Historia de la ciencias; 2)

Essays on Tafalla and his work *Flora Huayaqulensis: sive descriptiones et icones plantarum huayaquilensium secundum systema linnaeanum digestae.* (Madrid: Instituto ad Conservandam Naturam; Horto Regio Matritense = Real Jardín Botánico, 1989). Tafalla's work publishes results of a royal botanical expedition to the coast and southern highlands between 1799–1808, and includes 217 facsimiles of color drawings of plants. The findings of this expedition (a continuation of the Ruiz and Pavón botanical expedition) were previously unknown. The other members of the expedition and "coauthours" of the work were botanist Juan Agustín Manzanilla and painters Xavier Cortés and José Gabriel Rivera. See also item **2208.** [MTH]

2210 Estupiñán Viteri, Tamara. Los protocolos notariales en el estudio de los precios de la Real Audiencia de Quito, siglos XVI-XVII. (*Am. Lat. Hist. Econ. Bol. Fuentes*, 5, enero/junio 1996, p. 31–38)

Discusses the strengths and limitations of notarial records as a source for reconstructing the heretofore neglected history of prices in Ecuador. Also comments on the status of economic historiography of the Audiencia of Quito. Unfortunately, author does not possess an adequate grasp of the corresponding literature, paradigms, or methodologies. [MTH]

2211 FONSAL: El Fondo de Salvamento del Patrimonio Cultural, 1992–1996. Quito: Distrito Metropolitano de Quito, FONSAL, 1996. 187 p.: bibl., ill.

Reports on activities of the municipal program to restore the historical center of Quito. Magnificantly illustrated. [MTH]

2212 Freile Granizo, Carlos. Un caso de centralismo en la colonia: el Hospital de Quito pretende impedir que funcione el de Riobamba, 1772–1781. (*Quitumbe/Quito*, 10, junio 1996, p. 71–86)

Relates a minor incident in the history of hospitals, and therefore also of medicine, in Ecuador: a late-18th-century attempt by Quito authorities and the Bethlemites, who ran Quito's hospital, to force the closing of the hospital in Riobamba. [MTH]

2213 Freile Granizo, Carlos. Examen de aptitud para confesar tomado por el Obispo de Quito, Pedro de la Peña, en 1574. (*Quitumbe/Quito*, 8, junio 1994, p. 43–55, bibl.)

Examines Bishop De la Peña's utilization of episcopal authority to license the hearing of confessions. Exemplifies the prelate's concerns and approach by reproducing the examination of Diego Lobato, a mestizo and the first "Ecuadorian-born" priest. An essay in intellectual as well as ecclesistical history. [MTH]

2214 Freile Granizo, Carlos. Mons. José Pérez Calama, Obispo de Quito, 1740–1793. (*Rev. Inst. Hist. Ecles. Ecuat.*, 13, 1993, p. 51–94)

New appreciation of the episcopal, catechismal, and intellectual labors of a truly distinguished and enlightened prelate, based on research in the Archivo General de Indias and on Pérez Calama's writings. [MTH]

2215 Guerra Moscoso, Sabrina. Los "ilegítimos" de la sociedad colonial. (*Quitumbe/Quito*, 9, junio 1995, p. 21–35, bibl.)

Working paper focuses on mestizos in the Audiencia of Quito, the majority of whom may have been "illegitimate," according to quantitative and qualitative analysis of a not necessarily representative sample (40) of petitions of declaration of *mestizaje* presented from 1731–97. See also items **2189, 2206, 2223, 2264,** and **2267.** [MTH]

2216 Guerra Moscoso, Sabrina. La secularización de doctrinas y la participación indígena, siglo XVIII: Guano y Alangasí. (*Memoria/MARKA*, 5, 1995, p. 35–88, bibl.)

Studies "secularization" of parishes of Alangasí and Guano, the latter in 1754 and not at all peacefully. Examines the role of indigenous peoples as well as diocesan clergy and religious and civilian authorities in the process. [MTH]

2217 Herzog, Tamar. La administración como un fenómeno social: la justicia penal de la ciudad de Quito, 1650–1750. Madrid: Centro de Estudios Constitucionales, 1995. 352 p.: bibl., ill., maps. (Historia de la sociedad política)

Examines system of criminal justice in Quito from second half of 17th to first half of 18th centuries. Methodologically sophisticated, yet eminently readable. Based on extensive archival research in Spain and Ecuador. A novel, exceptionally important, multivariant contribution to the administrative, institutional, and social history of the colony. Originally presented in French as author's doctoral dissertation in 1994. See also item **2220.** [MTH]

2218 Herzog, Tamar. Mediación, archivos y ejercicio: los escribanos de Quito, siglo XVII. Frankfurt am Main: Vittorio Klostermann, 1996. 180 p.: appendices, bibl. (Studien zur Europäischen Rechtsgeschichte; 82)

Social and institutional history of the notaries of Quito focuses primarily on the 17th century. A wholly original work and, for the Audiencia of Quito, a pioneering study. [MTH]

2219 Herzog, Tamar. Los ministros de la audiencia de Quito: 1650–1750. Quito: Ediciones Libri Mundi, 1995. 171 p.

Biographical dictionary of members (i.e., presidents and *oidores*) of the Audiencia from second half of 17th to first half of 18th centuries, organized alphabetically. Entries provide career and family data, and sources. A basic reference work. [MTH]

2220 Herzog, Tamar. El rescate de una fuente histórica: los libros de visita de cárcel—el caso de Quito, 1738–1750. (*Anu. Estud. Am.*, 52:2, 1995, p. 251–261)

Brief essay on the inspection records of jails as a source of social as well as administrative and penal history, based primarily on reports for Sept. 1738-Sept. 1740. See also item **2217.** [MTH]

2221 Hidalgo Nutri, Fernando. Historia del paisaje natural ecuatoriano. (*Cultura/Quito*, 1, enero/marzo 1997, p. 2–10, ill.)

Essay on history of landscapes, with a special focus on the colonial period, reflects some original research. Examines a theme neglected in the natural history and historiography of Ecuador. [MTH]

2222 Hurtado, Consuelo. Cofradía del Rosario: espacio aglutinador de la elite quiteña en el siglo XVIII. (*Memoria/MARKA*, 4, 1994, p. 163–186, bibl.)

Original study examines religious, social, and economic activities of the Cofradía del Rosario, a Dominican sodality in Quito. Membership was based on class, not on gender or race, and was limited for the most part to members of the local elite, including titled nobility. [MTH]

2223 Ibarra, Alexia. La condición del mestizaje en el contexto de las Reformas Borbónicas, segunda mitad del siglo XVIII. (*Quitumbe/Quito*, 9, junio 1995, p. 55–75)

Brief analysis of 274 petitions of declaration of *mestizaje* presented between 1780–1815, and of the impact of the Decree of 1764. See also items **2189, 2206, 2215, 2264,** and **2267.** [MTH]

Jara, Álvaro. El financiamiento de la defensa en Cartagena de Indias: los excedentes de las Cajas de Bogota y de Quito, 1761–1802. See item **2169.**

2224 Jurado Noboa, Fernando. Los pulperos de Quito en 1631. (*Bol. Acad. Nac. Hist./Quito*, 67:143/144, 1984, p. 245–257)
Preliminary analysis of the 1631 list of *pulperos*, or shopkeepers, in Quito. See also item **2238.** [MTH]

2225 Jurado Noboa, Fernando. Las quiteñas. Quito: Dinediciones, 1995. 367 p.: bibl., ill. (Col. Siempre)
History of women of the capital from pre-Incan times through first half of 20th century. Looks at women from all walks of life and several ethnic groups. Rich in vignettes and anecdotes. [MTH]

2226 Keeding, Ekkehart. La Ilustración en Quito y su influjo en la Independencia. (*Bol. Acad. Nac. Hist./Quito*, 67:143/144, 1984, p. 182–190)
Spanish precis of Keeding's major work *Das Zeitalter der Aufklärung in der Provinz Quito* (1993), focusing on the Enlightenment in the Audiencia of Quito during the late colonial and independence periods.

2227 Kennedy, Alexandra. La fiesta barroca en Quito. (*Procesos/Quito*, 9, 1996, p. 1–20, bibl.)
Working paper on public celebrations during second half of 17th to first half of 18th centuries focuses particularly on festivals commemorating the birth, ascension to the throne, and death of Spanish kings. Examines the participation of indigenous peoples in such festivals and elucidates mentalities of Spaniards and Incas. [MTH]

2228 Landázuri N., Cristóbal. Las visitas y numeraciones del siglo XVI como fuentes para la historia andina. (*Memoria/MARKA*, 5, 1995, p. 273–299, bibl.)
Delineates and discusses 16th-century *visitas* of Ecuadorian pueblos. [MTH]

2229 Latorre, Octavio. La expedición a la Canela y el descubrimietno del Amazonas. Quito: O. Latorre, 1995. 246 p.: bibl., ill. (some col.).
Popular account of Orellana's discovery of the Amazon maintains that cinnamon drew the Spaniards down from the Andes and into the Oriente region of Ecuador. [MTH]

2230 Latorre, Octavio. Thomás de Berlanga y el descubrimiento de Galápagos. Quito: O. Latorre T., 1996. 314 p.: appendix, bibl., ill.
Three-part study includes: 1) a biography of the ecclesiastic Berlanga (1507–51), a major figure in the early history of Panama and Peru; 2) an ethnohistory of the Galapagos; and 3) an appendix of Berlanga's "documentos y cartas." [MTH]

Lavallé, Bernard. Bibliografía francesa sobre el Ecuador, 1968–1993: ciencias humanas, sociales y de la tierra. See item **2113.**

2231 Lavallé, Bernard. Quito et la crise de l'Alcabala, 1580–1600. Paris: Editions du Centre national de la recherche scientifique, 1992. 213 p.: bibl., map. (Col. de la Maison des pays ibériques; 50)
This first study in over 100 years of the sales tax protest of 1592–93 is detailed, sophisticated, and well researched. Places protest within economic and social, as well as political context, and considerably enhances knowledge of late-16th-century developments in Quito and the northern and central highlands. [MTH]

2232 Laviana Cuetos, María Luisa. La renta del tabaco en Guayaquil colonial. (*Rev. Ecuat. Hist. Econ.*, 9, 1994, p. 13–136, appendix, tables)
Original, complete, and definitive study of the Administración Principal, Factoría General y Fábrica de la Real Renta del Tabaco, established in Guayaquil in 1778. Includes appendix of primary materials. [MTH]

2233 León, Natalia. Género, matrimonio y sociedad criolla en Cuenca durante la segunda mitad del siglo XVIII. (*Procesos/Quito*, 10, 1997, p. 21–41, bibl.)
Exploratory essay on the concepts of women's honor, marriage patterns, and family violence in Cuenca during the late colonial period. [MTH]

2234 León Borja de Szászdi, Dora. El Cedulario de la Gobernación de Yaguarsongo y Pacamoros. (*Bol. Acad. Puertorriq. Hist.*, 13:44, julio 1992, p. 73–152, appendix, map)
Utilizes the 1571–1643 *cedulario* of the Gobernación de Yaguarsongo y Paca-

moros to detail the history of the *gober-nación* and to elucidate the career of its first governor, Juan de Salinas. Founded during the gold rush of the 1550s, the *gobernación* and its several "cities" (Sevilla de Oro, Logroño, Santiago de las Montañas, etc.) all but disappeared during the 1590s Shuar attacks. [MTH]

2235 Lucena Salmoral, Manuel. La crisis minera de Zaruma, Ecuador, a fines de la colonia: la visita de 1811. (*Rev. Eur.*, 57, Dec. 1994, p. 53–68, appendices, tables)

Well-researched study of late-1700s to early-1800s mining crisis is based primarily on the recently published account of the 1811 inspection. Elucidates many aspects of the economic situation of Zaruma, a town almost entirely dependent upon gold mining for its existence. [MTH]

2236 Lucena Salmoral, Manuel. La enseñanza en Quito durante la segunda mitad del siglo XVIII. (*in* Congreso Internacional de Historia de América, *5th, Granada, Spain, 1992.* El Reino de Granada y el Nuevo Mundo. Granada, Spain: Diputación Provincial de Granada, 1994, v. 3, p. 551–556)

Somewhat superficial review of the state of education in Quito during the period. [MTH]

2237 Lucena Salmoral, Manuel. Entre la escolástica y el despotismo ilustrado: reformismo universitario en Quito en vísperas de la independencia. (*in* Congreso Internacional de Universidades, *Madrid, 1992.* La universidad ante el Quinto Centenario: actas. Madrid: Editorial Complutense, 1992, p. 193–207)

Original study of late colonial period attempts by Bishop Pérez de Calama and President Barón de Carondelet to reform the Universidad Real de Santo Tomás, the ancestor of Quito's Universidad Central. Informative and well done. [MTH]

2238 Lucena Salmoral, Manuel. Las tiendas de la ciudad de Quito, circa 1800. (*Procesos/Quito*, 9, 1996, p. 125–137)

Analysis of 1795 and 1802 registers of shopkeepers. Important contribution given the paucity of research on *quiteño* commercial activities. See also item **2224.** [MTH]

2239 Luna Tamayo, Milton. Estado, regionalización y lucha política del Ecuador, 1800–1869. (*Rev. Arch. Nac. Hist. Azuay*, 7, 1987, p. 105–127)

Thoughtful essay on regionalism, incipient nationalism, and civil strife during the late colonial, independence, and early national periods. [MTH]

2240 "Las Manufacturas de la Provincia de Quito" de Juan de Larrea y Villavicencio, 1802. Introducción y transcripción de Christian Büschges. (*Procesos/Quito*, 9, 1996, p. 139–143)

Reprint of a brief but highly informative early-19th-century description of manufactures in northern and central highlands by a major *hacendado* and *obrajero* of the late colonial and independence periods. [MTH]

2241 Marchán Romero, Carlos. La sierra centro-norte del Ecuador: su delimitación geográfico-conceptual y su economía en el siglo XVII. (*Rev. Ecuat. Hist. Econ.*, 12, 1995, p. 59–90)

Less than half of this article is given over to the 17th century; the remainder consists of general remarks on the regions (northern highlands vis-à-vis central highlands) and on 18th- and 19th-century economic developments. Work is important for its attempt to establish a paradigm of the economic history of the region. [MTH]

2242 Martínez Borrero, Juan; Carmen Ugalde de Valdivieso; and Juan Cordero Iñiguez. De lo divino y lo profano: arte cuencano de los siglos XVIII y XIX. Cuenca, Ecuador: Ediciones del Banco Central del Ecuador, 1997. 231 p.: bibl., ill. (some col.).

Magnificently illustrated history of the 18th- and 19th-century art of Cuenca focuses primarily on the religious. Based largely on the collections of the monasteries of Carmen and the Concepción. A historiographic first for Ecuador. [MTH]

2243 Martínez Flores, Alexandra. Territorialidad indígena y lucha por la tierra en los Corregimientos de Ibarra y Otavalo, 1800–1820. (*Quitumbe/Quito*, 7, 1990, p. 63–80, tables)

Significant study of demographic and economic history of the *corregimientos* of Ibarra and Otavalo during late colonial period. Emphasizes struggle of indigenous communities to retain their lands. [MTH]

2244 Molestina Zaldumbide, María del Carmen. Excavaciones en el Convento Máximo de San Agustín de Quito. (*Mus. Hist.*, 63, 1996, p. 60–88, bibl., ill.)

Preliminary report on archeological excavations focuses on the use of brickwork and *botijuelas* (olive or wine jars) as fill, especially in 16th and 17th centuries. [MTH]

Morelli, Federica. Doing historical research in Quito: a guide to archives and libraries. See item **2114.**

2245 Moreno Egas, Jorge. La cofradía y la hermandad de los maestros tejedores de Quito. (*Rev. Inst. Hist. Ecles. Ecuat.*, 13, 1993, p. 105–124)

Working paper on the Cofradía de Nuestra Señora de la Purificación, based on sodality's record book of 1751–1834. [MTH]

2246 Moreno Egas, Jorge. Los jesuitas en Barbacoas. (*Rev. Inst. Hist. Ecles. Ecuat.*, 12, 1992, p. 21–34)

New data on the establishment of the Jesuit mission and indigenous pueblo of Mira in Barbacoas in 1630s. Based on research in the Archivo del Cabildo Metropolitano de Quito, heretofore a little-used repository of primary sources on Church history in Ecuador. [MTH]

2247 Moscoso C., Lucía. Aproximación al estudio de los diezmos en la Real Audiencia de Quito. (*Quitumbe/Quito*, 8, junio 1994, p. 127–140)

Preliminary study of tithes in the Audiencia of Quito. [MTH]

Navarro, José Gabriel. Estudios históricos. See item **2127.**

2248 Nueva historia del Ecuador. v. 15, Documentos de la historia del Ecuador. Coordinación del volumen de Cecilia Durán, Alexandra Martínez y Cecilia Ortiz. Quito: Corporación Editora Nacional; Grijalbo, 1995. 1 v.

This final volume in the series consists entirely of basic and well-known, but not always easily obtainable, primary sources. [MTH]

2249 Ortiz de la Tabla Ducasse, Javier. Los núcleos urbanos del Ecuador colonial: siglos XVI-XVII. (*in* Ciencia, vida y espacio en Iberoamérica. Madrid: Consejo Superior de Investigaciones Científicas, 1989, v. 2, p. 415–437)

Reviews the role of Spanish cities and towns in the Audiencia of Quito during 16th and 17th centuries. Stresses the hegemony of the city of Quito and examines economic and demographic developments. [MTH]

2250 Palomeque, Silvia. Continuidad y cambio entre la colonia y la república: estudio de los circuitos mercantiles y de las especializaciones productivas regionales en Cuenca, Ecuador. (*in* Circuitos mercantiles y mercados en Latinoamérica, siglos XVIII-XIX. México: Instituto de Investigaciones Dr. José María Luis Mora; Instituto de Investigaciones Históricas UNAM, 1995, p. 235–290, graphs, tables)

Quantitative study of Cuenca's trade with Lima, Guayaquil, Loja, northern Peru, Quito, and southern Colombia during the late colonial, independence, and early national periods. A major contribution to the economic history of the southern highlands. See also *HLAS 54:2686.* [MTH]

2251 Paniagua Pérez, Jesús. Un intento de reactivación económica en el Quito del siglo XVII: la fábrica de loza fina. (*Estud. Hist. Soc. Econ. Am.*, 12, 1995, p. 93–105)

Original essay on a little-known event in the economic history of Quito: the attempt by two *peninsulares*, Salvador Sánchez Pareja and Manuel Díez de la Peña, to establish and operate a porcelain factory from late 1760s-1788. [MTH]

2252 Paniagua Pérez, Jesús and María Isabel Viforcos Marinas. El poder económico del clero secular cuencano en la segunda mitad del siglo XVII. (*Estud. Hist. Soc. Econ. Am.*, 13, 1996, p. 59–77, tables)

Examines the "economic power" of parish priests in Cuenca, 1650–1700. Focuses on their sources of income, including real estate and moveable goods. Important contribution to socioeconomic as well as ecclesiastical history of the southern highlands. [MTH]

2253 **Poloni, Jacques.** Compras y ventas de tierras por los indios de Cuenca en el siglo XVII: elementos de coyuntura económica y de estratificación social. (*Memoria/MARKA*, 3, 1993, p. 1–39, bibl., maps, tables)

Spanish-language version of article previously published in French (see *HLAS 56:2359*). [MTH]

2254 **Porras P., María Elena.** La elite quiteña a mediados del siglo XVIII. (*Quitumbe/Quito*, 7, 1990, p. 37–53)

Well-documented study of the economic base of the Quito elite circa 1750. [MTH]

2255 **Proaño, Luis Octavio.** Nuestra Señora de la Merced en la colonia y en la República del Ecuador. Quito: L.O. Proaño, 1993. 806 p.: bibl., ill., index.

History of the cult of Our Lady of Mercy in Ecuador, especially in those cities where the Mercedarians established convents and churches, from early colonial times through the late-20th century. Well-researched and heavily documented. See also item **2256**. [MTH]

2256 **Proaño, Luis Octavio.** La Recolección Mercedaria de El Tejar. Quito: L.O. Proaño, 1994. 404 p.: bibl., ill., index.

Thoroughly researched study of the art, architecture, and history of the Retreat House of El Tejar, one of the major gems of "colonial" Quito. Emphasizes spiritual influence of the House and of its founder, Father Francisco de Jesús Bolaños. See also item **2255**. [MTH]

Puga, Miguel A. La gente ilustre de Quito. See item **2633**.

2257 **Puga, Miguel A.** Quito de ayer, Quito de siempre. Quito: Sociedad Amigos de la Genealogía, 1993. 283 p.: ill. (Col. Medio milenio; 11)

Together with Puga's earlier *Crónicas del Quito antiguo* (1991), provides anecdotal account of various aspects of city's history from prehispanic times through early-20th century. Based on secondary studies and published sources. [MTH]

2258 **Quishpe B., Jorge Marcelo.** Guía documental del Archivo Parroquial de Pifo. (*Memoria/MARKA*, 4, 1994, p. 269–307)

Well-done guide to holdings of the parish archives of Pifo, one of the five *pueblos* of the *alfoz* (district) of Quito. [MTH]

Relaciones y visitas a los Andes, siglo XVI. See item **2179**.

2259 **Revelo, Luis Alberto.** El estanco de aguardiente a finales del período colonial, 1765–1822. (*Quitumbe/Quito*, 8, junio 1994, p. 141–156, bibl.)

Student paper on cane liquor monopoly includes archival data. [MTH]

2260 **Ruf, Thierry.** Urcuquí a mediados del siglo XVII: preguntas sobre la formación de identidades. (*Memoria/MARKA*, 3, 1993, p. 189–225, bibl., ill., map, tables)

Quantitative study of the 1646 *visita* of the *repartimiento* of Urcuquí as published in *Numeraciones del Repartimiento de Otavalo* (see *HLAS 48:2709*). Important contribution to the demographic, economic, ethnic, and social history of the northern highlands. [MTH]

2261 **Soasti, Guadalupe.** Obraje colonial y mita obrajera. (*Quitumbe/Quito*, 8, junio 1994, p. 71–85, bibl., tables)

Delineates assignment of indigenous labor to the *obrajes* (textile factories) of Chambo and Licto in the central highlands during first half of the colonial period. [MTH]

2262 **Tapia Tamayo, Amílcar.** Doctrinas de la antigua Provincia de los Pastos. (*Memoria/SEIHGE*, 2, 1991/92, p. 211–260, bibl.)

Primarily a novel and original study of the Mercedarian *doctrinas* of Tulcán, Huaca, Tusa, and Puntal in the modern province of Carchi from 16th–18th centuries. Important contribution to ecclesiastical and local history of the northern highlands. Exceptionally well researched. Reprinted in author's *Pueblos y doctrinas de la antigua Provincia de los Pastos*(see *HLAS 56:2376*). [MTH]

2263 **Tardieu, Jean-Pierre.** Noirs et nouveaux maîtres dans les "vallées sanglantes" de l'Équateur, 1778–1820. Saint-Denis, Réunion: Université de la Réunion, Faculté des lettres et sciences humaines; Paris: Éditions L'Harmattan, 1997. 201 p.: bibl., maps, tables

Exceptionally solid study of the exploitation of black slaves in the Chota-Mira River Basin, especially on former Jesuit estates, during the late colonial period. Also examines blacks' reaction to mistreatment, including recourse to judicial authorities in Quito and the establishment of *palenques*. A major contribution to the socioeconomic history of the northern highlands and of Afro-Ecuadorians. [MTH]

2264 Terán Najas, Rosemarie. Los rasgos de la configuración social en la Audiencia de Quito. (*Quitumbe/Quito*, 9, junio 1995, p. 11–19)

Overview of the social structure and social change in the colony from the Spanish conquest to the eve of independence focuses particularly on mestizos. See also items **2189, 2206, 2215, 2223,** and **2267**. [MTH]

2265 Terán Najas, Rosemarie and María Elena Porras P. Las cofradías seráficas: estudios de casos. (*Quitumbe/Quito*, 8, junio 1994, p. 57–69, bibl.)

Student paper on Franciscan-sponsored brotherhoods throughout the Audiencia of Quito is based on research in the Archivo General de la Orden Fransicana in Quito. [MTH]

2266 Valencia Sala, Gladys. El mayorazgo en la Audiencia de Quito. Quito: Abya-Yala, 1994. 133 p.

Author's master's thesis, based on research in the Archivo Nacional de Historia, exemplifies institutionalization of entitled estates through a case study of the properties of the Sánchez de Orellana family (or the marqueses de Solanda). [MTH]

Vega Vega, Wilson. Bibliografía del Dr. Carlos Manuel Larrea. See item **2116**.

Vega Vega, Wilson. José María Vargas: bibliografía. See item **2117**.

2267 Vela, María Susana. Mulato "conocido y reputado por tal." (*Quitumbe/Quito*, 9, junio 1995, p. 77–88, bibl.)

Student paper on racial passing during Ecuador's late colonial period. Interestingly, "mulattoes" found it legally and socially advantageous to petition to be recognized as "mestizos." Based on archival research. See also items **2189, 2206, 2215, 2223,** and **2264**. [MTH]

2268 Villalba F., Jorge. La intervención de la Iglesia de Quito en la revolución de las alcabalas, 1592–1593. (*Rev. Inst. Hist. Ecles. Ecuat.*, 9, 1988, p. 35–72)

Re-examines the role of the clergy, especially the Jesuits, in the sales tax protest of 1592–93. Attributes the outbreak of violence to abuses and shortsightedness on the part of President Barros. [MTH]

2269 Wakefield, Celia. Searching for Isabel Godin. Chicago: Chicago Review Press, 1994. 200 p.: ill., index, map.

Popular account of the Mission geodésique of 1735 and of Isabel Godin's 1769 trek from her native Riobamba to the mouth of the Amazon to rejoin her husband, whom she had not seen in 20 years. An enjoyable read, but marred by inadequate research. [MTH]

PERU

Advis V., Patricio. Noticias de cronistas e historiadores sobre la travesia de los Andes realizada por la hueste de Almagro durante la jornada de Chile. See item **2398**.

2270 Águila Bartra, Herlinda del. Tarapoto y Cumbaza en las postrimerías del siglo XVIII. (*Rev. Arch. Arzobispal Arequipa*, 2, 1995, p. 83–99, bibl.)

Consists of research notes on Tarapoto (founded as a Spanish city in 1782) and Cumbaza (circa 1790) extracted from a coeval *expediente* on the dispute between the secular priest to whom the "mother parish" of Lamas had been assigned and the Franciscans, operating out of Ocopa, in the missions of the northern interior. [MTH]

2271 Aldana Rivera, Susana. "Malos vecinos" en Paita, década de 1810: competencia mercantil en la sociedad norteña colonial peruana. (*CLAHR/Albuquerque*, 5:3, Summer 1996, p. 261–286, maps)

Important article on a little-studied topic, the role of indigenous peoples in the colonial market economy. Work focuses on marketplace competition between Andeans, Europeans, and mestizos in Peruvian north coastal area. Also examines the socioeconomic consequences of racial blurring and the continuing struggle over land rights. [MTH]

2272 Arellano Hoffmann, Carmen. El Intendente de Tarma Juan Ma. de Galvez y su juicio de residencia 1791: aspectos de la corrupción en una administración serrana del Perú. (*Histórica/Lima*, 20:1, julio 1996, p. 29–57, bibl., tables)

Analyzes judicial review of the first *intendente* of Tarma, demonstrating that the *intendentes* were not necessarily less involved in local economies and societies or less self-interested than their *corregidor* predecessors had been. [MTH]

2273 Arrelucea Barrantes, Maribel. Conducta y control social colonial: estudio de las panaderías limeñas en el siglo XVIII. (*Rev. Arch. Gen. Nac.*, 13, 1996, p. 133–150, bibl., maps)

Focuses on the related questions of control of worker behavior and working conditions, and slave responses thereto, in Lima bakeries in the 1700s. Apparently a substantial number of the slaves employed were convicts on "work release." A novel contribution to social history of the late colonial period. [MTH]

2274 Assadourian, Carlos Sempat. Transiciones hacia el sistema colonial andino. México: Colegio de México, Fideicomiso Historia de las Américas; Lima: Instituto de Estudios Peruanos, 1994. 304 p.: bibl. (Serie Estudios históricos, 1019–4533; 15)

Anthology of previously published essays on the demographic, economic, and social history of the Andean region during early colonial period. All six essays examine "el complicado proceso de transición al sistema colonial desarrollado en el espacio regido antes por el inca." In the lead essay, Assadourian makes a strong case for the argument that warfare (nearly continuous from the death of Huayna Capac through the rebellion of the *encomenderos*), and not epidemics, was the primary reason for the initial population decline of the Tahuatinsuyu. [MTH]

2275 Bataillon, Marcel. La colonia: ensayos peruanistas. Recopilación de Alberto Tauro. Lima: Univ. Nacional Mayor de San Marcos, 1995. 202 p.: bibl. (Serie Historia. Biblioteca universitaria)

Useful anthology of Bataillon's multifaceted writings focuses on ideological, historiographic, and religious aspects of the Spanish conquest and ensuing civil wars. Bataillon (1895–1977), a scientific historian, insisted on the fullest possible reconstruction of events, based on all available documentation. His work prompted a number of revisionist interpretations of early colonial period events. [MTH]

2276 Benavides, María A. El Archivo Parroquial de Yanque. (*Bol. Inst. Riva-Agüero*, 17, 1990, p. 47–70, bibl., map)

Guide to the holdings of an important repository for the study of the historical demography and ethnohistory of southern Peru. Now housed in the Archivo Arzobispal de Arequipa, this repository holds parish registers of 16 *pueblos* from the 17th-early 20th centuries, as well as records of a number of *visitas* to Collaguas. Also discusses previous research based on these materials. [MTH]

2277 Benito Rodríguez, José Antonio. La modélica gestión del Contador de Cruzada de Lima, Gonzalo de la Maza. (*Hisp. Sacra*, 48:97, 1996, p. 199–230)

Reports on the career of Gonzalo de la Maza (c. 1560–1628), the accountant of the Bula de Cruzada in Peru for many years and an almost forgotten figure of the early colonial period. A scrupulous public servant, Maza often has been referred to as a friend and benefactor of Saint Rose of Lima; however, the details of his life and career have been largely unknown. [MTH]

2278 Cahill, David. Financing health care in the Viceroyalty of Peru: the hospitals of Lima in the late colonial period. (*Americas/Franciscans*, 52:2, Oct. 1995, p. 123–154, tables)

Novel study of the financial status of the 11 hospitals within the city and *cercado* of the City of Kings during the late colonial period. Impressive contribution to economic and social, as well as public health, history of Lima in the 1700s. [MTH]

2279 Cahill, David. Popular religion and appropriation: the example of Corpus Christi in eighteenth-century Cuzco. (*LARR*, 31:2, 1996, p. 67–110, bibl.)

Sophisticated analysis of the observance of Corpus Christi in Cuzco. Examination of both indigenous and Spanish perceptions and manipulations of the celebration elucidates social, economic and political, as well as religious, aspects of colonial fiestas. [MTH]

2280 Campos, F. Javier. Historia de la imagen y del monasterio de Ntra. Sra. del Prado de Lima, de Agustinas Recoletas. (*Rev.*

Agust., 37:113, mayo/agosto 1996, p. 565–659, bibl., tables)

Exceptionally detailed, thoroughly documented, but "other-worldly" study of devotion to an image of the Virgin Mary popular in colonial Lima; and of the Monasterio de Nuestra Señora del Prado, an Augustinian monastery for women that came to be associated with the icon. Unfortunately, work is more "hagiographical" than historical. [MTH]

2281 Cañedo-Argüelles Fábrega, Teresa. Cacicazgo y poder en el Valle de Moquegua, siglos XVII y XVIII. (*Rev. Arch. Arzobispal Arequipa*, 1, 1994, p. 17–30)

Brief but thought-provoking essay on the redefinition of traditional lordships and the restructuring of agencies of power in the Moquegua Valley during middle and late colonial periods. See also item **2282**. [MTH]

2282 Cañedo-Argüelles Fábrega, Teresa. Las reducciones indígenas en Moquegua: estrategias de producción y sus efectos en el medio ambiente. (*Rev. Arch. Arzobispal Arequipa*, 2, 1995, p. 135–154, facsim.)

Examines continuity and change in the agricultural base of indigenous communities in the Moquegua Valley from 16th–18th centuries, and the impact of those changes on the environment. Important contribution to the little-known ecological history of the colonial period. See also item **2281**. [MTH]

2283 Castañeda Delgado, Paulino and **Pilar Hernández Aparicio.** La Inquisición de Lima. v. 2, 1635–1696. Madrid: Deimos, 1989. 1 v.: bibl.

Second of projected three-volume history of the Inquisition in Peru. Comprehensive, detailed, objective, and thoroughly researched, work treats whole purview of the Holy Office, not just the persecution of Jews and Protestants. Examines and illuminates multiple aspects of daily life such as bigamy, clerical improprieties, and popular superstitions, as well as the institution itself and its staff. For annotation of vol. 1, see *HLAS 54:2364*. [MTH]

2284 Chalco Pacheco, Edgar. La tenencia de la tierra en Arequipa: un problema de merced en el Valle de Siguas, siglo XVI. (*Rev. Arch. Arzobispal Arequipa*, 2, 1995, p. 73–82, bibl.)

Case study of mid-16th-century land dispute is based on an incomplete *expediente*; however, it is known that the disputed land remained in the hands of Europeans. [MTH]

2285 Challco Huamán, Sonia. Composición y tenencia de tierras: valle de Paucartambo-Cuzco; Ss. XVI-XVIII. Lima: Univ. Nacional Mayor de San Marcos, Seminario de Historia Rural Andina, 1994. 135 p.: ill.,

Publishes, with a brief introduction, a mid-18th-century lawsuit regarding the hacienda of Cusipatta/Umamarca and the mortgage *censo* held on it by the Monasterio de Santa Cathalina in Cuzco. Reproduces documents from as early as 1595. A primary source for reconstructing agrarian history of the Altiplano. [MTH]

2286 Charney, Paul. Negotiating roots: Indian migrants in the Lima Valley during the colonial period. (*CLAHR/Albuquerque*, 5:1, Winter 1996, p. 1–20)

Attempts to bring together and analyze fragmented data on the circumstances of migration, to establish indigenous people's ability to control their destiny, and "to reveal new aspects of the Spanish colonizers' exploitation of the Indians." Interesting, but not well focused. [MTH]

Chávez, Fabiola. Iniciación y sueño entre las *parteras* de la sierra de Piura, Ayabaca. See *HLAS 57:1187*.

2287 Chocano Mena, Magdalena. Linaje y mayorazgo en el Perú colonial. (*Rev. Arch. Gen. Nac.*, 12, 1995, p. 129–146, table)

Detailed study of the ancestry of Fernando Carrillo de Albornoz de la Presa y Salazar, the Conde de Monteblanco, a principal member of the aristocracy of the late colonial period. Also examines relationships among wealth, status, and power. [MTH]

2288 Damian, Carol. The Virgin of the Andes: art and ritual in colonial Cuzco. Miami Beach, Fla.: Grassfield Press, 1995. 110 p.: bibl., ill. (some col.), map.

Reconstructs the history of the Virgin of Cuzco who, as a fusion of indigenous Andean and Spanish Christian beliefs and practices, represents both the Virgin Mary and Pachamama. Includes background chapters on Andean and Spanish beliefs and art. Major, mostly original work illuminates multiple aspects of the outlooks of both peoples as reflected in their religious iconography during the colonial period. Magnificently illustrated. [MTH]

2289 Dougnac Rodríguez, Antonio. El derecho de aguas indiano según Ambrosio Cerdán y Pontero. (*Rev. Hist. Derecho Ricardo Levene*, 30, 1995, p. 41–86)

Analyzes Cerdán y Pontero's exceptionally important and apparently unique 1793 *Tratado sobre las aguas de los valles de Lima.* Important source for reconstructing the history of not only the Superintendencia General de Aguas and the Jueces de Agua, but also the water distribution and irrigation control system itself, much of which dated from pre-Incan times. [MTH]

2290 Fernández Villegas, Oswaldo. Ladrones, abigeos y delincuentes de la costa norte del Perú a fines del siglo XVII. (*Bol. Lima*, 17:97, enero 1995, p. 5–10)

Publishes a 1691 *expediente* regarding the theft by two slaves of 240 pesos and some clothes from the *cacique* of Llacila, in the jurisdiction of Piura. Lacks introduction and notes. [MTH]

2291 Fernández Villegas, Oswaldo and **Mariene Farfán N.** La muerte de Luisa Puchupay: un homicidio de 1656. (*Bol. Lima*, 16:91/96, 1994, p. 16–24, bibl.)

Publishes, with introduction, a 1656 *expediente* regarding the homicide of the indigenous Luisa Puchupay in the *pueblo* of Catacaos, a crime that probably would not have concerned Spanish authorities at all had the victim not been a member of the household of the *kuraka* of Narigualá. [MTH]

2292 Flores Araoz, José *et al.* Santa Rosa de Lima y su tiempo. Lima: Banco de Crédito del Perú, 1995. 373 p.: bibl., col. ill., indexes, maps. (Col. Arte y tesoros del Perú)

A sumptuous work on Rose of Lima consists of three scholarly (not at all hagiographic) essays. The first, by Luis Eduardo Wuffarden and Pedro Guibovich Pérez, recreates ambience of late-16th- and early-17th-century Lima in exquisite detail; the second, by Ramón Mujica Pinilla, re-examines mysticism and the "intellectual sources" of Isabel de Flores y Oliva (1586–1617) and the impact of her beliefs and spiritual practices; and the third, by José Flores Araoz, looks at the iconography of the saint. Lavishly illustrated.

Includes previously unstudied art work such as series of oil paintings by heretofore unknown Laureano Dávila, a member of the Quito School, for the Monasterio de Santa Rosa in Santiago de Chile in 1700s. A splendid contribution to the religious, intellectual, and art history of the colonial period. See also items **2301** and **2304**. [MTH]

2293 Galende Díaz, Juan Carlos. El libro de los virreyes del Perú: una fuente documental para la historia de América. (*Anu. Estud. Am.*, 52:1, 1995, p. 215–228)

Detailed description of a codex preserved in the Archivo Central de la Subdirección de Historia Militar, Archivos y Bibliotecas del Servicio Histórico Militar (Madrid). Manuscript consists of a title page and 14 portraits with legends (on parchment leaves) of 16th-, 17th-, and 18th-century viceroys. [MTH]

2294 González del Riego E., Delfina. Fragmentos de la vida cotidiana a través de los procesos de divorcio: la sociedad colonial limeña en el siglo XVI. (*Histórica/Lima*, 19:2, dic. 1995, p. 197–217, bibl.)

Demonstrates that ecclesiastically sanctioned dissolution of marriages occurred in colonial Lima. Work is flawed by inadequate analysis. [MTH]

2295 González Rodríguez, María de la Paz. La acción educativa de España en Perú: el Virrey Toledo y la promoción del indio, 1569–1581. (*Arch. Ibero-Am.*, 56:221/222, enero/junio 1996, p. 191–278, appendices, bibl., ill., maps, photos)

Probably the most detailed study available of the "educational labor" undertaken by Viceroy Toledo "on behalf of" Andeans. Worth reading for information provided, but author's interpretations lack objectivity. [MTH]

2296 González Sánchez, Carlos Alberto. Los libros de los españoles en el Virreinato del Perú: siglos XVI y XVII. (*Rev. Indias*, 56:206, enero/abril 1996, p. 7–47)

Working paper on ongoing research into the inventories of the libraries of Spanish emigrants to the Viceroyalty of Peru in the 16th and 17th centuries. Research is based on the "Autos de Bienes de Difuntos" record group in the Archivo General de Indias. Lists of imprints appear in at least one-third of the inventories of emigre estates. [MTH]

2297 Guía del Archivo Histórico de Límites. Lima: Archivo Histórico de Límites, 1994. 47 p.: ill., maps.

The Archivo Histórico de Límites, founded in 1896, contains materials pertaining to national boundaries and miscellaneous materials from the colonial period. Unfortunately, the guide provides little description of the holdings. [MTH]

2298 Gutiérrez Arbulú, Laura. Los diezmos del Obispado de Arequipa a principios del siglo XVII. (*Rev. Arch. Arzobispal Arequipa*, 1, 1994, p. 45–82)

Publishes, with brief introduction, a 1623 "Quenta y razón de lo que han valido las rentas diezmales de todo el Obispado de la ciudad de Arequipa..." Undoubtedly an important primary source, but one that requires expert analysis and interpretation. [MTH]

2299 Gutiérrez Arbulú, Laura. Indice de los documentos del Archivo General de Indias sobre el comercio peruano en el siglo XVIII. (*Bol. Inst. Riva-Agüero*, 17, 1990, p. 71–146)

Describes 359 documents dating from the 1700s preserved in the Archivo General de Indias relating to the Viceroyalty's trade with the mother country and with other colonies and countries. Documents are indexed by name (including corporate body) and by year. [MTH]

2300 Gutiérrez Arbulú, Laura. Los primeros inventarios del Archivo Arzobispal de Lima. (*Rev. Arch. Gen. Nac.*, 12, 1995, p. 33–38)

Brief but fascinating account of the early history of the Archivo Arzobispal de Lima. [MTH]

2301 Hampe Martínez, Teodoro. El proceso de canonización de Santa Rosa: nuevas luces sobre la identidad criolla en el Perú colonial. (*Bol. Lima*, 17:99, junio/agosto 1995, p. 25–38, appendix, photo)

Hypothesizes that the canonization of the Rose of Lima was driven "por la identidad o autoconciencia de los criollos, deseosos de consolidar su posición mediante el reconocimiento supremo de la Iglesia;" but concludes that the relatively prompt declaration of the sainthood (1670) of Isabel de Flo-

res y Oliva (1586–1617) was the result of "la suma de expresiones de los más diversos estamentos de la población andina." See also items **2292** and **2304**. [MTH]

2302 Hampe Martínez, Teodoro. Recent works on the Inquisition and Peruvian colonial society, 1570–1820. (*LARR*, 31:2, 1996, p. 43–65, bibl.)

Cogent review of major works "published since the 1950s on the activities of the tribunal of the Santo Oficio de la Inquisición of Lima." Focuses especially on ways in which the studies elucidate and illuminate the social history of the Viceroyalty. [MTH]

2303 Hampe Martínez, Teodoro. El renacentismo del Inca Garcilaso revisitado: los clasicos greco-latinos en su biblioteca y en su obra. (*Histórica/Lima*, 18:1, julio 1994, p. 69–94, bibl.)

Novel and important analysis of the Greek and Roman works owned by the Inca Garcilaso de la Vega and the use he made of them in his writings as a man of the Renaissance. [MTH]

2304 Hampe Martínez, Teodoro. Los testigos de Santa Rosa. (*Rev. Arch. Gen. Nac.*, 13, 1996, p. 151–171)

Lists and analyzes prosopographically the 210 persons who testified during the canonization process of Saint Rose of Lima. Reaffirms thesis developed in item **2301,** but at the same time stresses that Flores y Oliva was neither a member nor a benefactress of the popular classes inasmuch as she belonged to an established, albeit impoverished, family and was an agent of "el protonacionalismo y la conciencia criolla," at least after death. See also item **2292.** [MTH]

2305 Hampe Martínez, Teodoro. Universo intelectual de un "extirpador de idolatrías:" la biblioteca de Francisco de Avila, 1648. (*Hist. Cult./Lima*, 22, 1993, p. 119–143, bibl.)

Analyzes the private library, as inventoried upon his death in 1647, of the priest who initiated the campaign to eradicate, once and for all, Andean religious beliefs and practices. At 3,108 volumes, Avila's was one of the largest collections in colonial Spanish America, not just in Peru. [MTH]

2306 **Heras, Julián.** Inventarios de las iglesias franciscanas del Valle del Mantaro, 1752. (*Bol. Inst. Riva-Agüero*, 17, 1990, p. 147–196)

Publishes, with a brief introduction, the 1752 inventories of the missionary parishes of Concepción, San Jerónimo de Tunan, Apata, Matahuasi, Cincos, Mito, and Orcotuna. Such inventories are important primary sources for the study of parishes, convents, and *cofradías;* they also delineate holdings, and sometimes the status, of the parishes' archives. [MTH]

2307 **Heras, Julián.** El P. Fernando Rodriguez Tena (+1781), historiador franciscano del Perú, siglo XVIII. (*Arch. Francisc. Hist.*, 85:1/4, Jan./Dec. 1992, p. 581–613)

Reassesses the scope and importance of a prolific, but neglected, 18th-century Franciscan chronicler. Although Father Tena continued the work of Diego Córdova Salinas (his far better known predecessor), none of Tena's extensive works (at least 13 vols.) have been published. Nevertheless, his chronicles include some new data on the activities of the Franciscans in Peru in the 1700s. [MTH]

2308 **Historia general del Perú.** v. 5, El virreinato. Lima: Editorial Brasa, 1994. 1 v.: bibl., index.

New digest of the history of the Viceroyalty of Peru emphasizes Peru proper. Includes chapters by Guillermo Lohmann Villena on institutions, José Antonio del Busto Duthurburu on the viceroys and governors, Eusebio Quiroz Paz Soldán on economic and social aspects, Armando Nieto Vélez on the Catholic Church, Jorge Cornejo Polar on literary developments, and Luis Eduardo Wuffarden on the arts. The illustrations, unfortunately, are so poorly reproduced as to be almost worthless. [MTH]

2309 **Honores Gonzales, Renzo.** Litigando en la Audencia: el devenir de un "pleyto." (*Hist. Cult./Lima*, 22, 1993, p. 27–45, bibl.)

Examines civil suit process before the Audiencia of Lima as a court of first instance. Focuses on the use of the court by Spaniards and Andeans, especially *encomenderos* and *caciques,* and on how such actions reflected their mental outlooks. [MTH]

2310 **Huertas, Lorenzo.** Fundación de la villa de Santiago de Miraflores de Zaña: un modelo hispano de planificación urbana. (*Hist. Cult./Lima*, 22, 1993, p. 145–205, bibl., facsims., maps, photo, tables)

Zaña, on Peru's north coast, was founded in 1563, destroyed by a flood in 1720, and never rebuilt. The *villa* served as an agricultural and manufacturing center. Relates the foundation and early years of the *villa,* and reconstructs the history of its layout, public buildings, ecclesiastical structures, and private homes. Also details multiple aspects of the *villa's* administrative, demographic, economic, and social structures. [MTH]

2311 **Iwasaki Cauti, Fernando.** Luisa Melgarejo de Soto y la alegría de ser tú testigo, Señor. (*Histórica/Lima*, 19:2, dic. 1995, p. 219–250, bibl.)

Reappraises the life and character of Luisa Melgarejo de Soto, a friend and confidant of Saint Rose of Lima. Although extolled by hagiographers of Saint Rose, Luisa was investigated by the Inquisition for, among other things, having been her husband's lover for some years preceding their marriage. Fascinating article. [MTH]

2312 **Laserna Gaitán, Antonio Ignacio.** El último intento de reforma de los monasterios femeninos en el Perú colonial: el auto del Arzobispo Parada de 1775. (*Anu. Estud. Am.*, 52:2, 1995, p. 263–287)

Solid study of the apparently last attempt made during the colonial period to reform the governance of women's religious orders in Lima. At issue was not only the nuns' lax behavior but also access to and control of the considerable wealth and income of the city's 14 convents. [MTH]

2313 **Lohmann Villena, Guillermo.** Juan de Hevia Bolaño: nuevos datos y nuevas disquisiciones. (*Histórica/Lima*, 18:2, dic. 1994, p. 317–333, bibl.)

Provides new data and raises new questions regarding a late-16th, early-17th-century lawyer, judge, and legal commentator whom the author has studied for over 60 years. [MTH]

2314 **Lohmann Villena, Guillermo.** Más documentos para la historia de la imprenta en Lima, 1602–1690. (*Rev. Arch. Gen. Nac.*, 12, 1995, p. 77–98, appendices)

Publishes with little commentary 13 documents from the 1660s related to the history of the press and books in Lima. These sources relate the publication history of both known and unknown works. [MTH]

2315 MacCormack, Sabine. "En los tiempos muy antiguos...": como se recordaba el pasado en el Perú de la colonia temprana. (*Procesos/Quito*, 7, 1995, p. 3–33, ill.)

Preview of a larger study in preparation on Andean (both indigenous and European) perceptions of the past at the time of the Spanish Conquest. Important contribution for understanding the evolution of mental outlooks. Well worth reading. [MTH]

2316 Málaga Núñez Zeballos, Alejandro. Archivo Arzobispal de Arequipa: guía. Arequipa, Peru: UNSA, 1994. 279 p.: bibl., ill. (some col.), index.

Well-done guide to the holdings of the recently reorganized and inventoried Archivo. In accordance with current Canon Law, this repository consolidates pre-20th-century records of the Curia proper, the Ecclesiastical Chapter, and the vicarates and parishes of the Archdiocese. Altogether, the Archivo holds 115.3 linear meters of materials dating from at least as early as 1602. [MTH]

2317 Mazzeo, Cristina Ana. Repercusiones y consecuencias de la aplicación del comercio libre en la elite mercantil limeña a fines del siglo XVIII. (*Rev. Indias*, 55:203, enero/abril 1995, p. 101–126, graphs, tables)

Relates effects, not entirely negative, of the Bourbon reforms on Lima's merchants. Some *peruleros* such as José Antonio Lavalle Cortés amassed fortunes during the late colonial period, trading in cacao and cascarilla bark from Ecuador, copper from Chile, and slaves from Africa. Compilation of time series for Lima's imports and exports during years covered, in order to put Lavalle's remarkable success in context, makes this an exceptionally important study. [MTH]

2318 Millones, Luis. Perú colonial: de Pizarro a Tupac Amaru II. Lima: Fondo Editorial de COFIDE, 1995. 250 p.: bibl. (Nuestra historia. Asuntos culturales COFIDE)

Collection of 22 essays covers colonial period in chronological order. Rreflects on various aspects of social, especially ethnic,

events of 16th, 17th, and 18th centuries. Worth reading for the multiple, occasionally novel, insights offered. [MTH]

Miño Grijalva, Manuel. La manufactura colonial: la constitución técnica del obraje. See item **1174.**

2319 Moreyra Paz Soldán, Manuel. Estudios históricos. v. 1–3. Lima: Pontificia Univ. Católica del Perú, Instituto Riva-Agüero, 1994. 3 v.: bibl., ill., maps.

Useful anthology of many important works by this pioneering economic historian (1894–1986), who was director of the prestigious *Revista histórica* of the Instituto Histórico del Perú for many years (1953–79). Vol. 1 reprints author's *Estudios sobre el tráfico marítimo en la época colonial* and *El Tribunal del Consulado de Lima*; vol. 2, various of his studies on *oidores* and viceroys, especially the viceregency of Count Monclova; and vol. 3, his classic, *La moneda colonial en el Perú*. [MTH]

2320 O'Phelan Godoy, Scarlett. La gran rebelión en los Andes: de Túpac Amaru a Túpac Catari. Cuzco, Peru: Centro de Estudios Regionales Andinos Bartolomé de las Casas, 1995. 237 p.: bibl., maps. (Archivos de historia andina, 20)

Anthology of six essays on the indigenous uprisings of 1780–82 by a leading authority. Three of the essays do not appear to have been previously published: no. 3, on elite trade and power in Cuzco following the uprisings; no. 5, on the ritual calendar of the uprisings; and no. 6, on the relationship between the uprisings and the Bourbon reforms. Essay no. 2, previously published, deals with the Inca nobility's attitude toward and role in the rebellion. For annotations of nos. 1 and 4, see *HLAS 54:2398* and *HLAS 56:2444*. [MTH]

2321 O'Phelan Godoy, Scarlett. Un siglo de rebeliones anticoloniales: Perú y Bolivia 1700–1783. Cuzco, Peru: Centro de Estudios Regionales Andinos Bartolomé de Las Casas, 1988. 351 p.: bibl., index, map. (Archivos de historia andina; 9)

Spanish-language version of previously published work (see *HLAS 50:703*). Solid study of the economic causes of the 1700s indigenous uprisings. [MTH]

2322 Ortiz Sotelo, Jorge. El Capitán de Fragata Agustín de Mendoza y Arguedas, primer capitán de puerto de Callao. (*Derroteros Mar Sur*, 2:2, 1994, p. 69–78)

Delineates the life and career of the first harbor master of Callao. Mendoza y Arguedas assumed the office in 1792 and held it until 1801, when he retired for health reasons. [MTH]

2323 Ortiz Sotelo, Jorge. Francisco Ruiz Lozano: General de la Mar del Sur, cosmógrafo mayor y primer catedrático de matemáticas de Lima, 1607–1677. (*Derroteros Mar Sur*, 1:1, 1993, p. 69–103, appendix)

Detailed, well-researched biography of the 17th-century mariner, mapmaker, mathematician, and merchant. Includes appendix of Ruiz Lozano's commercial and financial transations from 1660–71, as recorded in the notarial registers of Juan Fernández Algaba. [MTH]

2324 Ortiz Sotelo, Jorge. Rosendo Porlier y Pascual de Herazo y Ayeata: dos peruanos en la Antártida. (*Rev. Hist. Naval*, 13:48, 1995, p. 45–56)

Relates the lives and careers of the two Peruvian officers who died in Sept. 1819 when the *San Telmo*, the first known ship of any flag to have reached Antarctica, sank off the Shetland Islands. [MTH]

2325 Paniagua Pérez, Jesús. Cofradías limeñas: San Eloy y la Misericordia, 1597–1733. (*Anu. Estud. Am.*, 52:1, 1995, p. 13–35, map)

Clarifies and amplifies the history of two distinct religious brotherhoods, San Eloy and Nuestra Señora de Misericordia, both of which were affiliated with the Church of San Agustín, and which sometimes have been confused by scholars. San Eloy was the fraternity of silversmiths in Lima. [MTH]

2326 Pardo Sandoval, Teresa. Impresos peruanos del siglo XVI: ornamentación, tipografía y encuadernación. (*Bol. Inst. Riva-Agüero*, 17, 1990, p. 207–267, bibl.)

Notable attempt to write a history of the early Peruvian press. Examines fonts and illustrations, including vignettes, initials, and other devices employed by Antonio Ricardo, the first printer of Lima, and period bindings. At least two typefaces appear to have been designed by Ricardo himself and cast locally. [MTH]

2327 Pease G.Y., Franklin. Un memorial de un curaca del siglo XVII. (*Bol. Inst. Riva-Agüero*, 17, 1990, p. 197–205, bibl.)

Publishes, with a brief commentary, a petition presented to the Consejo de las Indias, ca. 1668, by Jerónimo Lorenzo Limaylla, an ethnic lord of Jauja who was in Spain to pursue honors and entitlements. Part of a larger body of documents author is preparing on Lorenzo Limaylla. [MTH]

2328 Peralta Barnuevo, Pedro de. Peralta Barnuevo and the discourse of loyalty: a critical edition of four selected texts. Edited, annotated, and introduced by Jerry M. Williams. Tempe: ASU Center for Latin American Studies Press, Arizona State Univ., 1996. 216 p.: bibl., ill., index.

Well-edited edition, with critical commentary, of four of author's texts, which are major sources for understanding the intellectual and political climate of the Viceroyalty of Peru during first half of the 18th century. Peralta Barnuevo (1663–1743) was a friend and confidant of viceroys as well as a major figure in intellectual circles. His life and writings have been largely overlooked until recently. For another study of Peralta Barnuevo's writing, see *HLAS 56:3465*. [MTH]

2329 Quijada, Mónica. De la Colonia a la República: inclusión, exclusión y memoria histórica en el Perú. (*Histórica/Lima*, 18:2, dic. 1994, p. 365–382, bibl.)

Re-examines the selective incorporation and exaltation of Incan past into the national consciousness during the late colonial and early national periods, as manifested in the *Mercurial peruano*, congressional decrees, and publications of such 19th-century intellectuals as Bartolomé Herrera, Manuel de Oriozola, and Sebastian Lorente. [MTH]

2330 Rabí Ch., Miguel. Un capítulo inédito: el traslado del Hospital del Espíritu Santo de Lima a Bellavista, 1750. (*Asclepio/Madrid*, 47:1, 1995, p. 123–133)

Research notes on the history of the mariners' hospital in Lima during the late colonial, independence, and early national periods. The proposed relocation to Bellavista never took place. Work is important as evidence that many aspects of the history of medicine in Spanish America remain to be researched. See also item **2331**. [MTH]

2331 Rabí Ch., Miguel. El Hospital del Espíritu Santo y la protección de la gente de mar, siglos XVI a XIX. (*Rev. Arch. Gen. Nac.*, 13, 1996, p. 85–94)

Additional notes on the mariners' hospital in Lima focus especially on its foundation in 1575 and its early years. See also item **2330**. [MTH]

2332 Ramírez, Susan E. Exchange and markets in the sixteenth century: a view from the north. (*in* Ethnicity, markets, and migration in the Andes: at the crossroads of history and anthropology. Edited by Brooke Larson and Olivia Harris with Enrique Tandeter. Durham, N.C.: Duke Univ. Press, 1995, p. 135–164)

Careful review of evidence recovered to date for the possible existence of "merchants" and "money" in the northern part of the Tahuantinsuyu (i.e., from Chincha through Pasto). Maintains that *mindaláes* were agents of a "long-distance exchange mechanism" and that the Spanish were responsible for the introduction of "a European commercial, profit-oriented system." [MTH]

2333 Rice, Prudence M. Wine and "local Catholicism" in colonial Moquegua, Peru. (*CLAHR/Albuquerque*, 4:4, Fall 1995, p. 369–404, appendix, photos, tables)

Historical archeological study of local religious practices is based largely on the analysis of inscriptions of religious themes on *tinajas* or "the huge...earthenware jars used to store and ferment wine at the haciendas." [MTH]

2334 Rodríguez Mateos, Joaquín. Las cofradías de Perú en la modernidad y el espíritu de la contrarreforma. (*Anu. Estud. Am.*, 52:2, 1995, p. 15–43, ill.)

Re-examines religious brotherhoods in the Archdiocese of Lima during the early colonial period. Differentiates between urban and rural *cofradías*. Based on some archival research, but concerned more with constructing a paradigm than with providing new data. Views *cofradías* as instruments of economic and social control as well as agencies for the propagation of the faith and indoctrination. [MTH]

2335 Sala i Vila, Núria. Y se armó el tole tole: tributo indígena y movimientos sociales en el Virreinato del Perú, 1790–1814. Ayacucho, Peru: Instituto de Estudios Regionales José María Arguedas, 1996. 320 p.: bibl., maps.

Revisionist study of the late colonial period focuses on reform of the tribute system following Túpac Amaru rebellion (1780–83); the response of *caciques*, indigenous *pueblos*, and specific groups such as the Yanaconas; and indigenous participation in the Angulo and Pumacahua rebellions (1814–16). Exceptionally well documented and researched. [MTH]

2336 Salas de Coloma, Miriam. Fuentes y derroteros para el estudio de los obrajes en el Perú colonial. (*Am. Lat. Hist. Econ. Bol. Fuentes*, 4, julio/dic. 1995, p. 9–15)

Reviews studies and highlights sources for reconstructing the history of *obrajes* in colonial Peru. See also item **2337**. [MTH]

2337 Salas de Coloma, Miriam. Transformación del paisaje ganadero del centro-sur-este andino con la llegada del conquistador español, siglos XVI-XVIII. (*in* International Congress of Americanists, *48th, Stockholm, 1994*. Colonización agrícola y ganadera en América, siglos XVI-XVIII: su impacto en la población aborigen. Quito: Ediciones Abya-Yala, 1995, p. 225–267, tables, map)

Delineates the transformation of agricultural landscape, especially the displacement of indigenous communities and cameloids of the Huamanga district (modern Ayacucho) during the colonial period, as textile manufacturing and sheep wool production increasingly became the motor of the conquerers' economy. Also a significant contribution to the history of *obrajes*. See also item **2336**. [MTH]

2338 San Cristóbal, Antonio. La construcción de la Iglesia de la Soledad. (*Hist. Cult./Lima*, 22, 1993, p. 205–241, facsim., ill., photo)

Well-researched and documented study of the construction and vicissitudes of the Church of la Soledad, situated next to San Franciso in Lima. Dating from 1669, church was originally a baroque structure but, according to author, was "bastardized" in early 1800s by the neoclassicist Master Matías. [MTH]

2339 San Cristóbal, Antonio. Ignacio Martorell y las torres de la Catedral de Lima. (*Histórica/Lima*, 19:2, dic. 1995, p. 295–318, bibl.)

Demonstrates that the architect Ignacio Martorell designed and built (in the 1790s) the present-day towers of the Cathedral of Lima. Well documented. [MTH]

2340 Sánchez-Concha Barrios, Rafael. La historia del derecho en el Perú: perspectivas de medio siglo, 1950–1993. (*Histórica/Lima*, 19:2, dic. 1995, p. 319–345, bibl.)

Reviews the historiography of law in Peru during the second half of the 20th century. Also surveys the study of history inasmuch as many noteworthy Peruvian historians, present and past, were trained in both law and history. Well worth reading. [MTH]

2341 Stavig, Ward. "Living in offense of our Lord": indigenous sexual values and marital life in the colonial crucible. (*HAHR*, 75:4, Nov. 1995, p. 597–622)

Pioneering study of sexual and marital beliefs and practices among indigenous peoples in the provinces of Quispicanchis and Canas y Canchis, in the Cuzco region, during the second half of the colonial period. Based on research in the archdiocesan and departmental archives of Cuzco. [MTH]

2342 Stern, Steve J. The variety and ambiguity of native Andean intervention in European colonial markets. (*in* Ethnicity, markets, and migration in the Andes: at the crossroads of history and anthropology. Edited by Brooke Larson and Olivia Harris with Enrique Tandeter. Durham, N.C.: Duke Univ. Press, 1995, p. 73–100, tables)

Excellent analysis of the ways in which Andeans appear to have interacted with European economic systems, especially with the "market." Proposes several promising venues for additional research, making the point that immersion in time and place through mastery of the sources, rather than methodology, provides the answers historians seek in their research. [MTH]

2343 Szemiński, Jan. The last time the Inca came back: messianism and nationalism in the great rebellion of 1780–1783.

(South and Meso-American native spirituality: from the cult of the feathered serpent to the theology of liberation. New York: Crossroad, 1993, p. 279–299, bibl.)

Focuses on the ideology of the Túpac Amaru movement, indigenous perceptions of "the Inca," the religious or mythological aspects of the man and the movement, and post-independence perceptions of Túpac Amaru (referred to as "Thupa Amaro" by Szemiński). Well written and insightful. [MTH]

Tandeter, Enrique. Población y economía en los Andes, siglo XVIII. See item **2394.**

Tandeter, Enrique; Vilma Milletich; and **Roberto Schmit.** Flujos mercantiles en el Potosí colonial tardío. See item **2396.**

2344 Urrutia Ceruti, Jaime. Mercancías y tejidos en Huamanga, 1779–1818. (*in* Circuitos mercantiles y mercados en Latinoamérica, siglos XVIII-XIX. México: Instituto de Investigaciones Dr. José María Luis Mora; Instituto de Investigaciones Históricas UNAM, 1995, p. 56–86, graphs, tables)

Quantitative study of commerce and textile production of Huamanga during the late colonial period is based on customs records from the Archivo General de la Nación. [MTH]

2345 Varón Gabai, Rafael. Francisco Pizarro and his brothers: the illusion of power in sixteenth-century Peru. Translated by Javier Flores Espinoza. Norman: Univ. of Oklahoma Press, 1997. 352 p.: bibl., ill., index, maps, tables.

Based on author's doctoral dissertation, work reconstructs and analyzes the making of the financial empire of the conquerer of Peru and his brothers. Painstaking study examines and elucidates multiple aspects of both the economic and sociopolitical history of the Perus and Spain in the 16th century. See also item **2346.** [MTH]

2346 Varón Gabai, Rafael. Negocios y gobierno de los Pizarro del Perú: un ensayo de interpretación. (*Histórica/Lima*, 18:2, dic. 1994, p. 417–433)

Publishes conclusions and therefore serves as a preview to author's dissertation. See item **2345.** [MTH]

2347 Vicente, Camilo Gustavo and **Luis Linci Jara.** Historia de Moyobamba. (*Rev. Arch. Gen. Nac.*, 12, 1995, p. 161–174, bibl., facsims.)

Archival notes and facsimiles of documents on the foundation of Moyobamba in 1549 and on its founder, Juan Pérez de Guevara. [MTH]

2348 Wuffarden, Luis Eduardo and **Pedro Guibovich Pérez.** El clérigo Juan López de Vozmediano, comitente de Martínez Montañes en Lima. (*Bol. Inst. Riva-Agüero*, 17, 1990, p. 419–430)

Research notes on a heretofore unknown middle colonial period clergyman and patron of the arts, especially of religious paintings and sculpture. [MTH]

2349 Zárate, Agustin de. Historia del descubrimiento y conquista del Perú. Edición, notas y estudio preliminar de Franklin Pease G.Y. y Teodoro Hampe Martínez. Lima: Pontificia Univ. Católica del Perú, Fondo Editorial, 1995. 539 p.: bibl., ill., indexes. (Col. clásicos peruanos)

Eminently scholarly and probably definitive edition of Zárate's well known 1555 chronicle of the discovery and conquest of the Perus incorporates author's corrections from 2nd, or 1577 edition. The introductory studies by Pease G.Y. and Hampe Martínez on Zárate, and on his work and the multiple editions and versions thereof, are exceptionally informative. Editors have added name and place indexes. [MTH]

2350 Zevallos Quiñones, Jorge. Los fundadores y primeros pobladores de Trujillo del Perú. v. 1–2. Trujillo, Peru: Fundación Alfredo Pinillos Goicochea, 1996. 2 v.: bibl., indexes.

Vol. 1 consists of biographies of the 31 founders of Trujillo and of 23 of the town's first settlers. Vol. 2 literally transcribes 59 primary sources related to these individuals. Rich in detail, well researched, documented, and indexed. Significant contribution to the history of the north coast during the early colonial period. [MTH]

2351 Zevallos Quiñones, Jorge. Pretendientes a la encomienda de Chicama en 1583. (*Bol. Inst. Riva-Agüero*, 17, 1990, p. 373–381)

Notes on the 43 individuals who petitioned to be granted the encomienda of Chi-

cama when it became vacant in 1583. Notwithstanding these individuals' merits or needs, the crown "repossessed" Chicama and its rents. [MTH]

ALTO PERÚ

Assadourian, Carlos Sempat. Transiciones hacia el sistema colonial andino. See item **2274.**

2352 Baptista Morales, Javier. Los misioneros jesuitas de Mojos. (*Yachay/ Cochabamba*, 12:21, 1995, p. 69–90, bibl.)

Sketches the lives and careers of Jesuits posted to the Mojos missions from the late-16th century to Order's expulsion in 1768. Includes some new data culled from the Jesuit archives in Rome. See also item **2381.** [MTH]

2353 Barnadas, Josep M. Nuevas luces sobre dos escritores potosinos: Luis Capoche y García de Llanos, 1589–1613. (*Anuario/Sucre*, 1996, p. 123–142, tables)

Publishes and comments on the significance of new archival data on Capoche, author of *Relación general del asiento y Villa Imperial de Potosí* (1585); and García de Llanos, author of a still unpublished 1609–10 account of the Red Mountain. [MTH]

2354 Block, David. Fuentes para la historia de Moxos. (*Anuario/Sucre*, 1994/95, p. 153–162)

Succinct work discusses and describes archival sources, published materials, and secondary literature for the reconstruction of the Mojos, or *departamento* of El Beni, during colonial and national periods. [MTH]

2355 Bravo Guerreira, Concepción. Las misiones de Chiquitos: pervivencia y resistencia de un modelo de colonización. (*Rev. Complut. Hist. Am.*, 21, 1995, p. 29–55, bibl., map, table)

Addresses little-known post-expulsion history of the Jesuit missions in the Chiquitos. Well-researched essay focuses on the history of the missions under the governorship of the Bishop of Santa Cruz during the late-18th and early-19th centuries. Also examines demographic, economic, and social developments among indigenous peoples of the province of Chiquitos (*departamento* of Santa Cruz). [MTH]

2356 Bridikhina, Eugenia. La vida urbana de los negros en La Paz en el siglo XVIII. (*in* Reunión Anual de Etnología, *8th?, La Paz?, 1994.* Actas. La Paz: Museo Nacional de Etnografía y Folklore, 1995, t. 1, p. 23–32, bibl.)

Examines the lives of black slaves and free blacks in Potosí and La Paz in the 17th and 18th centuries. Reflects some original research. [MTH]

2357 Brockington, Lolita Gutiérrez. La dinámica de la historia regional: el caso de Mizque (Cochabamba) y "la puente de 1630." (*Hist. Cult./Lima,* 22, 1993, p. 75–104, facsim., map, table)

Reports on the construction of a bridge across the "Río Grande" of Mizque in 1630 and its impact on the economy of the region, a major agricultural area during the colonial period. A detailed and wholly original preview of the author's forthcoming larger study on the *corregimiento* of Mizque. See also item **2358.** [MTH]

2358 Brockington, Lolita Gutiérrez. Trabajo, etnicidad y raza: el afro-boliviano en el corregimiento de Mizque, 1573–1787. (*Anuario/Sucre,* 1996, p. 107–122, map, tables)

Wholly original study of the demographic and economic presence of black slaves and freedmen in the *corregimiento* of Mizque during the colonial period. See also item **2357.** [MTH]

2359 Calzavarini, Lorenzo. Guía de fuentes franciscanas en el Archivo y Biblioteca Nacionales de Bolivia. (*Anuario/Sucre,* 1994/95, p. 201–207)

Highlights Franciscan sources preserved in the Archivo y Biblioteca Nacionales de Bolivia. [MTH]

2360 Cunietti-Ferrando, Arnaldo J. Historia de la Real Casa de Moneda de Potosí durante la dominación hispánica, 1573–1825. v. 1, 1573–1825. Buenos Aires: Impr. de Pellegrini, 1986 [i.e., 1995]. 267 p.: bibl., ill.

In press for nine years due to financial reasons, work is first part of a projected two-volume history of the Casa Real de Moneda de Potosí. Written by a numismatist for fellow numismatists; of interest to specialists only. [MTH]

2361 Diez de Medina, Francisco Tadeo. Diario del alzamiento de indios conjurados contra la Ciudad de Nuestra Señora de La Paz, 1781. Edición de María Eugenia del Valle de Siles. Prólogo de Gunnar Mendoza L. 2. ed. La Paz: Banco Boliviano Americano, 1994. 346 p.: bibl., ill. (some col.), indexes, maps (some col.).

The first complete edition of this extraordinarily detailed and exceptionally important eyewitness account of the 1781 siege of La Paz by the forces of Túpac Katari. Well edited and indexed. For annotation of first half of Diez de Medina's diary, see *HLAS 44:2738.* [MTH]

2362 Fernández Alonso, Serena. Minería peruana y rerformismo estatal: las ordenanzas del Real Banco de San Carlos de la Villa de Potosí. (*in* Minería americana colonial y del siglo XIX. México: Instituto Nacional de Antropología e Historia, 1994, p. 31–42, table)

Re-examines the impact of Real Banco de San Carlos on mining credit and output at Potosí. Concludes that although conditions in general improved, the changes introduced failed to transform the structure. [MTH]

2363 Frigerio, José Oscar. La rebelión criolla de la Villa de Oruro: principales causas y perspectivas. (*Anu. Estud. Am.,* 52:1, 1995, p. 57–90)

Examines the causes of the Feb. 10, 1781, uprising of Oruro creole miners against their *chapetón* exploiters, mostly merchants. Researched and drafted independently of Oscar Cornblit's more or less simultaneously published work (see *HLAS 56:2475*). [MTH]

2364 Gato Castaño, Purificación. Aproximación a la figura del ilustrado aragonés, José Antonio de San Alberto, 1727–1804. (*Anuario/Sucre,* 1996, p. 163–178)

Precis of ecclesiastical labors, especially in education, of José Antonio de San Alberto, the enlightened archbishop of Charcas (1785–1804). Based on author's previous work, see item *HLAS 54:2523.* [MTH]

2365 Gavira Márquez, Concepción. Caja Real, reforma y minería en Oruro, 1776–1810. (*Anuario/Sucre,* 1996, p. 199–227)

Re-examines the impact of Bourbon reforms on mining centers, specifically in

Oruro. Demonstrates that Oruro, unlike Potosí, did not benefit from programs such as the Real Banco de San Carlos; however, some residents of Oruro benefited from their appointment to Real Hacienda posts which they manipulated to their own advantage. [MTH]

2366 González Casasnovas, Ignacio. Debates y proyectos en la administración colonial sobre el papel de la economía minera altoperuana: la mita de Potosí en las postrimerías del siglo XVII, 1681–1692. (*in* Minería americana colonial y del siglo XIX. México: Instituto Nacional de Antropología e Historia, 1994, p. 13–29, bibl.)

Reassesses attempts by the Conde de Monclova to reform the "mita de Potosí." Concludes that the Viceroy's reforms probably had little impact on the mining sector, but that they may have benefited the indigenous communities responsible for supplying Potosí with labor. Based on considerable archival research and appropriate secondary literature. [MTH]

Grieshaber, Erwin P. Los padrones de la contribución indígena como fuente demográfica: posibilidades y limitaciones. See item **2721.**

2367 Inch C., Marcela. La biblioteca de Juan de Lizarazu: Potosí, siglo XVIII. (*Anuario/Sucre,* 1994/95, p. 229–245, bibl., index)

Analyzes the private library of Juan de Lizarazu (d. 1783), one of the richest men of late colonial Potosí. [MTH]

2368 Just, Estanislao. Apuntes para una historia del seminario y clero chuquisaqueño, 1538–1609. (*Yachay/Cochabamba,* 11:19/20, 1994, p. 147–182, facsims.)

Chronologically ordered notes for the reconstruction of the early history of the diocesan seminary of La Plata (modern Sucre) and of the first clergy of the diocese. [MTH]

2369 Just, Estanislao. La misión jesuítica de Santa Cruz de la Sierra en la correspondencia de sus misioneros, 1587–1608. (*Yachay/Cochabamba,* 12:21, 1995, p. 39–68, bibl.)

Chronologically ordered notes on the early years of Jesuit missions in Santa Cruz de la Sierra, based on *cartas anuas.* [MTH]

2370 Larson, Brooke and **Rosario León.** Markets, power, and the politics of exchange in Tapacarí, c. 1780 and 1980. (*in* Ethnicity, markets, and migration in the Andes: at the crossroads of history and anthropology. Edited by Brooke Larson and Olivia Harris with Enrique Tandeter. Durham, N.C.: Duke Univ. Press, 1995, p. 224–255)

Larson, a historian, and León, an anthropologist, join forces to compare the late-18th- and late-20th-century marketplaces of the Tapacarí region. Authors noted significant shifts "in power balances and terms of exchange" between San Agustín de Tapacarí and the outlying "villages and *estancias* of the southern and western highlands" of the region. [MTH]

2371 Lema, Ana María. Coca y rebelión: la coca yungueña a fines del siglo XVIII. (*Rev. Mus. Nac. Etnogr. Folk.,* 3:3, 1991, p. 67–89)

Brief but well-researched economic study of the *partido* of Chulumani, one of the primary coca-producing regions, during and after the Túpac Katari rebellion. [MTH]

2372 Libros registros-cedularios de Charcas, 1563–1717: catálogo. v. 1–4. Buenos Aires: Instituto de Investigaciones de Historia del Derecho, 1992. 4 v. (Edición de fuentes de derecho indiano en conmemoración del V centenario del descubrimiento de América; 5–8)

First four volumes of a projected five-volume set, the last of which is supposed to include an index. Work abstracts, in chronological order, the contents of royal decrees and orders dispatched to the Audiencia of Charcas between 1563 and 1717. A major set of primary sources. The Instituto de Investigaciones de Historia del Derecho also has published the three-volume set *Libros registros-cedularios del Río de la Plata, 1534–1717* (1984–91), and has announced future publication of similar volumes for Tucumán and Paraguay. [MTH]

2373 López Beltrán, Clara. La buena vecindad: las mujeres de elite en la sociedad colonial del siglo XVII. (*Colon. Lat. Am. Rev.,* 5:2, Dec. 1996, p. 219–236, bibl.)

Pioneering study of creole and peninsular women in La Paz during the middle colonial period. Delineates their role as "faithful" wife, "proper" mother, "dutiful" daughter, and "devout" nun, and examines various ways in which women contributed to the perpetuation of the elite. Also touches on "deviant" behavior. See also items **2374** and **2376**. [MTH]

2374 López Beltrán, Clara. El círculo del poder: matrimonio y parentesco en la elite colonial de La Paz. (*Anuario/Sucre,* 1996, p. 143–162, graphs)

Detailed, well-researched, original study of marriage politics of the European elite of La Paz, especially of the Gutiérrez de Escobar and Ramírez de Vargas families, during the 16th and 17th centuries. See also items **2373** and **2376**. [MTH]

2375 López Beltrán, Clara. Estructura económica de una sociedad colonial: Charcas en el siglo XVII. Presentación de Marcello Carmagnani. La Paz: Centro de Estudios de la Realidad Económica y Social, 1988. 326 p.: bibl., ill. (Estudios históricos; 7)

Economic and demographic study of the 17th century that has substantially advanced the knowledge and reshaped the interpretations of the middle colonial period. Well researched and solidly documented. [MTH]

2376 López Beltrán, Clara. Intereses y pasiones de los *vecinos* de La Paz en el siglo XVII: la elite provinciana en Charcas, virreinato del Perú. (*Anu. Estud. Am.,* 52:1, 1995, p. 37–56, tables)

Examines the composition and perpetuation of the La Paz elite in 1600s. See also items **2373** and **2374**. [MTH]

2377 Loza, Carmen Beatriz. Fuentes de subempadronamiento de la población de Charcas: una medida de la exhaustividad de registro en las visitas de Sonqo, La Paz, 1568/1569–1570. (*Anuario/Sucre,* 1994/95, p. 187–200, graphs, tables)

Analyzes two early, recently published *visitas* of Sonqo to demonstrate that a comparison of nominative lists for the same place from different years will correct for underregistration, provided that such registers were compiled within a few years of each other. [MTH]

2378 Loza, Carmen Beatriz. Monetización del tributo en La Paz: comparación del perfil de las tasas de nueve repartimientos de Juan Remón, 1563 y 1575. (*Anuario/Sucre,* 1996, p. 83–105, graphs, tables)

Detailed study of the conversion of tribute in kind to tribute in species. Utilizes for purposes of exemplification the 1563 (Conde de Nieva) and 1575 (Toledo) tribute schedules of the encomienda of Juan Remón, a *vecino feudatorio* of La Paz. [MTH]

2379 Medrano, Lilia Inés Zanotti de and **Ieda Neli Garcia.** Educação, religião e estado: um documento de 1788 sobre a educação indígena de Moxos, Bolívia. (*Not. Bibliogr. Hist.,* 28:160, jan./março 1996, p. 18–30)

Publishes and analyzes the 1788 *Carta fácil, breve y compendiosa,* designed to instill loyalty and obedience to the monarchy among the indigenous of the Mojos region. The extent to which the document was understood remains to be determined. [MTH]

2380 Meruvia, Fanor. La coca en Pocona: ocaso de una encomienda y emergencia en chacaras privadas, siglo XVI. (*Búsqueda/Cochabamba,* 3:4/5, julio 1993, p. 193–277, bibl., tables)

Extraordinarily well-detailed, wholly original, multifaceted study of coca production in *yungas* of Pocona from Incan times through the early 17th century. The encomienda of Pocona dates from 1538, if not earlier. The *chacaras,* or small farms, that eventually replaced the encomiendas emerged ca. 1579. An exceptionally important contribution to economic, demographic, and local history of early colonial period Bolivia. See also item **2390**. [MTH]

O'Phelan Godoy, Scarlett. La gran rebelión en los Andes: de Túpac Amaru a Túpac Catari. See item **2320**.

O'Phelan Godoy, Scarlett. Un siglo de rebeliones anticoloniales: Perú y Bolivia 1700–1783. See item **2321**.

2381 Perez Diez, Andres A. Jesuítas en moxos: el conocimiento lingüistico. (*in* Simpósio Nacional de Estudos Missioneiros, *8th, Santa Rosa, Brazil, 1991.* As missões jesuítico-guaranis: cultura e sociedade; anais. Santa Rosa, Brazil: Faculdade de Filosofia, Ciências e Letras Dom Bosco, 1991, p. 62–74, bibl.)

Brief but cogent review of the linguistic knowledge and contributions of the Jesuit missionaries assigned to the Mojos. Useful analysis and listing. See also item **2352**. [MTH]

Platt, Tristán. Los Guerreros de Cristo: cofradías, misa solar, y guerra regenerativa en una doctrina Macha, siglos XVIII-XX. See *HLAS 57:1092.*

2382 Presta, Ana María. Encomienda, familia, y redes en Charcas colonial: los Almendras, 1540–1600. (*Rev. Indias*, 57:209, enero/abril 1997, p. 21–53, map)

Reconstructs and analyzes the role of kinship and regional support in the amassing and retention of wealth and socioeconomic status by the Almendras, one of the leading early colonial period *encomendero* families. [MTH]

2383 Presta, Ana María. Hacienda y comunidad: un estudio en la provincia de Pilaya y Paspaya, siglos XVI-XVIII. (*ANDES Antropol. Hist.*, 1, primer semestre 1990, p. 31–45, bibl.)

Examines relationship between a Jesuit hacienda and nearby Aymara-speaking indigenous communities in the Pilaya and Paspaya region of Alto Perú. Finds that indigenous communities continued to maintain control over hacienda pasture land, eventually regaining the land after expulsion of the Jesuits. Questions supposed continual extension of haciendas at the expense of communal lands, as well as the idea that indigenous pueblos provided a reserve labor force for Spanish haciendas. [SMS]

2384 Presta, Ana María. Las propiedades del Colegio de la Compañia de Jesús de Tarija. (*Anuario/Sucre*, 1996, p. 179–198, graph, tables)

Quantitative study of the rural estates of the Jesuit *colegio* of Tarija focuses on the most profitable hacienda, the wine-producing San Francisco Xavier del Saladillo, for which account ledgers have survived from 1726–30. [MTH]

2385 Rossells, Beatriz. La gastronomía en Potosí y Charcas: siglos XVIII y XIX; 800 recetas de la cocina criolla. La Paz: Embajada de España, Fundación "Mario Mercado Vaca Guzmán", 1995. 319 p.: bibl., ill. (some col.), index.

Work is not only a compendium of cookbooks and recipe collections from the 18th and 19th centuries but, more importantly, a study of eating, banquet, and party customs of Bolivians of the period. Major contribution to the emerging history of private life in the Andes. Cookbooks and recipes date from 1776, 1820, 1880, and 1917. [MTH]

2386 Saignes, Thierry. Indian migration and social change in seventeenth-century Charcas. (*in* Ethnicity, markets, and migration in the Andes: at the crossroads of history and anthropology. Edited by Brooke Larson and Olivia Harris with Enrique Tandeter. Durham, N.C.: Duke Univ. Press, 1995, p. 167–195)

Easy-to-read essay on migration and the gradual transition from a hierarchical society founded on filiation, ascription, kinship, and estate to one based on residence, achievement, territoriality, and class. The primary sources and data-based analysis challenge facile assumption that Indian flight and absenteeism were acts of "resistance." Also adds complexity to the topic of the dissolution of ethnic identity and its replacement by a generic "Indian" identity. [S. Ramirez]

2387 Santamaría, Daniel J. Intercambios comerciales internos en el Alto Perú colonial tardío. (*Rev. Complut. Hist. Am.*, 22, 1996, p. 239–273, tables)

Quantifies patterns of trade between "peripheral" regions of Mizque, Vallegrande, and Santa Cruz de la Sierra, and "nuclear" regions such as La Paz and Potosí, during the late colonial period. Includes price data. Major contribution inasmuch as economic history of "secondary" areas is less well known than that of the mining center. [MTH]

2388 Santamaría, Daniel J. Recaudación y políticas tributarias en Charcas, fines del siglo XVIII. (*Rev. Indias*, 57:209, enero/abril 1997, p. 85–111, appendix, tables)

Quantifies collection of indigenous tributes in whole of Charcas, *intendencia* by *intendencia*, for years 1780–1810. Fills a major gap in the history of tributes. Includes useful appendix delineating and defining categories of tributes. [MTH]

2389 Santos Escobar, Roberto. Estructura de lo cotidiano de La Paz: la caja de agua en el siglo XVIII. (*Etnología/La Paz*, 15:19, 1991, p. 81–89)

Working paper on 18th-century water distribution system in La Paz. Some original research. [MTH]

2390 **Schramm, Raimund.** Paces y guerra, coca y sal: recursos naturales y planteamientos étnicos en el Anti de Pocona—corrigimiento de Mizque, siglos XVI y XVII. (*in* International Congress of Americanists, *48th, Stockholm, 1994*. Colonizacíon agrícola y ganadera en América, siglos XVI-XVIII: su impacto en la población aborigen. Quito: Ediciones Abya-Yala, 1995, p. 331–350)

Research notes on the relationships between ethnic groups and on the exploitation of natural resources in a *yunga* during the early colonial period. Of interest to specialists. See also item **2380.** [MTH]

2391 **Serrano, Carlos.** Cronología sobre la explotación de las vetas del Cerro Rico. (*Anuario/Sucre*, 1996, p. 69–82, bibl.)

Establishes a provisional chronology of the exploitation of lode-bearing veins of the Red Mountain. Task is made difficult because sources show different names for the same veins and because some of the names have fallen into disuse. [MTH]

2392 **Shimko, Susana** and **Gladys Mercado.** Comercio de coca en la yunga boliviana en el siglo XVIII: una estrategia de control en el uso de la coca. (*in* Congreso Nacional de Historia Argentina, *Buenos Aires, 1995*. Actas. Buenos Aires: Comisión Post Congreso Nacional de Historia Argentina, 1997, v. 1, p. 179–186, bibl., map)

Somewhat pedestrian piece is significant for calling attention to an early 18th-century proposal to monopolize the coca trade. [MTH]

Stern, Steve J. The variety and ambiguity of native Andean intervention in European colonial markets. See item **2342.**

2393 **Szemiński, Jan.** De unos herreros españoles entre los chiriguanos. (*Reflejos/Jerusalem*, 4, dic. 1995, p. 87–91, ill., table)

Questions extent to which the prolonged presence of Europeans (in this case, blacksmiths) among relatively isolated, independent groups such as the Chiriguanos resulted in acculturation. [MTH]

2394 **Tandeter, Enrique.** Población y economía en los Andes, siglo XVIII. (*Rev. Andin.*, 13:1, 1995, p. 7–42, bibl., graph)

Reviews the state and movement of the population and the economy of the highlands of the Perus in the 18th century. Based on author's reading of historiography on the two themes and his ongoing research on the demographic and economic history of the communities of Sacaca and Acasio in the prov. of Chayanta. Especially important is presentation and discussion of parish register and tithe data for the two *pueblos*. [MTH]

2395 **Tandeter, Enrique.** Los trabajadores mineros y el mercado. (*Anuario/Sucre*, 1996, p. 53–68)

Re-examines relationship between labor (supply) and market (demand) at Potosí throughout the colonial period. Author makes a number of interesting points, one of which is that "la evolución de los precios durante la segunda mitad del siglo XVIII, así como estudios particulares de áreas productoras, sugieren que la demanda interna no creció al ritmo de la población global ni en las ciudades ni en las comunidades indígenas." [MTH]

2396 **Tandeter, Enrique; Vilma Milletich;** and **Roberto Schmit.** Flujos mercantiles en el Potosí colonial tardío. (*in* Circuitos mercantiles y mercados en Latinoamérica, siglos XVIII-XIX. México: Instituto de Investigaciones Dr. José María Luis Mora; Instituto de Investigaciones Históricas UNAM, 1995, p. 13–55, graphs, tables)

Re-examines the flow of trade to and from Potosí during the late colonial period. In contrast to previously held ideas, authors demonstrate that 1) production of silver continued to increase from 1780–1800, as did production and import of principal products of districts of La Paz, Arequipa, and Cuzco; 2) the economic crisis of Potosí and the Altiplano did not begin until early 1800s; and 3) no correlation between silver production and regional prices for period 1780–1810 appears to exist. Exceptionally important piece substantially alters conventional picture of economic conditions in southern Peruvian and Bolivian highlands following Túpac Amaru and Catari rebellions. [MTH]

2397 Villarías-Robles, Juan J.R. and **David M. Pereira Herrera.** El emplazamiento de Canata y la fundación de la villa de Oropesa: una contribución a la geografía histórica del valle de Cochabamba, Bolivia, en los siglos XV y XVI. (*Rev. Andin.*, 13:1, 1995, p. 199–236, appendix, bibl., maps)

Well-researched and documented study includes many new details regarding the preexisting indigenous town of Canata and the initial Spanish settlement and early history of Oropesa (subsequently Cochabamba). Includes appendix of primary sources. For geographer's comment, see *HLAS 57:2686.* [MTH]

CHILE

2398 Advis V., Patricio. Noticias de cronistas e historiadores sobre la travesia de los Andes realizada por la hueste de Almagro durante la jornada de Chile. (*Contrib. Hist.*, 4, 1994, p. 103–127, bibl.)

The script for a television program produced by the Universidad Católica de Chile as part of its "Al Sur del Mundo" series, work reconstructs routes taken by followers of Almargo (consisting of eight factions or groups) from Cuzco to the Valley of Aconcagua from June 1535-Jan. 1536. Based on chronicles and histories of the conquest and colonization of Peru and Chile. [MTH]

2399 Almarza, Sara. El contorno de un hombre: carta de José Antonio de Rojas a su padre. (*Mapocho/Santiago*, 39, primer semestre 1996, p. 181–189, facsim.)

Reproduces and analyzes a 1781 letter written by then 14-year-old Rojas to his father. Shows private correspondence to be a useful tool for establishing and elucidating the mentality of early Spanish-Americans. [MTH]

2400 Benavente Aninat, Maria Antonia and **Carmen Bermejo Lorenzo.** Síntesis histórica de la funebria en Chile. (*Rev. Chil. Hist. Geogr.*, 162, 1996, p. 137–162, bibl.)

Useful review of funeral and burial practices during the colonial and national periods. [MTH]

2401 Boccara, Guillaume. Notas acerca de los dispositivos de poder en la sociedad colonial-fronteriza: la resistencia y la transculturación de los Reche-Mapuche del cen-

tro-sur de Chile, XVI-XVII. (*Rev. Indias*, 41:208, sept./dic. 1996, p. 659–695, maps)

Argues that the Mapuches did not exist as a distinct group during the early colonial period; that they came into existence through acculturation and amalgamation of preexisting ethnic groups during the second half of the 18th century; and that the preexisting group in central Chile was the Reche. Also claims that warfare was not replaced by "peace," as revisionist frontier historians of the 1980s and 1990s such as Sergio Villalobos have proposed (see, for example, item **2415**); rather, the Spaniards changed their tactics for achieving submission and domination of the indigenous groups. See also item **2403.** [MTH]

2402 Cavieres Figueroa, Eduardo. Epidemias, medicina y sociedad colonial: la plaga de 1779–1780 en Chile. (*Cuad. Hist./Santiago*, 10, dic. 1990, p. 87–108, graphs, tables)

Sheds light on the epidemic of 1779–80 by quantifying its impact through judicious analysis of registers of burials. Quantitatively and qualitatively sophisticated, yet eminently readable. [MTH]

2403 Foerster, Rolf. Jesuitas y mapuches, 1593–1767. Santiago: Editorial Universitaria, 1996. 397 p.: bibl., ill., map. (Col. Imagen de Chile)

Examines ways in which Jesuit missions impacted and recreated not only Mapuche identity but also Chilean identity itself. This postmodernistic, qualitative study is an important work that casts the Jesuits, the Mapuche, and Chilean colonial society in new, thought-provoking ways. See also item **2401.** [MTH]

2404 Larrain, José Manuel. Los términos de intercambio en una economía colonial: el caso de Chile en los siglos XVII-XVIII. (*Am. Lat. Hist. Econ. Bol. Fuentes*, 5, enero/junio 1996, p. 51–66, appendix, bibl.)

Re-evaluates terms of trade during the second half of colonial period, utilizing the price data that has become available mainly through author's own research. Conclusions are: 1) prices prevalent in Santiago were valid indicators of fluctuations in the international market; and 2) in the 18th century, Chile enjoyed a favorable balance of trade (much

more so than in the second half of the 17th).
[MTH]

2405 León Solís, Leonardo. Conflictos de
poder y guerras tribales en Araucanía
y Las Pampas: la Batalla de Tromen, 1774.
(*Historia/Santiago*, 29, 1995/96, p. 185–233)

Rescues from neglect a major chapter
in the internal history of the Mapuches: the
internecine Battle of Tromen. Fought after
Toqui Ayllapangui's rise to tribal power, the
battle was one of the bloodiest ever recorded
in Mapuche history and apparently increased
the power of the "*caciques* of peace." [MTH]

2406 Licata, Rosa. La Sociedad de los Hospi-
cianos Chilenos en la segunda mitad
del siglo XVIII. (*Rev. Interam. Bibliogr.*, 44:3,
1994, p. 481–500)

Analyzes social thought of the late colonial and early national period social reformer Manuel de Salas (1754–1841). [MTH]

Martínez Busch, Jorge. La influencia de Fray
Francisco de Vitoria O.P. en Chile, 1550–
1650: apuntes para una historia. See item
5200.

2407 Mejías-López, William. Francisco
Núñez de Pineda y Bascuñán, re-
formista seguidor de Ercilla. (*Rev. Interam.
Bibliogr.*, 43:1, 1993, p. 117–135)

Examines the pro-Araucanian leanings
of Núñez de Pineda y Bascuñán, author of
Cautiverio feliz. [MTH]

2408 Peña Alvarez, Sergio. La Parroquia de
San Antonio del Mar, Barraza, 1680–
1824: historia religiosa, social y económica
de una jurisdicción eclesiástica del valle del
Limarí, Norte Chico, Chile. Santiago: Fondo
de Desarrollo de la Cultura y las Artes, Ministerio de Educación, 1994. 90 p.: appendix,
bibl., ill., maps.

Well-researched and documented history of San Antonio del Mar, an ecclesiastical parish in the North Chico, from its earliest beginnings through the end of the
colonial period. Written by a professionally
trained scholar. Includes documentary appendix. [MTH]

2409 Pinto Rodríguez, Jorge. La familia en
una sociedad del Chile colonial: las
modalidades alternativas al vínculo matrimonial en el Norte Chico, 1700–1800. (*in*
Demografía, familia e inmigración en España
y América. Santiago: Univ. de Chile; Univ. de

Santiago de Chile; Univ. Católica de Valparaíso; Univ. Metropolitana de Ciencias de
la Educación; Embajada de España, 1992,
p. 91–116, tables)

Examines concubinage, common law
and more casual unions, prostitution, the
"theft" of women, and rape, practices which
the author maintains were more common
than marriage in Norte Chico in the 1700s
because economic conditions, especially labor mobility, did not favor traditional families. Cites interesting cases and conclusions
may be correct; but given the high rate of illegitimacy in other socioeconomically stable
regions of Spanish America during and following the colonial period, arguments need
to be re-examined and refined. [MTH]

**2410 Relaciones económicas del Reino de
Chile, 1780.** Estudio preliminar y edición de Francisco de Solano. Madrid: Consejo
Superior de Investigaciones Científicas; Centro de Estudios Históricos; Depto. de Historia
de América, 1994. 268 p.: bibl., indexes.
(Col.Tierra nueva e cielo nuevo; 34)

Publishes for the first time a major set
of economic descriptions presented individually by province, compiled circa 1780 by *corregidores* and other local officials in conjunction with the *visita* of Tomás Alvarez de
Acevedo. Invaluable sources for study of the
economy and demography of Chile during
the late-18th century at the local level. Well
edited and indexed. [MTH]

2411 Rosati Aguerre, Hugo. El imperio español y sus fronteras: Mapuches y
Chichimecas en la segunda mitad del siglo
XVI. (*Historia/Santiago*, 29, 1995/96, p. 391–
404)

Comparative study of the Araucanian
and Chichimeca frontiers in the early colonial period is interesting for its re-examination of the theses of Frederick Jackson
Turner and Walter Prescott Webb regarding
the role of the frontier in Chilean and Mexican history. [MTH]

2412 Salinas Meza, René. La violencia
conyugal y el rol de la mujer en la sociedad chilena tradicional: siglos XVIII y XIX.
(*in* Demografía, familia e inmigración en España y América. Santiago: Univ. de Chile;
Univ. de Santiago de Chile; Univ. Católica de
Valparaíso; Univ. Metropolitana de Ciencias

de la Educación; Embajada de España, 1992, p. 117–133, table)

An exceptionally important study that analyzes the various kinds of domestic violence reported in the 307 cases of petition for separation preserved in the archives of the Tribunal Eclesiástico de Santiago between 1700 and 1900. Also examines the role assigned to women in pre-20th-century Chile and the attitudes of ecclesiastical authorities towards spousal abuse and obligations of the "dutiful" wife. [MTH]

2413 Vargas, Juan Eduardo. Financiamento del ejército de Chile en el siglo XVII. (*in* Estudios (nuevos y viejos) sobre la frontera. Madrid: Consejo Superior de Investigaciones Científicas, Centro de Estudios Históricos, Depto. de Historia de América, 1991, p. 361–405, tables)

Quantifies financing the army during 1600s. Focuses on the issue of the subsidy (*situado*). Based on archival research in Spain and Chile. [MTH]

2414 Villalobos Celis, Hernán. El explorador Don José Santiago de Cerro y Zamudio. (*Rev. Chil. Hist. Geogr.*, 160, 1992/93, p. 261–270, maps)

Highlights the expeditions of the virtually forgotten Cerro y Zamudio, who explored possible overland routes between Talca and Buenos Aires in the early-19th century. [MTH]

2415 Villalobos R., Sergio. Tres siglos y medio de vida fronteriza chilena. (*in* Estudios (nuevos y viejos) sobre la frontera. Madrid: Consejo Superior de Investigaciones Científicas, Centro de Estudios Históricos, Depto. de Historia de América, 1991, p. 289–359, bibl.)

Revisionist study of the history of frontier life and war with the Araucanians that ended in 1883. Notwithstanding the "bloody" beginning of the war during the Spanish conquest and colonization of Chile, author concludes that there was no formidable uprising and the conflict was resolved through discussions, threats, and minor skirmishes. See also items **738** and **2401.** [MTH]

Villalobos R., Sergio. La vida fronteriza en Chile. See item **738.**

RIO DE LA PLATA

2416 Acevedo, Alba María. Acción apostólica de los laicos y de la Iglesia en Mendoza durante los siglos XVII y XVIII. (*in* 500 años de Hispanoamérica: congreso internacional, 1492–1992. Mendoza, Argentina: Univ. Nacional de Cuyo, Facultad de Filosofía y Letras, 1996, t. 1, p. 71–105, bibl.)

Reviews various actions undertaken by the clergy and lay population to Christianize the poor, isolated, and overwhelmingly indigenous population of Mendoza. Requests to state and Church authorities for aid seemed to be never-ending. [SMS]

2417 Acevedo, Alba María. Las manifestaciones públicas de religiosidad en la Mendoza colonial. (*Rev. Hist. Am. Argent.*, 17:33/34, 1993/94, p. 83–126)

Religious architecture, rituals and sacraments, feasts and processions, and special communal and private devotions to specific saints are examined in this discussion of religiosity in colonial Mendoza. A wealth of detail but little critical analysis. [SMS]

2418 Acevedo, Edberto Oscar. La Intendencia del Paraguay en el Virreinato del Río de la Plata. Buenos Aires: Ediciones Ciudad Argentina, 1996. 464 p.: bibl., index. (Monografías históricas)

Continuation of Acevedo's work on the *intendencias* of the Río de la Plata looks at the organizational aspects of the institution as well as the impact of the *intendente* on the local economy, society, and religion. Well-researched work. [SMS]

2419 Aguirre, Susana and **Marta Petit.** La contratación de aprendices en la actividad artesanal en la ciudad de Buenos Aires durante el Virreinato: su análisis de los registros notariales. (*in* Temas de historia argentina 1. La Plata, Argentina: Facultad de Humanidades y Ciencias de la Educación, Univ. Nacional de La Plata, 1994, p. 7–15)

Study of artisan apprentice contracts found in the Escribanía records of the Archivo General de la Nación. Analiza conditions of apprenticeship, including stipulations about clothing, medical care, and occasionally, salary. [SMS]

2420 Alemán, Bernardo E. Santa Fe y sus aborigenes. v. 1. Santa Fe, Argentina: Junta Provincial de Estudios Históricos, 1994. 1 v.: bibl., maps.

Overview of three centuries of Spanish reactions to indigenous populations in a crucial frontier zone, including *reducciones,* warfare, construction of forts, and the creation of a local militia. Organizes volume by indigenous group, looking first at the original inhabitants; then at a series of invading tribes including Calchaquies, Guaycurues, Charruas, Pampas and Araucanians. [SMS]

Almeida, Luís Ferrand de. Portugal, o Brasil e o comércio do Rio da Prata, 1640–1680. See item **3152.**

2421 Alvarez Kern, Arno. Cultura européia e indígena no Rio da Prata nos séculos XVI/XVIII. (*Estud. Ibero-Am. /Porto Alegre,* 19:2, dez. 1993, p. 5–18)

Following discussion of cultural exchange between indigenous peoples and Europeans, article concentrates on the Jesuit missions, "one of the most extraordinary examples of cultural synthesis in colonial America." [SMS]

2422 Alvarez Pantoja, María José. La actividad comercial y participación social en el siglo XVIII rioplatense. (*in* 500 años de Hispanoamérica: congreso internacional, 1492–1992. Mendoza, Argentina: Univ. Nacional de Cuyo, Facultad de Filosofía y Letras, 1996, t. 1, p. 137–151)

Study of the first fleet sent to Buenos Aires by the Spanish government after the signing of the Treaty of Utrecht (1713). The small fleet, organized by a Basque merchant and shipowner who had already sent ships to the Río de la Plata, arrived in Buenos Aires with merchandise shipped by 65 different individuals including churchmen and a handful of women. [SMS]

2423 Araujo, José Joaquín de. Guía de forasteros en la ciudad y Virreynato de Buenos-Ayres: ediciones facsimilares de 1792 y 1803. Buenos Aires: Honorable Senado de la Nación, Comisión de Cultura; Academia Nacional de la Historia, 1992. 229 p.

Facsimile edition of two published guides to the civilian and ecclesiastical government of the region. This edition finally makes the 1792 and 1803 guides easily accessible. [SMS]

2424 Archivo General de la Nación (Argentina). Bandos de los virreyes y gobernadores del Río de la Plata, 1741–1809: catálogo cronológico y temático. Adaptación e índices de Graciela Swiderski. Buenos Aires: Archivo General de la Nación, 1997. 297 p.: ill., index. (Col. Referencia. Serie Descriptores; 5)

Fine research tool catalogs gubernatorial and viceregal edicts by date of declaration and indexes them topically, such as "Celebraciones" and "Marina," and onomastically. Especially useful for social and municipal history of Buenos Aires. [LRG]

2425 Areces, Nidia R. *et al.* Relaciones interétnicas en Santa Fe la Vieja: sociedad y frontera. (*Rev. Junta Prov. Estud. Hist. Santa Fe,* 59, 1993, p. 71–106, bibl.)

After discussing early history of original frontier outpost of Santa Fe, authors examine the "ambigious and contradictory" relationship between this region and the local indigenous populations. Located in a region disputed between Spain, Portugal, several indigenous nations, and the Jesuits, the local inhabitants supplied themselves with laborers by ransoming indigens captured by the Charruas. [SMS]

2426 Azcuy Ameghino, Eduardo. El latifundio y la gran propiedad colonial rioplatense. Buenos Aires: F.G. Cambeiro, 1995. 236 p.: bibl., map. (Col. Estudios coloniales y de la independencia americana)

Marxist interpretation of late colonial history stresses the creation of a colonial landowning elite backed by the Spanish crown in their massive appropriation of land, and the corresponding growth of social conflict in the countryside. Author's work stands in dramatic opposition to that of Garavaglia, Gelman, and Mayo, who stress the existence of a large group of small landowners in the region. [SMS]

2427 Azcuy Ameghino, Eduardo *et al.* Poder terrateniente, relaciones de producción y orden colonial. Buenos Aires: F. García Cambeiro, 1996. 258 p.: bibl. (Col. Estudios coloniales y de la independencia americana)

Series of articles by the "Azcuy Group" of economic historians on rural landowners in the 18th-century Buenos Aires region. In contrast to the "Garavaglia-Gelman School," Azcuy and company stress power of large *hacendados* in controlling land, labor, and justice. Interesting, controversial, and well-documented work. [SMS]

2428 Barba, Fernando Enrique. Frontera ganadera y guerra con el indio durante el siglo XVIII. Buenos Aires: Univ. Nacional de La Plata, Facultad de Humanidades y Ciencias de la Educación, 1995. 64 p.: bibl. (Serie Estudios/investigaciones; 25)

Two articles on the colonial frontier examine 1) rural population growth in the early 18th century; and 2) attempts to improve protection of the rural population undertaken from mid-century on. Unfortunately, neither article deals directly with indigenous warfare. [SMS]

2429 Bellotto, Manoel Lelo. Espanha e o Vice-Reinado do Rio da Prata: a consolidação do comércio livre no triênio 1787–1789. (*Anu. Estud. Am.*, 53:1, 1996, p. 53–72, appendix, tables)

Examines legal trade between Montevideo and Spain during first three years in which Comercio Libre legislation was actually in effect. Using material from the Archivo General de Indias, presents data on types of ships, products exported, and values of gold and silver leaving the region. [SMS]

2430 Bentancur, Arturo Ariel. La primera burocracia montevideana, 1724–1814. (*in* Ediciones del Quinto Centenario. Montevideo: Univ. de la República, 1992, v. 2, p. 15–68)

Overview of the creation of a government bureaucracy in Montevideo begins with city's founding in 1724 and continues through "modernization" of 1778. Stresses lack of administrative capability and widespread corruption among Montevideo's officials. A solid study. [SMS]

2431 Bentancur, Arturo Ariel. El puerto de Montevideo en la mira de dos potencias europeas: efectos de la alternancia mercantil franco-británica sobre el último tramo colonial, 1797–1814. (*in* Tordesillas y sus consecuencias: la política de las grandes potencias europeas respecto a América Latina, 1494–1899. Frankfurt: Vervuert; Madrid: Iberoamericana, 1995, p. 69–90)

Fine article concentrates on maritime commerce in Montevideo during the French corsairs period (1797–1806) and following the period of British commercial ascendency

(1806–1814). First period is seen as one of risky but lucrative trading opportunities; the British period produces even greater trade as Montevideo becomes a mandatory stop on the way to or from Buenos Aires. Lastly, Buenos Aires' 1810 independence proves fatal for Montevideo, a result of losing its hinterland and being forced into greater dependence on British suppliers. [SMS]

2432 Bertocchi Morán, Alejandro N. Andrés de Oyarvide y la carta esférica del Río de la Plata. (*Rev. Hist. Naval*, 13:51, 1995, p. 75–91, bibl., facsim., maps, photo)

Brief biography of Oyarvide, a naval officer who accompanied Ceballos to Montevideo in 1777 and remained in the region, participating in the demarcation commission and then surveying and charting the Atlantic coast of present-day Uruguay. [SMS]

2433 La Biblioteca porteña del obispo Azamor y Ramirez, 1788–1796. Introducción y edición de Daisy Rípodas Ardanaz. Buenos Aires: PRHISCO-CONICET, 1994. 199 p.

Survey of books owned by the Bishop of Buenos Aires (1788–96). In addition to a brief introduction about the library and a list of more than 1,200 volumes with bibliographic citations, Ripodas provides a facsimile of two lists of the churchman's books (1787 and 1798). Important document for the intellectual history of the period. [SMS]

2434 Birocco, Carlos María. Historia de un latifundio rioplatense: las estancias de Riblos en Areco, 1713–1813. (*Anu. Estud. Am.*, 53:1, 1996, p. 73–99)

Contributing to a revision of the Garavalgia school of rural historiography, Birocco analyzes one of the largest estancias in the Buenos Aires region, that of Miguel de Riblos and descendants. Examines the problems of maintaining a large property intact in a region devoid of *mayorazgos* throughout the 18th century. [SMS]

2435 Boleda, Mario. Demografía histórica del noroeste argentino (I): dinámica demográfica hacia fines del siglo XVIII. Salta, Argentina: Grupo de Estudios Socio-Demográficos, 1992. 42 p.: bibl., graphs, tables. (Cuadernos del GREDES; 15)

Attempts to trace demographic patterns of the indigenous population of northern Argentina and Chile in the late-18th century. Uses three nominative lists and model life tables to estimate birth rates, fertility, and mortality. One of the more interesting findings is that women had a greater life expectancy than men. [SMS]

2436 Cardiel, José. Breve relación de las misiones del Paraguay. Estudio preliminar de Ernesto J.A. Maeder. Buenos Aires: Secretaría de Cultura de la Nación; Ediciones Theoría, 1994. 188 p.: bibl., ill., maps. (Col. Identidad nacional; 28)

A reprint of the strong defense of the Jesuit missions written by a priest who served in several missions throughout the La Plata region and was himself expelled from the region in 1768. Cardiel's classic work combines a detailed description of the mission and the work of the missionaries with a strong defense of Jesuit activities. See also item **2469.** [SMS]

2437 Carrazzoni, José Andrés. La mula: el fulgurante animal del siglo XVII. (*Todo es Hist.*, 28:332, marzo 1995, p. 8–28, bibl., ill., photos)

Popular overview of the importance of mules as a means of colonial commercial transport. Wars of independence destroyed the colonial mule trade, but the animal came to play an important military role throughout the 19th century. Only the coming of the railroad banished the mule to the poor sectors of the Argentine economy. [SMS]

2438 Cartas y documentos coloniales de Mendoza. Recopilación de Juan Draghi Lucero. Mendoza, Argentina: Ediciones Culturales de Mendoza, 1993. 168 p.

Reprints a selection of colonial documents preserved in the Archivo Administrativo e Histórico de Mendoza. Documents include personal letters, commercial correspondence, documents relating to problems with flooding and water supply, wills, and military correspondence. Offers no explanation of criteria used for selection of these materials. [SMS]

2439 Delgado, Mariela N. and **Marisa G. Martínez García.** Relevamiento documental en el Archivo y Biblioteca Históricos de Salta. Salta, Argentina: Grupo de Estudios Socio-Demográficos, Univ. Nacional de Salta, 1993. 59 p.: appendix, table. (Cuadernos del GREDES; 16)

Index of colonial materials relating to demography held by the Archivo y Biblioteca Históricos de Salta. Documents mentioned range from royal decrees to city finances to tribute paid by indigenous groups. [SMS]

2440 Estudios de historia colonial rioplatense. Coordinación de Carlos A. Mayo. La Plata?: Editorial de la Univ. Nacional de La Plata, 1995? 83 p.: bibl. (Col. Institutos)

Three articles by younger historians include Barreneche on murder and murderers in late colonial Buenos Aires; Troisi on promotion and career patterns among members of the regular ecclesiatical orders; and Sansón on the relationship of the work of noted Uruguayan historian Pivel Devoto to the creation of Uruguayan identity. [SMS]

2441 Estudios sobre la Real Ordenanza de Intendentes del Río de la Plata. Dirección de José M. Mariluz Urquijo. Buenos Aires: Instituto de Investigaciones de Historia del Derecho, 1995. 271 p.

Series of articles by institutional and legal historians look at the effect of the Real Ordenanza de Intendentes in the Río de la Plata. In addition to chapters examining each of the jurisdictions of the *intendentes* (*hacienda, justicia, guerra, gobierno*), the importance of the reform and its effect on the coming of independence are also considered. [SMS]

2442 Ferreiro, Juan Pablo. Tierras, encomiendas y élites: el caso de Jujuy en el siglo XVII. (*Anu. Estud. Am.*, 52:1, 1995, p. 189–214, tables)

Analysis of late-16th- to early-17th-century Jujuy encomenderos. Identifies 18 individuals and provides information on the location of their encomiendas. Finds that some encomenderos are linked to each other by family ties while others are tied to local merchants, and that all claim to be of noble lineage. [SMS]

2443 Fundación Vasco-Argentina Juan de Garay (Argentina). Departamento Estudios Historicos. Los Vascos en América: investigación sobre asentamientos vascos en el territorio argentino, siglos XVI a XIX. v. 1–4. Buenos Aires: Fundación Vasco-Argentina Juan de Garay, Departamento Estudios Históricos, 1991–1999. 4 v.: bibl.

Massive project tracing Basques who emigrated to Argentina from 16th-18th centuries is organized by provinces. Most contributors developed genealogies that vary from sketchy to detailed. Includes a few transcriptions of documents containing lists of settlers. [SMS]

2444 Gabbi, Alicia Virginia and **Elvira Martín de Codoni.** Mendoza en sus testamentos. v. 1, siglos XVI, XVII y XVIII. Mendoza, Argentina: Editorial de la Facultad de Filosofía y Letras de la Univ. Nacional de Cuyo, 1996. 1 v.: index.

Catalog of colonial wills, powers of attorney to draw up a will, and estate inventories found in the Archivo Histórico de la Provincia de Mendoza. Each entry provides basic information on the person making the will, as well as the names of executors and witnesses. [SMS]

Gallo, Klaus. De la invasión al reconocimiento: Gran Bretaña y el Río de la Plata, 1806–1826. See item **2897.**

2445 Gálvez, Lucía. Guaraníes y jesuitas de la tierra sin mal al paraíso. Ilustraciones de Oscar Rojas. Buenos Aires: Editorial Sudamericana, 1995. 412 p.: bibl., ill. (Sudamericana joven. Ensayo; 5)

Overview of the Jesuit missions among the Guarani stresses everyday life. Beginning with Tupí-Guaraní life at the time of the conquest, author traces the missions through their "heroic age" (1609–37), the period of *bandeirante* attacks (1628–41), and era of consolidation and demographic growth (1641–1750). Each section contains sidebars with relevant documents. [SMS]

2446 Garavaglia, Juan Carlos and **Jorge D. Gelman.** Rural history of the Río de la Plata, 1600–1850: results of a historiographical renaissance. (*LARR*, 30:3, 1995, p. 75–105, bibl.)

Review article of the "new" *rioplatense* rural history and contributions to it over the past 10 years. Stresses works that expand existing knowledge of rural production, markets, the relationship of the estancia to its work force, and the large subsistence peasant population in the Pampas. Essential for anyone interested in this important revision of Argentine historiography. [SMS]

2447 García Cortés, Carlos. En el II Centenario de Fr. Sebastián Malvar Pinto, O.F.M., 1730–1795: Obispo de Buenos Aíres

y e Obispo de Compostela. (*Estud. Francisc.*, 96:412/413, enero/agosto 1995, p. 165–195)

Brief biography of the Spanish-born Franciscan who served as Bishop of Buenos Aires from 1778–83 and then as Archbishop of Santiago de Compostela. [SMS]

2448 Ghirardi de Hillar, María Mónica. Matrimonio y familia de españoles en la Córdoba del siglo XVIII. (*Cuad. Hist. Poblac.*, 1, 1994, p. 57–84, appendix, graphs, map, tables)

Solid study of marriage patterns of Spanish immigrants in 18th-century Córdoba is based on *expedientes matrimoniales*, parish registers, and census data. Finds that the majority of immigrants who married were men who wed *criollas* of the local elite, although there were exceptional cases of Spaniards marrying *casta* women. Includes demographic analysis of the Spanish group. [SMS]

2449 Godoy, Marilyn. La conquista amorosa en tiempos de Irala. Asunción: BASE Investigaciones Sociales, 1994. 225 p.: bibl.

Examines the impact of the conquest on Guarani women. Written by an anthropologist using only secondary sources, work considers women in both Spanish towns and Jesuit missions. In spite of much generalization, work is interesting. [SMS]

2450 González Rissotto, Rodolfo and **Susana Rodríguez Varese.** Contribución al estudio de al influencia guaraní en la formación de la sociedad uruguaya. (*Rev. Hist./Montevideo*, 88:166, mayo 1994, p. 125–136, tables)

Demographic data on births, marriages, and deaths of Guarani residing on local missions, as well as on other Paraguayans and indigens, taken from four parishes in present-day Uruguay (Viboras, Minas, Melo and Paysandú). [SMS]

2451 González Rodríguez, Jaime. La censura franciscana del *Gobierno de los regulares* de Pedro José de Parras, OFM. (*Arch. Francisc. Hist.*, 85:1/4, Jan./Dec. 1992, p. 489–579, appendix, tables)

Short biography of Pedro José Parras, Franciscan who, after a lengthy residence in Buenos Aires and Paraguay, authored *Gobierno de los regulares*, a critique of his order's negligence in America. Parras, who also participated in a reform of the Univ. de Córdoba, was severely criticized by Spanish Franciscans. [SMS]

2452 Guerrero Soriano, Cándido P. Produccíon, evolución económica y análisis decimal: un estudio sobre el Río de la Plata en el siglo XVIII. (*Anu. Estud. Am.*, 51:1, 1994, p. 91–122, graphs)

Study of economic growth is based on tithe records for four principal collection zones in the Río de la Plata (Buenos Aires, Corrientes, Montevideo, and Santa Fé), which are compared to global hacienda data. [SMS]

2453 Gullotta, Víctor Gabriel. San Francisco Solano: una historia para contar; 1580–1993. Quilmes, Argentina: El Monje Editor, 1994. 269 p.: bibl., ill.. (Col. Nuestra historia)

Local study traces the creation of estancias in the rural district known as La Magdalena from 16th–19th centuries. [SMS]

2454 Herrera de Flores, Marta B. Los Jesuitas terratenientes en Mendoza. (*Todo es Hist.*, 28:331, feb. 1995, p. 64–77, bibl., map, photos)

Highlights Jesuits' important economic role in Mendoza. Arriving in 1610 (only 30 years after the founding of the city), the Jesuits were granted several large rural properties which they developed as an estancia, as well as lands closer to the city which were used to raise wheat. [SMS]

2455 Jolicoeur, Luis. Las reducciones jesuíticas de Paraguay. (*Yachay/Cochabamba*, 10:18, 1993, p. 71–118, ill.)

Examines Jesuit missions of Paraguay in the context of *reducciones* in Spanish America. Stresses legal, organizational, and political ramifications of the missions, but neglects to provide information on the daily lives of the indigenous population living within these missions. [SMS]

2456 Larrandart, Mirta Susana. El Comandante D. Lorenzo Morlote: un glorioso marino oriental de la emancipación, descendiente de fundadores canarios de Montevideo. (*Rev. Inst. Estud. Geneal. Uruguay*, 18, 1994, p. 33–42, bibl, ill.)

Biography and genealogy of a Montevideo-born sailor who supported Buenos Aires independence and rose to the rank of mid-level naval official. [SMS]

2457 López de Albornoz, Cristina. Arrieros y carreteros tucumanos: su rol en la articulación regional, 1786–1810. (*ANDES Antropol. Hist.*, 6, 1994, p. 89–122, appendices, graphs, tables)

Study of Tucumán drovers and carters, a group composed primarily of creoles and mestizos who prospered with the growing trade between Buenos Aires and Potosí. Tucumán profited from its extensive forests which provided raw material for the production of large wooden carts, and from the nearby pastureland favorable for raising oxen and mules. Author also has amassed salary information for individuals employed in transportation. [SMS]

2458 López de Albornoz, Cristina. La mano de obra libre: peonaje y conchabo en San Miguel de Tucumán a fines del siglo XVIII. (*Poblac. Soc.*, 1, dic. 1993, p. 17–33, bibl., tables)

Study of free and semi-free labor in rural Tucumán based on hacienda records of the Junta Municipal de las Temporalidades de San Miguel de Tucumán. Confirms existence of a growing mixed-blood population of subsistence peasants who supplemented their income by working as seasonal contract laborers (*conchabados*) on large estancias. A very fine article. [SMS]

2459 Lozier Almazán, Bernardo P. Beresford, Gobernador de Buenos Aires. Buenos Aires: Editorial Galerna, 1994. 302 p.: bibl.

Biography of William Carr Beresford, the British military officer and Governor of Buenos Aires who accompanied Popham in the British invasion of the city. Beresford, who seems to have treated the local population with consideration and respect, is traced from his birth and early career through his governorship and defeat to his later role in the Braganza court of Rio de Janeiro. [SMS]

2460 Luna, Félix. Historia integral de la Argentina. v. 1, El mundo del descubrimiento. Buenos Aires: Planeta, 1994. 1 v.: bibl.

Vol. 1 of a general, popular history of Argentina presents overview of indigenous civilization and the Spanish conquest of America, with a few chapters specifically on Argentina. Lively, well-informed, and lavishly illustrated. Luna also makes good use of sidebars to introduce documents, firsthand accounts, and excerpts from scholarly studies. [SMS]

2461 Luna, Félix. Historia integral de la Argentina. v. 2, El sistema colonial. Buenos Aires: Planeta, 1995. 1 v.

Vol 2. of Luna's popular history of Argentina concentrates on 16th and 17th centuries. Social and economic history are stressed, but culture is also given some prominence. Moreover, Argentina is placed within the wider context of colonial Latin American developments. Like other volumes in the series, well written and well illustrated. [SMS]

2462 Machón, Jorge Francisco. La reducción de guayanás del Alto Paraná: San Francisco de Paula. Jardín América, Argentina: J.F. Machón, 1996. 140 p.: bibl., ill., map.

Documents the rather pathetic history of San Francisco de Paula, a Dominican mission founded in 1768 among the Guayanás. The mission limped along until its destruction in 1800 by hostile Tupí tribes. Entire story serves as indirect testimony to earlier Jesuit perseverance and success. [SMS]

2463 Maeder, Ernesto J.A. Asimetría demográfica entre las reducciones franciscanas y jesuíticas de guaraníes. (*Rev. Complut. Hist. Am.,* 21, 1995, p. 71–83, map, tables)

Comparison of the Franciscan and Jesuit Guarani missions seeks to understand why the former failed to flourish. Among other factors, author sees the greater isolation of the Jesuits and their more peaceful missionizing practices as explaining their greater success. While the Franciscan mission population stagnated, the Guarani, under Jesuit tutulage, enjoyed almost constant growth, in part due to their younger population profile. [SMS]

2464 Maeder, Ernesto J.A. Misiones del Paraguay: conflictos y disolución de la sociedad guaraní, 1768–1850. Madrid: Editorial MAPFRE, 1992. 298 p.: bibl., ill., index. (Col. Realidades americanas 11. Col. MAPFRE 1492)

Important study of Guarani mission population from the expulsion of the Jesuits to the mid-19th century. Examines demography, economy, society, and everyday life of the Guarani, as well as the effects of the wars of independence and division of the mission zone between Argentina and Paraguay. [SMS]

2465 Mapas, planos, croquis y dibujos sobre Cuyo durante el período hispánico, 1561–1810. Recopilación de Pedro Santos Martínez. Mendoza, Argentina: Ediciones Culturales de Mendoza; Junta de Estudios Históricos de Mendoza, 1994. 177 p.: bibl., chiefly ill.

Brief historical overview is followed by rather poorly reproduced maps, sketches, and architectual drawings related to the Cuyo district (including Mendoza and San Juan), culled from archives in Spain and America. Largest number of illustrations are either general maps or road maps, although sketches of urban and rural *terrenos* are also numerous. Perhaps most interesting are drawings for bridges, *colegios*, and churches. Worthwhile catalog deserves better quality reproductions. [SMS]

2466 Marioni Berra, Alcira. Coronda en el acontecer político, social y económico del siglo XVIII. (*Rev. Junta Prov. Estud. Hist. Santa Fe,* 59, 1993, p. 261–301, bibl., maps)

Brief history of Coronda, a rural area along the Buenos Aires-Santa Fé road. [SMS]

2467 Martínez de Sánchez, Ana María. Indumentaria, "ser" y "parecer," en la Córdoba del setecientos. (*in* Páginas sobre Hispanoamérica colonial: sociedad y cultura. Buenos Aires: PRHISCO-CONICET, 1994, v. 1, p. 13–39)

Interesting article on clothing examines how race, social class, conceptions of decency, corporative membership, and even death affected what men and women were allowed to wear as well as what they actually put on their backs. [SMS]

2468 Martínez de Sánchez, Ana María. La vida cotidiana en Córdoba: el abasto de carne, 1783–1810. Córdoba, Argentina: Centro de Estudios Históricos, 1995. 135 p.: bibl., ill., index.

Based primarily on *cabildo* sources, this misnamed study concentrates on the Córdoba town council's efforts to ensure an adequate meat supply for the city. Also discusses related subjects including meat suppliers, local infrastructure (slaughterhouse and pens), ambulatory vendors, and the problem of cattle rustling. [SMS]

2469 Martínez Martín, Carmen. Las reducciones de los pampas, 1740–53: aportaciones etnogeográficas al sur de Buenos

Aíres. (*Rev. Complut. Hist. Am.*, 20, 1994,
p. 145–167)
Study of the short-lived Jesuit missions in the Pampas and Patagonian regions
concentrates on writing and cartography of
the Jesuit missionaries Cardiel and Falkner.
For ethnohistorian's comment, see item **680**.
See also item **2436**. [SMS]

2470 Mata de López, Sara E. Consideración
acerca de la mano de obra rural en la
jurisdicción de Salta a fines del siglo XVIII.
(*ANDES Antropol. Hist.*, 6, 1994, p. 79–88,
bibl.)
Brief but interesting article analyzes
two rural districts of Salta—the Calchaquí
and Lerma valleys. While labor force in the
former was heavily influenced by indigenous
peoples serving in the encomienda, the population of the latter was primarily Afromes-
tizo, with a good number of people entering
into seasonal labor contracts. Suggests existence of a salaried free labor market with
little or no debt peonage. See also item **2471**.
[SMS]

2471 Mata de López, Sara E. Estructura
agraria: la propiedad de la tierra en el
Valle de Lerma, Valle Calchaqui y la frontera
este, 1750–1800. (*ANDES Antropol. Hist.*, 1,
primer semestre 1990, p. 47–87, graphs,
maps, tables)
Comparison of the Calchaquí and
Lerma valley regions, and the frontier, concentrates on land values, rental prices, land
market, and peasant access to land. Finds
that Lerma Valley had a more complex land
structure and was more sensitive to economic developments in both Potosí and
Buenos Aires, as well as to demands for
food production in the city of Salta itself.
See also item **2470**. [SMS]

2472 Maziel, Juan Baltasar. De la justicia
del tratado de límites de 1750. Estudio
preliminar por José María Mariluz Urquilo.
Buenos Aires: Academia Nacional de la Historia, 1988. 204 p.: bibl., ill. (Col. del quinto
centenario del descubrimiento de América; 3)
This reprint of Maziel's anti-Jesuit
treatise and defense of the Spanish-Portuguese
boundary treaty is introduced by a fine essay
by Mariluz Urquijo stressing the place of this
jurist within the small intellectual community of mid-18th-century Buenos Aires.
[SMS]

**2473 Meliá, Bartomeu and Liane Maria
Nagel.** Guaraníes y jesuitas en tiempo
de las misiones: una bibliografía didáctica.
Asunción: Centro de Estudios Paraguayos
Antonio Guasch; Santo Angelo, Brazil: Centro de Cultura Missioneira; 1995. 305 p.: ill.,
indexes.
Interesting and useful annotated bibliography on the Jesuit mission experience
among the Guarani. Topics include contemporary sources, ideological interpretations,
mission architecture, and mission society;
each topic is preceded by a brief overview.
[SMS]

2474 Morrone, Francisco C. La disolución
del grupo afro-argentino. (*Desmemo-
ria/Buenos Aires*, 3:10, feb./mayo 1996,
p. 8–22, tables)
After reviewing the history and numbers of slaves imported into the Rio de la
Plata, briefly looks at *mestizaje*, disease, and
war as the reasons for the disappearance of
the black population. [SMS]

2475 Neumann, Eduardo. A participação
guarani missioneira na vida colonial
rio-platense. (*Estud. Ibero-Am./Porto Alegre*,
21:1, julho 1995, p. 37–48, bibl.)
Based almost exclusively on published
primary and second sources, article stresses
various types of Guarani settlement in the
Platine Basin: Jesuit missions, missions of
other religious orders, and nonmission indigenous peoples. Sees Guarani as providers
of goods and labor in a region lacking skilled
artisans. [SMS]

2476 Oyarzabal, Guillermo Andres. Las juntas de gobierno españolas: su influencia en los movimientos políticos previos a
los procesos de emancipación en el Río de
Plata, 1808–1810. (*Cuad. Sur Hist./Bahía
Blanca*, 26, 1996, p. 88–103, bibl.)
Based entirely on secondary sources
and printed documents, argues that from
1808–10 the local *mentalité* in the Río de la
Plata was transformed by a new appreciation
of the importance of America. While proof of
this transformation is sketchy, author sees
this change as crucial in paving the way to
independence. [SMS]

2477 Palomeque, Silvia. Intercambios mercantiles y participación indígena en la
"Puna de Jujuy" a fines del período colonial.

(ANDES Antropol. Hist., 6, 1994, p. 13–48, appendices, bibl., tables)

Using *alcabala* records, focuses on those regions of the Puna outside the Marquesado de Tojo. Stresses indigenous participation in trade (including wool, coca, coffee, cattle, and silver) and the participation of some merchants with indigenous surnames in this trade. [SMS]

2478 Pistoia, Benita Honorato. Los Franciscanos en el Tucumán y en el Norte Argentino, 1566–1973. Salta, Argentina: B.H. Pistoia, 1989. 132 p.: bibl., map.

History of the Franciscans in northern Argentina and Paraguay from 16th–20th centuries is written by a member of the order. Using a wide variety of sources, stresses missionary activity of the Franciscans. [SMS]

2479 Pistone, J. Catalina. Las vaquerías en Santa Fe. *(Rev. Junta Prov. Estud. Hist. Santa Fe*, 59, 1993, p. 341–377, bibl., ill.)

Based primarily on the minutes of the Santa Fe cabildo, reviews development of herds of wild cattle on the *pampas* as well as local government's role in granting permission for periodic round-ups *(vaquerías)*. The importance of drought, the gradual creation of privately-owned ranches, and growing 18th-century demand for hides are all considered as reasons for the decline of the *vaquerías*. [SMS]

2480 Porro Girardi, Nelly Raquel and **Estela Rosa Barbero.** Lo suntuario en la vida cotidiana del Buenos Aires virreinal: de lo material a lo espiritual. Buenos Aires: PRHISCO-CONICET, 1994. 493 p.: bibl., ill.

First study to examine the material culture in colonial Buenos Aires, volume discusses uses of silver, jewelry, and religious images. Chapters on jewelry, for example, examine esthetic, religious, funerary, and practical aspects of a wide range of silver, gold, and lesser metal objects. Includes detailed descriptions of these objects. [SMS]

2481 Punta, Ana Inés. La tributación indígena en Córdoba en la segunda mitad del siglo XVIII. *(ANDES Antropol. Hist.*, 6, 1994, p. 49–78, tables)

Uses encomienda and tribute records to examine Bourbon shift from system of indigenous peoples serving encomienda to paying monetary tribute. Although author doubts that local administration controlled

mechanisms effective enough to force indigens to pay the expected tribute, she believes that the new system forced indigenous peoples off their traditional lands and, at times, into new frontier communities. [SMS]

2482 Quevedo, Júlio R. A Guerra Guaranítica: a rebelião colonial nas missões. *(Estud. Ibero-Am./Porto Alegre*, 20:2, dez. 1994, p. 5–26, bibl.)

Studies Guaranitica War within context of indigenous rebellions. Examines first and second campaigns, and concludes that rebellion failed because the Luso-Spanish troops had more modern arms and superior fortifications, and were constantly present in the area. [SMS]

2483 Ras, Norberto. Crónica de la frontera sur. Buenos Aires: Academia Nacional de Agronomía y Veterinaria, 1994. 626 p.: bibl., maps. (Serie de la Academia Nacional de Agronomía y Veterinaria; 11)

Interesting volume presents wealth of information on a variety of subjects related to the frontier (indigenous society, labor, the Church, frontier society). Organized chronologically and stressing facts rather than interpretation, discusses subjects ranging from weather conditions to cattle rustling. [SMS]

2484 Reichel, Heloísa Jochims and **Ieda Gutfreind.** As raízes históricas do Mercosul: a Região Platina colonial. São Leopoldo, Brazil: Editora Unisinos, 1996. 213 p.: bibl., maps.

Discusses natural geographic union of the "Região Platina" and the values and habits established in that area during the colonial period as historical basis for late-20th-century emergence of the free trade zone. [J. Meznar]

2485 Reiter, Frederick J. They built Utopia: the Jesuit missions in Paraguay, 1610–1768. Potomac, Md.: Scripta Humanistica, 1995. 401 p.: bibl., ill., indexes, maps. (Scripta Humanistica; 116)

Relates story of Jesuit ouster from Spain and Paraguay beginning with state demands for indigenous soldiers in 1734, moving through Jesuit resistance to the border treaties between Spain and Portugal and the growing anti-Jesuit movement in the court of Charles III. Author attempts to liven up the story by creating dramatic conversations, but work is based on research in primary and secondary sources. [SMS]

2486 Rivarola Paoli, Juan Bautista. El régimen jurídico de la tierra. Asunción: Mach III, 1993. 373 p.: bibl., ill., maps.

Social and legal history of land ownership in Paraguay discusses encomiendas, haciendas, *latifundios,* and *reducciones.* Also examines cattle raising within the region. A solid study. [SMS]

2487 Saá, Víctor. San Luis, ciudad cabildo: 1594–1800. 2a. ed. San Luis, Argentina: Fondo Editorial Sanluiseño; Gobierno de la Provincia de San Luis, 1995. 110 p.: bibl. (Col. IV centenario; 40–3)

Originally published in 1971, this reissued but rather sketchy study of the cabildo of the city of San Luis de Loyola Neva Medina de Rioseco includes brief discussions of the role of the cabildo in local defense, water rights, and indigenous policy. [SMS]

2488 Santamaría, Daniel J. La Iglesia en el Jujuy colonial, siglos XVII y XVIII. (*in* Jujuy en la historia: avances de investigación. Jujuy, Argentina: Facultad de Humanidades y Ciencias Sociales, Univ. Nacional de Jujuy, 1995, v. 2, p. 27–42, bibl.)

After reviewing the social and economic role of the secular and regular clergy in Jujuy, concludes that, except for missionary activities, the Church had a minor impact on the political life of the region. [SMS]

2489 Santamaría, Daniel J. Las relaciones económicas entre tobas y españoles en el Chaco occidental, siglo XVIII. (*ANDES Antropol. Hist.,* 6, 1994, p. 273–300, bibl.)

Describes relations between the Spanish and various so-called Toba peoples in the western Chaco, and examines the internal economy of the Tobas and the economic effects of trade and warfare along the frontier. Important contribution to a growing literature emphasizing Spanish-indigenous exchange along the colony's multiple frontiers. [SMS]

2490 Sanz Tapia, Angel. El final del Tratado de Tordesillas: la expedición del Virrey Cevallos al Río de la Plata. Valladolid, Spain: Junta de Castilla y León; Sociedad V Centenario del Tratado de Tordesillas, 1994. 437 p.: bibl., maps.

Detailed study of the 1776 Cevallos expedition to the Río de la Plata, sent to block Portuguese expansion in the region and wrest control of Colonia da Sacramento. Describes military aspects of the campaign (which included a large naval component and several army regiments); also examines political, administrative, and economic import of this major event. [SMS]

2491 Schaposchnik, Ana Edith. Aliados y parientes: los diaguitas rebeldes de Catamarca durante el Gran Alzamiento. (*Histórica/Lima,* 18:2, dic. 1994, p. 383–416, bibl., maps)

Interesting analysis of the patterns of alliance among indigenous groups involved in the Diaguita uprising of 1630–43. Finds that the *malfines* were the principal group involved in the uprising, although they enjoyed support from the *ingamanas,* inhabitants of the Calchaquí Valley region. [SMS]

2492 Schulkin, Augusto I. Nuevos elementos para la historia del coronel español Benito Chain. (*Bol. Hist. Ejérc.,* 287/290, 1993, p. 7–18)

Biography of a Spanish military man who had an outstanding career in late-colonial Montevideo and Buenos Aires, including service against Charrúa raids and a role in the reconquest of Buenos Aires. An opponent of independence, Chain was imprisoned and then eventually repatriated back to Spain. [SMS]

2493 Serrera Contreras, Ramón María; Luisa Vila Vilar; and María Concepción Hernández-Díaz Tapia. El aragonés Cosme Bueno y la *Descripción geográfica del Río de la Plata, 1768–1776.* Huesca, Spain: Instituto de Estudios Altoaragoneses, Diputación de Huesca, 1996. 285 p.: bibl.

Reprint of Bueno's description of the interior regions of the La Plata Viceroyalty, including Chile, Alto Perú, Tucumán, and Chaco, follows a solid introduction. From Lima, the doctor/scientist gathered information for the Crown. In addition to a brief overview of the geography and climate, Bueno usually gave cursory information on population, government, and Church. [SMS]

2494 Several, Rejane da Silveira. A Guerra Guaranítica: um estudo de caso. (*Biblos/Rio de Janeiro,* 7, 1995, p. 103–109, bibl.)

Bibliographic note underlining the importance for scholars of a published report by the Spanish captain Francisco Graell. Includes excerpts of the report, which provides details of the region as well as of the war over the seven missions. [SMS]

2495 Silva, Hernán A. El comercio entre España y el Río de la Plata, 1778–1810. Madrid: Banco de España, Servicio de Estudios, 1993. 148 p.: bibl. (Estudios de historia económica, 0213–2702; 26)

Using Spanish, Argentine, and Uruguayan sources, presents thorough study of trade between the Río de la Plata region and Spain during the period of so-called "Free Trade." After discussing the effects of the new trading system and analyzing trade to various regions of Spain, describes how European conflicts forced a restructuring of trade after 1796. [SMS]

2496 Silva, Hernán A. La participación de los primeros navíos neutrales norteamericanos en el tráfico rioplatense y su incidencia en el sistema comercial. (*Cuad. Sur Soc. Econ. Polít.*, 25, 1995, p. 47–59, tables)

Ostensibly a study of US trade with Río de la Plata in 1790s, concentrates on cargo brought into Buenos Aires by the first "Anglo-American" ships and the immediate political consequences of their arrival. [SMS]

2497 Stella, Roseli Santaella. Entre a situação legal e a de fato: o comércio de Buenos Aires com o Brasil no século XVI. (*Cuad. Sur Hist./Bahía Blanca*, 26, 1996, p. 16–32, bibl.)

In spite of the host of legal impediments cited, shows that Portuguese merchants established themselves in the Río de la Plata during the reign of Philip II and carried on a lucrative, albeit illegal, trade into the 17th century. [SMS]

2498 Stoffel, Edgard Gabriel. El Sínodo de Asunción del año 1603 y la evangelización de los naturales. (*Rev. Junta Prov. Estud. Hist. Santa Fe*, 59, 1993, p. 379–407, bibl.)

Stressing Church's early concern with converting the many indigenous groups within the jurisdiction of the Río de la Plata bishopric, and the very limited success, discusses the 1603 Synod and its deep concern with instituting evangelization. Sees this meeting as resulting in the first pastoral plan for the *rioplatense* region, although there is

no discussion of the plan's impact on local reality. [SMS]

2499 Tandeter, Enrique. El período colonial en la historiografía argentina reciente. (*Entrepasados/Buenos Aires*, 4:7, 1994, p. 67–84, ill.)

Reviews Argentine colonial historiography against the backdrop of modern Argentine politics since the 1950s. Tandeter's concentration on both Marxist and French influences leads him to overemphasize economic history and ignore all but a handful of foreign scholars. [SMS]

2500 Tanodi de Chiapero, Branka María. La escritura en Córdoba del Tucumán, 1573–1650. Córdoba, Argentina: Univ. Nacional de Córdoba, 1994. 342 p.: bibl., ill.

Useful guide might help unravel specific paleography problems for anyone working in pre-18th-century Córdoba. After a brief history of various handwriting styles of the time, reviews the writing style of each *escribano*. Also includes section on writing styles of other residents. [SMS]

2501 Tejerina, Marcela Viviana. El comercio hispano-lusitano a fines del siglo XVII: una propuesta alternativa para analizar la presencia portuguesa en el Río de la Plata. (*Cuad. Sur Hist./Bahía Blanca*, 26, 1996, p. 60–74, bibl.)

Based on 1786 seizure of a Portuguese slave ship, article stresses that this case proves both the continuation of Portuguese commercial presence after the supposed end of special permissions and the existence of important trading connections between Portuguese and Spanish merchants in the Río de la Plata in late-18th century. [SMS]

2502 Ulloa, Mónica E. Migración y hogar en el Jujuy colonial, 1718–1778. (*in* Jujuy en la historia: avances de investigación. Jujuy, Argentina: Facultad de Humanidades y Ciencias Sociales, Univ. Nacional de Jujuy, 1995, v. 2, p. 43–56, bibl., graphs, tables)

Uses parish marriage records and nominative lists to analyze immigration and suggest how this affected household composition. Underlines the importance of Spanish male migration, the fluid nature of the population, and the relatively large number of female-headed households. [SMS]

2503 **Varanda, Atanasio.** Miscelánea histórico-política. Estudio preliminar de José M. Mariluz Urquijo. Buenos Aires: Academia Nacional de la Historia, 1994. 252 p.: bibl. (Col. del quinto centenario del descubrimiento de América; 7)

First published version of Varanda's report to the Crown on the implementation of the 1750 boundary treaty and on Jesuit resistance to turning over their missions to the Portuguese. Varanda, a military officer who served in the Río de la Plata from 1752–61, belonged to the anti-Jesuit camp. Prefaced by Mariluz Urquijo's fine introduction. [SMS]

2504 **Vega Castillos, Uruguay R.** La marcha de Cevallos por las tierras del este, 1763. (*Bol. Hist. Ejérc.*, 287/290, 1993, p. 43–91, bibl., tables)

After a brief history of early life of Pedro de Cevallos, the Spanish military man sent to the Río de la Plata as governor and charged with drawing up the new demarcation line between Spanish and Portuguese America, recounts the movement of Cevallos and his troops through present-day Uruguay. [SMS]

Vitar, Beatriz. Las fronteras "bárbaras" en los virreinatos de Nueva España y Perú. See item **2130.**

2505 **Zenarruza, Jorge G.C.** Crónicas: útiles para una futura historia de Jujuy, estado federal argentino. v. 1–3. Buenos Aires: Instituto de Estudios Iberoamericanos, 1994. 3 v.: bibl., ill. (Publicación del Instituto de Estudios Iberoamericanos; año 14, v. Serie histórica; 1–3)

Massive genealogy of early Spanish families of Jujuy includes assorted other documents. Overriding goal of this work is to disprove Mario Javier Saban's contention that some of the conquistadores of the region were of *marrano* descent. [SMS]

19th and 20th Centuries
Venezuela

PETER S. LINDER, *Assistant Professor of History, New Mexico Highlands University*

THE OVERALL QUALITY OF VENEZUELAN HISTORIOGRAPHY continues to improve. While political studies still dominate the materials reviewed for this volume, significant works also have appeared in economic history. Perhaps the most significant trend observed is the ongoing proliferation of excellent regional studies on varying topics and themes. The professionalization of historical study in Venezuela noted in earlier volumes has resulted in an increasingly critical spirit of inquiry and an overall increase in quality.

Historians of Venezuela remain preoccupied with the independence era. The bicentennial of the birth of Gen. Antonio José de Sucre has occasioned the publication (or republication) of a number of works dealing with this key figure. Perhaps the best of these is Hoover's study (item **2536**), originally published in 1975 (see *HLAS 40:3322*). Also worthy of mention is Polanco Alcántara's thoughtful biography of Francisco de Miranda (item **2549**).

Postindependence 19th-century politics and ideology continues to be the focus of much interesting work. Banko has traced the evolution of federalist thought from the wars of independence to the era of Guzmán Blanco (item **2507**). A documentary collection also contributes to the study of the origins of Venezuelan federalism in the early-19th century (item **2537**).

Twentieth-century political history continues to undergo significant revision.

As noted by Ellner, studies of 20th-century politics have become less overtly polemical and have come to challenge established views of both dictatorships and democratic regimes (item **2525**). Studies by Rangel (item **2551**) and Berríos Berríos (item **2508**) provide insights into the nationalist and anti-imperialist character of the Cipriano Castro regime. Campíns argues that the Medina Angarita government was democratic in character and criticizes its overthrow by Acción Democrática (AD) and the military (item **2513**). Blanco Muñoz accuses the Betancourt government of using excessive force in putting down a military uprising in Puerto Cabello on June 2, 1962 (item **2509**). Sosa Abascal published a series of works detailing the evolution of Betancourt's political thought in the late 1930s and early 1940s (items **2553, 2554,** and **2555**).

Interesting works in economic history also deserve mention. Briceño analyzes transportation and commerce on the Orinoco River and its tributaries (item **2512**), while Flores explores the relationship between commercial interests and the Guzmán Blanco administration (item **2529**).

A key recent development has been the proliferation of high-quality regional and local studies. Such works demonstrate the tremendous economic, social, and political variability of Venezuela in the 19th and 20th centuries and challenge traditional centrist visions. Yarrington's important work examines the connections between political power and agrarian change in Duaca, Lara state in the 19th and 20th centuries (item **2561**). Faculty and students of the University del Zulia's Centro de Estudios Históricos and graduate program in Venezuelan history continue to promote research and writing in regional history. A new journal of Zulian history, *Palafitos,* is planned for the near future, while a number of important studies using Zulia's archives have been published. For example, Urdaneta examines the role of municipal government and regional leaders in preserving Zulian autonomy in the 19th century (item **2558**). Cardozo Galué, meanwhile, analyzes Zulia's economy, society, and culture from the era of independence until the beginning of the 20th century (item **2516**).

2506 **1945–1947: del golpe militar a la constituyente.** Caracas: Ediciones Centauro, 1992. 165 p.: ill. (Papeles de archivo. Cuadernos de divulgación histórica; 9)

Presents a useful collection of reprinted documents about the military revolt that toppled Medina Angarita and brought Acción Democrática (AD) to power in 1945. Includes accounts of the coup from various perspectives and decrees of the provisional government.

2507 **Banko, Catalina.** Las luchas federalistas en Venezuela. Caracas: Monte Avila Editores Latinoamericana: Centro de Estudios Latinoamericanos Rómulo Gallegos, 1996. 223 p.: bibl. (Estudios. Serie Historia)

Study of federalism as a political ideology in Venezuela from independence to 1870. Argues that federalism developed in Venezuela as a response to internal problems and concerns. Also notes irony that federalist victories brought autocrat Antonio Guzmán Blanco to power.

2508 **Berríos Berríos, Alexi.** Cipriano Castro frente al imperialismo. Caracas: Fondo Editorial Tropykos, 1996. 78 p.: bibl.

Study of the Cipriano Castro regime, focusing on the confrontations with foreign powers and business interests. Portrays Castro as a nationalist, influenced by Santanderian liberalism.

2509 **Blanco Múñoz, Agustín.** La violencia en la Venezuela reciente, 1958–1980: proyecto. v. 5, Venezuela, 1962–1963: el porteñazo, tragica expresión de una aventura. Caracas: Fundación Cátedra Pio Tamayo, 1991. 1 v.: bibl., indexes. (Col. Historia actual / Cátedra "Pio Tamayo", Centro de Estudios de Historia Actual; 5)

Fifth volume in a series on violence in Venezuela after 1935. Analysis of military revolt in Puerto Cabello on June 2, 1962. Argues that the government of Rómulo Betancourt used excessive force in suppressing the uprising of the 2nd Battalion, Infantería de Marina. Also deems incident a decisive victory against armed insurgency seeking to topple Betancourt's government.

2510 Botello, Oldman. Historia regional del estado Aragua. Maracay, Venezuela: Gobernación del Estado Aragua: Academia Nacional de la Historia, 1995. 323 p.: bibl. (Biblioteca de autores y temas aragüeños; 1)

Published under the auspices of the Academia Nacional de la Historia. A fairly standard narrative of the history of Aragua, focusing primarily on military and political events. Based on archival research, contains useful documentary annexes.

2511 Briceño, Olga. Bajo esos techos rojos. Introducción de Juan Uslar Pietri. Caracas: Monte Avila Editores Latinoamericana, 1993. 223 p. (Documentos. Serie Difusión)

Spanish version or translation of well-known work *Cocks and Bulls in Caracas*, first published in English during World War II, describing daily life in Caracas.

2512 Briceño, Tarcila. Comercio por los ríos Orinoco y Apure durante la segunda mitad del siglo XIX. Caracas: Gobernación del Estado Bolívar, Dirección de Educación, Comisión de Historia Regional: Fondo Editorial Tropykos, 1993. 231 p.: appendix, bibl., ill., maps.

Based on a variety of primary sources, a useful study of development of riverine traffic on Río Orinoco and tributaries. Argues that regional economic development evolved from the production of hides and cattle to the production of gold. Also notes that economic development was driven and conditioned largely by growth of Ciudad Bolívar.

2513 Campíns, Héctor. El presidente Medina: de la represión a la libertad. Caracas: Planeta Biblioteca Andina, 1993. 229 p. (Colección Biblioteca andina)

Study of Medina Angarita regime. Asserts that Medina's government was democratic and nationalist in character. Critical of 1945 coup that brought Acción Democrática (AD) to power, contending that foreign oil companies played a complicit role.

2514 Capriles Ayala, Carlos. Décadas de historia de Venezuela: génesis de la república, 1831–1840, v. 1. Caracas: Consorcio de Ediciones Capriles, 1995. 1 v.: bibl., ill.

Compares contemporary Venezuelan political situation with conditions immediately after independence. Extremely critical of post-1958 political leadership as unqualified to lead and chosen by a "semi-literate" electorate.

2515 Carciente, Jacob. Presencia sefardí en la historia de Venezuela. Prólogo de Santos Rodulfo Cortés. Caracas: Centro de Estudios Sefardíes de Caracas, 1997. 194 p.: bibl., index. (Biblioteca popular sefardí; v. no. 14)

Discusses Sephardic Jewish community in Venezuela. Argues that the long-term Sephardic presence in Venezuela dates back to the colonial era. Also argues that Sephardic success in business resulted from group identity and solidarity.

2516 Cardozo Galué, Germán. Historia zuliana: economía, política y vida intelectual en el siglo XIX. Maracaibo, Venezuela: Univ. del Zulia, 1998. 1 v.

Collection of essays explores 19th-century Zulian history. Argues that the region's development is derived from its geographic and historical peculiarity, and that the relationship between Zulia and the national state was a contentious and contingent one, with the national state seeking unsuccessfully to establish effective control.

2517 Carrera Damas, Germán. La disputa de la independencia y otras peripecias del método crítico en historia de ayer y de hoy. Caracas: Ediciones Ge, 1995. 260 p.: bibl.

Collection of essays on selected topics of Venezuelan history ranges from the wars of independence to the regime of Juan Vicente Gómez. Work is intended to promote critical thought among Venezuelan historians.

2518 Carrera Damas, Germán. Juan Vicente Gómez: an essay in historical comprehension. (*in* Political culture, social movements and democratic transitions in South America in the XXth century. Edited by Fernando J. Devoto and Torcuato S. Di Tella. Milano: Fondazione Giangiacomo Feltrinelli, 1997, p. 245–262)

Revisionist analysis of the problems inherent in the historical evaluations of the Gómez regime. Advocates a more critical and balanced analysis of the era, the regime, and the man.

2519 Cartay Angulo, Rafael and **Alicia Chueco.** La tecnologia culinaria domestica en Venezuela, 1820–1980. Mérida, Venezuela: Univ. de Los Andes-Fundación Polar; Caracas: Area Economía Agroalimentaria, 1994. 98 p.: bibl., ill. (Sistema alimentario venezolano. Estudios especiales)

Relying primarily on a review of newspaper advertising, work presents a fascinating exploration of the impact of urbanization and modernization on technology and methods of food preparation and storage in Venezuela.

2520 Castellanos, Rafael Ramón. Caudillismo y nacionalismo: de Guzmán Blanco a Gómez; vida y acción de José Ignacio Lares. Caracas: Italgráfica, 1994. 668 p.: appendices, bibl., index.

Biographical study details the career of a Trujillan politician who served in various political and administrative posts during late-19th and early-20th centuries. Offers useful insights into the nature of regional politics during a crucial period in Venezuelan history.

2521 Castillo Lara, Lucas G. El General Ramón Guerra: un ilustre sancasimiereño. (*Bol. Acad. Nac. Hist./Caracas,* 78:309, enero/marzo 1995, p. 57–85)

Laudatory study of the life of one of San Casimiro's most famous sons, Ramón Guerra. Traditional narrative approach and very partisan, but useful as a study of politics and conflict after the Federal Wars.

2522 Castillo Lara, Lucas G. La raigambre salesiana en Venezuela: cien años de la primera siembra. Caracas: Academia Nacional de la Historia, 1995. 97 p.: bibl. (Biblioteca de la Academia Nacional de la Historia. Estudios, monografías y ensayos; 167)

Discusses early educational activities of Salesian religious and teaching order in Venezuela, beginning with their arrival in 1894.

2523 4F en 60 días y 4 diarios. v. 1–3 in 5. Maracaibo, Venezuela: Univ. del Zulia, Vicerrectorado Académico, 1992. 3 v.: facsims., indexes, ports. (Col. Documentos; 1)

Massive collection of articles and editorials from the Venezuelan press about the attempted military coup of Feb. 4, 1992 that brought Hugo Chávez to national prominence. Very useful for contemporary Venezuelan politics and history.

2524 Documentos de la insurrección de José Leonardo Chirinos. Caracas: Fundación Historia y Comunicación, 1994. 269 p.: ill., indexes, map. (Colección Abraxas; 1)

Useful collection of primary documents transcribed from the Archivo General de Indias de Sevilla, relating to a 1796 slave rebellion in Coro.

2525 Ellner, Steve. Venezuelan revisionist political history, 1908–1958: new motives and criteria for analyzing the past. (*LARR,* 30:2, 1995, p. 91–121, bibl.)

Useful essay points out challenges raised to official and traditional versions of 20th-century political history. Argues that revisionism reflects "a concern for objectivity and professionalism that represents an advance over years of politically inspired or influenced historiography." For political scientist's comment, see *HLAS 57:3456.*

2526 Ewell, Judith. Venezuela and the United States: from Monroe's hemisphere to petroleum's empire. Athens: University of Georgia Press, 1996. 267 p.: bibl., index. (The United States and the Americas)

Valuable work explores the evolution of US-Venezuelan relations in terms of "core cultural values" and disparities of power. Argues that the relationship between Venezuela and the US should take into account the vision and values of Venezuela, and that US relations with Venezuela represent a microcosm of all outstanding issues between Latin America and its northern neighbor.

2527 Falcón, Fernando. La política militar de Carlos III y su impacto en el proceso de independencia de Venezuela. (*Mundo Nuevo/Caracas,* 17:3/4, julio/dic. 1994, p. 253–270)

General study drawn from published sources concentrates on role of the colonial militia, its connections with the colonial elite, and the consequent implications for the independence movements. [J. Britton]

2528 Filippi, Alberto. Bolívar y la Santa Sede: religión, diplomacia, utopía, 1810–1983. Prólogo de Baltazar Porras Cardozo. Caracas: Editorial Arte, 1996. 227 p.: appendix, bibl.

Pro-clerical in orientation, argues that Bolívar sought a "direct" relationship with the papacy, without subordination of Church to state as had been the case under the Bourbons. Also asserts that Bolívar sought to promote Catholicism in order to stabilize post-independence society. Useful documentary appendix.

2529 Flores, Carmen Elena. Los comerciantes financistas y sus relaciones con el gobierno Guzmancista 1870–1888. Caracas: Academia Nacional de la Historia, 1995. 376 p.: bibl., ill. (Biblioteca de la Academia Nacional de la Historia. Fuentes para la historia republicana de Venezuela; 60)

Investigates evolving relationship between Venezuelan commercial interests and Guzmán Blanco's government, 1870–1888. Argues that merchants and the centralizing Guzmán regime had complementary interests that facilitated cooperation. Merchants supplied capital for state-building and infrastructural improvements, while regime provided a modicum of political stability. Relies primarily on official documents.

2530 Fombona de Certad, Ignacia. Armando Zuloaga Blanco: voces de una Caracas patricia. Caracas: Academia Nacional de la Historia: Banco del Caribe, 1995. 544 p.: bibl. (Biblioteca de la Academia Nacional de la Historia. Estudios, monografías y ensayos; 168)

Combines oral history, correspondence, and analysis of period novels in order to reconstruct elite life in Caracas in the waning years of the Gómez regime (1918–1930).

2531 Fortique, José Rafael. Crónicas médicas de la independencia venezolana. Caracas: Academia Nacional de la Historia, 1989. 229 p.: bibl. (Biblioteca de la Academia Nacional de la Historia. Estudios, monografías y ensayos; 113)

Argues that physicians, as members of the best-educated segment of criollo society, played a significant role in promoting Venezuelan independence.

2532 García Ponce, Antonio. Los pobres de Caracas, 1873–1907: un estudio de la pobreza urbana. Caracas: Instituto Municipal de Publicaciones, Alcaldía de Caracas, 1995. 416 p.: bibl.

Study focuses on the poorest segment of the Caracas population. Based on census materials and other unpublished statistical sources (e.g. burial records), argues that the high incidence of poverty—61.6 percent in 1891—was not a significant political issue.

González Escorihuela, Ramón. Las ideas políticas en el Táchira: de los años 70 del siglo XIX a la segunda década del siglo XX. See item **5150.**

2533 Los grandes períodos y temas de la historia de Venezuela: V centenario. Recopilación de Luis Cipriano Rodríguez. Caracas: Instituto de Estudios Hispanoamericanos, Decanato de la Facultad de Humanidades y Educación, Univ. Central de Venezuela, 1993. 383 p.: bibl., index.

A quincentenary history of Venezuela, consisting of a series of essays, each dealing with a specific period and topics of importance to students of Venezuelan history. Useful, but basic.

2534 Grases, Pedro. Manuel Pérez Vila, 1922–1991: vida y presencia en Venezuela. Bibliografía de sus obras elaborada por Horacio Jorge Becco. Caracas: Fundación Mendoza: Fundación Boulton: Fundación Polar, 1993. 115 p.: bibl., ill., index.

Brief biography of Manuel Pérez Vila, including a bibliography detailing his many contributions to Venezuelan historiography.

2535 Harwich Vallenilla, Nikita. Imaginario colectivo e identidad nacional: tres etapas en la enseñanza de la historia de Venezuela. (Latinoamérica: enseñanza de la historia, libros de textos y conciencia histórica. Buenos Aires: Alianza Editorial; FLACSO; Frankfurt: Georg Eckert Instituts, 1991, p. 77–102, tables)

Argues that the teaching of history has served to legitimize Venezuelan governments from independence to the regimes of the early-20th century.

2536 Hoover, John P. Sucre, soldado y revolucionario. Traducción de Francisco Rivera. Caracas: Presidencia de la República, 1995. 372 p.: bibl., ill. (Bicentenario del nacimiento de Antonio José de Sucre)

Reissue of one of the best biographies of Sucre, originally published by the Univ. de Cumaná in 1975. Traditional narrative approach, solidly researched using Venezuelan archives. See also *HLAS 40:3322.*

2537 Ideas de la Federación, 1811–1900. v. 1–2. Caracas: Monte Avila Editores, 1995. 2 v.: bibl. (Biblioteca del pensamiento venezolano José Antonio Páez; 7)

Useful documentary collection chronicles the evolution of federalism in Venezuela from independence to 1864. In a preliminary study, the author seeks to define authentically Venezuelan roots of federalism, arguing that the ideology evolved in Venezuela as a result of colonial experiences. Also observes tension between philosophical leanings toward federalism and the exigencies of 19th-century politics.

2538 Irwin G., Domingo. Relaciones civiles-militares en Venezuela, 1830–1910: una visión general. Caracas: Litobrit C.A., 1996. 166 p.: bibl., ill.

Study of relations between the Venezuelan military and political authorities from 1830–1910. Argues that 19th-century political conflicts interrupted military professionalization until the beginning of the Gómez administration.

2539 Materiales para el estudio de la cuestión agraria en Venezuela. v. 2, 1822–1860 mano de obra: opinion. Estudios preliminares de John V. Lombardi y Carmen Gómez. Caracas: Univ. Central de Venezuela, Facultad de Humanidades y Educación, 1979. 1 v.: bibl., indexes. (Ediciones de la Facultad de Humanidades y Educación; 5)

Addition to an extremely important series of volumes devoted to the development of Venezuelan agriculture. Contains reprinted government decrees, proclamations, and newspaper articles reflecting diverse opinions about agricultural problems following independence.

2540 Méndez Sereno, Herminia Cristina. La iglesia católica en tiempos de Guzmán Blanco. Caracas: Academia Nacional de la Historia, 1995. 282 p.: bibl. (Biblioteca de la Academia Nacional de la Historia. Fuentes para la historia republicana de Venezuela; 62)

Examines relationship between the Holy See and the Venezuelan government under Antonio Guzmán Blanco. Argues that frictions were the result of opposing goals and orientations, a process leading to the Venezuelan Church's subordination to the Venezuelan state and the elimination of monastic orders and ecclesiastical *fueros.*

2541 Mendible Z., Alejandro. La familia Río Branco y la fijación de las fronteras entre Venezuela y Brasil: dos momentos definitorios en las relaciones entre Venezuela y Brasil: El Tratado de Límites de 1859 y la gestión del barón de Río Branco, 1902–1912. Caracas: Academia Nacional de la Historia, 1995. 243 p.: bibl., ill., maps. (Biblioteca de la Academia Nacional de la Historia. Fuentes para la historia republicana de Venezuela; 64)

Study of evolving relations between Venezuela and Brazil in 19th and early 20th centuries. Sees Río Branco's actions as shaping relations between the two nations. The 1859 treaty solved colonial-era disputes, while Río Branco used international situations between 1902–1912 to assert Brazilian dominance in Amazon basin, while simultaneously professionalizing Brazil's foreign ministry.

2542 Mérida a través del tiempo: siglos XIX y XX; política, economía y sociedad. Recopilación de Rita Giacalone. Mérida, Venezuela: Univ. de Los Andes, Consejo de Publicaciones, Consejo de Desarrollo Científico, Humanístico y Tecnológico, 1996. 305 p.: bibl., ill., maps (Colección Ciencias sociales. Serie Historia)

Collection of essays prepared by the students, faculty, and alumni of Univ. de los Andes explores the evolving relations between Mérida and the rest of Venezuela. Essays are uneven in quality and utility.

2543 Ochoa, Rigel. Puertos y salubridad en Venezuela, 1908–1935. (*Tierra Firme,* 15:57, enero/marzo 1997, p. 57–72)

Useful article connects early public health efforts and improvements in port facilities with the Gómez regime's efforts to promote trade with the industrialized world. Based on published primary sources.

2544 Olivieri, Antonio. Apuntes para la historia de la publicidad en Venezuela. Caracas: Ediciones Fundación Neumann, 1992. 285 p.: bibl., ill. (some col.).

A fascinating description of the history of advertising in Venezuela, discussing the evolution of both advertisements and the advertising industry.

2545 Papeles clandestinos del Partido Democrático Nacional, 1937–1941: documentos del archivo de Juan Bautista Fuenmayor. Caracas: Ediciones de la Presidencia de la República, 1995. 794 p. (Colección Tiempo vigente; 10)

Useful collection of documents dealing with politics in Venezuela after the death of Juan Vicente Gómez, and the evolution of the Partido Democrático Nacional, predecesor to Acción Democrática (AD). Challenges categorization of this early political organization as a "class party," while drawing distinctions between it and the Venezuelan Communist Party.

2546 Pino Iturrieta, Elías. La reputación de Doña Fulana Castillo: un caso de honor y recogimiento de el siglo XIX venezolano. (*Tierra Firme*, 14:56, oct./dic. 1996, p. 533–553)

Uses the case of an Apuran woman to illustrate the tension between colonial attitudes toward women and the ideal of male honor, and more "modern" attitudes about women's roles in society.

2547 Pino Iturrieta, Elías. El siglo XIX en Venezuela: sugerencias para una nueva interpretación. (*in* Cincuenta años de historia en México: en el cincuentenario del Centro de Estudios Históricos. México: Colegio de México, Centro de Estudios Históricos, 1991, v. 1, p. 57–76)

Historiographic essay challenges prevailing trend in Venezuelan historiography; argues for continuity between the era of independence and the rest of the 19th century and against the view of the post-independence era as unrelievedly bleak and disastrous.

2548 Pla, Alberto J. La internacional comunista y América Latina: sindicatos y política en Venezuela, 1924–1950. Rosario, Argentina: Ediciones Homo Sapiens: Centro Estudios de Historia Obrera, UNR, 1996. 368 p.: bibl., map. (Estudios sociales)

Study of union movements—particularly oil workers' syndicates—in Venezuela to 1950. Argues that the Communist Party was the dominant force in the labor movement in its early decades. Based largely on oral histories and union publications; presents a somewhat simplistic vision of Gen. Juan Vicente Gómez as a tool of the oil companies.

2549 Polanco Alcántara, Tomás. Francisco de Miranda: bosquejo de una biografía; don Juan o don Quijote? Caracas: Editorial Melvin, 1996. 779 p.: bibl.

Generally sympathetic biography of Francisco de Miranda; author asserts that he was the crucial figure of the early movement for independence. Useful introduction provides a discussion of the historiography of this key national figure.

2550 Polanco Alcántara, Tomás. Simón Bolívar: ensayo de interpretación biográfica a través de sus documentos. Caracas: EG, 1994. 1033 p.: bibl.

Prize-winning Venezuelan historian challenges the idealized image of Bolívar by portraying him as a human being "who had virtues and made mistakes, who had strong passions and realized extraordinary achievements." Scholarly, readable biography based primarily on Bolívar's own writings. [J. Rausch]

2551 Rangel, Domingo Alberto. Cipriano Castro: semblanza de un patriota. San Cristóbal: Tipografía Cortés, 1995. 185 p.

Generally positive biography of Castro. Argues that, despite his many flaws, Castro was a true patriot and an opponent of North American domination.

Rojas, Reinaldo. La economía de Lara en cinco siglos: una aproximación a su estudio. See *HLAS 57:1971.*

2552 Schuyler, George W. Perspectives on Venezuelan democracy. (*Lat. Am. Perspect.*, 23:3, Summer 1996, p. 10–29, bibl.)

Perceptive discussion of recent Venezuelan political history. Argues that, since 1958, Venezuelan democracy has suffered from structural limitations. Attributes recent political upheavals to a "participatory crisis" and the transition to a more market-oriented capitalist economy that has impoverished an ever-greater number of Venezuelans.

2553 Sosa Abascal, Arturo. El programa nacionalista: izquierda y modernización, 1937–1939. 2a ed. corr. Caracas: Editorial Fundación Rómulo Betancourt, 1994. 319 p.: bibl. (Colección Tiempo vigente; 3)

Edited collection of columns written by Rómulo Betancourt in the late 1930s, reflecting the evolution of his thinking on economic and financial issues.

2554 Sosa Abascal, Arturo. Rómulo Betancourt y el Partido del Pueblo, 1937–1941. Caracas: Editorial Fundación Rómulo Betancourt, 1995. 618 p.: bibl. (Colección Tiempo vigente; 9)

A study of the origins of the Acción Democrática (AD) party in the years following the death of Gómez, and an investigation of the political career and style of Betancourt and other early leaders and personalities of the party. Also examines the origins and early nature of the party itself. Based largely on documents from the Rómulo Betancourt Archives and on documents and statements also published elsewhere.

2555 Sosa Abascal, Arturo. Rómulo Betancourt y el partido mínimo, 1935–1937. Caracas: Editorial Fundación Rómulo Betancourt, 1995. 99 p.: bibl. (Colección Tiempo vigente; 9)

A study of the early political formation of Rómulo Betancourt in his first period of overt political activity between the death of Gen. Juan Vicente Gómez and the repression unleashed by the López Contreras administration in 1937. Makes use of documents from Betancourt's archives. Details the evolution of Betancourt's political views from his support of the Popular Front to his break with the Venezuelan Communist Party.

2556 Tavera-Marcano, Carlos Julio. Historia de la propiedad territorial en los valles de Aragua, 1590–1830. Maracay, Venezuela: Gobernación del Estado Aragua: Academia Nacional de la Historia, 1995. 488 p.: bibl., index, map. (Biblioteca de autores y temas aragüeños; 5)

Detailed discussion of the evolution of landholdings in Aragua, from an adjunct to encomienda to major source of wealth and dominant institution in rural Venezuela.

Views land tenure issues as crucial to an understanding of Venezuelan history.

2557 Torres, Gumersindo. Memorias de Gumersindo Torres: un funcionario incorruptible en la dictadura del General Gómez. Prólogo de Elias Pino Iturrieta. Recopilación de José Agustín Catalá. Caracas: Edición especial de la Presidencia de la República, 1996. 229 p., 24 p. of plates: ill.

Presents edited memoirs of Gumersindo Torres. A man of apparent probity, Torres was also a faithful servant of the Gómez regime. Insights into inner workings of the gomecista state and the early development of Venezuela's oil industry.

2558 Urdaneta, Arlene. Autonomía y federalismo en el Zulia. Maracaibo: Secretaría de Gobierno, Dirección de Acervo Histórico del Estado Zulia: Biblioteca Temas de Historia de Zulia: Secretaría de Cultura del Estado Zulia: Fondo Editorial Tropykos, 1998. 198 p.: bibl.

Revisionist study of 19th-century politics in the western state of Zulia. Argues that the economic and political elite of Maracaibo used federalist ideology and institutions to promote regional autonomy and their own interests in the face of attempts by the national state to exercise effective central control.

2559 Vélez Boza, Fermín. Biografía del Dr. Fernando Bolet, 1818–1888: primer médico, cientifica, social, y en la alimentación. Caracas: Instituto Nacional de Nutrición de Venezuela, 1995. 179 p.: bibl., ill.

A study of the life and contribution of a Catalan-descended doctor of the 19th century who sought to improve public health and nutrition in Petare, along with combating epidemics, promoting agriculture and honey production. Interesting in its portrayal of health issues in rural Venezuela in the 19th century.

2560 Villegas Astudillo, Reinaldo. Simón Rodríguez: maestro y pensador de América. Valencia, Venezuela: Univ. de Carabobo, Centro de Estudios de las Américas y del Caribe, 1996. 268 p.: bibl. (Colección "Pensadores de América")

Book deals with an Enlightenment figure, the "other" teacher of Simón Bolívar. Argues that Rodríguez's ideas and contribution have been unreported and unlauded, both in terms of shaping of American thought and the development of the philosophy of education. Also argues for Rodríguez as a model to combat pernicious outside influences, by which the author means American capitalism.

2561 Yarrington, Doug. A coffee frontier: land, society, and politics in Duaca, Venezuela, 1830–1936. Pittsburgh, Pa.: Univ. of Pittsburgh Press, 1997. 267 p.: bibl., ill., index, maps. (Pitt Latin American series)

Meticulously researched and well written, this regional study details the evolution of rural society in the Lara region. Argues that coffee production in Duaca produced a large and autonomous peasantry, but in the early 20th century local elites used their connections with the centralizing state to monopolize land and resources, curtailing the autonomy of smallholders.

Colombia and Ecuador

JANE M. RAUSCH, *Professor of History, University of Massachusetts-Amherst*

THIS TWO-YEAR REVIEW PERIOD saw the publication of some superb historiographic and bibliographic studies in Colombia and Ecuador. The most notable event of the period—the 1995 bicentennial commemoration of the birth of Antonio José de Sucre—inspired, especially in Ecuador, an outpouring of books and articles reassessing the meaning of his career and his assassination. Other patriots, whose lives spanned the independence and early national periods, also received renewed attention on both sides of the border. Colombian monographs continue to reflect the fine scholarship that has characterized the field of history since the development of graduate programs at major Colombian universities. It is refreshing to observe that, after a long delay, similar developments in Ecuadorian universities are generating some excellent research.

Beginning with Colombian historiography, Londoño and Durán's bibliography of 376 memoirs and autobiographies written by Colombians from 1817–1996 is an essential guide to many previously obscure sources (item **2587**). The five-volume *Historia General del Huila* (item **2564**), a departmental version of the *Nueva Historia de Colombia*, which includes multidisciplinary essays by faculty, students, and aficionados on *huilense* topics ranging from preconquest to the present, reveals the value of a regional focus when studying a country composed of loosely united regions. Among several historiographical articles, the late Germán Colmenares' analysis of the weaknesses in Colombian school texts is especially intriguing (item **2573**). Finally, the long-awaited, *Entre la legitimidad y la violencia* by Marco Palacios (item **2593**), is a stimulating one-volume synthesis of Colombian history providing a fine counterpart to David Bushnell's *The Making of Modern Colombia* reviewed in *HLAS 52.*

Turning to the 19th century, several biographies obliterate the line that is often drawn between the independence and early national periods. Moreno de Angel's authoritative study of José María Córdoba (item **2591**) describes an able general and patriot who was murdered for rebelling against Bolívar's dictatorship in 1829. Lofstrom's analysis of the youthful years of Tomás Cipriano Mosquera (item **2586**) offers a unique but persuasive psychological approach, while Castrillón Arboleda (item **2572**) presents a fuller portrait of this statesman, military officer, and revolutionary. In a two-volume study, Malcom Deas (item **2575**) explores the life and writings of British entrepreneur Guillermo Wills, an active participant in New Granadan affairs between 1826 and 1875. Also providing insight into this era are Mantilla Ruiz's monograph on the role of the Franciscans in Colombian independence (item **2589**), and Spanish translations of two previously unpublished PhD dissertations: Gilmore's study of federalism (item **2580**), and Young's examination of university reform (item **2609**).

There are four important contributions to the intellectual history of the late-19th century: Martínez's study of the impact of European nationalism on the writings of Samper, Núñez, and Holguín (item **2590**); Múnera's collection of essays by *costeño* intellectuals and their impact on 19th-century political thought (item **2578**); Deas' article exploring the role played by grammarians and philologists in the Conservative Party from 1885–1930 (item **2574**); and Bermúdez Q.'s gendered analysis of the image of the "ideal woman" as portrayed in periodicals published during the Olimpo Radical (item **2568**).

Twentieth-century topics include regionalism, foreign policy, politics, and violence. Noteworthy among the regional studies is Posada Carbó's well-researched survey of the Colombian Caribbean from 1870–1950 (item **2597**). Donadío's concise narrative of Colombia's war with Peru in 1932, meanwhile, is based on a thorough examination of archives in Washington DC, London, Rome, and Bogotá (item **2577**). There are two perceptive biographies of Camilo Torres: Pérez Ramírez seeks to dispel the myths surrounding his career and death (item **2595**), while Villanueva Martínez argues that the priest did not become a revolutionary because of disillusionment with the Catholic Church, but rather because his "dramatic contact with national reality" led him to see armed struggle as the only way to effect structural change (item **2608**).

Turning now to Ecuador, Núñez Sánchez has produced an extraordinarily helpful survey of works by Ecuadorian and foreign historians associated with the "Nueva Historia" movement that began in the 1970s. His 70-page bibliography will be indispensable to researchers (item **2627**). Another useful bibliography is Himiob A.'s list of 1,680 primary and secondary sources concerning Sucre (item **2620**). Two other books spawned by the Sucre bicentennial are especially notable: the first, *Sucre, soldado y estadista* (item **2637**), is a collection of well-researched conference papers originally presented in Quito by scholars representing the Gran Colombian nations, while the second, *Juan José Flores en Berruecos* (item **2612**) reviews the events leading to Sucre's assassination, concluding that Flores, not José María Obando, ordered his murder.

For the later 19th century, Chiriboga's reproduction and analysis of 64 photographs taken between 1860–1920 offers a striking visual record of indigenous people (item **2616**), while *Imágenes e imagineros* explores the construction of white-mestizo identity through an examination of the iconography of Sierra and Amazonian indigenous peoples (item **2626**). In another collaborative volume, *Historia y region en el Ecuador: 1830–1930*, seven scholars trace the history of Oriente, Cuenca, Quito, and Guayaquil provinces and examine the economic and political connections among them (item **2612**). Esvertit Cobes' account of the attempt by the governor of Oriente to colonize the upper Napo river in 1884 is a thoughtful study that illuminates Ecuador's frontier policies in the Amazon (item **2617**).

Finally, for the liberal era (1895–1912), Ayala Mora's narrative synthesis based on his Oxford PhD dissertation should stand as the definitive work for some time (item **2614**), while Henderson's analysis of the government's collapse in 1925 challenges simplistic dependency theory explanations by stressing the domestic ramifications of the cocoa-dominated economy (item **2619**).

COLOMBIA

2562 Abel, Christopher. External philanthropy and domestic change in Colombian health care: the role of the Rockefeller Foundation, ca. 1920–1950. (*HAHR*, 75:3, Aug. 1995, p. 339–376, tables)

Detailed review of Rockefeller Foundation activities in health care and medicine in Colombia between 1920–50. Explores the connections between international goals and national expectations. Concludes that the foundation did achieve "some tangible, beneficial, and enduring accomplishments that were consistent with the gradualist outlook of Colombian governments and the aims of reformist U.S. foreign policymakers."

2563 Acevedo C., Darío. La mentalidad de las élites sobre la violencia en Colombia, 1936–1949. Bogotá: Instituto de Estudios Políticos y Relaciones Internacionales; El Ancora Editores, 1995. 224 p.: bibl., ill.

Analysis of public discourse of political and religious elite shows how conservative and liberal leaders "consciously and unconsciously created a climate of intolerance, insecurity, and conflict" that contributed to outbreak of La Violencia. Special attention paid to editorials and cartoons published in *El Tiempo* and *El Siglo* from 1948–49.

Afanador Ulloa, Miguel Angel. Amnistías e indultos: la historia reciente, 1948–1992. See *HLAS* 57:3367.

2564 Amézquita, Carlos Eduardo et al. Historia general del Huila. v. 1, Espacio, época prehispánica, conquista, colonia. v. 2, Comuneros, independencia, política (siglos XIX y XX), violencia contemporánea. v. 3, Economía (siglos XIX y XX), movimientos sociales, colonización, gobierno. v. 4, Educación, vida cotidiana, mujer, salud, cocina tradicional, diversiones. v. 5, Literatura, arte, arquitectura, ciencia, religión, mitos y leyendas. Neiva, Colombia: Instituto Huilense de Cultura; Fondo de Autores Huilenses; Gobernación del Depto. del Huila; Academia Huilense de Historia, 1995–1996. 5 v.: bibl., ill., maps.

Ground-breaking, comprehensive multivolume history of the Huila dept. from preconquest to the present. Work is the product of the collaboration of diverse university faculty and regional specialists who utilized archival, published, and oral sources to write monographic essays on individual topics. Vol. 1 covers preconquest through the colonial era; vol. 2 covers independence through the 20th century; vol. 3 covers economic topics, social movements, colonization, government; vol. 4 covers education, daily life, women, health, diversions; vol. 5 covers literature, art, architecture. Essential reference for regional history.

2565 Arciniegas, Germán. Bolívar y Santander, vidas paralelas. Selección y epílogo de Juan Gustavo Cobo Borda. Bogotá: Planeta, 1995. 301 p. (Memoria de la historia)

Selected excerpts from books, essays, and speeches by Arciniegas about Bolívar and Santander arranged to compare the careers and personalities of the two leaders, as well as their impact on the country. Also presents a synthesis of opposing trends in early national history.

2566 Ayala Diago, Cesár Augusto. Nacionalismo y populismo: ANAPO y el discurso político de la oposición en Colombia, 1960–1966. Bogotá: Linea de Investigación en Historia Política, Univ. Nacional, 1995. 262 p.: bibl.

Political scientist analyzes opposition to the National Front to show why a liberal faction did not consolidate within the ANAPO movement. Draws on contemporary documents and interviews to discuss renewal of Colombian nationalism, the electoral campaign of 1965–66, and the legislative and presidential elections of 1966.

2567 Ayala Diago, Cesár Augusto. Resistencia y oposición al establecimiento del Frente Nacional: los orígenes de la Alianza Nacional Popular, ANAPO; Colombia, 1953–1964. Bogotá: Univ. Nacional de Colombia, Facultad de Ciencias Humanas, Departamento de Historia, 1996. 371 p.: bibl., ill.

Traces the development of ANAPO from 1953–64 as a protest movement against the bi-partisan National Front. Penetrating analysis of *rojismo* and *anapismo:* their ideology, discourse, and proposals. Also examines the influence of Catholic doctrine and foreign ideologies from Asia, Africa, and the Cuban Revolution.

2568 Bermúdez Q., Suzy. El bello sexo: la mujer y la familia durante el Olimpo Radical. Bogotá: Ediciones Uniandes; ECOE Ediciones, 1993. 212 p., 18 leaves of plates: bibl., ill. (Col. La flor y el colibrí)

Traces the elaboration of the image of the ideal woman or "fair sex" during the Olimpo Radical (1849–85) by analyzing magazine and newspaper articles, and comparing those written by men with those written by women. Well-researched and well-written with excellent illustrations.

2569 Bucana, Juana B. de. La iglesia evangélica en Colombia: una historia. Bogotá: Asociación Pro-Cruzada Mundial, 1995. 249 p.: bibl., index.

Descriptive history of evangelical Protestants from their first failed efforts to their participation in the 1991 Constitutional Assembly. Author, an English missionary who became a Colombian citizen, omits discussion of groups not "clearly evangelical" such as Seventh Day Adventists and United Pentecostal Church. Pioneering work on a movement of growing importance.

2570 Calderón Mosquera, Carlos. Investigaciones históricas y temas económicos. Cali, Colombia: Editorial Claridad, 1993. 214 p.: bibl.

Collection of essays by an Afro-Colombian economist, lawyer, and historian. Subjects range from role of blacks in Colombian history to problems of credit development and banking policy. Primarily of interest as evidence of growing willingness on part of elites to challenge racism and to identify with African aspects of Colombian culture.

2571 Cappelletti, Angel J. El anarquismo en Colombia. (*Actual/Mérida*, 29, dic. 1994, p. 31–64)

Surveys anarchism in Colombia from early-19th century to the 1920s. Shows that the movement lacked the importance of its Argentine and Brazilian counterparts, but nevertheless produced influential activist-thinkers such as Biofilo Panclasta (Vicente Lizcano) and played a significant role in some memorable social struggles.

2572 Castrillón Arboleda, Diego. Tomás Cipriano de Mosquera. Bogotá: Planeta, 1994. 723 p.: bibl.

Statesman, military officer, and revolutionary, Mosquera (1798–1878) was a pivotal figure in the 19th century. This scholarly biography draws on a range of archival materials to present him as a complex leader in the transition of Colombia from colony to republic. Not a definitive work, but an important assessment.

2573 Colmenares, Germán. La batalla de los manuales en Colombia. (*in* Latinoamérica: enseñanza de la historia, libros de textos y conciencia histórica. Buenos Aires: Alianza Editorial; FLACSO; Frankfurt: Georg Eckert Instituts, 1991, p. 122–134)

Analyzes the weaknesses of standard history texts used in Colombia schools. Discusses the contributions of the so-called "new historians" after 1942, and then shows how the attempt to incorporate new approaches in school texts in the 1980s has provoked debate over the role of the study of history in public education.

2574 Deas, Malcolm D. Gramática y poder: la hegemonía de los letrados. (*Mundo Nuevo/Caracas*, 17:1/2, enero/junio 1994, p. 41–58)

Innovative investigation of the unique role played by grammarians and philologists in Colombian politics between 1885–30. Examines the connection between such academic endeavors and conservative presidents and legislators, and argues that the politicians' emphasis on linguistic purity served as a bridge to Colombia's Spanish heritage.

2575 Deas, Malcolm D. Vida y opiniones de Mr. William Wills. v. 1–2. Bogotá: Banco de la República, 1996. 2 v. (Col. bibliográfica)

Biography of Guillermo Wills (1805–75) who arrived in New Granada in 1826 and remained to become a prominent entrepreneur with ties to the Colombian and British communities. Vol. 1 assesses Wills' career and influence. Vol. 2 is a collection of his public writings on economic issues, roads, and politics.

2576 Deas, Malcolm D. and **Fernando Gaitán Daza.** Dos ensayos especulativos sobre la violencia en Colombia. Traducido por Juan Manuel Pombo. Prólogo de Armando Montenegro. Bogotá: FONADE; DNP, 1995. 436 p.: bibl., ill.

Two book-length "essays" analyze La Violencia. Historian Deas presents a historical and comparative meditation on political violence, while economist Gaitán Daza uses new methodologies to study current violence, and to disprove earlier theories that attempted to explain its high incidence.

2577 Donadío, Alberto. La guerra con el Perú. Bogotá: Planeta, 1995. 306 p.: bibl., ill., maps.

Authoritative narrative of Colombia's 1932 war with Peru over the Amazonian town of Leticia. Argues that the conflict was a by-product of the rubber trade aggravated by "the legendary lack of definition of international boundaries." Based on a thorough examination of archives in Washington, London, Rome, and Bogotá.

2578 Ensayos costeños: de la colonia a la república, 1770–1890. Recopilación de Alfonso Múnera. Bogotá: Colcultura, 1994. 477 p. (Biblioteca de autores costeños; 2)

Representative essays by Narváez y la Torre, de Pombo, García del Río, Madiedo, and Núñez. Collection is designed to acquaint new generations with essential historical texts and to demonstrate "the singular presence of the costeño intellectual in the elaboration of national political thought."

2579 Francisco Antonio Zea y su proyecto de integración ibero-americana. Recopilación de Lautaro Ovalles. Caracas: Academia Nacional de la Historia, 1994. 279 p.: bibl. (Biblioteca de la Academia Nacional de la Historia. Fuentes para la historia republicana de Venezuela; 59)

Archival documents relating to a plan for reconciliation between Spain and America that Zea presented to Spain's ambassador in London. The plan, which called for recognition of Colombian independence and a federation between Spain and her former colonies, was rejected but stands as an early attempt at Hispanic American integration.

2580 Gilmore, Robert Louis. El federalismo en Colombia, 1810–1858. v. 1–2. Bogotá: Sociedad Santanderista de Colombia;

Univ. Externado de Colombia, 1995. 2 v.: bibl., ill., maps.

Spanish translation of previously unpublished PhD dissertation based on seven years of research in Bogotá archives and completed at Univ. of California Berkeley in 1949. Deals with regional struggles for local autonomy and events that gave rise to controversy, debate, conflict, and civil wars from 1810–50.

2581 Green, W. John. Vibrations of the collective: the popular ideology of Gaitanismo on Colombia's Atlantic Coast, 1944–1948. (*HAHR*, 76:2, May 1996, p. 283–311)

Stimulating essay synthesizes data gleaned from personal interviews, published sources, and previously unexplored local archives to challenge conclusions of standard biographies on Gaitán. Seeks to demonstrate that the major tenets of gaitanismo as it developed in Cartagena, Barranquilla, and Santa Marta "reflected popularly-held notions which Gaitán identified, articulated and eventually came to symbolize."

2582 Gutiérrez Sanín, Francisco. Curso y discurso del movimiento plebeyo, 1849–1854. Prólogo de Gonzalo Sánchez. Bogotá: Instituto de Estudios Políticos y Relaciones Internacionales; Ancora Editores, 1995. 241 p.: bibl.

Analysis of the popular movement of 1849–54 through its political culture and representative images. Challenges earlier interpretations by so-called "new historians." According to Gonzalo Sánchez, this monograph by an anthropologist is "the most important contribution to the study of nineteenth-century artisans" since the classic works of Colmenares.

Herrera Angel, Marta. Population, territory and power in eighteenth century New Granada: *pueblos de indios* and authorities in the province of Santafe. See *HLAS* 57:2603.

2583 Hincapié Borda, Alicia. Tras la imagen y la presencia de Policarpa. Bogotá?: s.n., 1996. 160 p.: bibl., ill. (some col.).

Shows the enduring presence of independence-era revolutionary heroine Policarpa Salavarrieta (1796–1817) through a compilation of paintings and sculptures assembled to mark the bicentennial of her birth. Includes bibliography, genealogy, brief biography, and representations of her image on stamps and in heraldry.

2584 Hincapié Silva, César. Inmigrantes extranjeros en el desarrollo del Quindío: ¿quiénes vinieron? ¿quiénes se quedaron?; historia económica. Ed. 1995. Armenia, Colombia: Editorial QuinGráfica, 1996. 371 p.: bibl., ill.

Uses oral tradition and printed sources to describe non-Colombians—groups and individuals—who visited, lived, or worked in El Quindío from colonial times to present. An astonishing number of nationalities are represented. By highlighting their contributions to the development of the region, the author introduces often-overlooked aspect of Colombian history.

2585 König, Hans-Joachim. Los caballeros andantes del patriotismo: la actitud de la Academia Nacional de la Historia Colombiana frente a los procesos de cambio social. (*in* Latinoamérica: enseñanza de la historia, libros de textos y conciencia histórica. Buenos Aires: Alianza Editorial; FLACSO; Frankfurt: Georg Eckert Instituts, 1991, p. 135–154)

Balanced assessment of impact of Academia National de la Historia Colombiana on the study of national history after 1902. Suggests that while the emphasis on developing patriotism may have been appropriate in the early decades, by the 1930s this stance was a disservice to historical understanding.

2586 Lofstrom, William Lee. La vida íntima de Tomás Cipriano de Mosquera, 1798–1830. Bogotá: Banco de la República; El Ancora Editores, 1996. 253 p.: bibl., ill., index, maps.

Psycho-biography of Mosquera' youth covering 1798–1825. Mines previously unexplored archives of personal and family correspondence to explain why a man "who for reasons inherent to his character, his ancestry, his personality and the influences of his youth, did not succeed in fulfilling the role he aspired to play in Colombian history."

2587 Londoño, Patricia and Mario Jurisch Durán. Diarios, memorias y autobiografías en Colombia: la biblioteca sumergida. (*Bol. Cult. Bibliogr.*, 32:40, 1995, bibl., ill., tables)

Bibliography of 376 diaries, memoirs, and autobiographies written by Colombians between 1817–1996. Works included are organized alphabetically by title. Also provided are discussions of the various authors' backgrounds and the themes that are addressed. Since it is often argued that such firsthand accounts do not exist in Colombia, this study makes a real contribution.

Londoño de la Cuesta, Juan Luis. Distribución del ingreso y desarrollo económico: Colombia en el siglo XX. See *HLAS 57:1994.*

2588 López Garavito, Luis Fernando. Historia de la hacienda y el tesoro en Colombia, 1821–1900. Bogotá: Banco de la República, 1992. 371 p.: bibl., ill. (Col. bibliográfica/Banco de la República. Historia y teoría económica)

Economics professor and former Tesorero General de la República traces the history of Ministeries of Finance and Treasury through myriad reforms in the 19th century. Indispensable for those charting the evolution of Colombian tax, budget, customs, or credit policies. Contains bibliography, but lacks index.

2589 Mantilla Ruiz, Luis Carlos. Los franciscanos en la independencia de Colombia. (*Arch. Ibero-Am.*, 57:225/226, enero/dic. 1997, p. 297–337)

Leading Franciscan scholar uses material from provincial archive to discuss varying responses of Franciscans to the crisis posed by the War of Independence, and to show the war's impact on the community in 1820s. Balanced approach includes profiles of royalists and patriots, and excerpts from sermons and other original documents.

2590 Martínez, Frédéric. En los orígenes del nacionalismo colombiano: europeísmo e ideología nacional en Samper, Núñez y Holguín, 1861–1894. (*Bol. Cult. Bibliogr.*, 32:39, 1995, p. 27–59, ill., maps, photos)

By analyzing the *mediación cultural* embraced by Samper, the *cosmopolitismo patriótico* of Núñez, and *autencidad nacional* of Holguín, this work demonstrates how the ideas of 19th-century European nationalists influenced the development of Colombian nationalist ideology.

Martínez Carreño, Aída. La prisión del vestido: aspectos sociales del traje en América. See item **794.**

2591 **Moreno de Angel, Pilar.** José María Córdova. Bogotá: Planeta, 1995. 635 p.: bibl., index. (Col. Biografías)

Authoritative biography of Córdova (1799–1829) who fought at Pichincha and Ayacucho and was murdered for rebelling against the Bolivarian dictatorship in 1829. Uses materials from British, French, Mexican, and Colombian archives. Describes Córdova as an able general and a committed patriot steadfastly opposed to the establishment of a monarchy.

2592 **Pabón Villamizar, Silvano *et al.*** Ensayos de historia regional. Bucaramanga, Colombia: Escuela de Historia, UIS, 1995. 203 p.: bibl. (Col. de historia regional)

Seven essays, five examining the postcolonial period, based on master's theses by graduates of the Univ. Industrial de Santander's Escuela de Historia. High quality research and writing reflects the growing professionalization of regional history. Topics include slavery, liberalism, railroads, and the events of April 9, 1946, in Bucaramanga.

2593 **Palacios, Marco.** Entre la legitimidad y la violencia: Colombia, 1875–1994. Bogotá: Grupo Editorial Norma, 1995. 386 p.: bibl., ill., maps. (Col. Vitral)

Palacios' long-awaited and indispensable synthesis of Colombian history. Lacks footnotes, but includes extensive, up-to-date bibliography. Concludes that it is urgent and not impossible for Colombia to develop a political system capable of resolving modern conflicts without relying on myths or manipulation.

2594 **Palacios, Marco.** La gobernabilidad en Colombia: aspectos históricos. (*Anál. Polít./Bogotá*, 29, sept./dic. 1996, p. 3–19)

Stimulating analysis of Colombian history within the context of such global developments as the French Revolution and the collapse of Soviet Union. Concludes that in the 1990s popular "social, civil and political perceptions" of Colombia's constitutions and legal texts became a source of political and social frustration that discouraged Colombians from accepting the responsibilities of citizenship.

2595 **Pérez Ramírez, Gustavo.** Camilo Torres Restrepo: profeta para nuestro tiempo. Colaboración de Jaime Díaz Castañeda. Aporte de Fernando Torres Restrepo.

Bogotá: Indo-American Press Service, 1996. 390 p.: bibl., ill.

Compelling biography by a colleague seeking to dispel myths about the career and death of Torres without idealizing him. First section surveys his life, the second considers his legacy as a Christian, social scientist, and revolutionary. Based on family archives and personal correspondence. Extensive bibliography.

2596 **Posada Carbó, Eduardo.** Civilizar las urnas: conflicto y control en las elecciones colombianas, 1830–1930. (*Bol. Cult. Bibliogr.*, 32:39, 1995, p. 3–25, ill., photos)

Well-written essay reviews electoral campaigns over a 100-year-period showing that at all levels they were commonly accompanied by violence. Author examines different explanations for this phenomenon and discusses its impact on the history of the republic.

2597 **Posada Carbó, Eduardo.** The Colombian Caribbean: a regional history, 1870–1950. Oxford, England; New York: Clarendon Press, 1996. 310 p.: bibl., ill., index, maps. (Oxford historical monographs)

Revised PhD dissertation examines from a regional perspective the social, economic, and political development of the departments of Bolívar, Magdalena, Atlántico, and Guajira between 1870–1950. Topics include agriculture, cattle, rural and urban environments, transportation, external influences, politics, and the relationship between the region and the nation. Well-researched and clearly written.

2598 **Puyo Vasco, Fabio.** Bogotá. Madrid: Editorial MAPFRE, 1992. 339 p.: bibl., ill., index, maps, tables. (Col. Ciudades de Iberoamérica; 9. Col. MAPFRE 1492)

Straightforward introduction to history of Bogotá from colonial times to present. Shows how daily life changed over the centuries and how the city continually redefined itself by integrating people and customs from other parts of the country. Helpful maps, tables, bibliography, and capsule biographies of famous Bogotanos.

2599 **Rausch, Jane M.** Colombia: territorial rule and the Llanos frontier. Gainesville: Univ. Press of Florida, 1999. 296 p.: bibl., ill., index, maps.

Fascinating and well-researched account of the efforts by the three Colombian presidents who ruled during the so-called "Liberal Republic" (1930–46) to develop and incorporate the vast expanses of territory to the east of the Andes known commonly as the Llanos. Concludes that although some progress was made in the more accessible departments of Meta, Arauca, and Casanare, the reforms "did not change the basic structure of the Llanos frontier or its relationship to the highlands as it had been developing over the previous three centuries" (p. 216). Instead, the advent of the Violencia largely halted efforts and reinforced status of eastern Colombia as a haven for people fleeing from conflict elsewhere. Essential reading for anyone wishing to better understand why the Llanos became the focus of the Colombian drug trade and the main stronghold of the country's largest guerrilla force. [L. Boudon]

2600 **Romero Beltrán, Arturo.** Historia de la medicina colombiana: siglo XIX. Antioquia, Colombia: Colciencias; Univ. de Antioquia, 1996. 227 p.: ill.

Survey of medical practices and related scientific developments from 1810 to turn of the century. Chronological approach shows influence of European theories on domestic advances. Includes footnotes, but lacks bibliography and index.

2601 **Ruiz Martínez, Eduardo.** Los hombres del veinte de julio. Bogotá: Fundación Univ. Central, 1996. 532 p.: bibl., ill., index.

Useful reference work summarizes events leading up to the declaration of independence on July 20, 1810. Also presents short biographies of the 53 signatories.

2602 **Sanclemente, Carlos.** El presidente Sanclemente: un magistrado ejemplar. Bogotá: Academia Colombiana de Historia, 1996. 209 p.: bibl., ill. (Biblioteca de historia nacional; 145)

Great-grandson has written a sympathetic biography of former president Carlos Sanclemente. Elected in 1898, he was deposed on July 31, 1900 by a conservative coup that installed José Manuel Marroquín. Uses archival and family documents, some of which are reprinted.

2603 **Serret, Félix.** Viaje a Colombia, 1911–1912. Traducción y prólogo de Luis Carlos Mantilla Ruiz. Bogotá?: Instituto Colombiano de Cultura-Colcultura, Biblioteca Nacional de Colombia, 1994. 294 p.: ill., map. (Biblioteca V Centenario Colcultura. Viajeros por Colombia)

Spanish translation of a rare but informative travel account originally written in French. Serret, an engineer, spent 140 days in 1911 traveling from Buenaventura to Puerto Colombia by railroad, mule, and steamship. Good descriptions of Cali, Cartagena, and travel along the Magdalena River.

2604 **Sofer, Doug.** Power boost: Colombia and the United States during the early years of the Violence, 1946–1953. (SECOLAS Ann., 26, March 1995, p. 98–118)

Argues that US military and economic aid to Colombia between 1946–53 strengthened the power and autonomy of the armed forces, and created a cycle that increased anti-government activity and, ultimately, contributed to destabilizing Colombian politics.

2605 **Torres del Río, César.** Grandes agresiones contra Colombia. Bogotá: Ediciones Martínez Roca, 1994. 283 p.: bibl. (Col. Grandes)

Dependista historian examines incidents of foreign aggression against Colombia including the loss of Panama, war with Peru, Venezuelan border conflict, German actions during World War II, and the North American war against drugs. Condemns passivity of Colombian masses and willingness of leaders to give in when challenged. Calls for new sovereignty by democratic majority.

2606 **Tovar Pinzón, Hermes.** La humanización de la guerra, los pueblos y la independencia de Colombia. (Rev. Cienc. Hum./Pereira, 2:5, sept. 1995, p. 95–111)

Historian examines the refusal of towns in the Guajira Peninsula to accept the conditions of an 1820 peace treaty signed by Morillo and Bolívar. Seeks to show that even the most remote villages exercised influence on the direction of events.

2607 **Valencia Llano, Alonso.** Las luchas sociales y políticas del periodismo en el Estado Soberano del Cauca: ensayo. Cali, Colombia: Univ. del Valle, Facultad de Humanidades, Depto. de Historia, 1994. 154 p.: bibl. (Col. de autores vallecaucanos)

Examines newspapers published in Cauca between 1863–80. Attributes their ephemeral existence to shortages of presses, type, ink, paper, journalists, and a reading public but argues that newspapers nevertheless played an important role in promotion and development of political and social projects.

2608 Villanueva Martínez, Orlando.
Camilo: acción y utopía. Bogotá: Linea de Investigación en Historia Política, Univ. Nacional, 1995. 256 p.: bibl., ill.

Thoughtful biography based on a thorough command of primary sources. Argues that Torres did not become a revolutionary because of disillusionment with the Church, but that his ideological formation and "dramatic contact with national reality" led him to endorse armed struggle as the only way to effect fundamental structural change.

2609 Young, John Lane. La reforma universitaria de la Nueva Granada: 1820–1850. Traducción de Gloria Rincón Cubides. Bogotá: Instituto Caro y Cuervo; Univ. Pedagógica Nacional, 1994. 206 p.: bibl. (Serie Educación y desarrollo; 2)

Spanish translation of previously unpublished PhD dissertation completed at Columbia Univ. Reviews efforts to reform higher education in early national era. Describes students, professors, academic programs, and methods of financing. Helpful comparison with developments in other Latin American countries and the US. Excellent introduction to an important topic.

Zuluaga Gómez, Víctor. Vida, pasión y muerte de los indígenas de Caldas y Risaralda. See *HLAS 57:1145*.

ECUADOR

Aguilar, Paúl et al. Enfoques y estudios históricos: Quito a través de la historia. See item **2185.**

2610 Almeida, Mónica. Phoenicians of the Pacific: Lebanese and other Middle Easterners in Ecuador. (*Americas/Franciscans*, 53:1, July 1996, p. 87–111, table)

Examines the experiences of Lebanese, Syrian, and Palestinian immigrants to Ecuador from 1850 to the present. Argues that among other factors, their "surprising resilience" enabled them to integrate themselves into Ecuadorian society and to play an important role in the country's social, economic, and political life. Good introduction to a neglected topic.

2611 Almeida Guzmán, Patricio. Ingresos por diezmos, alcabalas, aduanas y tasas portuarias, 1830–1900. (*Rev. Ecuat. Hist. Econ.*, 12, 1995, p. 221–234, bibl.)

Provides national-level time series of tithes, sales taxes, customs duties, and port duties as reported in the quasi-annual reports of the Ministerio de Hacienda for first 70 years of the national period. Although sources of revenue are defined, the methodology used to compile these series is not explained. [M.T. Hamerly]

Arias Altamirano, Luis. Iglesias parroquiales de la Arquidiócesis de Guayaquil. See item **2110.**

2612 Aristizábal, Armando. Juan José Flores en Berruecos: síntesis de una infamia. Quito: Casa de la Cultura Ecuatoriana, 1995. 321 p.: bibl.

Ecuadorian historian reviews several hypotheses concerning the assassination of Antonio José de Sucre at Berruecos (Nariño). Concludes that it was Juan José Flores, not José María Obando, who ordered Sucre's murder. Despite distracting polemical style, the work provides a good overview of the historical debate.

2613 Arosemena, Guillermo. Los Coronel: grandes comerciantes guayaquileños del siglo XIX. (*Rev. Ecuat. Hist. Econ.*, 12, 1995, p. 91–145)

Reconstructs commercial and financial activities of Coronel family in Guayaquil from early-19th to early-20th centuries. Important contribution to economic history of first half of the national period and to history of entrepreneurs in Ecuador. [M.T. Hamerly]

Arosemena, Guillermo. El fruto de los dioses. See *HLAS 57:2018*.

2614 Ayala Mora, Enrique. Historia de la revolución liberal ecuatoriana. Quito: Corporación Editora Nacional, 1994. 406 p.: bibl., ill., index. (Col. Temas; 5)

Indispensable synthesis of the Liberal era (1895–1912) by Ecuador's preeminent historian based on his Oxford PhD dissertation. Examines conditions leading to 1895 revolution, developments during liberal hegemony, the structure and program of the liberal state, and the nature of the conservative opposition. Includes footnotes and bibliography.

2615 Bustos L., Guillermo. Notas sobre economía y sociedad en Quito y la sierra centro norte durante las primeras décadas del siglo XX. (*Quitumbe/Quito,* 7, 1990, p. 101–117, tables)

Working paper on demography, economy, and society of northern and central highlands during first third of 20th century. [M.T. Hamerly]

Cevallos García, Gabriel. Historia nacional del Ecuador, edición bilingüe = bilingual edition. See item **2202.**

2616 Chiriboga, Lucía and **Silvana Caparrini.** Identidades desnudas; Ecuador 1860–1920: la temprana fotografía del indio de los Andes. Quito: ILDIS, 1994. 144 p.: bibl., ill. (some col.).

Sixty-four photographs of Indians taken between 1860–1920 illustrate how photographers portrayed indigenous people. Introductory essays trace the history of photography in 19th-century Ecuador and analyze the photographic styles of the works presented. An extraordinarily touching document.

Cipolletti, María Susana. Lacrimabili statu: indianische Sklaven in Nordwestamazonien, 17.-20. Jahrhundert. See item **2204.**

2617 Esvertit Cobes, Natalia. La colonia oriental: un proyecto de colonización fracasado en la Amazonía ecuatoriana, 1884–1885. (*Bol. Am.,* 36:46, 1996, p. 99–109, bibl.)

Interesting study of the efforts of the governor of Oriente prov. to establish a colony on the upper Napo river. Uses archival materials and places the episode in the larger context of the relationship of the Quito government with the Amazon frontier.

2618 Gamara, María del Pilar. La frontera nómada: frentes y fronteras económicas en el proceso cauchero ecuatoriano, 1870-1920. (*Procesos/Quito,* 9, 1996, p. 39–79, graphs, map, tables)

This study, a first in Ecuadorian historiography, examines Ecuador's participation in late-19th–early-20th-century rubber boom. Examines politics and economics of production and extraction of rubber. Also demonstrates feasibility of completing archival research on the Oriente in that location. [M.T. Hamerly]

2619 Henderson, Paul. Cocoa, finance, and the state in Ecuador, 1985–1925. (*Bull. Lat. Am. Res.,* 16:2, May 1997, p. 169–186, tables)

Author challenges simplistic dependency theory explanations by synthesizing results of recent scholarship and his own research to analyze the development of Ecuador's cocoa-dominated economy. Also examines how governments and business interests tried to come to terms with adverse circumstances confronting cocoa exports between 1914–25.

2620 Himiob A., Santos. Sucre, época & épica, 1795–1995: bibliografía del general en jefe y gran mariscal de Ayacucho Antonio José de Sucre; homenaje en el bicentenario de su nacimiento. Caracas: Biblioteca Nacional, 1995. 145 p.: indexes.

Based on a review of library and archival holdings in Venezuela, Colombia, Ecuador, Peru, and Argentina, this bibliography contains 1,680 primary and secondary sources concerning Sucre. This indispensable resource is indexed by chronology and subject.

2621 Historia y región en el Ecuador: 1830–1930. Edición de Juan Maiguashca. Quito: Corporación Editora Nacional, 1994. 436 p.: bibl., ill., maps. (Biblioteca de ciencias sociales; 30)

Essays by seven international scholars seek to establish the historical origins of Ecuadorian regionalism by tracing the history of Oriente, Cuenca, Quito, and Guayaquil prov. and then examining the economic and political connections between them. Solid scholarly work based on archival and other primary documents.

Jurado Noboa, Fernando. Las quiteñas. See item **2225.**

Keeding, Ekkehart. La Ilustración en Quito y su influjo en la Independencia. See item **2226.**

2622 Kreuter, Maria-Luise. Wo liegt Ecuador?: Exil in einem unbekannten Land 1938 bis zum Ende der fünfziger Jahre. Berlin: Metropol, 1995. 320 p.: bibl., ill. (Reihe Dokumente, Texte, Materialien; Bd. 18)

Valuable study of Jewish refugees in Ecuador emphasizes those who, unlike members of the intellectual and scientific community, escaped from Europe late and had fewer options for host countries. Sources include 40 volumes of Quito's Jewish newspaper, published and unpublished work by the refugees, and 50 extensive interviews. Concentrates on immigrants' professional and social acculturation; their contributions to Ecuador; their cultural, religious, and social organizations; and relations within the Jewish community, with gentile victims of the Nazi regime, and with the existing German colony. [C.K. Converse]

Lavallé, Bernard. Bibliografía francesa sobre el Ecuador, 1968–1993: ciencias humanas, sociales y de la tierra. See item **2113.**

2623 Loor, Wilfrido. Estudios históricos. Selección y recopilación de Jorge Salvador Lara. Estudios introductorios de Fernando Jurado Noboa y Jorge Salvador Lara. Quito Aymesa: Academia Nacional de Historia, 1996. 738 p.: bibl. (Col. Grupo Aymesa; 16)

Reprints several of Loor's major, long out-of-print studies, most notably: *Guayaquil y Manabí en 1820* (see *HLAS 42:2921*); *La Provincia de Guayaquil en lucha por su independencia* (see *HLAS 40:3370*); and *García Moreno: apuntes para su biografía.* Inclusion of last title is providential, as few scholars had access to, or even were aware of, this quasi-book, which originally appeared in the Guayaquil weekly *La Verdad* from Oct. 7, 1955-Sept. 13, 1956. Loor (1892–1984) was a leading authority on the theocratic dictator. Includes useful biobibliographical sketch of Loor by Jurado Noboa. [M.T. Hamerly]

Luna Tamayo, Milton. Estado, regionalización y lucha política del Ecuador, 1800–1869. See item **2239.**

"Las Manufacturas de la Provincia de Quito" de Juan de Larrea y Villavicencio, 1802. See item **2240.**

2624 Martínez, Nicolás Guillermo. Ascensiones y exploraciones en los Andes ecuatorianos. Quito: Ediciones Abya-Yala; Nuevos Horizontes, 1994. 308 p.: bibl., ill. (Col. Tierra incógnita; 11. Pioneros y precursores del andinismo ecuatoriano; 1)

Accounts originally published in Quito between 1915–33 by Martínez Holguín describing his explorations in the Ecuadorian Andes. The introduction by Rodríguez Castelo provides biographical data on Martínez, one of the first Ecuadorian climbers, and evaluates his scientific observations and his descriptions of the expeditions.

Morelli, Federica. Doing historical research in Quito: a guide to archives and libraries. See item **2114.**

2625 Moscoso, Martha. Organización económica, autoridad indígena y conflicto en la comunidad de Jima, Sur-Este de los Andes ecuatorianos, siglo XIX. (*ANDES Antropol. Hist.*, 2/3, segundo semestre 1990/primer semestre 1991, p. 105–115)

Anthropologist draws on archival sources to trace the transformation of Jima, an Indian community in Azuay Province, during the 19th century. Emphasizes the collapse of collective land ownership and the indigenous authority system.

2626 Muratorio, Blanca. Imágenes e imagineros. Edición de Blanca Muratorio. Quito: FLACSO-Sede Ecuador, 1994. 293 p.: bibl., ill. (Serie Estudios-Antropología)

Five anthropologists study the iconography of Indians of the Sierra and Amazonia by examining 19th- and 20th-century narrative and visual texts produced by travelers, ethnologists, missionaries, and creole elite. Essays show how Europeans and Ecuadorans dealt with "internalization of the Other Indian" in the construction of white-mestizo identity.

Nueva historia del Ecuador. See item **2248.**

2627 Núñez, Jorge. La historiografía ecuatoriana contemporánea: 1970–1994. Quito: Ediciones de la FAU, 1994. 135 p.: bibl.

Informative survey of contributions by Ecuadorian and foreign historians associated with movement known as "Nueva Historia" that began in the 1970s. Assesses strengths and weaknesses of new work as well as problems facing continued professionalization of the discipline.

2628 Ospina, Pablo. Imaginarios nacionalistas: historia y significados nacionales en Ecuador, siglos XIX y XX. (*Procesos/Quito*, 9, 1996, p. 111–124)

Critical review of role of history, especially of officially sponsored histories, in the formation of nationalism in Ecuador. Emphasizes boundary dispute issue and views of indigenous peoples. [M.T. Hamerly]

2629 Páez Cordero, Alexei. Los orígenes de la izquierda ecuatoriana: notas sobre movimientos sociales e ideología. (Quitumbe/Quito, 7, 1990, p. 81–99)

Relatively objective and sophisticated analysis of origins of the Ecuadorian left in 1920s. Focuses on economic and social conditions as well as ideological developments. Stresses need for a more intensive, multidisciplinary study of events of the period, especially the general strike of Nov. 7, 1922. [M.T. Hamerly]

Palomeque, Silvia. Continuidad y cambio entre la colonia y la república: estudio de los circuitos mercantiles y de las especializaciones productivas regionales en Cuenca, Ecuador. See item **2250**.

2630 Peñaloza Bretel, Marco Antonio. La investigación historiográfica sobre la hacienda serrana ecuatoriana del siglo XIX. (Procesos/Quito, 7, 1995, p. 35–58, bibl.)

Solid review of the mostly recent and relatively limited work on history of rural estates in the highlands in 1800s. Includes useful bibliography. [M.T. Hamerly]

2631 Peralta, José. Notas sueltas para servir a mis memorias políticas. Ed. especial por el centenario de la Revolución Liberal. Quito: Namur Editores, 1995. 446 p.: bibl., ill., index.

Peralta (1855–1937) wrote this previously unpublished memoir in 1916 while exiled in Lima. Recounts his experiences in the Liberal Revolution of 1895 and as Minister of Foreign Relations, Public Instruction, and Hacienda in the two administrations of Eloy Alfaro (1897–1901) and (1906–11). Well-edited with introduction, annotations, and index.

2632 Pineo, Ronn F. Social and economic reform in Ecuador: life and work in Guayaquil. Gainesville: Univ. Press of Florida, 1996. 227 p.: bibl., ill., index, map.

Important addendum to increasing volume of work in English on post-independent

Ecuador adds appreciably to knowledge of demographic, economic, and social history of Guayaquil for period 1870–1925. However, work is not comprehensive as author seems unaware of some recent literature and the availability of data from 1861 census. For economist's comment, see HLAS 57:2051. [M.T. Hamerly]

2633 Puga, Miguel A. La gente ilustre de Quito. v. 1–2. Quito: Editorial Delta; Sociedad de Amigos de la Genealogía, 1994–1995. 2 v. (Col. Ecuador mestizo; 11–12)

Biographical sketches of 190 illustrious quiteños, mostly from national period including some still living. Useful reference work; exceptionally strong on artists and musicians. [M.T. Hamerly]

Puga, Miguel A. Quito de ayer, Quito de siempre. See item **2257**.

2634 Quito según los extranjeros: la ciudad, su paisaje, gentes y costumbres observadas por los visitantes extranjeros; siglos XVI-XX. Introducción, compilación y notas de Manuel Espinosa Apolo con la colaboración de María Páez. Quito: Centro de Estudios Felipe Guamán Poma, 1996. 195 p.: bibl., ill.

Useful anthology of descriptions of Quito from the 16th century to 1944 excerpted from travel accounts by 25 foreign visitors. Selections arranged chronologically and thematically. Almost half of the book deals with the post-1810 era. Includes introductory essay and brief biographies of the travelers.

2635 Rosero, Rocío. José Joaquín Olmedo: ¿patriota, político o desertor—?, 1800–1847. Quito: Eskeletra Editorial, 1994. 599 p.: bibl., index. (Historia)

Well-written biography of Olmedo (1780–1847), Ecuadorian poet, liberal politician, and lawyer. Analysis of his still-unedited letters emphasizes his multifaceted career and demonstrates that he was "the civilian founder of the Republic." Includes some little-known but important documents.

2636 Sáenz, Manuela. Manuela. Quito?: s.n., 1995? 219 p.: col. ill.

Curious volume reproduces so-called "lost" Quito, Paita, and Bucaramanga diaries of Manuela Sáenz (which may or may not be authentic) together with a selection of her letters. Also contains a brief biography by

Carlos Alvarez Saá and an imaginary interview with her conducted by Rodrigo Villacís Molina.

Sampedro V., Francisco. El espacio territorial ecuatoriano de 1830 a 1995, con la Guerra del Cenepa desatada por el Perú: auténtica historia de límites. See *HLAS 57:2633*.

2637 **Sucre, soldado y estadista.** Edición de Enrique Ayala Mora. Bogotá: Planeta; Quito: Univ. Andina Simón Bolívar, 1996. 319 p.: bibl. (Col. Biografías)

  Ten well-researched essays by Ecuadorian, Peruvian, Bolivian, and Colombian scholars provide fresh insights into Sucre's career and significance. Written for a conference held in Ecuador to mark the bicentennial of Sucre's birth. A valuable set of essays, but Ayala Mora's analysis of the evidence concerning Sucre's assassination is of special interest.

Urdaneta, Alberto. Alberto Urdaneta, vida y obra. See item **336.**

Vega Vega, Wilson. Bibliografía del Dr. Carlos Manuel Larrea. See item **2116.**

Vega Vega, Wilson. José María Vargas: bibliografía. See item **2117.**

Peru

DANIEL M. MASTERSON, *Professor, United States Navel Academy, Annapolis, Maryland*

IN *HLAS 54* AND *HLAS 56*, reviewer Nils P. Jacobsen noted the growing diversity and maturity of the historical scholarship on Republican Peru. He also commented on the increasingly cosmopolitan nature of the literature with the development of the "new political history" which drew upon the work of European, particularly French, historians. Also significant were the additions of discourse analysis and hegemony, which emerged in literature on Latin American history more than a decade after these themes came to dominate the historical literature on modern Europe and to a lesser extent the US. As is often the case with trends in historical interpretation, reliance on these approaches has waned in recent years. Additionally, dependency theory and Marxist structuralism no longer dominate the literature as they did in previous decades. This may well reflect the failure of statist economic policies throughout Latin America and the collapse of the Soviet Union, but it is still too early to be certain that these will be lasting trends.

  Some past mainstays of historical scholarship continue to garner careful attention. During the last years of the 20th century, studies of local and regional history, often sponsored by municipalities or departmental governments, continued to appear. Intellectual, political and, more recently, better-quality social histories are appearing regularly. As noted earlier, many of these studies are now less paradigmatic than in the past. Immigration histories, which have always been uneven with the exception of the Italians and the Chinese, are now becoming rapidly focused on the Japanese, although some interesting studies on smaller immigrant groups, such as the Croatians, are finally beginning to appear. The Alberto Fujimori phenomenon, as well as financial support from the Japanese community, particularly the JINAI Cultural Center in Lima, helps explain the surge of interest in Peru's relatively small *nikkei* (overseas Japanese) community. As might be expected, the Japanese-Peruvian scholars in Peru are responsible for much of the best work on the topic. Still, significant regional histories of the Japanese by non-*nikkei* scholars are beginning to emerge. The Peruvian *nikkei* have kept meticulous records, greatly aiding scholarship by members of their own community and by foreign historians as well.

There remains much scholarly space for the history of slavery in Peru. Blanchard's work on slavery and abolition has been followed most notably by Hunefelt's analysis of Lima's slaves and their resistance patterns, but has not yet been augmented by works of similar magnitude. The 19th-century social and political evolution of Peru, a field that has not received the attention it deserves until recently, continues to mature with the appearance of excellent studies on the rise of Civilismo and the role of the peasantry in the transition from colonial to republican rule.

The 1995 renewal of hostilities between Peru and Ecuador over their long-standing border dispute produced a flood of scholarship by both professional and amateur Peruvian scholars and the government. Some of these studies are founded on solid scholarship and merit mention in this review. Looking at the history of militarism, the military governments of Generals Juan Velasco Alavarado and Francisco Morales Bermudez are now a generation in the past. The deluge of literature on the military prompted by the *docenio* (12-year military rule) and its unprecedented and controversial reforms is now a mere trickle, but important monographs continue to emerge. In a broader sense, serious historical scholarship on the Peruvian military for both the 19th and 20th century was nearly absent for this review period.

As Jacobsen reported in *HLAS 56*, the history of women and gender has yet to appear as a mature field of study. Biographical studies, always a mainstay of Peruvian historiography, have not been significant in the past few years. Aside from the expected studies of Peru's Marxist icon, José Carlos Mariátegui, and the valuable but abbreviated biographies of prominent Peruvians by the Lima publisher BRASA, this field has suffered, possibly as a result of the greater diversity of historical scholarship. The historical literature on peasant consciousness and resistance in the republican era is still a field requiring further study. Important studies on peasant resistance and adaption in Ica, and on liberalism and traditional Indian communities provides evidence that this is still an area of serious scholarly concern. Significantly, very few biographies of APRA leader Victor Raul Haya de la Torre have been published two decades after his death. This may be explained in part by the decline of APRA as a significant political force in Peru in the aftermath of the Alan García's presidential debacle of the late 1980s.

General, and to a lesser extent, diplomatic histories of Peru continue to appear. Notable among these general works is a valuable anthology that is especially useful in the classroom. A number of other general studies demonstrate especially fine scholarship.

Klarén's very recently published Oxford history of Peru (item **2667**), will stand as the standard survey of Peru for decades to come. The broad range of his research is quite impressive. Unlike most studies in the Oxford series, which heavily stress economic developments, often at the expense of social and political aspects, Klarén's work offers a more balanced account. In addition, significant attention is paid to the role of the military in 20th-century affairs. The bibliography is a model of completeness and will be a valuable aid to scholars. Clayton's diplomatic history of Peruvian-US relations completes the first dozen of such studies in the University of Georgia series (item **2646**). It is a particularly vital work of scholarship because it transcends the traditional diplomatic history to include important social and economic themes, especially the unbalanced relationships between powerful US corporations such as Grace and the International Petroleum Company and the Peruvian state. Peru's troubled relationship with the US military through the Sendero Luminoso era also is given close attention. Wagner de Reyna's diplomatic history of Peru through the early decades of the 20th century offers useful background information on the lingering border disputes with Colombia and Ecuador and the formulation of international policy with non-Latin American nations (item **2707**). Also valuable to historians is the comprehensive anthology edited by Starn, Degregori, and Kirk that begins with the Chavin culture and works its way through to the modern cocaine economy and important aspects of contemporary Peruvian popular culture (see *HLAS 57:1215*).

In the realm of local and regional history, Doering and Lohman Villena's history of Lima published in the MAPFRE series is dated (item **2658**), but represents one of the best urban histories of the past decade by two of Peru's finest historians. Complementing this study of Lima is the excellent anthology edited by Panfichi and Portocarrero (item **2681**), which covers the century after 1850 and, as such, does not touch upon the mass migrations from the sierra which were about to occur. Historians of early-19th-century Peru will find the work by Santos-Granero and Barclay on the *selva central*, now offered in translation through Smithsonian Institution Press, extremely valuable with regard to the history of land-use patterns in this Peruvian frontier province (item **2696**). Other regional works of particular note are Huertas Vallejos' examination of the Sechura region (item **2662**) and Villegas Romero's study of Arequipa in the early-19th century (item **2706**). Scholars studying the history of cotton agriculture will find the work by Cueto and Lossio helpful, especially their emphasis on scientific innovations (item **2650**).

The study of the Japanese experience in Peru will rest for years to come on the excellent scholarship of the late Japanese-Peruvian sociologist, Fukumoto (item **2655**). Emphasizing social themes such as family stability and changes in cultural attitudes through four generations, Fukumoto still offers valuable quantitative materials drawn from the 1989 Japanese self-census in Peru. Morimoto, who was the chief administrator of that self-census, has updated an earlier study that also merits careful attention (item **2679**). Rocca Torres has written the only comprehensive regional history of the Japanese in Peru (item **2695**). One of the most compelling autobiographies by any Peruvian immigrant is Higashide's account of his challenging life in Japan, Peru, and the US (item **2660**). First published in Japanese, the book is now available in English through the University of Washington Press. An annotated book of photographs of Peru's Japanese compiled and edited by Watanabe, Morimoto, and Chambi bears mention because of its particular value to specialists and the poignancy of many of its photographs (item **2708**). Ortíz Sotelo's study of the small Croatian community, through the lens of one particular Croatian family, provides an interesting and relatively fresh approach to immigration history in Peru (item **2687**).

Valuable works dealing with Peru's evolving political and social culture in the 19th century continue to appear. The highly useful study by McEvoy explores the nation's search for the illusive "political ideal," particularly during the early part of the Civilista era (item **2676**). This work is complemented by that of German historian Mücke, who deftly examines the first decade of the Partido Civil (item **2680**). Thurner's monograph examines Republican nation-building from the perspective of its implications for the peasant population of highland Peru (item **2703**). Issues of resistance and cultural adaption are framed in the context of the 1885 Atusparia uprising and peasant political culture. Thurner's article in the *Hispanic American*

Historical Review explores similar themes but focuses on the relationship between Atusparia and the military caudillo Andrés Cáceres (item **2702**). Jacobsen presents a convincing analysis of the failure of liberalism to draw indigenous communities into the modern world of individualism and acquisitive capitalism (item **2664**). Peloso's valuable work on the peasantry of the Pisco valley in Ica analyzes the changing role of cotton plantation workers over the course of generations, detailing altered worker-planter relationships due to modernization (item **2690**).

Of the rush of books appearing on military, diplomatic, and legal aspects of Peru's border conflict with Ecuador since 1996, two of the most balanced and thoroughly researched accounts are those by Denegri Luna and Yepes (items **2653** and **2709,** respectively). The former concentrates on the long-term historical and diplomatic aspects of the dispute, while the latter examines attempts to politically validate the 1942 Rio de Janeiro settlement through legal means and US assistance.

Studies of the military and Sendero Luminoso have continued to diminish in the late 1990s. After more than a decade of reflection, it appears that the rapid decline of Sendero Luminoso following the capture of leader Abimael Guzmán in Sept. 1992 seriously undermined the Maoist paradigm and its applicability to Peru. Nevertheless, as the years have unfolded careful research has resulted in fewer, but more evenly balanced studies reflecting Peruvian impressions and memories of the civil war. Very useful for understanding the phenomenon of Sendero Lumunoso and critical issues related to the rise of the quasi-Maoist group is the anthology by Stern, *Shining and other paths: war and society in Peru, 1980–1995,* which contains, among others, valuable essays by Starn on the *Rondas Campesinas* (peasant defense brigades) (item **2697**), Mallon on antecedents to the movement in the Velasco era agrarian reforms (item **2669**), and Coral Cordero on the role of women in the conflict (item **2648**). Among its many strong points, the compelling account of the Shining Path's women sets the work by Kirk apart from most studies of the movement (item **2666**). Reflecting upon both Mariátegui's legacy and the Maoist paradigm of Sendero Luminoso, Masterson's analysis debates the peasant origins of and its ideological links to orthodox Maoism (item **2672**). The short but focused work by Mauceri on state policy and civil- military relations places great emphasis on the failure of "state populism" of the military and failed civilian governments before the 1990s in opening the doors for Sendero Luminoso (item **2673**). Tapia effectively examines the failed strategies of both the military and Sendero Luminoso before the capture of Guzmán in 1992 (item **2700**). Though flawed by a heavy offering of questionable statistical tables, the work by Fujimori's military chief of staff, De Bari Hermoza Ríos, will be of some use to scholars studying the Peruvian military's perspective during the conflict with Sendero Luminoso (item **2651**).

Turning to the rather slim biographical offerings, two in particular should draw the serious attention of scholars. Tamariz Lúcar's study of General Manuel A. Odría is one of the best to appear thus far (item **2699**). Additionally, Stein offers an intriguing look at the early life of José Carlos Mariátegui set around a 1917 ceremony in a Lima cemetery (item **2698**). Drawing upon Freud and literary theorists, the study provides a sophisticated analysis. Finally, as the Fujimori era enters its second decade, we continue to await a balanced and well-researched biography of the controversial Japanese-Peruvian president, Alberto Fujimori. Nevertheless, just as occurred with the extended rule of Gen. Velasco, useful anthologies of Fujimori's political and economic policies are now appearing. Editors Cameron and Mauceri strike a nice balance between these issues (item **2693**) and include an especially fine essay by Degregori on the post-Sendero era, among others (item **2652**). Another anthology edited by Crabtree and Thomas emphasizes the "political economy" of the Fujimori regime (item **2654**). Despite Fujimori's success in reversing the economic chaos of the García years, several contributors in this volume are deeply critical of the implications of his economic policies. Nevertheless, with reliable data still unavailable for the last years of the 20th century, assessments offered in this work may be tempered by time as the new century unfolds.

2638 Aguirre, Carlos. The Lima penitentiary and the modernization of criminal justice in nineteenth-century Peru. (*in* The birth of the penitentiary in Latin America: essays on criminology, prison reform, and social control. Austin: Univ. of Texas Press, 1996, p. 44–77)

Significant article analyzes conceptual changes in the criminal justice system and penal reform in late-19th-century Peru. First opened in 1862, the Lima penitentiary is described as the symbol of a state seeking greater centralization as the age of caudillismo reaches its apex. The construction of the penitentiary and better-organized urban police units are seen as only a part of the broader attempt by Peru's elite to create a more Europeanized society, while repressing new social tensions created by the recent abolition of slavery and evolving labor patterns on the nation's haciendas.

2639 Aldana Rivera, Susana. Un norte diferente para la independencia peruana. (*Rev. Indias*, 57:209, enero/abril 1997, p. 141–164)

Offers useful bibliographical review of the early independence movement and then shifts discussion to the struggle in northern Peru. Discusses economic consequences of military operations, particularly in Lambayeque and in the city of Trujillo. Also briefly discusses links between the struggle against royalists in the north and in present-day Ecuador.

2640 Aljovín, Cristóbal. Violencia y legitimidad: las revoluciones entre 1827 y 1841. (*Apuntes/Lima*, 39, segundo semestre 1996, p. 113–127, bibl.)

Well-researched overview of the emergence of early-19th-century caudillismo amid the violence and political instability following independence. Emphasizes the *golpes de estado* of such early caudillos as Santa Cruz, Gamarra, and Vivanco. Makes noteworthy argument that there was never an institutional military golpe until the movement of Gen.

Juan Velasco Alvarado in 1968. Concludes with the role of the military in politics, stressing how differing interest groups divided the nation's standing army and retarded its unity and professional development.

2641 Aparicio Vega, Manuel Jesús. De Vilcabamba a Camisea: historiografía de la Provincia de La Convención. Cusco, Peru: Univ. Nacional de San Antonio Abad del Cusco, 1999. 551 p.: bibl., ill. (Serie Ediciones especiales UNSAAC. Siglo XX; 2)

Highly detailed study of Peru's key province of La Convención, site of much peasant unrest and resistance movements. Like many of the regional histories reviewed here, this study relies heavily on a geographic and cultural format. Population patterns, bolstered by very useful statistics, are discussed in depth. Nearly devoid of any substantive political history, however, and, therefore, barely discusses much of the political unrest of the late 1950s-60s. Nevertheless, a comprehensive economic and cultural introduction to this region of Peru.

2642 Belaunde Moreyra, Antonio. Nuestro problema con Ecuador. Lima: Ariel, 1995. 352 p.: bibl., ill., maps.

Study prompted by border conflict between Peru and Ecuador in early 1995. Author has extensive diplomatic experience representing the Peruvian government. Explores major 20th-century issues, in particular the Rio Protocol of 1942. Decries Ecuador's "revisionist" efforts in the early 1960s to alter and eventually reject the provisions of the treaty. Reflects the consistent position of the Peruvian government regarding the enforcement of the Rio Protocol and should be viewed from this perspective. Extensive bibliography useful to specialists.

2643 Blanchard, Peter. The *transitional man* in nineteenth-century Latin America: the case of Domingo Elías of Peru. (*Bull. Lat. Am. Res.*, 15:2, May 1996, p. 157–176, bibl.)

Valuable article analyzes political career of early-19th-century landowner from Ica who was eventually named prefect of Lima by the caudillo Vivanco and later became provisional president. Described as fostering "liberal and enlightened" ideals, Elías also enacted progressive policies in his agricultural holdings. In the midst of the fierce struggles between military strongmen, this Ica *hacendado* is seen as the bridge to civilian political leadership following the age of Castilla.

2644 Burt, Jo-Marie. Shining Path and the "decisive battle" in Lima's barriadas: the case of Villa El Salvador. (*in* Shining and other paths: war and society in Peru, 1980–1995. Edited by Steve J. Stern. Durham, NC: Duke Univ. Press, 1998, p. 267–306)

Excellent extended article analyzes Shining Path's brutal and failed policies in one of Lima's largest *pueblos jóvenes*. Traces evolution of Lima's squatter settlements from the 1940s onward, focusing on the evolution of Villa El Salvador since the early 1970s. Places significant emphasis on Villa El Salvador mayor María Elena Moyano's resistance to Shining Path and the impact of her brutal assassination by that group. Concludes that Shining Path was not interested in building a mass base of popular support in Lima but, rather, in exploiting government weaknesses at all levels through the use of terror and intimidation so as to hasten the collapse of the Peruvian state.

2645 Cameron, Maxwell A. Political and economic origins of regime change in Peru: the eighteenth brummaire of Alberto Fujimori. (*in* The Peruvian labyrinth: polity, society, economy. Edited by Maxwell A. Cameron and Philip Mauceri. Foreword by Cynthia McClintock and Abraham Lowenthal. University Park, Pa.: Pennsylvania State Univ. Press, 1997, p. 70–106, bibl.)

Traces evolution of state-led development in Peru beginning in earnest with the Velasco regime in late 1960s. Critiques over-reliance on external borrowing, dependence on publically owned firms, and dramatic alienation of local private sector. Sees deconstruction of statist economy by Fujimori regime in early- to mid-1990s as problematic due to consistent refusal to allow for meaningful institution-building to maintain these reforms in place in a similar fashion to Peru's

neighbor, Chile. Morever, Cameron sees the "dismal pattern" of per capita GDP growth as a significant sign that the Fujimori economic reforms are not reaching the average Peruvian. For review of entire volume, see item **2693.**

2646 Clayton, Lawrence A. Peru and the United States: the condor and the eagle. Athens: University of Georgia Press, 1999. 363 p.: bibl., index. (The United States and the Americas)

Badly needed updated history of Peruvian-US relations from the series edited by Lester Langley on Latin American-US relations. Traces evolution of diplomatic, military and economic relations between the two nations from independence to late in second term of Fujimori presidency. Emphasizes dominant economic impact of such corporate giants as Cerro de Pasco, Grace, and the International Petroleum Company. Especially interesting and innovative sections of the study are discussions of "company towns," the Cornell University Vicos agrarian project (begun in the early 1950s), and the folksy critique of the Fujimori government's drug policy. Offers a highly useful bibliographical essay that will be helpful to both specialist and student alike, in which pertinent web sites are included. Well-suited for classroom use.

2647 Contreras, Carlos. Modernizarse o descentralizar: la difícil disjuntiva de las finanzas peruanas durante la era del guano. (*Bull. Inst. fr. étud. andin.*, 25:1, 1996, p. 125–150, appendix, bibl., maps, photos, tables)

Helpful article for 19th-century specialists discusses Peruvian fiscal structure from independence to the War of the Pacific. Divides era into six periods. Sees varying fiscal policies as largely ineffective in modernizing the state. Argues that the principal debate was over the predominance of direct versus indirect taxes. Suggests that the military defeat in the War of the Pacific marked the end of "the colonial tributary structure."

2648 Coral Cordero, Isabel. Women in war: impact and responses. (*in* Shining and other paths: war and society in Peru, 1980–1995. Edited by Steve J. Stern. Durham, NC: Duke Univ. Press, 1998, p. 345–374)

Probing article on the impact of the civil war on women and gender relations in Peru. Effective discussions of important issues of collective self-help actions such as communal soup kitchens and the "glass of milk" programs for children that emerged during the height of the economic crisis during the late García presidency and under "Fujishock." The role of women in Shining Path forms a central aspect, and the contradictory nature of the movement's leadership toward its women adherents is expertly explained. Concludes that, through the crucible of the war, women in Peru were able to substantially change their status from dependent and nearly "invisible" to "protagonistic social actors" during the Fujimori administration.

2649 Cosamalón A., Jesús A. La "union de todos": teatro y discurso político en la independencia, Lima, 1820–21. (*Apuntes/ Lima*, 39, segundo semestre 1996, p. 129–143)

Interesting article examines the nature of the discourse on independence as expressed in the language of plays presented in Lima during 1820–21. As might be expected, theatergoers were primarily from the elite and the stage language of the productions was largely reflective of their desire for a continuation of the colonial system rather than radical political change.

2650 Cueto, Marcos and Jorge Lossio. Innovación en la agricultura: Fermín Tangüis y el algodón en el Perú. Lima: Univ. del Pacífico, Centro de Investigación: Cosapi Organización Empresarial, 1999. 163 p.: bibl., ill.

Useful discussion of technological advances in agriculture in the Huaral region in the early 20th century. Special emphasis is placed on the expansion of cotton culture in the region. However, it neglects to discuss the role of Japanese immigrants in expanding cotton agriculture in the period after 1930.

2651 De Bari Hermoza Ríos, Nicolás. Fuerzas armadas del Perú: lecciones de este siglo. Perú: Editores & Impresores, 1996. 383 p.: bibl., col. ill.

This book by the now discredited Armed Forces Chief of Staff during the Fujimori regime in the mid-to-late 1990s is not a contemporary analysis of the nation's military establishment, but rather a statistics-laden discussion of the war against Sendero Luminoso. Offers pages of government statistics on terrorist acts, focusing on the urban terrorist campaign begun in the late 1990s. There is little analysis of the military's controversial role in the civil war, particularly on the question of human rights violations and how the military dealt with the Civil Defense Brigades. These two key topics need fuller elaboration by historians intimately familiar with the military and Sendero Luminoso campaign. Dramatic photographs of car bombings and police assassinations.

2652 Degregori, Carlos Iván. After the fall of Abimael Guzmán: the limits of Sendero Luminoso. (*in* The Peruvian labyrinth: polity, society, economy. Edited by Maxwell A. Cameron and Philip Mauceri. Foreword by Cynthia McClintock and Abraham Lowenthal. University Park, Pa.: Pennsylvania State Univ. Press, 1997, p. 79–91, bibl.)

Insightful article on the inner workings of Sendero Luminoso leadership before and after the capture of the movement's leader in 1992. Stresses the nearly complete political, intellectual, and symbolic control Guzmán held over the rank and file. Argues that the Sendero Rojo, the military component of the movement led by Senderistas who avoided capture, would have little hope of replicating the success of the original movement because its leader, Comrade Feliciano, lacks the charisma and intellectual stature of Guzmán. Assessment was borne out by the quick decline of Sendero Luminoso and the eventual capture of Comrade Feliciano by Peruvian authorities. For review of entire volume, see item **2693.**

2653 Denegri Luna, Félix. Perú y Ecuador: apuntes para la historia de una frontera. Lima: Bolsa de Valores de Lima: Instituto Riva-Agüero, Pontificia Univ. Católica del Perú, 1996. 378 p.: bibl., col. maps (some folded), indexes.

This treatment of the extended border controversy seeks to present a balanced account of the dispute through a detailed history of diplomatic negotiations, treaties, and military conflicts surrounding this issue since the colonial period. Many maps detailing various stages of the border negotiations over the course of nearly three centuries. Also available in an English translation. Represents the final work of the now deceased owner of Peru's finest private library.

2654 Fujimori's Peru: the political economy. Edited by John Crabtree and Jim Thomas. London: Institute of Latin American Studies, 1998. 293 p.: bibl., ill., index.

Anthology examines economic aspects of the first term of the Fujimori presidency. Contains a trenchant critique of the reforms of the Japanese-Peruvian president by Kisic, who argues that, despite the dismantling of the statist economy and the opening to all levels of foreign investment, Peru's economic growth still depends on primary product exports, particularly the mining sector. Thorp's chapter on tax reform demonstrates the administration's desire to deal with that long-standing problem in the Peruvian economy. The uncertain labor question which marked the second Fujimori term is addressed by Thomas, while Crabtree approaches his analysis of the Fujimori regime from the perspective of a "neopopulist" critique. Degregori, Coronel, and Del Pino deal effectively with the impact of Fujimori's policies on traditional poverty-plagued Ayacucho. Useful for specialists of contemporary Peru.

2655 Fukumoto Sato, Mary Nancy. Hacia un nuevo sol: japoneses y sus descendientes en el Perú; historia, cultura e identidad. Peru: Asociación Peruano Japonesa del Perú, 1997. 602 p.: bibl., ill. (some col.), col. maps.

Outstanding study of the Japanese in Peru will remain the standard work for many years to come. The late author, a sociologist by training, approaches the work from a carefully constructed historical perspective, going back to the beginning of the Japanese presence as sugar workers in Peru's coastal haciendas in 1899. Calls upon sociological methods, weaving discussions of occupational patterns, diet, religious customs and family into this masterful work. Employing statistics from the Japanese community's self-census of 1989, offers important information on intermarriage and the retention of traditional customs through four generations of Japanese in Peru. Concludes with a preliminary assessment of the Peruvian Japanese who have migrated to Japan in the past decade to serve as "guest workers," largely in factories and other blue collar jobs. Highly recommended to all scholars of the Japanese in Latin America and of immigration in general. See also item **2679.**

2656 González Carré, Enrique; Yuri Gutiérrez Gutiérrez; and **Jaime Urrutia Ceruti.** La ciudad de Huamanga: espacio, historia y cultura. Ayacucho, Peru: Univ. Nacional de San Cristóbal de Huamanga: Concejo Provincial de Huamanga: Centro Peruano de Estudios Sociales, 1995. 271 p.: bibl., ill., maps.

Solid history of the city of Huamanga published by the university that was the center of higher learning in the region during the 19th century and then became the staging ground for Sendero Luminoso's recruitment activities in the late 1960s and 1970s. The authors examine the fate of the *yanaconas* in the surrounding region from the 16th century onward. Chapter three deals with the emerging influence of the mestizo class in the city and the burgeoning merchant class. Chapter five discusses how Huamanga became a poverty-stricken backwater as the country began to slowly modernize in the 19th century. Chapter six provides an overview of the 20th century as a useful backdrop for those interested in the foundations of poverty and underdevelopment that gave rise to the violence in the late-20th century. Offers local history that has wider implications for Peruvian national affairs.

2657 Guerra Martinière, Margarita. La ocupación de Lima, 1881–1883. v. 2, Aspectos económicos del Gobierno de García Calderón. Lima: Pontificia Univ. Católica del Perú, Dirección Académica de Investigación, Instituto Riva-Agüero, 1991–1996. 1 v.: bibl., indexes.

Carefully researched study of the economic impact of the Chilean occupation of Lima during the War of the Pacific. Looks at banking and the roles of emerging Spanish and Chinese merchants. Concludes that the economic "ruin" of Lima by the end of the occupation was nearly complete. Suggests that the economic issues of the Chilean occupation were so profound that they played a significant role in delaying the final settlement of the War of the Pacific claims until 1929.

2658 Günther Doering, Juan and **Guillermo Lohmann Villena.** Lima. Madrid: Editorial MAPFRE, 1992. 340 p.: bibl., ill., indexes, maps. (Colecciones MAPFRE 1492)

Despite being well beyond the reviewing time frame, this excellent history of the city of Lima by two of Peru's finest historians deserves careful attention by urban historians and generalists as well. Tracing Lima's history from its origins in the 16th century, examines the city from the perspective of its various barrios. Also emphasizes key social and political issues that dominated Lima's public affairs. The emergence of the *pueblos jovenes* in the years following the Odría regime is given careful attention.

2659 Heras, Julián. Restauración y actividades de los franciscanos del Perú a partir del siglo XIX. (*Arch. Ibero-Am.*, 57:225/226, enero/dic. 1997, p. 263–296, appendix)

Excellent, well-researched and highly significant article on the 19th-century history of the Franciscans in Peru. The author, a Franciscan himself, focuses on such issues as the evolution of the church leadership, the evolving role of the Franciscan sponsored convents, schools and missionaries, both foreign and domestic. Accompanied by a valuable index and list of the primary church leaders of the 19th century. Highly recommended.

2660 Higashide, Seiichi et al. Adios to tears: the memoirs of a Japanese-Peruvian internee in U.S. concentration camps. Seattle, Wa: Univ. of Washington Press, 2000. 259 p.

English translation and first privately published edition of a valuable book on Japanese immigration and internment during WWII. Initially published in Japanese to a limited readership. This informative study, candidly and insightfully written, details the formative period of Japanese migration to Peru and, just as importantly, the trying experience of the author, his family, and 1,800 other Japanese-Peruvians who were interned in the US during WWII. Excellent memoir portrays Asian immigrant experience of cultural adaption in Latin America. Insightful forward by the late C. Harvey Gardiner, who wrote extensively on the Japanese in Latin America and Peru, in particular.

2661 Holguín, Oswaldo. La historia del Perú al trasluz: balances, 1910–1960. (*in* Encuentro Internacional de Peruanistas, *1st, Lima, 1996.* Encuentro Internacional de Peruanistas: estado de los estudios histórico-sociales sobre el Perú a fines del siglo XX. Lima: UNESCO; Univ. de Lima; Fondo de Cultura Económica, 1998, v. 1, p. 419–437, bibl.)

Useful historiographic essay on some of Peru's leading historians from 1910–1960. Included in the author's discussion, among others, are Riva Agüero, Gonzales Prada, Luis Alberto Sánchez, Basadre and the 1940s Marxist historian Alberto Tauro. The commentary on these historians' main works is helpful for the non-specialist and the author cites representative passages from their works that are well chosen. Good supplemental reading on modern Peru.

2662 Huertas Vallejos, Lorenzo. Sechura: identidad cultural a través de los siglos. Sechura, Peru: Municipalidad de Sechura, 1995. 343 p.: bibl., ill. (some col.), maps, photos.

Primarily a geographical study of the Peruvian province of Sechura, but does offer general historical background of use to regional scholars. Also discusses aspects of the economic development of the region which adds to the significance of this regional study. Enhanced by well-chosen photographs and a helpful bibliography.

2663 Hunefeldt, Christine. Contribución indígena, acumulación mercantil y reconformación de los espacios políticos en el sur peruano, 1820–1890. (*in* Circuitos mercantiles y mercados en Latinoamérica, siglos XVIII-XIX. México: Instituto de Investigaciones Dr. José María Luis Mora; Instituto de Investigaciones Históricas UNAM, 1995, p. 522–561)

Scholarly article on the role of the indigenous population in the economic development of the Puno region from independence through the War of the Pacific. Pays particular attention to the impact of the campesino rebellion in the Puno area during the War of the Pacific. Views the war as an important turning point in reconfiguring the relationship between Puno's elites and the campesino class regarding working relationships and modes of production. Essential article for understanding the changes in peasant mentality in an important and often unique area of Peru, given its Aymara population.

2664 Jacobsen, Nils. Liberalism and Indian communities in Peru, 1821–1920. (*in* Liberals, the Church, and Indian peasants: corporate lands and the challenge of reform in nineteenth-century Spanish America. Edited by Robert H. Jackson. Albuquerque: Univ. of New Mexico Press, 1997, p. 123–170, bibl.)

Excellent discussion of how 19th-century liberalism and the concept of individual land ownership failed as a formula for integrating the Indian population into modernizing Peru. Attributes the failure to the expansion of latifundia by highly aggressive hacendados in the highland that continued well into the 20th century. In a pattern similar to Mexico, Indian communities struggled to retain their communal lands, and their efforts were extolled by such pro-indigenous writers in the 20th century as Castro Pozo, Valcarcel and Mariátegui. Includes a well-constructed critique of Mariátegui's analysis of the extent to which the indigenous population rejected the liberal ideal. Concludes that such variables as the market and demography must be considered among other factors in understanding the indigenous mentality.

2665 Jochamowitz, Luis. Hombres, minas y pozos: 1896–1996; un siglo de minería y petróleo en el Perú. Lima: Sociedad Nacional de Minería y Petróleo, 1996. 129 p.: ill., photos.

Lavish study of the principal mining and petroleum companies operating in Peru during most of the 20th century. Primarily a "pictorial" or coffee-table book with no source material listed; however, the photographs are extremely useful for gathering images of the degree of modernization of mining and petroleum operations and for working conditions of the labor forces.

2666 Kirk, Robin. The monkey's paw: new chronicles from Peru. Amherst: Univ. of Massachusetts Press, 1997. 215 p.: bibl., ill., photos.

Journalistic account, set in a careful historical setting, of the impact of the Sendero Luminoso- inspired civil war from 1983 to the mid-1990s. Focuses on the civil defense brigades, Sendero's women in their prison setting, and campesino refugees in Lima who have fled their highland villages as a result of the war. Based on extensive interviews by a journalist who is fully familiar with the topic. One of the best sources for testimonials about the war from those most effected by it. Should not be overlooked by specialists seeking clear insights into the at-

titudes of both senderistas and those the movement terrorized.

2667 Klarén, Peter F. Peru: society and nationhood in the Andes. New York: Oxford Univ. Press, 2000. 494 p.: bibl., maps, photos, tables. (Latin American histories)

This latest work in the Oxford country study series on Latin America is an excellent addition to the collection. Scholars of Peru, specialists and non-specialists alike will benefit from the balanced discussion of economic, social, and political issues from the pre-Columbian period to the Fujimori administration. The 19th century and particularly the guano age and the Aristocratic Republic are given significant attention. Civil-military relations, often a somewhat neglected topic in surveys such as this, are also carefully analyzed. As with all the books in the Oxford series, this study offers a highly useful glossary, as well as maps, tables, some rare photos, and a thorough bibliography. Appropriate for classroom use.

2668 Lausent-Herrera, Isabelle. Los caucheros y comerciantes chinos en Iquitos a fines del siglo XIX, 1880–1900. (in Las raíces de la memoria: América Latina, ayer y hoy, quinto encuentro debate = Amèrica Llatina, ahir i avui, cinquena trobada debat. Coordinación de Pilar García Jordán et al. Barcelona: Univ. de Barcelona, 1996, p. 467–481, bibl.)

Well-researched article by a specialist on Asians in Peru details the activities of a small colony of Chinese that settled in Iquitos at the end of the 19th century. Establishing themselves initially as rubber-gatherers in the region, the Chinese soon moved into commerce as many did throughout Latin America after their initial experience in agriculture or mining. This same pattern is followed by the Japanese in Peru and Bolivia more than two decades later.

Málaga Núñez Zeballos, Alejandro. Archivo Arzobispal de Arequipa: guía. See item **2316.**

2669 Mallon, Florencia E. Chronicle of a path foretold?: Velasco's revolution, vanguardia revolucionaria and "shining omens" in the indigenous communities of Andahuaylas. (in Shining and other paths: war and society in Peru, 1980–1995. Edited by Steve J. Stern. Durham, NC: Duke Univ. Press, 1998, p. 84–116)

Highly informative study of the weak-

nesses of the Velasco regime's agrarian reform program in Andahuaylas prov. in the
mid-1970s. Makes a compelling argument
that the Velasco reforms opened a "space"
for expected reforms that was subsequently
not filled by successive military or civilian
governments. Further, argues that Sendero
Luminoso (and by implication, other leftist
movements such as the Tupac Amaru) was in
large measure born out of frustration generated when expectations for change were, in
senderista minds, betrayed by Peru's central
governments. Specifically, the failure of massive land invasions by the peasantry in Andahuaylas in 1973–74 created an extremely
fertile climate for the early campaign of
Sendero Luminoso. Clearly recognizes, however, how little Sendero Luminoso's leaders
understood the peasantry and, in the end,
created only one more illusion of a better
life.

2670 Marcone, Mario. Indígenas e inmigrantes durante la republica aristocrática: población e ideología civilista.
(*Histórica/Lima*, 19:1, julio 1995, p. 73–93,
bibl.)
    Discusses Positivist outlook of the
civilista leadership and their notion that the
nation could never modernize with its large
indigenous population. As with Brazil, European immigration was seen as a way of "colonizing" the nation with more "progressive"
peoples. Leans heavily on Fransisco Graña's
1908 study of immigration to develop the
thesis. Useful bibliography is worth careful
consultation.

2671 Martínez, Ascensión. Las relaciones
entre el Perú y España, 1880–1930. (*in*
Encuentro Internacional de Peruanistas, 1st,
Lima, 1996. Encuentro Internacional de Peruanistas: estado de los estudios histórico-
sociales sobre el Perú a fines del siglo XX.
Lima: UNESCO; Univ. de Lima; Fondo de
Cultura Económica, 1998, v. 1, p. 439–466)
    Standard approach to diplomatic rela-
tions between Peru and Spain. Covers a range
of pertinent topics, including the Treaty of
Peace and Amity, signed in Paris in 1879,
subsequent commercial relations, Spanish
immigration to Peru, and the treatment of
Spaniards in Peru, primarily during the era of
Leguía. Well-researched in Peruvian, Spanish,
and US sources. Should be consulted by students of international relations.

2672 Masterson, Daniel M. In the shining
path of Mariátegui, Mao Tse-tung or
presidente Gonzalo: Peru's Sendero Luminoso in historical perspective. (*in* Revolution
and revolutionaries: guerrilla movements in
Latin America. Edited by Daniel Castro,
Wilmington, DE: Scholarly Resources, 1999,
p. 171–190)
    Argues that Sendero Luminoso was
never truly a Maoist movement with a peasant base but rather a guerrilla/terrorist front
with a disenchanted mestizo leadership that
had been alienated by Peru's historic racial
barriers to social mobility. Briefly discusses
Mariátegui's Marxist vision for Peru and
notes how little Sendero Luminoso adhered
to that vision. Traces roots of Abimael
Guzmán's revolutionary resolve to the failed
Aprista revolt in October 1948. Concludes
that Sendero Luminoso violated primary
Maoist principles when its leadership abandoned the war in the countryside and turned
to an urban terrorist campaign in the late-
1980s. Based upon Peruvian military intelligence materials, Sendero Luminoso publications and interviews with military
personnel.

2673 Mauceri, Philip. The transition to democracy and the failures of institution
building. (*in* The Peruvian labyrinth: polity,
society, economy. Edited by Maxwell A.
Cameron and Philip Mauceri. Foreword by
Cynthia McClintock and Abraham Lowenthal. University Park, Pa.: Pennsylvania State
Univ. Press, 1997, p. 13–36)
    Examines period from the mid-1970s
to the beginning of the failed second term of
Belaúnde Terry. Notes most significantly
that the transition from military government
to civilian rule was not intended to established the foundations for strong political institutions that were largely demobilized during the 12-year military government. Rather,
concludes that the transition to civilian democratic rule essentially offered a framework
for the military to ease itself from power
rather than build a stronger civil society.
This tendency continued with three succeeding civilian presidents, as is discussed in the
volume. For review of entire volume, see
item **2693**.

2674 McEvoy, Carmen. El legado castillista.
(*Histórica/Lima*, 10:2, dic. 1996,
p. 211–241, bibl.)

Generally well-researched overview of the Ramon Castilla era during the mid-19th century argues that the legacy of Castilla's long rule continued well into the Civilista ra by means of the long list of Castilla's appointed deputies who tended to remain in power and perpetuate what the author refers to as the "Patrimonial State of Castilla." Notes that the "legacy" of Castilla seemed to be most long-lasting in Southern Peru. Useful for the study of the lasting impact of patronage and caudillismo in the 19th century.

2675 McEvoy, Carmen. El motín de las palabras: la caída de Bernardo Monteagudo y la forja de la cultura política limeña, 1821–1822. (*Bol. Inst. Riva-Agüero,* 23, 1996, p. 89–139, bibl.)

Sophisticated study of the language of the debate between advocates of independence and continued colonialism by one of Peru's most talented historians. Through a study of the Lima press, seeks to define the nature of Lima's "political culture" during the formative years of the independence movement in Peru. The debate seemed to be drawn over the more conservative concept of a "cultural nation" and the more liberal concept of a "contractual state." Monteagudo, who dominated Lima's politics for much of this period, advocated a Burkean concept of a sociocultural context for the new nation. For this, he was eventually condemned and fell from favor. Excellent scholarship adds to an understanding of the independence movement at the intellectual as well as the local level. Rich bibliography draws upon both English and Spanish sources that are theoretical as well as factually oriented.

2676 McEvoy, Carmen. La utopía republicana: ideales y realidades en la formación de la cultura política peruana, 1871–1919. Lima: Pontificia Univ. Católica del Perú, Fondo Editorial, 1997. 467 p.: bibl.

A culmination of the author's earlier research and writing on the tone and content of Peru's 19th-century "political culture." This sizeable study focuses on the Civilista era and argues that there existed a concerted attempt by a group of "vanguard intellectuals" at the Lima Univeristy to create a cultural consensus regarding the nature of citizenship in their nation. The War of the Pacific did not completely deter these efforts to define the characteristics and responsibilities of citizenship. Notes that the campaign was renewed during the civilian presidency of Nicolás de Piérola during the late 1890s. Not made fully clear whether this Lima vanguard in its search for illusive concept of citizenship, which still remains in question today, may not have been looking to one of Europe's most concrete models, the Napoleonic Civil Code.

2677 Melis, Antonio. Del *complot comunista* a la ruptura con Haya. (*Anu. Mariateg.,* 10:10, 1998, p. 13–31, bibl., facsims.)

Useful compilation of Mariátegui's correspondence regarding the political conflict with APRA leader Víctor Raúl Haya de la Torre in 1928. These letters, dating from Dec. 1927-Sept. 1928, detail Mariátegui's growing disenchantment with the evolution of APRA toward a more middle-class revisionist movement of the left with continental aspirations, rather than a Peruvian political party with Marxist foundations. The correspondence is helpful for students of the early APRA and Mariátegui's well-known, but not completely understood, differences with Haya del la Torre.

2678 Miller, Rory. La historia de los negocios en el Perú. (*in* Empresa e historia en América Latina: un balance historiográfico. Bogotá: Colciencias; TM editores, 1996, p. 171–194, bibl.)

Helpful article by British historian begins with a brief overview of the literature on commercial operations and the building of a transportation infrastructure citing key representative sources, many from British historians. Work then presents an overview of the role of primarily foreign corporations and their impact on the Peruvian economy beginning in the mid-19th century. Interweaves useful suggestions of the best sources on the Peruvian economy and offers an excellent bibliography of North American, British, and Peruvian scholars on that subject.

2679 Morimoto, Amelia. Los japoneses y sus descendientes en el Perú. Lima: Fondo Editorial del Congreso del Perú, 1999. 255 p.: bibl., ill., tables.

Sweeping recent analysis of the Japanese in Peru by the nation's current leading scholar on the topic. The author directed the highly comprehensive community self-census in 1989 and edited the narrative record of that census, published in 1991. Offers useful background material on the Meiji era in Japan as a foundation for the immigration experience beginning in Peru in 1899. Effectively reviews various epochs of the settlement experience from plantation labor to urban commerce. After discussing the trauma of World War II and the cultural rebuilding of the postwar era, examines the generational tensions within the Japanese community and the question of *nikkei* (overseas Japanese) perceived cultural identity. The bibliography and statistical tables are helpful to specialists. Along with the Fukumoto study (see item **2655**), this analysis offers a nearly complete picture of the Japanese community in Peru through the late 1990s.

2680 Mücke, Ulrich. Der Partido Civil in Peru 1871–1879: zur Geschichte politischer Parteien und Repräsentation in Lateinamerika. Stuttgart, Germany: Franz Steiner Verlag, 1998. 384 p. (Studien zur modernen Geschichte; Bd. 50)

This meticulously researched and well-written study was awarded the 1997 Kurt Hartwig-Siemens Prize by the Scientific Foundation of Hamburg. Using a wealth of previously unavailable and untapped sources, including Manuel Pardo's bookkeeping accounts and political correspondence, presents a convincing argument that, prior to the War of the Pacific, the Partido Civil met all the prerequisites of a viable political party: bourgeois, liberal, and able to survive its leader's assassination in 1878. [C.K. Converse]

2681 Mundos interiores: Lima 1850–1950. Recopilación de Aldo Panfichi H. and Felipe Portocarrero S. Lima: Univ. del Pacífico, Centro de Investigación, 1995. 442 p.: bibl., ill.

Extremely valuable edited volume on a formative period in the capital city's growth and development. Includes articles by Aguirre on the penal system, Elmore on health and sanitation, Italian immigrants in Lima by Bonfiglio, textile workers by Sanborn, and religion and family by Portocarrero. A must read for all specialists in Latin American urbanization.

2682 Muñoz, Hortensia. Human rights and social referents: the construction of new sensibilities. (*in* Shining and other

paths: war and society in Peru, 1980–1995. Edited by Steve J. Stern. Durham, NC: Duke Univ. Press, 1998, p. 447–469, bibl.)

Fine discussion of the creation of spontaneous human rights movements in Peru during the civil war of the 1980s through the mid-1990s. Argues that the increasing brutality of the war during the administrations of Belaúnde, García, and Fujimori generated such fear, rage, and anger that the spontaneous human rights movements arose in a fashion similar to the mothers groups in Argentina and Chile during the 1970s. Sees the violent repression of the 1986 Sendero-led prison riots as the turning point in shifting the locus of the human rights movement from Ayacucho to Lima, where it attracted far more international attention.

2683 Muñoz Cabrejo, Fanni. Las diversiones y el discurso modernizador: los intentos de formación de una cultura burguesa en Lima, 1890–1912. (*Allpanchis/Cusco*, 29:49, primer semestre 1997, p. 55–85, bibl., table)

Argues that the primary discourse of Lima's elites regarding the values and future of their nation were largely drawn from the Positivist tradition then prevailing in Europe. The nation's leadership, based on the Civilista tradition, continued to try to formulate a consensus on the nation's political culture. Drawing on the early work of Klarén, article describes the Lima elites primarily as nationalists, materialists, and utilitarians, who strongly attacked the "feudal Hispanic tradition." Among the most prominent members of this group were José Pardo, Javier Prado, Augusto B. Leguía, and Francisco Calderón de la Barca. The bibliography is useful, but some sources are dated. Still, this is a work that will be helpful for understanding the turn-of-the-century elite thought regarding the future of the nation.

2684 Obando, Enrique. Civil-military relations in Peru, 1980–1996: how to control and coopt the military (and the consequences of doing so). (*in* Shining and other paths: war and society in Peru, 1980–1995. Edited by Steve J. Stern. Durham, NC: Duke Univ. Press, 1998, p. 384–410)

Despite the kitsch title, this article offers one of the best analyses of the Peruvian military's troubled approach to a transition to military rule while simultaneously conducting a failing war again guerrilla/terror-ists. Author is one of the few Peruvian intimately knowledgeable about the inner workings of the Peruvian military in the post-1980 period. This is demonstrated by his lengthy discussion of the disenchantment of a group of mid-level army officers know as COMACA (Commanders, Majors and Cap-tains), the core of the opposition to the highly politicized military policies of the Alan García administation. Remarkably candid and illuminating discussion of civil-military relations during the first Fujimori administration, particularly on drug-trafficking and its impact on the internal affairs of the armed forces. Recommended for those with interest in civil-military rela-tions in Latin America.

2685 Orrego Penagos, Juan Luis. San Martín en Pisco: la historia de un valle costeño durante las guerras de Independen-cia. (*Bol. Inst. Riva-Agüero*, 23, 1996, p. 155–171, bibl., graph, tables)

Examines the economic and material aspects of the War of Independence in the Pisco valley as a result of the campaign of San Martín. Well-researched in Peru's Archivo General de la Nación. Presents lists and discussion of land tenure in the re-gion and the later development of the 41 principal haciendas in the Pisco area. Con-cludes with an analysis of the war's impact on the region's formerly flourishing wine trade and the subsequent emergence of a sugar economy.

2686 Ortiz Sotelo, Jorge. Identidad nacional: criollos al servicio de la Armada es-pañola y españoles al servicode la Armada peruana durante la emancipación. (*Rev. Hist. Naval*, 14:53, 1996, p. 71–78)

Author is the leading authority on naval history and maritime affairs in Peru. In this brief study of Spanish sailors serving on Peruvian naval vessels and Peruvians enlist-ing in the royalist navy, he discusses the complex reasons, both personal and national-istic, for these sailors to break ranks. Argues that the lack of a true national identity in Peru is reflected in the transitory nature of naval service. Similarly, the Spanish navy, still recovering from the trauma of Trafalgar, saw a low level of loyalty among its con-script sailors.

2687 Ortiz Sotelo, Jorge. Los Kisic de cibaca en el Perú. Prólogo de Drago Kisic. Lima: Enserfin Editores, 1998. 312 p.: bibl., ill., maps, photos.

Study of Croatian immigration to Peru through the lens of the Kisic family history, originally linked to small mining operations in central Peru and from there to the devel-opment of Satipo in the department of Junín. The Croatians eventually became involved in agricultural activity in the Chancay valley desert north of Lima, paralleling the Japanese in that same region. Useful study of the im-pact of smaller but cohesive immigrant groups and their assimilation into Peruvian society.

2688 Pakkasvirta, Jussi. Un continente, una nación?: intelectuales latinoameri-canos, comunidad política y las revistas cul-turales en Costa Rica y en el Perú, 1919–1930. Helsinki: Academia Scientiarum Fen-nica, 1997. 236 p.: bibl., maps, photos. (Suo-malaisen Tiedeakatemian toimituksia. Sarja Humaniora, 1239–6982; nide 290 = Annales Academiae Scientiarum Fennicae. Ser. Hu-maniora; tom. 290)

Seeks to gauge the debate between continentalism versus incipient nationalism by analyzing two of the leading intellectual journals in Latin America during the 1920s: Mariátequi's *Amauta* and the Costa Rican García Monge's *Reportario Americano*. Links emerging continentalism, as expressed by the intellectuals in these journals, with Arielismo, Aprismo, and most importantly indigenismo. Book's findings have applica-tion for present-day differing self-perceptions of nation and ethnicity.

2689 Parker, David S. Civilizing the city of kings: hygiene and housing in Lima, Peru. (*in* Cities of hope: people, protests, and progress in urbanizing Latin America, 1870–1930. Edited by Ronn Pineo and James A. Baer. Boulder, Colo.: Westview Press, 1998, p. 153–178)

Highly sophisticated discussion of the failure of Lima's municipal leaders to deal with poor hygiene and epidemic disease. Ar-gues that, while some of the *higienienistas* were generally well intentioned, they were significantly impeded by their social Darwin-ist concept of race, linking sickness and poor living conditions with racial inferiority. Thus the flood of Asians (both Chinese and Japanese) who settled in Lima from the late-1870s until World War II were nearly universally unwelcomed. The violent anti-Japanese riots in Lima in May 1940 attest to these claims. Notes the substantial material progress made during the long rule of Augusto B. Leguía, but concludes that by mid-century there were no victors in the long struggle against poor public health. The terrible cholera outbreak in the early 1990s in Lima bears witness to the well-crafted conclusions.

2690 Peloso, Vincent C. Peasants on plantations: subaltern strategies of labor and resistance in the Pisco valley, Peru. Durham, N.C.: Duke Univ. Press, 1999. 251 p.: bibl., index, maps, photos, tables.

Superb case study of plantation labor after the abolition of slavery examines the Hacienda San Francisco Solano de Palto in the Pisco Valley. According to the author, peasants involved in cotton production did not submit to the usually assumed forms of domination and exploitation. Rather, they adopted a variety of strategies including long-term labor contracts and direct negotiations with landowners that led to the more widespread use of *yanocanaje* in this region. An illuminating, carefully constructed study of the plantation records of Hacienda Palto first made available during the agrarian reform campaign of the Velasco government in the early 1970s. Succeeds in placing this case study in the broader context of subaltern studies in an international setting. Strongly recommended.

2691 Peñaloza Jarrín, José Benigno. Huancayo: historia, familia y región. Lima: Pontificia Univ. Católica del Perú, Instituto Riva-Agüero, 1995. 497 p.: bibl., ill.

Excellent political and social history of the city of Huancayo and its environs. Draws upon many primary documents in the Peruvian Archivo General de la Nación and many regional sources. The Helpful bibliography for regional and local historians of Peru. Also includes significant information from censuses and military records from the prehispanic era to the 1970s.

2692 Peralta Ruiz, Victor. Elecciones, constitucionalismo y revolución en el Cusco, 1809–1815. (*Rev. Indias*, 56:206, enero/abril 1996, p. 99–131, bibl., table)

Interesting and useful study of the relationship between the upper levels of colonial administration in Peru and the Cabildo of Cuzco during the last decades of Spanish rule. Pays particular attention to the small scale uprising of August 1814 that undermined the growing influence of the Cabildo. First-rate research relying heavily on the Actas del Cabildo for the city, Spanish archival sources, and appropriate secondary materials.

The Peru reader: history, culture, politics. See *HLAS 57:1215.*

2693 The Peruvian labyrinth: polity, society, economy. Edited by Maxwell A. Cameron and Philip Mauceri. Foreword by Cynthia McClintock and Abraham Lowenthal. University Park, Pa.: Pennsylvania State Univ. Press, 1997. 272 p.: bibl., ill., index.

Highly useful anthology dealing with the complex social, political and economic issues dominating Peru during the past three decades. Individual authors discuss the evolution of peasant communities in the sierra, the difficulties of transition from extended military to civilian rule after 1980, the dynamics of Fujimori's political leadership, the status of trade unions, the decline of Sendero Luminoso, and the troubling issue of human rights in contemporary Peru. Bibliography provides valuable guide to key issues of contemporary Peru. For reviews of individual chapters, see items **2652** and **2673**.

Quijada, Mónica. De la Colonia a la República: inclusión, exclusión y memoria histórica en el Perú. See item **2329**.

Rabí Ch., Miguel. Un capítulo inédito: el traslado del Hospital del Espíritu Santo de Lima a Bellavista, 1750. See item **2330**.

2694 Reyes, Alejandro. La familia Montero: empresarios nacionales, siglo XIX. (*in* Encuentro Internacional de Peruanistas, *1st, Lima, 1996.* Estado de los estudios histórico-sociales sobre el Perú a fines del siglo XX. Lima: UNESCO; Univ. de Lima; Fondo de Cultura Económica, 1998, v. 1, p. 501–532, bibl., tables)

Thorough and necessary study of the economic activities of the Montero family in Peru. Beginning with Don Juan Montero Núñez in the early-19th century, the family amassed landholdings from the Chancay Valley to the Pisco region. Details the economic activities of various haciendas and discusses the family's diversification into mining and railroad construction. Employs records from the Archivo General de la Nación, personal papers, and the records of the Henry Meiggs railroad-building venture. Highly effective case study.

2695 Rocca Torres, Luis. Japoneses bajo el sol de Lambayeque. Lima: Univ. Nacional "Pedro Ruiz Gallo", Facultad de Ciencias Histórico Sociales y Educación, 1997. 402 p.: appendices, bibl., ill., photos, tables.

Model regional historical study of Peru's Japanese in the Lambayeque area. Valuable work for scholars seeking to write regional or local histories of immigrant populations. Author, known previously for his work on Afro-Peruvians, based his study on interviews and local records of the Japanese community in Lambayeque. Addresses occupational questions, generational discontinuity through intermarriage with non-Japanese partners, the impact of local Japanese community organizations, and the influence of WWII on the Japanese in northern Peru. Many photographs taken through the 1990s add to this superb study.

Sánchez-Concha Barrios, Rafael. La historia del derecho en el Perú: perspectivas de medio siglo, 1950–1993. See item **2340.**

2696 Santos-Granero, Fernando and **Frederica Barclay.** Selva central: history, economy, and land use in Peruvian Amazonia. Translated by Elisabeth King. Washington, DC: Smithsonian Institution Press, 1998. 351 p.: bibl., graphs, ill., index, maps, tables.

Carefully researched and written history of the Peruvian Amazon region emphasizes early settlement patterns, land use, missionary work, and various crops. Particular attention is paid to coffee, fruit crops, and timber in this regional economy. Eschews the political aspects of border disputes or border locations that have historically troubled this region. Highly recommended as a study with a primary emphasis for geographers.

2697 Starn, Orin. Villagers at arms: war and counterrevolution in the central-south Andes. (*in* Shining and other paths: war and society in Peru, 1980–1995. Edited by Steve J. Stern. Durham, N.C.: Duke Univ. Press, 1998, p. 224–253)

Significant article on the evolution of Peru's *Rondas Campesinas* (Civil Defense Brigades) by a leading authority. Peru's peasantry spontaneously organized 3,500 *Rondas* by the early 1990s as the first line of defense against the violence of Sendero Luminoso. Thoughtfully critiques the controversial role of the civil defense brigades in their early years when many were recruited or coerced into military action by the Peruvian armed forces, which was incapable of confronting Sendero Luminoso without the help of the peasantry. Focuses on the village of Cangari-Viru Viru and reflects years of fieldwork. Thet *Rondas* were as much or more responsible for the defeat of Sendero Luminoso in the highlands as Peru's armed forces, especially in the violence-ridden Apurímac Valley. Extremely useful for understanding a poorly identified element of the conflict against Sendero Luminoso, and the capability of Peru's peasantry to deal with adversity through communal mobilization.

2698 Stein, William W. Dance in the cemetery: Jose Carlos Mariategui and the Lima Scandal of 1917. Lanham, Md.: Univ. Press of America, 1997. 271 p.: appendices, bibl., index.

Interesting use of the illegal night performance of a Swiss dancer in the cemetery to establish the focus for an excellent political biography of Mariátegui's early career. The young Peruvian Marxist was in attendance at the ceremony and many of the participants were subsequently arrested, including Mariátegui. According to Stein, this "tectonic experience" set the young writer and leftist on the path to a greater militancy and resistance to existing conditions in Peruvian society. Highly psycho-analytic approach. Author brings a deep understanding of Peru and the peasantry to this unique analysis.

2699 Tamariz Lúcar, Domingo. La ronda del general: testimonios inéditos del Cuartelazo de 1948. Lima: J. Campodonico Editor, 1998. 174 p.: bibl., ill., index, photos.

Despite the title, which refers to Gen. Manuel A. Odría's coup against President José Bustamante y Rivero in October 1948, this short anthology is compromised of interviews and primary documents that shed light on an important military leader who was a contemporary of Juan Perón and sought to copy many of the Argentine leader's populist methods. There are few biographies of Odría that are especially helpful to scholars, and this volume is not a true biography. But the interviews and the early background on the general's career before he served in Busta-mante y Rivero's cabinet and then betrayed him are illuminating. Rare photographs of the Odría era.

2700 Tapia, Carlos. Las fuerzas armadas y Sendero Luminoso: dos estrategias y un final. Lima: Instituto de Estudios Peru-anos, 1997. 160 p.: bibl., tables (Serie Ide-ología y política, 1019–455X; 8)

A good overview of the Peruvian mili-tary's strategic approaches to the conflict with Sendero Luminoso from the early 1980s until immediately after the capture of the movement's leader in 1992. Cites General Clemente Noel's highly unsuccessful cam-paign in Ayacucho in the mid-1980s as an ex-ample of the army's early and unrealistic at-tempt to adopt a modification of the failed "strategic hamlet" approach used by the US in Vietnam. Only after nearly a decade did the armed forces adopt a somewhat standard-ized "counter-subversive campaign." A close examination of government documents al-lows the author to competently discuss the critical role of the intelligence service in de-feating Sendero Luminoso. Lacks thorough consideration of the role of the rural-based *Rondas Campesinas.*

2701 Thorndike, Guillermo. Los imperios del sol: una historia de los japoneses en el Perú. Lima: Editorial BRASA, 1996. 231 p.: ill. (Collección BRASA/Thorndike)

Not as scholarly as other similar stud-ies, this volume emphasizes personal histo-ries, especially the commercial and commu-nity leaders of the Japanese in Lima. Pays close attention to the May 1940 anti-Japanese riots in Lima and the deportation of Japanese-Peruvians to US internment camps during WW II. Devotes much attention to Fujimori's rise to power, including some background on his early life. Dozens of photographs add significantly to the value of this study. Upon its publication, and before the appearance of the Morimoto and Fukumoto books (items **2655** and **2679**), the JINNAI center offered this volume as the best survey of the Japa-nese experience in Peru.

2702 Thurner, Mark. Atusparia and Cáceres: rereading representations of Peru's late nineteenth-century "national problem." (*HAHR*, 77:3, Aug. 1997, p. 409–441)

Uses meeting of indigenous rebel leader Pedro Pablo Atusparia and criollo Gen. Andres Cáceres in June 1886 to illustrate al-ternative ways of assessing Peru's "national problem" of indigenous integration and its implications for modernization. Discusses complex nature of the national discourse among criollo and indigenous communities regarding these issues. Interestingly, con-trasts the meeting of these two military lead-ers with that of Zapata and Villa in Mexico City after the fall of Victoriano Huerta.

2703 Thurner, Mark. From two republics to one divided: contradictions of post-colonial nationmaking in Andean Peru. Durham, N.C.; London: Duke Univ. Press, 1997. 203 p.: bibl., index, map. (Latin Amer-ica otherwise: languages, empires, nations)

Culmination of author's work on the Peruvian peasantry and its conflicts with the Eurocentric view of nationhood held by the majority of Peru criollo leadership. An espe-cially important book for 19th-century spe-cialists as well as those scholars examining the evolution of the role of the indigenous population in Peruvian society. As in item **2702,** author focuses on the 1885 Atusparia rebellion, which suggests a pragmatic and se-lective approach to Andean politics that can-not be categorized within the context of the assumed evolution of the liberal nation-state nor the subsequently more dominant de-pendency theories. Intelligent study con-tributes significantly to Andean peasant poli-tics during Peru's formative years. The work would have benefitted from a separate bibli-ography.

2704 Vargas Valente, Virginia et al. El movimiento feminista y el Estado: los avatares de la agenda propia. (*Social. Par-ticip.*, 80, dic. 1997, p. 25–60, facsims.)

Valuable overview of the history of the feminist movement in Peru within a broader Latin American context. Traces early history of the movement to the "Derechos de Mujer" agenda first initiated in the mid-1960s, and further to the Segundo Encuentro Feminista Latinoamerica y Caribe (Lima, July 1983). Carefully discusses the political and social objectives of Peruvian feminism, which are set mainly in an organizational context. The role of pragmatic and informal women's groups during the 1990s such as *vaso de leche* organizations is, however, not examined.

2705 Velázquez Castro, Marcel. José María de Pando y la consolidación del *sujeto esclavista* en el Perú del siglo XIX. (*Bol. Inst. Riva-Agüero*, 23, 1996, p. 303–325, bibl.)

Highly informative analysis of the discourse over slavery in early republican Peru, as seen through the legalistic arguments of one of the principals in the debate, José María de Pando. Links question of slavery to that of nascent nation-building and modernization. Employs a wide array of secondary sources to construct a useful wider argument. Extremely helpful analysis for scholars seeking to clarify the early-19th century debate over slavery within Peru's emerging legal structure.

2706 Villegas Romero, Arturo. Un decenio de la historia de Arequipa, 1830–1840. Peru: Edición Fundación Gloria, 1985. 515 p.: bibl.

Voluminous and well-researched history of Arequipa during the early decades of the Republican era. Valuable local study details power struggles of the early caudillos drawing on regional archival sources, newspapers, and pertinent secondary sources. Also delves into representative literary trends in the city to develop the cultural perspective.

2707 Wagner de Reyna, Alberto. Historia diplomática del Perú, 1900–1945. Lima: Fondo Editorial del Ministerio de Relaciones Exteriores, 1997. 463 p.: bibl., index, maps.

Useful review of Peru's foreign policy, primarily with its Latin American neighbors, during a difficult time in the nation's diplomatic and military relations with surrounding nations. Covers the era of the Tacna and Arica settlement with Chile, the Leticia dis-

pute with Colombia, and the border war with Ecuador and subsequent Rio de Janeiro Protocol (Jan. 1942). Peru's close cooperation with the US during WW II is a key point of discussion. Can be seen as an updated and Peruvian version of James Carey's study written nearly 30 years ago and covering the same time frame.

2708 Watanabe, José; Amelia Morimoto; and Óscar Chambi. La memoria del ojo: cien años de presencia japonesa en el Perú. Lima: Congreso de la República del Perú, 1999. 243 p.: photos.

While not a scholarly work, this beautiful book of photographs of the Japanese experience in Peru from the 1890s to the present offers invaluable images of daily life, cultural events, school work, and the hard times of deportation and internment during World War II. Compiled by the leading authorities on the Japanese in Peru and one of the nation's most prominent photographers, this lavish volume was published by the Peruvian government as a testimony to the role of the Japanese immigrant in Peruvian society. As such, it marks a complete evolution from the dark days of more than half a century ago.

2709 Yepes, Ernesto. Mito y realidad de una frontera: Perú-Ecuador, 1942–1949; un testimonio inédito del Departamento de Estado, el informe McBride. 2. ed. Lima: Ediciones Análisis, 1996. 253 p.: appendices, bibl., maps.

Study of the attempt by Peru, with the assistance of the US government under the auspices of the McBride Commission, to firmly define and mark the border between Peru and Ecuador which had been determined under significant pressure at the Rio de Janeiro Conference of January 1942. Author is one of Peru's most prominent emerging diplomatic historians. The McBride Commission's work was largely completed with the assistance of the US Air Force and a number of airmen lost their lives flying the aerial photography missions. The book's significance lies in the fact that the Peruvian government relied heavily on the McBride Commission's findings to validate its position when the dispute over the border with Ecuador flared again in 1995.

Bolivia

ERICK D. LANGER, *Professor of History, Georgetown University*

OVER THE PAST FEW YEARS, the 19th century has increasingly become a legitimate period of research in Bolivian history. New contributions for the independence era continue to appear (items **2735** and **2742**), as well as the reproduction of *El Cóndor de Bolivia,* Bolivia's first newspaper (item **2717**). Controversy swirled in particular around one book: In *La mesa coja,* Javier Mendoza asserts that the independence revolution in La Paz was not as radical as first believed and that the presumed revolutionary declaration was apocryphal (item **2735**). The document was put together in the late-19th century as a way for the La Paz elites to claim primacy over the constitutional capital, Sucre. For months in 1997, this book was the focus of many newspaper articles in the Bolivian press.

The insights gained in the last decade redefining 19th-century Bolivia have finally taken root (for example, items **2741** and **2743**). Political history focuses on the debate over protectionism and internal markets, which has become an important touchstone for understanding the economic dynamics of the century. The rising interest in Manuel Isidoro Belzu, a controversial 19th-century caudillo who implemented protectionist policies, demonstrates this development most clearly (items **2714, 2737,** and **2738**). Meanwhile, land tenure patterns continue to stimulate debate (items **2720, 2726,** and **2732**), as does the role of indigenous communities in Bolivian history, ranging from understanding the conceptual basis of the treatment of indigenous peoples to indigenous education and hereditary rights (items **2714, 2716, 2715, 2725,** and **2744**).

Another popular topic in this chapter (not restricted to the 19th century) is mining, including studies on both the mining companies and owners (items **2929** and **2746**) and on the workers themselves (items **2712, 2713,** and **2728**). The publication of the complete works of long-time labor activist and scholar, Guillermo Lora, will be an important source of 20th-century labor history (item **2733**). Political history received a boost from the vigorous publication record of Marta Irurozqui (items **2723, 2724,** and **2725**), as well as from publications of more established scholars such as Roberto Querejazu Calvo (item **2739**) and Ferran Gallego (item **2719**).

The Catholic Church merits greater attention, both as an institution (item **2747**) and with regard to the missions (items **2729** and **2732**). However, the history of the vast tropical lowlands, despite some interesting contributions, remains woefully under- represented (items **2722** and **2740**).

2710 **Albarracín Millán, Juan.** El poder financiero de la gran minería boliviana. La Paz: Ediciones AKAPANA, 1995. 327 p.: bibl., ill., index. (Los republicanos en la historia de Bolivia; 2)

By documenting the rise of Simón I. Patiño, who dominated 20th-century Bolivian tin production, shows how the state fell under the financial power of the tin barons.

The Bolivian state concentrated almost exclusively on mining, to the detriment of other economic and social sectors.

2711 **Antezana Salvatierra, Alejandro Vladimir.** Los liberales y el problema agrario de Bolivia, 1899–1920. La Paz: Plural Editores; Centro de Información para el Desarrollo, 1996. 330 p.: bibl., ill. (Col. Historia agraria)

Highly polemical but useful volume on agrarian legislation. Good compilation of important agrarian legislation of the first decades of the 20th century. Does not consider many important works and views liberals' actions as negative.

Aristizábal, Armando. Juan José Flores en Berruecos: síntesis de una infamia. See item **2612.**

Block, David. Fuentes para la historia de Moxos. See item **2354.**

2712 Boeger, Andrew. Dependencia y resistencia: el caso de la Mina Chojlla, 1944–1952. (*Rev. Mus. Nac. Etnogr. Folk.*, 5, 1995, p. 6–24, graphs)

Important contribution to labor history shows that mine workers were conscious of declining world position of the Mina Chojlla of Wolfram and did not strike because they feared the mine might be shut down. Instead, workers controlled their time and bodies through widespread absenteeism, and forged links with the Movimiento Nacional Revolucionario party and the National Miners' Federation.

2713 Cajías de la Vega, Magdalena. Los mineros en la historia contemporanea de Bolivia, 1900–1990: tercera parte; sindicalismo revolucionario y utopía socialista, 1965–1971. (*Estud. Boliv.*, 2, 1996, p. 49–98)

Condensation of a larger work. Good summary of events in the labor history of most turbulent years of Bolivian mining labor activism.

2714 Calderón Jemio, Raúl Javier. En defensa de la dignidad: el apoyo de los ayllus de Umasuyu al proyecto belcista durante su consolidación, 1848–1849. (*Estud. Boliv.*, 2, 1996, p. 99–110)

Case study of altiplano communities shows how the Aymara Indians supported Manuel Isidoro Belzu because he was seen as supportive of Indian causes. Asserts that this support was important for the populist Belzu regime.

2715 Choque Canqui, Roberto. La educación indigenal boliviana: el proceso educativo indígena-rural. (*Estud. Boliv.*, 2, 1996, p. 125–181)

A masterful summary of the history of providing education to the Quechua- and Aymara-speaking Indians in Bolivia, from the colonial period to 1994. Concentrates on 20th century, when formal rural education for Indians was introduced.

2716 Choque Canqui, Roberto and **Esteban Ticona Alejo.** Jesús de Machaqa: la marka rebelde. v. 2, Sublevación y masacre de 1921. La Paz: CEDOIN; CIPCA, 1996. 1 v.: ill., maps. (Cuadernos de investigación; 46 Col. Historia y documento)

Completely revised and expanded edition of 1986 work analyzes one of the most important indigenous rebellions and its repression in 20th-century Bolivia. Extensive documentary and testimonial sections provide excellent sources. For ethnologist's comment, see *HLAS 57:1073*.

2717 *El Condor* de Bolivia. La Paz: Banco Central de Bolivia; Archivo y Biblioteca Nacionales de Bolivia; Academia Boliviana de la Historia, 1995. 134 p.

Facsimile copy of Bolivia's first newspaper and official organ of Antonio José de Sucre's administration. Great source for politics of early independence period and government's point of view.

2718 Farcau, Bruce W. The Chaco War: Bolivia and Paraguay, 1932–1935. Westport, Conn.: Praeger, 1996. 264 p.: bibl., index, map.

Highly readable political and military account of the war that devastated both Paraguay and Bolivia. Based exclusively on published sources, emphasizes Bolivian actions more than those of Paraguay.

2719 Gallego, Ferran. Expansión y ruptura del orden liberal en Bolivia, 1900–1932. (*Anu. Estud. Am.*, 53:1, 1996, p. 153–173)

Combines economic and political analysis of the periods of Liberal and Republican party rule. Shows how new sectors, such as leftist labor movement and radicalized students, helped bring epoch of liberalism to a close in Bolivia. Largely based on secondary sources.

Gamarra, Eduardo A. and **James M. Malloy.** The patrimonial dynamics of party politics in Bolivia. See *HLAS 57:3506.*

2720   Grieshaber, Erwin P. La expansión de
la hacienda en el departamento de La
Paz, Bolivia, 1850–1920: una revisión cuanti-
tativa. (*ANDES Antropol. Hist.*, 2/3, segundo
semestre 1990/primer semestre 1991, p. 33–
83, appendices, tables)

Important effort to quantify expansion
of haciendas at the expense of Indian communities. The economic boom in La Paz in
the early-20th century, and more importantly, favorable political conditions, made
possible the rapid acquisition of Indian lands.

2721   Grieshaber, Erwin P. Los padrones de
la contribución indígena como fuente
demográfica: posibilidades y limitaciones.
(*Anuario/Sucre*, 1994/95, p. 177–185, table)

Summarizes 19th-century *padrones* in
the Archivo Nacional de Bolivia; discusses
subset known as *padrones de contribución
indígena* as source of demographic, economic, and social data; and critiques Herbert
S. Klein's *Haciendas and ayllus: rural society
in the Bolivian Andes in the eighteenth and
nineteenth centuries* (see *HLAS 56:2480*).
Significant methodological and historiographic contribution. [M.T. Hamerly]

2722   Hollweg, Mario Gabriel. Alemanes en
el oriente boliviano: su aporte al desarrollo de Bolivia. v. 1, 1535–1918. Santa Cruz
de la Sierra, Bolivia: s.n., 1995. 1 v.: bibl., ill.,
index, maps.

Detailed, encyclopedic enumeration of
Germans in the tropical lowlands of Bolivia.
Shows importance of Germans for trade and
industry in Santa Cruz. Indispensable source
for researching Germans in Bolivia.

2723   Irurozqui, Marta. La armonía de las desigualdades: elites y conflictos de
poder en Bolivia, 1880–1920. Madrid: Consejo Superior de Investigaciones Científicas;
Cusco: Centro de Estudios Regionales Andinos Bartolomé de las Casas, 1994. 237 p.:
bibl., maps. (Archivos de historia andina,
1022–0879; 18)

Useful interpretation of the La Paz
elites' rise to power. Provides description of
political conflict between the Sucre/Potosí
and La Paz elites before the Federalist War of
1899. After La Paz's victory in the war,
shows through literary analysis how the new
government viewed Indians, mestizos, and
the Catholic Church.

2724   Irurozqui, Marta. Ebrios, vagos y anal-
fabetos: el sufragio restringido en Bolivia, 1826–1952. (*Rev. Indias*, 61:208,
sept./dic. 1996, p. 697–742)

First in-depth study of the history of
suffrage in Bolivia shows that the lower orders attempted (and failed) to gain full citizenship before 1952 by utilizing elite rhetoric rather than pressing for radical change in
the exclusivist rules for suffrage.

2725   Irurozqui, Marta. El negocio de la
política: indios y mestizos en el discurso de la elite boliviana, 1900–1920. (*in*
Del discurso colonial al proindigenismo: ensayos de historia latinoamericana. Edición de
Jorge Pinto Rodríguez. Temuco, Chile: Ediciones Univ. de la Frontera, 1996, p. 116–140)

After the triumph in the Federalist
War of 1899, the La Paz elites debated how to
create a Bolivian nation-state with a highland Indian majority. Through their racist
views, they made the Indians exceptional but
also placed them in a hierarchy in which the
creole elites were superior.

2726   Jackson, Robert H. Community and
hacienda in the Bolivian highlands:
changing patterns of land tenure in Arque
and Vacas. (*in* Liberals, the Church, and Indian peasants: corporate lands and the challenge of reform in nineteenth-century Spanish America. Edited by Robert H. Jackson.
Albuquerque: Univ. of New Mexico Press,
1997, p. 193–206, tables)

Microstudies of land tenure patterns
in different Cochabamba districts show that
government policies had widely different effects, due to economic and social factors.

2727   Langer, Erick D. Los archivos históricos no tradicionales en Bolivia: una
lista incompleta. (*Anuario/Sucre*, 1994/95,
p. 291–299)

Lists numerous archives with rich research potential, almost all of which date
from the 19th century. [M.T. Hamerly]

2728   Langer, Erick D. The barriers to proletarianization: Bolivian mine labour,
1826–1918. (*in* "Peripheral" labour?: studies
in the history of partial proletarianization.
Edited by Shahid Amin and Marcel van der
Linden. Cambridge, England; New York:
Cambridge Univ. Press, 1997, p. 25–49)

Bolivian mine labor systems must

consider majority small mining operations and regional differences in access to workers. As a result, during the 19th and 20th centuries processes of proletarianization varied widely, especially among the important mining/hacienda complexes in the southern part of the country.

2729 Langer, Erick D. Caciques y poder en las misiones franciscanas entre los Chiriguanos durante la rebelión de 1892. (*Siglo XIX/Monterrey,* 3:9, Jan./June 1994, p. 82–103)

Calls for a reinterpretation of the "civilizing" function of Catholic missions in Latin America. Unlike the traditional view of missions, the great Chiriguano rebellion of 1892 in southeastern Bolivia showed that in the Franciscan missions, old chiefs held the balance of power rather than the missionaries.

2730 Langer, Erick D. Foreign cloth in the lowland frontier: commerce and consumption of textiles in Bolivia, 1830–1930. (*in* The allure of the foreign: imported goods in postcolonial Latin America. Edited by Benjamin Orlove. Ann Arbor: Univ. of Michigan Press, 1997, p. 93–112)

In contrast to conventional wisdom, claims that the Chiriguanos played a significant political and economic role in the 19th- and early-20th-century eastern lowlands. Not only were they substantial consumers of European textiles, but they were paid regularly by government officials and cattle ranchers not to engage in raids. [M.T. Hamerly]

2731 Langer, Erick D. Indígenas y exploradores en el Gran Chaco: relaciones indio-blancas en la Bolivia del siglo XIX. (*Anuario/Sucre,* 1996, p. 309–330)

Well-researched and written essay on impact of Bolivian expeditions in the Gran Chaco in 1800s, and on indigenous peoples' resistance to these incursions. Compares these 19th-century expeditions with the 16th-century Spanish conquest. [M.T. Hamerly]

2732 Langer, Erick D. and **Robert H. Jackson.** Liberalism and the land question in Bolivia, 1825–1920. (*in* Liberals, the Church, and Indian peasants: corporate lands and the challenge of reform in nineteenth-century Spanish America. Edited by Robert H. Jackson. Albuquerque: Univ. of New Mexico Press, 1997, p. 171–192)

Compares Bolivian state's differential actions toward corporate lands of the Catholic Church and lands of the Indian communities. Suggests that early expropriation of most Church lands and the survival of Indian lands was because the Indians had greater power to resist the elite's liberal impulses.

2733 Lora, Guillermo. Obras completas. v. 1–15. La Paz: Ediciones Masas, 1996. 15 v.

Important source for the life and times of Guillermo Lora, the Trotskyist intellectual and labor leader. Complete collection includes both published and unpublished writings, pamphlets, and manifestos.

2734 Martin Schmid, 1694–1772: Missionar, Musiker, Architekt; ein Jesuit aus der Schweiz bei den Chiquitano-Indianern in Bolivien; Ausstellung im Historischen Museum Luzern, 15. Juni bis 11. September 1994 [Martin Schmid, 1694–1772: missionary, musician, architect; a Jesuit from Switzerland with the Chiquitano Indians in Bolivia; exhibit held at the Historisches Museum Luzern, June 15-September 11, 1994]. Edited by Eckart Kühne. Luzern, Switzerland: Historisches Museum Luzern; Zurich, Switzerland: Jesuitenmission Zurich, 1994. 192 p.: bibl., ill. (some col.), map.

Well-organized, illustrated catalog describes in detail objects exhibited at the Historisches Museum Luzern. Together with essays based on Schmid's letters, book provides historical insights into the legacy of Jesuit missionary work. [C.K. Converse]

2735 Mendoza Pizarro, Javier. La mesa coja: historia de la proclama de la Junta uitiva del 16 de julio de 1809. La Paz: PIEB/SINERGIA, 1997. 334 p.: bibl., ill., index.

Highly controversial book asserts that the 1809 revolutionary proclamation was in fact a copy of one from La Plata (present-day Sucre). The La Paz elite manufactured this proclamation in the late-19th century in an effort to claim rights to being the capital city of Bolivia instead of Sucre.

2736 **Mitre, Antonio.** Los hilos de la memoria: ascensión y crisis de las casas comerciales alemanas en Bolivia, 1900–1942. La Paz: Grupo Editorial Anthropos, 1996. 128 p.: bibl., ill., plates.

Short study focuses on the importance of German firms in Bolivia and the effects of both world wars on the firms.

2737 **Ortiz Mesa, Luis Javier.** Poder y sociedad en Los Andes: Manuel Isidoro Belzu, un caudillo popular, Bolivia, 1848–1855. (*Anu. Colomb. Hist. Soc. Cult.*, 22, 1995, p. 75–94)

Solid summary of the political career and ideology of one of the most important 19th-century Bolivian caudillos. Incorporates most recent 19th-century research on social and economic conditions.

2738 **Pérez, Carlos.** Cascarilleros y comerciantes en cascarilla durante las insurrecciones populistas de Belzu en 1847 y 1848. (*Hist. Cult./La Paz*, 24, 1997, p. 197–213)

Asserts that the caudillo Manuel Isidoro Belzu was able to gain support and mobilize La Paz by promising to overcome the Ballivián administration's monopoly of the cinchona bark trade, the source for quinine, which was in the hands of the Argentine firm Jorge Tesanos Pinto and Company.

2739 **Querejazu Calvo, Roberto.** Aclaraciones históricas sobre la Guerra del Pacífico. La Paz: Librería Editorial Juventud, 1995. 265 p.

Collection of previously published short articles on the War of the Pacific by one of Bolivia's preeminent historians is useful for a basic understanding of the Bolivian position. Unfortunately, does not contain scholarly apparatus (source citations, etc.).

2740 **Recasens, Andreu Viola.** Tierra de nadie: representaciones del espacio y cultura de frontera en los territorios caucheros bolivianos, 1880–1930. (*Rev. Andin.*, 12:2, 1994, p. 529–545, bibl.)

Intriguing perspective about how the rubber boom engendered in the Bolivian tropical northeast. Author posits a "frontier culture" that exalted the individual, failed to foster long-term thinking, and allowed the taking of public goods for private gain and unrestricted exploitation of nature for immediate profit.

2741 **Rodríguez Ostria, Gustavo.** Estado nacional, mercado interior y elites regionales: los casos de Cochabamba y Santa Cruz en Bolivia, 1880–1930. (*ANDES Antropol. Hist.*, 2/3, segundo semestre 1990/primer semestre 1991, p. 11–32, bibl.)

Uses case studies of Santa Cruz and Cochabamba regions to revise proposition of conflict only between the internal market and export/import complex during 19th and early-20th centuries, showing that the internal market was not homogeneous. Instead, regions within Bolivia benefitted or suffered as the internal market changed.

Rossells, Beatriz. La gastronomía en Potosí y Charcas: siglos XVIII y XIX; 800 recetas de la cocina criolla. See item **2385.**

Sampedro V., Francisco. El espacio territorial ecuatoriano de 1830 a 1995, con la Guerra del Cenepa desatada por el Perú: auténtica historia de límites. See *HLAS 57:2633.*

2742 **Siles Salinas, Jorge.** La independencia de Bolivia. Madrid: Editorial MAPFRE, 1992. 406 p.: appendices, bibl., ill., index. (Col. Independencia de Iberoamérica; 10. Col. MAPFRE 1492)

A fine summary of the political history of the independence period, mainly based on secondary sources. Includes useful annotated bibliography of works on this era.

2743 **Soux, María Luisa.** Coca, mercado regional y políticas republicanas persistencia de circuitos comerciales coloniales. (*ANDES Antropol. Hist.*, 2/3, segundo semestre 1990/primer semestre 1991, p. 93–103, bibl., graphs)

Shows that, unlike other products, the colonial market for coca leaves remained much the same throughout the republican period, into the second half of the 20th century.

2744 **Soux, María Luisa.** Individuo, familia y comunidad: el derecho sucesorio entre los comunarios de La Paz, 1825–1850. (*Estud. Boliv.*, 2, 1996, p. 437–465, bibl.)

Important effort to understand hereditary rights among altiplano Indians by examining changing rights during a life cycle. Shows how community ties loosened during this period and were replaced by the family as the major unit of reference.

2745 Spitzer, Leo. Hotel Bolivia: the culture of memory in a refuge from Nazism. New York: Hill and Wang, 1998. 254 p.: bibl., ill., index.

As much a reminiscence as a scholarly work, Spitzer examines his childhood, born of German Jewish refugees in Bolivia. Tells how his parents came to Bolivia and describes their life in the new country. Emphasizes memory and the place of dispossessed German Jews in a foreign country, with Bolivian context in 1940s taking a back seat.

2746 Stang, Gudmund. Compañía Corocoro de Bolivia, 1873–1923: a Chilean copper-mining venture in Bolivia seen in the context of the contemporary development of the industry. (*Iberoamericana/Stockholm*, 23:1/2, 1993, p. 3–38, tables)

A curious effort to use the Corocoro mining enterprise, Chilean-owned but located in Bolivia, as a case study to understand reasons for failure of the native Chilean copper industry in late-19th century. Despite author's prejudices against Bolivian society, a useful study for understanding this mining complex.

2747 Valda Palma, Roberto. Historia de la Iglesia de Bolivia en la República. La Paz: Impr. Publicidad Papiro, 1995. 407 p.: bibl.

Useful institutional history of the Bolivian Catholic Church, written under official Church auspices. Good balance between discussion of the 19th and 20th centuries.

Chile

WILLIAM F. SATER, *Professor of History, California State University, Long Beach*

SCHOLARS HAVE FINALLY TURNED their attention to post-1920s Chile. Vial Correa added another volume to his authoritative multipart history of the period, this time focusing on Ibáñez's first regime, 1891–1973 (item **2794**). Collier and Sater have written a more general treatment of Chile which, while less specialized than Vial's work, covers a longer period, 1804–1994 (see *HLAS 56:2882*).

Silva (item **2788**) and Ibáñez Santa María (item **2769**) contend that former President Carlos Ibáñez del Campo created a corps of technicians who made Chile's industrialization possible and who created the Corporación de Fomento de la Producción (CORFO). It appears, however, that Ibáñez may well have been more deserving of his nickname, "the mule" (coined by Arturo Alessandri), than the title "General of Hope." As Etchepare Jenson notes, Ibáñez's second regime foundered because he failed to recognize that the rules of the political game had changed (item **2761**). Fermandois' investigation into Gustavo Ross Santa María, the "Minister of Hunger," provides superb insights into the latter's economic policies and US responses (item **2762**). Arancibia Clavel, Góngora Escobedo, and Vial Correa offer the first biography of former President Jorge Alessandri (item **2748**). Using interviews, they provide insights into the man who was the last representative of Chile's old mainstream parties.

Certain well-studied topics continue to attract attention, at times breaking new ground as scholars delve deeper into previously explored theories or utilize untapped sources of information. The essays by Pinto and Reyes in Luis Ortega's edited volume on the 1891 Revolution are noteworthy for their explanation of why the northern miners turned against José Manuel Balmaceda (item **2767**). Scholarly interest in the Allende period seems to be fading, but those still interested will profit from a splendid two-volume compilation of editorials and cartoons that appeared in the Chilean press from 1970–73 (item **2774**).

Economic history appears to have displaced political history as the primary area of research. Pinto Vallejos, a preeminent economic historian specializing in the history of nitrates, describes how mining, particularly the *salitreras,* not only stimulated Chile's economic growth and the adoption of technology, but also helped transform campesinos into laborers (items **2778** and **2779**).

Although called the *sueldo de Chile,* copper, unlike nitrates, has not attracted a high level of scholarly attention, perhaps because it did not become one of the most important aspects of the Chilean economy until well into the 20th century. In his work, Cavieres Figueroa attributes this deficiency to the Chilean failure to invest in the mines (item **2752**). As the outstanding collection of articles by Villalobos and Sagrado demonstrates, many intellectuals favored economic protectionism (item **2760**). In a similar vein, Grez Toso has compiled a book of essays on what became known as the *"cuestion social"*—a discussion of Chile's social and economic ills (item **2754**). His work demonstrates that these issues vexed the country's intellectuals long before the 1880s, the more commonly cited start of the debate. Wagner's collection of statistical data, while not riveting, nonetheless provides economic historians with an essential tool (item **2797**). Historians would certainly have benefitted further if the author had carried his study into the post-1930 period.

Krebs, Muñoz, and Valdivieso offer an interesting history of Santiago's Catholic Univ., emphasizing structural change rather than intellectual currents (item **2772**). Similarly, Cruz-Coke's overview of the professionalization and modernization of the medical profession opens new vistas. Regrettably, he ended his research well short of the 1950s (item **2753**).

Studies of marginalized social groups continue to attract the attention of historians. Góngora Escobedo describes the composition and working conditions of Santiago's prostitute population (item **2764**). Initially, he notes, the state sought to regulate the sex trade in the interest of public health, but later the exploitation of prostitutes became the more salient issue.

Military history remains popular. William Sater and Holger Herwig indicate that Emil Körner's vaunted reforms proved at best ephemeral (item **2787**) while Vergara Quiroz's work on the social background of the army's officer corps is excellent (item **2793**). Regrettably, he ended his research long before the end of the 19th century. Bringing the study up to date would have been useful.

Ethnic history has retained its newly discovered popularity. Estrada Turra's edited volume explains a great deal about Spanish immigration to Chile (item **2771**), while the rarely studied, but nonetheless important *Turcos,* as well as the similarly understudied Jews, attracted the attention of Rebolledo Hernández (item **2782**) and McGee Deutsch (item **2773**). It will be interesting to see if scholars continue to devote more attention to Chile's lesser known *colonias.*

Studies on gender have finally appeared among the works reviewed this biennium. Salinas Meza describes the diverging images of masculine and feminine honor, as well as the suffrage movement (item **2786**). However, as Supplee notes, any solidarity among women disappeared once they became enfranchised (item **2790**). Ideally, the study of women, as with the less-favored ethnic groups, will continue to attract scholarly attention. Still, the past years have been fruitful: historians cast their eyes on more recent events while continuing in-depth research on economic themes and opening up new areas for investigation.

2748 Arancibia Clavel, Patricia; Alvaro Góngora Escobedo; and Gonzalo Vial Correa. Jorge Alessandri, 1896–1986: una biografía. Santiago?: Zig-Zag, 1996. 441 p.: bibl., ill., index. (Memorias y biografías)

Biography of a leading Chilean politician describing his political career, presidency, and postcoup activities. Uses interviews with various contemporaries to provide scholars with a good place to begin a study of Alessandri and his years in office.

2749 Araya Ferrière, Pamela. Número, tipos y singularidades del empleo ferroviario hacia fines del siglo XIX. (*Rev. Hist. /Concepción*, 4:4, 1994, p. 97–132, tables)

The introduction of railroads created a new, more complex service as well as administrative jobs. What resulted was a complicated hierarchy in which foreigners sometimes staffed the highest positions and where employees received wages based on the technical nature of their position and years of service, both relatively new concepts to Chile.

Benavente Aninat, Maria Antonia and **Carmen Bermejo Lorenzo.** Síntesis histórica de la funebria en Chile. See item **2400.**

2750 Brahm García, Enrique. La discusión en torno al régimen de gobierno en Chile, 1830–1840. (*Rev. Estud. Hist. Juríd.*, 16, 1994, p. 35–56)

The defeat of the Liberals at Liracy did not end support for either the republican form of government or for democracy in Chile. Even supposedly Conservatives and men like Mariano Egaña favored both although, in truth, they had a severely skewed vision of these ideas. Interesting but not a revolutionary study.

2751 Cavieres Figueroa, Eduardo. Aislar el cuerpo y sanar el alma: el régimen penitenciario chileno, 1843–1928. (*Ibero-Am. Arch.*, 21:3/4, 1995, p. 303–328)

The government tried a combination of solitary confinement, prayer, and education to redeem its prison population. Because it lacked the financial resources to implement serious reform and educate its prison population, the state had to settle on housing and guarding the inmates.

2752 Cavieres Figueroa, Eduardo. Comercio chileno y comerciantes ingleses, 1820–1880: un ciclo de historia económica.

Valparaíso: Univ. Católica de Valparaíso, Vicerrectoría Académica, Instituto de Historia, 1988. 259 p.: bibl., ill., maps. (Serie Monografías históricas; 2)

Chile's copper mining sector suffered because it lacked capital and infrastructure and had to process poorer quality ores. It also suffered from competition and wild price variations. The industry continued to function although London, and British merchants dominated the copper trade as well as other sectors of the economy. A well-researched study.

2753 Cruz-Coke, Ricardo. Historia de la medicina chilena. Santiago: Editorial Andres Bello, 1995. 584 p.: bibl., ill., index.

An all-encompassing study of the development of medicine in Chile from precolonial times to 1927. Although stressing the development of various medical institutions, education, and professional journals, it also mentions the contributions of specific physicians. An all too brief overview of an important sector.

2754 La *cuestión social* en Chile: ideas y debates precursores, 1804–1902. Recopilación y estudio crítico de Sergio Grez Toso. Santiago: Dirección de Bibliotecas, Archivo y Museos, Centro de Investigaciones Diego Barros Arana, 1995. 577 p.: bibl., index. (Fuentes para la historia de la república; 7)

Superb compilation of essays which prove, contrary to traditional notions, that Chileans became preoccupied with "the social question" long before the 1880s. These works, which provide a penetrating analysis of Chile's social and economic problems, are preceded by an excellent introductory essay examining the various solutions propounded by the various critics.

2755 Culver, William W. and **Cornel J. Reinhart.** Alianzas y competencia por el control del Estado: políticas mineras en Chile y Estados Unidos de Norteamérica, 1850–1900. (*in* Minería americana colonial y del siglo XIX. México: Instituto Nacional de Antropología e Historia, 1994, p. 43–54, table)

Chile had the means of competing on the world copper market until the late 1880s. Unfortunately, the lack of a national policy, which could have facilitated investment, as well as created a better pro-mining environment, led the Chileans to abandon copper to foreign, particularly US interests.

2756 Culver, William W. and **Cornel J. Reinhart.** Las barras chilenas de cobre y el surgimiento del Estado liberal en Chile. (*in* Reunión de Historiadores de la Minería Latinoamericana (II), *1st, Zacatecas, Mexico, 1990. Empresarios y política minera. México: Instituto Nacional de Antropología e Historia, 1992, p. 57–63*)

Although presumably espousing economic liberalism, miners in Chile still sought state protection. Eventually local miners utilized foreign skills and local coal and ore to nurture the copper industry. The combination of private enterprise and state involvement meant that the copper industry had to compete against foreign mines.

2757 David Lebón, F. Jorge. Trigo en Chile: una historia desconocida. Santiago: Ediciones del Día, 1993. 641 p.: bibl., ill.

A detailed study, not simply of wheat production, but also of the milling industry. Includes information on the production of wheat, its sale, export, importation, domestic consumption, and prices, plus an extensive list of the various laws governing the production of wheat and bread. Not riveting but still essential reading for scholars interested in agriculture.

Díaz Melián, Mafalda Victoria. La presidencia del Dr. Miguel Juárez Celman: algunas notas de su administración en 1889; proyecto de tratado de comercio con Chile. See item **2876.**

2758 Durruty, Ana Victoria. Salitre, harina de luna llena. Antofagasta, Chile: s.n., 1993. 332 p.: bibl., ill.

Invaluable work on nitrates, particularly for the post-Ibáñez period; the development and collapse of COSACH; and the subsequent creation of Soquimich, which Allende nationalized and the junta returned to private hands. Excellent because it combined a general history of the nitrate industry while emphasizing the post-1930 period.

2759 Echenique Celis, Antonia and **Concepción Rodríguez Gómez.** Historia de la Compañía de Acero del Pacífico, S.A. v. 1, Huachipato, consolidación del proceso siderúrgico chileno, 1905–1950. Santiago: Compañía de Acero del Pacífico, 1990. 1 v.: bibl., ill., maps.

An attractive work tracing the growth of the Chilean steel industry, from the establishment of the unsuccessful El Corral complex to the development of the heavy industry complex at Huachipato. Places the industry within context of Chile's overall economic development. A good source which may facilitate additional research.

2760 Ensayistas proteccionistas del siglo XIX. Recopilación de Sergio Villalobos R. y Rafael Sagredo Baeza. Santiago: Dirección de Bibliotecas, Archivos y Museos, Centro de Investigaciones Diego Barros Arana, 1993. 315 p.: bibl. (Fuentes para la historia de la república; 6)

An excellent collection of essays, written by men from various social and economic classes, analyzing the Chilean economy. The articles, which advocated the establishment of protectionism in 19th-century Chile demonstrates that free trade was not the prevailing economic doctrine. A particularly useful study because it provides the reader easy access to these essential works.

2761 Etchepare Jensen, Juan Antonio. Ibáñez y su revolución de 1952. (*Política/Santiago*, 26, mayo 1991, p. 61–95, tables)

Ibáñez triumphed in the 1952 presidential election by winning over an electorate disillusioned with traditional parties and their failed nostrums. Unfortunately, Ibáñez's support quickly disintegrated, leaving the general to face a well-organized and uncooperative opposition. During his regime, some important political changes occurred—although not due to Ibáñez's efforts—including the emergence of the PDC. Excellent overview of a critical period.

2762 Fermandois H., Joaquín. Abismo y cimiento: Gustavo Ross y las relaciones entre Chile y Estados Unidos, 1932–1938. Santiago: Ediciones Univ. Católica de Chile, 1997. 335 p.: bibl., ill., index. (Investigaciones)

Splendid work on the pre-Popular Front era, particularly the activities of Gustavo Ross Santa María and the election of Aguirre Cerda. Ross managed to improve the economy and reduce Chile's foreign debt through a variety of schemes, including fleecing the foreign bond holders. Relying heavily on primary sources, this is required reading for political and diplomatic historians.

2763 Fischer, Ferenc. La expansión indirecta de la ciencia militar alemana en América Latina del Sur: la cooperación militar entre Alemania y Chile y las misiones militares germanófilas chilenas en los países latinoamericanos, 1885–1914. (*in* Tordesillas y sus consecuencias: la política de las grandes potencias europeas respecto a América Latina, 1494–1899. Frankfurt: Vervuert; Madrid: Iberoamericana, 1995, p. 243–260)

Chile's military missions in Ecuador, Paraguay, Venezuela, Colombia, and Central America, as well as its training of cadets from these nations in the *Escuela Militar*, indirectly spread German influence among Latin American military forces. It also made these nations into markets for German military equipment and weapons.

Fraga, Rosendo. Roca y Chile. See item **2891.**

2764 Góngora Escobedo, Alvaro. La prostitución en Santiago, 1813–1931: visión de las elites. Prologo de Gonzalo Vial Correa. Santiago: Dirección de Bibliotecas Archivos y Museos; Centro de Investigaciones Diego Barros Arana, 1994. 259 p.: bibl., ill. (Col. Sociedad y cultura; 8)

Chileans tried to regulate prostitution, essentially for reasons of public health. Only later did the government and private organizations attack the phenomenon for its exploitation of the sex worker. This innovative and well-researched study traces the spread of the sex industry and explains the origin and plight of its participants. Also discusses the state's involvement and the prostitutes' income, origins, and working conditions.

2765 González Miranda, Sergio. Hombres y mujeres de la Pampa: Tarapacá en el ciclo del salitre. v. 1. Iquique, Chile: Taller de Estudios Regionales, 1991. 1 v.: bibl., ill., maps. (Ediciones especiales Camanchaca; 2)

An excellent work, often employing interviews, describing life in the *salitreras:* the various social classes, the jobs they performed, the process of extraction, as well as production, transportation, and the methods employed to recruit labor. Includes sections on the infamous system of *fichas* and the *pulperías.* Essential work based on rich sources.

2766 Grez Toso, Sergio. La trayectoria histórica del mutualismo en Chile, 1853–1990: apuntes para su estudio. (*Mapocho/Santiago*, 35, primer semestre 1994, p. 293–315)

Beginning in the mid-19th century, Mutual aid societies provided a means for workers to protect themselves and their families. When anarchism, socialism, as well as different political parties obtained government legislation to help the workers, the mutualist system collapsed.

Güenaga, Rosario. Santa Cruz y Magallanes: historia socioeconómica de los territorios de la Patagonia Austral, Argentina y Chile. See item **2914.**

2767 La guerra civil de 1891: 100 años hoy. Edición de Luis Ortega. Santiago: Univ. de Santiago de Chile, 1993. 195 p.: bibl., ill.

Essays dealing with the Balmaceda period include immigration, frontier life, and historiography. Particularly meritorious are the works of Reyes, who blamed Balmaceda's repression for driving the nitrate workers into the Congressional camp, and Pinto, who concurred, but who noted that the workers quickly began revering the man they helped overthrow. A new look at an old topic.

2768 Huerta, María Antonieta. Otro agro para Chile: historia de la reforma agraria en el proceso social y político. Santiago: CISEC-CESOC, 1989. 413 p.: bibl., ill., maps.

Agrarian reform, which began because of government involvement, subsequently became the hobby horse first of the left and then the Centrist parties. The UPs accelerated program, while abolishing the hacienda and creating rural unions, also reduced productivity. Good overview of the issue of agrarian reform.

2769 Ibáñez Santa María, Adolfo. El líder en los gremios empresariales y su contribución al desarrollo del Estado moderno durante la década de 1930. (*Historia/Santiago*, 28, 1994, p. 183–216)

CORFO succeeded because it could draw upon the technical expertise of the private sector which, in cooperation with the state, had systematically encouraged Chile's mining, industrial, and agrarian sectors. Although beginning in the 1920s, these technocrats became more prominent in the Great Depression, providing key leadership at critical moments.

2770 **Illanes O., María Angélica.** *Ausente, señorita:* el niño chileno, la escuela para pobres y el auxilio, 1890–1990; hacia una historia social del siglo XX en Chile. Colaboración profesional de Luis Moulián. Santiago: Junta Nacional de Auxilio Escolar y Becas, 1991. 328 p.: bibl., ill.

Superb study on the attempt by Chile's educational establishment to improve the lot of children and its involuntary abandonment of this role after 1973. By incorporating new materials, the book benefits the social historian by providing a wealth of information on the growth and impact of the educational establishment on Chile's youth.

2771 **Inmigración española en Chile.** Edición de Baldomero Estrada Turra. Santiago: Univ. de Chile; Univ. de Santiago de Chile; Univ. Católica de Valparaíso; Univ. Metropolitana de Ciencias de la Educación; Embajada de España, 1994. 191 p.: bibl. (Serie Nuevo Mundo: Cinco Siglos, 0176–7571; 8)

A series of excellent essays focused on Spanish immigrants who resided in Antofagasta, Santiago, Valparaíso, Concepción, and Magallanes. Beginning with the mid-18th century, they describe the composition of the Spanish population, often their place of origin, their occupations, marriage patterns, as well as social, charitable, religious, and economic institutions.

2772 **Krebs, Ricardo; M. Angélica Muñoz; and Patricio Valdivieso.** Historia de la Pontificia Universidad Católica de Chile, 1888–1988. v. 1–2. Santiago: Ediciones Univ. Católica de Chile, 1994. 2 v. (1272 p.): bibl., ill.

A monumental effort tracing the evolution of the Catholic Univ. from its inception to the late 1980s when it had established branches throughout the country. Covering the entire university, the work describes the growth of *La Católica*, the formation of different departments, and the results of each rector's term of office.

Lavrin, Asunción. Women, feminism, and social change in Argentina, Chile, and Uruguay, 1890–1940. See item **3121.**

2773 **McGee Deutsch, Sandra.** Anti-Semitism and the Chilean Movimiento Nacional Socialista, 1932–1941. (*in* The Jewish diaspora in Latin America: new studies on

history and literature. New York: Garland Publ., 1996, p. 161–181, bibl.)

Chile's National Socialist Movement, unlike its German model, only briefly espoused anti-Semitism (1935–37), and it never considered Jews biologically inferior. When they sought to identify themselves with local forces, the Nacistas may have abandoned Jew-baiting but anti-Semitism did not disappear.

Mezzano Lopetegui, Silvia. Chile e Italia: un siglo de relaciones bilaterales, 1861–1961. See *HLAS 57:4389.*

2774 **Los mil días de Allende.** v. 1–2. Santiago: Centro de Estudios Públicos, 1997. 2 v.: ill., indexes.

Marvelous collection of newspaper editorials, reflecting different political opinions, on the Allende period. Also contains numerous pictures as well as documents plus various political cartoons. A godsend to scholars who wish to avoid grimy archives.

2775 **Nazer Ahumada, Ricardo.** José Tomás Urmeneta: un empresario del siglo XIX. Santiago: Dirección de Bibliotecas, Archivos y Museos, Centro de Investigaciones Diego Barros Arana, 1994. 289 p.: bibl., ill. (Col. Sociedad y cultura; 7)

Well-researched biography of a man who exemplified the ability of Chilean miners to diversify economically by spreading their investments throughout the entire economy. Urmeneta demonstrates the skills of Chilean capitalism, investing the profits from mines in smelting, railroads, utilities, industrial factories, flour mills, and banks.

2776 **Norambuena Carrasco, Carmen.** Las sociedades de socorros mútuos y de beneficiencia: otra fuente para el estudio de la imigración a Chile. (Colección nuestra patria es América: migraciones y vida urbana. Recopilación de Jorge Núñez Sánchez. Quito: Editora Nacional, 1992, v. 9, p. 43–63, tables)

Mutual benefit societies, particularly those identifying with specific ethnic groups, provided an excellent research tool to study the history and the composition of certain immigrant communities. In this case, the composition, sex, and place of origin of Chile's Spanish community is explored. Useful model for scholars interested in ethnic or social history.

Orlove, Benjamin S. Meat and strength: the moral economy of a Chilean food riot. See *HLAS 57:1114.*

2777 Pereira L., Teresa. El Partido Conservador, 1930–1965: ideas, figuras y actitudes. Santiago: Fundación Mario Góngora, 1994. 470 p.: bibl., ill.

The Conservative Party flourished thanks to its discipline and organization. The rise of a left wing among the Churchmen, the defection of the Falange, coupled with a general discontent with political parties, electoral reform, and an independent peasantry, eventually shattered its cohesion. An inability to distinguish reform from extremism completed the process of decay. Important political study worth reading.

2778 Pinto Vallejos, Julio. Cortar raíces, criar fama: el peonaje chileno en la fase inicial del ciclo salitrero, 1850–1879. (*Siglo XIX/Monterrey*, 3:9, mayo/agosto 1994, p. 107–134)

The 1890 *salitre* strike was important because it marked the transition of peasants into the proletariat. This transformation began as *peones* moved northward from Chile's Central Valley, where they worked in *salitreras, guano* mines, and built railroads. In the process, the *peones* became part of the wage economy and developed a new identity.

2779 Pinto Vallejos, Julio. El mercado minero como estímulo para la primera etapa de industrialización nacional: Chile, 1850–1914. (*in* Circuitos mercantiles y mercados en Latinoamérica, siglos XVIII-XIX. México: Instituto de Investigaciones Dr. José María Luis Mora; Instituto de Investigaciones Históricas UNAM, 1995, p. 397–441, graphs, map, tables)

Mining in the north stimulated the creation and growth of Chilean industries. It also set an example by adopting new technologies. Rather than try to remain competitive, Chile's elites instead relied upon foreign technologies, workers, and capital. Unfortunately, dependency on the volatile mining sector proved dangerous to Chile's economy.

2780 Pinto Vallejos, Julio. Minería e industrialización: la economía del norte chileno y los inicios de la industria nacional, 1850–1914. (Minería americana colonial y del siglo XIX. México: Instituto Nacional de Antropología e Historia, 1994, p. 55–67)

Chileans settled in Bolivia as part of a larger migration from the Chilean countryside, first to the cities and then to foreign nations. Bolivia's *guaneras, salitreras,* and silver mines attracted Chileans who often clashed with local authorities and each other. This process integrated the former *campesinos* into a money economy which they could not achieve in Chile.

2781 Poblete, Olga. Una mujer, Elena Caffarena. Santiago: Ediciones la Morada/Editorial Cuarto Propio, 1993. 110 p.: bibl., ill. (Serie Ensayo)

A flattering but brief study of Caffarena stressing her role in the politics of the Chilean left, the women's suffrage movement, the law, and resistance to the Pinochet regime. Sometimes anecdotal, it nonetheless includes some primary sources, placing Caffarena in the vanguard of the progressive movement in Chile. Good starting point for research.

2782 Rebolledo Hernández, Antonia. La *turcofobia:* discriminación antiárabe en Chile, 1900–1950. (*Historia/Santiago*, 28, 1994, p. 249–272, bibl.)

Unfortunately for them, Arabs migrated to Chile just when the nation had become more xenophobic. Even before the "Turcos" arrived, Chileans had manifested anti-Arab sentiments, the result of certain preconceived and erroneous notions. Lampooned and without diplomatic protection, the Chilean-Arab community did not come into its own until the 1952 election of Ibáñez. Interesting as one of the few studies to focus on this important but often overlooked immigrant community.

2783 Rojas Flores, Jorge. La dictadura de Ibáñez y los sindicatos, 1927–1931. Santiago: Dirección de Bibliotecas, Archivos y Museos, Centro de Investigaciones Diego Barros Arana, 1993. 190 p.: bibl., ill. (Col. Sociedad y cultura; 6)

Utilizing primary sources, many taken from parts of the Minister of Labor's heretofore unexamined archives, Rojas shows that Ibáñez pursued two policies: 1) repressing political activities of unions, and 2) using the power of the state to incorporate the working class into Chilean society. Ibáñez, in short, substituted the government for the old liberal laissez-faire policies.

2784 Saavedra Fuentes, Marcelo.
Movimiento Nacionalista y proyecto
de desarrollo, 1910–1920. (*Rev. Hist./Concepción*, 4:4, 1994, p. 133–167)
The Movimiento Nacionalista, which
culminated in the National Party, analyzed
Chile's socioeconomic realities and called for
economic nationalism, monetary and tax reforms, a return to the presidential form of
government, and compulsory education.
Demonstrates that demands for reforms often associated with Alessandri had, in fact,
developed earlier.

2785 Sagredo Baeza, Rafael. Fuentes e historiografía de la manufactura e industria
textil: Chile, siglo XIX. (*Am. Lat. Hist. Econ.
Bol. Fuentes*, 4, julio/dic. 1995, p. 29–36,
bibl.)
Places the textile industry within the
context of Chile's economic development
while providing scholars with a short bibliography of various sources. Not earth shattering but still useful.

2786 Salinas Meza, René. El ideario femenino chileno, entre la tradición y la
modernidad: siglos XVIII al XX. São Paulo:
Centro de Estudos de Demografia Histórica
da América Latina, Univ. de São Paulo,
Faculdade de Filosofia, Letras e Ciências
Humanas, 1993. 91 p.: bibl. (Estudos
CEDHAL; 8)
Using clerical records, one essay described the contrasting concepts of honor of
men and women in early Chile as well as the
phenomenon of domestic violence. Other
studies chronicle the suffrage movement and
women's slow integration into the educational system. Employing a variety of essentially primary sources, author opens new
vistas.

Salinas Meza, René. La violencia conyugal y
el rol de la mujer en la sociedad chilena tradicional: siglos XVIII y XIX. See item **2412.**

2787 Sater, William F. and Holger H. Herwig. The grand illusion: the prussianization of the Chilean Army. Lincoln: Univ.
of Nebraska Press, 1999. 247 p.: bibl., index.
(Studies in war, society, and the military)
Well-researched and welcome work on
the German efforts to train the Chilean army
during the Parliamentary Regime (1891–
1924). Argues convincingly that what appeared outwardly to be a Prussian-style military was in reality an ill-fed, poorly equipped
military force rife with corruption and low
on morale. Many of the German trainers,
themselves, contributed to the malaise by
seeking profits from weapons sales and land
deals. Oddly, perhaps, the Chilean army continues to display the influences of the German era. [L. Boudon]

2788 Silva, Patricio. State, public technocracy and politics in Chile, 1927–1941.
(*Bull. Lat. Am. Res.*, 13:3, Sept. 1994,
p. 281–297)
State involvement in fomenting industry occurred as early as the 1920s, when
Ibáñez appointed Pablo Ramírez to oversee
the government's economic policy. Henceforth, trained engineers acted as mediators,
exercising power in formulating and implementing economic policy while acting independently of political parties.

Stang, Gudmund. Compañía Corocoro de Bolivia, 1873–1923: a Chilean copper-mining
venture in Bolivia seen in the context of the
contemporary development of the industry.
See item **2746.**

2789 Subercaseaux, Bernardo. Historia del
libro en Chile, alma y cuerpo. Santiago: Editorial Andrés Bello, 1993. 266 p.:
bibl., ill., indexes.
Chileans did not produce many books
until the emergence of a middle class, which
created a market. This in turn lead to the formation of various private editorial houses.
After the 1973 coup, those editorial houses
which survived had to reorient their efforts
to win market space which had become increasingly crowded by the rise of publishing
being produced by various private *centros.*
Useful for intellectual historians.

2790 Supplee, Joan. Women and the
counter-revolution in Chile. (*in*
Women and revolution in Africa, Asia, and
the New World. Edited by Mary Ann
Tétreault. Colombia, South Carolina: Univ.
of South Carolina Press, 1994, p. 394–412)
Women voters lost their sense of solidarity once they became enfranchised. Females seemed more involved with the PDC
than the left which alienated them since it
emphasized class rather than gender. The

women, encouraged and sometimes organized by the PDC, spearheaded opposition to Allende. While initially supporting Pinochet, many eventually turned on him.

Sznajder, Mario. El nacionalsocialismo chileno de los años treinta. See item **5203.**

Tierra del Fuego en cuatro textos: del siglo XVIII al XX. See item **3061.**

Valdés, Ximena; Loreto Rebolledo G.; and **Angélica Willson Aedo.** Masculino y femenino en la hacienda chilena del siglo XX. See *HLAS 57:5185.*

2791 Valdivia Ortiz de Zárate, Verónica. La milicia republicana: los civiles en armas, 1932–1936. Santiago: Dirección de Bibliotecas, Archivos y Museos; Centro de Investigaciones Diego Barros Arana, 1992. 132 p.: bibl., ill. (Col. Sociedad y cultura; 2)

A well-researched study of the *Milicia Republicana,* the white guard that served to restore order following the turbulent days of 1931–32. Alessandri and the military used the group to buttress authority. Once the political situation had normalized, the group was disbanded, although it still influenced politics.

2792 Venegas Valdebenito, Hernán. La huelga grande del carbón, 1920. (*Rev. Chil. Hist. Geogr.,* 160, 1992/93, p. 225–249, tables)

This strike, which spread to and crippled Chile's economy, was important because it forced the central government, for the first time, to become involved in the resolution of the labor problem. The stoppage also galvanized the workers, increasing their sense of class consciousness, and altering the nature of the political process.

2793 Vergara Quiroz, Sergio. Historia social del ejército de Chile. v. 1, Ejército, sociedad, y familia en los siglos XVIII y XIX. v. 2, Los oficiales y sus familias en el siglo XIX. Santiago: Univ. de Chile, Vicerrectoría Académica y Estudiantil, Depto. Técnico de Investigación, 1993. 2 v.: bibl., ill. (Serie de programas de desarrollo; 4)

A careful analysis of the army's officer corps, its origins, education, social status, activities, and families. Vol. 2 provides extensive biographical information, including whom they married and their offspring. Un-

fortunately, the work does not cover the entire 19th century. Extensively researched, using primary sources, albeit sometimes turgidly written.

2794 Vial Correa, Gonzalo. Historia de Chile, 1891–1973. v. 4, La dictadura de Ibáñez, 1925–1931. Santiago: Editorial Fundación, 1996. 1 v.: bibl., ill., indexes.

A superb addition to his ongoing multivolume study of post-1891 Chile. This time Vial investigated the impact of Ibáñez's regime on Chile's economic and political development, its public administration, and the growth of the state. Provides an analysis of the dictator and the men who surrounded him. Essential for scholars. For comment on vol. 2, see *HLAS 46:3147.* For comment on vol. 3, see *HLAS 52:2617.*

2795 Vicealmirante Lord Thomas Alexander Cochrane. v. 1, Mando y organización naval. v. 2, Génesis, desarrollo y consecuencias del primer crucero. Chile: Armada de Chile, 1994. 2 v.: ill. (Archivo histórico naval; 1)

Two-volume compilation of documents from Lord Cochrane, first admiral of Chile's navy. A marvelous source for naval historians dedicated to the early national period.

2796 Volk, Steven S. Crecimiento sin desarrollo: los propietarios mineros chilenos y la caída de la minería en el siglo XIX. (*in* Minería americana colonial y del siglo XIX. México: Instituto Nacional de Antropología e Historia, 1994, p. 69–118, bibl., tables)

A well-researched article demonstrating the different goals of the rebels of 1851 and 1859 as well as the participation of the mining sector. The 1851 rebellion was a class war while that of 1859 enjoyed the support of large-scale miners. Clearly the mining interests were neither monolithic nor, as was claimed, radical.

2797 Wagner, Gert. Trabajo, producción y crecimiento: la economía chilena, 1860–1930. Santiago: Pontificia Univ. Católica de Chile, Instituto de Economía, 1992. 162, 55 p.: bibl., index. (Documento de Trabajo, 0716–7334; 150)

Essential work providing detailed statistical information on Chile's population, size of work force, type of work performed, salaries, prices charges, agricultural and pastoral activity and productivity. There is also a smaller section on mining. Extraordinarily useful.

2798 Zárate Campos, María Soledad. Vicious women, virtuous women: the female delinquent and the Santiago de Chile correctional house, 1860–1900. (*in* The birth of the penitentiary in Latin America: essays on criminology, prison reform, and social control. Austin: Univ. of Texas Press, 1996, p. 78–100)

Female prisoners supposedly received gender-based punishment, different from that which their male counterparts had to endure. Nuns, who acted as warders, tried not only to bring the women back to the path of virtue, but also to inculcate into them supposed womenly virtues as well.

2799 Zilci K., Sonia. La ordenanza de aduanas de 1864. (*Cuad. Hist./Santiago,* 10, dic. 1990, p. 109–125, tables)

Intent upon raising revenues, Reyes created a new customs code which ceased to protect domestic industry. Over the years, however, provisions were made to permit duty-free importation of items in order to help local industries. Clearly, free trade lasted but a short time.

Argentina, Paraguay, and Uruguay

JOEL HOROWITZ, *Professor of History, Saint Bonaventure University*
THOMAS WHIGHAM, *Professor of History, University of Georgia*

ARGENTINA

WHILE THE NUMBER OF SCHOLARLY PUBLICATIONS dedicated to 19th-century Argentine history fell slightly during the 1990s, the field has nonetheless moved in some new and exciting directions. Innovative studies in social and intellectual history have appeared, but the most impressive advances have occurred in political history, where young scholars have scouted territories that their seniors left untouched, or reconceptualized older dynamics. Provincial and regional histories, often based on documents drawn from little-known archives, have also made a strong showing this biennium.

The myriad efforts of Argentine elites to construct a modern nation out of a backward and isolated colony have provided material for several studies. Tulio Halperín Donghi's perceptive article on Deán Funes illustrates how the Hispanic past affected the revolutionary mind set in 1810 (item **2919**). José Carlos Chiaramonte argues a similar point in his thoughtful piece on the origins of the state in the Plata, although in this instance, he stresses how Spanish notions of sovereignty led to divisiveness in the aftermath of independence (item **2853**). The political uncertainty of the 1820s took the form of constant intrigue and fear, and soon demands for social order found a broad expression throughout the region, as suggested in Carlos S. Segreti's study of Argentine monarchists (item **3050**).

Caudillismo, not monarchy, was the result. In this context, historians have often portrayed the Rosas regime (1829–52) in stark black and white terms, with little depth or subtlety in their analyses. Jorge Myers' brilliant examination of Rosista political rhetoric, however, presents a far more incisive appraisal of the *Restaurador*, his supporters, and his detractors (item **2985**). The men who counted themselves in the latter group have received thorough, almost encyclopedic, treatment from William Katra (item **2937**), Tulio Halperín Donghi (item **3016**) and, more parenthetically, Alberto Rodolfo Lettieri (item **2950**). Donald S. Castro, in focusing on the solutions these modernizers proposed, provides a welcome summary of the politics of Argentine immigration (item **2848**).

The 19th-century economy, always a major feature in Argentine historiography, is here represented with several useful publications. Carlos Marichal's look at fiscal policy (item **2965**) works well in conjunction with Lyman L. Johnson's insightful piece on the distribution of wealth (item **2930**). The same could be said for Marcela Ferrari's extensively researched article on banking (item **2885**), and María Alejandra Irigoin's study of finances (item **2928**). Thomas Whigham has written extensively on provincial trade (item **3072**).

Argentine military history has not grown significantly, but two works of note have been produced: Julio Mario Luqui Lagleyze on the royalist forces during the independence wars (item **2960**), and Miguel Angel de Marco on the 1864–70 Paraguayan War (item **2964**).

Argentine biography, which in previous years has centered narrowly on San Martín, Rosas, Sarmiento, and various provincial caudillos, has now followed the lead of Nicholas Shumway and others and has branched out to include key intellectual figures. Alberto A. Rivera's article on Martin de Moussy, the French geographer of the Misiones, marks him as a rising scholar in the field (item **3026**). For her part, Josefa Emilia Sabor's account of Pedro de Angelis, the Italian bibliophile who became a valued publicist for Rosas, is a *tour de force* describing an important though understudied figure and his times (item **3038**). [TW]

The writing on the history of Argentina since the 1880s continues to be extremely impressive both in quality and quantity. Almost all of it is done by Argentines and a significant percentage is well researched and raises interesting questions. A problem for historians wishing to consult this body of work is that much appears in journals or in collective books of articles with limited circulation. This is not a new problem and one for which there is no ready solution. Equally disturbing is a growing trend among large commercial publishing houses. These presses are increasingly printing histories, particularly biographies, intended for popular audiences, without any indication of sources. While it is reassuring that there is still a market for history and some of these works are well done, their value for historians is severely limited by the inability to divine the sources of any findings.

Some of these biographies and histories were clearly written with the goal of helping to revive older political traditions. Fraga has continued his attempts to revalidate conservative politics with his biography of Julio A. Roca (item **2890**), whom he calls the most important conservative politician of the first half of the 20th century. While less clearly attempts to revive a political tradition, there have been published popular biographies of three key members of the Socialist Party, Alicia Moreau de Justo, Alfredo Palacios, and Nicolás Repetto (items **2857, 2903,** and **2998,** respectively). Two of the works were published by writers who had been active in Socialist politics.

There also has been a steady outflow of works on the 1960s and 1970s, much of it memoirs or histories which are at least partly based on personal experiences. The quality, as is to be expected, varies widely but provides increasingly large amounts of documentation for future studies. In addition, there have been a number of scholarly works. Gordillo has given us an important study of the creation in the 1960s of a culture of resistance and confrontation among Córdoba's working class (item **2913**). Moyano and Pozzi have done important studies of guerrilla experiences (items **2983** and **3012**). There continues to be a need for more scholarly examination of how and why Argentina fell into the abyss. Perhaps it is still too soon for most to be willing to confront that unpleasant past.

An important trend that has become even more prominent in the last biennium is the growing attention on areas away from the city of Buenos Aires. This salutary refocusing of attention partially just reflects the reality of the country, but it also reflects the dramatic improvements in some of the interior universities. These universities sometimes have published the works that their students and professors have produced.

We now have many areas of historiographical strength away from the capital. Many of the fine studies of rural economic conditions have focused on the southeastern region of Buenos Aires province because of the work being done at the Univ. Nacional del Centro de la Provincia de Buenos Aires in Tandil. With the publication of Gordillo's book on working class culture in Córdoba in the 1960s and the earlier work by James Brennan (*HLAS 56:2979*), we now know more about the working-class and unions in Córdoba in the 1960s than we do about other regions of the country. Gordillo and Brennan provide exemplary models for the type of studies that need to be done elsewhere.

An emerging and welcome trend is what can be labeled the new political history. The authors attempt to study how politics actually functioned, how votes and political support were mobilized. Politics becomes more closely tied to other aspects of life. Alonso (items **2802** and **2803**) and Sabato (items **3037** and **3036**) have continued to expand their pioneering work on elections in the city of Buenos Aires before the electoral reform law of 1912. While the two authors are not in complete agreement, it is now obvious that past generalizations about such elections are no longer viable. Excellent examples that combine political history and social history with attention focused on civic associations can be found in the works of Gutiérrez and Romero (item **2915**) and of Privitellio (item **3015**). Studies based away from the capital can be found in *Los caminos de la democracia* (item **2844**).

In a somewhat more traditional vein, there have been intensive studies of political parties in the interior. Vidal has done a close study of the Radical Party in Córdoba from 1912–30, examining the impact of internal problems and why they occurred (item **3070**). Lacoste has looked at both the Radical (item **2947**) and the Socialist (item **2946**) Parties in Mendoza. In addition, Potash has written a worthy successor to his previous books on the army, this time covering the period from 1962–73 (item **3011**). Caterina has given us an examination of the Liga Patriótica based on a wide use of primary sources (item **2850**).

Probably the most influential and important sector of Argentine society that traditionally has been ignored by most serious scholars is the Roman Catholic Church. Fortunately this has ended. Zanatta has explored the growing role of the Church in the 1930s, especially its relationship with the army (item **3011**). Caimari has studied the Church's relationship with the Perón regime and, with a well-researched effort, has been able to revise many of the traditional views (item **2842**). Burdick provides us with extensive information on the Movement of Priests for the Third World (item **2839**).

There continues to be a sizeable outflow of works on immigrants and the communities they created, though the number of publications seems to have decreased somewhat from recent years. The emphasis of these works continues to diversify. Bjerg (item **2825**) and Cibotti (item **2855**) deal with how different nationalities—Danes and Italians—developed and maintained a sense of identity. Jozami, meanwhile, studies the number of Muslims that were present in Argentina (item **2934**). Klich writes on different aspects of immigration to Argentina in the post-World War II era (items **2939, 2940,** and **2941**).

Studies of the rural economy of Buenos Aires province, especially the southeastern sector, continue to appear in considerable numbers. They are slowly altering our vision of the nature of the rural economy. The relationships between estancieros and tenants were more complex than previously thought. Important work is also being done on other provinces, both in the humid pampas and beyond, although in much less quantity. For example, Paz has examined the evolution of landholding among the indigenous peasantry of the puna of Jujuy between 1875 and 1910 (item **3001**), while Maluendres has given us an overview of wheat farming in its first decades in La Pampa (item **2962**). A hint of a crucial avenue for future studies is Stoffel's short book on the Grandes Almacenes Ripamonti which sold a wide variety of goods to the population of rural Santa Fe (item **3055**). While more suggestive than definitive, it indicates that it is possible to study merchants who provided credit and goods to the countryside.

The greatest departure from *HLAS 56* is a burst of publication on historiography. It is impossible to say why this occurred but it may reflect both a sense of how far the profession has come since the end of the last military dictatorship and a realization that it is time to take stock of the profession's past before pushing on. While not strictly historiographical, *Pensar la Argentina,* perhaps the most interesting of these works, is a series of eight interviews with scholars who write about Argentina's past (half are not, disciplinarily speaking, historians) (item **3003**). There are two overviews of the writing of Argentine history by groups of historians. *La Junta de Historia* is a commemorative volume on the 100th anniversary of the founding of the Academia Nacional de la Historia and covers the period until 1938 (item **2936**); the other, *La historiografía argentina,* has an emphasis on the renovation of the profession in the 1960s (item **2924**). The interest in this supposedly golden era of the writing of history (though it is clearly inferior to today's production) is also reflected in two articles on the influence of the French *Annales* school on the writing of history in Argentina (items **2874** and **2943**). A key participant in that epoch, Tulio Halperín Donghi, has had reprinted a series of historiographical essays composed over many decades (item **2920**). Several works also examine different aspects of the historical production. A fine example is Lobato and Suriano's examination of writing about the working class (item **2953**).

The level of the writing on the period since 1880 continues to be extremely high. The range of topics is wide, though lacunae exist. The first Peronist era, 1946–55, tends to be under-represented. Probably due to the current state of the Argentine publishing industry, there has been a serious lack of monographs that could pull together the many fine shorter studies that have been appearing and create new paradigms. Despite these problems, one can safely say that the quality of the historiograpical production is higher than it has ever been and shows no signs of flagging. [JH]

PARAGUAY

The 1989 collapse of the Stroessner dictatorship ushered in an unprecedented period of political change and self-reflection in Paraguay. While this has resulted in a plethora of books dedicated to national politics, it has not brought a concomitant expansion in new historical works, and there seem to be relatively few on the horizon. Nonetheless, thanks in part to the efforts of European and North American historians, the 1990s witnessed the appearance of several benchmark studies of 19th-century Paraguay.

In social history a major step forward has been made with the publication in German of Barbara Potthast-Jutkeit's monumental study of women and the family from the time of Dr. Francia through the 1870s (item **3092**). The book argues forcefully that patterns of illegitimacy in Paraguay long predate the Paraguayan War. Another German-language publication of interest is Heinz Joachim Domnick's careful consideration of German responses to that war (item **3083**).

One study that addresses the 1864–70 conflict is Augusto Ocampos Caballero's helpful account of Solano López in Spain (and subsequent Spanish-Paraguayan relations) (item **2830**).

In economic history, Thomas Whigham's article on Paraguayan cotton promotion provides a new backdrop to understanding Paraguay's place in world trade in the mid-19th century (item **3101**). His major study on regional trade, which centers on the export of yerba mate, tobacco, hides, and timber from the time of the viceroyalty until 1870, suggests a different approach to economic questions by placing Paraguay in its greater regional context and offering broad comparisons with northeastern Argentina (item **3102**). [TW]

URUGUAY

Unlike Argentina and Paraguay, where 19th-century historical publication has been limited but impressive, in Uruguay, it is barely holding its own, with only three monographs and a handful of articles worthy of mention during this biennium.

Two of the three book-length studies are biographies. Alfonso Fernández Cabrelli has produced a third volume on José Gervasio Artigas that manages to avoid the usual hagiographical overtones (item **3115**). Of somewhat lesser stature, though still worth reading, is Aristides I. Madere Larrosa's account of Blanco leader Manuel Oribe (item **3124**). Carlos Zubillaga has contributed the last of the three outstanding monographs, in this case, a brief but solid examination of Spanish immigration to Uruguay in the 1800s (item **3132**).

In addition to the above studies, special attention should also be paid to two minor works on Uruguayan political history: Ana Frega's interesting article on state formation in the Plata (item **3116**), and Fernando López Alves' competent piece on the origins of liberalism in Uruguay (item **3122**). Finally, Juan Manuel Casal's essay on the early Urugayan army (item **3109**) offers fresh ways of looking at the institution. [TW]

While the historical production on the 20th century is also meager in quantity, the quality tends to be very high. Unlike Argentina, almost all the noteworthy offerings are published in books, several of which are quite innovative. Caetano and Rilla have written a history of modern Uruguay combining text with documents, and short biographies (item **3107**). Chasteen has given us a study of the caudillos Aparacio and Gumercindo Saravia which tells us a great deal about life in the border area between Uruguay and Rio Grande do Sul and also about the role of a caudillo (item **3110**). Well written, the book alternates between descriptions of specific events and discussions of larger topics. [JH]

ARGENTINA

2800 Acerbi, Norberto. Vida y obra del Dr. Eduardo Wilde: la construcción del estado nacional roquista. Buenos Aires: Original & Copia, 1995. 172 p.: bibl., ill.

This sympathetic political biography attempts to restore Wilde to the place that the author feels he deserves in the construction of a strong national state. Emphasizes his role during the administration of Roca and Juárez Celman. [JH]

2801 Acuña, Marcelo Luis. Alfonsín y el poder económico: el fracaso de la concertación y los pactos corporativos entre 1983 y 1989. Buenos Aires: Corregidor, 1995. 429 p.: bibl.

Examines in great detail economic policy-making during the presidency of Alfonsín. Sees the administration's ultimate failure occurring due to the attempts to make social pacts with the corporatist bodies representing labor, agriculture, and industry. Author believes that the administration lost its credibility by attempting policies that had little chance of success. [JH]

2802 Alonso, Paula. Politics and elections in Buenos Aires, 1890–1898: the performance of the Radical Party. (*J. Lat. Am. Stud.*, 25:3, Oct. 1993, p. 465–487, graphs, tables)

An important contribution to the ongoing re-examination of the nature of elections prior to the Ley Sáenz Peña. Argues convincingly that elections in the city of Buenos Aires in the 1890s were not only hotly contested and reasonably fair, but that the Radical Party did well. Also examines social base of Radical Party support. Important both for its examination of the nature of elections and also for the history of the early period of the Radical Party. [JH]

2803 Alonso, Paula. Voting in Buenos Aires before 1912. Buenos Aires: Univ. Torcuato Di Tella, 1995. 24 p.: graph, tables. (Documentos de trabajo; 21)

Part of the ongoing revisionism related to the nature of politics prior to the Sáenz Peña Law of 1912. States that the break in political practices created by the electoral law reform was much less sharp than has been argued. The voting rate in the city of Buenos Aires was higher than normally as-

sumed, in part reflecting the modernization of political habits after 1890. [JH]

2804 Alvarez Gila, Oscar. La formación de la colectividad inmigrante vasca en los países del Río de la Plata, siglo XIX. (*Estud. Migr. Latinoam.*, 10:30, 1995, p. 299–331.)

A suggestive analysis of Basque immigration to the Platine countries in the late-19th century. Shows that while French and Spanish Basques in the Old World normally espoused separate and quite distinct identities, in the Río de la Plata, the two groups came together as a single *colectividad* with its own character and political agenda. [TW]

2805 Amaral, Samuel. Free trade and regional economies: San Juan and Mendoza, 1780–1820. (*in* Revolution and restoration: the rearrangement of power in Argentina, 1776–1860. Edited by Mark D. Szuchman and Jonathan C. Brown. Lincoln: Univ. of Nebraska Press, 1994, p. 124–149, tables)

Nicely crafted economic history of the Cuyo region from the end of the Bourbon era to 1820. Shows that the Cuyan economy was less affected by free trade than by climate, plague, primitive technology, and especially civil war. Includes tables on wine and brandy exports. [TW]

América Latina: planteos, problemas, preguntas. See *HLAS 57:4534*.

2806 Archivo del brigadier general Nazario Benavides. v. 1. San Juan, Argentina: Editorial Fundación Univ. Nacional de San Juan, 1994. 1 v.: bibl., ill.

A useful compendium of documents by and about the Sanjuanino caudillo taken from provincial and national archives. [TW]

2807 Arcondo, Aníbal B. En el reino de Ceres: la expansión agraria en Córdoba, 1870–1914. Córdoba: Univ. Nacional de Córdoba, Facultad de Ciencias Económicas, Instituto de Economía y Finanzas, 1996. 170 p.: bibl., ill., maps.

An excellent study of agriculture and land usage in Córdoba during the "agrarian revolution" at the turn of the century. Argues that in Córdoba, unlike, for example, in Santa Fe, economic and political conditions favored a relative balance between agrarian and ranching sectors, much to the benefit of the provincial elite. [TW]

2808 Arguindeguy, Pablo E. and **Horacio Rodríguez.** Guillermo Brown: apostillas a su vida. Buenos Aires: Instituto Browniano, 1994. 358 p.: bibl., ill., index.

A highly detailed, though uncritical, biography of the founder of the Argentine navy. Uses unusual archival and genealogical sources. [TW]

2809 Armus, Diego. La idea del verde en la ciudad moderna: Buenos Aires, 1870–1940. (*Entrepasados/Buenos Aires*, 5:10, 1996, p. 9–22, ill.)

Examines the idea of the city park as it developed between 1870–1940. Why did people want parks? What purpose were they to serve? This is a combination of intellectual and urban history, based on a wide range of sources. [JH]

2810 Balsa, Javier. La Gran Depresión y los productores rurales del sur triguero de la Pampa Argentina. (*Can. J. Lat. Am. Caribb. Stud.*, 19:37/38, 1994, p. 189–225, graphs, map, tables)

Studies impact of the Great Depression on medium-sized farmers of the partido of Tres Arroyos in the southern wheat belt of Buenos Aires prov. Looks at the social structure as it existed prior to 1929 and how the farmers managed to continue producing despite hard times brought about by economic collapse. Also hypothesizes about long run impact of the depression on Argentina's agricultural decline. Much of the work is based on interviews with older farmers. [JH]

2811 Balsa, Javier. El impacto de la Gran Depresión en la estructura agraria pampeana: un estado de cuestión. (*in* Estudios de historia rural III. Buenos Aires: Facultad de Humanidades y Ciencias de la Educación, 1993, p. 59–77, bibl.)

Reviews literature on the rural economy of the pampas during the 1920s and 1930s. Focuses on the impact of the depression while also clarifying conditions existing prior to its start. Presents different perspectives. [JH]

2812 Bandieri, Susana. Historia regional y relaciones fronterizas en los Andes meridionales: el caso del Neuquén, Argentina. (*Siglo XIX/Monterrey*, 4:12, mayo/agosto 1995, p. 49–73, map)

Good overview of border relations in the northern part of Argentine Patagonia.

Notes that Neuquén traditionally provided foodstuffs for Chilean cities, then saw natural market disrupted by political rivalries between the two countries starting in the early-20th century. Based on secondary sources. For sociologist's comment, see *HLAS* 57:5115. [TW]

2813 Barbero, María Inés. Treinta años de estudios sobre la historia de empresas en la Argentina. (*Ciclos Hist. Econ. Soc.*, 5:8, primer semestre 1995, p. 179–200)

Interesting historiographical piece looks at trends in writings about enterprises in Argentina. Emphasizes industrial firms, but the definition of *empresas* is loose as it encompasses works on organizations such as the Unión Industrial Argentina (UIA). Compares themes in Argentine historiography to trends in writing elsewhere. [JH]

2814 Barrancos, Dora. La escena iluminada: ciencias para trabajadores, 1890–1930. Buenos Aires: Plus Ultra, 1996. 259 p.: bibl., ill.

Looks at the Sociedad de Luz, an organization for popular education in Buenos Aires controlled by the Socialist Party. Examines the organization and the scientific ideas that it taught. [JH]

2815 Barrancos, Dora. El proyecto de *extensión universitaria* en la Argentina: el movimiento obrero entre 1909 y 1918. (*in* Movimientos sociales en la Argentina, Brasil y Chile, 1880–1930. Buenos Aires: Editorial Biblos; Fundación Simón Rodríguez, 1995, p. 77–112, table)

Looks at one part of a project, based on a Spanish model, that aimed at educating workers in Argentina. Element of a larger study on worker education. [JH]

2816 Baschetti, Roberto. Bibliografía de y sobre Eva Perón, 1943–1993. Buenos Aires: R. Baschetti, 1995. 79 leaves. (Bibliográficas, 0328–3283; 1)

An extensive bibliography of work directly relating to Eva Perón, with little annotation. Useful for beginning work. [JH]

2817 Baschetti, Roberto. La interna peronista. v. 1–2. Buenos Aires: R. Baschetti, 1996. 2 v. (82 leaves). (Bibliográficas, 0328–3283; 11–12)

Bibliography of internal conflicts within the Peronist movement largely in the 1970s-80s. [JH]

2818 Baschetti, Roberto. La resistencia peronista: 1955–1973. Buenos Aires: R. Baschetti, 1995. 33 leaves. (Bibliográficas, 0328–3283; 5)

Extensive bibliography deals with Peronist resistance. [JH]

2819 Beato, Guillermo. Grupos sociales dominantes: México y Argentina, siglos XIX-XX. Córdoba, Argentina: Univ. Nacional de Córdoba, 1993. 207 p.: bibl., ill.

Part of a larger study comparing the bourgeois elites in Mexico and Argentina. Work is composed of four articles. Three are roughly parallel examinations of the economic activities that produced the local bourgeoisie in the late-19th and early-20th centuries. While based on archival sources, they are necessarily brief and suggestive. The regions covered are the Mexican state of Jalisco, the Argentine province of Córdoba, and the Argentine territory of Chubut. Fourth article looks at how the merchant community in Córdoba gathered political power in the first half of the 19th century. [JH]

2820 Benejam, Luis Armando. Historia del deporte en Tucumán: origenes, grandes evoluciones y anecdotas hasta 1968/1970, aislados toques actuales, el estado del deporte en 1965, la medicina del deporte en su origen y en la actualidad, periodismo deportivo. v. 1–2. Argentina: s.n., 1995. 2 v. (515 p.): bibl., ill.

This two-vol. collection offers a mine of information on sports, organizations, clubs, and the winners of championships in the prov. of Tucumán. Lacks interpretation, but useful for those looking for obscure facts. [JH]

2821 Bertoni, Lilia Ana. Nacionalidad o cosmopolitismo: la cuestión de las escuelas de las colectividades extranjeras a fines del siglo XIX. (*Anu. IEHS*, 11, 1996, p. 179–199)

Examines late-19th-century education debate in Argentina, which questioned whether immigrant communities should be permitted separate standards for schooling with different curricula. [TW]

2822 Biagini, Hugo Edgardo. Intelectuales y políticos españoles a comienzos de la inmigración masiva. Buenos Aires: Centro Editor de América Latina, 1995. 198 p.: bibl., ill. (Biblioteca Política argentina; 481)

Perceptive study examines ideological and cultural factors of Spain's late-19th-century interest in Argentina. Balances presentation of general intellectual history themes with a series of succinct biographical sketches of key individuals, such as Justo López de Gomara and Serafín Alvarez Peral. [J. Britton]

2823 Bianchi, Susana. Catolicismo y peronismo: la educación como campo de conflicto, 1946–1955. (*Anu. IEHS*, 11, 1996, p. 147–178)

Balanced and thoughtful article examines peronists' view of the role of the Catholic Church in education. While most Peronists at first welcomed the increased presence of the Church in the classroom, the relationship became more complex as the peronists began to project an educational vision of their own that clashed with Catholic values. [JH]

2824 Bisio, Carlos A. Aporte a la bibliografía rioplatense: un impreso protestante sobre la diferenciación religiosa británica en el Plata, 1832. (*Boletín/Buenos Aires*, 2, oct. 1996, p. 75–82)

Short examination of a rare pamphlet detailing religious debates in the British community of Buenos Aires during the early Rosas period. [TW]

2825 Bjerg, María M. Entre Sofie y Tovelille: las escuelas de la comunidad danesa frente al problema de la identidad nacional de las generaciones nacidas en la Argentina, 1886–1930. (*Rev. Indias*, 56:206, enero/abril 1996, p. 133–165)

Looks at how the sizeable Danish community based in and around Tandil dealt with the question of ethnic identification of their Argentine children. Focuses principally on how schools were used to preserve a sense of Danishness. [JH]

2826 Blacha, Noemí M. Girbal de. Explotación forestal, riesgo empresario y diversificación económica: las inversiones argentinas en el Gran Chaco, 1905–1930. (*Rev. Hist. Am.*, 116, julio/dic. 1993, p. 29–57, maps, tables)

Examines beginning of exploitation by Argentine-based companies of the *quebracho* forest reserves of both the Argentine and the

Paraguayan Chaco. These companies were principally interested in the export of tannin. Ties the investment to the opportunities for large profits and the shrinking opportunities for such in the Pampas region. [JH]

2827 Blanco, Mónica Alejandra. Una aproximación al funcionamiento de los arrendamientos rurales en el sudeste bonaerense, 1940–1960. (*in* Problemas de la historia agraria: nuevos debates y perspectivas de investigación. Tandil, Argentina: Instituto de Estudios Histórico Sociales (IEHS), 1995, p. 297–321, bibl., graphs, map, table)

A study of the contracts for renting land in a southeastern *partido* (Juárez) from 1940–60. The contracts are examined in light of changing legislation. [JH]

2828 Boleda, Mario and María Cecilia Mercado. Introducción a la demografía histórica del noroeste argentino. Salta, Argentina: Grupo de estudios socio-demográficos, 1991. 60 p.: bibl., graphs, maps, tables. (Cuadernos del GREDES; 11)

Summarizes demographic trends in northwestern Argentina. Well documented, with statistical information drawn from local and provincial archives. [TW]

2829 Bonasso, Miguel. El presidente que no fue: los archivos ocultos del peronismo. 2. ed. Buenos Aires: Planeta, 1997. 651 p.: bibl., ill. (Espejo de la Argentina)

A well-written history of the period during which Héctor Campora was Perón's chief delegate in Argentina and the period during which he was president. The author, a journalist, was an advisor of Campora, and writes from that perspective. The principal sources, aside from numerous interviews, are the private collection of documents of Campora and of his Minister of Interior Esteban Righi. Lacks footnotes. [JH]

2830 Bosch, Beatriz. Juan María Gutiérrez, canciller de la Confederación Argentina, 1854–1856. Buenos Aires: Consejo Argentino para las Relaciones Internacionales, 1993. 34 p.: bibl., ill. (Los diplomáticos; 6)

The noted biographer of Justo José de Urquiza here traces two years in the career of his foreign minister, Juan María Gutiérrez. As Bosch observes, in that short time, Gutiérrez concluded six international treaties, opened relations with the Holy See,

and began negotiations that led to Spain's recognition of the Argentine Republic. [TW]

2831 Botana, Natalio R. and Ezequiel Gallo. De la república posible a la república verdadera: 1880–1910. Buenos Aires: Compañía Editora Espasa Calpe Argentina: Ariel, 1997. 693 p.: bibl. (Ariel historia)

Part of a collection examining the development of political thought in Argentina through the publication of selections of important writings on politics. Authors have put together an interesting collection of excerpts of important and representative thinkers. Many are those one would expect to find, but others are important revelations. The introduction provides an intellectual history of the period. [JH]

2832 Bou, María Luisa et al. A hacha, cuña y golpe: recuerdos de pobladores, Río Grande, Tierra del Fuego. Argentina: s.n., 1995. 595 p.: ill. (some col.).

A series of well-done interviews with early settlers in the city of Río Grande in Tierra del Fuego, with a solid introduction and numerous photographs. The memories of those who remember the early days of the city are particularly interesting. [JH]

2833 Bravo, María Celia. Cañeros, industriales y mecanismos de arbitraje azucareros en la década del '20. (*Poblac. Soc.*, 1, dic. 1993, p. 35–46, graphs)

Looks at the position of the cane growers vis-à-vis the processors during the crisis of the 1920s. Argues that the growers were less strong than posited by some recent works. [JH]

2834 Brennan, James P. *Clasismo* and the workers: the ideological-cultural context of *Sindicalismo de Liberación* in the Cordoban automobile industry, 1970–1975. (*Bull. Lat. Am. Res.*, 15:3, Sept. 1996, p. 293–308, bibl.)

Examines why some union leaders in Córdoba broke with traditional peronismo to follow the clasista pattern. In some aspects—especially regarding culture—author moves beyond his 1994 book (see *HLAS 56:2979*). [JH]

2835 Brennan, James P. Industrial sectors and union politics in Latin American labor movements: light and power workers in

Argentina and Mexico. (*LARR*, 30:1, 1995, p. 39–68, bibl.)

Brennan states that the nature of the industry needs to be considered in studies of labor unions. To illustrate his point, he describes the different trajectories of light and power workers during several decades in Buenos Aires and Córdoba in Argentina, and in Mexico. He ties their policy differences to the different structures and problems of the electrical industry. For Mexican historian's comment, see item **1397**. [JH]

2836 Brown, Jonathan C. Revival of the rural economy and society in Buenos Aires. (*in* Revolution and restoration: the rearrangement of power in Argentina, 1776–1860. Edited by Mark D. Szuchman and Jonathan C. Brown. Lincoln: Univ. of Nebraska Press, 1994, p. 240–272)

Examines the changing character of labor relations and forms of production in rural areas around Buenos Aires from late colonial times to the last decades of the 19th century. Shows how elites and state authorities developed strategies for the economy that promoted a broad expansion of the export sector. [TW]

2837 Buenos Aires, 1880–1930: la capital de un imperio imaginario. Recopilación de Horacio Vázquez Rial. Madrid: Alianza Editorial, 1996. 443 p.: bibl., ill. (Memoria de las ciudades)

Beautifully produced compilation of essays on the society and city life of Buenos Aires at the turn of the century. Urban historians will appreciate Juan José Sebreli's piece on the middle-class "habitat" and Ernesto Goldar's on "la mala vida." [TW]

2838 Buenos Aires ayer: testimonios gráficos de una ciudad; 1854–1930. Proyecto y dirección general de Manrique Zago = Buenos Aires yesteryear: a city in pictures; 1854–1930. English version by Harold Sinnot and Flaviana Penna. Buenos Aires: M. Zago, 1994. 190 p.: chiefly ill.

A series of interesting, well-presented photographs, mostly from the 1890s-1930, stored in the Museo de la Ciudad or the Archivo General de la Nación in Buenos Aires. The text, in both Spanish and English, is adequate, but does not give full historical

context. Does not explain how pictures were chosen. [JH]

2839 Burdick, Michael A. For God and the fatherland: religion and politics in Argentina. Albany: State Univ. of New York Press, 1995. 283 p.: bibl., index. (SUNY series in religion, culture, and society)

Title is somewhat misleading. While the work presents information on the conflict between church and state in the 1880s and examines the Perón regime's relationship with the Church, the heart of the book is much more tightly defined. Presents a detailed and sympathetic picture of the Movement for Priests of the Third World, a leftist tendency within the Church that favored peronism, during the 1960s-70s. [JH]

2840 Burzaco, Ricardo. Infierno en el Monte Tucumano: Argentina, 1973–1976. Buenos Aires: RE Editores, 1994. 162 p.: bibl., ill. (some col.), maps.

Study of military operations in the mountains of Tucuman against the Ejército Revolucionario del Pueblo (ERP) guerrillas. Written from the perspective of the military. [JH]

2841 Cabezas, Horacio. Villa María y su radicalismo. Córdoba, Argentina: Imprenta Brignone, 1991. 730, 24 p.: bibl., ill.

Provides details of the evolution of the Radical Party in the city of Villa María, Córdoba from 1901 until the military coup of 1943. Pays particular attention to hometown political activist Amadeo Sabattini. Work is a collection of data of varied types. Gives some information on the province as well. Offers little analysis. [JH]

2842 Caimari, Lila M. Perón y la Iglesia Católica: religión, Estado y sociedad en la Argentina, 1943–1955. Buenos Aires: Ariel Historia, 1995. 390 p.: bibl.

A sophisticated and intelligent investigation of the relationship between Perón, his regime, and the Catholic Church. The wide-ranging study, based on extensive research, reveals a much more complex relationship than has been previously hypothesized. For political scientist's comment, see *HLAS* 57:3692. [JH]

2843 Calvimonte, Luis Q. and **Alejandro Moyano Aliaga.** El antiguo camino real al Perú en el norte de Córdoba. Prólogo de

Jorge A. Maldonado. Córdoba, Argentina: Ediciones del Copista, 1996. 246 p.: bibl., ill., maps.

Interesting examination of the caravan route linking Córdoba province with Upper Peru. Anecdotal in tone with many details on independence-era political figures. [TW]

2844 Los caminos de la democracia: alternativas y prácticas políticas, 1900–1943. Recopilación de Julio César Melón Pirro and Elisa Pastoriza. Prólogo de Fernando Devoto. Buenos Aires: Editorial Biblos, 1996. 268 p.: bibl., ill., maps.

A series of solid articles on political history. Contains articles on Brazil and Uruguay, and one on *La Nación's* views. The rest are studies on the provincial level (three on Santa Fe, two on Buenos Aires, and one on Córdoba) and on the municipal level (two on Mar del Plata and one on Campana). [JH]

2845 Cane, James. "Unity for the defense of culture": the AIAPE and the cultural politics of Argentine antifascism, 1935–1943. (*HAHR*, 77:3, Aug. 1997, p. 443–469)

Examines development and evolution of an anti-Fascist organization composed of intellectuals. Claims that the organization laid the foundation for left-wing nationalism. [JH]

2846 Cano Rossini, Lelia. La mujer mendocina de 1800: una revolución cultural en marcha. 2. ed. Mendoza, Argentina: Ediciones Culturales de Mendoza, 1996. 368 p.: bibl., ill., index.

History of Mendocino women during the 19th century that is useful for those interested in the daily lives of Argentine women. One particularly valuable section discusses the role of North American headmistresses who helped develop primary and secondary educational institutions in the province of Mendoza. [TW]

2847 Cansanello, Oreste C. De súbditos a ciudadanos: los pobladores rurales bonaerenses entre el antiguo régimen y la modernidad. (*Bol. Inst. Hist. Ravignani,* 11, primer semestre 1995, p. 113–139, map, tables)

Suggestive essay on the politics of rural *vecinos* in Buenos Aires prov. during the first third of the 19th century. Argues convincingly that behind a new rhetoric of citizenship and representative institutions, the

traditional power-brokers continued to dominate the countryside. [TW]

2848 Castro, Donald S. The development and politics of Argentine immigration policy, 1852–1914: to govern is to populate. San Francisco: Mellen Research Univ. Press, 1991. 310 p.: bibl., index. (A Distinguished dissertation; v. 22)

A readable and highly informative history of immigration policy in Argentina. Shows that immigrants came to the country because of perceived economic opportunities, rather than because of specific government recruitment programs. Based on the author's 1970 doctoral dissertation. [TW]

2849 Castro Boedo, Emilio. Estudios sobre la navegación del Bermejo y la colonización del Chaco, 1872. San Salvador, Argentina: Univ. Nacional de Jujuy, 1995. 224 p. (Biblioteca de Historia y Antropología; 3)

Reissue of a classic work, first published in 1872, that details the early exploration and settlement of the Argentine Chaco, Salta, Jujuy, and riverine areas of eastern Bolivia. Worth reading for its descriptions of indigenous peoples and languages, flora and fauna, and landforms. [TW]

2850 Caterina, Luis María. La Liga Patriótica Argentina: un grupo de presión frente a las convulsiones sociales de la década del veinte. Buenos Aires: Corregidor, 1995. 333 p.: bibl., ill.

Re-examines the right-wing nationalist group using extensively primary sources. In a thoughtful manner, places the Liga in its time and judges its impact. [JH]

2851 Cecchini de Dallo, Ana María. Urbanización y arraigo de la población en el sistema de colonización de Santa Fe: segunda mitad del siglo XIX. (*Rev. Junta Prov. Estud. Hist. Santa Fe,* 59, 1993, p. 107–141, bibl., maps)

A short, detailed study of townships established as part of colonization efforts in 19th-century Santa Fe. Colonies addressed include Esperanza, San Carlos, San Jerónimo, Helvecia, California, Cayastá, Rafaela, and Chabas. [TW]

2852 Cejas Minuet, Monica and Mirta Pieroni. Mujeres en las naciones afroargentinas de Buenos Aires. (*Am. Negra,* 8, dic. 1994, p. 133–145, bibl.)

A thin but suggestive account of women's roles within the various Afro-Argentine benevolent societies of Buenos Aires during the mid-19th century. [TW]

2853 Chiaramonte, José Carlos. Acerca del orígen del estado en el Río de la Plata. (*Anu. IEHS*, 10, 1995, p. 27–50)

An impressive study of political ideology and the origins of the state in postcolonial Rio de la Plata. Argues that in forging a new political order, the patriots made considerable use of precedents from the *ancien régime*; notes that the civil strife that followed independence resulted from the conflicting sovereignties of various Platine cities, with the predominance of Buenos Aires by no means recognized by other communities (again, very much in the tradition of metropolitan Spain). [TW]

2854 Chiaramonte, José Carlos; Marcela Ternavasio; and Fabián Herrero. Vieja y nueva representación: los procesos electorales en Buenos Aires, 1810–1820. (*in* Historia de las elecciones en Iberoamérica, siglo XIX: de la formación del espacio político nacional. Coordinación de Antonio Annino. Buenos Aires: Fondo de Cultura Económica, 1995, p. 19–63, map)

An insightful and readable account of political institutions and electioneering practices in newly independent Argentina. Notes that the recently installed system of indirect elections failed to bring about necessary reforms in the province's main representative body, the Cabildo, which resulted in its being abolished as an anachronistic infringement on popular rule. [TW]

2855 Cibotti, Ema. Periodismo político y política periodística: la construcción pública de una opinión italiana en el Buenos Aires finisecular. (*Entrepasados/Buenos Aires*, 4:7, 1994, p. 7–25, ill.)

Examines how the Italian-language press helped create an Italian community in Buenos Aires at the end of the 19th century. Uses as its theoretical focus Benedict Anderson's *Imagined Communities* (1991). [JH]

2856 Cibotti, Ema. Sufragio, prensa y opinión pública: las elecciones municipales de 1883 en Buenos Aires. (*in* Historia de las elecciones en Iberoamérica, siglo XIX: de la formación del espacio político nacional. Coordinación de Antonio Annino. Buenos

Aires: Fondo de Cultura Económica, 1995, p. 141–175)

A tautly written study of the 1883 municipal elections in Buenos Aires, which pitted Autonomists against Liberals; the results of the vote confirmed President Roca's domination of porteño politics. Cibotti shows how the election was decided in the local press before a single ballot was cast. [TW]

2857 Cichero, Marta. Alicia Moreau de Justo. Buenos Aires: Planetas, 1994. 224 p.: bibl., ill. (Mujeres argentinas)

A popular biography that deals more with Moreau de Justo's personal life than her political life. Essentially stops with the death of Juan B. Justo. Also includes fragments from various interviews with the subject of the book. [JH]

2858 Cirigliano, Gustavo F.J. Por qué vino Ud., Clara J. Armstrong, a la Argentina? Argentina: s.n., 1996. 92 p.: bibl., ill.

A short account of the 65 North American schoolmistresses contracted by the Argentine government between 1869–98 to found and operate teaching colleges in the country. The project was the brainchild of Domingo F. Sarmiento, who intended to bring to Argentina the educational reforms initiated in the US by his friend Horace Mann. [TW]

2859 Civit de Ortega, Josefina. Don Emilio Civit, político y gobernante. v. 1–2. Mendoza, Argentina: Ediciones Culturales de Mendoza: Junta de Estudios Históricos de Mendoza, 1994. 2 v. (538 p.).

An extensive biographical treatment of a key Mendocino statesman who, between 1880s and 1910s, helped define conservative politics in Cuyo. Draws background material principally from family sources. [TW]

2860 Clementi, Hebe. El protagonismo de La Boca, 1850–1890. Buenos Aires: Ediciones Letra Buena, 1994. 102 p.: bibl. (Colección Temas de historia)

A brief but incisive history of the port district of Buenos Aires, and especially of the Italian immigrants who gave the district its particular flavor. Coverage is limited to the early period, when the railroads first linked La Boca to the rest of the nation. [TW]

**2861 Comunidad Judía de Buenos Aires,
1894–1994.** Buenos Aires: Milá: Asociación Mutual Israelita Argentina, 1995. 303 p.: bibl., ill.

An official history commemorating the centenary of organized Jewish life in Argentina. Examines history of the organized segment of Jewish life in a manner to be expected from such a work. Contains many photographs. [JH]

2862 Conti, Viviana E. Articulación mercantil en los albores del siglo XIX. (*in* Jujuy en la historia: avances de investigación. Jujuy, Argentina: Facultad de Humanidades y Ciencias Sociales, Univ. Nacional de Jujuy, 1995, v. 2, p. 97–115, bibl.)

Studies trade patterns in the Jujuy and Salta region in the wake of the War of the Pacific. Finds that trade shifted from the traditional exchange with Bolivia to provisioning the growing nitrate industry of northern Chile. The latter continued until the depression of the 1930s. [JH]

2863 Conti, Viviana E. and Daniel J. Santamaría. Mecanismos de intercambio en períodos de transición: el caso de los arrendamientos de dos estancias de la Puna jujeña, 1813–1819. (*Anu. Estud. Am.*, 51:1, 1994, p. 123–142, graphs, map, table)

Argues that indigenous peasants of Jujuy continued to operate within a money economy, though at a much reduced level, even after the independence wars had wrecked the mercantilist order elsewhere in the Plata. Payments for leaseholds, for instance, were still being made in silver as late as 1819. [TW]

2864 Contreras Pérez, Francisco. Recluta masiva de emigrantes andaluces y su inserción social en Argentina, siglo XIX: nuevas notas para su estudio. (*Anu. Estud. Am.*, 53:2, 1996, p. 173–197, tables)

Examines role of the Agencia de Emigración Señores Acebal Díaz y Cía and the Italo-Argentine Shipping Company in recruiting Andalucian emigrants to Argentina as laborers, starting in 1889. [TW]

2865 Cosmelli Ibáñez, José Luis. Historia de la cultura argentina. Buenos Aires: Librería "El Ateneo" Editorial, 1992. 802 p.: bibl., ill., index, maps.

A well-constructed and readable encyclopedic treatment of Argentine culture. Arranged in three chronological sections, the book's various chapters cover architecture, literature, the plastic arts, the sciences, education, medicine, philosophy, theater, music, journalism, historiography, and folklore. Coverage is weakest on the post-1960 period (the author tends to discount the contribution of nontraditional artists and scholars, and to ignore that of individuals like Ernesto J. A. Maeder and Carlos Sempat Assadourian, whose ouevre was produced outside of Buenos Aires). [TW]

2866 Crasemann Collins, Christiane. Urban interchange in the Southern Cone: Le Corbusier (1929) and Werner Hegemann (1931) in Argentina. (*JSAH*, 54:2, June 1995, p. 208–227, maps, photos)

An interesting examination of the impact on and visits to Argentina of two famous urbanists, Le Corbusier and Hegemann, with a decided emphasis on the latter. While largely a work on the intellectual history of urban planning, article also addresses the nature of Buenos Aires, as well as the hopes of those who wanted to transform it. Part of a larger work on Hegemann and partially based on his papers. [JH]

2867 Cresto, Juan José. Antecedentes del Pacto de San José de Flores: la Confederación Argentina y Buenos Aires, 1852–1859. Buenos Aires: Editorial Puma, 1994. 126 p.: bibl.

Classic work provides an in-depth description of Argentine politics in the 1850s, especially of the complex events leading up to the signing of the Pact of San José de Flores. Cresto is particularly adept at fleshing out the role of Entrerriano strongman Justo José de Urquiza. [TW]

2868 Cresto, Juan José. Gravitación pública de Mitre, 1892–1905. (*Anales/Buenos Aires*, 1992, p. 81–125)

Unusual study of Bartolomé Mitre's life as a publicist, politician, and scholar in the last decade of his life. The former president fell easily into the role of senior statesman, though he remained more controversial than is suggested here. [TW]

2869 Cuccorese, Horacio Juan. San Martín, catolicismo y masonería. Buenos Aires: Fundación Mater Dei, 1993. 160 p.: bibl.

Examines San Martín's purported links

to the Masonic Orders. After carefully weighing available historical evidence and tallying opinions of Bartolomé Mitre, Estanislao Zeballos, and others, concludes that San Martín was a liberal Catholic with only tenuous connections to the Argentine lodges. [TW]

2870 Cuccorese, Horacio Juan. San Martín y la libertad. Buenos Aires: Ediciones Macchi, 1992. 107 p.: bibl.

An erudite analysis of San Martín's notions of political freedom. Sketches Enlightenment philosophies that influenced he future liberator as a young student in Spain, and the idealism he carried with him throughout the wars for independence. Concludes that San Martín's selfless dedication in pursuit of a nearly utopian sense of liberty was precisely what marked him as a national hero. [TW]

2871 Cúneo, Dardo. El periodismo de la disidencia social, 1858–1900. Buenos Aires: Centro Editor de America Latina, 1994. 109 p. (Biblioteca Política argentina; 473)

A brief but fascinating look at the early journalism of the Argentine workers' movements (socialist, anarchist, syndicalist). Based on research in the Biblioteca Nacional and the Biblioteca Obrera Juan B. Justo in Argentina, and the International Institute of Social History in Amsterdam. [TW]

2872 Darío Salas, Rubén. Elites rioplatenses, sistema representativo y cabildo, 1810–1827. (in Vida pública y vida privada: actas de las primeras jornadas de historia argentina y americana; Buenos Aires, 5 al 7 de junio de 1996. Buenos Aires: Facultad de Filosofía y Letras de la Pontificia Univ. Católica Argentina Santa María de los Buenos Aires, 1996, p. 253–281)

Analysis of political debates among porteño elites in the first decade of independence regarding the character, powers, and justification of representative government destined to replace the former monarchical system. The North American and British models were the precedents most commonly discussed. Portrays the abolition of the aristocratic Cabildo as a triumph for those favoring new representative institutions for Argentina. [TW]

2873 Dellaferrera, Nelson C. Apuntes para la historia de la Audencia episcopal del Tucumán, 1688–1888. (Rev. Hist. Derecho, 21, 1993, p. 97–131)

A study of church law as seen through two centuries of deliberations of the ecclesiastical high courts in the Episcopate of Tucumán. Includes interesting data on bigamy cases (taken from the records of the Inquisition) and on church-state relations (taken from the records of the *Tribunal Eclesiástico Castrense*). [TW]

2874 Devoto, Fernando J. Itinerario de un problema: "Annales" y la historiografía argentina, 1929–1965. (Anu. IEHS, 10, 1995, p. 155–175)

A thoughtful examination of the influence of the Annales school of history on Argentine historians. Focuses on the institutional connections between Paris and historians in Buenos Aires, especially the ties that developed between Fernand Braudel and José Luis Romero and Romero's students. A key source is the papers of Braudel. Shows both the influence and limits of that influence. [JH]

2875 Díaz Araujo, Enrique. Mariano Fragueiro. Mendoza, Argentina: Editorial de la Facultad de Filosofía y Letras de la Univ. Nacional de Cuyo, 1994. 293 p.: bibl. (Hombres olvidados de la organización nacional; 2)

Useful analytic treatment of the life and work of Mariano Fragueiro (1795–1872), governor of Córdoba and author of *Cuestiones argentinos* and *Organización de crédito*, perhaps the two most influential works on the political and economic regeneration of Argentina in the 1850s. [TW]

2876 Díaz Melián, Mafalda Victoria. La presidencia del Dr. Miguel Juárez Celman: algunas notas de su administración en 1889; proyecto de tratado de comercio con Chile. (Bol. Acad. Puertorriq. Hist., 13:44, julio 1992, p. 19–45, facsim.)

Surveys the 1889 achievements of the Juárez Celman administration in the fields of immigration, trade, diplomacy, ranching, education, and the military. Based on Chilean records. [TW]

2877 Dictaduras y utopías en la historia reciente de la educación argentina, 1955–1983. Dirección de Adriana Puiggrós.

Buenos Aires: Editorial Galerna, 1997. 402 p.: bibl. (Historia de la educación en la Argentina; 8)

Part of an excellent collected work on the history of education in Argentina. This, the last volume, examines competing ideologies in education during the period between the fall of Perón and the return of democracy after the last military dictatorship. [JH]

2878 La educación en las provincias, 1945–1985. Dirección de Adriana Puiggrós. Coordinación del tomo VII de Edgardo Ossanna. Buenos Aires: Editorial Galerna, 1997. 472 p.: bibl., ill. (Historia de la educación en la Argentina; 7)

Part of an excellent collected work on the history of Argentine education. Looks at changes in education in nine provinces over varied time span, mainly from Peronism to the 1980s. [JH]

2879 Eickhoff, Georg. El 17 de octubre al revés: la desmovilización del pueblo peronista por medio del renunciamiento de Eva Perón. (*Desarro. Econ.,* 36:142, julio/sept. 1996, p. 635–660)

Contrasts the demonstration intended to make Eva Perón vice president in 1951 with the demonstrations of Oct. 17, 1945. Sees the 1951 event as a step towards demobilizing the populace in contrast to the earlier event. [JH]

2880 Endrek, Emiliano. Escuela, sociedad y finanzas en una autonomía provincial: Córdoba, 1820–1829. Córdoba, Argentina: Junta Provincial de Historia de Córdoba, 1994. 437 p.: bibl., ill. (Libros de la Junta Provincial de Historia de Córdoba, 0327–554; 14)

Impressive study of primary education in Córdoba prov. during Juan Bautista Bustos years. Covers church influences, construction and operation of schools, curricula, finances, and the government's role in promotion and direction of education. Includes a large selection of archival documents. [TW]

2881 Enz, Daniel. Rebeldes y ejecutores: historias, violencia y represión en la década del '70 en Entre Ríos. Argentina?: D. Enz, 1995. 526 p.: bibl., ill., index.

A gripping account of military repression in Entre Ríos in the wake of the 1976 coup. Discusses different incidents, attempting to describe the general situation. Work lacks footnotes, making it difficult to judge the sources of information. [JH]

2882 Fanesi, Pietro Rinaldo. El exilio antifascista en la Argentina. v. 1–2. Buenos Aires: Centro Editor de América Latina, 1994. 2 v. (191 p.): bibl. (Biblioteca política Argentina; 474–475)

Studies the politics of the exiled Italian anti-Fascist community largely through the activities of one important but not crucial figure, Albani Corneli. Uses Corneli's correspondence and a wealth of other material to reconstruct political activity. The perspective is oriented to Italy but author is well versed on Argentine history. [JH]

2883 Farberman, Judith. Familia, ciclo de vida y economía doméstica: el caso de Salavina, Santiago del Estero en 1819. (*Bol. Inst. Hist. Ravignani,* 12, segundo semestre 1995, p. 33–59, graphs, tables)

Thoughtful analysis of family structure and *dependientes* within families in a small Santiagueño *curato* in 1819. The scarcity of land in this wheat-producing district led to late marriages, outward migration of young men, and a high incidence of female retainers integrated into landowning families. Offers an excellent discussion of the varying degrees of dependency. [TW]

2884 Fernández, Alejandro E. Inmigración y sus redes comerciales: un estudio de caso sobre los catalanes de Buenos Aires a comienzos de siglo. (*Estud. Migr. Latinoam.,* 11:32, abril 1996, p. 25–60, graphs)

Uses a case study to examine the importance of trade between Spain and Argentina, and the link between that trade and immigration. Majority of the article is based on a case study of a single olive oil exporting company. Compares that experience with a textile firm. [JH]

2885 Ferrari, Marcela P. El Banco Hipotecario de la provincia de Buenos Aires y el estímulo a la producción rural, 1872–1890. (*Anu. IEHS,* 10, 1995, p. 219–242, map, tables)

Interesting case study of Argentine financing during the heyday of cereal expansion. The Banco Hipotecario, the chief mortgage bank of the prov. of Buenos Aires, was instrumental in supplying agricultural credit not just to the great landowners but also to more humble owners of rural properties. [TW]

2886 Los ferrocarriles en la Argentina, 1857–1910. Notas biográficas por Norberto J. Iannuzzi. Buenos Aires: Fundación Museo Ferroviario, 1994. 235 p.: ill., maps.

A reprint of two articles on the development of the railroad system printed in the second decade of the 20th century: "Los ferrocarriles argentinos en 1910: historia de su desarrollo" by Emilio Schickenkendantz, and "Historia del desarrollo de los ferrocarriles argentinos" by Emilio Rebuelto. Both discuss the building of the railroad network. [JH]

2887 Fitz-Gibbon, Spencer. Not mentioned in despatches: the history and mythology of the battle of Goose Green. Cambridge, England: Lutterworth Press, 1995. 208 p.: bibl., index, maps.

A critical reassessment of the Goose Green battle of the Malvinas/Falklands War based on primary and secondary English-language sources. Attributes much of British success to Argentine failure to pursue more mobile tactics. [JH]

2888 Follari, Rodolfo S. El noventa en San Luis: autonomistas y radicales en 1890. Buenos Aires: Ediciones Ciudad Argentina, 1995. 501 p.: bibl., ill. (Monografías históricas)

A detailed examination of the provincial reaction to the national political and economic crisis of 1890. Based largely on archival sources and local newspapers, offers valuable regional perspective on a national crisis. [JH]

2889 Fradkin, Raúl O. Tulio Halperín Donghi y la formación de la clase terrateniente porteña. (*Anu. IEHS,* 11, 1996, p. 71–107)

Thorough analysis of Halperín Donghi's contributions to the study of Argentine landholding elites in the early-19th century. Recommended for the specialist. [TW]

2890 Fraga, Rosendo. El hijo de Roca. Buenos Aires: Emecé Editores, 1994. 254 p., 8 p. of plates: bibl., ill.

A political biography that attempts to revive the image of the conservative politician and vice president who the author claims is the most important conservative

politician of the first half of the century. Part of the author's drive is to improve the image of the conservatives. Based on papers in the Archivo General de la Nación, periodicals, and a limited number of secondary sources. Does not include footnotes. [JH]

2891 Fraga, Rosendo. Roca y Chile. Buenos Aires: Editorial Centro de Estudios Unión para la Nueva Mayoría, 1996. 98 p.: bibl.

Straightforward narrative of Argentine-Chilean relations during the two Roca administrations (1880–86 and 1898–1904). [TW]

2892 Francioni, Alberto P. Gobernadores de Santa Fe, 1815–1995: biografía. Santa Fe, Argentina: Impr. Todograf, 1995. 506 p.: ill. (some col.), index.

A useful source for basic information on Santa Fe's governors. [JH]

2893 Fúrlong Cárdiff, Guillermo. Vida y obra de Fray Francisco de Paula Castañeda: un testigo de la naciente patria argentina, 1810–1830. San Antonio de Padua, Argentina: Ediciones Castañeda, 1994. 732 p.: bibl. (Colección Perspectiva nacional; 9)

A posthumous work by the father of Argentine ecclesiastical history, this detailed study traces the life and deeds of Castañeda (1776–1832), a Franciscan orator, missionary, educator, and writer, who played a minor role in the revolutionary period. Thorough use of newspaper sources. [TW]

2894 Galafassi, Guido P. Aproximación al proceso histórico de asentamiento, colonización y producción en el delta del Paraná. (*Estud. Soc./Santa Fe,* 6:11, segundo semestre 1996, p. 139–160, bibl.)

A thorough overview of the intertwining process of economic development and change with the peopling of the delta. Shows why this is the one region near the city of Buenos Aires in which population has been dropping for several decades after a period of rapid growth. [JH]

2895 Galasso, Norberto. Mariano Moreno: "el sabiecito del sur." Buenos Aires: Ediciones del Pensamiento Nacional, 1994. 138 p.: bibl.

Revisionist treatment of the Argentine revolutionary figure, whom the author portrays as the proponent of a radical but failed attempt to bring about true "national sovereignty and social redemption." [TW]

2896 Galasso, Norberto. La Revolución de Mayo: el pueblo quiere saber de qué se trató. Buenos Aires: Ediciones del Pensamiento Nacional, 1994. 87 p.: bibl.

Revisionist critique of Bartolomé Mitre's "official history" of the May Revolution. Claims that the latter interpretation, which Galasso characterizes as "liberal" and pro-English, deliberately ignores the popular nationalist thrust of many revolutionary leaders, particularly Manuel Moreno. [TW]

2897 Gallo, Klaus. De la invasión al reconocimiento: Gran Bretaña y el Río de la Plata, 1806–1826. Buenos Aires: A-Z Editora, 1994. 252 p.: bibl. (Serie Ciencias sociales)

Most studies of early Anglo-Argentine diplomacy have concentrated narrowly on trade questions, and on the 1806–07 invasions. The present work is decidedly more ambitious. By chronicling all the exploratory diplomacy that led to Britain's recognition of the Argentine Federation in 1825, Gallo has filled several gaps in the existing literature. He credits the innovative policies of Rivadavia—and the farsighted interest shown by George Canning—with opening the door. [TW]

2898 Gallo, Klaus. Political instability in post-independent Argentina, 1810–1827. Buenos Aires: Univ. Torcuato Di Tella, 1995. 34 p. (Working paper; 25)

Poorly translated, but perceptive account of political infighting and the rise of the military in Argentina (and particularly Buenos Aires). Argues that the adventurism of army officers in the early national period prevented the evolution of stable political institutions. Also stresses the militarization of elites as a key factor in government instability as well as the well-known problem of the city versus the provinces. No new ground broken. [TW]

2899 Galmarini, Hugo R. Los españoles esquilmados. (*Todo es Hist.*, 29:343, feb. 1996, p. 8–19, facsims.)

Useful examination of the role played by forced contributions and confiscations in sustaining the patriot cause in Argentina during the 1810s. Notes that Spanish merchants, whose loyalty to the new regime was always suspect, were particular targets of such exactions—and often responded by abandoning the country at the first opportunity. [TW]

2900 Gandía, Enrique de. Belgrano, Mitre y Alberdi. (*An. Acad. Nac. Cienc. Morales*, 23, 1994, p. 193–212)

The dean of Argentine historians discusses how Bartolomé Mitre and Juan Bautista Alberdi used the historical figure of Belgrano as a symbol in forwarding their own, rather distinct, visions of Argentine nationalism. [TW]

2901 Garavaglia, Juan Carlos. Tres estancias del sur Bonaerense en un periodo de "transición," 1790–1834. (*in* Problemas de la historia agraria: nuevos debates y perspectivas de investigación. Tandil, Argentina: Instituto de Estudios Histórico Sociales (IEHS), 1995, p. 79–123, graphs, maps, tables)

Detailed economic analysis of ranching in the south of Buenos Aires prov. in the early national period. Finds that slave labor still played a major role in estancias just north of the Patagonian frontier. [TW]

2902 García Belsunce, César A. Una ventana al pasado. Rosario, Argentina: Instituto de Historia Política Argentina, 1994. 359 p.: bibl., ill., 1 map.

The former head of the Archivo General de la Nación here offers 11 essays on various historical topics, ranging from *diezmos* and agricultural production in the viceregal period, to prohibitions of marriage between Europeans and Americans in the United Provinces in the early national era, to the construction of the Buenos Aires-Rosario railroad in the 1880s. [TW]

2903 García Costa, Víctor O. Alfredo Palacios: entre el clavel y la espada; una biografía. Buenos Aires: Planeta, 1997. 388 p.: bibl., ill., index. (Historia argentina)

A political biography by a historian long active in the Socialist Party. While clearly well informed, the work lacks footnotes. The coverage after Palacios' expulsion from the Socialist Party in 1915 is spotty. [JH]

2904 Gartner, Mariana. La condición de la mujer a través de los testimonios de época, 1810–1820: comunicación. (*in* Vida pública y vida privada: actas de las primeras jornadas de historia argentina y americana; Buenos Aires, 5 al 7 de junio de 1996. Buenos Aires: Facultad de Filosofía y Letras de la Pontificia Univ. Católica Argentina Santa María de los Buenos Aires, 1996, p. 283–293, bibl.)

Suggests that the roots of educational reform for Argentine women (usually associated with the Rivadavia and Sarmiento periods) can actually be found in the second decade of the 19th century. [TW]

2905 Gayol, Sandra. Sargentos, cabos y vigilantes: perfil de un plantel inestable en el Buenos Aires de la segunda mitad del siglo XIX. (*Bol. Am.*, 36:46, 1996, p. 133–151)

Theoretical piece examines the role of the night watchman in fostering social order in Buenos Aires. [TW]

2906 Gelman, Jorge D. Unos números sorprendentes: cambio y continuidad en el mundo agrario bonaerense durante la primera mitad del siglo XIX. (*Anu. IEHS*, 11, 1996, p. 123–145, graphs)

Makes use of little-known agrarian censuses to test traditional notions of country life in Buenos Aires prov. Concludes that the number of small estancieros was greater than previously assumed. [TW]

2907 Glatz, Markus. Schweizerische Einwanderer in Misiones: ein Beispiel ausländischer Siedlungskolonisation in Argentinien im 20. Jahrhundert [Swiss immigrants in Misiones: an example of foreign settlements in Argentina during the 20th century]. Frankfurt am Main; New York: P. Lang, 1997. 332 p.: bibl., ill., maps. (Hispano-Americana, 17)

This study of the economic impact of Swiss immigrants in Misiones during 1856–1939 emphasizes their initial social and economic differences as well as their development and contribution to market-oriented agriculture which contributed to the integration of Misiones into the Argentine national economy. Of particular interest to immigration studies are the sections about the individual Swiss communities of Oro Verde, Santo Pipo, Colón, Eldorado, and Línea Chuchilla. [C. Converse]

2908 Goldar, Ernesto. Buenos Aires, vida cotidiana en la década del 50. 2. ed. Buenos Aires: Plus Ultra, 1992. 181 p.: bibl.

Attempts to present the popular lifestyle of the porteños in the 1950s. Covers many aspects of life but focuses on the middle class. Finds little sense of change over the decade. Presents an interesting portrait. [JH]

Goldman, Noemí. Historia y lenguaje: los discursos de la Revolución de Mayo. See item **5262.**

2909 Goñi Demarchi, Carlos A.; José Nicolás Scala; and Germán W. Berraondo. Yrigoyen y la Gran Guerra: aspectos desconocidos de una gesta ignorada. Buenos Aires: Ediciones Ciudad Argentina, 1998. 278 p.: bibl.

Re-examines Yrigoyen's position on World War I. Strongly pro-Yrigoyen, partially based on British records. [JH]

2910 González, Marcela. Peones y milicias—destino involuntario de la poblacíon marginal: Córdoba en la segunda mitad del siglo XIX. (*Res Gesta*, 34, enero/dic. 1995, p. 173–187)

Argues that the expansion of state power in Córdoba left the poor of the province with only two real options: service in the militia or contracted labor in ranches or agricultural colonies. [TW]

2911 González Arzac, Alberto. Caudillos y constituciones. Buenos Aires: Instituto de Investigaciones Históricas Juan Manuel de Rosas, 1994. 128 p.: bibl., ill. (Colección Estrella federal; 3)

A brief but informative look at efforts to provide a framework for constitutional rule during the heyday of Argentine caudillismo. Includes full text of proposed 1834 constitution for the province of Buenos Aires. [TW]

2912 González Bernaldo, Pilar. Social imagery and its political implications in a rural conflict. (*in* Revolution and restoration: the rearrangement of power in Argentina, 1776–1860. Edited by Mark D. Szuchman and Jonathan C. Brown. Lincoln: Univ. of Nebraska Press, 1994, p. 177–207)

Unusual study of the rural rebellion in Buenos Aires prov. that brought about the fall of the Unitarian regime and the subsequent installation of the Rosas dictatorship. Rejects traditional thesis that rural mobilization was based on patron-client ties, and argues persuasively that country people responded instead to a complex set of motivations reflective of pre-existing social tensions. [TW]

2913 Gordillo, Mónica R. Córdoba en los '60: la experiencia del sindicalismo combativo. Córdoba, Argentina: Univ. Nacional de Córdoba, 1996. 296 p.: bibl. (Colección Manuales de cátedra)

Intelligent examination of the creation of a culture of resistance and confrontation among the working class in Córdoba between 1955–69. Attempts to explain why workers became radicalized. Based on printed, archival, and oral history sources. [JH]

Guber, Rosana. Las manos de la memoria. See *HLAS 57:1057.*

2914 Güenaga, Rosario. Santa Cruz y Magallanes: historia socioeconómica de los territorios de la Patagonia Austral, Argentina y Chile. México: Instituto Panamericano de Geografía e Historia, Comisión de Historia, 1994. 257 p.: bibl., ill. (Pub.; no. 475)

Influenced by Frederick Jackson Turner's work on the US frontier, work contrasts development of the southern-most Patagonian provinces of Argentina and Chile from mid-19th century until 1925. Concentrates on economic and demographic changes. [JH]

2915 Gutiérrez, Leandro H. and **Luis Alberto Romero.** Sectores populares, cultura y política: Buenos Aires en la entreguerra. Buenos Aires: Editorial Sudamericana, 1995. 212 p.: bibl. (Colección Historia y cultura)

Compiles a series of important articles describing the creation of what can be called a civic culture among the popular sectors of Buenos Aires. Combines political, social, and cultural history. [JH]

2916 Guy, Donna J. Mothers alive and dead: multiple concepts of mothering in Buenos Aires. (*in* Sex and sexuality in Latin America. New York: New York Univ. Press, 1997, p. 155–173)

Suggestive discussion of how the political order in 19th-century Buenos Aires defined and manipulated overlapping concepts of motherhood. Shows how the religious-based image of the passive mother gave way to the image of an active mother, committed to the emotional nurturing of her children. [TW]

2917 Halperín Donghi, Tulio. Argentina en el callejón. Buenos Aires: Ariel, 1995. 264 p.

Reprints a series of works written between 1955–64 dealing with the post-1930 era. In addition to the well-known work mentioned in the title, there are four others, some previously difficult to find. As the author points out, the works reflect the epoch of their composition but they still remain illuminating. [JH]

2918 Halperín Donghi, Tulio. The Buenos Aires landed class and the shape of Argentine politics, 1820–1930. (*in* Agrarian structure & political power: landlord & peasant in the making of Latin America. Pittsburgh, Pa.: Univ. of Pittsburgh Press, 1995, p. 39–66)

A chapter from a book examining the efficacy of Barrington Moore's classical work *Social Origins of Dictatorship and Democracy* (1966) in Latin America countries. Argues that the Argentine case is sufficiently different than the model to make the book a less than helpful tool. In the pampas not only did a peasantry not exist, but the chapter argues that the state functioned at various times as an independent actor. The argument is highly nuanced, as is customary with this author. [JH]

2919 Halperín Donghi, Tulio. The colonial *letrado* as a revolutionary intellectual: Deán Funes as seen through his *Apuntamientos para una biografía.* (*in* Revolution and restoration: the rearrangement of power in Argentina, 1776–1860. Edited by Mark D. Szuchman and Jonathan C. Brown. Lincoln: Univ. of Nebraska Press, 1994, p. 54–73)

Uses figure of Gregorio Funes to illustrate the contradictory legacy of Enlightenment ideas among intellectuals of revolutionary Argentina. While he categorically rejected the absolutism of Spain (and the reactionary social values that kept it in place), Funes nonetheless worried that the uncritical importation of English liberal values would damage the new political order he was trying to create. Recommended. [TW]

2920 Halperín Donghi, Tulio. Ensayos de historiografía. Buenos Aires: El Cielo por Asalto, 1996. 189 p.: bibl.

A collection of 12 previously printed,

insightful essays on historiography with a focus on how historians are shaped by the world around them. The time of their writing varies over three decades. They deal with mostly Argentine authors but also with international trends. [JH]

2921 Halperín Donghi, Tulio. Mitre y la formulación de una historia nacional para la Argentina. (*Anu. IEHS*, 11, 1996, p. 57–69)

Finely wrought study of Bartolomé Mitre's contribution to the development of an empirically based "national" interpretation of Argentine history. Argues that this interpretation provided the best defense for the liberal-democratic and constitutionalist order that Mitre sought to inaugurate in the country. [TW]

2922 Herrero, Fabián. Buenos Aires, año 1816: una tendencia confederacionista. (*Bol. Inst. Hist. Ravignani*, 12, segundo semestre 1995, p. 7–32, maps, tables)

Examination of political elites in 1815–16 posits a strong but short-term tendency in favor of confederation before the Congress of Tucumán. An excellent study supported by tables and analyses of various groupings of elites. Highly recommended for students of revolutionary Buenos Aires. [TW]

2923 Herz, Enrique Germán. Pellegrini, ayer y hoy. Buenos Aires: Editorial Centro de Estudios Unión para la Nueva Mayoría, 1996. 568 p., 8 p. of plates: bibl., ill. (Colección Estudios; no. 30)

Useful biographical treatment of Argentine president (1890–92). Based on secondary sources. [TW]

2924 La historiografía argentina en el siglo XX. v. 1–2. Buenos Aires: Centro Editor América Latina, 1993–94. 2 v.: bibl. (Los fundamentos de las ciencias del hombre; 86, 125)

A series of interesting and well-developed essays on the historiography of Argentina in the 20th century. Among the topics discussed are the Nueva Escuela Histórica, revisionism, and the renovation of the profession in the 1960s. On the latter there are separate essays discussing the changes in Buenos Aires, Rosario, and La Plata. [JH]

2925 Homenaje al Dr. Edmundo Correas. Recopilación de Pedro Santos Martínez. Mendoza: Junta de Estudios Históricos de Mendoza: Ediciones Culturales de Mendoza, 1994. 350 p.: bibl., ill.

Volume commemorates the life and work of Edmundo Correas (1901–91), perhaps the best-known historian of Mendoza. Includes several essays on Argentine culture, diplomacy, and political theory. [TW]

2926 Hora, Roy. Terratenientes y política en Buenos Aires: la experiencia de la Liga Agraria, 1892–1923. (*Anos 90*, 4, dez. 1995, p. 7–30, bibl.)

An interesting study of a little-known organization of Buenos Aires estancieros who wanted, as a class, to be more involved in politics. Points out why and how estancieros as a class failed to control politics, even as they became richer. [JH]

2927 Iriani, Marcelino. "Buenos vecinos": integración social de los vascos en Tandil, 1840–1880. (*Estud. Migr. Latinoam.*, 11:32, abril 1996, p. 85–110, graphs, tables)

Minor study of Basque immigrants in a small community in the Bonaerense countryside. Suggests that the integration of the immigrant group occurred when the majority of Argentines adopted Basque perspectives and folkloric appraisals of Basque identity. [TW]

2928 Irigoin, María Alejandra. Moneda impuestos e instituciones: la estabilización de la moneda corriente en el estado de Buenos Aires durante las décadas de 1850 y 1860. (*Anu. IEHS*, 10, 1995, p. 189–218, bibl., tables)

Excellent study of government finances in Buenos Aires during the province's short period as a breakaway state during the 1850s and early 1860s. Shows how the Bonaerense regime adopted fiscal policies that resulted in a stability unseen for more than 20 years. This positive picture did not long endure after reintegration with the rest of Argentina, however, for new military expenditures associated with the Paraguayan War—and bad banking decisions—soon set the economy on a new downward spiral. [TW]

2929 Irisarri, María Jimena. Avance de la frontera sur: la expedición de rosas en 1833; comunicación. (*in* Vida pública y vida privada: actas de las primeras jornadas de historia argentina y americana; Buenos Aires, 5 al 7 de junio de 1996. Buenos Aires: Facultad de Filosofía y Letras de la Pontificia Univ. Católica Argentina Santa María de los Buenos Aires, 1996, p. 57–76, bibl.)

Speculative piece discusses the role of the frontier in Argentine history, and how the frontier was affected by Rosa's 1833 expedition beyond the Río Colorado. [TW]

2930 Johnson, Lyman L. Distribution of wealth in nineteenth-century Buenos Aires province: the issue of social justice in a changing economy. (*in* The political economy of Spanish America in the age of revolution, 1750–1850. Albuquerque: Univ. of New Mexico Press, 1994, p. 197–213)

Analyzes probate inventories from 1800, 1829–30, and 1854–55 to discern shifts in wealth distribution in the province of Buenos Aires. Notes that policies of the Rosas government promoted inequality by siphoning wealth from the rural and urban masses, urban commercial and artisanal sectors, and small farmers, and then transferring it to the ranching elite. The concentration of wealth in the latter sector was accomplished at a substantial cost in terms of social justice. [TW]

2931 Johnson, Lyman L. The military as catalyst of change in late colonial Buenos Aires. (*in* Revolution and restoration: the rearrangement of power in Argentina, 1776–1860. Edited by Mark D. Szuchman and Jonathan C. Brown. Lincoln: Univ. of Nebraska Press, 1994, p. 27–53)

A focused and well-written analysis of the colonial militia of Buenos Aires in the first decades of the 19th century. Suggests that the level of military expenditures under the last viceroys increased local labor costs and thereby contributed to the structural weakness of the porteño economy just before independence. [TW]

2932 Jones, Kristine L. Indian-Creole negotiations on the southern frontier. (*in* Revolution and restoration: the rearrangement of power in Argentina, 1776–1860. Edited by Mark D. Szuchman and Jonathan C. Brown. Lincoln: Univ. of Nebraska Press, 1994, p. 103–123)

Detailed account of indigenous-white relations along the southern Platine frontier between independence and the 1860s. Notes that the first post-Rosas governments refused to continue the annuities previously assigned

to indigenous peoples, which set the stage for three decades of open hostility. This outcome sharply contrasted with the earlier political and economic interdependence that had existed between indigenous peoples and whites. [TW]

2933 José de San Martín, libertador de América. Dirección editorial de Manrique Zago. Buenos Aires: Instituto Nacional Sanmartiniano, 1995. 223 p.: bibl., ill. (some col.).

Sumptuously illustrated biography of Argentina's liberator with chapters by 48 historians and public figures, many of whom are affiliated with the Instituto Nacional Sanmartiniano. [TW]

2934 Jozami, Gladys. The manifestation of Islam in Argentina. (*Americas/Franciscans,* 53:1, July 1996, p. 67–85, tables)

A study of the number of Muslims in Argentina. Takes a conservative position in regard to the size of the community. Also contains insights into the problems of assimilation and acceptance. [JH]

2935 Jujuy: diccionario general. v. 1–12. Jujuy, Argentina: Ediciones Gobierno de la Provincia de Jujuy, 1992–93. 12 v. (6054 p.): bibl.

A historical dictionary of people, places, institutions, and associations related to Jujuy prov. For those working on the province, this is an extremely useful reference tool. [JH]

2936 La Junta de Historia y Numismática Américana y el movimiento historiográfico en la Argentina, 1893–1938. v. 1. Buenos Aires: Academia Nacional de la Historia, 1995. 1 v.: bibl., ill. (some col.).

Commemorates the centenary of the founding of the Academia Nacional de la Historia. Most of the volume is a series of institutional histories of the organization presented in chronological order from its founding until it changed its name to Academia Nacional de la Historia in 1938. Followed by a series of essays on key historiographical themes of the period: La Nueva Escuela Histórica; European influences and models; the Instituto de Investigaciones Históricas; the historical school of La Plata; revisionism; and La Sociedad de Historia Argentina. Also includes lists of members, corresponding members, and lectures given to the organization. [JH]

2937 Katra, William H. The Argentine generation of 1837: Echeverría, Alberdi, Sarmiento, Mitre. Madison, N.J.: Fairleigh Dickinson Univ. Press, 1996. 367 p.: bibl., index.

An informative and well-written study of the Generation of 1837, whose members were instrumental in forging a modern liberal nation out of a near-empty, unorganized Argentine polity. Uses chronological approach, following the ideas and public profiles of these men through five decades of political tumult. Study is especially strong in its detailed treatment of the bitter debates and problematic relations between the various pensadores. Based not only on standard published sources, but also on archival documentation and little-known newspaper articles of the era. For philosophy specialist's comment, see item **5267**. [TW]

2938 Kelly, Kevin. Rosas and the restoration of order through populism. (*in* Revolution and restoration: the rearrangement of power in Argentina, 1776–1860. Edited by Mark D. Szuchman and Jonathan C. Brown. Lincoln: Univ. of Nebraska Press, 1994, p. 208–239)

Describes Rosas as a primitive populist who enjoyed success precisely because he rose above his class origins and appealed directly to various segments of Argentine society—indigenous peoples, blacks, urban workers, gauchos, and estancieros alike. [TW]

2939 Klich, Ignacio. The chimera of Palestinian resettlement in Argentina in the early aftermath of the first Arab-Israeli war and other similarly fantastic works. (*Americas/Franciscans*, 53:1, July 1996, p. 15–43, table)

Discusses aborted plans to move Palestinians to Argentina in the late 1940s-early 1950s. Compares these attempts with similar earlier ideas by German and Polish governments. Work reveals a good deal about Argentine official attitudes towards immigration. [JH]

2940 Klich, Ignacio. Jewish settlement in Argentina: a view from Jerusalem. (*Am. Jew. Arch.*, 46:1, Spring/Summer 1994, p. 101–126)

A review essay of Haim Avni's *Argentina and the Jews: A History of Jewish Immigration* (see *HLAS 52:2633*), but also much more. In reality, it is an evaluation of current knowledge of Jews in Argentina, using critiques of Avni's book as starting points. Well done. [JH]

2941 Klich, Ignacio. La pericia científica alemana en el amanecer del proyecto nuclear argentino y el papel de los inmigrantes judíos. (*Bol. Inst. Hist. Ravignani*, 10, segundo semestre 1994, p. 61–89)

Part of author's ongoing study of Jewish immigration to Argentina in the 1930s-40s. Looks at why, despite government anti-Semitism, Jewish scientists were invited to participate in the founding of the Argentine nuclear program. Argues that this was due mostly to the respect in which "German" science was held. [JH]

2942 Klich, Ignacio. The role of the United States in securing Latin America sanctuary for alleged war criminals: the case of Walter Schreiber. (*Patterns Prejud.*, 31:3, 1997, p. 51–77)

Presents an overview of the existing information on the number of German war criminals who fled to Argentina. Then examines the case of Walter Schreiber and draws conclusions from it. Schreiber, a German military doctor who probably was involved with inhumane experiments, had been recruited to work for the US Air Force but when his past became public knowledge and therefore embarrassing, the US helped to place him in Argentina. [JH]

2943 Korol, Juan Carlos. La influencia de los "Annales" en la historiografía argentina de la década del 60. (*CLIO/Buenos Aires*, 1, 1993, p. 124–135, bibl.)

Examines how the Annales school influenced the writing of Argentine history in the 1960s. [JH]

2944 Korol, Juan Carlos. Tulio Halperín Donghi y la historiografía argentina y latinoamericana. (*Anu. IEHS*, 11, 1996, p. 49–56)

Insightful analysis of the writings of Tulio Halperín Donghi. [JH]

2945 Lacoste, Pablo. La generación del '80 en Mendoza. Mendoza, Argentina: EDIUNC, 1995. 244 p.: bibl. (Estudios; no. 9)

Between 1880–1914, the province of

Mendoza underwent an impressive spate of modernization. As this fine study points out, this transformation expressed itself in political, social, economic, and intellectual terms. In focusing on the Mendocino elites, the author sees the Generation of 1880 as launching a cultural assault on all aspects of the colonial past. While this wrenched the province into the modern world, it left much undone. [TW]

2946 Lacoste, Pablo. El socialismo en Mendoza y en la Argentina. v. 1–2. Buenos Aires: Centro Editor de América Latina, 1993. 2 v. (281 p.): bibl. (Biblioteca Política argentina; 417–418)

Attempts to dispel myth that socialism in Argentina never went beyond Buenos Aires. Looks at growth of socialism in Mendoza with a particular emphasis on its political control in the 1930s of the *comuna* of Godoy Cruz. [JH]

2947 Lacoste, Pablo. La Unión Cívica Radical en Mendoza y en la Argentina, 1890–1946: aportes para el estudio de la inestabilidad política en la Argentina. Prólogo de Félix Luna. Mendoza, Argentina: Ediciones Culturales de Mendoza, 1994. 366 p.: bibl., ill., index.

A detailed account of the conflictive and unique Radicalism of Mendoza. Includes both Lecinismo and more traditional varieties. Political history based on a wide use of sources. [JH]

2948 Laise, Juan Rodolfo. 400 años de la Iglesia en San Luis. San Luis: Kartel Publicidad, 1994. 456 p.: ill. (some col.).

A potentially useful commemorative and institutional history. Lacks analysis. [JH]

2949 Landaburu, Roberto E. Irlandeses, Eduardo Casey, vida y obra. Venado Tuerto, Argentina: Asociación Mutual de Venado Tuerto, 1995. 220 p.: bibl., ill.

Interesting account of Irish colonization in Santa Fe prov. and of Edward Casey (1847–1906), a key pioneer and promoter, who made possible much of the colonization. Of particular interest is the decription of Casey's work at Venado Tuerto, still a major farming and sheepraising center today. [TW]

Lavrin, Asunción. Women, feminism, and social change in Argentina, Chile, and Uruguay, 1890–1940. See item **3121**.

2950 Lettieri, Alberto Rodolfo. La construcción del consenso en los inicios del sistema político moderno argentino, 1862–1868. (*Anu. Estud. Am.*, 52:2, 1995, p. 151–177)

A suggestive analysis of Argentine political culture during the Mitre period. Argues that the creation of a political consensus was necessary to the realization of an elite-based national project. Ironically, the elaboration of this same consensus involved the use of authoritarian methods. [TW]

2951 Lettieri, Alberto Rodolfo. La formación del sistema político moderno: legitimidad, opinión pública y discurso parlamentaria; Argentina, 1862–1868. Buenos Aires: Instituto de Historia Argentina y Americanan Dr. Emilio Ravignani, Facultad de Filosofía y Letras, Univ. de Buenos Aires, 1995. 30 p. (Cuadernos del Instituto Ravignani; 8)

Fascinating account of public opinion and politics in Argentina during the Mitre administration. Argues that the construction of a political consensus was possible despite fraudulent elections and a continued antagonism among political elites. [TW]

2952 Levaggi, Abelardo. Tratados entre gobiernos argentinos e indios del Chaco. (*Folia Hist. Nordeste*, 11, 1993, p. 31–63)

Despite its title, this well-crafted account of indigenous-white relations in 19th-century Gran Chaco also covers the Misiones territory. Based on archival documentation from Corrientes, Salta, and Santa Fe. [TW]

2953 Lobato, Mirta Zaida and Juan Suriano. Historia del trabajo y de los trabajadores en la Argentina: aproximaciones a su historiografía. (*in* Trabajo y empleo: un abordaje interdisciplinario. Buenos Aires: Editorial Universitaria de Buenos Aires, Programa del Area de Investigación sobre Trabajo y Empleo, 1996, p. 143–175, bibl.)

A well-developed examination of trends in writings on the history of the working class during the second half of the 20th century. Concentrates on the production within Argentina. [JH]

2954 López, Manuel. Cartas entre padre e hijo. v. 2, Correspondencia entre José Victorio López y Manuel López, 1846–1850. Córdoba, Argentina: Centro de Estudios

Históricos, 1994. 1 v. (t. 2: Serie documental; no. 4)

Useful compilation of previously unpublished correspondence from the military commander of Villa Nueva to his father, the Rosista governor of Córdoba (1835–52). Letters drawn from the Archivo Histórico de la Provincia de Córdoba. [TW]

2955 López, Mario Justo. Historia de los ferrocarriles nacionales—incluyendo los de Santa Fé, Entre Ríos y Córdoba, 1866–1886. Buenos Aires?: Lumiere, 1994. 439 p.: bibl., ill., index, maps.

A scholarly overview of Argentine railroads during the third quarter of the 19th century. Criticizes previous studies for reducing the story of railroads to a subcategory of British imperialism while ignoring the construction and early operation of the railroads as historical themes. [TW]

2956 Lozano, C. Fernanda Gil; Facundo Bianchini; and Carlos Salomone. Palacios, Fidel y el triunfo de 1961. (*Todo es Hist.*, 29:341, dic. 1995, p. 8–27, photos)

Interesting piece examines ironic impact of Castro's Cuban Revolution on the Argentine Socialist Party. The fervor created by the revolution helped narrowly elect Alfredo Palacios to the Senate from the city of Buenos Aires. The ideological passions that Cuba created also splintered the party soon afterwards. [JH]

2957 Ludueña, Felipe. Historia de YPF y de la labor parlamentaria que le ha dado sustento. Buenos Aires: H. Senado de la Nación, Secretaria Parlamentaria, Dirección Publicaciones, 1993. 396 p.: bibl., ill. (some col.), maps.

An official history of the oil company Yacimientos Petrolíferos Fiscales (YPF) commissioned by the Senate at the time of its privatization. Potentially useful. [JH]

2958 Luna, Félix. Historia integral de la Argentina. v. 6, La nación argentina. Buenos Aires: Planeta, 1996. 1 v.: bibl., ill. (some col.), maps (some col.).

Written by long-time editor of *Todo es Historia*, this is a highly polished popular history of Argentina in the 1850s-60s. Topics covered include the rise and fall of Urquiza, the beginnings of porteño domination under Mitre, the Paraguayan War, and the Montonero rebellions. Recommended for the general reader. [TW]

2959 Luqui Lagleyze, Julio Mario. Los cuerpos militares en la historia argentina: organización y uniformes; 1550–1950. Rosario, Argentina: Instituto Nacional Sanmartiniano, 1995. 296 p.: bibl.

A detailed examination of Argentine military organization and uniforms from the early colonial period until the time of Perón. Useful mainly for the specialist. [TW]

2960 Luqui Lagleyze, Julio Mario. El Ejército Realista en la guerra de independencia: estudio orgánico y sociológico del Ejército Real. Buenos Aires: Instituto Nacional Sanmartiniano, 1995. 237 p.: bibl., ill.

A highly detailed description of the Spanish military in the Plata at the time of the independence wars. Includes a myriad of information on the officer corps, logistics, uniforms, armaments, even musical bands, but does not live up to the "organic and sociological study" of its title. [TW]

2961 Maestro, M. Cecilia. El papel de las fuerzas armadas durante el gobierno de Arturo Frondizi: las intervenciones militares entre 1958 y 1962. Buenos Aires: Univ. del Salvador, Facultad de Ciencias Sociales, Instituto de Investigación en Ciencias Sociales, 1994. 112 p.: bibl. (Serie Investigaciones del IDICSO; no. 6)

Presents new information based on material from the personal archives of President Frondizi. [JH]

2962 Maluendres, Sergio D. Los agricultores de los márgenes de la región pampeana; mitos y "realidades": el caso del Territorio Nacional de la Pampa. (*in* Problemas de la historia agraria: nuevos debates y perspectivas de investigación. Tandil, Argentina: Instituto de Estudios Histórico Sociales (IEHS), 1995, p. 183–209, bibl., tables)

Looks at the so-called black legend of agriculture in La Pampa in the first decades of wheat farming. Then shows how much legend overstates the case. Combines detailed study of existing secondary literature with some primary sources. [JH]

2963 Manuel Belgrano: los ideales de la patria. Dirección editorial de Manrique Zago. Buenos Aires: Manrique Zago Ediciones, 1995. 197 p.: bibl., ill. (some col.).

Lavishly produced biography of the Argentine who carried the patriot cause to the interior provinces, Paraguay, and Upper Peru. Includes brief, thoughtful pieces on such topics as iconography, genealogy, economic and political thought, military organization, and Belgrano's relations with women. [TW]

2964 Marco, Miguel Angel de. La Guerra del Paraguay. Buenos Aires: Planeta, 1995. 351 p.: bibl., ill. (Historia argentina)

A noted Santafecino historian produces a fine comprehensive history of the 1864–70 Triple Alliance War, one of the best works on the topic since the 1921 multivolume study of Juan Beverina. Thoroughly depicts Argentine soldier's daily life while on campaign. Based mainly on secondary sources. [TW]

2965 Marichal, Carlos. Liberalism and fiscal policy: the Argentine paradox, 1820–1862. (*in* Liberals, politics, and power: state formation in nineteenth-century Latin America. Edited by Vincent C. Peloso and Barbara A. Tenenbaum. Athens: Univ. of Georgia Press, 1996, p. 90–110)

Fascinating analysis of the interplay between fiscal policy and political reform in Buenos Aires through 1866. Argues persuasively that fiscal measures cannot be understood without a clear knowledge of the political systems under which they operated; *aduana* policies cannot themselves identify a regime as liberal or otherwise. [TW]

2966 Martínez de Gorla, Dora Noemí. La colonización del riego en las zonas tributarias de los ríos, Negro, Neuquén, Limay y Colorado. Buenos Aires: Corregidor, 1994. 159 p.: bibl., maps.

A detailed examination of the process of building irrigation systems in upper Patagonia and colonizing the area. Coverage ranges from the 1880s–1930s. Based on archival sources and newspapers. [JH]

2967 Martinic Beros, Mateo. Inmigrantes malvineros en Magallanes. (*An. Inst. Patagon./Ser. Cienc. Hum.*, 24, 1996, p. 21–41, appendices, bibl., tables)

This interesting study of Kelper immigration to the Magallanes region of Chilean Patagonia (1880–1920) demonstrates that though the Falklands are islands, they share certain socioeconomic and demographic patterns with the South American mainland. [TW]

2968 Masés, Enrique *et al.* El mundo del trabajo: Neuquén, 1884–1930. Prólogo de Ricardo Falcón. Neuquén, Argentina: G. E. Hi. So., 1994. 163 p.: bibl.

An accomplished examination of social, economic, and cultural aspects of workers in Neuquén. A feasible topic due to the small numbers under study. [JH]

2969 Mateu, Ana María. Poder y relaciones políticas y económicas en Mendoza, Argentina, 1880–1920. (*Anu. Estud. Am.*, 53:2, 1996, p. 199–226)

Attempts to tie social and economic changes produced by the development of the wine industry to political changes that occurred with the Ley Sáenz Peña and the ensuing victory of Lecinas. Based on both primary and secondary sources. [JH]

2970 Matthews, Abraham. Crónica de la colonia galesa de la Patagonia. Traducción directa del galés por F.E. Roberts. Buenos Aires: Ediciones Alfonsina, 1995. 155 p.

An informative eyewitness account of early Welsh colonization in Chubút written at the turn of the century by a Protestant clergyman who was among the first immigrants. Translated from the Welsh. [TW]

2971 Mattini, Luis. Hombres y mujeres del PRT-ERP: la pasión militante. 2. ed. La Plata, Argentina: Editorial de la Campana, 1995. 502 p.: bibl. (Colección Campana de palo)

An interesting and critical analysis of the activities of the PRT-ERP from its founding to the death of its leader, Mario Santucho, in 1976. Includes some information on later events. Presents insider's account as author was a key leader of the movement; the sources are also mostly internal ones, though there is no scholarly apparatus. For political scientist's comment on first edition, see *HLAS 55:3557*. [JH]

2972 Mazzei, Daniel Horacio. Medios de comunicación y golpismo: el derrocamiento de Illia, 1966. Buenos Aires: Grupo Editor Universitario, 1997. 155 p.: bibl., ill. (Biblioteca de temas argentinos)

Looks at how the Azul faction of the

army used the media to manipulate public opinion and prepare support for the 1966 coup. After providing a broad overview, the work then focuses on two magazines and a writer for each one. Examines in great detail *Primera Plana* and Mariano Grondona, and studies in less detail *Confirmado* and Mariano Montemayor. A sophisticated piece. [JH]

2973 McLean, David. War, diplomacy and informal empire: Britain and the republics of La Plata, 1836–1853. London; New York: British Academic Press; New York: Distributed by St. Martin's Press in US and Canada, 1995. 241 p.: bibl., index.

Essentially an update on John Frank Cady's now-classic *Foreign Intervention in the Río de la Plata, 1838–50* (1929). Challenges utility of the "informal empire" concept in explaining Britain's sloppy handling of its Platine interests in the mid-19th century. McClean is more comfortable with English-language materials (which includes an array of documents from the PRO), than he is with those sources written in Spanish. [TW]

2974 Meding, Holger M. *Der Weg:* eine deutsche Emigrantenzeitschrift in Buenos Aires, 1947–1957. Berlin: Wissenschaftlicher Verlag Berlin, 1997. 179 p.: appendices, bibl., index.

In a well-researched study and analysis of the German postwar journal *Der Weg*, published during the Perón era, Meding captures publication's essence in his choice of representative topics. These range from speculative revisionism at best to bizarre justifications of Hitler's actions and the genocide of millions at worst. The emigre journal's extremism and lack of finances led to its demise in 1957. A list of contributors is included. [C.K. Converse]

2975 Menéndez, Susana. En búsqueda de las mujeres: percepciones sobre género, trabajo y sexualidad, Buenos Aires, 1900–1930. Amsterdam: CEDLA, 1997. 204 p.: bibl. (Latin America studies; 79)

Study of porteño discourse on women and work in the first decades of the 20th century. Analyzes publications by male and female leaders, feminists, and social reformers; and political debates, poems, novels, plays, and songs, to show how the representations and perceptions of women in a changing soci-

ety generated public discussion, concern, and tension. [R. Hoefte]

2976 Mercado Luna, Ricardo. Los rostros de la ciudad golpeada. La Rioja, Argentina: Editorial Canguro, 1995. 192, 7 p.: bibl., ill.

Looks at the political impact on the province of La Rioja of the successful coups in the 20th century. [JH]

2977 Mercante, Domingo Alfredo. Mercante: el corazón de Perón. Prólogo de Héctor Masnatta. Buenos Aires: Ediciones de la Flor, 1995. 235 p.: ill.

A biography, written by his son, of Domingo Mercante, Perón's right-hand man during his rise to power and then governor of the province of Buenos Aires. Contains some interesting information on the power struggles within the Perón regime. While based on the son's memories, as well as privately held documents, there is little new here. [JH]

2978 Moncaut, Carlos Antonio. Estancias viejas: historia; audacia, coraje y aventura. v. 1–2. City Bell, Argentina: Editorial "El Aljibe," 1996. 2 v. (787 p.): bibl., ill. (some col.), indexes, maps.

Attractive collection of information on gauchos includes materials on estancia life, immigration, and gauchesco poetry. [TW]

2979 Montequín, Adriana. Sector público y sistema tributario argentina, 1914–1932. (*Ciclos Hist. Econ. Soc.,* 5:9, segundo semestre 1995, p. 133–165)

Studies the changing economic situation and budget priorities of the first Radical period and the first years of the neoconservative era and their impact on the tax structure. Looks at both the national government and the provincial governments taken as a unit. Focuses on the creation of an income tax. [JH]

2980 Monterisi, María Teresa. Inmigrantes italianos en el crecimiento y transformación de Córdoba, 1880–1914. (*Rev. Econ./ Córdoba,* 45:75, oct./dic. 1994, p. 161–227, maps, tables)

A preliminary report on the impact of Italian immigrants on the growth of the city of Córdoba. Although much of the data is still largely undigested, the report does provide interesting facts and information. [JH]

2981 Moreyra, Beatriz Inés. Crecimiento demográfico y expansión económica en el espacio pampeano cordobés durante el modelo primário-exportador, 1880–1930. (*in* América Latina contemporânea: desafios e perspectivas. Organização de Eliane Geraindo Dayrell e Zilda Márcia Gricoli Iokoi. Rio de Janeiro: Expressão e cultura; São Paulo: Edusp, 1996, p. 241–269, graphs, tables)

Interesting study demonstrates the interplay between demography and the expansion of agriculture in the humid pampas of the prov. of Córdoba. Contains useful tables. [JH]

2982 Morrone, Francisco C. Los negros en el Ejército: declinación demográfica y disolución. Buenos Aires: Centro Editor de América Latina, 1995. 129 p.: bibl. (Biblioteca Política argentina; 484)

Short but incisive analysis of Afro-Argentine populations during and after the independence wars. Argues that militia service provided blacks with an alternative to continued servitude, but also insured that they would be in the forefront of the fighting (and, thus, saw their numbers radically reduced by mid-century). During the Paraguayan War, Afro-Argentines continued to serve in the army, but were no longer segregated in separate units. [TW]

2983 Moyano, María José. Argentina's lost patrol: armed struggle, 1969–1979. New Haven, Conn.: Yale Univ. Press, 1995. 226 p.: bibl., ill., index, map.

An excellent analysis of Argentine guerrilla movements in the 1960s-70s based on a wide range of printed sources and extensive interviews with members of the groups. Rather than describing all the activities of the various groups, this study attempts to explain the rationale for their behavior. [JH]

2984 Muñoz Moraleda, Ernesto. Los grupos políticos españoles y su influencia en los sucesos rioplatenses, 1809–1820. Buenos Aires: Tall. Gráf. Segunda Edición, 1993. 137 p.: bibl., index.

Suggestive account of political trends in Spain and their impact on Platine politics in the early national period. Sees a correlation between the Spanish liberal ideologies and those of the Argentine Unitarios, and a parallel correlation between Spanish traditionalists and the Platine caudillos (Cornelio Saavedra, Artigas, and the subsequent federals). [TW]

2985 Myers, Jorge. Orden y virtud: el discurso republicano en el régimen rosista. Buenos Aires: Univ. Nacional de Quilmes, 1995. 310 p.: bibl. (La ideología argentina)

Impressive analysis of the republican rhetoric of the 1829–52 Rosas government. Maintains that the language of republicanism among Rosista publicists was in fundamental conflict with modern scientific concerns (something that was untrue of Rosas's Unitario opponents). Includes a fascinating anthology of writings by various figures in the Rosas camp. Highly recommended. For philosophy specialist's comment, see item **5275.** [TW]

2986 Nari, Marcela María Alejandra. Feminismo y diferencia sexual: análisis de la "Encuesta Feminista Argentina" de 1919. (*Bol. Inst. Hist. Ravignani*, 12, segundo semestre 1995, p. 61–86)

An interesting study of a 1919 survey of key figures (both men and women) in the political, cultural, and academic worlds on their views on feminism and what it should mean in Argentina. While the survey was not scientific and the answers were qualitative, it does provide an overview of the thoughts of a number of influential people on the roles that women should play in society. [JH]

2987 Nario, Hugo. Mesías y bandoleros pampeanos. Buenos Aires: Editorial Galerna, 1993. 143 p.: bibl.

Examines banditry and bandit leadership on the Bonaerense pampas in the 19th and early-20th centuries. Given the dearth of documentation, author depends principally on folkloric sources, which are woven into a tentative analysis that is more anthropological than historical. [TW]

2988 Newton, Ronald C. German Nazism and the origins of Argentine anti-Semitism. (*in* The Jewish diaspora in Latin America: new studies on history and literature. New York: Garland Publ., 1996, p. 199–217, bibl.)

A thoughtful, if preliminary essay, on the development of modern anti-Semitism in Argentina and the German role. Covers period from 1930–45. Argues that German role was relatively small. [JH]

2989 Newton, Ronald C. The 'Nazi menace' in Argentina revisited. (*Patterns Prejud.*, 31:3, 1997, p. 7–15)

A succinct re-examinaiton of Newton's views on the extent of the Nazi threat in Argentina, largely based on his 1992 book (see *HLAS* 52:2741). Places discussion in the context of recent increased attention to German activity in Argentina and other countries. [JH]

2990 Nicolau, Juan Carlos. El comercio de ultramar por el puerto de Buenos Aires, 1810–1850. (*Invest. Ens.*, 44, enero/dic. 1994, p. 303–320, graph, tables)

A short but very useful analysis of oceanic commerce through the port of Buenos Aires during the early national period. Finds that trade was dominated by British and North American carriers, and continually increased even when hampered at times by war and blockade. Imports usually outpaced exports, leading to a continual drain of specie from Buenos Aires. The tables, which cover customs receipts, nationality of carriers, and value of trade, are particularly valuable. [TW]

2991 Nicolau, Juan Carlos. Proteccionismo y libre comercio en Buenos Aires, 1810–1850. Córdoba, Argentina: Centro de Estudios Históricos, 1995. 128 p.: bibl. (Cuaderno, 0327–604X; no. 15 y 16)

This fine economic history deals with regional trade in the Lower Plata, and with the decades-long debate between protectionists and free traders. By 1850s, Nicolau observes, the landed elite of Buenos Aires had successfully prevented any changes in the system of open trade that had so benefited their interests. [TW]

2992 Nicolini, Esteban Alberto. El comercio en Tucumán, 1810–1815: flujos de mercancías y dinero y balanzas comerciales. (*Poblac. Soc.*, 2, dic. 1994, p. 47–79, bibl., graphs, tables)

Detailed survey of commercial trends in Tucumán in the immediate aftermath of independence. Methodologically sophisticated, the article traces the reorientation of trade away from the province's partners in Alto Peru, Chile, and Paraguay, and toward Buenos Aires. [TW]

2993 Oberman, Gerardo C.C. Antiquum peractum sit: la historia de la inmigración holandesa en la Argentina y los orí-genes del movimiento reformado, 1888–1910. Buenos Aires: Tall. Gráf. EDIGRAF, 1993. 222 p.: bibl., ill.

Written by a minister of the Reformed church, work studies Dutch immigration between 1888–1910 and the founding of the Reformed church in Argentina. Focuses on Buenos Aires and Rosario. Based largely on primary material. [JH]

2994 O'Donnell, Pacho. Monteagudo: la pasión revolucionaria. Buenos Aires: Planeta, 1995. 233 p.: bibl. (Colección Historia argentina)

Well-written study of Bernardo Monteagudo (1789–1824), the Tucumano revolutionary and friend of San Martín and Bolívar. Alternately described as a genius and an opportunist, Monteagudo was one of the most controversial figures of the early independence period (and the various opinions of him are well reflected in the more than 100 p. of documents included herein). Lacks clear references. [TW]

2995 Oggier, Gabriel. Las familias de San Jerónimo Norte: las que poblaron la colonia, sus hijos y sus nietos, 1858–1922. v. 1–2. Santa Fe, Argentina: SERV GRAF, 1993. 2 v.: ill., indexes, maps.

Encyclopedic treatment of the Swiss colonists who founded and operated Santa Fe's colony of San Jerónimo Norte. Recommended for specialist on immigration. [TW]

2996 Oliveira Cézar, Lucrecia de. Aristóbulo del Valle. Buenos Aires: Instituto Bonaerense de Numismática y Antigüedades: Ediciones de Arte Gaglianone, 1993. 103 p.: bibl., ill. (some col.) (Coleccionistas argentinos)

A richly illustrated pamphlet details life and accomplishments of one of Argentina's first collectors of European art. Del Valle (1845–96) had comprehensive tastes and his collection ran the gamut from Renaissance Spanish portraits to an "*arlequin dansant*" by Degas. [TW]

2997 Palacio, Juan Manuel. Jorge Sábato y la historiografía rural pampeana: el problema del otro. (*Entrepasados/Buenos Aires*, 5:10, 1996, p. 46–66, ill.)

Starting from Jorge Sábato's ideas about rural development, author looks at key questions about the *chacareros* of the humid pampas, drawing on evidence from the wheat areas of southern Buenos Aires. Discusses current state of research and makes suggestions for future investigation. [JH]

2998 Pan, Luis. El mundo de Nicolás Repetto. Buenos Aires: Grupo Editor Latinoamericano, 1996. 473 p. (Colección Estudios políticos y sociales)

Presents scattered information on Repetto and the Socialist Party, especially on Juan B. Justo. Written by a former militant in the party. [JH]

2999 Pasquali, Patricia. Algo más sobre Pavón y la resistencia federal. (*Invest. Ens.*, 44, enero/dic. 1994, p. 321–363)

Well-researched examination of Santafecino politics in the immediate aftermath of the crucial 1861 battle between Urquiza and Mitre. [TW]

3000 Pasquali, Patricia. Juan Lavalle: un guerrero en tiempos de revolución y dictadura. Buenos Aires: Planeta, 1996. 406 p., 16 p. of plates: bibl., ill. (Historia argentina)

Well-crafted, readable biography of a key Unitarian general (1797–1841). [TW]

3001 Paz, Gustavo L. Tierra y resistencia campesina en la puna de Jujuy, 1875– 1910. (*ANDES Antropol. Hist.*, 6, 1994, p. 209–234, bibl., tables)

Archivally based investigation of the evolution of landholding and demands for land by the indigenous peasantry of the puna of Jujuy after their failed revolt in 1874. Paz makes clear that the destruction of traditional forms of economic relationships is complex and that the provincial government played a major role in it. [JH]

3002 Pellichi, Pedro María et al. Misioneros del Chaco Occidental: escritos de franciscanos del Chaco Salteño, 1861–1914. Introducción, notas y selección de textos por Ana A. Teruel. Jujuy: Centro de Estudios Indígenas y Coloniales, 1995. 145 p.: bibl., 1 map. (Biblioteca de historia y antropología; 4)

An excellent compilation of little-known Franciscan writings on the order's missionary work in the western Chaco. Includes detailed descriptions of the society and customs of the Chiriguano, Toba, and Mataco Indians. [TW]

3003 Pensar la Argentina: los historiadores hablan de historia y política. Buenos Aires: Ediciones El Cielo por Asalto: Imago

Mundi, 1994. 220 p. (Colección La cultura argentina)

A series of fascinating interviews with writers about Argentina's past. Solid questions address interviewees' intellectual development and visions of the past. Includes interviews with Halperín, James, Terán, Sabato, Botana, Chiaramonte, Sarlo, and Torre. [JH]

3004 Perdía, Roberto Cirilo. La otra historia: testimonio de un jefe montonero. Argentina: Grupo Agora, 1997. 431 p.: bibl., ill. (Documentos de la Argentina)

A history/memoir of the Peronist left-wing guerrillas by one of their leaders. Perdía went from Catholic militancy to the FAP to the Montoneros. While there is evidence of research, the insider's perspective is what makes this an interesting piece. [JH]

3005 Perón, Eva. In my own words. Translated from the Spanish by Laura Dail. Introduction by Joseph A. Page. New York: New Press, 1996. 119 p.: ill.

Translation of a text supposedly written by Eva Perón on her deathbed, but not published until 1987. The authenticity of the work has been questioned and it is highly unlikely that she wrote all of it. If it is hers, it displays the sharper aspects of her personality that are missing from the works that she claimed to author. Includes a useful introduction. [JH]

3006 Petrocelli, Héctor B. Las Misiones Orientales: parte del precio que pagó Urquiza para derrocar a Rosas. Buenos Aires: Instituto de Investigaciones Históricas Juan Manuel de Rosas, 1995. 127 p.: bibl., ill. (Colección Estrella federal; 9)

Argues that in order to gain Brazilian help in ousting Rosas, the Entrerriano caudillo Justo José de Urquiza gave up all Argentine claims to a huge section of the Misiones territory (what today makes up the western portion of Brazil's Paraná, Santa Catarina, and Rio Grande do Sul). [TW]

Pistoia, Benita Honorato. Los Franciscanos en el Tucumán y en el Norte Argentino, 1566–1973. See item **2478.**

3007 Pistone, J. Catalina. La esclavatura negra en Santa Fe. Argentina: Junta Provincial de Estudios Históricos de Santa Fe, 1996. 86 p.: bibl., ill.

A short look at black slavery in the

town and province of Santa Fe. Focuses mainly on legal questions, abolitionism, and participation in the early Argentine military. Based in part on archival documentation. [TW]

3008 Plotkin, Mariano Ben. Freud, politics, and the porteños: the reception of psychoanalysis in Buenos Aires, 1910–1943. (*HAHR*, 77:1, Feb. 1997, p. 45–74, bibl.)

Examines the reception of psychoanalysis in Argentina before its institutionalization. Looks at the introduction of pyschoanalysis and its co-existence with other intellectual traditions. The hardening of intellectual debates made this more difficult over time. [JH]

3009 La población de Córdoba en 1813: publicación homenaje a la memoria del profesor Ceferino Garzón Maceda. Presentación y notas a cargo de Aníbal Arcondo. Córdoba, Argentina: Facultad de Ciencias Económicas, Instituto de Economía y Finanzas, 1995. 163 p.: bibl. + 1 computer disk (3 $\frac{1}{2}$ in.).

Finely wrought analysis of Córdoba's 1813 census. Includes 120 pages of tables and documents. [TW]

3010 Población y trabajo en el noroeste argentino: siglos XVIII y XIX. Recopilación de Ana A. Teruel. San Salvador de Jujuy, Argentina: Univ. Nacional de Jujuy, Unidad de Investigación en Historia Regional, 1995. 190 p.: bibl., ill. (Colección Arte-ciencia. Serie Jujuy en el pasado)

Impressive compilation of eight studies on population movement, labor acquisition, and indigenous-white relations in northwestern Argentina (provinces of Jujuy, Tucumán, Salta, Santiago de Estero, and Chaco). Based on solid archival research. [TW]

3011 Potash, Robert A. The army & politics in Argentina. v. 3, 1962–1973; From Frondizi's fall to the Peronist restoration. Stanford, Calif.: Stanford Univ. Press, 1996. 1 v.: bibl., facsim., ill., index, ports.

Third volume of in-depth analysis of the army. Format is similar to previous two volumes. There is, however, more emphasis on the internal maneuvering which characterizes the period. The detail is based on information provided by the participants. A worthy successor to the other studies and essential for analysis of the period. For reviews of vol. 1, see *HLAS 31:7229* and *HLAS 32:2599a*. [JH]

3012 Pozzi, Pablo A. "Los perros": la cultura guerrillera del PRT-ERP. (*Taller/Buenos Aires*, 1:2, nov. 1996, p. 101–124)

After reviewing existing literature on the ERP and guerrilla movements in general, Pozzi looks at the guerillas themselves, their reasons for joining the movements, and their outlook and attitudes. Information comes principally from about 70 interviews carried out by author. A useful piece. [JH]

3013 Un precursor de la colonización del Chubut: documentos sobre la actuación de Enrique Líbanus Jones en el Chubut. Recopilación de Clemente I. Dumrauf. Viedma, Argentina: Fundación Ameghino, 1991. 93 p.: map. (Biblioteca de la Fundación Ameghino. Textos ameghinianos)

Compilation of documents, some taken from the AGN, some from early porteño newspapers, and some taken from published sources, on the 1850s exploration of southern Patagonia. [TW]

3014 Prieto, Adolfo. Los viajeros ingleses y la emergencia de la literatura argentina, 1820–1850. Buenos Aires: Editorial Sudamericana, 1996. 189 p.: bibl. (Colección Historia y cultura)

A solid examination of English travel literature and its impact on the development of an Argentine intelligentsia in the 19th century. Argues that certain images of national reality—the Pampa, the slaughterhouse, the gaucho on his horse—were transmitted from the accounts of English travelers into the writings of Alberdi, Echeverría, Marmol, and Sarmiento, who went on to create a national literature. [TW]

3015 Privitellio, Luciano de. ¿Quien habla por la ciudad?: la política porteña y el affaire CHADE, 1932–1936. (*Entrepasados/ Buenos Aires*, 4:6, 1994, p. 49–64)

An excellent examination of the nature of politics in the city of Buenos Aires during the 1930s. Looks at controversies surrounding the electrical utility CHADE. Highlights, in particular, the role of *sociedades de fomento* (neighborhood associations) and their relationship with political parties. [JH]

3016 **Proyecto y construcción de una nación: 1846–1880.** v. 2. Buenos Aires: Compañia Editora Espasa Calpe Argentina: Ariel, 1995. 622 p.: bibl. (Ariel historia)

An excellent compilation of texts by 31 Argentine political commentators and polemecists from the 1846–80 era. Authors include Mitre, Sarmiento, Alberdi, Echeverría, José Hernández, and Vicente F. López. In his preliminary study, Halperín Donghi notes that only Argentina realized a measure of the material and political progess to which the rest of the continent aspired—and this reflected in no small part the farsightedness of its political thinkers. For annotation of vol. 1, see *HLAS 44:3340.* [TW]

3017 **Quesada, Juan Isidro.** Injerencia argentina en la guerra civil uruguaya de 1836–1838. (*Invest. Ens.,* 44, enero/dic. 1994, p. 381–420)

Discusses involvement of Juan Manuel de Rosas in the Uruguayan Civil War of 1836–39. Though ostensibly a supporter of Manuel Oribe, Rosas in fact preferred to dominate Uruguay through military surrogates—Lavalleja and Urquiza—who in turn aided the Oribe forces. Of particular interest is the description of the siege of Paysandú, which makes use of a little-known diary by a Blanco defender of the town, Colonel Antonio Toll. [TW]

3018 **Quevedo, Hugo Orlando.** El Partido Peronista en La Rioja. v. 3, 1972–1976: Crisis interna, triunfo y caída del justicialismo; la época de la derecha y la izquierda. Córdoba, Argentina: Lerner, 1992. 1 v.: bibl., ill.

Useful third volume of a detailed history of the Peronist Party in the province of La Rioja. Presents large amounts of material. Lacks serious interpretation. [JH]

3019 **Ramos, Jorge Abelardo.** La nación inconclusa: de las repúblicas insulares a la Patria Grande. Montevideo: Ediciones de La Plaza, 1994. 344 p.: bibl. (Colección Testimonios)

Compilation of 23 essays on Latin American political, historical, and literary themes by a well-known Argentine Marxist historian and social commentator. Works stress thesis of Francisco Miranda: that, in order to combat the forces of imperialism, the Latin American states must unite in a single nation. [TW]

3020 **Rato de Sambuccetti, Susana Irene.** La lucha por el poder hegemónico en Entre Ríos, 1881–1883: la elección del Gobernador Racedo y el traslado de la capital. (*Res Gesta,* 34, enero/dic. 1995, p. 201–255, tables)

Fascinating microhistorical account of Entrerriano politics, focusing on the decision to move the provincial capital from Concepción del Uruguay to Paraná. [TW]

3021 **Ratto, Silvia.** Indios amigos e indios aliados: origenes del "Negocio Pacífico" en la provincia de Buenos Aires (1829–1832). Buenos Aires: Instituto de Historia Argentina y Americana Dr. Emilio Ravignani, Facultad de Filosofía y Letras, Univ. de Buenos Aires, 1994. 34 p.: bibl., map. (Cuadernos del Instituto Ravignani; 5)

Brief but penetrating analysis of indigenous-white relations in Buenos Aires prov. in the early Rosas period. Shows how the government, in providing regular supplies of cattle and foodstuffs to friendly Pampas Indians, paved the way for a common resistance to other indigenous groups who had invaded the region from Chile. [TW]

3022 **Recalde, Héctor.** La salud de los trabajadores en Buenos Aires, 1870–1910: a través de las fuentes médicas. Buenos Aires: Grupo Editor Universitario. GEU, 1997. 347 p.: bibl. (Biblioteca de temas argentinos)

Examines how the medical profession viewed and tried to act on workers' health conditions in Buenos Aires. Includes discussion of impact of working conditions and housing on health and on the problems of tuberculosis and alcoholism. [JH]

3023 **Rein, Raanan.** Another front line: Francoists and anti-Francoists in Argentina, 1936–1949. (*Patterns Prejud.,* 31:3, 1997, p. 17–33)

Summarizes Spanish Civil War's impact in Argentina during the war itself and then more briefly during its aftermath, especially the early Perón years. Emphasizes the complexity of the reaction. [JH]

3024 **Remedi, Fernando Javier.** Condiciones de vida material de la población rural cordobesa, 1900–1914: un aporte a su estudio. Córdoba, Argentina: Centro de Estudios Históricos, 1996. 52 p.: bibl. (Cuaderno, 0327–604x; no. 19)

Brief introduction to the material culture of the Córdoba countryside at the beginning of the 20th century. Topics covered in short chapters include access to potable water, diseases and health care, cost of living, and social mobility. [TW]

3025 Representaciones inconclusas: las clases, los actores y los discursos de la memoria, 1912–1946. Recopilación de Waldo Ansaldi, Alfredo R. Pucciarelli, and José César Villarruel. Buenos Aires: Biblos, 1995. 383 p.: bibl.

A series of solid articles from the perspective of historical sociology. Includes articles on politics and the intersection of the state and the economy. [JH]

3026 Rivera, Alberto A. Martin de Moussy y su "Memoria histórica sobre la decadencia y ruina de las misiones jesuiticas en el seno del Plata. Su estado en 1856". (*Folia Hist. Nordeste,* 10, 1991, p. 249–264)

Excellent account of the French explorer whose three-vol. *Description Geographique et Statistique de la Confédération Argentine: 1860–1864* is still regarded as one of the best works on Argentine geography. Includes a facsimile copy of the Frenchman's report on the Misiones territory. [TW]

3027 Rocchi, Fernando. En busca del empresario perdido: los industriales argentinos y las tesis de Jorge Federico Sábato. (*Entrepasados/Buenos Aires,* 5 : 10, 1996, p. 67–88, ill., table)

An examination of Sábato's thesis about entrepreneurs, especially the belief that their financial interests were diversified, in commerce and service as well as industry and agriculture. Examines and amplifies this idea by looking at entrepreneurial activities during period of agricultural expansion. Based on primary and secondary sources. [JH]

3028 Rodil, Marta. Puerto perdido: vida y testimonios de su gente; documentación escrita, gráfica y fotográfica; testimonios literarios. Santa Fe, Argentina: Univ. Nacional del Litoral, 1994. 206 p.: bibl., ill.

An interesting series of oral histories with ordinary people who lived and worked in the old ports of the city of Santa Fe. Contains some literary fragments as well as old photographs. [JH]

3029 Rojo, Roberto. Heroes y cobardes en el ocaso federal. Buenos Aires: Ediciones COMFER, 1994. 222 p.: bibl., ill.

A well-researched, though modest account of the various *Montonero* movements launched against the Argentine national government between 1860–74. Focuses on the province of La Rioja and especially on the figure of Felipe Varela, for whom Rojo shows a marked sympathy. [TW]

3030 Rosal, Miguel A. El interior frente a Buenos Aires: flujos comerciales e integración económica, 1831–1850. (*Secuencia/México,* 31, enero/abril 1995, p. 51–111, bibl., graphs, ill., tables)

Well-informed examination of internal trade networks in Argentina, and especially of the influence of the porteño market in determining the character and volume of provincial exports. Excellent tables. [TW]

3031 Rosal, Miguel A. Negros y pardos en Buenos Aires: 1811–1860. (*Anu. Estud. Am.,* 51 : 1, 1994, p. 165–184, graph, table)

A brief but engaging look at blacks and pardos in Buenos Aires in the early national period. Especially good on Afro-Argentine landholders, who are presented as capable entrepreneurs and moneylenders, and as organizers (and chief backers) of benevolent associations. [TW]

3032 Rosal, Miguel A. and **Roberto Schmit.** Comercio, mercados e integración económica en la Argentina del siglo XIX. Buenos Aires: Instituto de Historia Argentina y Americana Dr. Emilio Ravignani, Facultad de Filosofía y Letras, Univ. de Buenos Aires, 1995. 118 p.: bibl., ill., map. (Cuadernos del Instituto Ravignani, 0524–9767; 9)

Two studies on Argentine domestic trade during the first half of the 19th century. The first study, by Rosal, addresses commercial relations between the Interior and Littoral provinces and the port of Buenos Aires between 1831–50. The second, by Schmit and Rosal, is backdated to the late colonial period and concentrates narrowly on trade within the Littoral. Both studies make use of intricate statistical registers compiled from archives in Buenos Aires (but not, unfortunately, from provincial archives). [TW]

3033 Ruffini de Grané, Martha. Un aspecto de la relación Yrigoyen-Crotto: agro política en la provincia de Buenos Aires. (Estudios de historia rural III. Buenos Aires: Facultad de Humanidades y Ciencias de la Educación, 1993, p. 33–58)

In the context of the political struggle between the Radical Party governor of

Buenos Aires prov., 1918–21, and President Yrigoyen, this article examines agricultural policies during an extremely conflictive era. [JH]

3034 Ruibal, Beatriz Celina. El honor y el delito: Buenos Aires a fines del siglo XIX. (*Entrepasados/Buenos Aires*, 6:11, 1996, p. 35–44, ill.)

Readable, suggestive essay on crimes of passion, hysteria, and concepts of feminine honor in turn-of-the-century Buenos Aires. Focuses on one notorious murder case. [TW]

3035 Ruiz Moreno, Isidoro. La revolución del 55. v. 1, Dictadura y conspiración. v. 2, Cómo cayó Perón. Buenos Aires: Emecé Editores, 1994. 2 v.: bibl., ill., index, maps.

Examines revolts against Perón in 1955. Looks at both their nature and their cause. Based on ample documentation, mainly oral history, the author clearly favors those trying to overthrow Perón and most of his sources lean in the same direction. Written for a popular audience. [JH]

3036 Sabato, Hilda. Elecciones y prácticas electorales en Buenos Aires, 1860–1880: ¿sufragio universal sin ciudadanía política? (*in* Historia de las elecciones en Iberoamérica, siglo XIX: de la formación del espacio político nacional. Coordinación de Antonio Annino. Buenos Aires: Fondo de Cultura Económica, 1995, p. 107–142)

A detailed and subtle analysis of electoral practices in the city of Buenos Aires during the late-19th century. Notes that porteño politics had an ambiguous character; despite legal universal suffrage, voting was, in practice, quite restricted. Recommended. [TW]

3037 Sabato, Hilda. Participación política y ciudadanía en la historiografía política argentina. (*Anos 90*, 1:1, maio 1993, p. 85–102, bibl.)

Explores two themes. First examines the return of politics to the forefront of historical studies, especially in Argentina. The author ties this trend to the political events of the last several decades. Second, the author briefly analyzes her previous work on electoral processes in Buenos Aires between the 1860s-80s, arguing that elections did not tie civil society to the political system. This work forms a part of the larger re-examina-tion of the nature of politics at the end of the 19th century. [JH]

3038 Sabor, Josefa Emilia. Pedro de Angelis y los orígenes de la bibliografía argentina: ensayo bio-bibliográfico. Buenos Aires: Ediciones Solar, 1995. 460 p.: bibl., index. (Biblioteca "Dimensión argentina")

Brilliant examination of the Italian bibliographer who lent his considerable talents to the Rosas regime in the mid 1800s. Though de Angelis might have had questionable politics, his contribution to Latin American scholarship was tremendous; he assembled and organized a vitally important collection of books, maps, documents, and pamphlets on the early history of the Plata still used today. Sabor's prize-winning study is part biography, part bibliographical essay, and wholly erudite. Recommended. [TW]

3039 Sáenz Quesada, María. Mariquita Sánchez: vida política y sentimental. Buenos Aires: Editorial Sudamericana, 1995. 347 p.: bibl., ill., index.

This extensively documented study of Mariquita Sánchez de Thompson y Mendeville captures the sense and intricacy of upper-class life in Buenos Aires in the early 1800s. Sánchez (1786–1868) knew many of the key figures of Argentine independence personally, and, as a member of the highest porteño elite, was as privy to their intrigues as to their ideals. This narrative works equally well as intimate biography and as introduction to early national politics. [TW]

3040 Sahni, Varun. Not quite British: a study of external influences on the Argentine navy. (*J. Lat. Am. Stud.*, 25:3, Oct. 1993, p. 489–513, appendix, graphs, tables)

Argues that the Argentine navy was not as affected by British influence as has often been argued. Supports argument by examining rules of discipline, naval doctrine, training of officers abroad and at home, and, above all, where ships and planes were procured. Evidence clearly shows that while the British had some impact, the influences on the navy were coming from a number of different countries. For political scientist's comment, see *HLAS 57:3766*. [JH]

3041 Salessi, Jorge. Médicos maleantes y maricas: higiene, criminología y homosexualidad en la construcción de la nación argentina; Buenos Aires, 1871–1914. Rosario,

Argentina: B. Viterbo Editora, 1995. 413 p.: bibl. (Estudios culturales)

Pathbreaking study of homosexuality in Buenos Aires in the late-19th and early-20th centuries. Drawing upon a wealth of information (much of it from government medical and criminal reports), Salessi shows how state officials and scientists placed homosexuality into the category of "disease"—a malady, which, like yellow fever, could be eradicated through proper public health measures. The subtleties and contradictions of their determination, and the basic unfairness of a system that saw machismo as the norm, make for fascinating reading. [TW]

3042 Salvatore, Ricardo D. The breakdown of social discipline in the Banda Oriental and the Littoral, 1790–1820. (in Revolution and restoration: the rearrangement of power in Argentina, 1776–1860. Edited by Mark D. Szuchman and Jonathan C. Brown. Lincoln: Univ. of Nebraska Press, 1994, p. 74–102)

Thought-provoking study of rural workers in the Lower Plata during the revolutionary age. Argues that the breakdown of social discipline that accompanied independence wars can be traced as much to workers' discontent with landholder authority as to the disintegration of the old elite (and the consequent rise of caudillismo). [TW]

3043 Salvatore, Ricardo D. Fiestas federales: representaciones de la República en el Buenos Aires rosista. (*Entrepasados/Buenos Aires*, 6:11, 1996, p. 45–68, ill.)

Fascinating examination of patriotic demonstrations and public celebrations during the Rosas era. Shows how these events recast terms like "freedom" and "equality" into notions politically useful to the *Restaurador*. [TW]

3044 Sartelli, Eduardo. Del asombro al desencanto: la tecnología rural y los vaivenes de la agricultura pampeana. (Problemas de la historia agraria: nuevos debates y perspectivas de investigación. Tandil, Argentina: Instituto de Estudios Histórico Sociales (IEHS), 1995, p. 125–154, tables)

Interesting article examines conventional views connecting problems of Argentine agriculture with technology, essentially arguing that they are invalid. For example, contends that development of mechanization was not due to high cost of labor, but rather,

agriculture would have been impossible without mechanization because of the small population. [JH]

3045 Schaller, Enrique César. La distribución de la tierra y el poblamiento en la provincia de Corrientes, 1821–1860. Resistencia, Argentina: Instituto de Investigaciones Geohistóricas, 1995. 277 p.: bibl., maps. (Cuadernos de geohistoria regional, 0325–8246; no. 31)

A first-rate, thorough analysis of land tenancy and economic development in 19th-century Corrientes. Based on a wide array of documents from the provincial archive. [TW]

3046 Schaller, Enrique César. La política de tierras en la provincia de Corrientes, 1850–1900. (*Folia Hist. Nordeste*, 11, 1993, p. 93–133, table)

Thorough, well-written description of landholding policies and debates in 19th-century Corrientes. Provides details on emphyteusis, sale of public lands, and state-sponsored colonization. [TW]

3047 Schwarcz, Alfredo José. Trotz allem—: die deutschsprachigen Juden in Argentinien [Despite everything: German-speaking Jews in Argentina]. Translated from the Spanish by Bernardo and Inge Schwarcz. Wien, Austria: Böhlau, 1995. 323 p.: bibl., ill.

Valuable contribution to immigration history examines background, economic integration, degree of adaptation and/or assimilation, interaction with older Jewish groups, retention of culture and language, and social and cultural institutions of German-speaking Jews in Argentina. Covers three groups of refugees who entered Argentina between 1933–45: immigrants over 18, under 18, and immigrants' children born in Argentina or neighboring countries. The author, a psychologist specializing in gerontology, was assisted by social scientists and supported by Jewish organizations. [C.K. Converse]

3048 Segreti, Carlos S.A. La acción política de Güemes. Córdoba, Argentina: Centro de Estudios Históricos, 1991. 104 p.: bibl. (Cuaderno; no. 1)

Brief study emphasizes popular support enjoyed by Martín Güemes, the Salteño caudillo of the early independence period. Argues that Güemes had a political vision more broadly "national" in character than is generally recognized. [TW]

3049 **Segreti, Carlos S.A.** Federalismo rioplatense y federalismo argentino: el
federalismo de Córdoba en los comienzos de
la época independiente, 1810–1829. Palabras
prévias de Dardo Pérez Guilhou. Córdoba,
Argentina: Centro de Estudios Históricos,
1995. 146 p.: bibl. (Cuaderno; no. 7 y 8)

Solid study of Córdoba's contribution
to the development of the political order in
early independent Argentina. Suggests that
the province had to balance the political interests of the Littoral and Interior and in so
doing forged its own particular variation of
federalism. [TW]

3050 **Segreti, Carlos S.A.** La máscara de la
monarquía: contribución al estudio
crítico de las llamadas gestiones monár-
quicas bajo la Revolución de Mayo, 1808–
1819. Córdoba, Argentina: Centro de Estudios Históricos, 1994. 312 p.: bibl.

Thoughtful examination of royalist intrigues and monarchist sympathies within
the Argentine revolutionary elite just after
independence. Segreti makes it clear that although the republican option was that which
won out in the end, this was by no means inevitable, and many sincere revolutionaries
regarded monarchy as an appropriate solution to the political chaos of their times.
[TW]

3051 **Senkman, Leonardo.** La Argentina
neutral de 1940 ante los refugiados
españoles y judios. (*Ciclos Hist. Econ. Soc.*,
5:9, segundo semestre 1995, p. 53–76)

Places in perspective a comparison of
the treatment of Jewish and Spanish refugees
in 1940, a crucial year. Shows that whether
politicians were pro-allied, neutralist, or pro-
German, dominant political forces considered most refugees to be undesirable. The
only major exception was the Basques, who
were encouraged to come due to the influence of the pro-Basque lobby, which included
much of the elite. [JH]

3052 **Serafín, Albino A.** 1955 revolución
libertadora: gobierno y partido de la
U.C.R.I. Buenos Aires: Narvaja, 1994. 290 p.:
bibl.

Looks at rise and fall of the UCRI, especially its time in power under Frondizi.
Special attention is paid to Córdoba. The
author, a political militant, had ties to elements of the party. [JH]

3053 **Serrano, Mario Arturo.** Arequito: por
qué se sublevó el Ejército del Norte?
Buenos Aires: Círculo Militar, 1996. 264 p.:
bibl., port. (Biblioteca del oficial; vol. 762)

Military historian examines the 1820
mutiny of the Auxiliary Army of Upper Peru,
an event that opened the door for all subsequent coups and *cuartelazos* that the country
suffered until the advent of Rosas. Based on
secondary sources. [TW]

Silva, Hernán A. El comercio entre España y
el Río de la Plata, 1778–1810. See item **2495.**

3054 **Solveira, Beatriz Rosario.** Las relaciones con Rusia durante las presiden-
cias de Yrigoyen y Alvear, 1916–1930. Córdoba, Argentina: Centro de Estudios
Históricos, 1995. 75 p.: bibl. (Cuaderno,
0327–604X; no. 9)

A short overview of diplomatic relations between Russia (and later the Soviet
Union) and Argentina. Based largely on
records of the Argentine foreign ministry.
Does not deal with extralegal relations produced by the Comintern. [JH]

3055 **Stoffel, Leticia María.** Ripamonti:
un hito en la historia de los comerciantes de la Pampa Gringa. Rafaela, Argentina: Fondo Editorial Municipal, 1994.
173 p.: bibl., ill. (Trabajo de investigación
histórica; 9)

Uses family and company archives
to examine the Ripamonti family and their
business, the Grandes Almacenes Ripamonti,
based in Rafaela, Santa Fe, with branches
elsewhere. The stores sold everything from
food to clothing to farm machinery. Combines history of the immigrant founding family with fortunes of the company. Important
information on a crucial aspect of rural life.
[JH]

Svampa, Maristella. El dilema argentino: civilización o barbarie; de Sarmiento al revisionismo peronista. See item **5285.**

Tandeter, Enrique. El período colonial en la
historiografía argentina reciente. See item
2499.

3056 **Tcach, César.** Neoperonismo y resistencia obrera en la Córdoba libertadora, 1955–1958. (*Desarro. Econ.*, 35:137,
abril/junio 1995, p. 63–82, tables)

Through an examination of politics in

the period directly after the overthrow of Perón, author highlights importance of neoperonist political parties. Demonstrates that the neoperonist parties were not an isolated phenomenon by showing their ties to wider sectors. [JH]

3057 Tedeschi de Brunet, Sonia. Los últimos años de una institución colonial: el cabildo de Santa Fe y su relación con otros espacios político-institucionales entre 1819 y 1832. (*Rev. Junta Prov. Estud. Hist. Santa Fe*, 59, 1993, p. 409–429, bibl.)

Traces decline of the Cabildo of Santa Fe in the face of pressure from the provincial legislature and Governor Estanislao López. Suggests that institutional rivalries in the early national period opened the door to caudillismo. [TW]

3058 Ternavasio, Marcela. Nuevo régimen representativo y expansión de la frontera política: las elecciones en el estado de Buenos Aires, 1820–1840. (*in* Historia de las elecciones en Iberoamérica, siglo XIX: de la formación del espacio político nacional. Coordinación de Antonio Annino. Buenos Aires: Fondo de Cultura Económica, 1995, p. 65–105, maps, tables)

Argues that political instability in the province of Buenos Aires during the early national period cannot be reduced to a conflict of economic interests or to jealousies among caudillos. Instead, it derived from the electoral reform law of 1821, which enfranchised all freeborn men in the provincial interior (who until then represented no threat to the traditional elites, but who afterwards gave solid support to Rosas and his plans to reorder political power in Buenos Aires). [TW]

3059 Teruel, Ana A. La incidencia de la tenancia de la tierra en la formación del mercado de trabajo rural en la provincia de Jujuy, 1870–1910. (*Poblac. Soc.*, 2, dic. 1994, p. 161–187, graphs, tables)

Well-crafted article describes land tenure and rural labor in late-19th-century Jujuy. Notes that land usage patterns were rather complex, with impoverished smallholders eking out a precarious living in the highlands, forcing wealthier lowland sugar growers to import laborers from Bolivia and other neighboring provinces. [TW]

3060 Terzaga, Alfredo. Claves de la historia de Córdoba. Río Cuarto, Argentina: Univ. Nacional de Río Cuarto, 1996. 344 p.: bibl.

A compilation of essays on the social and political history of the province of Córdoba written by an important local historian and literary critic. [TW]

3061 Tierra del Fuego en cuatro textos: del siglo XVIII al XX. Recopilación de Eduardo Bitlloch. Buenos Aires: Univ. de Buenos Aires, Facultad de Filosofía y Letras, Museo Etnográfico "Juan B. Ambrosetti," 1994. 93 p.: bibl., map. (Cuadernos de trabajo, 0327-7607; no. 2. Serie Documentos)

Compilation of little-known descriptive texts on Tierra del Fuego, two written by a Spanish naval officer in the 1780s, one by a French physician in 1884, and one by an Italian ethnographer in 1913. Useful for information on the early Fuegian peoples. [TW]

3062 Tobares, Jesús Liberato. Noticias para la historia de los pueblos de San Luis. San Luis, Argentina: Fondo Editorial Sanluiseño, Gobierno de la Provincia de San Luis, 1996. 287 p.: bibl. (Colección Investigación; 47–10)

Encyclopedic study of the small communities of an oft-forgotten province. Could benefit from including map. [TW]

3063 El trotskismo obrero e internacionalista en la Argentina. v. 2, Palabra obrera y la Resistencia, 1955–1959. Buenos Aires: Editorial Antídoto, 1995. 297 p.

Second vol. of official history of the Trotskyist faction led by Nahuel Moreno (formerly the Grupo Obrero Marxista and currently known as Movimiento al Socialismo—MAS). Based on party documents, interviews, as well as newspapers and secondary sources. Interesting perspective on the quarrels within international Trotskyism and, more importantly, on developments within the Argentine labor movement as it adjusted to the overthrow of Perón. For annotation of vol. 1, see *HLAS 56:3140*. [JH]

3064 Urquiza, Fernando Carlos. ¿Construir al estado o al ciudadano?: aproximación a las ideas de Pedro de Angelis sobre la organización política argentina, 1827–1856. (*Secuencia/México*, 36, sept./dic. 1996, p. 33–66, bibl., ill.)

Summary of the political thought of

the Italian-born De Angelis, the only major intellectual to affiliate explicitly with the Rosas regime. [TW]

3065 Vázquez-Presedo, Vicente. Estadísticas históricas argentinas. Suplemento 1970–1990. Buenos Aires: Academia Nacional de Ciencias Económicas, Instituto de Economía Aplicada, 1994. 347 p.

A supplement to the previously published volume covering 1873–1973. Attempts to use the same series as the previous volume but made adjustments according to change in sources. Adjustments were also made to reflect increased interest in Mercosur countries. Contains a very useful set of statistics. [JH]

3066 Vera de Flachs, María Cristina. La ciencia y los científicos alemanes en la Córdoba del XIX. (*Invest. Ens.*, 44, enero/dic. 1994, p. 463–481)

Discusses educational contributions of Hermann Burmeister and other German scientists to 19th-century Córdoba. [TW]

3067 Vera de Flachs, María Cristina. Españoles en Argentina: redes sociales e inserción ocupacional, Córdoba, 1840–1930. Córdoba, Argentina: Ediciones del Copista, 1996. 146 p.: bibl., ill.

Reviews 90 years of Spanish immigration in Córdoba, especially good on the contributions of wealthy Spaniards to the provincial economy. Well-developed study useful for the historian of population movements. [TW]

3068 Vera de Flachs, María Cristina and **Remedios Ferrero Micó.** Finanzas y poder político en las universidades hispanoamericanas: el caso de Córdoba 1613–1854. Córdoba, Argentina: Ediciones del Copista, 1996. 172 p.: bibl., ill.

Ambitious study of university financing at Córdoba, one of the most venerable institutions of higher learning in South America. Points out that the university's survival depended on elite support, while elite status often depended on a university degree. [TW]

3069 Verbitsky, Horacio. El vuelo. 2. ed. Buenos Aires: Planeta, 1995. 205 p.: bibl. (Espejo de Argentina)

Well-known and prolific journalist presents the story of Francisco Scilingo, the retired naval officer who disclosed many

Dirty War activities, especially concerning the disposal of bodies, carried out by the navy's Escuela de Mecánica during the last military regime. Includes a long interview with Scilingo as well as other supporting documents. For a review of the English-language translation, see item **4684.** [JH]

3070 Vidal, Gardenia. Radicalismo de Córdoba, 1912–1930: los grupos internos, alianzas, conflictos, ideas, actores. Córdoba, Argentina: Univ. Nacional de Córdoba, 1995. 403 p.: bibl.

Presents a detailed investigation of the Radical Party in the province of Córdoba from the opening of the political system to the Sept. 1930 coup. Argues that the constant fracturing of the party kept it from being a dominant party or even an efficient opposition party. Looks at causes of internal tensions: ideology, party organization, etc. [JH]

3071 Villa, Oscar Jorge and **Alicia Fernández.** Revolución, prensa y propaganda en el Río de la Plata, 1810–1815. (*Deslindes/Montevideo*, 4/5, dic. 1994, p. 13–54)

A nuanced account of the early press and its effect on political culture in the Plata. Discusses elaboration of an "ethical code" within the press, which later served Artigas and others as revolutionary propaganda. [TW]

3072 Whigham, Thomas. Trade and conflict on the rivers: Corrientes, 1780–1840. (*in* Revolution and restoration: the rearrangement of power in Argentina, 1776–1860. Edited by Mark D. Szuchman and Jonathan C. Brown. Lincoln: Univ. of Nebraska Press, 1994, p. 150–176)

Discusses how the vagaries of political change affected commercial development of Corrientes prov. in the revolutionary age. Notes that merchant elite in the province managed to conduct business in a steady if limited fashion even during the worst of times, and, unlike merchants in other provinces, retained a measure of political power. [TW]

3073 Yankelevich, Pablo. La diplomacia imaginaria: Argentina y la Revolución Mexicana 1910–1916. Mexico: Secretaría de Relaciones Exteriores, 1994. 181 p.: bibl.

Based on diplomatic archives in Mexico and Argentina, examines Argentina's official reaction to the Mexican Revolution.

Pays particular attention to the ABC powers' attempt to negotiate a settlement between the US and Mexico. [JH]

3074 Zanatta, Loris. Del estado liberal a la nación católica: iglesia y ejército en los orígenes del peronismo, 1930-1943. Traducción de Judith Farberman. Buenos Aires: Univ. Nacional de Quilmes, 1996. 413 p.: bibl., index. (Política, economía y sociedad)

Looking for the roots of authoritarianism in the period between the two world wars, author studies growing interconnection between the army and the Catholic Church. Examines growing role of Catholic Church in the society of the 1930s and the importance of this presence. [JH]

3075 Zimmermann, Eduardo A. Los liberales reformistas: la cuestión social en la Argentina, 1890-1916. Buenos Aires: Editorial Sudamericana; Univ. de San Andrés, 1995. 250 p.: bibl.

Excellent examination of responses by intellectuals and politicians to the problems created by the so-called "social question" of massive immigration. Looks at intellectual responses, as well as legislative attempts to deal with a variety of problems, such as public health concerns and anarchism. For philosophy specialist's comment, see item **5292**. [JH]

PARAGUAY

3076 Amaral, Raúl. Los presidentes del Paraguay, 1844-1954: crónica política. Prólogo del Dr. Domingo M. Rivarola. Asunción: Centro Paraguayo de Estudios Sociológicos, 1994. 347 p.: bibl., ill. (Biblioteca de estudios paraguayos; v. 50)

A detailed look at Paraguayan presidents before Gen. Stroessner. Amaral's previous work has concentrated on cultural history, and much attention in this case is given to such matters as journalism, literary trends, and educational development under the various presidents. Political historians and biographers, especially those interested in lesser-known figures, will find the study very useful. [TW]

3077 Areces, Nidia R. Concepción "peligrosa" y "descubierta" de la frontera norte paraguaya: espacio étnico y socio-

político, 1773-1840. (*Rev. Hist./São Paulo,* 133, segundo semestre 1995, p. 59-74, bibl.)

Imaginative article places late colonial and early national period Paraguay in a center-periphery framework with the base of political power in Asunción, and the social-ethnic dynamism of the colony/nation in the far north around Concepción. Portrays local elites as the key link between the state, especially under Dr. Francia, and the peripheral populations of the region. [TW]

3078 Areces, Nidia R. Espacio, sociedad y política en Concepción, frontera norte del Paraguaya, durante el gobierno del doctor Francia. (*in* América Latina contemporânea: desafios e perspectivas. Organização de Eliane Geraindo Dayrell e Zilda Márcia Gricoli Iokoi. Rio de Janeiro: Expressão e cultura; São Paulo: Edusp, 1996, p. 603-618)

Introduction to Paraguayan government indigenous policy on the northern frontier during the early Francia period. Argues that by 1821 Francia had decided to subordinate the Mbayá and Guaná, assimilating these Indians into Paraguayan society. Unequal alliances, trade, war, and employment of indigenous peoples on cattle ranches were some of the measures adopted to carry out this assimilation. [TW]

Blacha, Noemí M. Girbal de. Explotación forestal, riesgo empresario y diversificación económica: las inversiones argentinas en el Gran Chaco, 1905-1930. See item **2826**.

3079 Caballero Aquino, Ricardo. Iglesia y Estado en la era liberal. Asunción: Archivo del Liberalismo, 1991. 74 p. (Cuadernos Históricos; 4:23)

A relatively even-handed presentation, despite being published by the Liberals. Much is based on the memoir of Bishop Juan Sinforiano Bogarín. Emphasizes the poverty of both Church and state, while demonstrating that the Church was dependent on the state. [JH]

3080 Chamorro, Graciela. Kurusu ñe'ëngatu: palabras que la historia no podría olvidar. Prefacio de Bartomeu Melià. Asunción: Centro de Estudios Antropológicos, Univ. Católica; São Leopoldo, Brazil: Instituto Ecuménico de Posgrado, Escuela Superior de Teología: Consejo de Misión entre Indios, 1995. 235 p.: bibl., ill. (Biblioteca paraguaya de antropología; v. 25)

Part history, part ethnography, this attractive study examines the identity and world view of the Kaiová, a Guaraní-speaking indigenous group of Mato Grosso do Sul. Argues that for this group, history and time are defined through ritual song and sacred words, which in turn can be interpreted to understand the processes of colonization, religious syncretism, and economic exploitation. [TW]

3081 Cooney, Jerry W. and Thomas Whigham. Paraguayan commerce and the outside world, 1770–1850. (*in* The political economy of Spanish America in the age of revolution, 1750–1850. Albuquerque: Univ. of New Mexico Press, 1994, p. 215–241)

Overview of Paraguayan commercial history from the beginnings of the Viceroyalty to the time of Carlos Antonio López. Stresses the importance of credit (in the form of *libranzas*) and state sponsorship of commodity exporters in promoting external trade. [TW]

3082 Debernardi, Enzo. Apuntes para la historia política de Itaipú. Asunción: Editorial Gráfica Continua, 1996. 613 p.: bibl.

Former Paraguayan director of the Binational Hydroelectric Complex of Itaipú provides an historical summary of the Alto Paraná region and the Itaipú project. [TW]

3083 Domnick, Heinz Joachim. Der Krieg der Tripel-Allianz in der deutschen Historiographie und Publizistik: zur Erforschung des historischen Lateinamerikabildes im 19. und 20. Jahrhundert. Frankfurt; New York: Peter Lang, 1990. 291 p.: bibl. (Europäische Hochschulschriften. Reihe III, Geschichte und ihre Hilfswissenschaften, 0531–7320; Bd. 420 = Publications universitaires européennes. Série III, Histoire, sciences auxiliaires de l'histoire; vol. 420 European university studies. Series III, History and allied studies; vol. 420)

Far-ranging study of German reactions, both scholarly and diplomatic, to the Triple Alliance War. Makes deft use of documents from state archives in Bonn, Freiburg, Bremen, Hamburg, and Muenster. [TW]

3084 Doratioto, Francisco Fernando Monteoliva. A participação brasileira no golpe de estado de 1894 no Paraguai: a missão cavalcanti. (*Textos Hist. / Brasília,* 2:4, 1994, p. 145–174, bibl.)

A detailed examination of Brazilian intrigues in Paraguay in the 1890s and of the plot that brought about the overthrow of President Juan Gualberto González. Makes many of the same arguments as Harris G. Warren, who wrote a similar piece for the *Luso-Brazilian Review* (*Brazil and the Cavalcanti Coup of 1894 in Paraguay,* 19:2, Winter 1982, p. 221–236). [TW]

3085 Escobar, Ticio. A gravura popular, outra imagem da guerra. (*in* A Guerra do Paraguai: 130 anos depois. Organização da Maria Eduarda Castro Magalhães Marques. Rio de Janeiro: Relume Dumará, 1995, p. 121–129, ill.)

Interesting descriptive piece on the striking woodcut illustrations adorning *El Centinela* and *Cabichuí,* two Paraguayan newspapers published during the 1864–70 Triple Alliance War. [TW]

Farcau, Bruce W. The Chaco War: Bolivia and Paraguay, 1932–1935. See item **2718.**

3086 Lambert, Peter. Mechanisms of control: the Stroessner regime in Paraguay. (*in* Authoritarianism in Latin America since independence. Westport, Conn.: Greenwood Press, 1996, p. 93–108)

A broad overview of how Alfredo Stroessner controlled Paraguay. Argues that the length of time Stroessner spent in power was not inevitable, but instead resulted largely from his political skill and his ability to implement means of control. [JH]

3087 Laterza Rivarola, Gustavo. Historia del municipio de Asunción: desde sus comienzos hasta nuestros días. Asunción: GG Servicios Gráficos, 1995. 477 p.: bibl., index.

One of the best urban histories to come out of Paraguay since F.R. Moreno's *Ciudad de Asunción* (1926; for review of 1968 reprint, see *HLAS 38:2983*). Shows more interest than earlier work in city planning, transport, municipal governance, and the political dynamics of various barrios. A particularly well-developed theme is Asunción's metamorphosis under the Stroessner dictatorship. [TW]

Marco, Miguel Angel de. La Guerra del Paraguay. See item **2964.**

3088 Ocampos Caballero, Augusto. Emancipación y diplomacia: misión de Solano Lopéz en Madrid. Asunción: Editora Ricor Grafic, 1995. 236 p.: bibl., ill.

Sheds light on a little-known aspect of Francisco Solano López's 1853 European tour and his successful effort to gain Spanish recognition of Paraguay's independence. Makes good use of Spanish archival documents, several of which are transcribed here (perhaps the most interesting being a series of Spanish diplomatic dispatches from Buenos Aires, Montevideo, and Rio de Janeiro during the Triple Alliance War). [TW]

3089 Paniagua, Felino. Con los pies descalzos: entre el polvo y la sed. Asunción?: s.n., 1994. 165 p.

A straightforward, personal account of the Chaco War written by a soldier in the war. [JH]

3090 El Paraguay bajo el doctor Francia: ensayos sobre la sociedad patrimonial, 1814–1840. Recopilación de Thomas Whigham y Jerry W. Cooney. Asunción: El Lector, 1996. 179 p.: bibl. (Biblioteca paraguaya)

A series of six solid articles on the Francia period written by Whigham, Cooney (three), John Hoyt Williams, and Barbara Potthast-Jutkeit. Three are reprints while the others are new. [JH]

3091 Pesoa, Manuel. General doctor Benigno Ferreira: su biografía, insertada en la historia del Paraguay. Asunción: Intercontinental Editora, 1995. 357 p.: ill.

Informative but disjointed biography of Ferreira (1846–1920), a key figure among anti-López exiles during the 1860s, and later a member of the Legión Paraguaya, head of the postwar National Guard, and eventually president (1906–08). Repeats dubious claim that the Standard Oil Company engineered the outbreak of the Chaco War. [TW]

3092 Potthast-Jutkeit, Barbara. "Paradies Mohammeds" oder "Land der Frauen"?: zur Rolle von Frau und Familie in Paraguay im 19 Jahrhundert. Cologne; Weimar; Vienna: Böhlau Verlag, 1994. 520 p.: bibl., graphs, ill., maps, photos, tables. (Lateinamerikanische Forschungen; Bd. 21; 940341921)

Brilliant examination of women and the family in 19th-century Paraguay. Basing conclusions on a thorough reading of archival documents, shatters older nationalist interpretations of the role of women during and after the Triple Alliance War (1864–70). Especially good on demographic questions. Highly recommended. [TW]

3093 Querejazu Calvo, Roberto. Aclaraciones históricas sobre la Guerra del Chaco. La Paz: Librería Editorial "Juventud," 1995. 206 p.

A series of well-written newspaper essays by a Bolivian historian on the Chaco War. [JH]

3094 Rivarola, Milda. La contestación al orden liberal: la crisis del liberalismo en la preguerra del Chaco. Asunción: Centro de Documentación y Estudios, 1993. 113 p.: bibl. (Documento de trabajo; no. 40)

A short but well-done examination, supplemented with attached documents, of the challenge to liberalism that occurred within the governing elite in the decade before the Chaco War. [JH]

3095 Rivarola, Milda. Placeras y mercaderas: la versión europea de la vida cotidiana en la antigua Asunción. (*Rev. Hist./São Paulo*, 129/131, agôsto/dez. 1993-agôsto/dez. 1994, p. 133–139)

A short but well-written descriptive piece on Asuncena marketwomen as seen in the eyes of 19th-century European travelers. [TW]

3096 Rodríguez-Alcalá, Guido. Justicia penal de Francia. Asunción: RP Ediciones, 1997. 169 p.: index.

Brief, well-researched examination of criminal justice under the Francia dictatorship (1814–40). Argues that Francia's legal system was little more than a cover for corruption and personal vengeance. Includes useful documentary index. [TW]

3097 Salum-Flecha, Antonio. Derecho diplomático del Paraguay: de 1869 a 1994. 5. ed., corr. y aum. Asunción: Ediciones Comuneros, 1994. 285 p.: bibl., maps.

Fifth edition of a classic work on Paraguayan diplomacy, updated to the 1990s. Especially strong on the complicated negotiations surrounding the Gran Chaco dispute of the 1920s-30s. [TW]

3098 Scavone Yegros, Ricardo. Orígenes de las relaciones paraguayo-bolivianas. (*Hist. Parag.*, 35, 1995, p. 253–290)

Good summary analysis of Paraguayan-Bolivian diplomacy in the 1840s–50s. Covers early claims made by the two countries on the Gran Chaco region, as well as questions of river navigation, trade, and regional politics. Based on archival documentation from both La Paz and Asunción repositories. [TW]

3099 Viola, Alfredo. Los carceles en la época dictatorial. (*Anuario/Asunción*, 10:10, 1993, p. 119–145)

Intriguing descriptions of crime and prison life in Paraguay during the Francia dictatorship. Draws heavily on documents from the Archivo Nacional de Asunción. [TW]

3100 Viola, Alfredo. Relaciones del estado con la Iglesia durante la dictadura del Dr. Francia. (*Anuario/Asunción*, 10:10, 1993, p. 47–56)

Descriptive piece on church-state relations in Paraguay between 1814–40. Based on archival documentation. [TW]

3101 Whigham, Thomas. Paraguay and the world cotton market: the "crisis" of the 1860s. (*Agric. Hist.*, 68:3, Summer 1994, p. 1–15)

Interesting examination of Paraguay's attempt to use the world-wide scramble for new sources of cotton after the start of the US Civil War to break its own commercial isolation. Argues that Paraguay's expectations were unrealistic, but in any case were interrupted by warfare. [JH]

3102 Whigham, Thomas. The politics of river trade: tradition and development in the Upper Plata, 1780–1870. Albuquerque: Univ. of New Mexico Press, 1991. 274 p.: bibl., ill., index.

Argues that development of commerce along the inland rivers of the Plata was radically affected by politics in the 19th century. First section discusses trade structures in Paraguay and Corrientes, and merchant elites and political coalitions in the Plata generally. Second section offers detailed analyses of processing and sale of four commodities: yerba mate, tobacco, hides, and timber. [TW]

URUGUAY

3103 Ares Pons, Roberto *et al.* Los partidos uruguayos y su historia. v. 1. Montevideo: Fundación de Cultura Universitaria: Instituto de Ciencia Política, 1990. 1 v.: bibl. (Serie política nacional)

Useful compilation of 34 essays and selections from works by various Uruguayan and Argentine authors on the Blanco and Colorado parties in the 19th century. [TW]

3104 Barrán, José Pedro; Alción Cheroni; and Thomas Glick. La Ley de Aduanas de 1888: contexto social y proyección histórica. Montevideo: Univ. de la República, Facultad de Humanidades y Ciencias, Depto. de Publicaciones, 1992. 77 p.: bibl.

Series of three essays on the tariff law of 1888. The first analyzes why and how the law was passed; the second examines the scientific and technological vision of those who pressed for reform. The third, responding to a point raised in the congressional debate, compares Uruguay with the Massachusetts of that period. [JH]

3105 Bazzano, Daniel *et al.* Breve visión de la historia de la Iglesia en el Uruguay. Montevideo: OBSUR: Librería San Pablo, 1993. 146 p.: bibl.

Brief institutional history of the Catholic Church in Uruguay by authors who stress their role as believers. Sympathetic to changes that came to the Church after the Second Vatican Council. [JH]

3106 Bertino, Magdalena. Capitales y empresarios en los orígenes de la industria textil uruguaya y sus relaciones con la región. (*Hoy Hist.*, 11:65, sept./oct. 1994, p. 15–24, facsims.)

Outlines early development of Uruguayan textile industry, looking particularly at sources of capital. Shows connection with similar events in Argentina and Brazil. [JH]

3107 Caetano, Gerardo and **José Rilla.** História contemporánea del Uruguay: de la colonia al MERCOSUR. Montevideo: Editorial Fin de Siglo, 1994. 396 p.: bibl., ill. (Colección CLAEH)

Impressive attempt to write a history of Uruguay using new techniques. Concentrates principally on the 20th century. Combines traditional text with documents, short biographies, and detailed descriptions of events and institutions. [JH]

3108 Camou, María Magdalena and **Adela Pellegrino.** Una fotografía instantánea de Montevideo. (*in* Ediciones del Quinto Centenario. Montevideo: Univ. de la República, 1992, v. 2, p. 125–190, tables)

A demographic history of life in Montevideo in 1858–59 based on a registration of houses and their inhabitants done in that period. Uses numerous tables to present key information. [JH]

3109 Casal, Juan Manuel. Ejército y violencia en el Uruguay del siglo XIX. (*Humanas/Porto Alegre,* 16:2, julho/dez. 1993, p. 7–24, bibl., table)

Suggestive analysis of military violence directed by the 19th-century Uruguayan army towards itself, in the form of floggings and other punishments for infractions defined in the *Ordenanzas españolas;* and towards society at large, in the form of "legitimate" warfare, forced recruiting, and other kinds of legalized violence. Though sociological in tone, this essay includes many details of interest to the historian. [TW]

3110 Chasteen, John Charles. Heroes on horseback: a life and times of the last gaucho caudillos. Albuquerque: Univ. of New Mexico Press, 1995. 241 p.: bibl., index, maps. (Diálogos)

An extremely well-written examination of the lives of the caudillos Aparacio and Gumercindo Saravia which throws light on the political and economic world of the border areas of Uruguay and Rio Grande do Sul, and on Uruguayan politics in general. More importantly, it attempts, with a great deal of success, to examine the different roles of the caudillo in Spanish and Portuguese America and broadens the reader's understanding of caudillismo. For Brazilian historian's comment, see item **3250.** [JH]

3111 Comisión Nacional Archivo Artigas (Uruguay). Archivo Artigas. v. 27. Montevideo: Impresores A. Monteverde y Cía. S.A., 1993. 450 p.

Another volume of the famous series of archival documents on the Artigas period, covering the years 1815–16. Indispensible for scholars of the Platine region in the early-19th century. [TW]

3112 Cures, Oribe *et al.* El Uruguay de los años treinta: enfoques y problemas. Montevideo: Ediciones de la Banda Oriental, 1994. 218 p.: bibl.

Part of a larger project intended to tie Terrismo to Uruguay's past; the six essays are preliminary reports on large projects carried out on the 1930s. Essays cover the government's relationship with ITT; the Terra government's relationship with the Federación Rural and the *vendedores ambulantes;* human rights; and primary and secondary education under Terra. [JH]

3113 Dutrénit Bielous, Silvia. Uruguay: una historia breve. Colaboración de Ana Buriano Castro. México: Instituto de Investigaciones Dr. José María Luis Mora, 1994. 406 p.: bibl., maps.

Excellent overview of Uruguayan politics and economics during the 19th century. Written for a Mexican audience, the study includes a helpful comparative chronology of the two countries from the conquest to 1910. [TW]

3114 Ediciones del quinto centenario. v. 1, Estudios antropológicos. Montevideo: Univ. de la República, 1992. 1 v.: bibl., ill., maps.

Impressive compilation of nine essays on Uruguayan reality, most of which focus on the indigenous past or on the role of the immigrant. Other topics include social relations on the Uruguay-Brazil frontier, the prehistoric demography of Alaska and Siberia, and traditional children's games in Montevideo. [TW]

3115 Fernández Cabrelli, Alfonso. Artigas: el hombre frente al mito. v. 3, Artigas, de la cumbre al exilio. Montevideo?: s.n., 1995? 1 v.: bibl., ill., maps.

Third volume of a detailed biography of Artigas by a key historian of the Masonic Movement in the Plata. Argues that too many studies have offered only hagiographies of the Uruguayan chieftain, though, in fact, he attains his greatest stature when looked at as a man of flesh and blood. Includes extensive archival citations. For annotation of vol. 1, see *HLAS 56:3185.* [TW]

3116 Frega, Ana. Los pueblos y la construcción del estado en el crisol de la Revolución: apuntes para su estudio en el Río de la Plata, 1810–1820. (*Cuad. CLAEH*, 69, junio 1994, p. 49–63)

Discusses state formation in the Plata after independence wars. Maintains that the only two variations of federalism, the porteño and the Artiguista, could possibly have given birth to a nation-state in the region. Further argues that the Artiguista option, although ultimately defeated, represented a viable and more popular approach to nation-building. [TW]

3117 Geymonat, Roger. El templo y la escuela: los valdenses en el Uruguay. Prólogo de Gerardo Caetano. Montevideo: Cal y Canto: OBSUR, 1994. 297 p.: bibl., maps.

A well-documented, impressively written study of Waldensian immigration to Uruguay. Hardworking and pious without being fanatical, the Waldensians came to the Plata in the mid-19th century to escape the poverty of their Piedmontese villages, and proceeded to establish a series of prosperous agricultural colonies along the río Uruguay. As the author indicates, these settlements were models of social cohesion, where school and church played equal roles in everyday life. [TW]

3118 Giudice, Gerardo. Frugoni. Montevideo: Proyección, 1995. 401 p.

Sympathetic political biography of Frugoni, who was the leader of the Socialist Party in Uruguay for many years. Lacks scholarly apparatus. [JH]

3119 Jacob, Raúl. Bunge y Born en Uruguay, 1915–1945. (*Ciclos Hist. Econ. Soc.*, 5:8, primer semestre 1995, p. 29–54, graph, tables)

Discusses growth of the agro-industrial, multinational corporation that began investing in Uruguay in an effort to secure its hold on the market for flour in southern Brazil. Following the model that it had developed in Argentina, Bunge y Born moved into industrial production in the 1930s-40s. [JH]

3120 José Batlle y Ordóñez: documentos para el estudio de su vida y de su obra. ser. 1, pt. 2, v. 1–2, El joven Batlle, 1856–85, 1886–87. Montevideo: Poder Legislativo, Cámara de Representantes, 1989–1994. 2 v.

Continuation of a long-term project to publish a significant number of documents by and about Batlle. These two vols. cover his youth, education, his visit to Europe (1879–81), and his early journalistic work with *El Espíritu Nuevo* and *La Razón*. [TW]

3121 Lavrin, Asunción. Women, feminism, and social change in Argentina, Chile, and Uruguay, 1890–1940. Lincoln, Neb.: Univ. of Nebraska Press, 1995. 480 p.: bibl., ill., index. (Engendering Latin America; v. 3)

Compendium of information on the early feminist movement in the three countries. Includes discussion of women's suffrage and the right to divorce, among other issues. [JH]

3122 López Alves, Fernando. The authoritarian roots of liberalism: Uruguay, 1810–1886. (*in* Liberals, politics, and power: state formation in nineteenth-century Latin America. Edited by Vincent C. Peloso and Barbara A. Tenenbaum. Athens: Univ. of Georgia Press, 1996, p. 111–133)

Well-written summary of political trends in 19th-century Uruguay argues convincingly that the many civil wars permitted the state to achieve a high level of autonomy, which in turn ushered in the rule of liberalism. [TW]

3123 Luzuriaga, Juan Carlos and **Loreley de los Santos.** Paso Morlán: la protesta armada de 1935. Montevideo: Ediciones de la Banda Oriental, 1994. 119 p.: bibl., maps.

Discusses 1935 revolt by members of both the Colorados and the Nacionalists against the Terra government. Compares it to past revolts, especially those in the 19th century, and speculates on its long-term impact. [JH]

3124 Medere Larrosa, Aristides I. Oribe y su tiempo. v. 1. Montevideo: Tall. Gráf. Barreiros y Ramos, 1994. 1 v.

First half of a detailed biography of the Oriental caudillo Manuel Oribe. Could benefit from endnotes or references to sources. [TW]

3125 Perdomo, Jesús. El último chasque: Francisco de los Santos; realidad o mito? Rocha, Uruguay: Intendencia Municipal de Rocha; Montevideo: Editorial Fin de Siglo, 1994. 185 p.: bibl., ill., maps.

Interesting, almost folkloric account

of Francisco de los Santos, a minor figure in Artigas' army about whom many improbable tales have been spun. Fails to resolve the many questions and inconsistencies in the Santos story, but does offer some insights into the role of the African in 19th-century Uruguay. [TW]

3126 Porrini, Rodolfo and **Mariela Salaberry.** León Duarte: conversaciones con Alberto Márquez y Hortencia Pereira. Montevideo: Editorial Compañero, 1993. 126 p. (Biblioteca popular del pensamiento socialista Gerardo Gatti. Cuadernos de memoria popular)

León Duarte, a union leader in FUNSA, was disappeared in 1976. This work presents interviews with Alberto Márquez, a fellow worker and union activist, and with Hortencia Pereira, Duarte's wife and fellow worker. An interesting portrait of union activity at the grassroots level in the 1960s-70s. [JH]

Quesada, Juan Isidro. Injerencia argentina en la guerra civil uruguaya de 1836–1838. See item **3017.**

3127 Ribeiro, Ana. Historiografía nacional, 1880–1940: de la épica al ensayo sociológico. Montevideo: Ediciones de la Plaza, 1994. 83 p.: bibl.

Winner of a competition by the Academia Nacional de Letras for studies of historiography between 1880–1940. The author had previously won the organization's contest for 1940–90 (see *HLAS 56:3207*). While not forming a united work, the books do present a thoughtful analysis of the writing of history in Uruguay. [JH]

3128 Rosenthal, Anton. Steetcar workers and the transformation of Montevideo: the general strike of May 1911. (*Americas/Franciscans,* 51:4, April 1995, p. 471–494)

Ties Montevideo's first general strike to protest among streetcar workers and to the changes produced by rapid modernization. Underlines importance of the streetcar to everyday life in Montevideo and other cities. Hypothesizes the importance of transport workers in early general strikes throughout Latin America and calls for a rethinking of the nature of such strikes. [JH]

3129 Salaberry, Mariela. Mariana, tu y nosotros: diálogo con María Ester Gatti. Montevideo: Ediciones de la Banda Oriental, 1993. 152 p.: ill.

Revealing discussion with a mother of a Uruguayan woman who was disappeared in Argentina and had her baby adopted by a member of the Argentine security forces. Discusses the attempts, ultimately successful, to find the child. Work is revealing about societies of both Argentina and Uruguay, especially the latter. [JH]

3130 Schroeder Otero, Juan Bautista. El pacto del club naval. Montevideo: Arca, 1994. 72 p.

The civilian Minister of Educación y Cultura in 1984 recounts his role in the Club Naval negotiations between the military and the political parties, resulting in an agreement about the nature of the transition to civilian rule. Copies of some pertinent documents included. [JH]

Silva, Hernán A. El comercio entre España y el Río de la Plata, 1778–1810. See item **2495.**

3131 Villegas, Juan. Influjo de Ira Mayhew en la educación del pueblo de José Pedro Varela. Montevideo: HEGIL Impresos, 1989. 123 p.: bibl.

Short but incisive study discusses the impact in Uruguay of mid-19th century US educational theories, and more specifically, the influence of American educationalist Ira Mayhew on Uruguayan thinker José Pedro Varela. [TW]

Wiliman, Claudio. Las raíces cristianas en el pensamiento del Partido Nacional del Uruguay. See item **5243.**

3132 Zubillaga, Carlos. Hacer la América: estudios históricos sobre la inmigración española al Uruguay. Montevideo: Editorial Fin de Siglo, 1993. 123 p.: bibl., ill. (Colección Raíces)

Brief but fascinating account of Spanish immigration to Uruguay. Concentrates not only on questions of labor and the integration of Spaniards into the Uruguayan work force, but also on such specialized topics as republican-monarchist rivalries among the immigrants, the activities of the Spanish consul in promoting immigration to Uruguay, and Gallego journalism in Montevideo. [TW]

3133 **Zubillaga, Carlos.** Inmigración española y participación política en Uruguay. (*Estud. Migr. Latinoam.*, 11:32, abril 1996, p. 3–24, tables)

Shrewd analysis of Spanish immigration to Uruguay in the 1880s-90s. Points out that political instability and the lack of civil guarantees caused a low level of naturalization among this group. [TW]

3134 **Zubillaga, Carlos.** Pan y trabajo: organización sindical, estrategias de lucha y arbitraje estatal en Uruguay, 1870–1905.

Montevideo: Librería de la Facultad de Humanidades y Ciencias de la Educación, 1996. 185 p.: bibl., ill.

Well-documented study examines key questions for the early labor movement. Looks at such protounions as cooperatives and mutual aid associations, the nature of early unions, attempts at creating confederations, and the role of leaders. Also examines the nature of protests and union demands, as well as the political response to early unionism. [JH]

BRAZIL

DAIN BORGES, *Associate Professor of History, University of Chicago*
DAVID MCCREERY, *Professor of History, Georgia State University*
JOAN E. MEZNAR, *Associate Professor of History, Eastern Connecticut State University*

COLONIAL PERIOD

SEVERAL RECENT GUIDES to archives supply valuable assistance to those engaged in research on colonial Brazil. A special issue of the journal *Acervo* highlights material related to Brazil in Portuguese archives (items **3163, 3150, 3185, 3178,** and **3202**). Carlos de Araújo Moreira Neto's useful guide on Brazilian indigenous peoples describes materials housed in repositories in 11 Brazilian states and several European countries (item **3191**). In addition, Aluísio Fonseca de Castro has compiled an annotated guide to materials in the Arquivo Público do Pará dealing with indigenous labor (item **3158**).

Two excellent collections of essays bring together examples of some of the finest Brazilian historical scholarship. The beautifully produced and illustrated volume on private life in colonial Brazil edited by Fernando Novais demonstrates the continued rewards of exploring "everyday life" (item **3177**). João José Reis and Flávio dos Santos have also compiled outstanding essays from diverse interpretive perspectives on runaway slave communities throughout Brazil (item **3180**).

Interest in the role of religion and religious orders in shaping colonial society appears to be growing (items **3151, 3198, 3208, 3201,** and **3224**). Thomas Cohen's work on Antonio Vieira situates Jesuit activity in Brazil within a broader international and cultural context (item **3161**). Inquisition records prove to be useful sources for insight into the world of Old Christians as well as New Christians in Rio de Janeiro (item **3217**) and northeast Brazil (items **3183** and **3192**).

While social and economic concerns continue to dominate research, Shawn Miller's article on fuelwood in Bahia demonstrates that addressing such environmental issues can enrich our understanding of the history of colonial Brazil (item **3189**). [JM]

NATIONAL PERIOD

Recent years have seen a publishing boom in general introductions to Brazil and surveys of Brazilian history, finally replacing out-of-print or outdated introductions, such as Wagley (see *HLAS 27:2993*) and Burns (see *HLAS 34:2902*). In Spanish, there is Iglesias on political history (item **3143**) and Queiroz on São Paulo (item **3146**). Offerings in English are richer. First, paperback compilations of the state-of-the-art essays in Bethell's *Cambridge History of Latin America* made available overviews of specific periods (see *HLAS 52:2911* and *HLAS 52:2981*). Now there are introductions to contemporary Brazil by Page (item **3308**), Eakin (item **3261**) and Levine (item **3291**), and one-volume histories by Skidmore (item **3148**), Fausto (item **3139**), and Levine (item **3144**). *The Brazil Reader*, edited by Levine and Crocitti, provides a rich collection of documents and articles useful for students and general readers (item **3137**).

These introductory surveys suggest a poor fit between the general public's preoccupations and the concerns of professional historians. The surveys concentrate heavily on political history since 1930, economic development, and popular culture. Historians' research agendas and debates on Brazil since 1922 are vague, beyond a continuing fascination with Getúlio Vargas' reforms. Research agendas on 19th- and early 20th-century topics are much better defined, but aside from their concentration on marginal social types, they are not entirely oriented toward the topics emphasized in introductions to Brazil.

Social history continues to dominate recent historiographical production on the Empire and Old Republic, much of it in the form of revised *mestrado* and doctoral theses from the 1980s. "Marginals" occupy much of this attention. Several pieces, for example, look at the lives of foreign prostitutes and pimps (items **3248, 3284,** and **3303**), street vendors in Salvador (item **3331**), and army recruits suspected of sodomy (item **3237**). Bretas' study of police in Rio examines social control from the perspective of elites and their agents (item **3241**). There is the usual attention to "popular resistance" in its varied forms: riots, e.g., Reis (item **3317**); rebels and revolts, e.g., da Cunha and Villa on Canudos (items **3258** and **3340,** respectively), Dias on the Balaiada (item **3260**), and Silveira on the Cabanagem (item **3265**); and lastly, Ferraz's linking of "enlightenment liberalism" and postindependence revolts in Pernambuco (item **3329**).

Groups viewed as slightly less deviant, but certainly more dangerous, were ex-slaves, the urban poor (item **3269**), and the incipient working class. Particularly impressive works on slavery are Xavier on ex-slaves before and after abolition (item **3345**) and Castro on meanings of "freedom" (item **3247**). Workers receive scant attention, other than Pesavento on Porto Alegre (item **3312**), essays in the two *História econômica* volumes (items **3253** and **3254**), and occasional mention in Chalhoub (item **3249**), Rocha (item **3320**), and Meade (item **3300**).

Only slightly less marginal than prostitutes and *libertos* were the European immigrants Brazil began to seek urgently after the end of the international slave trade in 1850 (see Graden, item **3276** and Chaiban, item **3262** on the end of the trade). The Portuguese, in their traditional roles as *caixeiros* and merchants, are the subject of two *mestrado* theses published as a book (item **3299**), but the Germans receive more attention, as colonists, in Rodowicz-Oswiecimsky's first-person narrative (item **3321**), in Seyferth's study of the Itajahy/Brusque colony (item **3327**), and as reluctant participants in the Federalist Revolution (item **3319**). Boni has organized a third volume in a series on the Italian immigration experience (item **3314**; for review of first two volumes, see *HLAS 54:3402*), and Lesser has a short piece on discontent Jewish farmers (item **3290**). Immigration, exile, and assimilation remain the strongest single topic in 20th-century social history, with many amateur and commemorative histories of communities. Of note are studies of Syrians (item

3336), Jews (items **3245** and **3284**), Spaniards (items **3234, 3273,** and **3281**), and Portuguese (item **3294**).

Slaves, of course, were anything but marginal to 19th-century Brazil (item **3323**) and continue to attract very much of the scholarly attention given the Empire. Interesting new studies address kinship, including two that focus on the Fazenda Resgate (items **3136** and **3267**), as well as others that describe how slaves and ex-slaves used kinship to make their lives better, or at least more tolerable (items **3272** and **3304**). Historians continue to write about slave resistance: Machado (item **3296**) on the turbulence of the 1880s, Araujo (item **3230**) and Gomes (item **3275**) on quilombos, and Mello (item **3302**) and Chasteen (item **3251**) on street culture and samba. Other entries on slavery treat health (item **3330**), slaves and ex-slaves in the army in general (item **3283**) and the Paraguayan War specifically (item **3332**), the attitudes of slaves and masters towards work (item **3293**), and freedmen's opportunities in life (item **3282**).

Many recent books cluster around the problem of turn-of-the-century reform in Brazilian cities, particularly in Rio de Janeiro. Meade (item **3300**), Chalhoub (item **3249**), and Rocha (item **3320**) each address, in slightly different ways, the efforts of elites in the late Empire and Old Republic to "modernize" Rio de Janeiro by demolishing slum housing, undertaking public health campaigns, and, not incidentally, moving the poor out of the city's center. Lanna takes up these same topics for Santos (item **3287**), Lapa for Campinas (item **3288**), and Ponte for Fortaleza (item **3313**).

No clear central themes, other than immigration, emerge from the social history research on Brazil since 1922. Nevertheless, there were some excellent studies, such as Owensby on the middle class and its political mentalities in São Paulo and Rio (item **3307**) and the 20th-century essays in the outstanding collection on women since colonial times edited by Del Priore (item **3142**).

Although economic history continues to be, in general, a weak area in the study of Brazil, suffering from an absence of theory and a paucity of empirical research, several exceptional works have appeared recently. These include Florentinos' history of the Africa-Rio de Janeiro slave trade (item **3267**), papers in the Congresso volumes (items **3253** and **3254**), Motta's analysis of the marginalization of small-scale coffee producers in early-19th century São Paulo (item **3305**), and Takeya's extensively researched and beautifully produced analysis of French trade and investment in Ceará (item **3334**). Caldeira describes the activities of Mauá (item **3242**), Barickman compares the sugar industries of Bahia and Pernambuco (item **3235**), Galliza analyzes modernization in Paraiba (item **3271**), and Aleixo studies sugar in turn-of-the-century Mato Grosso (item **1929**). Schulz offers a new look at the *Encilhamento* (item **3324**). Economic topics in 20th-century Brazil were treated mainly as they drifted into labor history, in Weinstein's notable study of industrial policy and vocational training (item **3343**), Antonacci's revised thesis on the IDORT (item **3229**), and Welch's solid monograph on rural labor unions (item **3344**).

Apart from Chasteen's deservedly well-received study of border politics at the end of the century (item **3250**) and Topik's entry in the generally neglected arena of US-Brazil relations (item **3335**), this has not been a particularly good biennium for political history. Azevedo compares abolitionist ideologies more than politics (item **3232**). The *coronéis* are still with us, at least on the frontier (items **3255** and **3342**) and pursuing the Prestes Column (item **3301**), while Schulz provides a useful overview of army politics after the Paraguayan War (item **3325**). Debe's as yet incomplete life of Washington Luis is the best of an unpromising crop of political biographies (item **3259**), though Faria does use the career of Joaquim Murtinho to highlight the emptiness of Old Republic politics (item **3264**). But the field suffers broadly from a shortage of both serious monographs and interpretive writing, and the inadequacies of the political and economic history available for the Empire/Old Republic in turn make it difficult to adequately and effectively undertake the study of recent favorites: social history and history of memory and the "imagination."

Political history of Brazil since 1922 continues to focus on the Vargas eras. There is a useful biographical essay on Vargas, well fitted for teaching, by Levine (item **3292**) and a cluster of biographies of Oswaldo Aranha as ideologue and diplomat (items **3244, 3286,** and **3279**). Vargas' propaganda policies continue to attract interest (items **3274** and **3309**). Almost all serious work on politics between 1930–64 is based on the CPDOC archives—much of it, in fact, is sponsored by CPDOC; opening of the secret police archives will broaden perspectives (item **3231**). Aside from the essays in Gomes (item **3339**), work on Vargas is still largely apologetic or accusatory. Historical work on politics after 1964 is scarce. Welch on São Paulo rural labor unions is a notable exception (item **3344**). Soares and D'Araujo on regime policies (item **3341**) and Sosnowski and Schwartz on culture under authoritarianism (item **3240**) collect multidisciplinary research.

Historians and anthropologists made some important contributions to understanding 20th- century religious change. Souza on Paraty (item **3333**) and Nagle on Recife (item **3306**) view social and political change through festivals. Marin attempts to debunk the image of Helder Câmara as a reforming archbishop (item **3298**), and Lehmann makes an outstanding comparison of Pentecostal and Catholic social and political messages (item **3289**), as does Chesnut in a fine study of Pentecostal converts and church politics in Belém since 1910 (item **3252**).

Historians were willing to study themselves this biennium. Studies of intellectuals, the professions, and historiography in the 20th century were abundant. Publication of memoirs by Calmon (item **3243**), correspondence by Rodrigues (item **3322**), political papers of Freyre (item **3270**) and Ramos (item **3316**), and field notes by Azevedo (item **3233**), added evidence. Gomes provides an interesting study of historians during the Estado Novo (item **3274**), and Gutfreind does likewise in her study of Rio Grande regionalists (item **3140**). The second volume of Miceli's team research on social science institutions (item **3280**) is a valuable contribution, as is Schwarcz's intriguing study on racial ideas in museums and cultural institutes (item **3326**). [DB and DM]

GENERAL

3135 Arquivos & coleções fotográficas da Fundação Joaquim Nabuco. Organização de Ruth de Miranda Henriques Medeiros. Recife, Brazil: Fundação Joaquim Nabuco, Editora Massangana, 1995. 149 p.: bibl., ill., indexes. (Série Obras de consulta; 15)

Illustrated archival guide to splendid photograph collections with a Pernambuco focus includes many documenting social life and folklore. [DB]

3136 Bertran, Paulo. História da terra e do homem no Planalto Central: ecohistória do Distrito Federal; do indígena ao colonizador. Brasília: Solo Editores, 1994. 314 p.: bibl., ill., index, maps.

Interlaces a modest amount of text with extensive reproductions of documents, diagrams and maps, and photographs related to the history of the Distrito Federal, from prehistory to early-19th century. Includes information on *sesmarias* (land grants) and land settlement, ecohistory, trade routes, mining, travelers' accounts, and taxes. [DM]

3137 **The Brazil reader: history, culture, politics.** Edited by Robert M. Levine and John J. Crocitti. Durham, N.C.: Duke Univ. Press, 1999. 1 v.: bibl., index. (Latin American readers)

Indispensable introduction to Brazil for students and general readers includes short scholarly articles, interviews, documents, photographs, and many autobiographical pieces. Begins with precontact indigenous peoples, but about half deals with Brazil since 1945. Topics include indigenous peoples, slavery, Vargas and labor, political protest, women, race relations, marginal groups, and popular culture. Overarching themes are mobility and repression. [DB]

3138 **Cordeiro, Helio Daniel.** Os marranos e a diáspora sefardita: estudo introdutório sobre a identidade étnica criptojudaica. São Paulo: Editora Israel, 1995. 79 p.: bibl.

A pioneering "think piece" on the Jewish community in Brazil. Little historical depth in the text, but bibliography is extensive. [J. Britton]

3139 **Fausto, Boris.** A concise history of Brazil. Translated by Arthur Brakel. Cambridge, England; New York: Cambridge Univ. Press, 1999. 362 p.: bibl., ill., index, maps.

Excellent one-volume history of Brazil by leading Brazilian social historian is suitable for advanced students and sophisticated general readers. Emphasizes political and economic history. Treats colonial and 19th-century history seriously as political history; one-third of book covers 1930–80. Unlike other recent one-volume histories, such as those by Skidmore (see item **3148**) and Levine (see item **3144**), work does not cover contemporary events (1980–90), and the evaluation of the transition from 1964 dictatorship to electoral politics is reticent. Often narrates events by synthesizing differing interpretations in historiography of key issues: nature of Portuguese imperial state, reasons for 19th-century Brazilian territorial unity, relation between slavery and peasantry. Good summary discussion of demography and class structure, but little overt explanation of political culture and almost no references to folkways and the arts. Also see item **3291**. [DB]

Gomes, Heloisa Toller. As marcas da escravidão: o negro e o discurso oitocentista no Brasil e nos Estados Unidos. See item **4345**.

3140 **Gutfreind, Ieda.** A historiografia riograndense. Porto Alegre, Brazil: Editora da Univ. Federal do Rio Grande do Sul, 1992. 162 p.: bibl.

Exploration of eight historians' writings finds they stress either Portuguese or Spanish (Río de la Plata) origins of the province. From 1920s-1960s historians tended to favor nationalist version of Portuguese roots, a Farrapos rebellion that was federalist rather than separatist, and a *gaúcho* cowboy-type of non-Hispanic identity. Interesting for historians of contemporary separatism. [DB]

3141 **História da técnica e da tecnologia no Brasil.** Organização de Milton Vargas. São Paulo: Editora UNESP, Fundação para o Desenvolvimento da UNESP; Centro Estadual de Educação Tecnológica Paula Souza, 1995. 412 p.: bibl., ill., maps. (Col. Biblioteca básica)

Collected articles survey aspects of technology related to engineering profession. Pt. 1 touches on indigenous and colonial technology, emphasizing 19th-century engineering schools and public works. Pt. 2 focuses on the 20th century up to 1945, examining engineering education, technological research, electricity, and steel. Pt. 3 examines post-1945 military and armaments, telecommunications, energy, computing, and nuclear sectors. Little on agricultural technology. Like Telles' work (see item **3149**), a helpful starting place for research, although essays are short on bibliography. [DB]

3142 **História das mulheres no Brasil.** Organização de Mary Del Priore. Coordenação de Carla Beozzo Bassanezi. São Paulo: Editora Contexto; Editora Unesp Fundação, 1997. 678 p.: bibl., ill.

Highly recommended sampler of 20 essays by leading Brazilian historians and anthropologists. Some authors succinctly summarize their own books; others take on new topics. Not a balanced survey as treatment of periods and topics is uneven. Essays on colonial period are skewed toward sexuality; 19th century is poorly represented; and 20th-century essays emphasize working-class women. However, these emphases reflect trends in historiography. Overall quality is excellent; and many of the 20th-century essays are particularly accessible, fresh, and humorous. Good illustrations. [DB]

3143 Iglésias, Francisco. Historia política de Brasil, 1500–1964. Madrid: Editorial MAPFRE, 1992. 365 p.: bibl., ill., indexes. (Col. Realidades americanas; 4)

Spanish-language survey of political history for general readers is good on colonial institutions, thin on 19th century. [DB]

3144 Levine, Robert M. The history of Brazil. Westport, Conn.: Greenwood Press, 1999. 208 p.: bibl., ill., index, map. (The Greenwood histories of the modern nations series, 1096–2905)

Relatively bland historical introduction for general readers emphasizes economic development, social inequality, and apparent inability of reforms to address inequality. Begins in 1500, but more than half of volume is devoted to post-1930 Brazil and contemporary issues. Getúlio Vargas is central both as a reformist turning point in politics and as a representative enigma. Useful, but much less piquant and heartfelt than author's *Brazilian legacies* (item **3291**). See also items **3139** and **3148**. [DB]

Morón, Guillermo. Hispanoamérica y Brasil en la historia general de América. See item **804.**

3145 Pinto, Emanuel Pontes. Rondônia: evolução histórica. Rio de Janeiro: Expressão e Cultura, 1993. 216 p.: bibl., ill., maps.

Serviceable, brief survey history of frontier state up to 1945 is based mostly on secondary literature and printed chronicles. Good maps. About half deals with era since construction of Madeira-Mamoré railroad. [DB]

3146 Queiroz, Suely Robles Reis de. São Paulo. Madrid: Editorial MAPFRE, 1992. 315 p.: bibl., ill., index, maps. (Col. Ciudades de Iberoamérica; 3. Col. MAPFRE 1492)

Spanish-language introductory survey of city's history, from village to megalopolis,

1554–1990. Includes annotated bibliography and timeline. [DB]

Rodrigues, José Honório and **Ricardo Antônio Silva Seitenfus.** Uma história diplomática do Brasil, 1531–1945. See *HLAS 57:4509.*

3147 Sedução do horizonte. Organização, pesquisa e introdução de Laís Corrêa de Araujo. Belo Horizonte, Brazil: Sistema Estadual de Planejamento, Fundação João Pinheiro, Centro de Estudos Históricos e Culturais, 1996. 241 p.: ill. (some col.). (Col. Centenário)

Luxury album anthologizes excerpts from literary and journalistic appreciations of Belo Horizonte. Includes superb historical photographs. [DB]

3148 Skidmore, Thomas E. Brazil: five centuries of change. New York: Oxford Univ. Press, 1999. 254 p.: bibl., index. (Latin American histories)

Indispensable introductory survey of Brazilian history, 1500–1998. Pre-1930 history is treated as background. Second half is an outstanding narrative of politics and economic policy from 1930-present. Accessible to students and general readers. Particularly interesting are the book's final chapters, which seem to be addressed more to the conscience of the Brazilian ruling class than to foreign readers. Includes bibliographical essay, but one much less dense than typically found in Oxford Univ. Press one-volume histories of Latin American nations. See also items **3139, 3144,** and **3291.** [DB]

3149 Telles, Pedro Carlos da Silva. História da engenharia no Brasil. v. 1–2. 2a ed. rev. e ampliada. Rio de Janeiro: Clube de Engenharia, 1993. 2 v.: bibl., ill., indexes, maps.

Broad but shallow coverage of engineering education, professional associations, public works, civil construction, urban reforms, railroads and port works, industrial technology, leading engineers, and technology and inventions, from late-18th century through ca. 1930–50. Vol. 2 on 20th century has chapters on electricity, reinforced concrete, and highways. Useful as a reference tool for researchers, although bibliographic references are not always complete. See also item **3141.** [DB]

COLONIAL

3150 Abrantes, Maria Luísa Meneses.
Fontes para a história do Brasil colonial existentes no Arquivo Histórico Ultramarino. (*ACERVO/Rio de Janeiro*, 10:1, jan./junho 1997, p. 17–28, graphs, maps)
Good description of the organization of the archive and the materials it contains. Of use to historians of Brazil. [JM]

3151 Aguiar, Marcos Magalhães de.
Capelães e vida associativa na Capitania de Minas Gerais. (*Varia Hist.*, 17, março 1997, p. 80–105)
Investigates role of priests who served as chaplains of black and mulatto brotherhoods in Minas Gerais. Concludes that, although they performed this service for pay, they also sympathized with brotherhoods and served as "cultural intermediaries" who legitimized practices of black and mulatto brotherhoods. [JM]

3152 Almeida, Luís Ferrand de. Portugal, o
Brasil e o comércio do Rio da Prata, 1640–1680. (*in* Congresso das Academias da História Ibero-Americanas, *4th, Lisbon and Porto, Portugal, 1994.* Actas. Lisboa: Academia Portuguesa da História, 1996, p. 383–392)
Describes economic concerns leading to the establishment of Colonia do Sacramento in 1680. After 1640, war between Portugal and Spain cut off Spanish silver supply to Brazil. Portuguese settled Colonia do Sacramento to foster clandestine trade with Buenos Aires and thus replenish their supply of Andean silver. [JM]

3153 Azevedo, Esterzilda Berenstein de. Ingenios hidráulicos de caña de azúcar en Brasil. (*in* Seminario Internacional sobre la Caña de Azúcar, *6th, Motril, Spain, 1994.* Agua, trabajo y azúcar: actas. Granada, Spain: Diputación Provincial de Granada, 1996, p. 261–274, map, photos)
Brief history of the water-powered mills that made possible the large-scale production of sugar in Brazil. [JM]

3154 Barreto, Abílio. Belo Horizonte:
memória histórica e descritiva. v. 1, História antiga. Ed. atualizada, rev. e anotada. Belo Horizonte: Sistema Estadual de Planejamento, Fundação João Pinheiro, Centro de Estudos Históricos e Culturais;

Prefeitura de Belo Horizonte, Secretaria Municipal de Cultura, 1995. 1 v.: bibl., indexes. (Col. Mineiriana. Série Clássicos)
This new edition of a 1928 history of the city of Belo Horizonte includes the transcription of interesting land registry records. [JM]

3155 Bassanezi, Maria Silvia C. Beozzo.
Considerações sobre os estudos do celibato e da idade ao casar no passado brasileiro. (*in* Encontro de Estudos Populacionais, *9th, Caxambú, Brazil, 1994.* Memorias. Belo Horizonte, Brazil: Associação Brasileira de Estudos Populacionais (ABEP), 1994?, v. 1, p. 381–396, bibl., tables)
Diversity marked the experience of free men and women making marriage decisions throughout Brazil. Finds that marriage age fluctuated more for men than for women and that material conditions seemed to determine who married and when. [JM]

3156 Bergad, Laird W. Demographic change
in a post-export boom society: the population of Minas Gerais, Brazil, 1776–1821. (*J. Soc. Hist.*, 29:4, Summer 1996, p. 895–932, graphs, map, tables)
Examines demographic transformations as Minas Gerais moved from gold mining to a more diversified economy. Finds that population centers shifted to the south; that the free black and mulatto population grew; and that after a significant decline, the slave population of Minas Gerais appears to have stabilized around 1808, moving toward natural reproduction. [JM]

3157 O Brasil dos viajantes. Texto de Ana
Maria de Moraes Belluzzo. Lisboa: Fundação das Descobertas, Centro Cultural de Belém, 1995. 67 p.: bibl., ill. (some col.).
Catalog of an exposition of travelers' art highlights Brazil from early-16th century through 19th-century Romantic period. [JM]

3158 Castro, Aluisio Fonseca de. Manuscritos sobre a Amazônia colonial: repertório referente à mão-de-obra indígena do fundo Secretaria do Governo; colônia e império. (*An. Arq. Público Pará*, 2:1, 1996, p. 9–121)
Brief annotations of 960 pieces of correspondence to and from the Secretaria da Capitania do Governo do Pará and Secretaria da Presidência da Província dealing with indigenous labor between 1750–1807. This in-

teresting overview of a significant sample of manuscripts in the Arquivo Público do Pará provides a good perspective on indigenous participation in local society. [JM]

3159 Centurião, Luiz Ricardo Michaelsen. A cidade na América colonial portuguesa. (*Estud. Ibero-Am./Porto Alegre*, 22:1, junho 1996, p. 121–133, bibl.)

Sees cities, the centers of royal administration, as responsible for Brazil's territorial unity. [JM]

3160 Coelho, Duarte. Cartas de Duarte Coelho a El Rei. Coordenação de José Antônio Gonsalves de Mello e Cleonir Xavier de Albuquerque e Costa. Prefácio de Leonardo Dantas Silva. 2a. ed. Recife, Brazil: Fundação Joaquim Nabuco, Editora Massangana, 1997. 137 p.: bibl., ill. (Série Descobrimentos; 7)

Five letters from Duarte Coelho, donatary captain of Pernambuco, to João III, King of Portugal. All but the first letter are photographically reproduced; all are transcribed in original orthography; and all are also printed (and annotated) in updated Portuguese. Excellent source for early history of one of the few successful colonization efforts in early-16th-century Brazil. [JM]

3161 Cohen, Thomas M. The fire of tongues: António Vieira and the missionary church in Brazil and Portugal. Stanford, Calif.: Stanford Univ. Press, 1998. 262 p.: bibl., index.

This important contribution to the biographical literature on Antonio Vieira demonstrates how his experiences in Brazil, and his detention by the Inquisition in Portugal, convinced him that the missionary enterprise must be separated from Portugal's imperial project. Vieira concluded that the Jesuits' special talents (especially their talent for languages) equipped them to build the Christian church in the New World. [JM]

3162 Couto, Jorge. A construção do Brasil: ameríndios, portugueses e africanos, do início do povoamento a finais de quinhentos. Lisboa: Edições Cosmos, 1995. 408 p.: bibl., indexes, maps. (Cosmos História; 11)

History of 16th-century Brazil provides a thorough survey of Portuguese expansion in America. [JM]

3163 Dias Farinha, Maria do Carmo Jasmins and **Maria de Lurdes Henrique.** No V centenário da chegada dos portugueses ao Brasil: reviver o patrimônio comum; contribuição do Instituto dos Arquivos Nacionais/Torre do Tombo, Lisboa. (*ACERVO/Rio de Janeiro*, 10:1, jan./junho 1997, p. 3–15, map, photos)

Essential reading, especially as an introduction to material in the Torre do Tombo archive. Excellent survey of materials pertaining to Brazil, and good description of the different collections. [JM]

3164 Domingues, Ângela. Ameríndios do norte do Brasil na segunda metade do século XVIII: as contradições da liberdade. (*Rev. SBPH*, 12, 1997, p. 17–30)

Based on the 1755 law granting full freedom to the indigenous peoples of Grão Pará, discusses status of indigenous peoples and blacks in late colonial north Brazil. After the Portuguese Crown promised freedom to ensure indigenous peoples' loyalty against other Europeans attempting to establish themselves in the region, Portuguese settlers turned to African slaves to replace indigenous labor. [JM]

3165 Ferreira, Manoel Rodrigues. A fundação da Vila de Piratininga, depois Vila de São Paulo de Piratininga, hoje Cidade de São Paulo: uma escola de sertanismo. (*Rev. Inst. Hist. Geogr. São Paulo*, 92, 1996, p. 7–26)

Claims the Vila de São Paulo de Piratininga was founded to prepare and train Martim Affonso de Souza's men to explore the region for the great riches it supposedly held. Eventually, men trained in this school of *sertanismo* discovered new sources of wealth and contributed to a better understanding of Brazil's hinterland. [JM]

Florentino, Manolo Garcia. Em costas negras: uma história do tráfico atlântico de escravos entre a Africa e o Rio de Janeiro, séculos XVIII e XIX. See item **3267.**

3166 Florentino, Manolo Garcia and **José Roberto Góes.** Comércio negreiro e estratégias de socialização parental entre os escravos do agro-fluminense, 1790–1830. (*in* Encontro de Estudos Populacionais, *9th, Caxambú, Brazil, 1994.* Memorias. Belo Horizonte, Brazil: Associação Brasileira de Estudos Populacionais (ABEP), 1994?, v. 1, p. 365–380, bibl., graphs, tables)

Finds that nuclear families predominated during a period of stability in the slave trade (1790–1808), while matrifocal families increased with expansion of the slave traffic (1808–26). Nuclear families once again became the norm after 1826, when the British increased pressure to end the African slave trade to Brazil. [JM]

3167 Fragoso, João Luís Ribeiro and **Manolo Garcia Florentino.** O arcaísmo como projeto: mercado atlântico, sociedade agrária e elite mercantil no Rio de Janeiro, c.1790-c.1840. Rio de Janeiro: Diadorim, 1993. 118 p.: bibl.

Explores continuity of skewed income distribution in Brazil by examining consistent reproduction of a colonial economy defined here as the growing enrichment of the mercantile elite and the constant pauperization of the free poor. [JM]

3168 Freitas, Décio. A revolução dos malês: insurreições escravas. 2. ed. rev. Porto Alegre, Brazil: Editora Movimento, 1985. 103 p.: bibl. (Col. Documentos brasileiros; 11)

Examines slave insurrections in early-19th-century Salvador as the first and only urban slave revolts in the New World. Argues that slave life in the city, and the circulation of ideas from Haiti and elsewhere, made possible this type of revolt. See review of first edition (1976) in *HLAS 40:3978.* [JM]

3169 Furtado, Júnia Ferreira. Considerações sobre estratégias e formas de sobrevivência da mulher escrava nos setecentos. (*Cad. Filos. Ciênc. Hum.*, 5:9, out. 1997, p. 104–109, bibl.)

Stresses complexity of social relations within slave system. Claims slavery did not simply transform slaves into instruments of production, but that it also provided space for slave women to reduce the coercion of enslavement, and even to participate in a market economy in a fairly autonomous manner. [JM]

3170 Gandavo, Pero de Magalhães. Tratado da terra do Brasil. 5a. ed.; História da Província Santa Cruz a que vulgarmente chamamos Brasil, 1576. 12a. ed. Edição conjunta, organização e apresentação de Leonardo Dantas Silva. Recife, Brazil: Fundação Joaquim Nabuco, Editora Massangana, 1995. 128 p.: bibl., ill. (Série Descobrimentos; 5)

This first formal "history" of Brazil was written to encourage the Portuguese poor to settle Brazil. Good overview of social and economic life in early-16th-century Brazil. [JM]

3171 Garcia, Paulo. Cipriano Barata, ou, A liberdade acima de tudo. Prefácio de Nelson Werneck Sodré. Rio de Janeiro: Topbooks, 1997. 193 p.: bibl., ill.

An effort to resurrect the memory of Cipriano Barata, portrayed as a forgotten Brazilian hero who was relegated to oblivion by "official history." Describes Barata as a true liberal who fought for individual freedom (he participated in the Tailors' Conspiracy of 1798) and saw the state as the great enemy of freedom. [JM]

3172 Golin, Tau. A expedição: imaginário artístico na conquista militar dos Sete Povos jesuíticos e guaranis. Porto Alegre, Brazil: Editora Sulina, 1997. 125 p.: bibl., ill., maps.

Iberian court life came to southern Brazil with the military expeditions sent to subdue the Jesuit missions in the 1750s. This fascinating description of the pomp of European war in the backlands of southern Brazil includes glimpses of song, dance, theater, medieval ritual, and sumptuous banquets where Guarani musicians provided entertainment. Includes reproductions of documents and beautifully designed maps. [JM]

3173 Gomes, Flávio dos Santos. Nas fronteiras da liberdade: mocambos, fugitivos e protesto escravo na Amazônia colonial. (*An. Arq. Público Pará*, 2:1, 1996, p. 125–152)

Ranging well beyond the colonial period and the Amazon region, situates actions of black Brazilians in late-18th and 19th centuries in the context of international political rivalries and differing views of African slavery. Demonstrates that slaves and *quilombolas* were not passive recipients of outside views, but used knowledge of international events to promote their own interests. [JM]

3174 Guimarães, Geraldo. São João del-Rei: século XVIII; história sumária. São João del-Rei, Brazil: G. Guimarães, 1996. 147 p.: bibl., ill., index, maps.

Describes development of the town of São João del-Rei from its early-18th-century founding to the Inconfidência Mineira, with special attention to the emergence of a gold rush society. [JM]

3175 Herson, Bella. Cristãos-novos e seus descendentes na medicina brasileira, 1500–1850. São Paulo: Edusp, 1996. 422 p.: bibl., ill.

Study of doctors and medical practices in colonial Brazil claims most doctors were New Christians. [JM]

3176 Higgins, Kathleen J. Gender and the manumission of slaves in colonial Brazil: the prospects for freedom in Sabará, Minas Gerais, 1710–1809. (*Slavery Abolit.*, 18:2, Aug. 1997, p. 1–29, graphs, table)

Excellent article analyzes changes in manumission of slaves from height of gold boom in early-18th century to the economic bust at century's end. Evidence from manumission records points to significant differences between 1710–59, when men predominated in both free and slave population, and from 1760–1809, when more women had become economically active in Minas Gerais. [JM]

3177 História da vida privada no Brasil. v. 1, Cotidiano e vida privada na América portuguesa organização de Laura de Mello e Souza. São Paulo: Companhia das Letras, 1997. 1 v.: bibl., ill. (some col.), indexes, maps.

Excellent essays by top scholars (F. Novais, L. de Mello e Souza, L. Mezan Algranti, L. Mott, R. Vainfas, M. del Priore, L. Villalta, and I. Jancso) focus on economic, political, and social issues related to private life in colonial Brazil. Beautifully illustrated and engagingly written. Highly recommended. [JM]

3178 Leme, Magarida Ortigão Ramos Paes. O Arquivo da Casa da Moeda de Lisboa: seu interesse para a história do Brasil colonial, 1686–1822. (*ACERVO/Rio de Janeiro*, 10:1, jan./junho 1997, p. 47–56, tables)

Describes some of the materials in this archive, including important sources for those interested in the history of Brazilian mining. [JM]

3179 Libby, Douglas Cole. Notas sobre a produção têxtil brasileira no final do século XVIII: novas evidências de Minas Gerais. (*Estud. Econ./São Paulo*, 27:1, 1997, p. 97–125, bibl., tables)

Using a set of loom inventories for Minas Gerais elaborated in 1786, article suggests that cottage textile industry may have been quite significant in late colonial Brazil. (For English-language version, see *LARR*, 32:1, 1997, p. 88–108.) [JM]

3180 Liberdade por um fio: história dos quilombos no Brasil. Organização de João José Reis e Flávio dos Santos Gomes. São Paulo: Companhia das Letras, 1996. 509 p.: bibl., ill., maps.

Excellent collection of essays highlights recent interpretive currents in the study of runaway slaves. While providing several perspectives on Palmares, the collection also examines runaway slave communities in the Amazon region, Maranhão, Pernambuco, Bahia, Rio Grande do Sul, Rio de Janeiro, Goiás, Mato Grosso, and Minas Gerais. Highly recommended. [JM]

3181 Lyra, Maria de Lourdes Viana. A utopia do poderoso império: Portugal e Brasil; bastidores da política, 1798–1822. Rio de Janeiro: Sette Letras, 1994. 256 p.: bibl., ill.

Examines why Portuguese Brazil became a unified empire (and not a kingdom) following independence, whereas Spanish America broke apart into republican states. Argues that by 1820, when the Portuguese had abandoned the Enlightenment vision of a powerful Portuguese empire in which Brazil would play an important role, Brazilians shifted the discourse from emancipation within the empire to independence and the creation of a "powerful empire" of their own. [JM]

3182 Macedo, Francisco Ribeiro de Azevedo. Conquista pacífica de Guarapuava. Curitiba, Brazil: Prefeitura Municipal de Curitiba, 1995. 294 p.: bibl., ill., map. (Col. Farol do saber)

Excellent account of a settlement expedition in early-19th century highlights its potential, its problems, the presence of indigenous peoples, and Brazilian society on the march. [JM]

3183 Maia, Angela Maria Vieira. A sombra do medo: cristãos velhos e cristãos novos nas capitanias do açúcar. Rio de Janeiro: Oficina Cadernos de Poesia, 1995. 277 p.: bibl.

Finds that during first 80 years of Brazil's colonial period, New Christians became integrated at many different social levels. They coexisted peacefully with Old Christians, even intermarrying, until the denunciations and confessions provoked by the 1591 visit of the Portuguese inquisitor to northeast Brazil shattered that community. [JM]

3184 Martins, Tarcisio José. Quilombo do Campo Grande: a história de Minas roubada do povo. São Paulo: A Gazeta Maçônica, 1995. 318 p.: bibl.

Highlights participation of free blacks and slaves in colonial Minas Gerais. Based on an 18th-century document, author maps out 25 important *quilombos* in Minas Gerais, some with more than 200 houses. Believes that after 1725 and 1735, the *imposto por capitação* forced many of the unprotected poor to seek refuge in *quilombos*. [JM]

3185 Meireles, Maria Adelaide and **Luís Cabral.** Documentos relativos ao Brasil existentes na Biblioteca Pública Municipal do Porto. (*ACERVO/Rio de Janeiro*, 10:1, jan./junho 1997, p. 29–46, bibl., ill., map)

Describes manuscripts (almost all copies) related to Brazil. Most deal with physical aspects of the new lands, and most date from the 18th century. The collection also includes some maps, architectural plans of churches and convents, and several literary manuscripts related to religious orders. [JM]

3186 Mello, Carl Egbert Hansen Vieira de. O Rio de Janeiro no Brasil quinhentista. São Paulo: Editora Giordano, 1996. 235 p.: bibl., ill., maps.

Focuses on presence of Europeans in Guanabara Bay during 16th century and on the interplay of European politics in the region. [JM]

3187 Mello, Evaldo Cabral de. Rubro veio: o imaginário da restauração pernambucana. 2a. ed. rev. e aum. Rio de Janeiro: Topbooks, 1997. 473 p.: bibl., index.

Carefully researched study links nativist sentiment in northeast Brazil to the memory, bolstered by historiography, of the expulsion of the Dutch from Pernambuco. [JM]

3188 Mesquita Samara, Eni de and **Dora Isabel Paiva da Costa.** Family, patriarchalism, and social change in Brazil. (*LARR*, 32:1, 1997, p. 212–225)

A review article of monographs by Muriel Nazzari, Alida Metcalf, Dain Borges, and Angela Mendes de Almeida. Finds that all give a nuanced treatment of multiple family patterns in Brazil. Metcalf and Nazzari stress economic, while Borges and Almeida highlight ideological underpinnings of Brazilian patriarchalism. [JM]

3189 Miller, Shawn W. Fuelwood in colonial Brazil: the economic consequences of fuel depletion for the Bahian Recôncavo, 1549–1820. (An expanding world; 17) (*in* Agriculture, resource exploitation, and environmental change. Edited by Helen Wheatley. Aldershot, Great Britain; Brookfield, Vt.: Variorum, 1997, p. 135–159, map, photo, tables)

Demonstrates that the need for fuelwood, a critical economic commodity in the Recôncavo, helped to shape Bahian society. Competition for firewood provoked social tensions, especially as supply dwindled. Although scarcity was apparent by 1650, lack of concern with conservation set the stage for a greater crisis in the 19th century. [JM]

3190 Monteiro, John Manuel. Negros da terra: índios e bandeirantes nas origens de São Paulo. São Paulo: Companhia das Letras, 1994. 300 p.: bibl., ill. (some col.), index, maps (some col.).

Excellent social history of São Paulo from 16th-18th century. Addresses role of indigenous peoples in the socioeconomic history of colonial Brazil, the myth of the *bandeirante*, and importance of nonexport products in the formation of Brazilian society. For anthropologist's comment, see *HLAS 57:968*. [JM]

3191 Moreira Neto, Carlos de Araújo. Fontes documentais sobre índios dos séculos XVI-XIX. Madrid: Fundación Histórica Tavera, 1996. 130 p.: bibl. (Documentos Tavera; 2)

Valuable source lists repositories (museums, public libraries, and public archives) of material related to indigenous peoples in 11 Brazilian states and in Portugal, Spain, England, and the Netherlands. [JM]

3192 Mott, Luiz Roberto de Barros. A Inquisição em Sergipe. Aracajú, Brazil: Governo de Sergipe, Secretaria de Estado da Cultura e Meio Ambiente, Fundação Estadual de Cultura, 1989. 100 p.: bibl., ill. (Col. Jackson da Silva Lima)

Traces references to Sergipe and its residents in Inquisition records of the Lisbon tribunal from the first visit of inquisitors to Brazil in 1591 to the end of the Portuguese Inquisition in 1821. Claims the Inquisition shaped colonial society, and that the records of that institution help to reconstruct social relations within colonial Sergipe. [JM]

3193 Moura, Carlos Francisco. O ensino em Mato Grosso no século XVIII e no início do século XIX. (*Rev. Inst. Hist. Geogr. Bras.*, 156:390, jan./março 1996, p. 117–135)

Focusing on Cuiabá, describes training in engineering, medicine, military arts, and secondary schools that prepared students to enter university in Portugal. Also provides a list of the *matogrossenses* enrolled in the Univ. de Coimbra. [JM]

3194 Mourão, Gonçalo de Barros Carvalho e Mello. A Revolução de 1817 e a história do Brasil: um estudo de história diplomática. Belo Horizonte, Brazil: Editora Itatiaia Limitada, 1996. 289 p.: bibl. (Col. Reconquista do Brasil; 2a. sér., 182)

Uses diplomatic sources and diplomatic archives (Foreign Office in London and Itamaraty in Brazil) to provide an international vision of Brazil's 1817 Revolution. [JM]

3195 Nardi, Jean-Baptiste. O fumo brasileiro no período colonial: lavoura, comércio e administração. São Paulo: Editora Brasiliense, 1996. 432 p.: bibl., ill., maps.

Thorough study of Brazilian tobacco production between 1570–1830 highlights its connections to the colonial system through the Crown monopoly, the slave trade, and the development of Brazil's internal market and local industry. [JM]

3196 Netto, José Antonio Souza Pinto. A conquista do Rio Grande. Texto e fotografia de José Antonio Souza Pinto Netto = The conquest of Rio Grande. Text and photo-

graphs by José Antonio Souza Pinto Netto. Rio de Janeiro: AC&M Editora, 1990? 118 p.: bibl., ill. (some col.), maps. (O continente de São Pedro; 1)

Nicely illustrated bilingual (Portuguese and English) text describes ways in which rivalry between Portuguese and Spanish prompted the colonization of southern Brazil. Second part follows Domingos Filgueira, who set out in 1703 to establish a land route between Brazil and Colonia do Sacramento. [JM]

3197 Neumann, Eduardo. Porto Alegre colonial: uma ocupação luso-platina. (*Estud. Ibero-Am./Porto Alegre*, 23:1, junho 1997, p. 81–95)

Discusses local and international problems related to Portuguese efforts to settle what became Rio Grande do Sul. [JM]

3198 Nunes, Mari Thétis. A educação na colônia: os Jesuítas. (*Rev. Inst. Hist. Geogr. Bras.*, 156:389, out./dez. 1995, p. 661–674)

Discusses Jesuit control of education in Brazil between 1549–1749. By educating sons of rising bourgeoisie and directing them to enter either the priesthood or a Portuguese university, Jesuits in Brazil provided cultural continuity between the colony and the mother country. [JM]

3199 Oliveira, André Frota. A fortificação holandesa do Camocim. Fortaleza, Brazil: Expressão Gráfica e Editora, 1995. 148 p.: bibl., ill., maps.

Attempts to establish that the Dutch fort of Camocim was built on the outskirts of what is today the town of Granja. Provides a brief history of the Dutch invasion of Ceará. [JM]

3200 Paiva, Eduardo França. Escravos e libertos nas Minas Gerais do século XVIII: estratégias de resistência através dos testamentos. São Paulo: Annablume: Faculdades Integradas Newton Paiva, 1995. 240 p.: bibl., ill. (Selo universidade; 43. História)

Uses approximately 400 wills of female freed slaves to provide insight into 18th-century Minas Gerais society. Sees evidence of resistance to enslavement through the adoption of some the practices of the master class, which ultimately allowed slaves to gain freedom, and thus tempered the inherent violence of slavery. [JM]

3201 Paiva, Eduardo França. A viagem insólita de um cristão das Minas Gerais: um documento e um mergulho no imaginário colonial. (*Rev. Bras. Hist.*, 16:31/32, 1996, p. 353–363)

Uses three *requerimentos* to explore the meanings of life, death, power, and religion in late colonial Brazil. Highlights the document in which the petitioner, attempting to recover his job, claimed his soul had been to heaven where he had spoken with God and the Virgin Mary. Includes transcripts of these fascinating documents. [JM]

3202 Paixão, Judite Cavaleiro. Fontes do Tribunal de Contas de Portugal para a história do Brasil Colônia. (*ACERVO/Rio de Janeiro*, 10:1, jan./junho 1997, p. 57–70, graphs)

Brief history of the Tribunal de Contas and its functions. The historical archives of this Portuguese audit office include valuable materials for studying the financial administration of colonial Brazil. Describes a variety of sources (especially rich after 1750), including material related to the confiscation of Jesuit property following the expulsion of that order from Portugal and its colonies. [JM]

3203 Palacin, Luiz. O século do ouro em Goiás, 1722–1822: estrutura e conjuntura numa capitania de Minas. 4a. ed. Goiânia, Brazil: UCG Editora, 1994. 150 p.: bibl., col. ill.

Based on long-term archival research, provides a good view of the growth and decline of colonial society in a region where the initial quest for gold was followed by unsuccessful attempts to find alternative sources of wealth. [JM]

3204 Pinto, Emanuel Pontes. Aventura e pioneirismo: a viagem precursora de Manuel Félix de Lima pelo Rio Guaporé, em 1742. (*Rev. SBPH*, 12, 1997, p. 3–16, bibl.)

Describes the journey of Manuel Félix de Lima from Mato Grosso to Belém do Grão-Pará, demonstrating that it was shorter and safer to travel from Cuiabá to Belém than from Cuiabá to São Paulo. Arrested in Belém and sent to Portugal for navigating a forbidden route, Félix de Lima convinced the king of the need to encourage occupation along the right bank of the Guaporé river. [JM]

3205 Rabello, David. Os diamantes do Brasil: na regência de Dom João, 1792–1816; um estudo de dependência externa. São Paulo: Editora Arte & Ciência: UNIP, 1997. 278 p.: bibl., ill., maps. (Universidade aberta; 19. História)

Examines significance of the royal diamond monopoly for the Portuguese economy during critical period that culminated in the flight of the Portuguese court to Brazil. [JM]

3206 Raposo, Luciano. Barrocas famílias: vida familiar em Minas Gerais no século XVIII. São Paulo: Editora Hucitec, 1997. 198 p.: bibl., ill. (Estudos históricos; 30)

Examination of the family in 18th-century Minas Gerais is based on evidence found in the *devassas episcopais*. Finds that authorities' insistence on promoting church-sanctioned unions and legitimate families in the region was met with both resistance and accommodation. Concludes that the traditional (patriarchal and conservative) *mineiro* family emerged after 19th-century transition from mining to plantations. [JM]

Reichel, Heloísa Jochims and **Ieda Gutfreind.** As raízes históricas do Mercosul: a Região Platina colonial. See item **2484.**

3207 Reis, José Carlos. Varnhagen, 1853–7: o elogio da colonização portuguesa. (*Varia Hist.*, 17, março 1997, p. 106–131, bibl.)

Addresses Varnhagen's contributions to a new history of Brazil based on documentary evidence. However, in response to Robert Southey's negative description of Portuguese Brazil, Varnhagen focused on the Portuguese "heroes" who civilized that "wild" region. [JM]

3208 Rema, Henrique Pinto. As missões católicas portuguesas no Atlântico Sul no século XVII. (*Cuad. CENDES*, 12:28, enero/abril 1995, p. 493–552)

Describes the seven missionary dioceses of the South Atlantic in the 18th century. Lists clergy and missionary orders in each diocese. Work is favorable toward missionaries who, the author believes, promoted more just and Christian societies in Brazil and in Africa. [JM]

3209 Rosário, Irari de Oliveira. Três séculos e meio da história postal brasileira, 1500–1843. Rio de Janeiro: ECT-Gepro-RJ, 1993? 153 p.: bibl., ill.

Traces development of communications between Portugal and Brazil beginning with the letter from Pero Vaz de Caminha to the King of Portugal. [JM]

3210 Rubert, Arlindo. História da Igreja no Rio Grande do Sul. v. 1, Época colonial, 1626–1822. Porto Alegre, Brazil: EDIPUCRS, 1994. 1 v.: bibl., ill., indexes, map. (Col. Teologia; 2)

This regional church history is based on material collected from archives in Rome, Lisbon, Rio de Janeiro, and many local archives in Rio Grande do Sul. Interesting portrayal of the place of this "frontier" church in the political struggles of colonial Brazil. [JM]

3211 Russell-Wood, A.J.R. Colonial Brazil: the gold cycle, c. 1690–1750. (*in* Mines of silver and gold in the Americas. Edited by Peter Bakewell. Aldershot, Great Britain; Brookfield, Vt.: Variorum, 1997, p. 322–383, map, table)

Discusses ramifications of the discovery of gold in Brazil for Portugal, Brazil, and the rest of the world. Pays special attention to social, political, and economic issues. [JM]

3212 Salazar, Guilherme de Alencastro. Um capítulo da história da Companhia das Indias Ocidentais no Brasil: suas moedas obsidionais cunhadas no Recife. Recife, Brazil: Editora Universitária UFPE, 1994? 376 p.: ill.

Coins minted by the Dutch West India Company in Recife in 1640s to pay their soldiers serve as the basis for recounting the story of the Dutch in Brazil. [JM]

3213 Salvador, José Gonçalves. A capitania do Espírito Santo e seus engenhos de açúcar: 1535–1700, a presença dos cristãos-novos. Vitória, Brazil: SPDC/UFES, DEC, 1994? 103 p.: bibl., ill., map. (Col. Cultura UFES; 26)

Broad history of Espírito Santo emphasizes role of New Christians in the region. [JM]

3214 Santos, Corcino Medeiros dos. Evasão da prata espanhola para o Brasil. (*Rev. Inst. Hist. Geogr. Bras.*, 156:390, jan./março 1996, p. 7–72, tables)

Describes role of Peruvian silver in 17th-century Brazil. Claims Rio de Janeiro became the center for British contraband of Spanish silver. By 18th century, wars between Britain and Spain allowed for more active Brazilian contraband through the Rio de la Plata. [JM]

3215 Santos, Ricardo Evaristo dos. El Brasil filipino: 60 años de presencia española en Brasil, 1580–1640. Traducción de Mario Merlino. Madrid: Editorial MAPFRE, 1993. 263 p.: bibl., ill., indexes. (Colecciones MAPFRE 1492)

Discusses positive aspects of Spanish rule (1580–1640) in Brazil: the Tordesillas line lost its earlier significance; *ordenações filipinas* shaped Brazilian law; Spain's "Golden Age" influenced Brazil's literary culture; missionary activity increased and diversified; and Spanish political troubles provoked the Dutch invasion, resulting in the growth of Brazilian nationalism. [JM]

3216 Scisínio, Alaôr Eduardo. Dicionário da escravidão. Rio de Janeiro: L. Christiano Editorial, 1997. 331 p.: bibl., map.

Composed of more than 1,500 entries, this eclectic dictionary provides fascinating evidence of the enormous impact of African slavery on Brazilian culture. Entries include food (fruits, vegetables, herbs), illnesses, slave remedies, insurrections, ancestral beliefs, punishments, religious syncretism, slave ethnicities and dances, and slave legislation. An extensive entry on "Bibliography" is noteworthy. [JM]

Silva, Ligia Maria Osório. Terras devolutas e latifúndio: efeitos da lei de 1850. See item **3328.**

3217 Silva, Lina Gorenstein Ferreira da. Heréticos e impuros: a inquisição e os cristãos-novos no Rio de Janeiro, século XVIII. Rio de Janeiro: Prefeitura da Cidade do Rio de Janeiro, Secretaria Municipal de Cultura, Depto. Geral de Documentação e Informação Cultural, Divisão de Editoração, 1995. 217 p.: bibl., ill. (Col. Biblioteca carioca; v. 39. Série Publicação científica)

Addresses role of New Christians in urban Rio de Janeiro during a period of economic expansion in southeast Brazil. Concludes that the Inquisition, active in Rio de

Janeiro after 1703, shattered the unity of the New Christian community. [JM]

3218 Silva, Maria Beatriz Nizza da. Cultura Luso-Brasileira, 1772–1808. (*Arquipél. Hist.*, 2, 1997, p. 193–207)

Describes shared culture of Brazilian and Portuguese literate elite trained at Univ. de Coimbra who served the Portuguese Crown in Portugal, Africa, and Brazil. However, because there were so few seminaries in Brazil, and because university training was not required of priests, religious life proved less homogeneous in the Portuguese empire. [JM]

3219 Silva, Maria Beatriz Nizza da. Mulheres brancas no fim do período colonial. (*Cad. Pagu*, 4, 1995, p. 75–96)

Describes multifaceted experiences of white women at the end of the colonial period, ranging from different work options (sugar mill administrators, laundresses, cooks, beggars) to strategies for escaping bad marriages. Population growth (including the arrival of many foreigners after 1808) meant the number of white women in Brazil was far greater and more diverse just before independence than it had been earlier in the colonial period. [JM]

3220 Silva, Maria Beatriz Nizza da. Mulheres e patrimônio familiar no Brasil no fim do período colonial. (*ACERVO/Rio de Janeiro*, 9:1/2, jan./dez. 1996, p. 85–98, ill.)

Concludes that white women actively participated in generating, maintaining, and inheriting wealth at the end of the colonial period. [JM]

3221 Torre Reyes, Carlos de la. Pedro de Teixeria y el redescubrimiento del Amazonas. (*in* Congresso das Academias da História Ibero-Americanas, 4th, Lisbon and Porto, Portugal, 1994. Actas. Lisboa: Academia Portuguesa da História, 1996, p. 429–442)

After depicting challenges faced by the first Europeans to sail the Amazon River, recounts story of Pedro de Teixeira, a Portuguese nobleman who "rediscovered" the Amazon in the 1630s, sailing from Maranhão to Quito and back. [JM]

3222 Vangelista, Chiara. Las relaciones hispano-portuguesas en el norte de Mato Grosso, siglos XVIII-XIX. (*in* Las raíces de la memoria: América Latina, ayer y hoy, quinto encuentro debate = Amèrica Llatina, ahir i avui, cinquena trobada debat. Coordinación de Pilar García Jordán *et al.* Barcelona: Univ. de Barcelona, 1996, p. 409–424)

Focuses on second half of the 18th century, when the Portuguese established claims to Mato Grosso by appointing a governor and building cities and fortifications. But the lure of gold soon faded, and the independence of Brazil and Bolivia removed the geopolitical importance of that region. [JM]

3223 Venturelli, Isolde Helena Brans. Thomas Jefferson and the Vendek Mission. Washington: s.n., 1993. 34 leaves.

Discusses efforts of Brazilian patriots in France to persuade Thomas Jefferson (then US ambassador in Paris) to secure aid from the US for the Brazilian independence movement. [JM]

3224 Vilela, Magno. Uma questão de igualdade—: Antônio Vieira. Rio de Janeiro: Relume Dumará, 1997. 207 p.: bibl.

Uses the sermons of Antonio Vieira to address the question of slavery and Christian equality. Credits Vieira with taking a discussion of the injustices of slavery to the Portuguese court; but, convinced that slavery was essential for the success of Portuguese Brazil, Vieira could not promote the ultimate end of the institution. [JM]

3225 Viotti, Hélio Abranches. Ensino público em São Paulo entre 1551 e 1759. (*Rev. Inst. Hist. Geogr. São Paulo*, 92, 1996, p. 66–72)

Describes program in Jesuit schools as classical education, modeled on European content and methods. Superiors in Brazil, conscious of tensions between teaching vocation and missionary calling, never abandoned teaching. [JM]

3226 Weech, J. Friedrich von. A agricultura e o comércio do Brasil no sistema colonial: a situação atual do Brasil e o seu sistema colonial, sobretudo em relação à agricultura e ao comércio, destinado especialmente a imigrantes. São Paulo: Martins Fontes, 1992. 187 p.: bibl.

Written by a German military officer who emigrated to Brazil, this guide (originally published in 1828) was meant to aid other German immigrants, especially farmers. [JM]

NATIONAL

3227 Aleixo, Lúcia Helena Gaeta. Vozes no silêncio: subordinação, resistência e trabalho em Mato Grosso, 1888–1930. Cuiabá, Brazil: EdUFMT, 1995. 320 p.: bibl.

Examines state control and worker resistance in late-19th- and early-20th-century Mato Grosso, focusing on industrial work force in the sugar mills. After turn of the century, domination by traditional *coroneis* gave way to manipulation by the mills and growing state intervention, e.g., "vagrancy" laws. Good description of local sugar industry. [DM]

3228 Almeida, Carla Maria C. Minas Gerais de 1750 a 1850: bases da economia e tentativa de periodização. *(LPH Rev. Hist., 5, 1995, p. 88–111, graphs, tables)*

Summary of a *mestrado* thesis uses post-mortem records and travelers' accounts to show that the mid-18th century decline of mining, rather than provoking a collapse, reinforced the existing subsistence economy and prompted increased agricultural and handicraft production for local sale and for the expanding Rio market. [DM]

Almeida, Lúcio Flávio de. Ideologia nacional e nacionalismo. See item **5205.**

3229 Antonacci, Maria Antonieta. A vitória da razão (?): o IDORT e a sociedade paulista. São Paulo: Editora Marco Zero; Brasília: Programa Nacional do Centenário da República e Bicentenário da Inconfidência Mineira, MCT, 1993. 285 p.: bibl. (Biblioteca da República)

Institutional and ideological history of São Paulo's Instituto de Organização Racional do Trabalho (IDORT) describes its mission to promote technical training and rationalize industrial management, factory routines, and personnel practices. Institute's journal and ideas were influential in reorganization of state bureaucracy and in foundation of semi-official vocational training program Serviço Nacional de Aprendizagem Industrial (SENAI). For a broader view of industrial policy, see item **3343.** [DB]

3230 Araujo, Mundinha. Insurreição de escravos em Viana, 1867. Prefácio de Joel Rufino dos Santos. São Luís, Brazil: SIOGE, 1994. 239 p.: bibl., ill.

Slave insurrections and *quilombos* in mid-19th century Maranhão were linked to the effects of Paraguayan War on the province: the state withdrew regular troops and National Guards to fight in the south; draft evaders and deserters disrupted local society; and slaves had the idea that the war was in some manner linked to their freedom. Includes extensive quotes from newspapers, government documents, and trial records. [DM]

3231 Arquivo Público do Estado do Rio de Janeiro. Secretaria de Estado de Justiça. DOPS: a lógica da desconfiança. Rio de Janeiro: Arquivo Público do Estado do Rio de Janeiro, 1993. 57 p.: bibl., ill.

Preliminary essays and archival notes from the team organizing secret police archives (1933–83), which were opened in 1993. Archive includes voluminous investigative files on political suspects. [DB]

3232 Azevedo, Celia Maria Marinho de. Abolitionism in the United States and Brazil: a comparative perspective. New York: Garland Pub., 1995. 200 p.: bibl., index. (Studies in African American history and culture)

First book-length comparison of abolitionist movements, based on published sources and secondary literature, argues that slaveholders' and slaves' different views in the two places stemmed from Americans' religious inspiration, Brazilians' location inside slave territory, and white Americans' respect for a vocal black community. The crucial difference was American push through abolitionism toward reconstruction, in contrast to the Brazilian single-issue focus on abolition. Narrower in analysis of Brazilian ideology than Azevedo's own pioneering book on 19th-century debates over labor and social control (see *HLAS 52:2971*), and doesn't fully confront revisionist arguments that Brazilian slave resistance, more than abolitionists, precipitated formal abolition. [DB]

3233 Azevedo, Thales de. Os italianos no Rio Grande do Sul: cadernos de pesquisa. Caxias do Sul, Brazil: Editora da Univ. de Caxias do Sul, 1994. 507 p.: bibl., ill., index.

Transcribed field notebooks, archival notes, and news clippings, 1955–59 and 1973, from noted anthropologist's fieldwork in Italian settlements. Includes rich anecdotes on themes of acculturation, family and marriage, language, church and religion, ethnicity and race relations, and land use and tenure. These notes formed the basis of his work *Italianos e gaúchos* (see *HLAS 40:4062*). [DB]

3234 Bacelar, Jeferson Afonso. Galegos no paraíso racial. Salvador, Brazil: Centro Editorial e Didático; CEAO; Ianamá, 1994. 188 p.: bibl., ill., maps.

Useful overview of Spanish Galician immigration to Bahia, 1900–50, discusses Spanish causes, work and austerity ethic, families, and associations. Argues that during this period lack of integration and a niche as bakers and grocers made them white scapegoats of racial tensions. [DB]

3235 Barickman, B.J. Persistence and decline: slave labour and sugar production in the Bahian Recôncovo, 1850–1888. (*J. Lat. Am. Stud.*, 28:2, May 1996, p. 581–633)

In Bahia sugar production stagnated after 1850 and declined dramatically with abolition, the result of failure of local planters to make the transition from slave to free labor. Peasant and ex-slave access to land for subsistence agriculture and small-scale cash cropping made it difficult to coerce them into work on the sugar *fazendas*. [DM]

3236 Bastos Filho, Jayme de Araujo. A Missão Militar Francesa no Brasil. Rio de Janeiro: Biblioteca do Exército Editora, 1994. 173 p.: bibl., ill. (Publicação / Biblioteca do Exército Editora; 609. Col. General Benício; 299)

Summary account of French advisory missions from 1918–1940 that influenced officer training, logistics, and strategy. [DB]

3237 Beattie, Peter M. Conflicting penile codes: modern masculinity and sodomy in the Brazilian military, 1860–1916. (*in* Sex and sexuality in Latin America. New York: New York Univ. Press, 1997, p. 65–85)

Looks at attitudes toward sodomy in the military. As part of German-influenced reform, the army sought to make itself an honorable place "unencumbered with innuendos of deviance." Homosexual relations, if a sin, were not a state or army problem so long as they remained private and consensual, but demanded intervention if they involved force or public displays. [DM]

3238 Beattie, Peter M. The house, the street, and the barracks: reform and honorable masculine social space in Brazil, 1864–1945. (*HAHR*, 76:3, Aug. 1996, p. 439–473)

Popular resistance to 19th-century Brazilian practice of impressment into the military was widespread. The people hated the abuses; the *coroneis* fought threats to their control; and "honorable families" resented intrusion of the "street" into the "house," as well as forced service with social inferiors. [DM]

3239 Bierrenbach, Julio de Sá. 1954–1964: uma década política. Rio de Janeiro: Domínio Público, 1996. 239 p.: bibl., ill., index, map.

Political memoir explaining events leading to 1964 coup is written by officer who was secondary figure then, but who later became Ministro da Marinha and a member of the Superior Tribunal Militar during military governments. [DB]

3240 Brasil: o trânsito da memória. Organização de Saúl Sosnowski e Jorge Schwartz. São Paulo: Edusp; College Park: Univ. of Maryland, 1994. 226 p.: bibl., ill.

Papers, mostly opinion pieces, from a 1988 conference on Brazilian culture emphasize cultural impact of 1964–85 dictatorships. Useful as sampling of thought of leading academic social and cultural critics at the cusp of transition to democracy. Loose theme of remembering cultural costs of authoritarianism. [DB]

3241 Bretas, Marcos Luiz. A guerra das ruas: povo e polícia na cidade do Rio de Janeiro. Rio de Janeiro: Arquivo Nacional, 1997. 124 p.: bibl.

Arquivo Nacional prizewinner looks at history of the police and their relations with the people in turn-of-the-century Rio de Janeiro. Not an account of the *vencidos*, but rather of elites or, at least, of the elite's chief repressive arm in the city that seeks to show how and why domination worked. [DM]

3242 Caldeira, Jorge. Mauá: empresário do Império. São Paulo: Companhia das Letras, 1995. 557 p.: bibl., ill., index.

Impressive biography of leading mid-19th-century banker and entrepreneur. [DB]

3243 Calmon, Pedro. Memórias. Rio de Janeiro?: Editora Nova Fronteira, 1995. 440 p.: bibl., index.

Memoir by a leading historian focuses on his youth, family, political friendships, and travel anecdotes. Little about his ideas on history and education. [DB]

3244 Camargo, Aspásia; João Hermes Pereira de Araújo; and Mário Henrique Simonsen. Oswaldo Aranha: a estrela da revolução. Apresentaçã de Francisco Iglésias. São Paulo: Editora Mandarim, 1996. 442 p.: bibl.

Collection of three essays on Aranha deal with his role in the 1930 revolution, his diplomatic ventures with the US and the UN, and his two terms as Ministro da Fazenda. Based on secondary literature and Aranha archive at Centro de Pesquisa e Documentação de Historia Contemporânea do Brasil (CPDOC). See also items **3279** and **3286.** [DB]

3245 Carneiro, Maria Luiza Tucci. Brasil, um refúgio nos trópicos: a trajetória dos refugiados do nazi-fascismo = Brasilien, Fluchtpunkt in den Tropen: Lebenswege der Flüchtlinge des Nazi-Faschismus. Tradução de Dieter Strauss e Angel Bojadsen. São Paulo: Estação Liberdade; Instituto Goethe, 1996. 254 p.: bibl., ill., map.

Well-illustrated catalog of exhibition on refugees from Nazi Germany includes documents, letters, and art by exiles. [DB]

Carone, Edgard. Da esquerda à direita. See *HLAS 57:3862.*

3246 Carrara Junior, Ernesto and **Hélio Meirelles.** A indústria química e o desenvolvimento do Brasil, 1500–1889. v. 1–2. São Paulo: Metalivros, 1996. 2 v.: bibl., ill., index.

Offers general information on legislation and tariff policies, together with detailed material on chemical processes, patents, and concessions for specific industries, e.g., textiles, mining, glass, leather, etc. Focuses on 19th century. [DM]

3247 Castro, Hebe Maria Mattos de. Das cores do silêncio: os significados da liberdade no sudeste escravista, Brasil, século XIX. Rio de Janeiro: Arquivo Nacional, 1995. 426 p.: bibl., ill. (Prêmio Arquivo Nacional de Pesquisa)

What did freedom mean to former slaves and to their former masters? Focusing on the North Fluminense, author finds that the *libertos* rejected the term *negro* because it marked them as ex-slaves; they preferred *pardo*, which they saw not in terms of whitening but of social mobility and acceptance as citizens. For many elites, by contrast, the Republic was born "without people" ("citizens") and had to be filled with immigrants. Massively researched. [DM]

3248 Caulfield, Sueann. The birth of Mangue: race, nation, and the politics of prostitution in Rio de Janeiro, 1850–1942. (*in* Sex and sexuality in Latin America. New York: New York Univ. Press, 1997, p. 86–100)

A history of Mangue, a "zone" of tolerated prostitution in Rio de Janeiro associated with poor, often foreign, prostitutes. Prostitution, as opposed to pimping, was not illegal but police were pressured to keep it out of the public eye by forcing it into areas such as Mangue. By the 1940s, the tendency was away from brothel prostitution toward more independent activity. [DM]

3249 Chalhoub, Sidney. Cidade febril: cortiços e epidemias na corte imperial. São Paulo: Companhia das Letras, 1996. 250 p.: bibl., ill. (some col.), index.

Well-researched and theoretically informed study of origins and application of the "ideology of hygiene" in turn-of-the-century Rio de Janeiro. Gives particular attention to effects of destruction of slums (seen as centers of yellow fever infection) and to 19th-century development of popular resistance to small pox vaccination. [DM]

3250 Chasteen, John Charles. Heroes on horseback: a life and times of the last gaucho caudillos. Albuquerque: Univ. of New Mexico Press, 1995. 241 p.: bibl., index, maps. (Diálogos)

Well-written study of 19th-century *caudillismo* and border politics looks at both leaders and followers during the 1893–94 Federalist War and subsequent uprisings in Uruguay. The *caudillos* were charismatic leaders who embodied the values and aspirations of the rural masses on both sides of the border, values represented by the "myth of the *patriada.*" For Uruguayan historian's comment, see item **3110.** [DM]

3251 Chasteen, John Charles. The prehistory of Samba: carnival dancing in Rio de Janeiro, 1840–1917. (*J. Lat. Am. Stud.,* 28:1, Feb. 1996, p. 29–47)

Samba today is not simply the descendent of *batuque,* but rather was influenced by various intermediate 19th-century music and dances, including the *congo, lundu, fandango,* polka, and *maxixe,* and various street drumming groups. The Estado Novo converted samba from one of many regional expressions into the national tradition. [DM]

3252 Chesnut, R. Andrew. Born again in Brazil: the Pentecostal boom and the pathogens of poverty. New Brunswick, N.J.: Rutgers Univ. Press, 1997. 203 p.: bibl., ill., index.

Outstanding history of growth of Pentecostal churches in Belém, Pará, 1910–93, focuses on Assemblies of God. Based on church administrative documents and interviews with converts, work stresses experience of faith cures of socially and biologically "sick" slum dwellers as major motive for conversions. Also discusses church leaders in politics. Superb first-person accounts of spiritual experience make this an excellent introduction to Latin American Pentecostalism for students. [DB]

3253 Congresso Brasileiro de História Econômica, *1st, São Paulo, 1993.* História econômica da independência e do Império: Organização de Tamás Szmrecsányi e José Roberto do Amaral Lapa. São Paulo: Editora Hucitec; FAPESP; Associação Brasileira de Pesquisadores em História Econômica, 1996. 324 p.: bibl., ill., map.

Companion volume to item **3254.** Among chapter titles are "Origens da Economia Nacional (covering state building and political economy); "Do Trabalho Escravo ao Trabalho Livre" (debates over the slave trade and over indemnification); "A Construção da Infra-Estrutura" (port and railroad construction, economic diversification, foreign capital); and "Mercado Interno e Primeiras Indústrias" (industrialization in Minas Gerais, Rio de Janeiro, and Bahia). [DM]

3254 Congresso Brasileiro de História Econômica, *1st, São Paulo, 1993.* História econômica da primeira república.

Organização de Sérgio S. Silva e Tamás Szmrecsányi. São Paulo: Editora Hucitec; FAPESP; Associação Brasileira de Pesquisadores em História Econômica, 1996. 413 p.: bibl., map.

Excellent collection of essays by Brazilian and foreign authors originating from a 1993 conference. Among chapter titles are "O Brasil na América Latina" (general essays on coffee, rubber, and business history); "A Questão da Terra" (land appropriation and disputes); "O Processo de Industrialização" (covering immigrants and labor supply, the textile industry, foreign investment); and " O Mundo do Trabalho" (surveying labor markets). See also item **3253.** [DM]

3255 Corrêa, Valmir Batista. Coronéis e bandidos em Mato Grosso, 1889–1943. Campo Grande, Brazil: Editora UFMS, 1995. 189 p.: bibl., ill., maps.

In Mato Grosso the violent *coronel* politics typical of the Old Republic were aggravated by proximity of the international frontier, by continued *gaucho* migration to the south of the state, and by the Cuiabá oligarchy's control of state politics. In 1920s urbanization and arrival of the railroad shifted the economic center to Campo Grande, undercutting both the *coroneis* and Cuiabá, while in the 1930s the Estado Novo repressed free-lance violence. Relies heavily on oral tradition. [DM]

3256 Correspondência passiva de Francisco Glicério. Organização de Fernando Antonio Abrahão. Campinas, Brazil: Centro de Memória, UNICAMP, 1996. 207 p.: indexes. (Col. Instrumentos de pesquisa; 2)

Transcribes 200 letters to São Paulo Republican leader Francisco Glicério from 1878–1915, mostly terse political correspondence dating from 1882–89. Includes correspondence from Campos Salles, Prudente de Moraes, son-in-law Herculano de Freitas, and others. Only a sample from papers still held privately. [DB]

3257 Cultura e sviluppo: un'indagine sociologica sugli immigrati italiani e tedeschi nel Brasile meridionale. A cura di Renzo Gubert. Milano, Italy: F. Angeli, 1995. 508 p.: bibl. (Col. di sociologia; 252)

Questionnaire research by team of sociologists exploring attitudes of small farmers of Italian and German descent in Santa

Catarina and Rio Grande do Sul finds correlation between traditional values (about family, etc.) and attitudes conducive to development. Concludes that strong religiosity, rather than Catholic or Protestant affiliation, correlates with prodevelopment outlook. Historians might be able to collate this data with 1960s questionnaire research. [DB]

3258 Cunha, Euclides da. Canudos e outros temas. Introdução geral, seleção, cronologia e apresentações finais de Olímpio de Souza Andrade. Apresentação, notas e estabelecimento do texto definitivo a cargo de Cyl Gallindo. 3a ed., rev. e ampliada. Brasília: Subsecretaria de Edições Técnicas; Casa de Pernambuco, 1994. 261 p.: bibl.

Expanded re-edition of Cunha's newspaper reportage covers expedition against Canudos. Includes various newspaper articles on related topics, with several developed later in *Os sertoes*. Introductions discuss and provide context for each piece. [DM]

3259 Debes, Célio. Washington Luís. v. 1, 1869–1924. São Paulo: Imprensa Oficial do Estado: Instituto Histórico e Geográfico de S. Paulo, 1994. 1 v.: bibl., ill. (Col. Centenário; 1)

Vol. 1 of a biography, based on newspapers, government documents, and recently opened family papers, examines Luís' life up to 1924 and the presidency of São Paulo state. Traces the paradigmatic career of an Old Republic politician from law school through local judgeship and municipal politics to state and federal office. At the same time, argues that Luís was unusually interested in introducing political, administrative, and economic reforms. Uncritical. [DM]

3260 Dias, Claudete Maria Miranda. Balaios e bem-te-vis: a guerrilha sertaneja. Teresina, Brazil: Prefeitura Municipal de Teresina, Fundação Cultural Monsenhor Chaves, 1995. 224 p.: bibl.

Argues that the Balaiada was not, as it often is portrayed, a race war but instead was a popular, cross-class uprising that opposed a bad government and sought land and "liberty." Forced recruiting to put down revolts in other provinces, together with a sharp downturn in economic conditions, touched off the uprising. Focuses on Piauí. [DM]

Doratioto, Francisco Fernando Monteoliva. A participação brasileira no golpe de estado de 1894 no Paraguai: a missão cavalcanti. See item **3084.**

3261 Eakin, Marshall Craig. Brazil: the once and future country. New York: St. Martin's Press, 1997. 301 p.: bibl., index, map.

Lucid introduction to Brazil by leading US historian covers history, regional differences, social relations and popular culture, political history and contemporary political institutions through 1992, and economic development. Theme of frustrated potential reflects Brazilian mood of economic and political crisis ca. 1985–93. More helpful explanation of economic and political institutions than Levine's *Brazilian legacies* (see item **3291**), but less detail on the popular culture that may intrigue visitors. See also item **3308.** [DB]

3262 El-Kareh, Almir Chaiban. Imigração e marginalização: a política imigratória do governo imperial brasileiro nos anos 1850. (*Rev. Ciênc. Hist.*, 11, 1996, p. 205–220)

The 1850s was perceived as a period of tremendous change in Brazil, in large part because of the abolition of the international slave trade and the beginning of large-scale, sponsored immigration. Cholera deaths in 1855–56 increased demand for immigrant coffee workers, but private companies abused the immigrants' hopes, and the state inadequately policed this new traffic. [DM]

3263 Falci, Miridan Britto Knox. Escravos do sertão: demografia, trabalho e relações sociais; Piauí, 1826–1888. Teresina, Brazil: Fundação Cultural Monsenhor Chaves, 1995. 333 p.: bibl., ill.

Pioneering study of slave demography in Piauí, based on censuses, slave inventories, and official reports. Includes discussion of government-owned ranches (*fazendas nacionais*). [DB]

3264 Faria, Fernando Antonio. Arquivo de sombras: a privatização do Estado brasileiro nos anos iniciais da Primeira República. Rio de Janeiro: Sette Letras, 1996. 91 p.: bibl.

Uses career of Joaquim Murtinho— would-be entrepreneur, Mato Grosso politician, and government minister—to explore federal politics of the Old Republic. Finds a "deliberate suppression of the boundary between public and private" to facilitate individual gain during this period. Murtinho's brief service as Ministro da Indústria, Viação e Obras Públicas, for example, was devoted entirely to using government power to benefit special interests. [DM]

3265 Ferraz, Socorro. Liberais & liberais: guerras civis em Pernambuco no século XIX. Recife, Brazil: Editora Universitária UFPE, 1996? 229 p.: bibl.

Sees the Cabanagem not as a race or class uprising, but as a broad-based "popular revolution in the Amazon," a movement that brought together members of all groups and classes against an imperial policy that gave "foreigners," i.e., Portuguese and English mercenaries, provincial political and administrative power. See also item **3329.** [DM]

3266 Ferreira, Marieta de Moraes. Em busca da idade de ouro: as elites políticas fluminenses na Primeira República, 1889–1930. Rio de Janeiro: Editora UFRJ; Edições Tempo Brasileiro, 1994. 167 p.: bibl.

Efforts in Rio de Janeiro to develop an axis of federal power as an alternative to the São Paulo-Minas Gerais domination failed. Personalism and political and economic differences divided local elites, while proximity of the federal capital meant that Rio politicians tended to be more absorbed with national concerns and patronage than with state interests. [DM]

3267 Florentino, Manolo Garcia. Em costas negras: uma história do tráfico atlântico de escravos entre a Africa e o Rio de Janeiro, séculos XVIII e XIX. Rio de Janeiro: Arquivo Nacional, 1995. 300 p.: bibl., ill. (Prêmio Arquivo Nacional de Pesquisa)

Detailed treatment of the Africa-Rio de Janeiro slave trade from the 1790s-1830s, based on extensive archival research in Brazil. The trade was "the most important sector of endogenous [capital] accumulation in the colony," and the traders were the empresarial elites of the local socioeconomic hierarchy. Includes extensive quantitative material. [DM]

3268 Florentino, Manolo Garcia and José Roberto Góes. Parentesco e família entre os escravos no século XIX: um estudo de caso. (*Rev. Bras. Estud. Popul.*, 12:1/2, jan./dez. 1995, p. 151–167, bibl., graphs)

Case study of kinship relations among slaves, using materials from the Fazenda Resgate, São Paulo. Marriage, birth, and death records show that the slaves were at once immersed in a "vast" kinship network, a network they consciously sought to develop and use, and were also caught up in conflicts among themselves, conflicts more complex than simply master-slave or African-Creole. See also item **3318.** [DM]

3269 Fraga Filho, Walter. Mendigos, moleques e vadios na Bahia do século XIX. São Paulo: Editora Hucitec; Salvador, Brazil: EDUFBA, 1996. 188 p.: bibl., ill. (Estudos históricos; 26)

Social history of poverty in 19th-century Salvador looks at the urban geography and calendar of poverty, survival strategies of the poor, and state policies. The tendency over time was to increasingly criminalize poverty and unemployment, to repress independent activities such as begging, and, as slavery collapsed, to attempt to force the poor into regular work under elite/state control. [DM]

3270 Freyre, Gilberto. Discursos parlamentares. Seleção, introdução e comentários de Vamireh Chacon. Brasília: Câmara dos Deputados, Centro de Documentação e Informação, Coordenação de Publicações, 1994. 318 p.: bibl., ill., indexes. (Perfis parlamentares; 39)

Selected congressional speeches and debates by famous sociologist and one-term congressman. Includes text and debates of 1948 bill to found the Instituto Joaquim Nabuco de Pesquisas Sociais; also includes Northeast regionalist, propresidentialist, antiracist, and antideath penalty declarations. [DB]

3271 Galliza, Diana Soares de. Modernização sem desenvolvimento na Paraíba, 1890–1930. João Pessoa, Brazil: Idéia, 1993. 211 p.: bibl., ill, maps.

State elites under the Old Republic were divided politically between the northeast and the southwest and economically between the coastal sugar producers and the cotton and cattle *fazendeiros* of the interior, while the economy itself suffered a persistence of traditional work relations and distribution of income even as the forces of production modernized. A well-researched doctoral dissertation on the economic history of a neglected part of Brazil. [DM]

3272 García Alaniz, Anna Gicelle. Ingênuos e libertos: estratégias de sobrevivência familiar em épocas de transição, 1871–1895. Campinas, Brazil: Centro de Memória, Unicamp, 1997. 107 p.: bibl. (Coleção Campiniana; 11)

Compares situation of *libertos* from 1871–90s in Campinas and Itu. The more rural Itu enjoyed a relatively stable situation with the law working more or less as envisioned, whereas in Campinas the more fluid environment threatened the *libertos* and their families with becoming lost among the general urban poor. The key institution in these years was *tutela*, by which the *libertos* and their families gained some security and ex-masters formalized control over the childrens' labor. [DM]

Gareis, Maria da Guia Santos. Industrialização no Nordeste, 1880–1920. See *HLAS* 57:2352.

3273 Gattaz, André Castanheira. Braços da resistência: uma história oral da imigração espanhola. São Paulo: Xamã, 1996. 275 p.: bibl., ill.

Revised MA thesis on post-1945 migration from Spain to São Paulo is told through history of anti-Franco association Centro-Gallego Democrático Espanhol, ca. 1945–73. Transcribes eight substantial oral history interviews. [DB]

3274 Gomes, Angela Maria de Castro. História e historiadores: a política cultural do Estado Novo. Rio de Janeiro: Fundação Getulio Vargas Editora, 1996. 220 p.: bibl., ill.

Essays on historians and historiography. Analyzes two journals, *Autores e Livros* and *Cultura Política,* and the Estado Novo's successful cultural policy to promote a nationalist historiography that minimized diversity and conflict. [DB]

3275 Gomes, Flávio dos Santos. Histórias de quilombolas: mocambos e comunidades de senzalas no Rio de Janeiro, século XIX. Rio de Janeiro: Arquivo Nacional, 1995. 431 p.: bibl., ill. (Prêmio Arquivo Nacional de Pesquisa)

A study of *quilombos* near Iguaçu and Vassouras, Rio de Janeiro, seeks to under-

stand internal organization of escaped slave settlements and their relations with their neighbors, and to show how their existence affected slavery and slave relations in the area. *Quilombos* were not necessarily isolated or marginalized; rather, they commonly interacted with their free peasant neighbors and even with slaves, even as the authorities persisted in attempts to destroy them. [DM]

3276 Graden, Dale T. "Uma lei... até de segurança pública": resistência escrava, tensões sociais e o fim do tráfico internacional de escravos para o Brasil, 1835–1856. (*Estud. Afro-Asiát.,* 30, dez. 1996, p. 113–149, bibl., graphs, tables)

The fear that slave resistance was becoming more common and dangerous because of the large number of slaves imported in the late 1840s, coupled with disease epidemics linked to the slave traffic, contributed to Brazil's 1850 decision to abolish the international slave trade. (For English-language version, see *HAHR,* 76:2, May 1996.) [DM]

3277 Häuptli, Rudolf. Pioniere der wirtschaftlichen und sozialen Entwicklung im brasilianischen Nordosten: die Wasserkraftgesellschaft des São Francisco; Pionierphase, Expansion und Umbruch, 1948–1974. Frankfurt am Main; New York: P. Lang, 1996. 303 p.: bibl., maps. (Hispano-Americana, 0943–6022; Bd. 13)

A detailed study of the development of the Companhia Hidro Elétrica do São Francisco (CHESF) which became the first mixed (private-state) enterprise in the energy sector. An entrepreneurial, market-oriented endeavor with minimal bureaucratic interference, CHESF not only served as a pioneer project, but also had an important social impact on the region. However, centralization of electrical power distribution and the increased emphasis on growth and profits, beginning in the 1960s, resulted in neglect of the social and natural environment. [C.K. Converse]

3278 Heynemann, Cláudia B. Floresta da Tijuca: natureza e civilização no Rio de Janeiro, século XIX. Rio de Janeiro: Prefeitura da Cidade do Rio de Janeiro, Secretaria Municipal de Cultura, Depto. Geral de Documentação e Informação Cultural, Divisão de Editoração, 1995. 195 p.: bibl., ill. (Col. Biblioteca carioca; 38. Série Publicação científica)

The elites of Rio de Janeiro undertook to reforest Tijuca in 1860s-70s not only for such practical reasons as protection of the city's water supply and ensuring availability of building supplies, but also because they saw it as part of a "discourse" of progress and civilization "that had European nations as the paradigm." The forest domesticated nature while making trees part of the city. [DM]

3279 Hilton, Stanley E. Oswaldo Aranha: uma biografia. Rio de Janeiro: Editora Objetiva, 1994. 501 p.: bibl., ill.

Important biography of leader of 1930 revolution presents his career as framed by repeated failures to attain presidency; personal loyalty to and liberal dissent from Getúlio Vargas; and diplomatic achievements in consolidating 1940s Brazilian-US alliance and later at the UN. Solidly based on archives of the Centro de Pesquisa e Documentação de Historia Contemporânea do Brazil (CPDOC); engages historiographical debates only indirectly. See also items **3244** and **3286.** [DB]

3280 História das ciências sociais no Brasil. v. 2. São Paulo: IDESP; Vértice; FINEP, 1995. 1 v.

Vol. 2 of important collection of coordinated essays on quantitative and institutional history of social sciences. Useful primarily for specialized scholars. For annotation of vol. 1, see *HLAS 54:3366.* See also item **3326.** [DB]

Iyda, Massako. Cem anos de saúde pública: a cidadania negada. See *HLAS 57:5263.*

3281 Klein, Herbert S. La inmigración española en Brasil: siglos XIX y XX. Colombres, Spain: Archivo de Indianos, 1996. 163 p.: bibl., ill. (Cruzar el charco; 16)

Statistical overview of Spanish migration expands on author's previous article. See *HLAS 54:3332.* [DB]

3282 Klein, Herbert S. and **Clotilde Andrade Paiva.** Freedmen in a slave economy: Minas Gerais in 1831. (*J. Soc. Hist.*, 29:4, Summer 1996, p. 933–962, tables)

Uses manuscript censuses from two towns in Minas Gerais to argue that in first half of 19th century freedmen's occupational and social patterns differed little from those of free white population; freedmen were not a marginal group denied access to resources. Includes extensive statistical tables. For Portuguese-language version, see Estud. Econ./ São Paulo, 27:2, 1997, p. 309–335. [DM]

3283 Kraay, Hendrik. "O abrigo da farda": o exército brasileiro e os escravos fugidos, 1800–1881. (*Afro-Asia/Salvador*, 17, 1996, p. 29–56)

Some slaves ran away and enlisted in the army to escape their captivity, while others found themselves pressed against their will into service. Despite its abolitionist reputation, the Army, at least until the 1880s, commonly upheld property rights regarding slaves; however, the complexities of military law and the demand for clear proof of ownership often frustrated owners' attempts to retrieve their property. [DM]

3284 Kushnir, Beatriz. Baile de máscaras: mulheres judias e prostituição; as polacas e suas associações de ajuda mútua. Rio de Janeiro: Imago Editora, 1996. 258 p.: bibl., ill., maps.

Revised MA thesis on mutual aid associations, synagogues, and cemeteries of Jewish prostitutes in Rio de Janeiro and São Paulo focuses on what these institutions reveal about the daily lives of prostitutes within an immigrant community, rather than on themes of white slavery and prostitution. For a broader view of prostitution focused on São Paulo, see *HLAS 54:3407.* [DB]

3285 Lacerda Paiva, Cláudio. Uma crise de agosto: o atentado da Rua Toneleros. Rio de Janeiro: Editora Nova Fronteira, 1994. 313 p.: bibl.

Little new information in this journalistic account of the assassination scandal that led to Getúlio Vargas' suicide. Includes extensive quotations and excerpts from interviews and police and judicial documents. [DB]

3286 Lago, Luiz Aranha Corrêa do. Oswaldo Aranha, o Rio Grande e a Revolução de 1930: um político gaúcho na República Velha. Rio de Janeiro: Editora Nova Fronteira, 1995. 433 p.: bibl., ill., index, map.

Meticulous, even-handed study of leader of 1930 revolution written by his grandson, an economic historian, and based on primary documents including family archives not previously open to researchers. Emphasizes both family context and Aranha's meteoric rise in Rio Grande do Sul state politics between 1925–30. Supports arguments that Vargas' group carried the styles and policies of that state into the national sphere, although work does not follow Aranha's career past 1930. See also items **3244** and **3279**. [DB]

3287 Lanna, Ana Lúcia Duarte. Uma cidade na transição: Santos; 1870–1913. São Paulo: Editora Hucitec; Santos, Brazil: Prefeitura Municipal de Santos, 1996. 270 p.: bibl., ill., index, maps. (Estudos históricos; 25)

After 1870 the state undertook the systematic reform of Santos and other similar cities, addressing elites' fears about public health and vice, making physical changes to modernize and organize what had been a "colonial space," and attempting to tighten labor laws and their enforcement to better control newly freed slaves and recent immigrants. [DM]

3288 Lapa, José Roberto do Amaral. A cidade: os cantos e os antros; Campinas, 1850–1900. São Paulo: Edusp, 1996. 361 p.: bibl., photos.

Comprehensive treatment of modernization of late-19th-century Campinas examines how conflicts between traditional *senhorial* values and those of a rising commercial/capitalist bourgeoisie played out in social, economic, and built relations of the city. Because of the costs of "recycling," it proved preferable to "make invisible" (i.e., camouflage or destroy) buildings and remove persons that did not fit the new image. Thoroughly researched, with many excellent photographs. [DM]

3289 Lehmann, David. Struggle for the spirit: religious transformation and popular culture in Brazil and Latin America. Cambridge, Mass: Polity Press, 1996. 1 v.: bibl., index.

Sophisticated study of religion and political culture compares rhetoric of "the people" in the practices of Catholic Christian Base Communities and Pentecostal or Neo-Pentecostal congregations. Concludes that *basista* communities build small but powerful dissident elites among the poor, understandable in traditional terms of the rela-

tion between elite and popular culture, while *crente* congregations lead masses of the poor to break radically with what is rhetorically "popular" and thus with familiar Brazilian political bargains. [DB]

3290 Lesser, Jeffrey H. Colonial survival and foreign relations in Rio Grande do Sul, Brazil: the Jewish Colonization Association colony of Quatro Irmãos, 1904–1925. (*in* The Jewish diaspora in Latin America: new studies on history and literature. New York: Garland Publ., 1996, p. 143–160, bibl., table)

Argues that planned Jewish immigration failed in the 1920s because the immigrants preferred to leave the isolated rural settlements for the cities; because non-Jewish renters and wage workers invaded the colonies; and because the Jews found themselves caught in the middle when local political violence erupted, with no way to protect themselves and no place to turn for help. [DM]

3291 Levine, Robert M. Brazilian legacies. Armonk, N.Y.: M.E. Sharpe, 1997. 209 p., 8 p. of plates: bibl., ill., index, map. (Perspectives on Latin America and the Caribbean)

Engaging, highly personal introduction to contemporary Brazilian society by a leading US historian adopts a bottom-up perspective, emphasizing frustrations of popular aspirations to dignity and justice. Essays on various topics—race, mobility, marginal "outsiders" (includes women), informal political culture and corruption, coping strategies of the poor, and popular culture. Draws on a rich array of scholarly perspectives, personal anecdotes, and newspaper clippings. [DB]

3292 Levine, Robert M. Father of the poor?: Vargas and his era. New York: Cambridge Univ. Press, 1997. 193 p.: bibl., ill., index, map.

Biographical essay on Getúlio Vargas, dictator and elected president 1930–45 and 1951–54, focuses on inconsistencies in his claim to be a social reformer. Includes a creative collection of documents and photographs showing Vargas' many images. Extremely useful for students. [DB]

3293 Libby, Douglas Cole. Sociedade e cultura escravistas como obstáculos ao desenvolvimento econômico: notas sobre o

Brasil oiticentista. (*Estud. Econ./São Paulo*, 23:3, set./dez. 1993, p. 445–476, bibl.)

Slaves and ex-slaves proved themselves quite capable of carrying out complicated industrial tasks, but neither they nor their masters saw value in the work process as such or the worth of close supervision and rational management. In the interior, distances between markets granted local handicraft producers an effective monopoly, undercutting interest in rationalizing or expanding production. [DM]

3294 Lobo, Eulália Maria Lahmeyer. Portugueses en Brasil en el siglo XX. Madrid: Editorial MAPFRE, 1994. 439 p.: bibl., indexes, tables. (Col. Portugal y el mundo; 5. Col. MAPFRE 1492)

Helpful but uneven overview of Portuguese migration to Brazil, 1888–1970, by leading economic historian. Dual emphasis on causes and patterns of emigration and on Portuguese presence in Brazilian arts, with glimpses of social history of Portuguese businesses, associations, and families in Brazil. Identifies three periods: boom (1888–1930), decline (1930–50), and revival (1950–70). Indispensable for its tables alone, which display statistics from censuses, offical reports, and secondary literature. [DB]

3295 Ludwig, Sabine. In Blumenau und Pomerode: bei Deutschen im Süden Brasiliens. Würzburg, Germany: Bergstadtverlag, 1997. 132 p.: ill. (some col.).

For this useful contribution to German-Brazilian immigration history, author interviews 15 second- and third-generation German descendants and the Brazilian mayor of Blumenau. Searching questions concerning retention of culture and language, and economic activity and assimilation including the period of German Nazi influence, produce some candid answers. [C.K. Converse]

3296 Machado, Maria Helena Pereira Toledo. O plano e o pânico: os movimentos sociais na década da abolição. Rio de Janeiro: Editora UFRJ; São Paulo: EDUSP, 1994. 259 p.: bibl., ill.

Focuses on role of slave resistance, e.g., revolts, flight, messianic movements, land invasions, etc., and on efforts of urban ex-slaves and mixed bloods in the abolitionist process. The authorities and the press played down such activities for fear of panicking the white population, but by the 1880s there was clear evidence of a growing loss of social control and a spreading fear of a breakdown in public order. [DM]

3297 Manthorne, Katherine E. O imaginário brasileiro para o público norte-americano do século XIX. (*Rev. USP*, 30, junho/agôsto 1996, p. 60–71, bibl., ill.)

Short survey of 19th-century images of Brazil, particularly Rio de Janeiro and the Amazon, as evidenced in the output of foreign artists and travelers. There was a tendency to associate the American tropics with an idealized "Garden of Eden," emphasizing romance and beauty, often in the interest of promoting expansionism. Reproduces interesting period paintings. [DM]

3298 Marin, Richard. Dom Helder Camara, les puissants et les pauvres: pour une histoire de l'Eglise des pauvres dans le Nordeste brésilien, 1955–1985. Paris: Editions de l'atelier/Editions ouvrières, 1995. 366 p.: bibl., ill., index, maps. (Eglises/sociétés, 1151–8634)

A corrective to hagiographies, argues that Dom Helder Câmara's symbolic importance was inflated by critics' demonizing rhetoric and by statements he issued abroad while silenced in Brazil, 1970–77. First, the antiquated structure of the Archdiocese of Recife-Olinda (1964–69), and then the crisis of the priesthood (1970–85), limited the impact of his reforms. Recife was not much different from other dioceses in level of state repression or depth of reform. [DB]

3299 Martinho, Lenira Menezes and **Riva Gorenstein.** Negociantes e caixeiros na sociedade da Independência. Rio de Janeiro: Prefeitura da Cidade do Rio de Janeiro, Secretaria Municipal de Cultura, Turismo e Esportes, Depto. Geral de Documentação e Informação Cultural, Divisão de Editoração, 1992. 258 p.: bibl. (Biblioteca carioca; 24)

Summary of two *mestrado* theses examining early-19th-century Portuguese immigrants in Rio de Janeiro. Portuguese merchants quickly incorporated themselves into the new national elites after independence, a process they helped finance. Similarly, *caixeiros*, substituting in part for an absent national bourgeoisie, gained social and economic mobility by allying themselves with elites to repress lower-order demands. [DM]

3300 Meade, Teresa A. "Civilizing" Rio: reform and resistance in a Brazilian city, 1889–1930. University Park: Pennsylvania State Univ. Press, 1997. 212 p.: bibl., ill., index, map.

Conflicts during the Old Republic between Rio de Janeiro's lower orders and their employers, the transit companies, and the state about the effects of "modernization" resulted in many losses, but also a few victories for the poor. Such popular protests have been marginalized by a historiography that tends to label them "pre-modern" and to privilege workplace organization and protest over community protest. [DM]

3301 Meirelles, Domingos. As noites das grandes fogueiras: uma história da Coluna Prestes. 2a. ed. Rio de Janeiro: Editora Record, 1995. 765 p.: bibl., ill., map.

Journalistic reconstruction of Prestes Column of military rebels, 1924–27, emphasizes human drama and camaraderie. Based on interviews conducted in 1974 and primary documents, but only lightly footnoted. [DB]

3302 Mello, Marco Antônio Lirio de. Reviras, batuques e carnavais: a cultura de resistência dos escravos em Pelotas. Pelotas, Brazil: UFPel, Editora Universitária, 1994. 163 p.: bibl.

Part of a larger project on late-19th-century slave and *liberto* resistance in Pelotas (Rio Grande do Sul). Newspaper evidence shows cultural resistance in areas such as religion and carnival and in leisure activities such as *reviras* (dances), card games, and amorous encounters—in effect, the author argues, "counterfeit liberty." See also item **3330**. [DM]

Mendible Z., Alejandro. La familia Río Branco y la fijación de las fronteras entre Venezuela y Brasil: dos momentos definitorios en las relaciones entre Venezuela y Brasil: El Tratado de Límites de 1859 y la gestión del barón de Río Branco, 1902–1912. See item **2541**.

3303 Menezes, Lená Medeiros de. Os estrangeiros e o comércio do prazer nas ruas do Rio, 1890–1930. Rio de Janeiro: Arquivo Nacional, Orgão do Ministério da Justiça, 1992. 117 p.: bibl., ill. (Prêmio Arquivo Nacional de Pesquisa; 2)

Testimony in 189 deportation cases of pimps provides information on foreign participation in commercial sex in Rio de Janeiro between 1907–30. For the elites, a greatly expanded demand for foreign prostitutes was part of the "modernization" and "Europeanization" of the city. [DM]

Moraes, João Quartim de. A esquerda militar no Brasil. See *HLAS 57:3928.*

3304 Moreira, Paulo Roberto Staudt. Faces da liberdade, máscaras do cativeiro: experiências de liberdade e escravidão, percebidas através das Cartas de Alforria; Porto Alegre, 1858–1888. Porto Alegre, Brazil: EDIPUCRS, 1996. 136 p.: bibl. (Col. História; 12)

Explores lives of blacks in last decades of slavery, based on letters of freedom issued in Rio Grande do Sul from 1858–87. A confused situation prevailed in the urban areas where status of "free" and "slave" overlapped; some, e.g., *libertos*, did not know their own status. This situation blocked development of a free labor market. [DM]

3305 Motta, José Flávio and Nelson Nozoe. Cafeicultura e acumulação. (*Estud. Econ./São Paulo,* 24:2, maio/agôsto 1994, p. 253–320, bibl., tables)

Sophisticated analysis, based on manuscript censuses, of capital accumulation among early-19th-century coffee pioneers in Bananal, São Paulo. As production of the crop moved from an experiment at the turn of the century to commercial predominance by the 1830s, ownership of land and slaves concentrated production in the hands of a few, effectively marginalizing small, non-slave-owning producers. [DM]

3306 Nagle, Robin. Claiming the Virgin: the broken promise of liberation theology in Brazil. New York: Routledge, 1997. 224 p.: bibl., index, maps.

Compact anthropological case study of liberation theology in a shantytown parish of Recife under a conservative bishop. Uses 1991 dispute over the feast of the Virgin of the Immaculate Conception to elicit conflicting narratives over relationship between religion, social life, and politics. Interesting emphasis on expression of social and political tensions in church ritual. See also item **3333**. [DB]

Ninomiya, Masato. O centenário do Tratado de Amizade, Comércio e Navegação entre Brasil e Japão. See *HLAS 57:4502.*

3307 Owensby, Brian Philip. Intimate ironies: modernity and the making of middle-class lives in Brazil. Stanford, Calif.: Stanford Univ. Press, 1999. 332 p.: bibl., index.

Superb analysis of middle-class mentalities in Rio de Janeiro and São Paulo, 1920–50. Describes emergence of middle class, then argues that its members rejected political parties and leaders, but embraced the state's social service mission and social service jobs. Using a wide range of documents, sensitively explores reasons for political ambivalence and cult of domestic life. [DB]

3308 Page, Joseph A. The Brazilians. Reading, Mass.: Addison-Wesley, 1995. 540 p.: bibl., index, map.

Introduction to Brazil by a law professor who has been an engaged visitor since the 1960s. Themes of race, political power, violence, environment, religious diversity, and popular culture are made accessible through biographical profiles. Balances exuberance and indignation better than most recent introductions, but at a length that may exhaust the general reader. See Levine's work (item **3291**) or Eakin's (item **3261**) for more succinct introductory studies. [DB]

3309 Paulo, Heloísa. Estado Novo e propaganda em Portugal e no Brasil: o SPN/SNI e o DIP. Coimbra, Portugal: Livraria Minerva, 1994. 181 p.: bibl., ill. (Minerva-História; 11)

Compact, well-researched comparison of activities of propaganda agencies of Estado Novo of Salazar in Portugal and Vargas in Brazil, with some discussion of their cooperative projects. Based primarily on publications and documents of agencies. [DB]

3310 Peard, Julyan G. Tropical disorders and the forging of a Brazilian medical identity, 1860–1890. (*HAHR,* 77:1, Feb. 1997, p. 1–44)

Efforts by doctors of the Escola Tropicalista Bahiana, Salvador, to apply scientific methods to Brazil's tropical medical problems in second half of 19th century were largely ignored by other doctors and the general public, in favor of European racist theo-

ries of "degeneration". Subsequent histories also have ignored their work, focusing instead on turn-of-the-century activities of foreign public health foundations. [DM]

3311 Pedro, Joana Maria. Mulheres honestas e mulheres faladas: uma questão de classe. Prefácio de Maria Odila Leite da Silva Dias. Florianópolis, Brazil: Editora da UFSC, 1994. 210 p.: bibl.

Social history of turn-of-the-century Florianópolis explores prevailing stereotypes of women, how these contrasted with their actual situation, and how both changed with time and social pressures. Based on newspapers and archives, book is rich in detail but lacks conclusions. [DM]

3312 Pesavento, Sandra Jatahy. Os pobres da cidade: vida e trabalho, 1880–1920. Porto Alegre, Brazil: Editora da Univ., Univ. Federal do Rio Grande do Sul, 1994. 149 p.: bibl., ill. (Síntese rio-grandense; 18–19)

Broad treatment, based on extensive archival and newspaper research, of development of an urban working class in late-19th-century Porto Alegre. Details difficult living and working conditions of the poor and development of group identity and class consciousness. Also looks at elite reform campaigns meant to "moralize" the lower orders. [DM]

3313 Ponte, Sebastião Rogério. Fortaleza belle époque: reformas urbanas e controle social, 1860–1930. Fortaleza, Brazil: Fundação Demócrito Rocha, 1993. 208 p.: bibl., ill.

Revised MA thesis based on official reports, newspapers, chronicles, and reformist tracts links urban beautification and sanitation reforms to elite project of "disciplining" workers. Interesting as counterpoint to better-studied case of Rio de Janeiro in Needell (*HLAS 50:2705*) and Meade (*HLAS 52:3066*). [DB]

3314 A presença italiana no Brasil: atas. v. 3. Porto Alegre, Brazil: Escola Superior de Teologia; Torino, Italy: Fondazione Giovanni Agnelli, 1996. 1 v.: bibl., ill., maps. (Col. Imigração italiana)

Presents 38 papers, organized topically, on Italian immigration to Brazil. Topics include "Italians before the Great Immigration," "Family and Women," "Health and Criminality," and "Culture and Identity."

Quality varies, but many are well researched and argued. Papers intended for a conference that ultimately failed to take place. For annotation of vols. 1–2, see *HLAS 54:3402.* [DM]

3315 Prutsch, Ursula. Die österreichische Auswanderung nach Brasilien am Beispiel Rio Grande do Suls, 1820–1938, und ihr Verschwinden in der Immigrationsgeschichte. (*Ibero-Am. Arch.*, 24:1/2, 1998, p. 31–59, tables)

Examines available literature on Austrian-Brazilian immigration and concludes that research methodology must be adapted to reconstruct Austrian emigration history. Approximately 93,000 Austrians (including Germans, Italians, Slovenes, Croats, Czechs, Slovacs, Serbs, Poles, Ruthenes, Rumanians, Ukrainians, and Hungarians) who immigrated to Brazil between 1820–1938 were not listed as such due to their multi-ethnic and multilingual origins and the changing status of the Austro-Hungarian Empire. [C.K. Converse]

3316 Ramos, Graciliano. Relatórios. Organização de Mário Hélio. Rio de Janeiro: Editora Record, 1994. 140 p.

Three reports by major novelist during his term as mayor of Palmeira dos Indios contain terse and sarcastic commentary on small-town politics ca. 1929. Includes appreciations by critics. [DB]

3317 Reis, João José and Márcia Gabriela D. de Aguiar. "Carne sem osso e farinha sem caroço": o motim de 1858 contra a carestia na Bahia. (*Rev. Hist./São Paulo*, segundo semestre, 1996, p. 133–159, bibl., ill.)

An 1858 food riot in Salvador, which became entangled with a disturbance at a girls' home, provides a lens with which to examine relations among provincial and city governments, merchants, and the urban poor: the president and the merchants supported free trade and markets, whereas the town council and the urban masses favored regulated trade and prices. A wide range of social and political issues turned a dispute over food prices into a riot. [DM]

3318 Resgate: uma janela para o oitocentos. Organização de Hebe Maria Mattos de Castro e Eduardo Schnoor. Fotografias de Johny Salles e Márcia Kranz. Rio de Janeiro: Topbooks, 1995. 252 p.: bibl., ill. (some col.).

Excellent microhistory of Fazenda Resgate, a 19th-century plantation in the municipality of Bananal, São Paulo, based on family and government records. Includes chapters on development of the *fazenda*, the economy of the municipality, construction of the main house, the business activities of the owners, and family and kinship links among the slaves. Complemented by many photographs. See also item **3268.** [DM]

3319 A revolução federalista e os teuto-brasileiros. Organização de Arthur Blásio Rambo e Loiva Otero Félix. Porto Alegre, Brazil: Editora da Univ. Federal do Rio Grande do Sul; São Leopoldo, Brazil: Editora Unisinos, 1995. 185 p.: bibl.

Fourteen essays by nine authors, mostly faculty members at universities and *faculdades* in Rio Grande do Sul, on German participation in the Federalist Revolution. Essays treat, among other topics, role of the Catholic Church and evangelical churches, attitudes toward the revolution in the German language press, forced and voluntary participation in the fighting, and the historical memory of the events among the colonists. [DM]

Ribeiro, Carlos Antonio Costa. Cor e criminalidade: estudo e análise da justiça no Rio de Janeiro, 1900–1930. See *HLAS 57:5285.*

3320 Rocha, Oswaldo Porto and Lia de Aquino Carvalho. A era das demolições: cidade do Rio de Janeiro, 1870–1920. 2a ed. Rio de Janeiro: Prefeitura da Cidade do Rio de Janeiro, Secretaria Municipal de Cultura, Depto. Geral de Documentação e Informação Cultural, Divisão de Editoração, 1995. 183 p.: bibl., ill. (Col. Biblioteca carioca; 1. Série Publicação científica)

Combines two *mestrado* theses from 1986 on urban problems in turn-of-the-century Rio de Janeiro. Public health campaigns and land speculation undertaken at the urgings of elites prompted demolition of centrally located slums, forcing out and marginalizing the poor and aggravating their health and housing problems. State-sponsored *vilas operárias* were an inadequate response to these problems. [DM]

3321 Rodowicz-Oświecimsky, Theodor. A colônia Dona Francisca no sul do Brasil. Tradução de Júlio Chella. Florianópolis, Brazil: Editora DAUFSC; FCC Edições;

Joinville, Brazil: Fundação Cultural de Joinville, 1992. 111 p.: ill.

Translation of an 1853 book in German on the colony that would eventually become Joinville, Santa Catarina. Author resided in the colony from 1851–52 and his report shows clearly the problems caused by false publicity, poor planning and leadership, and failures of support and infrastructure. A detailed and valuable look at early colonization. [DM]

3322 Rodrigues, Lêda Boechat and **José Octávio.** José Honório Rodrigues: um historiador na trincheira. Rio de Janeiro: Civilização Brasileira, 1994. 323 p.: bibl., index.

Collection of excerpts from correspondence of leading historian and archivist, edited with comments by his widow. Includes biographical and critical essays by Octávio. Letters reveal breadth, more than depth, of his relationships with historians in Brazil and US. For more on his life and historiographical ideas see *HLAS 30:2369a* and his interview in *HAHR*, 64:2, May 1984. [DB]

3323 Salles, Ricardo. Nostalgia imperial: a formação da identidade nacional no Brasil do Segundo Reinado. Rio de Janeiro: Topbooks, 1996. 212 p.: bibl.

Extended essay based on secondary sources sees slavery as the social and political *matriz* for 19th-century formation of the nation. Dismissing popular nostalgia for "empire as time of greatness," author argues that this epoch was an elite creation resulting in an exclusionary "nation without people" that set antidemocratic social and cultural patterns that persist today. [DM]

Samara, Eni de Mesquita. A mulher e a família na historiografia latino-americana recente. See item **814.**

Santos, Murillo. O caminho da profissionalização das forças armadas. See *HLAS 57:3956.*

3324 Schulz, John. A crise financeira da abolição, 1875–1901. Tradução de Afonso Nunes Lopes. São Paulo: Edusp: Instituto Fernand Braudel, 1996. 167 p.: bibl.

The end of slavery opened modernization opportunities for Brazil, opportunities squandered in the short run by the irresponsible activities and policies of the government. The *Encilhamento* was not the result

of inexperience but of reckless efforts to compensate the *fazendeiro* class for the impact of abolition, an exception to the generally prudent and successful Brazilian monetary policy of the preceding century. [DM]

3325 Schulz, John. O Exército na política: origens da intervenção militar, 1850–1894. São Paulo: Edusp, 1994. 224 p.: bibl.

As a group, the military in the 1870s–80s was alienated from traditional elites by the corruption of the Paraguayan War and by slave-catching demands. But the military's political efforts after 1889 were disastrous, prompting a withdrawal into military professionalism in the second half of 1890s. Includes a statistical appendix on the makeup of the officer class. [DM]

3326 Schwarcz, Lilia Moritz. The spectacle of the races: scientists, institutions, and the race question in Brazil, 1870–1930. Translated by Leland Guyer. New York: Hill and Wang, 1999. 358 p.: bibl., ill., index, maps.

Clever survey of differing ideas about race and Brazil's racial formation that emerged in cultural institutions such as natural history museums, historical institutes, medical schools, and law schools. May overstate compartmentalization of Brazilian elites, but overturns vision of monolithic elite ideology. Developed out of the team research on social sciences presented in Miceli's work (see *HLAS 54:3366* and item **3280**). [DB]

3327 Seyferth, Giralda. Colonização e conflito: estudo sobre "motins" e "desordens" numa região colonial de Santa Catarina no século XIX. Rio de Janeiro: Programa de Pós-Graduação em Antropologia Social, Museu Nacional-UFRJ, 1988. 72 p.: bibl. (Comunicação; 10)

Short working paper on conflicts between the German—later Irish, Italian, and French—settlers and the administration of the Colônia Itajahy/Brusque. Problems included demarcation of lots, bureaucratic delays in titling, low wages for those seeking day labor, dependence on merchant credit, the arrival of too many immigrants without adequate planning, factional conflicts among the colonists, difficulties in adapting to the climate, and high mortality rates. [DM]

3328 Silva, Ligia Maria Osório. Terras devolutas e latifúndio: efeitos da lei de 1850. Campinas, Brazil: Editora da Unicamp, 1996. 373 p.: bibl., ill. (Col. Repertórios)

Comprehensive survey of land legislation and policy from colonial period to end of 19th century focuses primarily on origins and effects of the 1850 law. The law failed to regularize the land situation in the countryside because the central regime could or would not enforce it; state land laws after 1889 were similarly ineffective. [DM]

Silveira, Helder Gordim da. Brasil e Argentina: a guerra sul-americana nas projeções da razão estratégica, 1933–35. See *HLAS* 57:4518.

3329 Silveira, Itala Bezerra da. Cabanagem: uma luta perdida—. Belém, Brazil: Secretaria de Estado da Cultura, 1994. 249 p.: bibl., ill.

"Liberalism" in early-19th-century Pernambuco was a European transplant without an organic basis in the local situation, a transplant that served chiefly as a vehicle for personalism and regionalism and a brake on the development of the nation-state. Examination of provincial revolts between 1821–48 shows how each exploited different facets of "liberalism" for local purposes. See also item **3265.** [DM]

3330 Simão, Ana Regina Falkembach. A saúde do escravo em Pelotas, 1822–1850. (*in* Negros e índios: história e literatura. Porto Alegre, Brasil: EDIPUCRS, 1994, p. 147–155, bibl., tables)

Death notices and admission records to the Santa Misericórdia de Pelotas (Rio Grande do Sul) show that some 40 percent of slave deaths were among children under 10, and the most common cause was measles. Few older slaves or women turned up in the hospital records, suggesting that they may have been considered less valuable. The most common cause of death for adults was *moléstia interna.* See also item **3302.** [DM]

3331 Soares, Cecília Moreira. As ganhadeiras: mulher e resistência negra em Salvador no século XIX. (*Afro-Asia/ Salvador*, 17, 1996, p. 57–71, table)

Examines activities of free and slave female street vendors in 19th-century Salvador. Street selling could be a satisfactory arrangement for both owners, who shared in the slave income, and slaves, who earned the means to buy their freedom. The state tried with limited success to regulate the trade and to collect revenue. [DM]

3332 Sousa, Jorge Prata de. Escravidão ou morte: os escravos brasileiros na Guerra do Paraguai. Rio de Janeiro: MAUAD: ADESA, 1996. 135 p.: bibl., ill.

Cartorial evidence from Rio de Janeiro suggests that traditional sources have underestimated the number of slaves recruited into the army for the Paraguayan War. *Voluntários da pátria* were less often volunteers then either ex-slaves forcibly recruited or slaves sold at a profit by private owners to the state or furnished as substitutes. Spotty evidence from other provinces tends to confirm this. [DM]

3333 Souza, Marina de Mello e. Parati: a cidade e as festas. Rio de Janeiro: Editora UFRJ; Tempo Brasileiro, 1994. 261 p.: bibl., ill.

Revised MA thesis on social life of Parati (Rio de Janeiro state) as reflected in transformations of its religious festivals. Finds continual change in dates and character of festivals, but notes a turning point around 1959 when traditional brotherhoods were closed down and tourism became a dominant business in the town. Based on church archives, newspapers, interviews, and fieldwork. Compare Nagle's work (item **3306**). [DB]

Summerhill, William. Transport improvements and economic growth in Brazil and Mexico. See item **1357.**

3334 Takeya, Denise Monteiro. Europa, França e Ceará: origens do capital estrangeiro no Brasil. São Paulo: Editora Hucitec; Natal, Brazil: Editora UFRN, 1995. 201 p.: bibl., ill., maps. (Estudos históricos; 21)

Excellent case study of the commercial house of Boris Frères, installed in Ceará in 1872. Pt. 1 gives background of the company in France and surveys French trade with Brazil. Pt. 2 focuses specifically on Ceará, giving overview of the local economy and then detailing consolidation, expansion, and eventual decline of the French firm. Thoroughly researched in French and Brazilian archives. [DM]

3335 Topik, Steven. Trade and gunboats: the United States and Brazil in the Age of Empire. Stanford, Calif.: Stanford Univ. Press, 1996. 301 p.: bibl., ill., index, maps.

Late-19th-century US commercial policies were chiefly business-driven but met with little success in Brazil because US business leaders were largely ignorant of market conditions there. Brazil, for its part, was disappointed in its hopes for privileged access to the US sugar market. These commercial and diplomatic relations, even though imperfectly realized, did support development of republican institutions in Brazil. [DM]

3336 Truzzi, Oswaldo. De mascates a doutores: sírios e libaneses em São Paulo. São Paulo: IDESP, Editora Sumaré, 1992. 127 p.: bibl., ill. (Série Imigração, 0103–7730; 2)

Presents data on Syrian and Lebanese mobility from commercial to liberal professions in São Paulo, 1880–1950, with overview of migration, population, family strategies, and associations. Based on secondary literature, newspapers, and interviews. [DB]

3337 Vale, Brian. Independence or death!: British sailors and Brazilian independence, 1822–25. London; New York: I.B. Tauris, 1996. 219 p.: bibl., ill., index, maps.

A "blood and thunder" narrative of Lord Cochrane's career in Brazil and, more broadly, of the activities of British sailors in the Brazilian independence movement and in the postindependence consolidation of central control. Based on archives in Brazil and Great Britain. Generally, the employment of mercenaries in these conflicts served the Empire well. [DM]

3338 Vargas, Getúlio. Diário. v. 1, 1930–1936; v. 2, 1937–1942. São Paulo: Siciliano; Rio de Janeiro: Fundação Getulio Vargas, Editora, 1995. 2 v.: bibl., ill., indexes.

Possibly a daybook intended to aid memoirs—certainly not a reflective, intimate diary. Records incidents and meetings of Brazil's president, 1930–45. Entries in vol. 1 are richer than those in vol. 2. Well-indexed for reference. Indispensable reference tool for biographers and political historians, but too bland and unforthcoming for most readers. [DB]

3339 Vargas e a crise dos anos 50. Organização de Angela Maria de Castro Gomes. Rio de Janeiro: Relume Dumará, 1994? 271 p.: bibl., ill.

Collection of multidisciplinary essays, many exploratory in tone, on Vargas' administration and its legacy. Good cluster of essays on aspects of 1954 crisis. [DB]

3340 Villa, Marco Antonio. Canudos: o povo da terra. São Paulo: Editora Atica, 1995. 278 p.: bibl., ill., maps. (Ensaios; 141)

Useful survey rejects idea that Canudos was a manifestation of messianism and sees it instead as a protest of the rural poor against the destruction of their community and in support of a world free of landowners and *coroneis*. For this reason, the death of Conselheiro did not end the revolt. Incorporates most modern scholarship and a few primary sources, but is not aware of R. Levine's *Vale of tears* (see *HLAS 54:3342*). [DM]

3341 21 anos de regime militar: balanços e perspectivas. Organização de Gláucio Ary Dillon Soares e Maria Celina d'Araujo. Rio de Janeiro: Editora da Fundação Getúlio Vargas, 1994. 309 p.: bibl., ill., map.

Ten solid essays, mostly by prominent political scientists, on various aspects of 1964–85 government: regime and parties, regime and labor unions, elections, economy, and businessmen. [DB]

3342 Weingartner, Alisolete Antônia dos Santos. Movimento divisionista em Mato Grosso do Sul, 1889–1930. Porto Alegre, Brazil: Edições EST, 1995. 83 p.: bibl.

Efforts during the Old Republic to separate the south of Mato Grosso to create another state had their roots, at least in part, in the resentment of local elites against the privileges granted the Companhia Matte Larangeira. With the arrival of the railroad and the spread of cattle ranching, the south was the dynamic part of the state's economy and the *coroneis* resented Cuiabá's control. [DM]

3343 Weinstein, Barbara. For social peace in Brazil: industrialists and the remaking of the working class in São Paulo, 1920–1964. Chapel Hill: Univ. of North Carolina Press, 1996. 435 p.: bibl., ill., index.

Outstanding history of São Paulo industrialists' attempt to modernize industry by remaking the working class. Based on a wide range of documents, the work focuses on vocational training programs sponsored by the state-chartered, but industry-run, Serviço Nacional de Aprendizagem Industrial and on the industrial social services institute, Serviço Social da Indústria, from 1940s-1960s. Argues that workers and industrialists converged on rationalizing project of improving workers' skills, but diverged on politics where workers followed populists and industrialists conspired for more managerial, authoritarian government. Essential contribution to history of relationships between labor, elites, and state, revising arguments such as Cardoso's (see *HLAS 27:2319*) that Brazilian bourgeoisie lacked a "project." See also item **3229.** [DB]

3344 Welch, Cliff. The seed was planted: the São Paulo roots of Brazil's rural labor movement, 1924–1964. University Park: Pennsylvania State Univ. Press, 1999. 412 p.: bibl., ill., index, maps.

Argues that rural land and labor activism extend back to 1920s, at least in São Paulo state. Details interaction of rural workers with Vargas state, the Partido Comunista Brasileiro, Catholic Church, and other actors, and workers' responses to repression after 1964. Important antidote to generally ahistorical analyses of contemporary Movimento dos Trabalhadores Rurais Sem Terra. [DB]

3345 Xavier, Regina Célia Lima. A conquista da liberdade: libertos em Campinas na segunda metade do século XIX. Campinas, Brazil: Centro de Memória, Unicamp, 1996. 165 p.: bibl., ill. (Col. Campiniana; 6)

What happened to slaves after abolition? Work attempts to look beyond stereotypes of ex-slaves as marginalized victims to an examination of how they made their lives and constituted their families, how they "constructed" and "were constructed" by history. There were tremendous variations in the Campinas area. Based on laborious reconstruction of life histories of slaves, ex-slaves, and masters from a wide range of sources. [DM]

LITERATURE

SPANISH AMERICA
General

SARA CASTRO-KLARÉN, *Professor of Romance Languages and Literatures, Johns Hopkins University, with the assistance of Christian Fernández*

AS I WRITE THIS ESSAY in July 2000, I have already resigned as contributing editor to this section of the *Handbook of Latin American Studies*. It has been more than a positive experience, and it is with nostalgia that I look upon years of voraciously reading the many collections of essays and theoretical works that I have reviewed for the biennial *HLAS* humanities volume. I want to take this opportunity to thank the many people who work in the field of bibliography and who, by doing so, sustain it. The *Handbook* is a wonderful and creative endeavor and it is my ardent hope that it will go on well into the new century, for there is nothing more rewarding than the pleasure of new learning. I also want to thank the Library of Congress, and especially the Librarian, James Billington, for having invited me to contribute to this major task of surveying and assessing the scholarship in the field. To the staff of the Hispanic Division, of which I was chief for a few years in the early 1980s, also my appreciation.

The amount of space devoted to Spanish American general literature has not decreased, but the volume of scholarship has grown so much that I have had to be ever more selective in choosing materials to review. Nevertheless, I see in these two years the continuation of several trends and the breaking of some new ground. Among the continuing trends, one must indicate the many studies on women writers. These studies contain relatively new approaches in that the thematics vary, but the basic ideas continue to sustain the rationale for each study. A certain unproductive repetition of themes has begun to appear, as has a consistent choice of the same five or six women writers, effectively eclipsing the variety and abundance of other, less politically correct or, globally speaking, "occidental," marketable writers. A similar tendency can, of course, be detected with the writers of the boom. Regardless of the essay topic, the text analyzed is most often one of the handful of canonical writers which now always includes Borges. The exception seems to be José María Arguedas, whose dilemmas and heterogeneous world seem to inspire ever new and productive thinking on the key question in Latin American culture: the colonial legacy, or better put, in the words of Walter Mignolo, the colonial difference from which such texts are enunciated.

Neil Larsen's *Reading North by South: on Latin American Literature, Culture, and Politics* (item **3364**), along with other books not reviewed this biennium, for example, Beatriz Sarlo's *Escenas de la vida postmoderna* (1994), Walter Mignolo's *The Darker Side of the Renaissance* (1995; see *HLAS 56:3414* and *4633*), Vicky Unruh's *Latin American Vanguards: The Art of Contentious Encounters*

(1994), and Diana S. Goodrich's *Facundo and the Construction of Argentine Culture* (1996), represent the best of a theoretical reorientation that is revitalizing the field by entering into deep debates about many unexplored issues. Closer at hand and within the parameters of what is included here, it is important to note the forceful appearance of gay studies in the work of David William Foster (items **355;** **3356;** and, an edited volume, item **3349**). Along with Sylvia Molloy, he is leading the way into the gay problematization of literary and cultural studies. Notable also is the variety of anthologies and collected studies that are making an attempt to reintroduce the essay, once a vital form in Latin America, into the teaching canon (items **3346, 3374,** and **3379**).

Finally, it is important to note that some of the most sophisticated studies continue to emerge from reconfigured colonial studies which, in many ways, ask scholars of the contemporary period and historians of literature to take a fresh look at the archives and the ways in which the canon, led by modernist criteria, has been awkwardly formed.

3346 Antología del ensayo latinoamericano.
v. 1–2. Buenos Aires: O.R. Sánchez
Teruelo, 1994. 2 v.: bibl., ill., indexes.

Excellent anthology with far-reaching temporal scope. Intelligent rather than encompassing selection criteria. Required companion to the essay volumes edited by Meyer (item **3374**) and by Stabb (item **3379**). Recommended as point of departure for all essay studies.

3347 Apropiaciones de realidad en la novela hispanoamericana de los siglos XIX y XX. Recopilación de Hans-Otto Dill *et al.* Frankfurt: Vervuert, 1994. 560 p.: bibl., index. (Editionen der Iberoamericana. Serie A, Literaturgeschichte und -kritik; 3)

Impressive project, begun in 1989 before German reunification, carried out by German scholars on Latin America. Examines the relationship between the universe represented in Latin American novels and the historical reality of the 19th and 20th centuries. Proposes that, from its beginnings, the Latin American novel strove to depict political, artistic, and social realities. This is not to suggest simple mimesis. The novel transforms the reality it seeks to represent, which begs the questions: what is reality and where is it best represented? In the novel, historical writing, journalism, folk traditions, or some other discursive mode?

3348 Asedios a la heterogeneidad cultural: libro de homenaje a Antonio Cornejo Polar. Recopilación de José Antonio Mazzotti y U. Juan Zevallos Aguilar. Philadelphia: Asociación Internacional de Peruanistas, 1996. 525 p.: bibl., ill.

Important collection of articles in honor of Cornejo Polar. Many essays explore the ramifications of Cornejo Polar's concept of heterogeneity for Latin American culture and literature. Others focus on several major topics in Andean culture such as the work of the Inca Garcilaso de la Vega, Vallejo, and Arguedas. A third group examines the critical and theoretical work of Cornejo Polar. Useful retrospective on critical trends of the last 30 years as seen through the prism of Andean literature.

3349 Bodies and biases: sexualities in Hispanic cultures and literatures. Edited by David William Foster and Roberto Reis. Minneapolis: Univ. of Minnesota Press, 1996. 440 p.: bibl., index. (Hispanic issues; v. 13)

Essays study sexuality in several literary and cultural manifestations in the Hispanic world on both sides of the Atlantic from the Golden Age in Spain to the present. Examines sexuality in *Don Quijote* and watercolors painted by Gustavo Adolfo Becquer and his brother. Various essays also examine Latin American novels, magazines, and the bolero. Considers topics such as the concept of "hispanidad," ethnicity, and nation in relation to diverse manifestations of sexuality.

3350 Burgos, Fernando. Vertientes de la modernidad hispanoamericana. Caracas: Monte Avila Editores Latinoamericana, 1995. 269 p.: bibl. (Estudios. Serie Literatura)

Important essay examines modernity in Spanish-American narrative discourse. Finds unexpected relationship between authors and tendencies that appear distant in time and sociohistoric location. Based in textual analysis, the study links patterns in phonetic, morphosyntactic, and rhetorical aspects to the concept of modernity. Pays special attention to sociological and historical background of texts studied.

Cosmelli Ibáñez, José Luis. Historia de la cultura argentina. See item **2865.**

3351 D'Alessandro Bello, María Elena. La novela urbana en Latinoamérica durante los años 1945 a 1959. Caracas: Fundación CELARG, 1994. 218 p.: bibl.

Ambitious project to establish the model that Latin American novelists constructed in order to write "urban," as opposed to regional or rural novels. The period covered (1945–59) begins with the end of World War II and ends with the Cuban Revolution. Despite claims of a historical approach, author makes use of an immanent study of: *El falso cuaderno de Narciso Espejo, La vida breve, Rosaura a las diez, La región más transparente,* and *Coronación.*

3352 Domecq, Brianda. Mujer que publica—mujer pública. México: Editorial Diana, 1994. 296 p.: bibl., index.

Presents essays originally published in diverse journals and newspapers. Includes European writers, such as George Sand, Inés Arredondo, and Virginia Woolf, as well as Mexican and other Latin American women writers.

3353 Fagundo, Ana María. Literatura femenina de España y las Américas. Madrid: Editorial Fundamentos, 1995. 267 p.: bibl. (Espiral hispano-americana; 26)

Collection of previously published essays offers a panoramic, textual analysis of diverse novels, poetry, and testimony. Capricious mix of well-known writers such as Emily Dickinson, Carmen Martín Gaite, and Olga Orozco with less-known authors.

3354 Fernández, Teodosio; Selena Millares; and Eduardo Becerra. Historia de la literatura hispanoamericana. Madrid: Editorial Universitas, 1995. 467 p.: bibl., index.

The challenges of writing a history of Spanish-American literature—an immense body of works combined with the complexity and heterogeneity of the literary discourses—is met here by giving greater attention to the process of formation and cultural and poetic moments at the expense of individual authors. Offers a corrective to most histories in that it begins with the "literary" manifestations in Amerindian civilizations. Covers the novel, poetry, theater, and the essay from the colonial period to the present.

3355 Foster, David William. Cultural diversity in Latin American literature. Albuquerque: Univ. of New Mexico Press, 1994. 178 p.: bibl., index.

Foster continues the same line of study initiated in 1985 with the publication of *Alternative voices in the Latin American narrative* (see HLAS 48:5657). Questions body of literary criticism devoted exclusively to the study of major Latin American authors. Seeks to broaden understanding of the history of lettered production in Latin America by examining a more diverse body of works. Studies gay culture, children's and women's literature, and Argentine Jewish theater as representative of a national consciousness. Carefully researched and clearly written. For work by Foster on Latin American gay literature, see item **3356.**

3356 Foster, David William. Sexual textualities: essays on queer-ing Latin American writing. Austin: Univ. of Texas Press, 1997. 180 p.: bibl., index. (Texas Pan American series)

Author continues his work on gay studies by questioning the makeup of the canon and the occlusion of the queering rhetoric. Includes essays on homoerotic writing by Chicano authors, lesbian desire in representations of Evita, feminine pornography in Latin America, and the crisis of masculinity in Argentine fiction. Very well researched; theoretically sound and provocative. Required reading in queer studies. See also *HLAS 48:5657* and item **3355** by the same author.

3357 Grandis, Rita de. Polémica y estrategias narrativas en América Latina: José María Arguedas, Mario Vargas Llosa, Rodolfo Walsh, Ricardo Piglia. Rosario, Argentina: B. Viterbo Editora, 1993. 156 p.: bibl. (Tesis)

Arguedas, Vargas Llosa, Walsh, and Piglia constitute the focus of a study that questions the formation of the canons that define national literatures. How do criteria for inclusion or exclusion form part of a historico-cultural or political culture that defines the canon? Studies cultural and political forms that institutionalize "literature."

3358 **Las huellas de la memoria: entrevistas a escritores latinoamericanos.** Buenos Aires: Beas Ediciones, 1994. 207 p.

In this series of interviews, writers reflect on their memories, fears, ambitions, and hopes. Alfredo Bryce Echenique, Carlos Monsiváis, Elena Poniatowska, Carlos Fuentes, and Luisa Valenzuela converse in this very personal book.

3359 **International Institute of Ibero-American Literature. Congreso. *29th, Barcelona, 1992.*** Actas del XXIX Congreso del Instituto Internacional de Literatura Iberoamericana: Barcelona, 15–19 de junio de 1992. v. 1–3. Barcelona: PPU, 1994. 3 v. in 4: bibl., ill.

Sequel to the many publications in commemoration of the Quinto Centenario of the so-called discovery of America. Half of the papers are devoted to the study of colonial discourses, chroniclers, relaciones, and informaciones of the first encounter between Spaniards and Amerindian civilizations. Others attempt to establish comparison between the literary discourses of Spanish America and Spain. Lacks new insight.

3360 **International Institute of Ibero-American Literature. Congreso. *30th, Pittsburgh, Pa., 1994.*** Tradición y actualidad de la literatura iberoamericana: actas del XXX Congreso del Instituto Internacional de Literatura Iberoamericana. v. 1–2. Pittsburgh, Penn.: Univ. of Pittsburgh, 1995. 2 v.: bibl., ill.

A diverse collection of articles on diferent subjects, authors, genres, and countries that address the question of sexuality— women, homosexual desire, "transgressive" sexual desires and practices in film, literature, and art. Some essays break new ground.

3361 **Jehenson, Myriam Yvonne.** Latin-American women writers: class, race, and gender. Albany: State Univ. of New York Press, 1995. 201 p.: bibl., index. (SUNY Series in feminist criticism and theory)

Study examines class, race, and gender in literature, concentrating on 1950s. Offers comparison with European writers, which helps to illuminate our understanding of Julieta Campos, Luisa Valenzuela, Cristina Peri Rosi, Helena Perente Cunha, Rigoberta Menchú, Domitila Barrios, and Carolina María de Jesus.

3362 **Jornadas Andinas de Literatura Latino Americana, *1993.*** Memorias. La Paz: Plural Editores: Facultad de Humanidades y Ciencias de la Educación, UMSA, 1995. 831 p.: bibl., ill. (Colección Academia; no. 3)

Important volume gathers memorias from the first JALLA congress. The term "literature" cannot encompass all the topics gathered here: history, painting, linguistics, and ethnology are strong participants, hence the importance of the volume. Studies include Amerindian civilizations, chronicles of the conquest, colonial and post-colonial discourses, and indigenismo. Several theoretical perspectives and debates are represented in the work of Walter Mignolo, Tomás Escajadillo, Juan Zevallos, Santiago López, Teresa Gisbert, Miguel Angel Huamán, Ricardo Kaliman, Martín Lienhard, Julio Noriega, and Sara Castro-Klaren.

3363 **Lagos-Pope, María-Inés.** En tono mayor: relatos de formación de protagonista femenina en Hispanoamérica. Santiago: Editorial Cuarto Propio, 1996. 170 p.: bibl. (Serie Ensayo)

As much as in other countries, there is a bildungsroman novel in Spanish America like the ones of Güiraldes, Vargas Llosa, and Pacheco. However, less studied is the same genre of novel written by women. Examines growing pains and search for freedom in a patriarchal society in the works of Elena Poniatowska, Rosario Castellanos, Claribel Alegría, Rosario Ferré, and Beatriz Guido. Interesting contribution to the growing body of studies on these writers.

3364 **Larsen, Neil.** Reading north by south: on Latin American literature, culture, and politics. Minneapolis: Univ. of Minnesota Press, 1995. 234 p.: bibl., index.

Seminal work deals with the import and political consequences of the most influential approaches to the study of Latin American literature in the US. Chief virtue resides in scholarly method: a deep investigation of the theoretical foundations of major contributions. Essays demonstrate how many important approaches lack theoretical rigor due to a failure to investigate the philosophical grounding of the ideas deployed in the literary studies. A crucial book for serious critics. Absolutely required for all work on the boom and critical approaches that brought it about and maintain it; as well as for colonial discourse, *testimonio,* hegemony and ideology, and "invention" approaches.

3365 Latin American identity and constructions of difference. Edited by Amaryll Beatrice Chanady. Minneapolis: Univ. of Minnesota Press, 1994. 254 p.: bibl., index. (Hispanic issues; v. 10)

Required reading for those interested in Latin American identity. Authors recognize difficulty of the pregnancy of the moment—globalization and diaspora—in which the topic is being discussed. In the introduction, Chanady offers an excellent historical review of the topic. Essays by Enrique Dussel, José Rabasa (see item **3432**), François Perus, and Iris Zavala are especially noteworthy.

3366 Literatura revolucionaria hispanoamericana: antología. Recopilación de Mirza L. González. Madrid: Editorial Betania, 1994. 477 p.: bibl. (Colección Antologías)

Fills an important gap in the field. Intelligently conceived work gathers for the first time the key texts on revolution in Spanish America. Can be used as a reference book or as a textbook for courses on Spanish American literature and culture. Includes texts from Mexico, South America, and the Caribbean.

3367 Literatura y política en América Latina: actas del congreso, Salerno 6–8 de mayo de 1993. Recopilación de Rafael di Prisco and Antonio Scocozza. Caracas: Casa de Bello, 1995. 408 p.: bibl.

Conference papers by a number of European scholars focus on the role of literature in the political life of Latin America and how the role has changed in a new world order. Includes work on García Márquez, Neruda, Gallegos, and Jorge Amado.

3368 López, Amadeo. La conscience malheureuse dans le roman hispano-américain contemporain: littérature, philosophie et psychanalyse. Préface de Marcos Aguinis. Postface de Nestor Braunstein. Paris: L'Harmattan, 1994. 374 p.: bibl., indexes. (Recherches et documents. Amériques latines)

Fresh insights in the work of Vargas Llosa, García Márquez, Benedetti, Fuentes, Rulfo, and Roa Bastos. Concludes that these authors are intelligent and demonstrate knowledge of texts and command of a method that includes perspectives of psychoanalysis (Freud and Lacan), as well as phenomenology (Merleau Ponty) and philosophy (Hegel and Nietszche).

3369 Macías, Sergio. Presencia árabe en la literatura latinoamericana: ensayo. Santiago: Zona Azul, 1995. 106 p.: bibl. (Colección La aventura de la palabra; 2)

Survey emphasizes diversity of Latin American culture. Arabs have been present in Latin American culture since the first Spaniards arrived with Columbus, and many more came with the conquistadors. From Quevedo, Cervantes, and Borges, Macías shows that the great majority of Latin American writers have written some lines on the Arab culture.

3370 Martínez Gómez, Juana and **Almudena Mejías Alonso.** Hispanoamericanas en Madrid, 1800–1936. Madrid: Horas y Horas: Dirección General de la Mujer, Comunidad de Madrid, 1994. 221 p.: bibl., ill., index. (Mujeres en Madrid)

The presence of Spanish American writers in Spain and mainly in Madrid has not been sufficiently studied, and even less is known of the presence of women intellectuals in Spain. Women were in fact very active in culture and politics, including Gertrudis Gómez de Avellaneda, Mercedes Cabello de Carbonera, and Clorinda Matto de Turner. Provides solid basic information.

3371 Mujer y cultura en la colonia hispanoamericana. Edición de Mabel Moraña. Pittsburgh: Instituto Internacional de Literatura Iberoamericana, Univ. of Pittsburgh, 1996. 330 p.: bibl., ill. (Serie Biblioteca de América)

Excellent collection of articles dedicated to the representation of women in colonial Spanish America. Confronts the absence of women's voices in Spanish American colonial times, extending beyond the usual use of women-authored texts. Examines representations of women in the chronicles, such as the coyas in Guaman Poma and La Perricholi in Ricardo Palma. For a review of the chapter by Stacey Schlau examining race, class, gender, and the Inquisition, see item **3442**. For comment by colonial literature specialist, see item **3469**.

3372 Pérez, Alberto Julián. Modernismo, vanguardias, posmodernidad: ensayos de literatura hispanoamericana. Buenos Aires: Corregidor, 1995. 318 p.: bibl.

Groups several essays on literary modernism and avant garde, analyzed with a postmodernist theoretical criteria. Focuses on Rubén Darío's modernism, the avant-garde contribution to refashioning the concept of literature, and the figure of Borges as narrator and critic. Noteworthy essay deals with laughter and irony in Borges.

3373 The postmodern in Latin and Latino American cultural narratives: collected essays and interviews. Edited by Claudia Ferman. New York: Garland Pub., 1996. 245 p.: bibl., index. (Garland reference library of the humanities; v. 1728. Latin American studies; v. 3)

Collection of essays reaffirms that the debate over postmodernity in Latin America is alive and well. The book mixes a series of essays with interviews by well-known scholars working in Latin America and the US. Topics range from cultural esthetics to globalization.

3374 Reinterpreting the Spanish American essay: women writers of the 19th and 20th centuries. Edited by Doris Meyer. Austin: Univ. of Texas Press, 1995. 246 p.: bibl. (The Texas Pan American series)

Reading these essayists is essential for gaining an understanding of Latin American literature and culture. Work focuses on feminine perspective, and in doing so, proposes a reinterpretation of the history of the genre. Includes analyses of better-known women writers: Clorinda Matto de Turner, Gabriela Mistral, Alfonsina Storni, Magda Portal, Eduarda Mansilla, Victoria Ocampo, and Rosario Ferré. Major contribution to both the study of the essay and to the work of the

women included. Work could have benefitted from the inclusion of less-frequently studied women, since the classic feminist list is becoming repetitive, and, as with work on boom writers, it has nearly reached the point of exhaustion. See also items **3346** and **3379**.

3375 Rincón, Carlos. La no simultaneidad de lo simultáneo: postmodernidad, globalización y culturas en América Latina. Bogotá: Editorial Univ. Nacional, 1995. 245 p.: bibl. (EUN—Ciencias Humanas)

Survey of last 30 years of postmodernist debate from Latin American perspective includes topics such as globalization, recent economic developments, and social and discursive formations in architecture and urbanism. Engages the terms post-history and post-colonial. Uses work of García Márquez, Fuentes, and Rodríguez Juliá to examine the problem of the postmodern.

3376 Robinett, Jane. This rough magic: technology in Latin American fiction. New York: P. Lang, 1994. 284 p.: bibl., index. (Worcester Polytechnic Institute studies in science, technology, and culture; vol. 13)

Despite author's claim that the relation of technology and the arts is a new topic, it was a major concern for the avant-garde as well as Walter Benjamin and W.T. Adorno. Nevertheless, the consideration of technology in the making of magic realism is innovative.

3377 Semana Internacional en Homenaje a Pedro Henríquez Ureña en el Cincuentenario de su Muerte 1946–1996, *Santo Domingo, 1996.* Ponencias. Recopilación de Jorge Tena Reyes. Santo Domingo: Secretaría de Estado de Educación, Bellas Artes y Cultos de la República Dominicana, 1996. 724 p.: bibl., ill., index.

A well-deserved homage to Henríquez Ureña (1884–1946) on the 50th anniversary of his death. Henríquez Ureña began, in a way, the study of Latin American literature as a field consisting of major and minor masters, periods, and genres that crossed the borders of the emergent national literatures. This series of papers studies his life and works. Also includes articles by some of his contemporaries: Alfonso Reyes, José Vasconcelos, Amado Alonso, Anderson Imbert, and Juan Ramón Jiménez.

3378 Spitta, Silvia. Between two waters: narratives of transculturation in Latin America. Houston, Tex.: Rice Univ. Press, 1995. 246 p.: bibl., ill., index.

Departs from the Cuban Fernando Ortiz's cultural theory of transculturation. Modifies Ortiz, following Angel Rama, to include all of Latin America, not just Cuba, as a culture defined and articulated by transculation processes. Chooses four moments— Cabeza de Vaca's *Naufragios*, extirpation of idolatries, the Cuzco School of Painting, and José María Arguedas—providing interesting discussions of each, relying on existing scholarship. Important here is the project's ambition and the series of works examined. The triumphalist tone of the proponents of transculturation has lately been dampened by forceful critiques of Rama's work and the implicit asymmetry of any transculturative situation. Important resource.

3379 Stabb, Martin S. The dissenting voice: the new essay of Spanish America, 1960–1985. Austin: Univ. of Texas Press, 1994. 152 p.: bibl., index. (The Texas Pan American series)

Covers period dominated by the boom in the novel, in which all other genres and authors were eclipsed by a handful of novels. Restores many important texts and key aspects of Latin American culture to their rightful place. One of the singularities of this book is that it includes publications that would not be classified in a traditional canon of essay. Enriches the corpus of an already heterogeneous literature. Some authors studied are Paz, Vargas Llosa, Fuentes, Cortazar, and García Márquez. Work is well written and clearly conceptualized. Required consultation for the period and the essay. See also items **3346** and **3374.**

3380 Tierney-Tello, Mary Beth. Allegories of transgression and transformation: experimental fiction by women writing under dictatorship. Albany: State Univ. of New York Press, 1996. 286 p.: bibl., index.

The Latin American dictatorships of the 1970s-80s (dirty wars against civilian population) coincided with the period of women's liberation. Vol. deals with incursion and participation of women in all levels of society, but especially in the literary-political sphere. Work is concerned with how women writers responded to these regimes in Chile, Argentina, Brazil, and Uruguay through the literature of Cristina Peri Rosi, Diamela Eltit, Nélida Piñon, and Reyna Roffé. Theoretically well grounded in feminist and political theory and extremely well written, this lucid book represents a breakthrough in women's studies and a welcome respite from the feminist canon which has overworked the texts of a small number of women writers. Recommended as a point of departure for new studies on women.

3381 Vento, Arnoldo Carlos. La generación Hijo pródigo: renovación y modernidad. Lanham, Md.: Univ. Press of America, 1996. 301 p.: bibl.

Literary and cultural magazines in Latin America are of great importance for the understanding of literary and esthetic periods, and the introduction and diffusion of new works and their reception: *Martin Fierro* in Argentina, *Contemporaneos* in Mexico, *Amauta* in Peru, and *El Hijo Pródigo* in Mexico. Pays close attention to the contents of the 42 issues published from April 15, 1943-Sept. 15, 1946, with a note on the contents of each article. All studies of Mexican culture of the period should first consult this compendium and analysis.

Colonial Period

JENNIFER L. EICH, *Associate Professor of Modern Languages and Literatures, Loyola Marymount University*

THE FIELD OF COLONIAL LATIN AMERICAN LITERARY and cultural studies continued to expand during this biennium, in part due to the marking of two historical milestones which served as umbrella themes for international and domestic conferences and symposia as well as points of departure for individual research and writing. The first event was the 500th anniversary of the encounter between Europe and the Americas, which earlier in the decade had prompted scholars to re-examine traditional texts and to reconsider works previously deemed of secondary or extra-literary interest. The second event was the commemoration of the 300th anniversary of the death of the Mexican intellectual and prodigy, Sor Juana Inés de la Cruz (1648–95). Moreover, scholarly and general reader interest was generated in the colonial Spanish-American era itself as well as in those who lived in and wrote during the period.

Sor Juana's life and works, which now consistently attract the interest of scholars and students in many disciplines, and general readers, served as a theme for a number of conferences, symposia, and congresses in Latin America, Europe, and the US. Published proceedings from these symposia contributed in significant ways to the body of critical studies on the Hieronymite nun (items **3455** and **3477**). These authoritative, well-researched, and often intriguing studies, written by senior and junior scholars, cast new light on Sor Juana's poetry and prose as well as on some of the shadows in her life. This latter clarity emanates in part from the work of investigators who reflected upon or published newly discovered documents and brought forth new information about the nun herself (item **3447**) and her contemporaries. New anthologies and editions of the Hieronymite nun's writings have been published (items **3461, 3464,** and **3465**), along with works attributed to her (items **3453** and **3462**). Perhaps most significant, however, are the critical studies that take a new approach to her writings. Some works are comparative and creative in nature (items **3386, 3404, 3405,** and **3411**) whereas others are more informative, especially with regard to previously unknown writings (items **3391, 3443,** and **3444**). Yet traditional studies also continue to enlighten us about Sor Juana's works (items **3385, 3434, 3459, 3431, 3446, 3437,** and **3438**) and other writers who engaged in discourse with her (item **3395**). Finally, the increasingly widespread and often interdisciplinary interest in the Mexican nun's work has led to noteworthy translations of her works (item **3460**).

A welcome consequence of the critical and general interest in Sor Juana's writings is a new focus on colonial women's writings in general. Historians and literary critics have organized symposia that illuminate the lives and works of other colonial women authors and the broader topic of women's writings. Some organizers edited and published symposia proceedings (items **3457** and **3469**) that contain scholarly contributions that are significant and often represent pioneering research. Equally important was the appearance of anthologies of essays treating colonial women, especially religious women's lives and their writings, and the sociocultural and literary restrictions they faced (items **3401, 3402, 3412, 3414,** and **3469**). Other scholars offer us well-documented editions of unpublished texts (see *HLAS 56:3442* and item **3471**).

Significantly, critical interest in recuperating texts by and giving voice to the marginalized extended beyond women to other minority groups. Literary studies of monolingual or bilingual and bicultural indigenous texts (items **3388** and **3407**) and indigenous utilization of European rhetorical models (see *HLAS 56:3455*) are splendid examples of this new direction in scholarship. This new interest was also evidenced in editions of unpublished manuscripts treating syncretic and Indo- and Hispano-American beliefs (item **3450**). Other scholars published works by authors formerly ignored or by those whose texts were unknown (items **3458** and **3473**).

The escalating interest in colonial Spanish-American writings, reflected in the continued hiring of colonial specialists at universities and colleges across the US, has generated an awareness of the importance of the literary and social history and culture of the period. Recent notable books and articles, whose theoretical and/or critical frameworks concentrate on the social and cultural discourses of the colonial era, reflect this perception (items **3389, 3398, 3409, 3422, 3424, 3433, 3449,** and **3456**). Fundamental literary, sociocultural, and bibliographical histories of the colonial period were published (items **3452, 3454, 3470,** and **3472**), while other significant studies re-evaluated literary genres such as drama (items **3383, 3399,** and **3409**) and the concept of genre itself (item **3435**). Still other contributions derive from scholarly study of minor texts by canonic authors such as Bernardo de Balbuena (items **3439** and **3451**) or of texts written by seminal intellectual figures such as Sigüenza y Góngora (item **3417**), fray Servando Teresa de Mier (item **3441**) and Pedro de Peralta Barnuevo (item **3448**).

Primary and secondary historiographical and literary texts receive rekindled interest, resulting in new editions of works by canonic authors such as the Inca Garcilaso de la Vega (items **3421, 3426, 3475,** and **3476**). New works examine previously unpublished documents (item **3382**), those formerly considered outside the scope of literary analysis (item **3392**), and even offer suggestions on how to read these lesser-known works (item **3428**). Other studies re-evaluate canonic texts in light of a new theoretical understanding of hybrid texts—those that mix history and literature, for example (items **3394, 3430,** and **3432**).

Ultimately, interest in the Americas generated studies of colonial-era works by Peninsular Spanish and European authors who included American topics and/or themes in their visual and written texts (items **3396, 3397, 3400, 3408, 3415,** and **3467**). One rather interesting study turns the mirror around and looks at representations of Europe in Colombian travel writings (item **3419**).

Most conclusively, the increasing interest and importance of colonial-era writers and their works can be seen in the number of contemporary Latin American writers whose works treat literary and historical figures and events from their nation's colonial past. These cross-cultural and diachronic perspectives offer new and intriguing texts to the scholar and the student as well as the general and interdisciplinary reader.

INDIVIDUAL STUDIES

3382 Ahern, Maureen. Testimonio oral, memoria y violencia en el diario de Diego Pérez de Luxan: Nuevo México 1583. (*Rev. Crít. Lit. Latinoam.*, 21:41, 1995, p. 153–163)

Fascinating example of new critical interest in unstudied historical/literary texts. Examines the roles of memory, oral history, and writing in Diego Pérez de Luxán's unpublished camp diary kept during the expedition of Antonio de Espejo to New Mexico (1582–83). The diary represents an "alternative" discourse itself while also giving voice to the Indian informants and interpreters who testified to the true nature of the Spanish acquisition of northern frontier territories and the natives' assimilation of Spanish cultural signs.

3383 Arango L., Manuel Antonio. El teatro religioso colonial en la América hispana. Barcelona: Puvill Libros, 1997. 168 p.: bibl. (Biblioteca universitaria Puvill. Historia y cultura de Hispanoamérica; 4)

Concise examination of colonial Spanish-American religious theater includes definitions, describes beginning of theatrical forms popular in Spain and Spanish America, records names, offers brief biographies of principal dramatists, and lists works presented during colonial period. Basic reference work on colonial theater for both students and scholars.

3384 Arenal, Electa and Stacey Schlau. Thin lines, bedeviled words: monastic and inquisitional texts by colonial Mexican women. (*in* Estudios sobre escritoras hispánicas en honor de Georgina Sabat-Rivers. Edición e introducción de Lou Charnon-Deutsch. Madrid: Editorial Castalia, 1992, p. 31–44)

Well-researched and documented article presents ways that colonial women, primarily female lay religious and nuns, resisted religious and social restrictions. Notes success of some women just as the lack of it for others is underscored in references to inquisitional records of women tried for heresy and other religious crimes. Essential article for scholars of colonial women's literature. Useful to generalists, specialists in literature and history, and students of all levels.

3385 Arroyo Hidalgo, Susana. *El primero sueño* de sor Juana: estudio semántico y retórico. México: Univ. Nacional Autónoma de México, Instituto de Investigaciones Filológicas: Instituto Tecnológico y de Estudios Superiores de Monterrey, 1993. 209 p.: bibl., ill. (Cuadernos del Seminario de Poética; 16)

Formalist study of the rhetoric and semantics of Sor Juana's masterpiece. Full text of *El primero sueño* included in an appendix along with a brief bibliography of works consulted. Well done but useful only to specialists and linguists.

3386 Atamoros de Pérez Martínez, Noemí. Nueva iconografía sor Juana Inés de la Cruz: 1695–1995, trescientos años de inmortalidad. ed. conmemorativa. México: Hoechst Marion Roussel, 1995. 100 p.: bibl., col. ill.

Fascinating book. First section is an introduction that traces the historic and artistic antecedents for colonial and conventual iconography and features paintings of Sor Juana by her contemporaries. Second section includes a brief biography as well as contemporary images of Sor Juana and artistic representations inspired by her work and life.

3387 Atamoros de Pérez Martínez, Noemí. Sor Juana Inés de la Cruz. 2. ed. Toluca, Mexico: Instituto Mexiquense de Cultura, 1995. 86 p. (Biblioteca Sor Juana Inés de la Cruz)

Reprint of 1975 biography of Sor Juana (see *HLAS 40:6404*) that focuses on the human preoccupations and daily life of the Hieronymite nun with reference to her works and sociohistorical context. Of interest to scholars, students, and general readers.

3388 Ballón Aguirre, Enrique. Identidad y alteridad en un motivo etnoliterario amerindio e indioeuropeo: la doncella fecundada. (*Rev. Andin.*, 13:1, 1995, p. 43–102, bibl., graphs, tables)

Comparative study that examines

three cultural variants of an ethnic and literary myth: Mesoamerican (myth of Ixquic from the *Popol-Vuh*), Andean (myth of Cahuillaca from the *Manuscrito de Huarochirí*), and Greek and Latin (myth of Danaë). Analysis employs structuralist and anthropological theories. Also includes four critiques of Ballón Aguirre's article and his response.

3389 Baudot, Georges. México y los albores del discurso colonial. México: Nueva Imagen, 1996. 390 p.: bibl. (Colección Raíces del hombre)

Study divided into six sections examines initial encounter between Europe and the Americas, American men and resistance, transculturation and colonial discourse, Malintzin's discourse, Sor Juana Inés de la Cruz, and writers on the margins of New Spain discourse. Essays chronologically focus on the concept of alterity during precolumbian times, the encounter, and the subsequent formation of Spanish-American colonial institutions. Helpful to cultural and literary scholars, historians, and advanced students.

3390 Beggs, Donald. Sor Juana's feminism: from Aristotle to Irigaray. (*in* Hypatia's daughters: fifteen hundred years of women philosophers. Edited by Linda López McAlister. Bloomington, In.: Indiana Univ. Press, 1996, p. 108–127, bibl.)

Examines the Aristotelian, Thomistic, and Neoplatonist underpinnings of Sor Juana's *Respuesta* to understand the Hieronymite's feminism. Draws on theoretical arguments by Irigaray, Showalter, and Harding. Intellectually attractive study of Sor Juana's protofeminist standpoint. Useful to graduate students and specialists.

3391 Bénassy-Berling, Marie-Cécile. La mitificación de sor Juana Inés de la Cruz en el mundo hispánico: finales del siglo XVII-principios del siglo XVIII. (*Rev. Indias*, 55:205, sept./dic. 1995, p. 541–550)

Brief study traces impact of Sor Juana Inés de la Cruz's writings in America and Europe, referring to texts written by the nun's contemporaries and by authors who composed texts in her honor in subsequent years. Refers to texts not included in her original study *Humanisme et religion chez Sor Juana Inés de la Cruz, La femme et la culture au*

XVIIe siècle (1982) and to other documents that have been discovered recently.

3392 Bolaños, Alvaro Félix. Antropofagia y diferencia cultural: construcción retórica del canibal del Nuevo Reino de Granada. (*Rev. Iberoam.*, 61:170/171, 1995, p. 81–93)

Analysis of early Spanish chroniclers' characterizations of Americans as cannibals to justify conquest, enslavement, and/or slaying of autochtonous peoples. Specifically examines official and historical documents written between 1602–04 that recorded Spanish raids into Colombian territory of Pijao Indians designed to find and destroy a market where human flesh was bought and sold.

3393 Bolaños, Alvaro Félix. The historian and the Hesperides: Fernández de Oviedo and the limitations of imitation. (*Bull. Hisp. Stud.*, 72:3, 1995, p. 273–288)

Excellent analysis of how Fernández de Oviedo's discussion of the Hesperides Islands and their link with the West Indies early in *Historia general y natural de las Indias* demonstrates the constraints inherent in his rigid imitation of Pliny, limitations he overcomes in later chapters. In these later pages, the author states, Oviedo's use of direct methods offers "luminious and impressive descriptions of nature in the Americas and accounts of the Spanish expansion in the New World."

3394 Browne, Walden. When worlds collide: crisis in Sahagún's *Historia universal de las cosas de la Nueva España*. (*CLAHR/Albuquerque*, 5:2, Spring 1996, p. 101–149, facsims., table)

Extended examination of Sahagún's interpretation of the conversion crisis of the mid-16th century and the historical role of the first Franciscans in New Spain. Using James Lockhart's idea of "double mistaken identity," author studies Sahagún's attitudes towards the crisis and contrasts them with those of the Franciscan missionaries.

3395 Buxó, José Pascual. El enamorado de sor Juana: Francisco Álvarez de Velasco Zorrilla y su *Carta laudatoria—1698—*a sor Juana Inés de la Cruz. México: Univ. Nacional Autónoma de México, 1993. 234 p.: bibl., ill. (Serie Estudios de cultura literaria novohispana; 2)

Modern edition, bibliographical review of prior critical works, and sensitive and erudite analysis of this Colombian poet's panegyric to the Mexican intellectual. Valuable contribution to New Spain poetic studies and Sor Juanista criticism.

3396 Cabarcas Antequera, Hernando. Bestiario del Nuevo Reino de Granada: la imaginación animalística medieval y la descripción literaria de la naturaleza americana. Bogotá: Instituto Caro y Cuervo: Colcultura, Biblioteca Nacional de Colombia, 1994. 196 p.: bibl., ill. (some col.). (Biblioteca "Daniel Samper Ortega"; 1)

Three-part study examines how depictions of American fauna and flora, described in diverse works by both European and American chroniclers, reflect medieval ideology and classification of the world. Illustrations add invaluable component. Valuable resource for specialists and students.

3397 Castedo, Leopoldo. Chile, utopías de Quevedo y Lope de Vega: notas sobre América en el Siglo de Oro español. Prólogo de Armando Uribe. Santiago: LOM Ediciones, 1996. 127 p.: bibl. (Colección Sin norte)

Collection of impressionistic compositions of varying length treats diverse texts, primarily dramatic or poetic, that reveal a thematic, authorial, or topical connection between Spain and the Americas during the Siglo de Oro. Second part of book contains selections of texts discussed in first section. Useful only to the specialist.

3398 Castro-Klaren, Sara. El orden del sujeto en Guamán Poma. (*Rev. Crít. Lit. Latinoam.*, 21:41, 1995, p. 121–134)

Foucauldian analysis, informed by Spivak's writings on self-representation by the colonial subaltern, describes how Guamán Poma positions himself in his text as the "colonial hinge" between his European and American readers. Looks at visual and textual elements. Of interest to specialists and graduate students of literature and literary theory.

3399 Cevallos, Francisco Javier. Imitatio, aemulatio, elocutio: hacia una tipología de las poéticas de la época colonial. (*Rev. Iberoam.*, 61:172/173, 1995, p. 501–515, bibl.)

Introductory article highlights gap left

by traditional studies of Hispanic poetry and colonial Spanish-American poetics. Examines colonial Spanish-American theoretical treatises on literature and texts that include studies of poetics. Well-written with a comprehensive bibliography. Interesting and useful for scholars and students.

3400 Dadson, Trevor J. Libros y lecturas sobre el Nuevo Mundo en la España del Siglo de Oro. (*Histórica/Lima*, 18:1, julio 1994, p. 1–26, bibl.)

Interesting article about the literary effect that the New World had on the thousands of Spaniards who did not emigrate, and the types of books read by the emigres. Author reviewed 90 personal libraries (listed at end) of Spanish figures of note in political, literary, and historical sectors as well as lists of books sent to the New World. Useful information for scholars of different disciplines, students, and general public.

3401 Eich, Jennifer L. The mystic tradition and Mexico: Sor María Anna Agueda de San Ignacio. (*Let. Fem.*, 22:1/2, 1996, p. 19–32, bibl.)

Biographical and bibliographical introduction to this 18th-century Dominican nun, reputed to be the only New Spain female mystic to have her writings published during her lifetime. Her masterpiece, *Marabillas del divino amor, selladas con el sello de verdad,* was published along with Jesuit Fr. Joseph Bellido's biography in 1756. Of interest to scholars and students in diverse disciplines.

3402 Eich, Jennifer L. A question of authority: one eighteenth-century woman's answer. (*Dieciocho Hisp. Enlight.*, 20:1, 1997, p. 61–76, bibl.)

Study of the four mystical-theological treatises of the 18th-century Mexican mystic and Dominican nun Sor María Anna Agueda de San Ignacio. Examines the nun's use of different rhetorical devices and narrative techniques to present herself as a figure of authority in theological, mystical, and spiritual matters. Useful to scholars and students.

3403 Fernández Canel, Josefina. En torno al proceso genético de la identidad cultural en la literatura colonial hispanoamericana, siglos XVI y XVII. (*Islas/Santa Clara*, 107, enero/abril 1994, p. 60–73)

Reviews traditional theorists' claims

that Spanish-American letters were nonexistent prior to the 20th century, then refutes their assertions by demonstrating that the theme of the Americas was present from the beginning of the colonial era. Textual references limited to canonic authors and their texts, especially poetic works.

3404 Glantz, Margo. Sor Juana Inés de la Cruz: ¿hagiografía o autobiografía? Mexico: Grijalbo; Univ. Nacional Autónoma de México, 1995. 230 p.: bibl.

Interesting and intellectually engaging scholarly essays, some already published elsewhere, that examine Sor Juana's life, times, and works which scholars consider autobiographical, in order to identify more closely her place in colonial 17th-century Mexican society and letters. Highly recommended for scholars and students of the nun's life and works, and for anyone interested in literary genres, colonial history, or women's studies.

3405 Glantz, Margo. Sor Juana Inés de la Cruz: saberes y placeres. Toluca, Mexico: Gobierno del Estado de México, Instituto Mexiquense de Cultura, 1996. 177 p.: bibl., col. ill.

Excellent and unique bio-literary study of Sor Juana combines rigorous but accessible analysis with marvelous reproductions of illustrations (paintings, photographs, and original printings of colonial texts) to recreate the nun's milieu for today's readers. Highly recommended to specialists and students, and of interest to general reader.

3406 González Pizarro, José Antonio. La teorización sobre la realidad y el arte de narrar en los escritos de la conquista y colonia de América: hacia la conformación de la literatura hispanoamericana. Chile: Univ. Católica del Norte, Facultad de Humanidades, Depto. de Educación y Ciencias Sociales, 1992. 53 p.: bibl., ill.

Introductory monograph to the art of narrative in the Americas and its formation as an entity apart from Spanish literature using the concept of "reality" and the "*real maravilloso.*" Includes extensive citations from primary texts and other critics' works along with references to historical documents and literary texts.

3407 Harrison, Regina. The language and rhetoric of conversion in the Viceroyalty of Peru. (*Poetics Today*, 16:1, 1995, p. 1–27, bibl.)

Well-written and fascinating study of linguistic process of Spanish hegemony in the Viceroyalty of Peru through a study of four Andean Spanish-Quechua dictionaries printed in 16th and 17th centuries. Highlights how alternative lexicons allowed Quechua speakers to resist structures of domination and to preserve their ethnic identity.

3408 Las Indias (América) en la literatura del Siglo de Oro: homenaje a Jesús Cañedo. Pamplona, Spain: Gobierno de Navarra, Depto. de Educación y Cultura; Kassel: Edition Reichenberger, 1992. 312 p.: bibl., ill. (Estudios de literatura; 14)

Collection of essays provides engaging analysis of the perception of the Americas in Spanish literature. Includes Dadson's inventory of books pertaining to the New World contained in 67 personal libraries in Spain (starting with that of Isabel la Católica) and therefore is especially useful to scholars and archival researchers.

3409 Johnson, Julie Greer. Satire and early Spanish American theater. (*CHISPA / New Orleans*, 16, 1995, p. 173–183, bibl.)

Excellent history of the development of colonial Spanish-American secular and religious drama, and the ways in which it reacted to and was influenced by Spanish literature. Examines how colonial dramatists included satiric elements in order to defy civil and religious censorship, and how they wrote theatrical pieces that permitted them to express their American distinctiveness.

3410 Johnson, Julie Greer. Satire in colonial Spanish America: turning the New World upside down. Austin: Univ. of Texas Press, 1993. 203 p.: bibl., index. (The Texas Pan American series)

Contemporary theory (Bakhtin, Hutcheon, Todorov) combined with careful and extensive readings of primary and secondary colonial Spanish-American and Spanish works provides historians, literary critics, and students with an important guide and outstanding resource. Johnson's analyses of these texts and her discussion of literary influences illuminate the colonial works examined while also indicating the themes and literary styles that inspire contemporary Spanish-American writers. Very valuable book for specialist, students, and of interest to general reader.

3411 Kothe, Ana. The tantalizing absence of gender reference in the *Prólogo al lector* by Sor Juana Inés de la Cruz. (*in* Feminism in multi-cultural literature. Lewiston, NY: The Edwin Mellen Press, 1996, p. 123–136, bibl.)

Close textual reading and theoretical study of Sor Juana's lack of gender reference in the prologue she wrote for the second edition of her collection of poetry published in 1690. Well written and comparative, referring to norms followed by European and Spanish male poets and women writers of the period.

3412 Lavrin, Asunción. Espiritualidad en el claustro novohispano del siglo XVII. (*Colon. Lat. Am. Rev.*, 4:2, 1995, p. 155–179, bibl.)

Interesting and well-documented review of the political, religious, ideological, and sociocultural elements that informed the different types of writings of New Spain nuns and female lay religious writers, with special attention paid to the religious writings of Sor Juana Inés de la Cruz. For historian's comment, see *HLAS 56:1178*.

3413 Lavrin, Asunción. Sor Juana Inés de la Cruz: obediencia y autoridad en su entorno religioso. (*Rev. Iberoam.*, 61:172/173, 1995, p. 605–622)

Lavrin's illuminating historical contextualization of colonial-era conventual and religious norms draws on documents held in Mexican and Spanish archives (pastoral writings; personal, ecclesiastical, and conventual letters; religious rules and constitutions; inquisitional records, etc.). This sociocultural framework then informs her analysis of Sor Juana's (dis)obedience of pastoral authority in the *Respuesta*. Essential reading for scholars and students working in history, literature, sociology, and women's studies.

3414 Lavrin, Asunción. La vida femenina como experiencia religiosa: biografía y hagiografía en Hispanoamérica colonial.

(*Colon. Lat. Am. Rev.*, 2:1/2, 1993, p. 27–51, bibl.)

Well-researched and informative article studies relationship between male confessor and his female confessant by looking at themes characteristic of biographies of nuns who lived in New Spain. Useful to historians, literary critics, students of all levels, and readers interested in women's and/or cultural studies. For historian's comment, see *HLAS 56:903*.

3415 Lerzundi, Patricio. Arauco en el teatro del Siglo de Oro. Valencia, Spain: Albatros Hispanófila Ediciones, 1996. 165 p.: bibl. (Albatros Hispanófila; 59)

The theme of the Arauco serves as the focus for this study of six dramatic works from the Siglo de Oro. Provides a literary and critical history of the works, analyzes their portrayal of Spaniards and *araucanos*, gives the versification and function of different strophe types, and includes a linguistic analysis, focusing on Americanisms, along with an extended bibliography.

3416 López Chávez, Juan and Marina Arjona Iglesias. Lexicometría y fonometría del *Primero sueño* de sor Juana Inés de la Cruz. México: Univ. Nacional Autónoma de México, 1994. 146 p.

Statistical analysis of lexicon used in *Primero sueño*, part of a series of linguistic studies of literary works by Mexican authors. Useful only to specialists and linguists.

3417 Lorente Medina, Antonio. La prosa de Sigüenza y Góngora y la formación de la conciencia criolla mexicana. México: Fondo de Cultura Económica; Madrid: Univ. Nacional de Educación a Distancia, 1996. 238 p.: bibl., index. (Sección de lengua y estudios literarios)

Well-documented and methodical study is divided into five parts: *Theatro de Virtudes Políticas, Libra Astronómica y Philosóphica, Parayso Occidental, Piedad heroyca de Don Fernando Cortés*, and historical chronicles that Sigüenza authored including *Infortunios de Alonso Ramírez* and *Mercurio Volante*. Analyzes sources, form, and content of the works. Noteworthy final chapter focuses on the ideological and cultural implications of Sigüenza's works. Of interest to scholars and students.

3418 Luciani, Frederick. Anecdotal self-invention in Sor Juana's *Respuesta a Sor Filotea*. (*Colon. Lat. Am. Rev.*, 4:2, 1995, p. 73–83, bibl.)

Well-done and engaging study of how autobiographical anecdotes contained in Sor Juana's work must be viewed cautiously in light of their rhetorical function and self-fashioning nature. Yet author compellingly shows text "is a self-reflexive act, a giant emblem of the intellectual woman." Of interest to scholars, students, and general readers.

3419 Martínez, Frédéric. Représentations de l'Europe et discours national dans les récits de voyages colombiens, 1850–1900. (*Bull. Inst. fr. étud. andin.*, 24:2, 1995, p. 281–294, bibl.)

Well-documented article looks at travelogues published and/or written during the latter half of the 19th century by Colombians traveling in Europe. Author convincingly demonstrates the importance of these texts for understanding the concept of nationalism and "*extranjerismo*." Useful and interesting to scholars, students, and the general public.

3420 Maza, Francisco de la. La ruta de sor Juana de Nepantla a San Jerónimo. 2. ed. Toluca, Mexico: Instituto Mexiquense de Cultura, 1995. 98 p.: bibl. (Visiones y tentaciones. II)

Describes geography and architecture of places where Sor Juana lived or visited. Focuses on natural and urban characteristics of the sites and sociohistorical aspects of colonial life. Of interest to specialist.

3421 Mazzotti, José Antonio. Coros mestizos del Inca Garcilaso: resonancias andinas. Lima: Bolsa de Valores de Lima: Otorongo Producciones; México: Fondo de Cultura Económica, 1996. 384 p.: bibl., ill. (some col.). (Sección de obras de historia)

Multidisciplinary work offers "new" reading of the Inca Garcilaso's two-part masterpiece. Looks at "indigenous" influences of Quechua oral traditions, especially those found in Cuzco among the upper class, and use of a formulaic question/answer format in his analysis of the *Comentarios reales*. Study of the *Historia del Perú* looks at semantic and symbolic aspects that create a syncretic topology and the iconografic transformation of particular symbols. An interesting study that merits a central place among Andean and Garcilasan studies. Extensive bibliography.

3422 Meléndez, Mariselle. El perfil económico de la identidad racial en los *Apuntes* de las indias caciques del Convento de Corpus Christi. (*Rev. Crít. Lit. Latinoam.*, 23:46, 1997, p. 115–133, bibl.)

Discusses how economics serves as a narrative motif and organizational framework for the cultural images of eight *cacique* nuns presented in these biographical notes. Meléndez aptly demonstrates how the anonymous author of the text constructs an identity for these women based on a racial, socioeconomic, and religious status that defends their noble indigenous lineage.

3423 Meléndez, Mariselle. The reevaluation of the image of the *mestizo* in *El lazarillo de ciegos caminantes.* (*Indiana J. Hisp. Lit.*, 2:2, Spring 1994, p. 171–184, bibl.)

Interesting and well-organized study of how the central figure of Concolorcorvo constitutes an intertextual and symbolic response to the figure of the Inca Garcilaso de la Vega, effectively undermining his authority and credibility as a truthful narrator, "historian and as a *mestizo.*"

3424 Meléndez, Mariselle. Sexuality and hybridity in *El lazarillo de ciegos caminantes.* (*Lat. Am. Lit. Rev.*, 24:47, Jan./June 1996, p. 41–57, bibl.)

Excellent study in which the critic interprets the text as a treatise on sexuality and convincingly shows that the author's image of the female colonial subject reveals and reinforces negative societal attitudes towards racial hybridity.

3425 Mignolo, Walter. Decires fuera de lugar: sujetos dicentes, roles sociales y formas de inscripción. (*Rev. Crít. Lit. Latinoam.*, 21:41, 1995, p. 9–31)

Intriguing reflection on philosophical, linguistic, and theoretical underpinnings of speech forms and constitution of a speaking subject in Andean and Mesoamerican chronicles. Suggests that understanding these cultural and linguistic phenomena offers a lesson to a contemporary world, one that is characterized by technologic and scientific universalization coexistent with regionalized speech that is articulated in terms of identities and differences.

3426 Miró Quesada Sosa, Aurelio. El Inca Garcilaso. Lima: Pontificia Univ. Católica del Perú, Fondo Editorial, 1994. 407 p.: appendices, bibl., ill., index.

Literary and well-documented biography includes three interesting biographical appendices: his mother's testament; a family description drawn from his writings; and documentary references to a son. Represents a new trend in study of colonial letters. Useful to literary scholars, historians, and appealing to general public.

3427 Moraña, Mabel. *La endiablada,* de Juan Mogrovejo de la Cerda: testimonio satírico-burlesco sobre la perversión de la utopia. (*Rev. Iberoam.*, 61:172/173, 1995, p. 555–572)

Examines from a theoretical perspective how *La endiablada* criticizes and surpasses its Peninsular models. According to author, text exemplifies Baroque literary constructions that simultaneously supported hegemonic ideology, yet expressed an emerging heterodox "identidad criolla protonacional." Useful to specialists and literary critics.

3428 Moraña, Mabel. Fundación del canon: hacia una poética de la historia en la Hispanoamérica colonial. (*Rev. Crít. Lit. Latinoam.*, 22:43/44, 1996, p. 17–43, bibl.)

Analysis of historiographic projects from the Viceroyalties of Peru and New Spain undertaken during or about the colonial period, focusing on poetic and ideological elements such as cultural appropriation and recuperation of texts. Presents an excellent interpretation of how to read Latin American historiographic texts such as Eguiara y Eguren's *Bibliotheca Mexicana* or Beristáin de Souza's *Biblioteca hispanoamericana septentrional.*

3429 Moraña, Mabel. Poder, raza y lengua: la construcción étnica del Otro en los villancicos de sor Juana. (*Colon. Lat. Am. Rev.*, 4:2, 1995, p. 139–154, bibl.)

Study of Sor Juana's use of a polyphonic, multicultural discourse in her *villancicos* to articulate issues of gender, race, and power. The Hieronymite nun used ethnic and cultural differences to "re-present" the social situation of the Viceroyalty or in Bakhtinian terms, American heteroglossia. Of interest to scholars and students of cultural, ethnic, subaltern and women's studies, and literary criticism.

3430 Orquera, Yolanda Fabiola. Los castillos decrépitos: o la "Historia verdadera" de Bernal Díaz del Castillo; una indagación de las relaciones entre cultura popular y cultura letrada. Tucumán, Argentina: Facultad de Filosofía y Letras, Univ. Nacional de Tucumán, 1996. 270 p.: bibl.

Interesting theoretical and cultural study of the change in historiography from the traditional premise of a moral questioning of and reflection on events to a cultural and testimonial work. Asserts change occurred after Europe's encounter with the Americas and that Díaz's work exemplifies this change.

3431 Pérez Amador Adam, Alberto. El precipicio de Faetón: nueva edición, estudio filológico y comento de *Primero sueño* de sor Juana Inés de la Cruz. Frankfurt: Vervuert; Madrid: Iberoamericana, 1996. 239 p.: bibl. (Editionen der Iberoamericana. Serie A, Literaturgeschichte und -kritik = Ediciones de Iberoamericana. Série A, Historia y crítica de la literatura; 9)

Along with a carefully researched edition of the *Primero sueño*, work includes a study designed to introduce a first-time reader to the subtleties of this primary text by Sor Juana, translated previously and for the first time into German by the same author. Basic resource for the specialist and student of the Mexican Hieronymite's intellectual masterpiece. Extensive bibliography.

3432 Rabasa, José. On writing back: alternative historiography in *La Florida del Inca.* (*in* Latin American identity and constructions of difference. Edited by Amaryll Beatrice Chanady. Minneapolis: Univ. of Minnesota Press, 1994, p. 130–148, bibl.)

Engaging and theoretically adept study of the concepts of "civilization" and "barbarism" and "the noble savage" inherent in early colonial historiography. Discussion then leads to Rabasa's analysis of the Inca Garcilaso de la Vega's representation of self and identity ("porque soy indio") in his writings, especially in his version of Hernando de Soto's expedition, *La Florida del Inca.* Worth-

while article for scholars and students of history, literature, anthropology, and American/Ethnic studies. For review of entire work, see item **3365.**

3433 Rabasa, José. "Porque soy indio": subjectivity in *La Florida del Inca.* (*Poetics Today*, 16:1, 1995, p. 79–108)

Well-researched and thoughtful discussion of the modern Western episteme revealed in chronicles of the Americas (esp. Sahagún, Fernández de Oviedo, and Las Casas) and their depictions of Spaniards and Indians. Second section treats Garcilaso de la Vega's subjective positioning as an Indian author and demonstrates how his works, especially *La Florida*, created an acceptable "minority" discourse in Western historiography.

3434 Rivas, Gerardo. Voluntad de ser. México: Univ. Nacional Autónoma de México, Coordinación de Humanidades, Dirección General de Publicaciones, 1995. 222 p.: bibl. (Biblioteca de letras)

Focusing on the traditions of Western thought permeating the culture of New Spain, Rivas offers a philosophical/literary analysis of the theme of love in Sor Juana's poetry. Well-conceived and reflective, this study is of interest to scholars and students of Spanish-American poetic texts and themes.

3435 Ross, Kathleen. Cuestiones de género en *Infortunios de Alonso Ramírez.* (*Rev. Iberoam.*, 61:172/173, 1995, p. 591–603, bibl.)

Interesting study of how Carlos de Sigüenza y Góngora's work, examined in the light of his other writings such as *Parayso Occidental* and *Piedad heroica de don Fernando Cortés* and Bernal Díaz del Castillo's *Historia verdadera*, represents a parodic and hybrid text representative of a changing colonial reality.

3436 Ruptura de la conciencia hispanoamericana: época colonial. Recopilación de José Anadón. México: Fondo de Cultura Económica, 1993. 214 p.: bibl. (Sección de lengua y estudios literarios)

Collection of well-documented essays that are either theoretical discourses on historiography or literary studies of individual writers and/or works. Authors attempt to identify "una ruptura cultural" in order to identify the individuals/texts studied as

American offspring versus European descendant. Very useful to scholars and students.

3437 Sabat de Rivers, Georgina. Imágenes técnicas y mecánicas en la poesía de sor Juana. (*in* "Por amor de las letras": Juana Inés de la Cruz—le donne e il sacro *Venezia, 1996*. Atti del Convegno di Venezia, 26–27 gennaio 1996. Edited by Susanna Regazzoni. Rome: Bulzoni Editore, 1996, p. 43–56, bibl.)

Well-documented study of the technical and mechanical images and references used by Sor Juana in her poetry and prose that indicate the status and scope of the sciences (e.g., physics, cosmology, mechanics) in her time. Useful to specialists and students.

3438 Sabat de Rivers, Georgina. Love in some of Sor Juana's sonnets. (*Colon. Lat. Am. Rev.*, 4:2, 1995, p. 101–123, bibl.)

Excellent and beautifully translated study that reviews the development and traditions of Western love poetry before offering reader a thematic analysis of Sor Juana's love sonnets, which the author divides into orthodox or idealistic and heterodox or problematic. Indispensable work for scholars, specialists, students of all levels, and general readers.

3439 Sabat de Rivers, Georgina. Las obras menores de Balbuena: erudición, alabanza de la poesía y crítica literaria. (*Rev. Crít. Lit. Latinoam.*, 22:43/44, 1996, p. 89–101, bibl.)

Genre and thematic study of three minor works by Bernardo de Balbuena that set forth his theories about poetry. Argues that they show an early expression of *criolla* consciousness and demonstrate his pride as a poet who acclimated to and identified with the Americas.

3440 Sainz de Medrano, Luis. Sor Juana Inés de la Cruz en la crítica española. (*Cuad. Hispanoam. Complement.*, 16, nov. 1995, p. 5–24, bibl.)

Interpretive reading of Spanish literary figures and three Mexican and US literary critics (Octavio Paz, Georgina Sabat de Rivers, Elías Rivers), published by Spanish presses, who have studied Sor Juana primarily during the 20th century. Useful to Sor Juana scholars and bibliographers only.

3441 Sánchez de Abrego, Consuelo; Felipe C. Martínez Alcántara; and Leonardo Contreras López. Fray Servando Teresa de Mier: vida y obra. Monterrey, Mexico: Subsecretaría de Cultura del Gobierno del Estado de Nuevo León, 1994. 133 p.: bibl.

Publication of three essays selected from 20 submitted in celebration of the 230th anniversary of the birth of this son of Nuevo León. Essays examine the priest's life, works, and intellectual preoccupations in detail and chronological order. Useful resource for students and scholars of this notable figure.

3442 Schlau, Stacey. Yo no tengo necesidad que me lleven a la inquisición: las ilusas María Lucía Celis y María Rita Vargas. (*in* Mujer y cultura en la colonia hispanoamericana. Edición de Mabel Moraña. Pittsburgh: Instituto Internacional de Literatura Iberoamericana, Univ. of Pittsburgh, 1996, p. 183–193, bibl.)

Well-written article looks at cases of two poor urban *criollas* who, along with their confessor, were tried by Holy Office of the Inquisition for spiritual improprieties. Convincingly reveals how Christian rules of behavior, which also governed intimate aspects of one's personal life, varied according to class, race, and gender. For reviews of the entire book, see items **3469** and **3371.**

3443 Schmidhuber de la Mora, Guillermo. Sor Juana, dramaturga: sus comedias de "falda y empeño." Puebla, Mexico: Benemérita Univ. Autónoma de Puebla: Consejo Nacional para la Cultura y las Artes, 1996. 217 p.: bibl.

Critical study of the structures and language of three secular dramatic works that the author attributes to Sor Juana, along with a compilation of previous critical works treating New Spain baroque drama and theater. Includes a copy of the *Protesta de fe* written by Sor Juana and recently discovered by the author.

3444 Schmidhuber de la Mora, Guillermo. Un texto desconocido de sor Juana. (*Cuad. Hispanoam. Complement.*, 16, nov. 1995, p. 25–30)

Examines two important conventual texts: *Testamento místico*, by Sor Juana's confessor Antonio Núñez de Miranda, and *Protesta de la fe y renovación de los votos religiosos que hizo y dejó escrita con su sangre...*, an unknown text by Sor Juana included in her confessor's work. Sees the latter work as an influential piece in understanding Sor Juana.

3445 Soriano Vallès, Alejandro. La invertida escala de Jacob: filosofía y teología en *El sueño* de sor Juana Inés de la Cruz. Prólogo de José Pascual Buxó. Sor Juana Inés de la Cruz: signo del amor y otros demonios en nuestra cultura. Ádgar Fernando Carbajal López. Toluca, Mexico: Instituto Mexiquense de Cultura, 1996. 165 p.: bibl. (Visiones y tentaciones. II)

Publication of essays that received first and second place in the *Concurso Nacional de Ensayo Sor Juana Inés de la Cruz, 1995*, convened by the Instituto Mexiquense de Cultura to honor the 300th anniversary of the death of Sor Juana. Of interest to specialists.

3446 Tapia Méndez, Aureliano. Doña Iuana Ynes de Asuage ante la historia: biografías y autobiografía de sor Juana Inés de la Cruz. Monterrey: Producciones al Voleo el Troquel, 1996. 107 p.: bibl. (Colección Historia y letras; no. 6)

Study of contemporary and modern biographies written about the Mexican nun divided into chapters that treat themes or methods of analysis that distinguish the individual works. Analyzes her personal anxieties as they are revealed in a letter to her confessor and the *Respuesta*. Useful to specialist.

3447 Trabulse, Elías. Los años finales de sor Juana: una interpretación, 1688–1695. Chimalistac, Mexico: Centro de Estudios de Historia de México Condumex, 1995. 38 p.: facsim. (Colección Conferencias / Centro de Estudios de Historia de México Condumex)

Fascinating text brings to light new facts and documents that elucidate areas previously shadowed in the Hieronymite nun's life, such as her successful financial activities after her renunciation of literary pursuits in 1692. Highly recommended to anyone interested in Sor Juana's life and works.

3448 Williams, Jerry M. Peralta Barnuevo's *Diálogo político. La verdad y la justicia*, 1724: a transcription with introduction and notes. (*Dieciocho Hisp. Enlight.*, 18:2, Fall 1995, p. 119–156, bibl.)

Briefly introduces readers to the life, literary and political interests, and cultural context of Pedro de Peralta Barnuevo (1663–1743). Well-written essay includes a complete transcription of the Peruvian's treatise *Diálogo político: la verdad y la justicia* in addition to an authoritative and substantial bibliography of Peralta Barnuevo's works and critical texts that treat them. Useful to colonial scholars and graduate students.

3449 Zamora, Margarita. América y el arte de la memoria. (*Rev. Crít. Lit. Latinoam.*, 21:41, 1995, p. 135–148)

Examines cultural erasure of collective/individual memories and histories of natives during European colonization of the Americas. Looks specifically at writings by Sor Juana Inés de la Cruz and el Inca Garcilaso de la Vega. Despite difference in types of writing, Zamora admirably demonstrates that authors' texts show effects of colonialism on the colonial subject, yet also demonstrate recuperation of an esthetic/literary identity through creative and alternative cultural constructions.

TEXTS, EDITIONS, ANTHOLOGIES

3450 Anaya, José Lucas. La milagrosa aparición de Nuestra Señora María de Guadalupe de México. Estudio, edición y notas de Alejandro González Acosta. México: Univ. Nacional Autónoma de México, 1995. 344 p.: bibl., ill. (Serie Estudios de cultura literaria novohispana; 4)

Publication of 18th-century poem about history of Mexico and the formation of the Virgen of Guadalupe cult written after the Jesuits' expulsion in 1767. Taken from unedited manuscript previously thought lost but recently located at the Biblioteca del Museo Nacional de Antropología in Mexico. Contains extensive and excellent introduction to text, author, and Guadalupan literature.

3451 Balbuena, Bernardo de. Siglo de Oro en las selvas de Erífile. Edición, introducción y notas de José Carlos González Boixo. Xalapa, Mexico: Univ. Veracruzana, Centro de Investigaciones Lingüístico-Literarias, Instituto de Investigaciones Humanísticas, 1989. 323 p.: bibl., facsims. (Clásicos mexicanos; 2)

Brief review of Balbuena's life and

works, analysis of the form and content of each *égloga*, and abbreviated bibliography precede González Boixo's annotated text of this pastoral novel written in narrative and verse form. Useful to scholars, educators, and students.

3452 Buxó, José Pascual. Impresos novohispanos en las bibliotecas públicas de los Estados Unidos de América, 1543–1800. México: Univ. Nacional Autónoma de México, Instituto de Investigaciones Bibliográficas, 1994. 285 p., 28 p. of plates: facsims. (Serie Guías)

Extremely valuable resource for colonial scholars and students of diverse disciplines. Book offers researchers an impressive and accessible listing of materials, printed in New Spain during the 16th, 17th and 18th centuries, now held in collections and archives located in the US. Work anticipates restoration to Mexican Biblioteca Nacional of same items via photocopies and microfilms, as well as bibliographies of materials held in Spanish-American and European collections. Highly recommended.

3453 Buxó, José Pascual. El oráculo de los preguntones: atribuido a sor Juana Inés de la Cruz. México: Coordinación de Difusión Cultural, Univ. Nacional Autónoma de México: Ediciones del Equilibrista, 1991. 111 p.: bibl.

Extensive and well-documented introduction precedes edition of the 24 questions with 12 answers for each, all in verse, attributed to Sor Juana. Of interest to scholars and graduate students.

3454 The Cambridge history of Latin American literature. v. 1, Discovery to Modernism. Cambridge; New York: Cambridge Univ. Press, 1996. 670 p.: bibl., indexes.

Primary and vital resource for literary specialists, historians, students of all levels, and general readers interested in this period. Leading scholars write about diverse genres (narrative, essay, poetry, theater) and cultural interests and ideas (intellectual life, historiography, Viceregal culture, Mesoamerican indigenous peoples and cultures). Literature articles include analysis and discussion of canonic and previously marginalized authors and treat representative works, genres, and literary and philosophical currents. Extremely useful, well written, and interesting.

3455 Coloquio Internacional Sor Juana Inés de la Cruz y el Pensamiento Novohispano, *Toluca, Mexico, 1995.* Memoria. Toluca, Mexico: Univ. Autónoma del Estado de México: Instituto Mexiquense de Cultura, 1995. 532 p.: bibl., ill. (some col.). (Biblioteca Sor Juana Inés de la Cruz)

Proceedings of symposium sponsored by the Instituto Mexiquense de Cultura in conjunction with the Univ. Autónoma del Estado de México in Mexico in April, 1995. Forty articles, written by established and junior scholars from Mexico and abroad, treat diverse themes and topics related to the 17th-century nun using traditional and innovative methods of analysis. Important and very useful collection for specialists and students. For historian's comment, see *HLAS 56:1134.*

3456 Congreso de Manifestaciones Religiosas en el Mundo Colonial Americano, *1st, Tlaxcala, Mexico, 1991.* Manifestaciones religiosas en el mundo colonial americano. v. 1–2. México: Centro de Estudios de Historia de México Condumex; INAH, Dirección de Estudios Históricos; Univ. Iberoamericana, Depto. de Historia, 1993. 2 v.: bibl.

Interesting and well-written collection of seven essays focusing on different elements that characterized the Catholic faith and its adherents in different geographical areas of the Americas (New Spain, Peru, and New Granada) at distinct times during the colonial period. Of interest to historians, literary scholars, and graduate students. For historian's comment, see item **2119.**

3457 Congreso Internacional El Monacato Femenino en el Imperio Español, *2nd, México, 1995.* El monacato femenino en el imperio español: monasterios, beaterios, recogimientos y colegios; memoria. Coordinación de Manuel Ramos Medina. México: Centro de Estudios de Historia de México, 1995. 596 p.: bibl.

Excellent collection of essays by distinguished scholars in honor of noted scholar and historian Josefina Muriel. Topics treated include specific women writers, the founding of convents and female religious orders, and the education and culture of colonial-era women. Highly recommended. For historian's comment, see *HLAS 56:838.*

3458 Corvera, Juan Bautista. Obra literaria. Edición y estudio de Sergio López Mena. México: Univ. Nacional Autónoma de México, Instituto de Investigaciones Filológicas, Centro de Estudios Literarios, 1995. 177 p.: bibl. (Letras de la Nueva España; 1)

Study of the life and works of a man some scholars consider the first New Spain dramatist. Includes editions of three plays, epistles, and poetic texts, found in an Inquisition legajo in the Archivo General de la Nación in Mexico, that López Mena maintains were authored by Corvera. Useful to specialists and students.

3459 Los empeños: ensayos en homenaje a sor Juana Inés de la Cruz. Dirección de Sergio E. Fernández; colaboración de Mauricio Beuchot *et al.* México: Univ. Nacional Autónoma de México, Coordinación de Humanidades, Dirección General de Publicaciones, 1995. 238 p.: bibl.

Critical and literary essays by *sorjuanistas* and established scholars compiled in honor of the 300th anniversary of the death of the *décima musa*. Essays treat diverse works and biographical themes traditionally studied in her life and writings. Useful to scholars and students.

3460 Juana Inés de la Cruz, Sor. The answer: including a selection of poems = La respuesta. Critical edition and translation by Electa Arenal and Amanda Powell. New York: Feminist Press at the City Univ. of New York, 1994. 196 p.: bibl., index.

Outstanding edition and translation into English of Sor Juana's intellectual *tour de force*. Includes an excellent introduction, chronology, notes, and critical commentary. Both scholarly remarks and Sor Juana's work are essential reading for scholars, specialists, students of all levels, and the general reader. For translation specialist's comment, see *HLAS 56:4611.*

3461 Juana Inés de la Cruz, Sor. Carta athenagorica de la madre Juana Ynes de la Cruz religiosa profesa de velo, y choro en el muy religioso Convento de San Geronimo de la ciudad de Mexico cabeza de la Nueva España, qve imprime, y dedica a la misma sor, Phylotea de la Cruz [pseud.] su estudiosa aficionada en el Convento de la Santissima Trinidad de la Puebla de los Angeles. Chimalistac, Mexico: Centro de Estu-

dios de Historia de México Condumex, 1995. 36 p.: bibl. + 1 commentary volume (59 p.).

Elegantly packaged and beautiful facsimile edition of the 1690 work. Includes an excellent and erudite introduction to the text by Elías Trabulse, one of the most renowned Mexican experts on the Hieronymite nun. Of interest to scholars, students, and desirable for special collections of works on or about Sor Juana.

3462 Juana Inés de la Cruz, Sor. Enigmas ofrecidos a la Casa del Placer por Juana Inés de la Cruz. Edición y prólogo de Antonio Alatorre. México: Colegio de México, 1995. 80 p.

A hand-printed edition of 20 riddles published in Lisbon by the Casa do Prazer in 1693. The Casa, a cloistered group of Portuguese nuns who enjoyed secular verse, communicated via writing and exchanges of books and manuscripts. They also hand-copied manuscripts and distributed them. Alatorre proposes that these riddles are likely the last texts Sor Juana wrote; his edition is faithful to the original, without answers or commentary. Highly recommended for scholars and students of Sor Juana's works.

3463 Juana Inés de la Cruz, Sor. Inundación castálida. Introducción y reseña histórica de Aureliano Tapia Méndez. Recopilación de Tarsicio Herrera Zapién. Toluca, Mexico: Instituto Mexiquense de Cultura, 1995. 57, 365 p.

Unabridged edition and brief historical study of the first volume of Sor Juana's works, originally published in 1689 in Madrid.

3464 Juana Inés de la Cruz, Sor. Obra selecta. Selección y prólogo de Margo Glantz. Cronología y bibliografía de María Dolores Bravo Arriaga. Caracas: Biblioteca Ayacucho, 1994. 3 v.: bibl. (Biblioteca Ayacucho)

Three components make this anthology an excellent resource for scholars, students, and general readers: an extended and remarkable introduction to the Hieronymite nun's life and writings and the historical period and culture in which she lived, well-chosen and varied selections of her writings, and valuable annotations of the works included. Highly recommended.

3465 Juana Inés de la Cruz, Sor. Obras completas de sor Juana Inés de la Cruz. Edición, prólogo y notas de Alfonso Méndez Plancarte. México: Fondo de Cultura Económica, 1994. 4 v.: bibl., ill., indexes. (Biblioteca americana; 18, 21, 27, 32. Serie de literatura colonial)

Reprint of classic edition of Sor Juana's complete works edited by Méndez Plancarte (vols. 1–3) and Salceda (vol. 4). Still regarded as an authoritative text. Includes introduction to each volume, careful annotations of textual variants, and chronological and bibliographical dates. Primary reference for scholars, students, and general readers.

3466 Juana Inés de la Cruz, Sor. Segundo tomo de las obras de sor Juana Inés de la Cruz. Y, La segunda Celestina. Introducción de Fredo Arias de la Canal. Prólogo de Guillermo Schmidhuber de la Mora. México: Frente de Afirmación Hispanista, 1995. 552 p.: ill.

Facsimile versions of the second volume of Sor Juana's works and her *loa* written for *La segunda Celestina,* as well as the play written by Spanish dramatist don Agustín de Salazar y Torres, believed by some scholars to have been finished by Sor Juana. Also includes a study and facsimile copy of her *Protesta de la fe,* discovered by Schmidhuber.

3467 Lengua y literatura en la época de los descubrimientos: actas del coloquio internacional, Würzburg, 1992. Coordinación de Theodor Berchem y Hugo Laitenberger. Valladolid, Spain: Junta de Castilla y León, Consejería de Cultura y Turismo, 1994. 272 p.: bibl., ill. (Estudios de lengua y literatura)

Collection of essays written in Spanish, Portuguese, and Italian. Literary articles treat the topic of the Indies in European poetry and narratives; linguistic studies examine influence of Spanish language in Columbus' writings and Spanish America. Selected drawings by Guamán Poma de Ayala counterbalance the Eurocentric vision of articles.

3468 Maldonado Macías, Humberto Antonio. Hombres y letras del Virreinato: homenaje a Humberto Maldonado Macías. Presentación de Fernando Curiel Defossé; prólogo de José Quiñones Melgoza; semblanza biográfica de Lourdes Franco Bagnouls; edición, selección e índice de José Quiñones Melgoza y María Elena Victoria Jardón. México: Univ. Nacional Autónoma de México, Instituto de Investigaciones Filológicas, Centro de Estudios Literarios, 1995. 390 p.: bibl., indexes. (Letras de la Nueva España; 2)

Seventeen essays collected posthumously, most already published elsewhere. Meticulously researched, well-documented, and interesting articles cover diverse genres and study canonic New Spain authors (González de Eslava, Sor Juana) along with innovative and significant cultural topics such as New Spain's artistic relations with Spain and the Pacific Rim.

3469 Mujer y cultura en la colonia hispanoamericana. Edición de Mabel Moraña. Pittsburgh: Instituto Internacional de Literatura Iberoamericana, Univ. of Pittsburgh, 1996. 330 p.: bibl., ill. (Serie Biblioteca de América)

Compilation of well-researched and documented essays divided into "Inscripciones del mito," "Intertextos del humanismo," "Cuerpo y escritura en la clausura monacal," "Sor Juana Inés," and "Otras imágenes." Essays study sociohistorical context, lives, and works by or about canonic and previously marginalized colonial-era women. Requisite text for the study of colonial women's literature. Of interest to scholars and students. For a review of a chapter by Stacey Schlau that examines race, class, gender, and the Inquisition, see item **3442.** For comment by general literature specialist, see item **3371.**

3470 Orjuela, Héctor H. Historia crítica de la literatura colombiana. v. 1–3. Bogotá: Editorial Kelly, 1992. 3 v.: bibl., indexes.

Introduction briefly reviews previous histories of Colombian literature and other books that trace evolution of literature in Colombia. Traditional diachronic periodization of generational literary movements with attention to the sociocultural and historic processes that figure in distinct literary genres and representative texts. Study of canonic authors and their works with some figures and texts previously judged secondary. Valuable history of Colombian letters, although inclusion of very few female authors and/or their works is surprising.

3471 Ovando, Leonor de. Poesías. Estudio preliminar y notas por Iride María Rossi de Fiori. Salta, Argentina: Fundación García Arevalo: Univ. Católica de Salta, 1993. 65 p.: bibl., ill. (Biblioteca de textos universitarios. II, Sección general. Serie Divulgación; 1)

Brief contextualization and study of six poems by this almost-unknown Dominican nun from Santo Domingo. Poetic texts were taken from anthologies edited by Menéndez y Pelayo and Pedro Henríquez Ureña, both previous works based on an unpublished anthology compiled by Sor Leonor's contemporary, Spanish poet Eugenio de Salazar.

3472 Oviedo, José Miguel. Historia de la literatura hispanoamericana. v. 1, De los orígenes a la emancipación. Madrid: Alianza Editorial, 1995. 386 p.: bibl., index. (Alianza universidad textos; 151)

Well-conceived and contextualized study of colonial and 19th-century Spanish-American literature. Examines indigenous, Spanish, and Spanish-American narrative and poetic texts. Presents study of authors and literary periods (Baroque, Enlightenment, neoclassic, and Romantic periods). Thematic sections have selected bibliographies; volume includes onamastic index and general bibliography. Highly recommended.

3473 Teatro mexicano: historia y dramaturgia. v. 3, Autos, coloquios y entremeses del siglo XVI. México: Consejo Nacional para la Cultura y las Artes, 1992–1995. 124 p.: bibl., ill.

Third in a series, this useful anthology includes dramatic texts by an anonymous author, Juan Pérez Ramírez, and Fernán González de Eslava. Solórzano briefly introduces the authors, dramatic forms, and material treated in the texts, and examines the ideological function of colonial-era theater, while giving a literary/critical history and bibliography of Mexican theater.

3474 Trejo, Pedro de. Cancionero. Edición y estudio de Sergio López Mena. México: Univ. Nacional Autónoma de México,

Instituto de Investigaciones Filológicas, Centro de Estudios Literarios, 1996. 271 p.: bibl. (Letras de la Nueva España; 3)

Well-annotated edition of restant poetry of Pedro de Trejo, a Spanish poet born in Plascencia who lived much of his life in Nueva Galicia. Prosecuted by the Inquisition, Trejo was sentenced to cease writing and to be burned at the stake. Extensive introduction to the inquisitional record of Trejo's case and a brief overview of his surviving poetic works. Useful to scholars and students.

3475 Vega, Garcilaso de la. Comentarios reales: selección. Edición de Enrique Pupo-Walker. Madrid: Cátedra, 1996. 315 p.: bibl., ill., index. (Colección Letras hispánicas; 410)

Excellent introduction to the life and works of Garcilaso de la Vega that includes a superb analysis of classic and contemporary critical studies. Representative selections taken from *Diálogos de amor*, *La Florida*, the *Comentarios reales* and *Historia general del Perú*. Complete index to latter two works included as an appendix. Highly recommended.

3476 Vega, Garcilaso de la. El Inca Garcilaso de la Vega: antología. Noticia preliminar y selección de Aurelio Miró Quesada Sosa. Lima: Biblioteca Nacional del Perú, 1996. 380 p.: bibl., port. (Biblioteca básica peruana; 9)

Brief introduction presents highlights of the Inca Garcilaso's life and works. Selections are well chosen and the volume is accessible to students, scholars, and general readers.

3477 Y diversa de mí misma entre vuestras plumas ando: homenaje internacional a sor Juana Inés de la Cruz. Coordinación de Sara Poot Herrera y Elena Urrutia. Edición de Sara Poot Herrera. México: El Colegio de México, 1993. 408 p.: bibl.

Superb collection of articles by scholars who participated in the Sor Juana symposium held in Mexico in 1993. Authors look at the nun's diverse works, many previously overlooked, as well as different themes treated by Sor Juana. Highly recommended.

20th Century Prose Fiction
Mexico

JOSÉ MANUEL GARCÍA-GARCÍA, *Associate Professor of Spanish, New Mexico State University*

INTRODUCCIÓN SOMBRÍA PERO OPTIMISTA

En la República de las Letras mexicanas la "Generación de los 50" y la "Generación del '68" (ver *HLAS 56*) siguen trabajando unidas para imaginar una mejor literatura nacional. Los jóvenes de la "Generación Postista" han resultado, sin querer, los apadrinados por generaciones de los "viejos." Las estrategias comerciales y de fama de los chicos del Boom Latinoamericano de los años 60, de promoverse primero en la Península Madre (Barcelona y Madrid), están siendo reutilizadas por los mexicanos para enriquecer su currículum profesional. Es una especie de retro-colonización (¿característica postcolonial?) en la que, regla no dicha, primero hay que publicar en España o ganarse algún premio de alguna valía en ese país, para luego venir a invertir en tierras mexicanas el místico valor de uso de ese prestigio acumulado. Los que la están haciendo en España, tiene asegurados más premios (aunque sean locales), más publicaciones, más reconocimientos, trabajo seguro en los mejores suplementos de los diarios del país o de las mejores revistas de la ciudad de México como, por ejemplo, *Letras Libres,* y la serie de revistas publicadas bajo el presupuesto de Conaculta y organismos culturales descentralizados. Después del caudillismo de Octavio Paz, vino el reacomodo de los grupos y mafias y cárteles culturales. Y los jóvenes de la "Generación Postista" tuvieron que tomar partido; vivir fuera del presupuesto (y de las miras de los grupos culturales del Distrito Federal de México-Barcelona-Madrid) es un error histórico, o al menos, un vacío curricular.

Un ejemplo es que el desaparecido grupo de la "Literatura del Crack," promovido por Cohen a mediados de la década de 1990 (Volpi, Chávez, Padilla, Palou, y Urroz), coronó sus esfuerzos cuando uno de sus miembros, el talentoso Jorge Volpi Escalante, autor de *A pesar del oscuro silencio* (1992), *La paz de los sepulcros* (1995), *El temperamento melancólico* (1996), *Sanar tu piel amarga* (1997), y la triunfadora *En busca de Klingsor* (1999) obtiene el Premio Biblioteca Breve de la Editorial Seix Barral, un premio silenciado por 27 años). Y hablaron los antiguos: Luis Goytisolo y Guillermo Cabrera Infante, con Pere Gimferrer, Susana Fortes, y el editor de Seix Barral, Basilio Baltasar, fueron los miembros del jurado. Para Goytisolo, la novela está escrita de tal modo que no se reconoce la nacionalidad del autor, mientras que Cabrera Infante aseguró que es "una novela alemana escrita por un español." Volpi confirmó esto al asegurar: "He intentado no seguir el realismo mágico, pero tampoco he querido asesinarlo con el realismo duro de influencia norteamericana con que mi generación le respondió" (*España Hoy,* 16 de abril de 1999). Por su parte, Carlos Fuentes (además de su ejercicio vitalicio de diplomático de *Todo México* en la televisión norteamericana, y de trabajo en la "Biblioteca Carlos Fuentes"), ha declarado que puede morir en paz porque ya tiene un sucesor a su reino: Jorge Volpi. El caso Volpi ("abogado de profesión y secretario del procurador general de Justicia") es un modelo para obtener la fama y el reconocimiento que los jóvenes escritores mexicanos merecen.

Otro hecho destacable

También cabe destacar el "boom" mexicano de publicaciones en torno al tema de la masacre del '68. Los clásicos pero añejos libros "del 68" no bastan: Luis González de Alba, *Los días y los años* (*HLAS 34:3399*); Elena Poniatowska, *La noche de Tlatelolco* (*HLAS 35:7533*); Carlos Monsiváis, *Días de guardar* (1970); José Revueltas, *México 68: juventud y revolución* (*HLAS 44:2246*); Ramón Ramírez, *El movimiento estudiantil* (*HLAS 33:4679*); Sergio Zermeño, *México: una democracia utópica* (1978); Juan Miguel de Mora, *T-68, Tlatelolco 68: ¡por fin toda la verdad!* (1998); el utilísimo de Gonzalo Martré, *El movimiento popular estudiantil de 1968 en la novela mexicana* (1986); Héctor Aguilar Camín et al., *Pensar el 68*, coordinado por Hermann Bellinghausen (1988). Luego vino la nueva generación: Daniel Cazés, *Crónica 1968* (1993); Jaime Cruz Galdeano, *Proyecto 68* (1993); Raúl Alvarez Garín, *La estela de Tlatelolco: una reconstrucción histórica del movimiento estudiantil del 68* (1998); Renward García Medrano, *El 2 de octubre de 1968, en sus propias palabras* (1998); Jorge Volpi, *La imaginación y el poder: una historia intelectual de 1968* (item **3511**); Julio Scherer García y Carlos Monsiváis, *Parte de Guerra: Tlatelolco 1968: documentos del General Marcelino García Barragán* (item **3508**).

Los descentralizados

Los esfuerzos por descentralizar la cultura están siendo compensados con una mayor difusión de libros escritos fuera de la ciudad de México. Hay revistas como *Fronteras* y organismos paraestatales que buscan publicar a los del terruño, los provincianos olvidados de los poderosos "chilangos,". Hay cientos de novelas y poemarios de tirajes de mil y pobre difusión, pero que buscan su lugar en el abigarrado mosaico cultural mexicano. Al norte de la ciudad de México, una de las revistas académicas que impulsa esta descentralización (aunque no sea su propuesta explícita) es la excelente *Revista Mexicana Contemporánea*, editada por los profesores Fernando García Núñez y Luis Arturo Ramos de la Univ. of Texas at El Paso. También los esfuerzos de cientos de anónimos activistas culturales de las "provincias" mexicanas están comenzando a dar sus frutos, en revistas como *Solar* en Chihuahua.

Pero el proceso de descentralización de la cultura y la difusión de la literatura "de provincia," es sin embargo un proceso lento y con lamentables retrocesos. Un ejemplo: en 1999 un grupo de periodistas-académicas escribieron el libro testimonial *El silencio que la voz de todas quiebra: mujeres y víctimas de Ciudad Juárez* (item **3482**). En este libro contabilizaban 137 casos de mujeres violentamente asesinadas en Ciudad Juárez entre 1993–98. Las autoras recurrieron a las principales editoriales mexicanas y a las instituciones descentralizadas. Por fin, publicaron en una editorial chihuahuense, *Azar*. El libro tuvo un gran éxito: entrevistas en EE.UU., primeras planas, entrevistas con la clásica Poniatowska, etc. Las editoriales del Distrito Federal definitivamente se equivocaron; anteriormente habían publicado dos libros del DF: el de Gregorio Ortega, *Las muertas de Ciudad Juárez* (1999), que es un largo e ineficaz argumento en defensa de Abdel Latif Sharif, ya sentenciado como asesino de una de las juarenses. Y el libro de Victor Ronquillo, *Las muertas de Juárez* (1999), es machista, sádico y de pésima investigación periodística. Al paso en que va todo, es buena recomendación que las provincias no viajen al DF, sino a Madrid o a Barcelona para publicar sus libros.

El homenaje

El 12 de marzo del 2000, murió el escritor Jesús Gardea. La República (siguiendo la vieja metáfora) de las Letras Mexicanas está de luto. En novela y cuento, Gardea creó unas obras de gran calidad literaria: *Los viernes de Lautaro* (item

3496 and *HLAS 44:5171*), *Septiembre y los otros días* (item **3491**), *El sol que estás mirando* (item **3493**), *La canción de las mulas muertas* (item **3488**), *El tornavoz* (item **3495**), *De alba sombría* (*HLAS 48:5177*), *Los músicos y el fuego* (item **3490** and *HLAS 48:5178*), *Sóbol* (*HLAS 48:5179*), *Soñar la guerra* (*HLAS 48:5180*), *Las luces del mundo* (*HLAS 50:3096*), *Antología de cuentos* (*HLAS 52:3481*), *El diablo en el ojo* (item **3489**), *El agua de las esferas* (1992), *El árbol cuando se apague (novela)*, *La ventana hundida* (1992), *Difícil de atrapar: cuentos* (*HLAS 56:3492*), *Juegan los comensales* (1998), *Donde el gimnasta* (1999), *Reunión de cuentos* (1999). El FCE ha reunido 20 años de trabajo cuentístico de Gardea. Al momento de morir, Gardea tenía dos libros por publicar, *El biombo y los frutos, Casa de Anfibia* y un manuscrito de novela. El estilo de Gardea es de una pericia lírica, paciencia minuciosa en el detalle, en la saturación de contrastes de sombras, luces, brillos, y sonidos. A partir de *Sóbol*, será más marcado su uso de laconismos poéticos y trastocamientos sintácticos. La literatura de Gardea no es definitivamente para lectores "light," ni para arrullar el infantilismo literario o la pereza mental de nadie. Por eso, con su muerte, México y la mítica hispanoamérica ha perdido un gran escritor, un gran estilista. Como un homenaje de nuestra parte, reseñaré algunos de sus libros en este envío. En estas líneas que me restan, le doy las gracias a Juana Gamero de Coca por su ayuda [las entradas que llevan las iniciales [JG] corresponden a Juana Gamero]; aunque la versión final (estilo, tono, síntesis, yerrores) son responsabilidad únicamente mía.

PROSE FICTION

3478 Aguilera Garramuño, Marco Tulio et al. Cuentos eróticos mexicanos. México: Extassy, 1995. 250 p.: ill. (Extassy)

Hay relatos muy buenos: el de Oscar de la Borbolla, "Los teléfonos eróticos," donde las mujeres aburren con sus pujidos y frases sin mayor imaginación. El de Josefina Estrada, "Las memorias de Madam Lú," donde la claridosa Lú habla de las desventuras de su profesión. Se incluyen excelentes relatos de Avilés Fabila, José Luis Cuevas, Mónica Lavín, Ignacio Solares, y Hernán Lauro Zavala.

3479 Avilés Fabila, René. Fantasías en carrusel, 1969–1994. 2. ed. México: Fondo de Cultura Económica, 1995. 651 p. (Colección popular; 518)

Reunión de cuentos fantásticos-cortos-ultracortos. Hay relatos acerca de arte, literatura, vampiros, fantasmas, animales mitológicos, científicos locos, parodias bíblicas, mitos modernos, oficios perdidos y cuentos de hadas. Es la antología de un Borges que tira más a Monterroso, con algo de Arreola, definitivamente Avilés Fabila.

3480 Avilés Fabila, René. Todo el amor: 1970–1995. 2. ed. México: Editorial Aldus: Univ. Autónoma Metropolitana,

Unidad Xochimilco, Coordinación de Extensión Universitaria, 1996. 307 p. (Molinos de viento)

Una selección de cuentos, algunos de ellos supercortos. Todos con el tema del amor: el amor erótico, el desamor, el amor finito. En el relato "La lluvia no mata las flores" es un buen ejemplo: un hombre se obsesiona por una mujer que acaba de ver en un autobús. El hombre se siente traicionado por no conseguir la atención que de ella esperaba. En "Regreso a casa" una mujer busca derrotar su soledad, e inicia una peligrosa relación con un extraño.

3481 Beltrán, Rosa. La corte de los ilusos. México: Grupo Editorial Planeta, 1995. 260 p.

Excelente novela histórica. Trata de la coronación de Agustín de Iturbide como Emperador de México y la caída de su imperio. Hay un constante uso de la parodia y de la sátira. [JG]

3482 Benítez, Rohry et al. El silencio que la voz de todas quiebra: mujeres y víctimas de Ciudad Juárez. Chihuahua, México: Ediciones del AZAR, 1999. 163 p.: bibl., ill., map.

Libro testimonial, collage de géneros: entrevistas, crónicas, citas, resultados de investigación de campo, verdadero archivo y empatía narrativa, ensayística, y relatos que nos permite ver a través de los ojos de siete de las 137 muchachas sacrificadas en Ciudad Juárez los últimos cinco años. Es un libro que nos reeduca sentimentalmente. Al eliminar el sensacionalismo, rehumaniza a las Desaparecidas, nos dice de ellas, a través de ellas, lo que debemos oír para entender la verdadera dimensión de la tragedia de esta ciudad fronteriza mexicana. Es el mejor y único libro que ofrece una visión objetiva del feminicidio juarense.

3483 Bermejo Mora, Edgardo. Marcos' fashion: o de cómo sobrevivir al derrumbe de las ideologías sin perder el estilo. México: Océano, 1996. 90 p. (El día siguiente)

Es la pseudoposmoderna historia de amor entre una modelo internacional y el subcomandante Marcos. Las malditas trasnacionales se han fijado en el tercermundo y buscan lanzar al mercado un (inverosímil) estilo de verano a-lo-guerrillero-Marcos; envían a una superbarbi a conquistar la firma y el corazón comercialista de Marcos. Este, en un arranque de fantasía burguesa, acepta la seducción imperialista con cara de mujer, y la juventud podrá lucir atuendos de reboltosos chiapanecos de moda.

3484 Bullé-Goyri, Rafael. Bodega de minucias. Xalapa, Mexico: Univ. Veracruzana, 1996. 255 p. (Ficción)

Anécdotas en breves cuadros de costumbres—¡kafkianas! Las viñetas más disfrutables: "Hacia una calcetología comparada" (el recuento paródico de la función histórica del calcetín). Y "Breves notas sobre los aztecas" (la enumeración de supuestas causas de la derrota azteca).

3485 Cerda, Martha. Las mamás, los pastores y los hermeneutas. Monterrey, Mexico: Ediciones Castillo, 1995. 82 p.: ill. (Colección Más allá; 10)

Dos secciones; la primera con 17 cuentos, la segunda con tres. Cerda hace una recreación literaria sobre la versión bíblica de la creación del mundo y del ser humano. Destaca el cuento: "Farsa en un acto," en el que un músico provinciano reflexiona acerca de la mediocridad de su entorno artístico. [JG]

3486 De amores marginales: 16 cuentos mexicanos. Recopilación de Mario Muñoz. Xalapa, Mexico: Univ. Veracruzana,

1996. 200 p. (Ficción / Universidad Veracruzana)

Interesante (pero aburrida) colección de cuentos "marginales" (no tanto, lo marginal aquí sirve como gancho comercial). Están los clásicos gays: Jorge López P, ("Doña Herlinda y su hijos"), y Luis Zapata ("De amor es mi negra pena"). Y los no-gays (pero excelentes) Ignacio Betancourt ("El hábito oculto"), y Fidencio González M. ("Juego de ajedrez"). En realidad es una antología sin buen balance estético; hay textos perfectamente excluibles.

3487 Escalante, Beatriz et al. La luna de miel según Eva. Recopilación de Beatriz Escalante. Fotografías de Gabriela Bautista. México: Selector, 1996. 166 p.: ill. (Colección Aura)

El tema es la Luna de Miel y las antologadas se explayan sabrosamente. Berta Hiriart escribe acerca de una mujer que toma la decisión de casarse después de ir de espía-antropóloga a hoteles de recién casados. Fernanda de Teresa, por su parte, nos cuenta el erótico encuentro de una joven con un mulato "olor a tamarindo," mientras su (recién adquirido) marido duerme con la mona. Otras antologadas: Laura Esquivel, Ethel Krauze, Guadalupe Loaeza, Ángeles Mastreta, y Elena Poniatowska.

3488 Gardea, Jesús. La canción de la mulas muertas. México: Editorial Oasis, 1981. 107 p. (Lecturas de milenio; 3)

El drama se desata a partir de un juego de dominó en el que se enfrentan dos personajes (hombres poderosos de Placeres): Leónidas y Fausto. Este último pierde su fábrica de refrescos. Ambos están condenados a vivir con sus odios en el pueblo, hasta que Fausto se suicida y Leónidas se deja matar. El ambiente sofocante de Placeres y la soledad de los personajes son descritos en un estilo cada vez más poético y hermético.

3489 Gardea, Jesús. El diablo en el ojo. México: Editora y Distribuidora Leega, 1989. 133 p. (Programa cultural de las fronteras)

Estilo hermético, neobarroco, similar al de la novela *Sóbol* (1985). El narrador observa a través del ojo del diablo (el mal, la ira), y descubre cómo un grupo de hombres se persiguen, se matan, establecen complicidades y venganzas. El ejercicio neobarroco va al extremo de dedicarle diez páginas al acto de encender el motor de un auto. El lector descuidado se pierde fácilmente en el laberinto de torcimientos sintácticos y de omisiones y supuestos del narrador.

3490 Gardea, Jesús. Los músicos y el fuego. México: Ediciones Océano, 1985. 107 p.

Entre el "infierno sofocado" de Placeres y el limbo del desierto de ese pueblo, ocurre la historia de grupo de hombres que pelean por unas baratijas robadas. El lenguaje de Gardea se hace más elíptico, se "minimaliza." Y aunque el tema en sí es absurdo, los personajes no lo son, en tanto son la conciencia reflexiva (y emotiva) entre el desierto y sus efectos en los hombres. En esta novela, deja de importar lo que se cuenta; lo importante es cómo se describe el infierno que a los personajes les ha tocado vivir.

3491 Gardea, Jesús. Septiembre y los otros días. México: Editorial J. Mortiz, 1980. 152 p. (Serie del volador)

Diez cuentos donde el tono poético tradicional del autor es desplazado por un tono más realista y menos ambiguo. Destacan: "Septiembre y los otros días," cuento de carácter autobiográfico. Y "Más frío que el viento," donde los personajes luchan inútilmente contra las inclemencias del frío. Con esta obra, Gardea obtuvo el premio Xavier Villaurrutia, 1980.

3492 Gardea, Jesús. Sóbol. México: Grijalbo, 1985. 120 p. (Colección Narrativa)

La crítica afirma que esta novela es la parteaguas en la obra de Gardea. Se pierde definitivamente el interés por lo que se cuenta. La historia se puede resumir en que un aprendiz de brujo (Tolinga) le roba una cucharilla al vagabundo Sóbol. Éste planea con sus cómplices matar a su enemigo. El lenguaje se hace oscuro, se pierde la clara distinción entre lo literal y lo metafórico. Las descripciones de las acciones se alargan y saturan con descripciones de ambientes, efectos de luz y emociones de los personajes. La mejor definición de este estilo de Gardea es el neobarroco.

3493 Gardea, Jesús. El sol que estás mirando. México: Fondo de Cultura Económica, 1981. 97 p. (Letras mexicanas)

Narración de estilo realista, con descripciones poéticas del mítico pueblo de Placeres. Un hombre (David Gálvez) recuerda su niñez, las anécdotas formativas, y las batallas de generaciones por vencer las inclemencias del desierto y civilizar el pueblito de Placeres.

3494 Gardea, Jesús. Soñar la guerra. Oaxaca, Mexico: Editorial Oasis, 1984. 104 p. (Colección Lecturas del milenio; 15)

El narrador-personaje, Asís, sueña una guerra en la que mal organiza a un puñado de hombres en contra del gobierno. Su guerra fracasa; Asís muere y vuelve a Placeres para contarnos las consecuencias de su guerra. En esta novela, el estilo de Gardea es similar al de *La canción de las mulas muertas*, aunque se nota más el tortuoso determinismo existencial de las inclemencias del desierto.

3495 Gardea, Jesús. El tornavoz. México: J. Mortiz, 1983. 145 p. (Serie del volador)

Considerada la mejor de las novelas de Gardea. Es una mezcla de fantasía y realidad del pueblo de Placeres. El místico y loco tío Cándido habla con los ángeles y los santos. Cándido muere y visita a su sobrino, Isidro Paniagua, que enloquece también. El hijo de Isidro, Jeremías, crece en un mundo realmaravilloso (o magicorealista) de milagros y conversaciones con Cándido. Este quiere estar en un tornavoz (el interior de la cúpula de la iglesia del pueblo), donde pueda dialogar a gusto con todos los santos del lugar. Al final de la novela se logra el milagro.

3496 Gardea, Jesús. Los viernes de Lautaro. Portada de Anhelo Hernández. México: Siglo Veintiuno Editores, 1986. 165 p. (La Creación literaria)

Son 19 cuentos de excelente estilo narrativo, una mezcla de tono poético, sintaxis trastocada, diálogos breves, ambiguos, y que apuntan a realides poéticas o visiones sensoriales del mundo. Destacan los cuentos "Los viernes de Lautaro," en el que un hombre vive a mitad del desierto de Chihuahua y se dedica a realizar rituales solitarios en homenaje a su mujer muerta. En este cuento se refleja el tema obsesivo de Gardea: el sol, el calor de los desiertos. "En la caliente boca de la noche," un cuento de suspenso que culmina en el terror de un personaje devorado por insectos nocturnos del desierto. Y "Como el mundo," un hombre violento es dejado morir por sus cansados familiares; el hombre es tan gordo que muere como un cerdo pegado a la taza del escusado. Este libro tiene una segunda edición en Lecturas Mexicanas, Siglo XXI Editores—Secretaría de

Educación Pública, 1986. Ver también *HLAS 44:5171.*

3497 Gargallo, Francesca. Los pescadores de Kukulkán. México: Editorial Aldus, 1995. 67 p. (Colección La torre inclinada)
Noveleta de ambiente marítimo. Se describen las desventuras de cuatro pescadores que van del Caribe al Pacífico a través del Canal de Panamá. En los pescadores se representa el miedo y la visión de la pérdida de toda esperanza y pertenencia. [JG]

3498 Gomís, Anamari. La portada del sargento Pimienta. México: Aguilar, León y Cal Editores, 1994. 137 p. (Cal y arena)
Once cuentos con heroínas femeninas y detalle en la mención de firmas de ropa y peinados de moda. Es un retrato de los nuevos ricos mexicanos. Destacan los cuentos: "Bateador emergente," historia en la que el protagonista se encuentra atrapado en un ascensor y ve como su destino se desmorona por causas del azar. "Recóndita armonía," trata de las diversas emociones y perspectivas de una mujer ante la muerte de su marido. [JG]

3499 Jacobs, Bárbara. Juego limpio: ensayos y apostillas. México: Aguilar, Altea, Taurus, Alfaguara, 1997. 158 p. (Textos de escritor)
Antología de ensayos escritos a lo largo de 20 años. Aquí están: el "Manipulador Leonard Woolf" (editor de los diarios de la Woolf); "Un signo de puntuación" (exprese la coma riendo como si sonriera); y "El primer recuerdo de un escritor" (citas de autores que hablan de sus primeros recuerdos). Como Monterroso, el tono es humorístico y la intención didáctica.

3500 Krauze, Ethel. Intermedio para amar. México: Selector, 1996. 223 p. (Colección Aura)
Cuentos de *Intermedio para mujeres* (1982; see *HLAS 48:5187*) y *El lunes te amaré* (México: Océano, 1987). Mencionaré dos: "Hasta que la muerte nos separe" que relata la unión de una pareja despareja: jipiteca y gramatólogo, y "Ochichornia" que describe la vida de un paquidérmico fanático del fútbol que logra escapar de la familia al meterse (¡literalmente!) a "un juego de fut que pasaba por tele."

3501 Mejía, Raúl. Banquetes. Chimalistac, Mexico: Consejo Nacional para la Cultura y las Artes, 1995. 117 p. (Fondo editorial tierra adentro; 104)
Fino, sencillo, y claro estilo. Destacan los cuentos: "La verdadera historia de Coquis y la Estrella de Belén" (ex-jipiteca sabe la fecha real en que apareció la Estrella de Belén), y "El alma de los pasos" (reflexiones y apuros de un hombre obsesionado por la limpieza de sus zapatos).

3502 Padilla Suárez, Ignacio. La catedral de los ahogados. México: Univ. Autónoma Metropolitana, 1995. 159 p. (Colección Molinos de viento; 86. Serie/Narrativa)
Libro Premio "Juan Rulfo" para Primera Novela, 1994. En esta obra todo termina donde comenzó, representando la irracionalidad y la soledad de la existencia humana. El protagonista de la novela vive rescribiendo la historia de su vida una y otra vez. [JG]

3503 Puga, María Luisa. La reina. México: Seix Barral, 1995. 191 p. (Biblioteca breve)
Novela dedicada al poder determinista de la belleza. Ana Cecilia es una mujer bellísima, prisionera de las miradas y expectativas de los demás. Su belleza es tal que por el hecho de existir, de estar ahí, determina la vida de los que la rodean, mientras ella sufre de una soledad profundamente dolorosa. La novela está escrita desde la perspectiva de un testigo enamorado. [JG]

3504 Ramírez Heredia, Rafael. Con M de Marilyn. México: Alfaguara, 1997. 287 p.
Novela escrita en el estilo sobriorealista, trama detectivesco. La patética vida loca de Marilyn Monroe sirve de enlace para la recreación de ambientes defeños de mediados de siglo. La nostalgia por la ciudad perdida compite con el acartonamiento melodramático de la Monroe.

3505 Ramírez Heredia, Rafael. De tacones y gabardina. México: Aguilar, Altea, Taurus, Alfaguara, 1996. 120 p. (Alfaguara)
Consta de seis cuentos policíacos con lenguaje coloquial-realista. Destacan los cuentos "Danzón dedicado" (original de la película *Salón México*), en el que una joven embarazada abandona su casa y se inicia en la prostitución. Además, el cuento "Junto a

Tampico", en el que seguimos los pasos de un detective mediocre y hiperenamorado de una joven mujer. [JG]

3506 Rocío de historias: cuentistas de Filosofía y Letras. Recopilación de Dolores Gómez Antillón. Chihuahua: Facultad de Filosofía y Letras, U.A.Ch., 1996. 236 p.

Los egresados de Filosofía se ponen a literaturizar. Destacan: Humberto Payán con "Tu cuerpo fragmentado" (una esposa "sufre de accidentes" cada vez que el marido le pide el divorcio). Y Oscar Robles con "Que tanta belleza no se pudra" (un periodista reflexiona acerca del amor y la crueldad cuando se entera de que su ex-amante ha sido asesinada).

3507 Sáinz, Gustavo. La muchacha que tenía la culpa de todo. Monterrey, Mexico: Ediciones Castillo, 1995. 99 p. (Colección Más allá; 13)

Es una novela escrita con preguntas, una larga lista de preguntas sin respuesta. El lector, además, se ve dentro de otro interrogatorio, el que se le hizo a una prisionera (¿por la inquisición?). Dominan los temas del poder de la palabra y las interrogantes de quién tiene la culpa del dolor y de la incomprensión. [JG]

3508 Scherer García, Julio and **Carlos Monsiváis.** Parte de guerra, Tlatelolco 1968: documentos del general Marcelino García Barragán; los hechos y la historia. México: Nuevo Siglo/Aguilar, 1999. 269 p.: ill., maps.

El Monsiváis de *Días de guardar* y de *Amor perdido,* se une al campeón del periodismo honesto, Julio Scherer García, para crear este magnífico libro de crónicas, narrativas, entrevistas, documentos, y testimonios acerca de las personalidades del Poder que ordenaron la masacre de Tlatelolco.

3509 Solares, Ignacio. Columbus. México: Alfaguara, 1996. 180 p.

En la nebulosa memoria de un hombre lerdo se recupera la historia aquella de Villa y su (patética) toma de Columbus. El ambiente de la historia se desarrolla en una imaginaria Ciudad Juárez de los años 30, en un prostíbulo lleno de "freaks" amorosas, y clientes gringos—etílicos, y amoríos sofocantemente dependientes del personaje central de la novela.

3510 Solares, Ignacio. Muérete y sabrás: cuentos. México: Editorial Joaquín Mortiz, 1995. 133 p. (Serie del volador)

Son 16 cuentos de diversos temas, desde el miedo a la muerte hasta el dolor a la soledad. En el relato "La mesita del fondo," el protagonista es tratado como si no existiera por el resto de la familia. En "Los miedos," el protagonista trata de sobreponerse a sus miedos. En "Muérete y sabrás," una pareja se obsesiona con la idea de la vida eterna (o circular). [JG]

3511 Volpi Escalante, Jorge. La imaginación y el poder: una historia intelectual de 1968. México: Ediciones Era, 1998. 455 p.: bibl. (Biblioteca Era)

Formidable investigación acerca de las opiniones de los intelectuales en torno del movimiento estudiantil de 1968. Sorprenden las declaraciones de los intelectuales europeos y mexicanos acerca del estallido de vitalidad, imaginación, creatividad, e ingenuidad de los jóvenes estudiantes contra el Poder.

3512 Zacatecas: cielo cruel, tierra colorada; poesía, narrativa, ensayo y teatro, 1868–1992. Selección, prólogo y notas de Severino Salazar. México: Consejo Nacional para la Cultura y las Artes, 1994. 406 p.: bibl. (Letras de la república)

Conaculta cumple con difundir las literaturas surgidas al margen del Distrito Federal. Y Salazar nos ofrece un panorama de la literatura de Zacatecas. En la antología se incluye a clásicos y neoclásicos: Ramón López Velarde, Mauricio Magdaleno y José de Jesús Sampedro. Excelente.

3513 Zapata, Luis. La más fuerte pasión. México: Océano, 1995. 227 p. (Tiempo de México)

Larguísimo diálogo de dos homosexuales: Santiago (gay cuarentón), se enamora de Arturo, un joven que busca protección, seguridad, y viajes. Hay cachondeos telefónicos, celos, melodramas, y broncas entre Arturo y su Protector. Es el mismo rollo del Vampiro de la Colonia aquella.

LITERARY CRITICISM AND HISTORY

Vizcaíno, Fernando. Biografía política de Octavio Paz, o, La razón ardiente. See *HLAS* 57:3126.

Central America

WILFRIDO H. CORRAL, *Professor of Literature, University of California at Davis*

TOWARD THE END OF THE 20TH CENTURY, Central American literature tended to represent a distancing from the immediate national and regional referents that were largely responsible for the previous preponderance of testimonial discourse. This disposition was a historical necessity appropriated by critics for purposes the authors may not have intended. Thus, the reaction to David Stoll's accusations regarding the veracity of Rigoberta Menchú's writings has become an enterprise that is still growing as of the publication of this essay. Nevertheless, the power of literature that can be equally committed and still produce esthetic pleasure is alive and well, as seen in works by Augusto Monterroso (items **3532, 3533, 3534,** and **3535**) and Sergio Ramírez (items **3539** and **3540**), by far two of the most important Latin American writers at the beginning of the 21st century. Both authors illustrate how true literary value can overcome an endemic problem for Central American authors: the curse of national editions and minimal distribution. Most translations into English are done by courageous, smaller publishers, and conceivably, demanding commitment as the writer's exclusive task (see Monteforte, item **3531**) greatly contributes to a lack of exposure.

Writers such as Gioconda Belli serve as strong voices for the diversity of Central American literature, and women authors are certainly a force with which to be reckoned. However, there is no equality in the sense that both male and female authors tend to textualize their own gender's concerns, thereby falling into sexist themes or victimology. Coupled with these concerns are narratives devoted to racial hybridity (see Liano, item **3528**). Naturally, an accounting of the late-1970s and early-1980s exile experience was also to be expected (see Horra, item **3526,** and Schrijver, item **3545**), but the results have been uneven.

Perhaps the most consistent genre is still the short story, and its practitioners are on a par with writers elsewhere in the Americas. In this genre, Alfonso Chase is recognized as canonical. With his novel *El pavo real y la mariposa* (item **3521**), a major contribution to the type of historical novels that recreate the 19th and early-20th centuries, Chase should find a larger public, were it not for the national edition limitations mentioned above.

Tatiana Lobo's *Calypso* (item **3529**) is more promising as a novel than Belli's *Waslala: memorial del futuro* (item **3518**). Nevertheless, and more importantly, both are typical of the quandary in which Central Americans now find themselves: should they write lyrical allegories of sad historical conditions that possibly will never change (as does Belli) or should they not give in to the exoticism that sells well abroad, especially in the US, and write with a more cosmopolitan bent (as does Lobo)? This dichotomy seems to have been resolved by Rodrigo Rey Rosa, whose *Ningún lugar sagrado* (item **3541**) is a subtle, generic combination similar to the works of Monterroso and Ramírez. It appears that very few authors of recent generations, in their predictable (and in some cases accurate) desire to commit literary parricide, have given in to misguided "globalizing" impulses without noticing the richness of the Central American world. For this reason, Ricardo Roque Baldovinos' recovery and sorely needed edition of Salarrué's narrative is a major event (item **3543**), as are Jorge Eduardo Arellano's wonderful study of Darío's *Los raros* (item

3548) and his useful albeit limited *Diccionario de escritores centroamericanos* (item **3547**). The search for Central American identity is not the template anymore, which may be a sign of better things to come, despite the region's enduring and troubling social conditions, and devastating and continuous natural disasters.

PROSE FICTION

3514 Alemán, Adolfo. Cuentos completos. Edición de Oscar Acosta. Tegucigalpa: Editorial Iberoamericana; Editorial Guaymuras, 1996. 206 p. (Col. Fragua)

Alemán (1928–70) is, with David Moya Posas, Pompeyo del Valle, Armando Zelaya, and Oscar Acosta, one of the most important Honduran short story writers of the 20th century, a national literature that has not found a niche in Central America. This volume includes the three collections he published between 1959–67. Generally focusing on the tribulations and disappointments of country life, stories such as "Cuando sea Ministro," "Un Caso para el Dr. Morán," and "El Jarrón de los Mayas" show the complexity of which this talented writer was capable.

3515 Altamirano, Carlos Luis. Cuentos del 56. San José: Editorial Costa Rica, 1996. 160 p.

Recreates, in 14 "short stories," the legendary Costa Rican national campaign against the much-fictionalized and hated American mercenary William Walker. Altamirano's enhancement of peasant heroism is a result of both patriotism and literary treatment. The protagonists are the "people," and an integral part of the book is the sense of Central American unity against the invader.

3516 Alvarado-Watkins, Martha I. Honduras, adiós. Tegucigalpa: Editorial Guaymuras, 1996. 68 p.

Brief, fictionalized (she calls herself Mercedes), and fragmented memoir of the author's early life in Honduras. Uses conventional literary device of finding papers in dusty boxes in an attic to situate the story. Relies heavily on author's nostalgic memory of her adolescence.

3517 Angulo, Carlos Darío. Juegos de ceniza. San José: Editorial Realidad, 1996. 224 p.

Juan El Orangután, the anticommu-nist, French Legion protagonist, emigrates to Costa Rica after participating in the failed Bay of Pigs invasion. A seducer, Juan travels far and wide, yet always returns to Costa Rica or Nicaragua, usually for a woman. The story covers the years 1963–94, and the action moves from China to Moscow, where Juan dies and is incinerated. Attempts to textualize the effects of globalization; however, insubstantial asides and frequent uses of magical realism derail the effort.

3518 Belli, Gioconda. Waslala: memorial del futuro. Managua: Anamá Ediciones Centroamericanas, 1996. 379 p.

Belli typically combines fact and fiction in her novels. This futuristic novel may have the fortune of Fuentes' *Terra nostra*: a great failed attempt at an epic. Here, Belli experiments with the style of a *roman à clef* since the protagonists, Don José and Doña María, are based on the canonical poet José Coronel Urtecho and his wife, María Kautz. Toxic waste combined with smugglers, drugs, civil wars, and the magic realism of the mythical Waslala (naturally founded by poets) provide the setting for Belli's utopian message. The love between the journalist Rafael and the beautiful Melissandra, and the adventures that ensue, will appeal to a global audience.

3519 Canivell Arzú, Mariá Odette. María Isabel. Guatemala: Editorial Palo de Hormigo, 1995. 332 p. (Novela de fin de siglo; 3)

Canivell Arzú is a prime example of why more attention should be paid to the few exisiting Guatemalan women novelists. Her novel is a family saga, and its 11 chapters, excursus, and epilogue, framed by María Isabel's childhood and death, are generally dialogues that showcase the lives of the rich. Rants against neoliberalism are undermined by excessive attention to characters like the dysfunctional Lord Killarney, foreign locales, and the epilogue's attempt to gather narrative loose ends. Yet, the novel is successful in the sense that writing about this type of Central American family in literature is unusual.

3520 Chase, Alfonso. El hombre que se quedó adentro del sueño: relatos. San José: Editorial Univ. Estatal a Distancia, 1994. 79 p. (Col. Vieja y nueva narrativa costarricense; 13)

Chase is still the best known of Costa Rican short story writers, and in these nine stories, he returns to the literature of the fantastic vein, which first brought him notice outside of Costa Rica. This is particularly evident in the title story, "Quimera," and "Super Nova." The last text is an Ars Poetica in which he compares the conceptualization of his stories to that of the Uruguayan Felisberto Hernández.

3521 Chase, Alfonso. El pavo real y la mariposa. San José: Editorial Costa Rica, 1996. 301 p.

Set mainly in San José between 1885–89, with frequent jumps to other years and locales, Chase's historical novel deftly details the dialectic established between an authoritarian figure (José Joaquín Rodríguez) and a valiant intellectual (Manuelita Brenes y Peralta), who was Chase's relative. The founding of political parties and intrigues, as well as most of Costa Rica's insurgents and founding figures, appear in this novel. Brenes y Peralta's New York apartment is a refuge for Spanish American intellectuals like Vasconcelos, Mistral, Antonieta Rivas Mercado, Salomón de la Selva, Pedro Albizú Campos, Rómulo Gallegos, and Manuel Ugarte. Some of the events are apocryphal, but Chase's subtle intertwining of history, letters, psychological insights, and obvious research make this one of the best novels of this period.

3522 Chinchilla Núñez, Leonor. Voces en el tiempo. San José: Editorial Costa Rica, 1996. 63 p.

The narrative voice in this short novel about family values does not indicate how those values can be complicated by the subjectivity of friendship, solidarity, and patriotic "love of the land." Although Aunt Nice and the grandmother play a significant role in the narrator's life, the novel's six parts are ruled, in every sense, by men. Attempts to include "slice of life" connections with Costa Rican history are never fully developed.

3523 Darío, Rubén. Cuentos completos. Edición y notas de Ernesto Mejía Sánchez. Estudio introductorio de Raimundo Lida. Adiciones y cronología de Julio Valle-Castillo. Managua: Editorial Nueva Nicaragua, 1993. 436 p.

A reprint of the classic edition of Darío's stories published in 1950 by Mejía Sánchez, with a brilliant and erudite preliminary study by Raimundo Lida (see *HLAS 16:2619*). Valle-Castillo, who originally published this "second edition" in 1987 after Mejía Sánchez's death in 1985, adds "Historia de Mar," "Primera Impresión," and seven other stories, all discovered by Mejía Sánchez. He also adds a chronology whose template appears to be the one done for the Biblioteca Ayacucho 1994 edition of Darío's *Poesías*. The 1950 Mexican Fondo de Cultura Económica edition of *Cuentos completos*, reprinted in 1983, is still available, but this edition may be more accessible to Central Americans.

3524 Delgado Aburto, Leonel. Road movie y otros cuentos. Managua: Editorial Zorrillo, 1996. 91 p. (Col. Tío Conejo; 2)

"Boston es Peor" and the title story are this collection's true short stories. The first one is a dream-like sequence in which the main character describes how she faces the threats of some purported assassins. Unfortunately, the story never comes together. Among the shorter pieces, "Hijo Pródigo" is a convincing recreation of the impact of the revolutionary 1980s on two young lovers. Between the fantastic and a critique of provincial life, the stories fall into a solipsism used excessively in literary works.

3525 Duncan, Quince. Un señor de chocolate: treinta relatos de la vida de Quince. Heredia, Costa Rica: Programa de Publicaciones e Impresiones, Univ. Nacional, 1996. 113 p.

Duncan is one of the best known Costa Rican writers from the Caribbean coast, a section of the continent that is less known and written about in fiction or poetry. Full of bittersweet humor and colloquialisms, this is a delightful, and frequently tragic, autobiographical text. Duncan recreates anecdotally his life as a black man in his country and in his travels, encountering subtle racism at almost every step.

3526 Horra, Raúl de la. Se acabó la fiesta: novela. Guatemala: Editorial Artemis & Edinter, 1996. 183 p.

An uneven first novel that seems autobiographical, it is also a humorous description of the cultural differences a Guatemalan exiles faces in Paris where, like the author, the protagonist has gone to study psychology. Set in the 1970s, its attempts at a Bildungsroman are encumbered by excessive psychological language, uneven character development, and reliance on localized speech for humor.

3527 Kugler, Rosi. Como un árbol seco. Managua: SI Mujer, 1996. 223 p.: bibl.

This is a testimonial retelling of 12 years in the life of a woman. At times moving, it is primarily a denunciation of child sexual abuse. Unfortunately Kugler does not achieve a proper balance in her narrative, and the fictionalization she uses to protect the innocent undermine her endeavor.

3528 Liano, Dante. El misterio de San Andrés. México: Editorial Praxis, 1996. 400 p. (Col. El río)

Liano, a critic in his own right and long-time collaborator of Rigoberta Menchú, is one of the two best Guatemalan prose writers of his generation, along with Rodrigo Rey Rosa. In this historical novel which explores hybrid cultures, the main character Benito enters what can best be described as an "Asturias world." Colloquial language, bookish references, and irony (chapter XI set in a bordello is hilarious) combine to provide what is actually a bittersweet recreation of the Patzicía massacre.

3529 Lobo, Tatiana. Calypso. San Pedro, Costa Rica: Farben Grupo Editorial Norma, 1996. 267 p.

Lobo, a Chilean who for all literary intents and purposes is Costa Rican, is also the author of the well-received Asalto al paraíso (1992). The three parts of Calypso, a light-hearted novel, center on the precarious love affairs of Amanda, Eudora, and Matilda. Their lives offer an opportunity to portray the unheralded and ignored diversity of Costa Rican culture, and above all, its rhythm. There are memorable characters like "El Africano" in the first part, who may be "El Zambo's" double in the last part. Magic realism, marijuana, and Bob Marley's music, as well as the characters' hippie-like wanderings in Central America, make this an enjoyable if not committed novel.

3530 Méndez Vides. Mujeres tristes. Guatemala: Ediciones del Cadejo, 1995. 157 p.

Méndez Vides, a Guatemalan poet best known for his novel Las catacumbas (see HLAS 52:3592), collects 13 stories/vignettes focusing on the sad condition of women. In that regard, absences and ruptures are expected, yet the nucleus of these stories is the author's attempts at a new realism. For example, in "Nueva York," about a Guatemalan woman down on her luck in New York City, the author plays with stereotypes, not devoid of reverse racism, about Americans and Asians. When the character Margarita sees the Asian leave in a limousine, she is sad, not because she expected racial understanding from him, but because he is more fortunate than she. The stories' locales change, but the pessimism imposed by the narrative voice remains.

3531 Monteforte Toledo, Mario. La cueva sin quietud. Guatemala: Librerías Artemis-Edinter, 1996. 211 p.: ill.

Monteforte Toledo uses his fiction to unveil the ravages of capitalism and imperialism on Central America. Included here are 15 short stories from the period 1939–48, all previously published, but newly reworked by Monteforte. The best stories are those in the section entitled "Cuentos raros," centered on intellectual experiences derived from his readings. Other stories now seem dated, and most politicize human situations. Generally works divide characters into good (indigenous people) and evil (anyone who is white, especially Americans).

3532 Monterroso, Augusto. Los buscadores de oro. Barcelona: Editorial Anagrama, 1993. 110 p. (Narrativas Hispánicas/Anagrama; 145)

An undisputed master of the short story, this Honduran-born Guatemalan is the Central American writer who has deservedly attracted the greatest attention in Europe and Latin America during the last years. This first installment of his memoirs-cum-Künstlerroman covers his infancy up to 1936. His brilliant blending of both esthetic (early readings, music) and everyday experiences in a quirky, literate family, prove why writers as different as Issamov, Calvino, Fuentes, García Márquez, and Vargas Llosa acknowledge Monterroso as a master of contemporary prose. There is no other writer like Monterroso, nor does there appear to be one on the horizon of the 21st century.

3533 Monterroso, Augusto. Complete works & other stories. Translated by Edith Grossman. Introduction by Will H. Corral. Austin: Univ. of Texas Press, 1995. 152 p.: bibl. (Texas Pan American series)

Award-winning translation of most of Monterroso's stories, this critically acclaimed selection offers ample proof of how the writer has earned a place next to Quiroga, Borges, and Cortázar as a short story master. Ever disrespectful of genres and movements, a subtle evangelist of the new, Monterroso put an end to the myth of Latin American literary "tropicalism" (a term coined by Angel Rama). The range of these "stories" covers his initial commitment to social criticism (tempered by a larger concern for the esthetic) and his subsequent prose template for variants of what critics call "microstories," i.e., aphoristic vignettes or fragments. A prime example of the latter is the much anthologized (and analyzed) one-line story "The Dinosaur." In sum, this second book by Monterroso to appear in English (his fables were translated in 1971) is a brilliant introduction to a complex and highly readable prose stylist, a cosmopolitan writer who puts exoticism in its proper place. For translation specialist's comment, see item **4617**.

3534 Monterroso, Augusto. Tríptico. México: Fondo de Cultura Económica, 1995. 417 p.

Generous selection of author's "essays," this work includes pieces from "Movimiento perpetuo" (1972), "La palabra mágica" (1983), and "La letra e" (1987). The first collection also included some "short stories." Shows how Monterroso weaves many discourses with an incredible wit—at times mistakenly interpreted as sarcasm or irony. The last of Tríptico's three parts is a brilliant diary, bookish, quirky, sometimes snobbish (full of "dead white males"), and thus utterly humanistic. A necessary collection whose importance is underlined by the many critical books published about Monterroso in the 1990s.

3535 Monterroso, Augusto. La vaca. Madrid: Alfaguara, 1999. 149 p.

Monterroso assembles a few of the "essays" and articles he published after Tríptico (see item **3534**). His commitment to progressive ideas is unquestioned, and here he shows how a master imparts lessons. Equally unquestionable is his commitment to Western literature and its undeniable importance to Latin America. We read about Mayakovski, Virginia Woolf, Julian Barnes, Erasmus, Thomas Moore, and John Aubrey. Yet he always returns to Latin American masters (actually his peers): Borges, Rulfo, Onetti, Neruda. This book is proof that Monterroso does not repeat himself. There are wonderful essays on the advantages of underdevelopment and the theory of the short story. This collection ought to be translated immediately.

3536 Morera, Rosibel. Los héroes impuros: novela. San José: Editorial Costa Rica, 1995. 224 p.

Excellent novel that falls within the now-common practice of recovering colonial discourse in contemporary Spanish American narrative. Different from other works that fictionalize the "history" of the chroniclers' stories, Morera chooses to fictionalize the conquistadors, mainly Pizarro and Núñez de Balboa. They interact with Piedra Ceñuda/Esperanza, a sort of Malinche/Doña Marina, who guides them. But Cima, Napa, and other native women have a different purpose: to undo the myths about the discovery and subsequent colonialization of the Americas. Thus, the fable moves from Central to South America, and Amerindians and Spaniards are represented in their complexity, not as binary oppositions. Yet, the narrative sees both as poetic and surreal heroes, a choice which sometimes undermines the narrative thread.

3537 Murillo, Catalina. Largo domingo cubano. San José: Litografía e Imprenta LIL, 1995. 75 p.

Murillo's short novel centers on an old Costa Rican woman, Doña Berta, and her lyrical recollection of an affair with Don Carlos, an erudite Cuban. Her memories provide the frame for ideological threads about the differences between socialist and capitalist systems, the latter being privileged by the narrator, who is a younger, perhaps more cynical version of Doña Berta.

3538 Quesada, Uriel. Larga vida al deseo: relatos. San José: Editorial Univ. Estatal a Distancia, 1995. 117 p. (Col. Vieja y nueva narrativa costarricense; 24)

Quesada's third short story collection is made up of seven *microrelatos* and two longer pieces. Among the textualization of dreams and their relations to the everyday, the Cortazarian "Cómo Preparar la Vajila para un Desastre" is extremely witty, and the lack of local color reveals a very promising writer.

3539 Ramírez, Sergio. Un baile de máscaras. 1. ed. en México. México: Aguilar, Altea, Taurus, Alfaguara, 1995. 230 p. (Alfaguara hispánica)

In many senses a forerunner to his *Margarita, está linda la mar* (see item **3540**), this is the most riskily (and pleasantly) autobiographical of Ramírez's novels so far. He writes seemingly not about himself, but rather about the adults and the world that surround a child born in 1942, like he was. A rural masked ball is the fable's center, but the message is a nostalgic view of the music and popular culture that leave a permanent imprint on the young boy. Abundantly humorous (there is a boxing match between a blasphemous singer named Quevedo and Christ), rich in dialogue and characters who move in and out of time and space, and a treatise on onomastics. The novel's seven chapters emphasize without cynicism the richness of a close family.

3540 Ramírez, Sergio. Margarita, está linda la mar. Madrid: Santillana/Alfaguara, 1998. 373 p.

As he did in *Castigo divino* (1988), the great Nicaraguan novelist is fascinatingly concerned with creating a cultural context as well as recovering the intellectual templates of Central American mentalities. In 1907, when Darío purportedly writes "Margarita, the sea is beautiful" on a little girl's fan, and 1956, where a gathering of inexperienced, romantic intellectuals also plots to kill Anastasio Somoza, are the poles of this prize-winning novel. In between, Ramírez subtly weaves a national master narrative that, by emphasizing the humanity rather than the

myths that have sustained it, shows readers the hidden side of public figures. He manages to give a *modernista*, musical tinge to his language, thereby doubling the readers' attempts at deciphering its message. Fifteen years in the making, *Margarita, está linda la mar* is a masterpiece.

3541 Rey Rosa, Rodrigo. Ningún lugar sagrado. Barcelona: Seix Barral, 1998. 125 p. (Biblioteca breve)

In this collection of short stories, the Guatemalan writer Rey Rosa, one of the most highly touted fiction writers of his generation, textualizes in fascinating fashion the cultural constraints that most effect him. Most of the nine stories take place in Manhattan. Particularly attractive, and not only because of its epistolary/essay hybrid, is "Negocio para el milenio," which is the author's wry response to the phenomenal success of a private prison enterprise. Guatemala seems to be a distant memory, briefer pieces such as "El Chef," "Vídeo," and "Coincidencia" accurately capture the metropolitan ambience, even though the author's view of urban violence is frequently clichéd.

3542 Rodríguez, Ileana. Women, guerrillas, and love: understanding war in Central America. Translated by Ileana Rodríguez with Robert Carr. Minneapolis: Univ. of Minnesota Press, 1996. 199 p.: bibl., index.

The 14 chapters posit a regendering of revolutionary poetics, which is accomplished by reworking concepts such as "(new)man," "woman," and "subaltern." The predictability of Rodríguez's arguments and dated historical referents do not detract from solid analyses, like those in chapter eight regarding Mario Roberto Morales' "El esplendor de la pirámide" and those in the next chapter on Oreamuno's "La ruta de su evasión." The author focuses on her strength—narratives from Cuba and her native Nicaragua.

3543 Salarrué. Narrativa completa. Prólogo, compilación y notas de Ricardo Roque Baldovinos. 1. ed., Ed. conmemorativa del centenario de su natalicio. San Salvador: Dirección de Publicaciones e Impresos/ CONCULTURA, 1999. 3 v.: bibl., ill. (Col. Orígenes)

Centennial edition of an under-rated

short story writer and novelist, Roque's wonderful edition will help to recover this Salvadoran master of the esoteric and the oral tradition. Generally considered the best Salvadoran writer of the 20th century, rightly admired by Gabriela Mistral, Salarrué mixed the vernacular and the fantastic without disdain for perverse psychologies. Each work has a solid examination of variants by Roque, and longer works like *El señor de la burbuja* (1927) and the tales of *O-Yarkandal* (1929/ 1971), both included in vol. 1, put in perspective the avant-garde initiatives of other Spanish American writers of the period. In vol. 2, Roque revises and provides the fullest collection of Salarrué's folkloric tales *Cuentos de cipotes* (1945/1971; see *HLAS 38:6579* and *HLAS 40:6653*), which complement the complicated and rich stories for which he is best known, *Cuentos de barro* (1934), included in vol. 1. Vol. 3, also edited masterfully by Roque, includes Salarrué's last stories; a short novel; and his longest work, *Catleya luna* (1974/1980; see *HLAS 40:6652*), written in the 1950s according to Roque, but published much later.

3544 Sarasqueta de Jordán, Edith. Piedras sin rostro. Panamá: Impresora de la Nación, 1996. 272 p.: ill.

Bonifatti, Moretti, and Watson are the characters around whom Sarasueta de Jordán weaves a tale of intrigue and corruption. The novel fictionalizes the assassination of a man reminiscent of John F. Kennedy, although in this version he has 12 sons. This thriller ultimately fizzles, and readers are subjected to moralizing and a loyalty to a main character with no flaws. What does impress is the earthiness with which the author infuses her novel, a register generally unknown in Latin America.

3545 Schrijver, Guido de. El apartamento y otros cuentos del exilio. Guatemala: Disop, 1995. 107 p.

Three short stories and five shorter pieces make up what could have been a "short story cycle," i.e., a collection held together by a common theme or character. There is no index, and the only unifying thread appears to be the foibles of Central Americans exiled in Europe. This collection exhibits clichés about cultural misunderstanding, victimization, and resentment, especially during the 1970s and early 1980s.

3546 Soto, Rodrigo. Dicen que los monos éramos felices. San Pedro de la Bosch, Costa Rica: Farben Grupo Editorial Norma, 1995. 163 p.

These 15 stories demonstrate this Costa Rican author's preference for urban, postmodern locales and existential problems. The longer pieces, such as "Los Dos Caminos," "Mayke Goris Viene a Centroamérica a Decir Adiós," and "Un Día en la Playa" contain complex characters and surreal settings and would be well placed in any anthology of Spanish American short stories.

LITERARY CRITICISM AND HISTORY

3547 Arellano, Jorge Eduardo. Diccionario de escritores centroamericanos. Managua: ASDI-Bibliotecas Nacionales de Centroamérica y Panamá, 1997. 154 p.: bibl., ill.

Provides a biographical and bibliographical compendium of Central American writers. The brief entries for Costa Rica (65), El Salvador (55), Guatemala (74), Honduras (65), Nicaragua (78), and Panama (65) cover mainly 20th-century writers (the earliest is Nicaraguan Mariano Barreto, 1856–1927). Each national section is preceded by commentaries on that country's most important writers, thus for Guatemala there are no entries for Asturias or Arévalo Martínez but rather a note about each. Despite his attention to Panama, the youngest Central American state, Arellano has omitted discussion of the important colonial and 19th-century literatures for Nicaragua and Guatemala. Although flawed, this work is necessary given the paucity of Central American publications of this kind and limited access to them.

3548 Arellano, Jorge Eduardo. Los raros: una lectura integral. Managua: Instituto Nicaragüense de Cultura, 1996. 216 p.: bibl., ill.

Arellano is the most important Nicaraguan critic today, and one of the most visible in Central America due to his tireless work. Although there are excellent individual articles on Rubén Darío's precursory and still influential "biographies" known as *Los raros* (1896/1905), Arellano provides the first thorough study of that collection's complexity, which is really a study of modernity. This is an amazingly rich study of forerunners and imitators, of the book's Spanish American and European reception, its cultural context, and internal coherence. Excellent, fair-minded, and exhaustive analysis. Absolutely required reading.

3549 Craft, Linda J. Novels of testimony and resistance from Central America. Gainesville: Univ. Press of Florida, 1997. 237 p.: bibl., index.

In seven chapters, Craft argues for a new, generic recognition for what used to be known as "political novels." Discussion is generally convincing, well-researched, and occasionally revealing. The first two chapters and their conclusions are similar to accepted scholarly arguments. Craft is at her best when analyzing works by Claribel Alegría, Manlio Argueta, and Belli, in that order. More attention could have been given to Sergio Ramírez's development, which does not fit into the author's thesis, and to Rigoberto Menchú. A noteworthy error: Monterroso never wrote a book titled "Mr. Taylor & Co." (the actual title story is from the 1950s). The title refers to a Cuban selection of his stories.

3550 Medina Durón, Juan Antonio. Historia general de la literatura hondureña y glosario de términos literarios. Tegucigalpa?: s.n., 1995? 113 p.: appendices, bibl.

Its three chapters cover, respectively and briefly, the colonial period (up to the neoclassic movement), the 19th century, and the 20th century. The bibliographies for the first two periods lack substance. Three appendices by other critics deal with the 19th-century Padre Reyes (author of *pastorelas*), Honduran literature in general, and the essay as a written form.

3551 Noguerol Jiménez, Francisca. La trampa en la sonrisa: sátira en la narrativa de Augusto Monterroso. Sevilla, Spain: Univ. de Sevilla, 1995. 252 p.

First full European treatment of Monterroso's work up to *Los buscadores de oro* (see item **3532**). This is a revised version of

the author's very competent doctoral dissertation. Argues that Monterroso's writing is imbued with satire. This is a serious endeavor, particularly in the third and fourth chapters in which textual analysis dominates. Analysis of Monterroso's apocryphal and parodic "novel" *Lo demás es silencio: la vida y la obra de Eduardo Torres* (1978) is excellent: accurate in its study of sources and intertextual references.

3552 Pasos Marciacq, Ricardo. De la mujer la belleza y el arte: nicaraocalli teote Güegüense. Managua?: Ediciones Univ., 1993. 69 p.: bibl., ill. (Col. Tlatolli)

Purported recovery of an epic poem about the indigenous cacique called Nicarao (Nicaragua) and the Spanish conquerors, Pasos' lyrical narrative attempts to distinguish "historical truth" from fiction. Since his work is a hybrid of both types of discourse, aided and abetted by real and fictional document fragments, glossaries, and digressions, Pasos' attempt to explain the meaning of terms like güegüense and others (thereby forcing and recovering patriotism) ultimately fails.

3553 Urbina, Nicasio. La estructura de la novela nicaragüense. Managua: Anamá Ediciones Centroamericanas, 1995. 150 p.: bibl.

After Jorge Eduardo Arellano, Urbina is one of the better (and among the very few) interpreters of nonpolitical Nicaraguan literature. This work focuses on the conventional novel. His approach is predominantly narratological, and despite the formal limits of that methodology, Urbina's solid knowledge of Nicaraguan literary history rescues many 1920s and 1930s novels. The older works help contextualize the contemporary novels that are his corpus. Narratological terminology overwhelms the book's three short parts, so we learn mostly about Aguilar, Ramírez, Chávez Alfaro, and other representative novelists.

Hispanic Caribbean

EDNA ACOSTA-BELÉN, *Distinguished Service Professor of Latin American and Caribbean Studies and Women's Studies, and Director of the Center for Latino, Latin American, and Caribbean Studies (CELAC), at the University at Albany, SUNY*

UVA DE ARAGÓN, *Acting Director, Cuban Research Institute, Florida International University*

PUERTO RICO

IN RECENT YEARS PUERTO RICAN LETTERS and literary criticism reflect some new trends. One of the most obvious developments among Spanish-speaking writers is their incursion into the English-language market. Because of Puerto Rico's current colonial relationship with the US, most island Puerto Ricans are exposed to the formal study of the English language throughout their schooling and in their professional training, in addition to being native speakers of Spanish. This bilingualism has become even more important today with the globalization of the world economy, prevalent commuter migration patterns between the island and the continental US, and the transnational connections maintained by island Puerto Ricans with the US Puerto Rican communities.

The "crossover" writing of some Puerto Rican authors has yielded some important works in recent years. Bilingual island writers such as Rosario Ferré, well known in Latin America and the Caribbean for her prose fiction works, has written two novels in English: *The House on the Lagoon* (*HLAS 56:3563*) and *Eccentric Neighborhoods* (1998). She then proceeded to rewrite these novels in Spanish, rather than having them translated. Such is the case of the Spanish versions, *La casa de la laguna* (item **3566**) y *Vecindarios excéntricos* (item **3567**). A few prior works by Ferré had already caught the attention of English translators and were available to the US market. But the author's last two novels are a good example of how bilingual writers increasingly are trying to penetrate the wider US market by using their creativity to produce similar, but not necessarily the same, literary works in each language.

On the other hand, Puerto Rican writers born or raised in the US, who write primarily, although not exclusively, in English, are finding an audience in the Spanish-speaking world. Major publishing houses are commissioning their works to Spanish translators and even establishing editorial divisions that promote the work of US Latino writers in Spanish-speaking countries (e.g., Vintage Español). They are following the steps of smaller ethnic presses, such as Arte Público Press and Bilingual Press, which for many years have played a leading role in making some of this literature available in both languages. Prose fiction works originally published in English, such as *La línea del sol* (1996) and *Bailando en silencio* (item **3581**) by Judith Ortiz Cofer, *Cuando era puertorriqueña* (*HLAS 56:3585*) and *Casi una mujer* (item **3589**) by Esmeralda Santiago, and *Por estas calles bravas* (item **3591**) by Piri Thomas are good examples of this crossover trend.

The area of literary criticism is showing the increasing influence of poststructuralist theories, with postmodern, postcolonial, and feminist approaches at the vanguard. Interdisciplinary academic fields such as Puerto Rican, Latino, women's, gay and lesbian, and cultural studies have allowed humanists and social scientists to blur the boundaries of their respective disciplines and produce more provocative interdisciplinary interpretations of cultural and artistic production, particularly as it relates to identity issues.

The notion of a Puerto Rican literature that surpasses island borders to include Puerto Rican writers born or raised in the US is reflective of the commuter migratory experience of Puerto Ricans as well as that of other Latin American and Caribbean (im)migrants. This is a pattern that is also developing in the literature of other US Latino groups vis-à-vis their countries of origin. The traditional literary canons of their Latino countries of origin are being challenged to include the work of migrants who might write primarily in English or bilingually. While there is a long tradition of Latin American or Caribbean writing in exile by authors who lived in the US or other parts of the world, their works were mostly written in Spanish and are studied as part of their respective countries' national literatures. However, this has not been the case with more permanent (im)migrants to the US or with their US-born or raised offspring.

Studies such as *From Bomba to Hip-Hop: Puerto Rican Culture and Latino Identity* (item **3601**) by Juan Flores and *Listening to Salsa: Gender, Latino Popular Music, and Puerto Rican Cultures* (item **3597**) by Frances Aparicio are excellent examples of how leading literary critics are paying increasing attention to the interconnections between the cultural minority experiences of Puerto Ricans, the construction of their identities, and the creativity manifested in different artistic realms—literature, music, visual arts, performance—especially, in popular culture.

In *El arte de bregar* (item **3600**), Arcadio Díaz Quiñones, a leading critic, provides a series of insightful essays about language and writing, and how these are constituted, manipulated, and adapted to the diverse colonial spaces of Puerto Ricans. In *Partes de un todo* (item **3598**), literary critic Efraín Barradas, one of the pioneers of the study of US Puerto Rican letters, collects some of his most important essays on the emergence and development of this body of literature. The issue of Puerto Rican/Latino representation in a variety of texts/contexts—the media, literature, performance—are the focus of two major works: *Latin Looks: Images of Latinas and Latinos in the U.S. Media*, edited by Clara Rodríguez (item **3603**); and Alberto Sandoval- Sánchez's *José, Can You See?: Latinos On and Off Broadway* (item **3607**). These books provide a much needed sustained critique of Anglo-American discourse and representations of Latinos/as.

Journals such as the *Latino(a) Research Review* (formerly the *Latino Review of Books*) continue to promote the kinds of interdisciplinary approaches and "border crossings" that link the works of US Latino writers, artists, and scholars with those of their counterparts in their native countries. [EA-B]

CUBA AND THE DOMINICAN REPUBLIC

La narrativa cubana está en alza. Así lo muestran los importantes premios literarios otorgados recientemente a varios autores cubanos, como el Premio Cervantes a Guillermo Cabrera Infante, el Alfaguara a Alberto Diego, el Gijón a Matías Montes Huidobro y el Azorín a Daína Chaviano, estos tres últximos por novelas. Otra señal del creciente interés por la literatura cubana es el continuado éxito de ventas de Zoé Valdés con su última novela *Café Nostalgia* (item **3592**). Como todos los cubanos, los escritores de la isla viven, escriben y publican en los cuatro puntos cardinales del mundo. La selección a continuación mostrará obras publicadas de Barcelona a Miami, de Madrid a La Habana, de North Carolina a México, de Austin a Leuven, Bélgica. También han aparecido un buen número de trabajos críticos en inglés así como la antología de cuentos *The Voice of the Turtle* (item **3595**).

En cuanto a la temática, puede señalarse que aún está presente la novela policíaca, tan en auge dentro de la isla hace algunos años, como lo muestran *¿Quién mató a Iván Ivanovich?* de Humberto Arenal (item **3557**) y *Máscaras* de Leonardo Padura (item **3582**). El intimismo, las relaciones personales, el amor, dan aliento a algunas obras como *Salmos paganos* de Alberto Garrandés (item **3568**) y *A Tarzán con seducción y engaño* de Humberto Arenal (item **3556**). La narrativa cubana, sin embargo, no parece poder escapar la realidad sociopolítica del país, que aparece como un constante telón de fondo, que nos lleva por igual a un mundo marginal de "rockeros", que al fervor religioso de los que hacen peregrinaciones al Rincón de San Lázaro o a la desfachatez de dos adolescentes que se someten a abortos como si se tomaran un refresco. Los recuerdos de la infancia y el despertar de la adolescencia continúan siendo temas recurrentes como lo comprueban *La ruta del mago* de Carlos Victoria (item **3594**) y *Techo a cuatro aguas* de Luis Marré (item **3575**), a lo que se le añade un nuevo matiz—la aguda identificación con un grupo, una generación—en obras como *Café Nostalgia* de Zoé Valdés (item **3592**) e *Informe contra mí mismo* de Eliseo Alberto (item **3554**).

En cuanto al estilo, la variedad es amplia, pues nos encontramos con deliciosas prosas poéticas—la que exhibe Antonio José Ponte en *Las comidas profundas* (item **3584**), es un buen ejemplo—y, en el otro extremo, el crudo realismo de Zoé Valdés. Siguen floreciendo el cuento y las narraciones breves, y se observa asimismo un interés por el género de las memorias. En las re-ediciones y la crítica, se observa una preferencia por autores del siglo XX de reconocido prestigio.

La narrativa dominicana continúa muy apegada a la realidad sociopolítica del país. Se advierte un esfuerzo serio de ir construyendo un canon literario adscrito a medidas más rigurosas de valoración. El cuento sigue prevaleciendo como género. También es notable el número de mujeres escritoras. De particular interés es la publicación de obras escogidas de la feminista Abigail Mejías Solière (item **3576**). [UA]

PROSE FICTION

3554 Alberto, Eliseo. Informe contra mí mismo. México: Aguilar, Altea, Taurus, Alfaguara, 1997. 293 p. (Extra Alfaguara)

Cuenta la historia de la generación nacida en los 50 en Cuba y que se quedó en la isla. La generación que bebió Triple C en el Gato Tuerto, que no se perdía un concierto de Silvio, y a la que "le tocó en suerte vivir el arco del proceso revolucionario, desde la ilusión hasta el desencanto." Escrito en una prosa entre irónica y tierna, directa y profunda, filosa y sensible, irreverente y afianzada en cubanísimas raíces. Esta memoria incorpora cartas, retratos de familia, y cuentos. Una aguda radiografía de los cubanos, su improvisación, chivatería, sandunga, compadreo, piña, despelote, chisme, truquito, guapería, vacilón, choteo, no cojan lucha, chapucería, dale a quien no te dio, sálvese quien pueda y el hacer siempre las cosas a nuestra manera.

3555 Antología del cuento dominicano. Recopilación de Diógenes Céspedes. Santo Domingo: Editora de Colores, 1996. 340 p.: bibl.

Veintiséis narraciones cortas de autores que van desde el clásico Juan Bosch hasta otros más jóvenes, todos acompañados de una nota biobibliográfica y un juicio valorativo. Se incluye un capítulo que pasa revista a otras antologías dominicanas del mismo género y un interesante muestrario de los mecanismos de plagio de escritores que se han inspirado, con poca fortuna, en textos de autores extranjeros.

3556 Arenal, Humberto. A Tarzán, con seducción y engaño: novela. La Habana: Editorial Letras Cubanas, 1995. 250 p.

La búsqueda de la felicidad y de una razón existencial a través de la relación de una pareja sirven de base a esta narración que se adentra en el debatido e imponderable tema del amor.

3557 Arenal, Humberto. ¿Quién mató a Iván Ivánovich?: divertimento novador. La Habana: Ediciones Unión, Unión de Escritores y Artistas de Cuba, 1995. 100 p. (La rueda dentada)

Novela policial con humor criollo. La investigación de la misteriosa muerte de un ruso desnudo en una habitación de un hotel le da la vuelta al mundo en una prosa rica en intertextualidad y remozadas frases de cajón.

3558 Balseros, historia oral del éxodo cubano del '94. Entrevistas, transcripción y compilación por Felicia Guerra. Traducción al inglés e introducción por Tamara Alvarez-Detrell. Miami, Fla.: Ediciones Universal, 1997. 187 p.: ill., map. (Colección Cuba y sus jueces)

Transcripciones de entrevistas con varios "balseros" muchos de los que se echaron al mar en 1994. Narran las razones de sus salidas, la vida diaria, las condiciones de la salud pública y educación en la isla, así como la travesía marítima, la estancia en los campamentos y sus esperanzas de futuro.

3559 Betancourt, Luis A. Maceta. Madrid: Vosa, 1996. 105 p. (Los libros de la medianoche; 11)

Con la Cuba actual como telón de fondo, una novela sobre el mundo del delito. Una visión crítica de un país cercado donde sin embargo todavía la pasión persiste.

3560 Bobes León, Marilyn. Alguien tiene que llorar. La Habana: Casa de las Américas; Colombia: Instituto Colombiano de Cultura, 1995. 69 p.

En estos relatos entrelazados, merecedores del Premio Las Américas 1995, se destaca el dominio del oficio, una variedad de registros en el protagonismo femenino y la complejidad de las relaciones humanas. Llama la atención el factor generacional, temática de creciente presencia en la narrativa cubana.

3561 Cañellas, Miguel R. Primer juego y otros cuentos. Havana: Ediciones Unión, 1996. 62 p.

Relatos breves que traducen el universo de aulas, enamoramientos, inquietudes, compañerismo, miedo, y rivalidades que informan el agridulce transcurrir de la adolescencia.

3562 Carpentier, Alejo. El amor a la ciudad. Madrid: Santillana, 1996. 187 p. (Textos de escritor)

Deliciosas crónicas sobre La Habana hechas con amor y humor. Carpentier recorre sus calles y plazas, su puerto y la noche, sus cambiantes rostros de ciudad provinciana o cosmopolita, pequeño burguesa o prerevolucionaria. Esta recopilación de artículos periodísticos y breves ensayos salpica la descripción de la capital cubana con pintorescas anécdotas de personajes famosos o desconoci-

dos. La prosa de Carpentier se desviste de su disfraz barroco para traducir, con el paso ligero de un caminante feliz, sus andanzas por la ciudad portuaria.

3563 Díaz Mantilla, Daniel. Las palmeras domésticas. La Habana: Casa Editora Abril, 1996. 39 p.

Un inquietante relato de viajeros al Rincón, "rockeros" y balseros que huyen de una ciudad invisible, mágica y decadente al borde de un malecón o un abismo.

3564 Diego, Eliseo. Cuentos escogidos. Selección y notas de Redys Puebla Borrero. La Habana: Editorial Letras Cubanas, 1995. 157 p.

Recopilación de cuentos del ganador del Premio Juan Rulfo 1993, extraídos de distintos libros publicados a lo largo de más de 40 años (1942–89). Una muestra de la versatilidad del autor y de su absoluto dominio de la técnica del cuento, aunque el poeta siempre asoma en estas narraciones donde la ironía y la ternura se combinan con lo fantástico y lo grotesco. Son de especial interés los cuentos muy breves, que por su concisión y capacidad de sorpresa dejan una fuerte impresión al lector.

3565 Fernández Revuelta, Alina. Alina: memorias de la hija rebelde de Fidel Castro. Barcelona: Plaza & Janés, 1997. 250 p.: ill., index, ports., table.

Testimonio de la compleja vida de la hija natural de Fidel Castro, producto de sus breves amores con Naty Revuelta. El texto huye del panfleterismo fácil y del ajuste de cuentas familiares. Se transparentan claramente, sin embargo, los conflictos de la narradora con sus progenitores, con el régimen que encabeza su padre y con su propia identidad. Recrea con la fuerza de la vivencia y de un punto de mira privilegiado ciertos aspectos de la realidad cubana.

3566 Ferré, Rosario. La casa de la laguna. New York: Vintage Books, 1997. 430 p.: table. (Vintage español)

Narrates lives of several generations of a wealthy island family and how their social world contrasts with that of less-privileged Puerto Ricans, including those who are black or racially mixed. Female characterizations are always important in Ferré's narratives as women face lingering patriarchal values and search for their own survival strategies. The house near the lagoon serves as the main stage where some of the conflicts and contradictions of Puerto Rican society are carried out or revealed.

3567 Ferré, Rosario. Vecindarios excéntricos. New York: Vintage Español/ Vintage Books, 1999. 452 p.: ill., index.

Attempts to portray social dislocations of a Puerto Rican society transformed by the Spanish-Cuban-American War and US intervention through the lives of two island families. Ferré captures the decadence of the old Spanish world and the ascent of a new dominant class with a different outlook and values as they impact the lives of her characters.

3568 Garrandés, Alberto. Salmos paganos. La Habana: Ediciones Unión, Unión de Escritores y Artistas de Cuba, 1996. 96 p. (La rueda dentada)

La identidad y el destino, un triángulo amoroso y pavoroso, y el dilema de la percepción del mundo son los temas de los tres relatos que componen este libro luminoso y sombrío como los atardeceres junto a un mar de invierno.

3569 Heras León, Eduardo. La noche del capitán. México: Coordinación de Difusión Cultural, Dirección de Literatura/ UNAM, 1995. 223 p. (Textos de difusión cultural. Serie Rayuela internacional)

Estos 21 relatos escritos entre 1969–90 forman un retablo del acontecer cubano, desde los campos de batalla de Playa Girón hasta la desolación de un joven en espera de una beca de estudios en una Habana donde todos sus parientes se han ido y donde todavía son sutilmente palpables las diferencias de edad, clase, y raza.

3570 Hernández-Chiroldes, J. Alberto. A diez pasos del paraíso. Miami, Fla.: Universal, 1996. 214 p. (Colección Caniquí)

Diez cuentos que oscilan entre Cuba y los EE.UU., la adolescencia y el exilio, la nostalgia y su deconstrucción. Estas narraciones cortas no siempre cuentan con los finales sorprendentes que recomendaba Poe, pero se destacan, sin embargo, por la hábil (re)creación de ambientes y personajes.

3571 Lockward, Angel. Crónica de una página en blanco. Dominican Republic: s.n., 1997. 249 p.

Seis relatos donde se mezcla lo sexual y lo político. Páginas que de tanto intentar acercarse a la realidad se alejan peligrosamente de la buena literatura.

3572 Lockward, Angel. El gabinete de la sombra: novela. Santo Domingo: Editora de Colores, 1997. 253 p.

La historia de un hombre que encontró en el amor una razón para cambiar es el eje de la trama de esta novela. Su tema central es la debilidad de las instituciones en los países latinoamericanos. Los crímenes y robos que encubren la ambición y la corrupción en el manejo del poder público son los hilos que sustentan esta narración, que se instala fácilmente en los cánones de la literatura continental, tan ligada a la realidad sociopolítica.

3573 López Velaz, Elio Fidel. El reverso de la moneda. La Habana: Casa Editora Abril, 1996. 117 p.

En esta primera novela de este joven autor se perfilan dos maneras de asumir la vida, dos actitudes vitales, dos talantes psicológicos, dos hermanos que se unen en un discurso narrativo y una realidad compartida.

3574 Lozada, Angel. La patografía. México: Planeta, 1998. 1 v.

Provocative novel about the almost taboo subject of homosexuality in Puerto Rican culture and society. Belongs to the *bildungsroman* genre since it narrates the childhood and adolescence of a Puerto Rican protagonist growing with the conflicts stemming from his sexual orientation and surrounded by an environment of religious hypocrisy and bigotry. These prejudices allegorically transform the man into a gigantic *pato*. The term *pato* (literally, duck) is a derogatory term used throughout the Spanish-speaking world to refer to homosexuals.

3575 Marré, Luis. Techo a cuatro aguas. La Habana: Ediciones Unión, 1996. 88 p. (Noveleta)

El cuaderno de un joven de campo que anota su asombro ante la vida, su despertar sexual, relatos de familia, secretos de los abuelos, la fascinación con la naturaleza. Tiene el encanto de la difícil facilidad de lo sencillo.

3576 Mejía, Abigail. Obras escogidas. Recopilación de Arístides Incháustegui y Blanca Delgado Malagón. Santo Domingo:

Secretaría de Estado de Educación, Bellas Artes y Cultos, 1995. 2 v.: bibl., ill., index.

Sorprendente recopilación de textos-cuentos, ensayos, críticas literarias, perfiles biográficos—de esta escritora, activista feminista y pedagoga que murió en 1941, un año después de que fueron reconocidos en Santo Domingo los derechos civiles de la mujer.

3577 Menéndez, Ricardo. La "seguridad" siempre llama dos veces—: y los orichas también. Miami, Fla.: Ediciones Universal, 1997. 318 p. (Colección Caniquí)

Narración que va de Cuba a Estados Unidos, del exilio a la isla, de novela de suspenso a crónica de la violencia política, de una historia de amor al mundo misterioso de los *ñáñigos*, de la realidad a la ficción, de la vida cotidiana a las pesadillas de una compleja red de inteligencia y contrainteligencia. Todo en una prosa amena y sin pretensiones puesta al servicio de la narración.

3578 Mozo, Emilio M. Discretos aportes. Prólogo de Alfredo Pérez Alencart y epílogo de Carmen Ruiz Barrionuevo. Salamanca, Spain: Cátedra de Poética "Fray Luis de León," Univ. Pontificia, 1997. 99 p.: ill. (Colección "Fedro" de relato; 1)

Una serie de relatos breves, basados en recuerdos de infancia, que van creando un universo propio, donde la visión infantil se ve empañada por la pobreza, las humillaciones y la triste ironía. La visión retrospectiva del autor le añade un velo de esa nostalgia de exilio que bordea peligrosamente con la distorsión de la realidad.

3579 Mozo, Emilio M. Shakespeare tropical. Salamanca, Spain: Cátedra de Poética "Fray Luis de León", Univ. Pontifícia de Salamanca, 1997. 83 p.: port. (Colección "Fedro" de relato; 2)

En prosa alegórica, engañosamente poética, sin puntuación ni mayúsculas, como en un largo, incesante monólogo, un dictador tropical—toda semejanza con la realidad es pura coincidencia—narra sus asombros, debilidades, soledades, muerte, resurrección, engaños, indignaciones, abusos, y epitafio.

3580 Nieto, Benigno S. Los paraísos artificiales. Miami, Fla: Ediciones Universal, 1997. 484 p. (Coleccion caniqui)

Novela que se adentra en el drama de la ilusión y desilusión de dos parejas cuya trayectoria en la Revolución afecta sus vidas de formas diversas y dramática. La prosa es sobria y exacta, y la tensión entre la lealtad y la frustración se revela con ironía y ternura.

3581 Ortiz Cofer, Judith. Bailando en silencio: escenas de una niñez puertorriqueña. Traducción de Elena Olazagasti-Segovia. Houston, Tex.: Piñata Books, 1997. 159 p.

Collection of short stories and poems based on author's life experiences with her relatives in a small Puerto Rican town and in the Puerto Rican community of Paterson, N.J. The selected poems and stories are linked by author's memories of growing up between two cultures and the influence of her mother and grandmother in her personal development as a writer and storyteller.

3582 Padura, Leonardo. Máscaras. Barcelona: Tusquets Editores, 1997. 233 p. (Colección Andanzas; 292)

Esta novela, que obtuvo el Premio Internacional de Novela "Café Gijón" de 1995, fue editada anteriormente en España por Tusquets Editores, y ha sido traducida a diversos idiomas. Es la tercera de la tetralogía que se ha propuesto el autor bajo el título general *Las cuatro estaciones*. Trama de corte policial—la investigación del asesinato de un trasvesti que aparece muerto en el Bosque de La Habana—*Máscaras* penetra en un mundo en que nada es lo que parece.

3583 Pérez, Jorge Angel. Lapsus calami. La Habana: Ediciones Unión, 1996. 84 p.

Colección de cuentos breves, algunos muy breves, de penetrante humor y profunda ironía. Metáforas plurivalentes, planteamientos atrevidos y un dominio de las técnicas narrativas colocan a este volumen en una zona aún poco explorada en la narrativa cubana.

3584 Ponte, Antonio José. Las comidas profundas. Ilustrado con dibujos de Ramón Alejandro. Angers, France: Editions Deleatur, 1997. 43 p.: ill. (Colección Baralanube)

Deliciosas prosas poéticas en torno al tema de las comidas en Cuba. Libro con sabor y saber impregnado del aroma de la tierra. Comidas cruzadas entre la vigilia y el sueño, la realidad y la fantasía. Desde un país en "período especial" este recorrido gastronómico-literario es un *tour de force* de la imaginación, un estilete subversivo que entretiene el hambre colectivo con el poder de la letra de molde sazonada de cultura y poesía.

3585 Rivera, Martha. He olvidado tu nombre. Santo Domingo: Casa de Teatro, 1997. 139 p.

La vida y la muerte voluntaria de dos amigas, dos hermanas, espejo y reflejo de sí mismas y del mundo de fin de siglo que las rodea.

3586 Rizik, Marisela. El tiempo del olvido. Eugene, Or.: Multicultural Media, 1996. 280 p.

La historia de dos mujeres—Lorenza y Hermi—fragmentadas, cuyos destinos se bifurcan en las márgenes del silencio. El mundo de afuera, contaminado de represión ideológica y autoritaria, sirve para enmarcar este rito del desconsuelo.

3587 Rodríguez Soriano, René. La radio y otros boleros. Santo Domingo: Biblioteca Nacional, 1996. 116 p. (Colección Orfeo. Serie Cuento; 1)

Estos relatos no pueden escapar el trasfondo histórico de la era de Trujillo, tan presente en la narrativa dominicana, pero esta vez la mirada es oblicua, y la fantasía desborda la realidad.

3588 Rubio Albert, Carlos. Saga. New York: Zinnia Books, 1997. 186 p.

En una prosa neobarroca, asentada en los preceptos establecidos por tantos de sus compatriotas como Carpentier, Lezama Lima, y Sarduy, Rubio Albert ha creado un texto de gran originalidad, abierto a múltiples lecturas, siempre con un hálito de magia y sensualidad.

3589 Santiago, Esmeralda. Casi una mujer. Traducción de Nina Torres-Vidal. New York: Vintage Español, 1999. 312 p.

Author's third novel and a long-awaited sequel to her first autobiographical novel, *Cuando era puertorriqueña* (see *HLAS 56:3585*). She continues to chronicle her life as she leaves her childhood behind and enters adult life where her American values increasingly clash with those of her Puerto Rican parents. Most of all, this novel helps understand how Esmeralda Santiago, the writer was formed and became a writer.

3590 Sarduy, Severo. Cartas. Selección, prólogo y notas de Manuel Díaz Martínez. Madrid: Editorial Verbum, 1996. 61 p.: ill. (Ensayo)

Estas cartas, documentos, poemas—en la tipografía de aquellas viejas Olivettis—y fotos amarillosas por los años y la nostalgia, no sólo dan una visión de la amistad entre Sarduy y su destinatario, sino que reflejan París a través de los ojos de un poeta exiliado y una Cuba vista a la distancia con tanta perplejidad ante su inexplicable "burocracia" como melancolía—melancolía creadora, pero melancolía al fin—por sus esencias.

3591 Thomas, Piri. Por estas calles bravas. Traducido por Suzanne Dod Thomás. New York: Vintage Books, 1998. 368 p. (Vintage español)

Long-overdue translation of classic novel *Down these mean streets* (New York: Knopf, 1967), which was important for the development of US Puerto Rican literature. This *bildungsroman* focuses on the adolescent life of the author, a black Puerto Rican growing up in Spanish Harlem in the 1960s. The novel introduces important issues of racial discrimination, intergenerational and ethnic conflict, and the overall marginalization of Puerto Ricans during those years.

3592 Valdés, Zoé. Café Nostalgia. Barcelona: Planeta, 1997. 361 p. (Colección Autores españoles e hispanoamericanos)

Un collage que reúne—a partes desiguales—la recreación de la vida de un grupo de adolescentes en una Cuba de apagones y abortos, nostalgias de exilio, denuncias políticas, fragmentos eróticos y una historia de amor, tan inverosímil y rocambolesca como sólo puedo suceder en la vida real. El estilo mezcla los juegos de palabras a lo Cabrera Infante con diálogos insulsos, que recuerdan las novelas de la España de los 1950s. Lo cubano y lo cotidiano contrastan con ámbitos parisinos y un tímido afán cosmopolita que no acaba de cuajar.

3593 Victoria, Carlos. El resbaloso y otros cuentos. Miami, Fla.: Ediciones Universal, 1997. 167 p. (Colección Caniquí)

Siete historias que van de la isla al exilio. Sombríos los temas, luminoso el lenguaje. La voz narradora se confunde con la del propio escritor. Son desgarrones de vida, contados en tono menor, como conviene para narrar realidades terribles.

3594 Victoria, Carlos. La ruta del mago. Miami, Fla: Ediciones Universal, 1997. 154 p. (Coleccion caniqui)

El despertar sexual de la adolescencia y la desaparición de un mundo se entremezclan en esta novela que se desarrolla en Camagüey en los primeros años de la revolución. El autor nos deja ver el reverso de un tapiz donde las vidas de personas pequeñas y marginales son examinadas por la pupila precoz de Abel. Hay una dosis precisa de erotismo que se revela en la recién estrenada hombría del protagonista y en el fiero instinto de supervivencia de unos seres humanos al borde de un abismo tan temible por su altura como por ser desconocido. Todo en una prosa clara y exacta.

3595 The voice of the turtle: an anthology of Cuban stories. Edited by Peter Bush. London: Quartet Books, Ltd., 1997. 1 v.

Antología de cuentos cubanos del siglo veinte desde la primera generación hasta el presente. Aparecen autores de la isla y de la diáspora. La labor de traducción es notable. Un excelente panorama de la narrativa cubana.

LITERARY CRITICISM AND HISTORY

3596 Acosta-Belén, Edna *et al. Adiós, Borinquen querida:* la diáspora puertorriqueña, su historia y sus aportaciones. Albany, N.Y.: State Univ. of New York (SUNY) at Albany, Center for Latino, Latin American, and Caribbean Studies (CELAC), 2000. 182 p.

Comprehensive overview of the historical, cultural, political, and socioeconomic presence of Puerto Ricans in the US and other countries. Gives special attention to Puerto Rican contributions to literature and the visual and performing arts.

3597 Aparicio, Frances R. Listening to salsa: gender, Latin popular music, and Puerto Rican cultures. Hanover, N.H.: Univ. Press of New England, 1998. 290 p.: bibl., ill., index. (Music/culture)

Insightful study of Afro-Caribbean salsa music among Puerto Ricans relates different meanings in salsa lyrics to issues of gender, race, class, and national identities, both in Puerto Rico and Latino communities in the US. Aparicio, a literary critic, uses a postmodern approach to analyze diverse musical texts.

3598 Barradas, Efraín. Partes de un todo: ensayos y notas sobre literatura puertorriqueña en los Estados Unidos. San Juan: Editorial de la Univ. de Puerto Rico, 1998. 221 p.: bibl.

Collection of the best-known essays by one of the pioneer critics of US Puerto Rican literature. Some essays outline various stages in the historical development of Puerto Rican letters in the US while others focus on individual writers such as Bernardo Vega, Jesús Colón, Julia de Burgos, Pedro Pietri, Sandra María Esteves, Rosario Morales, Aurora Levins Morales, Martín Espada, Nicholasa Mohr, and Esmeralda Santiago.

3599 Di Pietro, Giovanni. Las mejores novelas dominicanas; & Bibliografía de la novela dominicana. San Juan: Isla Negra Editores, 1996. 75 p. (Visiones y cegueras)

Este breve ensayo que recorre la novelística dominicana desde Enriquillo (1882) de Manuel de Jesús Galván hasta nuestros días representa una rápida introducción a una narrativa muy poco conocida y aún menos valorada. La bibliografía ofrece la clasificación y primera edición de los textos más relevantes.

3600 Díaz Quiñones, Arcadio. El arte de bregar. San Juan: Ediciones Callejón, 2000. 303 p.

The leading essay of this collection discusses subtleties of language including its usage, how it assumes multiple meanings, and how it can be manipulated in certain contexts within the Puerto Rican colonial experience. Other essays are mainly author's insights on specific historical events or profiles of notable figures. Topics discussed include a tribute to writer José Luis González upon his death; a commentary on the 1998 centennial of the Spanish-Cuban-American War; a profile of José Martí as writer, warrior, and martyr of Cuban independence; and a description of artist Lorenzo Homar's formative years in New York.

3601 Flores, Juan. From bomba to hip-hop: Puerto Rican culture and Latino identity. New York: Columbia Univ. Press, 2000. 265 p.: bibl., ill., index. (Popular cultures, everyday lives)

Essential reading for understanding both national and panethnic issues that influence cultural expression and the construction of Puerto Rican identity in the US.

Analyzes distinctiveness of Puerto Rican culture in New York in relation to that of other US Latino groups. Theoretically grounded essays address many of the contradictions behind the complex process of identity construction among Puerto Ricans and other Latinos. Focuses on popular music and literature.

3602 Fornet, Ambrosio. Las máscaras del tiempo. La Habana: Letras Cubanas, 1995. 187 p.: bibl.

El volumen recoge prólogos, artículos y conferencias escritas a lo largo de 30 años. Además de trabajos críticos sobre autores extranjeros—Kafka, Tomás Carrasquilla, Benedetti—aporta igualmente juicios sobre obras de Jesús Díaz, Raúl Roa, y Alejo Carpentier. Este conjunto ofrece también al lector una visión, aunque incompleta, de los presupuestos literarios del crítico cubano.

3603 Latin looks: images of Latinas and Latinos in the U.S. media. Edited by Clara E. Rodríguez. Boulder, Colo.: Westview Press, 1997. 288 p.: bibl., ill., index.

Collection of essays provides a sustained critique of stereotypical images and representations of Puerto Ricans and other Latinos in US film, television, and printed media. Authors of individual chapters are experts in media and/or performance studies. Contributes to a better understanding of Latino cultural experiences in US society.

3604 Lie, Nadia. Transición y transacción: la revista cubana Casa de las Américas, 1960–1976. Gaithersburg, Md: Hispamérica; Leuven, Belgium: Leuven UP, 1996. 310 p.: bibl.

Un estudio de una etapa crucial de esta revista, central para comprender las corrientes de pensamiento latinoamericano de la década de los 1960s. La autora destaca la inserción de este discurso latinoamericano en la cultura cubana. El trabajo incluye una amplia documentación, una nutrida bibliografía, y fragmentos de entrevistas.

3605 Moya Pons, Frank. Bibliografía de la literatura dominicana, 1820–1990. Santo Domingo: Comisión Permanente de la Feria Nacional del Libro, 1997. 2 v.: bibl.

Monumental obra bibliográfica que se nutre del rastreo en 44 bibliotecas dominicanas y 10 extranjeras. Se anotan 2,777 obras de literatura y se ofrecen interesantes estadísticas por género (tanto literario como humano).

3606 Ramos Rosado, Marie. La mujer negra en la literatura puertorriqueña: cuentística de los setenta; Luis Rafael Sánchez, Carmelo Rodríguez Torres, Rosario Ferré y Ana Lydia Vega. San Juan: Editorial de la Univ. de Puerto Rico, 1999. 397 p.: bibl.

Important critical study on the presence of black women in Puerto Rican letters. Focuses on the short fiction writings of several Puerto Rican authors of the 1960s-70s who tried to capture the experiences of Afro-Puerto Ricans in their narratives, including Luis Rafael Sánchez, Rosario Ferré, Carmelo Rodríguez Torres, Ana Lydia Vega, and Carmen Lugo Filippi.

3607 Sandoval-Sánchez, Alberto. José, can you see?: Latinos on and off Broadway. Madison, Wis.: Univ. of Wisconsin Press, 1999. 275 p.: bibl., ill., index.

In-depth study of Latino representations and images in theater deconstructs ethnic, racial, gender, and sexual stereotypes ingrained in dominant American ideologies. Also recognizes Latino contributions to the stage.

3608 South Atlantic Quarterly, 96:1, Winter 1997. Bridging enigma: Cubans on Cuba. Edited by Ambrosio Fornet. Durham, N.C.: Duke Univ. Press.

Esta colección de ensayos—casi todos traducidos del español—de intelectuales cubanos y algunos jóvenes académicos norteamericanos ofrece una visión panorámica de la cultura cubana actual así como un enfoque novedoso de algunos temas históricos. Aunque, en conjunto, puede observarse un reconocimiento honesto de la problemática cubana en el "período especial," también salta a la vista cuán unida continúa la cultura de la isla a las políticas del estado. Entre los autores, se encuentran algunas de las figuras más destacadas de la intelligentsia cubana como Roberto Fernández Retamar, Lisandro Otero, Cintio Vitier, y Graciela Pogolotti.

3609 Souza, Raymond D. Guillermo Cabrera Infante: two islands, many worlds. Austin: Univ. of Texas Press, 1996. 195 p.: bibl., ill., index. (Texas Pan American series)

Reseña biográfica, entrevistas con el autor, sus parientes y amigos, fotos de familia y juicios críticos conforman este texto que ofrece una visión íntima del escritor habanero residente en Londres y de los ambientes y circunstancias que han influido su escritura.

3610 West, Alan. Tropics of history: Cuba imagined. Westport, Conn.: Bergin & Garvey, 1997. 214 p.: bibl., index.

Ensayos (en inglés) sobre importantes figuras literarias del siglo XX—Nancy Morejón, Alejo Carpentier, Virgilio Piñera, Dulce María Loynaz, José Lezama Lima, y Severo Sarduy—y la creación imaginativa de Cuba y su historia a través de sus textos. Los capítulos finales contienen un apretada síntesis histórica que ayudan al lector no familiarizado con el país a situar a estos escritores y su obra dentro de su contexto.

Andean Countries

CÉSAR FERREIRA, *Associate Professor of Spanish, University of Oklahoma*
GILBERTO GÓMEZ-OCAMPO, *Associate Professor of Spanish, Wabash College*

COLOMBIA AND VENEZUELA

IN THE LAST BIENNIUM, Colombian novelists increasingly have turned their attention to social consequences of the drug trade. Two established writers examine the violence that has resulted from drug trafficking: Darío Jaramillo Agudelo's *Novela con fantasma* (item **3644**) and Plinio Apuleyo Mendoza's *Cinco días en la isla* (item **3646**). The reissue of *Sin remedio* by Antonio Caballero (item **3642**), an extremely pessimistic vision of Colombian society, confirms a renewed interest in finding a meaning to Colombia's many problems. Other reissues such as Alvaro Mutis' *Siete novelas* (item **3647**) and the late Pedro Gómez Valderrama's *Cuentos completos* (item **3643**) demonstrate the continued prominence of these two writers. Critic Luz Mary Giraldo's timely compilation of short stories by younger writers attests to the genre's vitality among a new generation of writers (item **3613**). Elmo Valencia's *Islanada,* for years a much talked-about novel, finally appears in print (item **3649**).

In Venezuela, young writers who published noteworthy works are Antonio López Ortega (item **3699**), Juan Carlos Chirinos (item **3698**), and Armando Luigi Castañeda (item **3697**), while José Balza's latest collection confirms his status as an established writer (item **3695**). The reissues of Rufino Blanco Fombona's *Cuentos americanos* (item **3696**) and Mariano Picón Salas *Odisea de tierra firme* (item **3700**), not available for decades, fill an important editorial void. Two outstanding and complementary works of literary criticism were published by María Celina Núñez (item **3632**) and Juan Liscano (item **3631**). [GG]

PERU, ECUADOR, BOLIVIA

A pesar de atravesar por un difícil panorama económico que repercutió sobre las actividades en el campo cultural, Ecuador, Bolivia, y Perú lograron mantener una producción literaria variada y de calidad en los últimos años.

En Ecuador, escritores canónicos como Jorge Enrique Adoum, Eliécer Cárdenas, y Alicia Yánez Cossío añadieron valiosas entregas a sus respectivas bibliografías. Jorge Velasco Mackenzie también presentó una sólida novela histórica. Es preciso destacar los valiosos aportes de Javier Vásconez en libros como *El viajero de Praga* y *La sombra del apostador* (items **3665** and **3615**); Vásconez se postula como un protagonista de la historia literaria ecuatoriana reciente, siendo uno de los pocos escritores ecuatorianos cuyos libros tienen trascendencia internacional.

Eliécer Cárdenas, Jorge Dávila Vázquez, Iván Egüez, Gilda Holst, y Abdón Ubidia demostraron que el cuento ecuatoriano goza de gran calidad. A los aportes individuales de estos escritores se suma una excelente antología de cuentistas ecuatorianos, editada por Raúl Vallejo, que da cuenta de las diversas vertientes del relato breve en el fin de siglo (item **3656**). En el área de la crítica, Antonio Sacoto publicó un importante trabajo que incluye los títulos más relevantes de la novela ecuatoriana en los últimos 30 años (item **3614**).

En Bolivia, Manfredo Kempff y Edmundo Paz Soldán mostraron ser dos de los escritores más destacados de la literatura contemporánea de su país. Este último se perfila como un autor de trascendencia internacional, y dueño de una obra narrativa que ha sido premiada en diversos concursos literarios de prestigio. Debe mencionarse, además, una valiosa antología del cuento boliviano, realizada por Manuel Vargas, que incluye nombres canónicos de la narrativa boliviana junto con un gran número de escritores jóvenes (item **3633**).

En el Perú, la novela confirmó pasar por uno de sus mejores momentos en la década del noventa con considerables aportes de dos de sus más destacados escritores: Mario Vargas Llosa y Alfredo Bryce Echenique. Vargas Llosa mostró su reconocido oficio con la publicación de *Los cuadernos de don Rigoberto* (item **3690**), así como una gran lucidez crítica en libros como *Cartas a un novelista* (item **3689**) y su estudio sobre José María Arguedas, *La útopía arcaica* (item **3630**). Bryce Echenique añadió dos novelas a su extensa bibliografía y dos nuevos volúmenes de cuentos, siendo uno de los narradores peruanos más leídos en el Perú y en el extranjero (items **3675, 3671, 3673,** and **3674**). Otra figura importante en el fin de siglo es Edgardo Rivera Martínez, cuya novela *Libro del amor y de las profecías* confirma su gran calidad artística y lo convierte en un clásico de las letras peruanas (item **3684**). Asimismo, Jaime Bayly, Abelardo Sánchez, y Alonso Cueto demostraron con creces su talento entre los novelistas de una nueva generación. Es importante mencionar también el protagonismo que adquirieron las escritoras peruanas Pilar Dughi, Leyla Bartet, y Fietta Jarque, quienes entregaron importantes volúmenes que reafirmaron su calidad y oficio.

Varios trabajos críticos a cargo de Ricardo González-Vigil, Jorge Marcone, Miguel Gutiérrez, y Carmen María Pinilla se incorporaron a una variada lista de autores y temas, subrayando la gran heterogeneidad que caracterizó la producción literaria peruana de los noventa. [CF]

LITERARY CRITICISM AND HISTORY
Colombia

3611 Escobar Mesa, Augusto. Ensayos y aproximaciones a la otra literatura colombiana. Bogotá: Fundación Univ. Central, 1997. 466 p.: bibl. (Colección 30 años Universidad Central; 3)

A valuable volume that studies authors who, until now, have received little or no critical attention. The "other" literature studied here ranges from Sofía Ospina (1892–1974) and other Medellín-based authors to more contemporary novelists such as Arturo Echeverri Mejía, Manuel Mejía Vallejo, and Armando Romero (b. 1944). A useful leitmotiv in Escobar Mesa's analysis is the treatment of violence as a pervasive presence in the work of the various authors studied. [GG]

3612 González, Fernando. Fernando González. Recopilación de Luis Eduardo Yepes. Medellín: Editorial Colina, 1996. 120 p. (Colección Algunas verdades)

Anthology of excerpts from the work of González includes a short biography and a useful introduction to a writer who, with León de Greiff, has been credited with inaugurating modern literature in Colombia. The excerpts, unfortunately, are given out of context and are not properly documented, detracting from the book's usefulness. [GG]

3613 Nuevo cuento colombiano, 1975–1995. Selección y prólogo de Luz Mary Giraldo B. México: Fondo de Cultura Económica, 1997. 300 p. (Tierra firme)

A careful selection of stories by 23 writers from Darío Ruíz Gómez (b. 1937) to Mario Mendoza (b. 1964). Includes only one female author, Marvel Moreno, but otherwise the selection is balanced. Work complements *El cuento colombiano*, edited by Eduardo Pachón Padilla (see *HLAS 50:3375*). Giraldo illustrates the main tendencies in the Colombian short story, most notably "romper con el macondismo y el ruralismo." [GG]

Ecuador

3614 Sacoto, Antonio. La novela ecuatoriana, 1970–2000. Quito: Ministerio de Educación y Cultura, Sistema Nacional de Bibliotecas, 2000. 456 p.: bibl. (Colección Libros sobre libros)

Excelente estudio sobre la novela en Ecuador en los últimos 30 años. Además de una útil introducción sobre la nueva novela latinoamericana y ecuatoriana, el autor revisa textos claves que han forjado la tradición novelística del país andino (Egüez, Adoum, Cardenas, Yánez Cossío, Vásconez, entre otros). Se incluye una bibliografía mínima sobre el tema a manera de consulta. [CF]

3615 Vásconez, Javier. La sombra del apostador. Mexico: Alfaguara, 1999. 227 p.

Novela que se ambienta en el microcosmos de un hipódromo como metáfora del caos en el que está sumida la nación ecuatoriana. El amor, la muerte y la lucha implacable por el poder comparten un espacio común en el relato. [CF]

Peru

3616 Asedios a Julio Ramón Ribeyro. Recopilación de Ismael P. Márquez y César Ferreira. Lima: Pontificia Univ. Católica del Perú, Fondo Editorial, 1996. 320 p.: bibl.

Recopilación de ensayos críticos sobre uno de los escritores más leídos de la segunda mitad del siglo XX en el Perú. Además

de textos donde el autor reflexiona sobre su propio quehacer literario, se incluyen lecturas críticas sobre todos los géneros que cultivó Ribeyro. [CF]

3617 Bryce Echenique, Alfredo. A trancas y barrancas. Madrid: Espasa, 1996. 338 p. (Textos escogidos)

Recopilación de artículos periodísticos de Bryce que dan cuenta de su vida en Europa, su preocupación por la realidad peruana y sus lecturas de diversos escritores norteamericanos, europeos y latinoamericanos. [CF]

3618 Cornejo Polar, Antonio. Los universos narrativos de José María Arguedas. 2. ed. Lima: Editorial Horizonte, 1997. 279 p.: bibl. (Crítica literaria; 12)

Nueva edición de este estudio seminal sobre la obra de José María Arguedas, autor canónico del indigenismo peruano, en versión corregida y aumentada. [CF]

3619 El cuento peruano, 1980–1989. Selección, prólogo y notas de Ricardo González Vigil. Lima: PETROPERU; Ediciones Copé, 1997. 677 p.: bibl.

Nuevo volumen que forma parte de una vasta antología del relato en el Perú. El libro es un importante muestrario de los mejores representantes del cuento en la década de los años ochenta. Se incluyen comentarios informativos sobre los autores y su obra, así como una útil bibliografía sobre el tema. [CF]

3620 De lo andino a lo universal: la obra de Edgardo Rivera Martínez. Recopilación de César Ferreira y Ismael P. Márquez. Lima: Pontificia Univ. Católica del Perú, Fondo Editorial, 1999. 295 p.: bibl.

Recopilación de ensayos críticos sobre la obra de uno de los narradores contemporáneos más importantes del Perú. Durante la última década, la novela *País de Jauja* (ver *HLAS 56:3738*) convirtió a Rivera Martínez en un clásico de las letras peruanas. Este volumen reúne ensayos críticos sobre toda la obra del escritor andino, así como reflexiones del propio autor sobre su quehacer literario. [CF]

3621 Fuente, José Luis de la. Más allá de la modernidad: los cuentos de Alfredo Bryce Echenique. Valladolid, Spain: Secretariado de Publicaciones e Intercambio Científico, Univ. de Valladolid, 1998. 278 p.: bibl. (Literatura; no. 40)

Abarcador estudio sobre la cuentística de Bryce Echenique. Incluye una amplia bibliografía sobre toda la obra del escritor peruano. [CF]

3622 Gutiérrez, Miguel. Celebración de la novela. Lima: Peisa, 1996. 256 p.: index. (Serie del río hablador)

Interesante ensayo que examina textos y novelistas protagónicos de la narrativa peruana contemporánea y su diálogo con la tradición novelesca. También es un tributo a grandes novelistas extranjeros. [CF]

3623 Marcone, Jorge. La oralidad escrita: sobre la reivindicación y re-inscripción del discurso oral. Lima: Fondo Editorial de la Pontificia Univ. Católica, 1997. 292 p.: bibl.

Excelente estudio sobre el fenómeno de la oralidad en la narrativa de Vargas Llosa, *El hablador* (ver *HLAS 54:4029* y *HLAS 52:5012* para reseñas de la novela original y la traducción al inglés); Bryce Echenique, *La última mudanza de Felipe Carrillo* (ver *HLAS 54:4000*); y Gregorio Martínez, *Canto de sirena* (ver HLAS 42:5363). [CF]

3624 Mario Vargas Llosa: opera omnia. Recopilación de Ana María Hernández de López. Madrid: Editorial Pliegos, 1994? 439 p.: bibl. (Pliegos de ensayo; 96)

Excelente recopilación de textos críticos sobre la producción de Vargas Llosa. El volumen da cuenta del amplio interés que su obra mantiene entre sus lectores. [CF]

3625 Morote, Herbert. Vargas Llosa, tal cual. Lima: J. Campodónico, 1998. 305 p.: bibl., index. (Colección del sol blanco)

Combativo ensayo que polemiza con las memorias políticas de Vargas Llosa, *El pez en el agua* (ver *HLAS 54:4030*), publicadas luego de su frustrada campaña a la presidencia del Perú en 1990. [CF]

3626 Niño de Guzmán, Guillermo. La búsqueda del placer: notas sobre literatura. Lima: J. Campodónico Editor, 1996. 358 p.: bibl., ill., index. (Colección del sol blanco)

Recopilación de artículos literarios de este importante periodista y escritor peruano. El autor dedica múltiples ensayos a la novela peruana y latinoamericana, así como a la poesía peruana. Otras secciones del libro versan sobre novelistas norteamericanos, europeos y japoneses. [CF]

3627 Pinilla, Carmen María. Arguedas: conocimiento y vida. San Miguel, Perú: Fondo Editorial, Pontificia Univ. Católica del Perú, 1994. 284 p.: bibl.

Valioso estudio sobre la obra de José María Arguedas. A partir de un cuidadoso análisis de la biografía del autor, Pinilla analiza el imaginario de Arguedas y su intención por fundir su interés entre la literatura y la antropología. [CF]

3628 Ricardo Palma: escritor continental. Las huellas de Palma en hispanoamericanos. Compilación de Estuardo Núñez. Lima: Fondo Editorial, Banco Central de Reserva del Perú, 1998. 470 p.: bibl.

Estudio que demuestra que la tradición, el género literario creado por Palma, tuvo una gran acogida entre escritores latinoamericanos de su época. El autor presenta una muestra de lo más representativo de la tradición en Hispanoamerica en escritores de 19 países. [CF]

3629 Rodríguez Rea, Miguel Angel. Tras las huellas de un crítico: Mario Vargas Llosa, 1954–1959. Lima: Fondo Editorial, Pontificia Univ. Católica del Perú, 1996. 231 p.: bibl.

El compilador de este libro comenta los artículos críticos, entrevistas a escritores y reseñas de libros publicados por Vargas Llosa en diarios de Perú y España desde 1954 hasta 1959. El libro nos permite conocer las ideas, gustos y prejuicios en la etapa de formación del prestigioso novelista peruano. [CF]

3630 Vargas Llosa, Mario. La utopía arcaica: José María Arguedas y las ficciones del indigenismo. México: Fondo de Cultura Económica, 1996. 359 p.: bibl. (Colección Tierra firme)

Polémico ensayo sobre la obra de José María Arguedas, uno de los más importantes escritores del indigenismo peruano. Entre otras opiniones, Vargas Llosa defiende la noción de que la escritura de Arguedas fue en gran medida el producto de su capacidad para fabular sobre los indios y el mundo andino. [CF]

Venezuela

Fauquié Bescós, Rafael. La voz en el espejo. See *HLAS 57:4543.*

3631 Liscano, Juan. Panorama de la literatura venezolana actual. 2a ed. Caracas: Alfadil Ediciones, 1995. 356 p.: bibl., index. (Colección Trópicos; 54)

Liscano finds contemporary Venezuelan literature to be "somehow rural." He studies changes fueled by generational successions and more recently by the cultural industry and international literary tastemakers. Emphasizes contemporary writers and movements, but includes a brief study of the pervasive influence of Andrés Bello and Simón Rodríguez. [GG]

3632 Núñez, María Celina. Del realismo a la parodia: marcas para un mapa de la narrativa venezolana de los '90. Caracas: Editorial Memorias de Altagracia: Grupo Editorial Eclepsidra, 1997. 63 p.: bibl. (Colección Fuegos bajo el agua)

Brief analyses of fiction of the 1980s-90s that ranges from the realism of Gustavo Infante to the experimentalism of Lourdes Sifontes. Posits that in the 1990s both approaches have tended to merge in a "tercera vertiente," of postmodern writing, as in the work of Carlos Arribas, Dinapiera Di Donato, Cristina Policastro, and Miguel Gomes. [GG]

PROSE FICTION
Bolivia

3633 Antología del cuento boliviano moderno. Compilación de Manuel Vargas. La Paz: Editorial Acción, 1995. 269 p.

Antología de cuarenta cuentistas que le permite obtener al lector un panorama de la literatura boliviana contemporánea y sus tendencias más recientes. El volumen incluye nombres canónicos (Cerruto, Urzagasti, Shimose), así como un amplio número de narradores jóvenes (Paz Soldán, Bruzonic, Padilla Osinaga), nacidos en la década del sesenta. [CF]

3634 Arnal Franck, Ximena. Visiones de un espacio. Bolivia: Ediciones Piedra Libre, 1994. 99 p.

Novela de corte psicológico donde el relato juega con la noción del espacio doméstico y el espacio citadino para desembocar en un mundo de introspección. [CF]

3635 Kempff Suárez, Manfredo. Margarita Hesse. La Paz: Alfaguara, 1997. 181 p.

En una sociedad machista y conservadora, la protagonista de esta novela se enfrenta a los rígidos códigos morales y al poder. Escandaliza a toda una ciudad cuando, en un desvarío aparente, narra sus amores adúlteros con los políticos. La novela es un retrato agudo de la historia política de Bolivia y de su clase dirigente. [CF]

3636 Montes, José Wolfango. Ese indiscreto código de los amantes: novela. Bolivia: s.n., 1992. 212 p.

Una mujer escribe un libro donde cuenta detalles vergonzosos del pasado de su ex-marido, un político en plena campaña electoral, que hará lo imposible por impedir su publicación. Los entretelones del poder y sus protagonistas son exhibidos con una punzante ironía. [CF]

3637 Montes, José Wolfango. Trópico de corrupción: novela. Bolivia: s.n., 1993. 121 p.

Novela de corte detectivesco donde conviven un traficante perseguido, un policía, un burgués corrupto, una muchacha de vida fácil y una vasta galería de personajes marginales. El autor logra un retrato de la sociedad boliviana contemporánea gracias a una prosa ágil y efectiva. [CF]

3638 Paz Soldán, Edmundo. Amores imperfectos. La Paz: Alfaguara, 1998. 236 p.

Conjunto de 23 narraciones que van del relato brevísimo al cuento de corte más clásico. "Dochera" es uno de los textos más logrados del libro. El amor es una obsesión constante en muchos personajes de Paz Soldán, un ideal escurridizo que, una vez poseído, se resquebraja debido a la debilidad, el olvido, y la traición. [CF]

3639 Paz Soldán, Edmundo. Sueños digitales. La Paz: Alfaguara, 2000. 238 p. (Alfaguara)

Excelente novela que muestra las posibilides de representación que ofrece el mundo de la imagen digital y de la tecnología. La intención de modificar el turbio pasado de un presidente y, por ende, la historia de todo un país sirve de telón de fondo de este novedoso relato. [CF]

3640 Rocha Monroy, Enrique. Gardel—y el zorzal, cada día canta mejor: novela. La Paz: Editorial Pucara, 1997. 299 p.: ill.

Biografía novelada de Carlos Gardel, el

cantante más famoso en la historia del tango. Tras repasar la vida del cantautor argentino, el novelista explora la figura mítica del autor en su lugar de origen, así como en el resto de Latinoamérica. [CF]

3641 Vallejo de Bolívar, Gaby. Encuentra tu ángel y tu demonio. Cochabamba, Bolivia: Editorial "Los Amigos del Libro," 1998. 174 p. (Colección Literatura de hoy; no. 667)

Novela de sensaciones y sentidos que narra la vida de Isaura, su protagonista. El relato centra su atención en el cuerpo femenino. Desde allí, su protagonista poco a poco explora y descubre su identidad sexual y amorosa. [CF]

Colombia

3642 Caballero, Antonio. Sin remedio. Bogotá: Seix Barral, 1996. 565 p.

In a novel that mixes humor and tragedy with great dexterity, Caballero depicts some of Colombia's recent social and political upheavals with ferocious nihilism. The author, also known as a satirical cartoonist and a political columnist, suggests that his country's problems, like the antihero he has created, have no solution, that is, they are *sin remedio*. [GG]

3643 Gómez Valderrama, Pedro. Cuentos completos. Bogotá: Editorial Santillana, 1996. 400 p. (Alfaguara)

This volume includes Gómez Valderrama's last collection, *Las alas de los muertos* (1992), until now, unpublished. Gómez, one of the last members of the *Mito* group, wrote fiction anchored in historical events. The stories are tersely rendered in a language of great precision and elegance, with many references to the European Renaissance. [GG]

3644 Jaramillo Agudelo, Darío. Novela con fantasma. Bogotá: Editorial Norma, 1997. 181 p. (Colección La otra orilla)

Despite its conventional narrative, the characters in Jaramillo's fourth novel display an acute sense of self-awareness. The novel deals with a millionaire who discovers love late in life, and compares the power of wealth to power of love in the context of a social background marked by corruption and violence. The novel succeeds in its depiction of a society where even love is the victim of violence. [GG]

3645 Mejía Mejía, Juan Diego. El cine era mejor que la vida. Bogotá: Instituto Colombiano de Cultura, 1997. 201 p. (Premios nacionales de cultura, 1996)

Mejía's second novel is an evocation of childhood in Medellín and of the solace the protagonist finds in movies which set free his imagination and offer a vicarious form of romance. He ultimately develops a sense of reality that is more satisfying than the reality outside the movie house. The novel won the 1996 Premio Nacional. [GG]

3646 Mendoza, Plinio Apuleyo. Cinco días en la isla. Bogotá: Grupo Editorial Norma, 1997. 490 p. (Colección El Dorado)

Mendoza's novel deals with the deterioration in Colombia as a result of the corrupting power and wealth of the drug mafia. Set in Barranquilla, the protagonist returns from Paris in search of friends and relatives. The novel compares the sophistication of established families to the tastelessness of the ascending rich. An acerbic view of the mafia's role in Colombia in recent years. [GG]

3647 Mutis, Alvaro. Siete novelas: empresas y tribulaciones de Maqroll el Gaviero. Bogotá: Editorial Santillana, 1995. 717 p. (Alfaguara)

Collects in one volume the seven novels describing the saga of Maqroll el Gaviero from "La nieve del almirante" (1986) to "Tríptico de mar y tierra" (1993). The reader follows Maqroll's life of errancy and adventure, but eventually a powerful sense of dejá vu takes hold as Mutis overuses the exoticism that originally made his fiction so refreshing. [GG]

3648 Romero, Armando. La piel por la piel. Caracas: Monte Avila Editores Latino americana, 1997. 204 p. (Continentes)

This novel is the second in a trilogy by Romero, one of the youngest members of the *nadaista* movement. It narrates the story of a rambling writer who ends up in Mérida, Venezuela, a college town. One of the achievements of Romero's novel is the humorous depiction of university life, a topic rarely explored in Latin American fiction. [GG]

3649 Valencia, Luis Ernesto. Islanada. Bogotá: Editorial Big Bang, 1996. 360 p. Short but very useful forewords by

Gonzalo Arango and Jotamario Arbeláez precede the first edition of this mythical novel. Since 1967 it has been an underground point of reference, marking the literary innovation brought about by the *nadaísta* movement. *Islanada* is the fictional account of a trip around Colombia that culminates in an expedition to the Pacific Ocean in search of an unknown island where a group of artists intends to escape from a world ruled by pragmatism. "La obra cumbre del abismo," according to Arbeláez, it is a whimsical narrative full of irony and parody—a truly innovative novel in the context of Colombian narrative. In true *nadaísta* spirit, the work strongly rejects Colombia's cultural traditions, and marks an important generational rift. [GG]

Ecuador

3650 **Adoum, Jorge Enrique.** Ciudad sin ángel. México: Siglo Veintiuno Editores, 1995. 205 p. (La creación literaria)

Novela que tiene como trasfondo el París de los años sesenta. La política latino americana, el arte, la literatura y el amor, así como los encuentros y desencuentros entre Europa y América son algunos de sus temas. [CF]

3651 **Adoum, Jorge Enrique.** Ecuador: señas particulares—ensayo. 6. ed. Quito: Eskeletra Editorial, 2000. 347 p. (Ensayo)

Lúcido ensayo sobre la identidad cultural del Ecuador escrito por uno de los intelectuales más relevantes de ese país. El libro se ocupa tanto de la identidad individual de sus habitantes, a menudo determinada por las zonas geográficas del Ecuador, así como de un concepto más abarcador de una imagen de la nación ecuatoriana. [GG]

3652 **Cabrera, María Dolores.** Más allá de la piel: cuentos. Quito: Editorial El Conejo, 1998. 71 p.

Colección de cuentos en los que sus muchas protagonistas femeninas indagan sobre sí mismas con sutileza e imaginación. La incertidumbre de la existencia, el mundo onírico e incluso la alucinación sirven como claves para ingresar en los universos íntimos de los personajes. [CF]

3653 **Cárdenas Espinosa, Eliécer.** La incompleta hermosura: relatos. Ecuador: Nueva Editorial, Casa de la Cultura Ecuatoriana "Benjamín Carrión", 1996. 183 p.

Colección de relatos de este importante narrador ecuatoriano en la que sus personajes viven marcados por la angustia, la desesperanza y la muerte. Frente a estos sentimientos de derrota surgen la vitalidad y la maravilla de la memoria para eternizar una mirada y un gesto que redima sus existencias. [CF]

3654 **Carrión, Carlos.** Una guerra con nombre de mujer: novela. 2. ed. Quito: Editorial Ecuador, 1995. 224 p.: ill.

Novela que narra la historia de la muerte de un prestamista en un pueblito perdido en un mítico país llamado Ecuador. Mientras el pueblo celebra su desaparición en una fiesta disparatada, una venganza de amor se añade a los acontecimientos. La presencia del humor se manifiesta a través de una prosa irreverente y burlona. [CF]

3655 **Chiriboga, Argentina.** Jonatás y Manuela. Quito: Abrapalabra Editores, 1994. 166 p.

Novela surgida de un rito africano que exhuma los orígenes de la negritud en el Ecuador para luego centrarse en la presencia vivificadora de Jonatás, la esclava que acompañó toda la vida a Manuela Sáenz, la compañera del Libertador Simón Bolívar. [CF]

3656 **Cuento ecuatoriano de finales del siglo XX: antología crítica.** Estudio, selección y notas por Raúl Vallejo Corral. 2. ed. Quito: Libresa, 1999. 399 p. (Colección Antares; 30)

Excelente recopilación que refleja un vasto panorama de la producción del cuento ecuatoriano. Además de incluir a los nombres canónicos de la literatura ecuatoriana en los últimos 30 años, el compilador presenta una serie de autores nuevos que cultivan el género. [CF]

3657 **Dávila Vázquez, Jorge.** Cuentos breves y fantásticos. Quito: Editorial El Conejo, 1994. 165 p. (Colección Grandes autores ecuatorianos)

Excelente conjunto de microcuentos donde la fantasía y la sorpresa son otra forma de nombrar la realidad. Merece destacarse el

lenguaje ágil e imaginativo de un narrador
con oficio. [CF]

3658 Egüez, Iván. Cuentos gitanos. Quito:
Abrapalabra Editores, 1997. 164 p.

Excelente volumen de cuentos, cuyos
protagonistas son cíngaros, payasos, artistas,
y enanos como símbolos de la marginalidad y
la intolerancia que la sociedad ejerce sobre
los más débiles. El mundo lúdico y astral, la
fatalidad, el amor, y la ventura resultan
temas recurrentes en los relatos. [CF]

3659 Holst, Gilda. Turba de signos. Quito:
Abrapalabra Editores, 1995. 151 p.

Colección de cuentos con situaciones
y personajes enlazados por el vértigo de una
época conflictiva. El amor y sus tribulaciones
son temas recurrentes en estos relatos. [CF]

3660 Manzano, Sonia. Y no abras la ventana
todavía: zarzuela ligera sin divisiones
aparentes. Quito: Editorial El Conejo: Libresa, 1994. 139 p. (Colección Bienal de novela ecuatoriana)

Novela ambientada en el Guayaquil de
los años 50. La voz interior del relato evoca
el universo de los "intelectuales" que
repasan el mundo desde el espacio cerrado de
una librería y una radio, desde la cual se
proyecta el sujeto femenino. Con el uso de
un lenguaje de ecos modernistas, se retrata la
feminidad desde una óptica novedosa. [CF]

3661 Miraglia, Liliana. Un close up prolon-
gado. Quito: Abrapalabra Editores,
1996. 123 p.

Conjunto de cuentos que intenta revelar los excesos de significación que tiene la
rutina cotidiana y todo aquello que rodea si-
lenciosamente a sus personajes. En esa dimensión se esconden la risa y la tragedia en
medio de una prosa imaginativa y lúdica.
[CF]

3662 Reece Dousdebés, Alfonso. El nume-
rario. Quito: Editorial El Conejo, 1996.
322 p. (Colección Bienal de novela ecuatoriana)

Novela narrada en forma de diario de
viaje. Una organización católica fundamen-
talista recluta a un joven en el Ecuador de los
años 60; a su entusiasmo religioso inicial
sigue una decepción por los métodos mate-
rialistas del grupo para conseguir donaciones
y nuevos adeptos. Determinaciones sociales,
psíquicas y teológicas se unen en un relato
sobre el fanatismo religioso. [CF]

3663 Ubidia, Abdón. El palacio de los espe-
jos: nuevos divertinventos. Quito: Editorial El Conejo, 1996. 120 p.

Robots biológicos, máquinas que gra-
ban recuerdos, clones personales y sociedades
secretas son algunos de los temas de este libro marcado por su sentido lúdico de la realidad. En medio de su fantasía múltiple, está
presente la idea de que la mente humana no
puede mirar más allá de sus propios miedos,
deseos e incertidumbres. [CF]

3664 Vaca-Acevedo, Galo. De regreso al
ombligo. 2. ed., corr. y aum. Quito:
Editorial de la Casa de la Cultura Ecuato-
rianas, 1997. 228 p.

Colección de cuentos que narra las experiencias de los migrantes ecuatorianos en
el extranjero. El exilio en un mundo cultural
ajeno es el detonante que hará pasar a los personajes por un proceso de aprendizaje sobre
su propia identidad. [CF]

3665 Vásconez, Javier. El viajero de Praga.
México: Alfaguara, 1996. 303 p.

Novela de corte existencialista en la
que el doctor Kronz, protagonista de otros
relatos del autor, deambula entre Quito,
Barcelona y Praga, perdido entre la abulia
y la búsqueda de sentidos que mitiguen el
absurdo ineludible de la vida. Destaca la intensidad psicológica de la prosa de este excelente escritor. [CF]

3666 Velasco Mackenzie, Jorge. En nombre
de un amor imaginario. Quito: Editorial El Conejo, 1996. 293 p. (Colección Bienal
de novela ecuatoriana)

Bajo el telón de una historia de amor
se desarrolla una novela histórica situada en
el siglo XVIII que tiene como trasfondo el origen del Ecuador como concepto científico y
como país. Su autor fue premiado con el
primer premio de la IV Bienal de la Novela
Ecuatoriana el año de su publicación. [CF]

3667 Yánez Cossío, Alicia. El cristo feo.
Quito: Abrapalabra Editores, 1995.
216 p.

Novela que cuenta la vida de Ordalisa,
una empleada indígena. El mundo personal
de la protagonista, marcado por la pobreza, se
enfrenta con los patrones ricos a quienes
sirve. Un cristo imaginario sirve de símbolo
y guía para su tono crítico. A ratos el texto
resulta algo maniqueo, sin distancia irónica
para narrar los acontecimientos de la trama.

No obstante, destaca el oficio de esta importante escritora ecuatoriana para retratar la distancia entre los miembros privilegiados de la sociedad y los humildes que buscan un espacio en la misma. [CF]

Peru

3668 Bartet, Leyla. Me envolverán las sombras. Lima: Peisa, 1998. 125 p. (Serie del río hablador)

El amor, la enfermedad, la muerte y la presencia del pasado son los temas a partir de los cuales se engarzan las anécdotas de estos cuentos, marcados por la desolación y el desencanto. [CF]

3669 Bartet, Leyla. Ojos que no ven. Lima: Peisa, 1997. 110 p. (Serie del río hablador)

Cuentos en los que el autor demuestra una hábil utilización de la descripción, el diálogo, y la narración. Muchos de estos textos giran en torno a protagonistas femeninos, presentados por un narrador que sabe transmitir con efectividad sensaciones y misterios, dándole una interesante ambigüedad a la psicología de los personajes. [CF]

3670 Bayly, Jaime. Fue ayer y no me acuerdo. Lima: Peisa, 1996. 329 p. (Serie del río hablador)

Novela que tiene como protagonista a un joven de la alta burguesía limeña que, envuelto en un mundo de drogas, sexo y una dudosa moralidad, trata de reivindicar su compleja personalidad y su vocación de escritor. [CF]

3671 Bryce Echenique, Alfredo. La Amigdalitis de Tarzán. Lima: Peisa; Alfaguara, 1998. 245 p.

Novela que cuenta la frustrada historia amorosa entre un cantautor peruano y una mujer salvadoreña de clase alta en Europa. El relato presenta un formato epistolar, con una acentuada presencia de la voz femenina. [CF]

3672 Bryce Echenique, Alfredo. Antología personal. San Juan: Editorial de la Univ. de Puerto Rico, 1995. 495 p.

Antología de textos de este importante novelista peruano que sirve de excelente muestrario para conocer su obra novelística, su producción cuentística, su actividad periodística y sus memorias. [CF]

3673 Bryce Echenique, Alfredo. Cuentos completos. Madrid: Santillana, 1995. 479 p.

Recopilación de toda la obra cuentística de este importante narrador peruano hasta 1986. Se incluyen los textos *Huerto cerrado, La felicidad ja, ja,* y *Magdalena peruana y otros cuentos,* así como otros inéditos. [CF]

3674 Bryce Echenique, Alfredo. Guía triste de París. Lima: Alfaguara; Peisa, 1999. 187 p.

Nueva colección de cuentos de este importante narrador peruano. Todos los relatos versan sobre los encuentros y desencuentros de personajes peruanos y latino americanos que viajan hasta la capital francesa en busca de sus mitos. Una vez allí sólo se toparán con aventuras que desembocan en la soledad y la desilusión. [CF]

3675 Bryce Echenique, Alfredo. Reo de nocturnidad. Barcelona: Editorial Anagrama, 1997. 273 p. (Narrativas hispánicas; 22)

Novela que narra la historia de Max Gutiérrez, un profesor peruano en Francia, y sus tribulaciones amorosas. Se destaca en el relato la exploración pesadillesca del mundo de los sueños. [CF]

3676 Colchado Lucio, Oscar. Rosa Cuchillo. Lima: Univ. Nacional Federico Villarreal, Editorial Universitaria, 1997. 217 p.

Novela que tiene lugar en dos mundos: el de la realidad visible y el del otro lado de la muerte. Entre ambos espacios se tejen dos historias: la primera es la de una guerra fraticida y atroz situada en Ayacucho, en la sierra peruana, fundada en la historia reciente del Perú. La otra es una historia mítica basada en la cosmovisión andina. En busca de su hijo y deambulando entre entre lo real y lo mítico, el lector sigue los destinos de Rosa Cuchillo, la protagonista. [CF]

3677 Cueto, Alonso. Pálido cielo. Lima: Peisa, 1998. 227 p. (Serie del río hablador)

Nueva colección de relatos de este prolífico escritor. Una atmósfera melancólica y obnubilada cobija un abanico de personajes indecisos y fracasados que deambulan por el mundo marcados por una tediosa existencia. [CF]

3678 **Dughi M., Pilar.** Ave de la noche. Lima: Asociación Peruano Japonesa del Perú; Peisa, 1996. 140 p. (Serie del río hablador)

Seres perturbados, víctimas en su mayoría de la fatalidad, son los protagonistas de estos quince relatos que merecieron un primer premio en un importante concurso de cuentos en el Perú. [CF]

3679 **Dughi M., Pilar.** Puñales escondidos. Lima: Banco Central de Reserva del Perú, Fondo Editorial, 1998. 202 p.

Novela policial que narra los manejos turbios, intrigas y otras realidades del mundo del dinero en un banco. El tono psicológico del relato le da una densidad singular a la trama. El libro ganó un importante concurso de novela en el Perú: el Premio BCRP Novela Corta 1997. [CF]

3680 **Elmore, Peter.** Enigma de los cuerpos. Lima: Peisa, 1995. 318 p. (Serie del río hablador)

Andrés Saldívar, un joven periodista encargado de la sección cultural de un diario limeño, recibe el encargo de ocuparse de unos misteriosos crímenes. Elmore se vale de esta trama policial para mostrar un descarnado retrato de la Lima de la década de los ochenta. [CF]

3681 **González Viaña, Eduardo.** Correo de Salem. Lima: Mosca Azul Editores, 1998. 195 p.

Crónicas sobre las costumbres "americanas" narradas por un "latino" en los Estados Unidos. Estos textos relatan las aventuras y desventuras de un peruano que parecen dirigidas a lectores que aspiran a convertirse en inmigrantes en busca del sueño americano. [CF]

3682 **Jarque, Fietta.** Yo me perdono. Madrid: Alfaguara/Santillana, 1998. 356 p. (Extra Alfaguara)

Novela histórica que transcurre en el Cusco del siglo XVII durante la conquista española. Utilizando las voces de cuatro personajes, la novelista describe la realidad de esa región andina a través de epístolas, monólogos interiores, descripciones detalladas, y confesiones que representan la vida de los sacerdotes, la frivolidad de los cortesanos de la época, y la imposición ideológica en las artes y la religión. [CF]

3683 **Rivera Martínez, J. Edgardo.** A la hora de la tarde y de los juegos. Lima: Peisa, 1996. 91 p. (Serie del río hablador)

Colección de microrelatos que narran con aire de nostalgia experiencias infantiles en la ciudad andina de Jauja. Muchos de los textos logran transmitir un ambiente mágico y de intenso lirismo. [CF]

3684 **Rivera Martínez, J. Edgardo.** Libro del amor y de las profecías: novela. Lima: Peisa; Arango Editores, 1999. 551 p. (Serie del río hablador)

Excelente novela de uno de los narradores peruanos más importantes de la década del noventa. Desde la ciudad andina de Jauja, el protagonista Juan Esteban Uscamayta emprende la escritura de un diario impulsado por el deseo de entablar un diálogo de amor imaginario con Urganda, su inalcanzable y enigmática amada. Novela de gran aliento donde el amor, la nostalgia, el humor, y la reflexión comparten un mismo espacio. [CF]

3685 **Sánchez León, Abelardo.** La soledad del nadador. Lima: Peisa, 1996. 466 p. (Serie del río hablador)

Benjamín Hassler forma parte del equipo peruano que concurre a las Olimpíadas de Berlín en 1936, pero, por un azar que la historia registra, no llega a participar. Durante décadas rememorará este instante en que pudo alcanzar la gloria. Además de ser un penetrante retrato humano, esta novela es una visión del Perú durante la vida del protagonista en el siglo XX. [CF]

3686 **Solari Swayne, Enrique.** Juanito de Huelva. Lima: Peisa, 1995. 98 p. (Serie del río hablador)

Un español y un peruano se enfrentan en Berlín a la tragedia de la segunda guerra mundial. Es importante señalar el logrado dramatismo que alcanza el relato bajo la pluma de este autor canónico del teatro. [CF]

3687 **Tocilovac, Goran.** Trilogía Parisina. Lima: Peisa, 1996. 355 p. (Serie del río hablador)

La lectura de este volumen nos conduce por las sinuosidades de una historia policial. El lector tendrá todas las variantes para resolver el caso de los sucesivos asesinatos de mujeres, cuyo elemento común es haber tenido en su pasado una relación amorosa con uno de los personajes principales del relato. [CF]

3688 Vallejo, César. Novelas y cuentos completos. Prólogo, edición y notas de Ricardo González Vigil. Lima: Petroperú; Ediciones Copé, 1998. 425 p.: bibl.

Valiosa edición que incluye toda la obra narrativa de este importante poeta peruano. La narrativa vallejiana está orientada en una primera instancia, hacia la exploración vanguardista (*Escalas, Fabla salvaje, Contra el secreto profesional*), seguida de un marcado realismo social (*El tungsteno, Paco Yunque,* y *Hacia el reino de los Sciris*). [CF]

3689 Vargas Llosa, Mario. Cartas a un joven novelista. Barcelona: Ariel/Planeta, 1997. 157 p. (La línea del horizonte)

Creando un interlocutor epistolar imaginario, Vargas Llosa se dirige a un aspirante a novelista y reflexiona sobre el género de la novela. [CF]

3690 Vargas Llosa, Mario. Los cuadernos de don Rigoberto. Madrid: Alfaguara, 1997. 384 p.

Libro en el que el autor retoma los personajes de una novela anterior, *Elogio de la madrastra,* para narrar el triángulo amoroso entre un joven precoz, Fonchito, Lucrecia, su madrastra, y el ex-esposo de ésta, Don Rigoberto. [CF]

3691 Vargas Llosa, Mario. La Fiesta del Chivo. Madrid: Alfaguara, 2000. 518 p.

Novela histórica sobre los últimos días del gen. Rafael Leonidas Trujillo en la República Dominicana en 1961. El hilo conductor de la novela es el retorno a la isla de Urania Cabral, hija de un senador del régimen trujillista, luego de muchos años de la muerte del dictador. Mientras Urania visita a su padre moribundo, la narración reconstruye el fin de una era haciendo un recuento de una serie de personajes históricos, entre ellos, el sempiterno presidente de la República Dominicana, Joaquín Balaguer y ascenso político. La crueldad del poder y la maldad humana destacan en este gran relato, una de las mejores novelas del novelista peruano.

3692 Vargas Llosa, Mario. Una historia no oficial. Recopilación de Miguel García-Posada. Madrid: Editorial Espasa Calpe, 1997. 358 p.: bibl.

Antología de la obra novelística del escritor peruano. Incluye un útil prólogo sobre el universo del autor a cargo de un importante crítico español. [CF]

3693 Váscones, Violeta. En la cresta de la ola. Lima: Fondo Editorial, Banco Central de Reserva del Perú, 1998. 100 p.

Mujeres idealizadas e inalcanzables son vistas con fascinación por miradas jóvenes masculinas, sensibles y tímidas, en esta interesante colección de cuentos. [CF]

3694 Zorrilla, Zein. Dos más por Charly. Presentación de Martín Lienhard; colofón de Manuel J. Baquerizo. Lima: Lluvia Editores, 1996. 165 p. (Colección Sahumerio. Serie Novela; 1)

La alienación cultural y el anhelo frustrado de ascenso social son los temas del entramado narrativo de la primera novela de este escritor andino. El cambio de nombre del castizo "Carlos" por el de "Charly" manifiesta una transformación de la mentalidad del protagonista, así como un grado de transculturación del inmigrante andino motivada por su contacto con culturas foráneas. [CF]

Venezuela

3695 Balza, José. La mujer de la roca: ejercicios narrativos. México: Ediciones Sin Nombre, 1997. 83 p. (Los libros de la oruga)

Balza's latest collection of short narratives enchants the reader with its explorations of shifting borders and boundaries: the country and the city, cinema and literature, and old age and the memory of youth. Another accomplished example of Balza's mature art, most remarkably "Historia de alguien." [GG]

3696 Blanco-Fombona, Rufino. Cuentos americanos. Prólogo de Oscar Rodríguez Ortiz. Caracas: Monte Avila Editores Latinoamericana, 1997. 173 p. (Eldorado)

This is the first edition of Blanco's short stories since 1913. A late *modernista* who sought to contribute to the development of a national literature and on several occasions was candidate for the Nobel prize, Blanco's narratives share lyrical qualities and a stern realism. Most noteworthy in this collection is his portrayal of Juan Vicente Gómez's dictatorship. [GG]

3697 Castañeda, Armando Luigi. La crisis de la modernidad: auto sacramental. Caracas: Editorial Troya: Editorial Memorias de Altagracia: Grupo Editorial Eclepsidra, 1997. 132 p. (Narrativa)

This is a short but dense novel that epitomizes postmodern writing in contemporary Venezuelan literature. Castañeda uses Bocaccio's and Cervantes' views on the novel to justify the mixing of many rhetoric conventions, enhancing the artificiality of literature in a text that parodies an interpretive essay but deviates onto different paths, some not quite successful. [GG]

3698 Chirinos, Juan Carlos. Leerse los gatos. Caracas: Editorial Memorias de Altagracia: Grupo Editorial Eclepsidra, 1997. 79 p. (Narrativa)

These stories deal with the fictionality of literature. Their characters exist in a continuum of reality-fiction with no clear divide between the two, as in "Agnus Rey," set in the times of Alexander the Great, or "Guerrero árabe," which occurs in medieval times. Chirinos' fascination with language and its relative inability to represent reality is successfully conveyed. [GG]

3699 López Ortega, Antonio. Calendario y otros textos. 2a ed., corr. y aum. Caracas: Monte Avila Editores Latinoamericana: Equinoccio, Ediciones de la Univ. Simón Bolívar, 1997. 227 p. (Continentes)

In carefully constructed prose poems that play with reflexivity and identity, López elicits secret meanings from the apparently trivial, revealing the ability of art to transcend the fugacity of life. López derides "the encyclopedic efforts of the novel," a similar distrust of the novel that he had shown in his *Cartas de relación* (1982). [GG]

3700 Picón-Salas, Mariano. Odisea de tierra firme: relatos de Venezuela. Mérida, Venezuela: Dirección de Cultura del Estado Mérida, 1995. 120 p. (Solar de clásicos merideños)

Much better known for his essays and autobiographical writings, Picón reconstructs the history of Venezuela from the 18th-early 20th century in this work. Written at the height of the *costumbrista* and realist period, this reissue of his 1931 novel will allow a reassessment of the narrative quality of one of Venezuela's major writers. [GG]

Chile

JOSÉ PROMIS, *Professor of Latin American Literature and Literary Criticism, University of Arizona*

LA NOVELA CHILENA SUFRIÓ la desaparición de su más destacado representante durante el bienio 1996–97. José Donoso, Premio Nacional de Literatura, falleció a fines de 1996, seguido unos meses después por su esposa, Pilar Donoso, autora de *Los de entonces* (1987), una interesante contribución a la *Historia personal del Boom* (ver *HLAS 52:3801*). Poco antes de morir, Donoso concluyó con grandes penurias físicas la redacción de su novela *El mocho* (item **3716**), una síntesis donde se acumulan los temas que lo obsesionaron a lo largo de toda su extensa producción narrativa. El influjo de la visión literaria de Donoso sobre las generaciones actuales se manifiesta en varios relatos publicados durante este bienio, particularmente en aquellos que continúan la temática de la *casa* como espacio privilegiado para representar los conflictos trascendentales de la sociedad chilena. *Una casa vacía* (item **3709**) puede considerarse como novela paradigmática de la preferencia que Donoso impuso sobre los novelistas más jóvenes como Cerda y que ofrece un interesante campo de estudio para la investigación literaria.

Durante este bienio, la narrativa chilena exhibe varias características definidas. En primer lugar, una inequívoca tendencia hacia la apertura geográfica que ciertos críticos de la literatura llaman *cosmopolitismo contemporáneo* de la narrativa nacional. Si bien algunos lo consideran un reflejo artístico de la apertura de Chile hacia el mercado internacional y de la prosperidad económica del país, otros críticos lo interpretan como el único efecto positivo del exilio, ya que muchos relatos ambientados en Europa y EE.UU. pertenecen a escritores que sufrieron dicha experiencia. Tal es el caso del autor de los excelentes cuentos de *El funeral de la felicidad* (item **3737**), que pueden citarse como ejemplo representativo. Además, el período del gobierno militar continúa siendo el referente privilegiado para muchos narradores, en especial para los pertenecientes a la llamada "generación post-golpe." A diferencia de la narrativa publicada en años anteriores, el interés tiende a concentrarse ahora en las consecuencias de dicho régimen una vez desaparecido del ámbito político nacional. Un significativo repertorio de motivos literarios refleja esta preocupación, entre los que pueden citarse como más frecuentes el viaje y la búsqueda del padre, las experiencias adolescentes caracterizadas por sentimientos de desorientación y orfandad, y el contraste entre los idealismos del pasado con la fractura y la asfixia del presente. Significativas son también, en este mismo aspecto, tres tendencias que tienen como factor común enfrentarse de manera crítica o escéptica a las verdades oficiales: el interés que algunos novelistas de prestigio manifiestan por el escrutinio del "alma nacional" que se transparenta, por ejemplo, en *El humor brujo* (item **3705**), y que responde sin duda a la preocupación que despierta la denuncia de muchos sociólogos acerca de la pérdida de dicha identidad en el mundo de la economía global en que Chile se ha insertado; la desacralización del discurso oficial de la historia de Chile que se produce al interpretarlo a la luz de posibilidades imaginarias alternativas, como ocurre, por ejemplo, en *Déjame que te cuente* (item **3723**) o la parodización de las actitudes redentoras del pasado inmediato que representa muy bien la novela *Cien pájaros volando* (item **3710**). No menos significativa de la recuperación de una tradición cultural castigada durante el gobierno militar es la re-edición de relatos considerados clásicos de la narrativa social chilena, de los cuales se recogen varios ejemplos en las anotaciones.

Es necesario destacar también dos corrientes narrativas cuyo volumen y calidad aumenta durante el bienio. La narrativa femenina de tendencia feminista se manifiesta a través de la publicación de un número considerable de cuentos y novelas, entre las cuales hay que destacar la primera novela de García-Huidobro, *Hasta ya no ir* (item **3724**), una pequeña obra maestra. El éxito de ventas de relatos como *Tinta roja* (item **3722**) de Fuguet, y de relatos policiales como los de Ampuero (item **3702**), demuestra que la novela de entretención, desconocido en Chile hasta hace unos años atrás, sigue ganando espacio en las preferencias de los lectores, fenómeno que sin duda despertará el interés de los sociólogos de la literatura.

PROSE FICTION

3701 **Allende, Isabel** *et al.* Salidas de madre. Prólogo de Alejandra Rojas. Santiago: Planeta, 1996. 210 p. (Biblioteca del sur)

Volumen que contiene 20 cuentos de escritoras chilenas actuales donde el tema compartido de la relación madre e hija permite indagar acerca de los problemas de la identidad femenina y de la diferencia genérica. Aporta una reseña bio-bibliográfica de las autoras incluidas.

3702 **Ampuero, Roberto.** El alemán de Atacama. Santiago: Planeta, 1996. 251 p.

Tercera novela en que aparece la figura de Cayetano Brulé, un cubano que sobrevive precariamente como detective privado en Valparaíso. Excelente relato con gran cuidado por el detalle en la creación de ambientes, que utiliza la trama de la novela policial para analizar subterráneos desequilibrios sociales y políticos.

3703 Ampuero, Roberto. El hombre golondrina: y otros cuentos. Santiago: Seix Barral, 1997. 185 p. (Biblioteca breve)

El volumen reúne relatos breves escritos por el autor a lo largo de varios años. Además de exhibir una excelente calidad en su construcción narrativa, permiten observar el proceso de formación literaria de uno de los novelistas más populares en Chile.

3704 Azócar, Pablo. El señor que aparece de espaldas. Santiago: Aguilar Chilena de Ediciones, 1997. 310 p. (Alfaguara)

El motivo del viaje mítico es transformado en la búsqueda de un misterioso hermano fallecido, en un relato donde nada es lo que pareciera ser, pero que revela al final la exasperante complejidad del individuo. El título proviene de un poema de Gonzalo Rojas que ilumina el sentido final de las peripecias narradas.

3705 Blanco, Guillermo. El humor brujo: novela. Santiago: Planeta, 1996. 151 p. (Biblioteca del sur)

El título parodia el nombre del ballet flamenco con que Manuel de Falla sacó a luz las pasiones larvadas del alma gitana. La novela pretende, gracias a la mirada irónica que caracteriza a los relatos del autor, llegar a la imagen más profunda de lo que se denomina en el texto como el "alma chilena."

3706 Bolaño, Roberto. Estrella distante. Barcelona: Editorial Anagrama, 1996. 157 p. (Narrativas hispánicas; 210)

Relato que se desarrolla a partir del catálogo de autores nazis imaginado por el autor en su libro anterior *La literatura nazi en América*. La atención se concentra aquí sobre uno de ellos, Carlos Ramírez Hoffman, para denunciar la impunidad del horror y el sentido tragicómico de los destinos humanos.

3707 Bolaño, Roberto. La literatura nazi en América. Barcelona: Seix Barral, 1996. 237 p.: bibl.

Uno de los relatos más extraños y sorprendentes de la novela chilena actual, que asume la forma de un diccionario donde con gran minuciosidad y maestría narrativa se describen las biografías de una serie de intelectuales nazis de América y Europa. El catálogo pretende borrar la distancia que se asigna a la realidad y a la imaginación y, con ello, a la diferencia entre lo verdadero y lo falso.

3708 Bombal, María Luisa. Obras completas. Introducción y recopilación de Lucía Guerra-Cunningham. Santiago: Editorial Andrés Bello, 1996. 456 p.

Recopilación de las novelas y cuentos de la escritora chilena acompañada con otros escritos diversos que se reúnen bajo los títulos "Crónicas poéticas," "Otros escritos" y "Testimonios," donde se recogen cartas, entrevistas y declaraciones autobiográficas. La introducción sitúa la obra de M.L. Bombal dentro de los contextos ideológicos actuales.

3709 Cerda, Carlos. Una casa vacía. Santiago: Aguilar Chilena de Ediciones, 1996. 324 p. (Alfaguara)

La atracción hacia la "casa" es indudable en la novela escrita por un discípulo de José Donoso, pero aquí su espacio es transformado en lugar de torturas cometidas durante los años del gobierno militar. Una voz narrativa solidaria con el dolor de las víctimas investiga la manera como la sombra del pasado se proyecta sobre la vida cotidiana de sus habitantes actuales.

3710 Collyer, Jaime. Cien pájaros volando. Santiago: Planeta, 1995. 274 p. (Biblioteca del sur)

La fe en la existencia de verdades únicas es desacralizada paradójicamente con la historia de un antropólogo que viaja a estudiar las costumbres de una pequeña comunidad campesina en un inexistente valle de la Cordillera de los Andes. Relato al servicio de las ideas críticas sobre la modernidad, su título anuncia el carácter limitado y fragmentario de cualquier posible interpretación de los fenómenos históricos.

3711 Collyer, Jaime. El infiltrado. 2da. edición. Santiago: Editorial Sudamericana, 1997. 211 p.

Reedición de uno de los relatos más representativos de la novela chilena durante la década de los ochenta. La culpa, tema que se reitera en ese momento, sirve en este texto para representar con acierto una atmósfera de amargura, escepticismo y sofocación existencial.

3712 Costamagna, Alejandra. En voz baja. Santiago: LOM Ediciones, 1996. 172 p. (Opus uno)

Novela que representa muy bien la búsqueda del padre, motivo que los narradores más jóvenes utilizan con significativa frecuencia. Una adolescente que vivió el golpe militar durante su niñez indaga por su padre desaparecido a través de las palabras y de los silencios de los adultos.

3713 Cuentos extraviados. Santiago: Alfaguara, 1997. 288 p.

Relatos ganadores del Concurso de Cuentos Paula 1997. Demuestran el interés que existe entre los escritores chilenos actuales hacia la apertura de espacios y de experiencias individuales, así como también hacia la representación de conflictos humanos que tradicionalmente habían quedado al margen de las posibilidades de narración en la literatura chilena.

3714 Díaz Arrieta, Hernán. La sombra inquieta. 4a. ed. Santiago: Editorial Universitaria, 1997. 176 p. (Col. premios nacionales de literatura)

Unica novela que el autor publicó, cuando tenía 24 años, antes de dedicarse exclusivamente a la crítica literaria. Texto largamente agotado, es una novela de intriga social, en clave, que destaca los rasgos de la sensibilidad característicos del que fuera después el más famoso de los críticos literarios chilenos.

3715 Díaz Eterović, Ramón. Correr tras el viento. Santiago: Planeta, 1997. 192 p. (Biblioteca del sur)

Una serie de personajes de diferentes ascendencias étnicas que viven en la región magallánica de Punta Arenas son envueltos en los ecos de la guerra que tiene lugar en Europa a comienzos del siglo. Novela de intriga con que el autor se aparta de los conflictos policiales que identifican a su narrativa dentro de la literatura chilena actual.

3716 Donoso, José. El Mocho. Santiago: Aguilar Chilena de Ediciones, 1997. 193 p. (Alfaguara)

Novela póstuma que el autor terminó de escribir poco antes de su fallecimiento. En apretada síntesis reaparecen los motivos más característicos que recorren como obsesiones permanentes toda su narrativa anterior, para configurar una vez más el mundo de postri-

merías típicamente donosiano que se inicia en *Coronación* (1957), su primera novela y que queda definitivamente clausurado en ésta.

3717 Drago, Gonzalo. El purgatorio. Santiago: LOM Ediciones, 1996. 150 p.

Reedición de una de las novelas clásicas de la llamada "Generación de 1938," de la cual el autor fue uno de sus más destacados representantes.

3718 Edwards, Jorge. El origen del mundo. Barcelona: Tusquets Editores, 1996. 166 p. (Col. Andanzas; 277)

Siguiendo una línea narrativa que lo ha alejado de la representación realista de sus primeras novelas, el autor recupera el tema del triángulo amoroso dándole un giro inesperado que pone en juicio los mecanismos racionales con que algunos personajes juzgan el comportamiento humano.

3719 Emar, Juan. Un año. Santiago: Editorial Sudamericana, 1996. 119 p. (Biblioteca claves de Chile)

La reedición de esta novela escrita alrededor de 1935 y prácticamente ignorada por la crítica de su tiempo y la posterior, permite comprobar la sorprendente actualidad de la prosa de su autor, a la que con toda justicia podría denominársele desconstruccionista.

3720 Eytel, Guido. Casas en el agua. Santiago: LOM Ediciones, 1997. 162 p. (Col. Entre mares)

Tres voces alternadas relatan la fundación de San Estanislao de Rucaco en la araucanía chilena durante los años siguientes a la guerra contra Perú y Bolivia. Se origina así un cuarto discurso virtual que desacraliza al de la historia oficial y saca a luz el otro lado de la realidad, los aspectos oscuros y silenciados de la pacificación de la araucanía desechados por aquélla.

3721 Franz, Carlos. El lugar donde estuvo el paraíso. Buenos Aires: Planeta, 1996. 264 p.

Primer finalista en el Premio Planeta de Novela 1996. Constituye un excelente asedio narrativo a la temática de la culpa que el autor inauguró con su novela *Santiago Cero* (1990). Ubicada en la zona amazónica, exhibe una impecable construcción discursiva y una convincente profundidad en la manera como el autor presenta los complicados vericuetos de las pasiones humanas.

3722 Fuguet, Alberto. Tinta roja. Santiago: Aguilar Chilena de Ediciones, 1996. 414 p.

Incesante historia de aventuras de un aprendiz de periodista. Constituye un excelente ejemplo de la narrativa de entretención que cultivan hoy numerosos escritores chilenos y que como tal no puede desconocerse como una tendencia dominante y significativa en el momento actual de la novela chilena.

3723 Gallardo, Juanita. Déjame que te cuente. Santiago: Planeta, 1997. 251 p.: bibl. (Memoria de Chile. Personajes)

Novela referida a un episodio de la vida de Bernardo O'Higgins que la historiografía oficial se empeña en disimular, cuando no en olvidar completamente: su relación amorosa con una joven provinciana de la que nació el hijo del libertador de Chile que después habría de morir oscuramente en Lima. Convincente y atractiva recreación imaginaria de un hecho escamoteado por la historia.

3724 García-Huidobro, Beatriz. Hasta ya no ir. Santiago: LOM Ediciones, 1996. 91 p. (Col. Entre mares. Novela)

Historia de una niña de provincias cuya ingenuidad natural la convierte en víctima de las deformaciones de un adulto. Esta situación narrativa permite desplegar una novedosa visión del mundo campesino, cuya belleza esconde el acoso despiadado de los patrones sobre la indefensión de la servidumbre, a través de un lenguaje de sorprendente elegancia estilística y poética capacidad evocativa. Una de las mejores novelas del bienio 1996–97.

3725 Gómez, Sergio. Partes del cuerpo que no se tocan. Santiago: Planeta, 1997. 210 p.

Cuentos que relatan las experiencias a veces minúsculas de los habitantes de un suburbio imaginario de las afueras de Santiago para demostrar que no existe identidad entre la trascendencia de los problemas individuales y la reducción del espacio donde tienen lugar. Un regreso al criollismo urbano desde un punto de vista contemporáneo.

3726 González Vera, José Santos. Vidas mínimas. 9a ed. Santiago: LOM Ediciones, 1997. 107 p. (Col. clásicos de la novela social chilena)

Publicada por primera vez en 1923, esta novela inauguró una de las primeras reacciones contra la visión criollista con base en el positivismo que imperaba por esos años en la literatura chilena, destacando la fuerza de la interioridad humana antes que el determinismo del medio sobre el comportamiento individual.

3727 Lafourcade, Enrique. Cristianas viejas y limpias. Santiago: Planeta, 1997. 291 p.

Historia aparentemente banal de dos ancianas que viven en un pueblo del sur de Chile y que son enviadas a conocer a Juan Pablo II durante su visita al país. El autor reafirma su fe en la inconquistable belleza del espíritu y la esperanza en las posibilidades de salvación humana que ha venido comunicando en toda su extensa narrativa anterior.

3728 López-Aliaga, Luis. Fiesta de disfraces. Santiago: Mondadori; Grijalbo Mondadori, 1997. 235 p. (Literatura Mondadori)

Dos adolescentes pertenecientes a la llamada "generación post-golpe" avanzan hacia la madurez marcados por sentimientos de desorientación, ajenidad, soledad y ausencia de progenitores. Relato representativo del tema de la orfandad que se reitera en la novela chilena actual.

3729 Manns, Patricio. El corazón a contraluz. Buenos Aires: Emecé Editores, 1996. 297 p. (Grandes novelistas)

Historia alucinante, contradictoria y dolorosa del encuentro siempre renovado de la tierra con su conquistador, narrada con un magnífico discurso que convierte alternativamente al dolor en expresión lírica, en tragedia cósmica o en épica cotidiana. Una de las novelas más sobresalientes del bienio 1996–97.

3730 Marín, Germán. Las cien águilas. Santiago: Planeta, 1997. 385 p.: bibl. (Historia de una absolución familiar. Biblioteca del sur)

Segundo volumen de la trilogía *Historia de una absolución familiar.* El destino de una estirpe es relatado por un narrador de personalísima fisonomía que se desprende de su tradicional dominio sobre el lenguaje para transformarse en una voz itinerante que puede incluso negarse a sí misma, con lo cual acepta la contradicción, la duda y el silencio como aspectos de la verdad comunicada por su discurso.

3731 Maturana, Andrea. El daño. Santiago: Alfaguara, 1997. 230 p.

Relato cuyo argumento se sostiene sobre el motivo del viaje mítico. Dos muchachas emprenden un viaje al sur de Chile buscando reencontrarse consigo mismas después de haber sufrido sendas dilapidaciones por parte de los hombres, el padre en un caso y un amante, en el otro. El tratamiento del tema es un interesante ejemplo de la actual narrativa feminista chilena.

3732 Missana, Sergio. El invasor. Santiago: Planeta, 1997. 212 p. (Biblioteca del sur)

Utilizando el tema del amor fraterno y basándose en hechos efectivamente ocurridos, el autor recrea con maestría y dominio la atmósfera y las circunstancias que rodearon la matanza obrera de Santa María de Iquique ocurrida a comienzos del presente siglo. Un buen ejemplo de la narrativa que recupera el pasado nacional para reinterpretarlo mediante el discurso imaginario.

3733 Oses, Dario. La bella y las bestias. Santiago: Planeta, 1997. 327 p.

Esta novela confirma a su autor como una figura destacada de la narrativa actual. Una historia de adulterio con ribetes de aventura policial y narración fantástica sirve para desarrollar una parodia de los discursos donde las virtudes burguesas triunfan inexorablemente sobre los obstáculos a la felicidad.

3734 Parra, Marco Antonio de la. Grandes éxitos: y otros fracasos. Santiago: Planeta, 1996. 207 p. (Biblioteca del sur)

Diez cuentos publicados anteriormente y seis inéditos que tienen como propósito común sacar a luz las verdades escondidas, viscerales, que se ocultan bajo el disfraz de comportamientos legalizados por los hábitos, por las exigencias impuestas o por los mitos que hemos creado a nuestro alrededor.

3735 Río, Ana María del. A tango abierto. Santiago: Aguilar Chilena de Ediciones, 1996. 335 p. (Alfaguara)

Desarrollo del conflicto entre el antes y el ahora, entre las ilusiones que existían previas al golpe militar de 1973 en contraste con la derrota y la clausura posteriores, relatado mediante una sobresaliente composición que le confiere a esta novela un lugar destacado en el bienio 1996–97.

3736 Rivera Letelier, Hernán. Himno del ángel parado en una pata. Santiago: Planeta, 1996. 205 p. (Biblioteca del sur)

Premio de Novela del Consejo Nacional del Libro y la Lectura 1996. Historia de un niño criado en la región de las salitreras chilenas a quien el narrador observa deambulando por las calles de la ciudad de Antofagasta para transformarlo en símbolo de la dramática soledad de los marginados sociales.

3737 Riveros Olavarría, Patricio. El funeral de la felicidad. Santiago: Planeta, 1997. 231 p. (Biblioteca del sur)

Cuentos de buena factura literaria que ejemplifican muy bien la apertura y el cosmopolitismo de temas y asuntos que exhibe el relato chileno actual: algunos se ambientan en Europa, otros en Cuba y el resto en Chile. Breves y directos, enfocan una estrategia simple que demuestra la identidad de los problemas humanos, no importa donde ocurran.

3738 Rodríguez Elizondo, José. La pasión de Iñaki. Santiago: Editorial Andrés Bello, 1996. 213 p.

Un psiquiatra que ha sido asesor del gobierno militar y una periodista estadounidense viven una historia de amor ambientada principalmente en el momento crítico en que se recupera la democracia en Chile. Se acentúan las ideologías enemigas, las pasiones, la desconfianza y las ambiciones personales. Se trasluce un escepticismo característico de muchas novelas actuales.

3739 Román, Jose. El espejo de tres caras. Santiago: Planeta, 1996. 191 p. (Biblioteca del sur)

Relato que representa adecuadamente la llamada novela negra chilena y el uso de un discurso común entre la literatura y el film que se encuentra también en otras novelas de los últimos años. El enigma de un asesinato frustrado abre una historia de traiciones y devociones que ilustra lo que fue la atmósfera nacional bajo el gobierno militar.

3740 Sepúlveda, Luis. Patagonia express: apuntes de viaje. Barcelona: Tusquets Editores, 1995. 178 p.: 1 map. (Col. Andanzas; 252)

La extraordinaria capacidad para contar historias que caracteriza al autor queda de manifiesto en un relato donde se hace difícil distinguir la memoria de los recuerdos efectivamente vividos y la transformación artística que experimentan en la imaginación del narrador. Excelente recreación de personajes inusuales y de ambientes característicos de la Patagonia, representados con todo su atractivo natural.

3741 Serrano, Marcela. El albergue de las mujeres tristes. Santiago: Alfaguara, 1997. 393 p.

Se recuperan en esta novela algunas situaciones de anteriores relatos de la autora. Varias mujeres llevan sus problemas personales a una casa de reposo en el sur de Chile. De sus diálogos nace una imagen adecuadamente construida de la situación de desmedro que vive la mujer en la sociedad patriarcal contemporánea.

3742 Skármeta, Antonio. No pasó nada. Santiago: Editorial Sudamericana, 1997. 88 p.

Publicada por primera vez en 1983, trae un interesante prólogo donde el autor se refiere a la gestación de esta novela y de *Ardiente paciencia* (*El cartero de Neruda*). Historia del exilio, su protagonista es un adolescente ubicado en el margen de dos mundos

radicalmente distintos. Excelente ejemplo del período inicial de la prosa skarmetiana.

3743 Subercaseaux, Elizabeth. Matrimonio a la chilena. 2. ed. Santiago: Aguilar Chilena de Ediciones, 1997. 233 p. (Alfaguara)

La situación desventajosa de la mujer en una sociedad dominada por el machismo se representa a través de imágenes de perfil caricaturesco en un discurso que asume conscientemente la forma y la agilidad del lenguaje televisivo. Buen ejemplo de la narrativa chilena de tendencia feminista que se impone en el país durante los últimos años.

3744 Varas, José Miguel. Exclusivo. Santiago: Planeta, 1996. 225 p. (Biblioteca del sur)

Ocho excelentes relatos con protagonistas que pertenecen al mundo de los marginados sociales y cuyas vidas son focalizadas para recordar que los seres insignificantes o repudiados comparten con los demás idénticas actitudes y sentimientos universales. Estas narraciones confirman a su autor como uno de los mejores cuentistas chilenos actuales.

3745 Volpe Mossotti, Enrique. Responso para un bandolero. Santiago: LOM Ediciones, 1996. 151 p. (Col. Entre mares. Novela)

Un auténtico bandolero chileno, Segundo Catalán, apodado El Corralero, que aterrorizó a los santiaguinos durante la primera mitad del siglo, es convertido en un símbolo de extraordinaria calidad literaria que permite contrastar una existencia en vías de extinción con el explosivo desarrollo de la postmodernidad urbana.

River Plate Countries

MAGDALENA GARCÍA-PINTO, *Associate Professor of Spanish and Director of Women's Studies, University of Missouri-Columbia*
MARÍA CRISTINA GUIÑAZÚ, *Associate Professor of Spanish, Lehman College, City University of New York*
CLAIRE MARTIN, *Professor of Spanish, California State University, Long Beach*

ARGENTINA

LOS TEXTOS AQUÍ RESEÑADOS corresponden al período 1993–97. Predomina en estos años la publicación de novelas, hecho que no resulta extraño si se tiene en cuenta la preferencia de los lectores por este género. Algunas tendencias prolongan las de años anteriores.

Varias novelas históricas ambientadas a partir de mediados del siglo XIX expanden el imaginario público en relación con la etapa de la fundación nacional. Desde perspectivas variadas y en tonos diferentes postulan tramas que combinan el quehacer público con la vida privada de los grandes personajes. Centradas en torno a Rosas (items **3836** and **3835**), a Urquiza (item **3819**) y a Melgarejo (item **3813**) sugieren relaciones con la historia del siglo XX, sobre todo, con el fracaso de la democracia que desembocó en los nefastos golpes de estado. Si bien todas ellas utilizan técnicas pertinentes a la ficción, las novelas de Andrés Rivera desbordan la reconstrucción histórica con la inclusión de procedimientos que recalcan su carácter ficticio. Por otra parte, la novelización del pasado, contextualizado en el ambiente histórico y cultural de la colonia le da a la novela de Julio Torres, *El oro de los Césares* (item **3856**), una riqueza y complejidad afines a las fabulaciones de Carpentier o Posse.

El fin de siglo figura, aunque no siempre explícitamente, en novelas que echan una mirada sobre los acontecimientos del siglo XX. *Adiós, Buenos Aires* de Néstor Galo (item **3793**) deja traslucir el babélico caos productivo de las oleadas inmigratorias a partir de 1870. En la novela de Mabel Pagano, *Agua de nadie,* los personajes entretejen las historias personales con la historia colectiva (item **3827**). En un tono más crítico, *Brüll* de Marcelo Caruso revé el terror de los años de dictadura (item **3768**) mientras que *La máquina de escribir* abarca numerosos relatos heteróclitos que relevan más de la literatura que de la historia nacional (item **3815**). De modo más específico en cuanto a la presencia de la política en la ficción, el estudio crítico de Nuria Girona Fibla (item **3894**) completa lo que las novelas callan analizándolas a través de la visión caleidoscópica que le prestan Lyotard, Foucault, Hayden White, Barthes y otros.

Se debe mencionar que varios textos, entre ellos algunos de los ya mencionados, coinciden en adoptar como punto de partida una situación de aislamiento sofocante debida a causas diversas: desastre natural, voluntad propia o evento fantástico. A pesar de que los recursos y los tonos narrativos respectivos varían—*El cuarto hostil* pertenece a la corriente fantástica (item **3767**), *Brüll* utiliza la técnica policial (item **3768**), *Cuando caiga el día* pone en juego elementos de la novela gótica (item **3804**), y *Agua de nadie* emplea la primera persona de tono nostálgico (item **3827**)—los personajes comparten un mismo sentimiento de impotencia pesimista que halla desahogo en la construcción de relatos.

Cabe destacar dentro del mismo género las metanarrativas de Susana Silvestre (item **3851**), la ya señalada de Teresa Caballero, *El cuarto hostil* (item **3767**), y los textos de César Aira, incluyendo sus relatos cortos (items **3746** y **3748**). Mientras que las dos primeras acercan los procesos de la creación literaria a una aventura extraño-fantástica, el segundo explora, con la práctica de diferentes estilos, su contacto con la realidad. Así, al modo de Duchamps, personaje del primer relato de *Taxol* (item **3748**), convierte textos cotidianos en objetos literarios. Finalmente, la novela de Reina Roffé pertenece a la corriente feminista ya que se ocupa de las luchas internas de un sujeto femenino moderno en busca de una identidad que lo represente (item **3837**).

En relación con los cuentos de este período hay que mencionar los relatos de Cristina Peri Rossi que incursionan en la temática sexual adjudicándole un tono celebratorio, muy nuevo, sobre todo en lo concerniente a la mujer (item **3830**). José M. Brindisi, por su parte, desarrolla problemas de índole existencialista en relatos que expresan la soledad, tema al que aluden también varias de las novelas mencionadas más arriba (item **3766**). Por último, algunos de los cuentos de Guillermina Piñeyro, irónicos, si se los contrapone al título de la colección, *Todo en orden,* denuncian las tácticas de terror impuestas por las dictaduras militares (item **3831**).

Entre los escritores noveles es importante señalar el dominio narrativo demostrado tanto por la novela de Miguel Sedoff (item **3847**) como por los cuentos de Claudia Soláns (item **3852**). [MCG and CEM]

PARAGUAY

En este período se destaca la novela de Roa Basto, *Madama Sui,* en la cual este maestro examina la vida de una mujer en su función de trabajadora sexual de uso exclusivo de la autoridad (item **3865**). Roa Bastos inaugura con esta ficción un tema que se ha explorado mínimamente en las letras hispanoamericanas. En el área de la historiografía literaria de este país, marcamos tres proyectos importantes de Méndez-Faith (item **3896**), Kallsen (item **3898**) y Pérez-Maricevich (item **3899**), que vienen a llenar algunos de los muchos vacíos que existen en la periodización, compilación, y crítica de las letras paraguayas. Esta es un área que ofrece innumerables proyectos a los interesados en la literatura de Paraguay. [MGP]

URUGUAY

Continúa la prolífica e interesante producción literaria de Rafael Courtoisie (items **3874** y **3875**) junto a la publicación de la obra ensayística de Mario Benedetti (item **3870**), quien también ha incursionado en la escritura autobiográfica con *Andamios* (item **3868**). Continúa la exploración de temas que tienen como centro los efectos del terrorismo de estado en la vida y cultura del país. Finalmente, la figura y en particular los sucesos anteriores a la muerte de la poeta Delmira Agustini continúa siendo un imán para la imaginación masculina. En este bienio Omar Prego (items **3889** y **3890**) y Guillermo Giucci (item **3879**) han publicado novelas en Montevideo, y Pedro Orgambide una novela en Buenos Aires (item **3901**). [MGP]

PROSE FICTION
Argentina

3746 Aira, César. La abeja. Buenos Aires: Emecé Editores, 1996. 170 p. (Escritores argentinos)

En un primer plano narrativo, inverosímilmente a cargo de voces infantiles, alternan otros en los que las situaciones insólitas colindan con los comentarios sobre el acto de narrar. La complejidad de la trama confunde las categorías de lo real y lo ficticio y desafía los hábitos de lectura. [MCG]

3747 Aira, César. La liebre. Buenos Aires: Emecé Editores, 1991. 251 p. (Escritores argentinos)

Novela. Aunque ambientada en las pampas argentinas durante el período Rosista, la narración de aventuras extrañas excede ampliamente cualquier reconstrucción histórica. Tal como dice un personaje: "Estas cosas sólo pasan en las novelas... Pero las novelas sólo pasan en la realidad." [MCG]

3748 Aira, César. Taxol: precedido de Duchamp en México y La broma. Buenos Aires: Simurg, 1997. 106 p.

Tres relatos variados que acercan la ficción al ensayo. Elaborados en torno a episodios reducidos a lo mínimo, sus recursos difieren de los que caracterizan la novelística del autor. Sin embargo, las elucubraciones de las voces narrativas que investigan las relaciones entre realidad, imaginación y ficción aclaran y reafirman aspectos de su obra anterior. [MCG]

3749 Ali-Brouchoud, Francisco Javier. La circunfeérica. Misiones, Argentina: Editorial Universitaria, Univ. Nacional de Misiones, 1993. 128 p. (Libros arribeños)

El espacio de esta novela es un encuentro entre toda una ideología del arte de la narración y el experimento que se genera a base del lenguaje. Esa novela busca zafarse de moldes y parámetros y desafiar así la comodidad del tiempo lineal, del desarrollo de la trama y de la evolución de los personajes sujetos a un ambiente claramente estipulado. [CEM]

3750 Alvarez Tuñón, Eduardo. El diablo en los ojos: novela. Buenos Aires: Editorial Galerna, 1994. 168 p.

A raíz de un transplante de ojos, el protagonista se encuentra prisionero de un pacto con la viuda del dueño de sus ojos. Lo que se inicia como un ritual absurdo, pero inocente, poco a poco se va apoderando del protagonista. Novela de un lirismo metafísico intenso e inquietante. [CEM]

3751 Andahazi, Federico. El anatomista. 2. ed. Buenos Aires: Planeta, 1997. 277 p.

Novela. Recrea muy bien el ambiente del siglo XVI con sus prejuicios y creencias. El descubrimiento del anatomista lo enfrenta con la condena inquisitorial. El tema erótico de la novela causó el retiro del premio de la Fundación Amalia Lacroze de Fortabat hecho que duplica en el siglo XX el castigo renacentista de la ficción. [MCG]

3752 Anderson Imbert, Enrique. Amoríos (y un retrato de dos genios). Buenos Aires: El Francotirador Ediciones, 1997. 167 p.

El arte de la escritura es subvertido por el humor y la ironía en esta novela ágil en la cual un profesor de literatura y un grupo de estudiantes tratan de descifrar el misterio de un escritor olvidado que se resiste al juego de la fama. [CEM]

3753 Anderson Imbert, Enrique. Reloj de arena. Buenos Aires: El Francotirador Ediciones, 1995. 158 p.

Anderson Imbert superpone dos resúmenes de relatos pertenecientes a la cuentística universal para enfatizar la ambigüedad y la ironía que manan de este juego de dobles, pareados a veces arbitrariamente. [CEM]

3754 Arias, Abelardo. El, Juan Facundo. Buenos Aires: Editorial Galerna, 1995. 212 p.: bibl.

En el "Prólogo" el autor define su texto acertadamente como "una suerte de antología histórica novelada," una "especie de revisión literaria." Efectivamente, esta biografía de Facundo Quiroga que no elude la ficción dialoga con la de Sarmiento a la que corrige y completa con otras fuentes añadiendo mayor complejidad al personaje. Explica el surgimiento del caudillo como resultado de la situación política del momento. [MCG]

3755 Arlt, Roberto. Aguafuertes porteñas. Introducción de Rita Gnutzmann. Buenos Aires: Corregidor, 1995. 189 p.

Reedición de los textos que publicados en El Mundo entre 1928–1935 documentan la situación político-social del momento. Esta edición organiza su heterogeneidad agrupándolos según los temas tratados. Desfilan en ellos toda suerte de personajes, predominando los de la clase obrera y de la pequeña burguesía, sin eludir los tipos cómicos. Los precede una excelente introducción de Rita Gnutzmann. [MCG]

3756 Arlt, Roberto. El criador de gorilas; Un viaje terrible. Introducción y notas de Teodosio Fernández. Madrid: Alianza Editorial, 1994. 225 p.: bibl. (Sección Literatura)

Reedición de los cuentos y de la "nouvelle" originariamente publicados en 1941. Extremadamente útil por cuanto se trata de textos agotados, esta edición hecha por T. Fernández incluye una introducción así como una bibliografía. [MCG]

3757 Atanasiú, Andrés Homero. Preludio y muerte de amor. Buenos Aires: Grupo Editor Latinoamericano, 1994. 307 p. (Colección Escritura de hoy)

Esta novela entrelaza dos relatos: el del personaje principal, un escritor de fama y el del narrador, biógrafo del anterior. La relación entre ambos da pie a la inclusión de comentarios críticos y teóricos sobre la creación literaria y sobre la función de la palabra en dicha labor. [MCG]

3758 Belgrano Rawson, Eduardo. No se turbe vuestro corazón. Buenos Aires: Editorial Sudamericana, 1994. 245 p. (Colección Narrativas argentinas)

Las vidas de los habitantes de un pueblo se vuelven testimonio de la violencia y de la crueldad. El humor esconde el horror del acto arbitrario y cobarde; la broma disimula la necedad humana. Esta lograda novela contiene ecos de la triste historia nacional en su trama pícara y desgarradora. [CEM]

3759 Bellomo, Gabriel. Historias con nombre propio. Buenos Aires: Libros de Tierra Firme, 1994. 93 p. (Colección de narrativas Los Oficios terrestres; 7)

Incluye 15 cuentos de valor variado. Desarrollados cada uno en torno a un protagonista principal describen, con economía, su lucha contra la adversidad del medio en que viven. Cubren una gran variedad de técnicas que abarcan desde la pesquisa policial hasta el drama psicológico. [MCG]

3760 Bernatek, Carlos. La pasión en colores. Buenos Aires: Planeta, 1994. 245 p. (Biblioteca del sur. Novela)

Un joven provinciano inicia un viaje sin retorno al llegar a Buenos Aires. Es esta la historia de un individuo perdido entre personajes cuyas vidas apenas lo tocan, y sin embargo, dejan en él una impronta profunda. Todo en él lo destina a un último acto salvaje, el cual también llegará a enterrarse en el pasado. [CEM]

3761 Bianciotto, Horacio. Las murallas. Córdoba, Argentina: Vestal Ediciones, 1993. 94 p.: ill.

Incluye 12 relatos muy cortos. Desde perspectivas variadas narran experiencias extrañas que, a modo de metáforas cifran las vidas de los personajes. [MCG]

3762 Bini, Rafael. La venganza de Killing. Buenos Aires: Ediciones Ultimo Reino, 1993. 199 p.

Primera novela del autor. César Aira acertadamente la califica "de línea ciberpunk, multimedia, procedente del comic, la ciencia ficcion burroughsiana, el rock, y en general los fenómenos socioculturales agrupados bajo el nombre de posmodernismo." Con originalidad, desafía la reducción a esquemas simples. Premio Fundación Antorchas 1992. [MCG]

3763 Bioy Casares, Adolfo. De jardines ajenos: libro abierto. Edición al cuidado de Daniel Martino. Buenos Aires: Temas Grupo Editorial, 1997. 320 p. (Colección Temas de literatura)

Antología de expresiones y comenta-

rios del habla popular que se relaciona con los estilos de las novelas del autor. Con gran sentido del humor comenta sobre los registros orales de las distintas clases sociales. Indispensable para los estudiosos de la obra de Bioy. [MCG]

3764 Bioy Casares, Adolfo. Memorias. v. 1, Infancia, adolescencia, y cómo se hace un escritor. Barcelona: Tusquets Editores, 1994. 1 v.: ill. (Colección Andanzas; 210)

Autobiografía. Narrada en base a anécdotas entretenidas ilustrada, en un registro diferente, el hábil manejo de la prosa que caracteriza al autor. A los recuerdos de juventud siguen los de amistades, comentarios de lecturas y viajes. Ocupan un lugar especial los gustos compartidos con Silvina Ocampo y Borges, así como los "desencuentros" divertidos con Victoria Ocampo. En sección aparte figuran "Historia de mi familia" que detalla su genealogía e "Historia de mis libros" de gran valor para el estudio y comprensión de su obra. [MCG]

3765 Borges, Jorge Luis. El tamaño de mi esperanza. 2. ed. Buenos Aires: Seix Barral, 1993. 137 p. (Biblioteca breve)

Reedición del libro publicado originariamente en 1926 y cuya reedición fue prohibida por el autor. Resulta de gran interés puesto que prefigura los temas desarrollados posteriormente. Permite asimismo establecer grandes diferencias en cuanto al lenguaje y al estilo empleados. Incluye una "Inscripción" explicativa de María Kodama. [MCG]

3766 Brindisi, José María. Permanece oro. Buenos Aires: Editorial Sudamericana: Fondo Nacional de las Artes, 1996. 205 p. (Colección Narrativas argentinas)

Diez cuentos. La mayoría de los relatos en primera persona narran desde un punto de vista personal e intimista situaciones extrañas en que la realidad, el sueño y el delirio se superponen. La soledad, la búsqueda de la identidad propia y la revisión de culpas pasadas constituyen las cargas ineludibles de los personajes. Premio Fondo Nacional de las Artes, 1993. [MCG]

3767 Caballero, Teresa. El cuarto hostil. Buenos Aires: Corregidor, 1995. 175 p.

La contraposición de diversas voces y perspectivas en esta novela compone un registro narrativo cercano al de lo extraño-maravilloso. Se trata de un metatexto que narra su propia historia de manera original. [MCG]

3768 Caruso, Marcelo. Brüll. Buenos Aires: Planeta, 1996. 239 p. (Biblioteca del sur)
Primera novela del autor. La imagen de una inundación de magnitud bíblica—¿recuerdo de El matadero?—enmarca la narración. La combinación de técnicas del relato policial y de la novela de horror resulta eficaz en la creación de una extensa alegoría del país sumido en el terror político de las décadas de los 70 y 80. Premio de Novela Fortabat. [MCG]

3769 Castillo, Abelardo. La casa de ceniza. Buenos Aires: Emecé Editores, 1994. 142 p. (Escritores argentinos)
Novela gótica estructurada bajo un plan de intranquilizadora cerebralidad. El narrador atrapado en el delirio de un artista soberbio y demente, se enfrenta a una verdad enloquecedora sobre el espíritu humano en toda su belleza y su maldad. [CEM]

3770 Chernov, Carlos. Anatomía humana. Buenos Aires: Editorial Planeta Argentina, 1993. 393 p. (Biblioteca del sur)
Novela. A partir de una situación absurda—la muerte de la mayoría de los hombres—narra las aventuras de uno de los sobrevivientes. Libre de las trabas de lo verosímil, combina sobriedad y humor en la creación de ambientes delirantes en los que la imaginería sexual rige todos los comportamientos. Premio de Novela Planeta Biblioteca del Sur 1993. [MCG]

3771 Clucellas, María Isabel. Los que esperan. Buenos Aires: El Francotirador Ediciones, 1994. 269 p.: maps.
Desde el primer siglo de la era cristiana, los múltiples personajes de esta novela peregrinan por el mundo en búsqueda de su propia verdad. Las religiones y las culturas en las cuales crecen y se nutren, se revelan como caras de la misma moneda. El último personaje, una mujer argentina, desanda los pasos de los peregrinos que la anteceden en busca de respuestas. [CEM]

3772 Colombres, Adolfo. La gran noche. Buenos Aires: Ediciones Letra Buena, 1993. 202 p.: ill. (Colección Letras/novela)
Africa y Latinoamérica se anudan mediante el lenguaje en una narrativa que emula con ironía el arquetípico viaje. A través de una multiplicidad de niveles narrativos y de un idioma permeado, contaminado e inasible, se concretiza la alienación del ser en su encuentro con la otredad. [CEM]

3773 Colombres, Adolfo. Tierra incógnita. Buenos Aires: Ediciones del Sol: Distribución exclusiva, Ediciones Colihue, 1994. 206 p. (La Línea de sombra. Serie azul)
El encuentro entre un hombre retraído y huraño y una joven sin rumbo marca el inicio de la inquietante búsqueda de sí mismos durante una travesía marina poblada de misterios y revelaciones. [CEM]

3774 Conti, Haroldo. Cuentos completos. Buenos Aires: Emecé Editores, 1994. 355 p. (Escritores argentinos)
Colección que reúne en orden cronológico los cuentos anteriormente publicados en libros y revistas. Bajo el subtítulo de "Homenajes" aparecen cuatro composiciones recordatorias de amistades. [MCG]

3775 Cortázar, Julio. Cuentos completos. v. 1–2. Madrid: Alfaguara, 1994. 2 v. (Colección Unesco de obras representativas. Serie iberoamericana)
Publicada en 1994 en conmemoración del décimo aniversario de la muerte del autor, esta edición en dos volúmenes abarca la totalidad de su obra cuentística. Desde la poco conocida primera colección La otra orilla, publicada en 1945, hasta Deshoras de 1982 permite seguir el itinerario narrativo del autor, experimentador de estructuras y tramas que van de lo fantástico al juego lingüístico, pasando por el compromiso social y la crítica irónica. Las precede un "Prólogo" de Vargas Llosa, homenaje al maestro por las audacias con que ha renovado el género. [MCG]

3776 Cortázar, Julio. Final del juego. Edición de Jaime Alazraki. Madrid: Anaya & Mario Muchnik, 1995. 229 p.: bibl. (Escritores de América)
A cargo de Jaime Alazraki, esta edición cuidadosamente anotada reproduce la segunda, de 1964 incluyendo un total de dieciocho relatos. Añade un glosario de argentinismos así como un artículo crítico del editor. [MCG]

3777 Crespo, Enriqueta. El juego de la mirada. Buenos Aires: Corregidor, 1994. 125 p. (Plástica y literatura)

En cada breve narrativa encontramos el juego de las miradas que esconden el profundo dolor de la inquietud, de la ignorancia de sí mismo y de los otros. Los personajes de Crespo, anonadados por la rutina, buscan sin tregua algún indicio de la vida que soñaron y que parece escapárseles. [CEM]

3778 Cross, Esther. La divina proporción y otros cuentos. Buenos Aires: Emecé Editores, 1994. 139 p. (Escritores argentinos)

Incluye 14 cuentos impecablemente estructurados. La gran destreza en el manejo del humor, la parodia y la crueldad así como de los recursos fantásticos crea situaciones y ambientes extraños ingeniosamente montados. [MCG]

3779 Cuentistas argentinos de fin de siglo. v. 1–2 y estudio preliminar. Buenos Aires: Editorial Vinciguerra, 1997. 2 v.: bibl. (Colección Nuevo cauce)

El proceso de selección, inevitablemente arbitrario en una colección de este tipo, lo es aún más en esta edición cuyo criterio requería que los autores estuvieran vivos en el momento de publicación. Reúne las muestras de 84 autores, algunos canónicos que publican desde antes de mediados de siglo, otros, noveles y desconocidos. Esa amplitud aparente no impide omisiones importantes. Los precede un estudio preliminar de María Rosa Lojo que comenta sumariamente los textos antologados. [MCG]

3780 Deane Reddy, Teresa. La suerte al sur. Buenos Aires: Francotirador Ediciones, 1994. 126 p.

La novela sigue las tendencias por la corriente indigenista y se desarrolla en torno a personajes que encarnan valores opuestos. Enmarcado en un paisaje idílico de repercusiones míticas, el drama sobrepasa lo personal y adquiere valor social. [MCG]

3781 Denevi, Marco. Falsificaciones. Buenos Aires: Ediciones Corregidor, 1996. 172 p.

La colección de "falsificaciones" o versiones originales de hechos y personajes históricos, legendarios, bíblicos y literarios demuestra la pirotecnia intelectual de Denevi, quien con un guiño cómplice reescribe la materia prima narrativa universal. [CEM]

3782 Di Marco, Rubén A. Vecino de carpa. Buenos Aires: Corregidor, 1994. 159 p.

Novela ácida y despiadada sobre las relaciones entre los sexos. Di Marco hace alarde de un conocedor uso, entre irónico y humorístico, del vernáculo argentino. La lucha degarradora y cruenta entre los personajes por el dominio y el poder a través de la conquista sexual, dejan un sabor amargo y ahondan el profundo desamparo del ser. [CEM]

3783 Diaconú, Alina. Qué nos pasa, Nicolás? Buenos Aires: Editorial Atlántida, 1995. 194 p. (Voces del Plata)

Contiene 18 cuentos. Primer libro de cuentos de la autora que incluye algunos publicados anteriormente. Con gran economía en el lenguaje y con una perspectiva casi distante relatan situaciones que bordean el horror. Los conflictos internos de los personajes involucran la soledad, la falta de dinero y las relaciones humanas desesperanzadas. Prólogo de María Kodama. [MCG]

3784 Diosdado, Ana. Igual que aquel príncipe. Madrid: Ediciones Temas de Hoy, 1994. 210 p. (Nueva novela romántica; 6)

Novela. Ambientada en México durante la época de la independencia articula diestramente los episodios íntimos de la vida de una familia con instancias posibles de la guerra. El cruce entre los ámbitos de lo privado y lo público crea interés y permite la contraposición de los roles masculinos y femeninos. El espacio conventual figura como el único que provee la clandestinidad necesaria para las hacedoras de la historia. [MCG]

3785 Doallo, Beatriz Celina. Cuentos de aquí y de allá. Buenos Aires: Faro Editorial, 1993. 125 p. (Cuento)

Colección de cuentos donde los personajes emergen a través del lenguaje regional, y se ubican dentro de un paisaje rico en matices, profundo de significados. La condición humana se dibuja en los detalles nimios, en el giro de una frase con tonada, en el silencio digno y enigmático de ciertos tipos. [CEM]

3786 Donato, Ada. Había una vez—. Rosario, Argentina: Editorial Municipal, 1994. 140 p.

Colección de cuentos inéditos escritos entre 1955–93. Estos veinte relatos se ofrecen como un desafío a la linearidad temporal, y a la existencia de una dimensión única y comprobable. Lo real, lo imaginario, lo maravilloso dentro de lo cotidiano, las supersticiones, el delirio son planos desde los cuales la autora nos invita a cuestionar el absurdo de la certidumbre de lo real. [CEM]

3787 Esquivel, Eva. Trampa para no morir. Buenos Aires: Torres Agüero Editor, 1994. 163 p.

El libro se compone de dos series: "Trampas breves" contiene veintidós relatos que por su brevedad y temática se asemejan a poemas narrativos en prosa. Comentan actitudes sociales, expresiones lingüísticas, imágenes, recuerdos y evocan estados de ánimo. La segunda serie, "Trampas extensas" abarca catorce relatos de valor variado que combinan imaginación y humor negro. "No me esperes Kay (1)" y "Strip tease" recibieron respectivamente el Primer Premio del Concurso Literario de Cuento y Poesía "Enrique Pezzoni" 1992 y del Concurso Pablo Rojas Paz 1991. [MCG]

3788 Feinmann, José Pablo. Los crímenes de Van Gogh. Buenos Aires: Planeta, 1994. 306 p. (Biblioteca del sur)

Novela policial de gran originalidad. El protagonista se propone "abrir un nuevo espacio en la realidad", objetivo que logra fundiendo en ella grandes dosis de ficción. Las reminiscencias de decorados, guiones y personajes del cine integradas a los ambientes de la Argentina actual lleva a cuestionar el "snobismo" de la imitación ciega de todo lo norteamericano. Los personajes se convierten en los actores de un libreto ajeno. [MCG]

3789 Fernández, A. Daniel. Edipo en gris: gris de niebla, de perla envanecida, de muela de plomo, barata, mendicante. Buenos Aires: Corregidor, 1994. 123 p.

El mito de Edipo y el complejo freudiano dan lugar a una narrativa psicológica en la cual madre e hijo manejan los hilos de una relación secreta. La tensión afectiva, la manipulación de los sentimientos y la seducción de lo prohibido siguen a los personajes, en continuo movimiento entre la ciudad y el campo. [CEM]

3790 Ferreyra, Gustavo Alejandro. El amparo. Buenos Aires: Editorial Sudamericana, 1994. 267 p. (Colección Narrativas argentinas)

Adolfo ocupa un cargo inusitado: es el receptor de carozos. Esta novela inquietante, misteriosa y sobria se desarrolla en una mansión habitada por un amo y decenas de sirvientes. Los corredores esconden habita-

ciones-cárceles donde la vida parece tomar lugar sólo en la mente del personaje. El miedo, el desprecio, el odio y la paranoia son los compañeros infatigables de Adolfo. [CEM]

3791 Fresán, Rodrigo. Trabajos manuales. Buenos Aires: Planeta, 1994. 286 p. (Biblioteca del sur)

Colección de relatos unidos por el tenue hilo de un personaje-idea, Forma, que nos zarandea de una realidad a una ficción en una alocada carrera contra la estupidez y la uniformidad complaciente. La sucesión de mini-ensayos y relatos tiene como punto de mira el ridículo y deshumanizante mundo paralelo al cual nos sometemos todos en algún momento. [CEM]

3792 Galmarini, Hugo R. Crónica del desencuentro: el amor, el poder y los negocios; Buenos Aires 1820–1840. Buenos Aires: Grupo Editor Latinoamericano: Distribuidor exclusivo, Emecé Editores, 1995. 406 p.: bibl. (Colección Controversia)

Novela histórica. De modo ameno y con rigor investigativo relata en detalle las peripecias de la organización nacional comenzada a partir de la batalla de Cepeda. Narra el proceso que conduce a la ruptura de relaciones entre facciones diferentes y a la asunción de Rosas al poder. Integra la "petite histoire" a la relación del establecimiento de sociedades políticas, sociales y económicas. Las notas a final de capítulo documentan las fuentes consultadas. [MCG]

3793 Galo, Néstor. Adiós, Buenos Aires. Argentina: Editorial Otium, 1992. 272 p.: bibl., ill.

Novela histórica ubicada al principio de las oleadas inmigratorias en la Argentina del siglo pasado. La masacre de Tandil (1872) reúne a los personajes en torno a las tensiones entre los elementos extranjeros y los gauchos. La versión histórica de este suceso figura en John Lynch's *Massacre in the pampas, 1872* (1998). [CEM]

3794 Gambaro, Griselda. Después del día de fiesta. Buenos Aires: Seix Barral, 1994. 197 p. (Biblioteca breve)

Tristán se lanza a la calle como todos los días a un mundo en el cual convergen la belleza y el horror de la maldad. El odio, el egoísmo, la envidia y el prejuicio hacen batalla frente a un personaje observador y medio poeta. Con el poeta Leopardi en busca de su hermana y los grupos de negros que invaden la laguna, la alegoría de la eterna lucha entre el bien y el mal, la belleza y la fealdad adquiere un nuevo impacto entre lírico y extraño. [CEM]

3795 Gandolfo, Elvio E. Ferrocarriles argentinos. Buenos Aires: Aguilar, Altea, Taurus, Alfaguara, 1994. 166 p. (Alfaguara literaturas)

Con un título en apariencia apoético para una colección de cuentos, el autor ofrece diez relatos cuyos temas triviales se transforman en una excelente narración, atravesados por el humor, la tensión de un encuentro imprevisto y como si la vida diaria en su trivialidad y tensión fuera tan efímera como un viaje en tren, como lo sugiere el texto del último cuento de la colección, en el sentido que el ritmo del tren y su rutina configuran una metáfora de la existencia para la mayoría de los habitantes del planeta. [MGP]

3796 García Hamilton, José Ignacio. Vida de un ausente: la novelesca biografía del talentoso seductor Juan Bautista Alberdi. Buenos Aires: Editorial Sudamericana, 1993. 335 p.: bibl.

La historia argentina, desde sus albores republicanos hasta fines del siglo pasado, va surgiendo a medida que se desarrolla la vida de Juan Bautista Alberdi. Esta novela histórica desenmascara los lazos familiares que se repiten como ecos en la historia nacional. [CEM]

3797 Giardinelli, Mempo. Imposible equilibrio. Barcelona: Planeta, 1995. 235 p. (Colección Nueva narrativa)

Novela. La importación de hipopótamos al Chaco inicia con hilaridad una serie de aventuras que hacen reflexionar sobre la situación argentina del presente. El empleo del lenguaje coloquial junto a la descripción de ambientes provincianos contrapesan la inverosimilitud y posibilitan la crítica de carácter político. [MCG]

3798 Gómez, Albino. Si no volvemos a vernos. Buenos Aires: Editorial de Belgrano, 1996. 362 p.

Entretejida a modo de contrapunto, la historia de un amor nuevo se levanta a la sombra de los trágicos acontecimientos de la historia argentina desde 1974 a 1976. La brutalidad se opone a la belleza de las ideas y del amor sin poder anularlas. [CEM]

3799 Gorodischer, Angélica. Prodigios. Barcelona: Editorial Lumen, 1994. 174 p. (Femenino singular; 19)

La casa del poeta Novalis acoge las vidas de varias mujeres durante el siglo diecinueve. Con humor, ironía y un firme manejo de la atmósfera en que se desarrolla la acción, Gorodischer ofrece una trama misteriosa y secreta de estos destinos atrapados entre los muros de la vieja casona. [CEM]

3800 Gorodischer, Angélica. Técnicas de supervivencia. Rosario, Argentina: Editorial Municipal, 1994. 105 p.

Ocho cuentos. Aunque inéditos, pertenen a distintos períodos de la producción de la autora y fueron seleccionados por ella como muestra antológica. La diversidad de las técnicas empleadas enfatiza un elemento común, la capacidad crítica que revela la culminación de una crisis íntima. [MCG]

3801 Guebel, Daniel. Matilde. Buenos Aires: Editorial Sudaméricana, 1994. 167 p. (Colección Narrativas argentinas)

Novela psicológica en la cual los amores no correspondidos toman un rumbo cruel y despiadado. La ironía de la incomunicación o la comunicación fatalmente errada, apuntan a un plano de relaciones humanas que bordean en el ridículo y en el dolor. [CEM]

3802 Gusmán, Luis. La música de Frankie. Buenos Aires: Editorial Sudamericana, 1993. 139 p. (Colección Narrativas argentinas)

Dos hombres en una cárcel reconstruyen, a partir de vestigios, sus vidas. Las revelaciones se tornan mentiras, evocan la vergüenza, el miedo y el odio de una vida trunca por la falta de amor a sí mismos. Los recuerdos de los prisioneros, entrelazados por el crimen y la muerte, revelan inexorablemente la crueldad inherente del ser humano librado a sus pasiones. [CEM]

3803 Heker, Liliana. Frescos de amor. Buenos Aires: Editorial Planeta Argentina, 1995. 182 p. (Seix Barral)

Empleando la primera persona y en una prosa altamente poética, la protagonista busca otorgar sentido a su existencia. Las meditaciones, unidas a los procedimientos de montaje cinematográfico adoptados en la narración, deconstruyen un mundo caótico que confirma la enajenación propia. [MCG]

3804 Khedayan, Marcos. Cuando caiga el día: novela. Buenos Aires: Planeta, 1996. 193 p.

Primera novela del autor. Según un marco que se asemeja al del *Decamerón* reúne una serie de cuentos fantásticos de tono gótico. Este joven escritor novel da pruebas de un buen manejo de la narrativa. [MCG]

3805 Lagunas, Alberto. Diario de un vidente y otras alucinaciones. Rosario, Argentina: Editorial Municipal, 1994. 232 p.

Incluye 24 cuentos. A los relatos de la primera edición se agregan otros, previos, seleccionados de *Fogatas de Otoño* antologías y periódicos. Los precede una introducción de Inés Santa Cruz, sugerente de pautas de lectura. Primer Premio Concurso Internacional de Narrativa Losada 1980. [MCG]

3806 Lamborghini, Osvaldo. Tadeys. Recopilación de César Aira. Barcelona: Ediciones del Serbal, 1994. 376 p.: ill. (Novelas y cuentos; 12)

Narraciones de carácter novelesco en que se demuestra la originalidad creadora del autor. Esta obra, póstuma e incompleta, compilada por C. Aira incluye un "Dossier" y una "Tercera parte" de documentos relacionados con ella. El compilador ha respetado con fidelidad las variantes y las notas del texto. Una "Nota" introductoria ofrece datos esclarecedores acerca de la edición. [MCG]

3807 Linck, Delfina. Te busca y te nombra. Buenos Aires: Ediciones B, Grupo Zeta, 1994. 419 p. (América, tiempos modernos)

Primera novela de la autora. Entreteje una trama compleja que integra, una en otra, las historias de dos mujeres marginadas. Monólogos, diálogos, citas de tangos, alusiones literarias e históricas componen de modo original un texto que, además, narra su propia historia. A la búsqueda mítica de la madre se añade la labor escritural que pretende crear un relato coherente a partir de fragmentos. [MCG]

3808 Lojo de Beuter, María Rosa. La pasión de los nómades. Buenos Aires: Editorial Atlántida, 1994. 216 p. (Voces del Plata)

Rosaura y Merlín, personajes legendarios y anacrónicos se trasladan a Buenos Aires. Allí conocen a Lucio Victorio Mansilla, quien se ha escapado del paraíso para observar a su país. Con este personaje, la narración recorre en forma inversa la historia nacional pasada y la enfrenta al presente con humor e ironía. [CEM]

3809 López Echagüe, Hernán. La resaca. Rosario, Argentina: B. Viterbo Editora, 1994. 125 p. (Ficciones)

Un ex-revolucionario argentino encuentra en el dueño de un bar en São Paulo un interlocutor mudo y distante a quien narrar, entre copa y porro, la amargura y el desencanto de una vida desamparada, dura y finalmente desperdiciada. Los horrores de una época infame se trasladan a la prosa hiriente y cruel con la que el personaje reconstruye su vida. [CEM]

3810 Loreti, Miguel. Entrada a paraíso. Buenos Aires: Grupo Editor Latinoamericano: Distribuidor exclusivo, Emecé Editores, 1995. 134 p. (Colección Escritura de hoy)

Incluye 11 relatos. El predominio de la estructura dialogada y la fluidez de un lenguaje cuidadosamente equilibrado plantean discontinuidades entre personajes, temas y situaciones. Cuestionan los límites inciertos que enlazan categorías diversas: fantasías, relaciones humanas, conceptos. Premio Fondo Nacional de las Artes 1994. [MCG]

3811 Lysyj, Viviana. Erotópolis: erotic rocks. Buenos Aires: Ediciones de la Flor, 1994. 154 p. (Colección Narrativa)

Incluye 35 cuentos de valor que celebran explícitamente el erotismo femenino. La saturación de la expresión junto a los comentarios literarios y a las referencias a la cultura "pop" crean un barroquismo que realza el placer de la palabra. Irreverencia y humor se combinan para subvertir las voces tradicionales del género, usualmente masculinas. [MCG]

3812 Marechal, Leopoldo. Adán Buenosayres. Edición, introducción y notas de Pedro Luis Barcia. Madrid: Editorial Castalia, 1994. 979 p.: bibl., ill., index. (Clásicos Castalia; 210)

Reedición de la novela publicada por primera vez en 1947. Pedro Luis Barcia ha anotado prolijamente la edición a la que inicia con un estudio excelente sobre la misma. La completan varias fotografías y un índice de palabras argentinas. [MCG]

3813 **Martelli, Juan Carlos.** Melgarejo.
Buenos Aires: Perfil Libros, 1997.
223 p. (Las novelas de la historia)
Esta novela histórica es un relato de
las aventuras políticas y amorosas de quien
fuera el dictador boliviano más cruel del siglo
XIX. La alternancia de la primera y tercera
persona en la narración resulta efectiva para
dar la visión intimista del personaje junto a
otra, exterior, mayormente crítica. [MCG]

3814 **Martínez, Tomás Eloy.** Santa Evita.
Buenos Aires: Planeta, 1995. 398 p. (Biblioteca del sur)
Novela. Con una pertinacia casi obsesiva la voz narrativa persigue la trayectoria
del cuerpo de Eva Duarte de Perón. Las voces
de una galería de personajes transmiten la
fascinación ejercida por su figura y explican
su "canonización" en la imaginería popular.
La imposibilidad de discernir entre historia y
ficción produce un relato alucinante que re-
vivifica de manera indiscutible la categoría
de lo "real maravilloso." [MCG]

3815 **Martini, Juan Carlos.** La máquina de
escribir. Buenos Aires: Seix Barral,
1996. 313 p. (Biblioteca breve)
Una proliferación de pequeñas historias fragmentarias constituyen esta novela
que hace de los juegos del lenguaje y del humor paródico sus mayores recursos. El fin de
siglo sirve de punto de partida para la revisión de una colección disparatada de personajes, películas, novelas y hechos históricos. [MCG]

3816 **Masetto, Antonio dal.** Gente del bajo.
Buenos Aires: Planeta, 1995. 269 p.
(Biblioteca del sur)
Contiene 64 relatos breves, muchos de
los cuales habían sido publicados anteriormente. La estructura del diálogo, predominante, junto a la repetición de los tipos de
personajes sirven de vehículo para recrear el
mundo del Bajo. Los relatos dan una visión
masculina que integra el humor y la personalidad del hombre del barrio. [MCG]

3817 **Masetto, Antonio dal.** La tierra incom-
parable. Buenos Aires: Editorial Planeta, 1994. 273 p. (Biblioteca del sur)
La novela continúa una temática explorada anteriormente por el autor. A su
regreso a Italia después de una estadía de
cuarenta años como inmigrante en Argentina, una anciana coteja sus recuerdos con

la realidad del presente. El relato de viajes
vuelto meditación sobre la pérdida irrevoca-
ble del pasado evoca con precisión y nostalgia las memorias de una vida. Premio Planeta
Biblioteca del Sur 1994. [MCG]

3818 **Medrano, Carmen.** La buena gente. Argentina: Grupo Editor Latinoamericano, 1994. 133 p.: ill. (Colección Escritura
de hoy)
Periodista, crítica de arte, cuentista,
Carmen Medrano ofrece en esta colección de
cuentos breves y bien estructurados una posibilidad de evasión dentro de lo cotidiano. El
elemento sorpresivo, el humor recatado y el
acecho de un dolor o de un misterio planean
en la superficie de cada uno de sus cuentos. [CEM]

3819 **Miguel, María Esther de.** El general, el
pintor y la dama. Buenos Aires: Planeta, 1996. 318 p.
La autora incursiona nuevamente en la
novela histórica, tomando esta vez como protagonistas a Justo José de Urquiza y al pintor
uruguayo Juan Manuel Blanes. Entrelaza con
destreza la investigación minuciosa y las pasiones personales en la recreación del ambiente romántico rioplatense del siglo pasado. Premio Planeta 1996. [MCG]

3820 **Montergous, Gabriel.** Polo y los dispersos. Buenos Aires: Grupo Editor Latino
américano, 1995. 201 p. (Colección Escritura
de hoy)
Segundo Premio. Fondo Nacional de
las Artes. Novela 1994. Montergous demuestra de manera convincente su dominio del
arte de narrar en una novela que nos seduce
con sus personajes, y su visión crítica y a la
vez humana de los errores del pasado. [CEM]

3821 **Mujeres: imágenes argentinas.** Selección y prólogo de María Gabriela
Mizraje. Buenos Aires: Ediciones Instituto
Movilizador de Fondos Cooperativos, 1993.
128 p. (Desde la gente)
Esta antología reúne cartas, poesías,
ensayos, selecciones autobiográficas, cuentos, y recetas gastronómicas provenientes de
gran variedad de fuentes. Ilustra la escritura
de mujeres argentinas a lo largo de los siglos
XIX y XX e incluye nombres tan dispares
como Juana Manuela Gorriti, Emma de la
Barra, Victoria Ocampo, Eva Perón y Hebe de
Bonafini, entre muchos otros. Los precede un

prólogo de María Gabriela Mizraje con datos biográficos sobre las autoras. [MCG]

3822 Narradoras argentinas, 1852–1932. Recopilación de Lily Sosa de Newton. Buenos Aires: Editorial Plus Ultra, 1995. 268 p.: bibl., ill. (Colección Las mujeres)

La antología reúne 25 textos femeninos, escritos entre 1852–1932. Da una muestra excelente de la riqueza de géneros tratados: cuento, novela, ensayo. Junto a autoras de gran divulgación incluye a otras de menor difusión que merecen ser estudiadas. Guía útil por cuanto ofrece datos biográficos sobre las autoras así como una introducción explicativa sobre los diferentes períodos. [MCG]

3823 Neder, María Olga. Entre los huecos. Buenos Aires: Ediciones del Dock, 1994. 105 p.

Incluye 12 cuentos de valor variado. Estructurados en torno a interrupciones, ausencias y discontinuidades narran episodios extraños que suscitan expectativas e impresiones profundas en los personajes. [MCG]

3824 Newland, Carlos and **Cristina Corti Maderna.** Inquisición en Luxán: la histórica búsqueda del tesoro de Sobremonte. Buenos Aires: Grupo Editor Latinoamericano, 1993. 149 p.: bibl., ill. (Colección Escritura de hoy)

Novela histórica. Se estructura en torno a dos narrativas: la de la búsqueda del tesoro colonial por parte de los ingleses durante la primera invasión se inserta en la que historia la elaboración del texto en el presente. El cruce de ambas combina de manera interesante la tecnología detectivesca con la descripción de los ambientes y personajes del pasado. La bibliografía del final provee las fuentes investigativas. [MCG]

3825 Nicastro, Laura Diana. Libro de los amores clandestinos. Buenos Aires: Grupo Editor Latinoamericano: Distribuidor exclusivo, Emecé Editores, 1995. 112 p. (Colección Escritura de hoy)

Contiene 18 relatos. Como lo sugiere el título se trata de historias en que la estructura de la pareja binaria se bifurca en otra de tres o en que relaciones de esperanzas truncas se resuelven en postergaciones perennes y venganzas tardías. [MCG]

3826 Orozco, Olga. La luz es un abismo. Montevideo: Vintén Editor, 1993. 57 p.

Contiene tres relatos que evocan el mundo infantil recuperado en la memoria adulta. La experiencia poética de la autora permea la maleabilidad de su prosa, siempre justa en la expresión del suspenso ante sensaciones y sentimientos nuevos. Surgen de allí preguntas que, por la falta de respuestas, implantan la duda sobre la familiaridad de lo cotidiano. [MCG]

3827 Pagano, Mabel. Agua de nadie. Buenos Aires: Editorial Almagesto, 1995. 160 p. (Colección Relatos)

A partir de una situación de desastre natural y en base a una estructura bien tensionada crea un microcosmos del país. Surgen los testimonios y las críticas que, a cargo de personajes de clase media, comentan los cambios ocurridos en la Argentina desde los tiempos de Yrigoyen. Premio "Dr. Alfredo A. Roggiano," 1993. [MCG]

3828 Pagano, Mabel. Lo peor ya pasó: cuentos. Buenos Aires: Editorial Almagesto, 1996. 152 p.

Incluye 14 cuentos. A pesar de la gran variedad de registros permea en todos ellos un romanticismo vital que evoca el pasado desde las perspectivas de los olvidados de las grandes historias. Sean los protagonistas un bracero, una mujer de la primera fundación de Buenos, un judío inmigrante o una condenada, cada uno de ellos testimonia una experiencia desesperanzada. Primer premio en el certamen "Eduardo Mallea." [MCG]

3829 Paoletti, Mario. A fuego lento. Murcia, Spain: V Centenario, Comisión de Murcia, 1993. 247 p. (Colección Carabelas. Narrativa; 2)

Novela testimonial en la que el narrador nos encierra en su miserable prisión para hacernos sentir todo el horror y la angustia de la injusticia. Los días y sus interminables noches desfilan y nos introducen a las tácticas de la supervivencia, empleadas por aquellos que no pierden la esperanza. El humor y la ironía permean este relato desgarrador, que es a la vez un himno a la reciedumbre humana. [CEM]

3830 Peri Rossi, Cristina. Desastres íntimos. Barcelona: Editorial Lumen, 1997. 167 p. (Palabra en el tiempo; 243. Novela)

Contiene nueve relatos. Con el rigor y la maestría que caracterizan su prosa, la autora elabora tramas que exploran las diversas modalidades del erotismo. El humor junto a la sexualidad explícita los convierten en fuertes desafíos de las convenciones tanto genérico-sociales como literarias. [MCG]

3831 Piñeyro, Guillermina. Todo en orden. Buenos Aires: Correo Latino, 1992? 75 p.

Incluye 20 relatos. Con economía y precisión detallan los recuerdos, asociaciones e imágenes sensoriales que marcan los momentos de crisis y las relaciones frustradas. Dos excepciones, "Nexo" y "Ficción," evocan escenas del terror institucionalizado de las décadas del 70 y 80. [MCG]

3832 Posse, Abel. La pasión según Eva. Buenos Aires: Emecé Editores, 1994. 324 p.: bibl. (Escritores argentinos)

Biografía novelada de Eva Duarte de Perón. Combina textos fragmentarios de procedencia variada. En una "Nota" el autor explica: "Todas las circunstancias son históricas. Todas las palabras, o casi todas, surgen de versiones reconocidas, de declaraciones o de textos." Esa totalidad, sin embargo, resulta en la configuración de un personaje cuya desmesura anula toda visión crítica. El mito cautiva las versiones que se tejen a su alrededor. [MCG]

3833 Rabanal, Rodolfo. Cita en Marruecos. Buenos Aires: Seix Barral, 1996. 238 p. (Biblioteca breve)

Novela. En primera persona, explora las relaciones del protagonista con su pasado personal y con la realidad que lo rodea. El deseo y el erotismo confrontan fuerzas ajenas conducentes al descubrimiento de la imposibilidad de crear un ambiente utópico, alejado de las sacudidas político-sociales. [MCG]

3834 Raschella, Roberto. Diálogos en los patios rojos. Buenos Aires: Paradiso Ediciones, 1994. 202 p. (Paradiso narrativa)

El diálogo entre consciencias, entre destinos, y entre generaciones se transforma en una especie de lírica bilingüe, en la cual el italiano se entremezcla al castellano. El resultado de este amalgama lingüístico es una compenetración de la historia individual inserta en la nacional. [CEM]

3835 Rivera, Andrés. En esta dulce tierra. Buenos Aires: Alfaguara, 1995. 122 p. Reedición de la novela de 1984 (ver

HLAS 50:3465). Los episodios se engarzan con nitidez en una trama de raíz histórica que evoca el régimen de terror de Juan Manuel de Rosas. Hacia el final, la multiplicidad de registros altera la vertiente documental para acercarla a lo fantástico. [MCG]

3836 Rivera, Andrés. El farmer. Buenos Aires: Aguilar, Altea, Taurus, Alfaguara, 1996. 122 p.

Novela histórica. Desde su exilio en Southampton, el protagonista, Juan Manuel de Rosas rememora los episodios y los personajes de la política argentina del siglo XIX. El punto fuerte de la narración radica en la creación de una perspectiva personal, a veces intimista, de la cual emergen comentarios casi premonitorios de hechos y personajes del siglo presente. [MCG]

3837 Roffé, Reina. El cielo dividido. Buenos Aires: Editorial Sudamericana, 1996. 173 p. (Colección Narrativas argentinas)

Esta novela, muy bien narrada, trata una problemática actual—la identidad relacionada con varios temas que la definen y modifican: la sexualidad, el lugar donde se vive y las relaciones con los demás. Indaga, sobre todo, la amistad y el amor entre mujeres. [MCG]

3838 Ruiz Guiñazú, Magdalena. Huésped de un verano. 2. ed. Buenos Aires: Planeta, 1994. 207 p.: ill.

Primera novela de la autora. Prolijamente traza la crónica de una familia de la clase media alta en el verano de 1946. De la yuxtaposición de las diferentes voces narrativas—cada una sondea su drama personal—surge el panorama general de una época en la que reinan las opresiones sociales, religiosas, y políticas. [MCG]

3839 Saccomanno, Guillermo. Animales domésticos. Buenos Aires: Planeta, 1994. 237 p. (Biblioteca del sur. Cuentos)

La clase media actual argentina, con sus pequeñeces arbitrarias, sus sueños truncados, su heroicos y solitarios actos de valentía, y sus violencias cotidianas, constituye el núcleo de esta novela. Saccomanno obtiene de las miserias individuales y del lenguaje personal un atisbo de la humanidad escondida detrás de tanta apariencia. [CEM]

3840 Sáenz, Dalmiro. La mujer del vientre de oro. Buenos Aires: Emecé Editores, 1996. 224 p. (Escritores argentinos)

Sáenz ha creado personajes alucinantes, despiadados, y magnéticos en esta novela policial que revela de sorpresa en sorpresa las motivaciones criminales de un grupo de seres implacables. [CEM]

3841 Saer, Juan José. La pesquisa. Buenos Aires: Seix Barral, 1994. 175 p. (Biblioteca breve)

Con gran maestría narrativa la novela integra varios relatos en otro, mayor, que les sirve de marco. En base a la estructura del diálogo lleva a cabo indagaciones diversas que prolongan la tradición iniciada por Poe y que relaciona la actividad detectivesca con la lectura. [MCG]

3842 Salas, Martha. Juegos del atardecer y otros cuentos. Buenos Aires: Grupo Editor Latinoamericano: Distribuidor exclusivo, Emecé Editores, 1994. 166 p. (Colección Escritura de hoy)

Reúne 21 cuentos, algunos publicados anteriormente. Divididos en tres secciones "Cuento de cuentos," "Cuentos históricos" y "Cuentos de la revista *Barrio Norte*" dan muestra de una gran variedad de temas y registros. "Epílogo" incluye dos composiciones que en primera persona y haciendo uso de una prosa poética, fijan memorias e impresiones elusivas. [MCG]

3843 Santa Cruz, Yima. Echada del paraíso. Buenos Aires: Grupo Editor Latinoamericano, 1993. 265 p. (Colección Escritura de hoy)

Tres mujeres, cuyos destinos entrelazados exigen una verdad, buscan en el quehacer rutinario de sus vidas las respuestas a los interrogantes que poco a poco se animan a formular. [CEM]

3844 Santini, Alejandro. Las posibilidades infinitas. Buenos Aires: Torres Agüero Editor, 1994. 223 p.

Jorge Chanin, filósofo e investigador, es el protagonista de esta colección de cuentos. Su oficio lo lleva a solucionar los males y problemas ajenos mediante el uso de métodos esotéricos. [CEM]

3845 Santoro, Osvaldo. Cementerio de caracoles. Buenos Aires: Grupo Editor Latinoamericano: Distribudor exclusivo,

Emecé Editores, 1995. 140 p. (Colección Escritura de hoy)

Primera novela del autor. Desde una perspectiva futurista—el año 2008—el narrador rememora diversos tiempos de su pasado. Experimenta su vida como escindida por la culpa y la impotencia que perviven en él desde la desaparición de su amante durante la dictadura militar. [MCG]

3846 Scalona, Marcelo E. El camino del otoño. Buenos Aires: Corregidor, 1995. 157 p.

Novela. Ante la inminencia del fin del mundo, un bibliotecario debe cumplir con la misión de elegir los mejores trescientos libros de la historia universal de la literatura. Así se teje una trama ingeniosa que con gran pericia narrativa cuestiona y denuncia los fundamentos de todo intento por establecer límites dentro de la cultura. Ridiculiza las listas e índices que nunca pasarán de ser meras antologías. [MCG]

3847 Sedoff, Miguel. Todos aquellos días. Rosario, Argentina: Editorial Municipal, 1995. 196 p.

Primera novela del autor. La yuxtaposición de relatos personales resulta muy efectiva en el desarrollo de los temas tratados: la soledad, el despertar erótico, y la amistad. El ambiente juvenil de la Argentina de los últimos años está presentado según un movimiento de carácter cinematográfico. Primer Premio "Concurso de narradores jóvenes de Rosario." [MCG]

3848 Shua, Ana María. Cuentos judíos con fantasmas & demonios. Ilustrado por Mariza Dias Costa. Gilberto Sato, director de arte. Buenos Aires: Grupo Editorial Shalom, 1994. 166 p.: bibl., ill.

Ocho relatos. Destinada a un público juvenil, esta colección de mitos, leyendas y cuentos abarca algunos relatos originales de la autora y otros adaptados de fuentes diversas. Organizada con interés didáctico a cada relato sigue un "entrecuento" que explica su genealogía; se añade una introducción general esclarecedora de las tradiciones tratadas. [MCG]

3849 Shua, Ana María. El libro de los recuerdos. Buenos Aires: Editorial Sudamericana, 1994. 203 p.

Novela. El humor y el lenguaje coloquial son los recursos primordiales en la reconstrucción de la historia de una familia de origen judío-polaco. En base a las conflictivas versiones orales de sus integrantes logra memoriar los secretos, los triunfos y los fracasos compilados por tres generaciones sucesivas. [MCG]

3850 Silvestre, Susana. Mucho amor en inglés. Buenos Aires: Emecé Editores, 1994. 191 p. (Escritores argentinos)

En esta novela, la protagonista inserta en la narración de la vida propia las historias fragmentarias de otras mujeres. El monólogo interior sirve de vehículo para los relatos que, aunque variados, expresan un sentimiento común de enajenación. [MCG]

3851 Silvestre, Susana. No te olvides de mí. Buenos Aires: Espasa Calpe, 1995. 238 p.

Nuestra lectura del texto corre paralela a la lectura incierta que lleva a cabo la protagonista. En esa estructura que absorbe al lector en la ficción se incluye un collage diverso que abarca relatos y escenas teatrales. La especularidad resultante de esa estrategia textual produce un efecto de extrañeza. [MCG]

3852 Soláns, Claudia. El entierro del diablo: cuentos. Buenos Aires: Editorial Galerna, 1996. 139 p. (Colección La rosa de cobre)

Estos 10 relatos constituyen la primera publicación de la autora. El monólogo interior bien armado, la descripción de ambientes psicológicos opresores, la transición efectiva entre situaciones opuestas demuestran el dominio de la autora en manejar la prosa. Nota con precisión las tenues alteraciones que trastornan situaciones familiares y cotidianas. Premio Fondo Nacional de las Artes 1995. [MCG]

3853 Soler, Gustavo. La pequeña batalla de "Empalme Graneros". Buenos Aires: Corregidor, 1994. 191 p.

Novela. El relato del primer ataque guerrillero ocurrido el 5 de mayo de 1969 inicia la crónica de quienes participaron en él. Delaciones, prisión, tortura y actos de traición marcan sus destinos y prefiguran los horrores de la guerra posterior. [MCG]

3854 Tello, Antonio. El hijo del arquitecto. Madrid: Anaya & Mario Muchnik, 1993. 117 p. (Analectas)

Novela que roza de continuo la poesía mediante el uso de un lenguaje cargado de imágenes poderosas. La arquitectura, la creación, la expresión del deseo de trascendencia están a la base del impulso generacional que lleva de padre a hijo a la repetición inimitable del gesto creador a partir de la piedra. [CEM]

3855 Tizón, Héctor. Luz de las crueles provincias. Buenos Aires: Alfaguara, 1995. 201 p.

Novela. La primera parte ambientada a principios de siglo narra las luchas y frustraciones de una pareja de inmigrantes. La segunda detalla la vida del hijo en quien permanece un sentimiento de extranjería existencial. Comprueba hacia el final la imposibilidad de continuidad narrativa de toda historia hecha de olvidos y ausencias. [MCG]

3856 Torres, Julio. El oro de los Césares: historia de las siete muertes del hijo de la María de Toledo; novela. Buenos Aires: Corregidor, 1996. 381 p.: ill.

Novela histórica rica en datos ornados de un lenguaje erudito y fantasioso. América y Europa se hermanan en la prosa que recrea armoniosamente la época colonial. [CEM]

3857 Urbanyi, Pablo. Silver. Buenos Aires: Editorial Atlántida, 1994. 383 p. (Voces del Plata)

Silver, un mono de Gabón, es llevado a Stanford Univ. por una pareja de sociólogos. Allí, en ese ambiente "enriquecido", el primate se humaniza, adquiere los gestos, los hábitos, el habla y la plena conciencia de vivir una vida como un sueño. Silver relata su historia a un narrador que se presta en tanto que testigo y escribe para documentar el absurdo de la vida humana vivida por un simio. Finalista del Premio Planeta de 1993. [CEM]

3858 Vasser, Rafael. Las trampas del deseo. Buenos Aires: Cangrejal Editores, 1993. 125 p.: ill. (Serie Bienal; v. 2)

Novela premiada en la Nueva Bienal de Arte Joven 1991. Queda en ella el sello experimental de la novela de los sesenta. La convergencia de espacios y destinos, el humor y la ironía, la explosión de un lenguaje flexible, y la multiplicidad de perspectivas hacen de esta novela un texto minado por donde el lector debe negociar su camino. [CEM]

3859 **Verolin, Irma.** El puño del tiempo. Buenos Aires: Emecé Editores, 1994. 308 p. (Escritores argentinos)

Premio Emecé 1993/94. Una joven evoca su casa y su familia desde la década de los años cincuenta. Estos personajes al borde del ridículo, obsesionados por otras realidades y otros sueños pasan por la imaginación de la narradora dejando en ella su impronta. [CEM]

Paraguay

3860 **Garcete, Carlos.** El caballo del comisario: cuentos. Asunción: Arandurã Editorial, 1996. 119 p.

Esta colección de diez cuentos del autor, exiliado paraguayo en Buenos Aires, es ejemplo de su maestría en el género. Su estilo es deliberadamente contestatario en la confrontación con la realidad de su país, el trasfondo de este literatura que da cuenta de lo que ocurre en las vidas de la gente pero que no se nombra. Su obra comenzó a publicarse en 1987. Entre los cuentos que han sido aclamados por su excelencia cito: "La muerte tiene color" y "El collar sobre el río." [MGP]

3861 **Hernáez, Luis.** Donde ladrón no llega. Asunción: El Lector, 1996. 189 p. (Biblioteca paraguaya)

Novela situada durante el proceso de expulsión de los jesuítas de las colonias españolas, en la que el autor prefiere examinar la vida cotidiana de aquellos habitantes en vez de centrarse alrededor de un "gran hecho histórico" como suele ocurrir con las novelas históricas. Es una novela sobre la "historia chica" que busca interrogar una época remota que dejó importantes marcas en la historia general de las colonias. [MGP]

3862 **Moreno de Gabaglio, Luisa.** Ecos de monte y de arena. Asunción: Editora Litocolor, 1992. 113 p.: bibl., ill.

Reedición de esta obra de 1975 del influyente y excéntrico escritor que comenzó a escribir en la década de los sesenta. Esta edición incluye una bibliografía bastante completa del autor que muestra la gama de intereses y la diversidad de sus publicaciones. [MGP]

3863 **Pedrozo, Amanda** and **Mabel Pedrozo.** Mujeres al teléfono y otros cuentos. Asunción: El Lector, 1996. 148 p. (Colección literaria)

Una edición de 25 cuentos cortos de estas autoras paraguayas en los que se trabajan personajes del interior del país o de la zona periférica de Asunción. [MGP]

3864 **Plá, Josefina.** Cuentos completos. Edición, introducción y bibliografía de Miguel Angel Fernández. Asunción: El Lector, 1996. 451 p.: bibl. (Biblioteca paraguaya)

Esta edición de la destacada escritora paraguaya, a cargo de M.A. Fernández, incluye una breve introducción a la obra y una bibliografía crítica sobre la misma. Esta compilación incluye dos textos inéditos que datan de 1926 y 1960. Contiene los siguientes subtítulos: "La mano en la tierra," "El espejo y el canasto," "La pierna de Severina," "Anécdotas del folklore naciente," "La muralla robada,""Cuentos folklóricos y fantásticos, "Cuentos de la tierra," "Anécdotas," "Folklóricos," "Varios," y "Textos no incluidos en volumen." [MGP]

3865 **Roa Bastos, Augusto Antonio.** Madama Sui. Asunción: El Lector, 1995. 300 p. (Colección literaria; 27)

Otra gran novela del escritor paraguayo sobre una mujer que vivió en Asunción en los años sesenta. Esta vez el novelista ha escogido una mujer para el papel protagónico. El destino y drama de Madama Sui es estar a disposición del dictador para satisfacer sus necesidades sexuales. Roa Bastos crea y explora este personaje en vías de transformación y de liberación en el entorno de una sociedad patriarcal cuyos códigos revelan una constante subyugación de las mujeres. [MGP]

3866 **Roa Bastos, Augusto Antonio.** Metaforismos. Buenos Aires: Seix Barral, 1996. 151 p. (Biblioteca breve)

El autor explica que el título surgió de "aforismos llevados más allá del aforismo, más allá de la metáfora y aforismo." Recoge en este libro una selección de sentencias, máximas, proverbios, paradojas, parábolas, epigramas, epifonemas, pensamientos, divagaciones, etc., seleccionados de sus obras y de otros materiales inéditos. Priman sobre todo fragmentos de "Yo El Supremo." [MGP]

3867 **Vera, Saro.** Seis relatos de un campesino. Asunción: Editora Litocolor, 1995. 199 p.

El autor que se desempeñó como cura

párroco en Caazapá, recoge en estos cuentos testimonios de la experiencia guerrillera de los años sesenta en los límites de su parroquia desde las voces de los campesinos de la región. Son textos que pueden utilizarse para la construcción de la memoria colectiva del pueblo paraguayo. [MGP]

Uruguay

3868 Benedetti, Mario. Andamios. Buenos Aires: Seix Barral, 1996. 349 p. (Biblioteca Mario Benedetti)

Novela autobiográfica del prolífico escritor e importante crítico cultural, en la que examina la complejidad de los exilios a través de numerosos encuentros y desencuentros que trazan el mapa de la peripecia internacional. En lo que el autor titula "Andamio preliminar," Benedetti declara que no está muy seguro de que este texto sea una novela sino una colección de andamios sobre los que se pueden subir o bajar estatuas. [MGP]

3869 Benedetti, Mario. Cuentos completos: 1947–1994. Buenos Aires: Seix Barral, 1994. 615 p.: ill. (Biblioteca mayor)

Precedido de un inteligente prólogo de José Emilio Pacheco, se recoge en este volumen la obra cuentística de este prolífico novelista, cuentista, periodista, crítico y activista de la cultura, que se iniciara en 1945. [MGP]

3870 Benedetti, Mario. El ejercicio del criterio: obra crítica 1950–1994. Buenos Aires: Seix Barral, 1996. 589 p.: bibl.

Esta colección de ensayos y otros escritos del autor también aparecieron en Seix Barral, Buenos Aires (1996). La variedad de temas da cuenta de la apasionada y continua práctica de la escritura que refleja el compromiso intelectual e ideológico con su cultura. [MGP]

3871 Burel, Hugo. El elogio de la nieve. Montevideo: Editorial Fin de Siglo, 1995. 82 p. (Colección Deletras)

Distinguido con el prestigioso Premio Juan Rulfo 1995, Burel, cuentista y novelista a partir de 1983, es el primer escritor uruguayo en recibir esta distinción por el cuento "El elogio de la nieve". Este volumen contiene el excelente cuento premiado y una novela corta titulada "El vendedor de sueños." [MGP]

3872 Campodónico, Luis. 33 cuentos. Postfacio de Ana María Rodríguez Villamill. Montevideo: Arca, 1995. 135 p.: bibl.

Colección póstuma de 33 cuentos inéditos del escritor uruguayo seguidos de un excelente "Posfacio" de Ana María Rodríguez Villamil y cuya escritura contribuyó a dar nueva forma a la literatura uruguaya de su generación, en la que predominaron los elementos insólitos y fantásticos desde una nueva conceptualización de estos instrumentos creativos. [MGP]

3873 Campodónico, Miguel Angel. Invención del pasado. Montevideo: Planeta, 1996. 199 p. (Biblioteca del sur)

Séptima novela del autor, este seductor título alude al proyecto de reconstruir la historia de Montevideo a través de la experiencia vital de una familia de inmigrantes italianos, los Angiulli, cuya debacle tiene lugar durante los años de la dictadura. [MGP]

3874 Courtoisie, Rafael. Cadáveres exquisitos. Montevideo: Planeta, 1995. 188 p.: bibl. (Biblioteca del sur)

Joven autor de una trilogía publicada entre 1990–95, ofrece ahora estos quince relatos reunidos bajo el sugestivo bretoniano título. Exhiben estos cuentos tanto una prosa altamente trabajada como una fina concepción de la ironía y del humor para la construcción de un mundo literario original, de gran elaboración creativa, características todas que responden a la conocida actividad surrealista a la cual alude el titulo de la colección. [MGP]

3875 Courtoisie, Rafael. El mar de la tranquilidad. Montevideo: Ediciones de la Banda Oriental, 1995. 53 p.: bibl.

Colección de cuentos del notable y siempre prolífico escritor en la cual sobresalen la madurez de los temas seleccionados y el manejo del lenguaje. Es un volumen breve organizado en dos partes que contienen siete textos la primera, y la segunda, tres. [MGP]

3876 Echavarren Welker, Roberto. Ave roc. Montevideo: Editorial Graffiti, 1994. 250 p. (Colección de narrativa los centauros)

Conocido por sus trabajos de crítica literaria y por su poesía, Echavarren incursiona con gran logro el campo de la ficción narrativa en esta novela cuyo personaje central está modelado en la vida del rockero

Morrison. Es asimismo una novela sobre un personaje de nuestra época en su conexión íntima con la cultura popular en la cual el rock es el género más prominente. [MGP]

3877 Faget, Julio. Modelo para un crimen. Montevideo: Pontosur, 1992. 128 p.

A partir de acontecimientos reales ocurridos entre los años 1978–1986, este relato policiaco de Faget construye dos líneas narrativas que constituyen dos perspectivas acerca del asesinato de una modelo acaecido en el centro de Montevideo. Una interesante contribución al creciente género de la narrativa policiaca latinoamericana. [MGP]

3878 Freire, Silka. Mauricio Rosencof: el delirio imaginante. Montevideo: Arca, 1994. 160 p.: bibl.

Tesis doctoral sobre el teatro del dramaturgo uruguayo cuya obra de denuncia de la realidad uruguaya a través de recursos interpretativos que el autor estudia abarca su obra hasta 1988. [MGP]

3879 Giucci, Guillermo. Fiera de amor: la otra muerte de Delmira Agustini. Montevideo: Vintén Editor, 1995. 87 p.

Novela sobre los eventos que imaginariamente precedieron a la muerte de Delmira Agustini. [MGP]

3880 Hamed, Amir. Troya blanda. Montevideo: Editorial Fin de Siglo, 1996. 569 p. (Colección Deletras)

Novela histórica sobre el siglo diecinueve latinoamericano, examina la Guerra Grande durante el sitio a la ciudad de Montevideo, en cuyo escenario circulan las figuras de Juan Manuel de Rosas, Bartolomé Mitre, Oribe y otros criollos junto a Napoleón, el Papa Pío IX, el ubicuo Garibaldi, el paraguayo Solano López y Karl Marx. [MGP]

3881 Lago, Sylvia. Días dorados, días en sombra: cuentos, 1965–1995. Montevideo: Planeta, 1996. 363 p. (Biblioteca del sur)

Reúne una muestra de la obra cuentística (20 cuentos) de 30 años de producción de esta escritora que ha sido reconocida por su talento narrativo en el que enfoca el mundo de la alta burguesía, las relaciones familiares y las amorosas. Los textos están organizados en tres conjuntos titulados "Presagios," "Certezas" y "Lazos." [MGP]

3882 Levrero, Mario. El alma de Gardel. Montevideo: Ediciones Trilce, 1996. 93 p.

Novela corta de este talentoso narrador cuyo protagonista reflexiona sobre la relación y significado de los objetos y personas que lo rodean y con los que tiene una conexión que el narrador desde su perspectiva juega a adjudicarles un halo de misterio. [MGP]

3883 Levrero, Mario. El portero y el otro. Prólogo de Elvio E. Gandolfo. Montevideo: Arca, 1992. 187 p.

Con un prólogo de Elvio E. Gandolfo sobre la obra de este autor, esta colección de cuentos abre con una breve explicación de Levrero sobre la selección, seguida de 14 cuentos escritos en distintas épocas de su vida en Montevideo y luego en Buenos Aires. Este desplazamiento marca también un cambio en su escritura. [MGP]

3884 Onetti, Juan Carlos. Confesiones de un lector. Madrid: Santillana, 1995. 353 p.

Edición de artículos periodísticos del escritor uruguayo compilados por su hijo, el periodista Jorge Onetti, muestran al Onetti lector en sus reflexiones sobre los libros que admiraba y que le interesaban leer. Este volumen agrega una dimensión más al perfil del admirado escritor uruguayo. [MGP]

3885 Onetti, Juan Carlos. Periquito el aguador y otros textos, 1939–1984. Montevideo: Cuadernos de Marcha: Intendencia Municipal de Montevideo, 1994. 195 p.

Colección de cuentos aparecidos en el Semanario Marcha compilados por María Angélica Petit, quien señala en el prólogo que el volumen reúne la totalidad de la escritura no ficcional de J.C. Onetti, publicada en Marcha a través de los años. [MGP]

3886 Paternain, Alejandro. La ciudad de los milagros. Montevideo: Editorial Fin de Siglo, 1995. 198 p. (Colección Deletras)

Novela histórica sobre el sitio a Montevideo de 1843, uno de los eventos de la Guerra Grande. Es interesante la doble perspectiva que el autor desarrolla: en un plano el tema recrea la dimensión histórica desde la perspectiva actual del proceso de filmación de una miniserie sobre este acontecimiento histórico, y la segunda perspectiva se instala

en el año 1843, en el momento del
sitio. [MGP]

3887 Ponce de León, N. Baccino. Un amor
en Bangkok. Montevideo: BP, 1994.
260 p. (Colección Laberinto)

Segunda novela del autor de la acla-
mada novela Maluco, narra las aventuras de
un personaje modelado en el Ulises nave-
gante en un condensado fragmento temporal
de unas horas en el curioso viaje por el
pasado uruguayo. [MGP]

3888 Porzecanski, Teresa. La piel del alma.
Montevideo: Seix Barral, 1996. 222 p.

La quinta novela de esta excelente y
reconocida escritora, relata una serie de historias que tienen lugar en momentos históricos y geográficos distintos: la ciudad de Montevideo en una apacible prosperidad y la
ciudad de Toledo a fines del siglo quince, período en el que la ortodoxia católica apadrinó
la violencia contra los judíos sefardíes.
[MGP]

3889 Prego, Omar. Delmira. Montevideo:
Alfaguara, 1996. 258 p.

Novela que trata de reconstruir los últimos días de la poeta uruguaya en los que
se inmiscuyen comentarios del autor en
relación con los comentarios de su abuelo
que dice haber sido testigo de algunos eventos en la vida de Agustini. [MGP]

3890 Prego, Omar. Para sentencia. Montevideo: Ediciones Trilce, 1994. 138 p.

Esta novela examina los comportamientos humanos provocados por el clima
de terror impuestos a los habitantes de una
sociedad sometida a un régimen dictatorial.
Es una obra bien lograda que conmueve a sus
lectores de manera significativa. [MGP]

3891 Rodríguez Barilari, Elbio. La mitad del
infinito: cuentos. Prólogo de Jorge
Ruffinelli. Montevideo: Ediciones de la Banda
Oriental, 1994. 76 p. (Lectores de Banda
Oriental; 6. ser., 16)

En el prólogo a esta colección de cuentos, J. Ruffinelli señala que la obra narrativa
del autor iniciada en 1985, y que cuenta con
tres títulos anteriores, lo ha establecido
como un narrador de primera fila. Los cuentos de este volumen están conectados a la
motivación central de explorar el infinito a
través de la dimensión temporal, cíclica, o
del futuro incierto. [MGP]

3892 Rosencof, Mauricio. El bataraz. Hon-
darribia, Spain: Argitaletxe Hiru, 1993.
175 p. (Iru; 2)

Este es un texto novelado en el cual el
autor trabaja un material narrativo derivado
de su experiencia personal como participante
de la guerrilla Tupamara contra el régimen
militar del Uruguay y de su posterior y
tremenda experiencia en la cárcel. [MGP]

3893 Somers, Armonía. El hacedor de girasoles: tríptico en amarillo para un
hombre ciego. Montevideo: Linardi y Risso,
1994. 60 p.

Publicación póstuma de la admirable
Armonía Somers editada por Alberto Risso
que contiene los siguientes cuentos: "Un
cuadro para El Bosco," "Un remoto sabor a
cal," "El hacedor de girasoles," "Ultima entrevista a una mujer que nos ha rechazado" y
"La carta de El Cabildo." [MGP]

LITERARY CRITICISM
AND HISTORY
Argentina

3894 Girona Fibla, Nuria. Escrituras de la
historia: la novela argentina de los
años ochenta. Valencia, Spain: Depto. de
Filología Española, Facultad de Filología,
Univ. de Valencia, 1995? 175 p.: bibl. (Anejo
no. 17 de la revista Cuadernos de filología)

Estudio crítico que indaga los límites
entre la historia y la ficción en la novelística
de las últimas décadas. En base a las teorías
literarias de la segunda mitad del siglo, que
le prestan autoridad y rigor, formula acercamientos interesantes a novelas de T. Eloy
Martínez, O. Soriano, A. Rivera, M. Lynch,
M. Traba, y R. Piglia. [MCG]

3895 Lichtblau, Myron I. The Argentine
novel: an annotated bibliography. Lanham, Md.: Scarecrow Press, 1997. 1111 p.

Recopilación de gran magnitud que
cubre las novelas publicadas entre 1788–
1990. Anota prolijamente reimpresiones,
reediciones y traducciones. Cita convenien-
temente las reseñas que provienen de fuentes
previas. Incluye también una selección de
trabajos críticos. Guía de gran utilidad para
los estudiosos del género. [MCG]

Prieto, Adolfo. Los viajeros ingleses y la emergencia de la literatura argentina, 1820–1850. Ver item **3014.**

Paraguay

3896 Breve antología de la literatura paraguaya. Recopilación de Teresa Méndez-Faith. Asunción: El Lector, 1994. 329 p. (Colección literaria; 21)

Precedida de un brevísimo prólogo de Raúl Amaral, esta antología fue concebida como complemento del *Breve diccionario de la literatura paraguaya* (Asunción: El Lector, 1994), en la cual su autora reúne textos representativos de esta literatura cuya información es de difícil acceso muchas veces. Por esta razón, una antología realizada con buen criterio es bienvenida para contribuir a dar una muestra más cabal de la actividad literaria en Paraguay. [MGP]

3897 Castro, Claude. Historia y ficción: *Caballero* de Guido Rodríguez Alcalá. Asunción: Editorial Don Bosco, 1997. 242 p.: bibl.

Originariamente escrito en francés como tesis de doctorado de la Univ. de Toulouse, es un interesante estudio de un texto que trata el tema de la Guerra Grande o la Guerra de la Triple Alianza que tuvo tanta repercusión en la historia y el desarrollo del Paraguay. Este estudio está estructurado en dos partes: la primera examina el trasfondo histórico del conflicto; la segunda es un análisis de la estructura narrativa y otros elementos importantes de esta obra. [MGP]

3898 Kallsen, Margarita. Los poetas paraguayos y sus obras. Asunción: s.n., 1996. 178 p.: indexes.

Bienvenido volumen de referencia bibliográfica de la obra poética con 904 citas de libros y folletos sobre autores y autoras paraguayos y sobre su poesía. Otro esfuerzo para la recolección de la información sobre cultura literaria del Paraguay. [MGP]

3899 Pérez-Maricevich, Francisco. La poesía y la narrativa en el Paraguay. Asunción: El Lector, 1996. 143 p.: bibl. (Biblioteca paraguaya)

Ensayo que intenta una sistematización de la literatura paraguaya. Está organizado en cinco capítulos que incluyen una bibliografía selecta y una lista anotada de las revistas literarias paraguayas. [MGP]

Uruguay

3900 Cipriani, Carlos. A máscara limpia: el carnaval en la escritura uruguaya de dos siglos. v. 1, Crónicas, memorias, testimonios. Montevideo: Ediciones de la Banda Oriental, 1994. 1 v.: bibl., ill.

Interesante volumen de textos de narradores uruguayos que exploran el tema del carnaval, entre los que se cuenta a Roberto de las Carreras, Julio Herrera y Reissig, Mario Benedetti, y Mauricio Rosencof entre otros. La selección va precedida por una introducción informativa del editor. [MGP]

3901 Orgambide, Pedro G. Horacio Quiroga: una historia de vida. Buenos Aires: Planeta, 1994. 268 p.: bibl., ill. (Biografías del sur)

Este es el segundo libro que Orgambide dedica al gran cuentista uruguayo. En esta biografía se traza la trayectoria del escritor y de su escritura a lo largo de 15 capítulos que aportan una nueva perspectiva. Incluye una bibliografía selecta. [MGP]

Poetry

FRANCISCO CABANILLAS, *Associate Professor of Spanish, Bowling Green State University*
MIGUEL GOMES, *Associate Professor of Spanish, University of Connecticut*
PEDRO LASTRA, *Professor Emeritus, State University of New York, Stony Brook*
ELIZABETH MONASTERIOS, *Associate Professor of Spanish, State University of New York, Stony Brook*
JOSÉ MIGUEL OVIEDO, *Trustee Professor of Spanish, University of Pennsylvania*

OSCAR RIVERA-RODAS, *Professor of Spanish, University of Tennessee, Knoxville*
OSCAR SARMIENTO, *Associate Professor of Spanish, State University of New York at Potsdam*
JACOBO SEFAMÍ, *Associate Professor of Spanish, University of California, Irvine*
LILIÁN URIBE, *Associate Professor of Spanish, Central Connecticut State University*

GENERAL

EN ESTE PERÍODO se han publicado antologías dedicadas a momentos de gran interés en el proceso literario hispanoamericano: C.V. de Vallejo dispone una muestra muy útil e informada del romanticismo, etapa poco atendida por los estudiosos y lectores actuales (item **3903**); M.G. Grunfeld y J. González Suárez entregan sendas selecciones de la poesía de vanguardia (items **3904** y **3918**). El trabajo de Grunfeld es importante por la amplitud de su contenido, que considera la inclusión de los poetas vanguardistas más representativos de Brasil. Entre las antologías temáticas debe destacarse la que M. Ruano dedica a la poesía amorosa en Hispanoamérica (item **3929**). De las numerosas antologías nacionales, igualmente destinadas a ilustrar períodos, grupos, géneros o temas, dan cuenta pormenorizada las notas regionales que siguen a ésta.

Entre los estudios sobresalen el de K.H. Gauggel sobre el tema del cisne en el modernismo (item **4127**) y el sugestivo y polémico libro de S. Reisz, que revisa la actualidad de la poética y de la poesía feminista (item **4135**).

Particular y estimulante atención crítica merecieron los poetas G. Baquero (item **3931**), J. Lezama Lima (item **4138**). J. Sabines (item **4147**), L. Lloréns Torres (item **4139**), J. Coronel Urtecho (item **4151**), J. Pasos (item **4155**), J.A. Silva (items **4140** y **4141**), C. Vallejo (item **4146**), J. L. Ortiz (item **4065**) y E. Lihn (items **4144** y **4143**).

En un orden semejante deben mencionarse significativos premios internacionales discernidos a poetas hispanoamericanos: Alvaro Mutis fue galardonado con el Premio Reina Sofía de Poesía Iberoamericana, en 1997; también en España, Emilio Adolfo Westphalen mereció el Premio Miguel Hernández en 1998; el mismo año, el Premio Juan Rulfo fue otorgado a Olga Orozco, y los Premios José Hernández y Octavio Paz a Gonzalo Rojas.

La nota sombría de estos últimos años ha sido la desaparición de poetas tan importantes como José Coronel Urtecho (1994), Jorge Teillier y Enrique Molina (1996), Dulce María Loinaz y Gastón Baquero (1997), y Octavio Paz (1998). [PL]

MEXICO

Octavio Paz falleció el domingo 19 de abril de 1998. Los periódicos del mundo anunciaron el acontecimiento en su primera plana, puesto que se trataba de uno de los grandes escritores de este siglo. Paz es, quizá, el pensador y poeta más importante que ha dado México. De sus *Obras completas* (Fondo de Cultura Económica; véase *HLAS 56:4161*), sólo quedan por salir los vols. 12 a 14.

Continúan publicándose antologías voluminosas de diferentes estados de la República (items **3905** y **3945**). Pero en este período destacan antologías dedicadas a grupos, género sexual o momentos específicos: la de Palley (item **3915**) dedicada a las mujeres, la que recopila poemas sobre la masacre de 1968 (item **3928**), o la que por primera vez presenta poetas judíos mexicanos de lengua yidish (item **4156**).

También aparecen nuevas ediciones de poetas conocidos, como Salvador Díaz Mirón (item **3997**), José Gorostiza (item **4014**), Carlos Pellicer (item **4072**); o nuevas compilaciones de Rubén Bonifaz Nuño (item **3970**), Alberto Blanco (item **3968**),

Jaime García Terrés (item **4007**), Francisco Hernández (item **4018**), Gabriel Zaid (item **4121**) y la bellísima y lujosa edición de Jaime Sabines (item **4147**).

Aunque los poetas nacidos en los años 20 y 30 publican antologías o compilaciones de su obra, los libros verdaderamente nuevos pertenecen a los nacidos de los años 40 en adelante. A poetas como Huerta (item **4023**), Yáñez (ítem **4120**), Alberto Blanco (item **3968**), José Joaquín Blanco (item **3969**), Francisco Hernández (item **4018**), Aguilar Mora (item **3948**), y Boullosa (item **3971**), se les suman las voces de los más jóvenes que revitalizan a su modo el género poético: Baranda (item **3959**), Piña Williams (item **4077**), D'Aquino (item **3976**), Cano (item **3976**), Ostrosky (item **4066**), Leñero (item **4030**), Ramírez (item **4014**), Vidales (item **4112**) y Villareal (item **4115**). La multiplicidad y tratamiento de los temas elimina la posibilidad de ver rasgos que den unidad a la poesía de nuestros días.

Para la fortuna de la poesía, México cuenta con un buen número de editoriales que se preocupan por seguir publicando libros de versos: Fondo de Cultura Económica (serie Letras Mexicanas), Editorial Era, El Tucán de Virginia, Editorial Aldus, Ediciones sin Nombre, UNAM (El Ala del Tigre), UAM (a través de sus colecciones Margen de poesía de la revista *Casa del Tiempo*, y Molinos de Viento), CONACULTA (en sus series Práctica Mortal, Los Cincuenta, y Fondo Editorial Tierra Adentro). [JS]

CENTROAMÉRICA

Esta "entrega" de poesía centroamericana está marcada por un acontecimiento de singular importancia para la historia de la poesía latinoamericana: la muerte de José Coronel Urtecho (1906–94), líder del movimiento de vanguardia nicaragüense. José Emilio Pacheco señaló ese movimiento como la "*otra* vanguardia," entendiendo por ello el surgimiento de propuestas que modelaron *desde adentro* el curso de la historia literaria y cultural latinoamericana. De Coronel Urtecho se reseña en este número lo que seguramente fueron sus últimas "miradas" a la poesía nicaragüense en particular y latinoamericana en general: *Libro de conversaciones sobre libros.* Se trata de una conversación (en la que intervienen Luz Marina Acosta y Julio Valle-Castillo) extremadamente útil y novedosa en torno al discurso poético y sus posibilidades de articulación cultural (item **4151**).

También destacan tres libros extraordinariamente originales y provocativos. El primero, *Variaciones en clave de Mí*, pertenece a una figura de reconocida trayectoria internacional: Claribel Alegría (item **3951**). Los otros dos son muestras prometedoras de la joven poesía centroamericana: *El reino de la Zarza*, del hondureño Leonel Alvarado (Premio Unico de Poesía del Certamen Literario Latinoamericano EDUCA, 1993 (item **3952**) y *La furia del musgo* (1995), del costarricense Orlando Gei Brealey (item **4008**).

En la categoría "Antología" destacan: *Poetas Modernistas Nicaragüenses 1880–1930*, de Julio Valle-Castillo (item **3940**) y *Antología General de la Poesía Nicaragüense*, de Jorge Eduardo Arellano (item **3907**). También importantes son los distintos esfuerzos que se han hecho en este período por difundir la obra de poetas como Roque Dalton y Joaquín Pasos. Del primero nos llega *Roque Dalton: Antología* de Juan Carlos Berrio (item **3995**), y del segundo *Poemas de un joven*, con prólogo de Ernesto Cardenal y *Prosas de un joven* (dos vols.), magnífica edición crítica de Julio Valle-Castillo (item **4155**).

Otros poetas antologados y "revisados" son el costarricense Isaac Felipe

Azofeifa, *Poesía Reunida* (item **3957**); el nicaragüense Fanor Téllez, *Edad Diversa*, *1983- 1990* (item **4106**); el hondureño Roberto Sosa, *Antología Personal* (item **4099**) y el guatemalteco Roberto Obregón, *Recuento de Poesía* (item **4059**), cuya prematura muerte, a los 33 años, todavía resuena en algún lugar de la memoria. [EM]

EL CARIBE

Durante el último lustro de los años 90, se destaca la publicación de antologías, quizás como una urgencia de agrupar y reagrupar el estado de la poesía antes de que culmine el siglo. En el caso cubano, la necesidad de repensar la poesía es dramática; más de una decena de antologías, la mayoría publicada fuera de la isla, se da a la tarea de cartografiarla desde múltiples criterios. El énfasis en la poesía cubana publicada en las dos últimas décadas, sin que por ello domine una manera de inscribirla en el contexto poético, reclama la mayor atención. Esta producción poética finisecular de la isla se plantea como una continuidad recreadora de la tradición (item **3914**); como un rompimiento con la poesía de los años 60 y 70 (item **3926**); como una estética agónica centrada en la temática del amor (item **3919**); como una manifestación con tres ejes: el vínculo origenista, la articulación con el lector y la experiencia escritural (item **3920**); como una vitalidad lírica (item **3924**); como una poética de alejamiento ante lo social y de acercamiento a lo individual (item **3927**); como una incidencia de voces desprendidas que denuncian el adulterio moral (item **3930**); como una poética de la agresividad (item **3943**). En algunos casos, la antología persigue delinear la contemporaneidad—esa que, dividida en cuatro momentos, surge a partir de 1959—de la poesía en Cuba (item **3912**); en otros, la antología se circunscribe a los que viven y mantienen una obra sistemática en la isla (item **3938**). No podían faltar las propuestas transnacionales, ya como diálogo entre la isla y el exilio estadounidense (item **3934**), así como antología de la diáspora en general (item **3932**).

En el caso dominicano, tres antologías se ocupan de agrupar y reagrupar la poesía. De éstas, una contempla la poesía dominicana escrita fuera de la isla, en Nueva York (item **3942**). De las dos restantes, una provee una suma poética de la poesía dominicana escrita en la isla durante los dos últimos siglos (item **3916**); la otra se ocupa de replantear el acontecer poético durante el siglo XX (item **3909**). En el caso puertorriqueño, una antología se ocupa de la poesía de los siglos XIX y XX escrita en español, ofreciendo una amplia selección de poetas en cada estadio; de particular interés resulta la muestra de poetas de la segunda mitad del siglo XX (item **3906**).

Como parte del proceso del diálogo cubano, se publica un homenaje a Gastón Baquero (item **3931**) que reúne ensayos escritos dentro y fuera de la isla. Los 500 años de la fundación de América dan lugar a un poemario conjunto entre cuatro poetas (entre ellos, Marcio Veloz Maggiolo) y un artista dominicano (item **4152**). El estudio de Emilio Bejel sobre la poesía de Lezama Lima se traduce al español (item **4138**); la actitud de Luis Lloréns Torres frente al paisaje se plantea en un estudio (item **4139**); se recopila el romancero cubano (item **3921**).

La poesía femenina y feminista cuenta con varias publicaciones (items **3953**, **3984**, **4005**, **4110**, and **4001**). Entre los consagrados, se destaca el proceso de recuperación de la poesía de Pedro Mir (items **4044** and **4043**). Entre los poetas con antecedentes establecidos, cabe mencionar tres poemarios: el de José Mármol (item **4033**), el de Joserramón Melendes (item **4041**) y el de José Pérez Olivares (item **4075**).

En cuanto al trabajo editorial, se destaca la colección "Allí y Ahora" de la Univ. de Puerto Rico, entre cuyos poemarios publicados señalamos el de Rosa Vanessa Otero (item **4067**), así como también la editorial Isla Negra y el poemario de Juan Carlos Quintero-Herencia (item **4081**). Tanto en el caso de Cuba como en el de la República Dominicana y Puerto Rico, las nuevas o novísimas propuestas pertenecen a la poesía escrita a partir de los años 80. [FC]

COLOMBIA Y VENEZUELA

En este período se destacan los títulos de dos poetas no consagrados: Blanca Strepponi y Héctor Jaimes (items **4103, 4102,** y **4025**). La primera, desde la aparición de *Poemas visibles* (1988), ha publicado una serie de poemarios que definen a la perfección las principales tendencias líricas del decenio de 1990: de la confesión íntima y sentimental—típica de la poesía urbana de los ochenta—a la mirada objetiva y fría de quienes contemplan el espectáculo del mundo con horror contenido. El segundo continúa, pero a la vez remoza, una tradición poética conceptista e intelectual que se había interrumpido con el auge de los coloquialismos.

En lo que respecta a re-ediciones y a obras de autores que ya ocupan un lugar indiscutible en la historia poética colombo-venezolana, debe mencionarse, en primer lugar, la nueva versión de obras completas como las de Juan Sánchez Peláez (item **4091**), el volumen también abarcador de Raúl Gómez Jattin (item **4013**), la reaparición de *Nocturnos y otros sueños* de Fernando Charry Lara (item **3983**)—con el agregado dialógico de dibujos de Fernando Botero—y la nueva puesta en circulación de los *Poemas de amor* de Darío Jaramillo Agudelo (item **4027**), luego de su reciente triunfo en el campo de la novela. La calidad y el ritmo de producción de Eugenio Montejo, por otra parte, se mantienen con la publicación de *Adiós al siglo XX* (item **4049**), y nuevas compilaciones de su obra. Asimismo, Juan Liscano y Vicente Gerbasi (items **4031** y **4011**), este último póstumamente, añaden títulos a su ya extensa labor.

En el área de las antologías y los estudios descuella el trabajo de Julio Miranda en torno a la lírica de mujeres venezolanas, *Poesía en el espejo* (item **3935**), Ricardo Cano Gaviria pone en circulación la que será, probablemente, la biografía más exhaustiva de José Asunción Silva, *Una vida en clave de sombra* (item **4140**) y sobre la obra del mismo autor, se compila un sólido conjunto de aproximaciones críticas que aparece respaldado por la Casa de la Poesía Silva, de Bogotá (item **4141**).

Mención aparte merece el proyecto que se ha trazado y ha ido llevando a cabo el fondo editorial Pequeña Venecia, de Caracas: pocas colecciones de poesía han logrado, como ésta, armonizar ininterrumpidamente la producción local con la latinoamericana en general—y con la internacional, debidamente traducida y presentada por poetas hispanoamericanos. [MG]

BOLIVIA Y ECUADOR

Las consideraciones de la producción poética boliviana de los últimos años necesitan ser referidas a la actividad de imprentas y editoriales. Uno de los fenómenos más interesantes de la poesía de este país en el último período fue la aparición de poetas poco conocidos, pero de edad madura y con una obra que demuestra asimismo madurez y experiencia. No se trata de la aparición espontánea de nuevos valores, sino de un hecho editorial: el incremento de editoriales e imprentas nuevas y, además instaladas en medios fuera de los centros principales del país. Poetas maduros pero poco conocidos porque no tuvieron acceso a los medios editoriales comenzaron a publicar su obra, en un ambiente de recepción lectora alentador. Tales son los casos de Aguirre Gainsborg y Carvalho (items **3949** y **3979**), quienes, según sus respectivas obras, estuvieron dedicados a la literatura desde hace varias décadas. Este fenómeno editorial es entendible, puesto que en Bolivia no se advierte la existencia de una institución que respalde editorialmente la publicación y difusión de la obra poética de nuevos valores o autores con poco acceso a editoriales. Hay que exceptuar los esfuerzos limitados de algunas universidades estatales. Tampoco, al parecer, poetas consagrados gozan del apoyo editorial estatal o privado, como los casos de Bedregal y Cardona (items **3961** y **3978**) quienes en los últimos años re- editaron su obra en ediciones aparentemente financiadas personalmente. Del mismo modo, las publicaciones de jóvenes poetas de calidad indudable como Medina y Quiroga (items **4040** y **4082**) tampoco tienen respaldo institucional.

En el Ecuador, a diferencia de lo expuesto respecto a Bolivia, se debe destacar el papel importante que realiza la Casa de la Cultura en la edición y difusión de la poesía nacional , así como editoriales privadas con un fondo bibliográfico ya consistente. Dentro de ese ambiente de fomento y apoyo a la tarea poética, llama notablemente la atención la presencia de mujeres jóvenes en el cultivo de la poesía erótica y sexual, como los casos de Castillo (item **3981**) y Quevedo (items **4078** y **4079**), mediante una expresión franca y directa de calidad. Es una poesía articulada sobre una estructura de expresión y pensamiento muy definida que cuida tres aspectos básicos: la instancia femenina de la experiencia erótica como fenómeno corporal y anímico, la reflexión de los efectos de esa experiencia en el nivel intelectivo, y la búsqueda del lenguaje más adecuado mediante expresiones claras y simples, pero con efecto poético. Estos casos permiten afirmar, además, que el tema erótico en la poesía latinoamericana del siglo XX ha sido sometido a una renovación de calidad en los últimos años gracias al aporte de discursos femeninos. Otras representantes distinguidas de la poesía femenina ecuatoriana son autoras ya conocidas como Vascones y Vanegas (items **4109** y **4108**) o poco conocidas como Márquez Moreno (item **4034**). Por lo demás, en el panorama ecuatoriano participan activamente tanto poetas consagrados como nuevos. [ORR]

PERU
Una significativa porción de libros aquí anotados son recopilaciones, antologías o re-ediciones de obras poéticas correspondientes a épocas anteriores. Entre las primeras, sin duda deben destacarse las de Antonio Cisneros (item **3985**), Luis Hernández (item **4020**) y Marco Martos (item **4036**) los tres pertenecientes a la misma generación. Entre las recientes antologías publicadas en el Perú, la de icardo Silva-Santisteban puede considerarse entre las mejores y más completas, aunque precisamente no cubre la generación arriba aludida (item **3908**). De los poetas de la promoción del año 50, Francisco Bendezú ha re-editado *Cantos,* una colección que se había vuelto inhallable (item **3963**). De los poetas más jóvenes, seleccionamos dos breves volúmenes de Edgar O'Hara (item **4060**). Finalmente, registramos dos obras vinculadas a Vallejo: la que recoge las actas de un homenaje realizado en Lima por el centenario de su nacimiento; y la edición facsimilar de *Escalas melografiadas* (item **4157**), hecha a partir de un ejemplar con correcciones a mano del autor. Hay que considerar este hallazgo como uno de los más importantes sobre la crucial época limeña del poeta, antes de su definitivo viaje a Europa. [JMO]

CHILE
Entre los libros publicados en el período sobresale *Trece lunas* de Gonzalo Millán que ofrece una mirada de conjunto a una sólida, incisiva y diestra obra poética (item **4042**). Se destacan, entre los poetas más recientes, Jorge Montealegre con

Bien común por su vigilia irónica de la modernidad (item **4048**) y *Crónicas maravillosas* de Tomás Harris por su elocuencia pesadillesca de largo aliento (item **4016**).
Por otra parte, Gonzalo Rojas mantiene la intensidad de su obra previa con *Río Turbio* (item **4088**) y Nicanor Parra sorprende en *Discursos de sobremesa* con parodias
discursivas de múltiples tonalidades contraculturales (item **4068**).

En términos de ediciones, la de *Cuadernos de Temuco* de Víctor Farías (item
4056) nos regresa a los años de formación de Pablo Neruda; la *Defensa del ídolo* que
realiza Pedro Lastra nos revela las poderosas visiones de Omar Cáceres (item **3973**).
En términos de re-ediciones, Naín Nómez re-edita *Los gemidos*, libro genésico de
la obra de Pablo de Rokha (item **4089**) y Jaime Quezada *Poema de Chile*, periplo de
intenso retorno rememorativo a Chile de Gabriela Mistral (item **4045**).

La obra de Enrique Lihn recibe atención destacada: en el detallado y fundamental estudio de Carmen Foxley *Enrique Lihn: escritura excéntrica y modernidad* (item **4144**); en la vigilante revisión de la reflexión crítica de Lihn que lleva a
cabo Juan Zapata Gacitúa en *Enrique Lihn: la imaginación en su escritura crítico-
reflexiva* (see *HLAS 56:4156*); en la inteligencia ensayística de Luis Correa-Díaz de
Lengua muerta: poesía, post-literatura & erotismo en Enrique Lihn (item **4143**), y
en la fructífera recopilación de los ensayos del poeta en *El circo en llamas*, realizada
por G. Marín (item **4153**).

La poesía de Pedro Lastra recibe un incisivo estudio a partir de múltiples
perspectivas en *La precaución y la vigilancia: la poesía de Pedro Lastra* de Edgar
O'Hara (item **4148**).

La muerte de Jorge Teillier en 1996 cierra un momento de redescubrimiento
del mapa maravilloso del sur chileno. [OS]

ARGENTINA, URUGUAY Y PARAGUAY

La proximidad del fin del siglo ha motivado la publicación de varias antologías. Algunas de ellas han tenido como propósito esencial la reunión de las figuras más destacadas del siglo (items **3923**, **3937** y **3936**), mientras que otras han intentado agrupar poetas de las últimas promociones (items **3910** y **3917**). El criterio revisionista
que subyace en ambos casos resulta de particular interés para señalar la evolución y
tendencias de este corto siglo.

La producción editorial de este período revela también la reaparición de textos y autores claves. De particular interés resulta la edición de *Poesía reunida* de
Roa Bastos (item **4086**) que motivará sin duda merecidos estudios sobre esta zona
poco explorada de la creación del escritor paraguayo. La aparición de *Obra completa* de Juan L. Ortiz (item **4065**) constituye uno de los aportes editoriales más
importantes del período, en lo que respecta a poesía argentina. La importancia e
influencia de este poeta entrerriano en reconocidos poetas argentinos posteriores es
un trabajo de investigación aún pendiente que sin duda la edición de este volumen
posibilitará. Las antologías personales de poetas consagrados como Alfonsina Storni
(item **4101**), Juan Gelman (items **4009** y **4010**), Roberto Juárroz (item **4028**), Enrique
Molina (item **4046**) y Olga Orozco, dan cuenta del enorme interés crítico que sus
obras continúan suscitando. En el marco de la poesía uruguaya han sido las publicaciones de varios integrantes de la generación del '45 las que han sobresalido. Tal es
el caso de la labor poética (item **3964**) y crítica (item **4122**) de Mario Benedetti; el
nuevo poemario de Amanda Berenguer (item **3965**); y la publicación de las obras
completas—o casi—de Idea Vilariño (item **4113**) e Ida Vitale (item **4117**).

Entre los escritores más jóvenes sobresalen las voces de María Negroni (item
4055) en Argentina , Rafael Courtoisie (item **3990**) y Jorge Ernesto Olivera-Olivera

(item **4062**) en Uruguay. Se advierte en todos ellos una poderosa imaginería que con un no menos lúcido despliegue de humor da cuenta del espacio finisecular y los personajes/máscaras/fantasmas que lo pueblan. Son voces altamente promisorias. [LU]

ANTHOLOGIES

3902 **Acuña Aguero, Julio *et al.*** Instrucciones para salir del cementerio marino: antología del Taller de Literatura Activa "Eunice Odio," 1985–92. San José: Editorial El Quijote, 1995. 183 p.

Esta entrega de poesía costarricense reúne trabajos de los integrantes del *Taller de Poesía Activa de Eunice Odio*, fundado en 1986 por jóvenes poetas como Gabriel Sánchez y José Luis Amador. Desde su fundación, este Taller se propuso la inmensa tarea de llevar adelante una propuesta poética distinta a las que hasta ese momento se habían dado en Costa Rica. No buscan sus integrantes la difusión de una estética concreta, sino más bien la posibilidad de "salir" al encuentro de metáforas no convencionales y de horizontes ideológicos nuevos, marcados por la experiencia que dejó la guerra del Golfo, la caída del Muro, las luchas universitarias y la locura de querer vivirlo todo. El volumen está organizado en cuatro secciones (Fuego, Aire, Agua, Tierra), Melania Portilla (1966), José Gabriel Sánchez Jiménez (1955), Demetrio Polo-Cheva (1948) y Gustavo Induni (1968), entre otros. [EM]

3903 **Antología de la poesía del romanticismo hispanoamericano, 1820–1890.** Recopilación de Catharina V. de Vallejo. Miami: Ediciones Universal, 1993. 432 p.: bibl., indexes. (Colección Textos)

Util antología de un periodo poco atendido por la crítica. La introducción, las informaciones bibliográficas y la selección no pretenden ser exhaustivas, pero proporcionan un buen panorama de la actividad literaria en un tiempo de búsqueda de la expresión hispanoamericana. Incluye 28 poetas de Argentina, Bolivia, Colombia, Cuba, Ecuador, México, Perú, República Dominicana, Uruguay y Venezuela. [PL]

3904 **Antología de la poesía latinoamericana de vanguardia, 1916–1935.** Recopilación de Mihai G. Grünfeld. Madrid, Spain: Hiperión, 1995. 558 p.: bibl., ill. (Poesía Hiperión; 253)

Importante contribución en un área de estudios de gran interés. Además de las figuras canónicas de la vanguardia incluye textos, notas y referencias bibliográficas de numerosos poetas brasileños e hispanoamericanos menos difundidos, pero de indudable significación en el proceso poético continental desde los años 20 y 30. De consulta indispensable. [PL]

3905 **Antología de poesía contemporánea de Tabasco.** Villahermosa, Mexico: Sociedad de Escritores Tabasqueños "Letras y Voces de Tabasco," 1995. 487 p.

Tabasco ha dado poetas de primera magnitud como Carlos Pellicer, José Gorostiza y Juan Carlos Becerra. Esta antología recopila obra de 41 escritores. El prologuista explica que no se adoptó ningún criterio de selección, por lo que se incluyeron los textos que los poetas enviaron. El volumen, por ende, es muy desigual en cuanto a la calidad de los poemas, el espacio dedicado a cada escritor y su cohesión total. Pero de todos modos, el libro es útil en tanto que presenta voces y tonos muy distintos a los generados en la capital del país. [JS]

3906 **Antología de poesía puertorriqueña.** v. 1, Romanticismo. v. 2, Modernismo y postmodernismo. v. 3, Contemporánea. v. 4, Contemporánea. San Juan: Tríptico Editores, 1993. 4 v.

Concebida para un público hispanoamericano deseoso de familiarizarse con toda la poesía puertorriqueña, esta antología contiene una amplia selección de poetas, desde Mariana Bibiana Benítez en el siglo XIX hasta Mayra Santos Febres, que empieza a publicar a principios de 1990. Sin embargo, deja fuera la poesía puertorriqueña escrita en inglés. [FG]

3907 **Antología general de la poesía nicaragüense.** Introducciones, selección y notas de Jorge Eduardo Arellano. Managua: Instituto Nicaragüense de Cultura; Ediciones Distribuidora Cultural, 1994. 499 p.: ill.

Esta es la segunda *Antología general de la poesía nicaragüense* preparada por Jorge Eduardo Arellano. En relación a la primera, publicada en 1984, el editor ha incrementado considerablemente tanto el número de autores como el de composiciones, y ha cubierto casi cinco siglos de poesía. Se aprecia, además, que junto a los poetas consagrados aparecen algunas muestras de poesía prehispánica y poemas de poetas menores y desconocidos. Lo que decepciona del trabajo es la falta de rigor en las presentaciones que se hace de sus distintas secciones y el no haber incluido a ningún poeta nacido después de la década del cincuenta. Llama también la atención la ausencia de Darío, justificada en Nicaragua con el ya clásico argumento de que su presencia "trasciende fronteras geográficas y niveles estéticos". [EM]

3908 Antología general de la poesía peruana. Recopilación de Ricardo Silva-Santisteban. Lima: Biblioteca Nacional del Perú, 1994. 623 p.: bibl., ill. (Biblioteca básica peruana; 18)

El compilador reúne en este volumen los textos fundamentales de la poesía peruana, comenzando con la de los Incas hasta los poetas de la generación de los años 50. La selección es rigurosa (como puede verse por los criterios señalados en las pp. 35–36) y presenta a voces muy conocidas, al lado de otras usualmente marginadas por las antologías nacionales. [JMO]

3909 Antología histórica de la poesía dominicana del siglo XX, 1912–1995. Estudio y selección de Franklin Gutiérrez. New York: Ediciones Alcance, 1995. 446 p.: bibl.

A partir del primer brote vanguardista dominicano—el "Vedrinismo" de Vigil Díaz—que lo fue también en toda la América Latina, hasta la Generación de los 80, que empieza a publicar al finalizar el periodo de 12 años de Joaquín Balaguer (1978), en esta antología, a diferencia de las demás, la periodización difiere: por un lado, descarta el concepto de "generación" ante los poetas de 1948 y, por el otro, plantea los "Independientes del 48" y la "generación del 60." Contiene un estudio panorámico de los "movimientos, grupos, tendencias, manifiestos y enunciados de la poesía dominicana del siglo XX." [FC]

3910 Arbeleche, Jorge et al. Muestra de poesía. Asunción: Arandurã Editorial: Ediciones de la Banda Oriental, 1995. 86 p.

Muestrario breve pero representativo que tiene además el valor de incluir varios textos inéditos de estos autores. Cada poeta realizó su propia selección. [LU]

3911 La casa en la poesía venezolana del siglo XX, 1900–1950. Selección, notas y prólogo de Elí Galindo. Ilustraciones de Alirio Rodríguez. Caracas: Fondo Editorial Orlando Araujo; Banco de los Trabajadores de Venezuela, 1993. 215 p.: col. ill.

Amplia compilación que abarca poemas escritos entre 1900 y 1950 e incluye reproducciones de Alirio Rodríguez. De suma utilidad para el investigador interesado en la configuración de cosmovisiones en la poesía venezolana. La muestra incluye tanto textos pertenecientes a poetas mayores de indiscutible calidad (José Antonio Ramos Sucre, Vicente Gerbasi, Juan Liscano, Juan Sánchez Peláez) como piezas en deuda con su época o de interés por pertenecer a escritores de gran valor, pero cuyos logros se localizan más bien en otros géneros (Arturo Uslar Pietri, Miguel Otero Silva). [MG]

3912 Con una súbita vehemencia: antología de poesía contemporánea en Cuba. Selección y prólogo de Juan Nicolás Padrón Barquín. La Habana: Editorial José Martí: Split Quotation, 1996. 323 p.: bibl.

Tras un "acercamiento a lo esencial-inédito o a lo fundamental nuevo en la poesía," esta antología reúne a los más destacados poetas cubanos que, a partir de la contemporaneidad en Cuba (1959–1994), han concebido su obra en la isla. La contemporaneidad en Cuba se define en cuatro momentos poéticos: de 1959 a 1968 (mística revolucionaria y pasión épica; de 1968 a 1976 (intransigencia política y radicalismo poético); de 1979 a 1989 (institucionalidad hacia la democratización y preocupación ética); de 1989 hasta 1994 (período especial e incursión en la posmodernidad). [FC]

3913 Cuarenta poetas se balancean: poesía venezolana, 1967–1990, antología. Recopilación de Javier Lasarte Valcárcel. Caracas: Fundarte: Alcaldía del Municipio Libertador, 1991. 349 p.: bibl. (Colección Latinoamericana; no. 1)

La muestra antológica más completa de poesía venezolana de la segunda mitad del siglo XX. El antólogo posee una formación doble que contribuye a la precisión crítica y simultánea sugestividad estética de su trabajo: si por una parte no es ajeno a la disciplina universitaria—se desempeña, de hecho, como profesor en la Univ. Simón Bolívar—, por otra, es también poeta y ha sido miembro de agrupaciones que han signado la más reciente poesía de su país. La antología arranca de los años sesenta y llega a 1990, incluyendo obras ya consagradas y otras en cierne. [MG]

3914 Cuba, maestros y novísimos de la poesía: en un abrir y cerrar del siglo. Selección y prólogo de Carlos Martí Brenes *et al.* Buenos Aires: Ediciones Instituto Movilizador de Fondos Cooperativos, 1997. 127 p. (Desde la gente)

Esta antología, dirigida al público argentino, le plantea al lector la posibilidad de contrastar la poesía cubana de la primera mitad del siglo con la que se publica a partir de los ochenta. De ese contraste no se vislumbra un rompimiento apocalíptico sino una labor recreadora de los novísimos, que reciclan y recontextualizan el legado purista, vanguardista, social, origenista y conversacionalista que les ofrece la tradición poética cubana. [FC]

3915 De la vigilia fértil: antología de poetas mexicanas contemporáneas. Selección, prólogo y notas de Julian Palley. Colaboración de Aralia López González. México: UNAM, Coordinación de Difusión Cultural, Dirección de Literatura; Irvine, Calif.: Univ. of California, Irvine, 1996. 316 p.: bibl. (Textos de difusion cultural. Serie Antologías)

Esta recopilación reúne 26 voces de mujeres nacidas entre 1928 y 1962. Además de poetas contemporáneas frecuentemente incluidas en antologías generales, como Coral Bracho, Elva Macías, Elsa Cross, Gloria Gervitz, Carmen Boullosa o Myriam Moscona, Palley agrega nombres menos conocidos como Aura María Vidales, Teresa Riggen o Patricia Medina. Util introducción y la selección de poemas es suficientemente generosa como para apreciar el amplio espectro de tonos y estilos por el que pasa esta poesía: desde el feminismo combatiente, la protesta social, hasta la sofisticación del lenguaje amoroso y las búsquedas místicas. [JS]

3916 Dos siglos de literatura dominicana: siglos XIX-XX. v. 1–2, Poesía. Santo Domingo: Comisión Oficial para la Celebración del Sesquicentenario de la Independencia Nacional, 1996. 2 v.: bibl., ill. (Colección Sesquicentenario de la independencia nacional; v. 10)

Primera suma poética de la poesía dominicana. Incluye la producción desde el siglo XIX—cuando, según Manuel Rueda, empieza la poesía dominicana—hasta la actualidad de poetas como Soledad Bravo, José Marmol y Tomás Castro. [FC]

3917 Freidemberg, Daniel *et al.* Poetas: autores argentinos de fin de siglo. Presentación de Francisco Madariaga. Selección y prólogo de Juano Villafañe. Buenos Aires: Ediciones Instituto Movilizador de Fondos Cooperativos, 1995. 126 p. (Desde la gente)

La muestra incluye a poetas de distintas promociones desde Daniel Freidemberg (1945) hasta José Villa (1966). Si bien el criterio de selección es poco claro, el prólogo resulta útil por las consideraciones teóricas que surgen de los debates críticos sobre la poesía argentina actual. Los poetas más significativos son: Freidemberg, Bellesi, Carrera, Perlongher, Gruss, y Boccanera. Una ausencia lamentable es la de María Negroni. [LU]

3918 González Suárez, Julián. Antología poética de la vanguardia hispanoamericana. Managua: Ediciones Distribuidora Cultural, 1994. 168 p.: bibl. (Colección Letras universales)

Util información contextualizadora sobre el desarrollo y establecimiento de la vanguardia; la muestra antológica de los autores representativos del momento es igualmente atinada, valores que hacen del libro una estimable guía para estudiantes y lectores interesados en el tema. [PL]

3919 Jugando a juegos prohibidos. Recopilación de Eliana Dávila. La Habana: Editorial Letras Cubanas, 1992. 177 p.

Esta antología reúne a un grupo de poetas cubanos que empezaron a publicar a mediados de los ochenta, y que terminaron nucleados alrededor de la Asociación "Hermanos Saiz." Los caracteriza un "obstinado antropocentrismo," una pluralidad temática, un sentido casi agónico de la eticidad. Concretamente, la antología plantea "retomar" el tema del amor, "una vertiente en apariencia desterrada de nuestra literatura nacional." [FC]

3920 Mapa imaginario: dossier, 26 nuevos poetas cubanos. Recopilación de Rolando Sánchez Mejías. Havana: Embajada de Francia en Cuba: Instituto Cubano del Libro, 1995. 297 p.: ill.

Se plantea en esta antología una muestra de la poesía cubana reciente, al igual que una nueva manera de cartografiar el panorama poético de la isla ajena a las designaciones generacionales y a las propuestas emancipatorias de la historia. Se persigue "inventar un precario mapa" de los imaginarios poéticos con tres puntos cardinales: el de los poetas que continúan el legado origenista, el de los que aspiran a la "articulación significativa" con el lector, y el de los que se ciñen a la poesía como "experiencia de escritura." [FC]

3921 Mariscal, Beatriz. Romancero general de Cuba. México: Colegio de México, Centro de Estudios Lingüísticos y Literarios, 1996. 303 p.: bibl., ill. (some col.), index. (Serie Estudios de lingüística y literatura; 31)

Se reúnen en esta publicación tanto los textos inéditos del Archivo Menéndez Pidal y de los fondos de José María Chacón y Calvo de la Biblioteca Hispánica de Madrid, como todos aquellos textos publicados de que tiene conocimiento la autora. El romancero cubano se agrupa en cinco categorías: la mujer como objeto de la acción; el hombre como sujeto de la acción; romances de tema religioso; los animales protagonistas. [FC]

3922 Medusario: muestra de poesía latino americana. Selección y notas de Roberto Echavarren, José Kozer, and Jacobo Sefamí. Prólogos de Roberto Echavarren and Néstor Perlongher. Epílogo de Tamara Kamenszain. México: Fondo de Cultura Económica, 1996. 496 p.: bibl. (Colección Tierra firme)

No es del todo clara la "Razón de este libro", a pesar de la nota inicial así titulada. Prólogos de R. Echavarren y N. Perlongher intentan delinear los rasgos neobarrocos de la escritura poética actual, pero la abigarrada selección de los 22 autores convocados no hace atractivo ese camino. Muy justo y meritorio el amplio espacio concedido a J.C. Becerra, R. Hinostroza y Marosa di Giorgio. [PL]

3923 Mujeres: las mejores poetas uruguayas del siglo XX. Selección de poetas y prólogo de Washington Benavides. Montevideo: Ministerio de Educación y Cultura, Instituto Nacional del Libro, 1993. 398 p.: bibl. (Colección "Brazo corto")

Representativa antología de poetas uruguayas del siglo XX. La selección es muy acertada y las notas que anteceden los textos junto con la ficha bibliográfica que acompaña a la mayoría de las escritoras resulta muy útil. [LU]

3924 Nuevos juegos prohibidos: jóvenes poetas de Cuba. Selección y nota introductoria de Mayra Hernández Menéndez. La Habana: Editorial Letras Cubanas, 1997. 124 p.

Esta antología reúne a 24 poetas cubanos nacidos a partir de 1960, cuyo trabajo se inscribe en la poesía cubana de finales de los ochenta y principios de los noventa. Se propone recoger el nuevo decir poético de la época, tanto en términos estéticos como estilísticos, para corroborar la vitalidad de la poesía en Cuba, marcada por un "aliento lírico." [FC]

3925 Otros contemporáneos: Octavio G. Barreda, Anselmo Mena, Enrique Asúnsolo, Enrique Munguía. Recopilación de Luis Mario Schneider. México: UNAM, Coordinación de Humanidades, Instituto de Investigaciones Bibliográficas, 1995. 267 p.: bibl., ill.

Este volumen pretende recuperar poetas que, según el crítico Schneider, debieron pertenercer al grupo de Contemporáneos. El libro reúne la poesía completa de estos cuatro escritores prácticamente ignorados en las historias de la poesía mexican—salvo Barreda, quien sí es conocido por su labor como editor de las revistas literarias más importantes de los treinta y cuarenta. Quizá resulte prácticamente imposible introducir nuevos nombres a un grupo tan conocido por la crítica, pero el volumen es útil en tanto enseña la sensibilidad de la época. [JS]

3926 El pasado del cielo: la nueva y novísima poesía cubana. Selección, prólogo y notas de Víctor Rodríguez Núñez. Medellín: Alejandría Editores, 1994. 257 p. (Colección La isla en peso; 1)

Esta antología reúne a dos generaciones de poetas cubanos: los nuevos que surgieron a finales de los setenta, y los novísimos que, entre los ochenta y noventa, sucedieron a aquéllos. Entre ambas generaciones, que comparten una poética, se testimonia el rompimiento con la poesía de los setenta. Ambas generaciones plantean una "poesía de la soledad del que busca compañía, monólogo que no ansía otra cosa que el diálogo." [FC]

3927 **Poemas transitorios: antología de nuevos poetas cubanos.** Selección, prólogo y notas de Arsenio Cicero Sancristobal. Mérida: Dirección de Cultura y Extensión ULA, Consejo de Publicaciones ULA, Ediciones Mucuglifo, 1992. 137 p.: ill.

Esta selección de 5 poetas (Ramón Fernández Larrea, Marilyn Bobes, José Pérez Olivares, Reina María Rodríguez y Alex Fleites Rodríguez), destinada al público venezolano, ofrece un panorama de la poesía cubana que, a mediados de los años 70, se aleja del panfleto político para asumir—sin desdeñar cierto conversacionalismo—el papel que le corresponde al poeta: "ser una voz profundamente individual en la que puedan reconocerse los demás." [FC]

3928 **Poemas y narraciones sobre el movimiento estudiantil de 1968.** Recopilación de Marco Antonio Campos y Alejandro Toledo. Ciudad Universitaria, México: UNAM, Coordinación de Humanidades, Dirección General de Publicaciones, 1996. 282 p.: bibl.

La masacre estudiantil el 2 de octubre de 1968 fue un momento clave en la historia intelectual y política de México. Este volumen reúne poemas de 29 escritores y 10 narraciones. El libro es muy rico, en tanto presenta múltiples versiones de los acontecimientos a través de formas y estéticas variadísimas. Pero aun así, se queda corto en cuanto que el 68 dio mucho más, una literatura vastísima que sería imposible compilar en un solo libro. [JS]

3929 **Poesía amorosa latinoamericana.** Prólogo, selección y notas de Manuel Ruano. Caracas: Biblioteca Ayacucho, 1994. 240 p.: bibl. (Colección Claves de América; 18)

Esta antología se caracteriza por la amplitud de la muestra: 120 poemas de otros tantos autores, desde el siglo XVI. La inclusión de un poema precolombino y de textos del Conde de Lautréamont, J. Laforgue, J. Supervielle y Saint-John Perse es aporte novedoso. Muy útil el apéndice bibliográfico, pero la disposición de los poemas en 3 apartados es un tanto gratuita e innecesaria. [PL]

3930 **Poesía cubana de los años 80.** Recopilación de Alicia Llarena. Introducción de A. Llarena y O. Sánchez. Madrid: Ediciones La Palma, 1994. 241 p.: bibl. (El archipiélago; 2)

Muestra de 14 poetas cubanos de la isla cuya poesía, sin constituir "un nexo generacional insoslayable que unifique la voz poética," converge en cierto inconformismo latente, en cierta "ruptura providencial" con las generaciones anteriores. Desde lo lírico, se denuncia el adulterio moral. Los dos artículos introductorios—79 páginas en total—contextualizan la poesía de los 80. [FC]

3931 **Poesía cubana hoy.** Madrid: Editorial Grupo Cero, 1995. 127 p.: ill. (Colección Poesía hoy)

En esta antología se intenta incluir a un gran número de poetas cubanos actuales (64), de modo que el lector, sobre todo español, tenga acceso al panorama poético de la Cuba de los noventa, incluso cuando ello implique una muestra reducida de poemas por cada autor. La antología no parte de un criterio estético o temático que clasifique la producción poética. [FC]

3932 **Poesía cubana: la isla entera; antología.** Recopilación de Felipe Lázaro y Bladimir Zamora. Madrid: Editorial Betania, 1995. 382 p.: bibl., ill. (Colección Antologías)

Esta antología persigue continuar el proyecto de unificación de la poesía cubana en la isla y en el exilio, un proyecto que inició Orlando Rodríguez Sardiña en 1973, *La última poesía cubana.* Incluye a aquellos poetas de la "plural geografía de Cuba" nacidos a partir de 1940, independientemente de la estética o el credo político, pues se trata de mostrar la pluralidad y la heterogeneidad de esa poesía cubana. [FC]

3933 **La poesía de la rebelión.** Guatemala: Editorial O. de León Palacios, 1994. 88 p.: ill. (Colección "Para que todo el pueblo lea"; no. 14)

En ocasión del cincuentenario de la Revolución Guatemalteca del 20 de octubre de 1944, la Editorial Oscar de León Palacios publicó esta colección de poesía "rebelde" que reúne muestras de doce poetas representativos de cien años de insurrección popular. En algunos casos, los poetas antologados provienen de elites criollas cultas que no siempre saben captar el ritmo interno de la realidad popular e indígena de Guatemala. Esto sucede, por ejemplo, con el poeta del siglo XIX Ismael Cerna, con el modernista Rafael Arévalo Martínez y con algunos representantes de la generación del cuarenta. Pero conforme la antología se va acercando al presente, algunas voces van adquiriendo la fuerza que da el testimonio, la crónica y la literatura conversacional y empiezan a distanciarse de sintaxis y formalidades conservadoras. Destacan, en este grupo, Miguel Angel Vázquez (generación del cuarenta) y José Luis Villatoro. [EM]

3934 La poesía de las dos orillas: Cuba, 1959–1993; antología. Selección y prólogo de León de la Hoz. Madrid: Libertarias/Prodhufi, 1994. 428 p.: bibl. (Poesía)

Tras una esquematización de la poesía cubana—que de la Hoz plantea en términos de movimientos, en vez de generaciones (movimiento de los '60, "lo conversacional;" de los '70, agotamiento de lo conversacional; de los '80, síntesis; del exilio, sin una estructura poética dominante)—esta antología es uno de varios intentos por agrupar en un solo libro lo más representativo de la poesía cubana "de las dos orillas" a partir de la Revolución. [FC]

3935 Poesía en el espejo: estudio y antología de la nueva lírica femenina venezolana, 1970–1994. Recopilación de Julio Miranda. Caracas: FUNDARTE: Alcaldía de Caracas, 1995. 335 p.: bibl. (Colección Delta; no. 36)

A Julio Miranda debe la crítica literaria venezolana algunos de los trabajos más ambiciosos y sistemáticos acerca de la segunda mitad del siglo XX. A sus volúmenes dedicados a la narrativa y a la lírica en general, ahora agrega éste, en el que se analizan las tendencias colectivas de veintiséis poetas nacidas entre 1920 y 1970. Se describe y propone como definitoria una serie de rasgos— "brevedad," "la casa como tema," "extranjeridad," "máscaras"—y se selecciona con acierto lo más representativo del *corpus* inicialmente pautado en el prólogo. [MG]

3936 Poesía paraguaya de ayer y de hoy. v. 1. Paraguay: Intercontinental Editora, 1995. 1 v.: bibl., ill., index.

Útil volumen que incluye a poetas del siglo XIX y XX cuya obra está escrita mayoritariamente en español. El prólogo pasa revista de los principales periodos y autores representativos de la literatura paraguaya. [LU]

3937 Poesía uruguaya siglo 20: antología. Recopilación de Walter Rela. Montevideo: Alfar, 1994. 304 p.

Útil obra de referencia que sin embargo adolece de la falta de un claro criterio de selección. [LU]

3938 Poetas cubanos actuales. Selección, prólogo y notas de Daniuska González. Miranda, Venezuela: Ateneo de Los Teques: Colegio Universitario de Los Teques "Cecilio Acosta": Ateneo de Petare, 1995. 136 p. Colección Ateneo de Los Teques; no. 25

En esta antología, confeccionada para el público venezolano, la actualidad de la poesía cubana no excluye a los poetas establecidos, como Dulce María Loynaz, Cintio Vitier, Fina García-Marruz, Miguel Barnet. Poetas actuales son todos aquellos que viven y mantienen una obra sistemática "sin importar su reconocimiento o no." La antología no persigue agrupar a los diferentes poetas ni a sus respectivas estéticas, si bien la nota introductoria advierte al lector de estas diferencias. [FC]

3939 Poetas en Antioquia, 1966–1826. Selección, presentación y notas de Luis Iván Bedoya M. Medellín: Biblioteca Pública Piloto de Medellín, 1991. 201 p.: bibl. (Publicaciones especiales / Biblioteca Pública Piloto de Medellín)

Aunque falta un acercamiento crítico detenido a cada uno de los autores incluidos, esta antología puede constituir, sin duda, una valiosa introducción a la poesía antioqueña para el lector no colombiano, La muestra, además de extensa—cronológicamente va de 1826 a 1966 y contiene piezas de 80 autores—mantiene cierto rigor estético. [MG]

3940 Poetas modernistas de Nicaragua, 1880–1930. Recopilación de Julio Valle-Castillo. Managua: Editorial Nueva Nicaragua, 1993. 446 p.: bibl., ill.

El propósito de esta antología es el mismo que guió su primera edición, en 1978: ensanchar el horizonte del modernismo nicaragüense, generalmente limitado a la figura de Darío, y dar a conocer obras y autores que no han recibido la atención que seguramente merecen. "En arte lo excelente es enemigo de lo bueno," subraya el editor, Julio Valle-Castillo, y captura en estas pocas palabras los alcances de su trabajo. Además de Darío, que encabeza la serie, doce son los

poetas antologados, desde Román Mayorga
Rivas (1861–1925) hasta Antenor Sandino
Hernández (1899–1969). La gran ausencia es
Salomón de la Selva, a quien Valle-Castillo
no considera modernista sino más bien "el
primer poeta moderno de Mesoamérica" y
como tal, le dedica un libro aparte. El volumen cuenta además con un valioso estudio
introductorio que sitúa apropiadamente el
conjunto modernista nicaragüense. [EM]

**3941 Premio de Poesía Aguascalientes: 30
años.** v. 1–3. México: Joaquín Mortiz,
1997. 3 v. (Summa literaria mexicana)
Recopilación de todos los libros ganadores de este Premio (antes conocido como
Premio Nacional de Poesía), sin duda el
galardón más importante para la poesía en
México. A 30 años de su fundación, sigue
marcando la pauta de las voces más originales y singulares, ajustándose a los modos
del decir de las nuevas generaciones, como se
puede comprobar con el simple repaso de algunos de los poetas premiados: Juan Bañuelos, José Emilio Pacheco, Eduardo Lizalde,
Coral Bracho, Francisco Hernández, Efraín
Bartolomé, José Luis Rivas, Myriam
Moscona, Elsa Cross y Eduardo Milán. [JS]

**3942 Tertuliando: dominicanas y amiga[o]s
= Hanging out: Dominican women and
friends: bilingual text(o)s bilinguales, 1994–
1996.** v. 1. Santo Domingo: Comisión Permanente de la Feria Nacional del Libro, 1997. 1
v.: bibl.
Esta antología persigue dos propósitos
complementarios. Por un lado, se plantea
textualizar el trabajo literario (poemas y relatos) de la naciente comunidad de mujeres
dominicanas residentes en Nueva York, para
quienes escribir implica, además de hacer literatura, ir forjando las bases de una nueva
cultura. Por el otro, cuestiona la exclusión de
lo dominicano en el vigoroso espacio de la
literatura latina en Estados Unidos. [FC]

**3943 Tras la huella de lo imposible: an-
tología de nuevos poetas cubanos,
según la tendencia de la agresividad.** Selección y prólogo de Raúl Dopico Echevarría.
Guadalajara: Secretaría de Cultura de Jalisco,
1994. 143 p. (Colección Orígenes)
Se incluye una muestra de los llamados poetas de la Tercera Generación cuyo trabajo, marcado por el legado poético de
Rolando Escardó, Fayad Jamís y Roque Dal-

ton, plantea una nueva estética al margen de
la poesía social que dominó en los años setenta. En su lugar, surge una poesía de tonos
duros—libros coléricos—de factura compleja, entre lo reflexivo y lo sentencioso, polémica, paradójica, de tonos filosóficos y
místicos, donde sobresalen temas como la
muerte, la soledad, el amor, la patria, los héroes y Dios. [FC]

**3944 Veinticinco años de poesía chilena,
1970–1995.** Recopilación de Teresa
Calderón, Lila Calderón, y Tomás Harris.
México: Fondo de Cultura Económica, 1996.
467 p.: bibl. (Colección Tierra firme. Poetas
chilenos)
Esta antología se divide en dos secciones: la dedicada a poetas de los 60 incluye
a 14 poetas (13 hombres y una mujer). Un
arte poética introduce la selección de cada
poeta que se cierra con citas de reseñas críticas. Testimonio de la pluralidad de propuestas de la poesía chilena reciente que, en sus
mejores momentos, indaga con igual pericia
en el poema breve o extenso. [OS]

**3945 La voz ante el espejo: antología general
de poetas yucatecos.** Recopilación de
Rubén Reyes Ramírez. Mérida, Mexico: Gobierno del Estado de Yucatán, 1995. 2 v.: bibl.
La primera parte reúne poemas de 28
escritores nacidos entre 1900 y 1959; la segunda recoge obra de 17 creadores jóvenes.
Libro útil para el especialista, pero demasiado amplio para el lector común. A pesar de
algunos textos con temas mayas o de ciertas
evocaciones de sitios de la memoria, mucha
de esta poesía ha sido generada en la Ciudad
de México, donde muchos de estos escritores
se radicaron. Entonces, la dificultad en este
tipo de antologías reside en ver si se puede
distinguir una poesía que singularmente se
pueda identificar como yucateca. [JS]

BOOKS OF VERSE

3946 Acevedo, Rafael. Instrumentario. San
Juan: Isla Negra Editores, 1996. 120 p.
Poeta de la nueva poesía puertorriqueña—Acevedo dirigió la revista *Filo de
Juego* (1983–87)—este poemario asume "Los
animales de la palabra" para hacer una poesía
vinculada en múltiples contextos (literarios,
míticos, familiares, sociales, políticos, sexuales) sin ampararse en otra ideología que no
sea la imaginación poética. Una imaginación

crítica ante el estado, las instituciones, los héroes, que tampoco cree en los atropellos del nuevo orden neoliberal. [FC]

3947 Agosín, Marjorie. Las chicas desobedientes. Madrid: Ediciones Torremozas, 1997. 62 p. (Colección Torremozas; 129)

Segunda edición (primera en 1988) de poemas que incorporan a personajes mujeres en encrucijadas de vida o muerte. Dimensiones históricas y étnicas relevantes como la muerte de la última yámana se mezclan a una peculiar intensidad lírica del sujeto femenino. [OS]

3948 Aguilar Mora, Jorge. Stabat Mater. México: Ediciones Era, 1996. 60 p. (Biblioteca Era)

Mejor conocido por sus ensayos y sus novelas, Aguilar Mora (Chihuahua, 1946) es también autor de tres libros de poesía. Se podría argüir que este volumen conforma un solo poema, dividido en 33 fragmentos sin numeración ni título. "Stabat Mater" se refiere a un poema medieval que intenta representar el dolor de la Virgen al pie de la cruz. Aguilar Mora hace de cada uno de sus textos una exploración acerca del dolor y en un agudo cuestionamiento de la espiritualidad y de la fe, a través de diferentes voces que hablan pero no se escuchan las unas a las otras. [JS]

3949 Aguirre Gainsborg de Méndez, Aída. Instantes de una vida. La Paz: Editorial Offset Boliviana, 1995. 170 p.: ill.

Este volumen revela a una poeta boliviana poco conocida, pero que su obra merece ser leída. Su poesía se caracteriza por un tono sereno y contemplativo. Para esta autora, poetizar es reflexionar sobre aspectos físicos y metafísicos de la existencia del ser humano. La misma reflexión que a veces denuncia la dificultad de alcanzar el saber se convierte en motivo poético. [ORR]

3950 Ak'abal, Humberto. Hojas del árbol pajarero. México: Editorial Praxis, 1995. 108 p.: ill.

Terse, decidedly conversational haiku-like poetry collection by an indigenous Guatemalan, this book will surprise readers who may expect it to provide direct political commentary. Ak'abal's concerns are elsewhere, and if it is true that nature is present in the book's four subdivisions, especially in the onomatopoetic use of language, the poet focuses more on dangerously sentimental (for poetry) aspects of everyday life. [W. Corral]

3951 Alegría, Claribel. Variaciones en clave de mí. Madrid: Libertarias/Prodhufi, 1993. 78 p. (Poesía)

Este poemario es sin duda un aporte notable a la literatura latinoamericana. La poesía que aquí aparece es simplemente extraordinaria. El placer, y también la turbación que provoca la lectura de estos poemas dicen mucho acerca de los alcances de una poética que, como pocas, ha sabido superar esas dicotomías tan conflictivas que plantea una aproximación ideológica al poema frente a otra, más bien estética. Claribel Alegría le cumple a ambas. Sus poemas poseen, en igual medida, la perturbación metafísica de una Alejandra Pizarnik y la dimensión ideológica de un Sandino. Especialmente interesante es el tratamiento que aquí recibe la intertextualidad, que desde el *collage* literario articula críticas muy concretas a las historia y culturas latinoamericanas. En uno de los poemas, titulado "Ira Demetrae" leemos: "tres meses de sequía/...después/ indiferencia/...les cederé a los machos/...hasta que Zeus se arrepienta/ de su doble moral/ hasta que estés conmigo/ todo el año/ y decretemos juntas/ la primavera eterna." [EM]

3952 Alvarado, Leonel. El reino de la zarza. San José: Editorial Universitaria Centroamericana, 1994. 69 p. (Colección Séptimo día)

Este poemario ha recibido, por decisión unánime, el Premio Unico de Poesía del Certamen Literario Latinoamericano EDUCA 1993. El jurado, compuesto por los poetas Isaac Felipe Azofeifa (Costa Rica), Juan Bañuelos (México) y Roberto Sosa (Honduras), señala a Leonel Alvarado como "una sobresaliente promesa de la mejor poesía hondureña de hoy." Y no se equivoca. Los poemas premiados son evidentemente la promesa de una poesía renovada y lúcida en sus planteamientos. Renovada porque sabe poner la mirada allí donde pocos la han puesto: la dimensión poética del pensamiento prehispánico. Lúcida porque entiende las presiones del tiempo y el horror de la historia. [EM]

3953 Alvarez, Soledad. Vuelo posible. Santo Domingo: s.n., 1994. 75 p.

Incluida en la *Antología de la literatura dominicana* (1988) de José Alcántara Almanzar, la poesía de Alvarez aborda, desde un lirismo femenino, el espacio del amor desde la corporalidad del deseo que, ante el paso del tiempo y ante la presencia de la soledad—también, la certeza de la muerte— busca, a veces como un recurso de la memoria, un momento de unidad donde la amante y el amado se fundan "sin distancia de lo que nos rodea." [FC]

3954 Aquino, Alfonso D'. Tanagra. México: Consejo Nacional para la Cultura y las Artes, Dirección General de Publicaciones, 1996. 81 p. (Práctica mortal)

Alfonso D'Aquino (México, 1959) es continuador de la poesía que se cuestiona a sí misma, la poesía crítica, cuyo principal propulsor es Octavio Paz. En este caso, el pajarito cantor (tanagra) evoca el mundo cubocreacionista de Vicente Huidobro. La primera sección, "Lluvia," tiene varios ejercicios al estilo de los caligramas; las otras dos ("Arborescente" y "Musca") acuden a la metáfora del pájaro como poeta, tantas veces expuesta por la tradición. [JS]

3955 Arráiz Lucca, Rafael. El abandono y la vigilia: poemas. México: Fondo de Cultura Económica, 1992. 158 p. (Colección Tierra firme)

En los poemas de Arráiz Lucca—de los cuales este volumen ofrece una muestra generosa—se sintetizan varias de las tendencias que definen a la poesía venezolana de los últimos dos decenios del siglo XX: el respeto por un canon postvanguardista (en el que Nicanor Parra y José Emilio Pacheco no ocupan lugares secundarios); la necesidad de regresar a la historia personal para compensar las lagunas de la historia colectiva y, más concretamente, la nacional; los nostálgicos esfuerzos de una imaginería esencialmente prosaica, la del mundo moderno y la de lo cotidiano, por recuperar la musicalidad del verso antiguo. Atención detenida merece el prólogo de José Balza, que ve en la estructuración de este volumen un "rapto whitmaniano." [MG]

3956 Astudillo y Astudillo, Rubén. De la tierra, el fuego y los recuerdos. Quito: Subsecretaría de Cultura, Sistema Nacional de Bibliotecas, 1995. 99 p. (Colección País secreto)

Este volumen es una reedición del titulado *Poemas* (1982), cuyo autor es uno de los poetas de mayor prestigio en el Ecuador. El título que este volumen presenta ahora procede del primer poema. Otros tres poemas (*Mientras leo tus cartas, Palabras para gloriar la aurora,* y *Canción del reencuentro plural*) completan el volumen. De indudable calidad, la poesía de Astudillo (1938) se caracteriza por recuperar modalidades afines a la poesía vanguardista hispanoamericana en la configuración de sus imágenes y disposición de sus versos. [ORR]

3957 Azofeifa, Isaac Felipe. Poesía reunida. Estudio preliminar, notas y bibliografía de Carlos Francisco Monge. San José: Editorial Costa Rica, 1995. 544 p.: bibl., index.

Hay que celebrar esta iniciativa de recoger la obra poética de un poeta costarricense que, como Isaac Felipe Azofeifa (1909), es poco conocido fuera de su país de origen. El responsable de la edición, Carlos Francisco Monge, ha logrado un texto que resalta por la seriedad del estudio crítico que acompaña a los poemas y la inclusión de una bibliografía completa tanto de la obra de Azofeifa como de la crítica que se ha ocupado de ella. El lector tendrá la oportunidad de apreciar una poesía que, gestada originalmente en el modernismo latinoamericano, ha sabido recrearse al contacto con los distintos logros de la vanguardia, la poesía social, conversacional, el exteriorismo y el postmodernismo de las últimas década. Además de la obra poética publicada en forma de libro, el editor ha incluido poemas publicados en revistas y periódicos. [EM]

3958 Báez, Marcelo. Puerto sin rostros. Quito: Eskeletra Editorial, 1996. 203 p. (Poesía)

Un sentimiento de incertidumbre obliga a este joven poeta ecuatoriano (1969) a un enfrentamiento constante con el lenguaje y el poema. Con una doble atención hacia su propia escritura y hacia el espacio de la ciudad en que vive, Báez se entrega al hacer poético observando el espacio físico de su transcurrir y el lenguaje por el que lo expresa. De este modo, también comenta su propia manifestación desde un nivel metalingüístico. Esta segunda actitud más racional que la primera asume modalidad crítica respecto al lenguaje y a la escritura poética en general. [ORR]

3959 Baranda, María. Moradas imposibles. México: Ediciones Sin Nombre: Juan Pablos Editor, 1997. 58 p. (Cuadernos de la salamandra)

La poesía de María Baranda (pseudónimo de Alicia Meza, 1962) evoca el trabajo sumamente elaborado de la argentina Olga Orozco, con versos que lindan ante el abismo y la iluminación. Precisamente, en este pequeño volumen el epígrafe de Orozco enmarca la ansiedad frente al tiempo, el vacío, el exilio, y a la vez sentirse redimida por una especie de designio de los dioses. La elocuencia de esta voz apunta a Baranda como uno de los escritores mexicanos más interesantes de nuestros días. [JS]

3960 Bedoya Ramírez, Josué. Hoyos negros. México: Univ. Autónoma Metropolitana, Unidad Xochimilco; 1995. 66 p. (Mantícora)

La poesía de Ramírez (México, 1963) mantiene un intenso equilibrio entre la agonía de un yo (casi nunca expuesto en su subjetividad) y una fría relación de imágenes impersonales que se esbozan con neutralidad. Por ejemplo: "Moscas, / arcos en el aire, / un bote de cerveza la cúpula del mediodía." El ambiente "sentimental" del yo se deriva de la descripción de la imagen. [JS]

3961 Bedregal, Yolanda. Convocatorias. Ecuador?: s.n., 1994. 56 p.

Nueva colección de textos de una de las poetas bolivianas más conocidas. Una intención religiosa se advierte en la totalidad de este breve volumen. Bedregal (1918) lleva a su poesía temas del imaginario cristiano, con un afán de renovar las creencias al respecto, convencida de que la época actual—según afirma ella misma, en una nota final—es "fecunda en técnica y espiritualmente estéril." [ORR]

3962 Bellessi, Diana. Crucero ecuatorial: tributo del mudo. Buenos Aires: Libros de Tierra Firme, 1994. 84 p.: ill. (Colección de poesía Todos bailan; 182)

Reedición de estos libros de principios de los 80. Predomina, en el primero, el tema del viaje y el carácter testimonial del discurso. Del segundo poemario sobresale la parte titulada "Jade" que reúne poemas-homenaje a mujeres. [LU]

3963 Bendezú, Francisco. Cantos. 2. ed. Lima: Lluvia Editores, 1994. 83 p.: col. ill. (Colección Hojas de hierba)

Nueva edición de un libro poético originalmente publicado en 1971 y que es una expresión de la "poesía pura" que cultivó este miembro del grupo de poetas de la década del 50. El libro es un homenaje a la "pintura metafísica" de Giorgio De Chirico, cuyas ilustraciones acompañan el volumen. [JMO]

3964 Benedetti, Mario. El olvido está lleno de memoria. Montevideo: Cal y Canto, 1995. 177 p.

Este nuevo volumen reafirma la continuidad de una poesía que parte de la circunstancia inmediata para revelar las complejidades de lo real. [LU]

3965 Berenguer, Amanda. La botella verde: analysis situs. Montevideo: Cal y Canto, 1995. 73 p.

Desde ese sitio sitiado que es la botella, el hablante observa y se interroga por el mundo de afuera. Dede allí, recorre una genealogía cultural que le acompaña—desde el exterior—en ese topos aislado y aislante. [LU]

3966 Bignozzi, Juana. Interior con poeta. Buenos Aires: Libros de Tierra Firme, 1993. 48 p. (Colección de poesía Todos bailan; 137)

Predomina el tono elegíaco que acompaña una temática del desencanto, de la pérdida: la vida como desarraigo. [LU]

3967 Biseo, Luciana. Voceando con la pupila izquierda: 1993–1995. San José: TECNOSPA, 1995. 97 p.: ill.

En esta colección de poemas Luciana Biseo explora las posibilidades de lo que podría llamarse una "estética de la memoria." Su escritura, sólida y abiertamente identificada con el quehacer de las mujeres, sondea las diferentes "memorias" que éstas registran a través de su experiencia. Son Memorias del deseo y Memorias metafísicas. Quizás el rasgo más meritorio de esta poesía sea la maestría con que la autora trabaja la articulación sintáctica de sus poemas, que exigen lecturas sostenidas, sin la concesión de la pausa. Como si de verdaderas "memorias" se tratara. [EM]

3968 Blanco, Alberto. El corazón del instante. México: Fondo de Cultura Económica, 1998. 545 p. (Letras mexicanas)

Recopilación de la poesía completa de Blanco (México, 1951), salvo que el autor prescinde del orden cronológico y reorganiza los textos con los mismos criterios de muchos de sus volúmenes individuales. Blanco está obsesionado por los ciclos y las totalidades: este amplio volumen tiene 12 capítulos (o libros) con que se engloban sus exploraciones de lo sagrado en los terrenos de lo cotidiano. El volumen, además, cuenta con varios libros inéditos: "Paisajes en el oído," "Este silencio," "El corazón del instante," "La raíz cuadrada del cielo" y "Antipaisajes y poemas vistos." [JS]

3969 Blanco, José Joaquín. Garañón de la luna. México: Univ. Autónoma Metropolitana, 1995. 66 p. (Colección Molinos de viento; 83. Serie/Poesía)

Más conocido como ensayista, Blanco (México, 1951) es autor de varios libros de poesía. Este volumen explora un estado de ánimo nocturno, fuertemente influido por los humores impredecibles de la luna llena. Ciertas imágenes se emparentan con esta veta lunar: una violencia intermitente; una sexualidad expresada a través de metáforas de mar conmocionado, y una subyugación a partir del embrujo pasional. [JS]

3970 Bonifaz Nuño, Rubén. Versos, 1978–1994. México: Fondo de Cultura Económica, 1996. 351 p. (Letras mexicanas)

En 1979, Bonifaz Nuño (Veracruz, 1923) había reunido en De otro modo lo mismo su poesía completa hasta la fecha. Este volumen complementa al anterior y podría considerarse el segundo tomo. Poco conocido en el extranjero, el poeta tiene fuerte influencia entre los escritores jóvenes en México. Depuración de la forma, sabiduría clásica (él es, a su vez, traductor de poesía latina), y simultáneamente incorporación de lo coloquial mexicano. En este volumen destaca Del templo de su cuerpo, donde se recrean las diez sefirot de la cábala judía, en combinación con las letras del alfabeto. [JS]

3971 Boullosa, Carmen. La delirios. México: Fondo de Cultura Económica, 1998. 86 p. (Letras mexicanas)

Después de La salvaja (1989), parecía que Boullosa (México, 1954) había abandonado la poesía, puesto que publicó ocho novelas a partir de entonces. Este libro prueba que la versatilidad de Boullosa (además ha escrito teatro, y cuentos para niños) no demerita su calidad. Los delirios continúa la filiación femenina de su trabajo anterior, pero siempre a partir de una subversión de lo que significa ese género. Algunos de estos poemas largos y densos (léanse Jardín Elíseo, Niebla, Sangre) son incursiones cadenciosas en el ánima que habita en seres alucinados. [JS]

3972 Burgos, Julia de. Julia de Burgos: amor y soledad. Selección de Manuel de la Puebla. Madrid: Ediciones Torremozas, 1994. 71 p.: ill. (Colección Torremozas; 104)

Con esta selección de 31 poemas—"A Julia de Burgos," "Río Grande de Loíza," "Casi alba," "Dadme mi número," "Poema para mi muerte"—destinada al público español, de la Puebla recoge lo mejor y más representativo de Julia, a quien compara con Martí y Sor Juana en el prólogo. Contiene una útil introducción a la vida (trágica) y a la obra ("un fuerte, doloroso e intenso proceso interior") de la poeta puertorriqueña. [FC]

3973 Cáceres, Omar. Defensa del ídolo. Edición de Pedro Lastra. Prólogo de Vicente Huidobro. Santiago: LOM Ediciones, 1996. 70 p.: ill. (Colección Entre mares. Poesía)

Excelente rescate de figura enigmática de la poesía chilena fallecida a los treinta y nueve años. Los poemas—escritos en 1934—tienen el peso de lo onírico y exhiben una perplejidad angustiosa ante cierta existencia fantasmal: "... lo qu'él busca, aquéllos por quienes él ahora llora,/lo que ama, se ha ido también lejos, alcanzándose!". [OS]

3974 Calderón, Teresa. Imágenes rotas. Santiago: Red Internacional del Libro, 1995. 81 p.: ill.

Textos de corte aforístico que tematizan las rupturas trágicas de una existencia quebrada: suicidio, alcoholismo, depresión, muerte. "La vida es cruel y es mucha." [OS]

3975 Calzadilla, Juan. El fulgor y la oquedad. Mérida, Venezuela: Ediciones MUCUGLIFO, Dirección Sectorial de Literatura CONAC, 1994. 42 p.

Fiel a su propia trayectoria como poeta, Calzadilla nos ofrece una nueva entrega de su escritura fragmentaria. El atractivo también en esta ocasión esta en la ambigüedad fundamental del hablante lírico, que si unas veces formula solemnemente sus apotegmas, otras parece sugerir una lectura irrespetuosa de ellos. Fuente de metadiscursos inagotables y consecuentemente humorísticos, la voz textual se describe a sí misma como "boceto" y a sus líneas como "borrones." [MG]

3976 Cano, Kenia. Tiempo de hojas. Chimalistac, Mexico: Consejo Nacional para la Cultura y las Artes, 1995. 78 p. (Fondo editorial tierra adentro; 108)

Cano (Cuernavaca, México, 1972) es una de las nuevas voces de la poesía mexicana. En este volumen destaca su sagacidad, a través de ritmos bien logrados en algunos textos (el mejor del libro es "No se apaga"), a la vez que una irrupción irónica, mordaz, en poemas breves en forma de aforismos: "Pluma: Artefacto estúpido para decir tonterías." [JS]

3977 Cárdenas, Rolando. Obra completa. Recopilación y prólogo de Ramón Díaz Eterovic. Santiago: Ediciones La Gota Pura, 1994. 220 p.: bibl., ill.

Desde una exploración sin pausa del espacio de lo familiar se emprende una progresiva incursión del evasivo lar de la memoria—Punta Arenas—a través de una activa rememoración de trazos claves. Poemas que mantienen una misma intensidad y rescatan como pocos el mundo de la provincia. [OS]

3978 Cardona Torrico, Alcira. Rayo y simiente. La Paz: Editorial Benavides, 1995. 172 p.: ill.

Esta es la segunda edición del libro publicado originalmente en 1961. Cardona (1926) es una de las poetas más importantes de la poesía boliviana contemporánea. Escritora consagrada en su país, ha elaborado en este libro un discurso poético de notable fuerza expresiva y preocupación social. Esta nueva edición no introduce ninguna modificación con relación a la primera. [ORR]

3979 Carvalho, Ruber. Ahí te dejo el mar—con otras cosas: poemas. Santa Cruz, Bolivia: Ediciones Mavarú, 1993. 49 p.

Este es el segundo poemario de un poeta boliviano (1938) que sólo en los últimos años ha dado a la publicidad su obra literaria. Esta nueva colección presenta a un poeta interesado en las preocupaciones universales

del ser humano pero desde una instancia geográfica y nacional propia. El poeta acude a motivos históricos y culturales de su propio país para incorporarlos en la construcción del lenguaje poético. [ORR]

3980 Castelvecchi, Gladys. Por costumbre: poemas. Montevideo: Ediciones de la Banda Oriental, 1995. 66 p. (Poetas uruguayos)

Sobre el efecto destructor de la costumbre que homogeiniza lo real, que diluye los límites entre el sueño y la vigilia, entre lo ordinario y lo extraordinario. Sobresale el poema "Leyes." [LU]

3981 Castillo, Silvia del. Cuerpo de luna. Quito: s.n., 1994. 61 p.: ill.

Un joven valor en la poesía femenina ecuatoriana. Testimonio emocional a través de la experiencia de los cuerpos en la relación amorosa y sexual. Lenguaje poético que acude a la palabra directa y a la expresión despojada de eufemismos para relatar el deseo, describir o meditar la experiencia amorosa por el encuentro de los cuerpos. La elección de los versículos permite a la autora una aproximación al relato poético efectivo. La perspectiva femenina y el talento de la joven autora renuevan el tratamiento de los motivos. [ORR]

3982 Cervantes, Francisco. Regimiento de nieblas. México: Editorial Aldus, 1994. 94 p.: col. ill. (Colección Aldus. Los poetas)

Cervantes (Querétaro, Mexico, 1938) continúa con su pasión por la lengua portuguesa (es uno de los lectores más informados de literatura brasileña en México), y por el espacio del pasado lusitano. En sus poemas siempre afloran personajes históricos y sitios evocados y seguramente inventados por la imaginación poética como la ciudad de Lisboa. Eso se combina con una desazón del sujeto al enfrentarse a sí mismo. [JS]

3983 Charry Lara, Fernando. Nocturnos y otros sueños. Prólogo de Vicente Aleixandre. Ilustraciones de Fernando Botero. Bogotá: Ancora Editores, 1991. 110 p.: ill.

Este poemario se publicó por primera vez en 1949. No obstante, la nueva edición aporta una novedad significativa: las ilustraciones que en 1951 hizo Fernando Botero, como prueba de aprecio y amistad, sobre el ejemplar que Charry Lara le regaló. Como señala Vicente Aleixandre en el prólogo de la edición original, aquí reproducido, los temas del poeta bogotano son eternos: "el amor la esperanza, la pena, el deseo, el sueño." Los dibujos de Botero se convierten en una magnífica lectura al transmitir, mediante su esquematismo casi onírico, la pureza sensorial e introspectiva de los versos. [MG]

3984 Chaviano, Daína. Confesiones eróticas y otros hechizos. Madrid: Editorial Betania, 1994. 64 p. (Colección Betania de poesía)

Dividido en tres partes ("Memoria de la posesa;" "Galería privada;" "Confesiones eróticas"), este poemario, además de una confesión, es una reivindicación de la sexualidad femenina que se plantea como poseedora del deseo y también, como constructora del objeto sexual. La poesía de Chaviano ha sido incluida en la antología de poesía erótica femenina, *El placer en la palabra: literatura erótica femenina de América Latina* (1991). [FC]

3985 Cisneros, Antonio. Poesía reunida, 1961–1992. Lima: Editora Perú, 1996. 338 p.

Bajo este título genérico, usado por muchos poetas—entre ellos, Alí Chumacero y Gioconda Belli—el conocido poeta peruano (Lima, 1942) recoge su obra producida entre 1961 y 1992, o sea desde *Destierro* hasta *Las inmensas preguntas celestes*. La edición es de gran formato y viene precedida por un prólogo de Julio Ortega, que comienza con una afirmación que suena algo desmesurada: "Antonio Cisneros es el poeta peruano más influyente en el ámbito de su lengua." A las recopilaciones y antologías que ya existen, ésta añade otra oportunidad de revisar en conjunto la obra de este importante y renovador poeta. [JMO]

3986 Cobián, Ricardo. Un día me quedé solo: balada. San Juan: Instituto de Cultura Puertorriqueña, 1993. 46 p.: ill.

Poesía de trazos rápidos donde prevalece la imagen plástica; confesión desde lo cotidiano, desde lo lúdico y también desde lo onírico de la pérdida amorosa, ante la cual responde la poesía: "El arte de pensarte es/soñarte cada noche." Junto al poeta, Cobián provee también las ilustraciones. [FC]

3987 Cobo Borda, Juan Gustavo. El animal que duerme en cada uno y otros poemas. Bogotá: El Ancora Editores, 1995. 174 p.

Nueva compilación de la obra poética de su autor, que incorpora una serie de textos inéditos hasta el momento. Destacables, entre otros poemas recientes, son "Larga duración," "Querido Gerbasi," "Entrega" y "La sangre y el rito," donde, a los procedimientos ya muy codificados de la antipoesía que dominaba en la labor inicial de Cobo Borda, se agrega un *pathos* menos calculado y muy conveniente poéticamente. [MG]

3988 Contramaestre, Carlos. Tanatorio. Caracas: Tierra de Gracia Editores, 1993. 55 p. (Colección Rasgos comunes)

Tanto en su obra pictórica como en sus libros de poesía, Contramaestre es un cultivador constante de lo que Angel Rama llamaba "informalismo;" una variante del expresionismo que en la Venezuela de los años 1960 y 1970 mezclaba la desesperación existencialista con la alucinante podredumbre material y espiritual del subdesarrollo. En esto, el artista se mantiene fiel a la estética de *El techo de la ballena*, círculo del cual fue miembro fundador. *Tanatorio* refuerza muchas de las tendencias previas del autor para transformarse en una ambigua celebración de la muerte. Aunque desde el punto de vista lírico poco aporta este poemario si se tiene en cuenta lo que, partiendo del mismo material, ya han hecho Enrique Lihn, Oscar Hahn o Gonzalo Rojas en otros puntos del continente, *Tanatorio* puede ser un volumen aprovechable para evaluar la anacrónica persistencia de poéticas vanguardistas en el fin de siglo venezolano. [MG]

3989 Cos Causse, Jesús. Los años, los sueños: poesía, 1970–1994. Recopilación y prólogo de Pedro Correa Vásquez. Panamá: Ediciones de la Revista Littera, 1995. 64 p.: ill.

El poeta aquí antologado es el cubano Jesús Cos Causse (1945). El antologador y prologuista es el escritor panameño Pedro Correa Vásquez. Como muchas de las antologías poéticas centroamericanas y caribeñas, carece ésta de una apropiada presentación y de un aparato crítico serio y necesario para que el lector extranjero sitúe la producción del antologado dentro de su literatura nacional. Al margen de estos detalles, Correa Vásquez entrega una selección de poemas que permite apreciar de cerca la excelencia de la poesía cubana contemporánea. Los poemas antologados están tomados de los cinco poemarios publicados de Cos Causse:

Con el mismo violín (1970), *El último trovador* (1975), *Las islas y las luciérnagas* (1981), *Balada de un tambor y otros poemas* (1988) y *Concierto de Jazz* (1944). [EM]

3990 Courtoisie, Rafael. Textura. Montevideo: Ediciones de la Banda Oriental, 1994. 41 p.

R.C. sigue revelando su poderosa imaginación y el dominio majestuoso de la palabra en este texto que ganó el premio Plural (México) de 1991. Es una de las voces más sobresalientes de las nuevas promociones de poesía latinoamericana. [LU]

3991 Crespo, Luis Alberto. Más afuera. Caracas: Monte Avila Editores Latino americana, 1993. 50 p. (Altazor)

Este libro profundiza y depura la obra anterior de Crespo, en la que, característicamente, la recreación de un espacio árido y vacío se encarga de retratar el desarraigo espiritual de la voz lírica. Esta vez, con más claridad, los elementos espaciales se diluyen hasta el extremo de que sólo el lenguaje resulta habitable. Precariamente, eso sí: la sintaxis descoyuntada nos indica que sus dominios no son ni seguros ni estables. Sobre esa ausencia veremos construirse una trama erótica cuyo final será, por supuesto, infeliz. *Más afuera* se convierte, de esta manera, en el mejor ejemplo del melancólico nihilismo con el que podemos identificar la poesía de Crespo. [MG]

3992 Cros, Fernando. Crónica del hombre solo. San Juan: Editorial de la Univ. de Puerto Rico, 1997. 93 p. (Aquí y ahora; 29)

Entre la soledad y la escritura, la dualidad y la nada, el tiempo y la memoria, la unidad y la diversidad, la vida y la muerte, este poemario constituye una reflexión sostenida de estos temas imperecederos mediante un lenguaje limpio, calibrado. La segunda parte del poemario se vuelve al minimalismo: "Cierro los ojos y nace la noche." [FC]

3993 Cuevas, José Angel. Poesía de la comisión liquidadora. Santiago: LOM Ediciones, 1997. 69 p. (Colección Entres mares)

Una poética post-democracia que cuestiona la historia reciente desde una marginalidad quebrada en lo ideológico y cuya exasperación produce la intensidad de un sujeto sarcástico y casi al borde del energúmeno en

duelo por la modernidad radical extraviada. [OS]

3994 Daher Canedo, Gary Rover. Desde el otro lado del oscuro espejo. La Paz: Editorial Acción, 1995. 65 p.

Este es el cuarto poemario de este poeta boliviano (1956) cuyo lenguaje se caracteriza por construcciones irracionales y subjetivas. La ausencia de control sobre la expresión recuerda los experimentos de la década de 1920. Incierto y desorientado respecto a su propio sentido, esta escritura deja a la lectura sólo el efecto de la incertidumbre. [ORR]

3995 Dalton, Roque. Roque Dalton: antología. Selección de Juan Carlos Berrio. Tafalla, Spain: Txalaparta, 1995. 199 p.: bibl., ill. (Ravel; 3)

Esta antologia reúne gran parte de la producción poética de Dalton (1935–75), desde *La ventana en el rostro* hasta *Poemas clandestinos*. La selección, en general acertada, y la brevísima y poco elaborada presentación, están a cargo de Juan Carlos Berrio. La "novedad" del volumen radica en la inclusión de una serie de textos testimoniales que, intercalados entre poema y poema, ofrecen distintas versiones de cómo "vieron" a Roque Dalton su hijo, Juan José Dalton, Eduardo Galeano, Cintio Vitier, María Gravina Tellechea, Jesús Díaz, Omar Cabezas, Ernesto Cardenal, Miguel Mármol y Arqueles Morales. Se suma a este "homenaje" un poema de Mario Benedetti. Lo que definitivamente le falta a esta antología es el aparato crítico que la convertiría en un texto fundamental para el conocimiento de una de los más destacadas figuras de la poesía salvadoreña del siglo XX. [EM]

3996 Delgado, Susy. Sobre el beso del viento. Asunción: Arandurã Editorial, 1995. 76 p.

El tiempo y la ausencia son los ejes temáticos centrales de este libro de tono reflexivo y coloquial a la vez. La atmósfera íntima y cotidiana de los poemarios anteriores de esta prolífica escritora paraguaya es también una constante de este libro. [LU]

3997 Díaz Mirón, Salvador. Poesía completa. Recopilación y introducción de Manuel Sol. México: Fondo de Cultura Económica, 1997. 641 p.: bibl., ill., index. (Letras mexicanas)

Desde la recopilación de Antonio Castro Leal de 1941 (aunque corregida y revisada en ediciones subsecuentes), la poesía de Díaz Mirón (Veracruz, 1853–1928) se había mantenido ignorada (salvo algunas excepciones) por la crítica reciente. Esta edición de Manuel Sol contiene una larga introducción sobre la vida y la obra de Díaz Mirón, una bibliografía detallada, la poesía completa y un apéndice con documentos de diversa índole. [JS]

3998 Díaz Pimienta, Alexis. Cuarto de mala música. Murcia, Spain: Consejería de Cultura y Educación, Dirección General de Cultura, Editora Regional de Murcia, 1995. 92 p. (Poesía; 53)

Ganador del IX Premio Antonio Oliver Belmás, ex aequo, en 1994, este poemario es una excelente muestra de la novísima poesía cubana, a la que le ha tocado testimoniar la realidad inaplazable del cambio. Poesía inscrita en la intimidad del individuo frente a la historia, en la maleabilidad del tiempo, en el amor, en la muerte y en la necesidad de rescatar lo inaplazable de la humanidad: "y el que no arriesgue su opinión, no juega." [FC]

3999 Espina, Eduardo. La caza nupcial. Buenos Aires: Ediciones Ultimo Reino, 1993. 185 p.: ill.

El sensualismo verbal de esta poesía representa la tendencia neobarroca o neomodernista de las últimas promociones. A ello se suma la arbitraria ilación de una imaginación torrentosa. [LU]

4000 Fernández Retamar, Roberto. Cosas del corazón y otros poemas. Selección y notas de Mario Benedetti. Buenos Aires: Espasa Calpe, 1997. 82 p. (A viva voz; 15)

Este poemario contiene una colección de poemas de amor escritos a lo largo de cuarenta años. Frente a la hipocresía, el caos, los vuelcos de la historia, Fernández Retamar protege "el sentido generoso del amor," un sentido que abarca desde el amor carnal hasta el que, como en el político, se establece con los trabajadores, con la España republicana y con Nicaragua. [FC]

4001 Ferré, Rosario. Antología personal: 1992–1976. Puerto Rico: Editorial Cultural, 1994. 165 p.

Compuesta de tres poemarios anteriores—*Las dos Venecias*, 1992; *Fábula de la garza desangrada*, 1982; *Papeles de Pandora*, 1976—esta antología le permite al lector rastrear el periplo poético de Ferré, quizás menos importante que la narrativa, desde las propuestas juveniles de los setenta hasta las propuestas más seguras de su lugar en la literatura puertorriqueña. [FC]

4002 Flax, Hjalmar. Razones de envergadura: poemas nuevos y selectos. Selección y prólogo de Julio Marzán. Madrid: Editorial Verbum, 1995. 200 p.: ill. (Poesía)

Con este quinto poemario, Flax reafirma su espacio en la poesía puertorriqueña, en la que viene publicando desde 1969. Más que una propuesta diferente, aquí se plantea la madurez tanto de estilo como de visión. Un estilo marcado por la tradición de la antipoesía; una mirada poética marcada por la ironía, la autocrítica, el malabarismo verbal minimalista, la extrañeza, la cotidianidad, el intimismo. [FC]

4003 Fornerín, Miguel Angel. Yo soy esta ciudad: la espía que me amo. San Juan: Isla Negra, 1996. 76 p.: ill.

Dos poemarios en un breve libro de poesía -la ciudad imaginaria de un poeta imaginario; el amor imaginado de una pareja ausente- convergen en el imaginario de un joven poeta puertorriqueño para quien el espacio de la imaginación—de la poesía—es más amplio que el número de las páginas. Entre la ciudad imaginada y el amor imaginario, la agonía del poeta y la locura del amor. [FC]

4004 Galib, Hamid. Los presagios. San Juan: Univ. Interamericana de Puerto Rico, 1991. 71 p.: ill. (Colecciones Libros-homines)

Cinco presagios, una visión. Búsqueda—a través de lo angélico del niño, de la palabra como aproximación, de la infinitud del cielo, de la injusticia del dolor y de la oscuridad de la noche—de la Belleza. Una reflexión lírica entre la vida y la muerte, mediante un lenguaje sobrio pero sugerente. [FC]

4005 Galliano, Alina. La geometría de lo incandescente (en fija residencia). Coral Gables, Fla.: Iberian Studies Institute, North-South Center, Univ. of Miami, 1992. 49 p. (Letras de oro)

Ganador del concurso Letras de Oro (1992), este poemario de Galliano—poeta del exilio cubano—rastrea los espacios del sujeto enamorado, geometrías interiores de un "yo," desde una fijeza "incandescente" que devora, transformándolo, al ser amado: un "tú" que define como "el punto en la espiral / de lo inaudito." [FC]

4006 Galván, Kyra. Netzahualcóyotl recorre las islas. México: UNAM, Coordinación de Humanidades, Dirección General de Publicaciones, 1996. 120 p. (El ala del tigre)

Dentro de las nuevas generaciones de poetas, Kyra Galván (México, 1956) destaca por un sentido del humor que se despliega a partir de un uso anticonvencional del lenguaje. Este volumen es un recorrido por sitios reales y ficticios: de Inglaterra ("Tierra de los pelo amarillo") a Japón, al islote de la Ciudad de México, a "Subjetilandia," a la "Isla de las Mujeres," hasta terminar en la "Isla de los que no cupieron." Divertida e irónica, esta poesía se lee con deleite y con la sonrisa a flor de labios. [JS]

4007 García Terrés, Jaime. Obras. Tomo 1, Las manchas del sol, poesía, 1953–1994. México: El Colegio Nacional: Fondo de Cultura Económica, 1995. 1 v.: index. (Letras mexicanas)

García Terrés (México, 1924–97) ocupó puestos importantes en el ámbito cultural mexicano. Como se puede ver por este volumen, *Las manchas del sol, poesía, 1953–1994,* su obra poética es vasta a pesar de haber comenzado a publicarla tardíamente. Quizás ayude a difundir su obra internacionalmente. En esta edición se agregan sus espléndidas traducciones de poesía en griego, inglés, francés, alemán e italiano; y se incluye, además, su antología *100 imágenes del mar.* [JS]

4008 Gei Brealey, Orlando. La furia del musgo: poesía. San José: Editorial Costa Rica, 1995. 54 p.

La excelencia de estos poemas, merecedores del Primer Premio en el Certamen Nacional de la Juventud 1984, hace pensar que Orlando Gei Brealey (San José, 1966) es una verdadera promesa de la poesía costarricense contemporánea. La colección que aquí se reseña es, como sugiere el título, una "poética de la furia" cimentada en la herencia vallejiana pero al mismo tiempo independizada de ella. Más que el lenguaje, más que el motivo, prima en estos poemas el grito, la mirada que corta y que, en su violencia creadora, alcanza a encallar en algún lugar habitable. [EM]

4009 Gelman, Juan. Antología poética. Edición de Jorge Fondebrider. Buenos Aires: Espasa Calpe, 1994. 237 p.: bibl., ill. (Colección Austral. Biblioteca de literatura hispanoamericana)

La selección hecha por Jorge Fondebrider muestra cabalmente las obsesiones temáticas, las características expresivas y la evolución de la poesía gelmaniana. El prólogo y las referencias bibliográficas enriquecen el texto. [LU]

4010 Gelman, Juan. Hacia el sur y otros poemas. Selección y notas de Mario Benedetti. Buenos Aires: Espasa Calpe, 1995. 89 p. (A viva voz; 7)

Muestra antológica, a cargo de Mario Benedetti, de todos los poemarios de Gelman hasta *Carta a mi madre* inclusive. [LU]

4011 Gerbasi, Vicente. Los oriundos del paraíso. Caracas: Monte Avila Editores Latinoamericana, 1994. 55 p. (Altazor)

La obra de Gerbasi, una de las más consistentes y ricas de la poesía venezolana del siglo XX, todavía espera el debido reconocimiento más allá de las fronteras de su país. Este último poemario confirma que hasta el final de sus días el poeta sostuvo sus intuiciones originales; sus textos exploran ámbitos genesíacos, elementales, pero asimismo elegíacos, en los que la ensoñación revela los paralelos entre la historia personal y la configuración verbal de una imagen del mundo circular y perfecta. [MG]

4012 Gil, Pedro. Delirium tremens: poesía. Manta, Ecuador: Univ. Laica "Eloy Alfaro" de Manabí, 1993. 51 p.

Este joven poeta ecuatoriano (1971) introduce de una manera efectiva el chiste y la ironía en un lenguaje poético que se destaca por su novedad y calidad. Hay sin duda una actitud audaz e irreverente por las convenciones, que no resta calidad a su expresión. Su ironía revela preocupaciones genuinas por situaciones humanas y sociales. [ORR]

4013 Gómez Jattin, Raúl. Poesía: 1980–1989. Barcelona: Grupo Editorial Norma, 1995. 191 p. (Colección Poesía)

En la tradición hispánica pocas veces se ha abordado la poesía erótica con el desenfado y la inocencia que sólo puede proporcionar el recurso a un tono infantil. En efecto, hay algo "magicorrealista" en los versos de Gómez Jattin, no según la confusa conceptualización proveniente de la crítica literaria latinoamericana, sino según la acepción inicial que Franz Roh daba al término: un arte que pretende ver el universo con ojos nuevos; que ansía devolverle el vigor paradisíaco que el transcurso del tiempo le ha hecho perder. Este volumen abarca casi totalmente un decenio de la producción lírica de su autor; en una nota introductoria se apuntan las omisiones. [MG]

4014 Gorostiza, José. Poesía completa. Nota y recopilación de Guillermo Sheridan. México: Fondo de Cultura Económica, 1996. 259 p. (Letras mexicanas)

José Gorostiza (1901-73) es autor de uno de los grandes poemas mexicanos del siglo XX: *Muerte sin fin* (1939). Esta edición amplía la hecha en 1971, al incluir los poemas no coleccionados y los inconclusos. La nota de Sheridan (uno de los mejores críticos actuales en el examen del grupo Contemporáneos) se concentra en la descripción de su labor desempolvadora de los manuscritos del poeta. Para los entusiastas de Gorostiza, la edición crítica de Edelmira Ramírez hecha para la Colección Archivos (1988) sigue siendo de mayor utilidad, puesto que reúne muchísimo material crítico y bibliográfico. [JS]

4015 Granizo Ribadeneira, Francisco. Muerte y caza de la madre. Quito: Banco Central del Ecuador, 1990. 139 p. (Biblioteca de la revista Cultura; 8)

Buena muestra de uno de los poetas ecuatorianos más importantes, que cuida de elaborar por igual tanto el contenido como las formas del lenguaje poético. El volumen reúne una buena selección de textos de formas libres y métricas tradicionales, cuyo contenido, sin embargo, revela un buen conocimiento de la poesía contemporánea. [ORR]

4016 Harris, Tomás. Crónicas maravillosas. La Habana: Casa de las Américas, 1996. 179 p. (Poesía)

Extensa colección en que el personaje de Bergman, Antonius Block, se desplaza a la deriva en un universo multiforme y caótico, de fuertes tonalidades pesadillescas, donde los tiempos y las culturas se entrecruzan para formar una épica onírica y agónica. [OS]

4017 Harris, Tomás. Los 7 náufragos. Santiago: Red Internacional del Libro, 1995. 98 p.

El libro contiene cinco extensos poemas que fusionan momentos de la historia chilena reciente con la historia de la conquista a la manera de una fantasmagoría de lo siniestro y del horror. Como el Aguirre de Werner Herzog, el sujeto—situado en el siglo XXII—navega enloquecidamente por un paisaje infernal sin término escribiendo su crónica pesadillesca. [OS]

4018 Hernández, Francisco. Poesía reunida: 1974-1994. México: UNAM, Coordinación de Humanidades: Ediciones del Equilibrista, 1996. 579 p. (Colección Poemas y ensayos. Nueva época)

Libro voluminoso que consolida a Hernández (San Andrés Tuxtla, Veracruz, 1946) como uno de los poetas más importantes de su generación. Continuador del estilo coloquialista de Jaime Sabines, este poeta se destaca por su uso del humor, un ritmo que va desde los destellos del poemínimo, hasta las prosas de cadencia marina. En sus últimos libros, trata tres rebeldes que bordean entre el genio y la locura: Robert Schumann, Friedrich Hölderlin y George Trakl; poemas que dialogan y reinventan el espacio de la imaginación poética. [JS]

4019 Hernández, José. Martín Fierro. Edición, introducción y notas de Angel J. Battistessa. Madrid: Editorial Castalia, 1994. 358 p.: bibl., ill. Clásicos Castalia; 209

Cuidada edición de este clásico de la literatura gauchesca. La introducción señala las distintas etapas de la poesía gauchesca, destaca elementos biográficos de Hernández y características generales del poema. Las notas y referencias también son útiles. Para comentario del especialista de filosofía, ver item **5287**. [LU]

4020 Hernández, Luis. Trazos de los dedos silenciosos: antología poética. Selección, prólogo y notas de Edgar O'Hara. Lima: Petróleos del Perú: J. Campodónico, 1995. 313 p.

Luis Hernández (Lima, 1941–Bs. As., 1977) es, por la rareza de su obra y por su temprana y trágica muerte, una figura mítica de la poesía peruana, pero es completamente desconocido fuera de su país. Esta antología, prologada, seleccionada y anotada por Edgar O'Hara, reúne lo mejor de su obra, aquí ordenada según un criterio temático, no cronológico. [JMO]

4021 Hernández Ramos, Dionisio. El sueño de la batanda: cuentos y leyendas zoque del istmo. Oaxaca, Mexico: Instituto Oaxaqueño de las Culturas, Fondo Estatal para la Cultura y las Artes del Estado de Oaxaca, 1994. 79 p.: ill. (Stidxacanu. Colección Narrativa)

La poesía de inspiración en los mitos indígenas es más frecuente en Centroamérica: Asturias, Cuadra, Cardenal, por ejemplo. Este libro recoge viejas historias del pueblo zoque de Zanatepec (en la frontera de Oaxaca y Chiapas). Poesía que canta y cuenta a la vez, Hernández Ramos reconstruye el pasado mítico de fundación, con ritmos que rememoran la rica literatura de los antiguos mesoamericanos. [JS]

4022 Hinojosa, Joaquín. Huellas sin tiempo. Cochabamba, Bolivia: ODEC-RUNAWASI, 1994. 110 p.

Poesía testimonial sobre la experiencia de un autor boliviano bajo las dictaduras militares de Bolivia y Chile. Los textos han sido escritos desde la perspectiva de las víctimas de los crímenes cometidos por los regímenes de Banzer y Pinochet en los años de 1970. No se trata sólo de experiencias individuales sino también colectivas y populares. Este volumen se integra, sin duda, al subgénero de la poesía latinoamericana de testimonio político-social de la década de 1970, subgénero que merece ser estudiado. [ORR]

4023 Huerta, David. La sombra de los perros. México: Editorial Aldus, 1996. 78 p.: ill. (Colección Aldus. Los poetas)

Incurable (1987), uno de los poemas más portentosos de la lírica mexicana, se caracterizaba por un verso largo, denso, acumulante, al estilo del cubano Lezama Lima. Pero Huerta (México, 1949) transita por muchos caminos más en el ejercicio de la poesía, incluyendo textos fulminantes, brevísimos. En este último libro, se explora la imagen a partir de una sola palabra (todos los títulos así constituidos) y su evocación poética; muchos de estos textos sugieren separaciones amorosas que provocan ciertas angustias en el hablante. [JS]

4024 Jaffé, Verónica. El largo viaje a casa. Caracas: FUNDARTE, Alcaldía de Caracas, 1994. 60 p. (Colección Cuadernos de difusión; no. 222. Poesía)

Después de El arte de la pérdida (1991), este libro viene a afianzar la presencia ya importante de Verónica Jaffé en el escenario poético venezolano. Estructurado como texto de viajes—el hablante se denomina incluso "el viajero"—la sucesión de espacios progresa paralela al diálogo con otras poetas, cuyos versos, traducidos, se intercalan en el discurso de una voz que oscila entre la realidad fotográfica y el ensueño. Asunto esencial, articulador de ese orbe ambiguo, es la amistad entre mujeres. [MG]

4025 Jaimes, Héctor. Salvoconducto. Caracas: Fondo Editorial Tropykos, 1996. 74 p. (Colección Paria; 11)

Segundo libro de poemas de su autor (nacido en 1964), y, ciertamente, prueba fehaciente de su progresiva madurez literaria. Ajeno tanto a los clichés de lo urbano como a los facilismos de la imaginería proveniente de los medios de comunicación de masas, tan comunes en la poesía venezolana de los años ochenta, la voz lírica echa mano de una dicción precisa, a veces epigramática, en la que el tono intelectual y una recatada reflexión sobre la vida íntima conviven armónicamente. [MG]

4026 James, Miguel. La casa caramelo de la bruja. Caracas: FUNDARTE, Alcaldía de Caracas, 1993. 83 p. (Colección Cuadernos de difusión; no. 202. Poesía)

Pese al escaso reconocimiento crítico de su obra, en ésta, así como en sus colecciones anteriores—Mi novia Itala como flores (1988) y Albanela, Tuttifrutti, Blanca y otras (1990)—Miguel James incluye algunos de los poemas más originales y provocativos que se hayan escrito en Venezuela en la segunda mitad del siglo XX. El tono ingenuo con que la vida erótica, la rutina urbana, la literatura y la cultura de masas se mezclan, crea un discurso irreverente, pero a la vez espiritual.[MG]

4027 Jaramillo Agudelo, Darío. Poemas de amor. Bogotá: El Áncora Editores, 1996. 1 v.

Este poemario, editado por primera vez en 1986, reeditado en 1990 y que ahora se reimprime por séptima vez, es una magnífica prueba no sólo de la existencia de un público interesado en poesía, sino de la solidez y los logros en ese género de su autor, que recientemente ha experimentado el éxito también como novelista por sus Cartas cruzadas (1995). Los versos de Jaramillo Agudelo tienen sus fuentes en la antipoesía, pero de ella se apartan para expresar las necesidades de un hablante lírico poco interesado en las prédicas o el humor gratuito; una voz meditabunda y reflexiva que no le teme a la confesión o al desahogo sentimental. [MG]

4028 Juarroz, Roberto. Poesía vertical. v. 1. Buenos Aires: Emecé, 1993. 1 v.
El volumen incluye desde la primera (1958) hasta la séptima (1982) Poesía vertical. La austeridad del título elegido por Juarroz para identificar su poesía contrasta con la riqueza de la misma. [LU]

4029 Lander, Astrid. La distancia por dentro. Caracas: Dirección de Cultura, Univ. Central de Venezuela, 1994. 56 p. (Colección Letras de Venezuela; 118. Serie Poesía)
Este volumen, al que se le concedió el premio de la Bienal Ramón Palomares 1994, es el primero de su autora (nacida en 1962) y el inicio de una carrera poética que promete ser innovadora en el ámbito venezolano. Lejos del lenguaje de la poesía urbana de los años ochenta, la voz lírica aúna a un libro de viajes geográficos los trayectos menos previsibles de un aprendizaje sentimental, que a veces adopta las posturas intemporales de la erótica medieval trovadoresca—muchas de las composiciones, de hecho, conscientemente o no—actualizan los recursos de las *cantigas de amigo*. [MG]

4030 Leñero, Carmen. La fiera transparente. México: Consejo Nacional para la Cultura y las Artes, 1997. 84 p. (Práctica mortal)
Leñero (México, 1959) muestra una versatilidad en este volumen que va desde el aforismo de una sola línea ("Nadie alcanza con su muerte el final") hasta el poema largo ("Cementerio de elefantes"), que se construye combinando versos y prosa poética, estableciendo un diálogo entre el afuera y el adentro de la muerte. La metaforización de la bestia que acecha, y los diálogos con la luna— que recuerdan remotamente a Lugones—son otros de sus temas explorados. [JS]

4031 Liscano, Juan. El origen sigue siendo: poemas, 1987–1990. Caracas: Alfadil Ediciones, 1993. 45 p. (Colección Orinoco; 42)
Este volumen, que recoge poemas escritos entre 1987–90, no cambia la percepción crítica que pueda tenerse de una obra ya abultada, sino que confirma los principios estéticos que durante años se han hecho

patentes en los poemas del autor: gusto por el verso meditativo, apropiado para las "aventuras del pensamiento;" asuntos elevados y ya prestigiados—en esta ocasión, el lenguaje como fuente de ser y conocimiento—; transparencia verbal que acerca el poema al habla sin por ello hacer concesiones al coloquialismo. [MG]

4032 López-Adorno, Pedro. Concierto para desobedientes. Río Piedras, P.R.: Editorial Plaza Mayor, 1996. 99 p. (Biblioteca de autores de Puerto Rico. Poesía)
Inscrito entre movimientos musicales clásicos, este poemario de ascendencia barroca, y por lo tanto, de ostensible peso lingüístico, se orquesta a partir de cuatro ejes temáticos, todos endosados por la desobediencia poética ante el silencio, el amor, el engaño, la realidad. Lo serio y lo irreverente, lo culto y lo popular: el concierto de la poesía y el desconcierto que el irreverente poetiza para su diversión y crítica. [FC]

4033 Mármol, José. Deus ex machina: poemas. Santo Domingo: Casa de Teatro, 1994. 102 p.: ill.
Ganador del Premio de Poesía Casa de Teatro (1994), este poemario de Mármol— una propuesta surrealista desde la prosa poética—articula el espacio del deseo, de la ciudad, de los barrios, del burdel, de la música, de la pintura y del conocimiento trastocado por lo poético. Antologado en publicaciones como *Novísima poesía dominicana* (1985) y *El paisaje dominicano, pintura y poesía* (1992), la poesía de Mármol asume lo poético como el "milagro que maravilla cosas, encanta los sonidos, retuerce la sintaxis del color." [FC]

4034 Márquez Moreno, Inés. Camino de mediodía. Cuenca, Ecuador: Casa de la Cultura Ecuatoriana, Núcleo del Azuay, 1994. 182 p.
Con este volumen, la Casa de la Cultura Ecuatoriana presenta a una poeta desconocida, pero de calidad indudable. El volumen reúne textos escritos en casi medio siglo, pero que mantienen notable uniformidad. Inspirada en una contemplación tierna de situaciones cotidianas y domésticas, esta poesía se expresa por un lenguaje apropiado a esa percepción. Delicadeza y claridad son sus características principales. [ORR]

4035 Marrero, Marisol. Velaje. Caracas: Dirección de Cultura, Univ. Central de Venezuela, 1994. 72 p. (Colección Letras de Venezuela; 116. Serie Poesía)

La obra poética de Marrero comienza en 1979 con *Desmembrando la noche*, libro al que han seguido, entre otros, *Segmentos de memoria* (1982) y *Carsinva* (1993). *Velaje* prueba la definitiva madurez de su autora, aquí expresada a través de un antiguo tópico, el de las imágenes de marinería aplicadas a la existencia humana; sólo que, ahora, el correlato es específicamente erótico. Sobriedad y contención caracterizan a estos versos, que se apartan de toda estridencia. [MG]

4036 Martos, Marco. Leve reino: obra poética, 1965–1996. Lima: Peisa, 1996. 255 p. (Alma matinal)

Amplia recopilación de la obra poética de Marco Martos (Piura, 1942), uno de los mejores poetas peruanos de la generación de 1970. Recoge su producción entre 1965–96 y permite al lector que no pudo leer en su momento sus libros (siete están incluidos) descubrir una voz lírica realmente original e intensa, pese a su tono sencillo y equilibrado. [JMO]

4037 Mata, Andrés. Poesías completas. Prólogo de Arturo Uslar Pietri. Revisión y cuidado de José Ramón Medina. Caracas: Monte Avila Editores Latinoamericana: Diario El Universal, 1994. 234 p. (Documentos. Serie Difusión)

La reedición de un volumen de 1956 constituye una aportación valiosísima para reevaluar la poesía venezolana escrita hacia 1900. En Mata, uno de sus exponentes más característicos, se hacen notorias las tendencias que han condenado a la lírica modernista venezolana al olvido: la persistencia de la sensiblería romántica hispánica; las fórmulas rimbombantes; el escaso experimentalismo métrico. No obstante, aquí y allá, se destacan notas asombrosas que presagian el humor y las osadías de la futura antipoesía. Memorables, en este sentido, son los primeros versos de su "Psalmo," escrito en las postrimerías del siglo XIX: "¡ O. K., Dante, Tú lo dices: / no hay mayor desventura / que recordar en tiempos de amargura / las épocas felices !" [MG]

4038 Matos Paoli, Francisco. Decimario de Antonio Valero. San Juan, P.R.: s.n., 1995. 87 p.

Un canto, sobre todo, a la lucha por la libertad, al compromiso político del puertorriqueño Antonio Valero (1790–1863), cuya biografía se poetiza en décimas que lo ensalzan por su americanismo bolivariano. [FC]

4039 Maturo, Graciela. Cantos de Orfeo y Eurídice. Córdoba, Argentina: Ediciones del Copista, 1996. 61 p.: ill. (Colección Resonancia americana; 2)

Este volumen es la reedición de *Canto a Eurídice* y de *Orfeo canta*. La temática de los mitos celebra poéticamente y con gran intensidad una de las pasiones críticas de esta escritora. [LU]

4040 Medina, Javier. Nómada inmóvil: relictos de un viaje a la tierra del anochecer, 1966–1976. La Paz: Hisbol, 1994. 42 p.

Nueva voz en la poesía boliviana más reciente. Familiarizado con el pensamiento de la modernidad, este joven poeta busca e intenta una nueva expresión conocedora de que los códigos del pensamiento contemporáneo se apoyan paradójicamente en la falta de certeza en el pensar y el lenguaje. Motivos y conceptos claves y propios de este pensamiento del siglo XX son incorporados a la expresión poética en textos breves con aciertos notables. [ORR]

4041 Melendes, Joserramón. Desimos désimas. Con Andrés Jiménez, el Jíbaro. 3a ed. Río Piedras, P.R.: qeAse, 1996. 194 p.: ill., index + 1 computer laser optical disc (4 ¾ in.). (Perfil; año 1, núm. 3)

Esta nueva edición—que le añade a las dos anteriores una parte nueva—de este reconocido poeta de los setenta, se plantea como una celebración de la segunda década de la primera edición. Una celebración y una continuidad: aquí la poesía continúa siendo, desde su grafía crítica, una crítica ante la historia política de Puerto Rico, dominada en los noventa por la ideología de los "Nueborricos." [FC]

4042 Millán, Gonzalo. Trece lunas. Prólogo por Waldo Rojas. Santiago: Fondo de Cultura Económica Chile, 1997. 345 p. (Tierra firme. Poetas chilenos)

Magistral obra reunida de Millán que incluye cinco libros escritos desde 1965 a 1986: *Relación personal, Dragón que se muerde la cola, Vida, La ciudad* y *Virus*. Insistencia productiva en el poema breve de estructura articulada con meticulosa inteligencia que va desde el recuento amoroso al autoascultamiento a la metapoética crítica. Como contrapunto, el poema extenso—en *La ciudad*—(de)vela el horizonte traumático del autoritarismo pinochetista desde los ecos de una repetición sintáctica al infinito. [OS]

4043 Mir, Pedro. Poesías (casi) completas. Prólogo de Jaime Labastida. México: Siglo Veintiuno Editores, 1994. 214 p. (La creación literaria)

Declarado poeta nacional dominicano en 1993, la poesía de Mir carece, según el prólogo de Labastida, del reconocimiento que se merece. Esta antología persigue mostrar la continuidad del poeta joven de los *Primeros versos* en la obra del aclamado poeta político de *Viaje a la muchedumbre* y *El huracán Neruda*. [FC]

4044 Mir, Pedro. Primeros versos. Santo Domingo: Taller, 1993. 71 p.: ill. (Biblioteca Taller; no. 294)

Esta colección de 22 poemas—escritos entre 1937–47—recoge las primeras publicaciones de Mir en la prensa dominicana que, tras su exilio en 1947, quedaron olvidadas. En ellos se prefigura al poeta social de *Hay un país en el mundo* (1968) y *Viaje a la muchedumbre* (1971). [FC]

4045 Mistral, Gabriela. Poema de Chile. Revisión, ordenación y prólogo de Jaime Quezada. Santiago: Editorial Universitaria, 1996. 263 p.: bibl., ill. (Colección Premios nacionales de literatura; 10)

Nueva edición (la primera es de 1967) de crucial colección de la poeta. Dos personajes, una mujer y un niño indígena, recorren un Chile lleno de claves genéricas, étnicas y políticas en dirección a un origen decisivo: el sur chileno. Las voces del niño y la mujer en contrapunto subrayan la dimensión dramática de la mujer como fantasma o "trascordada." [OS]

4046 Molina, Enrique. Orden terrestre. Buenos Aires: Seix Barral, 1995. 335 p. (Biblioteca breve)

Esta antología recoge textos de todos los libros publicados por Molina hasta *Hacia una isla incierta* (1992). Se cierra con poemas no aparecidos previamente en libros y otros inéditos. El prólogo es una verdadera poética. [LU]

4047 Montaño Balderrama, Celso. Eternidades celestes: poesía. Cochabamba, Bolivia: Impr. Offset "Cueto", 1993. 106 p.

El autor de este libro es un joven valor descubierto en un certamen literario estudiantil de la Univ. Mayor de San Andrés, La Paz. Este libro demuestra el ímpetu incontenible con el que su autor se entrega a la escritura poética. Ese ímpetu, orientado por la espontaneidad y la sinceridad expresiva, desborda convenciones y normas del sistema del lenguaje así como deconstruye referentes tradicionales del pensar. En estas alteraciones radica la novedad de su poesía, de enunciados expansivos e intensos. Los motivos del amor y el erotismo, que predominan en el volumen, coadyuvan en la efusión expresiva. [ORR]

4048 Montealegre, Jorge. Bien común: poemas de Jorge Montealegre. Santiago: Editorial Asterión, 1995. 91 p.

Legado poético que el sujeto, inserto en los avatares históricos del siglo que termina, decide compartir con la generación venidera. Complejo panorama de las interacciones culturales contemporáneas, el libro cuestiona irónicamente la exaltación dogmática de una modernidad exitista e indiferente postulando un intercambio político-cultural flexible y abierto. [OS]

4049 Montejo, Eugenio. Adiós al siglo XX. Caracas: Ediciones Aymaría, 1992. 52 p.

Poesía del cosmos—han dicho algunos de sus mejores críticos—de equilibrio y simplicidad expresiva ejemplares en el contexto hispánico, la de Montejo examina en esta ocasión las vivencias de un hablante que se enfrenta al "fin" "si algún fin existe: es decir," con irónica distancia, aunque no menos con elegancia y melancolía. [MG]

4050 Montejo, Eugenio. Antología. Prólogo por Francisco José Cruz Pérez. Caracas: Monte Avila Editores Latinoamericana, 1996. 187 p. (Altazor)

Este, como todos sus otros libros, confirma que el autor es una de las voces esenciales de la poesía hispánica de la segunda mitad del siglo XX. Al atractivo de ofrecer una compilación extensa de sus versos—en este sentido semejante a las publicadas anteriormente por Laia y el F.C.E.—el presente volumen añade algunas composiciones inéditas o poco conocidas, como *Nostalgia de Bolívar* (1976), que sabia y discretamente se ocupa de una figura que en poetas menos aptos se prestaría a clichés. Digno de mención es el sensato prólogo de Cruz Pérez, que comenta sin rigidez ni compromisos académicos una obra de engañosa transparencia. [MG]

4051 Morejón, Nancy. Paisaje célebre: poemas 1987–1992. Caracas: FUNDARTE, Alcaldía de Caracas, 1993. 49 p. (Colección Breves; no. 42)

Finalista en el Concurso Internacional de Poesía "Pérez Bonalde" de Caracas, este poemario parte de una relación estrecha con la luz—"Me gusta contemplar las cosas en el trópico"—que deviene diálogo con la pintura (Marcelo Pogolotti, Antonio Eiriz, Ana Mendieta) al igual que con los claroscuros habaneros. [FC]

4052 Muñiz-Huberman, Angelina. La memoria del aire. México: UNAM, Facultad de Filosofía y Letras, Coordinación de Humanidades, 1995. 88 p. (Colección especial)

Conocida por sus novelas donde se explora el tema del judío desterrado de España, Angelina Muñiz (Hyéres, Francia, 1936; naturalizada en México) acude aquí a una especie de diario lírico en que la persona va refiriendo los sucesos de su interioridad. Es también un yo en continuo diálogo con su mundo. El libro culmina con una sección dedicada a la experiencia de la muerte asumida en el plano de la cotidianeidad. [JS]

4053 Mutis, Alvaro. Antología personal: poesía. Prólogo de Octavio Paz. Buenos Aires: Editorial Argonauta, 1995. 145 p.: ill. (Biblioteca de poesía; 4)

Esta selección abarca desde los primeros poemas de los años cuarenta hasta *Un homenaje y siete nocturnos* (1986) e incluye tres peomas dispersos. El conjunto capta a la perfección los rasgos que definen la poética de Mutis: la convivencia de lo lírico y lo narrativo; la desesperanza que resumen sus personajes errantes y sin centro; una cosmovisión de raigambre expresionista, en la que el espacio se tiñe de dicha desesperanza y se torna asfixiante. Acompaña a esta edición el ensayo de Octavio Paz incluido en *Puertas al campo*. [MG]

4054 Negro, Héctor. Ciudad de los flacos aires. Buenos Aires: Torres Agüero Editor, 1994. 143 p. (Memoria del tiempo)

Como otros integrantes de la generación argentina del 1960, Negro circunscribe su poesía al espacio ciudadano y recurre a las realizaciones del habla coloquial. [LU]

4055 Negroni, María. El viaje de la noche. Barcelona: Editorial Lumen, 1994. 83 p. (Poesía; 81)

El volumen marca una nueva etapa en la poesía de esta importante escritora argentina. El tema del viaje se acompaña con ricas imágenes de gran intensidad. Este es su sexto poemario. [LU]

4056 Neruda, Pablo. Cuadernos de Temuco, 1919–1920. Edición y prólogo de Víctor Farías. Buenos Aires: Seix Barral, 1996. 230 p.

Tres cuadernos de poesía escritos por Neruda en el Liceo de Hombres de Temuco que contienen la mayor cantidad de poemas iniciales en que lo erótico y lo religioso se vinculan, según Farías, "en interacción casi obsesiva" (20). Textos que anteceden y prefiguran la publicación de *Crepusculario*. [OS]

4057 Nieves Mieles, Edgardo. El amor es una enfermedad del hígado. San Juan: Comisión Puertorriqueña para la Celebración del Quinto Centenario del Descubrimiento de América y Puerto Rico, 199-? 118 p.: ill.

Un tributo al amor, y a la tradición literaria que lo ha abordado a lo largo de la historia, con un lenguage fresco, lúdico, vivaz e irreverente, que simplifica la complejidad de la poesía. La cotidianidad de la experiencia amorosa y sus mitos, se presenta desde ángulos inesperados; al poeta le gusta hablar como si no fuera poesía: "yo no vomito estrellas. Tampoco poesía, es cierto." [FC]

4058 Nisttahuz, Jaime. La humedad es una sombra y otros poemas. La Paz: Ediciones O' la Piut, 1992. 1 v.: ill.

Este es un intento de construir un poema extenso, como lo sugiere el mismo autor boliviano en una nota inicial en que refiere la historia del mismo poema. El texto está dividido en 29 secciones, cuyo discurso se caracteriza por su fragmentación. Cada sección está integrada por un conjunto de enunciados poéticos con diversos motivos, pero que logran mantener un tono meditativo sobre el acontecer y las preocupaciones temporales del ser humano. Otros 14 textos completan el volumen. [ORR]

4059 Obregón, Roberto. Recuento de poesía. Guatemala: Editorial Cultura, 1995. 252 p. (Colección poesía guatemalteca del siglo XX; no. 7. Serie Rafael Landívar)

Reunir la poesía completa del poeta guatemalteco Roberto Obregón (1940–73) es una iniciativa que hay que celebrar. Son pocos los poetas que en tan corto lapso de vida logran una obra tan intensa y sólida. Sus libros (seis en total) son exploraciones bien articuladas de las posibilidades que tiene la poesía para resemantizar la historia y la cultura oficial al contacto con el fondo indígena y popular que configura gran parte de la realidad latinoamericana. Al mismo tiempo, cala hondo en la construcción de lo que podría llamarse una metafísica poética enunciada en código guatemalteco. Hay que lamentar la falta de una introducción o prefacio que presente la obra y suscintamente la comente. [EM]

4060 O'Hara Gonzales, Edgar. En una casa prestada: Seattle, 1990–1992. Lima: J. Campodónico, 1995. 72 p.

Aunque el primero de estos libros está escrito en prosa (*En una casa prestada*) y el otro en verso (*Hacia qué linderos*, ver item **4061**), la unidad de tono permite que puedan considerárseles en verdad una sola colección. Ambos corresponden a su experiencia en Estados Unidos—específicamente en Seattle, donde ejerce la docencia universitaria—y reflejan los descubrimientos y nostalgias de la vida inserta en una cultura extranjera, que evocan, con ironía, imágenes del pasado familiar, los contrastes ambientales y humanos, y sobre todo los ritmos de un lenguaje perdido. O'Hara (Lima, 1954), fecundo tanto como poeta que como crítico, publica copiosamente dentro y fuera de su país. [JMO]

4061 O'Hara Gonzales, Edgar. Hacia qué linderos: Seattle, 1990–1993. Lima: J. Campodónico, 1995. 64 p.

Ver la resena en item **4060**.

4062 Olivera Olivera, Jorge Ernesto. Poemas del Desierto de Mojave. Soria: Ediciones de la Excma. Diputación Provincial de Soria, 1994. 110 p. (Colección "Leonor" y "Gerardo Diego" de poesía)

Olivera (1964) explora—con singular lirismo—las manifestaciones del imaginario contemporáneo. Pájaros y ángeles, fotografías y puentes son símbolos recurrentes de este poemario que expresa una visión profundamene desesperanzada del mundo. [LU]

4063 Orozco, Olga. Antología poética. Buenos Aires: Fondo Nacional de las Artes, 1996. 116 p. (Poetas argentinos contemporáneos; 6)

Incluye poemas representativos desde su primer poemario *Desde lejos* (1946) hasta *Con esta boca, en este mundo*. Ver item **4064**. [LU]

4064 Orozco, Olga. Con esta boca, en este mundo. Buenos Aires: Editorial Sudaméricana, 1994. 93 p.

Este libro reafirma la riqueza imaginativa y simbólica así como la intensidad poética de esta importante escritora argentina. El título del volumen es un evidente homenaje a Alejandra Pizarnik. [LU]

4065 Ortiz, Juan L. Obra completa: incluye En el aura del sauce. Introducción y notas de Sergio Delgado. Textos de Juan José Saer *et al.* Santa Fe, Argentina: Centro de Publicaciones, Univ. Nacional del Litoral, 1996. 1121 p.: bibl., ill.

Volumen de gran interés. El prólogo y los demás estudios destacan la importancia e influencia de Ortiz en la poesía argentina posterior, los puntos de contacto con poetas como González Tuñón o Enrique Molina, sus características estilísticas, etc. Las notas agregan importante información bibliográfica. En "Poesía inédita" se incluyen distintos borradores o versiones de poemas lo cual resulta muy revelador del proceso de escritura o composición de Ortiz. [LU]

4066 Ostrosky, Jennie. Palabras olvidadas somos. México: Univ. Autónoma Metropolitana, 1998. 28 p. (Margen de poesía; 67)

Además de narradora, Ostrosky (México, 1955) ha publicado tres poemarios. Este pequeño volumen traza la maravilla y ruina del amor. Habla desde un espacio mítico que trasluce un tiempo inmemorial y arquetípico: "Cargo algo de mujer que ha esperado / por siglos a cazador, marino o guerrero / al varón que ha de retornar al lecho." Aún hacia el final, dada la separación de los amantes, en un medio de destrucción total, apocalíptica, la hablante se mantiene fiel al amor como modo de desafiarlo todo. [JS]

4067 Otero, Rosa Vanessa. En el fondo del caño: genealogía. San Juan: Editorial de la Univ. de Puerto Rico, 1997. 92 p.: ill. (Aquí y ahora; 28)

Una de las nuevas voces de la poesía puertorriqueña, la de Otero comparte con la de los nuevos poetas un posicionamiento de la voz poética: se trata de hacer poesía desde la experiencia de "lo propio", una experiencia que aquí se articula, primero, con lo personal (quien escribe es la poeta de la familia), y después con lo familiar (genealogía) y lo social (el arrabal aludido en el título). Ni erótico ni violento, en este poemario la visión lírica, sosegada pero cortante, se sabe literaria ("Esto es un poemario"); una ostensible conciencia de clase ("Hija de obrero soy") reconstruye críticamente, aunque sin "alzar": la voz, la historia personal, familiar y social como desafío ante el olvido político de la historiografía oficial. [FC]

4068 Parra, Nicanor. Discursos de sobremesa. Concepción, Chile: Cuadernos Atenea, 1997. 174 p.: ill. (Serie Literatura)

Antipoemas que utilizan como contexto el premio Juan Rulfo y el Doctorado de la Univ. de Concepción otorgados al antipoeta. "Discurso de Guadalajara" sitúa a Rulfo como paradigma del escritor latinoamericano del margen; "Also Sprach Altazor" sitúa a Huidobro como articulador flexible de intercambios culturales; "Discurso del Bío Bío" realiza una cáustica desconstrucción de la institucionalización del antipoeta como doctorado. [OS]

4069 Parra, Sergio. Poemas de Paco Bazán. Santiago: Mosquito Editores, 1993. 75 p. (La estocada sorpresiva)

El sujeto alcoholizado y extraviado de estos poemas revela con precisión de cirujano los detalles a través de los cuales su desastre contínuo se potencia. El libro es un registro de apuntes cotidianos sobre la figura masculina del extraño en la sociedad de la modernidad y el éxito. [OS]

4070 Paso, Fernando del. Sonetos del amor y de lo diario. México: Editorial Vuelta, 1997. 85 p.: ill.

Fernando del Paso (México, 1935) es muy conocido por sus excelentes novelas.

Pero se inició en la literatura como poeta. Este volumen reproduce su primer libro (de 1958) y agrega otros sonetos escritos posteriormente. Paso se divierte con las formas de la tradición, parodiándolas: "Esto que ves, mester de cetrería," por ejemplo, juega con el celebre verso de Sor Juana, y al mismo tiempo con la frase "mester de clerecía." Muchos de estos poemas tienen como punto de referencia alguna imagen o texto clásico. [JS]

4071 Paz Castillo, Fernando. Obras completas. Caracas: Ediciones La Casa de Bello, 1995. 11 v.: bibl., indexes. (Colección Zona tórrida)

Los 11 vols. que integran esta edición incluyen 10 que contienen sus ensayos, crónicas y testimonios y uno que reúne su poesía. Paz Castillo fue un minucioso observador de la literatura venezolana del siglo XX y sus escritos abarcan desde el modernismo hasta los años 1970. Si bien sus reflexiones jamás están fundamentadas en métodos críticos rigurosos, sus impresiones y semblanzas resultan invariablemente provechosas para conocer el clima intelectual de su país durante casi cien años. [MG]

4072 Pellicer, Carlos. Poesía completa. v. 1–3. México: Consejo Nacional para la Cultura y las Artes: UNAM: Ediciones del Equilibrista, 1996. 3 v.: index. (Biblioteca Carlos Pellicer)

A la edición de la poesía de Pellicer (Tabasco, 1897–1977) de 1981, ésta agrega más de 385 poemas inéditos. El primer volumen reúne los libros de Pellicer en orden cronológico de aparición, de 1921 a 1949; el segundo continúa de 1956 a la fecha de su muerte, e incluye también los "poemas no coleccionados (1922–75);" el tercero recoge la poesía inicial escrita entre 1911–21. Recopilación necesaria e importante en el panorama de la poesía mexicana del siglo XX. [JS]

4073 Pérez, Floridor. Memorias de un condenado a amarte. Santiago: Ediciones Reencuentro, 1993. 87 p.: ill. (Colección poesía; v. 1)

La relación amorosa del poeta se presenta desde una variedad de situaciones cotidianas, las cuales adquieren tonalidades humorísticas y dramáticas que se producen en el choque de varios subtextos y la reescritura que hace el poeta. En sus mejores momentos los poemas describen situaciones cotidianas o absurdas de manera precisa. [OS]

4074 Pérez, Israel. Contemporáneos del tiempo. Santo Domingo: Editora Búho, 1995. 93 p.

Poemas cortos, en general, reflexiones poéticas que fluyen entre múltiples tópicos, desde lo filosófico y lo literario hasta lo cotidiano, con lirismo y precisión, para testimoniar la experiencia inapelable del tiempo, la soledad, el amor, el silencio, la angustia, la poesía: "Soy el escriba del agua." [FC]

4075 Pérez Olivares, José. Cristo entrando en Bruselas. Sevilla: Renacimiento, 1994. 52 p.

Como en poemarios anteriores, incluso mucho más, en éste la poesía surge del diálogo con la pintura: una aproximación al cuadro (Picasso, Goya, Ensor) que desata en el poeta una reflexión un diálogo, una descripción, una celebración, una apología, una defensa del arte: "porque él hace fuerte a los que aman, / a los que buscan algo / que otros no pueden encontrar." Diálogo en el que también se descubre la poesía: "Escribir es tocar a plenitud el lado oscuro de las cosas." [FC]

4076 Peri Rossi, Cristina. Aquella noche. Barcelona: Editorial Lumen, 1996. 102 p. (Poesía; 90)

Poesía de la situaciones cotidianas con un predominante tono dialógico. Sobresale el poema "Deseo." [LU]

4077 Piña Williams, Víctor Hugo. Transverbación. México: Editorial Aldus, 1994. 86 p.: 1 col. ill. (Colección Aldus. Los poetas)

Desde su página mensual en la revista *Casa del Tiempo*, ya Piña Williams (México, 1958) nos tenía acostumbrados a sus juegos con el lenguaje. Heredera de la poesía lúdica modernista de un Herrera y Reissig, de las jitanjáforas caribeñas, de las paronomasias de Villaurrutia, o del trabajo visual y fónico de los concretistas brasileños, esta poesía se inserta en una de las tendencias actuales mas imponentes en Latinoamérica: el neobarroco. Ejemplo "Lo que la sílaba soba y desova/ es el pulso larvoso de la nada." El libro es loable por su amplitud de registros y por su excelente manejo del ritmo y de la paronomasia. [JS]

4078 Quevedo, Aleyda. La actitud del fuego. Quito: Ediciones de Los Lunes, 1994. 80 p.: ill.

Primer poemario de una joven autora ecuatoriana (1972) que se enfrenta al tema de la relación amorosa completa. El discurso atiende por igual las manifestaciones emotivas y físicas, mediante un lenguaje que redescubre desde una voz femenina joven la atracción, el deseo y la sexualidad humana con naturalidad y sorpresa. [ORR]

4079 Quevedo, Aleyda. Algunas rosas verdes. Quito: Subsecretaría de Cultura, Sistema Nacional de Bibliotecas, 1996. 101 p. (Colección País secreto; 12)

Segundo poemario de una joven poeta (1972) que sorprende a sus lectores con un lenguaje poético que rehúye de la complejidad sintáctica y metafórica. Por el contrario, con un lenguaje directo y claro poetiza sobre la complejidad, aún en los actos más simples y cotidianos, de las relaciones del hombre y la mujer. Muy consciente de su condición femenina, su poesía no abandona esa instancia definida de enunciación. [ORR]

4080 Quino Márquez, Humberto. Crítica de la pasión pura. Bolivia: Papeles de Acracia Ediciones, 1993. 78 p.: ill. (Libros de la banda armada)

Lenguaje poético que busca la economía del lenguaje en la brevedad de versos y textos, escritor con enunciados afirmativos. Su contenido está impulsado por una constante reflexión sobre situaciones comunes y domésticas, con sorna y una intención que busca asombrar con rudeza. No obstante, la expresión poética mantiene una actitud constante de gravedad ante la vida por sus reiteraciones sobre motivos relacionados con la muerte. Su autor es uno de los poetas jóvenes de Bolivia. [ORR]

4081 Quintero-Herencia, Juan Carlos. La caja negra. San Juan, P.R.: Isla Negra Editores, 1996. 88 p.

Miembro fundador y co-editor de la revista *Filo de Juego* (1984–87), Quintero-Herencia pertenece a las nuevas voces de la poesía puertorriqueña. Heterogéneo, crítico, reivindicador, caribeño, este poemario articula lo culto, lo popular, la literatura, la música, la política, la historia, a través de un lenguaje indagador que abre nuevas y viejas realidades oscuras. [FC]

4082 Quiroga, María Soledad. Ciudad blanca. La Paz: P.A.P., 1993. 133 p.

Este libro ratifica la incorporación de su autora (1957) a la literatura boliviana contemporánea. Persistente y efectivo, este discurso crea sobre todo un espacio deshabitado donde los objetos pierden su materialidad y volumen. Las cosas de su mundo poético son transformadas ineludiblemente en aire, luz, niebla, altura, transparencia y otros referentes que remiten reiteradamente a formas de lo inmaterial. No obstante, este proceso no impide que la poeta realice su pensamiento poético sobre aspectos concretos que le conciernen. [ORR]

4083 Ramírez Monagas, Bayardo. En otro reinos. Prólogo de Juan Liscano. Caracas: Monte Avila Editores, 1993. 210 p.: ill. (Colección Las Formas del fuego. Poesía)

Caso notable para historiadores literarios, la poesía de Ramírez Monagas parece totalmente ajena a los movimientos que hoy en día dominan la escena literaria hispanoamericana y le imponen sus gustos. Los poemas aquí recogidos en un primer momento parecen anacrónicas resurrecciones de la poesía orientalista de José Manuel Tablada, pero pronto se distinguen de ella por la clara conciencia de ámbitos mistéricos, dotados de un sugestivo hermetismo conceptual que no empaña la limpidez lingüística del verso. [MS]

4084 Rica, Eduardo de la. Tiempos y aire de Cuenca. Cuenca, Spain: Excmo. Ayuntamiento de Cuenca, 1996. 116 p. (Papeles de Júcar; 15)

Nuevo libro de uno de los poetas más destacados del Ecuador. Rica (Cuenca, 1914) ha escrito la mayor parte de estos textos sobre motivos referidos a su provincia natal. Sin embargo, su poesía trasciende las motivaciones locales y gana universalidad plena mediante un lenguaje que instala una atmósfera de serenidad mediante versos pulidos y medidos con el rigor del poeta conocedor de la métrica tradicional, a la que renueva en construcciones contemporáneas. [ORR]

4085 Rivera, Silvia Tomasa. Vuelo de sombras. México: Aguilar, León y Cal Editores, 1994. 203 p. (Cal y arena)

Libro que reúne dos poemarios anteriores (*Duelo de espadas* y *Apuntes de abril*) y agrega otro inédito (*Aguila arpía*). Rivera (Veracruz, 1955) le da la lozanía a la nueva poesía mexicana con sus textos sensuales, que incorporan la experiencia de la costa, incitada a través de un ambiente animal y selvático. De allí que hablar de la ciudad se convierta en un ejercicio metafórico en donde el mundo de lo natural funcione siempre en lo subyacente de lo visto. [JS]

4086 Roa Bastos, Augusto Antonio. Poesías reunidas. Recopilación de Miguel Angel Fernández. Asunción: El Lector, 1995. 311 p.: bibl. (Colección Poesías; 1)

De gran interés es este volumen que permite reencontrarnos con un aspecto relegado—aunque no abandonado—en la creación de Roa Bastos. Se incluyen aquí poemas desde 1934 hasta los textos de *Silenciario* y la reproducción de tres ensayos del escritor paraguayo sobre la poesía. [LU]

4087 Rodríguez Arcos, Galo Edmundo. Homenaje a los días sin nombre: poesía. Quito: Fondo Editorial, Casa de la Cultura Ecuatoriana, 1994. 161 p.: ill. (Colección Pachacamac)

Rodríguez Arcos (1944) es un poeta ecuatoriano nacido en Ambato. Su poesía acude con preferencia a objectos naturales sencillos para reelaborar un lenguaje metafórico y simbólico que, sin embargo, no se cierra en representaciones herméticas. Por el contrario, es una poesía de referentes claros que remiten a una atmósfera de frescura y optimismo. [ORR]

4088 Rojas, Gonzalo. Río turbio. Madrid: Hiperión, 1996. 84 p. (Poesía Hiperión; 282)

Rojas inserta en momentos decisivos algunos poemas anteriores de exacta factura junto con un número importante de poemas recientes. El intenso erotismo se aúna otra vez a una percepción aguda de la fugacidad de la existencia. El poeta pasa ahora revista a los escritores desaparecidos de su generación como un lúcido sobreviviente del siglo que termina. [OS]

4089 Rokha, Pablo de. Los gemidos. 2. ed. Santiago: Lom Ediciones, 1994. 372 p.: ill., map. (Colección Entre mares)

Reedición de libro seminal de 1922 que incluye un clarificador ensayo de Naim

Nómez y el registro fotográfico del poeta. En su introducción Nómez dice que el libro se organiza como "una serie de cantos temáticos cuyo eje estructural es un sujeto capaz de alcanzar el conocimiento de las cosas por intermedio del dolor, antes de desaparecer en la nada." [OS]

4090 Sanabria Santaliz, Edgardo. Las horas púrpura. Puerto Rico?: Editorial Cultural, 1994. 200 p.

Esta antología personal—narrativa, ensayos y poemas—incluye trabajos conocidos, como "El día que el hombre pisó la luna," así como también material inédito. Miembro de la generación del setenta puertorriqueña, a Sanabria Santaliz lo marca y lo distingue una sensibilidad religiosa. Aquí la aparición de la poesía se plantea como una acercamiento a lo espiritual. [FC]

4091 Sánchez Peláez, Juan. Poesía. 2a. ed. Caracas: Monte Avila Editores Latino americana, 1993. 230 p. (Altazor)

Publicada por primera vez en 1984, circula nuevamente esta compilación de la obra completa del autor, corregida y ampliada con textos recientes. El hecho es digno de atención, pues Sánchez Peláez ocupa una posición privilegiada en la poesía venezolana por haber introducido en ella definitivamente, en los 1950, las enseñanzas del surrealismo y haber posibilitado, en consecuencia, las profundas reformas de la tradición que se verifican en toda la segunda mitad del siglo en ese país. [MG]

4092 Sansón Argüello, Mariana. Zoo fantástico. Managua: INC: BANIC: INCH, 1994. 57 p.: ill.

La apropiación del mundo animal constituye, en la tradición poética nicaragüense, un género conocido y revisitado recientemente por poetas como Cuadra (*Zoo*, 1962) y Solís (*Zoo*, 1993). Lo que ya no es tan común es darle a estas composiciones un sesgo antropo-fantástico inspirado en la ciencia ficción y en motivos indígenas que luego cristalizan en creaciones plásticas impredecibles, por cuanto le dan representación a seres recién creados en el poema, como los "Jilocondos", los "Timeques", el "Quezalpa", los "Soxil", las "Hortalá", etc. La poesía de Sansón Argüello explora (no siempre con éxito) estas provocativas posibilidades, y en muchos casos la propuesta teórica supera al poema. [EM]

4093 Santelices Quesada, Gonzalo. Vida de un vendedor de fotocopiadoras. Madrid: Huerga & Fierro Editores, 1996. 74 p. (Fenice poesía; 7)

Poemas de formato epigramático que encuentran en la palabra justa y un humor delicado la precisa representación de una situación existencial sin melodrama. "Soy un vendedor de fotocopiadoras / a quien la vida ha dispensado / un trato correcto." [OS]

4094 Santiago-Delpín, Eduardo A. Exodo. San Juan: Editorial de la Univ. de Puerto Rico, 1998. 91 p. (Aquí y ahora; 37)

Dividido en dos partes—en la segunda domina el haiku—este poemario se define como una búsqueda incesable de la "tierra prometida": el Amor en todas sus vertientes. Búsqueda esperanzada, convencida de que, después de la entropía final, está nuevamente el amor: "La semilla, / bajo las hojas secas, / Paciente espera." [FC]

4095 Sepúlveda, Arnaldo. El libro de sí. San Juan: Instituto de Cultura Puertorriqueña, 1993. 101 p.

Poesía entre islas—Puerto Rico y Manhattan—que, desde el español, recoge el espacio neoyorquino de la ciudad, que es también el espacio de una sintaxis tensa, de una escritura donde el "yo" es el primer pronombre. [FC]

4096 Sifontes Greco, Lourdes C. Oficios de auriga. Caracas: FUNDARTE: Alcaldía de Caracas, 1992. 77 p. (Cuadernos de difusión; no. 158)

La de su autora (nacida en 1961) es una de las voces poéticas más inconfundibles de la literatura venezolana reciente. Sifontes Greco suma a un decir de remota procedencia simbolista un interés patente en desdibujar toda ingenua referencialidad mediante alusiones transtextuales que inscriben a sus poemas en un orbe intelectual. Particularmente logradas son las piezas donde el hablante medita acerca de la condición femenina con un tono racional y objetivo, para nada en deuda con los discursos judiciales. [MG]

4097 Silva Acevedo, Manuel. Canto rodado. Santiago: Editorial Universitaria, 1995. 102 p. (Colección El Poliedro y el mar)

Este libro reúne los textos de *Lobos y ovejas* y una nueva colección de poemas dividida en cinco secciones: Señal de ceniza. La primera parte explora el universo contradictorio de las pulsiones del inconsciente a través de personajes bíblicos claves, y la segunda describe la agonía religiosa de un sujeto que, como Job, intenta encarnar trascendentemente su propia muerte. [OS]

4098 Silva Estrada, Alfredo. Acercamientos: antología poética, 1952–1991. Prólogo de Rafael Castillo Zapata. Caracas: Monte Avila Editores Latinoamericana, 1992. 220 p. (Altazor)

Con el título de *Acercamientos* han aparecido ya dos compilaciones de la obra de Silva Estrada. Esta tercera entrega suma a las anteriores varias composiciones nuevas, que ayudan a trazar una trayectoria poética uniforme y perseverante en sus logros iniciales. La de Silva Estrada es una poesía que, como pocas, apuesta a la disolución de los entornos referenciales y la inmersión del decir en un mundo verbal, en el que el artificio de la imaginación levanta sólidas estructuras espaciales habitadas por la intuición y la pureza. Esta edición viene acompañada por un lúcido prólogo de Rafael Castillo Zapata. [MG]

4099 Sosa, Roberto. Antología personal. San José: Editorial Universitaria Centroamericana, 1995. 124 p. (Colección Séptimo día)

Sosa (Honduras, 1930) es uno de los poetas vivos más representativos de la poesía centroamericana. Los poemas que aparecen en esta colección son los que él mismo considera de mayor pertinencia a la hora de hacer un balance de lo escrito a lo largo de una vida. Pero al margen de lo que el mismo Sosa pueda argumentar, las composiciones que aquí aparecen son una muestra estupenda de una obra iniciada en 1959, con *Caligramas*, y que el poeta ha sabido conservar viva y activa. Especialmente logrados son aquellos poemas que, como "Canción para un gato muerto" o "Sin nombre" llevan la tensión metafórica hasta sus límites más creativos. [EM]

4100 Sotomayor, Aurea María. La gula de la tinta: poesía, 1973–1993. San Juan: Editorial Postdata, 1994. 245 p.: ill. (Serie Circe)

Esta publicación reúne poemarios previamente publicados, como *Sitio de la memoria* (1983), a la vez que incluye trabajos inéditos, como *Detalles de la filiación* (1975) y *Ojeras de su pulso* (1986–89). La poesía aquí es una reflexión minuciosa—a veces aforística, siempre densa—de temas como la ausencia, el deseo, el cuerpo, la palabra, el amor, la amistad, la producción y reproducción del sentido, la imagen poética, la fuga filosófica. [FC]

4101 Storni, Alfonsina. Antología mayor. Presentación de Jorge Rodríguez Padrón. Madrid: Hiperión, 1994. 318 p.: bibl., ill. (Poesía Hiperión; 237)

Impecable muestra antológica de esta escritora que ha despertado nuevamente el interés de la crítica. La selección está precedida de un valioso estudio de Rodríguez Padrón. [LU]

4102 Strepponi, Blanca. El jardín del verdugo. Caracas: Fondo Editorial Pequeña Venecia, 1992. 29 p.: ill. (Poesía y reflexión poética)

Variando los contextos históricos del *Diario de John Roberton*, la poeta recurre aquí a diversas situaciones del pasado y el presente en las que manifestaciones patentes del mal y la locura—cruzadas contra los cátaros, asesinos que descansan junto a la mujer amada, la objetividad con que un verdugo saudita se refiere a los pormenores de su profesión—se abordan con una frialdad cuyo principal efecto es fortalecer la transmisión de una profunda inquietud por los aspectos más estremecedores del alma humana. [MG]

4103 Strepponi, Blanca. Las vacas. Caracas: Fondo Editorial Pequeña Venecia, 1995. 35 p.: ill. (Fondo Editorial Pequeña Venecia; 45)

Después de *Poemas visibles* (1988), *Diario de John Roberton* (1990) y *El jardín del verdugo* (1992), este poemario confirma que la obra poética de Strepponi es una de las más sólidas del ámbito hispanoamericano. La nota característica de sus versos radica en la sorprendente capacidad expresiva que la restricción y el tono compuesto y racional pueden aportar a temas que incluyen el horror, la desesperanza y la muerte, así como la historia o las menudencias de lo cotidiano. En *Las vacas*, se amplían los registros temáticos para dar cabida a los misterios venidos del inconsciente, que no por ello prescinden del arte y del diálogo con la poesía moderna. [MG]

4104 Sylvester, Santiago E. Santiago Sylvester: antología poética. Buenos Aires: Fondo Nacional de las Artes, 1996. 115 p. (Poetas argentinos contemporáneos; 9)

Los poemas aquí reunidos muestran la evolución, el desplazamiento de la ciudad y sus habitantes a un entorno más íntimo donde reside el sujeto poético, sin que el tono se vuelva intimista. La inclusión de un poema inédito—"el punto más lejano"—añade interés a esta antología. [LU]

4105 Teillier, Jorge. En el mudo corazón del bosque. Santiago: Fondo de Cultura Económica, 1997. 56 p.: ill. (Cuadernos de La Gaceta; 94)

Libro póstumo del poeta de los lares que incluye algunos poemas sobresalientes en que todavía muertes y maravillas se dan cita y nos sorprenden: "Una bandada de cuervos / se dispersa ante un balazo. Bajo un esplendoroso trigal / yace el difunto Vincent van Gogh." [OS]

4106 Téllez, Fanor. Edad diversa: 1983–1990. Managua: Fondo Editorial, Banco Central de Nicaragua, 1993. 270 p. (Colección Artes y letras; no. 1)

La poesía de Téllez se sitúa voluntariamente en el polo opuesto al exteriorismo revolucionario practicado por gran parte de los poetas nicaragüenses contemporáneos. Como él mismo sostiene en las páginas inaugurales de este volumen, su poesía busca huir de "la congelación de un lenguaje y de un discurso exclusivamente inspirados en la Trinidad Estado-Partido-Hueste." Busca, por tanto, otras metáforas de la libertad. En general, los poemas que componen esta colección logran tales propósitos y ofrecen una poética de propuestas sólidas y originales. Lo que no logran los poemas de Téllez es superar esas dicotomías (tan arraigadas en algunos poetas centroamericanos) entre una poesía de propuesta estética y otra de horizonte político. [EM]

4107 Valera Mora, Víctor. Obras completas. Prólogo de Javier Lasarte V. Caracas: FUNDARTE, Alcaldía de Caracas, 1994. 350 p. (Colección Delta; no. 32)

Destaca en esta compilación la rigurosa edición y el prólogo de Javier Lasarte, quien describe y analiza con gran lucidez el repertorio poético de Valera Mora, desde sus entusiasmos stalinistas hasta sus incursiones en el erotismo. La violencia de su decir se constata tanto en el plano referencial como en el enunciativo mismo, donde se percibe la paulatina desintegración del hablante poético presa de la angustia ante una realidad no comprensible con el auxilio de muletas ideológicas. La deuda de Valera Mora con la antipoesía es absoluta ("Un golpe de chigüire en el azar / jamás podrá abolir el codillo"), pero sirve de dramático contraste con la candidez de sus preferencias políticas. [MG]

4108 Vanégas Coveña, Sara Beatriz. Poemar. Cuenca, Ecuador: Casa de la Cultura Ecuatoriana "Benjamín Carrión," Núcleo del Azuay, 1994. 157 p.

Una de las voces más originales de Ecuador. A través de un discurso fracturado, que acude tanto al verso como a la prosa poética, sus textos recuperan su sentido diseminando en un espacio sugerente de alucinaciones indefinidas, pero de tensa expectativa. Con un interlocutor presente implícitamente, la voz poética oscila entre la soledad y la comunicación sobre motivos amorosos. [ORR]

4109 Váscones, Carmen. Memorial a un acantilado. Quito: Editorial El Conejo, 1994. 87 p. (Colección Metáfora)

Nueva colección de una de las poetas más destacadas del Ecuador. Incluye una introducción firmada por Eliécer Cárdenas, quien destaca acertadamente el carácter y el contenido de este discurso en una búsqueda de los sentidos del amor y el deseo, de la soledad y la muerte. La búsqueda de sentidos y contención, asimismo, dan como resultado una poesía sugerente que no concluye en la afirmación. Breves y medidos, sus enunciados acuden a la reescritura en un afán poético constante por lograr una expresión cabal. [ORR]

4110 Vázquez Arce, Carmen. Memoria de papel. Río Piedras, P.R.: Ediciones Huracán, 1992. 70 p.

El cuerpo como texto; la memoria como espacio donde el amor—real e inventado—se hace inevitablemente literatura. Poesía, testimonio del deseo que surge del cuerpo inscrito en la cultura del pene. Contradiscurso erótico. Desde un reclamo femenino de igualdad erótica, este primer poemario de Vázquez Arce se ubica en la marginalidad de los discursos que le cantan a la libertad, sexual y también la que se le exige a los discursos del poder. Amor, erotismo y poesía, un ejercicio democrático que la voz poética asume desde una feminidad cómplice y crítica ante el machismo. [FC]

4111 Vergara Díaz-Granados, Luis Aurelio. Luis Aurelio Vergara: obra poética. Santa Marta, Colombia: Instituto de Cultura Magdalena, 1993. 306 p.: ill. (Instituto de Cultura Magdalena; 4)

Rescate de la obra casi olvidada de un postmodernista colombiano, en el que se evidencian todas las desigualdades de ese momento estético continental: por una parte, el anacrónico desconocimiento de las vanguardias internacionales; por otra, la resurrección en el siglo XX de una poesía patriótica (un buen ejemplo: "Ante la estatua del general Francisco de Paula Santander") ya estéticamente exhausta cien años antes. Valiosa aportación para calibrar con objetividad histórica el valor y la audacia de otros contemporáneos suyos como Luis Carlos López o Porfirio Barba-Jacob. [MG]

4112 Vidales, Aura María. Cantos para el guerrero. México: Instituto Nacional de Bellas Artes, Centro Nacional de Información y Promoción de la Literatura, 1995. 51 p. (Letras nuevas)

Vidales (México, 1958) hereda un estilo de construcción poética sumamente depurado. Sus poemas de amor (el guerrero también es alguien apellidado así) son diálogos en donde se describe, primero, una escena en tercera persona, para después incorporar la voz de un yo apasionado: "Soy letanía, lámpara, luciérnaga en vela. / Mi flama es cárcel, dardo. / Quemo." Vidales también ha aprendido el decir enigmático y sucinto (véase el primer verso de esta cita), por lo que sus textos evocan cierta tonalidad barroquizante. [JS]

4113 Vilariño, Idea. Poesía, 1945–1990. Montevideo: Cal y Canto, 1994. 293 p.: bibl., ill.

Reorganización casi completa de la obra de esta valiosa poeta uruguaya de la generación del 45. Su poesía—austera y rica a su vez en procedimientos rítmicos—gira obsesivamente en torno a los temas del amor y lo nocturno. [LU]

4114 Villagra Marsal, Carlos. El júbilo difícil: poesía 1986–1995. Edición, prólogo y notas de Raúl Amaral. Asunción: Editorial Don Bosco, 1995. 169 p.: ill.

Muestra antológica de este integrante de la generación paraguaya del 50. [LU]

4115 Villarreal, José Javier. Portuaria. México: Ediciones Era, 1997. 100 p. (Biblioteca Era)

Cuando se trata de provincia, los poetas mexicanos que mayor influencia han ejercido han sido los del sur (de Chiapas y Tabasco, por ejemplo). Villarreal (Tijuana, 1959) es, quizás, la nueva voz del norte, ya reconocido con el Premio de Poesía de Aguascalientes en 1987. En este libro, se funde la textura del verso largo, elaborado y barroco, con la continuidad de la historia y la política que emanan de la región fronteriza: combinación bastante singular en la poesía mexicana actual. [JS]

4116 Villasís Endara, Carlos. Las raíces del sol: poema cíclico. Quito: IADP, 1995. 166 p. (Colección Creaciones literarias. Subcolección Poesía; v. 6)

Este volumen, de un poeta ecuatoriano consagrado en su país, encierra un conjunto de textos inspirados en pasajes de la historia precolombina de las naciones andinas. Los poemas, además de poetizar paisajes históricos de la civilización inca, propone una reflexión sobre el sometimiento de aquellas naciones al coloniaje europeo en el siglo XVI. El volumen incluye un poema titulado "De los sueños y la gloria," diálogo de voces no identificadas sobre el mismo tema de la conquista, texto premiado en un concurso nacional ecuatoriano. [ORR]

4117 Vitale, Ida. Obra poética. v. 1. Montevideo: Arca, 1992. 1 v.

Este primer tomo incluye su obra poética desde *La luz de esta memoria* (1949) hasta *Jardín de Sílice* (1980) inclusive. Una de las más importantes figuras de la generación del 45, su obra se caracteriza por una inclaudicable vigilancia ante la palabra. [LU]

4118 Wiethüchter, Blanca. El rigor de la llama. Bolivia: Ediciones Centro Simón I. Patiño, 1994. 63 p.

Lenguaje subjetivo e individualista por

el que la autora trata de realizar una reflexión introspectiva, que no muestra ni sus fines ni sus alcances al lector. El discurso no llega a desarrollarse ante la ausencia de propósitos explícitos o sugeridos, y el efecto que recibe el lector es que ese discurso se interrumpe incompleto en cada texto, para reiniciar su ciclo en textos subsiguientes, que tampoco definen su sentido. No se puede dejar de advertir la influencia que dejó en esta autora la poesía de Jaime Sáenz, que ciertamente es única y personal y, por ello mismo, inimitable. [ORR]

4119 **Wiezell, Elsa.** Rumbo al arco iris. Asunción: Impr. Salesiana, 1995. 53 p.

Perteneciente a la generación paraguaya del 50, su poesía se caracteriza por un marcado tono intimista y la recurrencia al tema de la pérdida. [LU]

4120 **Yáñez, Ricardo.** Dejar de ser. México: Ediciones Era, 1994. 70 p. (Biblioteca Era. Poesía)

En la poesía de Yáñez (Guadalajara, 1948) persiste una búsqueda espiritual: muchos de sus textos son reelaboraciones de la lucidez que deriva de la poesía mística o de las transparencias de lo sagrado en Octavio Paz. El título de este volumen, por ejemplo, es un variación a San Juan de la Cruz. Algunos de los poemas se reducen a la celebración del ser: "Las flores son el puro agradecimiento a la luz." [JS]

4121 **Zaid, Gabriel.** Reloj de sol. Madrid: Ave del Paraíso, 1995. 115 p. (Colección Es un decir; 6)

Libro que recoge poesía de libros publicados entre 1958–92. Según el propio Zaid (Nueva León, México, 1934), se trata de su "poesía completa," indicando obviamente que éstos son los textos con los que se siente más satisfecho. La poesía de Zaid se caracteriza por una ironía que se burla de todo, a la vez que deja traslucir una velada espiritualidad. [JS]

GENERAL STUDIES

4122 **Benedetti, Mario.** Poetas de cercanías. Montevideo: Cal y Canto, 1994. 186 p.: bibl.

Recopilación de trabajos generales sobre poesía latinoamericana y también sobre poetas contemporáneos de distintos países de América Latina. Todos los trabajos aquí reunidos ya habían aparecido previamente en distintas publicaciones. [LU]

4123 **Bronx, Humberto.** Historia de la poesía antioqueña. Colombia: s.n., 1993. 325 p.: bibl., ill. (Historia de la literatura antioqueña; v. 1)

Curioso acercamiento a la exégesis literaria, de una especie en vías de extinción: crítica *naive,* pero no por ello carente de interés—compila, de hecho, con exhaustividad ejemplar, la mayor cantidad impresa de lugares comunes acerca de diversos poetas colombianos. Destacan el tratamiento de la homosexualidad de Porfirio Barba Jacob y la sección titulada "Poetisas antioqueñas," donde leemos razonamientos como "La mujer es un ser iluminado; un vaso de hermosura que recibe la forma divina del ser." La inclusión antológica de poetas poco conocidos podría convertirse en un valioso argumento para quienes decidan defender la elaboración de estrictos cánones literarios. [MG]

4124 **Cobo Borda, Juan Gustavo.** El coloquio americano. Medellín: Editorial Univ. de Antioquia, 1994. 412 p.: bibl. (Otraparte; 9)

Diversos estudios sobre prosa y poesía hispanoamericanas. Volumen algo irregular, pero tienen valor informativo o crítico las páginas dedicadas a B. Sanín Cano y G. Arciniegas; la figura de Bolívar en la narrativa de los últimos años; la relación de A. Reyes y J.L. Borges; los poetas L. de Greiff, J. Zalamea, V. Gerbasi y G. Baquero. [PL]

4125 **Cobo Borda, Juan Gustavo.** Historia portátil de la poesía colombiana. Bogotá: TM Editores, 1995. 315 p.: bibl.

Este volumen recoge, corrige y amplía ensayos precedentes, pero también añade trabajos que se ocupan del quehacer poético colombiano de principios de los años noventa. Sin duda, una de las miradas críticas más estimulantes a un panorama rico y lleno de contrastes. Cobo Borda combina su conocimiento personal de muchos de los poetas estudiados con útiles remisiones bibliográficas. De destacar son las secciones dedicadas al nadaísmo y a las promociones que lo siguen. [MG]

4126 **Conversaciones con la poesía argentina.** Compilación de Jorge Fondebrider. Buenos Aires: Libros de Tierra Firme,

1995. 415 p.: index. (Coleccíon Sobre la poesía y los poetas)

Lúcidas entrevistas a importantes poetas argentinos; se destacan los diálogos con Fernández Moreno y Edgar Bayle. Dos ausencias lamentables son las de Enrique Molina y Olga Orozco. [LU]

4127 Gauggel, Karl Hermann. El cisne modernista: sus orígenes y supervivencia. New York: P. Lang, 1997. 584 p.: bibl., index. (Currents in comparative Romance languages and literatures, 0893–5963; vol. 35)

Investigación exhaustiva del tema. De interés para el especialista por la información rica y a menudo novedosa desplegada en el libro, desde los orígenes remotos del símbolo. Trabajo importante. Habría ganado considerablemente con una jerarquización más rigurosa de los datos y comentarios sobre R. Darío, E. González Martínez y demás poetas del periodo. [PL]

4128 Hija del día: artes poéticas nicaragüenses. Compilación e introducción de Julio Valle-Castillo. Managua: Editorial Nueva Nicaragua, 1994? 352 p.

La reflexión sobre el trabajo poético y la conciencia que de éste pueda tenerse constituye el corpus de esta nueva antología crítica de Julio Valle-Castillo. De aquí el criterio que determina la inclusión o exclusión de un poeta: únicamente figuran aquellos que han escrito artes poéticas. Una lectura detenida de estas poéticas no puede dejar de observar que la extraordinaria diversidad de la poesía nicaraguense difícilmente puede, como pretende el editor, unificarse bajo el signo de un "arte poético nacional." Estas muestras sugieren lo contrario: la invialibilidad de un proyecto nacional único y la urgencia de repensar al país en lo que éste tiene de multicultural y diverso. [EM]

4129 Moscona, Myriam. De frente y de perfil: semblanzas de poetas. Fotografías de Rogelio Cuéllar. México: Ciudad de México, Depto. del Distrito Federal, 1994. 327 p.: ports.

Hermoso y bellamente editado, este libro—casi como uno de arte—es el que se pone para admirar en la mesa de la sala. Moscona incluye 75 semblanzas de poetas nacidos entre 1898 y 1959. Básicamente, el diseño del libro implica una reseña biográfica acompañada por comentarios del escritor o por fragmentos de poemas, en cierto modo construyendo la imagen de la persona que está detrás de los textos que leemos. Más que utilidad académica, este libro tiene como virtud capturar el entorno anímico de los poetas retratados. [JS]

4130 O'Hara Gonzales, Edgar. Isla Negra no es una isla: el canon poético chileno a comienzos de los 80. Valdivia, Chile: Barba de Palo, 1996. 147 p.: bibl., ports. (Colección "Guillermo Araya" de monografías, ensayos y estudios)

Excelentes entrevistas realizadas en 1980 y 1981 a Enrique Lihn, Oscar Hahn, David Turkeltaub, Nicanor Parra, Gonzalo Rojas, Raúl Zurita, Manuel Silva Acevedo, y Jorge Teillier. Estimulantes reflexiones en torno a las respectivas poéticas de cada uno de los autores de acuerdo al contexto histórico-cultural de los años 80. [OS]

4131 Oviedo y Pérez de Tudela, Rocío. Narciso en la laguna: nueva poesía mexicana. (*Cuad. Hispanoam.*, 549/550, marzo/abril 1996, p. 101–122, bibl.)

Después de una breve introducción sobre la poesía de los sesenta, este artículo se concentra de modo panorámico en la poesía producida en México a partir de Tlatelolco y durante los setenta y los ochenta. La crítica escoge ciertos marcos referenciales (mitos, espacios, tiempo) para hacer referencia al trabajo de más de veinte escritores de distintas generaciones. La dificultad de esta propuesta radica en tratar de darle cohesión a un grupo tan variado de poetas. [JS]

4132 La poesía folklórica de Venezuela. Recopilación de Luis Felipe Ramón y Rivera. Caracas: Monte Avila Editores, 1992. 383 p.: bibl. (Documentos)

Reedición de un trabajo publicado en 1988 que se ha convertido en aportación imprescindible para los estudios antropológicos de la cultura venezolana. Si bien el análisis textual nunca llega a ir a fondo en las piezas recogidas, limitado a clasificaciones genológicas no debidamente sustentadas desde el punto de vista teórico, el valor y la amplitud de la compilación son innegables y confirman el tesón como investigador de Ramón y Rivera. [MG]

4133 La poesía nueva en el mundo hispánico: los últimos años. Madrid: Visor Libros, 1994. 291 p.: bibl. (Biblioteca filológica hispánica; 16)

Con méritos diferentes, los 19 trabajos incluidos constituyen un atendible balance del proceso poético en las diversas áreas idiomáticas de la península y de Iberoamérica, desde 1960. Los estudios iberoamericanos han estado a cargo de R.H. Herrera (Argentina), O. Rivera-Rodas (Bolivia), A.C. Secchin (Brasil), S. Millares (reseña la situación de la poesía centroamericana), J. G. Cobo Borda (Colombia), T. Fernández (Cuba), H. Montes Brunet (Chile), H. Rodríguez Castelo (Ecuador), F. Albizúrez Palma (Guatemala), A. Chouciño Fernández (México), J.C. Rovira (Nicaragua), J. Ortega (Perú), J. Pla (Paraguay), A. Villanueva (Uruguay), y J. Liscano (Venezuela). [PL]

4134 Poesía y poética del grupo Orígenes. Recopilación de Alfredo Chacón. Caracas: Biblioteca Ayacucho, 1994. 369 p.: bibl. (Biblioteca Ayacucho; 182)

Considerada como una de las mejores revistas culturales de la lengua española de 1944 a 1956, *Orígenes* fue también una estética y una agenda de promoción cultural, que además de la literatura incluía la música y la pintura tanto de las Américas como de Europa. La centralidad de Lezama Lima, los nexos internacionales, el culto a la amistad como modus operandi, las revistas que anteceden el surgimiento de *Orígenes (Verbum, Espuela de Plata, Nadie Parecía)*, el descubrimiento de la imagen, la presencia de Juan Ramón Jiménez, los contrastes entre Lezama y Virgilio Piñera, son, entre otros tópicos, discutidos en la introducción. [FC]

4135 Reisz, Susana. Voces sexuadas: género y poesía en Hispanoamérica. Lérida, Spain: Asociación Española de Estudios Literarios Hispanoamericanos: Edicions de la Universitat de Lleida, 1996. 217 p.: bibl. (Serie América; 1)

Páginas invitadoras al diálogo sobre un tema de gran actualidad. Suscitarán también polémicas, pues la autora asume riesgos interpretativos que no dejarán indiferentes a sus críticos (su lectura de "Trilce IX", por ejemplo). Son notables la coherencia de la argumentación y la brillantez expositiva. Sus aproximaciones a la obra de Susana Thenon y a la producción poética femenina del Perú son aportes sobresalientes. [PL]

4136 Yarza, Pálmenes. Una ojeada al modernismo en la lírica venezolana. Caracas: Centauro, 1994. 284 p.: bibl.

La obvia superioridad estética de la prosa modernista explica hasta cierto punto por qué la poesía venezolana de la misma época cuenta con escasos trabajos críticos de conjunto. El presente volumen, por ello, cubre notorios vacíos bibliográficos. Pese a la vaguedad metodológica implícita en una labor que a menudo se adentra en el campo de las semblanzas y las impresiones, la de Yarza tiene a su favor la disposición de rescatar nombres que corren el peligro de ser definitivamente olvidados. [MG]

SPECIAL STUDIES

4137 Alonso, Raúl *et al*. Alberto Girri: homenaje. Recopilación de Alina Diaconú. Buenos Aires: Fondo Nacional de las Artes: Editorial Sudamericana, 1993. 156 p.: bibl., ill.

Se reúnen aquí textos que evocan y celebran la figura de este escritor central dentro de la poesía argentina del siglo XX. Se destacan los trabajos de Arturo Carrera, Alina Diaconú y Olga Orozco. [LU]

4138 Bejel, Emilio. José Lezama Lima, poeta de la imagen. Madrid: Huerga & Fierro Editores, 1994. 206 p.: bibl. (Teoría y crítica; 2)

Este estudio, traducción del mismo estudio publicado en inglés en 1990, plantea un análisis del sistema poético de Lezama a partir de la relación entre la imagen y el sujeto poético, la escritura, la naturaleza y la historia. El sistema poético de Lezama implica también una manera de leer la literatura y la cultura americanas: una lectura integradora de los retazos de otras culturas. [FC]

4139 Cabrera de Ibarra, Palmira. Luis Lloréns Torres: ante el paisaje. San Juan: Editorial Yaurel, 1990. 147 p.: bibl.

Este estudio propone analizar "la actitud del poeta ante el paisaje," directamente relacionado con los dos temas más importantes de la poesía de Lloréns: el amor y la patria. Tres etapas conforman la relación paisaje-poesía: una etapa descriptiva, otra interpretativa y, finalmente, una en la que el paisaje es interiorizado. [FC]

4140 Cano Gaviria, Ricardo. José Asunción Silva, una vida en clave de sombra. Caracas: Monte Avila Editores, 1992. 537 p.: bibl., ill. (Documentos)

La de Cano Gaviria es, indudablemente, la contribución más valiosa de los últimos años a la ya extensa bibliografía en torno al mayor de los poetas colombianos. El rigor con que se seleccionan las fuentes disponibles y la objetividad con que se cotejan sus datos permiten al biógrafo poner fin a la larga serie de discursos legendarios—las mistificaciones—que han perseguido a Silva desde antes de su suicidio en 1896. La clave estructuradora elegida es la de ceñirse a una "biografía literaria" que estudia la evolución estética y mental del poeta, jalonada, desde luego, por los tres ámbitos sociales que conoció: el bogotano, el parisino y el caraqueño. El resultado constituye una sabia combinación de lo textual y lo extratextual, nunca alcanzada del todo antes de la aparición de este volumen. [MG]

4141 Carranza, María Mercedes; J. Eduardo Jaramillo-Zuluaga; and Anna María Rodríguez. Memoria del congreso: "Silva, su obra y su Época." Bogotá: Casa de Poesía Silva, 1997. 402 p.: bibl., ill.

Este volumen recoge las ponencias que 23 investigadores y escritores presentaron en mayo de 1996 en Bogotá, con motivo del centenario de la muerte de José Asunción Silva. La índole de los trabajos es naturalmente heterogénea y va de la crítica más especializada a ensayos en extremo personales. El conjunto es indispensable para familiarizarse con la recepción de Silva durante los últimos decenios. Destaca la exhaustiva bibliografía preparada por Jaramillo-Zuluaga. [MG]

4142 Celebración de la existencia: homenaje internacional al poeta cubano Gastón Baquero. Recopilación de Alfonso Ortega Carmona y Alfredo Pérez Alencart. Salamanca: Cátedra de Poética "Fray Luis de León," Univ. Pontificia de Salamanca, 1994. 276 p.: bibl., ill.

Este homenaje al poeta cubano, que desde 1959 reside en Madrid, reúne ensayos, entre otros, de cubanos de dentro y de fuera de Cuba que, en abril 1993, se dieron cita en Salamanca. La gama de artículos es amplia; el mestizaje, la identidad cultural, la poesía como salvación, el hermetismo, las magias, el vitalismo, la presencia de César Vallejo, Eliseo Diego y José Gorostiza en la poesía de Baquero, y otros. Incluye también una entrevista. [FC]

4143 Correa-Díaz, Luis. Lengua muerta: poesía, post-literatura & erotismo en Enrique Lihn. Providence, R.I.: INTI, 1996. 115 p.: bibl.

Estimulante ensayo sobre la escritura de Lihn cuyo eje crítico, el libro postumo *Diario de Muerte,* se vincula a la vertiente erótica de *Al bello aparecer de este lucero* como a su otra faz. Se subraya el valor singular de la escritura del diario dentro de la producción de Lihn—su intensidad negativa—y el quiebre que realiza de los géneros literarios y del principio metafísico del concepto de "obra." [OS]

4144 Foxley R., Carmen. Enrique Lihn: escritura excéntrica y modernidad. Santiago: Editorial Universitaria, 1995. 345 p.: bibl. (Colección El saber y la cultura. Temas de literatura)

Fundamental estudio de conjunto que incorpora la obra poética de Lihn al horizonte de preocupaciones literario-culturales del proyecto neobarroco (Severo Sarduy) que busca desplazar las carencias, los quiebres incesantes de la modernidad latinoamericana. En la tendencia manierista del barroco (Arnold Hauser), Foxley encuentra una descripción singularmente adecuada para caracterizar esta obra, destacando el valor crítico de las manipulaciones estilísticas y la carga intelectual con su juego de complejidades de tendencia elitista. Foxley sitúa a Lihn como un lector crítico de la vanguardia, y subraya ciertas estrategias: la rememorización (Heidegger) como viaje de redescubrimiento y no como retorno acrítico a una encrucijada del pasado, y la "hibris discursiva" por la cual se violenta tanto la linealidad del discurso como la posición monolítica del sujeto vanguardista. Se distinguen cinco ciclos en la obra de Lihn: 1) el sujeto poético todavía centrado es asediado por la incertidumbre y el sarcasmo; 2) se reemplaza al sujeto por una multiplicidad de personajes y una fuerte actividad rememorativa desplaza los ejes del discurso; 3) notas de viajes, en que el discurso se produce como profusión exuberante de códigos aleatorios; 4) crónicas de la ciudad, radiografía del Santiago autoritario y esperpéntico; 5) coloquios de amor y muerte, sobre la precariedad de Eros y la disputa con la muerte desde un matiz confesional. [OS]

4145 Gordon, Samuel. Carlos Pellicer: breve biografía literaria. México: Consejo Nacional para la Cultura y las Artes: Ediciones Del Equilibrista, 1997. 106 p., 24 p. of plates: bibl. (Biblioteca Carlos Pellicer)

Gordon es uno de los críticos más importantes en relación a la obra de Carlos Pellicer. Este libro traza el itinerario biográfico del poeta tabasqueño; se citan cartas, poemas y documentos inéditos que contribuyen a una mejor comprensión de esta obra. También se incluyen un "Anexo fotográfico" y un cuaderno cronológico. [JS]

4146 Intensidad y altura de César Vallejo.
Recopilación de Ricardo González Vigil. Lima: Pontificia Univ. Católica del Perú, Fondo Editorial, 1993. 341 p.: bibl.

El volumen contiene los discursos y ponencias leídos en el homenaje que, por el centenario del nacimiento de Vallejo, organizó la Univ. Católica del Perú en 1992. Los 15 textos cubren una variedad de asuntos (biografía, recepción de la obra, estética, temas, métrica, narrativa y teatro) a cargo de investigadores peruanos, a excepción del español Julio Vélez, quien murió poco después de asistir a este coloquio. [JMO]

4147 Jaime Sabines: algo sobre su vida.
Mexico: Carla Zarebska, 1994. 356 p.: bibl., ill. (some col.).

Para los entusiastas de Jaime Sabines (Tuxtlan Gutiérrez, Chiapas, 1926), este libro es una joya bibliográfica, en el sentido del excelente diseño gráfico, con papeles de diferentes texturas y colores; reproducciones facsimilares de documentos, libros, manuscritos de poemas, etc. El volumen está dividido cronológicamente, de acuerdo con la vida de Sabines, y se incluyen en cada sección fotos, poemas alusivos y fragmentos de entrevistas. [JS]

4148 O'Hara Gonzales, Edgar. La precaución y la vigilancia: la poesía de Pedro Lastra. Valdivia, Chile: Barba de Palo, 1996. 132 p., 13 p. of plates: bibl., facsims. (Colección "Guillermo Araya" de ensayos, monografías, estudios)

Excelente introducción al trabajo poético, a las preocupaciones culturales y a las interacciones literarias de Lastra. Las claves de su poética se estudian de manera informada e inteligente. Se incluye una extensa entrevista al poeta y una sección documental con 10 cartas -entre ellos de Arguedas

y de Lihn- y una dedicatoria de Salazar Bondy. [OS]

4149 Paoletti, Mario. El aguafiestas: la biografía de Mario Benedetti. Buenos Aires: Seix Barral, 1995. 268 p.: bibl., ill.

El libro desmerece la estatura intelectual de Benedetti a lo cual se agrega una escritura bastante descuidada. [LU]

4150 Santos Molano, Enrique. El corazón del poeta: los sucesos reveladores de la vida y la verdad inesperada de la muerte de José Asunción Silva. 3. ed. Bogotá: Presidencia de la República, 1997. 1305 p.: bibl. (Biblioteca familiar de la Presidencia de la República)

Esta biografía de Silva, aparecida por primera vez en 1992, se reedita ahora luego de las aportaciones de Ricardo Cano Gaviria, Héctor Orjuela y Fernando Vallejo en el mismo campo de investigación. Las ampliaciones y enmiendas de la presente versión son substanciales, aunque la tesis central del libro—hay más posibilidades de un asesinato que de un suicidio en el caso de Silva—sigue intacta. [MG]

MISCELLANEOUS

4151 Coronel Urtecho, José; Luz Marina Acosta; and Julio Valle-Castillo. Libro de conversaciones sobre libros. Fotos de Luis Rocha y Rossana Lacayo. Managua: Editorial Nueva Nicaragua, 1994 159 p.: ill.

¿Documental cultural? ¿Etica de la conversación? Difícil (e innecesario) catalogar la naturaleza de este espléndido libro de conversaciones. El *conversador* es el desaparecido líder de la vanguardia nicaragüense, J. Coronel Urtecho (1906–94), y los interlocutores: L.M. Acosta y J. Valle-Castillo. Las conversaciones versan sobre libros que en opinión de Coronel Urtecho han modelado el curso de la historia literaria y cultural de Centroamérica: *Recolección a mediodía*, de E. Mejía Sánchez (considerado como uno de los tres pilares de la poesía nicaragüense contemporánea); *El estrecho dudoso y Homenaje a los indios americanos*, de E. Cardenal, (por cuanto supieron repensar y replantear la historia americana); *El alba de oro*, de S. Ramírez, texto de investigación histórica que reivindica la oratoria revolucionaria frente a la retórica demagógica, y *La montaña es algo más que una inmensa estepa verde*, de O. Cabezas, por cuanto plantea la función del testimonio y la crónica en sociedades posrevolucionarias. [EM]

4152 Hernández Rueda, Lupo *et al.* La ciudad y el amor. Dominican Republic: Editorial Punto Creativo, 1997. 124 p.: ill.

Cuatro escritores dominicanos (L. Hernández Rueda, M. Veloz Maggiolo, T. Raful y T. Castro Burdiez) y un dibujante (D. Blanco) celebran y *cerebran* los 500 años de la fundación de Santo Domingo y también, por extensión, de América. Mediante lo mítico, lo histórico, lo político, lo cotidiano, lo popular, lo literario, la modernidad, se plasma una visión poética de la ciudad desde la desolación primigenia hasta el internet y el telecable. [FC]

4153 Lihn, Enrique. El circo en llamas: una crítica de la vida. Recopilación de Germán Marín. Santiago: LOM Ediciones, 1997. 694 p. (Colección Texto sobre texto)

Edición de los textos de crítica literaria que Lihn (1929–88) escribiera desde los 22 años. El libro está dividido en 7 secciones—encabezadas por una página que describe fotografías familiares—: "Almas de doble filo", sobre poetas chilenos de comienzos, mediados y finales de siglo; "Prólogos," textos escritos tanto para encabezar libros de autores chilenos—poetas y narradores—como antologías; "Par lui-même", sobre aspectos biográficos claves del poeta como su problemática vida infantil y adolescente en el Liceo Alemán y la relación con su abuela materna; "El compromiso, esa vieja palabra sartreana" sobre la voluntad constantemente democratizadora de la cultura y del hacer político del poeta; "Memorabilia" sobre el viaje de Lihn a Europa en 1965—período de *Poesía de paso*—con textos para periódicos, un texto sobre un personaje olvidado y esencial—Helio Rodríguez—y una sorprendente carta a Gabriela Mistral; "Gerardo de Pompier" con textos de y sobre Pompier, el alterego atrabiliario y pasatista de Lihn que da curso inicial a su verborrea (con la ayuda de Marín) en el fervor político cultural de 1969 y que el poeta recupera y lleva a la madurez durante el autoritarismo de los años 60; "Narradores y otras páginas" con artículos sobre Kafka—escritos en Cuba antes del caso

Padilla—y sobre narradores latinoamericanos como Cortázar, Rulfo, Carpentier, y Edwards. En suma, efectiva labor de rescate de artículos publicados e inéditos de Lihn que, de otra manera, se perderían en el anonimato de la dispersión. [OS]

4154 Novo, Salvador. Viajes y ensayos. v. 1. México: Fondo de Cultura Económica, 1996. 1 v.: bibl. (Letras mexicanas)

Quizás Novo (México, 1904–74) sea más importante como ensayista que como poeta. Este amplio volumen comprueba la agudeza y la ironía de este escritor, a partir de la selección de los temas (véanse, por ejemplo, los ensayos sobre la leche, el pan, la "H" y las aves en la poesía castellana) y los modos de presentarlos. Reúne todos los ensayos: desde los de juventud hasta el divertido *Las locas, el sexo, los burdeles*, publicado dos años antes de su muerte. Libro recomendable tanto para los especialistas como para aquellos que busquen una prosa entretenida y graciosa. [JS]

4155 Pasos, Joaquín. Prosas de un joven. Recopilación y prólogo de Julio Valle-Castillo. Ilustraciones de Joaquín Zavala Urtecho *et al.* Managua: Editorial Nueva Nicaragua, 1995. 2 v.: ill.

A Valle-Castillo debemos esta magnífica edición crítica de la obra en prosa de un destacado integrante del movimiento vanguardista nicaragüense: Joaquín Pasos (1914–47). El estudio de Valle-Castillo (casi 50 páginas) merece la mayor consideración, por cuanto aporta significativamente al conocimiento de una obra que sería incomprensible sin una adecuada contextualización histórica y literaria. Con su acostumbrada claridad argumentativa Valle-Castillo advierte que la obra de Pasos es (como en general la vanguardia de su tiempo) el producto de una élite intelectual cerrada, excluyente y localista que tuvo, sin embargo, la lucidez de enfrentar sus límites y prever el fracaso del proyecto histórico que ofrecían las clases aristocráticas nicaragüenses. Esa crisis, en opinión de Valle-Castillo, "fue la verdadera enfermedad que mató a Joaquín Pasos a los 33 años." A casi 50 años de su muerte, este volumen le da al lector la oportunidad de apreciar el pensamiento crítico de Pasos. [EM]

4156 **Tres caminos: el germen de la literatura judía en México.** Introducción, selección y traducción de Becky Rubinstein. Mexico: Ediciones El Tucán de Virginia, 1997. 141 p. (Colección Zona; Poemas)

Antología de tres poetas judíos emigrantes de Europa del Este a México, y de lengua idish: I. Berliner, J. Glantz y M. Glikovsky. Obviamente, la barrera lingüística impidió que estos escritores se dieran a conocer y se integraran al panorama de la literatura mexicana de los años 30, 40 y 50. Las notas de Rubinstein debieron haberse ceñido con mayor rigor a proporcionar datos al lector: fechas de nacimiento y muerte, fichas bibliográficas, etc. El libro es una contribución afortunada, puesto que da la visión del emigrante que entremezcla los sentimientos de extrañeza y adoración por las nuevas tierras. [JS]

4157 **Vallejo, César.** Escalas melografiadas. Arequipa, Peru: UNSA, 1994. 356 p.: bibl.

La presente edición es el resultado de un importante descubrimiento: el ejemplar de este libro narrativo de Vallejo, con correcciones de su propia mano, que encontró el hispanista francés, Claude Couffon. Aparte de la reproducción facsimilar del mencionado ejemplar (que perteneció al padre del poeta), la edición incluye el texto que ahora cabe considerar definitivo y el publicado en 1923. En vez de incluir este último, presentar los dos primeros frente a frente habría bastado y resultado más cómodo para el lector; también es de lamentar que la edición de un texto valioso como éste sea tan modesta y tan poco accesible a los investigadores interesados. [JMO]

Drama

MARIO A. ROJAS, *Associate Professor of Modern Languages, Catholic University of America*
SANDRA M. CYPESS, *Professor of Spanish, University of Maryland*

LA CANTIDAD DE RESENCIONES que contiene esta sección evidencia el creciente interés por la escritura dramática desarrollada en los últimos años en Hispanoamérica. En Sudamérica, dramaturgos ya establecidos, como Enrique Buenaventura, Jorge Díaz, Griselda Gambaro, Carlos Gorostiza, Marco Antonio de la Parra, Ricardo Monti, Eduardo Rovner, Rodolfo Santana, Eduardo Sarlós, Carlos Varela, y Egon Wolf continúan produciendo textos de gran calidad. Hay otros dramaturgos que empiezan a situarse entre los mejores, como Carlos María Alsina, Daniel Veronese, Arístides Vargas, César de María, Mario Cura, Javier Daulte, y Marcelo Ramos, que merecen una seria atención crítica de sus obras. Cabe mencionar, de modo especial, los textos de autoras como Estela Caicedo, Xiomara Moreno, Blanca Omar, Amanda Patrarca, Josefina Plá, que presentan sus ideas en torno a la situación cultural de la mujer e intentan borrar estereotipos, a la vez que proponen nuevos modelos de mujer contemporánea. Entre los estudios teóricos sobre teatro de dramaturgas es de especial interés el de Consuelo Morel.

También hay muchas antologías tanto del teatro del siglo XIX como del XX. Unas son compendios de obras de un mismo autor (items **4160, 4163, 4176, 4184, 4186, 4197, 4203, 4217, 4235,** y **4256**), otras ordenadas en torno a un lugar geográfico, sea país o región (items **4164, 4165, 4178, 4264, 4268,** y **4270**), en tanto que algunas están estructuradas más bien alrededor de una temática o de una forma teatral determinada (items **4261** y **4270**). Estos volúmenes son importantes porque coleccionan lo mejor de un autor o grupo de autores y porque dan a conocer nombres de escritores que aún no han logrado la visibilidad que se merecen. Entre los temas trabajados, algunos autores siguen preocupándose de temas o géneros recurrentes, como es el caso del drama histórico en las obras de Guerrero, Kaufmann, Magrini, Méndez Ballester, Balboa, Peredo Néstor, Ramos Perea, Reyes Carlos y de nuevas imágenes de mujeres que se proyectan en las obras de Estela Caicedo, Miriam Echeverría, Elizabeth Shön, Elisa Lerner, Mariela Romero, Lidia Febrijen y Blanca Omar. Otros temas de más actualidad están atrayendo la atención de algunos dramaturgos pendientes del referente histórico-social de sus respectivos países o de la región latinoamericana, como es el caso del neoliberalismo económico y sus efectos en América Latina planteado en las obras de Briski, Daneri, y Santana.

En México se siguen publicando autores de varias generaciones, nuevas ediciones de textos escritos por dramaturgos consagrados como Emilio Carballido, Vicente Leñero, Maruxa Vilalta, Tomás Urtusástegui, junto con algunos de la llamada "nueva dramaturgia" como Víctor Hugo Rascón Banda, Sabina Berman, y jóvenes como Benjamín Gómez Jiménez, Lorena Padrón, y Fernando Muñoz. Otra publicación importante es el Teatro inédito de Virgilio Piñera que contiene cinco obras del conocido escritor cubano que testimonian de nuevo su rol en el desarrollo del teatro de tendencias absurdistas en América Latina. "El no" sobre todo es una farsa sin referencia específica que tiene, sin embargo, claras alusiones políticas.

En Centroamérica, es de notar la importancia de temas históricos, especialmente del impacto de las muchas revoluciones en la vida de la gente ordinaria. Alfredo Valessi, en su Teatro de ira, por ejemplo, nos recuerda en sus referencias la trayectoria histórica de Nicaragua, la motivación de los argentinos como Gambaro o Pavlovsky, cuyas obras sirven de testimonio para no olvidar toda la historia sangrienta de intervenciones militares de su país, no sólamente la de la llamada guerra sucia. De igual manera ,Valessi, Hermenegildo Torrero Jaramillo de Panamá, Ileana Zambrana Piñeda de Costa Rica, y Mario Monteforte Toledo de Guatemala ejemplifica los dramaturgos que escriben con claros propósitos políticos.

En el campo de la crítica teatral hemos revisado, más que trabajos monográficos que pueden encontrarse en revistas especializadas, estudios teóricos que proponen o emplean pautas metodológicas para el estudio sincrónico o diacrónico de la escritura dramática hispanoamericana. En particular, nos referimos a los libros de Pelletieri y Villegas. También hemos consignado antologías, con estudios de diversos autores seleccionados de ponencias presentadas en prestigiosos congresos realizados en Hispanoamérica o en Europa (items **4294, 4316, 4317 y 4319**). Entre las revistas, las dos publicadas en los Estados Unidos, Gestos y Latin American Theatre Review, y otras que vienen de Latinoamérica, como Apuntes de Chile, Siglo XXI y Teatro al Sur de Argentina, continúan siendo valiosas fuentes de información de la producción teatral hispanoamericana, tanto de textos escritos como performativos.

Cabe destacar la publicación de trabajos teóricos de la revista Gestos, en cuya lista ha aparecido el libro de María de la Luz Hurtado y de Juan Villegas. Es de notar también la labor editorial de Galerna y Corregidor de Buenos Aires y Fundarte y Monte Avila en Venezuela, que siguen difundiendo estudios críticos muy importantes (items **4285, 4290, 4294, y 4315**). Finalmente, además de congresos sobre teatro hispanoamericano que se realizan en España, Latinoamérica y los Estados Unidos, es necesario mencionar los festivales de teatro que tienen lugar en estas regiones, entre ellos el FIT de Cádiz y el FITEI de Oporto, donde se realizan foros académicos sobre las obras presentadas que conducen a importantes publicaciones.

PLAYS

4158 Ahunchain, Alvaro. Cómo se deshace un país adolescente. Montevideo: Arca, 1993. 136 p. (Colección Las tablas)

Contiene tres obras del autor. La homónima al título del libro trata de las distintas formas de presión que ejercen los adultos en un adolescente quien, a pesar de resistirse, termina doblegándose. Todos los trabajos son bien elaborados, originales y polémicos. De interés es el prólogo en que el autor reflexiona sobre su obra. [MR]

4159 Alfonso, Enrique. Obras teatrales. v. 1– 4. Santa Cruz, Bolivia: Auspiciada por la Cooperativa de Ahorro y Crédito San Martín de Porres, 1993–1994. 4 v.: ill.

Se incluyen 13 piezas costumbristas de este destacado autor y actor de Santa Cruz. De especial interés es *Cañoto* (1978), un drama histórico basado en la vida del patriota de la independencia José Manuel Baca. [MR]

4160 Alsina, Carlos María. El sueño in- móvil. La Habana: Casa de las Améri- cas, 1996. 38 p. (Teatro)

Breve drama en que, mediante el uso de elementos realistas y fantásticos y un en- treverado juego de voces y coordenadas tem- porales, se va develando un misterio. La soledad, el incesto y la negación del amor son los motivos que modulan este texto que busca una nueva forma dramática. Excelente. Véase también item **4161**. [MR]

4161 Alsina, Carlos María. Teatro completo. v. 1. Buenos Aires: Torres Agüero Edi- tor, 1996. 1 v. (Colección Telón abierto; 12)

Contiene 5 obras del autor, entre ellas *Ladran, Che*, en que dialogan Don Quijote y el Che Guevara. Otra, *El pañuelo*, es un breve monólogo de una madre que habla con su hijo desaparecido en la dictadura. La mejor es el *El sueño inmóvil*. Véase item **4160**. [MR]

4162 Amaro Sánchez, Angel and **Carlos Canales.** P*E*P*E*; Vamos a seguir bailando. San Juan: Instituto de Cultura Puertorriqueña, 1993. 119 p. (Colección de teatro; 2)

Obras de dos dramaturgos de la gen- eración de los ochenta. *Pepe* tiene como pro- tagonistas a adolescentes. La violencia de sus vidas culmina en un asesinato. *Vamos a seguir bailando* gira en torno a la explotación de una prostituta que también termina en un asesinato. Ambos autores prueban nuevas formas teatrales y comparten una preocu- pación por la realidad puertorriqueña de las últimas décadas. [MR]

4163 Andrade Rivera, Gustavo. Obra dramática. Neiva, Colombia: Instituto Huilense de Cultura, 1994. 197 p.: ill. (Colec- ción bibliográfica. Dramaturgia)

Este volumen contiene las siete obras del autor, todas de breve extensión. La mayo- ría estructura sus conflictos a partir de la vio- lencia, cuya representación se hace más vívida en aquellas piezas relacionadas direc- tamente con el entorno histórico del autor. *El propio veredicto* concluye con un final de tipo brechtiano que demanda la intervención del público. [MR]

4164 Antología de teatro cubano. v. 5. La Habana: Editorial Pueblo y Educación, 1990. 1 v.: bibl.

Se antologan seis textos escritos des- pués del triunfo de la revolución. En su mayoría se amoldan a la convención realista- costumbrista de simple estructura dramática y fluidos diálogos salpicados de humor, desti- nados a una recepción popular. En ellas se plantean conflictos creados por la tensión de lo viejo y lo nuevo, por el machismo, o la reafirmación de valores nacionales. Por su temática cabe destacar el texto de Eugenio Hernández, en que la santería es el eje estruc- tural y semántico. [MR]

4165 Antología del teatro venezolano del siglo XIX. Introducción, selección y notas de José de la Cruz Rojas U. 2a. ed. Mérida, Venezuela: Dirección de Cultura del Estado Mérida: Consejo Nacional de la Cultura, 1994. 199 p. (Solar de teatro)

La primera obra incluida en un drama histórico protagonizado por Lope de Aguirre, un expedicionario español que se convertirá en el jefe de un grupo rebelde contra la co- rona española. La segunda, es un drama cos- tumbrista sobre un médico que se enamora de la hermana de uno de sus pacientes. Tanto esta obra como la primera son obras románti- cas, con el retoricismo típico de esta conven- ción literaria. [MR]

4166 Argentine Jewish theatre: a critical an- thology. Edited and translated by Nora Glickman and Gloria F. Waldman. Lewis- burg, Pa.: Bucknell Univ. Press, 1996. 346 p.: bibl., ill.

Excelente traducción de seis obras de dramaturgos judíos argentinos que va de *Aarón the Jew* de S. Eichelbaum (1926) a *Lost belongings* de D. Raznovich (1988). En ellas aparecen temas iterativos en la literatura de la diáspora e identidad cultural. Un valioso aporte para el estudio de la dramaturgia argentina. Para el comentario de la especialista en traducción, ver item **4548**. [MR]

4167 Balboa Echeverría, Miriam. Doña Catalina: obra de teatro en dos actos. Buenos Aires: Feminaria Editora, 1996. 62 p. (Colección Literatura y crítica)

Esta obra breve es una libre recreación de un personaje histórico aunque sin subvertir la imagen estampada en la historia-leyenda. A la pieza se añade un esbozo biográfico de la legendaria chilena que la historiografía ha presentado desde una perspectiva misógina. [MR]

4168 Barrera Gutiérrez, Juan. Marujita: comedia social en tres actos. La Paz: Librería Editorial "Juventud", 1994. 107 p.: ill. (Colección de teatro)

Comedia costumbrista en que la protagonista, una humilde chola, para sorpresa de muchos, logra recibirse de abogada, rompiendo así con el estereotipo de la chola-criada. [MR]

4169 Beltzer, Julio. La rosa. Santa Fe, Argentina: Centro de Publicaciones, Univ. Nacional del Litoral, 1996. 55 p.

Drama en torno a un asesinato. El autor intercala distintas voces enunciadas en tiempos y espacios diferentes. La historia que se construye es fragmentada y difícil de armar. [MR]

4170 Bizzio, Sergio. Gravedad. Rosario, Argentina: B. Viterbo Editora, 1996. 87 p.

Excelente y original obra que presenta las peripecias de tres astronautas que deben permanecer en su nave espacial, que son visitados por un marciano y finalmente aniquilados por fuerzas terretres enemigas. [MR]

4171 Blanchet, Martín. Las señoritas de Siam. Madrid: Sociedad General de Autores de España, 1994? 74 p. (Teatro / Sociedad General de Autores de España; 48)

Obra excelente sobre hermanas siamesas que explora la situación límite de una vida obligadamente compartida y pone en evidencia lo que el autor llama "las vísceras del ser humano," típico que le hace cometer las más terribles atrocidades. [MR]

4172 Borrero, Víctor. Tres mujeres contra el mundo. Lima: El Lagarto de Oro, 1995. 67 p.

Obra centrada en la figura de Flora Tristán, una connotada mujer peruana decimonónica, a quien el autor hace dialogar con mujeres posteriores en la historia, que comparten sus ideales sociales y políticos. [MR]

4173 Briski, Norman. Teatro del actor: obras de Norman Briski. Estudio preliminar de Jorge Dubatti. Buenos Aires: Atuel, 1996. 191 p. (Colección Los argentinos)

Se plantean problemas del des-exilio, la falta de solidaridad social, la pérdida de utopías y el solopsismo que caracterizan la era postmoderna y cibernética. Briski es un destacado actor, director y dramaturgo. Sus obras se distinguen por su lenguaje simbólico, metafórico y poético. Excelentes piezas breves con interesantes propuestas escénicas. [MR]

4174 Buenaventura, Enrique. Máscaras y ficciones. Selección e introducción de Carlos Vázquez Zawadski. Cali, Colombia: Ediciones Univ. del Valle, 1992. 314 p.: bibl., ill. (Colección Autores vallecaucanos)

Contiene tres obras dramáticas del autor, una adaptación de "Tirano Banderas" de Ramón del Valle Inclán, seis ensayos sobre el teatro de Bertolt Brecht, siete canciones, nueve textos poéticos y tres cuentos. Volumen muy útil para los estudiosos del *Nuevo teatro colombiano* dirigido por el autor. Algunos de los textos son inéditos. [MR]

4175 Caicedo Estela, Andrés. Teatro. Cali, Colombia: Univ. del Valle, 1997. 152 p.

Contiene todas las obras teatrales de la autora, la mayoría escritas cuando todavía era una adolescente. Los temas se relacionan con esta etapa de vida. En ellas se observan rasgos del existencialismo y la estética absurdista. La más lograda de las obras antalogadas es *El mar*, una libre adaptación de *El cuidador* de Harold Pinter. [MR]

4176 Castillo, Abelardo. Teatro completo. Buenos Aires: Emecé Editores, 1995. 298 p. (Escritores argentinos)

El autor se inspira en personajes bíblicos o en figuras de la cultura occidental. Sin perder los rasgos esenciales de sus modelos,

620 / Handbook of Latin American Studies v. 58

los recrea libremente para conseguir una sólida estructura dramática. Una de las obras, *Israfel*, recrea la vida de Edgar Alan Poe. Excelente teatro. [MR]

4177 Castillo, Julio and **Osvaldo Facio.** Cúneo, o, La inmolación de la poesía: obras en dos actos. Mendoza, Argentina: Ediciones Culturales de Mendoza, 1995. 77 p.

Presenta el estado de alienación del hombre contemporáneo ante un mundo caótico del que trata de huir usando como arma la belleza de las palabras. La obra culmina en lo que podría ser una inmolación redentora o un simple acto de escapismo. [MR]

4178 Concurso de Teatro. Teatro, obras premiadas. Santo Domingo: Casa de Teatro, 1991. 1 v.

Se incluyen siete obras. De interés es *Por Hora y a Piece Work* de Elizabeth Ovalle, que recibió el primer premio, y que se desarrolla en una fábrica confeccionadora de ropa de Nueva York y termina con el cierre de la fábrica y la consecuente deportación de mujeres dominicanas que trabajaban allí ilegalmente. [MR]

4179 Contreras Soto, Eduardo *et al.* El rencor y otros filos. México: Univ. Autónoma del Estado de México, 1996. 220 p. (Colección La abeja en la colmena; 36)

Es una colección de siete obras en un acto, de variada calidad. En "Ganarás la vida," Contreras Soto basa su texto en la poesía de León Felipe. Fernando Martínez Monroy presenta "Los nombres de ambición," una relectura de las motivaciones de Carlos V de España para emprender las empresas de la conquista. Usando diapositivas, compara a Carlos con el Presidente George Bush y todos los líderes que tienen ambiciones imperialistas, para condenarlos. Otros textos, como "Cementerio de moscas" de Humberto Florencia y "Panteón de amores" de Jesús Angulo juegan con la frontera entre realidad y fantasía al modo de Juan Rulfo. [SC]

4180 Copi. Una visita inoportuna. Ed. del Teatro Municipal General San Martín. Buenos Aires: Teatro Municipal General San Martín, 1993. 89 p.: bibl., ill. (Colección Las obras y sus puestas; 3)

Excelente obra, un juego metateatral, paródico y farsesco. El texto se acompaña de una introducción de Osvaldo Pelletieri, un texto de Mirta Arlt sobre la puesta realizada en el Teatro San Martín de 1992 y entrevistas a la directora Maricarmen Arno y al escenógrafo Jorge Ferrari. [MR]

4181 Córdova Saavedra, Armando. Patíbulo y Calvario: drama en tres actos. La Paz: Ediciones Casa de la Cultura, Alcaldía Municipal, 1993. 103 p.: ill.

Obra trágica de contenido social sobre la violación de los derechos humanos que sufren trabajadores mineros debido a dictaduras y golpes militares. [MR]

4182 Cortázar, Julio. Adiós, Robinson y otras piezas breves. Madrid: Santillana, 1995. 170 p. (Biblioteca Cortázar)

Obras breves escritas entre la década de los 40s y 70s. Se destacan por su lenguaje poético y el uso de elementos del teatro del absurdo. La más interesante, por su vigencia, es *Adiós, Robinson*, en la que, desde una época contemporánea se reviven los personajes de la obra de Defoe. [MR]

4183 Cortés, Hernando. Estación desamparados. Lima: CONCYTEC, 1993. 68 p.

Obra realista sobre la vida urbana y rural, estructurada en tres episodios que, aunque autónomos, se unen por la presencia de personajes marginados y por su ambientación espacial en las inmediaciones de la Estación Desamparados de Lima. [MR]

4184 Cura, Mario. Teatro. v. 1–2. Buenos Aires: Ediciones Sum, 1995. 2 v.

Uno de los principales exponentes de la nueva dramaturgia argentina. Sus obras se caracterizan por su lenguaje poético y la visión de un mundo interiorizado. *Compañeros del alma* se vincula directamente con el referente histórico, la Argentina de la post-dictadura. Excelente teatro. [MR]

4185 Daneri, Alberto. Hijos de la niebla. Buenos Aires: Torres Agüero Editor, 1995. 142 p.

La acción transcurre entre 1982–85. Dos hermanos nombrados como El y Ella intentan vanamente recuperarse de los traumatizantes efectos de la dictadura y de la post-dictadura. Se registran en la obra el desencanto actual de la utopías, la entrega sin resistencia al enajenamiento de las políticas económicas neoliberales, el consumismo, la inestabilidad laboral y los bajos salarios.

Pieza bien estructurada dramáticamente. Contiene una valiosa introducción y epílogo en que el autor expresa sus ideas sobre el teatro y su propia obra. [MR]

4186 Díaz, Jorge. Antología subjetiva. Santiago: Red Internacional del Libro, 1996. 583 p.: ill.

Contiene 16 obras seleccionadas por el mismo autor en que se excluye *El Cepillo de dientes*, la más conocida de todas y que ha encasillado al autor como un discípulo de Ionesco. En esta selección el autor muestra cuán alejado está del mundo de su modelo francés y tan cerca de Latinoamérica, región en que los seres se debaten en conflictos creados por la búsqueda de su identidad y agobiados por el poder hegemónico. [MR]

4187 Díaz Vargas, Henry. La sangre más transparente. Bogotá: Colcultura, 1992. 84 p. (Premios nacionales '92. Literatura)

El conflicto se desarrolla a partir del extraño encuentro entre un padre y su hijo a quien ha abandonado al nacer. El lugar de los hechos es Medellín. En la obra se refleja la violencia que se vive en Colombia. [MR]

4188 Diego Pizarro, Casto de. Teatro desde el sur. Buenos Aires: Editorial Vinciguerra, 1992. 221 p.

Obra de gran calidad con personajes cuyas motivaciones vitales y acciones no están totalmente definidas. La violencia y ambigüedad de las situaciones dramáticas conducen a un final igualmente enigmático. [MR]

4189 Diosdado, Ana. Cristal de Bohemia. Madrid: Sociedad General de Autores y Editores, 1996. 90 p. (Teatro; 69)

Obra de estilo farsesco muy bien escrita. Después de varios años, antiguos personajes de un elegante lenocinio se encuentran en la casa donde habían trabajado por muchos años. Todo ha sido planeado por el hijo de un aristócrata y la *madame* que quiere encontrar a sus padres y vengarse de ellos. [MR]

4190 Domínguez, Franklin. Obras premiadas. Santo Domingo: Biblioteca Nacional, 1993. 313 p. (Colección Orfeo. 2da. etapa. Serie Teatro; no. 2)

Recoge una selección de la obras del autor en que destacan *Lisístrata Odia la*

Política, estrenada en 1968, basada en la comedia de Aristófanes y *El primer voluntario de Junio*, sobre los movimientos guerrilleros de resistencia durante la dictadura de Trujillos y que está basada en la obra *Inmolación* de Juan Enrique Puigsubirá-Miniño. [MR]

4191 Dorfman, Ariel. La muerte y la doncella. Buenos Aires: Ediciones de la Flor, 1992. 100 p. (Teatro / Ariel Dorfman; 1)

Una mujer flagelada durante una dictadura se encuentra insólitamente con su torturador. Olvidar el pasado y perdonar a los verdugos o someterlos a un merecido castigo es la disyuntiva que plantea la obra. Excelente. [MR]

4192 Dubatti, Jorge. Así se mira el teatro de hoy: selección de obras de Mario Cura, Javier Daulte y Marcelo Ramos. Buenos Aires: Beas Ediciones, 1994. 212 p.: bibl., ill. (Colección Así se hace—)

Las tres obras de diferente concepción dramática son una muestra de la nueva dramaturgia argentina. *Tres mañanas* de Cura, con su simbolismo y complejos personajes difiere cualquier interpretación definitiva, en tanto que en *Obito* de Dualde, más contextualizada, relaciona metafóricamente los mecanismos del crimen con la dictadura. El tono ligero de la obra de Ramos *Salven al cómico*, no impide que trate problemas de candente actualidad. Prólogo y obras de gran calidad. [MR]

4193 Duque Mesa, Fernando. Antología del teatro experimental en Bogotá. v. 1. Bogotá: Instituto Distrital de Cultura y Turismo, 1995. 1 v.: bibl.

Contiene una larga introducción de Duque Mesa sobre las distintas corrientes del teatro colombiano desde los setenta en adelante. Aunque informativa no alcanza un rigor académico. La segunda parte contiene textos de autores como Santiago García, Carlos José Reyes y varios de Duque Mesa. [MR]

4194 Enríquez Gamón, Efraín. Francia, un hombre interminable. Asunción: El Lector, 1994. 138 p.: bibl.

Drama histórico de carácter biográfico sobre la vida y gobierno dictatorial de José Gaspar Rodríguez de Francia, conocido simplemente como Doctor Francia, quien gobernó Paraguay desde su independencia por 27 años. [MR]

4195 Ferrari, Carlos. El insólito caso de Miss Piña Colada; La nena se casa. Puerto Rico: Editorial Cultural, 1994. 242 p.

Includes the title play plus "La nena se casa: comedia cruel en dos actos," both of which show the extremes—economic ruin and death—to which Puerto Rican families will go in order to maintain their status in upper-class society. Well-timed scenes and clever dialogue provide a humorous, but sobering, vision of contemporary socioeconomic realities in Puerto Rico. [SC]

4196 Ferreira, Ramón. Teatro: donde está la luz; Un color para este miedo; El hombre inmaculado; El mar de cada día. Miami, Fla.: Ediciones Universal, 1993. 223 p.: ill. (Colección Teatro)

Estas obras fueron escritas entre 1952–59. En ellos son tratados temas como la discriminación racial e historias de familias de pescadores. *El hombre inmaculado* es considerada por la crítica como la mejor por su simbología y la cuidada caracterización de los personajes. Tiene como referente la dictadura de Fulgencio Batista. [MR]

4197 Freire, Susana. Teatro completo. v. 1. Buenos Aires: Torres Agüero Editor, 1995. 1 v. (Colección Telón abierto; 10)

Contiene cinco obras cuyos protagonistas son seres marginados, víctimas de una situación económica, política y social, que se mueven en espacios lúgubres y claustrofóbicos, siempre con el miedo de ser heridos o castigados. La mejor lograda de las obras es *Punto inicial.* [MR]

4198 García Alonso, Jorge. Teatro. Buenos Aires: Libros de Tierra Firme, 1994. 206 p. (Colección de teatro Babilonia; 2)

Incluye cinco obras, todas excelentes. En las más recientes *Al amigo más fiel* (1994) y *Rifar el corazón* (1993), se estudian con un cierto humor las relaciones humanas en que ambiguamente se confunden delirio y razón, poder y sumisión. [MR]

4199 Gavlovski E., Johnny. Ruido de piedras: teatro. Caracas: Pomaire, 1995. 43 p. (Colección Escena viva)

La obra tiene como tema central la represión fascista que asoló Europa y que posteriormente se reflejó en las dictaduras de países latinoamericanos, especialmente en los del cono sur, en las décadas de los 70s y 80s. [MR]

4200 Gené, Juan Carlos. Teatro. v. 1. Buenos Aires: Ediciones de la Flor, 1994. 1 v.: bibl.

De especial interés son *Golpes a mi puerta,* en que una monja prefiere el martirio en vez de renunciar al papel social y apostólico de la Iglesia Popular Latinoamericana y *Memorial del cordero asesinado,* que muestra las circunstancias ominosas que llevaron a la muerte de García Lorca. *Ulf* tiene como protagonista a dos ancianos cirqueros, quienes rememoran un pasado que sus frágiles mentes sólo recuperan fragmentariamente. [MR]

4201 Giani, Camilo A. Cacho: drama en tres actos, 1980–1995. Buenos Aires: Corregidor, 1996. 60 p. (Teatro)

Drama psicológico-social de una familia en que un joven es el primer miembro en recibir un título universitario desde que inmigraran a la Argentina sus abuelos, pero que por las condiciones económicas del país, puede verse obligado a emigrar a Australia y repetir la historia de sus ancestros. [MR]

4202 Godínez, Jorge. Qué lindo ser feo: tres comedias. Guatemala: Editorial Oscar de León Palacios, 1993. 219 p.

Three plays explore the search for a meaningful existence in the face of contemporary social injustice and life's misfortunes. "Electro Show," set in a mental hospital, examines our responsibility for our own behavior and the impossibility of erasing the world's evils. "Concierto a dos bocas" deals with the artist's existential dilemma: to pursue fame or to be faithful to one's moral and ethical principles. "La consiga" explores the vice of alcoholism. Dialogue contains numerous Guatemalan idiomatic expressions, which are explained in a glossary at the end of the play. [SC]

4203 Gorostiza, Carlos. Teatro. v. 3. Buenos Aires: Ediciones de la Flor, 1996. 1 v.

Se incluyen cinco de las primeras obras del autor, escritas entre 1949–68. Entre las más conocidas figuran *Los prójimos, El pan de la locura* y *El Puente.* Se manifiesta en ella una tendencia que dominará en sus obras posteriores: su preocupación por problemas sociales, económicos y políticos de la Argentina, que representa, sin ambages, transparentando su compromiso político. Teatro ejemplar. [MR]

4204 Guerra, Ibrahim. A 2.50 la Cuba libre: vivencias, angustias y finales de cinco mesoneras; La última noche de Fedora; Fedora, la Vampira, en la casa de Dios. Venezuela: Compañía Nacional de Investigación Teatral, 1992. 90 p. (Teatro hiperrealista)

En ambas obras, la especial configuración del espacio teatral del autor/director, reúne a actores y espectadores compartiendo el mismo lugar. En la primera obra en un bar y, en la segunda, en un *night club* de mala muerte en donde se juntan seres marginados, mujeres y trasvestíes, cuyo crudo lenguaje e inevitable cercanía crean un extraño ambiente. Excelentes obras. [MR]

4205 Guerrero Risco, Héctor. Qori Ocllo: drama histórico en cinco actos; Cosco-Yúcay, Perú, 1539. Lima: Distribuye, Jr. Pachitea, 1994. 128 p.: ill.

La obra transcurre en tiempos de Francisco Pizarro. En ella se reivindica la figura de la reina *Qori Ocllo*, la esposa principal de *Maco Inca*, apenas citada por la historia. Obra de interés histórico y antropológico. Los densos y largos diálogos se entremezclan con canciones andinas. [MR]

4206 Guglielmino, Osvaldo. Teatro. Buenos Aires: Corregidor, 1995. 143 p.

La labor social de Eva Perón, la construcción al comienzo del siglo XX de un tren transandino que unirá la Patagonia chileno-argentina y las circunstancias políticas y sociales que motivaron la Guerra de las Malvinas son los tres temas que se desarrollan respectivamente en las obras que componen este volumen. [MR]

4207 Halley Mora, Mario. Teatro breve para uso didáctico en la iniciación teatral. Selección e introducción de Rudi Torga. Asunción: El Lector, 1996. 179 p.: ill. (Colección Teatro; 3)

Comedias y dramas escritos en un estilo realista e inspirados en la vida cotidiana del Paraguay. [MR]

4208 Hermosillo, Jaime Humberto and **Arturo Villaseñor.** Intimidades en un cuarto de baño: guión cinematográfico; Encuentro inesperado: guión cinematográfico. Xalapa, Mexico: Univ. Veracruzana, 1992. 60, 81 p.: ill. (Ficción)

Contiene dos guiones cinematográficos: "Intimidades en un cuarto de baño" y "Encuentro inesperado." La acción del primero tiene lugar en un cuarto de baño, en el cual entran todos los personajes y delatan allí aspectos malogrados de su vida, el simbolismo del cuarto de baño es múltiple. "Encuentro inesperado" refiere a la llegada de una joven misteriosa a la casa de la estrella de cine, Pilar Landeros. [SC]

4209 Ibáñez, Roberto. Teatro completo. v. 1. Buenos Aires: Torres Agüero Editor, 1995. 1 v. (Colección Telón abierto; 8)

Contiene cinco obras que fluctúan entre el realismo, el grotesco y el absurdismo y que, en un lenguaje directo, plantean situaciones circunstanciales e interiores del hombre contemporáneo. Entre los temas tratados figuran rupturas generacionales, el conformismo e inadaptación social y la contaminación ambiental. [MR]

4210 Kaufmann, Jacobo. Carvajal: el testamento de Joseph Lumbroso. Buenos Aires: Corregidor, 1994. 93 p.: bibl.

Drama histórico que relata la vida de Luis de Carvajal, El Mozo, autodenominado Joseph Lumb Roso y en que se revela el proceso inquisitorial a que es sometido, que finalmente lo lleva a la hoguera. Entre las voces individuales de los agentes principales de la acción se intercalan coros que relatan o comentan los hechos acontecidos. [MR]

4211 Korz, Sergio. Como los dioses. Buenos Aires: Editorial Eiffel, 1996. 124 p.

Obra en dos actos, de carácter filosófico, desafiante e irreverente. El autor, en una inversión de lo conocido, presenta a Dios como un ser degradado, hecho a imagen y semejanza del hombre, arrepentido de haberle dado a éste el libre albedrío. [MR]

4212 Larriera, Teófilo. El gran teatro y mi pequeña vida. Buenos Aires: Ediciones Extimas, 1992. 218 p.: bibl., ill. (some col.).

Además de dos obras de teatro, *Sí mi Coronel* y *El Caralisa*, el volumen contiene textos poéticos y viñetas autobiográficas del autor que reconstruyen momentos de su vida en que expresa su visión personal sobre la historia del teatro argentino. *Sí mi Coronel* fue escrita después de la muerte del Che Guevara e incursiona sobre la realidad política latinoamericana de entonces. [MR]

4213 Leñero, Vicente. Los perdedores: siete obras breves de temas deportivos. Introducción de Juan Villoro. México: Ediciones El Milagro: Consejo Nacional para la Cultura y las Artes, 1996. 119 p.: ill. (Teatro)

Como indica el título, el gran maestro del teatro documental, reúne en esta edición obras que reflejan lo lúdico de la vida urbana por medio de imágenes deportivas; una de las más destacadas es "Pelearán diez rounds," que imagina la vida matirmonial como una pelea de box. [SC]

4214 Magrini, César. 1841: drama histórico en 9 cuadros; Yo, Victoria: ensayo de unipersonal. Buenos Aires: Ediciones Braga, 1993. 175 p. (Nalidra en Acuario)

La acción de la primera obra sucede durante el gobierno de Juan Manuel de Rosas. El conflicto se estructura adoptando como eje semántico los mitos griegos de Edipo y Electra. La segunda es un unipersonal que presenta, en 19 escenas distintas, facetas de la vida personal, social, intelectual de la conocida escritora argentina Victoria Ocampo. [MR]

4215 María, César de. Teatro. Lima: Lluvia Editores, 1995. 177 p.

Contiene tres dramas. Sus personajes son del mundo de los marginados: payasos pobres, locos, ciegos, ancianas que se debaten en un mundo hostil amenazados por fuerzas externas, pero también por la maldad o la locura que habita en ellos mismos. De las tres obras, todas de superior calidad, *Escorpiones mirando al cielo* es tal vez la mejor lograda, un grupo de ancianas dementes, de diferentes procedencias, comparten una vieja mansión donde mueren en un acto de autodestrucción. [MR]

4216 Masciángioli, Jorge. Sagrario y la tierra hechizada: oratorio trágico; tres actos y siete cuadros. Buenos Aires: Grupo Editor Latinoamericano: Distribuidor exclusivo, Emecé Editores, 1993. 121 p.: bibl. (Colección Escritura de hoy)

Obra bien escrita. Plantea el problema típico del terrateniente latinoamericano que convive, además de con su esposa legítima, con otras mujeres campesinas que trabajan en su hacienda. El planteamiento del autor sobre esta situación, aunque focalizado en la perspectiva las afectadas, es muy controversial. [MR]

4217 Matas, Julio. Juegos y rejuegos: teatro. Miami, FL: Ediciones Universal, 1992. 96 p. (Colección Teatro)

Contiene seis obras que, aunque breves, crean situaciones de gran suspenso con hechos extraños o imprevistos que determinan o modifican la conducta de los personajes y llevan ya a previsibles o a ambiguos desenlaces. Se destacan en la colección, *El cambio, Juego de damas* y *Así se conquistó el mundo.* [MR]

4218 Medina, Roberto Nicolás. Teatro. v. 1–2. Buenos Aires: Torres Agüero Editor, 1994–1995. 2 v. (Colección Telón abierto; 3, 9)

Se compendian siete obras. En ellas el autor utiliza la sátira, la parodia, el melodrama y el grotesco para demontar mitos y arraigadas ideologías. Entre ellas se distingue *Una sombra en el pajonal*, en que se usan técnicas brechtianas y paródicamente se reconstruyen episodios de radioteatro gauchesco y *Los generales mueren de aburrimiento*, cuya crítica al militarismo se hace a partir del anquilosado discurso de un general anacrónico que revive el ideal de civilización sarmentino. [MR]

4219 Méndez Ballester, Manuel. Las turbias aguas del pasado: tragedia política puertorriqueña en cuatro actos. San Juan: First Publishing of Puerto Rico, 1994. 96 p.

Una reflexión sobre la historia de Puerto Rico y el estado de su dependencia colonial. El protagonista, un rebelde independentista, es acribillado en Nueva York por la policía federal de los Estados Unidos. [MR]

4220 Meza Wevar, Gustavo. Murmuraciones acerca de la muerte de un juez y dos murmuraciones más. Santiago: LOM Ediciones, 1995. 184 p. (Colección Entre mares)

Contiene tres obras, todas de excelente calidad. La mejor lograda es *Cartas de Jenny*, cuya tensión psicológica se desarrolla en torno a una madre posesiva que intenta, tenazmente, evitar separarse de su hijo. [MR]

4221 Mier Rivas, Adolfo. Rutuchi. La Paz: Librería Editorial "Juventud," 1992. 78 p.

Drama costumbrista que presenta la vida un joven indígena que se ve envuelto en el narcotráfico. Se plantea el profundo significado religioso-cultural del suceso. [MR]

4222 Molina, Silvia. Circuito cerrado. México: Coordinación de Difusión Cultural, Dirección de Literatura/UNAM, 1995.

67 p. (Textos de difusión cultural. Serie La carpa)

Con gran destreza, Molina estudia la psicología de una familia mexicana marcada por muchos problemas graves, entre otros, abusos sexuales, incluyendo una relación incestuosa. Es una obra seria, sensitiva, que se aprovecha de una imagen dramática innovadora al usar la televisión para reproducir los eventos ocultos que pasan y para comentar la mirada "patriarcal" que afecta las relaciones familiares. [SC]

4223 Monteforte Toledo, Mario. Los gringos. Guatemala: s.n., 1994. 49 p.

Although set on a Guatemalan banana plantation during the late 1950s-early 1960s, the play has present-day implications in its treatment of US involvement in Guatemalan politics, and the different responses by US and Guatemalan citizens to the US-backed overthrow of the government. [SC]

4224 Monti, Ricardo. Teatro. v. 1. Buenos Aires: Corregidor, 1995. 1 v.: bibl. (Colección Dramaturgos argentinos contemporáneos; 8)

En las tres obras de la selección, el autor emplea un lenguaje alusivo y ambiguo en que el mito, el símbolo, la metáfora y la alegoría son recursos fundamentales para una revisión/recuento de la historia argentina. La densidad y complejidad de los textos, las técnicas dramáticas empleadas y la ambigüedad de planteamientos requieren de un lector/espectador instruido capaz de descodificar los signos culturales y teatrales desplegados. Excelente teatro. [MR]

4225 Moreno, Xiomara. Perlita blanca como sortija de señorita; Geranio; Manivela: teatro. Caracas: Fundarte, Alcaldía de Caracas, 1992. 131 p. (Cuadernos de difusión; no. 180)

Tres obras en un acto. La autora profundiza en la psicología de los personajes para mostrar sus frustraciones y lo absurdo de su existencia, Sin imponer patrones éticos, deja que los personajes se expresen en su propia ambigüedad y confusión. [MR]

4226 Moreno, Xiomara. Ultimo piso en Babilonia. Caracas: Fundarte Alcaldía de Caracas, 1995. 41 p. (Colección Cuadernos de Difusión; no. 228)

Original obra cuyos protagonistas son seres marginados, una prostituta, una artista de cabaret y una lesbiana, que fortuitamente convergen en un piso derruido y abandonado. Cada personaje, en una especie de autoconfesión, relata sus perversiones y miserias. [MR]

4227 Muñoz, Fernando. Soy Jasón, tengo 28 años; Las niñas grandes no lloran y otras obras de teatro. Mexico: Gobierno del Estado de Yucatán, Instituto de Cultura de Yucatán, 1993. 150 p.

Incluye "Soy Jasón, tengo 28 años," "Las niñas grandes no lloran," "Viví sin conocerte, puedo vivir sin ti;" "Tríptico minihistórico: La función debe comenzar, Terapia ocupacional, Kiki de Montparnasse." Estas obras recrean la vida de las clases adineradas mexicanas e incluyen muchos motivos típicos tanto de la cultura popular como del mundo literario. "Las niñas grandes no lloran" recuerda el tercer acto de "El eterno femenino" en su presentación de un grupo de amigas de la clase alta mexicana y cómo enfrentan los problemas sociales contemporáneos, como el SIDA, el divorcio y el lesbianismo, entre otros. [SC]

4228 Navajas Cortés, Esteban. Fantasmas de amor que rondaron el veintiocho: obra dramática escrita en trece jornadas. Bogotá: Colcultura, 1995. 88 p. (Premios nacionales de cultura, 1994)

Obra en torno al movimiento obrero ocurrido en las plantaciones bananeras colombianas en 1928. La acción obrera es seguida desde el recinto de una casa de baile. De especial interés es la caracterización interior de los personajes. [MR]

4229 La nueva dramaturgia mexicana. Selección e introducción de Vicente Leñero. México: Ediciones El Milagro: Consejo Nacional para la Cultura y las Artes, 1996. 597 p.: ill. (Nuestro teatro)

La introducción de Leñero es muy valiosa y aporta mucha información sobre el trabajo general de cada uno de los nueve dramaturgos y la trayectoria de sus carreras. Incluye obras de Víctor Hugo Rascón Banda (Playa azul), Jesús González Dávila (Crónica de un desayuno); Leonor Azcárate (Trabajo sucio), Tomás Urtusástegui (Cupo limitado), Sabina Berman (Muerte súbita), Miguel Angel Tenorio (Travesía guadalupana), Oscar Liera, (El jinete de la Divina Providencia), Guillermo Schmidhuber (Por las tierras de

Colón), y Gerardo Velásquez (Los heraldos negros). [SC]

4230 Omar, Blanca. Teatro. v. 1. Buenos Aires: Ediciones Amaru, 1995. 1 v.: ill.
Obras breves en que sobresale *Alfonsina*, un drama unipersonal de 11 cuadros que recrea libremente la vida de la poeta argentina. La autora maneja hábilmente el monólogo teatral en un bien logrado lenguaje poético. [MR]

4231 Orgambide, Pedro G. Don Fausto: teatro. Buenos Aires: Asociación Amigos del Complejo Teatral Enrique Santos Discépolo: Secretaría de Cultura de la Municipalidad de la Ciudad de Buenos Aires, 1995. 52 p.: ill.
Obra ligera, en un acto, que revive la leyenda de Fausto en un ambiente campesino, en que un viejo rico negocia su alma con el diablo para lograr seducir a una muchacha. Se acompaña de canciones de estilo folklórico argentino. [MR]

4232 Oteiza, Alberto M. Luz roja: pieza teatral en ocho cuadros. Argentina: Ediciones Olimpo, 1994. 133 p.: ill.
Obra cuyo protagonista es el ejecutivo de una empresa multinacional que es víctima del propio presidente de dicha empresa. La acción transcurre a fines de los setenta, años de gran tensión política y económica en la Argentina. La honestidad del personaje principal no puede sobreponerse a la corrupción reinante que lo impelen al crimen y eventualmente a su muerte. [MR]

4233 Pais, Carlos. Teatro completo. v. 1. Buenos Aires: Torres Agüero Editor, 1992. 1 v. (Colección "Telón abierto"; v. 2)
Se compendian cuatro de las mejores obras del dramaturgo. Aunque estrechamente relacionadas con su contexto social, su concepción surrealista hace que trascienda la mímesis referencial. La cosificación del ser humano, su deseo de evasión y el miedo al acosamiento político, social y existencial son temas que el autor universaliza a partir de la realidad argentina. [MR]

4234 Parra, Marco Antonio de la and **José Urbistondo.** Tristán & Isolda: bolero estático. Et in toxico ego. Valladolid: Caja España, 1994? 79 p.: ill.
En la primera obra se usa como correlato el mito clásico; dos antiguos amantes se encuentran en un bar para recordar sus relaciones íntimas que no pueden borrar de su memoria. La segunda se desarrolla en un hospicio de locos, donde las acciones demenciales son peores en los que cuidan a los pacientes. [MR]

4235 Patarca M., Amanda. Teatro completo. v. 1. Buenos Aires: Torres Agüero, 1996. 1 v. (Colección Telón abierto; 11)
Uno de los temas recurrente es el desamor que se manifiesta a distintos niveles en relaciones familiares y sociales. Dos ejemplos son el hijo adoptivo que se lanza contra los padres que lo han "comprado" y contra la madre que lo ha abandonado; y la soledad en que muere una anciana en un hospital mientras su hija atiende sus asuntos de negocio. Excelente teatro, profundo en sus personajes, su lenguaje y construcción dramática. [MR]

4236 Peña, Edilio. Regalo de Van Gogh; Los amantes de Sara; Ese espacio peligroso. Caracas: Monte Avila Editores, 1991. 93 p. (Colección Teatro)
Las tres obras reflejan el talento del autor, uno de los más destacados de Venezuela. En ellas se plantean atrevidas situaciones dramáticas determinadas por motivaciones sexuales. La última, de composición absurdista, presenta el desgaste vital de una pareja. [MR]

4237 Peña Castellón, José. Obras teatrales costumbristas de los valles cruceños. Organización y publicación de Javier Rivas Osinaga. Santa Cruz, Bolivia: J. Rivas Osinaga, 199-. 103 p.: ill.
Contiene cuatro obras cuya acción está situada en la región oriental de Bolivia. En un tono cómico y didáctico, el autor registra las costumbres y sociolectos típicos del lugar. Además de alusiones a las costumbres, hay referencias al gobierno y su política en relación a las provincias del país. [MR]

4238 Peredo, Néstor. Boquerón, o, "La gran batalla." La Paz: Librería Editorial "Juventud," 1996. 148 p. (Colección de teatro)
Drama histórico-realista que relata la defensa y posterior rendimiento del Fortín Boquerón, que tuvo lugar en 1932 durante la guerra entre Bolivia y Paraguay, conocida como la Guerra del Chaco. [MR]

4239 Peredo, Néstor. Illimani: comedia en un acto dividido en tres cuadros. La Paz: Librería Editorial "Juventud," 1994. 87 p.

Una adaptación del cuento homónimo de Marcelo Cárdenas Rodríguez. Obra de simple estructura realista que tiene como asunto central el reencuentro de un hombre con su hija y su mujer. Plantea, aunque tangencialmente, preocupaciones ecológicas. [MR]

4240 Peredo, Néstor. Los repiques de Santo Domingo: relato tradicional recogido por Manuel María Lara. El gesto: cuento homónimo de Gastón Suárez. La Paz: Librería Editorial "Juventud," 1994. 76 p. (Colección de teatro)

Obras breves de sencillo argumento. La primera tiene como protagonista a un hacendado rico que, por su afan de notoriedad, pierde sus bienes que pasan a manos de los dominicos. [MR]

4241 Pérez-Barrón, Rafael. Teatro breve. Tijuana, Mexico: Taller Teatral Aristófanes, 1994. 375 p.: appendices, bibl., ill. (Colección Diez años, 1983–1993)

El fundador del taller teatral Aristófanes de Baja California ofrece una colección de sus piezas de un acto, de naturaleza didáctica la mayoría, con temas variados: del papel histórico de Flores Magón, avisos en contra del fumar, textos ecológicos, etc. Pérez-Barrón es también actor, director y maestro, así es que añade unos apéndices que incluyen un resumen de la historia del teatro y los varios géneros teatrales, se método stanislavski, los pasos básicos de director de escena y una bibliografía. [SC]

4242 Petre, Juan Carlos de. El teatro desconocido. Maracaibo, Venezuela: Univ. del Zulia, Dirección de Cultura, Catedra Libre "Teatro Latinoamericano y del Caribe", 1996. 111 p.: bibl., ill. (Colección YanamA)

Conjunto de ensayos en que el autor, avalado por una experiencia de treinta años, se refiere a los aspectos más importantes que inciden en el proceso o creación de una puesta en escena. Desde 1976, Petre es director y creador de TEATRO ALTOSF. [MR]

4243 Piñera, Virgilio. Teatro inédito. La Habana: Editorial Letras Cubanas, 1993. 193 p.

Este volumen recoge cinco obras inéditas que fueron escritas en las décadas del 60 y 70: *El no, La niñita querida, Una caja de zapatos vacía, Nacimiento de palabras* y *El trac.* Muestra la gran capacidad de Piñera de crear dramas alegóricos que refieren a la vez a la política cubana y a la existencia absurda del ser humano contemporáneo. *El no* y *Una caja de zapatos vacía* en particular llaman mucho la atención. [SC]

4244 Plá, Josefina. Teatro escogido. v. 1. Asunción: El Lector, 1996. 1 v.: bibl. (Col. Teatro; 2)

Contiene seis obras, casi todas de carácter realista-naturalista. En algunas se destaca el personaje femenino, cuya caracterización anticipa la imagen de mujer emancipada de los movimientos feministas. La obra mejor lograda de la colección es *Alcestes,* basada en la tragedia de Eurípides del mismo nombre. [MR]

4245 Prieto, Ricardo. La buena vida. Montevideo: Arca, 1994. 148 p. (Colección Las tablas)

Además de la piezas que titula el volumen incluye *Se alquila.* Ambas obras de un acto presentan a familias de la clase media de Montevideo luchando por sobreponerse a sus precarias condiciones, aun recurriendo a situaciones extremas, como la prostitución. [MR]

4246 Puig, Manuel. La tajada; Gardel, uma lembrança. Rosario, Argentina: Beatriz Viterbo Editora, 1998. 222 p. (Ficciones)

El primer texto es un guión de cine escrito en 1960; se trata de un melodrama basado en la vida de una actriz (cuya figura evoca a Eva Perón) que apasionadamente intenta socavar y subvertir el orden patriarcal. El segundo, uno de las últimos del autor, también melodramático, se ambienta en el Buenos Aires de 1915, y relata la relación de Gardel con prostitutas polacas. [MR]

4247 Rascón Banda, Víctor Hugo. Contrabando. México: Ediciones El Milagro, 1993. 79 p.: ill. (Teatro)

Este drama experimental recrea unos eventos de Santa Rosa, pequeño pueblo fronterizo invadido por el narcotráfico. Un escritor, llamado Víctor Banda, sólo se asemeja al dramaturgo en su ambigüedad: puede ser o no un poeta de regreso a su pueblo; es o no es un agente. Sirve de testigo para que tres mujeres cuenten sus historias, en largos monólogos que exponen su carácter a la vista de todos. [SC]

4248 Relatos de historia en tu imaginación.
v. 2. Querétaro, Mexico: H. Ayuntamiento de Querétaro, Coordinación de Publicaciones, 1994. 1 v.

Consiste en una serie de escenas que dramatizan la historia, costumbres y leyendas de Querétaro y que se desarrollan en "Las Posadas," "El día de muertos, la leyenda de Chucho el Roto," "Don Félix Osores." Los personajes incluyen un grupo de jóvenes cuyo guía en estas lecciones históricas es Mario, descrito como un muerto que sigue hablando con los jóvenes. [SC]

4249 Reyes, Carlos José. El carnaval de la muerte alegre: periplo de Balboa y Pedrarias. Bogotá: Panamericana Editorial, 1996. 173 p.: ill.

Drama histórico sobre la fundación de Santa María la Antigua del Darién protagonizado por Vasco Núñez de Balboa. Los hechos históricos metateatralmente se confunden con una fiesta de carnaval. Consta de 26 episodios en que el primero y el último enmarcan los hechos pasados. [MR]

4250 Rivarola Matto, Juan Bautista. El niño santo; Vidas y muerte de Chirito Aldama. Asunción: Arandurã Editorial, 1994. 146 p.: ill. (Arandurã teatro)

Obras de corte realista. La primera se sitúa en el siglo pasado durante la guerra paraguayo-brasileña y posteriormente contra la Alianza, con el protagonismo de Carlos Antonio López; es presentada desde la perspectiva de mujeres que padecen los efectos de la guerra. La segunda obra es de carácter mítico, con la muerte y el diablo como las figuras principales. [MR]

4251 Rivera Saavedra, Juan. Las armas de Dios; El paraíso encontrado. Lima: Auspicia CONCYTEC, 1990. 66 p.: ill. (Ediciones Pegaso. Teatro)

En *Las armas de Dios*, la naturaleza castiga al hombre. En *El paraíso encontrado*, una variación del mito del Edén, es el hombre quien tienta a otro y el espacio de las acciones es una ciudad convulsionada por la violencia. [MR]

4252 Rodríguez Fernández, Arturo. Dramas y comedias en ocho obras teatrales. Santo Domingo: Banco de Reservas de la

República Dominicana, 1996. 371 p.: ill. (Colección Banreservas. Serie Literatura; v. 3)

Se recoje en esta excelente edición lo mejor de la producción de las obras del autor nacido en 1948. Obras muy amenas y de pulida construcción dramática. Se destacan entre ellas *El viaje chino* y *Todos menos Elizabeth.* Ésta, aunque contiene elementos absurdistas, trata con humor el enigma detectivesco haciendo más grata su recepción. [MR]

4253 Rodríguez Muñoz, Alberto. Teatro. Buenos Aires: Ediciones Corregidor, 1994. 95 p.

Contiene tres obras del autor. La mejor lograda es *El canto de la vida,* cuyos personajes, para dar plenitud a su existencia, trascienden la realidad. [MR]

4254 Rodríguez Silva, Isidro. Las muñecas tambien se mueren: obras para teatro. Managua: Nueva Nicaragua, 1996. 79 p.: ill.

A collection of two one-act plays and a monologue focusing on the decadence of contemporary Nicaragua. The title play, containing meta-theatrical elements, deals with the violent psychological impact of social unrest on the younger generation. "Toda mujer feliz se suicida por la tarde" explores a mother/daughter relationship and the impossibility of forgetting past memories. In "A la sombra de una luz oscura" a woman uses her imagination to reveal herself at different ages, and finally chooses insanity to escape a reality that is too cruel. [SC]

4255 Rovner, Eduardo. Teatro. v. 2. Buenos Aires: Ediciones de la Flor, 1996. 1 v.

El volumen incluye las primeras obras del autor. En un lenguaje en que se combina el realismo, la metáfora y la estética del teatro del absurdo, el autor desarrolla conflictos de relaciones de poder que logra plasmar en impactantes imágenes. En esta obra se anticipan la sátira social y el humor que caracterizarán sus obras posteriores. Las piezas breves son particularmente apropiadas para estudiantes de teatro. [MR]

4256 Rovner, Eduardo. Tinieblas de un escritor enamorado. Bogotá: Colcultura, 1995. 61 p. (Gestus. Separata dramatúrgica)

Entre las obras del autor, ésta es una de las mejores. Un hombre viaja al más allá en busca de su amada. Este motivo argumental básico se entronca con los orígenes de la imaginería occidental, con el mito griego de

Orfeo y Eurídice, por ejemplo. Pero si bien hay una intertextualidad lejana, el lenguaje metafórico y polisémico alude igualmente a momentos recientes de la historia argentina. [MR]

4257 Rueda, Manuel. La trinitaria blanca: teatro. 2. ed. Dominican Republic: Librería La Trinitaria, 1992. 119 p.

La trama gira en torno a los prejuicios familiares y sociales de una mujer. Obra realista con un desarrollo profundo de los personajes y una acción dramática bien diseñada. [MR]

4258 Ruíz Ortíz, Ernesto. El juego de la verdad. San Juan: Editorial Asombro, 1995. 226 p.

Obra de más de 200 p. centrada en un trágico incidente protagonizado por dos parejas. En vez de acotaciones escénicas hay un narrador, que como el omnisciente de una novela, constantemente suspende la acción para comentar los actos y pensamientos de los personajes. [MR]

4259 Santana, Rodolfo. Nunca entregues tu corazón a una muñeca sueca y otras obras de teatro. Caracas: FUNDARTE/Alcaldía de Caracas, 1996. 305 p. (Colección Delta; no. 41)

Contiene cinco obras muy bien estructuradas dramáticamente, en que el autor, en un teatro de carácter filosófico más que de denuncia, presenta situaciones típicas de la vida contemporánea latinoamericana, en que nuevas prácticas económicas, el derrumbe de orientaciones ideológicas y la esquizofrenia de un mundo fragmentado están aniquilando los valores humanos y solidarios. En *Obra para dormir a un público*, Santana tematiza el proceso teatral mismo, que, de no cambiar, puede convertirse en lo que sugiere el título. [MR]

4260 Sarlós, Eduardo. La x con una pata rota. Montevideo: Arca, 1993. 128 p.: ill. (Colección Las tablas)

El volumen tiene dos obras, la que titula el libro y *Mujeres en el armario*. La primera consta de cinco escenas y la segunda de un acto. La primera está centrada en la especial relación entre un travesti y una anciana judía, setentona que habla con acento iddisch. En la segunda, dos hermanas, de mediana edad que han tenido vidas diferentes, se revelan desconocidos momentos de su vida. [MR]

4261 Schön, Elizabeth et al. Las Risas de nuestras medusas: teatro venezolano escrito por mujeres. Selección y estudio preliminar de Susana Castillo. Caracas: Fundarte, Alcaldía de Caracas, 1992. 119 p. (Cuadernos de difusión; no. 184)

Antología de obras breves de cuatro dramaturgas venezolanas, Shön, Elisa Lerner, Mariela Romero y Lidia Febrijen en que se proyecta una nueva imagen de mujer y se revisan roles sociales y culturales. Contiene estudios sobre la importancia del teatro feminista venezolano contemporáneo. [MR]

4262 Serrano, Carlos Luis. Teatro: Diana Durbin se equivoca, Raquel Liberman—una historia de Pichincha, Varieteblue. Rosario, Argentina: Editorial Fundación Ross, 1992. 214 p.

Excelentes obras del autor de Rosario, Argentina. El melodrama, el kitsch, la historia y el metateatro son los principales recursos dramáticos empleados por el autor. Mención especial merece *Raquel Liberman*, que se sitúa en los años 1920s y en donde desde una historia personal se describe la vida prostibularia de la época. [MR]

4263 Tapia y Rivera, Alejandro. La cuarterona: drama original en tres actos. San Juan: Instituto de Cultura Puertorriqueña: Editorial de la Univ. de Puerto Rico, 1993. 146 p.: bibl. (Colección puertorriqueña; 5)

Obra decimonónica romántico-realista que tiene como motivo estructurante el amor funesto concretado, en este caso, en el lazo sanguíneo y la discriminación racial. [MR]

4264 Teatro. San Juan: Instituto de Cultura Puertorriqueña, Programa de Publicaciones y Grabaciones, 1992. 167 p. (Colección de teatro; 1)

La obra de Ramos-Perea se sitúa a fines del siglo XIX antes de la invasión norteamericana. Presenta el ambiente teatral de la época en que se vivía un romanticismo peninsular pasatista, el cual contrastaba con las ideas anarquistas que llegaban a Puerto Rico. En la obra se critica a la prensa periodística que, en complicidad con la hegemonía cultural destruía, con sus ácidos comentarios, las obras que no correspondían al gusto elitista. La obra de Jaime Carreo se centra en un personaje que regresa a Puerto Rico después de vivir muchos años en Nueva York. [MR]

4265 Teatro breve: Premio Faiga 1997.
Buenos Aires: Federación Argentina de la Industria Gráfica y Afines: Fundación El Libro, 1997. 158 p.

Cinco obras muy bien escritas de autores que experimentan con nuevas formas dramáticas para tratar temas conocidos. Un buen ejemplo es *Memorias de Praga* de Héctor Levy-Daniel cuyo protagonista, que está en un manicomio, reconstruye en *bashbacks* su vida en Praga durante la segunda guerra mundial, su relación con su novia judía, y el homicidio contra su propio padre, quien había delatado a la familia de su novia. [MR]

4266 Teatro cartagenero contemporáneo.
Cartagena, Colombia: Alcaldía Mayor de Cartagena, Instituto Distrital de Recreación, Cultura y Deporte, 1994. 189 p.: ill.

Se antalogan diez obras de breve extensión que desarrollan diferentes temáticas y tendencias estéticas que han sido llevadas a la escena por grupos de Cartagena. Cabe mencionar *Sueños en blanco y negro* de E. Pachón, una adaptación libre de "Los sueños" de Francisco de Quevedo. Se incluye también la obra de teatro infantil en un acto *Juguemos al circo.* [MR]

4267 Teatro joven de México: antología. Del taller de Hugo Argüelles. Chimalistac, Mexico: Consejo Nacional para la Cultura y las Artes, 1992. 2 v. (Fondo editorial tierra adentro; 51–52)

Incluye obras de Lorena Padrón (Mexican Arias), Enrique Castillo (Gladiadores perdidos en la niebla), Alberto Castillo (El Edipo imaginario), Víctor Hugo García Rodríguez (Los trenes del mar), y Gerardo Luna (Corazón de melón). A través del humor y sarcasmo, usando un vocabulario popular y regional, tratan temas de la familia mexicana, la juventud y su rebelión contra los valores tradicionales, y la excesiva importancia de la madre en la cultura mexicana. [SC]

4268 Teatro uruguayo de hoy, 1987–1994: antología. Noticia histórico-crítica y selección de Walter Rela. Montevideo: Editorial Proyección, 1994. 283 p.: bibl.

Una selección de las mejores obras del teatro uruguayo actual, entre las que pueden citarse *Miss Mártir* de Dino Armas, *Garúa* de Ricardo Prieto, *Escenas de la vida de Su Majestad, la Reina Isabel* de Eduardo Sarlós y

Sin lugar de Carlos Manuel Varela. La introducción del investigador Rela aporta una valiosa información sobre el ambiente teatral uruguayo y contextualiza las obras compendiadas. [MR]

4269 Teatro: cinco autores cubanos. Selección y prólogo de Rine Leal. Jackson Heights, N.Y.: Ollantay Press, 1995. 277 p.: bibl. (Colección Teatro; v. 1)

Contiene obras de cubanos escritas en el exilio, excepto *Las monjas* de Eduardo Manet. *Fefu y sus amigas* de María Irene Fornés ofrece una interesante puesta de múltiples y simultáneos espacios que son recorridos por el público. *Nadie se va del todo* de Pedro R. Monge Rafuls y *Balada de un invierno en la Habana* abordan el tema del retorno del exiliado y el reencuentro con el lugar de origen. La quinta obra es *La fiesta* de José Triana. [MR]

4270 Teatro: monólogos de hoy. Prólogo de Roberto Cossa. Selección de Bernardo Carey. Buenos Aires: Ediciones Instituto Movilizador de Fondos Cooperativos, 1995. 126 p. (Desde la gente)

Excelente colección de monólogos de autores contemporáneos argentinos entre los que se incluyen *El despojamiento* de G. Gambaro, *Criatura* de E. Griffero, *Potestad* de E. Pavlovsky, y *El timbre* de B. Roitman. Además contiene *Estrella negra* de la uruguaya A. Genta; y el cuento de R. Piglia, *Mi amigo,* que fue puesto en escena. Recomendable para estudiantes de teatro. [MR]

4271 Torrero Jaramillo, Hermenegildo. Recuerdos del inmortal: drama a Bolívar en el bicentenario. Panamá: Impresora Real, 1993. 95 p.: ill.

Intended for children in Panamanian schools, this didactic drama presents important events in Simón Bolívar's life. By quoting famous speeches made by Bolívar, the characters comment on the failure of the liberator's ideals in present-day Panama and the lack of unity among Latin American countries. [SC]

4272 Torres, Ana María. Un día raro: obra en un acto. Buenos Aires: Torres Aguero Editor, 1995. 59 p.

Obra bien estructurada que se desarrolla en distintos planos simultáneos o alternativos. Un hombre en estado agónico se sumerge en un mundo de fantasía del que emerge la mujer que siempre amó. [MR]

4273 Vaca Pereyra, Raúl. El buri. Santa Cruz de la Sierra, Bolivia: ABC Casa Editora, 1994. 87 p.

Obra de carácter costumbrista que escenifica un Santa Cruz de antaño. Se describe una fiesta pueblerina o "buris," en que se mezclaban bandas de músicos, bailes, y coplas. [MR]

4274 Valessi, Alfredo. Teatro de la ira. Managua: Ediciones del Siglo/JEA: Fondo de Artistas Independientes/ASDI, 1995. 101 p.

The title of this trilogy of plays expresses the impact that events in Nicaragua have had on the younger postwar generation. In "Oscura raíz del grito," a young woman struggles when presented with the opportunity to seek revenge on the man who raped her. "Destino manifiesto," set in 1855, dramatizes the collaboration between the Church and Nicaraguan upper classes with the US forces led by William Walker. "El predicador," set in the late 1970s with flashbacks to 1966, features a family in conflict about the meaning of national progress and the costs of pursuing it. [SC]

4275 Varela, Carlos Manuel. La esperanza no bebe petróleo. Montevideo: Arca, 1993. 160 p. (Colección Las tablas)

Contiene *Las gaviotas no beben petróleo* y *La Esperanza, S.A.* En la primera, en que la metáfora supera a la simple anécdota, una madre dominante y perversa impide la relación feliz de su hijo con su esposa. En la segunda, un viudo y sus hijos, conviven en un precario presente sin poder librarse de un pasado que cargan como la piedra de Sísifo. Varela es uno de los más talentosos dramaturgos contemporáneos de Uruguay. [MR]

4276 Vargas, Arístides. Teatro. Quito: Eskeletra Editorial, 1997. 236 p.

Las tres obras del volumen son de excelente calidad, con personajes marginados que sueñan o tratan de recordar un pasado fragmentado y ambiguo y encontrar una razón a su existencia. Se destaca el lenguaje poético del autor, lleno de imágenes y significados connotativos. [MR]

4277 Vargas Llosa, Mario. Ojos bonitos, cuadros feos. Lima: Peisa, 1996. 91 p.

Un crítico de arte homosexual es acosado por el novio de una pintora que se ha suicidado probablemente por la mala crítica que recibió en su primera exposición. Obra bien escrita y muy amena. [MR]

4278 Vázquez Díaz, René. El último concierto. Madrid: Editorial Betania, 1992. 75 p. (Colección Teatro)

This play, written by a Cuban living in Sweden, explores the relationship between an abducted editor who comes from an upper-class family, and his Maraxist abductors. Forced to live in close quarters, the characters discover that they have much in common despite their differing ideologies. [SC]

4279 Veronese, Daniel. Cuerpo de prueba: textos teatrales. Buenos Aires: Centro Cultural Ricardo Rojas, Secretaría de Extensión Universitaria y Bienestar Estudiantil, Oficina de Publicaciones del CBC, Univ. de Buenos Aires, 1997. 376 p. (Libros del Rojas)

El autor es uno de los principales exponentes del nuevo teatro argentino. Representa la dramaturgia posmoderna que pretende librarse de ataduras ideológicas o intelectuales para explorar nuevas formas de expresión teatral con planteamientos filosóficos nunca definitivos. En este conjunto de 14 obras se incluye *Cámara Gesell,* que es la que mejor representa esta búsqueda de una nueva teatralidad. [MR]

4280 Veronese, Daniel. Formas de hablar de las madres de los mineros, mientras esperan que sus hijos salgan a la superficie. Buenos Aires: Ediciones Florida Blanca, 1995. 63 p.

Sin recurrir al aparente naturalismo que parece sugerir el título, en esta obra, si bien el esquema de la acción refleja un contenido social, lo que importa son las ambivalentes relaciones entre víctimas y victimarios. Excelente texto. [MR]

4281 Vilalta, Maruxa. Jesucristo entre nosotros. México: Fondo de Cultura Económica, 1995. 159 p.: bibl. (Colección popular; 515)

Estrenada en 1994, esta pieza de trece cuadros o escenas continúa la línea temática de obras precedentes como "Una voz en el desierto." Un Jesucristo moderno toma varios papeles, ya sea como modesto empleado de oficina, niño indigente, soldado que condena la violencia, camillero que salva de la muerte a un enfermo desahuciado. Al enfrentarse con narcotraficantes o soldados, vuelve a ser crucificado por los problemas modernos. [SC]

4282 Winer, Víctor. Teatro completo. v. 1. Buenos Aires: Torres Agüero, 1995. 1 v. (Col. Telón abierto; 7)

Contiene cinco obras. El autor ausculta las motivaciones interiores que inducen a sus personajes a buscar relaciones humanas que muchas veces terminan en un nudo ciego. El poder que uno ejerce sobre otro hace que no se arribe a un desenlace feliz. La obra mejor lograda del volumen es *Luna de miel en Hiroshima*. [MR]

4283 Wolff, Egon. Invitación a comer; Cicatrices. Santiago: Editorial Universitaria, 1995. 185 p. (Colección Los Contemporáneos)

Dos obras de excelente calidad en que se demuestra lo propuesto por el autor en el prólogo: que con el uso y poder de la palabra se pueden construir textos que ayuden a rescatar al espectador que ha abandonado el teatro debido a que el lenguaje es relegado a un plano secundario. En la primera obra se plantean varios problemas contemporáneos: relaciones de parejas, de generaciones, de socios de negocio. La segunda, muestra un juego en que se trata de revivir el argumento de una novela, y termina en la destrucción de una joven inocente. [MR]

4284 Zambrana Pineda, Ileana. Tinoco: días de tiranía. San José, Costa Rica: Euroamericana de Ediciones, 1994. 176 p.

Set in the 1930s with flashbacks to the Tinoco dictatorship in Costa Rica (1917–19), this historical drama features the Tinoco Granados brothers as protagonists. This well-structured play explores the struggle to maintain power and the different perspectives of those involved in the historical events. [SC]

THEATER CRITICISM AND HISTORY

4285 Azparren Giménez, Leonardo. La máscara y la realidad: comportamientos del teatro venezolano contemporáneo. Caracas: FUNDARTE, Alcaldía de Caracas, 1994. 109 p.: bibl. (Colección Delta; no. 35)

Contiene crítica periodística y académica. El más extenso de los ensayos es "Comportamientos del teatro venezolano contemporáneo" en que el autor revisa algunos modelos teóricos de la historia del teatro, para luego desde su propio modelo, historiar el teatro venezolano desde 1958 a 1993. Muchos de los artículos incluidos habían aparecido en revistas o periódicos. [MR]

4286 Barrios, Alba Liá; Carmen Mannarino; and Enrique Izaguirre. Dramaturgia venezolana del siglo XX: panorama en tres ensayos. Caracas: Centro Venezolano del ITI-UNESCO, 1997. 470 p.: bibl., charts.

El libro consta de tres partes a cargo de distintos autores. La primera abarca de 1890–1945; la segunda de 1950–69; la tercera de 1970–90. En ellas se destacan los dramaturgos más importantes de cada periódo. En la última parte, hay cinco nombres que, de acuerdo a Izaguirre, marcan hito en el teatro venezolano comporáneo: R. Santana, I. Cabrujas, F.L. Viloria, N. Caballero, I. Chocrón. [MR]

4287 Cabral, Fermín *et al*. Itinerario del autor dramático iberoamericano. San Juan: Editorial LEA, 1997. 222 p.: ill.

Contiene ensayos de Rodolfo Santana, Eduardo Rovner, Mauricio Kartún, Marco Antonio de la Parra, Ramón Ramos-Perea, Fermín Cabal y Guillermo Schmidhuber, integrantes del G.E.D.I. (*Grupo de Estudios Dramatúrgicos Iberoamericano*). Los autores exponen los propósitos y prácticas de su escritura. Este libro es útil para jóvenes dramaturgos y académicos interesados en estos escritores y en las nuevas tendencias del teatro iberoamericano. [MR]

4288 Cánepa Guzmán, Mario. Armando Moock: 1894–1942. Chile: Ediciones Astrid, 1996. 123 p.: ill.

Relación biográfica del dramaturgo chileno, con algunas notas periodísticas sobre su producción teatral. Se incluye *Del brazo y por la calle*, comedia en tres actos con dos personajes, estrenada en Buenos Aires en 1939. [MR]

4289 Cánepa Guzmán, Mario. Historia de los teatros universitarios. Santiago: Ediciones Mauro, 1995. 291 p.: bibl., ill.

Contiene una valiosa información sobre obras, actores y directores que han participado en los distintos grupos de teatro universitario. Gran parte del libro está dedicado al Teatro Experimental de la Univ. de Chile y al Teatro de Ensayo de la Univ. Católica. [MR]

4290 Castagnino, Raúl Héctor. José Antonio Saldías. Buenos Aires: Corregidor, 1992. 157 p.

Nacido en 1891, Saldías escribe dramas sobre acontencimientos sociales y políticos de mediados del siglo XX en la Argentina. En su estudio Castagnino incluye tres secciones con referencias bibliográficas sobre el autor, su producción teatral y su narrativa. Se compilan cinco obras representativas, *El candidato del pueblo, El divino tesoro, La bohemia loca, No hay tierra como mi tierra,* y *Mire que chiquito es el mundo.* [MR]

4291 Cordones-Cook, Juanamaría. ¿Teatro negro uruguayo?: texto y contexto del teatro afro-uruguayo de Andrés Castillo. Montevideo: Editorial Graffitti, 1996. 167 p.: appendix, bibl., ill., music. (Colección de ensayo Criterios)

Edición crítica de tres obras de Andrés Castillo, quien, aunque blanco, plantea en sus obras temas sociales y étnicos que recogen el folklore, carnaval y leyendas de los negros del Uruguay. En una extensa introducción, la autora expone su metodología y relaciona el contenido de las obras con su referente histórico y social. Al final hay un apéndice musical con letras de canciones y una partitura. [MR]

4292 Discépolo, Armando. Obra dramática de Armando Discépolo. v. 3. Buenos Aires: Editorial Galerna, 1996. 1 v.: bibl. (Arte para todos)

Contiene cinco obras correspondientes a la etapa de la producción dramática del Discépolo que Pelletieri denomina como "El periódo canónico de la dramática de Armando Discépolo," en que el dramaturgo perfeccionó los procedimientos del sainete, el grotesco criollo y el grotesco ortodoxo. Importante fuente para especialistas del teatro argentino. [MR]

4293 Documentos para la historia del teatro en Venezuela: siglos XVI, XVII y XVIII. Recopilación de Leonardo Azparren Giménez. Caracas: Monte Avila Editores Latinoamericana, 1996. 333 p.: bibl. (Documentos. Serie documental)

Este volumen incluye parte de una historia del teatro venezolano. Contiene documentos oficiales y otros consignados en libros de autores de la época, que permiten situar en un contexto histórico cultural, no sólo los textos literarios y espectáculos teatrales, sino también fiestas y otros hechos parateatrales que ayudarán a comprender mejor la dinámica social del momento y sus proyecciones actuales. [MR]

4294 La dramaturgia en Iberoamérica: teoría y práctica teatral. Recopilación de Osvaldo Pelletieri y Eduardo Rovner. Buenos Aires: Galerna: GETEA-CITI, 1998. 190 p.: bibl. (Tendencias del teatro actual en Iberoamérica y Argentina; no. 2)

Se reúnen artículos sobre teatro argentino, brasileño, chileno, costarricense, cubano, mexicano, uruguayo, puertorriqueño y español. Todos los artículos dan una visión panorámica del teatro de los '80s y '90s en Latinoamérica, con la excepción de uno que se dedica al estudio de una obra del costarricense Daniel Gallegos. [MR]

4295 Gambaro, Griselda. Teatro. v. 6. Buenos Aires: Ediciones de la Flor, 1996. 1 v.

Se reúnen varias obras de la autora, en su mayoría breves, en los que, con el lenguaje poético y metafórico que caracteriza la escritura de la autora, se plantean temas de carácter universal, pero sin perder de vista la realidad argentina. *La casa sin sosiego* es un libreto para ópera de cámara. [MR]

4296 Hurtado, María de la Luz. Teatro chileno y modernidad: identidad y crisis social. Irvine, Calif.: Ediciones de Gestos, 1997. 215 p.: bibl. (Colección Historia del teatro; 2)

Desde una perspectiva multidisciplinaria, que incluye la sociología, antropología cultural y semiótica teatral, se estudian las transformaciones experimentadas por el teatro chileno, en especial a partir del siglo XIX hasta la primera mitad del siglo, en su respuesta a los diferentes proyectos modernizadores de carácter eurocéntrico aplicados en Chile. Importante fuente de referencia para estudios puntuales sobre teatro chileno. [MR]

4297 Lagos, María Soledad. Creación colectiva: teatro chileno a fines de la década de los 80. Frankfurt: Lang, 1994. 264 p.: bibl.

(Europäische Hochschulschriften. Reihe XXIV, Ibero-romanische Sprachen und Literaturen, 0721–3565; Bd. 42 = Publications universitaires européennes. Série XXIV, Lenguas y literaturas iberorrománicas; v. 42 = European university studies. Series XXIV, Ibero-Romance languages and literatures; v. 42)

Se emplean enfoques teóricos diferentes según las exigencias de las seis obras estudiadas. De acuerdo a la autora, en el corpus elegido se observa una nueva estética donde los signos no verbales, la imagen visual en especial, se destaca sobre los signos verbales. A pesar de la renovación estética, la temática de los textos de creación sigue relacionándose con las condiciones contextuales del momento histórico de su producción. [MR]

4298 Martínez Moreno, Carlos. Crítica teatral. v. 1–3. Montevideo: República Oriental del Uruguay, Cámara de Senadores, Secretaría, 1994. 3 v.

Tomo I contiene una selección de artículos de crítica teatral publicados en el diario *El País* 1938–44 y en la revista *Cine Radio Actualidad* 1942. Tomo II contiene artículos publicados en el Semanario *Marcha* entre 1944–56 y Tomo III artículos aparecidos también en el Seminario *Marcha* entre 1957–60 y en el Diario *La Jornada*, (México) 1985. Una valiosa documentación para el estudio de la actividad teatral uruguaya, del trabajo directoral y actoral de importantes figuras de la escena uruguaya y de las obras de autores universales montadas en Uruguay. [MR]

4299 Matilla Jimeno, Alfredo. De teatro: artículos periodísticos de Alfredo Matilla Jimeno. San Juan: Instituto de Cultura Puertorriqueña, 1993. 327 p.: bibl., index.

Compilación de artículos de crítica musical y teatral de un exiliado político español radicado en Puerto Rico. Estos artículos, aparecidos en el periódico *El Mundo* entre los años 1949–60, dan cuenta de la actividad teatral de Puerto Rico en el período en que se privilegiaban las obras extranjeras. [MR]

4300 Mitos en el teatro latinoamericano. Recopilación de Perla Zayas de Lima. Buenos Aires: Instituto de Artes del Espectáculo, Facultad de Filosofía y Letras, UBA, 1996? 58 p.: bibl. (Cuadernos de teatro; no. 10)

Contiene siete ensayos en que se estudia el proceso de mitificación/demitificación de obras de autores como Ricardo Monti, Juan Carlos Gené, Marco Antonio de la Parra y José Ignacio Cabrujas. Se tratan igualmente el teatro callejero y otras formas populares de expresión teatral. [MR]

4301 Morel, Consuelo. Identidad femenina en el teatro chileno. Colaboración de Jaime Coloma. Santiago: Ediciones "Apuntes," Teatro U.C, 1996. 238 p.: bibl., ill. (Serie Teatro y psicología, 0716–4440)

Se seleccionan 15 obras estudiadas desde una perspectiva psicoanalítica, atendiendo a la identidad del personaje femenino y su relación con el sexo opuesto y la sociedad. Se incluyen piezas, escritas entre 1922–90, de conocidos autores como Armando Mook, Miguel Acevedo Hernández, Isidora Aguirre, Luis Alberto Heiremans y Marco Antonio de la Parra. [MR]

4302 Ostuni, Omar. Por los teatros del interior: crónicas y hechos que revelan historias desconocidas del teatro uruguayo. Montevideo: Asociación de Teatros del Interior, 1993. 178 p.: bibl.

Un valioso aporte para la historia del teatro uruguayo en que se revisa, con testimonios de sus agentes, la riquísima actividad teatral realizada en el interior del Uruguay desde 1858 en adelante. Contiene un detallado itinerario de las actividades de la Asociación de Teatros del Interior. [MR]

4303 Parra, Marco Antonio de la. Cartas a un joven dramaturgo. Santiago: Dolmen Ediciones, 1995. 140 p. (Mundo abierto)

Se exponen ideas del autor sobre lo que debería ser una nueva dramaturgia, en donde se debe armonizar un lenguaje poético e ingenioso con un auscultamiento profundo de la historia y la tradición y un redescubrimiento de la emoción que sitúe al ser humano en el centro de la escena. La intención del autor es la de incentivar la creatividad de dramaturgos jóvenes. [MR]

4304 Pellettieri, Osvaldo. Una historia interrumpida: teatro argentino moderno, 1949–1976. Buenos Aires: Editorial Galerna, 1997. 285 p.: bibl.

Mediante la utilización de una rigurosa metodología, el autor estudia los cambios semánticos, estéticos, de producción y recepción en el período más importante del desarrollo del teatro argentino que fue interrumpido en 1976 por el régimen dictatorial. El foco del libro está en la etapa que el autor denomina "microsistema emergente de los sesenta", la cual tuvo dos vertientes principales: el realismo reflexivo y la nueva vanguardia. [MR]

4305 Pignataro Calero, Jorge. La aventura del teatro independiente uruguayo: crónica de seis décadas. Montevideo: Cal y Canto, 1997. 180 p.: bibl.

Después de definir el concepto de teatro independiente, el autor distingue tres fases en el proceso histórico del teatro independiente uruguayo: el teatro de libertad (1930–60), el teatro de regresión (1960–64) y el de la libertad recuperada (1965–96). Hay una valiosa información sobre grupos y obras representadas. [MR]

4306 Pignataro Calero, Jorge. Directores teatrales del Uruguay: 50 retratos. Montevideo: Editorial Proyección, 1994. 250 p.: bibl., ill.

Otra contribución del autor para la historia del teatro uruguayo que se organiza a partir de la semblanza de destacados directores del siglo XX. [MR]

4307 Plá, Josefina. Cuatro siglos de teatro en el Paraguay: el teatro paraguayo desde sus orígenes hasta hoy, 1544–1988. v. 3, El teatro paraguayo en el siglo XX. Asunción: Univ. Católica Nuestra Señora de la Asunción, Depto. de Teatro, 1994. 1 v.: bibl.

Aunque el libro tiene un listado que llega hasta fines de los sesenta, se enfoca en el desarrollo del teatro paraguayo desde 1901 hasta el final de la década de los cuarenta. Contiene información sobre grupos, puestas y actores que puede ser útil para los interesados en la dramaturgia paraguaya. [MR]

4308 Rela, Walter. Teatro uruguayo, 1808–1994: historia. Montevideo: Academia Uruguaya de Letras, 1994. 347 p.: bibl., index.

En un acucioso registro de datos, se estudian las principales tendencia teatrales y de creadores, entre los que se destacan Florencio Sánchez y Ernesto Herrera. Igualmente se mencionan las compañías teatrales que dieron vida al teatro de este largo período. Una importante contribución a la historia del teatro uruguayo, que incluye bibliografía, índice de autores y tabla cronológica de los estrenos de obras. [MR]

4309 Ríos, Edda de los. Dos caras del teatro paraguayo. Prólogo de Richard Salvat. Asunción: Agencia Española de Cooperación Internacional, 1994. 70 p.: bibl.

Breve libro dividido en dos partes. En la primera se hace una somera revisión de expresiones teatrales aborígenes y españolas y, en la segunda, se relata la importante labor que ha tenido la mujer paraguaya en la historia, aun cuando su participación en el teatro haya sido relegada al papel de mera espectadora. Interesantes pero esquemáticas reflexiones. [MR]

4310 Rojas, Margarita and **Flora Ovares.** En el tinglado de la eterna comedia. Tomo II, Teatro costarricense 1930–1950. Heredia, Costa Rica: EUNA, 1995. 1 v.: bibl., ill.

Continues to trace the development of Costa Rican theater to the mid-20th century. Alfredo Casto was the most prolific dramatist of this period and this study is primarily devoted to analyzing his works. Concludes with a discussion of the theater's relationship to *el movimiento vanguardista* and an interesting commentary on female characters and patriarchal discourse in plays from this time period. For review of Tomo I, see item **4311.** [SC]

4311 Rojas, Margarita *et al.* En el tinglado de la eterna comedia. Tomo I, Teatro costarricense 1890–1930. Heredia, Costa Rica: EUNA, 1995. 1 v.: bibl., ill.

A careful study that situates the development of Costa Rican theater within the cultural and historical context of the early-20th century. Focuses on dramatists' generational conflicts regarding the characteristics of a "national theater" and their use of the family to represent national identity. For review of Tomo II, see item **4310.** [SC]

4312 Sansone de Martínez, Eneida. El teatro en el Uruguay en el siglo XIX: historia de una pasión avasallante. v. 1, Desde los orígenes a la Independencia. Montevideo: Editorial Surcos, 1995. 1 v.: bibl., ill., map.

Relación de la actividad teatral uruguaya decimonónica en que se incluyen salas, grupos y actores famosos. Aunque la autora sostiene que este libro está destinado a un público amplio más que al estudioso, contiene datos que pueden abrir muchas pistas de investigación. [MR]

4313 **Situación del teatro uruguayo contemporáneo: tendencias escénicas, el
público, la dramaturgia.** Recopilación de
Roger Mirza. Montevideo: Ediciones de la
Banda Oriental: Instituto Internacional del
Teatro: UNESCO, Sección Uruguay, 1996.
120 p.: bibl.

El libro se divide en tres partes. La
primera, contiene ensayos sobre las tendencias escénicas en la postrimerías del siglo XX
en que se estudian manifestaciones teatrales
convencionales y populares, sus cruces y
problemas. En la segunda, se estudian los
productores y receptores de espectáculos
teatrales; la tercera parte, la más breve,
plantea los problemas que enfrentaba la dramaturgia nacional en ese momento. Los ensayos no son sólo de críticos sino también de
dramaturgos. [MR]

4314 **Sterling, Aura Luisa.** Para una corriente teatral en el Huila. Colombia: Ediciones Samán, 1992. 142 p.: bibl.

De interés especial es el Capítulo III
del libro en que la autora realiza un breve estudio de *Juan Gil,* la única obra dramática de
José Eustasio Rivera y de Gustavo Andrade
Rivera, dos autores de la escasa producción
teatral del Huila. [MR]

4315 **Teatro latinoamericano de los setenta:
autoritarismo, cuestionamiento y
cambio.** Recopilación de Osvaldo Pellettieri.
Buenos Aires: Corregidor, 1995. 317 p.: bibl.
(Colección Imagen del drama)

Contiene ensayos de dramaturgos de
Argentina, Chile, Centroamérica, Uruguay,
Venezuela y México en que colaboran estudiosos de Latinoamérica, Canadá y los Estados Unidos. Tiene dos artículos introductorios: uno de Pellettieri sobre la modernidad
dramática latinoamericana y otro de Blas
Matamoro sobre la realidad social de los setenta. La tematización en las obras de represión de las dictaduras de la década es tratada
en varios de los ensayos. [MR]

4316 **El teatro y su crítica.** Recopilación de
Osvaldo Pellettieri. Buenos Aires:
Galerna: Facultad de Filosofía y Letras (UBA),
1998. 296 p.: bibl. (Colección Estudios de
teatro argentino i iberoamericano)

Selección de ensayos sobre teoría

teatral, teatro latinoamericano y español,
con una sección especial destinada al teatro
de Buenos Aires, otra al de las provincias
argentinas y una última parte que explora
la relación del teatro con otras artes. Entre
los dramaturgos estudiados se incluyen S.
Berma, I. Chocrón, G. Gómez-Peña, G.
Gambaro, D. Veronese, L. Marechal y R.
Arlt. [MR]

4317 **El teatro y sus claves: estudios sobre
teatro argentino e iberoamericano.** Recopilación de Osvaldo Pellettieri. Buenos
Aires: Galerna: Facultad de Filosofía y Letras,
UBA, 1996. 303 p.: bibl. (Colección Estudios
de teatro argentino e iberoamericano)

Importante colección de estudios con
planteamientos teóricos aplicados a textos
escritos y espectáculos de Argentina y de
otros países iberoamericanos. Estos artículos
fueron presentados como ponencias en el *III
Congreso Internacional de Teatro Ibero
americano y Argentino* realizado en Buenos
Aires, en agosto de 1994, con el auspicio de
GETEA y la UBA. [MR]

4318 **Torres Cárdenas, Edgar Guillermo.**
Praxis artística y vida política del
teatro en Colombia, 1955–1980. Tunja, Colombia: Magister en Historia, Escuela de Posgrado de la Facultad de Educación, Univ.
Pedagógica y Tecnológica de Colombia, 1990.
96 p.: bibl., ill. (Nuevas lecturas de historia,
0121–165X; 11)

Teatro, política y militancia son los
temas que el autor explora en este breve trabajo. Se refiere a los factores que indujeron la
adaptación del teatro brechtiano en Colombia. Se ejemplifica con el teatro de Enrique
Buenaventura, Pablo Azcárate, Mejía Duque
y Santiago García. [MR]

4319 **Variaciones sobre el teatro latinoamericano: tendencias y perspectivas.** Recopilación de Alfonso de Toro y Klaus Pörtl.
Frankfurt: Vervuert; Madrid: Iberoamericana,
1996. 247 p.: bibl. (Teoría y práctica del
teatro; vol. 5)

Contiene nueve ensayos, en que se
combinan teoría y práctica, presentados en
un encuentro de la *Asociación de Hispanistas Alemanes* realizado en Augsburg en
marzo de 1993. Hay artículos sobre el teatro

de Pavlovsky, Cabrujas, el teatro chileno, el ecuatoriano y sobre la posmodernidad teatral latinonamericana. [MR]

4320 Villegas Morales, Juan. Para un modelo de historia del teatro. Irvine, Calif.: Gestos, 1997. 206 p.: bibl. (Colección Teoría; 1)

Se revisan y replantean modelos teóricos expuestos en un libro anterior del autor. Más que la consideración de variantes internas de textos escritos o de espectáculos, se propone aquí considerar parámetros contextuales que pueden explicar no sólo variaciones textuales intrínsecas, sino también la dinámica de su producción y recepción. La propuesta teórica del autor permite la inclusión de textos que en las historias quedaban al margen de la hegemonía cultural. [MR]

4321 Yáñez, Ruben. Hoy es siempre todavía: medio siglo en el teatro, la enseñanza y otros trabajos. Montevideo: Cal y Canto, 1996. 240 p.

Libro autobiográfico de uno de los más distinguidos directores del teatro uruguayo que relata su relación profesional con varios grupos: el Teatro Independiente, el Teatro del Pueblo, la Comedia Nacional y sobre todo, El Galpón, que Yáñez dirigió dentro del Uruguay y en su exilio en México. Termina el libro con reflexiones acerca del derrumbe de las ideologías progresistas y el avance del neoliberalismo económico en América Latina. [MR]

4322 Zayas de Lima, Perla. Carlos Somigliana: teatro histórico-teatro político. Prólogo de Roberto Cossa. Argentina: Ediciones Fray Mocho, 1995. 189 p.: bibl.

La autora estudia los textos dramáticos y las puestas y recepción del teatro de Somigliana, un exponente de la generación de los 1960s, relacionándolos con el entorno cultural y social y a la luz de cuatro temas "nacionales": los intelectuales, el poder, el teatro y la vanguardia y la ciudad de Buenos Aires. [MR]

BRAZIL
Novels

REGINA IGEL, *Associate Professor, Department of Spanish and Portuguese, University of Maryland, College Park*

HAPPY BIRTHDAY, BRAZIL! In 2000, official quincentenary celebrations in several regions of the country honored the arrival of the first Portuguese settlers in the new land and the subsequent 500 years of Brazilian history and culture. In the literary realm, novelists too looked to the Brazilian historical landscape, recreating it in fictional terms, either by recounting past romantic interludes, as in *Paraguaçu e Caramuru: paixão e morte da nação tupinambá: romance* by Assis Brasil (item **4330**), or by uncovering personal aspects of public figures, as in *Anna e outros amores de Tiradentes* by Joaquim Borges (item **4329**) and *Joaquina, filha do Tiradentes* by Maria José de Queiroz (item **4373**). Characterizing many of the historical novels is a *roman à clef* aspect in which actual members of Brazilian society and history interact with fictional characters, as in *Noturno, 1894* by Raimundo Caruso, who recreates aspects of the consolidation of the Brazilian republic, including hypothetical dialogues about poet Cruz e Souza (item **4334**). Fictionalized depictions of historical events also reach beyond Brazilian borders, as in Antônio Olinto's novel of war in northern Africa, *Alcacer-Kibir*, the title taken from the infamous region from which King Sebastian of Portugal disappeared (item **4368**).

Revolutions and armed struggles provide the background for several novels portraying the conflict that typified the history of Brazil's southern region. *O exílio na terra dos muitos: o romance da fundação do Rio Grande* by Antônio Hohlfeldt features the development of the 1742 soldiers' revolution in Rio Grande do Sul (item **4346**). The combatant south is also described in Antonio A. Fagundes' *Destino de Tal: novela gauchesca*, which concerns the 1923 war between Chimangos and Maragatos (item **4341**). Revolutions in Santa Catarina, another southern state, are depicted in two novels, *O bruxo do Contestado* by Godofredo de Oliveira Neto and *O dragão vermelho do Contestado* by A. Sanford de Vasconcelos (items **4369** and **4388**). Both explore the messianic-political battle led by a monarchist monk in the first quarter of the 20th century. A further portrayal of the embattled southern region is set against the background of the Triple Alliance War; in *Netto perde sua alma* by Tabajara Ruas, the protagonist is a wounded Brazilian general, unable to move from his hospital bed, but mentally alert enough to plant strategic gossip in his ward (item **4381**).

The north and northeastern areas are also visited by authors reconstituting history. Many of these novels explore the history of racial, cultural, and gender relations in Brazil. *Tróia negra: a saga dos Palmares* by Jorge Landmann recounts the ferocious attacks of the Portuguese army against a colony of slaves who escaped from the region's sugarcane plantations (item **4352**). An exploration of the lives of African slaves in colonial-era Brazil is Heloísa Maranhão's novel, *Rosa Maria Egipcíaca da Vera Cruz: a incrível trajetória de uma princesa negra entre a prostituição e a santidade*, which realistically depicts the slaves' use of the language of their birthplace, Benin (item **4359**).

Esther Largman focuses on another aspect of colonial race relations in her tale of a Brazilian native taken to Holland as a slave by his Dutch owner, the Prince Mauritz von Nassau in *Jan e Nassau: trajetória de um índio cariri na Corte holandesa* (item **4353**). The Dutch prince appears in another novel, *Treliças: balas e gozos na corte de Nassau* by Virgílio Moretzsohn, whose mysterious and sensual protagonist, Ana Pais, overcomes the prejudices of her time through her role in the war against the Dutch and through her abilities as a businesswoman (item **4364**). *Os rios inumeráveis* by Alvaro Cardoso Gomes examines the cultural conflicts between Europeans and indigenous peoples through 500 years of Brazilian history; the stories are told in language that typifies each of the five centuries (item **4344**).

Another group of novels examines the lives of Middle Easterners in Brazil—a significant immigrant group whose history has only recently been uncovered and revealed in a variety of literary and historical works. The ubiquitous Jorge Amado delves into this world in his *A descoberta da América pelos turcos: romancinho*, where the "turcos" are Syrian and Lebanese immigrants arriving in Brazil in the first quarter of the 20th century (item **4326**). Also focusing on this group of settlers is Ana Miranda's *Amrik* (item **4361**), a narrative with a highly original structural frame in which a woman recalls the arrival of her foreign ancestors in São Paulo. Another novel about a descendant of Lebanese immigrants, *O papagaio e o doutor* (item **4360**) by Betty Milan, tells of the personal conflicts, painfully revealed through psychoanalysis, of a young Brazilian-born woman torn between the Lebanese world of her parents and her own dual identity. Domingos Pellegrini Júnior also focuses on immigrants in *Terra vermelha* (item **4371**), which tells of the first settlers in northern Paraná. The novel's narrative is shared by a grandfather and his grandson, though they are not aware that their stories are complementary.

The same exploration of the past reflected in these novels can also be found in narratives with a more sociological bent, such as *A superfície das águas* by Hilda

Simões L.C. Acevedo (item **4323**). This novel portrays the decadence of a family of the oligarchy of Rio Grande do Sul with links to both Getúlio Vargas, depicted as a fascist-totalitarian, and his good friend Felinto Müller. Former President Vargas also looms in the background of *A morte do presidente: ou, A amiga de mamãe* by Maria Alice Barroso (item **4327**). Another period of dictatorship (1964–85) is re-examined in *A ilha no espaço* by Osman Lins (item **4356**). In this allegorical narrative of mysterious deaths and disappearances of tenants in an apartment building, the protagonist remains in his apartment, isolated and alone, as if on an island.

The many re-editions of renowned novels issued this biennium offer reminders that the past is part of the present: a third edition of Clarice Lispector's *A cidade sitiada,* a reworking of the novel's second edition, has been published (item **4357**); José Lins do Rego's *Cangaceiros* is in its ninth edition since it was first published in 1953 (item **4374**); with his new novel, *Ópera dos fantoches,* Autran Dourado provides a reconstruction of *Tempo de Amar,* originally published in 1952 (item **4340**); and *Três casas e um rio* by Dalcídio Jurandir, now in its third edition, provides a view of the splendors and miseries of Amazonian dwellers in the island of Marajó (item **4348**).

Two new novels offer further literary explorations of the Amazon region: Paulo Jacob's *Amazonas, remansos, rebojos e banzeiros,* which depicts the Amazon river, its *caboclo* population, and the natural wonders of the area (item **4347**); and Benedicto Monteiro's *Como se faz um guerrilheiro,* in which the protagonist boasts of his virility, which he demonstrates by impregnating seven women in this novel's intriguing, symbolic comparison to the river's prowess (item **4363**).

Other novels published as Brazil celebrates its 500th year keep their gaze on contemporary and future society. Soccer is the main theme of *Uma vez Flamengo* by Antonio Luis Mendes de Almeida, which reveals the illicit wheeling and dealing of professional sports barely hidden by the façade of vibrant players and cheerful spectators (item **4324**). At the turn of the millennium, a glimpse into the future of the narrating art is provided by *Piritas siderais: romance cyberbarroco* by Guilherme Kujawski, who uses Internet lingo and its hermetic terminology in the configuration of this cybernovel (item **4349**).

Many critical studies of informative value enriched Brazilian studies these past years, such as Heloísa Toller Gomes' *As marcas da escravidão: o negro e o discurso oitocentista no Brasil e nos Estados Unidos,* a comparative study on race relations in Brazil and in the US that examines selected religious, political, and literary discourses within a determined span of time (item **4345**). Also of a comparative nature, but within the limits of Brazil, is Teoberto Landim's *Seca: a estação do inferno* (item **4351**), in which the author contrasts different dimensions of the drought in fiction, examining works by José de Alencar, Rodolfo Teófilo, Rachel de Queiroz, and Graciliano Ramos, among others. José Ramos Tinhorão also takes a comparative approach with his *Os romances em folhetins no Brasil, 1830 à atualidade* (item **4384**). He studies novels published in daily or weekly magazines and newspapers in the 19th century, contrasting them to contemporary "soap operas," characterized by a sequence of daily theater episodes shown on television.

The availability of the *Inventário do arquivo de Clarice Lispector,* a gift to the Casa de Rui Barbosa in Rio de Janeiro by one of the author's sons, will surely enrich future studies by providing a glimpse of the author's personal world: it comprises a splendid mix of mementos and collected items such as theater tickets and restaurant menus, along with reviews and critiques of her books that she kept in shoe boxes, drawers, or simply left spread out in her apartment (item **4343**).

Examining this selected array of novels and studies, it is possible to see the rich contribution that authors, literary critics, and others within the fictional realm have made to scholars, academicians, students, and the readership at large, all beneficiaries of a special moment in Brazilian literary history, the celebration of its first 500 years of existence.

4326 Acevedo, Hilda Simões Lopes Costa. A superfície das águas. Porto Alegre, Brazil: Instituto Estadual do Livro, 1997. 223 p. (Col. 2000)

Set against the background of the decadence of the *gaúcho* oligarchy in Brazil, narrative focuses on the consequences for the Pelotas family involved in the politics of the state of Rio Grande do Sul. Novel's *roman à clef* characters include Getúlio Vargas and Felinto Müller, both associated with totalitarian regimes. Relates the apprehensions and hopes of the Brazilian people, as well as describing individual deceptions and losses. With a preface by Assis Brasil, this well-written and structured novel reveals a talented author newly arrived on the Brazilian literary scene.

4324 Almeida, Antonio Luiz Mendes de. Uma vez Flamengo... Rio de Janeiro: Relume Dumará, 1995. 236 p.

This novel explores Brazilian soccer from behind the scenes: the politics of contracts, player trades, and the control of revenues. The press and the paying public are seen as distant and unwilling partners in games played far from the stadium's fields.

4325 Almeida, Roniwalter Jatobá de. Tiziu. São Paulo: Scritta, 1994. 134 p. (Brasilis)

Novel's title refers to a little bird that jumps up and down in place. Its habitat extends from São Paulo to parts of the Amazon. Narrator symbolically links this bird's movements to the route of a northeasterner who, like millions of others in the last 40 years of the 20th century, migrates to São Paulo in search of wealth and happiness. Just as the *tiziu* bird returns to its starting place, the protagonist also moves back to his hometown after 25 years of poverty. The city of São Miguel Paulista and its ill-famed Nitroquímica factory on the outskirts of São Paulo, which once was the principal destination of northern and northeastern migrants, appears prominently in this sad and realistic account of a life fed by illusions and fragmented by disillusion.

4326 Amado, Jorge. A descoberta da América pelos turcos: romancinho. Ilustrações e arte gráfica de Pedro Costa. Rio de Janeiro: Editora Record, 1994. 171 p.: ill.

Author seems to repeat himself in this arabesque version of the discovery of the Americas, revisiting the cocoa plantations in the south of Bahia and filling them with pseudo-poets, this time reciting their verses in Arabic. Despite their Arab dress and names, Amado's depictions of Syrian and Lebanese nationals and their descendants, known rather generically as *turcos* in Brazil, seem too familiar, particularly during visits to Amado's established milieu of the whorehouse and its residents-for-life. Perhaps more important than this presentation of worn characters during the first quarter of the 20th century is Amado's introduction to the novel; here the reader glimpses Amado's viewpoint vis-à-vis such subjects as author's rights, editions, re-editions, among others.

4327 Barroso, Maria Alice. A morte do presidente, ou, A amiga de mamãe. Rio de Janeiro: Editora Record, 1994. 222 p.

Narrative is a rich and flowing source of information on the historical and political period dominated by Carlos Lacerda and Getúlio Vargas. What seems to remain unchanged between mid-20th century and the end of century are the racial prejudices suffered by an inter-racial couple, the social criticism of a wife and mother who attempts to pursue her intellectual curiosity, and a mother's sense of loss as her daughter matures. Alternately told through the voice of the daughter and a narrator.

4328 Boos Júnior, Adolfo. Um largo, sete memórias: e mais uma, coletiva, inquisitorial, contraditória e, muitas vezes, perturbadora. Florianópolis, Brazil: Editora da UFSC, 1997. 237 p.: bibl.

Fiction and history (bibliography included) converge and run parallel through a narrative comprised of memories of seven characters, all of whom lived in Santa Catarina state at the time of slavery. The rigors of the slaves' conditions and the stern grip of their owners contrasts with the generosity of a humble shoemaker, an abolitionist ahead of his time.

4329 Borges, Joaquim. Anna e outros amores de Tiradentes. Rio de Janeiro: JC Editora, 1995. 98 p.: bibl., ill. (Col. Romance histórico)

Historical novel involves Tiradentes, the man who first fought for Brazilian independence from Portugal. Lovers, wife, and children were part of Tiradentes' multifaceted posture as husband, father, and politician (among other roles), and as failed revolutionary to mediocre soldier to a hero praised for the last 300 years. Author, claiming to be among the descendants of the man known as The Martyr of Independence, narrates several aspects of his amorous life through the imaginary voices of the women who filled it.

4330 Brasil, Assis. Paraguaçu e Caramuru: paixão e morte da nação tupinambá: romance. Rio de Janeiro: Rio Fundo Editora, 1995. 304 p.

Perhaps the most fascinating "love story" in Brazilian history is the interlude between Diogo Álvares Correia, a Portuguese adventurer, and Paraguaçu, a young indigenous princess of the Tupinambá nation. Using quotes from established historians of the period (1510–86), author depicts the colonization of Bahia and the adventures of Caramuru ("the dragon of the sea", as Correia was named by the indigenous peoples) and Fred Staden, his companion during the Atlantic crossing and after the shipwreck that led to the romance between the European and the native woman. Battles among indigenous peoples and between them and pirates of many origins, acts of piracy, and other epic episodes form part of novel's extended view of the 16th century.

4331 Brasil, Luiz Antonio de Assis. Concerto campestre. Porto Alegre, Brazil: L&PM Editores, 1997. 174 p.

Based on a 19th-century episode, the narrative depicts a young woman who becomes pregnant out of wedlock, her hardhearted father, and her lover. The reconstruction of the legend is framed by an idyllic and pastoral atmosphere filled with musical connotations, hence the title of the novel.

4332 Buarque de Hollanda, Chico. Benjamim. São Paulo: Companhia das Letras, 1995. 165 p.

This work by the renowned composer, singer, playwright, and recently turned novelist is a shattering rendering of the desolation of urban life. Protagonist Benjamim Zambraia thinks, feels, rebels, and screams, all within his mind, never uttering a sound. However, author reveals the inner life of this character with dexterity and refinement, elevating him to a symbolic portrayal of introspection and communication, of shyness and boldness. For comment on English translation, see item **4694.**

4333 Carrero, Raimundo. A história de Bernarda Soledade: a tigre do Sertão. Recife, Brazil: Edições Bagaço, 1993. 125 p.

Re-edition of one of the author's early novels. Narrative is introduced by famed writer Ariano Suassuna, who places novel within the Movimento Armorial that he founded in 1970. This movement identified and helped stimulate Northeastern literature, and Northeastern arts in general, as carriers of historical traits linked to the Medieval and Baroque ages. Carrero's novel conveys epic stances in the conquest of territory, as carried out by a woman. The female protagonist, a heroic warrior, is surrounded by paraphernalia from the Middle Ages such as banners, martyrdom, and battle scenes, depicted through dynamic events taking place in the Northeastern *sertão*. She regards the birth of a daughter as a defeat—preferring a boy whom she could turn into a "real" tiger of the backlands. Her demeanor is reversed when a nephew is born.

4334 Caruso, Raimundo C. Noturno, 1894: romance. Belo Horizonte, Brazil: Editora UFMG; Secretaria Municipal de Cultura de Belo Horizonte, 1993. 234 p.

Historical novel, awarded the Prêmio Cidade de Belo Horizonte for 1989, focuses on consolidation of the newly proclaimed Republic of Brazil in the city of Nossa Senhora do Desterro (modern Florianópolis). Author quotes from archives and other sources, inserting imaginary dialogues about poet Cruz e Souza, while revisiting the system of military government. Use of figures from Brazilian history gives the work a *roman à clef* quality.

4335 Celina, Lindanor. Eram seis assinalados: romance. Belém, Brazil: Editora Cejup, 1994? 248 p.

As critic Fábio Lucas indicates in the preface, "the theme of *Eram seis assinalados* is nothing less than a discourse on freedom." The main character, young Irene, becomes a woman who defies the deterministic ambiance of her little town. Relates her story of heroism and personal suffering and sacrifices, as she struggles against the social control exercised by her narrow-minded and conservative community.

4336 Cony, Carlos Heitor. O piano e a orquestra. São Paulo: Companhia das Letras, 1996. 306 p.: map.

A burlesque tone prevails in this narrative filled with histrionics of an individual challenging God. Novel's development focuses on a moment of epiphany for the protagonist who creates a dialectical confrontation between good and evil.

4337 Cony, Carlos Heitor. Quase memória: quase-romance. São Paulo: Companhia das Letras, 1995. 213 p.

Author reminisces about life with his father, also a journalist. Narrative encompasses a partial history of journalism in Brazil, relating encounters and conflicts between ethical and unethical opportunities and between honest news and marketable episodes that are published in the newspapers. Semi-autobiographical.

4338 Costa, Flávio Moreira da. O equilibrista do arame farpado. Rio de Janeiro: Editora Record, 1996. 206 p.

Carnivalesque and postmodernist are some of the possible qualifiers for this picaresque novel. Its structure involves both an orderly and chaotic array of themes, scenarios, and displacement of characters. The protagonist, Captain Poeira (Captain Dust), mutates from main character to narrator in mid-novel, following a string of incidents, some humorous and others not. Seemingly independent of each other, these incidents are also juxtaposed and inter-related by events of the captain's life of adventures and search for balance.

4339 Dantas, Francisco José Costa. Os desvalidos. São Paulo: Companhia das Letras, 1993. 221 p.

In a language close to the Brazilian northern oral tradition, narrative conveys life in the backlands for landlords, politicians, and cowboys. The periods immediately preceding and following the 1938 death of Lampião, the notorious *cangaceiro* (the outlaw of the fields), constitute the time frame for this epic, which describes raids on farms and the love between Maria Bonita and her husband Felipe, a relationship torn apart by Lampião.

4340 Dourado, Autran. Ópera dos fantoches. Rio de Janeiro: F. Alves, 1995. 251 p.

Revisits *Tempo de amar* (see *HLAS* 32:4730), one of the author's first novels. Characters and plot are reshaped and reformulated, though still echoing persona and drama of the former novel. Present work establishes a new construct, a revitalization of language that introduces a new mode of writing.

4341 Fagundes, Antonio Augusto. Destino de Tal: novela gauchesca. Porto Alegre, Brazil: Editora AGE, 1992. 141 p.

The large *estâncias*, the hills, and the *pampas* of Rio Grande do Sul form the background of the infamous war between the Chimangos and the Maragatos in 1923. Narrative follows most stages of the local battle.

4342 Fontes, Oleone Coelho. Cristais em chamas. Petrópolis, Brazil: Vozes, 1993. 472 p.

Encyclopedic narrative presents a panoramic view of the miserable life endured by the *garimpeiros* (seekers of gold and precious stones) in the backlands of Brazil. Includes stories, legends, narratives, chronicles, and religious sermons that circulate among the workers. Though of interest for the contrasts between the beauty of the gems and the poverty of the hunters, and between the applications of quartz for the comfort of part of the society and the backward lifestyle of the poor, novel is encumbered by an excessive representation of regional oral literature.

4343 Fundação Casa de Rui Barbosa (Brazil). Arquivo-Museu de Literatura Brasileira. Inventário do Arquivo Clarice Lispector. Rio de Janeiro: Ministério da Cultura, Fundação Casa de Rui Barbosa, Centro de Memória e Difusão Cultural, Arquivo-Museu de Literatura Brasileira, 1994. 110 p.: bibl., index. (Inventário do arquivo; 5)

Lispector's personal items were donated by one of her sons to the Casa de Rui Barbosa in Rio de Janeiro. Publication is an inventory of those donations, listing books previously owned by the author as well as letters received from prominent literary figures of Brazil during her lifetime. Also included are newspaper articles on her work, which she personally collected. Other miscellaneous items such as theater tickets, cancelled checks, menus of some restaurants abroad, and rental receipts are also part of her legacy, and help us to imagine other dimensions of her persona.

4344 Gomes, Álvaro Cardoso. Os rios inumeráveis. Prefácio de José Paulo Paes. Rio de Janeiro: Topbooks, 1997. 432 p.

Nine narratives address various aspects of Brazilian history through the 500 years since the collision of European and indigenous cultures in the coastal and backland areas of the country. Stories reflect Portuguese grammar structure and vocabulary that were predominant during the time period. Intriguing and innovative, novel reveals many dimensions of Brazilian identity, all linked by the metaphoric and emblematic image of "innumerable rivers" running throughout the land.

4345 Gomes, Heloisa Toller. As marcas da escravidão: o negro e o discurso oitocentista no Brasil e nos Estados Unidos. Rio de Janeiro: Editora UFRJ; EDUERJ, 1994. 199 p.: bibl.

Comparative study on race relations and on social and individual images of blacks in the US and Brazil. Examines selected religious, political, and literary discourses from an interdisciplinary perspective. Supported by theories of Michael Foucault and Jacques Derrida on discourse formation and intertextuality, demonstrates the ideological concepts of the colonizers, showing how these were later replaced by scientific theories that supported the ruling classes in neglecting, mistreating, and dehumanizing the non-white population in the two countries.

4346 Hohlfeldt, Antônio. O exílio na terra dos muitos: o romance da fundação do Rio Grande. Belo Horizonte, Brazil: Editora Lê, 1992. 103 p. (Romances da história)

Historical novel focuses on a 1742 soldiers' revolution in Rio Grande do Sul. No particular hero emerged from that rebellion,

the motive for which was a simple demand for bread. The Portuguese Crown seemed to have forgotten about even the existence of these humble subjects. Some credit the event as the seed for subsequent revolutions leading to an independent state in that region.

4347 Jacob, Paulo. Amazonas, remansos, rebojos e banzeiros. Rio de Janeiro: Nórdica, 1995. 87 p.

Massive linguistic, pictorial, and descriptive novel emulates possible impact of the Amazonian forest on humans living in that milieu—the waters, sounds, animals, insects, humidity, heat, coldness, shade, and brightness. The leitmotif of the narrative is the immense *samaumeira* tree that for centuries served as a point of reference for both mariners and land travelers. The gradual disappearance of the tree due to predators infuses the novel with a nostalgic feeling of abandonment and sadness comparable to the feelings experienced by the indigenous population when forced to leave the area at the foot of the Andes, fleeing the Spaniards, and entering the forest so aptly described here.

4348 Jurandir, Dalcídio. Três casas e um rio: romance. 3a. ed. Belém, Brazil: Edições CEJUP, 1994. 396 p.

Third edition of third volume of a trilogy (the first two are *Chove nos campos de Cachoeira*, see *HLAS 7:4962* and *Marajó* see *HLAS 13:2327*). The splendiferous Amazonian landscape is evident throughout the narrative, encompassing life in a small village on the island of Marajó. Author's skills include his determined approach to the Amazonian world as an integral part of humankind with its psychological and other conflicts, and his avoidance of the exoticism that usually accompanies texts related to that region.

4349 Kujawski, Guilherme. Piritas siderais: romance cyberbarroco. Rio de Janeiro: F. Alves, 1994. 136 p. (Col. Pedra de toque; 1)

Trailblazing novel for its innovative language and characters, both derived from Internet lingo. As if copied and pasted, the crypto-language practiced by Internet users in Brazil is used to interesting effect in this cybernovel. Between the parody and the burlesque, narrative challenges the reader's sense of boundaries and may foreshadow a confusing future for personal communication in the 21st century.

4350 Lage, Tarcísio. Os muros de Jerusalém. São Paulo: Estação Liberdade, 1993. 175 p.: bibl.

Using eschatological language, narrator creates an archetypical character who engages in dialogue with pictures of dead relatives, friends, and acquaintances. From these exchanges, novel conveys the significant political and repressive events of Brazilian dictatorship (1964–85), rites of passage in the life of a male character, and an insight to his world view as a political exile who lives until 2015.

4351 Landim, Teoberto. Seca: a estação do inferno. Fortaleza, Brazil: UFC, Casa de José de Alencar, Programa Editorial, 1992. 246 p.: bibl. (Col. Alagadiço novo; 35)

Study focuses on theme of drought in eight Brazilian novels. In *O sertanejo*, José de Alencar invents a landscape of desert. In *Os retirantes*, José do Patrocínio emphasizes people's mystical engagement, which contrasts with the scientific approach of Rodolfo Teófilo in *A fome*. Rachel de Queiroz assumes the spirituality of Patrocínio in *O quinze*, while Graciliano Ramos, in *Vidas secas*, presents a comprehensive vision of drought through individual dreams and introspective characters against the backdrop of a harsh nature that pushes humans to the edge of sanity. Author emphasizes the birth of a corrupt "industry" of the drought, manipulated by politicians, and the ever-persevering religious attitudes of the humble people who endure the absence of rain for extended periods of time.

4352 Landmann, Jorge. Tróia negra: a saga dos Palmares. São Paulo: Editora Mandarim, 1998. 422 p.

Narrative relates attack of Portuguese colonizers on the Quilombo de Palmares, a self-sufficient farm worked mainly by former slaves who escaped from sugarcane plantations in 17th-century Brazil. Located in a region between Pernambuco and Alagoas, the farm grew to a population of 30,000; all of its inhabitants eventually were killed in one of the cruelest massacres of blacks during Brazil's colonial period. Zumbi, a Brazilian black born in the Quilombo, sustained farm's defense for years as a military strategist

without equal. His heroic resistance is remembered with a holiday in his honor on Nov. 19, the date of his death (1695). Novel provides a fictional framework for these and other historical facts.

4353 Largman, Esther. Jan e Nassau: trajetória de um índio cariri na Corte holandesa. Rio de Janeiro: Imago, 1996. 260 p.: bibl. (Série Diversos)

The court of Prince Mauritz von Nassau upon his return to Holland is seen through the eyes of Jan, a young Brazilian. Like other Dutchmen of his time, Nassau held indigenous men as servants; however, Jan was his favorite and Nassau attended to his education. The imaginary encounter of the civilized European and the "barbaric" Amerindian cultures is depicted through descriptions of salons attended by travelers to the New World, rabbis, nobles, businessmen, and philosophers, such as Baruch Spinoza. The friendship between Nassau and the boy grows throughout the years and continues after Jan returns to Brazil to try and find his familial roots. Atmosphere constructed by author is guided by a rich and reliable bibliography.

4354 Lehmann, Elvira Vigna. O assassinato de bebê Martê. São Paulo: Companhia das Letras, 1997. 124 p.

A fragmented and circular narrative tells of two women passing through stages in life: from riches to rags, from a small town to a big city, from a heterosexual marriage to lesbianism. Novel is an extended reflection on life filled with the irony of appearances and delusions.

4355 Lima, Jorge de. Calunga. 4a. ed.? Rio de Janeiro: Civilização Brasileira, 1997. 142 p.

Lima's novels are being republished; hence the author of *Invenção de Orfeu* (see *HLAS 18:2799*) and the poem "Essa Negra Fulô" is becoming recognized as a novelist. Present work depicts conditions of Brazil's Northeast. A native of the region, protagonist Lula Bernardo prospers elsewhere and returns to his old home, the area of lakes, lagoons, and ponds where poverty, misery, and disease prevail. Social realism novel is rich in vivid descriptions of the ignorance of the people, their submission to a perverted landowner, and the destructive and emblematic role of a *calunga*—a whirling, sucking movement of the waters.

4356 Lins, Osman. A ilha no espaço. São Paulo: Editora Moderna, 1997. 75 p.

The allegorical island is actually a 1960s Recife apartment. Once tenants begin to die of unknown causes, survivors, including the wife and daughter of protagonist, leave the building. He remains alone on the "island," trying to find a solution to his fear of becoming another victim. The story is a veiled accusation of military dictatorship for the sudden disappearances occurring during that period. Short narrative was adapted for Brazilian television.

4357 Lispector, Clarice. A cidade sitiada. Rio de Janeiro: Rocco, 1998. 201 p.

Revised edition of Lispector's third novel is based on its second edition, the last one reformulated by the author.

4358 Lopes, Geraldo. O massacre da Candelária. São Paulo: Scritta, 1994. 140 p. (História imediata)

Based on a true story that shook Brazil, and indeed the world, this novel is a literary/journalistic cry for justice following a massacre of destitute youngsters in Rio de Janeiro. Narrative focuses on an eight-year-old boy living in the slums of Rio with his working parents. Story expands to include lives of other boys, young men, and young women whose only options in life are crime and narcotics. Author concentrates on the youths who were gunned down while asleep on the steps of the Candelária Church.

4359 Maranhão, Heloísa. Rosa Maria Egipcíaca da Vera Cruz: a incrível trajetória de uma princesa negra entre a prostituição e a santidade. Rio de Janeiro: Editora Rosa dos Tempos, 1997. 238 p.

Afro-Brazilian novel whose characters are African slaves in colonial Brazil. They speak together in Portuguese and in the language spoken in Benin, their birthplace. Author creates an atmosphere of transmutation between herself and Rosa Maria, the protagonist, a woman of noble origin sold as a slave before becoming an heiress to a fortune in gold. Novel portrays an intriguing side of colonial Brazil from the viewpoint of the *senzala* (slave headquarters) inhabitants.

4360 Milan, Betty. O papagaio e o doutor. Rio de Janeiro: Editora Record, 1998. 202 p.

First-person narrative reflects personal problems based on a search for identity by Seriema, a Brazilian-born descendant of Lebanese immigrants. Traveling to Paris, she submits herself to intense psychoanalytic sessions, descriptions of which form the main chapters of the novel. During the sessions, she reflects on her sense of inner and geographic displacement, her search for a home country, her sense of confusion from speaking a language (Portuguese) that is not the idiom of her parents, and the difficulties of disclosing her most intimate troubles in French, the language of her parents' former colonizers. Article by Michèle Sarde is included in this edition, revised by the author following publication of the French version.

4361 Miranda, Ana Maria. Amrik: romance. São Paulo: Companhia das Letras, 1997. 205 p.: bibl.

Focuses on a woman who dances her sorrows away and feeds a love story in her dreams, novel depicts Syrian and Lebanese immigrants in their first decades of adjustment to life in São Paulo. Original narrative structure is characterized by short chapters and a sequence of words apparently disconnected from main story, which refers to a woman recalling her Oriental heritage and reinventing the present in order to survive it.

4362 Miranda, Ana Maria. A última quimera. São Paulo: Companhia das Letras, 1995. 292 p.

Fiction and history converge to construct a profile of poet Augusto dos Anjos. Like Salieri who was overshadowed by Mozart, Dos Anjos was overshadowed by the personality of Olavo Bilac. Narrative focuses on both authors, comparing the dark and somber life of the author of "Eu" to Bilac, the radiant "poet of the stars."

4363 Monteiro, Benedicto. Como se faz um guerrilheiro: novela. Belém, Brazil: Editora Cejup, 1995? 88 p.

Innovative language reflects origin of narrator, born and raised in the Amazonian jungle. Framed by the rainforest and immersed in its vast world of rivers, male protagonist shows off his "macho" accomplishments, telling of the seven women from different backgrounds who he impregnated. In the same vein of male superiority, he claims that his children should be like him and tries, through his actions, to demonstrate the character they should develop: courageous, strong, and free—like the surrounding natural world.

4364 Moretzsohn, Virgílio. Treliças: balas e gozos na corte de Nassau. Rio de Janeiro: Leviatã, 1994. 155 p.

Historical novel set in the period of the 17th-century Dutch attack on Bahia. In the midst of naval battles and land clashes, a young Brazilian woman, Ana Pais, astounds her contemporaries by marrying a man who is 40 years her senior. Moreover, becoming a rich widow shortly after the nuptials, she further shocks the local society by audaciously taking control of her deceased husband's business. Novel conveys the sense of mystery and sensuality enveloping the atmosphere of war, ambition, and greed during the time that Nassau ruled the Brazilian Northeast.

4365 Nascimento, Esdras do. Minha morte será manchete: romance. Rio de Janeiro: Editora Revan, 1994. 203 p.

This recipient of many literary awards recycles a detective story in which a recurrent triangle—husband, wife, and her lover—is involved in an unquestionable crime that received a questionable solution. Skillful author retains mystery while depicting many aspects of contemporary middle-class life in Rio de Janeiro.

4366 Nejar, Carlos. O túnel perfeito: romance. Rio de Janeiro: Relume Dumará, 1994. 159 p.

The "perfect tunnel" is an ironic allegory related to the earth and its inhabitants. Referring to some of the greatest thinkers of Western civilization, narrator depicts fragmented biographies of friends, acquaintances, and unknown people, in an effort to extract a lesson or an answer to existential problems. The human search through the tunnel becomes the tunnel itself, made of individual openings and closures of thoughts and attitudes. Poetic allusions point to an intricate and imaginary construction that, while containing many channels of communication, does not offer a way out of the tunnel.

4367 Noll, João Gilberto. A céu aberto. São Paulo: Companhia das Letras, 1996. 164 p.

Story revolves around two boys in search of a father who is fighting in an undefined war in an undisclosed location. Vagueness replaces precision; imagery takes the place of analysis; and a chaotic tension between past and present preclude a future definition of the characters, who range from perverted old military men to masturbating couples to the narrator who appears to be in search of a sense of order in the midst of chaos.

4368 Olinto, Antônio. Alcacer-Kibir: romance. Belém, Brazil: Editora Cejup, 1997? 168 p.

Fictional account of facts surrounding the 1578 Christian-Moorish battle where King Sebastian of Portugal disappeared. Throughout the text, narrator interjects to present results of his research in Morocco and Lisbon. Includes comments on the emergence of the messianic movement that engulfed Portugal for centuries after the disappearance of the king who did not leave an heir to the throne.

4369 Oliveira Neto, Godofredo de. O bruxo do Contestado: romance. Rio de Janeiro: Editora Nova Fronteira, 1996. 205 p.

Narrative revolves mostly around the Contestado Insurrection (1912–16), a messianic-political battle led by a monarchist monk against the New Republic's army in Santa Catarina. Narrator's voice expresses problems he faces as author while writing about his main characters, Gerd Runnel and his small family (wife and a retarded daughter). Describes folk traditions of German descendants in southern Brazil and adds passages in documentary style related to members of that community who nurtured and acted on their empathy for Nazism during WWII.

4370 Pallottini, Renata. Ofícios & amargura: romance. São Paulo: Scipione Cultural, 1998. 142 p.

The name "Clara" is a sort of leitmotif to this peripatetic novel set in several South American countries. A theater critic reveals his personal fears, weaknesses, and, on another level, his ignorance of Latin American cultures.

4371 Pellegrini Júnior, Domingos. Terra-vermelha. São Paulo: Editora Moderna, 1998. 511 p.

A compelling and fascinating narrative of life among immigrant pioneers in northern Paraná early in the 20th century. Protagonist Old José is in a hospital bed for the last seven days of his life. His grandson narrates the family's history, and what he does not know is completed by the old man's memory. The narrators do not realize that they are partners in recounting their family's saga, including the years of working the red soil which demanded the sweat and blood of immigrants and their descendants before allowing its fruits to grow and be harvested.

4372 Prado, Adélia. O homem da mão seca. São Paulo: Editora Siciliano, 1994. 181 p.

Introspection, self-analysis, and trivialization of mystical raptures are among the characteristics of Prado's fiction; these are evident in the present work. Her narrative is closer to a theatrical setting; characters are unfolded by narrator's predictable stage arrangements.

4373 Queiroz, Maria José de. Joaquina, filha do Tiradentes. Ed. integral com posfácio da autora. Rio de Janeiro: Topbooks, 1997. 352 p.

Named after her father (Joaquim José da Silva Xavier), Joaquina, the unknown, historically suppressed illegitimate daughter of Tiradentes, lived with her mother following the final punishment of Brazil's "Martyr of Independence." In a study accompanying this edition, and intended as a warning to teachers and historians about the difference between a historical and a fictional novel, author clarifies that Joaquina did exist, but not exactly as she, the author, created her. Indeed, the story, as partially narrated by Joaquina, mixes history and fiction creating a scenario that might have existed, with elaborate dialogues, details of landscape, and descriptions of the anguish shared by mother, daughter, their friends, and others. Verses from *Romanceiro da Inconfidência* by Cecília Meireles (see *HLAS 38:7487*) are interspersed in the narrative. As a *roman à clef*, narrative includes historical figures such as the painter Van Leyden, a Dutchman who lived in Brazil in the 18th century. For

review of an earlier edition of this work, see *HLAS 52:4562*.

Rago, Margareth. A sexualidade feminina entre o desejo e a norma: moral sexual e cultural literária feminina no Brasil, 1900–1932. See *HLAS 57:5284*.

4374 Rego, José Lins do. Cangaceiros: romance. Estudo de Antonio Carlos Villaça. 9a. ed. Rio de Janeiro: J. Olympio Editora, 1992. 248 p.: bibl., port.

With an introduction by Villaça, this 9th edition of *Cangaceiros* retains the same interest as an epic of the Brazilian *sertão* as it did when first published in 1953 (see *HLAS 19:5325*). Author uncovered the state of abandon of the Northeast rural population left at the mercy of the *cangaceiros*, the outlaws of the *sertão*. At the same time, in a realistic mode he conveys some of their opposing traits: spirituality and cruelty, lyricism and rawness. The fictional intimacy of the author with his mercurial characters filled the imagination of Brazilians and then worldwide readers following translation of the novel into German, French, and Spanish.

4375 Rezende, Rodolfo Motta. Terra, céu e Aruanda. Rio de Janeiro: Civilização Brasileira, 1994. 180 p.

Novel won first prize in the Concurso Literário Civilização Brasileira for 1994. Explores the convergence of religions in Brazil, specifically among Catholics, Protestants, and followers of candomblé, an African religion practiced in Brazil. A mystical atmosphere seems to float through the narrative, which is otherwise a realistic portrayal of an apparently sleepy little town.

4376 Ribeiro, Edgard Telles. Branco como o arco-íris. São Paulo: Companhia das Letras, 1998. 134 p.

From simple things such as the beauty of fog floating over a pond and memories of a childhood spent away from Brazil, narrative action advances into a densely filled analysis of intricate relationships with women ranging from friends to strangers to paramours, some framed by narrator's attempts to recreate a new love from the ashes of old ones. Novel also deals with feelings of a man immersed in questions rooted in the realization that his father, his old buddy, is sinking into the fog of Alzheimer's disease.

4377 Ribeiro, Edgard Telles. As larvas azuis da amazônia: novela. São Paulo: Companhia das Letras, 1996. 100 p.

Pluralistic novel wherein four characters take turns voicing their interpretations of family activities. A young couple Daniel and Débora live together with his parents. The mother, paralyzed and mute after a stroke, reveals her thoughts to her nurse, who informs reader that her patient is aware of household events, including the affair between her husband and her daughter-in-law. Novel's structure, fragmented among characters, skillfully reveals and hides the façade and subterranean passages in this story of a middle-class urban family.

4378 Ribeiro, Rita. Ana Jansen: obra de ficção inspirada na vida de Ana Joaquina Jansen Pereira. Rio de Janeiro: Editora Record, 1995. 238 p.

Historical and biographical novel of Ana Joaquina Jansen Pereira of São Luís, Maranhão. Perhaps the least-known person of the Second Empire, Ana Jansen, a leader of her time, is redeemed in this narrative that captures in detail the way of life in Maranhão. Plays and poetry by Gonçalves Dias entertained local society, while republican ideas were nurtured by many.

4379 Rocha, Sidney. Sofia, uma ventania para dentro. Recife, Brazil: Governo do Estado de Pernambuco, Secretaria de Educação, Cultura e Esportes, Fundação do Patrimônio Histórico e Artístico de Pernambuco; Companhia Editora de Pernambuco, 1994. 121 p.

Though all novels are composed of words, Rocha's work, winner of the 1992 Prêmio Osman Lins de Literatura, *is* words. Sofia, the female protagonist, is the mythical being and the magnet that forms the thoughts and images conveyed by the narrator into words. Significant people and signifiers are erected around an allegory, Sofia, whose name, as the critic Mário Hélio states in his essay included in the volume, is based on the Hebrew roots *ein-sof*, meaning infinite. The constant wind corresponding to the main character is the core of this allegorical novel.

4380 Ruas, Tabajara. O fascínio. Rio de Janeiro: Editora Record, 1997. 141 p.

Detective story with all necessary components—crime, blood, and sheriff—with homosexuals and prostitutes as victims. Aspects of the history of Rio Grande do Sul are intertwined with legends involving elements of a supposed after-life existence. Author's *oeuvre* includes novels better structured and formulated than present one, which seems to be written for a harried reader in search of some thrilling novelties.

4381 Ruas, Tabajara. Netto perde sua alma. 2a. ed. Porto Alegre, Brazil: Mercado Aberto, 1995? 164 p.

Background of this narrative is the Paraguayan War (1865–70). Story takes place mostly in a hospital ward where an injured Brazilian general's bed is his outpost for observing the destinies of his roommates and for mentally returning to his past. He also plots to get rid of a doctor in the hospital.

4382 Santos, Claïr de Mattos. As águas de escorpião: romance. Rio de Janeiro: Civilização Brasileira, 1994. 274 p.

Twin sisters, one noted for her beauty and the other for her lack of it, find themselves on different life paths. Belonging to contemporary middle-class urban society of Rio de Janeiro, their activities disclose worldviews held by the highly educated young professionals of the city. Plot recalls *telenovelas*.

4383 Santos, João Felício dos. Cristo de lama: romance do Aleijadinho de Vila Rica. São Paulo: Círculo do Livro, 1993. 141 p.

Reconstructing the times of the Brazilian sculptor who brought universal recognition to Minas Gerais, author focuses on the diamond mining cycle and the world it made: from the rudimentary treatment of Aleijadinho's leprosy, to the elegant evenings at the homes of local nobility, to the political, public, and veiled talks about slavery. The famed Xica da Silva was a prominent topic in those talks.

4384 Tinhorão, José Ramos. Os romances em folhetins no Brasil, 1830 à atualidade. São Paulo: Livraria Duas Cidades, 1994. 99 p.: bibl.

Important contribution to the study of

folhetins (novels published in installments in daily and weekly newspapers or magazines). Author examines the *folhetins* from their appearance in the Brazilian press to their contemporary resurgence as television soap operas. Includes exhaustive annotated bibliography.

4385 Torero, José Roberto. Galantes memórias e admiráveis aventuras do virtuoso conselheiro Gomes, o Chalaça. São Paulo: Companhia das Letras, 1994. 222 p.

Novel is based on a fictional diary by "Chalaça," the irreverent and manipulative insider of the Court of Dom Pedro I. As Dom Pedro's secretary, he is remembered in history as having had a bad influence on the private life of the first Emperor of Brazil.

4386 Trevisan, João Silvério. Ana em Veneza. São Paulo: Editora Best Seller: Círculo do Livro, 1994. 579 p.

Roman à clef narrative relates encounter of the Brazilian musician Alberto Nepomuceno, the Mann family (parents and children, two of them who would become renowned authors), and Ana, their maid, a former Afro-Brazilian slave who accompanied the Brazilian-born Mrs. Mann. Mingling historical events with the musician's personal interpretation of the European scene, novel reveals intense research in areas of European and Brazilian music. A dense psychological analysis of the meaning of exile for the musician, the maid, and her employer is a strong component of the narrative.

4387 Utéza, Francis. JGR: metafísica do grande sertão. Tradução de José Carlos Garbuglio. São Paulo: EDUSP, 1994. 459 p.: bibl., ill. (some col.), index, maps.

Dense study explores esoteric dimensions of João Guimarães Rosa's *Grande sertão: veredas* (see *HLAS 20:4389*), translated into English with the title *The devil to pay in the backlands* (see *HLAS 26:2008*). Study provides the deep and comprehensive metaphysical analysis of Rosa's great novel which had been lacking up to now. Author, a French Brazilianist, conveys how Taoism, Hinduism, and other Oriental and Western metaphysical and spiritual positions on life are elements in the narratives of *Grande sertão*.:

4388 Vasconcellos, A. Sanford de. O dragão vermelho do Contestado. Florianópolis, Brazil: Editora Insular, 1998. 325 p.

Fictional and historical re-examination of the episode known as the Guerra do Contestado, an insurrection of landless *caboclos* (1912–16) against unbearable exploitation by landowners, a traditional clergy, biased laws, and an oblivious state. Novel deals with facts through a fantastic perspective, revealing the role of magicians, healers, and the charismatic presence of monarchist monk João Maria in the rebellion that took place in the region known today as Irani, in Santa Catarina.

4389 Vianna, Isolina Bresolin. Masmorras da Inquisição: memórias de Antônio José da Silva, o judeu; romance histórico. São Paulo: Editora e Livraria Sêfer, 1997. 139 p.

Fictional biography of a martyr of the Portuguese Inquisition, based on historical facts. Novel is a development of author's Ph.D. dissertation, recreating the atmosphere of the times, with dialogue reflecting the language spoken in the 17th century. Narrative concludes that nothing proved that Antônio José da Silva, a Jew, was a Judaizer.

Short Stories

M. ANGÉLICA GUIMARÃES LOPES, *Associate Professor, University of South Carolina*

BETWEEN 1994–97, THE BRAZILIAN SHORT STORY demonstrated its usual vigor. Several established writers published significant collections (items **4391, 4404, 4407, 4410, 4412, 4416, 4426,** and **4425**), while promising new authors—in many cases prize-winners—joined them (items **4405, 4409,** and **4423**). At the same time, concern for literature and literary history is evident in current editions (items **4390, 4396, 4406,** and **4415**).

The general direction continues as in recent decades, following Mario de Andrade's modernist tenets of the 1920s. The stories reviewed here deal with the writers' reality, employ colloquial Portuguese in dialogue as well as in narrative, and exhibit the authors' awareness of and openness to national and international literary paths. The late-1990s fiction not only conveys Brazil and its people (and nature), but also enriches and strengthens the Portuguese language by using an established lexicon coupled with a newer one (consisting of popular or scientific and technical expressions, as in Tavares' science fiction).

A significant development regarding style and structure has been the recent influence of cinema on fiction. Because of pace and angles, this fiction is much closer to the usual contemporary movie than to stories of 50 years ago. This cinematic connection is easily perceived in the stories of Galiano (item **4400**), Lerner (item **4403**), and Volpato (item **4427**), who write for and about the movies.

Thematically, the Brazilian short story examines different aspects of Brazilian life, including the lives of immigrants. Following Scliar's and Rawet's examples, two São Paulo writers, Cytrynowicz (item **4394**) and Reibscheid (item **4414**), depict Jewish life in that metropolis. Fischer tells about *"vida alamoa,"* i.e., the activities of German Brazilians in the temperate, subtropical south (item **4399**). Another reality and a separate region, the extreme north—Amazonia with its past (rainforest legends) and present (mining and other devastation) is at the heart of tales by Feio (item **4397**) and Silva (item **4419**), and to a lesser extent, Orico (item **4411**) and Savary (item **4417**).

Cities are also represented in these collections: Rio de Janeiro (items **4422** and **4400**), São Paulo (items **4394** and **4414**), Belo Horizonte (item **4409**), Porto Alegre (item **4405**), and Vitória (item **4408**). Gullar's "imaginary cities" cover a broad geographical and chronological spectrum (item **4401**): many offer recognizable Brazilian traits of overpopulation and the shock of wealth juxtaposed with poverty.

Established trends such as black, gay, and women's literature continue to be represented in notable works reviewed for *HLAS 58*. Cuti (item **4393**) and Silveira (item **4420**) depict a wide range of black Brazilian life. Two major writers offer collections of great distinction clearly labeled as gay literature, although given their skillful writing and universal sentiments, these works should not be limited to a particular genre or readership (items **4416** and **4425**). Regarding women's literature, stories by Arnaud (item **4392**), Lunardi (item **4405**), and Savary (item **4417**) are works from a homogeneous female perspective, uniting implicit author and protagonist.

Another notable trend represented in *HLAS 58* is science fiction, which has not been as consistent as black, gay, and women's literature in the 1990s. Tavares (item **4423**) and Gullar (item **4401**) show their powers of invention and their skill. Both works remind the reader that good science fiction is not limited to extraterrestrial matter and that these works can be highly literary.

From a geographical perspective, the Brazil's south and southeast printed the great majority of outstanding works included in *HLAS 58*, which is hardly surprising given that the two regions are the most populous and have the most active publishing houses. However, Veiga, the dean of story writers, represents the centerwest with panache (item **4426**). Two collections are by authors from the northeast (items **4392** and **4423**), a region that is generally more prolific from a literary viewpoint. As mentioned previously, four books depict the north.

Orico (item **4411**), Gullar (item **4401**), and Savary (item **4417**) are among the writers recognized in other areas who are not generally practitioners of short fiction. Both Gullar's and Savary's works evince the poetic exercise for which they are well known.

4390 Abreu, Caio Fernando. Inventário do ir-remediável. 2a. ed. Porto Alegre, Brazil: Editora Sulina, 1995. 158 p. (Narrativas)

Distinguished author, aware of approaching death, presents second edition of prize-winning collection. Theme is traumatic military period (1964–84); and style is allegorical, used to evade censorship. A writer's writer, author was 21 when he first published *Inventário do irremediável* (original title, opposed to new, "avoidable voyage").

4391 Alves, Henrique L. Caminhos do desejo. São Paulo: Sindicato dos Jornalistas Profissionais no Estado de São Paulo: Imprensa Oficial do Estado, 1995. 81 p.: ill.

By São Paulo veteran prize-winning journalist, fiction writer, and literary critic, these stories present realistic characters in dramatic episodes. Collection is an impressive literary work well-deserving of Amnesty and Human Rights Award for insight and concern with contemporary Brazilian social problems.

4392 Arnaud, Marília. A menina de Cipango: contos. João Pessoa, Brazil: A União Editora, 1994. 103 p.

Sensitive, understated and humorous, Northeastern author from Paraiba state tells well-crafted stories from a young girl's viewpoint.

4393 Cuti. Negros em contos. Belo Horizonte, Brazil: Mazza Edições, 1996. 143 p.: bibl.

Stories focusing on Afro-Brazilian characters in São Paulo prove author's keen ethnic concern and powers of perception and invention. Touches upon many aspects of racism in Brazil. Able characterization despite structurally and stylistically uneven stories.

4394 Cytrynowicz, Roney. A vida secreta dos relógios e outras histórias. São Paulo: Scritta, 1994. 77 p. (Brasilis)

Collection is young historian and economist's first published literary endeavor.

Employs nostalgia and suspense in fashioning imaginative tales of Jewish immigrant life in São Paulo's Bom Retiro district. Awarded prestigious Paraná State Short Fiction Prize.

4395 Degrazia, José Eduardo. A orelha de bugre: minicontos. Porto Alegre, Brazil: Movimento, 1998. 1 v.

Entertaining collection by poet who also writes children's literature. *Savage's ear* offers very brief, ironic and often philosophical tales, employing metamorphoses, other metaphors, and developed puns as narrative devices.

4396 Duque Estrada, Luís Gonzaga. Horto de mágoas: contos. 2a ed. Rio de Janeiro: Prefeitura da Cidade do Rio de Janeiro, Secretaria Municipal de Cultura, Depto. Geral de Documentação e Informação Cultural, Divisão de Editoração, 1996. 151 p.: bibl., ill. (Coleção Biblioteca carioca; v. 40 Série Literatura)

Exemplary scholarly second edition of collection originally published in 1911. *Garden of Sorrows"* prints 12 original stories with 2 studies of author, his biography, bibliography, glossary and notes. Although generally good fiction, hermetic plots, arcane words, and often convoluted syntax may deter timid readers.

4397 Feio, Mário. Os arariaras: contos e lendas marajoaras. Belém, Brazil: Gráfica Sto. Antonio, 1995. 262 p.: map.

Carefully told tales of Marajó Island focus on protagonists and on nature. Narrators are often local characters whose difficult lives are due more to greedy landowners than to dangerous beasts and jungle. Some stories have an epic tinge in their depiction of communal or individual struggle.

4398 Figueiredo, Rubens. O livro dos lobos. Rio de Janeiro: Rocco, 1994. 148 p.

Attaining precision through poetic allusions, these skillful stories build a universe that perceives nuances, shadows and doubts through a technique of compact detail accretion. Everyday happenings enveloped by shadows have a Kafkaesque significance. Excellent collection by a novelist.

4399 Fischer, Luís Augusto. O edifício do lado da sombra. Porto Alegre, Brazil: Artes e Ofícios, 1996. 84 p.

Erudite collection, by undeniably talented, sensitive, and humorous author, pays homage to literature through elegant epigraphs and allusions. Ludic aspect permeates collection and is conveyed through numerous mirror games. Imbedded poetry volume is most surprising.

4400 Galiano, Iterbio. Olhos do tempo. Rio de Janeiro: Litteris Editora, 1994. 160 p.

Combining *crônicas* and stories, these pieces present episodes in Rio's old Catumbi and Santa Teresa districts. Keen-eyed, moviemaker author depicts characters with lively style: boys playing on streets, young political revolutionaries meeting, and man filming documentary in women's sanitarium.

4401 Gullar, Ferreira. Cidades inventadas. Rio de Janeiro: J. Olympio Editora, 1997. 107 p.: bibl., ill.

With woodcuts by R. Grilo, beautiful book presents 23 "invented cities" from author-poet's imagination. Wise, ironic, and ludic, collection reminds reader of Iberian descriptions of voyages, Rabelais, Voltaire, Swift, Lewis Carroll, Wells, Orwell, Borges, Calvino, and Rubião. Superbly written stories flow unhindered by puns and occasional mock-scholarly apparatus.

4402 Leiradella, Cunha de. Síndromes & síndromes: e conclusões inevitáveis; contos. Rio de Janeiro: Relume Dumará, 1997. 81 p.

Stories by minimalist master exhibit great vitality because or in spite of brevity. "Syndrome" as the first word in each title establishes parallel. First four stories are minimalist: all have protagonist couple, laconic dialogues, gestures, and descriptions. Final story is a contrast: long narrative in 16th-century Portuguese.

4403 Lerner, Jaime. Entre quatro paredes. Porto Alegre, Brazil: Prefeitura de Porto Alegre, 1995. 135 p.: ill. (some col.).

Wide variety of competent, intelligent, and ironic tales by writer and movie maker

deal with several characters in a Southern metropolis. Title is Brazilian translation for Sartre's play, *Huis clos (No Exit)*. Book is elegantly illustrated with author's photographs: a pair of eyes for each story.

4404 Lobo, Luiza. Sexameron: novelas sobre casamentos. Rio de Janeiro: Relume Dumará, 1997. 113 p.

With title as pun on Bocaccio's and Marguerite of Navarre's famous books as well as on its own theme of sex, inventive collection is also couched in these two authors' narrative mode. Here the Great Plague that sends anonymous literary characters out of Rio into a mansion in city's devastated outskirts is unnamed AIDS.

4405 Lunardi, Adriana. As meninas da Torre Helsinque: histórias. Porto Alegre, Brazil: Prefeitura de Porto Alegre: Mercado Aberto, 1996. 139 p.

Elegant, psychological stories by new writer from Rio Grande de Sul focus on young female characters in unusual circumstances: a molested young girl becomes a murderess, an artist's model is set with a peculiar task, and friend is betrayed by friend. Author is a talent to watch.

4406 Magalhães, Adelino. Sebastianópolis: antologia de contos. Rio de Janeiro: Prefeitura da Cidade do Rio de Janeiro, Secretaria Municipal de Cultura, Depto. Geral de Documentação e Informação Cultural, Divisão de Editoração, 1994. 272 p.: bibl. (Coleção Biblioteca carioca; v. 30. Série Literatura)

Title is facetious name for São Sebastião do Rio de Janeiro, founded in 1500s. The 17 stories were published by precursor of modernism between 1916–39. Creates superb portrait of Rio focusing on poor, young, and dispossessed. Work is surrealistic and expressionistic, and includes autobiography, "Plenitude."

4407 Martins, Anna Maria. Retrato sem legenda. São Paulo: Editora Siciliano, 1995. 75 p.

By one of the finest story writers of her generation, the best tales in *Portrait without a label* convey author's literary skill, sensitivity, and powers of implication.

4408 Mazzini, Roberto. Navegantes: contos. Vitória, Brazil: Instituto Histórico e Geográfico do Espírito Santo, 1997. 1 v.

From coastal Southeast, "Sailor" stories depict *capixaba* nature as well as natives. Not regional, however, in narrow sense of local color as a major trait. Conveys universal sentiment: despair of impossible love, children's awareness of incipient sexual attraction, etc. Unusually perceptive and fine fiction by sports writer.

4409 Mendes, Francisco de Morais. Escreva, querida. Belo Horizonte, Brazil: Mazza Edições, 1996. 126 p.

Excellent volume deserves literary prizes garnered. Presents dramatic urban stories with large casts of characters in metropolis. Broaches family relationships with enviable perception, irony and respect. Remarkable treatment of crowds, including traffic jams; unusual and effective focus on facial and hand gestures.

4410 Nepomuceno, Eric. Coisas do mundo: contos. São Paulo: Companhia das Letras, 1994. 171 p.

Hybrid prize-winning collection unites pieces of a *crônica* nature (i.e., little action and much commentary). Mystery and surprise elements pervade low-key, well-crafted stories.

4411 Orico, Osvaldo. A vida imita os contos. Prefácio de Jorge Amado. Rio de Janeiro: Editora Record, 1995. 176 p.: bibl.

Posthumous pieces by eminent educator and intellectual who was also politician and diplomat were collected by daughter, actress, and singer Vanja Orico. Realistic tales take place in author's native Amazônia and Rio. Many are anecdotal, some are historical recreations of Brazil in the 1930s, 1950s and 1960s.

4412 Pellegrini Júnior, Domingos. Tempo de guerra: contos. São Paulo: Companhia das Letras, 1997. 158 p.

Complex, exemplary stories by distinguished author work classical metaphor of living as fighting. "Civil War" examines homeless bands roaming across Paraná state obliquely through dogs that accompany them. "Frost" recounts war between coffee planters and nature. Excellent, erotic "A Cup

of Sugar" focuses on seduction and love. Splendid collection.

4413 Queiroz, Maria José de. Amor cruel, amor vingador. Rio de Janeiro: Editora Record, 1996. 139 p.

One novella and five shorter tales present passion crimes, each the result of "cruel, vengeful love," in a declared Freudian line. Written with authority and elegance, each tale has a final twist in the tradition of a well-made thriller. Ably fashions vocabulary and syntax according to setting.

4414 Reibscheid, Samuel. Breve fantasia. São Paulo: Scritta, 1995. 217 p. (Brasilis)

Author-physician's first foray into fiction recreates São Paulo's Jewish district. Witty, often sardonic and Rabelaisian in detail, collection conveys sentiment and nostalgia. Includes Yiddish glossary.

4415 Rubião, Murilo. Contos reunidos. São Paulo: Editora Atica, 1998. 279 p.

First complete edition of stories by Brazilian master of fantastic, whose influence continues to be felt by writers and readers. Superb collection with biblical quotes as epigraphs includes unpublished "A Diáspora," which author rewrote until his death, after he had left original manuscript in a taxi.

4416 Santiago, Silviano. Keith Jarrett no blue note: improvisos de jazz. Rio de Janeiro: Rocco, 1996. 147 p.

Impressive *Jazz Improvisations* are accomplished stories with Jarrett's songs as titles. Introspective and retrospective, follows Machado de Assis' and Proust's memorialist paths as character/narrator recasts old loves in cities of his youth against snowy Midwestern US background. Although presented as "gay stories," range is universal.

4417 Savary, Olga. O olhar dourado do abismo: contos. Teresópolis, Brazil: Impressões do Brasil Editora, 1997. 138 p.

Many of these elegant, perceptive, and brief tales deal with almost ineffable feelings, and in others with Amazonian lore—all suited to poetic approach and language. *Golden look from the abyss* unites irony and mythology: the look belongs to a goat. Collection won several prestigious awards.

4418 Seixas, Heloisa. Pente de vênus: histórias do amor assombrado. Porto Alegre, Brazil: Editora Sulina, 1995. 244 p. (Narrativas)

First collection by imaginative, competent writer creates dense atmosphere fraught with fear, memory, and passion in which characters remember or discover themselves. Echoes of Poe and Kafka in characters obsessed by their sorrows and apparently insoluble problems.

4419 Silva, Renato Ignácio da. Cascalhos da promessa: aventuras no garimpo do mal. São Paulo: RENIG-Editora e Assessoria Publicitária, 199-? 182 p.: ill.

Adventures in hell's strip mining are ecologically inspired stories and part of series on Amazon region. Main title is mining camp's name, "Gravel of Promise." Technically traditional first story provides extensive data on nature and mining as well as a certain humor. In all, book is more journalistic than literary. Of special interest to mining aficionados.

4420 Silveira, Maria Helena Vargas da. Odara: fantasia e realidade. Porto Alegre, Brazil: s.n., 1993. 67 p.: bibl., ill.

Competent stories on black Brazilians in southernmost Rio Grande do Sul mix reality and history (such as 1888 Emancipation) with fiction. Tone is semi-didactic in book devoted to preserving ethnic traits, especially religious African traditions. Includes glossary and recommended bibliography on Afro-Brazilian topics.

4421 Sobreiro Júnior, Valter. A sombra que avança até Valério e outras sombras: contos. Porto Alegre, Brazil: Tchê!, 1995. 87 p.

Forceful stories are at times hermetic and abrupt in inner transitions. Interesting technique guides careful and slow development of unusual plots such as servant helping master poison tyrannical mother and general's aged daughter becoming a weapons smuggler.

4422 Sodré, Muniz. Rio, Rio: contos. Rio de Janeiro: Relume Dumará, 1995. 142 p.

Often including or ending in anecdote, well-made, intelligent, and ironic stories were critically acclaimed and make for pleasant reading. Rio's Southern beach districts from Copacabana and Ipanema to Barra da Tijuca serve as settings.

4423 Tavares, Braulio. A espinha dorsal da memória: mundo fantasmo. Rio de Janeiro: Rocco, 1996. 158 p.

Some of these skillful, entertaining stories won an important science fiction prize; others are new. Imaginative, poetic, and dramatic plots deal with imaginary worlds and with pre-history and the middle ages.

4424 Torres, Paulo. Todos estes anos: contos. Vitória, Brazil: Nemar Editora, 1994. 101 p.

All these years refers to mid-1960s, an era of political repression and hippie counterculture experienced by journalist-author. Fast pace and montage symbolize video clips and insinuate disorientation brought about by alcohol and other drugs.

4425 Trevisan, João Silvério. Troços & destroços: contos. Rio de Janeiro: Editora Record, 1997. 157 p. (Contraluz)

Rubbish and wreckage presents adolescent boys in throes of sexual anguish which often ends in despair or death. Bitter, somber, and perceptive collection portrays homosexual characters, situations, and viewpoint. Distinguished book is expectedly classified as "gay literature," a growing category in Brazil.

4426 Veiga, José J. Objetos turbulentos: contos para ler à luz do dia. Rio de Janeiro: Bertrand Brasil, 1997. 157 p.

One of Brazil's finest contemporary authors describes "turbulent objects," beginning as old, often discarded objects, and looming large as they irrevocably change owners' lives. Advises that tales should be read by light of day, obliquely warning readers of fantastic nature. Texture, depth, and irony of daily life are notable.

4427 Volpato, Cadão. Ronda noturna. São Paulo: Iluminuras, 1995. 95 p.

"Night patrol" collects five concise, elegant, and humorous stories, three of which are variations on theme of family. Style and approach mirror journalistic and cinematic practice.

Crônicas

CHARLES A. PERRONE, *Professor of Portuguese and Luso-Brazilian Literature and Culture, University of Florida*

AS THE NEW MILLENNIUM BEGINS and the shapes of communication media inevitably change, definitions of *crônica*—a brief composition about an aspect of contemporary life—continue to be reworked, as can be noted in the prefaces and afterwords of some current collections. Carlos Lacerda describes this literary-journalistic type as "esse discretear luminoso e calmo sobre as coisas que vão passando à beira do caminho" [that calm and luminous chat about things that happen by the side of the road] (quoted in item **4439**). While by necessity and practice the literary, editorial, and bibliographical senses of what *crônica* may mean to readers, writers, and publishers are more fluid than those of the standard genres of literature, a consensus remains. Poet Ledo Ivo wrote that we [the literate Brazilian public] all presume to know, through direct experience as newspaper readers, what a *crônica* is, or are able to recognize one, even when it is masked as criticism of customs or political reflection, or is clearly sliding toward the essay ("Os dias que passam," *Estado de São Paulo*, 3/23/1981). Given the thematic and tonal variety of today's production, an informed and experienced reader might say, "I can't give a perfect definition, but I know it when I see it," and wonder whether certain publications titled, subtitled, self-classified, or otherwise described as *crônica* indeed fall within the bounds of this genre. Acknowledging gray areas and blurred lines, new publications are questioned as encroachments on the *crônica* and are regarded more as opinion columns, political analysis, or commentary, especially when consistently heavier tones pervade the writing (items **4429**, **4438**, **4442**, and **4458**).

As for the staying power of the *crônica*, writers and publishers who title or register a borderline book as a volume of *crônicas* indicate enhanced confidence in the genre. The widening of definitions is a symptom of the growth of the genre and the consolidation of its late-century manifestations. Lyric (poetry) and epic (fiction) may be losing readership in the age of electronic media, but *crônica* has maintained public interest, growing in availability as newspaper websites continue to appear. In addition to works by new authors, notable reprints also still appear, notably the "classics" of Rachel de Queiroz (items **4454** and **4455**). Publishers gather the newspaper work of noteworthy modern figures—such as Rodrigues (item **4457**) and Antônio Maria (item **4430**)—and of salient turn-of-the-century writers—Machado de Assis (item **4445**), Bilac (item **4431**), and João do Rio (item **4443**). In the late 20th century, poets and fiction writers continued to double as *cronistas;* the present group (in addition to the venerable Queiroz) includes Ribeiro (item **4456**), Abreu (item **4428**), João Antônio (item **4440**), and the friends of Plínio Doyle (item **4449**). These literary associations and historical editions further suggest a diversified readership.

A general market interest is evident in the access Brazilian migrant communities abroad have to *crônicas*, which now appear on the Internet and in Portuguese-language periodicals in Japan and Portugal and in US states such as Florida, New York, and Massachusetts. Favorite readings are naturally included in Internet editions of metropolitan dailies, but *crônicas* also are posted ad hoc to news and discussion groups, or simply passed along by avid readers sharing the textual experience. The brevity of the genre naturally facilitates consumption in the fast-paced digital world.

Appearance on the ever-changing Internet again raises the question of the fundamentally ephemeral journalistic nature of the *crônica* and its continuation in book form. Ledo Ivo asserted that publishing books of *crônicas* was the authors' way of saving themselves from the perishable quality of the genre and of giving a lasting image to the attentive reader. This concept may have been true in previous generations, but now more collections are being published at the initiative of editors and cultural promoters, rather than by the authors themselves. There are also several examples of *crônicas* written not just for newspapers or magazines, but in anticipation of a subsequent anthology or for direct inclusion in a made-to-order book.

The latter type of *crônica* is found in volumes produced both through local municipal and regional state interest in the genre as a vehicle of self-promotion, self-discovery and civic pride. Of the publications reviewed for *HLAS 58*, nine items are from state capitals other than the metropolitan centers of Rio de Janeiro, São Paulo and Brasília. The case of Vitória is exemplary (item **4453**). Quantitatively, Rio Grande do Sul is a leader in such promotion (items **4435** and **4459**), including a specific regional ethnic case of bilingualism (item **4444**). Elsewhere, Germanic heritage is central (item **4433**), and an example from the remote state of Acre focuses on Middle Eastern ancestry (item **4441**).

As communication technology expands and the pace of modern life quickens, so do the thematic and geographical bounds of the *crônica* broaden. Concurrently, the 1990s saw a growing presence of international and travel motifs. Whether in the US (items **4446** and **4460**) or Europe (items **4434, 4437, 4439,** and **4456**), *cronistas* go beyond mere touristic curiosity to provide a meeting place between foreign and Brazilian experiences.

Finally, new scholarly interest should be noted. Less than two decades ago, Ledo Ivo also said that academic curiosity in this area was so scant that it did not even merit the label "curiosity." Though today, as Eduardo Portella said years ago, there is still no theory of the *crônica*, there are more critical editions and studies. Pereira's effort joins the group of general studies (item **4451**), while specific historical interest in the previously-mentioned turn-of-the-century authors are well served by the work of Gledson (item **4445**), Dimas (item **4431**), and Levin (item **4443**). Such contributions should inspire additional serious studies as we embark upon the third century of the *crônica*.

4428 Abreu, Caio Fernando. Pequenas epifanias: crônicas, 1986/1995. Porto Alegre, Brazil: Sulina, Livraria, Editora e Distribuidora, 1996. 188 p.

Pieces previously published in São Paulo and Porto Alegre daily newspapers by flamboyant figure of contemporary literature. Good example of fiction writer doubling as *cronista*.

4429 Alves, Márcio Moreira. Manual do cronista aprendiz. Rio de Janeiro: Editora Revan, 1995. 215 p.

Collected articles by sharp-witted and sharp-tongued columnist aspire to condition of *crônica* as popular genre. Spanning 1960s-90s, works illustrate what one observer calls "the art of political communication." Novelist Antonio Callado notes utility of collection as historical vision of modern Brazil. Others compare author to Portuguese chroniclers of early colonial period.

4430 Antônio Maria. Com vocês, Antônio Maria. São Paulo: Paz e Terra, 1994. 268 p.: ill.

Selection exemplifies *crônica* as a simple, unpretentious form, pleasant but rarely profound. Thematic sections, with titles drawn from memorable phrases by author, concern love, admired public figures, Copacabana neighborhood, food, and, interestingly, letters from readers.

4431 Bilac, Olavo. Vossa insolência: crônicas. São Paulo: Companhia das Letras, 1996. 415 p.: bibl. (Retratos do Brasil; 6)

With introduction, organization, and notes by Prof. Antônio Dimas, volume represents a unique contribution to current work in field, emphasizing historical role of this particularly significant author. Bilac, prince of Brazilian poets, succeeded Machado de Assis as *cronista* in Rio's press. Titles are organized thematically (people, cinema, literature, city life, politics, etc.), with special note on the Canudos campaign.

4432 Blanc, Aldir. Um cara bacana na 19a. contos, crônicas e poemas. Rio de Janeiro: Editora Record, 1996. 238 p.: ill.

Graphically attractive volume includes *crônicas* accompanied by narrative song lyrics, stories, and lyrical verse by one of Rio's most beloved popular writers, commemorating his 50th birthday.

4433 Blumenau, alles blau. v. 1. Florianópolis, Brazil: Paralelo 27, 1992. 1 v.: ill. (Série Crônicas Barriga-verde)

Prime example of municipal self-promotion via *crônica*. First group is a historical curiosity, 12 impressions from 1947 of this Germanic city by a military author. Also includes compositions solicited from local writers and editor-observer's own *crônicas*. Volume is interspersed with advertisements, as in a commercial magazine.

4434 Celina, Lindanor. Diário da ilha: crônicas. Belém, Brazil: Edições CEJUP, 1992. 239 p.

Published in a state capital, collection is international in scope. Travel diary focuses on Greece, with memories of Brazil from afar.

4435 A cidade de perfil. Porto Alegre, Brazil: Unidade Editorial Porto Alegre, 1994. 166 p. (Série Coruja)

In addition to nostalgic views of city, gaúcho-centric profiles by local authors deal with economic growth and current affairs. One moving title concerns the death of favorite daughter, vocalist Elis Regina.

4436 Colasanti, Marina. Eu sei, mas não devia. Rio de Janeiro: Rocco, 1996. 188 p.

In addition to common theme of daily city life, new *crônicas* concern women's issues, love, contemporary artists, street children, and, in keeping with a recent trend, travel. Colasanti's intelligence is complemented by a constant ethical sense.

4437 Congílio, Mariazinha. Por este mundão afora: crônicas de viagem. São Paulo: Editora Pannartz, 1991. 136 p.

In the introduction to her 13th book of *crônicas*, Congílio notes the inclusion of her work in the original pedagogical volume, *Crônicas brasileiras* (1971). These newly collected anecdotes, illustrating a recent editorial tendency to favor travel literature, reveal a typically familiar tone, but are not consistently engaging.

4438 Freire, Roberto. Tesudos de todo o mundo, uni-vos! São Paulo: Editora Siciliano, 1995. 245 p.

These sui generis compositions are self-cataloged as *crônicas*, but they lie in a gray area of genre, closer to brief essays or long opinion columns. Freire, a therapist by profession, is an anarchist thinker who takes an informed but informal approach to topics such as soccer, sex, and national politics.

4439 Guerra, Jacinto. O gato de Curitiba: crônicas e histórias acontecidas pelo mundo afora. Brasília, Brazil: Thesaurus, 1994. 155 p.: ill.

With five separate presentations or prefaces, Guerra approaches, with descriptive force, both real and imaginary places in Brazil, from Paraná to Amazonas, and abroad. Small, mid-size, and large cities all concern him.

4440 João Antônio. Casa de loucos. 4a. ed. Rio de Janeiro: Rocco, 1994. 151 p.

Fourth printing of lively short book with just 12 titles highlights personal portraits (including Noel Rosa and Darcy Ribeiro) and presents often satirical dramatizations of urban life and customs.

4441 Kalume, Jorge. Crônicas do Acre antigo. Brasília, Brazil: s.n., 1991. 75 p.: ill.

Career politician (former governor, federal deputy) writes about northern region, in particular old Acre, especially Xapuri and Lebanese immigrants.

4442 Konder, Rodolfo. O rio da nossa loucura. São Paulo: Editora Saraiva, 1994. 104 p.

Traces evolution of Konder's thought since the verge of *abertura* (political opening) in late 1970s. Generally more serious commentary, these *crônicas* consider such topics as torture and Amnesty International, encompassing author's leftist perspective.

4443 Levin, Orna Messer. As figurações do dândi: um estudo sobre a obra de João do Rio. Campinas, Brazil: Editora da UNICAMP, 1996. 228 p.: bibl., ill. (Coleção Viagens da voz)

Valuable critical study, based on master's thesis, regarding decadent and turn-of-the-century styles in fictional work of one of period's most noted writers, best known for his *crônicas*. Significant inclusion of genre in wide-ranging literary analysis.

4444 Luzzatto, Darcy Loss. Stòrie de la nostra gente. Porto Alegre, Brazil: Sagra-DC Luzzatto Editores: Massolin de Fiori Società Taliana, 1991. 110 p.: ill. (Série Imigração italiana; 09)

Illustrated volume is a unique bilingual (Portuguese/Venetian Italian) collection about immigrant communities in Rio Grande do Sul, with expected themes of coming from the "old country" and making a new life in Brazil. Interesting title for immigration studies and sociolinguistics since it includes several prefaces by Italian academics.

4445 Machado de Assis. A semana: crônicas, 1892–1893. São Paulo: Editora Hucitec, 1996. 3 v.: bibl., ill., index. (Literatura brasileira)

Distinguished English scholar John Gledson organizes, introduces, and annotates 83 *crônicas* in first volume of journalistic publications of Brazil's premier author. Vols. 1–3 cover all 243 *crônicas* published in last decade of 19th century in *A Gazeta.*

4446 Matta, Roberto da. Torre de Babel: ensaios, crônicas, críticas, interpretações e fantasias. Rio de Janeiro: Rocco, 1996. 265 p.

These *crônicas* and other pieces by noted cultural anthropologist turned journalist often deal comparatively with Brazil and US, falling within the paradigm of travel and commentary. Pervasive concerns are customs, national character, and modern social history; soccer, music, and political vagaries complete the panorama.

4447 Medeiros, Martha. Geração bivolt. Porto Alegre, Brazil: Artes e Ofícios, 1995. 126 p.

Medeiros, a young author from Porto Alegre, is a reader of international feminism and media stars. Work deals with male-female relations, modern behavior, and even androgyny in title piece. Engages readers thematically despite somewhat flat prose.

4448 Mendonça, Antonio Penteado. Crônicas da cidade. São Paulo: Edições GRD, 1996. 224 p.

To combat the notion that the *crônica* essentially belongs to Rio de Janeiro, Mendonça brings together his pieces about São Paulo, its people, and history. Thematic variety compensates somewhat for uninspired prose.

4449 O Natal no Sabadoyle. Organização de Olímpio José Garcia Matos. Ed. comemorativa. São Paulo: M. Ohno Editor, 1994. 123 p.: ill. (some col.).

Collection of annual Christmas-time texts (1972–94)—some in verse, most in prose and qualifying as special-occasion *crônicas*—about preceding year's Saturday gatherings of intellectuals at home of Plínio Doyle, who commissioned the pieces. Including two contributions by Carlos Drummond de Andrade, provides excellent opportunity to study literary elite of Rio.

4450 Neves, Dom Lucas Moreira. O homem descartável e outras crônicas. Rio de Janeiro: Editora Record, 1995. 206 p. (Col. Univ. Católica do Salvador)

The archbishop of Salvador avails himself of the secular Brazilian literary tradition of *crônica* to write about religious themes: the Christ figure, the pope, the Church as institution; and the values of modern life in general.

4451 Pereira, Wellington. Crônica: arte do útil ou do fútil?; ensaio sobre a crônica no jornalismo impresso. João Pessoa, Brazil: Idéia, 1994. 159 p.

Brief study recapitulates evolution of *crônica* genre and its function in journalism.

4452 Pernidji, Joseph Eskenazi. Girassóis de Van Gogh: crônicas. Rio de Janeiro: Imago, 1993. 165 p. (Série Diversos)

Pernidji, a lawyer by profession, offers colloquial, impressionistic prose contemplating human characters and situations, often playing with reality, fictionality, or plausibility of episodes.

4453 Prefeitura Municipal de Vitória, Secretaria Municipal de Cultura e Esporte. Escritos de Vitória. v. 1, Crônicas. Vitória, Brazil: A Secretaria, 1993. 1 v.: ill.

First (slim) volume of a series about the capital of Espírito Santo state includes commissioned *crônicas*, which are mostly proud and nostalgic in tone, but often seem contrived. Perfect example of a regional collection with institutional initiative and support.

4454 Queiroz, Rachel de. Um alpendre, uma rede, um açude: 100 crônicas escolhidas. 6a. ed. São Paulo: Editora Siciliano, 1994. 261 p.

Sixth printing of original 1958 volume—with curiously titled pieces from 1940s and 1950s—demonstrates wide interest in genre and author. With no index or page breaks between selected *crônicas*, book comprises an almost-novel like constant flow.

4455 Queiroz, Rachel de. O caçador de tatu: 57 crônicas escolhidas. 2a. ed. São Paulo: Editora Siciliano, 1994. 146 p.

Reprint of a 1967 collection is a sign of the popularity of both author and genre. In her treatment of multifarious rural, urban, local, national and international topics, Queiroz invariably reveals an affective dimension.

4456 Ribeiro, João Ubaldo. Um brasileiro em Berlim: crônicas. Rio de Janeiro: Editora Nova Fronteira, 1995. 159 p.

Excellent current example of a noted writer residing abroad and sharing experiences with readers in Brazil in the form of *crônicas*. Aside from considerations of cultural exchange, includes numerous memories of Northeast, confirming Ribeiro's talent and reputation established in short fiction and novels.

4457 Rodrigues, Nelson. A cabra vadia: novas confissões. São Paulo: Companhia das Letras, 1995. 300 p.: index. (Coleção das obras de Nelson Rodrigues; 9)

Vol. 9 of complete works of a great phrase-maker, one of the most celebrated Brazilian authors since 1980, includes 80 short *crônicas* selected by biographer Ruy Castro. Focuses on 1968, a turbulent and historically significant year. Conservative-minded Rodrigues views ongoing events and social unrest with a sometimes irritating sarcasm but characteristically admirable force of style. Among most cited are Mao Tse-Tung, Che Guevara, Dom Helder Câmara, and protest singer Geraldo Vandré, in context of noted popular-music festivals of 1968.

4458 Sarney, José. Sexta-feira, Folha. São Paulo: Editora Siciliano, 1994. 398 p.: index.

Despite self-classification as *crônicas*, only a few of these 300 pieces by former president deal with people or places in a fashion closer to character of the genre. Most are personal documents about presidential politics and recent history.

4459 Tostes, Theodemiro. Bazar e outras crônicas. 2a. ed. Porto Alegre, Brazil: Fundação Paulo do Couto e Silva: Instituto Estadual do Livro, 1994. 288 p.: ill. (Coleção LetraSul; vol. 3)

This volume, sponsored by Rio Grande do Sul state, contains reprints of over 100 short pieces published in 1930s by poet-journalist Tostes. Most of the lyrical vignettes consider themes and places other than local culture or the state's capital city of Porto Alegre. One of the final entries, "Da crônica e do leitor," is a whimsical consideration of the genre and potential readers.

4460 Veríssimo, Luís Fernando. América. Porto Alegre, Brazil: Artes e Ofícios, 1994. 129 p.: ill.

With 1994 World Cup Soccer as a point of departure, most pieces concern American customs, exemplifying travel motifs in the genre. The articles, while generally more serious (i.e., without comic intentions) than is common in Veríssimo's repertory, do not compare favorably with US travel literature of author's father, novelist Érico Veríssimo.

4461 Veríssimo, Luís Fernando. Comédias da vida privada: 101 crônicas escolhidas. 2a ed. Porto Alegre, Brazil: L&PM Editores, 1994. 326 p.

After Drummond, Veríssimo is Brazil's most accomplished, prolific, and successful current *crônista* (cf. the number of reprints of his works). Selection reveals characteristic humor, stylistic grace, and engaging approaches. Focuses on middle-class life in bars, family situations, courtship, and other aspects of male-female relationships.

Poetry

NAOMI HOKI MONIZ, *Associate Professor of Portuguese, Georgetown University*

IN THE LAST 20 YEARS, globalization and democratization, combined with the pervasiveness of media and communications technology, have resulted in tremendous changes in the cultural life of Brazil, and in the production, distribution, and consumption of its culture. Brazilian poetry has not been impervious to these alterations; poetic works are exhibiting a wider range of views and approaches and demonstrating a renewal of older forms. Contemporary Brazilian poetry conveys the fluidity and movement of the present, while portraying the utopian ideal as empty, disappointing, or even abandoning attempts to define a perfect society. Perhaps poetry has entered a "post-utopian" era as expressed by the poet and rock singer Arnaldo Antunes. Despite these trends, no single new style or movement has established itself as paramount. Lack of consensus about the social role of literature makes it difficult to find a common poetic language that unifies a diverse group of writers.

Some of the aforementioned issues are analyzed in Charles Perrone's *Seven Faces: Brazilian Poetry Since Modernism* (item **4502**), a survey of poetry produced in Brazil from the 1950s to the late-1980s. This work and Gonzalez and Treece's *The Gathering of Voices: the Twentieth Century Poetry of Latin America* (1992) are among the few English-language studies about the new generation of Brazilian poetry. Contemporary Brazilian poetry exhibits, in its various stages—*tropicalismo, marginal,* post-Concretism, and postmodernism—tendencies that have different forms of resistance, nonconformity, and formal innovation. In general, contemporary poets have been practicing the major themes of earlier groups, particularly those found in the works of the "Geração de 60;" and post-Concretist works: 1) the obligatory *points de répere,* i.e., points of reference in their own language, that is their lyric inheritance; 2) the use of the epic and long narrative poems; and 3) metapoetics or the exploration of the nature and function of poetry.

Democratization has led to a movement away from a unified critical libertarian political perspective to a fragmented body of voices—feminist, racial, and ethnic, among others—demanding a share of the public space. Additionally, there is an acute awareness of marketing forces, and the inter-relationship of media, art, and culture. The Concretist movement anticipated this point of view with its critical exploration of the relationship between advertising and new media technology, poetry, and popular music (for example, the poetry of Vinicius de Moraes, MPB or *tropicalismo,* and even in rock, among singers/poets like Antunes).

In the 1990s and as the end of the millennium approached, several prominent themes were evident in the "novíssima poesia brasileira." First among these themes is self-knowledge, the "search for the self," or the formation of the subject, together with its opposite, the "loss of self " or the dissolution of the subject. The second theme, poetry as its own subject, is more reflexive, less centered in self-expression and less autobiographical as it questions the subject itself, the implied reader, and the idea of reality in poetry. The third theme, modern urban life as a disaster, reflects the explosion of large urban centers. A fourth theme explores the persistence of the *topos* of the poetic search, a key myth of modern poetry. This poetic odyssey is found in two opposing theoretical camps of Brazilian poetry: Haroldo de Campos' *Sobre Finismundo: a último viagem*, which narrates a journey through literary history (item **4477**), and Alexei Bueno's *A via estreita*, a search for history in its totality, which is linked to the modernist ideology that the structure and content of poetry is created through history. Bueno stands out as one of the pre-eminent poets of the "novissima geração," a unique poet within the typically aris-tocratic diction and references of this group, and, as noted by Stegagno-Picchio, the "last of the classics" with roots in the Luso-Brazilian tradition. Fifth, in addition to Bueno's metaphysical search, a number of poets have preserved a type of spiritual poetry, especially in the Northeast with the influence of Jorge de Lima and, in the South, thanks to the gaúcho poet Nejar. Nejar, the author of *Arca da Aliança* is also considered a classic modern poet, according to Octavio Paz (item **4498**). Finally, race has become synonymous with community for Afro-Brazilians and the commingling of these ideas figures prominently within their poetry.

As we enter a new millennium, there is a need for coalitions that transcend differences of color, culture, and class to ensure political and economic advance-ment. There is a need to explore our diverse personal histories and to examine our multifaceted heritage to relieve racial and ethnic conflict and resolve issues of iden-tity, providing a kind of "healthy ethnocentrism."

Finally, it is important to note that during this biennium, two great names in Brazilian literature—Carlos Drummond de Andrade and João Guimarães Rosa—had their works *Farewell* and *Magma* published for the first time (items **4463** and **4508**, respectively).

4462 Aguilar, José Roberto. Hércules Pas-tiche. São Paulo: Iluminuras, 1994. 167 p.: ill. (some col.).

Text uses as a motif the 12 works (*athloi*) of Hercules transposed to a contem-porary urban setting in the figure of a CEO. Poetry and lyrics from the cult band Per-fomática are inserted among 16 paintings that function as romance. Includes introduc-tion by Haroldo de Campos titled "As Tra-balheiras Inventivas de Aguilar."

4463 Andrade, Carlos Drummond de. Farewell. Rio de Janeiro: Editora Record, 1996. 142 p.: bibl., ill.

Book of poems published after author's death in 1987. All but two of the 49 poems have not been previously published. "Filmes de Greta Garbo" was inspired by a book given to Andrade by his grandson Luís Mau-rício because of a passion for this silent

movie diva. "Elegia ao Tucano Morto" is in honor of his grandson Pedro. Preface by Humberto Werneck, "O Ninho da Poesia."

4464 Andrade, Mário de. Balança, trombeta e battleship, ou, O descobrimento da alma. Edição genética e crítica de Telê An-cona Lopez. Projeto gráfico de Hélio de Almeida. São Paulo: Instituto Moreira Salles; Instituto de Estudos Brasileiros, USP, 1994. 179 p.: bibl., ill. (some col.).

Important book for understanding the creator of Macunaíma. Author travels in the Amazon with two young women, Balançã e Trombeta, collecting material for his work.

4465 Archanjo, Neide. Pequeno oratório do poeta para o anjo. Rio de Janeiro: N. Archanjo, 1997. 16 leaves: col. ill. + 1 com-pact disc.

Author employs classic diction in the tradition of Cecilia Meirelles and Stella

662 / Handbook of Latin American Studies v. 58

Leonardos. The angel is the muse, like her own name. Archangel is beautiful and terrible, as in Rilke's *Duino elegies.*

4466 Barreto, Antonio Carlos. O dossiê do Fonseca. Teresina, Brazil: Gráfica e Editora Júnior, 1991. 275 p.: ill., index.

Barreto has researched the work of one of the most famous and popular poets: *repentista,* guitarist, and singer Domingos Martins Fonseca. Very useful study includes biography, songs, and a glossary of all characters, episodes, objects, and folk customs mentioned in them.

4467 Beça, Anibal. Banda da asa: poemas reunidos. Rio de Janeiro: Sette Letras; Ministerio da Cultura, Fundação Biblioteca Nacional, Depto. Nacional do Livro; São Paulo: Univ. de Mogi das Cruzes, 1998. 474 p.: ill.

Born in Manaus, author is a member of the esthetic movement "Clube da Madrugada" that began in 1955 as a latter-day manifesto of the Brazilian Modernism of 1922. Work includes poems from *Suite para os habitantes da noite* (1994 Nestlé Prize for Literature) and *Ter/na colheita* (1988), as well as other poems.

4468 Benevides, Artur Eduardo. Escadarias na aurora. Fortaleza, Brazil: UFC, Casa de José de Alencar, Programa Editorial, 1997. 173 p. (Col. Alagadiço novo; 102)

Benevides, who is from Ceará, is a poet with a great affinity for the classic spiritual traditions of Western poetry. In this work, his landscape covers Delfos, Saxonia, Elsinor, La Mancha, Verona, and Tarragona.

4469 Bonvicino, Régis R. Primeiro tempo: reunindo os livros *Sósia da cópia, Régis Hotel* e *Bicho papel.* São Paulo: Editora Perspectiva, 1995. 105 p.: ill. (Signos; 18)

Work's three parts include poems of the author's first phase. Author belongs to the new generation of the Concretist movement that came after Paulo Leminski, the *tropicalia,* and pop culture. This movement expresses urban life with caustic irony.

4470 Bueno, Alexei. Entusiasmo. Rio de Janeiro: Topbooks, 1997. 59 p.

Final work in a trilogy that includes *A via estreita* (1995) and *A juventude dos deuses* (1996). In this age of cultural change, neither esthetic or ideological formalism nor

thematic hegemony exist, which this work illustrates. Uses romantic pathos to describe the long, mythical voyage into the *carioca* bohemian night, sordidly treading Apolinean lines into the Bacchean abyss. Introduction by Miguel Sanches Neto is titled "O Polo Dionisíaco."

4471 Bueno, Wilson. Pequeno tratado de brinquedos. Curitiba, Brazil: Fundação Cultural de Curitiba; São Paulo: Iluminuras, 1996. 74 p. (Col. Catatau)

This work, part of the Catatau collection organized by the poet Paulo Leminski, includes an essay by Leo Gilson Ribeiro, "As Metamorfoses de Wilson Bueno." Title sums up this poet's protean character: from the jazzy tone of his short stories in *Bolero's Bar* (1986); to the animal poetry of *Manual of Zoophilia* (1991); to the soap opera as in *Mar paraguaio* (1992); to the present work of *tanka,* a Japanese genre of five verses with 31 syllables.

4472 Cabral, Astrid. De déu em déu: poemas reunidos, 1979–1994. Rio de Janeiro: Sette Letras; Ministério da Cultura, Fundação Biblioteca Nacional, Depto. Nacional do Livro; São Paulo: Univ. de Mogi das Cruzes, 1998. 422 p.: bibl., ill.

Collection of poems written from 1979–94, with a critical introduction by Antônio Paulo Graça. As did many of the writers who described specific experiences of women's lives (such as Adélia Prado, Susana Vargas, and Ana Cristina César), Cabral brings not only sensibility but also new ways to express lyrically these experiences. In the poem "Ponto de Cruz," a domestic, modern-day Brazilian Penelope, embroidering "ponto em cruz," shops for love and returns home, unlike Ulysses who was cast upon different shores by winds and singing sirens.

4473 Cabral de Melo Neto, João. A educação pela pedra e depois. Rio de Janeiro: Editora Nova Fronteira, 1997. 385 p.

Second volume in reissue of author's works covers period 1962–90s. Section entitled "Sevilha Andando" (1987–93) includes the poem "Sevilha Revisitada" (1992). See also item **4474.**

4474 Cabral de Melo Neto, João. Serial e antes. Rio de Janeiro: Editora Nova Fronteira, 1997. 325 p.

First of two-volume reissue of author's

poems written over a period of 40 years covers 1940–61. (Second vol. is annotated in item **4473**.) The division was established by the author, and the volumes were published a year before his death. This volume includes a preface by the poet and his wife, Marly de Oliveira. Begins with "Pedra do Sono" (1940–41) and concludes with "Serial" (1959–61). Research on author's earliest works is based on 1968 edition (see *HLAS 32:4833*), according to his wish.

4475 *Cadernos Negros.* Vol. 21, 1998. Afro-Brazilian poems. São Paulo: Quilombhoj.

Anthology organized by Quilombhoje, a pioneer group of Afro-Brazilian poets founded in 1978. Collection includes works by 16 poets from various states, five of whom are women. Cuti, Esmeralda Ribeiro, Lepê Correia, and Míriam Alves are the best known. Authors of both rural and urban backgrounds demonstrate the variety and strength of the Afro-Brazilian experience.

4476 **Campos, Augusto de.** Despoesia. São Paulo: Editora Perspectiva, 1994. 131 p.: ill. (some col.). (Col. Signos; 17)

Collection of poems in two parts: "Expoemas" (1980–84) and "Intraduções" (1979–93). In a "desfacio," Campos claims he had not published for 15 years, the last work being an anthology of 30 years of poetry, *Viva vaia* (see *HLAS 52:4683*). "Expoemas" has 13 compositions with richly colored illustrations silkscreened by Omar Guedes to a more rustic homemade "mini-contralivropoema," xerographically published in 1990 ("Não"). In this period, he experimented with various media formats: videotext, holograms, neon, laser, clip-poems, computer graphics—everything but a book. The second part, "Intraduções," has 50 poems.

4477 **Campos, Haroldo de.** Sobre Finismundo: a última viagem. Rio de Janeiro: Sette Letras, 1997. 58 p.

In an introductory note, author explains the genesis of his latest poem as an allegory of the search for adventure, compared with the lack of adventure of contemporary modern life , i.e., contrasting the Homeric seafaring Odyssus with the urban Joycean Ulysses. Work is inspired by a canto from *Dante's Inferno* about the last voyage of Odyssus. Story's basic framework is a semilogical model: the violation of interdiction, the adversary of which is destiny or God, with elements from the medieval Greco-Latin tradition.

4478 **Capinan, José Carlos.** Confissões de Narciso: poemas. Rio de Janeiro: Civilização Brasileira, 1995. 102 p.

In this work, which was not written but dictated into a tape recorder, the poet shows another face to his more familiar, socially engaged side by dwelling more in the psychological transformation and rediscovers his ego, "Narciso."

4479 **Capinan, José Carlos.** Inquisitorial. Ensaio introdutório de José Guilherme Merquior. Rio de Janeiro: Civilização Brasileira, 1995. 98 p.

Book has three parts: 1) "Aprendizagem" (1962–64); 2) "Inquisitorial" (1965); and 3) "Algum Exercício" (1959–64). A poet-lyricist, Capinan was among the *tropicalismo* vanguard that critically revised Brazilian culture through music and introduced new models of postmodernist sensibility of plurality. Introductory essay, by critic Merquior, is titled "Capinan e a Nova Lírica."

4480 **Cassas, Luís Augusto.** Opera barroca: guia erótico-poético & serpentário-lírico da cidade de São Luís do Maranhão. Rio de Janeiro: Imago, 1998. 266 p.: ill. (some col.).

Cassas celebrates and criticizes his hometown São Luís, the old Brazilian Athens, in the same way as London was celebrated by Eliot, Dublin by Joyce, and Rio de Janeiro by Lima Barreto. Thus this is "uma ópera de escárnio e maldizer," as the poet deplores the abandonment of and indifference to the previously beautiful capital founded by French Huguenots and cradle of poets Gonçalves Dias and Ferreira Gullar. His verse summarizes the cycles of this city.

4481 **Cassas, Luís Augusto.** O *shopping* de Deus & a alma do negócio: poemossaurus rex. Rio de Janeiro: Imago, 1998. 198 p.

Cassas is at the center of two tendencies represented by Ferreira Gullar (social poetry) and Nauro Machado (existentialism), similar to Murillo Mendes and Jorge de Lima. In this work, he searches for a reconciliation between the material and the spiritual world, mixing elevated tone with humor and meditation with puns. Irony prevails in his search for unity between his two loves: God and the world. Book is dedicated "para aqueles que amam Deus e aqueles que amam o mundo."

4482 Chacal. Muito prazer. Ed. comemorativa 25 anos. Rio de Janeiro: Sette Letras, 1997. 63 p.

Poesia marginal expressed the experience of modern urban youth with an antiestablishment stance that had its origins in Rimbaud's late-19th-century *poète maudit.* Chacal, one of the typical voices of this poetry, led the hippie counterculture call of "sex, drugs, and rock and roll." He also affiliated himself with Oswald de Andrade's disregard for form and metrics, a poetry of the moment ("flash"—Oswald's "Kodak").

4483 Colasanti, Marina. Gargantas abertas. Rio de Janeiro: Rocco, 1998. 122 p.

Work opens and closes with two poems in Italian as an introduction to these poems inspired by poet's travels and especially reminiscences of Italy, where she grew up. The poem "Em Que Espelho" dialogues with Cecília Meirelles' poem "Retrato," from which it borrows the title. In Meirelles' verse "Em que espelho ficou perdida minha face?" Colasanti searches for her dead mother's face and her own. The women in the fields, the washerwomen of her childhood, or the women portrayed by Vermeer, Cranach, or Artemisia, personify their passion and rage and survive as modern-day "Salomés," carrying in the tray "nem prata, nem Batista / um copo d'água."

4484 Couto, Rui Ribeiro. Rui Ribeiro Couto no seu centenário. Organização de Vasco Mariz. Rio de Janeiro: Academia Brasileira de Letras, 1998. 194 p. (Col. Afrânio Peixoto da Academia Brasileira de Letras; 36)

Includes preface by Arnaldo Niskier and an essay on Couto's poetry by Mariz. Covers various genres in which Couto wrote: 40 poems selected from his early *penumbrismo* work *Jardim das confidências* (1915–19) and later work *Longe* (1947–60), six short stories, and crônicas. Also includes 11 reviews by critics such as Mário de Andrade, Manuel Bandeira, Carlos Drummond de An-

drade, and José Lins de Rego. Author occupies a special place among Brazilian poets, as Mário de Andrade notes, for his "suburban lyricism;" or as Carlos Drummond de Andrade reiterates, for his "tenderness, sweetness, and humor without corrosiveness."

4485 Duarte, Sebastião Moreira. Calendário lúdico: quasipoemas transversos. São Luís, Brazil: Sotaque Norte Editora, 1998. 107 p.

Title appears to be a pun on the liturgical calendar. Work moves through a quoditian life permeated by God's presence, notably in the second part, "Novena de Natal."

4486 Espínola, Adriano. Beira-sol. Rio de Janeiro: Topbooks, 1997. 83 p.

Espínola belongs to the expressionistic poetry tradition, although he is a late bloomer. His poems are a mental adventure through the city and memory. "Em Trânsito" is a poem wherein he realizes the sordid poem dreamed by Manuel Bandeira. In this collection, the poet tries to encapsulate the senses of things and beings in the coastline urban cities. Divided into two parts: "Claridade" and "O Cão dos Sentidos."

4487 Fraga, Myriam. Femina. Salvador, Brazil: Fundação Casa de Jorge Amado; COPENE, 1996. 131 p. (Col. Casa de palavras. Série Poesia)

First part is about mythical and historical women throughout the ages, such as Europa and the bull, Carmen Miranda, Jeanne d'Arc, Judith, Penelope, and Salomé. Second part is a "calendar," with poems that feature women/animal myths: the Sphinx, the Harpies, the Medusa, and the Succubus. Classical-style poems of a feminine universe reinvented through myths using the mirror, labyrinth, and scissors weave a textured cloth of female poetry.

4488 Franco, Aninha. Brechó. Salvador, Brazil: Fundação Casa de Jorge Amado; COPENE, 1996. 146 p.: ill. (Col. Casa de palavras. Série Poesia)

"Brechó" in Portuguese means second-hand store, a sampling of everything. Concrete poem "Poderia Ser" opens the book, followed by "Bilhetes"—hand-written notes, then by a poem called "Toda uma festa que se inicia com a madrugada em quartos de motel barato." "Palcos" has "cânticos" of the seven sins, or odes. Work ends with a play of

14 scenes about Salvador, drugs, and the petit bourgeoisie.

4489 Fróes, Leonardo. Vertigens: obra re-unida, 1968–1998. Edição fixada e re-vista pelo autor, com textos introdutórios de José Thomaz Brum, Ciro Barroso e Ivan Jun-queira. Rio de Janeiro: Rocco, 1998. 330 p.: bibl.

Critical edition of collected works re-vised by the author. Fróes has translated Shelley, Swift, and Eliot, and some works on the natural sciences. His poems are perme-ated by classical readings and by philosophi-cal affinity to the Enlightenment. Nature is represented in the poems of this mountain climber and amateur naturalist, reminding the reader of the German romantics.

4490 Gil, Gilberto. Gilberto Gil: todas as le-tras; incluindo letras comentadas pelo compositor. Organização de Carlos Rennó. Textos de Arnaldo Antunes e José Miguel Wisnik. Edição gráfica de João Baptista da Costa Aguiar. São Paulo: Companhia das Le-tras, 1996. 390 p.: ill., indexes.

Includes comments from Arnaldo An-tunes' "O Receptivo" and José Miguel Wis-nick's "O Dom da Ilusão." Also includes more than 400 texts of Gil's songs, 80 of which have comments by him and 94 of which have not been previously published.

4491 Jesus, Carolina Maria de. Antologia pessoal. Organização de José Carlos Sebe Bom Meihy. Revisão de Armando Fre-itas Filho. Rio de Janeiro: Editora UFRJ, 1996? 235 p.: bibl.

Organized and introduced by José Car-los Sebe Bom Meihy, these poems are written by the famous *Child of the dark* author (see *HLAS 25:4740*).

4492 Kolody, Helena. Luz infinita. Curitiba, Brazil: Museu-Biblioteca Ucranianos em Curitiba da União Agrícola Instrutiva, Clube Ucraíno-Brasileiro, Organização Femi-nina, 1997. 204 p.: ill., index.

Bilingual edition in Portuguese and Ukranian. Kolody is from Paraná, where some Ukranian immigrants have settled. Her poems address such topics as the immigrant experience and regional landscape. A Slavic religious lyricism can be detected throughout her work.

4493 Leonardos, Stella. Romanceiro do Con-testado. Florianópolis, Brazil: Editora da UFSC, 1996. 235 p.

This is part of her Brazil-project to sing the Romanceiro of Dom Sebastião, Anita Garibaldi, memorial de Aleidinho, and others. The Rebellion of the Condestado happened in Santa Catarina state during 1912–16, inspiring movies, painters, and playwriters.

4494 Lopes, Nei. Incursões sobre a pele. Rio de Janeiro: Artium Editora, 1996. 124 p.

Lopes is known primarily as a com-poser of sambas in Rio de Janeiro and by his work in the Quilombo Samba School. His is an Afro-Brazilian voice that celebrates his culture in lyrics and music. Book is divided methodologically into five thematic blocks that cover the African diaspora and slavery and the celebration of Angolan and Nago myths. Preface by Domingos Proença Filho.

4495 Lucinda, Elisa. O semelhante. Rio de Janeiro: Editora Record, 1998? 224 p.: ill.

Title represents the way Lucinda views issues of race, gender, class, and na-tion: not the *Other* but the *Same,* in the voices of Zumbi and Grande Othelo, and in "Mulata Exportação." National identity is represented in "Por Mea Copa Mea Máxima Copa" and "Deus, o Cara."

4496 Luft, Lya Fett. Secreta mirada. São Paulo: Editora Mandarim, 1997. 262 p.

Although Luft is best known as a fiction writer, here she returns to her first vocation as a poet, declaring: "This is a book about love." Presents 41 songs, each intro-duced by an epigraph from poets such as Rilke, Drummond, Meirelles, and Fernando Pessoa, and followed by a reflection on lyri-cal prose and a poem. Includes personal rec-ollections, the experiences of many of her characters, and the testimony of others.

4497 Moriconi, Italo. Ana Cristina César: o sangue de uma poeta. Rio de Janeiro: Relume Dumará; Rio Arte, 1996. 150 p.: bibl., ill. (Perfis do Rio)

Part of the collection of profiles *Perfis do Rio,* among which are those of Clarice Lispector, Antonio Maria, and Grande Otelo, who became emblems of the city. Ana Cristina César is the object as poet, journalist, academic, and participant in the intellectual battles and cultural debates of the time.

4498 Nejar, Carlos. Arca da aliança. Guarapari, Brazil: Nejarim Editora, Paiol da Aurora, 1995. 83 leaves. (Col. Os viventes)

Edition commemorates 35 years of this poet's writing (1960–95). Biblical themes range from Genesis to St. John's Apocalypse, 4:3. Twenty-two poems are based on the Old Testament and the remaining 16 on the New Testament.

4499 Oliveira, Jelson. Terra de livres. São Paulo: M. Ohno Editor, 1997. 60 p.

Born in Rio Grande do Sul, Jelson is a university student and a member of the Pastoral Land Commission in Paraná. In this work, he presents a mosaic of the plight of the MST (landless peasant movement) in 39 places throughout Brazil as "land of the free." From Eldorado in Pará to São Miguel das Missões in Rio Grande do Sul, to Promissão in São Paulo to Xapuri in Acre, he presents a dramatic picture of these forgotten places in the hinterland, and links them to past rebellions: Contestado, Canudos, Trombas, and Formoso.

4500 Oliveira, Marly de. Antologia poética. Organização e prefácio de João Cabral de Melo Neto. 2a. impressão. Rio de Janeiro: Editora Nova Fronteira, 1997. 250 p.: bibl.

Oliveira has mastered all the techniques and imprints them with her own touch. In the introduction, Cabral notes her interesting decasyllables, breaking away from traditional forms. Of Oliveira's 17 works, he has chosen 10: poems from *Cerco da primavera* (1957); *A suave pantera* (1962); *Sangue na veia* (1967; see *HLAS 36:7110*); *Invocação de Orfeu* (1979; see *HLAS 46:6253*); *A incerteza das coisas* (1984); *Retrato* (1986); *Vertigem* (1986); *O banquete* (1988); *O deserto jardim* (1990; see *HLAS 54:4895*); and six poems never before published.

4501 Peres, Fernando da Rocha. Mr. Lexo-Tan e outros poemas. Apresentação de Luciana Stegagno Picchio. Salvador, Brazil: Fundação Casa de Jorge Amado; COPENE, 1996. 111 p.: ill. (Col. Casa de palavras. Série Poesia.)

Includes 68 poems "to clear complications and block anxiety." Demonstrates abstract texture, the lightness of the idea behind the concrete opaqueness of an object.

Objects transcend into metaphors and metonyms inspired by Carlos Drummond de Andrade, Fernando Pessoa, João Cabral de Melo Neto, Pedro Nava, and José Saramago.

4502 Perrone, Charles A. Seven faces: Brazilian poetry since modernism. Durham, N.C.: Duke Univ. Press, 1996. 234 p.: bibl., ill., index.

Study of Brazilian poetry from 1950–90 examines its "seven faces" (a pun on Drummond's poem of the same name), phases, and trends. Introductory chapter reviews movement's initial phases and sets the stage for what follows: the legacy of the Modernist movement. Chapters 2–6 cover Concrete poetry and other vanguard groups, the lyricism of popular music, and different types of 1970s youth poetry. Also examines social and esthetic tensions in contemporary Brazilian poetry.

4503 A poesia mineira no século XX: antologia. Organização, introdução e notas de Assis Brasil. Rio de Janeiro: Imago, 1998. 310 p.: bibl., ill. (Col. Poesia brasileira)

Selection includes symbolists from the late Alphonsus Guimarães to Eric Ponty (b. 1968). Minas Gerais has produced the largest number of great poets, including the greatest, Carlos Drummond de Andrade, whose poems unfortunately are not included here due to copyright restrictions. Murillo Mendes, Affonso Romano de Sant'Anna, Adélia Prado, and others are represented with two poems each and a brief biography.

4504 Portugal, Claudius Hermann. Aguas. Salvador, Brazil: Fundação Casa de Jorge Amado; COPENE, 1996. 128 p. (Col. Casa de palavras. Série Poesia.)

Born in Bahia, Portugal is a journalist and editor of the magazine *Exu*. He has worked in diverse media such as musicals, soap operas, and theater. He is a vanguard poet and produces Concrete poetry representing experiences of street kids (*funkeiros* and *rapeiros*).

4505 Portugal, Claudius Hermann. Duende. Salvador, Brazil: IWE; Fundação Casa de Jorge Amado, 1995. 122 p. (Casa de palavras)

A Bahian *duende* is a lyricist, historian, playwright, and editor. In this work, a *triálogo caleidoscópico* takes place between authoritarian figures (bishop, judge, and general) and a libertarian woman embodied by the *duende*. Uses graphic design to create a new poetic language with objects from daily life such as old magazines and empty bottles. Also explores the drama of children without a future.

4506 Risério, Antonio. Fetiche. Salvador, Brazil: Fundação Casa de Jorge Amado, 1996. 103 p.: ill. (some col.), col. map. (Col. Casa de palavras. Série Poesia)

Risério is a critic and vanguardist with influences of Dada and Concrete poetry and this work is his first book of poems. In "Alguns Toques," author talks about the genesis of the book. "Via Papua" is based on other texts such as Malinowski's "Argonauts of the Western Pacific." Author uses old Chinese proverbs and makes a collage of Brazilian rivers. He plays with the sound similarities between Yoruba and Japanese and plays with words like *yume-ya, xogum, axogum,* Kioto/Ketu, and Mairi (a Tupi village).

4507 Roquette-Pinto, Claudia. Saxífraga. Rio de Janeiro: Salamandra Consultoria Editorial, 1993. 39 leaves.

The title is based on a famous verse by William Carlos Williams, "Saxifraga é minha flor que fende / as rochas." Roquette-Pinto, like the "objectivists," isolates the object from its original pedestrian context and unveils in its being-there, *da-sein*. Her voice also has precious baroque images that have a protean quality and continually change.

4508 Rosa, João Guimarães. Magma. Rio de Janeiro: Editora Nova Fronteira, 1997. 146 p.: ill.

Prize-winning work includes 24 poems and comments by Guilherme de Almeida. Contains four *haiku* poems: "Imensidão," "Romance I," "Egoísmo," and "Mundo Pequeno." According to Almeida: "*Magma* é poesia centrífuga, universalizadora, capaz de dar ao resto do mundo, síntese perfeitado que temos e somos. Há aí, vivo de beleza, todo o Brasil: sua terra, a sua gente, a sua alma, o seu bem e o seu mal."

4509 Salomão, Waly. Algaravias; Câmara de ecos. São Paulo: Editora 34, 1996. 82 p.: ill.

Among the early *tropicalistas*, Sa-

lomão's merit, according to Davi Arrigucci in the cover presentation, is to bring into Brazilian poetry the decentering and problematic situation of the poet in the contemporary world, summed up in the verse "me segura que me vai dar um troço." His book presents four themes: the private semipersonal reflection about poetry, the personal and national myths, and voyages.

4510 Sena, Davino Ribeiro de. O jaguar no deserto. Recife, Brazil: Bagaço, 1997. 86 p.

Sena presents "Jaguar," a retired major and ferocious macho who philosophizes about life while persecuting bandits—narcotraffickers, kidnappers, thieves, killers—and who is himself killed in an ambush. Dead, he returns to his apartment in Bairro das Graças and listens to the objects of his life. Recife is the "desert of the dead" and the major has the final word, living in the desert of the urban milieu of the Northeast. Jaguar is a *nordestino* of the *Sargento Getúlio* (João Ubaldo Ribeiro) race, a *delegado* now reflecting on his life which is narrated by domestic objects, plants, and the landscape surrounding him.

4511 Sisterolli, Maria Luzia dos Santos. Da lira ao ludus: travessia; leitura da poética de Gilberto Mendonça Teles. São Paulo: Annablume, 1998. 229 p.: bibl. (Selo universidade; 68. Poesia)

Study is divided into three phases: 1) "Da Lira à Lírica," concerned with sound and meaning, centered in the lyric "I;" 2) "Do Logos à Linguagem," focusing on the poet in relation to the world and to the construction of a language; and 3) "Do lúdico ao Interlúdico," about a magic play (*ludus*—with words).

4512 Wamosy, Alceu. Poesia completa. Porto Alegre, Brazil: EDIPUCRS; Instituto Estadual do Livro; Alves Editores, 1994. 154 p. (Col. Memória)

Symbolist poet was born in Uruguaiana, Rio Grande do Sul, and died in 1923. Work includes 110 poems published for the first time in one anthology, divided into three parts: 1) "Flâmulas"—sonetos de estréia—and "Alegrete;" 2) "Na Terra Virgem;" and 3) "Coroa de Sonho."

Drama

SEVERINO J. ALBUQUERQUE, *Associate Professor of Portuguese, University of Wisconsin-Madison*

IN THE MID-1990S, *encenadores* remain at the forefront of Brazilian theater. Criticism has duly reflected the prevalence of an *encenador*-oriented theater, with its leading name, Gerald Thomas, as the subject of an important work, *Um encenador de si mesmo* (item **4536**). A key predecessor of the *encenador* figure, Polish-born Zbigniew Ziembinski, is the focus of a seminal biography, published posthumously in 1995 by another Polish émigre to Brazil, Yan Michalski (item **4544**).

Since *encenadores* like Thomas and others show little concern or support for the work of younger Brazilian playwrights, the 1990s saw a relative scarcity of good original plays. Still, a few new works deserve the attention of theater students. Of note among published texts is the anthology, *Cinco textos do teatro brasileiro contemporâneo* (item **4519**), which includes works by Miguel Falabella and Mauro Rasi, the two leading names in comedy and light theater in the late 1980s-90s. Falabella's contribution to this collection ("A partilha") and Rasi's *Pérola* (item **4528**) are among the top grossing plays of the last 10 years in Brazil. Less known, but nevertheless worthy of attention, are younger playwrights such as Luiz Fernando Botelho, whose award-winning works, *Reis andarilhos* (item **4516**) and *Menino minotauro* (item **4515**), blend children's theater, classical mythology, and the folklore of Northeastern Brazil; and Vera Karam and Arines Ibias, whose plays, *Dona Otília lamenta muito* (item **4522**) and *Fogo cruzado* (item **4521**), are part of the same series, *Teatro: textos e roteiros*, an important joint initiative of commercial publishers and the Instituto Estadual do Livro on behalf of quality theater for young audiences in the state of Rio Grande do Sul.

Also noteworthy among new plays are Roberto Athayde's attempt at historical drama, *Carlota Rainha* (item **4513**); and Plínio Marcos' *A dança final* (item **4526**) and especially, his intriguing experiment, *O assassinato do anão do caralho grande* (1986). A long overdue publication, the complete verse drama of the late Vinicius de Moraes has been carefully edited by Carlos Augusto Calil in *Teatro em versos* (item **4527**). In *Exu, o cavaleiro da encruzilhada*, Zora Seljan continues her theatrical exploration of African-Brazilian themes (item **4529**). Equally significant is the publication of plays by two important names in 19th-century Brazilian theater, *Uma pupila rica* (item **4524**), the recently discovered manuscript of a comedy that Joaquim Manoel de Macedo wrote in 1840, and *Raimundo* (item **4518**), a historical drama by the lesser-known, but definitely notable Santa Catarina-born playwright, Alvaro August de Carvalho; these two publications are part of an ongoing effort to make available to contemporary audiences and the reading public a number of texts and documents from a vital period in the history of Brazilian theater.

Three broad topics seem to dominate theater criticism in the period under scrutiny. The first, black theater, is the subject of three books, two of which were originally written as doctoral dissertations and later published without major editing: Miriam G. Mendes' *O negro e o teatro brasileiro* (item **4543**) and Leda Martins' *A cena em sombras* (item **4542**). Martins' book is clearly the more solid of the two; Mendes' work, a companion piece to her 1982 book on blacks in 19th-century

Brazilian theater, though well-researched, is marred by shoddy writing and unconvincing argumentation.

Politically committed theater, the second topic, has occupied four noted critics in recent years. In *Teatro da militância*, Silvana Garcia has penned a key contribution to the study of the intersection of popular theater and leftist politics (item **4539**). Equally important is Camargo Costa's *A hora do teatro épico no Brasil*, which bravely challenges previously accepted notions of the nature of epic theater in Brazil (item **4534**). Two other significant works are compilations, in one case a series of interviews on the repression of engaged theater in Pernambuco in the 1960s and 1970s (item **4530**), and the other a collection of essays and short pieces on popular and political theater in Brazil and elsewhere (item **4545**).

The study of the theater is the third theme, and one that has absorbed the attention of such established authors as Oswald de Andrade, Oduvaldo Vianna Filho, and Plínio Marcos. The critical approaches used in their books is as varied as the interests and orientations of the several playwrights and thus range from the thematic (item **4547**) to the psychoanalytic, and from application of cultural studies (item **4535**) to cultural anthropophagy (item **4540**).

Finally, the mid-1990s also saw the publication of reference works (item **4533**), biographies (items **4532** and **4544**), lengthy interviews with key figures (item **4531**), as well as difficult to locate research materials, such as documentation on the theater scene outside of traditional centers (items **4538** and **4546**).

PLAYS

4513 Athayde, Roberto. *Carlota Rainha.* Rio de Janeiro: AGIR, 1994? 179 p. (Teatro moderno)

Historical drama by author of the acclaimed *Apareceu a Margarida* (see *HLAS 38:7526*). First installment of a planned tetralogy titled *A casa de Bragança*, on the royal family that ruled Portugal and Brazil from mid-17th through the early-20th centuries.

4514 *Bailei na curva*. 2a ed. Porto Alegre, Brazil: Mercado Aberto, 1994? 168 p. (Série Vamos fazer teatro; 4)

New edition of one of the best plays of the 1980s. In the play, Grupo do Jeito Que Dá, led by Júlio César Conte, traces the lives of a group of young people from the 1964 military coup to the early 1980s.

4515 Botelho, Luiz Felipe. *Menino minotauro.* Recife, Brazil: Governo do Estado de Pernambuco, Secretaria de Educação, Cultura e Esportes, Fundação do Patrimônio Histórico e Artístico de Pernambuco; Companhia Editora de Pernambuco, 1994. 89 p.

Winner of the Hermilo Borba Filho Theatre Award for 1992, *Menino minotauro* is representative of this young playwright's

interest in revisiting and updating the mythology of different eras and places.

4516 Botelho, Luiz Felipe. *Reis andarilhos.* Recife, Brazil: Governo do Estado de Pernambuco, Secretaria de Educação, Cultura e Esportes, Fundação do Patrimônio Histórico e Artístico de Pernambuco, Companhia Editora de Pernambuco, 1994. 88 p.

Skillful dramatic use of themes drawn from the *bumba-meu-boi* folklore tradition of Brazil's Northeast. Awarded the Hermilo Borba Filho Theatre Award in 1993.

4517 Carrano, Austregésilo. Textos: teatro. São Paulo: Scarpitta Gráfica e Editora, 1994. 198 p.

Collection of six mostly disappointing pieces by an activist for mental health care reform in Brazil. First text is the dramatic version of Carrano's autobiographical novel *Canto dos malditos* (1990), about his own experience as a patient in mental health clinics.

4518 Carvalho, Alvaro Augusto de. *Raimundo*: drama em cinco atos. Florianópolis, Brazil: FCC Edições; Editora da UFSC, 1994. 167 p.: bibl. (Memória literária—Santa Catarina; 2. Teatro)

New edition of a 19th-century work

by an important, if little-studied author. Text had long been unavailable, as copies of the first edition became rarities soon after its 1868 publication.

4519 5 textos do teatro contemporâneo brasileiro. Rio de Janeiro: Shell Brasil, 1993. 217 p.: ill.

Corporate-sponsored, privately distributed anthology presents five plays from late 1980s-early 1990s, including top-grossing *A partilha* by Miguel Falabella and *A cerimônia do adeus*, an engaging early work by Mauro Rasi. Other texts are Flávio de Souza's *Fica comigo esta noite*, Geraldo Carneiro's *A bandeira dos cinco mil réis*, and Paulo César Coutinho's "*Lucrécia, o veneno dos Bórgia.*

4520 Freire, Roberto. *3/4.* Rio de Janeiro: Guanabara Koogan, 1993. 91 p.

Collected plays by the militant physician and playwright. The title is a play on the meaning of *quarto*, which translates as both "three-fourths" and "three rooms," in this case an allusion to the titles of the three plays in this collection: *Quarto de empregada* or the maid's room, *Quarto de estudante* or the student's room, and *Quarto de hotel* or the hotel room.

4521 Ibias, Arines. *Fogo cruzado.* Porto Alegre, Brazil: L&PM Editores; Instituto Estadual do Livro, 1994. 87 p. (Teatro, textos & roteiros; 12)

Dramatic treatment of Jerônimo Jardim's 1992 novel *Sob fogo cruzado.* Antiwar pamphleteering directed at a younger public.

4522 Karam, Vera. *Dona Otília lamenta muito.* Porto Alegre, Brazil: Tchê!; Instituto Estadual do Livro, 1994. 96 p. (Teatro, textos & roteiros; 11)

Seven comic sketches by one of the most promising new playwrights active in regional theater. Collection borrows its title from the strongest of these short pieces.

4523 Levinson, Bruno and **Daniel Herz.** *A entrevista*; seguida de, *Cartão de embarque.* Rio de Janeiro: Relume-Dumará, 1994. 128 p.

Two one-act plays staged in 1992 and 1994 by the vibrant group Atores de Laura. Ordinary situations (a job interview and a journalist's trip) are given impressive dramatic impact in this debut of a promising duo.

4524 Macedo, Joaquim Manuel de. *Uma pupilla rica:* comédia em 5 actos por Dr. Manoel Joaquim de Macedo, 1840. Rio de Janeiro: Fundação Biblioteca Nacional, Ministério da Cultura; Itaboraí, Brazil: Prefeitura Municipal de Itaboraí, Secretaria Municipal de Educação e Cultura, Depto. Geral de Cultura, 1995. 189 p.

First edition of previously unpublished comedy by the popular 19th-century playwright and novelist. Work ably illustrates Macedo's skill in combining romanticism and realism in his theater.

4525 Marcos, Plínio. *O assassinato do anão do caralho grande:* noveleta policial e peça teatral. São Paulo: Geração Editorial, 1996. 142 p.

Set in a struggling circus, this somewhat absurd mystery is presented twice, first as a novella and then as a play.

4526 Marcos, Plínio. *A dança final.* São Paulo: Maltese, 1994. 51 p.

Marcos returns to the two-character format he mastered with his first major hit, *Dois perdidos numa noite suja* (see *HLAS 42:6375*). Here, a man and a woman prepare for their 25th anniversary celebration as they discuss the failure of their relationship.

4527 Moraes, Vinícius de. Teatro em versos. Organização, introdução e notas de Carlos Augusto Calil. São Paulo: Companhia das Letras, 1995. 259 p., 8 p. of plates.

Five verse plays by the celebrated poet and lyricist. Includes *Orfeu da Conceição*, later adapted as the script for the film *Black Orpheus.* Careful edition and helpful introduction by Calil.

4528 Rasi, Mauro. *Pérola.* Rio de Janeiro: Editora Record, 1995. 143 p.

The story of a woman (the title character was loosely based on author's mother) and an era, the play has garnered public and critical acclaim for Rasi, the strongest and most consistent voice in contemporary Brazilian comedy.

4529 Seljam, Zora. *Exu, o cavaleiro da encruzilhada.* Rio de Janeiro: Editora Grafline, 1993. 63 p.

Another Yoruba-themed work by a distinguished author of African-Brazilian theater, this work is the first of such plays to include some touches of comedy. Preface by Antônio Olinto provides information on 1991 London premiere of the English version of *Exu*.

THEATER CRITICISM AND HISTORY

4530 Baccarelli, Milton J. O teatro em Pernambuco (trocando a máscara). Prefácio de José Mário Austregésilo. Recife, Brazil: Governo do Estado de Pernambuco, Secretaria de Educação, Cultura e Esportes, Fundação do Patrimônio Histórico e Artístico de Pernambuco; Companhia Editora de Pernambuco, 1994. 184 p.

Study of the political repression of theater in the state of Pernambuco from 1964–84. Essentially a series of interviews with key figures of the period conducted by the late critic and theater professor.

4531 Bastidores: entrevistas a Simon Khoury. v. 1–6. Rio de Janeiro: Leviatã, 1994. 6 v.

Series of lengthy, often revealing interviews with major actors, directors, and playwrights is invaluable tool for research on 20th-century Brazilian theater.

4532 Britto, Sérgio. Fábrica de ilusão: 50 anos de teatro. Rio de Janeiro: FUNARTE; Salamandra, 1996. 261 p.: ill.

Large, carefully produced volume is part autobiography, part study of the major productions in the career of the esteemed actor and director.

4533 Campos, Geir. Glossário de termos técnicos do espetáculo. Niterói, Brazil: Univ. Federal Fluminense, Editora Universitária, 1989. 161 p.: bibl., indexes.

Provides multilingual (German, Spanish, French, English, Italian) equivalents and Portuguese definitions of stage-related terms.

4534 Costa, Iná Camargo. A hora do teatro épico no Brasil. Rio de Janeiro: Graal, 1996. 233 p.: bibl., index. (Estudos de cultura)

Provocative study of epic theater in Brazil. Concludes that most Brazilian works generally accepted as epic theater do not in fact belong in the category.

4535 Damasceno, Leslie Hawkins. Cultural space and theatrical conventions in the works of Oduvaldo Vianna Filho. Detroit,

Mich. Wayne State Univ. Press, 1996. 290 p., 17 p. of plates: bibl., ill., index. (Latin American literature and culture series)

Combines textual analysis and cultural production studies to trace career of a major political and esthetic voice of the 1960s-70s. Best critical study to date of the theater of Oduvaldo Vianna Filho. For review of Spanish-language version, see *HLAS 56:4490*.

4536 Um encenador de si mesmo: Gerald Thomas. Organização de Sílvia Fernandes e J. Guinsburg. São Paulo: Editora Perspectiva, 1996. 295 p.: bibl., ill. (some col.). (Col. Signos; 21)

Collection of essays by and about the important if controversial *encenador*. Pt. 1 is largely a compilation of articles by Thomas published in the Brazilian press from 1986–95; pt. 2 contains writings by several distinguished critics.

4537 Flores, Moacyr. O negro na dramaturgia brasileira, 1838–1888. Porto Alegre, Brazil: EDIPUCRS, 1995. 100 p.: bibl. (Col. História; 5)

Disappointing survey of 19th-century theater is mostly a compilation of plot summaries of abolitionist plays and other works featuring black characters, with little critical acumen.

4538 Franco, Aninha. O teatro na Bahia através da imprensa, século XX. Salvador, Brazil: Fundação Casa de Jorge Amado, 1994. 407 p.: bibl., ill. (Casa de palavras. Memória)

Each chapter focuses on one decade of the 20th century (through the 1990s), providing a wealth of information and detail on a vast number of productions staged in Salvador.

4539 Garcia, Silvana. Teatro da militância: a intenção do popular no engajamento político. São Paulo: Editora Perspectiva; Editora da Univ. de São Paulo, 1990. 208 p.: bibl., ill. (Col. Estudos; 113. Teatro)

Excellent study of agitprop and politically engaged popular theater in Brazil. Pays close attention to little-studied groups outside the mainstream.

4540 Gardin, Carlos. O teatro antropofágico de Oswald de Andrade: da ação teatral ao teatro de ação. São Paulo: Annablume,

1993. 196 p.: bibl., ill. (Selo universidade; 3. Teatro)

Interesting approach to Oswald's trilogy (*O homem e o cavalo, O rei da vela, A morta*) relies on the cultural cannibalist metaphor (the theater absorbs/ingests other texts, media, cultures) previously used by David George and other critics.

4541 Magaldi, Sábato. O texto no teatro. São Paulo: Editora Perspectiva; Editora da Univ. de São Paulo, 1989. 481 p. (Col. Estudos; 111. Teatro)

Compilation of 86 reviews of foreign plays emphasizes printed text over staging considerations. Most of these pieces were published in the prestigious *Suplemento Literário do Estado de São Paulo* during Magaldi's tenure as head theater critic.

4542 Martins, Leda Maria. A cena em sombras. São Paulo: Editora Perspectiva, 1995. 217 p.: bibl., ill. (Debates; 267. Teatro)

Originally written as the author's doctoral dissertation, this carefully researched and clearly argued comparative study of black theater in Brazil and the US is a welcome addition to the scarce bibliography on the subject.

4543 Mendes, Miriam Garcia. O negro e o teatro brasileiro. São Paulo: Editora Hucitec; Rio de Janeiro: Instituto Brasileiro de Arte e Cultura; Brasília: Fundação Cultural Palmares, 1993. 207 p.: bibl., ill. (Teatro; 25)

Originally written as author's doctoral dissertation, this posthumously published work is a companion piece to Mendes first book, *A personagem negra no teatro brasileiro* (see *HLAS 46:6313*). Provides important information on the group Teatro Experimental do Negro (TEN) and on African-Brazilian theater in general.

4544 Michalski, Yan. Ziembinski e o teatro brasileiro. Edição de Fernando Peixoto e Johana Albuquerque. São Paulo: Editora Hucitec; Rio de Janeiro: Ministério da Cultura/FUNARTE, 1995. 517 p.: bibl., ill., index. (Teatro; 30)

Published posthumously, this critical biography is the best study to date of the contributions of the Polish-born director who is generally associated with the creation of modern Brazilian theater. Carefully edited by Fernando Peixoto with the assistance of Johana Albuquerque.

4545 Peixoto, Fernando. Teatro em questão. São Paulo: Editora Hucitec, 1989. 263 p., 16 p. of plates: ill. (Teatro; 17)

This volume, part of a substantial series by the distinguished actor, director, and critic, focuses on the period 1960–86. Previous works in the series are *Teatro em pedaços* (*HLAS 44:6156*), *Teatro em movimento* (*HLAS 50:4090*), and *Um teatro fora do eixo* (*HLAS 56:4052*).

4546 Santos, Jorge Fernando dos. BH em cena: teatro, televisão, ópera e dança na Belo Horizonte centenária. Belo Horizonte, Brazil: Livraria Del Rey Editora, 1995. 230 p.: ill., index.

Each of book's four sections focuses on one of the four media in the subtitle. Pt. 1 provides difficult-to-obtain information on the theater scene in Brazil's third largest city. Other sections illustrate the close ties between theater and the other media; this is especially true of the strong dance scene in Belo Horizonte.

4547 Vieira, Paulo. Plínio Marcos: a flor e o mal. Petrópolis, Brazil: Editora Firmo, 1994. 188 p.: bibl., ill.

Useful survey of Marcos' career through the late 1980s. Pts. 2 and 3 provide plot summaries and analyses of each play.

TRANSLATIONS INTO ENGLISH FROM THE SPANISH AND THE PORTUGUESE

CAROL MAIER, *Professor of Spanish, Kent State University*
DAPHNE PATAI, *Professor of Portuguese, University of Massachusetts, Amherst*

MAUREEN AHERN, *Professor of Spanish, Ohio State University*
KATHLEEN ROSS, *Associate Professor of Spanish, New York University*

TRANSLATIONS FROM THE SPANISH

TO REFER TO CHARACTERISTICS discernible within a single biennium as "trends" would be rash. When certain characteristics, however, are observed in two or three biennia, it seems relatively safe to consider them ongoing. For instance, in the current period under review, several phenomena associated with the translation of Latin American literature into English were discussed previously in *HLAS 54* and *HLAS 56*.

Notable among those phenomena is one particularly troubling trend: the increasing number of translations published with little or no information about the author or context of the original work. In fact, one might surmise, especially in the case of fiction, where some novels have been altered or "adapted," that many publishers are making a deliberate effort to replace the original works with translations more likely to appeal to North American readers.

The extent to which such "silencing" is truly a marketing strategy and the extent to which it can be attributed to the rising cosmopolitanism of Latin American literature[1] is impossible to determine. Nevertheless, there is a sharp contrast between the packaging and promotion of Latin American literature in translation and the current interest in translation theory and criticism, the growth of translation studies as an interdisciplinary field, and the need for works in translation on the part of scholars, teachers, and students. This contrast makes it difficult to celebrate the high quality of many translations without remarking, for example, on the changes undergone in such cases as Alicia Kozameh's *Steps under Water* (item 4638)[2] or Elena Poniatowska's *Tinísima* (item 4648), or noting that the works that see translation and the translators chosen often seem to depend less on poetics than on politics, as David William Foster has explained very well in "The Politics of Spanish Language Translation in the United States" (item 4721).

Fortunately, however, it is not only commercial presses that publish literature in translation. A significant number of both university and independent presses continue to publish work by authors who are not well known to English-language readers or who, for other reasons, are not considered commercially viable. These presses are far more apt to include ancillary materials than are the larger, commercial houses. This is not always the case, of course, if only because, like some publishers and some readers, there are translators who insist that a translation must be able to stand alone as a new "original." But more often than not, non-commercial situations offer the reader fuller access to the context of a work and to the conditions under which it was written. Both the Univ. of Nebraska Press and the Univ. of Texas Press, for instance, have long histories of publishing translations, as does the Univ. of Pittsburgh Press, where the titles in its "Colección Archivos" series routinely include several critical essays and extensive background material (see *Canaima;* item 4635). For its part, the independent Curbstone Press publishes a periodic newsletter, provides teachers with discussion guides for some of its titles, and offers other instructional materials on its website (*http://www.curbstone.org/*).

In addition, some university and independent presses make possible the publication of landmark texts in Latin American arts and history. Noteworthy examples include César Paternosto's *Piedra abstracta: la escritura Inca* in Esther Allen's elegant translation *The Stone and the Thread: Andean Roots of Abstract Art* from the Univ. of Texas Press (*HLAS 56:315*) and the outstanding bilingual edition of

Subcomandante Marcos' retelling of a folktale published by Cinco Puntos Press (item **4616**). Both of these titles might well be considered works of literature.

With respect to other ongoing phenomena, it is heartening to see not only an increasing number of contributions in the "Bibliography, Theory, and Practice" section but also the outstanding work on translation by critics and translators themselves, for instance Ilan Stavans' essays in *Art and Anger*, Eliot Weinberger's *Written Reactions*, and Alastair Reid's *Oases*.[3]

Other characteristics observed across genres include the retranslation of both canonical and contemporary work (for example, Miguel Barnet's *Biografía de un cimarrón* (item **4668**), Rómulo Gallegos' *Canaima* (item **4635**), Clorinda Matta de Turner's *Aves sin nido* (item **4642**), and Ángeles Mastretta's *Arráncame el corazón* (item **4641**)). It is also interesting to note that during the biennium several selections appeared in different translations in two collections. Finally, the translation of work by women authors has continued to increase, particularly of fiction.

As occurs in many biennia, numerous anthologies were under review. They comprise a rich mix of perspectives and foci that include special issues of journals and individual volumes devoted to a particular topic, such as a theme, a country, or the work of a single author. Although the nature and quality of the anthologies vary widely, it would be safe to say that, as a group, they seem to strive for a kind of "wrapping up," for a broad overview of the 20th century. Two additional characteristics worth noting are the attention to women writers, as in Margaret Sayers Peden's collection of work by Sor Juana Inés de la Cruz (item **4586**) and Delia Poey's *Out of the Mirrored Garden* (item **4559**), as well as the quality of the translations in Peter Bush's *The Voice of the Turtle* (item **3595**) and *Grand Street 61* (item **4556**). Lest one wonder if such collections find the readers they aim to inform, Brad Morrow, the editor of a special issue of the journal *Conjunctions* (item **4554**), sold several hundred copies of his volume at the 1996 Miami Book Fair. In fact, the anthology was so popular that when members of the audience of a Sunday morning panel to mark the book's publication were asked why they weren't at church, one woman responded: "We are."[4]

In the case of poetry, it seems appropriate to mention the outstanding contributions by referring to their translators, given the genre's reputation of being difficult to translate, if not "untranslatable." Indeed, some of the work is not of high quality; but Stephen Kessler's work with Julio Cortázar (item **4577**) and William S. Merwin's versions of poems by Jaime Sabines (item **4597**) are certainly worthy of high praise. Other notable volumes include Harriet de Onís' *Poemas sin nombre*, by Dulce de Loynaz (item **4587**), Christine Jacox Kyle's *Poemas de las madres; The mothers' poems*, by Gabriela Mistral (item **4591**), and Cynthia Steele and David Lauer's *City of Memory*, by José Emilio Pacheco (item **4596**).

Translations in the categories of both brief fiction and theater saw an increase during the biennium. This is particularly significant with respect to theater, as few Latin American works from this genre find their way into English. Most of the translations reviewed here are of high quality, so that the genre as a whole, including *Women Writing Women* (item **4568**) and *Argentine Jewish Theatre* (item **4166**) deserves special mention. There are also excellent examples of work in the translation of brief fiction, for example Edith Grossman's translations of Augusto Monterroso (item **4617**), Lillian Lorca de Tagle's translations of Jaime Collyer (item **4607**), Alberto Manguel's versions of Julio Cortázar (item **4608**), and Cynthia Steele's work with Inés Arredondo (item **4602**).

Like the anthology, the novel is such a heterogenous genre that translations of fiction works cannot be grouped neatly. There continues to be, however, a preponderance of material from Argentina, Chile, and Mexico, which makes work from countries whose literature is virtually unknown to North American readers particularly welcome. This is especially true when the works contain both excellent translations and extensive background material, as in the case of *Canaima* (item **4635**). It is interesting to note that there are few titles by writers who could truly be called "canonical," although there are certainly translations of work by other relatively well-known writers such as Antonio Skármeta (item **4658**) and Paco Ignacio Taibo II (items **4659** and **4660**). In addition, there are some excellent translations of novels by women writers, for example Anna Diegel's *Hagiography of Narcisa the Beautiful*, by Mireya Robles (item **4653**), Dolores M. Koch's *The Angel of Galilea*, by Laura Restrepo (item **4651**), and Margaret Sayers Peden's *Señora Honeycomb*, by Fanny Buitrago (item **4626**). A further example would be Ronald Christ's translation of *Lumpérica* by Diamela Eltit, titled *E. Luminata* (item **4629**), which must be singled out for Christ's excellent translation and his exceptional translator's essay. Translations of three novels by Eltit were published during the biennium, making her work widely available in English for the first time.

Essays in translation published during the biennium show a clear leaning toward the issues of politics and social justice, sometimes based on *testimonio* (Agosín, Alegría and Flakoll, Mellibovsky, Verbitsky) and sometimes on the author's personal experience (Agosín, Fuentes, González, Martí, Ramírez, Vargas Llosa). Much of this work provides a look back over the events of the 1970s and 1980s in Argentina, Chile, and Nicaragua. Three editions of 19th-century volumes were published: the well-known Manzano Cuban slave narrative in a bilingual, edited version (item **4668**); and two different translations of Argentine Lucio Victorio Mansilla's *Una excursión a los indios ranqueles* (items **4674** and **4675**). All areas of the region are covered, with the Southern Cone most heavily represented either by topic or author's national origin. Ospina's volume is the only one in a more philosophical vein, following the tradition of essay as literature (item **4679**). The letters written to Torres-Rioseco comprise an interesting source for literary scholars (item **4673**), while Angel Rama's *The Lettered City* is a key work of cultural criticism and a most valuable addition to the bibliography in English (item **4680**). Two anthologies of essays, by Stavans and Meyer respectively, which include works from the 19th and 20th centuries (items **4560** and **4563**), were also published during the biennium, with the latter devoted to the writing of women.

It is a pleasure to note both an increase in individual articles devoted to translation and the publication of such fine bibliographical and reference works as Kathy S. Leonard's *Index to Translated Short Fiction by Latin American Women in English Anthologies* (item **4723**) and the *Encyclopedia of Latin American Literature* (item **4720**). The encyclopedia is outstanding not only for the extensive entries about individual authors but also for the comprehensive articles about a wide variety of topics (for example, both feminism and feminist literary theory, négritude, Nahuatl literature, and translation) as well as genres and places; a single reservation here would concern the absence of an entry or entries about gay and lesbian topics. Two additional works on translation must also be mentioned: *Searching for Recognition*, Irene Rostagno's historical work about Latin American literature in English-language translation (item **4728**) and *Traducción como cultura*, one of the few collections of essays about translation available in Spanish (item **4731**).

The reviews in this section (with the exception of work in "Essays, Interviews, and Reportage," prepared by Ross, and "Bibliography, Theory, and Practice," prepared by Maier), have been prepared by the three contributing editors for Spanish translations (Ross, Ahern, and Maier); their respective contributions are indicated by their initials following the annotations. As explained in *HLAS 56*, the reviews contain comments about the quality of translations, but are focused primarily on the content of the volumes and the various kinds of materials that accompany them. Given the need for such materials on the part of scholars, teachers, and students—not to mention general readers—, the reviewers cannot but wonder why background information is so often absent and how translators and reviewers might encourage more publishers and editors to include such material. [CM, with MA and KR]

TRANSLATIONS FROM THE PORTUGUESE

The number of translations considered here is greater than in previous volumes, due in part to the somewhat longer than usual span of time—1997–99—covered by *HLAS 58*. But that is not the whole story. A glance at the range of works translated and the publishers involved (in England and the US) suggests a new and dynamic interest in Brazilian literature.

Translations of classics are appearing through Oxford Univ. Press' Library of Latin America, which is dedicated to making available previously neglected works of major 19th- century authors. Machado de Assis may hardly seem to count as a forgotten author, but considering his relative obscurity compared to his European counterparts, it is not so surprising to find his works among Oxford's new translations. Nevertheless, new publications lead to a peculiar situation in which Machado is repeatedly discovered by critics who have no knowledge of his existing reputation. For example, in a recent issue of *Review: Latin American Literature and Arts* (61, Fall 2000), Maria Di Battista lauds Machado for his modernism and tells us that *Quincas Borba* "secures" Machado's place "as an illustrious forerunner of Joyce and Beckett." This honor in fact belongs to Machado's *Brás Cubas*— and in any case it is hardly news. This is the fate of Brazilian literature, endlessly consigned to "discovery" or "rediscovery."

The same problem attends the very welcome endeavors of several smaller presses that are bringing out contemporary Brazilian authors. The result is a varied and exciting literary scene, introducing Brazilian writers such as J.G. Noll, Rubem Fonseca, Patrícia Melo, Chico Buarque, and Ana Cristina Cesar to a potentially large audience. Still, *The Times* (London), in its reviews of these works, invariably treats Brazilian literature as something that has just arrived, as if these writers had achieved overnight success. The reviews reaffirm the general sense that Brazilian literature is a new phenomenon, even as the talents of its practitioners are ostensibly celebrated. A column conveying such a view appeared in *The Times* (May 31, 1997), under the title "Hot on the Samba Beat." In it, Liz Calder asserts that "fiction can open windows on the world like nothing else. So while I hope Brazil wins the next five World Cups, let it be made clear that this astounding nation has much more to offer than football." Can one be more patronizing? Another review from *The Times* (May 15, 1997), by James Woodall, also dealing with the translations brought out by the London publisher Bloomsbury (which organized a British reading tour for several Brazilian writers), informs us that "the energy of Latin American letters is not confined to Buenos Aires or Mexico City. The modern Brazilian novel has arrived." Arrived where?

In the US, the Univ. of New Mexico Press is making a major contribution with volumes big and small through its Jewish Latin America Series edited by Ilan

Stavans: Moacyr Scliar's collected short fiction—brilliantly translated by Eloah Giacomelli—weighs in at nearly 500 pages (item **4691**), while Samuel Rawet's stories form a slender but very welcome book, excellently translated by Nelson Vieira (item **4689**). Oxford continues its translations of 19th-century Latin American works, and Bloomsbury Publishing in London has an active program on Brazil (with many of its titles subsequently published in the US by Ecco Press in Hopewell, NJ), as does Boulevard/Babel in London. Although these publishers' works have been receiving significant press attention in England, the American editions are not often reviewed in leading US newspapers.

The present crop of books (including a few reprints of existing translations) also highlights the talents of many translators, old and new. Especially prominent these days is Clifford H. Landers, a Political Science professor who is working indefatigably to bring Brazilian literature, both past and present, to the public. Of the present batch, he has translated six novels, many short stories (usually published in small journals, not included here for review), and a few poems. Landers has four more volumes projected for publication in 2001, as well as his own book *Literary Translation: A Practical Guide.* His inspired and nuanced translations will set a standard for future translators because of their visibility and number. Landers continues to be associated in particular with Rubem Fonseca, just as David S. George is known for his translations of Edla van Steen's works.

Two historians, Robert M. Levine and José Carlos Sebe Bom Meihy, have carried out a particularly intriguing project in recent years. They have unearthed and published several additional works by Carolina Maria de Jesus, as well as a close and unexpurgated edition of her notebooks, some of which appeared in an earlier incarnation as *Quarto de Despejo* (*Child of the Dark*). The two have also published their own studies of this fascinating figure and her reception in Brazil and abroad (items **4709**, **4710**, and **4711**.)

Paulo Coelho's inspirational New Age fictions and semifictions continue to appear in English, still seeking the book that will make him the bestseller in the US that he has been in other countries, where millions of copies of his books have been sold. After working for some years with Alan R. Clarke, the translator who "introduced" him to the US market (items **4695** and **4708**), Coelho has opted for new translators—Margaret Jull Costa (who began translating José Saramago's work after the death of Giovanni Pontiero) and Landers (items **4696** and **4697**).

All in all, with a large variety of works appearing and many translators involved, Brazilian translations into English present a lively and promising picture. Whether a market exists to sustain such efforts remains to be seen. [DP]

NOTES:

1 In this context, see Bill Vourvoulias, "Where are the Butterflies? A Survey of Recent Japanese and Latin American Fiction," *Culture Front,* 6:2, 1997, p. 12–15, 93.

2 See Alicia Partnoy, "Silence and Survival," *The Women's Review of Books,* 15:2, 1997, p. 26.

3 Ilan Stavans, *Art and Anger: Essays on Politics and the Imagination,* Albuquerque: Univ. of New Mexico Press, 1995; Alastair Reid, *Oasis: Poems and Prose,* Edinburgh, UK: Canongate Books, 1997; Eliot Weinberger, *Written Reactions: Poetics, Politics, Polemics,* NY: Marsilio, 1996.

4 David Streitfield, "Letter from the Miami Book Fair," *Book World* (*The Washington Post*), Dec. 29, 1996, p. 15.

ANTHOLOGIES

4548 Argentine Jewish theatre: a critical anthology. Edited and translated by Nora Glickman and Gloria F. Waldman. Lewisburg, Pa.: Bucknell Univ. Press, 1996. 346 p.: bibl., ill.

Scholarly compilation of eight plays spanning seven decades (1920s-80s). Contemporary writers include Goldenberg, Halac, Dragún, and Raznovich. Short but informative introduction, biographical prefaces, notes (often explaining Yiddish terms), and bibliography make volume especially good for classroom use. Accompanying materials stress several recurring themes of this diverse group of plays. For drama specialist's comment, see item **4166.** [KR]

4549 Bellessi, Diana and **Ursula K. Le Guin.** The twins, the dream: two voices = Las gemelas, el sueño: dos voces. Houston, Tex.: Arte Público Press, 1996. 225 p.

Fascinating collaboration between Diana Bellessi (Argentina) and Ursula K. Le Guin (US), each of whom translates a collection of poems by the other. The two poets worked in close consultation with each other, especially in the case of Le Guin, whose knowledge of Spanish is admittedly minimal. Bilingual format except for authors' introductions which are printed without translation. [CM]

4550 Birmingham-Pokorny, Elba D. An English anthology of Afro-Hispanic writers of the twentieth century. Miami: Ediciones Universal, 1994. 126 p. (Col. Ebano y canela)

Introductory, bilingual anthology intended for students of Spanish-American literature, civilization, and culture. Work might be useful for this purpose given its focus on Afro-Hispanic contributions to Spanish-American literature, a topic too little researched and studied. Selections are very brief however, and many of the translations are quite awkward. [CM]

4551 Boricuas: influential Puerto Rican writings—an anthology. Edited by Roberto Santiago. Translated by Roberto Santiago et al. New York: One World, 1995. 357 p.: ill., index.

Selection of poetry, stories, drama, and essays by 40 Puerto Rican writers, late-19th—late-20th centuries. Organized into thematic categories such as "History and Politics" and "Anxiety and Assimilation." Introduction by Santiago makes clear his goal, that the book "will provide us with answers to our innermost questions of identity." Majority of texts originally written in English or "Spanglish"; translations from Spanish range from good to excellent. [KR]

4552 Bridges to Cuba = Puentes a Cuba. Edited by Ruth Behar. Translated by David Frye et al. Ann Arbor: Univ. of Michigan Press, 1995. 421 p.

Groundbreaking anthology of artwork, drama, fiction, interviews, and poetry by authors both within and outside Cuba. Wide, provocative range of perspectives. Highlights include Ruth Behar's introductory and closing essays, interviews with Nancy Morejón, and essays by María de los Angeles Torres and Alan West. Majority of translations by David Frye. See also items **4587, 4578,** and **4600.** [CM]

4553 A century of Cuban writers in Florida: selected prose and poetry. Edited with an introduction by Carolina Hospital and Jorge Cantera. Sarasota, Fla.: Pineapple Press, 1996. 238 p.: bibl., index.

Prose and poetry by 33 writers, arranged in chronological groups from 19th century to present. Interesting introduction by editors explores long history of contact and cultural ties between Florida and Cuba. Selection includes well-known figures (Martí, Cabrera, Padilla) alongside less famous ones. Some texts originally written in English. Literary quality of texts is uneven, but volume is useful for the classroom. [KR]

4554 Conjunctions. Vol. 27, 1996. The Archipelago: new Caribbean writing. New York: Conjunctions.

Rich collection of artwork, drama, essays, fiction, and poetry assembled to address such "simple yet impossible questions" as *What is the Caribbean?* and *What are its literatures?* Selections by Antonio Benítez-Rojo, Juan Bosch, García Márquez, Mayra Montero, Senel Paz, Severo Sarduy, and Arturo Uslar-Pietri, among others. Also includes many works by English-language writers. [CM]

4555 Cruel fictions, cruel realities: short stories by Latin American women writers. Edited and translated by Kathy S.

Leonard. Pittsburgh, Pa.: Latin American Literary Review Press, 1997. 131 p.: bibl.

Nineteen stories by 12 writers from across the region, almost all little-known or never before translated into English. Stories share common theme of human cruelty in different forms (political, personal, religious, etc.). Includes translator's introduction, biographical pages on each author, and extensive bibliography. Some compelling stories. Solid translations, if sometimes too similar in voice. [KR]

4556 Grand Street. Vol. 61, 1997. All-American. New York: Grand Street Publications.

Large special issue whose contents (there is no editorial introduction or statement) suggest a redefinition of "American" literature and the visual arts. Selections include work by both North and South American artists and writers working in English, French, Portuguese, and Spanish. Many translators; translations excellent for the most part. [CM]

4557 Manoa: A Pacific Journal of International Writing. Vol. 8, No. 1, Summer 1996. New writing from the Pacific coast of South America. Honolulu: Univ. of Hawaii Press.

Issue includes selections from Chile, Colombia, and Peru, as well as Okinawa and North America. Poetry selections, chosen by James Hoggard, include work by new and well-established poets. Stories, all by women, "reflect the tendency...to depict a world of instability, a consciousness wounded and troubled." Many translations; great variance in quality. [CM]

4558 Masterworks of Latin American short fiction: eight novellas. Edited by Cass Canfield, Jr. Introduction by Ilan Stavans. New York: Icon Editions, 1996. 385 p.

Translations of works by eminent writers (Cabrera Infante, Carpentier, Cortázar, García Márquez, Guimarães Rosa, Felisberto Hernández, Mutis, Ana Lydia Vega) reprinted from previous editions. Accomplished, excellent translators in all cases. Strong locating introduction by Stavans describes trajectory of novella in Latin America, historical antecedents, and current practices. Short bio-bibliographies of authors.

Unusual volume for its varied selection of writers. [KR]

4559 Out of the mirrored garden: new fiction by Latin American women. Edited by Delia Poey. New York: Anchor Books, 1996. 222 p.: bibl.

Collection of 17 stories, most not previously published in English, by writers from across the region. Some are well-known in translation (Campos, Peri Rossi, Mastretta, Poniatowska); others less so (Kociancich, Boullosa). Varied styles and story content. Stories strong and translations generally excellent. Includes a short introduction by Poey, biographical paragraphs, and a short bibliography. [KR]

4560 The Oxford book of Latin American essays. Edited by Ilan Stavans. New York: Oxford Univ. Press, 1997. 518 p.: bibl., index.

Seventy-seven essays—only 12 by women—include works written in Spanish and Portuguese between 1849 (Bello) and 1994 (Subcomandante Marcos). The broad definition of essay allows for inclusion of pieces such as Borges' "Pierre Menard," usually defined as fiction. Historical introduction by Stavans; bio-bibliographical notes for authors. Many pieces translated expressly for this volume. Consistently high level of translation. [KR]

4561 The Oxford book of Latin American short stories. Edited by Roberto González Echevarría. New York: Oxford Univ. Press, 1997. 481 p.: bibl., index.

Includes 53 stories spanning evolution of short fiction in Brazil as well as Hispanic America across a broad range of writing from colonial era and 19th century to modern favorites such as Lugones, Quiroga, Lima Barreto, Borges, Cortázar, Rulfo, Ribeyro, Castellanos, Lispector, Ferré, and Monterroso, in versions by distinguished translators. An essay by the editor traces evolution of the genre. Brief headnotes for each period and author and a short bibliography provide ample contextualization. Recommended for classroom use. [MA]

4562 Paz, Senel. Strawberry & chocolate. Introduction, translations, and interview by Peter R. Bush. London: Bloomsbury, 1995. 197 p.: bibl., ill., ports.

By including not only an informative

introduction and an interview with Senel Paz, but also translations of the screenplay for the film *Fresa y chocolate* (*Strawberry and Chocolate*), and of the story *El lobo, el bosque y el hombre nuevo* (*The wolf, the woods, and the new man*) on which that film was based, editor-translator Peter Bush chronicles origins of a landmark event in Cuban culture. Fine translations. For comment on original story, see *HLAS 54:3838.* [CM]

4563 Rereading the Spanish American essay: translations of 19th and 20th century women's essays. Edited by Doris Meyer. Austin: Univ. of Texas Press, 1995. 324 p. (The Texas Pan American series)

Companion volume to *Reinterpreting the Spanish American essay* (see item **3374**), this anthology collects work of 22 essayists including Gómez de Avellaneda, Ocampo, Peri Rossi, Castellanos, and others less known. Many treat topics related to women. Excellent translations; short introductory essays on each writer. First-rate contribution to revisionist literary history. [KR]

4564 The silver candelabra and other stories: a century of Jewish Argentine literature. Edited and translated by Rita Mazzetti Gardiol. Pittsburgh, Pa.: Latin American Literary Review Press, 1997. 187 p.: bibl.

Translations of 20 stories by 12 writers, including immigrants, first (b. early-20th century) and second (b. 1930s-40s) generation. Variety of styles and subjects, some treating Jewish life and culture. Useful historical introduction by Gardiol; biographical page on each author; bibliography. Well-chosen stories and generally good translations. [KR]

4565 Spanish-American poetry: a dual-language anthology. Edited and translated by Seymour Resnick. Mineola, N.Y.: Dover Pub., 1996. 59 p.

Brief volume of selections ranging from colonial period (Ercilla, Sor Juana) to Neruda. Some longer poems are represented by very short excerpts. Poems have been included with pedagogical purposes in mind, as "popular poems that have endured" that lend themselves to memorization and recitation. Accurate, though uninspired literal translations. *En face*, with short biographical information on each writer. [KR]

4566 Twentieth century Latin American poetry: a bilingual anthology. Edited by Stephen Tapscott. Austin: Univ. of Texas Press, 1996. 418 p. bibl., ill., index. (The Texas Pan American series)

Large anthology includes work by 58 poets. Extensive, but general, introduction. Poets arranged chronologically from José Martí to Marjorie Agosín. Volume includes few surprises and relatively few women. Bilingual format. Many translators; great fluctuation in quality. For detailed discussion of translations, see Charles Tomlinson in *Times Literary Supplement*, May 9, 1997; and Eliot Weinberger in *Sulfur*, 40, Spring 1997. [CM]

4567 What is secret: stories by Chilean women. Edited by Marjorie Agosín. Fredonia, N.Y.: White Pine Press, 1995. 303 p. (Secret weavers series; 9)

Thirty-three authors and 37 texts represent powerful voices "spoken from a woman's threshold" throughout 20th century. Twenty-two translators achieve a competent level with a wide variety of themes and styles. Editor's introduction orients reader to stories' Chilean context. Short notes on authors and translators. Recommended for classroom use. [MA]

4568 Women writing women: an anthology of Spanish-American theater of the 1980s. Edited by Teresa Cajiao Salas and Margarita Vargas. Introduction by Margarita Vargas. Albany: State Univ. of New York Press, 1997. 468 p.: bibl., ill., index. (SUNY series in Latin American and Iberian thought and culture)

Translations of eight plays by acclaimed women playwrights: Isidora Aguirre (Chile), Sabina Berman (Mexico), Myrna Casas (Puerto Rico), Teresa Marichal (Puerto Rico), Diana Raznovich (Argentina), Mariela Romero (Venezuela), Beatriz Seibel (Argentina), and Maruxa Vilalta (Mexico). Introductory essay and bio-bibliographical notes on each author offer ample contextualization supplemented by a useful bibliography of primary and secondary sources. Lively translations by editors and Kirsten Nigro produce stageworthy scripts. Outstanding collection highly recommended for classroom and dramatic use. [MA]

TRANSLATIONS FROM
THE SPANISH
Poetry

4569 Agosín, Marjorie. Melodious women. Translated by Monica Bruno. Pittsburgh, Pa.: Latin American Literary Review Press, 1997. 160 p. (Discoveries)

English-only volume of 86 poems, most dealing with female historical figures or other lesser-known women. Poetic voice often autobiographical. Translations convey a "portrait of both the diversity and unity of the female experience" through simple, direct language; poems at times are rather repetitive. No bibliographical or introductory material. [KR]

4570 Agosín, Marjorie. Starry night: poems. Translated by Mary G. Berg. Fredonia, N.Y.: White Pine Press, 1996. 103 p.

Berg's fine translation of *Noche estrellada,* a meditation on van Gogh's luminous paintings of the south of France, won the 1995 Letras de Oro Prize for Poetry. Translation conserves original's vivid chromatic metaphors. Lacking the Spanish texts, a table of contents, or a painting reproduction, work's format does not do justice to these poems. [MA]

4571 Agosín, Marjorie. Toward the splendid city. Translated by Richard Schaaf. Tempe, Ariz.: Bilingual Press/Editorial Bilingüe, 1994. 139 p.

Collection divided into four sections, each devoted to a different city but unified by the poet's quest for splendor amid suffering and injustice. No ancillary material; translations are excellent, however. Bilingual format (Spanish on the right, English on the left) is provocative. [CM]

4572 Alegría, Claribel. Umbrales = Thresholds; poems. Translated by Darwin J. Flakoll. Willimantic, Conn.: Curbstone Press, 1996. 69 p.

Bilingual edition of nine poems, all of which relate experiences of passage and increased, at times painful, awareness. English versions are highly readable, even "rereadable" (*Sojourner,* Feb. 1997); however, they often lack the alliterative precision and nuances of the Spanish. No commentary of any kind provided. [CM]

4573 Bennett, John M. Prime sway: a transduction of *Primero Sueño* by Sor Juana Inés de la Cruz. Responses by Blaster Al Ackerman, Jake Berry, Jim Leftwich, and Joe Napora. Illustrations by Joel Lipman. Norman, Okla.: Texture Press, 1996. 48 p.: ill.

Bennett's "transduction" of Sor Juana's *Primero sueño* was written "...pretending I don't know Spanish and writing it out (reading it) as if it were English." The reader shares in the creative process by assuming the role of writer. "Transduction...is the process of applying inappropriate sets of memory to a text, as when Bennett reads Sor Juana's Spanish while utilizing his memory of English and ignoring his memory of Spanish" (Leftwich, p. 33). Resulting palimpsest is a jolting modern rebounding of Sor Juana's voice. Includes responses by other poets, and readings. [MA]

4574 Blanco, Alberto. Dawn of the senses: selected poems of Alberto Blanco. Edited by Juvenal Acosta. Introduction by José Emilio Pacheco. San Francisco: City Lights Books, 1995. 215 p. (Pocket poets series; 52)

Extensive bilingual collection of translations by 12 translators, among them Edith Grossman, Reginald Gibbons, and Mark Schafer. Brief introductory remarks by José Emilio Pacheco are supplemented by a more complete biographical endnote on Blanco and his work as poet, translator, and professor. [CM]

4575 Burgos, Julia de. Song of the simple truth: obra completa poética; the complete poems. Compiled and translated by Jack Agüeros. Willimantic, Conn.: Curbstone Press, 1997. 523 p.: bibl.

Book is invaluable both for its introduction to the life and work of Burgos and as a complete bilingual edition of her poems. Agüeros knows Burgos' work intimately, and his introduction is highly informative. Translations are less then satisfying, but this volume makes all of Burgos' poems available in English for the first time. [CM]

4576 Cardenal, Ernesto. Quetzalcóatl. Translated by Clifton Ross. Berkeley, Calif.: New Earth Publications, 1993. 59 p.

In this poem (see *HLAS 52:4033* for review of original Spanish-language version), Cardenal fuses oral rhythms of the ancient myth of the Feathered Serpent who created man, nature, and arts to his vision of present and future Central America. The sensitive translation, *en face* format, and brief introduction recommend this work for classroom use. [MA]

4577 Cortázar, Julio. Save twilight: selected poems by Julio Cortázar. Translated by Stephen Kessler. San Francisco: City Lights Books, 1997. 169 p. (Pocket poets series; 53)

Selections from Cortázar's 1984 collection *Salvo el crepúsculo* (see *HLAS 50:3601*), including prose commentaries from that volume. *En face*. Highly accomplished, colloquial translations. Short translator's preface; biographical note. Selection "attempts to represent the range of Cortázar's poetic accomplishment" without traditional organization, following original volume's method. Excellent contribution to bibliography. [KR]

4578 Cruz Varela, María Elena. El ángel agotado = The exhausted angel. Madrid?: Fundación Liberal José Martí, 1992. 143 p.

Selection of moving poems by Cuban poet reflects her struggle to subvert official language, her disenchantment with Cuba's revolutionary government, and her incarceration. Unidentified translator has served poorly not only Cruz Varela's poetry but also Nicasio Silva's critical essay and Liva Clavijo's prologue. For more satisfying translations, see Ruth Behar's translation of "El Muro" ("The Wall") in *Bridges to Cuba* (see item **4552**) and Mairym Cruz-Bernal's work in *Ballad of the blood* (see item **4579**). [CM]

4579 Cruz Varela, María Elena. Balada de la sangre: los poemas de María Elena Cruz Varela. Traducidos por Mairym Cruz-Bernal con Deborah Digges = Ballad of the blood: the poems of María Elena Cruz Varela. Translated and edited by Mairym Cruz-Bernal and Deborah Digges. Hopewell, N.J.: Ecco Press, 1996. 119 p.

Intense, intimate, often dark collection of poems by dissident Cuban poet imprisoned in early 1990s and now living in Puerto Rico. Translations replicate this highly personal poetic voice with mixed success. *En face*. Useful biographical introduction by Cruz-Bernal. See also item **4578**. [KR]

4580 Dalton, Roque. Small hours of the night: selected poems of Roque Dalton. Edited by Hardie St. Martin. Translated by Jonathan Cohen *et al*. Willimantic, Conn.: Curbstone Press, 1996. 201 p.: bibl.

English-only edition of poems written from exile, prison, and on the run by the Salvadoran revolutionary whose life and word urged love as well as change. Selected from 10 of his collections including two posthumous manuscripts, but none are from *Poemas clandestinos* (1980). The vital force of the intimate, conversational Spanish challenges the translators. Introductory essays by Ernesto Cardenal, Claribel Alegría, and Hardie St. Martin recommend work for the classroom and the general reader. [MA]

4581 Fernández, Pablo Armando. Learning to die: the poetry of Pablo Armando Fernández. Selected, translated, and with an introduction by John Brotherton. La Habana: Instituto Cubano del Libro; Editorial José Martí, 1995. 225 p.

Bilingual selection of poems by a major Cuban poet written between 1947–78 about loneliness in New York, his struggle for integration into the Revolution, and coming to terms with the power of love. Introduction and translator's note, but no table of contents or index. Careful translation at times lacks force of conversational Spanish register. [MA]

4582 Futoransky, Luisa. The duration of the voyage: selected poems. Edited and translated by Jason Weiss. San Diego, Calif.: Junction Press, 1997. 95 p.

First English translation of well-known Argentine novelist and poet, resident in Paris since 1981. Collected poems from six volumes spanning 1972–97 treat topics including travel, Jewish culture, and exile. *En face*. Highly cosmopolitan, cerebral poems, translated effectively by Weiss. Back-cover biographical information; no other locating material. [KR]

4583 Gelman, Juan. Unthinkable tenderness: selected poems. Edited and translated by Joan Lindgren. Foreword by Eduardo Galeano. Berkeley: Univ. of California Press, 1997. 191 p.: appendices.

English-only collection includes poems from the two volumes of Gelman's *Interrupciones* (see *HLAS 52:4077–4078*) plus other material, covering work of last 30 years. Moving, consistently translated selection emphasizes poet's response to dictatorship, exile, and disappearance. Useful editor's preface; chronological and biographical appendices. Some notes and explanation of translator's approach to Gelman's work. [KR]

4584 Huidobro, Vicente. The poet is a little god: creationist verse. Translated from the Spanish by Jorge García-Gómez and introduced by Gary Kern. 2nd ed., thoroughly rev. Riverside, Calif.: Xenos Books, 1996. 181 p.: bibl., ill.

En face edition includes poems from *El espejo de agua* (1916), the entire collection of *Poemas árticos,* and the extended poem *Ecuatorial* (both 1918). Informative, if tendentious, introductory essay by Kern; short selected bibliography. Rather literal translations are accurate, not inspired. [KR]

4585 Isaacson, José. Desde el mundo de Borges. Versión inglesa de William Shand. Buenos Aires: Marymar Ediciones, 1994. 75 p.: ill.

En face edition of a cycle of nine poems by the Argentine Isaacson (b. 1922) published to observe 95th anniversary of Borges' birth. Interesting double voice of Isaacson as Borges, writing about his life and art. Thoughtful translation follows introspective tone of the Spanish. Useful biblio-biographical information (in Spanish and English) on flaps and back cover. [KR]

4586 Juana Inés de la Cruz, Sor. Poems, protest, and a dream: selected writings. Translated with notes by Margaret Sayers Peden. Introduction by Ilan Stavans. New York: Penguin Books, 1997. 254 p.: bibl.

This *en face* annotated edition of selected writings of the Mexican poet includes the *Respuesta* to the Bishop of Puebla (1691) and a broad selection of her poetry and dramatic texts: nine love sonnets; segments from *Primero sueño,* Villancico VI to Saint Catherine, and *Loa para el auto sacramental de el divino Narciso;* and Leonor's speech from the play *Los empeños de una casa.* Peden's "Translator's Note" explains her translation strategy of "moving backwards" towards the poet's place and time, which skillfully captures the full flavor of the baroque past. Stavans' extensive "Introduction" and "Suggestions for Further Reading" provide orientation to Sor Juana's masterpieces and their social and intellectual contexts. Highly recommended for classroom and general use. See also item **4613.** [MA]

4587 Loynaz, Dulce María. Poems without name. Translated by Harriet De Onís. La Habana: Editorial José Martí; Ediciones ARTEX, 1993. 289 p.

Virtually the only available English translations of the work of an important Cuban poet, prose writer, and critic awarded the Cervantes Prize in 1992. Loynaz's contribution to 20th-century literature awaits extensive translation and critical study. In the meantime, De Onís' careful, sensitive—if not consistently poetically successful—versions provide good introduction. See also comments by Ruth Behar and Pablo Armando Fernández in *Bridges to Cuba* (item **4552**). [CM]

4588 Manrique, Jaime. My night with Federico García Lorca = Mi noche con Federico García Lorca. Translated by Edith Grossman and Eugene Richie. Hudson, N.Y.: Groundwater Press, 1995. 89 p.

Bilingual, autobiographical collection of a Colombian-born "transcultural dweller" (Ilan Stavans, *Washington Post Book World,* June 17, 1997) living in the US. Poems record gay writer's childhood, adolescence, and coming of age. In addition to Grossman and Richie, Manrique himself contributes a translation: the book's pivotal poem, which is also its most affective. [CM]

4589 Martí, José. Versos sencillos = Simple verses. Translated, with an introduction, by Manuel A. Tellechea. Houston, Tex.: Arte Público Press, 1997. 123 p. (Recovering the U.S. Hispanic Literary Heritage)

First complete translation (according to cover notes) of Martí's famous work (see *HLAS 5:3875*). *En face.* Useful, although uncritical, biographical introduction. No notes or bibliography. Rhymed translations, often stilted and forced, capture little of the beauty and simplicity of originals. More useful for the Spanish text than the translations. [KR]

4590 Miranda, Verónica. Estudio erótico = Erotic study. Prólogo por Luis Benítez. Traducción de Angela McEwan. Tarzana, Calif.: Luz Bilingual Pub., 1996. 73 p.: ill. (Col. Luz bilingüe)

Bilingüe edition of *haiku*-like poems in which "eroticism is insinuated rather than overt." A self-published book, as Miranda (born in Argentina and now resident in Los Angeles) is president of Luz Bilingual. Some poems are interesting for their playful use of

Spanish, but this is largely lost in translation. Prologue in Spanish only. A very slim collection. [KR]

4591 Mistral, Gabriela. Poemas de las madres = The mothers' poems. Translated by Christiane Jacox Kyle. Paintings by Sara Adlerstein González. Introduction by Margaret Sayers Peden. Cheney, Wash.: EWU Press, 1996. 39 p.: ill. (some col.).

Beautiful bilingual edition of the prose poems that exemplify "Mistral's sense of sisterhood with all women," first published in *Desolación* in 1922 and revised by Mistral in the 1950 edition upon which these translations are based. Twelve powerful paintings by a leading Chilean artist and superb English renditions capture the multilayered imagery, cadences, and "sense of otherness." Eloquent introductory essay and translator's note. Highly recommended. [MA]

4592 Montejo, Victor. Sculpted stones = Piedras labradas. Translated by Victor Perera. Willimantic, Conn.: Curbstone Press, 1995. 107 p.

Poems written between 1982–92 by the Guatemalan folklorist after leaving his country for the US. Themes include violence of war, exile, continuity with the past, and love for homeland. Lyrical, direct voice captured skillfully and movingly by translations. *En face;* no supporting material beyond short biographical paragraph and a few notes. [KR]

4593 Morábito, Fabio. Toolbox. Translated by Geoff Hargreaves. Introduction by Jaime Moreno Villarreal. Illustrations by Bernardo Recamier. Riverside, Calif.: Xenos Books, 1996. 103 p.: bibl., ill.

Fascinating collection of 12 prose poems, each accompanied by a pen-and-ink illustration by Bernardo Recamier. Morábito presents a set of tools for assembling the world based on John Cage's "scratch," describing the tools' distinct yet multiple, at times overlapping and even dangerous, uses. Translations unfortunately more prosodic than poetic. [CM]

4594 Neruda, Pablo. Ceremonial songs = Cantos ceremoniales. Translated by Maria Jacketti. Pittsburgh, Pa.: Latin American Literary Review Press, 1996. 141 p. (Discoveries)

First complete English-language publication of 10 songs published nearly four de-

cades ago (see *HLAS 28:2152*) in which the great Chilean laureate explores "landscapes of the heart and mind." Competent translations in a bilingual edition. Lacks both an introduction and translator's note. [MA]

4595 Neruda, Pablo. Odes to opposites. Selected and illustrated by Ferris Cook. Translated by Kenneth Krabbenhoft. Boston: Little, Brown, 1995. 149 p.

Second impressive collection of Neruda's *Odes* by skilled team of translator Krabbenhoft and artist Ferris Cook whose fine pencil drawings add a third "dimension" to the bilingual format. Intriguing selection of 11 pairs of *Odes* with opposing themes. Contrasting illustrations for each pair. For comment on first *Odes* collection, see *HLAS 56:4545*. [CM]

4596 Pacheco, José Emilio. City of memory and other poems. Translated by Cynthia Steele and David Lauer. San Francisco: City Lights Books, 1997. 195 p.

Includes full texts of *Miro la tierra* (see *HLAS 50:3647*) and *Ciudad de la memoria* (see *HLAS 52:4144*), translated by Lauer and Steele, respectively. Useful translators' prefaces, introduction, biographical note on author. *En face.* Major themes are Mexico City and the 1985 earthquake. Effective translations; very different styles of Lauer and Steele offer an interesting tool for teaching. [KR]

4597 Sabines, Jaime. Selected poems of Jaime Sabines: pieces of shadow. Translated by W.S. Merwin. Foreword by Mario del Valle. México: Papeles Privados, 1995. 205 p.

This splendid bilingual edition brings the voice of a great modern Mexican poet into English through that of a major North American poet and translator. The "Foreword" and "Translator's Note" present a broad selection ranging from early books of the 1950s through *Tarumba* and the last poems from 1995. Forceful translation captures the power, anger, and spontaneity of this searing verse. Highly recommended for classroom and general reading. [MA]

4598 Segovia, Tomás. Partición = Partition. Translated by Myra S. Gann. York, S.C.: Spanish Literature Publications Co., 1996. 162 p.: port.

Poetry and prose poems by Spanish-born poet (1927) who spent much of his youth in Mexico's Spanish exile community. Collection comprises three books previously published individually, of which *The nomad's notebook* is particularly moving. Informative, thoughtful introduction by translator, whose versions would be stronger if she had tried to be less literally "faithful." [CM]

4599 Sepúlveda-Pulvirenti, Emma. Death to silence = Muerte al silencio. Translated by Shaun T. Griffin. Houston, Tex.: Arte Público Press, 1997. 97 p.

Poems of death, sexuality, poetics, protest, witness, and exile by Argentine-born (1950) poet raised in Chile and now living in the US. Brief introduction by Alicia Galaz-Vivar Weldon describes poems; short biographical notes for author and translator. Literal, at times overly literal, translations. [CM]

Spanish-American poetry: a dual-language anthology. See item **4565.**

4600 West, Alan. Dar nombres a la lluvia = Finding voices in the rain. Translated by Alan West and Mark Schafer. Madrid: Editorial Verbum, 1995. 135 p. (Poesía)

Bilingual collection by Cuban-born (1953) poet, essayist, writer, and translator, whose family has resided in Puerto Rico since 1963. Many translations by poet himself, which makes possible an interesting bilingual reading in terms of language, memory, repression, sexuality, flight, and exile. *En face.* See also West's "My Life with Fidel Castro" in *Bridges to Cuba* (item **4552**). [CM]

4601 Zamora Delgado, Juan Carlos. Hoy que regresan mis ventanas = Today my windows are back; Hay quien ya no podrá venir = He won't be able to come back now. Traducción de Agustín Zamora. Miami, Fla.: Senda Pub., 1993. 162 p. (Senda poesía)

Double volume, each *en face*, of lyrical-philosophical poems on daily existence by exiled Cuban author (b. 1960) now living in US. Essentially home-made volume has frequent typos and missing words. Spanish poetry, if not especially original, employs polished language. English version is at times unreadable and generally awkward. [KR]

Brief Fiction and Theater

4602 Arredondo, Inés. Underground river and other stories. Translated by Cynthia Steele. Foreword by Elena Poniatowska. Lincoln: Univ. of Nebraska Press, 1996. 128 p. (Latin American women writers)

Outstanding collection of stories chosen from Arredondo's *Obras completas* (1991), translated by Cynthia Steele, Elena Poniatowska, and the author. Informative essay by Steele, foreword by Poniatowska, and Steele's fine translation provide a welcome introduction to a body of work that deserves a wider readership in both Spanish and English. Highly recommended. [CM]

4603 Asturias, Miguel Angel. The mirror of Lida Sal: tales based on Mayan myths and Guatemalan legends. Translated by Gilbert-Alter-Gilbert. Introduction by Gerald Martin. Pittsburgh, Pa.: Latin American Literary Review Press, 1997. 126 p. (Discoveries)

First English-language edition of *El espejo de Lida Sal* (see *HLAS 30:3268*), in which the Nobel laureate melds Mayan and Guatemalan myth and folklore in 10 stories whose hallucinatory prose challenges the reader. "Everything unfolds in a land of natural dreamscapes...The imagination reels." Although lacking a table of contents and translator's note, the superb translation recommends the work for classroom use. [MA]

4604 Benedetti, Mario. Blood pact and other stories. Edited by Claribel Alegría and Darwin J. Flakoll. Willimantic, Conn.: Curbstone Press, 1997. 213 p.

Translations of 27 stories from over 40 years of writing by one of Latin America's favorite authors whose prose creates powerful surprises and compelling humor out of "the terrors lurking in 'ordinary people' and things" in Montevideo. Fine editing and translating by Louise Popkin and 14 other translators, but lacking an introduction. [MA]

4605 Campos, Julieta. Celina or the cats. Translated by Leland H. Chambers. Pittsburgh, Pa.: Latin American Literary Review Press, 1995. 140 p. (Discoveries)

Translation of *Celina o los gatos* (1968), a collection of five short stories linking the cat with mystery, reality, and narrative by the Cuban-born narrator who resides in Mexico. Her introductory essay explores symbolism of cats in life and art. Skillfull translations of four stories by Chambers and another by Kathleen Ross recommend the collection. [MA]

4606 Chocrón, Isaac E. Three plays by Isaac Chocrón. Translation and critical study by Barbara Younoszai and Rossi Irausquin-Johnson. Foreword by Isaac Chocrón. New York: Lang, 1995. 234 p.: bibl., ill. (Taft Memorial Fund and Univ. of Cincinnati studies in Latin American, Chicano, and US Latino theater; 4)

Accomplished translation (according to the translators, the first into English of works by this contemporary Venezuelan playwright) of *OK* (see *HLAS 34:4003*), *La máxima felicidad* (see *HLAS 40:7254*), and *Clipper* (see *HLAS 54:4565*). Interesting themes of alternative family structures, gender roles, Jews in Latin America, and homosexuality. Clear and concise locating introduction by the translators. Useful bibliography; no notes to translations themselves. [KR]

4607 Collyer, Jaime. People on the prowl: short stories. Translated by Lillian Tagle. Pittsburgh, Pa.: Latin American Literary Review Press, 1996. 156 p. (Series Discoveries)

Wonderful translation of Chilean writer's *Gente al acecho* (1992) comprised of 15 stories and an author's epilogue. Varied themes are neo-Borgesian in cosmopolitan historical and intellectual content, but richer in humor. Tagle's mastery of the text is evident in her engaging work. Cover biography; no further supporting material. [KR]

4608 Cortázar, Julio. Unreasonable hours. Translated by Alberto Manguel. Toronto: Coach House Press, 1995. 157 p. (Passport books)

Seven stories from Cortázar's volume *Deshoras* (see *HLAS 48:5600*). Useful afterword by Manguel places work in biographical, literary, and political context. Powerful, often fantastic narrations told from different points of view, compellingly translated by Manguel. Important contribution to Cortázar bibliography in English. [KR]

4609 Di Benedetto, Antonio. Animal world: stories. Translated by Herbert Edward Francis. Afterword by Jorge García-Gómez.

Grand Terrace, Calif.: Xenos Books, 1996. 1 v.: bibl.

Powerful stories by Argentine writer from *Mundo animal*, his first collection, influenced by Borges, Kafka, and others. Di Benedetto explains that he wants to "intern" readers in "the mysteries of life," something which his complexly plotted tales of the transformation of human beings-become animals accomplish provocatively. Adequate, although at times stilted, translations. Bilingual edition. For comment on original work, see *HLAS 36:4342*. [CM]

4610 Galeano, Eduardo H. Walking words. Woodcuts by José Francisco Borges. Translated by Mark Fried. New York: W.W. Norton, 1995. 328 p.: ill.

Striking collaboration between Galeano's tales rooted in the oral tradition and Brazilian artist José Francisco Borges' woodcuts in the *cordel* tradition is given a rich third dimension by Fried's imaginative translation of *Palabras andantes*. Readers will have to look elsewhere for introductory material, but in effect the book introduces and explains itself. For comment on original work, see *HLAS 56:3869*. [CM]

4611 Garro, Elena. First love; and Look for my obituary; two novellas. Translated by David Unger. Willimantic, Conn.: Curbstone Press, 1997. 1 v.

Excellent translation of *Busca mi esquela* and *Primer amor*, two novellas awarded the 1996 Sor Juana Inés de la Cruz Prize. Provocative, haunting fiction whose author deserves to be studied and read for works other than her *Recuerdos del porvenir* (see *HLAS 28:1843*). [CM]

4612 Jaramillo Levi, Enrique. The shadow: thirteen stories in opposition. Translated by Samuel A. Zimmerman. Pittsburgh, Pa.: Latin American Literary Review Press, 1996. 119 p.

Short vignettes of narrators coming to terms with their angst, identities, and realities. Zimmerman's translations of the Panamanian writer's flowing style are adequate but the reader needs an introduction. [MA]

4613 Juana Inés de la Cruz, Sor. The house of trials. A translation of *Los empeños de una casa* by David Pasto. New York: Peter Lang, 1996. 150 p.: bibl. (Ibérica; 21)

First complete English translation of

Sor Juana's brilliant *comedia, Los empeños de una casa* (1940), in which she subverts the conventions of gender and Golden Age drama to suit her own feminine perspectives. Castaño, the male character disguised as a woman, performs the construction of gendered identity. Notes help with the 17th-century references and baroque Spanish. Bibliography of primary and secondary sources. This script served for premier productions in March 1996 at Oklahoma City Univ. and at the International Siglo de Oro Theater Festival in El Paso. The annotated translation is clear but its modern registers lose the baroque flavor and wit of the original, in contrast to Peden's translation. See item **4586**. [MA]

Juana Inés de la Cruz, Sor. Poems, protest, and a dream: selected writings. See item **4586**.

4614 Leñero, Vicente. No one knows anything. Introduction and translations by Myra S. Gann. Potsdam, N.Y.: Danzón Press, 1995. 120 p. (Contemporary Mexican drama in translation; 2)

Vol. 2 of series *Contemporary Mexican drama in translation*. Excellent translation of a 1988 work by the well-known writer Leñero. Short introduction (reprinted from Vol. 1) locates trajectory of 1980s Mexican theater. Two-page introduction to play explains its style of "hyperrealism," production history, and original staging. No further notes or bibliography. [KR]

4615 Levinson, Luisa Mercedes. The two siblings and other stories. Translations by Sylvia Ehrlich Lipp. Prologue by Luisa Valenzuela. Pittsburgh, Pa.: Latin American Literary Review Press, 1996. 157 p.

Twenty-three stories by Argentine author from volumes published between 1967–81, selected by the translator. Short prologue by Luisa Valenzuela (Levinson's daughter); personal note by Lipp. Texts, showing influence of Borges, are cosmopolitan in character, often with fantastic or nightmarish twists, some with arresting plots. [KR]

4616 Marcos, subcomandante. The story of colors = La historia de los colores. Illustrated by Domitila Domínguez. Translated by Anne Bar Din. El Paso, Tex.: Cinco Puntos Press, 1999. 1 v. (unpaged): col. ill.

Beautiful bilingual retelling for children of a folktale from Chiapas that explains how colors were created, why people differ in color and ways of thinking, and why the macau sports all the colors. Excellent translation; stunning illustrations. A remarkable book. [CM]

4617 Monterroso, Augusto. Complete works & other stories. Translated by Edith Grossman. Introduction by Will H. Corral. Austin: Univ. of Texas Press, 1995. 152 p.: bibl. (Texas Pan American series)

Monterroso's *microcuentos* defy social and literary categories in this collection of brilliant satires that combine the first English-language versions of *Obras completas y otros cuentos* (1959) and *Movimiento perpetuo* (1972). Corral's "Before and After Augusto Monterroso" and Grossman's competent translations make this volume an excellent introduction to one of Latin America's greatest living writers. Highly recommended for classroom and general use. For literature specialist's comment, see item **3533**. [MA]

4618 Piglia, Ricardo. Assumed name. Translated by Sergio Gabriel Waisman. Pittsburgh, Pa.: Latin American Literary Review Press, 1995. 160 p. (Discoveries)

Complete translation of *Nombre falso*, for which Sergio Gabriel Waisman earned a Eugene M. Kayden Meritorious Achievement Award in 1995. Given the stature of Piglia's writing and its potential interest to English-language scholars and students of contemporary Argentine literature, one wishes for more extensive introductory and bibliographical material. For comment on original work, see *HLAS 40:6936*. [CM]

4619 Ramos, Luis Arturo. Los viejos asesinos. [Old assassins.] Translated by Tim Richards. México: Grupo Editorial Eón, 1996. 143 and 144 p. (E narrativa; 1)

Ten detective stories from the early collections *Los viejos asesinos* (see *HLAS 48:5205*) and *Del tiempo y otros lugares* (see *HLAS 44:5193*) by an author from Veracruz. The inventive translation won the Eugene M. Kayden National Translation Award in 1994. Includes original Spanish text. Without introduction. [MA]

4620 Rey Rosa, Rodrigo. The Pelcari Project = Cárcel de árboles. Translated by Paul Bowles. Tiburon, Calif.: Cadmus Editions, 1997. 117 p.

En face edition of a 1992 novella by the Guatemalan writer. Gripping, highly original, allegorical tale of a dehumanizing neuropsychological "project" carried out on prisoners in a jungle. Elegant work by Bowles, translator of several other works by the author. Short afterword by Bowles; biographical note. [KR]

4621 Santos Febres, Mayra. Urban oracles: stories. Translated by Nathan Budoff and Lydia Platon Lázaro. Cambridge, Mass.: Lumen Editions, 1997. 129 p.

Fifteen short stories and vignettes in Caribbean settings by a prize-winning Puerto Rican narrator. Competent translation of the idiomatic Spanish, but lacks a needed introduction. [MA]

4622 Stavans, Ilan. The one-handed pianist and other stories. Albuquerque: Univ. of New Mexico Press, 1996. 196 p.

Translations of eight stories and a novella from two books: *La pianista manca* (1991) and *Talia y el cielo* (1979; rev. 1989). Work treats identity, literary influence, writer's coming of age: themes Stavans details in an autobiographical epilogue. "Wonderful fables for the Aeonic Age reader" (Don Webb: *American Book Review*, June/July 1997, p. 17). Excellent translations by author and several others. [CM]

Novels

4623 Abad Faciolince, Héctor Joaquín. The joy of being awake. Translated by Nathan Budoff. Cambridge, Mass.: Lumen Editions, 1996. 202 p.

Excellent translation of Colombian Abad Faciolince's *Asuntos de un hidalgo disoluto* (see *HLAS 56:3663*). Novel's sometimes black humor reviews life of its elderly protagonist, as dictated to his secretary. Many references to cultural, political, and historical issues in Colombia and Europe. Short biography of author; no other locating material. [KR]

4624 Aguilar, Rosario. The lost chronicles of Terra Firma. Translated by Edward Waters Hood. Fredonia, N.Y.: White Pine Press, 1997. 186 p. (The secret weavers series; 10)

A Nicaraguan journalist weaves past and present into a historical novel about the Spanish conquest of Central America from perspective of six women of the period—three Spanish, two Amerindian, and one mestiza—involved in that violent conflict of cultures. Narrator intersperses her own life in the transition from the Sandinistas to the government of Violeta Chamorro with that of her women characters. Skillful feminocentric recreation and a seamless natural translation make a compelling read. First published as *La niña blanca y los pájaros sin pies* (1992). Afterword by Ann González provides context. [MA]

4625 Bencastro, Mario. A shot in the cathedral. Translated by Susan Giersbach Rascón. Houston, Tex.: Arte Público Press, 1996. 215 p.

Prizewinning novel *Disparo en la catedral* follows a San Salvador journalist through an eight-month period leading up to and following Archbishop Romero's assassination. Verbatim texts of Romero's homilies incorporated into text. Bencastro's work as a playwright evident in copious dialogue. Competently translated. No supporting materials, but good for classroom use given historical context. [KR]

4626 Buitrago, Fanny. Señora honeycomb: a novel. Translated by Margaret Sayers Peden. New York: HarperCollins, 1996. 232 p.

Buitrago enjoys an international reputation, but this is the first of her works to be translated into English. Translation is a highly inventive one in which Peden has created a playful, lush language appropriate to the erotic and culinary ambience of original work, *La señora de la miel* (1993). Teachers and students might wish for an introduction to the cultural traditions and society that are the target of Buitrago's irony. [CM]

4627 Bullrich, Silvina. Tomorrow I'll say, Enough. Translated by Julia Shirek Smith. Pittsburgh, Pa.: Latin American Literary Review Press, 1996. 189 p. (Discoveries)

First long work in English by the Argentine Bullrich, published as *Mañana digo basta* (1968). Diary format follows a woman's summer spent alone following her 49th birthday, with reflections on women's roles, art, love, and family. Somewhat dated discussion of lesbianism and sexuality. Competent translation. Short biography of author on back cover. Interesting for classroom use. [KR]

4628 Cerda, Martha. Señora Rodríguez and other worlds. Translated by Sylvia Jiménez-Andersen. Durham, N.C.: Duke Univ. Press, 1997. 133 p. (Latin America in translation/en traducción/em tradução)

Cerda's *Señora Rodríguez and other worlds* is a playful, parodic, and often sarcastic tale of a woman, her magical purse, and the other worlds that may or may not be closely linked to the protagonist. Novel or collection of short stories? Both English- and Spanish-language critics are uncertain. The translator gives no hints either. For comment on original work, see *HLAS 56:3477.* [CM]

4629 Eltit, Diamela. E. Luminata. Translated by Ronald Christ. Santa Fe, N.M.: Lumen, Inc. 1997. 234 p.

Superb translation of *Lumpérica* (1983). Text of novel is framed by author's foreword and translator's afterword, both of which reflect on the writing of literature under military dictatorship; the novel's metaphoric, poetic narration; and the translator's methods for dealing with the challenges inherent to this work. Important contribution to contemporary literature in translation and a tour-de-force by Christ. [KR]

4630 Eltit, Diamela. The fourth world. Translated and with foreword by Dick Gerdes. Lincoln: Univ. of Nebraska Press, 1995. 113 p. (Latin American women writers)

Gerdes' brief but informative introduction makes clear that he has been a sensitive reader of *El cuarto mundo.* The two narrators, although twins—one male, one female, tell different tales and use language very differently. Translation is competent, but Gerdes' own language lacks the dynamic energy of Eltit's, perhaps because he follows the Spanish structures so closely. For comment on original work, see *HLAS 52:3777.* [CM]

4631 Eltit, Diamela. Sacred cow. Translated by Amanda Hopkinson. London; New York: Serpent's Tail, 1995. 106 p.

Eltit's *Vaca sagrada* (see *HLAS 54:4047*), an intense narrative of erotic desire set against the backdrop of political repression in Chile, treats themes of sexual violence, power relationships, the domination of women, and female fantasy. Well translated by Hopkinson. However, this first translation of an Eltit novel includes no locating materials beyond a very short author's biography on the back flap. [KR]

4632 Esquivel, Laura. The law of love. Translated by Margaret Sayers Peden. New York: Crown Publishers, 1996. 266 p.: col. ill., sound disc (digital; 4 ¾ in.).

Fusion of science fiction and adventure-romance attempts to produce a multimedia "event" that narrates through comic-strip panels and period music on accompanying CD (see *HLAS 56:3484*). New Age tracts, precolumbian poetry, Puccini arias, and tedious plots never achieve narrative coherence in spite of Peden's adequate translation. [MA]

4633 Fuentes, Carlos. Diana, the goddess who hunts alone. Translated by Alfred J. Mac Adam. New York: Farrar, Straus and Giroux, 1995. 217 p.

Fuentes' novel (see *HLAS 56:3488*) recounts a 1970 love affair between a Mexican writer and a North American movie actress against the backdrop of FBI political repression and its brutal consequences. Reflections on sex, love, literature, Latin and North American culture, and Cold War politics. Excellent translation by Mac Adam. No supporting materials. [KR]

4634 Fuguet, Alberto. Bad vibes. Translated by Kristina Cordero. New York: St. Martin's Press, 1997. 308 p.

Translation of *Mala onda* (see *HLAS 54:4049*), Fuguet's first, controversial novel that follows 10 days in the life of an upper-class Chilean teenager at the time of the 1980 referendum on Pinochet's power. Excellent translation captures a youth culture of privilege, drugs, sex, and angst caught in the midst of brutal political forces. No locating materials in volume, although book jacket relates narrative to Chilean politics and history. [KR]

4635 Gallegos, Rómulo. Canaima. Translated by Will Kirkland. Pittsburgh, Pa.: Univ. of Pittsburgh Press, 1996. 348 p.: bibl.

(The Pittsburgh editions of Latin American literature)

This new English translation of *Canaima* should be welcomed by all readers of Gallegos. In addition to Kirkland's translation (based on Charles Minguet's 1991 critique of the novel in Spanish), work contains his engaging and provocative translator's essay; an informative introduction by Michael John Doudoroff; essays by five specialists and Venezuelan writers who provide varied perspectives on the novel; and a glossary of terms that readers will find invaluable. For comment on earlier translation, see *HLAS 50:4277*. [CM]

4636 Gerchunoff, Alberto. Jewish gauchos of the pampas. Translated by Prudencio de Pereda. Foreword by Ilan Stavans. Albuquerque: Univ. of New Mexico Press, 1998. 149 p. (Jewish Latin America)

Reprint, with minor changes, of the 1955 translation of Gerchunoff's 1910 classic volume about Jewish immigrants in rural Argentina. Twenty-six vignettes, with some inter-related characters, tell stories of customs, love, death, religion, prejudice, and assimilation. Skillful translation captures bilingual (Spanish-Yiddish) flavor of original. Stavans' essay provides useful historical and literary background. [KR]

4637 Güiraldes, Ricardo. Don Segundo Sombra. Translated by Patricia Owen Steiner. Critical ed. coordinated by Gwen Kirkpatrick. Pittsburgh, Pa.: Univ. of Pittsburgh Press, 1995. 302 p.: bibl. (Col. Archivos)

New translation of 1926 Argentine classic, accompanied by extensive critical materials. Seven essays by scholars including Gwen Kirkpatrick and Beatriz Sarlo treat historical, literary, and biographical topics. Steiner discusses novel's setting, writing, and reception, but does not reflect on translation process itself nor on differences between this work and 1935 version by Harriet De Onís (see *HLAS 1:2119*). Glossary and bibliography. Valuable teaching tool. [KR]

4638 Kozameh, Alicia. Steps under water: a novel. Translated by David E. Davis. Foreword by Saúl Sosnowski. Berkeley: Univ. of California Press, 1996. 149 p.

Translation of *Pasos bajo el agua*, with brief introductory notes (dated 1987 and 1996) by author and foreword by Sosnowski,

who describes the military dictatorship under which Kozameh lived and was imprisoned. A powerful, moving book in both languages; however, bilingual readers no doubt will miss Kozameh's drawings done during her imprisonment, and may regret the alterations to the original intended to make the book more attractive and accessible to readers in English. For comment on original work, see *HLAS 52:3838*. [CM]

4639 Levinson, Luisa Mercedes. In the shadow of the owl. Translated by Sylvia Ehrlich Lipp. Barcelona: Salvat, 1989. 211 p. (Letras de oro)

A la sombra del búho, novel by the Argentine Levinson, has three parts set respectively in 1800s, 1960s, and 1980s. Epic-type story, reminiscent of García Márquez and Isabel Allende, follows members of a family, especially its women, through various generations. Interesting historical detail in first part. Competent translation. No locating or prefatory materials whatsoever. [KR]

4640 Mastretta, Angeles. Lovesick. Translated by Margaret Sayers Peden. New York: Riverhead Books, 1997. 292 p.

Set against the backdrop of the Mexican Revolution, this romance knits the passion of a strong, independent woman into the history of a country, much in the manner of the 19th-century *costumbrista* tradition. Which of two men and their opposing paths will she choose? Peden's seamless translation of the richly detailed prose make for a page-turner. In its first publication under the title *Mal de amores* (1996), work was awarded the 1997 Rómulo Gallegos international prize for fiction. [MA]

4641 Mastretta, Angeles. Tear this heart out. Translated by Margaret Sayers Peden. New York: Riverhead Books, 1997. 293 p.

Excellent, highly colloquial translation of *Arráncame la vida* (see *HLAS 48:5193*), set in post-revolutionary Mexico. Peden has created a sparkling, irreverent Catalina, Mastretta's first-person protagonist who narrates her coming of age through a marriage to a retired general much older than herself. No background information. For historical introduction, see Ann Wright's translation of this novel, *Mexican bolero* (*HLAS 54:5031*). [CM]

4642 Matto de Turner, Clorinda. Birds without a nest: a novel; a story of Indian life and priestly oppression in Peru, Translation by J.G.H. (1904); emended by Naomi Lindstrom (1996). Austin: Univ. of Texas Press, 1996. 181 p.: bibl. (Texas Pan American series)

Much-needed new English-language version of *Aves sin nido* (1889). Work comprises Lindstrom's excellent introduction to the novel and her emendation of the first English translation (by J.G. Hudson, 1904). Lindstrom explains that she restored and translated author's preface and the other material excised or suppressed by the previous translator; returned chapters to their original order; and, in some instances, made the English more accurate or precise. Highly recommended. [CM]

4643 Montero, Mayra. In the palm of darkness: a novel. Translated by Edith Grossman. New York: HarperCollins Publishers, 1997. 181 p.: map.

Translation of *Tú, la oscuridad,* a work by a Cuban-born author now living in Puerto Rico. English-language readers may wish for some background information about Montero or the context of her novel. However, they will find helpful a map of Haiti (not included in Spanish original) that will enable them to follow the protagonist's search for an extinct red frog. For comment on original work, see *HLAS 56:3572*. [CM]

4644 Moyano, Daniel. The flight of the tiger. Translated and with an afterword by Norman Thomas di Giovanni. London: Serpent's Tail, 1995. 175 p.

El vuelo del tigre (1981?), an allegorical, satirical novel by the Argentine Moyano, recounts the militaristic takeover of an Andean village. Bizarre, often surreal plot; oppressors are percussionists, villagers resist through music. Useful translator's afterword sets work in political and historical context of Argentina's Dirty War. Skillful, knowledgeable translation. [KR]

4645 Onetti, Juan Carlos. Past caring? Translated by Peter R. Bush. London: Quartet Books, 1995. 194 p.

Bush's affecting translation of Onetti's last novel (*Cuando ya no me importe*) immediately draws one into the world of a narrator so desperate for a job that he'll take absolutely anything: "There is no crust of bread too stale for me." Information about Onetti and the role of the imaginary Santamaría in his work would have been helpful. For comment on original work, see *HLAS 54:4182*. [CM]

4646 Otero, Lisandro. The situation. Translated by Eileen Shea. La Habana: Editorial José Martí, 1994. 266 p.

Ruthless reconstruction of Havana's middle class from beginning of the Republic in 19th century to Batista period. The 1982 reprint (see *HLAS 48:5401*) received that year's Casa de las Américas Prize. Notes assist the reader with culture-specific terms. [MA]

4647 Paso, Fernando del. Palinuro of Mexico. Translated by Elisabeth Plaister. Normal, Ill.: Dalkey Archive Press, 1996. 557 p.

The gargantuan epic of medical student Palinuro's quest for the relationships between knowledge, myth, history, and art as he journeys through the real and imaginary realms of Mexico's cultural body. Original published in 1977 (see *HLAS 42:5203*) and winner of numerous international awards. Translation is inventive and "reads like hypertext" (*New York Times Book Review,* 11 Aug. 1996). Lacks the introduction needed to bring its huge dimensions of slapstick and satire within reader's grasp. [MA]

4648 Poniatowska, Elena. Tinisima. Translated by Katherine Silver. New York: Farrar, Straus, and Giroux, 1996. 357 p.: ill.

Long though it is, this English version of *Tinísima,* Poniatowska's novel based closely on the life of Italian photographer Tina Modotti (1896–1942), represents a considerable abridgment of the original. Implicitly, however, the textual recreation is the work of Poniatowska herself, who signs the acknowledgments, thanks Katherine Silver (whose translation is excellent), and writes a new dedication for the book. For comment on original work, see *HLAS 54:3727*. [CM]

4649 Ramos, Luis Arturo. Within these walls. Translated by Samuel A. Zimmerman. Pittsburgh, Pa.: Latin American Literary Review Press, 1997. 221 p. (Series Discoveries)

Translation of *Intramuros* (see *HLAS 48:5204*). Plot explores process of acclimation to a new country through the lives of two generations of Spanish immigrants to Veracruz. Serious tone and well translated by Zimmerman, work treats questions of memory and time. Very short, locating translator's note; no other locating material. [KR]

4650 Rebolledo, Francisco. Rasero: a novel. Translated by Helen R. Lane. Baton Rouge: Louisiana State Univ. Press, 1995. 552 p. (The Pegasus Prize for Literature)

Translation of *Rasero* (1993) received the Pegasus Prize for Literature. Set in 18th-century Europe, Rebolledo's ambitious first novel tells of a young Spaniard in search of wisdom who travels to Paris and experiences the Enlightenment, with all its contradictions. [CM]

4651 Restrepo, Laura. The angel of Galilea. Translated by Dolores M. Koch. New York: Crown Publishers, 1997. 193 p.

Originally titled *Dulce compañía* (1995), novel set in Bogotá tells the first-person story of a woman journalist's involvement with the people of a poor barrio and the man they call an angel. Ironic, often humorous details of daily life in Colombia combine with passionate descriptions of madness, religion, and love. Excellent translation by Koch. Short author's biography; no other locating material. [KR]

4652 Reyes, Luis Eduardo. Modelo antiguo: a novel of Mexico City. Translated by Sharon Franco and Joe Hayes. El Paso, Tex.: Cinco Pintos Press, 1997. 184 p.

Engaging, idiomatic translation of *Modelo antiguo* (1992) is first translation into English of work by Mexican playwright, script writer, and novelist Reyes. In this novel, his first-person narrator, a taxi driver, is hired by a fatally ill old woman who wants to be driven around Mexico City so she can die in her car. No ancillary information. [CM]

4653 Robles, Mireya. Hagiography of Narcisa the beautiful. Translated by Anna Diegel. Columbia, La.: Readers International, 1996. 188 p.

Satirical, darkly comic novel set in 1950s Cuba (see *HLAS 48:5405*) depicts a nuclear family through the eyes of Narcisa, the unwanted ugly duckling. Explores inequality inherent in gender roles and oppression of women in Cuban society. Story narrated without paragraph or chapter breaks for entire length; fast-paced translation. Glossary of Cuban terms; author's biographical note. Excellent text for women's studies classes. [KR]

4654 Rodríguez Juliá, Edgardo. The renunciation: a novel. Translated by Andrew Hurley. New York: Four Walls Eight Windows; Paris: UNESCO Pub., 1997. 135 p.

Andrew Hurley's fine translation makes available this acclaimed Puerto Rican novelist's *La renuncia del héroe Baltasar* (1974), the fictive chronicles of an arranged marriage plotted to save Puerto Rico from certain slave rebellion. Interspersed lectures, letters, and documents reconstruct conflicts of class and race set in Island's colonial past. Occasional footnotes, but an introduction would have added insights for the nonspecialized reader. [MA]

4655 Sención, Viriato. They forged the signature of God. Translated by Asa Zatz. Willimantic, Conn.: Curbstone Press, 1995. 250 p.: map.

Los que falsificaron la firma de Dios (1992), a chilling picture of internal politics in the Dominican Republic, became that country's best-selling ever work of fiction. Tracing the lives of three seminarians persecuted by Church and state, allegory and gallows humor portray political power gone awry. A lively translation, but no introduction. [MA]

4656 Sepúlveda, Luis. The name of a bullfighter. Translated by Suzanne Ruta. New York: Harcourt Brace, 1996. 211 p.

Readers may be unfamiliar with Ariel Dorfman and Paco Ignacio Taibo III (with whom Sepúlveda is compared in the brief blurb on the book's cover), but no doubt they easily will become engrossed in the world of *The name of the bullfighter*, thanks to Suzanne Ruta's ability to translate a novel's genre as well as its words. For comment on original work, see *HLAS 56:3796*. [CM]

4657 Shua, Ana María. Patient. Translated by David William Foster. Pittsburgh, Pa.: Latin American Literary Review Press, 1997. 122 p. (Discoveries)

Appropriately colloquial, idiomatic

translation of prolific Argentine writer's novel *Soy paciente*. A humerous satire on the state's health care system, novel may remind readers of Ken Kesey's *One flew over the cuckoo's nest*. No accompanying materials, which is unfortunate since Shua's work is not yet well known in English. For comment on original work, see *HLAS 44:5543*. [CM]

4658 Skármeta, Antonio. Love-fifteen. Translated by Jonathan Tittler. Pittsburgh, Pa.: Latin American Literary Review Press, 1996. 126 p. (Series Discoveries)

Translation of Chilean author's *Match ball* (see *HLAS 54:4061*), a *Lolita*-esque story of a middle-aged man's obsession with a teenage tennis star. Told in first person, novel's black humor is set among the European upper classes, with cosmopolitan, especially German and Spanish, cultural references. Competent translation by Tittler. Back-cover notes; no other locating material. [KR]

4659 Taibo, Paco Ignacio. Leonardo's bicycle. Translated by Martin Michael Roberts. New York: Mysterious Press, 1995. 453 p.

Another entertaining, fast-paced detective story (1996), featuring protagonist José Daniel Fierro. Novel set alternately in today's Mexico City and Ciudad Juárez, Renaissance Italy, and modern Barcelona follows a suspenseful plot combined with political and social commentary. Excellent colloquial translation; no notes. Author's endnote sheds light on some characters and references. [KR]

4660 Taibo, Paco Ignacio. Return to the same city. Translated by Laura Dail. New York: Mysterious Press, 1996. 178 p.

Regreso a la misma ciudad y bajo la lluvia (1989) is another Héctor Belascoarán Shayne caper in the hilarious series of venality and violence as told by Mexico's favorite one-eyed detective in this wild, *noir* vision of Mexican reality. Dail's translation transmits the inventive dead-pan humor. No supplementary material beyond the jacket. [MA]

4661 Ubidia, Abdón. Wolves' dream. Translated by Mary Ellen Fieweger. Pittsburgh, Pa.: Latin American Literary Review Press, 1996. 268 p.

Sueño de lobos (1986) won the 1986 José Mejía award for the best work of fiction in Ecuador. Set in Quito in early 1980s at the end of the oil boom, four petty cons and an insomniac accountant join forces to plot a bank heist that becomes a nightmare. Adequate translation, but no introduction. [MA]

4662 Valdés, Zoé. Yocandra in the paradise of nada: a novel of Cuba. Translated by Sabina Cienfuegos. New York: Arcade Pub.; Boston: Little, Brown, 1997. 157 p.: bibl.

Yocandra, the first-person narrator, was born (like Valdés herself) in Havana in 1959. Now a dispirited, outspoken woman living in Cuba, narrator writes of a reality of "nothing" that contrasts poignantly with that of a *gusana* friend in Madrid with whom she exchanges letters. This colloquial, idiomatic translation of *La nada cotidiana* reflects work's humor and word play. Brief but helpful translator's notes. For comment on original work, see *HLAS 56:3589*. [CM]

4663 Vargas Llosa, Mario. Death in the Andes. Translated by Edith Grossman. New York: Farrar, Straus and Giroux, 1996. 275 p.

In this novel (see *HLAS 56:3743*), simultaneous plot lines ranging from an investigation by Corporal Lituma of a mysterious disappearance, to his deputy's love affair with a prostitute, to an Andean community terrorized by Shining Path guerrillas, and the alternating first- and third-person narrators all obscure coherence. Grossman's lazy translation needlessly retains large doses of original Spanish lexicon. An introduction, maps, and a translator's note are badly needed to orient readers not familiar with Peru. [MA]

Essays, Interviews, and Reportage

4664 Agosín, Marjorie. Ashes of revolt: essays. Fredonia, N.Y.: White Pine Press, 1996. 182 p.: bibl. (Human rights series; 4)

Includes 22 short essays, most related to culture and politics in Chile before, during, and after the Pinochet dictatorship; more than half previously published in English between 1990–95. Many treat questions of women's oppression and resistance to power. Several pieces are autobiographical in nature. Includes endnotes to many essays and translators' biographies. Translations all of high quality. [KR]

4665 Agosín, Marjorie. Tapestries of hope, threads of love: the arpillera movement in Chile, 1974–1994. Translated by

Celeste Kostopulos-Cooperman. Photographs by Emma Sepulveda and Ted Polumbaum. Albuquerque: Univ. of New Mexico Press, 1996. 142 p.: bibl., ill. (some col.).

Moving, beautifully produced volume records work of the Chilean *arpilleristas* during and after Pinochet. Long essay by Agosín focuses on Chilean history, the movement that spawned these tapestries, and her personal involvement with it over two decades. Excellent translation. Includes 45 full-color plates with explanatory captions, followed by testimonies of the tapestry makers themselves. For political scientist's comment, see *HLAS 57:3605.* [KR]

4666 Alegría, Claribel and **Darwin J. Flakoll.** Death of Somoza. Translated by Darwin J. Flakoll. Willimantic, Conn.: Curbstone Press, 1996. 161 p.

Gripping story of planning and execution of Somoza's 1980 assassination, as told to Alegría and Flakoll in 1983 by the Argentine guerrillas who carried it out. Well-translated inverviews woven into narration lend aspect of a thriller in suspense and drama. Much historical and political background on both Nicaragua and Argentina. Excellent for classroom use. For historian's comment on Spanish-language original, see *HLAS 56:1690.* [KR]

4667 Alegría, Claribel and **Darwin J. Flakoll.** Tunnel to Canto Grande. Translated by Darwin J. Flakoll. Willimantic, Conn.: Curbstone Press, 1996. 193 p.

Translation of *Fuga de Canto Grande* (see *HLAS 55:3359*). Records 1990 interviews conducted by authors with members of the Peruvian Movimiento Revolucionario Túpac Amaru who had escaped from prison only weeks earlier. Skillful narration provides excellent historical background. Flakoll's translation is good, although at times a bit stiff. Dynamism of story makes for compelling reading. [KR]

4668 Barnet, Miguel. Biography of a runaway slave. Translated by W. Nick Hill. Rev. ed. Willimantic, Conn.: Curbstone Press, 1994. 217 p.: bibl.

Valuable new version of *Biografía de un cimarrón* includes Hill's expert translation; brief but informative preface about Esteban Montejo (the book's first-person narrator); Barnet's afterword (which replaces, albeit partially, his original introduction), in which he explains his understanding of *literatura testimonal;* and a glossary of terms. Original work was first translated as *Autobiography of a runaway slave* by Jocasta Innes (1968). For annotation of original work, see *HLAS 32:1944.* [CM]

4669 Bello, Andrés. Selected writings of Andrés Bello. Translated by Frances M. López-Morillas. Edited by Ivan Jaksic. Oxford, England; New York: Oxford Univ. Press, 1997. 295 p.

Contains translations of a broad selection of poetry, essays, and speeches illustrating richness and complexity of Bello's thought as a key intellectual figure in the construction of a new political order in postindependence Latin America. Extracted from *Obras completas* (see *HLAS 48:5125*), most selections are unabridged. Eloquent yet accessible translations. Jaksiác's essay analyzes Bello's blueprint for nation-building, language, education, history, and law, and includes notes and chronology. Highly recommended for the classroom and the general reader. [MA]

4670 Betanzos, Juan de. Narrative of the Incas. Translated and edited by Roland Hamilton and Dana Buchanan from the Palma de Mallorca manuscript. Austin: Univ. of Texas Press, 1996. 344 p.: bibl., ill., index, maps.

Work is first complete English translation of original manuscript of this key document about early Andean societies. *Suma y narración de los yngas* was written in the 1550s by a Spanish interpreter of Quechua who drew on oral traditions of Inca history including eyewitness testimony of the war between Huascar and Atahualpa and events of the conquest. The richness of the colloquial narrative of informants from Atahualpa's family, probably dictated from the Quechua, begs for a more extensive introductory essay. Informative translators' note discusses their use of both the original manuscript at the March Foundation Library in Palma de Mallorca and the Escorial partial manuscript. Recommended for classroom and general use. For ethnohistorian's comment, see item **624.** [MA]

4671 Fuentes, Carlos. A new time for Mexico. Translated by Marina Gutman Castañeda and the author. New York: Farrar, Straus and Giroux, 1996. 216 p.

Series of 12 essays on Mexican culture, history, and politics, originally published as *Nuevo tiempo mexicano* (1994). Time and memory are recurring motifs connecting essays. Some autobiographical chapters. Several centered on Mexico's 1994 political crossroads are somewhat dated given the outcome of the 2000 elections. Fluent translation; no supporting or introductory materials. [KR]

4672 González, Luisa. At the bottom: a woman's life in Central America. Translated by Regina Pustan. Berkeley, Calif.: New Earth Publications, 1994. 121 p.

Translation of *A ras del suelo* (1977), Gonzalez's best-selling autobiography. Born in 1904, she became a schoolteacher; later a writer and editor, and a well-known member of the Partido Comunista de Costa Rica. Account follows her life to 1932, ending with militancy in the Party. Direct, unsentimental portrayal of working-class poverty; clear translation. Many useful explanatory notes by Pustan; short locating introduction. [KR]

4673 Literary and cultural journeys: selected letters to Antonio Torres-Rioseco. Edited by Carlota Caulfield and Miguel Ángel Zapata. Translated by Rosalie Torres-Rioseco and Rose Passalacqua. Oakland, Calif.: Mills College Center for the Book, 1995. 231 p.: ill.

Letters written to (but not by) the distinguished Chilean literary scholar between 1921–67 by 25 well-known Latin American and Spanish cultural figures such as G. Mistral, A. Reyes, and M. Azuela. *En face* bilingual presentation, competently translated with useful explanatory notes. Introduction, chronology, illustrations. Interesting history of international literary connections. [KR]

4674 Mansilla, Lucio Victorio. An expedition to the Ranquel Indians. Translated by Mark McCaffrey. Austin: Univ. of Texas Press, 1997. 418 p.: bibl., index, maps. (Texas Pan American series)

Translation of 1870 *Una excursión a los indios ranqueles,* letters recounting Mansilla's visit with the Ranquel nation of Argentina. Translator made some cuts to the text for fluency, but their location is not indicated to the reader. Short introduction, notes, map, and glossary give historical and cultural background. Narrative flow emphasized through organization into five parts,

each with short preface. Highly accomplished literary prose. See also item **4675.** [KR]

4675 Mansilla, Lucio Victorio. A visit to the Ranquel Indians. Translated by Eva Gillies. Lincoln: Univ. of Nebraska Press, 1997. 453 p.: bibl., ill., maps.

Another translation of *Una excursión a los indios ranqueles* (see item **4674**). Extensive, well-informed introduction for historical background; detailed notes, maps, illustrations from archival photographs. Translation of complete text, including chapter titles. Translation literal in nature but still highly readable; somewhat less fluent and literary than that of McCaffrey. Excellent for classroom use. [KR]

4676 Manzano, Juan Francisco. The autobiography of a slave. Introduction and modernized Spanish version by Ivan A. Schulman. Translated by Evelyn Picon Garfield. Bilingual ed. Detroit, Mich.: Wayne State Univ. Press, 1996. 135 p.: bibl., ill. (Latin American literature and culture series)

En face bilingual edition of only extant Latin American slave narrative written during slavery era (see *HLAS 40:6692*). Original Spanish punctuation, spelling, and syntax corrected and modernized by Schulman; translation is of this new version of text. Introduction, notes, chronology give extensive background. Excellent for undergraduate classroom use. Scholars may prefer original text. [KR]

4677 Martí, José. Thoughts: on liberty, social justice, government, art, and morality. Selection, translation, and introduction by Carlos Ripoll. 3rd. ed. rev. Miami?: Endowment for Cuban American Studies, Cuban-American National Foundation; New York: Editorial Dos Ríos, 1995. 48 p.

Previously published in 1980 and 1985, volume consists of 215 short (one paragraph or less) "thoughts," grouped by subject. Short introduction by Ripoll gives biographical information on Martí and states the political, anti-Castro aim of the anthology. English translations are fluent. [KR]

4678 Mellibovsky, Matilde. Circle of love over death: testimonies of the mothers of the Plaza de Mayo. Translated by Maria and Matthew Proser. Willimantic, Conn.: Curbstone Press, 1997. 249 p.

Translation of moving volume (1990)

narrating history of the Argentine mothers' resistance movement, as told by member Mellibovsky. Mothers' testimonies of their children's lives and disappearances are interwoven with group's story. Covers period from Dirty War to early Menem presidency. Translations colloquial and effective. Some notes; useful explanatory list of Argentine names and terms. [KR]

4679 Ospina, William. Too late for man: essays. Translated by Nathan Budoff. Cambridge, Mass.: Brookline Books, 1995. 105 p. (New voices from Latin America)

Translations of six essays (1994) by Colombian poet and essayist. Texts make philosophical and literary references while examining the meaning of human existence in a technological, materialistic world at century's end. Perspective broad, sometimes concentrating on Latin American issues. Excellent translation. Brief author's biography; very short translator's introduction. [KR]

4680 Rama, Angel. The lettered city. Edited and translated by John Charles Chasteen. Durham, N.C.: Duke Univ. Press, 1996. 141 p.: bibl., ill., index. (Post-contemporary interventions)

Extremely influential cultural analysis by Uruguayan author published posthumously in 1984 (see *HLAS 50:3069*). Chasteen's very good English translation includes entire text with original notes, along with useful locating introduction and index. Important contribution to the literature and an excellent volume for classroom use. [KR]

4681 Ramírez, Sergio. Hatful of tigers: reflections on art, culture, and politics. Translated by Darwin J. Flakoll. Willimantic, Conn.: Curbstone Press, 1995. 135 p.

Vignettes by the Nicaraguan author and political leader, divided into "Before" and "After" the 1979 Sandinista Revolution. Originally published as *Estás en Nicaragua* (1985), with title taken from Cortázar poem; Cortázar's work and trips to Nicaragua are organizing motifs. Well translated, but no notes to explain names and places to the uninitiated reader; no other locating material. [KR]

4682 Sarduy, Severo. Christ on the Rue Jacob. Translated by Suzanne Jill Levine and Carol Maier. San Francisco: Mercury House, 1995. 166 p.

Sarduy's "inventory of marks," both physical and mnemonic, is a collection of 26 essays that, in Sarduy's words, "outline a possible autobiography." Afterword by collaborative translators Suzanne Jill Levine and Carol Maier. For comment on original work, see *HLAS 54:3842*. [CM]

4683 Vargas Llosa, Mario. Making waves. Edited and translated by John King. New York: Farrar, Straus and Giroux, 1997. 338 p.: bibl., index.

Translations of 46 short articles comprising a collection of Vargas Llosa's writings from early 1960s-93, chosen for their diversity of topics. Presented in chronological order with some grouped thematically; political and literary development stressed. Locating foreword, index. Excellent translations. Compelling selection, with most recent pieces from *Desafíos a la libertad* (see *HLAS 56:3742*). [KR]

4684 Verbitsky, Horacio. The flight: confessions of an Argentine dirty warrior. Translated by Esther Allen. New York: New Press; W.W. Norton, 1996. 207 p.: bibl.

Best-selling account of retired naval officer Francisco Scilingo regarding torture and murder of political prisoners during the Argentine military dictatorship. Excellent and gripping translation includes a new epilogue; afterword places these human rights violations in a worldwide context. Useful identifying list of historical figures and persons mentioned in the text. For historian's review of the Spanish-language version, see item **3069**. [KR]

TRANSLATIONS FROM THE PORTUGUESE
Poetry

4685 Nothing the sun could not explain: 20 contemporary Brazilian poets. Edited by Michael Palmer, Regis Bonvicino, and Nelson Ascher. Foreword by João Almino. Los Angeles: Sun & Moon Press, 1997. 305 p.

Valuable bilingual anthology of the "post-concrete" generation of Brazilian poets, as João Almino calls them, translated with varying degrees of success by Regina Alfarano, Martha Black Jordan, John Milton, Michael Palmer, Charles Perrone, and Dana Stevens. [DP]

4686 **Outras praias: 13 poetas brasileiros emergentes = Other shores: 13 emerging Brazilian poets. Coordenação de Ricardo Corona.** São Paulo: Iluminuras, 1998. 293 p.: bibl.

Bilingual anthology introduces 13 poets born between 1945–66. Unfortunately, the state of Paraná is over-represented with seven poets, and only four other states are represented at all, thus ignoring much of the richness and variety of Brazilian poetry today. [DP]

Salgado, Sebastião. Terra: struggle of the landless. See item **4714.**

Brief Fiction and Theater

4687 **Carneiro, João Emanuel** and **Marcos Bernstein.** Central Station. Translated by John Gledson. Introduction by Walter Salles. London: Bloomsbury, 1999. 115 p.

Translation of screenplay for Walter Salles' prize-winning film (*Central do Brasil*) about a woman who works in Rio's largest train station writing letters for illiterate people. Through her work she meets a young boy whose mother dies tragically. The woman and the boy then set out together on a journey to Brazil's Northeast in search of the child's father. A good translation that occasionally lacks the vivacity of real speech. [DP]

4688 **Noll, João Gilberto.** Hotel Atlântico. Translated by David Treece. London: Boulevard Books, 1997. 151 p.

Translations of two novellas, *Hotel Atlântico* (see *HLAS 54:4743*) and *Harmada* (see *HLAS 56:4332*), introduce Noll to English-language readers. Both works are surreal, first-person narratives of sex, decay, and death. The translations, although at times stilted, are generally effective in conveying Noll's evocative tone and style, which varies from staccato to obsessively long and repetitious sentences. [DP]

The Oxford book of Latin American short stories. See item **4561.**

4689 **Rawet, Samuel.** The prophet and other stories. Translated and with introduction by Nelson H. Vieira. Albuquerque: Univ. of New Mexico Press, 1998. 111 p.: bibl. (Jewish Latin America)

Called the "pioneer of Brazilian-Jewish

writing" starting with a 1957 volume, Rawet (1929–84) until now has had only two of his short stories translated into English. Vieira has chosen 12 stories from four collections and excellently conveys Rawet's dense, hermetic, and often elliptical style. A long overdue volume. [DP]

4690 ***Review: Latin American literature and arts.*** No. 53, 1996. New writing and arts from Brazil. New York: Americas Society, Inc.

Contains an enticing selection of poetry, prose, and art from contemporary Brazil, with an introductory essay on "Brazilian Literature in the 1990s" by Wilson Martins. While it is laudable that the *Review* would devote an entire issue to Brazil—which, as editor Alfred Mac Adam notes, is often "given short shrift," the translators' names have been omitted throughout the issue, a practice not in evidence in other issues of this journal. [DP]

4691 **Scliar, Moacyr.** The collected stories of Moacyr Scliar. Translated by Eloah F. Giacomelli. Introduction by Ilan Stavans. Albuquerque: Univ. of New Mexico Press, 1999. 475 p. (Jewish Latin America; 7)

Superb volume consists of Scliar's six collections of stories published between 1968–89, three of which have never before been rendered into English. Excellently translated, work conveys in fluent, evocative prose Scliar's enormous success in this difficult form. Stories range from biblical parables, through magical realism, to fantastic and humorous accounts. Concludes with a short autobiographical essay. [DP]

4692 **Urban voices: contemporary short stories from Brazil.** Edited, and with introduction and notes, by Cristina Ferreira Pinto. Lanham, Md.: Univ. Press of America, 1999. 250 p.

Excellent collection of long and very short stories by 17 contemporary Brazilian writers, rendered into English by 13 translators including Clifford E. Landers and Adria Frizzi. Though quality of translations varies, volume as a whole is first-rate. [DP]

Novels

4693 **Almeida, Manuel Antônio de.** Memoirs of a militia sergeant: a novel. Translated from the Portuguese by Ronald W.

Sousa. Foreword by Thomas H. Holloway. Afterword by Flora Süssekind. New York: Oxford Univ. Press, 1999. 184 p.: bibl. (Library of Latin America)

Excellent translation of a Brazilian classic first published as a serial in 1852–53. Sousa captures the vivacity and wit of the original while effectively evoking mood and historical milieu of free lower classes of Rio de Janeiro in early-19th century. Outstanding accompanying essays. [DP]

4694 Buarque de Hollanda, Chico. Benjamin. Translated by Clifford E. Landers. London: Bloomsbury, 1997. 150 p.

Buarque's second novel is the disturbing tale of an exmodel who, in the seconds before dying, relives his life as if it were a film. A tale of obsession and urban chaos, expertly and lovingly translated, with great attention to the dense descriptive passages of the original. For comment on Portuguese-language original, see item **4332**. [DP]

4695 Coelho, Paulo. By the River Piedra I sat down and wept. Translated by Alan R. Clarke. San Francisco: HarperSanFrancisco, 1996. 210 p.

The story of a young Spanish woman, Pilar, and her encounter with her lost love, an unnamed spiritual seeker who comes to worship the feminine face of God. Clarke's translation is, as usual, somewhat hurried and condensed as if he's impatient with Coelho's admittedly belabored and self-consciously poetical style. [DP]

4696 Coelho, Paulo. The fifth mountain. Translated by Clifford E. Landers. New York: HarperFlamingo, 1998. 245 p.

In this retelling and extensive extrapolation of the story of the Hebrew prophet Elijah, Coelho situates his New Age prose in an appropriate biblical setting. An excellent and faithful translation willing to follow the rhythms and belabored biblical style of the original. [DP]

4697 Coelho, Paulo. Veronika decides to die. Translated by Margaret Jull Costa. New York: HarperCollins Publishers, 1999. 210 p.

Another of Coelho's spiritual journeys, this time by the 24-year-old protagonist who, after a failed suicide attempt, rediscovers in an insane asylum in Slovenia the preciousness and precariousness of life. Costa's trans-

lation is competent, but cannot save Coelho's novel from its by now familiar and conventionally inspirational tone and message. [DP]

4698 Fonseca, Rubem. Vast emotions & imperfect thoughts. Translated by Clifford E. Landers. Hopewell, N.J.: Ecco Press, 1998. 312 p.

A complex narrative, at once comic and serious, told by a movie director protagonist who accidentally gets involved in a murder and becomes obsessed with Isaac Babel's fiction. Another outstanding translation by Landers, retaining structure and tone of the original while eliminating some redundancies. For comment on original work, see *HLAS 54:4734.* [DP]

4699 Machado de Assis. Dom Casmurro. Translated by John Gledson. Preface by John Gledson. Afterword by João Adolfo Hansen. New York: Oxford Univ. Press, 1997. 258 p.: bibl. (Library of Latin America)

At last, a new translation of Machado's masterpiece that is complete (unlike Scott-Buccleuch's 1992 version—see *HLAS 54:5078*—which omitted key chapters) and highly readable. Gledson produces a much-needed, graceful and accurate translation, attentive to Machado's tone and rhythms. Hansen's Afterword is excellent. [DP]

4700 Machado de Assis. Epitaph of a small winner. Translated by William L. Grossman. Introduction by Louis de Bernières. London: Bloomsbury, 1997. 209 p.

Reprint of Grossman's 1952 translation (see *HLAS 18:2767*) of *Memórias póstumas de Brás Cubas*. De Bernières' useful though brief introduction to this edition somewhat compensates for Grossman's very outdated translator's introduction. [DP]

4701 Machado de Assis. Philosopher or dog? Translated by Clotilde Wilson. Introduction by Louis de Bernières. London: Bloomsbury, 1997. 271 p.

Reprint of Wilson's 1954 translation (*HLAS 19:5304*) of *Quincas Borba (HLAS 5:4076*). De Bernières' introduction is virtually identical to that in item **4700**. [DP]

4702 Machado de Assis. The posthumous memoirs of Brás Cubas. Translated by Gregory Rabassa. Foreword by Enylton de Sá

Rego. Afterword by Gilberto Pinheiro Passos. New York: Oxford Univ. Press, 1997. 219 p. (Library of Latin America)

New translation of Machado's famous novel is for the most part faithful and readable. However, work has occasional odd errors and omissions, and fails to give sufficient attention to Machado's rhythm and syntax. Given Rabassa's vast experience as a translator, it is hard not to suspect that carelessness and haste explain the mistakes and lapses. Also poorly edited and inadequately proofread. [DP]

4703 Machado de Assis. Quincas Borba. Translated by Gregory Rabassa. Introduction by David T. Haberly. Afterword by Celso Favaretto. New York: Oxford Univ. Press, 1998. 290 p.: bibl. (Library of Latin America)

Updated translation of another Machado classic, with excellent accompanying essays, is a welcome addition to his work available in English. Rabassa provides a more informal, less strained tone than Wilson's 1954 version (see *HLAS 19:5304*). [DP]

4704 Melo, Patrícia. In praise of lies. Translated by Clifford E. Landers. London: Bloomsbury, 1999. 187 p.

Thoroughly enjoyable satire of the craft of writing fiction, the publishing industry, and the narrator's transformation from mediocre plagiarist to successful author of self-help books, set against a background of murder and poisonous snakes. Landers' inventive yet faithful translation catches the wit and humor of the original *Elogio da mentira* (1998). [DP]

4705 Melo, Patrícia. The killer. Translated by Clifford E. Landers. Hopewell, N.J.: Ecco Press, 1997. 217 p.

Melo's prize-winning novel (*Matador*) is a thriller about a man who accidentally becomes a hired killer and a local hero. Once again Landers achieves an excellent result: colloquial, entirely readable, and authentic, with just the right tone for its narrator whose language one reviewer has called "racy hoodlum-speak." [DP]

4706 Soares, Jô. A samba for Sherlock. Translated by Clifford E. Landers. New York: Pantheon, 1997. 271 p.: bibl., map.

Translation of the well-known comedian and comic writer's first novel, *Xangô de*

Baker Street (1995). A playful tale full of intriguing historical details about Rio in 1886 when Sarah Bernhardt visited for the first time, includes all sorts of actual historical figures, political and literary, along with Sherlock Holmes and Dr. Watson, and awards Brazil credit for originating the notion of "serial killer." Translation is fluent and fun to read, with occasional excessive literalisms and at times awkward explanations for readers unfamiliar with Brazil. [DP]

4707 Steen, Edla van. Early mourning. Translated by David Sanderson George. Pittsburgh, Pa.: Latin American Literary Review Press, 1996. 142 p. (Discoveries)

Prize-winning novel written as a multilayered series of 21 brief chapters depicting São Paulo life from dusk to dawn one September. Beautifully translated and brilliantly titled, with great fidelity to terse and compelling tone of original, *Madrugada* (1992). [DP]

Essays, Interviews, and Reportage

4708 Coelho, Paulo. The valkyries: an encounter with angels. Translated by Alan R. Clarke. San Francisco: HarperSanFrancisco, 1995. 245 p.

In this autobiographical tale, we follow Coelho and his wife Chris on a 40-day spiritual journey through the Mojave Desert in search of the eternal feminine. Translation has an uncertain feel and suffers from too much editing, pruning, and rearranging of the original as well as occasional misreading. [DP]

4709 Jesus, Carolina Maria de. Bitita's diary: the childhood memoirs of Carolina Maria de Jesus. Edited by Robert M. Levine. Translated by Emanuelle Oliveira and Beth Joan Vinkler. Armonk, N.Y.: M.E. Sharpe, 1998. 163 p.: bibl., ill. (Latin American realities)

Carolina (1915–77), whose childhood nickname was Bitita, evokes the hardships of her early life in 1920s-30s rural Minas Gerais. Volume was written in 1970s and posthumously published, first in French in 1982 and finally in Portuguese in 1986. This very careful translation aims to retain inconsistencies and nonstandard grammar of the original. Valuable introduction and afterword by Levine. [DP]

4710 Jesus, Carolina Maria de. I'm going to have a little house: the second diary of Carolina Maria de Jesus. Translated by Melvin S. Arrington Jr. and Robert M. Levine. Afterword by Robert M. Levine. Lincoln: Univ. of Nebraska Press, 1997. 181 p. (Engendering Latin America; 4)

Never before published in English, Carolina's second diary, written in 1960–61, describes her life in the first year after the sudden (and, as it turned out, temporary) fame of *Quarto de despejo* (see *HLAS* 25:4741). Translated faithfully into English, evokes the often awkward style adopted by Carolina. Excellent afterword and notes. [DP]

4711 Jesus, Carolina Maria de. The unedited diaries of Carolina Maria de Jesus. Edited by Robert M. Levine and José Carlos Sebe Bom Meihy. Translated by Nancy P.S. Naro and Cristina Mehrten. New Brunswick, N.J.: Rutgers Univ. Press, 1999. 233 p.: bibl., ill., index.

Important volume attempts to lay to rest doubts about authorship of Carolina's best-selling *Quarto de despejo* (see *HLAS* 25:4741), translated as *Child of the dark* (see *HLAS* 25:4740). Diary entries cover years 1958–66. Translations aim to reproduce tone and register of the original, without embellishment or correction, and are followed by a fascinating discussion of Carolina's significance. [DP]

4712 Levine, Robert M. and **José Carlos Sebe Bom Meihy.** The life and death of Carolina Maria de Jesus. Albuquerque: Univ. of New Mexico Press, 1995. 162 p.: bibl., ill., index, map. (Diálogos)

Important companion to items **4709, 4710,** and **4711.** Two historians retrace Carolina's life, especially in the years following the short-lived success of *Quarto de despejo* (*Child of the dark*), and reflect on what her life story reveals about race in Brazil. Includes extensive interviews with Carolina's children. [DP]

4713 Lispector, Clarice. Selected cronicas. Translated by Giovanni Pontiero. New York: New Directions Pub. Corp., 1996. 212 p. (A New Directions paperbook; 834)

Translations of chronicles first published between 1967–73 in Lispector's weekly column for *Jornal do Brasil* and representing about two-thirds of the volume *A*

descoberta do mundo (*HLAS 48:6221*). That work was translated by Pontiero under title *Discovering the world* (*HLAS 54:5084*). [DP]

4714 Salgado, Sebastião. Terra: struggle of the landless. Preface by José Saramago. Poetry by Chico Buarque de Hollanda. Translated by Clifford E. Landers. London: Phaidon, 1997. 143 p.: photos.

Salgado's stunning photographs of Brazil's landless rural population (estimated at nearly five million) includes an impassioned and biting preface by Saramago, three poems by Chico Buarque, and extensive captions. Ably translated. A beautiful and disturbing book. [DP]

BIBLIOGRAPHY, THEORY, AND PRACTICE

4715 Bueno, Salvador. Antecedentes de la traducción literaria en Cuba. (*Cuad. Hispanoam.*, 576, junio 1998, p. 41–47)

Brief but informative overview of translators from José María Heredia to Nicolás Guillén, and of their principal contributions. Bueno begins with Enrique José Varona's remarks about Cuban efforts to rectify Spain's historical neglect of translation, and his article provides an excellent point of departure for future study. [CM]

4716 Carrión, M. María. Geographies, (m)other tongues and the role of translation in Giannina Braschi's *El imperio de los sueños.* (*Tulsa Stud. Women's Lit.*, 20:1, 1990, p. 167–191)

Excellent essay examines Braschi's parodic, performative Spanish and her effort to problematize and explore the imperial domination of a single, universal, and uniform Spanish (Castilian). Studying Braschi's effort from the perspective of translation, Carrión traces and elucidates the Puerto Rican writer's esthetics and her contribution. For comment on English translation of Braschi's original work, see *HLAS 56:4574.* [CM]

4717 Congreso Internacional de Traducción e Interpretación de Soria, 1st, Soria, Spain, 1993. La traducción de lo inefable: actas. Coordinación de Antonio Bueno García, Manuel Ramiro Valderrama y Juan Miguel Zarandona Fernández. Soria, Spain: Depto. de Publicaciones del Colegio Universitario de Soria, 1994. 483 p.: bibl.

Many of the papers included here may be of interest to translators of Latin American literatures, although only one addresses the subject specifically: linguist Ramiro Valderrama's essay detailing the many challenges that Julio Cortázar's *Libro de Manuel* (*HLAS 38:6732*) would offer a translator. (For review of English translation—*A manual for Manuel,* see *HLAS 42:6629.*) Ana Sofía Ramírez's essay about Cuban authors living in the US is also pertinent. [CM]

4718 Durán Luzio, Juan. Michel de Montaigne: ante sus censores hispánicos. (*Rev. Chil. Lit.,* 50, 1997, p. 51–64)

Fascinating essay about three forms of censorship that have prevented a complete translation of Michel de Montaigne's essay into Spanish: those practiced by the Inquisition; by the 17th-century translator as his own self-censor; and by Franco's censors, *ultrahispánicos,* who in the 20th century restored previous excisions but made others of their own. [CM]

4719 Encuentros Complutenses en Torno a la Traducción, *5th, Madrid, 1994.* Actas. Edición de Rafael Martín-Gaitero. Madrid: Editorial Complutense, 1995. 759 p.: bibl., ill.

Nearly every aspect of translation is discussed in these plenaries and papers, and many may interest translators of Latin American literature even though none relates directly to Latin America. See, for example, the plenary lectures, or essays such as Lidia Tallefer de Haya's piece on feminist translators. [CM]

4720 Encyclopedia of Latin American literature. Edited by Verity Smith. London; Chicago: Fitzroy Dearborn, 1997. 926 p.: bibl., indices, map.

Invaluable for translators as well as scholars, students, and teachers. Bibliography following each entry includes information about work in translation; numerous lesser-known writers and countries are covered well; long thematic entries discuss such individual topics. Dick Gerdes' "Translation," for example, offers a fine overview of work and trends in both Brazil and Spanish America. Highly recommended. [CM]

4721 Foster, David William. The politics of Spanish language translation in the United States. (*Point Contact,* 4:2, Fall 1995, p. 63–72)

Foster develops two topics: the shared linguistic features of English and Spanish, and their (paradoxically) distinct statuses in the US; the hegemonic status of English affects both the sociology and structure of Spanish. Insightful comments; important article for translators and teachers. [CM]

4722 Hintz, Suzanne S. Rosario Ferré: a search for identity. New York: Lang, 1995. 275 p.: bibl., index. (Wor(l)ds of change: Latin American and Iberian literature; 12)

Entire book will interest scholars and students of Ferré's writing, but Chapter 6, "Ferré's Search for Identity in English Translation," should also interest translators. Hintz compares Ferré's translations in *The youngest doll* (*HLAS 54:5000*) and *Sweet diamond dust* (*HLAS 52:4993*) with original works (*Papeles de Pandora* and *Maldito amor,* respectively), and shows that Ferré significantly altered her work, softening or even eliminating numerous explicitly erotic and anti-North American passages. [CM]

4723 Index to translated short fiction by Latin American women in English language anthologies. Compiled by Kathy S. Leonard. Westport, Conn.: Greenwood Press, 1997. 120 p.: bibl., indices. (Bibliographies and indexes in women's studies, 0742–6941; 25)

Excellent resource for locating translations of brief fiction by Latin American women includes three cross-reference indices: an anthology index covering 165 volumes published between 1938–96, which gives full bibliographical information and tables of contents; an autobiographical author index; and an index of authors by their individual countries. Highly recommended. [CM]

4724 Jaffe, Janice A. Translation and prostitution: Rosario Ferré's *Maldito amor* and *Sweet diamond dust.* (*Lat. Am. Lit. Rev.,* 23:46, 1995, p. 66–80)

Jaffe agrees with Suzanne Hintz (see item **4722**) that Rosario Ferré "prostituted herself" (Jaffe's words) as a Puerto Rican writer in her translation of *Maldito amor* (*Sweet diamond dust*). She argues, however, that Ferré worked deliberately and carefully to redefine metaphors of gender in an effort to free Puerto Ricans from the secondary status given them by "dualistic representations of identity." [CM]

4725 Landers, Clifford E. Latin America and translation: three contributions to knowing "The Other". (*LARR*, 30:3, 1995, p. 254–263)
Thorough, thoughtful review essay examines Suzanne Jill Levine's *The subversive scribe* (see *HLAS 54:5095*) and *Translating Latin America: culture as text* (see *HLAS 54:5101*), and John Milton's *O poder da tradução*. See also item **4726**. [CM]

4726 Levine, Suzanne Jill. La escribiente subversiva (I). (*Cuad. Marcha*, 11:120, oct. 1996, p. 64–69)
Transcribes a section of Ruben Gallo's forthcoming Spanish translation of Levine's work *The subversive scribe*. See also item **4725**. For comment on original work, see *HLAS 54:5095*. [CM]

4727 Mafla-Bustamante, Cecilia. A study of the English translations of Jorge Icaza's *Huasipungo*. (*in* The knowledges of the translator: from literary interpretation to machine classification. Edited by Malcolm Coulthard and Patricia Anne Odber de Baubeta. Lewiston, N.Y.: The Edwin Mellen Press, 1996, p. 259–278, bibl.)
Comparative examination of two English-language translations of *Huasipungo*: Marvyn Savill's *Huasipungo* (1962) and Bernard Dulsey's *The Villagers* (see *HLAS 26:1603*). Author's principal interest lies in the translation of the two varieties of Ecuadorian Andean speech found in Icaza's two versions of the novel: the 1934 version (see *HLAS 1:2131*) used by Savill and the 1953 version used by Dulsey. Useful, informative article for translators, scholars, and students. [CM]

4728 Rostagno, Irene. Searching for recognition: the promotion of Latin American literature in the United States. Westport, Conn.: Greenwood Press, 1997. 159 p.: bibl, index. (Contributions to the study of world literature, 0738-9345; 72)

Significant book for history of Latin American literature in English-language translation. Focusing on Waldo Frank's contributions, Rostagno chronicles changing North American attitudes toward Latin American literature. Other chapters deal with Blanche and Alfred Knopf, the serial *El Corno Emplumado*, the impact(s) of the Cuban Revolution, and the Center for Inter-American Relations. The take of any "promotion," however, is far more complicated than Rostagno indicates. [CM]

4729 Sillato, María del Carmen. "Com/posiciones" de Juan Gelman, o como traducir los rastros de la realidad. (*Hispamérica/Gaithersburg*, 24:72, 1995, p. 3–14)
Study of Juan Gelman's "translations" of work by his own heteronyms, and of conventional poetry from Biblical poems to Sephardic poetry of the Renaissance. Even in the latter, however, Sillato shows that Gelman takes considerable liberties with the original poems in order to engage the reader in the "visión exiliar" at the root of them all. [CM]

4730 Stewart, Jon. Borges on language and translation. (*Philos. Lit.*, 19:2, 1995, p. 320–329)
In his provocative reading of "Averroes' Search," Stewart argues that through this story Borges maintains that both translation and true cross-cultural understanding are impossible. Limited by the epistemological categories of culture, neither Averroes nor any of us is able to overcome barriers impenetrable by imagination, technology, or erudition. [CM]

4731 Traducción como cultura. Recopilación de Lisa Bradford. Rosario, Argentina: B. Viterbo Editora, 1997. 189 p.: bibl. (Tesis/ensayo)
Essays by translators and scholars from Argentina and US working under auspices of the Univ. Nacional de Mar del Plata. Translation is addressed with respect to both general issues such as gender and exile, and specific writers such as Borges and T.S. Eliot. Recommended for translators, scholars, and students. [CM]

4732 Western translation theory: from Herodotus to Nietzsche. Edited by Douglas Robinson. Manchester, England: St. Jerome Pub., 1997. 337 p.: bibl., indices.

Robinson's extensive anthology of comments by translators, scholars, and writers includes only one text written originally in Spanish (Don Quixote's famous remarks about Flemish tapestries viewed from the wrong side). Even so, the selections and Robinson's introductions should prove valuable to all translation scholars and students. [CM]

MUSIC

General

4733 Cosmología y música en los Andes.
Edición de Max Peter Baumann. Frankfurt am Main: Vervuert; Madrid: Iberoamericana, 1996. 567 p.: bibl., ill., index. (Bibliotheca Ibero-Americana; 55)

A collection of 26 essays in Spanish and English on the relationship between music and cosmology in the Andes. Sections deal with cosmology in the areas of dualism, ceremonial myth and ritual, traditional religious festivals, song texts, tradition, and modernity. Baumann treats symbolic dualism and cosmology in Andean music, while Schechter focuses on Quichua *sanjuán* as cultural macro- and microcosm. Schlegelberger highlights cosmological aspects in Andean religion, and Vokral treats the social context of carnival song texts. Cánepa Koch writes on identity and modernity in Andean dance. [WC]

4734 Ficher, Miguel. Latin American classical composers: a biographical dictionary. Compiled and edited with Martha Furman Schleifer and John M. Furman. Lanham, Md.: Scarecrow Press, 1996. 422 p.: bibl.

Although the authors of this condensed biographical dictionary claim to have restricted the entries to "composers who have written in the classical or cultivated tradition," a few composers of salon music are also included. Compiles brief biographical information on 377 composers from Argentina, 30 from Bolivia, 171 from Brazil, 77 from Chile, seven from Paraguay, and 42 from Uruguay; also provides short lists of works. Despite the undeniable need for a reference work such as this, the brevity of treatment given to major names makes it of very limited use for specialists. [CM]

4735 Figueroa Hernández, Rafael. Salsa and related genres: a bibliographical guide. Westport, Conn.: Greenwood Press, 1992. 121 p.: bibl., indexes. (Music reference collection, 0736–7740; 38)

Well-organized, detailed bibliography covers the general topic of salsa, including styles, genres, musicians, and instruments. Appropriate indices make the volume highly useful. [AL]

4736 Gómez, Zoila and **Victoria Eli Rodríguez.** Música latinoamericana y caribeña. La Habana: Editorial Pueblo y Educación, 1995. 436 p.: bibl., ill.

An extensive study of the development of music in Latin America, especially in the Caribbean. Traces musical development in the broadest sense from colonial times to the later-20th century, exploring trends such as aleatoric music. [AL]

4737 Pinto, Arturo Kike. El waqra phuku. (*Bol. Lima*, 17:99, junio/agosto 1995, p. 10–14, ill., map, music)

Brief study of the origin, construction, and music of the Andean *waqra phuku* or natural horn trumpet. Musical examples are useful. Unfortunately, no photos of the instrument are provided. [JR]

Mexico

JAMES RADOMSKI, *Assistant Professor, Music, California State University, San Bernardino*

INTEREST IN THE SCHOLARLY STUDY of Mexican music continues to grow, as evidenced by significant musicological conferences: *After Columbus: The Musical Journey* at California Polytechnic State Univ. in 1992, and the *International Conference on Mexican Music* at the Univ. of Kansas in 1997. Recent scholarship reflects the richness of Mexican musical culture: from indigenous music traditions and Renaissance colonial music through the popular music of the 18th and 19th centuries on to the most recent art music—not to mention rock and popular music—of the 20th century.

Among Mexican writers, there is a continued fascination with the *mariachi* phenomenon, from historical, anthropological, and musical perspectives. Significant works by Jesús Flores y Escalante and Pablo Dueñas Herrera (item **4752**), Alvaro Ochoa (item **4764**), and Jorge Chamorro Escalante (item **4745**) have appeared on this topic.

Groundbreaking contributions in the area of 20th-century art music were seen in the first volume of the *Diccionario de compositores mexicanos de música de concierto, Siglo XX,* compiled by Eduardo Soto Millán (item **4774**) and *La composición en México en el siglo XX* by Yolanda Moreno Rivas (item **4762**).

Important periodicals published in the US dealing with Mexican music include the *Revista de Música Latino Americana/Latin American Music Review* edited by Gerard Behague and the *Inter-American Music Review* edited by Robert Stevenson. Vol. 7 (1994–95) of *Ars Musica Denver,* edited by Paul Laird and Craig Russell, brought together significant essays from the 1992 *After Columbus* conference (items **4746, 4766,** and **4769**).

4738 Alcaraz, José Antonio. Reflexiones sobre el nacionalismo musical mexicano. México: Editorial Patria, 1991. 187 p.: ill.

After a brief introductory chapter surveying musical nationalism in Europe, the author presents chapters on José Rolón, Julián Carrillo, Candelario Huízar, Carlos Chávez, Silvestre Revueltas, Luis Sandi, Blas Galindo, Miguel Bernal Jiménez, José Pablo Moncayo, and Carlos Jiménez Mabarak, focusing on specific nationalistic works by each musician.

4739 Antología de la marimba en América. Recopilación de César Pineda del Valle. Verdadera evolución de la marinbah maya de Carlos R. Asturias Gómez. Guatemala: Librería Artemis-Edinter, 1994. 376 p.: bibl., ill.

Proposes to present a comprehensive collection on the origins of the marimba: Chiapas, Guatemala, and Cuba. Includes

short articles by over 30 scholars, writers, and musicians. A large portion of the work is dedicated to the complicated theories of Carlos R. Asturias Gómez about the Mayan marinbah. Useful for those interested in the marimba or Mayan music.

4740 Berrones, Guillermo. Ingratos ojos míos: Miguel Luna y la historia de El Palomo y El Gorrión. Monterrey, Mexico: Centro de Información de Historia Regional, Univ. Autónoma de Nuevo León, 1995. 159 p.: ill.

Reminiscences of the career of norteño artists Cirilo (El Palomo) and Miguel (El Gorrión) Luna Franco based on a series of conversations with the latter. Offers an intimate glimpse of a group that flourished in the 1960s. Lyrics of various *corridos* included.

4741 Carlos Chávez 1899–1978: iconografía. Investigación iconográfica y documental de Gloria Carmona. México: Consejo Nacional para la Cultura y las Artes,

Instituto Nacional de Bellas Artes, 1994. 167 p.: appendix, bibl., discography, ill.

Valuable collection of photos, prints, and sketches tracing the composer's life and career. Minimal text, but includes a useful chronology. Also includes an appendix listing positions held; orchestras and concerts directed as guest-conductor; academic activities; publications by Chávez; honors and awards; and a discography.

4742 Carredano, Consuelo. Felipe Villanueva, 1862–1893. México: CENIDIM, 1992. 171 p.: bibl., discography, ill., music.

Excellent study of the composer's life and musical style. Includes numerous illustrations, musical examples, catalog of works, and a discography.

4743 Castañeda, Daniel Perez and **Vicente T. Mendoza.** Instrumental precortesiano. Mexico: Univ. Nacional Autónoma de México, 1991. 1 v.: bibl., ill. (part fold., part col.), index, music.

Reprint of seminal scientific study on precolumbian percussion instruments. Essential tool for serious scholars. Bibliography cites over 100 obscure 19th- and early-20th-century sources.

4744 Chamorro Escalante, Jorge Arturo. Presencia africana en la música de México. (*Am. Negra*, 12, dic. 1996, p. 61–75, bibl., ill., music)

Analyzes African traits in the *son mexicano* according to a three-part scheme: 1) basic rhythmic foundation; 2) middle rhythmic framework; and 3) rhythmic embellishments. Gives examples and cites scholarly works to support arguments.

4745 Chamorro Escalante, Jorge Arturo. La transregionalización del mariachi tradicional: de Michoacán a Colima y de Jalisco a Michoacán. (*Relaciones/Zamora*, 60, otoño 1994, p. 123–139, bibl., map, music)

Authoritative ethnomusicological study of mariachi style, texts, and performers, and their interactions across various regions.

4746 Corona Alcalde, Antonio. The popular music from Veracruz and the survival of instrumental practices of the Spanish baroque. (*Ars Musica Denver*, 7:2, Spring 1995, p. 39–68, map, music)

Discusses parallels between baroque music and modern popular/folk music in Veracruz as a means of understanding 17th-century performance practice.

4747 Dávalos Amaya, Guillermo. Belisario de Jesús García de la Garza, su obra musical. Monterrey, Mexico: Gobierno del Estado de Nuevo León, Univ. Regiomontana, 1992. 160 p.: bibl., music.

Authoritative study of popular Nuevo Leónese composer (1892–1952). Author had access to recordings, photos, and manuscripts in the possession of the composer's children. Includes biographical notes; catalog of published scores, piano rolls, 78 RPM and 33 $\frac{1}{3}$ RPM records; song lyrics, and sheet music facsimiles. Also contains brief biographies and articles collected from various periodicals.

4748 Díez de Urdanivia, Fernando. Mi historia secreta de la música. Presentación de Luis Herrera de la Fuente. México: Luzam, 1991. 147 p.: index.

Personal reminiscences (mostly from the 1950s-60s) of musicians and other performers as told to noted journalist.

4749 Figueroa Hernández, Rafael. Luis Angel Silva Melón. Xalapa, Mexico: R. Figueroa Hernández, 1994. 95 p.: bibl., ill.

Popular biography, told in first person, of an important proponent of *son mexicano* from the 1950s-80s.

4750 Figueroa Hernández, Rafael. Salsa mexicana: transculturación e identidad. Xalapa, Mexico: ConClave, 1996. 128 p.: bibl., ill., index.

Transculturation provides a theoretical context for this scholarly work. Placing Mexico within the Caribbean cultural complex, the author begins his study with considerations of African-Hispanic music in the Antilles, and then discusses African-Mexican music, specifically, Mexican salsa. Salsa is examined from an historical perspective with reference to important groups and performers.

4751 Flores Longoria, Samuel. Alberto Cervantes y la historia del bolero en México. Monterrey, Mexico: Ediciones Castillo, 1994. 134 p.: bibl., ill., index.

A useful overview of the bolero in Mexico. Twelve pages discuss the dance's origins and popularization in 19th-century Mexico. The rest of the largely anecdotal work focuses on the composer Alberto Cervantes (b. 1923), drawing upon interviews in 1980–94. Some texts and music of Cervantes' boleros included. Also includes useful lists of Mexican boleros by Cervantes and others.

4752 Flores y Escalante, Jesús and **Pablo Dueñas Herrera.** Cirilo Marmolejo: historia del mariachi en la Ciudad de México. México: Asociación Mexicana de Estudios Fonográficos; Dirección General de Culturas Populares, 1994. 150 p.: bibl., ill., indexes. (Archivo histórico testimonial)

Authors consider Cirilo Marmolejo, founder of the "legendary" Mariachi Coculense de Cirilo Marmolejo, to be the "principal introducer" of mariachi music in Mexico City, a process which began around 1919. This study traces the family back to the 17th century, providing facsimiles of baptismal certificates and letters. Briefly deals with other mariachi groups from the early-20th century. Presents a valuable discography of Marmolejo and other groups from 1908–37.

4753 González Quiñones, Jaime. La verdadera fecha de la muerte de Manuel de Sumaya. (*Lat. Am. Music Rev.,* 13:2, Fall/Winter 1997, p. 317–319)

Transcribes a death certificate from the Cathedral of Oaxaca as proof that the composer died on Dec. 21, 1755. Argues for the spelling of the name with S instead of Z.

4754 Hacer música: Blas Galindo, compositor. Guadalajara, Mexico: Univ. de Guadalajara, Dirección de Publicaciones, 1994. 85 p.: ill. (Cuadernos de arte; 2–1994)

Biography, autobiography, and reflections prepared with the help of the composer shortly before his death in 1993. Includes letters from Aaron Copland, Carlos Chávez, Serge Koussevitsky, Robert Stevenson, and others. Also includes a catalog of works and a biographical chronology.

4755 Herrera Sánchez, Raymundo. Folía sin sol: de cómo utilizó y traicionó Cuauhtémoc Cárdenas Solórzano y otros a los Niños Cantores de Morelia. Morelia, Mexico: Editorial de Escritores y Autores de Morelia, 1989. 323 p.: bibl., ill.

Polemic denouncing the secularization of the Morelia choirboys school by the revolutionary government. Strangely interspersed

with a biographical account of the career of the castrato Carlo Broschi (Farinelli).

4756 Hess, Carol A. Silvestre Revueltas in Republican Spain: music as political utterance. (*Lat. Am. Music Rev.,* 13:2, Fall/Winter 1997, p. 278–296, bibl.)

Discusses the enthusiastic reception of Revueltas' tour of Republican Spain in 1937 with the leftist organization LEAR (Liga de Escritores y Artistas Revolucionarios) and considers how his works fit the regnant revolutionary esthetic and political ideologies.

4757 Jara Gámez, Simón; Aurelio Rodríguez Yeyo; and **Antonio Zedillo Castillo.** De Cuba con amor—: el danzón en México. México: Grupo Azabache; Consejo Nacional para la Cultura y las Artes, Culturas Populares, 1994. 259 p.: bibl., ill.

History of Cuban danzón in Mexico (earliest reference 1882) with background on earlier dances. Includes a note on sung danzón and 50 p. on the danzón in Cuba.

4758 Koegel, John. Spanish and Mexican dance music in early California. (*Ars Musica Denver,* 7:1, Fall 1994, p. 31–55, music, photos)

Scholarly consideration of musical and sociological aspects of the fandango, baile, and jarabe. Draws upon the valuable descriptions of everyday California life in the 1840s in Antonio Coronel's *Casas de California* (1897).

4759 Koegel, John. Village musical life along the Río Grande: Tomé, New Mexico, since 1739. (*Lat. Am. Music Rev.,* 13:2, Fall/Winter 1997, p. 173–251, ill., photos)

Useful addition to the study of Hispanic-American sacred and secular music in the 18th and 19th centuries. Discusses *Once misas mexicanas,* a surprising example of an early Latin folk Mass tradition from Tomé and other villages, and *Cánticos espirituales,* "the most important 19th-century Spanish language hymnbook of the Southwest."

4760 Lanz, Joaquín. Los cantos al Niño Dios. Campeche, Mexico: H. Ayuntamiento de Campeche, 1992. 88 p.: bibl., ill. (Col. Barlovento. Miscelánea)

Collection of 27 traditional Christmas carols from Campeche with harmonic realization. Introduction surveys the history of music and Christmas traditions in Campeche.

4761 Mauleón Rodríguez, Gustavo. Música en el virreinato de la Nueva España: recopilación y notas, siglos XVI y XVII. Puebla, Mexico: Univ. Iberoamericana, Golfo Centro; Lupus Inquisitor, 1995. 181 p.: bibl., ill.

Brief, well-documented survey of the history of 16th- and 17th-century Mexican colonial music draws upon primary and secondary sources. Includes bibliography and useful discography.

4762 Moreno Rivas, Yolanda. La composición en México en el siglo XX. México: Consejo Nacional para la Cultura y las Artes, 1994. 237 p.: appendices, bibl., ill., index, photos. (Cultura contemporánea de México)

An important contribution to the study of 20th-century Mexican art music. Introduction sketches the 16th-18th-century origins of Mexican art music and discusses 19th-century composers such as Aniceto Ortega, Melesio Morales, Ricardo Castro, and Julio Ituarte. Then proceeds to the 20th century, examining the contributions of composers such as Manuel Ponce, Carlos Chávez, and Silvestre Revueltas, through Manuel Enríquez, Mario Lavista and other composers active in the early 1990s. Numerous photos and color plates accompany the narrative. Useful appendices include: "14 composers talk about aesthetics and their work;" brief biographies of 60 composers; and chronological lists of important 20th-century works by Mexican and non-Mexican composers.

4763 Nuestra gente—nuestra música: testimonios de los músicos populares de la Comarca Lagunera. Durango, Mexico: Secretaría de Educación, Cultura y Deporte, Dirección General de Culturas Populares, 1994. 167 p.: ill. (Col. Identidad duranguense)

Useful collection of anecdotal biographical/autobiographical essays dealing with folk and popular musicians who flourished in the Lagunera region (states of Durango and Coahuila) from the 1940s-60s: Gerónimo Morales Gaspar (to whom the volume is dedicated); Andrés Olvera Gómez (and the Conjunto de Cuerdas "Casino Torreón"); Gilberto Gallegos Joven; José Macías Salas; Alfonso Arreola Palacios; Gregorio Treviño

Alzalde; Salvador Enríquez; Alfredo Medina Nevárez; Pedro Palacios Gurrola; Amador Vaquera Cabrera; Bernardo Suárez Botello; Jesús Gallegos Joven; Armando Ramos Martínez; Manuel Ortiz Ríos; Adela Campos Navarro; Antonio García García; José Flores Simental; Adolfo Macías Salas; Antonio Lopez Moreno; Nicolás Meraz Alvarado; Irineo García Esparza; Apolinar Rodríguez Meza; and Nestor Mesta Chairez.

4764 Ochoa Serrano, Alvaro. Mitote, fandango y mariacheros. Zamora, Mexico: El Colegio de Michoacán, 1994. 124 p.: bibl., ill. (Colección Ensayos)

Well-documented study traces indigenous, Spanish, and African threads in the music of Michoacán from the early "Agustino" ensemble through the valona, malagueña, tambora, fandango, and mariachi.

4765 Olguín, Enriqueta M. Hacer guitarritas. Pachuca, Mexico: Centro de Investigaciones y Estudios sobre el Estado de Hidalgo, Coordinación de Investigación y Posgrado, Univ. Autónoma del Estado de Hidalgo, 1994. 55 p.: bibl., ill. (Col. Sociedad y pensamiento)

Surveys tradition of craftsmanship (shell inlay) of guitars and other instruments and objects in the barrio of El Nith, town of Ixmiquilpan, in the state of Hidalgo. Author draws from interviews with local artisans between 1987-93.

4766 Osorio Bolio de Saldívar, Elisa. Gabriel Saldívar y Silva: the legacy of a Mexican maestro. Translated by Astrid Kristine Topp Russell. (*Ars Musica Denver*, 7:2, Spring 1995, p. 5-12)

Reflections on the life and contributions of the eminent Mexican musical scholar by his wife.

4767 Perfiles yucatecos. Mérida, Mexico: Museo de la Canción Yucateca, 1995. 225 p.: ill., index.

Useful collection of brief biographies, accompanied by oil portrait from the museum, and song texts of 30 composers, 18 lyricists, and five singers from Yucatán.

4768 Ramos Aguirre, Francisco. Historia del corrido en la frontera tamaulipeca, 1844-1994. Victoria, Mexico: Fondo Nacional para la Cultura y las Artes, 1994. 266 p.: appendix, ill.

Journalistic survey of the *corrido* in Tamaulipas. No music, some lyrics. Brief biographies of *corrido* artists in appendix.

4769 Russell, Craig H. New jewels in old boxes: retrieving the lost musical heritages of colonial Mexico. (*Ars Musica Denver*, 7:2, Spring 1995, p. 13–38, facsims., table)

Erudite discussion of 18th-century works in the Saldívar Archive by Sebastián de Aguirre and Santiago de Murcia together with an anonymous violin method.

4770 Russell, Craig H. Tesoro de la música polifónica en México, VII. (*Inter-Am. Music Rev.*, 15:2, Summer/Fall 1996, p. 123–132, music)

A review of *Archivo musical de la Catedral de Oaxaca: cantadas y villancicos de Manuel de Sumaya; revisión, estudio y transcripción*, edited by Aurelio Tello (see *HLAS 56:4770*). A useful introduction to the composer Manuel de Zumaya (Sumaya) and his music, additionally providing an overview of previous Zumaya scholarship.

4771 Santiago de Murcia's Códice Saldívar no. 4: a treasury of secular guitar music from baroque Mexico. v. 1, Commentary. Urbana: Univ. of Illinois Press, 1995. 1 score (1 v.): appendix, bibl., ill., index. (Music in American life)

Authoritative study includes detailed description of the manuscript, background on "Music for Dance and Theater in Seventeenth- and Eighteenth-Century Spain," discussion of individual dances supported by historical data and musical examples, and a biography of the composer. Appendix provides valuable list of sources for individual dances. Thorough bibliography of primary and secondary sources, detailed index.

4772 Simpatía por el rock: industria, cultura y sociedad. Recopilación de Miguel Ángel Aguilar, Adrián de Garay, y José Hernández Prado. México: Univ. Autónoma Metropolitana, Unidad Azcapotzalco, 1993. 196 p.

Collection of essays on sociological, musical, and esthetic aspects of rock from a series of roundtable discussions held at the Univ. Autónoma Metropolitana, Unidad Azcapotzalco and Iztapalapa from Nov. 16–18, 1992.

4773 Sosa, José Octavio. La ópera en Guadalajara. Prólogo de Eduardo Lizalde. Guadalajara, Mexico: Secretaría de Cultura de Jalisco, 1994. 179 p.: bibl., ill., indexes, photos.

Chronology of operas, concerts, and artists at the Teatro Degollado in Guadalajara from its opening in 1866 through 1993. Abundant period engravings and photographs. Name index included.

4774 Soto Millán, Eduardo. Diccionario de compositores mexicanos de música de concierto, Siglo XX. v. 1, A-H. México: Sociedad de Autores y Compositores de Música; Fondo de Cultura Económica, 1996. 1 v.: ill. (Vida y pensamiento de México)

An extremely valuable contribution to the study of Mexican art music in the 20th century. The entry for each composer contains a photograph portrait, short biography, list of works (by genre and date), discography, and published scores. Thoroughly researched (with the help of some of the composers themselves) and beautifully organized. Useful introduction by Robert Stevenson.

4775 Stevenson, Robert. Colonial treasure in the Puebla Cathedral music archive. (*Inter-Am. Music Rev.*, 15:1, Winter/Spring 1996, p. 39–51)

Catalog of compositions by named composers in the Puebla Cathedral archive is introduced by an informative discussion of the value of individual composers and works represented in the collection.

4776 Stevenson, Robert. Ignacio Jerusalem, 1707–1769: Italian parvenu in eighteenth-century Mexico, part one. (*Inter-Am. Music Rev.*, 16:1, Summer/Fall 1997, p. 57–61)

With scholarly detail, the career of this important composer of sacred and secular music is traced from his appointment as titular *maestro de capilla* at the Mexico City Cathedral in 1750 until his death.

4777 Stevenson, Robert. Sor Juana Inés de la Cruz's musical rapports: a tercentenary remembrance. (*Inter-Am. Music Rev.*, 15:1, Winter/Spring 1996, p. 1–21, facsims., music)

Meticulously documented study of the musical world surrounding this brilliant 17th-century figure, including details of the musical life at convents in Puebla and Mexico City and musical connections with composers such as Mexico City Cathedral *maestros de capilla* José de Agurto y Loaysa and Antonio Salazar, Puebla Cathedral *maestro de capilla* Miguel Matheo de Dallo y Lana, and Oaxaca Cathedral *maestro de capilla* Matheo Vallados, all of whom set to music villancico texts of Sor Juana.

4778 Stevenson, Robert. Sor Juana's Mexico City musical coadjutors. (*Inter-Am. Music Rev.*, 15:1, Winter/Spring 1996, p. 23–37, facsims., music)

Authoritative study details the life and works of Mexico City *maestros de capilla* José de Loaysa y Agurto (fl. 1647–1695) and Antonio de Salazar (1650–1715).

4779 Tomlinson, Gary. Ideologies of Aztec song. (*J. Am. Musicol. Soc.*, 48:3, Fall 1995, p. 343–379)

Laborious discussion of the problems in understanding Aztec song which result from the bias of Eurocentric paradigms.

4780 Velasco, Xavier. Una banda nombrada Caifanes. México: Dragón, 1990. 95 p.: ill. (Col. Por las eléctricas penumbras del rock)

Anecdotal history of the rock group Caifanes.

4781 Villanueva, René. Cantares de la memoria: recuerdos de un folklorista. México: Grupo Editorial Planeta, 1994. 402 p.: ill. (Espejo de México)

Popular history of the group Los Folkloristas from its beginnings in 1966 to the present, told in the first person by one of the group's members, with nostalgic reflections on the leftist folk music scene throughout Latin America.

Central America and the Caribbean

ALFRED E. LEMMON, *Director and Assistant Professor, Music, Williams Research Center, Historic New Orleans Collection*

THE WORKS ON CENTRAL AMERICA AND THE CARIBBEAN selected for review this biennium reflect a healthy trend in the development of the region's musicological studies. The appearance of a luxurious edition of colonial music, published in a format and style usually reserved for scholarly editions of the European masters, is a milestone. Compilers of colonial music anthologies have frequently seen superb work appear in less than ideal formats and, therefore, the publication of Robert Snow's *A New-World Collection of Polyphony for Holy Week and the Salve Service: Guatemala City, Cathedral Archive, Music MS 4* should be celebrated (item **4801**), as should the efforts of others who have labored to create scholarly editions of Latin American colonial music.

Articles on Latin American music continue to appear in a wide variety of journals. The essay of Alfred E. Lemmon and John A. Crider in *Mesoaméerica* is a reflection of the journal's willingness to publish essays on Central American music with some regularity (item **4799**). The editors of *American Music* should likewise be commended for including the essays by Warren R. Pinckney, Jr. dealing with Barbados and the Virgin Islands (items **4788** and **4789**). The growing inclination of journals to accept articles on musical topics indicates that solid research is being conducted on the region.

It is heartening to see colonial music of the Caribbean and Central America receiving attention from performance groups, and equally encouraging to see the subsequent appearance of superb recordings. The *Exaudi Choir* of Cuba, under the direction of María Felicia Peréz, was featured in two recordings of Esteban Salas (1725–1803) on the Jade label. *Cuban Baroque Sacred Music: Esteban Salas* (Jade 35808–2) and *Un Barroco Cubano del Siglo SVIII: Esteban Salas* (Jade 35746–2) are superior recordings of excellent music. They reflect the renewed interest in Salas seen in Robert Stevenson's *Inter-American Music Review* essay (item **4812**) and Victoria Eli Rodríguez's article in *Revista Musical de Venezuela* (item **4811**).

The growing number of scholars in the Caribbean and Central America with appropriate academic credentials is a welcome trend. Olive Lewin's article "The UMH Contribution to the English, French, and Dutch-Speaking Caribbean," presented at the 15th Congress of the International Musicological Society and published in *Revista de Musicología* (see *HLAS 56:4724*) documents this tendency and examines the impact of "The Universe of Music: A History," a project of UNESCO's International Music Council. The project is the work of authors native to the Caribbean and has helped to stimulate musicological research in the region.

The sheer volume of material, together with its increasingly high quality, is welcome. Also promising is the wide range of music currently under study, from art music to folk music to popular music. In light of this surge of interest in musical topics, it is encouraging that reprints of exemplary works are newly available, for example, Fernando Ortiz's trilogy concerning the Afro-Cuban musical experience (item **4810**).

The number of entries selected for *HLAS 58*, slightly greater than in previous years, is an indication of the strength of current research and the number of publications issued on the music of Central America and the Caribbean. While it was impossible to include each work published this biennium, an attempt was made to ensure equal representation of topics and regions.

THE CARIBBEAN (EXCEPT CUBA)

4782 Blérald-Ndagano, Monique. Musiques et danses créoles au tambour de la Guyane Française. Cayenne, French Guiana: Ibis Rouge Editions, 1996. 228 p.: bibl., discography, ill. (some col.). (Col. Espaces guyanais)

An examination of the songs and dance of French Guiana. Discussions of the musical instruments, the prominence of song in daily life, rhythm, choreography, and costume are supplemented by excellent photographs, a glossary, and musical examples and texts.

4783 Developments in Caribbean music: papers presented at the Seminar for National Liaison Officers of the Caribbean Inter-Cultural Music Institute. Music in Belize by Gina Scott. Music in the Commonwealth of the Bahamas by Veronica Ingraham. Music in Jamaica by Maureen Rowe. Music in St. Kitts & Nevis by Alphonsus Bridgewater. Music in Antigua & Barbuda by Robert Margetson. Music in Montserrat by Leslie Thomas. Music in the Commonwealth of Dominica by Pearle Christian. Music in St. Lucia by Cypriani Norville. Music in Barbados by Janice Millington-Robertson. Music in St. Vincent and the Grenadines by Joffre Venner. Music in Grenada by Derick Clouden. Music in Trinidad & Tobago by Mungal Patasar. Music in Guyana by Bill Pilgrim. St. Augustine, Trinidad and Tobago: Caribbean Inter-Cultural Institute, Creative Arts Centre, Univ. of the West Indies, 1991. 66 p.: bibl., ill.

An examination of the indigenous, African, and European musical heritages, with the resulting retention and "creolization," of the Caribbean nations of Cuba, Puerto Rico, the Dominican Republic, Haiti (and the French Caribbean), Jamaica, Trinidad, and the East Indians population. A discussion of musical styles and forms reveals the universality and diversity, ethnicity, and impact on North America of this continent of islands. Particularly valuable is a glossary of musical terms used throughout the Caribbean.

4784 Leymarie, Isabelle. Musiques caraïbes. Paris?: Cité de la musique; Arles: Actes sud, 1996. 174 p.: bibl., discography, ill., index + 1 digital sound disc (4 ¾ in.). (Musiques du monde)

An exploration of origins and sources of traditional Caribbean music, emphasizing Afro-Cuban and Afro-Latin music. Musical instruments, dance, and the influence of Catholicism and voodoo are examined. Accompanied by a 45-minute CD with extensive notes on the musical extracts.

Lowe, Agatha. Themes of war, politics and health education in calypso music. See *HLAS 57:4860.*

4785 Manuel, Peter; Kenneth Bilby; and **Michael Largey.** Caribbean currents: Caribbean music from rumba to reggae. Philadelphia: Temple Univ. Press, 1995. 288 p.: bibl., ill., index, maps.

A guide to the cultural festivals, traditional culture, musical forms, dances, instruments, music education, government institutions concerned with music, and copyright mechanisms in Belize, the Bahamas, Jamaica, St. Kitts & Nevis, Antigua and Barbado, Montserrat, Dominica, St. Lucia, Barbados, St. Vincent and the Grenadines, Grenada, Trinidad & Tobago, and Guyana.

4786 McDaniel, Lorna. The concept of nation in the Big Drum Dance of Carriacou, Grenada. (*in* Musical repercussions of 1492: encounters in text and performance. Edited by Carol E. Robertson. Washington: Smithsonian Institution Press, 1992, p. 395–411, bibl., music)

A thorough examination of the Big Drum Dance, which most often is performed at funeral observances. It may also be performed at wedding receptions, the launching of a new boat, or the christening of a new house. The musical ensemble includes three male drummers and several female singer-dancers. The songs have a strict vocal monophony (accompanied by drums), and are in call-and-response form.

4787 Menéndez Maysonet, Guillermo. Catálogo temático de la música de Felipe Gutiérrez y Espinosa, 1825–1899. Río Piedras: Sección de Musicología, Centro de Investigaciones Históricas, Univ. de Puerto Rico, Recinto de Río Piedras, 1993. 243 p.: index, music.

Detailed catalog of the musical compositions (both sacred and secular) of Felipe Gutiérrez y Espinosa (1825–99), *maestro de capilla* of the Cathedral of San Juan from 1858–98. The catalog is particularly useful due to an abundance of musical examples.

Muñoz Tábora, Jesús. La cultura garífuna en el contexto musical Afro Caribe. See *HLAS 57:4881.*

4788 Pinckney, Warren R., Jr. Jazz in Barbados. (*Am. Music/Society,* 12:1, Spring 1994, p. 58–87, ill.)

Excellent examination of the assimilation of American-style jazz in Barbados. Both jazz and calypso were inherited by Barbadians from other cultures; Barbadian jazz is usually viewed as a response to and product of British colonialism. Both music types, however, have gained popular acceptance and official recognition as evidenced by the sponsorship of the Barbadian/Caribbean Jazz Festivals by the National Cultural Foundation.

4789 Pinckney, Warren R., Jr. Jazz in U.S. Virgin Islands. (*Am. Music/Society,* 10:4, Winter 1992, p. 441–467, photos)

A review of sociomusicological factors underlying the evolution of American jazz in the Virgin Islands from the 1920s-80s. Explores inter-relationships between mainland and Virgin Island jazz currents. Also presents a general chronicle of the musical heritage of the Virgin Islands beginning with the *bamboula,* a dance/drumming tradition that African slaves brought to the islands in the 18th century.

Quintero Rivera, Angel G. El tambor oculto en el cuatro: la melodización de ritmos y la etnicidad cimarroneada en la caribeña cultura de la contraplantación. See *HLAS 57:4900.*

4790 Stuempfle, Stephen. The steelband movement: the forging of a national art in Trinidad and Tobago. Barbados: Press Univ. of the West Indies, 1995. 307 p.: bibl., discography, ill., index, maps.

Tracing the steelband from the Trinidadian tamboo bamboo band, this chronicle begins in the 1930s with young performers of African descent. In the 1940s, civic leaders gave encouragement, and by independence from Britain in 1962, the steelband had become a national symbol. Details the steelband repertoire, ranging from calypsos to favored European selections.

4791 Surinaamse noten = Surinamese notes. Edited by Wim Hoogbergen and Hans Ramsoedh. Nijmegen, The Netherlands: Stichtring Instituut ter Bevordering van de Surinamistick (IBS) te Nijmegen, 2000. 136 p.: bibl., ill., table. (OSO: Tijdschrift voor Surinaamse taalkunde, letterkunde en geschiedenis; Vol. 19, No. 1)

Special issue devoted to Suriname music. The often-exceedingly descriptive articles discuss creolization and Afro-Surinamese music (including music by Maroons), developments in traditional and modern Javanese-Surinamese and Indian-Surinamese music, classical music and choral singing, and Suriname music in the Netherlands. [R. Hoefte]

4792 Wolf, Tim de. Discography of music from the Netherlands Antilles and Aruba: including a history of the local recording studios. Zutphen, The Netherlands: Walburg Pers, 1999. 128 p.: ill.

Overview of Dutch Antillian music on gramophone records. Discusses historical and technical aspects of disc recording in Antillian and Aruban studios. More than half of the text is devoted to a discography of recordings made between 1945–60. Includes summaries in Dutch and Aruban and Curaçaoan Papiamentu. [R. Hoefte]

CENTRAL AMERICA

4793 Brisset, Demetrio. Supervivencias actuales del baile de la conquista en Guatemala. (*Rev. Indias,* 55:203, enero/abril 1995, p. 203–221)

A well-documented examination of the *baile de la conquista* as represented in recent years in Guatemala, particularly in Cakchiquel, Tzutuhil, and Quiché communities. Contains descriptions of regional differences of the dance throughout Latin America, origins of the dance, and historiographical notes.

4794 Ingram, Jaime. Noventa años de música en Panamá. (*Rev. Univ./Panamá,* 52/53, enero/marzo 1995, p. 75–105)

A summary of musical activity in Pan-ama during the 20th century, beginning with the inauguration of the Teatro Nacional (1908) with Verdi's *Aida.* Traces Panama's musical development through its history of composers, institutions, perfumeries, and teachers. The essay is enhanced by listings of compositions and biographical data on musicians.

4795 Jorge, Bernarda. El canto de tradición oral de República Dominicana. Santo Domingo: Banco de Reservas de la República Dominicana, 1996. 207 p.: bibl., ill., music. (Col. Banreservas. Serie Arte y Cultura; 2)

After examining the diverse ethnic and cultural influences on the music of the Dominican Republic, the author studies popular religious songs, songs for entertainment, work songs, and children's songs. Texts and music are included, as well as a catalog of folk music arranged by type and location.

4796 Lehnhoff, Dieter. Elementos indígenas y africanos en el villancico guatemalteco del siglo XVI. (*Rev. Music. Venez.,* 12:30/31, 1992, p. 203–209)

Traces the evolution of the villancico in Guatemala, as enriched by indigenous and African influences, from the 16th-18th centuries.

Lehnhoff, Dieter. El maestro de capilla durante la época colonial en Guatemala. See item **1645.**

4797 Lehnhoff, Dieter. Música sacra e instrumental en la ciudad de Guatemala a principios del siglo XIX. (*An. Acad. Geogr. Hist. Guatem.,* 67, 1993, p. 159–174, bibl., discography)

An examination of religious and instrumental music in Guatemala City during the first half of the 19th-century. The wealth of musical activity in Guatemala, as well as the sources for its history, is underscored by the use of unpublished writings of musicians Vicente Sáenz and José Eulalia Samayoa.

4798 Lemmon, Alfred E. Antonio Literes y José de Nebra: el inicio de la presencia italiana en el archivo musical de la catedral de Guatemala. (Domenico Zipoli: itinerari iberoamericani della musica italiana nel Settecento: atti del convegno internazionale; Prato, 30 settembre-2 ottobre 1988. A cura di Mila De Santis. Firenze: L.S. Olschki, 1994, p. 265–272)

A preliminary catalog of works by Antonio Literes and José de Nebra. Lists Italian composers present in the musical archive of the Cathedral of Guatemala.

4799 Lemmon, Alfred E. and **John A. Crider.** Un antiguo libro guatemalteco de reglamentos para músicos. (*Mesoamérica/Plumsock*, 16:30, dic. 1995, p. 389–403)

Civil documents remain an underutilized source in the study of colonial Spanish-American cathedral music. The authors present a series of documents from the Archivo General de Centro-America that consists of a formal denunciation by one group of Guatemalan church musicians against another faction. The documents describe fee structures and attempts to establish qualifications for musicians and standards for musical performances.

4800 Luján Muñoz, Luis. Las memorias inéditas de José Eulalio Samayoa: posible primer escrito autobiográfico conservado en Guatemala. (*An. Acad. Geogr. Hist. Guatem.*, 68, 1994, p. 153–174, bibl., ill.)

An examination of the unpublished "Memorias" of the 19th-century Guatemalan symphonist, José Eulalio Samayoa (b. 1781). An outline is presented of this 40 p. manuscript, rich in personal data about Samayoa, his musical activity and political involvement.

4801 A New-World collection of polyphony for Holy Week and the Salve service: Guatemala City, Cathedral Archive, music MS 4. Edited with an introduction by Robert J. Snow. Chicago: Univ. of Chicago Press, 1996. 1 score (486 p.): bibl., facsims., indexes. (Monuments of Renaissance music; 9)

Perhaps the most luxurious edition of Latin American colonial music to date, the volume describes in detail life in the Guatemala cathedral (1524–1606), presents an inventory of Guatemalan choirbooks, and reviews the liturgical and musical background for Holy Week music and music for the Salve Service and Compline. In addition to presenting transcriptions of Guatemalan Cathedral MS 4, each composition is given an individual commentary. Among composers represented are Santos de Alisseda, Antón de España, Pedro Bermúdez, Juan de Carbantes, Hernando Franco, Francisco Guerrero, Cristóbal de Morales, Giovanni Pierluigi da Palestrina, Francisco de Peñalosa, and Alonso de Trujillo. An overview of this topic can be seen in Robert Snow's article "Guatemala" (Revista de Musicología 16:3, 1993, p. 1209–1215).

4802 Orquesta Sinfónica de Panamá: periodo del director titular, maestro Eduardo Charpentier De Castro, 1966–1988. Panamá: Orquesta Sinfónica Nacional, 1994. 132 p.: bibl., ill.

A well-organized, detailed chronicle of the Orquesta Sinfónica de Panamá under the directorship of Eduardo Charpentier de Castro (1966–88). Includes a detailed biography of Charpentier and an examination of the musical repertoire for the period.

4803 Valerio Hernández, Jubal. Una historia de tres ciudades: ensayo biográfico sobre Carlos Härtling, autor de la música del Himno Nacional de Honduras. Tegucigalpa: Mejores Ideas, 1994. 108 p.: bibl., ill., music.

Detailed biography of German-born composer Carlos Härtling, (1869–1920), who immigrated to Honduras. In addition to advancing musical education and performing organizations in the country, he wrote the Honduran national anthem.

4804 Zárate, Dora Pérez de. Sobre nuestra música típica. Panamá: Editorial Universitaria, 1996. 103 p.: bibl., ill.

An illustrated, descriptive guide to the instruments used by Panamanian folk musicians.

CUBA

4805 Barreiro Lastra, Hugo. Los días cubanos de Juventino Rosas. Prólogo de Abel Prieto. Guanajuato, Mexico: Gobierno del Estado de Guanajuato, 1994. 262 p.: bibl., ill. (Nuestra cultura)

Juventino Rosas y Cadenas (1868–94), universally known as the composer of *Sobre las olas*, spent the last 175 days of his life presenting concerts in Cuba. Rosas' activity in Cuba and his acclaimed performances at the 1893 Chicago exposition are traced in detail.

4806 Faulín, Ignacio. Silvio Rodríguez: canción cubana. Valencia, Spain: Editorial la Máscara, 1995. 238 p.: bibl., ill. (Todas las músicas)

A detailed biography of Cuban singer Silvio Rodríguez (b. 1946) that traces not only his musical development, but also his relation to Cuban political currents. Presents particularly detailed information on recording and texts.

4807 León, Carmela de. Ernesto Lecuona: el maestro. La Habana: Editora Musical de Cuba, 1995. 223 p.: bibl., discography, ill. (Col. Testimonio. Estudios musicológicos)

Containing a biography of internationally popular Cuban composer Ernesto Lecuona (1895–1963), this work is particularly valuable because of the extensive listing of his compositions. The catalog of his works includes publication information, as well as date of copyright registration.

4808 Moore, Robin. Nationalizing blackness: afrocubanismo and artistic revolution in Havana, 1920–1940. Pittsburgh, Pa.: Univ. of Pittsburgh Press, 1997. 332 p.: bibl., ill., index. (Pitt Latin American series)

An examination of Cuban society through the music of the 1920s-30s when it began to embrace Afro-Cuban culture. Traces how the African element of Cuban society became associated with national identity. Among topics examined are carnival bands, *son* music, cabaret rumba, and blackface theater shows. The highly documented volume is enhanced by the inclusion of relevant legislation concerning music, and a listing of sextets in Havana between 1920–45 by barrio.

Muñoz Tábora, Jesús. La cultura garífuna en el contexto musical Afro Caribe. See *HLAS 57:4881.*

4809 Orovio, Helio. Diccionario de la música cubana: biográfico y técnico. 2. ed. corr. y aum. La Habana: Editorial Letras Cubanas, 1992. 516 p.: ill.

Augmented second edition of a highly useful dictionary containing information on, but not limited to, Cuban institutions, instruments, musical forms, musicians, and performance groups.

4810 Ortiz, Fernando. La africanía de la música folkórica de Cuba. Havana: Letras Cubanas, 1993. 363 p.: bibl., ill.

A reprint of this extensive study of Afro-Cuban music examines the musical traditions of the African population in Cuba, including rhythmic and melodic features, instrumentation, and vocal characteristics. It must be studied in conjunction with Ortiz's *Los bailes y el teatro de los negros en el folklore de Cuba* (1993) and *Los instrumentos de la música afrocubana* (1995), both of which have been reprinted. The three works have also been reprinted in Spain (Madrid: Editorial Música Mundana Maqueda, 1997).

4811 Rodríguez, Victoria Eli. Un tesoro aún inexplorado: la capilla de música de Santiago de Cuba. (*Rev. Music. Venez.,* 16:34, mayo/agosto 1997, p. 65–75, bibl.)

Three cities in Cuba have particularly rich musical archives: Havana, Matanzas, and Santiago de Cuba. In Santiago de Cuba, the Museo Ecclesiástico of the Cathedral has the oldest musical sources in the nation. To demonstrate the wealth of materials in the Museo, the author reviews sources detailing the contribution of Pablo Hernández Balaguer and the musical legacy of Esteban Salas (1725–1803), the most important Cuban musician of the 18th century.

4812 Stevenson, Robert. Esteban Salas y Castro, 1725–1803: Cuba's consummate cathedral composer. (*Inter-Am. Music Rev.,* 15:2, Summer/Fall 1996, p. 73–102)

An examination of Salas y Castro through the musicological literature, the early attempts at establishing a *Capilla Musical* in Santiago de Cuba's cathedral, an outline of Salas' musical career, and a catalog of his works and his legacy.

Andean Countries

WALTER AARON CLARK, *Professor of Musicology, University of Kansas*

THE APPEARANCE OF THE NEW EDITION of *Die Musik in Geschichte und Gegenwart* (1994) in most respects fulfills the high expectations surrounding its publication. Entries on Latin American countries and topics are detailed and authoritative (the previous edition virtually ignored Latin America), with leading scholars like Stevenson and Béhague contributing many of the entries. The encyclopedia is divided into two parts: subjects (Sachteil) and biographies (Personenteil). The first part is nearly complete (up to Q); the second will appear in installments thereafter. For entries on Colombia and Peru, see items **4824** and **4830,** respectively. The second edition of the *New Grove Dictionary of Music and Musicians* will be published in 2000. It will be available in both book and electronic formats and retains its distinction as the foremost reference source on music in any language.

Also worthy of mention is the *Latin American Classical Composers: A Biographical Dictionary* (item **4734**). The work is somewhat disappointing in the summary nature of the biographies and works lists, and in the absence of many minor composers. The third edition of the ethnomusicology textbook *Worlds of Music* (1996) retains the excellent chapter on Latin America written by John Schechter, though some might quibble with its emphasis on Ecuador at the expense of any mention of Mexico, Brazil, Cuba, or Argentina. More balanced, but less detailed coverage of Latin America is found in another world-music textbook, *Excursions in World Music,* 2nd ed., by Bruno Nettl *et al.,* 1997.

In general, musicological research on Andean countries, especially Ecuador, remains underdeveloped. This is particularly true of the art-music traditions in those countries. Nevertheless, several recently published dissertations are notable for their high quality, offering a promise of more fine scholarship in the future:

Aileen Martina, "The traditional bambuco in nineteenth and twentieth-century Colombian composition" (Univ. of North Texas, 1994).

Dale J. Bonge, "Samuel Martí (1906–1975), a Mexican ethnomusicologist: his work, theses and contributions (Biography, Archaeology)" (Michigan State Univ., 1996).

Ana María Ochoa, "Plotting musical territories (Bandola, Nueva Cultura, Gustavo Adolfo Renjifo, Colombia, Social Movements)" (Indiana Univ., 1996).

BOLIVIA

4813 Cavour Aramayo, Ernesto. Instrumentos musicales de Bolivia. La Paz: Producciones Cima, 1994. 438 p.: bibl., ill., photos.

Includes photographs, drawings, and descriptions of Bolivian musical instruments of indigenous, African, and creole derivation. Very useful for students and specialists. [C. Magaldi]

4814 Cespedes, Gilka Wara. Huayno, saya, and chuntunqui: Bolivian identity in the music of Los Kjarkas. (*Lat. Am. Music Rev.,* 14:1, 1993, p. 52–101)

Focuses on Los Kjarkas, a pop group ensemble from Cochabamba. Discusses the group's appropriation of native genres and its dual mission of using music as a cultural symbol and as a means of asserting Bolivian identity. Also explores issues of commercialism in "world music." [C. Magaldi]

4815 Gerard-Ardenois, Arnaud and **Marcos Clemente J.** Ayrachis del sur de Bolivia: un primer ensayo. (*in* Reunión Anual de Etnología, 9th, *La Paz?, 1995.* Actas. La Paz: Museo Nacional de Etnografía y Folklore, 1995?; t. 2, p. 107–134, bibl., graphs, ill., music, photos, tables)

Ethnographic study reports on the construction and performance practice of the Ayrichi panpipe from southern Bolivia, focusing on instrument construction, tuning systems, and scales produced by different instruments. Computer analysis aids in the study of the panpipe's sounds. Includes transcriptions and descriptions of dance choreographies. [C. Magaldi]

4816 Gutiérrez Condori, Ramiro. Instrumentos musicales tradicionales en la comunidad artesanal Walata Grande, Bolivia. (*Lat. Am. Music Rev.*, 12:2, 1991, p. 124–159)

Ethnographic study deals with technical aspects of building musical instruments in the community of Walata Grande, describing the tools used by peasant artisans. For an updated version, see *HLAS 57:1083*. [C. Magaldi]

4817 Huseby, Gerardo V.; Irma Ruiz; and Leonardo J. Waisman. Un panorama de la música en Chiquitos. (*in* Las misiones jesuíticas de Chiquitos. Edición y recopilación de Pedro Querejazu. La Paz: Fundación BHN, Línea Editorial; La Papelera, 1995, p. 659–676, photos)

Invaluable report covering 300 years of musical activities in Chiquitos. Documentation attests to the survival of musical tradition of the Jesuits well into the 1850s, and to the coexistence of the missionary repertory with native musical practices and with popular urban dances. Describes the musical repertory maintained in the Chiquitos archive; noteworthy is a substantial number of compositions in the vernacular (*chiquitano*). Also examines how the Jesuit tradition is reflected in contemporary music-making in Chiquitos. [C. Magaldi]

4818 Illari, Bernardo. ¿Existe un repertorio de San Felipe Neri de Sucre? (*Anuario/Sucre*, 1994/95, p. 163–175, appendix, facsim.)

Discusses the collection of music that was located at San Felipe Neri in Sucre. Since most of the manuscripts predate the establishment of San Felipe in 1795 and are not appropriate to the liturgy celebrated there, they were probably not used for performances at that institution.

4819 Illari, Bernardo. Un fondo desconocido de música antigua de Sucre: catálogo comentado. (*Anuario/Sucre*, 1996, p. 377–402)

A carefully annotated catalog of previously overlooked 18th- and 19th-century music manuscripts originally in the possession of Sucre Cathedral and now housed in the Archivo Nacional de Bolivia. This important collection includes villancicos, hymns, sequences, Lamentations, Passions, Masses, and motets, as well as instrumental works and opera excerpts.

4820 Nawrot, Piotr. El barroco musical en las reducciones jesuíticas. (*Anuario/Sucre*, 1994/95, p. 57–71, music)

Excerpt from the author's D.M.A. dissertation "Vespers Music in the Paraguay Reductions" (Catholic Univ. of America, 1993; published in Spanish as "Música de vísperas en las reducciones de Chiquitos, Bolivia, 1691–1767." La Paz: Secretaría Nacional de la Cultura, 1994). Provides invaluable information on 17th- and 18th-century music and performance practices in Jesuit missions in the Provincia del Paraguay and in Chiquitos (today northeastern Bolivia). Includes transcriptions of Juan de Araujo's *Si el amor* and the anonymous *Cánite, pláudite* (for violin and continuo) from Sucre's Cathedral and the Archivo de Chiquitos respectively. [C. Magaldi]

4821 Nawrot, Piotr. Música renacentista y barroca en los archivos de Bolivia. (*Anuario/Sucre*, 1996, p. 361–375)

Sources of Renaissance and baroque music in Bolivia at the Archivo Nacional, Chiquitos, San Ignacio de Moxos, Monasterio de Santa Clara de Cochabamba, Potosí, Curia de la Provincia Boliviana de la Compañía de Jesús (La Paz), La Paz Cathedral, La Recoleta de Sucre, as well as Bolivian manuscripts now held outside the country. For related information, see *HLAS 56:4682* and item **4820**.

Rondón, Víctor. Música jesuita en Chile en los siglos XVII y XVIII: primera aproximación. See item **4867**.

4822 Solomon, Thomas. *Coplas de todos santos* in Cochabamba: language, music, and performance in Bolivian Quechua song dueling. (*J. Am. Folk.*, 107:3, 1994, p. 378–414)

Analyzes a Quechua song duel from Cochabamba dept.; addresses how the performers create and recreate their own agendas and expectations through improvised *coplas* during the event. [C. Magaldi]

4823 Stobart, Henry. Flourishing horns and enchanted tubers: music and potatoes in highland Bolivia. (*Br. J. Ethnomusicol.*, 3, 1994, p. 35–48)

Discusses the relationship between

musical performance and potato cultivation in a rural Andean community of the Northern Potosí people. The potato is viewed as a symbolic object central to the structuring of musical expression. [C. Magaldi]

COLOMBIA

4824 Béhague, Gerard. Kolumbien. (*in* Die Musik in Geschichte und Gegenwart. Kassel: Bärenreiter, 1996, Sachteil 5, columns 465–482)

Exemplary treatment of folk music organized by geographic region followed by a chronological discussion of Colombian art music. Includes some musical examples.

4825 Chavarriaga Montoya, Lyndon Alberto. Cultura musical campesina caldense. Manizales, Colombia: Editorial Rodrigo, 1994? 54 p.: bibl., ill., 1 map (folded), photos, tables.

Brief but systematic study of the folk music of Caldas, Colombia. The *corrido*, *ranchera*, *vals*, and *pasillo* are especially popular (*paseo*, *merengue*, *joropo*, and *bambuco* less so), and this study traces their character and diffusion, performers, and concert venues. Does not include musical examples.

4826 Ochoa, Ana María. Counterpoints of time and space in el *Concierto de los Colores.* (*J. Lat. Am. Cult. Stud.*, 6:1, June 1997, p. 51–63)

Postmodern analysis of the 1994 premiere of Colombian composer Juan Rodríguez's *Concierto de los Colores*, a work for a monophonic choir of 200 children accompanied by symphonic wind band. The muddled prose tends to obscure any useful information.

4827 Valverde, Umberto and **Rafael Quintero.** Abran paso: historia de las orquestas femeninas de Cali. Fotos especiales de Fernell Franco. Cali, Colombia: Centro Editorial, Univ. del Valle, 1995. 137 p.: bibl., ill., photos.

A strictly journalistic account of all-female bands in Cali, Colombia, with an emphasis on contemporary groups and soloists. Amply illustrated with photographs that reveal the youth-oriented character of this phe-nomenon, which nonetheless has its roots in Havana of the 1930s.

ECUADOR

Costales, Piedad Peñaherrera de and **Alfredo Costales Samaniego.** Lo indígena y lo negro. See *HLAS 57:5021.*

Puga, Miguel A. La gente ilustre de Quito. See item **2633.**

4828 Stevenson, Robert. Atahuallpa's realm: the quest for musical identity in Ecuador. (*in* Music in performance and society: essays in honor of Roland Jackson. Edited by Malcolm Cole and John Koegel. Warren, Mich.: Harmonie Park Press, 1997, p. 425–436)

Magisterial summary of music in Ecuador from the prehispanic period to modern times. Though disrupted periodically by political upheaval and poverty, the musical life of Ecuador has flourished through the centuries, particularly in Quito, and has been enriched by autochthonous rural traditions as well as by immigrant European musicians.

PERU

Música, danzas y máscaras en los Andes. See *HLAS 57:1209.*

4829 Rodríguez Amado, Gustavo. Música y danzas en las fiestas del Perú. 1. ed. en español. Arequipa, Peru: Univ. Nacional de San Agustín; Univ. Católica de Santa María, 1995. 253 p.: bibl., ill., photos.

Discusses the various types of festival music and dance in Peru. Descriptions are organized by region or festival, including, for example, the altiplano, Cusco, Holy Week, and Christmas. Discusses music and dance of the coastal regions and Afro-Peruvian genres. Does not contain musical examples.

4830 Romero, Raúl R. Peru. (*in* Die Musik in Geschichte und Gegenwart. Kassel: Bärenreiter, 1997, Sachteil 7, columns 1547–5898)

Explores precolumbian music and instruments, regional folklore, and art music of Peru from colonial to modern times.

4831 Varallanos, José. El harahui y el yaraví: dos canciones poplares peruanas. Lima: Editorial Argos, 1989. 184 p.: bibl.

A diminutive study of the history,

texts, and music of two popular Peruvian songs, the *harahui* and *yaraví*. They evolved during the colonial epoch and remain a vital expression of the Andean mestizo spirit. Discusses outstanding examples, composers, and performers. Includes footnotes and bibliography, but no musical examples or index.

4832 Vásquez Rodríguez, Chalena and **Abilio Vergara Figueroa.** Ranulfo, el hombre. Lima: Centro de Desarrollo Agropecuario, 1990. 319 p.: bibl., ill. (some col.).

Deals with the life and music of the poet and composer Ranulfo Fuentes Rojas (b. 1940). Begins with a biographical portrait, followed by an intelligent discussion of his poetic and musical language. Ample citation of texts and music. Contains color plates of art works by Edilberto Jiménez Quispe.

VENEZUELA

4833 Arvelo Ramos, Alberto. El cuatro. Fotografía de J.J. Castro. Textos especialmente preparados para esta edición por Luis Felipe Ramón y Rivera. Caracas: J.J. Castro Fotografía Infrarroja, 1992. 163 p.: bibl., ill., photos.

The texts by Arvelo and Ramón y Rivera form a lyric reflection on the history and cultural significance of the cuatro (a four-string guitar) in Venezuela. Numerous photographs by Castro vividly illuminate the text. Includes some interview material with cuatro performers.

4834 Bendahán, Daniel. Siete músicos venezolanos. Caracas: Depto. de Relaciones Públicas de Lagoven, 1990. 90 p.: bibl., ill., index. (Cuadernos Lagoven)

Brief biographies of seven celebrated Venezuelan musicians: Pedro Elías Gutiéres, Andrés Delgado Pardo, Angel Mottola, Joaquín Silva Díaz, Vicente Martucci, Primo Casale, and Pedro Antonio Ríos Reyna. Though aimed at a nonspecialist readership, the work concludes with a bibliography and index.

4835 Bracho Reyes, José Gregorio. El culto a San Benito en el sur del lago de Maracaibo: una propuesta de acercamiento desde la antropología de la música. (*Bol. Am.*, 37:47, 1997, p. 45–75, bibl.)

Attacks the "old guard" (Isabel Aretz and Luis Felipe Ramón y Rivera) of Venezuelan musicology for its "eurocentric" preoccupation with the "musical product" and its indifference to cultural context. Includes 19 p. of historical background on the region under consideration, followed by the author's methodology for studying the music.

4836 Quintana Moreno, Hugo José. Estudio preliminar sobre el primer Método de Guitarra publicado en Venezuela, 184? (*Anu. Estud. Boliv.*, 3:3, 1994, p. 277–314, bibl.)

Study of an anonymous guitar method that apparently dates from the 1840s and is now in the collections of the National Library of Venezuela. A lengthy (26 p.) history of the guitar precedes discussion of the method itself, whose three parts span notation, technique, and original compositions.

4837 Ramón y Rivera, Luis Felipe. Memorias de un andino. Caracas: Fundación Internacional de Etnomusicología y Folklore (FINIDEF), 1992. 130 p.: ill.

Autobiography of the eminent Venezuelan musicologist Ramón y Rivera (1913–93). Born to a family of modest means in San Cristóbal, he became an accomplished musician and leading authority on the folk music of Venezuela. The narrative, however, goes only to 1945, focusing on his early career as a performing musician and educator.

4838 Ramón y Rivera, Luis Felipe and **Isabel Aretz.** La música típica del Táchira: el folklore tachirense. Caracas: Biblioteca de Autores y Temas Tachirenses, 1996. 147 p.: bibl., ill., index. (Biblioteca de Autores y Temas Tachirenses; 129)

Opens with a general essay on folk music in Táchira, Venezuela. Dance music occupies the greatest portion of the book; songs of various types are treated next. Both are illustrated with transcriptions. Ends with a discussion of the instruments, mostly chordophones, used in the music. Useful index of musical examples.

Southern Cone and Brazil

CRISTINA MAGALDI, *Assistant Professor of Music, Towson University*

THE RECENT PUBLICATIONS ON MUSIC emanating from the Southern Cone countries are notable in terms of their large quantity and high quality. Especially noteworthy is the proliferation of periodical literature, a consequence of the growing number of graduate programs in music at Latin American universities. While seminal articles continue to spring from the well-established *Revista Musical Chilena* (Univ. del Chile, Santiago, Chile) and *Revista Brasileira de Música* (Univ. Federal do Rio de Janeiro, Brazil), important contributions by young scholars have appeared in new music periodicals such as the *Revista Música* (Univ. de São Paulo, Brazil) (items **4884** and **4909**). In addition, nonmusical periodicals continue to include significant studies on music (items **4815** and **4820**). Highlighting a growing interest in the music of the Southern Cone countries, an unprecedented number of English-language articles have appeared in North American music periodicals other than the two specialized journals *Latin American Music Review* and *Inter-American Music Review* (items **4861, 4903, 4904,** and **4906**). Additionally, edited works on general topics regarding Latin America regularly have included chapters on music (items **4817** and **4908**).

Colonial music has received special attention, particularly studies of 17th- and 18th-century musical practices in Jesuit missions. Excellent works in this area include Gerardo Huseby *et al.* (item **4817**), Piotr Nawrot (items **4820** and **4821**), and Victor Rondón (item **4867**). A significant contribution to Brazilian colonial music is Régis Duprat's scholarly edition of the music holdings of the Museu da Inconfidência in Ouro Preto, Minas Gerais (item **4896**). Other welcome additions to the literature are Rogério Budasz's article on José de Anchieta's poetry (item **4878**), Duprat's study on André da Silva Gomes (item **4886**), Maurício Dottori's essay on chapel masters in Rio de Janeiro (item **4884**), and Jaime Diniz's study on chapel masters in Bahia (item **4883**).

Nineteenth-century music has received less attention. Nonetheless, two outstanding works are Mônica Vermes' study on Alberto Nepomuceno's piano music (item **4909**) and Esteban Buch's book on patriotic music in Argentina (item **4841**). Biographical and analytical studies continue to dominate this area, with significant contributions by Iván Barrientos Garrido (item **4863**), Samuel Claro Valdes (item **4864**), and José Maria Neves (item **4897**). Despite the 1996 commemorations of Carlos Gomes' death (1836–96), no significant new research on the Brazilian composer has appeared. However, Marcus Góes' biographical/analytical study (item **4890**) and the second edition of Gomes' biography by Juvenal Fernandes (item **4888**) provide valuable data.

Studies on 20th-century art music are scarce. Ilza Nogueira's analysis of Ernst Widmer's work provides fresh insight to the composer's music (item **4898**). Also, the revised edition of Mariz's history of Brazilian art music includes information on the younger generation of Brazilian composers (item **4893**).

Studies on popular music form a large segment of the recent publications from Argentina and Brazil. A particularly outstanding publication is Ricardo Risetti's book on bolero in Buenos Aires (item **4857**). While rock in Argentina has received significant attention in studies by Pablo Vila (item **4860**) and Eduardo Berti (item **4840**), Argentine authors continue to emphasize the history of tango. Among the noteworthy works in this area are Simon Collier *et al.* (item **4845**) and Hector Luis Goyena (item **4849**).

The invaluable survey (in English) of Brazilian popular music by Chris McGowan and Ricardo Pessanha (item **4894**) is now available in a revised and expanded edition (item **4895**). Stephen Thomas Walden's dissertation "Brasilidade: Brazilian Rock Nacional in the Context of National Cultural Identity" (Univ. of Georgia, Athens, 1996) is a welcome addition to companion works in Portuguese on Brazilian rock by Goli Guerreiro (item **4891**) and Arthur Dapieve (item **4882**). Also welcome is Hermano Vianna's major new analysis of the urban samba (item **4910**).

Traditional music continues to receive a great deal of attention. Significant studies have appeared in *Reunión Anual de Etnología, Actas* (Bolivia) (item **4815**). Also worth mentioning is the 1994 issue of *Revista Musical Chilena*, which pays homage to the composer/singer Margot Loyola by including a reprint of her interviews with Magdalena Vicuña.

ARGENTINA

4839 Alvarez, Eliseo and **Daniela Basso.** Carlos Gardel: biografía autorizada. Buenos Aires: De la Urraca, 1995. 191 p.: bibl., ill.

Describes Gardel's activities outside Buenos Aires and the changes to his image as he became an international figure; includes information on Gardel's life in Montevideo, Bogotá, New York, and Paris.

4840 Berti, Eduardo. Rockología: documentos de los '80. Buenos Aires: Beas Ediciones, 1994. 173 p.: bibl., ill.

Describes the development of rock in Argentina's political context and compares it with rock in the international scene; includes interviews with Argentine rock leaders such as Fito Páez, Charly García, the group Soda Stereo, as well as with emerging rock groups.

4841 Buch, Esteban. O juremos con gloria morir: historia de una épica de estado. Buenos Aires: Editorial Sudamericana, 1994. 211 p.: bibl.

Traces the path of the Argentine national anthem and describes the emergence of Argentine national identity through patriotic music. Based on extensive investigation of primary sources, this exemplary study contributes significantly to the available research on 19th-century musical manifestations in Argentina.

4842 Buenos Aires, ciudad tango. Proyecto editorial y dirección de Manrique Zago. Fotografía de Jorge Salatino. Coordinación editorial de Amanda Varela. Coordinación literaria de Oscar del Priore. Colaboración especiales de León Benarós *et al.* Producción gráfica de Héctor Fossati y Silvia Varela. Buenos Aires: M. Zago Ediciones, 1986. 122 p.: ill. (some col.).

Richly illustrated coffee-table book includes a short history of the tango. Of limited use to specialists.

4843 Cantares tradicionales del Tucumán: antología. Recopilación de Juan Alfonso Carrizo. Prólogo de Alberto Rouges. Ilustración de Guillermo Buitrago. 2. ed. San Salvador de Jujuy, Argentina: Univ. Nacional de Jujuy, 1994. 213 p.: bibl., ill., index, music. (Col. Arte-ciencia: Serie Jujuy en el passado)

This reprint of the 1934 publication compiles traditional lyrics, including romances, coplas, and glosas, and transcriptions of melodies collected by the author in the region of Tucumán. For original publication information, see *HLAS 5:1592.*

4844 Carretero, Andrés M. Tango: testigo social. Buenos Aires: Librería General de Tomás Pardo, 1995. 141 p.: bibl.

Briefly describes the social and ethnic conditions that made possible the emergence of tango in Buenos Aires in the 19th and early-20th century.

4845 Collier, Simon et al. Tango!: the dance, the song, the story. Special photography by Ken Haas. New York: Thames and Hudson, 1995. 208 p.: bibl., ill. (some col.), index.

Exquisite publication, written by respected scholars and artist, combines scholarly research with a pleasant writing style. Covers tango's history from early-19th century to the present, addressing tango's spread into Europe and North America and its "golden age" in Buenos Aires from the 1920s-50s; also discusses topics such as tango and "machismo," and the tango revival in film, theater, and literature. Includes an extended bibliography and discography. Richly illustrated with facsimiles, reproductions of drawings, paintings, and photographs. For review by Pablo Vila, see *Lat. Am. Music Rev.*, Vol. 18, No. 1, 1997, p. 113–123.

Cosmelli Ibáñez, José Luis. Historia de la cultura argentina. See item **2865.**

4846 Ferrer, Horacio Arturo. The golden age of tango: an illustrated compendium of its history. English version by Alejandro Tiscornia. Buenos Aires: Manrique Zago, 1996. 215 p.: ill. (some col.).

Published by the Argentine Dept. of Culture and the National Academy of Tango, this beautifully produced coffee-table book is an abridged version of the author's *El libro del tango* (see *HLAS 46:7032*). Written in English to serve as a gift from Argentine authorities to foreign visitors, the work is richly illustrated and covers over 100 years of tango history. Lacking a bibliography and source citations, it is of limited use to specialists.

4847 Galasso, Norberto. Atahualpa Yupanqui: el canto de la patria profunda. Buenos Aires?: Ediciones del Pensamiento Nacional, 1992. 218 p.: bibl. (Col. Los Malditos)

Biographical study addresses Yupanqui's fight for popular causes, his life in exile, his performances of Argentine traditional songs, his use of folk material in compositions, and the political content of his lyrics.

4848 García, Miguel A. Indicios, sociabilización y *performance* en las danzas nocturnas de los wici del Chaco argentina. (*Lat. Am. Music Rev.*, 17:1, 1996, p. 21–41)

Deals with the indigenous *wici* group in the Chaco region; attempts to reconstruct an extinct musical performance through written reports and old recordings, and to compare it with present practices.

4849 Goyena, Hector Luis. El tango en la escena dramática de Buenos Aires durante la década del veinte. (*Lat. Am. Music Rev.*, 15:1, 1994, p. 93–109)

Explores two modalities of tangos presented in Buenos Aires theaters in the 1920s. Tangos included in sainetes and creole zarzuelas were performed by instrumental groups very different from the *orquestas típicas*. Tangos included in *teatros de cabaret* retained the instrumentation in vogue in contemporary *orquestas*, including the *bandoneon*.

4850 Huet, Héctor. Carlos Gardel: el detalle que faltaba. Buenos Aires: Corregidor, 1995. 126 p.: bibl., ill.

Provides a useful list of Gardel's songs and recordings organized by genre, and a list of musicians who performed with him. Includes an invaluable comparison between the trajectory of Gardel's career and those of Agustín Magaldi and Ignacio Corsini.

4851 Longoni, Matias and **Daniel Vecchiarelli.** El Polaco: la vida de Roberto Goyeneche. Buenos Aires: Atuel, 1996. 319 p.: bibl., ill. (Col. Los Argentinos)

This biography of tango singer Goyeneche (1925–94) is based on interviews with fellow musicians and friends. Useful for those interested in the singer's life and in tango in general.

4852 López Ruiz, Oscar. Piazzolla loco loco loco: 25 años de laburo y jodas conviviendo con un genio. Buenos Aires: Ediciones de la Urraca, 1994. 285 p.: ill.

A member of Quinteto Nuevo Tango, the author reports on his personal experiences with Astor Piazzolla, with whom he toured extensively beginning in 1961. Based solely on the author's recollections, the book includes no bibliographical references.

4853 Ostuni, Ricardo A. Repatriación de Gardel. Prólogo de Horacio Ferrer. Epílogo de Hipólito Paz. Buenos Aires: Ediciones Club de Tango, 1995. 316 p.: bibl., ill.

Claiming that the image of Gardel is a major component of Argentine identity, the author attempts to shed light on the mysteries surrounding the singer's life.

4854 Pérez Bugallo, Rubén. Catálogo ilustrado de instrumentos musicales argentinos. Buenos Aires: Ediciones del Sol,

1993. 163 p.: bibl., ill., photos. (Biblioteca de cultura popular; 19)

Brief study describes traditional instruments of indigenous and creole derivation; includes drawings, pictures, and photographs.

4855 Pérez Bugallo, Rubén. Pillantun, estudios de etno-organología patagónica y pampeana. Buenos Aires: Búsqueda de Ayllu, 1993. 187 p.: bibl., ill. (Col. Arte y comunicación)

Organology of traditional instruments from the Pampas and Patagonia; includes descriptions of musical instruments by 18th- and 19th-century European travelers.

4856 Pujol, Sergio Alejandro. Discépolo: una biografía argentina. Buenos Aires: Emecé Editores, 1996. 385 p.: bibl., ill., index.

Biographical study describes the life of tango composer Enrique Santos Discépolo (1901–51) in the sociopolitical context of early-20th-century Argentina. Also offers invaluable information on the lives of musicians who contributed to the national and international fame of tango.

4857 Risetti, Ricardo. De corazón a corazón: memorias del bolero en la Argentina. Buenos Aires: Corregidor, 1996. 335 p.: bibl., ill.

Offers an excellent overview of the history of Argentine popular music from the 1940s- 50s. Traces the emergence and development of bolero in Argentina, compares it with the genre in Mexico and Cuba, and indicates parallels between the history of the bolero and that of the tango. Also includes biographies of prominent Argentine bolero singers, short surveys on Latin American artists who performed in Buenos Aires, and a lengthy discography.

Rondón, Víctor. Música jesuita en Chile en los siglos XVII y XVIII: primera aproximación. See item **4867.**

Savigliano, Marta E. Tango and the political economy of passion. See *HLAS 57:1066.*

4858 Scarabino, Guillermo. Alberto Ginastera: técnicas y estilo, 1935–1950. Buenos Aires: Pontificia Univ. Católica Musicales, Facultad de Artes y Ciencias Musicales, Instituto de Investigación Musicológica Carlos Vega, 1996. 144 p.: music. (Cuaderno de estudio; 2)

This revised version of the author's master's thesis (Eastman School of Music, 1967) is an analytical study of Ginastera's style in the period 1935–54. Focuses on the composer's use of tonality, melody, harmonic, rhythm, and form. The purported aim of the work is to fill the gap left by studies that focus solely on "biographical and historical details."

4859 Valenti Ferro, Enzo. 100 años de música en Buenos Aires: de 1890 a nuestros días. Buenos Aires: Ediciones de Arte Gaglianoil, 1992. 556 p.: bibl., ill., index.

Reports on musicians, orchestras, operas, and ballet companies that performed in Buenos Aires from 1900-present. Lists premieres, but lacks citations, and is therefore of limited use as a reference work.

4860 Vila, Pablo. Argentina's *rock nacional:* the struggle for meaning. (*Lat. Am. Music Rev.,* 10:1, 1989, p. 1–28)

Describes *rock nacional* as a musical fusion with ties throughout its development to rock and roll, blues, punk, jazz, classical, and folk music; discusses the ideology and identity of *rock nacional* in the Argentinian context. See also *HLAS 50:4386* and *HLAS 50:4387.*

4861 Vila, Pablo. Tango to folk: hegemony construction and popular identities in Argentina. (*Stud. Lat. Am. Pop. Cult.,* 10, 1991, p. 107–139)

Focuses on the popularity of traditional musical genres in Argentina since the 1950s. In the first half of the century tango represented an identity constructed from experiences of European migration and middle-class upward mobility. After the 1950s, however, a new emphasis on traditional music resulted from urban migration and working-class upward mobility.

CHILE

4862 Aracena, Beth K. Viewing the ethnomusicological past: Jesuit influences on Araucanian music in colonial Chile. (*Lat. Am. Music Rev.,* 18:1, 1997, p. 1–29)

A survey of travelers' and Jesuits' reports that attempts to reconstruct Araucanian and Jesuit music practices in colonial Chile. The author points out the relevance of historical and ethnomusicological studies that "put together elements of a musical culture... previously silenced by colonial attitudes."

4863 Barrientos Garrido, Iván. Luigi Stefano Giarda: una luz en la historia de la música chilena. (*Rev. Music. Chil.*, 50:186, julio/dic. 1996, p. 40–72, bibl., photos)

Focuses on the life of the Italian cellist and composer Luigi Stefano Giarda (1868–1952). The author makes wide use of primary sources dealing with Giarda's career in Europe, first as a cellist in the Teatro La Scala in Milan and later as a concert virtuoso. Also explores his activities in Chile where he established residency in 1905. Offers an excellent picture of Chilean concert life in the first half of the 20th century.

4864 Claro Valdés, Samuel. Rosita Renard, pianista chilena: su primera estada en los Estados Unidos, 1916–1920. (*Nassarre/Zaragoza*, 12:2, 1996, p. 69–83, bibl.)

Published posthumously, this short article is an excerpt of the author's biography of Rosita Renard. Surveys the international career of the Chilean virtuoso pianist through newspaper reviews of her concerts in the US, including brief references to repertory. Also compares Renard's international success with that of Teresa Carreño (Caracas, 1853-New York, 1917).

4865 González, Juan Pablo. Evocación, modernización y reivindicación del folclore en la música popular chilena: el papel de la performance. (*Rev. Music. Chil.*, 50:185, 1996, p. 25–37)

Compares the uses of folklore in three types of Chilean popular music: música típica (1927), neofolclore (1963), and nueva canción (1965). Examines the role of performance in the construction of meaning and function in Chilean nueva canción.

Pérez Bugallo, Rubén. Pillantun, estudios de etno-organología patagónica y pampeana. See item **4855**.

4866 Pérez de Arce, José. Polifonía en fiestas rituales de Chile central. (*Rev. Music. Chil.*, 50:185, 1996, p. 38–59)

Based on ethnographic research done in 1992–95, the article investigates the role of music in the "fiestas de chinos." Focuses on the instrumental sounds, particularly in the polyphony resulting from the superimposition of instrumental groups of flutes and drums.

4867 Rondón, Víctor. Música jesuita en Chile en los siglos XVII y XVIII: primera aproximación. (*Rev. Music. Chil.*, 51:188, julio/dic. 1997, p. 7–39, bibl.)

Lengthy survey of sources revealing musical activities of Jesuits in 17th- and 18th-century Chile. Compares music-making in missions in Paraguay, Argentina, and Bolivia, unveiling similarities in missionary practices. Well-documented study, includes one transcription. For transcriptions of 19 missionary songs see the author's *19 canciones misionales en mapudúngún contenidas en el "Chilidúgú [1777] del misionero jesuita en la Araucanía Bernardo de Havestadt"* (Santiago, Univ. de Chile, Revista Musical Chilena, FONDART, 1997).

4868 Schindler, Helmut. Una canción mapuche de Carlos Painenao para el Año Nuevo. (*Anthropos/Freiburg*, 92:1/3, 1997, p. 129–138, bibl., photos)

Ethnographic study includes a short introduction that describes the available literature on the history of Mapuche song; provides a translation of the lyrics of a Mapuche song for the New Year with a brief description of the text.

PARAGUAY

Rondón, Víctor. Música jesuita en Chile en los siglos XVII y XVIII: primera aproximación. See item **4867**.

URUGUAY

4869 Ayestarán, Lauro. Las músicas primitivas en el Uruguay. Montevideo: Arca, 1994. 148 p.: bibl., ill.

Brief study compiles reports from European travelers describing indigenous and African musical practices in 17th–19th-century Uruguay.

4870 Erro, Eduardo. Alfredo Zitarrosa: su historia *casi* oficial. Montevideo: Arca, 1996. 239 p.: discography, ill.

This biographical study relies on sources from the musician's personal archive, reports of friends, and press releases; discusses Zitarrosa's participation in the Canto Popular Uruguayo, his life in exile, and his return to Uruguay. Includes a list of works and discography.

4871 Pinto, Guilherme de Alencar. Razones locas: el paso de Eduardo Mateo por la música uruguaya. Montevideo: Metro; Ediciones de la Pluma, 1994. 332 p.: bibl., ill., indexes.

Compiles interviews with fellow musicians and friends of Eduardo Mateo (1940–90), and at the same time summarizes 30 years of popular music in Uruguay, from Candombe-beat in the 1960s to jazz and rock in the 1980s. Exemplary study, includes reference section, discography, bibliography, and a very useful index.

4872 Trigo, Abril. Candombe and the reterritorialization of culture. (*Callaloo/ Baltimore*, 16:3, 1993, p. 716–728)

Focuses on Candombe, Uruguay's African-based rhythm and dance music rooted in carnival festivities. Discusses Candombe function as a symbol of national identity and as a means of resistance against the military dictatorship in the 1970s.

4873 Trigo, Abril. Words and silences in Uruguayan *canto popular*. (*Stud. Lat. Am. Pop. Cult.*, 10, 1991, p. 215–238)

Studies the Uruguayan *canto popular*, a movement that emerged in reaction to the 1973 military coup embracing aspects of tango, Candombe, jazz, and rock. Analyzes three examples of *canto popular*.

BRAZIL

4874 Alves, Luciane. Raul Seixas e o sonho da sociedade alternativa. São Paulo: Martin Claret, 1993. 191 p.: bibl., ill. + 1 poster (col.).

Brief biography of the Brazilian rock star of the 1970s-80s places his music within the Brazilian sociopolitical context. Includes transcriptions of interviews and song lyrics.

4875 Andrade, Mário de. Introdução à estética musical. Estabelecimento do texto, introdução e notas de Flávia Camargo Toni. São Paulo: Editora HUCITEC, 1995. 170 p.: bibl., ill. (Mariodeandradiando; 4)

Compilation of Andrade's writings on musical esthetics. Part of a series of publications edited by Flávia Camargo Toni aimed at making Andrade's collection available for study (for other works edited by Toni, see *HLAS 52:5119* and *HLAS 54:5167*). This book undoubtedly adds to our understanding of Andrade's ideas, revealing his reliance on works by German musicologists such as Hugo Riemann and E. Hanslick.

4876 Araújo, Mozart de. Rapsódia brasileira: textos reunidos de um militante do nacionalismo musical. Introdução por Jairo Severiano. Seleção, prefácio e notas por Vicente Salles. Fortaleza, Brazil: Univ. Estadual do Ceará, 1994. 223 p.: bibl., ill.

Compilation of Mozart de Araújo's (1904–88) writings on music. Although the eminent Brazilian musicologist published only one book during his lifetime (an important study on the 18th-century modinha, see *HLAS 32:5033*), he left seminal articles scattered in several music periodicals, books, and liner notes in recordings. Compiled by musicologist Vicente Salles, Araujo's complete works are finally available for study in this most welcome publication. Includes a chronology of Araújo's life.

4877 Browning, Barbara. Samba: resistance in motion. Bloomington: Indiana Univ. Press, 1995. 214 p.: bibl., ill., index. (Arts and politics of the everyday)

Relying on literary theories, the author discusses the role of dance and the body in Afro-Brazilian secular and sacred practices. Ethnographic study addresses samba academies, candomblé, capoeira, and carnival dances.

4878 Budasz, Rogério. A presença do Cancioneiro Ibérico na Lírica de José de Anchieta: um enfoque musicológico. (*Lat. Am. Music Rev.*, 17:1, 1996, p. 42–77)

Focuses on Anchieta's poetry, analyzing the introduction of religious subjects into secular texts. Well-documented study, this is a significant contribution to the understanding of Anchieta's versions *a lo divino* and its relation to popular Iberian *cancioneros*.

4879 Cabral, Sérgio. Elisete Cardoso, uma vida. 2a ed. Rio de Janeiro: Lumiar Editora, 1993? 404 p.: ill.

This biography of Elisete Cardoso (1920–90) is a compilation of interviews with members of Cardoso's family, friends, and musicians who worked with the singer. Through the interviews, the author also highlights musical life in Rio de Janeiro from the golden age of radio shows to the emergence and dominance of TV in the 1960s. Includes discography but lacks bibliography.

4880 Cezimbra, Márcia; Tessy Callado; and Tárik de Souza. Tons sobre Tom. Rio de Janeiro: Editora Revan, 1995? 197 p.: bibl., ill., index.

Compilation of interviews with family, friends, and musicians who worked with Tom Jobim, as well as interviews with the composer himself. Addresses Jobim's life and works, his early career in Rio de Janeiro, and the popularity of bossa nova. Includes a list of Jobim's compositions organized alphabetically by title but lacking dates.

Chasteen, John Charles. The prehistory of Samba: carnival dancing in Rio de Janeiro, 1840–1917. See item **3251.**

4881 Corrêa, Sérgio Nepomuceno Alvim.
Lorenzo Fernandez: catálogo geral. Rio de Janeiro: RIOARTE/Instituto Municipal de Arte e Cultura, 1992. 80 p.: bibl., ill.

Biographical study and catalog of works by Fernández (1897–1948). Continuation of a series published by FUNARTE (see *HLAS 28:3048a* for Corrêa's catalog of Alberto Nepomuceno's work).

4882 Dapieve, Arthur. Brock: o rock brasileiro dos anos 80. Rio de Janeiro, Brazil: Editora 34, 1995. 215 p.: ill., index. (Col. Ouvido musical)

Historical account of the rise of rock in Brazilian cities in the 1980s. Provides useful information on the most popular Brazilian rock groups such as Barão Vermelho, Paralemas do Sucesso, Titãs, RPM, and Legião Urbana. Includes a selected discography and index, but no bibliography.

4883 Diniz, Jaime C. Mestres de Capela da Misericórdia da Bahia, 1647–1810. Salvador, Brazil: Centro Editorial e Didático da UFBA, 1993. 150 p.: bibl., ill.

Published posthumously and edited by Manuel Veiga, this work adds to a long list of musicological writings by Diniz that focus on three centuries of musical activities in the states of Pernambuco and Bahia (see *HLAS 50:4398, HLAS 36:4538, HLAS 32:5046, HLAS 34:5033,* and *HLAS 46:7059*). Based on primary sources, this study includes biographies of 20 chapel masters active at the Santa Casa da Misericórdia in Bahia, and provides excerpts of documents. (See review in *Inter-Am. Music Rev.,* Vol. 13, No. 2, 1993, p. 159–160.)

4884 Dottori, Maurício. Achegas para a história dos mestres de capela do Rio de Janeiro colonial. (*Rev. Músic./São Paulo,* 7:1/2, maio/nov. 1996, p. 37–46)

Reveals important information concerning the appointment of chapel masters in colonial Rio de Janeiro. Brief study based on documentation retrieved from the Chancelarias da Ordem de Cristo currently held in the Torre do Tombo in Lisbon.

4885 Dreyfus, Dominique. Vida do viajante: a saga de Luiz Gonzaga. Prefácio de Gilberto Gil. São Paulo: Editora 34, 1996. 349 p.: ill. (Col. Ouvido musical)

Biographical study based on the author's personal contact with composer and performer Luiz Gonzaga (1912–89), as well as on testimonies from the composer himself. While focusing on Gonzaga's career, the book also offers valuable information for the student interested in the history of Brazilian popular music (see also item **4905**). Includes no bibliography or index, but provides an excellent discography and a list of Gonzaga's compositions.

4886 Duprat, Régis. Música na Sé de São Paulo colonial. São Paulo: Paulus; Sociedade Brasileira de Musicologia, 1995. 231 p.: bibl., ill., map.

Updates his previous publications on the history of music in São Paulo cathedral (see *HLAS 32:2820, HLAS 32:5048,* and *HLAS 40:9045*) and the biographies of chapel masters. Most welcome is the inclusion of a thematic catalog of the music manuscripts of André da Silva Gomes (1752–1844). Very useful for specialists.

4887 Echeverria, Regina. Furacão Elis. Nova ed., rev. e ampliada. São Paulo: Editora Globo, 1994. 253 p.: ill.

Detailed biography of the famous singer. Includes a useful discography (by Maria Luiza Kfouri), but no bibliography. Makes only a few corrections to the 1985 edition.

4888 Fernandes, Juvenal. Do sonho à conquista: Carlos Gomes. Prefácio de Francisco Mignone. 2. ed. São Paulo: Imprensa Oficial do Estado, 1994? 253 p., 32 p. of plates: bibl., ill. (some col.), index.

Ten years after its first edition, Fernandes' biography of Carlos Gomes continues to be one of the most complete sources on the composer's life and work. Includes reproductions of documents and other primary sources, as well as photos and facsimiles. Unfortunately, this second edition was neither expanded nor updated.

4889 Galinsky, Philip. Co-option, cultural resistance, and Afro-Brazilian identity: a history of the *pagode* samba movement in Rio de Janeiro. (*Lat. Am. Music Rev.*, 17:2, 1996, p. 120–149)

Overview of the musical movement *pagode*. Compares the older *pagode,* derived from a tradition bound in the Afro-Brazilian cultural lineage, with the new *pagode,* modeled on an internationalized Black Brazilian esthetic; emphasizes the earlier movement as a means of reinforcing Afro-Brazilian identity and cultural resistance.

4890 Góes, Marcus. Carlos Gomes: a força indômita. Belém, Brazil: Secretaria de Estado de Cultura (SECULT), 1996. 462 p.: bibl., ill. (some col.), index.

Excellent biographical study of Carlos Gomes based on primary and secondary sources. Includes facsimiles of 19th-century printed materials describing the reception given to Gomes' operas in Europe. Analyzes his most famous operas to show their "Brazilian character."

4891 Guerreiro, Almerinda. Retratos de uma tribo urbana: rock brasileiro. Salvador, Brazil: Centro Editorial e Didático da UFBA, 1994. 154 p.: bibl.

Based on the author's master's thesis in anthropology at the Univ. de São Paulo, the work relates the development of rock in Brazil to contemporary international pop music. Particularly relevant are chapter two, dealing with social and cultural analysis of rock in Brazil, and chapter three, a historical account of rock in Brazil from the 1960s to the early 1990s.

4892 Lenharo, Alcir. Cantores do rádio: a trajetória de Nora Ney e Jorge Goulart e o meio artístico de seu tempo. Campinas, Brazil: Editora da Unicamp, 1995. 306 p.: bibl., ill. (Col. Viagens da voz)

Examines the career of two famous Brazilian singers, placing their accomplishments within the social, political, and cultural context of the golden years of Brazilian radio, the 1940s-50s. An exemplary study highlighting an important, but overlooked, stage in the development of Brazilian popular music.

4893 Mariz, Vasco. História da música no Brasil. 4a. ed., rev. e ampliada. Rio de Janeiro: Civilização Brasileira, 1994. 468 p.: bibl., index.

This revised and expanded edition (see *HLAS 50:4409* for review of 1983 edition) provides updated biographies and lists the most recent compositions by contemporary composers. The newly written last chapter introduces the works of the young generation of Brazilian art music composers.

4894 McGowan, Chris and **Ricardo Pessanha.** The Brazilian sound: samba, bossa nova, and the popular music of Brazil. New York: Billboard Books, 1991. 215 p.: bibl., ill., index, map.

Perhaps the best survey in English of Brazilian popular music. Covers from 19th-century genres such as *modinhas* up to 1980s Brazilian rock. Includes invaluable descriptions of styles, musical instruments, and short biographical data on composers and singers. Reviewed in *Notes,* Vol. 50, No. 1, 1993, p. 200–201. Useful introduction to Brazilian music. For comment on updated edition, see item **4895.**

4895 McGowan, Chris and **Ricardo Pessanha.** The Brazilian sound: samba, bossa nova, and the popular music of Brazil. New ed. Philadelphia: Temple University Press, 1998. 248 p.: bibl., ill., index.

Revised and updated edition of the 1991 publication (see item **4894**). Welcome additions are an expanded coverage of *axé* music and other musical styles from Bahia, and information on recent Brazilian artists and musical styles.

4896 Música do Brasil colonial. Organização de Régis Duprat. Coordinação técnica de Carlos Alberto Baltazar. São Paulo: Editora da Univ. de São Paulo; Ouro Preto, Brazil: Museu da Inconfidência, 1994. 1 score (142 p.).

Following publication of a thematic catalog of the music manuscript holdings in the Museu da Inconfidência (see *HLAS 54:5166*), the authors continue their remarkable study of the school of Minas Gerais. Preceding Carlos Alberto Baltazar's and Conceição Rezende's transcriptions is a short introduction by Duprat describing three works by José Joaquim Emerico Lobo de Mesquita and one by Marcos Coelho Neto. Provides modern music editions.

4897 Neves, José Maria. Brasílio Itiberê: vida e obra. Curitiba, Brazil: Fundação Cultural de Curitiba; Farol do Saber, 1996. 124 p.: bibl., ill., index.

Biographical and analytical study draws largely on secondary sources. Addresses works other than *A Sertaneja*, the piano piece for which Itiberê is most widely known. Includes a useful catalog of works.

4898 Nogueira, Ilza Maria Costa. Ernst Widmer: perfil estilístico. Salvador, Brazil: Univ. Federal da Bahia, Escola de Música, 1997. 198 p.: bibl., ill.

Much awaited study on Swiss-Brazilian composer Ernst Widmer (1927–90). The first part surveys the composer's compositional output, while five studies in the second part analyze the musical form, orchestration, and motivic elaboration of selected pieces. Includes musical examples, list of works, discography, and bibliography.

4899 Perrone, Conceição *et al.* A música de Jamary de Oliveira: estudos analíticos. Porto Alegre: Setor Gráfico do CPG-Música/UFRGS, 1994. 148 p.: bibl., music.

Festschrift commemorating the Bahian composer's 50th birthday, includes three analytical studies by Oliveira himself, analytical studies of the composer's output by Brazilian scholars, and a biographical article by Conceição Perrone.

4900 Pinto, Tiago de Oliveira. Musical difference, competition, and conflict: the Maracatu groups in the Pernambuco carnival, Brazil. (*Lat. Am. Music Rev.,* 17:2, 1996, p. 97–119)

Describes carnival in the state of Pernambuco emphasizing the Maracatu groups. Includes information on the organization of carnival competitions, their musical repertory, and the religious affiliations of the parading groups. Also explores the role of state regulations during carnival time.

4901 Pinto, Tiago de Oliveira. Pernambuco carnival and its formal organizations: music as expression of hierarchies of power in Brazil. (*Yearb. Tradit. Music,* 26, 1994, p. 20–37)

Overview of the different categories of musical associations in the Pernambuco carnival, including their traditions and musical repertories.

4902 Reily, Suzel Ana. Macunaíma's music: national identity and ethnomusicological research in Brazil. (*in* Ethnicity, identity, and music: the musical construction of place. Edited by Martin Stokes. Oxford, England; Providence, RI: Berg, 1994, p. 71–96)

Summary of Mário de Andrade's views on nationalism and music as expressed in his 1928 novel, *Macunaíma*. One of the few studies in English to explore Andrade's ideas about music, this essay is also valuable for situating his views within the context of Brazilian ethnomusicology.

4903 Reily, Suzel Ana. *Música sertaneja* and migrant identity: the stylistic development of a Brazilian genre. (*Pop. Music,* 11:3, 1992, p. 337–358)

Based on four years of research conducted in São Bernardo do Campo, São Paulo, this excellent study outlines the stylistic development of *música sertaneja* (country music). Provides fresh insight into the role of the music in articulating the social identity of migrants from Brazil's southeastern regions now living in the industrial center of greater São Paulo.

4904 Reily, Suzel Ana. Tom Jobim and the bossa nova era. (*Pop. Music,* 15:1, 1996, p. 1–16)

Traces the development of bossa nova and briefly discusses its role in reformulating the language of Brazilian popular music. Focuses on the life and works of Antonio Carlos Jobim.

Santos, Jorge Fernando dos. BH em cena: teatro, televisão, ópera e dança na Belo Horizonte centenária. See item **4546.**

4905 Tinhorão, José Ramos. Pequena história da música popular: da modinha à lambada. 6. ed., rev. e aum. São Paulo: Art Editora, 1991. 294 p.: bibl.

This revised and expanded edition includes a chapter on the history of the lambada. As with other publications by Tinhorão (see *HLAS 54:5176* and *HLAS 54:5177*), this book includes valuable information on the social aspects of Brazilian popular music, particularly during the colonial period. The new edition continues to lack an index and musical examples. See *HLAS 50:4418* for review of 1986 edition.

4906 Treece, David. Guns and roses: bossa nova and Brazil's music of popular protest, 1958–68. (*Pop. Music,* 16:1, 1997, p. 1–29)

Traces the trajectory of Brazilian popular music from bossa nova to protest song, focusing on the role of music in socioeconomic transformations, and on the political and cul-

730 / Handbook of Latin American Studies v. 58

tural upheaval in the decade leading up to 1968. Excellent study that addresses not only songs' lyrics, but also musical structures, instrumental styles, and modes and conditions of performances.

Trevisan, João Silvério. Ana em Veneza. See item **4386.**

4907 Ulhôa, Martha. Musical style, migration, and urbanization: some considerations on Brazilian *música sertaneja* [country music]. (*Stud. Lat. Am. Pop. Cult.*, 12, 1993, p. 75–94)

Provides a historical account of the changes in musical style and lyric content of *música sertaneja*, from the rurally oriented *modas-de-viola* of the 1930s to the urban *baladas* of the 1980s. Discusses the dissemination of *música sertaneja* through records, radio, and television. Selected discography included.

4908 Ulhôa, Martha. Tupi or not Tupi MPB: popular music and identity in Brazil. (*in* The Brazilian puzzle: culture and the borderlands of the western world. Edited by David J. Hess. New York: Columbia Univ. Press, 1995, p. 159–179)

Borrowing the concept of *anthropophagy* from modernist Oswald de Andrade, the author briefly surveys Brazilian popular music leading up to MPB (música popular brasileira) to argue that Brazilian musicians ritualistically capture other people's musical traits and incorporate them into their own music.

4909 Vermes, Mônica. A produção para piano a duas mãos de Alberto Nepomuceno: características gerais e proposta de um novo catálogo. (*Rev. Músic./São Paulo*, 7:1/2, maio/nov. 1996, p. 59–91)

Excellent and well-documented study of Nepomuceno's piano works. Questions the accepted view of Nepomuceno as a "nationalistic" composer, pointing out that only a small and atypical portion of his work has been analyzed. In the majority of his pieces for piano, nationalistic elements do not prevail. Includes a catalog of Nepomuceno's piano works for two hands, short descriptions of selected pieces, and a useful discography.

4910 Vianna, Hermano. O mistério do samba. Rio de Janeiro: J. Zahar Editor; Editora UFRJ, 1995. 193 p.: bibl. (Col. Antropologia social)

Exemplary study, based on author's dissertation in anthropology (Univ. Federal do Rio de Janeiro, 1994), focuses on social aspects of the urban samba, offering an account of the genre's early popularity. The dissemination of samba as a national product of Brazil in the 1930s-40s not only reflected the interests of a specific social and ethnic group, but was also the result of a set of complex interactions among the lower classes, intellectuals, politicians, art music composers, and foreign visitors.

PHILOSOPHY: LATIN AMERICAN THOUGHT

JUAN CARLOS TORCHIA ESTRADA, *Independent Consultant, Hispanic Division, Library of Congress, Washington, DC*
CLARA ALICIA JALIF DE BERTRANOU, *Professor, Facultad de Filosofía y Letras, Universidad Nacional de Cuyo, Mendoza, Argentina*

EL TÍTULO DE ESTA SECCIÓN, que reúne las nociones de 'Filosofía' y 'Pensamiento', refleja el contenido actual, pero a la vez representa la etapa final de ciertos cambios por los que ese contenido fue pasando a través del tiempo. Como cualquier otra sección del *Handbook,* la presente ha reflejado la marcha de las disciplinas que cubre y, naturalmente, la del propio *Handbook.* Veamos, brevemente, cómo eso ha ocurrido.

Regular o irregularmente, en América Latina siempre hubo alguna forma de ejercicio de la filosofía, desde los comienzos coloniales. Muy temprano en el proceso de colonización, los frailes de las diversas órdenes religiosas crearon en sus conventos los estudios que necesitaban sus novicios, que incluían la enseñanza de la filosofía dentro de la carrera de Artes. Las primeras universidades fueron también relativamente tempranas en el tiempo, y reforzaron con su prestigio el tipo de estudios propios de la época, trasplantados de la Península y de contenido escolástico. En el siglo XVIII, la escolástica colonial sigue vigente, pero afectada por el avance de la filosofía y la física modernas. El siglo XIX, etapa de lucha por la independencia, de guerras civiles y de la modernización de los países hispanoamericanos, no fue muy favorable a la estabilidad de las instituciones, y consiguientemente a la filosofía, en tanto ésta es transmisible por la enseñanza. Desde fines del siglo XIX y comienzos del XX, la práctica de la filosofía se incrementó notablemente en Iberoamérica, lo que se hace muy visible a partir de la década del 40 del siglo XX. Muchas veces se ha señalado cómo, a partir de esa década, aumentó el número de personas vinculadas a la filosofía, el de las cátedras dedicadas a ella, el de las publicaciones sobre esos temas, el de las revistas filosóficas, así como la vinculación entre los actores de ese desarrollo. Francisco Romero, que llamó a ese proceso de ampliación e incrementación etapa de la "normalidad filosófica" (en el sentido de actividad regular y no excepcional), se hubiera asombrado, de vivir en el año 2000, de la magnitud, en calidad, pero sobre todo en extensión, que esa supuesta normalidad ha adquirido.

Pero ese aumento en la atención dedicada a la filosofía, con el consiguiente refuerzo de sus recursos institucionales, es sólo uno de tres fenómenos que confluyen al mismo tiempo. El segundo fue el interés por hacer la historia de la filosofía de cada país, o de los principales por lo menos. Fue natural que, cuando la dedicación a la filosofía en América Latina alcanzó en aquel momento la madurez señalada, sus representantes se interesaran por los antecedentes históricos de su actividad, es decir, por la tradición histórica a la que pertenecían. Pioneras fueron, en ese sentido, las obras de Arturo Ardao para Uruguay, de Samuel Ramos para México, de Cruz Costa para Brasil, pero pronto a ellas les siguieron otras.

El tercer fenómeno consistió en que, precisamente en esa época, cuando quienes practican la filosofía así vigorizada se sienten continuadores de la gran tradición filosófica occidental, aparece un movimiento que pone el énfasis en lo propio y regional y habla, por aquel entonces, de la necesidad de destacar y profundizar la "filosofía americana"—se entiende, "latinoamericana." Los artículos con que Leopoldo Zea da origen a esa tendencia son precisamente de los primeros años de la década de 1940. Por parte de quienes estaban habituados a profesar la filosofía dentro de la tradición europea como fuente y madre del pensamiento filosófico hubo, en el primer momento, sorpresa y desconfianza con respecto a esa propuesta de innovación, lo que dio lugar a diferencias polémicas. De todas maneras, a partir de estos comienzos el movimiento "americanista" o "latinoamericanista" crecerá considerablemente, tendrá entre sus ingredientes principales la extensa y reconocida obra de Leopoldo Zea y la de muchos otros, dará lugar más tarde a la filosofía de la liberación, y continuará en la actualidad bajo diferentes formas, casi siempre tomando franca distancia de la filosofía "académica" o "profesional." Esta última, la que se ocupa de problemas filosóficos sin vinculación (intencionada, al menos) con asuntos de la región, también seguirá su marcha, con homóloga indiferencia por las posiciones "latinoamericanistas." Salvo excepciones, terminará por no haber examen de contraste entre las dos orientaciones, que seguirán su camino ignorándose mutuamente. Aceptamos que nuestro resumen es simple hasta lo simplista, pero no podemos desbordar nuestro muy específico asunto con mayores desarrollos, especialmente cuando se trata de un tema que reclama una serena y cuidadosa historia.

Ahora bien, este nuevo movimiento "americanista," que es el tercer factor confluyente en la década de 1940, influyó también en la historiografía, en la mirada histórica sobre el pasado filosófico latinoamericano. Desde la perspectiva de esta corriente se observó entonces que, si se utilizaba como medida de apreciación para crear esa historia solamente la presencia de la filosofía profesional o sistemática, quedaban huecos en la línea que se perseguía. Sin mayor atención hacia la escolástica colonial, se advertía que en el siglo XIX era poco lo que se encontraba de filosofía en sentido estricto, excepto hacia el final del siglo, cuando adviene el positivismo. Esto significaba la siguiente alternativa: o aceptar que en ciertos períodos no había habido filosofía en América Latina, o cambiar el criterio de la búsqueda y rastrear expresiones que, aunque no fueran plenamente *filosóficas* (como aquellas a las que la historia de la filosofía europea, especialmente en el caso de los grandes sistemas, nos tenía acostumbrados), fueran sin embargo expresiones de ideas o ideologías, bañadas en más o en menos por contenidos filosóficos, tan imprecisos como pudieran ser, pero de todas maneras válidos para comprender qué se había pensado en América Latina sobre el ordenamiento de la sociedad, la política, la educación y la realidad histórica en general. Este segundo enfoque prevaleció, y para satisfacerlo se usó, por caminos que no es posible indicar aquí, la noción de *pensamiento*, más amplia que la de *filosofía*, y que la comprende como si fuera su género próximo. En esto tuvo mucho que ver, sin ser el único, José Gaos, el filósofo español "transterrado" a México. La fórmula a la que se arribó fue: no nos faltó filosofía; lo que ocurre es que 'filosofía' se definió de un modo que excluye buena parte de la que se hizo en Hispano-América (ambos lados del Atlántico), que tiene caracteres menos precisos, pero igualmente válidos. Con ello se establecieron dos conceptos complementarios: el de historia de la filosofía, más restringido, y el de historia del "pensamiento" o historia de las ideas, más amplio y más flexible, y que en su mayor generalidad abarca la historia de la filosofía propiamente dicha. Con independencia del juicio general que pueda emitirse sobre el movimiento latino americanista, esta consecuencia historiográfica suya es un legado positivo, porque todo un escenario de ideas, ideologías y corrientes que interpretaron la realidad latinoamericana y trataron de actuar sobre ella fue descubierto y explorado, lo que no hubiera ocurrido con una mirada filosófica más restringida. Martí, Sarmiento, Bolívar, Montalvo o Rodó no podían quedar fuera de una historia del *pensamiento* latinoamericano, aunque ninguno de ellos fue filósofo propiamente dicho. Se dirá que esos temas ya estaban cubiertos dentro de la historia del ensayo hispanoamericano, pero aun así hay que reconocer que se trataba, en los casos mencionados, de ensayo de ideas, que no tenía por qué quedar exclusivamente en manos del historiador de la literatura.[1]

El desarrollo interno de la sección de filosofía en relación con el par 'historia de la filosofía' / 'historia de las ideas', fue el que a continuación se resume. Para comenzar, es interesante señalar que la Sección de Filosofía (que así se llamaba entonces), se incorpora al *Handbook* precisamente en el año 1940, simbólico de la incrementación filosófica de la que antes se habló. Y, por supuesto, la fecha no fue casual. Los materiales correspondientes al período 1939–49 (etapa atendida por Risieri Frondizi) fueron casi exclusivamente filosóficos en sentido estricto. Desde 1953 (cuando la Sección pasa a manos de Aníbal Sánchez Reulet), se crea una nueva subsección de *Historia de las Ideas*, cuya incorporación estaba indicando ya el reconocimiento de una realidad. Se incluyeron a partir de ahí dos tipos de materiales: 1) los de naturaleza propiamente filosófica, agrupados según disciplinas (Gnoseología, Metafísica, Filosofía Social y Política, etc.), incluyendo también artículos o libros de autores latinoamericanos sobre temas de historia de la filosofía europea (Filosofía Antigua y Medieval, Filosofía Moderna, etc.); y 2) materiales relacionados con América Latina, fueran sobre la filosofía desarrollada en la región o sobre su historia de las ideas, en el sentido antes señalado. Este arreglo estuvo vigente entre el número 20 (1953) y el 44 (1982).

El número inmediato posterior, el 46 (1984), refleja un cambio considerable, resultado de una decisión de política editorial, según la cual se suprimieron las entradas de artículos o libros propiamente filosóficos (es decir, escritos sobre filósofos y corrientes europeas y sobre la temática propia de las disciplinas filosóficas) y se mantuvieron solamente los que se referían a la historia de la filosofía y de las ideas en general en América Latina. O en otras palabras, se mantuvo lo que aludía a América Latina, pero no lo que era filosofía sin referencia a la región. O, todavía, con ejemplos: ya no se incluían artículos o libros de autores latinoamericanos sobre Aristóteles o sobre el existencialismo, por ejemplo, ni tampoco la producción filosófica original de esos autores en, digamos, metafísica o filosofía de la historia; pero sí se recogía un libro o artículo sobre Antonio Caso o Alejandro Korn, porque trataba de filosofía latinoamericana, y un examen del liberalismo en México, del marxismo de Mariátegui o del nacionalismo brasileño, porque era historia más amplia de las ideas.

A pesar de esta reducción de temas o asuntos, la cantidad de entradas se duplicó en el número 56 (1999) en relación con el 46 (1984). Y previamente se había duplicado entre el número 20 (1953) y el 44 (1982). Dada la limitación de espacio del volumen impreso del *Handbook* (la versión *online* no tiene ese problema), esta Sección nunca pudo incluir todo el material aprovechable, dejando siempre, para el próximo número, un rezago o *backlog*, que sólo podrá eliminarse con una más intensa selectividad. En cualquier caso, lo dicho anteriormente explica el contenido actual de la Sección,[2] y ofrece un rápido recorrido de su historia en relación con la marcha del pensamiento latinoamericano en los últimos 60 años.

Sin que se noten grandes cambios en la producción, a continuación se dan indicaciones sobre aspectos destacados del material reunido, según las correspondientes subsecciones.

GENERAL

Son siempre abundantes los trabajos de índole general, entendiendo por tales los que por su asunto, abarcan la región en su conjunto. En su mayoría no son monográficos o de investigación detallada, sino más bien interpretaciones generales, tomas de posición, expresiones de pensamiento político (en un sentido amplio), lo cual no les quita interés para nuestro propósito de perfilar el panorama de las ideas y las ideologías en Latinoamerica.

Las reuniones, de temática muy amplia y numerosas ponencias, contienen siempre mucho material de naturaleza general, y por su misma profusión no es posible, en el breve espacio de una anotación, dar idea aproximada del contenido que tienen. En lo que toca al presente volumen, cabe recordar aquí por lo menos dos de esas reuniones, que se concretaron en sendas publicaciones con los títulos de: *A 500 años: América Latina se descubre a sí misma* (item **4911**) y *Pensar desde América: vigencia y desafíos actuales* (item **5025**). Casi todas las reuniones que se organizan en el ámbito de la filosofía o de las humanidades, en general, tienen títulos muy abarcadores, a veces más llamativos que verdaderamente representativos del contenido, y consiguientemente el material es muy diverso. Se debo indicar, con independencia de lo que este número y otros de este *Handbook* puedan incluir, que ya casi no es posible seguir la pista de las reuniones que se realizan, porque, a las que se convocan para toda la región (en el Continente o en otras partes del mundo), se suman las de ámbito más restringido, y como no siempre se publican actas, muchas no dejan huella por escrito. En cuanto a otras publicaciones similares a los que estamos considerando, es de particular interés para conocer la situación de la enseñanza y la investigación filosófica en América Latina el volumen colectivo, resultado de una reunión auspiciada por la Unesco y la Universidad de Lima (item **4962**), y tiene buen valor monográfico *Newton en América* (item **4947**), producto de un simposio en el Tercer Congreso Latinoamericano de Historia de las Ciencias y la Tecnología.

Entre las contribuciones más destacadas de autores individuales recordamos: Arturo Ardao, *Romania y América Latina,* (item **4918**), que se sitúa en la serie de investigaciones del autor sobre el nombre de América Latina, pero que va mucho más allá, especialmente en lo que se refiere a los orígenes culturales de Latinoamérica. (En *HLAS 56:1000,* se ha dado noticia también de *España en el origen del nombre América Latina,* de la misma serie.) En *El laberinto de los tres minotauros,* José M. Briceño Guerrero reúne sus escritos en torno a una especie de filosofía de la historia de América Latina (item **4927**); partes de este libro recibieron anteriormente anotación en *HLAS 44:7504* y *HLAS 46:7507.* La obra de Mariano Picón Salas, *Europa-América: preguntas a la esfinge* (item **5028**), es re-edición póstuma de escritos de este valioso ensayista que se habían publicado originalmente hace medio siglo. Hallamos asimismo varios artículos de Leopodo Zea (items **5059, 5062** y **5063**) y un valioso ensayo de Octavio Paz (item **5024**). Parcialmente es trabajo de interpretación general la obra *Introducción al pensamiento filosófico latinoamericano* (item **4991**).

La visión de América Latina desde el ángulo de la modernidad y la postmo-dernidad se mantiene presente. De un autor que es referencia obligada en el tema de la modernidad como problema para Latinoamérica, José Joaquín Brunner, recor-damos *Cartografías de la modernidad* (item **4928**). El tema se encuentra también, aunque sin ser el único, en *El complejo de Próspero: ensayos sobre cultura, moder-nidad y modernización en América Latina* (item **4944**). El mismo asunto es visto desde la perspectiva de la cultura en Néstor García Canclini, *Hybrid Cultures: Strategies for Entering and Leaving Modernity* (item **4976**). Brunner y García Can-clini se cuentan entre los colaboradores del volumen colectivo, *The Postmodernism Debate in Latin America*, obra en la cual algunos autores vinculan el asunto a la situación de la izquierda latinoamericana (item **5030**). En el *HLAS 56* habíamos señalado, dentro de este mismo tema, sendos libros de H.C.F. Mansilla (ver *HLAS 56:4876*) y de Aníbal Quijano (ver *HLAS 56:4895*).

Sigue vigente la cuestión de la conquista de América, con los encontrados juicios que son tradicionales en el asunto. Ernesto Garzón Valdés presenta una só-lida pieza de buen razonamiento sobre el tema (item **4978**), y dos *scholars* (Jacques Lafaye y James Lockhart) hacen una contribución conjunta muy iluminadora en el caso de los orígenes del México moderno (item **4997**). Otro artículo analítico y equilibrado es el de Celina Lértora Mendoza (item **4998**). Se reitera el tema de Fray Bartolomé de Las Casas, y consiguientemente el de Ginés de Sepúlveda: se reco-gen dos volúmenes resultado de sendos congresos: 1) sobre Las Casas, Congreso Teológico Internacional (item **4949**); y 2) sobre Sepúlveda, Congreso Internacional sobre el Quinto Centenario del Nacimiento del Dr. Juan Ginés de Sepúlveda (item **4946**). Debe agregarse el libro de Mauricio Beuchot sobre Las Casas y los derechos humanos (item **4922**), y una visión desde el punto de vista actual: el volumen *El pensamiento lascasiano en la conciencia de América y Europa* (item **5053**). Entre otros buenos materiales sobre estos temas se encuentra un resumen no prescindible de polémica, por parte de José Juan Arrom (item **4919**), y un artículo muy atendible sobre Sepúlveda, de Francisco Castilla Urbano (item **4935**), autor también de un excelente libro sobre Vitoria.

En lo que respecta a la filosofía latinoamericana, es más frecuente encon-trar, y así ha sido también el caso en ediciones anteriores de este *Handbook*, el tratamiento del problema de su existencia, naturaleza y finalidad, que estudios historiográficos sobre ella en su conjunto. No faltan voces que señalan que no tiene sentido cuestionar la existencia de lo que ya ha adquirido tan visible volumen; pero naturalmente, la cuestión de la interpretación va más allá de esa comprobación de hecho. En cuanto a los materiales de esta entrega, una visión general de las distin-tas posiciones ante el problema de la filosofía latinoamericana puede hallarse en el libro de E.V. Demenchonok, *Filosofía latinoamericana: problemas y tendencias* (item **4953**), y en el artículo de José Rubén Sanabria, "En torno a la filosofía latino americana" (item **5044**). Participa parcialmente de esta temática, por los autores que trata, pero va más allá de ella, como puede apreciarse por la anotación corre-spondiente, la obra de Ofelia Schutte, *Cultural Identity and Social Liberation in Latin American Thought* (item **5048**). También se relacionan con este problema, aunque son más amplios, el libro de Arturo A. Roig, *Rostro y filosofía de América Latina* (item **5039**), y el de Raúl Fornet Betancourt, *Hacia una filosofía intercul-tural latinoamericana* (item **4970**). El artículo de este último autor, "Balance y per-spectivas del estudio del pensamiento latinoamericano en América y Europa" (item **4969**) se refiere a la metodología del estudio del pensamiento latinoamericano, y ofrece una oportuna comparación con la Europa del Este el trabajo de Eugeniusz

Górski, "Filosofía y sociedad en el pensamiento europeo oriental y latinoamericano" (item **4981**). Se encontrarán también buenos trabajos expositivos sobre otros temas: la Ilustración en el pensamiento latinoamericano (item **5042**); el exilio filosófico español en México (item **5046**); y la filosofía latinoamericana del siglo XX (item **5054**). Por último, debe señalarse el valioso libro del P. Ismael Quiles, *Filosofía latinoamericana en los siglos XVI a XVIII* (item **5032**). Sobre este tema de la filosofía latinoamericana se puede ver también *HLAS 56*, Introducción, p. 714.

La filosofía de la liberación no tiene, por lo menos con ese nombre, una presencia tan frecuente como en el pasado, en parte porque sus cultores, dentro del mismo espíritu, han derivado a otros temas afines. En esta entrega puede encontrarse una discusión de Enrique Dussel con Karl-Otto Apel (item **4957**); un análisis de la filosofía de la liberación desde el punto de vista del marxismo (item **4982**); y un número especial de la revista *Islas*, de Cuba, dedicada al tema (item **4993**). En cuanto a la teología de la liberación, señalamos un libro que se ocupa de su presente y su futuro (item **5052**); un artículo de Enrique Dussel que reseña 30 años de esta corriente (item **4959**); dos que se refieren a su naturaleza (items **4996** y **5026**); además de comparaciones con la cuestión de la modernidad (item **5002**), con la doctrina social de la Iglesia (item **4913**) y con la religiosidad popular (item **4930**). Las menciones a estas tendencias se pueden ver en el *HLAS 56* en la Introducción, p. 714.

Sobre la izquierda y el marxismo en América Latina, hay referencias al futuro de la izquierda (item **4925**) y del socialismo (item **5027**); a su giro hacia la democratización (item **4964**); a la crisis del marxismo (item **4940**); a su historia en la región (item **4968**); y a la relación entre marxismo y antimarxismo, desde el punto de vista del marxismo-leninismo clásico (item **4983**). Finalmente, se encontrará un análisis del trotskismo en América Latina (item **4942**). Lugar aparte merece el libro de conjunto, *La utopía desarmada*, de Jorge Castañeda (item **4934**).

Lo que no es frecuente, dos libros se dedican a Ortega y Gasset: uno muy amplio sobre su presencia en Hispanoamérica, de Tzvi Medin (item **5012**), y otro más enfocado a encontrar en Ortega la paternidad del "pensamiento de la liberación," este último de José Luis Gómez-Martínez (item **4979**).

MÉXICO
La obra de mayor envergadura desde el punto de vista histórico es el estudio sobre Vasco de Quiroga por José Aparecido Gómes Moreira (item **5078**). Se encuentran asimismo oportunas antologías, a saber: una reunión de escritos del positivista mexicano José Torres Orozco (item **5098**); una antología del liberalismo mexicano (item **5067**) y otra de Narciso Bassols (item **5070**); y una sólida obra sobre Eguiara y Eguren, con estudios críticos y reproducción de textos (item **5086**). Se ha re-editado el clásico libro de Miguel León Portilla sobre la filosofía náhuatl (item **5088**). Por último, entre los trabajos dedicados a autores individuales señalamos sendos libros sobre Luis Villoro (item **5075**) y Alejandro Rossi (item **5073**).

AMÉRICA CENTRAL Y PANAMA
Se destacan dos contribuciones: un libro sobre un aspecto del positivismo hispanoamericano poco frecuente, a saber, las ideas positivistas y liberales de Ramón Rosa, en Honduras (item **5107**); y un artículo que ejercita una mirada crítica y de conjunto sobre la historia del pensamiento en Panamá, por un autor que se ha ocupado de esa historia a menudo y desde un enfoque marxista (item **5109**).

CARIBE INSULAR

Como en el *HLAS 56*, en este caso es visible la cantidad proporcionalmente amplia de entradas correspondientes a la República Dominicana, situación que no se había dado en años anteriores. Debe recordarse en primer lugar uno de los mejores libros escritos sobre Pedro Henríquez Ureña, el de Enrique Zuleta Alvarez (item **5145**). Se encontrarán también una antología de Juan Bosch (item **5114**) y un artículo sobre la evolución de su pensamiento político (item **5129**). Entre otros materiales, se incluyen obras sobre dos figuras del siglo XIX, Pedro Francisco Bonó (item **5123**) y Juan Pablo Duarte (item **5132**), y otra del XVIII, Antonio Sánchez Valverde (item **5139**).

En cuanto al número de entradas en términos absolutos, y como es habitual en esta subsección, la mayor cantidad corresponde a Cuba. Casi todos son artículos. Reciben especial atención la Revolución cubana (items **5111** y **5127**) y el marxismo en Cuba, (items **5131, 5133, 5136** y **5141**). También se encuentran varios artículos sobre José Martí.Y por último, otros temas de historia de las ideas en Cuba están presentes, destacándose un libro sobre el liberalismo cubano (item **5118**).

Sobre Eugenio María de Hostos se hallarán varios artículos, pero se destaca un libro sobre el tema de la mujer (item **5137**). Estos materiales se suman a los señalados en *HLAS 56*, p. 715-716. Hay, último, tres artículos sobre el pensamiento político de los países del Caribe actualmente de habla inglesa (items **5125, 5126** y **5142**).

VENEZUELA

En el caso de este país, la obra más saliente e importante es el excelente libro de Angel J. Cappelletti, *Positivismo y evolucionismo en Venezuela* (item **5147**). Véanse también otras dos buenas contribuciones de Elena Plaza (items **5153** y **5154**), una autora ya reconocida por sus estudios sobre el positivismo venezolano.

COLOMBIA

Como contribuciones a la historia de las ideas en este país deben resaltarse trabajos sobre autores como: José Félix Restrepo (item **5156**), José Manuel Rivas Sacconi (item **5158**), Francisco José de Caldas (item **5161**) y las relaciones entre Eugenio María de Hostos y José M. Samper (item **5160**).

ECUADOR

Se destaca aquí una obra antológica con textos de autores positivistas: *Pensamiento positivista ecuatoriano* (item **5168**) y otra sobre Fray Vicente Solano: *Configuración y presencia del pensamiento conservador ecuatoriano* (item **5169**).

PERÚ

Como en otras oportunidades, en la presente entrega aproximadamente la mitad de las entradas correspondientes a Perú se refieren a José Carlos Mariátegui, y debe observarse que las contribuciones, en esta oportunidad, son libros y no artículos. Hay una edición de sus *Escritos juveniles* (item **5181**); volúmenes colectivos sobre él (items **5171** y **5182**); y de autores individuales. Entre estos último corresponde mencionar: el de César Germaná (item **5177**); un libro originariamente publicado en ruso (item **5178**); y el de Estuardo Núñez sobre la experiencia europea de Mariátegui (item **5184**). Algunos se refieren especialmente al socialismo o al marxismo del autor peruano y a su significado para la izquierda latinoamericana (items **5175,**

5179, 5189 y **5192**) en tanto otro establece relaciones entre su obra y el movimiento "Sendero Luminoso" (item **5193**). Sobre Perú en general deben recordarse dos enfoques de cierta amplitud temática: sobre la modernidad peruana (item **5172**) y sobre el siglo XX en el país (item **5186**).

BOLIVIA Y PARAGUAY
Siempre escasa la producción sobre estos países, hallamos, en el caso de Bolivia, un breve estudio sobre el trotskismo y una justa apreciación de la valiosa obra del filósofo e historiógrafo Guillermo Francovich (item **5195**). En cuanto al segundo país, es de interés una visión de la cultura paraguaya actual (item **5235**).

CHILE
Se encuentran artículos sobre autores importantes: Alberto Edwards (item **5198**), Mario Góngora (item **5199**), el abate Juan Ignacio Molina (item **5201**) y el filósofo católico Clarence Finlayson (item **5197**). La influencia del positivismo en la interpretación de la historia de Chile es otro de los buenos trabajos recogidos (item **5202**).

BRASIL
Como ocurrió en el *HLAS 56* (véase p. 717), se hallarán en esta entrega varias contribuciones sobre Gilberto Freyre. Entre ellas, un libro que examina etapas dentro de la obra de Freyre (item **5207**), y artículos que de una manera u otra comparan a este autor con otros, especialmente con Buarque de Holanda (items **5215** y **5228**).

Hay varios trabajos sobre la filosofía en Brasil, un tema bien cultivado en el país. Algunos son enfoques generales, como por ejemplo, los surgidos de los Encuentros Nacionales de Profesores e Investigadores de Filosofía, en los que sobresalen autores como Antonio Paim, Ubiratan Macedo y Ricardo Vélez Rodríguez (items **5216** y **5217**). Otros están dedicados a figuras particulares: José Guilherme Merquior (item **5219**); Newton da Costa (item **5222**); Miguel Reale (item **5225**); Caio Prado Junior (item **5226**); Lima Vaz (item **5230**). Otros se dedican al pensamiento político en Brasil, analizando doctrinas (items **5221, 5227** y **5229** (marxismo), y **5205** (populismo)), o autores en particular: Tancredo Neves (item **5211**); Oliveira Viana (item **5212**); Alberto Torres (item **5223**); Joaquim Pimenta (item **5234**). Por último, indicamos tres entradas dedicadas al pensamiento católico: items **5204, 5208** y **5209**.

ARGENTINA
Encontramos tres relevantes contribuciones a la historia de la filosofía en la Argentina: de Angel J. Cappelletti, *Filosofía argentina del siglo XX* (item **5250**); de Francisco Leocata, *Las ideas filosóficas en Argentina* (item **5269**); y la extensa obra de Alberto Caturelli sobre la filosofía en Córdoba (item **5251**). Otros títulos dignos de destacarse y que entran en el campo de las ideas más allá de lo restringidamente filosófico son: una buena antología de escritos del historiador José Luis Romero (item **5279**); un volumen colectivo sobre el pensamiento político argentino contemporáneo (item **5246**); una revisión de la llamada generación del 80 (item **5247**); un libro muy logrado sobre el reformismo social de grupos liberales de fines del siglo XIX y comienzos del XX (item **5292**); una amplia visión histórica de la antítesis de origen sarmientino, "civilización y barbarie" (item **5285**); y dos obras sobre temas correlacionados: una interpretación de la generación de 1837, desde un ángulo que

refleja opiniones políticas actuales (item **5267**) y un examen de Esteban Echeverría, miembro prominente de esa generación (item **5264**).Otros asuntos que se reiteran son: la interpretación del peronismo (orígenes (item **5248**); ideología (item **5257** y **5261**)); el nacionalismo (en general (item **5288**); sobre Julio Irazusta (item **5256** y **5282**)); y la teoría del discurso aplicada a casos concretos de ideología en la Argentina (Revolución de Mayo (item **5262**); discurso republicano (item **5275**); léxico iluminista (item **5290**)).

URUGUAY

Aunque poco numerosos, los materiales recogidos sobre Uruguay incluyen algunas publicaciones importantes: la re-edición, con apéndices ampliados, del clásico libro de Arturo Ardao, *Filosofía pre-universitaria en el Uruguay* (item **5236**), además de un volumen de homenaje a este autor (item **5242**); una importante obra sobre el darwinismo en Uruguay (item **5237**); y un libro ampliamente informativo sobre Rodó (item **5240**).[3]

NOTES:

1 Quizás José Gaos, que en todos los demás respectos era un perfecto filósofo "profesional" o "académico", discípulo cercano de Ortega y Gasset, conocedor a fondo de la historia de la filosofía y traductor de Husserl, Heidegger y tantos más, intentó una operación de salvataje de la "filosofía" latinoamericana y, de paso, de la española, en tanto ambas no respondían, en algunos aspectos, a la fórmula clásica de la historia de la filosofía en otros países europeos. Pero cualquiera haya sido la motivación de Gaos, el resultado ha beneficiado a la visión histórica del pensamiento latinoamericano.

2 Para una descripción puede verse la Introducción al vol. 52, 1993, del *Handbook* (p. 751).

3 Las entradas que llevan las iniciales [CJB] corresponden a Clara Jalif de Bertranou. Las que no tienen ninguna indicación, corresponden a J.C. Torchia Estrada.

GENERAL

4911 A 500 años—: América Latina se descubre a sí misma; actas de las jornadas de reflexión. Recopilación de Susana B. Becerra y Mabel Cardello de Sottano. Mendoza, Argentina: EDIUNC, 1993. 191 p.: bibl. (Serie América Latina; 3)

Materiales correspondientes a un encuentro realizado en 1992 en la Univ. Nacional de Cuyo (Argentina). Las colaboraciones responden a tres "paneles" (Vo. Centenario; Identidad Cultural de América Latina; y Latinoamérica y el Nuevo Orden Mundial). Además se reproducen once ponencias, algunos de cuyos autores son: Adriana Arpini, Alejandra Ciriza, Estela Fernández, Liliana Giorgis y Oscar Zalazar.

4912 Ainsa, Fernando. América Latina: más allá de sus antinomias. (*Cuad. Am.*, 32:2, marzo/abril 1992, p. 33–48)

Se exploran los aspectos através de los cuales América Latina podría superar antiguas antinomias. Esos aspectos seían: la transformación productiva y la democratización política; la restitución de la responsabilidad, la iniciativa y las decisiones al conjunto de la sociedad; la apertura al resto del mundo; y el diálogo intercultural y la convivencia interétnica. [CJB]

4913 América Latina y la doctrina social de la Iglesia: diálogo latinoamericano-alemán. v. 1, Reflexiones metodológicas. Buenos Aires: Ediciones Paulinas, 1992. 1 v.: bibl., indexes.

De sumo interés para esta Sección es la comparación entre la doctrina social de la Iglesia y la teología de la liberación. Un artículo se dedica especialmente a ese tema, pero hay también alusiones a este asunto en otros trabajos.

4914 Amo, Julián. La obra impresa de los intelectuales españoles en América, 1936–1945: facsímil. Madrid: ANABAD; Fundación Españoles en el Mundo; IBERIAB, 1994. 239 p.: maps. (Col. Documentos)

En 1950, Stanford Univ. publicó una bibliografía con el mismo título que la presente obra, preparada en la entonces Hispanic Foundation de la Biblioteca del Congreso de los Estados Unidos. Esa valiosa bibliografía se reproduce ahora en edición facsímil y se le agregan 15 índices y cuatro mapas que naturalmente incrementan su utilidad. Debe considerarse, sin embargo, que el volumen representa solamente la producción de los primeros diez años de los intelectuales españoles referidos, siendo obvio, en muchos de ellos, el aporte posterior a la fecha límite elogida.

4915 Andrés Gallego, José. Recapitulación centenaria II: 1492–1992, América como filosofía. (*Hisp. Sacra,* 44:89, enero/junio 1992, p. 11–20)

El tema del artículo, continuación de otro que apareció en el volumen anterior, es el muy reiterado de los *justos títulos* y la Escuela de Salamanca, pero el presente texto no es repetitivo y presenta algunos materiales de interés para el lector.

4916 Araya Rivas, Fernando. La trilogía cultural del desarrollo en América Latina. (*Rev. Pensam. Centroam.,* 46:210, enero/marzo 1991, p. 26–53, bibl.)

Ambicioso intento que en los límites de un ensayo quiere, entre otras cosas, "formular algunos lineamientos génerales de la teoría de la cultura en perspectiva latino americana;" "presentar los perfiles culturales, socio-económicos y científico-tecnológicos de la región;" "elaborar un conjunto de propuestas tendientes a encauzar la evolución futura de la interacción cultura-desarrollo."

4917 Arciniegas, Germán. América Ladina. Recopilación de Juan Gustavo Cobo Borda. México: Fondo de Cultura Económica, 1993. 432 p.: bibl. (Col. Tierra firme)

Selección de ensayos de asunto americanista del reconocido escritor colombiano. El acertado prólogo de Cobo Borda intenta una imagen total de Arciniegas y su obra, repasando sus primeros libros y sus escritos más recientes. El resultado es "un gran fresco de América Ladina, no Latina, que Arciniegas ha terminado por trazar."

4918 Ardao, Arturo. Romania y América Latina. Montevideo: Biblioteca de Marcha; Univ. de la República Oriental del Uruguay, 1991. 159 p.: bibl., index.

Síntesis histórica del concepto y el nombre de 'Romania', tal como ha sido visto en la Antigüedad, la Edad Media, la época moderna y, epecialmente, en el siglo XIX. Si bien al final se establece el enlace con "la idea y el nombre" de 'América Latina' (siendo por eso el libro complemento de su obra anterior *Génesis de la idea y el nombre de América Latina,* ver *HLAS 44:7501)* no podría dejar de destacarse el valor de la larga aclaración histórica sobre el tema de la Romania en general. Finalmente explica el autor, cómo de lo 'románico' se pasa a la acentuación de lo 'latino', y cómo el latinismo europeo es, si no creador, por lo menos inspirador del concepto de 'América Latina.'

4919 Arrom, José Juan. Las primeras imágenes opuestas y el debate sobre la dignidad del indio. (*in* De palabra y obra en el nuevo mundo. Vol. 1, Imágenes interétnicas. Madrid: Siglo Veintiuno Editores, 1992, p. 63–85)

Buen resumen de la polémica Las Casas/Sepúlveda, con interesantes datos etnográfico-históricos sobre los indios taínos, fuente de la primera imagen del indio. Razonables reflexiones sobre el mestizaje cultural.

4920 Barloewen, Constantin von. Cultural history and modernity in Latin America: technology and culture in the Andes Region. Providence, R.I.: Berghahn, 1995. 218 p.: bibl.

Preconiza la necesidad de tomar en cuenta las culturas tradicionales ante las necesidades de la modernización, especialmente en el orden de lo científico-tecnológico.

4921 Beuchot, Mauricio. La defensa del indígena por Bartolomé de las Casas en su *Historia de las Indias.* (*Mem. Acad. Mex. Hist.,* 34, 1991, p. 83–93)

Buen resumen de las tesis de Las Casas y de su argumentación sobre el tema.

4922 Beuchot, Mauricio. Los fundamentos de los derechos humanos en Bartolomé de las Casas. Proemio de Silvio Zavala.

Barcelona: Anthropos, 1994. 174 p.: bibl. (Biblioteca A; 3. Conciencia)

Artículos previamente publicados, pero precedidos de una introducción general escrita especialmente para el volumen. Casi todos los trabajos están elaborados atendiendo a temas filosóficos, especialmente los siguientes: "Antropología Filosófica y Dignidad Humana en Bartolomé de las Casas;" "La Conciencia Filosófica de la Identidad del Indio Americano en Bartolomé de las Casas;" "Las Casas y las Formas Lógicas de la Argumentación" (un tema poco frecuente); "Fundamentos Filosóficos de la Justicia. Las Casas en Seguimiento de Vitoria y Santo Tomás."

4923 Biagini, Hugo Edgardo. La filosofía latinoamericana a partir de su historia. (*Anu. Estud. Am.*, 49:1, suplemento 1992, p. 3–45, appendix)

En parte es revisión de algunos momentos de la historiografía latinoamericana y en parte se expresan opiniones y criterios prescriptivos sobre ella. Entre los autores tratados se encuentran: Francisco García Calderón, Aníbal Sánchez Reulet, Alejandro Korn, José Ingenieros, Francisco Romero, Risieri Frondizi y Arturo Andrés Roig, quien representa para Biagini, un cambio con respeto a todo lo anterior. Contiene un apéndice sobre la historiografía de la década de 1940 de gran utilidad.

4924 Bolívar y el mundo de los libertadores. México: Univ. Nacional Autónoma de México, Coordinación de Humanidades, Centro Coordinador y Difusor de Estudios Latinoamericanos, 1993. 244 p.: bibl. (Nuestra América; 34)

Conjunto de trabajos cuyo origen fue el bicentenario del nacimiento de Bolívar. Sobre el Libertador escriben Charles Minguet, Leopoldo Zea, Ricaurte Soler, Margarita Vera, Angel Gutiérrez, Felícitas López Portillo. Sobre el proceso de independencia: Harold E. Davis, Carlos Stoetzer, Juan Manuel de la Serna, François Chevalier, Mario Contreras. Hay artículos sobre Juan Germán Roscio (Domingo Miliani), Fray Servando Teresa de Mier (Manuel Calvillo), José del Valle (Jorge M. García Laguardia), Morelos (Abelardo Villegas), Hidalgo (Carlos Herrejón Peredo). Otros artículos: Juan A. Ortega y Medina, "Disociación Imperial y Unificación Latino americana;" Ignacio Sosa, "El Héroe y sus Usos en la Historia;" Arturo A. Roig, "La Ilustración y la 'Primera Independencia;'" Lucía Sala de Touron, "Algunos Rasgos Específicos del Pensamiento Artiguista;" Arturo Ardao, "Unión y Denominación antes de la Insurgencia de 1810." [CJB]

4925 Borón, Atilio. La crisis en América Latina: nuevos desafíos para la izquierda. (*in* Estrategias para el desarrollo de la democracia: en Perú y América Latina. Lima: Instituto de Estudios Peruanos, 1990, p. 291–338)

Desde una posición de marxismo abierto y dispuesto a constante revisión, encuentra que la función de la izquierda latino americana es rechazar igualmente la propuesta neoliberal y el populismo, y lograr mayor poder real para la "sociedad civil." La manera de obtener este resultado no se hace explícita en el artículo.

4926 Brett, Stephen Francis. Slavery and the Catholic tradition: rights in the balance. New York: P. Lang, 1994. 237 p.: bibl. (American university studies. Series V, Philosophy; 157)

Es de interés para esta sección el tratamiento de la cuestión de la esclavitud en la teología de Francisco de Vitoria y de Domingo de Soto. También se estudia a Santo Tomás y se comparan los tres autores.

4927 Briceño Guerrero, José M. El laberinto de los tres minotauros. Caracas: Monte Avila Editores Latinoamericana, 1994. 303 p. (Estudios)

Reúne tres libros que en su conjunto componen una especie de filosofía de la historia de América Latina. Los libros aludidos son: *La identificación americana con la Europa segunda* (1977) (ver *HLAS 44:7504*); *Discurso salvaje* (Venezuela: Fundarte, 1980); y *Europa y América en el pensar mantuano* (1981) (ver *HLAS 46:7507*) que representan tres discursos o tres mentalidades que conviven en el latinoamericano. Como bien afirma el autor, no es un *estudio* sino una amplia *interpretación* en la cual se buscan las mentalidades subyacentes que podían explicar muchos hechos históricos, ideológicos y de pensamiento.

4928 Brunner, José Joaquín. Cartografías de la modernidad. Santiago: Dolmen Ediciones, 1994? 212 p.: bibl. (Mundo abierto)

De esta obra, cuyo autor ha escrito con frecuencia sobre el tema de la modernidad en general, deben destacarse tres artículos de inspiración sociológica sobre América Latina: "América Latina en la Encrucijada de la Modernidad;" "Tradicionalismo y Modernidad en la Cultura Latinoamericana;" y "Escenificaciones de la Identidad Latino americana."

4929 Camacho, Luis A.; Edgar Roy Ramírez Briceño; and Luis Fernando Araya. Cultura y desarrollo desde América Latina: tres enfoques. San José: Editorial de la Univ. de Costa Rica, 1993. 116 p.: bibl. (Col. Identidad cultural)

Buena parte del libro se dedica a la relación entre cultura y desarrollo en general. El último de los trabajos, "La Reconstitución del Paradigma Socio-cultural Latinoamericano," se refiere al caso específico de la región.

4930 Candelaria, Michael R. Popular religion and liberation: the dilemma of liberation theology. Albany: State Univ. of New York Press, 1990. 194 p.: bibl., index. (SUNY series in religion, culture, and society)

El tema del libro es la ambivalencia de la religiosidad popular para la teología de la liberación y para la liberación misma. Enfoca el asunto en dos posiciones de opuesta apreciación de la religiosidad popular: la de Juan Carlos Scannone y la de Juan Luis Segundo. Concede gran importancia a la religiosidad popular.

4931 Cantolla B., Enrique. Ser lo que somos: notas sobre cultura hispánica, modernidad y desarrollo. (Contribuciones, 3, julio/sept. 1991, p. 116–125, bibl.)

Con inevitable esquematismo, caracteriza la "cosmovisión" de raíz medieval que sería válida para todo el mundo hispánico, y la que corresponde al mundo sajón de Inglaterra y Estados Unidos. Concluye que América Latina, sin abandonar sus rasgos fundamentales, se beneficiaría al asimilar los aspectos políticos del otro paradigma.

4932 Capel, Horacio. El asociacionismo científico en Iberoamerica: la necesidad de un enfoque globalizador. (Interciencia/Caracas, 17:3, May/June 1992, p. 168–176, bibl.)

De interés para la historia de las cien-cias en América Latina, en lo que repecta a las sociedades científicas.

4933 Cardoso, Fernando Henrique. Desafios da social-democracia na América Latina. (Novos Estud. CEBRAP, 28, out. 1990, p. 29–49)

Expresa el credo social-democrático de Cardoso, unos años antes de ser Presidente de Brasil. Es un análisis de lo que podría ser la social-democracia latinoamericana en comparación con la europea, y diferenciada del Estado patrimonialista, el populismo y el neoliberalismo económico. Aunque en gran parte programático, contiene elementos de interpretación de la realidad social y política latinoamericana y de las diversas tendencias que se han presentado en el siglo veinte. Para el comentario del politólogo, ver HLAS 53:3212.

4934 Castañeda, Jorge G. La utopía desarmada. 2a ed. corr. y aum. México: Joaquín Mortiz, 1995. 579 p.: bibl., index. (Contrapuntos)

Esta segunda edición de la versión española es precedida de un prólogo que confronta las tesis originales del libro con los acontecimientos más recientes, especialmente el movimiento de Chiapas, cuyo examen ocupa la mayor parte de dicho prólogo y tiene un valor en sí como análisis. Según el autor, aquellas tesis (agotamiento de la vía revolucionaria, función reformista de la izquierda) quedan corroboradas, lo cual no impide que puedan reclamarse condiciones más justas dentro del esquema imperante. Para el comentario del politólogo sobre la edición original de este libro (en inglés), ver HLAS 55:2732.

4935 Castilla Urbano, Francisco. Juan Ginés de Sepúlveda: en torno a una idea de civilización. (Rev. Indias, 52:195/196, mayo/dic. 1992, p. 329–348)

El autor, que lo es también de un excelente libro sobre Francisco de Vitoria (ver HLAS 56: 4843), trata en este artículo de desentrañar el modelo de "civilización" que servía a Sepúlveda como eje de su doctrina, y del cual se siguieron las consecuencias de su posición frente al indio americano. La comprensión, ya que no justificación, de ese modelo permite evitar los estereotipos que pesan sobre una figura que sólo se recuerda usualmente como el opositor de Las Casas. Parte de la tesis es distinguir entre subordinación por servidumbre y esclavitud natural. Para el comentario del historiador, ver *HLAS 56:825.*

4936 Castro-Gómez, Santiago. Filosofía e identidad latinoamericana: exposición y crítica de una problemática. (*Rev. Cuba. Cienc. Soc.,* 8:27, enero/junio 1992, p. 58–77, bibl.)

Ágil ensayo articulado en tres partes: 1) Reconstrucción histórica de la filosofía de lo latinoamericano; 2) Presentación de las diferentes respuestas dadas al problema; 3) Crítica de las mismas. Establece la necesidad de "una racionalidad que permita el diálogo intercultural" y posibilite "llevar a cabo una política solidaria... con los intereses de toda la humanidad." Sólo ése puede ser el sentido actual de filosofar "en perspectiva latino americana." [CJB]

4937 Castro Leiva, Luis. El arte de hacer una revolución feliz. (*Cah. Am. lat.,* 10, 1990, p. 91–122)

Se toma el caso de la revolución de la Independencia, pero el objetivo no es historiográfico, sino semántico o lingüístico: "recrear la historia de una experiencia conceptual" (la del concepto de 'revolución'); "Nuestro propósito será recrear las condiciones históricas del proceso conceptual o intelectual que nos permitió, por vez primera, concebir la idea de revolución."

4938 Cerutti-Guldberg, Horacio. Hacia la utopía de nuestra América. (*Ibero-Am. Arch.,* 18:3/4, 1992, p. 455–465, bibl.)

Intento de aproximarse a una teoría de la utopía, tema que el autor ha frecuentado en trabajos anteriores. Distingue tres sentidos de la noción de 'utopía': el cotidiano, del género y epistémico. En el tercer sentido lo utópico sería un ejercicio acerca de los límites de lo posible o "un esfuerzo *plus ultrico* por rebasar lo imposible," ante la necesidad de transformar lo intolerable y desocultar lo velado. [CJB]

4939 Chaparro, Máximo. América Latina: liberación y filosofía. Guaranda, Ecuador: Editorial de la Univ. Estatal de Bolívar, 1992. 196 p.: bibl.

Algunos artículos se refieren a la Argentina, otros a América Latina en general y otros al tema de Dios. Cuando se trata de Argentina se muestra representante de la crítica al liberalismo argentino que caracterizó al período de la unificación y organización nacional en la segunda mitad del siglo XIX; de allí las frecuentes críticas a Sarmiento y el apoyo buscado en autores como Arturo Jauretche o Juan José Hernández Arregui. Entre los artículos dedicados a América Latina podría destacarse el que lleva por título "América Latina y la posibilidad de la filosofía," donde se afirma que una de las principales funciones de la filosofía latino americana es repensar la filosofía occidental desde la propia cultura, lo que le da un sentido de liberación.

4940 Chilcote, Ronald H. Post-Marxism: the retreat from class in Latin America. (*Lat. Am. Perspect.,* 17:2, Spring 1990, p. 3–24, bibl., tables)

Ensayo preliminar a un número especial de la revista *Latin American Perspectives.* El tema es la crisis del marxismo y las reformas nuevas de esta corriente que se separan del marxismo clásico en algunos de sus aspectos, según han sido desarrolladas o adaptadas en América Latina. Hay referencia al contenido de los artículos que componen el número y a numerosa literatura sobre el asunto.

4941 Ciriza, Alejandra and Estela Fernández. Hacia una interpretación del discurso independentista. (*Rev. Filos. Univ. Costa Rica,* 30:71, junio 1992, p. 97–101)

Tras examinar varias interpretaciones de la Independencia, concluyen que tuvo decisiva importancia por parte de los sectores dirigentes la "resemantización" de "ideas movilizadoras" como "libertad" e "igualdad." Por estas ideas se involucraron en el proceso los grupos populares, los mismos que percibían después, para su desventaja, la división entre ellos y la minoría ilustrada.

4942 Coggiola, Osvaldo. El trotskismo en América Latina. Buenos Aires: Ediciones Magenta, 1993. 77 p.: bibl.

Como breve narrativa de síntesis, sigue las vicisitudes del trotskismo latino americano desde sus comienzos hasta la actualidad. Se ponen de manifesto sus dificultades frente a los partidos comunistas pro-soviéticos y sus luchas internas y correspondientes divisiones. También los problemas que debió enfrentar con motivo de la aparición de fenómenos obreros como el peronismo y movimientos de izquierda como la Revolución Cubana. Indica que, a pesar de insertarse en la vida político-social latinoamericana, el trotskismo es por esencia un movimiento internacional. Para el comentario sobre la edición original, en portugués, ver *HLAS 50:4553.*

4943 Coloquio Internacional sobre el Ensayo en América Latina, *México, 1993.*
El ensayo en nuestra América: para una reconceptualización. México: Univ. Nacional Autónoma de México, 1993. 595 p.: bibl. (Col. El ensayo iberoamericano; 1)

Hay dos tipos de trabajos: los que se refieren al ensayo en sí mismo o su teoría, y los de contenido histórico. A la primera categoría corresponden los de Cerutti Guldberg sobre el valor del ensayo para la expresión latinoamericana, y los de Liliana Weinberg sobre ensayo y paradoja. Algunos de los de contenido crítico o histórico pertenecen a los siguientes autores: Francesca Gargallo (El Feminismo en México); José Luis Gómez Martínez (Pensamiento de la Liberación); Clara A. Jalif de Bertranou (Fenomenología en América Latina); Mario Magallón Anaya (Vasconcelos); Domingo Miliani (Arturo Uslar Pietri); Salvador Morales (Martí); María Ramírez Fierro (Simón Rodríguez); Rafael Rojas (Ensayo en Cuba en el Siglo XIX); Enrique Ubieta Gómez (Cinto Vitier y Fernández Retamar); Norma Villagómez Rosas (Calibán en Latinoamérica); Janusz Wojcieszak (Ensayo y Filosofía en el Caso Latinoamericano).

4944 El complejo de Próspero: ensayos sobre cultura, modernidad y modernización en América Latina. Montevideo: Vintén Editor, 1993. 300 p.: bibl.

Obra interesante y de viva discusión sobre la posible interpretación de América Latina en su pasado y su presente, y sobre su inclusión o exclusión de la modernidad. Gira en torno a la obra de Richard Morse *El espejo de Próspero: un estudio de la dialéctica del Nuevo Mundo* (México: Siglo XXI, 1982). Hay artículos de los compiladores, del propio Morse, de José Guilherme Merquior, Simon Schwartzman, y Luiz Weneck Vianna.

4945 Congreso de Estudios Latinoamericanos, *1st, La Plata, Argentina, 1991.*
Homenaje a José Martí: actas. La Plata, Argentina: Secretaría de Extensión, Facultad de Humanidades y Ciencias de la Educación,

Univ. Nacional de La Plata, 1994. 435 p.: bibl., ill.

La mayoría de las ponencias se refieren a Martí; pero las hay también sobre temas de literatura e ideología latinoamericanas. Entre las primeras destacamos, por razones de interés para la historia de las ideas, "La Polisemia Prohibida: la Recepción de José Martí como Sismógrafo de la Vida Política y Cultural" (ver item **5120**); y "Ecos Martianos en el Latinoamericanismo de un Argentino: Manuel Ugarte" (Adriana Arpini). Entre las segundas: "América Latina en los Años Setenta: Surgimiento del Antiintelectualismo como Tópico de los Intelectuales de Izquierda" (Claudia Gilman). Se incluyen dos ponencias sobre Ezequiel Martínez Estrada.

4946 Congreso Internacional sobre el V Centenario del Nacimiento del Dr. Juan Ginés de Sepúlveda, *Pozoblanco, Spain, 1991.* Actas. Organizado y patrocinado por el Excmo. Ayuntamiento de Pozoblanco. Pozoblanco, Spain: Excmo. Ayuntamiento de Pozoblanco; Córdoba, Spain: Excma. Diputación Provincial de Córdoba, Area de Cultura, 1993. 339 p.: bibl.

El volumen intenta abarcar la totalidad de la obra y significación de Sepúlveda, y no sólo su famosa controversia con Las Casas. Interesan particularmente el trabajo inicial, a cargo de Angel Losada, reconocido especialista en Sepúlveda, "Evolución del Moderno Pensamiento Filosófico-Histórico sobre Juan Ginés de Sepúlveda," y los varios artículos de la parte correspondiente a los "Estudios sobre Sepúlveda Referentes a Temas Americanos." En general se manifiesta una tendencia revisionista de la imagen tradicional de Sepúlveda frente a Las Casas.

4947 Congreso Latinoamericano de Historia de las Ciencias y la Tecnología, *3rd, México, 1992.* Newton en America: simposio. Recopilación de Celina Ana Lértora Mendoza. Buenos Aires: FEPAI, 1995. 101 p.: bibl.

Volumen monográficamente muy valioso. Autores y temas: María de la Paz Ramos Lara: "Mecánica Newtoniana en Nueva España;" Juan M. Espinoza y Patricia Aceves: "Antonio de León y Gama, México, Siglo XVIII;" Luis Carlos Arboleda y Diana Soto Arango: "Newton en España y la Nueva

Granada"; Libertad Díaz Molina: "Newton en Cuba"; Celina Ana Lértora Mendoza: "Bibliografía Newtoniana en el Río de la Plata, Siglo XVIII".

4948 Congreso Nacional de Filosofía (Argentina), *7th*, *Río Cuarto, Argentina, 1993*. Actas. Edición de Alfredo Sergio Burgos. Río Cuarto, Argentina: Univ. Nacional de Río Cuarto, 1994. 850 p.: bibl.

Contiene una sección especial sobre Filosofía Latinoamericana, donde hay ponencias de los siguientes autores: Carlos Alemián, Abelardo Barra Ruatta, Alberto Buela y Oscar Wingartz Plata. Además, sobre Arturo A. Roig (dos artículos, uno de Estela Fernández y otro de Marisa Muñoz, Dante Ramaglia y Oscar Zalazar); sobre ensayo y fenomenología en América Latina (Clara Alicia Jalif de Bertranou); sobre Agustín Alvarez (Dante Ramaglia); y sobre Simón Rodríguez (Oscar Salazar). De otras secciones destacamos una ponencia de Arturo A. Roig sobre la historia de las ideas y la filosofía latino americana, y otras dos, una sobre Mariátegui (Néstor Kohan) y la segunda sobre Andrés Mercado Vera (Isabel Luchetta). [CJB]

4949 Congreso Teológico Internacional, *Lima, 1992*. Las Casas entre dos mundos . Lima: Instituto Bartolomé de las Casas; CEP, 1993. 433 p.: bibl. (CEP; 135. Col. Bartolomé de las Casas; 4)

Contiene los trabajos presentados al Congreso Teológico Internacional realizado en Lima en 1992, organizado por el Instituto Bartolomé de las Casas, que dirige el Padre Gustavo Gutiérrez. Hay ponencias sobre teología, evangelización, defensa de los indios, influye de Las Casas en el Perú y también sobre el Quinto Centenario en general. Entre los autores se cuentan Gustavo Gutiérrez, Helen Rand Parish y Rolena Adorno. Hay un total de 26 ponencias.

4950 Cruz Kronfly, Fernando. La sombrilla planetaria: ensayos sobre modernidad y postmodernidad en la cultura. Bogotá: Planeta, 1994. 215 p. (Col. Pensamiento)

Varios de los artículos son de tema literario, pero reflejan más la meditación del ensayista que el lenguaje técnico del crítico. Entran en la categoría de ensayo de ideas los dos primeros, que se ocupan de la modernidad, la postmodernidad y sus consecuencias sociales. Sobre esta última materia se encon-

trarán observaciones, interrogantes y reflexiones con algunos atisbos acertados. El estilo es vivaz y de fácil comunicación.

4951 De Roux, Rodolfo R. Violencia y persuación. (*Cristianismo Soc.*, 29:110, 1991, p. 37–46)

Se refiere a los problemas teórico-teológicos y a la práctica y alcance real de la evangelización de América. Con buena información, sin inútiles defensas ni críticas extemporáneas, pero tampoco sin dejar de ejercitar el juicio, es un artículo de lectura recomendable.

4952 Dembicz, Andrzej. Más allá de los 500 años: una perspectiva polaca. (*Cuad. Am.*, 32:2, marzo/abril 1992, p. 71–76)

Breve referencia a algunas actividades llevadas a cabo en Polonia con motivo del Quinto Centenario. [CJB]

4953 Demenchonok, Eduard Vasilévich. Filosofía latinoamericana: problemas y tendencias. Bogotá: Editorial El Buho, 1990. 289 p.: bibl.

Desde el punto de vista temático, el libro abarca prácticamente todo lo que se incluye bajo el llamado problema de la filosofía latinoamericana: su posibilidad, especificidad, autenticidad, sus orígenes, rasgos esenciales, etc. En cuanto a autores, se exponen con mayor extensión los postpositivistas Korn y Vaz Ferreira y, entre los más actuales, José Gaos, Leopoldo Zea, Arturo A. Roig, Enrique Dussel, y Marquínez Argote. Se plantea la cuestión del método de la investigación histórico-filosófica. Se critican las posiciones de la CEPAL. Por último, el libro dedica extensa atención a la filosofía de la liberación, sus orígenes y los problemas que actualmente se le plantean. Toda la temática está abordada en sintonía con el latinoamericanismo filosófico actual.

4954 El desafío neoliberal: el fin del tercermundismo en América Latina. Recopilación de Barry B. Levine. Contribuciones de Mario Vargas Llosa, *et al.* Barcelona: Grupo Editorial Norma, 1992. 518 p.: bibl., indexes. (Literatura y ensayo)

Aunque la mayoría de los artículos se refieren a asuntos de política económica, los hay de índole general, como el de Peter L. Berger, "América Latina Bajo una Perspectiva Cultural Comparativa" y el de Barry B. Levine, "Un Manifiesto Liberal para América

Latina en una Era de Desencanto". Otro motivo para su inclusión en este bibliografía es la actualidad de esta corriente económico-ideológica en las discusiones sobre el presente y el futuro de América Latina, como lo fue en su momento el marxismo y lo es aún la Teología de la Liberación. Los países especialmente tratados son Chile, México, Colombia, Brasil, Venezuela, Perú y el área del Caribe. Para el comentario del especialista de relaciones internacionales, ver *HLAS* 55:3874.

4955 Díaz Cid, Manuel Antonio and Fidencio Aguilar Víquez. Sociedades de pensamiento e independencia. Puebla, Mexico: Ediciones de la Univ. Popular Autónoma del Estado de Puebla, 1990? 177 p.: bibl., ill., maps.

Contribución a la historia de la masonería en la época de la Independencia. Abundante en datos, más bien en estilo de crónica, para el caso de Nueva Granada, Venezuela, Río de la Plata, Chile y Perú. Para el comentario del historiador, ver item **1000**. [CJB]

4956 Donoso, Antón. Latin American applied philosophy. (*LARR*, 27:2, 1992, p. 237–257)

Ensayo bibliográfico que revisa varias obras generales, colectivas y antológicas sobre la filosofía latinoamericana. Algunos de los autores incluidos son: Alain Guy, Jorge Gracia, y Raúl Fornet Betancourt. Estima que el concepto de "filosofía aplicada" es atribuible a la filosofía latinoamericana y por esa vía puede justificar la atención de los medios académicos.

4957 Dussel, Enrique D. La introducción de la *transformación de la filosofía* y América Latina. (*Reflexão/Campinas*, 16:47, maio/agosto 1990, p. 7–58)

Extenso paralelo entre el pensamiento de Karl-Otto Apel y la filosofía de la liberación del autor.

4958 Dussel, Enrique D. 1492: análisis ideológico de las diferentes posiciones. (*Cristianismo Soc.*, 29:110, 1991, p. 7–20)

Desde su posición, frecuentemente reiterada en sus escritos, el autor hace del destino—histórico y futuro—del Otro (indio, negro, campesino, marginado, etc.) la fuente de sentido para juzgar la intromisión europea en América a partir de 1492. Desde esa perspectiva juzga a las otras posiciones, que encuentra representadas con expresiones como: invención de América, descubrimiento, encuentro, conquista, evangelización.

4959 Dussel, Enrique D. Recent Latin American theology. (*in* The Church in Latin America, 1492–1992. Turnbridge Wells, England: Burns & Oats; Maryknoll, N.Y.: Orbis Books, 1992, p. 391–402)

Síntesis de la marcha de la teología de la liberación desde 1959 hasta 1991, por uno de sus principales adherentes.

4960 El ensayo hispanoamericano del siglo XX. Recopilación de John Skirius. 3. ed. México: Fondo de Cultura Económica, 1994. 634 p.: bibl. (Col. Tierra firme)

Encabezada por un ensayo sobre el ensayo, esta amplia antología, cuyo objetivo principal es el ensayo literario, acoge también autores cercanos a la filosofía y a la literatura de ideas, como González Prada, Rodó y Vasconcelos. Precede a los textos de cada autor una breve introducción. [CJB]

4961 El ensayo iberoamericano: perspectivas. México: Univ. Nacional Autónoma de México, Dirección General de Asuntos del Personal Académico, Centro Coordinador y Difusor de Estudios Latino americanos, 1995. 251 p.: bibl. (Col. El ensayo iberoamericano; 4)

Contiene materiales literarios, políticos, teológicos, feministas y sobre teoría del ensayo (especialmente, sobre este último tema, los artículos de Liliana Weinberg y José Luis Gómez Martínez). Relacionados con la historia de las ideas encontramos varias contribuciones sobre Simón Rodríguez; una apreciación de la obra del autor panameño Ricarte Soler (Mario Magallón Anaya); y otra sobre Darcy Ribeiro (Jesús Serna Moreno).

4962 La enseñanza, la reflexión y la investigación filosóficas en América Latina y el Caribe. Madrid: Tecnos; París: UNESCO, 1990. 247 p.: bibl. (Semilla y surco. Serie de sociología.)

Volumen muy útil, que contiene información sobre el tema en 12 países latinoamericanos y del Caribe de habla inglesa. En casi todos hay una presentación breve de la "tradición filosófica" del país correspondiente. Un capítulo especial se dedica a la lógica, la epistemología y el análisis filosófico en la región. Algunos de los autores son

Eduardo Rabossi, Fermando Salmerón, Ricaurte Soler y Eduardo Vázquez. El contenido debiera compararse con el de *La enseñanza de la filosofía en la universidad hispanoamericana* (ver *HLAS 28:3211* y *HLAS 33:4511*) para observar los cambios que pudieran haber ocurrido.

4963 Ette, Ottmar. La puesta en escena de la mesa de trabajo en Raynal y Humboldt. (*Cuad. Am.*, 46:4, julio/agosto 1994, p. 29–68, ill.)

Trabajo de interpretación sobre las relaciones entre los textos y las ilustraciones aparecidas en las primeras ediciones de la *Histoire des deux Indes* del abate Guillaume-Thomas Raynal (1713–1796) y la iconografía de época sobre Alexander von Humboldt (1769–1859). [CJB]

4964 Fadéev, Dmitri. El socialreformismo en América Latina: orígenes y perspectivas. (*Am. Lat./Moscow*, 1, enero 1991, p. 24–32, ill.)

Interesa, teniendo en cuenta la publicación en que aparece, que se trata de una apreciación fáctica, sin críticas ideológicas, al giro de la izquierda latinoamericana hacia formas más democráticas. La fecha de publicación puede tener que ver con eso.

4965 Fernández, Estela. Nativos y extranjeros, civilizados y bárbaros: el juego semántico de las oposiciones categoriales en los escritos mirandinos. (*Rev. Hist. Am.*, 110, julio/dic. 1990, p. 109–124)

El análisis se realiza por la vía de la semántica de ciertos conceptos dentro del contexto histórico, pero el trabajo es, en realidad, una crítica, desde un punto de vista actual, del significado que Miranda dio a esos conceptos.

4966 Fernández, Estela and **Alejandra Ciriza.** Notas a propósito de la Ilustración Americana. (*Rev. Hist. Am.*, 110, julio/dic. 1990, p. 71–98)

Bien elaborado, contribuye a la discusión de las relaciones entre Ilustración española y la americana, la influencia de la francesa, la distinción entre la Ilustración e independencia y la función de los intelectuales y el pensamiento político. Al tratar esos temas discute diversas interpretaciones.

4967 Fernández Delgado, Miguel Angel. El utopismo de Fray Bartolomé de las Casas: las experiencias de la Verapaz. (*Cuad. Am.*, 49, enero/feb. 1995, p. 146–164)

Reflexiones sobre la utopía y su distinción respecto de la ideología; sobre lo que llama "proyectos de evasión" y "proyectos de reconstrucción" según la utopía que se proponga; y la experiencia lascasiana de la Verapaz, con las posibles razones por las que fracasó. [CJB]

4968 Fernández Díaz, Osvaldo. Historia e ideología en el pensamiento marxista latinoamericano. (*Am. Lat./Moscow*, 8, 1991, p. 25–29)

Contiene una periodización de la historia del marxismo en América Latina. Afronta el problema de cómo la región fue vista por Marx y por el marxismo en general. Una de las conclusiones es que el marxismo no ha pensado aún apropiadamente a América Latina.

4969 Fornet-Betancourt, Raúl. Balance y perspectivas del estudio del pensamiento latinoamericano en América y Europa. (*Rev. Filos./México*, 25:75, sept./dic. 1992, p. 273–288)

Con acierto señala algunos hábitos con los que el europeo ha visto el pensamiento latinoamericano (y en los cuales han caído también algunos latinoamericanos). Ellos son: consideración del modelo europeo de filosofía como paradigmático; tendencia reduccionista que ha llevado a ver la incidencia europea en América con prescindencia de las formas americanas propias; consideración de las ideas filosóficas como procesos puros, aislados de sus contextos. Dado el carácter limitativo de estos enfoques, el autor propone un programa de "desoccidentalización de la filosofía" como "forma concreta de diálogo intercultural." [CJB]

4970 Fornet-Betancourt, Raúl. Hacia una filosofía intercultural latinoamericana. San José: Editorial Depto. Ecuménico de Investigaciones, 1994. 124 p.: bibl. (Col. universitaria)

El libro presenta la posibilidad de una filosofía intercultural, que se basaría a su vez en un diálogo intercultural, entendido éste como alternativa histórica para transformar los modos de pensar vigentes. [CJB]

4971 Fornet-Betancourt, Raúl. Para un balance crítico de 500 años de cristianismo en América Latina: ¿cuál ha sido el aporte del cristianismo al cambio social en América Latina? (*Cristianismo Soc.*, 29:110, 1991, p. 47–52)

Declarativamente es una nueva increpación a la Iglesia Católica por su actuación en la conquista de América. Como apoyo se exponen las posiciones del peruano Francisco de Paula G. Vigil (*Defensa de la autoridad de los gobiernos y de los obispos contra las pretensiones de la Curia Romana*, Lima: J. Huidobro Molina, 1848) y de José Martí (diversos escritos).

4972 Fornet-Betancourt, Raúl. La problemática de los valores en la tradición filosófica latinoamericana del siglo XX. (*Rev. Agust.*, 36:110, mayo/agosto 1995, p. 571–596)

Revisa las concepciones axiológicas de Alejandro Korn, Antonio Caso, José Vasconcelos, Samuel Ramos, Francisco Romero, Juan Llambías de Azevedo y Risieri Frondizi. Se atribuye a este último el haber superado la dualidad subjetivismo/objetivismo. [CJB]

4973 Fuente de la Ojeda, A.G. V Centenario: fiesta de la hispanidad. Barcelona: A.G. Fuente de la Ojeda, 1991. 166 p.: ill.

Obra polémica y exaltada en defensa de España y su acción en América.

4974 Fuentes, Carlos. Imagining America. (*Diogenes/Philosophy*, 160, Winter 1992, p. 5–19)

En materia y forma, debe suponerse una de las mejores obras escritas con motivo del fin del milenio y el Quinto Centenario. Equilibrada y lúcida en la visión del pasado y positiva en la perspectiva del futuro. Por encima de las disputas ideológicas, sin ser por esta falta de contenido. Con gran énfasis en el valor de la cultura latinoamericana.

4975 Gallardo, Helio. 500 años: fenomenología del mestizo; violencia y resistencia. San José: Editorial Departamento Ecuménico de Investigaciones, 1993. 183 p.: bibl. (Col. Análisis)

La primera parte se compone de artículos aparecidos en la prensa sobre (o más bien en contra de) la conquista de América. La segunda se refiere a la actitud "ladina" en las sociedades latinoamericanas y en ella se encuentran críticas a—entre otros—Rodó y Octavio Paz.

4976 García Canclini, Néstor. Hybrid cultures: strategies for entering and leaving modernity. Translated by Christopher L. Chiappari and Silvia L. López. Foreword by Renato Rosaldo. Minneapolis: Univ. of Minnesota Press, 1995. 293 p.: bibl., ill., index.

El libro es una especie de sociología de la cultura aplicada a América Latina. Aunque los temas son muy concretos, el enfoque del autor tiende a ser filosófico. Tradición y modernidad son los dos ejes de la obra, pero esta caracterización dista mucho de captar toda su complejidad.

4977 García Laguardia, Jorge Mario. La polémica sobre el Nuevo Mundo: nacionalismo e hispanoamericanismo; una respuesta ilustrada centroamericana. (*Cuad. Am.*, 4:5(23), sept./oct. 1990, p. 138–172)

La Sociedad Económica de Amigos del País (Guatemala) habría dado la primera respuesta centroamericana a las negaciones del Nuevo Mundo que provenían, especialmente, de De Pauw, mostrando los recursos de la región. Un segundo momento de esta conciencia americana se habría dado a partir de 1808, en la lucha por la independencia. Se destaca en este sentido el Proyecto de Confederación, del cual José Cecilio del Valle sería figura ejemplar. Se incluye un apéndice bibliográfico que completa la documentación contenida en el artículo. [CJB]

4978 Garzón Valdés, Ernesto. La polémica de la justificación ética de la conquista. (*Estud. Filos. Hist. Let.*, 27, invierno 1991/92, p. 23–40)

Modelo de razonamiento analítico aplicado a un tema en el cual, desde el siglo XVI hasta hoy, han abundado las posiciones interesadas o extremas, y en último caso no racionales. Se organiza según tres niveles de discusión: la explicación, la justificación, la excusa. Considera que la mayor relevancia de la polémica de la conquista reside en que de alguna manera es actual, si se advierte que la desfavorable condición del indio no ha cambiado en gran medida.

4979 Gómez-Martínez, José Luis. Pensamiento de la liberación: proyección de Ortega en Iberoamérica. Madrid: EGE Ediciones, 1995. 232 p.: bibl. (Col. Cultura y pensamiento iberoamericano)

Ensayo que se propone mostrar la presencia de las tesis de Ortega y Gasset en la reflexión sobre la identidad de América Latina en el siglo XX y, particularmente, sus derivaciones en el "pensamiento de la liberación," con especial énfasis en la perspectiva de Leopoldo Zea. [CJB]

4980 Gómez Muller, Alfredo. Sobre la legitimidad de la conquista de América: Las Casas y Sepúlveda. (*Ideas Valores,* 85/86, agosto 1991, p. 3–18)

Resumen de las tesis de ambos contendientes, sus fuentes y su argumentación. En un análisis final la diferencia se reconduce a contrapuestas modalidades de evangelización. Desde una obvia posición actual, el autor considera que la propuesta de Las Casas es la legítima porque toma en cuenta la realidad del Otro.

4981 Górski, Eugeniusz. Filosofía y sociedad en el pensamiento europeo oriental y latinoamericano. (*Cuad. Am.,* 7:41, sept./ oct. 1993, p. 76–92)

Valioso intento de comparar las estructuras sociales y la filosofía de los países del Centro y el Este europeos y los de América Latina. Se hallan similitudes en el papel dependiente y periférico con respecto a Europa Occidental y en los planteos filosóficos correspondientes, especialmente en su dimensión práctica, social e histórica. [CJB]

4982 Guadarrama González, Pablo. Las alternativas sociales en América Latina y la filosofía de la liberación. (*Islas/Santa Clara,* 96, mayo/agosto 1990, p. 89–102)

Desde la posición marxista-leninista del autor, se reitera, para la filosofía de la liberación, la misma apreciación que se aplica a otros pensadores del pasado considerados "progresistas:" bueno y loable pero no suficiente. Sin embargo, el análisis de las diferentes variantes de la filosofía de la liberación resulta útil, con prescindencia del juicio de conjunto que no es difícil anticipar. Acierta también en señalar que esa corriente, a pesar de querer insertarse en la praxis, suele quedarse en el plano declarativo.

4983 Guadarrama González, Pablo. Marxismo y antimarxismo en América Latina. La Habana: Editora Política; México: Ediciones El Caballito, 1994. 217 p.: bibl. (Col. Marxismo vivo; 1)

El eje del criterio valorativo del libro reside en considerar que ser marxista en América Latina es ser marxista-leninista orgánico, diferenciado de cualquier otra posición que pueda recibir la calificación de "marxista." En función de ello se juzgan todas las formas de antimarxismo, con las características polémicas previsibles, y los antecedentes del marxismo-leninismo que se han dado en la historia de la región. El último capítulo está dedicado a la Revolución Cubana, la cual es vista desde los fundamentos señalados. Para el tema de la filosofía latinoamericana destacamos el parágrafo: "Por Qué y Para Qué Filosofar en América Latina."

4984 Guerra, François-Xavier. L'Amérique latine face à la Révolution française. (*Caravelle/Toulouse,* 54, 1990, p. 7–20, bibl.)

Es un artículo de presentación de un número especial sobre América Latina y la Revolución Francesa, que es a la vez un análisis independiente y muy atendible del tema en cuestión.

4985 Hernández González, Manuel. La Ilustración en Canarias y su proyección en América. Las Palmas, Spain: Cabildo Insular de Gran Canaria, 1993. 73 p.: bibl. (Col. Guagua; 76)

El interés de este breve libro para la historia de las ideas en América (incluye las relaciones con las colonias norteamericanas) reside en la estrecha conexión de las Islas Canarias con Hispanoamérica en la época colonial—especialmente con Venezuela y Cuba—y en el hecho de que el autor coloca las ideas de reforma ilustrada en el contexto económico y social.

4986 Herrera Alamos, Claudio. Reflexiones generales sobre desarrollo, cultura e integración en América Latina. (*Integr. Latinoam.,* 15:155, abril 1990, p. 3–18, bibl.)

Buena síntesis de los problemas involucrados en el tema. Recalca la importancia de la complejidad étnico-cultural de la región. Contiene propuestas para la cooperación regional en materia de políticas culturales.

4987 Humboldt, Alexander von. Breviario del Nuevo Mundo. Presentación de Oscar Rodríguez Ortiz. Caracas: Biblioteca Ayacucho, 1993. 165 p.: bibl. (Col. La Expresión americana; 12)

Breve antología de los escritos de

Humboldt sobre América, con una presentación. [CJB]

4988 Ibero-América 500 años después, identidad e integración: contribución a la I Cumbre Iberoamericana, Guadalajara, México, 1991. México: Univ. Nacional Autónoma de México, 1993. 169 p.: bibl. (Cuadernos de cuadernos, 0188-7815; 3. Cuadernos americanos. Nueva época)

Recoge algunas de las ponencias presentadas al simposio. Interesan particularmente las que se refieren a los temas de identidad e integración. Algunos de los autores son: Leopoldo Zea, Juan Antonio Ortega y Medina, Carlos Bosch García, Elsa Cecilia Frost y Abelardo Villegas. [CJB]

4989 The Indian in Spanish America: centuries of removal, survival, and integration; a critical anthology. v. 1-2. Lancaster, Calif.: Labyrinthos, 1994- . 2 v.: bibl., ill.

Se trata de una valiosa antología, que en algunos aspectos va más allá de la estricta cuestión del indio para extenderse, por ejemplo, a temas históricos de educación. El primer volumen contiene textos clásicos de documentos, cronistas de Indias, viajeros y figuras como Las Casas, Sahagún, Vitoria y Acosta, entre otros. El segundo recoge textos de la época independiente, entre ellos de Bolívar, Sarmiento, González Prada, Alejandro Deustua, Mariátegui, Martí, Juárez, Gabino Barreda, Vasconcelos, Manuel Gamio y Samuel Ramos. El Estudio Preliminar de Himelblau se refiere solamente a algunos autores del segundo volumen. Una primera versión de este Estudio Preliminar fue adelantada en publicación aparte en 1993.

4990 Instituto Jacques Maritain de Cuba (University of Miami). Pensadores hispano-americanos. Miami, Fla.: Ediciones Universal, 1995. 218 p.: bibl. (Col. Polymito)

Contiene siete conferencias sobre las siguientes figuras: Andrés Bello (Guillermo de Zéndegui); José Cecilio del Valle (Gonzalo Facio); Juan Bautista Alberdi (Luis A. Gómez-Domínguez); Francisco Bilbao (Alberto J. Varona); Eugenio María de Hostos (Luis M. Oraa); Manuel González Prada (Uva de Aragón Clavijo); José Vasconcelos (Rosa Leonor Whitmarsh). [CJB]

4991 Introducción al pensamiento filosófico latinoamericano: ¿qué es esto, filosofía?, ¿qué es esto, Latinoamérica?, ¿qué es esto, filosofía latinoamericana? v. 1-2. México: Centro de Investigación en Ciencias Sociales y Humanidades, 1990. 2 v.: bibl.

Selección de textos. El primer volumen esta dedicado a la filosofía en general y contiene escritos de varios filósofos europeos y, entre los latinoamericanos, Francisco Romero. El segundo contiene textos sobre la interpretación de América Latina. Sus autores: César Fernández Moreno, Augusto Tamayo Vargas, José Lezama Lima, Roberto Fernández Retamar, Lourdes Arizpe y Benjamín Carrión. En función de las tres preguntas del título, se supone que habría un tercer volumen, dedicado a la filosofía latinoamericana.

4992 Iriarte Aniz, Cándido. Ferrater Mora, 1912-1991: filósofo continuista-integracionista. (*Estud. Filos.*, 41:116, enero/abril 1992, p. 131-146)

Síntesis de datos biográficos, obra y características filosóficas de uno de los mayores representantes de la filosofía de habla española del siglo XX.

4993 Islas. No. 99, mayo/agosto 1991. Santa Clara, Cuba: Univ. Central de Las Villas.

Número dedicado a la filosofía de la liberación. En 16 artículos, los autores tratados son, entre otros: Rodolfo Kusch, Carlos Cullen, Juan Carlos Scannone, Mario Casalla, Silvio Maresca, Osvaldo Ardiles, Arturo A. Roig, Enrique Dussel y Horacio Cerutti Guldberg (Argentina); Augusto Salazar Bondy y Francisco Miró Quesada (Perú); Yamandú Acosta y Carlos Mato (Uruguay); Miguel Manzanera (Bolivia); Germán Marquínez Argote (Colombia); Leopoldo Zea (México); y Alejandro Serrano Caldera (Nicaragua). También se revisa la situación en Brasil y Ecuador (en este último más bien, en el campo de la historia de las ideas). Al final hay una visión de balance crítico, uno de cuyos principales elementos es la relación con el marxismo. El número de la revista en general, y en especial el referido balance final, constituyen una visión de conjunto descriptivo-crítico de la filosofía de la liberación que no ha sido frecuente con tal extensión.

4994 Janik, Dieter. La noción de sociedad en el pensamiento de Lizardi y sus contemporaneos. (*Cah. Am. lat.*, 10, 1990, p. 39-48)

Sobre las diferencias en el concepto de

"sociedad" en Fernández de Lizardi, Ignacio de Herrera (Colombia), Bolívar, Juan Bautista Alberdi y Esteban Echeverría.

4995 Kohut, Karl. Fernández de Oviedo, historiador y literato: humanismo, cristianismo e hidalguía. (*Estud. Latinoam./Poland*, 15, 1992, p. 55–116, bibl., ill., plate)

Aunque todo el artículo es de muy buena factura, interesa aquí principalmente la parte correspondiente a la evangelización de los indios.

4996 Koval, Boris. La teología de la liberación: contra la falsa resignación. (*Am. Lat./Moscow*, 8, 1991, p. 17–23)

Con simpatía y sin intensa acentuación del marxismo, destaca el aspecto de preocupación moral terrena de la Teología de la Liberación, tanto en sus fundamentos doctrinarios como en la directa acción social, al punto de afirmar que no podría verse exclusivamente como una doctrina teológica.

4997 Lafaye, Jacques and **James Lockhart.** A scholarly debate: the origins of modern Mexico; *indigenistas* vs. *hispanistas*. (*Americas/Franciscans*, 48:3, Jan. 1992, p. 315–330)

El título es general para dos artículos individuales, breves y de intención sintética que, aunque provenientes de especialistas, merecerían difundirse al amplio público, especialmente para compensar los estereotipos del Vo. Centenario. El primero (de Lafaye) se refiere a las visiones "negra" y "dorada" de la conquista. El segundo (de Lockhart) resume la valiosa investigación del autor sobre el contacto cultural entre las poblaciones española y náhuatl. Para el comentario del historiador colonial, ver *HLAS 54:1137*.

4998 Lértora Mendoza, Celina Ana. Cinco siglos de cultura hispanoamericana: visión retro-prospectiva. (*Rev. Filos./México*, 25:75, sept./dic. 1992, p. 289–306)

Intento de clarificar la cultura nacida en 1492 y las categorías con que ella ha sido pensada y puede pensarse prospectivamente. El artículo es analítico y equilibrado, y tiende a eliminar simplificaciones. En algunos aspectos se opone a estereotipos críticos muy divulgados del "Encuentro" de dos mundos, así como a la concepción más difundida de la filosofía latinoamericana.

4999 Levaggi, Abelardo. Notas sobre la vigencia de los derechos indígenas y la doctrina indiana. (*Rev. Complut. Hist. Am.*, 17, 1991, p. 79–91)

Ejemplos bien elegidos de ciertos autores y sus respectivas opiniones sobre la validez o invalidez de la estructura normativa (o "derecho") de las culturas indígenas, y sus consecuencias para el derecho indiano. Algunos de esos autores: Las Casas, Vitoria, Alonso de Zorita, Vasco de Quiroga, Fernando de Santillán, Juan de Matienzo, Polo de Ondegardo, Garcilaso de la Vega, Sarmiento de Gamboa, Juan de Torquemada, Solórzano Pereira. El interés por este asunto decae a mediados del siglo XVII, con Solórzano como punto límite.

5000 Lizcano, Manuel. España en el pensamiento hispanoamericano a la hora del reajuste del mundo. (*Cuad. Am.*, 32:2, marzo/abril 1992, p. 49–63)

Reflexiona sobre el papel que le correspondería representar al mundo ibérico en "la hora del reajuste del mundo" y a las puertas del siglo XXI. Recoge, asimismo, opiniones de escritores hispanoamericanos sobre la representación de España y sus aportes a la cultura americana. [CJB]

5001 López y Rivas, Gilberto. Nación y pueblos indios en el neoliberalismo. México: Plaza y Valdés Editores, 1995. 171 p.: bibl.

En general, los artículos del libro reiteran—y tienden a fundamentar—la necesidad de la "autonomía" de los pueblos indios dentro del Estado-nación. En ese contexto se destaca y defiende la rebelión surgida en el Estado de Chiapas, México.

5002 Löwy, Michael. Modernidad y crítica de la modernidad en la Teología de la Liberación. (*Cuad. Am.*, 5:6, nov./dic. 1991, p. 229–252)

Expone las líneas principales de la crítica que la teología de la liberación formula a la modernidad en su versión capitalista: individualismo, modernización económica, culto del progreso técnico e ideología del desarrollo. Crítica que, a diferencia de las teologías progresistas, no acepta pensar la historia a partir de esos elementos ambivalentes. [CJB]

Magallón Anaya, Mario. Martí: a cien años de *Nuestra América*. Ver item **5128.**

5003 Malamud, Carlos. El espejo quebrado: la imagen de España en América de la independencia a la transición democrática. (*Rev. Occident.*, 131, abril 1992, p. 180–198)
Síntesis de una obra más amplia sobre el asunto. Repasa las apreciaciones sobre España en dos momentos: el siglo XIX con posterioridad a la Independencia, y en la actualidad. Para comentarios del historiador, ver *HLAS 56:741*.

5004 Mansilla, H.C.F. Aspectos antidemocráticos y antipluralistas en la cultura política latinoamericana. (*Rev. Estud. Polít.*, 74, oct./dic. 1991, p. 17–42)
Severa disección de las debilidades de la democracia latinoamericana, entre las cuales el autor encuentra: el antipluralismo, el centralismo, el autoritarismo, el caudillismo, el estatismo y la empleomanía. Todo ello configuraría un "monismo políticocultural." Gran parte de la explicación de estos fenómenos residiría en la herencia islámica e hispano-católica. El análisis se muestra independiente de las actitudes políticas e ideológicas más corrientes.

5005 Mansilla, H.C.F. La crítica contemporánea a las ilusiones de la modernidad. (*Cuad. Marcha*, 10:105, junio 1995, p. 11–14)
Este artículo se vincula con otros escritos del autor, en los cuales ha analizado la modernidad y los efectos de la posmodernidad, con especial referencia a América Latina. [CJB]

5006 Mansilla, H.C.F. El dilema de la identidad nacional y del desarrollo autóctono en una era de normas y metas universalistas. (*Social. Particip.*, 50, junio 1990, p. 1–16)
El eje (y la utilidad) del artículo reside en mostrar diversas reacciones, en el Tercer Mundo, frente a la hegemonía, imposición o condición modélica de la cultura occidental y sus consecuencias económico-tecnológicas. Entre esas reacciones se consideran: la teoria de la dependencia, el marxismo, el populismo y los fundamentalismos religiosos. El breve sumario no responde bien al contenido.

5007 Mansilla, H.C.F. El disciplinamiento social como factor del desarrollo histórico. (*Folia Humaníst.*, 30:325, marzo/abril 1992, p. 117–132)
Primera parte de un artículo en el que

se discute la evolución moderna y actual de Europa y Norteamérica como paradigmas normativos de evolución histórica. Por contraposición se propone una revalorización de tradiciones culturales y formas de organización premodernas en las sociedades periféricas de Asia, Africa y América Latina. [CJB]

5008 Mansilla, H.C.F. La ensayística latino americana y la cuestión de la identidad colectiva. (*Síntesis/Madrid*, 13, enero/abril 1991, p. 15–37)
La ensayística latinoamericana es vista en cuanto a su contenido de pensamiento. La divide en tres grandes direcciones: 1) las corrientes antiliberales, en la que incluye autores como Leopoldo Zea y Augusto Salazar Bondy junto con Mariátegui, Lucas Alamán, Jorge Abelardo Ramos, Eduardo Galeano, Mario Benedetti, Fernández Retamar y expresiones de "la reivindicación de lo americano" y de la teoría de la dependencia; 2) las corrientes pro-occidentales, donde entran las manifestaciones de la modernización latino americana, como las de Alberdi y Sarmiento, por ejemplo; 3) las corrientes críticas, donde incluye a Rodó, Octavio Paz y Carlos Rangel. Se advierte que el autor es crítico de las manifestaciones latinoamericanistas más difundidas y prevalecientes.

5009 Mansilla, H.C.F. La herencia iberocatólica y la esfera pólíticoinstitucional en América Latina. (*Social. Particip.*, 54, junio 1991, p. 45–69)
Tras largas consideraciones apoyadas en abudantes fuentes se concluye que tanto las grandes culturas autóctomas de América como la tradición iberocatólica no favorecieron en América Latina los hábitos democráticos, la tolerancia del disenso y el espíritu crítico, y en cambio fomentaron el centralismo y el autoritarismo burocraticista.

5010 Maresca, Silvio Juan. Topología y máscara en el fin de la confrontación. (*Rev. Filos. Latinoam. Cienc. Soc.*, 7:17, marzo 1992, p. 7–25, bibl.)
Reflexiones muy personales de un representante de la originaria filosofía de la liberación, que toma en cuenta la situación del mundo actual y cómo los cambios ocurridos habían afectado a dicha corriente filosófica. Pareciera que en lugar de "filosofía de la li-

beración" se prefiere hablar de "filosofía latino americana." Es obvia en la posición actual del autor la elaboración de ciertas tesis de Nietzsche.

5011 Martínez Torrón, Diego. Los liberales románticos españoles ante la descolonización americana, 1808–1833. Madrid: Editorial MAPFRE, 1992. 318 p.: bibl., indexes. (Col. MAPFRE 1492. Col. Relaciones entre España y América; 8)

La tesis principal es la necesidad de revalorar el liberalismo español, en general y como causa contribuyente a la independencia de las colonias. Temas principales son las Cortes de Cádiz, manifestaciones en la prensa y autores individuales como Manuel José Quintana, Alvaro Flores Estrada y José María Blanco White. Coincide con ciertas posiciones del historiador de las ideas José Luis Abellán. La investigación está basada en un vasto material. Se nota en este autor, como en otros recientes, cierto cansancio ante las tradicionales críticas a España por su pasado colonialista, aunque no tiene en absoluto el tono defensivo de los nostálgicos de la España imperial. Veáse también item **5018.**

5012 Medin, Tzvi. Ortega y Gasset en la cultura hispanoamericana. México: Fondo de Cultura Económica, 1994. 318 p.: bibl. (Sección de obras de filosofía)

Libro muy valioso y completo sobre la presencia e influencia de Ortega en Hispanoamérica, y las reacciones, favorables y contrarias, que originó, aun después de su muerte. De hecho es también útil para seguir la marcha del pensamiento filosófico latino americano durante buena parte del siglo veinte.

5013 Melgar Bao, Ricardo. Las utopías indígenas y la posmodernidad en América Latina. (*Cuad. Am.*, 8:1, enero/feb. 1994, p. 64–79, bibl.)

Resumen y balance de las distintas posiciones frente a las utopías indígenas— entre las que se destaca la del estudioso peruano Alberto Flores Galindo—y los nuevos desafíos que plantean a la luz de distintos documentos producidos en Guatemala en 1991 con motivo del II Encuentro del Movimiento Quinientos Años de Resistencia Indígena y Popular. [CJB]

5014 Memorias del III Simposio Internacional sobre Pensamiento Filosófico Latinoamericano. (*Islas/Santa Clara*, 102, mayo/agosto 1992, p. 5–20)

Util para tener una idea de las ponencias que se presentaron al Simposio (Santa Clara, Cuba, 1992). La crónica correspondiente a la filosofía de la liberación es más detallada respecto de las conclusiones a que se arribó.

5015 Méndez Salcedo, Ildefonso. Dos estudios sobre Montesquieu y Bolívar. Caracas: M.A. García e Hijo 1995 77 p.: bibl., ill.

Contiene dos trabajos: uno sobre Montesquieu y otro sobre "La Influencia de Montesquieu en el Pensamiento de Simón Bolivar." En este segundo se persiguen las huellas de *El espíritu de las leyes* en los escritos y la correspondencia del Libertador.

5016 Merino Medina, Augusto. Notas sobre cultura, modernidad y política en el mundo de habla hispana. (*Contribuciones*, 3, julio/sept. 1991, p. 130–138)

Tras consideraciones sobre la historia de España relacionadas con su acción e influencia en América, la principal conclusión es que el mundo hispánico no ha resuelto el ajuste con la cultura de la Ilustración, es decir, con la modernidad, ni hay posibilidades de una completa asimilación. Lo último tampoco es deseable para el autor, por ser mejor alternativa mantenerse dentro de la propia tradición y adoptar desde ella los valores modernos con criterio selectivo. La conclusión es semejante a la del artículo de Enrique Cantolla. Veáse también item **4931.**

5017 Miró Quesada, Francisco. Philosophy and the birth of Latin America. (*Diogenes/Philosophy*, 154, Summer 1991, p. 47–69, bibl.)

Por un lado explica el desarrollo de la filosofía latinoamericana, en sus etapas y su relación con la realidad histórica. Por otro, destaca la condición que esa filosofía tiene y debe tener como filosofía de la liberación.

5018 Murillo, Fernando. América y la dignidad del hombre: los derechos del hombre en la filosofía de la historia de América. Madrid: Editorial MAPFRE, 1992. 321 p.: bibl., index. (Col. MAPFRE 1492. Col. Relaciones entre España y América; 18)

El propósito es mostrar el lugar que la

unidad y la dignidad del género humano tienen en la antropología cristiana, y cómo el hecho americano, tanto en la época de la colonización como en la de la independencia, se convierte en una vía para su realización. En la segunda parte se plantea el problema de las influencias intelectuales y filosóficas en las ideas independentistas. Es parte de una literatura que se enfrenta a la acción de España sin las nostalgias del antiguo imperio pero tampoco sin pedir disculpas por ella. Semejante en este sentido a la actitud que muestra el libro de Martínez Torrón. Ver item **5011.**

Neira, Hernán. El espejo del olvido: la idea de América en las *Memorias* de Juan Bautista Túpac Amaru. Ver item **5183.**

5019 Núñez, Jorge. Orígenes del pensamiento nacional en América Latina. (*in* Colección nuestra patria es América: nación, estado y conciencia nacional. Recopilación de Jorge Nuñez Sánchez, Quito: Editora Nacional, 1992, v. 2, p. 27–51, bibl.)
Aunque basado en una bibliografía mínima, es útil como narrativa sintética del siglo XVIII latinoamericano en lo que se refiere a las reformas borbónicas, la posición de los criollos y la influencia de la Revolución Francesa.

5020 Ortega, Julio. Identidad y postmodernidad en América Latina. (*Social. Particip.*, 70, junio 1995, p. 41–52, ill.)
Texto de una conferencia que analiza, con perspectiva histórica, las definiciones de identidad en el desarrollo cultural de América Latina y su necesaria ampliación a la luz de la postmodernidad. [CJB]

5021 Osuna, Antonio. Ideario político-religioso de las Leyes de Indias. (*Estud. Filos.*, 41:118, 1992, p. 391–432)
Los dos principales temas son: el papel de la fe católica en la legislación; y la cuestión de los títulos del dominio sobre la Indias. Artículo muy útil a pesar de ser un asunto muchas veces tratado. Muestra el papel fundamental que jugó, en todo el fenómeno americano de la época, el convencimiento del valor supremo de la propia religión. De particular interés lo que dice sobre la Bulas alejandrinas.

5022 Palma, Norman. Del deber-ser frente a la negatividad histórica de la realidad latinoamericana. (*Cuad. Am.*, 4:2(20), marzo/abril 1990, p. 34–41)

Señala aspectos formales y de hecho que debeían darse para superar lo que llama "la negatividad histórica de la realidad latino americana." El deber-ser de Latinoamérica se alcanzaría con el estado de justicia, aquel en el cual las prácticas sociales estaían guiadas por principios de orden universal: el bien, la verdad, la justicia. [CJB]

5023 Parker, Christián. Christianity and the cultural identity of Latin America on the threshold of the 21st century. (*Soc. Compass*, 39:4, Dec. 1992, p. 571–583)
La religión no es la esencia de la cultura, pero el cristianismo, entendido como factor cultural, puede ser la base de una nueva civilización en América Latina, siempre que sean predominantes la cultura indígena y la popular.

5024 Paz, Octavio. La democracia: lo absoluto y lo relativo. (*Rev. Occident.*, 130, marzo 1991, p. 5–25)
Páginas que se inscriben en la mejor tradición del ensayo latinoamericano de ideas. Su tema es una meditación del presente, que se retrotrae a la conquista de América, los orígenes y las características de la modernidad, el eje revolucionario que va desde el Pueblo de la Revolución francesa hasta el Proletariado y el Comité Central del marxismo institucionalizado, la democracia actual y sus debilidades, lo absoluto y lo relativo en la existencia humana.

5025 Pensar desde América: vigencia y desafíos actuales. Coordinación y prólogo de Dina V. Picotti C. Buenos Aires: Catálogos, 1995 349 p.: bibl.
Contiene 30 ponencias presentadas a una reunión aparentemente realizada en 1993. Todas las contribuciones tienen referencia directa o indirecta a América Latina. Se abre con tres trabajos que prodían considerarse metodológicos: el de Daniel Toribio, que propone bases para una adecuada historia del pensamiento latinoamericano; el de Arturo A. Roig, que consiste en una visión retrospectiva de los fundamentos que este importante autor utilizó en su labor historiográfica; y el de Celina Lértora Mendoza, que cuestiona críticamente conceptos como los de 'unidad latinoamericana', 'linealidad de la historia' y 'sentido de la historia'. Algunos temas de la reunión fueron: postmodernidad, tecnociencia, antropología y hermenéutica, arte latinoamericano y experiencia religiosa.

Entre los autores se cuentan: Miguel Wiñazki, Aníbal Fornari, Mario Casalla, Gustavo Cirigliano, Graciela Maturo, Julio de Zan y Hugo Biagini.

5026 Pérez García, Antonio. Sobre la teología de la liberación. (*Razón Fe*, 226:1127/1128, sept./oct. 1992, p. 297–310, bibl.)

Reflexiones sobre la teología de la liberación en la que se señalan algunos de sus rasgos principales; dentro de los que se destaca el hecho de que sería un fenómeno cultural emparentado con el resto de la cultura latinoamericana contemporánea. [CJB]

5027 Pí Esquijarrosa, Manuel and **Gilberto Valdés Gutiérrez.** El paradigma socialista: su perdida autenticidad en América Latina. La Habana: Editorial de Ciencias Sociales; Buenos Aires: A.B.R.N. Producciones Gráficas, 1994. 63 p.: bibl. (Pinos nuevos. Ensayo)

El texto es más positivo para el socialismo de lo que sugiere el título. Es una reflexión sobre el futuro del marxismo, con aplicación a América Latina, desde el ambiente marxista cubano. Refleja la confusión provocada por la actual crisis de esa doctrina y tiende a su reconstitución en la praxis futura. En algunos aspectos se muestra flexibilidad, como en la posible combinación de planificación y mercado. En otros, la posición es más tradicional, como cuando se insiste en la función del Partido como "vanguardia."

5028 Picón-Salas, Mariano. Europa-América: preguntas a la esfinge de la cultura y otros ensayos. Selección de Guillermo Sucre. Introducción de Adolfo Castañón. Notas y variantes de Cristian Alvarez. Caracas: Monte Avila Editores Latino americana, 1996. 316 p.: appendix, bibl. (Biblioteca Mariano Picón-Salas; 5)

Este libro se publicó por primera vez (incluyendo el material de otro aparecido diez años antes en Chile) en México (ver *HLAS 14:2441*). En la presente y bien cuidada edición, se reproduce agregándole diez ensayos de tema hispanoamericano. Es parte de una encomiable iniciativa: reeditar los escritos de Mariano Picón-Salas en doce volúmenes.

5029 El populismo en España y América. Recopilación de José Alvarez Junco y Ricardo González Leandri. Madrid: Editorial Catriel, 1994. 255 p.: bibl. (Col. Ensayo)

Dos artículos tienen intención de clarificación conceptual (José Alvarez Junco, "El Populismo como Problema") o analítica (Carlos de la Torre, "Los Significados Ambiguos de los Populismos Latinoamericanos"). Otros se refieren específicamente a España (Eduardo González Calleja); a Argentina (Juan Carlos Torre, Ricardo González Leandri y Mariano Plotkin, todos sobre el peronismo); a Bolivia (Ferrán Gallego, sobre el Movimiento Nacionalista Revolucionario); a Brasil (Waldo Ansaldi); a Chile (Jean Grugel); a Ecuador (Carlos de la Torre, velasquismo); y a Perú (Aldo Mariátegui, el APRA). Volumen útil sobre un tema no siempre bien definido.

5030 The postmodernism debate in Latin America. Edited by John Beverley, Michael Aronna, and José Miguel Oviedo. Durham, N.C.: Duke Univ. Press, 1995. 322 p.: bibl., index.

Grupo de artículos en torno a los conceptos de modernidad y postmodernidad aplicados a América Latina. Los compiladores vinculan esta temática con la crisis de la izquierda y su futuro, aunque no todos los artículos señalan esa dirección. Contribuyen: José Joaquín Brunner, Néstor García Canclini, Martín Hopenhayn, Aníbal Quijano (registrado en *HLAS 56:4895*). Por razones no muy claras, los editores decidieron cerrar el volumen con la primera declaración del Ejército Zapatista de Liberación Nacional (EZLN).

5031 Queralto, Ramon. Síntesis doctrinal del pensamiento de Bartolomé de las Casas. (*Rábida/Huelva*, 9, marzo 1991, p. 84–90, ill., photo)

La acción de Las Casas y su motivación práctica son bien conocidas, pero no se comprenden sin reconocer la existencia de presupuestos teóricos o "razones teórico-filosóficas" que el dominico tomó de ciertas fuentes y elaboró orgánicamente. Cuáles fueron esos supuestos y su consecuente aplicación, según el juicio del autor, es el contenido del presente artículo, resumen de una obra más extensa.

5032 Quiles, Ismael. Filosofía latinoamericana en los siglos XVI a XVIII. Buenos Aires: Ediciones Depalma, 1989. 171 p.: bibl., index. (Obras de Ismael Quiles, S.J.; 18)

Conjunto de valiosos trabajos, la mayoría previamente publicados y procedentes de la década del 50. Los autores estudiados con mayor detalle son Fray Alonso de la Veracruz y Antonio Rubio. Hay también estudios sobre la escolástica latinoamericana en general y sobre Chile, Venezuela y Argentina. De interés para una antigua controversia en torno a la filosofía colonial es el artículo: "La Libertad de Investigación Filosófica en la Época Colonial."

5033 500 años del ensayo en Hispanoamérica: antología anotada. Recopilación e introducción de Cathy Maree. Pretoria: Univ. of South Africa, 1993. 489 p.: bibl., index. (Studia originalia ; 16)

Antología del ensayo hispanoamericano y sobre el tema de Hispanoamérica (o sus países individuales). Pensado principalmente para uso de cátedra. Si se excluyen los siempre posibles comentarios sobre faltantes o sobrantes (por ejemplo, por qué la ausencia de Mariano Picón-Salas), es un trabajo bien elaborado y con el necesario aparato de aclaraciones didácticas.

5034 Rigolot, François. Montaigne: lector europeo de América. (*Cuad. Am.*, 46:4, julio/agosto 1994, p 69–81)

Se interroga sobre el origen y la originalidad de la perspectiva de Montaigne en su encuentro con el Nuevo Mundo. Montaigne coloca en un cono de relatividad lo que se pueda decir de las costumbres de América y halla su par en la propia Europa. Con esto suprimirá la alteridad radical del Nuevo Mundo y mostrará, al mismo tiempo, la frágil frontera entre "civilización" y "barbarie." [CJB]

5035 Rivadeneira Vargas, Antonio José. Dialéctica integradora de Bolívar en América Latina. Bogotá: Publicaciones de la Univ. Central, 1989. 369 p.: bibl. (Pensamiento latinoamericano; 9)

El tema de la integración latinoamericana se enfoca en el contexto de los conceptos de dependencia y libertad. En ese sentido se contrastan el monroísmo y el panamericanismo, por un lado, y la "integración en la libertad", de origen bolivariano, por el otro. Se destaca la figura latinoamericanista de José María Torres Caicedo. La segunda parte del libro es documental, conteniendo textos históricos de Bolívar, de tratados internacionales y de organismos de integración.

5036 Rodríguez Ozán, María Elena. Las ideologías de los inmigrantes europeos en América Latina. (*Cuad. Am.*, 7:41, sept./oct. 1993, p. 122–130)

Se refiere especialmente a la inmigración hacia el Cono Sur de América a fines del siglo XIX y comienzos del XX. De esos grupos analiza la acción de anarquistas y socialistas, destacando su error de querer reproducir en un ambiente diferente las formas de acción política de los países europeos. [CJB]

5037 Roig, Arturo Andrés. Figuras y símbolos de Nuestra América. (*Cuad. Am.*, 6:4, julio/agosto 1992, p. 171–179, bibl.)

Excelentes páginas que representan una antigua preocupación del autor y concluyen con el simbolismo de las Madres de Plaza de Mayo (Argentina). Estas habían realizado la "locura" de Antígona, pero a diferencia de la figura clásica, encerrada en oscuras leyes de la naturaleza, expresaían la lucha por la subjetividad creadora de una nueva eticidad. [CJB]

5038 Roig, Arturo Andrés. El pensamiento latinoamericano y su aventura. v. 1–2. Buenos Aires: Centro Editor de América Latina, 1994. 2 v.

Nueva recopilación de artículos de este destacado autor, que lo confirman en sus opiniones sobre la interpretación de América Latina y su pensamiento.

5039 Roig, Arturo Andrés. Rostro y filosofía de América Latina. Mendoza, Argentina: EDIUNC, 1993. 228 p.: appendix, bibl. (Serie América Latina; 2)

El contenido se agrupa en dos grandes temas: "Entre la Civilización y la Barbarie," con un artículo metodológico, dos sobre Argentina (Sarmiento, Alberdi) y uno sobre Ecuador (Montalvo); y "Una Filosofía para la Liberación," en general sobre el tema de la filosofía latinoamericana. El volumen está precedido por un estudio de Ofelia Schutte sobre el pensamiento de Roig. Contiene también el texto de dos entrevistas al autor, sumamente reveladoras de su posición. Se cierra con un apéndice bibliográfico que contiene publicaciones de Roig entre 1986 y 1992.

5040 Rojas Bez, José. Visión de América en Ortega y Gasset. (*Islas/Santa Clara*, 101, enero/abril 1992, p. 183–196)

Exposición comentada de los escritos y opiniones de Ortega sobre América, especialmente en relación con las famosas afirmaciones de Hegel sobre el particular. [CJB]

5041 Rojas Osorio, Carlos. Cien años de filosofía en América Latina. (*Plural/ San Juan*, 9/10:1/2, 1991/92, p. 9–25, bibl.)

Rápido panorama de la filosofía latino americana desde mediados del siglo XIX a mediados del siglo XX. Se consideran los autores más consagrados, desde Andrés Bello a José Vasconcelos. Al final se señala la necesidad de superar el enfoque histórico de la filosofía latinoamericana basado en las escuelas europeas, y se llama la atención sobre las influencias de filósofos latinoamericanos entre sí, ejemplificándolo con el caso de José Victorino Lastarria y las menciones que sobre él hacen Varona, Hostos y Ramón Rosa.

5042 Rojas Osorio, Carlos. El impacto de la Ilustración en el pensamiento latino americano. (*Torre/Río Piedras*, 5:número extraordinario, 1991, p. 139–155)

Señala la presencia de autores como Rousseau, Voltaire, Montesquieu y Raynal. Examina especialmente el pensamiento de Mariano Moreno (1778–1811), miembro de la Primera Junta de Buenos Aires, y el de Bolívar.

5043 Romero Baró, José María. Alain Guy y la idea de finitud en la filosofía latino americana. (*Rev. Filos./México*, 24:72, sept./dic. 1991, p. 276–294)

Busca las influencias determinantes en el pensamiento de Alain Guy, autor que se ha ocupado mucho del pensamiento español e hispanoamericano. Interesa la extensión concedida en el artículo a la discusión de Guy sobre autores como Francisco Romero y Samuel Ramos.

5044 Sanabria, José Rubén. En torno a la filosofía latinoamericana. (*Rev. Filos./México*, 25:75, sept./dic. 1992, p. 360–417)

El artículo intenta una visión muy extensa de este recurrente tema. Están representados numerosos autores que lo han tratado: Risieri Frondizi, José Gaos, Luis Villoro, Alejandro Rossi, Augusto Salazar Bondy, Alberto Wagner de Reyna, Jorge Millas, Aníbal Sánchez Reulet, Samuel Ramos, Leopoldo Zea (a quien el autor estima como muy importante), Francisco Miró Quesada, Arturo A. Roig y varios representantes de la filosofía de la liberación. Para esta última el autor tiene algunas observaciones críticas.

5045 Sánchez-Gey Venegas, Juana. El modernismo filosófico en América. (*Cuad. Am.*, 7:41, sept./oct. 1993, p. 109–121)

Se analiza la inserción de José Enrique Rodó en el modernismo y se afirma el carácter eticista de su pensamiento. Para la autora el modernismo tendría tres componentes principales: la propuesta moral, la estética y el reconocimiento de España. [CJB]

5046 Sánchez Vázquez, Adolfo. Exilio y filosofía: la aportación de los exiliados españoles al filosofar latinoamericano. (*Cuad. Am.*, 5:6, nov./dic. 1991, p. 139–153, bibl.)

Visión panorámica del aporte de los "transterrados" españoles a la filosofía latino americana. Desfilan los nombres de José Gaos, Joaquín Xirau, Juan David García Bacca, María Zambrano, José Gallegos Rocafull, Eugenio Imaz, Jaime Serra Hunter, Eduardo Nicol y Luis Recaséns Siches, entre otros. [CJB]

5047 Saranyana, Josep-Ignasi. Influencia de la conmemoración del Quinto Centenario en la teología latinoamericana. (*Scr. Theol.*, 24:1, enero/abril 1992, p. 177–196)

Tomando como tema el valor que, dentro de la teología de la liberacion, y de variadas maneras, se atribuye a la primitiva u originaria evangelización de Iberoamérica, disiente de autores como Enrique Dussel, Gustavo Gutiérrez, Pablo Richard y Clodovis Boff, entre otros.

5048 Schutte, Ofelia. Cultural identity and social liberation in Latin American thought. Albany: State Univ. of New York Press, 1993. 313 p.: bibl., index. (SUNY series in Latin American and Iberian thought and culture)

El libro tiene dos grandes temas: la identidad cultural, sobre la que se expresan opiniones balanceadas entre los extremos posibles, y la "liberación social", entendida en general como liberación con respecto a estructuras opresivas. El itinerario de estos temas se cumple partiendo de consideraciones teóricas preliminares para desarrollar luego capítulos críticos sobre autores como José Carlos Mariátegui, Leopoldo Zea, Samuel Ramos, Augusto Salazar Bondy, Arturo A. Roig y Francisco Miró Quesada, y corrientes como la teología de la liberación, la filosofía de la liberación y el pensamiento feminista. Posiblemente en el tratamiento de este último tema se muestren con mayor intensidad las opiniones personales de la autora.

Schvarz, Niko. América Latina y el retoñar de la utopía: la concepción de Rodney Arismendi sobre la revolución continental, de cara al siglo XXI. See item **5239.**

5049 Schvarzberg, Oscar. El americanismo y su errática historia. México: Instituto Panamericano de Geografía e Historia, 1995. 70 p.: bibl. (Pub. / Instituto Panamericano de Geografía e Historia; 480)

En cuanto a estructura, no se trata de una historia formal del americanismo (en realidad, hispanoamericanismo), sino de un ensayo. La parte más destacada y menos conocida es la que el autor dedica a las tensiones conflictivas entre los países bolivarianos y la Argentina, representadas, aunque no exclusivamente, por las posiciones de Bolívar y Bernardino Rivadavia.

5050 Sepúlveda Muñoz, Isidro. Comunidad cultural e hispano-americanismo, 1885–1936. Prólogo de Javier Tusell. Madrid: Univ. Nacional de Educación a Distancia, 1994. 331 p.: bibl. (Aula abierta; A.A.67)

Obra muy completa sobre el tema, dentro de la época delimitada. Examina las dos modalidades ideales de unión entre España y la América española: el panhispanismo, en general de carácter conservador, y lo que el autor denomina el hispano-americanismo progresista. En la parte correspondiente a las bases conceptuales de estas corrientes hay capítulos de interés sobre el anti-hispanismo en Hispanoamérica, las consecuencias de la expansión norteamericana, el indigenismo y la leyenda negra, entre otros. La bibliografía es de particular valor. Aunque la mayor parte del material se refiere a España, importa para la historia de las ideas en América Latina.

5051 Squella, Agustín. Presencia de Bobbio en Iberoamérica. Valparaíso, Chile: EDEVAL, 1993. 84 p. (Col. Temas / Univ. de Valparaíso, Facultad de Derecho y Ciencias Sociales; 18)

Lo más importante del libro es una exposición—clara y sucinta—de las posiciones de Norberto Bobbio en teoría del derecho, filosofía política y concepción de la democracia; pero también se refiere a quienes han difundido a Bobbio en América Latina y a sus seguidores y simpatizantes en varios países latinoamericanos.

5052 Tamayo-Acosta, Juan José. Presente y futuro de la teología de la liberación. Madrid: San Pablo, 1994. 213 p.: bibl. (Teología siglo XXI; 4)

El punto de partida o motivación del libro es negar que la teología de la liberación se encuentre en vías de desaparición. Señala sin embargo la omisión de esa corriente en la Asamblea del Episcopado Latinoamericano que tuvo lugar en Santo Domingo en 1992. En dos capítulos centrales reitera el cuerpo conceptual básico de la teología de la liberación y los ajustes que se encuentran realizando en función de las nuevas circunstancias del mundo. Concluye formulando la pregunta de si es posible una teología semejante en Europa.

5053 Universidad Nacional Autónoma de México. Centro de Investigaciones Humanísticas de Mesoamérica y el Estado de Chiapas. El pensamiento lascasiano en la conciencia de América y Europa. Recopilación de Pablo González Casanova Henríquez. San Cristóbal de Las Casas, Mexico: UNAM, Centro de Investigaciones Humanísticas de Mesoamérica y el Estado de Chiapas, 1994. 281 p.: bibl.

Casi todos los artículos tratan el tema vinculándolo a sus resonancias actuales, y ninguno en mayor medida que el que abre el volumen, a cargo de Pablo González Casanova: "Colonización y Emancipación Ayer y Hoy: Historia del Hambre." Algunos se ocupan de las bases filosóficas (Pablo Romo Cedano) y jurídicas (Rafael Márquez Piñero) del pensamiento lascasiano. El volumen concluye con una "conferencia magistral" de Joaquín Sánchez Macgregor sobre Colón y Las Casas.

5054 Vargas Lozano, Gabriel. La filosofía latinoamericana en el siglo XX. (*Lateinamerika/Rostock*, 25:2, 1990, p. 9–17)

Panorama del pensamiento filosófico latinoamericano desde el positivismo en adelante, dentro de los límites de un artículo no extenso. De la filosofía desarrollada en el siglo veinte encuentra predominantes el marxismo, el historicismo y la filosofía analítica. También presta atención a la filosofía de la liberación. Contiene apreciaciones, tanto sobre las corrientes mencionadas como, en forma de conclusiones, sobre el proceso total. Revela simpatías marxistas y estima que la filosofía latinoamericana "debe contribuir... al diseño de una sociedad racional, igualitaria y democrática que prefigure el cambio histórico."

5055 Vargas Lozano, Gabriel. Filosofía y autenticidad en la cultura latinoamericana hoy. (*Cuad. Am.*, 46:4, julio/agosto 1994, p. 163–171)

Básicamente trata del debate entre Luis Villoro y Leopoldo Zea en torno a dos modos de entender la filosofía y sus relaciones con la sociedad latinoamericana. A juicio del autor los desacuerdos existían por falta de una teoría de la filosofía, y enumera algunas de las condiciones de producción de esa metafilosofía. [CJB]

5056 Vargas Martínez, Gustavo. Bolivarismo y monroísmo cien años después. (*Cuad. Am.*, 4:5(23), sept./oct. 1990, p. 116–137)

Las ideas de Bolívar sobre la unidad americana no debían confundirse con el panamericanismo monroísta. El Libertador habría considerado que a Estados Unidos debía tratárselo como vecino forzoso, pero no facilitarle su intervención en asuntos internos del continente. [CJB]

5057 Weinberg, Gregorio. Viejo y nuevo humanismo. (*Cuad. Am.*, 7:38, marzo/abril 1993, p. 11–16)

Señala algunas de las limitaciones del "viejo" humanismo, con su carácter eurocéntrico, y propone un "nuevo" humanismo que superaría los reduccionismos para conformar una cosmovisión de fuerte carga social y ética. [CJB]

5058 Werz, Nikolaus. Aspectos del pensamiento político y cultural en Latinoamérica. (*Ibero-Am. Arch.*, 18:3/4, 1992, p. 429–443, bibl.)

El contenido, que no corresponde exactamente con el título, es una visión general de los 500 años, llegando hasta las últimas manifestaciones del siglo veinte. En general, es una exposición equilibrada. Una de las conclusiones del autor—de lengua alemana—es que pintar el pasado latinoamericano con colores demasiado oscuros puede no ser beneficioso para el futuro de la región.

5059 Zea, Leopoldo. América, vacío de Europa. (*Cuad. Am.*, 35:5, sept./oct. 1992, p. 11–20)

Consecuente con se línea de pensamiento el autor sostiene que América, tierra vacía para la Europa conquistadora, ha sido conformada por un crisol de razas y culturas e incorporada a un mundo que debe ser Casa Común del Hombre con sus diversas expresiones de identidad. [CJB]

5060 Zea, Leopoldo. Derecho a la diferencia: más allá de la tolerancia. (*Cuad. Am.*, 47, sept./oct. 1994, p. 11–21)

A raíz de la propuesta de organismos internacionales para declarar el año de 1995 como Año de la Tolerancia, el autor discute el concepto. Dice que no se trataría de tolerar lo diferente, sino de aceptar y comprender la diversidad. Como resultado propone declarar dicho año como Año del Derecho a la Diferencia. [CJB]

5061 Zea, Leopoldo. Latinoamérica y el problema de la modernidad. (*Cuad. Am.*, 46:4, julio/agosto 1994, p. 11–28)

Sobre el tema de las nuevas relaciones mundiales después de 1989, el rol de Estados Unidos y el caso particular de México. [CJB]

5062 Zea, Leopoldo. Más allá de los quinientos años. (*Cuad. Am.*, 32:2, marzo/abril 1992, p. 114–122)

Congruente con otros escritos del autor producidos con motivo del Quinto Centenario, la obra se cuestiona sobre lo que debería esperarse más allá de la fecha. Halla respuestas en el futuro que podían protagonizar en común los pueblos a ambos lados del Atlántico, en conjunto concebidos como mundo iberoamericano. [CJB]

5063 Zea, Leopoldo. Problemas de identidad e integración en Latinoamérica. (*Cuad. Am.*, 5:5, sept./oct. 1991, p. 48–57)

Trabajo de síntesis sobre el proceso de identidad latinoamericana y los vaivenes en su relación con España. Señala que ante el nuevo orden mundial los pueblos debeían guardar la solidaridad, con independencia de sus identidades. [CJB]

5064 Zea, Leopoldo. Sentido y proyección del descubrimiento de América. (*Cuad. Am.*, 14:3(21), mayo/junio 1990, p. 106–120)

El Quinto Centenario le sirve al autor

para reflexionar sobre el futuro de las Américas, de Europa y de la humanidad, haciéndose eco del mensaje de José Vasconcelos en favor de una "raza" capaz de "verdadera fraternidad y de visión realmente universal." [CJB]

MEXICO

5065 Abadie-Aicardi, Aníbal. La tradición salmantina en la Real y Pontificia Universidad de México, 1551-1821. (*Novahispania/México*, 2, 1996, p. 7-72)

Investigación de archivo que muestra la larga presencia de los estatutos de la Universidad de Salamanca en la vida de la Universidad de México.

5066 Aguila M., Marcos Tonatiuh. Daniel Cosío Villegas y Jesús Reyes Heroles: contrapuntos sobre el fracaso del liberalismo mexicano. (*Memoria/CEMOS*, 41, abril 1992, p. 5-18, bibl., photos)

Paralelo entre las dos figuras seleccionadas, con referencia al liberalismo, pero sobre todo a la Revolución Mexicana y al proceso político posterior a ella. Cosío Villegas resulta más intelectual y crítico cultural que político, y la inversa se da en Reyes Heroles.

5067 Antología del liberalismo social mexicano. Compilación y apuntes biográficos de Alejandro de Antuñano Maurer. México: Cambio XXI Fundación Mexicana, 1993. 249 p.: ill. (Textos fundamentales)

Oportuna reunión de textos, algunos de difícil acceso. Abarca desde Hidalgo en el siglo XIX hasta Francisco Villa en el XX, e incluye figuras como Morelos, Fernández de Lizardi, José María Luis Mora, Ignacio Ramírez, Benito Juárez, Francisco Madero, Ricardo Flores Magón y Venustiano Carranza, entre otros. También hay documentos, como el Programa del Partido Liberal Mexicano (1906). Muy útil la introducción, con rasgos biográficos de los autores seleccionados.

5068 Ardao, Arturo. La filosofía como compromiso de liberación. (*Cuad. Am.*, 6:4, julio/agosto 1992, p. 223-249)

Escrito para servir de prólogo al libro de Leopoldo Zea *La filosofía como compromiso de liberación* (Caracas: Biblioteca Ayacucho, 1991). [CJB]

5069 Basave Benítez, Agustín Francisco. México mestizo: análisis del nacionalismo mexicano en torno a la mestizofilia de Andrés Molina Enríquez. México: Fondo de Cultura Económica, 1992. 167 p.: bibl., index. (Sección de obras de historia)

El cuerpo central del libro lo compone el análisis de las ideas de Molina Enríquez sobre el mestizaje como fuente de identidad nacional. Según el autor, estas ideas no han sido percibidas debidamente. Resultan de interés la indicación de la raigambre positivista de Molina Enríquez y las comparaciones con otros autores latinoamericanos. Hay consideraciones sobre la apreciación del mestizaje antes y después de Molina Henríquez. El libro es de verdadero provecho para la historia de las ideas.

5070 Bassols, Narciso. Narciso Bassols, pensamiento y acción: antología. Compilación y estudio introductorio de Alonso Aguilar Monteverde. México: Fondo de Cultura Económica, 1995. 258 p.: bibl. (Vida y pensamiento de México)

Antología de escritos de Narciso Bassols (1897-1959), hombre público y político representante de la izquierda mexicana. El estudio introductorio es una narración y apreciación de la vida, la acción y las luchas políticas del personaje estudiado. Las *Obras* de Bassols fueron publicadas en 1964 (see *HLAS 30:1348*), por lo que este libro tiene más bien un sentido de difusión y revaloración.

Beggs, Donald. Sor Juana's feminism: from Aristotle to Irigaray. Ver **3390.**

5071 Beuchot, Mauricio. El conocimiento metafísico del absoluto en Fray Francisco Naranjo, O.P.—México, s. XVII. (*Novahispania/México*, 2, 1996, p. 147-160)

Fray Francisco Naranjo fue, aparentemente, el primero que escribió en español un comentario (parcial) a Santo Tomás. El presente artículo describe y comenta ese texto de Naranjo, que ha sido publicado recientemente en edición crítica por el propio Beuchot.

5072 Beuchot, Mauricio. Panorama de la historia de la filosofía novohispana. (*Mem. Acad. Mex. Hist.*, 33, 1989/90, p. 235-250)

Síntesis de la escolástica en la Nueva

España, desde los clásicos del siglo XVI hasta la apertura a la ciencia moderna en el XVIII, por uno de los mejores conocedores actuales del tema. Al parecer es anticipo de una extensa obra en preparación.

5073 Coloquio Lenguaje, Literatura y Filosofía, México, 1993. Lenguaje, literatura y filosofía: aproximaciones a Alejandro Rossi; memoria. México: Facultad de Filosofía y Letras, Instituto de Investigaciones Filosóficas, Univ. Nacional Autónoma de México; Ediciones del Equilibrista, 1994. 263 p.

Conjunto de artículos, en general breves, de homenaje a Alejandro Rossi, quien es parte del grupo filosófico analítico de México, pero también ha producido textos literarios. Entre los colaboradores se cuentan León Olivé, Víctor Flores Olea, Adolfo Sánchez Vázquez, Fernando Salmerón, Luis Villoro, Ramón Xirau, Enrique Krauze y Octavio Paz.

5074 Covo, Jacqueline. Une figure non conformiste du libéralisme mexicain: Isidoro Olvera. (in Minorités et marginalités en Espagne et en Amérique latine au XIXème siècle. Lille, France: Presses Univ. de Lille, 1990, p. 153–161)

Para la historia del liberalismo mexicano. Expone la posición de Isidoro Olvera en el Congreso Extraordinario Constituyente de 1856–57, sobre dos asuntos: la libertad religiosa, en la cual tuvo una posición moderada, y la propiedad de tierras, donde su tesitura fue mucho más radical y la autora la considera antecedente del Plan de Ayala.

5075 Epistemología y cultura: en torno a la obra de Luis Villoro. Edición de Ernesto Garzón Valdés y Fernando Salmerón. México: Univ. Nacional Autónoma de México, Instituto de Investigaciones Filosóficas, 1993. 366 p.: bibl.

Justificado y bien elaborado homenaje a uno de los más destacados filósofos latinoamericanos contemporáneos. Varios artículos se refieren a su obra *Creer, saber, conocer*; pero los hay también sobre temas como ideología y ética, y uno sobre la obra de Villoro como historiador, entre otros. Villoro responde a las objeciones expresadas en algunos trabajos en un artículo al final del volumen. Incluye también una bibliografía de Villoro.

5076 Fernández de Amicarelli, Estela. José Gaos y la ampliación metodológica en historia de las ideas. (*Cuad. Am.*, 4:2(20), marzo/abril 1990, p. 19–33)

Util trabajo, destinado a rescatar las etapas de la indagación en historia de las ideas: invención de textos; análisis y síntesis textuales; y articulación de la historia. En las tres etapas se apreciaría la presencia del sujeto, pues lo gnoseológico tendría su condición de posibilidad en un acto de afirmación de valores, intereses, afectos, que a su vez daían lugar a un "horizonte de comprensión" a partir del cual se mediaría la realidad y se constituiría la objetividad. La ampliación metodológica de la cual se habla es extraída de la obra de José Gaos *En torno a la filosofía mexicana* (ver *HLAS 18:3095*, *HLAS 19:5755*, and *HLAS 44:7541*), con apoyo en textos de Valentín Voloshinov y Arturo A. Roig. [CJB]

5077 Foro de la Juventud Positiva, 2nd, Guadalajara, Mexico, 1992. V centenario del nuevo mundo: afirmación de la mexicanidad. Guadalajara, Mexico: Univ. Autónoma de Guadalajara, 1992. 130 p.: ill.

Conjunto de conferencias o discursos, la mayoría de los cuales sostiene una apreciación favorable a España y a los valores de la colonización ibérica. Uno de ellos (autor: Antonio Caponnetto) es una crítica muy severa a la teología de la liberación. Entre los autores se encuentran: Silvio Zavala, Ernesto de la Torre Villar y Agustín Basave Fernández del Valle.

5078 Gomes Moreira, José Aparecido. Conquista y conciencia cristiana: el pensamiento indigenista y jurídico teológico de Don Vasco de Quiroga (+1565). Quito: Ediciones ABYA-YALA; México: CENAMI, 1990. 250 p.: bibl. (Col. 500 años; 28)

Es uno de los estudios más completos sobre Vasco de Quiroga. Presta gran atención a las fuentes, los antecedentes y los documentos de época que constituyen el contexto de los escritos y la acción de Vasco de Quiroga. Elude la visión hagiográfica que es frecuente en la apreciación de "Tata Vasco." La motivación interpretativa es actual y reitera una tónica conocida: tal como los cristianos del siglo XVI vieron en América la posibilidad de una nueva era para el cristianismo, también hoy se abre una "nueva era" para los pueblos colonizados y explotados del Tercer Mundo.

5079 Gómez-Martínez, José Luis. La nueva época de *Cuadernos Americanos* en el desarrollo del pensamiento mexicano. (*Cuad. Am.,* 6:1, enero/feb. 1992, p. 72–81)

Escrito con motivo de los cincuenta años de la revista Cuadernos Americanos, se refiere sucintamente a los años de fundación y al desenvolvimiento posterior de la publicación. [CJB]

5080 Gómez Serrano, Jesús. Notas sobre el liberalismo mexicano. (*Espacios Cult. Soc.,* 2:7, otoño/invierno 1991, p. 8–22, ill.)

Aunque preparado para una antología del liberalismo en Aguascalientes, da una visión general y clara del liberalismo mexicano. Entre los temas considerados dentro de esa corriente se encuentran: el sistema representativo; el régimen de libertades; la propiedad; el latifundismo; el desarrollo económico; la influencia norteamericana; la hispanofobia; los indios; la instrucción pública.

5081 Guadarrama González, Pablo. Urdimbres del pensamiento de Leopoldo Zea frente a la marginación y la barbarie. (*Cuad. Am.,* 37:1, enero/feb. 1993, p. 51–64)

Analiza el pensamiento de Zea en su libro *Discurso desde la marginación y la barbarie* (see *HLAS 52:5324*). Valora en el filósofo mexicano los siguientes aspectos: la elaboración de una filosofía de la historia; la fundamentación de un proyecto liberador para los países oprimidos y en especial América Latina; el esfuerzo por alcanzar un humanismo completo; la contribución a determinar la identidad cultural latinoamericana; y la especificidad de la reflexión filosófica latinoamericana. [CJB]

5082 Hale, Charles A. El renacimiento de la historia política y la Revolución Francesa en México. (*Cah. Am. lat.,* 10, 1990, p. 303)

Tomando como punto de partida la interpretación de la historia de México por parte de François-Xavier Guerra, revisa la influencia, durante la época liberal y aun del Porfiriato, de Benjamin Constant, Edouard Laboulaye e Hippolite Taine.

5083 Hernández Oramas, Roberto. Cultura e identidad nacional: una reflexión en torno a la filosofía en México, siglo XX. (*Is-*

las/Santa Clara, 102, mayo/agosto 1992, p. 144–151)

Rápido panorama, más descriptivo y sereno de lo que haían esperar ciertas opiniones políticas iniciales. Tras mencionar a Vasconcelos, Samuel Ramos y Narciso Bassols, reconoce tres grandes corrientes: la filosofía latinoamericana (Gaos, Zea y otros); el marxismo; y la filosofía analítica. Encuentra que el final del siglo muestra un relativo debilitamiento de las tres, lamenta el auge del postmodernismo y espera que se superen las dificultades que enfrenta el "pensamiento progresista."

5084 Ibargüengoitia, Antonio. Filosofía social en México: siglos XVI al XX; síntesis histórico-crítica. México: Univ. Iberoamericana, Filosofía, 1994. 224 p.: bibl. (Col. Sophia; 1)

Tras una primera parte teórica sobre el orden social y el bien común, en general y en el mundo contemporáneo, la segunda es una exposición sintética del pensamiento social de numerosos autores mexicanos desde la colonia hasta el siglo XX. Todavía en un último capítulo estos mismos autores se presentan en función de ciertos temas, como la libertad, la justicia, los valores sociales, etc.

5085 Ibargüengoitia, Antonio. El mestizaje y algunos puntos de vista de filósofos mexicanos. (*Rev. Univ. Medellín,* 55, julio/sept. 1990, p. 171–178, bibl.)

Se ocupa principalmente del filósofo hispano-mexicano Eduardo Nicol y su obra *El problema de la filosofía hispánica.* Ver *HLAS 25:5344.*

5086 Juan José de Eguiara y Eguren y la cultura mexicana. Coordinación y presentación de Ernesto de la Torre Villar. México: Univ. Nacional Autónoma de México, Coordinación de Humanidades, 1993. 176 p.: bibl. (Nueva biblioteca mexicana; 107)

Deben destacarse en primer lugar algunos de los apsectos documentales de la obra: un escrito teológico de Eguiara y Eguren traducido y presentado por Mauricio Beuchot; y "El Prólogo a las Selectas Disertaciones Mexicanas," traducido y con una introducción de Roberto Heredia Correa. Sin agotar la lista de las contribuciones indicamos que Ernesto de la Torre Villar tiene a su cargo la presentación del volumen y es autor de tres trabajos sobre Eguiara y Eguren, dos de ellos en relación con otras figuras: José

Antonio de Villaseñor y Sánchez, y Fray Juan de Zumárraga.

Lafaye, Jacques and **James Lockhart.** A scholarly debate: the origins of modern Mexico; *indígenistas* vs. *hispanistas*. Ver item **4997.**

5087 Lannoy, Jean-Louis de. La culture d'opposition des communautés indiennes du Mexique au 19ème siècle. (*in* Minorités et marginalités en Espagne et en Amérique latine au XIXème siècle. Lille, France: Presses Univ. de Lille, 1990, p. 197–210, bibl.)

Sintéticamente pero con claridad expone la situación de las poblaciones indígenas en México durante la Colonia y el siglo XIX. Una de las principales conclusiones es que tanto el racionalismo liberal como el darwinismo social de los positivistas, la modernización desarrollista y aun ciertas formas de marxismo se han caracterizado por la incomprensión de la realidad indígena, con los previsibles resultados negativos para esta última.

5088 León Portilla, Miguel. La filosofía náhuatl: estudiada en sus fuentes con un nuevo apéndice. Prólogo de Angel Ma. Garibay K. 7. ed. México: Univ. Nacional Autónoma de México, 1993. 461 p., 28 p. of plates: appendix, bibl., ill., index. (Serie Cultura náhuatl. Monografías; 10)

Reedición de una obra clásica. Publicada por primera vez en 1956, fue reseñada en el *HLAS 20:* 227 y *4767.* En esta edición se agrega un extenso apéndice, donde el autor discute una cuestión fundamental: críticas relacionadas con la autoridad de las fuentes utilizadas.

5089 Magallón Anaya, Mario. El filosofar de José Gaos: una aproximación. (*Cuad. Am.,* 32:2, marzo/abril 1992, p. 236–244)

El pensamiento de José Gaos (1900–69) estaría dominado por una constante: el tema de la filosofía. Esta, a su vez, se habría enriquecido con los cambios que le tocó vivir al filósofo. El artículo pone el acento en la idea de la filosofía como actividad personal y subjetiva, según la habría entendido Gaos. [CJB]

5090 Malpartida, Juan. América como utopía en la obra de Alfonso Reyes. (*Hoy Hist.,* 7:41, sept./oct. 1990, p. 15–20)

Ensayo inteligente, crítico, aunque respetuoso de la concepción de Reyes sobre América como utopía.

5091 Méndez Reyes, Salvador. El hispanoamericanismo de Lucas Alamán. (*Cuad. Am.,* 32:2, marzo/abril 1992, p. 228–235)

Revisión de las gestiones de Lucas Alamán (1792–1853) en pro de la unión de los países hispanoamericanos, realizadas en 1831. [CJB]

5092 Meyer, Jean A. Religión y nacionalismo. (*in* Coloquio de Antropología e Historia Regionales, *8th, Zamora, Mexico, 1986.* El nacionalismo en México. Zamora, Mexico: El Colegio de Michoacán, 1992, p. 703–718)

Relaciones entre la religión (católica) y la política en la historia de México, especialmente durante el siglo XIX.

5093 Morales Benítez, Otto. *Cuadernos Americanos:* una tribuna para la verdad y la libertad. (*Cuad. Am.,* 6:1, enero/feb. 1992, p. 41–71)

Pone de relieve la trayectoria y el valor de la revista Cuadernos Americanos en sus cincuenta años de vida. Destaca la labor de sus dos directores: el fundador, Jesús Silva Herzog, y Leopoldo Zea, el continuador. [CJB]

5094 Pedraza Reyes, Héctor. La reacción contra el positivismo en México, 1910–1967. (*Nóesis/UACJ,* 5:12, enero/junio 1994, p. 49–64, photos)

Traza un panorama muy general de lo ocurrido filosóficamente en México en el siglo veinte, reseña que utiliza para mostrar la superación del positivismo. Reacciona contra la filosofía analítica desarrollada recientemente en el país, y la confunde con una forma nueva de la orientación positivista tradicional.

5095 Pía León, Rafael. Para un retrato ideológico de Leopoldo Zea. (*Islas/Santa Clara,* 103, sept./dic. 1992, p. 143–149)

Si bien la filosofía de Zea no cumple con todos los requisitos de la posición socialista del autor, es vista con respetuosa simpatía, destacándose los aspectos positivos que desde aquella posición se advierten. Dentro de la brevedad, hay un intento de observar el desarrollo histórico del pensamiento e Zea.

5096 Portal, María Ana and **Xóchitl Ramírez.** Pensamiento antropológico en México: un recorrido histórico. México: Univ. Autónoma Metropolitana, Unidad Iztapalapa, 1995. 146 p.: bibl.. (Libros de texto, manuales de prácticas y antologías)

De utilidad para el lector general, da una visión didáctica del desarrollo de la antropología en México desde la Colonia hasta la actualidad.

5097 Quintanilla, Lourdes. El nacionalismo de Lucas Alamán. Guanajuato, Mexico: Gobierno del Estado de Guanajuato, 1991. 86 p. (Nuestra cultura; 1)

Es un intento de leer, en forma comprensiva (previa a toda crítica), aunque no necesariamente aprobatoria, los textos histórico-políticos de Alamán. Estima que un diálogo con él, con sus tesis (conservadoras) y con sus intenciones es necesario para comprender la historia de México. Se basa en las dos obras clásicas de Alamán: *Disertaciones sobre la historia de la República Mejicana* (1884–89), *Historia de Méjico desde los primeros movimientos que prepararon su independencia en el año 1808, hasta la época presente* (1849–52), aunque los títulos completos de estas obras y sus fechas de edición nunca aparecen en el ensayo.

5098 Torres Orozco, José. Veinte ensayos sobre filosofía y psicología. Morelia, Mexico: Univ. Michoacana de San Nicolás de Hidalgo, Centro de Estudios sobre la Cultura Nicolaita, 1993. 395 p.

Excelente iniciativa de publicar escritos éditos e inéditos de José Torres Orozco, uno de los últimos representantes del positivismo en México. Juan Hernández Luna presenta los aspectos biográficos del autor como su posición dentro del positivismo mexicano. Es de interés señalar que entre los escritos filosóficos hay varios dedicados a Nietzche. Entre los psicológicos, uno de 1922 se ocupa de Freud.

5099 Tovar de Teresa, Guillermo; Miguel León Portilla; and Silvio Arturo Zavala. La utopía mexicana del siglo XVI: lo bello, lo verdadero y lo bueno. México: Grupo Azabache, 1992. 108 p.: bibl., ill. (some col.), maps. (Arte novohispano; 1)

Con magníficas ilustraciones, reproduce tres trabajos: Guillermo Tovar de Teresa, "La Utopía del Virrey de Mendoza;" Miguel León Portilla, "Fray Juan de Zumárraga y las Lenguas Indígenas en México;" y Silvio Zavala, "La 'Utopía' de Tomás Moro en la Nueva España." Para el comentario del especialista de arte colonial, ver *HLAS 54:161.*

Vargas Lozano, Gabriel. Filosofía y autenticidad en la cultura latinoamericana hoy. Ver item **5055.**

5100 Vázquez Leos, J. Jesús E. Liberalismo y masonería en San Luis. San Luis Potosí, Mexico: s.n, 1994. 134 p.: ill.

Aunque es obra partidista y testimonial, y sin característica académica alguna, puede servir para la historia de la masonería en San Luis Potosí, México.

5101 Weckmann, Luis. El milenarismo de Fray Bernardino de Sahagún. (*Mem. Acad. Mex. Hist.*, 34, 1991, p. 205–217)

No se refiere solamente a Sahagún, sino a "los doce" franciscanos que actuaron en la Nueva España en los comienzos de la colonización, inmediatamente después de Pedro de Gante y sus dos compañeros flamencos. El tema es la influencia del teólogo medieval Joaquín de Floris y de sus ideas sobre el advenimiento del milenio, el descenso del Espíritu Santo, el comienzo de la edad de la perfección, etc., y su vinculación con la labor evangelizadora sobre los indios, la cual se realizaba con una premura fundada en la supuesta cercanía del fin de los tiempos. El autor considera a Fray Gerónimo de Mendieta como "el campeón de la idea milenarista." Ver también items **5102** y **5101.**

5102 Zaballa Beascoechea, Ana de and Josep-Ignasi Saranyana. La discusión sobre el joaquinismo novohispano en el siglo XVI en la historiografía reciente. (*Quinto Cent.*, 16, 1990, p. 173–189)

Crítica—moderada en el juicio pero detallada en el aspecto erudito—a algunas opiniones de autores como Marcel Bataillon, José Antonio Maravall, John L. Phelan y George Baudot sobre el supuesto joaquinismo (doctrinas teológicas de Joaquín de Fiore o Floris [1145–1202]) en los primeros franciscanos españoles que actuaron en la Nueva España. Para el comentario del historiador, véase *HLAS 54:1193.*

5103 Zafra Oropeza, Aurea. Agustín Rivera y Agustín de la Rosa ante la filosofía novohispana. Presentación de Luis Medina Ascensio. Prólogo de Ernesto de la Torre Villar. Guadalajara, Mexico: Sociedad Jalisciense de Filosofía, 1994. 358 p.: bibl., ill.

Agustín Rivera publicó en 1887 *Filosofía en la Nueva España*, obra muy crítica de la filosofía y la ciencia novohispanas. Agustín de la Rosa contestó defensivamente con *La instrucción en México durante su dependencia de España* (1888). El presente libro ofrece amplio detalle de esa polémica, hasta en los aspectos de técnica de la discusión, y es sin duda de utilidad. Sobre el tema recordamos también *Dos ideas sobre la filosofía en la Nueva España* (1959) de Juan Hernández Luna, reseñada en *HLAS 22:5836*, y extrañamente omitida en la bibliografía de la obra que comentamos.

5104 Zavala, Agustín Jacinto. La teoría de la formación de la sociedad en José Vasconcelos. (*Relaciones/Zamora*, 12:46, primavera 1991, p. 99–127)

Expone lo que podría denominarse la sociología "filosófica" o teoría de la sociedad en Vasconcelos, vista en el conjunto del sistema de dicho autor.

Zea, Leopoldo. Latinoamérica y el problema de la modernidad. Ver item **5061.**

AMÉRICA CENTRAL

5105 Bendaña, Alejandro. La mística de Sandino. Managua: Centro de Estudios Internacionales, 1994. 260 p.: bibl. (Col. Perspectiva; 3)

Biografía, apreciación y rastreo de las fuentes que contribuyeron al mundo conceptual de Sandino. Aproximadamente la mitad de la obra es de carácter documental.

5106 González Dobles, Jaime. La patria del tico: interpretación del ser costarricense. Presentación del Dr. Arnoldo Mora Rodríguez. San José: Editorial Antares; Logos Editorial, 1995. 188 p.: bibl.

Además de describir las características nacionales del costarricense, hay reflexiones sobre el fenómeno del patriotismo. Se aprovecha el aporte dado por autores nacionales como Luis Barahona Jiménez, Rodrigo Carazo, Omar Dengo y Constantino Láscaris, entre otros.

5107 Perdomo Interiano, Claudio Roberto. Pensamiento positivista y liberal de Ramón Rosa. Tegucigalpa: Mejores Ideas, 1994. 123 p.: bibl.

Sobre la forma en que Ramón Rosa (Honduras, 1848–93) asimiló y aplicó el positivismo de Comte y Stuart Mill y las ideas liberales. Se compara a Rosa con Bello, Sarmiento y Lastarria, y con el liberalismo mexicano, el liberalismo cubano, y el escritor centroamericano Antonio José Irisarri.

5108 Romero, Ramón. Filosofía e identidad en Honduras. (*Rev. Filos. Univ. Costa Rica*, 28:67/68, dic. 1990, p. 93–97)

En Honduras la identidad sólo podrá ser el resultado de un proyecto nacional actualmente inexistente debido a la condición neocolonial del país. El autor da indicaciones sobre la función que la filosofía podría tener en ese proyecto.

5109 Soler, Ricaurte. Tradición, reflexión y enseñanza de la filosofía en Panamá. (*Tareas/Panamá*, 79, sept/dic. 1991, p. 3–30)

En este artículo, que viene a resumir estudios anteriores—siempre atendibles—del autor, la posición marxista es lo que da personalidad a la apreciación de la historia filosófico-ideológica de Panamá, y a la vez lo que estrecha la visión para comprender otras posiciones. Particularmente valiosa la exposición sobre Justo Arosemena. Se ven con óptica sumamente crítica la "reacción antipositivista" y la más reciente "filosofía académica". A lo largo de todo el trabajo es visible el intento de correlacionar las ideas con la realidad económica, social y política.

CARIBE INSULAR

5110 Acosta de Arriba, Rafael. La revolución de 1868–1878 y el desarrollo de las ideas en Cuba. (*Rev. Cuba. Cienc. Soc.*, 9:26, julio/dic. 1991, p. 100–114, bibl.)

Sostiene que la guerra del decenio 1878–88 tenía un claro contenido ideológico independista y que no ha sido tenida en cuenta suficientemente en la elaboración de la historia de las ideas en Cuba. Critica, consiguientemente, algunas manifestaciones historiográficas anteriores. Es un artículo muy atendible. Para el comentario del historiador, ver *HLAS 56:1979.*

5111 Alonso Tejada, Aurelio. Marxismo y espacio de debate en la Revolución cubana. (*Temas/Habana*, 3, julio/sept. 1995, p. 34–43)

Analiza la evolución del marxismo como tema de debate dentro de la Revolución cubana. Durante los años sesenta se habría dado la asimilación del marxismo "dentro de un espectro de apertura." Durante los setenta se habría producido una "depuración oficializadora," nacida de la experiencia soviética. En la segunda mitad de los ochenta habría habido un proceso de rectificación. El derrumbe de la Unión Soviética pondría a Cuba "de cara al desafío definitivo." Véase también item **5141**. [CJB]

5112 Arpini, Adriana. La traza del krausismo en el pensamiento ético social de Eugenio María de Hostos. (*Rev. Hist. Am.*, 110, julio/dic. 1990, p. 99–107)

Considera que el krausismo fue predominante en el pensamiento de Hostos, por encima del positivismo. Lo muestra en su concepción del "Ideal de la Humanidad" y en el método de su *Sociología*.

5113 Borge Legrá, Félix. Las primeras manifestaciones del pensamiento filosófico en Cuba: la escolástica como teorización dominante en el período del criollismo. (*Islas/Santa Clara*, 96, mayo/agosto 1990. p. 150–156, bibl.)

El propósito declarado es realizar una interpretación desde el punto de vista marxista. Expone de modo general la escolástica en Cuba (siglos XVII y XVIII) y la conducta de las clases sociales predominantes. La necesaria relación entre ambas instancias (como base y superestructura, respectivamente), que es el objetivo del artículo, queda más bien postulada que mostrada históricamente.

5114 Bosch, Juan. Antología del pensamiento de Juan Bosch. v. 1. Santo Domingo: Editora Alfa y Omega, 1994. 1 v.: bibl.

Esta antología, parte de un proyecto más amplio, divide los materiales del político y escritor dominicano en dos grandes temas: el pensamiento filosófico-cultural y el pensamiento político.

5115 Castells, Ricardo. Fernández Retamar's "The Tempest" in a cafetera: from Ariel to Mariel. (*Cuba. Stud.*, 25, 1995, p. 165–182, bibl.)

Después de considerar el uso de los símbolos de *La Tempestad* de Shakespeare en Rubén Darío y José Enrique Rodó, critica duramente la interpretación de Calibán por parte de Roberto Fernández Retamar, a la cual estima como una simple defensa del go-

bierno cubano ante la opinión internacional por el llamado "Caso Padilla" (1971). [CJB]

5116 Chevannes, Barry. Healing the nation: Rastafari exorcism of the ideology of racism in Jamaica. (*Caribb. Q.*, 36:1/2, June 1990, p. 59–84, bibl., tables)

Sostiene la importancia del movimiento Rastafari en el incremento de la identidad africana de Jamaica y en la autoestima de los grupos de ese origen. Describe la situación previa a la influencia del movimiento Rastafari a partir de los años 20 y 30 del siglo XX y hasta los años de la década del 60, mostrando las creencias del grupo mencionado y su función en la vida religiosa y política de Jamaica. Para el comentario del sociólogo, ver *HLAS 53:5133*.

Congreso de Estudios Latinoamericanos, 1st, La Plata, Argentina, 1991. Homenaje a José Martí: actas. Ver item **4945**.

5117 Córdova Iturregui, Félix. Hostos y la Ilustración. (*Torre/Río Piedras*, 5:número extraordinario, 1991, p. 157–167)

Es fundamentalmente un ensayo sobre la idea del hombre en Hostos.

5118 Cuba, fundamentos de la democracia: antología del pensamiento liberal cubano desde fines del siglo XVIII hasta fines del siglo XX. Compilación y estudio introductorio de Beatriz Bernal. Prólogo de Carlos A. Montaner. Madrid: Fundación Liberal José Martí, 1994. 414 p.: bibl.

Bien presentada, con notas sobre cada autor, esta antología intenta mostrar el arraigo del pensamiento liberal en Cuba desde el siglo XVIII hasta la actualidad. Recoge textos de casi 60 autores, algunos clásicos como Francisco de Arango y Parreño, José Agustín Caballero, José de la Luz y Caballero, Félix Varela, José Martí, Enrique José Varona, Fernando Ortiz, Jorge Mañach, y muchos otros, incluidos autores muy recientes. Se tocan aspectos filosóficos, económicos, políticos y de la historia de Cuba.

5119 Díaz Soler, Luis M. El pensamiento abolicionista de Eugenio María de Hostos. (*in* Congreso Internacional de Historia Económica y Social de la Cuenca del Caribe, 1763–1898, 1st, San Juan, 1987. Actas. San Juan: Centro de Estudios Avanzados de Puerto Rico y el Caribe, 1992, p. 105–121)

Se refiere a la larga prédica y a la acción personal de Hostos en favor de la abolición de la esclavitud en las Antillas, y especialmente en Puerto Rico.

5120 Ette, Ottmar. La polisemia prohibida: la recepción de José Martí como sismógrafo de la vida política y cultural. (*Cuad. Am.*, 32:2, marzo/abril 1992, p. 196–211)

Interesante trabajo destinado a exponer los derroteros de la recepción de José Martí, utilizando la teoría de los campos del sociólogo francés Pierre Bourdieu. Se entiende la literatura cubana como un campo literario bipartito conformado por la literatura producida en la isla y la producida fuera de ella, con raíces que se remontaían al primer tercio del siglo XIX. En el interior del campo literario cubano distingue un subcampo de los estudios martianos, también bipartito, que habría servido de sismógrafo del acontecer político, económico e intelectual de Cuba. Véase también item **4945**. [CJB]

5121 Fernández Retamar, Roberto. Más de cien años de previsión: algunas reflexiones sobre el concepto martiano de "Nuestra América." (*Cuad. Am.*, 7:40, julio/agosto 1993, p. 65–76)

Señala el derrotero de la feliz expresión martiana "Nuestra América", que Martí acuñara durante su estancia en México, pero madurara en Guatemala. Ilustra con textos las ya clásicas observaciones del prócer cubano. Véase también items **5128** y **5144**. [CJB]

5122 Giorgis, Liliana. José Martí y la utopía de un "humanismo social." (*Cuad. Am.*, 6:4, julio/agosto 1992, p. 157–163)

Visión crítica de las categorías de 'lo humano' y 'humanidad' cuando son vistas sin tener en cuenta las mediaciones sociales, entramado desde el cual los seres humanos construyen su propia imagen. La autora sostiene la tesís de que esa crítica no sería aplicable a Martí. [CJB]

5123 González, Raymundo. Bonó, un intelectual de los pobres. Santo Domingo: Centro de Estudios Sociales Padre Juna Montalvo SJ, 1994. 156 p.: bibl.

Varios ensayos sobre Pedro Francisco Bonó (1828–1906), quien intervino en la vida política dominicana representando las ideas liberales pero mostró particular preocupación por las "clases trabajadoras". Por éstas últimas entendía, sin embargo, principalmente el campesinado, dadas las condiciones de la economía dominicana de la época. Se dan noticias de su actuación y escritos.

5124 González, Raymundo. Peña Batlle y su concepto histórico de la nación dominicana. (*Anu. Estud. Am.*, 48, 1991, p. 585–631)

Aunque de orígenes liberales, Peña Battle (1902–54) giró hacia ideas conservadoras e hispanistas. Su concepción de la nacionalidad dominicana se habría desarrollado en contraposición al pensamiento de Hostos y con franca animadversión hacia Haití. Fue miembro destacado del gobierno del General Trujillo.

Hoetink, H. Ideology, intellectuals, identity: the Dominican Republic 1880–1980; some preliminary notes. See *HLAS 57:4848.*

5125 Lewis, Rupert. J.J. Thomas and political thought in the Caribbean. (*Caribb. Q.*, 36:1/2, June 1990, p. 46–58, bibl.)

Sobre J.J. Thomas (1840–89), autor de *Froudacity: West Indian fables* (1889; ver *HLAS 32:3716*), que consiste en una polémica con el autor inglés James Anthony Froude, considerado en este artículo como de mentalidad imperialista, favorecedor de la expansión inglesa en el Caribe y de opinión muy desfavorable a la población de origen africano. Para el comentario del historiador, ver *HLAS 54:2045.*

5126 Lewis, Rupert. The writing of Caribbean political thought. (*Caribb. Q.*, 36:1/2, June 1990, p. 153–165, bibl.)

Detallada reseña de los libros de Gordon Lewis, *Main currents in Caribbean thought: the historical evolution of Caribbean society in its ideological aspects, 1492–1900* (see *HLAS 50:1513*); y de Denis Benn, *Ideology and political development: the growth and development of political ideas in the Caribbean, 1774–1983* (Mona, Jamaica: Univ. of the West Indies, 1987).

5127 Llerena, Mario. The myth and the mirage: six essays on revolution. Miami: Endowment for Cuban American Studies of the Cuban American National Foundation, 1995. 219 p.: bibl.

Aunque es una reflexión sobre el concepto de 'revolución' en general, la fuente de inspiración es la experencia de la Revolución Cubana, a la cual se dedica directamente el último capítulo. El autor identifica esta revolución con Fidel Castro y sus características y motivaciones personales.

5128 Magallón Anaya, Mario. Martí: a cien años de *Nuestra América*. (*Cuad. Am.*, 6:3, mayo/junio 1991, p. 127–136)

Propone interpretar los textos de Martí en lo que tienen de actualidad para pensar la situación latinoamericana contemporánea. Es parte de una serie de artículos publicados en la misma revista con motivo del centenario de la aparición del ensayo de José Martí, "Nuestra América." Véase también items **5121** y **5144**. [CJB]

5129 Maríñez, Pablo A. Evolución del pensamiento sociopolítico de Juan Bosch. (*Caribe Contemp.*, 21, julio/dic. 1990, p. 53–61)

El centro del artículo es el cambio verificado en el escritor y político dominicano, Juan Bosch, hacia fines de la década de los años 60, al abandonar su adhesión a la democracia representativa e inclinarse hacia cierta forma de marxismo. Esto ocurre después de que es derrocado como Presidente de la República Dominicana y de la intervención militar norteamericana en ese país, en 1965.

5130 Martínez Heredia, Fernando. El Ché y el socialismo de hoy. (*Casa Am.*, 33:189, oct./dic. 1992, p. 111–120)

Redactado para la reedición del libro *Ché, el socialismo y el comunismo* (ver *HLAS 54:5415*), es principalmente una reflexión sobre lo acontecido al socialismo, en general y en Cuba en particular. Hay críticas al "socialismo real" de la antigua Unión Soviética, frente al cual se recortaría, en forma antitética, la concepción socialista del Ché.

5131 Martínez Heredia, Fernando. Izquierda y marxismo en Cuba. (*Temas/Habana*, 3, julio/sept. 1995, p. 16–27)

Artículo con buena dosis de reflexión y crítica sobre los avatares del marxismo en Cuba. Esta doctrina ha atravesado por diversas etapas: algunas de mayor reflexión teórica, otras de apego acrítico al marxismo emanado de la Unión Soviética. Para el autor, se hace necesario la "recreación del concepto

de socialismo," elaborada desde el presente hacia el futuro. [CJB]

5132 Miniño Marión Landais, Manuel Marino. El pensamiento de Duarte en su contexto histórico e ideológico. Santo Domingo: Gobierno Dominicano, 1994. 102 p.: bibl. (Col. Sesquicentenario de la independencia nacional; 6)

Reproduce documentos que representan el pensamiento de Juan Pablo Duarte (1813–76), patriota dominicano.

5133 Mosquera, Gerardo. Estética y marxismo en Cuba. (*Cuad. Am.*, 5:5, sept./oct. 1991, p. 169–186, bibl.)

Prólogo a la edición cubana de la antología de Adolfo Sánchez Vázquez, *Estética y marxismo*, que se publicó por primera vez en 1970. Véase *HLAS 34:5331*. [CJB]

5134 Palazón, María Rosa. Utopía sobre las nacionalidades de *Nuestra América*. (*Cuad. Am.*, 6:3, mayo/junio 1991, p. 158–163)

Considera que una utopía sobre las nacionalidades debería proponer que los grupos nacionales se diferencien culturalmente, manteniendo sus peculiaridades, pero se igualen en sus derechos políticos, econónicos y sociales. [CJB]

5135 Pimentel, Miguel A. Poder y política en la era de Trujillo: filosofía y política, 1930–1961. v. 1. Santo Domingo: Imprenta Amiama, 1995. 1 v.: bibl.

Además de criticar duramente a la dictadura trujillista en general, se refiere, en la misma modalidad crítica, a los que llama "intelectuales orgánicos" de aquel régimen: ante todo, el filósofo Andrés Avelino, pero también Pedro Troncoso Sánchez y Antonio Fernández Spencer, entre otros. De particular interés es lo que refiere sobre la actitud oficial asumida en esa época contra el pensamiento educativo de Hostos.

5136 Ravelo Cabrera, Paul. Posmodernidad y marxismo en Cuba. (*Temas/Habana*, 3, julio/sept. 1995, p. 58–68)

Ante el hecho de que el debate sobre la posmodernidad ha sido tratado en el ámbito académico cubano por la fractura del paradigma tradicional marxista y la situación de "desencanto" e incertidumbre, el artículo propone pensar y promover la posmodernidad para a su vez repensar y renovar el marxismo como teoría filosófico-política de la contemporaneidad. [CJB]

5137 Rivera Nieves, Irma N. El tema de la mujer en el pensamiento social de Eugenio María de Hostos. San Juan: Decanato de Estudios Graduados e Investigación, Recinto de Río Piedras, Univ. de Puerto Rico; Instituto de Estudios Hostosianos, 1992. 102 p.: bibl.

Sobre las ideas de Hostos respecto de la mujer, mostradas en tres aspectos: la igualdad antropológica (o en general como ser humano); la igualdad moral; y la igualdad sexual. Dentro de una apreciación general positiva, señala también contradicciones en las afirmaciones del clásico puertorriqueño.

5138 Rojas Gómez, Miguel. Valor y significación de la filosofía racionalista de Medardo Vitier. (*Islas/Santa Clara*, 103, sept./dic. 1992, p. 85–107)

Expone y valora muy positivamente la obra de Vitier como historiador del pensamiento cubano. También se refiere al pensamiento filosófico de Vitier, el cual es visto dentro de la tradición "progresista" del país. Algunas objeciones previsibles desde el medio intelectual e ideológico del autor del artículo no ocultan la simpatía y el deseo de hacer la mayor justicia posible al personaje estudiado.

Rojas Osorio, Carlos. Eugenio M. de Hostos y José M. Samper. See item **5160.**

5139 Rossi, Máximo, Jr. Praxis, historia y filosofía en el siglo XVIII: textos de Antonio Sánchez Valverde, 1729–90. Santo Domingo: Taller, 1994. 213 p.: bibl.

Monografía sobre la figura poco conocida de Antonio Sánchez Valverde (1729–90), dominicano que entró en la polémica sobre la naturaleza del continente americano en defensa de la isla que era su patria, escribiendo, entre otras obras, *Idea del valor de la Isla Española* (1785) y *La América vindicada de la calumnia de haber sido la madre del mal venéreo*, publicada el mismo año que la anterior. El libro traza un panorama de la vida colonial en Santo Domingo, expone las dos obras mencionadas y proporciona una biografía de Sánchez Valverde. Util bibliografía.

5140 Sang Ben, Mu-Kien. Contradicciones en el liberalismo dominicano del siglo XIX: un contraste entre el discurso y la práctica. (*Cienc. Soc./INTEC*, 16:3, julio/sept. 1991, p. 240–251)

Sobre las ideas liberales de Ulises Francisco Espaillat, pensador y político dominicano, en el contexto de las luchas caudillistas de la época.

5141 Santana Castillo, Joaquín. Algunos problemas de la filosofía marxista y su enseñanza en Cuba. (*Temas/Habana*, 3, julio/sept. 1995, p. 28–33)

Distingue tres etapas en el desarrollo de la filosofía marxista en la vida académica de Cuba después de 1959: 1) En la década del 60 coexisten una interpretación que sigue el modelo soviético junto con lecturas de autores de la Revolución Cubana y de la liberación nacional del Tercer Mundo; 2) En la década del 70 predomina la interpretación soviética del marxismo-leninismo; 3) Desde los 80 en adelante, con la política de la Perestroika, se observa un giro hacia una interpretación teórica de la realidad cubana. Señala la necesidad de rescatar al socialismo como un fenómeno en el cual el hombre, al transformar la sociedad, se transforma a sí mismo. Véase también item **5111.** [CJB]

Steel, M.J. A philosophy of fear: the world view of the Jamaican plantocracy in a comparative perspective. Ver item **1923.**

5142 Stevens Arroyo, Antonio M. Catholicism as civilization: contemporary reflections on the political philosophy of Pedro Albizu Campos. San Germán: Inter-American Univ. of Puerto Rico, 1992. 20 p.: bibl. (Working papers / Caribbean Institute and Study Center for Latin America; 50)

Sobre las ideas políticas de Pedro Albizu Campos (1891–1965), dirigente del Partido Nacionalista de Puerto Rico, y sus fuentes en la filosofía de Balmes. Entre las conclusiones, afirma el autor que el pensamiento de Albizu Campos podría considerarse antecedente de la teología de la liberación.

5143 Ubieta Gómez, Enrique. Ensayos de identidad. La Habana: Editorial Letras Cubanas, 1993. 201 p.: bibl.

Contribución a la historia de las ideas y la historia intelectual en Cuba, durante el siglo XX. Además de un extenso ensayo, "Panhispanismo y Panamericanismo: Controversia sobre Identidad Cultural (1900–1922)," hay artículos sobre Juan Marinello,

Fernández Retamar, Cintio Vitier y el ensayismo en Cuba.

5144 Weinberg, Liliana Irene. Nuestro Martí. *(Cuad. Am.*, 6:3, mayo/junio 1991, p. 144–157)

Fino artículo de interpretación del ensayo "Nuestra América" de José Martí, en el que se analizan sus metáforas e imágenes y las dimensiones de sus elementos literarios. Véase también items **5121** y **5128**. [CJB]

5145 Zuleta Alvarez, Enrique. Pedro Henríquez Ureña y su tiempo: vida de un hispanoamericano universal. Buenos Aires: Catálogos, 1997. 446 p.: bibl., index.

Presenta la obra de Pedro Henríquez Ureña al hilo de su biografía. Muestra conocimiento integral de ambos aspectos y puede considerarse, en ese sentido, la mejor introducción al estudio del maestro dominicano. Véase también item **5146.**

5146 Zuleta Alvarez, Enrique. Teoría y práctica del mestizaje hispanoamericano: Pedro Henríquez Ureña. *(Cuad. Am.*, 32:2, marzo/abril 1992, p. 64–70)

Repasa textos del maestro dominicano para mostrar que consideraba el mestizaje racial y cultural como una esencial caracterización de la realidad iberoamericana. El mestizaje cultural, especialmente, habría dado lugar a una entidad nueva, distinta y más rica, que le habría permitido afirmarse en su originalidad propia y, al mismo tiempo, proyectarse a la universalidad. Véase también item **5145.** [CJB]

VENEZUELA

Bello, Andrés. Selected writings of Andrés Bello. See item **4669.**

5147 Cappelletti, Angel J. Positivismo y evolucionismo en Venezuela. Caracas: Monte Avila Editores Latinoamericana, 1992. 507 p.: bibl. (Pensamiento filosófico)

Libro sumamente valioso. Tras sendas visiones de conjunto, muy logradas, del positivismo en América Latina en general y en Venezuela en particular, siguen capítulos sobre: Adolfo Ernst; Rafael Villavicencio; Vicente Marcano; Lasandro Alvarado; Luis Razetti; Guillermo Delgado Palacios; Luis López Méndez; José Gil Fortoul; Laureano Vallenilla Lanz; César Zumeta y Manuel Arcaya. Tiende a hacer comparaciones con otras manifestaciones del positivismo latinoamericano.

5148 Encuentro de Cátedras José Martí de Venezuela, *1st, Mérida, Venezuela, 1991.* José Martí en Venezuela y Nuestra América. Mérida, Venezuela: Univ. de los Andes, Cátedra Latinoamericana José Martí; Dirección General de Cultura y Extensión; Instituto de Investigaciones Literarias Gonzalo Picón Febres, 1992. 127 p.: bibl.

Resultado del Primer Encuentro de Cátedras José Martí de Venezuela (1991). La mayoría de los trabajos versan sobre el ensayo "Nuestra América," que Martí publicó en 1891. Varios son expresiones de opiniones políticas. "Discurso Reflexivo y Discurso Literario en 'Nuestra América' de José Martí," tal vez sea uno de los que tiene más intención de estudio. El volumen también recuerda la fundación, por parte de Martí, de la *Revista Venezolana*, en 1881, cuando se encontraba en Venezuela.

5149 Fernández, Estela. La estructura categorial del discurso político venezolano: variaciones en la oposición civilización-barbarie; Francisco de Miranda y Simón Rodríguez, 1790–1850. *(Hoy Hist.*, 11:65, sept./oct. 1994, p. 57–71, facsims.)

Análisis de las variaciones categoriales en los discursos de Francisco de Miranda y Simón Rodríguez, que abarcan desde la etapa pre-independencia hasta la organización política de Venezuela. Es intento de la autora "leer," a través de esas variaciones, la historia de los conflictos sociales del período. [CJB]

5150 González Escorihuela, Ramón. Las ideas políticas en el Táchira: de los años 70 del siglo XIX a la segunda década del siglo XX. Caracas: Biblioteca de Autores y Temas Tachirenses, 1994. 235 p.: bibl., ill. (Biblioteca de Autores y Temas Tachirenses; 115)

Exposición general de la situación económica y social de la región del Táchira en el período seleccionado, mostrando las opiniones políticas, la situación de la prensa y de la educación, y destacando en capítulos especiales algunas figuras. De éstas quizás la más interesante desde el punto de vista de la historia de las ideas sea la de Carlos Rangel Lamus, periodista y educador, simpatizante de Nietzsche y Marx y de las ideas socialistas.

5151 López Palma, Jorge. Simón Rodríguez: utopía y socialismo. Caracas: Cátedra Pío Tamayo; Expediente, 1989. 126 p. (Col. Los no descubiertos; 3)

Con pensamiento y lenguaje marxistas, las ideas pedagógicas de Simón Rodríguez se consideran una utopía superestructural socialista, organizada sin embargo con el bagaje del pensamiento ilustrado y con conocimiento del socialismo utópico.

5152 Pérez Leyva, Leonardo. Algunas consideraciónes sobre la filosofía existencialista de Ernesto Mayz Vallenilla. (*Islas/ Santa Clara*, 96, mayo/agosto 1990, p. 27–33)

Examen crítico de algunos aspectos del pensamiento de Mayz Vallenilla, "desde una perspectiva materialista y dialéctica." Crítica escueta, sin mayor esfuerzo interpretativo, pero respetuosa.

5153 Plaza, Elena. Bases filosóficas del positivismo social venezolano. (*Bol. Acad. Nac. Hist./Caracas*, 73:291, julio/sept. 1990, p. 89–102)

Precisiones histórico-interpretativas sobre el positivismo venezolano y, especialmente, sobre su historiografía. Contribuye a un enfoque más afinado y perceptivo de la complejidad del fenómeno estudiado. Algunas observaciones son válidas para otros países y para precisar el concepto de historia de las ideas en América Latina. Es parte de una benéfica revisión del enfoque tradicional del pensamiento latinoamericano en su relación con la filosofía.

5154 Plaza, Elena. Por el origen de la vida: evolucionismo y creacionismo en Venezuela, 1904–1907. (*Bol. Acad. Nac. Hist./ Caracas*, 74:294, abril/junio 1991, p. 63–82, appendix)

Esta entrada corresponde a la segunda parte del artículo. (Para la primera, véase *HLAS 54:2599*). Muestra que la polémica que aquí se expone no fue tanto sobre teorías científicas como sobre la oposición general entre la concepción evolucionista (representada por Luis Razetti) y la creacionista, defendida por la jerarquía institucional de la religión católica—un fenómeno, por otra parte, ampliamente reiterado en América Latina. Es

particularmente útil el apéndice que contiene la cronología de los escritos que expresaron esta polémica entre 1904 y 1907.

5155 Suárez, Wagner Rafael. El pensamiento teológico de Mario Briceño-Iragorry. (*Montalbán/Caracas*, 23, 1991, p. 123–211, bibl.)

Por el detalle y la extensión es de hecho una monografía sobre el autor estudiado, representante del pensamiento católico en Venezuela en la primera mitad del siglo XX. Se ocupa de la biografía de Briceño-Iragorry, de su obra y del contexto eclesial y político en cada etapa de su vida. En sus últimos años defendió el compromiso del cristianismo con la justicia social, por lo cual el autor lo considera antecedente de la teología de la liberación.

COLOMBIA

Arciniegas, Germán. América Ladina. Ver item **4917.**

5156 Herrera Restrepo, Daniel. José Félix de Restrepo, filósofo ilustrado. (*Ideas Valores*, 85/86, agosto 1991, p. 19–38)

Valioso trabajo sobre Restrepo (1760–1832), que se refiere a su enseñanza y la adopción de ciertas tendencias propias de la Ilustración europea, aunque sin abandonar la posición religiosa tradicional. De particular interés es lo que se expone sobre dos manuales: uno de lógica, receptivo de las ideas de Port-Royal, y otro de física, que compendia mucho del saber científico de la época y del cual el autor de este artículo muestra que no fue, como se ha opinado, un mero resumen del manual de Nollet.

5157 Morales Benítez, Otto. El maestro Arciniegas, emancipador cultural del continente. (*Cuad. Am.*, 14:3(21), mayo/junio 1990, p. 167–185)

Texto de una conferencia sobre el maestro colombiano. Se exalta su figura de polígrafo, pero sobre todo de luchador por la democracia. Se lo considera "emancipador cultural del continente." [CJB]

5158 Ocampo López, Javier. José Manuel Rivas Sacconi y el humanismo colombiano. (*Bol. Acad. Colomb.*, 41:173, julio/sept. 1991, p. 68–82)

Apreciación integral de los estudios, la acción humanista y las obras de Rivas Sacconi (1917–91), autor de *El latín en Colombia* (ver *HLAS 15:2210*), y cuyo nombre está unido al del Instituto Caro y Cuervo.

5159 Quintero Esquivel, Jorge Eliécer. Ergotismo, Ilustración y utilitarismo en Colombia, siglos XVIII y XIX. (*Islas/Santa Clara*, 96, mayo/agosto 1990, p. 53–66)

Repaso de la secuencia: escolástica (aquí denominada ergotismo), Ilustración y benthamismo, dominantes en Colombia a lo largo de los siglos XVIII y XIX. La parte correspondiente a la Ilustración es la más útil.

5160 Rojas Osorio, Carlos. Eugenio M. de Hostos y José M. Samper. (*Ideas Valores*, 85/86, agosto 1991, p. 39–50)

Puntos de semejanza entre estos dos pensadores que se conocieron e intercambiaron correspondencia. Especialmente en lo que se refiere a la apreciación del método experimental y las concepciones de la ética, el derecho y la política. También se señalan las diferencias entre ambos.

5161 Saladino García, Alberto. El papel de Francisco José de Caldas en la divulgación de la ciencia moderna en Nueva Granada. (*Cuad. Am.*, 47, sept./oct. 1994, p. 217–224)

Da cuenta de la difusión científica realizada por el intelectual y político colombiano Francisco José de Caldas en los periódicos *Correo Curioso, Erudito*, y *Económico y Mercantil* (1801), y *Semanario del Nuevo Reino de Granada* (1808–09). [CJB]

5162 Uribe Uribe, Rafael. La Regeneración Conservadora de Nuñez y Caro. Antología y prólogo de Otto Morales Benítez. Bogotá: Instituto para el Desarrollo de la Democracia Luis Carlos Galán, 1995. 463 p.: ill., index. (Antología; 4)

Antología de escritos de Rafael Uribe Uribe (1859–1914), general y político colombiano perteneciente al Partido Liberal. Es parte de una serie de antologías de este personaje. El Prólogo es de hecho un extenso estudio preliminar.

5163 Uslar Pietri, Arturo. Arciniegas, 90. (*Rev. Nac. Cult./Caracas*, 52:282, julio/sept. 1991, p. 15–19)

Con excelente prosa, traza con simpatía, pero sin ditirambo, una bella y ajustada imagen de Germán Arciniegas en sus 90 años.

ECUADOR

5164 Cárdenas Reyes, María Cristina. La racionalidad ética. (*Rev. IDIS*, 27, junio 1991, p. 95–140)

Se trata de un capítulo del libro *José Peralta y la trayectoria del liberalismo ecuatoriano*, en vías de publicación cuando apareció este artículo. Es una exposición detallada. Interesa en especial lo que dice sobre el libro de Peralta *La esclavitud de la América Latina* (redactado en 1927 y publicado póstumamente en 1961; ver *HLAS 24:3444*), puesto en el contexto de la literatura sobre la apreciación de Estados Unidos en esa época.

5165 Estrella, Eduardo. La noción de identidad nacional en el pensamiento científico de Juan de Velasco. (*Bol. Acad. Nac. Hist./Quito*, 71:151/152, 1988 [i.e. 1991], p. 43–56, bibl.)

Juan de Velasco (Juan Manuel de Velasco y Peroche, 1727–92), jesuita expulso, fue autor de *Historia del Reino de Quito en la América Meridional*, cuyas primeras ediciones son póstumas y del siglo XIX. Este artículo muestra la pertenencia de Velasco al pensamiento de la Ilustración y su defensa del hombre americano frente a los escritos de Buffon y De Pauw, entre otros. Una de las afirmaciones del autor es que, en la mencionada obra, se encuentra la primera manifestación de la identidad nacional ecuatoriana.

5166 Paladines Escudero, Carlos. Ilustración francesa e ilustración ecuatoriana: lugares comunes, encuentros y desencuentros. (*in* Colección nuestra patria es América: nación, estado y conciencia nacional. Recopilación de Jorge Nuñez Sánchez. Quito: Editora Nacional, 1992, v. 2, p. 53–90)

Búsqueda de los caracteres distintivos de la "Ilustración" ecuatoriana y su lugar en la historiografía sobre el tema.

5167 El pensamiento de Fray Vicente Solano. (*Rev. IDIS*, 27, junio 1991, p. 141–167)

Se trata de un conjunto de artículos sobre Fray Vicente Solano (1791–1865), representante del pensamiento conservador ecuatoriano en el siglo XIX. Tras una introducción de María Cristina Cárdenas Reyes ("Presencia Histórica de Fray Vicente Solano"), contiene artículos de Miguel Díaz

Cueva, Leonardo Torres León, Edgard Cevallos Gualpa, y Mons. Luis Alberto Luna Tobar. Véase también item **5169.**

5168 Pensamiento positivista ecuatoriano.
Estudio introductorio y selección de Carlos Paladines Escudero y Samuel Guerra Bravo. Quito: Banco Central del Ecuador; Corporación Editora Nacional, 1982? 506 p.: bibl. (Biblioteca básica del pensamiento ecuatoriano; 16)

Valiosa antología, precedida por una exposición del positivismo europeo (Carlos Paladines Escudero) y otra sobre esa misma corriente en Ecuador (Samuel Guerra Bravo). Este último sostiene que el positivismo en el Ecuador fue "la ideología de la burguesía comercial-bancaria de Guayaquil que 'controló' el país entre 1895 y 1934." Los autores cuyos textos se incluyen son: Julio Endara, Juan H. Peralta, Julio Arauz y César H. Semblantes, todos del siglo XX.

5169 Seminario Configuración y presencia del pensamiento conservator ecuatoriano, *Cuenca, Ecuador, 1993.* Actas. Cuenca, Ecuador: IDIS-CONUP; Univ. de Cuenca, 1995. 137 p.: bibl.

Precedido por una breve reseña de las relaciones entre la Iglesia y el estado en Ecuador, y por una confrontación entre la teología tradicionalista y la teología de la liberación, siguen tres artículos sobre Fray Vicente Solano (1791–1895), por Jorge Salvador Lara, María Cristina Cárdenas Reyes y Juan J. Paz y Miño Cepeda.

5170 Tinajero Villamar, Fernando. Literatura y pensamiento en el Ecuador entre 1948 y 1970. (*in* El Ecuador de la postguerra: estudios en homenaje a Guillermo Pérez Chiriboga. Quito: Banco Central del Ecuador, 1992, v. 2, p. 573–599)

Podría decirse que el autor continúa la línea de su libro anterior, *De la evasión al desencanto,* (ver *HLAS 54:5449*). El propósito es estudiar la literatura y el pensamiento político en su relación "con la realidad" (léase: situación económica y vida política). Se presta mucha atención a grupos de izquierda con intereses culturales, especialmente de la década del 60. Uno de los autores que se considera representativo del período estudiado es Agustín Cueva (*Entre la ira y la esperanza,* 1967). El lector no ecuatoriano se hubiera beneficiado de menos so-

brentendidos respecto de la historia reciente del Ecuador.

PERU

5171 La aventura de Mariátegui: nuevas perspectivas. Edición de Gonzalo Portocarrero Maisch, Eduardo Cáceres y Rafael Tapia Rojas. Lima: Pontificia Univ. Católica del Perú, Fondo Editorial, 1995. 592 p.: bibl.

Este conjunto numeroso de artículos, resultado de una reunión sobre el tema, se caracteriza porque sus contribuciones son más "académicas" que otras que se dedican a la apreciación de este autor, de tan nutrida bibliografía en los últimos años. La temática es amplia: vida y pensamiento; la relación de Mariátegui con la filosofía, el arte y la cultura, la política, la etnicidad y el indigenismo; y Mariátegui desde nuestra época. La variedad de asuntos impide el resumen. Obra recomendable.

5172 Castro Carpio, Augusto. El Perú, un proyecto moderno: una aproximación al pensamiento peruano. Lima: Pontificia Univ. Católica del Perú, Instituto Riva-Agüero; Centro de Estudios y Publicaciones, 1994. 240 p.: bibl.

Sin propósito de ser una historia de las ideas o del pensamiento filosófico, el libro trata autores desde la Colonia hasta el siglo XX, en tanto representan etapas de la modernidad peruana. Considera que la condición moderna es la que ordena y explica el pensamiento peruano en su historia.

5173 Clément, Jean-Pierre. La Révolution française dans le *Mercurio Peruano.* (*Caravelle/Toulouse,* 54, 1990, p. 107–151, appendix)

Ilustra con oportunas citas la reacción negativa ante los hechos de la Revolución francesa expresada por el *Mercurio Peruano* hacia finales del siglo XVIII. La lista de los artículos (18 en total) aparece como apéndice.

Congreso Teológico Internacional, *Lima, 1992.* Las Casas entre dos mundos. Ver item **4949.**

5174 Espinoza Montesinos, Gustavo. Mariátegui y el optimismo histórico. Lima: s.n., 1994. 66 p.

Apreciación de Mariátegui por un miembro del Partido Comunista Peruano que polemiza con las otras interpretaciones (tanto las de extrema izquierda como las del marxismo no ortodoxo) y que hace de Mariátegui un pensador marxista-leninista. Por supuesto, no acepta las críticas a la Internacional Comunista y sus diferencias con Mariátegui.

5175 Fernández Díaz, Osvaldo. Mariátegui, o la experiencia del otro. Lima: Empresa Editora Amauta, 1994. 137 p.: bibl. (Presencia y proyección de la obra de Mariátegui)

Comentario a la obra y acción de Mariátegui. Resalta particularmente la significación de la revista *Amauta*. Afirma la actualidad del autor peruano para la izquierda latinoamericana. Mariátegui se habría distinguido por su preocupación por lo específico (el marxismo aplicado a la realidad peruana), pero también por la apertura hacia el "otro" (disposición a la confrontación y amplitud en la búsqueda, incluyendo en esto último la atención a otras corrientes, como el psicoanálisis, el pragmatismo, Nietzsche, Bergson, etc.). [CJB]

5176 García Salvattecci, Hugo. Visión de un apóstol: pensamiento del Maestro González Prada. Prólogo de Luis Alberto Sánchez. Lima: EMISA Editores, 1990. 472 p.: bibl.

Extenso ensayo-comentario sobre las ideas y las opiniones de González Prada, especialmente las vinculadas a la religión, la política, el anarquismo, el diagnóstico sobre Perú y la cuestión de la guerra con Chile.

5177 Germaná, César. El "socialismo indo-americano" de José Carlos Mariátegui: proyecto de reconstitución del sentido histórico de la sociedad peruana. Lima: Empresa Editora Amauta, 1995. 267 p.: bibl. (Serie Centenario)

El objetivo es destacar el "socialismo indo-americano" de Mariátegui, como algo que el *Amauta* vio inscrito en la realidad peruana y no como la aplicación de un modelo externo. Considera que este tema es el que articula la totalidad del pensamiento de Mariátegui. De particular interés las relaciones que señala con la llamada "generación del novecientos" peruana.

5178 Goncharova, Tatiana Viktorovna. La creación heroica de José Carlos Mariátegui. Lima: Empresa Editora Amauta, 1995. 166 p.: bibl. (Serie Centenario)

El libro apareció anteriormente en ruso, con motivo del centenario de Mariátegui (1994). Es un recorrido de las principales etapas de la vida del autor peruano y de su obra entre los que se destacan la preocupación por Perú, las relaciones con Haya de la Torre, la revista *Amauta* y la fundación del Partido Socialista.

5179 Guibal, Francis. Vigencia de Mariátegui. Lima: Empresa Editora Amauta, 1995. 234 p.: bibl. (Serie Centenario)

Conjunto de ensayos sobre Mariátegui y sus ideas, escritos con simpatía por un autor de formación europea. El punto de partida es la situación crítica del socialismo y el marxismo en la actualidad, situación que el autor considera superable.

5180 Instituto Andrés Townsend Ezcurra (Lima). Andrés Townsend Ezcurra, trayectoria de un pensamiento. Lima: Instituto Andrés Townsend Ezcurra, 1995. 102 p.

Textos de un cercano colaborador de Haya de la Torre. Algunos de ellos corresponden a la decadencia electoral del Aprismo, después de la presidencia de Alan García.

5181 Mariátegui, José Carlos. Escritos juveniles: la edad de piedra. v. 8, Voces. Lima: Biblioteca Amauta, 1994. 1 v. (Biblioteca Amauta)

Vol. 8 de los llamados *Escritos juveniles* de Mariátegui (véase también *HLAS 52:5390* y *HLAS 56:5020*). Los editores afirman que con este volumen "se completa la compilación de los textos de Mariátegui publicados antes de su viaje a Europa," pero al parecer no ha sido posible identificar todos los artículos de esta época. Los volúmenes anteriores de esta serie habían sido compilados y presentados por Alberto Tauro, cuyo fallecimiento impidió el prólogo que hubiera escrito para el presente volumen. Los escritos recogidos fueron publicados en la prensa periódica en 1918–19.

5182 Mariátegui: una verdad actual siempre renovada. Compilación e introducción de Roland Forgues. Lima: Empresa Editora Amauta, 1994. 171 p.: bibl.

Reúne trabajos que examinan a Mariátegui desde la literatura, la biografía, la interpretación de Perú, las relaciones y comparaciones con Vasconcelos, Haya de la Torre y Luis Alberto Sánchez, entre otros temas. El compilador afirma que las contribuciones reunidas "se inscriben dentro de la nueva línea de investigación abierta en el Perú por las reflexiones de Aníbal Quijano, Alberto Flores Galindo y César Germaná." Aparentemente el volumen es resultado de reuniones llevados a cabo en Francia.

5183 Neira, Hernán. El espejo del olvido: la idea de América en las *Memorias* de Juan Bautista Túpac Amaru. (*Rev. Indias*, 51:191, enero/abril 1991, p. 97–120)

Analiza las Memorias del quinto "nieto del último emperador del Perú" (medio hermano de José Gabriel Túpac Amaru), quien estuvo confinado en Ceuta y volvió a América para residir en Buenos Aires, en 1822. El análisis le sirve al autor para fundamentar una nueva ciencia, la "americología," que no se interesa en la comprobación de los hechos históricos, sino en los supuestos cosmovisionales que subyacen a las representaciones de los hechos. Un saber, por lo tanto, que se sitúa "en el campo de la semántica y de la epistemología," disciplinas que, según el autor, han sido ignoradas en la historiografía sobre América. Para el comentario del historiador, ver *HLAS 54:2395.*

5184 Núñez, Estuardo. La experiencia europea de José Carlos Mariátegui. 2. ed., aum. Lima: Empresa Editora Amauta, 1994. 130 p.: bibl.

Conjunto de artículos, algunos previamente publicados y otros inéditos. No se ocupa solamente de seguir la presencia de Mariátegui en varios países europeos, sino también la de otras influencias recibidas de Europa. Tal vez uno de los aspectos menos estudiados sea el caso de Alemania. También hay relatos testimoniales de las tertulias en la casa de Mariátegui. [CJB]

5185 Núñez, Estuardo. Olavide: testigo excepcional de la Revolución Francesa. (*Cuad. Am.*, 4:2(20), marzo/abril 1990, p. 62–67)

Exposición sucinta de la vida, los intereses y las actividades del pensador peruano Pablo de Olavide (1725–1803), observador atento y a la vez crítico de la Revolución Francesa, como se muestra en su obra *El evangelio en triunfo* (1797). [CJB]

5186 Pacheco Vélez, César. Ensayos de simpatía: sobre ideas y generaciones en el Perú del siglo XX. Lima: Univ. del Pacífico, 1993. 478 p.: bibl.

De lectura recomendable para los siguientes temas y autores: la influencia de Ortega y Gasset en el Perú; la generación del 90 o "arielista;" Riva Agüero; Víctor Andrés Belaúnde; Oscar Miró Quesada; César Vallejos; Luis E. Valcárcel; Jorge Basadre; Mario Alzamora Valdés; y la revista (tercer) *Mercurio Peruano* fundada en 1918 por Víctor Andrés Belaúnde.

5187 Peña, Milagros. The Sodalitium Vitae movement in Perú: a rewriting of liberation theology. (*Sociol. Anal.*, 53:2, Summer 1992, p. 159–173, bibl.)

Resulta instructivo sobre el movimiento Sodalitium Vitae y su "teología de la conciliación", que tiende a ser una vía intermedia entre la pasividad conservadora frente a las situaciones de pobreza y la actividad contestaria teológico-política de la teología de la liberación. Sin embargo, es también un frente opositor a esta segunda forma de teología y de acción.

5188 Ríos, Gregorio Salvador. Andecentrismo: en 500 años de choque intercultural. (*Social. Particip.*, 57, marzo 1992, p. 9–19)

Sobre la posibilidad de aprovechar las modalidades de la cultura indígena en el desarrollo del Perú ("el desarrollo endógeno y andecentrista").

5189 Rojas Gómez, Miguel. Mariátegui, la contemporaneidad y América Latina. Santa Clara, Cuba: Univ. Central de las Villas; Bogotá: Univ. INCCA de Colombia, 1994. 100 p.

Se enfatiza mayormente en el libro, en términos elogiosos, el carácter abierto del marxismo de Mariátegui, especialmente su contacto con otras corrientes filosóficas y aun con la religión. De ahí el tono que podría llamarse "revisionista" al mencionar despectivamente al "marxismo manualesco." De los tres artículos que contiene el libro, el tercero está dedicado a Mariátegui y la identidad latinoamericana.

5190 Rouillon, Guillermo. La creación heroica de José Carlos Mariátegui. v. 2, La edad revolucionaria, 1920–1930. Ed. homenaje a Guillermo Rouillon, 2. ed. Lima?: A. Picón, 1993. 1 v.

Para el comentario sobre el primer volumen de esta obra, ver *HLAS 40:9524.* Este segundo, publicación póstuma, muestra la vida y la obra de Mariátegui en el período 1919–30.

5191 Sánchez Pérez, Francisco. Paradojas de la identidad nacional peruana. (*Rev. Occident.*, 136, sept. 1992, p. 114–125, bibl.)

En clara exposición muestra las complejidades y dificultades que confronta la determinación de una identidad "peruana," debido a la estrucutura racial y social del país, a cómo esa estructura ha sido vivida por sus integrantes, y a las imágenes, a veces paradójicas, que se han construido sobre aquella identidad desde la Colonia hasta la actualidad.

5192 Walker Gogol, Eugene. Mariátegui y Marx: la transformación social en los países en vías de desarrollo. México: Univ. Nacional Autónoma de México, Centro Coordinación de Humanidades, Centro Coordinador y Difusor de Estudios Latinoamericanos, 1994. 89 p.: bibl., ill. (Serie Nuestra América; 44)

La interpretación gira en torno al paralelo entre el socialismo de Mariátegui, que toma en cuenta la realidad peruana y, dentro de ella al indígena, y los estudios de Marx sobre las sociedades no capitalistas y el modo de producción asiático.

5193 Wheat, Andrew. Shining Path's "Fourth Sword" ideology. (*J. Polit. Mil. Sociol.*, 18:1, Summer 1990, p. 41–55, bibl.)

Exposición de la ideología de "Sendero Luminoso," entendida como resultante de combinar la interpretación de Mariátegui respecto de la realidad peruana y las tácticas del maoísmo.

BOLIVIA

5194 García Fernández, Irsa Teresa. Aproximaciones para un estudio del trotskismo en Bolivia. (*Islas/Santa Clara*, 96, mayo/agosto 1990, p. 78–82, bibl.)

Muy breve, pero con datos básicos sobre partidos de izquierda y sobre figuras como Tristán Marof (nombre real: Gustavo Adolfo Navarro) y Guillermo Lora.

5195 Gómez Martínez, José Luis. Homenaje a Guillermo Francovich, 1901–1990. (*Cuad. Am.*, 5:3(27), mayo/junio 1991, p. 34–51)

Homenaje al pensador boliviano, fallecido en 1990, que destaca su personalidad de ensayista, dramaturgo e historiador de las

ideas. Incluye un apéndice bibliográfico de y sobre Francovich. [CJB]

CHILE

5196 Berrios C., Mario. La construcción de la idea de ciencia en América Latina. (*in* Colección nuestra patria es America: la cultura en la historia. Recopilación de Jorge Nuñez Sánchez. Quito: Editora Nacional, 1992, v. 8, p. 73–80)

Pese al título, se trata de la exposición de la obra que Claudio Gay (1800–73) realizó en Chile, elaborando un inventario de flora, fauna y minerales, en el cual dió cabida a la percepción y los usos locales de esos elementos. [CJB]

5197 Caiceo Escudero, Jaime and Elena Sánchez de Irarrázabal. Clarence Finlayson: sinopsis de la filosofía en Chile. Santiago?: Facultad de Filosofía, Pontificia Univ. Católica de Chile, 1988. 127 p.: bibl. (Textos, seminarios y ciclos de estudio)

Se compone de dos trabajos. Jaime Caiceo Escudero traza un panorama de las etapas de la filosofía en Chile, con generoso espacio para el pensamiento católico. Elena Sánchez de Irarrázabal se refiere a Clarence Finlayson (1913–54), destacado filósofo católico que enseñó en varios países de América Latina y en Estados Unidos, y es autor de *Dios y la filosofía* (ver HLAS 11:3904), entre otras obras.

5198 Cristi, Renato. El pensamiento conservador de Alberto Edwards. (*Estud. Públicos*, 44, primavera 1991, p. 141–180)

Trabajo extenso que sigue el pensamiento subyacente a las opiniones políticas y a la historiografía del autor de *La fronda aristocrática en Chile* (ver HLAS 2:2217). Muestra que Burke y Spengler se contaron entre los pensadores en que se inspiró Edwards. Artículo importante para el tema.

5199 Góngora Escobedo, Alvaro. El estado en Mario Góngora: una noción de contenido spengleriano. (*Historia/Santiago*, 25, 1990, p. 39–79, bibl.)

Clara y útil exposición de la influencia de Spengler en el historiador y pensador chileno Mario Góngora.

5200 Martínez Busch, Jorge. La influencia de Fray Francisco de Vitoria O.P. en Chile, 1550–1650: apuntes para una historia. Santiago: Zig-Zag, 1993. 139 p.: bibl. (Serie Estudios)

Proporciona útiles datos sobre la cuestión del indio durante la conquista y colonización del territorio de Chile. Las manifestaciones en favor de los indios se reconducen a las doctrinas de Vitoria, pues el autor se ocupa especialmente de los dominicos y de su vinculación con el convento de San Esteban de Salamanca.

5201 Pinedo, Javier. Reflexiones en torno al Abate Juan Ignacio Molina, la ilustración, y el ensayo sobre la historia natural de Chile. (*Universum/Talca*, 7, 1992, p. 21–40, bibl., ill., map)

El abate Juan Ignacio Molina (1740–1829) fue parte del grupo de los jesuitas expulsos. Escribió varias obras sobre Chile (donde había nacido), entre ellas dos ensayos, uno sobre la historia civil, y otro sobre la historia natural de ese país. El presente artículo se ocupa de la segunda de dichas obras. Expone su contenido buscando mostrar los recursos metódicos de la investigación de Molina, sus ideas científicas generales y el grado de asimilación de las doctrinas iluministas de la época, a las cuales combina, como es frecuente en la "Ilustración Católica," con la creencia religiosa.

5202 Pozo Ruiz, José Miguel. Historia de Chile y positivismo. (*Rev. Humanid./ Santiago*, 1, 1993, p. 107–115)

Analiza la influencia del positivismo en la historiografía clásica chilena. Concluye que aquél no tuvo la presencia que se le ha atribuido, dado que habría sido asumido de modo ingenuo, sin calar en una teoría sociológica o una filosofía de la historia. [CJB]

5203 Sznajder, Mario. El nacionalsocialismo chileno de los años treinta. (*Mapocho/ Santiago*, 32, primer semestre 1992, p. 169–193, bibl.)

Trabajo importante, con buena apoyatura bibliográfica, que reseña las actividades del Movimiento Nacional Socialista de Chile (MNS) y su diferenciación con respecto al nazismo alemán. Incluye una breve referencia a su estructura organizativa y a su participación en el golpe del 5 de septiembre de 1938. [CJB]

BRAZIL

5204 Albuquerque, Antonio Luiz Porto e. Utopia e crise social no Brasil, 1871–1916: o pensamento do padre Júlio Maria. Rio de Janeiro: Ministério da Cultura, Fundação Casa de Rui Barbosa, 1994. 218 p.: bibl.

El autor estudiado es Júlio César de Moraes Carneiro (1850–1916), quien, al ordenarse de presbítero, cambió su nombre al de Júlio Maria. El libro sigue la línea de pensamiento político-religiosa de este autor, convertido al catolicismo y defensor de la doctrina social de la Iglesia después de haber pasado por el liberalismo y el darwinismo social. Pero al estudiarlo se examina también el pensamiento brasileño de la época, en la medida en que se relaciona con el tema. Se afirma, sin embargo, que la preocupación social de Júlio Maria fue de origen teológico, fundada en la esperanza de la segunda venida de Cristo.

5205 Almeida, Lúcio Flávio de. Ideologia nacional e nacionalismo. São Paulo: EDUC, 1995. 214 p.: bibl.

Después de dos capítulos teóricos se estudia el populismo nacionalista del período 1930–64.

5206 Arantes, Paulo Eduardo. Um departamento francês de ultramar: estudos sobre a formação da cultura filosófica uspiana; uma experiência nos anos 60. São Paulo: Paz e Terra, 1994. 316 p.: bibl.

Mezcla de ensayo, comentario y memoria, recoge trabajos orgánicamente ensamblados sobre la acción de profesores franceses en la enseñanza de la filosofía en São Paulo durante la década de los años 60. Se destaca la obra de autores brasileños como Bento Padro Jr., Oswaldo Porchat, José Arthur Giannotti y Ruy Fausto. Un capítulo se dedica al historiador de la filosofía en Brasil, Joao Cruz Costa.

5207 Araújo, Ricardo Benzaquen de. Guerra e paz: *Casa-grande & senzala* e a obra de Gilberto Freyre nos anos 30. Rio de Janeiro: Editora 34, 1994. 215 p.: bibl.

Ensayo que compara *Casa-grande e senzala* con otras obras de Freyre de la década del 30, especialmente *Sobrados e mucambos*. Para el comentario del sociólogo, vea *HLAS 57:5212*.

5208 Azzi, Riolando. O estado leigo e o projeto ultramontano. São Paulo: Paulus, 1994. 138 p.: bibl. (História do pensamento católico no Brasil; 4)

Cuarto volumen de una historia del catoliscismo en el Brasil. Buena contribución, como otras del mismo autor sobre el tema. Muestra, en la época de la instalación de la República, la relación crítica entre la Iglesia (de orientación ultramontana) y el poder político. Indica también cómo la Iglesia trata de recuperar su posición anterior. Entre las ideas consideradas, se destacan la reacción de la jerarquía eclesiástica contra el liberalismo y el anarquismo, la prédica de la obediencia a los poderes constituidos, el tradicionalismo monárquico, el catolicismo liberal y el anticlericalismo liberal.

5209 Azzi, Riolando. A neocristandade: um projeto restaurador. São Paulo: Paulus, 1994. 166 p.: bibl. (História do pensamento católico no Brasil; 5)

Expone la aproximación, en la década de los años 20, entre la Iglesia Católica brasileña y el estado, unidos ambos en el combate contra las ideas socialistas. Sólo hacia mediados del siglo, afirma el autor, la Iglesia en Brasil comenzó a preocuparse por los problemas sociales.

5210 Calado, Adérito. A influencia de Ortega y Gasset no Brasil. (*Rev. Inst. Hist. Geogr. São Paulo*, 85, 1990, p. 75–84, bibl.)

Entre los autores que considera influídos por Ortega en Brasil señala los siguientes: Gilberto de Mello Kujawski, Ubiratan Macedo, Antonio Luís Machado Neto, Irineu Strenger, Hélio Jaguaribe, Roland Corbisier y Luis Washington Vita. También da otras indicaciones sobre la resonancia del filósofo español en Brasil.

Cardoso, Fernando Henrique. Livros que inventaram o Brasil. Ver *HLAS* 57:5226.

5211 Carvalho, José Maurício de. As idéias filosóficas e políticas de Tancredo Neves. Belo Horizonte, Brazil: Editora Itatiaia, 1994. 198 p.: appendix, bibl. (Col. Reconquista do Brasil; 2a. sér., 176)

Presenta el pensamiento que animó la prédica y la acción de Tancredo Neves, hombre público y político de Brasil. Destaca en Neves la creencia básica en el valor de la libertad dentro de un espiritualismo trascendente que rechaza el liberalismo ateo. Esta posición colorea sus ideas sobre la economía, la sociedad y la convivencia política. Señala que las raíces de esa ideología se encuentran en manifestaciones de pensamiento propias de Minas Gerais durante el siglo XIX.

5212 Carvalho, José Murilo de. A utopia de Oliveira Viana. (*Estud. Hist./Rio de Janeiro*, 4:7, 1991, p. 82–99, bibl.)

Aunque por el contenido desafía el resumen, puede decirse que la intención es revisar ("revisitar") la obra y el significado de Oliveira Viana, autor de *Populações meridionais do Brasil* (1920) y *Evolução do povo brasileiro* (São Paulo: Monteiro Lobado, 1923), muy elogiado antes de la primera mitad del siglo y muy criticado después. Considera su concepción de la naturaleza de la investigación histórica, sus fuentes intelectuales, y su utopía política. Oliveira Viana pertenecería a la corriente "iberista," contrapuesta al liberalismo. Hay comparaciones con el Vizconde de Uruguay, con Sérgio Buarque de Holanda y con Gilberto Freyre. Artículo de interés. Véase también item **5233.**

5213 Cavalcanti, Zaida-María Costa. Os verdes anos de Gilberto Freyre: germinações. (*Ciênc. Tróp.*, 18:2, julho/dez. 1990, p. 141–172, bibl.)

Aproximación biográfica que interesa para la obra Gilberto Freyre y su modalidad de escritor.

5214 Cesar, Constança Marcondes. A relação homem-natureza na filosofia brasileira contemporânea. (*Rev. Bras. Filos.*, 39:164, out./dez. 1991, p. 259–271)

Según la autora, dos corrientes del pensamiento filosófico brasileño actual acentúan los aspectos éticos, especialmente en relación con las obligaciones ante la naturaleza: la filosofía cristiana y la filosofía existencial. En el caso de la primera son autores destacados Alvino Moser y Josafá Carlos de Siqueira, con particular preocupación por la ecología. Dentro de la escuela existencialista de tendencia orteguiana, son tratados Gilberto de Mello Kujawski y Vicente Ferreira da Silva, este último con su "ética do telurismo." Ambas corrientes coincidían en la denuncia a la civilización técnica y la tendencia a la desacralización.

5215 Costa, Valeriano Mendes Ferreira.
Vertentes democráticas em Gilberto
Freyre e Sérgio Buarque. (*Lua Nova*, 26, 1992,
p. 219–248, bibl.)

Gilberto Freyre, con su búsqueda de
las raíces nacionales en el plano social (*Casa-
grande & senzala*, ver *HLAS 2:1635, HLAS
4:3353*, y *HLAS 12:2831*); y Buarque de
Holanda, con su método dialéctico o "con-
trapuntístico" (*Raizes do Brasil*, ver *HLAS
14:62a* y *HLAS 14:2262*), son vistos en
relación con las ideas democráticas y el pensamiento autoritario de la época. De hecho
hay comparaciones también con Alberto Torres y Oliveira Viana.

**5216 Encontro Nacional de Professores e
Pesquisadores da Filosofia Brasileira,
1st, Londrina, Brazil, 1989.** Anais. Coordenação de Leonardo Prota. Londrina, Brazil:
Centro de Estudos Filosóficos de Londrina;
Univ. Estadual de Londrina, 1989. 255 p.:
bibl.

El cuerpo principal de esta obra, en lo
que se refiere al interés de esta sección, está
compuesto por dos artículos: "O Modelo de
Pesquisa da Filosofia Brasileira," de Antonio
Paim y Ricardo Vélez Rodríguez; y "O Diálogo da Filosofia Brasileira com outras Filo-
sofias Nacionais", de Antonio Paim. Este último autor considera que son características
del pensamiento filosófico propiamente
brasileño aquellos esfuerzos que tienden a
"dar continuidad al diálogo que venimos
emprendiendo con las otras filosofías nacionales." Y entre ellos selecciona: la corriente culturalista, la fenomenológica, la orteguiana, la neopositivista de Leónidas
Hegenberg, y la de algunos existencialistas.
En materia de problemas tendría prioridad el
tema del hombre (con sus derivaciones hacia
la ética, la cultura y la política). También hay
en el volumen una parte dedicada a la enseñanza y a la investigación de la filosofía
brasileña.

**5217 Encontro Nacional de Professores e
Pesquisadores da Filosofia Brasileira,
2nd, Londrina, Brazil, 1991.** Anais. Coorde-
nação de Leonardo Prota. Londrina, Brazil:
Centro de Estudos Filosóficos de Londrina;
Univ. Estadual de Londrina, 1991. 2 v.: bibl.

Se encuentran varios artículos de interés, a saber: de Antonio Paim sobre el tema
de las filosofías nacionales; dos sobre Ortega
y Gasset, uno en comparación con Miguel

Reale y otro de Ubiratan Macedo, uno de los
mejores conocedores del filósofo español en
Brasil; otro sobre "Iberoamérica como Totalidad" de Ricardo Vélez Rodríguez; y dos dedicados a la influencia filosófica alemana en
Brasil: en forma panorámica (Creusa Ca-
palbo) y en especial sobre la fenomenología
(Antonio Paim).

5218 Fonseca, Edson Nery da. Gilberto
Freyre e sua cosmovisão cristocên-
trica. (*Ciênc. Tróp.*, 18:2, julho/dez. 1990,
p. 173–178, bibl.)

Breve indicación sobre el aspecto
cristocéntrico en la *Weltanschauung* de
Gilberto Freyre y su reflejo en su obra.

5219 Forum Merquior, Paris, 1990.
Merquior: memorial crítico. Brasília:
Instituto Tancredo Neves de Estudos Políti-
cos e Sociais, 1994. 174 p.: bibl.

En general, excelente homenaje a José
Guilherme Merquior, uno de los más brillan-
tes y sólidos intelectuales de Brasil en lo que
va del siglo. Además de artículos—entre
otros—de Sérgio Paulo Rouanet, Celso
Laufer y Roberto Campos, hay dos inéditos
de Merquior: un discurso de juventud (1963)
y su última conferencia (París, 1990).

5220 Gadotti, Moacir. Paulo Freire: uma
biobibliografia. São Paulo: Cortez
Editora; Instituto Paulo Freire Brasília:
UNESCO, 1996. 765 p.: bibl., ill., index.

Homenaje a Paulo Freire, con numerosas apreciaciones y juicios críticos. Contiene su bibliografía completa y lo escrito sobre su obra. Muestra la gran proyección de la
labor del pedagogo brasileño. [CJB]

5221 História do marxismo no Brasil. v. 2,
Os influxos teóricos. Organizado de
João Quartim de Moraes. Campinas, Brazil:
Editora da UNICAMP, 1995. 1 v.: bibl.

En este segundo volumen (de una serie
propuesta de cuatro) se incluyen estudios sobre: los primeros socialistas brasileños; la
evolución de la conciencia política de los
marxistas nacionales; el marxismo en la
economía de Brasil; el pensamiento marxista
en la filosofía de José Arthur Giannotti; y
sendos capítulos sobre Lukács y Trotsky en
Brasil. Para el comentario sobre el vol. 1, ver
HLAS 54:3413.

5222 Krause, Décio. A filosofia da ciência de
Newton C.A. da Costa. (*Rev. Bras. Filos.*, 34:158, abril/junho 1990, p. 117–144)

Visión general de la filosofía de la ciencia de Newton da Costa, destacándose especialmente el problema del conocimiento científico, el carácter histórico de la teoría de la ciencia, y los presupuestos metafísicos de la labor científica.

5223 Lemos, Maria Teresa Toríbio Brittes. Alberto Torres: contribuição para o estudo das idéias no Brasil. Rio de Janeiro: Quartet, 1995. 163 p.: bibl.

Busca determinar el pensamiento de Alberto Torres (1865–1917), "basándose en los principales conceptos que utilizó para interpretar los problemas brasileños." Se revisa la formación cientificista de Torres, sus ideas sobre las razas y la correspondiente aplicación a Brasil, y, de la misma manera, sus conceptos sobre el nacionalismo.

5224 Lorenzon, Alino. Influência do personalismo de Emmanuel Mounier no Brasil: subsídios e apontamentos para um estudo mais aprofundado. (*Rev. Filos. Bras.,* 5:1, junho 1992, p. 99–114, bibl.)

Además de algunos aspectos filosóficos, Mounier habría influido en otros de ética y de praxis. Entre los autores que recibieron esa orientación, señala a Alceu Amoroso Lima y el Padre Lima Vaz. Y en cuanto a movimientos de grupos, a la Juventud Universitaria Católica. Véase también item **5230.**

5225 Macedo, Ubiratan. Presença de Miguel Reale na cultura brasileira. (*Presença Filos.,* 16:1/4, 1991, p. 18–29)

Con sentido de homenaje, traza un acabado perfil de Reale, una de las máximas figuras de la filosofía brasileña. También señala su influencia en la vida filosófica de Brasil y en la cultura en general.

5226 Pádua, Elisabete Matallo Marchesini de. A filosofia de Caio Prado Júnior. (*Reflexão/Campinas,* 17:49, jan./abril 1991, p. 7–26)

De Caio Prado Júnior se examinan sus trabajos *Dialética do conhecimento* (ver *HLAS 18:3126*) y *Notas introdutórias à lógica dialética* (1959), pero previamente se sitúa la obra de este autor en el contexto de la historia del marxismo latinoamericano. Se encuentra que son figuras semejantes las de Sergio Bagú y José Carlos Mariátegui. En relación a este último se dice que sus *Siete ensayos de interpretación de la realidad pe-* ruana (1928) y el libro de Prado *Evolução política do Brasil* (1933) son los primeros ensayos de análisis de la formación social de América Latina basados en principios marxistas.

5227 Penna, José Osvaldo de Meira. A ideologia do século XX: ensaios sobre o nacional-socialismo, o marxismo, o terceiro-mundismo e a ideologia brasileira. 2a. ed. Rio de Janeiro: Instituto Liberal; Nordica, 1994. 254 p.: bibl., ill., index.

Desde un punto de vista liberal en lo político y lo económico, examina críticamente ideologías como el socialismo, el nacionalismo, el marxismo y el fascismo, entre otras. Con el mismo enfoque revisa críticamente el nacionalismo y otros aspectos ideológicos de Brasil, hasta fechas recientes. Un capítulo se dedica a la crítica de la teoría de la dependencia.

5228 Santos, Luis Antônio de Castro. O espírito da aldeia: orgulho ferido e vaidade na trajetória intelectual de Gilberto Freyre. (*Novos Estud. CEBRAP,* 27, julho 1990, p. 45–67)

Ensayo de enfoque psicológico, tendiente a mostrar características personales de Gilberto Freyre que habían perjudicado su obra posterior a 1950. Es, de paso, y en función de los intereses del autor, una comparación con las carreras intelectuales de Sergio Buarque de Holanda y Caio Prado Junior.

5229 Semeraro, Giovanni. A primavera dos anos 60: a geração de Betinho. Rio de Janeiro: Centro João XXIII; São Paulo: Edições Loyola, 1994. 209 p.: bibl. (Col. Estudos brasileiros; 3)

Es una historia de la juventud católica de izquierda en Brasil entre 1959 y 1964. Presenta el contexto histórico-político del movimiento, su acción y sus fundamentos doctrinarios; también sus limitaciones, su dispersión final y su legado. Escrito con gran simpatía hacia el grupo estudiado.

5230 Souza, Luiz Alberto Gómez de. Pe. Vaz, mestre de uma geração de cristãos. (*Síntese/Belo Horizonte,* 18:55, out./dez. 1991, p. 643–651)

Relato testimonial de los comienzos de la Juventud Universitaria Católica y su compromiso social en los años 60. Expresa, con un sentido de homenaje, la influencia ejercida por el filósofo jesuita Henrique Cláudio de Lima Vaz. Véase también item **5224**.

5231 Teixeira, António Braz. A idéia de Deus na filosofia brasileira do século XIX. (*Rev. Bras. Filos.*, 40:165, jan./março 1992, p. 21–34)

Sobre cómo es vista la teodicea en Silvestre Pinheiro Ferreira (1769–1846), Diego António Fejió (1784–1842), Domingo Gonçalves de Magalhães (1811–82), Tobias Barreto (1838–89) y Farias Brito.

5232 Vélez Rodriguez, Ricardo. O fenômeno do cientificismo na cultura brasileira. (*Rev. Bras. Filos.*, 39:161, jan/março 1991, p. 17–31)

'Cientificismo' no se entiende aquí como la posición filosófica que se constituye con una desmedida apreciación por la ciencia, sino como la estimación de la ciencia dentro de un proyecto nacional. Distingue cinco momentos en que se dio esa correlación: 1) la época pombalina; 2) las ideas de Frei Caneca (1774–1825); 3) el positivismo y el 'castilhismo;' 4) la época de Getúlio Vargas; y 5) los veinte años de dictadura siguientes al golpe de estado de 1964. En estos casos se trató de una búsqueda de la modernización o de asegurar la racionalidad del estado. Clarificador con respecto al fenómeno estudiado.

5233 Vianna, Luiz Werneck. Americanistas e Iberistas: a polêmica de Oliveira Viana com Tavares Bastos. (*Dados/Rio de Janeiro*, 34:2, 1991, p. 145–189)

Dicho de modo muy simplificado, se contrastan dos enfoques que se han dado de la realidad brasileña y su posible futuro: el americanismo y el iberismo. El primero se caracteriza porque quiere modificar la sociedad por medio de un sistema político (liberal), encuentra en la Colonia la fuente de muchos males, propone limitar los efectos negativos de la población existente con inmigración europea, y tiene por modelo a los Estados Unidos. El iberismo aprecia las estructuras sociales de la Colonia, el pasado y la singularidad del país, y acepta sólo una modernidad controlada. Uno de los aspectos de mayor interés en el artículo es que el contenido de estos enfoques se confrontan con actitudes como las de Sarmiento y Alberdi, en Argentina, y aun con interpretaciones como la de Richard Morse en *O espelho de*

Próspero (São Paulo: Companhia das Letras, 1988). Véase también item **5212**.

5234 Zaverucha, Jorge. A filosofia política de Joaquim Pimenta. (*Ciênc. Tróp.*, 20:2, julho/dez. 1992, p. 423–446, bibl.)

Sobre las ideas político-sociales de Joaquim Pimenta (nac. 1866), especialmente sobre la clase obrera y su posible organización, y en relación con el liberalismo, el socialismo, el anarquismo y la Iglesia. El autor encuentra contradictorio con las ideas de Pimenta que éste haya colaborado con el gobierno de Getúlio Vargas.

PARAGUAY

5235 Escobar, Ticio. Textos varios sobre cultura, transición y modernidad. Asunción: Agencia Española de Cooperación Internacional, Centro Cultural Español Juan de Salazar, 1992. 163 p.: ill.

Reflexiones actuales sobre el destino de la cultura en Paraguay después de los años de dictadura, enlazadas asimismo con consideraciones sobre el arte, la modernidad y el postmodernismo.

URUGUAY

5236 Ardao, Arturo. Filosofía pre-universitaria en el Uruguay: de la escolástica al socialismo utópico, 1787–1842. 2a ed. Montevideo: Fundación de Cultura Universitaria; Biblioteca de Marcha, 1994. 173 p.: appendices, bibl., index.

Oportuna reedición de una obra clásica sobre el pensamiento en Uruguay antes de la creación de la Universidad de la República (1849). Esta edición tiene aumentado el apéndice documental.

5237 Mañé Garzón, Fernando. Un siglo de darwinismo: un ensayo sobre la historia del pensamiento biológico en el Uruguay. Montevideo: Facultad de Medicina, Sección Historia de la Medicina, 1990. 347 p.: bibl., ill., index.

Extensa exposición de la recepción del darwinismo en el Uruguay, que llega hasta la actualidad. Salvo en épocas más recientes, las reacciones, en favor o en contra, fueron de índole ideológica más que científica, especialmente a partir del conocimiento de *The descent of man*. Las polémicas entre católicos y "evolucionistas" tienen, según el autor, su punto candente entre 1871–90. Le siguió un período de mayor apaciguamiento, en que la cuestión se consideró en función de los desarrollos de la ciencia biológica. Es obligado poner esta contribución en relación con la obra de Thomas Glick, *Darwin y el darwinismo: en el Uruguay y en América Latina* (ver *HLAS 56:5067*).

Memoria colectiva y políticas de olvido: Argentina y Uruguay, 1970–1990. Ver item **5273.**

5238 Michelena, Alejandro Daniel. Real de Azúa: itinerarios de un multiple ensayista. (*Hoy Hist.*, 8:46, julio/agosto 1991, p. 8–18)

Visión apreciativa de la obra del ensayista uruguayo, en sus aspectos de crítica literaria y cultural, de historiografía, de ensayo político y de interpretación de América Latina. En cuanto a este último aspecto, el autor a considera "obra abierta," es decir, de incitación para repensar el asunto.

Sánchez-Gey Venegas, Juana. El modernismo filosófico en América. Ver item **5045.**

5239 Schvarz, Niko. América Latina y el retoñar de la utopía: la concepción de Rodney Arismendi sobre la revolución continental, de cara al siglo XXI. Montevideo: Ediciones Fundación Rodney Arismendi, 1994. 160 p.: bibl., ill.

No es tanto un estudio del pensamiento de Arismendi (dirigente del Partido Comunista Uruguayo), como una extensa consideración sobre el futuro del socialismo democrático anti-imperialista en América Latina. Dentro de ese propósito trata de asimilar los acontecimientos que produjeron el derrumbe de la antigua Unión Soviética.

5240 Suiffet, Norma. José Enrique Rodó: su vida, su obra, su pensamiento. Montevideo: Ediciones la Urpila, 1995. 202 p.: bibl., index.

Ofrece amplia información sobre todos los aspectos de Rodó: su biografía, sus ideas filosóficas y políticas, sus escritos, su estilística, sus enseñanzas, su correspondencia. La bibliografía es considerable.

5241 Trigo, Abril. Un texto antropológico de Julio Herrera y Reissig. (*Cuad. Am.*, 32:2, marzo/abril 1992, p. 212–227, bibl.)

Introducción a un texto inédito del poeta modernista y escritor uruguayo Julio Herrera y Reissig (1875–1910). Se trata de "Los nuevos charrúas," que se refiere en corrosivas palabras a la influencia del medio físico en la conformación de los uruguayos y su civilización. En el texto de Herrera y Reissig se perciben huellas de Spencer, Guyau, Renan, Taine, Darwin y Buckle. [CJB]

5242 Universidad de la República (Uruguay). Facultad de Humanidades y Ciencias de la Educación. Ensayos en homenaje al doctor Arturo Ardao. Recopilación de Manuel A. Claps. Montevideo: Univ. de la República, Facultad de Humanidades y Ciencias de la Educación, Depto. de Publicaciones, 1995. 234 p.: bibl.

Contiene tres trabajos sobre Arturo Ardao: sobre la noción de sujeto (Yamandú Acosta); sobre la interpretación de Andrés Bello (Arturo A. Roig); y sobre su libro *Filosofía de lengua española* (ver *HLAS 36:5047*). Mencionamos algunas de las otras contribuciones: el tema de la historia de la filosofía latinoamericana (Horacio Cerutti Guldberg); el batllismo (Manuel A. Claps); el tema de Calibán (Roberto Fernández Retamar); el pensamiento de Pedro Figari (Juan Fló); la universidad latinoamericana en el siglo XVIII (Gregorio Weinberg); el pensamiento socialista en el Uruguay (Carlos Zubillaga). Es de lamentar que no se agregara al volumen una bibliografía de Ardao.

5243 Wiliman, Claudio. Las raíces cristianas en el pensamiento del Partido Nacional del Uruguay. (*Contribuciones/Buenos Aires*, 2, abril/junio 1991, p. 19–36, table)

Muestra, desde sus orígenes en el siglo XIX, las ideas y las tendencias ideológicas del Partido "Blanco" de Uruguay, ejemplificando la exposición con los actos históricos de dicho Partido. Hispanismo y catolicismo seían dos de sus principales rasgos, a diferencia de "la línea liberal-iluminista, antiespañola y anticatólica" que según el autor es propia del Partido "Colorado." Es también, en resumen, una historia del partido con documentos de hasta 1983.

ARGENTINA

5244 Ames, José Luiz. Da libertação à liberdade: crítica interna de alguns pontos da ética de Dussel. (*Reflexão/Campinas*, 17:49, jan./abril 1991, p. 72–108, bibl.)

Extenso y detenido análisis crítico de

las ideas éticas de Dussel. Como expresa el título, es una crítica interna, es decir, atendiendo a la coherencia propia de las partes de la doctrina.

5245 Arpini, Adriana. Ecos martianos en el latinoamericanismo de un argentino: Manuel Ugarte. (*Cuad. Am.*, 6:4, julio/agosto 1992, p. 164–170)

Relaciona a Manuel Ugarte (1878–1951) con los proyectos de unión latinoamericana del siglo XIX. Concluye que tanto Martí como Ugarte, al formular la pregunta por el ser latinoamericano buscaron una respuesta que, más allá de la caracterización geográfica u ontológica, implicaba una determinada valoración del sujeto que formula la pregunta. [CJB]

5246 Asociación de Investigación y Especialización sobre Temas Iberoamericanos (Madrid). El pensamiento político argentino contemporáneo. Edición de Aníbal Iturrieta. Buenos Aires: Grupo Editor Latino americano; Emecé Editores, 1994. 390 p.: bibl. (Col. Estudios políticos y sociales. Síntesis)

El libro fue pensado para el público español y su elaboración se remonta a la década de 1980. Aunque no cubre la totalidad del pensamiento político argentino, el panorama es representativo. Los aspectos estudiados son: el nacionalismo (Aníbal Iturrieta y Carlos Floria); José Ingenieros y José Luis Romero (Oscar Terán); el radicalismo (Félix Luna); Arturo Jauretche (Horacio J. Pereyra); el liberalismo (Ezequiel Gallo); el socialismo (José Aricó); el peronismo (Aníbal Iturrieta y Horacio Cerutti Guldberg); y el menemismo (Vicente Palermo). También hay un trabajo sobre las relaciones hispano-argentinas y una visión de conjunto del alfonsinismo. Contiene buena bibliografía.

5247 Biagini, Hugo Edgardo. La Generación del Ochenta: cultura y política. Buenos Aires: Editorial Losada, 1995. 173 p.: bibl. (Cristal del tiempo)

Es ampliación de su obra anterior, *Cómo fue la generación del 80* (ver *HLAS 44:7580*). No se limita a la mencionada generación, sino que en realidad se trata de trabajos sobre la época (aproximadamente 1870–1910). Entre los nuevos materiales hay artículos sobre la ciudad de Buenos Aires, el Cuarto Centenario del Descubrimiento de

América, y el Congreso Pedagógico Internacional de 1882. Un epílogo resume las relaciones entre la Generación del Ochenta y el país.

5248 Bianchi, Susana. La Iglesia Católica en los orígenes del peronismo. (*Anu. IEHS*, 5, 1990, p. 71–89)

Trabajo interesante y bien expuesto que distingue la posición de los diferentes grupos católicos argentinos frente al peronismo en sus comienzos. [CJB]

Botana, Natalio R. and Ezequiel Gallo. De la república posible a la república verdadera: 1880–1910. Ver item **2831.**

5249 Brieger, Pedro. Sacerdotes para el tercer mundo: una frustrada experiencia de evangelización. (*Todo es Hist.*, 25:287, mayo 1991, p. 10–28, bibl., facsims., photos)

Efectos de la encíclica *Populorum Progressio*, en conjunción con las tendencias político-sociales de la década de los años 60 y el populismo peronista, sobre un grupo considerable de sacerdotes argentinos cuya acción fue violentamente suprimida en la década siguiente.

Cane, James. "Unity for the defense of culture": the AIAPE and the cultural politics of Argentine antifascism, 1935–1943. Ver item **2845.**

5250 Cappelletti, Angel J. Filosofía argentina del siglo XX. Rosario, Argentina: Univ. Nacional de Rosario, 1995. 180 p.

Este valioso volumen contiene artículos sobre Alejandro Korn, Alberto Rougès, Alfredo Franceschi, Lisandro de la Torre, Vicente Fatone, Georg Nicolai, Rodolfo Mondolfo, Francisco Romero y Risieri Frondizi. Los artículos son más bien interpretativos que monográficos. El libro se abre con tres visiones de conjunto: sobre la historia de las ideas filosóficas en América Latina; sobre la periodización de esa historia; y sobre la filosofía argentina del siglo veinte. También contiene opiniones utilizables para la cuestión de la naturaleza de la filosofía latino americana.

5251 Caturelli, Alberto. Historia de la filosofía en Córdoba, 1610–1983. v. 1–3. Córdoba, Argentina: Gráficos Biffignandi, 1992. 3 v.: bibl., index. (La filosofía en la Argentina; pt. 1)

El grado de detalle a que llega la obra

puede apreciarse por el hecho de dedicar tres volúmenes a la filosofía en un sola ciudad, bien que ella fue de gran importancia cultural, especialmente en los siglos XVII y XVIII. A estos siglos está dedicado el vol. 1, en tanto el vol. 2 lo está al siglo XIX y el vol. 3 al siglo XX. La obra adquiere su mayor valor en la exposición de la filosofía colonial. En el balance total la presencia de la filosofía cristiana (católica) tiene gran predominancia.

Chaparro, Máximo. América Latina: liberación y filosofía. Ver item **4939.**

5252 Cohen Imach, Victoria. De utopías y desencantos: campo intelectual y periferia en la Argentina de los sesenta. Tucumán, Argentina: Univ. Nacional de Tucumán, Facultad de Filosofía y Letras, Instituto Interdisciplinario de Estudios Latinoamericanos, 1994. 508 p.: bibl., ill., map. (Publicación; 1493)

Los términos 'centro' y 'periferia' se refieren aquí a Buenos Aires y el resto del país, respectivamente. El tema del libro es de historia literaria, especialmente la recepción y apreciación de la literatura del interior argentino en los grandes medios del país; pero contiene información e interpretación sobre la vida cultural y política argentina entre 1955 y 1976.

Congreso de Estudios Latinoamericanos, 1st, La Plata, Argentina, 1991. Homenaje a José Martí: actas. Ver item **4945.**

Cosmelli Ibáñez, José Luis. Historia de la cultura argentina. Ver item **2865.**

5253 Cuyo: Anuario de Historia del Pensamiento Argentino. Nos. 8/9, 1991/92. Mendoza, Argentina: Univ. Nacional de Cuyo, Facultad de Filosofía y Letras, Instituto de Filosofía Argentina y Americana.

Principales artículos: Diego F. Pro, "La Cultura Filosófica de Vicente López;" Marta Pisi de Catalini, "La Teoría Egológica de Carlos Cossio y el Tridimensionalismo Jurídico de Miguel Reale;" Angélica Gabrielidis de Luna, "El Pensamiento Filosófico de Homero Mario Guglielmini;" Estela María Fernández, "La Construcción de la Identidad Americana en Torno a la Utopía Independentista en los Textos de Francisco de Miranda;" Ignacio Lucero, "El Pensamiento de Rodolfo Rivarola;" Adriana Arpini, "Desarrollo y Crisis del Historicismo como Metodología Para

Nuestra Historia de las Ideas;" José Ramón Pérez, "Homenaje al Dr. Nimio de Anquín." [CJB]

5254 Cuyo: Anuario de Historia del Pensamiento Argentino. No. 12, 1995. Mendoza, Argentina: Univ. Nacional de Cuyo, Facultad de Filosofía y Letras, Instituto de Filosofía Argentina y Americana.

Algunos artículos y notas de este número: Javier Pinedo Castro, "El Tema del Fin de la Historia y su Recepción en Chile" (sobre Francis Fukuyama); Estela Fernández y Alejandra Ciriza, "Simón Rodríguez, una Utopía Socialista en América;" Hugo E Biagini, "El Pensamiento Universitario de Arturo Roig." Además, hay notas sobre los estudios latinoamericanos en Polonia, de Marta Bronislawa Duda; sobre el libro *Quinientos años de historia, sentido y proyección* (ver *HLAS 56:4896*), de Rosa Licata; y un recuerdo de Eugenio Pucciarelli (1907–95), de J.C. Torchia Estrada. Por último, Rosa Licata presenta un texto inédito de Miguel Angel Virasoro escrito en los comienzos de la década de 1930. [CJB]

5255 Cuyo: Anuario de Historia del Pensamiento Argentino. No. 13, 1996. Mendoza, Argentina: Univ. Nacional de Cuyo, Facultad de Filosofía y Letras, Instituto de Filosofía Argentina y Americana.

Artículos y notas de esta entrega: J.C. Torchia Estrada, "El Padre Antonio Rubio y la Enseñanza de los Jesuitas en la Nueva España;" Clara Alicia Jalif de Bertranou, "Recepción y Elaboración de la Fenomenología en la Argentina;" Rosa Licata, "Hombre y Sociedad en la Pensamiento de Miguel Angel Virasoro;" Salvador E. Morales, "Utopía y Praxis Revolucionaria: las Alternativas de José Martí para América Latina;" Hugo E. Biagini, "Universidad e Integración Latino americana;" Herminia Solari, "Joaquín V. González: Algunas Consideraciones Alrededor de la Idea de Nación;" Alicia N. Salomone, "Mujeres e Ideas en América Latina: una Relación Problemática." Continuando con la acertada tradición de esta revista, se publica un texto inédito, en este caso de Agustín Alvarez, al cuidado de Dante Ramaglia. [CJB]

5256 Díaz Araujo, Enrique. La teoría política de Julio Irazusta. Buenos Aires: C.E.C.P.U.C.A. Ediciones, 1995. 121 p.: bibl.

Julio Irazusta (1899–1982) es recordado como iniciador del "revisionismo" histórico en Argentina y una de las figuras principales del nacionalismo en ese país. Aquí se lo estudia como pensador político, especialmente en su obra *La política, cenicienta del espíritu* (ver *HLAS 42:3367*). Contiene todos los elementos para una introducción al autor estudiado, cuyas tesis se miran con simpatía. Véase también item **5282**.

5257 Discursos pedagógicos e imaginario social en el peronismo, 1945–1955. Dirección de Adriana Puiggrós. Coordinación de Sandra Carli. Buenos Aires: Editorial Galerna, 1995. 308 p.: bibl. (Historia de la educación en la Argentina; 6)

Contiene materiales para el estudio de la educación en la época del primer peronismo, pero también sobre los antecedentes de esa época. Naturalmente recorre el libro la relación pedagogía/política. El volumen anterior de esta historia, *Peronismo: cultura política y educación, 1945–1955* (Buenos Aires: Editorial Galerna, 1993), también se ocupa del peronismo, en tanto otros previos de la serie (*Historia de la educación en la Argentina*) se remontan a los orígenes del sistema educativo argentino.

5258 Forment, Eudaldo. Filosofía inmanentista y filosofía cristiana de Iberoamérica. (*Rev. Filos./México*, 25:75, sept./dic. 1992, p. 320–341)

Exposición y elogio del filósofo argentino contemporáneo Alberto Caturelli. Destaca la crítica que, desde la posición católica del autor estudiado, se hace a las formas "inmanentistas" (no trascendentes) de la filosofía actual, y la extensión de aquélla al problema de América en la visión de Caturelli.

Franzé, Javier. El concepto de política en el socialismo argentino. Ver *HLAS 57:3717.*

5259 Frederick, Bonnie. A state of conviction, a state of feeling: scientific and literary discourses in the works of three Argentine writers, 1879–1908. (*Lat. Am. Lit. Rev.*, 19:38, July/Dec. 1991, p. 48–61, bibl.)

Sobre el lugar de ciertos conceptos científicos en los textos (algunos de ficción) de Eduardo L. Holmberg, Carlos Octavio Bunge y Eduardo Wilde. [CJB]

5260 Frydenberg, Julio and **Irene Frydenberg.** Anatole France en Buenos Aires. (*Todo es Hist.*, 25:291, sept. 1991, p. 81–91)

Crónica de la repercusión que tuvo en Buenos Aires la visita de Anatole France en 1909. Fuera de la reacción de los grupos católicos, se atiende más a los aspectos sociales que a los intelectuales, si bien los primeros son de gran interés anecdótico.

5261 Goldar, Ernesto. John William Cooke: de Perón al Che Guevara. (*Todo es Hist.*, 25:288, junio 1991, p. 10–40, bibl., facsims., photos)

El significado para la historia ideológica es que Cooke fue un ideólogo del peronismo, pero no de su corriente central, debido a su nacionalismo extremo, al comienzo, y a su giro hacia la izquierda revolucionaria, al final.

5262 Goldman, Noemí. Historia y lenguaje: los discursos de la Revolución de Mayo. Tucumán, Argentina: Centro Editor de América Latina, 1992. 168 p.: appendix, bibl. (Los fundamentos de las ciencias del hombre)

La principal contribución de la autora, además de consideraciones teóricas y de revisar la historiografía sobre el asunto, es el estudio de los discursos políticos de tres actores del movimiento de independencia en el Río de la Plata: Mariano Moreno, Juan José Castelli y Bernardo Monteagudo. Se completa con un muy útil apéndice documental de textos de estos autores.

5263 González, Alina. El pensamiento marxista en América Latina: la figura del teórico argentino José Aricó. (*Islas/Santa Clara*, 101, enero/abril 1992, p. 69–83)

Análisis crítico del pensamiento de José Aricó, que se propone caracterizar la posición de dicho autor en función de algunos escritos marcados por su ruptura con el Partido Comunista de la Argentina. [CJB]

5264 González, Liliana C. Repensando el *Dogma socialista* de Esteban Echeverría. Buenos Aires: Instituto Torcuato Di Tella, 1994. 117 p.: bibl. (Ciencias sociales)

El propósito declarado de la autora es comprender el pensamiento y el *Dogma socialista* de Echeverría (ver *HLAS 6:3365* y *HLAS 13:1051*), en función de su contexto histórico: situaciones, necesidades e ideas de la época. Para ello pasa revista a las interpretaciones de un grupo de autores (entre ellos Paul Groussac, José Ingenieros, Alfredo

Palacios y Tulio Halperín Donghi), y examina luego los conceptos fundamentales del *Dogma*. Concluye que Echeverría debe interpretarse y juzgarse por su propósito práctico frente a la situación del país y su futuro, cuyo objetivo principal fue el logro de un consenso social y programático. Manifiesta adhesión al enfoque y la metodología de Quentin Skinner. Libro claro y atendible.

5265 Huertas García-Alejo, Rafael. El delincuente y su patología: medicina, crimen y sociedad en el positivismo argentino. Madrid: Consejo Superior de Investigaciones Científicas, 1991. 199 p.: bibl. (Cuadernos Galileo de historia de la ciencia; 12)

Mucho del aspecto monográfico del libro gira en torno a la obra criminológica de José Ingenieros, según se manifiesta en sus trabajos sobre la simulación y en sus teorías de la "defensa social." También se examinan las opiniones médicas y psiquiátricas a que dio lugar el fenómeno inmigratorio y sus consecuencias sociales. Todo a lo largo del libro se reitera la afirmación de que los peritajes médicos que se utilizaban para asistir a la justicia, la labor de los asilos, la consideración de los inmigrantes y el saber psiquiátrico en general fueron formas que utilizó la burguesía para ejercer el control social y favorecer el capitalismo. Esa afirmación queda sobreimpuesta al material de estudio, como una imputación más que como una tesis o una hipótesis de trabajo que realmente se demuestra.

5266 Jornadas de Historia del Pensamiento Científico Argentino, 5th, Buenos Aires, 1990. Actas. Buenos Aires: Ediciones FEPAI, 1994. 259 p.: bibl.

Trabajos contenidos en este volumen y que son de interés para esta sección: Carlos Mato Fernández, "Historia de las Ciencias e Historia de las Ideas;" Hugo A. Klappenbach, "Los Orígenes del Psicoanálisis en la Argentina y la Psicología Experimental y Clínica de Principios de Siglo;" Beatriz Martino de Arocena y Elsa E. Pavón, "La Universidad de la Ciencia y la Paz en el Pensamiento de Joaquín V. González;" Luis A. Santaló, "La Historia de las Ciencias en la Argentina en la Década de los Años 80."

5267 Katra, William H. The Argentine generation of 1837: Echeverría, Alberdi, Sarmiento, Mitre. Madison, N.J.: Fairleigh

Dickinson Univ. Press; London; Cranbury, N.J.: Associated University Presses, 1996. 367 p.: bibl., index.

Narrativa comentada del pensamiento y la actuación de los personajes indicados en el subtítulo y otros. Es predominantemente un enfoque de historia política. Sin una tesis central, pero con opiniones políticamente "progresistas;" son ejemplos: lo que se dice sobre la posición "elitista" y "racista" de la generación de 1837 o sobre las opiniones de Sarmiento y Alberdi respecto a la distribución de las tierras públicas. Aun en los casos en que los temas originan opiniones encontradas la lectura es útil. Para el comentario del historiador, ver item **2937**.

5268 Kovadloff, Santiago. A propósito de la herencia colonial y su influjo en América Latina: España en Sarmiento. (*Integr. Latinoam.*, 15:155, abril 1990, p. 24–38)

Sobre la preocupación de Sarmiento por las modalidades españolas—consideradas por él como retardatarias del progreso—que todavía persistían en su época en Argentina, a pesar de la independencia. También examina la relación de Sarmiento con el romanticismo.

5269 Leocata, Francisco. Las ideas filosóficas en Argentina. v. 1–2. Buenos Aires: Centro Salesiano de Estudios, 1992–93. 2 v.: bibl. (Estudios proyecto; 5,12)

Se trata de la obra más completa hasta hoy sobre la historia de las ideas filosóficas en Argentina. El primer volumen cubre desde la colonia hasta los comienzos de la superación del positivismo. El segundo se dedica al siglo veinte, desde 1910 a 1943, y considera que los temas capitales de esta etapa son la vida y los valores, notándose una relación menos estrecha, por lo menos en lo aparente, entre el pensamiento filosófico y la vida político-social. Sería altamente recomendable que el autor completara este panorama hasta fines del siglo que concluye.

5270 Lettieri, Alberto Rodolfo. Vicente Fidel López: la construcción histórico-política de un liberalismo conservador. Buenos Aires: Editorial Biblos; Fundación Simón Rodríguez, 1995. 185 p.: bibl. (Col. Cuadernos Simón Rodríguez; 29)

Vicente Fidel López (1815–1903) es conocido por su *Historia de la República Argentina* y la polémica que sobre el tema historiográfico sostuvo con Bartolomé Mitre.

Aquí se estudia su pensamiento político y su acción que, según el autor, entran dentro de lo que puede denominarse "liberalismo conservador". Al estudio sigue un apéndice con textos de Vicente Fidel López.

5271 Malamud, Carlos. Las historias de una historia: la vida de Lisandro de la Torre según sus biógrafos o las peripecias de un centrista. Buenos Aires: Instituto Torcuato di Tella, 1991. 39 p. (Serie documentos de trabajo; 116)

Examina críticamente la labor de varios biógrafos de Lisandro de la Torre (1868–1939), respetado político argentino, pero sin una posición suficientemente definida de parte del autor.

5272 Martínez, Beatriz. Los fundamentos filosóficos de la Nueva Escuela Histórica a través de la polémica Ravignani-Carbia. (*Anu. Estud. Am.*, 44, 1987, p. 35–65, appendix)

De interés para la historia de la historiografía argentina en las tres primeras décadas del siglo XX. Las discusiones que se exponen no se limitan a asuntos de metodología histórica propiamente dicha, sino que se extienden a temas más amplios, como las doctrinas de Benedetto Croce sobre la historia. Este filósofo influyó también, hacia las mismas fechas, en el campo filosófico. [CJB]

5273 Memoria colectiva y políticas de olvido: Argentina y Uruguay, 1970–1990. Recopilación de Adriana J. Bergero y Fernando Reati. Rosario, Argentina: B. Viterbo Editora, 1997. 376 p.: bibl. (Estudios culturales)

Los artículos de esta colección son una reflexión sobre la función de la memoria en las sociedades latinoamericanas en el proceso de apertura democrática actual y de qué manera el terror afecta y se interroga en los objetos culturales contemporáneos. Contribuyen, A. Avellaneda, A.J. Bergero, H. Conteris, L. Edelman, G. Geirola, J. Graham Jones, D. Kordon, A. Kozameh, D. Lagos, M. Moraña, M. Morello-Frosch, M. Pianca, F. Reati, G. Remedi, S. Sosnowski, y A. Trigo. [M. García-Pinto]

5274 Montes Miranda, Jaime. La filosofía americanista de Rodolfo Kusch: el hombre americano entre el "ser alguien" y el "estar no más." (*Rev. Filos./Santiago*, 45/46, 1995, p. 65–70)

Breve glosa del pensamiento del filósofo argentino. [CJB]

5275 Myers, Jorge. Orden y virtud: el discurso republicano en el régimen rosista. Buenos Aires: Univ. Nacional de Quilmes, 1995. 310 p.: bibl. (La ideología argentina)

"Rosismo" se refiere a Juan Manuel de Rosas, gobernante argentino durante el siglo XIX. El "discurso" al que se atiende corresponde a lo expresado en la prensa periódica de la Provincia de Buenos Aires durante el período 1829–52. Afirma el autor que "el lenguaje político hablado por el rosismo fue esencialmente republicano." Para el comentario del historiador, ver item **2985**.

5276 Ocultismo y espiritismo en la Argentina. Buenos Aires: Centro Editor de América Latina, 1992. 143 p.: bibl. (Biblioteca Política argentina; 391)

Se caracteriza por el serio tratamiento sociológico del tema. Asunto menos conocido que el de las ideas en el sentido más habitual de la palabra. Se tratan el ocultismo, los Hare Krishna, las comunidades multiétnicas migrantes, el culto a la Madre María y el espiritismo, entre otros temas. Se encuentran relaciones entre el espiritismo y el positivismo y la ciencia experimental.

5277 Omil, Alba. Sábato: pensamiento y creación. Tucumán, Argentina: Ediciones del Gabinete, Secretaría de Post-grado, U.N.T., c1992. 137 p.: bibl.

Libro breve que es en realidad un ensayo extenso sobre el novelista y ensayista argentino. El propósito es "situar un punto de vista que abarque, en forma global, el pensamiento de Sábato como sustento de su creación artística."

5278 Peña, Roberto I. Los derechos naturales del hombre en la ideología del siglo XVIII rioplatense. (*Cuad. Hist./Córdoba*, 2, 1992, p. 11–31)

Afirma que en el siglo XVIII rioplatense "confluyen tres corrientes doctrinarias de cuya síntesis nacían las instituciones políticas y jurídicas" del nuevo estado independiente: "la Escolástica, el derecho natural racionalista y la Ilustración." El artículo sigue la presencia de esas tres corrientes en: los conceptos jurídicos; la enseñanza en la Universidad de Córdoba y las autoridades europeas en que esa enseñanza se basó; y la modalidad de "Ilustración Católica" en que se concretó la influencia ilustrada anterior a 1810.

Prieto, Adolfo. Los viajeros ingleses y la emergencia de la literatura argentina, 1820–1850. Ver item **3014.**

Proyecto y construcción de una nación: 1846–1880. Ver item **3016.**

5279 Romero, José Luis. Historia, sociedad, cultura y praxis política en José Luis Romero. Edición de Rafael Gutiérrez Girardot. Alicante, Spain: Generalitat Valenciana, Comissió per al V Centenari del Descobriment d'America; Instituto de Cultura Juan Gil-Albert, Diputación Provincial de Alicante, 1995. 151 p.: bibl. (Antología del pensamiento hispanoamericano; 10)

Antología de uno de los más importantes historiadores de Hispanoamérica. Aunque contiene artículos completos, pero no parte de sus obras principales, es altamente representativa de los intereses del autor. El Prólogo de Gutiérrez Girardot destaca, con franca simpatía pero también con justicia, los valores de José Luis Romero.

5280 Salinas, Alejandra. La guerra y la paz en Alberdi. (*Libertas/Buenos Aires,* 9:16, mayo 1992, p. 63–78, bibl.)

Exposición, principalmente de un escrito póstumo de Alberdi, *El crimen de la guerra.* Destaca la contribución de este autor al pensamiento liberal. [CJB]

5281 Scheines, Graciela I. Las metáforas del fracaso: desencuentros y utopías en la cultura argentina. Buenos Aires: Editorial Sudamericana, 1993. 204 p.: bibl.

Ensayo inteligente y de prosa ágil, que busca describir las características del argentino. Los materiales provienen de la vida política, el cine, el teatro, la literatura, el tango. Podría observarse que tiende a generalizar para la totalidad del país los rasgos del habitante de la ciudad de Buenos Aires. [CJB]

5282 Segovia, Juan Fernando. Julio Irazusta: conservatismo y nacionalismo en la Argentina. Prólogo de Carlos I. Massini Correas. Mendoza, Argentina: Editorial Idearium de la Univ. de Mendoza, 1992. 211 p.: bibl.

El tema principal es la concepción de la política en Julio Irazusta (1899–1982), pensador adherido al nacionalismo argentino. Pero la obra tiene un sentido integral, y trata aspectos de biografía intelectual y analiza las

influencias de autores como Maurras, Burke, de Maistre y Croce, que habían obrado sobre el pensamiento de Irazusta. Véase también item **5256.**

5283 Seibold, Jorge R. Nuevo punto de partida en la filosofía latinoamericana: las grandes etapas de la filosofía inculturada de J.C. Scannone. (*Stromata/San Miguel,* 47:1/2, enero/junio 1991, p. 193–204)

Muy útil para concocer la trayectoria del pensamiento teológico-filosófico de Scannone. También para los orígenes de la filosofía de la liberación en Argentina. [CJB]

5284 *Studia.* No. 1, 1990. Córdoba, Argentina: Univ. Nacional de Córdoba, Facultad de Filosofía y Humanidades.

Este número está dedicado al pensamiento de Joaquín Víctor González (1863–1923), político, escritor y fundador de la Univ. de La Plata. Norma Riquelme de Lobos se ocupa de la idea de "patria universal" en este autor, bajo la influencia del krausismo. Eduardo Patiño Porcel de Peralta estudia la tesis doctoral de González y sus raíces positivistas. El pensamiento educativo y su acción en la Univ. de La Plata es objeto del artículo de Mónica Bustos y Sandra Cazón. Beatriz Martino de Arocena y Elsa Pavón dedican su trabajo a la idea de ciencia en el autor estudiado. Por último, el tema de la inmigración y otros aspectos políticos son tratados por Marcela González de Martínez, Graciela Giordano de Rocca, y Lilians Romero Cabrera.

5285 Svampa, Maristella. El dilema argentino: civilización o barbarie; de Sarmiento al revisionismo peronista. Buenos Aires: El Cielo por Asalto; Imago Mundi, 1994. 315 p.: bibl. (Col. La Cultura argentina)

Persigue el peregrinaje de la imagen sarmientina, "civilización o barbarie", desde el *Facundo* de Sarmiento hasta la oposición peronismo-antiperonismo, pasando por la actitud de nacionalistas y positivistas frente a la inmigración europea, y la política de las primeras décadas del siglo XX.

5286 Tenorio Trillo, Mauricio. Bartolomé Mitre y Vicente Fidel López: el pensamiento historiográfico argentino en el siglo XIX. (*Secuencia/México,* 16, enero/abril 1990, p. 97–122, ill.)

Extenso y detallado análisis de la polémica historiográfica que sostuvieron

Mitre y López, ambos historiadores de la Argentina, tanto sobre el modo de escribir la historia en general como sobre la específica historia de ese país. Toma en cuenta también lo escrito por otros críticos e historiadores sobre el asunto. Abundancia de observaciones y opiniones más que una tesis central sobre la polémica.

5287 Trías, Manuel Bartolomé. Nacionalidad y destino, reflexiones sobre la argentinidad. Prólogo de Judith Botti de González Achával. Córdoba, Argentina: Sociedad Argentina de Filosofía, 1994. 150 p.: bibl. (Col. Perspectivas; 4)

Reflexión en tono de ensayo sobre las características del argentino. Por el contenido, es difícil el resumen y el señalamiento de los aciertos parciales. La reflexión es a ratos filosófica, correspondiendo a la formación intelectual del autor, que se revela en ciertas discusiones y en algunas fuentes que utiliza. Uno de los capítulos está dedicado a los rasgos hispánicos del argentino y otro al poema de José Hernández, *Martín Fierro*. Para el comentario del especialista de literatura, ver item **4019.**

5288 Tur Donatti, Carlos M. La utopía criolla en el siglo XX: cultura y política del nacionalismo restaurador en Argentina. (*Rev. Hist./Neuquén*, 2, nov. 1991, p. 21–51, bibl.)

De manera panorámica, sigue la línea del nacionalismo argentino que denomina "restaurador" y "contrarrevolucionario," aproximadamente entre 1930 y 1970, en especial durante el primer peronismo y posteriormente a su caída en 1955. No revisa solamente el campo de las ideas, sino también su manifestación en aspectos como la arquitectura y la pintura. Todo ello enfocando en lo posible el contexto de otras corrientes de pensamiento, particularmente la denominada "liberal."

5289 Universidad Nacional de Tucumán (Argentina). Secretaría de Ciencia y Técnica. Aportes para una historia de las ideas en Tucumán, 1810–1850. Tucumán, Argentina: Facultad de Filosofía y Letras, U.N.T., 1992. 147 p.: bibl. (Proyecto de Investigación; 206)

De los varios temas tratados, se relaciona con la historia de las ideas un artículo dedicado a Bernardo Monteagudo.

Urquiza, Fernando Carlos. ¿Construir al estado o al ciudadano?: aproximación a las ideas de Pedro de Angelis sobre la organización política argentina, 1827–1856. Ver item **3064.**

5290 Vallejos de Llobet, Patricia. El léxico ideológico del grupo rivadaviano. (*Invest. Ens.*, 42, enero/dic. 1992, p. 517–561, bibl.)

Extenso trabajo sobre el "léxico iluminista" en el Río de la Plata entre 1821 y 1830, tomando como fuentes las publicaciones periódicas de la época. "Grupo rivadaviano" alude a Bernardino Rivadavia (Ministro de Gobierno de la Prov. de Buenos Aires en las fechas antes señaladas) y sus seguidores. Se trata, por lo tanto, del análisis del vocabulario político y social de ese grupo.

5291 Vetter, Ulrich. Alejandro Korn: filosofía de la libertad. (*Am. Lat./Moscow*, 10, oct. 1990, p. 46–52)

Exposición de los principales elementos de la filosofía de Korn, con opiniones personales sobre ellos.

5292 Zimmermann, Eduardo A. Los liberales reformistas: la cuestión social en la Argentina, 1890–1916. Buenos Aires: Editorial Sudamericana; Univ. de San Andrés, 1995. 250 p.: bibl.

Obra bien realizada y de gran utilidad sobre la acción que tomaron grupos liberales frente a la "cuestión social" o "cuestión obrera," producida por la inmigración masiva entre 1890 y 1916. Esta acción fue paralela y a veces coordinada con el socialismo argentino, pero rechazó la prédica anarquista. Aspectos especiales que se examinan en detalle son las ideas de grupos intelectuales, la salud pública y la criminología. Presta contexto a la labor de intelectuales como Joaquín Víctor González, José Ingenieros, Juan Bautista Justo y Ernesto Quesada, entre otros. Para el comentario del historiador, ver item **3075.**

ABBREVIATIONS AND ACRONYMS

Except for journal abbreviations which are listed: 1) after each journal title in the
Title List of Journals Indexed (p. 801); and 2) in the *Abbreviation List of Journals
Indexed* (p. 815).

ALADI	Asociación Latinoamericana de Integración
a.	annual
ABC	Argentina, Brazil, Chile
A.C.	antes de Cristo
ACAR	Associação de Crédito e Assistência Rural, Brazil
AD	Anno Domini
A.D.	Acción Democrática, Venezuela
ADESG	Associação dos Diplomados de Escola Superior de Guerra, Brazil
AGI	Archivo General de Indias, Sevilla
AGN	Archivo General de la Nación
AID	Agency for International Development
a.k.a.	also known as
Ala.	Alabama
ALALC	Asociación Latinoamericana de Libre Comercio
ALEC	*Atlas lingüístico etnográfico de Colombia*
ANAPO	Alianza Nacional Popular, Colombia
ANCARSE	Associação Nordestina de Crédito e Assistência Rural de Sergipe, Brazil
ANCOM	Andean Common Market
ANDI	Asociación Nacional de Industriales, Colombia
ANPOCS	Associação Nacional de Pós-Graduação e Pesquisa em Ciências Sociais, São Paulo
ANUC	Asociación Nacional de Usuarios Campesinos, Colombia
ANUIES	Asociación Nacional de Universidades e Institutos de Enseñanza Superior, Mexico
AP	Acción Popular
APRA	Alianza Popular Revolucionaria Americana, Peru
ARENA	Aliança Renovadora Nacional, Brazil
Ariz.	Arizona
Ark.	Arkansas
ASA	Association of Social Anthropologists of the Commonwealth, London
ASSEPLAN	Assessoria de Planejamento e Acompanhamento, Recife
Assn.	Association
Aufl.	Auflage (edition, edición)
AUFS	American Universities Field Staff Reports, Hanover, N.H.
Aug.	August, Augustan
aum.	aumentada
b.	born (nació)
B.A.R.	British Archaeological Reports
BBE	Bibliografia Brasileira de Educação
b.c.	indicates dates obtained by radiocarbon methods
BC	Before Christ

bibl(s).	bibliography(ies)
BID	Banco Interamericano de Desarrollo
BNDE	Banco Nacional de Desenvolvimento Econômico, Brazil
BNH	Banco Nacional de Habitação, Brazil
BP	before present
b/w	black and white
C14	Carbon 14
ca.	*circa* (about)
CACM	Central American Common Market
CADE	Conferencia Anual de Ejecutivos de Empresas, Peru
CAEM	Centro de Altos Estudios Militares, Peru
Calif.	California
Cap.	Capítulo
CARC	Centro de Arte y Comunicación, Buenos Aires
CARICOM	Caribbean Common Market
CARIFTA	Caribbean Free Trade Association
CBC	Christian base communities
CBD	central business district
CBI	Caribbean Basin Initiative
CD	Christian Democrats, Chile
CDHES	Comisión de Derechos Humanos de El Salvador
CDI	Conselho de Desenvolvimento Industrial, Brasília
CEB	comunidades eclesiásticas de base
CEBRAP	Centro Brasileiro de Análise e Planejamento, São Paulo
CECORA	Centro de Cooperativas de la Reforma Agraria, Colombia
CEDAL	Centro de Estudios Democráticos de América Latina, Costa Rica
CEDE	Centro de Estudios sobre Desarrollo Económico, Univ. de los Andes, Bogotá
CEDEPLAR	Centro de Desenvolvimento e Planejamento Regional, Belo Horizonte
CEDES	Centro de Estudios de Estado y Sociedad, Buenos Aires; Centro de Estudos de Educação e Sociedade, São Paulo
CEDI	Centro Ecumênico de Documentos e Informação, São Paulo
CEDLA	Centro de Estudios y Documentación Latinoamericanos, Amsterdam
CEESTEM	Centro de Estudios Económicos y Sociales del Tercer Mundo, México
CELADE	Centro Latinoamericano de Demografía
CELADEC	Comisión Evangélica Latinoamericana de Educación Cristiana
CELAM	Consejo Episcopal Latinoamericano
CEMLA	Centro de Estudios Monetarios Latinoamericanos, Mexico
CENDES	Centro de Estudios del Desarrollo, Venezuela
CENIDIM	Centro Nacional de Información, Documentación e Investigación Musicales, Mexico
CENIET	Centro Nacional de Información y Estadísticas del Trabajo, Mexico
CEOSL	Confederación Ecuatoriana de Organizaciones Sindicales Libres
CEPADE	Centro Paraguayo de Estudios de Desarrollo Económico y Social
CEPA-SE	Comissão Estadual de Planejamento Agrícola, Sergipe
CEPAL	Comisión Económica para América Latina y el Caribe
CEPLAES	Centro de Planificación y Estudios Sociales, Quito
CERES	Centro de Estudios de la Realidad Económica y Social, Bolivia
CES	constant elasticity of substitution
cf.	compare
CFI	Consejo Federal de Inversiones, Buenos Aires
CGE	Confederación General Económica, Argentina
CGTP	Confederación General de Trabajadores del Perú
chap(s).	chapter(s)
CHEAR	Council on Higher Education in the American Republics
Cía.	Compañía

CIA	Central Intelligence Agency
CIDA	Comité Interamericano de Desarrollo Agrícola
CIDE	Centro de Investigación y Desarrollo de la Educación, Chile; Centro de Investigación y Docencias Económicas, Mexico
CIDIAG	Centro de Información y Desarrollo Internacional de Autogestión, Lima
CIE	Centro de Investigaciones Económicas, Buenos Aires
CIEDLA	Centro Interdisciplinario de Estudios sobre el Desarrollo Latinoamericano, Buenos Aires
CIEDUR	Centro Interdisciplinario de Estudios sobre el Desarrollo Uruguay, Montevideo
CIEPLAN	Corporación de Investigaciones Económicas para América Latina, Santiago
CIESE	Centro de Investigaciones y Estudios Socioeconómicos, Quito
CIMI	Conselho Indigenista Missionário, Brazil
CINTERFOR	Centro Interamericano de Investigación y Documentación sobre Formación Profesional
CINVE	Centro de Investigaciones Económicas, Montevideo
CIP	Conselho Interministerial de Preços, Brazil
CIPCA	Centro de Investigación y Promoción del Campesinado, Bolivia
CIPEC	Consejo Intergubernamental de Países Exportadores de Cobre, Santiago
CLACSO	Consejo Latinoamericano de Ciencias Sociales, Secretaría Ejecutiva, Buenos Aires
CLASC	Confederación Latinoamericana Sindical Cristiana
CLE	Comunidad Latinoamericana de Escritores, Mexico
cm	centimeter
CNI	Confederação Nacional da Indústria, Brazil
CNPq	Conselho Nacional de Pesquisas, Brazil
Co.	Company
COB	Central Obrera Boliviana
COBAL	Companhia Brasileira de Alimentos
CODEHUCA	Comisión para la Defensa de los Derechos Humanos en Centroamérica
Col.	Collection, Colección, Coleção
col.	colored, coloured
Colo.	Colorado
COMCORDE	Comisión Coordinadora para el Desarrollo Económico, Uruguay
comp(s).	compiler(s), compilador(es)
CONCLAT	Congresso Nacional das Classes Trabalhadoras, Brazil
CONCYTEC	Consejo Nacional de Ciencia y Tecnología (Peru)
CONDESE	Conselho de Desenvolvimento Econômico de Sergipe
Conn.	Connecticut
COPEI	Comité Organizador Pro-Elecciones Independientes, Venezuela
CORFO	Corporación de Fomento de la Producción, Chile
CORP	Corporación para el Fomento de Investigaciones Económicas, Colombia
Corp.	Corporation, Corporación
corr.	corrected, corregida
CP	Communist Party
CPDOC	Centro de Pesquisa e Documentação, Brazil
CRIC	Consejo Regional Indígena del Cauca, Colombia
CSUTCB	Confederación Sindical Unica de Trabajadores Campesinos de Bolivia
CTM	Confederación de Trabajadores de México
CUNY	City University of New York
CUT	Central Unica de Trabajadores (Mexico); Central Unica dos Trabalhadores (Brazil); Central Unitaria de Trabajadores (Chile; Colombia); Confederación Unitaria de Trabajadores (Costa Rica)
CVG	Corporación Venezolana de Guayana
d.	died (murió)

DANE	Departamento Nacional de Estadística, Colombia
DC	developed country; Demócratas Cristianos, Chile
d.C.	después de Cristo
Dec./déc.	December, décembre
Del.	Delaware
dept.	department
depto.	departamento
DESCO	Centro de Estudios y Promoción del Desarrollo, Lima
Dez./dez.	Dezember, dezembro
dic.	diciembre, dicembre
disc.	discography
DNOCS	Departamento Nacional de Obras Contra as Secas, Brazil
doc.	document, documento
Dr.	Doctor
Dra.	Doctora
DRAE	*Diccionario de la Real Academia Española*
ECLAC	UN Economic Commission for Latin America and the Caribbean, New York and Santiago
ECOSOC	UN Economic and Social Council
ed./éd.(s)	edition(s), édition(s), edición(es), editor(s), redactor(es), director(es)
EDEME	Editora Emprendimentos Educacionais, Florianópolis
Edo.	Estado
EEC	European Economic Community
EE.UU.	Estados Unidos de América
EFTA	European Free Trade Association
e.g.	*exempio gratia* (for example, por ejemplo)
ELN	Ejército de Liberación Nacional, Colombia
ENDEF	Estudo Nacional da Despesa Familiar, Brazil
ERP	Ejército Revolucionario del Pueblo, El Salvador
ESG	Escola Superior de Guerra, Brazil
estr.	estrenado
et al.	*et alia* (and others)
ETENE	Escritório Técnico de Estudos Econômicos do Nordeste, Brazil
ETEPE	Escritório Técnico de Planejamento, Brazil
EUDEBA	Editorial Universitaria de Buenos Aires
EWG	Europaische Wirtschaftsgemeinschaft. *See* EEC.
facsim(s).	facsimile(s)
FAO	Food and Agriculture Organization of the United Nations
FDR	Frente Democrático Revolucionario, El Salvador
FEB	Força Expedicionária Brasileira
Feb./feb.	February, Februar, febrero, febbraio
FEDECAFE	Federación Nacional de Cafeteros, Colombia
fev./fév.	fevereiro, février
ff.	following
FGTS	Fundo de Garantia do Tempo de Serviço, Brazil
FGV	Fundação Getúlio Vargas
FIEL	Fundación de Investigaciones Económicas Latinoamericanas, Argentina
film.	filmography
fl.	flourished
Fla.	Florida
FLACSO	Facultad Latinoamericana de Ciencias Sociales
FMI	Fondo Monetario Internacional
FMLN	Frente Farabundo Martí de Liberación Nacional, El Salvador
fold.	folded
fol(s).	folio(s)

FPL	Fuerzas Populares de Liberación Farabundo Marti, El Salvador
FRG	Federal Republic of Germany
FSLN	Frente Sandinista de Liberación Nacional, Nicaragua
ft.	foot, feet
FUAR	Frente Unido de Acción Revolucionaria, Colombia
FUCVAM	Federación Unificadora de Cooperativas de Vivienda por Ayuda Mutua, Uruguay
FUNAI	Fundação Nacional do Indio, Brazil
FUNARTE	Fundação Nacional de Arte, Brazil
FURN	Fundação Universidade Regional do Nordeste
Ga.	Georgia
GAO	General Accounting Office, Washington
GATT	General Agreement on Tariffs and Trade
GDP	gross domestic product
GDR	German Democratic Republic
GEIDA	Grupo Executivo de Irrigação para o Desenvolvimento Agrícola, Brazil
gen.	gennaio
Gen.	General
GMT	Greenwich Mean Time
GPA	grade point average
GPO	Government Printing Office, Washington
h.	hijo
ha.	hectares, hectáreas
HLAS	*Handbook of Latin American Studies*
HMAI	*Handbook of Middle American Indians*
Hnos.	hermanos
HRAF	Human Relations Area Files, Inc., New Haven, Conn.
IBBD	Instituto Brasileiro de Bibliografia e Documentação
IBGE	Instituto Brasileiro de Geografia e Estatística, Rio de Janeiro
IBRD	International Bank for Reconstruction and Development (World Bank)
ICA	Instituto Colombiano Agropecuario
ICAIC	Instituto Cubano de Arte e Industria Cinematográfica
ICCE	Instituto Colombiano de Construcción Escolar
ICE	International Cultural Exchange
ICSS	Instituto Colombiano de Seguridad Social
ICT	Instituto de Crédito Territorial, Colombia
id.	*idem* (the same as previously mentioned or given)
IDB	Inter-American Development Bank
i.e.	*id est* (that is, o sea)
IEL	Instituto Euvaldo Lodi, Brazil
IEP	Instituto de Estudios Peruanos
IERAC	Instituto Ecuatoriano de Reforma Agraria y Colonización
IFAD	International Fund for Agricultural Development
IICA	Instituto Interamericano de Ciencias Agrícolas, San José
III	Instituto Indigenista Interamericana, Mexico
IIN	Instituto Indigenista Nacional, Guatemala
ILDIS	Instituto Latinoamericano de Investigaciones Sociales
ill.	illustration(s)
Ill.	Illinois
ILO	International Labour Organization, Geneva
IMES	Instituto Mexicano de Estudios Sociales
IMF	International Monetary Fund
Impr.	Imprenta, Imprimérie
in.	inches
INAH	Instituto Nacional de Antropología e Historia, Mexico

INBA	Instituto Nacional de Bellas Artes, Mexico
Inc.	Incorporated
INCORA	Instituto Colombiano de Reforma Agraria
Ind.	Indiana
INEP	Instituto Nacional de Estudios Pedagógicos, Brazil
INI	Instituto Nacional Indigenista, Mexico
INIT	Instituto Nacional de Industria Turística, Cuba
INPES/IPEA	Instituto de Planejamento Econômico e Social, Brazil
INTAL	Instituto para la Integración de América Latina
IPA	Instituto de Pastoral Andina, Univ. de San Antonio de Abad, Seminario de Antropología, Cusco, Peru
IPEA	Instituto de Pesquisa Econômica Aplicada, Brazil
IPES/GB	Instituto de Pesquisas e Estudos Sociais, Guanabara, Brazil
IPHAN	Instituto de Patrimônio Histórico e Artístico Nacional, Brazil
ir.	irregular
IS	Internacional Socialista
ITESM	Instituto Tecnológico y de Estudios Superiores de Monterrey
ITT	International Telephone and Telegraph
Jan./jan.	January, Januar, janeiro, janvier
JLP	Jamaican Labour Party
Jr.	Junior, Júnior
JUC	Juventude Universitária Católica, Brazil
JUCEPLAN	Junta Central de Planificación, Cuba
Kan.	Kansas
km	kilometers, kilómetros
Ky.	Kentucky
La.	Louisiana
LASA	Latin American Studies Association
LDC	less developed country(ies)
LP	long-playing record
Ltd(a).	Limited, Limitada
m	meters, metros
m.	murió (died)
M	mille, mil, thousand
M.A.	Master of Arts
MACLAS	Middle Atlantic Council of Latin American Studies
MAPU	Movimiento de Acción Popular Unitario, Chile
MARI	Middle American Research Institute, Tulane University, New Orleans
MAS	Movimiento al Socialismo, Venezuela
Mass.	Massachusetts
MCC	Mercado Común Centro-Americano
Md.	Maryland
MDB	Movimiento Democrático Brasileiro
MDC	more developed countries
Me.	Maine
MEC	Ministério de Educação e Cultura, Brazil
Mich.	Michigan
mimeo	mimeographed, mimeografiado
min.	minutes, minutos
Minn.	Minnesota
MIR	Movimiento de Izquierda Revolucionaria, Chile and Venezuela
Miss.	Mississippi
MIT	Massachusetts Institute of Technology
ml	milliliter
MLN	Movimiento de Liberación Nacional

mm.	millimeter
MNC	multinational corporation
MNI	minimum number of individuals
MNR	Movimiento Nacionalista Revolucionario, Bolivia
Mo.	Missouri
MOBRAL	Movimento Brasileiro de Alfabetização
MOIR	Movimiento Obrero Independiente y Revolucionario, Colombia
Mont.	Montana
MRL	Movimiento Revolucionario Liberal, Colombia
ms.	manuscript
M.S.	Master of Science
msl	mean sea level
n.	nació (born)
NBER	National Bureau of Economic Research, Cambridge, Massachusetts
N.C.	North Carolina
N.D.	North Dakota
NE	Northeast
Neb.	Nebraska
neubearb.	neubearbeitet (revised, corregida)
Nev.	Nevada
n.f.	neue Folge (new series)
NGO	nongovernmental organization
NGDO	nongovernmental development organization
N.H.	New Hampshire
NIEO	New International Economic Order
NIH	National Institutes of Health, Washington
N.J.	New Jersey
NJM	New Jewel Movement, Grenada
N.M.	New Mexico
no(s).	number(s), número(s)
NOEI	Nuevo Orden Económico Internacional
NOSALF	Scandinavian Committee for Research in Latin America
Nov./nov.	November, noviembre, novembre, novembro
NSF	National Science Foundation
NW	Northwest
N.Y.	New York
OAB	Ordem dos Advogados do Brasil
OAS	Organization of American States
Oct./oct.	October, octubre, octobre
ODEPLAN	Oficina de Planificación Nacional, Chile
OEA	Organización de los Estados Americanos
OIT	Organización Internacional del Trabajo
Okla.	Oklahoma
Okt.	Oktober
ONUSAL	United Nations Observer Mission in El Salvador
op.	opus
OPANAL	Organismo para la Proscripción de las Armas Nucleares en América Latina
OPEC	Organization of Petroleum Exporting Countries
OPEP	Organización de Países Exportadores de Petróleo
OPIC	Overseas Private Investment Corporation, Washington
Or.	Oregon
OREALC	Oficina Regional de Educación para América Latina y el Caribe
ORIT	Organización Regional Interamericana del Trabajo
ORSTOM	Office de la recherche scientifique et technique outre-mer (France)
ott.	ottobre

out.	outubro
p.	page(s)
Pa.	Pennsylvania
PAN	Partido Acción Nacional, Mexico
PC	Partido Comunista
PCCLAS	Pacific Coast Council on Latin American Studies
PCN	Partido de Conciliación Nacional, El Salvador
PCP	Partido Comunista del Perú
PCR	Partido Comunista Revolucionario, Chile and Argentina
PCV	Partido Comunista de Venezuela
PD	Partido Democrático
PDC	Partido Demócrata Cristiano, Chile
PDS	Partido Democrático Social, Brazil
PDT	Partido Democrático Trabalhista, Brazil
PDVSA	Petróleos de Venezuela S.A.
PEMEX	Petróleos Mexicanos
PETROBRAS	Petróleo Brasileiro
PIMES	Programa Integrado de Mestrado em Economia e Sociologia, Brazil
PIP	Partido Independiente de Puerto Rico
PLN	Partido Liberación Nacional, Costa Rica
PMDB	Partido do Movimento Democrático Brasileiro
PNAD	Pesquisa Nacional por Amostra Domiciliar, Brazil
PNC	People's National Congress, Guyana
PNM	People's National Movement, Trinidad and Tobago
PNP	People's National Party, Jamaica
pop.	population
port(s).	portrait(s)
PPP	purchasing power parities; People's Progressive Party of Guyana
PRD	Partido Revolucionario Dominicano
PREALC	Programa Regional del Empleo para América Latina y el Caribe, Organización Internacional del Trabajo, Santiago
PRI	Partido Revolucionario Institucional, Mexico
Prof.	Professor, Profesor(a)
PRONAPA	Programa Nacional de Pesquisas Arqueológicas, Brazil
prov.	province, provincia
PS	Partido Socialista, Chile
PSD	Partido Social Democrático, Brazil
pseud.	pseudonym, pseudónimo
PT	Partido dos Trabalhadores, Brazil
pt(s).	part(s), parte(s)
PTB	Partido Trabalhista Brasileiro
pub.	published, publisher
PUC	Pontifícia Universidade Católica
PURSC	Partido Unido de la Revolución Socialista de Cuba
q.	quarterly
rev.	revisada, revista, revised
R.I.	Rhode Island
s.a.	semiannual
SALALM	Seminar on the Acquisition of Latin American Library Materials
SATB	soprano, alto, tenor, bass
sd.	sound
s.d.	*sine datum* (no date, sin fecha)
S.D.	South Dakota
SDR	special drawing rights
SE	Southeast

SELA	Sistema Económico Latinoamericano
SEMARNAP	Secretaria de Medio Ambiente, Recursos Naturales y Pesca, Mexico
SENAC	Serviço Nacional de Aprendizagem Comercial, Rio de Janeiro
SENAI	Serviço Nacional de Aprendizagem Industrial, São Paulo
SEP	Secretaría de Educación Pública, Mexico
SEPLA	Seminario Permanente sobre Latinoamérica, Mexico
Sept./sept.	September, septiembre, septembre
SES	socioeconomic status
SESI	Serviço Social da Indústria, Brazil
set.	setembro, settembre
SI	Socialist International
SIECA	Secretaría Permanente del Tratado General de Integración Económica Centroamericana
SIL	Summer Institute of Linguistics (Instituto Lingüístico de Verano)
SINAMOS	Sistema Nacional de Apoyo a la Movilización Social, Peru
S.J.	Society of Jesus
s.l.	*sine loco* (place of publication unknown)
s.n.	*sine nomine* (publisher unknown)
SNA	Sociedad Nacional de Agricultura, Chile
SPP	Secretaría de Programación y Presupuesto, Mexico
SPVEA	Superintendência do Plano de Valorização Econômica da Amazônia, Brazil
sq.	square
SSRC	Social Sciences Research Council, New York
STENEE	Empresa Nacional de Energía Eléctrica. Sindicato de Trabajadores, Honduras
SUDAM	Superintendência de Desenvolvimento da Amazônia, Brazil
SUDENE	Superintendência de Desenvolvimento do Nordeste, Brazil
SUFRAMA	Superintendência da Zona Franca de Manaus, Brazil
SUNY	State University of New York
SW	Southwest
t.	tomo(s), tome(s)
TAT	Thematic Apperception Test
TB	tuberculosis
Tenn.	Tennessee
Tex.	Texas
TG	transformational generative
TL	Thermoluminescent
TNE	Transnational enterprise
TNP	Tratado de No Proliferación
trans.	translator
UABC	Universidad Autónoma de Baja California
UCA	Universidad Centroamericana José Simeón Cañas, San Salvador
UCLA	University of California, Los Angeles
UDN	União Democrática Nacional, Brazil
UFG	Universidade Federal de Goiás
UFPb	Universidade Federal de Paraíba
UFSC	Universidade Federal de Santa Catarina
UK	United Kingdom
UN	United Nations
UNAM	Universidad Nacional Autónoma de México
UNCTAD	United Nations Conference on Trade and Development
UNDP	United Nations Development Programme
UNEAC	Unión de Escritores y Artistas de Cuba
UNESCO	United Nations Educational, Scientific and Cultural Organization
UNI/UNIND	União das Nações Indígenas
UNICEF	United Nations International Children's Emergency Fund

Univ(s).	university(ies), universidad(es), universidade(s), université(s), universität(s), università(s)
uniw.	uniwersytet (university)
Unltd.	Unlimited
UP	Unidad Popular, Chile
URD	Unidad Revolucionaria Democrática
URSS	Unión de Repúblicas Soviéticas Socialistas
US	United States
USAID	*See* AID.
USIA	United States Information Agency
USSR	Union of Soviet Socialist Republics
UTM	Universal Transverse Mercator
UWI	Univ. of the West Indies
v.	volume(s), volumen (volúmenes)
Va.	Virginia
V.I.	Virgin Islands
viz.	*videlicet* (that is, namely)
vol(s).	volume(s), volumen (volúmenes)
vs.	versus
Vt.	Vermont
W.Va.	West Virginia
Wash.	Washington
Wis.	Wisconsin
WPA	Working People's Alliance, Guyana
WWI	World War I
WWII	World War II
Wyo.	Wyoming
yr(s).	year(s)

TITLE LIST OF JOURNALS INDEXED

For journal titles listed by abbreviation, see *Abbreviation List of Journals Indexed*, p. 815.

ACERVO. Arquivo Nacional. Rio de Janeiro. (ACERVO/Rio de Janeiro)

Acervo: Revista Hondureña de Cultura. Instituto del Libro y el Documento, Ministerio de Cultura. Tegucigalpa. (Acervo/Tegucigalpa)

Actual. Dirección General de Cultura y Extensión, Univ. de Los Andes. Mérida, Venezuela. (Actual/Mérida)

Afro-Asia. Centro de Estudos Afro-Orientaís, Faculdade de Filosofia e Ciências Humanas, Univ. Federal da Bahia. Salvador, Brazil. (Afro-Asia/Salvador)

Agricultural History. Agricultural History Society; Univ. of California Press. Berkeley. (Agric. Hist.)

Allpanchis. Instituto de Pastoral Andina. Cusco, Peru. (Allpanchis/Cusco)

América Indígena. Instituto Indigenista Interamericano. México. (Am. Indíg.)

América Latina. Russian Academy of Sciences, Branch of World Economy Problems and of International Relations, Institute de Latin America. Moscow. (Am. Lat./Moscow)

América Latina en la Historia Económica: Boletín de Fuentes. Proyecto de Historia Económica, Instituto de Investigaciones Dr. José Luis Mora. México. (Am. Lat. Hist. Econ. Bol. Fuentes)

América Negra. Expedición Humana, Instituto de Genética Humana, Facultad de Medicina, Pontificia Univ. Javeriana. Bogotá. (Am. Negra)

American Anthropologist. American Anthropological Assn. Washington. (Am. Anthropol.)

American Ethnologist. American Ethnological Society, American Anthropological Assn. Washington. (Am. Ethnol.)

American Jewish Archives. Jacob Rader Marcus Center, American Jewish Archives. Cincinnati, Ohio. (Am. Jew. Arch.)

American Music. Society for American Music. Univ. of Illinois Press. Champaign, Ill. (Am. Music/Society)

The Americas: A Quarterly Review of Inter-American Cultural History. Catholic Univ. of America, Academy of American Franciscan History; Catholic Univ. of America Press. Washington. (Americas/Franciscans)

Anais do Arquivo Público do Pará. Arquivo Público do Estado do Pará. Belém, Brazil. (An. Arq. Público Pará)

Anales. Academia Nacional de la Historia. Buenos Aires. (Anales/Buenos Aires)

Anales de Antropología. Univ. Nacional Autónoma de México, Instituto de Investigaciones Históricas. México. (An. Antropol.)

Anales de la Academia de Geografía e Historia de Guatemala. Academia de Geografía e Historia de Guatemala. Guatemala. (An. Acad. Geogr. Hist. Guatem.)

Anales de la Academia Nacional de Ciencias Morales y Políticas. Academia Nacional de Ciencias Morales y Políticas. Buenos Aires. (An. Acad. Nac. Cienc. Morales)

Anales del Instituto de la Patagonia: Serie Ciencias Humanas. Instituto de la Patagonia, Univ. de Magallanes. Punta Arenas, Chile. (An. Inst. Patagon./Ser. Cienc. Hum.)

Anales del Museo de América. Museo de América, Dirección General de Bellas Artes y Bienes Culturales, Ministerio de Educación, Cultura y Deporte. Madrid. (An. Mus. Am.)

Análisis Político. Instituto de Estudios Políticos y Relaciones Internacionales, Univ. Nacional de Colombia. Bogotá. (Anál. Polít./Bogotá)

Ancient Mesoamerica. Cambridge Univ. Press. Cambridge, England; New York. (Anc. Mesoam.)

ANDES: Antropología e Historia. Centro Promocional de las Investigaciones en Historia y Antropología, Facultad de Humanidades, Univ. Nacional de Salta. Salta, Argentina. (ANDES Antropol. Hist.)

Annales des Antilles. Société d'histoire de la Martinique. Fort-de-France, Martinique. (Ann. Antill.)

Annales: histoire, sciences sociales. L'École des Hautes Études en Sciences Sociales. Paris. (Ann. hist. sci. soc.)

Annales historiques de la Révolution française. Société des Études Robespierristes. Paris. (Ann. hist. Révolut. fr.)

Annals of the Association of American Geographers. Assn. of American Geographers. Washington; Blackwell Publishers. Oxford, England; Malden, Mass. (Ann. Assoc. Am. Geogr.)

Anos 90: Revista do Programa de Pós-Graduação em História. Univ. Federal do Rio Grande do Sul, Programa de Pós-Graduação em História. Porto Alegre, Brazil. (Anos 90)

Anthropologica del Departamento de Ciencias Sociales. Depto. de Ciencias Sociales, Pontificia Univ. Católica del Perú. Lima. (Anthropologica/Lima)

Anthropos: International Review of Ethnology and Linguistics. Anthropos-Institut. Freiburg, Switzerland. (Anthropos/Freiburg)

Anuario. Instituto de Investigaciones Históricas Dr. José Gaspar Rodríguez de Francia. Asunción. (Anuario/Asunción)

Anuario. Instituto de Investigaciones Histórico-Sociales, Univ. Veracruzana. Xalapa, Mexico. (Anuario/Xalapa)

Anuario. Archivo y Biblioteca Nacionales de Bolivia. Sucre. (Anuario/Sucre)

Anuario Colombiano de Historia Social y de la Cultura. Depto. de Historia, Facultad de Ciencias Humanas, Univ. Nacional de Colombia. Bogotá. (Anu. Colomb. Hist. Soc. Cult.)

Anuario de Espacios Urbanos. Depto. de Evaluación del Diseño en el Tiempo, División de Ciencias y Artes para el Diseño, Univ. Autónoma Metropolitana—Unidad Azcapotzalco. México. (Anu. Espacios Urbanos)

Anuario de Estudios Americanos. Escuela de Estudios Hispano-Americanos, Consejo Superior de Investigaciones Científicas. Sevilla, Spain. (Anu. Estud. Am.)

Anuario de Estudios Bolivarianos. Univ. Simón Bolívar, Instituto de Investigaciones Históricas Bolivarium. Caracas. (Anu. Estud. Boliv.)

Anuario de Estudios Centroamericanos. Univ. de Costa Rica. San José. (Anu. Estud. Centroam.)

Anuario de Estudios Urbanos. Depto. de Evaluación del Diseño en el Tiempo, División de Ciencias y Artes para el Diseño, Univ. Autónoma Metropolitana—Unidad Azcapotzalco. México. (Anu. Estud. Urbanos)

Anuario de la Dirección de Etnología y Antropología Social del INAH. Dirección de Etnología y Antropología Social, Instituto Nacional de Antropología e Historia. México. (Anuario/INAH)

Anuario IEHS. Instituto de Estudios Histórico-Sociales, Facultad de Ciencias Humanas, Univ. Nacional del Centro de la Provincia de Buenos Aires. Tandil, Argentina. (Anu. IEHS)

Anuario IEI. Instituto de Estudios Indígenas, Univ. Autónoma de México. San Cristóbal de las Casas, Mexico. (Anu. IEI)

Anuario Instituto Chiapaneco de Cultura. Instituto Chiapaneco de Cultura. Tuxtla Gutiérrez, Mexico. (Anu. Inst. Chiapaneco Cult.)

Anuario Mariateguiano. Empresa Editora Amauta. Lima. (Anu. Mariateg.)

Apuntes. Centro de Investigación, Univ. del Pacífico. Lima. (Apuntes/Lima)

Archivo Español de Arte. Centro de Estudios Históricos, Depto. de Historia del Arte Diego Velázquez, Consejo Superior de Investigaciones Científicas. Madrid. (Arch. Esp. Arte)

Archivo Ibero-Americano: Revista Franciscana de Estudios Históricos. Franciscanos Españoles. Madrid. (Arch. Ibero-Am.)

Archivum Franciscanum Historicum. Collegio S. Bonaventura. Rome. (Arch. Francisc. Hist.)

Archivum Historicum Societatis Iesu. Institutum Scriptorum de Historia. Rome. (Arch. Hist. Soc. Iesu)

Arquipélago História: Revista da Universidade dos Açores. Univ. dos Açores. Ponta Delgada, Portugal. (Arquipél. Hist.)

Ars Musica Denver. Lamont School of Music, Univ. of Denver. Denver. (Ars Musica Denver)

Asclepio: Archivo Iberoamericano de Historia de la Medicina y Antropología Médica. Centro de Estudios Históricos, Consejo Superior de Investigaciones Científicas. Madrid. (Asclepio/Madrid)

Bermuda Journal of Archaeological and Maritime History. Bermuda Maritime Museum. Mangrove Bay, Bermuda. (Bermud. J. Archaeol. Marit. Hist.)

Biblos: Revista do Departamento de Biblioteconomia e História. Depto. de Biblioteconomia e História, Fundação Univ. do Rio Grande. Rio Grande, Brazil. (Biblos/ Rio de Janeiro)

Boletín. Sociedad de Estudios Bibliográficos Argentinos. Buenos Aires. (Boletín/ Buenos Aires)

Boletín Americanista. Sección de Historia de América y Africa, Depto. de Antropología Social y de Historia de América y Africa, Facultad de Geografía e Historia, Univ. de Barcelona. Barcelona. (Bol. Am.)

Boletín Antropológico. Museo Arqueológico, Centro de Investigaciones Etnológicas, Facultad de Humanidades y Educación, Univ. de los Andes. Mérida, Venezuela. (Bol. Antropol./Mérida)

Boletín Cultural y Bibliográfico. Biblioteca Luis-Angel Arango, Banco de la República. Bogotá. (Bol. Cult. Bibliogr.)

Boletín de Historia y Antigüedades. Academia Colombiana de la Historia. Bogotá. (Bol. Hist. Antig.)

Boletín de la Academia Colombiana. Academia Colombiana. Bogotá. (Bol. Acad. Colomb.)

Boletín de la Academia Nacional de Historia. Academia Nacional de Historia; La Prensa Catolica. Quito. (Bol. Acad. Nac. Hist./ Quito)

Boletín de la Academia Nacional de la Historia. Academia Nacional de la Historia. Caracas. (Bol. Acad. Nac. Hist./Caracas)

Boletín de la Academia Puertorriqueña de la Historia. Academia Puertorriqueña de la Historia. San Juan. (Bol. Acad. Puertorriq. Hist.)

Boletín de Lima: Revista Cultural Científica. Asociación Cultural Boletín de Lima A.C. Lima. (Bol. Lima)

Boletín del Instituto de Historia Argentina y Americana Dr. Emilio Ravignani. Univ. de Buenos Aires, Facultad de Filosofía y Letras. Buenos Aires. (Bol. Inst. Hist. Ravignani)

Boletín del Instituto Riva-Agüero: BIRA. Pontificia Univ. Católica del Perú, Instituto Riva-Agüero. Lima. (Bol. Inst. Riva-Agüero)

Boletín del Museo e Instituto Camón Aznar. Museo e Instituto de Humanidades Camón Aznar. Zaragoza, Spain. (Bol. Mus. Inst. Camón Aznar)

Boletín Histórico del Ejército. República Oriental del Uruguay, Comando General del Ejército, Estado Mayor del Ejército, Depto. de Estudios Históricos. Montevideo. (Bol. Hist. Ejérc.)

British Journal of Ethnomusicology. International Council for Traditional Music, UK Chapter. London. (Br. J. Ethnomusicol.)

Bulletin de l'Institut français d'études andines. l'Institut français d'études andines. Lima. (Bull. Inst. fr. étud. andin.)

Bulletin de la Société d'histoire de la Guadeloupe. Archives départementales avec le concours du Conseil général de la Guadeloupe. Basse-Terre, Guadeloupe. (Bull. Soc. hist. Guadeloupe)

Bulletin of Hispanic Studies. Institute of Hispanic Studies. Liverpool, England. (Bull. Hisp. Stud.)

Bulletin of Latin American Research. Society for Latin American Studies; Blackwell Publishers. Oxford, England. (Bull. Lat. Am. Res.)

Búsqueda: Revista Semestral de Ciencias Sociales. Univ. Mayor de San Simón, Facultad de Ciencias Económicas y Sociales. Cochabamba, Bolivia. (Búsqueda/ Cochabamba)

Caderno de Filosofia e Ciências Humanas. Depto. de Filosofia e Ciências Humanas, Faculdade de Ciências Humanas e Letras, Centro Universitário Newton Paiva. Belo Horizonte, Brazil. (Cad. Filos. Ciênc. Hum.)

Cadernos Negros. Editora Anita Ltda. São Paulo. (Cad. Negros)

Cadernos Pagu. Univ. Estadual de Campinas, Núcleo de Estudo de Gênero-PAGU. Campinas, Brazil. (Cad. Pagu)

Les Cahiers de l'Adminstration Outre-Mer. Univ. des Antilles, Centre de Recherche sur les Pouvoirs Locaux dans la Caraïbe.

Cayenne?, French Guiana. (Cah. Adm. Outre-Mer)

Cahiers des Amériques latines. Univ. de la Sorbonne nouvelle—Paris III, Institut des haute études de l'Amérique latine. Paris. (Cah. Am. lat.)

Callaloo. Johns Hopkins Univ. Press. Baltimore, Md. (Callaloo/Baltimore)

Canadian Journal of Latin American and Caribbean Studies = Revue canadienne des études latino-américaines et caraïbes. Univ. of Ottawa. Ontario, Canada. (Can. J. Lat. Am. Caribb. Stud.)

Caravelle: Cahiers du monde hispanique et luso-brésilien. Univ. de Toulouse, Institute d'études hispaniques, hispano-americaines et luso-brésiliennes. Toulouse, France. (Caravelle/Toulouse)

Caribbean Quarterly: CQ. Cultural Studies Initiative, Office of Vice Chancellor, Univ. of the West Indies. Mona, Jamaica. (Caribb. Q.)

Caribbean Studies. Univ. of Puerto Rico, Institute of Caribbean Studies. Río Piedras, Puerto Rico. (Caribb. Stud.)

El Caribe Contemporáneo. Univ. Nacional Autónoma de México, Facultad de Ciencias Políticas, Centro de Estudios Latinoamericanos. México. (Caribe Contemp.)

Caribena: cahiers d'études américanistes de la Caraïbe. Centre d'études et de recherches archéologiques. Martinique. (Caribena/Martinique)

Casa de las Américas. Casa de las Américas. La Habana. (Casa Am.)

Cespedesia. Depto. del Valle del Cauca. Cali, Colombia. (Cespedesia/Cali)

LA CHISPA: Selected Proceedings. Tulane Univ. New Orleans, La. (CHISPA/New Orleans)

Ciclos en la Historia, Economía y la Sociedad. Instituto de Investigaciones de Historia Económica y Social, Facultad de Ciencias Económicas, Univ. de Buenos Aires. Buenos Aires. (Ciclos Hist. Econ. Soc.)

Ciência & Trópico. Fundação Joaquim Nabuco; Editora Massangana. Recife, Brazil. (Ciênc. Tróp.)

Ciencia y Sociedad. Instituto Tecnológico de Santo Domingo. Santo Domingo. (Cienc. Soc./INTEC)

CLIO. Comité Argentino de Ciencias Históricas, Comité Internacional. Buenos Aires; Editorial Canguro. La Rioja, Argentina. (CLIO/Buenos Aires)

Clío. Univ. Autónoma de Sinaloa, Escuela de Historia. Culiacán, Mexico. (Clío/Culiacán)

Clio: Série Arqueológica. Univ. Federal de Pernambuco, Programa de Pós-Graduação em Historia. Recife, Brazil. (Clio Arqueol./Recife)

Clio: Série História do Nordeste. Univ. Federal de Pernambuco. Recife, Brazil. (Clio Hist./Recife)

Colonial Latin American Historical Review. Univ. of New Mexico, Spanish Colonial Research Center. Albuquerque, N.M. (CLAHR/Albuquerque)

Colonial Latin American Review. City Univ. of New York, City College, Dept. of Foreign Languages and Literatures, Simon H. Rifkind Center for the Humanities. New York; Carfax Publishing, Taylor & Francis, Ltd. Abingdon, England; Philadelphia, Pa. (Colon. Lat. Am. Rev.)

Conjunctions. Conjunctions. New York. (Conjunctions/New York)

Contribución Histórica. Museo Regional de Atacama. Copiapó, Chile. (Contrib. Hist.)

Contribuciones. Centro Interdisciplinario de Estudios Sobre el Desarrollo Latinoamericano, Fundación Konrad-Adenauer-Stiftung. Buenos Aires. (Contribuciones/Buenos Aires)

Contributions to Indian Sociology. Institute of Economic Growth. New Delhi, India; Sage Publications, Inc. Thousand Oaks, Calif. (Contrib. Indian Sociol.)

Correspondance. Univ. de Extremadura, Facultad de Filosofía y Letras, Centro de Estudios sobre la Bélgica Francófona. Cáceres, Spain; Communauté Française de Belgique, Archives et Musée de la Littérature. Brussels. (Correspondance/Cáceres)

Cristianismo y Sociedad. Junta Latinoamericana de Iglesia y Sociedad. Montevideo. (Cristianismo Soc.)

Cuadernos Americanos. Univ. Nacional Autónoma de México. México. (Cuad. Am.)

Cuadernos de Historia. Instituto de Historia del Derecho y de las Ideas Políticas. Córdoba, Argentina. (Cuad. Hist./Córdoba)

Cuadernos de Historia. Univ. de Chile, Facultad de Humanidades y Educación, Depto. de Ciencias Históricas. Santiago. (Cuad. Hist./Santiago)

Cuadernos de Historia: Serie Población. Univ. Nacional de Córdoba, Facultad de

Filosofía y Humanidades, Centro de Investigaciones. Córdoba, Argentina. (Cuad. Hist. Poblac.)

Cuadernos de Marcha. Montevideo. (Cuad. Marcha)

Cuadernos del CENDES. Univ. Central de Venezuela, Centro de Estudios del Desarrollo. Caracas. (Cuad. CENDES)

Cuadernos del CLAEH. Centro Latinoamericano de Economía Humana. Montevideo. (Cuad. CLAEH)

Cuadernos del Instituto Nacional de Antropología y Pensamiento Latinoamericano. Presidencia de la Nación, Secretaria de Cultura, Instituto Nacional de Antropología y Pensamiento Latinoamericano. Buenos Aires. (Cuad. Inst. Nac. Antropol. Pensam. Latinoam.)

Cuadernos del Sur: Ciencias Sociales. Univ. Autónoma Benito Juárez de Oaxaca, Instituto de Investigaciones Sociológicas. Oaxaca, Mexico. (Cuad. Sur/Oaxaca)

Cuadernos del Sur: Historia. Univ. Nacional del Sur, Depto. de Humanidades. Bahía Blanca, Argentina. (Cuad. Sur Hist./Bahía Blanca)

Cuadernos del Sur: Sociedad, Economía, Política. Editorial Tierra del Fuego. Buenos Aires. (Cuad. Sur Soc. Econ. Polít.)

Cuadernos Hispanoamericanos. Agencia Española de Cooperación Iberoamericana; Instituto de Cooperación Iberoamericana. Madrid. (Cuad. Hispanoam.)

Cuadernos Hispanoamericanos: Los Complementarios. Agencia Española de Cooperación Iberoamericana; Instituto de Cooperación Iberoamericana. Madrid. (Cuad. Hispanoam. Complement.)

Cuadernos Prehispánicos. Univ. de Valladolid, Seminario de Historia de América. Vallodolid, Spain. (Cuad. Prehispánicos)

Cuban Studies. Univ. of Pittsburgh Press. Pittsburgh, Pa. (Cuba. Stud.)

Cultura. Banco Central del Ecuador. Quito. (Cultura/Quito)

Cultural Anthropology: Journal of the Society for Cultural Anthropology. Society for Cultural Anthropology; American Anthropological Assn. Washington. (Cult. Anthropol.)

Current Anthropology. Univ. of Chicago Press. Chicago, Ill. (Curr. Anthropol.)

Cuyo: Anuario de Historia del Pensamiento Argentino. Univ. Nacional de Cuyo, Instituto de Filosofía, Sección de Historia del

Pensamiento Argentino. Mendoza, Argentina. (Cuyo/Mendoza)

Dados: Revista de Ciências Sociais. Instituto Universitários de Pesquisas do Rio de Janeiro, Univ. Candido Mendes. Rio de Janeiro. (Dados/Rio de Janeiro)

Derroteros de la Mar del Sur. Instituto de Estudios Histórico-Marítimos del Perú. Lima. (Derroteros Mar Sur)

Desarrollo Económico: Revista de Ciencias Sociales. Instituto de Desarrollo Económico y Social. Buenos Aires. (Desarro. Econ.)

Deslindes. Biblioteca Nacional. Montevideo. (Deslindes/Montevideo)

Desmemoria. Buenos Aires. (Desmemoria/Buenos Aires)

Dieciocho: Hispanic Enlightenment. Univ. of Virginia. Charlottesville. (Dieciocho Hisp. Enlight.)

Diogenes. International Council for Philosophy and Humanistic Studies. Paris; Blackwell Publishers. Oxford, England. (Diogenes/Philosophy)

Ecología Política: Cuadernos de Debate Internacional. Icaria Editorial; Fundación Hogar del Empleado. Barcelona, Spain. (Ecol. Polít.)

Entrepasados: Revista de Historia. Buenos Aires. (Entrepasados/Buenos Aires)

Espacios: Cultura y Sociedad. Instituto Cultural de Aguascalientes. Aguascalientes, Mexico. (Espacios Cult. Soc.)

Estudios Bolivianos. Univ. Mayor de San Andrés, Facultad de Humanidades y Ciencias de la Educación, Instituto de Estudios Bolivianos. La Paz. (Estud. Boliv.)

Estudios de Cultura Náhuatl. Univ. Nacional Autónoma de México, Instituto de Investigaciones Históricas. México. (Estud. Cult. Náhuatl)

Estudios de Historia Moderna y Contemporánea de México. Univ. Nacional Autónoma de México, Instituto de Investigaciones Históricas. México. (Estud. Hist. Mod. Contemp. Méx.)

Estudios de Historia Novohispana. Instituto de Investigaciones Históricas, Univ. Nacional Autónoma de México. México. (Estud. Hist. Novohisp.)

Estudios de Historia Social y Económica de América. Univ. de Alcalá de Henares. Madrid. (Estud. Hist. Soc. Econ. Am.)

Estudios del Hombre. Univ. de Guadalajara, Depto. de Estudios del Hombre. Guadalajara, Mexico. (Estud. Hombre)

Estudios: Filosofía, Historia, Letras. Instituto Tecnológico Autónomo de México, Depto. Académico de Estudios Generales. México. (Estud. Filos. Hist. Let.)

Estudios Filosóficos. Instituto Superior de Filosofía. Valladolid, Spain. (Estud. Filos.)

Estudios Franciscanos. Convento de Capuchinas. Barcelona, Spain. (Estud. Francisc.)

Estudios Fronterizos. Univ. Autónoma de Baja California, Instituto de Investigaciones Sociales. Mexicali, Mexico. (Estud. Front.)

Estudios Humanísticos: Geografía, Historia, Arte. Facultad de Filosofía y Letras, Univ. de León. León, Spain. (Estud. Humaníst. Geogr. Hist. Arte)

Estudios Jaliscienses. El Colegio de Jalisco. Zapopan, Mexico. (Estud. Jalisc.)

Estudios Latinoamericanos. Academia de Ciencias de Polonia, Instituto de Historia. Wrocław, Poland. (Estud. Latinoam./Poland)

Estudios Michoacanos. El Colegio de Michoacán. Zamora, Mexico. (Estud. Michoacanos)

Estudios Migratorios Latinoamericanos. Centro de Estudios Migratorios Latinoamericanos. Buenos Aires. (Estud. Migr. Latinoam.)

Estudios Públicos. Centro de Estudios Públicos. Santiago. (Estud. Públicos)

Estudios: Revista de Antropología, Arqueología e Historia. Instituto de Investigaciones Históricas, Antropológicas, y Arqueológicas, Escuela de Historia, Univ. de San Carlos de Guatemala. Guatemala. (Estudios/USAC)

Estudios Sociales. Centro de Estudios Sociales P. Juan Montalvo, SJ. Santo Domingo. (Estud. Soc./Santo Domingo)

Estudios Sociales: Revista de Investigación del Noroeste. Centro de Investigación en Alimentación y Desarrollo; El Colegio de Sonora; Univ. de Sonora. Hermosillo, Mexico. (Estud. Soc./Hermosillo)

Estudios Sociales: Revista Universitaria Semestral. Centro de Estudios Históricos, Facultad de Formación Docente en Ciencias, Univ. Nacional del Litoral. Santa Fe, Argentina; Centro de Publicaciones, Secretaría de Extensión, Univ. Nacional del Litoral. Santa Fe, Argentina. (Estud. Soc./Santa Fe)

Estudios Sociológicos. El Colegio de México, Centro de Estudios Sociológicos. México. (Estud. Sociol./México)

Estudos Afro-Asiáticos. Centro de Estudos Afro-Asiáticos. Rio de Janeiro. (Estud. Afro-Asiát.)

Estudos Econômicos. Fundação Instituto de Pesquisas Econômicas, Faculdade de Economia, Administração e Contabilidade, Univ. de São Paulo. São Paulo. (Estud. Econ./São Paulo)

Estudos Históricos. Centro de Pesquisa e Documentação de História Contemporânea do Brasil, Fundação Getulio Vargas. Rio de Janeiro. (Estud. Hist./Rio de Janeiro)

Estudos Ibero-Americanos. Pontifícia Univ. Católica do Rio Grande do Sul, Faculdade de Filosofia e Ciências Humanas, Depto. de História, Programa Pós-Graduação em História. Porto Alegre, Brazil. (Estud. Ibero-Am./Porto Alegre)

Estudos Leopoldenses. Univ. do Vale do Rio dos Sinos, Faculdade de Filosofia, Ciências e Letras. São Leopoldo, Brazil. (Estud. Leopold.)

Ethnohistory. American Society for Ethnohistory; Duke Univ., Durham, N.C. (Ethnohistory/Society)

Ethnology: An International Journal of Cultural and Social Anthropology. Univ. of Pittsburgh, Dept. of Anthropology. Pittsburgh, Pa. (Ethnology/Pittsburgh)

Etnología: Boletín del Museo Nacional de Etnografía y Folklore. Museo Nacional de Etnografía y Folklore. La Paz. (Etnología/La Paz)

Feminist Studies. Feminist Studies, Inc.; Univ. of Maryland. College Park, Md. (Fem. Stud.)

Fermentum: Revista Venezolana de Sociología y Antropología. Univ. de los Andes. Mérida, Venezuela. (Fermentum/Mérida)

Folia Histórica del Nordeste. Univ. Nacional del Nordeste, Facultad de Humanidades, Instituto de Historia; CONICET, Instituto de Investigaciones Geohistóricas; FUNDANORD. Resistencia, Argentina. (Folia Hist. Nordeste)

Folia Humanística. Editorial Glarma. Barcelona, Spain. (Folia Humaníst.)

Frontera Norte. El Colegio de la Frontera Norte. Tijuana, Mexico. (Front. Norte)

Gender & History. Blackwell Publishers. Abingdon, England; Williston, Vt. (Gend. Hist.)

Généalogie et histoire de la Caraïbe. Assn. de la généalogie et histoire de la Caraïbe. Le Pecq, France. (Généal. hist. Caraïbe)

Geographical Review. American Geographical Society. New York. (Geogr. Rev.)

Grand Street. Grand Street Publications. New York. (Grand Str.)

Guyana Historical Journal. Univ. of Guyana, Faculty of Arts, Dept. of History, History Society. Georgetown. (Guyana Hist. J.)

Haciendo Historia. México. (Haciendo Hist.)

Handbook of Latin American Studies CD-ROM: HLAS/CD. Library of Congress, Hispanic Division. Washington. Fundación Histórica Tavera; DIGIBIS. Madrid. (HLAS CD-ROM)

Hispamérica. Gaithersburg, Md. (Hispamérica/Gaithersburg)

Hispania. Consejo Superior de Investigaciones Científicas, Instituto de Historia, Depto. de Medieval Moderna y Contemporánea. Madrid. (Hispania/Madrid)

Hispania Sacra: Revista de Historia Eclesiástica de España. Consejo Superior de Investigaciones Científicas, Centro de Estudios Históricos. Madrid. (Hisp. Sacra)

Hispanic American Historical Review. Conference on Latin American History of the American Historical Assn.; Duke Univ. Press. Durham, N.C. (HAHR)

Historia. Instituto de Historia, Facultad de Historia, Geografia y Ciencia Política, Pontificia Univ. Católica de Chile. Santiago. (Historia/Santiago)

Historia Mexicana. Centro de Estudios Históricos, El Colegio de México. México. (Hist. Mex.)

Historia Paraguaya. Academia Paraguaya de la Historia. Asunción. (Hist. Parag.)

Historia Social. Univ. Nacional de Educación a Distancia Alzira-Valencia, Centro Francisco Tomás y Valiente, Fundación Instituto de Historia Social. Valencia, Spain. (Hist. Soc./Valencia)

Historia y Cultura. Museo Nacional de Arqueología, Antropología e Historia. Lima. (Hist. Cult./Lima)

Historia y Cultura. Sociedad Boliviana de Historia. La Paz. (Hist. Cult./La Paz)

Historia y Fuente Oral. Univ. de Barcelona, Depto. de Historia Contemporanea. Barcelona. (Hist. Fuente Oral)

Historia y Grafía. Depto. de Historia, Univ. Iberoamericana. México. (Hist. Graf.)

Histórica. Pontificia Univ. Católica del Perú, Depto. de Humanidades. Lima. (Histórica/Lima)

History Gazette. Univ. of Guyana, History Society. Turkeyen, Guyana. (Hist. Gaz.)

History of Religions. Univ. of Chicago. Chicago, Ill. (Hist. Relig.)

The History of the Family: an International Quarterly. JAI Press, Inc. Greenwich, Conn. (Hist. Fam.)

Hoy es Historia: Revista Bimestral de Historia Nacional e Iberoamericana. Editorial Raíces. Montevideo. (Hoy Hist.)

Humanas: Revista do Instituto de Filosofia e Ciências Humanas da Universidade Federal do Rio Grande do Sul. Univ. Federal do Rio Grande do Sul, Instituto de Filosofia e Ciências Humanas. Porto Alegre, Brazil. (Humanas/Porto Alegre)

Humanitas: Anuario del Centro de Estudios Humanísticos. Centro de Estudios Humanísticos, Secretaría de Extensión y Cultura, Univ. Autónoma de Nuevo León. Monterrey, Mexico. (Humanitas/Monterrey)

Ibero-Amerikanisches Archiv: Zeitschrift für Sozialwissenschaften und Geschichte. Ibero-Amerikanisches Institut. Berlin. (Ibero-Am. Arch.)

Iberoamericana: Nordic Journal of Latin American Studies/Revista Nórdica de Estudios Latinoamericanos. Stockholm Univ., Institute of Latin American Studies. (Iberoamericana/Stockholm)

Ideas y Valores. Univ. Nacional de Colombia, Instituto de Filosofía y Letras. Bogotá. (Ideas Valores)

Indiana Journal of Hispanic Literature. Indiana Univ. Bloomington, Ind. (Indiana J. Hisp. Lit.)

Integración Latinoamericana. Instituto para la Integración de América Latina, Depto. de Integración y Programas Regionales, Banco Interamericano de Desarrollo = Inter-American Development Bank. Buenos Aires. (Integr. Latinoam.)

Inter-American Music Review. Theodore Front Musical Literature, Inc. Van Nuys, Calif. (Inter-Am. Music Rev.)

Interciencia. Asociación Interciencia. Caracas. (Interciencia/Caracas)

The International History Review. Dept. of History, Simon Fraser Univ. Burnaby, British Columbia. (Int. Hist. Rev.)

Investigación Económica. Univ. Nacional Autónoma de México, Facultad de Economía. México. (Invest. Econ.)

Investigaciones y Ensayos. Academia Nacional de Historia. Buenos Aires. (Invest. Ens.)

Islas. Univ. Central de Las Villas, Facultad de Ciencias Sociales y Humanísticas, Depto. de Letras. Santa Clara, Cuba. (Islas/Santa Clara)

Itinerario. Centre for the History of European Expansion, Faculty of the School of Humanities, Univ. of Leiden. Leiden, The Netherlands. (Itinerario/Leiden)

Iztapalapa. Univ. Autónoma Metropolitana— Unidad Iztapalapa, División de Ciencias Sociales y Humanidades. México. (Iztapalapa/México)

Jahrbuch für Geschichte von Staat, Wirtschaft und Gesellschaft Lateinamerikas. Böhlau Verlag. Köln, Germany. (Jahrb. Gesch.)

JILAS: Journal of Iberian and Latin American Studies. Association of Iberian and Latin American Studies of Australasia; La Trobe Univ., School of History. Bundoora, Australia. (JILAS/Bundoora)

Jornadas de Historia de Occidente. Centro de Estudios de la Revolución Mexicana Lázaro Cárdenas. Jiquilpan, Mexico. (J. Hist. Occidente)

Journal of American Folklore. American Folklore Society. Arlington, Va. (J. Am. Folk.)

Journal of Anthropological Research. Univ. of New Mexico. Albuquerque, N.M. (J. Anthropol. Res.)

The Journal of Caribbean History. Univ. of the West Indies Press; Dept. of History, Univ. of the West Indies. Mona, Jamaica. (J. Caribb. Hist.)

Journal of Caribbean Studies. Assn. of Caribbean Studies. Coral Gables, Fla. (J. Caribb. Stud.)

The Journal of Economic History. Economic

History Assn.; Univ. of Arizona. Tucson. (J. Econ. Hist.)

Journal of Family History. Sage Periodicals Press. Thousand Oaks, Calif. (J. Fam. Hist.)

Journal of Latin American Cultural Studies: Travesía. Taylor & Frances Ltd., Carfax Publishing. Basingstoke, England; Levittown, Pa. (J. Lat. Am. Cult. Stud.)

Journal of Latin American Studies. Cambridge Univ. Press. Cambridge, England. (J. Lat. Am. Stud.)

Journal of Political and Military Sociology: JPMS. Northern Illinois Univ., Dept. of Sociology. DeKalb, Ill. (J. Polit. Mil. Sociol.)

Journal of Social History. George Mason Univ. Press. Fairfax, Va. (J. Soc. Hist.)

Journal of the American Musicological Society. American Musicological Society. Richmond, Va. (J. Am. Musicol. Soc.)

Journal of the Bahamas Historical Society. Bahamas Historical Society. Nassau, Bahamas. (J. Bahamas Hist. Soc.)

Journal of the West. Sunflower Univ. Press. Manhattan, Kan. (J. West)

Journal of World History. World History Assn.; Univ. of Hawaii Press. Honolulu. (J. World Hist.)

JSAH: Journal of the Society of Architectural Historians. Society of Architectural Historians. Chicago. (JSAH)

Lateinamerika. Univ. Rostock. Rostock, Germany. (Lateinamerika/Rostock)

The Latin American Anthropology Review. Society for Latin American Anthropology. Fairfax, Va. (Lat. Am. Anthropol. Rev.)

Latin American Indian Literatures Journal. Geneva College, Dept. of Foreign Languages. Beaver Falls, Pa. (Lat. Am. Indian Lit. J.)

Latin American Literary Review. Latin American Literary Review Press. Pittsburgh, Pa. (Lat. Am. Lit. Rev.)

Latin American Music Review = Revista de Música Latinoamericana. Univ. of Texas Press. Austin, Tex. (Lat. Am. Music Rev.)

Latin American Perspectives. Sage Publications, Inc. Thousand Oaks, Calif. (Lat. Am. Perspect.)

Latin American Research Review. Latin American Studies Assn.; Univ. of New Mexico, Latin American Institute. Albuquerque, N.M. (LARR)

Letras Femeninas. Asociación de Literatura Femenina Hispánica. Boulder, Colo. (Let. Fem.)

Leviatán: Revista de Hechos e Ideas. Fundación Pablo Iglesias. Madrid. (Leviatán/Madrid)

Libertas. Escuela Superior de Economía y Administración de Empresas. Buenos Aires. (Libertas/Buenos Aires)

LPH: Revista de História. Univ. Federal de Ouro Preto, Depto. de História. Mariana, Brazil. (LPH Rev. Hist.)

Lua Nova. Centro de Estudos de Cultura Contemporânea. São Paulo. (Lua Nova)

Maguaré. Univ. Nacional de Colombia, Depto. de Antropología. Bogotá. (Maguaré/Bogotá)

Manoa: A Pacific Journal of International Writing. Univ. of Hawaii Press. Honolulu. (Manoa/Honolulu)

Mapocho. Dirección de Bibliotecas, Archivos y Museos. Santiago. (Mapocho/Santiago)

Mélanges de la Casa de Velázquez. Casa de Velázquez. Madrid. (Mélanges/Madrid)

Memoria. Sociedad Ecuatoriana de Investigaciones Históricas y Geográficas. Quito. (Memoria/SEIHGE)

Memoria. MARKA: Instituto de Historia y Antropología Andina. Quito. (Memoria/MARKA)

Memoria: Boletín de CEMOS. Centro de Estudios del Movimiento Obrero y Socialista. México. (Memoria/CEMOS)

Memorias de la Academia Mexicana de la Historia. Academia Mexicana de la Historia. México. (Mem. Acad. Mex. Hist.)

Mesoamérica. Plumsock Mesoamerican Studies. South Woodstock, Vt.; Centro de Investigaciones Regionales de Mesoamérica. Antigua, Guatemala. (Mesoamérica/Plumsock)

Metapolítica: Revista Trimestral de Teoría y Ciencia de la Política. Centro de Estudios de Política Comparada. México. (Metapolítica/México)

Mexican Studies/Estudios Mexicanos. Univ. of California Press. Berkeley, Calif. (Mex. Stud.)

Montalbán. Univ. Católica Andrés Bello, Facultad de Humanidades y Educación, Institutos Humanísticos de Investigación. Caracas. (Montalbán/Caracas)

Mundo Nuevo. Univ. Simón Bolívar, Instituto de Altos Estudios de América Latina. Caracas. (Mundo Nuevo/Caracas)

Museo Histórico. Museo de Historia de la Ciudad de Quito. Quito. (Mus. Hist.)

Nassarre: Revista Aragonesa de Musicología. Diputación de Zaragoza, Sección Música Antigua, Institución Fernando el Católico. Zaragoza, Spain. (Nassarre/Zaragoza)

Nóesis: Revista de Ciencias Sociales y Humanidades. Dirección General de Investigación y Estudios Superiores, Univ. Autónoma de Ciudad Juárez. Ciudad Juárez, Mexico. (Nóesis/UACJ)

Notícia Bibliográfica e Histórica. Pontificia Univ. Católica de Campinas. Campinas, Brazil. (Not. Bibliogr. Hist.)

Noticiario de Historia Agraria. Seminario de Historia Agraria. Murcia, Spain. (Not. Hist. Agrar.)

Novahispania. Univ. Nacional Autónoma de México, Instituto de Investigaciones Filológicas. México. (Novahispania/México)

Novos Estudos CEBRAP. Centro Brasileiro de Análise e Planejamento. São Paulo. (Novos Estud. CEBRAP)

Nueva Sociedad. Editorial Nueva Sociedad. Caracas. (Nueva Soc.)

Nütram. Centro Ecuménico Diego de Medellín. Santiago. (Nütram/Santiago)

NWIG: New West Indian Guide/Nieuwe West Indische Gids. Royal Institute of Linguistics and Anthropology, KITLV Press. Leiden, The Netherlands. (NWIG)

Obradoiro de Historia Moderna. Univ. de Santiago de Compostela. Santiago de Compostela, Spain. (Obradoiro Hist. Mod.)

Op. Cit.: Boletín del Centro de Investigaciones Históricas. Univ. de Puerto Rico, Facultad de Humanidades, Depto. de Historia. Río Piedras, Puerto Rico. (Op. Cit./Río Piedras)

Paramillo. Univ. Católica de Táchira, Centro de Estudios Interdisciplinarios. San Cristóbal, Venezuela. (Paramillo/San Cristóbal)

Paraninfo. Instituto de Ciencias del Hombre Rafael Heliodoro Valle. Tegucigalpa. (Paraninfo/Tegucigalpa)

Patterns of Prejudice. Institute of Jewish Affairs. London. (Patterns Prejud.)

Philosophy and Literature. Johns Hopkins Univ. Press. Baltimore, Md. (Philos. Lit.)

Plantation Society in the Americas. Univ. of New Orleans, Dept. of History. New Orleans, La. (Plant. Soc. Am.)

Plural. Univ. de Puerto Rico, Administración de Colegios Regionales. San Juan. (Plural/San Juan)

Población y Sociedad. Fundación Yocavil. Tucumán, Argentina. (Poblac. Soc.)

Poetics Today. Duke Univ. Press. Durham, N.C. (Poetics Today)

Point of Contact. Punto de Contacto/Point of Contact, Inc. Syracuse, NY. (Point Contact)

Política. Univ. de Chile, Instituto de Ciencia Política. Santiago. (Política/Santiago)

Political Science Quarterly. The Academy of Political Science. New York. (Polit. Sci. Q.)

Politics & Society. Sage Publications, Inc. Thousand Oaks, Calif. (Polit. Soc./Marxism)

Popular Music. Cambridge Univ. Press. England. (Pop. Music)

Presença Filosófica. Sociedade Brasileira de Filósofos Católicos. Rio de Janeiro. (Presença Filos.)

Procesos. Corporación Editora Nacional. Quito. (Procesos/Quito)

Pumapunku. Centro de Investigaciones Antropológicas Tiwanaku. La Paz. (Pumapunku/La Paz)

Quinto Centenario. Univ. Complutense de Madrid, Facultad de Geografía e Historia, Depto. de Historia de América I. Madrid. (Quinto Cent.)

Quitumbe. Pontificia Univ. Católica del Ecuador, Facultad de Pedagogía, Depto. de Historia. Quito. (Quitumbe/Quito)

Rábida. Patronato Provincial del V Centenario del Descubrimiento de América. Huelva, Spain. (Rábida/Huelva)

Razón y Fe. La Compañía de Jesús. Madrid. (Razón Fe)

Reflejos. Hebrew Univ., Facultad de Humanidades, Depto. de Estudios Españoles y Latinoamericanos. Jerusalem. (Reflejos/Jerusalem)

Reflexão. Instituto de Filosofia, Pontifícia Univ. Católica de Campinas. Campinas, Brazil. (Reflexão/Campinas)

Relaciones. El Colegio de Michoacán. Zamora, Mexico. (Relaciones/Zamora)

Res Gesta. Univ. Católica Argentina, Facultad de Derecho y Ciencias Sociales, Instituto de Historia. Rosario, Argentina. (Res Gesta)

Review. Binghamton Univ., Fernand Braudel Center. Binghamton, New York. (Review/Binghamton)

Revista Agustiniana. American Theological Library Assn. Madrid. (Rev. Agust.)

Revista Andina. Centro Bartolomé de las Casas. Cuzco, Peru. (Rev. Andin.)

Revista Archivo Arzobispal de Arequipa. Arequipa, Peru. (Rev. Arch. Arzobispal Arequipa)

Revista Brasileira de Estudos de População. Associação Brasileira de Estudos Populacionais. São Paulo. (Rev. Bras. Estud. Popul.)

Revista Brasileira de Filosofia. Instituto Brasileiro de Filosofia. São Paulo. (Rev. Bras. Filos.)

Revista Brasileira de História. Associação Nacional de História. São Paulo. (Rev. Bras. Hist.)

Revista Centroamericana de Economía. Univ. Nacional Autónoma de Honduras, Programa de Postgrado Centroamericano en Economía y Planificación del Desarrollo. Tegucigalpa. (Rev. Centroam. Econ.)

Revista Chilena de Historia y Geografía. Sociedad Chilena de Historia y Geografía. Santiago. (Rev. Chil. Hist. Geogr.)

Revista Chilena de Literatura. Univ. de Chile, Facultad de Filosofía y Humanidades, Depto. de Literatura. Santiago. (Rev. Chil. Lit.)

Revista Colombiana de Antropología. Ministerio de Educación Nacional, Instituto Colombiano de Antropología. Bogotá. (Rev. Colomb. Antropol.)

Revista Complutense de Historia de América. Depto. de Historia de América I, Facultad de Geografía e Historia, Univ. Complutense de Madrid. Madrid. (Rev. Complut. Hist. Am.)

Revista Cubana de Ciencias Sociales. Centro de Estudios Filosóficos, Academia de Ciencias de Cuba. La Habana. (Rev. Cuba. Cienc. Soc.)

Revista da SBPH. Sociedade Brasileira de Pesquisa Histórica. Curitiba, Brazil. (Rev. SBPH)

Revista de Ciências Históricas. Univ. Portucalense. Porto, Portugal. (Rev. Ciênc. Hist.)

Revista de Ciencias Humanas. Univ. Tecnológica de Pereira. Pereira, Colombia. (Rev. Cienc. Hum./Pereira)

Revista de Ciencias Sociales. Univ. de Puerto Rico, Recinto de Río Piedras, Facultad de Ciencias Sociales, Centro de Investigaciones Sociales. Río Piedras, Puerto Rico. (Rev. Cienc. Soc./Río Piedras)

Revista de Ciencias Sociales. Facultad de Derecho y Ciencias Sociales, Univ. de Valparaíso. Valparaíso, Chile. (Rev. Cienc. Soc./Valparaíso)

Revista de Crítica Literaria Latinoamericana. Latinoamericana Editores. Lima. (Rev. Crít. Lit. Latinoam.)

Revista de Economía. Banco de la Provincia de Córdoba. Córdoba, Argentina. (Rev. Econ./Córdoba)

Revista de Estudios Histórico-Jurídicos. Escuela de Derecho, Facultad de Ciencias Jurídicas y Sociales, Univ. Católica de Valparaíso. Valparaíso, Chile. (Rev. Estud. Hist. Juríd.)

Revista de Estudios Políticos. Centro de Estudios Constitucionales. Madrid. (Rev. Estud. Polít.)

Revista de Filosofía. Depto. de Filosofía y Humanidades, Univ. de Chile. Santiago. (Rev. Filos./Santiago)

Revista de Filosofía. Univ. Iberoamericana, Depto. de Filosofía. México. (Rev. Filos./México)

Revista de Filosofía de la Universidad de Costa Rica. Editorial de la Univ. de Costa Rica. San José. (Rev. Filos. Univ. Costa Rica)

Revista de Filosofía Latinoamericano y Ciencias Sociales. Asociación de Filosofía Latinoamericana y Ciencias Sociales. Buenos Aires. (Rev. Filos. Latinoam. Cienc. Soc.)

Revista de Historia. Escuela de Historia, Univ. Nacional. Heredia, Costa Rica; Centro de Investigaciones Históricas de América Central, Univ. de Costa Rica. San José. (Rev. Hist./Heredia)

Revista de Historia. Univ. Centroamericana, Instituto de Historia de Nicaragua y Centroamérica. Managua. (Rev. Hist./Managua)

Revista de Historia. Depto. de Ciencias Históricas y Sociales, Univ. de Concepción, Chile. (Rev. Hist./Concepción)

Revista de Historia. Univ. Nacional de Comahue, Facultad de Humanidades, Depto. de Historia. Neuquén, Argentina. (Rev. Hist./Neuquén)

Revista de História. Univ. de São Paulo, Faculdade de Filosofia, Letras e Ciências Humanas, Depto. de História. São Paulo. (Rev. Hist./São Paulo)

Revista de Historia Americana y Argentina. Univ. Nacional de Cuyo, Instituto de Historia. Mendoza, Argentina. (Rev. Hist. Am. Argent.)

Revista de Historia Contemporánea. Univ de Sevilla, Depto. de Historia Contemporánea, Facultad de Geografía e Historia. Sevilla, Spain. (Rev. Hist. Contemp.)

Revista de Historia de América. Comisión de Historia, Instituto Panamericano de Geografía e Historia. México. (Rev. Hist. Am.)

Revista de Historia del Derecho. Instituto de Investigaciones Históricas del Derecho. Buenos Aires. (Rev. Hist. Derecho)

Revista de Historia del Derecho Ricardo Levene. Univ. de Buenos Aires, Facultad de Derecho y Ciencias Sociales; Instituto de Investigaciones Jurídicas y Sociales Ambrosio L. Gioja. Buenos Aires. (Rev. Hist. Derecho Ricardo Levene)

Revista de Historia Naval. Instituto de Historia y Cultura Naval Armada Española. Madrid. (Rev. Hist. Naval)

Revista de Historia Universal. Univ. Nacional de Cuyo, Facultad de Filosofía y Letras. Mendoza, Argentina. (Rev. Hist. Univ.)

Revista de Humanidades. Univ. Nacional Andrés Bello. Santiago. (Rev. Humanid./Santiago)

Revista de Indias. Consejo Superior de Investigaciones Científicas, Instituto de Historia, Depto. de Historia de América. Madrid. (Rev. Indias)

Revista de la Junta Provincial de Estudios Históricos de Santa Fe. Santa Fe, Argentina. (Rev. Junta Prov. Estud. Hist. Santa Fe)

Revista de Occidente. Madrid. (Rev. Occident.)

Revista del Archivo General de la Nación. Ministerio de Justicia, Instituto Nacional de Cultura. Lima. (Rev. Arch. Gen. Nac.)

Revista del Archivo Nacional de Historia, Sección del Azuay. Casa de la Cultura Ecuatoriana, Núcleo del Azuay. Cuenca, Ecuador. (Rev. Arch. Nac. Hist. Azuay)

Revista del Instituto de Estudios Genealógicos del Uruguay. Instituto de Estudios Genealógicos del Uruguay. Montevideo. (Rev. Inst. Estud. Geneal. Uruguay)

Revista del Instituto de Historia Eclesiástica Ecuatoriana. Instituto de Historia Eclesiástica Ecuatoriana. Quito. (Rev. Inst. Hist. Ecles. Ecuat.)

Revista del Museo Nacional de Etnografía y Folklore. MUSEF Editores. La Paz. (Rev. Mus. Nac. Etnogr. Folk.)

Revista del Pensamiento Centroamericano. Centro de Investigaciones y Actividades Culturales. Managua; Asociación Libro Libre. San José. (Rev. Pensam. Centroam.)

Revista do Instituto Histórico e Geográfico Brasileiro. Instituto Histórico e Geográfico Brasileiro. Rio de Janeiro. (Rev. Inst. Hist. Geogr. Bras.)

Revista do Instituto Histórico e Geográfico de São Paulo. São Paulo. (Rev. Inst. Hist. Geogr. São Paulo)

Revista do Museu de Arqueologia e Etnologia. Univ. de São Paulo, Museu de Arqueologia e Etnologia. São Paulo. (Rev. Mus. Arqueol. Etnol.)

Revista do Patrimônio Histórico e Artístico Nacional. Ministério da Cultura, Secretaria do Livro e da Leitura, Instituto do Patrimônio Histórico e Artístico Nacional. Rio de Janeiro. (Rev. Patrim. Hist. Artíst. Nac.)

Revista Ecuatoriana de Historia Económica. Banco Central del Ecuador, Centro de Investigación y Cultura. Quito. (Rev. Ecuat. Hist. Econ.)

Revista Española de Antropología Americana. Depto. de Historia de América II (Antropología de América), Facultad de Geografía e Historia, Univ. Complutense de Madrid. Madrid. (Rev. Esp. Antropol. Am.)

Revista Europea de Estudios Latinoamericanos y del Caribe = European Review of Latin American and Caribbean Studies. Center for Latin American Research and Documentation = Centro de Estudios y Documentación Latinoamericanos. Amsterdam; Royal Institute of Linguistics and Anthropology, Dept. of Caribbean Studies. Leiden, The Netherlands. (Rev. Eur.)

Revista Filosófica Brasileira. Univ. Federal do Rio de Janeiro, Depto. de Filosofía. Rio de Janeiro, Brazil. (Rev. Filos. Bras.)

Revista Histórica. Museo Histórico Nacional. Montevideo. (Rev. Hist./Montevideo)

Revista Iberoamericana. Instituto Internacional de Literatura Iberoamericana; Univ.

de Pittsburgh. Pittsburgh, Pa. (Rev. Iberoam.)

Revista IDIS. Univ. de Cuenca, Instituto de Investigaciones Sociales. Ecuador. (Rev. IDIS)

Revista Interamericana de Bibliografía = Review of Inter-American Bibliography. Organization of American States. Washington. (Rev. Interam. Bibliogr.)

Revista Latina de Pensamiento y Lenguaje = Revue latine sur la pensée et le langage. Sociedad Iberoamericana de Pensamiento y Lenguaje. México. (Rev. Lat. Pensam. Leng.)

Revista Mexicana de Política Exterior. Coordinación General, Instituto Matías Romero de Estudios Diplomáticos, Secretaría de Relaciones Exteriores. México. (Rev. Mex. Polít. Exter.)

Revista Música. Univ. de São Paulo, Depto. de Música. São Paulo. (Rev. Músic./São Paulo)

Revista Musical Chilena. Univ. de Chile, Facultad de Artes, Sección de Musicología. Santiago. (Rev. Music. Chil.)

Revista Musical de Venezuela. Consejo Nacional de la Cultura, Fundación Emilio Sojo. Caracas. (Rev. Music. Venez.)

Revista Nacional de Cultura. Consejo Nacional de Cultura; La Casa de Bello. Caracas. (Rev. Nac. Cult./Caracas)

Revista/Review Interamericana. Univ. Interamericana de Puerto Rico/Inter-American Univ. of Puerto Rico. San Germán, Puerto Rico. (Rev. Rev. Interam.)

Revista Universidad. Univ. de Panamá, Vicerrectoría de Extensión. Panamá. (Rev. Univ./Panamá)

Revista Universidad de Medellín. Univ. de Medellín, Colombia. (Rev. Univ. Medellín)

Revista USP. Univ. de São Paulo, Coordenadoria de Comunicação Social. São Paulo. (Rev. USP)

Revue de la Société haïtienne d'histoire et de géographie. Société haïtienne d'histoire et de géographie. Port-au-Prince. (Rev. Soc. haïti.)

Revue française d'histoire d'Outre-mer. Société française d'histoire d'Outre-mer. Paris. (Rev. fr. hist. Outre-mer)

Runa. Archivo para las Ciencias del Hombre; Univ. de Buenos Aires, Facultad de Filosofía y Letras, Instituto de Antropología. Buenos Aires. (Runa/Buenos Aires)

SA: Sociological Analysis. Assn. for the Sociology of Religion. Holiday, Fla. (Sociol. Anal.)

Saastun: Revista de Cultura Maya/Maya Culture Review. Univ. del Mayab, Instituto de Cultura Maya. Mérida, Mexico. (Saastun/Mérida)

Scripta Theologica. Univ. de Navarra, Facultad de Teología. Pamplona, Spain. (Scr. Theol.)

SECOLAS Annals: Journal of the Southeastern Council on Latin American. Southeastern Conference on Latin American Studies; Georgia Southern Univ., Statesboro, Ga. (SECOLAS Ann.)

Secuencia: Revista de Historia y Ciencias Sociales. Instituto Mora. México. (Secuencia/México)

Sefárdica. Centro de Investigación y Difusión de la Cultura Sefardí. Buenos Aires. (Sefárdica/Buenos Aires)

Serie Científica. Instituto Antártico Chileno. Santiago. (Serie Cient.)

Siglo XIX. Univ. Autónoma de Nuevo León, Facultad de Filosofía y Letras. Monterrey, Mexico. (Siglo XIX/Monterrey)

Síntese: Revista de Filosofia. Companhia de Jesus, Centro de Estudios Superiores, Faculdade de Filosofia. Belo Horizonte, Brazil. (Síntese/Belo Horizonte)

SÍNTESIS. Asociación de Investigación y Especialización sobre Temas Latinoamericanos; Sociedad Editorial SÍNTESIS. Madrid. (Síntesis/Madrid)

Slavery and Abolition. Frank Cass & Co. Ltd. London. (Slavery Abolit.)

Social and Economic Studies. Institute of Social and Economic Research, Univ. of the West Indies. Mona, Jamaica. (Soc. Econ. Stud.)

Social Compass: Revue Internationale de Sociologie de la Religion (International Review of Sociology of Religion). Sage Publications, Inc. Thousand Oaks, Calif. (Soc. Compass)

Socialismo y Participación. Centro de Estudios para el Desarrollo y Participación. Lima. (Social. Particip.)

The South Atlantic Quarterly. Duke Univ. Press. Durham, N.C. (South Atl. Q.)

Stromata. Univ. del Salvador, Filosofía y Teología. San Miguel, Argentina. (Stromata/San Miguel)

Studia. La Cátedra de Historia del Pensamiento y La Cultura Argentinos. Córdoba, Argentina. (Studia/Córdoba)

Studia Histórica: Historia Contemporánea. Ediciones Univ. de Salamanca. Spain. (Stud. Hist. Hist. Contemp.)

Studia Rosenthaliana. Amsterdam Univ. Press. Amsterdam, The Netherlands. (Stud. Rosenthaliana)

Studies in Latin American Popular Culture. Univ. of Arizona, College of Humanities. Tucson, Ariz. (Stud. Lat. Am. Pop. Cult.)

Taller: Revista de Sociedad, Cultura y Política. Asociación de Estudios de Cultura y Sociedad. Buenos Aires. (Taller/Buenos Aires)

Tareas. Centro de Estudios Latinoamericanos. Panamá. (Tareas/Panamá)

Temas Americanistas. Univ. de Sevilla, Servicio de Publicaciones. Sevilla, Spain. (Temas Am.)

Temas: Cultura, Ideología, Sociedad. Instituto Cubano del Libro. La Habana; Univ. of New Mexico, Latin American Institute, Cuban Project. Albuquerque, N.M. (Temas/Habana)

Textos de História. Univ. de Brasília, Pós-Graduação em História. Brasília. (Textos Hist./Brasília)

Tierra Firme. Editorial Tierra Firme. Caracas. (Tierra Firme)

Todo es Historia. Buenos Aires. (Todo es Hist.)

La Torre. Univ. de Puerto Rico. Río Piedras, Puerto Rico. (Torre/Río Piedras)

TRACE. Centre d'études mexicaines et centraméricaines. México. (TRACE/México)

Tulsa Studies in Women's Literature. Univ. of Tulsa. Tulsa, Okla. (Tulsa Stud. Women's Lit.)

La Universidad. Univ. de El Salvador. San Salvador. (Universidad/San Salvador)

Universum. Univ. de Talca. Talca, Chile. (Universum/Talca)

Varia História. Univ. Federal de Minas Gerais, Faculdade de Filosofia e Ciências Humanas, Depto. de História. Belo Horizonte, Brazil. (Varia Hist.)

Wani: Una Revista sobre la Costa Atlántica. Centro Investigaciones y Documentación de la Costa Atlántica. Managua. (Wani/Managua)

The Western Historical Quarterly. Western

History Assn.; Utah State Univ., Logan, Utah. (West. Hist. Q.)

World Development. Elsevier Science Ltd. (Pergamon Press). Oxford, England. (World Dev.)

Yachay. Univ. Católica Boliviana, Deptos. de Filosofía y Letras y Ciencias Religiosas. Cochabamba, Bolivia. (Yachay/Cochabamba)

Yaxkin. Instituto Hondureño de Antropología e Historia. Tegucigalpa. (Yaxkin/Tegucigalpa)

Yearbook. Conference of Latin Americanist Geographers; Univ. of Texas Press. Austin, Tex. (Yearbook/CLAG)

Yearbook for Traditional Music. International Council for Traditional Music. New York. (Yearb. Tradit. Music

ABBREVIATION LIST OF JOURNALS INDEXED

For journal titles listed by full title, see *Title List of Journals Indexed*, p. 801.

ACERVO/Rio de Janeiro. ACERVO. Arquivo Nacional. Rio de Janeiro.

Acervo/Tegucigalpa. Acervo: Revista Hondureña de Cultura. Instituto del Libro y el Documento, Ministerio de Cultura. Tegucigalpa.

Actual/Mérida. Actual. Dirección General de Cultura y Extensión, Univ. de Los Andes. Mérida, Venezuela.

Afro-Asia/Salvador. Afro-Asia. Centro de Estudos Afro-Orientaís, Faculdade de Filosofia e Ciências Humanas, Univ. Federal da Bahia. Salvador, Brazil.

Agric. Hist. Agricultural History. Agricultural History Society; Univ. of California Press. Berkeley.

Allpanchis/Cusco. Allpanchis. Instituto de Pastoral Andina. Cusco, Peru.

Am. Anthropol. American Anthropologist. American Anthropological Assn. Washington.

Am. Ethnol. American Ethnologist. American Ethnological Society, American Anthropological Assn. Washington.

Am. Indíg. América Indígena. Instituto Indigenista Interamericano. México.

Am. Jew. Arch. American Jewish Archives. Jacob Rader Marcus Center, American Jewish Archives. Cincinnati, Ohio.

Am. Lat. Hist. Econ. Bol. Fuentes. América Latina en la Historia Económica: Boletín de Fuentes. Proyecto de Historia Económica, Instituto de Investigaciones Dr. José Luis Mora. México.

Am. Lat./Moscow. América Latina. Russian Academy of Sciences, Branch of World Economy Problems and of International Relations, Institute de Latin America. Moscow.

Am. Music/Society. American Music. Society for American Music. Univ. of Illinois Press. Champaign, Ill.

Am. Negra. América Negra. Expedición Humana, Instituto de Genética Humana, Facultad de Medicina, Pontificia Univ. Javeriana. Bogotá.

Americas/Franciscans. The Americas: A Quarterly Review of Inter-American Cultural History. Catholic Univ. of America, Academy of American Franciscan History; Catholic Univ. of America Press. Washington.

An. Acad. Geogr. Hist. Guatem. Anales de la Academia de Geografía e Historia de Guatemala. Academia de Geografía e Historia de Guatemala. Guatemala.

An. Acad. Nac. Cienc. Morales. Anales de la Academia Nacional de Ciencias Morales y Políticas. Academia Nacional de Ciencias Morales y Políticas. Buenos Aires.

An. Antropol. Anales de Antropología. Univ. Nacional Autónoma de México, Instituto de Investigaciones Históricas. México.

An. Arq. Público Pará. Anais do Arquivo Público do Pará. Arquivo Público do Estado do Pará. Belém, Brazil.

An. Inst. Patagon./Ser. Cienc. Hum. Anales del Instituto de la Patagonia: Serie Ciencias Humanas. Instituto de la Patagonia, Univ. de Magallanes. Punta Arenas, Chile.

An. Mus. Am. Anales del Museo de América. Museo de América, Dirección General de Bellas Artes y Bienes Culturales, Ministerio de Educación, Cultura y Deporte. Madrid.

Anál. Polít./Bogotá. Análisis Político. Instituto de Estudios Políticos y Relaciones Internacionales, Univ. Nacional de Colombia. Bogotá.

Anales/Buenos Aires. Anales. Academia Nacional de la Historia. Buenos Aires.

Anc. Mesoam. Ancient Mesoamerica. Cambridge Univ. Press. Cambridge, England; New York.

ANDES Antropol. Hist. ANDES: Antropología e Historia. Centro Promocional de las Investigaciones en Historia y Antropología, Facultad de Humanidades, Univ. Nacional de Salta. Salta, Argentina.

Ann. Antill. Annales des Antilles. Société d'histoire de la Martinique. Fort-de-France, Martinique.

Ann. Assoc. Am. Geogr. Annals of the Association of American Geographers. Assn. of American Geographers. Washington; Blackwell Publishers. Oxford, England; Malden, Mass.

Ann. hist. Révolut. fr. Annales historiques de la Révolution française. Société des Études Robespierristes. Paris.

Ann. hist. sci. soc. Annales: histoire, sciences sociales. L'École des Hautes Études en Sciences Sociales. Paris.

Anos 90. Anos 90: Revista do Programa de Pós-Graduação em História. Univ. Federal do Rio Grande do Sul, Programa de Pós-Graduação em História. Porto Alegre, Brazil.

Anthropologica/Lima. Anthropologica del Departamento de Ciencias Sociales. Depto. de Ciencias Sociales, Pontificia Univ. Católica del Perú. Lima.

Anthropos/Freiburg. Anthropos: International Review of Ethnology and Linguistics. Anthropos-Institut. Freiburg, Switzerland.

Anu. Colomb. Hist. Soc. Cult. Anuario Colombiano de Historia Social y de la Cultura. Depto. de Historia, Facultad de Ciencias Humanas, Univ. Nacional de Colombia. Bogotá.

Anu. Espacios Urbanos. Anuario de Espacios Urbanos. Depto. de Evaluación del Diseño en el Tiempo, División de Ciencias y Artes para el Diseño, Univ. Autónoma Metropolitana—Unidad Azcapotzalco. México.

Anu. Estud. Am. Anuario de Estudios Americanos. Escuela de Estudios Hispano-Americanos, Consejo Superior de Investigaciones Científicas. Sevilla, Spain.

Anu. Estud. Boliv. Anuario de Estudios Bolivarianos. Univ. Simón Bolívar, Instituto de Investigaciones Históricas Bolivarium. Caracas.

Anu. Estud. Centroam. Anuario de Estudios Centroamericanos. Univ. de Costa Rica. San José.

Anu. Estud. Urbanos. Anuario de Estudios Urbanos. Depto. de Evaluación del Diseño en el Tiempo, División de Ciencias y Artes para el Diseño, Univ. Autónoma Metropolitana—Unidad Azcapotzalco. México.

Anu. IEHS. Anuario IEHS. Instituto de Estudios Histórico-Sociales, Facultad de Ciencias Humanas, Univ. Nacional del Centro de la Provincia de Buenos Aires. Tandil, Argentina.

Anu. IEI. Anuario IEI. Instituto de Estudios Indígenas, Univ. Autónoma de México. San Cristóbal de las Casas, Mexico.

Anu. Inst. Chiapaneco Cult. Anuario Instituto Chiapaneco de Cultura. Instituto Chiapaneco de Cultura. Tuxtla Gutiérrez, Mexico.

Anu. Mariateg. Anuario Mariateguiano. Empresa Editora Amauta. Lima.

Anuario/Asunción. Anuario. Instituto de Investigaciones Históricas Dr. José Gaspar Rodríguez de Francia. Asunción.

Anuario/INAH. Anuario de la Dirección de Etnología y Antropología Social del INAH. Dirección de Etnología y Antropología Social, Instituto Nacional de Antropología e Historia. México.

Anuario/Sucre. Anuario. Archivo y Biblioteca Nacionales de Bolivia. Sucre.

Anuario/Xalapa. Anuario. Instituto de Investigaciones Histórico-Sociales, Univ. Veracruzana. Xalapa, Mexico.

Apuntes/Lima. Apuntes. Centro de Investigación, Univ. del Pacífico. Lima.

Arch. Esp. Arte. Archivo Español de Arte. Centro de Estudios Históricos, Depto. de Historia del Arte Diego Velázquez, Consejo Superior de Investigaciones Científicas. Madrid.

Arch. Francisc. Hist. Archivum Franciscanum Historicum. Collegio S. Bonaventura. Rome.

Arch. Hist. Soc. Iesu. Archivum Historicum Societatis Iesu. Institutum Scriptorum de Historia. Rome.

Arch. Ibero-Am. Archivo Ibero-Americano: Revista Franciscana de Estudios Históricos. Franciscanos Españoles. Madrid.

Arquipél. Hist. Arquipélago História: Revista da Universidade dos Açores. Univ. dos Açores. Ponta Delgada, Portugal.

Ars Musica Denver. Ars Musica Denver. Lamont School of Music, Univ. of Denver. Denver.

Asclepio/Madrid. Asclepio: Archivo Iberoamericano de Historia de la Medicina y Antropología Médica. Centro de Estudios Históricos, Consejo Superior de Investigaciones Científicas. Madrid.

Bermud. J. Archaeol. Marit. Hist. Bermuda Journal of Archaeological and Maritime History. Bermuda Maritime Museum. Mangrove Bay, Bermuda.

Biblos/Rio de Janeiro. Biblos: Revista do Departamento de Biblioteconomia e História. Depto. de Biblioteconomia e História, Fundação Univ. do Rio Grande. Rio Grande, Brazil.

Bol. Acad. Colomb. Boletín de la Academia Colombiana. Academia Colombiana. Bogotá.

Bol. Acad. Nac. Hist./Caracas. Boletín de la Academia Nacional de la Historia. Academia Nacional de la Historia. Caracas.

Bol. Acad. Nac. Hist./Quito. Boletín de la Academia Nacional de Historia. Academia Nacional de Historia; La Prensa Catolica. Quito.

Bol. Acad. Puertorriq. Hist. Boletín de la Academia Puertorriqueña de la Historia. Academia Puertorriqueña de la Historia. San Juan.

Bol. Am. Boletín Americanista. Sección de Historia de América y Africa, Depto. de Antropología Social y de Historia de América y Africa, Facultad de Geografía e Historia, Univ. de Barcelona. Barcelona.

Bol. Antropol./Mérida. Boletín Antropológico. Museo Arqueológico, Centro de Investigaciones Etnológicas, Facultad de Humanidades y Educación, Univ. de los Andes. Mérida, Venezuela.

Bol. Cult. Bibliogr. Boletín Cultural y Bibliográfico. Biblioteca Luis-Angel Arango, Banco de la República. Bogotá.

Bol. Hist. Antig. Boletín de Historia y Antigüedades. Academia Colombiana de la Historia. Bogotá.

Bol. Hist. Ejérc. Boletín Histórico del Ejército. República Oriental del Uruguay, Comando General del Ejército, Estado Mayor del Ejército, Depto. de Estudios Históricos. Montevideo.

Bol. Inst. Hist. Ravignani. Boletín del Instituto de Historia Argentina y Americana Dr. Emilio Ravignani. Univ. de Buenos Aires, Facultad de Filosofía y Letras. Buenos Aires.

Bol. Inst. Riva-Agüero. Boletín del Instituto Riva-Agüero: BIRA. Pontificia Univ. Católica del Perú, Instituto Riva-Agüero. Lima.

Bol. Lima. Boletín de Lima: Revista Cultural Científica. Asociación Cultural Boletín de Lima A.C. Lima.

Bol. Mus. Inst. Camón Aznar. Boletín del Museo e Instituto Camón Aznar. Museo e Instituto de Humanidades Camón Aznar. Zaragoza, Spain.

Boletín/Buenos Aires. Boletín. Sociedad de Estudios Bibliográficos Argentinos. Buenos Aires.

Br. J. Ethnomusicol. British Journal of Ethnomusicology. International Council for Traditional Music, UK Chapter. London.

Bull. Hisp. Stud. Bulletin of Hispanic Studies. Institute of Hispanic Studies. Liverpool, England.

Bull. Inst. fr. étud. andin. Bulletin de l'Institut français d'études andines. l'Institut français d'études andines. Lima.

Bull. Lat. Am. Res. Bulletin of Latin American Research. Society for Latin American Studies; Blackwell Publishers. Oxford, England.

Bull. Soc. hist. Guadeloupe. Bulletin de la Société d'histoire de la Guadeloupe. Archives départamentales avec le concours du Conseil général de la Guadeloupe. Basse-Terre, Guadeloupe.

Búsqueda/Cochabamba. Búsqueda: Revista Semestral de Ciencias Sociales. Univ. Mayor de San Simón, Facultad de Ciencias Económicas y Sociales. Cochabamba, Bolivia.

Cad. Filos. Ciênc. Hum. Caderno de Filosofia e Ciências Humanas. Depto. de Filosofia e Ciências Humanas, Faculdade de Ciências Humanas e Letras, Centro Universitário Newton Paiva. Belo Horizonte, Brazil.

Cad. Negros. Cadernos Negros. Editora Anita Ltda. São Paulo.

Cad. Pagu. Cadernos Pagu. Univ. Estadual de Campinas, Núcleo de Estudo de Gênero-PAGU. Campinas, Brazil.

Cah. Adm. Outre-Mer. Les Cahiers de l'Adminstration Outre-Mer. Univ. des Antilles, Centre de Recherche sur les Pouvoirs Locaux dans la Caraïbe. Cayenne?, French Guiana.

Cah. Am. lat. Cahiers des Amériques latines. Univ. de la Sorbonne nouvelle—Paris III, Institut des haute études de l'Amérique latine. Paris.

Callaloo/Baltimore. Callaloo. Johns Hopkins Univ. Press. Baltimore, Md.

Can. J. Lat. Am. Caribb. Stud. Canadian Journal of Latin American and Caribbean Studies = Revue canadienne des études latino-américaines et caraïbes. Univ. of Ottawa. Ontario, Canada.

Caravelle/Toulouse. Caravelle: Cahiers du monde hispanique et luso-brésilien. Univ. de Toulouse, Institute d'études hispaniques, hispano-americaines et luso-brésiliennes. Toulouse, France.

Caribb. Q. Caribbean Quarterly: CQ. Cultural Studies Initiative, Office of Vice Chancellor, Univ. of the West Indies. Mona, Jamaica.

Caribb. Stud. Caribbean Studies. Univ. of Puerto Rico, Institute of Caribbean Studies. Río Piedras, Puerto Rico.

Caribe Contemp. El Caribe Contemporáneo. Univ. Nacional Autónoma de México, Facultad de Ciencias Políticas, Centro de Estudios Latinoamericanos. México.

Caribena/Martinique. Caribena: cahiers d'études américanistes de la Caraïbe. Centre d'études et de recherches archéologiques. Martinique.

Casa Am. Casa de las Américas. Casa de las Américas. La Habana.

Cespedesia/Cali. Cespedesia. Depto. del Valle del Cauca. Cali, Colombia.

CHISPA/New Orleans. LA CHISPA: Selected Proceedings. Tulane Univ. New Orleans, La.

Ciclos Hist. Econ. Soc. Ciclos en la Historia, Economía y la Sociedad. Instituto de Investigaciones de Historia Económica y Social, Facultad de Ciencias Económicas, Univ. de Buenos Aires. Buenos Aires.

Cienc. Soc./INTEC. Ciencia y Sociedad. Instituto Tecnológico de Santo Domingo. Santo Domingo.

Ciênc. Tróp. Ciência & Trópico. Fundação Joaquim Nabuco; Editora Massangana. Recife, Brazil.

CLAHR/Albuquerque. Colonial Latin American Historical Review. Univ. of New Mexico, Spanish Colonial Research Center. Albuquerque, N.M.

Clio Arqueol./Recife. Clio: Série Arqueológica. Univ. Federal de Pernambuco, Programa de Pós-Graduação em Historia. Recife, Brazil.

CLIO/Buenos Aires. CLIO. Comité Argentino de Ciencias Históricas, Comité Internacional. Buenos Aires; Editorial Canguro. La Rioja, Argentina.

Clío/Culiacán. Clío. Univ. Autónoma de Sinaloa, Escuela de Historia. Culiacán, Mexico.

Clio Hist./Recife. Clio: Série História do Nordeste. Univ. Federal de Pernambuco. Recife, Brazil.

Colon. Lat. Am. Rev. Colonial Latin American Review. City Univ. of New York, City College, Dept. of Foreign Languages and Literatures, Simon H. Rifkind Center for the Humanities. New York; Carfax Publishing, Taylor & Francis, Ltd. Abingdon, England; Philadelphia, Pa.

Conjunctions/New York. Conjunctions. Conjunctions. New York.

Contrib. Hist. Contribución Histórica. Museo Regional de Atacama. Copiapó, Chile.

Contrib. Indian Sociol. Contributions to Indian Sociology. Institute of Economic Growth. New Delhi, India; Sage Publications, Inc. Thousand Oaks, Calif.

Contribuciones/Buenos Aires. Contribuciones. Centro Interdisciplinario de Estudios Sobre el Desarrollo Latinoamericano, Fundación Konrad-Adenauer-Stiftung. Buenos Aires.

Correspondance/Cáceres. Correspondance. Univ. de Extremadura, Facultad de Filosofía y Letras, Centro de Estudios sobre la Bélgica Francófona. Cáceres, Spain; Communauté Française de Belgique, Archives et Musée de la Littérature. Brussels.

Cristianismo Soc. Cristianismo y Sociedad. Junta Latinoamericana de Iglesia y Sociedad. Montevideo.

Cuad. Am. Cuadernos Americanos. Univ. Nacional Autónoma de México. México.

Cuad. CENDES. Cuadernos del CENDES. Univ. Central de Venezuela, Centro de Estudios del Desarrollo. Caracas.

Cuad. CLAEH. Cuadernos del CLAEH. Centro Latinoamericano de Economía Humana. Montevideo.

Cuad. Hispanoam. Cuadernos Hispanoamericanos. Agencia Española de Cooperación Iberoamericana; Instituto de Cooperación Iberoamericana. Madrid.

Cuad. Hispanoam. Complement. Cuadernos Hispanoamericanos: Los Complementarios. Agencia Española de Cooperación Iberoamericana; Instituto de Cooperación Iberoamericana. Madrid.

Cuad. Hist./Córdoba. Cuadernos de Historia. Instituto de Historia del Derecho y de las Ideas Políticas. Córdoba, Argentina.

Cuad. Hist. Poblac. Cuadernos de Historia: Serie Población. Univ. Nacional de Córdoba, Facultad de Filosofía y Humanidades, Centro de Investigaciones. Córdoba, Argentina.

Cuad. Hist./Santiago. Cuadernos de Historia. Univ. de Chile, Facultad de Humanidades y Educación, Depto. de Ciencias Históricas. Santiago.

Cuad. Inst. Nac. Antropol. Pensam. Latinoam. Cuadernos del Instituto Nacional de Antropología y Pensamiento Latinoamericano. Presidencia de la Nación, Secretaria de Cultura, Instituto Nacional de Antropología y Pensamiento Latinoamericano. Buenos Aires.

Cuad. Marcha. Cuadernos de Marcha. Montevideo.

Cuad. Prehispánicos. Cuadernos Prehispánicos. Univ. de Valladolid, Seminario de Historia de América. Vallodolid, Spain.

Cuad. Sur Hist./Bahía Blanca. Cuadernos del Sur: Historia. Univ. Nacional del Sur, Depto. de Humanidades. Bahía Blanca, Argentina.

Cuad. Sur/Oaxaca. Cuadernos del Sur: Ciencias Sociales. Univ. Autónoma Benito Juárez de Oaxaca, Instituto de Investigaciones Sociológicas. Oaxaca, Mexico.

Cuad. Sur Soc. Econ. Polít. Cuadernos del Sur: Sociedad, Economía, Política. Editorial Tierra del Fuego. Buenos Aires.

Cuba. Stud. Cuban Studies. Univ. of Pittsburgh Press. Pittsburgh, Pa.

Cult. Anthropol. Cultural Anthropology: Journal of the Society for Cultural Anthropology. Society for Cultural Anthropology; American Anthropological Assn. Washington.

Cultura/Quito. Cultura. Banco Central del Ecuador. Quito.

Curr. Anthropol. Current Anthropology. Univ. of Chicago Press. Chicago, Ill.

Cuyo/Mendoza. Cuyo: Anuario de Historia del Pensamiento Argentino. Univ. Nacional de Cuyo, Instituto de Filosofía, Sección de Historia del Pensamiento Argentino. Mendoza, Argentina.

Dados/Rio de Janeiro. Dados: Revista de Ciências Sociais. Instituto Universitários de Pesquisas do Rio de Janeiro, Univ. Candido Mendes. Rio de Janeiro.

Derroteros Mar Sur. Derroteros de la Mar del Sur. Instituto de Estudios Histórico-Marítimos del Perú. Lima.

Desarro. Econ. Desarrollo Económico: Revista de Ciencias Sociales. Instituto de Desarrollo Económico y Social. Buenos Aires.

Deslindes/Montevideo. Deslindes. Biblioteca Nacional. Montevideo.

Desmemoria/Buenos Aires. Desmemoria. Buenos Aires.

Dieciocho Hisp. Enlight. Dieciocho: Hispanic Enlightenment. Univ. of Virginia. Charlottesville.

Diogenes/Philosophy. Diogenes. International Council for Philosophy and Humanistic Studies. Paris; Blackwell Publishers. Oxford, England.

Ecol. Polít. Ecología Política: Cuadernos de Debate Internacional. Icaria Editorial; Fundación Hogar del Empleado. Barcelona, Spain.

Entrepasados/Buenos Aires. Entrepasados: Revista de Historia. Buenos Aires.

Espacios Cult. Soc. Espacios: Cultura y Sociedad. Instituto Cultural de Aguascalientes. Aguascalientes, Mexico.

Estud. Afro-Asiát. Estudos Afro-Asiáticos. Centro de Estudos Afro-Asiáticos. Rio de Janeiro.

Estud. Boliv. Estudios Bolivianos. Univ. Mayor de San Andrés, Facultad de Humanidades y Ciencias de la Educación, Instituto de Estudios Bolivianos. La Paz.

Estud. Cult. Náhuatl. Estudios de Cultura Náhuatl. Univ. Nacional Autónoma de México, Instituto de Investigaciones Históricas. México.

Estud. Econ./São Paulo. Estudos Econômicos. Fundação Instituto de Pesquisas Econômicas, Faculdade de Economia, Administração e Contabilidade, Univ. de São Paulo. São Paulo.

Estud. Filos. Estudios Filosóficos. Instituto Superior de Filosofía. Valladolid, Spain.

Estud. Filos. Hist. Let. Estudios: Filosofía, Historia, Letras. Instituto Tecnológico Autónomo de México, Depto. Académico de Estudios Generales. México.

Estud. Francisc. Estudios Franciscanos. Convento de Capuchinas. Barcelona, Spain.

Estud. Front. Estudios Fronterizos. Univ. Autónoma de Baja California, Instituto de Investigaciones Sociales. Mexicali, Mexico.

Estud. Hist. Mod. Contemp. Méx. Estudios de Historia Moderna y Contemporánea de México. Univ. Nacional Autónoma de México, Instituto de Investigaciones Históricas. México.

Estud. Hist. Novohisp. Estudios de Historia Novohispana. Instituto de Investigaciones Históricas, Univ. Nacional Autónoma de México. México.

Estud. Hist./Rio de Janeiro. Estudos Históricos. Centro de Pesquisa e Documentação de História Contemporánea do Brasil, Fundação Getulio Vargas. Rio de Janeiro.

Estud. Hist. Soc. Econ. Am. Estudios de Historia Social y Económica de América. Univ. de Alcalá de Henares. Madrid.

Estud. Hombre. Estudios del Hombre. Univ. de Guadalajara, Depto. de Estudios del Hombre. Guadalajara, Mexico.

Estud. Humaníst. Geogr. Hist. Arte. Estudios Humanísticos: Geografía, Historia, Arte. Facultad de Filosofía y Letras, Univ. de León. León, Spain.

Estud. Ibero-Am./Porto Alegre. Estudos Ibero-Americanos. Pontificia Univ. Católica do Rio Grande do Sul, Faculdade de Filosofia e Ciências Humanas, Depto. de História, Programa Pós-Graduação em História. Porto Alegre, Brazil.

Estud. Jalisc. Estudios Jaliscienses. El Colegio de Jalisco. Zapopan, Mexico.

Estud. Latinoam./Poland. Estudios Latinoamericanos. Academia de Ciencias de Polonia, Instituto de Historia. Wrocław, Poland.

Estud. Leopold. Estudos Leopoldenses. Univ. do Vale do Rio dos Sinos, Faculdade de Filosofia, Ciências e Letras. São Leopoldo, Brazil.

Estud. Michoacanos. Estudios Michoacanos. El Colegio de Michoacán. Zamora, Mexico.

Estud. Migr. Latinoam. Estudios Migratorios Latinoamericanos. Centro de Estudios Migratorios Latinoamericanos. Buenos Aires.

Estud. Públicos. Estudios Públicos. Centro de Estudios Públicos. Santiago.

Estud. Soc./Hermosillo. Estudios Sociales: Revista de Investigación del Noroeste. Centro de Investigación en Alimentación y Desarrollo; El Colegio de Sonora; Univ. de Sonora. Hermosillo, Mexico.

Estud. Soc./Santa Fe. Estudios Sociales: Revista Universitaria Semestral. Centro de Estudios Históricos, Facultad de Formación Docente en Ciencias, Univ. Nacional del Litoral. Santa Fe, Argentina; Centro de Publicaciones, Secretaría de Extensión, Univ. Nacional del Litoral. Santa Fe, Argentina.

Estud. Soc./Santo Domingo. Estudios Sociales. Centro de Estudios Sociales P. Juan Montalvo, SJ. Santo Domingo.

Estud. Sociol./México. Estudios Sociológicos. El Colegio de México, Centro de Estudios Sociológicos. México.

Estudios/USAC. Estudios: Revista de Antropología, Arqueología e Historia. Instituto de Investigaciones Históricas, Antropológicas, y Arqueológicas, Escuela de Historia, Univ. de San Carlos de Guatemala. Guatemala.

Ethnohistory/Society. Ethnohistory. American Society for Ethnohistory; Duke Univ., Durham, N.C.

Ethnology/Pittsburgh. Ethnology: An International Journal of Cultural and Social Anthropology. Univ. of Pittsburgh, Dept. of Anthropology. Pittsburgh, Pa.

Etnología/La Paz. Etnología: Boletín del Museo Nacional de Etnografía y Folklore. Museo Nacional de Etnografía y Folklore. La Paz.

Fem. Stud. Feminist Studies. Feminist Studies, Inc.; Univ. of Maryland. College Park, Md.

Fermentum/Mérida. Fermentum: Revista Venezolana de Sociología y Antropología. Univ. de los Andes. Mérida, Venezuela.

Folia Hist. Nordeste. Folia Histórica del Nordeste. Univ. Nacional del Nordeste, Facultad de Humanidades, Instituto de Historia; CONICET, Instituto de Investigaciones Geohistóricas; FUNDANORD. Resistencia, Argentina.

Folia Humaníst. Folia Humanística. Editorial Glarma. Barcelona, Spain.

Front. Norte. Frontera Norte. El Colegio de la Frontera Norte. Tijuana, Mexico.

Gend. Hist. Gender & History. Blackwell Publishers. Abingdon, England; Williston, Vt.

Généal. hist. Caraïbe. Généalogie et histoire de la Caraïbe. Assn. de la généalogie et histoire de la Caraïbe. Le Pecq, France.

Geogr. Rev. Geographical Review. American Geographical Society. New York.

Grand Str. Grand Street. Grand Street Publications. New York.

Guyana Hist. J. Guyana Historical Journal. Univ. of Guyana, Faculty of Arts, Dept. of History, History Society. Georgetown.

Haciendo Hist. Haciendo Historia. México.

HAHR. Hispanic American Historical Review. Conference on Latin American History of the American Historical Assn.; Duke Univ. Press. Durham, N.C.

Hisp. Sacra. Hispania Sacra: Revista de Historia Eclesiástica de España. Consejo Superior de Investigaciones Científicas, Centro de Estudios Históricos. Madrid.

Hispamérica/Gaithersburg. Hispamérica. Gaithersburg, Md.

Hispania/Madrid. Hispania. Consejo Superior de Investigaciones Científicas, Instituto de Historia, Depto. de Medieval Moderna y Contemporánea. Madrid.

Hist. Cult./La Paz. Historia y Cultura. Sociedad Boliviana de Historia. La Paz.

Hist. Cult./Lima. Historia y Cultura. Museo Nacional de Arqueología, Antropología e Historia. Lima.

Hist. Fam. The History of the Family: an International Quarterly. JAI Press, Inc. Greenwich, Conn.

Hist. Fuente Oral. Historia y Fuente Oral. Univ. de Barcelona, Depto. de Historia Contemporanea. Barcelona.

Hist. Gaz. History Gazette. Univ. of Guyana, History Society. Turkeyen, Guyana.

Hist. Graf. Historia y Grafía. Depto. de Historia, Univ. Iberoamericana. México.

Hist. Mex. Historia Mexicana. Centro de Estudios Históricos, El Colegio de México. México.

Hist. Parag. Historia Paraguaya. Academia Paraguaya de la Historia. Asunción.

Hist. Relig. History of Religions. Univ. of Chicago. Chicago, Ill.

Hist. Soc./Valencia. Historia Social. Univ. Nacional de Educación a Distancia Alzira-Valencia, Centro Francisco Tomás y Valiente, Fundación Instituto de Historia Social. Valencia, Spain.

Historia/Santiago. Historia. Instituto de Historia, Facultad de Historia, Geografía y Ciencia Política, Pontificia Univ. Católica de Chile. Santiago.

Histórica/Lima. Histórica. Pontificia Univ. Católica del Perú, Depto. de Humanidades. Lima.

HLAS CD-ROM. Handbook of Latin American Studies CD-ROM: HLAS/CD. Library of Congress, Hispanic Division. Washington. Fundación Histórica Tavera; DIGIBIS. Madrid.

Hoy Hist. Hoy es Historia: Revista Bimestral de Historia Nacional e Iberoamericana. Editorial Raíces. Montevideo.

Humanas/Porto Alegre. Humanas: Revista do Instituto de Filosofia e Ciências Humanas da Universidade Federal do Rio Grande do Sul. Univ. Federal do Rio Grande do Sul, Instituto de Filosofia e Ciências Humanas. Porto Alegre, Brazil.

Humanitas/Monterrey. Humanitas: Anuario del Centro de Estudios Humanísticos. Centro de Estudios Humanísticos, Secretaría de Extensión y Cultura, Univ. Autónoma de Nuevo León. Monterrey, Mexico.

Ibero-Am. Arch. Ibero-Amerikanisches Archiv: Zeitschrift für Sozialwissenschaften und Geschichte. Ibero-Amerikanisches Institut. Berlin.

Iberoamericana/Stockholm. Iberoamericana: Nordic Journal of Latin American Studies/Revista Nórdica de Estudios Latinoamericanos. Stockholm Univ., Institute of Latin American Studies.

Ideas Valores. Ideas y Valores. Univ. Nacional de Colombia, Instituto de Filosofía y Letras. Bogotá.

Indiana J. Hisp. Lit. Indiana Journal of Hispanic Literature. Indiana Univ. Bloomington, Ind.

Int. Hist. Rev. The International History Review. Dept. of History, Simon Fraser Univ. Burnaby, British Columbia.

Integr. Latinoam. Integración Latinoamericana. Instituto para la Integración de América Latina, Depto. de Integración y Programas Regionales, Banco Interamericano de Desarrollo = Inter-American Development Bank. Buenos Aires.

Inter-Am. Music Rev. Inter-American Music Review. Theodore Front Musical Literature, Inc. Van Nuys, Calif.

Interciencia/Caracas. Interciencia. Asociación Interciencia. Caracas.

Invest. Econ. Investigación Económica. Univ. Nacional Autónoma de México, Facultad de Economía. México.

Invest. Ens. Investigaciones y Ensayos. Academia Nacional de Historia. Buenos Aires.

Islas/Santa Clara. Islas. Univ. Central de Las Villas, Facultad de Ciencias Sociales y Humanísticas, Depto. de Letras. Santa Clara, Cuba.

Itinerario/Leiden. Itinerario. Centre for the History of European Expansion, Faculty of the School of Humanities, Univ. of Leiden. Leiden, The Netherlands.

Iztapalapa/México. Iztapalapa. Univ. Autónoma Metropolitana—Unidad Iztapalapa, División de Ciencias Sociales y Humanidades. México.

J. Am. Folk. Journal of American Folklore. American Folklore Society. Arlington, Va.

J. Am. Musicol. Soc. Journal of the American Musicological Society. American Musicological Society. Richmond, Va.

J. Anthropol. Res. Journal of Anthropological Research. Univ. of New Mexico. Albuquerque, N.M.

J. Bahamas Hist. Soc. Journal of the Bahamas Historical Society. Bahamas Historical Society. Nassau, Bahamas.

J. Caribb. Hist. The Journal of Caribbean History. Univ. of the West Indies Press; Dept. of History, Univ. of the West Indies. Mona, Jamaica.

J. Caribb. Stud. Journal of Caribbean Studies. Assn. of Caribbean Studies. Coral Gables, Fla.

J. Econ. Hist. The Journal of Economic History. Economic History Assn.; Univ. of Arizona. Tucson.

J. Fam. Hist. Journal of Family History. Sage Periodicals Press. Thousand Oaks, Calif.

J. Hist. Occidente. Jornadas de Historia de Occidente. Centro de Estudios de la Revolución Mexicana Lázaro Cárdenas. Jiquilpan, Mexico.

J. Lat. Am. Cult. Stud. Journal of Latin American Cultural Studies: Travesía. Taylor & Frances Ltd., Carfax Publishing. Basingstoke, England; Levittown, Pa.

J. Lat. Am. Stud. Journal of Latin American Studies. Cambridge Univ. Press. Cambridge, England.

J. Polit. Mil. Sociol. Journal of Political and Military Sociology: JPMS. Northern Illinois Univ., Dept. of Sociology. DeKalb, Ill.

J. Soc. Hist. Journal of Social History. George Mason Univ. Press. Fairfax, Va.

J. West. Journal of the West. Sunflower Univ. Press. Manhattan, Kan.

J. World Hist. Journal of World History. World History Assn.; Univ. of Hawaii Press. Honolulu.

Jahrb. Gesch. Jahrbuch für Geschichte von Staat, Wirtschaft und Gesellschaft Lateinamerikas. Böhlau Verlag. Köln, Germany.

JILAS/Bundoora. JILAS: Journal of Iberian and Latin American Studies. Association of Iberian and Latin American Studies of Australasia; La Trobe Univ., School of History. Bundoora, Australia.

JSAH. JSAH: Journal of the Society of Architectural Historians. Society of Architectural Historians. Chicago.

LARR. Latin American Research Review. Latin American Studies Assn.; Univ. of New Mexico, Latin American Institute. Albuquerque, N.M.

Lat. Am. Anthropol. Rev. The Latin American Anthropology Review. Society for Latin American Anthropology. Fairfax, Va.

Lat. Am. Indian Lit. J. Latin American Indian Literatures Journal. Geneva College, Dept. of Foreign Languages. Beaver Falls, Pa.

Lat. Am. Lit. Rev. Latin American Literary Review. Latin American Literary Review Press. Pittsburgh, Pa.

Lat. Am. Music Rev. Latin American Music Review = Revista de Música Latinoamericana. Univ. of Texas Press. Austin, Tex.

Lat. Am. Perspect. Latin American Perspectives. Sage Publications, Inc. Thousand Oaks, Calif.

Lateinamerika/Rostock. Lateinamerika. Univ. Rostock. Rostock, Germany.

Let. Fem. Letras Femeninas. Asociación de Literatura Femenina Hispánica. Boulder, Colo.

Leviatán/Madrid. Leviatán: Revista de Hechos e Ideas. Fundación Pablo Iglesias. Madrid.

Libertas/Buenos Aires. Libertas. Escuela Superior de Economía y Administración de Empresas. Buenos Aires.

LPH Rev. Hist. LPH: Revista de História. Univ. Federal de Ouro Preto, Depto. de História. Mariana, Brazil.

Lua Nova. Lua Nova. Centro de Estudos de Cultura Contemporánea. São Paulo.

Maguaré/Bogotá. Maguaré. Univ. Nacional de Colombia, Depto. de Antropología. Bogotá.

Manoa/Honolulu. Manoa: A Pacific Journal of International Writing. Univ. of Hawaii Press. Honolulu.

Mapocho/Santiago. Mapocho. Dirección de Bibliotecas, Archivos y Museos. Santiago.

Mélanges/Madrid. Mélanges de la Casa de Velázquez. Casa de Velázquez. Madrid.

Mem. Acad. Mex. Hist. Memorias de la Academia Mexicana de la Historia. Academia Mexicana de la Historia. México.

Memoria/CEMOS. Memoria: Boletín de CEMOS. Centro de Estudios del Movimiento Obrero y Socialista. México.

Memoria/MARKA. Memoria. MARKA: Instituto de Historia y Antropología Andina. Quito.

Memoria/SEIHGE. Memoria. Sociedad Ecuatoriana de Investigaciones Históricas y Geográficas. Quito.

Mesoamérica/Plumsock. Mesoamérica. Plumsock Mesoamerican Studies. South Woodstock, Vt.; Centro de Investigaciones Regionales de Mesoamérica. Antigua, Guatemala.

Metapolítica/México. Metapolítica: Revista Trimestral de Teoría y Ciencia de la Política.

Centro de Estudios de Política Comparada. México.

Mex. Stud. Mexican Studies/Estudios Mexicanos. Univ. of California Press. Berkeley, Calif.

Montalbán/Caracas. Montalbán. Univ. Católica Andrés Bello, Facultad de Humanidades y Educación, Institutos Humanísticos de Investigación. Caracas.

Mundo Nuevo/Caracas. Mundo Nuevo. Univ. Simón Bolívar, Instituto de Altos Estudios de América Latina. Caracas.

Mus. Hist. Museo Histórico. Museo de Historia de la Ciudad de Quito. Quito.

Nassarre/Zaragoza. Nassarre: Revista Aragonesa de Musicología. Diputación de Zaragoza, Sección Música Antigua, Institución Fernando el Católico. Zaragoza, Spain.

Nóesis/UACJ. Nóesis: Revista de Ciencias Sociales y Humanidades. Dirección General de Investigación y Estudios Superiores, Univ. Autónoma de Ciudad Juárez. Ciudad Juárez, Mexico.

Not. Bibliogr. Hist. Notícia Bibliográfica e Histórica. Pontifícia Univ. Católica de Campinas. Campinas, Brazil.

Not. Hist. Agrar. Noticiario de Historia Agraria. Seminario de Historia Agraria. Murcia, Spain.

Novahispania/México. Novahispania. Univ. Nacional Autónoma de México, Instituto de Investigaciones Filológicas. México.

Novos Estud. CEBRAP. Novos Estudos CEBRAP. Centro Brasileiro de Análise e Planejamento. São Paulo.

Nueva Soc. Nueva Sociedad. Editorial Nueva Sociedad. Caracas.

Nütram/Santiago. Nütram. Centro Ecuménico Diego de Medellín. Santiago.

NWIG. NWIG: New West Indian Guide/ Nieuwe West Indische Gids. Royal Institute of Linguistics and Anthropology, KITLV Press. Leiden, The Netherlands.

Obradoiro Hist. Mod. Obradoiro de Historia Moderna. Univ. de Santiago de Compostela. Santiago de Compostela, Spain.

Op. Cit./Río Piedras. Op. Cit.: Boletín del Centro de Investigaciones Históricas. Univ. de Puerto Rico, Facultad de Humanidades, Depto. de Historia. Río Piedras, Puerto Rico.

Paramillo/San Cristóbal. Paramillo. Univ. Católica de Táchira, Centro de Estudios Interdisciplinarios. San Cristóbal, Venezuela.

Paraninfo/Tegucigalpa. Paraninfo. Instituto de Ciencias del Hombre Rafael Heliodoro Valle. Tegucigalpa.

Patterns Prejud. Patterns of Prejudice. Institute of Jewish Affairs. London.

Philos. Lit. Philosophy and Literature. Johns Hopkins Univ. Press. Baltimore, Md.

Plant. Soc. Am. Plantation Society in the Americas. Univ. of New Orleans, Dept. of History. New Orleans, La.

Plural/San Juan. Plural. Univ. de Puerto Rico, Administración de Colegios Regionales. San Juan.

Poblac. Soc. Población y Sociedad. Fundación Yocavil. Tucumán, Argentina.

Poetics Today. Poetics Today. Duke Univ. Press. Durham, N.C.

Point Contact. Point of Contact. Punto de Contacto/Point of Contact, Inc. Syracuse, NY.

Polit. Sci. Q. Political Science Quarterly. The Academy of Political Science. New York.

Polit. Soc./Marxism. Politics & Society. Sage Publications, Inc. Thousand Oaks, Calif.

Política/Santiago. Política. Univ. de Chile, Instituto de Ciencia Política. Santiago.

Pop. Music. Popular Music. Cambridge Univ. Press. England.

Presença Filos. Presença Filosófica. Sociedade Brasileira de Filósofos Católicos. Rio de Janeiro.

Procesos/Quito. Procesos. Corporación Editora Nacional. Quito.

Pumapunku/La Paz. Pumapunku. Centro de Investigaciones Antropológicas Tiwanaku. La Paz.

Quinto Cent. Quinto Centenario. Univ. Complutense de Madrid, Facultad de Geografía e Historia, Depto. de Historia de América I. Madrid.

Quitumbe/Quito. Quitumbe. Pontificia Univ. Católica del Ecuador, Facultad de Pedagogía, Depto. de Historia. Quito.

Rábida/Huelva. Rábida. Patronato Provincial del V Centenario del Descubrimiento de América. Huelva, Spain.

Razón Fe. Razón y Fe. La Compañía de Jesús. Madrid.

Reflejos/Jerusalem. Reflejos. Hebrew Univ., Facultad de Humanidades, Depto. de Estudios Españoles y Latinoamericanos. Jerusalem.

Reflexão/Campinas. Reflexão. Instituto de Filosofia, Pontifícia Univ. Católica de Campinas. Campinas, Brazil.

Relaciones/Zamora. Relaciones. El Colegio de Michoacán. Zamora, Mexico.

Res Gesta. Res Gesta. Univ. Católica Argentina, Facultad de Derecho y Ciencias Sociales, Instituto de Historia. Rosario, Argentina.

Rev. Agust. Revista Agustiniana. American Theological Library Assn. Madrid.

Rev. Andin. Revista Andina. Centro Bartolomé de las Casas. Cuzco, Peru.

Rev. Arch. Arzobispal Arequipa. Revista Archivo Arzobispal de Arequipa. Arequipa, Peru.

Rev. Arch. Gen. Nac. Revista del Archivo General de la Nación. Ministerio de Justicia, Instituto Nacional de Cultura. Lima.

Rev. Arch. Nac. Hist. Azuay. Revista del Archivo Nacional de Historia, Sección del

Azuay. Casa de la Cultura Ecuatoriana, Núcleo del Azuay. Cuenca, Ecuador.

Rev. Bras. Estud. Popul. Revista Brasileira de Estudos de População. Associação Brasileira de Estudos Populacionais. São Paulo.

Rev. Bras. Filos. Revista Brasileira de Filosofia. Instituto Brasileiro de Filosofia. São Paulo.

Rev. Bras. Hist. Revista Brasileira de História. Associação Nacional de História. São Paulo.

Rev. Centroam. Econ. Revista Centroamericana de Economía. Univ. Nacional Autónoma de Honduras, Programa de Postgrado Centroamericano en Economía y Planificación del Desarrollo. Tegucigalpa.

Rev. Chil. Hist. Geogr. Revista Chilena de Historia y Geografía. Sociedad Chilena de Historia y Geografía. Santiago.

Rev. Chil. Lit. Revista Chilena de Literatura. Univ. de Chile, Facultad de Filosofía y Humanidades, Depto. de Literatura. Santiago.

Rev. Ciênc. Hist. Revista de Ciências Históricas. Univ. Portucalense. Porto, Portugal.

Rev. Cienc. Hum./Pereira. Revista de Ciencias Humanas. Univ. Tecnológica de Pereira. Pereira, Colombia.

Rev. Cienc. Soc./Río Piedras. Revista de Ciencias Sociales. Univ. de Puerto Rico, Recinto de Río Piedras, Facultad de Ciencias Sociales, Centro de Investigaciones Sociales. Río Piedras, Puerto Rico.

Rev. Cienc. Soc./Valparaíso. Revista de Ciencias Sociales. Facultad de Derecho y Ciencias Sociales, Univ. de Valparaíso. Valparaíso, Chile.

Rev. Colomb. Antropol. Revista Colombiana de Antropología. Ministerio de Educación Nacional, Instituto Colombiano de Antropología. Bogotá.

Rev. Complut. Hist. Am. Revista Complutense de Historia de América. Depto. de

Historia de América I, Facultad de Geografía e Historia, Univ. Complutense de Madrid. Madrid.

Rev. Crít. Lit. Latinoam. Revista de Crítica Literaria Latinoamericana. Latinoamericana Editores. Lima.

Rev. Cuba. Cienc. Soc. Revista Cubana de Ciencias Sociales. Centro de Estudios Filosóficos, Academia de Ciencias de Cuba. La Habana.

Rev. Econ./Córdoba. Revista de Economía. Banco de la Provincia de Córdoba. Córdoba, Argentina.

Rev. Ecuat. Hist. Econ. Revista Ecuatoriana de Historia Económica. Banco Central del Ecuador, Centro de Investigación y Cultura. Quito.

Rev. Esp. Antropol. Am. Revista Española de Antropología Americana. Depto. de Historia de América II (Antropología de América), Facultad de Geografia e Historia, Univ. Complutense de Madrid. Madrid.

Rev. Estud. Hist. Juríd. Revista de Estudios Histórico-Jurídicos. Escuela de Derecho, Facultad de Ciencias Jurídicas y Sociales, Univ. Católica de Valparaíso. Valparaíso, Chile.

Rev. Estud. Polít. Revista de Estudios Políticos. Centro de Estudios Constitucionales. Madrid.

Rev. Eur. Revista Europea de Estudios Latinoamericanos y del Caribe = European Review of Latin American and Caribbean Studies. Center for Latin American Research and Documentation = Centro de Estudios y Documentación Latinoamericanos. Amsterdam; Royal Institute of Linguistics and Anthropology, Dept. of Caribbean Studies. Leiden, The Netherlands.

Rev. Filos. Bras. Revista Filosófica Brasileira. Univ. Federal do Rio de Janeiro, Depto. de Filosofía. Rio de Janeiro, Brazil.

Rev. Filos. Latinoam. Cienc. Soc. Revista de Filosofía Latinoamericano y Ciencias Sociales. Asociación de Filosofía Latinoamericana y Ciencias Sociales. Buenos Aires.

Rev. Filos./México. Revista de Filosofía. Univ. Iberoamericana, Depto. de Filosofía. México.

Rev. Filos./Santiago. Revista de Filosofía. Depto. de Filosofía y Humanidades, Univ. de Chile. Santiago.

Rev. Filos. Univ. Costa Rica. Revista de Filosofía de la Universidad de Costa Rica. Editorial de la Univ. de Costa Rica. San José.

Rev. fr. hist. Outre-mer. Revue française d'histoire d'Outre-mer. Société française d'histoire d'Outre-mer. Paris.

Rev. Hist. Am. Revista de Historia de América. Comisión de Historia, Instituto Panamericano de Geografía e Historia. México.

Rev. Hist. Am. Argent. Revista de Historia Americana y Argentina. Univ. Nacional de Cuyo, Instituto de Historia. Mendoza, Argentina.

Rev. Hist./Concepción. Revista de Historia. Depto. de Ciencias Históricas y Sociales, Univ. de Concepción, Chile.

Rev. Hist. Contemp. Revista de Historia Contemporánea. Univ. de Sevilla, Depto. de Historia Contemporánea, Facultad de Geografía e Historia. Sevilla, Spain.

Rev. Hist. Derecho. Revista de Historia del Derecho. Instituto de Investigaciones Históricas del Derecho. Buenos Aires.

Rev. Hist. Derecho Ricardo Levene. Revista de Historia del Derecho Ricardo Levene. Univ. de Buenos Aires, Facultad de Derecho y Ciencias Sociales; Instituto de Investigaciones Jurídicas y Sociales Ambrosio L. Gioja. Buenos Aires.

Rev. Hist./Heredia. Revista de Historia. Escuela de Historia, Univ. Nacional. Heredia, Costa Rica; Centro de Investigaciones Históricas de América Central, Univ. de Costa Rica. San José.

Rev. Hist./Managua. Revista de Historia. Univ. Centroamericana, Instituto de Historia de Nicaragua y Centroamérica. Managua.

Rev. Hist./Montevideo. Revista Histórica. Museo Histórico Nacional. Montevideo.

Rev. Hist. Naval. Revista de Historia Naval. Instituto de Historia y Cultura Naval Armada Española. Madrid.

Rev. Hist./Neuquén. Revista de Historia. Univ. Nacional de Comahue, Facultad de Humanidades, Depto. de Historia. Neuquén, Argentina.

Rev. Hist./São Paulo. Revista de História. Univ. de São Paulo, Faculdade de Filosofia, Letras e Ciências Humanas, Depto. de História. São Paulo.

Rev. Hist. Univ. Revista de Historia Universal. Univ. Nacional de Cuyo, Facultad de Filosofía y Letras. Mendoza, Argentina.

Rev. Humanid./Santiago. Revista de Humanidades. Univ. Nacional Andrés Bello. Santiago.

Rev. Iberoam. Revista Iberoamericana. Instituto Internacional de Literatura Iberoamericana; Univ. de Pittsburgh. Pittsburgh, Pa.

Rev. IDIS. Revista IDIS. Univ. de Cuenca, Instituto de Investigaciones Sociales. Ecuador.

Rev. Indias. Revista de Indias. Consejo Superior de Investigaciones Científicas, Instituto de Historia, Depto. de Historia de América. Madrid.

Rev. Inst. Estud. Geneal. Uruguay. Revista del Instituto de Estudios Genealógicos del Uruguay. Instituto de Estudios Genealógicos del Uruguay. Montevideo.

Rev. Inst. Hist. Ecles. Ecuat. Revista del Instituto de Historia Eclesiástica Ecuatoriana. Instituto de Historia Eclesiástica Ecuatoriana. Quito.

Rev. Inst. Hist. Geogr. Bras. Revista do Instituto Histórico e Geográfico Brasileiro. Instituto Histórico e Geográfico Brasileiro. Rio de Janeiro.

Rev. Inst. Hist. Geogr. São Paulo. Revista do Instituto Histórico e Geográfico de São Paulo. São Paulo.

Rev. Interam. Bibliogr. Revista Interamericana de Bibliografía = Review of Inter-American Bibliography. Organization of American States. Washington.

Rev. Junta Prov. Estud. Hist. Santa Fe. Revista de la Junta Provincial de Estudios Históricos de Santa Fe. Santa Fe, Argentina.

Rev. Lat. Pensam. Leng. Revista Latina de Pensamiento y Lenguaje = Revue latine sur la pensée et le langage. Sociedad Iberoamericana de Pensamiento y Lenguaje. México.

Rev. Mex. Polít. Exter. Revista Mexicana de Política Exterior. Coordinación General, Instituto Matías Romero de Estudios Diplomáticos, Secretaría de Relaciones Exteriores. México.

Rev. Mus. Arqueol. Etnol. Revista do Museu de Arqueologia e Etnologia. Univ. de São Paulo, Museu de Arqueologia e Etnologia. São Paulo.

Rev. Mus. Nac. Etnogr. Folk. Revista del Museo Nacional de Etnografía y Folklore. MUSEF Editores. La Paz.

Rev. Music. Chil. Revista Musical Chilena. Univ. de Chile, Facultad de Artes, Sección de Musicología. Santiago.

Rev. Músic./São Paulo. Revista Música. Univ. de São Paulo, Depto. de Música. São Paulo.

Rev. Music. Venez. Revista Musical de Venezuela. Consejo Nacional de la Cultura, Fundación Emilio Sojo. Caracas.

Rev. Nac. Cult./Caracas. Revista Nacional de Cultura. Consejo Nacional de Cultura; La Casa de Bello. Caracas.

Rev. Occident. Revista de Occidente. Madrid.

Rev. Patrim. Hist. Artíst. Nac. Revista do Patrimônio Histórico e Artístico Nacional. Ministério da Cultura, Secretaria do Livro e da Leitura, Instituto do Patrimônio Histórico e Artístico Nacional. Rio de Janeiro.

Rev. Pensam. Centroam. Revista del Pensamiento Centroamericano. Centro de

Investigaciones y Actividades Culturales. Managua; Asociación Libro Libre. San José.

Rev. Rev. Interam. Revista/Review Interamericana. Univ. Interamericana de Puerto Rico/Inter-American Univ. of Puerto Rico. San Germán, Puerto Rico.

Rev. SBPH. Revista da SBPH. Sociedade Brasileira de Pesquisa Histórica. Curitiba, Brazil.

Rev. Soc. haïti. Revue de la Société haïtienne d'histoire et de géographie. Société haïtienne d'histoire et de géographie. Port-au-Prince.

Rev. Univ. Medellín. Revista Universidad de Medellín. Univ. de Medellín, Colombia.

Rev. Univ./Panamá. Revista Universidad. Univ. de Panamá, Vicerrectoría de Extensión. Panamá.

Rev. USP. Revista USP. Univ. de São Paulo, Coordenadoria de Comunicação Social. São Paulo.

Review/Binghamton. Review. Binghamton Univ., Fernand Braudel Center. Binghamton, New York.

Runa/Buenos Aires. Runa. Archivo para las Ciencias del Hombre; Univ. de Buenos Aires, Facultad de Filosofía y Letras, Instituto de Antropología. Buenos Aires.

Saastun/Mérida. Saastun: Revista de Cultura Maya/Maya Culture Review. Univ. del Mayab, Instituto de Cultura Maya. Mérida, Mexico.

Scr. Theol. Scripta Theologica. Univ. de Navarra, Facultad de Teología. Pamplona, Spain.

SECOLAS Ann. SECOLAS Annals: Journal of the Southeastern Council on Latin American. Southeastern Conference on Latin American Studies; Georgia Southern Univ., Statesboro, Ga.

Secuencia/México. Secuencia: Revista de Historia y Ciencias Sociales. Instituto Mora. México.

Sefárdica/Buenos Aires. Sefárdica. Centro de Investigación y Difusión de la Cultura Sefardí. Buenos Aires.

Serie Cient. Serie Científica. Instituto Antártico Chileno. Santiago.

Siglo XIX/Monterrey. Siglo XIX. Univ. Autónoma de Nuevo León, Facultad de Filosofía y Letras. Monterrey, Mexico.

Síntese/Belo Horizonte. Síntese: Revista de Filosofia. Companhia de Jesus, Centro de Estudios Superiores, Faculdade de Filosofia. Belo Horizonte, Brazil.

Síntesis/Madrid. SÍNTESIS. Asociación de Investigación y Especialización sobre Temas Latinoamericanos; Sociedad Editorial SÍNTESIS. Madrid.

Slavery Abolit. Slavery and Abolition. Frank Cass & Co. Ltd. London.

Soc. Compass. Social Compass: Revue Internationale de Sociologie de la Religion (International Review of Sociology of Religion). Sage Publications, Inc. Thousand Oaks, Calif.

Soc. Econ. Stud. Social and Economic Studies. Institute of Social and Economic Research, Univ. of the West Indies. Mona, Jamaica.

Social. Particip. Socialismo y Participación. Centro de Estudios para el Desarrollo y Participación. Lima.

Sociol. Anal. SA: Sociological Analysis. Assn. for the Sociology of Religion. Holiday, Fla.

South Atl. Q. The South Atlantic Quarterly. Duke Univ. Press. Durham, N.C.

Stromata/San Miguel. Stromata. Univ. del Salvador, Filosofía y Teología. San Miguel, Argentina.

Stud. Hist. Hist. Contemp. Studia Histórica: Historia Contemporánea. Ediciones Univ. de Salamanca. Spain.

Stud. Lat. Am. Pop. Cult. Studies in Latin American Popular Culture. Univ. of Arizona, College of Humanities. Tucson, Ariz.

Stud. Rosenthaliana. Studia Rosenthaliana. Amsterdam Univ. Press. Amsterdam, The Netherlands.

Studia/Córdoba. Studia. La Cátedra de Historia del Pensamiento y La Cultura Argentinos. Córdoba, Argentina.

Taller/Buenos Aires. Taller: Revista de Sociedad, Cultura y Política. Asociación de Estudios de Cultura y Sociedad. Buenos Aires.

Tareas/Panamá. Tareas. Centro de Estudios Latinoamericanos. Panamá.

Temas Am. Temas Americanistas. Univ. de Sevilla, Servicio de Publicaciones. Sevilla, Spain.

Temas/Habana. Temas: Cultura, Ideología, Sociedad. Instituto Cubano del Libro. La Habana; Univ. of New Mexico, Latin American Institute, Cuban Project. Albuquerque, N.M.

Textos Hist./Brasília. Textos de História. Univ. de Brasília, Pós-Graduação em História. Brasília.

Tierra Firme. Tierra Firme. Editorial Tierra Firme. Caracas.

Todo es Hist. Todo es Historia. Buenos Aires.

Torre/Río Piedras. La Torre. Univ. de Puerto Rico. Río Piedras, Puerto Rico.

TRACE/México. TRACE. Centre d'études mexicaines et centraméricaines. México.

Tulsa Stud. Women's Lit. Tulsa Studies in Women's Literature. Univ. of Tulsa. Tulsa, Okla.

Universidad/San Salvador. La Universidad. Univ. de El Salvador. San Salvador.

Universum/Talca. Universum. Univ. de Talca. Talca, Chile.

Varia Hist. Varia História. Univ. Federal de Minas Gerais, Faculdade de Filosofia e Ciências Humanas, Depto. de História. Belo Horizonte, Brazil.

Wani/Managua. Wani: Una Revista sobre la Costa Atlántica. Centro Investigaciones y Documentación de la Costa Atlántica. Managua.

West. Hist. Q. The Western Historical Quarterly. Western History Assn.; Utah State Univ., Logan, Utah.

World Dev. World Development. Elsevier Science Ltd. (Pergamon Press). Oxford, England.

Yachay/Cochabamba. Yachay. Univ. Católica Boliviana, Deptos. de Filosofía y Letras y Ciencias Religiosas. Cochabamba, Bolivia.

Yaxkin/Tegucigalpa. Yaxkin. Instituto Hondureño de Antropología e Historia. Tegucigalpa.

Yearb. Tradit. Music. Yearbook for Traditional Music. International Council for Traditional Music. New York.

Yearbook/CLAG. Yearbook. Conference of Latin Americanist Geographers; Univ. of Texas Press. Austin, Tex.

SUBJECT INDEX

Aberastury, Gabriela, 262.

Abolition (slavery). Argentina, 3007. Brazil, 3232, 3296, 3304, 3324, 3345. British, 1980. British Caribbean, 1980, 1989. Capitalism, 1880. Caribbean Area, 2023. Cuba, 2002, 2026. Drama, 4537. Dutch Caribbean, 1880. France, 2023–2025, 2028. French Caribbean, 2023. Haiti, 1881. Jamaica, 1980. Martinique, 1973. Montserrat, 1942. Newspapers, 1989. Puerto Rico, 5119. Social Classes, 2026. Suriname, 1776, 1802, 1981, 1988. US, 3232.

Abstract Art. Andean Region, 697. Argentina, 284, 286, 289. Brazil, 428. Costa Rica, 229. Ecuador, 341. Inca Influences, 697.

Academia Brasileira de Letras, 4.

Academia Nacional de la Historia (Argentina), 2936.

Acción Democrática (Venezuela), 2506, 2545, 2554.

Acculturation. Argentina, 3047. Aztecs, 551. Barbados, 4788. Brazil, 3162. Costa Rica, 1736. Guatemala, 1736. History, 802. Incas, 551. Mexico, 464, 1257. Uruguay, 702.

Actors. Mexico, 5.

Adolescents. *See* Youth.

Adopte una Obra de Arte (program), 25.

Advertising. Venezuela, 2544.

African Influences, 796. Art, 442. Bolivia, 4813. Brazil, 442, 3216. Caribbean Area, 4783–4784. Central America, 1615. Costa Rica, 1686. Cuba, 259, 4808, 4810. Folk Music, 4810. Haiti, 1927. Mexico, 4744, 4750. Musical History, 4791, 4869. Musical Instruments, 4813. Musicology, 4744. National Characteristics, 4872. Popular Music, 4764, 4808. Saint-Domingue, 1927. Slaves and Slavery, 1897, 1910. Suriname, 4791. Uruguay, 4869, 4872. Villancicos, 4796. Virgin Islands, 4789.

Africans. Bahamas, 1822. Central America, 1615. Cultural History, 796. Political Ideology, 1927. Return Migration, 1011. Suriname, 1924.

Afro-Americans. *See* Africans; Blacks.

Aged. Nueva Granada, 2180.

Agosín, Marjorie, 4664–4665.

Agrarian Reform. *See* Land Reform.

Agricultural Colonies. Panama, 1689. Uruguay, 3117.

Agricultural Colonization. Argentina, 2966. Mexico, 1282, 1293.

Agricultural Credit. Argentina, 2885.

Agricultural Development. Argentina, 2810, 3044–3045. Chile, 2768. Cuba, 1856. Dominican Republic, 2093. Mexico, 580. Panama, 1655. Venezuela, 2150, 2539.

Agricultural Ecology. Barbados, 1969. Colonial History, 2282.

Agricultural Geography. Guadeloupe, 1896. Mexico, 1277.

Agricultural History. Venezuela, 2556.

Agricultural Industries. Uruguay, 3119.

Agricultural Labor, 1455. Argentina, 2901, 3059. Brazil, 3344, 3344, 4714. Costa Rica, 1687. Cuba, 2007. East Indians, 1990. Guyana, 1990. Mexico, 1277, 1340. Nicaragua, 1760. Nueva Granada, 2181. Pictorial Works, 4714. Slaves and Slavery, 2901. Viceroyalty of Río de la Plata, 2458.

Agricultural Policy. Argentina, 3033. Dominican Republic, 2093. Mexico, 1446.

Agricultural Productivity. Andean Region, 630. Chile, 2768. Mexico, 1179.

Agricultural Systems. Bermuda, 1872. Cuba, 1856.

Agricultural Technology. Argentina, 3044. Peru, 2650.

Agriculture. Argentina, 2807, 2902. Brazil, 728. Costa Rica, 1741. European Influences, 630. Indigenous Peoples, 728. Nicaragua, 1748. Peru, 2696. Venezuela, 2539.

Agroindustry. *See* Agricultural Industries.

Aguado, Pedro de, 2141.

Aguaruna (indigenous group), 708.

Aguascalientes, Mexico (city). Archives, 1376. Art Exhibitions, 200.

Aguascalientes, Mexico (state). Archives,

934. Indigenous Peoples/Portuguese, 3162. Indigenous Peoples/Spaniards, 924, 935, 1086, 4998. Latin America/Europe, 5034, 5059. Latin America/Spain, 831, 5003. Latin America/Sweden, 803. Maroons/Dutch, 1926. Nahuas/Spaniards, 4997.

Cultural Destruction, 5006. California, 1232. Indigenous Peoples, 808. Mexico, 1238.

Cultural Development, 763, 822, 4912, 4916, 4928, 4974, 4976. Cuba, 1853. Indigenous Influences, 5188. Literary Criticism, 4950. Mayas, 490. Modernization, 5005. Paraguay, 5235. Peru, 5188, 5191. Philosophy, 5055. Social Life and Customs, 5007. Social Structure, 5007. Spanish Influences, 5016.

Cultural Geography, 4997, 5062. Uruguay, 5241.

Cultural History, 773, 822, 2865, 4998. Argentina, 9, 2865, 5252, 5285. Catholicism, 5009. Costa Rica, 1729. Cuba, 1853. Historiography, 5025. Mexico, 1045, 1302, 1480, 1568. Nicaragua, 1622. Peru, 712, 2679, 2687, 2701. Puerto Rico, 1814. Spanish Influences, 5009, 5050. Suriname, 1795, 1988, 2103. The Netherlands, 1988. Uruguay, 3076.

Cultural Identity, 4916, 4974, 5037, 5059, 5063, 5134, 5245. Andean Region, 676. Argentina, 5281, 5287. Bolivia, 4814. Brazil, 454–455, 3323, 4889. Chile, 2403. Christianity, 5023. Collective Memory, 234. Cuba, 252, 5143. Dominican Republic, 5124. East Indians, 2031, 2098. Economic Development, 4929, 4931, 4986, 5006. Ecuador, 5165. Essays, 5008. Guyana, 2005. Honduras, 5108. Indigenous Peoples, 615, 659, 742. Jamaica, 5116. Liberation Theology, 5048. Mestizos and Mestizaje, 5146. Mexico, 1175, 1281, 1302, 1566, 5069, 5077, 5083. Modernization, 4928, 4931, 4944, 5016. Nahuas, 569. Peru, 2329, 2679, 5191. Philosophy, 4991, 5108. Political Philosophy, 4936. Popular Music, 4814. Post-Modernism, 5020. Precolumbian Civilizations, 643. Puerto Ricans, 4722, 4724. Puerto Rico, 2070, 2086, 4551. Technological Development, 4920. Trinidad and Tobago, 2098. Uruguay, 2440.

Cultural Policy, 4976. Brazil, 3274. Mexico, 1302. Nicaragua, 1622.

Cultural Property. Brazil, 435. Conservation and Restoration, 49. Mexico, 34–35.

Cultural Relations, 5060. Argentina/Chile, 2812. Argentina/Spain, 2822. Latin America/Europe, 5028, 5064. Latin America/Spain, 5050, 5062–5063. Mexico/Catalonia, 126.

Cumbaza, Peru (city). Colonial History, 2270.

Cuna (indigenous group), 736. Government, Resistance to, 1710. Land Tenure, 1710.

Cundinamarca, Colombia (dept.). Local History, 2583.

Currency. See Money Supply.

Customs. Chile, 2799. Law and Legislation, 3104. Uruguay, 3104.

Cuyo, Argentina (region). Historical Geography, 2465. History, 685. Maps and Cartography, 2465. Pictorial Works, 2465.

Cusco. See Cuzco.

Cuzco, Peru (city). Art Collections, 350. Colonial Art, 75. Colonial Painting, 93. Local History, 2692. Museums, 350. Religious Art, 120, 2288. Religious Life and Customs, 2279.

Cuzco, Peru (dept.). Ethnohistory, 619.

Damiani, Jorge, 360.

Dance. Argentina, 4844, 4851. Brazil, 3251, 4877. California, 4758. Caribbean Area, 4784. Guatemala, 4793. Indigenous Peoples, 629, 4829, 4848. Mexico, 4757, 4771. Peru, 4829.

Darío, Rubén, 3548.

de Angelis, Pedro, 3064.

de Gálvez, José, 1263.

De la Torre, Michael, 2191.

De l'esprit des loix, 5015.

De Loayza, Rodrigo, 623.

De Medina, Diego, 117.

De Olmos, Andrés, 568.

de Pineda, Juan Claudio, 1261.

De Salinas, Juan, 2234.

de Zorita, Alonso, 1119.

Death. Indigenous Peoples, 523. Mexico, 466, 523, 1164. Nahuas, 573. Precolumbian Civilizations, 692. Viceroyalty of Peru, 692.

Debien, Gabriel, 1820.

Debt. See Debt Crisis; Debt Relief; External Debt; Public Debt.

Debt Crisis. Women, 1034.

Decolonization. Historiography, 5011. Liberalism, 5011. Suriname, 2102.

Decorative Arts. Mexico, 55–57. Venezuela, 83.

Deforestation. Bolivia, 2740. Cuba, 2010. Guadeloupe, 1896.

Deities. Aztecs, 597. Mayas, 547.

Delgrès, Louis, 1808.

Democracy, 5004, 5051. Central America, 1703. Costa Rica, 1688, 1693, 1703, 1725. Essays, 5024. Historiography, 5024. Mexico, 1336.

Democratization, 1027, 4933. Costa Rica, 1693. Dominican Republic, 2051. Peru, 2673, 2693. Uruguay, 3130. Venezuela, 2506, 2509.

Demography. Agricultural Development, 2981. Argentina, 3009–3010. Bolivia, 2721. Brazil, 3139. Colonial History, 906. Ecuador, 2615. El Salvador, 1639. Indigenous Peoples, 1639. Precolumbian Civilizations, 745, 1639.

Dependency, 777. Brazil, 5227.

Deportation, French. French Guiana, 1868.

Deportation, Guadeloupean. Corsica, 1865.

Deportation, Haitian. Corsica, 1865.

Descripción geográfica del Río de la Plata, 1768–1776, 2493.

Desaparecidos. *See* Disappeared Persons.

Description and Travel. Andean Region, 713, 2624. Antigua and Barbuda, 1858. Brazil, 401, 403–404, 3157, 3226, 3297. Colombia, 729, 2603. Colonial History, 879. Costa Rica, 1731. Cuba, 1974. Ecuador, 2624, 2634. Europeans, 4855. Guatemala, 1724. Martinique, 1941. Mexico, 31, 1176, 1191, 1191, 1248, 1289. Nicaragua, 4681. Nueva Granada, 2179. Panama, 1659. Pictorial Works, 800. Puerto Rico, 1995. Saint-Domingue, 1928.

Description Geographique et Statistique de la Confédération Argentine: 1860–1864, 3026.

Dessalles, Pierre, 1964.

Development. Costa Rica, 1612.

Diaguita (indigenous group). Insurrections, 2491.

Díaz, Porfirio, 1276, 1278, 1295, 1311, 1322, 1335.

Dictators. Guatemala, 1718. Nicaragua, 1700. Paraguay, 3086.

Dictatorships. Central America, 1703. Costa Rica, 1703. Guatemala, 1718, 1742.

Dictionaries. Composers, 4774. Cuba, 4809. Honduras, 1637. Indigenous Peoples, 503. Music, 4734, 4809. Theater, 4533.

Dieties. Mexico, 547.

Díez de la Peña, Manuel, 2251.

Diplomatic History, 1018, 2104. Argentina, 2925, 3073. Brazil, 3194, 3244, 3279. Central America, 1706. Chile, 2762. Costa Rica, 1706, 1751. Germany, 1017. Guatemala, 1706. Mexico, 1020, 1273,

1296, 1382, 1394, 1402, 1474, 1500, 1562, 1583, 1592–1593. Paraguay, 3088, 3097. Peru, 2642, 2646, 2653, 2671, 2707. Spain, 1006, 1298. US, 2762. Venezuela, 2526, 2541.

Diplomats. Biography, 4897. Brazil, 4897. Mexico, 1469, 1488. US, 1706.

Dirty War (Argentina, 1976–1983), 298. Naval History, 3069.

Disappeared Persons. Argentina, 3069, 4678. Chile, 4665. Mexico, 3482. Uruguay, 3129.

Discourse Analysis. Argentina, 2975.

Discovery and Exploration, 4963. Amazon Basin, 2229. Argentina, 2460, 2849, 3026. Barbados, 1836. Bibliography, 950. Brazil, 3162, 3165, 3196, 3204, 3221. British, 856. Central America, 1631. Chile, 2398. Colombia, 642. Dutch, 1859. Ecuador, 2205. French, 758. French Caribbean, 1832. Historians, 857. Historiography, 857, 913. Intellectual History, 835. International Relations, 873. Law and Legislation, 635. Mexico, 1220, 1222, 1234, 1255. Peru, 636, 2349, 2398. Pictorial Works, 800. Puerto Rico, 1861. Sources, 1234. US, 1931, 1933. Venezuela, 2132, 2142.

Discurso desde la marginación y la barbarie, 5081.

Diseases. Bolivia, 2738. Brazil, 3249, 3310. Caribbean Area, 1854. Mexico, 1087. New Mexico, 1260. Slaves and Slavery, 3330.

Distribution of Wealth. *See* Income Distribution.

Distrito Federal, Brazil. Colonization, 3136. Historical Geography, 3136. Land Settlement, 3136.

Divisão de Ordem Política e Social—DOPS (Brazil), 3231.

Divorce. Venezuela, 2147.

Documentation Centers. *See* Libraries.

Dogma socialista, 5264.

Domestic Violence. *See* Family Violence.

Dominicans (religious order), 765. Chile, 5200. Colonial Painting, 111. History, 797. Mexico, 49, 546, 563, 1126, 1187, 1237, 1247, 1253. Peru, 115.

Don Segundo Sombra, 4637.

Dorado, El. *See* El Dorado.

Dorado, Puerto Rico (town). History, 1778. Popular Culture, 1778.

Dowry. Mexico, 1138.

Drake, Francis, *Sir*, 1095.

Drama. Argentina, 4166, 4548. Brazil, 4534, 4547. Literary Criticism, 4541.

Dramatists. Argentina, 4166, 4548. Brazil, 4531. Women, 4568.
Dreyfus, Alfred, 1965.
Droughts. Mexico, 1054.
Drug Abuse. Mexico, 1331.
Drug Utilization. Indigenous Peoples, 675.
Drugs and Drug Trade. *See* Drug Abuse; Drug Utilization.
Duarte, Juan Pablo, 5132.
Duarte, León, 3126.
Duclos, Arturo, 308.
Dundonald, Thomas Cochrane, *Earl of*, 2795, 3337.
Durán, Diego, 493, 515, 602.
Durango, Mexico (state). Biography, 4763. Minerals and Mining Industry, 1544. Musicians, 4763. Popular Music, 4763.
Dussel, Enrique D, 4957, 5244.
Dutch. Araucanía Region (Chile), 681. Brazil, 3187, 3199, 3212. Discovery and Exploration, 1859.
Dutch Caribbean. Abolition (slavery), 1880. African Influences, 1816. Archives, 1833. Bibliography, 1783. Commerce, 1845, 1852. Cults, 1816. Cultural History, 1789, 1812, 1817. Cultural Identity, 1812. Genealogy, 1833. Historiography, 2044. History, 2105. Human Geography, 1905. International Trade, 1855. Jews, 799. Literature, 1817. Maritime History, 1855. Moravians, 1897, 1905, 1910. Physical Anthropology, 1905. Political History, 1789. Religious Life and Customs, 1816. Repression, 1816. Slaves and Slavery, 1784–1785, 1792, 1827, 1852, 1897, 1905, 1910. Social History, 1833. Sources, 1833.
Dye and Dyeing. Guatemala, 1749. Mexico, 1117.
East Indians. Agricultural Labor, 1990. Caribbean Area, 1826. Cultural Identity, 2031, 2098. Guyana, 1990. Jamaica, 2031. Religious Life and Customs, 1826. Suriname, 2078. Trinidad and Tobago, 1775, 2006, 2089, 2098.
Echave Ibía, Baltasar, 51.
Echeverría, Esteban, 2937, 5264, 5267.
Ecology. Brazil, 5214.
Economic Assistance, US. Colombia, 2604. Puerto Rico, 2079.
Economic Conditions, 7. Argentina, 3010. Guatemala, 1696. Incas, 740–741. Indigenous Peoples, 1172. Mexico, 1106, 1133, 1176. Saint-Domingue, 1928. Uruguay, 3113.
Economic Development. Argentina, 2826,

2836, 2914. Brazil, 3156, 3246, 3257. Chile, 2785. Colombia, 2597. Colonial History, 887. Cultural Identity, 4929, 4931, 4986, 5006. Guatemala, 1718, 1766. Mexico, 1055, 1314, 1365, 1413, 1438, 1465, 1487, 1499. Paraguay, 3101. Peru, 2645, 2662. Puerto Rico, 2079. Textiles and Textile Industry, 2785. Uruguay, 3119.
Economic Forecasting, 11.
Economic Growth. Railroads, 1357.
Economic History, 11, 773, 793, 985. Argentina, 2835. Bahamas, 1800. Barbados, 1844, 2046. Bermuda, 1906. Bibliography, 1165. Bolivia, 2387, 2719–2720, 2737, 2741. Brazil, 3139, 3148, 3190, 3253–3254. British Caribbean, 1773. Central America, 1604, 1706. Chile, 2410, 2755, 2760, 2762, 2788, 2794, 2797. Colombia, 2588. Costa Rica, 1667, 1706. Cuba, 1856, 1863, 2082. Dominican Republic, 2093. Ecuador, 2241, 2613, 2615, 2618. Gender Relations, 1034. Guadeloupe, 1803, 1945, 2027. Guatemala, 1628, 1706, 1766. Guyana, 2054. Historiography, 777, 812. Honduras, 1602. Jamaica, 1977. Mexico, 1395, 2835. Nicaragua, 1748. Peru, 2645, 2657, 2667, 2678, 2685, 2694, 2696. Venezuela, 2131, 2156.
Economic Indicators. Barbados, 1844. Chile, 2410, 2797. Colonial History, 2410.
Economic Integration. Honduras, 1756.
Economic Liberalization. Chile, 2756. Peru, 2654.
Economic Models. Andean Region, 690. Historiography, 812.
Economic Planning. *See* Economic Policy.
Economic Policy. Argentina, 3025. Chile, 2762, 2783, 2788. Colonial History, 993. El Salvador, 1761. Mexico, 1436.
Economic Theory, 754. Mexico, 1369.
Economists. Argentina, 2875.
Ecuador. Congresses, 14. Economic History, 2260. Historiography, 716. Peru, 2642, 2653. Social History, 2260.
Education. Argentina, 2878, 3066. Guatemala, 1633. Mexico, 1053, 1425, 1442, 1458, 1492, 1499, 1577. Women, 1633.
Education and State. *See* Educational Policy.
Educational Models. Jesuits, 3225. Philosophy, 4962. Uruguay, 3131.
Educational Policy. Argentina, 2821, 2877, 5257. Aymara, 2715. Barbados, 2046. Bolivia, 2715. Chile, 2770. Martinique, 1973. Mexico, 1458, 1499. Nationalism, 2035.

velopment, 580. Coffee Industry and Trade, 580. Indigenous Peoples, 496. Land Settlement, 496. Land Use, 496. Livestock, 580. Peasants, 580. Sugar Industry and Trade, 580.

Hugues, Victor, 1892.

Huila, Colombia (dept.). History, 2564.

Huilliche (indigenous group). Land Tenure, 632.

Human Ecology. Amazon Basin, 611. Slaves and Slavery, 1911. Suriname, 1911.

Human Rights, 5053. Argentina, 1. Chile, 4664. Guatemala, 1764. Haiti, 2061. Peru, 2682. Uruguay, 3129.

Humanism, 5057. Colombia, 5158.

Humboldt, Alexander von, 4963, 4987.

Humor. Art, 418. Brazil, 418.

Hunting. Antarctica, 723.

Hurtado, Angel, 391.

Hydroelectric Power. Brazil, 3277.

Ianelli, Arcangelo, 415.

Ibáñez del Campo, Carlos, 2761, 2783, 2788, 2794.

Ica, Peru. Political History, 2643.

Iconography. Andean Region, 643. Argentina, 74. Aztecs, 458, 570. Codices, 458. Colonial Art, 23. Colonial History, 21, 957. Incas, 663. Indigenous Peoples, 653. Mexico, 464, 544. Mixtec, 508. Nahuas, 544. Precolumbian Civilizations, 639. Zapotecs, 508.

Ideology. Mexico, 1463, 1521, 1593.

Ideology and political development: the growth and development of political ideas in the Caribbean, 1774–1983, 5126.

Illia, Arturo Umberto, 2972.

Illness. *See* Diseases.

Illustrators. Brazil, 407. Mexico, 148.

Imán, Santiago, 1345.

Immigration. *See* Migration.

Immigrants. Acculturation, 3234. Argentina, 2821. Brazil, 432. Education, 2821.

Imperialism, 1013. Nicaragua, 1701. US, 3297.

Imperio de los sueños, 4716.

Import Substitution. Mexico, 1487.

Imports and Exports. *See* International Trade.

Inca Conquest, 666.

Inca Influences. Abstract Art, 697. Colonial Art, 103. Peru, 2329, 2343.

Incas. Acculturation, 551. Astronomy, 620, 724. Boundary Disputes, 726. Communication, 735. Cronistas, 663. Demography, 2274. Economic Conditions, 619, 739–741. Ethnohistory, 613, 637, 730. Histori-

cal Geography, 726. History, 624, 660, 677, 721–722, 4670. Iconography, 663. Kings and Rulers, 733. Land Tenure, 739. Mathematics, 709. Music, 735. Myths and Mythology, 676, 724. Oral History, 624, 4670. Political Conditions, 619. Political Systems, 739. Precolumbian Art, 645. Precolumbian Trade, 669. Relations with Indigenous Peoples, 650. Relations with Spaniards, 656. Religion, 705. Religious Life and Customs, 677. Rites and Ceremonies, 677, 705. Social Conditions, 551, 619. Social Life and Customs, 103, 613. Sovereignty, 656. Spanish Conquest, 725. Symbolism, 645.

Income Distribution. Brazil, 3167. Colonial History, 3167.

Income Tax. Argentina, 2979.

Indentured Servants. Barbados, 1914.

Independence Movements, 997, 1001, 1005, 1016. Argentina, 5262. Blacks, 2149. Brazil, 3181, 3223, 3337. British Influences, 1009. Central America, 1608. Cuba, 1862, 1951, 2004, 2016. Dominican Republic, 1867. Encomiendas, 996. Enlightenment, 999. Freemasonry, 999-1000, 1002. Mexico, 1089. Military Policy, 2527. Panama, 1755. Peru, 2639, 2675. Protestantism, 999. Venezuela, 2149, 2527, 2531, 2549. Viceroyalty of Río de la Plata, 2476.

Indians. *See* East Indians; Indigenous Peoples; West Indians.

Indigenismo and Indianidad, 742. Nicaragua, 1701.

Indigenous Architecture. *See* Vernacular Architecture.

Indigenous Art. Ecuador, 339. Exhibitions, 16. Mexico, 38.

Indigenous Influences. Caribbean Area, 4783. Cultural Development, 5188. Europe, 835. Food, 861. Uruguay, 2450. Villancicos, 4796.

Indigenous Languages, 746, 774. Colombia, 679. Colonial History, 990. Mexico, 459, 600, 1338. Nahuas (indigenous group), 459.

Indigenous Literature, 530.

Indigenous Music. Andean Region, 4737. Argentina, 4854. Aztecs, 4779. Bolivia, 4813, 4815. Caingua Indians, 3080. Chile, 4866, 4868. Colonial History, 932. Festivals, 4866. Mapuche, 4868. Musical History, 4869. Peru, 4829–4830. Uruguay, 4869.

Indigenous Peoples, 659, 850. Acculturation, 1265, 3078, 3080. Agriculture, 666. Ama-

Lora, Guillermo, 2733.
Lorenzo Limaylla, Jerónimo, 2327.
Los Teques, Venezuela (town). Church Records, 2139. Colonial History, 2139.
Louisiana, US (state). Slaves and Slavery, 1930.
Lucas, Eugenio, 251.
Lucas, Juan Francisco, 1360.
Machaca, Jesús de, 2716.
Machado de Assis, 4.
Machismo. *See* Sex Roles.
Macunaíma, 4902.
Madero, Francisco, 1448, 1503.
Madero Family, 1368.
Madrazo, Carlos A, 1372.
Madres de Plaza de Mayo (Argentina), 4678, 5037.
Magaldi, Agustín, 4850.
Magallanes, Chile (prov.). Mortuary Customs, 683.
Magic Realism (art). Venezuela, 388.
Main currents in Caribbean thought: the historical evolution of Caribbean society in its ideological aspects, 1492–1900, 5126.
Maize. *See* Corn.
Málaga, Spain (city). Commerce, 890. Maritime History, 890.
Malaria. Bolivia, 2738. Migration, 1035.
Maldonado, Tomás, 276.
Malinche. *See* Marina.
Malvar Pinto, Sebastián, 2447.
Malnutrition. *See* Nutrition.
Malvinas. *See* Falkland Islands.
Mannerism (art). Mexico, 51.
Mansilla, Lucio Victorio, 4675.
Manso de Velasco, José Antonio, 963.
Manufactures. Mexico, 1174. Peru, 1174.
Manufacturing. *See* Manufactures.
Manuscripts, 550. Aztecs, 482, 507, 583, 589, 1635. Bolivia, 4821. Brazil, 3185. Chol, 533. Mexico, 457, 494, 532–533, 583, 590, 606. Mixtec, 480. Musical History, 4886. Nahuas, 485, 606. Precolumbian Civilizations, 457, 459. Religious Life and Customs, 456. Viceroyalty of New Spain, 456–457.
Manzanillo, Mexico (city). Political History, 1513.
Manzano, Juan Francisco, 4676.
Maoism. Peru, 2672.
Mapa de Cuauhtinchan núm. 3, 606.
Maps and Cartography, 800. Colonial History, 900. Indigenous Peoples, 649. Uruguay, 2432. Viceroyalty of Río de la Plata, 2432.

Mapuche (indigenous group), 742. Colonial History, 2401, 2405, 2411. Cultural Identity, 2403. Indigenous Music, 4868. Jesuits, 2403. Land Tenure, 621. Musical History, 4868. Musical Instruments, 4855. Relations with Spaniards, 671, 2401. Social Conditions, 671. Warfare, 2405.
Maracaibo, Venezuela (city). Colonial History, 2154. Commerce, 2154. Economic History, 2154. Merchants, 2154.
Maranhão, Brazil (state). Slaves and Slavery, 3230.
Marcos, Plínio, 4547.
Margil de Jesús, Antonio, 1218.
Mari Brás, Juan, 2081.
Mariátegui, José Carlos, 2677, 2698, 5171, 5174–5175, 5177–5179, 5181–5182, 5184, 5189–5190, 5192–5193.
Marimba. Cuba, 4739. Guatemala, 4739. Mayas, 4739. Mexico, 4739.
Marina, 1071, 1137.
Marine Resources. Antarctica, 723.
Maritime History, 776. Chile, 2795. Commerce, 2990. Costa Rica, 1716. Cuba, 2014. Great Britain, 856. Martinique, 1894. Mexico, 1136, 1220, 1256, 1290. Mortality, 1999. Slaves and Slavery, 853. Spain, 886, 903, 984, 1022, 1290, 2014. The Netherlands, 1784, 1795, 1855.
Maritime Law. History, 1290. Mexico, 1290. Spain, 1290.
Markets. Andean Region, 2342. Bolivia, 2370. Costa Rica, 1625. Indigenous Peoples, 1172. Mexico, 1082, 1129, 1151.
Marmolejo, Cirilo, 4752.
Maroons. Brazil, 3180, 3184. Cultural Identity, 2032. Guadeloupe, 2033. Political Culture, 1926. Slaves and Slavery, 2033. Social History, 2032. Suriname, 1795, 1926.
Márquez, Alberto, 3126.
Márquez, Roberto, 166.
Marranos. Brazil, 3138, 3183, 3213, 3217. Physicians, 3175.
Marriage. Brazil, 3155. Chile, 2412. Colonial History, 945, 973, 2341, 3155. Costa Rica, 1624. Law and Legislation, 945. Mexico, 26, 543, 1125, 1226. Mixtec, 508. Nahuas, 543. Nueva Granada, 2180. Saint-Domingue, 1893. Trinidad and Tobago, 1775. Venezuela, 2138, 2147. Zapotecs, 508.
Martí, Agustín Farabundo, 1676.
Martí, José, 1951, 1966, 4677, 4945, 5120–5122, 5128, 5144, 5148, 5245, 5255.

Parati, Brazil (town). Festivals, 3333. Religious Life and Customs, 3333.
Pardo, Mercedes, 387.
Parera, Blas, 4841.
Parks and Reserves. Argentina, 2809.
Parlamento Latinoamericano, 1038.
Parliamentary Systems. *See* Political Systems.
Parra Mata, Manuel, 1549.
Parras, Pedro José, 2451.
Parroquia de San Antonio del Mar (Chile), 2408.
Partido Aprista Peruano. *See* APRA (Peru).
Partido Autonomista Puertorriqueño, 1959.
Partido Blanco. *See* Partido Nacional (Uruguay).
Partido Católico Nacional, 1319.
Partido Colorado (Uruguay), 5243.
Partido Comunista de Costa Rica, 1725.
Partido Comunista de Cuba, 2050.
Partido Comunista de El Salvador, 1676.
Partido Comunista de la Argentina, 5263.
Partido Comunista Mexicano, 1494.
Partido Comunista Peruano, 5174.
Partido Demócrata-Cristiano (Chile), 2790.
Partido Liberal Mexicano, 1369, 1566.
Partido Nacional (Uruguay), 5243.
Partido Revolucionario Cubano, 1976, 2011.
Partido Revolucionario de los Trabajadores (Argentina), 2971, 3012.
Partido Revolucionario Institucional (Mexico), 1372.
Partido Vanguardia Popular (Costa Rica), 1725.
Pasto, Colombia (city). Colonial History, 2161–2162.
Pasto (indigenous group), 666, 731–732.
Patagonia (region). Expeditions, 3013. Food, 701. Indigenous Peoples, 665, 710. Migration, 665. Precolumbian Trade, 691. Subsistence Economy, 691, 701.
Patiño, Simón I., 2710.
Patterson, Percival James, 2048.
Paz, La. *See* La Paz, Bolivia.
Paz, Senel, 4562.
Peabody Museum of Archaeology and Ethnology, 526.
Pearce, Robert, 404.
Peasant Movements. History, 787. Mexico, 1374, 1423, 1439.
Peasant Uprisings. Andean Region, 612. Haiti, 1975. Mexico, 1292, 1345, 4671. Peru, 2663.
Peasants. Artisanry, 4816. Bolivia, 2780. Chile, 2778, 2780. Costa Rica, 1625. Dominican Republic, 2093. El Salvador, 1673. Guatemala, 1696, 1699. Land Tenure,

1258. Medicinal Plants, 625. Mexico, 1053, 1192, 1389, 1405, 1423. Peru, 2663, 2690, 2697, 2703. Saint-Domingue, 1883. Strikes and Lockouts, 2778. Traditional Medicine, 625. Venezuela, 2561. Wages, 1143.
Peddlers. *See* Informal Sector.
Pedrarias, 1631.
Peixoto, Fernando, 4545.
Pellegrini, Carlos, 2923.
Pellicer, Carlos, 4145.
Pelotas, Brazil (town). Popular Culture, 3302. Slaves and Slavery, 3302, 3330.
Pelourinho, Brazil (neighborhood). Conservation and Restoration, 439.
Peña Batlle, Manuel Arturo, 5124.
Penal Colonies. Costa Rica, 1735. French Guiana, 1965, 2063.
Pentecostalism, 3289. Brazil, 3252, 3289.
People's Progressive Party (Guyana), 2072.
Peralta, José, 2631, 5164.
Peralta Barnuevo, Pedro de, 2328.
Péralte, Charlemagne, 2084.
Pereira, Hortencia, 3126.
Pérez, Antonio, 555.
Pérez Calama, Joseph, 2214, 2237.
Pérez de Guevara, Juan, 2347.
Pérez Vila, Manuel, 2534, 2534.
Periodicals. Argentina, 2974. Haiti, 1790. Mexico, 5093.
Pernambuco, Brazil (state). Carnival, 4900–4901. Colonial Administration, 3160. Colonization, 3160. Dutch, 3187. Historiography, 3187. Pictorial Works, 3135. Revolutions and Revolutionary Movements, 3194. Theater, 4530.
Perón, Eva, 2816, 2879, 3005, 3814, 3832.
Perón, Juan Domingo, 2818, 2977.
Peronism, 5285. Argentina, 2834, 2879, 3018, 3056, 5261. Bibliography, 2817–2818. Catholic Church, 5248. Education, 2823, 5257.
Perrigny Family, 1882.
Personal Narrative. *See* Oral Tradition; Autobiography.
Peru. Archaeology, 712. Boundaries, 2642. Chile, 2657. Colonial History, 2122. Croatia, 2687. Cultural Identity, 2329. Discovery and Exploration, 636. Ecuador, 2642, 2653, 2709. History, 664, 712, 721. Japan, 2679. Minerals and Mining Industry, 767. Slaves and Slavery, 2705. Spain, 2671, 2686. Spanish Conquest, 868. United States, 2646. Women, 942.
Petroleos Mexicanos (PEMEX), 1431.
Petroleum Industry and Trade. Argentina,

2563, 2566–2567, 2572, 2580, 2582, 2586, 2593, 2595–2596, 2604–2605, 2608. Costa Rica, 1617, 1688, 1693, 1706, 1725–1726, 1734, 1767. Cuba, 6, 1853, 2040. Curaçao, 2090. Dominican Republic, 1867, 2051. Ecuador, 2202, 2239, 2612, 2629, 2631, 2636. El Salvador, 1680, 1690, 1714, 1721, 1732, 1761–1762. Guatemala, 1607, 1628, 1677, 1681, 1697, 1699, 1706–1707, 1713, 1717, 1738, 1742. Guyana, 2054, 2094. Haiti, 1975, 2068, 2096–2097. Honduras, 1691, 1694–1695, 1759, 1770. Martinique, 1811, 2091. Mexico, 534, 608, 1052, 1269–1270, 1295, 1355, 1372, 1427, 1540, 1671, 2111, 4671. Montserrat, 1786. Nicaragua, 1611, 1622, 1679, 1685, 1700–1701, 1708, 1715, 1723, 1763, 4666, 4681. Panama, 1740, 1755. Peru, 2111, 2667, 2674, 2680. Puerto Rico, 1814, 1835, 1953, 2064, 2081. Saint-Domingue, 1909. Spain, 855. Suriname, 1776. Trinidad and Tobago, 1864. Venezuela, 1488, 2137, 2506, 2514, 2525, 2537, 2552.

Political Ideology, 4940, 4968. Argentina, 2853, 3043, 5246. Bolivia, 2737. Brazil, 5205, 5227. Colombia, 2567, 2581, 2590. Costa Rica, 5106. Cuba, 5111. Ecuador, 2629. Mexico, 1081, 1304, 1505, 4756. Music, 4756. Peru, 5193. Political Left, 4934. Popular Music, 4873. Uruguay, 3118. Venezuela, 2507, 2537, 2553, 2555.

Political Institutions, 4912. Argentina, 2854, 2898, 3057. Brazil, 3261. Guyana, 1794. Historiography, 811. Peru, 2673.

Political Integration, 1038, 5035. Central America, 4977. History, 792.

Political Left, 4925, 4942. Argentina, 5261. Bolivia, 5194. Chile, 2781. Democratization, 4964. Ecuador, 2629. Folk Music, 4781. Mexico, 5070. Modernization, 5030. Political Ideology, 4934.

Political Opposition. *See* Opposition Groups.

Political Participation. Argentina, 2926. Aymara, 2714. Black Carib, 1720. Bolivia, 2714. Chile, 2790. Guyana, 2107. Honduras, 1720. Indigenous Peoples, 2714. Mexico, 1530. Women, 1033, 1530, 2107, 2790.

Political Parties, 5239. Argentina, 2850, 2947, 2998, 3015. Bolivia, 5194. Chile, 2761, 2777, 2784, 2788. Colombia, 2567. El Salvador, 1721. Guatemala, 1738. Guyana, 2072. Mexico, 1319, 1372, 1494. Peru, 2677, 2680, 5180. Uruguay, 3103, 3118,

3123, 5243. Venezuela, 2525, 2545, 2554–2555.

Political Persecution. Brazil, 3240. Chile, 4665. El Salvador, 1673. Guatemala, 1707. Haiti, 2061. Panama, 1689.

Political Philosophy, 5039, 5051, 5254. Argentina, 5278. Brazil, 5205, 5211, 5221, 5223, 5233–5234. Chile, 5198. Cuba, 5110, 5113, 5118, 5138. Cultural Identity, 4936. Dominican Republic, 5140. Ecuador, 5170. Historiography, 5025. Mexico, 5067. Panama, 5109. Peru, 5172, 5177. Puerto Rico, 5142. Venezuela, 5149, 5151.

Political Prisoners. Argentina, 4684. Peru, 4667.

Political Psychology. Puerto Rico, 1970.

Political Reform. Argentina, 2965, 3058. Mexico, 1404.

Political Sociology. Argentina, 3025. Brazil, 3307, 3323. Dominican Republic, 2051. Puerto Rico, 2086.

Political Stability. Argentina, 2898, 2951. Uruguay, 3123, 3133.

Political Systems. Andean Region, 644. Argentina, 2872. Colombia, 2593. Costa Rica, 1725. Incas, 739. Indigenous Peoples, 644. Paraguay, 3094. Peru, 2673.

Political Theater. Brazil, 4530, 4539.

Political Theory, 811. Argentina, 2925. Costa Rica, 1725.

Political Thought, 4925, 4933, 5058. Argentina, 5282, 5288. Caribbean Area, 5125. Colombia, 2578. Cuba, 5110. Dominican Republic, 5114, 5129. Enlightenment, 2919. Marxism, 4968, 4983. Mexico, 1280, 1286, 1336, 5080. Nicaragua, 1692, 5105. Peru, 5171, 5176–5177. Puerto Rico, 2081. Uruguay, 5243, 5273.

Politicians. Argentina, 2800, 2868, 2890. Brazil, 3244, 3256, 3259, 3264, 3279, 3286. Colombia, 2563, 5162. Ecuador, 2635. El Salvador, 1676. Guadeloupe, 2045. Guyana, 2094. Haiti, 2097. Martinique, 2091. Mexico, 1300, 1323, 1355, 1381, 1575. Peru, 3625.

Polverel, Etienne, 1916.

Ponce Vaides, Federico, 1717.

Poor. Mexico, 1081.

Popayán, Colombia (city). Colonial History, 2166–2167. Economic History, 2159.

Popoloca (indigenous group). Land Tenure, 541.

Popular Art. Mexico, 133.

Popular Culture. Argentina, 2915, 5273, 5281. Audiencia of Quito, 2227. Biogra-

phy, 4874. Brazil, 4874, 4891. Colonial
History, 916. Feminism, 1028. Labor
Movement, 1309. Mexico, 1235, 1309,
1339. Slaves and Slavery, 3302. Uruguay,
5273.
Popular Education. *See* Nonformal Education.
Popular Literature. Mexico, 1356.
Popular Movements. *See* Social Movements.
Popular Music. African Influences, 4750,
4808. Argentina, 4840, 4860. Biography,
4780, 4806. Bolivia, 4814. Brazil, 4882,
4891–4892, 4894–4895, 4903–4908.
Chile, 4865. Colombia, 4827. Composers,
4747. Cuba, 4806, 4808. Cultural Identity,
4814. Dominican Republic, 4795. Folklore, 4865. Mexico, 4746–4747, 4750–
4752, 4763–4764, 4768, 4772, 4780. Musical History, 4752, 4772, 4860, 4871, 4882,
4894, 4905, 4907. Peru, 4831. Political Ideology, 4873. Protests, 4906. Trinidad and
Tobago, 4790. Tupi, 4908. Uruguay, 4871,
4873.
Popular Religion, 4930.
Popular Theater. Brazil, 4539. Colonial His-
tory, 916.
Population Studies. *See* Demography.
Populism, 5029. Argentina, 1030, 2938. Bo-
livia, 2714. Brazil, 1030, 5205. Colombia,
2566. Mexico, 1030. Spain, 5029. State-
Building, 1030.
Portes Gil, Emilio, 1379.
Portinari, Cândido, 424–425.
Porto Alegre, Brazil (city). Labor and Laboring
Classes, 3312. Slaves and Slavery, 3304.
Social Classes, 3312. Urban Sociology,
3312.
Portocarrero Lasso de la Vega, Melchor,
Conde de la Monclova, 2319.
Portraits. Ecuador, 2616. Indigenous Peoples,
2616. Mexico, 33, 134.
Ports. Argentina, 2990, 3028. Mexico, 1256.
Venezuela, 2543.
Portugal, Diogo Pinto de Azevedo, 3182.
Portuguese. Brazil, 3152, 3162–3163, 3170,
3196, 3205, 3221–3222, 3294, 3299. Brit-
ish Guiana, 1979. Elites, 3218. Guyana,
2003.
Portuguese Conquest, 3162–3163, 3172,
3197. Brazil, 3182. Historiography, 3207.
International Relations, 873.
Portuguese Influences. Brazil, 3218.
Portuguese Language. Dictionaries, 4533.
Theater, 4533.
Posada, José Guadalupe, 152, 156, 189, 1337.

Positivism, 5107. Chile, 5202. Costa Rica,
1735. Ecuador, 5168. Honduras, 1691,
1770. Mexico, 5094, 5098. Peru, 2670,
2683. Venezuela, 5147, 5153.
Posnansky, Arthur, 706.
Post-Modernism, 5005. Cuba, 5136. Cultural
Identity, 5020. Paraguay, 5235.
Postal Service. Brazil, 3209.
Postmodernism, 3373.
Potatoes. Bolivia, 4823. Ethnomusicology,
4823.
Potiguara (indigenous group), 646.
Potosí, Bolivia (city). Colonial Art, 114. Colo-
nial History, 2128. Silver, 114.
Potosí, Bolivia (dept.). Colonial History,
2395–2396.
Poverty. Haiti, 2049. Peru, 2656. Venezuela,
2532.
Prado Júnior, Caio, 5226, 5228.
Precolumbian Art. Andean Region, 643, 697.
Brazil, 659. Incas, 645. Mexico, 584.
Precolumbian Civilizations. Andean Region,
638, 661, 664, 676, 712. Brazil, 696. British
Caribbean, 1805. Codices, 600. Communication, 600. Cronistas, 698. Cultural Identity, 643. Death, 692. Demography, 1639.
El Salvador, 1639. Historiography, 638,
640. Iconography, 472. Irrigation, 662. Law
and Legislation, 711. Manuscripts, 457,
459. Mexico, 471. Musical Instruments,
4743. Nobility, 471. Political Conditions,
714. Political Development, 471. Sex
Roles, 460. Social Structure, 714. Tierra
del Fuego, 678. Uruguay, 702. Women,
460. Writing, 600.
Precolumbian Land Settlement Patterns. Bo-
livia, 2397. Mexico, 476.
Precolumbian Pottery. Huari Site, 639. Ti-
wanaku Site, 639.
Precolumbian Trade. Andean Region, 650,
690. Colombia, 668. Incas, 669. Indigenous
Peoples, 669. Mexico, 470. Patagonia, 691.
Tierra del Fuego, 678.
Prehistory. *See* Archaeology.
Presidential Systmes. *See* Political Systems.
Presidents. Argentina, 2876. Biography, 1768.
Bolivia, 2612, 2637, 2714, 2737–2738.
Brazil, 3259, 3338. Caribbean Area, 1671.
Central America, 1671. Chile, 2748, 2761.
Colombia, 2572, 2574, 2586, 2602. Costa
Rica, 1693. Guatemala, 1713, 1764. Mex-
ico, 1269, 1355, 1495, 1671. Nicaragua,
1685, 1715, 1723, 1768. Paraguay, 3091.
Uruguay, 3076.
Press. *See* Mass Media.

tory, 1050. Indigenous/Non-Indigenous Relations, 539. Mexican Revolution, 1414. Mining, 1050. Missionaries, 539.

Singers. Argentina, 4839, 4851, 4853. Biography, 4749, 4767, 4839, 4851, 4853, 4870, 4879, 4887, 4892. Brazil, 4879, 4887, 4892. Children, 4755. Mexico, 4749, 4749, 4767. Uruguay, 4870.

Siqueiros, David Alfaro, 161, 184, 204–205.

Slaves and Slavery, 761. African Influences, 1897, 1910. Antigua, 1850. Argentina, 2901, 3007. Audiencia of Quito, 2204, 2263. Aztecs, 591. Bahamas, 1800–1801, 1899, 1984. Baptists, 1904. Barbados, 1851, 1871. Belize, 1722. Bermuda, 1831. Bibliography, 756, 1792, 1827. Biography, 4668, 4676. Birth Rate, 1873. Bolivia, 2356, 2358. Brazil, 1825, 3164, 3166, 3168, 3173, 3176, 3180, 3184, 3200, 3216, 3224, 3230, 3232, 3235, 3247, 3253, 3263, 3267–3268, 3275–3276, 3283, 3293, 3296, 3302, 3304, 3318, 3330–3332, 5207. British, 1843, 1851. British Caribbean, 1773, 1805, 1873, 1879, 1888, 1978, 2017. British Guiana, 1983. Capitalism, 1796. Caribbean Area, 1793, 1825, 1843. Catholic Church, 1819, 3224, 4926. Catholicism, 1839. Colombia, 2173. Colonial Administration, 2146. Colonial History, 947–948. Cuba, 1972, 1982, 1992, 2015–2016, 4668, 4676. Cultural Collapse, 801. Cultural Geography, 801. Cultural Identity, 1930. Danish Caribbean, 1897, 1905, 1910. Demography, 801. Diseases, 3330. Dominican Republic, 1819. Dutch Caribbean, 1784–1785, 1852, 1903. Economic Development, 3293. Ecuador, 2204, 2263. Ethnic Groups and Ethnicity, 880. Family and Family Relations, 3166, 3268, 3318. French, 1857, 1908, 1916, 1918. French Caribbean, 1839, 1857, 1968. Great Britain, 1796. Guadeloupe, 1913, 2033. Haciendas, 927. Hispaniola, 1841. Historiography, 756, 770, 807, 877, 1997–1998. History, 796. Human Ecology, 1911. Indigenous Peoples, 883, 1841, 2204. Informal Sector, 3331. Insurrections, 1891, 2137, 3168. International Relations, 3173. Islamic Influences, 1936. Jamaica, 1834, 1904, 1923, 1936, 1977. Jesuits, 927. Kinship, 3268, 3318. Law and Legislation, 883, 2146, 3224. Maritime History, 853. Maroons, 2033. Martinique, 1891. Medical Care, 1983. Mexico, 1107, 1180. Military, 3283, 3332. Minerals and Mining Industry, 2129. Montserrat, 1786. Moravians, 1897.

Mortality, 910. Names, 1981. Paraguayan War, 3332. Peru, 2273, 2705, 2705. Pictorial Works, 1802. Popular Culture, 3302. Puerto Rico, 1838, 1997–1998. Quality of Life, 927. Religious Life and Customs, 927, 1936. Saint-Domingue, 1890, 1900, 1916, 1928. Saint Kitts and Nevis, 2030. Saint Martin, 1807. Saint Vincent, 2000. Sex Roles, 3169, 3176. Social Life and Customs, 1910. Sources, 770, 1792, 1827, 1972. Spaniards, 2146. Statistics, 1843. Suriname, 1776, 1795, 1802, 1911, 1981, 1986. The Netherlands, 1784–1785, 1859, 1915. Trinidad and Tobago, 1983. Urban Areas, 1998. US, 1825, 1904, 1930, 1984, 3232. Venezuela, 2137, 2146, 2524, 2524. Viceroyalty of Río de la Plata, 2474. Virgin Islands, 1792, 1827. Women, 880, 1850, 1871, 1873, 1890, 1900, 1968, 2017, 3169.

Smuggling. British, 1667. Caribbean Area, 1919. Colonial History, 2131. Costa Rica, 1667. Santo Domingo, 1842. Venezuela, 2131.

Sobalvarro, Orlando, 223.

Sobrados e mucambos, 5207.

Social History. Ecuador, 2615.

Social Change, 4912. El Salvador, 1721. Mexico, 1045. Nicaragua, 1679. Puerto Rico, 2064.

Social Classes. Argentina, 2926, 3042. Bahamas, 1800. Belize, 1722. Brazil, 3238, 3248–3249, 3313. Costa Rica, 1684, 1728. Dominican Republic, 1940. Guatemala, 1647, 1662. Housing, 1728. Military History, 3238. Nicaragua, 1763. Panama, 1740. Political Participation, 2926.

Social Conditions, 7, 11. Argentina, 2910. El Salvador, 1714. Haiti, 2049. Honduras, 1720. Mexico, 1058, 1106. Peru, 3617. Trinidad and Tobago, 2062. Venezuela, 2532.

Social Conflict. Argentina, 3042. Belize, 1722. Bolivia, 2723. British Guiana, 1979. Colonial History, 841. Cuba, 2002. Mexico, 1150, 1257. Missionaries, 1221. Uruguay, 3112.

Social Control. Mexico, 1103.

Social Customs. *See* Social Life and Customs.

Social Darwinism. Costa Rica, 1736. Guatemala, 1736.

Social Democracy. Brazil, 4933.

Social Development. Colombia, 2597.

Social History, 756, 773, 782, 793, 973, 5104. Andean Region, 629. Argentina, 2461, 3075, 4844, 5292. Bahamas, 1800. Barba-

Tacla, Jorge, 314.
Tacna, Peru (town). Churches, 94.
Tafalla, Juan, 2209.
Taller de Gráfica Popular (México), 203.
Tamaulipas, Mexico (state). Family and Family Relations, 1456. Landowners, 1456. Musicians, 4768. Political History, 1379. Popular Music, 4768.
Tamayo, Rufino, 136.
Tambu (cult). Curaçao, 1816. Dutch Caribbean, 1816.
Tango. Argentina, 4842, 4844, 4846, 4849, 4851, 4856. Pictorial Works, 4845.
Tangüis, Fermín, 2650.
Tarahumara (indigenous group). Ethnohistory, 502.
Tarapacá, Chile (prov.). Frontier and Pioneer Life, 738. Salt and Salt Industry, 2765.
Tarapoto, Peru (city). Colonial History, 2270.
Tarasco (indigenous group). Ethnohistory, 588.
Tavares Bastos, Aureliano Cândido, 5233.
Tax Evasion. Zoque, 581.
Taxation. Bolivia, 2721. Ecuador, 655, 2611. Indigenous Peoples, 514, 655, 672. Mexico, 532, 1131, 1134. Nahuas, 532. Nueva Granada, 2175. Peru, 2647, 2654. Spaniards, 532.
Teachers. Argentina, 2858.
Teatro Experimental do Negro (Brazil), 4543.
Technological Development. Brazil, 3141, 3149. Cultural Identity, 4920. Mexico, 1412.
Technology Transfer. Colonial History, 934.
Tehuantepec, Mexico (region). Caciquismo, 608. Indigenous Resistance, 608. Political History, 608.
Tehuelche (indigenous group). Musical Instruments, 4855. Social Life and Customs, 682.
Telecommunication. Mexico, 1291.
Teles, Gilberto Mendonça, 4511.
Ten Years' War (Cuba, 1868–1878), 1967.
Teotihuacán Site (Mexico). Ethnohistory, 640.
Teques, Venezuela. See Los Teques, Venezuela (city).
Tequila Industry. Mexico, 1493.
Terra, Gabriel, 3112.
Terrorism. El Salvador, 1673.
Texas, US (state). History, 1230.
Textbooks. Caudillos, 809. Colombia, 2573. Colonial History, 859. History, 789, 793, 806.
Textiles and Textile Industry. Audiencia of

Quito, 2194, 2196, 2199. Bolivia, 2730. Brazil, 3179. Chile, 304, 2785. Colonial History, 2194, 2196, 2199. Economic Development, 2785. Guatemala, 1702. Mayas, 511–512. Mexico, 1174, 1362. Peru, 1174, 2681. Uruguay, 3106. Women, 511.
Theater. Brazil, 4531–4532, 4545. Catholic Church, 1096. Dictionaries, 4533. Indigenous Peoples, 509. Missionaries, 568. Peru, 2649. Sources, 4531. Viceroyalty of New Spain, 509, 568.
Thomas, Aquinas, Saint, 4926.
Thomas, Gerald, 4536.
Thomas, J.J., 5125.
Tierra del Fuego (region). Description and Travel, 3061. Indigenous Peoples, 665, 719. Indigenous/Non-Indigenous Relations, 652, 699. Migration, 665. Missions, 652. Precolumbian Civilizations, 678. Precolumbian Trade, 678. Salesians, 719. Subsistence Economy, 678.
Tigua, Ecuador (village). Indigenous Art, 339.
Timucua (indigenous group). Architecture, 1934. Cultural Destruction, 1935. History, 1932. Relations with Europeans, 1935.
Tin Industry. Bolivia, 2710.
Tipu Site (Belize). Cultural Development, 490. Medical Care, 490. Sex Roles, 490.
Tiwanaku Site (Bolivia), 662. Ethnohistory, 640. Pottery, 639.
Tlatelolco, Mexico (zone). Aztecs, 599. Cultural History, 1366. Ethnohistory, 598. Excavations, 598. History, 482.
Tlaxcala, Mexico (city). Manuscripts, 1105. Social Life and Customs, 1105.
Tlaxcala, Mexico (state). Local History, 1075. Manuscripts, 532. Mexican Revolution, 1405. Municipal Government, 1328. Urbanization, 59.
Tlaxcalans (indigenous group), 467.
Toba (indigenous group). Relations with Spaniards, 2489.
Tobacco Industry and Trade. Audiencia of Quito, 2232. Brazil, 3195. Colonial History, 3195. Cuba, 1939. Mexico, 1200.
Tobacco Use. Cuba, 1939.
Toledo, Francisco, 207.
Toledo, Francisco de, Viceroy, 2295.
Tolima, Colombia (dept.). Colonial History, 2164. Urban History, 2164.
Toltecs (indigenous group). Myths and Mythology, 506.
Toluca, Mexico (city). Architecture, 1077. Archives, 1077. Local History, 1077.

2420, 2435, 2481, 2498. Indigenous Policy, 2481. Indigenous Resistance, 2482, 2491, 2494. Indigenous/Non-Indigenous Relations, 2420–2421, 2425, 2428, 2477, 2481, 2489. Insurrections, 2482, 2491. Intellectual History, 2433. Inter-Tribal Relations, 2425. International Relations, 2897. International Trade, 2495–2497, 2501. Jesuits, 2421, 2436, 2454, 2469, 2485, 2503. Labor Supply, 2470. Land Tenure, 2426–2427, 2434, 2471, 2486. Land Use, 2471. Landowners, 2426–2427, 2434. Libraries, 2433. Local History, 2453, 2466. Maps and Cartography, 2432. Maritime History, 2422, 2429, 2431. Marriage, 2448. Meat Industry, 2468. Migration, 2502. Military History, 2490, 2492, 2504. Missions, 2462, 2485. Murder, 2440. Peasants, 2446. Pictorial Works, 2465. Portuguese, 2497, 2501. Religious Life and Customs, 2417, 2480, 2498. Rites and Ceremonies, 2417. Rural Conditions, 2427, 2446. Slaves and Slavery, 2419, 2474. Social Conflict, 2426. Social Life and Customs, 2385. Sources, 2424. Spaniards, 2448. Transportation, 2437. Treaties, 2472, 2503. Wages, 2457. Warfare, 2482. Wars of Independence, 2492.

Viceroys. Mexico, 1127, 1144. Sources, 2293. Viceroyalty of Peru, 2293.

Vieira, Antônio, 3161, 3224, 3461.

Villa, Pancho, 3509.

Villa Obregón, Mexico (neighborhood). Description and Travel, 31.

Villancicos. African Influences, 4796. Bolivia, 4819. Guatemala, 4796. Indigenous Influences, 4796. Mexico, 4760, 4770, 4777.

Villanueva, Felipe, 4742.

Villareal, Antonio Ireneo, 1525.

Villarroel, Gaspar de, 928.

Villaseñor, Isabel, 155.

Villavicencio, Antonio, 1276.

Villoro, Luis, 5055, 5075.

Vinatea Reinoso, Jorge, 351.

Violence. Argentina, 2881, 2983. Central America, 1709. Colombia, 2563, 2576. Costa Rica, 1616. El Salvador, 1673, 1690. Honduras, 1632, 1759. Mexico, 1560, 1595. Nicaragua, 1754. Panama, 1689. Venezuela, 2509.

Virasoro, Miguel Angel, 5254–5255.

Virgin of Guadalupe. See Guadalupe, Our Lady of.

Virginity. See Sex and Sexual Relations.

Visitations (church work). Audiencia of Quito, 2228.

Vitier, Medardo, 5138.

Vitoria, Francisco de, 4926, 5200.

Vocabulario en lengua Tzendal, 546.

Volcanoes. French Caribbean, 1771. Guadeloupe, 1771. Martinique, 1771.

Voorhoeve, Jan, 2103.

Voting. Argentina, 2803, 3036, 3058. Bolivia, 2724. Colombia, 2596. Puerto Rico, 2047.

Wages. Chile, 2749, 2778. Mexico, 1199. Railroads, 2749.

Waldenses. Uruguay, 3117.

War of the Pacific (1879–1884), 2739. Peru, 2647, 2657, 2663, 2676, 2680, 5176.

War of the Triple Alliance. See Paraguayan War (1865–1870).

Warfare. Aztecs, 495, 515, 528. Chichimecs, 538. Chile, 2415. Indigenous Peoples, 744. Mexico, 538. Sex Roles, 528.

Wari. See Huari.

Wars of Independence, 995, 1001, 1005–1006, 1009, 1012, 1016, 2933, 4924. Argentina, 2893, 2895–2896, 2899, 2963, 2994, 3042, 3050. Bolivia, 2742. Central America, 1608. Colombia, 2579, 2589, 2591, 2601, 2606. Cuba, 1943, 1954, 1967, 1991, 2009, 5110. Ecuador, 2635. Freemasonry, 4955. Guerrillas, 1019. Haiti, 1901. Historiography, 1021, 4941. Mexico, 1060, 1090, 1285. Peru, 2639, 2649, 2685. Political Ideology, 1019. Political Philosophy, 4941. South America, 2620, 2637. Spaniards, 1991. Uruguay, 3125. Venezuela, 2550. Viceroyalty of Río de la Plata, 2960. Writing, 4937.

Washington Luís, 3259.

Water Resources Development. Suriname, 1911.

Water Rights. Mexico, 1153. New Mexico, 1266. Viceroyalty of Peru, 2289.

Water Supply. Mexico, 1361.

Watercolors. Brazil, 404.

W.E.B. Du Bois Institute for Afro-American Research, 770, 853, 910.

Weg, 2974.

West Indians. Costa Rica, 1686–1687. Soldiers, 2073. Suriname, 4791. World War I, 2074.

West-Indische Compagnie (The Netherlands), 1784, 1852, 3212.

Wheat. Chile, 2757. Mexico, 1179.

Widmer, Ernst, 4898.

Wiedemann, Guillermo, 337.

Wilde, Eduardo, 2800.

AUTHOR INDEX

Cappelletti, Angel J., 2571, 5147, 5250
Capriles Ayala, Carlos, 2514
Carabias Torres, Ana María, 873
Caraveo Estrada, Baudilio B., 1410
Carbajal López, Édgar Fernando, 3445
Carbó Darnaculleta, Margarita, 1411
Carciente, Jacob, 2515
Cardello de Sottano, Mabel, 4911
Cardenal, Ernesto, 4576
Cardenas, Claudia, 2774
Cárdenas, Eduardo, 1029
Cárdenas, Jorge, 319
Cárdenas, Rolando, 3977
Cárdenas Espinosa, Eliécer, 3653
Cárdenas García, Nicolás, 1412
Cárdenas Gutiérrez, Salvador, 1279
Cárdenas Reyes, María Cristina, 5164
Cárdenas Ruiz, Manuel, 1787
Cardiel, José, 2436
Cardona Torrico, Alcira, 3978
Cardoso, Fernando Henrique, 4933
Cardoza y Aragón, Luis, 1681
Cardozo Galué, Germán, 2516
Careaga Viliesid, Lorena, 1048
Caribbean Inter-Cultural Music Institute, 4783
Cariño Olvera, Martha Micheline, 1413
Carli, Sandra, 5257
Carlos Casas, Bernardo, 32
Carlos Chávez 1899–1978: iconografía, 4741
Carmichael, Trevor A., 2046
Carmona, Gloria, 4741
Carneiro, João Emanuel, 4687
Carneiro, Maria Luiza Tucci, 3245
Caron, Aimery, 1833
Caron, Peter, 1930
Carpentier, Alejo, 3562
Carpio Alfaro, Iván, 1677
Carr, Barry, 2050
Carrano, Austregésilo, 4517
Carranza, María Mercedes, 4141
Carrara Junior, Ernesto, 3246
Carrasco, Pedro, 475
Carrazzoni, José Andrés, 2437
Carredano, Consuelo, 4742
Carrera Damas, Germán, 2517–2518
Carrero, Jaime, 4264
Carrero, Raimundo, 4333
Carretero, Andrés M., 4844
Carrillo, Francisco, 641
Carrillo Cázares, Alberto, 1108–1110
Carrillo Padilla, José Domingo, 1629
Carrillo Rojas, Arturo, 1414
Carrión, Carlos, 3654

Carrión, M. María, 4716
Carrizo, Juan Alfonso, 4843
Carroll, Patrick, 761
Cartas de frontera: los documentos del conflicto interétnico, 631
Cartas y documentos coloniales de Mendoza, 2438
Cartay Angulo, Rafael, 861, 2519
Caruso, Marcelo, 3768
Caruso, Raimundo C., 4334
Carvalhal, Tania Franco, 4459
Carvalho, Alvaro Augusto de, 4518
Carvalho, José Maurício de, 5211
Carvalho, José Murilo de, 5212
Carvalho, Lia de Aquino, 3320
Carvalho, Ruber, 3979
Casa de América (Madrid), 255
Casa de las Américas (Cuba), 231
La Casa del Marqués de San Jorge, Santafé de Bogotá: colección de arte y objetos coloniales, 82
Casa do Pontal (Rio de Janeiro, Brazil), 429
La casa en la poesía venezolana del siglo XX, 1900–1950, 3911
Casablanca, Marie-Jeanne, 1950
Casal, Juan Manuel, 3109
Casanova Rosado, Aída Amine, 1057
Casanovas Codina, Joan, 1951
Casas, Bartolomé de las, 862–863
Casillas de Alba, Martín, 1415
Casimiro Castro y su taller, 137
Caso, Alfonso, 480
Cassá, Roberto, 1779, 2051
Cassas, Luís Augusto, 4480–4481
Castagnino, Raúl Héctor, 4290
Castañeda, Armando Luigi, 3697
Castañeda, Carmen, 1226
Castañeda, Daniel Perez, 4743
Castañeda, Jorge G., 2052, 4934
Castañeda Delgado, Paulino, 862, 2283
Castedo, Leopoldo, 302, 3397
Castelán Rueda, Roberto, 1280
Castellano Gil, José Manuel, 1952
Castellanos, José Alfredo, 1416
Castellanos, Justo Pedro, 5114
Castellanos, Rafael Ramón, 2520
Castells, Ricardo, 5115
Castelvecchi, Gladys, 3980
Castilla Urbano, Francisco, 864, 4935
Castillero Calvo, Alfredo, 61, 1630
Castillo, Abelardo, 3769, 4176
Castillo, Eduardo, 632
Castillo, Edward D., 1243
Castillo, Julio, 4177

Jiménez P., Blanca M., 1310
Jiménez Pelayo, Agueda, 1064
Jiménez Villalba, Félix, 663
Jiquilpan, 1920–1940: memoria pueblerina, 1471
João Antônio, 4440
Jochamowitz, Luis, 2665
Johansson K., Patrick, 522–523
Johns, Michael, 1311
Johnson, Howard, 1800–1801, 1899
Johnson, Julie Greer, 3409–3410
Johnson, Lyman L., 859, 2930–2931
Johnson, Whittington B., 1984
Johnston Aguilar, Mario René, 1643
Jolicoeur, Luis, 2455
Jones, Charles A., 785
Jones, Kristine L., 2932
Jones, Maldwyn Allen, 786
Jones, Oakah L., Jr, 1245
Jones Mathers, Constance, 2171
Jordán de Balmori, Helena, 135
Jorge, Bernarda, 4795
Jornadas Andinas de Literatura Latino Americana, 1993, 3362
Jornadas de Andalucía y América, 8th, Univ. de Santa María de la Rábida, Seville, 1988, 787
Jornadas de Andalucía y América, 10th, Univ. de Santa María de la Rábida, Sevilla, 1991, 907
Jornadas de Historia del Pensamiento Científico Argentino, 5th, Buenos Aires, 1990, 5266
Jornadas Presencia de España en América—Aportación Gallega, 1st, Pazo de Mariñán, Spain, 1987, 788
José Batlle y Ordóñez: documentos para el estudio de su vida y de su obra, 3120
José de San Martín, libertador de América, 2933
José Leonardo Chirino y la insurrección de la Serranía de Coro de 1795: insurrección de libertad o rebelión de independencia; memoria del simposio realizado en Mérida los días 16 y 17 de noviembre de 1995, 2137
Jose Luis Cuevas, el ojo perdido de Dios, 163
Joseph, de San Buenaventura, fray, 524
Joyas de la pintura mexicana: exposición temporal inaugural, 164
Joyce, Arthur A., 525
Joyce, Rosemary A., 526
Jozami, Gladys, 2934
Jrade, Ramón, 1472
Juan José de Eguiara y Eguren y la cultura mexicana, 5086

Juana Inés de la Cruz, Sor, 3385–3386, 3431, 3453, 3459–3466, 3477, 4573, 4586, 4613
Juárez, Abel, 1154
Juárez, Orient Bolívar, 1712, 1723
Juarroz, Roberto, 4028
Jugando a juegos prohibidos, 3919
Jujuy, Argentina (prov.), 2935
Jujuy: diccionario general, 2935
Jules, Didacus, 2053
Junta de Andalucía (Spain). Consejería de Cultura, 908
Junta de Estudios Históricos de Mendoza (Argentina), 2925
La Junta de Historia y Numismática Americana y el movimiento historiográfico en la Argentina, 1893–1938, 2936
Jurado Noboa, Fernando, 2224–2225, 2623
Jurandir, Dalcídio, 4348
Jurisch Durán, Mario, 2587
Just, Estanislao, 2368–2369

Kafka, Judith, 1900
Kahlo, Frida, 165, 167
Kalenberg, Angel, 360
Kallsen, Margarita, 3898
Kalume, Jorge, 4441
Kaplan, Charles D., 495
Karam, Vera, 4522
Karlen, Stefan, 1713
Karttunen, Frances E., 527
Katra, William H., 2937, 5267
Katz, Friedrich, 1473
Kaufmann, Jacobo, 4210
Kaulicke, Peter, 664
Kearney, Milo, 1065
Keeding, Ekkehart, 2226
Keen, Benjamin, 789
Kelly, Kevin, 2938
Kempff Suárez, Manfredo, 3635
Kennedy, Alexandra, 2227
Kessler, Stephen, 4577
Keune, Lou, 1714
Khedayan, Marcos, 3804
Khoury, Simon, 4531
King, Johannes, 2032
King, John, 4683
Kinloch Tijerino, Frances, 1611
Kinsbruner, Jay, 1985
Kiple, Kenneth F., 1854
Kirby, Peadar, 790
Kirk, Robin, 2666
Kirking, Clayton, 166
Kirkland, Will, 4635
Kirkpatrick, Gwen, 4637
Kitroeff, Alexander, 1031

Mexico. Dirección General de Culturas Populares Unidad Regional Norte-La Laguna, 1524

México en el mundo de las colecciones de arte, 174

Mexico. Secretaría de Hacienda y Crédito Público, 175, 178

Mexico. Secretaría de Relaciones Exteriores, 1382

Mexico. Sector Comunicaciones y Transportes, 1408

Meyer, Bárbara, 33

Meyer, Doris, 3374, 4563

Meyer, Eugenia, 798, 1406

Meyer, Jean A., 1225, 5092

Meyer Cosío, Francisco Javier, 1504

Meza Wevar, Gustavo, 4220

Miceli, Sergio, 3280

Michalski, Yan, 4544

Michel, Georges, 2084

Michelena, Alejandro Daniel, 5238

Michelena, Juan Antonio, 382

Michieli, Catalina Teresa, 685

Michoacán desde afuera: visto por algunos de sus ilustres visitantes extranjeros, siglos XVI al XX, 1069

Mier Rivas, Adolfo, 4221

Mignolo, Walter, 3425

Miguel, María Esther de, 3819

Los mil días de Allende, 2774

Milan, Betty, 4360

Milanich, Jerald T., 1935

Milbrath, Susan, 547

Millán, Gonzalo, 4042

Millares, Selena, 3354

Mille ans de civilisations mésoaméricaines: des Mayas aux Aztèques; mélanges en l'honneur de Jacques Soustelle, 548–549

Miller, Eugene D., 1726

Miller, Jeannette, 232

Miller, Rory, 2678

Miller, Shawn W., 3189

Milletich, Vilma, 2396

Milliet, Maria Alice, 420

Millon, Robert Paul, 1505

Millones, Luis, 688, 2318

Milwaukee Art Museum, 124

Minería y metalurgia: intercambio tecnológico y cultural entre América y Europa durante el período colonial español, 934

Minguet, Charles, 4924

Mínguez, Víctor, 1173

Miniño Marión Landais, Manuel Marino, 5132

Miño Grijalva, Manuel, 1174

Mir, Pedro, 4043–4044

Mira Caballos, Esteban, 935–936

Miraglia, Liliana, 3661

Miranda, Ana Maria, 4361–4362

Miranda, Julio E., 3935

Miranda, Verónica, 4590

Miranda Bastidas, Haidee, 2537

Miranda Godínez, Francisco, 1175

Mirelman, Victor A., 799

Miró Quesada, Francisco, 5017

Miró Quesada Sosa, Aurelio, 3426, 3476

Mirza, Roger, 4313

Missana, Sergio, 3732

Mistral, Gabriela, 4045, 4591

Mito y simbolismo en los Andes: la figura y la palabra, 103

Mitos en el teatro latinoamericano, 4300

Mitre, Antonio, 2736

Mizraje, María Gabriela, 3821

Moberg, Mark, 1727

Modernidade e modernismo no Brasil, 395

O Modernismo no Museu de Arte Brasileira: pintura, 421

Moguel, Josefina, 1506

Mohamed, Khalleel, 1979

Molestina Zaldumbide, María del Carmen, 2244

Molina, Enrique, 4046

Molina, Silvia, 4222

Molina Barbery, Plácido, 104

Molina Jiménez, Iván, 1610, 1613, 1728–1729

Molinari, Alina, 281

Momprodé, Electra L., 800

Monasterio de Carmelitas Descalzas (Córdoba, Argentina), 75

Moncaut, Carlos Antonio, 2978

La moneda en México, 1750–1920, 1325

Monge, Carlos Francisco, 3957

Monjarás-Ruiz, Jesús, 485

Monségur, Jean de, 1176

Monsiváis, Carlos, 128, 162, 3508

Montalvo de Morales, Ana Joaquina, 43

Montaño Balderrama, Celso, 4047

Monteagudo, María C. R. de, 911

Montealegre, Jorge, 4048

Monteforte Toledo, Mario, 3531, 4223

Monteiro, Benedicto, 4363

Monteiro, Jacinto, 937

Monteiro, John Manuel, 3190

Monteiro, Vicente do Rego, 422

Montejo, Eugenio, 4049–4050

Montejo, Víctor D., 4592

Montejo Arrechea, Carmen, 2085

Ramírez Briceño, Edgar Roy, 4929
Ramírez de Verger, Antonio, 975
Ramírez Flores, José, 1528
Ramírez Godoy, Guillermo, 191
Ramírez Heredia, Rafael, 3504–3505
Ramírez Meza, Benito, 1261
Ramírez Monagas, Bayardo, 4083
Ramírez Rancaño, Mario, 1529
Ramiro Valderrama, Manuel, 4717
Ramón, Armando de, 2128
Ramón y Rivera, Luis Felipe, 4132, 4833, 4837–4838
Ramos, Gabriela, 762
Ramos, Graciliano, 3316
Ramos, Jorge Abelardo, 3019
Ramos, Luis Arturo, 4619, 4649
Ramos, Marcelo, 4192
Ramos, María Elena, 385
Ramos Aguirre, Francisco, 4768
Ramos Arizpe, Guillermo, 1471
Ramos Escandón, Carmen, 1073, 1530
Ramos Garrido, Estrella, 954
Ramos Martínez, Alfredo, 170, 177
Ramos Medina, Manuel, 2119, 3456–3457
Ramos-Perea, Roberto, 4264
Ramos Pérez, Demetrio, 846, 872
Ramos Rosado, Marie, 3606
Ramos Sosa, Rafael, 115
Ramsoedh, Hans, 4791
Ranaboldo, Claudia, 625
Rangel, Domingo Alberto, 2551
Ranston, Jackie, 2076
Raposo, Luciano, 3206
Ras, Norberto, 2483
Raschella, Roberto, 3834
Rascón Banda, Víctor Hugo, 4247
Rasi, Mauro, 4528
Rathbone, Richard, 1011
Rathsam, Marilisa, 417
Rato de Sambuccetti, Susana Irene, 3020
Ratto, Silvia, 3021
Rausch, Jane M., 2599
Ravelo Cabrera, Paul, 5136
Ravines, Róger, 712, 721
Rawet, Samuel, 4689
Reati, Fernando O., 5273
Rebolledo, Francisco, 4650
Rebolledo Hernández, Antonia, 2782
Rebuelto, Emilio, 2886
Recalde, Héctor, 3022
Recasens, Andreu Viola, 2740
Recuento histórico bibliográfico de la minería en la región central de México, 1074
Recurrencias: arte argentino de la generación de los 80, 287

Redescubramos Lima: Iglesia de San Pedro, 116
Reece Dousdebés, Alfonso, 3662
Rego, José Lins do, 4374
Reibscheid, Samuel, 4414
Reichel, Heloísa Jochims, 2484
Reichel-Dolmatoff, Gerardo, 2177
Reily, Suzel Ana, 4902–4904
Rein, Raanan, 3023
Reinders Folmer-van Prooijen, C., 1915
Reinhart, Cornel J., 2755–2756
Reinterpreting the Spanish American essay: women writers of the 19th and 20th centuries, 3374
Reis, João José, 3180, 3317
Reis, José Carlos, 3207
Reis, Roberto, 3349
Reisz, Susana, 4135
Reiter, Frederick J., 2485
Rela, Walter, 352, 3937, 4268, 4308
Relaciones económicas del Reino de Chile, 1780, 2410
Relaciones geográficas de 1792, 1191
Relaciones y visitas a los Andes, siglo XVI, 713, 2179
Relatos de historia en tu imaginación, 4248
Religión, política y sociedad: el sinarquismo y la Iglesia en México; nueve ensayos, 1531
Rema, Henrique Pinto, 3208
Remedi, Fernando Javier, 3024
Remesal, Agustín, 955
Rendón Garcini, Ricardo, 1075
Rendón Seminario, Manuel, 338
Rennó, Carlos, 4490
Representaciones inconclusas: las clases, los actores y los discursos de la memoria, 1912–1946, 3025
Requena, Francisco, 2193
Rereading the Spanish American essay: translations of 19th and 20th century women's essays, 4563
Reséndez, Andrés, 1330
Reséndez Fuentes, Andrés, 1532
Resgate: uma janela para o oitocentos, 3318
Resnick, Seymour, 4565
La responsabilidad del historiador: homenaje a Moisés González Navarro, 1533
Restall, Matthew, 566–567
Restrepo, Laura, 4651
Restrepo Arcila, Roberto A., 714
Revelo, Luis Alberto, 2259
Reverón, Armando, 389
Review: Latin American literature and arts, 4690

Sarramone, Alberto, 718
Sartelli, Eduardo, 3044
Sater, William F., 2787
Saugera, Eric, 1918
Saunders, Gail, 2095
Saunders, Hartley Cecil, 1822
Savary, Olga, 4417
Scala, José Nicolás, 2909
Scalona, Marcelo E., 3846
Scannone, Juan Carlos, 4913
Scarabino, Guillermo, 4858
Scarzanella, Eugenia, 719
Scavone Yegros, Ricardo, 3098
Schaaf, Richard, 4571
Schafer, Mark, 4600
Schaller, Enrique César, 3045–3046
Schaposchnik, Ana Edith, 2491
Schávelzon, Daniel, 291
Scheines, Graciela I., 5281
Scheker O., Luis, 69
Schell, William, Jr, 1353
Scherer García, Julio, 3508
Schickendantz, Emilio, 2886
Schindler, Helmut, 4868
Schlau, Stacey, 3384, 3442
Schleifer, Martha Furman, 4734
Schmid, Catherine, 587
Schmid, Martin, 2734
Schmidhuber de la Mora, Guillermo, 3443–3444
Schmidt, Arthur, 1721
Schmidt, Hans, 2096
Schmidt, Nelly, 2023–2025, 2028
Schmidt, Peer, 600
Schmidt-Nowara, Christopher, 2026
Schmit, Roberto, 2396, 3032
Schmölz-Häberlein, Michaela, 1753
Schnakenbourg, Christian, 1945, 2027
Schneider, Luis Mario, 3925, 4072
Schnoor, Eduardo, 3318
Schoelcher, Victor, 2028
Schön, Elizabeth, 378, 4261
Schöondube, Otto, 588
Schoonover, Thomas D., 1551
Schoultz, Lars, 815
Schramm, Raimund, 2390
Schrijver, Guido de, 3545
Schroeder, Michael J., 1754
Schroeder, Susan, 477
Schroeder Otero, Juan Bautista, 3130
Schröter, Bernd, 825, 1017
Schuetz-Miller, Mardith K., 1255
Schulkin, Augusto I., 2492
Schüller, Karin, 825
Schulman, Ivan A., 4676

Schultz, Margarita, 313
Schulz, John, 3324–3325
Schutte, Ofelia, 5048
Schuyler, George W., 2552
Schvarz, Niko, 5239
Schvarzberg, Oscar, 5049
Schwaller, John F., 589
Schwarcz, Alfredo José, 3047
Schwarcz, Lilia Moritz, 3326
Schwartz, Jorge, 3240
Schwarzstein, Dora, 816
Scisínio, Alaôr Eduardo, 3216
Scliar, Moacyr, 4691
Scocozza, Antonio, 3367
Scott, Julius S., 1919
Secretaría de Desarrollo Turístico del Estado de Oaxaca, 49
Sedoff, Miguel, 3847
Sedução do horizonte, 3147
Seed, Patricia, 974
Sefamí, Jacobo, 3922
Segall, Lasar, 408, 427
Segovia, Juan Fernando, 5282
Segovia, Tomás, 4598
Segreti, Carlos S.A., 3048–3050
Segui, Antonio, 292–293
II Arte Atual Paraibana, 399
Seibold, Jorge R., 5283
Seis décadas de arte argentino, 294
Seixas, Heloisa, 4418
Sekou, Lasana M., 1807
Selig, Robert A., 1920
Seljam, Zora, 4529
Selser, Gregorio, 1018
Semana Internacional en Homenaje a Pedro Henríquez Ureña en el Cincuentenario de su Muerte 1946–1996, *Santo Domingo, 1996*, 3377
Semeraro, Giovanni, 5229
Seminario Balance Histórico del Estado Nación en Centroamérica, *San Salvador, 1993*, 1711
Seminario Configuración y presencia del pensamiento conservator ecuatoriano, *Cuenca, Ecuador, 1993*, 5169
Seminario Internacional de Etnohistoria del Norte del Ecuador y Sur de Colombia, *1st, Popayán and Cali, Colombia, 1994*, 720
Seminario sobre Historia de los Precios de Alimentos y Manufacturas Novohispanos *Villahermosa, Tabasco, Mexico 1990*, 1189
Semprún, José, 1019
Sena, Davino Ribeiro de, 4510
Sención, Viriato, 4655